CONSTITUTIONAL LAW AND POLITICS
VOLUME TWO

SIXTH EDITION

OTHER BOOKS BY DAVID M. O'BRIEN

Storm Center:
The Supreme Court in American Politics
7th ed.

Animal Sacrifice and Religious Freedom:
Church of Lukumi Babalu Aye
v. City of Hialeah

Privacy, Law, and Public Policy

The Public's Right to Know:
The Supreme Court and the First Amendment

The Politics of Technology Assessment:
Institutions, Processes and Policy Disputes
(with Donald Marchand)

Views from the Bench:
The Judiciary and Constitutional Politics
(with Mark Cannon)

What Process is Due?:
Courts and Science-Policy Disputes

Judicial Roulette

Abortion and American Politics
(with Barbara H. Craig)

The Politics of American Government
3rd ed.
(with Stephen J. Wayne, G. Calvin Mackenzie, and Richard Cole)

Supreme Court Watch

To Dream of Dreams:
Religious Freedom and Constitutional Politics in Postwar Japan
(with Yasuo Ohkoshi)

Judges on Judging
2d ed.

The Lanahan Readings on Civil Rights and Civil Liberties
2nd ed.

Judicial Independence in the Age of Democracy:
Critical Perspectives from Around the World
(with Peter Russell)

Government By the People
21st ed.
(with James MacGregor Burns, J. W. Peltason, Thomas E. Cronin, David B. Magleby, and Paul Light)

CONSTITUTIONAL LAW AND POLITICS

VOLUME TWO

Civil Rights and Civil Liberties

SIXTH EDITION

DAVID M. O'BRIEN

UNIVERSITY OF VIRGINIA

W • W • NORTON & COMPANY • NEW YORK

For Claudine, Benjamin, Sara, and Talia

W. W. Norton & Company has been independent since its founding in 1923, when William Warder Norton and Mary D. Herter Norton first published lectures delivered at the People's Institute, the adult education division of New York City's Cooper Union. The Nortons soon expanded their program beyond the Institute, publishing books by celebrated academics from America and abroad. By mid-century, the two major pillars of Norton's publishing program—trade books and college texts—were firmly established. In the 1950s, the Norton family transferred control of the company to its employees, and today—with a staff of four hundred and a comparable number of trade, college, and professional titles published each year—W. W. Norton & Company stands as the largest and oldest publishing house owned wholly by its employees.

Printed in the United States of America.
Composition by PennSet, Inc.
Manufacturing by the Courier Companies—Westford Division.
Book design by Martin Lubin Graphic Design.
Project editor: Dexter Gasque.
Production manager: Benjamin Reynolds.
Drawn art by John McAusland.

Library of Congress Cataloging-in-Publication Data

O'Brien, David M.
    Constitutional law and politics / David M. O'Brien.— 6th ed.
      p. cm.
    Includes bibliographical references and index.
    Contents: v. 1. Struggles for power and governmental accountability—
v. 2. Civil rights and civil liberties.

    ISBN 0-393-92565-X (v. 1 : pbk.) — ISBN 0-393-92566-8 (v. 2 : pbk.)

    1. Constitutional law—United States—Cases. 2. Constitutional history—
United States—Cases. 3. Political questions and judicial power—United
States—Cases. 4. Civil rights—United States—Cases. I. Title.

KF4541.A7027 2005
342.73—dc22

                                                        2005040573

W. W. Norton & Company, Inc., 500 Fifth Avenue, New York, N.Y. 10110
www.wwnorton.com

W. W. Norton & Company Ltd., Castle House, 75/76 Wells Street,
London W1T 3QT

2 3 4 5 6 7 8 9 0

CONTENTS

Cases [within brackets] are discussed and extensively quoted in the topic introductions.

ILLUSTRATIONS   xxv

PREFACE   xvii

ACKNOWLEDGMENTS   xxxi

THE UNITED STATES CONSTITUTION AND AMENDMENTS   1

CHAPTER 1 ■ *The Supreme Court, Judicial Review, and Constitutional Politics*   23

A. ESTABLISHING AND CONTESTING THE POWER OF JUDICIAL REVIEW   27
   ☐ HOW TO LOCATE DECISIONS OF THE SUPREME COURT   28
   [*Calder v. Bull*]   29
   ☐ CONSTITUTIONAL HISTORY: Decisions of the Supreme Court Overruled and Acts of Congress Held Unconstitutional, and State Laws and Municipal Ordinances Overturned, 1789–2004   36
   James Kent's Introductory Law School Lecture in 1794   40
   The Virginia and Kentucky Resolutions of 1798   43
   Marbury v. Madison   46
   Eakin v. Raub   56
   President Jackson's Veto Message of 1832   59
   President Roosevelt's Radio Broadcast, March 9, 1937   62

B. THE POLITICS OF CONSTITUTIONAL INTERPRETATION   67
   ☐ IN COMPARATIVE PERSPECTIVE: Written and Unwritten Constitutions: Britain's and Israel's Constitutions   69
   (1) The Text and Historical Context   76
   (2) In and Beyond the Text   86
   ☐ CONSTITUTIONAL HISTORY: What Is the Constitution? Could a Constitutional Amendment Violate the Constitution?   89

☐ THE DEVELOPMENT OF LAW: Comparative Constitutional Interpretation   96

CHAPTER 2 ■ *Law and Politics in the Supreme Court: Jurisdiction and Decision-Making Process* 103

A. JURISDICTION AND JUSTICIABLE CONTROVERSIES   104

☐ FIGURE 2.1 Avenues of Appeal: The two main routes to the Supreme Court   106

[*Frothingham v. Mellon*]   108

☐ FIGURE 2.2 Jurisdictional map of the U.S. Courts of Appeal and U.S. District Courts   109

[*Northeastern Florida Chapter of the Associated General Contractors of America v. City of Jacksonville, Florida*]   111

[*Wyoming v. Oklahoma*]   111

☐ THE DEVELOPMENT OF LAW: Other Important Rulings on Standing   112

☐ THE DEVELOPMENT OF LAW: Class Action Suits   117

[*Luther v. Borden*]   119

[*Colegrove v. Green*]   119

☐ INSIDE THE COURT: Standing and the Connecticut Birth Control Cases   120

[*Nixon v. United States*]   124

☐ INSIDE THE COURT: The Supreme Court's Reversal of Precedent in Historical Perspective   128

Flast v. Cohen   130

Valley Forge Christian College v. Americans United for Separation of Church and State, Inc.   137

Lujan v. Defenders of Wildlife   141

Baker v. Carr   145

Goldwater v. Carter   157

Elk Grove Unified School District v. Newdow   161

☐ CONSTITUTIONAL HISTORY: Rules for Judicial Self-Restraint and Avoiding Constitutional Questions   169

B. THE COURT'S DOCKET AND SCREENING CASES   170

C. THE RULE OF FOUR AND AGENDA SETTING   171

☐ CONSTITUTIONAL HISTORY: Figure 2.3. Docket and filings, 1800–2003   171

☐ IN COMPARATIVE PERSPECTIVE: The "European Model" of Constitutional Courts and Judicial Review   173

D. SUMMARILY DECIDED CASES   176

E. THE ROLE OF ORAL ARGUMENT   176

F. CONFERENCE DELIBERATIONS   178
   ☐ INSIDE THE COURT: On the Tentativeness of Votes and the Importance of Opinion Writing   180

G. POSTCONFERENCE WRITING AND CIRCULATION OF OPINIONS   182
   ☐ CONSTITUTIONAL HISTORY: FIGURE 2.4. Opinion writing, 1937–2004   184

H. OPINION DAYS AND COMMUNICATING DECISIONS   185
   ☐ INSIDE THE COURT: Voting Alignments in the Rehnquist Court, 1986–2002 Terms   186

I. THE IMPACT OF SUPREME COURT DECISIONS: COMPLIANCE AND IMPLEMENTATION   187
   ☐ CONSTITUTIONAL HISTORY: The Southern Manifesto: A Declaration of Constitutional Principles   190
   Linkletter v. Walker   200
   Griffith v. Kentucky   204
   Jaffree v. Board of School Commissioners of Mobile County   206
   Commonwealth of Kentucky v. Jeffrey Wasson   208
   ☐ THE DEVELOPMENT OF LAW: Other Recent State Supreme Court Decisions Declining to Follow the U.S. Supreme Court's Rulings   212

CHAPTER 3 ■ *Economic Rights and American Capitalism*   220

A. THE CONTRACT CLAUSE AND VESTED INTERESTS IN PROPERTY   222
   ☐ CONSTITUTIONAL HISTORY: John Locke on the Ends of Political Society and Government   223
   Fletcher v. Peck   226
   Trustees of Dartmouth College v. Woodward   229
   Charles River Bridge Co. v. Warren Bridge Co.   233

Home Building & Loan Association v. Blaisdell 240

City of El Paso v. Simmons 246

United States Trust Co. of New York v. State of New Jersey 249

B. THE DEVELOPMENT AND DEMISE OF A "LIBERTY OF CONTRACT" 252

[*Allgeyer v. Louisiana*] 256

[*Jacobson v. Massachusetts*] 259

Butchers' Benevolent Association v. Cresent City Livestock Landing & Slaughterhouse Co. (The Slaughterhouse Cases) 266

Munn v. Illinois 270

Lochner v. New York 273

Muller v. Oregon 279

West Coast Hotel Co. v. Parrish 281

Lincoln Federal Labor Union v. Northwestern Iron & Metal Co. 285

C. THE "TAKINGS CLAUSE" AND JUST COMPENSATION 286

Hawaii Housing Authority v. Midkiff 290

Nollan v. California Coastal Commission 293

Lucas v. South Carolina Coastal Council 296

□ THE DEVELOPMENT OF LAW: Other Important Rulings on the Takings Clause 301

CHAPTER 4 ■ *The Nationalization of the Bill of Rights* 304

A. THE SELECTIVE NATIONALIZATION OF GUARANTEES OF THE BILL OF RIGHTS PLUS OTHER FUNDAMENTAL RIGHTS 309

□ THE DEVELOPMENT OF LAW: The Selective Nationalization of the Bill of Rights plus Other Fundamental Rights 314

□ CONSTITUTIONAL HISTORY: Guarantees of the Bill of Rights That Have Not Been Applied to the States 316

□ THE DEVELOPMENT OF LAW: Approaches to Nationalization of the Bill of Rights under the Fourteenth Amendment 317

Barron v. The Mayor and City of Baltimore 319

The Slaughterhouse Cases (reprise) 321

Hurtado v. California   321

Palko v. Connecticut   326

Adamson v. California   329

Rochin v. California   334

☐ INSIDE THE COURT: The Theory and Drafting of Justice
Douglas's Opinion in *Griswold v. Connecticut*   337

Griswold v. Connecticut   339

Duncan v. Louisiana   347

☐ CONSTITUTIONAL HISTORY: The Second and Third
Amendments   353

B. THE RISE AND (PARTIAL) RETREAT OF THE "DUE
PROCESS REVOLUTION"   354

[O'Connor v. Donaldson]   355

[DeShaney v. Winnebago County Department of Social Services]   357

[Michael H. v. Gerald D.]   358

☐ THE DEVELOPMENT OF LAW: Other Recent Rulings on
Substantive and Procedural Due Process   364

BMW of North America v. Gore   369

County of Sacramento v. Lewis   374

☐ CONSTITUTIONAL HISTORY: Citizens, Noncitizens, "Enemy
Combatants," and Civil Rights in Wartime   379

CHAPTER 5 ■ *Freedom of Expression and
Association*   386

☐ CONSTITUTIONAL HISTORY: The 1735 Trial of John Peter
Zenger and Free Speech in the Colonies   389

A. JUDICIAL APPROACHES TO THE FIRST AMENDMENT   397

(1) Fifty Years of "Clear and Present Danger"   399

[Abrams v. United States]   399

[Whitney v. California]   400

[Yates v. United States]   402

[Scales v. United States]   403

*[Communist Party of the United States v. Subversives Activities
Control Board (SACB)]*   403

Schenck v. United States   405

Gitlow v. People of the State of New York   406

Dennis v. United States   412

Brandenburg v. Ohio   423

□ CONSTITUTIONAL HISTORY: Judicial Approaches to the First Amendment   425

(2) Judicial Line Drawing: *Ad Hoc* and Definitional Balancing   426

[*Chaplinsky v. New Hampshire*]   428

B. OBSCENITY, PORNOGRAPHY, AND OFFENSIVE SPEECH   430

(1) Obscenity and Pornography   431

[*Regina v. Hicklin*]   431

Roth v. United States and *Alberts v. California*   438

Stanley v. Georgia   442

□ INSIDE THE COURT: Letter from Justice Black to Justice Harlan, December 10, 1969   443

Miller v. California   444

Paris Adult Theatre I v. Slaton   449

New York v. Ferber   455

City of Erie v. Pap's A.M.   459

Reno v. American Civil Liberties Union   465

Ashcroft v. Free Speech Coalition   474

(2) Fighting Words and Offensive Speech   479

[*Packer Corporation v. Utah*]   480

[*Public Utilities Commission v. Pollak*]   481

[*Erzoznik v. City of Jacksonville*]   481

Cohen v. California   485

Federal Communications Commission v. Pacifica Foundation   489

Bethel School District No. 403 v. Fraser   495

R.A.V. v. City of St. Paul, Minnesota   499

Wisconsin v. Mitchell   508

Virginia v. Black   510

Rust v. Sullivan   517

□ IN COMPARATIVE PERSPECTIVE: Communitarianism, Feminism, and the Canadian Supreme Court's Rulings on Hate Speech and Pornography   522

C. Libel   526

[*Beauharnais v. Illinois*]   526

[*Milkovich v. Lorain Journal Co.*]   529

[*Time, Inc. v. Hill*]   531

☐ the development of law: Other Important Rulings on Libel   532

The New York Times Company v. Sullivan   534

Gertz v. Robert Welch, Inc.   540

Masson v. The New Yorker Magazine   546

Cox Broadcasting Corporation v. Cohn   549

D. Commercial Speech   551

[*Valentine v. Chrestensen*]   551

[*Central Hudson Gas & Electric Corp. v. Public Service Commission of New York*]   553

☐ the development of law: Other Important Rulings on Commercial Speech and the First Amendment   555

Bigelow v. Virginia   559

44 Liquormart, Inc. v. Rhode Island   564

Lorillard Tobacco Co. v. Reilly   572

E. Freedom of the Press   578

(1) The Doctrine of No Prior Restraint   580

Near v. State of Minnesota ex rel. Olson   583

New York Times Company v. United States   586

(2) Indirect Prior Restraints   594

Branzburg v. Hayes, In re Pappas, and *United States v. Caldwell*   597

Houchins v. KQED, Inc.   603

F. Regulating the Broadcast and Cable Media, and the Internet   606

Red Lion Broadcasting Co., Inc. v. Federal Communications Commission   612

Federal Communications Commission v. Pacifica Foundation (reprise)   614

Denver Area Educational Telecommunications Consortium, Inc. v. Federal Communications Commission   615

Reno v. American Civil Liberties Union (reprise)   620

Ashcroft v. American Civil Liberties Union   621

United States v. American Library Association   626

G. FAIR TRIAL/FREE PRESS CONTROVERSIES   630

[*Sheppard v. Maxwell*]   631

[*Nebraska Press Association v. Stuart*]   632

[*Gannett Co. v. DePasquale*]   632

[*Richmond Newspapers, Inc. v. Virginia*]   633

Globe Newspaper Company v. Superior Court for the County of Norfolk   635

H. SYMBOLIC SPEECH AND SPEECH-PLUS-CONDUCT   637

(1) Symbolic Speech   638

[*United States v. O'Brien*]   639

West Virginia State Board of Education v. Barnette   641

Tinker v. Des Moines Independent Community School District   650

Texas v. Johnson   653

(2) Speech-Plus-Conduct   660

[*Hague v. Committee for Industrial Organization (CIO)*]   660

☐ THE DEVELOPMENT OF LAW: Rulings Extending the Concept of a Public Forum   662

☐ THE DEVELOPMENT OF LAW: Places That Have Been Held Not to Be Public Forums   663

[*Hurley v. Irish-American Gay, Lesbian, and Bisexual Group of Boston*]   665

I. FREEDOM OF ASSOCIATION   666

[*Bell v. Maryland*]   670

National Association for the Advancement of Colored People v. Alabama   673

Roberts v. United States Jaycees   676

Boy Scouts of America v. Dale   679

CHAPTER 6 ■ *Freedom from and of Religion* 688

A. THE (DIS)ESTABLISHMENT OF RELIGION   697

☐ CONSTITUTIONAL HISTORY: Religious Displays in Public Places and the Establishment Clause   700

☐ THE DEVELOPMENT OF LAW: Major Rulings Upholding Governmental Aid or Support of Religion over Establishment Clause Objections   710

☐ THE DEVELOPMENT OF LAW: Major Rulings Striking Down Laws and Policies for Violating the Establishment Clause   713

Everson v. Board of Education of Ewing Township   716

Engel v. Vitale   723

Abington School District v. Schempp and *Murray v. Curlett*   728

Lemon v. Kurtzman, Earley v. DiCenso, and *Robinson v. DiCenso*   733

Wallace v. Jaffree   740

☐ INSIDE THE COURT: Justice Kennedy Switches Positions and the Outcome in *Lee v. Wiesman*   749

Lee v. Weisman   751

Zobrest v. Catalina Foothills School District   756

Board of Education of Kiryas Joel Village School District v. Grumet   760

Rosenberger v. The Rector and Visitors of the University of Virginia   769

Agostini v. Felton   781

Zelman v. Simmons-Harris   787

Elk Grove Unified School District v. Newdow (reprise)   798

B. FREE EXERCISE OF RELIGION   798

[United States v. Ballard]   800

☐ THE DEVELOPMENT OF LAW: Major Rulings Denying Free Exercise Claims   803

Sherbert v. Verner   806

☐ THE DEVELOPMENT OF LAW: Major Rulings Upholding Free Exercise Claims   810

Wisconsin v. Yoder   812

Employment Division, Department of Human Resources of Oregon v. Smith   816

Church of the Lukumi Babalu Aye v. City of Hialeah   825

City of Boerne v. Flores   832

Locke v. Davey   841

☐ IN COMPARATIVE PERSPECTIVE: The *Self-Defense Forces Enshrinement Case*, the Supreme Court of Japan, and Religious Minorities   845

CHAPTER 7 ■ *The Fourth Amendment Guarantee against Unreasonable Searches and Seizures*   850

A. REQUIREMENTS FOR A WARRANT AND REASONABLE SEARCHES AND SEIZURES   853

[*Chapman v. United States*]   854

[*Maryland v. Buie*]   855

Chimel v. California   858

Arizona v. Hicks   861

B. EXCEPTIONS TO THE WARRANT REQUIREMENT   864

[*Schneckloth v. Bustamonte*]   864

[*California v. Hodari D.*]   866

[*Florida v. Bostick*]   868

[*United States v. Verdugo-Urquidez*]   870

[*Gould v. United States*]   872

[*Warden v. Hayden*]   872

☐ INSIDE THE COURT: Memorandum from Justice William J. Brennan to Chief Justice Earl Warren on *Terry v. Ohio*   873

Terry v. Ohio   875

United States v. Sokolow   880

Illinois v. Wardlow   884

Bond v. United States   886

Minnesota v. Dickerson   888

United States v. Santana   892

County of Riverside v. McLaughlin   894

C. THE SPECIAL PROBLEMS OF AUTOMOBILES IN A MOBILE SOCIETY   897

[*Carroll v. United States*]   897

☐ THE DEVELOPMENT OF LAW: Automobiles and Border Patrol Searches   899

[*United States v. Chadwick*]   900

United States v. Robinson   903

Illinois v. Lidster   908

☐ INSIDE THE COURT: Memorandum from Justice Sandra Day O'Connor on *California v. Acevedo*   911

California v. Acevedo   912

Knowles v. Iowa   916

Atwater v. Lago Vista   918

D. OTHER GOVERNMENTAL SEARCHES IN THE ADMINISTRATIVE STATE   924

[*Frank v. Maryland*]   924

[*Camara v. Municipal Court*]   925

[*New York v. Burger*]   926

☐ THE DEVELOPMENT OF LAW: Searches by Government Officials in the Administrative State   928

National Treasury Employees Union v. Von Raab   931

Vernonia School District 47J v. Acton   938

Ferguson v. Charleston   944

Board of Education of Independent School District No. 92 of Pottawatomie City v. Earls   950

E. WIRETAPPING, BUGGING, AND POLICE SURVEILLANCE   954

[*Boyd v. United States*]   954

[*Silverman v. United States*]   956

[*United States v. White*]   959

☐ INSIDE THE COURT: Letter from Chief Justice Taft on *Olmstead v. United States*, Holmes, Prohibition, and the Supreme Court   961

Olmstead v. United States   962

Katz v. United States   965

California v. Ciraolo   969

Minnesota v. Carter   973

☐ THE DEVELOPMENT OF LAW: Other Important Rulings on Governmental Wiretapping and Electronic Surveillance   977

Kyllo v. United States 978

☐ THE DEVELOPMENT OF LAW: The USA PATRIOT Act of
2001, Wiretaps, and the Foreign Intelligence Surveillance
Court 983

F. THE EXCLUSIONARY RULE 985

[*Weeks v. United States*] 986

[*Wolf v. Colorado*] 986

[*Elkins v. United States*] 987

[*Stone v. Powell*] 988

Mapp v. Ohio 990

☐ INSIDE THE COURT: Letter from Justice Stewart to Justice Clark
on *Mapp v. Ohio* 992

Nix v. Williams 998

United States v. Leon and *Massachusetts v. Sheppard* 1003

Arizona v. Evans 1015

CHAPTER 8 ■ *The Fifth Amendment Guarantee against
Self-Accusation* 1018

☐ CONSTITUTIONAL HISTORY: The Accusatorial and Inquisitorial
Systems Compared in the Medieval Period 1021

A. COERCED CONFESSIONS AND POLICE
INTERROGATIONS 1027

[*Escobedo v. Illinois*] 1028

[*Edwards v. Arizona*] 1031

[*Minnick v. Mississippi*] 1031

[*Chapman v. California*] 1033

☐ INSIDE THE COURT: Chief Justice Earl Warren, *Miranda v.
Arizona*, and the Attack on the Court 1035

Miranda v. Arizona 1037

In re Gault 1048

Rhode Island v. Innis 1051

Duckworth v. Eagan 1055

Arizona v. Fulminante 1060

Dickerson v. United States 1064

Missouri v. Seibert 1070

United States v. Patane   1074

☐ THE DEVELOPMENT OF LAW: Other Court Rulings on Coerced Confessions and Limiting *Miranda*   1077

☐ IN COMPARATIVE PERSPECTIVE: The Right to Remain Silent and the Exclusion of Incriminating Statements in England, France, Germany, and Italy   1081

B. GRANTS OF IMMUNITY   1083

C. REAL VERSUS TESTIMONIAL EVIDENCE   1084

☐ THE DEVELOPMENT OF LAW: Rulings on Real versus Testimonial Evidence   1085

D. REQUIRED RECORDS, PRIVATE PAPERS, AND CUSTODIAL POSSESSION   1086

☐ THE DEVELOPMENT OF LAW: Rulings on Required Records and Private Papers   1089

CHAPTER 9 ■ *The Right to Counsel and Other Procedural Guarantees*   1091

A. THE RIGHT TO COUNSEL   1091

☐ THE DEVELOPMENT OF LAW: Rulings Extending the Right to Counsel throughout the Criminal Justice System   1094

Powell v. Alabama   1096

Gideon v. Wainwright   1099

Argersinger v. Hamlin   1103

B. PLEA BARGAINING AND THE RIGHT TO EFFECTIVE COUNSEL   1106

[*Strickland v. Washington*]   1107

☐ THE DEVELOPMENT OF LAW: Rulings on Plea Bargaining and Effective Counsel   1109

Bordenkircher v. Hayes   1112

C. INDICTMENT BY A GRAND JURY   1115

Hurtado v. California (reprise)   1117

D. THE RIGHT TO AN IMPARTIAL JURY TRIAL   1117

Duncan v. Louisiana (reprise)   1123

Batson v. Kentucky   1123

A. L. Lockhart v. McCree   1126

Williams v. Florida   1131

Burch v. Louisiana   1133

E.   A Speedy and Public Trial   1135

F.   The Right to Be Informed of Charges and to Confront Accusers   1136

G.   The Guarantee against Double Jeopardy   1139

Palko v. Connecticut (reprise)   1139

H.   The Guarantee against Excessive Bail and Fines   1143

I.   Indigents and the Criminal Justice System   1145

☐ the development of law: Other Rulings on Indigents and the Judicial System   1146

CHAPTER 10 ■ *Cruel and Unusual Punishment*   1149

A.   Noncapital Punishment   1152

[*Robinson v. California*]   1152

[*Hudson v. McMillian*]   1153

Ewing v. California   1156

B.   Capital Punishment   1161

☐ constitutional history: The Imposition and Execution of Capital Punishment   1165

☐ in comparative perspective: Capital Punishment around the World   1167

☐ inside the court: Justice Arthur Goldberg's Role in the Controversy over Capital Punishment and Opinion in *Rudolph v. Alabama*   1168

Furman v. Georgia, Jackson v. Georgia, and *Branch v. Texas*   1172

Lockett v. Ohio   1183

McCleskey v. Kemp   1189

☐ inside the court: Justice Scalia's Unpublished Memorandum on *McCleskey v. Kemp,* indicating that statistics show racial prejudice in death penalty sentencing   1190

Payne v. Tennessee   1200

Morgan v. Illinois 1204

Atkins v. Virginia 1206

☐ THE DEVELOPMENT OF LAW: Other Post-*Furman* Rulings on Capital Punishment 1213

☐ IN COMPARATIVE PERSPECTIVE: The South African Constitutional Court Declares Capital Punishment Unconstitutional 1218

CHAPTER 11 ■ *The Right of Privacy* 1222

A. PRIVACY AND REPRODUCTIVE FREEDOM 1226

[*Meyer v. Nebraska*] 1226

[*Skinner v. Oklahoma*] 1226

[*Eisenstadt v. Baird*] 1227

[*City of Akron v. Akron Center for Reproductive Health*] 1230

[*Webster v. Reproductive Health Services*] 1234

Buck v. Bell 1236

Griswold v. Connecticut (reprise) 1237

☐ INSIDE THE COURT: The Oral Argument and Decision-Making Process in *Roe v. Wade* 1237

Roe v. Wade 1242

Maher v. Roe 1251

☐ THE DEVELOPMENT OF LAW: Other Post-*Roe* Rulings on Abortion 1255

Rust v. Sullivan (reprise) 1258

☐ INSIDE THE COURT: Drafting the Opinion for the Court in *Planned Parenthood of Southeastern Pennsylvania v. Casey* 1259

Planned Parenthood of Southeastern Pennsylvania v. Casey 1260

Stenberg v. Carhart 1272

☐ THE DEVELOPMENT OF LAW: State Laws Regulating Abortion 1282

B. PRIVACY AND PERSONAL AUTONOMY 1285

[*Moore v. City of East Cleveland*] 1285

[*Whalen v. Roe*] 1287

☐ INSIDE THE COURT: Vote Switching in *Bowers v. Hardwick* and Justice Powell's April 8, 1986, Memorandum 1290

Commonwealth of Kentucky v. Wasson (reprise) 1292

Lawrence v. Texas   1293

Cruzan by Cruzan v. Director, Missouri Department of Health   1305

Washington v. Glucksberg and *Vacco v. Quill*   1313

CHAPTER 12 ■ *The Equal Protection of the Laws*   1325

[*Yick Wo v. Hopkins*]   1325

[*United States v. Carolene Products, Co.*]   1326

☐ THE DEVELOPMENT OF LAW: The Supreme Court's Evolving Equal Protection Standards and Tests   1330

[*City of Cleburne, Texas v. Cleburne Living Center*]   1332

A. RACIAL DISCRIMINATION AND STATE ACTION   1336

[*Strauder v. West Virginia*]   1338

☐ CONSTITUTIONAL HISTORY: *Loving v. Virginia* and Bans on Interracial Marriage   1343

☐ THE DEVELOPMENT OF LAW: Other Rulings on State Action   1346

[*Edmonson v. Leesville Concrete Co.*]   1348

[*Bob Jones University v. United States*]   1348

[*Runyon v. McCrary*]   1349

[*Patterson v. McLean Credit Union*]   1350

Dred Scott v. Sandford   1352

The Civil Rights Cases   1363

Plessy v. Ferguson   1372

Shelley v. Kraemer   1377

☐ CONSTITUTIONAL HISTORY: A Chronology of the Civil Rights Movement and the Court   1379

B. RACIAL DISCRIMINATION IN EDUCATION   1382

[*Missouri ex rel. Gaines v. Canada*]   1383

[*Sweatt v. Painter*]   1383

[*McLaurin v. Oklahoma State Regents*]   1383

[*Alexander v. Holmes County Board of Education*]   1387

[*Board of Education of Oklahoma City Public Schools v. Dowell*]   1390

Brown v. Board of Education of Topeka, Kansas (Brown I)   1395

☐ INSIDE THE COURT: William H. Rehnquist's Memorandum to Justice Robert Jackson on *Brown v. Board of Education*   1400

☐ INSIDE THE COURT: Justice Robert H. Jackson's Unpublished Memorandum on *Brown v. Board of Education*   1401

Bolling v. Sharpe   1406

Brown v. Board of Education of Topeka, Kansas (Brown II)   1407

Cooper v. Aaron   1410

Swann v. Charlotte-Mecklenburg Board of Education   1416

Milliken v. Bradley   1421

Freeman v. Pitts   1425

United States v. Fordice   1428

☐ THE DEVELOPMENT OF LAW: Other Rulings on School Desegregation   1432

C. AFFIRMATIVE ACTION AND REVERSE DISCRIMINATION   1435

[DeFunis v. Odegaard]   1436

Regents of the University of California v. Bakke   1442

☐ THE DEVELOPMENT OF LAW: Other Rulings on Affirmative Action and Reverse Discrimination   1452

City of Richmond v. J. A. Croson   1456

Northeastern Florida Chapter of the Associated General Contractors of America v. City of Jacksonville, Florida   1468

Adarand Constructors, Inc. v. Peña   1471

Gratz v. Bollinger   1483

Grutter v. Bollinger   1488

D. NONRACIAL CLASSIFICATIONS AND THE EQUAL PROTECTION OF THE LAWS   1497

(1) Gender-Based Discrimination   1497

[Muller v. Oregon]   1498

☐ CONSTITUTIONAL HISTORY: The Equal Rights Amendment   1500

☐ THE DEVELOPMENT OF LAW: Other Rulings Striking Down Gender-Based Distinctions under the Constitution   1501

☐ THE DEVELOPMENT OF LAW: Other Rulings Upholding Gender-Based Distinctions under the Constitution   1503

Frontiero v. Richardson 1505

Craig v. Boren 1509

Michael M. v. Superior Court of Sonoma County 1513

United States v. Virginia 1517

☐ THE DEVELOPMENT OF LAW: Rulings Dealing with Gender Discrimination and Statutory Interpretation 1529

(2) Discrimination against Gays and Lesbians 1533

Romer v. Evans 1534

Lawrence v. Texas (reprise) 1545

☐ IN COMPARATIVE PERSPECTIVE: Canadian Courts Forbid Discrimination against Homosexuals and Same-Sex Marriages 1545

(3) Wealth, Poverty, and Illegitimacy 1547

Shapiro v. Thompson 1549

San Antonio Independent School District v. Rodriguez 1553

☐ THE DEVELOPMENT OF LAW: Rulings on Residency Requirements, the Right to Interstate Travel, and Indigency 1560

☐ THE DEVELOPMENT OF LAW: Other Rulings Dealing with Illegitimate Children 1562

(4) Alienage and Age 1564

☐ THE DEVELOPMENT OF LAW: Rulings on the Classification of Aliens 1565

☐ THE DEVELOPMENT OF LAW: Recent Rulings on Age Discrimination 1567

Plyler v. Doe 1569

(5) Mental Illness and Retardation 1574

Heller v. Doe 1576

RESEARCHING LEGAL MATERIALS 1581

THE HOW, WHY, AND WHAT TO BRIEFING AND CITING COURT CASES 1583

MEMBERS OF THE SUPREME COURT OF THE UNITED STATES 1587

BIOGRAPHIES OF CURRENT JUSTICES   1591

GLOSSARY   1597

GENERAL INDEX   1605

INDEX OF CASES   1619

ILLUSTRATIONS

The Supreme Court, 2003   85
Figure 2.1 Avenues of Appeal   106
Figure 2.2 Jurisdictional Map of the U.S. Courts of Appeal and
U.S. District Courts   109
Page from Docket Book   177
Members of the Burger Court shaking hands before going on
the bench   179
The Justices' private conference room   189
"Hooverville" during the Great Depression   242
Cartoon depicting the Supreme Court's backlog of cases in 1883
due to the growing amount of litigation challenging government
regulation   257
Picketers from the National Association for the Advancement
of Colored People (NAACP) protesting lynching   312
Justice Benjamin Cardozo and Chief Justice Charles Evans
Hughes in 1937   326
Justices Oliver Wendell Holmes and Louis D. Brandeis   398
Benjamin Gitlow   407
A cross burning   422
Justice Hugo Black   428
Letter from Justice Black   443
Roger Baldwin, the founder of the American Civil Liberties
Union   466
John and Mary Beth Tinker   651
Gregory Johnson being arrested after setting fire to the
American flag   654
NAACP protesters at the time of *NAACP v. Alabama* (1958)   674
Crèche & Menorah   702
Memos from J. Sandra D. O'Connor   911
Dollee Mapp   991
Letter from Justice Stewart   992
An early "Impeach Earl Warren" sign in 1960   1047
The Scottsboro boys with their attorney Samuel S. Leibowitz   1093
Clarence Gideon in 1964   1100
Clarence Gideon's petition to the Supreme Court   1102
Justice Goldberg's Memo in *Rudolph v. Alabama*   1168

Justice Scalia's Unpublished Memorandum in *McCleskey v. Kemp* 1190
Justice William O. Douglas   1235
Norma Mc Corvey   1244
Demonstration on the steps of the Supreme Court protesting
rulings on abortion   1254
Memo from Justice Powell   1293
John Lawrence and Tyron Garner, who were arrested for
violating Texas's sodomy law   1294
The Klu Klux Klan hold a march on the nation's Capitol
in 1925   1339
Interracial marriage prohibition laws   1344
George McLaurin segregated and required to sit outside of
his classroom at the University of Oklahoma in 1948.   1384
"Separate but equal" in West Memphis, Tennessee, in the
early 1950s   1389
Linda Brown, at age nine, in 1952   1399
William H. Rehnquist's Memo on *Brown v. Board of Education*   1400
Justices Ruth Bader Ginsburg and Sandra Day O'Connor   1520
Justice William J. Brennan, Jr. in his chambers   1554

PREFACE

Because there is no dearth of casebooks, the appearance of another one needs a defense, or at least a further explanation of how it still differs from others. What distinguishes this casebook is its treatment and incorporation of material on constitutional history and American politics. Few casebooks pay adequate attention to the forces of history and politics on the course of constitutional law. Yet constitutional law, history, and politics are intimately intertwined.

The Constitution and Bill of Rights, of course, are political documents. Rooted in historic struggles and based on political compromises, their provisions and guarantees continue to invite competing interpretations and political contests over, for example, the separation of powers between Congress and the president, federalism, and civil rights and liberties. Because the Constitution says nothing about *who* should interpret it or about *how* it should be interpreted, constitutional law is animated by the politics of interpretation and the interpretation of politics. Neither do we have a single accepted theory of constitutional interpretation, nor do the justices write on a clean slate. Instead, we face constitutional choices and competing judicial and political philosophies.

The Supreme Court's decisions do not occur in a political vacuum, standing apart from history and the political struggles within the Court and the country. Virtually every major political controversy raises questions of constitutional law, no less than do technological changes and social movements and economic forces. The development and direction of constitutional law also shift (more or less quickly) with the Court's changing composition. Members of the Court, just as other citizens, differ in their readings of the Constitution. Moreover, major confrontations in constitutional law and politics, such as those over the powers of the national government, or slavery, school desegregation, and abortion, involve continuing struggles that run from one generation to another. In the course of those struggles, constitutional law evolves with changes in the Court and the country. The Constitution and the Bill of Rights bind the Court, other political institutions, and the people in an ongoing dialogue over the exercise of and limitations on governmental power.

By providing the historical context and explaining the political contests among the justices and between the Court and the country, this casebook aims to make constitutional law more accessible for students. History and politics are also important for students' analyzing of particular decisions and their relation to developments and changes in constitutional law and politics. They are crucial as well for students trying critically to evaluate competing interpretations and to appreciate the political consequences of alternative interpretations. And they are essential if students are to engage in the dialogue of constitutional law, confront constitutional choices, and come to terms with their and others' views of the Constitution and the Bill of Rights.

The casebook remains different in several ways. First, it comes in two very comprehensive, anthology-like volumes. Volume I, *Struggles for Power and Governmental Accountability*, deals with separation of powers, federalism, and the democratic process. Volume II, *Civil Rights and Civil Liberties*, is devoted to the enduring struggles to limit governmental power and guarantee civil rights and liberties. As a two-volume set, it not only includes more Court decisions than other casebooks but also permits more introductory background material. Instructors, therefore, have greater flexibility when assigning cases, and students will find useful the additional cases and guides to other cases and resources.

Second, two chapters dealing with the politics of constitutional interpretation and Supreme Court decision making contain material not usually found in casebooks. Chapter 1 goes beyond dealing with the establishment of the power of judicial review, and political criticisms of the Court's exercise of that power, to examining rival theories of constitutional interpretation. Students are introduced to differing judicial and political philosophies and referred to cases and opinions found in subsequent chapters that illustrate these different positions on constitutional interpretation. Chapter 2 combines an introduction to jurisdictional matters, such as standing, with a discussion of how the Court operates as an institution and in relation to other political institutions, which may help promote compliance with and implementation of its rulings, or thwart and even reverse them. In short, Chapter 1 prepares students for critically evaluating competing interpretations of constitutional provisions in subsequent chapters. And Chapter 2 prepares them for understanding the political struggles that take place within the Court as well as between the Court and other political institutions over its decisions. While the volumes together are designed for a two-semester course, both of these chapters, as well as The Constitution of the United States, are included in each volume for the convenience of teachers and students who might be involved in only one of the two-semester constitutional law course sequence.

As already noted, each chapter and subsection contains a lengthy introductory essay. These essays focus on particular provisions of the Constitution and the Bill of Rights, why they took the form they did, and what controversies surrounded them during the Founding period and later. Most begin with the debates at the Constitutional Convention of 1787 and those between the Federalists and Anti-Federalists during the ratification period, and then review subsequent cases and controversies. Besides providing a historical and political context for the cases in each chapter, the essays highlight the continuity and changes in the debates over constitutional law and politics that run from the Founding period to those rulings of the Rehnquist Court.

Something should also be said about the case excerpts. Most are preceded by "headnotes," short explanations of the facts and why the case was appealed to the Court. But, unlike the brief (and usually dry) headnotes typically found in casebooks, these reveal something about the personal and political struggles of those who appeal to the Court. Throughout, there is an attempt to help students understand the judicial and political process and appreciate how questions of constitutional law are embedded in everyday life. For this reason, students will also find excerpts from oral arguments before the Court and other materials bearing on the political struggles that they represent. Along with excerpts of the opinion announcing the decision of the Court, students will frequently encounter excerpts from separate concurring and dissenting opinions. These are included to help students appreciate the choices that the Court and they must make when interpreting the Constitution and the Bill of Rights. Related to this is a good suggestion made by a number of adopters of the first edition: the headnotes now record the actual Court vote.

In addition, each volume contains four types of boxes, which include materials that further place constitutional interpretation and law in historical and political perspective. One set of boxes, *CONSTITU-TIONAL HISTORY*, presents important background material, such as excerpts from John Locke on the connection between property and liberty and explanatory notes on the "Watergate crisis" and the battle over the Equal Rights Amendment. Another set, *THE DEVELOP-MENT OF LAW*, shows changes and patterns in constitutional law and refers students to other cases on topics of special interest. The third, *INSIDE THE COURT*, illustrates the internal dynamics of the Court when engaged in the process of constitutional interpretation and deciding cases. Finally, *IN COMPARATIVE PERSPECTIVE* boxes illustrate how courts around the world have dealt with similar constitutional controversies. These boxes are indicated by □ in the contents. Also included at the end of each volume are brief biographies of the current sitting justices.

This sixth edition updates the introductions, the cases, and the four types of boxes, as well as incorporates the highlights of the Court's terms through the 2003–2004 term. Along with adding a number of new boxes on *CONSTITUTIONAL HISTORY*, INSIDE THE COURT, *THE DEVELOPMENT OF LAW*, and *IN COMPARATIVE PERSPECTIVE*, this edition includes a number of other new features. RESEARCHING LEGAL MATERIALS provides a guide for students to access and to search for legal materials and law-related sources on the Internet. THE HOW, WHY, and WHAT TO BRIEFING and CITING COURT CASES discusses the how, why, and what to briefing and citing court decisions and opinions. In response to requests from adopters of past editions, the chapter titled "Economic Rights and American Capitalism" is included in both volumes; it appears as Chapter 9 in Volume I and remains Chapter 3 in Volume II. Besides maintaining the *Supreme Court Web Watch* (at http://www.wwnorton.com/scww/), with links to pertinent information on the Supreme Court and the Constitution, in order to keep the fourth edition up to date, I will continue to write, and Norton to publish each September, an annual supplement that we call *Supreme Court Watch*.

What follows will, it is hoped, enrich students' understanding of constitutional law, politics, and history, as well as open them to the possibilities in interpreting the Constitution and the Bill of Rights. But the Constitution is where students should begin their study, and it is assuredly where they will return again and again.

D. M. O.

ACKNOWLEDGMENTS

I am indebted to my students and colleagues for the favorable reception that they gave earlier editions, but I still owe a larger debt to Claudine, my wife, for giving me the freedom to work as I do and to enjoy life's pleasures with Benjamin, Sara, and Talia. I continue to be grateful for the inspiration and support of my teacher, C. Herman Pritchett, University of California, Santa Barbara, and my colleagues at the University of Virginia, Henry J. Abraham and David Klein. Ira Carmen, University of Illinois; Phillip Cooper, University of Vermont; Jerome Hanus, The American University; and Gerald Rosenberg, University of Chicago, read and made very helpful suggestions on the first edition for which I am grateful. Also, I thank Thomas Baker, Texas Tech University; Sue Davis, University of Delaware; Susan Fino, Wayne State University; Christine Harrington, New York University; and H. N. Hirsch, University of California, San Diego, for offering comments that helped shape the casebook early on in its development.

This sixth edition incurs even more debt. I very much appreciate the support and suggestions made by countless undergraduate and graduate students. In particular, several current and former graduate students deserve special recognition: Christopher Banks, Cindy Boyles, Stephen Bragaw, Steve Brown, John Blakeman, Richard Drew, Scott Gerber, Jeffrey Hockett, Robert Hume, Edward Kelly, Charles Kromkowski, William Mandel, Rick Mayes, Laura Mirsky, Darby Morrisroe, Stacy Nyikos, Gavin Reddick, James Staab, Jon Talotta, Stephen Tauber, and James Todd. Numerous colleagues around the country offered support and very helpful suggestions for changes and corrections that have improved this edition. Among many other colleagues, I am grateful to the following: John Q. Adams, Maria Antonini, Gordon Baker, Jack Barlow, John Brigham, Joseph Callahan, David Carrithers, Richard Claude, George F. Cole, Ronald Collins, Sheila Collins, Akiba Covitz, John Domino, Louis Fisher, Jack Fruchtman, Jr., Hal Goldman, Leslie Goldstein, Susan Grogan, Robert Hardgrave, Jr., Harry N. Hirsch, Milton Heumann, Elizabeth Hull, Sidney Heyman, Michael Horan, Carolyn Johnson, Robert M. Johnstone, Nancy Kassop, Paul Kens, Byron Lander, Susan Lawrence, James Lennertz, Robert Katzmann, J. Morgan Kousser, Thomas Lewis, Kevin McGuire, Pricilla Macadeo, David T. Mason, Eddie L. Meaders, Vincent Michelot, Lucas Morel, Bruce Murphy, Jill Norgren, Karen O'Connor, Jack W. Peltason, Marie Provine, Stephen Ross, John Scheb, Guy Scoffoni, David Skover, Rogers Smith, Neil Snortland, Donald Songer, Gene Straughan, Harold Sullivan, John Taylor, James Todd, and Mary Volcansek.

In preparing this sixth edition I benefited from the comments of several reviewers and remain indebted to John C. Blakeman, J. M. Bordelon, Steven Brown, Michelle D. Dearorff, Milton Heumann, Paul Kens, S. A. Dwyer-Shick, Cary Federman, Jack Fruchtman, Jr., David R. Manwaring, Wendy L. Martinek, W. McKercher, David Pogue, Alisa Rosenthal, Daniel E. Smith, Mark Caleb Smith, William R. Stevenson, Jr., Steve Tauber, and Paul Weber.

Finally, the generous support of the American Philosophical Society and the Earhart Foundation contributed to this project as well. Donald Fusting, a patient and wise editor, worked with me on the first two editions, as did Steve Dunn on the third, Sarah Caldwell on the fourth, Ann Marcy on the fifth edition, and Aaron Javsicas on the sixth. Work on these volumes, I should also acknowledge, was indirectly but significantly helped by the U.S. Fulbright Commission. The first edition was largely completed during 1987–1988 while I was a Fulbright Lecturer in Constitutional Studies at Oxford University. The third edition was completed while I was a Fulbright Research Fellow in Japan. And the fourth edition was completed while I held the Fulbright Chair in History and Political Science at the University of Bologna. I am thus deeply indebted to the Fulbright Commission and a number of scholars who made my stays so productive. In particular, I am grateful to Byron Shafer, Yasuo Ohkoshi, Vincent Michelot, and Tiziano Bonazzi. I am grateful as well for permission to reproduce materials here granted by the following individuals and organizations: Justices William J. Brennan, Jr., and Antonin Scalia; the curator of the Supreme Court of the United States; the Library of Congress; Justice Hans Linde of the Oregon State Supreme Court; the Supreme Court Historical Society; the National Portrait Gallery/Smithsonian Institution; *The New York Times*; the Roosevelt Library; Sygma/*New York Times Magazine*; Paula Okamoto; and Wide World Photos.

Constitutional Law and Politics

VOLUME TWO

SIXTH EDITION

THE UNITED STATES CONSTITUTION AND AMENDMENTS

We the people of the United States, in Order to form a more perfect Union, establish Justice, insure domestic Tranquility, provide for the common defence, promote the general Welfare, and secure the Blessings of Liberty to ourselves and our Posterity, do ordain and establish this Constitution for the United States of America.

ARTICLE I

SECTION 1. All legislative Powers herein granted shall be vested in a Congress of the United States, which shall consist of a Senate and House of Representatives.

SECTION 2. The House of Representatives shall be composed of Members chosen every second Year by the People of the several States, and the Electors in each State shall have the Qualifications requisite for Electors of the most numerous Branch of the State Legislature.

No Person shall be a Representative who shall not have attained to the Age of twenty five Years, and been seven Years a Citizen of the United States, and who shall not, when elected, be an Inhabitant of that State in which he shall be chosen.

[Representatives and [direct Taxes] shall be apportioned among the several States [which may be included within this Union,] according to their respective Numbers, which shall be determined by adding to the whole Number of free Persons, including those bound to Service for a

Term of Years, and excluding Indians not taxed, three fifths of all other Persons. *(This clause was changed by section 2 of the Fourteenth Amendment.)*] The actual Enumeration shall be made within three Years after the first Meeting of the Congress of the United States, and within every subsequent Term of ten Years, in such Manner as they shall by Law direct. The Number of Representatives shall not exceed one for every thirty Thousand, but each State shall have at Least one Representative; and until such enumeration shall be made, the State of New Hampshire shall be entitled to chuse three, Massachusetts eight, Rhode-Island and Providence Plantations one, Connecticut five, New-York six, New Jersey four, Pennsylvania eight, Delaware one, Maryland six, Virginia ten, North Carolina five, South Carolina five, and Georgia three.

When vacancies happen in the Representation from any State, the Executive Authority thereof shall issue Writs of Election to fill such Vacancies.

The House of Representatives shall chuse their Speaker and other Officers; and shall have the sole Power of Impeachment.

Section 3. The Senate of the United States shall be composed of two Senators from each State, [chosen by the Legislature thereof, *(This provision was changed by section 1 of the Seventeenth Amendment.)*] for six Years; and each Senator shall have one Vote.

Immediately after they shall be assembled in Consequence of the first Election, they shall be divided as equally as may be into three Classes. The Seats of the Senators of the first Class shall be vacated at the Expiration of the second Year, of the second Class at the Expiration of the fourth Year, and of the third Class at the Expiration of the sixth Year, so that one third may be chosen every second Year; [and if Vacancies happen by Resignation, or otherwise, during the Recess of the Legislature of any State, the Executive thereof may make temporary Appointments until the next Meeting of the Legislature, which shall then fill such Vacancies. *(This clause was changed by section 2 of the Seventeenth Amendment.)*]

No Person shall be a Senator who shall not have attained to the Age of thirty Years, and been nine Years a Citizen of the United States, and who shall not, when elected, be an Inhabitant of that State for which he shall be chosen.

The Vice President of the United States shall be President of the Senate, but shall have no Vote, unless they be equally divided.

The Senate shall chuse their other Officers, and also a President pro tempore, in the Absence of the Vice President, or when he shall exercise the Office of President of the United States.

The Senate shall have the sole Power to try all Impeachments. When sitting for that Purpose, they shall be on Oath or Affirmation. When the President of the United States is tried, the Chief Justice shall preside: And no Person shall be convicted without the Concurrence of two thirds of the Members present.

Judgment in Cases of Impeachment shall not extend further than to removal from Office, and disqualification to hold and enjoy any Office of honor, Trust or Profit under the United States: but the Party convicted shall nevertheless be liable and subject to Indictment, Trial, Judgment and Punishment, according to Law.

SECTION 4. The Times, Places and Manner of holding Elections for Senators and Representatives, shall be prescribed in each State by the Legislature thereof; but the Congress may at any time by Law make or alter such Regulations, except as to the Places of chusing Senators.

The Congress shall assemble at least once in every Year, and such Meeting shall be [on the first Monday in December, *(This provision was changed by section 2 of the Twentieth Amendment.)*] unless they shall by Law appoint a different Day.

SECTION 5. Each House shall be the Judge of the Elections, Returns and Qualifications of its own Members, and a Majority of each shall constitute a Quorum to do Business; but a smaller Number may adjourn from day to day, and may be authorized to compel the Attendance of absent Members, in such Manner, and under such Penalties as each House may provide.

Each House may determine the Rules of its Proceedings, punish its Members for disorderly Behaviour, and, with the Concurrence of two thirds, expel a Member.

Each House shall keep a Journal of its Proceedings, and from time to time publish the same, excepting such Parts as may in their Judgment require Secrecy; and the Yeas and Nays of the Members of either House on any question shall, at the Desire of one fifth of those Present, be entered on the Journal.

Neither House, during the Session of Congress, shall, without the Consent of the other, adjourn for more than three days, nor to any other Place than that in which the two Houses shall be sitting.

SECTION 6. The Senators and Representatives shall receive a Compensation for their Services, to be ascertained by Law, and paid out of the Treasury of the United States. They shall in all Cases, except Treason, Felony and Breach of the Peace, be privileged from Arrest during their Attendance at the Session of their respective Houses, and in going to and returning from the same; and for any Speech or Debate in either House, they shall not be questioned in any other Place.

No Senator or Representative shall, during the Time for which he was elected, be appointed to any civil Office under the Authority of the United States, which shall have been created, or the Emoluments whereof shall have been encreased during such time; and no Person holding any Office under the United States, shall be a Member of either House during his Continuance in Office.

Section 7. All Bills for raising Revenue shall originate in the House of Representatives; but the Senate may propose or concur with Amendments as on other Bills.

Every Bill which shall have passed the House of Representatives and the Senate, shall, before it become a Law, be presented to the President of the United States; If he approve he shall sign it, but if not he shall return it, with his Objections to that House in which it shall have originated, who shall enter the Objections at large on their Journal, and proceed to reconsider it. If after such Reconsideration two thirds of that House shall agree to pass the Bill, it shall be sent, together with the Objections, to the other House, by which it shall likewise be reconsidered, and if approved by two thirds of that House, it shall become a Law. But in all such Cases the Votes of both Houses shall be determined by yeas and Nays, and the Names of the Persons voting for and against the Bill shall be entered on the Journal of each House respectively. If any bill shall not be returned by the President within ten Days (Sundays excepted) after it shall have been presented to him, the Same shall be a Law, in like Manner as if he had signed it, unless the Congress by their Adjournment prevent its Return, in which Case it shall not be a Law.

Every Order, Resolution, or Vote to which the Concurrence of the Senate and House of Representatives may be necessary (except on a question of Adjournment) shall be presented to the President of the United States; and before the Same shall take Effect, shall be approved by him, or being disapproved by him, shall be repassed by two thirds of the Senate and House of Representatives, according to the Rules and Limitations prescribed in the Case of a Bill.

Section 8. The Congress shall have Power To lay and collect Taxes, Duties, Imposts and Excises, to pay the Debts and provide for the common Defence and general Welfare of the United States; but all Duties, Imposts and Excises shall be uniform throughout the United States;

To borrow Money on the credit of the United States;

To regulate Commerce with Foreign Nations, and among the several States, and with the Indian tribes;

To establish an uniform Rule of Naturalization, and uniform Laws on the subject of Bankruptcies throughout the United States;

To coin Money, regulate the Value thereof, and of foreign Coin, and fix the Standard of Weights and Measures;

To provide for the Punishment of counterfeiting the Securities and current Coin of the United States;

To establish Post Offices and post Roads;

To promote the Progress of Science and useful Arts, by securing for limited Times to Authors and Inventors the exclusive Right to their respective Writings and Discoveries;

To constitute Tribunals inferior to the supreme Court;

To define and punish Piracies and Felonies committed on the high Seas, and Offences against the Law of Nations;

To declare War, grant Letters of Marque and Reprisal, and make Rules concerning Captures on Land and Water;

To raise and support Armies, but no Appropriation of Money to that Use shall be for a longer Term than two Years;

To provide and maintain a Navy;

To make Rules for the Government and Regulation of the land and naval Forces;

To provide for calling forth the Militia to execute the Laws of the Union, suppress Insurrections and repel Invasions;

To provide for organizing, arming, and disciplining, the Militia, and for governing such Part of them as may be employed in the Service of the United States, reserving to the States respectively, the Appointment of the Officers, and the Authority of training the Militia according to the discipline prescribed by Congress;

To exercise exclusive Legislation in all Cases whatsoever, over such District (not exceeding ten Miles square) as may, by Cession of particular States, and the Acceptance of Congress, become the Seat of the Government of the United States, and to exercise like Authority over all Places purchased by the Consent of the Legislature of the State in which the Same shall be, for the Erection of Forts, Magazines, Arsenals, dock-Yards, and other needful Buildings;—And

To make all Laws which shall be necessary and proper for carrying into Execution the foregoing Powers, and all other Powers vested by this Constitution in the Government of the United States, or in any Department or Officer thereof.

SECTION 9. The Migration or Importation of such Persons as any of the States now existing shall think proper to admit, shall not be prohibited by the Congress prior to the Year one thousand eight hundred and eight, but a Tax or duty may be imposed on such Importation, not exceeding ten dollars for each Person.

The Privilege of the Writ of Habeas Corpus shall not be suspended, unless when in Cases of Rebellion or Invasion the public Safety may require it.

No Bill of Attainder or ex post facto Law shall be passed.

No Capitation, or other direct, Tax shall be laid, unless in Proportion to the Census or Enumeration herein before directed to be taken.

No Tax or Duty shall be laid on Articles exported from any State.

No Preference shall be given by any Regulation of Commerce or Revenue to the Ports of one State over those of another: nor shall Vessels bound to, or from, one State, be obliged to enter, clear, or pay Duties in another.

No Money shall be drawn from the Treasury, but in Consequence of Appropriations made by Law; and a regular Statement and Account of the Receipts and Expenditures of all public Money shall be published from time to time.

No Title of Nobility shall be granted by the United States: And no Person holding any Office of Profit or Trust under them, shall, without the Consent of the Congress, accept of any present, Emolument, Office, or Title, of any kind whatever, from any King, Prince, or foreign State.

SECTION 10. No State shall enter into any Treaty, Alliance, or Confederation; grant Letters of Marque and Reprisal; coin Money; emit Bills of Credit; make any Thing but gold and silver Coin a Tender in Payment of Debts; pass any Bill of Attainder, ex post facto Law, or Law impairing the Obligation of Contracts, or grant any Title of Nobility.

No State shall, without the Consent of the Congress, lay any Imposts or Duties on Imports or Exports, except what may be absolutely necessary for executing it's inspection Laws: and the net Produce of all Duties and Imposts, laid by any State on Imports or Exports, shall be for the Use of the Treasury of the United States; and all such Laws shall be subject to the Revision and Controul of the Congress.

No State shall, without the Consent of Congress, lay any Duty of Tonnage, keep Troops, or Ships of War in time of Peace, enter into any Agreement or Compact with another State, or with a foreign Power, or engage in War, unless actually invaded, or in such imminent Danger as will not admit of delay.

ARTICLE II

Section 1. The executive Power shall be vested in a President of the United States of America. He shall hold his Office during the Term of four Years, and, together with the Vice President, chosen for the same Term, be elected, as follows

Each State shall appoint, in such Manner as the Legislature thereof may direct, a Number of Electors, equal to the whole Number of Senators and Representatives to which the State may be entitled in the Congress: but no Senator or Representative, or Person holding an Office of Trust or Profit under the United States, shall be appointed an Elector.

[The Electors shall meet in their respective States, and vote by Ballot for two Persons, of whom one at least shall not be an inhabitant of the same State with themselves. And they shall make a List of all the Persons voted for, and of the Number of Votes for each; which List they shall sign and certify, and transmit sealed to the Seat of the Government of the United States, directed to the President of the Senate. The President of the Senate shall, in the Presence of the Senate and House of Representatives, open all the Certificates, and the Votes shall then be counted. The Person having the greatest Number of Votes shall be the President, if such Number be a Majority of the whole Number of Electors appointed; and if there be more than one who have such Majority, and have an equal Number of Votes, then the House of Representatives shall immediately chuse by Ballot one of them for President; and if no Person have a Majority, then from the five highest on the List the said House shall in like Manner chuse the President. But in chusing the President, the Votes shall be taken by States, the Representation from each State having one Vote; A quorum for this purpose shall consist of a Member or Members from two thirds of the States, and a Majority of all the States shall be necessary to a Choice. In every Case, after the Choice of the President, the Person having the greatest Number of Votes of the Electors shall be the Vice President. But if there should remain two or more who have equal Votes, the Senate shall chuse from them by Ballot the Vice President. *(This clause was superseded by the Twelfth Amendment.)*]

The Congress may determine the Time of chusing the Electors, and the Day on which they shall give their Votes; which Day shall be the same throughout the United States.

No Person except a natural born Citizen, or a Citizen of the United States, at the time of the Adoption of this Constitution, shall be eligible to the Office of President; neither shall any Person be eligible to that Office who shall not have attained to the Age of thirty five

Years, and been fourteen Years a Resident within the United States.

[In Case of the Removal of the President from Office, or of his Death, Resignation, or Inability to discharge the Powers and Duties of the said Office, the Same shall devolve on the Vice President, and the Congress may by Law provide for the Case of Removal, Death, Resignation or Inability, both of the President and Vice President, declaring what Officer shall then act as President, and such Officer shall act accordingly, until the Disability be removed, or a President shall be elected. (*This clause was modified by the Twenty-Fifth Amendment.*)]

The President shall, at stated Times, receive for his Services, a Compensation, which shall neither be increased nor diminished during the Period for which he shall have been elected, and he shall not receive within that Period any other Emolument from the United States, or any of them.

Before he enter on the Execution of his Office, he shall take the following Oath or Affirmation:—"I do solemnly swear (or affirm) that I will faithfully execute the Office of President of the United States, and will to the best of my Ability, preserve, protect and defend the Constitution of the United States."

SECTION 2. The President shall be Commander in Chief of the Army and Navy of the United States, and of the Militia of the several States, when called into the actual Service of the United States; he may require the Opinion, in writing, of the principal Officer in each of the executive Departments, upon any Subject relating to the Duties of their respective Offices, and he shall have Power to grant Reprieves and Pardons for Offences against the United States, except in Cases of Impeachment.

He shall have Power, by and with the Advice and Consent of the Senate, to make Treaties, provided two thirds of the Senators present concur; and he shall nominate, and by and with the Advice and Consent of the Senate, shall appoint Ambassadors, other public Ministers and Consuls, Judges of the supreme Court, and all other Officers of the United States, whose Appointments are not herein otherwise provided for, and which shall be established by Law: but the Congress may by Law vest the Appointment of such inferior Officers, as they think proper, in the President alone, in the Courts of Law, or in the Heads of Departments.

The President shall have Power to fill up all Vacancies that may happen during the Recess of the Senate, by granting Commissions which shall expire at the End of their next Session.

SECTION 3. He shall from time to time give to the Congress Information of the State of the Union, and recommend to their Consideration such Measures as he shall judge necessary and expedient; he may, on extraordinary Occasions, convene both Houses, or either of them, and in Case of Disagreement between them, with Respect to the Time of Adjournment, he may adjourn them to such Time as he shall think proper; he shall receive Ambassadors and other public Ministers; he shall take Care that the Laws be faithfully executed, and shall Commission all the Officers of the United States.

Section 4. The President, Vice President and all civil Officers of the United States, shall be removed from Office on Impeachment for, and Conviction of, Treason, Bribery, or other high Crimes and Misdemeanors.

ARTICLE III

Section 1. The judicial Power of the United States, shall be vested in one supreme Court, and in such inferior Courts as the Congress may from time to time ordain and establish. The Judges, both of the supreme and inferior Courts, shall hold their Offices during good Behaviour, and shall, at stated Times receive for their Services, a Compensation, which shall not be diminished during their Continuance in Office.

Section 2. The judicial Power shall extend to all Cases, in Law and Equity, arising under this Constitution, the Laws of the United States, and Treaties made, or which shall be made, under their Authority;—to all Cases affecting Ambassadors, other public Ministers and Consuls;—to all Cases of admiralty and maritime Jurisdiction;—to Controversies to which the United States shall be a Party;—to Controversies between two or more States;—between a State and Citizens of another State;—between Citizens of different States,—between Citizens of the same State claiming Lands under Grants of different States, and between a State, or the Citizens thereof, and foreign States, Citizens or Subjects.

In all Cases affecting Ambassadors, other public Ministers and Consuls, and those in which a State shall be Party, the supreme Court shall have original Jurisdiction. In all the other Cases before mentioned, the supreme Court shall have appellate Jurisdiction, both as to Law and Fact, with such Exceptions, and under such Regulations as the Congress shall make.

The Trial of all Crimes, except in Cases of Impeachment, shall be by Jury; and such Trial shall be held in the State where the said Crimes shall have been committed; but when not committed within any State, the Trial shall be at such Place or Places as the Congress may by Law have directed.

SECTION 3. Treason against the United States, shall consist only in levying War against them, or in adhering to their Enemies, giving them Aid and Comfort. No Person shall be convicted of Treason unless on the Testimony of two Witnesses to the same overt Act, or on Confession in open Court.

The Congress shall have Power to declare the Punishment of Treason, but no Attainder of Treason shall work Corruption of Blood, or Forfeiture except during the Life of the Person attainted.

ARTICLE IV

SECTION 1. Full Faith and Credit shall be given in each State to the public Acts, Records, and judicial Proceedings of every other State; And the Congress may by general Laws prescribe the Manner in which such Acts, Records and Proceedings shall be proved, and the Effect thereof.

SECTION 2. The Citizens of each State shall be entitled to all Privileges and Immunities of Citizens in the several States.

A Person charged in any State with Treason, Felony, or other Crime, who shall flee from Justice, and be found in another State, shall on Demand of the executive Authority of the State from which he fled, be delivered up, to be removed to the State having Jurisdiction of the Crime.

[No Person held to Service or Labour in one State, under the Laws thereof, escaping into another, shall, in Consequence of any Law or Regulation therein, be discharged from such Service or Labour, but shall be delivered up on Claim of the Party to whom such Service or Labour may be due. *(This clause was superseded by the Thirteenth Amendment.)*]

SECTION 3. New States may be admitted by the Congress into this Union; but no new State shall be formed or erected within the Jurisdiction of any other State; nor any State be formed by the Junction of two or more States, or Parts of States, without the Consent of the Legislatures of the States concerned as well as of the Congress.

The Congress shall have Power to dispose of and make all needful Rules and Regulations respecting the Territory or other Property belonging to the United States; and nothing in this Constitution shall be so construed as to Prejudice any Claims of the United States, or of any particular State.

Section 4. The United States shall guarantee to every State in this Union a Republican Form of Government, and shall protect each of them against Invasion; and on Application of the Legislature, or of the Executive (when the Legislature cannot be convened) against domestic Violence.

ARTICLE V

The Congress, whenever two thirds of both Houses shall deem it necessary, shall propose Amendments to this Constitution, or, on the Application of the Legislatures of two thirds of the several States, shall call a Convention for proposing Amendments, which, in either Case, shall be valid to all Intents and Purposes, as Part of this Constitution, when ratified by the legislatures of three fourths of the several States, or by Conventions in three fourths thereof, as the one or the other Mode of Ratification may be proposed by the Congress; Provided that no Amendment which may be made prior to the Year One thousand eight hundred and eight shall in any Manner affect the first and fourth Clauses in the Ninth Section of the first Article; and that no State, without its Consent, shall be deprived of its equal Suffrage in the Senate.

ARTICLE VI

All Debts contracted and Engagements entered into, before the Adoption of this Constitution, shall be as valid against the United States under this Constitution, as under the Confederation.

This Constitution, and the Laws of the United States which shall be made in Pursuance thereof; and all Treaties made, or which shall be made, under the Authority of the United States, shall be the supreme Law of the Land; and the Judges in every State shall be bound thereby, any Thing in the Constitution or Laws of any State to the Contrary notwithstanding.

The Senators and Representatives before mentioned, and the Members of the several State Legislatures, and all executive and judicial Officers, both of the United States and of the several States, shall be bound by Oath or Affirmation, to support this Constitution; but no religious Test shall ever be required as a Qualification to any Office or public Trust under the United States.

ARTICLE VII

The Ratification of the Conventions of nine States, shall be sufficient for the Establishment of this Constitution between the States so ratifying the Same.

DONE in Convention by the Unanimous Consent of the States present the Seventeenth Day of September in the Year of our Lord one thousand seven hundred and Eighty seven and of the Independence of the United States of America the Twelfth.

IN WITNESS whereof We have hereunto subscribed our Names.

AMENDMENT I

[*The first ten amendments (the Bill of Rights) were ratified December 15, 1791.*]

Congress shall make no law respecting an establishment of religion, or prohibiting the free exercise thereof; or abridging the freedom of speech, or of the press, or the right of the people peaceably to assemble, and to petition the Government for a redress of grievances.

AMENDMENT II

A well regulated Militia, being necessary to the security of a free State, the right of the people to keep and bear Arms, shall not be infringed.

AMENDMENT III

No Soldier shall, in time of peace be quartered in any house, without the consent of the Owner, nor in time of war, but in a manner to be prescribed by law.

AMENDMENT IV

The right of the people to be secure in their persons, houses, papers, and effects, against unreasonable searches and seizures, shall not be violated, and no Warrants shall issue, but upon probable cause, supported by Oath or affirmation, and particularly describing the place to be searched, and the persons or things to be seized.

AMENDMENT V

No person shall be held to answer for a capital, or otherwise infamous crime, unless on a presentment or indictment of a Grand Jury, except in cases arising in the land or naval forces, or in the Militia, when in actual service in time of War or public danger; nor shall any person be subject for the same offence to be twice put in jeopardy of life or limb, nor shall be compelled in any criminal case to be a witness against himself, nor be deprived of life, liberty, or property, without due process of law; nor shall private property be taken for public use, without just compensation.

AMENDMENT VI

In all criminal prosecutions, the accused shall enjoy the right to a speedy and public trial, by an impartial jury of the State and district wherein the crime shall have been committed; which district shall have been previously ascertained by law, and to be informed of the nature and cause of the accusation; to be confronted with the witnesses against him; to have compulsory process for obtaining Witnesses in his favor, and to have the assistance of counsel for his defence.

AMENDMENT VII

In Suits at common law, where the value in controversy shall exceed twenty dollars, the right of trial by jury shall be preserved, and no fact tried by a jury, shall be otherwise re-examined in any Court of the United States, than according to the rules of the common law.

AMENDMENT VIII

Excessive bail shall not be required, nor excessive fines imposed, nor cruel and unusual punishments inflicted.

AMENDMENT IX

The enumeration in the Constitution, of certain rights, shall not be construed to deny or disparage others retained by the people.

AMENDMENT X

The powers not delegated to the United States by the Constitution, nor prohibited by it to the States, are reserved to the States respectively, or to the people.

AMENDMENT XI

[Ratified February 7, 1795.]

The Judicial power of the United States shall not be construed to extend to any suit in law or equity, commenced or prosecuted against one of the United States by Citizens of another State, or by Citizens or Subjects of any Foreign State.

AMENDMENT XII

[Ratified June 15, 1804.]

The Electors shall meet in their respective states, and vote by ballot for President and Vice-President, one of whom, at least, shall not be an inhabitant of the same state with themselves; they shall name in their ballots the person voted for as President, and in distinct ballots the person voted for as Vice-President, and they shall make distinct lists of all persons voted for as President, and of all persons voted for as Vice-President, and of the number of votes for each, which lists they shall sign and certify, and transmit sealed to the seat of the government of the United States, directed to the President of the Senate;—The President of the Senate shall, in the presence of the Senate and House of Representatives, open all the certificates and the votes shall then be counted;—The person having the greatest number of votes for President, shall be the President, if such number be a majority of the whole number of Electors appointed; and if no person have such majority, then from the persons having the highest numbers not exceeding three on the list of those voted for as President, the House of Representatives shall choose immediately, by ballot, the President. But in choosing the President, the votes shall be taken by states, the representation from each state having one vote; a quorum for this purpose shall consist of a member or members from two-thirds of the states, and a majority of all the states shall be necessary to a choice. [And if the House of Representatives shall not choose a President whenever the right of choice shall devolve upon them, before the fourth day of March next following, then the Vice-President shall act as President, as in the case of the death or other constitutional disability of the President—*(This clause was superseded by section 3 of the Twentieth Amendment.)*]. The person having the greatest number of votes as Vice-President, shall be the Vice-President, if such number be a majority of the whole number of Electors appointed, and if no person have a majority, then from the two highest numbers on the list, the Senate shall choose the Vice-President; a quorum for the purpose shall consist of two-thirds of the whole number of Senators, and a majority of the whole number shall be necessary to a choice. But no person constitutionally ineligible to the office of President shall be eligible to that of Vice-President of the United States.

AMENDMENT XIII

[Ratified December 6, 1865.]

Section 1. Neither slavery nor involuntary servitude, except as a punishment for crime whereof the party shall have been duly convicted, shall exist within the United States, or any place subject to their jurisdiction.

Section 2. Congress shall have power to enforce this article by appropriate legislation.

AMENDMENT XIV

[Ratified July 9, 1868.]

Section 1. All persons born or naturalized in the United States, and subject to the jurisdiction thereof, are citizens of the United States and of the State wherein they reside. No State shall make or enforce any law which shall abridge the privileges or immunities of citizens of the United States; nor shall any State deprive any person of life, liberty, or property, without due process of law; nor deny to any person within its jurisdiction the equal protection of the laws.

Section 2. Representatives shall be apportioned among the several States according to their respective numbers, counting the whole number of persons in each State, excluding Indians not taxed. But when the right to vote at any election for the choice of electors for President and Vice President of the United States, Representatives in Congress, the Executive and Judicial officers of a State, or the members of the Legislature thereof, is denied to any of the male inhabitants of such State, being twenty-one years of age, and citizens of the United States, or in any way abridged, except for participation in rebellion, or other crime, the basis of representation therein shall be reduced in the proportion which the number of such male citizens shall bear to the whole number of male citizens twenty-one years of age in such State.

SECTION 3. No person shall be a Senator or Representative in Congress, or elector of President and Vice President, or hold any office, civil or military, under the United States, or under any State, who, having previously taken an oath, as a member of Congress, or as an officer of the United States, or as a member of any State legislature, or as an executive or judicial officer of any State, to support the Constitution of the United States, shall have engaged in insurrection or rebellion against the same, or given aid or comfort to the enemies thereof. But Congress may by a vote of two-thirds of each House, remove such disability.

SECTION 4. The validity of the public debt of the United States, authorized by law, including debts incurred for payment of pensions and bounties for services in suppressing insurrection or rebellion, shall not be questioned. But neither the United States nor any State shall assume or pay any debt or obligation incurred in aid of insurrection or rebellion against the United States, or any claim for the loss of emancipation of any slave; but all such debts, obligations and claims shall be held illegal and void.

SECTION 5. The Congress shall have power to enforce, by appropriate legislation, the provisions of this article.

AMENDMENT XV

[Ratified February 3, 1870.]

SECTION 1. The right of citizens of the United States to vote shall not be denied or abridged by the United States or by any State on account of race, color, or previous condition of servitude.

SECTION 2. The Congress shall have power to enforce this article by appropriate legislation.

AMENDMENT XVI

[Ratified February 3, 1913.]

The Congress shall have power to lay and collect taxes on incomes, from whatever source derived, without apportionment among the several States, and without regard to any census or enumeration.

AMENDMENT XVII

[Ratified April 8, 1913.]

The Senate of the United States shall be composed of two Senators from each State, elected by the people thereof, for six years; and each Senator shall have one vote. The electors in each State shall have the qualifications requisite for electors of the most numerous branch of the State legislatures.

When vacancies happen in the representation of any State in the Senate, the executive authority of such State shall issue writs of election to fill such vacancies: *Provided*, That the legislature of any State may empower the executive thereof to make temporary appointments until the people fill the vacancies by election as the legislature may direct.

This amendment shall not be so construed as to affect the election or term of any Senator chosen before it becomes valid as part of the Constitution.

AMENDMENT XVIII

[Ratified January 16, 1919.]

SECTION 1. After one year from the ratification of this article the manufacture, sale, or transportation of intoxicating liquors within, the importation thereof into, or the exportation thereof from the United States and all territory subject to the jurisdiction thereof for beverage purposes is hereby prohibited.

SECTION 2. The Congress and the several States shall have concurrent power to enforce this article by appropriate legislation.

SECTION 3. This article shall be inoperative unless it shall have been ratified as an amendment to the Constitution by the legislatures of the several States, as provided in the Constitution, within seven years from the date of the submission hereof to the States by the Congress.

AMENDMENT XIX

[Ratified August 18, 1920.]

The right of citizens of the United States to vote shall not be denied or abridged by the United States or by any State on account of sex.

Congress shall have power to enforce this article by appropriate legislation.

AMENDMENT XX

[Ratified January 23, 1933.]

SECTION 1. The terms of the President and Vice President shall end at noon on the 20th day of January, and the terms of Senators and Representatives at noon on the 3d day of January, of the years in which such terms would have ended if this article had not been ratified; and the terms of their successors shall then begin.

SECTION 2. The Congress shall assemble at least once in every year, and such meeting shall begin at noon on the 3d day of January, unless they shall by law appoint a different day.

SECTION 3. If, at the time fixed for the beginning of the term of the President, the President elect shall have died, the Vice President elect shall become President. If a President shall not have been chosen before the time fixed for the beginning of his term, or if the President elect shall have failed to qualify, then the Vice President elect shall act as President until a President shall have qualified; and the Congress may by law provide for the case wherein neither a President elect nor a Vice President elect shall have qualified, declaring who shall then act as President, or the manner in which one who is to act shall be selected, and such person shall act accordingly until a President or Vice President shall have qualified.

SECTION 4. The Congress may by law provide for the case of the death of any of the persons from whom the House of Representatives may choose a President whenever the right of choice shall have devolved upon them, and for the case of the death of any of the persons from whom the Senate may choose a Vice President whenever the right of choice shall have devolved upon them.

SECTION 5. Sections 1 and 2 shall take effect on the 15th day of October following the ratification of this article.

SECTION 6. This article shall be inoperative unless it shall have been ratified as an amendment to the Constitution by the legislatures of three-fourths of the several States within seven years from the date of its submission.

AMENDMENT XXI

[Ratified December 5, 1933.]

SECTION 1. The eighteenth article of amendment to the Constitution of the United States is hereby repealed.

SECTION 2. The transportation or importation into any State, Territory, or possession of the United States for delivery or use therein of intoxicating liquors, in violation of the laws thereof, is hereby prohibited.

SECTION 3. This article shall be inoperative unless it shall have been ratified as an amendment to the Constitution by conventions in the several States, as provided in the Constitution, within seven years from the date of the submission hereof to the States by the Congress.

AMENDMENT XXII

[Ratified February 27, 1951.]

SECTION 1. No person shall be elected to the office of the President more than twice, and no person who has held the office of President, or acted as President, for more than two years of a term to which some other person was elected President shall be elected to the office of the President more than once. But this Article shall not apply to any person holding the office of President when this Article was proposed by the Congress, and shall not prevent any person who may be holding the office of President, or acting as President, during the term within which this Article becomes operative from holding the office of President or acting as President during the remainder of such term.

SECTION 2. This article shall be inoperative unless it shall have been ratified as an amendment to the Constitution by the legislatures of three-fourths of the several States within seven years from the date of its submission to the States by the Congress.

AMENDMENT XXIII

[Ratified March 29, 1961.]

SECTION 1. The District constituting the seat of Government of the United States shall appoint in such manner as the Congress may direct:

A number of electors of President and Vice President equal to the whole number of Senators and Representatives in Congress to which the District would be entitled if it were a State, but in no event more than the least populous State; they shall be in addition to those appointed by the States, but they shall be considered, for the purposes of the election of President and Vice President, to be electors appointed by a State; and they shall meet in the District and perform such duties as provided by the twelfth article of amendment.

SECTION 2. The Congress shall have power to enforce this article by appropriate legislation.

AMENDMENT XXIV

[Ratified January 23, 1964.]

SECTION 1. The right of citizens of the United States to vote in any primary or other election for President or Vice President, for electors for President or Vice President, or for Senator or Representatives in Congress, shall not be denied or abridged by the United States or any State by reason of failure to pay any poll tax or other tax.

SECTION 2. The Congress shall have power to enforce this article by appropriate legislation.

AMENDMENT XXV

[Ratified February 10, 1967.]

SECTION 1. In case of the removal of the President from office or of his death or resignation, the Vice President shall become President.

SECTION 2. Whenever there is a vacancy in the office of the Vice President, the President shall nominate a Vice President who shall take office upon confirmation by a majority vote of both Houses of Congress.

SECTION 3. Whenever the President transmits to the President pro tempore of the Senate and the Speaker of the House of Representatives his written declaration that he is unable to discharge the powers and duties of his office, and until he transmits to them a written declaration to the contrary, such powers and duties shall be discharged by the Vice President as Acting President.

Section 4. Whenever the Vice President and a majority of either the principal officers of the executive departments or of such other body as Congress may by law provide, transmit to the President pro tempore of the Senate and the Speaker of the House of Representatives their written declaration that the President is unable to discharge the powers and duties of his office, the Vice President shall immediately assume the powers and duties of the office as Acting President.

Thereafter, when the President transmits to the President pro tempore of the Senate and the Speaker of the House of Representatives his written declaration that no inability exists, he shall resume the powers and duties of his office unless the Vice President and a majority of either the principal officers of the executive department or of such other body as Congress may by law provide, transmit within four days to the President pro tempore of the Senate and the Speaker of the House of Representatives their written declaration that the President is unable to discharge the powers and duties of his office. Thereupon Congress shall decide the issue, assembling within forty-eight hours for that purpose if not in session. If the Congress, within twenty-one days after receipt of the latter written declaration, or, if Congress is not in session, within twenty-one days after Congress is required to assemble, determines by two-thirds vote of both Houses that the President is unable to discharge the powers and duties of his office, the Vice President shall continue to discharge the same as Acting President; otherwise, the President shall resume the powers and duties of his office.

AMENDMENT XXVI

[Ratified July 1, 1971.]

Section 1. The right of citizens of the United States, who are eighteen years of age or older, to vote shall not be denied or abridged by the United States or by any State on account of age.

Section 2. The Congress shall have power to enforce this article by appropriate legislation.

AMENDMENT XXVII

[Ratified May 7, 1992.]

No law varying the compensation for the services of Senators and Representatives shall take effect until an election of Representatives shall have intervened.

I

THE SUPREME COURT, JUDICIAL REVIEW, AND CONSTITUTIONAL POLITICS

Judicial review is one of the greatest and most controversial contributions of the Constitution to the law and politics of government. Article III of the Constitution simply provides that "[t]he judicial Power of the United States, shall be vested in one supreme Court, and in such inferior Courts as the Congress may from time to time ordain and establish." Remarkably, that power is not further defined in the Constitution. But in the course of constitutional politics, *judicial review* has come to be the power of the Supreme Court and the federal judiciary to consider and overturn any congressional and state legislation or other official governmental action deemed inconsistent with the Constitution, Bill of Rights, or federal law.

Like other provisions of the Constitution, the three brief sections in Article III register compromises forged during the Constitutional Convention; the Constitution, as the renowned historian and editor of *The Records of the Federal Convention of 1787*, Max Farrand, observed, is "a bundle of compromises."[1] The first section of Article III makes clear that the Supreme Court is the only federal court constitutionally required. The convention left it for the First Congress to establish a system of lower federal courts, which it did with the Judiciary Act of 1789. Both the convention and the First Congress rejected proposals that would have left the administration of justice entirely in the hands of state courts (with appeals to the Supreme Court). Also rejected was

James Madison's proposal to join justices and executive branch officials in a "council of revision" with a veto power over congressional legislation. Agreement on the importance of guaranteeing judicial independence resulted in the first section of Article III also providing that federal judges "hold their Offices during good Behaviour," subject only to impeachment, and forbidding the diminution of their salaries. That guarantee reflects colonial opposition to royalist judges under the English Crown. One of the grievances listed in the Declaration of Independence as a justification for the Revolutionary War was that King George III had "made Judges dependent on his Will alone."[2] The two remaining sections of Article III specify the kinds of cases and controversies that the federal judiciary may hear (that is, jurisdiction) (see Vol. 1, Ch. 2) and empower Congress to punish individuals for treason.

The Framers, it is fair to say, failed to think through the power of judicial review and its ramifications for constitutional politics. "[T]he framers anticipated some sort of judicial review," noted political scientist Edward S. Corwin, but he added that "it is equally without question that the ideas generally current in 1787 were far from presaging the present role of the Court."[3] In a letter to Corwin, Max Farrand also concluded that "[t]he framers of the Constitution did not realize it themselves [how markedly different their conceptions of judicial review were]: they were struggling to express an idea and their experience was as yet insufficient."[4]

The Constitutional Convention left the power of the judiciary (and much else set forth in the Constitution) to be worked out in practice. As John Mercer, a delegate to the Constitutional Convention from Maryland, observed, "It is a great mistake to suppose that the paper we are to propose will govern the United States. It is the men whom it will bring into the government and interest in maintaining it that is to govern them. The paper will only mark out the mode and the form."[5] The Constitution, of course, is not self-interpreting and crucial principles—such as judicial review, separation of powers, and federalism—are presupposed rather than spelled out. Moreover, in creating separate institutions that share specific and delegated powers, the Constitution amounts to a prescription for political struggle and an invitation for an ongoing debate about enduring constitutional principles.

Almost immediately following the convention in 1787, controversy erupted over the powers granted the national government and in particular to the federal judiciary. Those opposed to the states' ratification of the Constitution, the Anti-Federalists, warned that "[t]here are no well defined limits of the Judiciary Powers, they seem to be left as a boundless ocean."[6] Fears that "the powers of the judiciary may be extended to any degree short of Almighty" were echoed by Thomas

Tredwell, among others, during New York's convention.[7] Robert Yates, one of the most articulate Anti-Federalists writing under the name of Brutus, attacked both the independence and the power of federal judges:

> There is no authority that can remove them, and they cannot be controuled [*sic*] by the laws of the legislature. In short, they are independent of the people, of the legislature, and of every power under heaven. Men placed in this situation will generally soon feel themselves independent of heaven itself. . . .
>
> And in their decisions they will not confine themselves to any fixed or established rules, but will determine, according to what appears to them, the reason and spirit of the constitution. The opinions of the supreme court, whatever they may be, will have the force of law; because there is no power provided in the constitution, that can correct their errors, or controul their adjudiciations. From this court there is no appeal.[8]

"This power in the judicial," charged Brutus, "will enable them to mould the government, into almost any shape they please."

Defenders of the Constitution countered that "the powers given the Supreme Court are not only safe, but constitute a wise and valuable part of the system."[9] In North Carolina's convention, Governor Johnston observed that "[i]t is obvious to every one that there ought to be one Supreme Court for national purposes."[10] During the fight for New York's ratification, Alexander Hamilton provided the classic defense of the judiciary as "the least dangerous branch." Responding to Brutus in *The Federalist*, No. 78, Hamilton argued,

> Whoever attentively considers the different departments of power must perceive, that in a government in which they are separated from each other, the judiciary, from the nature of its functions, will always be the least dangerous to the political rights of the constitution; because it will be least in a capacity to annoy or injure them. The executive not only dispenses the honors, but holds the sword of the community. The legislature not only commands the purse, but prescribes the rules by which the duties and rights of every citizen are to be regulated. The judiciary on the contrary has no influence over either the sword or the purse, no direction either of the strength or of the wealth of the society, and can take no active resolution whatever. It may truly be said to have neither Force nor Will, but merely judgment; and must ultimately depend upon the aid of the executive arm even for the efficacy of its judgments.
>
> If it be said that the legislative body are themselves the constitutional judges of their own powers, and that the construction they put upon them is conclusive upon other departments, it may be answered, that this cannot be the natural presumption, where it is not

to be collected from any particular provisions in the constitution. It is not otherwise to be supposed that the constitution could intend to enable the representatives of the people to substitute their *will* to that of their constituents. It is far more rational to suppose that the courts were designed to be an intermediate body between the people and the legislature, in order, among other things, to keep the latter within the limits assigned to their authority. The interpretation of the laws is the proper and peculiar province of the courts. A constitution is in fact, and must be, regarded by the judges as a fundamental law. It therefore belongs to them as to ascertain its meaning as well as the meaning of any particular act proceeding from the legislative body. If there should happen to be an irreconcilable variance between the two, that which has the superior obligation and validity ought of course to be preferred; or in other words, the constitution ought to be preferred to the statute, the intention of the people to the intention of their agents.

Nor does this conclusion by any means suppose a superiority of the judicial to the legislative power. It only supposes that the power of the people is superior to both; and that where the will of the legislature declared in its statutes, stands in opposition to that of the people declared in the constitution, the judges ought to be governed by the latter, rather than the former. . . .

If then the courts of justice are to be considered as the bulwarks of a limited constitution against legislative encroachments, this consideration will afford a strong argument for the permanent tenure of judicial offices, since nothing will contribute so much as this to that independent spirit in the judges, which must be essential to the faithful performance of so arduous a duty.

The Federalists' interpretation of Article III was advanced by others in the effort to win ratification. In Pennsylvania's convention, James Wilson, who was one of the first justices appointed by President George Washington, argued that

under this Constitution, the legislature may be restrained, and kept within its prescribed bounds, by the interposition of the judicial department. . . . [T]he power of the Constitution [is] paramount to the power of the legislature acting under that Constitution; for it is possible that the legislature, when acting in that capacity, may transgress the bounds assigned to it, and an act may pass, in the usual *mode*, notwithstanding that transgression; but when it comes to be discussed before *the judges*,—when they consider its principles, and find it to be incompatible with the superior power of the Constitution,—it is their duty to pronounce it *void*.[11]

In Connecticut, Oliver Ellsworth, another who was later appointed to the Court, declared, "If the general legislature should at any time overleap their limits, the judicial department is a constitutional check."[12]

Even among the Federalists, however, there were differing views of the judiciary's power. Alexander Hamilton and James Madison agreed that the Court would exercise some checking power over the states. The Court, in Madison's words, was "the surest expositor of . . . the [constitutional] boundaries . . . between the Union and its members."[13] But they were in less agreement on whether the Court had the power to check coequal branches, the Congress and the president. In *The Federalist*, Madison called the judiciary an "auxiliary precaution" against the possible domination of one branch of government over another. Later, during a debate in the First Congress in 1789, he observed that "in the ordinary course of Government, . . . the exposition of the laws and Constitution devolves upon the Judiciary." Still, Madison doubted that the Court's interpretation of the Constitution was superior to that given by Congress. "Nothing has been offered to invalidate the [view]," he argued, "that the meaning of the Constitution may as well be ascertained by the legislative as by the judicial authority."[14] The Court stood as a forum of last resort, Madison explained, but "this resort must necessarily be deemed the last in relation to the authorities of the other departments of the government; not in relation to the rights of the parties to the constitutional compact, from which the judicial, as well as the other departments, hold their delegated trusts."[15]

From the initial debate in the Constitutional Convention in 1787 to those between the Federalists and the Anti-Federalists over state ratification of the Constitution and into the First Congress, the power of judicial review and the meaning of other key provisions and principles of the Constitution have remained a continuing source of controversy in constitutional politics. And the Supreme Court has remained, as Justice Oliver Wendell Holmes observed, a "storm centre" of political controversy.

A | *Establishing and Contesting the Power of Judicial Review*

In its first decade, the Supreme Court had little business, frequent turnover in personnel, no chambers or staff, no fixed customs, and no institutional identity. When the Court initially convened on February 1, 1790, only Chief Justice John Jay and two other justices arrived at the Exchange Building in New York City. They adjourned until the next day when Justice John Blair arrived; the two other justices never arrived. With little to do other than admit attorneys to practice

■ HOW TO LOCATE DECISIONS
   OF THE SUPREME COURT

[The decisions of the Supreme Court are published in the *United States Reports* by the U.S. Government Printing Office. Each decision is referred to by the names of the appellant, the person bringing the suit, and the appellee, the respondent: hence, *McCulloch v. Maryland*. After the name of the case is the volume number in which it appears in the *United States Reports* and the page number on which the Court's opinion begins, followed by the year of the decision. *McCulloch v. Maryland*, 17 U.S. 316 (1819), thus may be found in volume 17 of the *United States Reports* beginning on page 316.

   Prior to the publication of the *United States Reports* in 1875, the Court's opinions used to be cited according to the name of the reporter of the Court, who published the Court's opinions at his own expense. Decisions thus would originally be cited as follows:

1789–1800	Dallas	(1–4 Dall., 1–4 U.S.)
1801–1815	Cranch	(1–9 Cr., 5–13 U.S.)
1816–1827	Wheaton	(1–12 Wheat, 14–25 U.S.)
1828–1842	Peters	(1–16 Pet., 26–41 U.S.)
1843–1860	Howard	(1–24 How., 42–65 U.S.)
1861–1862	Black	(1–2 Bl., 66–67 U.S.)
1863–1874	Wallace	(1–23 Wall., 68–90 U.S.)
1875–		(91– , U.S.)

The full citation for *McCulloch v. Maryland* is 4 Wheat. (17 U.S.) 316 (1819). But with volume 91 in 1875, the reporters' names were dropped, and decisions were then cited only by the volume number and the designation "U.S."

   In addition, two companies print editions of the Court's decisions. There is the *Lawyers' Edition*, published by the Lawyer's Cooperative, and *The Supreme Court Reports*, published by West Publishing Company. The *Lawyers' Edition* is cited as L.Ed. (e.g., 91 L.Ed. 575), and *The Supreme Court Reporter* is cited as S.Ct. (e.g., 104 S.Ct. 3005).

   See also Researching Legal Materials.

---

before its bar, the Court concluded its first sessions in less than two weeks.

   When the capital moved from New York City to Philadelphia in the winter of 1790, the Court met in Independence Hall and in the Old City Hall, until the capital again moved to Washington, D.C., in 1800. Most of the first justices' time was spent riding circuit. That is, each would travel throughout a particular area, or circuit, in the country. Under the Judiciary Act of 1789, they were required twice a year to hold court, in the company of local district judges, in a circuit to hear appeals from the federal district courts. Hence, the justices resided primarily in their circuits, rather than in Washington, and felt a greater allegiance to their circuits than to the Court.

The Court's uncertain status was reflected in the first justices' exercise of their power of judicial review. Although in its initial years the Court had few important cases, *Chisholm v. Georgia*, 2 Dall. (2 U.S.) 419 (1793), precipitated the country's first constitutional crisis. In that case, Justice James Wilson, who had been a delegate to the Constitutional Convention and Pennsylvania's ratifying convention, ruled that citizens of one state could sue another state in federal courts. That provoked an angry dissent from Justice James Iredell, a Southerner who had attended North Carolina's ratifying convention and a strong proponent of "states' rights." His dissent invited the adoption by Congress of the Eleventh Amendment in 1795, overturning *Chisholm* and guaranteeing sovereign immunity for states from lawsuits brought by citizens of other states. The outcry over *Chisholm* convinced Chief Justice John Jay that the Court would remain "the least dangerous branch." He resigned in 1795 to become New York's governor and later declined reappointment as chief justice.

The Court, though, in *Ware v. Hylton*, 3 Dall. (3 U.S.) 199 (1796), upheld the provisions of a federal treaty, the 1783 peace treaty with England, over state law. And *Hylton v. United States*, 3 Dall. (3 U.S.) 171 (1796), affirmed, over objections raised by the states, Congress's power to levy a carriage tax (and thus implicitly asserted the Court's power to nullify acts of Congress).

Still, two years later, *Calder v. Bull*, 3 Dall. (3 U.S.) 386 (1798), illustrates how uncertain and divided the justices were about exercising their power of judicial review. There the Court declined to assert its power when ruling that conflicts between state laws and state constitutions are matters for state, not federal, courts to resolve. But Justice Iredell maintained that a state law might run against principles of "natural justice" and the Court still have no power to strike it down. By contrast, Justice Samuel Chase contended that the Court had the power to overturn laws that violate fundamental principles, explaining,

> I cannot subscribe to the omnipotence of a State legislature, or that it is absolute and without controul; although its authority should not be expressly restrained by the Constitution, or fundamental laws of the State. The people of the United States erected their Constitution . . . to establish justice, to promote the general welfare, to secure the blessings of liberty;and to protect their persons and property from violence. . . . There are acts which the Federal,

or State, Legislature cannot do. . . . It is against all reason and justice to entrust a Legislature with SUCH [despotic] powers; and therefore, it cannot be presumed that they have done it. The genius, the nature, and the spirit of our State Governments, amount to a prohibition of such [unlimited] acts of legislation; and the general principles of law and reason forbid them.

Justice Chase was not alone in claiming that the judiciary had the power of judicial review. As an ardent Federalist, James Kent (1763–1847) staunchly defended the power of judicial review in his Introductory Law Lecture at Columbia University in 1794 (excerpted below). Like Alexander Hamilton, James Wilson, and other Federalists, Kent justified judicial review in terms of fundamental principles of constitutional government. But, unlike Hamilton's arguments in *The Federalist*, No. 78, Kent stressed the uniquely American basis for the doctrine of judicial review.

The uncertainty and controversy over the power of judicial review was, nevertheless, further underscored in 1798 with the passage of the Virginia and Kentucky Resolutions (excerpted below), in response to Congress's enactment of the Alien and Sedition Acts. Drafted by James Madison and Thomas Jefferson, the Virginia and Kentucky Resolutions not only contended that Congress had violated the First Amendment but claimed that state legislatures had the power to judge the constitutionality of federal laws. Jefferson went so far as to assert that states could nullify federal laws that they deemed unconstitutional. The "sovereign and independent" states, in his words, "have the unquestionable right to judge . . . and, that a nullification [by] those sovereignties, of all unauthorized acts done under the color of that instrument is the rightful remdy."

Jefferson remained opposed to the power of judicial review and the view that the Supreme Court's interpretation of the Constitution was binding on the other branches of government. In a 1819 letter to Spencer Roane, a Virginia state judge, Jefferson explained,

> My construction of the Constitution is . . . that each department is truly independent of the others, and has an equal right to decide for itself what is the meaning of the Constitution in the cases submitted to its action most especially where it is to act ultimately and without appeal. . . . Each of the three departments has equally the right to decide for itself what is its duty under the Constitution, without any regard to what the others may have decided for themselves under a similar question.[16]

Although less strident than Jefferson, Madison thought that the "true and safe construction" of the Constitution would emerge with the "uniform sanction of successive legislative bodies; through a period of years and under the varied ascendency of parties."[17]

Chief Justice John Marshall provided the classic justification for the power of judicial review in the landmark ruling in *Marbury v. Madison* (1803) (excerpted below; see also The How, Why, and What to Briefing and Citing Court Cases at the end of the book). Notice that Marshall's arguments draw on both general principles and the text of the Constitution and are not unassailable. In an otherwise unimportant state case, *Eakin v. Raub* (Pa., 1825) (excerpted below), for example, Pennsylvania Supreme Court Justice John Gibson expressly refutes Marshall's arguments. It does not inexorably follow from Marshall's claim that the Constitution created a limited government that *only* the judiciary should enforce those limitations. No more persuasive is the argument that judges have the power to authoritatively interpret the Constitution based on their taking an oath to uphold the document, because all federal and state officers take an oath to support the Constitution. Like Madison and Jefferson, Justice Gibson rejects *Marbury*'s implication that the judiciary has a monopoly (or supremacy) over interpreting the Constitution or, as Chief Justice Charles Evans Hughes later put it, "We are under a Constitution but the Constitution is what the judges say it is."[18] In providing a rationale for judicial self-restraint, Gibson embraces a theory of *tripartite* constitutional interpretation—namely, that each branch has the authority to interpret the Constitution.

Chief Justice Marshall's arguments based on the text of the Constitution fare better. In specifying that the "judicial Power shall extend to" cases and controversies "arising under this Constitution," Article III implies that constitutional questions may be decided by the judiciary. And, as Marshall points out, the Supremacy Clause of Article VI makes it clear that the Constitution is "the supreme Law of the Land." Judicial review is thus a logical implication of the Constitution, for as Justice Joseph Story observed,

> The laws and treaties, and even the constitution, of the United States, would become a dead letter without it. Indeed, in a complicated government, like ours, where there is an assemblage of republics, combined under a common head, the necessity of some controlling judicial power, to ascertain and enforce the powers of the Union is, if possible, still more striking. The laws of the whole would otherwise be in continual danger of being contravened by the laws of the parts. The national government would be reduced to a servile dependence upon the states; and the same scenes would be again acted over in solemn mockery, which began in the neglect, and ended in the ruin, of the confederation.[19]

Still and undeniably, the power of judicial review is not expressly provided for in the Constitution and its exercise remains a continuing source of controversy.

The immediate political controversy over the exercise of judicial review in *Marbury* in striking down a section of the Judiciary Act of 1789 was defused by Chief Justice Marshall's conclusion that the Court had no power to order the delivery of Marbury's commission. Though outraged by Marshall's assertion of judicial review, Madison and Jefferson had not been compelled by the Court to do anything. Jefferson continued to maintain that each branch of government could interpret the Constitution and to deny that the Court's interpretations were binding on the president's exercise of executive powers. In a letter to Mrs. John Adams in 1804, explaining his decision to pardon those tried and convicted under the Sedition Act of 1798, Jefferson wrote,

> The Judges, believing the law constitutional, had a right to pass a sentence of fine and imprisonment; because that power was placed in their hands by the Constitution. But the Executive, believing the law to be unconstitutional, was bound to remit the execution of it; because that power has been confided to him by the Constitution. The instrument meant that its co-ordinate branches should be checks on each other. But the opinion which gives to the Judges the right to decide what Laws are constitutional, and what not, not only for themselves in their own sphere of action, but for the Legislative and Executive also in their spheres, would make the Judiciary a despotic branch.[20]

Jefferson was not the last president to contest the authority of the Court. An irate President Andrew Jackson, on hearing of the decision in *Worcester v. Georgia*, 31 U.S. 515 (1832), holding that states could not pass laws affecting federally recognized Indian nations, reportedly declared, "John Marshall has made his decision, now let him enforce it."[21] Jackson elaborated his view in his Veto Message of 1832, explaining his vetoing of legislation rechartering the national bank (see Vol. 1, Ch. 6). Besides contending that *McCulloch v. Maryland*, 17 U.S. 316 (1819) (see Vol. 1, Ch. 6) was not binding on his actions, Jackson reiterated the position that

> [t]he Congress, the Executive, and the Court must each for itself be guided by its own opinion of the Constitution. Each public officer who takes an oath to support the Constitution swears that he will support it as he understands it, and not as it is understood by others. . . . The opinion of the judges has no more authority over Congress than the opinion of Congress has over the judges, and on that point the President is independent of both.[22]

Jackson's Veto Message drew an impassioned response from Senator Daniel Webster, who thundered in the halls of Congress that

> [t]he President is as much bound by the law as any private citizen. . . . He may refuse to obey the law, and so may a private citizen; but both do it at their own peril, and neither of them can settle the question of its validity. The President may say a law is unconstitutional, but he is not the judge. . . . If it were otherwise, there would be no government of laws; but we should all live under the government, the rule, the caprices of individuals. . . .

> [President Jackson's] message . . . converts a constitutional limitation of power into mere matters of opinion, and then strikes the judicial department, as an efficient department, out of our system. . . .

> [The message] denies first principles. It contradicts truths heretofore received as indisputable. It denies to the judiciary the interpretation of law.

Controversy over judicial review continues, but it bears emphasizing that Jefferson, Jackson, and subsequent presidents concede that the Court's rulings are binding for the actual cases decided and handed down. Technically, a decision of the Court is final only for the parties involved in the case. Yet, because the justices in their opinions give general principles for deciding a case and because they generally adhere to precedents (or tend to do so until the composition of the bench markedly changes), the Court's rulings are usually considered controlling for other similar cases and the larger political controversy they represent. But in major confrontations in constitutional politics—like those over the creation of a national bank, slavery, school desegregation, and abortion—the Court alone cannot lay those controversies to rest.

What presidents, Congress, the states, and others occasionally deny is *judicial supremacy* or the finality of the Court's interpretation of broad constitutional principles for resolving major political controversies. In his famous debates with Stephen Douglas, for instance, Abraham Lincoln denounced the Court's ruling in *Dred Scott v. Sandford*, 60 U.S. 393 (1857) (see Ch. 12), that blacks were not citizens of the United States. While Lincoln doubted that "we, as a mob, will decide [Dred Scott] to be free," he exclaimed that

> we nevertheless do oppose that decision as a political rule which shall be binding on the voter, to vote for nobody who thinks it wrong, which shall be binding on the members of Congress or the President to favor no measure that does not actually concur with the principles of that decision. . . . We propose so resisting it as to have it reversed if we can, and a new judicial rule established upon this subject.[23]

Later, in his first Inaugural Address in 1861, Lincoln elaborated,

> I do not forget the position assumed by some, that constitutional questions are to be decided by the Supreme Court; nor do I deny that such decisions must be binding in any case, upon the parties to a suit, as to the object of that suit, while they are also entitled to a very high respect and consideration, in all parallel cases, by all other departments of government. And while it is obviously possible that such a decision may be erroneous in any given case, still the evil effect following it, being limited to that particular case, with the chance that it may be over-ruled, and never become a precedent for other cases, can better be borne than could the evils of a different practice. At the same time the candid citizen must confess that if the policy of the government, upon vital questions, affecting the whole people, is to be irrevocably fixed by the decisions of the Supreme Court, the instant they are made, in ordinary litigation between parties, in personal actions, the people will have ceased, to be their own rulers, having to that extent, practically resigned their government, into the hands of that eminent tribunal. Nor is there, in this view, any assault upon the court, or the judges. It is a duty, from which they may not shrink, to decide cases properly brought before them; and it is no fault of theirs, if others seek to turn their decisions to political purposes.

In major confrontations with the Court, other presidents have taken similar positions to that of President Lincoln. During the constitutional crisis of 1937, resulting from the Court's invalidation of much of the early New Deal progressive economic legislation, President Franklin D. Roosevelt proposed that Congress expand the size of the Court from nine to fifteen justices, and thereby enable him to secure a majority sympathetic to his programs and policies. And in a "Fireside Chat" in March 1937 (see excerpt below), FDR followed in the footsteps of Jefferson, Jackson, and Lincoln in attacking the Court for becoming a "super-legislature."

Judicial supremacy over interpreting the Constitution remains controversial. In *Marbury*, however, Chief Justice Marshall did not lay claim to judicial supremacy, only that the Court, no less than the president and Congress, has the authority and duty to interpret the Constitution.[24] By contrast, in this century justices have often asserted the supremacy of their decisions. In *United States v. Butler*, 297 U.S. 1 (1936), Justice (and later Chief Justice) Harlan Stone claimed that "[w]hile unconstitutional exercise of power by the executive and legislative branches of government is subject to judicial restraint, the only check upon our own exercise of power is our own sense of self-restraint." In the wake of massive resistance to the Court's watershed ruling on school desegregation, in *Brown v. Board of Education*, 347 U.S. 483

(1954) (see Ch. 12), all nine justices took the unusual step of signing the opinion announcing *Cooper v. Aaron*, 358 U.S. 1 (1958) (see Ch. 12), which ordered the desegregation of schools in Little Rock, Arkansas. And they interpreted *Marbury* to have

> declared the basic principle that the federal judiciary is supreme in the exposition of the law of the Constitution. . . . It follows that the interpretation of the Fourteenth Amendment enunciated by this Court in the *Brown* case is the supreme law of the land, and Article VI of the Constitution makes it have binding effect on the States. . . . Every state legislator and executive and judicial officer is solemnly committed by oath taken pursuant to Article VI, 3 "to support this Constitution."

The Court likewise proclaimed itself the "ultimate interpreter of the Constitution" in *Baker v. Carr*, 369 U.S. 186 (1962) (excerpted in Ch. 2), when holding that courts could decide disputes over the malapportionment of state legislatures. And again citing *Marbury* in *Powell v. McCormack*, 395 U.S. 486 (1969) (see Vol. 1, Ch. 5), involving a controversy over the House of Representatives' exclusion of a duly elected representative, the Court declared that "it is the responsibility of this Court to act as the ultimate interpreter of the Constitution." The Rehnquist Court underscored its authority, in *City of Boerne v. Flores*, 521 U.S. 507 (1997) (excerpted in Ch. 6 of Vols. 1 and 2), when reasserting that Congress's power under the Fourteenth Amendment is only remedial, not definitive, and thus only the Court, and not Congress, has the power to define constitutional rights.

Despite the Court's occasional claims of judicial supremacy, the president, Congress, and the states may in various ways undercut and thwart compliance with, if not ultimately overturn, the Court's rulings (see Vol. 1, Ch. 2). By deciding only immediate cases, the Court infuses constitutional meaning into the larger surrounding political controversies by bringing them within the language, structure, and spirit of the Constitution. The Court may thus raise a controversial issue, as it did with school desegregation in *Brown* and with the right to abortion in *Roe*, to the national political agenda. But by itself the Court cannot lay those controversies to rest because its power, in Chief Justice Edward White's words, rests "solely upon the approval of a free people."[25] In areas of major and continuing political controversy, constitutional law is a kind of dialogue between the Court and the country over the meaning of the Constitution, and judicial review is more provisional than final.[26]

Even more than Chief Justice Marshall's arguments in *Marbury*, the establishment of judicial review turned on public acceptance and the forces of history. That is not to gainsay Marshall's contributions. He

■ CONSTITUTIONAL HISTORY

Decisions of the Supreme Court Overruled and Acts of Congress Held Unconstitutional and State Laws and Municipal Ordinances Overturned, 1789–2004*

Year	Supreme Court Decision Overruled	Acts of Congress Overturned	State Laws Overturned	Ordinances Overturned
1789–1800, Pre-Marshall				
1801–1835, Marshall Court	3	1	18	
1836–1864, Taney Court	4	1	21	
1865–1873, Chase Court	4	10	33	
1874–1888, Waite Court	13	9	7	
1889–1910, Fuller Court	4	14	73	15
1910–1921, White Court	5	12	107	18
1921–1930, Taft Court	6	12	131	12
1930–1940, Hughes Court	21	14	78	5
1941–1946, Stone Court	15	2	25	7
1947–1952, Vinson Court	13	1	38	7
1953–1969, Warren Court	45	25	150	16
1969–1986, Burger Court	52	34	192	15
1986– , Rehnquist Court	38	38	94	20

*| Note that in *Immigration and Naturalization Service v. Chadha* (1983), the Burger Court struck down a provision for a "one-house" legislative veto in the Immigration and Naturalization Act but effectively declared all one- and two-house legislative vetoes unconstitutional. While 212 statutes containing provisions for legislative vetoes were implicated by the Court's decision, *Chadha* is here counted as a single declaration of the unconstitutionality of congressional legislation. Note also that the Court's ruling in *Texas v. Johnson* (1989), striking down a Texas law making it a crime to desecrate the American flag, invalidated laws in forty-eight states and a federal statute. It is counted here, however, only once. This table includes cases through the 2003–2004 term.

had a keen understanding of the malleable nature of the young republic and the important role that the first generation would play in establishing the power of the national government. Marshall's long tenure (1801–1835) and that of others who served with him may have contributed as well. After *Marbury*, moreover, the Court did not again strike down another act of Congress or challenge a coequal branch of government until the 1857 ill-fated ruling in *Dred Scott*, which left the Court at a low ebb for two decades. Instead, the Marshall Court buttressed its own power by defending the interests of the national government against the states and striking down state laws.

Finally, social forces have shaped the Court's role in the kinds of cases and controversies brought to it for review. As already noted, the Court had little important business during its first decade. Over 40 percent of its business consisted in admiralty and prize cases (disputes over captured property at sea). About 50 percent raised issues of common law, and the remaining 10 percent dealt with matters like equity, including one probate case. By the late nineteenth century, the Court's business gradually changed in response to developments in American society. The number of admiralty cases, for instance, had by 1882 dwindled to less than 4 percent of the total. Almost 40 percent of the Court's decisions still dealt with either disputes of common law or questions of jurisdiction and procedure in federal courts. More than 43 percent of the Court's business, however, involved interpreting congressional statutes. Less than 4 percent of the cases raised issues of constitutional interpretation. The decline in admiralty and common-law litigation and the increase in statutory interpretation reflected the impact of the Industrial Revolution and the growing governmental regulation of social and economic relations. In the twentieth century, the trend continued. About 47 percent of the cases annually decided by the Court involve matters of constitutional law. Another 38 percent deal with the interpretation of congressional legislation. The remaining 15 percent involve issues of practice and procedure, administrative law, taxation, patents, and claims.

The Court is no longer "the least dangerous branch" or primarily concerned with correcting the errors of lower courts. In response to growing and changing litigation, the Court more frequently overturns prior rulings, congressional legislation, and state and local laws. The Court takes only "hard cases," involving major issues of legal policy and "not primarily to preserve the rights of the litigants," in the words of Chief Justice William Howard Taft: "The Supreme Court's function is for the purpose of expounding and stabilizing principles of law for the benefit of the people of the country, passing upon constitutional questions and other important questions of law for the public benefit."[27]

The Court and the country have changed with constitutional politics. From 1789 to the Civil War, the major controversies confronting the Court involved disputes between the national government and the states, and the Court employed its power to preserve the Union (see Vol. 1, Chs. 6 and 7). Between 1865 and 1937, during the Reconstruction and the Industrial Revolution, the dominant political controversy revolved around balancing regulatory interests and those of businesses, and the Court defended the interests of American capitalism and private enterprise (see Ch. 3). Only after 1937 did the Court begin to assume the role of "a guardian for civil liberties and civil rights" in defending the rights of minorities (see Chs. 4–12). The Court's role has changed with constitutional politics, as Harvard Law School professor Paul Freund nicely expressed by analogy, "As Hamlet is to one generation a play of revenge, to another a conflict between will and conscience, and to another a study in mother-fixation, so the Constitution has been to one generation a means of cementing the Union, to another a protectorate of burgeoning property, and to another a safeguard of basic human rights and equality before the law."[28]

NOTES

1. See Max Farrand, *The Framing of the Constitution* (New Haven, CT: Yale University Press, 1913); Max Farrand, ed., *The Records of the Federal Convention of 1787*, 4 vols. (New Haven, CT: Yale University Press, 1911); and John P. Roche, "The Founding Fathers: A Reform Caucus in Action," 55 *American Political Science Review* 799 (1961).

2. The Supreme Court has enforced the tenure and salary provisions in *Ex parte Milligan*, 4 Wall. 2 (1867) (see Vol. 1, Ch. 3), holding that civilians cannot be tried before military tribunals; in *O'Donoghue v. United States*, 289 U.S. 516 (1933), holding that judicial salaries cannot be reduced, even during the Great Depression; and *Northern Pipe Line Construction Co. v. Marathon Pipe Line Co.*, 458 U.S. 50 (1982), striking down a statute expanding the power of bankruptcy judges.

3. Edward S. Corwin, "The Constitution as Instrument and as Symbol," 30 *American Political Science Review* 1078 (1936).

4. Letter from Max Farrand to Edward Corwin, Jan. 3, 1939, in Edward Samuel Corwin Papers, Box 3, Princeton University Library, Princeton, NJ.

5. Quoted in James Madison, *Notes of Debates in the Federal Convention of 1787* (Athens: Ohio University Press, 1966), 455–456.

6. A Columbia Patriot, in *The Complete Anti-Federalist*, Vol. 4, ed. Herbert J. Storing (Chicago: University of Chicago Press, 1981), 276.

7. Thomas Tredwell, in *The Debates in the Several State Conventions on the Adoption of the Federal Constitution*, Vol. 4, ed., Jonathan Elliot (New York: Burt Franklin, 1974), 401.

8. Brutus, in *The Complete Anti-Federalist*, Vol. 2, ed. Storing, 438–439, 420, 422.

9. James Wilson, in *The Debates*, Vol. 2, ed. Elliot, 494.

10. Governor Johnston, in *The Debates*, Vol. 4, ed. Elliot, 142.

11. James Wilson, in *The Debates*, Vol. 2, ed. Elliot, 445–446.

12. Oliver Ellsworth, in *The Debates*, Vol. 2, ed. Elliot, 196.

13. Letter from James Madison to an unidentified person, Aug. 1834, reprinted in *Letters and Other Writings of James Madison*, Vol. 4 (Philadelphia, 1865), 350.

14. James Madison, in *Annals of Congress*, Vol. 1 (Washington, DC: Gales & Seaton, 1789), 500, 546–547.

15. James Madison, "Report on the Virginia Resolutions," in *The Debates*, Vol. 5, ed. Elliot, 549.

16. Thomas Jefferson, *The Works of Thomas Jefferson*, Vol. 12, ed. Paul Ford (New York: G. P. Putnam's Sons, 1904–1905), 137–138.

17. Quoted in Robert J. Morgan, *James Madison on the Constitution and the Bill of Rights* (Westport, CT: Greenwood Press, 1988), 196. For more on Jefferson's and Madison's views, see the discussion of the controversy over Congress's creating a national bank and *McCulloch v. Maryland*, 17 U.S. 316 (1819) (excerpted in Vol. 1, Ch. 6).

18. Charles Evans Hughes, *Address and Papers of Charles Evans Hughes* (New York: Columbia University Press, 1908), 139.

19. Joseph Story, *Commentaries on the Constitution*, (Durham, NC: Carolina Academic Press, 1987), reprint of 1833 ed.

20. Thomas Jefferson, Letter to John Adams, Sept. 11, 1804, as quoted in Charles Warren, *The Supreme Court in United States History*, Vol. 1 (Boston: Little, Brown, 1922), 265.

21. Quoted in Edward Corwin, *The Doctrine of Judicial Review* (Princeton, NJ: Princeton University Press, 1914), 22.

22. President's Veto Message (July 10, 1832), *A Compilation of the Messages and Papers of the Presidents*, Vol. 2, ed. J. Richardson (New York: Bureau of National Literature, 1917), 582.

23. Abraham Lincoln, *The Collected Works of Abraham Lincoln*, Vol. 2, ed. Roy Basler (New Brunswick, NJ: Rutgers University Press, 1953), 401.

24. See David M. O'Brien, "Judicial Review and Constitutional Politics: Theory and Practice," 48 *University of Chicago Law Review* 1070 (1981).

25. Quoted in David M. O'Brien, *Storm Center: The Supreme Court in American Politics*, 6th ed. (New York: W. W. Norton, 2002), 22.

26. See Paul Diamond, *The Supreme Court and Judicial Choice* (Ann Arbor: University of Michigan Press, 1989).

27. William H. Taft, *Hearings before the House Committee on the Judiciary*, 67th Cong., 2d sess., 1922, 2.

28. Paul Freund, "My Philosophy of Law," 39 *Connecticut Bar Journal* 220 (1965).

SELECTED BIBLIOGRAPHY

Corwin, Edward S. *The Doctrine of Judicial Review.* Princeton, NJ: Princeton University Press, 1914.

———. *Constitutional Revolution, Ltd.* Claremont, CA: Claremont Colleges, 1941.

Ellis, Joseph. *Founding Brothers: The Revolutionary Generation.* New York: Knopf, 2000.

Fisher, Louis. *Constitutional Dialogues.* Princeton, NJ: Princeton University Press, 1988.

Freund, Paul A. *The Supreme Court of the United States.* Cleveland, OH: World Publishing, 1961.

Hall, Kermit. *The Oxford Companion to the Supreme Court.* New York: Oxford University Press, 1992.

Lasser, William. *The Limits of Judicial Power.* Chapel Hill: University of North Carolina Press, 1988.

Levy, Leonard, ed. *American Constitutional History.* New York: Macmillan, 1989.

Nelson, William. *Marbury v. Madison: The Origins and Legacy of Judicial Review.* Lawrence: University of Kansas Press, 2000.

Warren, Charles. *The Supreme Court in United States History*, 3 vols. Boston: Little, Brown, 1922.

James Kent's Introductory Law School Lecture in 1794

James Kent (1763–1847) began a long legal career as a professor at Columbia University Law School in 1794. He later became a master of chancery and in 1804 the chief justice of New York's supreme court. His Columbia Law Lectures were later expanded into *Commentaries on the American Law* (1826–1830), which Justice Joseph Story called "our first judicial classic." Excerpted here is part of his "Introductory Lecture," which did not remain intact in his *Commentaries* but which uniquely justified judicial review in terms of established principles of republican government in America.

JAMES KENT: The British Constitution and Code of Laws, to the knowledge of which our Lawyers are so early and deeply introduced by the prevailing course of their professional inquiries, abounds, it is true, with invaluable Principles of Equity, of Policy, and of Social Order; Principles which cannot be too generally known, studied and received. It must however be observed at the same time, that many of the fundamental doctrines of their Government, and Axioms of their Jurisprudence, are utterly subversive of an Equality of Rights, and totally incompatible with the liberal spirit of our American Establishments. The Student of our Laws should be carefully taught to distinguish between the Principles of the one Government, and the Genius which presides in the other. He ought to have a correct acquaintance with genuine Republican Maxims, and be thereby induced to cultivate a superior regard for our own, and I trust more perfect systems of Liberty and Justice. . . .

The doctrine I have suggested, is peculiar to the United States. In the European World, no idea has ever been entertained (or at least until lately) of placing constitutional limits to the exercise of the Legislative Power. In England, where the Constitution has separated and designated the Departments of Government with precision and notoriety, the Parliament is still considered as transcendently absolute; and altho some Judges have had the freedom to observe, that a Statute made against natural equity was void, yet it is generally laid down as a necessary principle in their Law, that no Act of Parliament can be questioned or disputed. But in this country we have found it expedient to establish certain rights, to be deemed paramount to the power of the ordinary Legislature, and this precaution is considered in general as essential to perfect security, and to guard against the occasional violence and momentary triumphs of party. Without some express provisions of this kind clearly settled in the original compact, and constantly protected by the firmness and moderation of the Judicial department, the equal rights of a minor faction, would perhaps very often be disregarded in the animated competitions for power, and fall a sacrifice to the passions of a fierce and vindictive majority.

No question can be made with us, but that the Acts of the Legislative body, contrary to the true intent and meaning of the Constitution, ought to be absolutely null and void. The only inquiry which can arise on the subject is, whether the Legislature is not of itself the competent Judge of its own constitutional limits, and its acts of course to be presumed always conformable to the commission under which it proceeds; or whether the business of determining in this instance, is not rather the fit and exclusive province of the Courts of Justice. It is easy to see, that if the Legislature was left the ultimate Judge of the nature and extent of the barriers which have been placed against the abuses of its discretion, the efficacy of the check would be totally lost. The Legislature would be inclined to narrow or explain away the Constitution, from the force of the same propensities or considerations of temporary expediency, which would lead it to overturn private rights. Its will would be the supreme law, as much with, as without these constitutional safeguards. Nor is it probable, that the force of public opinion, the only restraint that could in that case exist, would be felt, or if felt, would be greatly regarded. If public opinion was in every case to be presumed correct and competent to be trusted, it is evident, there would have been no need of original and fundamental limitations. But sad experience has sufficiently taught mankind, that opinion is not an infallible standard of safety. When powerful rivalries prevail in the Community, and Parties become highly disciplined and hostile, every measure of the major part of the Legislature is sure to receive the sanction of that Party among their Constituents to which they belong. Every Step of the minor Party, it is equally certain will be approved by their immediate adherents, as well as indiscriminately misrepresented or condemned by the prevailing voice. The Courts of Justice which are organized with peculiar advantages to exempt them from the baneful influence of Faction, and to secure at the same time, a steady, firm and impartial interpretation of the Law, are therefore the most proper power in the Government to keep the Legislature within the limits of its duty, and to maintain the Authority of the Constitution. . . .

This power in the Judicial, of determining the constitutionality of Laws, is necessary to preserve the equilibrium of the government, and prevent usurpations of one part upon another; and of all the parts of government, the Legislative body is by far the most impetuous and powerful. A mere designation on paper, of the limits of the several departments, is altogether insufficient, and for this reason in limited Constitutions, the executive is armed with a negative, either qualified or complete upon the making of Laws. But the Judicial Power is the weakest of all, and as it is equally necessary to be preserved entire, it ought not in sound theory to be left naked without any constitutional means of defence. This is one reason why the Judges in this State are associated with the Governor, to form the Council of Revision, and this association renders some of these observations less applicable to our own particular Constitution, than to any other. The right of expounding the Constitution as well as Laws, will however be found in general to be the most fit, if not only effectual weapon, by which the Courts of Justice are enabled to repel assaults, and to guard against encroachments on their Chartered Authorities.

Nor can any danger be apprehended, lest this principle should exalt the Judicial above the Legislature. They are co-ordinate powers, and equally bound by the instrument under which they act, and if the former should at any time be prevailed upon to substitute arbitrary will, to the exercise of a rational Judgment, as it is possible it may do even in the ordinary course of judicial proceeding, it is not left like the latter, to the mere controul of public opinion. The Judges may be brought before the tribunal of the Legislature, and tried, condemned, and removed from office.

I consider then the Courts of Justice, as the proper and intended Guardians of our limited Constitutions, against the factions and encroachments of the Legislative Body. . . .

The Virginia and Kentucky Resolutions of 1798

In the spring of 1798, President John Adams and his Federalist dominated Congress enacted the Alien and Sedition Acts, regulating immigration and making criticism of the government a crime of seditious libel. The laws aimed at silencing partisan criticism by Jeffersonian-Republicans of the Adams administration's pro-British policies. Although Jeffersonian-Republicans were prosecuted under the laws, often receiving stiff penalties, no court ruled on the constitutionality of the laws or whether they violated the First Amendment's guarantee for freedom of speech and press. The Kentucky legislature adopted a resolution secretly written by Thomas Jefferson, and Virginia adopted a similar resolution drafted by James Madison. Prosecutions for seditious libel ended in 1801, when the laws expired and Jefferson became president. Over 160 years later, the Supreme Court in a landmark ruling on libel, in the *New York Times Company v. Sullivan*, 376 U.S. 254 (1964) (see Ch. 5), declared the Sedition Act and seditious libel unconstitutional and inconsistent with the First Amendment.

VIRGINIA RESOLUTIONS, DECEMBER 21, 1798

1. *Resolved,* That the General Assembly of Virginia doth unequivocally express a firm resolution to maintain and defend the Constitution of the United States, and the Constitution of this State, against every aggression, either foreign or domestic, and that it will support the government of the United States in all measures warranted by the former. . . .

3. That this Assembly doth explicitly and peremptorily declare that it views the powers of the Federal Government as resulting from the compact to which the States are parties, as limited by the plain sense and intention of the instrument constituting that compact; as no further valid than they are authorized by the grants enumerated in that compact; and that in case of a deliberate, palpable, and dangerous exercise of other powers not granted by the said compact, the States, who are the parties thereto, have the right, and are in duty bound, to interpose for arresting the progress of the evil, and for maintaining within their respective limits, the authorities, rights, and liberties appertaining to them.

4. That the General Assembly doth also express its deep regret that a spirit has in sundry instances been manifested by the Federal Government, to enlarge its powers by forced constructions of the constitutional charter which defines them; and that indications have appeared of a design to expound certain general phrases (which, having been copied from the very limited grant of powers in the former articles of confederation, were the less liable to be misconstrued), so as to destroy the meaning and effect of the particular enumeration, which necessarily explains and limits the general

phrases, and so as to consolidate the States by degrees into one sovereignty, the obvious tendency and inevitable result of which would be to transform the present republican system of the United States into an absolute, or at best, a mixed monarchy.

5. That the General Assembly doth particularly protest against the palpable and alarming infractions of the Constitution, in the two late cases of the "alien and sedition acts," passed at the last session of Congress, the first of which exercises a power nowhere delegated to the Federal Government; and which by uniting legislative and judicial powers to those of executive, subverts the general principles of free government, as well as the particular organization and positive provisions of the federal Constitution; and the other of which acts exercises in like manner a power not delegated by the Constitution, but on the contrary expressly and positively forbidden by one of the amendments thereto; a power which more than any other ought to produce universal alarm, because it is levelled against that right of freely examining public characters and measures, and of free communication among the people thereon, which has ever been justly deemed the only effectual guardian of every other right.

6. That this State having by its convention which ratified the federal Constitution, expressly declared, "that among other essential rights, the liberty of conscience and of the press cannot be cancelled, abridged, restrained, or modified by any authority of the United States," and from its extreme anxiety to guard these rights from every possible attack of sophistry or ambition, having with other States recommended an amendment for that purpose, which amendment was in due time annexed to the Constitution, it would mark a reproachful inconsistency and criminal degeneracy, if an indifference were now shown to the most palpable violation of one of the rights thus declared and secured, and to the establishment of a precedent which may be fatal to the other.

KENTUCKY RESOLUTIONS, NOVEMBER 10, 1798

1. *Resolved*, That the several states composing the United States of America, are not united on the principle of unlimited submission to their general government; but that by compact, under the style and title of a Constitution for the United States, and of amendments thereto, they constituted a general government for special purposes, delegated to that government certain definite powers, reserving, each state to itself, the residuary mass of right to their own self-government;and that whensoever the general government assumes undelegated powers, its acts are unauthoritative, void, and of no force: That to this compact each state acceded as a state, and is an integral party, its co-states forming as to itself, the other party: That the government created by this compact was not made the exclusive or final *judge* of the extent of the powers delegated to itself; since that would have made its discretion, and not the Constitution, the measure of its powers; but that, as in all other cases of compact among parties having no common judge, each party has an equal right to judge for itself, as well of infractions, as of the mode and measure of redress.

2. *Resolved*, That the Constitution of the United States having delegated to Congress a power to punish treason, counterfeiting the securities and current coin of the United States, piracies and felonies committed on the high

seas, and offences against the laws of nations, and no other crimes whatever,
. . . all other [of] their acts which assume to create, define, or punish crimes
other than those enumerated in the Constitution, are altogether void, and of
no force, and that the power to create, define, and punish such other crimes
is reserved, and of right appertains, solely and exclusively, to the respective
states, each within its own territory.

3. *Resolved*, That it is true as a general principle, and is also expressly declared by one of the amendments to the Constitution, that "the powers not
delegated to the United States by the Constitution, nor prohibited by it to
the states, are reserved to the states respectively, or to the people"; and that
no power over the freedom of religion, freedom of speech, or freedom of
the press, being delegated to the United States by the Constitution, nor prohibited by it to the states, all lawful powers respecting the same did of right
remain, and were reserved to the states, or to the people; that thus was
manifested their determination to retain to themselves the right of judging
how far the licentiousness of speech and of the press may be abridged without lessening their useful freedom, and how far those abuses which cannot
be separated from their use, should be tolerated rather than the use be destroyed; and thus also they guarded against all abridgment by the United
States of the freedom of religious opinions and exercises, and retained to
themselves the right of protecting the same, as this state by a law passed on
the general demand of its citizens, had already protected them from all human restraint or interference: and that in addition to this general principle
and express declaration, another and more special provision has been made
by one of the amendments to the Constitution, which expressly declares,
that "Congress shall make no law respecting an establishment of religion, or
prohibiting the free exercise thereof, or abridging the freedom of speech, or
of the press," thereby guarding in the same sentence, and under the same
words, the freedom of religion, of speech, and of the press, insomuch, that
whatever violates either, throws down the sanctuary which covers the others, and that libels, falsehoods, and defamations, equally with heresy and false
religion, are withheld from the cognizance of federal tribunals: that therefore
the act of the Congress of the United States, passed on the 14th day of July,
1798, entitled, "an act in addition to the act for the punishment of certain
crimes against the United States," which does abridge the freedom of the
press, is not law, but is altogether void and of no effect.

4. *Resolved*, That alien-friends are under the jurisdiction and protection
of the laws of the state wherein they are; that no power over them has been
delegated to the United States, nor prohibited to the individual states distinct
from their power over citizens; and it being true as a general principle, and
one of the amendments to the Constitution having also declared, that "the
powers not delegated to the United States by the Constitution, nor prohibited by it to the states, are reserved to the states respectively, or to the people," the act of the Congress of the United States, passed on the 22d day of
June, 1798, entitled "an act concerning aliens," which assumes power over
alien-friends not delegated by the Constitution, is not law, but is altogether
void and of no force. . . .

6. *Resolved*, That the imprisonment of a person under the protection of
the laws of this commonwealth, on his failure to obey the simple *order* of the
President, to depart out of the United States, as is undertaken by the said act,

entitled "an act concerning aliens," is contrary to the Constitution, one amendment to which has provided, that "no person shall be deprived of liberty without due process of law," and that another having provided, "that in all criminal prosecutions, the accused shall enjoy the right to a public trial by an impartial jury, to be informed of the nature and cause of the accusation, to be confronted with the witnesses against him, to have compulsory process for obtaining witnesses in his favour, and to have the assistance of counsel for his defence," the same act undertaking to authorize the President to remove a person out of the United States, who is under the protection of the law, on his own suspicion, without accusation, without jury, without public trial, without confrontation of the witnesses against him, without having witnesses in his favour, without defence, without counsel, is contrary to these provisions, also, of the Constitution, is therefore not law, but utterly void and of no force.

That transferring the power of judging any person who is under the protection of the laws, from the courts to the President of the United States, as is undertaken by the same act, concerning aliens, is against the article of the Constitution which provides, that "the judicial power of the United States shall be vested in courts, the judges of which shall hold their offices during good behaviour," and that the said act is void for that reason also; and it is further to be noted, that this transfer of judiciary power is to that magistrate of the General Government, who already possesses all the executive, and a qualified negative in all the legislative powers.

Marbury v. Madison

1 CR. (5 U.S.) 137 (1803)

This case grew out of one of the great early struggles over the course of constitutional politics. Shortly after the ratification of the Constitution, two rival political parties emerged with widely different views of the Constitution and governmental power. The Federalists supported a strong national government, including the power of the federal courts to interpret the Constitution. Their opponents, the Anti-Federalists and later the Jeffersonian-Republicans (who after the 1832 election became known as Democrats), remained distrustful of the national government and continued to favor the states and state courts. The struggle between the Federalists and the Jeffersonian-Republicans finally came to a head with the election of 1800. The Jeffersonians defeated the Federalists, who had held office since the creation of the republic and feared what the Jeffersonian-Republicans might do once in office.

Before leaving office, President John Adams and his Federalist-dominated Congress vindictively created a number of new judgeships and appointed all Federalists in the hope that they would counter the

Jeffersonians once in office. But with time running out before the inauguration of Thomas Jefferson as president in 1801, not all of the commissions for the new judgeships were delivered. John Marshall, who Adams had just appointed as chief justice, continued to work as secretary of state, delivering the commissions. But he failed to deliver seventeen commissions before Adams's term expired and left them for his successor as secretary of state, James Madison, to deliver. The Federalists' attempt to pack the courts infuriated the Jeffersonian-Republicans. And President Jefferson instructed Madison not to deliver the rest of the commissions.

William Marbury was one whose commission went undelivered. He decided to sue to force Madison to give him his commission. Specifically, he sought a *writ of mandamus*, which is simply a court order directing a government official (Madison) to perform a certain act (hand over the commission). Marbury argued that Section 13 of the Judiciary Act of 1789 had authorized the Supreme Court to issue such writs. He saw this as a way of getting back his commission and for the Marshall Court to take a stand against the Jeffersonians.

Marbury v. Madison was a politically explosive case for the Court and the country over the still-untested power of judicial review. The Court faced a major dilemma. On the one hand, if the Marshall Court ordered Marbury's commission, it was likely that Jefferson would refuse to comply. The Court would then be powerless, perhaps permanently. On the other hand, if the Court refused to issue the writ, it would appear weak and that would confirm the Jeffersonian argument that the courts had no power to intrude on the executive branch. Chief Justice Marshall's opinion, handed down on February 24, 1803, however, shrewdly asserted the power of judicial review and for the first time overturned part of an act of Congress but gave Jefferson no opportunity to retaliate and thus helped to defuse the political controversy surrounding the case. While Jeffersonians fervently disagreed with Marshall's ruling, there was little for them to do because Marshall had not ordered the delivery of Marbury's commission.

The Court's decision was unanimous.

☐ *Chief Justice MARSHALL delivers the opinion of the Court.*

At the last term on the affidavits then read and filed with the clerk, a rule was granted in this case, requiring the secretary of state to show cause why a *mandamus* should not issue, directing him to deliver to William Marbury his commission as a justice of the peace for the county of Washington, in the District of Columbia.

No cause has been shown, and the present motion is for a *mandamus*. The peculiar delicacy of this case, the novelty of some of its circumstances, and the real difficulty attending the points which occur in it, require a complete exposition of the principles on which the opinion to be given by the court is founded.

These principles have been, on the side of the applicant very ably argued at the bar. In rendering the opinion of the court, there will be some departure in form, though not in substance, from the points stated in that argument.

In the order in which the court has viewed this subject, the following questions have been considered and decided.

1st. Has the applicant a right to the commission he demands?

2d. If he has a right, and that right has been violated, do the laws of his country afford him a remedy?

3d. If they do afford him a remedy, is it a *mandamus* issuing from this court?

The first object of inquiry is,

1st. Has the applicant a right to the commission he demands?

His right originates in an act of congress passed in February, 1801, concerning the District of Columbia.

After dividing the district into two counties, the 11th section of this law enacts, "that there shall be appointed in and for each of the said counties, such number of discreet persons to be justices of the peace as the president of the United States shall, from time to time, think expedient, to continue in office for five years."

It appears, from the affidavits, that in compliance with this law, a commission for William Marbury, as a justice of the peace for the county of Washington, was signed by John Adams, then President of the United States; after which the seal of the United States was affixed to it; but the commission has never reached the person for whom it was made out.

In order to determine whether he is entitled to this commission, it becomes necessary to inquire whether he has been appointed to the office. For if he has been appointed, the law continues him in office for five years, and he is entitled to the possession of those evidences of office, which, being completed, became his property.

The 2d section of the 2d article of the constitution declares, that "the president shall nominate, and, by and with the advice and consent of the senate, shall appoint, ambassadors, other public ministers and consuls, and all other officers of the United States, whose appointments are not otherwise provided for."

The 3d section declares, that "he shall commission all the officers of the United States."

An act of congress directs the secretary of state to keep the seal of the United States, "to make out and record, and affix the said seal to all civil commissions to officers of the United States, to be appointed by the president, by and with the consent of the senate, or by the president alone; provided, that the said seal shall not be affixed to any commission before the same shall have been signed by the President of the United States."

These are the clauses of the constitution and laws of the United States, which affect this part of the case. They seem to contemplate three distinct operations:

1st. The nomination. This is the sole act of the president, and is completely voluntary.

2d. The appointment. This is also the act of the president, and is also a voluntary act, though it can only be performed by and with the advice and consent of the senate.

3d. The commission. To grant a commission to a person appointed, might, perhaps, be deemed a duty enjoined by the constitution. "He shall," says that instrument, "commission all the officers of the United States." . . .

The last act to be done by the president is the signature of the commission. He has then acted on the advice and consent of the senate to his own nomination. The time for deliberation has then passed. He has decided. His judgment, on the advice and consent of the senate concurring with his nomination, has been made, and the officer is appointed. . . .

It is . . . decidedly the opinion of the court, that when a commission has been signed by the president, the appointment is made; and that the commission is complete when the seal of the United States has been affixed to it by the secretary of state.

Where an officer is removable at the will of the executive, the circumstance which completes his appointment is of no concern; because the act is at any time revocable; and the commission may be arrested, if still in the office. But when the officer is not removable at the will of the executive, the appointment is not revocable, and cannot be annulled. It has conferred legal rights which cannot be resumed. . . .

Mr. Marbury, then, since his commission was signed by the president, and sealed by the secretary of state, was appointed; and as the law creating the office, gave the officer a right to hold for five years, independent of the executive, the appointment was not revocable, but vested in the officer legal rights, which are protected by the laws of his country.

To withhold his commission, therefore, is an act deemed by the court not warranted by law, but violative of a vested legal right.

This brings us to the second inquiry; which is,

2d. If he has a right, and that right has been violated, do the laws of this country afford him a remedy?

The very essence of civil liberty certainly consists in the right of every individual to claim the protection of the laws, whenever he receives an injury. One of the first duties of government is to afford that protection. In Great Britain the king himself is sued in the respectful form of a petition, and he never fails to comply with the judgment of his court. . . .

By the constitution of the United States, the president is invested with certain important political powers, in the exercise of which he is to use his own discretion, and is accountable only to his country in his political character and to his own conscience. To aid him in the performance of these duties, he is authorized to appoint certain officers, who act by his authority, and in conformity with his orders.

In such cases, their acts are his acts; and whatever opinion may be entertained of the manner in which executive discretion may be used, still there exists, and can exist, no power to control that discretion. The subjects are political. They respect the nation, not individual rights, and being intrusted to the executive, the decision of the executive is conclusive. . . .

But when the legislature proceeds to impose on that officer other duties; when he is directed peremptorily to perform certain acts; when the rights of individuals are dependent on the performance of those acts; he is so far the officer of the law; is amenable to the laws for his conduct; and cannot at his discretion sport away the vested rights of others.

The conclusion from this reasoning is, that where the heads of departments are the political or confidential agents of the executive, merely to execute the will of the president, or rather to act in cases in which the executive possesses a constitutional or legal discretion, nothing can be more perfectly clear than that their acts are only politically examinable. But where a specific duty is assigned by law, and individual rights depend upon the performance of that duty, it seems equally clear that the individual who considers himself injured, has a right to resort to the laws of his country for a remedy. . . .

It is, then, the opinion of the Court,

1st. That by signing the commission of Mr. Marbury, the President of the United States appointed him a justice of peace for the county of Washington, in the District of Columbia; and that the seal of the United States, affixed thereto by the secretary of state, is conclusive testimony of the verity of the signature, and of the completion of the appointment; and that the appointment conferred on him a legal right to the office for the space of five years.

2d. That, having this legal title to the office, he has a consequent right to the commission; a refusal to deliver which is a plain violation of that right, for which the laws of his country afford him a remedy.

It remains to be inquired whether,

3d. He is entitled to the remedy for which he applies. This depends on,

1st. The nature of the writ applied for; and,

2d. The power of this court.

1st. The nature of the writ. . . .

[T]o render the *mandamus* a proper remedy, the officer to whom it is to be directed, must be one to whom, on legal principles, such writ may be directed; and the person applying for it must be without any other specific and legal remedy.

1st. With respect to the officer to whom it would be directed. The intimate political relation subsisting between the President of the United States and the heads of departments, necessarily renders any legal investigation of the acts of one of those high officers peculiarly irksome, as well as delicate; and excites some hesitation with respect to the propriety of entering into such investigation. Impressions are often received without much reflection or examination, and it is not wonderful that in such a case as this the assertion, by an individual, of his legal claims in a court of justice, to which claims it is the duty of that court to attend, should at first view be considered by some, as an attempt to intrude into the cabinet, and to intermeddle with the prerogatives of the executive.

It is scarcely necessary for the court to disclaim all pretensions to such jurisdiction. An extravagance, so absurd and excessive, could not have been entertained for a moment. The province of the court is, solely, to decide on the rights of individuals, not to inquire how the executive, or executive officers, perform duties in which they have a discretion. Questions in their nature political, or which are, by the constitution and laws, submitted to the executive, can never be made in this court.

But, if this be not such a question; if, so far from being an intrusion into the secrets of the cabinet, it respects a paper which, according to law, is upon record, and to a copy of which the law gives a right. . . .

If one of the heads of departments commits any illegal act, under colour of his office, by which an individual sustains an injury, it cannot be pretended that his office alone exempts him from being sued in the ordinary mode of proceeding, and being compelled to obey the judgment of the law. How, then, can his office exempt him from this particular mode of deciding on the legality of his conduct if the case be such a case as would, were any other individual the party complained of, authorize the process?

It is not by the office of the person to whom the writ is directed, but the nature of the thing to be done, that the propriety or impropriety of issuing a *mandamus* is to be determined. . . .

This, then, is a plain case for a *mandamus*, either to deliver the commission, or a copy of it from the record; and it only remains to be inquired,

Whether it can issue from this court.

The act to establish the judicial courts of the United States authorizes the Supreme Court "to issue writs of *mandamus* in cases warranted by the principles and usages of law, to any courts appointed, or persons holding office, under the authority of the United States."★

The secretary of state, being a person holding an office under the authority of the United States, is precisely within the letter of the description, and if this court is not authorized to issue a writ of mandamus to such an officer, it must be because the law is unconstitutional, and therefore absolutely incapable of conferring the authority, and assigning the duties which its words purport to confer and assign.

The constitution vests the whole judicial power of the United States in one supreme court, and such inferior courts as congress shall, from time to time, ordain and establish. This power is expressly extended to all cases arising under the laws of the United States; and, consequently, in some form, may be exercised over the present case; because the right claimed is given by a law of the United States.

In the distribution of this power it is declared that "the supreme court shall have original jurisdiction in all cases affecting ambassadors, other public ministers and consuls, and those in which a state shall be a party. In all other cases, the supreme court shall have appellate jurisdiction."

It has been insisted, at the bar, that as the original grant of jurisdiction, to the supreme and inferior courts, is general, and the clause, assigning original jurisdiction to the supreme court, contains no negative or restrictive words, the power remains to the legislature, to assign original jurisdiction to that court in other cases than those specified in the article which has been recited; provided those cases belong to the judicial power of the United States.

★ Note that Chief Justice Marshall selectively quotes from Section 13 of the Judiciary Act of 1789, which he construes ostensibly to confer authority on the Court to hear Marbury's case under the Court's original jurisdiction and, in turn, declares unconstitutional. The relevant part of Section 13 reads:

> The Supreme Court shall also have appellate jurisdiction from the circuit courts and courts of the several states, in the cases herein after specifically provided for; and shall have power to issue writs of prohibition to the district courts, when proceeding as courts of admiralty and maritime jurisdiction, and writs of *mandamus*, in cases warranted by the principles and usages of law, to any courts appointed, or persons holding office, under the authority of the United States.

If it had been intended to leave it in the discretion of the legislature to apportion to the judicial power between the supreme and inferior courts according to the will of that body, it would certainly have been useless to have proceeded further than to have defined the judicial power, and the tribunals in which it should be vested. The subsequent part of the section is mere surplusage, is entirely without meaning, if such is to be the construction. If congress remains at liberty to give this court appellate jurisdiction, where the constitution has declared their jurisdiction shall be original; and original jurisdiction where the constitution has declared it shall be appellate; the distribution of jurisdiction, made in the constitution, is form without substance.

Affirmative words are often, in their operation, negative of other objects than those affirmed; and in this case, a negative or exclusive sense must be given to them, or they have no operation at all.

It cannot be presumed that any clause in the constitution is intended to be without effect; and, therefore, such a construction is inadmissible, unless the words require it.

If the solicitude of the convention, respecting our peace with foreign powers, induced a provision that the supreme court should take original jurisdiction in cases which might be supposed to affect them; yet the clause would have proceeded no further than to provide for such cases, if no further restriction on the powers of congress had been intended. That they should have appellate jurisdiction in all other cases, with such exceptions as congress might make, is no restriction; unless the words be deemed exclusive of original jurisdiction.

When an instrument organizing fundamentally a judicial system, divides it into one supreme, and so many inferior courts as the legislature may ordain and establish; then enumerates its powers, and proceeds so far to distribute them, as to define the jurisdiction of the supreme court by declaring the cases in which it shall take original jurisdiction, and that in others it shall take appellate jurisdiction; the plain import of the words seems to be, that in one class of cases its jurisdiction is original, and not appellate; in the other it is appellate, and not original. If any other construction would render the clause inoperative, that is an additional reason for rejecting such other construction, and for adhering to their obvious meaning.

To enable this court, then, to issue a *mandamus*, it must be shown to be an exercise of appellate jurisdiction, or to be necessary to enable them to exercise appellate jurisdiction.

It has been stated at the bar that the appellate jurisdiction may be exercised in a variety of forms, and that if it be the will of the legislature that a *mandamus* should be used for that purpose, that will must be obeyed. This is true, yet the jurisdiction must be appellate, not original.

It is the essential criterion of appellate jurisdiction, that it revises and corrects the proceedings in a cause already instituted, and does not create that cause. Although, therefore, a mandamus may be directed to courts, yet to issue such a writ to an officer for the delivery of a paper, is in effect the same as to sustain an original action for that paper, and, therefore, seems not to belong to appellate, but to original jurisdiction. Neither is it necessary in such a case as this, to enable the court to exercise its appellate jurisdiction.

The authority, therefore, given to the supreme court, by the act establishing the judicial courts of the United States, to issue writs of *mandamus* to public officers, appears not to be warranted by the constitution; and it becomes necessary to inquire whether a jurisdiction so conferred can be exercised.

The question, whether an act, repugnant to the constitution, can become the law of the land, is a question deeply interesting to the United States; but, happily, not of an intricacy proportioned to its interest. It seems only necessary to recognize certain principles, supposed to have been long and well established, to decide it.

That the people have an original right to establish, for their future government, such principles, as, in their opinion, shall most conduce to their own happiness is the basis on which the whole American fabric has been erected. The exercise of this original right is a very great exertion; nor can it, nor ought it, to be frequently repeated. The principles, therefore, so established, are deemed fundamental. And as the authority from which they proceed is supreme, and can seldom act, they are designed to be permanent.

This original and supreme will organizes the government, and assigns to different departments their respective powers. It may either stop here, or establish certain limits not to be transcended by those departments.

The government of the United States is of the latter description. The powers of the legislature are defined and limited; and that those limits may not be mistaken, or forgotten, the constitution is written. To what purpose are powers limited, and to what purpose is that limitation committed to writing, if these limits may, at any time, be passed by those intended to be restrained? The distinction between a government with limited and unlimited powers is abolished, if those limits do not confine the persons on whom they are imposed, and if acts prohibited and acts allowed, are of equal obligation. It is a proposition too plain to be contested, that the constitution controls any legislative act repugnant to it; or, that the legislature may alter the constitution by an ordinary act.

Between these alternatives there is no middle ground. The constitution is either a superior paramount law, unchangeable by ordinary means, or it is on a level with ordinary legislative acts, and, like other acts, is alterable when the legislature shall please to alter it.

If the former part of the alternative be true, then a legislative act contrary to the constitution is not law: if the latter part be true, then written constitutions are absurd attempts, on the part of the people, to limit a power in its own nature illimitable.

Certainly all those who have framed written constitutions contemplate them as forming the fundamental and paramount law of the nation, and, consequently, the theory of every such government must be, that an act of the legislature, repugnant to the constitution, is void.

This theory is essentially attached to a written constitution, and, is consequently, to be considered, by this court, as one of the fundamental principles of our society. It is not therefore to be lost sight of in the further consideration of this subject.

If an act of the legislature, repugnant to the constitution, is void, does it, notwithstanding its invalidity, bind the courts, and oblige them to give it effect? Or, in other words, though it be not law, does it constitute a rule as operative as if it was a law? This would be to overthrow in fact what was established in theory; and would seem, at first view, an absurdity too gross to be insisted on. It shall, however, receive a more attentive consideration.

It is emphatically the province and duty of the judicial department to say what the law is. Those who apply the rule to particular cases, must of necessity expound and interpret that rule. If two laws conflict with each other, the courts must decide on the operation of each.

So if a law be in opposition to the constitution; if both the law and the constitution apply to a particular case, so that the court must either decide that case conformably to the law, disregarding the constitution; or conformably to the constitution, disregarding the law; the court must determine which of these conflicting rules governs the case. This is of the very essence of judicial duty.

If, then, the courts are to regard the constitution, and the constitution is superior to any ordinary act of the legislature, the constitution, and not such ordinary act, must govern the case to which they both apply.

Those, then, who controvert the principle that the constitution is to be considered, in court, as a paramount law, are reduced to the necessity of maintaining that courts must close their eyes on the constitution, and see only the law.

This doctrine would subvert the very foundation of all written constitutions. It would declare that an act which, according to the principles and theory of our government, is entirely void, is yet, in practice, completely obligatory. It would declare that if the legislature shall do what is expressly forbidden, such act, notwithstanding the express prohibition, is in reality effectual. It would be given to the legislature a practical and real omnipotence, with the same breath which professes to restrict their powers within narrow limits. It is prescribing limits, and declaring that those limits may be passed at pleasure.

That it thus reduces to nothing what we have deemed the greatest improvement on political institutions, a written constitution, would of itself be sufficient, in America, where written constitutions have been viewed with so much reverence, for rejecting the construction. But the peculiar expressions of the constitution of the United States furnish additional arguments in favour of its rejection.

The judicial power of the United States is extended to all cases arising under the constitution.

Could it be the intention of those who gave this power, to say that in using it the constitution should not be looked into? That a case arising under the constitution should be decided without examining the instrument under which it arises?

This is too extravagant to be maintained.

In some cases, then, the constitution must be looked into by the judges. And if they can open it at all, what part of it are they forbidden to read or to obey?

There are many other parts of the constitution which serve to illustrate this subject.

It is declared that "no tax or duty shall be laid on articles exported from any state." Suppose a duty on the export of cotton, of tobacco, or of flour; and a suit instituted to recover it. Ought judgment to be rendered in such a case? Ought the judges to close their eyes on the constitution, and only see the law?

The constitution declares "that no bill of attainder or *ex post facto* law shall be passed."

If, however, such a bill should be passed, and a person should be prosecuted under it; must the court condemn to death those victims whom the constitution endeavors to preserve?

"No person," says the constitution, "shall be convicted of treason unless on the testimony of two witnesses to the same overt act, or on confession in open court."

Here the language of the constitution is addressed especially to the courts. It prescribes, directly for them, a rule of evidence not to be departed from. If the legislature should change that rule, and declare one witness, or a confession out of court, sufficient for conviction, must the constitutional principle yield to the legislative act?

From these, and many other selections which might be made, it is apparent, that the framers of the constitution contemplated that instrument as a rule for the government of courts, as well as of the legislature.

Why otherwise does it direct the judges to take an oath to support it? This oath certainly applies in an especial manner, to their conduct in their official character. How immoral to impose it on them, if they were to be used as the instruments, and the knowing instruments, for violating what they swear to support!

The oath of office, too, imposed by the legislature, is completely demonstrative of the legislative opinion on this subject. It is in these words: "I do solemnly swear that I will administer justice without respect to persons, and do equal right to the poor and to the rich; and that I will faithfully and impartially discharge all the duties incumbent on me as ————, according to the best of my abilities and understanding agreeably to the constitution and laws of the United States."

Why does a judge swear to discharge his duties agreeably to the constitution of the United States, if that constitution forms no rule for his government? if it is closed upon him, and cannot be inspected by him?

If such be the real state of things, this is worse than solemn mockery. To prescribe, or to take this oath, becomes equally a crime.

It is also not entirely unworthy of observation, that in declaring what shall be the *supreme law* of the land, *the constitution* itself is first mentioned; and not the laws of the United States generally, but those only which shall be made in *pursuance* of the constitution, have that rank.

Thus, the particular phraseology of the constitution of the United States confirms and strengthens the principle, supposed to be essential to all written constitutions, that a law repugnant to the constitution is void; and that *courts*, as well as other departments, are bound by that instrument.

The rule must be discharged.

Eakin v. Raub

12 SARGEANT & RAWLE 330 (PA., 1825)

In this case involving the power of the Pennsylvania Supreme Court to invalidate a state law, Justice John Bannister Gibson wrote a dissenting opinion aimed at refuting Chief Justice John Marshall's arguments for judicial review in *Marbury v. Madison* (1803) (see excerpt above). Note that Justice Gibson's criticism of *Marbury* was limited to the exercise of judicial review over coequal branches of government. While he contended that state courts had no power to overturn state laws deemed to violate the state constitution, Justice Gibson did not deny that state courts could strike down state laws that were inconsistent with federal law or the Constitution. Moreover, twenty years later, Justice Gibson repudiated the position taken in his opinion here. In *Norris v. Clymer*, 2 Pa. 277 (1845), he explained his change in "opinion for two reasons. The late convention (which drafted Pennsylvania's state constitution), by their silence, sanctioned the pretensions of the courts to deal freely with the Acts of the Legislature; and from experience of the necessity of the case."

☐ *Justice GIBSON, dissenting.*

I am aware, that a right [in the judiciary] to declare all unconstitutional acts void . . . is generally held as a professional dogma, but, I apprehend, rather as a matter of faith than of reason. I admit that I once embraced the same doctrine, but without examination, and I shall therefore state the arguments that impelled me to abandon it, with great respect for those by whom it is still maintained. But I may premise, that it is not a little remarkable, that although the right in question has all along been claimed by the judiciary, no judge has ventured to discuss it, except Chief Justice MARSHALL, and if the argument of a jurist so distinguished for the strength of his ratiocinative powers be found inconclusive, it may fairly be set down to the weakness of the position which he attempts to defend. . . .

I begin, then, by observing that in this country, the powers of the judiciary are divisible into those that are POLITICAL and those that are purely civil. Every power by which one organ of the government is enabled to control another, or to exert an influence over its acts, is a political power. . . .

The constitution and the right of the legislature to pass the act, may be in collision. But is that a legitimate subject for judicial determination? If it be, the judiciary must be a peculiar organ, to revise the proceedings of the legislature, and to correct its mistakes; and in what part of the constitution are we to look for this proud pre-eminence? Viewing the matter in the opposite direction, what would be thought of an act of assembly in which it should be declared that the supreme court had, in a particular case, put a wrong construction on the constitution of the United States, and that the judgment should therefore be reversed? It would doubtless be thought a usurpation of judicial power. But it is by no means clear, that to declare a law void which has been enacted according to the forms prescribed in the constitution, is not a usurpation of legislative power. . . .

But it has been said to be emphatically the business of the judiciary, to ascertain and pronounce what the law is; and that this necessarily involves a consideration of the constitution. It does so: but how far? If the judiciary will inquire into anything besides the form of enactment, where shall it stop? . . .

In theory, all the organs of the government are of equal capacity; or, if not equal, each must be supposed to have superior capacity only for those things which peculiarly belong to it; and as legislation peculiarly involves the consideration of those limitations which are put on the law-making power, and the interpretation of the laws when made, involves only the construction of the laws themselves, it follows that the construction of the constitution in this particular belongs to the legislature, which ought therefore to be taken to have superior capacity to judge of the constitutionality of its own acts. But suppose all to be of equal capacity in every respect, why should one exercise a controlling power over the rest? That the judiciary is of superior rank, has never been pretended, although it has been said to be co-ordinate. It is not easy, however, to comprehend how the power which gives law to all the rest, can be of no more than equal rank with one which receives it, and is answerable to the former for the observance of its statutes. Legislation is essentially an act of sovereign power; but the execution of the laws by instruments that are governed by prescribed rules and exercise no power of volition, is essentially otherwise. . . . It may be said, the power of the legislature, also, is limited by prescribed rules. It is so. But it is nevertheless, the power of the people, and sovereign as far as it extends. It cannot be said, that the judiciary is coordinate merely because it is established by the constitution. If that were sufficient, sheriffs, registers of wills, and recorders of deeds, would be so too. Within the pale of their authority, the acts of these officers will have the power of the people for their support; but no one will pretend, they are of equal dignity with the acts of the legislature. Inequality of rank arises not from the manner in which the organ has been constituted, but from its essence and the nature of its functions;and the legislative organ is superior to every other, inasmuch as the power to will and to command, is essentially superior to the power to act and to obey. . . .

Everyone knows how seldom men think exactly alike on ordinary subjects; and a government constructed on the principle of assent by all its parts, would be inadequate to the most simple operations. The notion of a complication of counter checks has been carried to an extent in theory, of which the framers of the constitution never dreamt. When the entire sovereignty was separated into its elementary parts, and distributed to the appropriate branches, all things incident to the exercise of its powers were committed to each branch exclusively. The negative which each part of the legislature may exercise, in regard to the acts of the other, was thought sufficient to prevent material infractions of the restraints which were put on the power of the whole; for, had it been intended to interpose the judiciary as an additional barrier, the matter would surely not have been left in doubt. The judges would not have been left to stand on the insecure and ever shifting ground of public opinion as to constructive powers; they would have been placed on the impregnable ground of an express grant. They would not have been compelled to resort to debates in the convention, or the opinion that was generally entertained at the time. . . .

The power is said to be restricted to cases that are free from doubt or difficulty. But the abstract existence of a power cannot depend on the clearness or obscurity of the case in which it is to be exercised; for that is a consideration that cannot present itself, before the question of the existence of the power shall have been determined; and, if its existence be conceded, no considerations of policy arising from the obscurity of the particular case, ought to influence the exercise of it. . . .

To say, therefore, that the power is to be exercised but in perfectly clear cases, is to betray a doubt of the propriety of exercising it at all. Were the same caution used in judging of the existence of the power that is inculcated as to the exercise of it, the profession would perhaps arrive at a different conclusion. The grant of a power so extraordinary ought to appear so plain, that he who should run might read. . . .

What I have in view in this inquiry, is the supposed right of the judiciary to interfere, in cases where the constitution is to be carried into effect through the instrumentality of the legislature, and where that organ must necessarily first decide on the constitutionality of its own act. The oath to support the constitution is not peculiar to the judges, but is taken indiscriminately by every officer of the government, and is designed rather as a test of the political principles of the man, than to bind the officer in the discharge of his duty; otherwise it is difficult to determine what operation it is to have in the case of a recorder of deeds, for instance, who, in the execution of his office, has nothing to do with the constitution. But granting it to relate to the official conduct of the judge, as well as every other officer, and not to his political principles, still it must be understood in reference to supporting the constitution, *only as far as that may be involved in his official duty;* and, consequently, if his official duty does not comprehend an inquiry into the authority of the legislature, neither does his oath. . . .

But do not the judges do a positive act in violation of the constitution, when they give effect to an unconstitutional law? Not if the law has been passed according to the forms established in the constitution. The fallacy of the question is, in supposing that the judiciary adopts the acts of the legislature as its own; whereas the enactment of a law and the interpretation of it are not concurrent acts, and as the judiciary is not required to concur in the enactment, neither is it in the breach of the constitution which may be the consequence of the enactment. The fault is imputable to the legislature, and on it the responsibility exclusively rests. . . .

But it has been said, that this construction would deprive the citizen of the advantages which are peculiar to a written constitution, by at once declaring the power of the legislature in practice to be illimitable. . . . But there is no magic or inherent power in parchment and ink, to command respect and protect principles from violation. In the business of government a recurrence to first principles answers the end of an observation at sea with a view to correct the dead reckoning; and for this purpose, a written constitution is an instrument of inestimable value. It is of inestimable value, also, in rendering its first principles familiar to the mass of people; for, after all, there is no effectual guard against legislative usurpation but public opinion, the force of which, in this country is inconceivably great. . . . Once let public opinion be so corrupt as to sanction every misconstruction of the constitution and abuse of power which the temptation of the moment may dictate, and the party which may happen to be predominant, will laugh at the puny efforts of a dependent power to arrest it in its course.

For these reasons, I am of [the] opinion that it rests with the people, in whom full and absolute sovereign power resides, to correct abuses in legislation, by instructing their representatives to repeal the obnoxious act. What is wanting to plenary power in the government, is reserved by the people for their own immediate use; and to redress an infringement of their rights in this respect, would seem to be an accessory of the power thus reserved. It might, perhaps, have been better to vest the power in the judiciary; as it might be expected that its habits of deliberation, and the aid derived from the arguments of counsel, would more frequently lead to accurate conclusions. On the other hand, the judiciary is not infallible; and an error by it would admit of no remedy but a more distinct expression of the public will, through the extraordinary medium of a convention; whereas, an error by the legislature admits of a remedy by an exertion of the same will, in the ordinary exercise of the right of suffrage—a mode better calculated to attain the end, without popular excitement. It may be said, the people would probably not notice an error of their representatives. But they would as probably do so, as notice an error of the judiciary; and, besides, it is a postulate in the theory of our government, and the very basis of the superstructure, that the people are wise, virtuous, and competent to manage their own affairs; and if they are not so, in fact, still every question of this sort must be determined according to the principles of the constitution, as it came from the hands of the framers, and the existence of a defect which was not foreseen, would not justify those who administer the government, in applying a corrective in practice, which can be provided only by convention. . . .

But in regard to an act of [a state] assembly, which is found to be in collision with the constitution, laws, or treaties of the *United States*, I take the duty of the judiciary to be exactly the reverse. By becoming parties to the federal constitution, the states have agreed to several limitations of their individual sovereignty, to enforce which, it was thought to be absolutely necessary to prevent them from giving effect to laws in violation of those limitations, through the instrumentality of their own judges. Accordingly, it is declared in the sixth article and second section of the federal constitution, that "This constitution, and the laws of the *United States* which shall be made in pursuance thereof, and all treaties made, or which shall be made under the authority of the *United States*, shall be the *supreme* law of the land; and the *judges* in every *state* shall be BOUND thereby: anything in the *laws* or *constitution* of any *state* to the contrary notwithstanding."

President Jackson's Veto Message of 1832

President Andrew Jackson distrusted banks and, as a westerner, opposed the policies of the Bank of the United States which limited credit for land speculation. When Congress rechartered the Bank in 1832, Jackson vetoed the bill with this message,★ drafted by Secretary of the Treasury (and later appointed as chief justice) Roger B. Taney. The controversy over the establishment of the national bank and its importance in shaping constitutional politics is dealt with further in Volume 1, Chapter 6.

☐ *To the Senate:*

The bill "to modify and continue" the act entitled "An act to incorporate the subscribers to the Bank of the United States" was presented to me on the 4th July instant. Having considered it with that solemn regard to the principles of the Constitution which the day was calculated to inspire, and come to the conclusion that it ought not to become a law, I herewith return it to the Senate, in which it originated, with my objections.

It is maintained by the advocates of the bank that its constitutionality in all its features ought to be considered as settled by precedent and by the decision of the Supreme Court. To this conclusion I can not assent. Mere precedent is a dangerous source of authority, and should not be regarded as deciding questions of constitutional power except where the acquiescence of the people and the States can be considered as well settled. So far from this being the case on this subject, an argument against the bank might be based on precedent. One Congress, in 1791, decided in favor of a bank; another in 1811, decided against it. One Congress, in 1815, decided against a bank, another, in 1816, decided in its favor. Prior to the present Congress, therefore, the precedents drawn from that source were equal. If we resort to the States, the expressions of legislative, judicial, and executive opinions against the bank have been probably to those in its favor as 4 to 1. There is nothing in precedent, therefore, which, if its authority were admitted, ought to weigh in favor of the act before me.

If the opinion of the Supreme Court covered the whole ground of this act, it ought not to control the coordinate authorities of this Government. The Congress, the Executive, and the Court must each for itself be guided by its own opinion of the Constitution. Each public officer who takes an oath to support the Constitution swears that he will support it as he understands it, and not as it is understood by others. It is as much the duty of the House of Representatives, of the Senate, and of the President to decide upon the constitutionality of any bill or resolution which may be presented to them for passage or approval as it is of the supreme judges when it may be brought before them for judicial decision. The opinion of the judges has no more authority over Congress than the opinion of Congress has over the judges, and on that point the President is independent of both. The authority of the Supreme Court must not, therefore, be permitted to control the Congress or the Executive when acting in their legislative capacities, but to have only such influence as the force of their reasoning may deserve.

But in the case relied upon the Supreme Court have not decided that all the features of this corporation are compatible with the Constitution. It is

★ From James D. Richardson, ed., *A Compilation of the Messages and Papers of the Presidents* (Washington, DC: Bureau of National Literature and Art, 1908), Vol. 2, 581–582.

true that the court have said that the law incorporating the bank is a constitutional exercise of power by Congress; but taking into view the whole opinion of the court and the reasoning by which they have come to that conclusion, I understand them to have decided that inasmuch as a bank is an appropriate means for carrying into effect the enumerated powers of the General Government, therefore the law incorporating it is in accordance with that provision of the Constitution which declares that Congress shall have power "to make all laws which shall be necessary and proper for carrying those powers into execution." Having satisfied themselves that the word *"necessary"* in the Constitution means *"needful," "requisite," "essential," "conducive to,"* and that "a bank" is a convenient, a useful, and essential instrument in the prosecution of the Government's "fiscal operations," they conclude that to "use one must be within the discretion of Congress" and that "the act to incorporate the Bank of the United States is a law made in pursuance of the Constitution"; "but," say they, *"where the law is not prohibited and is really calculated to effect any of the objects intrusted to the Government, to undertake here to inquire into the degree of its necessity would be to pass the line which circumscribes the judicial department and to tread on legislative ground."*

The principle here affirmed is that the "degree of its necessity," involving all the details of a banking institution, is a question exclusively for legislative consideration. A bank is constitutional, but it is the province of the Legislature to determine whether this or that particular power, privilege, or exemption is "necessary and proper" to enable the bank to discharge its duties to the Government, and from their decision there is no appeal to the courts of justice. Under the decision of the Supreme Court, therefore, it is the exclusive province of Congress and the President to decide whether the particular features of this act are *necessary* and *proper* in order to enable the bank to perform conveniently and efficiently the public duties assigned to it as a fiscal agent, and therefore constitutional, or *unnecessary* and *improper*, and therefore unconstitutional. . . .

The bank is professedly established as an agent of the executive branch of the Government, and its constitutionality is maintained on that ground. Neither upon the propriety of present action nor upon the provisions of this act was the Executive consulted. It has had no opportunity to say that it neither needs nor wants an agent clothed with such powers and favored by such exemptions. There is nothing in its legitimate functions which makes it necessary or proper. Whatever interest or influence, whether public or private, has given birth to this act, it can not be found either in the wishes or necessities of the executive department, by which present action is deemed premature, and the powers conferred upon its agent not only unnecessary, but dangerous to the Government and country. . . .

Experience should teach us wisdom. Most of the difficulties our Government now encounters and most of the dangers which impend over our Union have sprung from an abandonment of the legitimate objects of Government by our national legislation, and the adoption of such principles as are embodied in this act. Many of our rich men have not been content with equal protection and equal benefits, but have besought us to make them richer by act of Congress. By attempting to gratify their desires we have in the results of our legislation arrayed section against section, interest against interest, and man against man, in a fearful commotion which threatens to shake the foundations of our Union. It is time to pause in our career to review our principles, and if possible revive that devoted patriotism and spirit of compromise which distinguished the sages of the Revolution and the fathers of our Union. If we can not at once, in justice to interests vested under improvident legislation, make our Government what it ought to be, we can at least take a stand against all new grants of monopolies and exclusive privileges, against any prostitution of our Government to the advancement of the few at the expense of the many, and in favor of compromise and gradual reform in our code of laws and system of political economy.

I have now done my duty to my country. If sustained by my fellow-citizens, I shall be grateful and happy; if not, I shall find in the motives which impel me ample grounds for contentment and peace.

President Roosevelt's Radio Broadcast, March 9, 1937

During President Franklin D. Roosevelt's first term (1933–1937), the Supreme Court by a vote of five to four invalidated much of his New Deal program and plan for the country's economic recovery from the Great Depression. After his landslide reelection in November 1936, FDR proposed in February 1937 that Congress expand the size of the Court from nine to fifteen justices and thereby give him the chance to secure a majority sympathetic to his policies. On March 9, 1937, the Democratic president made the following radio address in an effort to marshal public support for his "Court-packing plan." But that same month, while the Senate Judiciary Committee was considering his proposal, Justice Owen Roberts, who had previously cast the crucial vote for overturning progressive economic legislation, switched sides and voted to uphold New Deal legislation. The Court's proverbial "switch-in-time-that-saved-nine" then contributed to the Democrat-dominated Senate's defeat of FDR's proposal. The constitutional crisis that loomed over the Court and the country in 1937 is discussed further in Volume 1, Chapter 6, and in this volume, Chapter 3.

Tonight, sitting at my desk in the White House, I make my first radio report to the people in my second term of office.★

I am reminded of that evening in March, four years ago, when I made my first radio report to you. We were then in the midst of the great banking crisis.

Soon after, with the authority of the Congress, we asked the Nation to

★ From 1937 *Public Papers and Addresses of Franklin D. Roosevelt* (1941), 122.

turn over all of its privately held gold, dollar for dollar, to the Government of the United States.

Today's recovery proves how right that policy was.

But when, almost two years later, it came before the Supreme Court its constitutionality was upheld only by a five-to-four vote. The change of one vote would have thrown all the affairs of this great Nation back into hopeless chaos. In effect, four Justices ruled that the right under a private contract to exact a pound of flesh was more sacred than the main objectives of the Constitution to establish an enduring Nation.

In 1933 you and I knew that we must never let our economic system get completely out of joint again—that we could not afford to take the risk of another great depression.

We also became convinced that the only way to avoid a repetition of those dark days was to have a government with power to prevent and to cure the abuses and the inequalities which had thrown that system out of joint.

We then began a program of remedying those abuses and inequalities—to give balance and stability to our economic system—to make it bombproof against the causes of 1929.

Today we are only part-way through that program—and recovery is speeding up to a point where the dangers of 1929 are again becoming possible, not this week or month perhaps, but within a year or two.

National laws are needed to complete that program. Individual or local or state effort alone cannot protect us in 1937 any better than ten years ago. . . .

The American people have learned from the depression. For in the last three national elections an overwhelming majority of them voted a mandate that the Congress and the President begin the task of providing that protection—not after long years of debate, but now.

The Courts, however, have cast doubts on the ability of the elected Congress to protect us against catastrophe by meeting squarely our modern social and economic conditions.

We are at a crisis in our ability to proceed with that protection. It is a quiet crisis. There are no lines of depositors outside closed banks. But to the far-sighted it is far-reaching in its possibilities of injury to America.

I want to talk with you very simply about the need for present action in this crisis—the need to meet the unanswered challenge of one-third of a Nation ill-nourished, ill-clad, ill-housed.

Last Thursday I described the American form of Government as a three horse team provided by the Constitution to the American people so that their field might be plowed. The three horses are, of course, the three branches of government—the Congress, the Executive and the Courts. Two of the horses are pulling in unison today; the third is not. Those who have intimated that the President of the United States is trying to drive that team, overlook the simple fact that the President, as Chief Executive, is himself one of the three horses.

It is the American people themselves who are in the driver's seat.

It is the American people themselves who want the furrow plowed.

It is the American people themselves who expect the third horse to pull in unison with the other two.

I hope that you have re-read the Constitution of the United States. Like the Bible, it ought to be read again and again.

It is an easy document to understand when you remember that it was called into being because the Articles of Confederation under which the original thirteen States tried to operate after the Revolution showed the need of a National Government with power enough to handle national problems. In its Preamble, the Constitution states that it was intended to form a more perfect Union and promote the general welfare; and the powers given to the Congress to carry out those purposes can be best described by saying that they were all the powers needed to meet each and every problem which then had a national character and which could not be met by merely local action.

But the framers went further. Having in mind that in succeeding generations many other problems then undreamed of would become national problems, they gave to the Congress the ample broad powers "to levy taxes . . . and provide for the common defense and general welfare of the United States."

That, my friends, is what I honestly believe to have been the clear and underlying purpose of the patriots who wrote a Federal Constitution to create a National Government with national power, intended as they said, "to form a more perfect union . . . for ourselves and our posterity." . . .

But since the rise of the modern movement for social and economic progress through legislation, the Court has more and more often and more and more boldly asserted a power to veto laws passed by the Congress and State Legislatures in complete disregard of this original limitation.

In the last four years the sound rule of giving statutes the benefit of all reasonable doubt has been cast aside. The Court has been acting not as a judicial body, but as a policy-making body.

When the Congress has sought to stabilize national agriculture, to improve the conditions of labor, to safeguard business against unfair competition, to protect our national resources, and in many other ways, to serve our clearly national needs, the majority of the Court has been assuming the power to pass on the wisdom of these Acts of the Congress—and to approve or disapprove the public policy written into these laws.

That is not only my accusation. It is the accusation of most distinguished Justices of the present Supreme Court. I have not the time to quote to you all the language used by dissenting Justices in many of these cases. But in the case holding the Railroad Retirement Act unconstitutional, for instance, Chief Justice Hughes said in a dissenting opinion that the majority opinion was "a departure from sound principles," and placed "an unwarranted limitation upon the commerce clause." And three other Justices agreed with him.

In the case holding the A.A.A. unconstitutional, Justice Stone said of the majority opinion that it was a "tortured construction of the Constitution." And two other Justices agreed with him.

In the case holding the New York Minimum Wage Law unconstitutional, Justice Stone said that the majority were actually reading into the Constitution their own "personal economic predilections," and that if the legislative power is not left free to choose the methods of solving the problems of poverty, subsistence and health of large numbers in the community, then "government is to be rendered impotent." And two other Justices agreed with him.

In the face of these dissenting opinions, there is no basis for the claim made by some members of the Court that something in the Constitution has compelled them regretfully to thwart the will of the people.

In the face of such dissenting opinions, it is perfectly clear, that as Chief Justice Hughes has said: "We are under a Constitution but the Constitution is what the Judges say it is."

The Court in addition to the proper use of its judicial functions has improperly set itself up as a third House of the Congress—a super-legislature, as one of the Justices has called it—reading into the Constitution words and implications which are not there, and which were never intended to be there.

We have, therefore, reached the point as a Nation where we must take action to save the Constitution from the Court and the Court from itself. We must find a way to take an appeal from the Supreme Court to the Constitution itself. We want a Supreme Court which will do justice under the Constitution—not over it. In our Courts we want a government of laws and not of men.

I want—as all Americans want—an independent judiciary as proposed by the framers of the Constitution. That means a Supreme Court that will enforce the Constitution as written—that will refuse to amend the Constitution by the arbitrary exercise of judicial power—amendment by judicial say-so. It does not mean a judiciary so independent that it can deny the existence of facts universally recognized.

How then could we proceed to perform the mandate given us? It was said in last year's Democratic platform "If these problems cannot be effectively solved within the Constitution, we shall seek such clarifying amendment as will assure the power to enact those laws, adequately to regulate commerce, protect public health and safety, and safeguard economic security." In other words, we said we would seek an amendment only if every other possible means by legislation were to fail.

When I commenced to review the situation with the problem squarely before me, I came by a process of elimination to the conclusion that short of amendments the only method which was clearly constitutional, and would at the same time carry out other much needed reforms, was to infuse new blood into all our Courts. We must have men worthy and equipped to carry out impartial justice. But, at the same time, we must have Judges who will bring to the Courts a present-day sense of the Constitution—Judges who will retain in the Courts the judicial functions of a court, and reject the legislative powers which the Courts have today assumed. . . .

What is my proposal? It is simply this: whenever a Judge or Justice of any Federal Court has reached the age of seventy and does not avail himself of the opportunity to retire on a pension, a new member shall be appointed by the President then in office, with the approval, as required by the Constitution, of the Senate of the United States.

That plan has two chief purposes. By bringing into the Judicial system a steady and continuing stream of new and younger blood, I hope, first, to make the administration of all Federal justice speedier and, therefore, less costly; secondly, to bring to the decision of social and economic problems younger men who have had personal experience and contact with modern facts and circumstances under which average men have to live and work. This plan will save our national Constitution from hardening of the judicial arteries.

The number of Judges to be appointed would depend wholly on the decision of present Judges now over seventy, or those who would subsequently reach the age of seventy.

If, for instance, any one of the six Justices of the Supreme Court now over the age of seventy should retire as provided under the plan, no additional place would be created. Consequently, although there never can be more than fifteen, there may be only fourteen, or thirteen, or twelve. And there may be only nine.

There is nothing novel or radical about this idea. It seeks to maintain the Federal bench in full vigor. It has been discussed and approved by many persons of high authority ever since a similar proposal passed the House of Representatives in 1869.

Why was the age fixed at seventy? Because the laws of many States, the practice of the Civil Service, the regulations of the Army and Navy, and the rules of many of our Universities and of almost every great private business enterprise, commonly fix the retirement age at seventy years or less.

The statute would apply to all the Courts in the Federal system. There is general approval so far as the lower Federal courts are concerned. The plan has met opposition only so far as the Supreme Court of the United States itself is concerned. If such a plan is good for the lower courts it certainly ought to be equally good for the highest Court from which there is no appeal.

Those opposing this plan have sought to arouse prejudice and fear by crying that I am seeking to "pack" the Supreme Court and that a baneful precedent will be established.

What do they mean by the words "packing the Court"?

Let me answer this question with a bluntness that will end all *honest* misunderstanding of my purposes.

If by that phrase "packing the Court" it is charged that I wish to place on the bench spineless puppets who would disregard the law and would decide specific cases as I wished them to be decided, I make this answer—that no President fit for his office would appoint, and no Senate of honorable men fit for their office would confirm, that kind of appointees to the Supreme Court.

But if by that phrase the charge is made that I would appoint and the Senate would confirm Justices worthy to sit beside present members of the Court who understand those modern conditions—that I will appoint Justices who will not undertake to override the judgment of the Congress on legislative policy—that I will appoint Justices who will act as Justices and not as legislators—if the appointment of such Justices can be called "packing the Courts," then I say that I and with me the vast majority of the American people favor doing just that thing—now.

Is it a dangerous precedent for the Congress to change the number of the Justices? The Congress has always had, and will have, that power. The number of Justices has been changed several times before—in the Administrations of John Adams and Thomas Jefferson,—both signers of the Declaration of Independence—Andrew Jackson, Abraham Lincoln and Ulysses S. Grant.

I suggest only the addition of Justices to the bench in accordance with a clearly defined principle relating to a clearly defined age limit. Fundamentally, if in the future, America cannot trust the Congress it elects to refrain from abuse of our Constitutional usages, democracy will have failed far beyond the importance to it of any kind of precedent concerning the Judiciary. . . .

It is the clear intention of our public policy to provide for a constant flow of new and younger blood into the Judiciary. Normally every President appoints a large number of District and Circuit Judges and a few members of the Supreme Court. Until my first term practically every President of the United States had appointed at least one member of the Supreme Court. President Taft appointed five members and named a Chief Justice—President Wilson three—President Harding four including a Chief Justice—President Coolidge one—President Hoover three including a Chief Justice.

Such a succession of appointments should have provided a Court well-balanced as to age. But chance and the disinclination of individuals to leave the Supreme bench have now given us a Court in which five Justices will be over seventy-five years of age before next June and one over seventy. Thus a sound public policy has been defeated.

I now propose that we establish by law an assurance against any such ill-balanced Court in the future. I propose that hereafter, when a Judge reaches the age of seventy, a new and younger Judge shall be added to the Court automatically. In this way I propose to enforce a sound public policy by law instead of leaving the composition of our Federal Courts, including the highest, to be determined by chance or the personal decision of individuals.

If such a law as I propose is regarded as establishing a new precedent—is it not a most desirable precedent?

Like all lawyers, like all Americans, I regret the necessity of this controversy. But the welfare of the United States, and indeed of the Constitution itself, is what we all must think about first. Our difficulty with the Court today rises not from the Court as an institution but from human beings within it. But we cannot yield our constitutional destiny to the personal judgment of a few men who, being fearful of the future, would deny us the necessary means of dealing with the present.

This plan of mine is no attack on the Court; it seeks to restore the Court to its rightful and historic place in our system of Constitutional Government and to have it resume its high task of building anew on the Constitution "a system of living law."

B | *The Politics of Constitutional Interpretation*

Constitutional interpretation and law, Justice Felix Frankfurter observed, "is not at all a science, but applied politics."[1] The Constitution, of course, is a political document and as a written document is not self-interpreting; its interpretation is political. *How* the Constitution should be interpreted is thus as controversial as the ongoing debate over *who* should interpret it.

For much of the nineteenth century, theories of constitutional interpretation were generally not debated.[2] The Court's interpretation of the Constitution, of course, remained politically controversial. Yet, the great debates between Jeffersonian-Republicans and Federalists centered on disagreements over fundamental principles of constitutional politics (the power and structure of government and guarantees for civil rights and liberties), rather than competing interpretive theories. Their struggle was over rival political philosophies and interpretations of the political system created by the Constitution. That struggle continues except that contemporary debates, within the Court and the legal community, tend to be more complex and linked to rival theories of constitutional interpretation that aim to justify or criticize the Court's exercise of judicial review.

In 1833, for example, Justice Joseph Story in his influential *Commentaries on the Constitution of the United States* saw no need to offer a theory of constitutional interpretation, explaining that

> [t]he reader must not expect to find in these pages any novel views and novel constructions of the Constitution. I have not the ambition to be the author of any new plan of interpreting the theory of the Constitution, or of enlarging or narrowing its powers by ingenious subtleties and learned doubts. . . . Upon subjects of government, it has always appeared to me, that metaphysical refinements are out of place. A constitution of government is addressed to the common sense of the people, and never was designed for trials of logical skill or visionary speculation.[3]

Story assumed that "[t]he first and fundamental rule in the interpretation of all instruments is, to construe them according to the sense of the terms and the intention of the parties."[4] This "plain meaning rule" was set forth by Chief Justice John Marshall in *Sturges v. Crowninshield*, 17 U.S. 122 (1819):

> [A]lthough the spirit of an instrument, especially of a constitution, is to be respected not less than its letter, yet the spirit is to be collected chiefly from its words. . . . [I]f, in any case, the plain meaning of a provision, not contradicted by any other provision in the same instrument, is to be disregarded, because we believe the framers of that instrument could not intend what they say, it must be one in which the absurdity and injustice of applying the provision to the case, would be so monstrous that all mankind would, without hesitation, unite in rejecting the application.

While the plain meaning of the Constitution for Story and Marshall was derived from a commonsense, rather than a literal, reading of the Constitution, Jeffersonian-Republicans nevertheless charged them with distorting the plain meaning of the document to advance their nationalistic political vision.

One reason political struggles in the nineteenth century did not in-

■ IN COMPARATIVE PERSPECTIVE

Written and Unwritten Constitutions: Britain's and Israel's Constitutions

What is a constitution? Does a constitution have to be written? Most of the world's 185 countries have written constitutions. Yet several do not, including Bosnia-Herzogovenia; Libya; New Zealand; Oman; Qatar; Saudi Arabia; Britain; and, at least until 1995, Israel. Furthermore, British legal scholars have long contended that Britain has a "historic constitution." By contrast, the Supreme Court of Israel declared its Basic Laws to constitute a constitution in 1995.

The British constitution, according to some legal scholars, is best understood not as an "unwritten" constitution but as a "historic constitution," a written and unwritten product of historical development, not of deliberate design; it is a romantic, pre-Enlightenment constitution. Parts of the British constitution are found in historic documents, such as the Magna Carta, the Act of Settlement, and the Parliament Acts. Still, as Vernon Bogdanor emphasizes:

> [T]here is a sense in which the British Constitution can be summed up in eight words: What the Queen in Parliament enacts is law. The essence of the British Constitution is thus better expressed in the statement that it is a historic constitution whose dominating characteristic is the sovereignty of Parliament, than in the statement that Britain has an unwritten constitution.

Because parliamentary sovereignty is at the heart of the British constitution, Bogdanor and others deem it "pointless to rationalise it in an enacted constitution which could forbid nothing, nor could it provide a list of basic freedoms which governments would be unable to infringe."[1]

In October 2000, however, Britain became subject to the European Convention on Human Rights, as a result of the going into effect of the Human Rights Act of 1998 which incorporates those guarantees into British law. British courts now have jurisdiction over human rights claims, though they still have no power to declare laws unconstitutional. If they find conflicts with legislation, they may issue declarations of incompatibility and the Parliament must decide whether to amend the legislation accordingly. Nonetheless, British judges are expected to increasingly look to rulings of the European Court of Justice on Human Rights and to those of high courts in other member states of the European Union.

When Israel was proclaimed a state in 1948, it was expected to eventually enact a written constitution.[2] But, due to initial opposition, the Knesset (parliament) in 1950 agreed, as a compromise, to the Harari Resolution, to build a constitution chapter by chapter through the enactment of Basic Laws. Accordingly, the Knesset enacted Basic Laws on The Knesset (1958); Israel Lands (1960); The President of the State (1964); The Government (1968); The State Economy (1975); Israel Defense Forces (1976); Jerusalem, The Capital of Israel (1980); The Judiciary (1984); and The State Comptroller (1988). These Basic Laws largely codified existing practices. But in 1992 the Knesset enacted two more dealing for the first time with human rights: the Basic Laws on Freedom of Occupation and on Human Dignity and Liberty. Notably, Section 5 of the Basic Law on Freedom of Occupation also stipulated that it could not be changed "except by a Basic Law enacted by a majority of the Knesset members."

Until the 1990s, the prevailing view in Israel was that the Knesset's sovereignty was virtually unlimited and that the Supreme Court would exercise only limited judicial review, invalidating legislation only when in conflict with specific provisions of a Basic Law. But, in *United Mizrachi Bank plc v. Migdal Cooperative Village* (1995),[3] the Supreme Court reversed a lower court's ruling and proclaimed Israel's Basic Laws a constitution. A district court had struck down, as a violation of the 1992 Basic Law on Human Dignity and Liberty, a Knesset law aimed at providing agricultural relief. It was the first time an Israeli court had asserted "American-style" substantive judicial review of legislation. On appeal, though reversing that court's decision, all but one of the nine justices agreed that the Knesset had the "constituent authority" to frame a constitution, binding on its own powers, and that it had done so when enacting the 1992 Basic Laws on human rights. Furthermore, the Supreme Court held that Israel's constitution authorized the judiciary's exercise of "American-style" judicial review.

In *United Mizrachi Bank*, the Israeli Supreme Court embraced a theory that its President (or chief justice) Aharon Barak had championed following the enactment of the 1992 Basic Laws. According to Chief Justice Barak:[4]

> Under these new Basic Laws, several human rights—among them Dignity, Liberty, Mobility, Privacy, Property—acquired a constitutional force above regular statutes. . . . A regular Knesset (Parliamentary) statute can no longer infringe upon these rights, unless it fulfills the requirements of the Basic Laws (the "limitations clause"), namely, it befits the values of the State of Israel, it was passed for a worthy purpose and the harm caused to the constitutional Human Right is proportional to the purpose. Thus, we became a constitutional democracy. We joined the democratic, enlightened nations in which human rights are awarded a constitutional force above regular statutes. Similar to the United States, Canada, France, Germany, Italy, Japan, and other western countries, we now have a constitutional defense for Human Rights. We too have the central chapter in any written constitution, the subject-matter of which is Human

Rights; we too have restrictions on the legislative power of the legislator; we too have judicial review of statutes which unlawfully infringe upon constitutionally protected human rights; we too have a written constitution, to which the Knesset in its capacity as legislator is subject and which it cannot alter. . . .

The Constitutional Revolution has led to a change in the judiciary's status. Great responsibilities have been imposed on it. It must fill the mould created by the "majestic generalities" in the new Basic Laws. The judiciary must be aware of the fundamental values of the people. It must balance them in accordance with the views of the "enlightened general public" in Israel. . . . Constitutional interpretation should not be formalistic or pedantic. It should be purposive. It should be done from a wide perspective and adopt a substantive approach. A constitution is a living organism. . . .

1. Vernon Bogdanor, "Britain: The Political Constitution," in Vernon Bogdanor, ed., *Constitutions and Democratic Politics* 53, 55 (Aldershot, England: Gower, 1988).

2. See Martin Edelman, *Courts, Politics, and Culture in Israel* (Charlottesville: University Press of Virginia, 1994); and Asher Arian, *The Second Republic: Politics in Israel* (Chatham, NJ: Chatham House, 1998).

3. A translation of and commentary on *United Mizrachi Bank plc v. Migdal Cooperative Village*, 48 (iv) P.D. 221 (1995), may be found in 31 *Israel Law Review* 754 (1997).

4. Aharon Barak, "The Constitutionalization of the Israeli Legal System as a Result of the Basic Laws and Its Effect on Procedural and Substantive Criminal Law," 31 *Israel Law Review* 3–23 (1997).

vite debates over competing theories of constitutional interpretation is that Federalists and Jeffersonian-Republicans largely professed acceptance of the English declaratory theory of law. This theory, or philosophy, of legal positivism holds that judges have no discretion, make no law, but simply discover and "declare" the law.[5] According to one of the most widely read English jurists, Sir William Blackstone, in his *Commentaries on the Laws of England* (1765–1768), judges were merely the "depositories of the laws; the living oracles" of law. Hamilton and Marshall considered themselves Blackstonians; judges, Hamilton wrote in *The Federalist*, No. 78, "may truly be said to have neither force nor will, but merely judgment."

By the late nineteenth century, the Blackstonian theory of law was under sharp attack. Oliver Wendell Holmes (1841–1935) was one of the first to debunk the idea that law is "a brooding omnipresence in the sky."[6] In his words, "The life of the law has not been logic; it has been experience. The felt necessities of the time, the prevalent moral and political theories, intuitions of public policy, avowed or unconscious, even the prejudices which judges share with their fellow-men, have had a good deal more to do than the syllogism in determining the rules by which men should be governed."[7] Holmes took it for granted that judges make law and pointed toward the empirical study of law: "The prophecies of what the courts will do in fact, and nothing more pretentious, are what I mean by the law."[8] Nor was Holmes alone in the revolt against legal formalism and the "mechanical jurisprudence" associated with the declaratory theory of judicial decision making.[9] Roscoe Pound (1870–1964), the founder of "sociological jurisprudence" and dean of Harvard Law School, encouraged the use of sociology and the study of law in relation to changing social forces. Unlike Holmes, though, Pound also encouraged judges to creatively mold law to the needs of society; judges should become "social engineers."[10]

One immediate consequence of this revolt against legal formalism was the innovation in legal argumentation that became known as "the Brandeis brief," after its author, a progressive legal reformer and later justice, Louis D. Brandeis. In 1908, in support of Oregon's law limiting working hours for women, Brandeis filed a brief in *Muller v. Oregon*, 208 U.S. 412 (1908), which included only two pages of legal argumentation, followed by ninety-seven pages of statistics and other social science data documenting the health risks for women working long hours. Drawing on social science in legal argumentation was necessary, claimed Brandeis, if law was to keep "pace with the rapid development of our political, economic, and social ideals."[11]

By the 1920s and 1930s a diverse group of law professors, political scientists, economists, and sociologists emerged calling themselves "American legal realists."[12] They further questioned the determinancy of formal legal rules and the facts of cases for judicial decision making, thereby underscoring that judges interpret (and manipulate) both legal rules and the facts when deciding cases.[13] Karl Llewellyn, one of the most influential legal realists, brought these insights to bear on constitutional interpretation when calling for a "jurisprudence of a living Constitution":

> A "written constitution" is a system of unwritten practices in which the Document in question, by virtue of men's attitudes, has *a little influence. Where it makes no important difference which way the decision goes,* the Text—in the absence of countervailing practice—is an excellent traffic light. . . . The view advanced here *sounds* unorthodox. It sounds unorthodox only because it puts into words the *tacit* doing of the Court, and draws from that doing conclusions not to be avoided by a candid child. . . . Whatever the Court has *said*, it has repeatedly turned to established governmental practice in search of norms. What the Court has *said*, it has shaped the living Constitution to the needs of the day as it felt them. The whole expansion of the due process clause has been an enforcement of the

majority's ideal of government-as-it-should-be, running free of the language of the Document.[14]

The Supreme Court was not immune from this change in legal thinking. On the bench sat Holmes (1902–1932), Brandeis (1916–1939), Benjamin Cardozo (1932–1938),[15] and Felix Frankfurter (1939–1962), among other legal progressives. Moreover, even judicial conservatives on the Court no longer denied that the process of interpreting the Constitution involves making law. As Chief Justice Harlan F. Stone, a political and judicial conservative, reflected in a letter to Edward Corwin, "I always thought the real villain in the play was Blackstone, who gave to both lawyers and judges artificial notions of the law which, when applied to constitutional interpretation made the Constitution a mechanical and inadequate instrument of government."[16] Justice Frankfurter, a former liberal professor at Harvard Law School who became an advocate of judicial self-restraint on the bench, elaborated his view in a letter to Justice Hugo Black:

> I think one of the evil features, a very evil one, about all this assumption that judges only find the law and don't make it, often becomes the evil of a lack of candor. By covering up the law-making function of judges, we miseducate the people and fail to bring out into the open the real responsibility of judges for what they do. . . .

> That phrase "judicial legislation" has become ever since a staple of a term of condemnation. I, too, am opposed to judicial legislation in its invidious sense; but I deem equally mischievous—because founded on an untruth and an impossible aim—the notion that judges merely announce the law which they find and do not themselves inevitably have a share in the law-making. Here, as elsewhere, the difficulty comes from arguing in terms of absolutes when the matter at hand is conditioned by circumstances, is contingent upon the everlasting problem of how far is too far and how much is too much. Judges as you well know, cannot escape the responsibility of filling in gaps which the finitude of even the most imaginative legislation renders inevitable. . . .

> So the problem is not whether judges make the law, but when and how and how much. Holmes put it in his highbrow way, that "they can do so only interstitially; they are confined from molar to molecular motions." I used to say to my students that legislatures make law wholesale, judges retail.[17]

Once constitutional interpretation was candidly conceded to be a lawmaking process, the Court and its commentators squarely faced what has been called the Madisonian dilemma and "the countermajoritarian difficulty" for judicial review. As former judge and unsuccessful 1987 Supreme Court nominee Robert Bork explains,

The United States was founded as what we now call a Madisonian system, one which allows majorities to rule in wide areas of life simply because they are majorities, but which also holds that individuals have some freedoms that must be exempt from majority control. The dilemma is that neither the majority nor the minority can be trusted to define the proper spheres of democratic authority and individual liberty. The first would court tyranny by the majority; the second tyranny by the minority.[18]

When overturning legislation, the Court exercises a countermajoritarian power and substitutes its interpretation of the Constitution for that of elected representatives. Theories or rationalizations of the Court's interpretation of the Constitution thus appear necessary to justify the Court's countermajoritarian role in American politics, especially in the last fifty years as the Court increasingly overturned legislation in defense of civil rights and liberties.

In addition, in the aftermath of the American legal realist movement, legal scholarship became more pluralistic and interdisciplinary. Again quoting Judge Bork:

> The fact is that the law has little intellectual or structural resistance to outside influences, influences that should properly remain outside. The striking, and peculiar, fact . . . is that the law possesses very little theory about itself. . . . This theoretical emptiness at its center makes law, particularly constitutional law, unstable, a ship with a great deal of sail but a very shallow keel, vulnerable to the winds of intellectual or moral fashion, which it then validates as the commands of our most basic compact.[19]

Legal scholars have always turned toward moral and political philosophy as a guide for constitutional interpretation and the Court's exercise of judicial review, but since World War II they have also called for the development of a "political jurisprudence" that would combine normative theory with empirical studies;[20] would draw on an economic approach to law, which would make rights turn on cost–risk–benefit analysis;[21] would look to theories of literary criticism;[22] and would advocate "legal pragmatism." Still others in the Critical Legal Studies movement attack theories of liberal legalism in an effort to deconstruct legal reasoning and law to show its drawbacks for minorities, women, and the poor.[23]

The rest of this section surveys and illustrates various theories of constitutional interpretation in terms of two broad approaches that have come to be known as *interpretivism* and *noninterpretivism*. Broadly speaking, interpretivists hold that constitutional interpretation should be limited solely to the text and historical context of particular provisions of the Constitution and Bill of Rights. By contrast, noninterpretivists maintain that constitutional interpretation frequently requires going beyond the text and historical context of specific provisions to articulate and apply broader principles of constitutional politics. Neither approach is inextricably linked to either a liberal or a conservative political philosophy; for example, a predominantly conservative Court in the late nineteenth century invented and wrote into constitutional law a "liberty of contract" to strike down progressive economic legislation (see Ch. 3), while in the twentieth century a more liberal Court proclaimed and enforced a "right of privacy" to overturn legislation restricting the use of contraceptives and the availability of abortions (see Ch. 11).

NOTES

1. Felix Frankfurter, in *Law and Politics*, ed. E. Prichard, Jr., and Archibald Macleish (New York: Harcourt, Brace, 1939), 6.

2. See Robert H. Bork, "Styles in Constitutional Theory," 1984 *Supreme Court Historical Society Yearbook* 53 (1985).

3. Joseph Story, *Commentaries on the Constitution of the United States* (Durham, NC: Carolina Academic Press, 1987), vi, reprint of 1833 ed.

4. Ibid., 135.

5. See, generally, Lord Lloyd, *Lloyd's Introduction to Jurisprudence*, 5th ed. (London: Stevens & Sons, 1985); H. L. A. Hart, *Essays in Jurisprudence and Philosophy* (Oxford, UK: Clarendon Press, 1983), Chs. 1–5, 13; William Nelson, *Americanization of the Common Law* (Cambridge, MA: Harvard University Press, 1975); and Morton Horwitz, *The Transformation of American Law, 1780–1860* (Cambridge, MA: Harvard University Press, 1977).

6. *Southern Pacific Co. v. Jensen*, 244 U.S. 205 (1916).

7. Oliver W. Holmes, *The Common Law* (Boston: Little, Brown, 1881), 1.

8. Oliver W. Holmes, "The Path of Law," 10 *Harvard Law Review* 39 (1897).

9. See, generally, Morton White, *Social Thought in America: The Revolt against Formalism* (New York: Viking Press, 1949); and Benjamin Twiss, *Lawyers and the Constitution* (Princeton, NJ: Princeton University Press, 1942).

10. See Roscoe Pound, *An Introduction to the Philosophy of Law* (New Haven, CT: Yale University Press, 1922).

11. Louis Brandeis, "The Living Law," 10 *Illinois Law Review* 461 (1916).

12. See Wilfred Rumble, *American Legal Realism* (Ithaca, NY: Cornell University Press, 1968).

13. See Jerome Frank, *Law and the Modern Mind* (New York: Coward-McCann, 1930), and *Courts on Trial* (Princeton, NJ: Princeton University Press, 1949).

14. Karl Llewellyn, "The Constitution as an Institution," 34 *Columbia Law Review* 39–40 (1934).

15. See Benjamin Cardozo's highly acclaimed *The Nature of the Judicial Process* (New York: Yale University Press, 1921).

16. Letter to E. Corwin, November 5, 1942, in Harlan F. Stone Papers, Box 10, Library of Congress, Washington, DC.

17. Letter to Justice Black, December 15, 1939, in Stone Papers, Box 13.

18. Bork, "Styles in Constitutional Theory," 53.

19. Robert H. Bork, "Tradition and Morality in Constitutional Law," in *Views from the Bench: The Judiciary and Constitutional Politics*, ed. Mark Cannon and David M. O'Brien (Chatham, NJ: Chatham House, 1985), 166.

20. See Martin Shapiro, "Political Jurisprudence," 52 *Kentucky Law Review* 294 (1964); Harry Stumpf, Martin Shapiro, David Danelski, Austin Sarat, and David O'Brien, "Whither Political Jurisprudence?: A Symposium," 36 *Western Political Quarterly* 533 (1983); and Rogers Smith, "Political Jurisprudence, the 'New Institutionalism,' and the Future of Public Law," 82 *American Political Science Review* 89 (1988).

21. See, for example, Richard Posner, *Economic Analysis of Law*, 2d ed. (Boston: Little Brown, 1977).

22. See William Bishin and Christopher Stone, *Law, Language and Ethics* (Mineola, NY: Foundation Press, 1972); John Brigham, *Constitutional Language* (Westport, CT: Greenwood Press, 1978); Leif Carter, *Contemporary Constitutional Lawmaking* (New York: Pergamon, 1985); James White, *The Legal Imagination* (Chicago: University of Chicago Press, 1973); James White, *When Words Lose Their Meaning* (Chicago: University of Chicago Press, 1984); Richard Posner, *Law and Literature: A Misunderstood Relation* (Cambridge, MA: Harvard University Press, 1988); and James White, *Justice as Translation* (Chicago: University of Chicago Press, 1990).

23. See David Kairys, ed., *The Politics of Law* (New York: Pantheon, 3d, 1998); and Editors of the Harvard Law Review, *Essays on Critical Legal Studies* (Cambridge, MA: Harvard Law Review Association, 1986).

■ (1) The Text and Historical Context

The Supreme Court has been criticized by presidents from Thomas Jefferson to Ronald Reagan and George W. Bush for departing from a "strict" or "literal" interpretation of the Constitution. During the 1968 presidential election campaign, for instance, Republican nominee Richard Nixon attacked the "liberal jurisprudence" of the Warren Court (1953–1969) and promised to appoint only strict constructionists to the bench. *Strict constructionists* hold that constitutional interpretation should be confined to the "four corners" of the document, the literal language of the text of the Constitution.

Within the Court, Chief Justice Roger Taney expressed a strong version of strict constructionism in *Dred Scott v. Sandford*, 60 U.S. 393 (1857) (see Ch. 12), when holding that blacks were not citizens of the United States within the meaning of "citizens" in Article III:

> No one, we presume, supposes that any change in public opinion or feeling, in relation to this unfortunate race [of blacks], in the civ-

ilized nations of Europe or in this country, should induce the court to give to the words of the Constitution a more liberal construction in their favor than they were intended to bear when the instrument was framed and adopted. . . .

It [the Constitution] speaks not only in the same words, but with the same meaning and intent with which it spoke when it came from the hands of its framers, and was voted on and adopted by the people of the United States. Any other rule of construction would abrogate the judicial character of this Court and make it the mere reflex of the popular opinion or passion of the day.

This version of strict constructionism unrealistically (or disingenuously) denies the basic choices involved in constitutional interpretation. For example, much turns on whether the Court analyzes church-state controversies from the perspective of the First Amendment's free exercise clause or its establishment clause (see Ch. 6). When applying the Fourth Amendment's guarantee against "unreasonable searches and seizures," the Warren Court chose to enforce strictly the requirements specified in that amendment's warrants and probable cause clauses. By contrast, the Burger Court (1969–1986), and the Rehnquist Court (1986–), tended to give less force to those requirements by relying instead on the justices' reading of what is "reasonable" under the amendment's reasonableness clause. Whether the Fourth Amendment is enforced primarily in terms of its reasonableness clause or its warrants and probable cause clauses represents a basic constitutional choice with important consequences for individual rights and law enforcement interests (see Ch. 7).

Justice Hugo Black claimed to be an "absolutist," a "literalist." In his words:

My view is, without deviation, without exception, without any if's, but's, or whereas, that freedom of speech means that government shall not do anything to people, or, in the words of the Magna Carta, move against people, either for the views they have or the views they express or the words they speak or write. Some people would have you believe that this is a very radical position, and maybe it is. But all I am doing is following what to me is the clear working of the First Amendment that "Congress shall make no law . . . abridging the freedom of speech or of the press."[1]

However, Justice Black acknowledged that the Constitution presents some interpretive problems and constitutional choices. In the controversy over the Court's application of the Bill of Rights to the states under the Fourteenth Amendment, for instance, Black became convinced that those guarantees were included in the amendment's privileges or immunities clause, whereas other justices contended that they were included in the Fourteenth Amendment's due process clause (see Ch. 4).

Justice Black's absolutism was in response to the Court's *balancing* of First Amendment freedoms against governmental interests in national security in cases like *Dennis v. United States*, 341 U.S. 494 (1951) (see Ch. 5), under the guise of the "clear and present danger" test. He opposed the Court's invention and use of such tests and metaphors. Still, much of constitutional law consists in metaphors created by the Court when explaining and applying constitutional provisions; consider the debates over executive privilege (see Vol. 1, Ch. 4), states' sovereignty (see Vol. 1, Ch. 7), the liberty of contract (see Ch. 3), the high wall of separation between church and state (see Ch. 6), or the controversy over whether the Constitution is color-blind (see Ch. 12).

Interpretivism is usually only the beginning, not the end, of constitutional interpretation. The most frequently contested guarantees of the Constitution are neither unambiguous nor amenable to a literal or strict interpretation. What is the literal meaning of the reasonableness clause of the Fourth Amendment or of the due process and equal protection clauses of the Fourteenth Amendment? Nor do interpretivists, like Justice Black, deny First Amendment protection for posters and songs on the ground that they are not strictly speaking "speech"; although Black drew a line at extending protection to speech-plus-conduct and "symbolic speech" (see Ch. 5).

Crucial provisions in the Constitution have what philosophers call an "open texture."[2] They are framed in general terms that are nonexhaustive of all future applications and have an essential incompleteness in dictating unforeseeable applications. The commerce clause in Article I, for example, gives Congress the power to regulate interstate commerce but fails to define *interstate commerce*. No one today, though, contends that interstate commerce should include only the methods of transportation available in 1787 or exclude modes of commerce, such as telecommunications, that were unforeseen by the Constitutional Convention.

These are only some of the problems with strict constructionism, as federal court of appeals Judge Richard Posner notes in an essay titled, "What Am I? A Potted Plant? The Case against Strict Constructionism." Moreover, Posner underscores that nothing in the Constitution commands the Court to construe either "strictly" or "broadly" the document:

> Even the decision to read the Constitution narrowly, and thereby "restrain" judicial interpretation, is not a decision that can be read

directly from the text. The Constitution does not say, "Read me broadly," "Read me narrowly." That decision must be made a matter of political theory, and will depend on such things as one's view of the springs of judicial legitimacy and of the relative competence of courts and legislatures in dealing with particular types of issues.[3]

Strict constructionism is incomplete as a theory of interpretation and inadequately deals with the fact that the Constitution was framed in generalities in order to express general principles. Because this is so, interpretivists often turn to the historical context of the Constitution. Consider, for example, the call for a *jurisprudence of original intention* by Ronald Reagan's attorney general, Edwin Meese III:

> As the "faithful guardians of the Constitution," the judges were expected to resist any political effort to depart from the literal provisions of the Constitution. The text of the document and the original intention of those who framed it would be the judicial standard in giving effect to the Constitution. . . . [But] it seems fair to conclude that far too many of the court's opinions are, on the whole, more policy choices than articulations of constitutional principle. The voting blocs, the arguments, all reveal a greater allegiance to what the court thinks constitutes sound public policy than a deference to what the Constitution—its text and intention—demands.[4]

Meese was not the first to contend that the text and the Framers' intent should solely guide constitutional interpretation.[5] Nonetheless, he sparked considerable debate and provoked Justice William J. Brennan to respond in a speech, observing,

> In its most doctrinaire incarnation, this view demands that Justices discern exactly what the Framers thought about the question under consideration and simply follow that intention in resolving the case before them. It is a view that feigns self-effacing deference to the specific judgments of those who forged our original social compact. But in truth it is little more than arrogance cloaked as humility. It is arrogant to pretend that from our vantage we can gauge accurately the intent of the Framers on application of principle to specific, contemporary questions. All too often, sources of potential enlightenment such as records of the ratification debates provide sparse or ambiguous evidence of the original intention. Typically, all that can be gleaned is that the Framers themselves did not agree about the application or meaning of particular constitutional provisions, and hid their differences in cloaks of generality. Indeed, it is far from clear whose intention is relevant—that of the drafters, the congressional disputants, or the ratifiers in the states?—or even whether the idea of an original intention is a coherent way of thinking about a jointly drafted document drawing its authority

from a general assent of the states. And apart from the problematic nature of the sources, our distance of two centuries cannot but work as a prism refracting all we perceive. . . .

We current Justices read the Constitution in the only way that we can: as Twentieth Century Americans. We look to the history of the time of framing and to the intervening history of interpretation. But the ultimate question must be, what do the words of the text mean in our time. For the genius of the Constitution rests not in any static meaning it might have had in a world that is dead and gone, but in the adaptability of its great principles to cope with current problems and current needs. What the Constitution's fundamentals meant to the wisdom of other times cannot be their measure to the vision of our time. Similarly, what those fundamentals mean for us, our descendants will learn, cannot be the measure to the vision of their time.[6]

As Justice Brennan suggests, there are methodological difficulties with a "jurisprudence of original intention." For one thing, determining "intent" is a subjective enterprise; it proposes to discover what the Framers had in mind when drafting and ratifying the Constitution. But as already noted, the Framers often disagreed and were forced to compromise on the language of the Constitution. At best, this approach considers the intentions of the drafters and ratifiers of the Constitution. And, who are "the Framers"? Should the views of only the thirty-nine signers of the document be considered, or should those of the other sixteen delegates who left before the Constitutional Convention concluded or refused to sign the document be considered as well? There are also compelling reasons for including the views of delegates to the thirteen state ratifying conventions, for as a result of those conventions the Bill of Rights was immediately added to the Constitution (see Ch. 4).

Problems with discovering the intentions of the Framers also arise because the proceedings of the Constitutional Convention were conducted in secrecy and records of that convention and those in the states are far from complete and reliable. Moreover, it is debatable that the Framers intended their intentions to limit or guide constitutional interpretation.[7] Not until 1819 were speeches, resolutions, and votes of the delegates to the Constitutional Convention published. Almost another decade passed before Jonathan Elliot began publishing his collection of the debates in the state ratifying conventions. James Madison, who took notes of the debates at the Constitutional Convention and whose notes provide the only full record, refused to allow the publication of his notes until 1840, after his death. Madison insisted that the intent and literal reading of the text would be a "hard rule of construction."

Instead, among the "obvious and just guides applicable to the Constn. of the U.S.," he listed

> 1. the evils & defects for curing which the Constitution was called for & introduced. 2. The comments prevailing at the times it was adopted. 3. The early, deliberate & continued practice under the Constitution as preferable to constructions adopted on the spur of occasions, and subject to the vicissitudes of party or personal considerations.[8]

In addition, it bears noting that in its first fifty years the Supreme Court infrequently cited works such as *The Federalist Papers* in its opinions. Between 1790 and 1839, *The Federalist Papers* were cited in only fifteen decisions; by comparison, since 1950 they were cited in more than 100 cases.[9]

Because of these difficulties, Chief Justice William Rehnquist, Justice Antonin Scalia, Judge Bork, and others associated with interpretivism and the "originalist" approach to constitutional interpretation more modestly contend that the Court should remain faithful to the "original understanding" or "original meaning"[10] of the governing principles or political philosophy of the Framers. They do not claim to be uncovering the Framers' subjective intentions but rather limiting the interpretation of constitutional provisions to those principles that the Framers might be fairly said to have embraced when drafting and ratifying the Constitution. Judge Bork explains that

> [a] major problem with the idea of original intention is that the Framers articulated their principles in light of the world they knew, a world very different in important respects from that in which judges must decide cases today. . . . In order to protect the freedoms the Framers envisaged, the judge must discern a principle in the applications the Framers thought of and then apply that principle to circumstances they did not foresee.[11]

Nor do Chief Justice Rehnquist, Justice Scalia, and Judge Bork claim that originalism eliminates the burden of making basic constitutional choices. Rather, they argue that this approach is superior to other noninterpretivist approaches because it ostensibly sharply limits the exercise of judicial review and thus proves more responsive to criticisms of the Court's countermajoritarian power. In Justice Scalia's words,

> The principal theoretical defect of nonoriginalism, in my view, is its incompatibility with the very principle that legitimizes judicial review of constitutionality. Nothing in the text of the Constitution confers upon the courts the power to inquire into, rather than passively assume, the constitutionality of federal statutes. . . . Quite to

the contrary, the legislature would seem a much more appropriate
expositor of social values, and *its* determination that a statute is
compatible with the Constitution should, as in England, prevail.[12]

Justice Scalia concedes that originalism poses methodological problems in practice but nonetheless claims that it is "the lesser evil" in
constitutional interpretation:

> [It] *is* true that it is often exceedingly difficult to plumb the origi-
> nal understanding of an ancient text. Properly done, the task re-
> quires the consideration of an enormous mass of material—in the
> case of the Constitution and its Amendments, for example, to men-
> tion only one element, the records of the ratifying debates in all the
> states. Even beyond that, it requires an evaluation of the reliability
> of that material—many of the reports of the ratifying debates, for
> example, are thought to be quite unreliable. And further still, it re-
> quires immersing oneself in the political and intellectual atmo-
> sphere of the time—somehow placing out of mind knowledge that
> we have which an earlier age did not, and putting on beliefs, atti-
> tudes, philosophies, prejudices and loyalties that are not those of
> our day. It is, in short, a task sometimes better suited to the histo-
> rian than the lawyer. . . .
>
> I can be much more brief in describing what seems to me the sec-
> ond most serious objection to originalism. In its undiluted form, at
> least, it is medicine that seems too strong to swallow. Thus, almost
> every originalist would adulterate it with the doctrine of *stare decisis*
> [which holds that prior decisions should be respected]. . . . But *stare
> decisis* alone is not enough to prevent originalism from being what
> many would consider too bitter a pill. What if some state should en-
> act a new law providing public lashing, or branding of the right
> hand, as punishment for certain criminal offenses? Even if it could
> be demonstrated unequivocally that these were not cruel and un-
> usual measures [which are forbidden under the Eighth Amendment]
> in 1791, and even though no prior Supreme Court decision has
> specifically disapproved them, I doubt whether any federal judge—
> even among the many who consider themselves originalists—would
> sustain them against an Eighth Amendment challenge. It may well
> be . . . that this cannot legitimately be reconciled with originalist
> philosophy—that it represents the unrealistic view of the Constitu-
> tion as a document intended to create a perfect society for all ages to
> come, whereas in fact it was a political compromise that did not pre-
> tend to create a perfect society even for its own age (as its toleration
> of slavery, which a majority of the founding generation recognized
> as an evil, well enough demonstrates). Even so, I am confident that
> public flogging and hand-branding would not be sustained by our
> courts, and any espousal of originalism as a practical theory of exe-
> gesis must somehow come to terms with that reality.[13]

Justice Scalia's discussion of public flogging and the Eighth Amendment is revealing not only in indicating that he is (in his words) "a faint-hearted originalist," because he would hold public flogging unconstitutional despite the fact that the Framers permitted that practice. The original understanding of constitutional guarantees, as Justice Anthony Kennedy observed during his 1987 Senate confirmation hearings, is a "necessary starting point," not an "adequate methodology" or "mechanical process" that "tells us how to decide a case."

What Scalia's discussion also points out is that crucial *concepts* in the Constitution give rise to competing *conceptions* and political philosophies.[14] Scalia would not limit the concept of cruel and unusual punishment in the Eighth Amendment to the Framers' conception of that punishment in 1791. Nor would Scalia go as far as Justice Brennan in interpreting the Eighth Amendment to bar capital punishment based on his "constitutional vision of human dignity" (see Ch. 10). But, why not? What divides justices like Scalia, Brennan, and Souter is their underlying judicial and political philosophies of the Constitution and the exercise of judicial review. So too, just as the Federalists and Anti-Federalists had competing political visions of the separation of powers and federalism, for example, even originalists such as Chief Justice Rehnquist and Justices Scalia and Thomas may have rival conceptions and interpretations of the separation of powers; see, for instance, *Morrison v. Olson*, 487 U.S. 654 (1988) (see Vol. 1, Ch. 4), and *McIntyre v. Ohio Elections Commission*, 514 U.S. 334 (1995) (see Vol. 1, Ch. 8).

An underlying problem for interpretivists and noninterpretivists is how broadly or narrowly they conceive and express the concept or principle of a constitutional provision. Consider, for example, the constitutional choices presented in interpreting and applying the Fourth Amendment and the equal protection clause of the Fourteenth Amendment.

The Fourth Amendment guarantees the people a right "to be secure in their persons, houses, papers, and effects against unreasonable searches and seizures." That guarantee was interpreted in *Olmstead v. United States*, 277 U.S. 438 (1928) (see Ch. 7), not to cover wiretaps because a majority of the Court limited the amendment's application to Framers' conception of "unreasonable searches and seizures," giving the lowest level of generality to the amendment's principle, so as to bar only actual physical trespass by police and the seizure of tangible materials. By contrast, dissenting Justice Louis Brandeis argued for a broader conception of the amendment and a more general principle of privacy in the home that would have extended the guarantees of the amendment to cover electronic surveillance. Almost forty years later, in *Katz v. United States*, 389 U.S. 347 (1967) (see Ch. 7), the Court finally embraced the broader principle of Fourth Amendment-protected privacy.

The Fourteenth Amendment guarantees "the equal protection of the laws." The principle of equality embodied there might be interpreted to bar only discrimination against blacks, because in the historical context of the post–Civil War period the Thirty-ninth Congress was indisputably primarily concerned with ensuring that states did not deny certain rights of newly freed blacks. However, the principle of equality has been given broader application and a higher level of generality so as to bar other kinds of racial discrimination against, for example, Hispanics and Asians. Even more broadly (as further discussed in Ch. 12), the amendment has been construed to forbid forms of nonracial discrimination against women and homosexuals. But how and on what basis may this broader application of the equal protection clause be defended and the Court's exercise of judicial review in this way justified?

In sum and in Judge Bork's words, "The question is always the level of generality the judge chooses when he states the idea or object of the Framers."[15] Interpretivists, no less than noninterpretivists, cannot evade making basic constitutional choices in their conceptions and formulations of the underlying principles of constitutional provisions.

NOTES

1. Hugo Black, *A Constitutional Faith* (New York: Knopf, 1968), 45.

2. See H. L. A. Hart, *The Concept of Law* (Oxford, UK: Clarendon Press, 1961), 124–132.

3. Richard Posner, "What Am I? A Potted Plant?" *The New Republic*, Sept. 28, 1987, 23.

4. Edwin Meese, "The Attorney General's View of the Supreme Court: Toward a Jurisprudence of Original Intention," in *Special Issue, Law and Public Affairs*, ed. Charles Wise and David O'Brien, 45 *Public Administration Review* 701 (1985).

5. See also Raoul Berger, *Government by Judiciary* (Cambridge, MA: Harvard University Press, 1977); and Walter Berns, *Taking the Constitution Seriously* (New York: Simon & Schuster, 1987).

6. William J. Brennan, Jr., "The Constitution of the United States: Contemporary Ratification," Georgetown University, Washington, DC (Oct. 12, 1985).

7. See H. Jefferson Powell, "The Original Understanding of Original Intent," 98 *Harvard Law Review* 885 (1985); and James Hutson, "The Creation of the Constitution: The Integrity of the Documentary Record," 65 *Texas Law Review* 1 (1986).

8. Quoted in Robert Morgan, *James Madison on the Constitution and the Bill of Rights* (Westport, CT: Greenwood Press, 1988), 196–197.

9. See James Wilson, "The Most Sacred Text: The Supreme Court's Use of *The Federalist Papers*," 1985 *Brigham Young University Law Review* 65 (1985).

The Supreme Court, 2003. (*Photo by Richard Strauss. Collection of the Supreme Court of the United States.*)

10. See Antonin Scalia, "Originalism: The Lesser Evil," 57 *Cincinnati Law Review* 849 (1989).

11. Robert Bork, "Foreword" to Gary McDowell, *The Constitution and Contemporary Constitutional Theory* (Cumberland, VA: Center for Judicial Studies, 1985), x.

12. Scalia, "Originalism," 854.

13. Scalia, "Originalism," 856–857.

14. On the distinction between concepts and conceptions, see Ronald Dworkin, *Taking Rights Seriously* (Cambridge, MA: Harvard University Press, 1977), 135–137.

15. Bork, "Foreword," x.

SELECTED BIBLIOGRAPHY

Amsterdam, Anthony, and Bruner, Jerome. *Minding the Law: How Courts Rely on Storytelling, and How Their Stories Change the Ways We Understand the Law—And Ourselves.* Cambridge, MA: Harvard University Press, 2000.

Barber, Sotirios. *The Constitution of Judicial Power.* Baltimore: Johns Hopkins University Press, 1993.

Berger, Raoul. *Government by Judiciary: The Transformation of the Fourteenth Amendment.* Cambridge, MA: Harvard University Press, 1977.

Berns, Walter. *Taking the Constitution Seriously.* New York: Simon & Schuster, 1987.

Bickel, Alexander. *The Morality of Consent.* New Haven, CT: Yale University Press, 1975.

Black, Hugo. *A Constitutional Faith.* New York: Knopf, 1968.

Bork, Robert. *The Tempting of America.* New York: Free Press, 1989.

Brandwein, Pamela. *Reconstructing the Reconstruction: The Supreme Court and the Production of Historical Truth.* Durham, NC: Duke University Press, 1999.

Crapanzano, Vincent. *Serving the Word: Literalism in America from the Pulpit to the Bench.* New York: New Press, 2000.

Cogan, Neil, ed. *The Complete Bill of Rights: The Drafts, Debates, Sources, & Origins.* New York: Oxford University Press, 1997.

Goldstein, Leslie. *In Defense of the Text.* Lanham: Rowman & Littlefield, 1991.

Harris, William F. *The Interpretable Constitution.* Baltimore: Johns Hopkins University Press, 1993.

Jaffa, Harry V. *Original Intent and the Framers of the Constitution.* Washington, DC: Regnery Gateway, 1994.

Levy, Leonard. *Original Intent and the Framers' Constitution.* Chicago: Ivan Dee, 2000.

Lynch, Joseph. *Negotiating the Constitution: The Earliest Debates over Original Intent.* Ithaca, NY: Cornell University Press, 1999.

Rakove, Jack. *Original Meanings: Politics and Ideas in the Making of the Constitution.* New York: Knopf, 1996.

———, ed. *Interpreting the Constitution: The Debate over Original Intent.* Boston: Northeastern University Press, 1990.

Scalia, Antonin. *A Matter of Interpretation: Federal Courts and the Law.* Princeton, NJ: Princeton University Press, 1997.

Thayer, Bradley. *Thayer's Legal Essays.* Boston: Boston Book Company, 1908.

Whittington, Keith. *Constitutional Interpretation: Textual Meaning, Original Intent, and Judicial Review.* Lawrence: University Press of Kansas, 1999.

■ (2) In and Beyond the Text

Noninterpretivism differs from interpretivism in the sources and kinds of argumentation marshaled in support of giving broader scope or higher levels of generality to constitutional principles. Whereas interpretivists confine analysis to the text and historical context of a provision, noninterpretivists tend to formulate more broadly the underlying principle of a constitutional provision. Noninterpretivists may turn to history and social science, for example, or appeal to natural law, natural rights, and moral or political philosophy, or call on process-oriented theories of judicial review and arguments about the structure of the Constitution.

Historical, economic, technological, and political changes are obviously relevant to constitutional interpretation. Yet, when and how should the Court use *history*? The Sixth Amendment, for instance, guarantees criminal defendants the right to a jury trial but does not define *jury*. When confronted with the question of whether juries must consist of twelve members, in *Thompson v. Utah*, 170 U.S. 343 (1882), the Court simply ruled that the Sixth Amendment incorporated the traditional common-law practice of twelve-member juries because that practice was firmly rooted in English history and familiar to the Framers of the Bill of Rights. The Court may also take *judicial notice* of historical events without the benefit of their being adjudicated, such as the fact that there was an economic depression in the 1930s. Chief Justice Morrison Waite drew heavily on history as a guide when upholding under the commerce clause the power of Congress, over that of the states, to regulate interstate telegraph lines, in *Pensacola Telegraph Co. v. Western Union Telegraph, Co.*, 96 U.S. 1 (1877):

> The powers thus granted are not confined to the instrumentalities of commerce . . . known or in use when the Constitution was adopted, but they keep pace with the progress of the country, and adapt themselves to the new developments of time and circumstance. They extend from the horse with its rider to the stagecoach, from the sailing-vessel to the steamboat . . . and from the railroad to the telegraph, as these new agencies are successively brought into use to meet the demands of increasing population and wealth. . . . As they were intrusted to the general government for the good of the nation, it is not only the right, but the duty, of Congress to see to it that intercourse among the States and the transmission of intelligence are not obstructed or unnecessarily encumbered by State legislation.

Justice Holmes took an even more expansive view of the use of history in the famous case dealing with the national government's treaty-making power in *Missouri v. Holland*, 252 U.S. 416 (1920) (see Vol. 1, Ch. 3). Note his observation that "[t]he case before us must be considered in light of our whole experience and not merely in that of what was said a hundred years ago."

The Court's reliance on history is not unproblematic, however.[1] Justices are not trained as historians and they may confront problems in evaluating different schools of history and the works of revisionist historians. More fundamentally, Chief Justice William Rehnquist, among others, cautions against turning to history because it encourages the notion that the "Constitution is a living document" and that the Court ought to keep the Constitution in "tune with the times." In Rehnquist's view, there are three serious flaws with the notion of a living Constitution:

> First, it misconceives the nature of the Constitution, which was designed to enable the popularly elected branches of government, not the judicial branch, to keep the country abreast of the times. Second, [it] ignores the Supreme Court's disastrous experiences when in the past it embraced contemporary, fashionable notions of what

a living Constitution should contain. Third, however socially desirable the goals to be advanced, . . . advancing them through a free-wheeling, non-elected judiciary is quite unacceptable in a democratic society.[2]

Social science may prove a no less controversial source of support for the Court's decisions. In the landmark school desegregation ruling in *Brown v. Board of Education*, 347 U.S. 483 (1954) (see Ch. 12), for example, the Court cited in footnote 11 several social science studies in support of overturning the racial doctrine of "separate but equal facilities." Among those studies was the Swedish economist and sociologist Gunnar Myrdal's book *An American Dilemma* (1944), the premier work on race relations in America. The Court's mention of *An American Dilemma* intensified the antagonism of powerful Southerners, such as the South Carolina governor and former Supreme Court Justice James F. Byrnes and Mississippi Senator James O. Eastland. They and others attacked the Court for citing the work of "foreign sociologists," bad social science research, and, most of all, for drawing on social science in the first place, instead of simply sticking to the text and historical context of the Constitution.

The Court's use of social science materials may raise questions about judicial competence and the legitimacy of basing decisions on social science evidence.[3] Consider *Williams v. Florida*, 399 U.S. 78 (1970) (see Ch. 9), upholding juries composed of fewer than twelve members, despite history and the ruling in *Thompson v. Utah* that the Sixth Amendment jury consisted "as it was at common law, of twelve persons, neither more nor less." *Williams* proved controversial because the Court held on the basis of psychological and sociological studies of small-group behavior that juries of fewer than twelve members were "functionally equivalent" to traditional twelve-member juries.

Natural law and *natural rights*, or what Edward Corwin termed, the "higher law" background of the Constitution, is an older tradition and source of constitutional interpretation.[4] The Framers took seriously natural law and natural rights in maintaining that individuals enjoy certain rights prior to the establishment of government and which may not be denied by government. Federalists, though, contended that the Constitution adequately safeguarded natural rights by creating a government of limited and specifically delegated powers. But the Anti-Federalists pushed for the addition of a bill of rights containing a statement of natural rights (see Ch. 4).

Although the natural rights tradition runs throughout much of constitutional law, controversy has ensnarled appeals to natural law and rights ever since Justices Iredell and Chase debated, in *Calder v. Bull*,

■ CONSTITUTIONAL HISTORY

What Is the Constitution? Could a Constitutional Amendment Violate the Constitution?

What is the Constitution? Could a constitutional amendment violate the Constitution or fundamental principles of a constitution? These questions continue to be debated, especially in countries such as Germany and India that have constitutional provisions forbidding, or their high courts have interpreted their constitutions to forbid, amendments infringing on fundamental principles such as "human dignity."

The German Constitutional Court, for instance, struck down a provision of its Constitution in the *Southwest Case*, 1 BverfGE 14 (1951).[1] After World War II, the occupation forces divided two states, Baden and Wurttemberg, into three for the purposes of administration. When the new Constitution of the Federal Republic of Germany went into effect in 1949, these three territories became Länder (states) with their own constitutions. Article 118 of Germany's Basic Law, however, provided that these three territories could be reorganized according to their own agreement or, if they failed to reach an agreement, by federal legislation and a referendum of the people. They were unable to reach an agreement and in 1951 the parliament passed two reorganization laws, creating a single Länder to be called Baden-Wurttemberg. Baden immediately challenged the constitutionality of these laws on the ground that they diminished Baden's status as a Länder and treated it unfairly and unequally by calling for a referendum of the people, instead of just its own population. In holding unconstitutional Article 118, the German court observed:

> An individual constitutional provision cannot be considered as an isolated clause and interpreted alone. A constitution has an inner unity, and the meaning of any one part is linked to that of other provisions. Taken as a unit, a constitution reflects certain overarching principles and fundamental decisions to which individual provisions are subordinate. Article 79, paragraph 3, makes it clear that the Basic Law agrees with the statement of the Bavarian Constitutional Court:

> That a constitutional provision itself may be null and void, is not conceptually impossible just because it is part of the constitution. There are constitutional principles that are so fundamental and to such an extent an expression of a law that precedes even the constitution that they also bind the framer of the constitution, and other constitutional provisions that do not rank so high may be null and void because they contravene these principles. . . .

From this rule of interpretation, it follows that any constitutional provision must be interpreted in such a way that it is compatible with those elementary principles and with the basic decisions of the framer of the constitution. This rule applies also to Article 118, sentence 2.

In the United States, some legal scholars also contend that the proposed constitutional amendment to forbid desecration of the American flag would violate the Constitution. Following the Supreme Court's ruling in *Texas v. Johnson* (excerpted in Ch. 5), holding that flag-burning is protected speech under the First Amendment, Congress passed the Federal Flag Protection Act of 1989. That statute was then struck down in *United States v. Eichman* (1990). Following those rulings, an attempt in 1995 to override the Court's decisions by means of a constitutional amendment failed to pass the Senate by three votes. In 1997, the House of Representatives passed another proposed constitutional amendment and the Senate was closely divided on whether to send it to the states for ratification. Moreover, 49 state legislatures, far more than the 38 required to amend the Constitution, had indicated that they would ratify a constitutional amendment outlawing flag-burning. The Senate, however, ended its session in 1998 without voting on the proposed amendment.

The constitutionality of constitutional amendments was raised previously in challenges to the validity of the Eighteenth and Nineteenth Amendments. The Eighteenth Amendment, ratified in 1919, prohibited the manufacturing, sales, and transportation of intoxicating liquors; it was later repealed by the Twenty-first Amendment in 1933. The Nineteenth Amendment, ratified in 1920, extended federal and state voting rights to women.

Shortly after the ratification of the Eighteenth Amendment, the Court consolidated seven lawsuits challenging the amendment's constitutionality in *The National Prohibition Cases, State of Rhode Island v. Palmer*, 253 U.S. 350 (1920). When arguing for Rhode Island, Herbert Rice contended that "the Amendment is an invasion of the sovereignty of the complaining State and her people . . ." Continuing, he argued:

> It is "This Constitution" that may be amended. "This Constitution" is not a code of transient laws but a framework of government and an embodiment of fundamental principles. By an amendment, the identity or purpose of the instrument is not to be changed; its defects may be cured, but "This Constitution" must remain. It would be the greatest absurdity to contend that there was a purpose to create a limited government and at the same time to confer upon that government a power to do away with its own limitations. . . .

> In the case of this so-called amendment, the representatives of the people of the United States have attempted, not to amend the Constitution of the United States, but to amend the constitution of every State in the Union. If the amending function is construed as

extensive with absolute sovereignty, then the basis of our political system is no longer the right of the people of a State to make and alter their constitution, for their political institutions are at the mercy of others and may be changed against their will. . . .

Attorneys Elihu Root and William D. Guthrie also sought to persuade the Court of the amendment's unconstitutionality, arguing:

> If, as contended by the defendants, the power of amendment vested in Congress and three-fourths of the state legislatures be absolute and unrestricted, then there would be no limitation whatever upon their legislative authority. They could then by amendment establish a state religion, or oppress or discriminate against any denomination, or authorize the taking away of life, liberty and property, without due process of law, etc., etc. This would destroy the most essential limitation upon power under the American system of government, which is that the rights of the individual citizen shall be protected by withholding from the legislative function the power to do certain things inconsistent with individual liberty. This was the reason of the irresistible demand for the first ten amendments. . . .

By contrast, Solicitor General Alexander King countered, first, that whether the amendment was within the amending power of Article V and whether it in fact had been ratified "are questions committed by the Constitution to the political branch and not to the judicial branch of the Government." Second, "It has always been understood that there is no limitation upon the character of amendments which may be adopted, except such limitations as are imposed by Article V itself. . . . The fact that the Eighteenth Amendment confers upon Congress a power which had previously belonged exclusively to the States does not prevent that Amendment from being within the amending power conferred by Article V of the Constitution." Finally, he concluded: "No State by any provision of its laws or its constitution can make the ratification of an amendment to the Constitution of the United States by its legislature subject to a referendum vote of the people. The only method of ratification mentioned in the Constitution is through representatives assembled either in the legislature or a convention called for that purpose."

The arguments of the solicitor general prevailed and in a brief opinion for the Court Justice Van Devanter stated only "the conclusions of the Court," not its reasoning. Subsequently, the Nineteenth Amendment was challenged on the grounds that it was enacted without Maryland's consent and that state's constitution limited suffrage to men. Writing for the Court in *Leser v. Garnett*, 258 U.S. 130 (1922), Justice Brandeis dismissed that claim as well.[2]

Still, some scholars continue to maintain that amendments, such as the proposed one outlawing flag desecration, might run afoul of underlying constitutional principles. For further discussion, see Walter Murphy, "An

Ordering of Constitutional Values," 53 *Southern California Law Review* 757 (1984); Sanford Levinson, ed., *Responding to Imperfection: The Theory and Practice of Constitutional Amendment* (Princeton: Princeton University Press, 1995); and the CONSTITUTIONAL HISTORY boxes in Volume I, Chapter 6.

1. The *Southwest Case* is translated and excerpted in Walter F. Murphy and Joseph Tanenhaus, eds., *Comparative Constitutional Law: Cases and Commentaries* (New York: St. Martin's Press, 1977). See also *Article 117 Case*, 3 BverfGE 225 (1953); *Privacy in Communications (Klass) Case*, 30 BverfGE 1 (1970); and Donald Kommers, ed., *The Constitutional Jurisprudence of the Federal Republic of Germany* (Durham, NC: Duke University Press, 2d ed., 1997).

2. See also *Schneiderman v. United States*, 320 U.S. 118 (1943).

---

3 Dall. 398 (1798), whether the Court has the power to strike down legislation based on principles of natural justice. Chief Justice John Marshall faced the problem of enforcing his own acceptance of natural rights against the claims of Spanish and Portuguese slave traders in *The Antelope Case*, 23 U.S. 66 (1825). Slaves had been seized by pirates, who were later captured by an American naval ship, and the slave traders and owners sued to recover their "property." Of slavery and the slave trade, Chief Justice Marshall observed "[t]hat it is contrary to the law of nature will scarcely be denied. That every man has a natural right to the fruits of his own labor, is generally admitted, and [that] no other person can rightfully deprive him of those fruits, and appropriate them against his will, seems to be the necessary result of this admission." But Marshall concluded that

> [w]hatever might be the answer of a moralist to this question, a jurist must search for its legal solution, in those principles of action which are sanctioned by the usages, the national acts, and the general assent, of that portion of the world of which he considers himself as a part, and to whose law the appeal is made. If we resort to this standard as the test of international law, the question . . . is decided in favor of the legality of the [slave] trade.

Other members of the Court, though, have sided with Justice Chase's position in *Calder* that with respect to "certain vital principles . . . [a]n act of the Legislature (for I cannot call it a *law*) contrary to the *great first principles* of the social compact, cannot be considered a *rightful exercise* of legislative authority" and, therefore, must be overturned. Consider the debate over fundamental rights and the formulations and standards used by the Court when interpreting the Fourteenth Amendment's due process clause (see Ch. 4). In *Hurtado v. California*, 110 U.S. 516 (1884) (see Ch. 4), for example, Justice Stanley Matthews speaks of the "wellsprings of justice." In *Adamson v. California*, 332 U.S. 46 (1947) (see Ch. 4), and *Rochin v. California*, 342 U.S. 165 (1952) (see Ch. 4), Justice Frankfurter invokes "the shocks the conscience test" and "fundamental fairness standard" for determining what process is due under the due process clause.

The principal criticism of "natural law formulations" is levied in opinions by Justice Hugo Black, particularly in his dissent from the Court's recognition of a right of privacy in *Griswold v. Connecticut*, 381 U.S. 481 (1965) (see Ch. 4), where he observes that

> [o]ne of the most effective ways of diluting or expanding a constitutionally guaranteed right is to substitute for the crucial word or words of a constitutional guarantee another word for the word or words, more or less flexible and more or less restricted in meaning. . . . Use of any such broad, unbounded judicial authority would make this Court's members a day-to-day constitutional convention.

This criticism of the Court for imposing its own substantive value choices applies as well to those arguing that the Court should draw on *moral* and *political philosophy*. Yet Professor Ronald Dworkin and other contemporary legal scholars call for "a fusion of constitutional law and moral theory" or political philosophy.[5] Contemporary legal scholarship is indeed marked by a proliferation of expressly normative theories that would rationalize and guide constitutional interpretation according to "abstract beliefs about morality and justice,"[6] the "voice of reason,"[7] "a moral patrimony" implicit in "our common heritage,"[8] "the circumstances and values of the present generation,"[9] "conventional morality,"[10] "public morality,"[11] "constitutional morality,"[12] "fundamental values,"[13] and the "essential principles of justice,"[14] or "the idea of progress."[15] But this movement toward more specialized and abstract theories of constitutional interpretation raises the ante for reaching consensus within the Supreme Court and the country.[16]

Interpretivists counter that the turn to moral and political philosophy only exacerbates the problems of constitutional interpretation and the countermajoritarian difficulty of judicial review. As Stanford University Law School professor John Hart Ely cleverly put it, "The Constitution may follow the flag, but is it really supposed to keep up with the *New York Review of Books*?"[17] Judge Bork raises other concerns:

> The abstract, universalistic style of legal thought has a number of dangers. For one thing, it teaches disrespect for the actual institutions of the American polity. These institutions are designed to achieve compromise, to slow change, to dilute absolutisms. They embody wholesome inconsistencies. They are designed, in short, to do things that abstract generalizations about the just society tend to bring into contempt.[18]

Interpreting the Constitution, nevertheless, presupposes a judicial and political philosophy and poses inescapable questions of substantive value choices. As Justice Brennan explains,

> Faith in democracy is one thing, blind faith quite another. Those who drafted our Constitution understood the difference. One cannot read the text without admitting that it embodies substantive choices; it places certain values beyond the power of any legislature. . . .
>
> To remain faithful to the content of the Constitution, therefore, an approach to interpreting the text must account for the existence of these substantive value choices, and must accept the ambiguity inherent in the effort to apply them to modern circumstances. The Framers discerned fundamental principles through struggles against particular malefactions of the Crown; the struggle shapes the particular contours of the articulated principles. But our acceptance of the fundamental principles has not and should not bind us to those precise, at times anachronistic, contours. Successive generations of Americans have continued to respect these fundamental choices and adopt them as their own guide to evaluating quite different historical practices. Each generation has the choice to overrule or add to the fundamental principles enunciated by the Framers; the Constitution can be amended or it can be ignored. Yet with respect to its fundamental principles, the text has suffered neither fate. . . .
>
> The Constitution on its face is, in large measure, a structuring text, a blueprint for government. And when the text is not prescribing the form of the government it is limiting the powers of that government. The original document, before addition of any of the amendments, does not speak primarily of the rights of man, but of the abilities and disabilities of government. When one reflects upon the text's preoccupation with the scope of government as well as its shape, however, one comes to understand that what this text is about is the relationship of the individual and the state. The text marks the metes and bounds of official authority and individual autonomy. When one studies the boundary that the text marks out, one gets a sense of the vision of the individual embodied in the Constitution.
>
> As augmented by the Bill of Rights and the Civil War Amendments, this text is a sparking vision of the supremacy of the human dignity of every individual. This vision is reflected in the very choice of democratic self-governance: the supreme value of a democracy is the presumed worth of each individual. . . . It is a vision that has guided us as a people throughout our history, although the precise rules by which we have protected fundamental human dignity have been transformed over time in response to both transformations of social conditions and evolution of our concepts of human dignity.[19]

Neither do alternative theories and modes of constitutional interpretation elude a dependence on political philosophy. Interpreting
the Constitution frequently requires, as Professor Charles L. Black, Jr.,
argues, "inference from the structure and relationships created by
the constitution in all its parts or in some principal part."[20] Chief Justice Marshall's watershed opinion in *McCulloch v. Maryland*, 4 Wheat.
(17 U.S.) 316 (1819) (see Vol. 1, Ch. 6), illustrates the role of *structural
analysis* of the Constitution. There, Marshall upheld the constitutionality of the national bank as a necessary and proper exercise of Congress's
powers based on inferences from the structure of federalism, instead of
relying on the necessary and proper clause per se. Still, Jeffersonian-
Republicans disagreed with the infusion of Marshall's nationalistic political philosophy into constitutional law. Moreover, differences rooted
in rival political philosophies over the structure of federalism persist in
the Court and the country (see Vol. 1, Ch. 6).

Nor do attempts to reconcile the exercise of the Court's power
with majoritarian democracy in terms of what has become known as
process-oriented theory of judicial review fare much better.[21] Justice Harlan
Stone initially suggested that the Court's role ought to be limited to
policing the political process and ensuring that it does not discriminate
against "discrete and insular minorities," in footnote 4 of *United States
v. Carolene Products Co.*, 304 U.S. 144 (1938) (see Ch. 12). In a book titled *Democracy and Distrust*, Professor Ely further developed the theory
that the Court's role should be limited to policing the democratic
process and facilitating the representation of minorities in the electoral
process: "[T]he general theory is one that bounds judicial review under
the Constitution's open-ended provisions by insisting that it can appropriately concern itself only with questions of participation, and not
with the substantive merits of the political choice under attack."[22] In
this way, Ely aims to justify the Court's supervision of the electoral
process (see Vol. 1, Ch. 8) and reconcile judicial review with democratic theory. But Ely fails to provide a general theory in saying nothing about how the Court should handle cases involving disputes over
presidential power and federalism, for example.[23] Moreover, the
process-oriented theory of judicial review has been criticized for too
sharply limiting the Court's role in protecting civil liberties and civil
rights. As Justice Robert Jackson in *West Virginia State Board of Education
v. Barnette*, 319 U.S. 624 (1943) (see Ch. 5), observes, "The very purpose of a Bill of Rights was to withdraw certain subjects from the vicissitudes of political controversy, to place them beyond the reach of
majorities and officials and to establish them as legal principles to be
applied by the courts" (see also Ch. 4).

Ultimately, what divides the justices, and sometimes the Court and the country, has less to do with interpretivism and noninterpretivism than fundamentally rival political philosophies and views of the role of the Court in American politics. It is not just that constitutional interpretation draws on the text, structure, history, doctrines, practices, and moral and political philosophy that is important, but how these sources and modes of analysis are employed. Admittedly, as Justice Scalia has noted, there may be a "sense of dissatisfaction" with finding that we "do not yet have an agreed-upon theory" of constitutional interpretation. "But it should come as no surprise."[24] That conclusion has also led the Chief Judge of the Court of Appeals for the Seventh Circuit and a prolific author and advocate of pragmatism, Richard A. Posner, to argue against the need for specialized constitutional theories to justify legal doctrines, and for more empirical research into the socioeconomic complexities underlying legal controversies.[25] To be sure, there is no denying that in constitutional politics there are no simple solutions but instead an invitation for reflection and enduring political struggles.

■ THE DEVELOPMENT OF LAW

Comparative Constitutional Interpretation

Comparative constitutional interpretation increasingly commands greater attention. Scholars, along with members of the Supreme Court and other high courts around the world, are debating the uses and misuses of comparative constitutional law and interpretation.[1]

Several factors contribute to this development. For one, in the latter half of the twentieth century the European Court of Justice and constitutional courts in Western European countries have increasingly asserted their power and employed comparative constitutional analysis (see the IN COMPARATIVE PERSPECTIVE box in Vol. 1, Ch. 6). Following the collapse of the former Soviet Union, constitutional courts in Central and Eastern Europe also turned to comparative constitutional law analysis when construing their new constitutions. High courts in Canada, Germany, and Japan also frequently look to decisions of the U.S. Supreme Court when interpreting similar provisions in their post–World War II constitutions and bills of rights (see the IN COMPARATIVE PERSPECTIVE boxes in Chs. 5 and 6). And the South African Constitution of 1996 and Bill of Rights specifically requires its judiciary to consider foreign and international law (see, for example, the IN COMPARATIVE PERSPECTIVE box in Ch. 10). In addition, bar associations along with business and human rights organizations promote international exchanges, and comparative constitutional analysis became much easier with Internet access to court decisions from around the world.

Within the Supreme Court, however, the justices disagree about the use of comparative constitutional analysis. Unlike courts in Canada, Japan, South Africa, and elsewhere, the Supreme Court generally resists comparative constitutional law in justifying its decisions. Justice Scalia, in particular, is unapologetic, observing in *Printz v. United States*, 521 U.S. 898 (1997) that "comparative analysis [is] inappropriate to the task of interpreting a constitution, though it was of course relevant to the task of writing one." By contrast, Justice Breyer, the strongest supporter of comparative constitutional analysis, responded in his dissent that comparative law "may . . . cast an empirical light on the consequences of different legal solutions to a common legal problem."[2] As a result, some foreign jurists have been highly critical of the U.S. Supreme Court for not paying more attention to comparative and international law, particularly with respect to human rights.[3]

Nonetheless, historically the Court has drawn on comparative law and experiences in several ways. First, such analysis has been employed to support the factual basis for the Court's rulings, highlighting relevant "constitutional facts." As a progressive attorney, before joining the Court, Louis D. Brandeis pioneered the idea in his famous "Brandeis brief." Filed in *Muller v. Oregon*, 208 U.S. 412 (1907), it cited, in support of Oregon's law restricting the number of hours that women could work, statutes and reports from Great Britain, France, Switzerland, Austria, Holland, Italy, and Germany. Brandeis did so to show the reasonableness of the legislation. In other words, the Court may take judicial notice of comparative law and experiences in its rulings. In striking down laws criminalizing homosexual sodomy in *Lawrence v. Texas* (2003) (excerpted in Ch. 11), for instance, Justice Kennedy cites in support a decision of the European Court of Human Rights. In *Atkins v. Virginia* (2002) (excerpted in Ch. 10), when holding that the execution of mentally retarded criminals violates the Eighth Amendment, Justice Stevens noted in a footnote that "within the world community, the imposition of the death penalty for crimes committed by mentally retarded offenders is overwhelmingly disapproved." But that reference invited a sharp rebuke from Chief Justice Rehnquist and Justice Scalia, who maintain that "the viewpoints of other countries simply are not relevant to interpreting constitutional standards."

Second, the Court sometimes uses comparative analysis in *dicta-dicta* that throws a comparative light on and ostensibly supports the interpretation given in the Court's opinion. Chief Justice Rehnquist, thus, in the doctor-assisted suicide ruling in *Washington v. Glucksberg*, 521 U.S. 702 (1997), cites comparative constitutional law in underscoring the importance of the issue, as have other justices in giving "kindred problems"[4] a comparative perspective. More frequently, such citations aim to buttress the Court's line drawing an announced principle based on our "traditions," especially historical and traditional links to English law and legal history; even Justice Scalia employs comparative constitutional analysis in this fashion.[5]

Third, closely related but more controversial are citations to developing

international and comparative constitutional law as basis for a new interpretation of provisions of the Constitution and Bill of Rights. One of the most
controversial illustrations, perhaps, is Justice Goldberg's 1963 opinion dissenting from the denial of *certiorari* in *Rudolph v. Alabama* (reproduced in the
INSIDE THE COURT box in Ch. 10), inviting challenges to the constitutionality of the death penalty.[6]

1. For justices' off-the-bench comments favorably addressing the use of comparative
constitutional law, see Stephen Breyer, Keynote Address, 97 *American Society for
International Law Proceedings* 265 (2003); Sandra Day O'Connor, "Broadening Our
Horizons: Why American Judges and Lawyers Must Learn about Foreign Law,"
International Observer 2 (June 1997); Sandra Day O'Connor, Keynote Address, 96
American Society for International Law Proceedings 348 (2002); Ruth Bader Ginsburg,
"Looking beyond Our Borders: The Value of a Comparative Perspective in Compar-
ative Adjudication," 40 *Idaho Law Review* 1 (2003); and Ruth Bader Ginsburg and
Deborah Hones Merritt, "Affirmative Action: An International Human Rights Dia-
logue," 21 *Cardozo Law Review* 253 (1999). See also David Fontana, "Refined Com-
parativism in Constitutional Law," 49 *U.C.L.A. Law Review* 539 (2001); Harold
Hongju Koh, "Paying 'Decent Respect' to World Opinion on the Death Penalty," 35
U.C. Davis Law Review 1085 (2002); Sujit Choudhry, "Globalization in Search of Justification: Towards a Theory of Comparative Constitutional Interpretation," 74 *Indiana Law Review* 819 (1999).

   For criticisms of the Supreme Court's use of comparative law in constitutional
interpretation, see Antonin Scalia, "Commentary," 40 *St. Louis University Law Journal*
1119 (1996); Robert H. Bork, *Coercing Virtue: The Worldewide Rule of Judges* (Washington, DC: American Enterprise Institute, 2003); and Roger Alford, "Misusing International Sources to Interpret the Constitution," 98 *American Journal of International
Law* 57 (2004).

2. See also *Knight v. Florida*, 528 U.S. 984 (1994), denying *certiorari* in two death
penalty appeals raising the issue of whether delays in executions violate the Eighth
Amendment. Justice Thomas filed an opinion dismissing comparative legal analysis as
"unnecessary" in response to an opinion filed by Justice Breyer, which cited comparative constitutional law decisions and contended that such "views are useful even
though not binding."

3. See, e.g., The Honourable Claire L'Heureux-Dube, Justice of the Supreme Court
of Canada, "The Importance of Dialogue: Globalization and the International Impact of the Rehnquist Court," 34 *Tulsa Law Journal* 15 (1998).

4. *State Tax Commission of Utah v. Aldrich*, 316 U.S. 174 (1942) (Frankfurter, J., con. op.).

5. See, e.g., *Loving v. United States*, 517 U.S. 748 (1996). See also *Rogers v. Richmond*,
365 U.S. 534, 541 (1961) (on the roots of our adversary system); *McGowan v. State of
Maryland*, 366 U.S. 101 (1961); *Thompson v. Oklahoma*, 487 U.S. 815, 868 (1988); and
McIntyre v. Ohio Elections Commission, 514 U.S. 334 (1995) (Scalia, J., dis. op.).

6. See also *Tropp v. Dulles*, 356 U.S. 86, 102–103 (1958); and *Thompson v. Oklahoma*,
487 U.S. 815 (1988).

NOTES

1. See Willard Hurst, "The Role of History," in *Supreme Court and Supreme Law*, ed.
Edmond Cahn (New York: Clarion Books, 1971); and Charles Miller, *The Supreme
Court and the Uses of History* (Cambridge, MA: Harvard University Press, 1969).

2. William Rehnquist, "The Notion of a Living Constitution," in *Views from the Bench: The Judiciary and Constitutional Politics*, ed. Mark Cannon and David O'Brien (Chatham, NJ: Chatham House, 1985), 191.

3. See Paul Rosen, *The Supreme Court and Social Science* (Urbana: University of Illinois Press, 1972); Wallace Loh, ed., *Social Research in the Judicial Process* (New York: Russell Sage Foundation, 1984); and David O'Brien, "The Seduction of the Judiciary: Social Science and the Courts," 64 *Judicature* 8 (1980).

4. See Edward S. Corwin, *The "Higher Law" Background of American Constitutional Law* (Ithaca, NY: Cornell University Press, 1955); Thomas Grey, "Do We Have an Unwritten Constitution," 27 *Stanford Law Review* 703 (1975); Robert Goldwin and William Schambra, eds., *How Does the Constitution Secure Rights?* (Washington, DC: American Enterprise Institute, 1985); Morton White, *The Philosophy of the American Revolution* (New York: Oxford University Press, 1978); and Symposium, "The Framers' Intent: An Exchange," 10 *University of Puget Sound Law Review* 343–369 (1987).

5. See Ronald Dworkin, *Taking Rights Seriously* (Cambridge, MA: Harvard University Press, 1977), 149; Ronald Dworkin, *A Matter of Principle* (Cambridge, MA: Harvard University Press, 1985); and Ronald Dworkin, *Law's Empire* (Cambridge, MA: Harvard University Press, 1986).

6. See G. Edward White, "Reflections on the Role of the Supreme Court: The Contemporary Debate and the Lessons of History," 63 *Judicature* 162 (1979); and Philip Bobbit, *Constitutional Fate* (New York: Oxford University Press, 1982).

7. Henry Hart, "Foreword: The Time Chart of the Justices," 73 *Harvard Law Review* 84 (1959).

8. Charles Black, "Old and New Ways in Judicial Review," address given at Bowdoin College, 1957.

9. Terrance Sandalow, "Constitutional Interpretation," 79 *Michigan Law Review* 1033 (1981). See also Joseph Grano, "Judicial Review and a Written Constitution in a Democratic Society," 28 *Wayne Law Review* 1 (1981); and Paul Brest, "The Misconceived Quest for the Original Understanding," 60 *Boston University Law Review* 204 (1980).

10. Harry Wellington, "Common Law Rules and Constitutional Double Standards: Some Notes on Adjudication," 83 *Yale Law Journal* 221 (1973). See also Michael Perry, *The Constitution, the Courts, and Human Rights* (New Haven, CT: Yale University Press, 1982); and Michael Perry, *Morality, Politics & Law* (New York: Oxford University Press, 1988).

11. Owen Fiss, "Objectivity and Interpretation," 34 *Stanford Law Review* 739 (1982).

12. Dworkin, *Taking Rights Seriously*, 149.

13. Kenneth Karst, "The Freedom of Intimate Association," 89 *Yale Law Journal* 624 (1980); and Richard Richards, "Human Rights as the Unwritten Constitution: The Problem of Change and Stability in Constitutional Interpretation," 4 *University of Dayton Law Review* 295 (1979).

14. Michael Michelman, "In Pursuit of Constitutional Welfare Rights: One View of Rawl's Theory of Justice," 121 *University of Pennsylvania Law Review* 962 (1979).

15. Alexander Bickel, *The Supreme Court and the Idea of Progress* (New York: Harper & Row, 1970).

16. See David O'Brien, " 'The Imperial Judiciary:' Of Paper Tigers and Socio-Legal

Indicators," 2 *Journal of Law & Politics* 1 (1985); and William Van Alstyne, "Interpreting *This* Constitution: The Unhelpful Contributions of Special Theories of Judicial Review," 35 *University of Florida Law Review* 209 (1983).

17. John Ely, *Democracy and Distrust* (Cambridge, MA: Harvard University Press, 1980), 58.

18. Robert Bork, "Tradition and Morality in Constitutional Law," in *Views from the Bench*, ed. Cannon and O'Brien, 169.

19. William Brennan, Jr., "The Constitution of the United States: Contemporary Ratification," speech given at Georgetown University, Oct. 12, 1985.

20. Charles Black, Jr., *Structure and Relationship in Constitutional Law* (Baton Rouge: Louisiana University Press, 1969).

21. See Laurence Tribe, "The Puzzling Persistence of Process-Based Constitutional Theories," 89 *Yale Law Journal* 1063 (1980); and Mark Tushnet, "Darkness on the Edge of Town: The Contributions of John Hart Ely," 89 *Yale Law Journal* 1037 (1980).

22. Ely, *Democracy and Distrust*, 181.

23. See David O'Brien, "Judicial Review and Constitutional Politics: Theory and Practice," 48 *University of Chicago Law Review* 1052 (1981).

24. Antonin Scalia, "Originalism: The Lesser Evil," 57 *Cincinnati Law Review* 850 (1989), 865.

25. Richard A. Posner, "Against Constitutional Theory," 73 *New York University Law* 1 (1998). See also R. Posner, *The Problematics of Moral and Legal Theory* (Cambridge: Belknap Press, 1999).

SELECTED BIBLIOGRAPHY

Agresto, John. *The Supreme Court and Constitutional Democracy.* Ithaca, NY: Cornell University Press, 1984.

Barber, Sotirios. *On What the Constitution Means.* Baltimore, MD: Johns Hopkins University Press, 1984.

Bickel, Alexander. *The Supreme Court and the Idea of Progress.* New York: Harper & Row, 1970.

———. *The Least Dangerous Branch.* New York: Bobbs-Merrill, 1961.

Black, Charles, Jr. *Decision According to Law.* New York: W. W. Norton, 1981.

———. *Structure and Relationship in Constitutional Law.* Baton Rouge: Louisiana State University Press, 1969.

———. *A New Birth of Freedom: Human Rights, Named and Unnamed.* New York: Grosset/Putnam, 1997.

Bobbitt, Philip. *Constitutional Fate.* New York: Oxford University Press, 1982.

Bork, Robert. *Coercing Virtue: The Worldwide Rule of Judges.* Washington, DC: American Enterprise Institute, 2003.

Choper, Jesse. *Judicial Review and the National Political Process.* Chicago: University of Chicago Press, 1980.

Corwin, Edward. *The "Higher Law" Background of American Constitutional Law.* Ithaca, NY: Cornell University Press, 1955.

Delgado, Richard, and Stefancic, Jean. *Critical Race Theory: The Cutting Edge.* Philadelphia: Temple University Press, 1999.

Devins, Neal, and Fisher, Louis. *The Democratic Constitution.* New York: Oxford University Press, 2004.

Dworkin, Ronald. *Taking Rights Seriously.* Cambridge, MA: Harvard University Press, 1977.

———. *Law's Empire.* Cambridge, MA: Harvard University Press, 1986.

———. *Freedom's Law: The Moral Reading of the American Constitution.* Cambridge, MA: Harvard University Press, 1996.

Ely, John. *Democracy and Distrust.* Cambridge, MA: Harvard University Press, 1980.

Erickson, Rosemary, and Simon, Rita. *The Use of Social Science Data in Supreme Court Decisions.* Urbana: University of Illinois Press, 1998.

Farber, Daniel, and Sherry, Suzanna. *Beyond All Reason: The Radical Assault on Truth in American Law.* New York: Oxford University Press, 1997.

———. *Desperately Seeking Certainty: The Misguided Quest for Constitutional Foundations.* Chicago: University of Chicago, 2003.

Fisher, Louis. *Constitutional Dialogues.* Princeton, NJ: Princeton University Press, 1988.

George, Robert P. *In Defense of Natural Law.* New York: Oxford University Press, 1999.

Gerber, Scott. *To Secure These Rights: The Declaration of Independence and Constitutional Interpretation.* New York: New York University Press, 1995.

Goldstein, Leslie, ed. *Feminist Jurisprudence.* Lanham, MD: Rowman & Littlefield, 1992.

Hirsch, H. N. *A Theory of Liberty.* New York: Routledge, 1992.

Hoffman, Daniel. *Our Elusive Constitution: Silences, Paradoxes, Priorities.* Albany: University of New York Press, 1996.

Kahn, Paul. *Legitimacy and History.* New Haven, CT: Yale University Press, 1992.

Kairys, David. *The Politics of Law.* 3d ed. New York: Pantheon Books, 1998.

Levinson, Sanford. *Constitutional Faith.* Princeton, NJ: Princeton University Press, 1988.

Lipkin, Justin. *Constitutional Resolutions: Pragmatism and the Role of Judicial Review in American Constitutionalism.* Durham, NC: Duke University Press, 2000.

MacKinnon, Catharine, *Toward a Feminist Theory of the State.* Cambridge, MA: Harvard University Press, 1989.

———. *Feminism Unmodified.* Cambridge, MA: Harvard University Press, 1987.

Miller, Charles. *The Supreme Court and the Uses of History,* Cambridge, MA: Harvard University Press, 1969.

Peretti, Terri Jennings. *In Defense of a Political Court.* Princeton, NJ: Princeton University Press, 1999.

Perry, Michael. *Morality, Politics & Law.* New York: Oxford University Press, 1988.

———. *The Constitution, the Courts, and Human Rights.* New Haven, CT: Yale University Press, 1982.

Posner, Richard. *The Problems of Jurisprudence.* Cambridge, MA. Harvard University Press, 1990.

――――. *The Problematics of Moral and Legal Theory.* Cambridge, MA: Belknap Press, 1999.

――――. *Law, Pragmatism, and Democracy.* Cambridge: Harvard University Press, 2003.

Redish, Martin. *The Constitution as Political Structure.* New York: Oxford University Press, 1995.

Rosen, Paul. *The Supreme Court and Social Science.* Urbana: University of Illinois Press, 1972.

Seidman, Louis, and Tushnet, Mark. *Remnants of Belief: Contemporary Constitutional Issues.* New York: Oxford University Press, 1996.

Smith, Rogers. *Liberalism and American Constitutional Law.* Cambridge, MA: Harvard University Press, 1985.

Tribe, Laurence. *Constitutional Choices.* Cambridge, MA: Harvard University Press, 1985.

Tribe, Laurence, and Dorf, Michael. *On Reading the Constitution.* Cambridge, MA: Harvard University Press, 1991.

Tushnet, Mark. *Red, White, and Blue: A Critical Analysis of Constitutional Law.* Cambridge, MA: Harvard University Press, 1988.

Wellington, Harry. *Interpreting the Constitution.* New Haven, CT: Yale University Press, 1990.

White, James. *Justice as Translation.* Chicago: University of Chicago Press, 1990.

――――. *When Words Lose Their Meaning.* Chicago: University of Chicago Press, 1984.

2

LAW AND POLITICS IN THE
SUPREME COURT:
JURISDICTION AND
DECISION-MAKING PROCESS

The supreme court is the only federal court in the United States to have complete power to decide what to decide, that is, which cases to hear. This power enables the Court to set its own agenda as well as to manage its docket. Like other courts, the Supreme Court, however, must await issues brought by lawsuits; it does not initiate its own. Also, like other social institutions, it is affected by social change. One hundred fifty years ago, the Court's docket did not include issues of personal privacy raised by electronic surveillance and computer data banks, for instance, or controversies over abortion and the patenting of organic life-forms. As technology develops and society changes, courts respond. Law evolves more or less quickly in response to social change. Another change occurring over the past several decades has been a substantial increase in the number of cases, the caseload, sent to the Court. Unable to hear them all, the Court assumed the power to pick which issues it will decide. The Court now functions like a roving commission in responding to social forces.

A │ *Jurisdiction and Justiciable Controversies*

Jurisdiction is the authorized power of a court to hear a case and to exercise judicial review. The Court's jurisdiction derives from three sources: (1) Article III of the Constitution, which defines the Court's original jurisdiction; (2) congressional legislation, providing the basis for hearing appeals of lower courts' decisions, or appellate jurisdiction; and (3) the Court's own interpretation of 1 and 2 together with its own rules for accepting cases.

Article III of the Constitution provides that the judicial power extends to all federal questions, that is, "all Cases, in Law and Equity, arising under this Constitution, the Laws of the United States, and Treaties." The Court also has original jurisdiction over specific kinds of "cases or controversies": those affecting ambassadors and other public ministers and consuls; disputes to which the United States is a party; disputes between two or more states, disputes between a state and a citizen of another state, if a state waives its sovereign immunity under the Eleventh Amendment; and disputes between a state (or its citizens) and foreign countries. The Court today has only about ten cases each term (the first Monday in October through June) coming on original jurisdiction. Most involve states suing each other over land and water rights, and they tend to be rather complex and carried over for several terms before they are finally decided.

Congress establishes (and may change) the appellate jurisdiction of the federal judiciary, including the Supreme Court. Most cases used to come as direct appeals, requiring obligatory review. But as the caseload increased, Congress expanded the Court's discretionary jurisdiction by replacing appeals with petitions for *certiorari* (a petition asking a court to inspect the proceedings and decision of a lower court), which the Court may in its discretion grant or deny. Prior to the Judiciary Act of 1925, which broadened the Court's discretionary jurisdiction, appeals amounted to 80 percent of the docket and petitions for *certiorari*, less than 20 percent. Today, well over 99 percent of the docket comes on *certiorari*.

Although most cases now come as *certiorari* (*cert.*) petitions, Congress provides that appellate courts may submit a writ of certification to the Court, requesting the justices to clarify or "make more certain" a point of federal law. The Court receives only a handful of such cases each term. Congress also gave the Court the power to issue certain extraordinary writs, or orders. In a few cases, the Court may issue writs of *mandamus* and prohibition, ordering lower courts or public officials to either do something or refrain from some action. In addition, the Court has the power to grant writs of *habeas corpus* ("produce the body"), enabling it to review cases by prisoners who claim that their constitutional rights have been violated and they are unlawfully imprisoned.

Congress also established the practice of giving the poor, or the indigent, the right to file without the payment of fees. When filing an appeal or petition for *certiorari*, indigents may file an affidavit requesting that they be allowed to proceed *in forma pauperis* ("in the manner of a pauper,") without the usual filing fees and forms. The Court sets both the rules governing filing fees and the form that appeals, *cert.* petitions, and other documents must take. Except for indigents, the Court requires $300 for filing any case and another $100 if a case is granted oral argument. Indigents are exempt as well from the Court's rules specifying particular colors and lengths of paper for various kinds of filings. All *cert.* petitions, for instance, must have a white color, whereas opposing briefs are light orange. Any document filed by the federal government has a gray cover. No petition or appeal may exceed thirty pages, and for those few cases granted oral argument, briefs on the merits of cases are limited to fifty pages.

The Constitution and Congress thus stipulate the kinds of cases and controversies the Court may consider. Yet, as Charles Evans Hughes, who later became chief justice (1930–1941), candidly remarked, "We are under the Constitution, but the Constitution is what the Judges say it is."[1] The Court has developed its own doctrines for denying a large number of cases review and for setting its own agenda. Specifically, the Court considers whether it has jurisdiction over a "case or controversy," and then whether that dispute is justiciable, or capable of judicial resolution. Justices thus may, or may not, deny a case if it (1) lacks adverseness or (2) is brought by parties who lack "standing to sue," or poses issues that either (3) are not "ripe," (4) have become "moot," or (5) involve a "political question." What all this means is discussed below.

■ ADVERSENESS AND ADVISORY OPINIONS

The Court generally maintains that litigants, those involved in a lawsuit, must be real and adverse in seeking a decision that will resolve their dispute and not some hypothetical issue. The requirement of real and adverse parties means that the Court will not decide so-called friendly suits (when the parties do not have adverse interests in the

Figure 2.1

Avenues of Appeal:
The two main routes to the Supreme Court.

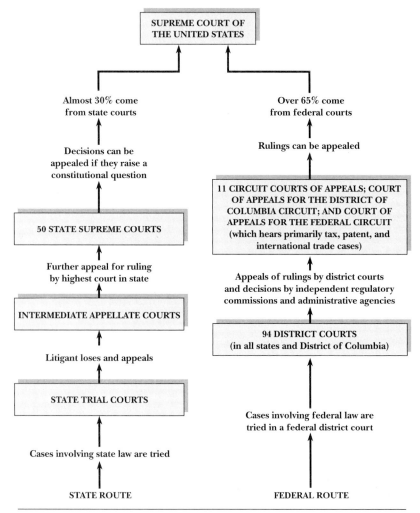

Note: In addition, some cases come directly to the Supreme Court from trial courts when they involve reapportionment or civil rights disputes. Appeals from the Court of Military Appeals also go directly to the Supreme Court. A few cases come on "original jurisdiction" and involve disputes between state governments.

outcome of a case). Nor will the Court give "advisory opinions" on issues not raised in an actual lawsuit. The Jay Court denied two requests
for advisory opinions: one in 1790 by Secretary of Treasury Alexander
Hamilton on the national government's power to assume state Revolutionary War debts, and the other in 1793 by Secretary of State Thomas
Jefferson for an interpretation of certain treaties and international law.
Chief Justice John Jay held that it would be improper for the Court to
judge such matters, because the president may call on cabinet heads for
advice. The Court continues to maintain that it is inappropriate "to
give opinions in the nature of advice concerning legislative action, a
function never conferred upon it by the Constitution and against the
exercise of which this court has steadily set its face from the beginning."[2]

Historically, justices have nevertheless extrajudicially advised attorneys, congressmen, and presidents. They occasionally even accuse each
other of including in opinions *dicta* (statements of personal opinion or
philosophy not necessary to the decision handed down) that is tantamount to "giving legal advice."[3] The Court, furthermore, upheld the
constitutionality of the Declaratory Judgment Act authorizing federal
courts to declare, or make clear, rights and legal relationships even before a legislature has mandated a law to take effect, although only in
"cases of actual controversy."[4]

■ STANDING TO SUE

Standing, like adverseness, is a threshold requirement for getting into
court. "Generalizations about standing to sue," as Justice William O.
Douglas discouragingly, but candidly, put it, "are largely worthless as
such."[5] Nonetheless, the basic requirement is that individuals show injury to a legally protected interest or right and demonstrate that other
opportunities for defending that claim (before an administrative tribunal or a lower court) have been exhausted. The claim of an injury "must
be of a personal and not official nature" and of "some specialized interest of [the individual's] own to vindicate, apart from political concerns
which belong to it."[6] The interest must be real as opposed to speculative
or hypothetical.

The injuries and legal interests claimed traditionally turned on a
showing of personal or proprietary damage. Typically, plaintiffs had suffered some "pocketbook" or monetary injury. But in the last thirty
years, individuals have sought standing to represent nonmonetary injuries and "the public interest."

The law of standing is a combination of judge-made law and congressional legislation, as interpreted by the Court. During Earl Warren's tenure as chief justice (1953–1969) the Court substantially lowered the threshold for standing and permitted more litigation of public policy issues. *Frothingham v. Mellon*, 262 U.S. 447 (1923), was the leading case on taxpayer suits until it was overturned in *Flast v. Cohen* (1968) (see excerpt below). In *Frothingham*, the Taft Court had denied taxpayers standing to challenge the constitutionality of federal legislation. Mrs. Frothingham, a taxpayer, had attacked Congress's appropriation of federal funds to the states for a maternal and infant care program. She claimed that Congress exceeded its power and intruded on "the reserved rights of the states" under the Tenth Amendment of the Constitution. Writing for the Court, Justice George Sutherland avoided confronting the merits of her claim by denying standing. He did so on the grounds that an individual taxpayer's interest in the financing of federal programs is "comparatively minute and indeterminable," when viewed in light of all taxpayers. Frothingham's "injury" was neither direct nor immediate and the issue raised was basically "political, not judicial." As Sutherland put it,

> [T]he relation of a taxpayer of the United States to the Federal Government is very different [from that relationship with state and local governments]. His interest in the moneys of the Treasury— partly realized from taxation and partly from other sources— is shared with millions of others; is comparatively minute and indeterminable; and the effect upon future taxation, or any payment out of the funds, so remote, fluctuating and uncertain, that no basis is afforded for an appeal to the preventive powers of a court of equity.

To gain standing, according to Sutherland, a taxpayer "must be able to show not only that the statute is invalid but that he has sustained . . . some direct injury as the result of its enforcement, and not merely that he suffers in some indefinite way in common with people generally."

Frothingham's "direct injury" test was met in *Pierce v. Society of Sisters*, 268 U.S. 510 (1925). There, a religious school won a court order barring the enforcement of Oregon's 1922 constitutional amendment requiring children between the ages of eight and sixteen to attend public schools. The Court affirmed on the grounds that the law directly damages the business and property interests of the school and because it "unreasonably interferes with the liberty of parents and guardians to direct the upbringing and education of children under their control."

The federal government relied on *Frothingham* to provide an absolute barrier to subsequent federal taxpayer suits until the Warren Court repudiated that view in *Flast v. Cohen* (1968) (see excerpt be-

FIGURE 2.2
Jurisdictional Map of the U.S. Courts of Appeal and U.S. District Courts

Note: The court of appeals for the federal circuit and the District of Columbia circuit are located in the District of Columbia
(*Administrative Office of the U.S. Courts, Washington, DC.*)

low). In his opinion for the Court, Chief Justice Warren created a two-pronged standard for granting standing to federal taxpayers: Taxpayers must show a logical relationship between their status as taxpayers and the challenged congressional statute as well as a connection between that status and the "precise nature of the constitutional infringement alleged."

The Burger Court (1969–1986) and the Rehnquist Court tightened the requirements for standing in some cases, but relaxed them in others. In 1972, in two sharply divided decisions, the Burger Court denied standing to a group challenging military surveillance of lawful political protests in public places and to the Sierra Club when challenging the construction of a ski resort in Mineral King National Park. In both *Laird v. Tatum*, 408 U.S. 1 (1972), and *Sierra Club v. Morton*, 405 U.S. 727 (1972), a bare majority found that the groups failed to show a "personal stake in the outcome" of the litigation. The following year, however, standing was granted to a group of law students attacking a proposed surcharge on railroad freight. The students contended that the surcharge would discourage the recycling of bottles and cans, and thus contribute to environmental pollution. In *United States v. Students Challenging Regulatory Agency Procedure* (SCRAP), 412 U.S. 669 (1973), the Burger Court granted standing, observing that "[a]esthetic and environmental well-being, like economic well-being, are important ingredients of the quality of life in our society, and the fact that particular environmental interests are shared by the many rather than the few does not make them less deserving of legal protection through the judicial process."

Plaintiffs, those bringing suit, must still claim a personal injury, but they now can act as surrogates for special interest groups. The personal injuries claimed thus embrace a public injury. Congress at the same time expanded the principle even more by providing that any individual "adversely affected or aggrieved" may challenge administrative decisions. Health, safety, and environmental legislation passed in the 1970s mandated such "citizen suits" and right to judicial review of regulatory action. Even when legislation does not provide for the citizen suits, individuals may claim personal injuries, or a "private cause of action," to gain access to the courts and to force agency compliance with the law.

The more conservative Burger and Rehnquist Courts have restricted standing requirements in several ways. First, they have refused to recognize new interests and injuries in granting standing. In *Linda R. S. v. Richard D.*, 410 U.S. 614 (1973), an unwed mother sought enforcement of child support under the Texas Penal Code because the local prosecutor refused to enforce the statute against fathers of illegitimate children. A majority of the Court ruled that she had no recognizable injury and no standing because she could not prove that payments stopped because that particular statute was unenforced.

In *Paul v. Davis*, 424 U.S. 693 (1976), the Court's majority rejected a claim of injury to personal reputation by an individual who objected to the circulation of a flyer to local merchants that carried his photograph along with that of other alleged "active shoplifters." Rehnquist dismissed the claim out of hand. But Justice William Brennan in dissent responded that "[t]he Court by mere fiat and with no analysis wholly excludes personal interest in reputation from the ambit of 'life, liberty, of property' under the Fifth and Fourteenth Amendments, thus rendering due process concerns *never* applicable to the official stigmatization, however, arbitrary." The Court went even further with its reinterpretation of the application of *Flast*'s test for taxpayer suits in *Valley Forge Christian College v. Americans United for Separation of Church and State, Inc.* (1982) (see excerpt below).

Almost two decades after the Court liberalized the law of standing so as to allow citizens' suits for environmental damages, a majority of the Rehnquist Court tightened standing requirements by raising new obstacles for citizens bringing environmental lawsuits. Writing for the majority in *Lujan v. Defenders of Wildlife*, 504 U.S. 555 (1992) (see excerpt below), Justice Scalia denied two environmentalists standing because they failed to show "imminent injury," or that they were in immediate danger of suffering a concrete harm that supported their filing a suit under the Endangered Species Act of 1973. Although Justice Stevens concurred, he would have granted standing, as would have the two dissenters, Justices Blackmun and O'Connor.

In another important ruling on standing, in *Northeastern Florida Chapter of the Associated General Contractors of America v. City of Jacksonville, Florida*, 508 U.S. 656 (1993) (see Ch. 12), the Rehnquist Court made it easier for whites to gain standing to challenge affirmative action and minority set-aside programs. With Justices O'Connor and Blackmun dissenting, the Court held that a building association could challenge a city's set-aside program, even though during the course of the litigation the city had repealed its program. Writing for the majority, Justice Thomas held that in asserting standing to sue a building association did not have to show that any of its members, in the absence of the program, would have received building contracts set aside for women and minorities. While the ruling makes it easier to bring suits attacking set-aside and affirmative action programs, the decision more generally invites lawsuits against governments over the administration of benefit programs by individuals who need not show they were actually denied or would have obtained benefits.

In *Wyoming v. Oklahoma*, 502 U.S. 437 (1992), however, a majority

■ THE DEVELOPMENT OF LAW

Other Important Rulings on Standing

CASE	VOTE	RULING
Schlesinger v. Reservists Committee to Stop the War, 418 U.S 208 (1974)	6:3	Held that members of an organization of present and past members of the military reserves opposed to the Vietnam War had no standing to file a class action suit against the secretary of defense attacking

the constitutionality of members of Congress holding commissions in the reserves and voting on appropriations for the war, as an alleged violation of Article I, Section 6, Clause 2, which declares that "no person holding any office under the United States, shall be a Member of either House during his continuance in office."

United States v. Richardson, 418 U.S. 166 (1974)	5:4	Denied taxpayer standing to bring suit against Congress's secret funding for the Central Intelligence Agency, as an alleged violation of Article I, Section 9, Clause 7,

which provides that "no Money shall be drawn from the Treasury, but in Consequence of Appropriations made by Law; and a regular Statement of Account of the Receipts and Expenditures of all public money shall be published from time to time."

Warth v. Seldin, 422 U.S. 490 (1975)	5:4	Denied standing to various organizations in Rochester, New York, seeking to sue officials of the suburban town of Pen-

field, claiming that the latter's zoning ordinance excluded low- and moderate-income persons from living in the town and violated their rights under the Bill of Rights. The Court held that the individuals and organizations failed to show that they had been "personally" injured.

Simon v. Eastern Kentucky Welfare Rights Organization, 426 U.S. 26 (1976)	9:0	Denied standing to indigents seeking to challenge federal tax regulations reducing the amount of free medical care hospitals must provide in order to receive certain tax benefits.

City of Los Angeles v. Lyons, 461 U.S. 95 (1983)	5:4	Held that an arrestee had standing to sue the city for damages incurred as a result of police subjecting him to a "choke hold," but that he had no standing to

seek an injunction against the police practice of using choke holds, because he failed to show that he might ever be subjected to a choke hold again.

CASE	VOTE	RULING
Allen v. Wright, 468 U.S. 737 (1984)	5:3	Denied standing to parents of black children attending public schools in districts around the country that were in the

process of desegregation to sue various government officials and present their contention that the IRS failed to fulfill its obligation under the law to deny tax-exempt status to private schools engaged in racial discrimination.

Renne v. Geary, 498 U.S. 890 (1991)	7:2	Held that a challenge to a section of California's constitution, which prohibits political parties from endorsing candi-

dates in nonpartisan elections for judgeships and local government offices, was nonjusticiable because members of the San Francisco County Republican and Democratic Central committees did not have standing and failed to present a ripe case in challenging the state's restrictions as a violation of their First Amendment freedoms. Justices Blackmun and Marshall dissented.

Lujan v. Defenders of Wildlife, 504 U.S. 555 (1992)	7:2	Writing for the Court, Justice Scalia denied standing to two environmentalists to bring a suit because they failed to show "imminent injury," or that they were in

immediate danger of suffering a concrete harm that supported their challenge to federal funding for projects in foreign countries, under the Endangered Species Act of 1973. Although Justice Stevens concurred, he would have granted standing, as would have dissenting Justices Blackmun and O'Connor.

Wyoming v. Oklahoma, 502 U.S. 437 (1992)	6:3	Expanded standing for states to sue one another, under the dormant commerce clause theory, on the grounds that one

state's regulations diminished the tax revenues of another. Dissenting Chief Justice Rehnquist and Justices Scalia and Thomas denounced the majority's expansive interpretation of standing under the commerce clause and warned that the ruling would invite a flood of litigation from the states.

Northeastern Florida Chapter of the Associated General Contractors of America v. City of Jacksonville, Florida, 508 U.S. 656 (1993)	7:2	Held that a building association had standing to challenge an affirmative action set-aside program for contractors, even though during the course of the litigation the city had repealed its program and the building association did not present any evidence that its members, in the

absence of the program, would have received building contracts set aside for women and minorities. Justices Blackmun and O'Connor dissented.

CASE	VOTE	RULING
Bennett v. Spear, 520 U.S. 154 (1997)	9:0	Held that property owners, no less than environmentalists, may assert standing to bring "citizen suits" under the Endan-

gered Species Act, and thereby challenge proposed environmental regulations. Writing for the Court, Justice Scalia ruled that the act's permitting
"any person" to sue should be broadly interpreted because "the overall subject matter of this legislation is the environment . . . a matter in which it is
common to think all persons have an interest." As a result, landowners have
new legal standing to challenge environmental regulations.

Raines v. Byrd, 521 U.S. 811 (1997)	7:2	Writing for the Court, Chief Justice Rehnquist held that several members of Congress who challenged the constitu-

tionality of the Line Item Veto Act of 1996, delegating to the president the
power of line-item vetoes, did not have standing to sue, because they did not
assert any personal injury and "the institutional injury [to Congress] they allege[d] is wholly abstract and widely dispersed." Dissenting Justices Stevens
and Breyer would have granted standing and reached the merits presented.

Friends of the Earth, Inc. v. Laidlaw Environmental Services, 528 U.S. 167 (2000)	7:2	Upheld the right of Friends of the Earth, Inc., to sue Laidlaw Environmental Ser- vices for failing to comply with the Clean Water Act by impermissibly dump- ing mercury into a South Carolina river

on 489 occasions from 1987 to 1995. Writing for the Court, Justice Ginsburg
held that the group had shown sufficient personal injury from their loss of
enjoyment of the river to gain standing to sue without also having to prove
"direct injury" to the river. The test for standing, in her words, is "not injury
to the environment but injury to the plaintiff." Moreover, Justice Ginsburg
ruled that the fact that fines won under such citizen suits go to the federal
government, not to the individuals bringing the suits, does not diminish the
personal injury at stake or deprive plaintiffs of standing. Justices Scalia and
Thomas dissented.

Alexander v. Sandoval, 532 U.S. 275 (2001)	5:4	Writing for the Court, Justice Scalia held that individuals do not have standing to sue in order to enforce compliance with Title VI of the Civil Rights Act, which

bars state and local governments from spending federal funds in a discriminatory manner, unless they can show that the *intent* of the institution—a
state, school district, hospital, etc.—was to discriminate. Previously, the Department of Justice and federal courts had held that, in most cases, individuals could sue upon showing that the *effect* of a particular practice or
policy—hiring or admissions rules, for example—worked to disadvantage

CASE	VOTE	RULING

minorities and women. Thus, the threshold for standing for private individuals to enforce state and local government compliance with Title VI was raised and the filing of so-called disparate-impact lawsuits limited. Justices Stevens, Souter, Ginsburg, and Breyer dissented.

Palazzolo v. Rhode Island, 533 U.S. 606 (2001)   6:3   Writing for the Court, Justice Kennedy held that once property owners take title to property that includes land-use restrictions, they have standing to challenge those restrictions, even if the restrictions were imposed years earlier. In Justice Kennedy's words, the government may not be relieved "of its obligation to defend any action restricting land use, no matter how extreme or unreasonable." Although inviting more challenges to environmental regulations, on the merits the Court reaffirmed that to prevail such challenges must demonstrate that the owner was deprived of all economic value of the land. Justice Ginsburg, joined by Justices Souter and Breyer, dissented, contending that the case was not "ripe" for decision.

---

of the Rehnquist Court expanded standing for states to challenge the constitutionality of other states' regulations under the commerce clause on the ground those regulations diminished the state's tax revenues. In order to promote local jobs and to increase tax revenues, in 1986 Oklahoma enacted a law requiring its public utilities to purchase at least 10 percent of the coal they used from mines within the state. As a result, Oklahoma's public utilities purchased less Wyoming-mined coal, and Wyoming lost revenues from severance taxes on coal that would have otherwise been sold to Oklahoma's public utilities. Writing for the Court, Justice White struck down Oklahoma's statute as a violation of the Commerce Clause, which "prohibits economic protectionism—that is, regulatory measures designed to benefit in-state economic interests by burdening out-of-state competitors." In doing so, he held that states could invoke the Court's original jurisdiction, granted in Article III, and rejected Oklahoma's argument that Wyoming was neither engaged in interstate commerce nor had asserted an injury or interest covered by the commerce clause. "It is beyond peradventure," Justice White claimed, "that Wyoming has raised a claim of 'sufficient seriousness and dignity.' Oklahoma, acting in its sovereign capacity, passed the act, which directly affects Wyoming's ability to collect severance tax revenues, an action undertaken in its sovereign capacity." Having granted Wyoming standing to sue on the basis of its loss of revenue, Justice White struck down Oklahoma's law, observing that "when a state statute clearly discriminates against interstate commerce, it will be struck down, unless the discrimination is demonstrably justified by a valid factor unrelated to economic protectionism, see, e.g., *Maine v. Taylor*, 477 U.S. 131 (1986)" (see Vol. 1, Ch. 7). By contrast, in a dissenting opinion joined by Chief Justice Rehnquist and Justice Thomas, Justice Scalia took strong exception to the majority's exercise of its original jurisdiction, granting of standing to Wyoming, and holding that a state's loss of revenue was within the "zone of interests" covered by the Commerce Clause. Wyoming, in his view, failed to assert a direct injury or an interest within the "zone-of-interests" embraced by the commerce clause; a state's interest in collecting taxes, as he put, was "only marginally related to the national market/free trade foundation of our jurisprudence" of applying the commerce clause in the absence of congressional legislation to strike state regulations deemed to burden interstate commerce.

Finally, the Court avoided the controversy over whether requiring schoolchildren to recite the Pledge of Allegiance violates the First Amendment by denying standing in *Elk Grove Unified School District v. Newdow* (2004) (excerpted below). Writing for the Court, Justice Stevens held that Michael A. Newdow, who challenged the policy on behalf of his daughter, even though he was not her legal custodian, lacked "prudential standing"—a Court-made rule. In other words, when legal claims are based on domestic relations law, a field largely left to states, "the prudent course is for the federal court to stay its hand rather than reach out to resolve a weighty question of federal constitutional law." But in concurring opinions, Chief Justice Rehnquist and Justices O'Connor and Thomas dismissed the ruling on "prudential standing" as "novel" and "like the proverbial excursion ticket—good for this day only." They would have granted standing and rejected Newdow's First Amendment claims. The controversy over the Pledge and the motto "In God We Trust" is nonetheless certain to continue and to return to the Court in another case.

■ Ripeness and Mootness

With these doctrines the Court wields a double-edged sword. Appellants, those appealing a lower court ruling, may discover that a case is dismissed because it was brought too early or because the issues are moot and the case was brought too late. Cases are usually rejected as not ripe if the injury claimed has not yet been realized, or if other avenues of appeal have not yet been exhausted. Petitioners raising a federal claim when appealing a state court ruling, for example, must ex-

- THE DEVELOPMENT OF LAW

Class Action Suits

The Federal Rules of Civil Procedure provide for "class action" suits—suits filed by an individual for himself and for all others who have suffered the same injury. This rule enables individuals who have suffered small monetary damages to bring lawsuits that they might not otherwise have brought because of the prohibitively high cost of litigation. Specifically, Rule 23 provides that

> [o]ne or more members of a class may sue or be sued as representative parties on behalf of all only if (1) the class is so numerous that joinder of all members is impracticable, (2) there are questions of law or fact common to the class, (3) the claims or defenses of the representative parties are typical of the claims or defenses of the class, and (4) the representative parties will fairly and adequately protect the interests of the class....
>
> In any class action maintained under [this Rule], the court shall direct to the members of the class the best notice practicable under the circumstances, including individual notice to all members who can be identified.

The scope of this rule, however, was limited by *Eisen v. Carlisle & Jacquelin*, 417 U.S. 156 (1974), holding that when a representative of a class action suit refuses to pay the cost of giving actual notice to all reasonably identifiable class members, federal courts are required to dismiss the suit. Here, representatives would have had to notify 2,250,000 class members at a cost of $225,000.

---

haust all appeals in the state courts and the Court will not exercise jurisdiction until a "final judgment" has been rendered by the highest court in the state. The Court underscored its adherence to that rule when it dismissed *Johnson v. California*, 124 S.Ct. 1833 (2004), because the petitioner failed to include (as required under the Court's rules) in an appendix to the petition for *certiorari* all opinions and final decisions in the case. Here, the state appellate court published only part of its decision (and, like other state and federal appellate courts in the last thirty years, withheld publication of part of its judgment, due to the mounting number of decisions annually handed down). Johnson included in the appendix only the published opinion and not the unpublished portion (which, like other unpublished opinions, was nonetheless available on Lexis). When the Court discovered from the unpublished opinion that the state appellate court's decision was not in all respects final, it dismissed the case. The Court thereby signaled petitioners to append any published and unpublished opinions of state high courts in order to establish that the decision appealed is indeed "final."

Alternatively, a case may be dismissed if pertinent facts or laws change so that there is no longer real adverseness or an actual case or controversy. The issue becomes moot because "there is no subject matter on which the judgment of the court can operate," and hence a ruling would not prove "conclusive" and final.[7] In practice both doctrines bend to the Court's will, because the requirement of ripeness permits the Court to avoid or delay deciding certain issues.

A finding of mootness likewise enables the Court to avoid, if not escape, deciding controversial political issues. *DeFunis v. Odegaard*, 416 U.S. 312 (1974), for example, involved a white student who was denied admission to the University of Washington Law School. The student claimed that the school's affirmative action program discriminated against him and allowed the entrance of minorities with lower LSAT test scores. After the trial judge ruled in his favor, he was admitted into law school but by the time his case reached the Supreme Court he was completing his final year and assured of graduation. Over four dissenters, the majority held that the case was moot. Yet, as the dissenters predicted, the issue would not go away. Within four years, the Burger Court reconsidered the issue of reverse discrimination in university affirmative action programs in *Regents of the University of California v. Bakke*, 438 U.S. 265 (1978) (see Ch. 12).

The issue of mootness could have presented a problem when the Burger Court ruled on abortion in *Roe v. Wade*, 410 U.S. 113 (1973) (see Ch. 11). There the Court struck down Texas's criminal statute prohibiting abortions, except when necessary to save a mother's life. When defending the law, the state's attorney general argued that the plaintiff was a single woman whose pregnancy had already resulted in birth by the time the case reached the Court, and hence her claim was moot. However, Justice Harry Blackmun, writing for the Court, rejected that view out of hand:

> [W]hen, as here, pregnancy is a significant fact in the litigation, the normal 266-day human gestation period is so short that the pregnancy will come to term before the usual appellate process is complete. If that termination makes a case moot, pregnancy litigation seldom will survive much beyond the trial stage, and appellate review will be effectively denied. Our law should not be that rigid. Pregnancy often comes more than once to the same woman, and in the general population, if man is to survive, it will always be with us. Pregnancy provides a classic justification for a conclusion of

nonmootness. It truly could be "capable of repetition, yet evading review."

■ POLITICAL QUESTIONS

Even when the Court has jurisdiction over a properly framed suit, it may decline to rule because it decides that a case raises a "political question" that should be resolved by other political branches. Like other jurisdictional doctrines, the political question doctrine means what the justices say it means.

The doctrine has its origin in Chief Justice Marshall's observation in *Marbury v. Madison*, 5 U.S. 137 (1803) (see Vol. 1, Ch. 1), that "[t]he province of the Court, is, solely, to decide on the rights of individuals. . . . Questions in their nature political, or which are, by the constitution and laws, submitted to the executive can never be made in this Court." Yet as the French commentator Alexis de Tocqueville noted in the 1830s, "Scarcely any political question arises in the United States that is not resolved, sooner or later, into a judicial question."[8] Litigation that reaches the Court is political, and the justices for political reasons decide what and how to decide cases on their docket.

The Taney Court first developed the doctrine in *Luther v. Borden*, 7 How. [48 U.S.] 1 (1849). There, the Court held that whether Rhode Island had a "republican form of government," as guaranteed by Article IV of the Constitution, was a question for Congress, not the Court, to decide. Subsequent rulings elaborated other reasons for the doctrine besides deference to separation of powers. The Court may lack information and resources needed for a ruling. In some areas, as in foreign policy and international relations, the Court lacks both adequate standards for resolving disputes and the means to enforce its decisions.

For many decades the Court relied on the doctrine to avoid entering the "political thicket" of state representation and apportionment, that is, the ways by which a state is divided geographically as a basis for representation in state and federal elections. When declining to rule on the malapportionment of Illinois's congressional districts in *Colegrove v. Green*, 328 U.S. 549 (1946), Justice Felix Frankfurter explained,

> We are of the opinion that the petitioners ask of this Court what is beyond its competence to grant. This is one of those demands on judicial power which cannot be met by verbal fencing about "jurisdiction." It must be resolved by considerations on the basis of which this Court, from time to time, has refused to intervene in contro-

■ INSIDE THE COURT

Standing and the Connecticut Birth Control Cases

Between 1943 and 1965, the Court continually refused standing to individuals attacking the constitutionality of a late nineteenth-century Connecticut statute. The law prohibited virtually all single and married individuals from using contraceptives and physicians from giving advice about their use. In *Tileston v. Ullman*, 318 U.S. 44 (1943), a doctor sued charging that the statute prevented him from giving information to patients. But the Court ruled that he had no real interest or personal injury because he had not been arrested.

More than a decade later in *Poe v. Ullman*, 367 U.S. 497 (1961), a doctor, C. Lee Buxton, and a patient were likewise denied standing on the ground that the law had not been enforced for more than eighty years, even though the state had begun to close birth control clinics. This time the justices split five to four and only Chief Justice Warren and Justices Clark and Whittaker joined Justice Frankfurter's opinion for the Court (Justice Brennan concurred in the decision but not in the opinion). There, Frankfurter observed that

> [t]he Connecticut law prohibiting the use of contraceptives has been on the State's books since 1879. . . . During more than three-quarters of a century since its enactment, a prosecution for its violation seems never to have been initiated, save in [one] case. . . . Neither counsel nor our own researches have discovered any other attempt to enforce the prohibition of distribution or use of contraceptive devices by criminal process. The unreality of these lawsuits is illuminated by another circumstance. We were advised by counsel for appellants that contraceptives are commonly and notoriously sold in Connecticut drug stores. Yet no prosecutions are recorded. . . .
>
> The various doctrines of "standing," "ripeness," and "mootness," which this Court has evolved with particular, though not exclusive, reference to such cases are but several manifestations—each having its own "varied application"—of the primary conception that federal judicial power is to be exercised to strike down legislation, whether state or federal, only at the instance of one who is himself immediately harmed, or immediately threatened with harm, by the challenged action. . . .

By contrast, dissenting Justices Douglas, Harlan, and Stewart disagreed. Notably, Justice Harlan's dissent in *Poe v. Ullman* would have granted standing and reached the merits of the case in a lengthy and influential opinion, observing that

I consider that this Connecticut legislation, as construed to apply to these appellants, violates the Fourteenth Amendment. I believe that a statute making it a criminal offense for married couples to use contraceptives is an intolerable and unjustifiable invasion of privacy in the conduct of the most intimate concerns of an individual's personal life. . . .

[I]t is not the particular enumeration of rights in the first eight Amendments which spells out the reach of Fourteenth Amendment due process, but rather, as was suggested in another context long before the adoption of that Amendment, those concepts which are considered to embrace those rights "which are . . . fundamental; which belong . . . to the citizens of all free governments," *Corfield v. Coryell*, for "the purposes [of securing] which men enter into society," *Calder v. Bull*. Again and again this Court has resisted the notion that the Fourteenth Amendment is no more than a shorthand reference to what is explicitly set out elsewhere in the Bill of Rights. . . .

Due process has not been reduced to any formula; its content cannot be determined by reference to any code. The best that can be said is that through the course of this Court's decisions it has represented the balance which our Nation, built upon postulates of respect for the liberty of the individual, has struck between that liberty and the demands of organized society. If the supplying of content to this Constitutional concept has of necessity been a rational process, it certainly has not been one where judges have felt free to roam where unguided speculation might take them. The balance of which I speak is the balance struck by this country, having regard to what history teaches are the traditions from which it developed as well as the traditions from which it broke. That tradition is a living thing. A decision of this Court which radically departs from it could not long survive, while a decision which builds on what has survived is likely to be sound. No formula could serve as a substitute, in this area, for judgment and restraint. . . .

Each new claim to Constitutional protection must be considered against a background of Constitutional purposes, as they have been rationally perceived and historically developed. Though we exercise limited and sharply restrained judgment, yet there is no "mechanical yardstick," no "mechanical answer." The decision of an apparently novel claim must depend on grounds which follow closely on well-accepted principles and criteria. The new decision must take "its place in relation to what went before and further [cut] a channel for what is to come." *Irvine v. California* (dissenting opinion).

Precisely what is involved here is this: the State is asserting the right to enforce its moral judgment by intruding upon the most intimate details of the marital relation with the full power of the criminal law. Potentially, this could allow the deployment of all the incidental machinery of the criminal law, arrests, searches and seizures; inevitably, it must mean at the very least the lodging of criminal charges, a public trial, and testimony as to the *corpus delicti* [the body of crime]. . . . In sum, the statute allows the State to enquire into, prove and punish married people for the private use of their marital intimacy. . . .

I think the sweep of the Court's decisions, under both the Fourth and Fourteenth Amendments, amply shows that the Constitution protects the privacy of the home against all unreasonable intrusion of whatever character. . . .

Finally, after Dr. Buxton and Estelle Griswold, executive director of Planned Parenthood League of Connecticut, were tried and found guilty of prescribing contraceptives to a married couple, the Court in *Griswold v. Connecticut* (1965) (excerpted in Ch. 4) struck down what Justice Potter Stewart called Connecticut's "uncommonly silly law." In his opinion for the Court, Justice Douglas explained why Buxton and Griswold were now granted standing:

> The appellants were found guilty as accessories and fined $100 each, against the claim that the accessory statute as so applied violated the Fourteenth Amendment. . . . We think that appellates have standing to raise the constitutional rights of married people with whom they had a professional relationship. *Tileston v. Ullman*, is different, for there the plaintiff seeking to represent others asked for a declaratory judgment. In that situation, we thought that the requirements of standing should be strict, lest the standards of "case or controversy" in Article III of the Constitution become blurred. Here those doubts are removed by reason of a criminal conviction for serving married couples in violation of an aiding-and-abetting statute. Certainly the accessory should have standing to assert that the offense which he is charged with assisting is not, or cannot constitutionally be a crime.

Griswold was limited to the privacy and marital decisions of couples. Consequently, in *Eisenstadt v. Baird*, 405 U.S. 438 (1972), to gain standing to claim that single individuals also have a right to acquire and use contraceptives, a doctor arranged to be arrested after delivering a public lecture on contraceptives and handing out samples to single women in the audience. The Court accepted the case and ruled that single women also have the right to acquire and use contraceptives.

versies. It has refused to do so because due regard for the effective working of our Government revealed this issue to be of a peculiarly political nature and therefore not meet for judicial determination.

This is not an action to recover for damages because of the discriminatory exclusion of a plaintiff from rights enjoyed by other citizens. The basis for the suit is not a private wrong, but a wrong suffered by Illinois as a polity. . . . In effect this is an appeal to the federal courts to reconstruct the electoral process of Illinois in order that it may be adequately represented in the councils of the Nation. Because the Illinois legislature has failed to revise its Congressional Representative districts in order to reflect great changes, during more than a generation, in the distribution of its population, we are asked to do this, for Illinois. . . .

Of course no court can affirmatively remap the Illinois districts so as to bring them more in conformity with the standards of fairness for a representative system. At best we could only declare the existing electoral system invalid. The result would be to leave Illinois undistricted and to bring into operation, if the Illinois legislature chose not to act, the choice of members for the House of Representatives on a state-wide ticket. The last stage may be worse than the first. . . .

Nothing is clearer than that this controversy concerns matters that bring courts into immediate and active relations with party contests. From the determination of such issues this Court has traditionally held aloof. It is hostile to the democratic system to involve the judiciary in the politics of the people. And it is not less pernicious if such judicial intervention in an essentially political contest be dressed up in the abstract phrases of the law.

The one stark fact that emerges from the study of the history of Congressional apportionment is its enrollment in politics, in the sense of party contests and party interests. The Constitution enjoins upon Congress the duty of apportioning Representatives "among the several States . . . according to their respective Numbers. . . ." Article I, Sec. 2. Yet, Congress has at times been heedless of this command and not apportioned according to the requirements of the Census. It never occurred to anyone that this Court could issue mandamus to compel Congress to perform its mandatory duty to apportion.

Still, whites, blacks, and other minorities in urban and suburban areas were often denied equal representation in Congress and state legislatures until the Court reversed itself in *Baker v. Carr* (1962) (excerpted below).

In *Goldwater v. Carter* (1979) (excerpted below), the Court issued an order vacating (overturning) a lower court decision in a dispute between several congressmen, headed by conservative Senator Barry Goldwater, and Democratic President Jimmy Carter over the termination of a defense treaty with Taiwan. There, Justices Lewis F. Powell and William Rehnquist took quite different views of the application of the "political questions" doctrine in controversies between Congress and the president.

The Court also reconsidered the "political question" doctrine in *Nixon v. United States*, 506 U.S. 224 (1993) (see Vol. 1, Ch. 5). There, the Rehnquist Court held that a former federal judge's challenge to the Senate's expedited impeachment procedure was nonjusticiable. While also upholding the constitutionality of the Senate's procedure in his opinion for the Court, Chief Justice Rehnquist appeared to go out of his way to justify the application of the doctrine and ostensible exercise of judicial self-restraint.

The doctrine's logic is admittedly circular. "Political questions are matters not soluble by the judicial process; matters not soluble by the judicial process are political questions. As an early dictionary explained," political scientist John Roche says, "violins are small cellos, and cellos are large violins."[9] Still, Columbia Law School professor Louis Henkin points out, even when denying review because of a political question, "the court does not refuse judicial review; it exercises it. It is not dismissing the case or the issue as nonjusticiable; it adjudicates it. It is not refusing to pass on the power of the political branches; it passes upon it, only to affirm that they had the power which had been challenged and that nothing in the Constitution prohibited the particular exercise of it."[10]

Another illustrative controversy over the "political question" doctrine that continues to dog the Court involves the justiciability of political gerrymandering (redrawing voting district lines by the majority party in a legislature to benefit incumbents and to disadvantage candidates and voters in opposing parties). In *Davis v. Bandemer*, 478 U.S. 106 (1986), a plurality held that political gerrymandering controversies were justiciable, but failed to provide a standard for adjudicating such disputes. Almost twenty years later in *Vieth v. Juderlirer*, 124 S.Ct. 1769 (2004) (excerpted in Vol. 1, Ch. 8), a plurality would have overruled *Davis v. Bandemer* and held that such controversies are nonjusticiable. But Justice Kennedy, who cast the deciding vote, would not go along with that and maintained that a standard for adjudicating the matter might still evolve. The four dissenters—Justices Stevens, Souter, Ginsburg, and Breyer—countered that such disputes were justiciable and proposed their own standards, but they could not agree on a standard for determining when political gerrymanders are unconstitutional.

■ *Stare Decisis* and Other Policies

The justices occasionally rely on other self-denying policies to avoid reaching issues as well. They, for example, may invoke what has been called the doctrine of *strict necessity*, and thereupon formulate and decide only the narrowest possible issue.

Another doctrine, *stare decisis* ("let the prior decision stand"), is also not a mechanical formula. It is rather a judicial policy that promotes "the certainty, uniformity, and stability of the law." Even conservative Justice George Sutherland recognized that members of the Court "are not infallible, and when convinced that a prior decision was not originally based on, or that conditions have so changed as to render the decision no longer in accordance with, sound reason, [they] should not hesitate to say so."[11] "*Stare decisis* is usually the wise policy," Justice Louis Brandeis remarked, "because in most matters it is more important that the applicable rule of law be settled than that it be settled right."[12] On constitutional matters, however, Justice Douglas among others emphasizes, "*stare decisis*—that is, established law—was really no sure guideline because what did . . . the judges who sat there in 1875 know about, say, electronic surveillance? They didn't know anything about it."[13]

The Rehnquist Court's deference to *stare decisis* has been a matter of controversy on and off the bench for several years. Indeed, Justice Scalia's sharp attack on a number of prior rulings prompted a response from retired Justice Lewis F. Powell, Jr., in his 1989 Leslie H. Arps Lecture, delivered to the Association of the Bar of the City of New York and entitled "*Stare Decisis* and Judicial Restraint." In Justice Powell's words:

> Those who would eliminate *stare decisis* in constitutional cases argue that the doctrine is simply one of convenience. . . . But elimination of constitutional *stare decisis* would represent explicit endorsement of the idea that the Constitution is nothing more than what five Justices say it is. This would undermine the rule of law. . . .
>
> It is evident that I consider *stare decisis* essential to the rule of law. . . . After two centuries of vast change, the original intent of the Founders is difficult to discern or is irrelevant. Indeed, there may be no evidence of intent. The Framers of the Constitution were wise enough to write broadly, using language that must be construed in light of changing conditions that could not be foreseen. Yet the doctrine of *stare decisis* has remained a constant thread in preserving continuity and stability.

But the debate over *stare decisis* continued and was especially sharp when by a six-to-three vote the Rehnquist Court overturned two of its own earlier decisions, in *Payne v. Tennessee*, 501 U.S. 808 (1991) (see Ch. 10), striking down the use of "victim impact statements" in death penalty cases. Note, however, that subsequently Justices O'Connor, Kennedy, and Souter balked at applying *Payne*'s analysis of *stare decisis* in

Planned Parenthood of Southeastern Pennsylvania v. Casey, 505 U.S. 833 (1992) (see Ch. 11). There, they gave the doctrine of *stare decisis* a new twist when justifying their refusal to overrule entirely the landmark abortion ruling in *Roe v. Wade* (1973) (see Ch. 11) and drew sharp criticism from Chief Justice Rehnquist and Justices Scalia, Thomas, and White.

In sum, *stare decisis* and the precedential value of the Court's jurisdictional doctrines and policies, as Justice Jackson in half-jest quipped, "are accepted only at their current valuation and have a mortality rate as high as their authors."[14]

■ Formal Rules and Practices

Except for government attorneys and members of the practicing bar, few people pay any attention to the technical Rules of the Court. Yet, they are an exercise of political power and determine the nation's access to justice. The rules govern the admission and activities of attorneys in filing appeals, petitions, and motions and conducting oral arguments. They stipulate the fees, forms, and length of filings. Most important, they explain the Court's formal grounds for granting and disposing of cases.

To expedite the process of deciding what to decide, the Court periodically revises its rules. For example, even after the Judiciary Act of 1925 expanded the Court's discretionary jurisdiction, the justices still felt burdened by mandatory appeals. Accordingly, in 1928 the Court required the filing of a jurisdictional statement explaining the circumstances of an appeal, the questions presented, and why the Court should grant review. The requirement also allowed the justices to screen appeals just like petitions for *certiorari*.

One of the reasons for granting *certiorari* given in the Court's rules is whether "a federal court of appeals has rendered a decision in conflict with the decision of another federal court of appeals on the same matter." This rule is especially advantageous for the federal government. The Department of Justice has a relitigation policy. If it receives an adverse ruling from a circuit court of appeals, it will relitigate the issue in other circuits to obtain favorable decisions and generate a conflict among the circuits, which then may be brought to the Court. The rule for granting circuit conflicts, however important, does not control the justices' actual practice of granting *certiorari*. The government and individuals often allege circuit conflicts simply in an effort to get their cases accepted. But most circuit conflicts are "tolerable" and need not be immediately decided. The justices often feel that conflicts should percolate in the circuits before they take them. Sometimes, the justices may want to avoid or delay addressing an issue that has created a conflict among the circuits. Most crucial in granting *certiorari* is simply that at least four justices agree on the importance of the issue presented.

NOTES

1. Charles E. Hughes, *Addresses of Charles Evans Hughes* (New York: Putnam's, 1916), 185–186.

2. *Muskrat v. United States*, 219 U.S. 346 (1911).

3. See *Duke Power Co. v. Carolina Environmental Study Group*, 438 U.S. 59 (1978); and *Bellotti v. Baird*, 443 U.S. 622 (1979).

4. *Aetna Life Insurance Co. v. Haworth*, 300 U.S. 277 (1937).

5. *Data Processing Service v. Camp*, 397 U.S. 150, 151 (1970).

6. *Braxton County Court v. West Virginia*, 208 U.S. 192 (1908); and *Coleman v. Miller*, 307 U.S. 433 (1931) (Frankfurter, J., dissenting opinion).

7. *Ex parte Baez*, 177 U.S. 378 (1900).

8. Alexis de Tocqueville, *Democracy in America*, Vol. 1, ed. P. Bradley (New York: Vintage, 1945), 288.

9. John Roche, "Judicial Self-Restraint," 49 *American Political Science Review* 768 (1955).

10. Louis Henkin, "Is There a 'Political Question' Doctrine?" 85 *Yale Law Journal* 606 (1976).

11. Draft of an opinion, George Sutherland Papers, Manuscript Room, Library of Congress.

12. *Burnet v. Coronado Oil*, 285 U.S. 393 (1932) (Brandeis, J., dissenting opinion).

13. William O. Douglas, interview on *CBS Reports*, Sept. 6, 1972, CBS News, transcript p. 13.

14. Robert Jackson, "The Task of Maintaining Our Liberties: The Role of the Judiciary," 39 *American Bar Association Journal* 962 (1953).

SELECTED BIBLIOGRAPHY

Banks, Christopher. *Judicial Politics in the D.C. Circuit Court*. Baltimore: Johns Hopkins University Press, 1999.

Brenner, Saul, and Spaeth, Harold. *Stare Indecisis*. New York: Cambridge University Press, 1995.

Clayton, Cornell, and Gillman, Howard, eds. *Supreme Court Decision-Making*. Chicago: University of Chicago Press, 1999.

Ivers, Gregg, and McGuire, Kevin T., eds. *Creating Constitutional Change*. Charlottesville: University of Virginia Press, 2004.

Kloppenberg, Lisa. *Playing It Safe: How the Supreme Court Sidesteps Hard Cases and Stunts the Development of the Law*. New York: New York University Press, 2001.

O'Brien, David. *Storm Center: The Supreme Court in American Politics.* New York: W. W. Norton, 7th ed., 2005.

Posner, Richard. *The Federal Courts.* Cambridge, MA: Harvard University Press, 1996.

Rowland, C. K., and Carp, Robert. *Politics & Judgment in Federal District Courts.* Lawrence: University Press of Kansas, 1996.

Stern, Robert, Gressman, Eugene, Shapiro, Steven, and Geller, Kenneth. *Supreme Court Practice.* 7th ed. Washington, DC: Bureau of National Affairs, 1993.

Sterns, Maxwell L. *Constitutional Process: A Social Choice Analysis of Supreme Court Decisionmaking.* Ann Arbor: University of Michigan Press, 2000.

Strum, Philippa. *The Supreme Court and "Political Questions": A Study in Judicial Evasion. Birmingham: University of Alabama Press, 1974.*

Urofsky, Melvin, ed. *100 Americans Making Constitutional History.* Washington, DC: C. Q. Press, 2004.

■ INSIDE THE COURT

The Supreme Court's Reversal of Precedent in Historical Perspective

The Supreme Court's reversal of prior rulings registers the politics of the changing composition of the high bench. Between 1791 and 1991, the Court reversed itself on average about once each term. Last century, though, reversals were more infrequent, if only because there were fewer decisions to overturn. There were just 32 reversals in the nineteenth century, whereas the Court has reversed itself 179 times in this century, and 166 of those reversals have been since 1937.

The year 1937, of course, was a turning point for the Court and the country. An economically conservative Court had struck down much of the early New Deal program and, after his landslide reelection, Democratic president Franklin D. Roosevelt proposed that the number of justices be changed from nine to fifteen, thereby enabling him to pack the Court. In the spring of 1937, however, the Court abruptly reversed itself, upholding major pieces of New Deal legislation, and the Senate defeated FDR's "Court-packing plan." Conservative Justice Willis Van Devanter then retired and FDR had the first of eight opportunities during the next six years to fill vacancies on the Court, as well as the opportunity to elevate Justice Harlan F. Stone to the chief justiceship. Between 1937 and 1946, the Roosevelt Court overturned some thirty precedents.

When the Court's composition changes dramatically in a short period of time, or a pivotal justice leaves the bench, the Court tends to overturn prior rulings. The Warren Court (1953–1969) was even more activist than the Roosevelt Court in reversing forty-five precedents. Yet its record shows how crucial the timing of one or two changes on the bench may prove for the direction of the Court. From the landmark school desegregation ruling in *Brown v. Board of Education*, 347 U.S. 483 (1954) (see Vol. 2, Ch. 12), to the appointment of Justice Potter Stewart in 1959, the Warren Court reversed only six precedents. With Justice Stewart's arrival, six more precedents were overturned in the following four years. In 1962, the Court's composition changed again with Democratic President John F. Kennedy's appointments of Justices Byron White and Arthur Goldberg. Over the following three years fourteen prior rulings were discarded, and in the remaining four years of the Warren Court another twenty were reversed, as constitutional law was pushed in ever more liberal and egalitarian directions.

During Chief Justice Warren F. Burger's tenure (1969–1986), the Court gradually became more conservative, particularly in the area of criminal procedure. As its composition changed, the Burger Court also continued reconsidering precedents although typically liberal ones, reversing a total of fifty-two prior rulings. After Republican president Richard M. Nixon made the last two of his four appointments, Justices Harry Blackmun and William Rehnquist, ten decisions were reversed between 1972 and 1975. A critical conservative mass comparable to the liberal bloc on the Warren Court, however, failed to emerge. Then, liberal Justice William O. Douglas retired and his seat was filled by Republican President Gerald R. Ford's sole appointee, Justice John Paul Stevens. Between 1975 and 1981 the Burger Court then reversed no fewer than twenty-two decisions. Following the arrival of Republican president Ronald Reagan's first appointee, Justice Sandra Day O'Connor, another twelve precedents were overturned in the last five terms of the Burger Court.

The Rehnquist Court has reversed twenty-seven decisions in the past decade. Notably, with each successive change in its composition the Rehnquist Court has also more actively reconsidered precedents laid down by its predecessors. In the year following Reagan's elevation of Justice Rehnquist to the chief justiceship and appointment of Justice Antonin Scalia, three precedents were reversed. After Reagan's fourth appointee, Justice Anthony Kennedy, joined the Court in 1987, another eight reversals came down in the 1987 to 1989 terms. Republican President George Bush's first appointee, Justice David H. Souter, then replaced the retired liberal Justice William J. Brennan. In the 1990 term, the Rehnquist Court overturned seven prior decisions. At the end of that term, Justice Thurgood Marshall announced his retirement and predicted, in *Payne v. Tennessee*, 501 U.S. 808 (1991), that the Rehnquist Court would reverse many earlier liberal rulings. With Bush's second appointee, Justice Clarence Thomas, on the bench, the Rehnquist Court reversed, in whole or in part, five decisions during the 1991 term. But compare the treatment of the doctrine of *stare decisis* in the opinions in *Payne* with those in *Planned Parenthood of Southeastern Pennsylvania v. Casey*, 505 U.S. 833 (1992).

The following table places the Rehnquist Court's reversals of precedents in historical perspective.[a]

COURT	NUMBER OF PRECEDENTS OVERTURNED
Marshall Court (1801–1836)	3
Taney Court (1836–1864)	4
Chase Court (1864–1873)	4
Waite Court (1874–1888)	13
Fuller Court (1888–1910)	4
White Court (1910–1921)	5
Taft Court (1921–1930)	6
Hughes Court (1930–1941)	21
Stone Court (1941–1946)	15
Vinson Court (1946–1953)	13
Warren Court (1953–1969)	45
Burger Court (1969–1986)	52
Rehnquist Court (1986–	38
Total	223

[a] This table updates data collected and analyzed by Christopher Banks. For a further discussion of the Supreme Court's reversal of precedents, see Christopher Banks, "The Supreme Court and Precedent: An Analysis of Natural Courts and Reversal Trends," 75 *Judicature* 262 (Feb/Mar. 1992). This table was updated through the 2003–2004 term by the author.

Flast v. Cohen

392 U.S. 83, 88 S.CT. 1942 (1968)

Florance Flast and several other taxpayers sought standing to challenge the constitutionality of the Elementary and Secondary Education Act of 1965. The act provided funding for instructional materials and purchase of textbooks for religious schools. Flast contended that the act violated the First Amendment's ban on the establishment of religion and guarantee for the free exercise of religion. In a federal district court in New York, she filed suit against Wilbur Cohen, the secretary of Health, Education, and Welfare, to enjoin the spending of funds authorized for religious schools. The district court denied standing and Flast appealed to the Supreme Court.

The Court's decision was eight to one, with the majority's opinion announced by Chief Justice Warren. There were concurrences by Justices Douglas, Stewart, and Fortas. Justice Harlan dissented.

■ *Chief Justice WARREN delivers the opinion of the Court.*

In *Frothingham v. Mellon* [262 U.S. 447] (1923), this Court ruled that a federal taxpayer is without standing to challenge the constitutionality of a federal statute. That ruling has stood for 45 years as an impenetrable barrier to suits against Acts of Congress brought by individuals who can assert only the interest of federal taxpayers. In this case, we must decide whether the *Frothingham* barrier should be lowered when a taxpayer attacks a federal statute on the ground that it violates the Establishment and Free Exercise Clauses of the First Amendment. . . .

This Court first faced squarely the question whether a litigant asserting only his status as a taxpayer has standing to maintain a suit in a federal court in *Frothingham v. Mellon*, supra, and that decision must be the starting point for analysis in this case. The taxpayer in *Frothingham* attacked as unconstitutional the Maternity Act of 1921, 42 Stat. 224, which established a federal program of grants to those States which would undertake programs to reduce maternal and infant mortality. . . . The Court noted that a federal taxpayer's "interest in the moneys of the Treasury . . . is comparatively minute and indeterminable" and that "the effect upon future taxation, of any payment out of the [Treasury's] funds, . . . [is] remote, fluctuating and uncertain." As a result, the Court ruled that the taxpayer had failed to allege the type of "direct injury" necessary to confer standing.

Although the barrier *Frothingham* erected against federal taxpayer suits has never been breached, the decision has been the source of some confusion and the object of considerable criticism. The confusion has developed as commentators have tried to determine whether *Frothingham* establishes a constitutional bar to taxpayer suits or whether the Court was simply imposing a rule of self restraint which was not constitutionally compelled. The conflicting viewpoints are reflected in the arguments made to this Court by the parties in this case. The Government has pressed upon us the view that *Frothingham* announced a constitutional rule, compelled by the Article III limitations on federal court jurisdiction and grounded in considerations of the doctrine of separation of powers. Appellants, however, insist that *Frothingham* expressed no more than a policy of judicial self-restraint which can be disregarded when compelling reasons for assuming jurisdiction over a taxpayer's suit exist. The opinion delivered in *Frothingham* can be read to support either position. . . .

To the extent that *Frothingham* has been viewed as resting on policy considerations, it has been criticized as depending on assumptions not consistent with modern conditions. For example, some commentators have pointed out that a number of corporate taxpayers today have a federal tax liability running into hundreds of millions of dollars, and such taxpayers have a far greater monetary stake in the Federal Treasury than they do in any municipal treasury. To some degree, the fear expressed in *Frothingham* that allowing one taxpayer to sue would inundate the federal courts with countless similar suits has been mitigated by the ready availability of the devices of class actions and joinder under the Federal Rules of Civil Procedure, adopted subsequent to the decision in *Frothingham*. . . .

The jurisdiction of federal courts is defined and limited by Article III of the Constitution. In terms relevant to the question for decision in this case, the judicial power of federal courts is constitutionally restricted to "cases" and "controversies." As is so often the situation in constitutional adjudication, those two words have an iceberg quality, containing beneath their surface simplicity submerged complexities which go to the very heart of our constitutional form of government. Embodied in the words "cases" and "controversies" are two complementary but somewhat different limitations. In part those words limit the business of federal courts to questions presented in an adversary context and in a form historically viewed as capable of resolution through the judicial process. And in part those words define the role assigned to the judiciary in a tripartite allocation of power to assure that the federal courts will not intrude into areas committed to the other branches of government. Justiciability is the term of art employed to give expression to this dual limitation placed upon federal courts by the case-and-controversy doctrine.

Justiciability is itself a concept of uncertain meaning and scope. Its reach is illustrated by the various grounds upon which questions sought to be adjudicated in federal courts have been held not to be justiciable. Thus, no justiciable controversy is presented when the parties seek adjudication of only a political question, when the parties are asking for an advisory opinion, when the question sought to be adjudicated has been mooted by subsequent developments, and when there is no standing to maintain the action. Yet it remains true that "[j]usticiability is . . . not a legal concept with a fixed content or susceptible of scientific verification. Its utilization is the resultant of many subtle pressures," *Poe v. Ullman* [367 U.S. 497 (1961)].

Part of the difficulty in giving precise meaning and form to the concept of justiciability stems from the uncertain historical antecedents of the case-and-controversy doctrine. For example, Justice FRANKFURTER twice suggested that historical meaning could be imparted to the concepts of justiciability and case and controversy by reference to the practices of the courts of Westminster when the Constitution was adopted. . . .

However, the power of English judges to deliver advisory opinions was well established at the time the Constitution was drafted. And it is quite clear that "the oldest and most consistent thread in the federal law of justiciability is that the federal courts will not give advisory opinions." Thus, the implicit policies embodied in Article III, and not history alone, impose the rule against advisory opinions on federal courts. When the federal judicial power is invoked to pass upon the validity of actions by the Legislative and Executive Branches of the Government, the rule against advisory opinions implements the separation of powers prescribed by the Constitution and confines federal courts to the role assigned them by Article III. However, the rule against advisory opinions also recognizes that such suits often "are not pressed before the Court with that clear concreteness provided when a question emerges precisely framed and necessary for decision from a clash of adversary argument exploring every aspect of a multifaceted situation embracing conflicting and demanding interests." Consequently, the Article III prohibition against advisory opinions reflects the complementary constitutional considerations expressed by the justiciability doctrine: Federal judicial power is limited to those disputes which confine federal courts to a role consistent with a system of separated powers and which are traditionally thought to be capable of resolution through the judicial process.

Additional uncertainty exists in the doctrine of justiciability because that doctrine has become a blend of constitutional requirements and policy considerations. And a policy limitation is "not always clearly distinguished from the constitutional limitation." . . . The "many subtle pressures" which cause policy considerations to blend into the constitutional limitations of Article III make the justiciability doctrine one of uncertain and shifting contours.

It is in this context that the standing question presented by this case must be viewed and that the Government's argument on that question must be evaluated. As we understand it, the Government's position is that the constitutional scheme of separation of powers, and the deference owed by the federal judiciary to the other two branches of government within that scheme, present an absolute bar to taxpayer suits challenging the validity of federal spending programs. The Government views such suits as involving no more than the mere disagreement by the taxpayer "with the uses to which tax money is put." According to the Government, the resolution of such disagreements is committed to other branches of the Federal Government and not to the judiciary. Consequently, the Government contends that, under no circumstances, should standing be conferred on federal taxpayers to challenge a federal taxing or spending program. An analysis of the function served by standing limitations compels a rejection of the Government's position.

Standing is an aspect of justiciability and, as such, the problem of standing is surrounded by the same complexities and vagaries that inhere in justiciability. . . .

Despite the complexities and uncertainties, some meaningful form can be given to the jurisdictional limitations placed on federal court power by the concept of standing. The fundamental aspect of standing is that it focuses on the party seeking to get his complaint before a federal court and not on the issues he wishes to have adjudicated. The "gist of the question of standing" is whether the party seeking relief has "alleged such a personal stake in the outcome of the controversy as to assure that concrete adverseness which sharpens the presentation of issues upon which the court so largely depends for illumination of difficult constitutional questions," *Baker v. Carr*, [369 U.S. 186] (1962). In other words, when standing is placed in issue in a case, the question is whether the person whose standing is challenged is a proper party to request an adjudication of a particular issue and not whether the issue itself is justiciable. Thus, a party may have standing in a particular case, but the federal court may nevertheless decline to pass on the merits of the case because, for example, it presents a political question. A proper party is demanded so that federal courts will not be asked to decide "ill-defined controversies over constitutional issues," *United Public Workers of America v. Mitchell*, 330 U.S. 75 (1947), or a case which is of "a hypothetical or abstract character," . . . So stated, the standing requirement is closely related to, although more general than, the rule that federal courts will not entertain friendly suits. . . .

When the emphasis in the standing problem is placed on whether the person invoking a federal court's jurisdiction is a proper party to maintain the action, the weakness of the Government's argument in this case becomes apparent. The question whether a particular person is a proper party to maintain the action does not, by its own force, raise separation of powers problems related to improper judicial interference in areas committed to other branches of the Federal Government. Such problems arise, if at all, only from the substantive issues the individual seeks to have adjudicated. Thus, in terms of Article III limitations on federal court jurisdiction, the question of standing is related only to whether the dispute sought to be adjudicated will be presented in an adversary context and in a form historically viewed as capable of judicial resolution. It is for that reason that the emphasis in standing problems is on whether the party invoking federal court jurisdiction has "a personal stake in the outcome of the controversy," *Baker v. Carr*, and whether the dispute touches upon "the legal relations of parties having adverse legal interests." A taxpayer may or may not have the requisite personal stake in the outcome, depending upon the circumstances of the particular case. Therefore, we find no absolute bar in Article III to suits by federal taxpayers challenging allegedly unconstitutional federal taxing and spending programs. There remains, however, the problem of determining the circumstances under which a federal taxpayer will be deemed to have the personal stake and interest that impart the necessary concrete adverseness to such litigation so that standing can be conferred on the taxpayer *qua* taxpayer consistent with the constitutional limitations of Article III. . . .

Whether such individuals have standing to maintain that form of action turns on whether they can demonstrate the necessary stake as taxpayers in the outcome of the litigation to satisfy Article III requirements.

The nexus demanded of federal taxpayers has two aspects to it. First, the taxpayer must establish a logical link between that status and the type of legislative enactment attacked. Thus, a taxpayer will be a proper party to allege the unconstitutionality only of exercises of congressional power under the taxing and spending clause of Art. I, § 8, of the Constitution. It will not be sufficient to allege an incidental expenditure of tax funds in the administration of an essentially regulatory statute. . . . Secondly, the taxpayer must establish a nexus between that status and the precise nature of the constitutional infringement alleged. Under this requirement, the taxpayer must show that the challenged enactment exceeds specific constitutional limitations imposed upon the exercise of the congressional taxing and spending power and not simply that the enactment is generally beyond the powers delegated to Congress by Art. I, § 8. When both nexuses are established, the litigant will have shown a taxpayer's stake in the outcome of the controversy and will be a proper and appropriate party to invoke a federal court's jurisdiction.

The taxpayer-appellants in this case have satisfied both nexuses to support their claim of standing under the test we announce today. Their constitutional challenge is made to an exercise by Congress of its power under Art. I, § 8, to spend for the general welfare, and the challenged program involves a substantial expenditure of federal tax funds. In addition, appellants have alleged that the challenged expenditures violate the Establishment and Free Exercise Clauses of the First Amendment. Our history vividly illustrates that one of the specific evils feared by those who drafted the Establishment Clause and fought for its adoption was that the taxing and spending power would be used to favor one religion over another or to support religion in general. James Madison, who is generally recognized as the leading architect of the religion clauses of the First Amendment, observed in his famous Memorial and Remonstrance Against Religious Assessments that "the same authority which can force a citizen to contribute three pence only of his property for the support of any one establishment, may force him to conform to any other establishment in all cases whatsoever." 2 *Writings of James Madison* 183, 186 (Hunt ed. 1901). The concern of Madison and his supporters was quite clearly that religious liberty ultimately would be the victim if government could employ its taxing and spending powers to aid one religion over another or to aid religion in general. The Establishment Clause was designed as a specific bulwark against such potential abuses of governmental power, and that clause of the First Amendment operates as a specific constitutional limitation upon the exercise by Congress of the taxing and spending power conferred by Art. I, § 8.

The allegations of the taxpayer in *Frothingham v. Mellon,* supra, were quite different from those made in this case, and the result in *Frothingham* is consistent with the test of taxpayer standing announced today. The taxpayer in *Frothingham* attacked a federal spending program and she, therefore, established the first nexus required. However, she lacked standing because her constitutional attack was not based on an allegation that Congress, in enacting the Maternity Act of 1921, had breached a specific limitation upon its taxing and spending power. The taxpayer in *Frothingham* alleged essentially that Congress, by enacting the challenged statute, had exceeded the general powers delegated to it by Art. I, § 8, and that Congress had thereby invaded the legislative province reserved to the States by the Tenth Amendment. To be sure, Mrs. Frothingham made the additional allegation that her tax liability would be increased as a result of the allegedly unconstitutional enactment, and she framed that allegation in terms of a deprivation of property without due process of law. However, the Due Process Clause of the Fifth Amendment does not protect taxpayers against increases in tax liability, and the taxpayer in *Frothingham* failed to make any additional claim that the harm she alleged resulted from a breach by Congress of the specific constitutional limitations imposed upon an exercise of the taxing and spending power. In essence, Mrs. Frothingham was attempting to assert the States' interest in their legislative prerogatives and not a federal taxpayer's interest in being free of taxing and spending in contravention of specific constitutional limitations imposed upon Congress' taxing and spending power.

We have noted that the Establishment Clause of the First Amendment does specifically limit the taxing and spending power conferred by Art. I, § 8. Whether the Constitution contains other specific limitations can be determined only in the context of future cases. However, whenever such specific limitations are found, we believe a taxpayer will have a clear stake as a taxpayer in assuring that they are not breached by Congress. Consequently, we hold that a taxpayer will have standing consistent with Article III to invoke federal judicial power when he alleges that congressional action under the taxing and spending clause is in derogation of those constitutional provisions which operate to restrict the exercise of the taxing and spending power. The taxpayer's allegation in such cases would be that his tax money is being extracted and spent in violation of specific constitutional protections against such abuses of legislative power. Such an injury is appropriate for judicial redress, and the taxpayer has established the necessary nexus between his status and the nature of the allegedly unconstitutional action to support his claim of standing to secure judicial review. Under such circumstances, we feel confident that the questions will be framed with the necessary specificity, that the issues will be contested with the necessary adverseness and that the litigation will be pursued with the necessary vigor to assure that the constitutional challenge will be made in a form traditionally thought to be capable of judicial resolution. We lack that confidence in cases such as *Frothingham* where a taxpayer seeks to employ a federal court as a forum in which to air his generalized grievances about the conduct of government or the allocation of power in the Federal System.

☐ *Justice HARLAN, dissenting.*

The problems presented by this case are narrow and relatively abstract, but the principles by which they must be resolved involve nothing less than the proper functioning of the federal courts, and so run to the roots of our constitutional system. The nub of my view is that the end result of *Frothingham v. Mellon* was correct, even though, like others, I do not subscribe to all of its reasoning and premises. Although I therefore agree with certain of the conclusions reached today by the Court, I cannot accept the standing doctrine that it substitutes for *Frothingham*, for it seems to me that this new doctrine rests on premises that do not withstand analysis. Accordingly, I respectfully dissent. . . .

The lawsuits here and in *Frothingham* are fundamentally different. They present the question whether federal taxpayers *qua* taxpayers may, in suits in which they do not contest the validity of their previous or existing tax obligations, challenge the constitutionality of the uses for which Congress has authorized the expenditure of public funds. These differences in the purposes of the cases are reflected in differences in the litigants' interests. An action brought to contest the validity of tax liabilities assessed to the plaintiff is designed to vindicate interests that are personal and proprietary. The wrongs alleged and the relief sought by such a plaintiff are unmistakably private; only secondarily are his interests representative of those of the general population. I take it that the Court, although it does not pause to examine the question, believes that the interests of those who as taxpayers challenge the constitutionality of public expenditures may, at least in certain circumstances, be similar. Yet this assumption is surely mistaken. . . .

Presumably the Court recognizes at least certain . . . hazards, else it would not have troubled to impose limitations upon the situations in which, and purposes for which, such suits may be brought. Nonetheless, the limitations adopted by the Court are, as I have endeavored to indicate, wholly untenable. This is the more unfortunate because there is available a resolution of this problem that entirely satisfies the demands of the principle of separation of powers. This Court has previously held that individual litigants have standing to represent the public interest, despite their lack of economic or other personal interests, if Congress has appropriately authorized such suits. Any hazards to the proper allocation of authority among the three branches of the Government would be substantially diminished if public actions had been pertinently authorized by Congress and the President. I appreciate that this Court does not ordinarily await the mandate of other branches of the Government, but it seems to me that the extraordinary character of public actions, and of the mischievous, if not dangerous, consequences they involve for the proper functioning of our constitutional system, and in particular of the federal courts, makes such judicial forbearance the part of wisdom. It must be emphasized that the implications of these questions of judicial policy are of fundamental significance for the other branches of the Federal Government.

Such a rule could readily be applied to this case. Although various efforts have been made in Congress to authorize public actions to contest the validity of federal expenditures in aid of religiously affiliated schools and other institutions, no such authorization has yet been given.

This does not mean that we would, under such a rule, be enabled to avoid our constitutional responsibilities, or that we would confine to limbo the First Amendment or any other constitutional command. The question here is not, despite the Court's unarticulated premise, whether the religious clauses of the First Amendment are hereafter to be enforced by the federal courts; the issue is simply whether plaintiffs of an *additional* category, heretofore excluded from those courts, are to be permitted to maintain suits. The recent history of this Court is replete with illustrations, including even one announced today that questions involving the religious clauses will not, if federal taxpayers are prevented from contesting federal expenditures, be left "unacknowledged, unresolved, and undecided."

Accordingly, for the reasons contained in this opinion, I would affirm the judgment of the District Court.

Valley Forge Christian College v. Americans United for Separation of Church and State, Inc.

454 U.S. 464, 102 S.Ct. 752 (1982)

Americans United for Separation of Church and State, an organization dedicated to the separation of religion from government, filed a suit in federal district court in Pennsylvania to stop the Department of Health, Education, and Welfare (now the Department of Education) from conveying as "surplus property" a closed and former army hospital to Valley Forge Christian College. Under the Federal Property and Administrative Services Act of 1949, the department has authority to sell surplus government property for educational use to nonprofit, tax-exempt educational institutions. Congress has the power to "dispose of and make all needful Rules and Regulations respecting the . . . Property belonging to the United States," under Article IV, Section 3, Clause 2. But Americans United for Separation of Church and State contended that the department's conveyance here abridged its members' First Amendment rights to religious freedom and "deprived [them] of the fair and constitutional use of [their] tax dollars." The district court dismissed the suit but the Court of Appeals for the Third Circuit reversed.

Thereupon, Valley Forge Christian College appealed to the Supreme Court.

The Court's decision was five to four, with the majority's opinion announced by Justice Rehnquist. Dissents were by Justices Stevens and Brennan, who was joined by Justices Blackmun and Marshall.

☐ *Justice REHNQUIST delivers the opinion of the Court.*

We need not mince words when we say that the concept of "Art. III standing" has not been defined with complete consistency in all of the various cases decided by this Court which have discussed it, nor when we say that this very fact is probably proof that the concept cannot be reduced to a one-sentence or one-paragraph definition. But of one thing we may be sure: Those who do not possess Art. III standing may not litigate as suitors in the courts of the United States. Article III, which is every bit as important in its circumscription of the judicial power of the United States as in its granting of that power, is not merely a troublesome hurdle to be overcome if possible so as to reach the "merits" of a lawsuit which a party desires to have adjudicated; it is a part of the basic charter promulgated by the Framers of the Constitution at Philadelphia in 1787, a charter which created a general government, provided for the interaction between that government and the governments of the several States, and was later amended so as to either enhance or limit its authority with respect to both States and individuals. . . .

[I]n *Flast v. Cohen*, [392 U.S. 83 (1968)], [t]he Court developed a two-part test to determine whether the plaintiffs had standing to sue. First, because a taxpayer alleges injury only by virtue of his liability for taxes, the Court held that "a taxpayer will be a proper party to allege the unconstitutionality only of exercises of congressional power under the taxing and spending clause of Art. I, § 8, of the Constitution." Second, the Court required the taxpayer to "show that the challenged enactment exceeds specific constitutional limitations upon the exercise of the taxing and spending power and not simply that the enactment is generally beyond the powers delegated to Congress by Art. I, § 8."

Unlike the plaintiffs in *Flast*, respondents fail the first prong of the test for taxpayer standing. Their claim is deficient in two respects. First, the source of their complaint is not a congressional action, but a decision by HEW to transfer a parcel of federal property. *Flast* limited taxpayer standing to challenges directed "only [at] exercises of congressional power." See *Schlesinger v. Reservists Committee to Stop the War*, [418 U.S. 208 (1974)] (denying standing because the taxpayer plaintiffs "did not challenge an enactment under Art. I, § 8, but rather the action of the Executive Branch").

Second, and perhaps redundantly, the property transfer about which respondents complain was not an exercise of authority conferred by the Taxing and Spending Clause of Art. I, § 8. The authorizing legislation, the Federal Property and Administrative Services Act of 1949, was an evident exercise of Congress' power under the Property Clause, Art. IV, § 3, cl. 2. Respondents do not dispute this conclusion, and it is decisive of any claim of taxpayer standing under the *Flast* precedent.

☐ *Justice BRENNAN, with whom Justice MARSHALL and Justice BLACKMUN join, dissenting.*

The opinion of the Court is a stark example of this unfortunate trend of resolving cases at the "threshold" while obscuring the nature of the underlying rights and interests at stake. The Court waxes eloquent on the blend of prudential and constitutional considerations that combine to create our misguided "standing" jurisprudence. *But not one word is said about the Establishment Clause right that the plaintiff seeks to enforce.* And despite its pat recitation of our standing decisions, the opinion utterly fails, except by the sheerest form of *ipse dixit*, to explain why this case is unlike *Flast v. Cohen* (1968), and is controlled instead by *Frothingham v. Mellon* (1923). . . .

It is at once apparent that the test of standing formulated by the Court in *Flast* sought to reconcile the developing doctrine of taxpayer "standing" with the Court's historical understanding that the Establishment Clause was intended to prohibit the Federal Government from using tax funds for the advancement of religion, and thus the constitutional imperative of taxpayer standing in certain cases brought pursuant to the Establishment Clause. The two-pronged "nexus" test offered by the Court, despite its general language, is best understood as "a determinant of standing of plaintiffs alleging only injury as taxpayers who challenge alleged violations of the Establishment and Free Exercise Clauses of the First Amendment," and not as a general statement of standing principles. The test explains what forms of governmental action may be attacked by someone alleging *only* taxpayer status, and, without ruling out the possibility that history might reveal another similarly founded provision, explains why an Establishment Clause claim is treated differently from any other assertion that the Federal Government has exceeded the bounds of the law in allocating its largesse. . . .

The nexus test that the Court "announced," sought to maintain necessary continuity with prior cases, and set forth principles to guide future cases involving taxpayer standing. But *Flast* did not depart from the principle that no judgment about standing should be made without a fundamental understanding of the rights at issue. The two-part *Flast* test did not supply the rationale for the Court's decision, but rather is exposition: That rationale was supplied by an understanding of the nature of the restrictions on government power imposed by the Constitution and the intended beneficiaries of those restrictions.

It may be that Congress can tax for *almost* any reason, or for no reason at all. There is, so far as I have been able to discern, but one constitutionally imposed limit on that authority. Congress cannot use tax money to support a church, or to encourage religion. That is "*the* forbidden exaction." *Everson v. Board of Education* [330 U.S. 1 (1947)]. In absolute terms the history of the Establishment Clause of the First Amendment makes this clear. History also makes it clear that the federal taxpayer is a singularly "proper and appropriate party to invoke a federal court's jurisdiction" to challenge a federal bestowal of largesse as a violation of the Establishment Clause. Each, and indeed every, federal taxpayer suffers precisely the injury that the Establishment Clause guards against when the Federal Government directs that funds be taken from the pocketbooks of the citizenry and placed into the coffers of the ministry.

A taxpayer cannot be asked to raise his objection to such use of his funds at the time he pays his tax. Apart from the unlikely circumstance in which the Government announced in advance that a particular levy would be used for religious subsidies, taxpayers could hardly assert that they were being injured until the Government actually lent its support to a religious venture. Nor would it be reasonable to require him to address his claim to those officials charged with the collection of federal taxes. Those officials would be without the means to provide appropriate redress—there is no practical way to segregate the complaining taxpayer's money from that being devoted to the religious purpose. Surely, then, a taxpayer must have standing at the time that he learns of the Government's alleged Establishment Clause violation to seek equitable relief in order to halt the continuing and intolerable burden on his pocketbook, his conscience, and his constitutional rights.

Blind to history, the Court attempts to distinguish this case from *Flast* by wrenching snippets of language from our opinions, and by perfunctorily applying that language under color of the first prong of *Flast*'s two-part nexus test. The tortuous distinctions thus produced are specious, at best: at worst, they are pernicious to our constitutional heritage.

First, the Court finds this case different from *Flast* because here the "source of [plaintiffs'] complaint is not a *congressional* action, but a decision by HEW to transfer a parcel of federal property." This attempt at distinction cannot withstand scrutiny. *Flast* involved a challenge to the actions of the Commissioner of Education, and other officials of HEW, in disbursing funds under the Elementary and Secondary Education Act of 1965 to "religious and sectarian" schools. Plaintiffs disclaimed "any intent[ion] to challenge . . . all programs under . . . the Act." Rather, they claimed that defendant-administrators' approval of such expenditures was not authorized by the Act, or alternatively, to the extent the expenditures were authorized, the Act was "unconstitutional and void." In the present case, respondents challenge HEW's grant of property pursuant to the Federal Property and Administrative Services Act of 1949, seeking to enjoin HEW "from making a grant of this and other property to the [defendant] so long as such a grant will violate the Establishment Clause." It may be that the Court is concerned with the adequacy of respondents' pleading; respondents have not, in so many words, asked for a declaration that the "Federal Property and Administrative Services Act is unconstitutional and void to the extent that it authorizes HEW's actions." I would not construe their complaint so narrowly.

More fundamentally, no clear division can be drawn in this context between actions of the Legislative Branch and those of the Executive Branch. To be sure, the First Amendment is phrased as a restriction on Congress' legislative authority; this is only natural since the Constitution assigns the authority to legislate and appropriate only to the Congress. But it is difficult to conceive of an expenditure for which the last governmental actor, either implementing directly the legislative will, or acting within the scope of legislatively delegated authority, is not an Executive Branch official. The First Amendment binds the Government as a whole, regardless of which branch is at work in a particular instance.

The Court's second purported distinction between this case and *Flast* is equally unavailing. The majority finds it "decisive" that the Federal Property and Administrative Services Act of 1949 "was an evident exercise of Congress' power under the Property Clause, Art. IV, § 3, cl. 2," while the Government action in *Flast* was taken under Art. I, § 8. The Court relies on *United States v. Richardson*, 418 U.S. [166] (1974), and *Schlesinger v. Reservists Committee to Stop the War*, 418 U.S. 208 (1974), to support the distinction between the two Clauses, noting that those cases involved alleged deviations from the requirements of Art. I, § 9, cl. 7, and Art. I, § 6, cl. 2, respectively. The standing defect in each case was *not*, however, the failure to allege a violation of the Spending Clause; rather, the taxpayers in those cases had not complained of the distribution of Government largesse, and thus failed to meet the essential requirement of taxpayer standing recognized in *Doremus [v. Board of Education*, 342 U.S. 429 (1952)].

It can make no constitutional difference in the case before us whether the donation to the petitioner here was in the form of a cash grant to build a facility, see *Tilton v. Richardson*, 403 U.S. 672 (1971), or in the nature of a gift of property including a facility already built. That this is a meaningless distinction is illustrated by *Tilton*. In that case, taxpayers were afforded standing to object to the fact that the Government had not received adequate assurance that if the property that it financed for use as an educational facility was later converted to religious uses, it would receive full value for the property, as the Constitution requires. The complaint here is precisely that, although the property at issue is actually being used for a sectarian purpose, the Government has not received, nor demanded, full value payment. Whether undertaken pursuant to the Property Clause or the Spending Clause, the breach of the Establishment Clause, and the relationship of the taxpayer to that breach, is precisely the same.

Plainly hostile to the Framers' understanding of the Establishment Clause, and *Flast's* enforcement of that understanding, the Court vents that hostility under the guise of standing, "to slam the courthouse door against plaintiffs who [as the Framers intended] are entitled to full consideration of their [Establishment Clause] claims on the merits." *Barlow v. Collins*, 397 U.S. 159 (1970) (BRENNAN, J., concurring in result and dissenting). Therefore, I dissent.

Lujan v. Defenders of Wildlife

504 U.S. 555, 112 S.CT. 2130 (1992)

Under the Endangered Species Act (ESA) of 1973, federal agencies are required to consult with the Department of Interior (DOI) to make sure that their policies and actions will not jeopardize endangered or threatened species or their habitats. For more than a decade DOI interpreted that act to apply to federally funded projects at home and abroad. But in 1986 the Reagan administration reversed course, announcing that the law no longer applied to projects overseas. Immediately, Defenders of Wildlife, other environmental groups, and their members challenged that reinterpretation of the law.

To gain standing to file a lawsuit, members of Defenders of Wildlife—its president, Joyce Kelly, and another member, Amy Skilbred—filed affidavits alleging that they would suffer injuries due to the failure of the Agency for International Development (AID) and other agencies to consult with DOI about a federally funded irrigation project on the Mahaweli River in Sri Lanka and a redevelopment project on the Nile River in Egypt. Those projects, they claimed, threatened endangered elephants and leopards in Sri Lanka and the crocodile and other species in Egypt. And when asserting their standing to sue and personal injuries, Kelly and Skilbred testified that they were environmentalists and had traveled to each site, although neither indicated specifically when she would again visit those sites. A federal district court dismissed the suit for lacking standing, but the Court of Appeals for the Eighth Circuit reversed.

The Bush administration appealed the appellate court's holding that Kelly and Skilbred had standing to sue under the ESA's provision conveying on citizens the right to sue the secretary of DOI for failure to consult with other federal agencies on projects potentially threatening to endangered species and their habitats, even though they failed to allege concrete injuries. Relying on *dicta* in several recent cases (see Justice Scalia's concurring opinion in *Gwaltney of Smithfield, Ltd. v. Chesapeake Bay Foundation*, 484 U.S. 49 [1987], and *Lujan v. National Wildlife Federation*, 497 U.S. 871 [1989]), the Bush administration asked the Court to sharply limit standing in such citizen suits.

The Court's decision was seven to two; the opinion was announced by Justice Scalia. Concurring opinions were delivered by Justice Kennedy, whom Justice Souter joined, and by Justice Stevens. Justice Blackmun dissented and was joined by Justice O'Connor.

☐ *Justice SCALIA delivers the opinion of the Court with respect to Parts I, II, III-A, and IV, and an opinion with respect to Part III-B in which Chief Justice REHNQUIST and Justices WHITE, KENNEDY, SOUTER, and THOMAS join.*

■ II

Over the years, our cases have established that the irreducible constitutional minimun of standing contains three elements: First, the plaintiff must have suffered an "injury in fact"—an invasion of a legally protected interest which is (a) concrete and particularized, *Warth v. Seldin*, 422 U.S. 490 (1975); *Sierra Club v. Morton*, 405 U.S. 727 (1972); and (b) "actual or imminent, not 'conjectural' or 'hypothetical.'" Second, there must be a causal connection between the injury and the conduct complained of—the injury has to be "fairly . . . traceable to the challenged action of the defendant, and not . . . the result [of] the independent action of some third party not before the court." *Simon v. Eastern Kentucky Welfare Rights Org.*, 426 U.S. 26 (1976). Third, it must be "likely," as opposed to merely "speculative," that the injury will be "redressed by a favorable decision."

When the suit is one challenging the legality of government action or inaction, the nature and extent of facts that must be averred (at the summary judgement stage) or proved (at the trial stage) in order to establish standing depends considerably upon whether the plaintiff is himself an object of the action (or foregone action) at issue. If he is, there is ordinarily little question that the action or inaction has caused him injury, and that a judgment preventing or requiring the action will redress it. When, however, as in this case, a plaintiff's asserted injury arises from the government's allegedly unlawful regulation (or lack of regulation) of someone else, much more is needed. In that circumstance, causation and redressability ordinarily hinge on the response of the regulated (or regulable) third party to the government action or inaction—and perhaps on the response of others as well. The existence of one or more of the essential elements of standing "depends on the unfettered choices made by independent actors not before the courts and whose exercise of broad and legitimate discretion the courts cannot presume either to control or to predict," *ASARCO Inc. v. Kadish*, 490 U.S. 605 (1989); and it becomes the burden of the plaintiff to adduce facts showing that those choices have been or will be made in such manner as to produce causation and permit redressability of injury. Thus, when the plaintiff is not himself the object of the government action or inaction he challenges, standing is not precluded, but it is ordinarily "substantially more difficult" to establish.

■ III

We think the Court of Appeals failed to apply the foregoing principles. . . . Respondents had not made the requisite demonstration of (at least) injury and redressability.

A. Respondents' claim to injury is that the lack of consultation with respect to certain funded activities abroad "increases the rate of extinction of endangered and threatened species." Of course, the desire to use or observe an animal species, even for purely aesthetic purposes, is undeniably a cognizable interest for purpose of standing. "But the 'injury in fact' test requires more than an injury to a cognizable interest. It requires that the party seeking review be himself among the injured." . . . [R]espondents had to submit affidavits or other evidence showing, through specific facts, not only that listed species were in fact being threatened by funded activities abroad, but also that one or more of respondents' members would thereby be "directly" affected apart from their " 'special interest' in the subject." . . .

We shall assume for the sake of argument that these affidavits contain facts showing that certain agency-funded projects threaten listed species—though that is questionable. They plainly contain no facts, however, showing how damage to the species will produce "imminent" injury to Mss. Kelly and Skilbred. That the women "had visited" the areas of the projects before the projects commenced proves nothing. . . .

Besides relying upon the Kelly and Skilbred affidavits, respondents propose a series of novel standing theories. The first, inelegantly styled "ecosystem nexus," proposes that any person who uses any part of a "contiguous ecosystem" adversely affected by a funded activity has standing even if the activity is located a great distance away. . . . [But to] say that the Act protects ecosystems is not to say that the Act creates (if it were possible) rights of action in persons who have not been injured in fact, that is, persons who use portions of an ecosystem not perceptibly affected by the unlawful action in question.

Respondents' other theories are called, alas, the "animal nexus" approach, whereby anyone who has an interest in studying or seeing the endangered animals anywhere on the globe has standing; and the "vocational nexus" approach, under which anyone with a professional interest in such animals can sue. Under these theories, anyone who goes to see Asian elephants in the Bronx Zoo, and anyone who is a keeper of Asian elephants in the Bronx Zoo, has standing to sue because the Director of AID did not consult with the Secretary regarding the AID-funded project in Sri Lanka. This is beyond all reason. . . .

B. The most obvious problem in the present case is redressability. Since the agencies funding the projects were not parties to the case, the District Court could accord relief only against the Secretary: He could be ordered to revise his regulation to require consulation for foreign projects. But this would not remedy respondents' alleged injury unless the funding agencies were bound by the Secretary's regulation, which is very much an open question. Whereas in other contexts the ESA is quite explicit as to the Secretary's controlling authority, with respect to consultation the initiative, and hence arguably the initial responsibility for determining statutory necessity, lies with the agencies. When the Secretary promulgated the regulation at issue here, he thought it was binding on the agencies. The Solicitor General, however, has repudiated that position here, and the agencies themselves apparently deny the Secretary's authority. . . .

A further impediment to redressability is the fact that the agencies generally supply only a fraction of the funding for a foreign project. AID, for example, has provided less than 10 percent of the funding for the Mahaweli Project. Respondents have produced nothing to indicate that the projects they have named will either be suspended, or do less harm to listed species, if that fraction is eliminated. . . .

We hold that respondents lack standing to bring this action.

☐ *Justice BLACKMUN, with whom Justice O'CONNOR joins, dissenting.*

I part company with the Court in this case in two respects. First, I believe that respondents have raised genuine issues of fact—sufficient to survive summary judgment—both as to injury and as to redressability. Second, I question the Court's breadth of language in rejecting standing for "procedural" injuries. I fear the Court seeks to impose fresh limitations on the constitutional authority of Congress to allow citizen-suits in the federal courts for injuries deemed "procedural" in nature. I dissent. . . .

To survive petitioner's motion for summary judgement on standing, respondents need not prove that they are actually or imminently harmed. They need show only a "genuine issue" of material fact as to standing. Federal Rules of Civil Procedure 56(c). This is not a heavy burden. A "genuine issue" exists so long as "the evidence is such that a reasonable jury could return a verdict for the nonmoving party respondents." *Anderson v. Liberty Lobby, Inc.*, 477 U.S. 242 (1986). "This Court's function is not itself to weigh the evidence and determine the truth of the matter but to determine whether there is a genuine issue for trial."

The Court never mentions the "genuine issue" standard. Rather, the Court refers to the type of evidence it feels respondents failed to produce, namely, "affidavits or other evidence showing, through specific facts" the existence of injury. The Court thereby confuses respondents' evidentiary burden (i.e., affidavits asserting "specific facts") in withstanding a summary judgment motion under Rule 56(e) with the standard of proof (i.e., the existence of a "genuine issue" of "material fact") under Rule 56(c). . . .

I think a reasonable finder of fact could conclude from the information in the affidavits and deposition testimony that either Kelly or Skilbred will soon return to the project sites, thereby satisfying the "actual or imminent" injury standard. . . .

By requiring a "description of concrete plans" or "specification of when the same day [for a return visit] will be," the Court, in my view, demands what is likely an empty formality. No substantial barriers prevent Kelly or Skilbred from simply purchasing plane tickets to return to the Aswan and Mahaweli projects. . . .

In conclusion, I cannot join the Court on what amounts to a slash-and-burn expedition through the law of environmental standing. In my view, "the very essence of civil liberty certainly consists in the right of every individual to claim the protection of the laws, whenever he receives an injury." *Marbury v. Madison*, 1 Cranch 137 (1803).

Baker v. Carr

369 U.S. 186, 82 S.Ct. 691 (1962)

In 1901, the Tennessee legislature apportioned both houses and provided for subsequent reapportionment every ten years on the basis of the number of people in each of the state's counties as reported in the census. But for more than sixty years proposals to redistribute legislative seats failed to pass, while the state's population shifted from rural to urban areas. Charles Baker and several other citizens and urban residents sued various Tennessee officials. Baker claimed that as an urban resident he was being denied the equal protection of the law under the Fourteenth Amendment. He asked the court to order state officials to hold either an at-large election or an election in which legislators would be selected from constituencies in accordance with the 1960 federal census. The federal district court dismissed the suit, conceding that Baker's civil rights were being denied but holding that the court could offer no remedy. Baker made a further appeal to the Supreme Court.

When the Supreme Court granted review in *Baker v. Carr*, it faced two central issues: first, whether the malapportionment of a state legislature is a "political question" for which courts have no remedy and, second, the merits of Baker's claim that individuals have a right to equal votes and equal representation. With potentially broad political consequences, the case was divisive for the Court and was carried over and reargued for a term. Allies on judicial self-restraint, Justices Frankfurter and Harlan were committed to their view, expressed in *Colegrove v. Green*, 328 U.S. 549 (1946), that the "Court ought not to enter this political thicket." At conference, Justices Clark and Whittaker supported their view that the case presented a nonjusticiable political question. By contrast, Chief Justice Warren and Justices Black, Douglas, and Brennan thought that the issue was justiciable. They were also prepared to address the merits of the case. The pivotal justice, Potter Stewart, considered the issue justiciable, but he refused to address the merits of the case. He voted to reverse the lower court ruling only if the Court's decision was limited to holding that courts have jurisdiction to decide such disputes. He did not want the Court to take on the merits of reapportionment in this case.

Assigned the task of drafting the opinion, Brennan had to hold on to Stewart's vote and dissuade Black and Douglas from writing opinions on the merits that would threaten the loss of the crucial fifth vote. After circulating his draft and incorporating suggested changes, he optimistically wrote Black, "Potter Stewart was satisfied with all of the changes. The Chief also is agreed. It, therefore, looks as though we have a court agreed upon this as circulated." It appeared that the decision would come down on the original five-to-four vote.

Clark, however, had been pondering the fact that in this case the population ratio for the urban and rural districts in Tennessee was more than nineteen to one. As he put it, "city slickers" had been "too long deprive[d] of a constitutional form of government." Clark concluded that citizens denied equal voting power had no political recourse; their only recourse was to the federal judiciary. Clark thus wrote an opinion abandoning Frankfurter and going beyond the majority to address the merits of the claim.

Brennan faced the dilemma of how to bring in Clark without losing Stewart, and thereby enlarge the consensus. Further negotiations were necessary but limited. Brennan wrote his brethren:

> The changes represent the maximum to which Potter will subscribe. We discussed much more elaborate changes which would have taken over a substantial part of Tom Clark's opinion. Potter felt that if they were made it would be necessary for him to dissent from that much of the revised opinion. I therefore decided it was

best not to press for the changes but to hope that Tom will be willing to join the Court opinion but say he would go further as per his separate opinion.

Even though there were five votes for deciding the merits, the final opinion was limited to the jurisdictional question.★

The Court's decision was six to two, with Justice Whittaker not participating and with the majority's opinion delivered by Justice Brennan. There were concurrences by Justices Douglas, Clark, and Stewart. Justice Frankfurter dissented and was joined by Justice Harlan.

☐ *Justice BRENNAN delivers the opinion of the Court.*

[W]e hold today only (a) that the court possessed jurisdiction of the subject matter: (b) that a justiciable cause of action is stated upon which appellants would be entitled to appropriate relief; and (c) because appellees raise the issue before this Court, that the appellants have standing to challenge the Tennessee apportionment statutes. Beyond noting that we have no cause at this stage to doubt the District Court will be able to fashion relief if violations of constitutional rights are found, it is improper now to consider what remedy would be most appropriate if appellants prevail at the trial.

JURISDICTION OF THE SUBJECT MATTER

The District Court was uncertain whether our cases withholding federal judicial relief rested upon a lack of federal jurisdiction or upon the inappropriateness of the subject matter for judicial consideration—what we have designated "nonjusticiability." The distinction between the two grounds is significant. In the instance of nonjusticiability, consideration of the cause is not wholly and immediately foreclosed: rather, the Court's inquiry necessarily proceeds to the point of deciding whether the duty asserted can be judicially identified and its breach judicially determined, and whether protection for the right asserted can be judicially molded. In the instance of lack of jurisdiction the cause either does not "arise under" the Federal Constitution, laws or treaties (or fall within one of the other enumerated categories of Art. III, § 2), or is not a "case or controversy" within the meaning of that section; or the cause is not one described by any jurisdictional statute. Our conclusion that this cause presents no nonjusticiable "political question" settles the only possible doubt that it is a case or controversy. . . .

The appellees refer to *Colegrove v. Green*, 328 U.S. 549 [(1946]), as authority that the District Court lacked jurisdiction of the subject matter. Appellees misconceive the holding of that case. The holding was precisely contrary to their reading of it. Seven members of the Court participated in the decision. Unlike many other cases in this field which have assumed without discussion that there was jurisdiction, all three opinions filed in Cole-

★ Sources of quotations are internal Court memos, located in the William J. Brennan, Jr., Papers, Library of Congress; and the Tom C. Clark Papers, University of Texas Law School.

grove discussed the question. Two of the opinions expressing the views of four of the Justices, a majority, flatly held that there was jurisdiction of that subject matter. Justice BLACK joined by Justice DOUGLAS and Justice MURPHY stated: "It is my judgment that the District Court had jurisdiction. . . ." Justice RUTLEDGE, writing separately, expressed agreement with this conclusion. . . . Indeed, it is even questionable that the opinion of Justice FRANKFURTER, joined by Justices REED and BURTON, doubted jurisdiction of the subject matter. . . .

JUSTICIABILITY

In holding that the subject matter of this suit was not justiciable, the District Court relied on *Colegrove v. Green, supra,* and subsequent *per curiam* cases. The court stated: "From a review of these decisions there can be no doubt that the federal rule . . . is that the federal courts . . . will not intervene in cases of this type to compel legislative reapportionment." We understand the District Court to have read the cited cases as compelling the conclusion that since the appellants sought to have a legislative apportionment held unconstitutional, their suit presented a "political question" and was therefore nonjusticiable. We hold that this challenge to an apportionment presents no nonjusticiable "political question." The cited cases do not hold the contrary.

Of course the mere fact that the suit seeks protection of a political right does not mean it presents a political question. Such an objection "is little more than a play upon words." Rather, it is argued that apportionment cases, whatever the actual wording of the complaint, can involve no federal constitutional right except one resting on the guaranty of a republican form of government, and that complaints based on that clause have been held to present political questions which are nonjusticiable.

We hold that the claim pleaded here neither rests upon nor implicates the Guaranty Clause and that its justiciability is therefore not foreclosed by our decisions of cases involving that clause. . . . To show why we reject the argument based on the Guaranty Clause, we must examine the authorities under it. But because there appears to be some uncertainty as to why those cases did present political questions, and specifically as to whether this apportionment case is like those cases, we deem it necessary first to consider the contours of the "political question" doctrine.

Our discussion, even at the price of extending this opinion, requires review of a number of political question cases, in order to expose the attributes of the doctrine—attributes which, in various settings, diverge, combine, appear, and disappear in seeming disorderliness. . . .

We have said that "In determining whether a question falls within [the political question] category, the appropriateness under our system of government of attributing finality to the action of the political departments and also the lack of satisfactory criteria for a judicial determination are dominant considerations." *Coleman v. Miller* [307 U.S. 433 (1939)]. The nonjusticiability of a political question is primarily a function of the separation of powers. Much confusion results from the capacity of the "political question" label to obscure the need for case-by-case inquiry. Deciding whether a matter has in any measure been committed by the Constitution to another branch of government, or whether the action of that branch exceeds whatever authority has been committed, is itself a delicate exercise in constitutional interpretation, and is a responsibility of this Court as ultimate interpreter of the Constitution. To demonstrate this requires no less than to analyze representative cases and to infer from them the analytical threads that make up the political question doctrine. We shall then show that none of those threads catches this case.

Foreign relations: There are sweeping statements to the effect that all questions touching foreign relations are political questions. Not only does resolution of such issues frequently turn on standards that defy judicial application, or involve the exercise of a discretion demonstrably committed to the executive or legislature; but many such questions uniquely demand single-voiced statement of the Government's views. Yet it is error to suppose that every case or controversy which touches foreign relations lies beyond judicial cognizance. Our cases in this field seem invariably to show a discriminating analysis of the particular question posed, in terms of the history of its management by the political branches, of its susceptibility to judicial handling in the light of its nature and posture in the specific case, and of the possible consequences of judicial action. . . .

Dates of duration of hostilities: Though it has been stated broadly that "the power which declared the necessity is the power to declare its cessation, and what the cessation requires," *Commercial Trust Co. v. Miller*, 262 U.S. 51 [(1923)], here too analysis reveals isolable reasons for the presence of political questions, underlying this Court's refusal to review the political departments' determination of when or whether a war has ended. Dominant is the need for finality in the political determination, for emergency's nature demands "A prompt and unhesitating obedience." *Martin v. Mott*, 12 Wheat. [(256 U.S.) 19 (1827)] [Calling up of militia.] . . . Further, clearly definable criteria for decision may be available. In such case the political question barrier falls away. . . .

Validity of enactments: In *Coleman v. Miller*, supra, this Court held that the questions of how long a proposed amendment to the Federal Constitution remained open to ratification, and what effect a prior rejection had on a subsequent ratification, were committed to congressional resolution and involved criteria of decision that necessarily escaped the judicial grasp. Similar considerations apply to the enacting process: "The respect due to coequal and independent departments," and the need for finality and certainty about the status of a statute contribute to judicial reluctance to inquire whether, as passed, it complied with all requisite formalities. *Field v. Clark*, 143 U.S. 649 [(1892)]. . . .

The status of Indian tribes: This Court's deference to the political departments in determining whether Indians are recognized as a tribe, while it reflects familiar attributes of political questions, also has a unique element in that "the relation of the Indians to the United States is marked by peculiar and cardinal distinctions which exist nowhere else. [The Indians are] domestic dependent nations. . . . Their relation to the United States resembles that of a ward to his guardian." *Cherokee Nation v. Georgia*, 5 Pet. 1 [(1831)]. Yet, here too, there is no blanket rule. . . .

It is apparent that several formulations which vary slightly according to the settings in which the questions arise may describe a political question, although each has one or more elements which identify it as essentially a function of the separation of powers. Prominent on the surface of any case held to involve a political question is found a textually demonstrable constitutional commitment of the issue to a coordinate political department; or a lack of judicially discoverable and manageable standards for resolving it; or the impossibility of deciding without an initial policy determination of a kind clearly for nonjudicial discretion; or the impossibility of a court's undertaking independent resolution without expressing lack of the respect due coordinate branches of government; or an unusual need for unquestioning adherence to a political decision already made; or the potentiality of embarrassment from multifarious pronouncements by various departments on one question.

Unless one of these formulations is inextricable from the case at bar, there should be no dismissal for nonjusticiability on the ground of a political question's presence. The doctrine of which we treat is one of "political questions," not one of "political cases." The courts cannot reject as "no law suit" a bona fide controversy as to whether some action denominated "political" exceeds constitutional authority. The cases we have reviewed show the necessity for discriminating inquiry into the precise facts and posture of the particular case, and the impossibility of resolution by any semantic cataloguing.

But it is argued that this case shares the characteristics of decisions that constitute a category not yet considered, cases concerning the Constitution's guaranty, in Art. IV, Section 4, of a republican form of government. . . . [Yet, we] shall discover that Guaranty Clause claims involve those elements which define a "political question," and for that reason and no other, they are nonjusticiable. In particular, we shall discover that the nonjusticiability of such claims has nothing to do with their touching upon matters of state governmental organization.

Republican form of government: Luther v. Borden, 7 How. 1 [(1848)], though in form simply an action for damages for trespass was, as Daniel Webster said in opening the argument for the defense, "an unusual case." The defendants, admitting an otherwise tortious breaking and entering, sought to justify their action on the ground that they were agents of the established lawful government of Rhode Island, which State was then under martial law to defend itself from active insurrection; that the plaintiff was engaged in that insurrection; and that they entered under orders to arrest the plaintiff. The case arose "out of the unfortunate political differences which agitated the people of Rhode Island in 1841 and 1842," and which had resulted in a situation wherein two groups laid competing claims to recognition as the lawful government. . . .

Chief Justice TANEY's opinion for the Court reasoned as follows: (1) If a court were to hold the defendants' acts unjustified because the charter government had no legal existence during the period in question, it would follow that all of that government's actions—laws enacted, taxes collected, salaries paid, accounts settled, sentences passed—were of no effect; and that "the officers who carried their decisions into operation [were] answerable as trespassers, if not in some cases as criminals." There was, of course, no room for application of any doctrine of *de facto* status to uphold prior acts of an officer not authorized *de jure*, for such would have defeated the plaintiff's very action. A decision for the plaintiff would inevitably have produced some significant measure of chaos, a consequence to be avoided if it could be done without abnegation of the judicial duty to uphold the Constitution.

(2) No state court had recognized as a judicial responsibility settlement

of the issue of the locus of state governmental authority. Indeed, the courts of Rhode Island had in several cases held that "it rested with the political power to decide whether the charter government had been displaced or not," and that that department had acknowledged no change.

(3) Since "[t]he question relates, altogether, to the constitution and laws of [the] . . . State," the courts of the United States had to follow the state courts' decisions unless there was a federal constitutional ground for overturning them.

(4) No provision of the Constitution could be or had been invoked for this purpose except Art. IV, § 4, the Guaranty Clause. Having already noted the absence of standards whereby the choice between governments could be made by a court acting independently, Chief Justice TANEY now found further textual and practical reasons for concluding that, if any department of the United States was empowered by the Guaranty Clause to resolve the issue, it was not the judiciary:

"Under this article of the Constitution it rests with Congress to decide what government is the established one in a State. For as the United States guarantee to each State a republican government, Congress must necessarily decide what government is established in the State before it can determine whether it is a republican or not. And when the senators and representatives of a State are admitted into the councils of the Union, the authority of the government under which they are appointed, as well as its republican character, is recognized by the proper constitutional authority. And its decision is binding on every other department of the government, and could not be questioned in a judicial tribunal. It is true that the contest in this case did not last long enough to bring the matter to this issue; and . . . Congress was not called upon to decide the controversy. Yet the right to decide is placed there, and not in the courts."

"So, too, as relates to the clause in the above-mentioned article of the Constitution, providing for cases of domestic violence. It rested with Congress, too, to determine upon the means proper to be adopted to fulfill this guarantee. . . . [B]y the act of February 28, 1795, [Congress] provided, that, 'in case of an insurrection in any State against the government thereof, it shall be lawful for the President of the United States, on application of the legislature of such State or of the executive (when the legislature cannot be convened) to call forth such number of the militia of any other State or States, as may be applied for, as he may judge sufficient to suppress such insurrection.'

"By this act, the power of deciding whether the exigency had arisen upon which the government of the United States is bound to interfere, is given to the President" [*Luther v. Borden*].

Clearly, several factors were thought by the Court in *Luther* to make the question there "political": the commitment to the other branches of the decision as to which is the lawful state government; the unambiguous action by the President, in recognizing the charter government as the lawful authority; the need for finality in the executive's decision; and the lack of criteria by which a court could determine which form of government was republican. . . .

But the only significance that *Luther* could have for our immediate purposes is in its holding that the Guaranty Clause is not a repository of judicially manageable standards which a court could utilize independently in order to identify a State's lawful government. The Court has since refused to resort to the Guaranty Clause—which alone had been invoked for the purpose—as the source of a constitutional standard for invalidating state action. . . .

We come, finally, to the ultimate inquiry whether our precedents as to what constitutes a nonjusticiable "political question" bring the case before us under the umbrella of that doctrine. A natural beginning is to note whether any of the common characteristics which we have been able to identify and label descriptively are present. We find none: The question here is the consistency of state action with the Federal Constitution. We have no question decided, or to be decided, by a political branch of government coequal with this Court. Nor do we risk embarrassment of our government abroad, or grave disturbance at home if we take issue with Tennessee as to the constitutionality of her action here challenged. Nor need the appellants, in order to succeed in this action, ask the Court to enter upon policy determinations for which judicially manageable standards are lacking. Judicial standards under the Equal Protection Clause are well developed and familiar, and it has been open to courts since the enactment of the Fourteenth Amendment to determine, if on the particular facts they must, that a discrimination reflects *no* policy, but simply arbitrary and capricious action.

This case does, in one sense, involve the allocation of political power within a State, and the appellants might conceivably have added a claim under the Guaranty Clause. Of course, as we have seen, any reliance on that clause would be futile. But because any reliance on the Guaranty Clause could not have succeeded it does not follow that appellants may not be heard on the equal protection claim which in fact they tender. . . .

We conclude that the complaint's allegations of a denial of equal protection present a justiciable constitutional cause of action upon which appellants are entitled to a trial and a decision. The right asserted is within the reach of judicial protection under the Fourteenth Amendment.

The judgment of the District Court is reversed and the cause is remanded for further proceedings consistent with this opinion.

Reversed and remanded.

☐ *Justice DOUGLAS, concurring.*

While I join the opinion of the Court and, like the Court, do not reach the merits, a word of explanation is necessary. I put to one side the problems of "political" questions involving the distribution of power between this Court, the Congress, and the Chief Executive. We have here a phase of the recurring problem of the relation of the federal courts to state agencies. More particularly, the question is the extent to which a State may weight one person's vote more heavily than it does another's.

So far as voting rights are concerned, there are large gaps in the Constitution. Yet the right to vote is inherent in the republican form of government envisaged by Article IV, Section 4 of the Constitution. . . .

Race, color, or previous condition of servitude is an impermissible standard by reason of the Fifteenth Amendment, and that alone is sufficient to explain *Gomillion v. Lightfoot*, 364 U.S. 339 [(1960)].

Sex is another impermissible standard by reason of the Nineteenth Amendment.

There is a third barrier to a State's freedom in prescribing qualifications of voters and that is the Equal Protection Clause of the Fourteenth Amendment, the provision invoked here. And so the question is, may a State weight the vote of one county or one district more heavily than it weights the vote in another?

The traditional test under the Equal Protection Clause has been whether a State has made "an invidious discrimination," as it does when it selects "a particular race or nationality for oppressive treatment." Universal equality is not the test; there is room for weighting. . . .

I agree with my Brother CLARK that if the allegations in the complaint can be sustained a case for relief is established. We are told that a single vote in Moore County, Tennessee, is worth 19 votes in Hamilton County, that one vote in Stewart or in Chester County is worth nearly eight times a single vote in Shelby or Knox County. The opportunity to prove that an "invidious discrimination" exists should therefore be given the appellants.

☐ *Justice CLARK, concurring.*

One emerging from the rash of opinions with their accompanying clashing of views may well find himself suffering a mental blindness. The Court holds that the appellants have alleged a cause of action. However, it refuses to award relief here—although the facts are undisputed—and fails to give the District Court any guidance whatever. . . . I believe it can be shown that this case is distinguishable from earlier cases dealing with the distribution of political power by a State, that a patent violation of the Equal Protection Clause of the United States Constitution has been shown, and that an appropriate remedy may be formulated. . . .

Although I find the Tennessee apportionment statute offends the Equal Protection Clause, I would not consider intervention by this Court into so delicate a field if there were any other relief available to the people of Tennessee. But the majority of the people of Tennessee have no "practical opportunities for exerting their political weight at the polls" to correct the existing "invidious discrimination." Tennessee has no initiative and referendum. I have searched diligently for other "practical opportunities" present under the law. I find none other than through the federal courts. The majority of the voters have been caught up in a legislative strait jacket. Tennessee has an "informed, civically militant electorate" and "an aroused popular conscience," but it does not sear "the conscience of the people's representatives." This is because the legislative policy has riveted the present seats in the Assembly to their respective constituencies, and by the votes of their incumbents a reapportionment of any kind is prevented. The people have been rebuffed at the hands of the Assembly; they have tried the constitutional convention route, but since the call must originate in the Assembly it, too, has been fruitless. They have tried Tennessee courts with the same result, and Governors have fought the tide only to flounder. It is said that there is recourse in Congress and perhaps that may be, but from a practical standpoint this is without substance. To date Congress has never undertaken such a task in any State. We therefore must conclude that the people of Tennessee are stymied and without judicial intervention will be saddled with the present discrimination in the affairs of their state government.

□ *Justice FRANKFURTER, with whom Justice HARLAN joins, dissenting.*

The Court today reverses a uniform course of decision established by a dozen cases, including one by which the very claim now sustained was unanimously rejected only five years ago. The impressive body of rulings thus cast aside reflected the equally uniform course of our political history regarding the relationship between population and legislative representation—a wholly different matter from denial of the franchise to individuals because of race, color, religion or sex. Such a massive repudiation of the experience of our whole past in asserting destructively novel judicial power demands a detailed analysis of the role of this Court in our constitutional scheme. Disregard of inherent limits in the effective exercise of the Court's "judicial Power" not only presages the futility of judicial intervention in the essentially political conflict of forces by which the relation between population and representation has time out of mind been and now is determined. It may well impair the Court's position as the ultimate organ of "the supreme Law of the Land" in that vast range of legal problems, often strongly entangled in popular feeling, on which this Court must pronounce. The Court's authority—possessed of neither the purse nor the sword—ultimately rests on sustained public confidence in its moral sanction. Such feeling must be nourished by the Court's complete detachment, in fact and in appearance, from political entanglements and by abstention from injecting itself into the clash of political forces in political settlements.

A hypothetical claim resting on abstract assumptions is now for the first time made the basis for affording illusory relief for a particular evil even though it foreshadows deeper and more pervasive difficulties in consequence. The claim is hypothetical and the assumptions are abstract because the Court does not vouchsafe the lower courts—state and federal—guidelines for formulating specific, definite, wholly unprecedented remedies for the inevitable litigations that today's umbrageous disposition is bound to stimulate in connection with politically motivated reapportionments in so many States. In such a setting, to promulgate jurisdiction in the abstract is meaningless. It is as devoid of reality as "a brooding omnipresence in the sky," for it conveys no intimation what relief, if any, a District Court is capable of affording that would not invite legislatures to play ducks and drakes with the judiciary. For this Court to direct the District Court to enforce a claim to which the Court has over the years consistently found itself required to deny legal enforcement and at the same time found it necessary to withhold any guidance to the lower court how to enforce this turnabout, new legal claim, manifests an odd—indeed an esoteric—conception of judicial propriety. One of the Court's supporting opinions, as elucidated by commentary, unwittingly affords a disheartening preview of the mathematical quagmire (apart from divers judicially inappropriate and elusive determinants) into which this Court today catapults the lower courts of the country without so much as adumbrating the basis for a legal calculus as a means of extrication. Even assuming the indispensable intellectual disinterestedness on the part of judges in such matters, they do not have accepted legal standards or criteria or even reliable analogies to draw upon for making judicial judgments. To charge courts with the task of accommodating the incommensurable factors of policy that underlie these mathematical puzzles is to attribute, however flatteringly, omnicompetence to judges. . . .

We were soothingly told at the bar of this Court that we need not worry about the kind of remedy a court could effectively fashion once the abstract constitutional right to have courts pass on a statewide system of electoral districting is recognized as a matter of judicial rhetoric, because legislatures would heed the Court's admonition. This is not only a euphoric hope. It implies a sorry confession of judicial impotence in place of a frank acknowledgment that there is not under our Constitution a judicial remedy for every political mischief, for every undesirable exercise of legislative power. The Framers carefully and with deliberate forethought refused so to enthrone the judiciary. In this situation, as in others of like nature, appeal for relief does not belong here. Appeal must be to an informed, civically militant electorate. In a democratic society like ours, relief must come through an aroused popular conscience that sears the conscience of the people's representatives. In any event there is nothing judicially more unseemly nor more self-defeating than for this Court to make *in terrorem* pronouncements, to indulge in merely empty rhetoric, sounding a word of promise to the ear, sure to be disappointing to the hope. . . .

From its earliest opinions this Court has consistently recognized a class of controversies which do not lend themselves to judicial standards and judicial remedies. To classify the various instances as "political questions" is rather a form of stating this conclusion than revealing of analysis. Some of the cases so labelled have no relevance here. But from others emerge unifying considerations that are compelling.

1. The cases concerning war or foreign affairs, for example, are usually explained by the necessity of the country's speaking with one voice in such matters. While this concern alone undoubtedly accounts for many of the decisions, others do not fit the pattern. It would hardly embarrass the conduct of war were this Court to determine, in connection with private transactions between litigants, the date upon which war is to be deemed terminated. But the Court has refused to do so. A controlling factor in such cases is that, decision respecting these kinds of complex matters of policy being traditionally committed not to courts but to the political agencies of government for determination by criteria of political expediency, there exists no standard ascertainable by settled judicial experience or process by reference to which a political decision affecting the question at issue between the parties can be judged. . . .

2. The Court has been particularly unwilling to intervene in matters concerning the structure and organization of the political institutions of the States. The abstention from judicial entry into such areas has been greater even than that which marks the Court's ordinary approach to issues of state power challenged under broad federal guarantees. . . .

3. The cases involving Negro disfranchisement are no exception to the principle of avoiding federal judicial intervention into matters of state government in the absence of an explicit and clear constitutional imperative. For here the controlling command of Supreme Law is plain and unequivocal. An end of discrimination against the Negro was the compelling motive of the Civil War Amendments. . . .

4. The Court has refused to exercise its jurisdiction to pass on "abstract

questions of political power, of sovereignty, of government." *Massachusetts v. Mellon*, 262 U.S. 447 [(1923)]. The "political question" doctrine, in this aspect, reflects the policies underlying the requirement of "standing": that the litigant who would challenge official action must claim infringement of an interest particular and personal to himself, as distinguished from a cause of dissatisfaction with the general frame and functioning of government—a complaint that the political institutions are awry. . . . What renders cases of this kind non-justiciable is not necessarily the nature of the parties to them, for the Court has resolved other issues between similar parties; nor is it the nature of the legal question involved, for the same type of question has been adjudicated when presented in other forms of controversy. The crux of the matter is that courts are not fit instruments of decision where what is essentially at stake is the composition of those large contests of policy traditionally fought out in non-judicial forums, by which governments and the actions of governments are made and unmade. . . .

5. The influence of these converging considerations—the caution not to undertake decision where standards meet for judicial judgment are lacking, the reluctance to interfere with matters of state government in the absence of an unquestionable and effectively enforceable mandate, the unwillingness to make courts arbiters of the broad issues of political organization historically committed to other institutions and for whose adjustment the judicial process is ill-adapted—has been decisive of the settled line of cases, reaching back more than a century, which holds that Art. IV, § 4, of the Constitution, guaranteeing to the States "a Republican Form of Government," is not enforceable through the courts. . . .

The present case involves all of the elements that have made the Guarantee Clause cases non-justiciable. It is, in effect, a Guarantee Clause claim masquerading under a different label. But it cannot make the case more fit for judicial action that appellants invoke the Fourteenth Amendment rather than Art. IV, § 4, where, in fact, the gist of their complaint is the same—unless it can be found that the Fourteenth Amendment speaks with greater particularity to their situation. We have been admonished to avoid "the tyranny of labels." Art. IV, § 4, is not committed by express constitutional terms to Congress. It is the nature of the controversies arising under it, nothing else, which has made it judicially unenforceable. Of course, if a controversy falls within judicial power, it depends "on how he [the plaintiff] casts his action," whether he brings himself within a jurisdictional statute. But where judicial competence is wanting, it cannot be created by invoking one clause of the Constitution rather than another. . . .

Appellants invoke the right to vote and to have their votes counted. But they are permitted to vote and their votes are counted. They go to the polls, they cast their ballots, they send their representatives to the state councils. Their complaint is simply that the representatives are not sufficiently numerous or powerful—in short, that Tennessee has adopted a basis of representation with which they are dissatisfied. . . . What is actually asked of the Court in this case is to choose among competing bases of representation—ultimately, really, among competing theories of political philosophy—in order to establish an appropriate frame of government for the State of Tennessee and thereby for all the States of the Union. . . .

To find such a political conception legally enforceable in the broad and unspecific guarantee of equal protection is to rewrite the Constitution. See *Luther v. Borden*, supra. Certainly, "equal protection" is no more secure a foundation for judicial judgment of the permissibility of varying forms of representative government than is "Republican Form." . . .

The notion that representation proportioned to the geographic spread of population is so universally accepted as a necessary element of equality between man and man that it must be taken to be the standard of a political equality preserved by the Fourteenth Amendment—that it is, in appellants' words "the basic principle of representative government"—is, to put it bluntly, not true. However desirable and however desired by some among the great political thinkers and framers of our government, it has never been generally practiced, today or in the past. It was not the English system, it was not the colonial system, it was not the system chosen for the national government by the Constitution, it was not the system exclusively or even predominantly practiced by the States at the time of adoption of the Fourteenth Amendment, it is not predominantly practiced by the States today. Unless judges, the judges of this Court, are to make their private views of political wisdom the measure of the Constitution—views which in all honesty cannot but give the appearance, if not reflect the reality, of involvement with the business of partisan politics so inescapably a part of apportionment controversies—the Fourteenth Amendment, "itself a historical product," *Jackman v. Rosenbaum Co.*, 260 U.S. 22 [(1922)], provides no guide for judicial oversight of the representation problem.

    ☐ *Justice HARLAN, with whom Justice FRANKFURTER joins, dissenting.*

I can find nothing in the Equal Protection Clause or elsewhere in the Federal Constitution which expressly or impliedly supports the view that state legislatures must be so structured as to reflect with approximate equality the voice of every voter. Not only is that proposition refuted by history, as shown by my Brother FRANKFURTER, but it strikes deep into the heart of our federal system. Its acceptance would require us to turn our backs on the regard which this Court has always shown for the judgment of state legislatures and courts on matters of basically local concern. . . .

Goldwater v. Carter

444 U.S. 996, 100 S.CT. 533 (1979)

In 1979, Senator Barry Goldwater and several other senators filed suit against President James ("Jimmy") Carter, challenging the constitutionality of Carter's termination of a defense treaty with Taiwan without the approval of the Senate. Underlying the case was the enduring support that the nation's conservative leadership extended toward Taiwan. A tiny island, Taiwan housed the Chinese nationalist government after it was forced out of the China mainland by the new communist government. Granting a petition for *certiorari* but without hearing oral arguments, the Court vacated a court of appeals ruling and remanded the case to a federal district court with directions to dismiss the complaint. In separate concurring opinions, Justice Powell rejects the application of the "political question" doctrine here, while Justice Rehnquist contends that it applies here and in other controversies over foreign policy. In his dissenting opinion, Justice Brennan rejects the idea that the question presented here is "political" and further discusses the scope of the judicial power.

The Court by a vote of eight to one ordered the appellate court's judgment vacated and remanded the case to the district court. There were concurrences by Justices Powell and Rehnquist, who was joined by Chief Justice Burger and Justices Stewart and Stevens. Justice Marshall concurred without filing or joining an opinion. Justice Brennan filed a dissent. Justice Blackmun, joined by Justice White, filed a dissent from the Court's refusal to hear oral arguments in the case.

☐ *Justice POWELL, concurring.*

Although I agree with the result reached by the Court, I would dismiss the complaint as not ripe for judicial review.

This Court has recognized that an issue should not be decided if it is not ripe for judicial review. Prudential considerations persuade me that a dispute between Congress and the President is not ready for judicial review unless and until each branch has taken action asserting its constitutional authority. Differences between the President and the Congress are commonplace under our system. The differences should, and almost invariably do, turn on political rather than legal considerations. The Judicial Branch should not decide issues affecting the allocation of power between the President and Congress until the political branches reach a constitutional impasse. Otherwise, we would encourage small groups or even individual Members of Congress to seek judicial resolution of issues before the normal political process has the opportunity to resolve the conflict.

In this case, a few Members of Congress claim that the President's action in terminating the treaty with Taiwan has deprived them of their constitutional role with respect to a change in the supreme law of the land. Congress has taken no official action. In the present posture of this case, we do not know whether there ever will be an actual confrontation between the Legislative and Executive Branches. Although the Senate has considered a resolution declaring that Senate approval is necessary for the termination of any mutual defense treaty, no final vote has been taken on the resolution. Moreover, it is unclear whether the resolution would have retroactive effect. It cannot be said that either the Senate or the House has rejected the President's claim. If the Congress chooses not to confront the President, it is not our task to do so. I therefore concur in the dismissal of this case.

Justice REHNQUIST suggests, however, that the issue presented by this case is a nonjusticiable political question which can never be considered by this Court. I cannot agree. In my view, reliance upon the political-question doctrine is inconsistent with our precedents. As set forth in the seminal case of *Baker v. Carr*, [369 U.S. 186] (1962), the doctrine incorporates three inquiries: (i) Does the issue involve resolution of questions committed by the text of the Constitution to a coordinate branch of Government? (ii) Would resolution of the question demand that a court move beyond areas of judicial expertise? (iii) Do prudential considerations counsel against judicial intervention? In my opinion the answer to each of these inquiries would require us to decide this case if it were ready for review. . . .

In my view, the suggestion that this case presents a political question is incompatible with this Court's willingness on previous occasions to decide whether one branch of our Government has impinged upon the power of another. Under the criteria enunciated in *Baker v. Carr*, we have the responsibility to decide whether both the Executive and Legislative Branches have constitutional roles to play in termination of a treaty. If the Congress, by appropriate formal action, had challenged the President's authority to terminate the treaty with Taiwan, the resulting uncertainty could have serious consequences for our country. In that situation, it would be the duty of this Court to resolve the issue.

☐ *JUSTICE REHNQUIST, with whom the CHIEF JUSTICE, Justice STEWART, and Justice STEVENS join, concurring.*

I am of the view that the basic question presented by the petitioners in this case is "political" and therefore nonjusticiable because it involves the authority of the President in the conduct of our country's foreign relations and the extent to which the Senate or the Congress is authorized to negate the action of the President. In *Coleman v. Miller*, 307 U.S. 433 (1939), a case in which members of the Kansas Legislature brought an action attacking a vote of the State Senate in favor of the ratification of the Child Labor Amendment, Chief Justice HUGHES wrote in what is referred to as the "Opinion of the Court":

> We think that . . . the question of the efficacy of ratifications by state legislatures, in the light of previous rejection or attempted withdrawal, should be regarded as a political question pertaining to the political departments, with the ultimate authority in the Congress in the exercise of its control over the promulgation of the adoption of the Amendment.
>
> The precise question as now raised is whether, when the legislature of the State, as we have found, has actually ratified the proposed amendment, the Court should restrain the state officers from certifying the ratification to the Secretary of State, because of an earlier rejection, and thus prevent the question from coming before the political departments. We find no basis in either Constitution or statute for such judicial action. Article V, speaking solely of ratification, contains no provision as to rejection.

Thus, Chief Justice HUGHES' opinion concluded that "Congress in controlling the promulgation of the adoption of a constitutional amendment has the final determination of the question whether by lapse of time its proposal of the amendment had lost its vitality prior to the required ratifications." . . .

I believe it follows *a fortiori* from *Coleman* that the controversy in the instant case is a nonjusticiable political dispute that should be left for resolution by the Executive and Legislative Branches of the Government. Here, while the Constitution is express as to the manner in which the Senate shall participate in the ratification of a treaty, it is silent as to that body's participation in the abrogation of a treaty. . . .

I think that the justifications for concluding that the question here is political in nature are even more compelling than in *Coleman* because it involves foreign relations—specifically a treaty commitment to use military force in the defense of a foreign government if attacked. In *United States v. Curtiss-Wright Corp.*, 299 U.S. 304 (1936), this Court said:

> Whether, if the Joint Resolution had related solely to internal affairs it would be open to the challenge that it constituted an unlawful delegation of legislative power to the Executive, we find it unnecessary to determine. The whole aim of the resolution is to affect a situation entirely external to the United States, and falling within the category of foreign affairs.

The present case differs in several important respects from *Youngstown Sheet & Tube Co. v. Sawyer*, 343 U.S. 579 (1952), cited by petitioners as authority both for reaching the merits of this dispute and for reversing the Court of Appeals. In *Youngstown*, private litigants brought a suit contesting the President's authority under his war powers to seize the Nation's steel industry, an action of profound and demonstrable domestic impact. Here, by contrast, we are asked to settle a dispute between coequal branches of our Government, each of which has resources available to protect and assert its interests, resources not available to private litigants outside the judicial forum. Moreover, as in *Curtiss-Wright*, the effect of this action, as far as we can tell, is "entirely external to the United States, and [falls] within the category of foreign affairs." Finally, as already noted, the situation presented here is closely akin to that presented in *Coleman*, where the Constitution spoke only to the procedure for ratification of an amendment, not to its rejection.

☐ *Justice BLACKMUN, with whom Justice WHITE joins, dissenting in part.*

In my view, the time factor and its importance are illusory; if the President does not have the power to terminate the treaty (a substantial issue that we should address only after briefing and oral argument), the notice of intention to terminate surely has no legal effect. It is also indefensible, without further study, to pass on the issue of justiciability or on the issues of standing or ripeness. While I therefore join in the grant of the petition for *certiorari*, I would set the case for oral argument and give it the plenary consideration it so obviously deserves.

☐ *Justice BRENNAN, dissenting.*

I respectfully dissent from the order directing the District Court to dismiss this case, and would affirm the judgment of the Court of Appeals insofar as it rests upon the President's well-established authority to recognize, and withdraw recognition from, foreign governments.

In stating that this case presents a non-justiciable "political question," Justice REHNQUIST, in my view, profoundly misapprehends the political-question principle as it applies to matters of foreign relations. Properly understood, the political-question doctrine restrains courts from reviewing an exercise of foreign policy judgment by the coordinate political branch to which authority to make that judgment has been "constitutional[ly] commit[ted]." *Baker v. Carr*. But the doctrine does not pertain when a court is faced with the *antecedent* question whether a particular branch has been constitutionally designated as the repository of political decisionmaking power. The issue of decisionmaking authority must be resolved as a matter of constitutional law, not political discretion; accordingly, it falls within the competence of the courts.

The constitutional question raised here is prudently answered in narrow terms. Abrogation of the defense treaty with Taiwan was a necessary incident to Executive recognition of the Peking Government, because the defense treaty was predicated upon the now-abandoned view that the Taiwan Government was the only legitimate political authority in China. Our cases firmly establish that the Constitution commits to the President alone the power to recognize, and withdraw recognition from, foreign regimes. That mandate being clear, our judicial inquiry into the treaty rupture can go no further.

Elk Grove Unified School District v. Newdow
124 S.Ct. 2301 (2004)

In 2000, Michael A. Newdow, an atheist, challenged the constitutionality of Elk Grove Unified School District's requirement that teachers lead their classes in reciting the Pledge of Allegiance. Because the Pledge contains the words "under God," he contended that the practice amounted to religious indoctrination and violates the First Amendment. At the time, his daughter was in kindergarten and Newdow was in a custody battle with her mother, Sandra Banning. Banning and Newdow were awarded shared "physical custody," but Banning had "exclusive legal custody." A federal district court dismissed Newdow's complaint, but the Court of Appeals for the Ninth Circuit reversed, holding Newdow had standing as a parent to sue and that the school district's policy violated the (Dis)establishment clause. Banning, then, filed a motion to have the case dismissed on the ground that she was the sole legal custodian and that she did not feel that it was in her daughter's interest to be a party to the suit. The Ninth Circuit, nonetheless, reaffirmed Newdow's standing to challenge allegedly unconstitutional governmental practices, and that under California law he retained the right to expose his child to his religious views, even though they contradicted her mother's Christian views. The school district appealed that decision to the Supreme Court, which granted review. Subsequently, Newdow filed a motion requesting Justice Scalia to recuse himself due to his off-the-bench comments criticizing the Ninth Circuit's ruling that the school district's policy violated the First Amendment.

The Ninth Circuit's decision was unanimously reversed, with Justice Scalia not participating. Justice Stevens delivered the opinion for the Court, holding that Newdow lacked "prudential standing" to raise the challenge on behalf of his daughter and declined to reach the merits of the case. In three separate concurring opinions, Chief Justice Rehnquist and Justices O'Connor and Thomas indicate that Newdow had standing and they would, though each for different reasons, uphold the school district's policy over First Amendment objections.

Justice STEVENS delivered the opinion of the Court.

As part of the nationwide interest in commemorating the 400th anniversary of Christopher Columbus' discovery of America, a widely circulated national magazine for youth proposed in 1892 that pupils recite the following affirmation: "I pledge allegiance to my Flag and the Republic for which it stands: one Nation indivisible, with Liberty and Justice for all." In the 1920's, the National Flag Conferences replaced the phrase "my Flag" with "the flag of the United States of America."

In 1942, in the midst of World War II, Congress adopted, and the President signed, a Joint Resolution codifying a detailed set of "rules and customs pertaining to the display and use of the flag of the United States of America." This resolution, which marked the first appearance of the Pledge of Allegiance in positive law, confirmed the importance of the flag as a symbol of our Nation's indivisibility and commitment to the concept of liberty.

Congress revisited the Pledge of Allegiance 12 years later when it amended the text to add the words "under God." The resulting text is the Pledge as we know it today: "I pledge allegiance to the Flag of the United States of America, and to the Republic for which it stands, one Nation under God, indivisible, with liberty and justice for all." . . .

We granted the School District's petition for a writ of *certiorari* to consider two questions: (1) whether Newdow has standing as a noncustodial parent to challenge the School District's policy, and (2) if so, whether the policy offends the First Amendment. . . .

The command to guard jealously and exercise rarely our power to make constitutional pronouncements requires strictest adherence when matters of great national significance are at stake. Even in cases concededly within our jurisdiction under Article III, we abide by "a series of rules under which [we have] avoided passing upon a large part of all the constitutional questions pressed upon [us] for decision." *Ashwander v. TVA*, 297 U.S. 288 (1936) (BRANDEIS, J., concurring).

Consistent with these principles, our standing jurisprudence contains two strands: Article III standing, which enforces the Constitution's case or controversy requirement; and prudential standing, which embodies "judicially self-imposed limits on the exercise of federal jurisdiction," *Allen* [*v. Wright*, 468 U.S. 737 (1984)]. . . . Although we have not exhaustively defined the prudential dimensions of the standing doctrine, we have explained that prudential standing encompasses "the general prohibition on a litigant's raising another person's legal rights, the rule barring adjudication of generalized grievances more appropriately addressed in the representative branches, and the requirement that a plaintiff's complaint fall within the zone of interests protected by the law invoked." *Allen.*

One of the principal areas in which this Court has customarily declined to intervene is the realm of domestic relations. Long ago we observed that "[t]he whole subject of the domestic relations of husband and wife, parent and child, belongs to the laws of the States and not to the laws of the United States." *In re Burrus*, 136 U.S. 586 (1890). [W]hile rare instances arise in which it is necessary to answer a substantial federal question that transcends or exists apart from the family law issue, in general it is appropriate for the federal courts to leave delicate issues of domestic relations to the state courts. . . .

Newdow's standing derives entirely from his relationship with his daughter, but . . . the interests of this parent and this child are not parallel and, indeed, are potentially in conflict.

Newdow's parental status is defined by California's domestic relations law. Our custom on questions of state law ordinarily is to defer to the interpretation of the Court of Appeals for the Circuit in which the State is located. In this case, the Court of Appeals, which possesses greater familiarity with California law, concluded that state law vests in Newdow a cognizable right to influence his daughter's religious upbringing. . . . Animated by a conception of "family privacy" that includes "not simply a policy of minimum state intervention but also a presumption of parental autonomy," the state cases create a zone of private authority within which each parent, whether custodial or noncustodial, remains free to impart to the child his or her religious perspective. . . .

In our view, it is improper for the federal courts to entertain a claim by a plaintiff whose standing to sue is founded on family law rights that are in dispute when prosecution of the lawsuit may have an adverse effect on the person who is the source of the plaintiff's claimed standing. When hard questions of domestic relations are sure to affect the outcome, the prudent course is for the federal court to stay its hand rather than reach out to resolve a weighty question of federal constitutional law. There is a vast difference between Newdow's right to communicate with his child —which both California law and the First Amendment recognize—and his claimed right to shield his daughter from influences to which she is exposed in school despite the terms of the custody order. We conclude that, having been deprived under California law of the right to sue as next friend, Newdow lacks prudential standing to bring this suit in federal court.

☐ *Chief Justice REHNQUIST, with whom Justice O'CONNOR joins, and with whom Justice THOMAS joins as to Part I, concurring in the judgment.*

The Court today erects a novel prudential standing principle in order to avoid reaching the merits of the constitutional claim. I dissent from that ruling. On the merits, I conclude that the Elk Grove Unified School District policy that requires teachers to lead willing students in reciting the Pledge of Allegiance, which includes the words "under God," does not violate the Establishment Clause of the First Amendment.

[T]he Court does not dispute that respondent Newdow satisfies the requisites of Article III standing. But curiously the Court incorporates criticism of the Court of Appeal's Article III standing decision into its justification for its novel prudential standing principle. The Court concludes that respondent lacks prudential standing, under its new standing principle, to bring his suit in federal court.

We have, in the past, judicially self-imposed clear limits on the exercise of federal jurisdiction. In contrast, here is the Court's new prudential standing principle: "[I]t is improper for the federal courts to entertain a claim by a plaintiff whose standing to sue is founded on family law rights that are in dispute when prosecution of the lawsuit may have an adverse effect on the person who is the source of the plaintiff's claimed standing." . . .

First, the Court relies heavily on *Ankenbrandt v. Richards*, 504 U.S. 689 (1992), in which we discussed both the domestic relations exception and the abstention doctrine. . . . We . . . conclude[ed] that the domestic relations exception only applies when a party seeks to have a district court issue a "divorce, alimony, and child custody decree." We further held that abstention was inappropriate because "the status of the domestic relationship ha[d] been determined as a matter of state law, and in any event ha[d] no bearing on the underlying torts alleged."

The Court['s] conclusion does not follow from *Ankenbrandt's* discussion of the domestic relations exception and abstention; even if it did, it would not be applicable in this case because, on the merits, this case presents a substantial federal question that transcends the family law. . . .

Although the Court may have succeeded in confining this novel principle almost narrowly enough to be, like the proverbial excursion ticket— good for this day only—our doctrine of prudential standing should be governed by general principles, rather than ad hoc improvisations. . . .

The phrase "under God" in the Pledge seems, as a historical matter, to sum up the attitude of the Nation's leaders, and to manifest itself in many of our public observances. Examples of patriotic invocations of God and official acknowledgments of religion's role in our Nation's history abound.

At George Washington's first inauguration on April 30, 1789, . . . "Washington put his right hand on the *Bible*, opened to Psalm 121:1: 'I raise my eyes toward the hills. Whence shall my help come.' The Chancellor proceeded with the oath: 'Do you solemnly swear that you will faithfully execute the office of President of the United States and will to the best of your ability preserve, protect and defend the Constitution of the United States?' The President responded, 'I solemnly swear,' and repeated the oath, adding, 'So help me God.' He then bent forward and kissed the Bible before him."

Later the same year, after encouragement from Congress, Washington issued his first Thanksgiving proclamation, which began: "Whereas it is the duty of all Nations to acknowledge the providence of Almighty God, to obey His will, to be grateful for his benefits, and humbly to implore his protection and favor—and whereas both Houses of Congress have by their joint Committee requested me 'to recommend to the People of the United States a day of public thanksgiving and prayer to be observed by acknowledging with grateful hearts the many signal favors of Almighty God especially by affording them an opportunity peaceably to establish a form of government for their safety and happiness.' "

Almost all succeeding Presidents have issued similar Thanksgiving proclamations. Later Presidents, at critical times in the Nation's history, have likewise invoked the name of God. . . .

The motto "In God We Trust" first appeared on the country's coins during the Civil War. [I]n 1956, Congress declared that the motto of the United States would be "In God We Trust."

Our Court Marshal's opening proclamation concludes with the words "God save the United States and this honorable Court." . . .

I do not believe that the phrase "under God" in the Pledge converts its recital into a "religious exercise" of the sort described in *Lee* [*v. Weisman*, 505 U.S. 577 (1992)]. Instead, it is a declaration of belief in allegiance and loyalty to the United States flag and the Republic that it represents. The phrase "under God" is in no sense a prayer, nor an endorsement of any religion. . . . Reciting the Pledge, or listening to others recite it, is a patriotic exercise, not a religious one; participants promise fidelity to our flag and our Nation, not to any particular God, faith, or church. . . .

When courts extend constitutional prohibitions beyond their previously recognized limit, they may restrict democratic choices made by public bodies. . . . The Constitution only requires that schoolchildren be entitled to abstain from the ceremony if they choose to do so. To give the parent of such a child a sort of "heckler's veto" over a patriotic ceremony willingly participated in by other students, simply because the Pledge of Allegiance contains the descriptive phrase "under God," is an unwarranted extension of the Establishment Clause, an extension which would have the unfortunate effect of prohibiting a commendable patriotic observance.

□ *Justice O'CONNOR, concurring in the judgment.*

I join the concurrence of THE CHIEF JUSTICE in full. Like him, I would follow our policy of deferring to the Federal Courts of Appeals in matters that involve the interpretation of state law, and thereby conclude that the respondent does have standing to bring his constitutional claim before a federal court. Like THE CHIEF JUSTICE, I believe that petitioner school district's policy of having its teachers lead students in voluntary recitations of the Pledge of Allegiance does not offend the Establishment Clause. But while the history presented by THE CHIEF JUSTICE illuminates the constitutional problems this case presents, I write separately to explain the principles that guide my own analysis of the constitutionality of that policy. . . .

When a court confronts a challenge to government-sponsored speech or displays, I continue to believe that the endorsement test "captures the essential command of the Establishment Clause, namely, that government must not make a person's religious beliefs relevant to his or her standing in the political community by conveying a message 'that religion or a particular religious belief is favored or preferred.' " *County of Allegheny v. American Civil Liberties Union, Greater Pittsburgh Chapter*, 492 U.S. 573 (1989) (opinion of O'CONNOR, J.).

Endorsement, I have explained, "sends a message to nonadherents that they are outsiders, not full members of the political community, and an accompanying message to adherents that they are insiders, favored members of the political community." In order to decide whether endorsement has occurred, a reviewing court must keep in mind two crucial and related principles.

First, because the endorsement test seeks "to identify those situations in which government makes adherence to a religion relevant . . . to a person's standing in the political community," it assumes the viewpoint of a reasonable observer. Given the dizzying religious heterogeneity of our Nation, adopting a subjective approach would reduce the test to an absurdity. Nearly any government action could be overturned as a violation of the Establishment Clause if a "heckler's veto" sufficed to show that its message was one of endorsement.

The Court has permitted government, in some instances, to refer to or commemorate religion in public life. . . . One such purpose is to commemorate the role of religion in our history. . . . For centuries, we have marked important occasions or pronouncements with references to God and invocations of divine assistance. Such references can serve to solemnize an occasion instead of to invoke divine provenance. . . .

This case requires us to determine whether the appearance of the phrase "under God" in the Pledge of Allegiance constitutes an instance of such ceremonial deism. Although it is a close question, I conclude that it does, based on my evaluation of the following four factors.

HISTORY AND UBIQUITY

The constitutional value of ceremonial deism turns on a shared understanding of its legitimate nonreligious purposes. That sort of understanding can exist only when a given practice has been in place for a significant portion of the Nation's history, and when it is observed by enough persons that it can fairly be called ubiquitous. By contrast, novel or uncommon references to religion can more easily be perceived as government endorsements because the reasonable observer cannot be presumed to be fully familiar with their origins. As a result, in examining whether a given practice constitutes an instance of ceremonial deism, its "history and ubiquity" will be of great importance. . . .

Absence of worship or prayer

"[O]ne of the greatest dangers to the freedom of the individual to worship in his own way [lies] in the Government's placing its official stamp of approval upon one particular kind of prayer or one particular form of religious services." *Engel v. Vitale*, 370 U.S. 421 (1962). Because of this principle, only in the most extraordinary circumstances could actual worship or prayer be defended as ceremonial deism. . . .

ABSENCE OF REFERENCE TO PARTICULAR RELIGION

"The clearest command of the Establishment Clause is that one religious denomination cannot be officially preferred over another." *Larson v. Valente*, 456 U.S. 228 (1982). . . . As a result, no religious acknowledgment could claim to be an instance of ceremonial deism if it explicitly favored one particular religious belief system over another.

The Pledge complies with this requirement. It does not refer to a nation "under Jesus" or "under Vishnu," but instead acknowledges religion in a general way: a simple reference to a generic "God." . . . The phrase "under God," conceived and added at a time when our national religious diversity was neither as robust nor as well recognized as it is now, represents a tolerable attempt to acknowledge religion and to invoke its solemnizing power without favoring any individual religious sect or belief system.

MINIMAL RELIGIOUS CONTENT

A final factor that makes the Pledge an instance of ceremonial deism, in my view, is its highly circumscribed reference to God. [T]he brevity of a reference to religion or to God in a ceremonial exercise can be important for several reasons. First, it tends to confirm that the reference is being used to acknowledge religion or to solemnize an event rather than to endorse religion in any way. Second, it makes it easier for those participants who wish to "opt out" of language they find offensive to do so without having to reject the ceremony entirely. And third, it tends to limit the ability of government to express a preference for one religious sect over another. . . .

Michael Newdow's challenge to petitioner school district's policy is a well-intentioned one, but his distaste for the reference to "one Nation under God," however sincere, cannot be the yardstick of our Establishment Clause inquiry. Certain ceremonial references to God and religion in our Nation are the inevitable consequence of the religious history that gave birth to our founding principles of liberty. It would be ironic indeed if this Court were to wield our constitutional commitment to religious freedom so as to sever our ties to the traditions developed to honor it.

  ☐ *Justice THOMAS, concurring in the judgment.*

Because I agree with THE CHIEF JUSTICE that respondent Newdow has standing, I would take this opportunity to begin the process of rethinking the Establishment Clause. I would acknowledge that the Establishment Clause is a federalism provision, which, for this reason, resists incorporation. Moreover, as I will explain, the Pledge policy is not implicated by any sensible incorporation of the Establishment Clause, which would probably cover little more than the Free Exercise Clause.

In *Lee* [*v. Weisman*], the Court held that invocations and benedictions could not, consistent with the Establishment Clause, be given at public secondary school graduations. . . . It brushed aside both the fact that the students were not required to attend the graduation, and the fact that they were not compelled, in any meaningful sense, to participate in the religious component of the graduation ceremony. The Court surmised that the prayer violated the Establishment Clause because a high school student could—in light of the "peer pressure" to attend graduation and "to stand as a group or, at least, maintain respectful silence during the invocation and benediction"—have "a reasonable perception that she is being forced by the State to pray in a manner her conscience will not allow."

Adherence to *Lee* would require us to strike down the Pledge policy, which, in most respects, poses more serious difficulties than the prayer at issue in *Lee*. A prayer at graduation is a one-time event, the graduating students are almost (if not already) adults, and their parents are usually present. By contrast, very young students, removed from the protection of their parents, are exposed to the Pledge each and every day.

Moreover, this case is more troubling than *Lee* with respect to both kinds of "coercion." First, although students may feel "peer pressure" to attend their graduations, the pressure here is far less subtle: Students are actually compelled.

Analysis of the second form of "coercion" identified in Lee is somewhat more complicated. It is true that since this Court decided *West Virginia Bd. of Ed. v. Barnette*, 319 U.S. 624 (1943), States cannot compel (in the traditional sense) students to pledge their allegiance. Formally, then, dissenters can refuse to pledge, and this refusal would be clear to onlookers. That is, students have a theoretical means of opting out of the exercise. . . . On *Lee*'s reasoning, *Barnette*'s protection is illusory, for government officials can allow children to recite the Pledge and let peer pressure take its natural and predictable course. Further, even if we assume that sitting in respectful silence could be mistaken for assent to or participation in a graduation prayer, dissenting students graduating from high school are not "coerced" to pray. At most, they are "coerced" into possibly appearing to assent to the prayer. The "coercion" here, however, results in unwilling children actually pledging their allegiance.

THE CHIEF JUSTICE would distinguish *Lee* by asserting "that the phrase 'under God' in the Pledge [does not] conver[t] its recital into a 'religious exercise' of the sort described in Lee." In *Barnette*, the Court addressed a state law that compelled students to salute and pledge allegiance to the flag. The Court described this as "compulsion of students to declare a belief." In its current form, reciting the Pledge entails pledging allegiance to "the Flag of the United States of America, and to the Republic for which it stands, one Nation under God." Under *Barnette*, pledging allegiance is "to declare a belief" that now includes that this is "one Nation under God." It is difficult to see how this does not entail an affirmation that God exists. Whether or not we classify affirming the existence of God as a "formal religious exercise" akin to prayer, it must present the same or similar constitutional problems.

To be sure, such an affirmation is not a prayer, and I admit that this might be a significant distinction. But the Court has squarely held that the government cannot require a person to "declare his belief in God." *Torcaso v. Watkins*, 367 U. S. 488 (1961). . . .

I conclude that, as a matter of our precedent, the Pledge policy is unconstitutional. I believe, however, that *Lee* was wrongly decided. *Lee* depended on a notion of "coercion" that . . . has no basis in law or reason. The kind of coercion implicated by the Religion Clauses is that accomplished "by force of law and threat of penalty." Peer pressure, unpleasant as it may be, is not coercion. But rejection of *Lee*-style "coercion" does not suffice to settle this case. Although children are not coerced to pledge their allegiance, they are legally coerced to attend school. Because what is at issue is a state action, the question becomes whether the Pledge policy implicates a religious liberty right protected by the Fourteenth Amendment.

I accept that the Free Exercise Clause, which clearly protects an individual right, applies against the States through the Fourteenth Amendment. But the Establishment Clause is another matter. The text and history of the Establishment Clause strongly suggest that it is a federalism provision intended to prevent Congress from interfering with state establishments. Thus, unlike the Free Exercise Clause, which does protect an individual right, it makes little sense to incorporate the Establishment Clause. In any case, I do not believe that the Pledge policy infringes any religious liberty right that would arise from incorporation of the Clause. Because the Pledge policy also does not infringe any free-exercise rights, I conclude that it is constitutional.

■ CONSTITUTIONAL HISTORY

Rules for Judicial Self-Restraint and Avoiding Constitutional Questions

Justice Louis D. Brandeis, concurring in *Ashwander v. Tennessee Valley Authority*, 297 U.S. 288 (1936), summarized some prudential rules for exercising judicial self-restraint and avoiding ruling on the constitutionality of congressional legislation:

> The Court developed, for its own governance in the cases confessedly within its jurisdiction, a series of rules under which it has avoided passing upon a large part of all the constitutional questions pressed upon it for decision. They are:
>
> 1. The Court will not pass upon the constitutionality of legislation in a friendly, non-adversary, proceeding, declining because to decide such questions "is legitimate only in the last resort, and as a necessity in the determination of real, earnest and vital controversy between individuals. . . .
>
> 2. The Court will not "anticipate a question of constitutional law in advance of the necessity of deciding it." *Liverpool, N.Y. & P. S. S. Co. v. Emigration Commissioners*, 113 U.S. 33 [(1885)]. . . .
>
> 3. The Court will not "formulate a rule of constitutional law broader than is required by the precise facts to which it is to be applied." *Liverpool*.
>
> 4. The Court will not pass upon a constitutional question although properly presented by the record, if there is also present some other ground upon which the case may be disposed of. Appeals from the highest court of a state challenging its decision of a question under the Federal Constitution are frequently dismissed because the judgment can be sustained on an independent state ground.

5. The Court will not pass upon the validity of a statute upon complaint of one who fails to show that he is injured by its operation. Among the many applications of this rule, none is more striking than the denial of the right of challenge to one who lacks a personal or property right.

6. The Court will not pass upon the constitutionality of a statute at the instance of one who has availed himself of its benefits.

7. "When the validity of an act of the Congress is drawn in question, and even if a serious doubt of constitutionality is raised, it is a cardinal principle that this Court will first ascertain whether a construction of the statute is fairly possible by which the question may be avoided." *Crowell v. Benson*, 285 U.S. 22 [(1932)].

B | *The Court's Docket and Screening Cases*

The justices' interpretation of their jurisdiction and rules governs access to the Court. But they also need flexible procedures for screening cases and deciding what to decide. This is because the Court's docket has grown phenomenally (see Figure 2.3).

When any appeal or *cert.* petition arrives at the Court it immediately goes to the clerk's office. Staff look at whether it satisfies requirements as to form, length, and fees and if the filing is from an indigent whether there is an affidavit stating that the petitioner is too poor to pay fees. All unpaid cases are assigned a number in the order they arrive, and placed on what is called the Miscellaneous Docket. Paid cases are also assigned a number but placed on the Appellate Docket. The clerk then notifies the other party, or respondent, in each case that he or she must file a brief in response within thirty days. After receiving briefs from respondents, the clerk circulates to the justices' chambers a list of cases ready for consideration and a set of briefs for each case.

For much of the Court's history every justice was responsible for reviewing each case. The justices did not work by panels or delegate responsibility for screening cases to others. That is no longer true. In 1972 the "*cert.* pool" was established. Eight of the justices now share their collective law clerks' memos on all paid and unpaid cases. The memos explain the facts, issues raised, and lower court ruling as well as recommend whether the case should be granted or denied. Those justices not joining the pool—now only Stevens—receive copies of unpaid cases along with other filings. Brennan examined each case himself, when he had time to do so. Stevens has his clerks screen all the cases and write memos on only those they think are important enough for him to consider.

C | *The Rule of Four and Agenda Setting*

When Congress gave the Court discretionary jurisdiction in the Judiciary Act of 1925, by substituting petitions for *certiorari* for mandatory appeals, the justices developed the informal "rule of four" to decide which petitions they would grant. During conference, at least four justices must agree that a case warrants oral argument and consideration by the full Court.

■ CONSTITUTIONAL HISTORY

Docket and filings, 1800–2003

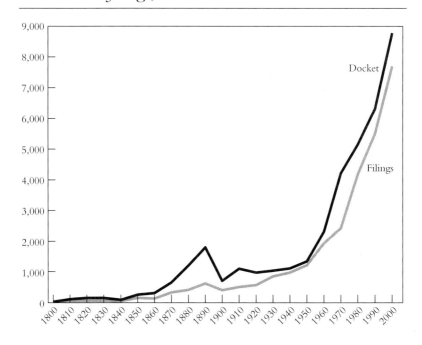

FIGURE 2.3

Source: David M. O'Brien, *Storm Center,* 7th ed. (W. W. Norton, 2005) and data from the U.S. Supreme Court through the 2003–2004 term.

The rule of four operates in a fraction of cases due to the increasing caseload, which is a result of a number of factors. Most important, institutional norms promote a shared conception of the role of the Court as a tribunal for resolving only issues of national importance. Justices agree that the overwhelming proportion of cases is "frivolous," and that there is a limited number of cases to which they may give full consideration.

The caseload and institutional norms push toward limiting the operation of the rule of four. But the rule remains useful, particularly if there is a bloc of justices who share the same ideological orientation. The rule of four thus enables a bloc of justices to work together in picking cases they want the Court to rule on.

Denial of *certiorari* is an important technique for managing the Court's caseload. But its meaning in particular cases may be far from clear. The Court has few fixed rules, and even the rule of four is not "an absolutely inflexible rule."[1] Although enabling the Court to manage its business, denials invite confusion and the suspicion, as Justice Jackson once observed, "that this Court no longer respects impersonal rules of law but is guided in these matters by personal impression which from time to time may be shared by a majority of the justices."[2]

The Court now decides only about 1 percent of the cases annually arriving on its docket.[3] That is far less than twenty-five years ago, when about 3 percent of a much smaller docket were granted and decided. A quarter of a century ago the docket was just reaching 5,000 cases and the justices decided between 150 and 180 cases a term. The docket now exceeds 9,000 yet the justices decide less than 100 a year. That is the same number decided by the Court in 1955 when the docket remained under 2,000. Even if the Court in the 1990s had continued to grant as many cases as it did in the 1970s and 1980s, the percentage granted would have declined, of course, due to the continued growth in the caseload. Still, the diminished plenary docket is striking and probably reflects a combination of factors internal and external to the Court, which undoubtedly contributed to the inflation of the plenary docket during the Burger Court years (1969–1986) and to its contraction thereafter. Early in his chief justiceship, Burger expanded the size of the oral argument calendar in order to accommodate more cases, because of his concern about the Court's declining supervisory capacity. During Burger's chief justiceship, the discipline imposed by the rule of four was also weakened by the emergence of the practice of casting Join-3 votes and the increased circulation of dissents from denial of review, especially by Justice White who drew attention to cases raising conflicts among the lower courts that the Court was not resolving. A Join-3 vote is a vote to provide a fourth vote if others vote to grant review, but is otherwise considered as voting to deny. In the 1970s and 1980s, Join-3

■ IN COMPARATIVE PERSPECTIVE

The "European Model" of Constitutional Courts and Judicial Review

In most European states, the institution and power of "American-style" judicial review has been rejected. Instead, institutions called constitutional courts have been established in Austria (1945), Italy (1948), the Federal Republic of Germany (1949), France (1958), Portugal (1976), Spain (1978), and Belgium (1985), as well as in many of the post-communist countries in Eastern Europe (after 1989), including the Czech Republic, Hungary, Poland, Romania, Russia, and Slovakia.

In contrast to the United States federal judiciary, which has general jurisdiction over issues of constitutional and statutory law, European courts have historically been subordinate to legislatures and denied jurisdiction over constitutional matters. The constitutional courts created in post–World War II Europe thus were an innovation, although their powers of judicial review differed from the American model in several key respects. European constitutional courts are (1) formally detached from the judiciary, (2) given exclusive jurisdiction over constitutional questions, and (3) authorized to exercise review as well as to issue advisory opinions at the request of other governmental institutions.

Unlike the U.S. federal judiciary's jurisdiction over only actual cases or controversies, European constitutional courts may exercise abstract and concrete constitutional review of legislation. *Abstract constitutional review* of legislation is initiated by elected officials or national and regional governmental bodies with respect to legislation that has been recently adopted that either (a) has not yet been put into force (as in France) or (b) has not yet been enforced, or has been suspended, pending review by the constitutional court (as in Germany, Italy, and Spain). In short, before controversial legislation goes into effect the constitutional court must pass on its constitutionality, and thereafter the legislation may be revised. *Concrete constitutional review* arises from litigation in the courts when ordinary judges are uncertain about the constitutionality or the application of a statute or ordinance; in such cases the judges refer the constitutional question or complaint to the constitutional court for resolution.

The principal features of the European model of constitutional courts and judicial review in France, Germany, Italy, and Spain are summarized on the following page.

	FRANCE	GERMANY	ITALY	SPAIN
Court and date of creation	Constitutional Council (1958)	Federal Constitutional Court (1949)	Italian Constitutional Court (1956)	Spanish Constitutional Court (1978)
JURISDICTION				
Abstract review	Yes	Yes	Yes	Yes
Authority to initiate abstract review of legislation	President, Presidential Assembly, or Senate	Federal and lander (state) governments or one-third of the Bundestag	National government (against regional laws); regional governments (against national laws)	Prime minister, president of the Parliament, 50 deputies or senators, executives of autonomous regions, and ombudsmen
Laws referred	National	Federal and lander legislation	National and regional legislation	National and regional legislation
Laws must be referred	Within 15 days of adoption	Within 30 days of adoption	Within 30 days of adoption	Within 90 days of adoption
Concrete review	No	Yes	Yes	Yes
Authority to initiate concrete review of legislation		Judiciary and individuals (after exhaustion of judicial remedies)	Judiciary	Judiciary, ombudsmen, and individuals (after exhaustion of judicial remedies)
COMPOSITION, RECRUITMENT, TENURE				
Number of judges	9	16	15	12
Recruitment	Named by the president (3), assembly (6),	Elected by the Bundestag (8) and Bundesrat (8)	Named by the president (5), judiciary (5); elected by the Parliament (5)	Named by the federal government (2), judiciary (2); elected by the Congress (4) and Senate (4)
Length of term	9 years	12 years	9 years	9 years

For further reading, see Louis Favoreau, "Constitutional Review in Europe," in Louis Henkin, ed., *Constitutionalism and Rights* (New York: Columbia University Press, 1990); Donald P. Kommers, *The Constitutional Jurisprudence of the Federal Republic of Germany*. 2d ed. (Durham, NC: Duke University Press, 1997); Alex Stone, *The Birth of Judicial Politics in France* (New York: Oxford University Press, 1992); Mary Volcansek, *Constitutional Politics in Italy: The Constitutional Court* (New York: St. Martin's Press, 2000); Alec Stone Sweet, *Governing with Judges: Constitutional Politics in Europe* (New York: Oxford University Press, 2000); and Carlo Guarnieri and Patrizia Pederzoli, *The Power of Judges: A Comparative Study of Courts and Democracy* (Oxford: Oxford University Press, 2002).

votes arguably lowered the threshold for granting cases, thereby weakening the self-discipline imposed by the rule of four and contributing to the inflation of the plenary docket.

As the Court's composition changed in the 1990s, so did the justices' voting practices when deciding what to decide: both Join-3 votes and dissents from denial became no longer commonplace and the justices became more tolerant of intercircuit conflicts. In addition, the Judicial Improvements and Access to Justice Act of 1988 eliminated virtually all remaining nondiscretionary appellate jurisdiction, thereby increasing the Court's "managerial capacity" for controlling the plenary docket by denying *cert.* to more cases. Finally, the institutionalization of the *cert.* pool over the last quarter of a century undoubtedly contributed to the shrinking plenary docket in several ways: more justices now rely, and rely to a greater degree than before, on their law clerks' *cert.* memos; there is, thus, less independent review of petitions by the justices themselves; and, as Stevens has suggested, the clerks tend to be "risk averse" when recommending that cases be granted.

NOTES

1. Potter Stewart, "Inside the Supreme Court," *The New York Times*, Oct. 1, 1979, p. 17A, col. 2.

2. *Brown v. Allen*, 344 U.S. 443, 535 (1953) (Jackson, J., concurring opinion).

3. This discussion draws on the author's analysis in "Join-3 Votes, the Rule of Four, the *Cert.* Pool, and the Supreme Court's Shrinking Plenary Docket," 13 *The Journal of Law & Politics* 779 (1997).

SELECTED BIBLIOGRAPHY

Pacelle, Richard L. *The Transformation of the Supreme Court's Agenda: From the New Deal to the Reagan Administration*. Boulder, CO: Westview Press, 1991.

Perry, H. W. *Deciding to Decide: Agenda Setting in the United States Supreme Court*. Cambridge, MA: Harvard University Press, 1991.

Provine, Doris Marie. *Case Selection in the United States Supreme Court.* Chicago: University of Chicago Press, 1980.

D | *Summarily Decided Cases*

Even before the 1988 Act to Improve the Administration of Justice, which eliminated virtually all mandatory appeals, the distinction between mandatory and discretionary review of appeals and *cert.* petitions had largely disappeared in the Court's process of deciding what to decide. The Court annually received between 300 and 400 appeals, and the overwhelming majority were summarily decided (without hearing oral arguments and full consideration). They simply dismissed them for want of jurisdiction or failure to present a substantial federal question, or they ordered the lower court ruling affirmed or reversed.

Summarily decided cases enabled the Court to cut down on its workload. But they also engendered confusion among the lower courts. Summary decisions take the form of rather cryptic orders or *per curiam* (unsigned) opinions. Like denials of *cert.* petitions, they invite confusion over how the Court views the merits of a case and the lower court ruling. The problem is one of the Court's own making. The Court holds that summarily decided cases do not have the same precedential weight as plenary decisions, but they are nonetheless binding on lower courts "until such time as the Court informs [them] that [they] are not." *Hicks v. Arizona,* 422 U.S. 322 (1975).

E | *The Role of Oral Argument*

The Court grants a full hearing—that is, oral argument—to only about 80 of the more than 9,000 cases on the docket each term. When cases are granted full consideration, attorneys for each side submit briefs setting forth their arguments and how they think the case should be decided. The clerk of the Court circulates the briefs to each chamber and sets a date for the attorneys to argue their views orally before the justices. After hearing oral arguments, in private conference the justices vote on how to decide the issues presented in a case.

For fourteen weeks each term, from the first Monday in October until the end of April, the Court hears arguments on Monday, Tuesday, and Wednesday about every two weeks. The importance of oral argument, Chief Justice Hughes observed, lies in the fact that often "the impression that a judge has at the close of a full oral argument accords

Court...CA - 2.................. Voted on......11/8...../...., 19.90.
Argued......10/30............, 19.90. Assigned ...11/13 CO........, 19.90. No. 89-1391
Submitted............................, 19...... Announced....5/23..., 19.91. Vide 89-1392

IRVING RUST, ETC., ET AL., Petitioners

vs.

LOUIS W. SULLIVAN, SECRETARY OF HEALTH AND HUMAN SERVICES

03/01/90 - Cert.

5/29/90 - cert. granted

HOLD FOR	CERT.			JURISDICTIONAL STATEMENT				MERITS		MOTION			
	G	D	G&R	N	POST	DIS	AFF	REV	AFF	G	D		
Rehnquist, Ch. J. *assigned*	✓								✓				
~~Brennan, J.~~		✓							✓				
White, J.	✓							✓					
Marshall, J.	✓												
Blackmun, J.	✓							✓					
Stevens, J.	✓							✓					*in part only*
O'Connor, J.	✓							✓	✓				
Scalia, J.	✓								✓				
Kennedy, J.									✓				
Souter, J.									✓				

19020-2-88

with the conviction which controls his final vote."[1] The justices hold conference and take their initial, often decisive, vote on cases within a day or two after hearing arguments. Oral arguments come at a crucial time. They focus the minds of the justices and present the possibility for fresh perspectives on a case. It is the only opportunity for attorneys to communicate directly with the justices. Two basic factors appear to control the relative importance of oral argument. As Justice Wiley Rutledge observed, "One is brevity. The other is the preparation with which the judge comes to it."[2] When the Court revised its rules in 1980, the justices underscored that "*[t]he Court looks with disfavor on any oral argument that is read from a prepared text.*" Central to preparation and delivery is a bird's-eye view of the case, the issues and facts, and the reasoning behind legal developments. Crisp, concise, and conversational presentations are what the justices want. An attorney must never forget, in Chief Justice Rehnquist's words, that "[h]e is not, after all, presenting his case to some abstract, platonic embodiment of appellate judges as a class, but . . . nine flesh and blood men and women." Oral argument is definitely not a "brief with gestures."[3]

Notably, in 2000 the Supreme Court created its own web site (at http:www.supremecourtus.gov) that makes available transcripts of oral arguments and the full text of its decisions and opinions, until they are officially published.

NOTES

1. Charles E. Hughes, *The Supreme Court of the United States* (New York: Columbia University Press, 1928), 61.

2. Wiley Rutledge, "The Appellate Brief," 28 *American Bar Association Journal* 251 (1942).

3. William Rehnquist, "Oral Advocacy: A Disappearing Art," Brainerd Currie Lecture, Mercer University School of Law, Oct. 20, 1983, msp. 4.

F | *Conference Deliberations*

The justices meet alone in conference to decide which cases to accept and to discuss the merits of those few cases on which they hear oral arguments. Throughout the term during the weeks in which the Court hears oral arguments, conferences are held on Wednesday afternoons to take up the four cases argued on Monday, and then on Fridays to discuss new filings and the eight cases for which oral argument was heard on Tuesday and Wednesday. In May and June, when the Court does not

Members of the Burger Court, in the tradition begun by Chief Justice Melville Fuller, shaking hands prior to going on the bench to hear oral arguments. (© *Yoichi Okamoto, Photo Researchers*)

hear oral arguments, conferences are held on Thursdays, from ten in the morning until four or four-thirty in the afternoon, with the justices breaking for a forty-five-minute lunch around twelve-thirty. A majority may vote to hold a special session during the summer months, when extraordinarily urgent cases arise.

Summoned by a buzzer five minutes before the hour, the justices meet in the conference room, located directly behind the courtroom itself and next to the chief justice's chamber. The oak-paneled room is lined with *United States Reports* (containing the Court's decisions). Over the mantel of an exquisite fireplace at one end hangs a portrait of Chief Justice Marshall. Next to the fireplace stands a large rectangular table where the justices sit. The chief justice sits at the one end and the senior associate justice (Stevens) at the other. Along the right-hand side of the chief justice, next to the fireplace, sit O'Connor, Scalia, and Kennedy; on the left-hand side, sit Souter, Thomas, Ginsburg, and Breyer, the most junior justice. The seating of the justices traditionally has been on the basis of seniority. But variations occur due to individual justices' preferences.

Two conference lists are circulated to each chamber by noon on Wednesday prior to the Friday conference. They structure conference

■ INSIDE THE COURT

On the Tentativeness of Votes and the Importance of Opinion Writing

In two controversial cases, involving claims by the press to a First Amendment right of access to visit and interview prisoners, Chief Justice Burger switched his vote after conference. During the conference discussion of *Pell v. Procunier* 417 U.S. 817 (1974) and *Saxbe v. Washington Post* 417 U.S. 843 (1974), the vote went five to four for recognizing that the press has a First Amendment right of access. But Burger later changed his mind and explained that the final outcome of the cases depended on how the opinions were written:

> This difficult case has few very clear cut and fixed positions but my further study over the weekend leads me to see my position as closer for those who would sustain the authority of the corrections administrators than those who would not! I would therefore reverse in 73–754, affirm in 73–918 and reverse in 73–1265.

> This is another one of those cases that will depend a good deal on "how it is written." The solution to the problem must be allowed time for experimentation and I fear an "absolute" constitutional holding adverse to administrators will tend to "freeze" progress.

The Court ultimately divided five to four but held that the press does not have a First Amendment right of access to interview inmates of prisons.

For other notable instances of vote switching that dramatically affected the outcome, see in Volume 1, Chapter 7, INSIDE THE COURT box and the discussion of *Garcia v. San Antonio Metropolitan Transit Authority*, 469 U.S. 528 (1985) (excerpted there); and in Volume 2, Chapter 6, the box INSIDE THE COURT: Justice Kennedy Switches Positions and the Outcome in *Lee v. Weisman*; and Chapter 11, the box INSIDE THE COURT: Vote Switching in *Bowers v. Hardwick* and Justice Powell's April 8, 1986, Memorandum. These examples illustrate how important postconference deliberations and communications among the chambers have become for the Court's decision making.

Source: Library of Congress, Justice William J. Brennan, Jr., Papers, Manuscripts Room.

discussion and enable the justices to get through their caseload. On the first list—Special List I, or the Discuss List—are jurisdictional statements, petitions for *certiorari*, and motions that are ready and worth discussing. The Discuss List typically includes between forty and fifty cases for each conference. Attached is a second list—Special List II, or what was called the Dead List—containing those cases considered unworthy of discussion. Any justice may request that a case be put on the Discuss List, and only after the chief's conference secretary has heard from all chambers do the lists become final. Over 90 percent of the cases on the conference lists are automatically denied without discussion, and most of those that do make the Discuss List are denied as well. The conference lists are an important technique for saving time and focusing attention on the few cases deemed worthy of consideration.

The significance of conference discussions has changed with the increasing caseload. Conference discussions do not play the role that they once did. When the docket was smaller in the nineteenth century, conferences were integral to the justices' collective deliberations. As the caseload grew, conferences became largely symbolic of past collective deliberations. They now serve only to discover consensus. There is no longer time to reach agreement and compromise on opinions for the Court. "In fact," Justice Antonin Scalia claims, "to call our discussion of a case a conference is really something of a misnomer. It's much more a statement of the views of each of the nine Justices."[1] More discussion, however, he admits would probably not contribute much or lead justices to change their minds when voting on cases. This is because the justices confront similar issues year after year and, as Chief Justice Rehnquist notes, "it would be surprising if [justices] voted differently than they had the previous time."[2]

The justices' votes are always tentative until the day the Court hands down its decision and opinion. Before, during, and after conference justices may use their votes in strategic ways to influence the disposition of a case.

NOTES

1. Antonin Scalia, comments at George Washington National Law Center, Feb. 16, 1988, quoted in "Ruling Fixed Opinions," *The New York Times*, Feb. 22, 1988, p. 16A.

2. William H. Rehnquist, quoted in David M. O'Brien, *Storm Center: The Supreme Court in American Politics*, 6th ed. (New York: W. W. Norton, 2002).

SELECTED BIBLIOGRAPHY

Dickson, Del. *The Supreme Court in Conference*. New York: Oxford University Press, 2001.

Matltzman, Forrest, Spriggs II, James F., and Wahlbeck, Paul. *Crafting Law on the Supreme Court: The Collegial Game*. Cambridge, MA: Cambridge University Press, 2000.

O'Brien, David M. *Storm Center: The Supreme Court in American Politics*, 7th ed. New York: W. W. Norton, 2005.

Schwartz, Bernard. *Decision: How the Supreme Court Decides Cases*. New York: Oxford University Press, 1996.

G | *Postconference Writing and Circulation of Opinions*

Opinions justify or explain votes at conference. The opinion for the Court is the most important and most difficult to write because it represents a collective judgment. Because conference votes are tentative, the assignment, drafting, and circulation of opinions is crucial to the Court's rulings. At each stage justices compete for influence in determining the Court's final decision and opinion.

By tradition, when the chief justice is in the majority, he assigns the Court's opinion. If the chief justice did not vote with the majority, then the senior associate justice who was in the majority either writes the opinion or assigns it to another. Chief justices may keep cases for themselves. This is in the tradition of Chief Justice Marshall, but as modified by the workload and other justices' expectations of equitable opinion assignments. In unanimous decisions and landmark cases the chief justice often self-assigns the Court's opinion.

Parity in opinion assignment now generally prevails. But the practice of immediately assigning opinions after conference as Hughes did, or within a day or two as Stone did, was gradually abandoned by the end of Vinson's tenure as chief justice. Warren and Burger adopted the practice of assigning opinions after each two-week session of oral arguments and conferences. With more assignments to make at any given time, they thus acquired greater flexibility in distributing the workload. They also enhanced their own opportunities for influencing the final outcome of cases through their assignment of opinions.

Writing opinions is the most difficult and time-consuming task of the justices. Justices differ in their styles and approaches to opinion writing. They now more or less delegate responsibility to their clerks for assisting in the preparation of opinions. Chief Justice Rehnquist, for example, usually has one of his clerks do a first draft, without bothering about style, and gives him about ten days to prepare it. Before having the clerk begin work, Rehnquist goes over the conference discussion with the clerk and explains how he thinks "an opinion can be written supporting the result reached by the majority."

Only after a justice is satisfied with an initial draft does the opinion circulate to the other justices for their reactions. The practice of circulating draft opinions is pivotal in the Court's decision-making process because all votes are tentative until the final opinion is handed down.

Final published opinions for the Court are the residue of conflicts and compromises among the justices. But they also reflect changing institutional norms. In historical perspective, changes in judicial norms have affected trends in opinion writing, the value of judicial opinions, and the Court's contributions to public law.

"The business of the Court," Justice Stewart once observed, "is to give institutional opinions for its decisions." The opinion for the Court serves to communicate an institutional decision. For much of the Court's history, there were few concurring opinions (those in which a justice agrees with the Court's ruling but not the reasons given in its opinion) and dissenting opinions (those in which justices disagree with the Court's ruling and give an alternative interpretation). It was also rare for a justice to write a separate opinion in which he or she concurred and dissented from parts of the opinion for the Court. But in the last forty years there has been a dramatic increase in the total number of opinions issued each term, as depicted in Figure 2.4. However, under Chief Justice Rehnquist's direction the Court has granted fewer cases plenary consideration and, hence, has annually handed down fewer opinions. In addition, in the 1990s the justices also cut back on writing separate dissenting opinions, except in cases deemed especially important and divisive. The dissenters, instead, joined one another in a single dissenting opinion more frequently than was the practice during the Burger Court years.

The increase in the number of opinions reflects in part that the justices are now more interested in merely the tally of votes than arriving at an institutional decision and opinion. The number of cases decided by a bare majority has thus grown in the last few decades. In addition, sometimes a bare majority for deciding a case a certain way cannot agree on an opinion for the Court's decision and the author of the opinion announcing the Court's decision must write for only a plurality.

In contrast to the author of an opinion for the Court, a justice writing separate concurring or dissenting opinions does not carry the burden of massing other justices. Dissenting opinions are more understandable and defensible. Dissenting opinions in the view of Chief Justice Charles Evans Hughes, who rarely wrote dissents, appeal "to the brooding spirit of the law, to the intelligence of a future day, when a later decision may possibly correct the error into which the dissenting judge believes the Court to have been betrayed."[1] The first Justice John M. Harlan's dissent from the doctrine of "separate but equal" in *Plessy v.*

■ CONSTITUTIONAL HISTORY

Opinion Writing, 1937–2004

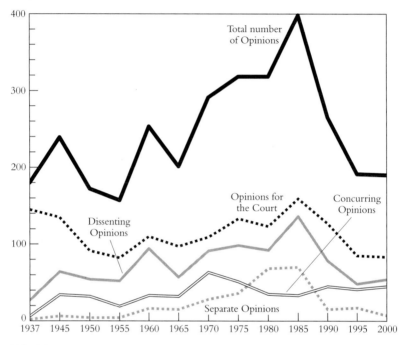

FIGURE 2.4

Source: David M. O'Brien, *Storm Center,* 7th ed. (W. W. Norton, 2005) and as updated by the author through the 2003–2004 term.

Ferguson, 163 U.S. 537 (1896) (see Vol. 2, Ch. 12), was eventually vindicated in *Brown v. Board of Education* (1954). Dissents may also appeal for more immediate legislative action: Justice James Iredell's dissent in *Chisholm v. Georgia,* 2 U.S. 419 (1793), invited the adoption of the Eleventh Amendment overturning the Court's decision; and the dissenters' arguments in *Dred Scott v. Sandford,* 60 U.S. 393 (1857) (see Vol. 2, Ch. 12), lent support to the passage of the Thirteenth, Fourteenth, and Fifteenth Amendments after the Civil War. A dissenting opinion is a way of undercutting the Court's decision and opinion. The threat of a dissent may thus be useful when trying to persuade the majority to narrow its holding or tone down the language of its opinion.

NOTE

1. Charles Evans Hughes, *The Supreme Court of the United States* (New York: Columbia University Press, 1928).

H | *Opinion Days and Communicating Decisions*

The justices announce their decisions in the courtroom, typically crowded with reporters, anxious attorneys, and curious spectators. When several decisions are to be handed down, the justices delivering the Court's opinions make their announcements in reverse order of seniority. Authors of concurring or dissenting opinions are free to give their views orally as well. By tradition there is no prior announcement as to when cases will be handed down. Most opinions are now announced in two to four minutes with justices merely stating the result in each case. In especially controversial cases, such as those concerning restrictions on abortion, justices may read portions of their opinions and, sometimes, dissents.

Justices appreciate that compliance with their decisions depends on public understanding of their opinions. And media coverage of the Court has grown in the last thirty years. On "Opinion Days," journalists now receive copies of the headnotes—prepared by the reporter of decisions—summarizing the main points of a decision. The Court has a public information office as well. The office serves primarily reporters (not members of the general public, whose inquiries are typically handled by the offices of the clerk, marshal, or curator) and provides space for a pressroom with sixteen assigned cubicles. The public information officer makes available all filings and briefs for cases on the docket, the Court's conference lists and final opinions, and speeches made by the justices.

SELECTED BIBLIOGRAPHY

Graham, Fred. *Happy Talk: Confessions of a TV Newsman.* New York: W. W. Norton, 1990.

MacKenzie, John P. *The Appearance of Justice.* New York: Scribner's, 1974.

O'Brien, David M., ed. *Judges on Judging: Views from the Bench.* Washington, D.C.: C. Q. Press, 2 ded., 2003.

Slotnick, Elliot E., and Segal, Jennifer A. *Television News and the Supreme Court.* New York: Cambridge University Press, 1998.

■ Inside the Court

Voting Alignments in the Rehnquist Court, 1986–2002 Terms

	REHNQUIST	WHITE	BLACKMUN	STEVENS	O'CONNOR	SCALIA	KENNEDY	SOUTER	THOMAS	BRENNAN	MARSHALL	GINSBURG	BREYER
Rehnquist	—	80.8	55.2	52.1	80.4	78.6	83.1	67.9	79.1	47.6	46.4	63.6	62.6
White	80.8	—	62.2	60.4	72.5	69.8	75.7	73.5	67.7	52.9	52.9		
Blackmun	55.2	62.2	—	72.0	58.4	49.1	57.6	64.8	44.4	77.4	77.0	68.2	76.3
Stevens	52.1	60.4	72.0	—	56.7	46.5	57.6	71.4	44.7	69.9	71.6	77.4	71.0
O'Connor	80.4	72.5	58.4	56.7	—	70.8	78.8	71.6	70.4	49.4	47.9	66.2	52.1
Scalia	78.6	69.8	49.1	46.5	70.8	—	75.7	59.3	87.0	47.5	45.0	54.4	65.6
Kennedy	83.1	75.7	57.6	57.6	78.8	75.7	—	70.4	73.8	53.7	51.2	66.9	52.1
Souter	67.9	73.5	64.8	71.4	71.6	59.3	70.4	—	56.0		54.6	84.5	82.1
Thomas	79.1	67.7	44.4	44.7	70.4	87.0	73.8	56.0	—			52.4	51.1
Brennan	47.6	52.9	77.4	69.9	49.4	47.5	53.7			—	95.0		
Marshall	46.4	52.9	77.0	71.6	47.9	45.0	51.2	54.6		95.0	—		
Ginsburg	63.6		68.2	77.4	66.2	54.4	66.9	84.5	52.4			—	81.5
Breyer	62.6		76.3	71.0	52.1	65.6	52.1	82.1	51.1			81.5	—

The above are average percentages. The percentages for each term are from Table 1 of the *Harvard Law Review*'s annual review of the Supreme Court's term in volumes 101–117 (1986–2003).

I | *The Impact of Supreme Court Decisions: Compliance and Implementation*

"By itself," political scientist Robert Dahl observed, "the Court is almost powerless to affect the course of national policy."[1] This is because the Court's rulings are not self-executing. Enforcement and implementation require the cooperation and coordination of all three branches of government.

Brown v. Board of Education (1954) (see Ch. 12), the public school desegregation case, dramatically altered the course of American life but also reflected the justices' awareness that their decisions are not self-executing. When striking down the "separate but equal" doctrine, which was practiced in segregated public school systems, the Warren Court waited a year after *Brown I* (1954) before issuing in *Brown II* its mandate for "all deliberate speed" in ending racial segregation in public education. The Court knew that there would be substantial public resistance to the social policy announced in *Brown I*. A rigid timetable for desegregation would have only intensified opposition. President Dwight Eisenhower refused to endorse the ruling for some time. Hence, implementation of *Brown* was deliberately slow and uneven. The Department of Justice had little role in ending school segregation before the passage of the Civil Rights Act of 1964 during Lyndon B. Johnson's presidency. For over three decades problems of implementing and achieving compliance with *Brown* persisted. Litigation by civil rights groups forced change, but it was piecemeal, costly, and modest. The judiciary alone could not achieve desegregation.

Public opinion serves to curb the Court when it threatens to go too far or too fast in its rulings. Life in the marble temple is not immune from shifts in public opinion.[2] But justices deny being directly influenced by public opinion. The Court's prestige rests on preserving the public's view that justices base their decisions on interpretations of the law, rather than on their personal policy preferences. Yet complete indifference to public opinion would be the height of judicial arrogance. In the highly controversial 1992 abortion ruling in *Planned Parenthood of Southeastern Pennsylvania v. Casey*, 505 U.S. 833 (1992) (see Vol. 2, Ch. 11), the justices engaged in an unusual debate over the influence of public opinion on the Court with the dissenters, Chief Justice Rehnquist and Justices Scalia, Thomas, and White, accusing the plurality (Justices O'Connor, Kennedy, and Souter) of bending to public opinion and following "not a principle of law . . . but the principle of Realpolitik."

Most of the Court's decisions do not attract widespread public attention. Most people find the Court remote and confusing or identify with its institutional symbols. The public perceives the Court as a temple of law rather than of politics—impartial and removed from the pressures of special partisan interests.[3] Issues such as school desegregation, school prayer, and abortion focus public attention and may mobilize public support or opposition for the Court. But those issues are also the most divisive within the country as well. Public opinion, therefore, tends to be diffuse and indirectly expressed by public officials and elected representatives.

Less concerned about public opinion than elected public officials, justices are sensitive to the attitudes of the Court's immediate constituents: the solicitor general, the attorney general and the Department of Justice, counsel for federal agencies, states' attorneys general, and the legal profession. Their responses to the Court's rulings help shape public understanding and determine the extent of compliance.

The solicitor general, attorney general, and agency counsel interpret the Court's decisions and advise the White House and agencies on compliance. Justices may find a favorable or unfavorable reception from the executive branch. The solicitor general decides which and what kinds of cases to take to the Court. In selecting cases he tries to offer the Court (or a majority) opportunities for pursuing their policy goals and those of the president.

The attorney general, cabinet heads, and agency counsel may likewise extend or thwart the Court's policies. They do so through their advisory opinions, litigation strategies, and development of agency policy and programs. The reactions of the fifty state attorneys general are no less important. Each has a pivotal role in advising governors, mayors, police chiefs, and others in his or her state. Their responses tend to reflect state and local reactions to the Court's rulings. Regional differences were evident in responses to the 1962 and 1963 school prayer decisions. In upholding separation of church and state, the Court struck down a state-composed prayer in *Engel v. Vitale*, 370 U.S. 421 (1962), and the reciting of the Lord's Prayer in public schools in *Abington School District v. Schempp*, 374 U.S. 203 (1963) (see Ch. 6). Long-standing practices of school prayer in the East and South were not to be easily relinquished. Voluntary school prayer, silent meditation, and "the objective study of the Bible and of religion" were viewed as still permissible. Where school prayer received support in state constitutions or legislation, state and local officials denied the legitimacy of the Court's decrees and refused to obey.

The justices do consider anticipated reactions of the immediate au-

The justices' private conference room. (*Photo by Franz Jantzen, Collection of the Supreme Court of the United States.*)

dience of the Court's rulings. One example is that of Chief Justice Warren's opinion in *Miranda v. Arizona*, 384 U.S. 436 (1966) (see Ch. 8), which held that police must read suspects their rights, granted them by the Fifth and Sixth Amendments, to remain silent and to consult and have the presence of an attorney during police questioning. A former attorney general in California, Chief Justice Warren knew full well that not all state attorneys general and police supported the Court's rulings on criminal procedure. He, therefore, strove to outline in *Miranda* a code for police procedures governing the interrogation of criminal suspects that police could not easily evade.

The Court's decisions have traditionally applied retroactively, permitting individuals to have retrials. In *Linkletter v. Walker* (1965) (see excerpt below), however, the Court refused to apply retroactively its controversial ruling in *Mapp v. Ohio*, 367 U.S. 643 (1961) (see Ch. 7), which extended to the states the Fourth Amendment exclusionary rule, forbidding the use at trial of evidence obtained in violation of the requirements for a proper search and seizure. The Court subsequently developed what became known as its *ambulatory-retroactive doctrine* in other areas of criminal law as well. "That doctrine," Justice Harlan explained, "was the product of the Court's disquietude with the impacts of its fast-moving pace in constitutional innovation in the criminal field." But he

■ CONSTITUTIONAL HISTORY

The Southern Manifesto: A Declaration of Constitutional Principles

Following the Supreme Court's landmark school desegregation rulings in *Brown v. Board of Education* (1954 and 1955) (see Ch. 12), 101 U.S. senators and representatives issued The Southern Manifesto, denouncing the decision and the Court for running afoul of established constitutional principles. The excerpt reprinted here comes from 102 *Congressional Record* 4515 (1956).

The Founding Fathers gave us a Constitution of checks and balances because they realized the inescapable lesson of history that no man or group of men can be safely entrusted with unlimited power. They framed this Constitution with its provisions for change by amendment in order to secure the fundamentals of government against the dangers of temporary popular passion or the personal predilections of public officeholders.

We regard the decision of the Supreme Court in the school cases as a clear abuse of judicial power. It climaxes a trend in the federal judiciary undertaking to legislate, in derogation of the authority of Congress, and to encroach upon the reserved rights of the States and the people.

The original Constitution does not mention education. Neither does the 14th amendment nor any other amendment. The debates preceding the submission of the 14th amendment clearly show that there was no intent that it should affect the system of education maintained by the States.

The very Congress which proposed the amendment subsequently provided for segregated schools in the District of Columbia.

When the amendment was adopted in 1868, there were 37 States of the Union. Every one of the 26 States that had any substantial racial differences among its people, either approved the operation of segregated schools already in existence or subsequently established such schools by action of the same law-making body which considered the 14th amendment. . . .

This interpretation [the doctrine of "separate but equal"], restated time and again, became a part of the life of the people of many of the States and confirmed their habits, customs, traditions, and way of life. It is founded on elementary humanity and common sense, for parents should not be deprived by Government of the right to direct the lives and education of their own children.

Though there has been no constitutional amendment or act of Congress changing this established legal principle almost a century old, the Supreme Court of the United States, with no legal basis for such action, undertook to exercise their naked judicial power and substituted their personal political and social ideas for the established law of the land.

This unwarranted exercise of power by the Court, contrary to the Constitution, is creating chaos and confusion in the States principally affected. It is destroying the amicable relations between the white and Negro races that have been created through 90 years of patient effort by the good people of both races. It has planted hatred and suspicion where there has been heretofore friendship and understanding.

Without regard to the consent of the governed, outside agitators are threatening immediate and revolutionary changes in our public-school system. If done, this is certain to destroy the system of public education in some of the States.

With the gravest concern for the explosive and dangerous condition created by this decision and inflamed by outside meddlers:

We reaffirm our reliance on the Constitution as the fundamental law of the land.

We decry the Supreme Court's encroachments on rights reserved to the States and to the people, contrary to established law, and to the Constitution.

We commend the motives of those States which have declared the intention to resist forced integration by any lawful means.

We appeal to the States and people who are not directly affected by these decisions to consider the constitutional principles involved against the time when they too, on issues vital to them, may be the victims of judicial encroachment.

Even though we constitute a minority in the present Congress, we have full faith that a majority of the American people believe in the dual system of government which has enabled us to achieve our greatness and will in time demand that the reserved rights of the States and of the people be made secure against judicial usurpation.

We pledge ourselves to use all lawful means to bring about a reversal of this decision which is contrary to the Constitution and to prevent the use of force in its implementation.

In this trying period, as we all seek to right this wrong, we appeal to our people not to be provoked by the agitators and troublemakers invading our States and to scrupulously refrain from disorder and lawless acts.

---

also objected that the doctrine merely rationalizes the Court's freedom "to act, in effect, like a legislature, making its new constitutional rules wholly or partially retroactive or only prospective as it deems wise."[4] In *Griffith v. Kentucky* (1987) (see excerpt below), Justice Blackmun further explains the Court's application of the doctrine of ambulatory retroactivity.

The Court directly and indirectly encourages interest groups and the government to litigate issues of public policy. The Court selects and decides "only those cases which present questions whose resolution will have immediate importance far beyond the particular facts and parties involved." Attorneys whose cases are accepted by the Court, Chief Justice Fred Vinson emphasized, "are, in a sense, prosecuting or defending class actions; that you represent your clients, but [more crucially] tremendously important principles, upon which are based the plans, hopes and aspirations of a great many people throughout the country."[5]

Interest groups from the entire political spectrum look to the Court to decide issues of public policy: from business organizations and corporations in the late nineteenth century to the Jehovah's Witnesses in the 1930s, to the ACLU and NAACP in the 1950s and 1960s, and to "liberal" women's rights groups and consumer and environmental protection groups—like the National Organization of Women (NOW), Common Cause, "Nader's Raiders," the Sierra Club, the Environmental Defense Fund, and the Natural Resources Defense Council—as well as to a growing number of conservative "public interest" law firms like the Pacific Legal Foundation, the Mountain States Legal Foundation, and the Washington Legal Foundation. "This is government by lawsuit," Justice Robert Jackson declared; "these constitutional lawsuits are the stuff of power politics in America."[6]

Interest group activities and public interest law firms offer a number of advantages for litigating policy disputes. They command greater financial resources than the average individual. A single suit may settle a large number of claims, and the issues are not as likely to be compromised or settled out of court. Interest group law firms typically specialize in particular kinds of lawsuits. They are, therefore, able to litigate more skillfully and over a longer period of time. There are also tactical opportunities. Litigants may be chosen to bring test cases, and those cases may be coordinated with other litigation and the activities of other organizations.

The Court is an instrument of political power, but the justices remain dependent on the attitudes and actions of their immediate constitutents, elected officials, and the dynamics of pressure-group politics and public opinion. Implementation and compliance largely depend on lower courts, Congress, and the president.

Compliance with the Court's decisions by lower courts is invariably uneven. They may extend or limit decisions in anticipation of later rulings by the high Court. Following the watershed ruling on privacy in *Griswold v. Connecticut*, 381 U.S. 479 (1965) (see Ch. 4), lower courts interpreted the newfound constitutional right of privacy to strike down a wide range of laws, from those limiting the length of male employees'

and students' hair to ones forbidding certain sexual acts between consenting adults and the use of marijuana, to laws requiring psychological
tests of applicants for government jobs, and to laws governing access to
financial and medical records. The Court reversed or would not approve the extension of the right of privacy in many of these areas.

A simple model of compliance is not very useful: Decisions handed
down by the Court are not necessarily or readily applied by lower
courts. Ambiguity and plurality or five-to-four decisions invite lower
courts to pursue their own policy goals. Crucial language in an opinion
may be treated as *dicta*. Differences between the facts on which the
Court ruled and the circumstances of a case at hand may be emphasized so as to distinguish or reach the opposite result of the Court's decision. Lower courts may thus effectively delay implementation and
compliance.

Open defiance is infrequent but not unprecedented. *Jaffree v. Board
of School Commissioners* (1983) (see excerpt below) is extreme but illustrative of lower court defiance. There, a federal district court judge in
Alabama directly challenged the legitimacy of the Court in its public
school prayer rulings. A majority of the Court rebuffed the lower court
when it decided an appeal of the ruling and struck down the "moment
of silence" law in *Wallace v. Jaffree*, 472 U.S. 38 (1985) (see Ch. 6).

As the Burger and Rehnquist Courts have moved in more conservative directions in areas of civil rights and liberties, state supreme
courts have increasingly refused to follow the Court's construction of
federal law and recognized new rights or extended protection on the
basis of state constitutions to claims that the Supreme Court has declined to embrace (see Vol. 1, Ch. 7). In *Bowers v. Hardwick*, 478 U.S. 186
(1986), for instance, a bare majority of the Court refused to extend the
constitutional right of privacy in a challenge to Georgia's law punishing
sodomy. But, in *Commonwealth of Kentucky v. Wasson*, 842 S.W.2d 487
(1992) (see excerpt below), Kentucky's supreme court expressly declined to follow *Bowers* when striking down its state law against homosexual sodomy. See also THE DEVELOPMENT OF LAW: Other
Recent State Supreme Court Decisions Declining to Follow the U.S.
Supreme Court's Rulings (in this section).

Major confrontations between Congress and the Court have occurred a number of times. With the election of Thomas Jefferson in
1800, Republicans gained control of Congress. Defeated President John
Adams and the outgoing Federalists in Congress passed the Judiciary
Act of 1801, creating new circuit court judgeships and stipulating that
when the next vacancy on the Court occurred it should go unfilled.
That attempt to maintain influence in the judiciary was quickly countered. In 1802, the Republican Congress repealed the Act of 1801,

abolishing the judgeships and returning the number of justices to six. Congress also postponed the Court's next term to preclude it from immediately hearing a challenge, in *Stuart v. Laird*, 5 U.S. 299 (1803), to its repealing legislation. When the Court decided *Stuart*, it upheld Congress's power to repeal the Judiciary Act of 1801. The Jeffersonian-Republicans then impeached Justice Samuel Chase for expounding federalist doctrine. Although the Senate acquitted him, it would not confirm nominees for federal judgeships unless they were Republicans.

The Marshall Court approved the expansion of national governmental power, but in response Congress in the 1820s and 1830s threatened to remove the Court's jurisdiction over disputes involving states' rights. After the Civil War, Congress succeeded in repealing the Court's jurisdiction over certain denials of writs of *habeas corpus*—orders commanding that a prisoner be brought before a judge and cause shown for his imprisonment. In *Ex parte McCardle*, 74 U.S. 506 (1869), the Court upheld the repeal of its jurisdiction and thus avoided deciding a controversial case attacking the constitutionality of Reconstruction legislation.

At the turn of the twentieth century, Progressives in Congress unsuccessfully sought to pressure the Court—dominated at the time by advocates of laissez-faire social and economic policy. They proposed requiring a two-thirds vote by the justices when striking down federal statutes and permitting Congress to overrule the Court's decisions by a two-thirds majority. The confrontation escalated with the Court's invalidation of President Franklin D. Roosevelt's early New Deal program passed by Congress in the 1930s. FDR retaliated by attempting to pack the Court by increasing the number of justices. Even though it was upset by the Court's invalidation of the New Deal, Congress would not accept FDR's Court-packing plan. It did, though, pass legislation allowing justices to retire, after ten years of service at age seventy, with full rather than half salary. Congress thus made retirement more financially attractive and gave FDR opportunities to appoint justices who shared his political philosophy.

Congress may pressure the Court in a number of ways. The Senate may try to influence judicial appointments, and justices may be impeached. More often, institutional and jurisdictional changes are used as weapons against the Court. Congress has tried to pressure the Court when setting its terms and size and when authorizing appropriations for salaries, law clerks, secretaries, and office technology. Only once, in 1802 when repealing the Judiciary Act of 1801 and abolishing a session for a year, did Congress actually set the Court's term to delay and influence a particular decision.

The size of the Court is not preordained, and changes generally reflect attempts to control the Court. The Jeffersonian-Republicans' quick repeal of the act passed by the Federalists in 1801 reducing the number of justices was the first of several attempts to influence the Court. Presidents James Madison, James Monroe, and John Adams all claimed that the country's geographical expansion warranted enlarging the size of the Court. But Congress refused to do so until the last day of Andrew Jackson's term in 1837. During the Civil War, the number of justices increased to ten ostensibly due to the creation of a tenth circuit in the West. This gave Abraham Lincoln his fourth appointment and a chance to secure a pro-Union majority on the bench. Antagonism toward President Andrew Johnson's Reconstruction policies following the Civil War led to a reduction from ten to seven justices. After General Ulysses S. Grant was elected president, Congress again authorized nine justices—the number that has prevailed. In the nineteenth century at least, Congress rather successfully denied presidents additional appointments to preserve the Court's policies and increased the number of justices as a way to change the ideological composition of the Court.

Although Article III of the Constitution forbids reducing justices' salaries, Congress may withhold salary increases as punishment, especially in times of high inflation. More direct attacks are possible. Under Article III, Congress is authorized "to make exceptions" to the appellate jurisdiction of the Court. That authorization has been viewed as a way of denying the Court review of certain kinds of cases. But Congress succeeded only once, with the 1868 repeal of jurisdiction over writs of *habeas corpus*, which the Court upheld in *Ex parte McCardle*, 7 Wall. (74 U.S.) 506 (1869).

Court-curbing legislation is not a very viable weapon. Rather than limiting judicial review, Congress has given the Court the power to set its own agenda and decide major issues of public law and policy—precisely the kinds of issues that Congress then seeks to deny the Court review. The Court has also suggested that it would not approve repeals of its jurisdiction that are merely attempts to dictate how particular kinds of cases should be decided.[7] Most proposals to curb the Court, of course, are simply that. During the McCarthy era, for instance, Republican Senator William Jenner spearheaded a drive to forbid review of cases challenging legislative committees investigating un-American activities. Another unsuccessful attempt was made in 1968 to amend the Omnibus Crime Control and Safe Streets Act so as to prevent the Court from reviewing state criminal cases raising *Miranda* issues.

Congress has had somewhat greater success in reversing the Court by constitutional amendment. Congress must pass a constitutional amendment that three-fourths of the states must then ratify. The process is cumbersome, and thousands of amendments to overrule the Court have failed. But four decisions have been overturned by constitutional amendment. *Chisholm v. Georgia*, 2 U.S. 419 (1793), holding that citizens of one state could sue in federal courts another state, was reversed by the Eleventh Amendment, guaranteeing sovereign immunity for states from suits by citizens of another state. The Thirteenth and Fourteenth Amendments, abolishing slavery and making blacks citizens of the United States, technically overturned the ruling in *Dred Scott v. Sanford* (1857) that blacks were not persons under the Constitution. With the ratification in 1913 of the Sixteenth Amendment, Congress reversed *Pollock v. Farmers' Loan and Trust Company*, 157 U.S. 429 (1895), which had invalidated a federal income tax. In 1970 an amendment to the Voting Rights Act of 1965 lowered the voting age to eighteen years for all elections. Although signing the act into law, President Richard Nixon had his attorney general challenge the validity of lowering the voting age by simple legislation, rather than by constitutional amendment. Within six months in *Oregon v. Mitchell*, 400 U.S. 112 (1970), a bare majority of the Court held that Congress exceeded its power by lowering the voting age for state and local elections. Less than a year later the Twenty-sixth Amendment was ratified extending the franchise to eighteen-year-olds in all elections.

More successful than Court curbing and amending the Constitution are congressional enactments and rewriting of legislation in response to the Court's rulings. Congressional reversals usually relate to both statutory and nonstatutory matters involving administrative policies.

Congress cannot overturn the Court's interpretations of the Constitution by mere legislation, as the Court underscored in *City of Boerne v. Flores*, 521 U.S. 507 (1997) (excerpted in Ch. 6). But Congress can enhance or thwart compliance with the Court's rulings. After the Warren Court's landmark decision in *Gideon v. Wainwright*, 372 U.S. 335 (1963) (see Ch. 9), that indigents have a right to counsel, Congress provided attorneys for indigents charged with federal offenses. By contrast, in the Crime Control and Safe Streets Act of 1968, Congress permitted federal courts to use evidence obtained from suspects who had not been read their *Miranda* rights, if their testimony appeared voluntary based on the "totality of the circumstances" surrounding their interrogation. Congress thus attempted to return to a pre-*Miranda* standard for police questioning of criminal suspects.

Congress indubitably has the power to delay and undercut implementation of the Court's rulings. On major issues of public policy Congress is likely to prevail or, at least, temper the impact of the Court's rulings. But the Court forges public policy not only when invalidating federal legislation. No less importantly, the Court makes policy by overturning state and local laws and practices. The continuing controversies over decisions striking down state laws on school desegregation, school prayer, and abortion are a measure of the Court's influence on American life.

Charged with the responsibility of taking "care that the laws be faithfully executed," the president is the chief executive officer under the Constitution. As the only nationally elected public official, the president represents the views of the dominant national political coalition. A president's obligation to faithfully execute the laws, including decisions of the Court, thus may collide with his own perceived electoral mandate.

The Court has often been the focus of presidential campaigns and power struggles. But presidents rarely openly defy particular decisions by the Court. Presidential defiance is, perhaps, symbolized by the famous remark attributed to Andrew Jackson: "John Marshall has made his decision, now let him enforce it." Jackson's refusal to enforce the decision in *Worcester v. Georgia*, 31 U.S. 515 (1832), which denied state courts jurisdiction over crimes committed on Indian lands, in fact simply left enforcement problems up to the courts and legislatures. During the Civil War however, Lincoln ordered his military commanders to refuse to obey writs of *habeas corpus* issued by Chief Justice Taney.

In major confrontations, presidents generally yield to the Court. Richard Nixon complied with the ruling in *New York Times Co. v. United States*, 403 U.S. 713 (1971) (see Vol. 1, Ch. 4), which struck down, as a prior restraint on freedom of the press, an injunction against the publication of the Pentagon Papers—a top secret report detailing the history of America's involvement in Vietnam. Then, during the Watergate scandal in 1974, Nixon submitted to the Court's decision in *United States v. Nixon*, 418 U.S. 683 (1974) (see Vol. 1, Ch. 4) ordering the release of White House tape recordings pertinent to the trial of his former attorney general John Mitchell and other presidential aides for conspiracy and obstruction of justice.

Although seldom directly defying the Court, in the short and long run presidents may undercut Supreme Court policymaking. By giving contradictory directives to federal agencies and assigning low priority for enforcement by the Department of Justice, presidents may limit the Court's decisions. Presidents may also make broad moral appeals in response to the Court's rulings, and those appeals may transcend their limited time in office. The Court put school desegregation and abortion on the national agenda. But President John F. Kennedy's appeal for civil rights captivated a generation and encouraged public acceptance of the Court's rulings. Similarly, President Ronald Reagan's opposition to abortion focused attention on "traditional family values" and served to legitimate resistance to the Court's decisions.

Presidential influence over the Court in the long run remains contingent on appointments to the Court. Vacancies occur on the average of one every twenty-two months. Four presidents—including Jimmy Carter—had no opportunity to appoint members of the Court. There is no guarantee how a justice will vote or whether that vote will prove sufficient in limiting or reversing past rulings with which a president disagrees. But through their appointments presidents may leave their mark on Supreme Court policymaking and possibly align the Court and the country or precipitate later confrontations.

For much of the Court's history, the work of the justices has not involved major issues of public policy. In most areas of public law and policy, the fact that the Court decides an issue is more important than what it decides. Relatively few of the major issues of public policy that arise in government reach the Court. When the Court does decide major questions of public policy, its rulings decide only the instant case and not the larger surrounding political controversies. Major confrontations in constitutional politics, like those over school desegregation and abortion, are determined as much by what is possible in a system of free government and pluralistic society as by what the Court says about the meaning of the Constitution. And on those controversial issues of public policy, constitutional law frames the political debate in the ongoing dialogue between the Court and the country. The Court's rulings and interpretation of the Constitution rest, in Chief Justice Edward White's words, "solely upon the approval of a free people."[8]

Notes

1. Robert Dahl, "Decision-Making in a Democracy: The Supreme Court as a National Policy-Maker," 6 *Journal of Public Law* 293 (1957).

2. See Richard Funston, "The Supreme Court and Critical Elections," 69 *American Political Science Review* 795 (1975); Jonathan Casper, "The Supreme Court and National Policymaking," 70 *American Political Science Review* 5066 (1976); William Mishler and Reginald Sheehan, "The Supreme Court as a Countermajoritarian Institution?" 87 *American Political Science Review* 87 (1993); and Thomas Marshall, *Public Opinion and the Supreme Court* (New York: Longman, 1989).

3. See, for example, Walter Murphy, J. Tananhaus, and D. Kastner, *Public Evaluations of Constitutional Courts* (Beverly Hills, CA: Sage, 1973).

4. *Williams v. United States*, 401 U.S. 675 (1971).

5. Fred Vinson, speech given before the American Bar Association, Sept. 7, 1949, reprinted in 69 S.Ct. vi (1949).

6. Robert Jackson, *The Struggle for Judicial Supremacy* (New York: Knopf, 1951), 287.

7. *United States v. Klein*, 80 U.S. 128 (1872).

8. Edward White, "The Supreme Court of the United States," 7 *American Bar Association Journal* 341 (1921).

Selected Bibliography

Abraham, Henry J. *The Judicial Process*, 7th ed. New York: Oxford University Press, 1998.

Barnes, Jeb. *Overruled? Legislative Overrides, Pluralism, and Contemporary Court-Congress Relations*. Pab Alto, CA: Stanford University Press, 2004.

Canon, Bradley, and Johnson, Charles. *Judicial Policies: Implementation and Impact*, 2d ed. Washington, DC: CQ Press, 1999.

Cardozo, Benjamin. *The Nature of the Judicial Process*. New Haven, CT: Yale University Press, 1921.

Cooper, Phillip. *Hard Judicial Choices*. New York: Oxford University Press, 1988.

Epstein, Lee, and Kobylka, Joseph. *The Supreme Court & Legal Change*. Chapel Hill: University of North Carolina Press, 1992.

Fisher, Louis, and Devins, Neal. *Political Dynamics of Constitutional Law*. 3d. ed. St. Paul, MN, 2001.

Friedman, Leon, and Israel, Fred. *The Justices of the United States Supreme Court 1789–1978: Their Lives and Major Opinions*, 5 vols. New York: Chelsea House, 1980.

Friesen, Jennifer. *State Constitutional Law*. New York: Matthew Bender, 1993.

Gates, John. *The Supreme Court and Partisan Realignment*. Boulder, CO: Westview, 1992.

Hall, Kermit, ed. *The Oxford Companion to the Supreme Court*. New York: Oxford University Press, 1992.

Lawrence, Susan. *The Poor in Court*. Princeton, NJ: Princeton University Press, 1990.

Marshall, Thomas. *Public Opinion and the Supreme Court*. Boston: Unwin Hyman, 1989.

McGuire, Kevin. *The Supreme Court Bar*. Charlottesville: University Press of Virginia, 1993.

Murphy, Walter. *Elements of Judicial Strategy*. Chicago: University of Chicago Press, 1964.

O'Brien, David M. *Storm Center: The Supreme Court in American Politics*, 7th ed. New York: W. W. Norton, 2005.

O'Connor, Karen, and Epstein, Lee. *Woman's Organizations' Use of the Courts*. Lexington, MA: Lexington Books, 1980.

Pacelle, Richard. *The Transformation of the Supreme Court's Agenda*. Boulder, CO: Westview, 1991.

Pickerill, J. Mitchell. *Constitutional Deliberation in Congress*. Durham: Duke University Press, 2004.

Rosenberg, Gerald. *The Hollow Hope*. Chicago: University of Chicago Press, 1991.

Segal, Jeffrey, and Spaeth, Harold. *The Supreme Court and the Attitudinal Model*. 2d ed. Cambridge, MA: Cambridge University Press, 2002.

Supreme Court Historical Society. *Yearbook*. Washington, DC: SCHS, 1976–present.

Linkletter v. Walker

381 U.S. 618, 85 S.Ct. 1731 (1965)

Victor Linkletter was tried and convicted in state court on evidence illegally obtained by police prior to *Mapp v. Ohio*, 367 U.S. 643 (1961) (see Ch. 7), which barred states from using illegally obtained evidence at trial under the Fourth Amendment's exclusionary rule. Linkletter contended that *Mapp* should apply retroactively and he should be retried with the illegally obtained evidence excluded. A federal district court disagreed and after a court of appeals affirmed that ruling, Linkletter appealed to the Supreme Court.

The Court's decision was seven to two; with the majority's opinion announced by Justice Clark. The dissent was by Justice Black, who was joined by Justice Douglas.

☐ *Justice CLARK delivered the opinion of the Court.*

In *Mapp v. Ohio*, 367 U.S. 643 (1961), we held that the exclusion of evidence seized in violation of the search and seizure provisions of the Fourth Amendment was required of the States by the Due Process Clause of the Fourteenth Amendment. In so doing we overruled *Wolf v. People of State of Colorado*, 338 U.S. 25 (1949), to the extent that it failed to apply the exclusionary rule to the States. This case presents the question of whether this requirement operates retrospectively upon cases finally decided in the period prior to *Mapp*. The Court of Appeals for the Fifth Circuit held that it did not, and we granted *certiorari* in order to settle what has become a most troublesome question in the administration of justice. We agree with the Court of Appeals. . . .

At common law there was no authority for the proposition that judicial decisions made law only for the future. Blackstone stated the rule that the duty of the court was not to "pronounce a new law, but to maintain and expound the old one." 1 Blackstone, Commentaries 69 (15th ed. 1809). . . .

In the case of the overruled decision, *Wolf v. People of State of Colorado*, supra, here, it was thought to be only a failure at true discovery and was consequently never the law; while the overruling one, *Mapp*, was not "new law but an application of what is, and theretofore had been, the true law." . . .

On the other hand, [the late-nineteenth century legal philosopher John] Austin maintained that judges do in fact do something more than discover law; they make it interstitially by filling in with judicial interpretation the vague, indefinite, or generic statutory or common-law terms that alone are but the empty crevices of the law. Implicit in such an approach is the admission when a case is overruled that the earlier decision was wrongly decided. However, rather than being erased by the later overruling decision it is considered as an existing juridical fact until overruled, and intermediate cases finally decided under it are not to be disturbed.

The Blackstonian view ruled English jurisprudence and cast its shadow over our own. . . . However, some legal philosophers continued to insist that such a rule was out of tune with actuality largely because judicial repeal oft-time did "work hardship to those who [had] trusted to its existence." CAR-DOZO, Address to the N.Y. Bar Assn. (1932). . . .

It is true that heretofore, without discussion, we have applied new constitutional rules to cases finalized before the promulgation of the rule. Petitioner contends that our method of resolving those prior cases demonstrates that an absolute rule of retroaction prevails in the area of constitutional adjudication. However, we believe that the Constitution neither prohibits nor requires retrospective effect. As Justice CARDOZO said, "We think the Federal Constitution has no voice upon the subject." . . .

Once the premise is accepted that we are neither required to apply, nor prohibited from applying, a decision retrospectively, we must then weigh the merits and demerits in each case by looking to the prior history of the rule in question, its purpose and effect, and whether retrospective operation will further or retard its operation. We believe that this approach is particularly correct with reference to the Fourth Amendment's prohibitions as to unreasonable searches and seizures. Rather than "disparaging" the Amendment we but apply the wisdom of Justice HOLMES that "[t]he life of the law has not been logic: it has been experience." Holmes, The Common Law 5 (Howe ed. 1963).

Since *Weeks v. United States*, 232 U.S. 383 (1914) this Court has adhered to the rule that evidence seized by federal officers in violation of the Fourth Amendment is not admissible at trial in a federal court. In 1949 in *Wolf v. People of State of Colorado*, supra, the Court decided that while the right to privacy—"the core of the Fourth Amendment"—was such a basic right as to be implicit in "the concept of ordered liberty" and thus enforceable against the States through the Fourteenth Amendment, "the ways of enforcing such a basic right raise questions of a different order. How such arbitrary conduct should be checked, what remedies against it should be afforded, the means by which the right should be made effective, are all questions that are not to be so dogmatically answered as to preclude the varying solutions which spring from an allowable range of judgment on issues not susceptible of quantitative solution."

Mapp was announced in 1961. The Court in considering "the current validity of the factual grounds upon which Wolf was based" pointed out that prior to *Wolf* "almost two-thirds of the States were opposed to the use of the exclusionary rule, now, despite the *Wolf* case, more than half of those since passing upon it . . . have wholly or partly adopted or adhered to the *Weeks* rule." . . .

We believe that the existence of the *Wolf* doctrine prior to *Mapp* is "an operative fact and may have consequences which cannot justly be ignored. The past cannot always be erased by a new judicial declaration." The thousands of cases that were finally decided on *Wolf* cannot be obliterated. The "particular conduct, private and official," must be considered. Here "prior determinations deemed to have finality and acted upon accordingly" have "become vested." And finally, "public policy in the light of the nature both of the [*Wolf* doctrine] and of its previous application" must be given its proper weight. In short, we must look to the purpose of the *Mapp* rule; the reliance placed upon the *Wolf* doctrine; and the effect on the administration of justice of a retrospective application of *Mapp*.

It is clear that the *Wolf* Court, once it had found the Fourth Amendment's unreasonable Search and Seizure Clause applicable to the States through the Due Process Clause of the Fourteenth Amendment, turned its attention to whether the exclusionary rule was included within the command of the Fourth Amendment. This was decided in the negative. It is clear that based upon the factual considerations heretofore discussed the *Wolf* Court then concluded that it was not necessary to the enforcement of the Fourth Amendment for the exclusionary rule to be extended to the States as a requirement of due process. *Mapp* had as its prime purpose the enforcement of the Fourth Amendment through the inclusion of the exclusionary rule within its rights. This, it was found, was the only effective deterrent to lawless police action. Indeed, all of the cases since *Wolf* requiring the exclusion of illegal evidence have been based on the necessity for an effective deterrent to illegal police action. We cannot say that this purpose would be advanced by making the rule retrospective. The misconduct of the police prior to *Mapp* has already occurred and will not be corrected by releasing the prisoners involved. Nor would it add harmony to the delicate state-federal relationship of which we have spoken as part and parcel of the purpose of *Mapp*. Finally, the ruptured privacy of the victims' homes and effects cannot be restored. Reparation comes too late. . . .

Finally, there are interests in the administration of justice and the integrity of the judicial process to consider. To make the rule of *Mapp* retrospective would tax the administration of justice to the utmost. Hearings would have to be held on the excludability of evidence long since destroyed, misplaced or deteriorated. If it is excluded, the witnesses available at the time of the original trial will not be available or if located their memory will be dimmed. To thus legitimate such an extraordinary procedural weapon that has no bearing on guilt would seriously disrupt the administration of justice. . . .

All that we decide today is that though the error complained of might be fundamental it is not of the nature requiring us to overturn all final convictions based upon it. After full consideration of all the factors we are not able to say that the *Mapp* rule requires retrospective application.

Affirmed.

    □ *Justice BLACK, with whom Justice DOUGLAS joins, dissenting.*

The Court offers no defense based on any known principle of justice for discriminating among defendants who were similarly convicted by use of evidence unconstitutionally seized. It certainly cannot do so as between Linkletter and Miss Mapp. The crime with which she was charged took place more than a year before his, yet the decision today seems to rest on the fanciful concept that the Fourth Amendment protected her 1957 offense against conviction by use of unconstitutional evidence but denied its protection to Linkletter for his 1958 offense. In making this ruling the Court assumes for itself the virtue of acting in harmony with a comment of Justice HOLMES that "[t]he life of the law has not been logic: it has been experience." Justice HOLMES was not there talking about the Constitution; he was talking about the evolving judge-made law of England and of some of our States whose judges are allowed to follow in the common law tradition. It should be remembered in this connection that no member of this Court has ever more seriously criticized it than did Justice HOLMES for reading its own predilections into the "vague contours" of the Due Process Clause. But quite apart from that, there is no experience of the past that justifies a new Court-made rule to perpetrate a grossly invidious and unfair discrimination against Linkletter simply because he happened to be prosecuted in a State that was evidently well up with its criminal court docket. If this discrimination can be excused at all it is not because of experience but because of logic—sterile and formal at that—not, according to Justice HOLMES, the most dependable guide in lawmaking. . . .

As the Court concedes, this is the first instance on record where this Court, having jurisdiction, has ever refused to give a previously convicted defendant the benefit of a new and more expansive Bill of Rights interpretation. I am at a loss to understand why those who suffer from the use of evidence secured by a search and seizure in violation of the Fourth Amendment should be treated differently from those who have been denied other guarantees of the Bill of Rights. . . .

One reason—perhaps a basic one—put forward by the Court for its refusal to give Linkletter the benefit of the search and seizure exclusionary rule is the repeated statement that the purpose of that rule is to deter sheriffs, policemen, and other law officers from making unlawful searches and seizures. The inference I gather from these repeated statements is that the rule is not a right or privilege accorded to defendants charged with crime but is a sort of punishment against officers in order to keep them from depriving people of their constitutional rights. In passing I would say that if that is the sole purpose, reason, object and effect of the rule, the Court's action in adopting it sounds more like law making than construing the Constitution. . . . [T]he undoubted implication of today's opinion that the rule is not a safeguard for defendants but is a mere punishing rod to be applied to law enforcement officers is a rather startling departure from many past opinions, and even from *Mapp* itself. *Mapp* quoted from the Court's earlier opinion in *Weeks v. United States*, supra, certainly not with disapproval, saying that the Court "in that case clearly stated that use of the seized evidence involved 'a denial of the constitutional rights of the accused.' " I have read and reread the *Mapp* opinion but have been unable to find one word in it to indicate that the exclusionary search and seizure rule should be limited on the basis that it was intended to do nothing in the world except to deter officers of the law. . . .

The Court says that the exclusionary rule's purpose of preventing law enforcement officers from making lawless searches and seizures "will not at this late date be served by the wholesale release of the guilty victims." It has not been the usual thing to cut down trial protections guaranteed by the Constitution on the basis that some guilty persons might escape. There is probably no one of the rights in the Bill of Rights that does not make it more difficult to convict defendants. But all of them are based on the premise, I suppose, that the Bill of Rights' safeguards should be faithfully enforced by the court without regard to a particular judge's judgment as to whether more people could be convicted by a refusal of courts to enforce the safeguards. Such has heretofore been accepted as a general maxim. . . .

The plain facts here are that the Court's opinion cuts off many defendants who are now in jail from any hope of relief from unconstitutional convictions . . . No State should be considered to have a vested interest in keeping prisoners in jail who were convicted because of lawless conduct by the State's officials. Careful analysis of the Court's opinion shows that it rests on the premise that a State's assumed interest in sustaining convictions obtained under the old, repudiated rule outweighs the interests both of that State and of the individuals convicted in having wrongful convictions set aside. It certainly offends my sense of justice to say that a State holding in jail people who were convicted by unconstitutional methods has a vested interest in keeping them there that outweighs the right of persons adjudged guilty of crime to challenge their unconstitutional convictions at any time. . . .

Griffith v. Kentucky

479 U.S. 314, 107 S.Ct. 708 (1987)

Justice Blackmun's opinion for the Court discusses the issues presented here.

The Court's decision was six to three, with the majority's opinion announced by Justice Blackmun. Justice Powell concurred. There were dissents by Chief Justice Rehnquist and Justice White, who were joined by Justice O'Connor.

☐ *Justice BLACKMUN delivered the opinion of the Court.*

Twenty-one years ago, this Court adopted a three-pronged analysis for claims of retroactivity of new constitutional rules of criminal procedure. See *Linkletter v. Walker*, 381 U.S. 618 (1965). In *Linkletter*, the Court held that *Mapp v. Ohio* [367 U.S. 643 (1961)], which extended the Fourth Amendment exclusionary rule to the States, would not be applied retroactively to a state conviction that had become final before *Mapp* was decided. The Court explained that "the Constitution neither prohibits nor requires retrospective effect" of a new constitutional rule, and that a determination of retroactivity must depend on "weigh[ing] the merits and demerits in each case." The Court's decision not to apply *Mapp* retroactively was based on "the purpose of the *Mapp* rule; the reliance placed upon the [previous] doctrine; and the effect on the administration of justice of a retrospective application of *Mapp*." . . .

Shortly after the decision in *Linkletter*, the Court held that the three-pronged analysis applied both to convictions that were final and to convictions pending on direct review. . . .

In *United States v. Johnson*, 457 U.S. 537 (1982), however, the Court shifted course. In that case, we reviewed at some length the history of the Court's decisions in the area of retroactivity and concluded, in the words of Justice HARLAN: " '[R]etroactivity' must be rethought." Specifically, we concluded that the retroactivity analysis for convictions that have become final must be different from the analysis for convictions that are not final at the time the new decision is issued. . . . The rationale for distinguishing between cases that have become final and those that have not, and for applying new rules retroactively to cases in the latter category, was explained at length by Justice HARLAN in *Desist v. United States*, 394 U.S. [244 (1969)] (dissenting opinion), and in *Mackey v. United States*, 401 U.S. 667 (1971) (opinion concurring in judgments). In *United States v. Johnson*, we embraced to a significant extent the comprehensive analysis presented by Justice HARLAN in those opinions.

In Justice HARLAN's view, and now in ours, failure to apply a newly declared constitutional rule to criminal cases pending on direct review violates basic norms of constitutional adjudication. First, it is a settled principle that this Court adjudicates only "cases" and "controversies." See U.S. Const., Art. III, § 2. Unlike a legislature, we do not promulgate new rules of constitutional criminal procedure on a broad basis. Rather, the nature of judicial review requires that we adjudicate specific cases, and each case usually becomes the vehicle for announcement of a new rule. But after we have decided a new rule in the case selected, the integrity of judicial review requires that we apply that rule to all similar cases pending on direct review. . . .

As a practical matter, of course, we cannot hear each case pending on direct review and apply the new rule. But we fulfill our judicial responsibility by instructing the lower courts to apply the new rule retroactively to cases not yet final. . . .

Second, selective application of new rules violates the principle of treating similarly situated defendants the same. . . .

In *United States v. Johnson*, our acceptance of Justice HARLAN's views led to the holding that "subject to [certain exceptions], a decision of this Court construing the Fourth Amendment is to be applied retroactively to all convictions that were not yet final at the time the decision was rendered." The exceptions to which we referred related to three categories in which we concluded that existing precedent established threshold tests for the retroactivity analysis. In two of these categories, the new rule already was retroactively applied: (1) when a decision of this Court did nothing more than apply settled precedent to different factual situations, and (2) when the new ruling was that a trial court lacked authority to convict a criminal defendant in the first place. . . .

The third category—where a new rule is a "clear break" with past precedent—is the one at issue in these cases. . . .

Under this exception, a new constitutional rule was not applied retroactively, even to cases on direct review, if the new rule explicitly overruled a past precedent of this Court, or disapproved a practice this Court had arguably sanctioned in prior cases, or overturned a long-standing practice that lower courts had uniformly approved. . . .

For the same reasons that persuaded us in *United States v. Johnson* to adopt different conclusions as to convictions on direct review from those that already had become final, we conclude that an engrafted exception based solely upon the particular characteristics of the new rule adopted by the Court is inappropriate.

First, the principle that this Court does not disregard current law, when it adjudicates a case pending before it on direct review, applies regardless of the specific characteristics of the particular new rule announced. . . .

Second, the use of a "clear break" exception creates the same problem of not treating similarly situated defendants the same. . . .

We therefore hold that a new rule for the conduct of criminal prosecutions is to be applied retroactively to all cases, state or federal, pending on direct review or not yet final, with no exception for cases in which the new rule constitutes a "clear break" with the past. . . .

Jaffree v. Board of School Commissioners of Mobile County

554 F.Supp. 1104 (1983)

Ishmael Jaffree challenged the constitutionality of Alabama's law authorizing teachers to lead students in a moment of "silent meditation or voluntary prayer" as a violation of the First Amendment guarantees for religious freedom. Federal District Court Judge Brevard Hand rejected Jaffree's complaint in an opinion sharply critical of the Supreme Court's rulings on the First Amendment establishment clause. His ruling was subsequently appealed by Jaffree and overturned by a court of appeals. Governor George Wallace then appealed that ruling to the Supreme Court in *Wallace v. Jaffree*, 472 U.S. 38 (1985) (see Ch. 6).

MEMORANDUM OPINION

☐*Chief Judge BREVARD HAND.*

The United States Supreme Court has previously addressed itself in many cases to the practice of prayer and religious services in the public schools. As courts are wont to say, this court does not write upon a clean slate when it addresses the issue of school prayer.

Viewed historically, three decisions have lately provided general rules for school prayer. In *Engel v. Vitale*, 370 U.S. 421 [(1962)], *Abington v. Schempp*, 374 U.S. 203 (1963), and *Murray v. Curlett*, 374 U.S. 203 (1963) the Supreme Court established the basic considerations. As stated, the rule is that "[t]he First Amendment has erected a wall between church and state. That wall must be kept high and impregnable. We could not approve the slightest breach." *Everson v. Board of Education*, 330 U.S. 1 (1947).

The principles enunciated in *Engel v. Vitale*, *Abington v. Schempp*, and *Murray v. Curlett* have been distilled to this: "To pass muster under the Establishment Clause, the governmental activity must, first, reflect a clearly secular governmental purpose; second, have a primary effect that neither advances nor inhibits religion; and third, avoid excessive government entanglement with religion. *Committee for Public Education & Religious Liberty v. Nyquist*, 413 U.S. 756 (1973)." . . .

In sum, under present rulings the use of officially-authorized prayers or Bible readings for motivational purposes constitutes a direct violation of the establishment clause. Through a series of decisions, the courts have held that the establishment clause was designed to avoid any official sponsorship or approval of religious beliefs. Even though a practice may not be coercive, active support of a particular belief raises the danger, under the rationale of the Court, that state-approved religious views may be eventually established. . . .

In the face of this precedent the defendants argue that school prayers as they are employed are constitutional. The historical argument which they advance takes two tacks. First, the defendants urge that the first amendment to the U.S. Constitution was intended only to prohibit the *federal government* from establishing a *national* religion. Read in its proper historical context, the defendants contend that the first amendment has no application to the states. The intent of the drafters and adoptors of the first amendment was to prevent the establishment of a national church or religion, and to prevent any single religious sect or denomination from obtaining a preferred position under the auspices of the federal government. . . .

Second, the defendants argue that whatever prohibitions were initially placed upon the federal government by the first amendment that those prohibitions were not incorporated against the states when the fourteenth amendment became law on July 19, 1868. The defendants have introduced the Court to a mass of historical documentation which all point to the intent of the Thirty-ninth Congress to narrowly restrict the scope of the fourteenth amendment. In particular, these historical documents, according to the defendants, clearly demonstrate that the first amendment was never intended to be incorporated through the fourteenth amendment to apply against the states. The Court [subsequently] examine[d] each historical argument in turn. . . .

[The Court concluded that] the establishment clause, as ratified in 1791, was intended only to prohibit the federal government from establishing a national religion. The function of the establishment clause was two-fold. First, it guaranteed to each individual that Congress would not impose a national religion. Second, the establishment clause guaranteed to each state that the states were free to define the meaning of religious establishment under their own constitutions and laws.

The historical record clearly establishes that when the fourteenth amendment was ratified in 1868 that its ratification did not incorporate the first amendment against the states. . . .

What is a court to do when faced with a direct challenge to settled precedent? In most types of cases "it is more important that the applicable rule of law be settled than that it be settled right." *Burnet v. Coronado Oil & Gas Co.*, 285 U.S. 393 (1932) (BRANDEIS, J., dissenting). This general rule holds even where the court is persuaded that it has made a serious error of interpretation in cases involving a statute. However, in cases involving the federal constitution, where correction through legislative action is practically impossible, a court should be willing to examine earlier precedent and to overrule it if the court is persuaded that the earlier precedent was wrongly decided. . . .

"[T]he ultimate touchstone of constitutionality is the Constitution itself and not what we have said about it." *Graves v. O'Keefe*, 306 U.S. 466 (1939)

(FRANKFURTER, J., concurring). "By placing a premium on 'recent cases' rather than the language of the Constitution, the Court makes it dangerously simple for future Courts using the technique of interpretation to operate as a 'continuing Constitutional Convention.' " *Coleman v. Alabama*, 399 U.S. 1 (1970) (BURGER, C.J.). . . .

This Court's review of the relevant legislative history surrounding the adoption of both the first amendment and of the fourteenth amendment, together with the plain language of those amendments, leaves no doubt that those amendments were not intended to forbid religious prayers in the schools which the states and their political subdivisions mandate. . . .

If the appellate courts disagree with this Court in its examination of history and conclusion of constitutional interpretation thereof, then this Court will look again at the record in this case and reach conclusions which it is not now forced to reach.

Commonwealth of Kentucky v. Jeffrey Wasson

Supreme Court of Kentucky, 842 S.W. 2d 487 (1992)

Jeffrey Wasson was arrested in a public parking lot and charged with soliciting an undercover police officer to engage in "deviate sexual intercourse." Under a Kentucky statute (KRS 510.100), "deviate sexual intercourse with another person of the same sex" is a criminal offense; the statute also provides that "consent of the other person shall not be a defense." At Wasson's trial, however, a district judge dismissed the charge and held that the statute violated provisions in the Kentucky Constitution that guarantee a "right of privacy" and the equal protection of the laws. A state appellate court affirmed and the Commonwealth of Kentucky appealed that ruling to its supreme court.

☐ *Opinion of the Court by Justice LEIBSON*

The Commonwealth maintains that the United States Supreme Court's decision in *Bowers v. Hardwick*, [478 U.S. 186 (1986)], is dispositive of the right to privacy issue; that the "Kentucky Constitution did not intend to confer any greater right to privacy than was afforded by the U.S. Constitution." Turning to the equal protection argument raised by a statute which criminalizes oral or anal intercourse between persons of the same sex, but not between persons of different sexes, which was not addressed in the *Bowers* case, the Commonwealth argues there is "a rational basis for making such a distinction." . . . The thrust of the argument advanced by the Commonwealth as a rational basis for criminalizing consensual intercourse between persons of the same sex, when the same acts between persons of the opposite sex are not punished, is that the level of moral indignation felt by the majority of society against the sexual preference of homosexuals justifies having their legislative representative criminalize these sexual activities. The Commonwealth believes that homosexual intercourse is immoral, and that what is beyond the pale of majoritarian morality is beyond the limits of constitutional protection.

The grounds stated by the District Court for striking down the statute as unconstitutional are: "KRS 510.100 clearly seeks to regulate the profoundly private conduct and in so doing impermissibly invades the privacy of the citizens of this state." . . . The Fayette Circuit Court "agreed with that conclusion," and further held the statute "unjustifiably discriminates, and thus is unconstitutional under Sections 2 and 3 of our Kentucky Constitution." These Sections are:

> "Section 2. Absolute and arbitrary power over the lives, liberty and property of freemen exists nowhere in a republic, not even in the largest majority.
>
> Section 3. All men, when they form a social compact, are equal. . . .'"

These Sections [together with other provisions of the Kentucky Constitution] express the guarantee of equal treatment provided by the law in our Kentucky Constitution. The lower courts' judgments limit their finding of unconstitutionality to state constitutional grounds. *Bowers v. Hardwick* speaks neither to rights of privacy under the state constitution nor to equal protection rights under either federal or state constitutions. *Bowers* addressed the constitutionality of a Georgia statute prohibiting acts of consensual sodomy between persons of the same sex or the opposite sex. Because the Georgia statute embraced both heterosexual and homosexual conduct, the *Bowers* opinion did not involve the Equal Protection Clause of the Fourteenth Amendment.

For reasons that follow, we hold the guarantees of individual liberty provided in our 1891 Kentucky Constitution offer greater protection of the right of privacy than provided by the Federal constitution as interpreted by the United States Supreme Court, and that the statute in question is a violation of such rights; and, further, we hold that the statute in question violates rights of equal protection as guaranteed by our Kentucky Constitution.

I. RIGHTS OF PRIVACY

No language specifying "rights of privacy," as such, appears in either the federal or State Constitution. The Commonwealth recognizes such rights exist, but takes the position that, since they are implicit rather than explicit, our Court should march in lock step with the United States Supreme Court in declaring when such rights exist. Such is not the formulation of federalism. On the contrary, under our system of dual sovereignty, it is our responsibility to interpret and apply our state constitution independently. We are not bound by decisions of the United States Supreme Court when deciding whether a state statute impermissibly infringes upon individual rights guaranteed in the State Constitution so long as state constitutional protection does not fall below the federal floor, meaning the minimum guarantee of individual rights under the United States Constitution as interpreted by the United States Supreme Court. . . .

Kentucky cases recognized a legally protected right of privacy based on our own constitution and common law tradition long before the United States Supreme Court first took notice of whether there were any rights of privacy inherent in the Federal Bill of Rights. . . .

[Moreover,] the United States Supreme Court is extremely reticent in extending the reach of the Due Process Clauses in substantive matters [pertaining to privacy]. . . . *Bowers v. Hardwick* decides that rights protected by the Due Process Clauses in the Fifth and Fourteenth Amendments to the United States Constitution do not "extend a fundamental right to homosexuals to engage in acts of consensual sodomy."

Bowers decides nothing beyond this. But state constitutional jurisprudence in this area is not limited by the constraints inherent in federal due process analysis. Deviate sexual intercourse conducted in private by consenting adults is not beyond the protections of the guarantees of individual liberty in our Kentucky Constitution simply because "proscriptions against that conduct have ancient roots." Kentucky constitutional guarantees against government intrusion address substantive rights. . . . [T]he Kentucky Constitution of 1891 . . . amplifies [its guarantee of individual liberty] with a Bill of Rights in 26 sections, the first of which states:

> "Section 1. All men are, by nature, free and equal, and have certain inherent and inalienable rights, among which may be reckoned:
>
> First: The right of enjoying and defending their lives and liberties. . . .
>
> Third: The right of seeking and pursuing their safety and happiness. . . .
>
> Section 2. Absolute and arbitrary power over the lives, liberty and property of freemen exists nowhere in a republic, not even in the largest majority." . . .

The leading case on this subject is *Commonwealth v. Campbell*, [133 Ky. 50 (1909)]. At issue was an ordinance that criminalized possession of intoxicating liquor, even for "private use." Our Court held that the Bill of Rights in the 1891 Constitution prohibited state action thus intruding upon the "inalienable rights possessed by the citizens" of Kentucky. Our Court interpreted the Kentucky Bill of Rights as defining a right of privacy, even though the constitution did not say so in that terminology. . . .

In the *Campbell* case our Court quoted at length from the "great work" *On Liberty* of the nineteenth-century English philosopher and economist, John Stuart Mill. . . . Mill's premise is that "physical force in the form of legal penalties," i.e., criminal sanctions, should not be used as a means to improve the citizen. The majority has no moral right to dictate how everyone else should live. Public indignation, while given due weight, should be subject to the overriding test of rational and critical analysis, drawing the line at harmful consequences to others. Modern legal philosophers who follow Mill temper this test with an enlightened paternalism, permitting the law to intervene to stop self-inflicted harm such as the result of drug taking, or failure to use seat belts or crash helmets, not to enforce majoritarian or conventional morality, but because the victim of such self-inflicted harm becomes a burden on society.

Based on the *Campbell* opinion, and on the Comments of the 1891

Convention Delegates, there is little doubt but that the views of John Stuart Mill, which were then held in high esteem, provided the philosophical underpinnings for the reworking and broadening of protection of individual rights that occurs throughout the 1891 constitution.

We have recognized protection of individual rights greater than the federal floor in a number of cases, most recently: *Ingram v. Commonwealth, Ky.*, 801 S.W.2d 321 (1900), involving protection against double jeopardy and *Dean v. Commonwealth, Ky.*, 777 S.W.2d 900 (1989), involving the right of confrontation. Perhaps the most dramatic recent example of protection of individual rights under the state constitution where the United States Supreme Court had refused to afford protection under the Federal Constitution is *Rose v. Council for Better Educ., Inc., Ky.*, 790 S.W.2d 186 (1989). In *Rose*, our Court recognized our Kentucky Constitution afforded individual school children from property poor districts a fundamental right to an adequate education such as provided in wealthier school districts, even though sixteen years earlier the United States Supreme Court held the Federal Constitution provided no such protection in *San Antonio Independent School District v. Rodriguez*, 411 U.S. 1 (1973). . . .

We view the United States Supreme Court decision in *Bowers v. Hardwick* as a misdirected application of the theory of original intent. To illustrate: as a theory of majoritarian morality, miscegenation was an offense with ancient roots. It is highly unlikely that protecting the rights of persons of different races to copulate was one of the considerations behind the Fourteenth Amendment. Nevertheless, in *Loving v. Virginia*, 388 U.S. 1 (1967), the United States Supreme Court recognized that a contemporary, enlightened interpretation of the liberty interest involved in the sexual act made its punishment constitutionally impermissible.

According to *Bowers v. Hardwick*, "until 1961, all fifty States outlawed sodomy, and today, twenty-five States and District of Columbia continue to provide criminal penalties for sodomy performed in private and between consenting adults." In the space of three decades half the states decriminalized this conduct. . . . Two states [New York and Pennsylvania] by court decisions hold homosexual sodomy statutes of this nature unconstitutional for reasons similar to those stated here. . . . Thus our decision, rather than being the leading edge of change, is but a part of the moving stream. . . .

II. EQUAL PROTECTION

As stated earlier, in *Bowers v. Hardwick*, the Equal Protection Clause was not implicated because the Georgia statute criminalized both heterosexual and homosexual sodomy. Unlike the due Process Clause analysis provided in *Bowers v. Hardwick*, equal protection analysis does not turn on whether the law (KRS 510.100) transgresses "liberties that are 'deeply rooted in this Nation's history and tradition.' " *Bowers v. Hardwick*. . . .

Certainly, the practice of deviate sexual intercourse violates traditional morality. But so does the same act between heterosexuals, which activity is decriminalized. Going one step further, all sexual activity between consenting adults outside of marriage violates our traditional morality. The issue here is not whether sexual activity traditionally viewed as immoral can be punished by society, but whether it can be punished solely on the basis of sexual preference. . . .

We need not speculate as to whether male and/or female homosexuals will be allowed status as a protected class if and when the United States Supreme Court confronts this issue. They are a separate and identifiable class for Kentucky constitutional law analysis because no class of persons can be discriminated against under the Kentucky Constitution. All are entitled to equal treatment, unless there is a substantial governmental interest, a rational basis, for different treatment.

In the final analysis we can attribute no legislative purpose to this statute except to single out homosexuals for different treatment for indulging their sexual preference by engaging in the same activity heterosexuals are now at liberty to perform. By 1974 there had already been a sea change in societal values insofar as attaching criminal penalties to extramarital sex. The question is whether a society that no longer criminalizes adultery, fornication, or deviate sexual intercourse between heterosexuals has a rational basis to single out homosexual acts for different treatment. Is there a rational basis for declaring this one type of sexual immorality so destructive of family values as to merit criminal punishment whereas other acts of sexual immorality which were likewise forbidden by the same religious and traditional heritage of Western civilization are now decriminalized? If there is a rational basis for different treatment it has yet to be demonstrated in this case.

The purpose of the present statute is not to protect the marital relationship against sexual activity outside of marriage, but only to punish one aspect of it while other activities similarly destructive of the marital relationship, if not more so, go unpunished. Sexual preference, and not the act committed, determines criminality, and is being punished. Simply because the majority, speaking through the General Assembly, finds one type of extramarital intercourse more offensive than another, does not provide a rational basis for criminalizing the sexual preference of homosexuals.

For the reasons stated, we affirm the decision of the Fayette Circuit Court, and the judgment on appeal from the Fayette District Court.

  ☐ *Justices LAMBERT, WINTERSHEIMBER, and REYNOLDS dissented.*

■ THE DEVELOPMENT OF LAW

Other Recent State Supreme Court Decisions Declining to Follow the U.S. Supreme Court's Rulings

Indiana v. Gerschoffer, 763 N.E.2d 960 (Ind., 2002) Held that a sobriety checkpoint for drivers violated the state constitution. See also *Brown v. State*, 653 N.E.2d 77 (Ind., 1995), holding that a warrantless search of defendant's car violated the state constitution.

Anchorage Police Department   Declined to follow *Vernonia School District*
Employees Association v.   *No. 47J v. Acton*, 515 U.S. 646 (1995), in
Municipality of Anchorage,   holding that random drug testing of
24 P.3d 547 (Als., 2001)   police and fire fighters violated the state
constitution.

Shadler v. Florida, 761 So.2d   Declined to follow *Arizona v. Evans*,
279 (Fla., 2000)   514 U.S. 1 (1995) (excerpted in Ch. 7) in
holding on state constitutional grounds
that the "good-faith" exception to the exclusionary rule does not apply to
arrests based on mistaken highway safety computerized records.

State v. Cline, 617 N.W.2d   Declined to follow *Illinois v. Krull*, 480
277 (Iowa, 2000)   U.S. 340 (1987), and *United States v. Leon*,
468 U.S. 897 (1984) (excerpted in Ch. 7),
in refusing to recognize a "good faith" exception to the exclusionary rule
as a matter of state constitutional law. See also *Iowa v. Gillespie*, 619 N.W.2d
345 (Iowa, 2000)

Powell v. State of Georgia,   The Georgia Supreme Court struck down
510 S.E.2d 18 (1998)   its state law criminalizing noncommercial, consensual sodomy and expressly re-
jected the ruling in *Bowers v. Hardwick*, 478 U.S. 186 (1986), which had
upheld that state's law. Other state courts have struck their state laws criminalizing sodomy. See also *Kentucky v. Wasson*, 842 S.W.2d 487 (Ky. 1992)
(excerpted in this chapter); *Michigan Organization for Human Rights v. Kelley*,
No. 88-815820 CZ (Mich. Cir. Ct., July 9, 1990); and *State v. Cogshell*,
997 S.W.2d 534 (Mo. App. W.D., July 6, 1999).

Commonwealth v. Labron,   The Pennsylvania Supreme Court re-
690 A.2D 228 (1997)   asserted, as a matter of state constitutional
law, its earlier holding that the automo-
bile exception to search warrant requirements does not justify a police search
unless there exists probable cause for the search and a warrantless search is
justified by the "exigencies of the circumstances," thereby declining to follow
the ruling in *Pennsylvania v. Labron*, 518 U.S. 938 (1996).

American Academy of   By a vote of four to three, the Supreme
Pediatrics v. Lungren,   Court of California refused to follow the
940 P.2d 797 (1997)   U.S. Supreme Court's rulings upholding
state restrictions on minors seeking abor-
tions by requiring them to obtain the permission of their parents or a judge.
Here, the court invalidated the parental consent and judicial-bypass requirement for infringing on minors' right of privacy under the California Constitution.

Gryczan v. Montana,
942 P.2d 112 (1997)

Like the Supreme Court of Kentucky in *Commonwealth of Kentucky v. Wasson*, 842 S.W. 2d (1992), the Montana Supreme Court refused to follow the ruling in *Bowers v. Hardwick*, 478 U.S. 186 (1986) (excerpted in Ch. 11) and struck down its state law criminalizing sodomy based on its state constitution. Besides those two, other state supreme courts have likewise invalidated their laws against sodomy. See, e.g., *Tennessee v. Sundquist*, 926 S.W.2d 250 (Tenn., 1996); *People v. Onofre*, 415 N.E.2d 936 (N.Y., 1980); and *Commonwealth v. Bonadio*, 415 A.2d 47 (Pa., 1980).

Smith v. Fair Employment and Housing Commission,
12 Cal. 4th 1143 (1996)

Among other state supreme courts refusing to follow the U.S. Supreme Court's ruling in *Employment Division, Department of Human Resources of Oregon v. Smith*, 494 U.S. 872 (1990) (excerpted in Ch. 6), the California Supreme Court held that its state constitution "afford[s] the same protection for religious exercise as the Federal Constitution [did] before [the U.S. Supreme Court's decision in] *Employment Division v. Smith*." State supreme courts in Alaska, Maine, Michigan, Minnesota, Ohio, New York, and Washington ruled likewise.

Sheff v. O'Neill,
238 Conn. 1 (1996)

Departing from the U.S. Supreme Court's holdings that only segregation brought about by intentional state action violates the Fourteenth Amendment, the Connecticut Supreme Court ruled that its state constitution explicitly bars unintentional racial segregation and guarantees a right to free and equal public education. In doing so, the state supreme Court found that *de facto* racial isolation and socioeconomic deprivation violated the right of equal opportunity to a free public education of students in Hartford, Connecticut. Whereas children from minority groups constitute 25 percent of the state's public school population, 92 percent of Hartford's public school students come from minority groups. "Because of the negative consequences of racial and ethnic isolation," the Court held unconstitutional a state law requiring that school districts coincide with municipal boundaries and ordered the state to integrate public schools across district lines.

Commonwealth of Pennsylvania v. Matos,
672 A.2d 769 (1996)

Rejecting the reasoning and result in *California v. Hodari D.*, 499 U.S. 621 (1991) (see Ch. 7), the Supreme Court of Pennsylvania held that under its state constitution, contraband discarded by a person fleeing a police officer was the fruit of an illegal search, because the officer possessed neither probable cause for an arrest nor a "reasonable suspicion" to stop the individual; and thus the contraband must be excluded as evidence against the accused. In the Court's words, "we reject *Hodari D.* as incompatible with the privacy rights guaranteed to the citizens of this Commonwealth under ... the Pennsylvania

Constitution." The Court noted as well that a number of other states had rejected the analysis in *Hodari D.*; those states include Connecticut, Hawaii, New Jersey, New York, and Oregon.

Florida v. White, 660
So. 2d 664 (1995)

Within months of the ruling in *Arizona v. Evans*, 514 U.S. 1 (see Ch. 7), which extended the "good faith exception" to the Fourth Amendment's exclusionary rule to police officers' reliance on mistaken computerized records of an outstanding arrest warrant, the Supreme Court of Florida decided otherwise in holding that the "failure of the police to maintain up-to-date and accurate computer records results in an illegal arrest and search" and that "evidence obtained as a result of the illegal arrest is subject to the exclusionary rule" of the state constitution.

Women of Minnesota v. Gomez,
542 N.W.2d 17 (1995)

In striking down its state's restrictions on public funding for therapeutic abortions, the Supreme Court of Minnesota observed that "in reaching our decision, we have interpreted the Minnesota Constitution to afford broader protection than the United States Constitution of a woman's fundamental right to reach a private decision on whether to obtain an abortion, and thus reject the United States Supreme Court's opinion on this issue in *Harris v. McRae*, 448 U.S. 297 (1980)." Appellate courts in California, Connecticut, Massachusetts, Michigan, and New Jersey have also struck down prohibitions on public funding for abortions not necessary to save a pregnant woman's life on the basis of their state constitutions.

*Montana v. Bullock and
Peterson*, 901 P.2d 61 (1995)

The Supreme Court of Montana ruled that under the state constitution individuals have "reasonable expectations of privacy" and standing to challenge the legality of a police search of property that they do not own, and thus declined to follow the U.S. Supreme Court's rulings in *Rakas v. Illinois*, 439 U.S. 128 (1978). Other state supreme courts have ruled likewise, including those in New Jersey, in *State v. Alston*, 440 A.2d 1311 (1981); in Arizona, in *State v. White*, 574 P.2d 840 (1978); and New Hampshire, in *State v. Alosa*, 623 A.2d 218 (1993).

*Torre Jenkins v. Chief Justice
of the District Court Department*,
416 Mass. 221 (1993)

The Massachusetts Supreme Court refused to follow the decision in *County of Riverside v. McLaughlin*, 500 U.S. 44 (1991) (see Ch. 7), that following a warrantless arrest individuals may be incarcerated for up to forty-eight hours before being given a hearing to determine the probable cause for their arrest.

*Rick Sitz v. Michigan
Department of State Police*,
443 Mich. 744 (1993)

The Supreme Court of Michigan refused to abide by the U.S. Supreme Court's holding, in *Michigan Department of State Police v. Sitz*, 496 U.S. 444 (1990), that Michigan state police's use of sobriety checkpoints did not violate the Fourth Amendment. When that case was remanded back to the state appellate court, the state supreme court held that the state's policy of indiscriminate suspicionless stopping of automobiles violates the state constitution's prohibition against unreasonable searches and seizures. The Supreme Court of Washington also held that police checkpoints violate the privacy rights guaranteed by its state constitution, in *City of Seattle v. Mesiani*, 755 P.2d 775 (1988).

Derricott v. Maryland, In *United States v. Sokolow*, 490 U.S. 1
611 A.2d 592 (1992) (1989) (see Ch. 7), the use of "drug courier profiles" by law enforcement officials was upheld over Fourth Amendment objections. But in *Derricott* the Court of Appeals of Maryland held that stopping and searching a car solely on the ground that the driver fit a "drug courier profile"—that is, was young, black, driving a sports car, and had a beeper—was not permissible under state constitutional law.

Gary v. Georgia, 422 S.E. 2d The Supreme Court of Georgia ruled
426 (1992) that provisions of the state constitution precluded the adoption of a "good-faith" exception to the exclusionary rule and declined to follow the rulings in *United States v. Leon*, 468 U.S. 902 (1984), and *Massachusetts v. Sheppard*, 468 U.S. 981 (1984) (see Ch. 7). Other state supreme courts that have refused to recognize a "good-faith exception" to the exclusionary rule as a matter of state constitutional law are in Connecticut, in *State v. Marsala*, 579 A.2d 58 (1990); Massachusetts, in *Commonwealth v. Upton*, 476 N.E.2d 548 (1985); Michigan, in *People v. Sundling*, 395 N.W.2d 308 (1986); New Jersey, in *State v. Novembrino*, 519 A.2d 820 (1987); New York, in *People v. Bigelow*, 488 N.E.2d 451 (1985); North Carolina, in *State v. Carter*, 370 S.E.2d 553 (1988); Pennsylvania, in *Commonwealth v. Edmunds*, 586 A.2d 887 (1991); Texas, in *Davis v. State*, 831 S.W.2d 426 (1992); and Vermont, in *State v. Oakes*, 598 A.2d 119 (1991).

New Jersey v. Hemple and Declining to follow *California v. Green-*
Hemple, 576 A.2d 793 *wood*, 486 U.S. 35 (1988), which held that
(1990) under the Fourth Amendment individuals do not have "reasonable expectations of privacy" in the contents of garbage bags left for collection in public areas, the Supreme Court of New Jersey ruled otherwise, observing that "When the United States Constitution affords our citizens less protection than does the New Jersey Constitution, we have not merely the authority to give full effect to the State protection, we have the duty to do so." The supreme courts of California and Hawaii have also ruled that their constitutions protect against warrantless searches of garbage in, respectively, *People of California v. Krivda*, 504 P.2d 457 (1973), and *State v. Tanaka*, 701 P.2d 1274 (1985).

In re T.W., 551 So.2d 1186 (1989)   In anticipation that the U.S. Supreme Court might overrule *Roe v. Wade*, 410 U.S. 113 (1973) (see Ch. 11), or significantly cut back on its upholding a woman's right to secure an abortion, as occurred in *Planned Parenthood of Southeastern Pennsylvania v. Casey*, 505 U.S. 833 (1992) (see Ch. 11), the Supreme Court of Florida interpreted a 1980 state constitutional amendment, providing that "Every natural person has the right to be let alone and free from government intrusion into his private life except as otherwise provided herein," to guarantee a woman the right to have an abortion and observed that its ruling "is beyond the reach" of the U.S. Supreme Court because the latter is "a bystander when it comes to interpreting state constitutions." Other state supreme courts have likewise ruled that their state constitutions protect a woman's right to abortion, including California, in *Committee to Defend Reproductive Rights v. Meyers*, 625 P.2d 779 (1981) (requiring state funding for abortions); Connecticut, in *Doe v. Maher*, 515 A.2d 134 (1986); Michigan, in *Doe v. Director of Michigan Department of Social Services*, 468 N.W. 2d 862 (1991); Massachusetts, in *Moe v. Secretary of Administration*, 417 N.E. 2d 387 (1981); Tennessee, in *Davis v. Davis*, 842 S.W. 588 (Tenn., 1992) (holding state constitution's right of privacy covered the choice not to procreate); and New Jersey, in *Right to Choose v. Byrne*, 450 A. 2d 925 (1982).

Edgewood Independent School District v. Kirby, 777 S.W.2d 391 (1989)   In a Fourteenth Amendment Equal Protection Clause challenge to disparities in Texas's system of public school financing, the U.S. Supreme Court held, in *San Antonio Independent School District v. Rodriguez*, 411 U.S. 1 (1973), that public education is not a "fundamental right" barring states from discriminatory public school financing. In *Edgewood Independent School District*, however, the Supreme Court of Texas ruled to the contrary, on the basis of its state constitution. Other state supreme courts have refused to follow *Rodriguez*; they include New Jersey [see *Robinson v. Cahill*, 303 A.2d 273 (N.J., 1973) to *Robinson VII*, 360 A.2d 400 (N.J., 1976)], California [*Serrano v. Priest*, 557 P.2d 929 (Cal., 1976)], Washington [*Seattle School Dist. No. 1 v. State*, 585 P.2d 71 (Wash., 1978)], West Virginia [*Pauley v. Kelly*, 255 S.E.2d 859 (W. Va., 1979)], and Wyoming [*Washakie County School Dist. No. 1 v. Herschler*, 606 P.2d 310 (Wyo., 1980)].

Witters v. State of Washington Commission for the Blind, 771 P.2d 1119 (Wash., 1989)   On remand, the Supreme Court of Washington refused to follow the ruling in *Witters v. Washington Dept. of Services for the Blind*, 474 U.S. 481 (1981), holding that a state scholarship given to a handicapped person who attended a religious college did not violate the First Amendment's disestablishment clause. It found that such financial assistance violated its state constitution.

People v. P.J. Video, Inc.,   In *New York v. P.J. Video, Inc.,* 475 U.S. 868
68 N.Y. 2d 296 (1986)   (1986), the U.S. Supreme Court reversed
a ruling by the New York Court of Ap-
peals, which had held that a state judge erred when issuing a search warrant
for the seizure of allegedly obscene videos, which were subject to First
Amendment protection and thus required a higher standard of probable
cause than the usual "fair probability" that evidence of a crime would be
found. When that case was remanded back to the state appellate court, the
latter reaffirmed its earlier ruling on the basis of independent state grounds
and refused to apply the "total of the circumstances/fair probability" test
announced in *Illinois v. Gates,* 462 U.S. 213 (1983).

Montana v. Johnson,   Departing from the ruling in *Fare v.*
719 P.2d 1248 (1986)   *Michael C.,* 442 U.S. 707 (1979), to the
application and scope of the rights set
forth in *Miranda v. Arizona,* 384 U.S. 436 (1966) (see Ch. 8), to a juvenile
who asked to see his probation officer, the Supreme Court of Montana held
that the right to counsel is broader under its state constitutional law than under federal constitutional law, observing that "we refuse to 'march lock-step'
with the United States Supreme Court where constitutional issues are concerned, even if the applicable State Constitution provisions are identical or
nearly identical to those of the United States Constitution."

Montana v. Solis,   Recognizing broader protection for in-
693 P.2d 518 (1984)   terests in privacy and against unreasonable
searches and seizures, the Supreme Court
of Montana rejected the "assumption of risk" rule laid down in *United States
v. White,* 401 U.S. 745 (1971) (see Ch. 7), with respect to recording of conversations by undercover police, observing that "This Court is not bound
by decisions of the United States Supreme Court where independent
grounds exist for reaching a contrary result," and noting that in *State v. Van
Hyem,* 630 P.2d 202 (1981), it had ruled "that independent state grounds existed for this Court to extend greater privacy rights, and thereby greater
protection against unreasonable search and seizure, than would be afforded
under the Federal Constitution."

South Dakota v. Neville,   In *South Dakota v. Neville,* 459 U.S. 553
346 N.W.2d 425 (1984)   (1983), the U.S. Supreme Court held that
the introduction as evidence of the de-
fendant's refusal to take a blood-alcohol test after being stopped by police for
failing to stop at a stop sign did not violate the Fifth Amendment privilege
against self-incrimination. On remand, however, the Supreme Court of
South Dakota ruled on the basis of its state constitution the defendant's refusal to submit to the test was inadmissible as evidence against him.

Washington v. Chrisman,
676 P.2d 419 (1984)

In *Washington v. Chrisman*, 455 U.S. 1 (1982), the U.S. Supreme Court reversed and remanded the decision of the Washington state supreme court that a campus police officer's warrantless entry and search of a dormitory room of two university students violated the Fourth Amendment, characterizing the decision as a "novel reading of the Fourth Amendment." On remand, the Supreme Court of Washington nonetheless found the officer's search to violate provisions of the state constitution.

People v. Long, 659
N.W. 2d 194 (1984)

On remand, the Michigan state supreme court reasserted on independent state grounds its earlier ruling on the impermissibility of a police officer's search of a driver after its previous decision was reversed in *Michigan v. Long*, 463 U.S. 1032 (1983) (excerpted in Vol. 1, Ch. 7).

Right to Choose v. Byrne,
450 A.2d 925 (N.J., 1982)

After the ruling in *Harris v. McRae*, 448 U.S. 297 (1980) that a congressional prohibition on the use of Medicaid funds for abortions did not violate the Fourteenth Amendment equal protection clause, the New Jersey Supreme Court held otherwise on the basis of its state constitution. State supreme courts in California, Connecticut, Massachusetts, Michigan, and Oregon have likewise upheld the right of indigent women to state-funded abortions.

For further reading see and compare Barry Latzer, *State Constitutions and Criminal Law* (New York: Greenwood, 1991); Jennifer Friesen, *State Constitutional Law* (New York: Matthew Bender, 1995); Matthew Bosworth, *Courts as Catalysts: State Supreme Courts and Public School Finance Equity* (Albany: State University of New York Press, 2001); and Charles Lopeman, *The Activist Advocate: Policy Making in State Supreme Courts* (New York: Praeger, 1999).

3

ECONOMIC RIGHTS AND AMERICAN CAPITALISM

Private property is not mentioned in the Constitution even though its protection was one of the central purposes of the Constitution. Sections 8 and 10 of Article I and Section 1 of Article IV govern various matters related to private property—taxes, duties, imposts, excises, commerce, bankruptcies, bills of credit, debts, the impairment of contracts, and the rights of authors and inventors. Yet private property did not receive specific protection until the ratification in 1791 of the Fifth Amendment. The due process and takings clauses of that amendment provide that "No person shall . . . be deprived of life, liberty, or property without due process of law; nor shall private property be taken for public use without just compensation."

Liberty and property were, nevertheless, closely tied together in the minds of the Framers of the Constitution. Property conditioned suffrage and was closely linked with representation (see Vol. 1, Chs. 5 and 8). When defending the Constitution in *The Federalist*, Alexander Hamilton sought to show that it would provide security "to liberty and to property." Noah Webster, a prominent New York publisher, even more bluntly claimed "that *property* is the basis of *power*" when differentiating America from England and Europe, where property was concentrated in the hands of a few:

> [I]n America, and here alone, we have gone at once to the *foundation of liberty*, and raised the people to their true dignity. Let the lands be possessed by the people in fee-simple, let the fountain be kept pure, and the streams will be pure of course. Our jealousy of *trial by jury, the liberty of the press, &c.*, is totally groundless. Such rights are inseparably connected with the *power* and *dignity* of the

people, which rest on their *property*. They cannot be abridged. All *other* [free] nations have wrested *property* and *freedom* from *barons* and *tyrants; we* begin our empire with full possession of property and all its attending rights.[1]

The Framers took to heart the teaching of the English philosopher John Locke, in his *Second Treatise of Government*, that property is a natural right—a right preceding the establishment of government—and its preservation one of the chief ends of government. On Locke's labor theory of value, property was but an extension of liberty. "The *labour* that was mine, removing [objects] out of that common state [of nature] they were in, hath *fixed* my *Property* in them," argued Locke. "Thus the Grass my Horse has bit; the Turfs my Servant has cut; and the Ore I have digg'd in any place where I have a right to them in common with others, become my *Property*."[2] No less influential than Locke on the Framers was Sir William Blackstone, who also maintained in his *Commentaries on the Laws of England* that property was an "absolute right, inherent in every Englishman."[3]

Given this background and understanding of the fundamental nature of property, it is perhaps not surprising that the Supreme Court emerged within a generation of the ratification of the Constitution as a defender of property rights and economic liberty. Through an expansive interpretation of the contract clause in the early nineteenth century, and the creation of a "liberty of contract" in the latter part of that century, the Court laid the basis in constitutional law for the growth of American capitalism.

Notes

1. Noah Webster, "An Examination into the Leading Principles of the Federal Constitution" (Oct. 10, 1787), in *The Founders' Constitution*, Vol. 1, ed. Philip Kurland and Ralph Lerner (Chicago: University of Chicago Press, 1987), 596–597.

2. John Locke, "Second Treatise of Government" (1689), in *Two Treatises of Government*, ed. Peter Laslett (New York: Mentor Books, 1960), 330.

3. Sir William Blackstone, *Commentaries on the Laws of England* (1765–1769) (Chicago: University of Chicago Press, 1979).

Selected Bibliography

Ely, James W. *The Guardian of Every Other Right: A Constitutional History of Property Rights*. New York: Oxford University Press, 1992.

Goldwin, Robert A., and Schambra, William A., eds. *How Capitalistic Is the Constitution?* Washington, DC: American Enterprise Institute, 1982.

Levy, Leonard. "Property as a Human Right." 5 *Constitutional Commentary* 169 (1988).

Paul, Ellen F., and Dickman, Howard. *Liberty, Property, and the Future of Constitutional Development.* Albany: State University of New York Press, 1990.

Pennock, J. Roland, and Chapman, John, eds. *Property.* New York: New York University Press, 1980.

A | *The Contract Clause and Vested Interests in Property*

Article I, Section 10, forbids the states from "impairing the Obligation of Contracts." That provision was ostensibly aimed at preventing the states from reneging on private contracts (such as loans made by banks) and passing laws favoring debtors, as was done in the 1780s in the aftermath of the Revolutionary War. As such, the guarantee presumably covered only private contracts. But in a series of rulings, the Marshall Court (1801–1836) broadly interpreted the contract clause to apply to public contracts (that is, contracts between a governmental agency and private individuals) and to safeguard vested interests in private property.

The famous "*Yazoo* case," *Fletcher v. Peck* (1810) (excerpted below), was the first important ruling of the Marshall Court in which the contract clause was turned into a guarantee for public contracts, in addition to a limitation on states' powers over private contracts. Notice that besides broadly construing the contract clause, Chief Justice Marshall notes that Georgia's law revoking its earlier land grants contravened "general principles, which are common to our free institutions, or by the particular provisions of the constitution of the United States." Chief Justice Marshall pushed his theory further two years later in *New Jersey v. Wilson*, 7 Cr. 164 (11 U.S.) (1812). New Jersey had made Indian lands tax-exempt, but when the land was sold to a non-Indian the state sought to tax the new owner. However, the Marshall Court ruled that the original contract with the Indians was still valid and the state could not tax the land. In one of the few cases involving private contracts, *Sturges v. Crowninshield*, 4 Wheat. (17 U.S.) 122 (1819), Chief Justice Marshall struck down a New York bankruptcy law as applied to a contract made before the law was passed. However, he found himself in the minority in *Ogden v. Sanders*, 12 Wheat. (25 U.S.) 213 (1827), when the Court upheld another bankruptcy law that had been enacted before a contested contract was made.

Next to *Fletcher v. Peck*, the second most important Marshall Court ruling on the contract clause is *Trustees of Dartmouth College v. Woodward* (1819) (see excerpt below). Again, the clause was expansively read to

■ CONSTITUTIONAL HISTORY

John Locke on the Ends of Political Society and Government

123. If Man in the State of Nature be so free, as has been said; If he be absolute Lord of his own Person and Possessions, equal to the greatest, and subject to no Body, why will he part with his Freedom? Why will he give up this Empire, and subject himself to the Dominion and Controul of any other Power? To which 'tis obvious to Answer, that though in the state of Nature he hath such a right, yet the Enjoyment of it is very uncertain, and constantly exposed to the Invasion of others. For all being Kings as much as he, every Man his Equal, and the greater part no strict Observers of Equity and Justice, the enjoyment of the property he has in this state is very unsafe, very unsecure. This makes him willing to quit a Condition, which however free, is full of fears and continual dangers: And 'tis not without reason, that he seeks out, and is willing to joyn in Society with others who are already united, or have a mind to unite for the mutual *Preservation* of their Lives, Liberties and Estates, which I call by the general Name, *Property*.

124. The great and *chief end*, therefore, of Mens uniting into Commonwealths, and putting themselves under Government, *is the Preservation of their Property*. To which in the state of Nature there are many things wanting.

First, There wants an *establish'd*, settled, known *Law*, received and allowed by common consent to be the Standard of Right and Wrong, and the common measure to decide all Controversies between them. For though the Law of Nature be plain and intelligible to all rational Creatures; yet Men being biassed by their Interest, as well as ignorant for want of study of it, are not apt to allow of it as a Law binding to them in the application of it to their particular Cases.

125. *Secondly*, In the State of Nature there wants a *known and indifferent Judge*, with Authority to determine all differences according to the established Law. For every one in that state being both Judge and Executioner of the Law of Nature, Men being partial to themselves, Passion and Revenge is very apt to carry them too far, and with too much heat, in their own Cases; as well as negligence, and unconcernedness, to make them too remiss, in other Mens.

126. *Thirdly*, In the state of Nature there often wants *Power* to back and support the Sentence when right, and to *give* it due *Execution*. They who by any Injustice offended, will seldom fail, where they are able, by force to make

good their Injustice: such resistance many times makes the punishment dangerous, and frequently destructive, to those who attempt it.

Source: John Locke, "Second Treatise of Government," in *Two Treatises of Government,* ed. Peter Laslett (New York: Mentor Books, 1960), ch. 5.

protect the vested interests in a corporate charter granted by the English Crown in 1769, prior to the Revolutionary War.

The Marshall Court's interpretation of the contract clause was controversial and was viewed as a severe limitation on states' regulatory powers. Yet it remained the dominant feature in the early development of constitutional law and the vehicle by which the power of judicial review was asserted and established. Indeed, political scientist Benjamin Wright found that the contract clause was used in almost 40 percent of the cases challenging state legislation before 1889 and that the Court and lower federal courts used it to strike down some seventy-five state laws.[1]

The Court under Chief Justice Roger Taney (1836–1864) maintained respect for proprietary interests but was more deferential to the powers of states. In its leading ruling on the contract clause, *Charles River Bridge Co. v. Warren Bridge Co.* (1837) (see excerpt below), notice that Chief Justice Taney emphasizes that "[w]hile the rights of private property are sacredly guarded, we must not forget that the community also have rights, and that the happiness and well-being of every citizen depends on their faithful preservation." Taney thus established the principle that public contracts were to be strictly construed on the recognition that states have an important role in promoting the general welfare and technological advances in the public interest.

Despite the expansive interpretation given the contract clause in the early and mid-nineteenth century, its protection for proprietary interests did not override state police powers or the power of eminent domain (the government's taking of private property for public use without just compensation) (see section C, in this chapter). Nor did it foreclose the possibility of state regulations aimed at promoting public morals, health, safety, and welfare. In *Stone v. Mississippi*, 101 U.S. 814 (1880), for instance, the Court unanimously upheld state police power over John Stone's claim of vested property rights. Stone had been granted by the Mississippi legislature a twenty-five-year franchise to sell lottery tickets, but two years later the state adopted a new constitution prohibiting the sale of lottery tickets. When Stone sought to evade prosecution for selling lottery tickets, the Court rejected his invocation of the contract clause, just as it did when state prohibition laws were attacked for infringing on contracts for the sale of beer,[2] and when employment contracts were superseded by workmen's compensation laws.[3]

As Justice Mahlon Pitney, in *Atlantic Coastline Railroad Co. v. City of Goldsboro*, 232 U.S. 548 (1914), explained for a unanimous Court, when affirming that states may delegate to cities the power to regulate health, safety, and welfare,

> [I]t is settled that neither the "contract" clause nor the "due process" clause has the effect of overriding the power of the state to establish all regulations that are reasonably necessary to secure the health, safety, good order, comfort, or general welfare of the community; that this power can neither be abdicated nor bargained away, and is inalienable even by express grant; and that all contract and property rights are held subject to its fair exercise.

Justice Pitney expressed the modern view of the contract clause. *Home Building & Loan Association v. Blaisdell* (1934) (see excerpt below) illustrates how far the Court in the twentieth century has moved away from its earlier application of the contract clause. There a bare majority of the Hughes Court upheld Minnesota's law, passed during the Great Depression, preventing the repossession of mortgaged property. The principle of judicial deference to legislative regulation of private contracts asserted in *Blaisdell* was reaffirmed in *City of El Paso v. Simmons* (1965) (see excerpt below). However, *United States Trust Co. of New York v. State of New Jersey* (1977) (see excerpt below) indicates that the Court gives heightened scrutiny and greater weight to claims under the contract clause in controversies involving a state's impairment of its own contracts.

Why did the Court's reliance on and enforcement of the contract clause decline in the late nineteenth and twentieth centuries? There are a number of reasons. For one thing, the Industrial Revolution brought a growth in the number of corporations and economic problems that could not be accommodated even with a broad reading of the contract clause. Second, the Court developed its contract clause jurisprudence in the absence of congressional legislation. But in the late nineteenth century Congress responded to the social and economic pressures that accompanied industrialization and urbanization. Finally, as discussed below, the Court invented and enforced a "liberty of contract" under the Fourteenth Amendment's due process clause in defense of vested property rights against progressive economic legislation.

Notes

1. Benjamin Wright, *The Contract Clause of the Constitution* (Cambridge, MA: Harvard University Press, 1938), 95.

2. See *Boston Beer Co. v. Massachusetts*, 97 U.S. 25 (1878).

3. *New York Central R. Co. v. White*, 243 U.S. 188 (1917).

Selected Bibliography

Ackerman, Bruce. *Private Property and the Constitution.* New Haven, CT: Yale University Press, 1977.

Kutler, Stanley I. *Privilege and Creative Destruction: The Charles River Bridge Case.* 2d ed. Baltimore, MD: Johns Hopkins University Press, 1990.

Magrath, C. Peter. *Yazoo: The Case of Fletcher v. Peck,* New York: W. W. Norton, 1967.

Stites, Francis. *Private Interest and Public Gain: The Dartmouth College Case.* Amherst: University of Massachusetts, 1972.

Wright, Benjamin. *The Contract Clause of the Constitution.* Cambridge, MA: Harvard University Press, 1938.

Fletcher v. Peck

6 Cr. (10 U.S.) 87 (1810)

Robert Fletcher sued John Peck for the breach of a covenant on land that Peck had sold him. The land was part of a larger land grant in 1795 of the Georgia legislature to four land-holding companies, which had bribed several members of the legislature to win passage of the land grant. The next year, however, the state enacted legislation declaring the 1795 law and all rights and claims to it null and void. Peck had acquired the land in 1800 and sold it three years later to Fletcher, at which time he claimed that all past sales of the land had been lawful. Fletcher, though, contended that because the original sale of the land had been declared invalid by the Georgia legislature, Peck could not legally sell the land and was guilty of breach of contract. A federal circuit court found in favor of Peck, and Fletcher appealed directly to the Supreme Court.

The Court's decision was six to one, and the opinion was announced by Chief Justice Marshall. A separate opinion was delivered by Justice Johnson.

☐ *Chief Justice MARSHALL delivered the opinion of the Court.*

The suit was instituted on several covenants contained in a deed made by John Peck, the defendant in error, conveying to Robert Fletcher, the plaintiff in error, certain lands which were part of a large purchase made by James Gunn and others, in the year 1795, from the state of Georgia, the contract for which was made in the form of a bill passed by the legislature of that state. . . .

Titles which, according to every legal test, are perfect, are acquired with that confidence which is inspired by the opinion that the purchaser is safe. If there be any concealed defect, arising from the conduct of those who had held the property long before he acquired it, of which he had no notice, that concealed defect cannot be set up against him. He has paid his money for a title good at law, he is innocent, whatever may be the guilt of others, and equity will not subject him to the penalties attached to that guilt. All titles would be insecure, and the intercourse between man and man would be very seriously obstructed, if this principle be overturned. . . .

If the legislature felt itself absolved from those rules of property which are common to all the citizens of the United States, and from those principles of equity which are acknowledged in all our courts, its act is to be supported by its power alone, and the same power may devest any other individual of his lands, if it shall be the will of the legislature so to exert it.

It is not intended to speak with disrespect of the legislature of Georgia, or of its acts. Far from it. The question is a general question and is treated as one. For although such powerful objections to a legislative grant, as are alleged against this, may not again exist, yet the principle, on which alone this rescinding act is to be supported, may be applied to every case to which it shall be the will of any legislature to apply it. The principle is this: that a legislature may, by its own act, devest the vested estate of any man whatever, for reasons which shall, by itself, be deemed sufficient. . . .

Is the power of the legislature competent to the annihilation of such title, and to a resumption of the property thus held?

The principle asserted is, that one legislature is competent to repeal any act which a former legislature was competent to pass; and that one legislature cannot abridge the powers of a succeeding legislature.

The correctness of this principle, so far as respects general legislation, can never be controverted. But, if an act be done under a law, a succeeding legislature cannot undo it. The past cannot be recalled by the most absolute power. Conveyances have been made; those conveyances have vested legal estates, and, if those estates may be seized by the sovereign authority, still, that they originally vested is a fact, and cannot cease to be a fact.

When, then, a law is in its nature a contract, when absolute rights have vested under that contract; a repeal of the law cannot devest those rights; and the act of annulling them, if legitimate, is rendered so by a power applicable to the case of every individual in the community. . . .

It is the peculiar province of the legislature to prescribe general rules for the government of society; the application of those rules to individuals in society would seem to be the duty of other departments. How far the power of giving the law may involve every other power, in cases where the constitution is silent, never has been, and perhaps never can be, definitely stated.

The validity of this rescinding act, then, might well be doubted, were Georgia a single sovereign power. But Georgia cannot be viewed as a single, unconnected, sovereign power, on whose legislature no other restrictions are imposed than may be found in its own constitution. She is a part of a large empire; she is a member of the American Union; and that Union has a constitution the supremacy of which all acknowledge, and which imposes limits to the legislatures of the several states, which none claim a right to pass. The constitution of the United States declares that no state shall pass any bill of attainder, ex post facto law or law impairing the obligation of contracts.

Does the case now under consideration come within this prohibitory section of the constitution?

In considering this very interesting question, we immediately ask ourselves what is a contract? Is a grant a contract?

A contract is a compact between two or more parties, and is either executory or executed. An executory contract is one in which a party binds himself to do, or not to do, a particular thing; such was the law under which the conveyance was made by the governor. A contract executed is one in which the object of contract is performed; and this, says Blackstone, differs in nothing from a grant. The contract between Georgia and the purchasers was executed by the grant. A contract executed, as well as one which is executory, contains obligations binding on the parties. A grant, in its own nature, amounts to an extinguishment of the right of the grantor, and implies a contract not to reassert that right. A party is, therefore, always estopped by his own grant.

Since, then, in fact, a grant is a contract executed, the obligation of which still continues, and since the constitution uses the general term contract, without distinguishing between those which are executory and those which are executed, it must be construed to comprehend the latter as well as the former. A law annulling conveyances between individuals, and declaring that the grantors should stand seized of their former estates, notwithstanding those grants, would be as repugnant to the constitution as a law discharging the vendors of property from the obligation of executing their contracts by conveyances. It would be strange if a contract to convey was secured by the constitution, while an absolute conveyance remained unprotected.

If, under a fair construction of the constitution, grants are comprehended under the term contracts, is a grant from the state excluded from the operation of the provision? Is the clause to be considered as inhibiting the state from impairing the obligation of contracts between two individuals, but as excluding from that inhibition contracts made with itself?

The words themselves contain no such distinction. They are general, and are applicable to contracts of every description. . . .

It is, then, the unanimous opinion of the court, that, in this case, the estate having passed into the hands of a purchaser for a valuable consideration, without notice, the state of Georgia was restrained, either by general principles, which are common to our free institutions, or by the particular provisions of the constitution of the United States, from passing a law whereby the estate of the plaintiff in the premises so purchased could be constitutionally and legally impaired and rendered null and void. . . .

☐ *Justice JOHNSON delivered a separate opinion.*

In this case I entertain . . . an opinion different from that which has been delivered by the court. . . .

[My] opinion . . . is not founded on the provision in the constitution of the United States, relative to laws impairing the obligation of contracts. It is much to be regretted that words of less equivocal signification had not been adopted in that article of the constitution. There is reason to believe, from the letters of Publius, which are well known to be entitled to the highest respect, that the object of the convention was to afford a general protection to individual rights against the acts of the state legislatures. Whether the words, "acts impairing the obligation of contracts," can be construed to have the same force as must have been given to the words "obligation and effect of contracts," is the difficulty in my mind.

There can be no solid objection to adopting the technical definition of the word "contract," given by Blackstone. The etymology, the classical signification, and the civil law idea of the word, will all support it. But the difficulty arises on the word "obligation," which certainly imports an existing moral or physical necessity. Now, a grant or conveyance by no means necessarily implies the continuance of an obligation beyond the moment of executing it. . . .

I enter with great hesitation upon this question, because it involves a subject of the greatest delicacy and much difficulty. The states and the United States are continually legislating on the subject of contracts, prescribing the mode of authentication, the time within which suits shall be prosecuted for them, in many cases affecting existing contracts by the laws which they pass, and declaring them to cease or lose their effect for want of compliance, in the parties, with such statutory provisions. All these acts appear to be within the most correct limits of legislative powers, and most beneficially exercised, and certainly could not have been intended to be affected by this constitutional provision; yet where to draw the line, or how to define or limit the words, "obligation of contracts," will be found a subject of extreme difficulty.

To give it the general effect of a restriction of the state powers in favor of private rights, is certainly going very far beyond the obvious and necessary import of the words, and would operate to restrict the states in the exercise of that right which every community must exercise, of possessing itself of the property of the individual, when necessary for public uses; a right which a magnanimous and just government will never exercise without amply indemnifying the individual, and which perhaps amounts to nothing more than a power to oblige him to sell and convey, when the public necessities require it.

Trustees of Dartmouth College v. Woodward
4 WHEAT. (17 U.S.) 518 (1819)

Dartmouth College was incorporated in 1769 under a charter granted by the English Crown, which authorized a twelve-member board of trustees to govern the college and to appoint their successors. The New Hampshire legislature, however, amended the charter in 1816 with legislation increasing the size of the board of trustees to twenty-one, establishing a board of overseers, and authorizing the governor to appoint new trustees and members of the board of overseers. The incumbent trustees refused to recognize the legislation as binding and sued William Woodward, the college's treasurer, to recover corporate property that was temporarily entrusted to him under the legislation. A trial court failed to resolve the question of the constitutionality of the legislation, but it was upheld by a state superior court. The trustees of Dartmouth

College then appealed to the Supreme Court. As was the practice through most of the nineteenth century, they hired a member of the Supreme Court's bar, Daniel Webster, to argue their case. As was also the practice, attorneys for both sides were given unlimited time to present their arguments. Webster was one of the greatest orators and rather dramatically concluded his argument before the bench, observing,

> Sir, you may destroy this little institution. It is weak. It is in your hands! I know it is one of the lesser lights in the literary horizon of the country. You may put it out. But if you do so, you must carry through your work. You must extinguish, one after another, all those great lights of science which, for more than a century, have thrown their radiance over our land.

> It is, Sir, as I have said, a small college and yet, there are those who love it. . . .

> Sir, I care not how others may feel, but, for myself, when I see my Alma Mater surrounded, like Caesar in the senate-house, by those who are reiterating stab on stab, I would not, for this right hand, have her turn to me, and say *et tu quoque, mi fili!*

The Court's decision was six to one; the opinion was announced by Chief Justice Marshall. Justices Washington and Story concurred, and Justice Duvall dissented.

☐ *Chief Justice MARSHALL delivered the opinion of the Court.*

It can require no argument to prove that the circumstances of this case constitute a contract. An application is made to the crown for a charter to incorporate a religious and literary institution. In the application, it is stated that large contributions have been made for the object, which will be conferred on the corporation as soon as it shall be created. The charter is granted, and on its faith the property is conveyed. Surely in this transaction every ingredient of a complete and legitimate contract is to be found.

The points for consideration are:

1. Is this contract protected by the constitution of the United States?

2. Is it impaired by the acts under which the defendant holds?

1. On the first point it . . . becomes, then, the duty of the court most seriously to examine this charter, and to ascertain its true character. . . .

From [a] review of the charter, it appears that Dartmouth College is an eleemosynary institution, incorporated for the purpose of perpetuating the application of the bounty of the donors, to the specified objects of that bounty; that its trustees or governors were originally named by the founder, and invested with the power of perpetuating themselves; that they are not public officers, nor is it a civil institution, participating in the administration of government; but a charity school, or a seminary of education, incorporated for the preservation of its property, and the perpetual application of that property to the objects of its creation.

Yet a question remains to be considered, of more real difficulty, on which more doubt has been entertained than on all that have been discussed. The founders of the college, at least those whose contributions were in money, have parted with the property bestowed upon it, and their representatives have no interest in that property. The donors of land are equally without interest, so long as the corporation shall exist. Could they be found, they are unaffected by any alteration in its constitution, and probably regardless of its form, or even of its existence. The students are fluctuating, and no individual among our youth has a vested interest in the institution, which can be asserted in a court of justice. Neither the founders of the college nor the youth for whose benefit it was founded, complain of the alteration made in its charter, or think themselves injured by it. The trustees alone complain, and the trustees have no beneficial interest to be protected. Can this be such a contract as the constitution intended to withdraw from the power of state legislation? Contracts, the parties to which have a vested beneficial interest, and those only, it has been said, are the objects about which the constitution is solicitous, and to which its protection is extended.

The court has bestowed on this argument the most deliberate consideration, and the result will be stated. Dr. Wheelock, acting for himself, and for those who, at his solicitation, had made contributions to his school, applied for this charter, as the instrument which should enable him, and them, to perpetuate their beneficent intention. It was granted. An artificial, immortal being, was created by the crown, capable of receiving and distributing forever, according to the will of the donors, the donations which should be made to it. On this being, the contributions which had been collected were immediately bestowed. These gifts were made, not, indeed, to make a profit for the donors, or their posterity, but for something in their opinion of inestimable value; for something which they deemed a full equivalent for the money with which it was purchased. The consideration for which they stipulated, is the perpetual application of the fund to its object, in the mode prescribed by themselves. Their descendants may take no interest in the preservation of this consideration. But in this respect their descendants are not their representatives. They are represented by the corporation. The corporation is the assignee of their rights, stands in their place, and distributes their bounty, as they would themselves have distributed it, had they been immortal. So with respect to the students who are to derive learning from this source. The corporation is a trustee for them also. Their potential rights, which, taken distributively, are imperceptible, amount collectively to a most important interest. These are, in the aggregate, to be exercised, asserted and protected, by the corporation. They were as completely out of the donors, at the instant of their being vested in the corporation, and as incapable of being asserted by the students, as at present. . . .

This is plainly a contract to which the donors, the trustees, and the crown (to whose rights and obligations New Hampshire succeeds), were the original parties. It is a contract made on a valuable consideration. It is a contract for the security and disposition of property. It is a contract, on the faith of which real and personal estate has been conveyed to the corporation. It is then a contract within the letter of the constitution, and within its spirit also, unless the fact that the property is invested by the donors in trustees for the promotion of religion and education, for the benefit of persons who are perpetually changing, though the objects remain the same, shall create a particular exception, taking this case out of the prohibition contained in the constitution.

It is more than possible that the preservation of rights of this description was not particularly in the view of the framers of the constitution when the clause under consideration was introduced into that instrument. It is probable that interferences of more frequent recurrence, to which the temptation was stronger, and of which the mischief was more extensive, constituted the great motive for imposing this restriction on the state legislatures. But although a particular and a rare case may not, in itself, be of sufficient magnitude to induce a rule, yet it must be governed by the rule, when established unless some plain and strong reason for excluding it can be given. It is not enough to say that this particular case was not in the mind of the convention when the article was framed, nor of the American people when it was adopted. It is necessary to go farther, and to say that, had this particular case been suggested, the language would have been so varied, as to exclude it, or it would have been made a special exception. The case being within the words of the rule, must be within its operation likewise, unless there be something in the literal construction so obviously absurd, or mischievous, or repugnant to the general spirit of the instrument, as to justify those who expound the constitution in making it an exception.

On what safe and intelligible ground can this exception stand? There is no exception in the constitution, no sentiment delivered by its contemporaneous expounders, which would justify us in making it. In the absence of all authority of this kind, is there, in the nature and reason of the case itself, that which would sustain a construction of the constitution, not warranted by its words? Are contracts of this description of a character to excite so little interest that we must exclude them from the provisions of the constitution, as being unworthy of the attention of those who framed the instrument? Or does public policy so imperiously demand their remaining exposed to legislative alteration, as to compel us, or rather permit us to say that these words, which were introduced to give stability to contracts, and which in their plain import comprehend this contract, must yet be so construed as to exclude it?

Almost all eleemosynary corporations, those which are created for the promotion of religion, of charity, or of education, are of the same character. The law of this case is the law of all. . . .

The opinion of the court, after mature deliberation, is, that this is a contract, the obligation of which cannot be impaired without violating the constitution of the United States. This opinion appears to us to be equally supported by reason, and by the former decisions of this court.

2. We next proceed to the inquiry whether its obligation has been impaired by those acts of the legislature of New Hampshire to which the special verdict refers.

From the review of this charter, which has been taken, it appears that the whole power of governing the college, of appointing and removing tutors, of fixing their salaries, of directing the course of study to be pursued by the students, and of filling up vacancies created in their own body, was vested in the trustees. On the part of the crown it was expressly stipulated that this corporation, thus constituted, should continue forever; and that the number of trustees should forever consist of twelve, and no more. By this contract the crown was bound, and could have made no violent alteration in its essential terms, without impairing its obligation. . . .

It has been already stated that the act "to amend the charter, and enlarge and improve the corporation of Dartmouth College," increases the number of trustees to twenty-one, gives the appointment of the additional members to the executive of the state, and creates a board of overseers, to consist of twenty-five persons, of whom twenty-one are also appointed by the executive of New Hampshire, who have power to inspect and control the most important acts of the trustees. . . .

The whole power of governing the college is transferred from trustees appointed according to the will of the founder, expressed in the charter, to the executive of New Hampshire. The management and application of the funds of this eleemosynary institution, which are placed by the donors in the hands of trustees named in the charter, and empowered to perpetuate themselves, are placed by this act under the control of the government of the state. The will of the state is substituted for the will of the donors in every essential operation of the college. This is not an immaterial change. The founders of the college contracted, not merely for the perpetual application of the funds which they gave, to the objects for which those funds were given; they contracted also to secure that application by the constitution of the corporation. They contracted for a system which should, as far as human foresight can provide, retain forever the government of the literary institution they had formed, in the hands of persons approved by themselves. This system is totally changed. The charter of 1769 exists no longer. It is reorganized; and reorganized in such a manner as to convert a literary institution, moulded according to the will of its founders, and placed under the control of private literary men, into a machine entirely subservient to the will of government. This may be for the advantage of this college in particular, and may be for the advantage of literature in general, but it is not according to the will of the donors, and is subversive of that contract, on the faith of which their property was given. . . .

It results from this opinion, that the acts of the legislature of New Hampshire, which are stated in the special verdict found in this cause, are repugnant to the constitution of the United States; and that the judgment on this special verdict ought to have been for the plaintiffs. The judgment of the State Court must therefore be reversed.

Charles River Bridge Co. v. Warren Bridge Co.
11 Pet. (36 U.S.) 420 (1837)

In 1785, the Massachusetts legislature incorporated the Charles River Bridge Company and authorized it to build a toll bridge over the Charles River. The company was obligated to pay Harvard College £200 annually as compensation in lieu of its right to operate a ferry that had been granted the college in 1650. In 1792, the charter was extended for another seventy years. But in 1832 the legislature incorporated the Warren Bridge Company and authorized it to build a bridge for free public use just 275 yards away from the Charles River Bridge. That prompted the owners of the Charles River Bridge Company to seek an injunction against the construction of the Warren Bridge. The Massachusetts Supreme Judicial Court dismissed the complaint and Charles River Bridge Company appealed to the Supreme Court.

The Court's decision was five to two, and the majority's opinion was announced by Chief Justice Taney. Justice McLean concurred. Dissent was by Justice Story, who was joined by Justice Thompson.

☐ *Chief Justice TANEY delivered the opinion of the Court.*

[On] what ground can the plaintiffs in error contend that the ferry rights of the college have been transferred to the proprietors of the bridge? If they have been thus transferred, it must be by some mode of transfer known to the law, and the evidence relied on to prove it can be pointed out in the record. How was it transferred? It is not suggested that there ever was in point of fact, a deed of conveyance executed by the college to the bridge company. Is there any evidence in the record from which such a conveyance may, upon legal principle, be presumed? The testimony before the court, so far from laying the foundation for such a presumption, repels it in the most positive terms. The petition to the Legislature in 1785, on which the charter was granted, does not suggest an assignment, nor any agreement or consent on the part of the college; and the petitioners do not appear to have regarded the wishes of that institution, as by any means necessary to insure their success. They place their application entirely on considerations of public interest and public convenience, and the superior advantages of a communication across Charles River by a bridge instead of a ferry. The Legislature, in granting the charter, show, by the language of the law, that they acted on the principles assumed by the petitioners. The preamble recites that the bridge "will be of great public utility;" and that is the only reason they assign for passing the law which incorporates this company. The validity of the charter is not made to depend on the consent of the college, nor of any assignment or surrender on their part; and the Legislature deal with the subject, as if it were one exclusively within their own power, and as if the ferry right were not to be transferred to the bridge company, but to be extinguished; and they appear to have acted on the principle that the State, by virtue of its sovereign powers and eminent domain, had a right to take away the franchise of the ferry; because in their judgment, the public interest and convenience would be better promoted by a bridge in the same place; and upon that principle they proceed to make a pecuniary compensation to the college for the franchise thus taken away. . . .

It does not, by any means, follow that because the legislative power in Massachusetts, in 1650, may have granted to a justly favored seminary of learning, the exclusive right of ferry between Boston and Charlestown, they would, in 1785, give the same extensive privilege to another corporation, who were about to erect a bridge in the same place. The fact that such a right was granted to the college cannot, by any sound rule of construction, be used to extend the privileges of the bridge company beyond what the words of the charter naturally and legally import. Increased population longer experienced in legislation, the different character of the corporations which owned the ferry from that which owned the bridge, might well have induced a change in the policy of the State in this respect; and as the franchise of the ferry and that of the bridge are different in their nature. . . .

[T]here is no rule of legal interpretation which would authorize the court to associate these grants together, and to infer that any privilege was intended to be given to the bridge company, merely because it had been conferred on the ferry. The charter to the bridge is a written instrument which must speak for itself, and be interpreted by its own terms.

This brings us to the Act of the Legislature of Massachusetts of 1785, by which the plaintiffs were incorporated by the name of "The Proprietors of the Charles River Bridge;" and it is here, and in the law of 1792, prolonging their charter, that we must look for the extent and nature of the franchise conferred upon the plaintiffs. . . .

"This, like many other cases, is a bargain between a company of adventurers and the public, the terms of which are expressed in the statute; and the rule of construction in all such cases, is now fully established to be this—that any ambiguity in the terms of the contract, must operate against the adventurers, and in favor of the public, and the plaintiffs can claim nothing that is not clearly given them by the act." And the doctrine thus laid down is abundantly sustained by the authorities referred to, in this decision. . . .

[T]he object and end of all government is to promote the happiness and prosperity of the community by which it is established, and it can never be assumed that the government intended to diminish its power of accomplishing the end for which it was created. And in a country like ours, free, active and enterprising, continually advancing in numbers and wealth; new channels of communication are daily found necessary, both for travel and trade, and are essential to the comfort, convenience, and prosperity of the people. A State ought never to be presumed to surrender this power, because, like the taxing power, the whole community have an interest in preserving it undiminished. And when a corporation alleges that a State has surrendered for seventy years its power of improvement and public accommodation, in a great and important line of travel, along which a vast number of its citizens must daily pass; the community have a right to insist, in the language of this court above quoted, "that its abandonment ought not to be presumed, in a case in which the deliberate purpose of the State to abandon it does not appear." The continued existence of a government would be of no great value, if by implications and presumptions, it was disarmed of the powers necessary to accomplish the ends of its creation, and the functions it was designed to perform, transferred to the hands of privileged corporations. The rule of construction announced by the court was not confined to the taxing power, nor is it so limited in the opinion delivered. On the contrary, it was distinctly placed on the ground that the interests of the community were concerned in preserving, undiminished, the power then in question; and whenever any power of the State is said to be surrendered or diminished, whether it be the taxing power or any other affecting the public interest, the same principle applies, and the rule of construction must be the same. No one will question that the interests of the great body of the people of the State, would, in this instance, be affected by the surrender of this great line of travel to a single corporation, with the right to exact toll, and exclude competition for seventy years. While the rights of private property are sacredly guarded, we must not forget that the community also have rights, and that the happiness and well being of every citizen depends on their faithful preservation.

Adopting the rule of construction above stated as the settled one, we proceed to apply it to the charter of 1785, to the proprietors of the Charles River Bridge. This act of incorporation is in the usual form, and the privileges such as are commonly given to corporations of that kind. It confers on them the ordinary faculties of a corporation, for the purpose of building the bridge; and establishes certain rates of toll, which the company are authorized to take. This is the whole grant. There is no exclusive privilege given to them over the waters of Charles River, above or below their bridge. No right to erect another bridge themselves, nor to prevent other persons from erecting one. No engagement from the State that another shall not be erected, and no undertaking not to sanction competition, nor to make improvements that may diminish the amount of its income. Upon all these subjects the charter is silent, and nothing is said in it about a line of travel, so much insisted on in the argument, in which they are to have exclusive privileges. No words are used from which an intention to grant any of these rights can be inferred. If the plaintiff is entitled to them, it must be implied simply from the nature of the grant, and cannot be inferred from the words by which the grant is made.

The relative position of the Warren Bridge has already been described. It does not interrupt the passage over the Charles River Bridge, nor make the way to it or from it less convenient. None of the faculties or franchises granted to that corporation have been revoked by the Legislature; and its right to take the tolls granted by the charter remains unaltered. In short, all the franchises and rights of property enumerated in the charter, and there mentioned to have been granted to it, remain unimpaired. But its income is destroyed by the Warren Bridge; which, being free, draws off the passengers and property which would have gone over it, and renders their franchise of no value. This is the gist of the complaint. For it is not pretended that the erection of the Warren Bridge would have done them any injury, or in any degree affected their right of property, if it had not diminished the amount of their tolls. In order, then, to entitle themselves to relief, it is necessary to show that the Legislature contracted not to do the act of which they complain; and that they impaired, or in other words violated, that contract, by the erection of the Warren Bridge.

The inquiry then is, does the charter contain such a contract on the part of the State? Is there any such stipulation to be found in that instrument? It must be admitted on all hands, that there is none—no words that even relate to another bridge, or to the diminution of their tolls, or to the line of travel. If a contract on that subject can be gathered from the charter, it must be by implication, and cannot be found in the words used. Can such an agreement be implied? The rule of construction before stated is an answer to the question. In charters of this description, no rights are taken from the public or given to the corporation, beyond those which the words of the charter, by their natural and proper construction, purport to convey. There are no words which import such a contract as the plaintiffs in error contend for, and none can be implied. . . .

Indeed, the practice and usage of almost every State in the Union, old enough to have commenced the work of internal improvement, is opposed to the doctrine contended for on the part of the plaintiffs in error. Turnpike roads have been made in succession, on the same line of travel; the latter ones interfering materially with the profits of the first. These corporations have, in some instances, been utterly ruined by the introduction of newer and better modes of transportation and traveling. In some cases railroads have rendered the turnpike roads on the same line of travel so entirely useless, that the franchise of the turnpike corporation is not worth preserving. Yet in none of these cases have the corporations supposed that their privileges were invaded, or any contract violated on the part of the State. . . .

If this court should establish the principles now contended for, what is to become of the numerous railroads established on the same line of travel with turnpike companies; and which have rendered the franchises of the turnpike corporations of no value? Let it once be understood that such charters carry with them these implied contracts, and give this unknown and undefined property in a line of traveling, and you will soon find the old turnpike corporations awakening from their sleep, and calling upon this court to put down the improvements which have taken their place. The millions of property which have been invested in railroads and canals, upon lines of travel which had been before occupied by turnpike corporations, will be put in jeopardy. We shall be thrown back to the improvements of the last century, and obliged to stand still until the claims of the old turnpike corporations shall be satisfied, and they shall consent to permit these States to avail themselves of the lights of modern science, and to partake of the benefit of those improvements which are now adding to the wealth and prosperity, and the convenience and comfort, of every other part of the civilized world. . . .

The judgment of the Supreme Judicial Court of the Commonwealth of Massachusetts, dismissing the plaintiffs' bill, must, therefore, be affirmed with costs.

☐ *Justice McLEAN concurred in a separate opinion, expressing his view that the case should be dismissed for lack of jurisdiction.*

☐ *Justice STORY, dissenting.*

I admit that where the terms of a grant are to impose burdens upon the public, or to create a restraint injurious to the public interest, there is sound reason for interpreting the terms, if ambiguous, in favor of the public. But at the same time, I insist that there is not the slightest reason for saying, even in such a case, that the grant is not to be construed favorably to the grantee, so as to secure him in the enjoyment of what is actually granted. . . .

This charter is not . . . any restriction upon the legislative power, unless it be true that because the Legislature cannot grant again what it has already granted, the legislative power is restricted. If so, then every grant of the public land is a restriction upon that power; a doctrine that has never yet been established, nor (as far as I know) ever contended for. Every grant of a franchise is, so far as that grant extends, necessarily exclusive; and cannot be resumed, or interfered with. All the learned judges in the State court admitted that the franchise of Charles River Bridge, whatever it be, could not be resumed or interfered with. The Legislature could not recall its grant or destroy it. It is a contract, whose obligation cannot be constitutionally impaired. In this respect, it does not differ from a grant of lands. In each case, the particular land, or the particular franchise, is withdrawn from the legislative operation. . . .

Then, again, how is it established that this is a grant in derogation of the rights and interests of the people? No individual citizen has any right to build a bridge over navigable waters; and consequently he is deprived of no right, when a grant is made to any other persons for that purpose. Whether it promotes or injures the particular interest of an individual citizen, constitutes no ground for judicial or legislative interference, beyond what his own rights justify. When, then, it is said that such a grant is in derogation of the rights and interests of the people, we must understand that reference is had to the rights and interests common to the whole people, as such (such as the right of navigation), or belonging to them as a political body; or, in other words, the rights and interests of the State. Now, I cannot understand how any grant of a franchise is a derogation from the rights of the people of the State, any more than a grant of public land. The right, in each case, is gone to the extent of the thing granted, and so far may be said to derogate from, that is to say, to lessen the rights of the people, or of the State. But that is not the sense in which the argument is pressed; for, by derogation, is here meant an injurious or mischievous detraction from the sovereign rights of the State. On the other hand, there can be no derogation from the rights of the people, as such, except it applies to rights common there before; which the building of a bridge over navigable waters certainly is not. If it had been said that the grant of this bridge was in derogation of the common right of navigating the Charles River, by reason of its obstructing, pro tanto, a free and open passage, the ground would have been intelligible. So, if it had been an exclusive grant of the navigation of that stream. But, if at the same time, equivalent public rights of a different nature, but of greater public accommodation and use, had been obtained; it could hardly have been said, in a correct sense, that there was any derogation from the rights of the people, or the rights of the State. It would be a mere exchange of one public right for another. . . .

No sound lawyer will, I presume, assert that the grant of a right to erect a bridge over a navigable stream, is a grant of a common right. Before such grant, had all the citizens of the State a right to erect bridges over navigable streams? Certainly they had not; and, therefore, the grant was no restriction of any common right. It was neither a monopoly, nor, in a legal sense, had it any tendency to a monopoly. It took from no citizen what he possessed before, and had no tendency to take it from him. It took, indeed, from the Legislature the power of granting the same identical privilege or franchise to any other persons. But this made it no more a monopoly than the grant of the public stock or funds of a State for a valuable consideration. Even in cases of monopolies, strictly so called, if the nature of the grant be such that it is for the public good, as in cases of patents for inventions, the rule has always been to give them a favorable construction in support of the patent. . . .

I have thus endeavored to answer, and I think I have successfully answered all the arguments (which indeed run into each other) adduced to justify a strict construction of the present charter. I go farther, and maintain not only that it is not a case for strict construction, but that the charter upon its very face, by its terms, and for its professed objects, demands from the court, upon undeniable principles of law, a favorable construction for the grantees. In the first place, the Legislature has declared that the erecting of the bridge will be of great public utility; and this exposition of its own motives for the grant requires the court to give a liberal interpretation, in order to promote, and not to destroy an enterprise of great public utility. In the next place, the grant is a contract for a valuable consideration, and a full and adequate consideration. The proprietors are to lay out a large sum of money (and in those times it was a very large outlay of capital) in erecting a bridge; they are to keep it in repair during the whole period of forty years; they are to surrender it in good repair at the end of that period to the State, as its own property; they are to pay, during the whole period, an annuity of two hundred pounds to Harvard College; and they are to incur other heavy expenses and burdens, for the public accommodation. In return for all these charges, they are entitled to no more than the receipt of the tolls during the forty years, for their reimbursement of capital, interest and expenses. With all this they are to take upon themselves the chances of success; and if the enterprise fails, the loss is exclusively their own. Nor let any man imagine that there was not, at the time when this charter was granted, much solid ground for doubting success. In order to entertain a just view of this subject, we must go back to that period of general bankruptcy, and distress and difficulty. The Constitution of the United States was not only not then in existence, but it was not then even dreamed of. The union of the States was crumbling into ruins, under the old confederation. Agriculture, manufactures and commerce were at their lowest ebb. There was infinite danger to all the States from local interests and jealousies, and from the apparent impossibility of a much longer adherence to that shadow of a government the Continental Congress. And even four years afterwards, when every evil had been greatly aggravated, and civil war was added to other calamities, the Constitution of the United States was all but shipwrecked in passing through the State conventions. It was adopted by very slender majorities. These are historical facts which required no coloring to give them effect, and admitted of no concealment to seduce men into schemes of future aggrandizement. I would even now put it to the common sense of every man, whether, if the Constitution of the United States had not been adopted, the charter would have been worth a forty years' purchase of the tolls. . . .

Now, I put it to the common sense of every man, whether if at the moment of granting the charter the Legislature had said to the proprietors—you shall build the bridge; you shall bear the burdens; you shall be bound by the charges; and your sole re-imbursement shall be from the tolls of forty years: and yet we will not even guaranty you any certainty of receiving any tolls. On the contrary, we reserve to ourselves the full power and authority to erect other bridges, toll or free bridges, according to our own free will and pleasure, contiguous to yours, and having the same termini with yours; and if you are successful we may thus supplant you, divide, destroy your profits, and annihilate your tolls, without annihilating your burdens: if, I say, such had been the language of the Legislature, is there a man living of ordinary discretion or prudence, who would have accepted such a charter upon such terms? I fearlessly answer no. . . .

Yet, this is the very form and pressure of the present case. It is not an imaginary and extravagant case. Warren Bridge has been erected, under such a supposed reserved authority, in the immediate neighborhood of Charles River Bridge; and with the same termini, to accommodate the same line of travel. For a half dozen years it was to be a toll bridge for the benefit of the proprietors, to re-imburse them for their expenditures. At the end of that period, the bridge is to become the property of the State, and free of toll, unless the Legislature should hereafter impose one. In point of fact, it has since become, and now is, under the sanction of the act of incorporation, and other subsequent acts, a free bridge without the payment of any tolls for all persons. So that, in truth, here now is a free bridge, owned by and erected under the authority of the Commonwealth, which necessarily takes away all the tolls from Charles River Bridge, while its prolonged charter has twenty years to run. And yet the act of the Legislature establishing Warren Bridge is said to be no violation of the franchise granted to the Charles River Bridge. . . .

To sum up, then, the whole argument on this head, I maintain that, upon the principles of common reason and legal interpretation, the present grant carries with it a necessary implication that the Legislature shall do no act to destroy or essentially to impair the franchise: that (as one of the learned judges of the State court expressed it) there is an implied agreement that the State will not grant another bridge between Boston and Charlestown, so near as to draw away the custom from the old one: and (as another learned judge expressed it) that there is an implied agreement of the State to grant the undisturbed use of the bridge and its tolls, so far as respects any acts of its own, or of any persons acting under its authority. In other words, the State, impliedly, contracts not to resume its grant, or to do any act to the prejudice or destruction of its grant.

Home Building & Loan Association v. Blaisdell
290 U.S. 398, 54 S.CT. 231 (1934)

In response to the social pressures arising from the economic depression in the early 1930s, Minnesota's legislature passed the Minnesota Moratorium Act of 1934. The law authorized state courts to postpone the payments of homeowners and farmers on mortgages to prevent their foreclosures. Under the act, John Blaisdell sought an extension of time on the payment of his mortgage to Home Building & Loan Association. But a trial court granted a motion to dismiss Blaisdell's petition. The Minnesota Supreme Court reversed and the trial court subsequently granted Blaisdell an extension of time on his mortgage payments. Home Building & Loan Association appealed, contending that Minnesota's moratorium law violated state and federal protections for private contracts and the taking of property without the due process of law.

The Court's decision was five to four; the majority's opinion was announced by Chief Justice Hughes. Justice Sutherland dissented and was joined by Justices Van Devanter, McReynolds, and Butler.

☐ *Chief Justice HUGHES delivered the opinion of the Court.*

In determining whether the provision for this temporary and conditional relief exceeds the power of the state by reason of the clause in the Federal Constitution prohibiting impairment of the obligations of contracts, we must consider the relation of emergency to constitutional power, the historical setting of the contract clause, the development of the jurisprudence of this Court in the construction of that clause, and the principles of construction which we may consider to be established.

Emergency does not create power. Emergency does not increase granted power or remove or diminish the restrictions imposed upon power granted or reserved. The Constitution was adopted in a period of grave emergency. Its grants of power to the federal government and its limitations of the power of the States were determined in the light of emergency, and they are not altered by emergency. What power was thus granted and what limitations were thus imposed are questions which have always been, and always will be, the subject of close examination under our constitutional system.

While emergency does not create power, emergency may furnish the occasion for the exercise of power. . . . The constitutional question presented in the light of an emergency is whether the power possessed embraces the particular exercise of it in response to particular conditions. . . .

In the construction of the contract clause, the debates in the Constitutional Convention are of little aid. But the reasons which led to the adoption of that clause, and of the other prohibitions of section 10 of article 1, are not left in doubt, and have frequently been described with eloquent emphasis. The widespread distress following the revolutionary period and the plight of debtors had called forth in the States an ignoble array of legislative schemes for the defeat of creditors and the invasion of contractual obligations. Legislative interferences had been so numerous and extreme that the confidence essential to prosperous trade had been undermined and the utter destruction of credit was threatened. "The sober people of America" were convinced that some "thorough reform" was needed which would "inspire a general prudence and industry, and give a regular course to the business of society." The *Federalist*, No. 44. It was necessary to interpose the restraining power of a central authority in order to secure the foundations even of "private faith." The occasion and general purpose of the contract clause are summed up in the terse statement of Chief Justice MARSHALL in *Ogden v. Saunders*, 12 Wheat. 213 [(1827)]. "The power of changing the relative situation of debtor and creditor, of interfering with contracts, a power which comes home to every man, touches the interest of all, and controls the conduct of every individual in those things which he supposes to be proper for his own exclusive management, had been used to such an excess by the state legislatures, as to break in upon the ordinary intercourse of society, and destroy all confidence between man and man. This mischief had become so great, so alarming, as not only to impair commercial intercourse, and threaten the existence of credit, but to sap the morals of the people, and destroy the sanctity of private faith. To guard against the continuance of the

"Hooverville," named after President Herbert Hoover, in New York City during the Great Depression. Hoover was president from 1928 to 1932, when he lost the presidential election to Democrat Franklin D. Roosevelt. The economic collapse that began in Hoover's first year as president led to the Great Depression. (*Corbis/Bettmann*)

evil, was an object of deep interest with all the truly wise, as well as the virtuous, of this great community, and was one of the important benefits expected from a reform of the government." . . .

The obligation of a contract is the law which binds the parties to perform their agreement. This Court has said that "the laws which subsist at the time and place of the making of a contract, and where it is to be performed, enter into and form a part of it, as if they were expressly referred to or incorporated in its terms." This principle embraces alike those which affect its validity, construction, discharge, and enforcement. . . .

Not only is the constitutional provision qualified by the measure of control which the state retains over remedial processes, but the state also continues to possess authority to safeguard the vital interests of its people. It does not matter that legislation appropriate to that end "has the result of modifying or abrogating contracts already in effect." Not only are existing laws read into contracts in order to fix obligations as between the parties, but the reservation of essential attributes of sovereign power is also read into contracts as a postulate of the legal order. The policy of protecting contracts against impairment presupposes the maintenance of a government by virtue of which contractual relations are worth while,—a government which retains adequate authority to secure the peace and good order of society. This principle of harmonizing the constitutional prohibition with the necessary residuum of state power has had progressive recognition in the decisions of this Court. . . .

The question is not whether the legislative action affects contracts incidentally, or directly or indirectly, but whether the legislation is addressed to a legitimate end and the measures taken are reasonable and appropriate to that end. . . .

Undoubtedly, whatever is reserved of state power must be consistent with the fair intent of the constitutional limitation of that power. The reserved power cannot be construed so as to destroy the limitation, nor is the limitation to be construed to destroy the reserved power in its essential aspects. They must be construed in harmony with each other. This principle precludes a construction which would permit the state to adopt as its policy the repudiation of debts or the destruction of contracts or the denial of means to enforce them. But it does not follow that conditions may not arise in which a temporary restraint of enforcement may be consistent with the spirit and purpose of the constitutional provision and thus be found to be within the range of the reserved power of the state to protect the vital interests of the community. It cannot be maintained that the constitutional prohibition should be so construed as to prevent limited and temporary interpositions with respect to the enforcement of contracts if made necessary by a great public calamity such as fire, flood, or earthquake. . . .

Where, in earlier days, it was thought that only the concerns of individuals or of classes were involved, and that those of the state itself were touched only remotely, it has later been found that the fundamental interests of the state are directly affected; and that the question is no longer merely that of one party to a contract as against another, but of the use of reasonable means to safeguard the economic structure upon which the good of all depends.

It is no answer to say that this public need was not apprehended a century ago, or to insist that what the provision of the Constitution meant to the vision of that day it must mean to the vision of our time. If by the statement that what the Constitution meant at the time of its adoption it means to-day, it is intended to say that the great clauses of the Constitution must be confined to the interpretation which the framers, with the conditions and outlook of their time, would have placed upon them, the statement carries its own refutation. It was to guard against such a narrow conception that Chief Justice MARSHALL uttered the memorable warning: "We must never forget, that it is *a constitution* we are expounding" (*McCulloch v. Maryland*, 4 Wheat. 316 [(1819)]) "a constitution intended to endure for ages to come, and, consequently, to be adapted to the various *crises* of human affairs." . . . When we are dealing with the words of the Constitution, said this Court in *Missouri v. Holland*, 252 U.S. 416 [(1920)], "we must realize that they have called into life a being the development of which could not have been foreseen completely by the most gifted of its begetters. . . . The case before us must be considered in the light of our whole experience and not merely in that of what was said a hundred years ago."

Nor is it helpful to attempt to draw a fine distinction between the intended meaning of the words of the Constitution and their intended application. When we consider the contract clause and the decisions which have expounded it in harmony with the essential reserved power of the states to protect the security of their peoples, we find no warrant for the conclusion that the clause has been warped by these decisions from its proper significance or that the founders of our government would have interpreted the clause differently had they had occasion to assume that responsibility in the conditions of the later day. The vast body of law which has been developed was unknown to the fathers, but it is believed to have preserved the essential content and the spirit of the Constitution. With a growing recognition of public needs and the relation of individual right to public security, the court has sought to prevent the perversion of the clause through its use as an instrument to throttle the capacity of the states to protect their fundamental interests. This development is a growth from the seeds which the fathers planted. It is a development forecast by the prophetic words of Justice Johnson in *Ogden v. Saunders*, already quoted. And the germs of the later decisions are found in the early cases of the *Charles River Bridge* [11 Pet. 420 (1837)] and the *West River Bridge* [*Co. v. Dix*, 6 How. (47 U.S.) 506 (1848)], which upheld the public right against strong insistence upon the contract clause. The principle of this development is, as we have seen, that the reservation of the reasonable exercise of the protective power of the state is read into all contracts, and there is no greater reason for refusing to apply this principle to Minnesota mortgages. . . .

Applying the criteria established by our decisions, we conclude:

1. An emergency existed in Minnesota which furnished a proper occasion for the exercise of the reserved power of the state to protect the vital interests of the community. The declarations of the existence of this emergency by the Legislature and by the Supreme Court of Minnesota cannot be regarded as a subterfuge or as lacking in adequate basis. . . .

2. The legislation was addressed to a legitimate end; that is, the legislation was not for the mere advantage of particular individuals but for the protection of a basic interest of society.

3. In view of the nature of the contracts in question—mortgages of unquestionable validity—the relief afforded and justified by the emergency, in order not to contravene the constitutional provision, could only be of a character appropriate to that emergency, and could be granted only upon reasonable conditions.

4. The conditions upon which the period of redemption is extended do not appear to be unreasonable. . . .

5. The legislation is temporary in operation. It is limited to the exigency which called it forth. While the postponement of the period of redemption from the foreclosure sale is to May 1, 1935, that period may be reduced by the order of the court under the statute, in case of a change in circumstances, and the operation of the statute itself could not validly outlast the emergency or be so extended as virtually to destroy the contracts.

We are of the opinion that the Minnesota statute as here applied does not violate the contract clause of the Federal Constitution. Whether the legislation is wise or unwise as a matter of policy is a question with which we are not concerned.

☐ *Justice SUTHERLAND dissenting, joined by Justices VAN DEVANTER, McREYNOLDS, and BUTLER.*

Few questions of greater moment than that just decided have been submitted for judicial inquiry during this generation. He simply closes his eyes to the necessary implications of the decision who fails to see in it the potentiality of future gradual but ever-advancing encroachments upon the sanctity of private and public contracts. . . .

A provision of the Constitution, it is hardly necessary to say, does not admit of two distinctly opposite interpretations. It does not mean one thing at one time and an entirely different thing at another time. If the contract impairment clause, when framed and adopted, meant that the terms of a contract for the payment of money could not be altered in invitum by a state statute enacted for the relief of hardly pressed debtors to the end and with the effect of postponing payment or enforcement during and because of an economic or financial emergency, it is but to state the obvious to say that it means the same now. . . .

[W]e are here dealing, not with a power granted by the Federal Constitution, but with the state police power, which exists in its own right. Hence the question is, not whether an emergency furnishes the occasion for the exercise of that state power, but whether an emergency furnishes an occasion for the relaxation of the restrictions upon the power imposed by the contract impairment clause; and the difficulty is that the contract impairment clause forbids state action under any circumstances, if it have the effect of impairing the obligation of contracts. That clause restricts every state power in the particular specified, no matter what may be the occasion. It does not contemplate that an emergency shall furnish an occasion for softening the restriction or making it any the less a restriction upon state action in that contingency than it is under strictly normal conditions.

The Minnesota statute either impairs the obligation of contracts or it does not. If it does not, the occasion to which it relates becomes immaterial, since then the passage of the statute is the exercise of a normal, unrestricted, state power and requires no special occasion to render it effective. If it does, the emergency no more furnishes a proper occasion for its exercise than if the emergency were nonexistent. And so, while, in form, the suggested distinction seems to put us forward in a straight line, in reality it simply carries us back in a circle, like bewildered travelers lost in a wood, to the point where we parted company with the view of the state court.

If what has now been said is sound, as I think it is, we come to what really is the vital question in the case: Does the Minnesota statute constitute an impairment of the obligation of the contract now under review? . . .

It is quite true . . . that "the reservation of essential attributes of sovereign power is also read into contracts"; and that the Legislature cannot "bargain away the public health or the public morals." General statutes to put an end to lotteries, the sale or manufacture of intoxicating liquors, the maintenance of nuisances, to protect the public safety, etc., although they have the indirect effect of absolutely destroying private contracts previously made in contemplation of a continuance of the state of affairs then in existence but subsequently prohibited, have been uniformly upheld as not violating the contract impairment clause. The distinction between legislation of that character and the Minnesota statute, however, is readily observable. . . .

[T]he statute denies appellant for a period of two years the ownership and possession of the property—an asset which, in any event, is of substantial character, and which possibly may turn out to be of great value. The statute, therefore, is not merely a modification of the remedy; it effects a material and injurious change in the obligation.

City of El Paso v. Simmons
379 U.S. 497, 85 S.Ct. 577 (1965)

Since 1876, Texas had offered land for sale to raise funds for public schools and to settle the state. Under its law, land could be bought with a down payment of one-fortieth of the purchase price and the annual payment of 3 percent interest. If a purchaser missed an interest payment, the land was forfeited to the state unless the purchaser paid the interest before a third party obtained title to the land. Under this program, Greenberry Simmons bought some forfeited land which he in turn forfeited to the state in 1947. Two days and five years later, however, Simmons offered to pay the interest and applied to have his land reinstated. The state denied his request, citing a 1941 amendment to its law barring the reinstatement of forfeited land after five years from the date of forfeiture. Texas then sold the land to the City of El Paso in 1955. And Simmons sued in federal district court for the return of the land title, claiming that Texas's 1941 amendment to its law violated the contract clause of the Constitution. A district court judge decided for the city but a federal appellate court reversed. The City of El Paso then appealed to the Supreme Court.

The Court's decision was eight to one, with the majority's opinion announced by Justice White. Justice Black dissented.

☐ *Justice WHITE delivered the opinion of the Court.*

The City seeks to bring this case within the long line of cases recognizing a distinction between contract obligation and remedy and permitting a modification of the remedy as long as there is no substantial impairment of the value of the obligation.

We do not pause to consider further whether the Court of Appeals correctly ascertained the Texas law at the time these contracts were made, or to chart again the dividing line under federal law between "remedy" and "obligation," or to determine the extent to which this line is controlled by state court decisions, decisions often rendered in contexts not involving Contract Clause considerations. For it is not every modification of a contractual promise that impairs the obligation of contract under federal law, any more than it is every alteration of existing remedies that violates the Contract Clause. . . .

The decisions "put it beyond question that the prohibition is not an absolute one and is not to be read with literal exactness like a mathematical formula," as Chief Justice HUGHES said in *Home Building & Loan Assn. v. Blaisdell*, 290 U.S. 398 [(1934)], The *Blaisdell* opinion, which amounted to a comprehensive restatement of the principles underlying the application of the Contract Clause, makes it quite clear that "[n]ot only is the constitutional provision qualified by the measure of control which the state retains over remedial processes, but the state also continues to possess authority to safeguard the vital interests of its people. It does not matter that legislation appropriate to that end 'has the result of modifying or abrogating contracts already in effect.' " . . .

Of course, the power of a State to modify or affect the obligation of contract is not without limit. . . . But we think the objects of the Texas statute make abundantly clear that it impairs no protected right under the Contract Clause. . . .

The circumstances behind the 1941 amendment are well described in the Reports of the Commissioner of the General Land Office. The general purpose of the legislation enacted in 1941 was to restore confidence in the stability and integrity of land titles and to enable the State to protect and administer its property in a businesslike manner. . . .

The State's policy of quick resale of forfeited lands did not prove entirely successful; forfeiting purchasers who repurchased the lands again defaulted and other purchasers bought without any intention of complying with their contracts unless mineral wealth was discovered. The market for land contracted during the depression. These developments hardly to be expected or foreseen, operated to confer considerable advantages on the purchaser and his successors and a costly and difficult burden on the State. . . .

Laws which restrict a party to those gains reasonably to be expected from the contract are not subject to attack under the Contract Clause, notwithstanding that they technically alter an obligation of a contract. The five-year limitation allows defaulting purchasers with a bona fide interest in their lands a reasonable time to reinstate. It does not and need not allow defaulting purchasers with a speculative interest in the discovery of minerals to remain in endless default while retaining a cloud on title. . . .

The measure taken to induce defaulting purchasers to comply with their contracts, requiring payment of interest in arrears within five years, was a mild one indeed, hardly burdensome to the purchaser who wanted to adhere to his contract of purchase, but nonetheless an important one to the State's interest. The Contract Clause does not forbid such a measure.

The judgment is reversed.

☐ *Justice BLACK, dissenting.*

I have previously had a number of occasions to dissent from judgments of this Court balancing away the First Amendment's unequivocally guaranteed rights of free speech, press, assembly and petition. In this case I am compelled to dissent from the Court's balancing away the plain guarantee of Art. 1. § 10, that

"No State shall . . . pass any . . . Law impairing the Obligation of Contracts . . . ,"

a balancing which results in the State of Texas' taking a man's private property for public use without compensation in violation of the equally plain guarantee of the Fifth Amendment, made applicable to the States by the Fourteenth, that

". . . private property [shall not] be taken for public use, without just compensation."

The respondent, Simmons, is the loser and the treasury of the State of Texas the ultimate beneficiary of the Court's action.

I do not believe that any or all of the things set out above on which the Court relies are reasons for relieving Texas of the unconditional duty of keeping its contractual obligations as required by the Contract Clause. At most the Court's reasons boil down to the fact that Texas' contracts, perhaps very wisely made a long time ago, turned out when land soared in value, and particularly after oil was discovered, to be costly to the State. As the Court euphemistically puts it, the contracts were "not wholly effectual to serve the objectives of the State's land program many decades later. Settlement was no longer the objective, but revenues . . ." among other things were. In plainer language, the State decided it had made a bad deal and wanted out. There is nothing unusual in this. It is a commonplace that land values steadily rise when population increases and rise sharply when valuable minerals are discovered, and that many sellers would be much richer and happier if when lands go up in value they were able to welch on their sales. No plethora of words about state school funds can conceal the fact that to get money easily without having to tax the whole public Texas took the easy way out and violated the Contract Clause of the Constitution as written and as applied up to now. If the values of these lands and of valid contracts to buy them have increased, that increase belongs in equity as well as in sound constitutional interpretation not to Texas, but to the many people who agreed to these contracts under what now turns out to have been a mistaken belief that Texas would keep the obligations it gave to those who dealt with it.

All this for me is just another example of the delusiveness of calling "balancing" a "test." With its deprecatory view of the equities on the side of Simmons and other claimants and its remarkable sympathy for the State, the Court through its balancing process states the case in a way inevitably destined to bypass the Contract Clause and let Texas break its solemn obligation. As the Court's opinion demonstrates, constitutional adjudication under the balancing method becomes simply a matter of this Court's deciding for itself which result in a particular case seems in the circumstances the more acceptable governmental policy and then stating the facts in such a way that the considerations in the balance lead to the result. Even if I believed that we as Justices of this Court had the authority to rely on our judgment of what is best for the country instead of trying to interpret the language and purpose of our written Constitution, I would not agree that Texas should be permitted to do what it has done here. But more importantly, I most certainly cannot agree that constitutional law is simply a matter of what the Justices of this Court decide is not harmful for the country, and therefore is "reasonable." James Madison said that the Contract Clause was intended to protect people from the "fluctuating policy" of the legislature. The *Federalist*, No. 44. Today's majority holds that people are not protected from the fluctuating policy of the legislature, so long as the legislature acts in accordance with the fluctuating policy of this Court.

United States Trust Co. of New York v. State of New Jersey
431 U.S. 1, 97 S.Ct. 1505 (1977)

In 1962, New York and New Jersey made an interstate compact limiting the Port Authority's ability to subsidize mass transit through bonds. But during the 1974 energy crisis, the New York and New Jersey legislatures repealed the covenant. The United States Trust Company of New York, a trustee and bondholder of the Port Authority, contended that repealing the covenant violated the contract clause and filed a lawsuit which a state court dismissed. The New Jersey Supreme Court affirmed and United States Trust Company of New York appealed to the Supreme Court.

The Court's decision was four to three, with Justices Powell and Stewart not participating and with the majority's opinion announced by Justice Blackmun. Chief Justice Burger concurred. Justice Brennan, joined by Justices White and Marshall, dissented.

☐ *Justice BLACKMUN delivered the opinion of the Court.*

This case presents a challenge to a New Jersey statute as violative of the Contract Clause of the United States Constitution. That statute, together with a concurrent, and parallel New York statute repealed a statutory covenant made by the two States in 1962 that had limited the ability of The Port Authority of New York and New Jersey to subsidize rail passenger transportation from revenues and reserves. . . .

The trial court concluded that repeal of the 1962 covenant was a valid exercise of New Jersey's police power because repeal served important public interests in mass transportation, energy conservation, and environmental protection. Yet the Contract Clause limits otherwise legitimate exercises of state legislative authority, and the existence of an important public interest is not always sufficient to overcome that limitation. . . .

Of course, to say that the financial restrictions of the 1962 covenant were valid when adopted does not finally resolve this case. The Contract Clause is not an absolute bar to subsequent modification of a State's own financial obligations. As with laws impairing the obligations of private contracts, an impairment may be constitutional if it is reasonable and necessary to serve an important public purpose. In applying this standard, however, complete deference to a legislative assessment of reasonableness and necessity is not appropriate because the State's self-interest is at stake. A governmental entity can always find a use for extra money, especially when taxes do not have to be raised. If a State could reduce its financial obligations whenever it wanted to spend the money for what it regarded as an important public purpose, the Contract Clause would provide no protection at all. . . .

Mass transportation, energy conservation, and environmental protection are goals that are important and of legitimate public concern. Appellees contend that these goals are so important that any harm to bondholders from repeal of the 1962 covenant is greatly outweighed by the public benefit. We do not accept this invitation to engage in a utilitarian comparison of public benefit and private loss. Contrary to Justice BLACK's fear expressed in sole dissent in *El Paso v. Simmons* [379 U.S. 497 (1965)], the Court has not "balanced away" the limitation on state action imposed by the Contract Clause. Thus a State cannot refuse to meet its legitimate financial obligations simply because it would prefer to spend the money to promote the public good rather than the private welfare of its creditors. We can only sustain the repeal of the 1962 covenant if that impairment was both reasonable and necessary to serve the admittedly important purposes claimed by the State.

The more specific justification offered for the repeal of the 1962 covenant was the States' plan for encouraging users of private automobiles to shift to public transportation. The States intended to discourage private automobile use by raising bridge and tunnel tolls and to use the extra revenue from those tolls to subsidize improved commuter railroad service. Appellees contend that repeal of the 1962 covenant was necessary to implement this plan because the new mass transit facilities could not possibly be self-supporting and the covenant's "permitted deficits" level had already been exceeded. We reject this justification because the repeal was neither necessary to achievement of the plan nor reasonable in light of the circumstances.

The determination of necessity can be considered on two levels. First, it cannot be said that total repeal of the covenant was essential; a less drastic modification would have permitted the contemplated plan without entirely removing the covenant's limitations on the use of Port Authority revenues and reserves to subsidize commuter railroads. Second, without modifying the covenant at all, the States could have adopted alternative means of achieving their twin goals of discouraging automobile use and improving mass transit. . . .

We also cannot conclude that repeal of the covenant was reasonable in light of the surrounding circumstances. In this regard a comparison with *El Paso v. Simmons*, supra, again is instructive. There a 19th century statute had effects that were unforeseen and unintended by the legislature when originally adopted. As a result speculators were placed in a position to obtain windfall benefits. The Court held that adoption of a statute of limitation was a reasonable means to "restrict a party to those gains reasonably to be expected from the contract" when it was adopted. . . .

By contrast, in the instant case the need for mass transportation in the New York metropolitan area was not a new development, and the likelihood that publicly owned commuter railroads would produce substantial deficits was well known. As early as 1922, over a half century ago, there were pressures to involve the Port Authority in mass transit. It was with full knowledge of these concerns that the 1962 covenant was adopted. . . .

During the 12-year period between adoption of the covenant and its repeal, public perception of the importance of mass transit undoubtedly grew because of increased general concern with environmental protection and energy conservation. But these concerns were not unknown in 1962, and the subsequent changes were of degree and not of kind. We cannot say that these changes caused the covenant to have a substantially different impact in 1974 than when it was adopted in 1962. And we cannot conclude that the repeal was reasonable in the light of changed circumstances.

We therefore hold that the Contract Clause of the United States Constitution prohibits the retroactive repeal of the 1962 covenant. The judgment of the Supreme Court of New Jersey is reversed.

It is so ordered.

☐ *Justice BRENNAN, with whom Justice WHITE and Justice MAR-SHALL join, dissenting.*

Decisions of this Court for at least a century have construed the Contract Clause largely to be powerless in binding a State to contracts limiting the authority of successor legislatures to enact laws in furtherance of the health, safety, and similar collective interests of the polity. In short, those decisions established the principle that lawful exercises of a State's police powers stand paramount to private rights held under contract. Today's decision, in invalidating the New Jersey Legislature's 1974 repeal of its predecessor's 1962 covenant, rejects this previous understanding and remolds the Contract Clause into a potent instrument for overseeing important policy determinations of the state legislature. At the same time, by creating a constitutional safe haven for property rights embodied in a contract, the decision substantially distorts modern constitutional jurisprudence governing regulation of private economic interests. . . .

One of the fundamental premises of our popular democracy is that each generation of representatives can and will remain responsive to the needs and desires of those whom they represent. Crucial to this end is the assurance that new legislators will not automatically be bound by the policies and undertakings of earlier days. In accordance with this philosophy, the Framers of our Constitution conceived of the Contract Clause primarily as protection for economic transactions entered into by purely private parties, rather than obligations involving the State itself. The Framers fully recognized that nothing would so jeopardize the legitimacy of a system of government that relies upon the ebbs and flows of politics to "clean out the rascals" than the possibility that those same rascals might perpetuate their policies simply by locking them into binding contracts.

Following an early opinion of the Court, however, that took the first step of applying the Contract Clause to public undertakings, *Fletcher v. Peck*, 6 Cranch 87 (1810), later decisions attempted to define the reach of the Clause consistently with the demands of our governing processes. The central principle developed by these decisions, beginning at least a century ago, has been that Contract Clause challenges such as that raised by appellant are to be resolved by according unusual deference to the lawmaking authority of state and local governments. . . .

This theme of judicial self-restraint and its underlying premise that a

State always retains the sovereign authority to legislate in behalf of its people was commonly expressed by the doctrine that the Contract Clause will not even recognize efforts of a State to enter into contracts limiting the authority of succeeding legislators to enact laws in behalf of the health, safety, and similar collective interests of the polity—in short, that that State's police power is inalienable by contract. . . .

I would not want to be read as suggesting that the States should blithely proceed down the path of repudiating their obligations, financial or otherwise. Their credibility in the credit market obviously is highly dependent on exercising their vast lawmaking powers with self-restraint and discipline, and I, for one, have little doubt that few, if any, jurisdictions would choose to use their authority "so foolish[ly] as to kill a goose that lays golden eggs for them," *Erie R. Co. v. Public Util. Comm'rs.*, [254 U.S. 394 (1921)]. But in the final analysis, there is no reason to doubt that appellant's financial welfare is being adequately policed by the political processes and the bond marketplace itself. The role to be played by the Constitution is at most a limited one. For this Court should have learned long ago that the Constitution—be it through the Contract or Due Process Clause—can actively intrude into such economic and policy matters only if my Brethren are prepared to bear enormous institutional and social costs. Because I consider the potential dangers of such judicial interference to be intolerable, I dissent.

B | *The Development and Demise of a "Liberty of Contract"*

Ratification of the Fourteenth Amendment in 1868 provided the Supreme Court with a new basis for protecting economic rights. The amendment overturned the Taney Court's ruling in *Dred Scott v. Sandford*, 60 U.S. 393 (1857) (see Ch. 12), that blacks were not citizens of the United States. Section 1 of the amendment aimed at ensuring that states would not deny blacks their citizenship by providing that "[n]o State shall make or enforce any law which shall abridge the privileges or immunities of citizens of the United States; nor shall any State deprive any person of life, liberty, or property, without due process of law; nor deny to any person within its jurisdiction the equal protection of the laws." The drafters of the amendment in the Thirty-ninth Congress thought that the privileges or immunities clause was the most important guarantee, because it expressly prohibited states from denying the privileges and immunities of being a citizen of the United States. Its importance is underscored by its almost literal repetition of the privileges and immunities clause of Article IV, Section 2, which provides that "[t]he Citizens of each State shall be entitled to all Privileges and Immunities of Citizens in the several States."

What counted among the privileges and immunities, however, was far from certain. In *Dred Scott*, Chief Justice Taney construed Article IV to protect only the privileges and immunities of citizens of states who were also citizens of the United States and who were temporarily in a state other than their own. The Fourteenth Amendment overturned this interpretation by extending citizenship to blacks, but offered no further clarification.

An obvious, although narrow, view is that the privileges or immunities clause simply forbids states from discriminating against citizens of other states.[1] Yet during the House and Senate debates on the amendment's adoption a frequently cited opinion was that of Justice Bushrod Washington. While sitting on a circuit court, he had interpreted the privileges or immunities clause in *Corfield v. Coryell*, 6 Fed. Cases 3230 (1825), upholding a New Jersey statute prohibiting nonresidents from gathering oysters in the state. Gathering oysters was not among the privileges and immunities of citizenship, but Washington added that citizens were guaranteed those rights "which are, in their nature, fundamental; which belong of right, to the citizens of all free governments." He listed (notably without mentioning the Bill of Rights) a rather wide-ranging set of fundamental rights; among others, he included the right to possess property, to travel from one state to another, to be protected by the government, to be exempt from higher taxes than paid by other citizens, and the right to bring suits in courts of law.

Whatever potential the Fourteenth Amendment's privileges or immunities clause had was soon dashed in *Butchers' Benevolent Association v. Cresent City Livestock Landing & Slaughterhouse Co.* (1873) (see excerpt below). When upholding a Louisiana law that created a monopoly on the operation of slaughterhouses, Justice Samuel Miller construed citizenship in the states and the United States to be distinct and separate and the Fourteenth Amendment to apply only to national citizenship. The independent butchers who opposed the legislative creation of a monopoly thus could not claim protection under the Fourteenth Amendment.

Four dissenters in *The Slaughterhouse Cases* disagreed. Justice Stephen Field rejected the majority's notion of dual citizenship, while Justice Joseph Bradley contended that the butchers had a right to practice their profession under the due process clauses of the Fifth and Fourteenth Amendments. Bradley was the only one to accept the interpretation of the amendment advanced by the butchers' attorney, John Campbell, a former member of the Court who resigned when his state seceded from the Union.

Campbell had argued that the Fourteenth Amendment had a grander purpose than just guaranteeing the rights of former slaves. Its due process clause guaranteed individual freedom, free enterprise, and laissez-faire individualism. His argument was an invitation for the Court to interpret the due process clause as something more than a mere procedural guarantee. Although Campbell failed to carry the day, his argument proved prophetic of what would come.

Due process was generally understood to mean "the law of the land," but the law of the land and due process were on the brink of transformation. The due process clauses of the Fifth and Fourteenth Amendments were rooted in the English common law, running back to the Magna Carta of 1215. The Magna Carta granted that "[n]o freeman shall be arrested, or imprisoned, or disseized, or outlawed, or exiled, or in any way molested; nor will [the Crown] proceed against him, unless by lawful judgment of his peers or by the law of the land." That guarantee was reaffirmed and reformed in the Petition of Right in 1628, which specified that freemen could "be imprisoned or detained only by the law of the land, or by due process of law, and not by the King's special command without any charge." Later, colonial charters and state constitutions incorporated this provision as well.

The Court's first opportunity to interpret the Fifth Amendment's due process clause had come in 1856. *Murray's Lessee v. Hoboken Land & Improvement Company*, 18 How. (59 U.S.) 272 (1856), upheld a congressional statute authorizing the Treasury Department to issue administrative warrants (without prior judicial approval) for the property of revenue collectors found to be indebted to the United States. The Taney Court rejected the claim that this amounted to the taking of property without due process because it found no conflict between this procedure and any guarantee of the Bill of Rights or settled common-law practices.

The following year in *Dred Scott*, Chief Justice Taney relied in part on the Fifth Amendment's due process clause when upholding slave-owners' proprietary interests in slaves. Taney thereby suggested that the due process of law included substantive rights as well as procedural guarantees. Moreover, state courts were beginning to acknowledge protection for property rights and economic liberties as a matter of due process of law. In *Wynehamer v. New York*, 13 N.Y. 378 (1856), New York's highest court struck down a law prohibiting the possession of liquor as a denial of due process of law.[2]

Campbell's due process argument and Justice Bradley's dissent in *The Slaughterhouse Cases* were thus early manifestations of the legal movement toward extending greater protection to economic liberties under constitutional guarantees other than that of the contract clause. In 1870, the Legal Tender Act of 1862 was invalidated, partially on the grounds that it deprived creditors of property without the due process of law, in *Hepburn v. Griswold*, 8 Wall. 608 (1870). Five years later, in *Loan Association v. Topeka*, 20 Wall. (87 U.S.) 655 (1875), a Kansas tax designed to help local industries was overturned, in Justice Miller's words, as an "unauthorized invasion of [the] private right [of property which grows] . . . out of the essential nature of free government."

By 1877, the Court under Chief Justice Morrison Waite (1874–1888) was prepared to acknowledge the due process clause's *substantive* protection for economic liberty. Although upholding Illinois's law regulating grain elevators as "clothed with the public interest" in *Munn v. Illinois* (1877) (see excerpt below), Waite conceded that economic legislation might constitute the taking of property without due process of law. And while he cautioned that "[f]or protection against abuses by legislatures, the people must resort to the polls, not to the courts," *Munn* signaled that the Court might be persuaded to supervise legislation regulating economic activities. In any event, the Court faced a growing stream of litigation attacking legislation on due process grounds. In *Davidson v. New Orleans*, 96 U.S. 97 (1878), Justice Miller was thus moved to complain that

> the docket of this court is crowded with cases in which we are asked to hold that State courts and State legislatures have deprived their own citizens of life, liberty, or property without due process of law. There is here abundant evidence that there exists some strange misconception of the scope of this provision as found in the Fourteenth Amendment. In fact, it would seem, from the character of many of the cases before us, and the arguments made in them, that the clause under consideration is looked upon as means of bringing to the test of the decision of this court the abstract opinions of every unsuccessful litigant in a State court of justice of the decision against him, and of the merits of the legislation on which such a decision may be founded.

"The great tides and currents which engulf the rest of men," as Justice Benjamin Cardozo observed, "do not turn aside in their course, and pass the judges by."[3] The country's economic expansion in the late nineteenth century was reinforced by the intellectual currents of Conservative Social Darwinism—the philosophy of the survival of the fittest as applied to social and economic relations and perpetuating the myth of rugged individualism and laissez-faire capitalism.

The Court was gradually infused with this philosophy of laissez-faire capitalism, as its composition changed between 1877 and 1890 with the elevation of corporate lawyers to the ranks of justices.[4] And its assumption of the guardianship of economic liberty manifested itself in various ways. Notably, in an otherwise uninteresting tax case, *Santa Clara County v. Southern Pacific Railroad Company*, 118 U.S. 398 (1886), corporations were

proclaimed to be "legal persons" entitled to full protection of the Fourteenth Amendment. Chief Justice Waite evidently thought this was so self-
evident that he did not bother to emphasize it in his opinion, and the
reporter of the Court's decisions decided on his own initiative that it mer-
ited special note in the headnotes accompanying the Court's opinion. The
significance of that ruling, of course, was not lost on lawyers for railroads,
corporations, and other businesses attacking government regulations.

Ten years after *Santa Clara County*, the Court explicitly held that
the Fourteenth Amendment's due process clause protects a substantive,
but unenumerated, "liberty of contract." *Allgeyer v. Louisiana*, 165 U.S.
578 (1897), invalidated a Louisiana law restricting the issuance of insurance policies and imposing a $1,000 fine on anyone having an illegal
policy. Allgeyer & Company had a maritime insurance policy with a
New York insurance firm in violation of Louisiana's law and appealed a
ruling of that state's supreme court upholding the law and a fine on
Allgeyer. When striking down the law, Justice Rufus Peckham boldly
announced the doctrine of a liberty of contract:

> The "liberty" mentioned in [the Fourteenth] Amendment means
> not only the right of the citizen to be free from the mere physical
> restraint of his person, as by incarceration, but the term is deemed
> to embrace the right of the citizen to be free in the enjoyment of
> all his faculties; to be free to use them in all lawful ways; to live and
> work where he will; to earn his livelihood by any lawful calling; to
> pursue any livelihood or avocation, and for that purpose to enter
> into all contracts which may be proper, necessary and essential to
> his carrying out to a successful conclusion the purposes above men-
> tioned.

Allgeyer ushered in what became known as the *Lochner* era of substantive due process economic protectionism, after one of the most notori-
ous rulings on the liberty of contract, *Lochner v. New York* (1905) (see
excerpt below). There, speaking for a bare majority, Justice Peckham
struck down New York's labor law limiting the number of hours bakers could work as an interference with their liberty of contract. And in
one of his most famous dissenting opinions, Justice Oliver Wendell
Holmes sharply criticized his brethren for reading their own conservative economic philosophy into the Constitution. Under the guise of a
liberty of contract and its substantive due process analysis, Holmes
charged, the Court had become a superlegislature in overseeing economic regulations.

Justice Holmes's dissent brought the insights of "American legal realism" to bear on the majority's ruling in *Lochner* and embodies the
principal liberal and progressive criticism of the *Lochner* era: the majority in *Lochner* was making rather than interpreting the law, and through

Cartoon depicting the Supreme Court's backlog of cases in 1883 due to the growing amount of litigation challenging government regulations. (*Puck Magazine/Library of Congress*)

its creation and enforcement of an unenumerated "liberty of contract" imposed its own conservative economic philosophy on the country. But, note that the other dissenting opinion filed in *Lochner* by Justice Harlan, and joined by Justices White and Day, represents a rival interpretation of the ruling in and the era associated with *Lochner*. Justice Harlan considered the liberty of contract a vital constitutional guarantee, rooted in the Reconstruction Amendments and the antislavery movement's emphasis on self-ownership. That liberty, though, as Harlan reminded his colleagues, remained subject to legislation aimed at promoting public health, safety, and general welfare. The majority in *Lochner*, on Harlan's view, mistakenly construed New York's law as a protectionist measure for bakery workers, rather than as a legitimate piece of health and safety legislation promoting the general welfare. That is why Justice Harlan marshalled empirical studies showing that working long hours in bakeries may indeed be injurious to workers' health. In other words, the majority in *Lochner* failed to see how New York's law promoted the general welfare and got carried away with its stand against protectionist legislation favoring one occupation or group over another.[5]

Lochner and the era that it represents, in sum, invites two rival interpretations. On the Holmesian view, *Lochner* represents the Court's purblind imposition of a laissez-faire economic philosophy against the growing forces of economic progressives. Alternatively, the *Lochner* era was a time of great class conflict and political struggles during which the Court tried to draw (not always successfully) a principled distinction between, on the one hand, legitimate economic legislation promoting health, safety, and the general welfare; and, on the other hand, economic legislation that was invalid because it was deemed to advance the special interests of particular groups or classes.

For four decades (from 1897 to 1937) the philosophy of laissez-faire capitalism and defensive stand against special interests' protective economic legislation held sway with a majority of the Court under Chief Justices Waite, Melville Fuller (1888–1910), Edward White (1910–1921), William Howard Taft (1921–1930), and Charles Evans Hughes (1930–1941). Never before or since were economic regulations more severely scrutinized. Close to 200 state and federal laws were overturned during the *Lochner* era.

The Court did not strike down all legislation, however, as Justice Harlan's dissent in *Lochner* emphasized. Where legislation sought to enforce health, safety, or moral standards with little or no impact on economic liberty, the Court deferred to the states and Congress. In *Mugler v. Kansas*, 123 U.S. 623 (1887), for instance, when sustaining a state prohibition law, Justice John Harlan explained that

> [t]here is no justification for holding that the State, under the guise merely of police regulation, is here aiming to deprive the citizen of his constitutional rights; for we cannot shut out of view the fact, within the knowledge of all, that the public health, the public morals, and the public safety, may be endangered by the general use of intoxicating drinks; nor the fact, established by statistics accessible to everyone, that the idleness, disorder, pauperism, and crime existing in the country are, in some degree at least, traceable to this evil.

But Harlan also cautioned that not every law enacted for the promotion of public welfare would survive or

> be accepted as a legitimate exertion of the police powers of the State. There are, of necessity, limits beyond which legislation cannot rightfully go. . . . The courts are not bound by mere forms, nor are they to be misled by mere pretenses. They are at liberty—indeed, are under a solemn duty—to look at the substance of things, whenever they enter upon the inquiry whether the legislature has transcended the limits of its authority. If, therefore, a statute purporting to have been enacted to protect the public health, the public morals, or the public safety, has no real or substantial relation to

those objects, or is a palpable invasion of rights secured by the fundamental law, it is the duty of the courts to so adjudge, and thereby give affect to the Constitution.

On this reasoning, the Court also upheld federal laws prohibiting the sale of liquor[6] and state laws banning sales and advertisements for cigarettes,[7] as well as zoning and land-use laws.[8]

The extent to which the Court was predisposed to defer to states when regulations had no direct economic impact is underscored in two further rulings during the *Lochner* era. In *Jacobson v. Massachusetts*, 197 U.S. 11 (1905), the Court refused to question the basis for a state law requiring smallpox vaccinations. In Justice Harlan's words:

> We must assume that when the statute in question was passed, the legislature of Massachusetts was not unaware of . . . opposing theories [of the effectiveness of vaccinations], and was compelled, of necessity, to choose between them. It was not compelled to commit a matter involving the public health and safety to the final decision of a court or jury. It is no part of the function of a court or a jury to determine which one of two modes was likely to be the most effective for the protection of the public against disease. That was for the legislative department to determine in the light of all the information it had or could obtain.

Nor was the Court inclined to scrutinize the basis for Virginia's law, passed in response to the eugenics movement, requiring the sterilization of those who were mentally defective or afflicted with epilepsy. It affirmed the compulsory sterilization of Carrie Buck, a seventeen-year-old, "feebleminded" female in a state mental institution, whose mother had also been an inmate and who had already given birth to a mentally defective child. Justice Holmes's opinion for the Court revealed not only his deference to legislatures but his acceptance of the tooth and claw of Social Darwinism. In *Buck v. Bell*, 274 U.S. 200 (1927) (excerpted in Ch. 11), he observed that

> [w]e have seen more than once that the public welfare may call upon the best citizens for their lives. It would be strange if it could not call upon those who already sap the strength of the State for these lesser sacrifices, often not felt to be such by those concerned, in order to prevent our being swamped with incompetence. It is better for all the world, if instead of waiting to execute degenerate offspring for crime, or to let them starve for the imbecility, society can prevent those who are manifestly unfit from continuing their kind. The principle that sustains compulsory vaccination is broad enough to cover cutting the Fallopian tubes. . . . Three generations of imbeciles are enough.

When legislation aimed at promoting health, safety, or welfare *and* directly affected economic activities, the Court did not automatically strike it down. But the Court had to be convinced of the reasonableness of the regulations. In *Holden v. Hardy*, 169 U.S. 366 (1898), with only Justices Peckham and David Brewer dissenting, the Court upheld Utah's law limiting the number of hours in a day miners could work in mines and smelters to eight.

In *Muller v. Oregon* (1908), (excerpted below), the Court unanimously approved a state law limiting the workday for women in industries to ten hours per day. There the Court was persuaded by what became known as "the Brandeis brief." When defending Oregon's law, the progressive and highly regarded labor lawyer, Louis Brandeis, filed an extraordinary brief, containing only two pages of legal argument and more than a hundred pages of statistics and social science studies showing how long hours of labor endangered the health of women and thus the reasonableness of the state's law.[9] (Notably, after Brandeis was named to the Court in 1916, he never cited social science materials when writing an opinion for the Court upholding state legislation. Instead, he only cited these materials when writing dissenting opinions, criticizing the majority for overturning state laws and showing the reasonableness of the legislation.)

Although upholding state regulations in cases like *Muller* and *Bunting v. Oregon*, 243 U.S. 426 (1917), sustaining a labor law limiting workdays to ten hours a day for men and women, the Court's prevailing practice was nevertheless to strike down economic regulations. The problem for the Court and the country was that while the development of the doctrine of a liberty of contract may have been in response, in Holmes's classic phrase, "to the felt necessities of the time," it ran against the political currents of the early twentieth century. Reform Social Darwinism had replaced Conservative Social Darwinism in teaching that humans not only adapt to the environment but may change it as well.[10] Under pressure from reformers, labor unions, and the progressive movement, legislatures were passing new laws in response to the plight of workers in sweatshops, child labor, and generally dismal working conditions as depicted in novels by Upton Sinclair. The justices were no longer in tune with the times. The Court and the country were on a collision course in constitutional politics.

In *Adair v. United States*, 208 U.S. 161 (1908), for example, the Court, with only Justices Holmes and Joseph McKenna dissenting, struck down a section of a congressional labor-relations law banning yellow-dog contracts—contracts signed by workers promising they would not join labor unions—and forbidding the firing of employees who belonged to unions. When approving of Adair's firing of O. B.

Coppage from the Louisville & Nashville Railroad Company because he was a union member, Justice Harlan disabused any thought of abandoning the liberty of contract:

> While . . . the right of liberty and property guaranteed by the Constitution against deprivation without due process of law is subject to such reasonable restraints as the common good or the general welfare may require, it is not within the functions of government—at least, in the absence of contract between the parties—to compel any person, in the course of his business and against his will, to accept or retain the personal services of another, or to compel any person, against his will, to perform personal services for another. The right of a person to sell his labor upon such terms as he deems proper is, in its essence, the same as the right of the purchaser of labor to prescribe the conditions upon which he will accept such labor from the person offering to sell it. So the right of the employee to quit the service of the employer, for whatever reason, is the same as the right of the employer, for whatever reason, to dispense with the services of such employee. It was the legal right of the defendant Adair,—however unwise such a course might have been,—to discharge Coppage because of his being a member of a labor organization, as it was the legal right of Coppage, if he saw fit to do so,—however unwise such a course on his part might have been,—to quit the service in which he was engaged, because the defendant employed some persons who were not members of a labor organization. In all such particulars the employer and the employee have equality of right, and any legislation that disturbs that equality is an arbitrary interference with the liberty of contract which no government can legally justify in a free land.

In *Coppage v. Kansas*, 236 U.S. 1 (1915), with Justices Holmes, Rufus Day, and Charles Evans Hughes dissenting, the Court struck down a state law outlawing yellow-dog contracts. The Kansas state supreme court had upheld the law and the conviction of T. B. Coppage for firing a switchman for the St. Louis & San Francisco Railway Company because the employee refused to give up his union membership. In another vintage expression of the doctrine of a liberty of contract, Justice Mahlon Pitney explained that

> it is said by the Kansas supreme court to be a matter of common knowledge that "employees, as a rule, are not financially able to be as independent in making contracts for the sale of their labor as are employers in making a contract of purchase thereof." No doubt; wherever the right of private property exists, there must and will be inequalities of fortune; and thus it naturally happens that parties negotiating about a contract are not equally unhampered by circumstances. This applies to all contracts, and not merely to that between employer and employee. Indeed, a little reflection will show that

wherever the right of private property and the right of a free contract coexist, each party when contracting is inevitably more or less influenced by the question whether he has much property, or little, or none; for the contract is made to the very end that each may gain something that he needs or desires more urgently than that which he proposes to give in exchange. And, since it is self-evident that, unless all things are held in common, some persons must have more property than others, it is from the nature of things impossible to uphold freedom of contract and the right of private property without at the same time recognizing as legitimate those inequalities of fortune that are the necessary result of the exercise of those rights. But the 14th Amendment, in declaring that a state shall not "deprive any person of life, liberty, or property without due process of law," gives to each of these an equal sanction; it recognizes "liberty" and "property" as coexistent human rights, and debars the states from any unwarranted interference with either.

And since a state may not strike them down directly, it is clear that it may not do so indirectly, as by declaring in effect that the public good requires the removal of those inequalities that are but the normal and inevitable result of their exercise. . . . The police power is broad, and not easily defined, but it cannot be given the wide scope that is here asserted for it, without in effect nullifying the constitutional guaranty.

In the 1920s the Court's defense of the liberty of contract reached the high-water mark and the controversy was exacerbated by the Great Depression. In *Adkins v. Children's Hospital*, 261 U.S. 525 (1923), a bare majority struck down the District of Columbia's minimum wage law for women and again made clear that *Lochner* was still alive. The minimum wage law, according to Justice Arthur Sutherland, was "simply and exclusively a price-fixing law." "Women," he added, "are legally as capable of contracting for themselves as men." In dissent, Chief Justice Taft maintained that *Muller*, not *Lochner*, should control the decision and questioned whether *Lochner* had not been "overruled *sub silentio*," that is, overruled without expressly saying so. But *Wolf Packing Co. v. Court of Industrial Relations*, 262 U.S. 522 (1923), with none other than Taft delivering the Court's opinion, underscored that economic liberty was a "preferred freedom," when striking down Kansas's law creating an industrial-relations court to handle labor-management disputes. And there remained a die-hard majority on the Court into the 1930s for defending the vestiges of laissez-faire capitalism. In *Morehead v. Tipaldo*, 298 U.S. 587 (1936), the four remaining justices from *Adkins's* majority—Sutherland, Pierce Butler, Willis Van Devanter, and James McReynolds—were thus joined by Owen Roberts in overturning New York's minimum wage law.

The controversy over the Court finally erupted into the most serious crisis in constitutional politics since *Dred Scott*. During President Franklin D. Roosevelt's first term, the Court invalidated most of his early New Deal programs thereby thwarting his plans for the country's recovery from the Great Depression. After FDR's landslide reelection in 1936, he boldly proposed judicial reforms that would allow him to expand the size of the Court to fifteen by appointing a new member for every justice over seventy years of age. Then in the spring of 1937 when the Senate Judiciary Committee was debating his Court-packing plan, the Court abruptly upheld major pieces of the New Deal legislation. The Court had become badly split five to four in striking down progressive New Deal legislation. Sutherland, McReynolds, Butler, and Van Devanter—the "Four Horsemen"—voted as a bloc against economic legislation for violating economic liberty, while Stone and Cardozo followed Brandeis in supporting progressive legislation. Hughes and Roberts were the swing votes, although the latter, more conservative justice, had cast the crucial fifth vote to strike down FDR's programs. Roberts, however, was persuaded by Hughes to change his mind. In March he abandoned the Four Horsemen in *West Coast Hotel Co. v. Parrish* (1937) (see excerpt below) to uphold Washington State's minimum wage law. Two weeks later, in *National Labor Relations Board v. Jones & Laughlin Steel Corporation*, 301 U.S. 1 (1937) (see Vol. 1, Ch. 6), Roberts again switched sides to affirm a major piece of New Deal legislation, the National Labor Relations Act.

The Court's "switch in time that saved nine" was widely speculated to have been due to FDR's Court-packing plan. But even though the rulings did not come down until the spring, Roberts had switched his vote at conference in December 1936, two months before FDR announced his plan. The reversal of the Court's position nonetheless contributed to the Senate Judiciary Committee's rejection of FDR's proposal in May. Then Van Devanter—one of the president's staunchest opponents—told the president that he would resign at the end of the next term. FDR had the first of eight appointments in the next six years to infuse his own political philosophy into the Court.

The Court's about-face in 1937 ended a constitutional crisis and an era. With the Court's abandonment of the liberty of contract and turning its back on substantive due process came a virtual abdication of judicial supervision of economic regulations. *Lincoln Federal Labor Union v. Northwestern Iron & Metal Co.* (1949) (see excerpt below), which expressly repudiated *Adair* and *Coppage*, is illustrative. As FDR's first appointee to the Court, Justice Hugo Black, in *Ferguson v. Skrupa*, 372 U.S. 726 (1963), exclaimed, "[I]t is up to legislatures, not courts, to decide on the wisdom and utility of legislation."[11] The Burger Court, when upholding a state law requiring employees to be compensated when on jury duty by their employers, in *Dean v. Gadsden Times Publishing Corporation*, 412 U.S. 543 (1973), underscored that "[i]f our recent cases mean anything, they leave debatable issues as respects business, economic, and social affairs to legislative decision. We could strike down this law only if we returned to the philosophy of *Lochner*, *Coppage*, and *Adkins* cases."

Since the 1937 revolution in constitutional politics, the Court has evolved a proverbial double standard: it gives economic regulation only minimal scrutiny, requiring only that it have some rational basis, while giving that affecting civil liberties heightened scrutiny, often upholding legislation only if the government's interest in regulation is compelling. And since 1937 the Court has assumed a special role in overseeing voting rights and access to the political process (see Vol. 1, Ch. 8); the freedom of speech, press, and association (see Vol. 2, Ch. 5); and invidious forms of racial and nonracial discrimination (see Vol. 2, Ch. 12).

It appears highly unlikely that the Court will once again heighten its scrutiny of economic legislation under the due process clause, let alone return to the days of the liberty of contract. Justice William Rehnquist, for example, in *United States Railroad Retirement Board v. Fritz*, 449 U.S. 166 (1980), rebuffed a due process attack on legislation eliminating railroad retirees' social security and retirement benefits with the observation that "[t]he plain language [of the statute] marks the beginning and end of our inquiry."

Finally, it bears noting that although the Court turned its back on the doctrine of a liberty of contract in 1937, it did not abandon reading substantive guarantees into the due process clause of the Fourteenth Amendment, as further discussed in Chapters 4 and 12.

Notes

1. For further discussion, see Charles Fairman, "Does the Fourteenth Amendment Incorporate the Bill of Rights?" 2 *Stanford Law Review* 5 (1949); and William Crosskey, "Charles Fairman, 'Legislative History,' and the Constitutional Limitations on State Authority," 22 *University of Chicago Law Review* 1 (1954).

2. See Edward Corwin, *Liberty against Government: The Rise, Flowering and Decline of a Famous Judicial Concept* (Baton Rouge: Louisiana State University Press, 1948).

3. Benjamin Cardozo, *The Nature of the Judicial Process* (New Haven, CT: Yale University Press, 1921), 168.

4. For further discussion, see Benjamin Twiss, *Lawyers and the Constitution: How Laissez Faire Came to the Supreme Court* (Princeton, NJ: Princeton University Press, 1942); Robert McCloskey, *American Conservatism in the Age of Enterprise* (Cambridge, MA: Harvard University Press, 1951); and James Willard Hurst, *Law and the Conditions of*

Freedom in the Nineteenth-Century United States (Madison: University of Wisconsin Press, 1956).

5. For further discussion, see Howard Gillman, *The Constitution Besieged: The Rise and Demise of Lochner Era Police Powers Jurisprudence* (Durham, NC: Duke University Press, 1993).

6. *Hamilton v. Kentucky Distilleries and Warehouse Co.*, 251 U.S. 146 (1919).

7. See *Austin v. Tennessee*, 179 U.S. 343 (1900); and *Packer Corporation v. Utah*, 285 U.S. 105 (1932).

8. A leading case is *Euclid v. Ambler Realty Co.*, 272 U.S. 365 (1926). See also *Welch v. Swasey*, 214 U.S. 91 (1909); *Cusack v. Chicago*, 242 U.S. 526 (1917); and *Berman v. Parker*, 348 U.S. 26 (1954).

9. Other rulings upholding labor laws for women include *Cotting v. Godard*, 183 U.S. 79 (1901); *German Alliance Insurance Co. v. Lewis*, 233 U.S. 389 (1914); and *Townsend v. Yeomans*, 301 U.S. 441 (1937).

10. For further discussion, see Morton White, *Social Thought in America: The Revolt against Formalism* (New York: Viking Press, 1949).

11. See also *Williamson v. Lee Optical of Oklahoma*, 348 U.S. 483 (1955); *Olsen v. Nebraska*, 313 U.S. 236 (1952); and Richard Funston, "The Double Standard of Constitutional Protection in the Era of the Welfare State," 90 *Political Science Quarterly* 261 (1975).

Selected Bibliography

Brigham, John. *Property and the Politics of Entitlement.* Philadelphia: Temple University Press, 1990.

Freyer, Tony. *Producers versus Capitalists: Constitutional Conflict in Antebellum America.* Charlottesville: University Press of Virginia, 1994.

Gillman, Howard. *The Constitution Besieged: The Rise and Demise of Lochner Era Police Powers Jurisprudence.* Durham, NC: Duke University Press, 1993.

Kens, Paul. *Judicial Power and Reform Politics: The Anatomy of Lochner v. New York.* Lawrence: University Press of Kansas, 1990.

Labbé, Ronand, and Lurie, Jonathan. *The Slaughterhouse Cases.* Lawrence: University Press of Kansas, 2003.

Leuchtenburg, William E. *The Supreme Court Reborn: The Constitutional Revolution in the Age of Roosevelt.* New York: Oxford University Press, 1995.

Miller, Arthur S. *The Supreme Court and American Capitalism.* New York: Free Press, 1968.

Paul, Arnold. *Conservative Crisis and the Rule of Law: Attitudes of Bench and Bar, 1887–1895.* Ithaca, NY: Cornell University Press, 1960.

Seigan, Bernard. *Economic Liberties and the Constitution.* Chicago: University of Chicago Press, 1980.

Twiss, Benjamin. *Lawyers and the Constitution: How Laissez Faire Came to the Supreme Court.* Princeton, NJ: Princeton University Press, 1942.

Butchers' Benevolent Association v. Cresent City Livestock Landing & Slaughterhouse Co. (The Slaughterhouse Cases)

16 WALL. (83 U.S.) 36 (1873)

In 1869 due to the pollution and the spread of cholera, the Louisiana legislature passed a law aimed at cleaning up the Mississippi River by prohibiting all slaughtering of livestock in the City of New Orleans and surrounding parishes except at one slaughterhouse, which was given an exclusive franchise for twenty-five years. The Butchers' Benevolent Association, a group of independent slaughterers, challenged the constitutionality of the legislation on the grounds that it violated the Thirteenth and Fourteenth Amendments by depriving them of their livelihood. A state court and the Louisiana State Supreme Court upheld the law, and the Butchers' Benevolent Association appealed to the Supreme Court.

Court's decision was five to four, with the majority's opinion announced by Justice Miller. Justices Field, Bradley, and Swayne dissented, joined by Chief Justice Chase.

    ☐ *Justice MILLER delivered the opinion of the Court.*

The plaintiffs . . . allege that the statute is a violation of the Constitution of the United States in these several particulars:

That it creates an involuntary servitude forbidden by the 13th article of amendment;

That it abridges the privileges and immunities of citizens of the United States;

That it denies to the plaintiffs the equal protection of the laws; and,

That it deprives them of their property without due process of law; contrary to the provisions of the 1st section of the 14th article of amendment.

This court is thus called upon for the first time to give construction to these articles. . . .

The most cursory glance at these articles discloses a unity of purpose, when taken in connection with the history of the times, which cannot fail to have an important bearing on any question of doubt concerning their true meaning. . . .

[N]o one can fail to be impressed with the one pervading purpose found in [the 13th, 14th and 15th Amendments], lying at the foundation of each, and without which none of them would have been even suggested; we mean the freedom of the slave race, the security and firm establishment of that freedom, and the protection of the newly made freemen and citizens from the oppressions of those who had formerly exercised unlimited dominion over him. It is true that only the 15th Amendment, in terms, mentions the negro by speaking of his color and his slavery. But it is just as true that each of the other articles was addressed to the grievances of that race, and designed to remedy them as the fifteenth.

We do not say that no one else but the negro can share in this protection. Both the language and spirit of these articles are to have their fair and just weight in any question of construction. Undoubtedly, while negro slavery alone was in the mind of the Congress which proposed the 13th article, it forbids any other kind of slavery, now or hereafter. . . .

The next observation is more important in view of the arguments of counsel in the present case. It is that the distinction between citizenship of the United States and citizenship of a state is clearly recognized and established. Not only may a man be a citizen of the United States without being a citizen of a state, but an important element is necessary to convert the former into the latter. He must reside within the state to make him a citizen of it, but it is only necessary that he should be born or naturalized in the United States to be a citizen of the Union.

It is quite clear, then, that there is a citizenship of the United States and a citizenship of a state, which are distinct from each other and which depend upon different characteristics or circumstances in the individual.

We think this distinction and its explicit recognition in this Amendment of great weight in this argument, because the next paragraph of this same section, which is the one mainly relied on by the plaintiffs in error, speaks only of privileges and immunities of citizens of the United States, and does not speak of those of citizens of the several states. The argument, however, in favor of the plaintiffs, rests wholly on the assumption that the citizenship is the same and the privileges and immunities guaranteed by the clause are the same.

The language is: "No state shall make or enforce any law which shall abridge the privileges or immunities of citizens of the United States." It is a little remarkable, if this clause was intended as a protection to the citizen of a state against the legislative power of his own state, that the words "citizen of the state" should be left out when it is so carefully used, and used in contradistinction to "citizens of the United States" in the very sentence which precedes it. It is too clear for argument that the change in phraseology was adopted understandingly and with a purpose.

Of the privileges and immunities of the citizens of the United States, and of the privileges and immunities of the citizen of the state, and what they respectively are, we will presently consider; but we wish to state here that it is only the former which are placed by this clause under the protection of the Federal Constitution, and that the latter, whatever they may be, are not intended to have any additional protection by this paragraph of the Amendment.

If, then, there is a difference between the privileges and immunities belonging to a citizen of the United States as such, and those belonging to the citizen of the state as such, the latter must rest for their security and protection where they have heretofore rested; for they are not embraced by this paragraph of the Amendment. . . .

In the Constitution of the United States, which superseded the Articles of Confederation, the corresponding provision is found in section two of the 4th article, in the following words: The citizens of each state shall be entitled to all the privileges and immunities of citizens of the several states.

There can be but little question that the purpose of both these provisions is the same, and that the privileges and immunities intended are the same in each. In the Article of the Confederation we have some of these specifically mentioned, and enough perhaps to give some general idea of the class of civil rights meant by the phrase. . . .

The constitutional provision there alluded to did not create those rights, which it called privileges and immunities of citizens of the states. It threw around them in that clause no security for the citizen of the state in which they were claimed or exercised. Nor did it profess to control the power of the state governments over the rights of its own citizens.

Its sole purpose was to declare to the several states, that whatever those rights, as you grant or establish them to your own citizens, or as you limit or qualify, or impose restrictions on their exercise, the same, neither more nor less, shall be the measure of the rights of citizens of other states within your jurisdiction. . . .

The argument has not been much pressed in these cases that the defendant's charter deprives the plaintiffs of their property without due process of law, or that it denies to them the equal protection of the law. The first of these paragraphs has been in the Constitution since the adoption of the 5th Amendment, as a restraint upon the Federal power. It is also to be found in some form of expression in the constitutions of nearly all the states, as a restraint upon the power of the states. This law, then, has practically been the same as it now is during the existence of the government, except so far as the present Amendment may place the restraining power over the states in this matter in the hands of the Federal government.

We are not without judicial interpretation, therefore, both state and national, of the meaning of this clause. And it is sufficient to say that under no construction of that provision that we have ever seen, or any that we deem admissible, can the restraint imposed by the state of Louisiana upon the exercise of their trade by the butchers of New Orleans be held to be a deprivation of property within the meaning of that provision.

"Nor shall any state deny to any person within its jurisdiction the equal protection of the laws."

In the light of the history of these amendments, and the pervading purpose of them, which we have already discussed, it is not difficult to give a meaning to this clause. The existence of laws in the states where the newly emancipated negroes resided, which discriminated with gross injustice and hardship against them as a class, was the evil to be remedied by this clause, and by it such laws are forbidden.

☐ *Justice FIELD, dissenting.*

The question presented is . . . nothing less than the question whether the recent Amendments to the Federal Constitution protect the citizens of the United States against the deprivation of their common rights by state legislation. In my judgment the 14th Amendment does afford such protection, and was so intended by the Congress which framed and the states which adopted it.

The counsel for the plaintiffs in error have contended, with great force, that the act in question is also inhibited by the 13th Amendment.

That Amendment prohibits slavery and involuntary servitude, except as a punishment for crime, but I have not supposed it was susceptible of a construction which would cover the enactment in question. I have been so accustomed to regard it as intended to meet that form of slavery which had previously prevailed in this country, and to which the recent Civil War owed its existence, that I was not prepared, nor am I yet, to give to it the extent and force ascribed by counsel. Still it is evident that the language of the Amendment is not used in a restrictive sense. It is not confined to African slavery alone. It is general and universal in its application. Slavery of white men as well as of black men is prohibited, and not merely slavery in the strict sense of the term, but involuntary servitude in every form. . . .

The first clause of the fourteenth amendment . . . recognizes in express terms, if it does not create, citizens of the United States, and it makes the citizenship dependent upon the place of the birth, or the fact of their adoption, and not upon the Constitution or laws of any state or the condition of their ancestry. A citizen of a state is now only a citizen of the United States residing in that state. The fundamental rights, privileges, and immunities which belong to him as a free man and a free citizen, now belong to him as a citizen of the United States, and are not dependent upon his citizenship of any state. . . .

The Amendment does not attempt to confer any new privileges or immunities upon citizens or to enumerate or define those already existing. It assumes that there are such privileges and immunities which belong of right to citizens as such, and ordains that they shall not be abridged by state legislation. If this inhibition has no reference to privileges and immunities of this character, but only refers, as held by the majority of the court in their opinion, to such privileges and immunities as were before its adoption specially designated in the Constitution or necessarily implied as belonging to citizens of the United States, it was a vain and idle enactment, which accomplished nothing, and most unnecessarily excited Congress and the people on its passage. With privileges and immunities thus designated no state could ever have interfered by its laws, and no new constitutional provision was required to inhibit such interference. The supremacy of the Constitution and the laws of the United States always controlled any state legislation of that character. But if the Amendment refers to the natural and inalienable rights which belong to all citizens, the inhibition has a profound significance and consequence.

What, then, are the privileges and immunities which are secured against abridgement by state legislation? . . .

The privileges and immunities designated are those which of right belong to the citizens of all free governments. Clearly among these must be placed the right to pursue a lawful employment in a lawful manner, without other restraint than such as equally affects all persons. . . .

This equality of right, with exemption from all disparaging and partial enactments, in the lawful pursuits of life, throughout the whole country, is the distinguishing privilege of citizens of the United States. To them, everywhere, all pursuits, all professions, all avocations are open without other restrictions than such as are imposed equally upon all others of the same age, sex and condition. The state may prescribe such regulations for every pursuit and calling of life as will promote the public health, secure the good order and advance the general prosperity of society, but when once prescribed, the pursuit or calling must be free to be followed by every citizen who is within the conditions designated, and will conform to the regulations. This is the fundamental idea upon which our institutions rest, and unless adhered to in the legislation of the country our government will be a Republic only in name. The 14th Amendment, in my judgment, makes it essential to the validity of the legislation of every state that this equality of right should be respected. . . .

I am authorized by Chief Justice CHASE, Justice SWAYNE and Justice BRADLEY, to state that they concur with me in this dissenting opinion.

☐ *Justice BRADLEY, dissenting.*

In my view, a law which prohibits a large class of citizens from adopting a lawful employment, or from following a lawful employment previously adopted, does deprive them of liberty as well as property, without due process of law. Their right of choice is a portion of their liberty; their occupation is their property. Such a law also deprives those citizens of the equal protection of the laws, contrary to the last clause of the section. . . .

It is futile to argue that none but persons of the African race are intended to be benefited by this Amendment. They may have been the primary cause of the Amendment, but its language is general, embracing all citizens, and I think it was purposely so expressed.

Munn v. Illinois

4 Otto (94 U.S.) 113, 24 L.Ed. 77 (1877)

In 1871 in response to the Granger movement—a movement to promote the interests of independent farmers in midwest states—and pressures to stop the exploitation of farmers by grain-elevator operators, Illinois's legislature enacted a law requiring operating licenses and setting the maximum rates that grain warehouses and elevators could charge for the storage of grain. Ira Munn was found in violation of the law and attacked its constitutionality as a violation of the commerce clause and the due process clause of the Fourteenth Amendment. The Illinois State Supreme Court, however, upheld Munn's conviction and Munn appealed to the Supreme Court.

The Court's decision was seven to two, with the majority's opinion announced by Chief Justice Waite. Justices Field and Strong dissented.

☐ *Chief Justice WAITE delivered the opinion of the Court.*

Every statute is presumed to be constitutional. The courts ought not to declare one to be unconstitutional, unless it is clearly so. If there is doubt, the expressed will of the Legislature should be sustained.

The Constitution contains no definition of the word "deprive," as used in the 14th Amendment. To determine its signification, therefore, it is necessary to ascertain the effect which usage has given it, when employed in the same or a like connection.

While this provision of the Amendment is new in the Constitution of the United States as a limitation upon the powers of the States, it is old as a principle of civilized government. It is found in Magna Charta, and, in substance if not in form, in nearly or quite all the constitutions that have been from time to time adopted by the several States of the Union. By the 5th Amendment, it was introduced into the Constitution of the United States as a limitation upon the powers of the National Government, and by the 14th, as a guaranty against any encroachment upon an acknowledged right of citizenship by the Legislatures of the States. . . .

This Act was passed at a time when Magna Charta had been recognized as the fundamental law of England for hundreds of years.

This great charter embodied the principle that no person shall be deprived of life, liberty or property, but by the judgment of his peers or the law of the land, which is an equivalent for the modern phrase, "due process of law." . . .

[I]t is apparent that, down to the time of the adoption of the 14th Amendment, it was not supposed that statutes regulating the use, or even the price of the use, of private property necessarily deprived an owner of his property without due process of law. Under some circumstances they may, but not under all. The Amendment does not change the law in this particular; it simply prevents the States from doing that which will operate as such a deprivation.

This brings us to inquire as to the principles upon which this power of regulation rests, in order that we may determine what is within and what without its operative effect. Looking, then, to the common law, from whence came the right which the Constitution protects, we find that when private property is "affected with a public interest, it ceases to be juris privati only." This was said by Lord Chief Justice Hale more than two hundred years ago, in his treatise De Portibus Maris, 1 Harg. I. Tr., 78, and has been accepted without objection as an essential element in the law of property ever since. Property does become clothed with a public interest when used in a manner to make it of public consequence, and affect the community at large. When, therefore, one devotes his property to a use in which the public has an interest, he, in effect, grants to the public an interest in that use, and must submit to be controlled by the public for the common good, to the extent of the interest he has thus created. He may withdraw his grant by discontinuing the use; but, so long as he maintains the use, he must submit to the control. . . .

It remains only to ascertain whether the warehouses of these plaintiffs in error, and the business which is carried on there, come within the operation of this principle. . . .

[I]t is difficult to see why, if the common carrier, or the miller, or the ferryman, or the innkeeper, or the wharfinger, or the baker, or the cartman, or the hackney-coachman, pursues a public employment and exercises "a sort of public office," these plaintiffs in error do not. They stand, to use again the language of their counsel, in the very "gateway of commerce," and take toll from all who pass. Their business most certainly "tends to a common charge, and is become a thing of public interest and use." Every bushel of grain for its passage "pays a toll, which is a common charge," and, therefore, according to Lord Hale, every such warehouseman "ought to be under public regulation, viz.: that he . . . take but reasonable toll." Certainly, if any business can be clothed "with a public interest, and cease to be *juris privati* only," this has been. It may not be made so by the operation of the Constitution of Illinois or this statute, but it is by the facts. . . .

We know that this is a power which may be abused; but that is no argument against its existence. For protection against abuses by Legislatures the people must resort to the polls; not to the courts. . . .

We come now to consider the effect upon this statute of the power of Congress to regulate commerce. . . . The warehouses of these plaintiffs in error are situated and their business carried on exclusively within the limits of the State of Illinois. They are used as instruments by those engaged in State as well as those engaged in interstate commerce, but they are no more necessarily a part of commerce itself than the dray or the cart by which, but for them, grain would be transferred from one railroad station to another. Incidentally they may become connected with interstate commerce, but not necessarily so. Their regulation is a thing of domestic concern and, certainly, until Congress acts in reference to their interstate relations, the State may exercise all the powers of government over them, even though in so doing it may indirectly operate upon commerce outside its immediate jurisdiction. We do not say that a case may not arise in which it will be found that a State, under the form of regulating its own affairs, has encroached upon the exclusive domain of Congress in respect to interstate commerce, but we do say that, upon the facts as they are represented to us in this record, that has not been done. . . .

The judgment is affirmed.

☐ *Justice FIELD, dissenting.*

I am compelled to dissent from the decision of the court in this case, and from the reasons upon which that decision is founded. The principle upon which the opinion of the majority proceeds is, in my judgment, subversive of the rights of private property, heretofore believed to be protected by constitutional guaranties against legislative interference, and is in conflict with the authorities cited in its support. . . .

There is nothing in the character of the business of the defendants as warehousemen which called for the interference complained of in this case. Their buildings are not nuisances; their occupation of receiving and storing grain infringes upon no rights of others, disturbs no neighborhood, infects not the air, and in no respect prevents others from using and enjoying their property as to them may seem best. The legislation in question is nothing less than a bold assertion of absolute power by the State to control, at its discretion, the property and business of the citizen, and fix the compensation he shall receive. . . .

The business of a warehouseman was, at common law, a private business, and is so in its nature. It has no special privileges connected with it, nor did the law ever extend to it any greater protection than it extended to all other private business. No reason can be assigned to justify legislation interfering with the legitimate profits of that business, that would not equally justify an intermeddling with the business of every man in the community, so soon, at least, as his business became generally useful.

I am of opinion that the judgment of the Supreme Court of Illinois should be reversed.

Lochner v. New York

198 U.S. 45, 25 S.Ct. 539 (1905)

Joseph Lochner was found guilty and fined $50 for violating an 1897 New York law prohibiting employers from having their employees work more than sixty hours a week in a bakery. Lochner's conviction was affirmed by two state courts and he applied for a writ of error from the Supreme Court.

The Court's decision was five to four; the majority's opinion was announced by Justice Peckham. Dissents were by Justices Holmes and Harlan, who was joined by Justices White and Day.

☐ *Justice PECKHAM delivered the opinion of the Court.*

The mandate of the statute, that "no employee shall be required or permitted to work," is the substantial equivalent of an enactment that "no employee shall contract or agree to work," more than ten hours per day; and, as there is no provision for special emergencies, the statute is mandatory in all cases. It is not an act merely fixing the number of hours which shall constitute a legal day's work, but an absolute prohibition upon the employer permitting, under any circumstances, more than ten hours' work to be done in his establishment. The employee may desire to earn the extra money which would arise from his working more than the prescribed time, but this statute forbids the employer from permitting the employee to earn it.

The statute necessarily interferes with the right of contract between the employer and employees, concerning the number of hours in which the latter may labor in the bakery of the employer. The general right to make a contract in relation to his business is part of the liberty of the individual protected by the 14th Amendment of the Federal Constitution. *Allgeyer v. Louisiana*, 165 U.S. 578 [(1897)]. Under that provision no state can deprive any person of life, liberty, or property without due process of law. The right to purchase or to sell labor is part of the liberty protected by this amendment, unless there are circumstances which exclude the right. There are, however, certain powers, existing in the sovereignty of each state in the Union, somewhat vaguely termed police powers, the exact description and limitation of which have not been attempted by the courts. Those powers, broadly stated, and without, at present, any attempt at a more specific limitation, relate to the safety, health, morals, and general welfare of the public. Both property and liberty are held on such reasonable conditions as may be imposed by the governing power of the state in the exercise of those powers, and with such conditions the 14th Amendment was not designed to interfere. . . .

The state, therefore, has power to prevent the individual from making certain kinds of contracts, and in regard to them the Federal Constitution offers no protection. If the contract be one which the state, in the legitimate exercise of its police power, has the right to prohibit, it is not prevented from prohibiting it by the 14th Amendment. Contracts in violation of a statute, either of the Federal or state government, or a contract to let one's property for immoral purposes, or to do any other unlawful act, could obtain no protection from the Federal Constitution, as coming under the liberty of person or of free contract. Therefore, when the state, by its legislature, in the assumed exercise of its police powers, has passed an act which seriously limits the right to labor or the right of contract in regard to their means of livelihood between persons who are *sui juris* (both employer and employee), it becomes of great importance to determine which shall prevail,—the right of the individual to labor for such time as he may choose, or the right of the state to prevent the individual from laboring, or from entering into any contract to labor, beyond a certain time prescribed by the state.

This court has recognized the existence and upheld the exercise of the police powers of the states in many cases which might fairly be considered as border ones, and it has, in the course of its determination of questions regarding the asserted invalidity of such statutes, on the ground of their violation of the rights secured by the Federal Constitution, been guided by rules of a very liberal nature, the application of which has resulted, in numerous instances, in upholding the validity of state statutes thus assailed. . . .

It must, of course, be conceded that there is a limit to the valid exercise of the police power by the state. . . . Otherwise the 14th Amendment would have no efficacy and the legislatures of the states would have unbounded power, and it would be enough to say that any piece of legislation was enacted to conserve the morals, the health, or the safety of the people; such legislation would be valid, no matter how absolutely without foundation the claim might be. The claim of the police power would be a mere pretext,—become another and delusive name for the supreme sovereignty of the state to be exercised free from constitutional restraint. . . . In every case that comes before this court, therefore, where legislation of this character is concerned, and where the protection of the Federal Constitution is sought, the question necessarily arises: Is this a fair, reasonable, and appropriate exercise of the police power of the state, or is it an unreasonable, unnecessary, and arbitrary interference with the right of the individual to his personal liberty, or to enter into those contracts in relation to labor which may seem to him appropriate or necessary for the support of himself and his family? Of course the liberty of contract relating to labor includes both parties to it. The one has as much right to purchase as the other to sell labor.

This is not a question of substituting the judgment of the court for that of the legislature. If the act be within the power of the state it is valid, although the judgment of the court might be totally opposed to the enactment of such a law. . . .

The question whether this act is valid as a labor law, pure and simple, may be dismissed in a few words. There is no reasonable ground for interfering with the liberty of person or the right of free contract, by determining the hours of labor, in the occupation of a baker. There is no contention that bakers as a class are not equal in intelligence and capacity to men in other trades or manual occupations, or that they are not able to assert their rights and care for themselves without the protecting arm of the state, interfering with their independence of judgment and of action. They are in no sense wards of the state. Viewed in the light of a purely labor law, with no reference whatever to the question of health, we think that a law like the one before us involves neither the safety, the morals, nor the welfare, of the public, and that the interest of the public is not in the slightest degree affected by such an act. The law must be upheld, if at all, as a law pertaining to the health of the individual engaged in the occupation of a baker. It does not affect any other portion of the public than those who are engaged in that occupation. Clean and wholesome bread does not depend upon whether the baker works but ten hours per day or only sixty hours a week. The limitation of the hours of labor does not come within the police power on that ground.

It is a question of which of two powers or rights shall prevail,—the power of the state to legislate or the right of the individual to liberty of person and freedom of contract. The mere assertion that the subject relates, though but in a remote degree, to the public health, does not necessarily render the enactment valid. The act must have a more direct relation, as a means to an end, and the end itself must be appropriate and legitimate, before an act can be held to be valid which interferes with the general right of an individual to be free in his person and in his power to contract in relation to his own labor. . . .

We think that there can be no fair doubt that the trade of a baker, in and of itself, is not an unhealthy one to that degree which would authorize the legislature to interfere with the right to labor, and with the right of free contract on the part of the individual, either as employer or employee. In looking through statistics regarding all trades and occupations, it may be true that the trade of a baker does not appear to be as healthy as some other trades, and is also vastly more healthy than still others. To the common understanding the trade of a baker has never been regarded as an unhealthy one. . . .

It seems to us that the real object and purpose were simply to regulate the hours of labor between the master and his employees (all being men, *sui juris*), in a private business, not dangerous in any degree to morals, or in any real and substantial degree to the health of the employees. Under such circumstances the freedom of master and employee to contract with each other in relation to their employment, and in defining the same, cannot be prohibited or interfered with, without violating the Federal Constitution.

☐ *Justice HOLMES, dissenting.*

This case is decided upon an economic theory which a large part of the country does not entertain. If it were a question whether I agreed with that theory, I should desire to study it further and long before making up my mind. But I do not conceive that to be my duty, because I strongly believe that my agreement or disagreement has nothing to do with the right of a majority to embody their opinions in law. It is settled by various decisions of this court that state constitutions and state laws may regulate life in many ways which we as legislators might think as injudicious, or if you like as tyrannical, as this, and which equally with this, interfere with the liberty to contract. Sunday laws and usury laws are ancient examples. A more modern one is the prohibition of lotteries. The liberty of the citizen to do as he likes so long as he does not interfere with the liberty of others to do the same, which has been a shibboleth for some well-known writers, is interfered with by school laws, by the Postoffice, by every state or municipal institution which takes his money for purposes thought desirable, whether he likes it or not. The 14th Amendment does not enact Mr. Herbert Spencer's *Social Statics*. The other day we sustained the Massachusetts vaccination law. *Jacobson v. Massachusetts*, 197 U.S. 11 [1905]. United States and state statutes and decisions cutting down the liberty to contract by way of combination are familiar to this court. *Northern Securities Co. v. United States*, 193 U.S. 197 [(1904)]. Two years ago we upheld the prohibition of sales of stock on margins, or for future delivery, in the Constitution of California. *Otis v. Parker*, 187 U.S. 606 [(1903)]. The decision sustaining an eight-hour law for miners is still recent. *Holden v. Hardy* [169 U.S. 366 (1898)]. Some of these laws embody convictions or prejudices which judges are likely to share. Some may not. But a Constitution is not intended to embody a particular economic theory, whether of paternalism and the organic relation of the citizen to the state or of *laissez faire*. It is made for people of fundamentally differing views, and the accident of our finding certain opinions natural and familiar, or novel, and even shocking, ought not to conclude our judgment upon the question whether statutes embodying them conflict with the Constitution of the United States.

General propositions do not decide concrete cases. The decision will depend on a judgment or intuition more subtle than any articulate major premise. But I think that the proposition just stated, if it is accepted, will carry us far toward the end. Every opinion tends to become a law. I think that the word "liberty," in the 14th Amendment, is perverted when it is held to prevent the natural outcome of a dominant opinion, unless it can be said that a rational and fair man necessarily would admit that the statute proposed would infringe fundamental principles as they have been understood by the traditions of our people and our law. It does not need research to show that no such sweeping condemnation can be passed upon the statute before us. A reasonable man might think it a proper measure on the score of health. Men whom I certainly could not pronounce unreasonable would uphold it as a first installment of a general regulation of the hours of work. Whether in the latter aspect it would be open to the charge of inequality I think it unnecessary to discuss.

☐ *Justice HARLAN, with whom Justices WHITE and DAY join, dissenting.*

[Granting] that there is a liberty of contract which cannot be violated even under the sanction of direct legislative enactment, but assuming, as according to settled law we may assume, that such liberty of contract is subject to such regulations as the State may reasonably prescribe for the common good and the well-being of society, what are the conditions under which the judiciary may declare such regulations to be in excess of legislative authority and void? Upon this point there is no room for dispute; for, the rule is universal that a legislative enactment, Federal or state, is never to be disregarded or held invalid unless it be, beyond question, plainly and palpably in excess of legislative power. . . .

Let these principles be applied to the present case. By the statute in question it is provided that, "No employee shall be required or permitted to work in a biscuit, bread or cake bakery or confectionery establishment more than sixty hours in any one week, or more than ten hours in any one day, unless for the purpose of making a shorter work day on the last day of the week; nor more hours in any one week than will make an average of ten hours per day for the number of days during such week in which such employee shall work."

It is plain that this statute was enacted in order to protect the physical well-being of those who work in bakery and confectionery establishments. It may be that the statute had its origin, in part, in the belief that employers and employees in such establishments were not upon an equal footing, and that the necessities of the latter often compelled them to submit to such exactions as unduly taxed their strength. Be this as it may, the statute must be taken as expressing the belief of the people of New York that, as a general rule, and in the case of the average man, labor in excess of sixty hours during a week in such establishments may endanger the health of those who thus labor. Whether or not this be wise legislation it is not the province of the court to inquire. Under our systems of government the courts are not concerned with the wisdom or policy of legislation. So that in determining the question of power to interfere with liberty of contract, the court may inquire whether the means devised by the State are germane to an end which may be lawfully accomplished and have a real or substantial relation to the protection of health, as involved in the daily work of the persons, male and female, engaged in bakery and confectionery establishments. But when this inquiry is entered upon I find it impossible, in view of common experience, to say that there is here no real or substantial relation between the means employed by the State and the end sought to be accomplished by its legislation. Nor can I say that the statute has no appropriate or direct connection with that protection to health which each State owes to her citizens, or that it is not promotive of the health of the employees in question, or that the regulation prescribed by the State is utterly unreasonable and extravagant or wholly arbitrary. Still less can I say that the statute is, beyond question, a plain, palpable invasion of rights secured by the fundamental law. Therefore I submit that this court will transcend its functions if it assumes to annul the statute of New York. It must be remembered that this statute does not apply to all kinds of business. It applies only to work in bakery and confectionery establishments, in which, as all know, the air constantly breathed by workmen is not as pure and healthful as that to be found in some other establishments or out of doors.

Professor Hirt in his treatise on the *Diseases of the Workers* has said: "The labor of the bakers is among the hardest and most laborious imaginable, because it has to be performed under conditions injurious to the health of those engaged in it. . . ." Another writer says: "The constant inhaling of flour dust causes inflammation of the lungs and of the bronchial tubes. The eyes also suffer through this dust, which is responsible for the many cases of running eyes among the bakers. The long hours of toil to which all bakers are subjected produce rheumatism, cramps and swollen legs. The intense heat in the workshops induces the workers to resort to cooling drinks, which together with their habit of exposing the greater part of their bodies to the change in the atmosphere, is another source of a number of diseases of various organs. Nearly all bakers are pale-faced and of more delicate health than the workers of other crafts, which is chiefly due to their hard work and their irregular and unnatural mode of living whereby the power of resistance against disease is greatly diminished. The average age of a baker is below that of other workmen; they seldom live over their fiftieth year, most of them dying between the ages of forty and fifty. During periods of epidemic diseases the bakers are generally the first to succumb to the disease, and the number swept away during such periods far exceeds the number of other crafts in comparison to the men employed in the respective industries. . . ."

We judicially know that the question of the number of hours during which a workman should continuously labor has been, for a long period, and is yet, a subject of serious consideration among civilized peoples, and by those having special knowledge of the laws of health. Suppose the statute prohibited labor in bakery and confectionery establishments in excess of eighteen hours each day. No one, I take it, could dispute the power of the State to enact such a statute. But the statute before us does not embrace extreme or exceptional cases. It may be said to occupy a middle ground in respect of the hours of labor. What is the true ground for the State to take between legitimate protection, by legislation, of the public health and liberty of contract is not a question easily solved, nor one in respect of which there is or can be absolute certainty. There are very few, if any, questions in political economy about which entire certainty may be predicated. . . .

We also judicially know that the number of hours that should constitute a day's labor in particular occupations involving the physical strength and safety of workmen has been the subject of enactments by Congress and by nearly all of the States. Many, if not most, of those enactments fix eight hours as the proper basis of a day's labor. . . .

If such reasons exist that ought to be the end of this case, for the State is not amenable to the judiciary, in respect of its legislative enactments, unless such enactments are plainly, palpably, beyond all question, inconsistent with the Constitution of the United States. We are not to presume that the State of New York has acted in bad faith. Nor can we assume that its legislature acted without due deliberation, or that it did not determine this question upon the fullest attainable information, and for the common good. We cannot say that the State has acted without reason nor ought we to proceed upon the theory that its action is a mere sham. Our duty, I submit, is to sustain the statute as not being in conflict with the Federal Constitution, for the reason—and such is an all-sufficient reason—it is not shown to be plainly and palpably inconsistent with that instrument. . . .

The judgment in my opinion should be affirmed.

Muller v. Oregon

208 U.S. 412, 28 S. Cᴛ. 324 (1908)

At the dawn of the twentieth century, the Progressive Movement, led by organizations such as the National Consumers' League (NCL), promoted legislation setting maximum working hours and minimum wages. After *Lochner v. New York* (1905), however, many such state laws appeared in jeopardy. When the owner of a laundry, Curt Muller, challenged the constitutionality of his conviction for violating Oregon's law limiting the number of hours women could work to ten hours per day, the NCL decided to make a "test case" out of the suit and recruited the well-known Progressive reformer and advocate Louis D. Brandeis to argue the case on appeal. In light of *Lochner*, his strategy was try to persuade the Court of the reasonableness of and factual basis for Oregon's law. Accordingly, he had the NCL gather extensive social, economic, and public health information on the effect of women working long hours. Nearly thirty reports from other countries and states were compiled and quoted in the 113-page brief submitted to the Court. It later became known as the "Brandeis brief" because it contained only two pages of legal arguments, the rest being data and expert opinion supporting the position that "Long hours of labor are dangerous for women primarily because of their special physical organization."

The Court's decision was unanimous in affirming the state supreme court's ruling upholding Oregon's law. Justice Brewer delivered the opinion of the Court.

☐ *Justice BREWER delivered the opinion of the court.*

It is the law of Oregon that women, whether married or single, have equal contractual and personal rights with men. [P]utting to one side the elective franchise, in the matter of personal and contractual rights they stand on the same plane as the other sex. Their rights in these respects can no more be infringed than the equal rights of their brothers. We held in *Lochner v. New York*, 198 U.S. 45 [(1905)], that a law providing that no laborer shall be required or permitted to work in a bakery more than sixty hours in a week or ten hours in a day was not as to men a legitimate exercise of the police power of the State, but an unreasonable, unnecessary and arbitrary interference with the right and liberty of the individual to contract in relation to his labor, and as such was in conflict with, and void under, the Federal Constitution. That decision is invoked by plaintiff in error as decisive of the question before us. But this assumes that the difference between the sexes does not justify a different rule respecting a restriction of the hours of labor.

It may not be amiss, in the present case, before examining the constitutional question, to notice the course of legislation as well as expressions of opinion from other than judicial sources. In the brief filed by Mr. Louis D. Brandeis, for the defendant in error, is a very copious collection of all these matters, an epitome of which is found in the margin.

In foreign legislation Mr. Brandeis calls attention to these statutes: Great Britain: Factories Act of 1844; Factory and Workshop Act of 1901. France, 1848; Act Nov. 2, 1892, and March 30, 1900. Switzerland, Canton of Glarus, 1848; Federal Law 1877. Austria, 1855; Acts 1897. Holland, 1889; art. 5, Sec. 1. Italy, June 19, 1902, art. 7. Germany, Laws 1891.

Then follow extracts from over ninety reports of committees, bureaus of statistics, commissioners of hygiene, inspectors of factories, both in this country and in Europe, to the effect that long hours of labor are dangerous for women, primarily because of their special physical organization. The matter is discussed in these reports in different aspects, but all agree as to the danger. It would of course take too much space to give these reports in detail. Following them are extracts from similar reports discussing the general benefits of short hours from an economic aspect of the question. In many of these reports individual instances are given tending to support the general conclusion. Perhaps the general scope and character of all these reports may be summed up in what an inspector for Hanover says: "The reasons for the reduction of the working day to ten hours—(a) the physical organization of women, (b) her maternal functions, (c) the rearing and education of the children, (d) the maintenance of the home—are all so important and so far reaching that the need for such reduction need hardly be discussed." . . .

The legislation and opinions referred to in the margin may not be, technically speaking, authorities, and in them is little or no discussion of the constitutional question presented to us for determination, yet they are significant of a widespread belief that woman's physical structure, and the functions she performs in consequence thereof, justify special legislation restricting or qualifying the conditions under which she should be permitted to toil. Constitutional questions, it is true, are not settled by even a consensus of present public opinion, for it is the peculiar value of a written constitution that it places in unchanging form limitations upon legislative action, and thus gives a permanence and stability to popular government which otherwise would be lacking. At the same time, when a question of fact is debated and debatable, and the extent to which a special constitutional limitation goes is affected by the truth in respect to that fact, a widespread and long continued belief concerning it is worthy of consideration. We take judicial cognizance of all matters of general knowledge.

It is undoubtedly true, as more than once declared by this court, that the general right to contract in relation to one's business is part of the liberty of the individual, protected by the Fourteenth Amendment to the Federal Constitution; yet it is equally well settled that this liberty is not absolute and extending to all contracts, and that a State may, without conflicting with the provisions of the Fourteenth Amendment, restrict in many respects the individual's power of contract. Without stopping to discuss at length the extent to which a State may act in this respect, we refer to the following cases in which the question has been considered: *Allgeyer v. Louisiana*, 165 U.S. 578 [(1897)]; *Lochner v. New York*.

That woman's physical structure and the performance of maternal functions place her at a disadvantage in the struggle for subsistence is obvious. This is especially true when the burdens of motherhood are upon her. Even when they are not, by abundant testimony of the medical fraternity continuance for a long time on her feet at work, repeating this from day to day, tends to injurious effects upon the body, and as healthy mothers are essential to vigorous offspring, the physical well-being of woman becomes an object of public interest and care in order to preserve the strength and vigor of the race.

Still again, history discloses the fact that woman has always been dependent upon man. . . . As minors, though not to the same extent, she has been looked upon in the courts as needing especial care that her rights may be preserved. Education was long denied her, and while now the doors of the school room are opened and her opportunities for acquiring knowledge are great, yet even with that and the consequent increase of capacity for business affairs it is still true that in the struggle for subsistence she is not an equal competitor with her brother. Though limitations upon personal and contractual rights may be removed by legislation, there is that in her disposition and habits of life which will operate against a full assertion of those rights. She will still be where some legislation to protect her seems necessary to secure a real equality of right. Doubtless there are individual exceptions, and there are many respects in which she has an advantage over him; but looking at it from the viewpoint of the effort to maintain an independent position in life, she is not upon an equality. Differentiated by these matters from the other sex, she is properly placed in a class by herself, and legislation designed for her protection may be sustained, even when like legislation is not necessary for men and could not be sustained. It is impossible to close one's eyes to the fact that she still looks to her brother and depends upon him. . . . Many words cannot make this plainer. The two sexes differ in structure of body, in the functions to be performed by each, in the amount of physical strength, in the capacity for long-continued labor, particularly when done standing, the influence of vigorous health upon the future well-being of the race, the self-reliance which enables one to assert full rights, and in the capacity to maintain the struggle for subsistence. This difference justifies a difference in legislation and upholds that which is designed to compensate for some of the burdens which rest upon her. . . .

For these reasons, and without questioning in any respect the decision in *Lochner v. New York*, we are of the opinion that it cannot be adjudged that the act in question is in conflict with the Federal Constitution, so far as it respects the work of a female in a laundry, and the judgment of the Supreme Court of Oregon is

Affirmed.

West Coast Hotel Co. v. Parrish
300 U.S. 379, 57 S.Ct. 578 (1937)

An employee of the West Coast Hotel Company, Elsie Parrish, sued to recover the difference between her wage and the minimum wage of

$14.50 per forty-eight-hour week as set by the Industrial Welfare Committee of Washington State. In 1913, Washington's legislature passed legislation to protect the health and welfare of women and minors by setting a minimum wage. But the trial court denied Parrish's claim. When the Washington Supreme Court reversed, attorneys for West Coast Hotel Company appealed to the Supreme Court, arguing that the law ran afoul of the Fourteenth Amendment's due process clause.

The Court's decision was five to four, with the majority's opinion announced by Chief Justice Hughes. Justice Sutherland dissented and was joined by Justices Van Devanter, McReynolds, and Butler.

☐ *Chief Justice HUGHES delivered the opinion of the Court.*

This case presents the question of the constitutional validity of the minimum wage law of the state of Washington. . . .

The appellant conducts a hotel. The appellee Elsie Parrish was employed as a chambermaid and (with her husband) brought this suit to recover the difference between the wages paid her and the minimum wage fixed pursuant to the state law. The minimum wage was $14.50 per week of 48 hours. The appellant challenged the act as repugnant to the due process clause of the Fourteenth Amendment of the Constitution of the United States. The Supreme Court of the state, reversing the trial court, sustained the statute and directed judgment for the plaintiffs. *Parrish v. West Coast Hotel Co.*, 185 Wash. 581, 55 P.(2d) 1083 [(1936)]. The case is here on appeal.

The appellant relies upon the decision of this Court in *Adkins v. Children's Hospital*, 261 U.S. 525 [(1923)], which held invalid the District of Columbia Minimum Wage Act (40 Stat. 960) which was attacked under the due process clause of the Fifth Amendment. . . .

The recent case of *Morehead v. New York ex rel. Tipaldo*, 298 U.S. 587 [(1936)], came here on *certiorari* to the New York court which had held the New York minimum wage act for women to be invalid. A minority of this Court thought that the New York statute was distinguishable in a material feature from that involved in the *Adkins* Case and that for that and other reasons the New York statute should be sustained. But the Court of Appeals of New York had said that it found no material difference between the two statutes and this Court held that the "meaning of the statute" as fixed by the decision of the state court "must be accepted here as if the meaning had been specifically expressed in the enactment." That view led to the affirmance by this Court of the judgment in the *Morehead* Case, as the Court considered that the only question before it was whether the *Adkins* Case was distinguishable and that reconsideration of that decision had not been sought. . . .

We think that the question which was not deemed to be open in the *Morehead* Case is open and is necessarily presented here. . . .

The principle which must control our decision is not in doubt. The constitutional provision invoked is the due process clause of the Fourteenth Amendment governing the states, as the due process clause invoked in the *Adkins* Case governed Congress. In each case the violation alleged by those attacking minimum wage regulation for women is deprivation of freedom of contract. What is this freedom? The Constitution does not speak of freedom of contract. It speaks of liberty and prohibits the deprivation of liberty without due process of law. In prohibiting that deprivation, the Constitution does not recognize an absolute and uncontrollable liberty. Liberty in each of its phases has its history and connotation. But the liberty safe-guarded is liberty in a social organization which requires the protection of law against the evils which menace the health, safety, morals, and welfare of the people. Liberty under the Constitution is thus necessarily subject to the restraints of due process, and regulation which is reasonable in relation to its subject and is adopted in the interests of the community is due process.

This essential limitation of liberty in general governs freedom of contract in particular. More than twenty-five years ago we set forth the applicable principle in these words, after referring to the cases where the liberty guaranteed by the Fourteenth Amendment had been broadly described. . . .

This power under the Constitution to restrict freedom of contract has had many illustrations. That it may be exercised in the public interest with respect to contracts between employer and employee is undeniable. Thus statutes have been sustained limiting employment in underground mines and smelters to eight hours a day; in requiring redemption in cash of store orders or other evidences of indebtedness issued in the payment of wages; in forbidding the payment of seamen's wages in advance; in making it unlawful to contract to pay miners employed at quantity rates upon the basis of screened coal instead of the weight of the coal as originally produced in the mine; in prohibiting contracts limiting liability for injuries to employees; in limiting hours of work of employees in manufacturing establishments; and in maintaining workmen's compensation laws. In dealing with the relation of employer and employed, the Legislature has necessarily a wide field of discretion in order that there may be suitable protection of health and safety, and that peace and good order may be promoted through regulations designed to insure wholesome conditions of work and freedom from oppression. . . .

This array of precedents and the principles they applied were thought by the dissenting Justices in the *Adkins* Case to demand that the minimum wage statute be sustained. The validity of the distinction made by the Court between a minimum wage and a maximum of hours in limiting liberty of contract was especially challenged. That challenge persists and is without any satisfactory answer. . . .

We think that the views thus expressed are sound and that the decision in the *Adkins* Case was a departure from the true application of the principles governing the regulation by the state of the relation of employer and employed. . . .

There is an additional and compelling consideration which recent economic experience has brought into a strong light. The exploitation of a class of workers who are in an unequal position with respect to bargaining power and are thus relatively defenseless against the denial of a living wage is not only detrimental to their health and well being, but casts a direct burden for their support upon the community. What these workers lose in wages the taxpayers are called upon to pay. The bare cost of living must be met. We may take judicial notice of the unparalleled demands for relief which arose during the recent period of depression and still continue to an alarming extent despite the degree of economic recovery which has been achieved. It is unnecessary to cite official statistics to establish what is of common knowledge through the length and breadth of the land. While in the instant case no factual brief has been presented, there is no reason to doubt that the state of Washington has encountered the same social problem that is present elsewhere. The community is not bound to provide what is in effect a subsidy for unconscionable employers. The community may direct its law-making power to correct the abuse which springs from their selfish disregard of the public interest. . . .

Our conclusion is that the case of *Adkins v. Children's Hospital,* supra, should be, and it is, overruled. The judgment of the Supreme Court of the state of Washington is affirmed.

Affirmed.

☐ *Justice SUTHERLAND*

Justice VAN DEVANTER, Justice McREYNOLDS, Justice BUTLER, and I think the judgment of the court below should be reversed.

It is urged that the question involved should now receive fresh consideration, among other reasons, because of "the economic conditions which have supervened"; but the meaning of the Constitution does not change with the ebb and flow of economic events. We frequently are told in more general words that the Constitution must be construed in the light of the present. If by that it is meant that the Constitution is made up of living words that apply to every new condition which they include, the statement is quite true. But to say, if that be intended, that the words of the Constitution mean today what they did not mean when written—that is, that they do not apply to a situation now to which they would have applied then—is to rob that instrument of the essential element which continues it in force as the people have made it until they, and not their official agents, have made it otherwise. . . .

The judicial function is that of interpretation; it does not include the power of amendment under the guise of interpretation. To miss the point of difference between the two is to miss all that the phrase "supreme law of the land" stands for and to convert what was intended as inescapable and enduring mandates into mere moral reflections.

If the Constitution, intelligently and reasonably construed in the light of these principles, stands in the way of desirable legislation, the blame must rest upon that instrument, and not upon the court for enforcing it according to its terms. The remedy in that situation—and the only true remedy—is to amend the Constitution. . . .

In the *Adkins* Case we . . . said that while there was no such thing as absolute freedom of contract, but that it was subject to a great variety of restraints, nevertheless, freedom of contract was the general rule and restraint the exception; and that the power to abridge that freedom could only be justified by the existence of exceptional circumstances. This statement of the rule has been many times affirmed; and we do not understand that it is questioned by the present decision.

Lincoln Federal Labor Union v. Northwestern Iron & Metal Co.

335 U.S. 525, 69 S.Ct. 251 (1949)

In 1946, Nebraska's constitution was amended to provide that

> [n]o person shall be denied employment because of membership in or affiliation with, or resignation or expulsion from a labor organization or because of refusal to join or affiliate with a labor organization; nor shall any individual or corporation or association of any kind enter into any contract, written or oral, to exclude persons from employment because of membership in or nonmembership in a labor organization.

Several labor unions challenged the constitutionality of this and other state right to work laws, claiming that they infringed on the First Amendment freedoms of speech and assembly and the Fourteenth Amendment's due process clause. The Nebraska State Supreme Court rejected their claims and the Lincoln Federal Labor Union appealed to the Supreme Court of the United States.

The Court's decision was unanimous, and the opinion was announced by Justice Black. Justices Frankfurter and Rutledge concurred.

☐ *Justice BLACK delivered the opinion of the Court.*

Many cases are cited by appellants in which this Court has said that in some instances the due process clause protects the liberty of persons to make contracts. But none of these cases, even those according the broadest constitutional protection to the making of contracts, ever went so far as to indicate that the due process clause bars a state from prohibiting contracts to engage in conduct banned by a valid state law. So here, if the provisions in the state laws against employer discrimination are valid, it follows that the contract prohibition also is valid. We therefore turn to the decisive question under the due process contention, which is: Does the due process clause forbid a state to pass laws clearly designed to safeguard the opportunity of non-union members to get and hold jobs, free from discrimination against them because they are non-union workers?

There was a period in which labor union members who wanted to get and hold jobs were the victims of widespread employer discrimination practices. Contracts between employers and their employees were used by employers to accomplish this anti-union employment discrimination. Before hiring workers, employers required them to sign agreements stating that the workers were not and would not become labor union members. Such anti-union practices were so obnoxious to workers that they gave these required agreements the name of "yellow dog contracts." This hostility of workers also prompted passage of state and federal laws to ban employer discrimination against union members and to outlaw yellow dog contracts. . . .

The *Allgeyer-Lochner-Adair-Coppage* constitutional doctrine was for some years followed by this Court. It was used to strike down laws fixing minimum wages and maximum hours in employment, laws fixing prices, and laws regulating business activities. . . .

This Court beginning at least as early as 1934, when the *Nebbia* [*v. New York*, 291 U.S. 902 (1931)] case was decided, has steadily rejected the due process philosophy enunciated in the *Adair-Coppage* line of cases. In doing so it has consciously returned closer and closer to the earlier constitutional principle that states have power to legislate against what are found to be injurious practices in their internal commercial and business affairs, so long as their laws do not run afoul of some specific federal constitutional prohibition, or of some valid federal law. Under this constitutional doctrine the due process clause is no longer to be so broadly construed that the Congress and state legislatures are put in a strait jacket when they attempt to suppress business and industrial conditions which they regard as offensive to the public welfare.

Appellants now ask us to return, at least in part, to the due process philosophy that has been deliberately discarded. Claiming that the Federal Constitution itself affords protection for union members against discrimination, they nevertheless assert that the same Constitution forbids a state from providing the same protection for non-union members. Just as we have held that the due process clause erects no obstacle to block legislative protection of union members, we now hold that legislative protection can be afforded non-union workers.

Affirmed.

C | The "Takings Clause" and Just Compensation

A final source for the Court's protection of proprietary interests is the Fifth Amendment's provision that "private property [shall not] be taken for public use, without just compensation." It is also one area of constitutional law in which the Rehnquist Court moved toward giving somewhat greater protection for property rights: *Nollan v. California Coastal Commission* (1987) (see excerpt below) and THE DEVELOPMENT OF LAW box in this section are illustrative. Also relevant is *Dames & Moore v. Regan*, 453 U.S. 654 (1981) (see Vol. 1, Ch. 3).

The takings clause broadly guarantees government the power of eminent domain—the power to take private property for public purposes—subject to the just compensation of the owners. But what is a "public purpose"? What constitutes the "taking" of property? And what amounts to "just" compensation?

The requirement that government put private property to public use has been rather loosely interpreted. The only limitations appear to be that government may not take property for the sole purpose of making money for itself or for a private enterprise. However, government may take property and then resell it to private companies for such purposes as urban renewal, the development of industrial parks, or shopping centers, and for use by (even privately owned) public utilities. In *Hawaii Housing Authority v. Midkiff*, 467 U.S. 229 (1984) (excerpted below), for example, the Burger Court approved a state land reform act. As a vestige of Hawaiian feudalism, 96 percent of the state was owned by seventy-two landowners or state and federal governments. In 1967, Hawaii's legislature authorized the use of the power of eminent domain to condemn residential lots and to sell and transfer ownership to existing tenants on the land. The Court unanimously rejected the contention that this program constituted a taking of private property for private, not public, purposes.

General benefit to the public, not public ownership, is what matters, and the Court tends to be highly deferential to legislatures as to what benefits the public. "Subject to specific constitutional limitations," as the Court observed in *Berman v. Parker*, 348 U.S. 26 (1954), "when the legislature has spoken, the public interest has been declared in terms well-nigh conclusive."

Private property does not have to be physically taken by the government for an individual to win compensation. However, *Loretto v. Teleprompter Manhattan CATV*, 458 U.S. 419 (1982), held that permanent physical occupation of property by the government is per se taking and *First English Evangelical Lutheran Church v. County of Los Angeles*, 482 U.S. 304 (1987), ruled that temporary land-use laws may constitute a taking of private property.

In the classic case of *United States v. Causby*, 328 U.S. 258 (1946), the Court upheld a demand for compensation by a farmer whose land was adjacent to a military airport. The noise of airplane flights over the farm rendered it virtually worthless and the Court upheld the farmer's claim that the government was using his farmland as an extension of its runway and had to pay for it.

Not everyone next to an airport or highway, however, may demand compensation because of the accompanying noise or, for that matter, inconvenience of government regulations. Instead, for property to be "taken" in a constitutional sense, an owner must show a nearly total loss of the use of the property. In *Pennsylvania Coal Co. v. Mahon*, 260 U.S. 393 (1922), Justice Holmes formulated a practical rule, when holding that "property may be regulated to a certain extent, [but] if regulation goes too far it will be recognized as a taking." There is no "brightline

rule," but rather, the burden is placed on the property owner of showing a virtually complete loss of the use of his or her property to win
compensation.

In another important ruling in *Penn Central Transportation Co. v. New
York*, 438 U.S. 104 (1978), the Burger Court affirmed a historic preser-
vation law prohibiting the owners of Grand Central Station in New
York City from building a high-rise office tower above the station.

Finally, the Court largely avoided controversies over whether a
property owner has received just compensation. In general, just compensation means what, in the absence of the government's acquisition
of the property, a willing buyer would pay, or the fair market value. As
the Court observed in *Backus v. Fort Street Union Depot Co.*, 169 U.S.
557 (1898): "All that is essential is that in some appropriate way, before
some properly constituted tribunal, inquiry shall be made as to the
amount of compensation, and when this has been provided there is that
due process of law which is required by the Federal Constitution."

Although the Rehnquist Court signaled renewed interest in, and
invited litigation over, takings-clause jurisprudence in its 1987 rulings
in *Nollan v. California Coastal Commission* (see excerpt below) and *First
English Evangelical Lutheran Church v. County of Los Angeles*, 482 U.S. 304
(1987), as well as revisited challenges to land-use regulations in several
other cases,[1] a majority of the Court appears unwilling to further extend *Nollan's* analysis. In the leading "takings clause" case after *Nollan,
Lucas v. South Carolina Coastal Council* (1992) (excerpted below), the
owner of beachfront property appealed a decision of the South Carolina Supreme Court that upheld a regulation barring the rebuilding of
houses on the shoreline. Writing for the majority in *Lucas*, Justice Scalia
held, on the one hand, that property owners who suffer total economic
loss of the value of their land may have a takings-clause claim. Historically, the Court recognized takings claims only when the government
actually took physical possession of a property, as in an eminent domain
proceeding. But, in *Nollan* and *Lucas*, the Court recognized regulatory
takings requiring the government to pay compensation when its regulations diminish the value of private property. In *Lucas*, Scalia held that
it is not enough for the government to defend its environmental, land-
use, and zoning regulations as in the "public interest." Governments
must also defend their regulations as necessary to avoid a public harm
or the "harmful or noxious use" of private property; thus a property
owner might be denied a permit to run a landfill operation because it
would result in flooding of nearby land. Because the state courts failed
to identify the public nuisances that would justify the building restrictions in this case, the court remanded *Lucas* for further consideration.

Justice Scalia's opinion, on the other hand, limited its takings-clause analysis to apply only when property owners are totally deprived of the economic value of their land. As he put it, "When the owner of real property has been called upon to sacrifice *all* economically beneficial uses in the name of the common good, that is, to leave his property economically idle, he has suffered a taking." That, however, significantly limited the Court's holding because, as dissenting Justice Stevens observed, "A land-owner whose property is diminished in value 95 percent recovers nothing, while an owner whose property is diminished 100 percent recovers the land's full value." Since most environmental and land-use regulations do not deprive property owners of all economic use or value of their property, Justice Scalia's analysis in *Lucas* is severely limited; for further discussion see THE DEVELOPMENT OF LAW box in this section. See also the Court's rulings on substantive due process and punitive damages awards in Chapter 4 and *BMW of North America v. Gore* (excerpted there).

NOTE

1. See also *Yee v. The City of Escondido, California*, 503 U.S. 519 (1992), holding that a rent-control ordinance did not amount to a takings per se. Writing for the Court, Justice O'Connor distinguished two kinds of takings–clause cases: (1) those in which the government has actually physically taken private property for public use and (2) those challenging regulations of the use of private property. The former generally requires compensation of the owners and "courts to apply a clear rule," whereas the latter requires courts to assess the purposes and economic effects of the regulations. And O'Connor reaffirmed that "[s]tates have broad power to regulate housing conditions in general and the landlord-tenant relationship in particular."

SELECTED BIBLIOGRAPHY

Ackerman, Bruce. *Private Property and the Constitution*. New Haven, CT: Yale University Press, 1977.

Ely, James W. *The Guardian of Every Other Right: A Constitutional History of Property Rights*. New York: Oxford University Press, 1992.

Epstein, Richard. *Takings: Private Property and the Power of Eminent Domain*. Chicago: University of Chicago Press, 1985.

Fischel, William. *Regulatory Takings: Law, Economics, and Politics*. Cambridge, MA: Harvard University Press, 1995.

Levy, Leonard. *A License to Steal: Forfeiture of Property*. Chapel Hill: University of North Carolina Press, 1996.

Siegan, Bernard. *Property and Freedom: The Constitution, The Courts, and Land-Use Regulation*. New Brunswick, NJ: Transaction Books, 1998.

Hawaii Housing Authority v. Midkiff

467 U.S. 229, 104 S.Ct. 2321 (1984)

The Hawaiian islands were originally settled by Polynesian immigrants from the western Pacific. These settlers developed an economy around a feudal land-tenure system in which one island high chief controlled the land and assigned it for development to subchiefs. Beginning in the early 1800s, Hawaiian leaders and American settlers attempted to divide the lands of the kingdom among the crown, the chiefs, and the common people. These efforts proved largely unsuccessful, however. Finally, in the mid-1960s the Hawaii legislature held hearings and discovered that while the state and federal governments owned almost 49 percent of the state's land, another 47 percent was owned by 72 landholders. The legislature concluded that such concentrated land ownership was responsible for skewing the state's land prices and injuring the public tranquillity and welfare. Accordingly, the legislature enacted legislation in order to compel the large landowners to break up their estates. The Land Reform Act of 1967 created a mechanism for condemning residential tracts and for transferring ownership of condemned land to lessees. Under the act's condemnation scheme, tenants living on single-family lots within development tracts at least five acres in size were entitled to ask the Hawaii Housing Authority (HHA) to condemn the property on which they lived. When twenty-five eligible tenants, or tenants on half of the lots in the tract, whichever was less, filed appropriate applications, the act authorized the HHA to hold a public hearing to determine whether the acquisition of the land would "effectuate the public purposes" of the law. If the HHA found that these purposes would be served, it was authorized to acquire the land, at prices set either by a condemnation trial or by negotiations with the landowners.

After HHA held a public hearing on the proposed acquisition of appellees' lands and found that such acquisition would effectuate the act's public purposes, it directed appellees to negotiate with certain lessees concerning the sale of the designated properties. When these negotiations failed, HHA ordered appellees to submit to compulsory arbitration as provided by the act. Rather than comply with this order, appellees filed suit in federal district court, asking that the act be declared unconstitutional. That court held that act to be constitutional under the Public Use Clause of the Fifth Amendment. But the Court of Appeals for the Ninth Circuit reversed, holding that the law violated the Fifth Amendment. The Hawaiian Housing Authority appealed and the Supreme Court granted review and reversed the appellate court.

The Court's decision, with Justice Marshall not participating, was unanimous and delivered by Justice O'Connor.

☐ *Justice O'CONNOR delivered the opinion of the Court.*

The Fifth Amendment of the United States Constitution provides, in pertinent part, that "private property [shall not] be taken for public use, without just compensation." These cases present the question whether the Public Use Clause of that Amendment, made applicable to the States through the Fourteenth Amendment, prohibits the State of Hawaii from taking, with just compensation, title in real property from lessors and transferring it to lessees in order to reduce the concentration of ownership of fees simple in the State. We conclude that it does not. . . .

The starting point for our analysis of the Act's constitutionality is the Court's decision in *Berman v. Parker*, 348 U.S. 26 (1954). In *Berman*, the Court held constitutional the District of Columbia Redevelopment Act of 1945. That Act provided both for the comprehensive use of the eminent domain power to redevelop slum areas and for the possible sale or lease of the condemned lands to private interests. In discussing whether the takings authorized by that Act were for a "public use," the Court stated:

> "We deal, in other words, with what traditionally has been known as the police power. An attempt to define its reach or trace its outer limits is fruitless, for each case must turn on its own facts. The definition is essentially the product of legislative determinations addressed to the purposes of government, purposes neither abstractly nor historically capable of complete definition. Subject to specific constitutional limitations, when the legislature has spoken, the public interest has been declared in terms well-nigh conclusive. In such cases the legislature, not the judiciary, is the main guardian of the public needs to be served by social legislation, whether it be Congress legislating concerning the District of Columbia . . . or the States legislating concerning local affairs. . . . This principle admits of no exception merely because the power of eminent domain is involved. . . ."

The Court explicitly recognized the breadth of the principle it was announcing, noting:

> "Once the object is within the authority of Congress, the right to realize it through the exercise of eminent domain is clear. For the power of eminent domain is merely the means to the end. . . . Once the object is within the authority of Congress, the means by which it will be attained is also for Congress to determine. Here one of the means chosen is the use of private enterprise for redevelopment of the area. Appellants argue that this makes the project a taking from one businessman for the benefit of another businessman. But the means of executing the project are for Congress and Congress alone to determine, once the public purpose has been established."

The "public use" requirement is thus coterminous with the scope of a sovereign's police powers. There is, of course, a role for courts to play in reviewing a legislature's judgment of what constitutes a public use, even when the eminent domain power is equated with the police power. But the Court in *Berman* made clear that it is "an extremely narrow" one. The Court in *Berman* cited with approval the Court's decision in *Old Dominion Co. v. United States*, 269 U.S. 55 (1925), which held that deference to the legislature's "public use" determination is required "until it is shown to involve an impossibility." . . . To be sure, the Court's cases have repeatedly stated that "one person's property may not be taken for the benefit of another private person without a justifying public purpose, even though compensation be paid." *Thompson v. Consolidated Gas Corp.*, 300 U.S. 55 (1937). Thus, in *Missouri Pacific R. Co. v. Nebraska*, 164 U.S. 403 (1896), where the "order in question was not, and was not claimed to be, . . . a taking of private property for a public use under the right of eminent domain," the Court invalidated a compensated taking of property for lack of a justifying public purpose. But where the exercise of the eminent domain power is rationally related to a conceivable public purpose, the Court has never held a compensated taking to be proscribed by the Public Use Clause. On this basis, we have no trouble concluding that the Hawaii Act is constitutional. The people of Hawaii have attempted, much as the settlers of the original 13 Colonies did, to reduce the perceived social and economic evils of a land oligopoly traceable to their monarchs. The land oligopoly has, according to the Hawaii Legislature, created artificial deterrents to the normal functioning of the State's residential land market and forced thousands of individual homeowners to lease, rather than buy, the land underneath their homes. Regulating oligopoly and the evils associated with it is a classic exercise of a State's police powers. We cannot disapprove of Hawaii's exercise of this power. . . .

The State of Hawaii has never denied that the Constitution forbids even a compensated taking of property when executed for no reason other than to confer a private benefit on a particular private party. A purely private taking could not withstand the scrutiny of the public use requirement; it would serve no legitimate purpose of government and would thus be void. But no purely private taking is involved in these cases. The Hawaii Legislature enacted its Land Reform Act not to benefit a particular class of identifiable individuals but to attack certain perceived evils of concentrated property ownership in Hawaii—a legitimate public purpose. Use of the condemnation power to achieve this purpose is not irrational. Since we assume for purposes of these appeals that the weighty demand of just compensation has been met, the requirements of the Fifth and Fourteenth Amendments have been satisfied. Accordingly, we reverse the judgment of the Court of Appeals, and remand these cases for further proceedings in conformity with this opinion.

Nollan v. California Coastal Commission
483 U.S. 825, 107 S.Ct. 3141 (1987)

James Nollan and several other owners of beachfront property filed a suit against the California Coastal Commission in 1982. They contended that its regulations governing the construction and reconstruction of buildings on beachfront property were unconstitutional. Specifically, they argued that its requirement, as a condition of receiving a building permit, that property owners transfer to the public an easement across their property constituted a taking of property under the Fifth and Fourteenth Amendments. The California Superior Court agreed but a state appellate court reversed, and Nollan appealed to the Supreme Court of the United States.

The Court's decision was five to four, with the majority's opinion announced by Justice Scalia. Dissents were by Justice Brennan, joined by Justice Marshall, and Justices Blackmun and Stevens.

☐ *Justice SCALIA delivered the opinion of the Court.*

We have long recognized that land use regulation does not effect a taking if it "substantially advance[s] legitimate state interests" and does not "den[y] an owner economically viable use of his land." *Agins v. Tiburon*, 447 U.S. 255 (1980). . . . Our cases have not elaborated on the standards for determining what constitutes a "legitimate state interest" or what type of connection between the regulation and the state interest satisfies the requirement that the former "substantially advance" the latter. They have made clear, however, that a broad range of governmental purposes and regulations satisfies these requirements. See *Agins v. Tiburon*, supra, (scenic zoning); *Penn Central Transportation Co. v. New York City* (landmark preservation); *Euclid v. Ambler Realty Co.*, 272 U.S. 365 (1926) (residential zoning); Laitos and Westfall, Government Interference with Private Interests in Public Resources, 11 Harv. Envtl.L.Rev. 1, 66 (1987). The Commission argues that among these permissible purposes are protecting the public's ability to see the beach, assisting the public in overcoming the "psychological barrier" to using the beach created by a developed shorefront, and preventing congestion on the public beaches. We assume, without deciding, that this is so—in which case the Commission unquestionably would be able to deny the Nollans their permit outright if their new house (alone, or by reason of the cumulative impact produced in conjunction with other construction) would substantially impede these purposes, unless the denial would interfere so drastically with the Nollans use of their property as to constitute a taking.

The Commission argues that a permit condition that serves the same legitimate police-power purpose as a refusal to issue the permit should not be found to be a taking if the refusal to issue the permit would not constitute a taking. We agree. . . . Although such a requirement, constituting a permanent grant of continuous access to the property, would have to be considered a taking if it were not attached to a development permit, the Commission's assumed power to forbid construction of the house in order to protect the public's view of the beach must surely include the power to condition construction upon some concession by the owner, even a concession of property rights, that serves the same end. If a prohibition designed to accomplish that purpose would be a legitimate exercise of the police power rather than a taking, it would be strange to conclude that providing the owner an alternative to that prohibition which accomplishes the same purpose is not.

The evident constitutional propriety disappears, however, if the condition substituted for the prohibition utterly fails to further the end advanced as the justification for the prohibition. When that essential nexus is eliminated, the situation becomes the same as if California law forbade shouting fire in a crowded theater, but granted dispensations to those willing to contribute $100 to the state treasury. While a ban on shouting fire can be a core exercise of the State's police power to protect the public safety, and can thus meet even our stringent standards for regulation of speech, adding the unrelated condition alters the purpose to one which, while it may be legitimate, is inadequate to sustain the ban. Therefore, even though, in a sense, requiring a $100 tax contribution in order to shout fire is a lesser restriction on speech than an outright ban, it would not pass constitutional muster. Similarly here, the lack of nexus between the condition and the original purpose of the building restriction converts that purpose to something other than what it was. The purpose then becomes, quite simply, the obtaining of an easement to serve some valid governmental purpose, but without payment of compensation. Whatever may be the outer limits of "legitimate state interests" in the takings and land use context, this is not one of them. In short, unless the permit condition serves the same governmental purpose as the development ban, the building restriction is not a valid regulation of land use but "an out-and-out plan of extortion." . . .

It is quite impossible to understand how a requirement that people already on the public beaches be able to walk across the Nollans' property reduces any obstacles to viewing the beach created by the new house. It is also impossible to understand how it lowers any "psychological barrier" to using the public beaches, or how it helps to remedy any additional congestion on them caused by construction of the Nollans' new house. We therefore find that the Commission's imposition of the permit condition cannot be treated as an exercise of its land use power for any of these purposes. . . .

Justice BRENNAN argues that imposition of the access requirement is not irrational. In his version of the Commission's argument, the reason for the requirement is that in its absence, a person looking toward the beach from the road will see a street of residential structures including the Nollans' new home and conclude that there is no public beach nearby. If, however, that person sees people passing and repassing along the dry sand behind the Nollans' home, he will realize that there is a public beach somewhere in the vicinity. The Commission's action, however, was based on the opposite factual finding that the wall of houses completely blocked the view of the beach and that a person looking from the road would not be able to see it at all. . . .

We are left, then, with the Commission's justification for the access requirement unrelated to land use regulation:

> "Finally, the Commission notes that there are several existing provisions of pass and repass lateral access benefits already given by past Faria Beach Tract applicants as a result of prior coastal permit decisions. The access required as a condition of this permit is part of a comprehensive program to provide continuous public access along Faria Beach as the lots undergo development or redevelopment."

That is simply an expression of the Commission's belief that the public interest will be served by a continuous strip of publicly accessible beach along the coast. The Commission may well be right that it is a good idea, but that does not establish that the Nollans (and other coastal residents) alone can be compelled to contribute to its realization. Rather, California is free to advance its "comprehensive program," if it wishes, by using its power of eminent domain for this "public purpose," see U.S. Const., Amdt. V; but if it wants an easement across the Nollans' property, it must pay for it.

Reversed.

☐ *Justice BRENNAN, with whom Justice MARSHALL joins, dissenting.*

The Court's conclusion that the permit rendition imposed on appellants is unreasonable cannot withstand analysis. First, the Court demands a degree of exactitude that is inconsistent with our standard for reviewing the rationality of a state's exercise of its police power for the welfare of its citizens. Second, even if the nature of the public access condition imposed must be identical to the precise burden on access created by appellants, this requirement is plainly satisfied. . . .

Imposition of the permit condition in this case represents the State's reasonable exercise of its police power. The Coastal Commission has drawn on its expertise to preserve the balance between private development and public access, by requiring that any project that intensifies development on the increasingly crowded California coast must be offset by gains in public access. Under the normal standard for review of the police power, this provision is eminently reasonable. Even accepting the Court's novel insistence on a precise *quid pro quo* of burdens and benefits, there is a reasonable relationship between the public benefit and the burden created by appellants' development. The movement of development closer to the ocean creates the prospect of encroachment on public tidelands, because of fluctuation in the mean high tide line. The deed restriction ensures that disputes about the boundary between private and public property will not deter the public from exercising its right to have access to the sea.

Furthermore, consideration of the Commission's action under traditional takings analysis underscores the absence of any viable takings claim. The deed restriction permits the public only to pass and repass along a narrow strip of beach, a few feet closer to a seawall at the periphery of appellants' property. Appellants almost surely have enjoyed an increase in the value of their property even with the restriction, because they have been allowed to build a significantly larger new home with garage on their lot. Finally, appellants can claim the disruption of no expectation interest, both because they have no right to exclude the public under state law, and because, even if they did, they had full advance notice that new development along the coast is conditioned on provisions for continued public access to the ocean. . . .

I dissent.

Lucas v. South Carolina Coastal Council
505 U.S. 1003, 112 S. CT. 2886 (1992)

In 1986, petitioner David H. Lucas paid $975,000 for two residential lots on the Isle of Palms in Charleston County, South Carolina, on which he intended to build single-family homes. In 1988, however, the South Carolina Legislature enacted the Beachfront Management Act, which had the effect of barring Lucas from building on the land. A state trial court found that this prohibition rendered Lucas's parcels "valueless," for which he was entitled to just compensation. On appeal, the state supreme court reversed and Lucas appealed to the U.S. Supreme Court.

The state supreme court's decision was reversed by a vote of six to three. Justice Scalia delivered the opinion for the Court. Justice Kennedy filed a concurring opinion. Justices Blackmun and Stevens filed separate dissenting opinions, and Justice Souter filed a statement indicating that case should have been dismissed as improvidently granted.

□ *Justice SCALIA delivered the opinion of the Court.*

Prior to Justice HOLMES's exposition in *Pennsylvania Coal Co. v. Mahon*, 260 U.S. 393 (1922), it was generally thought that the Takings Clause reached only a "direct appropriation" of property, *Legal Tender Cases*, 79 U.S. (12 Wall.) 457 (1871), or the functional equivalent of a "practical ouster of [the owner's] possession," *Transportation Co. v. Chicago*, 99 U.S. 635 (1879). Justice HOLMES recognized in *Mahon*, however, that if the protection against physical appropriations of private property was to be meaningfully enforced, the government's power to redefine the range of interests included in the ownership of property was necessarily constrained by constitutional limits. If, instead, the uses of private property were subject to unbridled, uncompensated qualification under the police power, "the natural tendency of human nature [would be] to extend the qualification more and more until at last private property disappeared." These considerations gave birth in that case to the oft-cited maxim that, "while property may be regulated to a certain extent, if regulation goes too far it will be recognized as a taking."

Nevertheless, our decision in *Mahon* offered little insight into when, and under what circumstances, a given regulation would be seen as going "too far" for purposes of the Fifth Amendment. In 70-odd years of succeeding "regulatory takings" jurisprudence, we have generally eschewed any " 'set formula' " for determining how far is too far, preferring to "engage in . . . essentially ad hoc, factual inquiries." *Penn Central Transportation Co. v. New York City*, 438 U.S. 104 (1978). We have, however, described at least two discrete categories of regulatory action as compensable without case-specific inquiry into the public interest advanced in support of the restraint. The first encompasses regulations that compel the property owner to suffer a physical "invasion" of his property. In general (at least with regard to permanent invasions), no matter how minute the intrusion, and no matter how weighty the public purpose behind it, we have required compensation. For example, in *Loretto v. Teleprompter Manhattan CATV Corp.*, 458 U.S. 419 (1982), we determined that New York's law requiring landlords to allow television cable companies to emplace cable facilities in their apartment buildings constituted a taking, even though the facilities occupied at most only 1 1/2 cubic feet of the landlords' property.

The second situation in which we have found categorical treatment appropriate is where regulation denies all economically beneficial or productive use of land. As we have said on numerous occasions, the Fifth Amendment is violated when land-use regulation "does not substantially advance legitimate state interests or denies an owner economically viable use of his land."

We have never set forth the justification for this rule. Perhaps it is simply, as Justice BRENNAN suggested, that total deprivation of beneficial use is, from the landowner's point of view, the equivalent of a physical appropriation. See *San Diego Gas & Electric Co. v. San Diego*, 450 U.S. [627] (1981). . . . We think . . . that there are good reasons for our frequently expressed belief that when the owner of real property has been called upon to sacrifice all economically beneficial uses in the name of the common good, that is, to leave his property economically idle, he has suffered a taking.

The trial court found Lucas's two beachfront lots to have been rendered valueless by respondent's enforcement of the coastal-zone construction ban. Under Lucas's theory of the case, which rested upon our "no economically viable use" statements, that finding entitled him to compensation. . . . The South Carolina Supreme Court, however, thought otherwise. In its view, the Beachfront Management Act was no ordinary enactment, but involved an exercise of South Carolina's "police powers" to mitigate the harm to the public interest that petitioner's use of his land might occasion. . . . In the court's view, these concessions brought petitioner's challenge within a long line of this Court's cases sustaining against Due Process and Takings Clause challenges the State's use of its "police powers" to enjoin a property owner from activities akin to public nuisances. See *Mugler v. Kansas*, 123 U.S. 623 (1887) (law prohibiting manufacture of alcoholic beverages).

For a number of reasons, however, we think the South Carolina Supreme Court was too quick to conclude that that principle decides the present case. The "harmful or noxious uses" principle was the Court's early attempt to describe in theoretical terms why government may, consistent with the Takings Clause, affect property values by regulation without incurring an obligation to compensate—a reality we nowadays acknowledge explicitly with respect to the full scope of the State's police power. . . . "Harmful or noxious use" analysis was, in other words, simply the progenitor of our more contemporary statements that "land-use regulation does not effect a taking if it 'substantially advances legitimate state interests' . . ."

The transition from our early focus on control of "noxious" uses to our contemporary understanding of the broad realm within which government may regulate without compensation was an easy one, since the distinction between "harm-preventing" and "benefit-conferring" regulation is often in the eye of the beholder. It is quite possible, for example, to describe in either fashion the ecological, economic, and esthetic concerns that inspired the South Carolina Legislature in the present case. One could say that imposing a servitude on Lucas's land is necessary in order to prevent his use of it from "harming" South Carolina's ecological resources; or, instead, in order to achieve the "benefits" of an ecological preserve. Whether one or the other of the competing characterizations will come to one's lips in a particular case depends primarily upon one's evaluation of the worth of competing uses of real estate. A given restraint will be seen as mitigating "harm" to the adjacent parcels or securing a "benefit" for them, depending upon the observer's evaluation of the relative importance of the use that the restraint favors. Whether Lucas's construction of single-family residences on his parcels should be described as bringing "harm" to South Carolina's adjacent ecological resources thus depends principally upon whether the describer believes that the State's use interest in nurturing those resources is so important that any competing adjacent use must yield.

When it is understood that "prevention of harmful use" was merely our early formulation of the police power justification necessary to sustain (without compensation) any regulatory diminution in value; and that the distinction between regulation that "prevents harmful use" and that which "confers benefits" is difficult, if not impossible, to discern on an objective, value-free basis; it becomes self-evident that noxious-use logic cannot serve as a touchstone to distinguish regulatory "takings"—which require compensation—from regulatory deprivations that do not require compensation. . . .

Where the State seeks to sustain regulation that deprives land of all economically beneficial use, we think it may resist compensation only if the logically antecedent inquiry into the nature of the owner's estate shows that the proscribed use interests were not part of his title to begin with. This accords, we think, with our "takings" jurisprudence, which has traditionally been guided by the understandings of our citizens regarding the content of, and the State's power over, the "bundle of rights" that they acquire when they obtain title to property. It seems to us that the property owner necessarily expects the uses of his property to be restricted, from time to time, by various measures newly enacted by the State in legitimate exercise of its police powers; "as long recognized, some values are enjoyed under an implied limitation and must yield to the police power." *Pennsylvania Coal Co. v. Mahon.* And in the case of personal property, by reason of the State's traditionally high degree of control over commercial dealings, he ought to be aware of the possibility that new regulation might even render his property economically worthless (at least if the property's only economically productive use is sale or manufacture for sale). In the case of land, however, we think the notion pressed by the Council that title is somehow held subject to the "implied limitation" that the State may subsequently eliminate all economically valuable use is inconsistent with the historical compact recorded in the Takings Clause that has become part of our constitutional culture.

Where "permanent physical occupation" of land is concerned, we have refused to allow the government to decree it anew (without compensation), no matter how weighty the asserted "public interests" involved, *Loretto v. Teleprompter Manhattan CATV Corp.*—though we assuredly would permit the government to assert a permanent easement that was a pre-existing limitation upon the landowner's title. We believe similar treatment must be accorded confiscatory regulations, i.e., regulations that prohibit all economically beneficial use of land: Any limitation so severe cannot be newly legislated or decreed (without compensation), but must inhere in the title itself, in the restrictions that background principles of the State's law of property and nuisance already place upon land ownership. A law or decree with such an effect must, in other words, do no more than duplicate the result that could have been achieved in the courts—by adjacent landowners (or other uniquely affected persons) under the State's law of private nuisance, or by the State under its complementary power to abate nuisances that affect the public generally, or otherwise.

On this analysis, the owner of a lakebed, for example, would not be entitled to compensation when he is denied the requisite permit to engage in a landfilling operation that would have the effect of flooding others' land. . . . Such regulatory action may well have the effect of eliminating the land's only economically productive use, but it does not proscribe a productive use that was previously permissible under relevant property and nuisance principles. The use of these properties for what are now expressly prohibited purposes was always unlawful, and (subject to other constitutional limitations) it was open to the State at any point to make the implication of those background principles of nuisance and property law explicit. In light of our traditional resort to "existing rules or understandings that stem from an independent source such as state law" to define the range of interests that qualify for protection as "property" under the Fifth and Fourteenth Amendments, this recognition that the Takings Clause does not require compensation when an owner is barred from putting land to a use that is proscribed by those "existing rules or understandings" is surely unexceptional. When, however, a regulation that declares "off-limits" all economically productive or beneficial uses of land goes beyond what the relevant background principles would dictate, compensation must be paid to sustain it.

The "total taking" inquiry we require today will ordinarily entail (as the application of state nuisance law ordinarily entails) analysis of, among other things, the degree of harm to public lands and resources, or adjacent private property, posed by the claimant's proposed activities, the social value of the claimant's activities and their suitability to the locality in question, and the relative ease with which the alleged harm can be avoided through measures taken by the claimant and the government (or adjacent private landowners) alike. The fact that a particular use has long been engaged in by similarly situated owners ordinarily imports a lack of any common-law prohibition (though changed circumstances or new knowledge may make what was previously permissible no longer so. So also does the fact that other landowners, similarly situated, are permitted to continue the use denied to the claimant.

It seems unlikely that common-law principles would have prevented the erection of any habitable or productive improvements on petitioner's land; they rarely support prohibition of the "essential use" of land. The question, however, is one of state law to be dealt with on remand. We emphasize that to win its case South Carolina must do more than proffer the legislature's declaration that the uses Lucas desires are inconsistent with the public interest, or the conclusory assertion that they violate a common-law maxim. . . . As we have said, a "State, by *ipse dixit*, may not transform private property into public property without compensation. . . ." *Webb's Fabulous Pharmacies, Inc. v. Beckwith*, 449 U.S. 155 (1980). Instead, as it would be required to do if it sought to restrain Lucas in a common-law action for public nuisance, South Carolina must identify background principles of nuisance and property law that prohibit the uses he now intends in the circumstances in which the property is presently found. Only on this showing can the State fairly claim that, in proscribing all such beneficial uses, the Beachfront Management Act is taking nothing.

The judgment is reversed, and the case is remanded for proceedings not inconsistent with this opinion.

□ *Justice BLACKMUN, dissenting.*

Today the Court launches a missile to kill a mouse.

The State of South Carolina prohibited petitioner Lucas from building a permanent structure on his property from 1988 to 1990. Relying on an unreviewed (and implausible) state trial court finding that this restriction left Lucas' property valueless, this Court granted review to determine whether compensation must be paid in cases where the State prohibits all economic use of real estate. According to the Court, such an occasion never has arisen in any of our prior cases, and the Court imagines that it will arise "relatively rarely" or only in "extraordinary circumstances." Almost certainly it did not happen in this case.

Nonetheless, the Court presses on to decide the issue, and as it does, it ignores its jurisdictional limits, remakes its traditional rules of review, and creates simultaneously a new categorical rule and an exception (neither of which is rooted in our prior case law, common law, or common sense). I protest not only the Court's decision, but each step taken to reach it. More fundamentally, I question the Court's wisdom in issuing sweeping new rules to decide such a narrow case. [T]he Court could have reached the result it wanted without inflicting this damage upon our Takings Clause jurisprudence. . . .

□ *Justice STEVENS, dissenting.*

In addition to lacking support in past decisions, the Court's new rule is wholly arbitrary. A landowner whose property is diminished in value 95% recovers nothing, while an owner whose property is diminished 100% recovers the land's full value. The case at hand illustrates this arbitrariness well. The Beachfront Management Act not only prohibited the building of new dwellings in certain areas, it also prohibited the rebuilding of houses that were "destroyed beyond repair by natural causes or by fire." Thus, if the homes adjacent to Lucas' lot were destroyed by a hurricane one day after the Act took effect, the owners would not be able to rebuild, nor would they be assured recovery. Under the Court's categorical approach, Lucas (who has lost the opportunity to build) recovers, while his neighbors (who have lost both the opportunity to build and their homes) do not recover. The arbitrariness of such a rule is palpable.

Moreover, because of the elastic nature of property rights, the Court's new rule will also prove unsound in practice. In response to the rule, courts may define "property" broadly and only rarely find regulations to effect total takings. This is the approach the Court itself adopts in its revisionist reading of venerable precedents. We are told that—notwithstanding the Court's findings to the contrary in each case—the brewery in *Mugler*—could be put to "other uses" and that, therefore, those cases did not involve total regulatory takings. . . .

Finally, the Court's justification for its new categorical rule is remarkably thin. The Court mentions in passing three arguments in support of its rule; none is convincing. First, the Court suggests that "total deprivation of feasible use is, from the landowner's point of view, the equivalent of a physical appropriation." This argument proves too much. From the "landowner's point of view," a regulation that diminishes a lot's value by 50% is as well "the equivalent" of the condemnation of half of the lot. Yet, it is well established that a 50% diminution in value does not by itself constitute a taking. Thus, the landowner's perception of the regulation cannot justify the Court's new rule.

Second, the Court emphasizes that because total takings are "relatively rare" its new rule will not adversely affect the government's ability to "go on." This argument proves too little. Certainly it is true that defining a small class of regulations that are per se takings will not greatly hinder important governmental functions—but this is true of any small class of regulations. The Court's suggestion only begs the question of why regulations of this particular class should always be found to effect takings. . . .

In short, the Court's new rule is unsupported by prior decisions, arbitrary and unsound in practice, and theoretically unjustified. In my opinion, a categorical rule as important as the one established by the Court today should be supported by more history or more reason than has yet been provided. . . .

■ THE DEVELOPMENT OF LAW

Other Important Rulings on the Takings Clause

CASE	VOTE	RULING
Agins v. City of Tiburon, 447 U.S. 255 (1980)	9:0	Relying on *Village of Euclid v. Ambler Realty Co.*, 272 U.S. 365 (1926), the Court approved a

San Francisco zoning ordinance requiring the construction of single-family homes on a minimum of one-acre lots, over the objections of owners of five

CASE	VOTE	RULING

acres of undeveloped land of great value because of its view of San Francisco Bay. The owners had contended the zoning restriction amounted to a taking of their property.

Loretto v. Teleprompter Manhattan CATV Corporation, 458 U.S. 419 (1982) — 6:3 — Affirmed a takings-clause challenge of a New York law prohibiting landlords from interfering with cable companies' installation of cables and boxes in their buildings and specifying that property owners may not demand compensation in excess of a limit set by a state commission. When so holding, the Court observed that "Teleprompter's cable installation on appellant's building constitutes a taking under the traditional test. The installation involved a direct physical attachment of plates, boxes, wires, bolts, and screws to the building, completely occupying space immediately above and upon the roof and along the building's exterior wall."

Keystone Bituminous Coal Association v. DeBenedictis, 480 U.S. 470 (1987) — 5:4 — Rejected the claims of a coal company attacking the constitutionality of a Pennsylvania law limiting the mining of more than 50 percent of the coal beneath government and commercial buildings, private residences, and cemeteries to ensure surface support.

First English Evangelical Lutheran Church v. County of Los Angeles, 482 U.S. 304 (1987) — 6:3 — Held that the just compensation clause was violated by an ordinance, passed after a major flood, that prohibited the construction and reconstruction of buildings on certain land affected by the flood. Writing for the majority, Chief Justice Rehnquist held that the ordinance constituted a taking of property, for which the city owed the owner just compensation.

Pennell v. City of San Jose, 485 U.S. 1 (1988) — 6:2 — Rejected an attack by landlords on a city rent control ordinance limiting rent increases to 18 percent and allowing tenants to demand a hearing as to whether a rent increase was "reasonable under the circumstances"—circumstances that included the tenant's hardship.

Dolan v. City of Tigard, 512 U.S. 374 (1994) — 5:4 — Writing for a bare majority, Chief Justice Rehnquist held that when government sets down land-use restrictions affecting private property it must show a "rough proportionality" between the restrictions and the harm to be prevented. Notably, the chief justice reaffirmed that the government may simply ban all de-

CASE	VOTE	RULING

velopment in flood plains, for instance, and that "no precise mathematical calculation" was required to justify land-use restrictions. As a result of *Dolan*, state and local governments must satisfy a two-pronged test: first, they must show that their restrictions serve a "legitimate public purpose" and, second, when imposing their restrictions they must undertake "some sort of individualized determination" establishing a "rough proportionality" between the restrictions and the harms to be averted.

Bennis v. Michigan,   5:4   Writing for the majority, Chief
516 U.S. 442 (1996)   Justice Rehnquist rejected the claim that the government violates due process and the Fifth Amendment's takings clause when it undertakes the forfeiture of an innocent person's property, which was used in an illegal activity. Justices Breyer, Kennedy, Souter, and Stevens dissented.

Phillips v. Washington Legal   5:4   In the 1980s, Texas and 48 other
Foundation, 524 U.S. 156   states established Interest on Law-
(1998)   yers Trust Account (IOLTA) programs. Under them, certain funds from clients received by attorneys are held in federally authorized "Negotiable Order of Withdrawal" accounts. The interest income of these accounts is paid to the state and used to finance legal services for low-income people. In a narrow ruling for a bare majority, Chief Justice Rehnquist held that the interest income does constitute "property" under the Fifth Amendment, but declined to rule on whether IOLTA programs constitute a "takings" and whether "just compensation" is required, because those issues had not been addressed by the lower courts.

Tahoe-Sierra Preservation   6:3   Upheld a three-year building
Council, Inc.v. Tahoe Regional   moratorium on construction sur-
Planning Agency, 535 U.S.   rounding Lake Tahoe in order
302 (2002)   for regional governments to develop natural resources preservation and development plans, over the claim that the temporary moratorium constituted a "categorical" takings under the Fifth Amendment and deprived developers of the economically viable use of their land. Chief Justice Rehnquist and Justices Scalia and Thomas dissented.

4

THE NATIONALIZATION OF
THE BILL OF RIGHTS

This chapter examines the constitutional basis for civil liberties and civil rights and the controversy over the nationalization of the Bill of Rights—that is, the Supreme Court's extension of those guarantees as limitations on the states. The original Constitution contained few explicit guarantees for civil liberties and civil rights. But with the adoption of the Bill of Rights, the first ten amendments to the Constitution, the basis for civil liberties and civil rights was laid. The Bill of Rights, however, limited the powers of only the national government, not the states. With the ratification of the Fourteenth Amendment in 1868, though, there was a new basis for applying the Bill of Rights to the states. Its due process clause provides that "No state shall . . . deprive any person of life, liberty, or property without due process of law." This chapter examines the controversy over the Supreme Court's reading into the Fourteenth Amendment's due process clause guarantees of the Bill of Rights to make them applicable to the states. Subsequent chapters examine how the Supreme Court has interpreted and applied specific provisions of the Bill of Rights. Chapter 5 considers the First Amendment's guarantees for free speech, press, and association and Chapter 6, its provisions for religious freedom. Chapters 7 through 10 then examine guarantees for the rights of the accused in the criminal justice system. Chapter 11 takes up the right of privacy and Chapter 12, the Fourteenth Amendment's guarantee for the equal protection of the laws.

Unamended, the Constitution contains only five provisions for civil liberties. Article 1 forbids Congress and the states from passing *ex post facto* laws (laws making some activity retroactively a crime) and bills of attainder (legislation punishing specific individuals or members of a group without a trial). It also provides that Congress may not, except in times of rebellion or invasion, suspend writs of *habeas corpus*. A writ of *habeas corpus* is an ancient order (which is Latin for "you should have the body") aimed at safeguarding against unlawful arrests and imprisonment of individuals. (A prisoner in jail may petition a court for a writ of *habeas corpus* that then requires the government to explain to a judge why the prisoner is being held, of what crimes he or she is accused, and the basis for continuing imprisonment.) In addition (as dealt with in Ch. 3), states are also forbidden in Article I from "impairing the Obligation of Contract," and in Article IV from denying the privileges and immunities of citizenship.

The Constitution was itself deemed to be a bill of rights, at least by the Federalists. James Wilson and Alexander Hamilton, among others, argued that civil rights and civil liberties would remain secure because the powers of the national government are limited to those expressly granted, and the states would continue to safeguard individuals' civil rights and liberties.

Those opposing the Constitution, the Anti-Federalists, were unpersuaded. They feared that the national government's power was too great and would further expand at the expense of the powers of (and the protections for individual liberty afforded by) the states. A leading New York Anti-Federalist, Brutus, for example, warned that the federal judiciary would "extend the limits of the general government gradually, and by insensible degrees . . . facilitate the abolition of the state governments."[1] Nor did the Anti-Federalists trust Congress, let alone the executive branch, to respect civil rights and liberties. As Richard Henry Lee wrote to Samuel Adams in 1787:

> The corrupting nature of power, and its insatiable appetite for increase, hath proved the necessity, and procured the adoption of the strongest and most express declarations of that *Residuum* of natural rights, which is not intended to be given up to Society; and which indeed is not necessary to be given for any good social purpose. In a government therefore, when the power of judging what shall be for the *general welfare*, which goes to every object of human legislation; and where the laws of such Judges shall be the *supreme Law of the Land*: it seems to be of the last consequence to declare in most explicit terms the reservations above alluded to.[2]

Although the Anti-Federalists unsuccessfully fought against the Constitution's ratification, they succeeded in insisting on the addition of the Bill of Rights. Delaware unanimously ratified the document on December 7, 1787. Within weeks Pennsylvania, New Jersey, Georgia, and

Connecticut gave their approval. Massachusetts followed in February 1788, but with a closely divided vote of 187 to 168. In the spring, Maryland and South Carolina gave their overwhelming endorsements. Then in June, close votes in New Hampshire and Virginia secured the requisite nine states for ratification. But the battle in the New York convention was fierce and crucial, for this large commercial state separated New England from the Southern states. Largely due to the leadership of Hamilton, a Federalist, New York finally voted in favor. The price of winning ratification there and in Massachusetts and Virginia, however, was agreement that the First Congress would adopt a declaration of rights and promptly send it to the states for ratification. North Carolina did not ratify until November 1789 and Rhode Island held out until May 1790.

During the debate over New York's ratification, Hamilton tried to popularize the counterarguments to those made by the Anti-Federalists. "[T]he Constitution itself, in every rational sense, and to every useful purpose, is a bill of rights," he insisted in *Federalist*, No. 84, when contending that the addition of a declaration of rights was "not only unnecessary . . . but would even be dangerous." In arguing that a bill of rights was unnecessary, Hamilton pointed to the Preamble of the Constitution:

> We the people of the United States, to secure the blessings of liberty to ourselves and our posterity, do *ordain* and *establish* this constitution for the United States of America." Here is a better recognition of popular rights than volumes of those aphorisms which make the principal figure in several of our state bills of rights, and which would sound much better in a treatise of ethics than in a constitution of government.

A bill of rights might also prove dangerous, Hamilton contended, because it

> would contain various exceptions to powers which are not granted; and on this very account, would afford a colourable pretext to claim more than were granted. For why declare that things shall not be done which there is no power to do? Why for instance, should it be said, that the liberty of the press shall not be restrained, when no power is given by which restrictions may be imposed? I will not contend that such a provision would confer a regulating power; but it is evident that it would furnish, to men disposed to usurp, a plausible pretence for claiming that power. They might urge with a semblance of reason, that the constitution ought not to be charged with the absurdity of providing against the abuse of an authority, which was not given, and that provision against restraining the liberty of press afforded a clear implication, that a power to prescribe

proper regulations concerning it, was intended to be vested in the national government.

Furthermore, Hamilton suggested the problems of which rights to include and exclude and how to define those rights specified in a declaration of rights:

> On the subject of the liberty of the press, as much has been said, I cannot forbear adding a remark or two: In the first place, I observe that there is not a syllable concerning it in the constitution of this state [New York], and in the next I contend that whatever has been said about it in that of any other state, amounts to nothing. What signifies a declaration that "the liberty of the press shall be inviolably preserved?" What is the liberty of the press? Who can give it any definition which would not leave the utmost latitude for evasion? I hold it to be impracticable; and from this, I infer, that its security, whatever fine declarations may be inserted in any constitution respecting it, must altogether depend on public opinion, and on the general spirit of the people and of the government.

Despite their success in securing the ratification of the Constitution, the Federalists failed to turn the tide of public opinion running in favor of a bill of rights. As Thomas Jefferson noted in a letter to James Madison on December 20, 1787, "a bill of rights is what the people are entitled to against every government on earth, general or particular, and what no just government should refuse, or rest on inference."[3] Madison was not initially inclined toward the addition of a declaration of rights.

In a letter to Jefferson, Madison gave four reasons for his ambivalence. First, he accepted the Federalists' argument that "the rights in question are reserved by the manner in which the federal powers are granted." Second, he feared "that a positive declaration of some of the most essential rights could not be obtained in the requisite latitude." In particular, "the rights of Conscience" might be narrowed by any formal-legal definition. Third, republican liberty was guarded against Congress by its constitutionally "limited powers" and "the jealousy" of the states. Finally, he maintained that "experience proves the inefficacy of a bill of rights on those occasions when its controul is most needed."[4]

Madison came to side with Jefferson and the Anti-Federalists and provided some of the strongest arguments for a bill of rights. They, too, worried about what to include and exclude in a bill of rights. In 1788, Madison explained that he had not viewed a bill of rights "in an important light . . . [b]ecause there is great reason to fear that a positive declaration of some of the most essential rights could not be obtained in the requisite latitude."[5] But Jefferson responded that "Half a loaf is better than no bread. If we cannot secure all our rights, let's secure what we can."[6] He and Madison, furthermore, came to view a bill of rights as putting into "the hands of the judiciary" an additional check on the coercive powers of government. "This is a body," observed Jefferson, "which if rendered independent, and kept strictly to their own department merits great confidence for their learning and integrity."[7]

In the First Congress in 1789, as a member of the House of Representatives Madison championed the cause of adding a declaration of rights to the Constitution. His aim was "to satisfy the public mind that their liberties will be perpetual, and this without endangering any part of the constitution."[8] With parliamentary skill, Madison steered the amendments through Congress and the Bill of Rights was ratified by the states in 1791. Madison, however, was forced to compromise and failed to achieve two goals. He had proposed that the amendments be incorporated into the body of the original Constitution, because he did not want them to be perceived as inferior or less important than the document itself. But he was defeated on that as well as on proposing that the amendments bind the states along with the national government.

NOTES

1. Brutus, in *New York Journal*, in *The Complete Anti-Federalist*, Vol. 2, ed. Herbert Storing (Chicago: University of Chicago Press, 1981), 441.

2. Richard Henry Lee to Samuel Adams (Oct. 5, 1787), in *The Founders' Constitution*, Vol. 1, ed. Philip Kurland and Ralph Lerner (Chicago: University of Chicago Press, 1987), 448.

3. Thomas Jefferson, *The Papers of Thomas Jefferson*, Vol. 12, ed. Julian Boyd (Princeton, NJ: Princeton University Press, 1950–), 440.

4. James Madison, *The Papers of James Madison*, Vol. 11, ed. R. Rutland (Charlottesville: University Press of Virginia, 1977), 295–298.

5. *Ibid.*

6. Jefferson, *The Papers of Thomas Jefferson*, Vol. 14, 659.

7. *Ibid.*

8. Madison, *The Papers of James Madison*, Vol. 12, 196–209.

SELECTED BIBLIOGRAPHY

Abraham, Henry, and Perry, Barbara. *Freedom and the Court: Civil Liberties and Civil Rights in the United States.* 7th ed. New York: Oxford University Press, 1998.

Cogan, Neil H. *The Complete Bill of Rights: The Drafts, Debates, Sources, & Origins.* New York: Oxford University Press, 1997.

Gillespie, Michael, and Lienesch, Michael, eds. *Ratifying the Constitution.* Lawrence: University Press of Kansas, 1989.

Goldwin, Robert A., and Schambra, William, eds. *How Does the Constitution Secure Rights?* Washington, DC: American Enterprise Institution, 1985.

Levy, Leonard W. *Original Intent and the Framers' Constitution.* New York: Macmillan, 1988.

———. *Origins of the Bill of Rights.* New Haven, CT: Yale University Press, 1999.

Rutland, Robert. *The Birth of the Bill of Rights, 1776–1791.* Chapel Hill: University of North Carolina Press, 1955.

Schwartz, Bernard, ed. *The Roots of the Bill of Rights,* 5 vols. New York: Chelsea House, 1980.

A | *The Selective Nationalization of Guarantees of the Bill of Rights plus Other Fundamental Rights*

The Bill of Rights did not limit the powers of the states until the twentieth century. The Supreme Court's nationalization—or application to the states—of the Bill of Rights and its interpretative basis for doing so remain controversial. The prevailing view of the Bill of Rights in the nineteenth century was well stated in 1833 by Chief Justice John Marshall. In *Barron v. The Mayor and City Council of Baltimore* (1833) (see excerpt below), after reviewing the history of the Bill of Rights, Marshall concluded there was "no expression indicating an intention to apply [guarantees of the Bill of the Rights] to the State governments. This court cannot so apply them."

Barron was reaffirmed in *Permoli v. New Orleans*, 3 How. (44 U.S.) 589 (1845), and in *Mattox v. United States*, 156 U.S. 237 (1894). As late as 1922 the Court maintained that "the Constitution of the United States imposes upon the states no obligation to confer upon those within its jurisdiction . . . the right to free speech" in *Prudential Insurance Company v. Cheek*, 259 U.S. 530 (1922). Indeed, despite the Court's eventual nationalization of most of the guarantees of the Bill of Rights, *Barron* has never been expressly overturned.

Ratification of the Fourteenth Amendment in 1868, however, changed the constitutional landscape and laid a new basis for applying the Bill of Rights to the states. It specifically denied the states the power to "make or enforce any law which shall abridge the privileges or immunities of citizens of the United States . . . [or] deprive any person of life, liberty, or property, without due process of law . . . [or] deny to any person within its jurisdiction the equal protection of the laws." Two of the principal leaders in the Thirty-ninth Congress proposing the amendment, Ohio Representative John A. Bingham and Michigan Senator Jacob M. Howard, suggested during floor debates that an objective was the extension of the Bill of Rights to the states (thereby overturning *Barron*). The Fourteenth Amendment, Senator Howard claimed, would bar the states from denying citizens their privileges and immunities guaranteed by the Constitution, including "the personal rights guaranteed and secured by the first eight amendments of the Constitution."[1]

Whether Congress intended the Fourteenth Amendment to incorporate and apply guarantees of the Bill of Rights to the states, however, is a long-running controversy. The record of the Thirty-ninth Congress and of the states' ratification of the Fourteenth Amendment is far from complete and unambiguous.[2] Justices, historians, and legal scholars are unlikely to agree on the historical basis for the Court's reading provisions of the Bill of Rights into the Fourteenth Amendment. Justices Felix Frankfurter and (the second) John Harlan, as well as some law professors, maintain that the amendment was not intended to apply the Bill of Rights to the states.[3] By contrast, Justices Hugo Black and William Douglas, along with other leading historians and legal scholars, championed an interpretation of the legislative record pointing in the opposite direction.[4] And it seems fair to conclude, as John Hart Ely put it, that "the legislative argument is one neither side can win."[5]

History, though, is not the only thing that divided the Court when interpreting the Fourteenth Amendment. No less important are the politics of interpretation and rival judicial and political philosophies. And those differences, as much as different readings of history, account for the continuing controversy over turning the Fourteenth Amendment into a vehicle for nationalizing the Bill of Rights.

When initially confronted with the question of extending the Bill of Rights to the states in *The Slaughterhouse Cases* (1873) (see Ch. 3), the justices split five to four. The majority rejected the view that the Fourteenth Amendment's privileges or immunities clause incorporated the Bill of Rights. Yet the four dissenters (Chief Justice Chase and Justices Bradley, Field, and Swayne) took the opposite view. The Court's narrow reading of the amendment, in Swayne's words, turned "what was meant for bread into stone."

The Slaughterhouse Cases, as dissenting Justice Field remarked, rendered the Fourteenth Amendment "a vain and idle enactment, which accomplished nothing, and most unnecessarily excited Congress and the people on its passage." The majority's opinion, however, dealt primarily with the privileges and immunities clause. And that left open the possibility that the Court might eventually be persuaded to incorporate or absorb the Bill of Rights into the amendment's due process clause.

With two exceptions in the late nineteenth century, the Court remained unmoved from its interpretation in *The Slaughterhouse Cases.* Both rulings involved the Fifth Amendment's prohibition against the taking of private property for public use without just compensation, and registered the Court's embrace of laissez-faire capitalism and the priority given to economic liberties (see THE DEVELOPMENT OF LAW box in this section and, there, *Missouri Pacific Railway Co. v. Nebraska* and *Chicago, Burlington & Quincy Railway Co. v. Chicago*).

Despite refusing to nationalize the Bill of Rights, the Court could not escape responsibility for giving meaning to the Fourteenth Amendment's due process clause. That meant coming up with standards or tests for determining what state practices and procedures denied individuals their rights under the Fourteenth Amendment due process clause. So long as the Court held that the due process clause did not include the guarantees afforded by the Bill of Rights, the justices had to create their own standards and rationalizations for what process is due under the Fourteenth Amendment.

The Court faced the question of what process is due in *Hurtado v. California* (1884) (see excerpt below). In holding that states need not honor the Fifth Amendment's requirement that individuals be indicted by a grand jury before being tried for a crime, Justice Mathews proclaimed the states free to experiment with their own criminal justice procedures. They, he said, were free "to draw on the wells of justice, so long as they don't go too far." On this standard, each case would have to be considered on its own merits. But as dissenting Justice John Marshall Harlan suggested, whether states ran afoul of the due process clause also turned on each justice's conception of what process is due, rather than on enumerated guarantees. In Harlan's opinion the Bill of Rights were incorporated lock, stock, and barrel into the due process clause. His position of *total incorporation*, nevertheless, failed to command a majority. Accordingly, state practices and procedures falling short of the requirements of the Bill of Rights were upheld. In *Maxwell v. Dow*, 176 U.S. 581 (1900), for example, the Court ruled that states were free to convict individuals before juries composed of less than twelve members and on less than a unanimous verdict. And *Twinning v. New Jersey*, 211 U.S. 78 (1908), held that states need not honor an accused's Fifth Amendment's privilege against self-incrimination.

Forty years passed before the Court was prepared to extend guarantees of the Bill of Rights to the states. Then when confronted with a spate of litigation challenging state laws punishing subversive speech, the Court merely assumed (in spite of its previous denials) that the First Amendment freedoms of speech and press limited the states, no less than the national government. In *Gilbert v. Minnesota*, 254 U.S. 652

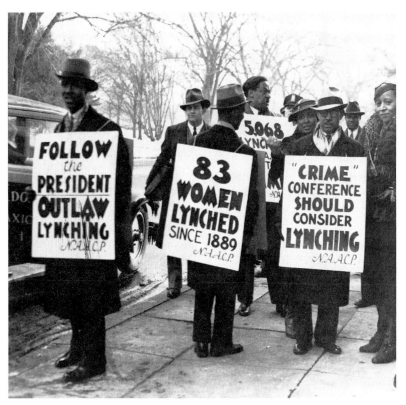

In 1909, the National Association for the Advancement of Colored People (NAACP) was founded to protest various forms of racial discrimination—discrimination in the criminal justice system, in voting rights, and in education and employment. In the 1920s and 1930s, one of the NAACP's major initiatives was to lobby Congress to enact a federal law against lynching, as well as to participate in bringing "test cases" like the famous *Scottsboro Boys Case, Powell v. Alabama* (1932) (excerpted in Ch. 9). But, because the NAACP was involved in lobbying, it was denied tax-exempt status by the Internal Revenue Service. As a result, in 1938 under the direction of Thurgood Marshall the NAACP's litigation activities were separated and carried forth with the formation of the NAACP Legal Defense and Educational Fund, Inc., known later as the LDF. Here, in 1934 NAACP members picket a crime conference in Washington, D.C., in protest of lynching. (Photo source: Corbis, 1934.)

(1920), the Court granted that individuals might challenge the constitutionality of state laws making it a crime falsely or maliciously to criticize the government. In *Gitlow v. New York*, 268 U.S. 652 (1925) (see Ch. 5), Justice Edward Sanford noted in *dictum* that "[w]e may and do assume that freedom of speech and of the press . . . are among the fundamental rights and liberties protected . . . from impairment by the states." By the 1940s, the other First Amendment freedoms were construed to be so fundamental as to constrain the states as well.

Still, in the area of criminal procedure, the Court remained reluctant to impose the guarantees of the Fourth through the Eighth Amendments on the states. Indicative of the Court's deference to the states is the infamous *Scottsboro Case, Powell v. Alabama,* 287 U.S. 32 (1932) (see Ch. 9). There nine black teenagers were tried and convicted for raping a white woman (a capital offense), without the representation of counsel, before an all-white jury in Scottsboro, Alabama. In ordering that they be retried and appointed an attorney, the Court ruled that they had been denied due process and subjected to a fundamentally unfair trial. But it declined to make the Fifth and Sixth Amendments applicable to the states. Instead, the Court relied on general principles of "natural justice" and "ordered liberty," as it also did in *Norris v. Alabama,* 294 U.S. 587 (1935), holding jury trials are required in criminal cases, and *Brown v. Mississippi,* 297 U.S. 278 (1936), holding that confessions coerced by third-degree police tactics violate due process.

In *Palko v. Connecticut* (1937) (excerpted below), Justice Benjamin Cardozo rationalized the selective application of some but not all guarantees of the Bill of Rights. According to his theory of *selective incorporation,* some rights are "so rooted in the traditions and conscience of our people as to be ranked as fundamental" and "implicit in the concept of ordered liberty." Among those he deemed applicable to the states were the First Amendment freedoms, the Fifth Amendment's eminent domain provision, and the Sixth Amendment right to counsel in capital cases. Other guarantees of the Bill of Rights were simply formal rights not binding on the states. Cardozo's honor roll of preferred freedoms thus created a constitutional double standard for enforcing the Bill of Rights.

Cardozo's theory of selective incorporation stood for almost twenty-five years, until the 1960s when the Warren Court forged a constitutional revolution in criminal procedure by extending virtually all of the guarantees of the Fourth through the Eighth Amendments to the states. In the 1940s and 1950s, the Court remained sharply divided over whether and how to nationalize the Bill of Rights.

The divisiveness within the Court arising from the debate over the nationalization of the Bill of Rights and the politics of interpretation is exemplified by *Adamson v. California* (1947) (see excerpt below). There Justice Reed, writing for the majority, adhered to the theory of selective incorporation. But concurring Justice Frankfurter maintained that the requirements of the due process clause in the Fifth Amendment and those of the due process clause in the Fourteenth Amendment were completely independent and that when enforcing the latter the justices should balance the rights of the accused against the interests of the states in prosecuting crime. Frankfurter urged the Court to look at

■ THE DEVELOPMENT OF LAW

The Selective Nationalization of the Bill of Rights plus Other Fundamental Rights

GUARANTEE/RIGHT	AMEND-MENT	YEAR	CASE
Public use and just compensation provisions condition the taking of private property by the government	5	1896	*Missouri Pacific Railway Co. v. Nebraska*, 164
		1897	U.S. 403
			Chicago, Burlington & Quincy Railway Co. v. Chicago, 166 U.S. 226
Freedom of speech	1	1927	*Fiske v. Kansas*, 274 U.S. 380 (also earlier in *dictum*: Gitlow v. New York, 268 U.S. 652 (1925); and Gilbert v. Minnesota, 254 U.S. 325) (1920)
Freedom of the press	1	1931	*Near v. Minnesota*, 283 U.S. 697
Fair trial and right to counsel in capital cases	6	1932	*Powell v. Alabama*, 287 U.S. 45
Freedom of religion	1	1934	*Hamilton v. Regents of the University of California*, 293 U.S. 245 (in *dictum*)
Freedom of assembly (and implicitly freedom to petition for redress of grievances)	1	1937	*De Jonge v. Oregon*, 299 U.S. 353
Free exercise of religion	1	1940	*Cantwell v. Connecticut*, 310 U.S. 296
Separation of church and state	1	1947	*Everson v. Board of Education*, 330 U.S. 1
Right to a public trial	6	1948	*In re Oliver*, 333 U.S. 257
Right against unreasonable searches and seizures	4	1949	*Wolf v. Colorado*, 338 U.S. 25
Freedom of association	1	1958	*NAACP v. Alabama*, 357 U.S. 449
Exclusionary rule	4	1961	*Mapp v. Ohio*, 367 U.S. 643

Ban against cruel and un-usual punishments	8	1962	*Robinson v. California,* 370 U.S. 660
Right to counsel in all felony cases	6	1963	*Gideon v. Wainwright,* 372 U.S. 335
Right against self-incrimination	5	1964	*Malloy v. Hogan,* 378 U.S. 1
Right to confront witness (and by implication the right to be informed of the nature and cause of the accusation)	6	1965	*Pointer v. Texas,* 380 U.S. 400
Right to privacy	penumbra of 1, 3, 4, and 5	1965	*Griswold v. Connecticut,* 381 U.S. 479
Right to impartial jury	6	1966	*Parker v. Gladden,* 385 U.S. 363
Right to speedy trial	6	1967	*Klopfer v. North Carolina,* 386 U.S. 213
Right to compulsory process for obtaining witnesses	6	1967	*Washington v. Texas,* 388 U.S. 14
Right to jury trial in nonpetty cases	6	1968	*Duncan v. Louisiana,* 391 U.S. 145
Right against double jeopardy	5	1969	*Benyton v. Maryland,* 395 U.S. 784
Right to counsel in all criminal cases involving a jail term	6	1972	*Argersinger v. Hamlin,* 407 U.S. 25

what *fundamental fairness* requires in each case when balancing these competing interests. Dissenting Justices Black and Douglas, however, countered that that standard was no improvement over the theory of selective incorporation; it was as ambiguous as other natural law formulations in giving the Court unbridled power. For that reason, along with his own reading of the history of the Fourteenth Amendment, Black continued to press for total incorporation. The two other dissenters in *Adamson,* Justices Frank Murphy and Wiley Rutledge, went further in advancing an even broader libertarian position, that of *total incorporation plus* any other fundamental rights not enumerated in the Bill of Rights.

In response to Justice Black's criticisms, Justice Frankfurter in *Rochin v. California* (1952) (excerpted below), invented a "shocks-the-con-

■ Constitutional History

Guarantees of the Bill of Rights That Have Not Been Applied to the States

Second Amendment "right of the people to keep and bear Arms."
Third Amendment limitation on the quartering of soldiers in a person's house.
Fifth Amendment right to indictment by a grand jury.
Seventh Amendment right to a jury trial in civil cases.
Eighth Amendment right against excessive fines and bail.

science" test for determining when police practices violate the due process clause. Yet as Black pointed out, it was no less subjective or un-problematic in application. Two years after *Rochin*, in Chief Justice Earl Warren's first term, the Court again relied on the test. But in *Irvine v. California*, 347 U.S. 128 (1954), the majority failed to find police bugging of an entire house for over a month, without obtaining a search warrant, to either violate the Fourth Amendment or shock their consciences.

The Warren Court remained until the 1960s split between Frankfurter's approach and Black's insistence on total incorporation. That intellectual struggle would not be decisively settled until the Court's composition changed. In *Mapp v. Ohio*, 367 U.S. 643 (1961) (see Ch. 7), the Court finally agreed to extend to the states the Fourth Amendment's exclusionary rule, requiring that illegally obtained evidence be excluded from use at trial. Then the following year Justices Frankfurter and Whittaker retired. With their replacements, Justices Byron White and Arthur Goldberg, there was finally a solid majority supporting the nationalization of the major guarantees of the Bill of Rights.

By the end of Chief Justice Warren's tenure in 1969, nearly all of the guarantees of the Bill of Rights were applied to the states. In addition, in *Griswold v. Connecticut* (1965) (see excerpt below), the Court created out of whole constitutional cloth a right of privacy, which Justice Douglas found in the penumbras, or shadows, of the First, Third, Fourth, Fifth, and Ninth Amendments, and made applicable to the states by the Fourteenth Amendment. While joining the decision announced in Douglas's opinion, concurring Justice Goldberg, joined by Chief Justice Warren and Justice Brennan, staked out yet another theory of incorporation—that of *selective incorporation plus* other fundamental

■ The Development of Law

Approaches to Nationalization of the Bill of Rights under the Fourteenth Amendment

Total incorporation of all guarantees—Justice Harlan's opinion, dissenting in *Hurtado v. California* (1884).

Selective incorporation of "preferred freedoms" and those rights "implicit in the concept of ordered liberty"—Justice Benjamin Cardozo's opinion in *Palko v. Connecticut* (1937).

Fundamental fairness and the selective application on a case-by-case basis—Justice Felix Frankfurter, concurring in *Adamson v. California* (1947).

Total incorporation plus other fundamental rights not expressly granted in the Bill of Rights—Justices Frank Murphy and Wiley Rutledge, dissenting in *Adamson v. California* (1947).

Selective incorporation plus other fundamental rights not expressly granted in the Bill of Rights—Justices Arthur Goldberg, Chief Justice Earl Warren, and Justice William J. Brennan, concurring in *Griswold v. Connecticut* (1965).

yet unenumerated rights. The Court in *Griswold* went too far for Justices Black and Stewart. In dissent, Black again warns that whenever the justices substitute their own interpretative language for that of the Constitution, they threaten to become "a day-to-day constitutional convention."

The controversy over the nationalization of the Bill of Rights continues. The divisions among the justices are further evident in the opinions issued in *Duncan v. Louisiana* (1968) (excerpted below). This ruling held that defendants charged in state courts with serious crimes are entitled to a trial by jury under the Sixth Amendment. Subsequently, the Burger Court in *Williams v. Florida*, 399 U.S. 78 (1970) (see Ch. 9) and *Apodaca v. Oregon*, 406 U.S. 404 (1972), respectively, ruled, that despite *Duncan*, states were free to use juries composed of fewer than the traditional twelve jurors, and to depart from the requirement that juries reach unanimous verdicts. In other areas, the more conservative Burger and Rehnquist Courts cut back and shifted the direction in which the Warren Court had pushed constitutional law in nationalizing the Bill of Rights.[6]

The Court's interpretative politics changed in the 1970s and 1980s with its changing composition. The Court's rulings extending to the states the rights of the accused afforded in the Bill of Rights made for a larger struggle in constitutional politics. They effectively raised the issue of "law and order" and "crime control" to the national political agenda as well. During their presidential campaigns, Richard Nixon, Ronald Reagan, and George Bush effectively criticized the Court for being soft on criminals. Subsequently, they appointed more conservative justices, which in turn changed the internal dynamics of the Court. The Rehnquist Court, though, did not turn back the constitutional clock on the incorporation of the Bill of Rights. Rather than disincorporate those guarantees, the Court (as further discussed in later chapters) in some cases limited their reach and carved out exceptions for state compliance with the commands of the Bill of Rights.[7]

NOTES

1. *Congressional Globe*, 39th Cong., 1st sess., 1865–1866, 2765.

2. For further discussion see, Howard J. Graham, "The 'Conspiracy Theory' of the Fourteenth Amendment," 47 *Yale Law Journal* 371 (1938); and Walter F. Murphy, "Constitutional Interpretation: The Art of the Historian, Magician, or Statesman?" 87 *Yale Law Journal* 1752 (1978).

3. Besides the cases discussed and reprinted here see, Felix Frankfurter, "Memorandum on 'Incorporation' of the Bill of Rights into the Due Process Clause of the Fourteenth Amendment," 78 *Harvard Law Review* 746 (1965); Charles Fairman, "Does the Fourteenth Amendment Incorporate the Bill of Rights?" 2 *Stanford Law Review* 1 (1949); Charles Fairman, "A Reply to Professor Crosskey," 22 *University of Chicago Law Review* 145 (1954); Raoul Berger, *Government by Judiciary: The Transformation of the Fourteenth Amendment* (Cambridge, MA: Harvard University Press, 1977).

4. See Hugo Black, "The Bill of Rights," 35 *New York University Law Review* 865 (1960); Alfred Avins, "Incorporation of the Bill of Rights: The Crosskey-Fairman Debates Revisited," 6 *Harvard Journal on Legislation* 1 (1968); William Crosskey, "Charles Fairman, 'Legislative History,' and the Constitutional Limitations on State Authority," 22 *University of Chicago Law Review* 1 (1954); Horace Flack, *The Adoption of the Fourteenth Amendment* (Baltimore, MD: Johns Hopkins University Press, 1908); and Jacobus tenBroek, *Equal under Law* (London: Collier Books, 1965).

5. John Hart Ely, *Democracy and Distrust: A Theory of Judicial Review* (Cambridge, MA: Harvard University Press, 1981), 27.

6. See, for example, *Argersinger v. Hamlin*, 407 U.S. 25 (1972) in Chapter 9.

7. However, see Rehnquist's dissenting opinion in *Wallace v. Jaffree*, 472 U.S. 38 (1985) (see Ch. 6), raising questions about the Court's extension of the First Amendment establishment clause to the states.

SELECTED BIBLIOGRAPHY

Amar, Akhil Reed. *The Bill of Rights: Creation and Reconstruction*. New Haven, CT: Yale University Press, 1998.

Berger, Raoul. *Government by Judiciary: The Transformation of the Fourteenth Amendment*. Cambridge, MA: Harvard University Press, 1977.

Cortner, Richard C. *The Supreme Court and the Second Bill of Rights: The Fourteenth Amendment and the Nationalization of Civil Liberties.* Madison: University of Wisconsin Press, 1981.

Flack, Horace. *The Adoption of the Fourteenth Amendment.* Baltimore, MD: Johns Hopkins University Press, 1908.

Graham, Howard. *Everyman's Constitution: Historical Essays on the Fourteenth Amendment, the "Conspiracy Theory," and American Constitutionalism.* Madison, WI: State Historical Society of Madison, 1968.

Kersch, Ken I. *Constructing Civil Liberties: Discontinuities in the Development of American Constitutional Law.* New York: Cambridge University Press, 2004.

tenBroek, Jacobus. *The Antislavery Origins of the Fourteenth Amendment.* Berkeley: University of California Press, 1951.

Barron v. The Mayor and City of Baltimore
7 Pet. (32 U.S.) 243, 8 L.Ed. 672 (1833)

John Barron inherited and was co-owner of a wharf in the eastern harbor of Baltimore. The wharf had been highly profitable because it was surrounded by some of the deepest water in the harbor. But city improvements (the diversion of certain streams and the paving of streets) resulted in large deposits of sand accumulating around the wharf. The waters became too shallow for ships to gain access to the wharf and Barron faced a major financial loss.

Barron sued the mayor and city council of Baltimore for damages in county court. He did so on the grounds that the Fifth Amendment forbids the states as well as the national government from taking private property for public use without just compensation. The trial court agreed and awarded Barron $4,500 in damages. That decision was reversed by an appellate court, and Barron appealed to the Supreme Court. When Barron's attorney appeared before the high bench, Chief Justice Marshall asked him to confine his argument to whether the Fifth Amendment was applicable to the states and thus gave the Court jurisdiction over the case. After hearing his arguments, the chief justice announced that the Court need not bother hearing the attorneys representing the city of Baltimore.

The Court's decision and opinion were unanimous.

☐ *Chief Justice MARSHALL delivered the opinion of the Court.*

The question thus presented is, we think, of great importance, but not of much difficulty.

The Constitution was ordained and established by the people of the

United States for themselves, for their own government, and not for the government of the individual States. Each State established a constitution for itself, and in that constitution provided such limitations and restrictions on the powers of its particular government as its judgment dictated. The people of the United States framed such a government for the United States as they supposed best adapted to their situation, and best calculated to promote their interests. The powers they conferred on this government were to be exercised by itself; and the limitations on power, if expressed in general terms, are naturally, and, we think, necessarily applicable to the government created by the instrument. They are limitations of power granted in the instrument itself; not of distinct governments, framed by different persons and for different purposes.

If these propositions be correct, the fifth amendment must be understood as restraining the power of the general government, not as applicable to the States. In their several constitutions they have imposed such restrictions on their respective governments as their own wisdom suggested; such as they deemed most proper for themselves. It is a subject on which they judge exclusively, and with which others interfere no farther than they are supposed to have a common interest.

The counsel for the plaintiff in error insists that the Constitution was intended to secure the people of the several States against the undue exercise of power by their respective State governments; as well as against that which might be attempted by their general government. In support of this argument he relies on the inhibitions contained in the tenth section of the first article.

We think that section affords a strong if not a conclusive argument in support of the opinion already indicated by the court.

The preceding section contains restrictions which are obviously intended for the exclusive purpose of restraining the exercise of power by the departments of the general government. Some of them use language applicable only to Congress, others are expressed in general terms. The third clause, for example, declares that "no bill of attainder or ex post facto law shall be passed." No language can be more general; yet the demonstration is complete that it applies solely to the government of the United States. . . .

If the original Constitution, in the ninth and tenth sections of the first article, draws this plain and marked line of discrimination between the limitations it imposes on the powers of the general government and on those of the States; if in every inhibition intended to act on State power, words are employed which directly express that intent, some strong reason must be assigned for departing from this safe and judicious course in framing the amendments, before that departure can be assumed.

We search in vain for that reason. . . .

Had the framers of these amendments intended them to be limitations on the powers of the State governments they would have imitated the framers of the original Constitution, and have expressed that intention. Had Congress engaged in the extraordinary occupation of improving the constitutions of the several States by affording the people additional protection from the exercise of power by their own governments in matters which concerned themselves alone, they would have declared this purpose in plain and intelligible language.

But it is universally understood, it is a part of the history of the day, that the great revolution which established the Constitution of the United States was not effected without immense opposition. Serious fears were extensively entertained that those powers which the patriot statesmen who then watched over the interests of our country, deemed essential to union, and to the attainment of those invaluable objects for which union was sought, might be exercised in a manner dangerous to liberty. In almost every convention by which the Constitution was adopted, amendments to guard against the abuse of power were recommended. These amendments demanded security against the apprehended encroachments of the general government—not against those of the local governments.

In compliance with a sentiment thus generally expressed, to quiet fears thus extensively entertained, amendments were proposed by the required majority in Congress, and adopted by the States. These amendments contain no expression indicating an intention to apply them to the State governments. This court cannot so apply them.

We are of opinion that the provision in the fifth amendment to the Constitution, declaring that private property shall not be taken for public use without just compensation, is intended solely as a limitation on the exercise of power by the government of the United States, and is not applicable to the legislation of the States. . . .

This court, therefore, has no jurisdiction of the case, and is dismissed.

The Slaughterhouse Cases

16 WALL. (83 U.S.) 36, 21 L.ED. 394 (1873)

See Chapter 3, where these cases are discussed and reprinted, in part.

Hurtado v. California

110 U.S. 516, 4 S.CT. 111 (1884)

On Saturday, February 4, 1882, Joseph Hurtado assaulted Jose Estuardo in a saloon brawl in Sacramento, California. He was arrested and scheduled for trial the following Monday. But the city attorney was unable to appear, the trial was postponed, and Hurtado released. He headed for a nearby bar. Later, Hurtado saw Estuardo approaching the bar and walked out and shot him in the chest. As Estuardo tried to flee, Hurtado shot him again in the back, and a third time as Estuardo lay on the ground. Hurtado was arrested and subsequently tried and convicted of murder, and sentenced to death.

If Hurtado had been tried in federal court, he would have been indicted by a grand jury before being tried for his crime. The Fifth Amendment requires indictment by a grand jury before a person accused of a capital offense may be tried. By contrast, the California Constitution of 1879 provided that prosecutions of criminal defendants could proceed on a prosecutor's filing a statement of information (a formal statement of accusation of the crimes committed, but not submitted to a grand jury). On appeal, Hurtado's attorney challenged the constitutionality of this procedure as a violation of the Fifth Amendment and the due process clause of the Fourteenth Amendment. After two state courts upheld his conviction, Hurtado petitioned the Supreme Court for a writ of error, claiming that the state had denied him his rights under the Bill of Rights. But the justices rejected that plea.

The Court's decision was seven to one, with Justice Field not participating; the majority's opinion was announced by Justice Matthews. Justice Harlan dissented.

☐ *Justice MATTHEWS delivered the opinion of the Court.*

It is claimed on behalf of the prisoner that the conviction and sentence are void, on the ground that they are repugnant to that clause of the fourteenth article of amendment to the constitution of the United States, which is in these words: "Nor shall any state deprive any person of life, liberty, or property without due process of law." The proposition of law we are asked to affirm is that an indictment or presentment by a grand jury, as known to the common law of England, is essential to that "due process of law," when applied to prosecutions for felonies, which is secured and guaranteed by this provision of the constitution of the United States, and which accordingly it is forbidden to the states, respectively, to dispense with in the administration of criminal law. . . .

[I]t is maintained that the phrase "due process of law" is equivalent to "law of the land," as found in the twenty-ninth chapter of *Magna Charta*; that by immemorial usage it has acquired a fixed, definite, and technical meaning; that it refers to and includes, not only the general principles of public liberty and private right, which lie at the foundation of all free government, but the very institutions which, venerable by time and custom, have been tried by experience and found fit and necessary for the preservation of those principles, and which, having been the birthright and inheritance of every English subject, crossed the Atlantic with the colonists and were transplanted and established in the fundamental laws of the state; that, having been originally introduced into the constitution of the United States as a limitation upon the powers of the government, brought into being by that instrument, it has now been added as an additional security to the individual against oppression by the states themselves; that one of these institutions is that of the grand jury, an indictment or presentment by which against the accused in cases of alleged felonies is an essential part of due process of law, in order that he may not be harassed and destroyed by prosecutions founded only upon private malice or popular fury.

It is urged upon us, however, in argument, that the claim made in behalf of the plaintiff in error is supported by the decision of this court in *Murray's Lessee v. Hoboken Land & Imp. Co.* [18 How. (59 U.S.) 272 (1856)]. There, Justice CURTIS, delivering the opinion of the court, after showing that due process of law must mean something more than the actual existing law of the land, for otherwise it would be no restraint upon legislative power, proceeds as follows: "To what principle, then, are we to resort to ascertain whether this process, enacted by congress, is due process? To this the answer must be twofold. We must examine the constitution itself to see whether this process be in conflict with any of its provisions. If not found to be so, we must look to those settled usages and modes of proceeding existing in the common and statute law of England before the emigration of our ancestors, and which are shown not to have been unsuited to their civil and political condition by having been acted on by them after the settlement of this country." . . .

We are to construe this phrase in the fourteenth amendment by the *usus loquendi* of the constitution itself. The same words are contained in the fifth amendment. That article makes specific and express provision for perpetuating the institution of the grand jury, so far as relates to prosecutions for the more aggravated crimes under the laws of the United States. It declares that "no person shall be held to answer for a capital or otherwise infamous crime, unless on a presentment or indictment of a grand jury, except in cases arising in the land or naval forces, or in the militia when in actual service in time of war or public danger; nor shall any person be subject for the same offense to be twice put in jeopardy of life or limb; nor shall he be compelled in any criminal case to be a witness against himself." It then immediately adds: "nor be deprived of life, liberty, or property without due process of law." According to a recognized canon of interpretation, especially applicable to formal and solemn instruments of constitutional law, we are forbidden to assume, without clear reason to the contrary, that any part of this most important amendment is superfluous. The natural and obvious inference is that, in the sense of the constitution, "due process of law" was not meant or intended to include, *ex vi termini*, the institution and procedure of a grand jury in any case. The conclusion is equally irresistible, that when the same phrase was employed in the fourteenth amendment to restrain the action of the states, it was used in the same sense and with no greater extent; and that if in the adoption of that amendment it had been part of its purpose to perpetuate the institution of the grand jury in all the states, it would have embodied, as did the fifth amendment, express declarations to that effect. Due process of law in the latter refers to that law of the land which derives its authority from the legislative powers conferred upon congress by the constitution of the United States, exercised within the limits therein prescribed, and interpreted according to the principles of the common law. In the fourteenth amendment, by parity of reason, it refers to that law of the land in each state which derives its authority from the inherent and reserved powers of the state, exerted within the limits of those fundamental principles of liberty and justice which lie at the base of all our civil and political institutions.

But it is not to be supposed that these legislative powers are absolute and despotic, and that the amendment prescribing due process of law is too vague and indefinite to operate as a practical restraint. It is not every act, legislative in form, that is law. Law is something more than mere will exerted as an act of power. It must be not a special rule for a particular person or a particular case, but, in the language of Mr. Webster, in his familiar definition, "the general law, a law which hears before it condemns, which proceeds upon inquiry, and renders judgment only after trial," so "that every citizen shall hold his life, liberty, property, and immunities under the protection of the general rules which govern society," and thus excluding, as not due process of law, acts of attainder, bills of pains and penalties, acts of confiscation, acts reversing judgments, and acts directly transferring one man's estate to another, legislative judgments and decrees, and other similar special, partial, and arbitrary exertions of power under the forms of legislation. Arbitrary power, enforcing its edicts to the injury of the persons and property of its subjects, is not law, whether manifested as the decree of a personal monarch or of an impersonal multitude. And the limitations imposed by our constitutional law upon the action of the governments, both state and national, are essential to the preservation of public and private rights, notwithstanding the representative character of our political institutions. The enforcement of these limitations by judicial process is the device of self-governing communities to protect the rights of individuals and minorities, as well against the power of numbers, as against the violence of public agents transcending the limits of lawful authority, even when acting in the name and wielding the force of the government....

Tried by these principles, we are unable to say that the substitution for a presentment or indictment by a grand jury of the proceeding by information after examination and commitment by a magistrate, certifying to the probable guilt of the defendant, with the right on his part to the aid of counsel, and to the cross-examination of the witnesses produced for the prosecution, is not due process of law. It is, as we have seen, an ancient proceeding at common law, which might include every case of an offense of less grade than a felony, except misprision of treason; and in every circumstance of its administration, as authorized by the statute of California, it carefully considers and guards the substantial interest of the prisoner. It is merely a preliminary proceeding, and can result in no final judgment, except as the consequence of a regular judicial trial, conducted precisely as in cases of indictments....

For these reasons, finding no error therein, the judgment of the supreme court of California is affirmed.

☐ *Justice HARLAN, dissenting.*

"Due process of law," within the meaning of the national Constitution, does not import one thing with reference to the powers of the states and another with reference to the powers of the general government. If particular proceedings, conducted under the authority of the general government, and involving life, are prohibited because not constituting that due process of law required by the Fifth Amendment of the Constitution of the United States, similar proceedings, conducted under the authority of a state, must be deemed illegal, as not being due process of law within the meaning of the

Fourteenth Amendment. The words "due process of law," in the latter amendment, must receive the same interpretation they had at common law from which they were derived, and which was given to them at the formation of the general government. What was that interpretation? . . .

"The words 'due process of law' were undoubtedly intended," said this Court, in *Murray's Lessee v. Hoboken, etc. Co.* [18 How (59 U.S.) 272 (1856)], "to convey the same meaning as the words 'by the law of the land' in Magna Charta." Whether the phrase in our American constitutions, national or state, be "law of the land" or "due process of law," it means in every case the same thing. . . .

It seems to me that too much stress is put upon the fact that the framers of the Constitution made express provision for the security of those rights which at common law were protected by the requirement of due process of law, and, in addition, declared, generally, that no person shall "be deprived of life, liberty or property without due process of law." The rights, for the security of which these express provisions were made, were of a character so essential to the safety of the people that it was deemed wise to avoid the possibility that Congress, in regulating the processes of law, would impair or destroy them. Hence, their specific enumeration in the earlier amendments of the Constitution, in connection with the general requirement of due process of law, the latter itself being broad enough to cover every right of life, liberty or property secured by the settled usages and modes of proceeding existing under the common and statute law of England at the time our government was founded. . . .

[I]t is a fact of momentous interest in this discussion, that, when the Fourteenth Amendment was submitted and adopted, the Bill of Rights and the constitutions of twenty-seven States expressly forbade criminal prosecutions, by information, for capital cases [including the California Constitution of 1849]; while, in the remaining ten States, they were impliedly forbidden by a general clause declaring that no person should be deprived of life otherwise than by "the judgment of his peers or the law of the land," or "without due process of law." It may be safely affirmed that, when that Amendment was adopted, a criminal prosecution, by information, for a crime involving life, was not permitted in any one of the States composing the Union. So that the court, in this case, while conceding that the requirement of due process of law protects the fundamental principles of liberty and justice, adjudges, in effect, that an immunity or right, recognized at the common law to be essential to personal security, jealously guarded by our national Constitution against violation by any tribunal or body exercising authority under the general government, and expressly or impliedly recognized, *when the Fourteenth Amendment was adopted*, in the Bill of Rights or Constitution of every State in the Union, is, yet, not a fundamental principle in governments established, as those of the States of the Union are, to secure to the citizen liberty and justice, and, therefore, is not involved in that due process of law required in proceedings conducted under the sanction of a State. My sense of duty constrains me to dissent from this interpretation of the supreme law of the land.

Justice Benjamin Cardozo and Chief Justice Charles Evans Hughes in 1937. Justice Cardozo's opinion in *Palko v. Connecticut* (1937) set the stage for the Court's selective nationalization of the Bill of Rights. (*Photo by Underwood & Underwood, Collection of the Supreme Court of the United States*)

Palko v. Connecticut
302 U.S. 319, 58 S.Ct. 149 (1937)

Frank Jacob Palko was a man wanted for killing two police officers in Bridgeport, Connecticut, in September 1935. He had been stopped by them for questioning about the burglary of a music store and when confronted shot them both and then escaped. A month later, he was arrested in New York and confessed to the Bridgeport murders. Palko was subsequently indicted by a grand jury on the charge of first-degree premeditated murder; tried before a jury, which found him guilty of second-degree murder; and sentenced to life imprisonment.

After his trial, the prosecution persisted in seeking the death penalty and appealed Palko's trial and sentence. Under Connecticut law, a criminal sentence could be appealed by the state if the trial judge made errors prejudicial to the prosecution and the judge granted his permission for an appeal. The prosecution objected to the judge's orders forbidding the use of Palko's confession as evidence and of certain questioning during the trial, as well as the judge's characterization of what constitutes premeditated murder in his instructions to the jury on the difference between first- and second-degree murder. The state supreme court of appeals agreed the trial judge had erred, reversed Palko's conviction, and ordered a retrial.

At Palko's second trial, his attorney objected that retrial violated the Fifth Amendment guarantee against holding a person in double jeopardy for the same offense. The trial judge overruled that objection. Palko was convicted for first-degree murder and sentenced to be electrocuted. After unsuccessfully appealing to the state supreme court, Palko's attorney petitioned the Supreme Court. In claiming that Palko's retrial violated the double jeopardy clause of the Fifth Amendment, he argued that historical evidence showed that the Bill of Rights was applicable to the states under the Fourteenth Amendment.

The Court's decision was eight to one; the majority's opinion was delivered by Justice Cardozo. Justice Butler dissented without opinion.

☐ *Justice CARDOZO delivered the opinion of the Court.*

The . . . appellant [contends] that whatever is forbidden by the Fifth Amendment is forbidden by the Fourteenth also. The Fifth Amendment, which is not directed to the States, but solely to the federal government, creates immunity from double jeopardy. No person shall be "subject for the same offense to be twice put in jeopardy of life or limb." The Fourteenth Amendment ordains, "nor shall any State deprive any person of life, liberty, or property, without due process of law." To retry a defendant, though under one indictment and only one, subjects him, it is said, to double jeopardy in violation of the Fifth Amendment, if the prosecution is one on behalf of the United States. From this the consequence is said to follow that there is a denial of life or liberty without due process of law, if the prosecution is one on behalf of the people of a state. . . .

We have said that in appellant's view the Fourteenth Amendment is to be taken as embodying the prohibitions of the Fifth. His thesis is even broader. Whatever would be a violation of the original bill of rights (Amendments 1 to 8) if done by the federal government is now equally unlawful by force of the Fourteenth Amendment if done by a state. There is no such general rule.

The Fifth Amendment provides, among other things, that no person shall be held to answer for a capital or otherwise infamous crime unless on presentment or indictment of a grand jury. This court has held that, in prosecutions by a state, presentment or indictment by a grand jury may give way to informations at the instance of a public officer. *Hurtado v. California*, 110 U.S. 516 [(1884)]. The Fifth Amendment provides also that no person shall be compelled in any criminal case to be a witness against himself. This court has said that, in prosecutions by a state, the exemption will fail if the state elects to end it. The Sixth Amendment calls for a jury trial in criminal cases and the Seventh for a jury trial in civil cases at common law where the value in controversy shall exceed $20. This court has ruled that consistently with those amendments trial by jury may be modified by a state or abolished altogether. . . .

On the other hand, the due process clause of the Fourteenth Amendment may make it unlawful for a state to abridge by its statutes the freedom of speech which the First Amendment safeguards against encroachment by the Congress (*De Jonge v. Oregon*, 299 U.S. 353 [(1937)] or the like freedom of the press (*Grosjean v. American Press Co.*, 297 U.S. 233 [(1936)]; *Near v. Minnesota*, 283 U.S. 697 [(1931)], or the free exercise of religion (*Hamilton v. Regents of University*, 293 U.S. 245 [(1934)], or the right of peaceable assembly, without which speech would be unduly trammeled . . . or the right of one accused of crime to the benefit of counsel (*Powell v. Alabama*, 287 U.S. 45 [(1932)]. In these and other situations immunities that are valid as against the federal government by force of the specific pledges of particular amendments have been found to be implicit in the concept of ordered liberty, and thus, through the Fourteenth Amendment, become valid as against the states.

The line of division may seem to be wavering and broken if there is a hasty catalogue of the cases on the one side and the other. Reflection and analysis will induce a different view. There emerges the perception of a rationalizing principle which gives to discrete instances a proper order and coherence. The right to trial by jury and the immunity from prosecution except as the result of an indictment may have value and importance. Even so, they are not of the very essence of a scheme of ordered liberty. To abolish them is not to violate a "principle of justice so rooted in the traditions and conscience of our people as to be ranked as fundamental." What is true of jury trials and indictments is true also, as the cases show, of the immunity from compulsory self-incrimination. *Twining v. New Jersey* [211 U.S. 78 (1908)]. This too might be lost, and justice still be done. . . .

We reach a different plane of social and moral values when we pass to the privileges and immunities that have been taken over from the earlier articles of the Federal Bill of Rights and brought within the Fourteenth Amendment by a process of absorption. These in their origin were effective against the federal government alone. If the Fourteenth Amendment has absorbed them, the process of absorption has had its source in the belief that neither liberty nor justice would exist if they were sacrificed. This is true, for illustration, of freedom of thought and speech. Of that freedom one may say that it is the matrix, the indispensable condition, of nearly every other form of freedom. With rare aberrations a pervasive recognition of that truth can be traced in our history, political and legal. So it has come about that the domain of liberty, withdrawn by the Fourteenth Amendment from encroachment by the states, has been enlarged by latter-day judgments to include liberty of the mind as well as liberty of action. The extension became, indeed, a logical imperative when once it was recognized, as long ago it was, that liberty is something more than exemption from physical restraint, and that even in the field of substantive rights and duties the legislative judgment, if oppressive and arbitrary, may be overridden by the courts. Fundamental too in the concept of due process, and so in that of liberty, is the thought that condemnation shall be rendered only after trial. The hearing, moreover, must be a real one, not a sham or a pretense. For that reason, ignorant defendants in a capital case were held to have been condemned unlawfully when in truth, though not in form, they were refused the aid of counsel. *Powell v. Alabama*. The decision did not turn upon the fact that the benefit of counsel would have been guaranteed to the defendants by the provisions of the Sixth Amendment if they had been prosecuted in a federal court. The decision turned upon the fact that in the particular situation laid before us in the evidence the benefit of counsel was essential to the substance of a hearing.

Our survey of the cases serves, we think, to justify the statement that the dividing line between them, if not unfaltering throughout its course, has been true for the most part to a unifying principle. On which side of the line the case made out by the appellant has appropriate location must be the next inquiry and the final one. Is that kind of double jeopardy to which the statute has subjected him a hardship so acute and shocking that our polity will not endure it? Does it violate those "fundamental principles of liberty and justice which lie at the base of all our civil and political institutions"? The answer surely must be "no." What the answer would have to be if the state were permitted after a trial free from error to try the accused over again or to bring another case against him, we have no occasion to consider. We deal with the statute before us and no other. The state is not attempting to wear the accused out by a multitude of cases with accumulated trials. It asks no more than this, that the case against him shall go on until there shall be a trial free from the corrosion of substantial legal error. This is not cruelty at all, nor even vexation in any immoderate degree. . . .

The judgment is affirmed.

Adamson v. California

332 U.S. 46, 67 S.Ct. 1672 (1947)

Admiral Dewey Adamson, a forty-three-year-old black man with a prior criminal record, was arrested and tried for breaking into the Los Angeles apartment of a sixty-four-year-old widow and then murdering her. At his trial, Adamson refused to testify in his own defense because of his prior criminal record. If he had, the prosecution could impeach his credibility as a witness based on his previous convictions for robbery and burglary. The Fifth Amendment guarantees the accused a right against self-incrimination and being "compelled in any criminal case to be a witness against himself." But California's state constitution permitted prosecutors to comment on a defendant's failure to testify. At Adamson's trial, the district attorney told the jury that Adamson's refusal to testify stripped him of a presumption of innocence. He told the jury in summation, "Counsel asked you to find this defendant not guilty. But does the defendant get on the stand and say, under oath, 'I am not guilty'? Not one word from him, and not one word from a single witness. I leave the case in your hands." The jury convicted Adamson on both counts. He was sentenced, as a habitual criminal, to life imprisonment on the burglary count and to death in the gas chamber on the murder count. Adamson's attorney appealed unsuccessfully to the state supreme court and then to the Supreme Court.

Adamson's attorney asked the Supreme Court to strike down California's law permitting prosecutorial comment. It penalized the defendant for exercising his Fifth Amendment rights which, he also argued, were applicable to the states under the Fourteenth Amendment's privileges or immunities clause and due process clause. That meant overturning *Twining v. New Jersey*, 211 U.S. 78 (1908), which upheld New Jersey's practice of allowing juries to draw unfavorable inferences from a defendant's failure to testify. But Adamson's attorney urged the Court to reconsider and adopt dissenting Justice Harlan's opinion there and in *Hurtado*. At conference, the justices voted five to three to affirm Adamson's conviction, with Justice Black initially passing because he was unsure prosecutorial comments violated the Fifth Amendment, although he was certain that the amendment and others of the Bill of Rights should apply to the states. In the end, Black joined the dissenters writing one of his major opinions disputing the majority's reading of the history and purposes of the Bill of Rights and the Fourteenth Amendment. Justice Reed's opinion for the majority paid little attention to the privileges or immunities claim and concentrated instead on the due process claim.

The Court's decision was five to four, and the majority's opinion was announced by Justice Reed. Justice Frankfurter concurred. Dissents were delivered by Justices Murphy and Black, joined by Justices Rutledge and Douglas.

☐ *Justice REED delivered the opinion of the Court.*

[The appellant contends that] the due process clause of the Fourteenth Amendment protects his privilege against self-incrimination. The due process clause of the Fourteenth Amendment, however, does not draw all the rights of the federal Bill of Rights under its protection. That contention was made and rejected in *Palko v. Connecticut* [302 U.S. 319 (1937)]. *Palko* held that such provisions of the Bill of Rights as were "implicit in the concept of ordered liberty" became secure from state interference by the clause. But it held nothing more. . . .

For a state to require testimony from an accused is not necessarily a breach of a state's obligation to give a fair trial. Therefore, we must examine the effect of the California law applied in this trial to see whether the comment on failure to testify violates the protection against state action that the due process clause does grant to an accused. The due process clause forbids compulsion to testify by fear of hurt, torture or exhaustion. It forbids any other type of coercion that falls within the scope of due process. California follows Anglo-American legal tradition in excusing defendants in criminal prosecutions from compulsory testimony. That is a matter of legal policy and not because of the requirements of due process under the Fourteenth Amendment. So our inquiry is directed, not at the broad question of the constitutionality of compulsory testimony from the accused under the due process clause, but to the constitutionality of the provision of the California law that permits comment upon his failure to testify. . . .

Generally, comment on the failure of an accused to testify is forbidden in American jurisdictions. . . . California, however, is one of a few states that permit limited comment upon a defendant's failure to testify. That permission is narrow. . . . This does not involve any presumption, rebuttable or irrebuttable, either of guilt or of the truth of any fact, that is offered in evidence.

It allows inferences to be drawn from proven facts. Because of this clause, the court can direct the jury's attention to whatever evidence there may be that a defendant could deny and the prosecution can argue as to inferences that may be drawn from the accused's failure to testify. . . . California has prescribed a method for advising the jury in the search for truth. However sound may be the legislative conclusion that an accused should not be compelled in any criminal case to be a witness against himself, we see no reason why comment should not be made upon his silence. It seems quite natural that when a defendant has opportunity to deny or explain facts and determines not to do so, the prosecution should bring out the strength of the evidence by commenting upon defendant's failure to explain or deny it. The prosecution evidence may be of facts that may be beyond the knowledge of the accused. If so, his failure to testify would have little if any weight. But the facts may be such as are necessarily in the knowledge of the accused. In that case a failure to explain would point to an inability to explain.

☐ *Justice FRANKFURTER, concurring.*

For historical reasons a limited immunity from the common duty to testify was written into the Federal Bill of Rights, and I am prepared to agree that, as part of that immunity, comment on the failure of an accused to take the witness stand as forbidden in federal prosecutions. . . .

But to suggest that such a limitation can be drawn out of "due process" in its protection of ultimate decency in a civilized society is to suggest that the Due Process Clause fastened fetters of unreason upon the States. . . .

Between the incorporation of the Fourteenth Amendment into the Constitution and the beginning of the present membership of the Court—a period of 70 years—the scope of that Amendment was passed upon by 43 judges. Of all these judges, only one, who may respectfully be called an eccentric exception, ever indicated the belief that the Fourteenth Amendment was a shorthand summary of the first eight Amendments theretofore limiting only the Federal Government, and that due process incorporated those eight Amendments as restrictions upon the powers of the States. . . .

The notion that the Fourteenth Amendment was a covert way of imposing upon the States all the rules which it seemed important to Eighteenth Century statesmen to write into the Federal Amendments, was rejected by judges who were themselves witnesses of the process by which the Fourteenth Amendment became part of the Constitution. Arguments that may now be adduced to prove that the first eight Amendments were concealed within the historic phrasing of the Fourteenth Amendment were not unknown at the time of its adoption. A surer estimate of their bearing was possible for judges at the time than distorting distance is likely to vouchsafe. Any evidence of design or purpose not contemporaneously known could hardly have influenced those who ratified the Amendment. Remarks of a particular proponent of the Amendment, no matter how influential, are not to be deemed part of the Amendment. What was submitted for ratification was his proposal, not his speech. Thus, at the time of the ratification of the Fourteenth Amendment the constitutions of nearly half of the ratifying States did not have the rigorous requirements of the Fifth Amendment for instituting criminal proceedings through a grand jury. It could hardly have occurred to these States that by ratifying the Amendment they uprooted their established methods for prosecuting crime and fastened upon themselves a new prosecutorial system. . . .

It may not be amiss to restate the pervasive function of the Fourteenth Amendment in exacting from the States observance of basic liberties. The Amendment neither comprehends the specific provisions by which the founders deemed it appropriate to restrict the federal government nor is it confined to them. The Due Process Clause of the Fourteenth Amendment has an independent potency, precisely as does the Due Process Clause of the Fifth Amendment in relation to the Federal Government. It ought not to require argument to reject the notion that due process of law meant one thing in the Fifth Amendment and another in the Fourteenth. The Fifth Amendment specifically prohibits prosecution of an "infamous crime" except upon indictment; it forbids double jeopardy; it bars compelling a person to be a witness against himself in any criminal case; it precludes deprivation of "life, liberty, or property, without due process of law." Are Madison and his contemporaries in the framing of the Bill of Rights to be charged with writing into it a meaningless clause? To consider "due process of law" as merely a shorthand statement of other specific clauses in the same amendment is to attribute to the authors and proponents of this Amendment ignorance of, or indifference to, a historic conception which was one of the great instruments in the arsenal of constitutional freedom which the Bill of Rights was to protect and strengthen. . . .

And so, when, as in a case like the present, a conviction in a State court is here for review under a claim that a right protected by the Due Process Clause of the Fourteenth Amendment has been denied, the issue is not whether an infraction of one of the specific provisions of the first eight Amendments is disclosed by the record. The relevant question is whether the criminal proceedings which resulted in conviction deprived the accused of the due process of law to which the United States Constitution entitled him. Judicial review of that guaranty of the Fourteenth Amendment inescapably imposes upon this Court an exercise of judgment upon the whole course of the proceedings in order to ascertain whether they offend those canons of decency and fairness which express the notions of justice of English-speaking peoples even toward those charged with the most heinous offenses. These standards of justice are not authoritatively formulated anywhere as though they were prescriptions in a pharmacopoeia. But neither does the application of the Due Process Clause imply that judges are wholly at large. The judicial judgment in applying the Due Process Clause must move within the limits of accepted notions of justice and is not to be based upon the idiosyncrasies of a merely personal judgement.

☐ *Justice MURPHY, with whom Justice RUTLEDGE joins, dissenting.*

While in substantial agreement with the views of Justice BLACK, I have one reservation and one addition to make.

I agree that the specific guarantees of the Bill of Rights should be carried over intact into the first section of the Fourteenth Amendment. But I am not prepared to say that the latter is entirely and necessarily limited by the Bill of Rights. Occasions may arise where a proceeding falls so far short of conforming to fundamental standards of procedure as to warrant constitutional condemnation in terms of a lack of due process despite the absence of a specific provision in the Bill of Rights.

☐ *Justice BLACK, dissenting.*

My study of the historical events that culminated in the Fourteenth Amendment, and the expressions of those who sponsored and favored, as well as those who opposed its submission and passage, persuades me that one of the chief objects that the provisions of the Amendment's first section, separately, and as a whole, were intended to accomplish was to make the Bill of Rights, applicable to the states. With full knowledge of the import of the *Barron* [*v. Baltimore* (1833)] decision, the framers and backers of the Fourteenth Amendment proclaimed its purpose to be to overturn the constitutional rule that case had announced. This historical purpose has never received full consideration or exposition in any opinion of this Court interpreting the Amendment. . . .

For this reason, I am attaching to this dissent, an appendix which contains a resumé, by no means complete, of the Amendment's history. In my judgment that history conclusively demonstrates that the language of the first section of the Fourteenth Amendment, taken as a whole, was thought by those responsible for its submission to the people, and by those who opposed its submission, sufficiently explicit to guarantee that thereafter no state could deprive its citizens of the privileges and protections of the Bill of Rights. Whether this Court ever will, or whether it now should, in the light of past decisions, give full effect to what the Amendment was intended to accomplish is not necessarily essential to a decision here. However that may be, our prior decisions, including *Twining* [*v. New Jersey*, 211 U.S. 78 (1908)], do not prevent our carrying out that purpose, at least to the extent of making applicable to the states, not a mere part, as the Court has, but the full protection of the Fifth Amendment's provision against compelling evidence from an accused to convict him of crime. And I further contend that the "natural law" formula which the Court uses to reach its conclusion in this case should be abandoned as an incongruous excrescence on our Constitution. I believe that formula to be itself a violation of our Constitution, in that it subtly conveys to courts, at the expense of legislatures, ultimate power over public policies in fields where no specific provision of the Constitution limits legislative power. . . .

I cannot consider the Bill of Rights to be an outworn 18th Century "strait jacket" as the *Twining* opinion did. Its provisions may be thought outdated abstractions by some. And it is true that they were designed to meet ancient evils. But they are the same kind of human evils that have emerged from century to century wherever excessive power is sought by the few at the expense of the many. In my judgment the people of no nation can lose their liberty so long as a Bill of Rights like ours survives and its basic purposes are conscientiously interpreted, enforced and respected so as to afford continuous protection against old, as well as new, devices and practices which might thwart those purposes. I fear to see the consequences of the Court's practice of substituting its own concepts of decency and fundamental justice for the language of the Bill of Rights as its point of departure in interpreting and enforcing that Bill of Rights. If the choice must be between the selective process of the *Palko* decision applying some of the Bill of Rights to the States, or the *Twining* rule applying none of them, I would choose the *Palko* selective process. But rather than accept either of these choices. I would follow what I believe was the original purpose of the Fourteenth Amendment—to extend to all the people of the nation the complete protection of the Bill of Rights.

Justice DOUGLAS joined in this opinion.

Rochin v. California

342 U.S. 165, 72 S.Ct. 205 (1952)

Antonio Richard Rochin was sitting in his bedroom when three Los Angeles county deputy sheriffs crashed through the door, armed, without a search or arrest warrant. He quickly grabbed and swallowed two morphine capsules lying on a nightstand. The deputies immediately tried to force him to vomit the pills by choking and sticking their fingers down his throat. When that failed, they rushed Rochin to a hospital, where a doctor inserted a tube and an emetic solution down his throat. At that, he finally vomited the pills into a pail. Rochin was later charged, tried, and convicted for violating a state narcotics law. His conviction was upheld on appeal by a state appellate court, and the California State Supreme Court denied a further appeal. Rochin's attorney petitioned the Supreme Court on the ground that the police denied Rochin's rights under the Fourth and Fifth Amendments and the due process clause of the Fourteenth Amendment. The petition was granted, and the Court reversed the two California State court rulings.

The Court's decision was unanimous; the opinion was announced by Justice Frankfurter, with Justice Minton not participating. Concurrences were by Justices Black and Douglas.

☐ *Justice FRANKFURTER delivered the opinion of the Court.*

In our federal system the administration of criminal justice is predominantly committed to the care of the States. The power to define crimes belongs to Congress only as an appropriate means of carrying into execution its limited grant of legislative powers. U.S. Const. Art. I, § 8, cl. 18. Broadly speaking, crimes in the United States are what the laws of the individual States make them, subject to the limitations of Art. I, § 10, cl. 1, in the original Constitution, prohibiting bills of attainder and *ex post facto* laws, and of the Thirteenth and Fourteenth Amendments.

These limitations, in the main, concern not restrictions upon the powers of the States to define crime, except in the restricted area where federal authority has pre-empted the field, but restrictions upon the manner in which the States may enforce their penal codes. Accordingly, in reviewing a State criminal conviction under a claim of right guaranteed by the Due Process Clause of the Fourteenth Amendment, from which is derived the most far-reaching and most frequent federal basis of challenging State criminal justice, "we must be deeply mindful of the responsibilities of the States for the enforcement of criminal laws, and exercise with due humility our merely negative function in subjecting convictions from state courts to the very narrow scrutiny which the Due Process Clause of the Fourteenth Amendment authorizes." . . .

However, this Court too has its responsibility. Regard for the requirements of the Due Process Clause "inescapably imposes upon this Court an exercise of judgment upon the whole course of the proceedings [resulting in a conviction] in order to ascertain whether they offend those canons of decency and fairness which express the notions of justice of English-speaking peoples even toward those charged with the most heinous offenses." These standards of justice are not authoritatively formulated anywhere as though they were specifics. Due process of law is a summarized constitutional guarantee of respect for those personal immunities which, as Justice CARDOZO twice wrote for the Court, are "so rooted in the tradition and conscience of our people as to be ranked as fundamental," or are "implicit in the concept of ordered liberty." *Palko v. State of Connecticut* [302 U.S. 319 (1937)].

The Due Process Clause places upon this Court the duty of exercising a judgment, within the narrow confines of judicial power in reviewing State convictions, upon interests of society pushing in opposite directions.

Due process of law thus conceived is not to be derided as resort to a revival of "natural law." To believe that this judicial exercise of judgment could be avoided by freezing "due process of law" at some fixed stage of time or thought is to suggest that the most important aspect of constitutional adjudication is a function for inanimate machines and not for judges, for whom the independence safeguarded by Article III of the Constitution was designed and who are presumably guided by established standards of judicial behavior. Even cybernetics has not yet made that haughty claim. To practice the requisite detachment and to achieve sufficient objectivity no doubt demands of judges the habit of self-discipline and self-criticism, incertitude that one's own views are incontestable and alert tolerance toward views not shared. But these are precisely the presuppositions of our judicial process. They are precisely the qualities society has a right to expect from those entrusted with ultimate judicial power.

Restraints on our jurisdiction are self-imposed only in the sense that there is from our decisions no immediate appeal short of impeachment or constitutional amendment. But that does not make due process of law a matter of judicial caprice. The faculties of the Due Process Clause may be indefinite and vague, but the mode of their ascertainment is not self-willed. In each case "due process of law" requires an evaluation based on a disinterested inquiry pursued in the spirit of science, on a balanced order of facts exactly and fairly stated, on the detached consideration of conflicting claims, on a judgment not *ad hoc* and episodic but duly mindful of reconciling the needs both of continuity and of change in a progressive society.

Applying these general considerations to the circumstances of the present case, we are compelled to conclude that the proceedings by which this conviction was obtained do more than offend some fastidious squeamishness or private sentimentalism about combatting crime too energetically. This is conduct that shocks the conscience. Illegally breaking into the privacy of the petitioner, the struggle to open his mouth and remove what was there, the forcible extraction of his stomach's contents—this course of proceeding by agents of government to obtain evidence is bound to offend even hardened sensibilities. They are methods too close to the rack and the screw to permit of constitutional differentiation. . . .

On the facts of this case the conviction of the petitioner has been obtained by methods that offend the Due Process Clause. The judgment below must be reversed.

Reversed.

☐ *Justice BLACK, concurring.*

Adamson v. People of State of California, 332 U.S. 46 [(1947)], sets out reasons for my belief that state as well as federal courts and law enforcement officers must obey the Fifth Amendment's command that "No person . . . shall be compelled in any criminal case to be a witness against himself." I think a person is compelled to be a witness against himself not only when he is compelled to testify, but also when as here, incriminating evidence is forcibly taken from him by a contrivance of modern science. . . .

In the view of a majority of the Court, however, the Fifth Amendment imposes no restraint of any kind on the states. They nevertheless hold that California's use of this evidence violated the Due Process Clause of the Fourteenth Amendment. Since they hold as I do in this case, I regret my inability to accept their interpretation without protest. But I believe that faithful adherence to the specific guarantees in the Bill of Rights insures a more permanent protection of individual liberty than that which can be afforded by the nebulous standards stated by the majority.

What the majority hold is that the Due Process Clause empowers this Court to nullify any state law if its application "shocks the conscience," offends "a sense of justice" or runs counter to the "decencies of civilized conduct." . . . We are further admonished to measure the validity of state practices, not by our reason, or by the traditions of the legal profession, but by "the community's sense of fair play and decency"; by the "traditions and conscience of our people"; or by "those canons of decency and fairness which express the notions of justice of English-speaking peoples." These canons are made necessary, it is said, because of "interests of society pushing in opposite directions." . . .

[O]ne may well ask what avenues of investigation are open to discover "canons" of conduct so universally favored that this Court should write them into the Constitution? All we are told is that the discovery must be made by an evaluation based on a disinterested inquiry pursued in the spirit of science, on a balanced order of facts." . . .

I long ago concluded that the accordion-like qualities of this philosophy must inevitably imperil all the individual liberty safeguards specifically enumerated in the Bill of Rights.

☐ *Justice DOUGLAS, concurring.*

I think that words taken from [Rochin's] lips, capsules taken from his stomach, blood taken from his veins are all inadmissible provided they are taken from him without his consent. They are inadmissible because of the command of the Fifth Amendment.

That is an unequivocal, definite and workable rule of evidence for state and federal courts. But we cannot in fairness free the state courts from that command and yet excoriate them for flouting the "decencies of civilized conduct" when they admit the evidence. That is to make the rule turn not on the Constitution but on the idiosyncrasies of the judges who sit here.

■ INSIDE THE COURT

The Theory and Drafting of Justice Douglas's Opinion in Griswold v. Connecticut

After the justices' conference, Chief Justice Earl Warren assigned Justice Douglas the task of drafting an opinion to announce the Court's decision in *Griswold v. Connecticut*. His initial draft, however, did not develop the theory that a constitutional right of privacy was based on penumbrae of various guarantees of the Bill of Rights, as eventually announced in *Griswold*. Rather, Douglas sought to justify the decision based on earlier cases recognizing a First Amendment right of associational privacy. The analogy and precedents, he admitted, "do not decide this case. . . . Marriage does not fit precisely any of the categories of First Amendment rights. But it is a form of association as vital in the life of a man or a woman as any other, and perhaps more so."

Both Black and Brennan strongly objected to Douglas's extravagant reliance on First Amendment precedents. In a three-page letter, Brennan detailed an alternative approach, as the following excerpt indicates:

> I have read your draft opinion in *Griswold v. Connecticut*, and, while I agree with a great deal of it, I should like to suggest a substantial change in emphasis for your consideration. It goes without saying, of course, that your rejection of any approach based on *Lochner v.*

New York is absolutely right. [In *Lochner*, a majority read into the Fourteenth Amendment a "liberty of contract" to strike down economic legislation. Although the Court later abandoned the doctrine of a liberty of contract, *Lochner* continues to symbolize the original sin of constitutional interpretation—that is, the Court's creation and enforcement of unenumerated rights.] And I agree that the association of husband and wife is not mentioned in the Bill of Rights, and that that is the obstacle we must hurdle to effect a reversal in this case.

But I hesitate to bring the husband-wife relationship within the right to association we have constructed in the First Amendment context. . . . In the First Amendment context, in situations like *NAACP v. Alabama*, privacy is necessary to protect the capacity of an association for fruitful advocacy. In the present context, it seems to me that we are really interested in the privacy of married couples quite apart from any interest in advocacy. . . . Instead of expanding the First Amendment right of association to include marriage, why not say that what has been done for the First Amendment can also be done for some of the other fundamental guarantees of the Bill of Rights? In other words, where fundamentals are concerned, the Bill of Rights guarantees are but expressions or examples of those rights, and do not preclude applications or extensions of those rights to situations unanticipated by the Framers.

The restriction on the dissemination and use of contraceptives, Brennan explained, "would, on this reasoning, run afoul of a right to privacy created out of the Fourth Amendment and the self-incrimination clause of the Fifth, together with the Third, in much the same way as the right of association has been created out of the First. Taken together, those amendments indicate a fundamental concern with the sanctity of the home and the right of the individual to be alone." "With this change of emphasis," Brennan concluded, the opinion "would be most attractive to me because it would require less departure from the specific guarantees and because I think there is a better chance it will command a Court."

Douglas subsequently revised his opinion and based the right of privacy on the penumbrae of the First, Third, Fourth, Fifth, Ninth, and Fourteenth Amendments. In the end, his opinion was joined by only a plurality of the Court. Justice Goldberg, joined by Chief Justice Warren and Justice Brennan, wrote a separate concurring opinion, as did Justices Harlan and White. Justices Black and Stewart each wrote separate dissenting opinions.

Source: Library of Congress, William J. Brennan, Jr., Letter of April 24, 1965, in Justice William J. Brennan, Jr., Papers.

Griswold v. Connecticut

391 U.S. 145, 85 S. CT. 1678 (1965)

Estelle Griswold, executive director of the Planned Parenthood League of Connecticut, and Dr. C. Lee Buxton were part of a movement to repeal Connecticut's 1879 law prohibiting the dissemination of information about and the use of contraceptives. In the 1940s, after unsuccessfully seeking a repeal of the law by the state legislature, the league turned to the courts for a declaratory judgment finding the law unconstitutional. When the state supreme court upheld the law, a doctor appealed its ruling to the Supreme Court. In *Tileston v. Ullman*, 318 U.S. 44 (1943) (discussed in Ch. 2), however, the Court ruled that the doctor had no standing alone, without his patients, to challenge the constitutionality of the law under the Fourteenth Amendment. Almost twenty years later, Dr. Buxton and two of his female patients, both of whom had previously experienced difficult pregnancies, decided again to ask the Court for a declaratory judgment striking down the law. Once again, in *Poe v. Ullman*, 367 U.S. 497 (1961) (discussed in Ch. 2), a majority of the Court denied standing, largely because the law (with one exception) had gone unenforced for more than three-quarters of a century. But four justices dissented and the next year two of the justices in the majority, Justices Frankfurter and Whittaker, retired. Because Justice Frankfurter's opinion in *Poe* had stressed the unenforceability of the law, Griswold and Buxton decided that they would have to get arrested to gain standing to challenge Connecticut's law. They opened a birth control clinic, ten days later were arrested, and subsequently convicted in state courts. They thereupon made another appeal to the Supreme Court, which granted review.

The Court's decision was seven to two, and the majority's opinion was announced by Justice Douglas. Concurrences were by Justice Goldberg, joined by Chief Justice Warren and Justice Brennan, and by Justices Harlan and White. Justices Black and Stewart dissented.

☐ *Justice DOUGLAS delivered the opinion of the Court.*

[W]e are met with a wide range of questions that implicate the Due Process Clause of the Fourteenth Amendment. Overtones of some arguments suggest that *Lochner v. State of New York*, 198 U.S. 45 [(1905)], should be our guide. But we decline that invitation as we did in *West Coast Hotel Co. v. Parrish*, 300 U.S. 379 [(1937)]; *Olsen v. State of Nebraska*, 313 U.S. 236 [(1941)]; *Lincoln Federal Labor Union v. Northwestern Co.*, 335 U.S. 525 [(1949)]; *Williamson v. Lee Optical Co.*, 348 U.S. 483 [(1955)]; [and] *Giboney v. Empire Storage Co.*, 336 U.S. 490 [(1949)]. We do not sit as a super-legislature to determine the wisdom, need, and propriety of laws that touch economic problems, business affairs, or social conditions. This law, however, operates directly on an intimate relation of husband and wife and their physician's role in one aspect of that relation.

The association of people is not mentioned in the Constitution nor in the Bill of Rights. The right to educate a child in a school of the parents' choice—whether public or private or parochial—is also not mentioned. Nor is the right to study any particular subject or any foreign language. Yet the First Amendment has been construed to include certain of those rights.

By *Pierce v. Society of Sisters*, [268 U.S. 510 (1925)], the right to educate one's children as one chooses is made applicable to the States by the force of the First and Fourteenth Amendments. By *Meyer v. State of Nebraska*, [262 U.S. 390 (1923)], the same dignity is given the right to study the German language in a private school. In other words, the State may not, consistently with the spirit of the First Amendment, contract the spectrum of available knowledge. The right of freedom of speech and press includes not only the right to utter or to print, but the right to distribute, the right to receive, the right to read; and freedom of inquiry, freedom of thought, and freedom to teach—indeed the freedom of the entire university community. *Sweezy v. State of New Hampshire*, 354 U.S. 234 [(1958)]. Without those peripheral rights the specific rights would be less secure. And so we reaffirm the principle of the *Pierce* and the *Meyer* cases.

In *NAACP v. State of Alabama* [357 U.S. 44 (1958)], we protected the "freedom to associate and privacy in one's associations," noting that freedom of association was a peripheral First Amendment right. Disclosure of membership lists of a constitutionally valid association, we held, was invalid "as entailing the likelihood of a substantial restraint upon the exercise by petitioner's members of their right to freedom of association." In other words, the First Amendment has a penumbra where privacy is protected from governmental intrusion. In like context, we have protected forms of "association" that are not political in the customary sense but pertain to the social, legal, and economic benefit of the members. . . .

Those cases involved more than the "right of assembly"—a right that extends to all irrespective of their race or idealogy. . . . The right of "association" like the right of belief (*West Virginia State Board of Education v. Barnette*, 319 U.S. 624 [(1943)], is more than the right to attend a meeting; it includes the right to express one's attitudes or philosophies by membership in a group or by affiliation with it or by other lawful means. Association in that context is a form of expression of opinion; and while it is not expressly included in the First Amendment its existence is necessary in making the express guarantees fully meaningful.

The foregoing cases suggest that specific guarantees in the Bill of Rights have penumbras, formed by emanations from those guarantees that help give them life and substance. See *Poe v. Ullman*, 367 U.S. 497 [(1961)] (dissenting opinion). Various guarantees create zones of privacy. The right of association contained in the penumbra of the First Amendment is one, as we have seen. The Third Amendment in its prohibition against the quartering of soldiers "in any house" in time of peace without the consent of the owner is another facet of that privacy. The Fourth Amendment explicitly affirms the "right of the people to be secure in their persons, houses, papers, and effects, against unreasonable searches and seizures." The Fifth Amendment in its Self-Incrimination Clause enables the citizen to create a zone of privacy which government may not force him to surrender to his detriment. The Ninth Amendment provides: "The enumeration in the Constitution, of certain rights, shall not be construed to deny or disparage others retained by the people."

The Fourth and Fifth Amendments were described in *Boyd v. United States*, 116 U.S. 616 [(1886)], as protection against all governmental invasions "of the sanctity of a man's home and the privacies of life."

We recently referred in *Mapp v. Ohio*, 367 U.S. 643 [(1961)], to the Fourth Amendment as creating a "right to privacy, no less important than any other right carefully and particularly reserved to the people." . . .

We have had many controversies over these penumbral rights of "privacy and repose." These cases bear witness that the right of privacy which presses for recognition here is a legitimate one.

The present case, then, concerns a relationship lying within the zone of privacy created by several fundamental constitutional guarantees. And it concerns a law which, in forbidding the *use* of contraceptives rather than regulating their manufacture or sale, seeks to achieve its goals by means having a maximum destructive impact upon that relationship. Such a law cannot stand in light of the familiar principle, so often applied by this Court, that a "governmental purpose to control or prevent activities constitutionally subject to state regulation may not be achieved by means which sweep unnecessarily broadly and thereby invade the area of protected freedoms." *NAACP v. Alabama.* . . . Would we allow the police to search the sacred precincts of marital bedrooms for telltale signs of the use of contraceptives? The very idea is repulsive to the notions of privacy surrounding the marriage relationship.

We deal with a right of privacy older than the Bill of Rights—older than our political parties, older than our school system. Marriage is a coming together for better or for worse, hopefully enduring, and intimate to the degree of being sacred. It is an association that promotes a way of life, not causes; a harmony in living, not political faiths; a bilateral loyalty, not commercial or social projects. Yet it is an association for as noble a purpose as any involved in our prior decisions.

Reversed.

☐ *Justice GOLDBERG, with whom the CHIEF JUSTICE and Justice BRENNAN join, concurring.*

I agree with the Court that Connecticut's birth-control law unconstitutionally intrudes upon the right of marital privacy, and I join in its opinion and judgment. Although I have not accepted the view that "due process" as used in the Fourteenth Amendment includes all of the first eight Amendments (see my concurring opinion in *Pointer v. Texas*, 380 U.S. 400 [(1965)], and the dissenting opinion of Justice BRENNAN in *Cohen v. Hurley*, 366 U.S. 117 [(1961)]. I do agree that the concept of liberty protects those personal rights that are fundamental, and is not confined to the specific terms of the Bill of Rights. My conclusion that the concept of liberty is not so restricted and that it embraces the right of marital privacy though that right is not mentioned explicitly in the Constitution is supported both by numerous decisions of this Court, referred to in the Court's opinion, and by the language and history of the Ninth Amendment. In reaching the conclusion that the right of marital privacy is protected, as being within the protected penumbra of specific guarantees of the Bill of Rights, the Court refers to the Ninth Amendment. I add these words to emphasize the relevance of that Amendment to the Court's holding. . . .

The language and history of the Ninth Amendment reveal that the Framers of the Constitution believed that there are additional fundamental rights, protected from governmental infringement, which exist alongside those fundamental rights specifically mentioned in the first eight constitutional amendments.

The Ninth Amendment reads, "The enumeration in the Constitution, of certain rights, shall not be construed to deny or disparage others retained by the people." The Amendment is almost entirely the work of James Madison. It was introduced in Congress by him and passed the House and Senate with little or no debate and virtually no change in language. It was proffered to quiet expressed fears that a bill of specifically enumerated rights could not be sufficiently broad to cover all essential rights and that the specific mention of certain rights would be interpreted as a denial that others were protected.

In presenting the proposed Amendment, Madison said:

> "It has been objected also against a bill of rights, that, by enumerating particular exceptions to the grant of power, it would disparage those rights which were not placed in that enumeration; and it might follow by implication, that those rights which were not singled out, were intended to be assigned into the hands of the General Government, and were consequently insecure. This is one of the most plausible arguments I have ever heard urged against the admission of a bill of rights into this system; but, I conceive, that it may be guarded against. I have attempted it, as gentlemen may see by turning to the last clause of the fourth resolution [the Ninth Amendment]." I Annals of Congress 439 (Gales and Seaton ed. 1834). . . .

While this Court has had little occasion to interpret the Ninth Amendment, "[i]t cannot be presumed that any clause in the constitution is intended to be without effect." *Marbury v. Madison*, 1 Cranch 137 [(1803)]. To hold that a right so basic and fundamental and so deep-rooted in our society as the right of privacy in marriage may be infringed because that right is not guaranteed in so many words by the first eight amendments to the Constitution is to ignore the Ninth Amendment and to give it no effect whatsoever. . . .

I do not mean to imply that the Ninth Amendment is applied against the States by the Fourteenth. Nor do I mean to state that the Ninth Amendment constitutes an independent source of rights protected from infringement by either the States or the Federal Government. Rather, the Ninth Amendment shows a belief of the Constitution's authors that fundamental rights exist that are not expressly enumerated in the first eight amendments and an intent that the list of rights included there not be deemed exhaustive. . . . The Ninth Amendment simply shows the intent of the Constitution's authors that other fundamental personal rights should not be denied such protection or disparaged in any other way simply because they are not specifically listed in the first eight constitutional amendments. . . .

In determining which rights are fundamental, judges are not left at large to decide cases in light of their personal and private notions. Rather, they must look to the "traditions and [collective] conscience of our people" to determine whether a principle is "so rooted [there] . . . as to be ranked as fundamental." *Snyder v. Com. of Massachusetts*, 291 U.S. 97 [(1934)]. The inquiry is whether a right involved "is of such a character that it cannot be denied without violating those 'fundamental principles of liberty and justice which lie at the base of all our civil and political institutions' . . ." *Powell v. State of Alabama*, 287 U.S. 45 [(1932)]. . . .

The entire fabric of the Constitution and the purposes that clearly underlie its specific guarantees demonstrate that the rights to marital privacy and to marry and raise a family are of similar order and magnitude as the fundamental rights specifically protected.

Although the Constitution does not speak in so many words of the right of privacy in marriage, I cannot believe that it offers these fundamental rights no protection. The fact that no particular provision of the Constitution explicitly forbids the State from disrupting the traditional relation of the family—a relation as old and as fundamental as our entire civilization—surely does not show that the Government was meant to have the power to do so. Rather, as the Ninth Amendment expressly recognizes, there are fundamental personal rights such as this one, which are protected from abridgment by the Government though not specifically mentioned in the Constitution. . . .

The logic of the dissents would sanction federal or state legislation that seems to me even more plainly unconstitutional than the statute before us. Surely the Government, absent a showing of a compelling subordinating state interest, could not decree that all husbands and wives must be sterilized after two children have been born to them. Yet by their reasoning such an invasion of marital privacy would not be subject to constitutional challenge because, while it might be "silly," no provision of the Constitution specifically prevents the Government from curtailing the marital right to bear children and raise a family. While it may shock some of my Brethren that the Court today holds that the Constitution protects the right of marital privacy, in my view it is far more shocking to believe that the personal liberty guaranteed by the Constitution does not include protection against such totalitarian limitation of family size, which is at complete variance with our constitutional concepts. . . .

In a long series of cases this Court has held that where fundamental personal liberties are involved, they may not be abridged by the States simply on a showing that a regulatory statute has some rational relationship to the effectuation of a proper state purpose. "Where there is a significant encroachment upon personal liberty, the State may prevail only upon showing a subordinating interest which is compelling," *Bates v. City of Little Rock*, 361 U.S. 516 [(1960)]. . . .

Although the Connecticut birth-control law obviously encroaches upon a fundamental personal liberty, the State does not show that the law serves any "subordinating [state] interest which is compelling" or that it is "necessary . . . to the accomplishment of a permissible state policy." The State, at most, argues that there is some rational relation between this statute and what is admittedly a legitimate subject of state concern—the discouraging of extramarital relations. It says that preventing the use of birth-control devices by married persons helps prevent the indulgence by some in such extra-marital relations. The rationality of this justification is dubious, particularly in light of the admitted widespread availability to all persons in the State of Connecticut, unmarried as well as married, of birth-control devices for the prevention of disease, as distinguished from the prevention of conception. . . . But, in any event, it is clear that the state interest in safeguarding marital fidelity can be served by a more discriminately tailored statute, which does not, like the present one, sweep unnecessarily broadly, reaching far beyond the evil sought to be dealt with and intruding upon the privacy of all married couples. . . . The law must be shown "necessary, and not merely rationally related to, the accomplishment of a permissible state policy." . . .

In sum, I believe that the right of privacy in the marital relation is fundamental and basic—a personal right "retained by the people" within the meaning of the Ninth Amendment. Connecticut cannot constitutionally abridge this fundamental right, which is protected by the Fourteenth Amendment from infringement by the States. I agree with the Court that petitioners' convictions must therefore be reversed.

☐ *Justice HARLAN, concurring.*

I fully agree with the judgment of reversal, but find myself unable to join the Court's opinion. The reason is that it seems to me to evince an approach to this case very much like that taken by my Brothers BLACK and STEWART in dissent, namely: the Due Process Clause of the Fourteenth Amendment does not touch this Connecticut statute unless the enactment is found to violate some right assured by the letter or penumbra of the Bill of Rights.

In other words, what I find implicit in the Court's opinion is that the "incorporation" doctrine may be used to *restrict* the reach of Fourteenth Amendment Due Process. For me this is just as unacceptable constitutional doctrine as is the use of the "incorporation" approach to *impose* upon the States all the requirements of the Bill of Rights as found in the provisions of the first eight amendments and in the decisions of this Court interpreting them.

In my view, the proper constitutional inquiry in this case is whether this Connecticut statute infringes the Due Process Clause of the Fourteenth Amendment because the enactment violates basic values "implicit in the concept of ordered liberty," *Palko v. State of Connecticut*, 302 U.S. 319 [(1937)]. For reasons stated at length in my dissenting opinion in *Poe v. Ullman*, [367 U.S. 497 (1961)], I believe that it does. While the relevant inquiry may be aided by resort to one or more of the provisions of the Bill of Rights, it is not dependent on them or any of their radiations. The Due Process Clause of the Fourteenth Amendment stands, in my opinion, on its own bottom. . . .

While I could not more heartily agree that judicial "self restraint" is an indispensable ingredient of sound constitutional adjudication, I do submit that the formula suggested for achieving it is more hollow than real. "Specific" provisions of the Constitution, no less than "due process," lend themselves as readily to "personal" interpretations by judges whose constitutional outlook is simply to keep the Constitution in supposed "tune with the times." . . .

Judicial self-restraint will not, I suggest, be brought about in the "due process" area by the historically unfounded incorporation formula long advanced by my Brother BLACK, and now in part espoused by my Brother STEWART. It will be achieved in this area, as in other constitutional areas, only by continual insistence upon respect for the teachings of history, solid recognition of the basic values that underlie our society, and wise appreciation of the great roles that the doctrines of federalism and separation of powers have played in establishing and preserving American freedoms. . . . Adherence to these principles will not, of course, obviate all constitutional differences of opinion among judges, nor should it. Their continued recognition will, however, go farther toward keeping most judges from roaming at large in the constitutional field than will the interpolation into the Constitution of an artificial and largely illusory restriction on the content of the Due Process Clause.

☐ *Justice WHITE, concurring.*

In my view this Connecticut law as applied to married couples deprives them of "liberty" without due process of law as that concept is used in the Fourteenth Amendment. I therefore concur in the judgment of the Court reversing these convictions under Connecticut's aiding and abetting statute.

☐ *Justice BLACK, with whom Justice STEWART joins, dissenting.*

The Court talks about a constitutional "right of privacy" as though there is some constitutional provision or provisions forbidding any law ever to be passed which might abridge the "privacy" of individuals. But there is not. There are, of course, guarantees in certain specific constitutional provisions which are designed in part to protect privacy at certain times and places with respect to certain activities. Such, for example, is the Fourth Amendment's guarantee against "unreasonable searches and seizures." But I think it belittles that Amendment to talk about it as though it protects nothing but "privacy." . . .

One of the most effective ways of diluting or expanding a constitutionally guaranteed right is to substitute for the crucial word or words of a constitutional guarantee another word or words, more or less flexible and more or less restricted in meaning. This fact is well illustrated by the use of the term "right of privacy" as a comprehensive substitute for the Fourth Amendment's guarantee against "unreasonable searches and seizures." "Privacy" is a broad, abstract and ambiguous concept which can easily be shrunken in meaning but which can also, on the other hand, easily be interpreted as a constitutional ban against many things other than searches and seizures. I have expressed the view many times that First Amendment freedoms, for example, have suffered from a failure of the courts to stick to the simple language of the First Amendment in construing it, instead of invoking multitudes of words substituted for those the Framers used. For these reasons I get nowhere in this case by talk about a constitutional "right of privacy" as an emanation from one or more constitutional provisions. I like my privacy as well as the next one, but I am nevertheless compelled to admit that government has a right to invade it unless prohibited by some specific constitutional provision. For these reasons I cannot agree with the Court's judgment and the reasons it gives for holding this Connecticut law unconstitutional. . . .

I think that if properly construed neither the Due Process Clause nor the Ninth Amendment, nor both together, could under any circumstances be a proper basis for invalidating the Connecticut law. I discuss the due process and Ninth Amendment arguments together because on analysis they turn out to be the same thing—merely using different words to claim for this Court and the federal judiciary power to invalidate any legislative act which the judges find irrational, unreasonable or offensive.

The due process argument which my Brothers HARLAN and WHITE adopt here is based, as their opinions indicate, on the premise that this Court is vested with power to invalidate all state laws that it considers to be arbitrary, capricious, unreasonable, or oppressive, or this Court's belief that a particular state law under scrutiny has no "rational or justifying" purpose, or is offensive to a "sense of fairness and justice." If these formulas based on "natural justice," or others which mean the same thing, are to prevail, they require judges to determine what is or is not constitutional on the basis of their own appraisal of what laws are unwise or unnecessary. The power to make such decisions is of course that of a legislative body. . . . I do not believe that we are granted power by the Due Process Clause or any other constitutional provision or provisions to measure constitutionality by our belief that legislation is arbitrary, capricious or unreasonable, or accomplishes no justifiable purpose, or is offensive to our own notions of "civilized standards of conduct." Such an appraisal of the wisdom of legislation is an attribute of the power to make laws, not of the power to interpret them. . . .

My Brother GOLDBERG has adopted the recent discovery that the Ninth Amendment as well as the Due Process Clause can be used by this Court as authority to strike down all state legislation which this Court thinks violates "fundamental principles of liberty and justice," or is contrary to the "traditions and [collective] conscience of our people." He also states, without proof satisfactory to me, that in making decisions on this basis judges will not consider "their personal and private notions." One may ask how they can avoid considering them. Our Court certainly has no machinery with which to take a Gallup Poll. . . .

I realize that many good and able men have eloquently spoken and written, sometimes in rhapsodical strains, about the duty of this Court to keep the Constitution in tune with the times. The idea is that the Constitution must be changed from time to time and that this Court is charged with a duty to make those changes. For myself, I must with all deference reject that philosophy. The Constitution makers knew the need for change and provided for it. Amendments suggested by the people's elected representatives can be submitted to the people or their selected agents for ratification. That method of change was good for our Fathers, and being somewhat old-fashioned I must add it is good enough for me. And so, I cannot rely on the Due Process Clause or the Ninth Amendment or any mysterious and uncertain natural law concept as a reason for striking down this state law. The Due Process Clause with an "arbitrary and capricious" or "shocking to the conscience" formula was liberally used by this Court to strike down economic legislation in the early decades of this century, threatening, many people thought, the tranquility and stability of the Nation. See, e. g., *Lochner v. State of New York*, 198 U.S. 45 [(1905)]. That formula, based on subjective considerations of "natural justice," is no less dangerous when used to enforce this Court's views about personal rights than those about economic rights. I had thought that we had laid that formula, as a means for striking down state legislation, to rest once and for all in cases like *West Coast Hotel Co. v. Parrish*, [300 U.S. 379 (1937)], and many other opinions.

☐ *Justice STEWART, whom Justice BLACK joins, dissenting.*

Since 1879 Connecticut has had on its books a law which forbids the use of contraceptives by anyone. I think this is an uncommonly silly law. . . . But we are not asked in this case to say whether we think this law is unwise, or even asinine. We are asked to hold that it violates the United States Constitution. And that I cannot do.

In the course of its opinion the Court refers to no less than six Amendments to the Constitution: the First, the Third, the Fourth, the Fifth, the Ninth, and the Fourteenth. But the Court does not say which of these Amendments, if any, it thinks is infringed by this Connecticut law.

We *are* told that the Due Process Clause of the Fourteenth Amendment is not, as such, the "guide" in this case. With that much I agree. . . .

As to the First, Third, Fourth, and Fifth Amendments, I can find nothing in any of them to invalidate this Connecticut law, even assuming that all those Amendments are fully applicable against the States. . . .

[And] to say that the Ninth Amendment has anything to do with this case is to turn somersaults with history. The Ninth Amendment, like its companion the Tenth, which this Court held "states but a truism that all is retained which has not been surrendered," *United States v. Darby*, 312 U.S. 100 [(1941)], was framed by James Madison and adopted by the States simply to make clear that the adoption of the Bill of Rights did not alter the plan that the *Federal* Government was to be a government of express and limited powers, and that all rights and powers not delegated to it were retained. . . .

What provision of the Constitution, then, does make this state law invalid? The Court says it is the right of privacy "created by several fundamental constitutional guarantees." With all deference, I can find no such general right of privacy in the Bill of Rights, in any other part of the Constitution, or in any case ever before decided by this Court.

Duncan v. Louisiana

391 U.S. 145, 88 S.Ct. 1444 (1968)

Gary Duncan, a nineteen-year-old black man, was driving in Plaquemines Parish, Louisiana, a community in which racial tensions ran high and opposition to school desegregation remained heated in 1966. He saw four white boys confronting two of his younger cousins and stopped to pick his cousins up. At that point, there apparently was some sort of exchange in which Duncan "touched" or "slapped" the arm of one of the white boys, Herman Landry, and then drove away. The head of a private school, established in opposition to the desegregation of the local public schools, saw the incident and called the sheriff. Duncan was intercepted and questioned by a deputy sheriff, but allowed to leave. Three days later, he was arrested on a charge of cruelty to minors. Believing that the arrest was racial harassment, Duncan's parents sought help from the Lawyers' Constitutional Defense Committee (LCDC), an organization providing attorneys for civil rights litigation. While the LCDC was initially reluctant to take what appeared to be a minor case, further developments led to an important ruling by the Supreme Court.

At Duncan's preliminary hearing, his attorney Richard Sobol moved to quash the charge since Louisiana's law governing cruelty to minors applied only to those with parental control or responsibility over an abused minor (which clearly did not apply to Duncan). Before the judge ruled on that motion, however, Landry's parents signed an affidavit charging Duncan with assault and battery. Duncan was re-arrested and scheduled for another trial on the battery charge, which carried a maximum sentence of two years in prison. This time, Sobol asked the judge for a jury trial on the grounds that the Sixth Amendment provision for jury trials applied to the states and that jury trials were required whenever an accused faces a serious charge and the possibility of being sentenced to six months or more in jail. That request was denied by the trial judge. The basis was thus laid for a test case for determining whether the Sixth Amendment applied to the states. Duncan was convicted for battery, fined $150, and sentenced to sixty days in prison. Sobol appealed Duncan's conviction to the supreme court of Louisiana, which upheld the lower court, and then to the Supreme Court. The fundamental issue in this case, as Duncan's attorney told the Court, is "whether the Due Process Clause of the Fourteenth Amendment secures the right to trial by jury in state criminal cases."

The Court's decision was seven to two, with the majority's opinion announced by Justice White. Justice Black, joined by Justice Douglas and Justice Fortas, concurred. Justice Harlan dissented and was joined by Justice Stewart.

    ☐ *Justice WHITE delivered the opinion of the Court.*

The Fourteenth Amendment denies the States the power to "deprive any person of life, liberty, or property, without due process of law." In resolving conflicting claims concerning the meaning of this spacious language, the Court has looked increasingly to the Bill of Rights for guidance; many of the rights guaranteed by the first eight Amendments to the Constitution have been held to be protected against state action by the Due Process Clause of the Fourteenth Amendment. That clause now protects the right to compensation for property taken by the State; the rights of speech, press, and religion covered by the First Amendment; the Fourth Amendment rights to be free from unreasonable searches and seizures and to have excluded from criminal trials any evidence illegally seized; the right guaranteed by the Fifth Amendment to be free of compelled self-incrimination; and the Sixth Amendment rights to counsel, to a speedy and public trial, to confrontation of opposing witnesses, and to compulsory process for obtaining witnesses.

The test for determining whether a right extended by the Fifth and Sixth Amendments with respect to federal criminal proceedings is also protected against state action by the Fourteenth Amendment has been phrased in a variety of ways in the opinions of this Court. The question has been asked whether a right is among those " 'fundamental principles of liberty and justice which lie at the base of all our civil and political institutions' "; whether it is "basic in our system of jurisprudence"; and whether it is "a fundamental right, essential to a fair trial." . . . Because we believe that trial by jury in criminal cases is fundamental to the American scheme of justice, we hold that the Fourteenth Amendment guarantees a right of jury trial in all criminal cases which—were they to be tried in a federal court—would come within the Sixth Amendment's guarantee. . . .

We are aware of prior cases in this Court in which the prevailing opinion contains statements contrary to our holding today that the right to jury trial in serious criminal cases is a fundamental right and hence must be recognized by the States as part of their obligation to extend due process of law to all persons within their jurisdiction. . . . Respectfully, we reject the prior *dicta* regarding jury trial in criminal cases.

The guarantees of jury trial in the Federal and State Constitutions reflect a profound judgment about the way in which law should be enforced and justice administered. A right to jury trial is granted to criminal defendants in order to prevent oppression by the Government. Those who wrote our constitutions knew from history and experience that it was necessary to protect against unfounded criminal charges brought to eliminate enemies and against judges too responsive to the voice of higher authority. The framers of the constitutions strove to create an independent judiciary but insisted upon further protection against arbitrary action. Providing an accused with the right to be tried by a jury of his peers gave him an inestimable safeguard against the corrupt or overzealous prosecutor and against the compliant, biased, or eccentric judge. If the defendant preferred the common-sense judgment of a jury to the more tutored but perhaps less sympathetic reaction of the single judge, he was to have it. Beyond this, the jury trial provisions in the Federal and State Constitutions reflect a fundamental decision about the exercise of official power—a reluctance to entrust plenary powers over the life and liberty of the citizen to one judge or to a group of judges. Fear of unchecked power, so typical of our State and Federal Governments in other respects, found expression in the criminal law in this insistence upon community participation in the determination of guilt or innocence. The deep commitment of the Nation to the right of jury trial in serious criminal cases as a defense against arbitrary law enforcement qualifies for protection under the Due Process Clause of the Fourteenth Amendment, and must therefore be respected by the States. . . .

Louisiana's final contention is that even if it must grant jury trials in serious criminal cases, the conviction before us is valid and constitutional because here the petitioner was tried for simple battery and was sentenced to only 60 days in the parish prison. We are not persuaded. It is doubtless true that there is a category of petty crimes or offenses which is not subject to the Sixth Amendment jury trial provision and should not be subject to the Fourteenth Amendment jury trial requirement here applied to the States. Crimes carrying possible penalties up to six months do not require a jury trial if they otherwise qualify as petty offenses. But the penalty authorized for a particular crime is of major relevance in determining whether it is serious or not and may in itself, if severe enough, subject the trial to the mandates of the Sixth Amendment. . . .

We need not, however, settle in this case the exact location of the line between petty offenses and serious crimes. It is sufficient for our purposes to hold that a crime punishable by two years in prison is, based on past and contemporary standards in this country, a serious crime and not a petty offense.

> *Justice BLACK, with whom Justice DOUGLAS joins, concurring.*

With this holding I agree for reasons given by the Court. I also agree because of reasons given in my dissent in *Adamson v. People of State of California* [322 U.S. 46 (1947)]. In that dissent I took the position that the Fourteenth Amendment made all of the provisions of the Bill of Rights applicable to the States. And I am very happy to support this selective process through which our Court has since the *Adamson* case held most of the specific Bill of Rights' protections applicable to the States to the same extent they are applicable to the Federal Government. Among these are the right to trial by jury decided today, the right against compelled self-incrimination, the right to counsel, the right to compulsory process for witnesses, the right to confront witnesses, the right to a speedy and public trial, and the right to be free from unreasonable searches and seizures. . . .

I want to emphasize that I believe as strongly as ever that the Fourteenth Amendment was intended to make the Bill of Rights applicable to the States. I have been willing to support the selective incorporation doctrine, however, as an alternative, although perhaps less historically supportable than complete incorporation. The selective incorporation process, if used properly, does limit the Supreme Court in the Fourteenth Amendment field to specific Bill of Rights' protections only and keeps judges from roaming at will in their own notions of what policies outside the Bill of Rights are desirable and what are not. And, most importantly for me, the selective incorporation process has the virtue of having already worked to make most of the Bill of Rights' protections applicable to the States. . . .

> *Justice HARLAN whom Justice STEWART joins, dissenting.*

The question in this case is whether the State of Louisiana, which provides trial by jury for all felonies, is prohibited by the Constitution from trying charges of simple battery to the court alone. In my view, the answer to that question, mandated alike by our constitutional history and by the longer history of trial by jury, is clearly "no." . . .

I have raised my voice many times before against the Court's continuing undiscriminating insistence upon fastening on the States federal notions of criminal justice, and I must do so again in this instance. With all respect, the Court's approach and its reading of history are altogether topsy-turvy.

I believe I am correct in saying that every member of the Court for at least the last 135 years has agreed that our Founders did not consider the requirements of the Bill of Rights so fundamental that they should operate directly against the States. They were wont to believe rather that the security of liberty in America rested primarily upon the dispersion of governmental power across a federal system. The Bill of Rights was considered unnecessary by some but insisted upon by others in order to curb the possibility of abuse of power by the strong central government they were creating.

The Civil War Amendments dramatically altered the relation of the Federal Government to the States. The first section of the Fourteenth Amendment imposes highly significant restrictions on state action. But the restrictions are couched in very broad and general terms: citizenship; privileges and immunities; due process of law; equal protection of the laws. . . . The question has been, Where does the Court properly look to find the specific rules that define and give content to such terms as "life, liberty, or property" and "due process of law"?

A few members of the Court have taken the position that the intention of those who drafted the first section of the Fourteenth Amendment was simply, and exclusively, to make the provisions of the first eight Amendments applicable to state action. This view has never been accepted by this Court. In my view, often expressed elsewhere, the first section of the Fourteenth Amendment was meant neither to incorporate nor to be limited to, the specific guarantees of the first eight Amendments. The overwhelming historical evidence demonstrates, to me conclusively, that the Congressmen and state legislators who wrote debated, and ratified the Fourteenth Amendment did not think they were "incorporating" the Bill of Rights.

Although I therefore fundamentally disagree with the total incorporation view of the Fourteenth Amendment, it seems to me that such a position does at least have the virtue, lacking in the Court's selective incorporation approach of internal consistency: we look to the Bill of Rights, word for word, clause for clause, precedent for precedent because it is said, the men who wrote the Amendment wanted it that way. . . .

Apart from the approach taken by the absolute incorporationists, I can see only one method of analysis that has an internal logic. That is to start with the words "liberty" and "due process of law" and attempt to define them in a way that accords with American traditions and our system of government. This approach, involving a much more discriminating process of adjudication than does "incorporation," is, albeit difficult, the one that was followed through out the 19th and most of the present century. It entails a "gradual progress of judicial inclusion and exclusion," seeking, with due recognition of constitutional tolerance for state experimentation and disparity, to ascertain those "immutable principles . . . of justice which inhere in the very idea of free government which no member of the Union may disregard." . . .

The relationship of the Bill of Rights to this "gradual process" seems to me to be twofold. In the first place it has long been clear that the Due Process Clause imposes some restrictions on state action that parallel Bill of Rights restrictions on federal action. Second, and more important than this accidental overlap, is the fact that the Bill of Rights is evidence, at various points, of the content Americans find in the term "liberty" and of American standards of fundamental fairness. . . .

Today's Court still remains unwilling to accept the total incorporationists' view of the history of the Fourteenth Amendment. This, if accepted, would afford a cogent reason for applying the Sixth Amendment to the States. The Court is also, apparently, unwilling to face the task of determining whether denial of trial by jury in the situation before us, or in other situations, is fundamentally unfair. Consequently, the Court has compromised on the ease of the incorporationist position, without its internal logic. It has simply assumed that the question before us is whether the Jury Trial Clause of the Sixth Amendment should be incorporated into the Fourteenth, jot-for-jot and case-for-case, or ignored. Then the Court merely declares that the clause in question is "in" rather than "out."

The Court has justified neither its starting place nor its conclusion. If the problem is to discover and articulate the rules of fundamental fairness in criminal proceedings, there is no reason to assume that the whole body of rules developed in this Court constituting Sixth Amendment jury trial must be regarded as a unit. The requirement of trial by jury in federal criminal cases has given rise to numerous subsidiary questions respecting the exact scope and content of the right. It surely cannot be that every answer the Court has given, or will give, to such a question is attributable to the Founders; or even that every rule announced carries equal conviction of this Court; still less can it be that every such subprinciple is equally fundamental to ordered liberty.

Examples abound. I should suppose it obviously fundamental to fairness that a "jury" means an "impartial jury." I should think it equally obvious that the rule, imposed long ago in the federal courts, that "jury" means "jury of exactly twelve," is not fundamental to anything: there is no significance except to mystics in the number 12. Again, trial by jury has been held to require a unanimous verdict of jurors in the federal courts, although unanimity has not been found essential to liberty in Britain, where the requirement has been abandoned. . . .

The argument that jury trial is not a requisite of due process is quite simple. The central proposition of *Palko* [*v. Connecticut*, 302 U.S. 319 (1937)], . . . is that "due process of law" requires only that criminal trials be fundamentally fair. As stated above, apart from the theory that it was historically intended as a mere shorthand for the Bill of Rights, I do not see what else "due process of law" can intelligibly be thought to mean. If due process of law requires only fundamental fairness, then the inquiry in each case must be whether a state trial process was a fair one. The Court has held, properly I think, that in an adversary process it is a requisite of fairness, for which there is no adequate substitute, that a criminal defendant be afforded a right to counsel and to cross-examine opposing witnesses. But it simply has not been demonstrated, nor, I think, can it be demonstrated, that trial by jury is the only fair means of resolving issues of fact. . . .

In sum, there is a wide range of views on the desirability of trial by jury, and on the ways to make it most effective when it is used; there is also considerable variation from State to State in local conditions such as the size of the criminal caseload, the ease or difficulty of summoning jurors, and other trial conditions bearing on fairness. We have before us, therefore, an almost perfect example of a situation in which the celebrated *dictum* of Justice BRANDEIS should be invoked. It is, he said, "one of the happy incidents of the federal system that a single courageous state may, if its citizens choose, serve as a laboratory. . . ." *New State Ice Co. v. Liebmann*, 285 U.S. 262 [(1932)]. This Court, other courts, and the political process are available to correct any experiments in criminal procedure that prove fundamentally unfair to defendants. That is not what is being done today: instead, and quite without reason, the Court has chosen to impose upon every State one means of trying criminal cases; it is a good means, but it is not the only fair means, and it is not demonstrably better than the alternatives States might devise.

I would affirm the judgment of the Supreme Court of Louisiana.

■ CONSTITUTIONAL HISTORY

The Second and Third Amendments

The Second and Third Amendments register the concerns of the revolutionary period during which state militias defeated the British and there was vehement opposition to the British practice of quartering troops in private homes. The Second Amendment states: "A well regulated Militia being necessary to the security of a free State, the right of the people to keep and bear Arms shall not be infringed." The Third Amendment provides that "No Soldier shall, in time of peace be quartered in any house, without the consent of the Owner, nor in time of war, but in a manner to be prescribed by law."

The guarantees of both amendments were part of some state constitutions and bills of rights, prior to the ratification of the Bill of Rights. Pennsylvania's Constitution of 1776, for example, provided in Article 13 of its Declaration of Rights "[t]hat the people have a right to bear arms for the defense of themselves and the state; and as standing armies in the time of peace are dangerous to liberty, they ought not to be kept up; And that the military should be kept under strict subordination to, and governed by, the civil power." Delaware's Declaration of Rights and Fundamental Rules of 1776 provided "[t]hat no Soldier ought to be quartered in any House in Time of Peace without the Consent of the Owner; and in Time of War in such Manner only as the Legislature shall direct."

Although the controversy over the right to bear arms has intensified in recent decades, neither amendment has been interpreted to limit state regulations; see *Presser v. Illinois*, 116 U.S. 252 (1886). Nor has the Supreme Court dealt extensively with either amendment. Indeed, the Third Amendment has only been cited in support of a constitutional right of privacy, in cases such as *Griswold v. Connecticut* (1965) (excerpted in this chapter and further discussed in Chapter 11).

The principal decision, *United States v. Miller*, 307 U.S. 174 (1939), construing the Second Amendment upheld a congressional statute, the National Firearms Act of 1934, requiring the registration of sawed-off shotguns. There, the Court reviewed the constitutional provisions pertaining to militias and observed: "With the obvious purpose to assure the continuation and render possible the effectiveness of such forces the declaration and guarantee of the Second Amendment were made. It must be interpreted and applied with that end in view." On that basis the Court concluded: "In the absence of any evidence tending to show that possession or use of a 'shotgun having a barrel of less than 18 inches in length' at this time has some reasonable relationship to the preservation or efficiency of a well regulated militia, we cannot say that the Second Amendment guarantees the right to keep and bear such an instrument. Certainly it is not within judicial notice that this weapon is any part of the ordinary military equipment or that its use could contribute to the common defense."

B | *The Rise and (Partial) Retreat of the "Due Process Revolution"*

The due process revolution forged during the Warren Court years by extending the major guarantees of the Bill of Rights to the states took on a life of its own. In the early 1970s, the Burger Court continued to expand the protection of the due process clause to require trial-type hearings prior to the infringement of individuals' rights and entitlements. Notably, in *Goldberg v. Kelly*, 397 U.S. 254 (1970), the Court held that the due process clause of the Fourteenth Amendment requires a trial-type hearing for recipients of Aid to Families with Dependent Children (AFDC) prior to the termination of their benefits under the AFDC program.

The Court subsequently extended due process-based requirements in *Wisconsin v. Constantineau*, 400 U.S. 208 (1971), for the public posting of the names of people deemed unfit to consume alcoholic beverages; *Richardson v. Wright*, 405 U.S. 208 (1972), requiring the opportunity to offer oral evidence and to cross-examine witnesses in a hearing before the termination of disability benefits; *Morrissey v. Brewer*, 408 U.S. 471 (1972), requiring a hearing before the revocation of parole; *Gibson v.*

Berryhill, 411 U.S. 609 (1973), requiring an impartial hearing by officers on a state optometry board; *Weinberger v. Hynson, Westcott & Dunning, Inc.*, 412 U.S. 609 (1973), requiring a hearing prior to the Food and Drug Administration's withdrawal of new drug applications; and *Arnett v. Kennedy*, 416 U.S. 134 (1974), holding that federal employees must be accorded minimal procedural guarantees as afforded by federal law before having their employment terminated.

In Justice William O. Douglas's last term after more than thirty-six years on the bench, a bare majority of the Court signaled that the due process revolution was coming to an end in *Goss v. Lopez*, 419 U.S. 565 (1975). There President Nixon's four appointees—Chief Justice Burger and Justices Blackmun, Powell, and Rehnquist—dissented from the majority's view that due process requires a conversation, and not a hearing, prior to the temporary suspension of students from school and that they must receive at least notice of the charges against them, an explanation of the evidence authorities have, and an opportunity to tell their side of the story. In Justice Byron White's words for the majority:

> Even truncated trial-type procedures might well overwhelm administrative facilities in many places and, in diverting resources, cost more than it would save in educational effectiveness. Moreover, further formalizing the suspension process and escalating its formality and adversary nature may not only make it too costly as a regular disciplinary tool but also destroy its effectiveness as part of the teaching process. On the other hand, requiring effective notice and informal hearing permitting the student to give his version of the events will provide a meaningful hedge against erroneous action.

The Burger Court's rulings on the substantive and procedural rights of individuals committed to mental institutions further illustrate its movement away from an expansive reading of the constitutional protection afforded by the due process clause. Along with *Goss v. Lopez* in 1975, the Burger Court held, in *O'Connor v. Donaldson*, 422 U.S. 563 (1975), that individuals who are not dangerous to others may not be confined in institutions against their will, if they can survive outside with the aid of relatives or friends and are not receiving special therapy. At the same time, the Court refused to embrace a constitutional "right to treatment." Kenneth Donaldson was confined to the Florida State Hospital, following commitment proceedings initiated by his father who said that he suffered from delusions. For almost fifteen years, Donaldson repeatedly requested to be released, claiming that he was not receiving any special treatment justifying his confinement and that he could survive outside the institution with the help of friends and relatives. But, the hospital superintendent, Dr. J. B. O'Connor, denied his release. Finally,

Donaldson filed a lawsuit charging that O'Connor was depriving him of his constitutional right to liberty under the Fourteenth Amendment. Following a trial, a jury agreed and awarded damages. O'Connor appealed, but the Court of Appeals for the Fifth Circuit affirmed, holding that Donaldson had "a constitutional right to receive such individual treatment as will give him a reasonable opportunity to be cured or to improve his mental health." O'Connor then made a further appeal to the Supreme Court.

Although declining to read a substantive "right to treatment" into the Fourteenth Amendment due process clause in *O'Connor v. Donaldson*, Justice Potter Stewart ruled that "a State cannot constitutionally confine without more a nondangerous individual who is capable of surviving safely in freedom by himself or with the help of willing and responsible family members or friends."

Subsequently, the Burger Court held that due process requires a standard of proof in civil commitment proceedings greater than the "preponderance of the evidence" standard used in other civil proceedings, but less rigorous than the "beyond a reasonable doubt" standard used in criminal cases. *Addington v. Texas*, 441 U.S. 418 (1979), created a new (middle level) standard requiring clear and convincing evidence to justify an individual's involuntary hospitalization. In cases involving the commitment of children to mental health institutions, the Court also held that a commitment hearing before a "neutral fact finder" (who, however, need not be legally trained) is required under the due process clause.[1] Notice, a hearing, and the opportunity to call and cross-examine witnesses before a neutral fact finder are also required before inmates in a state prison may be transferred to a mental institution.[2] Moreover, *Youngberg v. Romeo*, 457 U.S. 307 (1982), held that mentally retarded individuals still enjoy certain constitutionally protected liberty interests. In *Youngberg*, the Court unanimously ruled that individuals confined to state mental institutions may assert under the Fourteenth Amendment due process clause "constitutionally protected interests in the conditions of reasonable care and safety, reasonably nonrestrictive confinement conditions, and such training as may be required by these interests." Thus while *O'Connor v. Donaldson* declined to embrace a broad right to treatment under the due process clause, the Court nevertheless held that individuals have some constitutionally protected procedural and substantive liberty interests in commitment proceedings and in the conditions of their hospitalization.

With the Senate's confirmation of Justice Douglas's successor, Justice John Paul Stevens, the Court took a more restrictive, less expansive view of what process is due under the due process clause. In *Mathews v. Eldridge*, 424 U.S. 319 (1976), the Court held that an evidentiary hearing is not required prior to the termination of disability benefits. In a number of other cases, the Court denied claims to procedural guarantees under the due process clause: *Meachum v. Fano*, 427 U.S. 215 (1976), rejected a due process argument for a hearing prior to the transfer of a prisoner from one prison to another. *Bishop v. Wood*, 426 U.S. 341 (1976), approved the dismissal of a city police officer without a pretermination hearing. *Codd v. Velger*, 429 U.S. 624 (1977), held that a hearing need not be held for the dismissal of policemen who challenged materials placed in their files as damaging. *Dixon v. Love*, 431 U.S. 105 (1977), upheld Illinois's summary revocation of drivers' licenses for repeated traffic violations, holding that *Elridge* does not require a pretermination hearing. And in *Ingraham v. Wright*, 430 U.S. 651 (1977), the justices split five to four when holding that no hearing is necessary prior to the "paddling" of students in public schools. In *Board of Curators of University of Missouri v. Horowitz*, 435 U.S. 78 (1978), a bare majority of the Court affirmed that the dismissal of a medical student did not require an elaborate procedural hearing before the school's decision-making body. *Greenholtz v. Inmates*, 442 U.S. 1 (1979), ruled that an oral hearing for parole decisions was not needed and that a parole board could rely simply on the files on an inmate. *Barry v. Barchi*, 443 U.S. 55 (1979), upheld the summary dismissal of harness racing trainers.

The Burger Court, however, upheld claims for procedural due process in a few cases. In *Memphis Light, Gas & Water Division v. Craft*, 436 U.S. 1 (1978), for example, the Court held that the due process clause requires public utilities to establish an administrative procedure for hearing complaints before disconnecting gas, water, and electric services. And *Vitek v. Jones*, 445 U.S. 480 (1980), ruled that a hearing was required before the transfer of prisoners to state mental health institutions for involuntary commitment. *Cleveland Board of Education v. Loudermill*, 470 U.S. 532 (1985), also held that in the dismissal of an employee for cause the state must afford a hearing on the charges during the pretermination process.

The Burger and Rehnquist Courts, nevertheless, have tended to cut back on further readings of substantive rights into the due process clause. The due process clause has been interpreted only to prevent government "from abusing [its] power, or employing it as an instrument of oppression."[3]

As Chief Justice Rehnquist explains, in *DeShaney v. Winnebago County Department of Social Services*, 489 U.S. 189 (1989), "the Due Process Clauses generally confer no affirmative right to governmental aid, even where such aid may be necessary to secure life, liberty, or property interests of which the government itself may not deprive the individual." In *DeShaney* (with Justices Brennan, Blackmun, and Marshall dissenting) the Court held that

> [i]n the substantive due process analysis, it is the State's affirmative act of restraining the individual's freedom to act on his own behalf—through incarceration, institutionalization, or other similar restraint of personal liberty—which is the "deprivation of liberty" triggering the protections of the Due Process Clause, not its failure to act to protect his liberty interests against harms inflicted by other means.

In that case, Chief Justice Rehnquist rejected the claim of Melody DeShaney that welfare workers were liable for the repeated beatings by the natural father of her son, Joshua, which left the four-year-old boy brain damaged. As Chief Justice Rehnquist observed,

> [T]he harms Joshua suffered did not occur while he was in the State's custody, but while he was in the custody of his natural father, who was in no sense a state actor. While the State may have been aware of the dangers that Joshua faced in the free world, it played no part in their creation, nor did it do anything to render him any more vulnerable to them. That the State once took temporary custody of Joshua does not alter the analysis, for when it returned him to his father's custody, it placed him in no worse position than that in which he would have been had it not acted at all; the State does not become the permanent guarantor of an individual's safety by having once offered him shelter. Under these circumstances, the State had no constitutional duty to protect Joshua. . . .

> The people of Wisconsin may well prefer a system of liability which would place upon the State and its officials the responsibility for failure to act in situations such as the present one. They may create such a system, if they do not have it already, by changing the tort law of the State in accordance with the regular law-making process. But they should not have it thrust upon them by this Court's expansion of the Due Process Clause of the Fourteenth Amendment.

In another decision handed down in 1989, *Michael H. v. Gerald D.*, 491 U.S. 110 (1989), the Rehnquist Court split five to four in rejecting the substantive due process argument that the natural (unwed) father of the child of a married woman had a right to file to establish paternity and for visitation rights. Under California law, which the majority upheld, the legal husband of a married woman who bears a child is presumptively the legal father. Writing for a bare majority, Justice Antonin Scalia explained that

[i]n an attempt to limit and guide interpretation of the [Due Process] Clause, we have insisted not merely that the interest denominated as a "liberty" be "fundamental" (a concept that, in isolation, is hard to objectify), but also that it be an interest traditionally protected by our society. As we have put it, the Due Process Clause affords only those protections "so rooted in the traditions and conscience of our people as to be ranked as fundamental." *Snyder v. Massachusetts*, 291 U.S. 97 (1934). Our cases reflect "continual insistence upon respect for the teachings of history [and] solid recognition of the basic values that underlie our society. . . ." [Quoting *Griswold v. Connecticut.*]

[T]he legal issue in the present case reduces to whether the relationship between persons in the situation of Michael and Victoria has been treated as a protected family unit under the historic practices of our society, or whether on any other basis it has been accorded special protection. We think it impossible to find that it has. In fact, quite to the contrary, our traditions have protected the marital family. . . .

The presumption of legitimacy was a fundamental principle of the common law. . . .

[W]hat is at issue here is not entitlement to a state pronouncement that Victoria was begotten by Michael. It is no conceivable denial of constitutional right for a State to decline to declare facts unless some legal consequence hinges upon the requested declaration. What Michael asserts here is a right to have himself declared the natural father *and thereby to obtain parental prerogatives.* What he must establish, therefore, is not that our society has traditionally allowed a natural father in his circumstances to establish paternity, but that it has traditionally accorded such a father parental rights, or at least has not traditionally denied them. Even if the law in all States had always been that the entire world could challenge the marital presumption and obtain a declaration as to who was the natural father, that would not advance Michael's claim. Thus, it is ultimately irrelevant, even for purposes of determining *current* social attitudes towards the alleged substantive right Michael asserts, that the present law in a number of States appears to allow the natural father—including the natural father who has not established a relationship with the child—the theoretical power to rebut the marital presumption.

By contrast, dissenting Justice Brennan argued that

> it would be comforting to believe that a search for "tradition" involves nothing more idiosyncratic or complicated than poring through dusty volumes on American history. . . . "What the deeply rooted traditions of the country are is arguable." Indeed, wherever I would begin to look for an interest "deeply rooted in the country's traditions," one thing is certain: I would not stop (as does the plu-

rality) at Bracton, or Blackstone, or Kent, or even the American Law Reports in conducting my search. Because reasonable people can disagree about the content of particular traditions, and because they can disagree even about which traditions are relevant to the definition of "liberty," the plurality has not found the objective boundary that it seeks.

Even if we could agree, moreover, on the content and significance of particular traditions, we still would be forced to identify the point at which a tradition becomes firm enough to be relevant to our definition of liberty and the moment at which it becomes too obsolete to be relevant any longer. The plurality supplies no objective means by which we might make these determinations. Indeed, as soon as the plurality sees signs that the tradition upon which it bases its decision (the laws denying putative fathers like Michael standing to assert paternity) is crumbling, it shifts ground and says that the case has nothing to do with that tradition, after all. "What is at issue here," the plurality asserts after canvassing the law on paternity suits, "is not entitlement to a state pronouncement that Victoria was begotten by Michael." But that is precisely what is at issue here, and the plurality's last-minute denial of this fact dramatically illustrates the subjectivity of its own analysis.

It is ironic that an approach so utterly dependent on tradition is so indifferent to our precedents. Citing barely a handful of this Court's numerous decisions defining the scope of the liberty protected by the Due Process Clause to support its reliance on tradition, the plurality acts as though English legal treatises and the American Law Reports always have provided the sole source for our constitutional principles. They have not. Just as common-law notions no longer define the "property" that the Constitution protects, see *Goldberg v. Kelly*, 397, U.S. 254 [(1970)], neither do they circumscribe the "liberty" that it guarantees. On the contrary, " '[l]iberty' and 'property' are broad and majestic terms. . . ."

The plurality's interpretive method is more than novel; it is misguided. It ignores the good reasons for limiting the role of "tradition" in interpreting the Constitution's deliberately capacious language. In the plurality's constitutional universe, we may not take notice of the fact that the original reasons for the conclusive presumption of paternity are out of place in a world in which blood tests can prove virtually beyond a shadow of a doubt who sired a particular child and in which the fact of illegitimacy no longer plays the burdensome and stigmatizing role it once did. Nor, in the plurality's world, may we deny "tradition" its full scope by pointing out that the rationale for the conventional rule has changed over the years; instead, our task is simply to identify a rule denying the asserted interest and not to ask whether the basis for that rule— which is the true reflection of the values undergirding it—has changed too often or too recently to call the rule embodying that rationale a "tradition." Moreover, by describing the decisive question as whether Michael and Victoria's interest is one that has been "traditionally *protected by* our society," (emphasis added), rather than one that society traditionally has thought important (with or without protecting it), and by suggesting that our sole function is to "*discern* the society's views" (emphasis added), the plurality acts as if the only purpose of the Due Process Clause is to confirm the importance of interests already protected by a majority of the States. Transforming the protection afforded by the Due Process Clause into a redundancy mocks those who, with care and purpose, wrote the Fourteenth Amendment.

In construing the Fourteenth Amendment to offer shelter only to those interests specifically protected by historical practice, moreover, the plurality ignores the kind of society in which our Constitution exists. We are not an assimilative, homogeneous society, but a facilitative, pluralistic one, in which we must be willing to abide someone else's unfamiliar or even repellant practice because the same tolerant impulse protects our own idiosyncracies. Even if we can agree, therefore, that "family" and "parenthood" are part of the good life, it is absurd to assume that we can agree on the content of those terms and destructive to pretend that we do. In a community such as ours, "liberty" must include the freedom not to conform. The plurality today squashes this freedom by requiring specific approval from history before protecting anything in the name of liberty.

The document that the plurality construes today is unfamiliar to me. It is not the living charter that I have taken to be our Constitution; it is instead a stagnant, archaic, hidebound document steeped in the prejudices and superstitions of a time long past. *This* Constitution does not recognize that times change, does not see that sometimes a practice or rule outlives its foundations. I cannot accept an interpretive method that does such violence to the charter that I am bound by oath to uphold.

The question before us . . . is whether California has an interest so powerful that it justifies granting Michael *no* hearing before terminating his parental rights. . . .

Make no mistake: to say that the State must provide Michael with a hearing to prove his paternity is not to express any opinion of the ultimate state of affairs between Michael and Victoria and Carole and Gerald. In order to change the current situation among these people, Michael first must convince a court that he is Victoria's father, and even if he is able to do this, he will be denied visitation rights if that would be in Victoria's best interests. It is elementary that a determination that a State must afford procedures before it terminates a given right is not a prediction about the end result of those procedures.

In a separate dissenting opinion, Justice White observed,

California plainly denies Michael [due process] protection, by refusing him the opportunity to rebut the State's presumption that the mother's husband is the father of the child. California law not only deprives Michael H. of a legal parent-child relationship with his daughter Victoria but even denies him the opportunity to introduce blood-test evidence to rebut the demonstrable fiction that Gerald is Victoria's father. . . .

"The emphasis of the Due Process Clause is on 'process.' " *Moore v. East Cleveland*, 431 U.S. 494 (1977) (WHITE, J., dissenting). I fail to see the fairness in the process established by the State of California and endorsed by the Court today. Michael H. has evidence which demonstrates that he is the father of young Victoria. Yet he is blocked by the State from presenting that evidence to a court. As a result, he is foreclosed from establishing his paternity and is ultimately precluded, by the State, from developing a relationship with his child. "A fundamental requirement of due process is 'the opportunity to be heard.' *Grannis v. Ordean*, 234 U.S. 385 (1914). It is an opportunity which must be granted at a meaningful time and in a meaningful manner." *Armstrong v. Manzo*, 380 U.S. 545 (1965). I fail to see how appellant was granted any meaningful opportunity to be heard when he was precluded at the very outset from introducing evidence which would support his assertion of paternity. Michael H. has never been afforded an opportunity to present his case in any meaningful manner.

In addition, in *Washington v. Harper*, 494 U.S. 210 (1990), the Rehnquist Court held that mentally ill prison inmates may be treated with antipsychotic drugs against their will and without a prior judicial proceeding. In his opinion for the Court, Justice Kennedy held that such treatment does not violate substantive due process where the prisoner is deemed to be dangerous to himself or others and the treatment is in the prisoner's medical interest. Justice Kennedy also held that the due process clause does not require a judicial hearing prior to such treatment of prisoners. The requirements of "procedural due process," according to Justice Kennedy, are satisfied by prison policies requiring administrative panels, composed of corrections officials and medical professionals, to review decisions to treat prisoners with antipsychotic drugs. Justice Stevens, joined by Justices Brennan and Marshall, dissented.

However, in *Foucha v. Louisiana*, 504 U.S. 71 (1992) Justice White sharply divided the Court when commanding a bare majority for asserting substantive and procedural due process protection under the Fourteenth Amendment. There, he struck down Louisiana's law permitting the continued institutionalization of an individual who was criminally acquitted by reason of insanity and who subsequently regained his sanity but was still deemed to pose a threat to society. Chief Justice Rehnquist and Justice Scalia joined a bitter dissent written by Justice Thomas denouncing the majority's due process analysis, while Justice Kennedy dissented separately. However, in *Kansas v. Hendricks*, 521 U.S. 346 (1997) (see THE DEVELOPMENT OF LAW box in this section), writing for a bare majority, Justice Thomas rejected a substantive due process challenge to Kansas's 1994 law for institutionalizing sexual predators after they have served their prison time.

Notably, a bare majority of the Court revived economic substantive due process in holding that large punitive damages awards that are "grossly excessive" violate the Fourteenth Amendment in *BMW of North America v. Gore* (1996) (excerpted below); see also the other cases summarized in THE DEVELOPMENT OF LAW box in this section.

Finally, the Court underscored the continuing viability of and controversy over substantive due process in *County of Sacramento v. Lewis* (1998) (excerpted below). Although rejecting the specific claim presented, the Court did not entirely rule out substantive due process protection for innocent people injured by police action. Writing for the Court and drawing on the test first put forth in *Rochin v. California* (1952) (excerpted in Section A of this chapter), Justice Souter held that police who cause accidents that kill innocent bystanders during high-speed pursuit of criminal suspects are not liable unless their actions "shock the conscience." In his words, "Only a purpose to cause harm unrelated to the legitimate object of arrest will satisfy the element of arbitrary conduct shocking to the conscience, necessary for a due process violation." Notably, Chief Justice Rehnquist and Justices Breyer, Stevens, Kennedy, and Scalia each filed concurring opinions; the last justice, in particular, sharply disagreeing with Justice Souter's substantive due process analysis.

NOTES

1. See *Parham v. J. R.*, 442 U.S. 584 (1979).

2. See *Vitek v. Jones*, 445 U.S. 480 (1980).

3. *Davidson v. Cannon*, 474 U.S. 344 (1986). See also *Parratt v. Taylor*, 451 U.S. 527 (1981).

SELECTED BIBLIOGRAPHY

Keynes, Edward. *Liberty, Property, and Privacy: Toward a Jurisprudence of Substantive Due Process.* University Park: Pennsylvania State University Press, 1996.

Orth, John, V. *Due Process of Law: A Brief History.* University Press of Kansas, 2003.

Pennock, J. Roland, and Chapman, John, eds. *Due Process.* New York: New York University Press, 1977.

Strong, Frank. *Substantive Due Process of Law: A Dichotomy of Sense and Nonsense.* Durham, NC: Carolina Academic Press, 1986.

Sunstein, Cass; Hastie, Reid; Payne, John; Schkade, David; and Viscusi, W. Kip. *Punitive Damages: How Juries Decide.* Chicago: University of Chicago Press, 2002.

■ THE DEVELOPMENT OF LAW

Other Recent Rulings on Substantive and Procedural Due Process

CASE	VOTE	RULING
Sigert v. Gilley, 500 U.S. 226 (1991)	6:3	Reaffirmed the holding in *Paul v. Davis*, 424 U.S. 693 (1976), that injury to a person's reputa-

tion is neither a liberty interest protected by the due process clauses nor the constitutional right of privacy. Justices Blackmun, Marshall, and Stevens dissented.

Pacific Mutual Life Insurance Company v. Haslip, 499 U.S. 1 (1991)	8:1	Rejected a Fourteenth Amendment substantive due process challenge to the common law method for assessing punitive

damages against corporations for the fraudulent activities of their employees. Justice O'Connor dissented.

Foucha v. Louisiana, 504 U.S. 71 (1992)	5:4	Writing for the Court, Justice White struck down Louisiana's law permitting the continued in-

stitutionalization of an individual who was criminally acquitted by reason of insanity and who subsequently regained his sanity, but was still deemed to pose a threat to society. Chief Justice Rehnquist and Justices Kennedy, Scalia, and Thomas dissented.

Collins v. Harker Heights, 503 U.S. 115 (1992)	9:0	Unanimously rejected the claims of a city's sanitation worker's survivors that the Fourteenth

Amendment embraces the right of workers to be free from "unreasonable risk of harm."

Reno v. FlFs, 507 U.S. 292 (1993)	7:2	Rejected a substantive due process challenge to the Immigration and Naturalization Ser-

vice's policy of placing children entering the country illegally in detention centers, and releasing them only to parents or close relatives, pending their deportation hearings.

TXO Production Corporation v. Alliance Resources Corporation, 509 U.S. 443 (1993)	6:3	For the third time in five years, the Court revisited the issue of whether large punitive damage awards violate due process. At

issue was a jury's punitive damage award, along with $19,000 in actual dam-

CASE	VOTE	RULING

ages, to Alliance Resources, after the company countersued TXO Production Corporation for filing suit against it in order to force Alliance Resources to sell mineral rights to TXO. A jury found that TXO's initial suit was frivolous and awarded $10 million in punitive damages—approximately 526 times the amount of actual damages. Although upholding the award and rejecting a substantive due process challenge, the Court was badly splintered. Justice Stevens's opinion for the Court commanded only a plurality, with only Chief Justice Rehnquist and Justice Blackmun joining in its entirety. He reaffirmed the position, in *Pacific Mutual Life Insurance v. Haslip*, 498 U.S. 1306 (1991), that the Court could not "draw a mathematical bright line" between constitutionally acceptable and unacceptable jury awards. Instead of focusing on the disparity between punitive and compensatory awards, Justice Stevens maintained that the Court should focus on the general "reasonableness" of an award. Here, TXO's "bad faith" and "larger pattern of fraud, trickery, and deceit" justified the jury's award.

United States v. James Daniel Good Real Property, 510 U.S. 43 (1993) — 5:4 — Writing for the Court, Justice Kennedy ruled that convicted drug dealers must be given a hearing before the government seizes their property under forfeiture laws. Separate opinions, concurring and dissenting, were filed by Chief Justice Rehnquist and Justices O'Connor and Thomas.

Honda Motor Co. v. Oberg, 512 U.S. 415 (1994) — 7:2 — Writing for the Court, Justice Stevens struck down Oregon's limitation on judicial review of jury awards of punitive damages as a violation of due process. Justice Ginsburg, joined by Chief Justice Rehnquist, dissented.

Sandin v. Conner, 515 U.S. 472 (1995) — 5:4 — Writing for the majority, Chief Justice Rehnquist rejected a prison inmate's claim that officials deprived him of procedural due process when they refused to allow him to present witnesses during a disciplinary hearing that resulted in his isolated confinement for alleged misconduct. Justices Breyer, Ginsburg, Souter, and Stevens dissented.

Bennis v. Michigan, 516 U.S. 442 (1996) — 5:4 — Writing for the majority, Chief Justice Rehnquist rejected the claim that the government violates due process and the Fifth Amendment's taking clause when it undertakes the forfeiture of an innocent person's property, which was used in an illegal activity. Justices Breyer, Kennedy, Souter, and Stevens dissented.

Cooper v. Oklahoma, 517 U.S. 348 (1996) — 9:0 — Justice Stevens struck down Oklahoma's law presuming that a

CASE	VOTE	RULING

defendant is competent to stand trial unless proven incompetent by "clear and convincing evidence." Finding that the state's presumption and procedures violated "fundamental fairness" and due process, Justice Stevens reaffirmed that states may presume a defendant's competence and require proof of incompetence based on the lower standard of "the preponderance of the evidence."

United States v. Armstrong, **8:1**
517 U.S. 456 (1996)

Writing for the Court, Chief Justice Rehnquist reversed a lower federal court's holding that several black defendants, charged with drug trafficking, had met the threshold requirement for arguing that federal prosecutors engaged in the selective prosecution of blacks and for requiring the government to turn over records on its prosecutorial policies and practices. Their attorneys presented evidence that all of the defendants in twenty-four crack cocaine cases resolved in 1991 were black. However, the chief justice held that lower courts should defer to the government's interests in prosecutorial discretion and that under the federal rules of evidence and the equal protection component of the Fifth Amendment's due process clause, claimants must demonstrate that federal prosecution policy "had a discriminatory effect and that it was motivated by a discriminatory purpose."

BMW of North American v. **5:4**
Gore, 517 U.S. 559 (1996)

Writing for the Court, Justice Stevens held that a punitive damages award of 500 times the amount of the actual damages was "grossly excessive" and violated the Fourteenth Amendment's due process clause. Chief Justice Rehnquist and Justices Scalia, Ginsburg, and Thomas dissented.

Montana v. Egelhoff, 518 **5:4**
U.S. 37 (1996)

Writing for a plurality, Justice Scalia held that due process was not violated by a Montana law instructing juries that an intoxicated condition should not be considered in determining the mental state of a person accused of deliberate homicide.

Young v. Harper, 520 **9:0**
U.S. 193 (1997)

Writing for the Court, Justice Thomas held that the summary reinstitutionalization of a state prisoner who had been released under a preparole program, aimed at reducing prison overcrowding, deprived him of liberty without the due process of law under the Fourteenth Amendment and that the prisoner was entitled to the procedural protections for parole hearings set forth in *Morrissey v. Brewer,* 408 U.S. 471 (1972).

Kansas v. Hendricks, 521 **5:4**
U.S. 346 (1997)

Upheld Kansas's law providing for the involuntary civil commitment of sexual predators,

CASE	VOTE	RULING

even after they have served their prison sentences, over due process objections. Agreeing with that part of the Court's analysis, Justices Breyer, Ginsburg, Souter, and Stevens dissented on other grounds.

| *Sacramento County v. Lewis,* 523 U.S. 833 (1998) | 9:0 | Held that police who cause accidents that kill even innocent bystanders during high-speed |

pursuit of criminal suspects are not liable unless their actions "shock the conscience." As Justice Souter explained: "Only a purpose to cause harm unrelated to the legitimate object of arrest will satisfy the element of arbitrary conduct shocking to the conscience, necessary for a due process violation."

| *Chicago v. Morales,* 527 U.S. 41 (1999) | 6:3 | In an opinion for the Court joined only by a plurality, Justice Stevens held that an ordinance |

prohibiting "criminal street gang members" from loitering in public places was impermissibly vague in defining "loitering" and, therefore, failed to give citizens adequate notice of what was forbidden. Justices Scalia and Thomas filed dissenting opinions; Chief Justice Rehnquist joined the latter's dissent.

| *Troxel v. Granville,* 530 U.S. 57 (2000) | 6:3 | Reaffirming that the Fourteenth Amendment has a substantive component providing "height- |

ened protection against governmental interference with certain fundamental rights and liberty interests," including those of parents to make decisions concerning the care of their children, the Court held that Washington's statute allowing "any person" "at any time" to petition for visitation rights infringed on parents' "fundamental right to rear children."

| *Cooper Industries, Inc. v. Leatherman Tool Group, Inc.* 532 U.S. 424 (2001) | 8:1 | Held that due process requires federal appellate courts to use a *de novo*, rather than an abuse of discretion, standard when re- |

viewing for "grossly excessive" damage awards. A jury awarded Leatherman Tool Group $50,000 in compensatory damages and $4.5 million dollars in punitive damages for Cooper Industries' unfair competition and false advertising. Writing for the Court, Justice Stevens reasoned that *de novo* review was appropriate because determining whether damages awards are excessive requires courts to determine the reasonableness of the award based on the facts in each case. Justice Ginsburg dissented.

| *Dusenbery v. United States,* 534 U.S. 161 (2002) | 5:4 | Writing for the Court, Chief Justice Rehnquist upheld the forfeiture of private property of |

a prison inmate, who was served notice by certified mail and in the absence

CASE	VOTE	RULING

of a response to the notice of forfeiture, and held that due process does not require "actual notice," only "an attempt to provide actual notice" of forfeiture. Justices Ginsburg, Stevens, Souter, and Breyer dissented.

Kansas v. Crane,   7:2   In *Kansas v. Hendricks,* 521 U.S.
534 U.S. 407 (2002)   346 (1997) (excerpted in this
chapter) the Court upheld the state's Sexually Violent Predator Act, authorizing the continued civil commitment of convicted sexual offenders who have a "mental abnormality or personality disorder" that renders them dangerous to themselves or others. Subsequently, Kansas sought the continued commitment of Michael Crane, but the state supreme court ruled that due process requires a finding that the defendant "cannot control his dangerous behavior." Justice Breyer held that there must be a hearing and finding that a dangerous sexual offender lacks self-control, but also emphasized that under *Hendricks* there is no narrow or technical meaning of "lack of control" and that that depends on the circumstances and individual psychiatric evaluations. Justices Scalia and Thomas dissented.

Connecticut Department of   9:0   Writing for a unanimous Court,
Public Safety v. Doe, 538   Chief Justice Rehnquist held
U.S. 1 (2003)   that due process is not violated
by states' requiring convicted sex offenders to register personal information, including addresses and photographs, which are then posted on a web site, because the registry requirement is based on a prior conviction, not the sex offender's current dangerousness.

State Farm Mutual Automobile   6:3   Writing for the Court, Justice
Insurance v. Campbell,   Kennedy held that punitive
538 408 (2003)   damages awards must be propor-
tionate to the wrong committed and that "the wealth of a defendant cannot justify an otherwise unconstitutional punitive damages award." Here, the majority overturned a $145 million jury award against State Farm that was 145 times the amount of the injury as "an irrational and arbitrary deprivation of the property of the defendant." Justices Scalia, Thomas, and Ginsburg dissented.

Demore v. Kim,   5:4   Writing for the Court, Chief
538 U.S. 510 (2003)   Justice Rehnquist upheld a 1996
federal law authorizing the detention of immigrants, including permanent residents or "green card holders," who have committed certain crimes and served their sentences while the government decides whether to deport them. The majority rejected the due process claim that they are entitled to a hearing on whether they would

CASE	VOTE	RULING

jump bail or posed a danger to society. In the chief justice's words: "Congress may make rules as to aliens that would be unacceptable if applied to citizens." Justice Souter, joined by Justices Stevens and Ginsburg, filed an opinion in part concurring and dissenting that endorsed the substantive and procedural due process claim. In a separate opinion, Justice Breyer concurred and dissented in part.

| *Overton v. Bazetta*, 539 U.S. 126 (2003) | 9:0 | Held that prison regulations limiting inmate visitations do not violate freedom of associa- |

tion or substantive due process, and are rationally related to penal interests.

| *Sell v. United States*, 539 U.S. 166 (2003) | 6:3 | Writing for the Court, Justice Breyer held that antipsychotic drugs may be administered to a |

mentally-ill defendant without his or her consent if the forced medication (1) is necessary to an "important governmental interest," (2) significantly furthers that interest, (3) is medically necessary without a less intrusive alternative, and (4) is medically appropriate.

| *Lawrence v. Texas*, 539 U.S. 558 (2003) | 6:3 | Writing for the Court, Justice Kennedy invalidated Texas's law criminalizing homosexual sodomy; the case is excerpted in Chapter 11. |

BMW of North America v. Gore
517 U.S. 559, 116 S. Ct. 1589 (1996)

Dr. Ira Gore, Jr., purchased a BMW sedan for $40,750.88. After driving the car for about nine months, he took it to "Slick Finish" to make it look " 'snazzier than it normally would appear.' " Mr. Slick detected evidence that the car had been repainted. Convinced that he had been cheated, Gore sued BMW of North America (BMW), alleging that the failure to disclose that the car had been repainted constituted suppression of a material fact. He asked for $500,000 in compensatory and punitive damages. During the trial, BMW acknowledged that it had a policy of selling damaged new cars as "new" if the cost of repairing them was less than 3 percent of their retail price. Because the $601.37 cost of repainting Gore's car was only about 1.5 percent of its suggested retail price, BMW did not disclose the damage or repair. Gore countered that his repainted car was worth less than a car that had not been refinished. To prove his actual damages of $4,000, he relied on the testimony of a former BMW dealer who estimated that the value of a repainted BMW was approximately 10 percent less than the value of a new car that had not been damaged and repaired. To support his claim for punitive damages, Dr. Gore introduced evidence that since 1983 BMW had sold 983 refinished cars as new, including fourteen in Alabama, without disclosing that the cars had been repainted at a cost of more than $300 per vehicle. Using the actual damage estimate of $4,000 per vehicle, Gore argued that a punitive award of $4 million would provide an appropriate penalty for selling approximately 1,000 cars for more than they were worth. The jury returned a verdict finding BMW liable for compensatory damages of $4,000. In addition, the jury assessed $4 million in punitive damages, based on a determination that the nondisclosure policy constituted "gross, oppressive or malicious" fraud. On appeal, the Alabama Supreme Court rejected BMW's claim that the award exceeded the constitutionally permissible amount, but ruled that the jury improperly computed the amount of punitive damages by multiplying Gore's compensatory damages by the number of similar sales in other jurisdictions. The court held that "a constitutionally reasonable punitive damages award in this case is $2,000,000." BMW appealed that decision to the Supreme Court.

The state supreme court's decision was reversed by a five to four vote. Justice Stevens delivered the opinion for the Court. Justice Breyer filed a concurring opinion. Justice Scalia filed a dissenting opinion, which Justice Thomas joined. Justice Ginsburg filed a dissenting opinion, which Chief Justice Rehnquist joined. On remand, the state supreme court reduced the punitive award to $50,000.

    Justice STEVENS delivered the opinion of the Court.

The Due Process Clause of the Fourteenth Amendment prohibits a State from imposing a " 'grossly excessive' " punishment on a tortfeasor. *TXO Production Corp. v. Alliance Resources Corp.*, 509 U.S. 443 (1993). The wrongdoing involved in this case was the decision by a national distributor of automobiles not to advise its dealers, and hence their customers, of predelivery damage to new cars when the cost of repair amounted to less than 3 percent of the car's suggested retail price. The question presented is whether a $2 million punitive damages award exceeds the constitutional limit. . . .

Punitive damages may properly be imposed to further a State's legitimate interests in punishing unlawful conduct and deterring its repetition. *Gertz v. Robert Welch, Inc.*, 418 U.S. 323 (1974). In our federal system, States necessarily have considerable flexibility in determining the level of punitive damages that they will allow in different classes of cases and in any particular case. Most States that authorize exemplary damages afford the jury similar latitude, requiring only that the damages awarded be reasonably necessary to vindicate the State's legitimate interests in punishment and deterrence. Only when an award can fairly be categorized as "grossly excessive" in relation to these interests does it enter the zone of arbitrariness that violates the Due Process Clause of the Fourteenth Amendment. For that reason, the federal excessiveness inquiry appropriately begins with an identification of the state interests that a punitive award is designed to serve. We therefore focus our attention first on the scope of Alabama's legitimate interests in punishing BMW and deterring it from future misconduct.

No one doubts that a State may protect its citizens by prohibiting deceptive trade practices and by requiring automobile distributors to disclose presale repairs that affect the value of a new car. But the States need not, and in fact do not, provide such protection in a uniform manner. Some States rely on the judicial process to formulate and enforce an appropriate disclosure requirement by applying principles of contract and tort law. Other States have enacted various forms of legislation that define the disclosure obligations of automobile manufacturers, distributors, and dealers. The result is a patchwork of rules representing the diverse policy judgments of lawmakers in 50 States. . . .

We think it follows from these principles of state sovereignty and comity that a State may not impose economic sanctions on violators of its laws with the intent of changing the tortfeasors' lawful conduct in other States. Before this Court Dr. Gore argued that the large punitive damages award was necessary to induce BMW to change the nationwide policy that it adopted in 1983. But by attempting to alter BMW's nationwide policy, Alabama would be infringing on the policy choices of other States. To avoid such encroachment, the economic penalties that a State such as Alabama inflicts on those who transgress its laws, whether the penalties take the form of legislatively authorized fines or judicially imposed punitive damages, must be supported by the State's interest in protecting its own consumers and its own economy. Alabama may insist that BMW adhere to a particular disclosure policy in that State. Alabama does not have the power, however, to punish BMW for conduct that was lawful where it occurred and that had no impact on Alabama or its residents. Nor may Alabama impose sanctions on BMW in order to deter conduct that is lawful in other jurisdictions. . . .

When the scope of the interest in punishment and deterrence that an Alabama court may appropriately consider is properly limited, it is apparent—for reasons that we shall now address—that this award is grossly excessive.

Elementary notions of fairness enshrined in our constitutional jurisprudence dictate that a person receive fair notice not only of the conduct that will subject him to punishment, but also of the severity of the penalty that a State may impose. Three guideposts, each of which indicates that BMW did not receive adequate notice of the magnitude of the sanction that Alabama might impose for adhering to the nondisclosure policy adopted in 1983, lead us to the conclusion that the $2 million award against BMW is grossly excessive: the degree of reprehensibility of the nondisclosure; the disparity between the harm or potential harm suffered by Dr. Gore and his punitive damages award; and the difference between this remedy and the civil penalties authorized or imposed in comparable cases. We discuss these considerations in turn.

Perhaps the most important indicium of the reasonableness of a punitive damages award is the degree of reprehensibility of the defendant's conduct. This principle reflects the accepted view that some wrongs are more blameworthy than others. In *TXO*, both the West Virginia Supreme Court and the Justices of this Court placed special emphasis on the principle that punitive damages may not be "grossly out of proportion to the severity of the offense."

In this case, none of the aggravating factors associated with particularly reprehensible conduct is present. The harm BMW inflicted on Dr. Gore was purely economic in nature. The presale refinishing of the car had no effect on its performance or safety features, or even its appearance for at least nine months after his purchase. BMW's conduct evinced no indifference to or reckless disregard for the health and safety of others. . . .

Finally, the record in this case discloses no deliberate false statements, acts of affirmative misconduct, or concealment of evidence of improper motive. . . .

That conduct is sufficiently reprehensible to give rise to tort liability, and even a modest award of exemplary damages does not establish the high degree of culpability that warrants a substantial punitive damages award. Because this case exhibits none of the circumstances ordinarily associated with egregiously improper conduct, we are persuaded that BMW's conduct was not sufficiently reprehensible to warrant imposition of a $2 million exemplary damages award.

The second and perhaps most commonly cited indicium of an unreasonable or excessive punitive damages award is its ratio to the actual harm inflicted on the plaintiff. The principle that exemplary damages must bear a reasonable relationship to compensatory damages has a long pedigree. . . .

The $2 million in punitive damages awarded to Dr. Gore by the Alabama Supreme Court is 500 times the amount of his actual harm as determined by the jury. Moreover, there is no suggestion that Dr. Gore or any other BMW purchaser was threatened with any additional potential harm by BMW's nondisclosure policy. . . .

Comparing the punitive damages award and the civil or criminal penalties that could be imposed for comparable misconduct provides a third indicium of excessiveness. . . . In this case the $2 million economic sanction imposed on BMW is substantially greater than the statutory fines available in Alabama and elsewhere for similar malfeasance.

The maximum civil penalty authorized by the Alabama Legislature for a violation of its Deceptive Trade Practices Act is $2,000; other States authorize more severe sanctions, with the maxima ranging from $5,000 to $10,000. . . . Moreover, at the time BMW's policy was first challenged, there does not appear to have been any judicial decision in Alabama or elsewhere indicating that application of that policy might give rise to such severe punishment.

The sanction imposed in this case cannot be justified on the ground that it was necessary to deter future misconduct without considering whether less drastic remedies could be expected to achieve that goal. The fact that a multimillion dollar penalty prompted a change in policy sheds no light on the question whether a lesser deterrent would have adequately protected the interests of Alabama consumers. In the absence of a history of noncompliance with known statutory requirements, there is no basis for assuming that a more modest sanction would not have been sufficient to motivate full compliance with the disclosure requirement imposed by the Alabama Supreme Court in this case.

[W]e of course accept the Alabama courts' view that the state interest in protecting its citizens from deceptive trade practices justifies a sanction in addition to the recovery of compensatory damages. We cannot, however, accept the conclusion of the Alabama Supreme Court that BMW's conduct was sufficiently egregious to justify a punitive sanction that is tantamount to a severe criminal penalty.

The fact that BMW is a large corporation rather than an impecunious individual does not diminish its entitlement to fair notice of the demands that the several States impose on the conduct of its business. Indeed, its status as an active participant in the national economy implicates the federal interest in preventing individual States from imposing undue burdens on interstate commerce. While each State has ample power to protect its own consumers, none may use the punitive damages deterrent as a means of imposing its regulatory policies on the entire Nation.

[W]e are not prepared to draw a bright line marking the limits of a constitutionally acceptable punitive damages award. [H]owever, we are fully convinced that the grossly excessive award imposed in this case transcends the constitutional limit. . . .

　□ *Justice SCALIA, with whom Justice THOMAS joins, dissenting.*

Today we see the latest manifestation of this Court's recent and increasingly insistent "concern about punitive damages that 'run wild.' " *Pacific Mut. Life Ins. Co. v. Haslip*, 499 U.S. 1 (1991). Since the Constitution does not make that concern any of our business, the Court's activities in this area are an unjustified incursion into the province of state governments. . . .

I do not regard the Fourteenth Amendment's Due Process Clause as a secret repository of substantive guarantees against "unfairness"—neither the unfairness of an excessive civil compensatory award, nor the unfairness of an "unreasonable" punitive award. What the Fourteenth Amendment's procedural guarantee assures is an opportunity to contest the reasonableness of a damages judgment in state court; but there is no federal guarantee a damages award actually be reasonable. . . .

The most significant aspects of today's decision—the identification of a "substantive due process" right against a "grossly excessive" award, and the concomitant assumption of ultimate authority to decide anew a matter of "reasonableness" resolved in lower court proceedings—are of course not new. *Haslip* and *TXO* revived the notion . . . that the measure of civil punishment poses a question of constitutional dimension to be answered by this Court. Neither of those cases, however, nor any of the precedents upon which they relied, actually took the step of declaring a punitive award unconstitutional simply because it was "too big."

At the time of adoption of the Fourteenth Amendment, it was well understood that punitive damages represent the assessment by the jury, as the voice of the community, of the measure of punishment the defendant deserved. Today's decision, though dressed up as a legal opinion, is really no more than a disagreement with the community's sense of indignation or outrage expressed in the punitive award of the Alabama jury, as reduced by the State Supreme Court. . . .

One might understand the Court's eagerness to enter this field, rather than leave it with the state legislatures, if it had something useful to say. In fact, however, its opinion provides virtually no guidance to legislatures, and to state and federal courts, as to what a "constitutionally proper" level of punitive damages might be. . . .

[T]he Court identifies "three guideposts" that lead it to the conclusion that the award in this case is excessive: degree of reprehensibility, ratio between punitive award and plaintiff's actual harm, and legislative sanctions provided for comparable misconduct. The legal significance of these "guideposts" is nowhere explored, but their necessary effect is to establish federal standards governing the hitherto exclusively state law of damages. Apparently (though it is by no means clear) all three federal "guideposts" can be overridden if "necessary to deter future misconduct"—a loophole that will encourage state reviewing courts to uphold awards as necessary for the adequat[e] protect[ion]" of state consumers. By effectively requiring state reviewing courts to concoct rationalizations—whether within the "guideposts" or through the loophole—to justify the intuitive punitive reactions of state juries, the Court accords neither category of institution the respect it deserves.

Of course it will not be easy for the States to comply with this new federal law of damages, no matter how willing they are to do so. In truth, the "guideposts" mark a road to nowhere; they provide no real guidance at all. . . . For the foregoing reasons, I respectfully dissent.

Justice GINSBURG, with whom THE CHIEF JUSTICE joins, dissenting.

The Court, I am convinced, unnecessarily and unwisely ventures into territory traditionally within the States' domain, and does so in the face of reform measures recently adopted or currently under consideration in legislative arenas. The Alabama Supreme Court, in this case, endeavored to follow this Court's prior instructions; and, more recently, Alabama's highest court has installed further controls on awards of punitive damages. I would therefore leave the state court's judgment undisturbed, and resist unnecessary intrusion into an area dominantly of state concern. . . .

County of Sacramento v. Lewis
523 U.S. 1833, 118 S.Ct. 1708 (1998)

On May 22, 1990, James Smith, a Sacramento County sheriff's deputy, along with another officer, Murray Stapp, responded to a call to break up a fight. Upon returning to his patrol car, Stapp saw a motorcycle approaching at high speed. It was operated by Brian Willard and carried Philip Lewis as a passenger. Neither had anything to do with the fight that prompted the call to the police. Stapp turned on his rotating lights, yelled to the boys to stop, and pulled his patrol car closer to Smith's, attempting to pen the motorcycle in. Instead, Willard slowly maneuvered the cycle between the two police cars and sped off. Smith immediately began pursuit at high speed. They wove in and out of oncoming traffic, reaching speeds up to 100 miles an hour. The chase ended after the motorcycle tipped. By the time Smith slammed on his brakes, Willard was out of the way, but Lewis was not. The patrol car skidded into him at 40 miles an hour, propelling him some 70 feet down the road. Lewis was pronounced dead at the scene.

Lewis's parents sued the Sacramento County Sheriff's Department and Deputy Smith, alleging a deprivation of Philip Lewis's Fourteenth Amendment substantive due process right to life. The district court granted summary judgment for Smith, reasoning that even if he violated the Constitution, he was entitled to qualified immunity. The Court of Appeals for the Ninth Circuit reversed and the city appealed to the Supreme Court which granted review and reversed the appellate court.

The Court's decision was unanimous and opinion delivered by Justice Souter. Concurring opinions were filed by Chief Justice Rehnquist and Justices Breyer, Kennedy, Scalia, and Stevens.

☐ *Justice SOUTER delivered the opinion of the Court.*

The issue in this case is whether a police officer violates the Fourteenth Amendment's guarantee of substantive due process by causing death through deliberate or reckless indifference to life in a high-speed automobile chase aimed at apprehending a suspected offender. We answer no, and hold that in such circumstances only a purpose to cause harm unrelated to the legitimate object of arrest will satisfy the element of arbitrary conduct shocking to the conscience, necessary for a due process violation. . . .

Our prior cases have held the provision that "no State shall . . . deprive any person of life, liberty, or property, without due process of law," U.S. Const., Amdt. 14, Sec. 1, to "guarantee more than fair process," *Washington v. Glucksberg*, [521 U.S. 702] (1997), and to cover a substantive sphere as well, "barring certain government actions regardless of the fairness of the procedures used to implement them," *Daniels v. Williams*, 474 U.S. 327 (1986). . . .

Since the time of our early explanations of due process, we have understood the core of the concept to be protection against arbitrary action . . . *Hurtado v. California*, 110 U.S. 516 (1884).

We have emphasized time and again that "the touchstone of due process is protection of the individual against arbitrary action of government," *Wolff v. McDonnell*, 418 U.S. 539 (1974), whether the fault lies in a denial of fundamental procedural fairness, or in the exercise of power without any reasonable justification in the service of a legitimate governmental objective. While due process protection in the substantive sense limits what the government may do in both its legislative, see, e.g., *Griswold v. Connecticut*, 381 U.S. 479 (1965), and its executive capacities, see, e.g., *Rochin v. California*, 342 U.S. 165 (1952), criteria to identify what is fatally arbitrary differ depending on whether it is legislation or a specific act of a governmental officer that is at issue.

Our cases dealing with abusive executive action have repeatedly emphasized that only the most egregious official conduct can be said to be "arbitrary in the constitutional sense," *Collins v. Harker Heights*, 503 U.S. [112 (1992)], thereby recognizing the point made in different circumstances by Chief Justice MARSHALL, " 'that it is a constitution we are expounding,' " *McCulloch v. Maryland*, 4 Wheat. 316 (1819). . . .

To this end, for half a century now we have spoken of the cognizable level of executive abuse of power as that which shocks the conscience. We first put the test this way in *Rochin v. California*, where we found the forced pumping of a suspect's stomach enough to offend due process as conduct "that shocks the conscience" and violates the "decencies of civilized conduct." In the intervening years we have repeatedly adhered to *Rochin's* benchmark. . . .

It should not be surprising that the constitutional concept of conscience-shocking duplicates no traditional category of common-law fault, but rather points clearly away from liability, or clearly toward it, only at the ends of the tort law's spectrum of culpability. Thus, we have made it clear that the due process guarantee does not entail a body of constitutional law imposing liability whenever someone cloaked with state authority causes harm. . . .

Whether the point of the conscience-shocking is reached when injuries are produced with culpability falling within the middle range, following from something more than negligence but "less than intentional conduct, such as recklessness or 'gross negligence' " is a matter for closer calls. . . .

Rules of due process are not, however, subject to mechanical application in unfamiliar territory. Deliberate indifference that shocks in one environment may not be so patently egregious in another, and our concern with preserving the constitutional proportions of substantive due process demands an exact analysis of circumstances before any abuse of power is condemned as conscience-shocking. What we have said of due process in the procedural sense is just as true here:

> "The phrase [due process of law] formulates a concept less rigid and more fluid than those envisaged in other specific and particular provisions of the Bill of Rights. Its application is less a matter of rule. Asserted denial is to be tested by an appraisal of the totality of facts in a given case. That which may, in one setting, constitute a denial of fundamental fairness, shocking to the universal sense of justice, may, in other circumstances, and in the light of other considerations, fall short of such denial." *Betts v. Brady*, 316 U.S. 455 (1942).

Thus, attention to the markedly different circumstances of normal pretrial custody and high-speed law enforcement chases shows why the deliberate indifference that shocks in the one case is less egregious in the other (even assuming that it makes sense to speak of indifference as deliberate in the case of sudden pursuit). As the very term "deliberate indifference" implies, the standard is sensibly employed only when actual deliberation is practical, and in the custodial situation of a prison, forethought about an inmate's welfare is not only feasible but obligatory under a regime that incapacitates a prisoner to exercise ordinary responsibility for his own welfare. . . .

But just as the description of the custodial prison situation shows how deliberate indifference can rise to a constitutionally shocking level, so too does it suggest why indifference may well not be enough for liability in the different circumstances of a case like this one. We have, indeed, found that deliberate indifference does not suffice for constitutional liability (albeit under the Eighth Amendment) even in prison circumstances when a prisoner's claim arises not from normal custody but from response to a violent disturbance. . . .

Like prison officials facing a riot, the police on an occasion calling for fast action have obligations that tend to tug against each other. Their duty is to restore and maintain lawful order, while not exacerbating disorder more than necessary to do their jobs. They are supposed to act decisively and to show restraint at the same moment, and their decisions have to be made "in haste, under pressure, and frequently without the luxury of a second chance." A police officer deciding whether to give chase must balance on one hand the need to stop a suspect and show that flight from the law is no way to freedom, and, on the other, the high-speed threat to everyone within stopping range, be they suspects, their passengers, other drivers, or bystanders.

To recognize a substantive due process violation in these circumstances when only mid-level fault has been shown would be to forget that liability for deliberate indifference to inmate welfare rests upon the luxury enjoyed by prison officials of having time to make unhurried judgments, upon the chance for repeated reflection, largely uncomplicated by the pulls of competing obligations. . . . Just as a purpose to cause harm is needed for Eighth Amendment liability in a riot case, so it ought to be needed for Due Process liability in a pursuit case. Accordingly, we hold that high-speed chases with no intent to harm suspects physically or to worsen their legal plight do not give rise to liability under the Fourteenth Amendment, redressible by an action under Section 1983. . . .

The judgment below is accordingly reversed.

□ *Justice KENNEDY, with whom Justice O'CONNOR joins, concurring.*

I join the opinion of the Court, and write this explanation of the objective character of our substantive due process analysis. . . .

The Court decides this case by applying the "shocks the conscience" test first recognized in *Rochin v. California* and reiterated in subsequent decisions. The phrase has the unfortunate connotation of a standard laden with subjective assessments. In that respect, it must be viewed with considerable skepticism. As our opinion in *Collins v. Harker Heights* illustrates, however, the test can be used to mark the beginning point in asking whether or not the objective character of certain conduct is consistent with our traditions, precedents, and historical understanding of the Constitution and its meaning. As Justice SCALIA is correct to point out, we so interpreted the test in *Glucksberg*. In the instant case, the authorities cited by Justice SCALIA are persuasive, indicating that we would contradict our traditions were we to sustain the claims of the respondents.

That said, it must be added that history and tradition are the starting point, but not in all cases the ending point of the substantive due process inquiry. There is room as well for an objective assessment of the necessities of law enforcement, in which the police must be given substantial latitude and discretion, acknowledging, of course, the primacy of the interest in life which the State, by the Fourteenth Amendment, is bound to respect. I agree with the Court's assessment of the State's interests in this regard. Absent intent to injure, the police, in circumstances such as these, may conduct a dangerous chase of a suspect who disobeys a lawful command to stop when they determine it is appropriate to do so. There is a real danger in announcing a rule, or suggesting a principle, that in some cases a suspect is free to ignore a lawful police command to stop. No matter how narrow its formulation, any suggestion that suspects may ignore a lawful command to stop and then sue for damages sustained in an ensuing chase might cause suspects to flee more often, increasing accidents of the kind which occurred here. . . .

> ☐ *Justice SCALIA, with whom Justice THOMAS joins, concurring in the judgment.*

Today's opinion gives the lie to those cynics who claim that changes in this Court's jurisprudence are attributable to changes in the Court's membership. It proves that the changes are attributable to nothing but the passage of time (not much time, at that), plus application of the ancient maxim, "That was then, this is now."

Just last Term, in *Washington v. Glucksberg*, the Court specifically rejected the method of substantive-due-process analysis employed by Justice SOUTER in his concurrence in that case, which is the very same method employed by Justice SOUTER in his opinion for the Court today. . . .

Today, so to speak, the stone that the builders had rejected has become the foundation-stone of our substantive-due-process jurisprudence. The atavistic methodology that Justice SOUTER announces for the Court is the very same methodology that the Court called atavistic when it was proffered by Justice SOUTER in *Glucksberg*. In fact, if anything, today's opinion is even more of a throw-back to highly subjective substantive-due-process methodologies than the concurrence in *Glucksberg* was. Whereas the latter said merely that substantive due process prevents "arbitrary impositions" and "purposeless restraints" (without any objective criterion as to what is arbitrary or purposeless), today's opinion resuscitates the *ne plus ultra*, the Napoleon Brandy, the Mahatma Ghandi, the Celophane of subjectivity, th' ol' "shocks-the-conscience" test. According to today's opinion, this is the measure of arbitrariness when what is at issue is executive rather than legislative action. *Glucksberg*, of course, rejected "shocks-the-conscience," just as it rejected the less subjective "arbitrary action" test. A 1992 executive-action case, *Collins v. Harker Heights*, which had paid lip-service to "shocks-the-conscience," was cited in *Glucksberg* for the proposition that "our Nation's history, legal traditions, and practices . . . provide the crucial 'guideposts for responsible decisionmaking.' " In fact, even before *Glucksberg* we had characterized the last "shocks-the-conscience" claim to come before us as "nothing more than [a] bald assertion," and had rejected it on the objective ground that the petitioner "failed to proffer any historical, textual, or controlling precedential support for [his alleged due process right], and we decline to fashion a new due process right out of thin air." *Carlisle v. United States*, 517 U.S. 416 (1996).

Adhering to our decision in *Glucksberg*, rather than ask whether the police conduct here at issue shocks my unelected conscience, I would ask whether our Nation has traditionally protected the right respondents assert. The first step of our analysis, of course, must be a "careful description" of the right asserted. Here the complaint alleges that the police officer deprived Lewis "of his Fourteenth Amendment right to life, liberty and property without due process of law when he operated his vehicle with recklessness, gross negligence and conscious disregard for his safety." I agree with the Court's conclusion that this asserts a substantive right to be free from "deliberate or reckless indifference to life in a high-speed automobile chase aimed at apprehending a suspected offender."

Respondents provide no textual or historical support for this alleged due process right, and, as in *Carlisle*, I would "decline to fashion a new due process right out of thin air." Nor have respondents identified any precedential support. . . .

I would reverse the judgment of the Ninth Circuit, not on the ground that petitioners have failed to shock my still, soft voice within, but on the ground that respondents offer no textual or historical support for their alleged due process right. Accordingly, I concur in the judgment of the Court.

■ CONSTITUTIONAL HISTORY

Citizens, Noncitizens, "Enemy Combatants," and Civil Rights in Wartime

Shortly after the attacks on the World Trade Center and the Pentagon on September 11, 2001, President George W. Bush declared war against Al Qaeda forces in Afghanistan and international terrorism. He issued an order authorizing the indefinite detention of captured terrorists and their trial by military tribunals, without appeal. Bush's order invited controversy because the detainees were not treated as prisoners of war according to international law. Under the Third Geneva Convention of 1949, prisoners of war are entitled to an independent and impartial trial, the assistance of counsel, and the right of appeal. Less than two months later, Bush signed into law the 342-page USA PATRIOT Act. Its provisions expand surveillance by law enforcement agencies, provide for greater cooperation among federal agencies, and create new crimes. Civil libertarians and other critics contend that the government overreacted, especially in detaining immigrants and holding U.S. citizens as "enemy combatants."

In historical perspective, threats to national security have tended to be exaggerated and civil liberties curbed. When on the verge of war with France, in 1798 Congress enacted the Alien and Sedition Acts, empowering the president to expel any alien deemed dangerous. The Sedition Act made it unlawful to "write, print, utter or publish . . . any false, scandalous and malicious writing . . . against" the government. It led to twenty-five arrests, fifteen indictments, and ten convictions. All of them were Jeffersonian-Republican opponents of the Federalists, who were then in power. The laws expired in 1801 and the Supreme Court took the extraordinary step over 150 years later of declaring them unconstitutional in *New York Times Company v. Sullivan*, 376 U.S. 254 (1964) (excerpted in Ch. 5).

In 1798, Congress also enacted the Enemy Alien Act, still in effect, authorizing the president during a war to detain and expel citizens of a country with which we are at war. James Madison invoked it during the War of 1812; President Woodrow Wilson did so during World War I to arrest over 6,000 German nationals and hold about 2,300 in internment camps; and during World War II President Franklin D. Roosevelt invoked the law to classify almost one million foreigners as "enemy aliens."

World War I brought other restrictions, particularly for immigrants from East Europe and Russia. The Senate debated a bill that would have turned the country into a military zone and made it a crime to publish anything endangering national security, with trials by military tribunals, and convictions punishable by death. But President Wilson persuaded Congress to enact the less extreme Espionage Act of 1917, making it a crime to interfere with war efforts. Still, as amended in 1918, the law criminalized any "disloyal, profane, scurrilous or abusive" language about the government. Approximately 2,000 individuals were prosecuted under the law. By the time appeals reached the Court, World War I was over, but the "Red Scare" remained and most of the convictions were upheld. In *Schenck v. United States*, 249 U.S. 47 (1919) (excerpted in Ch. 5), Justice Oliver Wendell Holmes proposed his "clear and present danger" test for protecting speech, yet upheld the conviction, observing: "When a nation is at war many things that might be said in time of peace are such a hindrance to its effort that their utterance will not be endured so long as men fight." When another appeal reached the Court, *Abrams v. United States*, 250 U.S. 616 (1919), Justices Holmes and Louis D. Brandeis dissented and explained: "The power undoubtedly is greater in time of war than in time of peace because war opens dangers that do not exist at other times. But as against dangers peculiar to war, as against others, the principle of the right of free speech is always the same." (See also

Gitlow v. People of the State of New York, 268 U.S. 652 (1925), excerpted in Ch. 5.)

During World War II and the Cold War, the Court again did not seriously question wartime hysteria or the prosecution of "subversives." Notably, the Court upheld the convictions of leaders of the Communist Party under the Smith Act of 1940, in *Dennis v. United States*, 341 U.S. 494 (1951) (excerpted in Ch. 5). That law made it a crime "to organize any society . . . advocat[ing] . . . the overthrow or destruction of any government of the United States." Subsequently, Congress enacted the Internal Security Act of 1950 and the Communist Control Act of 1954, aimed at flushing out communists and others belonging to "subversive organizations."

The Cold War in the 1950s and 1960s also led to congressional "witch hunts." The House Un-American Activities Committee (HUAC), established in 1938 and not abolished until 1974, and the Senate Permanent Investigations Subcommittee, chaired by Wisconsin Senator Joseph R. McCarthy, subpoenaed hundreds of individuals to testify about alleged communist activities. In response to challenges to the investigations, the Court ruled that witnesses may refuse to answer vague and irrelevant questions; see *Watkins v. United States*, 354 U.S. 178 (1957); and *Barenblatt v. United States*, 360 U.S. 109 (1959) (both excerpted in Vol. 1, Ch. 5). But the Court was initially reluctant to check Congress or the executive branch. However, *United States v. Robel*, 389 U.S. 258 (1967), struck down a section of the Internal Security Act, making it unlawful for a member of a communist-action organization to work in a defense facility, for sweeping "too indiscriminately" and "literally establish[ing] guilt by association."

Besides limiting freedom of speech, press, and association, the government also detained and incarcerated immigrants and citizens, along with suspending other guarantees of the Bill of Rights. In *Ex parte Milligan*, 71 U.S. 2 (1866) (excerpted in Vol. 1, Ch. 3), the Court overruled President Abraham Lincoln's use of military courts to try civilians accused of disloyalty during the Civil War. Yet during World War II it upheld the internment of over 110,000 Japanese-Americans—70,000 of whom were U.S. citizens—as "enemy aliens" without evidence of their disloyalty, in *Korematsu v. United States*, 323 U.S. 214 (1944) (excerpted in Vol. 1, Ch. 3). On the same day *Korematsu* came down, though, the Court ruled, in *Ex parte Endo*, 323 U.S. 283 (1944), that, although the evacuation was permissible, the detention of loyal Japanese-Americans was unconstitutional.

During World War II the Court also approved the use of military tribunals to try eight German saboteurs, including one naturalized U.S. citizen, for sabotaging bridges and utility plants. In *Ex parte Quirin*, 317 U.S. 1 (1942), the Court ruled that the president has the "power . . . to carry into effect . . . all laws defining and punishing offenses against the law of nations, including those which pertain to the conduct of war." Chief Justice Stone added that there was no distinction between U.S. citizens and noncitizens deemed belligerents. As he put it: "citizenship in the United States of an enemy belligerent does not relieve him from the consequences of a belligerency which is unlawful."

At the end of World War II, the Court upheld the use of military commissions to try leaders of the Japanese Imperial Military in *In re Yamashita*, 327 U.S. 1 (1946). The Court also held, in *Johnson v. Eisentrager*, 339 U.S. 763 (1950), that federal courts have no jurisdiction over *habeas corpus* petitions filed by foreign nationals held overseas by U.S. military forces. In *Reid v. Covert*, 354 U.S. 1 (1957), though, the Court ruled that U.S. citizens who are dependents of military personnel stationed abroad may not be subject to courts-martial or denied rights guaranteed in the Bill of Rights. For that reason, John Walker Lindh, the young American captured fighting with the Taliban in Afghanistan, was accorded counsel and prosecuted in federal court.

In the aftermath of the September 11, 2001, terrorist attacks, the boundaries between the rights of citizens and noncitizens were once again blurred. International and constitutional law has long recognized that during wartime the government has special powers over foreign nationals from a country at war. The Bush administration advanced the position that the war against international terrorism was different because it was against Al Qaeda and other terrorists, not a nation. Over 3,000 foreign nationals from the Middle East were detained, and another 6,000 targeted for deportation. The administration rejected international criticism of its indefinite and incommunicado detention of about 650 foreign nationals as "enemy combatants" in Guantanamo Bay, Cuba. The administration initially distinguished between the rights of citizens and foreign nationals, but then blurred the line, drawing sharp criticism from commentators and some lower federal courts, for its treatment of U.S. citizens as "enemy combatants."

The line between the rights of citizens and foreign nationals has been breached in the past. The Constitution expressly distinguishes the rights of citizenship in certain respects: only citizens may run for elective federal office and their right to vote may not be denied discriminatorily. Yet, all other rights are not so literally limited. The Fourth Amendment guarantee against "unreasonable searches and seizures," for instance, extends to all "people." The Fifth and Fourteenth Amendment guarantees of due process and equal protection extend to all "persons," including resident foreign nationals.

Accordingly, the Court has held that neither the First nor the Fifth Amendment "acknowledges any distinction between citizens and resident aliens," *Kwong Hai Chew v. Colding*, 344 U.S. 590 (1953). The Court reaffirmed that "the Due Process Clause applies to all 'persons' within the United States, including aliens, whether their presence here is lawful, unlawful, temporary, or permanent," in *Zadvydas v. Davis*, 533 U.S. 678 (2001). It also has repeatedly held that equal protection is "universal in [its] application to all persons within the territorial jurisdiction, without regard to differences of . . . nationality," *Yick Wo v. Hopkins*, 118 U.S. 356 (1886); see also *Plyer v. Doe*, 457 U.S. 2002 (1982) (excerpted in Ch. 12, rejecting the denial of public education to children of illegal aliens).

At the same time, citizens and noncitizens are not similarly situated. Although the Court has held that state laws discriminating against aliens may be presumptively invalid, in *Graham v. Richardson*, 403 U.S. 365 (1971), it has permitted states to bar foreign nationals from public employment as police officers, schoolteachers, and probation officers; see *Foley v. Connelie*, 435 U.S. 291 (1978); *Ambach v. Norwick*, 441 U.S. 68 (1979); and *Cabell v. Chavez-Salido*, 454 U.S. 432 (1982).

The status of citizens and noncitizens diverges most sharply with respect to detention, deportation, and immigration. Citizens may not be expelled from the country, whereas noncitizens may be expelled for even minor infractions. As the Court observed in *Mathews v. Diaz*, 426 U.S. 67 (1976): "In the exercise of its broad power over naturalization and immigration, Congress regularly makes rules that would be unacceptable if applied to citizens." The Court has, thus, permitted the exclusion and expulsion of foreign nationals on the basis of their race and if they have committed certain crimes, in *Chae Chan Ping v. United States*, 130 U.S. 581 (1889); and *Yamataya v. Fisher*, 189 U.S. 861 (1903); as well as allowed their deportation because of political associations, in *Shaughnesy v. United States ex rel Mezei*, 345 U.S. 206 (1953).

In *United States v. Salerno*, 481 U.S. 739 (1987), the Court nonetheless blurred the line between citizens and noncitizens when upholding the pretrial detention for two years, without bail, of a citizen as "regulatory, not penal," and hence not a violation of due process. In *dictum*, referring to times of "war or insurrection," Chief Justice Rehnquist added that "the government may detain individuals whom the government believes to be dangerous." However, in *Zadvydas v. Davis*, 533 U.S. 678 (2001), the Court ruled that legal immigrant felons are entitled to due process and may not be held indefinitely—longer than six months—under deportation orders when countries refuse to take them back. Subsequently, though, a bare majority in *Demore v. Kim*, 538 U.S. 510 (2003), upheld a federal statute mandating preventive detention during deportation proceedings of foreign nationals accused of certain crimes, based on statistics showing that a high percentage of "criminal aliens" commit more offenses after their release and fail to reappear at deportation hearings.

The detentions and deportations of immigrants of Middle East origins in the aftermath of 9/11 gave rise to a new series of litigation. The Immigration and Naturalization Service's (INS) adoption of secret deportation hearings resulted in conflicting lower federal court rulings. The U.S. Court of Appeals for the Sixth Circuit held that the First Amendment guarantees a right of access for the press and the media to the proceedings, while Third and District of Columbia Circuit courts ruled contrariwise. The Supreme Court denied review of the latter decisions (for further discussion of claims to a right of access see Ch. 5).

A panel of the Court of Appeals for the Ninth Circuit also ruled against the administration's policy of indefinite detention, without appeal to federal courts, of foreign nationals deemed "enemy combatants," in *Gherebi v. Bush* (2003). The court found no support in the Congress's Authorization for Use of Military Force of 2001 or precedents, such as *Johnson v. Eisentrager*, for denying detainees access to the judicial process. In the words of the panel, "no lawful policy or precedent supports such a counter-intuitive and undemocratic procedure. . . . In our view, the government's position is inconsistent with fundamental tenets of American jurisprudence and raises serious questions under international law."

The Court had inexorably to consider appeals of the treatment of "enemy combatants," and to clarify the rights of foreign nationals, as well as U.S. citizens in the cases of Yaser Esam Hamdi and Joes Padilla. In its 2003–2004 term, the Court reviewed cases involving foreign nationals captured in Afghanistan and Pakistan, *Rasul v. Bush* (2004) (excerpted in Vol. 1, Ch. 3). Both posed the question of whether federal courts have jurisdiction over challenges to the legality of holding foreign nationals held in Guantanamo Bay. By a six-to-three vote the Court held that federal courts have jurisdiction over foreign nationals held in Guantanamo Bay, Cuba, and that such foreign nationals have the right to seek independent review of their detention.

The Court also granted the appeal of a U.S. citizen declared an "enemy combatant," Yaser Esam Hamdi. Hamdi was born in Baton Rouge, Louisiana, but moved as a child to his parents' homeland in Saudi Arabia, where he was raised. He eventually went to Afghanistan, where he was captured fighting alongside the Taliban. He was initially taken to Guantanamo, but once his U.S. citizenship was discovered he was designated an "enemy combatant" and moved to a brig in Norfolk, Virginia. Hamdi challenged his detention and denial of legal representation as a violation of the Fifth and the Fourteenth Amendments. Before the government could respond, a federal district court judge appointed a public defender and ordered the government to allow Hamdi to consult with an attorney. The Bush administration appealed and the Court of Appeals for the Fourth Circuit reversed. The appellate court, however, rejected the administration's position "that, with no meaningful judicial review, any American citizen alleged to be an enemy combatant could be detained indefinitely without charges or counsel on the government's say-so." Instead, the court sanctioned a deferential judicial review and remanded the case to the district court. On remand, the judge directed the government to respond to Hamdi's petition, and it did so with a two-page, nine-paragraph affidavit from the Special Advisor to the Under Secretary of Defense for Policy, Michael Mobbs, detailing only the most rudimentary facts of Hamdi's capture. The judge held that the affidavit fell short of supporting Hamdi's detention and ordered the government to turn over copies of all of his statements to interrogators. When the government objected, the judge certified for the Fourth Circuit's review the following question: "Whether the Mobbs Declaration, standing alone, is sufficient as a matter of law to allow a meaningful judicial review of Yaser Esam Hamdi's classification as an enemy combatant?" Back in the Fourth Circuit, Chief Judge J. Harvie Wilkinson relied on *Quirin* in reaffirming that courts should defer to the executive branch in cases involving national security and concluded that the Mobbs declaration was a sufficient basis to justify Hamdi's incarceration. In December 2003, the Bush administration decided to allow Hamdi to consult with an attorney, though maintaining that it could hold him without further judicial hearings. The Court subsequently granted an appeal and held in *Hamdi v. Rumsfeld* (2004) (excerpted in Vol. 1, Ch. 3) that the president had the power to detain U.S. citizens as enemy combatants, but also that Hamdi had the right to contest his detention before an independent tribunal.

Another U.S. citizen detained as an "enemy combatant," Jose Padilla, was seized under very different circumstances. Padilla was detained after deplaning, unarmed, from a flight in Chicago. He was initially held as a "material witness" for allegedly meeting with Al Qaeda operatives and conspiring to detonate a radioactive "dirty bomb." Subsequently, he was moved to a New York jail and then to a Navy brig in Charleston, South Carolina. There, he was held without being charged, denied access to a lawyer, and not given other guarantees of due process. Lawyers challenged the administration's denial of judicial review, access to a lawyer, and the opportunity to contest the detention. A federal district court asked the Court of Appeals for the Second Circuit to decide whether it had jurisdiction and to decide whether Padilla could be held as an "enemy combatant." A panel of the appellate court held that federal courts have jurisdiction and Padilla's detention was not authorized by the Constitution or Congress. Based on Justice Jackson's opinion in *Youngstown Sheet and Tube Co. v. Sawyer*, 343 U.S. 579 (1952) (excerpted in Vol. 1, Ch. 3), the panel ruled that the president has no inherent power to detain U.S. citizens outside of zones of combat. The panel also held that the president had no power to do so under Congress's Authorization for Use of Military Force Joint Resolution of 2001, or the Nondetention Act of 1971, which prohibits detentions of U.S. citizens without specific congressional authorization. But on appeal, a bare majority in *Rumsfeld v. Padilla*, 124 S.Ct. 2711 (2004), ruled that Padilla's lawyer should have filed the petition in a federal court in South Carolina, where Padilla is held, and not in New York. The four dissenters—Justices Stevens, Souter, Ginsburg, and Breyer—would have upheld the court's jurisdiction and held that Padilla had a right to consult with an attorney and to contest the basis for his detention.

5

FREEDOM OF EXPRESSION AND ASSOCIATION

A connection between freedom of speech, press, and association and the exigencies of a self-governing society was acknowledged by the colonists and the Framers of the Constitution and Bill of Rights. Yet in the seventeenth and eighteenth centuries those freedoms were more circumscribed than today and were still emerging from a protracted struggle that began in England in the Middle Ages.

Government censorship stems from the 1275 enactment of De Scandalis Magnatum, imposing penalties for any false talk about the king.1 The law punished what a later amendment in 1559 termed "seditious words" (criticism of the government subject to criminal penalties) for contributing to public disorder and lawlessness. In the sixteenth and seventeenth centuries, censorship expanded with the enforcement of Scandalum Magnatum by the King's Council, which sat in the "starred chambre" at Westminster and became infamously known as the Star Chamber. The Star Chamber was especially merciless in cases such as that of the *Trial of William Prynn*.2 Prynn had published a book expressing disdain for actors and acting, which was viewed as an attack on the queen, who had recently appeared in a play, and, therefore, as seditious libel against the government. Prynn was fined £10,000, sentenced to life imprisonment, branded on the forehead, and had his nose slit and his ears cut off!

The Star Chamber left a legacy of human tragedy and an imprint on the English heritage from which the drafters of the Bill of Rights drew their principles of free government. The Star Chamber was abolished in 1641, but its precedents continued to be applied by common-law courts. Criminal liability for slander remained a question of law, not of fact for juries to decide, and the truth or falsity of a publication was immaterial as a defense against prosecution. Partisan political publications (especially in the colonies) were discouraged both by the Licensing Act of 1662 and a tax on all newspapers imposed by the Stamp and Advertising Act of 1711.

By 1776 freedom of speech and press basically meant the absence of prior restraints or censorship. As the most influential eighteenth century legal commentator, Sir William Blackstone, authoritatively observed:

> The liberty of the press is indeed essential to the nature of a free state; but this consists in laying no *previous* restraints upon publications, and not in freedom from censure for criminal matter when published. Every freeman has an undoubted right to lay what sentiments he pleases before the public; but if he publishes what is improper, mischievous, or illegal, he must take the consequences of his own temerity.[3]

Blackstone assumed that the Parliament could punish licentious speech and press, and offered no principle or standard for protecting speakers and publishers from subsequent punishment for what they said or published.

In England and in the colonies, differences over what constituted liberty and licentiousness, truth and falsehood, and good motives and criminal intent perpetuated a tumultuous struggle for freedom of speech and press. In 1792, with the Fox Libel Act, English juries were finally given the power to determine the culpability of allegedly libelous publications, rather than being confined to deciding whether an individual had in fact published allegedly libelous materials. Not until Lord Campbell's Act in 1843 was truth accepted as a defense against libel indictments, and only after 1855 was the Stamp and Advertising Act abandoned.

Colonial governments could be just as suppressive as the English Crown and Parliament. Indeed restrictions on speech and press articulated in English common law were largely incorporated into colonial common law. "Colonial America was an open society dotted with closed enclaves," as political scientist John P. Roche concluded, "and one could generally settle in with his cobelievers in safety and comfort and exercise the right of oppression."[4]

While objecting to the prior censorship of the press, English and colonial libertarians did not seriously question the propriety of punishing seditious libel and licentious publications. Thus although poet John Milton exalted freedom of speech and press in *Areopagitica*, he refused to recognize such freedom for Protestants and deplored libel of Parliament.[5] So too, John Locke, whose writings were so influential for the

Framers, in *A Letter Concerning Toleration*, urged that "no opinions contrary to human society, or to those moral rules which are necessary to the preservation of civil society, are to be tolerated by the magistrate."[6]

Widely read in the colonies were the letters of two English Whig political journalists, John Trenchard and Thomas Gordon, who wrote under the pseudonym of "Cato." Benjamin Franklin, who himself ran a printing house, first published Cato's essays in 1721. When proclaiming freedom of speech and press as "the great bulwark of Liberty," Cato observed:

> The Administration of Government, is nothing else but the Attendance of the Trustees of the People upon the Interest, and Affairs of the People. And it is the Part and Business of the People, for whose sake alone all publick Matters are or ought to be transacted, to see whether they be well or ill transacted; so it is the Interest, and ought to be the Ambition of all honest Magistrates, to have their Deeds openly examined and publickly scanned.
>
> Freedom of Speech is ever the Symptom as well as the Effect of good Government.[7]

Although giving expression to the eighteenth-century libertarian vision of free speech and press, *Cato's Letters* did not challenge the common-law rejection of truth as a defense in libel actions. Like Milton and Locke, Cato accepted the common-law proscription of seditious libel. Even Cato's colonial protégé, John Peter Zenger, failed to repudiate the common law of seditious libel when defending an unbridled freedom of the press to criticize government.

The struggle for freedom of speech and press during the colonial period largely revolved around the application of accepted common-law principles as articulated by Blackstone. By the time of the ratification of the Constitution, however, libertarians, like James Madison, broke with Alexander Hamilton and others who continued to embrace the Blackstonian understanding of free speech and press.

In 1789, when the First Congress entertained amendments to the Constitution, Madison endeavored to give constitutional effect to his rejection of common-law principles. He urged the adoption of the following provision: "The people shall not be deprived or abridged of their right to speak, to write, or to publish their sentiments; and the freedom of the press, as one of the great bulwarks of liberty, shall be inviolable." Madison argued that "freedom of the press and the rights of conscience, those choicest privileges of the people, are unguarded in the British constitution." In England, Parliament was trusted to guard the people against the sovereign's unlawful acts. By contrast, Madison pointed out, in the United States the people are sovereign and their rights, therefore,

■ CONSTITUTIONAL HISTORY

The 1735 Trial of John Peter Zenger and Free Speech in the Colonies

Undoubtedly, the *cause célèbre* of colonial prosecutions was the trial of John Peter Zenger, publisher of *The New York Weekly Journal*. The *Journal*, like other colonial newspapers, was a partisan publication, and Zenger, poorly educated and neither an editor or writer for his paper, was part of a political faction that lost power when William Cosby became governor of New York. In 1734, Zenger published, along with several of Cato's essays, a series of satirical ballads attacking Governor Cosby. A year later, Zenger was tried for printing "many things tending to raise factions and tumults among the people of this province, inflaming their minds with contempt for his majesty's government, and greatly disturbing the peace thereof." In the penultimate trial before royal judges, Zenger's initial lawyers, James Alexander and William Smith, sought to use the trial to further discredit Cosby's administration, and went so far as to attack the chief justice for presiding at the trial. They were promptly disbarred from practicing law in the colony. An acclaimed Quaker attorney, Andrew Hamilton, came unsolicited from Philadelphia to Zenger's defense with an unprecedented challenge of the common-law principles governing freedom of speech and press. Hamilton contended that Zenger's publications were true and that if he was not permitted to demonstrate their truth as a defense, then the jury should acquit Zenger. The jury, already critical of Cosby's administration and the chief justice, found Zenger not guilty.

Zenger's trial popularized for colonists the struggle against governmental censorship in the form of prosecutions for sedition. Both sides of the Zenger controversy, however, accepted the common-law principle that freedom of speech and press did not permit licentiousness and seditious libel. What divided them was the issue of when and where to draw a line between permissible political commentary and licentious criticism of the government.

Sources: See Livingston Rutherford, *John Peter Zenger, His Press, His Trial, and a Bibliography of Zenger Imprints* (New York: Dodd, Mead, & Co., 1904); and Leonard Levy, ed., *Freedom of the Press from Zenger to Jefferson* (New York: Bobbs-Merrill, 1966).

had to be guaranteed against both the executive and the legislature. For these reasons, Madison not only rejected the application of Blackstonian common-law principles to freedom of speech and press but proposed as another constitutional amendment that "no State shall violate the equal rights of conscience, or the freedom of the press."

Madison advanced perhaps the broadest possible view of free speech and press. Considering a vigorous press essential to free government, he rejected the imposition of any sanctions for the licentiousness accompanying the exercise of free speech and press. In Madison's words:

> Among those principles deemed sacred in America, among those sacred rights considered as forming the bulwark of liberty, which the Government contemplates with awful reverence and would approach only with the most cautious circumspection, there is no one of which the importance is more deeply impressed on the public mind than the liberty of the press. That this *liberty* is often carried to excess; that it has sometimes degenerated into *licentiousness*, is seen and lamented, *but the remedy has* not yet been discovered. Perhaps it is an evil inseparable from the good with which it is allied; perhaps it is a shoot which cannot be stripped from the stalk without wounding vitally the plant from which it is torn. However desirable those measures might be which might correct without enslaving the press, they have never yet been devised in America.[8]

Still, as Madison acknowledged, his understanding of freedom of speech and press was not representative of that in the founding period.[9] Colonial experiences with censorship by the Crown had fostered agreement that free speech and press should be protected. Also, there was little debate in the First Congress on adopting a provision guaranteeing the freedom of speech and press. But those, including Thomas Jefferson, who feared the abuse of these freedoms also expected the states to continue common-law restrictions on libel and other licentious publications.

Madison's proposal for expressly prohibiting the states from limiting the freedom of speech and press did not survive. Ratified on December 15, 1791, the First Amendment provides, "Congress shall make no law respecting an establishment of religion, or prohibiting the free exercise thereof; or abridging the freedom of speech, or of the press; or the right of the people peaceably to assemble." The amendment was thought to protect only against prior restraint by the national government; it did not provide absolute immunity for what speakers or publishers might utter or print. Thus the First Amendment was in Hamiltonian terms superfluous (because the Constitution did not give Congress the power to regulate speech and press in the first place), whereas from Madison's vantage point it did not sufficiently safeguard individuals' freedom (particularly from state regulation) and from Jefferson's perspective the amendment simply reaffirmed both the limits of the national government's power and the reserved powers of the states.

Less than a decade later, a constitutional crisis over the First Amendment arose when Congress passed the Alien and Sedition Acts of 1798. The Sedition Act imposed criminal sanctions for "any false, scandalous writing against the government of the United States." It was passed by the Federalist Congress to censure political criticism and turn public opinion against the Jeffersonian-Republicans. The ensuing controversy revealed, once again, that the predominant view of freedom of speech and press was that the First Amendment incorporated traditional Blackstonian common-law principles, rather than broader libertarian principles.

The congressional reports on the repeal of the Sedition Act on February 25, 1799, amply illustrate the acceptance of Blackstonian principles. The constitutionality of the act was defended in the majority's report to Congress on four grounds. First, punishment of seditious libel did not constitute an abridgment of freedom of speech and press, because those freedoms never included "a license for every man to publish what he pleases without being liable to punishment." Second, although little more than a restatement of the first point, the laws of the states and national government never extended "to the publication of false, scandalous, and malicious writings against the Government." Third, the Sedition Act was "merely declaratory of the common law, and useful for rendering that law more generally known, and more easily understood." Fourth, the committee drew a distinction between the religious and the speech and press freedoms protected by the First Amendment. The amendment provides that "*Congress shall make no law respecting* an establishment of religion, *or prohibiting* the free exercise thereof,*" implying that the national government is absolutely barred from legislating on religious matters. By comparison, the amendment forbids Congress only from passing laws "*abridging* the freedom of speech, or of the press." From that language, the committee surmised that Congress was not precluded from passing legislation *respecting* speech and press.[10]

In the House of Representatives, Albert Gallatin and others had argued against the constitutionality of the Sedition Act on the grounds that "the States have complete power on the subject." Likewise, Thomas Jefferson, in the Kentucky Resolutions of 1798 and 1799 (see Ch. 1), insisted that the states alone possessed the power to initiate libel actions. But the minority report filed in Congress on the repeal of the Sedition Act drew on Madison's understanding of the importance of political speech and guaranteeing the freedom of political debate and criticism:

> The most important and necessary information for the people to receive is, of the misconduct of the Government; because their

good deeds, although they will produce affection and gratitude to public officers, will only confirm the existing confidence, and will, therefore, make no change in the conduct of the people. The question, whether the Government ought to have control over the persons who alone can give information throughout the country, is nothing more than this, whether men interested in suppressing information necessary for the people to have, ought to be entrusted with the power, or whether they ought to have a power which their personal interest leads to the abuse of?[11]

On this basis, Jeffersonian-Republicans and libertarians, who were a minority in Congress, rejected the majority's report on the constitutionality of the Sedition Act. But their arguments proved unpersuasive, in part because they were neither in complete agreement nor consistent in their views of the scope of freedom of speech and press. The Jeffersonian-Republicans waxed and waned in maintaining that the only permissible restrictions on speech and press could come from the states. And the continued prosecutions for seditious libel after the Sedition Act expired underscores how deeply rooted was the common-law understanding of the freedom of speech and press.

There were no prosecutions under the Sedition Act after 1801, when the act expired and Thomas Jefferson became president. But seditious libel remained a crime in common law. In 1804, President Jefferson wrote to Mrs. John Adams and explained his pardoning of those convicted under the Sedition Act, insisting that the "law [was] a nullity as absolute and as palpable as if Congress had ordered us to fall down and worship a golden image." Eloquent in describing his rage against the Federalists' prosecutions under the act, Jefferson was no less vengeful in recommending prosecutions by the states of Federalist editors![12] In New York courts, in *People v. Croswell*, 3 Johnson's (N.Y.) Cases 336 (1804), Republicans prosecuted a Federalist editor for seditious libel against President Jefferson. Three years later, they were still relying on state and federal courts to try individuals for seditious libel against the president. Not until 1812, in another action for libel against the president, did the Supreme Court finally rule that there was no federal common law of crimes, including the crime of seditious libel. *United States v. Hudson and Goodwin*, 1 Cr. 21 (1812).

In 1833, the most widely read commentator on the Constitution within a generation of the founding period and a Supreme Court justice, Joseph Story, observed that "there is a good deal of loose reasoning on the subject of the liberty of the press, as if its inviolability were constitutionally such." Story endorsed Blackstone's view of free speech and press, remained uncertain whether the First Amendment prohibited Congress from "punishing the licentiousness of the press," and had no doubt that the states could punish individuals for libelous and "other mischievous publications."[13]

By the late nineteenth century, another influential authority on the Constitution, Thomas Cooley, acknowledged that the press had assumed an increasingly important role in society as a result of technological innovations and urbanization. Cooley agreed with Madison that "repression of full and free discussion is dangerous in any government resting upon the will of the people." However, like Story, Cooley continued to view the First Amendment in terms of common-law principles and practices. The amendment, as he put it, guaranteed "a right to freely utter and publish whatever the citizen may please, and to be protected against any responsibility for so doing, except so far as such publications, from their blasphemy, obscenity, or scandalous character, may be a public offense, or as by their falsehood and malice they may injuriously affect the standing, reputation, or pecuniary interests of individuals."[14]

From the founding period and throughout the nineteenth century, the First Amendment was thus comprehended in terms of developing common-law principles and practices. That meant that Blackstone's definition of free speech and press served as the touchstone for understanding those freedoms. As we saw earlier, Blackstone's view was that liberty of speech and press meant the absence of prior restraints but also the permissibility of subsequent punishment for speech or print that was deemed "improper, mischievous or illegal." While Blackstone distinguished between liberty and licentiousness—or protected and unprotected communications—he failed to articulate the criteria for determining what and when speech and print constituted an abuse of liberty, assuming that common-law judges would defer to legislatures when defining the nature of licentiousness.

In the absence of constitutional restraints imposed by the Supreme Court under the First Amendment, the struggle for free speech and press became a legacy of suppression. In the nineteenth century, lower courts, legislatures, government officials, and ultimately the shifting tides of public opinion enjoyed broad power to punish speech and press and thereby the power to deprive the rights of minorities to express unpopular views.

After the public outcry against the Sedition Act, the national government in the first half of the nineteenth century largely left the suppression of licentious publications to the states. Beginning in the 1830s, the dissemination of information about slavery was punished in the North and the South by enthusiasts both of abolition and of the institution of slavery. In the North, crusading vigilantes fomented mob action, leading to the tarring and feathering, clubbing, whipping, and shooting of abolitionists. William Lloyd Garrison, for one, was stripped half naked and paraded through the streets of Boston. In Illinois, Elijah Lovejoy died at the hands of a mob, while resisting the destruction of his printing press. In the South, legislation punished abolitionist sentiments as "incendiary," "inflammatory," and "provoking servile insurrection." That legislation was reinforced by censorship of the mails. Censorship of the mails began in 1835 with the refusal of a Charleston, South Carolina, postmaster to deliver abolitionist mail in the South. The postmaster general, along with President Andrew Jackson and John C. Calhoun, endeavored to get Congress to pass a law authorizing such actions. Congress refused and passed a law to the contrary, at the urging of Daniel Webster and Henry Clay that such legislation would abridge free speech and press. But states effectively nullified federal law. During the Civil War, major newspapers in the North and the South criticized President Abraham Lincoln's conduct of the war, and Lincoln reluctantly ordered the New York *World* and the New York *Journal of Commerce* closed and their editors arrested.

While abolitionist sentiments sparked government censorship in the early nineteenth century, allegedly lewd and obscene materials were the object of censorship in the latter part of the century. In 1865, Congress authorized punishment for purveyors of obscenity and further expanded the law with the Comstock Act of 1873, named after Anthony Comstock, a tireless crusader against impure and lustful publications. Into this century, federal courts upheld congressional power to suppress obscene materials. Likewise, state courts affirmed bans against publishing, importing, mailing, and purchasing of pornographic materials, as well as supposedly objectionable books by noted authors such as Honoré de Balzac, Gustav Flaubert, James Joyce, and D. H. Lawrence, as well as Theodore Dreiser's *An American Tragedy!*

Along with a growing number of obscenity prosecutions, actions for criminal libel increased in the last quarter of the nineteenth century, with more than 100 prosecutions between 1890 and 1900. By the turn of the century, public opinion was aroused by the doctrines of socialism, anarchism, syndicalism, and the specter of violent revolution raised by radical political groups, especially Communists. The assassination of President William McKinley by a reputed anarchist dramatized for the public the dangers of such doctrines. Consequently, there was resumption of legislation punishing seditious libel. By the end of World War I, no less than thirty-two states had laws against criminal syndicalism or sedition; more than 1,900 individuals were prosecuted for seditious libel; and more than 100 newspapers, pamphlets, and other periodicals were censored.[15]

The Espionage Act of 1917 was the primary source of federal restrictions on speech and press in the early twentieth century. That act rested on the traditional dichotomy of liberty versus licentiousness in imposing criminal liability on any individual who, when the country was at war, would "make or convey false reports or false statements with the intent to interfere with the operations or success of the military or naval forces of the United States or to promote the success of its enemies," or to "willfully cause or attempt to cause insubordination, disloyalty, mutiny, or refusal of duty, in the military or naval forces of the United States," or to "willfully obstruct the recruiting or enlistment service of the United States, to the injury of the service of the United States."[16]

When challenges to the Espionage Act and other state laws punishing dissident and subversive individuals and groups finally reached the Supreme Court, the justices faced the vexing responsibility of giving meaning to the First Amendment by developing standards and tests for determining the scope of constitutionally protected free speech and press. As discussed in the next section and as the cases excerpted there illustrate, in the first half of the twentieth century the Court employed "the clear and present danger" test and other techniques of ad hoc balancing of free speech claims against competing governmental interests. In the second half of the twentieth century, however, the Court evolved a "two-level theory" or definitional balancing approach to the First Amendment: political and other kinds of speech receive full protection unless they fall into one of *four categories of unprotected speech* ("obscenity," "libel," "fighting words," and "commercial speech"). But as discussed and as the cases excerpted show in other sections of this chapter, more recently some of these categories ("fighting words" and "commercial speech," for instance) have been given expanded First Amendment protection, and depending on the *context*—public schools, airwaves and broadcasts versus the print media and the Internet—the Court has denied protection for indecent and offensive speech in balancing free speech claims against competing governmental interests.

In sum, the justices and the country remain locked in a dialogue over how free "free speech" should be and how it should be balanced with such competing governmental interests as promoting moral decency, national security, equality, and the social order. In other words, the Court and the country continue to debate why we value and should value free speech over other competing values. Is free speech valuable because it is *instrumental* to self-governance and the democratic process? Does free speech have *intrinsic value* because individual expression is related to self-determination and human dignity? Should speech be protected because we are agnostic and, as Justice Holmes in *Abrams v. United States*, 250 U.S. 616 (1919), observed, "the best test of truth is the power of the thought to get itself accepted in the competition of the market"? Or should we value free speech over governmental restrictions due to the "slippery slope" of governmental censorship?

NOTES

1. See Fredrick Siebert, *Freedom of the Press in England, 1476–1776* (Urbana: University of Illinois, 1965).

2. *Trial of William Prynn*, 3 Howell's State Trials 561 (1632).

3. Sir William Blackstone, *Commentaries on the Laws of England*, Vol. 4 (Oxford, UK: Clarendon Press, 1766), 151–152.

4. John P. Roche, *Shadow and Substance* (New York: Macmillan, 1964), 11.

5. John Milton, *Areopagitica*, in *The Works of John Milton*, Vol. 4, ed. William Haller (New York: Columbia University Press, 1931); and see William Clyde, *The Struggle for the Freedom of the Press from Caxton to Cromwell* (London: Oxford University Press, 1934).

6. John Locke, "A Letter Concerning Toleration," in *The Works of John Locke*, Vol. 4, 11th ed. (London: W. Otridge, 1905–1907), 45–46.

7. Cato, "Reflections on Libelling," in *Freedom of the Press from Zenger to Jefferson*, ed. Leonard Levy (New York: Bobbs-Merrill, 1966), 12.

8. *Annals of Congress: First Congress, 1789–1791*, Vol. 1 (Washington, DC: Gales and Seaton, 1834), 453; and James Madison, *The Writings of James Madison*, Vol. 6, ed. Haillard Hunt (New York: Putnam's Sons, 1906–1910), 336.

9. See James Madison to Edward Everett (Aug. 28, 1830), in Madison, *The Writings of James Madison*, Vol. 9, 383.

10. "Majority Report on Repeal of the Sedition Act," *Annals of Congress*, 5th Cong., 3d Sess., Feb. 25, 1799, 2987–2990.

11. Ibid., 3003–3014.

12. Letters from Thomas Jefferson to Abigail Adams (Sept. 11, 1804), and to Thomas McKean (Feb. 19, 1803) in *The Writings of Thomas Jefferson*, Vol. 8, ed. Paul Ford (New York: Putnam's Sons, 1892–1899), 310 and 218–219.

13. Joseph Story, *Commentaries on the Constitution of the United States* (Boston: Little, Brown, 1833), 735.

14. Thomas Cooley, *A Treatise on the Constitutional Limitations*, Vol. 2 (Boston: Little, Brown, 1868), 886 and 931–940.

15. See Fredrick Siebert, *The Rights and Privileges of the Press* (New York: D. Appleton-Century, 1934), 271; and James Paul and Murray Schwartz, *Federal Censorship: Obscenity in the Mail* (New York: Free Press, 1961), 17–24.

16. The Espionage Act of June 15, 1917, 40 Stat. 217. See also Act of May 16, 1918, 40 Stat. 553.

Selected Bibliography

Blanchard, Margaret. *Revolutionary Sparks: Freedom of Expression in Modern America.* New York: Oxford University Press, 1992.

Curtis, Michael K. *Free Speech, "The People's Darling Privilege": Struggles for Freedom of Expression in American History.* Durham, NC: Duke University Press, 2000.

Graber, Mark. *Transforming Free Speech: The Ambiguous Legacy of Civil Libertarianism.* Berkeley: University of California Press, 1991.

Levy, Leonard, ed. *Freedom of Press from Zenger to Jefferson.* New York: Bobbs-Merrill, 1966.

Levy, Leonard, *Emergence of a Free Press.* New York: Oxford University Press, 1985.

Meiklejohn, Alexander. *Political Freedom: The Constitutional Powers of the People.* New York: Harper & Row, 1948.

Nelson, Harold, ed. *Freedom of the Press from Hamilton to the Warren Court.* New York: Bobbs-Merrill, 1967.

Smith, James M. *Freedom's Fetters: The Alien and Sedition Laws and American Civil Liberties.* Ithaca, NY: Cornell University Press, 1956.

Smith, Jeffery. *Printers and Press Freedom.* New York: Oxford University Press, 1988.

Steele, Richard. *Free Speech in the Good War.* New York: St. Martin's, 1999.

A | *Judicial Approaches to the First Amendment*

When First Amendment challenges to state and federal sedition laws reached the Supreme Court in the aftermath of World War I, the convictions were upheld. This litigation, however, forced the Court to confront two long-avoided tasks: first, deciding whether the First Amendment applied equally against the states and the national government and, second, articulating standards for defining the scope of constitutionally protected free speech and press. Once the Court held the First Amendment applied to the states (see Ch. 3), it could no longer avoid the even more difficult task of giving constitutional meaning to the amendment. Initially, the Court took for granted that Blackstone's common-law principles governed the First Amendment's guarantees of free speech and press. But gradually members of the Court pressed for the development of constitutional principles that would define the scope of protected speech and press. By 1936, in *Grosjean v. American Press Co.*, 297 U.S. 233 (1936), Justice George Sutherland finally noted, as Madison more than a century before had urged, that constitutional principles (not the English common law) governed the scope of protected speech and press. In Sutherland's words,

Justices Oliver Wendell Holmes (left) and Louis D. Brandeis. In the 1920s, Justices Brandeis and Holmes dissented from the Court's upholding the convictions of individuals for expressing unpopular, and what was considered subversive, political ideas. In an effort to extend First Amendment protection for free speech, Justice Holmes invented the clear and present danger test. (*Underwood & Underwood, Collection of the Supreme Court of the United States*)

> It is impossible to concede that by the words "freedom of the press" the framers of the amendment intended to adopt merely the narrow view then reflected by the law of England that such freedom consisted only in immunity from previous censorship. . . . Undoubtedly, the range of a constitutional provision phrased in terms of the common law sometimes may be fixed by recourse to the applicable rules of law. But the doctrine which justifies such recourse, like other canons of construction, must yield to more compelling reasons whenever they exist.

Still, it took decades for the Court to respond to those "more compelling reasons" for breaking away from common-law principles and articulating the constitutional principles that now govern the application of the First Amendment. For the justices that meant reconciling rival interpretative approaches to the First Amendment and a political struggle within the Court, as well as between the Court and the country over the freedoms of speech and press.

■ (1) FIFTY YEARS OF "CLEAR AND PRESENT DANGER"

The surge of litigation challenging convictions under the Espionage Act and state sedition laws necessitated that the Court develop its own interpretative standards for protecting the freedom of speech and press. In *Schenck v. United States* (1919) (see excerpt below), Justice Oliver Wendell Holmes initially intimated what would become one of the best-known tests for defining the scope of constitutionally protected free speech and press: "*the clear and present danger" test*—" whether the words used are used in such circumstances and are of such a nature as to create a clear and present danger that they will bring about the substantive evils that Congress has a right to prevent." However, Holmes retreated and based his opinion on the old common-law presumption of the "reasonableness of legislation" and whether the proscribed speech had a "*bad tendency*"—"whether the statements contained in the [communication] had a natural tendency to produce the forbidden consequences."[1] Within a week, in two more unanimous rulings, Holmes again upheld convictions under the Espionage Act on the bad tendency standard.[2]

But in a fourth case in 1919, *Abrams v. United States*, 250 U.S. 616 (1919), Holmes broke with the majority over using the clear and present danger test as an alternative to the bad tendency test. *Abrams* involved the conviction of five individuals under the Espionage Act for distributing leaflets condemning the government's war effort and intervention in Russia and calling for a general strike of workers in protest. When rejecting the majority's reliance on the bad tendency test, in dissent with Justice Louis Brandeis, Holmes proclaimed that "only the emergency that makes it immediately dangerous to leave the correction of evil counsels to time warrants making any exception to the sweeping command, 'Congress shall make no law . . . abridging the freedom of speech.' " His dissent in *Abrams* was followed by four other biting dissents and one concurring opinion, establishing the foundations for the evolution of this most famous of judicial approaches to the First Amendment.[3]

In the 1920s, the Court continued to hold that the First Amendment did not protect speech and press that might have pernicious effects on society. *Gitlow v. People of the State of New York* (1925) (excerpted below) is illustrative. There Justice Edward Sanford reaffirmed the traditional common-law principles governing the punishment of subversive speech:

> Such utterances, by their very nature, involve danger to the public peace and to the security of the State. They threaten breaches of the peace and ultimate revolution. And the immediate danger is

none the less real and substantial, because the effect of a given utterance cannot be accurately foreseen. The State cannot reasonably be required to measure the danger from every such utterance in the nice balance of a jeweler's scale. A single revolutionary spark may kindle a fire that, smoldering for a time, may burst into a sweeping and destructive conflagration.

In another illustrious dissent in *Gitlow*, Holmes reiterated his clear and present danger test. Two years later, in *Whitney v. California*, 274 U.S. 357 (1927), involving the conviction of a Communist under a state syndicalism act, Brandeis endeavored to further sharpen the clear and present danger test. Even in the face of legislation, the First Amendment forbids restrictions short of demonstrating an *imminent* clear and present danger; in Brandeis's words, "Only an emergency can justify repression."

In the two decades following *Abrams*, the clear and present danger test was virtually abandoned. Under the leadership of Chief Justice Charles Evans Hughes in the 1930s, however, the Court also substantially undermined reliance on the reasonableness of legislation and bad tendency approach. A series of rulings extended First Amendment protection to pamphlets and leaflets,[4] and peaceful picketing,[5] because its guarantees were construed to safeguard "the liberty to discuss publicly and truthfully all matters of public concern without previous restraint or fear of subsequent punishment."[6]

In the 1940s, the clear and present danger test enjoyed a kind of renaissance, buttressed by the Hughes Court's precedents expanding the scope of the First Amendment. The test, though, was fundamentally transformed during the tenures of Chief Justices Harlan Stone and Fred Vinson (respectively, 1941–1946 and 1946–1953).

Holmes and Brandeis formulated the clear and present danger test as an evidentiary rule for determining the permissibility of applying statutory prohibitions in particular circumstances; it did not purport to establish a standard for reviewing the constitutionality of legislation per se. Moreover, they invoked the test only in cases involving alleged threats to national security.

By contrast, in the 1940s the Court turned the clear and present danger test into a standard for judging both the application and constitutionality per se of statutes. It also became a basis for reviewing a wide range of restrictions on speech and the press, including state laws restricting or prohibiting handbill distributions and solicitations,[7] and requiring compulsory saluting of the American flag,[8] as well as contempt-of-court convictions and individuals' speeches before public assemblies.[9]

As the scope of the First Amendment expanded in the 1940s, some justices pushed for an even more libertarian approach. Chief Justice Stone and Justices Black, Douglas, Murphy, and Rutledge claimed the amendment enjoyed a "preferred position," virtually foreclosing the possibility of upholding any restrictions on free speech and press. As Stone observed, "The First Amendment is not confined to safeguarding freedom of speech and freedom of religion against discriminatory attempts to wipe them out. On the contrary, the Constitution, by virtue of the First and Fourteenth Amendments, has put those freedoms in a *preferred position*."[10]

The reformulation of the clear and present danger test and articulation of the preferred position approach toward the First Amendment were not without opposition from within the Court. Throughout his twenty-three years on the bench (1939–1962), Justice Frankfurter criticized his colleagues for their "idle play on words" and "perversion" of the Holmesian-Brandeis formulation and ridiculed those embracing a "preferred position" for devising a "deceptive formula . . . [that] makes for mechanical jurisprudence."[11]

Divisions within the Court were further exacerbated by the political currents in the 1940s and 1950s. Beginning in the early 1940s, political passions again swept the country with dire warnings about fascism and communism. In 1940, Congress enacted the Alien Registration Act, or Smith Act, the first federal peacetime sedition act since the Alien and Sedition Acts of 1798. Less restrictive than the Sedition Act, the Smith Act made it a crime to advocate or to belong to any organization that advocated the forceful overthrow of the government. Subsequently, Congress required loyalty oaths and statements of non-Communist affiliation from public- and private-sector employees, with the Labor-Management Relations Act of 1947. The paranoia over Communists continued through the 1950s. Over President Harry Truman's veto, Congress passed the Internal Security Act of 1950, also known as the McCarran Act, which required members of the Communist Party to register with the U.S. attorney general. Senator Joseph McCarthy's subcommittee and the Special House Committee on Un-American Activities as well as numerous legislative committees held hearings and investigations of individuals' loyalty.

Bitterly divided, the Court affirmed the constitutionality of both the Smith Act and the McCarran Act in, respectively, *Dennis v. United States* (1951) (see excerpt below), and *Communist Party v. Subversive Activities Control Board*, 367 U.S. 203 (1961). *Dennis* remains the watershed case in which the Vinson Court's reformulation of the clear and present danger test rendered futile further reliance on the test.

Dennis was presaged by Chief Justice Vinson's opinion in *American Communications Association v. Douds*, 339 U.S. 382 (1950), upholding a requirement for the filing of non-Communist affidavits in the Labor-Management Relations Act. In their briefs before the Court, the unions argued that it was difficult "to conceive how the expression of belief, or the joining of a political party, without more, could ever constitute [a clear and present] danger." Chief Justice Vinson thought otherwise: the threat of communism was substantial, considerably greater than when Holmes proposed his clear and present danger test and, therefore, justified congressional action. No less important, Vinson indicated that the clear and present danger test was not a mechanical rule, but rather a balancing technique:

> [E]ven harmful conduct cannot justify restrictions upon speech unless substantial interests of society are at stake. But in suggesting that the substantive evil must be serious and substantial, it was never the intention of this Court to lay down an absolutist test measured in terms of danger to the Nation. When the effect of a statute or ordinance upon the exercise of First Amendment freedoms is relatively small and the public interest to be protected is substantial, it is obvious that a rigid test requiring a showing of imminent danger to the security of the Nation is an absurdity.

In Vinson's hands, the clear and present danger test became a balancing technique for rationalizing restrictions on speech and the press.[12]

The opinions in *Dennis* reveal the internal politics of the Vinson Court and the competing interpretive approaches toward the First Amendment. When a second opportunity to interpret the Smith Act arose with *Yates v. United States*, 354 U.S. 178 (1957), it was anticipated that the result would be different from that in *Dennis*. Oleta Yates and thirteen other second-string functionaries of the Communist Party were prosecuted shortly after *Dennis* was announced; each was found guilty, fined $10,000, and sentenced to five years in prison. By the time their appeal was granted in 1955, Vinson and his three supporters in *Dennis* were gone. President Dwight Eisenhower in 1953 had appointed Earl Warren as chief justice, and Justices Reed, Jackson, and Minton had been replaced by Whittaker, Harlan, and Brennan. Still, the Warren Court (with newly appointed Justices Whittaker and Brennan not participating) declined to strike down the Smith Act in *Yates*. However, it reversed five of the convictions and ordered retrials for the others, setting forth certain conditions for applying the Smith Act that made future convictions exceedingly difficult.

Justice Harlan's opinion for the Court in *Yates* abandoned the clear and present danger test and substituted instead a *balancing approach* according to which First Amendment freedoms were weighed against society's right of self-preservation. He claimed that was the essence of

Dennis in distinguishing between advocacy of abstract doctrines (which receives First Amendment protection) and the advocacy of violence and unlawful action. Two years later, he again provided the voice for a bare majority and reasserted his balancing approach to the First Amendment in *Barenblatt v. United States*, 360 U.S. 109 (1959) (see Vol. 1, Ch. 5).

By the 1960s, the clear and present danger test had evolved into a rhetorical technique and then gave way to Harlan's explicit balancing of First Amendment freedoms against legislative restrictions. Harlan's balancing approach, however, enjoyed the support only of a bare majority of the Court. In the early 1960s, the Warren Court was split five to four over balancing First Amendment freedoms, with Justice Potter Stewart as the swing vote. A bare majority, in *Scales v. United States*, 367 U.S. 203 (1961), upheld the Smith Act's prohibition on membership in subversive organizations, and in *Communist Party of the United States v. Subversives Activities Control Board (SACB)*, 367 U.S. 1 (1961), the registration requirements for all members of subversive organizations, as established by the Internal Security Act of 1950. In *Scales*, Harlan upheld the membership clause by distinguishing between mere, passive members (the "foolish, deluded, or perhaps merely optimistic") and those knowing, active members whose intent was "to bring about the overthrow of the government as speedily as circumstances would permit." Over the four dissenters' objections that the Court had legitimated "guilt by association," Harlan's opinion for the majority concluded that there was enough evidence that Scales was an "active" member engaged in illegal advocacy. In the second case upholding the SACB, Frankfurter performed the delicate task of writing an opinion for another bare majority. In both cases, Chief Justice Warren and Justices Black, Douglas, and Brennan dissented. One week later, though, Justice Stewart swung over to the dissenters' side to form a majority for reversing the conviction of an individual found in contempt for refusing to answer questions before a subcommittee of the House Committee on Un-American Activities, *Deutch v. United States*, 367 U.S. 456 (1961).

Following *Scales*, prosecutions for subversive activities under the Smith Act sharply declined, and by the mid-1960s (with the appointments of Abe Fortas and Thurgood Marshall as associate justices) there was a solid majority on the Warren Court for striking down portions of the McCarran Act. Because Congress refused to appropriate funds, the SACB was finally shut down in 1973, over the objections of President Richard Nixon, who as a congressman in 1950 had been one of its sponsors. A year later, the Special House Committee on Un-American Activities was abolished and its duties transferred to the House Judicial Committee.

In Chief Justice Earl Warren's last term, the Court handed down a *per curiam* opinion in *Brandenburg v. Ohio* (1969) (see excerpt below), finally laying to rest the long line of cases upholding convictions for so-called subversive speech and activities advocating unpopular political doctrines. Justices Black and Douglas gave their final requiem for the clear and present danger test in brief concurring opinions. But see and compare the Court's ruling on the constitutionality of criminalizing cross burning in *Virginia v. Black* (2003) (in Section B of this chapter).

Notes

1. *Pierce v. United States*, 252 U.S. 239 (1920).

2. *Debs v. United States*, 249 U.S. 211 (1919); and *Frowerk v. United States*, 249 U.S. 204 (1919).

3. See *Schaefer v. United States*, 251 U.S. 466 (1920); *Pierce v. United States*, 252 U.S. 239 (1920); *Gilbert v. Minnesota*, 254 U.S. 235 (1920); *Gitlow v. New York*, 268 U.S. 652 (1925); and *Whitney v. California*, 274 U.S. 357 (1927).

4. See *Lovell v. City of Griffin*, 303 U.S. 444 (1938); *Schneider v. New Jersey*, 308 U.S. 147 (1939); *Marsh v. Alabama*, 326 U.S. 296 (1940); *Cantwell v. Connecticut*, 310 U.S. 296 (1940); and *Cox v. New Hampshire*, 312 U.S. 569 (1941).

5. *Cantwell v. Connecticut*, 310 U.S. 296 (1940).

6. *Thornhill v. Alabama*, 310 U.S. 102 (1940).

7. See *Cantwell v. Connecticut*, 310 U.S. 296 (1940); *Douglas v. City of Jeanette*, 319 U.S. 157 (1943); *Jones v. Opelika*, 319 U.S. 103 (1943); *Murdock v. Pennsylvania*, 319 U.S. 105 (1943); and *Follet v. Town of McCormick*, 321 U.S. 573 (1944).

8. See and compare *Minersville School District v. Gobitus*, 310 U.S. 586 (1940), with *West Virginia Board of Education v. Barnette*, 319 U.S. 624 (1943).

9. *Bridges v. California*, 314 U.S. 252 (1941); *Pennekamp v. Florida*, 328 U.S. 331 (1946); *Craig v. Harney*, 331 U.S. 367 (1947) (contempt-of-court citations for publications concerning pending trials); and *Terminello v. Chicago*, 337 U.S. 1 (1949) (conviction for public speech).

10. *Jones v. Opelika*, 316 U.S. 584, 608 (1942) (Stone, J., dissenting opinion), adopted on rehearing, *Jones v. Opelika*, 319 U.S. 103 (1943).

11. See *Bridges v. California*, 314 U.S. 252, 295 (1941); *Craig v. Harney*, 331 U.S. 367, 391 (1947); and *Kovacs v. Cooper*, 336 U.S. 77, 96 (1949).

12. See *Niemotko v. Maryland*, 340 U.S. 268 (1951); and *Feiner v. New York*, 340 U.S. 315 (1951).

Selected Bibliography

Allen, David, and Jensen, Robert, eds. *Freeing the First Amendment: Critical Perspectives on Freedom of Expression*. New York: New York University Press, 1995.

Baker, C. Edwin. *Human Liberty and Freedom of Speech*. New York: Oxford University Press, 1989.

Black, Hugo. *A Constitutional Faith*. New York: Knopf, 1968.

Bollinger, Lee. *The Tolerant Society: Freedom of Speech and Extremist Speech in America.* New York: Oxford University Press, 1986.

Emerson, Thomas. *The System of Freedom of Expression.* New York: Random House, 1970.

Fiss, Owen. *The Irony of Free Speech.* Cambridge, MA: Harvard University Press, 1997.

Polenberg, Richard. *Fighting Faiths: The Abrams Case, the Supreme Court, and Free Speech.* New York: Viking, 1987.

Rabban, David. *Free Speech in Its Forgotten Years.* New York: Cambridge University Press, 1997.

Shiffrin, Steve. *The First Amendment, Democracy, and Romance.* Princeton, NJ: Princeton University Press, 1991.

Schenck v. United States
249 U.S. 47, 39 S.Ct. 247 (1919)

As secretary of the Socialist Party, Schenck was responsible for the printing, distributing, and mailing to men eligible for the draft leaflets that advocated opposition to the government's involvement in World War I and urged them to resist conscription. He was arrested, tried, and convicted in federal courts for violating the Espionage Act of 1917. That act was passed amid the so-called Red (communist) scare, prompted by economic dislocations due to the war and growing distrust of aliens and foreign-born radicals because of the Bolshevik revolution in Russia. Schenck's appeal was the first of several cases challenging the Espionage Act to reach the Supreme Court.

The Court's decision was unanimous, and the opinion was announced by Justice Holmes.

☐ *Justice HOLMES delivered the opinion of the Court.*

The document in question upon its first printed side recited the first section of the Thirteenth Amendment, said that the idea embodied in it was violated by the conscription act and that a conscript is little better than a convict. In impassioned language it intimated that conscription was despotism in its worst form and a monstrous wrong against humanity in the interest of Wall Street's chosen few. It said, "Do not submit to intimidation," but in form at least confined itself to peaceful measures such as a petition for the repeal of the act. The other and later printed side of the sheet was headed "Assert Your Rights." It stated reasons for alleging that anyone violated the Constitution when he refused to recognize "your right to assert your opposition to the draft," and went on, "If you do not assert and support your rights, you are helping to deny or disparage rights which it is the solemn duty of all citizens and residents of the United States to retain." It described the arguments on the other side as coming from cunning politicians and a mercenary capitalist press, and even silent consent to the conscription law as helping to support an infamous conspiracy. It denied the power to send our citizens away to foreign shores to shoot up the people of other lands, and added that words could not express the condemnation such cold-blooded ruthlessness deserves, &c., &c., winding up, "You must do your share to maintain, support and uphold the rights of the people of this country." Of course the document would not have been sent unless it had been intended to have some effect, and we do not see what effect it could be expected to have upon persons subject to the draft except to influence them to obstruct the carrying of it out. The defendants do not deny that the jury might find against them on this point.

But it is said, suppose that that was the tendency of this circular, it is protected by the First Amendment to the Constitution. Two of the strongest expressions are said to be quoted respectively from well-known public men. It well may be that the prohibition of laws abridging the freedom of speech is not confined to previous restraints, although to prevent them may have been the main purpose, as intimated in *Patterson v. Colorado*, 205 U.S. 454 [(1907)]. We admit that in many places and in ordinary times the defendants in saying all that was said in the circular would have been within their constitutional rights. But the character of every act depends upon the circumstances in which it is done. *Aikens v. Wisconsin*, 195 U.S. 194 [(1904)]. The most stringent protection of free speech would not protect a man in falsely shouting fire in a theatre and causing a panic. It does not even protect a man from an injunction against uttering words that may have all the effect of force. The question in every case is whether the words used are used in such circumstances and are of such a nature as to create a clear and present danger that they will bring about the substantive evils that Congress has a right to prevent. It is a question of proximity and degree. When a nation is at war many things that might be said in time of peace are such a hindrance to its effort that their utterance will not be endured so long as men fight and that no Court could regard them as protected by any constitutional right. It seems to be admitted that if an actual obstruction of the recruiting service were proved, liability for words that produced that effect might be enforced. The statute of 1917 in section 4 (Comp. St. 1918, § 10212d) punishes conspiracies to obstruct as well as actual obstruction. If the act, (speaking, or circulating a paper,) its tendency and the intent with which it is done are the same, we perceive no ground for saying that success alone warrants making the act a crime. . . .

Judgments affirmed.

Gitlow v. People of the State of New York
268 U.S. 652, 45 S.Ct. 625 (1925)

On November 8, 1919, police arrested Benjamin Gitlow, a twenty-eight-year-old son of Russian-Jewish immigrants, who a year before

Benjamin Gitlow and William Z. Foster, the Communist Workers' Party 1928 candidates for president and vice president, three years after the Supreme Court upheld Gitlow's conviction for publishing an article calling for workers to overthrow capitalism. (*Corbis/UPI*)

was elected to the New York legislature as a Socialist and who was well known as a leader of the left-wing faction of the Socialist Party—which would later form the American Communist Party. Gitlow was arrested and tried under the New York Criminal Anarchy Act of 1902, prohibiting the advocacy of criminal anarchy—"the doctrine that organized governments should be overthrown by force or violence, or by the assassination of the executive head or of any of the executive officials of government, or by any unlawful means." Gitlow's crime was publishing a pamphlet, *Left Wing Manifesto*, proclaiming the inevitability of a proletarian revolution. Although no evidence was introduced at trial that his publication had led to any unlawful action, Gitlow was convicted by a jury and given the maximum sentence of five to ten years in prison. Gitlow unsuccessfully appealed his conviction in state courts on the grounds that the New York law was unconstitutional under the First and Fourteenth Amendments. The recently formed American Civil Liberties Union (ACLU) then came to Gitlow's defense and appealed his case to the Supreme Court.

The Court's decision was seven to two, with the majority's opinion announced by Justice Sanford. Justice Holmes dissented and was joined by Justice Brandeis.

☐ *Justice SANFORD delivered the opinion of the Court.*

Benjamin Gitlow was indicted in the Supreme Court of New York, with three others, for the statutory crime of criminal anarchy. He was separately tried, convicted, and sentenced to imprisonment. . . .

The contention here is that the statute, by its terms and as applied in this case, is repugnant to the due process clause of the Fourteenth Amendment. Its material provisions are: . . .

"Sec. 161. *Advocacy of Criminal Anarchy.* Any person who:

"1. By word of mouth or writing advocates, advises or teaches the duty, necessity or propriety of overthrowing or overturning organized government by force or violence, or by assassination of the executive head or of any of the executive officials of government, or by any unlawful means; or,

"2. Prints, publishes, edits, issues or knowingly circulates, sells, distributes or publicly displays any book, paper, document, or written or printed matter in any form, containing or advocating, advising or teaching the doctrine that organized government should be overthrown by force, violence or any unlawful means, . . .

"Is guilty of a felony and punishable" by imprisonment or fine, or both. . . .

The defendant is a member of the Left Wing Section of the Socialist Party, a dissenting branch or faction of that party formed in opposition to its dominant policy of "moderate Socialism." Membership in both is open to aliens as well as citizens. The Left Wing Section was organized nationally at a conference in New York City in June, 1919, attended by ninety delegates from twenty different States. The conference elected a National Council, of which the defendant was a member, and left to it the adoption of a "Manifesto." This was published in The Revolutionary Age, the official organ of the Left Wing. The defendant was on the board of managers of the paper and was its business manager. He arranged for the printing of the paper and took to the printer the manuscript of the first issue which contained the Left Wing Manifesto, and also a Communist Program and a Program of the Left Wing that had been adopted by the conference. Sixteen thousand copies were printed, which were delivered at the premises in New York City used as the office of the Revolutionary Age and the headquarters of the Left Wing, and occupied by the defendant and other officials. . . .

There was no evidence of any effect resulting from the publication and circulation of the Manifesto.

No witnesses were offered in behalf of the defendant. . . .

The sole contention here is, essentially, that as there was no evidence of any concrete result flowing from the publication of the Manifesto or of circumstances showing the likelihood of such result, the statute as construed and applied by the trial court penalizes the mere utterance, as such, of "doctrine" having no quality of incitement, without regard either to the circumstances of its utterance or to the likelihood of unlawful consequences. . . .

The statute does not penalize the utterance or publication of abstract "doctrine" or academic discussion having no quality of incitement to any concrete action. It is not aimed against mere historical or philosophical essays. It does not restrain the advocacy of changes in the form of government by constitutional and lawful means. What it prohibits is language advocating, advising or teaching the overthrow of organized government by unlawful means. These words imply urging to action. . . .

The Manifesto, plainly, is neither the statement of abstract doctrine nor, as suggested by counsel, mere prediction that industrial disturbances and revolutionary mass strikes will result spontaneously in an inevitable process of evolution in the economic system. It advocates and urges in fervent language mass action which shall progressively foment industrial disturbances and through political mass strikes and revolutionary mass action overthrow and destroy organized parliamentary government. It concludes with a call to action in these words:

> "The proletariat revolution and the Communist reconstruction of society—*the struggle for these*—is now indispensable. . . . The Communist International calls the proletariat of the world to the final struggle!"

This is not the expression of philosophical abstraction, the mere prediction of future events; it is the language of direct incitement. . . .

For present purposes we may and do assume that freedom of speech and of the press—which are protected by the First Amendment from abridgment by Congress—are among the fundamental personal rights and "liberties" protected by the due process clause of the Fourteenth Amendment from impairment by the States. . . .

It is a fundamental principle, long established, that the freedom of speech and of the press which is secured by the Constitution, does not confer an absolute right to speak or publish, without responsibility, whatever one may choose, or an unrestricted and unbridled license that gives immunity for every possible use of language and prevents the punishment of those who abuse this freedom. . . .

That a State in the exercise of its police power may punish those who abuse this freedom by utterances inimical to the public welfare, tending to corrupt public morals, incite to crime, or disturb the public peace, is not open to question. . . .

By enacting the present statute the State has determined, through its legislative body, that utterances advocating the overthrow of organized government by force, violence and unlawful means, are so inimical to the general welfare and involve such danger of substantive evil that they may be penalized in the exercise of its police power. That determination must be given great weight. Every presumption is to be indulged in favor of the validity of the statute. *Mugler v. Kansas.* . . . And the case is to be considered "in the light of the principle that the State is primarily the judge of regulations required in the interest of public safety and welfare"; and that its police "statutes may only be declared unconstitutional where they are arbitrary or unreasonable attempts to exercise authority vested in the State in the public interest." *Great Northern Ry. v. Clara City* [246 U.S. 434 (1918)]. That utterances inciting to the overthrow of organized government by unlawful means, present a sufficient danger of substantive evil to bring their punishment within the range of legislative discretion, is clear. Such utterances, by their very nature, involve danger to the public peace and to the security of the State. They threaten breaches of the peace and ultimate revolution. And the immediate danger is none the less real and substantial, because the effect of a given utterance cannot be accurately foreseen. The State cannot reasonably be required to measure the danger from every such utterance in the nice balance of a jeweler's scale. A single revolutionary spark may kindle a fire that, smouldering for a time, may burst into a sweeping and destructive conflagration. It cannot be said that the State is acting arbitrarily or unreasonably when in the exercise of its judgment as to the measures necessary to protect the public peace and safety, it seeks to extinguish the spark without waiting until it has enkindled the flame or blazed into the conflagration. It cannot reasonably be required to defer the adoption of measures for its own peace and safety until the revolutionary utterances lead to actual disturbances of the public peace or imminent and immediate danger of its own destruction; but it may, in the exercise of its judgment, suppress the threatened danger in its incipiency. . . .

We cannot hold that the present statute is an arbitrary or unreasonable exercise of the police power of the State unwarrantably infringing the freedom of speech or press; and we must and do sustain its constitutionality.

This being so it may be applied to every utterance—not too trivial to be beneath the notice of the law—which is of such a character and used with such intent and purpose as to bring it within the prohibition of the statute. . . .

In other words, when the legislative body has determined generally, in the constitutional exercise of its discretion, that utterances of a certain kind involve such danger of substantive evil that they may be punished, the question whether any specific utterance coming within the prohibited class is likely, in and of itself, to bring about the substantive evil, is not open to consideration. It is sufficient that the statute itself be constitutional and that the use of the language comes within its prohibition.

It is clear that the question in such cases is entirely different from that involved in those cases where the statute merely prohibits certain acts involving the danger of substantive evil, without any reference to language itself, and it is sought to apply its provisions to language used by the defendant for the purpose of bringing about the prohibited results. There, if it be contended that the statute cannot be applied to the language used by the defendant because of its protection by the freedom of speech or press, it must necessarily be found, as an original question, without any previous determination by the legislative body, whether the specific language used involved such likelihood of bringing about the substantive evil as to deprive it of the constitutional protection. In such case it has been held that the general provisions of the statute may be constitutionally applied to the specific utterance of the defendant if its natural tendency and probable effect was to bring about the substantive evil which the legislative body might prevent. *Schenck v. United States*, [249 U.S. 47 (1919)]; *Debs v. United States*, [249 U.S. 211 (1919)]. And the general statement in the *Schenck* Case, [249 U.S. 47 (1919)], that the "question in every case is whether the words used are used in such circumstances and are of such a nature as to create a clear and present danger that they will bring about the substantive evils,"—upon which great reliance is placed in the defendant's argument—was manifestly intended, as shown by the context, to apply only in cases of this class, and has no application to those like the present, where the legislative body itself has previously determined the danger of substantive evil arising from utterances of a specified character. . . .

Affirmed.

▢ *Justice HOLMES, dissenting.*

Justice BRANDEIS and I are of the opinion that this judgment should be reversed. The general principle of free speech, it seems to me, must be taken to be included in the Fourteenth Amendment, in view of the scope that has been given to the word "liberty" as there used, although perhaps it may be accepted with a somewhat larger latitude of interpretation than is allowed to Congress by the sweeping language that governs or ought to govern the laws of the United States. If I am right then I think that the criterion sanctioned by the full Court in *Schenck v. United States*, applies:

> "The question in every case is whether the words used are used in such circumstances and are of such a nature as to create a clear and present danger that they will bring about the substantive evils that [the State] has a right to prevent." . . .

If what I think the correct test is applied it is manifest that there was no present danger of an attempt to overthrow the government by force on the part of the admittedly small minority who shared the defendant's views. It is said that this manifesto was more than a theory, that it was an incitement. Every idea is an incitement. It offers itself for belief and if believed it is acted on unless some other belief outweighs it or some failure of energy stifles the movement at its birth. The only difference between the expression of an opinion and an incitement in the narrower sense is the speaker's enthusiasm for the result. Eloquence may set fire to reason. But whatever may be thought of the redundant discourse before us it had no chance of starting a present conflagration. If in the long run the beliefs expressed in proletarian dictatorship are destined to be accepted by the dominant forces of the community, the only meaning of free speech is that they should be given their chance and have their way.

If the publication of this document had been laid as an attempt to induce an uprising against government at once and not at some indefinite time in the future it would have presented a different question. The object would have been one with which the law might deal, subject to the doubt whether there was any danger that the publication could produce any result, or in other words, whether it was not futile and too remote from possible consequences. But the indictment alleges the publication and nothing more.

Dennis v. United States

341 U.S. 494, 71 S.Ct. 857 (1951)

Eugene Dennis and ten other leaders of the American Communist Party were indicted under the Smith Act of 1940 for willfully and knowingly conspiring to teach and advocate the forceful and violent overthrow and destruction of the government. After a nine-month trial, Dennis and the others were found guilty and, thereafter, appealed their convictions in a federal appeals court. That court upheld their convictions with a scholarly opinion written by prominent Judge Learned Hand. Reviewing the evolution of the clear and present danger test since *Schenck*, Hand concluded that it was no more than a balancing technique. But he also ventured to give the test greater precision by adding that courts must consider "whether the gravity of the 'evil,' discounted by its improbability, justifies such invasion of free speech as is necessary to avoid the danger." According to Hand, restrictions on speech and press were permissible only if they posed a clear and, not merely present but, imminent and probable danger. As refashioned, the clear and present danger test was sharper than Justice Holmes's initial formulation, yet it permitted changing political circumstances to determine the scope of the First Amendment. Turning to international events and the threat of communism, Judge Hand could not imagine "a more probable danger, unless one must wait till the actual eve of hostilities." Dennis's attorneys promptly appealed Judge Hand's ruling to the Supreme Court. The Court granted review (with newly appointed Justice Tom Clark recusing himself, because he had been attorney general when the government began prosecuting Dennis).

The Court's decision was six to two, with Justice Clark not participating, and the plurality's opinion announced by Chief Justice Vinson. Concurrences were by Justices Frankfurter and Jackson, dissents by Justices Black and Douglas.

☐ *Chief Justice VINSON, with whom Justice REED, Justice BURTON, and Justice MINTON join, delivered the opinion of the Court.*

Petitioners were indicted in July, 1948, for violation of the conspiracy provisions of the Smith Act, 54 Stat. 671, 18 U.S.C. (1946 ed.) § 11, during the period of April, 1945, to July, 1948. . . . A verdict of guilty as to all the petitioners was returned by the jury on October 14, 1949. The Court of Appeals affirmed the convictions. We granted *certiorari* [to decide] . . . the following two questions: (1) Whether either § 2 or § 3 of the Smith Act, inherently or as construed and applied in the instant case, violates the First Amendment and other provisions of the Bill of Rights; (2) whether either

§ 2 or § 3 of the Act, inherently or as construed and applied in the instant case, violates the First and Fifth Amendments because of indefiniteness.

Sections 2 and 3 of the Smith Act provide as follows:

> "Sec. 2.
> "(a) It shall be unlawful for any person—
> "(1) to knowingly or willfully advocate, abet, advise, or teach the duty, necessity, desirability, or propriety of overthrowing or destroying any government in the United States by force or violence, or by the assassination of any officer of any such government. . . ."
> "Sec. 3. It shall be unlawful for any person to attempt to commit, or to conspire to commit, any of the acts prohibited by the provisions of . . . this title."

The indictment charged the petitioners with wilfully and knowingly conspiring (1) to organize as the Communist Party of the United States of America a society, group and assembly of persons who teach and advocate the overthrow and destruction of the Government of the United States by force and violence, and (2) knowingly and wilfully to advocate and teach the duty and necessity of overthrowing and destroying the Government of the United States by force and violence. . . .

The trial of the case extended over nine months, six of which were devoted to the taking of evidence, resulting in a record of 16,000 pages. Our limited grant of the writ of *certiorari* has removed from our consideration any question as to the sufficiency of the evidence to support the jury's determination that petitioners are guilty of the offense charged. Whether on this record petitioners did in fact advocate the overthrow of the Government by force and violence is not before us, and we must base any discussion of this point upon the conclusions stated in the opinion of the Court of Appeals, which treated the issue in great detail. That court held that the record in this case amply supports the necessary finding of the jury that petitioners, the leaders of the Communist Party in this country, were unwilling to work within our framework of democracy, but intended to initiate a violent revolution whenever the propitious occasion appeared. . . .

The obvious purpose of the statute is to protect existing Government, not from change by peaceable, lawful and constitutional means, but from change by violence, revolution and terrorism. That it is within the *power* of the Congress to protect the Government of the United States from armed rebellion is a proposition which requires little discussion. Whatever theoretical merit there may be to the argument that there is a "right" to rebellion against dictatorial governments is without force where the existing structure of the government provides for peaceful and orderly change. We reject any principle of governmental helplessness in the face of preparation for revolution, which principle, carried to its logical conclusion, must lead to anarchy. No one could conceive that it is not within the power of Congress to prohibit acts intended to overthrow the Government by force and violence. The question with which we are concerned here is not whether Congress has such *power*, but whether the *means* which it has employed conflict with the First and Fifth Amendments to the Constitution. . . .

[The petitioners attack] the statute on the grounds that by its terms it

prohibits academic discussion of the merits of Marxism Leninism, that it sti
fles ideas and is contrary to all concepts of a free speech and a free press. . . .

The very language of the Smith Act negates the interpretation which
petitioners would have us impose on that Act. It is directed at advocacy, not
discussion. Thus, the trial judge properly charged the jury that they could not
convict if they found that petitioners did "no more than pursue peaceful
studies and discussions or teaching and advocacy in the realm of ideas." . . .
Congress did not intend to eradicate the free discussion of political theories,
to destroy the traditional rights of Americans to discuss and evaluate ideas
without fear of governmental sanction. Rather Congress was concerned
with the very kind of activity in which the evidence showed these petitioners engaged.

But although the statute is not directed at the hypothetical cases which
petitioners have conjured, its application in this case has resulted in convictions for the teaching and advocacy of the overthrow of the Government by
force and violence, which, even though coupled with the intent to accomplish that overthrow, contains an element of speech. For this reason, we must
pay special heed to the demands of the First Amendment marking out the
boundaries of speech. . . .

The rule we deduce from [*Schenck v. United States* and the other Espionage Act] cases is that where an offense is specified by a statute in nonspeech or nonpress terms, a conviction relying upon speech or press as
evidence of violation may be sustained only when the speech or publication
created a "clear and present danger" of attempting or accomplishing the prohibited crime, e.g., interference with enlistment. The dissents, in emphasizing
the value of speech, were addressed to the argument of the sufficiency of the
evidence. . . .

Although no case subsequent to *Whitney* [*v. California*, 274 U.S. 421
(1927)] and *Gitlow* [*v. New York* (1925)] has expressly overruled the majority
opinions in those cases, there is little doubt that subsequent opinions have inclined toward the HOLMES-BRANDEIS rationale. . . . But . . . neither Justice HOLMES nor Justice BRANDEIS ever envisioned that a shorthand
phrase should be crystallized into a rigid rule to be applied inflexibly without regard to the circumstances of each case. Speech is not an absolute, above
and beyond control by the legislature when its judgment, subject to review
here, is that certain kinds of speech are so undesirable as to warrant criminal
sanction. . . .

In this case we are squarely presented with the application of the "clear
and present danger" test, and must decide what that phrase imports. We first
note that many of the cases in which this Court has reversed convictions by
use of this or similar tests have been based on the fact that the interest which
the State was attempting to protect was itself too insubstantial to warrant restriction of speech. . . . Overthrow of the Government by force and violence
is certainly a substantial enough interest for the Government to limit speech.
. . . If, then, this interest may be protected, the literal problem which is presented is what has been meant by the use of the phrase "clear and present
danger" of the utterances bringing about the evil within the power of Congress to punish.

Obviously, the words cannot mean that before the Government may act,
it must wait until the *putsch* is about to be executed, the plans have been laid

and the signal is awaited. If Government is aware that a group aiming at its overthrow is attempting to indoctrinate its members and to commit them to a course whereby they will strike when the leaders feel the circumstances permit, action by the Government is required. The argument that there is no need for Government to concern itself, for Government is strong, it possesses ample powers to put down a rebellion, it may defeat the revolution with ease needs no answer. For that is not the question. Certainly an attempt to overthrow the Government by force, even though doomed from the outset because of inadequate numbers or power of the revolutionists, is a sufficient evil for Congress to prevent. The damage which such attempts create both physically and politically to a nation makes it impossible to measure the validity in terms of the probability of success, or the immediacy of a successful attempt. In the instant case the trial judge charged the jury that they could not convict unless they found that petitioners intended to overthrow the Government "as speedily as circumstances would permit." This does not mean, and could not properly mean, that they would not strike until there was certainty of success. What was meant was that the revolutionists would strike when they thought the time was ripe. We must therefore reject the contention that success or probability of success is the criterion.

The situation with which Justices HOLMES and BRANDEIS were concerned in *Gitlow* was a comparatively isolated event, bearing little relation in their minds to any substantial threat to the safety of the community. . . . They were not confronted with any situation comparable to the instant one—the development of an apparatus designed and dedicated to the overthrow of the Government, in the context of world crisis after crisis.

Chief Judge Learned Hand, writing for the majority below, interpreted the phrase as follows: "In each case [courts] must ask whether the gravity of the 'evil,' discounted by its improbability, justifies such invasion of free speech as is necessary to avoid the danger." We adopt this statement of the rule. As articulated by Chief Judge Hand, it is as succinct and inclusive as any other we might devise at this time. It takes into consideration those factors which we deem relevant, and relates their significances. More we cannot expect from words.

Likewise, we are in accord with the court below, which affirmed the trial court's finding that the requisite danger existed. The mere fact that from the period 1945 to 1948 petitioners' activities did not result in an attempt to overthrow the Government by force and violence is of course no answer to the fact that there was a group that was ready to make the attempt. The formation by petitioners of such a highly organized conspiracy, with rigidly disciplined members subject to call when the leaders, these petitioners, felt that the time had come for action, coupled with the inflammable nature of world conditions, similar uprisings in other countries, and the touch-and-go nature of our relations with countries with whom petitioners were in the very least ideologically attuned, convince us that their convictions were justified on this score. And this analysis disposes of the contention that a conspiracy to advocate, as distinguished from the advocacy itself, cannot be constitutionally restrained, because it comprises only the preparation. It is the existence of the conspiracy which creates the danger. . . . If the ingredients of the reaction are present, we cannot bind the Government to wait until the catalyst is added. . . .

When facts are found that establish the violation of a statute, the protection against conviction afforded by the First Amendment is a matter of law. The doctrine that there must be a clear and present danger of a substantive evil that Congress has a right to prevent is a judicial rule to be applied as a matter of law by the courts. The guilt is established by proof of facts. Whether the First Amendment protects the activity which constitutes the violation of the statute must depend upon a judicial determination of the scope of the First Amendment applied to the circumstances of the case. . . .

[I]n the very case in which the phrase was born, *Schenck*, this Court itself examined the record to find whether the requisite danger appeared, and the issue was not submitted to a jury. And in every later case in which the Court has measured the validity of a statute by the "clear and present danger" test, that determination has been by the court, the question of the danger not being submitted to the jury.

The question in this case is whether the statute which the legislature has enacted may be constitutionally applied. In other words, the Court must examine judicially the application of the statute to the particular situation, to ascertain if the Constitution prohibits the conviction. We hold that the statute may be applied where there is a "clear and present danger" of the substantive evil which the legislature had the right to prevent.

☐ *Justice FRANKFURTER, concurring.*

Primary responsibility for adjusting the interests which compete in the situation before us of necessity belongs to the Congress. . . . We are to set aside the judgment of those whose duty it is to legislate only if there is no reasonable basis for it. . . .

"Great cases," it is appropriate to remember, "like hard cases make bad law. For great cases are called great, not by reason of their real importance in shaping the law of the future, but because of some accident of immediate overwhelming interest which appeals to the feelings and distorts the judgment. These immediate interests exercise a kind of hydraulic pressure which makes what previously was clear seem doubtful, and before which even well settled principles of law will bend." Justice HOLMES, dissenting in *Northern Securities Co. v. United States*, 193 U.S. 197 [(1904)].

This is such a case. Unless we are to compromise judicial impartiality and subject these defendants to the risk of an *ad hoc* judgment influenced by the impregnating atmosphere of the times, the constitutionality of their conviction must be determined by principles established in cases decided in more tranquil periods. . . .

First. Free-speech cases are not an exception to the principle that we are not legislators, that direct policy-making is not our province. How best to reconcile competing interests is the business of legislatures, and the balance they strike is a judgment not to be displaced by ours, but to be respected unless outside the pale of fair judgment. . . .

Second. A survey of the relevant decisions indicates that the results which we have reached are on the whole those that would ensue from careful weighing of conflicting interests. . . .

Third. Not every type of speech occupies the same position on the scale of values. There is no substantial public interest in permitting certain kinds of utterances: "the lewd and obscene, the profane, the libelous, and the insulting or 'fighting' words—those which by their very utterance inflict injury or tend to incite an immediate breach of the peace." *Chaplinsky v. State of New Hampshire*, 315 U.S. 568 [(1942)]. It is pertinent to the decision before us to consider where on the scale of values we have in the past placed the type of speech now claiming constitutional immunity.

The defendants have been convicted of conspiring to organize a party of persons who advocate the overthrow of the Government by force and violence. The jury has found that the object of the conspiracy is advocacy as "a rule or principle of action," "by language reasonably and ordinarily calculated to incite persons to such action," and with the intent to cause the overthrow "as speedily as circumstances would permit."

On any scale of values which we have hitherto recognized, speech of this sort ranks low. . . .

But there is underlying validity in the distinction between advocacy and the interchange of ideas, and we do not discard a useful tool because it may be misused. That such a distinction could be used unreasonably by those in power against hostile or unorthodox views does not negate the fact that it may be used reasonably against an organization wielding the power of the centrally controlled international Communist movement. The object of the conspiracy before us is so clear that the chance of error in saying that the defendants conspired to advocate rather than to express ideas is slight. Justice DOUGLAS quite properly points out that the conspiracy before us is not a conspiracy to overthrow the Government. But it would be equally wrong to treat it as a seminar in political theory.

These general considerations underlie decision of the case before us.

On the one hand is the interest in security. The Communist Party was not designed by these defendants as an ordinary political party. For the circumstances of its organization, its aims and methods, and the relation of the defendants to its organization and aims we are concluded by the jury's verdict. The jury found that the Party rejects the basic premise of our political system—that change is to be brought about by nonviolent constitutional process. The jury found that the Party advocates the theory that there is a duty and necessity to overthrow the Government by force and violence. It found that the Party entertains and promotes this view, not as a prophetic insight or as a bit of unworldly speculation, but as a program for winning adherents and as a policy to be translated into action. . . .

On the other hand is the interest in free speech. The right to exert all governmental powers in aid of maintaining our institutions and resisting their physical overthrow does not include intolerance of opinions and speech that cannot do harm although opposed and perhaps alien to dominant, traditional opinion. . . .

A public interest is not wanting in granting freedom to speak their minds even to those who advocate the overthrow of the Government by force. For, as the evidence in this case abundantly illustrates, coupled with such advocacy is criticism of defects in our society. . . . Suppressing advocates of overthrow inevitably will also silence critics who do not advocate overthrow but fear that their criticism may be so construed. No matter how clear we may be that the defendants now before us are preparing to overthrow our Government at the propitious moment, it is self-delusion to think that we can punish them for their advocacy without adding to the risks run by loyal citizens who honestly believe in some of the reforms these defendants advance. It is a sobering fact that in sustaining the convictions before us we can hardly escape restriction on the interchange of ideas. . . .

It is not for us to decide how we would adjust the clash of interests which this case presents were the primary responsibility for reconciling it ours. Congress has determined that the danger created by advocacy of overthrow justifies the ensuing restriction on freedom of speech. . . .

To make validity of legislation depend on judicial reading of events still in the womb of time—a forecast, that is, of the outcome of forces at best appreciated only with knowledge of the topmost secrets of nations—is to charge the judiciary with duties beyond its equipment.

☐ *Justice JACKSON, concurring.*

The Communist Party . . . does not seek its strength primarily in numbers. Its aim is a relatively small party whose strength is in selected, dedicated, indoctrinated, and rigidly disciplined members. From established policy it tolerates no deviation and no debate. It seeks members that are, or may be, secreted in strategic posts in transportation, communications, industry, government, and especially in labor unions where it can compel employers to accept and retain its members. It also seeks to infiltrate and control organizations of professional and other groups. Through these placements in positions of power it seeks a leverage over society that will make up in power of coercion what it lacks in power of persuasion.

The Communists have no scruples against sabotage, terrorism, assassination, or mob disorder; but violence is not with them, as with the anarchists, an end in itself. The Communist Party advocates force only when prudent and profitable. Their strategy of stealth precludes premature or uncoordinated outbursts of violence, except, of course, when the blame will be placed on shoulders other than their own. They resort to violence as to truth, not as a principle but as an expedient. Force or violence, as they would resort to it, may never be necessary, because infiltration and deception may be enough. . . .

The foregoing is enough to indicate that, either by accident or design, the Communist stratagem outwits the anti-anarchist pattern of statute aimed against "overthrow by force and violence" if qualified by the doctrine that only "clear and present danger" of accomplishing that result will sustain the prosecution.

The "clear and present danger" test was an innovation by Justice HOLMES in the *Schenck* case, reiterated and refined by him and Justice BRANDEIS in later cases, all arising before the era of World War II revealed the subtlety and efficacy of modernized revolutionary techniques used by totalitarian parties. In those cases, they were faced with convictions under so-called criminal syndicalism statutes aimed at anarchists but which, loosely construed, had been applied to punish socialism, pacifism, and left-wing ideologies, the charges often resting on far-fetched inferences which, if true, would establish only technical or trivial violations. They proposed "clear and present danger" as a test for the sufficiency of evidence in particular cases.

I would save it, unmodified, for application as a "rule of reason" in the kind of case for which it was devised. When the issue is criminality of a hot-headed speech on a street corner, or circulation of a few incendiary pamphlets, or parading by some zealots behind a red flag, or refusal of a handful of school children to salute our flag, it is not beyond the capacity of the judicial process to gather, comprehend, and weigh the necessary materials for decision whether it is a clear and present danger of substantive evil or a harmless letting off of steam. It is not a prophecy, for the danger in such cases has matured by the time of trial or it was never present. The test applies and has meaning where a conviction is sought to be based on a speech or writing which does not directly or explicitly advocate a crime but to which such tendency is sought to be attributed by construction or by implication from external circumstances. The formula in such cases favors freedoms that are vital to our society, and, even if sometimes applied too generously, the consequences cannot be grave. But its recent expansion has extended, in particular to Communists, unprecedented immunities. Unless we are to hold our Government captive in a judge-made verbal trap, we must approach the problem of a well-organized, nation-wide conspiracy, such as I have described, as realistically as our predecessors faced the trivialities that were being prosecuted until they were checked with a rule of reason.

I think reason is lacking for applying that test to this case.

If we must decide that this Act and its application are constitutional only if we are convinced that petitioner's conduct creates a "clear and present danger" of violent overthrow, we must appraise imponderables, including international and national phenomena which baffle the best informed foreign offices and our most experienced politicians. We would have to foresee and predict the effectiveness of Communist propaganda, opportunities for infiltration, whether, and when, a time will come that they consider propitious for action, and whether and how fast our existing government will deteriorate. And we would have to speculate as to whether an approaching Communist *coup* would not be anticipated by a nationalistic fascist movement. No doctrine can be sound whose application requires us to make a prophecy of that sort in the guise of a legal decision. The judicial process simply is not adequate to a trial of such far-flung issues. The answers given would reflect our own political predilections and nothing more.

The authors of the clear and present danger test never applied it to a case like this, nor would I. If applied as it is proposed here, it means that the Communist plotting is protected during its period of incubation; its preliminary stages of organization and preparation are immune from the law; the Government can move only after imminent action is manifest, when it would, of course, be too late.

The highest degree of constitutional protection is due to the individual acting without conspiracy. But even an individual cannot claim that the Constitution protects him in advocating or teaching overthrow of government by force or violence. I should suppose no one would doubt that Congress has power to make such attempted overthrow a crime. But the contention is that one has the constitutional right to work up a public desire and will to do what it is a crime to attempt. I think direct incitement by speech or writing can be made a crime, and I think there can be a conviction without also proving that the odds favored its success by 99 to 1, or some other extremely high ratio. . . .

Of course, it is not always easy to distinguish teaching or advocacy in the sense of incitement from teaching or advocacy in the sense of exposition or explanation. It is a question of fact in each case.

What really is under review here is a conviction of conspiracy, after a trial for conspiracy, on an indictment charging conspiracy, brought under a statute outlawing conspiracy. With due respect to my colleagues, they seem to me to discuss anything under the sun except the law of conspiracy. . . .

The Constitution does not make conspiracy a civil right. The Court has never before done so and I think it should not do so now. . . .

The reasons underlying the doctrine that conspiracy may be a substantive evil in itself, apart from any evil it may threaten, attempt or accomplish, are peculiarly appropriate to conspiratorial Communism. . . .

I do not suggest that Congress could punish conspiracy to advocate something, the doing of which it may not punish. Advocacy or exposition of the doctrine of communal property ownership, or any political philosophy unassociated with advocacy of its imposition by force or seizure of government by unlawful means could not be reached through conspiracy prosecution. But it is not forbidden to put down force or violence, it is not forbidden to punish its teaching or advocacy, and the end being punishable, there is no doubt of the power to punish conspiracy for the purpose.

☐ *Justice BLACK, dissenting.*

At the outset I want to emphasize what the crime involved in this case is, and what it is not. These petitioners were not charged with an attempt to overthrow the Government. They were not charged with overt acts of any kind designed to overthrow the Government. They were not even charged with saying anything or writing anything designed to overthrow the Government. The charge was that they agreed to assemble and to talk and publish certain ideas at a later date: The indictment is that they conspired to organize the Communist Party and to use speech or newspapers and other publications in the future to teach and advocate the forcible overthrow of the Government. No matter how it is worded, this is a virulent form of prior censorship of speech and press, which I believe the First Amendment forbids. I would hold § 3 of the Smith Act authorizing this prior restraint unconstitutional on its face and as applied. . . .

So long as this Court exercises the power of judicial review of legislation, I cannot agree that the First Amendment permits us to sustain laws suppressing freedom of speech and press on the basis of Congress' or our own notions of mere "reasonableness." Such a doctrine waters down the First Amendment so that it amounts to little more than an admonition to Congress. . . .

Public opinion being what it now is, few will protest the conviction of these Communist petitioners. There is hope, however, that in calmer times, when present pressures, passions and fears subside, this or some later Court will restore the First Amendment liberties to the high preferred place where they belong in a free society.

☐ *Justice DOUGLAS, dissenting.*

If this were a case where those who claimed protection under the First Amendment were teaching the techniques of sabotage, the assassination of the President, the filching of documents from public files, the planting of bombs, the art of street warfare, and the like, I would have no doubts. The freedom to speak is not absolute; the teaching of methods of terror and other seditious conduct should be beyond the pale along with obscenity and immorality. This case was argued as if those were the facts. . . . But the fact is that no such evidence was introduced at the trial. There is a statute which makes a seditious conspiracy unlawful. Petitioners, however, were not charged with a "conspiracy to overthrow" the Government. They were charged with a conspiracy to form a party and groups and assemblies of people who teach and advocate the overthrow of our Government by force or violence and with a conspiracy to advocate and teach its overthrow by force and violence. It may well be that indoctrination in the techniques of terror to destroy the Government would be indictable under either statute. But the teaching which is condemned here is of a different character.

So far as the present record is concerned, what petitioners did was to organize people to teach and themselves teach the Marxist-Leninist doctrine contained chiefly in four books: *Foundations of Leninism* by Stalin (1924); *The Communist Manifesto* by Marx and Engels (1848); *State and Revolution* by Lenin (1917); *History of the Communist Party of the Soviet Union* (1939).

Those books are to Soviet Communism what *Mein Kampf* was to Nazism. If they are understood, the ugliness of Communism is revealed, its deceit and cunning are exposed, the nature of its activities becomes apparent, and the chances of its success less likely. That is not, of course, the reason why petitioners chose these books for their classrooms. They are fervent Communists to whom these volumes are gospel. They preached the creed with the hope that some day it would be acted upon.

The opinion of the Court does not outlaw these texts nor condemn them to the fire, as the Communists do literature offensive to their creed. But if the books themselves are not outlawed, if they can lawfully remain on library shelves, by what reasoning does their use in a classroom become a crime? It would not be a crime under the Act to introduce these books to a class, though that would be teaching what the creed of violent overthrow of the Government is. The Act, as construed, requires the element of intent—that those who teach the creed believe in it. The crime then depends not on what is taught but on who the teacher is. That is to make freedom of speech turn not on *what is said*, but on the *intent* with which it is said. Once we start down that road we enter territory dangerous to the liberties of every citizen. . . .

Intent, of course, often makes the difference in the law. An act otherwise excusable or carrying minor penalties may grow to an abhorrent thing if the evil intent is present. We deal here, however, not with ordinary acts but with speech, to which the Constitution has given a special sanction. . . .

There comes a time when even speech loses its constitutional immunity. Speech innocuous one year may at another time fan such destructive flames that it must be halted in the interests of the safety of the Republic. That is the meaning of the clear and present danger test. When conditions are so critical that there will be no time to avoid the evil that the speech threatens, it is time to call a halt. Otherwise, free speech which is the strength of the Nation will be the cause of its destruction.

Yet free speech is the rule, not the exception. The restraint to be constitutional must be based on more than fear, on more than passionate opposition against the speech, on more than a revolted dislike for its contents. There must be some immediate injury to society that is likely if speech is allowed. The classic statement of these conditions was made by Justice BRANDEIS in his concurring opinion in *Whitney v. People of State of California*, 274 U.S. 357 [(1927)].

> "Fear of serious injury cannot alone justify suppression of free speech and assembly. Men feared witches and burnt women. It is the function of speech to free men from the bondage of irrational fears. To justify suppression of free speech there must be reasonable ground to fear that serious evil will result if free speech is practiced. There must be reasonable ground to believe that the danger apprehended is imminent. There must be reasonable ground to believe that the evil to be prevented is a serious one. Every denunciation of existing law tends in some measure to increase the probability that there will be violation of it. Condonation of a breach enhances the probability. Expressions of approval add to the probability. Propagation of the criminal state of mind by teaching syndicalism increases it. Advocacy of law-breaking heightens it still further. But even advocacy of violation, however, reprehensible morally, is not a justification for denying free speech where the advocacy falls short of

Brandenburg v. Ohio was perhaps the climax of the many Court decisions in the 1960s that significantly expanded First Amendment freedoms. Clarence Brandenburg was a member of the Ku Klux Klan who violated an Ohio syndicalism statute by advocating racial strife during a televised rally. (*Library of Congress*)

incitement and there is nothing to indicate that the advocacy would be immediately acted on. The wide difference between advocacy and incitement, between preparation and attempt, between assembling and conspiracy, must be borne in mind. In order to support a finding of clear and present danger it must be shown either that immediate serious violence was to be expected or was advocated, or that the past conduct furnished reason to believe that such advocacy was then contemplated."

Brandenburg v. Ohio
395 U.S. 444, 89 S.CT. 1827 (1969)

Clarence Brandenburg, the leader of a Ku Klux Klan group, was arrested, tried, and convicted under the Ohio Criminal Syndicalism statute for "advocat[ing] . . . the duty, necessity, or propriety of crime, sabotage, violence, or unlawful methods of terrorism as a means of accomplishing industrial or political reform" and for "voluntarily assembl[ing] with any society, group, or assemblage or persons formed to teach or advocate the doctrines of criminal syndicalism." He had addressed a small rally of hooded men, some of whom carried firearms, standing before a burning cross and declared, among other things, that if the president, Congress, and the Court continued "to suppress the white, Caucasian race, it's possible that there might have to be revengenance [*sic*] taken." The major evidence introduced against Brandenburg at trial were two films of his speeches at rallies. Brandenburg unsuccessfully appealed his conviction in a state appellate court and then to the state supreme court, which denied review. On further appeal to the Supreme Court, Brandenburg's case was granted review. At conference, the justices unanimously voted to overturn his conviction. Subsequently, Chief Justice Warren assigned Justice Abe Fortas to draft an opinion for the Court. But Justice Fortas was pressed into resigning in May, and hence the Court's opinion came on June 9 as an unsigned (*per curiam*) opinion.

The Court's decision was unanimous, and the opinion was announced *per curiam*, with Justice Fortas not participating. Concurrences were by Justices Black and Douglas.

PER CURIAM.

The appellant, a leader of a Ku Klux Klan group, was convicted under the Ohio Criminal Syndicalism statute for "advocat[ing] . . . the duty, necessity, or propriety of crime, sabotage, violence, or unlawful methods of terrorism as a means of accomplishing industrial or political reform" and for "voluntarily assembl[ing] with any society, group, or assemblage of persons formed to teach or advocate the doctrines of criminal syndicalism." Ohio Rev. Code Ann. § 2923.13. He was fined $1,000 and sentenced to one to 10 years' imprisonment. The appellant challenged the constitutionality of the criminal syndicalism statute under the First and Fourteenth Amendments to the United States Constitution, but the intermediate appellate court of Ohio affirmed his conviction without opinion. . . . We reverse.

The record shows that a man, identified at trial as the appellant, telephoned an announcer-reporter on the staff of a Cincinnati television station and invited him to come to a Ku Klux Klan "rally" to be held at a farm in Hamilton County. With the cooperation of the organizers, the reporter and a cameraman attended the meeting and filmed the events. Portions of the films were later broadcast on the local station and on a national network. . . .

One film showed 12 hooded figures, some of whom carried firearms. They were gathered around a large wooden cross, which they burned. No one was present other than the participants and the newsmen who made the film. Most of the words uttered during the scene were incomprehensible when the film was projected, but scattered phrases could be understood that were derogatory of Negroes and, in one instance, of Jews. . . .

The second film showed six hooded figures one of whom, later identified as the appellant, repeated a speech very similar to that recorded on the first film. The reference to the possibility of "revengeance" was omitted, and one sentence was added: "Personally, I believe the nigger should be returned to Africa, the Jew returned to Israel." Though some of the figures in the films carried weapons, the speaker did not. . . .

[The Court's] decisions have fashioned the principle that the constitutional guarantees of free speech and free press do not permit a State to forbid or proscribe advocacy of the use of force or of law violation except where such advocacy is directed to inciting or producing imminent lawless action and is likely to incite or produce such action. As we said in *Noto v. United States*, 367 U.S. 290 (1961), "the mere abstract teaching . . . of the moral propriety or even moral necessity for a resort to force and violence, is not the same as preparing a group for violent action and steeling it to such action." A statute which fails to draw this distinction impermissibly intrudes upon the freedoms guaranteed by the First and Fourteenth Amendments. It sweeps within its condemnation speech which our Constitution has immunized from governmental control.

Measured by this test, Ohio's Criminal Syndicalism Act cannot be sustained. The Act punishes persons who "advocate or teach the duty, necessity, or propriety" of violence "as a means of accomplishing industrial or political reform"; or who publish or circulate or display any book or paper containing such advocacy; or who "justify" the commission of violent acts "with intent to exemplify, spread or advocate the propriety of the doctrines of criminal syndicalism"; or who "voluntarily assemble" with a group formed "to teach or advocate the doctrines of criminal syndicalism." Neither the indictment nor the trial judge's instructions to the jury in any way refined the statute's bald definition of the crime in terms of mere advocacy not distinguished from incitement to imminent lawless action.

Accordingly, we are here confronted with a statute which, by its own

■ CONSTITUTIONAL HISTORY

Judicial Approaches to the First Amendment

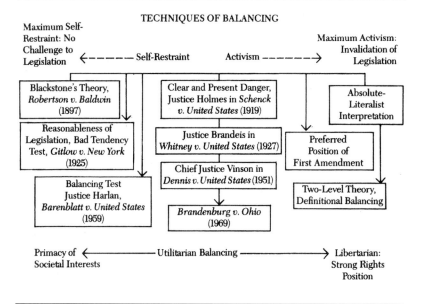

TECHNIQUES OF BALANCING

Maximum Self-Restraint: No Challenge to Legislation ←————— Self-Restraint   Activism ————→ Maximum Activism: Invalidation of Legislation

Blackstone's Theory, *Robertson v. Baldwin* (1897)

Clear and Present Danger, Justice Holmes in *Schenck v. United States* (1919)

Absolute-Literalist Interpretation

Reasonableness of Legislation, Bad Tendency Test, *Gitlow v. New York* (1925)

Justice Brandeis in *Whitney v. United States* (1927)

Preferred Position of First Amendment

Chief Justice Vinson in *Dennis v. United States* (1951)

Balancing Test Justice Harlan, *Barenblatt v. United States* (1959)

Two-Level Theory, Definitional Balancing

Brandenburg v. Ohio (1969)

Primacy of ←——————— Utilitarian Balancing ——————→ Libertarian: Societal Interests   Strong Rights Position

words and as applied, purports to punish mere advocacy and to forbid, on pain of criminal punishment, assembly with others merely to advocate the described type of action. Such a statute falls within the condemnation of the First and Fourteenth Amendments. The contrary teaching of *Whitney v. California*, [274 U.S. 357 (1927)], cannot be supported, and that decision is therefore overruled.

R̲eversed.

☐ *Justice BLACK, concurring.*

I agree with the views expressed by Justice DOUGLAS in his concurring opinion in this case that the "clear and present danger" doctrine should have no place in the interpretation of the First Amendment.

☐ *Justice DOUGLAS, concurring.*

While I join the opinion of the Court, I desire to enter a *caveat*. . . .

I see no place in the regime of the First Amendment for any "clear and present danger" test, whether strict and tight as some would make it, or freewheeling as the Court in *Dennis* [*v. United States* (1951)] rephrased it.

When one reads the opinions closely and sees when and how the "clear and present danger" test has been applied, great misgivings are aroused. First, the threats were often loud but always puny and made serious only by judges so wedded to the *status quo* that critical analysis made them nervous. Second, the test was so twisted and perverted in *Dennis* as to make the trial of those teachers of Marxism an all-out political trial which was part and parcel of the cold war that has eroded substantial parts of the First Amendment. . . .

The line between what is permissible and not subject to control and what may be made impermissible and subject to regulation is the line between ideas and overt acts.

The example usually given by those who would punish speech is the case of one who falsely shouts fire in a crowded theatre.

This is, however, a classic case where speech is brigaded with action. They are indeed inseparable and a prosecution can be launched for the overt acts actually caused. Apart from rare instances of that kind, speech is, I think, immune from prosecution.

■ (2) JUDICIAL LINE DRAWING: *Ad Hoc* AND DEFINITIONAL BALANCING

The internal struggle within the Court over rival interpretive approaches to the First Amendment registered not merely differences over the history and principles of free speech and press. There were profound differences as well in judicial self-perception and philosophy over the role of the Court in a constitutional democracy. How deferential should the Court be to legislative majorities in defining the line between constitutionally protected and unprotected speech and press? What standards and principles should guide the Court's line drawing?

The clear and present danger test was initially formulated as an alternative to the traditional presumption of the reasonableness of legislation and the bad tendency test, which was used by the Court to rationalize legislative restrictions on speech and press. Although potentially a basis for protecting free speech and press, the clear and present danger test gradually evolved into a balancing technique for upholding restrictions on speech and press. After fifty years, the clear and present danger test was laid to rest in *Brandenburg v. Ohio* (1969) (excerpted above), and since then survives primarily in *dicta*.[1] A majority of the Warren Court also eventually repudiated the *ad hoc* or case-by-case balancing approach advanced by Justice Harlan. Two years before *Brandenburg*, in a six-to-two decision (with Harlan and White in dissent and newly appointed Justice Thurgood Marshall not participating), Chief Justice Warren struck down as unconstitutional a provision of the McCarran Act forbidding any member of the Communist party to be employed in a defense facility. Joined by Black, Douglas, Stewart, Fortas, and Brennan in *United States v. Robel*, 389 U.S. 258 (1967), Warren used the occasion expressly to reject *ad hoc* balancing of First Amendment freedoms:

Faced with a clear conflict between a federal statute enacted in the interests of national security and an individual's exercise of his First Amendment rights, we have confined our analysis to whether Congress has adopted a constitutional means in achieving its concededly legitimate legislative goal. In making this determination we have found it necessary to measure the validity of the means adopted by Congress against both the goal it has sought to achieve and the specific prohibitions of the First Amendment. But we have in no way "balanced" those respective interests. We have ruled only that the Constitution requires that the conflict between congressional power and individual rights be accommodated by legislation drawn more narrowly to avoid the conflict.

Ad hoc balancing, whether under the clear and present danger test or as advocated by Harlan, was widely criticized within and without the Court for three principal reasons: (1) it was ambiguous and unpredictable in application, (2) it failed to establish a constitutional standard for adjudicating claims in a principled fashion, and (3) it tended to legitimate restrictions on speech and press because First Amendment claims were construed as simply private interests to be juxtaposed with public interests in self-preservation and punishing licentiousness.[2]

During his more than thirty years on the high bench, Justice Black remained one of the sharpest critics of balancing First Amendment freedoms and championed an "absolutist-literalist" interpretation. As he summarized his approach in 1968, when giving the James Carpenter Lectures at Columbia University School of Law,

My view is, without deviation, without exception, without any ifs, buts, or whereas, that freedom of speech means that government shall not do anything to people, or, in the words of the Magna Carta, move against people, either for the views they have or the views they express or the words they speak or write. Some people would have you believe that this is a very radical position, and maybe it is. But all I am doing is following what to me is the clear wording of the First Amendment that "Congress shall make no law . . . abridging the freedom of speech[,] or of the press."[3]

The Court's abandonment of *ad hoc* balancing is a measure of Black's contribution to the constitutional politics of the First Amendment. Still a majority of the Court has never been persuaded to embrace his absolutist-literalist position.

Instead of *ad hoc* balancing and Black's absolutism, the Court gradually developed a "principled, or definitional, balancing" approach to the First Amendment—that is, the Court has defined certain categories of speech as protected or unprotected per se. The Court's definitional-balancing approach to, or two-level theory of, the First Amendment

Justice Hugo Black in his chambers. Black was President Roosevelt's first appointee to the Court and a leader of the liberals on the Court. Justice Black is also known for his view that the First Amendment is absolute, that "Congress shall make no law . . . abridging the freedom of speech, or of the press" means what it says. (*Collection of the Supreme Court of the United States*)

was initially intimated by Justice Murphy, when writing for a unanimous Court in *Chaplinsky v. New Hampshire*, 315 U.S. 568 (1942). There the Court upheld the conviction under a statute forbidding the use of offensive or derisive language in public. Chaplinsky, at the time of his arrest for creating a public disturbance, called the arresting officer "a Goddamned racketeer" and "a damned Fascist." In contemplating these "fighting words," Murphy held that the First Amendment provides no protection for such words because they "are no essential part of any exposition of ideas." Certain categories of speech—the insulting or fighting words, the obscene, and libelous—have minimal, if any, social value and, therefore, are not worthy of constitutional protection. In Justice Murphy's words:

> There are certain well-defined and narrowly limited classes of
> speech, the prevention and punishment of which has never been

thought to raise any constitutional problem. These include the lewd and the obscene, the profane, the libelous, and the insulting or "fighting words"—those which by their very utterance inflict injury or tend to incite an immediate breach of the peace. It has been observed that such utterances are no essential part of any exposition of ideas, and are of such slight social value as a step to truth that any benefit that may be derived from them is clearly outweighed by the social interest in law and order.

Justice Murphy thus implied a two-level theory of the First Amendment: the amendment safeguards communications that have social value, but not those categories of (unprotected) speech that are "clearly outweighed by the social interest in order and morality."

Definitional balancing remains no less problematic than *ad hoc* balancing, because the Court must with some precision define the categories of and the standards for determining unprotected speech (fighting words, obscenity, libel, and commercial speech). Because of the Court's preoccupation with subversive political speech in the early part of the twentieth century and due to its deference to legislative and common-law proscriptions on speech and press, the task of further defining these categories of unprotected speech was largely avoided until the era of the Warren Court. Since then the Burger and Rehnquist Courts have faced the problems of refining and defining the tests for those narrow categories of speech that fall outside the scope of First Amendment protection. It is those and other problems of judicial line drawing that the following sections of this chapter address. But note that the Rehnquist Court is not of one mind on the application of categories of unprotected speech. Indeed, in the "hate-speech" case, *R.A.V. v. City of St. Paul, Minnesota*, 505 U.S. 377 (1992) (excerpted in Section B), concurring Justice Stevens draws into question the Court's definitional balancing or categorical approach to the First Amendment. See also *Virginia v. Black* (2003) (excerpted below) on the constitutionality of criminalizing cross burning.

NOTES

1. See, for example, *Detroit Edison Company v. National Labor Relations Board*, 440 U.S. 301 (1979); *Federal Communications Commission v. Pacifica Foundation*, 438 U.S. 726 (1978); *Landmark Communications, Inc. v. Virginia*, 435 U.S. 829 (1977); *Nebraska Press Association v. Stuart*, 427 U.S. 539 (1976); *Greer v. Spock*, 424 U.S. 828 (1976); *Pell v. Procunier*, 417 U.S. 817 (1974); *Cohen v. California*, 403 U.S. 15 (1971); and *Younger v. Harris*, 401 U.S. 37 (1971).

2. For criticism of the *ad hoc* balancing approach, see Thomas I. Emerson, "Toward a General Theory of the First Amendment," 72 *Yale Law Journal* 854 (1963); Laurent Frantz, "The First Amendment in the Balance," 71 *Yale Law Journal* 1424 (1962);

Robert McKay, "The Preference for Freedom," 34 *New York University Law Review* 1182 (1959); Samuel Krislov, "From *Ginzburg* to *Ginsberg*: The Unhurried Children's Hour in Obscenity Litigation," in *Supreme Court Review*, ed. Philip Kurland (Chicago: University of Chicago Press, 1968); and Harry Kalven, "Uninhibited, Robust, and Wide-Open—A Note on Free Speech and the Warren Court," 67 *Minnesota Law Review* 289 (1968). For defenses of balancing, see Wallace Mendelson, "On the Meaning of the First Amendment: Absolutes in the Balance," 50 *California Law Review* 821 (1962); and Dean Alfange, Jr., "The Balancing of Interests in Free Speech Cases: In Defense of an Abused Doctrine," 2 *Law in Transition Quarterly* 35 (1965).

3. Hugo L. Black, *A Constitutional Faith* (New York: Alfred Knopf, 1968), 45.

SELECTED BIBLIOGRAPHY

Berns, Walter. *Freedom, Virtue and the First Amendment.* Baton Rouge: Louisiana State University Press, 1957.
———. *The First Amendment and the Future of American Democracy.* New York: Basic Books, 1976.
Black, Hugo. *A Constitutional Faith.* New York: Alfred Knopf, 1968.
Bollinger, Lee C., and Stone, Geoffrey R., eds. *Eternally Vigilant: Free Speech in the Modern Era.* Chicago: University of Chicago Press, 2002.
Dodge, David. *Casualty of War: The Bush Administration's Assault on a Free Press.* New York: Prometheus Books, 2004.
Emerson, Thomas. *The System of Freedom of Expression.* New York: Random House, 1970.
Fish, Stanley. *There Is No Such Thing as Free Speech: And It's a Good Thing, Too.* New York: Oxford University Press, 1993.
Haiman, Franklyn S. *Speech and Law in a Free Society.* Chicago: University of Chicago Press, 1981.
Meiklejohn, Alexander. *Political Freedom: The Constitutional Powers of the People.* New York: Harper & Row, 1965.
Redish, Martin. *The Logic of Persecution: Free Speech and the McCarthy Era.*, Palo Alto: Stanford University Press, 2004.
Smolla, Rodney A. *Deliberate Intent: A Lawyer Tells the True Story of Murder by the Book*: New York: Crown Publishing Group, 2000.
Strum, Philippa. *When the Nazis Came to Skokie: Freedom for Speech We Hate.* Lawrence: University of Kansas Press, 1999.

B | *Obscenity, Pornography, and Offensive Speech*

The problem of defining and dealing with obscenity, pornography, and other offensive speech is a continuing controversy in the constitutional politics of interpreting the First Amendment. Perhaps, as political scientist Harry Clor proposed:

> In the ideal system of legal control . . . wise men would solemnly weigh three considerations: the moral evils of obscenity, the virtues of art, and the requirements of public consensus in a regime of rational liberty. Each consideration would be given its full weight in the light of the common good. No work which is grossly obscene would ever be publicly circulated in society. No work which is not obscene would ever be censored.[1]

But such an "ideal system," as Clor concedes, "cannot be achieved among us." In a pluralistic society, people disagree over what is obscene, pornographic, and offensive; no consensus is likely. "One man's vulgarity is another man's lyric," as Justice Harlan put it in *Cohen v. California*, (1971) (see excerpt below). Or as Justice Stewart quipped in *Jacobellis v. Ohio*, 378 U.S. 184 (1964), "I know it [pornography] when I see it." Yet, for that very reason, Justice Black and Harvard Law School professor Alan Dershowitz, among others, argued, "To deny constitutional protection to a genre of speech that is incapable of precise definition is to endanger all freedom of expression. . . . Pornography should be included within the protection of the First Amendment, if for no other reason than by excluding it we give too much definitional power to the voracious censor."[2]

The Supreme Court in maintaining that obscenity, pornography, and fighting words fall outside the scope of First Amendment protection continues to confront the vexing definitional problems presented by its own line drawing. So too, as the Court's composition has changed, the tests and boundaries drawn defining *obscenity* and other forms of constitutionally unprotected offensive speech have evolved.

■ (1) Obscenity and Pornography

From the late nineteenth to the twentieth century, federal courts upheld congressional and state power to suppress allegedly obscene materials by applying the extremely restrictive English common-law test set forth in *Regina v. Hicklin*, L.R. 2 Q.B. 360 (1868). The so-called *Hicklin* test was "whether the tendency of the matter charged as obscenity is to deprive and corrupt those whose minds are open to such immoral influences and into whose hands a publication of this sort might fall." Under this test, books by Honoré de Balzac, Gustave Flaubert, James Joyce, D. H. Lawrence, and Arthur Miller were banned based on isolated passages and the influence they might have on the weakest members of society (children and the mentally impaired). As Justice Frankfurter was moved to observe, "the incidence of this standard is to reduce the adult population of [the country] to reading only what is fit for children."[3]

Not until *Roth v. United States* and its companion case, *Alberts v. California* (1957) (excerpted below) was the *Hicklin* test finally repudiated. There with Justices Black, Douglas, and Harlan in dissent over the holding that obscenity is "utterly without redeeming social value" and without First Amendment protection, Justice Brennan proposed a constitutional test for obscenity—"whether to the average person, applying contemporary community standards, the dominant theme of the material taken as a whole appeals to the prurient interests." As the opinions of the dissenters point out, though, the *Roth* test was problematic. Who is an "average person," what are "contemporary community standards," how and where are those standards to be determined, and, finally, what is "prurient interest"?

The Warren Court subsequently expanded the *Roth* test in three other important rulings. In *Kingsley International Corporation v. Regents of University of New York*, 360 U.S. 684 (1959), overturning the denial of a license to exhibit the movie *Lady Chatterley's Lover*, Justice Stewart held that books and films could not be banned for "thematic obscenity"— their dealing primarily with sexual themes. In *Manual Enterprises, Inc. v. Day*, 370 U.S. 478 (1962), Justice Harlan interpreted the prurient interest element of *Roth* to require that materials appeal to prurient interests in a "patently offensive way." Again writing for the Court in *Jacobellis v. State of Ohio*, 378 U.S. 184 (1964), Justice Brennan reversed the convictions of the makers and distributors of a film *The Lovers* and added to the *Roth* test the requirement that a book or film must be shown to lack "redeeming social importance" according to "national contemporary standards." Finally, in *A Book Named "John Cleland's Memoirs of a Woman of Pleasure" v. Massachusetts*, 383 U.S. 413 (1966), Justice Brennan combined all three of the above requirements in holding that obscene materials are excluded from First Amendment protection only if they fail all three requirements—that is, they (1) have a prurient interest that (2) appeal in a patently offensive way and (3) lack a redeeming social value.

As a result of the Warren Court's rulings only hard-core pornography fell outside of the scope of protected speech. This encouraged the proliferation of sexually oriented publications during the 1960s, the decade of the sexual revolution, and, in turn, elevated pornography to an issue in national politics. In 1968, for example, one of the charges made against Justice Fortas during his ill-fated nomination to be chief justice was that he had sided with the majority on the Warren Court in expansively reading the protection afforded by the First Amendment. Richard Nixon then made an issue of pornography in his 1968 presidential election campaign, pledging to return law and order to the country and appoint only "strict constructionists" to the Court.[4]

The Warren Court responded to the increased legislation and law enforcement efforts to control the "explosion" in the dissemination of sexually oriented and pornographical materials. The Court, for instance, upheld the conviction of Ralph Ginzburg for pandering by advertising the sale and mailing of his magazine *Eros* from such places as Middlesex, New Jersey; Blue Balls, Montana; and Intercourse, Pennsylvania, in *Ginzburg v. United States*, 383 U.S. 463 (1966). Selective prosecutions and bans on the sales of sexually oriented magazines to minors were also upheld in *Ginsberg v. New York*, 390 U.S. 629 (1968), sustaining the conviction of Sam Ginsberg for selling two "girlie" magazines to a sixteen-year-old boy. In addition, permit systems and local censorship boards for screening sexually oriented films were approved so long as they afforded the film's distributors due process and abided by the Court's standards for determining what is obscene.[5]

However, even in Chief Justice Earl Warren's last term, the Court stood by its expansive reading of the First Amendment. *Stanley v. Georgia* (1969) (see excerpt below) struck down a statute prohibiting the possession of obscene materials even in an individual's own house; as Justice Marshall put it, "Whatever may be the justifications for other statutes regulating obscenity, we do not think they reach into the privacy of one's home."

The year after *Stanley*, however, President Nixon's first appointee, Chief Justice Warren Burger, came to the Court. Already critical of the Warren Court's rulings on obscenity, he quickly tried to persuade his colleagues that the *Roth* line of rulings should be reconsidered. Initially unsuccessful, Burger was forced to voice his disagreement in dissenting opinions, questioning the propriety of "the national community standard" for obscenity in *Hoyt v. Minnesota*, 399 U.S. 524 (1970), and criticizing the Court for becoming a "super-censorship board" in *Cain v. Kentucky*, 387 U.S. 319 (1970), and *Walker v. Ohio*, 398 U.S. 434 (1970).

By 1973, Nixon's last two appointees, Justices Lewis Powell and William Rehnquist, were on the Court. And Burger finally got a bare majority to agree on a new test for obscenity, giving states and localities greater flexibility and control over sexually oriented materials. In *Miller v. California* (1973) (excerpted below), Burger set out more concrete rules for obscenity prosecutions. While maintaining the prurient interest test, he redefined it as "whether the work depicts or describes, in a patently offensive way sexual conduct specifically defined by state law," thus inviting states precisely to define obscenity in legislation. He also rejected as too broad the utterly without redeeming social value test and devised his own more precise test—"whether the work, taken as a whole, lacks serious literary, artistic, political or scientific value." Finally, the contemporary community standards test was reinterpreted to mean local, not national standards.

Ten companion cases coming down on a five-to-four vote with *Miller* buttressed the Burger Court's renewed deference to states and localities in controlling sexually oriented materials. *Paris Adult Theatre I v. Slaton* (1973) (excerpted below), for example, limited the ruling in *Stanley v. Georgia*, by upholding state regulation of adult movie houses. Prior to *Paris Adult Theatre I*, the Court had held that the First Amendment and the right of privacy did not preclude searches of luggage for obscene materials by U.S. customs officials at airports in *United States v. 37-Photographs*, 402 U.S. 363 (1971). Subsequently, in *United States v. 12-1200 Foot Reels of Super 8Mm Film*, 413 U.S. 123 (1973), the Court held that an individual does not have a First Amendment or privacy right to purchase obscene materials.

The test for obscenity announced in *Miller* was problematic, and the four dissenters remained adamant in their opposition. But the politics of the Court had changed. As Justice Stevens, in an unusual concurring opinion to the denial of review of an appeal of one of the hundreds of obscenity convictions following *Miller*, explained, "[T]here is no reason to believe that the majority of the Court which decided *Miller v. California* . . . is any less adamant than the minority. Accordingly, regardless of how I might vote on the merits after full argument, it would be pointless to grant *certiorari* in case after case of this character only to have *Miller* reaffirmed time after time."[6]

The most troubling problems with *Miller* arose because obscenity prosecutions under the ruling turned on varying local community standards. At the federal level this allowed prosecutors to "forum shop," that is, they could initiate prosecutions in a district court in a geographical area with the most restrictive community standards. The Court declined to review this practice. At the state level, materials deemed obscene in one state might not be obscene in another. Consequently, the Court frequently cannot avoid rendering a final decision on the matter, notwithstanding that obscenity under *Miller* is determined according to local community standards. The Court thus held, in *Jenkins v. Georgia*, 418 U.S. 153 (1973), that the movie *Carnal Knowledge* was not obscene, despite lower court rulings to the contrary.

The Burger and Rehnquist Courts tried to clarify some of the ambiguous aspects of *Miller*. *Pinkus v. United States*, 436 U.S. 293 (1978), held that children are not part of the "community," but "sensitive persons" and deviant groups are and should be considered in determining whether sexually oriented materials run afoul of local community standards. In *Pope v. Illinois*, 481 U.S. 497 (1987), the Court ruled that *Miller*'s third prong—requiring the showing that a work lacks serious literary, artistic, political, or scientific value—be applied based on standards set by a "reasonable" person, not an "ordinary" person. In addition, in *New York v. Ferber* (1982) (see excerpt below) the Court unanimously, although with four separate concurring opinions, upheld New York's ban on child pornography. Subsequently, in *Osborne v. Ohio*, 495 U.S. 103 (1990), the Rehnquist Court upheld Ohio's statute banning the possession and viewing of child pornography. However, in *Ashcroft v. Free Speech Coalition* (2002) (excerpted below) the Court held that Congress may not make it a crime to create, distribute, or possess "virtual child pornography" generated by computer images of young adults or simulated images, rather than of actual children.

Besides trying to clarify the application of *Miller's* tests for obscenity, the Burger and Rehnquist Courts have been more receptive to restrictions on the availability of sexually oriented materials. Over First Amendment objections, for example, restrictions on the mailing of obscene materials have been upheld. *Rowan v. U.S. Post Office Department*, 397 U.S. 728 (1970), sustained a federal obscenity statute allowing individuals to request that the post office not deliver unsolicited mailings to their homes of materials they find offensive. *United States v. Reidel*, 402 U.S. 351 (1971) upheld a federal obscenity statute prohibiting the mailing of certain pornographic materials, but *Bolger v. Youngs Drug Product Corp.*, 463 U.S. 60 (1983), struck down another statute as applied to the unsolicited mailing of advertisements for contraceptives.

Restrictions on adult bookstores, nude dancing, and other forms of live sexually oriented entertainment have also been approved. *California v. LaRue*, 409 U.S. 109 (1972), sustained California's law prohibiting sexually explicit live entertainment and films in bars. Although striking down a law prohibiting nude dancers in places of adult-only entertainment in *Schad v. Borough of Mount Ephraim*, 452 U.S. 61 (1981), the Court upheld New York's prohibition on nude dancing on the basis of the state's power to regulate liquor under the Twenty-first Amendment.[7] *Arcara v. Cloud Books, Inc.*, 478 U.S. 697 (1986), also allowed the closing of an adult bookstore whose premises were used for the purpose of soliciting for prostitution.

One of the principal ways that cities and localities control and regulate adult theaters and nightclubs is through exclusionary zoning, that is, restricting the operation of such businesses to certain areas of a community. In *Young v. American Mini Theatres*, 327 U.S. 50 (1976), the justices (five to four) upheld the barring of adult theaters from within 1,000 feet of each other or 500 feet from a residential area. *Larkin v. Grendel's Den, Inc.*, 459 U.S. 116 (1982), however, struck down a Massachusetts statute giving the power to churches to veto applications for liquor licenses for running afoul of the First Amendment establishment clause. In *City of Renton v. Playtime Theatres, Inc.*, 475 U.S. 41 (1986), the Court approved the use of exclusionary zoning in regulating adult entertainment establishments. Subsequently, in *Barnes v. Glen Theatre, Inc.*, 501 U.S. 560 (1991), a bare majority of the Rehnquist Court upheld Indiana's ban on "totally nude dancing." But the Court was badly fragmented and almost a decade later it revisited the issue of First Amendment protection for nude dancing in *City of Erie v. Pap's A. M.* (2000) (excepted below), again upholding bans on totally nude dancing. There Justice O'Connor held that a ban on totally nude dancing was not aimed at regulating expression per se but instead at curbing the "secondary effects," such as prostitution, associated with adult entertainment establishments. On that basis, Justice O'Connor also upheld an ordinance barring more than one adult establishment from operating at the same location, but only a plurality joined her opinion in *City of Los Angeles v. Alameda Books, Inc.*, 535 U.S. 425 (2002).

By contrast, in *Reno v. American Civil Liberties Union*, 521 U.S. 844 (1997) (excerpted below), the Court struck down the Communications Decency Act of 1996, in which Congress had sought to protect minors from "obscene or indecent" material on the Internet. The following term, though, in *National Endowment for the Arts v. Finley*, 524 U.S. 569 (1998), the Court upheld a 1990 "public decency" amendment to the National Foundation for the Arts and Humanities Act, requiring the NEA to take "general standards of decency" into account when awarding grants to artists. Writing for Court, Justice O'Connor relied on and extended the ruling in *Rust v. Sullivan*, 500 U.S. 173 (1991) (excerpted in this chapter). However, in *Ashcroft v. Free Speech Coalition* (2002) (excerpted below) the Court struck down provisions of the Child Pornography Prevention Act of 1996 that criminalized the creation, possession, and distribution of "virtual child pornography." But see also, in Section F of this chapter, *Ashcroft v. American Civil Liberties Union*, 535 U.S. 564 (2002), upholding the use of "community standards" to define what material on the Internet is "harmful to minors" in the Child Online Protection Act of 1998, but also allowing the law to be enjoined from going into effect until other questions about its impact on free speech are resolved; and *United States v. American Library Association* (2003), upholding the Children's Internet Protection Act of 2001, authorizing public libraries that receive federal funding to install pornography filters on computers that provide public access to the Internet.

NOTES

1. Harry Clor, *Obscenity and Public Morality* (Chicago: University of Chicago Press, 1969), 272.

2. Alan Dershowitz, "What Is Porn?" *ABA Journal* 36 (November 1, 1986).

3. *Butler v. Michigan*, 352 U.S. 380 (1957).

4. See David M. O'Brien, *Storm Center: The Supreme Court in American Politics*, 7th ed. (New York: W. W. Norton, 2005), Ch. 2; and Bruce Murphy, *Fortas: The Rise and Ruin of a Supreme Court Justice* (New York: Morrow, 1988).

5. See, for example, *Kingsley Books v. Brown*, 354 U.S. 436 (1957) (city may get injunction against sale of indecent books with appeal and trial within two days); *Times Film Corporation v. City of Chicago*, 365 U.S. 43 (1961) (no absolute right to exhibit, even once, any and every kind of film; no prior censorship of permit system); *Bantam Books, Inc. v. Sullivan*, 372 U.S. 58 (1963) (held Rhode Island Committee on Morality constituted prior restraint in providing no hearing on books banned for youths); *A Quantity of Copies of Books v. Kansas*, 378 U.S. 205 (1964) (procedure for impoundment of books was unconstitutional); *Freedman v. Maryland*, 380 U.S. 51 (1965) (held state motion picture censorship statute failed to provide adequate safeguards against undue repression of speech); *Teitel Film Corporation v. Cusack*, 390 U.S. 139 (1968) (held censorship board for review of films was unconstitutional, where fifty days passed before completion of administrative process and no provision was made for prompt judicial decision); *Rabe v. Washington*, 405 U.S. 313 (1972) (held state's obscenity statute, proscribing showing of pictures at drive-ins, which could be shown in adult theaters, was unconstitutional and vague); *Heller v. New York*, 413 U.S. 483 (1973) (held because judge saw entire film before issuing warrant for seizure for obscene film, no adversary hearing prior to seizure was required); *Roaden v. Kentucky*, 413 U.S. 496 (1973) (holding seizure of film in public distribution without warrant was prior restraint and violated Fourth Amendment); *Southeastern Promotions, Ltd. v. Conrad*, 420 U.S. 546 (1975) (held denial of city-leased theater for production of *Hair* was prior restraint because it was imposed without procedural safeguards); *Vance v. Universal Amusement Co.*, 445 U.S. 308 (1980) (struck down as prior restraint restriction on an exhibition of obscene motion pictures). Most recently, in *City of Littleton v. Z. J. Gifts D-4, LLC*, 124 S.Ct. 2219 (2004), the Court reaffirmed that ordinances requiring the licensing of adult businesses must provide access to judicial review and a prompt judicial decision.

6. *Lies v. Oregon*, 425 U.S. 963 (1976).

7. *New York State Liquor Authority v. Bellanca*, 452 U.S. 714 (1981); reaffirmed in *City of Newport, Kentucky v. Iacobucci*, 479 U.S. 92 (1986).

Selected Bibliography

Arcand, Bernard. *The Jaguar and the Anteater*. New York: Verso, 1993.

Clor, Harry. *Obscenity and Public Morality*. Chicago: University of Chicago Press, 1969.

deGrazia, Edward. *Girls Lean Back Everywhere: The Law of Obscenity and the Assault on Genius*. New York: Random House, 1992.

Dooling, Richard. *Swearing, Free Speech, and Sexual Harassment*. New York: Random House, 1996.

Downs, Donald. *The New Politics of Pornography*. Chicago: University of Chicago Press, 1989.

Greenwalt, Kent. *Fighting Words: Individuals, Communities, and Liberties of Speech*. Princeton, NJ: Princeton University Press, 1995.

Hunt, Lynn, ed. *The Invention of Pornography*. New York: Zone Books, 1993.

Kendrick, Walter. *The Secret Museum: Pornography in Modern Culture*. New York: Viking, 1987.

MacKinnon, Catharine. *Only Words*. Cambridge, MA: Harvard University Press, 1993.

MacKinnon, Catharine, and Dworkin, Andrea. *In Harm's Way: The Pornography Civil Rights Hearings*. Cambridge, MA: Harvard University Press, 1997.

Paglia, Camille. *Sex, Art, and American Culture*. New York: Vintage, 1992.

Saunders, Kevin. *Violence as Obscenity: Limiting the Media's First Amendment Protection*. Durham, NC: Duke University Press, 1996.

Strossen, Nadine. *Defending Pornography*. New York: Scribner, 1995.

Williams, Susan H. *Truth, Autonomy, and Speech: Feminist Theory and the First Amendment*. New York: New York University Press, 2004.

Roth v. United States and *Alberts v. California*

354 U.S. 476, 77 S.CT. 1304 (1957)

Samuel Roth was charged with violating a federal statute making it a crime to send "obscene, lewd, lascivious, or filthy" materials or advertisements through the mail. He was convicted for advertising and selling a quarterly publication, *American Aphrodite*, dealing with literary erotica and containing nude photographs, but acquitted on the charge that the photographs were obscene. David Alberts was indicted and convicted under California's obscenity law for publishing pictures of "nude and scantily-clad women"; his works made no claim to literary aspirations. On their appeal of their convictions to the Supreme Court, their cases were consolidated in the Warren Court's landmark ruling and opinion by Justice Brennan, who was still in his freshman year, having arrived at the Court only nine months before.

The Court's decision was six to three in *Roth* and seven to two in *Alberts*, with the majority's opinion announced by Justice Brennan. Chief Justice Warren concurred. A separate opinion, concurring in *Alberts* and dissenting in *Roth*, was delivered by Justice Harlan. Justice Douglas dissented and was joined by Justice Black.

☐ *Justice BRENNAN delivered the opinion of the Court.*

Roth conducted a business in New York in the publication and sale of books, photographs and magazines. He used circulars and advertising matter to solicit sales. He was convicted by a jury in the District Court for the Southern District of New York upon 4 counts of a 26-count indictment charging him with mailing obscene circulars and advertising, and an obscene book, in violation of the federal obscenity statute. His conviction was affirmed by the Court of Appeals for the Second Circuit. . . .

Alberts conducted a mail-order business from Los Angeles. He was convicted . . . under a misdemeanor complaint which charged him with lewdly keeping for sale obscene and indecent books, and with writing, composing and publishing an obscene advertisement of them, in violation of the California Penal Code. The conviction was affirmed by the Appellate Department of the Superior Court of the State of California in and for the County of Los Angeles. . . .

The dispositive question is whether obscenity is utterance within the area of protected speech and press. . . .

All ideas having even the slightest redeeming social importance—unorthodox ideas, controversial ideas, even ideas hateful to the prevailing climate of opinion—have the full protection of the guaranties, unless excludable because they encroach upon the limited area of more important interests. But implicit in the history of the First Amendment is the rejection of obscenity as utterly without redeeming social importance. This rejection for that reason is mirrored in the universal judgment that obscenity should be restrained, reflected in the international agreement of over 50 nations, in the obscenity laws of all of the 48 States, and in the 20 obscenity laws enacted by the Congress from 1842 to 1956. This is the same judgment expressed by this Court in *Chaplinsky v. New Hampshire* [315 U.S. 568 (1942)]. We hold that obscenity is not within the area of constitutionally protected speech or press. . . .

[S]ex and obscenity are not synonymous. Obscene material is material which deals with sex in a manner appealing to prurient interest. The portrayal of sex, *e.g.*, in art, literature and scientific works, is not itself sufficient reason to deny material the constitutional protection of freedom of speech and press. Sex, a great and mysterious motive force in human life, has indisputably been a subject of absorbing interest to mankind through the ages; it is one of the vital problems of human interest and public concern. . . .

It is therefore vital that the standards for judging obscenity safeguard the protection of freedom of speech and press for material which does not treat sex in a manner appealing to prurient interest.

The early leading standard of obscenity allowed material to be judged merely by the effect of an isolated excerpt upon particularly susceptible persons. *Regina v. Hicklin*, [1868] L.R. 3 Q.B. 360. Some American courts adopted this standard but later decisions have rejected it and substituted this test: whether to the average person, applying contemporary community standards, the dominant theme of the material taken as a whole appeals to prurient interest. The *Hicklin* test, judging obscenity by the effect of isolated passages upon the most susceptible persons, might well encompass material legitimately treating with sex, and so it must be rejected as unconstitutionally restrictive of the freedoms of speech and press. On the other hand, the substituted standard provides safeguards adequate to withstand the charge of constitutional infirmity.

Both trial courts below sufficiently followed the proper standard. Both courts used the proper definition of obscenity. . . .

In summary, then, we hold that these statutes, applied according to the proper standard for judging obscenity, do not offend constitutional safeguards against convictions based upon protected material, or fail to give men in acting adequate notice of what is prohibited.

☐ *Chief Justice WARREN, concurring.*

The line dividing the salacious or pornographic from literature or science is not straight and unwavering. Present laws depend largely upon the effect that the materials may have upon those who receive them. It is manifest that the same object may have a different impact varying according to the part of the community it reached. But there is more to these cases. It is not the book that is on trial; it is a person. The conduct of the defendant is the central issue, not the obscenity of a book or picture. The nature of the materials is, of course, relevant as an attribute of the defendant's conduct, but the materials are thus placed in context from which they draw color and character. A wholly different result might be reached in a different setting.

☐ *Justice HARLAN, concurring in part and dissenting in part.*

In the final analysis, the problem presented by these cases is how far, and on what terms, the state and federal government have power to punish individuals for disseminating books considered to be undesirable because of their nature of supposed deleterious effect upon human conduct. Proceeding from the premise that "no issue is presented in either case concerning the obscenity of the material involved," the Court finds the "dispositive question" to be "whether obscenity is utterance within the area of protected speech and press," and then holds that "obscenity" is not so protected because it is "utterly without redeeming social importance." This sweeping formula appears to me to beg the very question before us. The Court seems to assume that "obscenity" is a peculiar *genus* of "speech and press," which is as distinctly recognizable, and classifiable as poison ivy is among other plants. On this basis the *constitutional* question before us simply becomes, as the Court says, whether "obscenity," as an abstraction is protected by the First and Fourteenth Amendments, and the question whether a *particular* book may be suppressed becomes a mere matter of classification, of "fact," to be entrusted to a fact-finder and insulated from independent constitutional judgment. But surely the problem cannot be solved in such a generalized fashion. Every communication has an individuality and "value" of its own. The suppression of a particular writing or other tangible form of expression is, therefore, an *individual* matter, and in the nature of things every such suppression raises an individual constitutional problem, in which a reviewing court must determine for *itself* whether the attacked expression is suppressable within constitutional standards. Since those standards do not readily lend themselves to generalized definitions, the constitutional problem in the last analysis becomes one of particularized judgments which appellate courts must make for themselves. . . .

I concur in the judgment of the Court in No. 61, *Alberts v. People of State of California.*

The question in this case is whether the defendant was deprived of liberty without due process of law when he was convicted for selling certain materials found by the judge to be obscene because they would have a "tendency to deprave or corrupt its readers by exciting lascivious thoughts or arousing lustful desire." . . .

Since the domain of sexual morality is pre-eminently a matter of state concern, this Court should be slow to interfere with state legislation calculated to protect that morality. It seems to me that nothing in the broad and flexible command of the Due Process Clause forbids California to prosecute one who sells books whose dominant tendency might be to "deprave or corrupt" a reader. I agree with the Court, of course, that the books must be judged as a whole and in relation to the normal adult reader.

What has been said, however, does not dispose of the case. It still remains for us to decide whether the state court's determination that this material should be suppressed is consistent with the Fourteenth Amendment; and that, of course, presents a federal question as to which we, and not the state court, have the ultimate responsibility. And so, in the final analysis, I concur in the judgment because, upon an independent perusal of the material involved, and in light of the considerations discussed above, I cannot say that its suppression would so interfere with the communication of "ideas" in any proper sense of that term that it would offend the Due Process Clause. I therefore agree with the Court that appellant's conviction must be affirmed.

I dissent in No. 582, *Roth v. United States.*

We are faced here with the question whether the federal obscenity statute, as construed and applied in this case, violates the First Amendment to the Constitution. To me, this question is of quite a different order than one where we are dealing with state legislation under the Fourteenth Amendment. I do not think it follows that state and federal powers in this area are the same, and that just because the State may suppress a particular utterance, it is automatically permissible for the Federal Government to do the same. . . .

The Federal Government has, for example, power to restrict seditious speech directed against it, because that Government certainly has the substantive authority to protect itself against revolution. But in dealing with obscenity we are faced with the converse situation, for the interests which obscenity statutes purportedly protect are primarily entrusted to the care, not of the Federal Government, but of the States. Congress has no substantive power over sexual morality. Such powers as the Federal Government has in this field are but incidental to its other powers, here the postal power, and are not of the same nature as those possessed by the States, which bear direct responsibility for the protection of the local moral fabric. . . .

Not only is the federal interest in protecting the Nation against pornography attenuated, but the dangers of federal censorship in this field are far greater than anything the States may do. It has often been said that one of the great strengths of our federal system is that we have, in the forty-eight States, forty-eight experimental social laboratories. Different States will have different attitudes toward the same work of literature. The same book which is freely read in one State might be classed as obscene in another. And it seems to me that no overwhelming danger to our freedom to experiment and to gratify our tastes in literature is likely to result from the suppression of a borderline book in one of the States, so long as there is no uniform nationwide suppression of the book, and so long as other States are free to experiment with the same or bolder books.

Quite a different situation is presented, however, where the Federal Government imposes the ban. The danger is perhaps not great if the people of one State, through their legislature, decide that "Lady Chatterley's Lover" goes so far beyond the acceptable standards of candor that it will be deemed offensive and non-sellable, for the State next door is still free to make its own choice. At least we do not have one uniform standard. But the dangers to free thought and expression are truly great if the Federal Government imposes a blanket ban over the Nation on such a book. The prerogative of the States to differ on their ideas of morality will be destroyed, the ability of States to experiment will be stunted. The fact that the people of one State cannot read some of the works of D. H. Lawrence seems to me, if not wise or desirable, at least acceptable. But that no person in the United States should be allowed to do so seems to me to be intolerable, and violative of both the letter and spirit of the First Amendment.

I judge this case, then, in view of what I think is the attenuated federal interest in this field, in view of the very real danger of a deadening uniformity which can result from nation-wide federal censorship, and in view of the fact that the constitutionality of this conviction must be weighed against the First and not the Fourteenth Amendment. So viewed, I do not think that this conviction can be upheld.

☐ *Justice DOUGLAS, with whom Justice BLACK joins, dissenting.*

I do not think that the problem can be resolved by the Court's statement that "obscenity is not expression protected by the First Amendment." . . . I reject too the implication that problems of freedom of speech and of the press are to be resolved by weighing against the values of free expression, the judgment of the Court that a particular form of that expression has "no redeeming social importance." The First Amendment, its prohibition in terms absolute, was designed to preclude courts as well as legislatures from weighing the values of speech against silence. The First Amendment puts free speech in the preferred position.

Stanley v. Georgia
394 U.S. 561, 89 S.Ct. 1243 (1969)

Robert Eli Stanley was charged in Fulton County, Georgia, for violating the state's law making it a crime to possess obscene materials. His arrest arose from a search of his home by police who had a warrant to seize evidence of bookmaking activities, but discovered in a desk drawer in Stanley's bedroom three reels of 8-millimeter film. After viewing the films in his living room, the police arrested Stanley, and he was later convicted for the possession of allegedly obscene materials in a state superior court. Stanley appealed a decision by the state supreme court upholding his conviction to the Supreme Court, which granted *certiorari.*

The Court's decision was unanimous, and the opinion was announced by Justice Marshall. Concurrences were by Justices Black and Stewart, who was joined by Justices Brennan and White.

■ INSIDE THE COURT

Letter from Justice Black to Justice Harlan, December 10, 1969

Because the Supreme Court held that obscene materials fall outside of the protection of the First Amendment, when hearing appeals of convictions under state and federal obscenity laws, the justices had to examine the evidence in each case, including screening sexually explicit films in a room in the basement of the Court. Because of Justice Hugo Black's absolutist interpretation of the First Amendment, he declined to join the other justices in screening allegedly obscene films, as the following letter indicates.

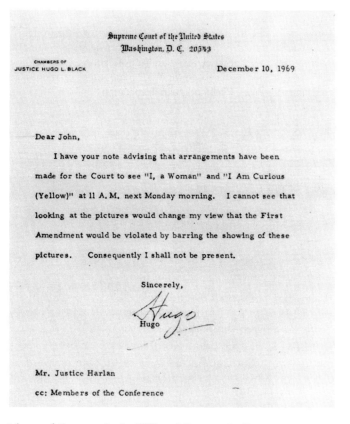

Source: Library of Congress, Justice William J. Brennan, Jr., Papers.

☐ *Justice MARSHALL delivered the opinion of the Court.*

[The] appellant is asserting . . . the right to read or observe what he pleases—the right to satisfy his intellectual and emotional needs in the privacy of his own home. He is asserting the right to be free from state inquiry into the contents of his library. Georgia contends that appellant does not have these rights, that there are certain types of materials that the individual may not read or even possess. Georgia justifies this assertion by arguing that the films in the present case are obscene. But we think that mere categorization of these films as "obscene" is insufficient justification for such a drastic invasion of personal liberties guaranteed by the First and Fourteenth Amendments. Whatever may be the justifications for other statutes regulating obscenity, we do not think they reach into the privacy of one's own home. If the First Amendment means anything, it means that a State has no business telling a man, sitting alone in his own house, what books he may read or what films he may watch. Our whole constitutional heritage rebels at the thought of giving government the power to control men's minds. . . .

We hold that the First and Fourteenth Amendments prohibit making mere private possession of obscene material a crime. *Roth* [*v. United States* (1957)] and the cases following that decision are not impaired by today's holding. As we have said, the States retain broad power to regulate obscenity; that power simply does not extend to mere possession by the individual in the privacy of his own home. Accordingly, the judgment of the court below is reversed and the case is remanded for proceedings not inconsistent with this opinion.

Miller v. California
413 U.S. 15, 93 S.CT. 2607 (1973)

By the 1970s, as a result of the *Roth* line of cases, there was a proliferation of sexually oriented materials and there were renewed attempts by states and localities to regulate and ban obscene and pornographical materials. That in turn meant a large number of appeals of obscenity convictions coming to the Supreme Court. In 1971–1972, there were more than sixty such cases on the Court's docket, and the justices heard oral arguments in eight cases in the 1972 term. One of these cases involved the conviction of Marvin Miller for violating California's obscenity law. He was found guilty of mailing unsolicited materials advertising adult books and films, which included pictures of men and women engaged in sexual acts and displaying their genitals.

When the justices discussed *Miller* and other obscenity cases in May and June 1972, they were dissatisfied with *Roth* yet pulled in opposite directions. In particular, Chief Justice Burger and Justice Brennan each wanted to take the Court in a different direction on the obscenity problem.

Chief Justice Burger had come to the Court in 1969 believing that the *Roth* line of cases was mistaken; it was too permissive and failed to give states and localities enough power over sexually explicit materials. He urged a reconsideration of *Roth* and tougher standards. "In short," as he put in a June 14, 1972, memorandum, "a little 'chill' will do some of the 'pornos' no great harm and it might be good for the country."

Justice Brennan, who authored *Roth* and other opinions in this area for the Warren Court, was no less concerned and had come to reevaluate his earlier position in *Roth*. In his view, however, *Roth* was mistaken in not going far enough; it allowed too much censorship. As he explained in a memorandum for the justices on May 22, 1972:

> With all respect, the Chief Justice's proposed solution to the obscenity quagmire will, in my view, worsen an already intolerable mess. I've been thinking for some time that only a drastic change in applicable constitutional principles promises a way out. I've decided that I shall use this case as a vehicle for saying that I'm prepared to make that change. I'll write in effect that it has proved impossible to separate expression concerning sex, called obscenity, from other expression concerning sex, whether the material takes the form of words, photographs or film; . . . that we should treat obscenity not as expression concerning sex except from First Amendment speech but as expression, although constituting First Amendment speech, that is regulable to the extent of legislating against its offensive exposure to unwilling adults and dissemination to juveniles.

Both Burger and Brennan began working on draft opinions in the hope of winning a majority over to their side. That proved impossible so late in the term, so *Miller* was carried over for reargument in the October 1972 term. Both continued to compete for votes, but in the end, on June 21, 1973, a bare majority accepted Burger's analysis and more restrictive tests for obscenity based on local community standards. Brennan's draft became a dissenting opinion.

The Court's decision was five to four, with the majority's opinion announced by Chief Justice Burger. Dissents were by Justices Douglas and Brennan, who was joined by Justices Stewart and Marshall.

☐ *Chief Justice BURGER delivered the opinion of the Court.*

This is one of a group of "obscenity-pornography" cases being reviewed by the Court in a re-examination of standards enunciated in earlier cases involving what Justice HARLAN called "the intractable obscenity problem." . . .

Appellant conducted a mass mailing campaign to advertise the sale of illustrated books, euphemistically called "adult" material. After a jury trial, he was convicted of violating California Penal Code § 311.2(a), a misdemeanor, by knowingly distributing obscene matter, and the Appellate Department, Superior Court of California, County of Orange, summarily affirmed the judgment without opinion. Appellant's conviction was specifically based on his conduct in causing five unsolicited advertising brochures . . . [containing] pictures and drawings very explicitly depicting men and women in groups of two or more engaging in a variety of sexual activities, with genitals often prominently displayed.

This case involves the application of a State's criminal obscenity statute to a situation in which sexually explicit materials have been thrust by aggressive sales action upon unwilling recipients who had in no way indicated any desire to receive such materials. . . .

[O]bscene material is unprotected by the First Amendment. . . . We acknowledge, however, the inherent dangers of undertaking to regulate any form of expression. State statutes designed to regulate obscene materials must be carefully limited. As a result, we now confine the permissible scope of such regulation to works which depict or describe sexual conduct. That conduct must be specifically defined by the applicable state law, as written or authoritatively construed. A state offense must also be limited to works which, taken as a whole, appeal to the prurient interest in sex, which portray sexual conduct in a patently offensive way, and which, taken as a whole, do not have serious literary, artistic, political, or scientific value.

The basic guidelines for the trier of fact must be: (a) whether "the average person, applying contemporary community standards" would find that the work, taken as a whole, appeals to the prurient interest; (b) whether the work depicts or describes, in a patently offensive way, sexual conduct specifically defined by the applicable state law; and (c) whether the work, taken as a whole, lacks serious literary, artistic, political, or scientific value. We do not adopt as a constitutional standard the "*utterly* without redeeming social value" test of *Memoirs v. Massachusetts* [383 U.S. 413 (1966)].

We emphasize that it is not our function to propose regulatory schemes for the States. That must await their concrete legislative efforts. It is possible, however, to give a few plain examples of what a state statute could define for regulation under part (b) of the standard announced in this opinion, *supra*:

> (a) Patently offensive representations or descriptions of ultimate sexual acts, normal or perverted, actual or simulated.
> (b) Patently offensive representation or descriptions of masturbation, excretory functions, and lewd exhibition of the genitals.

Sex and nudity may not be exploited without limit by films or pictures exhibited or sold in places of public accommodation any more than live sex and nudity can be exhibited or sold without limit in such public places. At a minimum, prurient, patently offensive depiction or description of sexual conduct must have serious literary, artistic, political, or scientific value to merit First Amendment protection. . . . For example, medical books for the education of physicians and related personnel necessarily use graphic illustrations and descriptions of human anatomy. In resolving the inevitably sensitive questions of fact and law, we must continue to rely on the jury system, accompanied by the safeguards that judges, rules of evidence, presumption of innocence, and other protective features provide, as we do with rape, murder, and a host of other offenses against society and its individual members.

Justice BRENNAN has abandoned his former position and now maintains that no formulation of this Court, the Congress, or the States can adequately distinguish obscene-material unprotected by the First Amendment from protected expression. . . .

[But under] the holdings announced today, no one will be subject to prosecution for the sale or exposure of obscene materials unless these materials depict or describe patently offensive "hard core" sexual conduct specifically defined by the regulating state law, as written or construed. We are satisfied that these specific prerequisites will provide fair notice to a dealer in such materials that his public and commercial activities may bring prosecution.

Justice BRENNAN also emphasizes "institutional stress" in justification of his change of view. Noting that "[t]he number of obscenity cases on our docket gives ample testimony to the burden that has been placed upon this Court," he quite rightly remarks that the examination of contested materials "is hardly a source of edification to the members of this Court." He also notes, and we agree, that "uncertainty of the standards creates a continuing source of tension between state and federal courts. . . ."

But today, for the first time since *Roth* was decided in 1957, a majority of this Court has agreed on concrete guidelines to isolate "hard core" pornography from expression protected by the First Amendment. Now we may abandon the casual practice of *Redrup v. New York*, 386 U.S. 767 (1967), and attempt to provide positive guidance to federal and state courts alike.

This may not be an easy road, free from difficulty. But no amount of "fatigue" should lead us to adopt a convenient "institutional" rationale—an absolutist, "anything goes" view of the First Amendment—because it will lighten our burdens. . . .

Under a National Constitution, fundamental First Amendment limitations on the powers of the States do not vary from community to community, but this does not mean that there are, or should or can be, fixed, uniform national standards of precisely what appeals to the "prurient interest" or is "patently offensive." These are essentially questions of fact, and our Nation is simply too big and too diverse for this Court to reasonably expect that such standards could be articulated for all 50 States in a single formulation, even assuming the prerequisite consensus exists. When triers of fact are asked to decide whether "the average person, applying contemporary community standards" would consider certain materials "prurient," it would be unrealistic to require that the answer be based on some abstract formulation. The adversary system, with lay jurors as the usual ultimate fact-finders in criminal prosecutions, has historically permitted triers of fact to draw on the standards of their community, guided always by limiting instructions on the law. To require a State to structure obscenity proceedings around evidence of a *national* "community standard" would be an exercise in futility. . . .

We conclude that neither the state's alleged failure to offer evidence of "national standards," nor the trial court's charge that the jury consider state community standards, were constitutional errors. Nothing in the First Amendment requires that a jury must consider hypothetical and unascertainable "national standards" when attempting to determine whether certain materials are obscene as a matter of fact. . . . It is neither realistic nor constitutionally sound to read the First Amendment as requiring that the people of Maine or Mississippi accept public depiction of conduct found tolerable in Las Vegas, or New York City. . . . People in different States vary in their tastes and attitudes, and this diversity is not to be strangled by the absolutism of imposed uniformity. . . . We hold that the requirement that the jury evaluate the materials with reference to "contemporary standards of the State of California" serves this protection purpose and is constitutionally adequate. . . .

In sum, we (a) reaffirm the *Roth* holding that obscene material is not protected by the First Amendment; (b) hold that such material can be regulated by the States, subject to the specific safeguards enunciated above, without a showing that the material is "*utterly* without redeeming social value"; and (c) hold that obscenity is to be determined by applying "contemporary community standards," . . . not "national standards." . . .

Vacated and remanded.

☐ *Justice DOUGLAS, dissenting.*

Today the Court retreats from the earlier formulations of the constitutional test and undertakes to make new definitions. This effort, like the earlier ones, is earnest and well intentioned. The difficulty is that we do not deal with constitutional terms, since "obscenity" is not mentioned in the Constitution or Bill of Rights. And the First Amendment makes no such exception from "the press" which it undertakes to protect nor, as I have said on other occasions, is an exception necessarily implied, for there was no recognized exception to the free press at the time the Bill of Rights was adopted which treated "obscene" publications differently from other types of papers, magazines, and books. So there are no constitutional guidelines for deciding what is and what is not "obscene." The Court is at large because we deal with tastes and standards of literature. What shocks me may be sustenance for my neighbor. What causes one person to boil up in rage over one pamphlet or movie may reflect only his neurosis, not shared by others. We deal here with a regime of censorship which, if adopted, should be done by constitutional amendment after full debate by the people. . . .

The idea that the First Amendment permits government to ban publications that are "offensive" to some people puts an ominous gloss on freedom of the press. That test would make it possible to ban any paper or any journal or magazine in some benighted place. . . . The idea that the First Amendment permits punishment for ideas that are "offensive" to the particular judge or jury sitting in judgment is astounding. No greater leveler of speech or literature has ever been designed. . . .

I do not think we, the judges, were ever given the constitutional power to make definitions of obscenity. If it is to be defined, let the people debate and decide by a constitutional amendment what they want to ban as obscene and what standards they want the legislatures and the courts to apply. Perhaps the people will decide that the path towards a mature, integrated society requires that all ideas competing for acceptance must have no censor. Perhaps they will decide otherwise. Whatever the choice, the courts will have some guidelines. Now we have none except our own predilections.

☐ *Justice BRENNAN, with whom Justice STEWART and Justice MARSHALL join, dissenting.*

In my dissent in *Paris Adult Theatre I v. Slaton*, 413 U.S. 49 [(1973)], I noted that I had no occasion to consider the extent of state power to regulate the distribution of sexually oriented material to juveniles or the offensive exposure of such material to unconsenting adults. . . . I need not now decide whether a statute might be drawn to impose, within the requirements of the First Amendment, criminal penalties for the precise conduct at issue here. For it is clear that under my dissent in *Paris Adult Theatre I*, the statute under which the prosecution was brought is unconstitutionally overbroad, and therefore invalid on its face.

Paris Adult Theatre I v. Slaton
413 U.S. 49, 93 S.Ct. 2628 (1973)

This ruling came down on June 21, 1973, with *Miller v. California* and three other obscenity decisions. The case originated with Atlanta's district attorney, Lewis Slaton, seeking an injunction against the showing of two allegedly obscene movies, *Magic Mirror* and *It All Comes Out in the End*, by Paris Adult Theatre I. The trial judge refused to issue an injunction on the ground that showing such movies to consenting adults in a commercial theater was constitutionally permissible under the First Amendment. On appeal, the Georgia state supreme court reversed on finding the movies to be hard-core pornography. The owners of Paris Adult Theatre I appealed to the Supreme Court.

The Court's decision was five to four, with the majority's opinion announced by Chief Justice Burger. Dissents were by Justices Douglas and Brennan, who was joined by Justices Stewart and Marshall.

☐ *Chief Justice BURGER delivered the opinion of the Court.*

We categorically disapprove the theory, apparently adopted by the trial judge, that obscene, pornographic films acquire constitutional immunity from state regulation simply because they are exhibited for consenting adults only. . . . Although we have often pointedly recognized the high importance of the state interest in regulating the exposure of obscene materials to juveniles and unconsenting adults, . . . this Court has never declared these to be the only legitimate state interests permitting regulation of obscene material. . . . In particular, we hold that there are legitimate state interests at stake in stemming the tide of commercialized obscenity, even assuming it is feasible to enforce effective safeguards against exposure to juveniles and to passersby. Rights and interests "other than those of the advocates are involved." These include the interest of the public in the quality of life and the total community environment, the tone of commerce in the great city centers, and, possibly, the public safety itself. The Hillink Minority Report of the Commission on Obscenity and Pornography indicates that there is at least an arguable connection between obscene material and crime. Quite apart from sex crimes, however, there remains one problem of large proportions aptly described by Professor Bickel:

> "It concerns the tone of the society, the mode, or to use terms that have perhaps greater currency, the style and quality of life, now and in the future. A man may be entitled to read an obscene book in his room, or expose himself indecently there. . . . We should protect his privacy. But if he demands a right to obtain the books and pictures he wants in the market, and to foregather in public places—discreet, if you will, but accessible to all—with others who share his tastes, *then to grant him his right is to affect the world about the rest of us, and to impinge on other privacies.* Even supposing that each of us can, if he wishes, effectively avert the eye and stop the ear (which, in truth, we cannot), what is commonly read and seen and heard and done intrudes upon us all, want it or not." *The Public Interest* 25–26 (Winter 1971). (Emphasis added.)

As Chief Justice WARREN stated, there is a "right of the Nation and of the States to maintain a decent society. . . ."

But, it is argued, there are no scientific data which conclusively demonstrate that exposure to obscene material adversely affects men and women or their society. It is urged on behalf of the petitioners that, absent such a demonstration, any kind of state regulation is "impermissible." We reject this argument. It is not for us to resolve empirical uncertainties underlying state legislation, save in the exceptional case where that legislation plainly impinges upon rights protected by the Constitution itself. . . . Although there is no conclusive proof of a connection between antisocial behavior and obscene material, the legislature of Georgia could quite reasonably determine that such a connection does or might exist. In deciding *Roth*, this Court implicitly accepted that a legislature could legitimately act on such a conclusion to protect "*the social interest in order and morality.*" . . .

If we accept the unprovable assumption that a complete education requires the reading of certain books, and the well nigh universal belief that good books, plays, and art lift the spirit, improve the mind, enrich the human personality, and develop character, can we then say that a state legislature may not act on the corollary assumption that commerce in obscene books, or public exhibitions focused on obscene conduct, have a tendency to exert a corrupting and debasing impact leading to antisocial behavior? . . .

It is asserted, however, that . . . state regulation of access by consenting adults to obscene material violates the constitutionally protected right to privacy enjoyed by petitioners' customers. Even assuming that petitioners have vicarious standing to assert potential customers' rights, it is unavailing to compare a theater, open to the public for a fee, with the private home of *Stanley v. Georgia* [394 U.S. 557 (1969)], and the marital bedroom of *Griswold v. Connecticut* [381 U.S. 479 (1965)].

Our prior decisions recognizing a right to privacy guaranteed by the

Fourteenth Amendment included "only personal rights that can be deemed 'fundamental' or 'implicit in the concept of ordered liberty.' . . ." This privacy right encompasses and protects the personal intimacies of the home, the family, marriage, motherhood, procreation, and child rearing. Nothing, however, in this Court's decisions intimates that there is any "fundamental" privacy right "implicit in the concept of ordered liberty" to watch obscene movies in places of public accommodation. . . .

It is also argued that the State has no legitimate interest in "control [of] the moral content of a person's thoughts," and we need not quarrel with this. But we reject the claim that the State of Georgia is here attempting to control the minds or thoughts of those who patronize theaters. Preventing unlimited display or distribution of obscene material, which by definition lacks any serious literary, artistic, political, or scientific value as communication, is distinct from a control of reason and the intellect. . . .

Finally, petitioners argue that conduct which directly involves "consenting adults" only has, for that sole reason, a special claim to constitutional protection. Our Constitution establishes a broad range of conditions on the exercise of power by the States, but for us to say that our Constitution incorporates the proposition that conduct involving consenting adults only is always beyond state regulation, is a step we are unable to take. Commercial exploitation of depictions, descriptions, or exhibitions of obscene conduct on commercial premises open to the adult public falls within a State's broad power to regulate commerce and protect the public environment. The issue in this context goes beyond whether someone, or even the majority, considers the conduct depicted as "wrong" or "sinful." The States have the power to make a morally neutral judgment that public exhibition of obscene material, or commerce in such material, has a tendency to . . . endanger the public safety, or to jeopardize in Chief Justice WARREN's words, the States' "right . . . to maintain a decent society."

☐ *Justice BRENNAN, with whom Justice STEWART and Justice MARSHALL join, dissenting.*

Our experience with the *Roth* approach has certainly taught us that the outright suppression of obscenity cannot be reconciled with the fundamental principles of the First and Fourteenth Amendments. For we have failed to formulate a standard that sharply distinguishes protected from unprotected speech, and out of necessity, we have resorted to . . . disposing of these cases through summary reversal or denial of certiorari [and] we have deliberately and effectively obscured the rationale underlying the decisions. It comes as no surprise that judicial attempts to follow our lead conscientiously have often ended in hopeless confusion. . . .

[A]fter 16 years of experimentation and debate I am reluctantly forced to the conclusion that none of the available formulas, including the one announced today, can reduce the vagueness to a tolerable level while at the same time striking an acceptable balance between the protections of the First and Fourteenth Amendments, on the one hand, and on the other the asserted state interest in regulating the dissemination of certain sexually oriented materials. Any effort to draw a constitutionally acceptable boundary on state power must resort to such indefinite concepts as "prurient interest," "patent offensiveness," "serious literary value," and the like. The meaning of these concepts necessarily varies with the experience, outlook, and even idiosyncrasies of the person defining them. Although we have assumed that obscenity does exist and that we "know it when [we] see it," *Jacobellis v. Ohio* [378 U.S. 184 (1964)] (STEWART, J., concurring), we are manifestly unable to describe it in advance except by reference to concepts so elusive that they fail to distinguish clearly between protected and unprotected speech. . . .

The severe problems arising from the lack of fair notice, from the chill on protected expression, and from the stress imposed on the state and federal judicial machinery persuade me that a significant change in direction is urgently required. I turn, therefore, to the alternatives that are now open.

1. The approach requiring the smallest deviation from our present course would be to draw a new line between protected and unprotected speech, still permitting the States to suppress all material on the unprotected side of the line. In my view, clarity cannot be obtained pursuant to this approach except by drawing a line that resolves all doubt in favor of state power and against the guarantees of the First Amendment. We could hold, for example, that any depiction or description of human sexual organs, irrespective of the manner or purpose of the portrayal, is outside the protection of the First Amendment and therefore open to suppression by the States. That formula would, no doubt, offer much fairer notice of the reach of any state statute drawn at the boundary of the State's constitutional power. And it would also, in all likelihood, give rise to a substantial probability of regularity in most judicial determinations under the standard. But such a standard would be appallingly overbroad, permitting the suppression of a vast range of literary, scientific, and artistic masterpieces. Neither the First Amendment nor any free community could possibly tolerate such a standard. Yet short of that extreme it is hard to see how any choice of words could reduce the vagueness problem to tolerable proportions, so long as we remain committed to the view that some class of materials is subject to outright suppression by the State.

2. The alternative adopted by the Court today recognizes that a prohibition against any depiction or description of human sexual organs could not be reconciled with the guarantees of the First Amendment. But the Court does retain the view that certain sexually oriented material can be considered obscene and therefore unprotected by the First and Fourteenth Amendments. To describe that unprotected class of expression, the Court adopts a restatement of the *Roth-Memoirs* definition of obscenity: "The basic guidelines for the trier of fact must be: (a) whether 'the average person, applying contemporary community standards' would find that the work, taken as a whole, appeals to the prurient interest . . . (b) whether the work depicts or describes, in a patently offensive way, sexual conduct specifically defined by the applicable state law, and (c) whether the work, taken as a whole, lacks serious literary, artistic, political, or scientific value." *Miller v. California.* In apparent illustration of "sexual conduct," as that term is used in the test's second element, the Court identifies "(a) Patently offensive representations or descriptions of ultimate sexual acts, normal or perverted, actual or simulated," and "(b) Patently offensive representations or descriptions of masturbation, excretory functions, and lewd exhibition of the genitals." . . .

In my view, the restatement [of *Roth's* standards] leaves unresolved the very difficulties that compel our rejection of the underlying *Roth* approach, while at the same time contributing substantial difficulties of its own. . . . And today's restatement will likely have the effect, whether or not intended, of permitting far more sweeping suppression of sexually oriented expression, including expression that would almost surely be held protected under our current formulation. . . .

It is beyond dispute that the [Court's new] approach can have no ameliorative impact on the cluster of problems that grow out of the vagueness of our current standards. Indeed, even the Court makes no argument that the reformulation will provide fairer notice to booksellers, theater owners, and the reading and viewing public. Nor does the Court contend that the approach will provide clearer guidance to law enforcement officials or reduce the chill on protected expression. Nor, finally, does the Court suggest that the approach will mitigate to the slightest degree the institutional problems that have plagued this Court and the state and federal judiciary as a direct result of the uncertainty inherent in any definition of obscenity.

Of course, the Court's restated *Roth* test does limit the definition of obscenity to depictions of physical conduct and explicit sexual acts. . . . But, just as the agreement in *Roth* on an abstract definition of obscenity gave little hint of the extreme difficulty that was to follow in attempting to apply that definition to specific material, the mere formulation of a "physical conduct" test is no assurance that it can be applied with any greater facility. . . .

If the application of the "physical conduct" test to pictorial material is fraught with difficulty, its application to textual material carries the potential for extraordinary abuse. Surely we have passed the point where the mere written description of sexual conduct is deprived of First Amendment protection. Yet the test offers no guidance to us, or anyone else, in determining which written descriptions of sexual conduct are protected, and which are not. . . .

I am convinced that a definition of obscenity in terms of physical conduct cannot provide sufficient clarity to afford fair notice, to avoid a chill on protected expression, and to minimize the institutional stress, so long as that definition is used to justify the outright suppression of any material that is asserted to fall within its terms.

3. I have also considered the possibility of reducing our own role, and the role of appellate courts generally, in determining whether particular matter is obscene. Thus, we might conclude that juries are best suited to determine obscenity *vel non* and that jury verdicts in this area should not be set aside except in cases of extreme departure from prevailing standards. . . . [Yet] the First Amendment requires an independent review by appellate courts of the constitutional fact of obscenity. That result is required by principles applicable to the obscenity issue no less than to any other area involving free expression. . . .

4. Finally, I have considered the view, urged so forcefully since 1957 by our Brothers BLACK and DOUGLAS, that the First Amendment bars the suppression of any sexually oriented expression. That position would effect a sharp reduction, although perhaps not a total elimination, of the uncertainty that surrounds our current approach. Nevertheless, I am convinced that it would achieve that desirable goal only by stripping the States of power to an extent that cannot be justified by the commands of the Constitution, at least

so long as there is available an alternative approach that strikes a better balance between the guarantee of free expression and the States' legitimate interests.

Our experience since *Roth* requires us not only to abandon the effort to pick out obscene materials on a case-by-case basis, but also to reconsider a fundamental postulate of *Roth*: that there exists a definable class of sexually oriented expression that may be totally suppressed by the Federal and State Governments. Assuming that such a class of expression does in fact exist, I am forced to conclude that the concept of "obscenity" cannot be defined with sufficient specificity and clarity to provide fair notice to persons who create and distribute sexually oriented materials, to prevent substantial erosion of protected speech as a byproduct of the attempt to suppress unprotected speech, and to avoid very costly institutional harms. Given these inevitable side effects of state efforts to suppress what is assumed to be *unprotected* speech, we must scrutinize with care the state interest that is asserted to justify the suppression. For in the absence of some very substantial interest in suppressing such speech, we can hardly condone the ill effects that seem to flow inevitably from the effort. . . .

The opinions in *Redrup* [*v. New York* (1967)] and *Stanley* [*v. Georgia* (1969)] reflected our emerging view that the state interests in protecting children and in protecting unconsenting adults may stand on a different footing from the other asserted state interests. . . .

But, whatever the strength of the state interests in protecting juveniles and unconsenting adults from exposure to sexually oriented materials, those interests cannot be asserted in defense of the holding of the Georgia Supreme Court in this case. That court assumed for the purposes of its decision that the films in issue were exhibited only to persons over the age of 21 who viewed them willingly and with prior knowledge of the nature of their contents. And on that assumption the state court held that the films could still be suppressed. The justification for the suppression must be found, therefore, in some independent interest in regulating the reading and viewing habits of consenting adults. . . .

In *Stanley* we pointed out that "[t]here appears to be little empirical basis for" the assertion that "exposure to obscene materials may lead to deviant sexual behavior or crimes of sexual violence." In any event, we added that "if the State is only concerned about printed or filmed materials inducing antisocial conduct, we believe that in the context of private consumption of ideas and information we should adhere to the view that '[a]mong free men, the deterrents ordinarily to be applied to prevent crime are education and punishment for violations of the law. . . .' "

Moreover, in *Stanley* we rejected as "wholly inconsistent with the philosophy of the First Amendment," the notion that there is a legitimate state concern in the "control [of] the moral content of a person's thoughts," and we held that a State "cannot constitutionally premise legislation on the desirability of controlling a person's private thoughts." That is not to say, of course, that a State must remain utterly indifferent to—and take no action bearing on—the morality of the community. The traditional description of state police power does embrace the regulation of morals as well as the health, safety, and general welfare of the citizenry. . . . But the State's interest in regulating morality by suppressing obscenity, while often asserted, remains essentially unfocused and ill defined. And, since the attempt to curtail unprotected speech necessarily spills over into the area of protected speech, the effort to serve this speculative interest through the suppression of obscene material must tread heavily on rights protected by the First Amendment. . . .

In short, while I cannot say that the interests of the State—apart from the question of juveniles and unconsenting adults—are trivial or nonexistent, I am compelled to conclude that these interests cannot justify the substantial damage to constitutional rights and to this Nation's judicial machinery that inevitably results from state efforts to bar the distribution even of unprotected material to consenting adults. I would hold, therefore, that at least in the absence of distribution to juveniles or obtrusive exposure to unconsenting adults, the First and Fourteenth Amendments prohibit the State and Federal Governments from attempting wholly to suppress sexually oriented materials on the basis of their allegedly "obscene" contents. Nothing in this approach precludes those governments from taking action to serve what may be strong and legitimate interests through regulation of the manner of distribution of sexually oriented material.

☐ *Justice DOUGLAS, dissenting.*

I am sure I would find offensive most of the books and movies charged with being obscene. But in a life that has not been short, I have yet to be trapped into seeing or reading something that would offend me. I never read or see the materials coming to the Court under charges of "obscenity," because I have thought the First Amendment made it unconstitutional for me to act as a censor. I see ads in bookstores and neon lights over theaters that resemble bait for those who seek vicarious exhilaration. As a parent or a priest or as a teacher I would have no compunction in edging my children or wards away from the books and movies that did no more than excite man's base instincts. But I never supposed that government was permitted to sit in judgment on one's tastes or beliefs—save as they involved action within the reach of the police power of government.

New York v. Ferber

458 U.S. 747, 102 S.CT. 3348 (1982)

Paul Ferber, the proprietor of a Manhattan adult bookstore, sold to an undercover police officer two films almost exclusively showing young boys masturbating. He was arrested, tried, and convicted under New York's law prohibiting anyone from knowingly promoting a sexual performance by a child under the age of sixteen by distributing materials depicting such activities. The New York Court of Appeals, however, overturned the conviction and found the statute overly broad and that it ran afoul of the First Amendment. The state, thereupon, appealed to the Supreme Court.

The Court's decision was unanimous, with the opinion announced by Justice White. Concurrences were by Justices Blackmun, O'Connor, Brennan, and Stevens.

☐ *Justice WHITE delivered the opinion of the Court.*

At issue in this case is the constitutionality of a New York criminal statute which prohibits persons from knowingly promoting sexual performances by children under the age of 16 by distributing material which depicts such performances. . . .

In *Miller v. California* [(1973)], a majority of the Court agreed that "a state offense must also be limited to works which, taken as a whole, appeal to the prurient interest in sex, which portray sexual conduct in a patently offensive way, and which, taken as a whole, do not have serious literary, artistic, political, or scientific value." Over the past decade, we have adhered to the guidelines expressed in *Miller*, which subsequently has been followed in the regulatory schemes of most states.

The *Miller* standard, like its predecessors, was an accommodation between the state's interests in protecting the "sensibilities of unwilling recipients" from exposure to pornographic material and the dangers of censorship inherent in unabashedly content-based laws. Like obscenity statutes, laws directed at the dissemination of child pornography run the risk of suppressing protected expression by allowing the hand of the censor to become unduly heavy. For the following reasons, however, we are persuaded that the States are entitled to greater leeway in the regulation of pornographic depictions of children.

First. It is evident beyond the need for elaboration that a state's interest in "safeguarding the physical and psychological well being of a minor" is "compelling." . . .

The legislative judgment, as well as the judgment found in the relevant literature, is that the use of children as subjects of pornographic materials is harmful to the physiological, emotional, and mental health of the child. That judgment, we think, easily passes muster under the First Amendment.

Second. The distribution of photographs and films depicting sexual activity by juveniles is intrinsically related to the sexual abuse of children in at least two ways. First, the materials produced are a permanent record of the children's participation and the harm to the child is exacerbated by their circulation. Second, the distribution network for child pornography must be closed if the production of material which requires the sexual exploitation of children is to be effectively controlled. . . .

Third. The advertising and selling of child pornography provides an economic motive for and is thus an integral part of the production of such materials, an activity illegal throughout the nation. . . . We note that were the statutes outlawing the employment of children in these films and photographs fully effective, and the constitutionality of these laws have not been questioned, the First Amendment implications would be no greater than that presented by laws against distribution: enforceable production laws would leave no child pornography to be marketed.

Fourth. The value of permitting live performances and photographic reproductions of children engaged in lewd sexual conduct is exceedingly modest, if not *de minimis.* We consider it unlikely that visual depictions of children performing sexual acts or lewdly exhibiting their genitals would often constitute an important and necessary part of a literary performance or scientific or educational work. As the trial court in this case observed, if it were necessary for literary or artistic value, a person over the statutory age who perhaps looked younger could be utilized. Simulation outside of the prohibition of the statute could provide another alternative. Nor is there any question here of censoring a particular literary theme or portrayal of sexual activity. The First Amendment interest is limited to that of rendering the portrayal somewhat more "realistic" by utilizing or photographing children.

Fifth. Recognizing and classifying child pornography as a category of material outside the protection of the First Amendment is not incompatible with our earlier decisions. . . .

[I]t is not rare that a content-based classification of speech has been accepted because it may be appropriately generalized that within the confines of the given classification, the evil to be restricted so overwhelmingly outweighs the expressive interests, if any, at stake, that no process of case-by-case adjudication is required. When a definable class of material, such as that covered by § 263.15, bears so heavily and pervasively on the welfare of children engaged in its production, we think the balance of competing interests is clearly struck and that it is permissible to consider these materials as without the protection of the First Amendment.

There are, of course, limits on the category of child pornography which, like obscenity, is unprotected by the First Amendment. As with all legislation in this sensitive area, the conduct to be prohibited must be adequately defined by the applicable state law, as written or authoritatively construed. Here the nature of the harm to be combatted requires that the state offense be limited to works that *visually* depict sexual conduct by children below a specified age. The category of "sexual conduct" proscribed must also be suitably limited and described.

The test for child pornography is separate from the obscenity standard enunciated in *Miller,* but may be compared to it for purpose of clarity. The *Miller* formulation is adjusted in the following respects: A trier of fact need not find that the material appeals to the prurient interest of the average person; it is not required that sexual conduct portrayed be done so in a patently offensive manner; and the material at issue need not be considered as a whole. We note that the distribution of descriptions of other depictions of sexual conduct, not otherwise obscene, which do not involve live performance or photographic or other visual reproduction of live performances, retain First Amendment protection. . . .

It is therefore clear that there is nothing unconstitutionally "under-inclusive" about a statute that singles out this category of material for proscription. It also follows that the State is not barred by the First Amendment from prohibiting the distribution of unprotected materials produced outside the State.

It remains to address the claim that the New York statute is unconstitutionally overbroad because it would forbid the distribution of material with serious literary, scientific or educational value or material which does not threaten the harms sought to be combatted by the State. . . .

The scope of the First Amendment overbreadth doctrine, like most exceptions to established principles, must be carefully tied to the circumstances in which facial invalidation of a statute is truly warranted. Because of the wide-reaching effects of striking a statute down on its face at the request of one whose own conduct may be punished despite the First Amendment, we have recognized that the overbreadth doctrine is "strong medicine" and have employed it with hesitation, and then "only as a last resort." We have, in consequence, insisted that the overbreadth involved be "substantial" before the statute involved will be invalidated on its face. . . .

The requirement of substantial overbreadth is directly derived from the purpose and nature of the doctrine. While a sweeping statute, or one incapable of limitation, has the potential to repeatedly chill the exercise of expressive activity by many individuals, the extent of deterrence of protected speech can be expected to decrease with the declining reach of the regulation. This observation appears equally applicable to the publication of books and films as it is to activities, such as picketing or participation in election campaigns, which have previously been categorized as involving conduct plus speech. . . .

Applying these principles, § 263.15 is not substantially overbroad. We consider this the paradigmatic case of a state statute whose legitimate reach dwarfs its arguably impermissible applications. . . . While the reach of the statute is directed at the hard core of child pornography, the Court of Appeals was understandably concerned that some protected expression, ranging from medical textbooks to pictorials in National Geographic would fall prey to the statute. How often, if ever, it may be necessary to employ children to engage in conduct clearly within the reach of the § 263.15 in order to produce educational, medical or artistic works cannot be known with certainty. Yet we seriously doubt, and it has not been suggested, that these arguably impermissible applications of the statute amount to more than a tiny fraction of the materials within the statute's reach. . . .

As applied to Paul Ferber and to others who distribute similar material, the statute does not violate the First Amendment as applied to the States through the Fourteenth. The decision of the New York Court of Appeals is reversed and the case is remanded to that Court for further proceedings not inconsistent with this opinion.

☐ *Justice BRENNAN, with whom Justice MARSHALL joins, concurring.*

I agree with much of what is said in the Court's opinion. . . .

But in my view application of § 263.15 or any similar statute to depictions of children that in themselves do have serious literary, artistic, scientific or medical value, would violate the First Amendment. As the Court recognizes, the limited classes of speech, the suppression of which does not raise serious First Amendment concerns, have two attributes. They are of exceedingly "slight social value," and the State has a compelling interest in their regulation. See *Chaplinsky v. New Hampshire* [315 U.S. 568] (1942). The First Amendment value of depictions of children that are in themselves serious contributions to art, literature or science, is, by definition, simply not "*de minimis.*" At the same time, the State's interest in suppression of such materials is likely to be far less compelling. For the Court's assumption of harm to the child resulting from the "permanent record" and "circulation" of the child's "participation," lacks much of its force where the depiction is a serious contribution to art or science.

City of Erie v. Pap's A.M.
529 U.S. 277, 120 S.CT. 1382 (2000)

Following the Supreme Court's ruling in *Barnes v. Glen Theatre, Inc.*, 501 U.S. 560 (1991), that Indiana's law against public nudity could apply to nude dancing in adult clubs and require dancers to wear G-strings and pasties instead of dancing totally nude, the city of Erie, Pennsylvania, enacted an ordinance making it an offense to appear in public in a "state of nudity." Two days after the law went into effect, Pap's A.M., the owner of Kandyland, a club that featured totally nude dancing, sought an injunction against the enforcement of the law. The trial court granted an injunction upon finding the ordinance unconstitutional, but an appellate court reversed. Subsequently, the Pennsylvania Supreme Court overruled that decision, holding that nude dancing was expressive conduct protected by the First Amendment. The state supreme court noted that that was the view of eight members of the Supreme Court in *Barnes*, counting four members in the majority and the four dissenters. But it also concluded that *Barnes* provided no clear precedent because the Court's decision was five to four and its plurality opinion fragmented the justices with four separate and conflicting opinions. Erie appealed and the Supreme Court granted review.

The Court reversed, and its decision was seven-and-a-half to two-and-a-half. Justice O'Connor delivered the opinion for the Court. Justice Scalia, joined by Justice Thomas, filed a concurring opinion. Justice Souter filed a separate opinion, concurring and dissenting in part. Justice Stevens filed a dissent, which Justice Ginsburg joined.

☐ *Justice O'CONNOR announced the judgment of the Court, delivered the opinion of the Court with respect to Parts I and II, and delivered an opinion with respect to Parts III and IV, in which Chief Justice REHNQUIST, Justice KENNEDY, and Justice BREYER joined.*

■ III

Being "in a state of nudity" is not an inherently expressive condition. As we explained in *Barnes* [*v. Glen Theatre, Inc.*, 501 U.S. 560 (1991)], however, nude dancing of the type at issue here is expressive conduct, although we think that it falls only within the outer ambit of the First Amendment's protection.

To determine what level of scrutiny applies to the ordinance at issue here, we must decide "whether the State's regulation is related to the suppression of expression." *Texas v. Johnson*, 491 U.S. 397 (1989). If the governmental purpose in enacting the regulation is unrelated to the suppression of expression, then the regulation need only satisfy the "less stringent" standard from [*United States v.*] *O'Brien* [391 U.S. 367 (1968)] for evaluating restrictions on symbolic speech. If the government interest is related to the content of the expression, however, then the regulation falls outside the scope of the *O'Brien* test and must be justified under a more demanding standard.

In *Barnes*, we analyzed an almost identical statute, holding that Indiana's public nudity ban did not violate the First Amendment, although no five Members of the Court agreed on a single rationale for that conclusion. We now clarify that government restrictions on public nudity such as the ordinance at issue here should be evaluated under the framework set forth in *O'Brien* for content-neutral restrictions on symbolic speech.

The ordinance here, like the statute in *Barnes*, is on its face a general prohibition on public nudity. By its terms, the ordinance regulates conduct alone. It does not target nudity that contains an erotic message; rather, it bans all public nudity, regardless of whether that nudity is accompanied by expressive activity. . . . As Justice SOUTER noted in *Barnes*, "on its face, the governmental interest in combating prostitution and other criminal activity is not at all inherently related to expression." In that sense, this case is similar to *O'Brien*. O'Brien burned his draft registration card as a public statement of his antiwar views, and he was convicted under a statute making it a crime to knowingly mutilate or destroy such a card. This Court rejected his claim that the statute violated his First Amendment rights, reasoning that the law punished him for the "noncommunicative impact of his conduct, and for nothing else." . . . So too here, the ordinance prohibiting public nudity is aimed at combating crime and other negative secondary effects caused by the presence of adult entertainment establishments like Kandyland and not at suppressing the erotic message conveyed by this type of nude dancing. Put another way, the ordinance does not attempt to regulate the primary effects of the expression, i.e., the effect on the audience of watching nude erotic dancing, but rather the secondary effects, such as the impacts on public health, safety, and welfare, which we have previously recognized are "caused by the presence of even one such" establishment. *Renton v. Playtime Theatres, Inc.*, 475 U.S. 41 (1986). . . .

[E]ven if Erie's public nudity ban has some minimal effect on the erotic message by muting that portion of the expression that occurs when the last stitch is dropped, the dancers at Kandyland and other such establishments are free to perform wearing pasties and G-strings. Any effect on the overall expression is *de minimis*. . . .

We conclude that Erie's asserted interest in combating the negative secondary effects associated with adult entertainment establishments like Kandyland is unrelated to the suppression of the erotic message conveyed by nude dancing. The ordinance prohibiting public nudity is therefore valid if it satisfies the four-factor test from *O'Brien* for evaluating restrictions on symbolic speech.

■ IV

Applying that standard here, we conclude that Erie's ordinance is justified under *O'Brien*. The first factor of the *O'Brien* test is whether the government regulation is within the constitutional power of the government to enact. Here, Erie's efforts to protect public health and safety are clearly within the city's police powers. The second factor is whether the regulation furthers an important or substantial government interest. The asserted interests of regulating conduct through a public nudity ban and of combating the harmful secondary effects associated with nude dancing are undeniably important. And in terms of demonstrating that such secondary effects pose a threat, the city need not "conduct new studies or produce evidence independent of that already generated by other cities" to demonstrate the problem of secondary effects, "so long as whatever evidence the city relies upon is reasonably believed to be relevant to the problem that the city addresses." *Renton v. Playtime Theatres, Inc.* Because the nude dancing at Kandyland is of the same character as the adult entertainment at issue in *Renton, Young v. American Mini Theatres, Inc.*, 427 U.S. 50 (1976), and *California v. LaRue*, 409 U.S. 109 (1972), it was reasonable for Erie to conclude that such nude dancing was likely to produce the same secondary effects. . . .

In any event, Erie also relied on its own findings. The preamble to the ordinance states that "the Council of the City of Erie has, at various times over more than a century, expressed its findings that certain lewd, immoral activities carried on in public places for profit are highly detrimental to the public health, safety and welfare, and lead to the debasement of both women and men, promote violence, public intoxication, prostitution and other serious criminal activity." The city council members, familiar with commercial downtown Erie, are the individuals who would likely have had first-hand knowledge of what took place at and around nude dancing establishments in Erie, and can make particularized, expert judgments about the resulting harmful secondary effects. Here, Kandyland has had ample opportunity to contest the council's findings about secondary effects—before the council itself, throughout the state proceedings, and before this Court. Yet to this day, Kandyland has never challenged the city council's findings or cast any specific doubt on the validity of those findings. . . .

The ordinance also satisfies *O'Brien*'s third factor, that the government interest is unrelated to the suppression of free expression. The fourth and final *O'Brien* factor—that the restriction is no greater than is essential to the furtherance of the government interest—is satisfied as well. The ordinance regulates conduct, and any incidental impact on the expressive element of nude dancing is *de minimis*. The requirement that dancers wear pasties and G-strings is a minimal restriction in furtherance of the asserted government interests, and the restriction leaves ample capacity to convey the dancer's erotic message. Justice SOUTER points out that zoning is an alternative means of addressing this problem. It is far from clear, however, that zoning imposes less of a burden on expression than the minimal requirement implemented here. In any event, since this is a content-neutral restriction, least restrictive means analysis is not required.

We hold, therefore, that Erie's ordinance is a content-neutral regulation that is valid under *O'Brien*. Accordingly, the judgment of the Pennsylvania

Supreme Court is reversed, and the case is remanded for further proceedings not inconsistent with this opinion.

☐ *Justice SCALIA, with whom Justice THOMAS joins, concurring in the judgment.*

I agree that the decision of the Pennsylvania Supreme Court must be reversed, but disagree with the mode of analysis the Court has applied.

The city of Erie self-consciously modeled its ordinance on the public nudity statute we upheld against constitutional challenge in *Barnes v. Glen Theatre, Inc.*, calculating (one would have supposed reasonably) that the courts of Pennsylvania would consider themselves bound by our judgment on a question of federal constitutional law. In *Barnes*, I voted to uphold the challenged Indiana statute "not because it survives some lower level of First Amendment scrutiny, but because, as a general law regulating conduct and not specifically directed at expression, it is not subject to First Amendment scrutiny at all." Erie's ordinance, too, by its terms prohibits not merely nude dancing, but the act—irrespective of whether it is engaged in for expressive purposes—of going nude in public. The facts that a preamble to the ordinance explains that its purpose, in part, is to "limi[t] a recent increase in nude live entertainment," that city councilmembers in supporting the ordinance commented to that effect, and that the ordinance includes in the definition of nudity the exposure of devices simulating that condition, neither make the law any less general in its reach nor demonstrate that what the municipal authorities really find objectionable is expression rather than public nakedness. As far as appears (and as seems overwhelmingly likely), the preamble, the council members' comments, and the chosen definition of the prohibited conduct simply reflect the fact that Erie had recently been having a public nudity problem not with streakers, sunbathers or hot-dog vendors, but with lap dancers. . . .

Moreover, even were I to conclude that the city of Erie had specifically singled out the activity of nude dancing, I still would not find that this regulation violated the First Amendment unless I could be persuaded (as on this record I cannot) that it was the communicative character of nude dancing that prompted the ban. When conduct other than speech itself is regulated, it is my view that the First Amendment is violated only "[w]here the government prohibits conduct precisely because of its communicative attributes." Here, even if one hypothesizes that the city's object was to suppress only nude dancing, that would not establish an intent to suppress what (if anything) nude dancing communicates. I do not feel the need, as the Court does, to identify some "secondary effects" associated with nude dancing that the city could properly seek to eliminate. (I am highly skeptical, to tell the truth, that the addition of pasties and G-strings will at all reduce the tendency of establishments such as Kandyland to attract crime and prostitution, and hence to foster sexually transmitted disease.) The traditional power of government to foster good morals (*bonos mores*), and the acceptability of the traditional judgment (if Erie wishes to endorse it) that nude public dancing itself is immoral, have not been repealed by the First Amendment.

☐ *Justice SOUTER, concurring in part and dissenting in part.*

Erie's stated interest in combating the secondary effects associated with nude dancing establishments is an interest unrelated to the suppression of expression under *United States v. O'Brien,* and the city's regulation is thus properly considered under the *O'Brien* standards. I do not believe, however, that the current record allows us to say that the city has made a sufficient evidentiary showing to sustain its regulation, and I would therefore vacate the decision of the Pennsylvania Supreme Court and remand the case for further proceedings. . . .

[T]he record before us today is deficient in its failure to reveal any evidence on which Erie may have relied, either for the seriousness of the threatened harm or for the efficacy of its chosen remedy. The plurality does the best it can with the materials to hand, but the pickings are slim. . . .

There is one point, however, on which an evidentiary record is not quite so hard to find, but it hurts, not helps, the city. The final *O'Brien* requirement is that the incidental speech restriction be shown to be no greater than essential to achieve the government's legitimate purpose. To deal with this issue, we have to ask what basis there is to think that the city would be unsuccessful in countering any secondary effects by the significantly lesser restriction of zoning to control the location of nude dancing, thus allowing for efficient law enforcement, restricting effects on property values, and limiting exposure of the public. The record shows that for 23 years there has been a zoning ordinance on the books to regulate the location of establishments like Kandyland, but the city has not enforced it. One councilor remarked that "I think there's one of the problems. The ordinances are on the books and not enforced. Now this takes place. You really didn't need any other ordinances." Another commented, "I felt very, very strongly, and I feel just as strongly right now, that this is a zoning matter." Even on the plurality's view of the evidentiary burden, this hurdle to the application of *O'Brien* requires an evidentiary response.

The record suggests that Erie simply did not try to create a record of the sort we have held necessary in other cases, and the suggestion is confirmed by the course of this litigation. The evidentiary question was never decided (or, apparently, argued) below, nor was the issue fairly joined before this Court. . . . Accordingly, although I join with the plurality in adopting the *O'Brien* test, I respectfully dissent from the Court's disposition of the case.

☐ *Justice STEVENS, with whom Justice GINSBURG joins, dissenting.*

Far more important than the question whether nude dancing is entitled to the protection of the First Amendment are the dramatic changes in legal doctrine that the Court endorses today. Until now, the "secondary effects" of commercial enterprises featuring indecent entertainment have justified only the regulation of their location. For the first time, the Court has now held that such effects may justify the total suppression of protected speech. Indeed, the plurality opinion concludes that admittedly trivial advancements of a State's interests may provide the basis for censorship. The Court's commendable attempt to replace the fractured decision in *Barnes v. Glen Theatre, Inc.,* with a single coherent rationale is strikingly unsuccessful; it is supported neither by precedent nor by persuasive reasoning.

The Court relies on the so-called "secondary effects" test to defend the ordinance. The present use of that rationale, however, finds no support whatsoever in our precedents. Never before have we approved the use of that doctrine to justify a total ban on protected First Amendment expression. On the contrary, we have been quite clear that the doctrine would not support that end.

In *Young v. American Mini Theatres, Inc.*, 427 U.S. 50 (1976), we upheld a Detroit zoning ordinance that placed special restrictions on the location of motion picture theaters that exhibited "adult" movies. The "secondary effects" of the adult theaters on the neighborhoods where they were located—lower property values and increases in crime (especially prostitution) to name a few—justified the burden imposed by the ordinance. Essential to our holding, however, was the fact that the ordinance was "nothing more than a limitation on the place where adult films may be exhibited" and did not limit the size of the market in such speech.

In *Renton v. Playtime Theatres, Inc.*, 475 U.S. 41 (1986), we upheld a similar ordinance, again finding that the "secondary effects of such theaters on the surrounding community" justified a restrictive zoning law. We noted, however, that "[t]he Renton ordinance, like the one in *American Mini Theatres*, does not ban adult theaters altogether," but merely "circumscribe[s] their choice as to location." Indeed, in both *Renton* and *American Mini Theatres*, the zoning ordinances were analyzed as mere "time, place, and manner" regulations. Because time, place, and manner regulations must "leave open ample alternative channels for communication of information," *Ward v. Rock Against Racism*, 491 U.S. 781 (1989), a total ban would necessarily fail that test. . . .

The reason we have limited our secondary effects cases to zoning and declined to extend their reasoning to total bans is clear and straightforward: A dispersal that simply limits the places where speech may occur is a minimal imposition whereas a total ban is the most exacting of restrictions. The State's interest in fighting presumed secondary effects is sufficiently strong to justify the former, but far too weak to support the latter, more severe burden. . . . The fact that this censorship may have a laudable ulterior purpose cannot mean that censorship is not censorship. For these reasons, the Court's holding rejects the explicit reasoning in *American Mini Theatres* and *Renton*. . . .

The Court's mishandling of our secondary effects cases is not limited to its approval of a total ban. It compounds that error by dramatically reducing the degree to which the State's interest must be furthered by the restriction imposed on speech, and by ignoring the critical difference between secondary effects caused by speech and the incidental effects on speech that may be caused by a regulation of conduct.

In what can most delicately be characterized as an enormous understatement, the plurality concedes that "requiring dancers to wear pasties and G-strings may not greatly reduce these secondary effects." To believe that the mandatory addition of pasties and a G-string will have any kind of noticeable impact on secondary effects requires nothing short of a titanic surrender to the implausible. . . .

Of course, the line between governmental interests aimed at conduct and unrelated to speech, on the one hand, and interests arising out of the effects of the speech, on the other, may be somewhat imprecise in some cases.

In this case, however, we need not wrestle with any such difficulty because Erie has expressly justified its ordinance with reference to secondary effects. Indeed, if Erie's concern with the effects of the message were unrelated to the message itself, it is strange that the only means used to combat those effects is the suppression of the message. For these reasons, the Court's argument that "this case is similar to *O'Brien*" is quite wrong. . . . The Court cannot have its cake and eat it too—either Erie's ordinance was not aimed at speech and the Court may attempt to justify the regulation under the incidental burdens test, or Erie has aimed its law at the secondary effects of speech, and the Court can try to justify the law under that doctrine. But it cannot conflate the two with the expectation that Erie's interests aimed at secondary effects will be rendered unrelated to speech by virtue of this doctrinal polyglot. . . .

The censorial purpose of Erie's ordinance precludes reliance on the judgment in *Barnes* as sufficient support for the Court's holding today. Several differences between the Erie ordinance and the statute at issue in *Barnes* belie the Court's assertion that the two laws are "almost identical." . . . To begin with, the preamble to Erie's ordinance candidly articulates its agenda, declaring: "Council specifically wishes to adopt the concept of Public Indecency prohibited by the laws of the State of Indiana, which was approved by the U.S. Supreme Court in *Barnes v. Glen Theatre Inc.*, for the purpose of limiting a recent increase in nude live entertainment within the City." . . .

It is clear beyond a shadow of a doubt that the Erie ordinance was a response to a more specific concern than nudity in general, namely, nude dancing of the sort found in Kandyland. Given that the Court has not even tried to defend the ordinance's total ban on the ground that its censorship of protected speech might be justified by an overriding state interest, it should conclude that the ordinance is patently invalid. For these reasons, as well as the reasons set forth in Justice WHITE's dissent in *Barnes*, I respectfully dissent.

Reno v. American Civil Liberties Union

521 U.S. 844, 117 S.CT. 2329 (1997)

When enacting the Communications Decency Act of 1996 (CDA), Congress sought to protect minors from harmful material on the Internet. The law, among other things, in Section 223(a) criminalized the "knowing" transmission of "obscene or indecent" messages to any recipient under 18 years of age. Section 223(d) prohibited the "knowing" sending or displaying to a person under 18 of any message "that, in context, depicts or describes, in terms patently offensive as measured by contemporary community standards, sexual or excretory activities or organs." Affirmative defenses were provided for those who take "good faith, . . . effective . . . actions" to restrict access by minors to the prohibited communications (Section 223(e)(5)(A)), and those who restrict

Roger Baldwin on the campus of Washington University, St. Louis, Missouri, in 1906. A Boston aristocrat and a Progressive Era social reformer, Baldwin founded the Civil Liberties Bureau of the American Union against Militarism in 1917 to defend draft resisters during World War I. In 1920, that organization was reorganized as the American Civil Liberties Union (ACLU), based on nationwide local chapters. The ACLU is credited with spearheading the drive to defend and to expand the scope of First Amendment freedoms in the twentieth century. (Photo Source: Mudd Library, Princeton University, Princeton, New Jersey)

---

such access by requiring certain designated forms of proof of age, such as a verified credit card or an adult identification number (Section 223(e)(5)(B)).

Following the law's enactment, the American Civil Liberties Union and a number of businesses and interest groups filed suit challenging the constitutionality of Sections 223(a)(1) and 223(d). Subsequently, a federal district court entered a preliminary injunction against enforcement of both challenged provisions and the government appealed to the Supreme Court.

The Court's decision was seven to two and its opinion delivered by Justice Stevens. Justice O'Connor filed an opinion concurring in the judgment in part and dissenting in part, which Chief Justice Rehnquist joined.

☐ *Justice STEVENS delivered the opinion of the Court.*

At issue is the constitutionality of two statutory provisions enacted to protect minors from "indecent" and "patently offensive" communications on the Internet. Notwithstanding the legitimacy and importance of the congressional goal of protecting children from harmful materials, we agree with the three-judge District Court that the statute abridges "the freedom of speech" protected by the First Amendment.

The Internet is an international network of interconnected computers. It is the outgrowth of what began in 1969 as a military program called "ARPANET," which was designed to enable computers operated by the military, defense contractors, and universities conducting defense-related research to communicate with one another by redundant channels even if some portions of the network were damaged in a war. While the ARPANET no longer exists, it provided an example for the development of a number of civilian networks that, eventually linking with each other, now enable tens of millions of people to communicate with one another and to access vast amounts of information from around the world. The Internet is "a unique and wholly new medium of worldwide human communication." . . .

Sexually explicit material on the Internet includes text, pictures, and chat and "extends from the modestly titillating to the hardest-core." These files are created, named, and posted in the same manner as material that is not sexually explicit, and may be accessed either deliberately or unintentionally during the course of an imprecise search. "Once a provider posts its content on the Internet, it cannot prevent that content from entering any community." Some of the communications over the Internet that originate in foreign countries are also sexually explicit.

Though such material is widely available, users seldom encounter such content accidentally. . . . For that reason, the "odds are slim" that a user would enter a sexually explicit site by accident. Unlike communications received by radio or television, "the receipt of information on the Internet requires a series of affirmative steps more deliberate and directed than merely turning a dial. A child requires some sophistication and some ability to read to retrieve material and thereby to use the Internet unattended."

Systems have been developed to help parents control the material that may be available on a home computer with Internet access. A system may either limit a computer's access to an approved list of sources that have been identified as containing no adult material, it may block designated inappropriate sites, or it may attempt to block messages containing identifiable objectionable features. "Although parental control software currently can screen for certain suggestive words or for known sexually explicit sites, it cannot now screen for sexually explicit images." Nevertheless, the evidence indicates that "a reasonably effective method by which parents can prevent their children from accessing sexually explicit and other material which parents may believe is inappropriate for their children will soon be available."

The problem of age verification differs for different uses of the Internet. The District Court categorically determined that there "is no effective way to determine the identity or the age of a user who is accessing material through e-mail, mail explorers, newsgroups or chat rooms." The Government offered no evidence that there was a reliable way to screen recipients and participants in such fora for age. Moreover, even if it were technologically feasible to block minors' access to newsgroups and chat rooms containing discussions of art, politics, or other subjects that potentially elicit "indecent" or "patently offensive" contributions, it would not be possible to block their access to that material and "still allow them access to the remaining content, even if the overwhelming majority of that content was not indecent."

Technology exists by which an operator of a Web site may condition access on the verification of requested information such as a credit card number or an adult password. Credit card verification is only feasible, however, either in connection with a commercial transaction in which the card is used, or by payment to a verification agency. Using credit card possession as a surrogate for proof of age would impose costs on non-commercial Web sites that would require many of them to shut down. For that reason, at the time of the trial, credit card verification was "effectively unavailable to a substantial number of Internet content providers." Moreover, the imposition of such a requirement "would completely bar adults who do not have a credit card and lack the resources to obtain one from accessing any blocked material." . . .

In arguing for reversal, the Government contends that the CDA is plainly constitutional under three of our prior decisions: (1) *Ginsberg v. New York*, 390 U.S. 629 (1968); (2) *FCC v. Pacifica Foundation*, 438 U.S. 726 (1978); and (3) *Renton v. Playtime Theatres, Inc.*, 475 U.S. 41 (1986). A close look at these cases, however, raises—rather than relieves—doubts concerning the constitutionality of the CDA.

In *Ginsberg*, we upheld the constitutionality of a New York statute that prohibited selling to minors under 17 years of age material that was considered obscene as to them even if not obscene as to adults. We rejected the defendant's broad submission that "the scope of the constitutional freedom of expression secured to a citizen to read or see material concerned with sex cannot be made to depend on whether the citizen is an adult or a minor." In four important respects, the statute upheld in *Ginsberg* was narrower than the CDA. First, we noted in *Ginsberg* that "the prohibition against sales to minors does not bar parents who so desire from purchasing the magazines for their children." Under the CDA, by contrast, neither the parents' consent—nor even their participation—in the communication would avoid the application of the statute. Second, the New York statute applied only to commercial transactions, whereas the CDA contains no such limitation. Third, the New York statute combined its definition of material that is harmful to minors with the requirement that it be "utterly without redeeming social importance for minors." The CDA fails to provide us with any definition of the term "indecent" as used in Section 223(a)(1) and, importantly, omits any requirement that the "patently offensive" material covered by Section 223(d) lack serious literary, artistic, political, or scientific value. Fourth, the New York statute defined a minor as a person under the age of 17, whereas the CDA, in applying to all those under 18 years, includes an additional year of those nearest majority.

In *Pacifica*, we upheld a declaratory order of the Federal Communications Commission, holding that the broadcast of a recording of a 12-minute monologue entitled "Filthy Words" that had previously been delivered to a live audience "could have been the subject of administrative sanctions." The Commission had found that the repetitive use of certain words referring to excretory or sexual activities or organs "in an afternoon broadcast when children are in the audience was patently offensive" and concluded that the monologue was indecent "as broadcast." The respondent did not quarrel with the finding that the afternoon broadcast was patently offensive, but contended that it was not "indecent" within the meaning of the relevant statutes because it contained no prurient appeal. After rejecting respondent's statutory arguments, we confronted its two constitutional arguments: (1) that the Commission's construction of its authority to ban indecent speech was so broad that its order had to be set aside even if the broadcast at issue was unprotected; and (2) that since the recording was not obscene, the First Amendment forbade any abridgment of the right to broadcast it on the radio.

In the portion of the lead opinion not joined by Justices POWELL and BLACKMUN, the plurality stated that the First Amendment does not prohibit all governmental regulation that depends on the content of speech. Accordingly, the availability of constitutional protection for a vulgar and offensive monologue that was not obscene depended on the context of the broadcast. Relying on the premise that "of all forms of communication" broadcasting had received the most limited First Amendment protection, the Court concluded that the ease with which children may obtain access to broadcasts, "coupled with the concerns recognized in *Ginsberg*," justified special treatment of indecent broadcasting.

As with the New York statute at issue in *Ginsberg*, there are significant differences between the order upheld in *Pacifica* and the CDA. First, the order in *Pacifica*, issued by an agency that had been regulating radio stations for decades, targeted a specific broadcast that represented a rather dramatic departure from traditional program content in order to designate when—rather than whether—it would be permissible to air such a program in that particular medium. The CDA's broad categorical prohibitions are not limited to particular times and are not dependent on any evaluation by an agency familiar with the unique characteristics of the Internet. Second, unlike the CDA, the Commission's declaratory order was not punitive; we expressly refused to decide whether the indecent broadcast "would justify a criminal prosecution." Finally, the Commission's order applied to a medium which as a matter of history had "received the most limited First Amendment protection" in large part because warnings could not adequately protect the listener from unexpected program content. The Internet, however, has no comparable history.

In *Renton*, we upheld a zoning ordinance that kept adult movie theaters out of residential neighborhoods. The ordinance was aimed, not at the content of the films shown in the theaters, but rather at the "secondary effects"—such as crime and deteriorating property values—that these theaters fostered: " 'It is the secondary effect which these zoning ordinances attempt to avoid, not the dissemination of "offensive" speech.' " According to the Government, the CDA is constitutional because it constitutes a sort of "cyberzoning" on the Internet. But the CDA applies broadly to the entire universe of cyberspace. And the purpose of the CDA is to protect children from the primary effects of "indecent" and "patently offensive" speech, rather than any "secondary" effect of such speech. Thus, the CDA is a content-based blanket restriction on speech, and, as such, cannot be "properly analyzed as a form of time, place, and manner regulation."

These precedents, then, surely do not require us to uphold the CDA and are fully consistent with the application of the most stringent review of its provisions. . . .

Neither before nor after the enactment of the CDA have the vast democratic fora of the Internet been subject to the type of government supervision and regulation that has attended the broadcast industry. More-over, the Internet is not as "invasive" as radio or television. The District Court specifically found that "communications over the Internet do not 'in-vade' an individual's home or appear on one's computer screen unbidden. Users seldom encounter content 'by accident.' " It also found that "almost all sexually explicit images are preceded by warnings as to the content," and cited testimony that " 'odds are slim' that a user would come across a sexu-ally explicit sight by accident." . . .

Regardless of whether the CDA is so vague that it violates the Fifth Amendment, the many ambiguities concerning the scope of its coverage ren-der it problematic for purposes of the First Amendment. For instance, each of the two parts of the CDA uses a different linguistic form. The first uses the word "indecent," while the second speaks of material that "in context, depicts or describes, in terms patently offensive as measured by contemporary com-munity standards, sexual or excretory activities or organs." Given the absence of a definition of either term, this difference in language will provoke un-certainty among speakers about how the two standards relate to each other and just what they mean. Could a speaker confidently assume that a serious discussion about birth control practices, homosexuality, the First Amendment issues raised by the Appendix to our *Pacifica* opinion, or the consequences of prison rape would not violate the CDA? This uncertainty undermines the likelihood that the CDA has been carefully tailored to the congressional goal of protecting minors from potentially harmful materials.

The vagueness of the CDA is a matter of special concern for two rea-sons. First, the CDA is a content-based regulation of speech. The vagueness of such a regulation raises special First Amendment concerns because of its obvious chilling effect on free speech. Second, the CDA is a criminal statute. In addition to the opprobrium and stigma of a criminal conviction, the CDA threatens violators with penalties including up to two years in prison for each act of violation. The severity of criminal sanctions may well cause speakers to remain silent rather than communicate even arguably unlawful words, ideas, and images. . . .

We are persuaded that the CDA lacks the precision that the First Amendment requires when a statute regulates the content of speech. In or-der to deny minors access to potentially harmful speech, the CDA effectively suppresses a large amount of speech that adults have a constitutional right to receive and to address to one another. That burden on adult speech is un-acceptable if less restrictive alternatives would be at least as effective in achieving the legitimate purpose that the statute was enacted to serve.

In evaluating the free speech rights of adults, we have made it perfectly clear that "sexual expression which is indecent but not obscene is protected by the First Amendment." *Sable* [*Communications v. Federal Communications Commission*, 492 U.S. 115 (1989)]. Indeed, *Pacifica* itself admonished that "the fact that society may find speech offensive is not a sufficient reason for sup-pressing it."

It is true that we have repeatedly recognized the governmental interest in protecting children from harmful materials. But that interest does not jus-tify an unnecessarily broad suppression of speech addressed to adults. As we have explained, the Government may not "reduce the adult population . . . to . . . only what is fit for children." "Regardless of the strength of the government's interest" in protecting children, "the level of discourse reaching a mailbox simply cannot be limited to that which would be suitable for a sandbox." *Bolger v. Young's Drug Products Corp.*, 463 U.S. 60 (1983).

In arguing that the CDA does not so diminish adult communication, the Government relies on the incorrect factual premise that prohibiting a transmission whenever it is known that one of its recipients is a minor would not interfere with adult-to-adult communication. The findings of the District Court make clear that this premise is untenable. Given the size of the potential audience for most messages, in the absence of a viable age-verification process, the sender must be charged with knowing that one or more minors will likely view it. Knowledge that, for instance, one or more members of a 100-person chat group will be minor—and therefore that it would be a crime to send the group an indecent message—would surely burden communication among adults. . . .

For the purposes of our decision, we need neither accept nor reject the Government's submission that the First Amendment does not forbid a blanket prohibition on all "indecent" and "patently offensive" messages communicated to a 17-year-old—no matter how much value the message may contain and regardless of parental approval. It is at least clear that the strength of the Government's interest in protecting minors is not equally strong throughout the coverage of this broad statute. Under the CDA, a parent allowing her 17-year-old to use the family computer to obtain information on the Internet that she, in her parental judgment, deems appropriate could face a lengthy prison term. Similarly, a parent who sent his 17-year-old college freshman [Child] information on birth control via e-mail could be incarcerated even though neither he, his child, nor anyone in their home community, found the material "indecent" or "patently offensive," if the college town's community thought otherwise.

The breadth of this content-based restriction of speech imposes an especially heavy burden on the Government to explain why a less restrictive provision would not be as effective as the CDA. It has not done so. The arguments in this Court have referred to possible alternatives such as requiring that indecent material be "tagged" in a way that facilitates parental control of material coming into their homes, making exceptions for messages with artistic or educational value, providing some tolerance for parental choice, and regulating some portions of the Internet—such as commercial Web sites—differently than others, such as chat rooms. Particularly in the light of the absence of any detailed findings by the Congress, or even hearings addressing the special problems of the CDA, we are persuaded that the CDA is not narrowly tailored if that requirement has any meaning at all. . . .

For the foregoing reasons, the judgment of the district court is affirmed.

☐ *Justice O'CONNOR, with whom the CHIEF JUSTICE joins, concurring in the judgment in part and dissenting in part.*

I write separately to explain why I view the Communications Decency Act of 1996 (CDA) as little more than an attempt by Congress to create "adult zones" on the Internet. Our precedent indicates that the creation of such zones can be constitutionally sound. Despite the soundness of its purpose, however, portions of the CDA are unconstitutional because they stray from the blueprint our prior cases have developed for constructing a "zoning law" that passes constitutional muster. . . .

The Court in *Ginsberg* concluded that the New York law created a constitutionally adequate adult zone simply because, on its face, it denied access only to minors. The Court did not question—and therefore necessarily assumed—that an adult zone, once created, would succeed in preserving adults' access while denying minors' access to the regulated speech. Before today, there was no reason to question this assumption, for the Court has previously only considered laws that operated in the physical world, a world with two characteristics that make it possible to create "adult zones": geography and identity. . . .

The electronic world is fundamentally different. Because it is no more than the interconnection of electronic pathways, cyberspace allows speakers and listeners to mask their identities. Cyberspace undeniably reflects some form of geography; chat rooms and Web sites, for example, exist at fixed "locations" on the Internet. Since users can transmit and receive messages on the Internet without revealing anything about their identities or ages, however, it is not currently possible to exclude persons from accessing certain messages on the basis of their identity.

Cyberspace differs from the physical world in another basic way: Cyberspace is malleable. Thus, it is possible to construct barriers in cyberspace and use them to screen for identity, making cyberspace more like the physical world and, consequently, more amenable to zoning laws. This transformation of cyberspace is already underway. Internet speakers (users who post material on the Internet) have begun to zone cyberspace itself through the use of "gateway" technology. Such technology requires Internet users to enter information about themselves—perhaps an adult identification number or a credit card number—before they can access certain areas of cyberspace much like a bouncer checks a person's driver's license before admitting him to a nightclub. Internet users who access information have not attempted to zone cyberspace itself, but have tried to limit their own power to access information in cyberspace, much as a parent controls what her children watch on television by installing a lock box. This user-based zoning is accomplished through the use of screening software (such as Cyber Patrol or SurfWatch) or browsers with screening capabilities, both of which search addresses and text for keywords that are associated with "adult" sites and, if the user wishes, blocks access to such sites. The Platform for Internet Content Selection (PICS) project is designed to facilitate user-based zoning by encouraging Internet speakers to rate the content of their speech using codes recognized by all screening programs. . . .

Although the prospects for the eventual zoning of the Internet appear promising, I agree with the Court that we must evaluate the constitutionality of the CDA as it applies to the Internet as it exists today. Given the present state of cyberspace, I agree with the Court that the "display" provision cannot pass muster. . . .

The "indecency transmission" and "specific person" provisions present a closer issue, for they are not unconstitutional in all of their applications. As discussed above, the "indecency transmission" provision makes it a crime to transmit knowingly an indecent message to a person the sender knows is under 18 years of age. The "specific person" provision proscribes the same conduct, although it does not as explicitly require the sender to know that the intended recipient of his indecent message is a minor. Appellant urges the Court to construe the provision to impose such a knowledge requirement and I would do so.

So construed, both provisions are constitutional as applied to a conversation involving only an adult and one or more minors—e.g., when an adult speaker sends an e-mail knowing the addressee is a minor, or when an adult and minor converse by themselves or with other minors in a chat room. In this context, these provisions are no different from the law we sustained in *Ginsberg*. Restricting what the adult may say to the minors in no way restricts the adult's ability to communicate with other adults. He is not prevented from speaking indecently to other adults in a chat room (because there are no other adults participating in the conversation) and he remains free to send indecent e-mails to other adults. The relevant universe contains only one adult, and the adult in that universe has the power to refrain from using indecent speech and consequently to keep all such speech within the room in an "adult" zone.

The analogy to *Ginsberg* breaks down, however, when more than one adult is a party to the conversation. If a minor enters a chat room otherwise occupied by adults, the CDA effectively requires the adults in the room to stop using indecent speech. If they did not, they could be prosecuted under the "indecency transmission" and "specific person" provisions for any indecent statements they make to the group, since they would be transmitting an indecent message to specific persons, one of whom is a minor. The CDA is therefore akin to a law that makes it a crime for a bookstore owner to sell pornographic magazines to anyone once a minor enters his store. Even assuming such a law might be constitutional in the physical world as a reasonable alternative to excluding minors completely from the store, the absence of any means of excluding minors from chat rooms in cyberspace restricts the rights of adults to engage in indecent speech in those rooms. The "indecency transmission" and "specific person" provisions share this defect.

But these two provisions do not infringe on adults' speech in all situations. I do not find that the provisions are overbroad in the sense that they restrict minors' access to a substantial amount of speech that minors have the right to read and view. Accordingly, the CDA can be applied constitutionally in some situations. . . .

[T]he constitutionality of the CDA as a zoning law hinges on the extent to which it substantially interferes with the First Amendment rights of adults. Because the rights of adults are infringed only by the "display" provision and by the "indecency transmission" and "specific person" provisions as applied to communications involving more than one adult, I would invalidate the CDA only to that extent. Insofar as the "indecency transmission" and "specific person" provisions prohibit the use of indecent speech in communications between an adult and one or more minors, however, they can and should be sustained. The Court reaches a contrary conclusion, and from that holding that I respectfully dissent.

Ashcroft v. Free Speech Coalition
534 U.S. 234, 122 S.Ct. 1389 (2002)

In 1996 Congress enacted the Child Pornography Prevention Act
(CPPA), making it a crime to create, distribute, or possess "virtual child
pornography" generated by computer images of young adults rather
than actual children. The constitutionality of the law was challenged by
the Free Speech Coalition—a coalition of artists, photographers, and
adult entertainment businesses. A federal district court upheld its provisions but the Court of Appeals for the Ninth Circuit reversed and
found that the CPPA violated the First Amendment. Attorney General John D. Ashcroft appealed that decision and the Supreme Court
granted review.

The decision of the appellate court was affirmed in a six-and-a-
half to two-and-a-half vote. Justice Kennedy delivered the opinion
for the Court. Justice Thomas filed a concurring opinion, indicating
that a more narrowly drawn statute might pass constitutional muster.
Chief Justice Rehnquist filed a dissenting opinion, which Justice Scalia
joined. Justice O'Connor filed a separate opinion in part concurring
and dissenting.

□ *Justice KENNEDY delivered the opinion of the Court.*

We consider in this case whether the Child Pornography Prevention Act
of 1996 (CPPA) abridges the freedom of speech. . . . By prohibiting child
pornography that does not depict an actual child, the statute goes beyond
New York v. Ferber, 458 U.S. 747 (1982), which distinguished child pornography from other sexually explicit speech because of the State's interest in protecting the children exploited by the production process. As a general rule,
pornography can be banned only if obscene, but under *Ferber*, pornography
showing minors can be proscribed whether or not the images are obscene
under the definition set forth in *Miller v. California*, 413 U.S. 15 (1973). . . .

The CPPA, however, is not directed at speech that is obscene; Congress
has proscribed those materials through a separate statute. Like the law in *Ferber*, the CPPA seeks to reach beyond obscenity, and it makes no attempt to
conform to the *Miller* standard. For instance, the statute would reach visual
depictions, such as movies, even if they have redeeming social value.

The principal question to be resolved, then, is whether the CPPA is
constitutional where it proscribes a significant universe of speech that is neither obscene under *Miller* nor child pornography under *Ferber*.

Before 1996, Congress defined child pornography as the type of depictions at issue in *Ferber*, images made using actual minors. The CPPA retains
that prohibition at 18 U.S.C. Sec. 2256(8)(A) and adds three other prohibited
categories of speech, of which the first, Sec. 2256(8)(B), and the third, Sec.
2256(8)(D), are at issue in this case. Section 2256(8)(B) prohibits "any visual

depiction, including any photograph, film, video, picture, or computer or computer-generated image or picture" that "is, or appears to be, of a minor engaging in sexually explicit conduct." The prohibition on "any visual depiction" does not depend at all on how the image is produced. The section captures a range of depictions, sometimes called "virtual child pornography," which include computer-generated images, as well as images produced by more traditional means. For instance, the literal terms of the statute embrace a Renaissance painting depicting a scene from classical mythology, a "picture" that "appears to be, of a minor engaging in sexually explicit conduct." The statute also prohibits Hollywood movies, filmed without any child actors, if a jury believes an actor "appears to be" a minor engaging in "actual or simulated . . . sexual intercourse."

These images do not involve, let alone harm, any children in the production process; but Congress decided the materials threaten children in other, less direct, ways. Pedophiles might use the materials to encourage children to participate in sexual activity. Furthermore, pedophiles might "whet their own sexual appetites" with the pornographic images, "thereby increasing the creation and distribution of child pornography and the sexual abuse and exploitation of actual children." Under these rationales, harm flows from the content of the images, not from the means of their production. In addition, Congress identified another problem created by computer-generated images: their existence can make it harder to prosecute pornographers who do use real minors. As imaging technology improves, Congress found, it becomes more difficult to prove that a particular picture was produced using actual children.

Section 2256(8)(C) prohibits a more common and lower tech means of creating virtual images, known as computer morphing. Rather than creating original images, pornographers can alter innocent pictures of real children so that the children appear to be engaged in sexual activity. Although morphed images may fall within the definition of virtual child pornography, they implicate the interests of real children and are in that sense closer to the images in *Ferber*. Respondents do not challenge this provision, and we do not consider it.

Respondents do challenge Sec. 2256(8)(D). Like the text of the "appears to be" provision, the sweep of this provision is quite broad. Section 2256(8)(D) defines child pornography to include any sexually explicit image that was "advertised, promoted, presented, described, or distributed in such a manner that conveys the impression" it depicts "a minor engaging in sexually explicit conduct." The statute is not so limited in its reach, however, as it punishes even those possessors who took no part in pandering. . . .

The CPPA's penalties are indeed severe. A first offender may be imprisoned for 15 years. A repeat offender faces a prison sentence of not less than 5 years and not more than 30 years in prison. While even minor punishments can chill protected speech, this case provides a textbook example of why we permit facial challenges to statutes that burden expression. With these severe penalties in force, few legitimate movie producers or book publishers, or few other speakers in any capacity, would risk distributing images in or near the uncertain reach of this law. . . .

Under *Miller v. California* the Government must prove that the work, taken as a whole, appeals to the prurient interest, is patently offensive in light of community standards, and lacks serious literary, artistic, political, or scientific value. The CPPA, however, extends to images that appear to depict a minor engaging in sexually explicit activity without regard to the *Miller* requirements. The materials need not appeal to the prurient interest. Any depiction of sexually explicit activity, no matter how it is presented, is proscribed. The CPPA applies to a picture in a psychology manual, as well as a movie depicting the horrors of sexual abuse. It is not necessary, moreover, that the image be patently offensive. Pictures of what appear to be 17-year-olds engaging in sexually explicit activity do not in every case contravene community standards.

The CPPA prohibits speech despite its serious literary, artistic, political, or scientific value. The statute proscribes the visual depiction of an idea—that of teenagers engaging in sexual activity—that is a fact of modern society and has been a theme in art and literature throughout the ages. Under the CPPA, images are prohibited so long as the persons appear to be under 18 years of age. This is higher than the legal age for marriage in many States, as well as the age at which persons may consent to sexual relations.

Both themes—teenage sexual activity and the sexual abuse of children—have inspired countless literary works. William Shakespeare created the most famous pair of teenage lovers, one of whom is just 13 years of age. See *Romeo and Juliet*, act I, sc. 2, l. 9 ("She hath not seen the change of fourteen years"). In the drama, Shakespeare portrays the relationship as something splendid and innocent, but not juvenile. The work has inspired no less than 40 motion pictures, some of which suggest that the teenagers consummated their relationship. Shakespeare may not have written sexually explicit scenes for the Elizabethan audience, but were modern directors to adopt a less conventional approach, that fact alone would not compel the conclusion that the work was obscene. . . .

In contrast to the speech in *Ferber*, speech that itself is the record of sexual abuse, the CPPA prohibits speech that records no crime and creates no victims by its production. Virtual child pornography is not "intrinsically related" to the sexual abuse of children, as were the materials in *Ferber*. While the Government asserts that the images can lead to actual instances of child abuse, the causal link is contingent and indirect. The harm does not necessarily follow from the speech, but depends upon some unquantified potential for subsequent criminal acts.

The Government says these indirect harms are sufficient because, as *Ferber* acknowledged, child pornography rarely can be valuable speech. This argument, however, suffers from two flaws. First, *Ferber*'s judgment about child pornography was based upon how it was made, not on what it communicated. The case reaffirmed that where the speech is neither obscene nor the product of sexual abuse, it does not fall outside the protection of the First Amendment.

The second flaw in the Government's position is that *Ferber* did not hold that child pornography is by definition without value. On the contrary, the Court recognized some works in this category might have significant value, but relied on virtual images—the very images prohibited by the CPPA—as an alternative and permissible means of expression: "[I]f it were necessary for literary or artistic value, a person over the statutory age who perhaps looked younger could be utilized. Simulation outside of the prohibition of the statute could provide another alternative." *Ferber*, then, not only referred to the distinction between actual and virtual child pornography, it relied on it as a reason supporting its holding. *Ferber* provides no support for a statute that eliminates the distinction and makes the alternative mode criminal as well.

The CPPA, for reasons we have explored, is inconsistent with *Miller* and finds no support in *Ferber*. The Government seeks to justify its prohibitions in other ways. It argues that the CPPA is necessary because pedophiles may use virtual child pornography to seduce children. There are many things innocent in themselves, however, such as cartoons, video games, and candy, that might be used for immoral purposes, yet we would not expect those to be prohibited because they can be misused. The Government, of course, may punish adults who provide unsuitable materials to children, see *Ginsberg v. New York*, 390 U.S. 629 (1968), and it may enforce criminal penalties for unlawful solicitation. The precedents establish, however, that speech within the rights of adults to hear may not be silenced completely in an attempt to shield children from it. *Butler v. Michigan*, 352 U.S. 380 (1957). . . .

In sum, Sec. 2256(8)(B) covers materials beyond the categories recognized in *Ferber* and *Miller*, and the reasons the Government offers in support of limiting the freedom of speech have no justification in our precedents or in the law of the First Amendment. The provision abridges the freedom to engage in a substantial amount of lawful speech. For this reason, it is overbroad and unconstitutional.

Respondents challenge Sec. 2256(8)(D) as well. This provision bans depictions of sexually explicit conduct that are "advertised, promoted, presented, described, or distributed in such a manner that conveys the impression that the material is or contains a visual depiction of a minor engaging in sexually explicit conduct." The parties treat the section as nearly identical to the provision prohibiting materials that appear to be child pornography. In the Government's view, the difference between the two is that "the 'conveys the impression' provision requires the jury to assess the material at issue in light of the manner in which it is promoted."

We disagree with this view. The CPPA prohibits sexually explicit materials that "conve[y] the impression" they depict minors. While that phrase may sound like the "appears to be" prohibition in Sec. 2256(8)(B), it requires little judgment about the content of the image. Under Sec. 2256(8)(D), the work must be sexually explicit, but otherwise the content is irrelevant. Even if a film contains no sexually explicit scenes involving minors, it could be treated as child pornography if the title and trailers convey the impression that the scenes would be found in the movie. The determination turns on how the speech is presented, not on what is depicted. While the legislative findings address at length the problems posed by materials that look like child pornography, they are silent on the evils posed by images simply pandered that way. . . .

The CPPA does more than prohibit pandering. It prohibits possession of material described, or pandered, as child pornography by someone earlier in the distribution chain. The provision prohibits a sexually explicit film containing no youthful actors, just because it is placed in a box suggesting a prohibited movie. Possession is a crime even when the possessor knows the movie was mislabeled. The First Amendment requires a more precise restriction. For this reason, Sec. 2256(8)(D) is substantially overbroad and in violation of the First Amendment.

For the reasons we have set forth, the prohibitions of Sections 2256(8)(B) and 2256(8)(D) are overbroad and unconstitutional. . . .

☐ *CHIEF JUSTICE REHNQUIST, with whom Justice SCALIA joins in part, dissenting.*

Congress has a compelling interest in ensuring the ability to enforce prohibitions of actual child pornography, and we should defer to its findings that rapidly advancing technology soon will make it all but impossible to do so.

I also agree with Justice O'CONNOR that serious First Amendment concerns would arise were the Government ever to prosecute someone for simple distribution or possession of a film with literary or artistic value, such as "Traffic" or "American Beauty." I write separately, however, because the Child Pornography Prevention Act of 1996 (CPPA) need not be construed to reach such materials. . . .

Other than computer generated images that are virtually indistinguishable from real children engaged in sexually explicit conduct, the CPPA can be limited so as not to reach any material that was not already unprotected before the CPPA. The CPPA's definition of "sexually explicit conduct" is quite explicit in this regard. It makes clear that the statute only reaches "visual depictions." . . . I think the definition reaches only the sort of "hard core of child pornography" that we found without protection in *Ferber*. So construed, the CPPA bans visual depictions of youthful looking adult actors engaged in actual sexual activity; mere suggestions of sexual activity, such as youthful looking adult actors squirming under a blanket, are more akin to written descriptions than visual depictions, and thus fall outside the purview of the statute. . . .

To the extent the CPPA prohibits possession or distribution of materials that "convey the impression" of a child engaged in sexually explicit conduct, that prohibition can and should be limited to reach "the sordid business of pandering" which lies outside the bounds of First Amendment protection. *Ginzburg v. United States*, 383 U.S. 463 (1966). . . .

For these reasons, I would construe the CPPA in a manner consistent with the First Amendment, reverse the Court of Appeals' judgment, and uphold the statute in its entirety.

☐ *Justice O'CONNOR, with whom THE CHIEF JUSTICE and Justice SCALIA join, concurring in the judgment and dissenting in part.*

Because the Government may already prohibit obscenity without violating the First Amendment, see *Miller v. California* (1973), what the Government asks this Court to rule is that it may also prohibit youthful-adult and virtual-adult pornography that is merely indecent without violating that Amendment. Although such pornography looks like the material at issue in *New York v. Ferber*, no children are harmed in the process of creating such pornography. Therefore, *Ferber* does not support the Government's ban on youthful-adult and virtual-child pornography. . . .

I also agree with the Court's decision to strike down the CPPA's ban on material presented in a manner that "conveys the impression" that it contains pornographic depictions of actual children ("actual-child pornography"). The Government fails to explain how this ban serves any compelling state interest. . . .

Finally, I agree with Court that the CPPA's ban on youthful-adult pornography is overbroad. . . .

I disagree with the Court, however, that the CPPA's prohibition of virtual-child pornography is overbroad. . . . Although Section 2256(8)(B) does not distinguish between youthful-adult and virtual-child pornography, the CPPA elsewhere draws a line between these two classes of speech. The statute provides an affirmative defense for those who produce, distribute, or receive pornographic images of individuals who are actually adults, Sec. 2252A(c), but not for those with pornographic images that are wholly computer generated. This is not surprising given that the legislative findings enacted by Congress contain no mention of youthful-adult pornography. Those findings focus explicitly only on actual-child pornography and virtual-child pornography. Drawing a line around, and striking just, the CPPA's ban on youthful-child pornography not only is consistent with Congress' understanding of the categories of speech encompassed by Section 2256(8)(B), but also preserves the CPPA's prohibition of the material that Congress found most dangerous to children.

In sum, I would strike down the CPPA's ban on material that "conveys the impression" that it contains actual-child pornography, but uphold the ban on pornographic depictions that "appea[r] to be" of minors so long as it is not applied to youthful-adult pornography.

■ (2) FIGHTING WORDS AND OFFENSIVE SPEECH

Although fighting words is a category of unprotected First Amendment speech, the Court so narrowly applies the category as virtually to eliminate it. Even an invitation to a brawl no longer appears excluded from First Amendment protection. The Court, for example, reversed the conviction of a man who while being arrested rather unambiguously invited a fight by calling a police officer a son of a bitch and threatening to kill him.[1] *Lewis v. New Orleans*, 415 U.S. 130 (1974), struck down an ordinance prohibiting the cursing of policemen, and *City of Houston, Texas v. Hill*, 482 U.S. 451 (1987), invalidated a law that made it unlawful to interfere with a police officer while performing his duties.

Offensive speech may convey a political statement and hence be entitled to protection. In *Watts v. United States*, 395 U.S. 705 (1969), for instance, the Court overturned the conviction of an individual who, at a protest rally against the Vietnam War, shouted, "If they ever make me carry a rifle, the first man I want to get is LBJ [President Lyndon Johnson]." The justices agreed (six to three) that the federal statute criminalizing threats against the life of the president must be strictly construed and the statement here was an expression of political views, rather than an actual threat. The Rehnquist Court, however, was more sharply split in *Rankin v. McPherson* 483 U.S. 378 (1987), holding that a public employee could not be fired for remarking during a private conversation, after hearing of the 1981 assassination attempt on President Reagan, "If they go for him again, I hope they get him." Dissenting Justice Scalia, joined by Chief Justice Rehnquist and Justices O'Connor and White, contended that such speech conveys no "public concerns" entitled to First Amendment protection.

The landmark ruling in *Cohen v. California* (1969) (see excerpt below) held that four-letter words, however offensive, are not per se excluded from First Amendment protection. Over the objections of three dissenters, Justice Harlan rejected arguments that privacy interests justified the conviction, under California's penal code punishing disturbances of the peace and offensive conduct, of an individual who wore a jacket emblazoned with the words *Fuck the Draft* in the corridor of a Los Angeles County courthouse. Notice that Harlan weighed the competing claims of privacy and free speech not on the basis of the content of the speech (whether some individuals regard certain speech as obscene or offensive), but in terms of the manner of the intrusion and the context in which individuals claim that they have reasonable expectations of privacy against being made a "captive audience" for offensive speech.

When weighing free speech claims against interests in privacy and safeguards against offensive intrusions, the Court considers the context and relative intrusiveness of different modes of communication. Justice Brandeis in *Packer Corporation v. Utah*, 285 U.S. 105 (1932), suggested this approach when upholding a statute forbidding all advertising of cigarettes on billboards and streetcar signs, but permitting such ads in newspapers, magazines, and storefront windows:

> Billboards, street car signs, and placards and such are in a class by themselves. . . . [They] are constantly before the eyes of observers on the streets and in street cars to be seen without the exercise of choice or violation on their part. Other forms of advertising are ordinarily seen as a matter of choice on the part of the observer. The young people as well as the adults have the message of the billboard thrust upon them by all the arts and devices that skill can produce. In the case of newspapers and magazines, there must be some seeking by the one who is to see and read the advertisement. The radio can be turned off, but not so the billboard or street car placard.

In the *Handbills Cases* of 1939, however, the Court ruled that Jehovah's Witnesses and others seeking to engage in religious or political canvassing could not be barred from ringing doorbells and knocking on the doors of private residencies.[2] As the Court, in *Martin v. City of Struthers*, 319 U.S. 141 (1943), observed, "[T]he ordinance was designed to protect a legitimate interest, that of privacy in the home, but in balancing the interests, the considerations of free speech and the free exercise of religion out-weighed this interest." Subsequently, the owners of a company town were forbidden from prohibiting the door-to-door circulation of religious and political literature.[3] Those rulings were reaffirmed in *Watchtower Bible & Tract Society of New York, Inc. v. Village of Stratton,* 536 U.S. 150 (2002).

By contrast, *Kovacs v. Cooper*, 336 U.S. 77 (1949), upheld an ordinance outlawing sound trucks emitting "loud and raucous noises" because their intrusiveness was such that an individual "is practically helpless to escape this interference with his privacy by loudspeakers." Two years later, *Breard v. Alexandria*, 341 U.S. 622 (1951), sustained a prohibition on solicitors, peddlers, and transient vendors of merchandise from going onto private property without the owner's permission. There the Court distinguished the solicitations for religious purposes from that of the door-to-door salesmen in finding that the latter did not outweigh the intrusion on individuals' privacy in their homes.

As in *Cohen*, the Court in *Public Utilities Commission v. Pollak*, 343 U.S. 451 (1952), ruled that individuals have greater privacy interests against offensive intrusions in their homes than in public places. There the Court sustained a privately owned transit company's use of radio loudspeakers in its streetcars and buses for the purpose of providing "music as you ride." In rejecting the arguments of patrons who found the music offensive and intrusive on their privacy, Justice Burton observed,

> The Court below has emphasized the claim that the radio programs are an invasion of the constitutional rights of privacy of the passengers. . . . This position wrongly assumes that . . . each passenger on a public vehicle regulated by the Federal Government [has] a right of privacy substantially equal to the privacy to which he is entitled in his own home. However complete his right of privacy may be at home, it is substantially limited by the rights of others when its possessor travels on a public thoroughfare or rides in a public conveyance.

Still, balancing free speech claims against interests in privacy and freedom from offensive speech is often difficult for the Court. Over the dissent of Chief Justice Burger and Justices White and Rehnquist, *Erzoznik v. City of Jacksonville*, 422 U.S. 205 (1975), struck down an ordinance making it a public nuisance to show any motion picture

containing nudity in a drive-in theater where the screen was visible
from a public street. In rejecting the privacy claims of homeowners
who could see the movie screen from their backyards and of drivers of
cars passing by on a highway, Justice Powell reasoned that

> [t]his discrimination cannot be justified as a means of preventing
> significant intrusions on privacy. The ordinance seeks to keep these
> films from being seen from public streets and places where the of-
> fended viewer can avert his eyes. In short, the screen of a drive-in
> theater is not "so unobtrusive as to make it impossible for an un-
> willing individual to avoid exposure to it." . . . Thus, we conclude
> that the limited privacy interest of persons on the public streets
> cannot justify this censorship of otherwise protected speech on the
> basis of its content.

Compare the reasoning in cases such as *Cohen* and *Erzoznik* with
that in Justice Stevens's plurality opinion and the dissenters' opinions
in *Federal Communications Commission v. Pacifica Foundation* (1976) (see
excerpt below). There a bare majority upheld the Federal Communication Commission's regulations banning indecent, but not obscene,
speech on the radio, in a case arising from a twelve-minute monologue
by satiric humorist George Carlin on seven dirty words that cannot be
said on the radio or television. In *Sable Communications v. Federal Communications Commission*, 492 U.S. 115 (1989), though, the Rehnquist
Court unanimously struck down a 1988 congressional statute banning
indecent telephone "dial-a-porn" services when holding that only
hard-core obscene messages may be outlawed. A fragmented Court also
struck down a similar requirement, under the Cable Television Consumer Protection and Competition Act of 1992, that cable companies
block access to sexually explicit material unless viewers request access
in advance and in writing. See *Denver Area Education Telecommunications Consortium, Inc. v. Federal Communications Commission*, 518 U.S. 727
(1996) (excerpted in Section F, in this chapter, regulating the Broadcast
and Cable Media, and the Internet).

Controversy over indecent and offensive speech has also led to
some important rulings on the rights of students in primary and secondary schools.[4] In *Board of Education, Island Trees Union Free School District v. Pico*, 457 U.S. 853 (1985), the Court ruled that local school
boards could not *remove* books from school libraries because they were
deemed offensive. Although not addressing the power of school boards
to select books for its libraries, Justice Brennan emphasized that "[o]ur
Constitution does not permit the official suppression of *ideas*. . . .
[L]ocal school boards may not remove books from school library

shelves simply because they dislike the ideas contained in those books and seek by their removal to prescribe what shall be orthodox in politics, nationalism, religion, or other matters of opinion."

In *Bethel School District No. 403 v. Fraser* (1986) (see excerpt below), however, the Court (voting seven to two) upheld the authority of a principal to discipline a student for using suggestive (possibly indecent, but not obscene) language in a speech at a student rally. Consider the opinions in this case with those in *Tinker v. Des Moines Independent Community School District*, 393 U.S. 503 (1969) (see Section H, in this chapter). Following *Bethel*, the Rehnquist Court upheld over First Amendment objections a high school principal's censorship of articles on teenage pregnancy scheduled to appear in a student newspaper.[5]

The Court also could not escape reviewing challenges to so-called hate-speech codes and laws enacted by more than thirty states and numerous localities and colleges in the late 1980s and 1990s. The laws basically took two forms: (1) some made it a crime to arouse "anger, alarm, or resentment in others on the basis of race, color, creed, religion, or gender"; while (2) others provided enhanced sentences for individuals found guilty of criminal assault or vandalism, mandating longer prison sentences for those convicted of such crimes when the victim was selected out of racial, religious, gender, or ethnic bias.

When confronted with an attack on the first kind of hate-speech law in *R.A.V. v. City of St. Paul, Minnesota*, 505 U.S. 377 (1992) (see excerpt below), the Court unanimously invalidated St. Paul's hate-speech ordinance. In announcing the decision Justice Scalia held that even within the category of fighting words—a category of unprotected speech—governments may not bar or penalize the expression of some but not other words, based on their content. Yet, only Chief Justice Rehnquist and Justices Kennedy, Souter, and Thomas agreed with Scalia's analysis and joined his opinion. In concurring opinions that read like dissents, Justices Blackmun, Stevens, and White, whom O'Connor joined, accused the majority of rewriting First Amendment doctrine. They would have overturned the ordinance as "fatally overbroad because it criminalizes not only unprotected expression but expression protected by the First Amendment."

Despite unanimity on the result in *R.A.V.*, the fragmentation of the justices contributed, perhaps, to the Court's willingness to revisit the controversy over hate-speech laws the following term in *Wisconsin v. Mitchell*, 508 U.S. 476 (1993) (see excerpt below). Here, unlike *R.A.V.*, the justices unanimously joined Chief Justice Rehnquist's opinion upholding the second sort of hate-speech law, which mandates longer sentences for individuals convicted of assault or vandalism when the crime was committed and the victim was selected because of racial, religious, gender, or ethnic bias. Subsequently, in *Virginia v. Black* (2003) (excerpted below), a majority of the Court indicated that a properly drawn statute criminalizing cross burning, if clearly aimed at punishing intimidation rather than political expression, would survive constitutional muster.

Finally, in recent years another major source of controversy has been governmental financing and grants for speech deemed offensive or politically objectionable. In *Rust v. Sullivan*, 500 U.S. 173 (1991) (excerpted below), a bare majority of the Rehnquist Court upheld the Reagan administration's regulation prohibiting family-planning clinics that receive federal funding from also providing medical counseling on abortion; compare the positions of Chief Justice Rehnquist and Justice Blackmun on the nature of free speech in that case. In *National Endowment for the Arts v. Finley*, 524 U.S. 569 (1998), the Court upheld a "public decency" amendment to the National Foundation for the Arts and Humanities Act, requiring the NEA to take "general standards of decency" into account when awarding grants to artists. See also *United States v. American Library Association*, 539 U.S. 126 (2003) (excerpted in Section F), upholding a federal statute requiring public libraries that receive federal funding for providing Internet access to install software to block obscene and pornographic images and to prevent minors from accessing such materials. *Rust*, however, was subsequently limited and distinguished in *Legal Services Corporation v. Velazquez*, 351 U.S. 533 (2001), striking down a restriction on the kinds of lawsuits that the federally funded Legal Services Corporation (LSC), which represent poor people, may engage in. Justice Kennedy distinguished *Rust* while reaffirming that the *Rust* ban on abortion counseling amounted to *governmental speech*, even though it was using private speakers to communicate its message. By contrast, the LSC program, like that challenged in *Rosenberger v. Rector and Visitors of the University of Virginia*, 515 U.S. 819 (1995) (excerpted in Ch. 6), was deemed to facilitate *private speech*, not to promote a governmental message.

Notes

1. *Gooding v. Wilson*, 405 U.S. 518 (1972).

2. *Schneider v. New Jersey*, 308 U.S. 147 (1939).

3. *Marsh v. Alabama*, 326 U.S. 501 (1946).

4. In *Papish v. Board of Curators*, 410 U.S. 15 (1973), the Court held that a graduate student could not be expelled from a university for distributing a publication that included a cartoon of the Statue of Liberty with the word "motherfucker."

5. *Hazelwood School District v. Kuhlmeier*, 482 U.S. 260 (1988).

SELECTED BIBLIOGRAPHY

Cleary, Edward J. *Beyond the Burning Cross: The First Amendment and the Landmark R.A.V. Case.* New York: Random House, 1994.

Dooling, Richard. *Blue Streak: Swearing, Free Speech, and Sexual Harassment.* New York: Random House, 1996.

Greenawalt, Kent. *Fighting Words: Individuals, Communities, and Liberties of Speech.* Princeton, NJ: Princeton University Press, 1995.

Jacobs, James, and Potter, Kimberly. *Hate Crimes: Criminal Law and Identity Politics.* New York: Oxford University Press, 1998.

Lawrence, Frederick. *Punishing Hate: Bias Crimes under American Law.* Cambridge, MA: Harvard University Press, 1999.

Matsuda, Mari; Lawrence, Charles; Delgado, Richard; and Crenshaw, Kimberle. *Words That Wound: Critical Race Theory, Assaultive Speech, and the First Amendment.* Boulder, CO: Westview Press, 1993.

Cohen v. California
403 U.S. 15, 91 S.Ct. 1780 (1971)

Justice Harlan's opinion for the Court recounts the facts that led to this important ruling announcing the First Amendment principle that four-letter words are not obscene per se and may express political ideas as well. His position was controversial within the Court, however. In a circulated but unpublished dissenting opinion, Chief Justice Burger protested "that this Court's limited resources of time should be devoted to such a case as this. It is a measure of a lack of a sense of priorities. . . . It is nothing short of absurd nonsense that juvenile delinquents and their emotionally unstable outbursts should command the attention of this Court. The appeal should be dismissed for failure to present a substantial federal question." By the time the decision came down, Burger decided to withhold his draft and to join with Justice Black in a dissenting opinion filed by Justice Blackmun.

The Court's decision was six to three, with the majority's opinion announced by Justice Harlan. Justice Blackmun dissented and was joined by Chief Justice Burger and Justice Black.

☐ *Justice HARLAN delivered the opinion of the Court.*

This case may seem at first blush too inconsequential to find its way into our books, but the issue it presents is of no small constitutional significance.

Appellant Paul Robert Cohen was convicted in the Los Angeles Municipal Court of violating that part of California Penal Code § 415 which prohibits "maliciously and willfully disturb[ing] the peace or quiet of any neighborhood or person . . . by . . . offensive conduct. . . ." He was given 30 days' imprisonment. The facts upon which his conviction rests are detailed in the opinion of the Court of Appeal of California, Second Appellate District, as follows:

> "On April 26, 1968, the defendant was observed in the Los Angeles County Courthouse in the corridor outside of division 20 of the municipal court wearing a jacket bearing the words 'Fuck the Draft' which were plainly visible. There were women and children present in the corridor. The defendant was arrested. The defendant testified that he wore the jacket knowing that the words were on the jacket as a means of informing the public of the depth of his feelings against the Vietnam War and the draft.
>
> "The defendant did not engage in, nor threaten to engage in, nor did anyone as the result of his conduct in fact commit or threaten to commit any act of violence. The defendant did not make any loud or unusual noise, nor was there any evidence that he uttered any sound prior to his arrest." . . .

In order to lay hands on the precise issue which this case involves, it is useful first to canvass various matters which this record does *not* present.

The conviction quite clearly rests upon the asserted offensiveness of the *words* Cohen used to convey his message to the public. The only "conduct" which the State sought to punish is the fact of communication. Thus, we deal here with a conviction resting solely upon "speech." . . .

[T]he state certainly lacks power to punish Cohen for the underlying content of the message the inscription conveyed. At least so long as there is no showing of an intent to incite disobedience to or disruption of the draft, Cohen could not, consistently with the First and Fourteenth Amendments, be punished for asserting the evident position on the inutility or immorality of the draft his jacket reflected. . . .

In the second place, as it comes to us, this case cannot be said to fall within those relatively few categories of instances where prior decisions have established the power of government to deal more comprehensively with certain forms of individual expression simply upon a showing that such a form was employed. This is not, for example, an obscenity case. Whatever else may be necessary to give rise to the States' broader power to prohibit obscene expression, such expression must be, in some significant way, erotic. *Roth v. United States*, 354 U.S. 476 (1957). It cannot plausibly be maintained that this vulgar allusion to the Selective Service System would conjure up such psychic stimulation in anyone likely to be confronted with Cohen's crudely defaced jacket.

This Court has also held that the States are free to ban the simple use, without a demonstration of additional justifying circumstances, of so-called "fighting words," those personally abusive epithets which, when addressed to the ordinary citizen, are, as a matter of common knowledge, inherently likely to provoke violent reaction. *Chaplinsky v. New Hampshire*, 315 U.S. 568 (1942). While the four-letter word displayed by Cohen in relation to the draft is not uncommonly employed in a personally provocative fashion, in this instance it was clearly not "directed to the person of the hearer." No individual actually or likely to be present could reasonably have regarded the words on appellant's jacket as a direct personal insult. Nor do we have here an instance of the exercise of the State's police power to prevent a speaker from intentionally provoking a given group to hostile reaction.

There is, as noted above, no showing that anyone who saw Cohen was in fact violently aroused or that appellant intended such a result.

Finally, in arguments before this Court much has been made of the claim that Cohen's distasteful mode of expression was thrust upon unwilling or unsuspecting viewers, and that the State might therefore legitimately act as it did in order to protect the sensitive from otherwise unavoidable exposure to appellant's crude form of protest. Of course, the mere presumed presence of unwitting listeners or viewers does not serve automatically to justify curtailing all speech capable of giving offense. While this Court has recognized that government may properly act in many situations to prohibit intrusion into the privacy of the home of unwelcome views and ideas which cannot be totally banned from the public dialogue, *e.g., Rowan v. United States Post Office Dept.*, 397 U.S. 728 (1970), we have at the same time consistently stressed that "we are often 'captives' outside the sanctuary of the home and subject to objectionable speech." The ability of government, consonant with the Constitution, to shut off discourse solely to protect others from hearing it is, in other words, dependent upon a showing that substantial privacy interests are being invaded in an essentially intolerable manner. Any broader view of this authority would effectively empower a majority to silence dissidents simply as a matter of personal predilections.

In this regard, persons confronted with Cohen's jacket were in a quite different posture than, say, those subjected to the raucous emissions of sound trucks blaring outside their residences. Those in the Los Angeles courthouse could effectively avoid further bombardment of their sensibilities simply by averting their eyes. And, while it may be that one has a more substantial claim to a recognizable privacy interest when walking through a courthouse corridor than, for example, strolling through Central Park, surely it is nothing like the interest in being free from unwanted expression in the confines of one's own home. Given the subtlety and complexity of the factors involved, if Cohen's "speech" was otherwise entitled to constitutional protection, we do not think the fact that some unwilling "listeners" in a public building may have been briefly exposed to it can serve to justify this breach of the peace conviction where, as here, there was no evidence that persons powerless to avoid appellant's conduct did in fact object to it, and where that portion of the statute upon which Cohen's conviction rests evinces no concern, either on its face or as construed by the California courts with the special plight of the captive auditor, but, instead, indiscriminately sweeps within its prohibitions all "offensive conduct" that disturbs "any neighborhood or person." . . .

Against this background, the issue flushed by this case stands out in bold relief. It is whether California can excise, as "offensive conduct," one particular scurrilous epithet from the public discourse, either upon the theory of the court below that its use is inherently likely to cause violent reaction or upon a more general assertion that the States, acting as guardians of public morality, may properly remove this offensive word from the public vocabulary.

The rationale of the California Court is plainly untenable. At most it reflects an "undifferentiated fear or apprehension of disturbance [which] is not enough to overcome the right to freedom of expression." *Tinker v. Des Moines Indep. Community School Dist.*, 393 U.S. 503 (1969). We have been shown no evidence that substantial numbers of citizens are standing ready to strike out physically at whoever may assault their sensibilities with execrations like that uttered by Cohen. There may be some persons about with such lawless and violent proclivities, but that is an insufficient base upon which to erect, consistently with constitutional values, a governmental power to force persons who wish to ventilate their dissident views into avoiding particular forms of expression. . . .

At the outset, we cannot overemphasize that, in our judgment, most situations where the State has a justifiable interest in regulating speech will fall within one or more of the various established exceptions, discussed above but not applicable here, to the usual rule that governmental bodies may not prescribe the form or content of individual expression. Equally important to our conclusion is the constitutional backdrop against which our decision must be made. The constitutional right of free expression is powerful medicine in a society as diverse and populous as ours. It is designed and intended to remove governmental restraints from the arena of public discussion, putting the decision as to what views shall be voiced largely into the hands of each of us, in the hope that use of such freedom will ultimately produce a more capable citizenry and more perfect polity and in the belief that no other approach would comport with the premise of individual dignity and choice upon which our political system rests. . . .

To many, the immediate consequence of this freedom may often appear to be only verbal tumult, discord, and even offensive utterance. These are, however, within established limits, in truth necessary side effects of the broader enduring values which the process of open debate permits us to achieve. That the air may at times seem filled with verbal cacophony is, in this sense not a sign of weakness but of strength. . . .

Against this perception of the constitutional policies involved, we discern certain more particularized considerations that peculiarly call for reversal of this conviction. First, the principle contended for by the State seems inherently boundless. How is one to distinguish this from any other offensive word? Surely the State has no right to cleanse public debate to the point where it is grammatically palatable to the most squeamish among us. Yet no readily ascertainable general principle exists for stopping short of that result were we to affirm the judgment below. For, while the particular four-letter word being litigated here is perhaps more distasteful than most others of its genre, it is nevertheless often true that one man's vulgarity is another's lyric. Indeed, we think it is largely because governmental officials cannot make principled distinctions in this area that the Constitution leaves matters of taste and style so largely to the individual.

Additionally, we cannot overlook the fact, because it is well illustrated by the episode involved here, that much linguistic expression serves a dual communicative function: it conveys not only ideas capable of relatively precise, detached explication, but otherwise inexpressible emotions as well. In fact, words are often chosen as much for their emotive as their cognitive force. We cannot sanction the view that the Constitution, while solicitous of the cognitive content of individual speech has little or no regard for that emotive function which practically speaking, may often be the more important element of the overall message sought to be communicated. . . .

Finally, and in the same vein, we cannot indulge the facile assumption that one can forbid particular words without also running a substantial risk of suppressing ideas in the process. Indeed, governments might soon seize upon the censorship of particular words as a convenient guise for banning the expression of unpopular views. We have been able, as noted above, to discern little social benefit that might result from running the risk of opening the door to such grave results.

It is, in sum, our judgment that absent a more particularized and compelling reason for its actions, the State may not, consistently with the First and Fourteenth Amendments, make the simple public display here involved of this single four-letter expletive a criminal offense. Because that is the only arguably sustainable rationale for the conviction here at issue, the judgment below must be reversed.

Reversed.

☐ *Justice BLACKMUN, with whom the CHIEF JUSTICE and Justice BLACK join, dissenting.*

I dissent [because] . . . Cohen's absurd and immature antics, in my view, was mainly conduct and little speech. . . . Further, the case appears to me to be well within the sphere of *Chaplinsky v. New Hampshire*, where Justice MURPHY, a known champion of First Amendment freedoms, wrote for a unanimous bench. As a consequence, this Court's agonizing over First Amendment values seems misplaced and unnecessary.

Federal Communications Commission v. Pacifica Foundation

438 U.S. 726, 98 S.Ct. 3026 (1978)

Justice Stevens explains the facts in this case, involving satiric humorist George Carlin and the FCC's regulation of indecent language on radio and television, at the outset of his plurality opinion announcing the decision of the Court.

The Court's decision was five to four, with the plurality's opinion announced by Justice Stevens. Justice Powell concurred and was joined by Justice Blackmun. Dissents were by Justices Brennan and Stewart, who were joined by Justices Marshall and White.

☐ *Justice STEVENS delivered the opinion of the Court, with whom the CHIEF JUSTICE and Justice REHNQUIST joined.*

This case requires that we decide whether the Federal Communications Commission has any power to regulate a radio broadcast that is indecent but not obscene.

A satiric humorist named George Carlin recorded a 12-minute monologue entitled "Filthy Words" before a live audience in a California theater. He began by referring to his thoughts about "the words you couldn't say on the public, ah, airwaves, um, the ones you definitely wouldn't say, ever." He proceeded to list those words and repeat them over and over again in a variety of colloquialisms. The transcript of the recording, which is appended to this opinion, indicates frequent laughter from the audience. [The words that Carlin said could not be said on television or the radio, were "shit, piss, fuck, cunt, cocksucker, motherfucker, and tits."]

At about 2 o'clock in the afternoon on Tuesday, October 30, 1973, a New York radio station, owned by respondent Pacifica Foundation, broadcast the "Filthy Words" monologue. A few weeks later a man, who stated that he had heard the broadcast while driving with his young son, wrote a letter complaining to the Commission. . . .

The complaint was forwarded to the station for comment. In its response, Pacifica explained that the monologue had been played during a program about contemporary society's attitude toward language and that, immediately before its broadcast, listeners had been advised that it included "sensitive language which might be regarded as offensive to some." Pacifica characterized George Carlin as "a significant social satirist" who "like Twain and Sahl before him, examines the language of ordinary people. . . . Carlin is not mouthing obscenities, he is merely using words to satirize as harmless and essentially silly our attitudes towards those words." Pacifica stated that it was not aware of any other complaints about the broadcast.

On February 21, 1975, the Commission issued a declaratory order granting the complaint and holding that Pacifica "could have been the subject of administrative sanctions." 56 F.C.C.2d 94, 99. The Commission did not impose formal sanctions, but it did state that the order would be "associated with the station's license file, and in the event that subsequent complaints are received, the Commission will then decide whether it should utilize any of the available sanctions it has been granted by Congress." . . .

The Commission characterized the language used in the Carlin monologue as "patently offensive," though not necessarily obscene, and expressed the opinion that it should be regulated by principles analogous to those found in the law of nuisance where the "law generally speaks to *channeling* behavior more than actually prohibiting it. . . . [T]he concept of 'indecent' is intimately connected with the exposure of children to language that describes, in terms patently offensive as measured by contemporary community standards for the broadcast medium, sexual or excretory activities and organs at times of the day when there is a reasonable risk that children may be in the audience." . . .

The United States Court of Appeals for the District of Columbia reversed. . . . [We now reverse that ruling and uphold the F.C.C.'s action.]

The question in this case is whether a broadcast of patently offensive words dealing with sex and excretion may be regulated because of its content. Obscene materials have been denied the protection of the First Amendment because their content is so offensive to contemporary moral standards. *Roth v. United States*, 354 U.S. 476 [(1957)]. But the fact that society may find speech offensive is not a sufficient reason for suppressing it. Indeed, if it is the speaker's opinion that gives offense, that consequence is a reason for according it constitutional protection. For it is a central tenet of the First Amendment that the government must remain neutral in the marketplace of ideas. If there were any reason to believe that the Commission's characterization of the Carlin monologue as offensive could be traced to its political content—or even to the fact that it satirized contemporary attitudes about four-letter words—First Amendment protection might be required. But that is simply not this case. These words offend for the same reasons that obscenity offends. Their place in the hierarchy of First Amendment values was aptly sketched by Justice MURPHY when he said: "Such utterances are no essential part of any exposition of ideas, and are of such slight social value as a step to truth that any benefit that may be derived from them is clearly outweighed by the social interest in order and morality." *Chaplinsky v. New Hampshire* [315 U.S. 568 (1942)]. . . .

Although these words ordinarily lack literary, political, or scientific value, they are not entirely outside the protection of the First Amendment. Some uses of even the most offensive words are unquestionably protected. See, *e.g., Hess v. Indiana*, 414 U.S. 105 [(1973)]. Indeed, we may assume, *arguendo*, that this monologue would be protected in other contexts. Nonetheless, the constitutional protection accorded to a communication containing such patently offensive sexual and excretory language need not be the same in every context. It is a characteristic of speech such as this that both its capacity to offend and its "social value," to use Justice MURPHY's term, vary with the circumstances. Words that are commonplace in one setting are shocking in another. To paraphrase Justice HARLAN, one occasion's lyric is another's vulgarity. Cf. *Cohen v. California*, [403 U.S. 15 (1971)].

In this case it is undisputed that the content of Pacifica's broadcast was "vulgar," "offensive," and "shocking." Because content of that character is not entitled to absolute constitutional protection under all circumstances, we must consider its context in order to determine whether the Commission's action was constitutionally permissible.

We have long recognized that each medium of expression presents special First Amendment problems. And of all forms of communication, it is broadcasting that has received the most limited First Amendment protection. Thus, although other speakers cannot be licensed except under laws that carefully define and narrow official discretion, a broadcaster may be deprived of his license and his forum if the Commission decides that such an action would serve "the public interest, convenience, and necessity." Similarly, although the First Amendment protects newspaper publishers from being required to print the replies of those whom they criticize, *Miami Herald Publishing Co. v. Tornillo*, 418 U.S. 241 [(1974)], it affords no such protection to broadcasters; on the contrary, they must give free time to the victims of their criticism. *Red Lion Broadcasting Co. v. FCC*, 395 U.S. 367 [(1969)].

The reasons for these distinctions are complex, but two have relevance to the present case. First, the broadcast media have established a uniquely pervasive presence in the lives of all Americans. Patently offensive, indecent material presented over the airwaves confronts the citizen, not only in public, but also in the privacy of the home, where the individual's right to be left alone plainly outweighs the First Amendment rights of an intruder. *Rowan v. Post Office Dept.*, 397 U.S. 728. [(1970)]. Because the broadcast audience is constantly tuning in and out, prior warnings cannot completely protect the listener or viewer from unexpected program content. To say that one may avoid further offense by turning off the radio when he hears indecent language is like saying that the remedy for an assault is to run away after the first blow. One may hang up on an indecent phone call, but that option does not give the caller a constitutional immunity or avoid a harm that has already taken place.

Second, broadcasting is uniquely accessible to children, even those too young to read. Although Cohen's written message might have been incomprehensible to a first grader, Pacifica's broadcast could have enlarged a child's vocabulary in an instant. Other forms of offensive expression may be withheld from the young without restricting the expression at its source. Bookstores and motion picture theaters, for example, may be prohibited from making indecent material available to children. We held in *Ginsberg v. New York*, 390 U.S. 629 [(1968)], that the government's interest in the "well-being of its youth" and in supporting "parents' claim to authority in their own household" justified the regulation of otherwise protected expression. The ease with which children may obtain access to broadcast material, coupled with the concerns recognized in *Ginsberg*, amply justify special treatment of indecent broadcasting.

It is appropriate, in conclusion, to emphasize the narrowness of our holding. This case does not involve a two-way radio conversation between a cab driver and a dispatcher, or a telecast of an Elizabethan comedy. We have not decided that an occasional expletive in either setting would justify any sanction or, indeed, that this broadcast would justify a criminal prosecution. The Commission's decision rested entirely on a nuisance rationale under which context is all-important. The concept requires consideration of a host of variables. The time of day was emphasized by the Commission. The content of the program in which the language is used will also affect the composition of the audience, and differences between radio, television, and perhaps closed-circuit transmissions, may also be relevant. As Justice SUTHERLAND wrote a "nuisance may be merely a right thing in the wrong place,—like a pig in the parlor instead of the barnyard." *Euclid v. Ambler Realty Co.*, 272 U.S. 365 [(1926)]. We simply hold that when the Commission finds that a pig has entered the parlor, the exercise of its regulatory power does not depend on proof that the pig is obscene.

The judgment of the Court of Appeals is reversed.

It is so ordered.

☐ *Justice POWELL, with whom Justice BLACKMUN joins, concurring in part.*

The issue . . . is whether the Commission may impose civil sanctions on a licensee radio station for broadcasting the monologue at two o'clock in the afternoon. The Commission's primary concern was to prevent the broadcast from reaching the ears of unsupervised children who were likely to be in the audience at that hour. In essence, the Commission sought to "channel" the monologue to hours when the fewest unsupervised children would be exposed to it. In my view, this consideration provides strong support for the Commission's holding. . . .

In most instances, the dissemination of this kind of speech to children may be limited without also limiting willing adults' access to it. Sellers of printed and recorded matter and exhibitors of motion pictures and live performances may be required to shut their doors to children, but such a requirement has no effect on adults' access. The difficulty is that such a physical separation of the audience cannot be accomplished in the broadcast media. . . .

A second difference, not without relevance, is that broadcasting—unlike most other forms of communication—comes directly into the home, the one place where people ordinarily have the right not to be assaulted by uninvited and offensive sights and sounds. . . . The Commission also was entitled to give this factor appropriate weight in the circumstances of the instant case. This is not to say, however, that the Commission has an unrestricted license to decide what speech, protected in other media, may be banned from the airwaves in order to protect unwilling adults from momentary exposure to it in their homes. Making the sensitive judgments required in these cases is not easy. But this responsibility has been reposed initially in the Commission, and its judgment is entitled to respect. . . .

In short, I agree that on the facts of this case, the Commission's order did not violate respondent's First Amendment rights. . . .

In my view, the result in this case does not turn on whether Carlin's monologue, viewed as a whole, or the words that constitute it, have more or less "value" than a candidate's campaign speech. This is a judgment for each person to make, not one for the judges to impose upon him. . . .

☐ *Justice BRENNAN, with whom Justice MARSHALL joins, dissenting.*

Without question, the privacy interests of an individual in his home are substantial and deserving of significant protection. In finding these interests sufficient to justify the content regulation of protected speech, however, the Court commits two errors. First, it misconceives the nature of the privacy interests involved where an individual voluntarily chooses to admit radio communications into his home. Second, it ignores the constitutionally protected interests of both those who wish to transmit and those who desire to receive broadcasts that many—including the FCC and this Court—might find offensive. . . .

Even if an individual who voluntarily opens his home to radio communications retains privacy interests of sufficient moment to justify a ban on protected speech if those interests are "invaded in an essentially intolerable manner," *Cohen v. California*, [403 U.S. 15 [(1971)], the very fact that those interests are threatened only by a radio broadcast precludes any intolerable invasion of privacy; for unlike other intrusive modes of communication, such as sound trucks, "[t]he radio can be turned off," *Lehman v. Shaker Heights*, 418 U.S. 298 (1974)—and with a minimum of effort. . . .

The Court's balance, of necessity, fails to accord proper weight to the interests of listeners who wish to hear broadcasts the FCC deems offensive. It permits majoritarian tastes completely to preclude a protected message from entering the homes of a receptive, unoffended minority. No decision of this Court supports such a result. Where the individuals constituting the offended majority may freely choose to reject the material being offered, we have never found their privacy interests of such moment to warrant the suppression of speech on privacy grounds. . . .

Most parents will undoubtedly find understandable as well as commendable the Court's sympathy with the FCC's desire to prevent offensive broadcasts from reaching the ears of unsupervised children. Unfortunately, the facial appeal of this justification for radio censorship masks its constitutional insufficiency. . . .

Because the Carlin monologue is obviously not an erotic appeal to the prurient interests of children, the Court, for the first time, allows the government to prevent minors from gaining access to materials that are not obscene, and are therefore protected, as to them. It thus ignores our recent admonition that "[s]peech that is neither obscene as to youths nor subject to some other legitimate proscription cannot be suppressed solely to protect the young from ideas or images that a legislative body thinks unsuitable for them." The Court's refusal to follow its own pronouncements is especially lamentable since it has the anomalous subsidiary effect, at least in the radio context at issue here, of making completely unavailable to adults material which may not constitutionally be kept even from children. This result violates in spades the principle of *Butler v. Michigan*, [352 U.S. 380 (1957)]. *Butler* involved a challenge to a Michigan statute that forbade the publication, sale, or distribution of printed material "tending to incite minors to violent or depraved or immoral acts, manifestly tending to the corruption of the morals of youth." Although *Roth v. United States* [357 U.S. 476 (1957)], had not yet been decided, it is at least arguable that the material the statute in *Butler* was designed to suppress could have been constitutionally denied to children. Nevertheless, this Court found the statute unconstitutional. Speaking for the Court, Justice FRANKFURTER reasoned:

> "The incidence of this enactment is to reduce the adult population of Michigan to reading only what is fit for children. It thereby arbitrarily curtails one of those liberties of the individual, now enshrined in the Due Process Clause of the Fourteenth Amendment, that history has attested as the indispensable conditions for the maintenance and progress of a free society." . . .

Where, as here, the government may not prevent the exposure of minors to the suppressed material, the principle of *Butler* applies *a fortiori*. . . .

☐ *Justice STEWART, with whom Justice BRENNAN, Justice WHITE, and Justice MARSHALL join, dissenting.*

I think that "indecent" should properly be read as meaning no more than "obscene." Since the Carlin monologue concededly was not "obscene," I believe that the Commission lacked statutory authority to ban it. Under this construction of the statute, it is unnecessary to address the difficult and important issue of the Commission's constitutional power to prohibit speech that would be constitutionally protected outside the context of electronic broadcasting.

Bethel School District No. 403 v. Fraser

478 U.S. 675, 106 S.Ct. 3159 (1986)

The facts in this case involving lewd speech at a school assembly are given in Chief Justice Burger's opinion for the Court, Justice Brennan's concurring opinion, and Justice Stevens's dissenting opinion. Notice how each emphasizes particular facts and views differently the context and circumstances that gave rise to this case.

The Court's decision was seven to two, with the majority's opinion announced by Chief Justice Burger. Concurrences were by Justices Blackmun and Brennan, dissents by Justices Marshall and Stevens.

☐ *Chief Justice BURGER delivered the opinion of the Court.*

On April 26, 1983, respondent Matthew N. Fraser, a student at Bethel High School in Bethel, Washington, delivered a speech nominating a fellow student for student elective office. Approximately 600 high school students, many of whom were 14-year-olds, attended the assembly. Students were required to attend the assembly or to report to the study hall. The assembly was part of a school-sponsored educational program in self-government. Students who elected not to attend the assembly were required to report to study hall. During the entire speech, Fraser referred to his candidate in terms of an elaborate, graphic, and explicit sexual metaphor.

Two of Fraser's teachers, with whom he discussed the contents of his speech in advance, informed him that the speech was "inappropriate and that he probably should not deliver it," and that his delivery of the speech might have "severe consequences." . . .

A Bethel High School disciplinary rule prohibiting the use of obscene language in the school provides:

> "Conduct which materially and substantially interferes with the educational process is prohibited, including the use of obscene, profane language or gestures."

The morning after the assembly, the Assistant Principal called Fraser into her office and notified him that the school considered his speech to have been a violation of this rule. . . . Fraser served two days of his suspension, and was allowed to return to school on the third day. . . .

This Court acknowledged in *Tinker v. Des Moines Independent Community School Dist.*, [393 U.S. 503 (1969)], that students do not "shed their constitutional rights to freedom of speech or expression at the schoolhouse gate." The Court of Appeals read that case as precluding any discipline of Fraser for indecent speech and lewd conduct in the school assembly. That court appears to have proceeded on the theory that the use of lewd and obscene speech in order to make what the speaker considered to be a point in a nominating speech for a fellow student was essentially the same as the wearing of an armband in *Tinker* as a form of protest or the expression of a political position.

The marked distinction between the political "message" of the armbands in *Tinker* and the sexual content of respondent's speech in this case seems to have been given little weight by the Court of Appeals. In upholding the students' right to engage in a nondisruptive, passive expression of a political viewpoint in *Tinker*, this Court was careful to note that the case did "not concern speech or action that intrudes upon the work of the schools or the rights of other students." . . .

It is against this background that we turn to consider the level of First Amendment protection accorded to Fraser's utterances and actions before an official high school assembly attended by 600 students.

The role and purpose of the American public school system was well described by two historians, saying "public education must prepare pupils for citizenship in the Republic. . . . It must inculcate the habits and manners of civility as values in themselves conducive to happiness and as indispensable to the practice of self-government in the community and the nation." . . .

These fundamental values of "habits and manners of civility" essential to a democratic society must, of course, include tolerance of divergent political and religious views, even when the views expressed may be unpopular. But these "fundamental values" must also take into account consideration of the sensibilities of others, and, in the case of a school, the sensibilities of fellow students. The undoubted freedom to advocate unpopular and controversial views in schools and classrooms must be balanced against the society's countervailing interest in teaching students the boundaries of socially appropriate behaviour. Even the most heated political discourse in a democratic society requires consideration for the personal sensibilities of the other participants and audiences. . . .

Surely it is a highly appropriate function of public school education to prohibit the use of vulgar and offensive terms in public discourse. Indeed, the "fundamental values necessary to the maintenance of a democratic political system" disfavor the use of terms of debate highly offensive or highly threatening to others. Nothing in the Constitution prohibits the states from insisting that certain modes of expression are inappropriate and subject to sanctions. The inculcation of these values is truly the "work of the schools." The determination of what manner of speech in the classroom or in school assembly is inappropriate properly rests with the school board. . . .

This Court's First Amendment jurisprudence has acknowledged limitations on the otherwise absolute interest of the speaker in reaching an unlimited audience where the speech is sexually explicit and the audience may include children. . . .

We hold that petitioner School District acted entirely within its permissible authority in imposing sanctions upon Fraser in response to his offensively lewd and indecent speech. Unlike the sanctions imposed on the students wearing armbands in *Tinker*, the penalties imposed in this case were unrelated to any political viewpoint. The First Amendment does not prevent the school officials from determining that to permit a vulgar and lewd speech such as respondent's would undermine the school's basic educational mission. A high school assembly or classroom is no place for a sexually explicit monologue directed towards an unsuspecting audience of teenage students. Accordingly, it was perfectly appropriate for the school to disassociate itself to make the point to the pupils that vulgar speech and lewd conduct is wholly inconsistent with the "fundamental values" of public school education.

☐ *Justice BRENNAN, concurring.*

Respondent gave the following speech at a high school assembly in support of a candidate for student government office:

> " 'I know a man who is firm—he's firm in his pants, he's firm in his shirt, his character is firm—but most . . . of all, his belief in you, the students of Bethel, is firm.
> " 'Jeff Kuhlman is a man who takes his point and pounds it in. If necessary, he'll take an issue and nail it to the wall. He doesn't attack things in spurts—he drives hard, pushing and pushing until finally—he succeeds.
> " 'Jeff is a man who will go to the very end—even the climax, for each and every one of you.
> " 'So vote for Jeff for A.S.B. vice-president—he'll never come between you and the best our high school can be.' " App. 47.

The Court, referring to these remarks as "obscene," "vulgar," "lewd," and "offensively lewd," concludes that school officials properly punished respondent for uttering the speech. Having read the full text of respondent's remarks, I find it difficult to believe that it is the same speech the Court describes. To my mind, the most that can be said about respondent's speech—and all that need be said—is that in light of the discretion school officials have to teach high school students how to conduct civil and effective public discourse, and to prevent disruption of school educational activities, it was not unconstitutional for school officials to conclude, under the circumstances of this case, that respondent's remarks exceeded permissible limits. Thus, while I concur in the Court's judgment, I write separately to express my understanding of the breadth of the Court's holding. . . .

In the present case, school officials sought only to ensure that a high school assembly proceed in an orderly manner. There is no suggestion that school officials attempted to regulate respondent's speech because they disagreed with the views he sought to express. Nor does this case involve an attempt by school officials to ban written materials they consider "inappropriate" for high school students, or to limit what students should hear, read, or learn about. Thus, the Court's holding concerns only the authority that school officials have to restrict a high school student's use of disruptive language in a speech given to a high school assembly.

☐ *Justice MARSHALL, dissenting.*

I agree with the principles that Justice BRENNAN sets out in his opinion concurring in the judgment. I dissent from the Court's decision, however, because in my view the school district failed to demonstrate that respondent's remarks were indeed disruptive.

☐ *Justice STEVENS, dissenting.*

"Frankly, my dear, I don't give a damn."

When I was a high school student, the use of those words in a public forum shocked the Nation. Today Clark Gable's four-letter expletive is less offensive than it was then. Nevertheless, I assume that high school administrators may prohibit the use of that word in classroom discussion and even in extracurricular activities that are sponsored by the school and held on school premises. For I believe a school faculty must regulate the content as well as the style of student speech in carrying out its educational mission. It does seem to me, however, that if a student is to be punished for using offensive speech, he is entitled to fair notice of the scope of the prohibition and the consequences of its violation. The interest in free speech protected by the First Amendment and the interest in fair procedure protected by the Due Process Clause of the Fourteenth Amendment combine to require this conclusion.

This respondent was an outstanding young man with a fine academic record. The fact that he was chosen by the student body to speak at the school's commencement exercises demonstrates that he was respected by his peers. This fact is relevant for two reasons. It confirms the conclusion that the discipline imposed on him—a three-day suspension and ineligibility to speak at the school's graduation exercises—was sufficiently serious to justify invocation of the School District's grievance procedures. More importantly, it indicates that he was probably in a better position to determine whether an audience composed of 600 of his contemporaries would be offended by the use of a four-letter word—or a sexual metaphor—than is a group of judges who are at least two generations and 3,000 miles away from the scene of the crime.

The fact that the speech may not have been offensive to his audience—or that he honestly believed that it would be inoffensive—does not mean that he had a constitutional right to deliver it. For the school—not the student—must prescribe the rules of conduct in an educational institution. But it does mean that he should not be disciplined for speaking frankly in a school assembly if he had no reason to anticipate punitive consequences.

One might conclude that respondent should have known that he would be punished for giving this speech on three quite different theories: (1) It violated the "Disruptive Conduct" rule published in the student handbook; (2) he was specifically warned by his teachers; or (3) the impropriety is so obvious that no specific notice was required. . . .

The fact that respondent reviewed the text of his speech with three different teachers before he gave it does indicate that he must have been aware of the possibility that it would provoke an adverse reaction, but the teachers' responses certainly did not give him any better notice of the likelihood of discipline than did the student handbook itself. In my opinion, therefore, the most difficult question is whether the speech was so obviously offensive that an intelligent high school student must be presumed to have realized that he would be punished for giving it. . . .

It seems fairly obvious that respondent's speech would be inappropriate in certain classroom and formal social settings. On the other hand, in a locker room or perhaps in a school corridor the metaphor in the speech might be regarded as rather routine comment. If this be true, and if respondent's audience consisted almost entirely of young people with whom he conversed on a daily basis, can we—at this distance—confidently assert that he must have known that the school administration would punish him for delivering it?

For three reasons, I think not. First, it seems highly unlikely that he would have decided to deliver the speech if he had known that it would result in his suspension and disqualification from delivering the school commencement address. Second, I believe a strong presumption in favor of free expression should apply whenever an issue of this kind is arguable. Third, because the Court has adopted the policy of applying contemporary community standards in evaluating expression with sexual connotations, this Court should defer to the views of the district and circuit judges who are in a much better position to evaluate this speech than we are.

R.A.V. v. City of St. Paul, Minnesota
505 U.S. 377, 112 S.CT. 2538 (1992)

Robert A. Viktora, a white teenager, and several other white youths burned a cross after midnight on the lawn of the only black family in a St. Paul, Minnesota, neighborhood. He was subsequently arrested and charged with violating a 1989 city ordinance making it a crime to place on public or private property a burning cross, swastika, or other symbol likely to arouse "anger, alarm, or resentment in others on the basis of race, color, creed, religion or gender." A state juvenile court, however, dismissed the complaint on the grounds that the ordinance was overly broad and unconstitutional. But the Minnesota State Supreme Court reversed upon concluding that the ordinance applied only to conduct "outside First Amendment protection." In determining that the ordinance only prohibited "fighting words," or speech that threatens "imminent lawless action"—categories of speech that have historically fallen outside of the scope of the First Amendment—the state court observed that "[t]he burning of a cross is itself an unmistakable symbol of violence and hatred based on virulent notions of racial supremacy. It is the responsibility, even the obligation, of diverse communities to confront such notions in whatever form they appear." The state high court also distinguished St. Paul's ordinance from Texas's flag-burning law, which was struck down by a bare majority in *Texas v. Johnson*, 491 U.S. 397 (1989) (see Ch. 5). St. Paul did not ban cross burning per se, the Minnesota court reasoned, "but only those displays that one knows or should know will create anger, alarm or resentment based on racial, ethnic, gender or religious bias." Robert A. Viktora appealed that ruling to the Supreme Court.

The Court's decision was unanimous; Justice Scalia announced the opinion. Justice O'Connor joined Justice White's concurrence, as did Justices Blackmun and Stevens who also delivered concurring opinions.

☐ *Justice SCALIA delivered the opinion of the Court.*

The First Amendment generally prevents government from proscribing speech, see, e.g., *Cantwell v. Connecticut*, 310 U.S. 296 (1940), or even expressive conduct, see, e.g., *Texas v. Johnson*, 491 U.S. 397 (1989), because of disapproval of the ideas expressed. Content-based regulations are presumptively invalid. From 1791 to the present, however, our society, like other free but civilized societies, has permitted restrictions upon the content of speech in a few limited areas, which are "of such slight social value as a step to truth that any benefit that may be derived from them is clearly outweighed by the social interest in order and morality." *Chaplinsky* [*v. New Hampshire*, 315 U.S. 568 (1942)]. We have recognized that "the freedom of speech" referred to by the First Amendment does not include a freedom to disregard these traditional limitations. Our decisions since the 1960's have narrowed the scope of the traditional categorical exceptions for defamation, and for obscenity, but a limited categorical approach has remained an important part of our First Amendment jurisprudence.

We have sometimes said that these categories of expression are "not within the area of constitutionally protected speech," or that the "protection of the First Amendment does not extend" to them. Such statements must be taken in context, however, and are no more literally true than is the occasionally repeated shorthand characterizing obscenity "as not being speech at all." What they mean is that these areas of speech can, consistently with the First Amendment, be regulated because of their constitutionally proscribable content (obscenity, defamation, etc.)—not that they are categories of speech entirely invisible to the Constitution, so that they may be made the vehicles for content discrimination unrelated to their distinctively proscribable content. Thus, the government may proscribe libel; but it may not make the further content discrimination of proscribing only libel critical of the government. . . .

The proposition that a particular instance of speech can be proscribable on the basis of one feature (e.g., obscenity) but not on the basis of another (e.g., opposition to the city government) is commonplace, and has found application in many contexts. We have long held, for example, that nonverbal expressive activity can be banned because of the action it entails, but not because of the ideas it expresses—so that burning a flag in violation of an ordinance against outdoor fires could be punishable, whereas burning a flag in violation of an ordinance against dishonoring the flag is not. Similarly, we have upheld reasonable "time, place, or manner" restrictions, but only if they are "justified without reference to the content of the regulated speech." *Ward v. Rock Against Racism*, 491 U.S. 781 (1989). And just as the power to proscribe particular speech on the basis of a noncontent element (e.g., noise) does not entail the power to proscribe the same speech on the basis of a content element; so also, the power to proscribe it on the basis of one content element (e.g., obscenity) does not entail the power to proscribe it on the basis of other content elements.

In other words, the exclusion of "fighting words" from the scope of the First Amendment simply means that, for purposes of that Amendment, the unprotected features of the words are, despite their verbal character, essentially a "nonspeech" element of communication. Fighting words are thus analogous to a noisy sound truck: Each is, as Justice FRANKFURTER recognized, a "mode of speech," *Niemotko v. Maryland*, 340 U.S. 268 (1951); both can be used to convey an idea; but neither has, in and of itself, a claim upon the First Amendment. As with the sound truck, however, so also with fighting words: The government may not regulate use based on hostility—or favoritism—towards the underlying message expressed. . . .

Even the prohibition against content discrimination that we assert the First Amendment requires is not absolute. It applies differently in the context of proscribable speech than in the area of fully protected speech. The rationale of the general prohibition, after all, is that content discrimination "raises the specter that the Government may effectively drive certain ideas or viewpoints from the marketplace," *Simon & Schuster* [*Inc. v. Members of the New York State Crime Victims Board*, 502 U.S. 105] (1992). But content discrimination among various instances of a class of proscribable speech often does not pose this threat.

When the basis for the content discrimination consists entirely of the very reason the entire class of speech at issue is proscribable, no significant danger of idea or viewpoint discrimination exists. Such a reason, having been adjudged neutral enough to support exclusion of the entire class of speech from First Amendment protection, is also neutral enough to form the basis of distinction within the class. To illustrate: A State might choose to prohibit only that obscenity which is the most patently offensive in its prurience—i.e., that which involves the most lascivious displays of sexual activity. But it may not prohibit, for example, only that obscenity which includes offensive political messages. And the Federal Government can criminalize only those threats of violence that are directed against the President—since the reasons why threats of violence are outside the First Amendment (protecting individuals from the fear of violence, from the disruption that fear engenders, and from the possibility that the threatened violence will occur) have special force when applied to the person of the President. . . . But the Federal Government may not criminalize only those threats against the President that mention his policy on aid to inner cities. And to take a final example, a State may choose to regulate price advertising in one industry but not in others, because the risk of fraud (one of the characteristics of commercial speech that justifies depriving it of full First Amendment protection, see *Virginia Pharmacy Bd. v. Virginia Citizens Consumer Council, Inc.*, 425 U.S. 748 (1976)) is in its view greater there.

Another valid basis for according differential treatment to even a content-defined subclass of proscribable speech is that the subclass happens to be associated with particular "secondary effects" of the speech, so that the regulation is "justified without reference to the content of the . . . speech," *Renton v. Playtime Theatres, Inc.*, 475 U.S. 41 (1986). A State could, for example, permit all obscene live performances except those involving minors. Moreover, since words can in some circumstances violate laws directed not against speech but against conduct (a law against treason, for example, is violated by telling the enemy the nation's defense secrets), a particular content-based subcategory of a proscribable class of speech can be swept up incidentally within the reach of a statute directed at conduct rather than speech. Where the government does not target conduct on the basis of its expressive content, acts are not shielded from regulation merely because they express a discriminatory idea or philosophy. . . .

Applying these principles to the St. Paul ordinance, we conclude that, even as narrowly construed by the Minnesota Supreme Court, the ordinance is facially unconstitutional. Although the phrase in the ordinance, "arouses anger, alarm or resentment in others," has been limited by the Minnesota Supreme Court's construction to reach only those symbols or displays that amount to "fighting words," the remaining, unmodified terms make clear that the ordinance applies only to "fighting words" that insult, or provoke violence, "on the basis of race, color, creed, religion or gender." Displays containing abusive invective, no matter how vicious or severe, are permissible unless they are addressed to one of the specified disfavored topics. Those who wish to use "fighting words" in connection with other ideas—to express hostility, for example, on the basis of political affiliation, union membership, or homosexuality—are not covered. The First Amendment does not permit St. Paul to impose special prohibitions on those speakers who express views on disfavored subjects. In its practical operation, moreover, the ordinance goes even beyond mere content discrimination, to actual viewpoint discrimination. Displays containing some words—odious racial epithets, for example—would be prohibited to proponents of all views. But "fighting words" that do not themselves invoke race, color, creed, religion, or gender—aspersions upon a person's mother, for example—would seemingly be usable ad libitum in the placards of those arguing in favor of race, color, etc. tolerance and equality, but could not be used by that speaker's opponents. One could hold up a sign saying, for example, that all "anti-Catholic bigots" are misbegotten; but not that all "papists" are, for that would insult and provoke violence "on the basis of religion." St. Paul has no such authority to license one side of a debate to fight freestyle, while requiring the other to follow Marquis of Queensbury Rules.

What we have here, it must be emphasized, is not a prohibition of fighting words that are directed at certain persons or groups (which would be facially valid if it met the requirements of the Equal Protection Clause); but rather, a prohibition of fighting words that contain (as the Minnesota Supreme Court repeatedly emphasized) messages of "bias-motivated" hatred and in particular, as applied to this case, messages "based on virulent notions of racial supremacy." . . .

The content-based discrimination reflected in the St. Paul ordinance comes within neither any of the specific exceptions to the First Amendment prohibition we discussed earlier, nor within a more general exception for content discrimination that does not threaten censorship of ideas. It assuredly does not fall within the exception for content discrimination based on the very reasons why the particular class of speech at issue (here, fighting words) is proscribable. As explained earlier, the reason why fighting words are categorically excluded from the protection of the First Amendment is not that their content communicates any particular idea, but that their content embodies a particularly intolerable (and socially unnecessary) mode of expressing whatever idea the speaker wishes to convey. St. Paul has not singled out an especially offensive mode of expression—it has not, for example, selected for prohibition only those fighting words that communicate ideas in a threatening (as opposed to a merely obnoxious) manner. Rather, it has proscribed fighting words of whatever manner that communicate messages of racial, gender, or religious intolerance. Selectivity of this sort creates the possibility that the city is seeking to handicap the expression of particular ideas. That possibility would alone be enough to render the ordinance presumptively invalid, but St. Paul's comments and concessions in this case elevate the possibility to a certainty. . . .

Let there be no mistake about our belief that burning a cross in someone's front yard is reprehensible. But St. Paul has sufficient means at its disposal to prevent such behavior without adding the First Amendment to the fire.

The judgment of the Minnesota Supreme Court is reversed, and the case is remanded for proceedings not inconsistent with this opinion.

☐ *Justice WHITE, with whom Justice BLACKMUN and Justice O'CONNOR join, and with whom Justice STEVENS joins except as to Part I(A), concurring in the judgment.*

I agree with the majority that the judgment of the Minnesota Supreme Court should be reversed. However, our agreement ends there.

[T]he majority casts aside long-established First Amendment doctrine without the benefit of briefing and adopts an untried theory. This is hardly a judicious way of proceeding, and the Court's reasoning in reaching its result is transparently wrong.

Today, . . . the Court announces that earlier Courts did not mean their repeated statements that certain categories of expression are "not within the area of constitutionally protected speech." The present Court submits that such clear statements "must be taken in context" and are not "literally true."

To the contrary, those statements meant precisely what they said: The categorical approach is a firmly entrenched part of our First Amendment jurisprudence. Indeed, the Court in *Roth* [*v. United States*, 354 U.S. 476 (1952)], reviewed the guarantees of freedom of expression in effect at the time of the ratification of the Constitution and concluded, "in light of this history, it is apparent that the unconditional phrasing of the First Amendment was not intended to protect every utterance."

In its decision today, the Court points to "nothing . . . in this Court's precedents warranting disregard of this longstanding tradition." Nevertheless, the majority holds that the First Amendment protects those narrow categories of expression long held to be undeserving of First Amendment protection—at least to the extent that lawmakers may not regulate some fighting words more strictly than others because of their content. The Court announces that such content-based distinctions violate the First Amendment because "the government may not regulate use based on hostility—or favoritism—towards the underlying message expressed." Should the government want to criminalize certain fighting words, the Court now requires it to criminalize all fighting words.

To borrow a phrase, "Such a simplistic, all-or-nothing-at-all approach to

First Amendment protection is at odds with common sense and with our jurisprudence as well." It is inconsistent to hold that the government may proscribe an entire category of speech because the content of that speech is evil, . . . but that the government may not treat a subset of that category differently without violating the First Amendment; the content of the subset is by definition worthless and undeserving of constitutional protection.

The majority's observation that "fighting words are quite expressive indeed" is no answer. Fighting words are not a means of exchanging views, rallying supporters, or registering a protest; they are directed against individuals to provoke violence or to inflict injury. Therefore, a ban on all fighting words or on a subset of the fighting words category would restrict only the social evil of hate speech, without creating the danger of driving viewpoints from the marketplace.

Therefore, the Court's insistence on inventing its brand of First Amendment underinclusiveness puzzles me. The overbreadth doctrine has the redeeming virtue of attempting to avoid the chilling of protected expression, but the Court's new "underbreadth" creation serves no desirable function. Instead, it permits, indeed invites, the continuation of expressive conduct that in this case is evil and worthless in First Amendment terms, until the city of St. Paul cures the underbreadth by adding to its ordinance a catch-all phrase such as "and all other fighting words that may constitutionally be subject to this ordinance."

Any contribution of this holding to First Amendment jurisprudence is surely a negative one, since it necessarily signals that expressions of violence, such as the message of intimidation and racial hatred conveyed by burning a cross on someone's lawn, are of sufficient value to outweigh the social interest in order and morality that has traditionally placed such fighting words outside the First Amendment. Indeed, by characterizing "fighting words as a form of debate," the majority legitimates hate speech as a form of public discussion.

Furthermore, the Court obscures the line between speech that could be regulated freely on the basis of content (i.e., the narrow categories of expression falling outside the First Amendment) and that which could be regulated on the basis of content only upon a showing of a compelling state interest (i.e., all remaining expression). By placing fighting words, which the Court has long held to be valueless, on at least equal constitutional footing with political discourse and other forms of speech that we have deemed to have the greatest social value, the majority devalues the latter category.

I(B)

In a second break with precedent, the Court refuses to sustain the ordinance even though it would survive under the strict scrutiny applicable to other protected expression. Assuming, arguendo, that the St. Paul ordinance is a content-based regulation of protected expression, it nevertheless would pass First Amendment review under settled law upon a showing that the regulation "is necessary to serve a compelling state interest and is narrowly drawn to achieve that end." *Simon & Schuster.* St. Paul has urged that its ordinance, in the words of the majority, "helps to ensure the basic human rights of members of groups that have historically been subjected to discrimination. . . ." The Court expressly concedes that this interest is compelling and is promoted by the ordinance. Nevertheless, the Court treats strict scutiny analysis as irrelevant to the constitutionality of the legislation. . . .

Although the First Amendment does not apply to categories of unprotected speech, such as fighting words, the Equal Protection Clause requires that the regulation of unprotected speech be rationally related to a legitimate government interest. A defamation statute that drew distinctions on the basis of political affiliation or "an ordinance prohibiting only those legally obscene works that contain criticism of the city government," would unquestionably fail rational basis review.

Turning to the St. Paul ordinance and assuming arguendo, as the majority does, that the ordinance is not constitutionally overbroad, there is no question that it would pass equal protection review. The ordinance proscribes a subset of "fighting words," those that injure "on the basis of race, color, creed, religion or gender." This selective regulation reflects the City's judgment that harms based on race, color, creed, religion, or gender are more pressing public concerns than the harms caused by other fighting words. In light of our Nation's long and painful experience with discrimination, this determination is plainly reasonable. Indeed, as the majority concedes, the interest is compelling. . . .

Although I disagree with the Court's analysis, I do agree with its conclusion: The St. Paul ordinance is unconstitutional. However, I would decide the case on overbreadth grounds. . . .

    ☐ *Justice STEVENS, with whom Justice WHITE and Justice BLACKMUN join as to Part I, concurring in the judgment.*

[M]y colleagues today wrestle with two broad principles: first, that certain "categories of expression [including 'fighting words'] are not within the area of constitutionally protected speech;" and second, that "content-based regulations [of expression] are presumptively invalid." Although in past opinions the Court has repeated both of these maxims, it has—quite rightly— adhered to neither with the absolutism suggested by my colleagues. Thus, while I agree that the St. Paul ordinance is unconstitutionally overbroad for the reasons stated in Part II of Justice WHITE's opinion, I write separately to suggest how the allure of absolute principles has skewed the analysis of both the majority and concurring opinions.

■ I

The Court today revises this categorical approach. It is not, the Court rules, that certain "categories" of expression are "unprotected," but rather that certain "elements" of expression are wholly "proscribable." To the Court, an expressive act, like a chemical compound, consists of more than one element. Although the act may be regulated because it contains a proscribable element, it may not be regulated on the basis of another (nonproscribable) element it also contains. Thus, obscene antigovernment speech may be regulated because it is obscene, but not because it is antigovernment. It is this revision of the categorical approach that allows the Court to assume that the St. Paul ordinance proscribes only fighting words, while at the same time concluding that the ordinance is invalid because it imposes a content-based regulation on expressive activity.

As an initial matter, the Court's revision of the categorical approach seems to me something of an adventure in a doctrinal wonderland, for the concept of "obscene antigovernment" speech is fantastical. The category of the obscene is very narrow; to be obscene, expression must be found by the trier of fact to "appeal to the prurient interest, . . . depict or describe, in a patently offensive way, sexual conduct, [and] taken as a whole, lack serious literary, artistic, political or scientific value." *Miller v. California*, 413 U.S. 15 (1973). "Obscene antigovernment" speech, then, is a contradiction in terms: If expression is antigovernment, it does not "lack serious . . . political . . . value" and cannot be obscene. . . .

I am, however, even more troubled by the second step of the Court's analysis—namely, its conclusion that the St. Paul ordinance is an unconstitutional content-based regulation of speech. Drawing on broadly worded *dicta*, the Court establishes a near-absolute ban on content-based regulations of expression and holds that the First Amendment prohibits the regulation of fighting words by subject matter. Thus, while the Court rejects the "all-or-nothing-at-all" nature of the categorical approach, it promptly embraces an absolutism of its own: within a particular "proscribable" category of expression, the Court holds, a government must either proscribe all speech or no speech at all. This aspect of the Court's ruling fundamentally misunderstands the role and constitutional status of content-based regulations on speech, conflicts with the very nature of First Amendment jurisprudence, and disrupts well-settled principles of First Amendment law. . . .

Our First Amendment decisions have created a rough hierarchy in the constitutional protection of speech. Core political speech occupies the highest, most protected position; commercial speech and nonobscene, sexually explicit speech are regarded as a sort of second-class expression; obscenity and fighting words receive the least protection of all. Assuming that the Court is correct that this last class of speech is not wholly "unprotected," it certainly does not follow that fighting words and obscenity receive the same sort of protection afforded core political speech. Yet in ruling that proscribable speech cannot be regulated based on subject matter, the Court does just that. Perversely, this gives fighting words greater protection than is afforded commercial speech. . . .

In sum, the central premise of the Court's ruling—that "content-based regulations are presumptively invalid"—has simplistic appeal, but lacks support in our First Amendment jurisprudence. To make matters worse, the Court today extends this overstated claim to reach categories of hitherto unprotected speech and, in doing so, wreaks havoc in an area of settled law. Finally, although the Court recognizes exceptions to its new principle, those exceptions undermine its very conclusion that the St. Paul ordinance is unconstitutional. Stated directly, the majority's position cannot withstand scrutiny.

■ II

Although I agree with much of Justice WHITE's analysis, I do not join Part I-A of his opinion because I have reservations about the "categorical approach" to the First Amendment. . . .

[T]his approach sacrifices subtlety for clarity and is, I am convinced, ultimately unsound. As an initial matter, the concept of "categories" fits poorly with the complex reality of expression. Few dividing lines in First Amendment law are straight and unwavering, and efforts at categorization inevitably give rise only to fuzzy boundaries. Our definitions of "obscenity" illustrate this all too well. The quest for doctrinal certainty through the definition of categories and subcategories is, in my opinion, destined to fail.

Moreover, the categorical approach does not take seriously the importance of context. The meaning of any expression and the legitimacy of its regulation can only be determined in context. Whether, for example, a picture or a sentence is obscene cannot be judged in the abstract, but rather only in the context of its setting, its use, and its audience. . . .

Perhaps sensing the limits of such an all-or-nothing approach, the Court has applied its analysis less categorically than its doctrinal statements suggest. The Court has recognized intermediate categories of speech (for example, for indecent nonobscene speech and commercial speech) and geographic categories of speech (public fora, limited public fora, nonpublic fora) entitled to varying levels of protection. The Court has also stringently delimited the categories of unprotected speech. While we once declared that "libelous utterances [are] not . . . within the area of constitutionally protected speech," *Beauharnais v. Illinois*, 343 U.S. 250 (1952), our rulings in *New York Times Co. v. Sullivan*, 376 U.S. 253 (1964); *Gertz v. Robert Welch, Inc.*, 418 U.S. 323 (1974), and *Dun & Bradstreet, Inc. v. Greenmoss Builders, Inc.*, 472 U.S. 749 (1985), have substantially qualified this broad claim. Similarly, we have consistently construed the "fighting words" exception set forth in *Chaplinsky* narrowly. . . . In short, the history of the categorical approach is largely the history of narrowing the categories of unprotected speech.

This evolution, I believe, indicates that the categorical approach is unworkable and the quest for absolute categories of "protected" and "unprotected" speech ultimately futile. . . .

■ III

Unlike the Court, I do not believe that all content-based regulations are equally infirm and presumptively invalid; unlike Justice WHITE, I do not believe that fighting words are wholly unprotected by the First Amendment. To the contrary, I believe our decisions establish a more complex and subtle analysis, one that considers the content and context of the regulated speech, and the nature and scope of the restriction on speech. Applying this analysis and assuming arguendo (as the Court does) that the St. Paul ordinance is not overbroad, I conclude that such a selective, subject-matter regulation on proscribable speech is constitutional. . . .

In sum, the St. Paul ordinance (as construed by the Court) regulates expressive activity that is wholly proscribable and does so not on the basis of viewpoint, but rather in recognition of the different harms caused by such activity. Taken together, these several considerations persuade me that the St. Paul ordinance is not an unconstitutional content-based regulation of speech. Thus, were the ordinance not overbroad, I would vote to uphold it.

Wisconsin v. Mitchell

508 U.S. 476, 113 S.CT. 2194 (1993)

One evening in 1989 Todd Mitchell and several other black men and youths were talking about a scene in the movie *Mississippi Burning* in which a white man beats a young black man. Later, as the group moved outside to the street, Mitchell asked them, "Do you all feel hyped up to move on some white people?" Shortly thereafter a young white boy appeared on the other side of the street. And as he walked by, Mitchell counted "one, two, three" and said: "There goes a white boy; go get him!" After rushing the boy, Mitchell and the others beat him unconscious and stole his tennis shoes.

Subsequently, Mitchell was convicted of battery, which carries a maximum sentence of two years imprisonment. But under Wisconsin's "hate-speech" law an enhanced sentence may be given whenever the defendant "intentionally selects the person against whom the crime . . . is committed . . . because of the race, religion, color, disability, sexual orientation, national origin or ancestry of that person." Accordingly, Mitchell was sentenced to four years imprisonment. His challenge to the state's "hate-speech" law was initially unsuccessful, but on appeal the state supreme court agreed that the law violated "the First Amendment directly by punishing what the legislature has deemed to be offensive thought." But that ruling was appealed by the state, and the Supreme Court granted review.

The Court's decision was unanimous. Chief Justice Rehnquist announced the opinion.

☐ *Chief Justice REHNQUIST delivered the opinion of the Court.*

The State argues that the statute does not punish bigoted thought, as the Supreme Court of Wisconsin said, but instead punishes only conduct. While this argument is literally correct, it does not dispose of Mitchell's First Amendment challenge. To be sure, our cases reject the "view that an apparently limitless variety of conduct can be labeled 'speech' whenever the person engaging in the conduct intends thereby to express an idea." *United States v. O'Brien*, 391 U.S. 367 (1968); accord, *R.A.V. [v. City of St. Paul, Minnesota*, 505 U.S. 377 (1992)]. Thus, a physical assault is not by any stretch of the imagination expressive conduct protected by the First Amendment. See *Roberts v. United States Jaycees*, 468 U.S. 609 (1984) ("Violence or other types of potentially expressive activities that produce special harms distinct from their communicative impact . . . are entitled to no constitutional protection").

But the fact remains that under the Wisconsin statute the same criminal conduct may be more heavily punished if the victim is selected because of his race or other protected status than if no such motive obtained. Thus, although the statute punishes criminal conduct, it enhances the maximum penalty for conduct motivated by a discriminatory point of view more severely than the same conduct engaged in for some other reason or for no reason at all. Because the only reason for the enhancement is the defendant's discriminatory motive for selecting his victim, Mitchell argues (and the Wisconsin Supreme Court held) that the statute violates the First Amendment by punishing offenders' bigoted beliefs.

Traditionally, sentencing judges have considered a wide variety of factors in addition to evidence bearing on guilt in determining what sentence to impose on a convicted defendant. Thus, in many States the commission of a murder, or other capital offense, for pecuniary gain is a separate aggravating circumstance under the capital-sentencing statute. . . .

[But] Mitchell argues that the Wisconsin penalty-enhancement statute is invalid because it punishes the defendant's discriminatory motive, or reason, for acting. But motive plays the same role under the Wisconsin statute as it does under federal and state antidiscrimination laws, which we have previously upheld against constitutional challenge.

Nothing in our decision last Term in *R.A.V.* compels a different result here. That case involved a First Amendment challenge to a municipal ordinance prohibiting the use of " 'fighting words' that insult, or provoke violence, 'on the basis of race, color, creed, religion or gender.' " Because the ordinance only proscribed a class of "fighting words" deemed particularly offensive by the city—i.e., those "that contain . . . messages of 'bias-motivated' hatred"—we held that it violated the rule against content-based discrimination. But whereas the ordinance struck down in *R.A.V.* was explicitly directed at expression (i.e., "speech" or "messages,") the statute in this case is aimed at conduct unprotected by the First Amendment. . . .

Finally, there remains to be considered Mitchell's argument that the Wisconsin statute is unconstitutionally overbroad because of its "chilling effect" on free speech. Mitchell argues (and the Wisconsin Supreme Court agreed) that the statute is "overbroad" because evidence of the defendant's prior speech or associations may be used to prove that the defendant intentionally selected his victim on account of the victim's protected status. Consequently, the argument goes, the statute impermissibly chills free expression with respect to such matters by those concerned about the possibility of enhanced sentences if they should in the future commit a criminal offense covered by the statute. We find no merit in this contention.

The sort of chill envisioned here is far more attenuated and unlikely than that contemplated in traditional "overbreadth" cases. We must conjure up a vision of a Wisconsin citizen suppressing his unpopular bigoted opinions for fear that if he later commits an offense covered by the statute, these opinions will be offered at trial to establish that he selected his victim on account of the victim's protected status, thus qualifying him for penalty-enhancement. To stay within the realm of rationality, we must surely put to one side minor misdemeanor offenses covered by the statute, such as negligent operation of a motor vehicle, for it is difficult, if not impossible, to conceive of a situation where such offenses would be racially motivated. We are left, then, with the prospect of a citizen suppressing his bigoted beliefs for fear that evidence of such beliefs will be introduced against him at trial if he commits a more serious offense against person or property. This is simply too speculative a hypothesis to support Mitchell's overbreadth claim. . . .

For the foregoing reasons, we hold that Mitchell's First Amendment rights were not violated by the application of the Wisconsin penalty-enhancement provision in sentencing him. The judgment of the Supreme Court of Wisconsin is therefore reversed, and the case is remanded for further proceedings not inconsistent with this opinion.

Virginia v. Black
538 U.S. 343, 123 S.Ct. 1536 (2003)

In 1998, Barry Elton Black led a Ku Klux Klan rally at which a twenty-five-foot cross was burned on private property with the owner's permission, but which was clearly visible to nearby homeowners and motorists on a state road. He was convicted, under Virginia's fifty-year old law making cross burning a crime, and fined $2,500. Also in 1998, Richard J. Elliott and Jonathan O'Mara burned a cross in the yard of James Jubilee, an African American, because they were angry with him. Both were convicted and sentenced to ninety days in jail and fined $2,500. On appeal in 2001, the Virginia Supreme Court overturned their convictions and struck down the state's law in holding that it ran afoul of the First Amendment's guarantee for freedom of expression. The state appealed and the Supreme Court granted *certiorari*.

Justice O'Connor's opinion for the Court commanded only a plurality, but by a vote of six to three the Court held that a properly drafted law punishing cross burning would survive a First Amendment challenge. Justice O'Connor's opinion, joined by Chief Justice Rehnquist and Justices Stevens and Breyer, held that state may make it a crime to burn a cross because it is "a particularly virulent form of intimidation." Justice Scalia, in a separate opinion in part concurring and dissenting, and Justice Thomas, in a dissenting opinion, agreed. However, Justice O'Connor also ruled that Virginia's law was unconstitutional because a section of the law dealing with jury instructions permitting an inference of intent to intimidate invited juries to ignore "all of the contextual factors that are necessary to decide whether a particular cross burning [was] intended to intimidate" instead of to express a political message. Justice Scalia disagreed with that part of her analysis and holding in contending that under the statute a jury could be properly instructed and the inference of intimidation rebutted. In his dissent, Justice Thomas contended that the plurality went too far and that cross burning could never receive First Amendment protection because its sole message was one of terror and lawlessness. Justice

Souter, joined by Justices Kennedy and Ginsburg, filed another separate opinion in part concurring and dissenting. These three justices agreed that Virginia's law was unconstitutional but maintained that the First Amendment forbids all content-based regulations of speech. Cross burning, in their view, was inherently symbolic and might convey not only a message of terror but also of political ideology. Accordingly, they would have held that any law punishing cross burning could not survive First Amendment scrutiny.

□ *Justice O'CONNOR announced the judgment of the Court and delivered the opinion of the Court with respect to Parts I, II, and III, and an opinion with respect to Parts IV and V, in which THE CHIEF JUSTICE, Justice STEVENS, and Justice BREYER join.*

In this case we consider whether the Commonwealth of Virginia's statute banning cross burning with "an intent to intimidate a person or group of persons" violates the First Amendment. We conclude that while a State, consistent with the First Amendment, may ban cross burning carried out with the intent to intimidate, the provision in the Virginia statute treating any cross burning as prima facie evidence of intent to intimidate renders the statute unconstitutional in its current form. . . .

■ II

Cross burning originated in the 14th century as a means for Scottish tribes to signal each other. . . . Cross burning in this country, however, long ago became unmoored from its Scottish ancestry. Burning a cross in the United States is inextricably intertwined with the history of the Ku Klux Klan.

The first Ku Klux Klan began in Pulaski, Tennessee, in the spring of 1866. Although the Ku Klux Klan started as a social club, it soon changed into something far different. The Klan fought Reconstruction and the corresponding drive to allow freed blacks to participate in the political process. Soon the Klan imposed "a veritable reign of terror" throughout the South. The Klan employed tactics such as whipping, threatening to burn people at the stake, and murder. The Klan's victims included blacks, southern whites who disagreed with the Klan and "carpetbagger" northern whites.

The activities of the Ku Klux Klan prompted legislative action at the national level. . . . Congress passed what is now known as the Ku Klux Klan Act. President Grant used these new powers to suppress the Klan in South Carolina, the effect of which severely curtailed the Klan in other States as well. By the end of Reconstruction in 1877, the first Klan no longer existed.

The genesis of the second Klan began in 1905, with the publication of Thomas Dixon's *The Clansmen: An Historical Romance of the Ku Klux Klan.* Dixon's book was a sympathetic portrait of the first Klan, depicting the Klan as a group of heroes "saving" the South from blacks and the "horrors" of Reconstruction. Although the first Klan never actually practiced cross burning, Dixon's book depicted the Klan burning crosses to celebrate the execution of former slaves. Cross burning thereby became associated with the first Ku Klux Klan. When D. W. Griffith turned Dixon's book into the movie The

Birth of a Nation in 1915, the association between cross burning and the Klan became indelible. . . .

From the inception of the second Klan, cross burnings have been used to communicate both threats of violence and messages of shared ideology. The first initiation ceremony occurred on Stone Mountain near Atlanta, Georgia. While a 40-foot cross burned on the mountain, the Klan members took their oaths of loyalty. This cross burning was the second recorded instance in the United States. The first known cross burning in the country had occurred a little over one month before the Klan initiation, when a Georgia mob celebrated the lynching of Leo Frank by burning a "gigantic cross" on Stone Mountain that was "visible throughout" Atlanta. . . .

The Klan continued to use cross burnings to intimidate after World War II. . . . The decision of this Court in *Brown v. Board of Education*, 347 U.S. 483 (1954), along with the civil rights movement of the 1950's and 1960's, sparked another outbreak of Klan violence. These acts of violence included bombings, beatings, shootings, stabbings, and mutilations. . . .

To this day, regardless of whether the message is a political one or whether the message is also meant to intimidate, the burning of a cross is a "symbol of hate." And while cross burning sometimes carries no intimidating message, at other times the intimidating message is the only message conveyed. . . .

In sum, while a burning cross does not inevitably convey a message of intimidation, often the cross burner intends that the recipients of the message fear for their lives. And when a cross burning is used to intimidate, few if any messages are more powerful.

■ III

The First Amendment affords protection to symbolic or expressive conduct as well as to actual speech. See, e.g., *R.A.V. v. City of St. Paul*, 505 U.S. [377 (1992)]; *Texas v. Johnson*, [491 U.S. 397 (1989)]; *United States v. O'Brien*, 391 U.S. 367 (1968); *Tinker v. Des Moines Independent Community School Dist.*, 393 U.S. 503 (1969).

The protections afforded by the First Amendment, however, are not absolute, and we have long recognized that the government may regulate certain categories of expression consistent with the Constitution. See, e.g., *Chaplinsky v. New Hampshire*, 315 U.S. 568 1942.

We have consequently held that fighting words—"those personally abusive epithets which, when addressed to the ordinary citizen, are, as a matter of common knowledge, inherently likely to provoke violent reaction"—are generally proscribable under the First Amendment. *Cohen v. California*, 403 U.S. 15 (1971). Furthermore, "the constitutional guarantees of free speech and free press do not permit a State to forbid or proscribe advocacy of the use of force or of law violation except where such advocacy is directed to inciting or producing imminent lawless action and is likely to incite or produce such action." *Brandenburg v. Ohio*, 395 U.S. 444 (1969). And the First Amendment also permits a State to ban a "true threat." *Watts v. United States*, 394 U.S. 705 (1969); accord, *R.A.V.* ("[T]hreats of violence are outside the First Amendment").

"True threats" encompass those statements where the speaker means to communicate a serious expression of an intent to commit an act of unlawful violence to a particular individual or group of individuals. The speaker need not actually intend to carry out the threat. Rather, a prohibition on true threats "protect[s] individuals from the fear of violence" and "from the disruption that fear engenders," in addition to protecting people "from the possibility that the threatened violence will occur." Intimidation in the constitutionally proscribable sense of the word is a type of true threat, where a speaker directs a threat to a person or group of persons with the intent of placing the victim in fear of bodily harm or death. . . .

The fact that cross burning is symbolic expression, however, does not resolve the constitutional question. The Supreme Court of Virginia relied upon *R.A.V.* to conclude that once a statute discriminates on the basis of this type of content, the law is unconstitutional. We disagree.

In *R.A.V.*, we held that a local ordinance that banned certain symbolic conduct, including cross burning, when done with the knowledge that such conduct would " 'arouse anger, alarm or resentment in others on the basis of race, color, creed, religion or gender' " was unconstitutional. We held that the ordinance did not pass constitutional muster because it discriminated on the basis of content by targeting only those individuals who "provoke violence" on a basis specified in the law.

We did not hold in *R.A.V.* that the First Amendment prohibits all forms of content-based discrimination within a proscribable area of speech. Rather, we specifically stated that some types of content discrimination did not violate the First Amendment. Indeed, we noted that it would be constitutional to ban only a particular type of threat: "[T]he Federal Government can criminalize only those threats of violence that are directed against the President . . . since the reasons why threats of violence are outside the First Amendment . . . have special force when applied to the person of the President." And a State may "choose to prohibit only that obscenity which is the most patently offensive in its prurience—i.e., that which involves the most lascivious displays of sexual activity." Consequently, while the holding of *R.A.V.* does not permit a State to ban only obscenity based on "offensive political messages," or "only those threats against the President that mention his policy on aid to inner cities," the First Amendment permits content discrimination "based on the very reasons why the particular class of speech at issue . . . is proscribable."

Similarly, Virginia's statute does not run afoul of the First Amendment insofar as it bans cross burning with intent to intimidate. Unlike the statute at issue in *R.A.V.*, the Virginia statute does not single out for opprobrium only that speech directed toward "one of the specified disfavored topics." . . .

The First Amendment permits Virginia to outlaw cross burnings done with the intent to intimidate because burning a cross is a particularly virulent form of intimidation. Instead of prohibiting all intimidating messages, Virginia may choose to regulate this subset of intimidating messages in light of cross burning's long and pernicious history as a signal of impending violence. Thus, just as a State may regulate only that obscenity which is the most obscene due to its prurient content, so too may a State choose to prohibit only those forms of intimidation that are most likely to inspire fear of bodily harm. A ban on cross burning carried out with the intent to intimidate is fully consistent with our holding in *R.A.V.* and is proscribable under the First Amendment.

■ IV

The Supreme Court of Virginia ruled in the alternative that Virginia's cross-burning statute was unconstitutionally overbroad due to its provision stating that "[a]ny such burning of a cross shall be prima facie evidence of an intent to intimidate a person or group of persons." . . . In this Court, as in the Supreme Court of Virginia, respondents do not argue that the prima facie evidence provision is unconstitutional as applied to any one of them. Rather, they contend that the provision is unconstitutional on its face. . . .

As construed by the jury instruction, the prima facie provision strips away the very reason why a State may ban cross burning with the intent to intimidate. The prima facie evidence provision permits a jury to convict in every cross-burning case in which defendants exercise their constitutional right not to put on a defense. And even where a defendant like Black presents a defense, the prima facie evidence provision makes it more likely that the jury will find an intent to intimidate regardless of the particular facts of the case. The provision permits the Commonwealth to arrest, prosecute, and convict a person based solely on the fact of cross burning itself. . . .

As the history of cross burning indicates, a burning cross is not always intended to intimidate. Rather, sometimes the cross burning is a statement of ideology, a symbol of group solidarity. . . . Thus, "[b]urning a cross at a political rally would almost certainly be protected expression." *R.A.V.* . . .

The prima facie provision makes no effort to distinguish among these different types of cross burnings. . . . For these reasons, the prima facie evidence provision, as interpreted through the jury instruction and as applied in Barry Black's case, is unconstitutional on its face. . . .

■ V

With respect to Barry Black, we agree with the Supreme Court of Virginia that his conviction cannot stand, and we affirm the judgment of the Supreme Court of Virginia. With respect to Elliott and O'Mara, we vacate the judgment of the Supreme Court of Virginia, and remand the case for further proceedings. It is so ordered.

☐ *Justice STEVENS, concurring.*

Cross burning with "an intent to intimidate" unquestionably qualifies as the kind of threat that is unprotected by the First Amendment. For the reasons stated in the separate opinions that Justice WHITE and I wrote in *R.A.V.*, that simple proposition provides a sufficient basis for upholding the basic prohibition in the Virginia statute even though it does not cover other types of threatening expressive conduct. With this observation, I join Justice O'CONNOR's opinion.

☐ *Justice THOMAS, dissenting.*

Although I agree with the majority's conclusion that it is constitutionally permissible to "ban . . . cross burning carried out with intent to intimidate," I believe that the majority errs in imputing an expressive component to the activity in question. In my view, whatever expressive value cross burning has, the legislature simply wrote it out by banning only intimidating conduct undertaken by a particular means. A conclusion that the statute prohibiting cross burning with intent to intimidate sweeps beyond a prohibition on certain conduct into the zone of expression overlooks not only the words of the statute but also reality. . . .

[T]his statute prohibits only conduct, not expression. And, just as one cannot burn down someone's house to make a political point and then seek refuge in the First Amendment, those who hate cannot terrorize and intimidate to make their point. In light of my conclusion that the statute here addresses only conduct, there is no need to analyze it under any of our First Amendment tests.

Even assuming that the statute implicates the First Amendment, in my view, the fact that the statute permits a jury to draw an inference of intent to intimidate from the cross burning itself presents no constitutional problems. Therein lies my primary disagreement with the plurality. . . .

Because I would uphold the validity of this statute, I respectfully dissent.

☐ *Justice* SCALIA, *with whom Justice* THOMAS *joins, concurring in part, concurring in the judgment in part, and dissenting in part.*

I agree with the Court that, under our decision in *R.A.V.*, a State may, without infringing the First Amendment, prohibit cross burning carried out with the intent to intimidate. Accordingly, I join Parts I–III of the Court's opinion. I also agree that we should vacate and remand the judgment of the Virginia Supreme Court so that that Court can have an opportunity authoritatively to construe the prima-facie-evidence provision of Section 18.2-423. I write separately, however, to describe what I believe to be the correct interpretation of Sec. 18.2-423, and to explain why I believe there is no justification for the plurality's apparent decision to invalidate that provision on its face.

In order to determine whether this component of the statute violates the Constitution, it is necessary, first, to establish precisely what the presentation of prima facie evidence accomplishes. . . . [P]resentation of evidence that a defendant burned a cross in public view is automatically sufficient, on its own, to support an inference that the defendant intended to intimidate only until the defendant comes forward with some evidence in rebuttal.

The question presented, then, is whether, given this understanding of the term "prima facie evidence," the cross-burning statute is constitutional. The Virginia Supreme Court answered that question in the negative. It stated that "[Sec.] 18.2-423 sweeps within its ambit for arrest and prosecution, both protected and unprotected speech." "The enhanced probability of prosecution under the statute chills the expression of protected speech sufficiently to render the statute overbroad."

This approach toward overbreadth analysis is unprecedented. We have never held that the mere threat that individuals who engage in protected conduct will be subject to arrest and prosecution suffices to render a statute overbroad. Rather, our overbreadth jurisprudence has consistently focused on whether the prohibitory terms of a particular statute extend to protected conduct; that is, we have inquired whether individuals who engage in protected conduct can be convicted under a statue, not whether they might be subject to arrest and prosecution. . . .

In deeming Sec. 18.2-423 facially invalid, the plurality presumably means to rely on some species of overbreadth doctrine. But it must be a rare species indeed. . . . The class of persons that the plurality contemplates could impermissibly be convicted under Sec. 18.2-423 includes only those individuals who (1) burn a cross in public view, (2) do not intend to intimidate, (3) are nonetheless charged and prosecuted, and (4) refuse to present a defense.

Conceding (quite generously, in my view) that this class of persons exists, it cannot possibly give rise to a viable facial challenge, not even with the aid of our First Amendment overbreadth doctrine.

I believe the prima-facie-evidence provision in Virginia's cross-burning statute is constitutionally unproblematic. . . .

☐ *Justice* SOUTER, *with whom Justice* KENNEDY *and Justice* GINSBURG *join, concurring in the judgment in part and dissenting in part.*

I agree with the majority that the Virginia statute makes a content-based distinction within the category of punishable intimidating or threatening expression, the very type of distinction we considered in *R.A.V.* I disagree that any exception should save Virginia's law from unconstitutionality under the holding in *R.A.V.* or any acceptable variation of it.

As the majority points out, the burning cross can broadcast threat and ideology together, ideology alone, or threat alone, as was apparently the choice of respondents Elliott and O'Mara.

The issue is whether the statutory prohibition restricted to this symbol falls within one of the exceptions to R.A.V.'s general condemnation of limited content-based proscription within a broader category of expression proscribable generally. Because of the burning cross's extraordinary force as a method of intimidation, the *R.A.V.* exception most likely to cover the statute is the first of the three mentioned there, which the *R.A.V.* opinion called an exception for content discrimination on a basis that "consists entirely of the very reason the entire class of speech at issue is proscribable." *R.A.V.* This is the exception the majority speaks of here as covering statutes prohibiting "particularly virulent" proscribable expression.

I do not think that the Virginia statute qualifies for this virulence exception as *R.A.V.* explained it. The statute fits poorly with the illustrative examples given in *R.A.V.*, none of which involves communication generally associated with a particular message, and in fact, the majority's discussion of a special virulence exception here moves that exception toward a more flexible conception than the version in *R.A.V.* I will reserve judgment on that doctrinal development, for even on a pragmatic conception of *R.A.V.* and its exceptions the Virginia statute could not pass muster, the most obvious hurdle being the statute's prima facie evidence provision. That provision is essential to understanding why the statute's tendency to suppress a message disqualifies it from any rescue by exception from *R.A.V.*'s general rule. . . .

[N]o content-based statute should survive even under a pragmatic recasting of *R.A.V.* without a high probability that no "official suppression of ideas is afoot," *R.A.V.* I believe the prima facie evidence provision stands in the way of any finding of such a high probability here. . . .

To the extent the prima facie evidence provision skews prosecutions, then, it skews the statute toward suppressing ideas. Thus, the appropriate way to consider the statute's prima facie evidence term, in my view, is not as if it were an overbroad statutory definition amenable to severance or a narrowing construction. The question here is not the permissible scope of an arguably overbroad statute, but the claim of a clearly content-based statute to an exception from the general prohibition of content-based proscriptions, an exception that is not warranted if the statute's terms show that suppression of ideas may be afoot. Accordingly, the way to look at the prima facie evidence provision is to consider it for any indication of what is afoot. And if we look at the provision for this purpose, it has a very obvious significance as a mechanism for bringing within the statute's prohibition some expression that is doubtfully threatening though certainly distasteful. . . .

I conclude that the statute under which all three of the respondents were prosecuted violates the First Amendment, since the statute's content-based distinction was invalid at the time of the charged activities, regardless of whether the prima facie evidence provision was given any effect in any respondent's individual case. In my view, severance of the prima facie evidence provision now could not eliminate the unconstitutionality of the whole statute at the time of the respondents' conduct. I would therefore affirm the judgment of the Supreme Court of Virginia vacating the respondents' convictions and dismissing the indictments. Accordingly, I concur in the Court's judgment as to respondent Black and dissent as to respondents Elliott and O'Mara.

Rust v. Sullivan
500 U.S. 173, III S. Ct. 1759 (1991)

In 1970, Congress enacted Title X of the Public Health Service Act, providing federal funding for family planning services and authorizing the secretary of the Department of Health, Education, and Welfare (now the Department of Health and Human Services [HHS]) to make grants to public and private organizations engaged in family-planning projects and to promulgate regulations for the administration of those grants. Section 1008 of the act also provided that "[n]one of the funds appropriated under this subchapter shall be used in programs where abortion is a method of family planning." In 1988, the Reagan administration's secretary of HHS set down new regulations attaching three principal conditions to the award of a grant of federal funds under Title X. First, the regulations specify that a "Title X project may not provide counseling concerning the use of abortion as a method of family planning or provide referral for abortion as a method of family planning." Second, the regulations broadly prohibit grant recipients from engaging in activities that "encourage, promote or advocate abortion as a method of family planning." Forbidden activities include lobbying for legislation that would increase the availability of abortion, developing or disseminating materials advocating abortion as a method of family planning, providing speakers to promote abortion, using legal action to make abortion available, and paying dues to any group that advocates abortion. Finally, the regulations require organizations that are engaged in family planning and receive federal funding to be organized so that they are "physically and financially separate" from prohibited abortion activities.

HHS's new regulations were immediately challenged in federal court by Dr. Irving Rust and several other doctors and recipients of federal funding for family-planning projects. They sued on behalf of themselves and their patients on several grounds: that the regulations were not authorized by Title X and that they violate the First and Fifth Amendment rights of doctors and clients. A federal district court, however, summarily decided in favor of the secretary of HHS, and a panel of the Court of Appeals for the Second Circuit affirmed that decision. Rust thereupon appealed to the Supreme Court. By a vote of five to four the Rehnquist Court upheld the ban on abortion counseling. Subsequently, under pressure from Congress to revise its regulations and after months of negotiations, the Bush administration's HHS issued a new regulation allowing doctors, but not nurses or clinic counselors, to advise women on abortion. However, on November 3, 1992, the day of the presidential election, a three-judge panel (coincidentally composed of Democratic appointees) on the Court of Appeals for the District of Columbia Circuit overturned that revised regulation. It did so, notably in an unpublished disposition in *National Family Planning and Reproductive Health Association, Inc. v. Sullivan*, on the grounds that the administration failed to comply with the Administrative Procedure Act's requirement that agencies provide an opportunity for public "notice and comment" before enacting new federal regulations. Two days after his inauguration, President Bill Clinton fulfilled a campaign promise and repealed the Reagan/Bush administration's ban on abortion counseling by organizations receiving federal funding. Subsequently, in January 2001 President George W. Bush reversed course with an executive order banning federal funding for overseas family-planning organizations that also provide abortion services.

The Court's decision was five to four, with Chief Justice Rehnquist announcing the majority's opinion. Justice Marshall joined Justice Blackmun's dissent, as did in part Justices Stevens and O'Connor, who also delivered dissenting opinions.

☐ *Chief Justice REHNQUIST delivered the opinion of the Court.*

We need not dwell on the plain language of the statute because we agree with every court to have addressed the issue that the language is ambiguous. The language of Sec. 1008—that "[n]one of the funds appropriated under this subchapter shall be used in programs where abortion is a method of family planning"—does not speak directly to the issues of counseling, referral, advocacy, or program integrity. If a statute is "silent or ambiguous with respect to the specific issue, the question for the court is whether the agency's answer is based on a permissible construction of the statute." *Chevron v. Natural Resources Defense Council*, 467 U.S. 837 (1984). . . .

The broad language of Title X plainly allows the Secretary's construction of the statute. By its own terms, Sec. 1008 prohibits the use of Title X funds "in programs where abortion is a method of family planning." Title X does not define the term "method of family planning," nor does it enumerate what types of medical and counseling services are entitled to Title X funding. Based on the broad directives provided by Congress in Title X in general and Sec. 1008 in particular, we are unable to say that the Secretary's construction of the prohibition in Sec. 1008 to require a ban on counseling, referral, and advocacy within the Title X project, is impermissible. . . .

There is no question but that the statutory prohibition contained in Sec. 1008 is constitutional. In *Maher v. Roe*, [432 U.S. 464 (1977)], we upheld a state welfare regulation under which Medicaid recipients received payments for services related to childbirth, but not for nontherapeutic abortions. The Court rejected the claim that this unequal subsidization worked a violation of the Constitution. We held that the government may "make a value judgment favoring childbirth over abortion, and . . . implement that judgment by the allocation of public funds."

To hold that the Government unconstitutionally discriminates on the basis of viewpoint when it chooses to fund a program dedicated to advance certain permissible goals, because the program in advancing those goals necessarily discourages alternate goals, would render numerous government programs constitutionally suspect. When Congress established a National Endowment for Democracy to encourage other countries to adopt democratic principles, it was not constitutionally required to fund a program to encourage competing lines of political philosophy such as Communism and Fascism. Petitioners' assertions ultimately boil down to the position that if the government chooses to subsidize one protected right, it must subsidize analogous counterpart rights. But the Court has soundly rejected that proposition. . . .

By requiring that the Title X grantee engage in abortion-related activity separately from activity receiving federal funding, Congress has, . . . not denied it the right to engage in abortion-related activities. Congress has merely refused to fund such activities out of the public fisc, and the Secretary has simply required a certain degree of separation from the Title X project in order to ensure the integrity of the federally funded program.

The same principles apply to petitioners' claim that the regulations abridge the free speech rights of the grantee's staff. Individuals who are voluntarily employed for a Title X project must perform their duties in accordance with the regulation's restrictions on abortion counseling and referral. . . .

We turn now to petitioners' argument that the regulations violate a woman's Fifth Amendment right to choose whether to terminate her pregnancy. We recently reaffirmed the long-recognized principle that " 'the Due Process Clauses generally confer no affirmative right to governmental aid, even where such aid may be necessary to secure life, liberty, or property interests of which the government itself may not deprive the individual.' " *Webster* [*v. Reproductive Health Services*, 492 U.S. 490 (1989)] quoting *De Shaney v. Winnebago County Dept. of Social Services*, 489 U.S. 189 (1989). . . .

That the regulations do not impermissibly burden a woman's Fifth Amendment rights is evident from the line of cases beginning with *Maher* and *McRae* and culminating in our most recent decision in *Webster*. Just as Congress' refusal to fund abortions in *McRae* left "an indigent woman with at least the same range of choice in deciding whether to obtain a medically necessary abortion as she would have had if Congress had chosen to subsidize no health care costs at all," and "Missouri's refusal to allow public employees to perform abortions in public hospitals leaves a pregnant woman with the same choices as if the State had chosen not to operate any public hospitals," *Webster*, Congress' refusal to fund abortion counseling and advocacy leaves a pregnant woman with the same choices as if the government had chosen not to fund family-planning services at all. The difficulty that a woman encounters when a Title X project does not provide abortion counseling or referral leaves her in no different position than she would have been if the government had not enacted Title X. . . .

☐ *Justice BLACKMUN, with whom Justice MARSHALL joins, with whom Justice STEVENS joins as to parts II and III, and with whom Justice O'CONNOR joins as to part I, dissenting.*

Until today, the Court never has upheld viewpoint-based suppression of speech simply because that suppression was a condition upon the acceptance of public funds. Whatever may be the Government's power to condition the receipt of its largess upon the relinquishment of constitutional rights, it surely does not extend to a condition that suppresses the recipient's cherished freedom of speech based solely upon the content or viewpoint of that speech. *Speiser v. Randall*, 357 U.S. 513 (1958) ("To deny an exemption to claimants who engage in certain forms of speech is in effect to penalize them for such speech. . . . The denial is 'frankly aimed at the suppression of dangerous ideas,' " quoted *American Communications Assn. v. Douds*, 339 U.S. 382 (1950)). This rule is a sound one. . . .

The Regulations are also clearly viewpoint-based. While suppressing speech favorable to abortion with one hand, the Secretary compels anti-abortion speech with the other. . . .

[I]t is of no small significance that the speech the Secretary would suppress is truthful information regarding constitutionally protected conduct of vital importance to the listener. One can imagine no legitimate governmental interest that might be served by suppressing such information. . . .

Contrary to the majority's characterization, this is not a case in which individuals seek government aid in exercising their fundamental rights. The Fifth Amendment right asserted by petitioners is the right of a pregnant woman to be free from affirmative government interference in her decision. *Roe v. Wade* and its progeny are not so much about a medical procedure as they are about a woman's fundamental right to self-determination. Those cases serve to vindicate the idea that "liberty," if it means anything, must entail freedom from governmental domination in making the most intimate and personal of decisions. By suppressing medically pertinent information and injecting a restrictive ideological message unrelated to considerations of maternal health, the government places formidable obstacles in the path of Title X clients' freedom of choice and thereby violates their Fifth Amendment rights.

☐ *Justice STEVENS, dissenting.*

In my opinion, the Court has not paid sufficient attention to the language of the controlling statute or to the consistent interpretation accorded the statute by the responsible cabinet officers during four different Presidencies and 18 years.

The relevant text of the "Family Planning Services and Population Research act of 1970" has remained unchanged since its enactment. The preamble to the Act states that it was passed:

> "To promote public health and welfare by expanding, improving, and better coordinating the family planning services and population research activities of the Federal Government, and for other purposes."

The declaration of congressional purposes emphasizes the importance of educating the public about family planning services. . . . In contrast to the statutory emphasis on making relevant information readily available to the public, the statute contains no suggestion that Congress intended to authorize the suppression or censorship of any information by any Government employee or by any grant recipient.

Section 6 of the Act authorizes the provision of federal funds to support the establishment and operation of voluntary family planning projects. The section also empowers the Secretary to promulgate regulations imposing conditions on grant recipients to ensure that "such grants will be effectively utilized for the purposes for which made." Sec. 300a-4(b). Not a word in the statute, however, authorizes the Secretary to impose any restrictions on the dissemination of truthful information or professional advice by grant recipients.

The word "prohibition" is used only once in the Act. Section 6, which adds to the Public Health Service Act the new Title X, covering the subject of population research and voluntary planning programs, includes the following provision:

"Prohibition of Abortion

SEC. 1008. None of the funds appropriated under this title shall be used in programs where abortion is a method of family planning."

Read in the context of the entire statute, this prohibition is plainly directed by conduct, rather than the dissemination of information or advice, by potential grant recipients.

The original regulations promulgated in 1971 by the Secretary of Health, Education and Welfare so interpreted the statue. . . . Conforming to the language of the governing statute, the regulations provided that "[t]he project will not provide abortions as a method of family planning." Like the statute itself, the regulations prohibited conduct, not speech. . . .

The entirely new approach adopted by the Secretary in 1988 was not, in my view, authorized by the statute. The new regulations did not merely reflect a change in a policy determination that the Secretary had been authorized by Congress to make. Rather, they represented an assumption of policymaking responsibility that Congress has not delegated to the Secretary. In a society that abhors censorship and in which policymakers have traditionally placed the highest value on the freedom to communicate, it is unrealistic to conclude that statutory authority to regulate conduct implicitly authorized the Executive to regulate speech.

☐ *Justice O'CONNOR, dissenting.*

In this case, we need only tell the Secretary that his regulations are not a reasonable interpretation of the statute; we need not tell Congress that it cannot pass such legislation. If we rule solely on statutory grounds, Congress retains the power to force the constitutional question by legislating more explicitly. It may instead choose to do nothing. That decision should be left to Congress; we should not tell Congress what it cannot do before it has chosen to do it.

▪ IN COMPARATIVE PERSPECTIVE

Communitarianism, Feminism, and the Canadian Supreme Court's Rulings on Hate Speech and Pornography

Since the enactment of the Canadian Charter of Rights and Freedoms in 1982, the Canadian Supreme Court has actively interpreted its provisions, frequently citing rulings of the U.S. Supreme Court in support of its decisions. Indeed, on the Charter's tenth anniversary, in an interview with the *Toronto Globe and Mail* (April 17, 1992), Chief Justice Antonio Lamer observed that the Charter had "Americanized" the Canadian Supreme Court.

When dealing with challenges to laws punishing hate speech and pornographic materials, however, the Canadian Supreme Court charted a different course, expressly rejecting the principal tenets of the U.S. Supreme Court's doctrine of free speech in favor of the more communitarian approach grounded in a theory of equality. In doing so, the Canadian Supreme Court embraced the controversial position advanced unsuccessfully in the United States by some American feminists, such as Catharine MacKinnon and Andrea Dworkin. MacKinnon also participated in filing "friend of the court" briefs for the Women's Legal Education and Action Fund in both of the major cases decided by the Canadian Supreme Court.

Notably, the Canadian Charter combines a commitment to social equality and multiculturalism with a guarantee for freedom of expression. Section 1 specifies that the Charter "guarantees the rights and freedoms set out in it subject only to such reasonable limits prescribed by law as can be demonstratively justified in a free and democratic society." Freedom of expression is guaranteed in Section 2(b)'s provision that "Everyone has the following fundamental freedoms: . . . freedom of thought, belief, opinion and expression, including freedom of the press and other media of communication." That guarantee, though, appears qualified by not only the first section but also a detailed provision for equality in Section 15, which reads:

(1) Every individual is equal before and under the law and has the right to the equal protection and equal benefit of the law without discrimination and, in particular, without discrimination based on race, national or ethnic origin, colour, religion, sex, age or physical or mental disability.

(2) Subsection (1) does not preclude any law, program or activity that has as its object the amelioration of conditions of disadvantaged individuals or groups including those that are disadvantaged because of race, national or ethnic origin, colour, religion, sex, age or mental or physical disability.

In addition, two other sections underscore the commitment to multiculturalism and gender equality. Section 27 provides that the Charter "shall be interpreted in a manner consistent with the preservation and enhancement of the multicultural heritage of Canadians." And Section 28 stipulates that, "Notwithstanding anything in this Charter, the rights and freedoms referred to in it are guaranteed equally to male and female persons."

In *Regina v. Keegstra*, 3 SCR 697 (1990), the Canadian Supreme Court confronted the application of those guarantees in a challenge to the constitutionality of a provision in the criminal code prohibiting the communication, other than in private conversation, of "hatred against any identifiable group . . . distinguished by colour, race, religion or ethnic origin." James Keegstra, a high school teacher, was tried and convicted for communicating anti-semitic teachings to his students. His conviction, however, was overturned by the Alberta Court of Appeals on the grounds that the provision punishing hate speech violated the Charter's guarantee for freedom of expression. That decision was in turn reversed by the Canadian Supreme Court which upheld Canada's hate-speech law. Writing for the majority, Chief Justice Dickson explained,

Where [section] 1 operates to accentuate a uniquely Canadian vision of a free and democratic society, however, we must not hesitate to part from the path taken in the United States. Far from requiring a less solicitous protection of *Charter* rights and freedoms, such independence of vision protects these rights and freedoms in a different way. As will be seen below, in my view the international commitment to eradicate hate propaganda and, most importantly, the special role given equality and multiculturalism in the Canadian Constitution necessitate a departure from the view, reasonably prevalent in America at present, that the suppression of hate propaganda is incompatible with the guarantee of free expression. . . .

In my opinion, a response of humiliation and degradation from an individual targeted by hate propaganda is to be expected. A person's sense of human dignity and belonging to the community at large is closely linked to the concern and respect accorded the groups to which he or she belongs. The derision, hostility and abuse encouraged by hate propaganda therefore have a severely negative impact on the individual's sense of self-worth and acceptance. This impact may cause target group members to take drastic measures in reaction, perhaps avoiding activities which bring them into contact with non-group members or adopting attitudes and postures directed towards blending in with the majority. Such consequences bear heavily in a nation that prides itself on tolerance and the fostering of human dignity. . . .

At the core of freedom of expression lies the need to ensure that truth and the common good are attained, whether in scientific and artistic endeavors or in the process of determining the best course to take in our political affairs. Since truth and the ideal form of political and social organization can rarely, if at all, be identified with absolute certainty, it is difficult to prohibit expression without impeding the free exchange of potentially valuable information. Nevertheless, the argument from truth does not provide convincing support for the protection of hate propaganda. Taken to its extreme, this argument would require us to permit the communication of all expression, it being impossible to know with *absolute* certainty which factual statements are true, or which ideas obtain the greatest good. The problem with this extreme position, however, is that the greater the degree of certainty that a statement is erroneous or mendacious, the less the value in the quest for truth. Indeed, expression can be used to the detriment of our search for truth; the state should not be the sole arbiter of truth, but neither should we overplay the view that rationality will overcome all falsehoods in the unregulated marketplace of ideas. There is very little chance that statements intended to promote hatred against an identifiable group are true, or that their vision of society will lead to a better world. To portray such statements as crucial to truth and the betterment of the political and social milieu is therefore misguided. . . .

The connection between freedom of expression and the political process is perhaps the linchpin of the s. 2(b) guarantee, and the nature of this connection is largely derived from the Canadian commitment to democracy. Nonetheless, expression can work to undermine our commitment to democracy where employed to propagate ideas anathemic to democratic values. Hate propaganda works in just such a way, arguing as it does for a society in which the democratic process is subverted and individuals are denied respect and dignity simply because of racial or religious characteristics. This brand of expressive activity is thus wholly inimical to the democratic aspirations of the free expression guarantee. . . .

Two years after handing down the ruling in *Keegstra*, the Canadian Supreme Court then faced, in *Regina v. Butler*, 1 SCR 452 (1992), a constitutional challenge to the criminal code's provision penalizing the possession and distribution of obscenity. The code defines obscenity as "any publication a dominant characteristic of which is the undue exploitation of sex, or of sex and any one or more of . . . crime, horror, cruelty, and violence, shall be deemed to be obscene." Donald Victor Butler challenged the constitutionality of that provision after he was tried for and convicted of selling "hard core" videotapes and magazines at his "adult video" store in Winnipeg, Manitoba. In rejecting his claim that the law ran afoul of the Charter's guarantee of freedom of expression, Justice Sopinka explained that

> In determining when the exploitation of sex will be considered "undue," the courts have attempted to formulate workable tests. The most important of these is the "community standard of tolerance" test. . . . The community standards test has been the subject of extensive judicial analysis. It is the standards of the community as a whole which must be considered and not the standards of a small segment of that community such as a university community where a film was shown. . . .
>
> [T]he community standards test is concerned not with what Canadians would not tolerate being exposed to themselves, but what they would not tolerate *other* Canadians being exposed to. . . . There has been a growing recognition in recent cases that material which may be said to exploit sex in a "degrading or dehumanizing" manner will necessarily fail the community standards test. . . .
>
> Among other things, degrading or dehumanizing materials place women (and sometimes men) in positions of subordination, servile submission or humiliation. They run against the principles of equality and dignity of all human beings. In the appreciation of whether material is degrading or dehumanizing, the appearance of consent is not necessarily determinative. Consent cannot save materials that otherwise contain degrading or dehumanizing scenes. Sometimes the very appearance of consent makes the depicted acts even more degrading or dehumanizing.
>
> This type of material would, apparently, fail the community standards test not because it offends against morals but because it is perceived by public opinion to be harmful to society, particularly to women. While the accuracy of this perception is not susceptible of exact proof, there is a substantial body of opinion that holds that the portrayal of persons being subjected to degrading or dehumanizing sexual treatment results in harm, particularly to women and therefore to society as a whole. . . .
>
> The courts must determine as best they can what the community would tolerate others being exposed to on the basis of the degree of harm that may flow from such exposure. Harm in this

context means that it predisposes persons to act in an anti-social manner as, for example, the physical or mental mistreatment of women by men, or what is perhaps debatable, the reverse. Anti-social conduct for this purpose is conduct which society formally recognizes as incompatible with its proper functioning. The stronger the inference of a risk of harm the lesser the likelihood of tolerance. The inference may be drawn from the material itself or from the material and other evidence. Similarly evidence as to the community standards is desirable but not essential.

In making this determination with respect to the three categories of pornography referred to above, the portrayal of sex coupled with violence will almost always constitute the undue exploitation of sex. Explicit sex which is degrading or dehumanizing may be undue if the risk of harm is substantial. Finally, explicit sex that is not violent and neither degrading nor dehumanizing is generally tolerated in our society and will not qualify as the undue exploitation of sex unless it employs children in its production. . . .

For further reading on Canadian constitutional politics, see Stephen Newman, ed., *Constitutional Politics in Canada and the United States* (Ithaca: State University of New York, 2004). On the debate over the censorship of pornography, see Catharine MacKinnon, *Only Words* (Cambridge, MA: Harvard University Press, 1993); Andrea Dworkin, *Intercourse* (New York: Free Press, 1987); and compare Nadine Strossen, *Defending Pornography: Free Speech, Sex, and the Fight for Women's Rights* (New York: Scribner, 1995).

C | *Libel*

Libel is defamation of character by print or visual presentation; slander is defamation by oral presentation. Libel prosecutions may be either criminal or civil. Criminal prosecutions for libel against the government and groups repair and maintain the peace and order of a community, whereas civil suits brought by victims of libel are for monetary damages.

English common law permitted prosecutions for seditious libel (libel of the government and government officials), as did the Alien and Sedition Act in 1798. But in the landmark libel ruling *New York Times v. Sullivan* (1964) (excerpted below), the Court had occasion to declare the Sedition Act and seditious libel unconstitutional and inconsistent with the First Amendment.

Some states also provided criminal penalties for group libel, attacks on groups. In *Beauharnais v. Illinois*, 343 U.S. 250 (1952), the Court upheld an Illinois law making it unlawful to publish or exhibit any writing or picture portraying the "depravity, criminality, unchastity, or lack of virtue of a class of citizens, of any race, color, creed or religion."

Beauharnais, head of the White Circle League, had circulated on the streets of Chicago a leaflet containing derogatory statements about blacks and urging the police to protect whites from their "rapes, knives, guns, and marijuana." But dissenting Justice Douglas warned that "Today a white man stands convicted for protesting in unseemly language against our decisions invalidating restrictive convenants. Tomorrow a Negro will be hauled before a court for denouncing lynch law in heated terms." Indeed, *Beauharnais* was widely criticized for failing to consider the close relationship between group libel and seditious libel, and allowing an important area of public discussion—the role of interest groups in American politics—to fall outside of First Amendment protection. Still, although in *Ashton v. Kentucky*, 384 U.S. 195 (1966), Justice Douglas struck down a criminal libel law as unconstitutionally vague, the Court has never expressly repudiated *Beauharnais* or the concept of group libel. Indeed, the Court often cites *Beauharnais* in support of maintaining that libel or defamation receives no First Amendment protection; thus, *Beauharnais* was cited approvingly in *R.A.V. v. City of St. Paul*, 505 U.S. 377 (1992) (see excerpt above), even though the Court struck down St. Paul's "hate-speech" law. Moreover, Justices Blackmun and Rehnquist, dissenting in *Smith v. Collin*, 436 U.S. 953 (1978), have underscored that "*Beauharnais* has never been overruled or formally limited in any way."

Civil libel suits may seek two kinds of damages: (1) compensatory damages as reimbursement for an individual's actual financial loss resulting from, for example, loss of employment or reputation as a result of being libeled; and (2) punitive damages awarded as compensation for mental suffering due to a libelous attack.

Awards for libel *by* public officials are virtually impossible to win. Members of Congress enjoy absolute immunity under the speech and debate clause, subject to the ruling in *Hutchinson v. Proxmire*, 443 U.S. 111 (1979) (see Vol. 1, Ch. 5). In *Barr v. Matteo*, 360 U.S. 564 (1959), the Court extended immunity to all federal administrative officials for statements made within the "outer perimeter" of their official duties.

Not until *New York Times v. Sullivan* (1964) (excerpted below) did the Court set down a constitutional standard for determining libel *of* public officials and "public figures." There Justice Brennan declared that public officials may win libel suits only on showing "actual malice," that is, "with knowledge that it was false or with reckless disregard of whether it was false or not."

The *New York Times* ruling proved controversial and makes it exceedingly difficult for public officials and public figures to win libel suits. Some critics, following Justices Black and Douglas in their concurring opinion in *New York Times*, argue that the Court did not go far enough toward safeguarding First Amendment freedoms and predict problems in applying the test. Other critics counter that the *New York Times* rule renders public officials defenseless against all but the most vicious attacks. As Justice Fortas observed in *St. Amant v. Thompson*, 390 U.S. 727 (1968), "The First Amendment does not require that we license shotgun attacks on public officials in virtually unlimited open-season. The occupation of public officeholder does not forfeit one's membership in the human race."

Following *New York Times*, the Court confronted the problems in defining "public officials" and "public figures" and over whether the actual malice test should apply to both. In *Rosenblatt v. Baer*, 383 U.S. 75 (1966), the Court held that a former ski instructor and county commissioner was a public figure, who had to prove actual malice in a libel suit over reports alleging his involvement in city corruption. A year later in two cases, *Associated Press v. Walker*, 388 U.S. 130 (1967), and *Curtis Publishing Company v. Butts*, 388 U.S. 130 (1967), both involving public figures, the Warren Court split five to four, with the chief justice as the swing vote.

In the *Associated Press* case, Edwin A. Walker, a well-known, retired, right-wing general, sought libel damages for a news report that he personally "took command" of a violent crowd protesting the enrollment of James Meredith, a black man, at the University of Mississippi. Walker claimed to have been libeled as a private individual and won a jury award of $500,000 in compensatory damages and $300,000 in punitive damages. However, the trial judge found no malice in the publication and struck down the latter award, which an appellate court affirmed. The Supreme Court unanimously reversed, but disagreed on the standard to be applied. Justices Brennan, Douglas, Black, and White, along with the chief justice, thought that the actual malice test should apply. But Justices Clark, Stewart, and Fortas joined an opinion by Justice Harlan allowing public figures (unlike public officials) to recover damages on showing only a "highly unreasonable conduct constituting an extreme departure from the standards of investigation and reporting ordinarily adhered to by responsible publishers." However, in *Curtis Publishing Company*, Harlan and three supporters in *Walker* were joined by Chief Justice Warren in upholding Wally Butts's libel award of $460,000 for an article in *The Saturday Evening Post*, alleging that Butts, a coach at the University of Georgia, conspired to rig a football game between his team and the University of Alabama. Although Butts, like Walker, was found to be a public figure, Harlan reasoned that here the publication was not "hot news" and, therefore, his standard of highly unreasonable conduct in the investigation and reporting of the story should apply. Although Chief Justice Warren concurred, he nevertheless agreed with the four dissenters that the actual malice test should apply to both public officials and public figures.

The Warren Court failed to reach complete agreement on the application of the actual malice test and, moreover, it never found a private individual who was not a public figure.[1] Finally, in *Gertz v. Robert Welch, Inc.* (1974) (excerpted below), the Burger Court found a "private individual" and announced a new libel standard for that category of persons—private individuals must prove only that a publisher was negligent in failing to exercise normal care in reporting. Two years later in *Time Inc. v. Firestone*, 424 U.S. 448 (1976), Justice Rehnquist reaffirmed that ruling in holding that a divorcée of the heir to the fortune of the Firestone Corporation was not a public figure, even though she had held news conferences about her divorce. *Time* magazine mistakenly referred to her as an "adulteress," when the divorce decree had not specifically found that she had committed adultery.[2]

In *Gertz*, Justice Powell emphasized that "under the First Amendment there is no such thing as a false idea. However pernicious an opinion may seem, we depend for its correction not on the conscience of judges and juries but on the competition of other ideas. But there is no constitutional value in false statements of fact." He, thereby, suggested that statements of "opinion" might be exempt from state libel laws. But in *Milkovich v. Lorain Journal Co.*, 497 U.S. 1 (1990), the Rehnquist Court rejected that implication. Michael Milkovich, Sr., a high-school wrestling coach, sued a small daily newspaper, owned by the Lorain Journal Company, for an article that asserted that he had lied under oath during an investigation of a melee in the school's gymnasium. The newspaper contended that its sportswriter was merely stating an "opinion" for which under *Gertz* he could not be held libel. Writing for the Court, however, Chief Justice Rehnquist rejected that interpretation of *Gertz*:

> [W]e do not think this passage from *Gertz* was intended to create a wholesale defamation exemption for anything that might be labeled "opinion." . . . Not only would such an interpretation be contrary to the tenor and context of the passage, but it would also ignore the fact that expressions of "opinion" may often imply an assertion of objective fact. . . .
>
> If a speaker says, "In my opinion John Jones is a liar," he implies a knowledge of facts which lead to the conclusion that Jones told an untruth. Even if the speaker states the facts upon which he bases his opinion, if those facts are either incorrect or incomplete, or if his assessment of them is erroneous, the statement may still imply a false assertion of fact. Simply couching such statements in terms of

opinion does not dispel these implications; and the statement, "In my opinion Jones is a liar," can cause as much damage to reputation as the statement, "Jones is a liar." . . .

Apart from their reliance on the *Gertz dictum*, respondents do not really contend that a statement such as, "In my opinion John Jones is a liar," should be protected by a separate privilege for "opinion" under the First Amendment. But they do contend that in every defamation case the First Amendment mandates an inquiry into whether a statement is "opinion" or "fact," and that only the latter statements may be actionable.

They propose that a number of factors developed by the lower courts (in what we hold was a mistaken reliance on the *Gertz dictum*) be considered in deciding which is which. But we think the "breathing space" which "freedoms of expression require in order to survive," [*Philadelphia Newspapers, Inc. v.*] *Hepps*, [475 U.S. 767 (1986)], (quoting *New York Times*), is adequately secured by existing constitutional doctrine without the creation of an artificial dichotomy between "opinion" and "fact."

Foremost, we think *Hepps* stands for the proposition that a statement on matters of public concern must be provable as false before there can be liability under state defamation law, at least in situations, like the present, where a media defendant is involved.

Thus, unlike the statement, "In my opinion Mayor Jones is a liar," the statement, "In my opinion Mayor Jones shows abysmal ignorance by accepting the teachings of Marx and Lenin," would not be actionable.

In other rulings the Court has made it somewhat easier for public officials and public figures, while somewhat more difficult for private individuals, to win libel awards. *Herbert v. Lando*, 441 U.S. 153 (1979), for example, held that at trial attorneys could probe the editorial process, questioning editors and reporters, to prove actual malice; members of the press have no privilege from testifying in libel cases and answering questions about editorial prepublication decisions. In *Philadelphia Newspapers, Inc. v. Hepps*, 475 U.S. 767 (1986), a bare majority agreed that private individuals bringing libel actions have the burden of showing the falsity in reports or stories that touch on matters of public concern. Subsequently, in *Masson v. The New Yorker Magazine*, 501 U.S. 496 (1991) (see excerpt below), the Rehnquist Court dealt with the complicated question of whether actual malice may be inferred in a libel suit based on evidence of fabricated quotations. Writing for the Court, Justice Kennedy held that the First Amendment does not provide a shield for writers who fabricate quotations.

The Court, however, continues to refuse to recognize in its First Amendment jurisprudence the difference between libel actions and suits over invasion of privacy. In tort law and common law, individuals may sue for basically four kinds of privacy interests: (1) intrusions into their private affairs, causing mental distress; (2) public disclosure of embarrassing facts damaging to their reputation; (3) publicity placing them in a false light; and (4) appropriation of their name or likeness without their permission.[3] In suits for invasion of privacy, unlike those for libel, truth is no defense; indeed, that is the basic difference between the two—truth is always a defense against libel, whereas in privacy suits it is the actual intrusion on, and truthful disclosure of, private affairs per se that causes mental suffering and injury to reputation.

In giving priority to First Amendment freedoms, the Court applies its tests for libel in cases involving invasion of privacy as well. As the Court explained, in *Time, Inc. v. Hill*, 385 U.S. 374 (1967), "We create a risk of serious impairment of the indispensable service of a free press in a free society if we saddle the press with the impossible burden of verifying to a certainty the facts associated with news articles with a person's name, picture, or portrait, particularly as related to nondefamatory matter." In this case, the Hill family sued *Life* magazine for a pictorial essay on the opening of a play, *The Desperate Hours*, which was based on the Hill family's experiences as hostages of three escaped convicts. The *Life* account, though, failed to differentiate between the truth and fiction in the play, and the Hills sued for invasion of privacy and portrayal of them in false light. The Court (with only Justice Fortas dissenting) reversed a lower court's award to the Hills on the grounds that the opening of the play was a matter of public interest.

Seven years later, in *Cantrell v. Forest City Publishing Company*, 419 U.S. 245 (1974), Margaret Cantrell and her children brought an invasion of privacy suit against the Forest City Publishing Company for a follow-up story on a bridge disaster that a year before had claimed the life of her husband. The story inaccurately portrayed the Cantrells as destitute after the bridge collapsed, and Mrs. Cantrell sued for invasion of privacy and misrepresentation. At trial, the judge instructed the jury to find the publisher liable on the *New York Times* actual malice test. On appeal, the Court refused to consider whether states may constitutionally apply more relaxed standards of liability for invasion of privacy than for libel.

In *Cox Broadcasting Corporation v. Cohn* (1975) (excerpted below), however, the Court struck down a privacy statute making it a misdemeanor to name or identify a rape victim, in a case brought by the father of a deceased rape victim against Cox Broadcasting Corporation for identifying his daughter as a rape victim in a television broadcast.[4] On a vote of six to three in *The Florida Star v. B.J.F.*, 491 U.S. 524 (1989), the justices also overturned a civil award against a newspaper for truthfully reporting, in violation of a state statute, the name of a rape victim. But there the Court suggested that *Cohn* was limited to actual public records.

NOTES

1. See *Greenbelt Co-op. v. Bresler*, 398 U.S. 6 (1970) (use of term *blackmail* when characterizing the conduct of a real estate developer, who was deemed to be a public figure, seeking zoning variances was not libel); *Monitor Patriot Co. v. Roy*, 401 U.S. 265, (1971) (held candidates for elective office were public officials or public figures subject to actual malice test); *Rosenbloom v. Metromedia*, 403 U.S. 29 (1971) (held that a distributor of nudist magazines, who was called a "smut peddler," but was later acquitted of obscenity charges, had to prove actual malice).

2. See also *Wolston v. Reader's Digest*, 443 US 157 (1979) (holding alleged KGB spy not a public figure).

3. See William Prosser, "Privacy," 48 *California Law Review* 383 (1960).

4. See, however, *Zacchini v. Scripps-Howard Broadcasting Corporation*, 433 U.S. 562 (1977) (holding five to four that the First Amendment does not immunize news media from a suit brought by a "human cannonball" for appropriation of names and likeness in media coverage of the stunt that arguably diminished its value).

SELECTED BIBLIOGRAPHY

Dennis, Everette, and Noam, Eli. *The Costs of Libel*. New York: Columbia University Press, 1989.

Forer, Louis. *A Chilling Effect: The Mounting Threat of Libel and Invasion of Privacy Actions to the First Amendment*. New York: W.W. Norton, 1987.

Gillmour, Donald. *Power, Publicity and the Abuse of Libel Law*. New York: Oxford University Press, 1992.

Lewis, Anthony. *Make No Law: The Sullivan Case and the First Amendment*. New York: Random House, 1991.

Smolla, Rodney. *Suing the Press: Libel, the Media, & Power*. New York: Oxford University Press, 1986.

―――. *Jerry Falwell v. Larry Flynt: The First Amendment on Trial*. New York: St. Martin's, 1988.

■ THE DEVELOPMENT OF LAW
Other Important Rulings on Libel

CASE	VOTE	HOLDING
Keeton v. Hustler Magazine, Inc., 465 U.S. 770 (1984)	6:3	Libel suits may be brought in any jurisdiction in which a mag-

CASE	VOTE	HOLDING
		azine is sold, allowing forum shopping.
Bose Corporation v. Consumers Union, 466 U.S. 485 (1984)	6:3	Actual malice test applies in libel suit against consumer magazine for review of loudspeakers.
Dun & Bradstreet, Inc. v. Greenmoss Builders, Inc., 472 U.S. 749 (1985)	6:3	Contractor need not prove actual malice in a suit against a credit reporting agency for issuing a false credit report to a bank.
Anderson v. Liberty Lobby 477 U.S. 242 (1986)	6:3	Libel actions should go to trial only if there is clear and convincing evidence of actual malice.
Philadelphia Newspapers, Inc. v. Hepps, 475 U.S. 767 (1986)	5:4	Held that private individuals bringing libel actions have the burden of showing the falsity in reports or stories that touch on

matters of public concern. The majority thus shifted the burden of showing falsity in stories of public concern to the plaintiff. Chief Justice Burger and Justices Stevens, White, and Rehnquist dissented.

Hustler Magazine v. Falwell, 485 U.S. 46 (1988)	9:0	Public figure forbidden from recovering damages for emotional distress due to advertisement parody.
Harte-Hanks v. Connaughton, 491 U.S. 657 (1989)	9:0	Upheld a $200 libel judgment for a lawyer who was a judicial candidate against a newspaper.
Milkovich v. Lorain Journal Co., 497 U.S. 1 (1990)	7:2	Held that there is no exception in the application of libel laws for statements of opinion, al-

though defendants may not be held liable for statements that cannot be proved true or false. The First Amendment, in Chief Justice Rehnquist's words, does not create "a wholesale defamation exemption for anything that might be labeled opinion."

The New York Times Company v. Sullivan

376 U.S. 254, 84 S.CT. 710 (1964)

Justice Brennan sets forth the pertinent facts at the outset of his opinion for the Court. The advertisement that gave rise to the litigation leading to this landmark ruling is reprinted here.

The Court's decision was unanimous, and the opinion was announced by Justice Brennan. Justices Black and Goldberg concurred and were joined by Justice Douglas.

    ☐ *Justice BRENNAN delivered the opinion of the Court.*

We are required in this case to determine for the first time the extent to which the constitutional protections for speech and press limit a State's power to award damages in a libel action brought by a public official against critics of his official conduct.

Respondent L. B. Sullivan is one of the three elected Commissioners of the City of Montgomery, Alabama. . . . He brought this civil libel action against the four individual petitioners, who are Negroes and Alabama clergymen, and against petitioner the New York Times Company, a New York corporation which publishes the *New York Times*, a daily newspaper. . . .

Respondent's complaint alleged that he had been libeled by statements in a full-page advertisement that was carried in the *New York Times* on March 29, 1960. Entitled "Heed Their Rising Voices," the advertisement began by stating that "As the whole world knows by now, thousands of Southern Negro students are engaged in widespread non-violent demonstrations in positive affirmation of the right to live in human dignity as guaranteed by the U.S. Constitution and the Bill of Rights." . . . The text concluded with an appeal for funds for three purposes: support of the student movement, "the struggle for the right-to-vote," and the legal defense of Dr. Martin Luther King, Jr., leader of the movement, against a perjury indictment then pending in Montgomery. . . .

Of the 10 paragraphs of text in the advertisement, the third and a portion of the sixth were the basis of respondent's claim of libel. They read as follows:

Third paragraph:

> "In Montgomery, Alabama, after students sang 'My Country, 'Tis of Thee' on the State Capitol steps, their leaders were expelled from school, and truckloads of police armed with shotguns and tear-gas ringed the Alabama State College Campus. When the entire student body protested to state authorities by refusing to re-register, their dining hall was padlocked in an attempt to starve them into submission."

Sixth paragraph:

> "Again and again the Southern violators have answered Dr. King's peaceful protests with intimidation and violence. They have bombed his home almost killing his wife and child. They have assaulted his person. They have arrested him seven times—for 'speeding,' 'loitering' and similar 'offenses.' And now they have charged him with 'perjury'—a *felony* under which they could imprison him for *ten years*. . . ."

Although neither of these statements mentions respondent by name, he contended that the word "police" in the third paragraph referred to him as the Montgomery Commissioner who supervised the Police Department, so that he was being accused of "ringing" the campus with police. He further claimed that the paragraph would be read as imputing to the police, and hence to him, the padlocking of the dining hall in order to starve the students into submission. As to the sixth paragraph, he contended that since arrests are ordinarily made by the police, the statement "They have arrested [Dr. King] seven times" would be read as referring to him. . . .

It is uncontroverted that some of the statements contained in the two paragraphs were not accurate descriptions of events which occurred in Montgomery. Although Negro students staged a demonstration on the State Capital steps, they sang the National Anthem and not "My Country, 'Tis of Thee." Although nine students were expelled by the State Board of Education, this was not for leading the demonstration at the Capitol, but for demanding service at a lunch counter in the Montgomery County Courthouse on another day. Not the entire student body, but most of it, had protested the expulsion, not by refusing to register, but by boycotting classes on a single day; virtually all the students did register for the ensuing semester. . . . Although the police were deployed near the campus in large numbers on three occasions, they did not at any time "ring" the campus, and they were not called to the campus in connection with the demonstration on the State Capitol steps, as the third paragraph implied. Dr. King had not been arrested seven times, but only four. . . .

Respondent made no effort to prove that he suffered actual pecuniary loss as a result of the alleged libel.★ . . .

The trial judge submitted the case to the jury under instructions that the statements in the advertisement were "libelous per se" and were not privileged, so that petitioners might be held liable if the jury found that they had published the advertisement and that the statements were made "of and concerning" respondent. The jury was instructed that, because the statements were libelous *per se*, "the law . . . implies legal injury from the bare fact of publication itself," "falsity and malice are presumed," "general damages need not be alleged or proved but are presumed," and "punitive damages may be awarded by the jury even though the amount of actual damages is neither found nor shown." [The jury found for the respondent and awarded $500,000 in damages.] . . .

★ Approximately 394 copies of the edition of the *Times* containing the advertisement were circulated in Alabama. Of these, about 35 copies were distributed in Montgomery County. The total circulation of the *Times* for that day was approximately 650,000 copies.

We reverse the judgment. We hold that the rule of law applied by the Alabama courts is constitutionally deficient for failure to provide the safeguards for freedom of speech and of the press that are required by the First and Fourteenth Amendments in a libel action brought by a public official against critics of his official conduct. We further hold that under the proper safeguards the evidence presented in this case is constitutionally insufficient to support the judgment for respondent.

■ I

We may dispose at the outset of two grounds asserted to insulate the judgment of the Alabama courts from constitutional scrutiny. The first is the proposition relied on by the State Supreme Court—that "The Fourteenth Amendment is directed against State action and not private action." That proposition has no application to this case. Although this is a civil lawsuit between private parties, the Alabama courts have applied a state rule of law which petitioners claim to impose invalid restrictions on their constitutional freedoms of speech and press. . . .

The second contention is that the constitutional guarantees of freedom of speech and of the press are inapplicable here, at least so far as the *Times* is concerned, because the allegedly libelous statements were published as part of a paid, "commercial" advertisement. The argument relies on *Valentine v. Chrestensen*, 316 U.S. 52 [(1942)], where the Court held that a city ordinance forbidding street distribution of commercial and business advertising matter did not abridge the First Amendment freedoms, even as applied to a handbill having a commercial message on one side but a protest against certain official action on the other. The reliance is wholly misplaced. . . .

The publication here was not a "commercial" advertisement in the sense in which the word was used in *Chrestensen*. It communicated information, expressed opinion, recited grievances, protested claimed abuses, and sought financial support on behalf of a movement whose existence and objectives are matters of the highest public interest and concern. . . . That the *Times* was paid for publishing the advertisement is as immaterial in this connection as is the fact that newspapers and books are sold. Any other conclusion would discourage newspapers from carrying "editorial advertisements" of this type, and so might shut off an important outlet for the promulgation of information and ideas by persons who do not themselves have access to publishing facilities—who wish to exercise their freedom of speech even though they are not members of the press. . . .

■ II

[W]e consider this case against the background of a profound national commitment to the principle that debate on public issues should be uninhibited, robust, and wide-open, and that it may well include vehement, caustic, and sometimes unpleasantly sharp attacks on government and public officials. The present advertisement, as an expression of grievance and protest on one of the major public issues of our time, would seem clearly to qualify for the constitutional protection. The question is whether it forfeits that protection by the falsity of some of its factual statements and by its alleged defamation of respondent.

Authoritative interpretations of the First Amendment guarantees have consistently refused to recognize an exception for any test of truth—whether administered by judges, juries, or administrative officials—and especially one that puts the burden of proving truth on the speaker. The constitutional protection does not turn upon "the truth, popularity, or social utility of the ideas and beliefs which are offered." . . .

Injury to official reputation error affords no more warrant for repressing speech that would otherwise be free than does factual error. Where judicial officers are involved, this Court has held that concern for the dignity and reputation of the courts does not justify the punishment as criminal contempt of criticism of the judge or his decision. This is true even though the utterance contains "half-truths" and "misinformation." Such repression can be justified, if at all, only by a clear and present danger of the obstruction of justice. . . .

If neither factual error nor defamatory content suffices to remove the constitutional shield from criticism of official conduct, the combination of the two elements is no less inadequate. This is the lesson to be drawn from the great controversy over the Sedition Act of 1798, 1 Stat. 596, which first crystallized a national awareness of the central meaning of the First Amendment. . . .

Although the Sedition Act was never tested in this Court, the attack upon its validity has carried the day in the court of history. Fines levied in its prosecution were repaid by Act of Congress on the ground that it was unconstitutional. Jefferson, as President, pardoned those who had been convicted and sentenced under the Act and remitted their fines. . . .

There is no force in respondent's argument that the constitutional limitations implicit in the history of the Sedition Act apply only to Congress and not to the States. It is true that the First Amendment was originally addressed only to action by the Federal Government. . . . But this distinction was eliminated with the adoption of the Fourteenth Amendment and the application to the States of the First Amendment's restrictions.

What a State may not constitutionally bring about by means of a criminal statute is likewise beyond the reach of its civil law of libel. The fear of damage awards under a rule such as that invoked by the Alabama courts here may be markedly more inhibiting than the fear of prosecution under a criminal statute. Alabama, for example, has a criminal libel law which subjects to prosecution "any person who speaks, writes, or prints of and concerning another any accusation falsely and maliciously importing the commission by such person of a felony, or any other indictable offense involving moral turpitude," and which allows as punishment upon conviction a fine not exceeding $500 and a prison sentence of six months. Presumably a person charged with violation of this statute enjoys ordinary criminal-law safeguards such as the requirements of an indictment and of proof beyond a reasonable doubt. These safeguards are not available to the defendant in a civil action. The judgment awarded in this case—without the need for any proof of actual pecuniary loss—was one thousand times greater than the maximum fine provided by the Alabama criminal statute, and one hundred times greater than that provided by the Sedition Act. . . . Whether or not a newspaper can survive a succession of such judgments, the pall of fear and timidity imposed upon those who would give voice to public criticism is an atmosphere in which the First Amendment freedoms cannot survive. . . .

The state rule of law is not saved by its allowance of the defense of truth. . . . A rule compelling the critic of official conduct to guarantee the truth of all his factual assertions—and to do so on pain of libel judgments virtually unlimited in amount—leads to a comparable "self-censorship." Allowance of the defense of truth, with the burden of proving it on the defendant, does not mean that only false speech will be deterred. . . . Under such a rule, would-be critics of official conduct may be deterred from voicing their criticism, even though it is believed to be true and even though it is in fact true, because of doubt whether it can be proved in court or fear of the expense of having to do so. They tend to make only statements which "steer far wider of the unlawful zone." The rule thus dampens the vigor and limits the variety of public debate. It is inconsistent with the First and Fourteenth Amendments.

The constitutional guarantees require, we think, a federal rule that prohibits a public official from recovering damages for a defamatory falsehood relating to his official conduct unless he proves that the statement was made with "actual malice"—that is, with knowledge that it was false or with reckless disregard of whether it was false or not. . . .

Such a privilege for criticism of official conduct is appropriately analogous to the protection accorded a public official when *he* is sued for libel by a private citizen. In *Barr v. Matteo*, 360 U.S. 564 [(1959)], this Court held the utterance of a federal official to be absolutely privileged if made "within the outer perimeter" of his duties. The States accord the same immunity to statements of their highest officers, although some differentiate their lesser officials and qualify the privilege they enjoy. But all hold that all officials are protected unless actual malice can be proved. The reason for the official privilege is said to be that the threat of damage suits would otherwise "inhibit the fearless, vigorous, and effective administration of policies of government" and "dampen the ardor of all but the most resolute, or the most irresponsible, in the unflinching discharge of their duties." Analogous considerations support the privilege for the citizen-critic of government. It is as much his duty to criticize as it is the official's duty to administer. As Madison said, "the censorial power is in the people over the Government, and not in the Government over the people." It would give public servants an unjustified preference over the public they serve, if critics of official conduct did not have a fair equivalent of the immunity granted to the officials themselves.

We conclude that such a privilege is required by the First and Fourteenth Amendments.

■ III

We hold today that the Constitution delimits a State's power to award damages for libel in actions brought by public officials against critics of their official conduct. Since this is such an action, the rule requiring proof of actual malice is applicable. . . .

[T]he proof presented to show actual malice lacks the convincing clarity which the constitutional standard demands, and hence that it would not constitutionally sustain the judgment for respondent under the proper rule of law. . . .

We also think the evidence was constitutionally defective in another re-spect: it was incapable of supporting the jury's finding that the allegedly li-belous statements were made "of and concerning" respondent. . . . There was no reference to respondent in the advertisement, either by name or official position. A number of the allegedly libelous statements—the charges that the dining hall was padlocked and that Dr. King's home was bombed, his person assaulted, and a perjury prosecution instituted against him—did not even concern the police; despite the ingenuity of the arguments which would at-tach this significance to the word "They," it is plain that these statements could not reasonably be read as accusing respondent of personal involvement in the acts in question. . . .

The judgment of the Supreme Court of Alabama is reversed and the case is remanded to that court for further proceedings not inconsistent with this opinion.

Reversed and remanded.

☐ *Justice BLACK, with whom Justice DOUGLAS joins, concurring.*

I base my vote to reverse on the belief that the First and Fourteenth Amendments not merely "delimit" a State's power to award damages to "public officials against critics of their official conduct" but completely pro-hibit a State from exercising such a power. The Court goes on to hold that a State can subject such critics to damages if "actual malice" can be proved against them. "Malice," even as defined by the Court, is an elusive, abstract concept, hard to prove and hard to disprove. The requirement that malice be proved provides at best an evanescent protection for the right critically to discuss public affairs and certainly does not measure up to the sturdy safe-guard embodied in the First Amendment. Unlike the Court, therefore, I vote to reverse exclusively on the ground that the *Times* and the individual defendants had an absolute, unconditional constitutional right to publish in the *Times* advertisement their criticisms of the Montgomery agencies and officials.

☐ *Justice GOLDBERG, with whom Justice DOUGLAS joins, concurring.*

In my view, the First and Fourteenth Amendments to the Constitution afford to the citizen and to the press an absolute, unconditional privilege to criticize official conduct despite the harm which may flow from excesses and abuses. The prized American right "to speak one's mind" about public offi-cials and affairs needs "breathing space to survive." The right should not de-pend upon a probing by the jury of the motivation of the citizen or press. The theory of our Constitution is that every citizen may speak his mind and every newspaper express its view on matters of public concern and may not be barred from speaking or publishing because those in control of govern-ment think that what is said or written is unwise, unfair, false, or malicious. In a democratic society, one who assumes to act for the citizens in an execu-tive, legislative, or judicial capacity must expect that his official acts will be commented upon and criticized. Such criticism cannot, in my opinion, be muzzled or deterred by the courts at the instance of public officials under the label of libel. . . .

Gertz v. Robert Welch, Inc.

418 U.S. 323, 94 S.CT. 2997 (1974)

Elmer Gertz was a Chicago lawyer hired to sue a policeman by a family whose son had been killed by the officer. The John Birch Society in its magazine *American Opinion* charged that Gertz was a "Leninist" and "Communist-fronter" and that the lawsuit against the policeman was part of a nationwide communist conspiracy to discredit law enforcement. Gertz sued Robert Welch, publisher of the magazine, for libel in federal district court. That court held for the publisher on applying the *New York Times v. Sullivan* actual malice rule. Gertz appealed to the United States Court of Appeals for the Seventh Circuit, which affirmed the lower court's ruling, and finally to the Supreme Court.

The Court's decision was five to four, and the majority's opinion was announced by Justice Powell. Justice Blackmun concurred. Dissents were by Chief Justice Burger and Justices Douglas, Brennan, and White.

☐ *Justice POWELL delivered the opinion of the Court.*

We begin with the common ground. Under the First Amendment there is no such thing as a false idea. However pernicious an opinion may seem, we depend for its correction not on the conscience of judges and juries but on the competition of other ideas. But there is no constitutional value in false statements of fact. Neither the intentional lie nor the careless error materially advances society's interest in "uninhibited, robust, and wide-open" debate on public issues. *New York Times Co. v. Sullivan*, [376 U.S. 254 (1964)]. They belong to that category of utterances which "are no essential part of any exposition of ideas, and are of such slight social value as a step to truth that any benefit that may be derived from them is clearly outweighed by the social interest in order and morality." *Chaplinsky v. New Hampshire* [315 U.S. 568] (1942).

Although the erroneous statement of fact is not worthy of constitutional protection, it is nevertheless inevitable in free debate. . . . And punishment of error runs the risk of inducing a cautious and restrictive exercise of the constitutionally guaranteed freedoms of speech and press. Our decisions recognize that a rule of strict liability that compels a publisher or broadcaster to guarantee the accuracy of his factual assertions may lead to intolerable self-censorship. . . . The First Amendment requires that we protect some falsehood in order to protect speech that matters.

The need to avoid self-censorship by the news media is, however, not the only societal value at issue. If it were, this Court would have embraced long ago the view that publishers and broadcasters enjoy an unconditional and indefeasible immunity from liability for defamation.

The legitimate state interest underlying the law of libel is the compensation of individuals for the harm inflicted on them by defamatory false-hood. We would not lightly require the State to abandon this purpose, for, as Justice STEWART has reminded us, the individual's right to the protection of his own good name

> "reflects no more than our basic concept of the essential dignity and worth of every human being—a concept at the root of any decent system of ordered liberty. The protection of private personality, like the protection of life itself, is left primarily to the individual States under the Ninth and Tenth Amendments. But this does not mean that the right is entitled to any less recognition by this Court as a basic of our constitutional system." *Rosenblatt v. Baer*, 383 U.S. 75 (1966) (concurring opinion). . . .

The *New York Times* standard defines the level of constitutional protection appropriate to the context of defamation of a public person. . . . For the reasons stated below, we conclude that the state interest in compensating-injury to the reputation of private individuals requires that a different rule should obtain with respect to them. . . .

[W]e have no difficulty in distinguishing among defamation plaintiffs. The first remedy of any victim of defamation is self-help—using available opportunities to contradict the lie or correct the error and thereby to minimize its adverse impact on reputation. Public officials and public figures usually enjoy significantly greater access to the channels of effective communication and hence have a more realistic opportunity to counteract false statements then private individuals normally enjoy. Private individuals are therefore more vulnerable to injury, and the state interest in protecting them is correspondingly greater.

More important than the likelihood that private individuals will lack effective opportunities for rebuttal, there is a compelling normative consideration underlying the distinction between public and private defamation plaintiffs. An individual who decides to seek governmental office must accept certain necessary consequences of that involvement in public affairs. He runs the risk of closer public scrutiny than might otherwise be the case. . . .

Those classed as public figures stand in a similar position. Hypothetically, it may be possible for someone to become a public figure through no purposeful action of his own, but the instances of truly involuntary public figures must be exceedingly rare. For the most part those who attain this status have assumed roles of especial prominence in the affairs of society. Some occupy positions of such persuasive power and influence that they are deemed public figures for all purposes. More commonly, those classed as public figures have thrust themselves to the forefront of particular public controversies in order to influence the resolution of the issues involved. In either event, they invite attention and comment.

Even if the foregoing generalities do not obtain in every instance, the communications media are entitled to act on the assumption that public officials and public figures have voluntarily exposed themselves to increased risk of injury from defamatory falsehood concerning them. No such assumption is justified with respect to a private individual. He has not accepted public office or assumed an "influential role in ordering society." He has relinquished no part of his interest in the protection of his own good name, and consequently he has a more compelling call on the courts for redress of injury inflicted by defamatory falsehood. Thus, private individuals are not only more vulnerable to injury than public officials and public figures: they are also more deserving of recovery.

For these reasons we conclude that the States should retain substantial latitude in their efforts to enforce a legal remedy for defamatory falsehood injurious to the reputation of a private individual. The extension of the *New York Times* test . . . would abridge this legitimate state interest to a degree that we find unacceptable. And it would occasion the additional difficulty of forcing state and federal judges to decide on an *ad hoc* basis which publications address issues of "general or public interest" and which do not—to determine, in the words of Justice MARSHALL, "what information is relevant to self-government," *Rosenbloom v. Metromedia, Inc.*, [403 U.S. 29 (1971)]. We doubt the wisdom of committing this task to the conscience of judges. . . .

We hold that, so long as they do not impose liability without fault, the States may define for themselves the appropriate standard of liability for a publisher or broadcaster of defamatory falsehood injurious to a private individual. This approach provides a more equitable boundary between the competing concerns involved here. It recognizes the strength of the legitimate state interest in compensating private individuals for wrongful injury to reputation, yet shields the press and broadcast media from the rigors of strict liability for defamation. At least this conclusion obtains where, as here, the substance of the defamatory statement "makes substantial danger to reputation apparent." This phrase places in perspective the conclusion we announce today. . . .

Our accommodation of the competing values at stake in defamation suits by private individuals allows the States to impose liability on the publisher or broadcaster of defamatory falsehood on a less demanding showing than that required by *New York Times*. This conclusion is not based on a belief that the considerations which prompted the adoption of the *New York Times* privilege for defamation of public officials and its extension to public figures are wholly inapplicable to the context of private individuals. Rather, we endorse this approach in recognition of the strong and legitimate state interest in compensating private individuals for injury to reputation. But this countervailing state interest extends no further than compensation for actual injury. For the reasons stated below, we hold that the States may not permit recovery of presumed or punitive damages, at least when liability is not based on a showing of knowledge of falsity or reckless disregard for the truth.

The common law of defamation is an oddity of tort law, for it allows recovery of purportedly compensatory damages without evidence of actual loss. Under the traditional rules pertaining to actions for libel, the existence of injury is presumed from the fact of publication. Juries may award substantial sums as compensation for supposed damage to reputation without any proof that such harm actually occurred. The largely uncontrolled discretion of juries to award damages where there is no loss unnecessarily compounds the potential of any system of liability for defamatory falsehood to inhibit the vigorous exercise of First Amendment freedoms. Additionally, the doctrine of presumed damages invites juries to punish unpopular opinion rather than to compensate individuals for injury sustained by the publication of a false fact. More to the point, the States have no substantial interest in securing for plaintiffs such as this petitioner gratuitous awards of money damages far in excess of any actual injury.

We would not, of course, invalidate state law simply because we doubt its wisdom, but here we are attempting to reconcile state law with a competing interest grounded in the constitutional command of the First Amendment. It is therefore appropriate to require that state remedies for defamatory falsehood reach no farther than is necessary to protect the legitimate interest involved. It is necessary to restrict defamation plaintiffs who do not prove knowledge of falsity or reckless disregard for the truth to compensation for actual injury. We need not define "actual injury," as trial courts have wide experience in framing appropriate jury instructions in tort actions. Suffice it to say that actual injury is not limited to out-of-pocket loss. Indeed, the more customary types of actual harm inflicted by defamatory falsehood include impairment of reputation and standing in the community, personal humiliation, and mental anguish and suffering. Of course, juries must be limited by appropriate instructions, and all awards must be supported by competent evidence concerning the injury, although there need be no evidence which assigns an actual dollar value to the injury.

We also find no justification for allowing awards of punitive damages against publishers and broadcasters held liable under state-defined standards of liability for defamation. In most jurisdictions jury discretion over the amounts awarded is limited only by the gentle rule that they not be excessive. Consequently, juries assess punitive damages in wholly unpredictable amounts bearing no necessary relation to the actual harm caused. And they remain free to use their discretion selectively to punish expressions of unpopular views. Like the doctrine of presumed damages, jury discretion to award punitive damages unnecessarily exacerbates the danger of media self-censorship, but, unlike the former rule, punitive damages are wholly irrelevant to the state interest that justifies a negligence standard for private defamation actions. They are not compensation for injury. Instead, they are private fines levied by civil juries to punish reprehensible conduct and to deter its future occurrence. In short, the private defamation plaintiff who establishes liability under a less demanding standard than that stated by *New York Times* may recover only such damages as are sufficient to compensate him for actual injury.

Notwithstanding our refusal to extend the *New York Times* privilege to defamation of private individuals, respondent contends that we should affirm the judgment below on the ground that petitioner is either a public official or a public figure. There is little basis for the former assertion. Several years prior to the present incident, petitioner had served briefly on housing committees appointed by the mayor of Chicago, but at the time of publication he had never held any remunerative governmental position. Respondent admits this but argues that petitioner's appearance at the coroner's inquest rendered him a "de facto public official." Our cases recognized no such concept. Respondent's suggestion would sweep all lawyers under the *New York Times* rule as officers of the court and distort the plain meaning of the "public official" category beyond all recognition. We decline to follow it. . . .

Petitioner has long been active in community and professional affairs.

He has served as an officer of local civic groups and of various professional organizations, and he has published several books and articles on legal subjects. Although petitioner was consequently well known in some circles, he had achieved no general fame or notoriety in the community. None of the prospective jurors called at the trial had ever heard of petitioner prior to this litigation, and respondent offered no proof that this response was atypical of the local population. We would not lightly assume that a citizen's participation in community and professional affairs rendered him a public figure for all purposes. Absent clear evidence of general fame or notoriety in the community and pervasive involvement in the affairs of society, an individual should not be deemed a public personality for all aspects of his life. It is preferable to reduce the public-figure question to a more meaningful context by looking to the nature and extent of an individual's participation in the particular controversy giving rise to the defamation.

In this context it is plain that petitioner was not a public figure. He played a minimal role at the coroner's inquest, and his participation related solely to his representation of a private client. He took no part in the criminal prosecution of Officer Nuccio. Moreover, he never discussed either the criminal or civil litigation with the press and was never quoted as having done so. He plainly did not thrust himself into the vortex of this public issue, nor did he engage the public's attention in an attempt to influence its outcome. We are persuaded that the trial court did not err in refusing to characterize petitioner as a public figure for the purpose of this litigation.

We therefore conclude that the *New York Times* standard is inapplicable to this case and that the trial court erred in entering judgment for respondent. Because the jury was allowed to impose liability without fault and was permitted to presume damages without proof of injury, a new trial is necessary. We reverse and remand for further proceedings in accord with this opinion.

It is so ordered.

◻ *Justice BLACKMUN, concurring.*

The Court today refuses to apply *New York Times* to the private individual, as contrasted with the public official and the public figure. . . . I sense some illogic in this. . . . [Still] I am willing to join, and do join, the Court's opinion and its judgment for two reasons:

1. By removing the specters of presumed and punitive damages in the absence of *New York Times* malice, the Court eliminates significant and powerful motives for self-censorship that otherwise are present in the traditional libel action. . . . By so doing, the Court leaves what should prove to be sufficient and adequate breathing space for a vigorous press. What the Court has done, I believe, will have little, if any, practical effect on the functioning of responsible journalism.

2. The Court was sadly fractionated in *Rosenbloom* [*v. Metromedia, Inc.,* 403 U.S. 29 (1971)]. A result of that kind inevitably leads to uncertainty. I feel that it is of profound importance for the Court to come to rest in the defamation area and to have a clearly defined majority position that eliminates the unsureness engendered by *Rosenbloom's* diversity. If my vote were not needed to create a majority, I would adhere to my prior view. A definitive ruling, however, is paramount.

☐ *Chief Justice BURGER, dissenting.*

I am frank to say I do not know the parameters of a "negligence" doctrine as applied to the news media. Conceivably this new doctrine could inhibit some editors, as the dissents of Justice DOUGLAS and Justice BRENNAN suggest. But I would prefer to allow this area of law to continue to evolve as it has up to now with respect to private citizens rather than embark on a new doctrinal theory which has no jurisprudential ancestry.

☐ *Justice DOUGLAS, dissenting.*

The Court describes this case as a return to the struggle of "defin[ing] the proper accommodation between the law of defamation and the freedoms of speech and press protected by the First Amendment." It is indeed a struggle, once described by Justice BLACK as "the same quagmire" in which the Court "is now helplessly struggling in the field of obscenity." I would suggest that the struggle is a quite hopeless one, for, in light of the command of the First Amendment, no "accommodation" of its freedoms can be "proper" except those made by the Framers themselves.

☐ *Justice BRENNAN, dissenting.*

I cannot agree . . . that free and robust debate—so essential to the proper functioning of our system of government—is permitted adequate "breathing space," when, as the Court holds, the States may impose all but strict liability for defamation if the defamed party is a private person and "the substance of the defamatory statement 'makes substantial danger to reputation apparent.' " I adhere to my view expressed in *Rosenbloom v. Metromedia, Inc.,* supra, that we strike the proper accommodation between avoidance of media self-censorship and protection of individual reputations only when we require States to apply the *New York Times Co. v. Sullivan* knowing-or-reckless-falsity standard in civil libel actions concerning media reports of the involvement of private individuals in events of public or general interest. . . .

☐ *Justice WHITE, dissenting.*

For some 200 years—from the very founding of the Nation—the law of defamation and right of the ordinary citizen to recover for false publication injurious to his reputation have been almost exclusively the business of state courts and legislatures. Under typical state defamation law, the defamed private citizen had to prove only a false publication that would subject him to hatred, contempt, or ridicule. Given such publication, general damage to reputation was presumed, while punitive damages required proof of additional facts. The law governing the defamation of private citizens remained untouched by the First Amendment because until relatively recently, the consistent view of the Court was that libelous words constitute a class of speech wholly unprotected by the First Amendment, subject only to limited exceptions carved out since 1964.

But now, using that Amendment as the chosen instrument, the Court, in a few printed pages, has federalized major aspects of libel law by declaring unconstitutional in important respects the prevailing defamation law in all or most of the 50 States. . . .

These are radical changes in the law and severe invasions of the prerogatives of the States. They should at least be shown to be required by the First Amendment or necessitated by our present circumstances. Neither has been demonstrated. . . .

Scant, if any, evidence exists that the First Amendment was intended to abolish the common law of libel, at least to the extent of depriving ordinary citizens of meaningful redress against their defamers. . . .

[T]he law has heretofore put the risk of falsehood on the publisher where the victim is a private citizen and no grounds of special privilege are invoked. The Court would now shift this risk to the victim, even though he has done nothing to invite the calumny, is wholly innocent of fault, and is helpless to avoid his injury. I doubt that jurisprudential resistance to liability without fault is sufficient ground for employing the First Amendment to revolutionize the law of libel, and in my view, that body of legal rules poses no realistic threat to the press and its service to the public. The press today is vigorous and robust. To me, it is quite incredible to suggest that threats of libel suits from private citizens are causing the press to refrain from publishing the truth. I know of no hard facts to support that proposition, and the Court furnishes none. . . .

Masson v. The New Yorker Magazine
501 U.S. 496, 111 S.CT. 2419 (1991)

Mr. Jeffrey Masson, a psychologist, was hired in 1980 as the projects director of the Sigmund Freud Archives. Subsequently, his research led him to challenge Freud's reasons for abandoning his "seduction theory," a controversial theory about adult emotional disorders rooted in childhood sexual abuse. His discussion of his research resulted in his dismissal from the archives in 1981. A year later Janet Malcolm interviewed Mr. Masson about the controversy, compiling more than forty hours of taped interviews. Her two-part article was published in 1983 in *The New Yorker* and republished as a book.

Mr. Masson sued Ms. Malcolm, *The New Yorker*, and the publisher for defamation. He charged that certain direct quotations were altered or fabricated, and all seriously damaged his reputation. Ms. Malcolm, for instance, quoted him as saying that if he had remained at the archives it "would have been a center of scholarship, but it would also have been a place of sex, women, and fun." That quote, however, did not appear in transcripts of the interviews. Nonetheless, a federal district court found for Ms. Malcolm, and a three-judge panel of the U.S. Court of Appeals for the Ninth Circuit by a two-to-one vote affirmed that decision. The majority held that actual malice could not be inferred if the word changes did not "alter the substantive content" or were "rational interpretations" of Mr. Masson's unambiguous statements. By contrast, dissenting Judge Alex Kozinski argued, "The right to deliberately alter quotations is not, in my view, a concomitant of a free press. . . . As I see it, when a writer uses quotation marks in reporting what someone else has said, she is representing that those are the speaker's own words or something very close to them." Mr. Masson appealed the decision of the Ninth Circuit to the Supreme Court, which granted review.

The Court's decision was seven to two. The majority's opinion was announced by Justice Kennedy. A separate opinion, in part dissenting and in part concurring, was delivered by Justice White and joined by Justice Scalia.

□ *Justice KENNEDY delivered the opinion of the Court.*

The First Amendment limits [states'] libel law in various respects. When, as here, the plaintiff is a public figure, he cannot recover unless he proves by clear and convincing evidence that the defendant published the defamatory statement with actual malice, i.e., with "knowledge that it was false or with reckless disregard of whether it was false or not." *New York Times Co. v. Sullivan*, 376 U.S. 254 (1964). Mere negligence does not suffice. . . .

Actual malice under the *New York Times* standard should not be confused with the concept of malice as an evil intent or a motive arising from spite or ill will. We have used the term actual malice as a shorthand to describe the First Amendment protections for speech injurious to reputation and we continue to do so here. But the term can confuse as well as enlighten. In this respect, the phrase may be an unfortunate one. In place of the term actual malice, it is better practice that jury instructions refer to publication of a statement with knowledge of falsity or reckless disregard as to truth of falsity. This definitional principle must be remembered in the case before us. . . .

A fabricated quotation may injure reputation in at least two senses, either giving rise to a conceivable claim of defamation. First, the quotation might injure because it attributes an untrue factual assertion to the speaker. An example would be a fabricated quotation of a public official admitting he had been convicted of a serious crime when in fact he had not.

Second, regardless of the truth or falsity of the factual matters asserted within the quoted statement, the attribution may result in injury to reputation because the manner of expression or even the fact that the statement was made indicates a negative personal trait or an attitude the speaker does not hold. . . .

The work at issue here, however, as with much journalistic writing, provides the reader no clue that the quotations are being used as a rhetorical device or to paraphrase the speaker's actual statements. To the contrary, the work purports to be nonfiction, the result of numerous interviews. . . .

The constitutional question we must consider here is whether, in the framework of a summary judgment motion, the evidence suffices to show that respondents acted with the requisite knowledge of falsity or reckless disregard as to truth or falsity. This inquiry in turn requires us to consider the concept of falsity; for we cannot discuss the standards for knowledge or reckless disregard without some understanding of the acts required for liability. We must consider whether the requisite falsity inheres in the attribution of words to the petitioner which he did not speak.

In some sense, any alteration of a verbatim quotation is false. But writers and reporters by necessity alter what people say, at the very least to eliminate grammatical and syntactical infelicities. If every alteration constituted the falsity required to prove actual malice, the practice of journalism, which the First Amendment standard is designed to protect, would require a radical change, one inconsistent with our precedents and First Amendment principles. Petitioner concedes this absolute definition of falsity in the quotation context is too stringent, and acknowledges that "minor changes to correct for grammar or syntax" do not amount to falsity for purposes of proving actual malice. We agree, and must determine what, in addition to this technical falsity, proves falsity for purposes of the actual malice inquiry. . . .

We reject the idea that any alteration beyond correction of grammar or syntax by itself proves falsity in the sense relevant to determining actual malice under the First Amendment. An interviewer who writes from notes often will engage in the task of attempting a reconstruction of the speaker's statement. That author would, we may assume, act with knowledge that at times she has attributed to her subject words other than those actually used. Under petitioner's proposed standard, an author in this situation would lack First Amendment protection if she reported as quotations the substance of a subject's derogatory statements about himself. . . .

We conclude that a deliberate alteration of the words uttered by a plaintiff does not equate with knowledge of falsity for purposes of *New York Times Co. v. Sullivan*, and *Gertz v. Robert Welch, Inc.*, unless the alteration results in a material change in the meaning conveyed by the statement. The use of quotations to attribute words not in fact spoken bears in a most important way on that inquiry, but it is not dispositive in every case.

Deliberate or reckless falsification that comprises actual malice turns upon words and punctuation only because words and punctuation express meaning. Meaning is the life of language. And, for the reasons we have given, quotations may be a devastating instrument for conveying false meaning. In the case under consideration, readers of *In the Freud Archives* may have found Malcolm's portrait of petitioner especially damning because so much of it appeared to be a self-portrait, told by petitioner in his own words. And if the alterations of petitioner's words gave a different meaning to the statements, bearing upon their defamatory character, then the device of quotations might well be critical in finding the word actionable. . . .

We apply these principles to the case before us. . . . The record contains substantial . . . evidence which, in a light most favorable to petitioner, would support a jury determination under a clear and convincing standard that Malcolm deliberately or recklessly altered the quotations.

First, many of the challenged passages resemble quotations that appear on the tapes, except for the addition or alteration of certain phrases, giving rise to a reasonable inference that the statements have been altered. Second, Malcolm had the tapes in her possession and was not working under a tight deadline. Unlike a case involving hot news, Malcolm cannot complain that she lacked the practical ability to compare the tapes with her work in progress. Third, Malcolm represented to the editor-in-chief of *The New Yorker* that all the quotations were from the tape recordings. Fourth, Malcolm's explanations of the time and place of unrecorded conversations during which petitioner allegedly made some of the quoted statements have not been consistent in all respects. Fifth, petitioner suggests that the progression from typewritten notes, to manuscript, then to galleys provides further evidence of intentional alteration.

Cox Broadcasting Corporation v. Cohn
420 U.S. 469, 95 S.Ct. 1029 (1975)

In August 1971, Martin Cohn's seventeen-year-old daughter was raped; she died as result of the incident. Subsequently, a television report on the incident and the arrest of six youths charged with her rape and murder identified Cohn's daughter as the victim, on the basis of police reports and other public records. Cohn thereupon sued the owner of the television station, Cox Broadcasting Corporation, under a Georgia privacy statute making it a misdemeanor to broadcast the name or identity of a rape victim. The trial judge rejected arguments of Cox Broadcasting Corporation that its broadcast was protected under the First and Fourteenth Amendments. On appeal, the state supreme court upheld Georgia's statute as a legitimate limitation on the First Amendment. Cox Broadcasting Corporation subsequently appealed that ruling to the Supreme Court.

The Court's decision was eight to one, and the majority's opinion was announced by Justice White. Concurrence was by Chief Justice Burger and Justices Powell and Douglas. Justice Rehnquist dissented.

☐ *Justice WHITE delivered the opinion of the Court.*

The issue before us in this case is whether, consistently with the First and Fourteenth Amendments, a State may extend a cause of action for damages for invasion of privacy caused by the publication of the name of a deceased rape victim which was publicly revealed in connection with the prosecution of the crime. . . .

Georgia stoutly defends both [Section] 26-9901 and the State's common-law privacy action challenged here. Its claims are not without force, for powerful arguments can be made, and have been made, that however it may be ultimately defined, there *is* a zone of privacy surrounding every individual, a zone within which the State may protect him from intrusion by the press, with all its attendant publicity. Indeed, the central thesis of the root article by Warren and Brandeis, The Right to Privacy, 4 *Harv.L.Rev.*

193, 196 (1890), was that the press was overstepping its prerogatives by publishing essentially private information and that there should be a remedy for the alleged abuses.

More compellingly, the century has experienced a strong tide running in favor of the so-called right of privacy. In 1967, we noted that "[i]t has been said that a 'right of privacy' has been recognized at common law in 30 States plus the District of Columbia and by statute in four States." *Time, Inc. v. Hill*, 385 U.S. 374 [(1967)]. . . .

In this sphere of collision between claims of privacy and those of the free press, the interests on both sides are plainly rooted in the traditions and significant concerns of our society. Rather than address the broader question whether truthful publications may ever be subjected to civil or criminal liability consistently with the First and Fourteenth Amendments, or to put it another way, whether the State may ever define and protect an area of privacy free from unwanted publicity in the press, it is appropriate to focus on the narrower interface between press and privacy that this case presents, namely, whether the State may impose sanctions on the accurate publication of the name of a rape victim obtained from public records—more specifically, from judicial records which are maintained in connection with a public prosecution and which themselves are open to public inspection. We are convinced that the State may not do so.

In the first place, in a society in which each individual has but limited time and resources with which to observe at first hand the operations of his government, he relies necessarily upon the press to bring to him in convenient form the facts of those operations. Great responsibility is accordingly placed upon the news media to report fully and accurately the proceedings of government, and official records and documents open to the public are the basic data of governmental operations. Without the information provided by the press most of us and many of our representatives would be unable to vote intelligently or to register opinions on the administration of government generally. With respect to judicial proceedings in particular, the function of the press serves to guarantee the fairness of trials and to bring to bear the beneficial effects of public scrutiny upon the administration of justice. . . .

[E]ven the prevailing law of invasion of privacy generally recognizes that the interests in privacy fade when the information involved already appears on the public record. The conclusion is compelling when viewed in terms of the First and Fourteenth Amendments and in light of the public interest in a vigorous press. The Georgia cause of action for invasion of privacy through public disclosure of the name of a rape victim imposes sanctions on pure expression—the content of a publication—and not conduct or a combination of speech and nonspeech elements that might otherwise be open to regulation or prohibition. The publication of truthful information available on the public record contains none of the indicia of those limited categories of expression, such as "fighting" words, which "are no essential part of any exposition of ideas, and are of such slight social value as a step to truth that any benefit that may be derived from them is clearly outweighed by the social interest in order and morality." *Chaplinsky v. New Hampshire*, 315 U.S. 568 (1942).

By placing the information in the public domain on official court records, the State must be presumed to have concluded that the public interest was thereby being served. Public records by their very nature are of interest to those concerned with the administration of government, and a public benefit is performed by the reporting of the true contents of the records by the media. The freedom of the press to publish that information appears to us to be of critical importance to our type of government in which the citizenry is the final judge of the proper conduct of public business. In preserving that form of government the First and Fourteenth Amendments command nothing less than that the States may not impose sanctions on the publication of truthful information contained in official court records open to public inspection.

We are reluctant to embark on a course that would make public records generally available to the media but forbid their publication if offensive to the sensibilities of the supposed reasonable man. Such a rule would make it very difficult for the media to inform citizens about the public business and yet stay within the law. The rule would invite timidity and self-censorship and very likely lead to the suppression of many items that would otherwise be published and that should be made available to the public. At the very least, the First and Fourteenth Amendments will not allow exposing the press to liability for truthfully publishing information released to the public in official court records. If there are privacy interests to be protected in judicial proceedings, the States must respond by means which avoid public documentation or other exposure of private information. Their political institutions must weigh the interests in privacy with the interests of the public to know and of the press to publish. Once true information is disclosed in public court documents open to public inspection, the press cannot be sanctioned for publishing it. In this instance as in others reliance must rest upon the judgment of those who decide what to publish or broadcast. . . .

Reversed.

D | *Commercial Speech*

In contrast with the toughening of obscenity standards, the Court has moved in the direction of extending greater protection to commercial speech, although not without sharp criticism. Commercial speech involves the advertising of goods and services, such as the costs of toothpaste or attorney's fees, as well as that of corporations and businesses that aim at influencing public policy.

That commercial speech should be "less protected" than other kinds of speech was first suggested in *Valentine v. Chrestensen*, 316 U.S. 52 (1942). There the Court upheld a New York ordinance prohibiting the distribution of "commercial and business advertising matter." Lewis Chrestensen was convicted under the ordinance for distributing handbills that on one side advertised his submarine and, on the other, printed the First Amendment as a protest against the ordinance. The justices unanimously held there was no "restraint on the government as respects purely commercial advertising." It remained unclear, though, whether commercial speech was unprotected per se (like obscenity) or simply less protected, and why it fell outside of First Amendment protection—was it the commercial motive, the content, or the method of distribution?

The problems with *Valentine* became more apparent in later cases. When confronted with the issue of whether the ad, "Heed Their Rising Voices," in *New York Times v. Sullivan* (1964) (see Section C in this chapter) fell under the commercial speech doctrine, Justice Brennan ducked the issue, observing that (unlike Chrestensen's handbill), *The New York Times* ad "communicated information, expressed opinion, recited grievances, protested claimed abuses, and sought financial support on behalf of a movement whose existence and objectives are matters of the highest public interest and concern. . . . That the *Times* was paid for publishing the advertisement is as immaterial in this connection as is the fact that newspapers and books are sold." In *New York Times v. Sullivan*, Brennan thus implied that the motive of a publisher might be used to define the scope of the First Amendment. But in *Pittsburgh Press v. Pittsburgh Commission on Human Rights*, 413 U.S. 376 (1973), the Court went the opposite way, suggesting that editorial motives may diminish a publication's status and First Amendment protection as well. There the *Pittsburgh Press* was found in violation of an ordinance against discriminatory hiring on the basis of gender, due to its carrying help-wanted advertisements in gender-designated columns. The publishers contended the First Amendment protected their editorial judgments; they had a right to decide whether to accept an ad in the first place and, once accepted, where to place it in the newspaper. A majority of the Court (with Chief Justice Burger and Justice Douglas dissenting) rejected that argument. Justice Powell, writing for the majority, found no impairment of editorial freedom and emphasized that "[t]he advertisements, as embroidered by their placement, signaled that the advertisers were likely to show an illegal sex preference in their hiring decisions."

In *Bigelow v. Virginia* (1975) (excerpted below) the Court finally limited *Valentine*, in holding that the "commercial aspects" and "publisher's motives of financial gain" in advertisements do not "negate all First Amendment guarantees." Compare the rationale for extending First Amendment protection to commercial speech given in Justice Blackmun's opinion with the competing arguments of Justice Rehnquist in his dissenting opinion.

Two years after *Bigelow*, a ban on lawyer advertising of routine legal services was struck down in *Bates v. State Bar of Arizona*, 433 U.S. 350 (1977). But the Court did not end the controversy over lawyer advertis-

ing in *Bates*. *In re Primus*, 436 U.S. 412 (1978), held that the First
Amendment protects lawyers who solicit clients for a nonprofit organization (there, the American Civil Liberties Union), but in *Ohralik v.
Ohio State Bar Association*, 436 U.S. 447 (1978), the Court upheld disciplining an attorney for ambulance chasing and soliciting clients on a
contingency basis (that is, if a lawyer wins the case for his client, he gets
a percentage of the award). In *Zauderer v. Office of Disciplinary Counsel of
Supreme Court of Ohio*, 471 U.S. 626 (1985), when holding that lawyers
may not be disciplined for advertising in newspapers, the Court ruled
that advertisements for contingency-fee services must disclose the difference between legal fees and costs (the latter are paid by the client regardless of the outcome of a case). *Shapero v. Kentucky Bar Association*,
486 U.S. 466 (1988), held that direct-mail solicitation by an attorney was
protected First Amendment–commercial speech, and that a state bar association could not prevent the lawyer from soliciting clients in this way.

The Court's expansion of First Amendment protection for commercial speech based on a public interest rationale came with strong
opposition from Chief Justice Rehnquist. As Justice Blackmun explained in *Virginia State Board of Pharmacy v. Virginia Citizen Consumer
Council*, 425 U.S. 748 (1976), "So long as we preserve a predominantly
free enterprise economy, the allocation of our resources in large measure will be made through numerous private economic decisions. It is a
matter of public interest that those decisions in the aggregate, be intelligent and well informed. To this end, the free flow of commercial information is indispensible." But, dissenting from that ruling, Rehnquist
retorted, "I cannot distinguish between the public's right to know the
price of drugs and its right to know the price of title searches or physical examinations or other professional services for which standardized
fees are charged."

Again, with only Justice Rehnquist dissenting in *Central Hudson Gas
& Electric Corp. v. Public Service Commission of New York*, 447 U.S. 557
(1980), the Burger Court upheld First Amendment protection for a public utility's promotional ads and set forth a four-factor test for protecting
commercial speech: (1) whether the speech concerns lawful activity and
is lawful; (2) whether the asserted governmental interest in banning the
speech is substantial; and, if so, (3) whether the regulation directly advances the government's interests; and (4) whether the regulation is no
more extensive than necessary to serve the government's interests.

Although Rehnquist failed to carry the Court in *Central Hudson*,
he massed a bare majority in *Posadas de Puerto Rico v. Tourism Company
of Puerto Rico*, 479 U.S. 328 (1986), for upholding Puerto Rico's ban on
advertising casino gambling to local residents. He did so largely on the
ground that Puerto Rico could ban gambling altogether and that this

power included the lesser power of regulating advertising for gambling.

However, subsequent rulings failed to follow *Posadas*. (For further discussion and a summary of other recent rulings, see "THE DEVELOPMENT OF LAW" below.) Finally, a decade after handing down *Posadas*, the Court reconsidered that ruling in *44 Liquormart v. Rhode Island* (excerpted below). In that case, Justice Stevens struck down a state's ban on advertising the price of liquor and threw into question other governmental attempts to regulate advertising for alcohol, tobacco, and other "vices." While Justice Stevens cast further doubt on the ruling and reasoning in *Posadas*, concurring Justices Scalia and Thomas also questioned the Court's continued use of *Central Hudson*. The First Amendment's protection for commercial speech was, again, reaffirmed in *Lorillard Tobacco Co. v. Reilly* (2001) (excerpted below), striking down state restrictions on advertising for tobacco products, as well as other recent rulings.

Selected Bibliography

Baker, C. Edwin. *Advertising and a Democratic Press*. Princeton, NJ: Princeton University Press, 1994.

Collins, Ronald, and Skover, David. *The Death of Discourse*. 2d ed. Boulder, CO: Westview, 2004.

Lessig, Lawrence. *Free Culture: How Big Media Uses Technology and the Law to Lock Down Culture and Control Creativity*. New York: Penguin Press, 2004.

Postman, Neil. *Amusing Ourselves to Death: Public Discourse in the Age of Show Business*. New York: Viking, 1985.

Shiner, Roger A. *Freedom of Commercial Expression*. New York: Oxford University Press, 2004.

Sunstein, Cass. *Democracy and the Problem of Free Speech*. New York: Free Press, 1994.

Twitchell, James. *Carnival Culture: The Trashing of Taste in America*. New York: Columbia University Press, 1992.

Twitchell, James. *Adcult USA: The Triumph of Advertising in American Culture*. New York: Columbia University Press, 1995.

■ THE DEVELOPMENT OF LAW

Other Important Rulings on Commercial Speech and the First Amendment

CASE	VOTE	HOLDING
Virginia State Board of Pharmacy v. Virginia Citizen Consumer Council, 425 U.S. 748 (1976)	7:1	Upheld advertising of prescription drug prices.
Bates v. State Bar of Arizona, 433 U.S. 350 (1977)	5:4	Struck down Arizona's disciplinary rule that restricted advertising by lawyers of

their services. Chief Justice Burger and Justices Powell and Stewart in part concurred and dissented. Justice Rehnquist dissented.

CASE	VOTE	HOLDING
First National Bank of Boston v. Bellotti, 435 U.S. 765 (1978)	5:4	Held corporations enjoy First Amendment protection in publicizing their views on an income tax referendum.
Friedman v. Rogers, 440 U.S. 1 (1979)	7:2	Upheld ban on advertising of optometrists under trade names.
Consolidated Edison Company v. Public Service Commission, 447 U.S. 530 (1980)	7:2	Upheld insertion of handbills on nuclear energy with billing statements.
Central Hudson Gas & Electric Corp. v. Public Service Commission of New York, 447 U.S. 557 (1980)	8:1	Upheld promotional ads of a public utility and electrical monopoly.
Bolger v. Youngs Drug Products Corporation, 463 U.S. 60 (1983)	9:0	Held unconstitutional a statute barring unsolicited mailings of ads for contraceptives.
Pacific Gas & Electric v. Public Utilities Commission of California, 475 U.S. 1 (1986)	5:4	A state may not force a public utility company to include in its newsletter the material of a third party.
Posadas de Puerto Rico Associates v. Tourism Company of Puerto Rico, 479 U.S. 328 (1986)	5:4	Over First Amendment objections, Justice Rehnquist upheld Puerto Rico's ban on advertising for gambling

CASE	VOTE	HOLDING

casinos to residents, while permitting such advertising to residents of the fifty states. Writing for a bare majority, Justice Rehnquist reasoned that, because Puerto Rico could completely ban gambling, it could regulate and restrict advertising for gambling operations.

| *Board of Trustees of the State University of New York v. Fox,* 492 U.S. 469 (1989) | 6:3 | Held that officials of a university did not violate students' First Amendment free speech rights by ban- |

ning Tupperware parties in dormitories; commercial speech need not meet the least drastic means test that applies when reviewing regulations of noncommercial speech.

| *Peel v. Attorney Registration and Disciplinary Commission of Illinois,* 496 U.S. 91 (1990) | 5:4 | In a plurality opinion, Justice Stevens held that Illinois had improperly censured an attorney for printing on his |

letterhead that he was a certified civil trial specialist, because the letterhead was nondeceptive and protected commercial speech. Justices White, O'Connor, and Scalia, along with Chief Justice Rehnquist, dissented.

| *Edenfield v. Fane,* 507 U.S. 761 (1993) | 8:1 | Struck down a ban on soliciting by certified public accountants (CPAs) on the |

ground that "[s]olicitation by a CPA does not entail the coercive force of the personal presence of a trained advocate." Writing for the majority, Justice Kennedy distinguished prior rulings that limited protection for attorneys' solicitations on the ground that "a CPA is not a professional trained in the art of persuasion" and CPAs solicit business in ways conducive to long-term relationships with their clients, rather than engaging in "high pressure sales tactics." Only Justice O'Connor dissented.

| *United States v. Edge Broadcasting Company,* 509 U.S. 418 (1993) | 7:2 | Under federal law, lottery advertisements are generally prohibited, but broadcasters |

may advertise state-run lotteries on stations licensed in a state that conducts lotteries. A North Carolina company, Edge Broadcasting Company, challenged the application of those restrictions because it wanted to broadcast advertisements for Virginia's lottery. As the company broadcasts close to the Virginia and North Carolina border, approximately 90 percent of Edge's listeners reside in the former state, though it is licensed in the latter. Writing for the majority Justice White applied the four-factor test for commercial speech set forth in *Central Hudson Gas & Electric Corp. v. Public Service Commission of New York,* 447 U.S. 557 (1980), and upheld the federal restrictions as applied to

CASE	VOTE	HOLDING

Edge Broadcasting Company, since they advanced the federal government's interest in supporting nonlottery states' antigambling policies and did so in an effective and nonexcessive way. Justices Stevens and Blackmun dissented.

Ibanez v. Florida Department of   7:2   Struck down Florida's ban
Professional Regulation, 512 U.S.   on the use of the appella-
136 (1994)   tions CPA (certified public
accountant) and CFP (certified financial planner) on lawyers' business cards and letterheads, as well as telephone listings. Writing for the majority, Justice Ginsburg reaffirmed that states may "ban such speech only if it is false, deceptive, or misleading," and rejected Florida's claim that the use of "CPA" in advertisements was "inherently misleading." By contrast, dissenting Justice O'Connor, along with Chief Justice Rehnquist, contended that, "States may prohibit inherently misleading speech entirely."

City of Ladue v. Gilleo, 512   9:0   Struck down an ordinance
U.S. 43 (1994)   that banned homeowners
                                       from posting any signs, ex-
cept for real estate sale signs, on their property. In 1990, during the United States' clash with Iraq, Margaret Gilleo ran afoul of the law by placing an 8½-by-11-inch sign, "For Peace in Gulf," in a second-floor window of her home. Writing for the Court, Justice Stevens held that the ordinance was overinclusive and too restrictive of the freedoms guaranteed by the First Amendment.

Rubin v. Coors Brewing Co., 514   9:0   Writing for the Court,
U.S. 476 (1995)   Justice Thomas affirmed a
                                       lower court's striking down
the provisions of a 1935 federal statute imposing labeling restrictions on the alcohol content of malt beverages. Under federal law, the disclosure of alcohol is required on distilled spirits and wines, while the alcohol content of beer could be shown on billboards but not on bottle labels. The government had defended its labeling restrictions on the ground that they prevented "strength wars" in advertising the sale of beer. The Court, however, held that the government's interest failed the test set forth in *Central Hudson Gas & Electric Corp. v. Public Service Commission of New York*, 447 U.S. 557 (1980), requiring the government's interest in regulating commercial speech to be "substantial" and "not more extensive than is necessary to serve that interest."

Florida Bar v. Went For It, 515   5:4   Writing for the majority,
U.S. 618 (1995)   Justice O'Connor upheld
                                       Florida's prohibition on per-

sonal lawyers from making written solicitations to victims or victims' relatives within thirty days of an accident or natural disaster, upon concluding that the government's interests in the restriction met the test set forth in *Central Hudson*. By contrast, dissenting Justices Ginsburg, Kennedy, Souter, and Stevens strongly disagreed with the majority's analysis and failure to recognize the First Amendment's protection for attorney advertising.

Glickman v. Wileman Brothers & Elliott, Inc., 521 U.S. 457 (1997)	5:4	Upheld regulations pursuant to the Agricultural Marketing Agreement Act of 1937 requiring fruit producers to

contribute financially toward generic advertising for fruit in certain markets. Wileman Brothers & Elliott, Inc., challenged the constitutionality of that regulation as compelled speech in violation of the First Amendment's protection for commercial speech. In rejecting that claim, Justice Stevens observed that "requiring respondents to pay the assessments cannot be said to engender any crisis of conscience. None of the advertising in this record promotes any particular message other than encouraging consumers to buy California tree fruit."

Greater New Orleans Broadcasting Association v. United States, 527 U.S. 173 (1999)	9:0	In *United States v. Edge Broadcasting Co.*, 509 U.S. 418 (1993), the Court upheld the application of a

section of the Communications Act of 1934, forbidding the broadcasting of advertisements for gambling, to bar a radio station in North Carolina, where lotteries are illegal, from broadcasting ads for Virginia's lotteries. Here, however, the Court held that the prohibition infringed on First Amendment interests as applied to radio and television broadcasts for private casino gambling in Louisiana, where gambling is legal. Writing for the Court, Justice Stevens emphasized that federal law regulating gambling advertisements is inconsistent and crosscutting. Among the numerous exceptions to the Communications Act's ban on advertisements of gambling, for instance, were Congress's 1975 exemption of the broadcasting of ads for state-run lotteries and its 1988 exemption of those for gambling operations run by Native American tribes. Because of these exemptions to, and the incoherence of, federal law, Justice Stevens ruled that the government failed to satisfy the four-factor test for regulating commercial speech laid down in *Central Hudson Gas & Electric Corp. v. Public Service Commission of New York*, 447 U.S. 557 (1980). Chief Justice Rehnquist and Justice Thomas filed concurring opinions.

Los Angeles Police Department v. United Reporting Publishing Corporation, 528 U.S. 32 (1999)	7:2	Writing for the Court, Chief Justice Rehnquist upheld a California law that

CASE	VOTE	HOLDING

permits police departments to give journalists, scholars, and others access to arrest records, but forbids their release to companies that would use the information for commercial purposes; the law was enacted to safeguard privacy interests and to protect arrestees and victims from solicitations, lawyers and, other businesses.

United States v. United Foods, 6:3 Writing for the Court, Jus-
533 U.S. 405 (2001) tice Kennedy struck down
a 1990 federal statute mandating that mushroom handlers pay an assessment that was used to fund advertisements promoting the sale of mushrooms. In holding that the law violates the First Amendment, the Court distinguished *Glickman v. Wileman Brothers & Elliott, Inc.*, 521 U.S. 457 (1997), upholding the constitutionality of a series of agricultural marketing orders that required producers of certain California fruits to pay a fee used for product advertising. In *Glickman*, according to Justice Kennedy, the mandated fee was part of a larger regulatory marketing scheme, whereas here the forced subsidy for generic advertising was not part of a larger economic regulatory scheme and, thus, ran afoul of the First Amendment protection for commercial speech, relying on *Abood v. Detroit Board of Education*, 431 U.S. 209 (1977).

Lorillard Tobacco Co. v. Reilly, 5:4 Writing for the Court,
533 U.S. 525 (2001) Justice O'Connor held that
federal regulations of cigarette advertising preempted Massachusetts's regulations, and that the state's regulation of advertisements for smokeless tobacco products violated the First Amendment.

Thompson v. Western States Medical 5:4 Writing for the Court, Jus-
Center, 535 U.S. 357 (2002) tice O'Connor struck down
a federal restriction on the advertising of "compound drugs." Chief Justice Rehnquist and Justices Stevens, Ginsburg, and Breyer dissented.

Bigelow v. Virginia
421 U.S. 809, 95 S.Ct. 2222 (1975)

Justice Blackmun in his opinion for the Court sets forth the facts in this case involving a Virginia State prohibition against advertising the availability of abortion services and clinics, even those in other states.

The Court's decision was seven to two, and the majority's opinion was announced by Justice Blackmun. Dissent was by Justice Rehnquist, who was joined by Justice White.

☐ *Justice BLACKMUN delivered the opinion of the Court.*

An advertisement carried in appellant's newspaper led to his conviction for a violation of a Virginia statute that made it a misdemeanor, by the sale or circulation of any publication, to encourage or prompt the procuring of an abortion. The issue here is whether the editor-appellant's First Amendment rights were unconstitutionally abridged by the statute. . . .

The Virginia Weekly was a newspaper published by the Virginia Weekly Associates of Charlottesville. . . . Jeffrey C. Bigelow, was a director and the managing editor and responsible officer of the newspaper.

On February 8, 1971, the Weekly's Vol. V, No. 6, was published and circulated under the direct responsibility of the appellant. On page 2 of that issue was the following advertisement:

> "UNWANTED PREGNANCY
> LET US HELP YOU
> Abortions are now legal in New York
> There are no residency requirements.
> FOR IMMEDIATE PLACEMENT IN
> ACCREDITED HOSPITALS AND
> CLINICS AT LOW COST
> Contact
> WOMEN'S PAVILION
> 515 Madison Avenue
> New York, N.Y. 10022
> or call any time
> (212) 371-6670 or (212) 371-6650
> AVAILABLE 7 DAYS A WEEK
> STRICTLY CONFIDENTIAL. We
> will make all arrangements for you
> and help you with information and
> counseling."

It is to be observed that the advertisement announced that the Women's Pavilion of New York City would help women with unwanted pregnancies to obtain "immediate placement in accredited hospitals and clinics at low cost" and would "make all arrangements" on a "strictly confidential" basis; that it offered "information and counseling"; that it gave the organization's address and telephone numbers; and that it stated that abortions "are now legal in New York" and there "are no residency requirements." Although the advertisement did not contain the name of any licensed physician, the "placement" to which it referred was to "accredited hospitals and clinics."

Bigelow was charged with [and convicted for] violating . . . [a statute that provided]:

"If any person, by publication, lecture, advertisement, or by the sale or circulation of any publication, or in any other manner, encourage or prompt the procuring of abortion or miscarriage, he shall be guilty of a misdemeanor." [The Supreme Court of Virginia upheld Bigelow's conviction.] . . .

The central assumption made by the Supreme Court of Virginia was that the First Amendment guarantees of speech and press are inapplicable to paid commercial advertisements. Our cases, however, clearly establish that speech is not stripped of First Amendment protection merely because it appears in that form. . . .

The appellee, as did the Supreme Court of Virginia, relies on *Valentine v. Chrestensen*, 316 U.S. 52 (1942), where a unanimous Court, in a brief opinion, sustained an ordinance which had been interpreted to ban the distribution of a handbill advertising the exhibition of a submarine. The handbill solicited customers to tour the ship for a fee. The promoter-advertiser had first attempted to distribute a single-faced handbill consisting only of the advertisement, and was denied permission to do so. He then had printed, on the reverse side of the handbill, a protest against official conduct refusing him the use of wharfage facilities. The Court found that the message of asserted "public interest" was appended solely for the purpose of evading the ordinance and therefore did not constitute an "exercise of the freedom of communicating information and disseminating opinion." . . .

But the holding is distinctly a limited one: the ordinance was upheld as a reasonable regulation of the manner in which commercial advertising could be distributed. The fact that it had the effect of banning a particular handbill does not mean that *Chrestensen* is authority for the proposition that all statutes regulating commercial advertising are immune from constitutional challenge. The case obviously does not support any sweeping proposition that advertising is unprotected *per se*.

This Court's cases decided since *Chrestensen* clearly demonstrate as untenable any reading of that case that would give it so broad an effect. In *New York Times Co. v. Sullivan*, [376 U.S. 254 (1964)], a city official instituted a civil libel action against four clergymen and the *New York Times*. The suit was based on an advertisement carried in the newspaper criticizing police action against members of the civil rights movement and soliciting contributions for the movement. The Court held that this advertisement, although containing factually erroneous defamatory content, was entitled to the same degree of constitutional protection as ordinary speech. . . .

The principle that commercial advertising enjoys a degree of First Amendment protection was reaffirmed in *Pittsburgh Press Co. v. Human Rel. Comm'n*, 413 U.S. 376 (1973). There, the Court, although divided sustained an ordinance that had been construed to forbid newspapers to carry help-wanted advertisements in sex-designated columns except where based upon a bona fide occupational exemption. The Court did describe the advertisements at issue as "classic examples of commercial speech," for each was "no more than a proposal of possible employment." But the Court indicated that the advertisements would have received some degree of First Amendment protection if the commercial proposal had been legal. . . .

The legitimacy of appellant's First Amendment claim in the present case is demonstrated by the important differences between the advertisement presently at issue and those involved in *Chrestensen* and in *Pittsburgh Press*. The advertisement published in appellant's newspaper did more than simply propose a commercial transaction. It contained factual material of clear "public interest." Portions of its message, most prominently the lines, "Abortions are now legal in New York. There are no residency requirements," involve the exercise of the freedom of communicating information and disseminating opinion.

Viewed in its entirety, the advertisement conveyed information of potential interest and value to a diverse audience—not only to readers possibly in need of the services offered, but also to those with a general curiosity about, or genuine interest in, the subject matter or the law of another State and its development, and to readers seeking reform in Virginia. . . .

Advertising, like all public expression, may be subject to reasonable regulation that serves a legitimate public interest. To the extent that commercial activity is subject to regulation, the relationship of speech to that activity may be one factor, among others, to be considered in weighing the First Amendment interest against the governmental interest alleged. Advertising is not thereby stripped of all First Amendment protection. The relationship of speech to the marketplace of products or of services does not make it valueless in the marketplace of ideas. . . .

If . . . this statute were upheld . . . Virginia might exert the power sought here over a wide variety of national publications or interstate newspapers carrying advertisements similar to the one that appeared in Bigelow's newspaper or containing articles on the general subject matter to which the advertisement referred. Other States might do the same. The burdens thereby imposed on publications would impair, perhaps severely, their proper functioning. We know from experience that "liberty of the press is in peril as soon as the government tries to compel what is to go into a newspaper." The policy of the First Amendment favors dissemination of information and opinion, and "[t]he guarantees of freedom of speech and press were not designed to prevent 'the censorship of the press merely, but any action of the government by means of which it might prevent such free and general discussion of public matters as seems absolutely essential.' . . ."

We conclude that Virginia could not apply Va. Code Ann. § 18.1-63 (1960), as it read in 1971, to appellant's publication of the advertisement in question without unconstitutionally infringing upon his First Amendment rights. The judgment of the Supreme Court of Virginia is therefore reversed.

☐ *Justice REHNQUIST, with whom Justice WHITE joins, dissenting.*

Since the Court concludes, apparently from two lines of the advertisement, that it conveyed information of value to those interested in the "subject matter or the law of another State and its development" and to those "seeking reform in Virginia," and since the ad relates to abortion, elevated to constitutional stature by the Court, it concludes that this advertisement is entitled to something more than the limited constitutional protection traditionally accorded commercial advertising. Although recognizing that "[a]dvertising, like all public expression, may be subject to reasonable regulation that serves a legitimate public interest," the Court for reasons not entirely clear to me concludes that Virginia's interest is of "little, if any, weight." . . .

If the Court's decision does, indeed, turn upon its conclusion that the advertisement here in question was protected by the First and Fourteenth

Amendments, the subject of the advertisement ought to make no difference. It will not do to say, as the Court does, that this advertisement conveyed information about the "subject matter or the law of another State and its development" to those "seeking reform in Virginia," and that it related to abortion, as if these factors somehow put it on a different footing from other commercial advertising. This was a proposal to furnish services on a commercial basis, and since we have always refused to distinguish for First Amendment purposes on the basis of content, it is no different from an advertisement for a bucket shop operation or a Ponzi scheme which has its headquarters in New York. If Virginia may not regulate advertising of commercial abortion agencies because of the interest of those seeking to reform Virginia's abortion laws, it is difficult to see why it is not likewise precluded from regulating advertising for an out-of-state bucket shop on the ground that such information might be of interest to those interested in repealing Virginia's "blue sky" laws. . . .

[T]he advertisement appears to me, as it did to the courts below, to be a classic commercial proposition directed toward the exchange of services rather than the exchange of ideas. . . . Whatever slight factual content the advertisement may contain and whatever expression of opinion may be laboriously drawn from it does not alter its predominantly commercial content. . . . I am unable to perceive any relationship between the instant advertisement and that for example in issue in *New York Times Co. v. Sullivan*. . . .

Assuming *arguendo* that this advertisement is something more than a normal commercial proposal, I am unable to see why Virginia does not have a legitimate public interest in its regulation. The Court apparently concedes . . . that the States have a strong interest in the prevention of commercial advertising in the health field—both in order to maintain high ethical standards in the medical profession and to protect the public from unscrupulous practices.

Without denying the power of either New York or Virginia to prohibit advertising such as that in issue where both publication of the advertised activity and the activity itself occur in the same State, the Court instead focuses on the multistate nature of this transaction. . . .

The source of this rigid territorial limitation on the power of the States in our federal system to safeguard the health and welfare of their citizens is not revealed. . . . [W]e have consistently recognized that irrespective of a State's power to regulate extraterritorial commercial transactions in which its citizens participate it retains an independent power to regulate the business of commercial solicitation and advertising within its borders.

Were the Court's statements taken literally, they would presage a standard of the lowest common denominator for commercial ethics and business conduct. . . . Loan sharks might well choose States with unregulated small loan industries, luring the unwary with immune commercial advertisements. And imagination would place the only limit on the use of such a "no-man's land" together with artificially created territorial contacts to bilk the public and circumvent long-established state schemes of regulation.

44 Liquormart, Inc. v. Rhode Island

517 U.S. 484, 116 S.CT. 1495 (1996)

In 1956, Rhode Island enacted two prohibitions against advertising the retail price of alcoholic drinks. The first prohibits "advertising in any manner whatsoever" of the price of alcoholic drinks, with the exception of price tags, and the second categorically forbids any ads making "reference to the price of any alcoholic beverages." In 1991, complaints from competitors about an ad placed by 44 Liquormart in a newspaper generated enforcement proceedings under the statute. Notably, the ad did not state the price of any alcoholic beverages and, indeed, noted that "State law prohibits advertising liquor prices." Rather, the ad listed 44 Liquormart's low prices for peanuts, potato chips, and Schweppes mixers and identified various brands of packaged liquor as well as including the word "WOW" in large letters next to pictures of vodka and rum bottles. Subsequently, after being fined $400, 44 Liquormart filed a suit seeking a declaratory judgment that the state's restrictions violated the First Amendment. A federal district court agreed that the advertising ban was unconstitutional because it did not "directly advance" the government's interest in reducing alcohol consumption and was "more extensive than necessary to serve that interest." But a federal appellate court reversed this decision and 44 Liquormart appealed to the Supreme Court.

The Court's decision was unanimous and the opinion was delivered by Justice Stevens. Justices Scalia, Thomas, and O'Connor filed concurring opinions.

> ☐ *Justice STEVENS delivered the opinion of the Court with respect to Parts I, II, and VII, in which Justices SCALIA, KENNEDY, SOUTER, THOMAS, and GINSBURG joined; the opinion of the Court with respect to Part VIII, in which Justices SCALIA, KENNEDY, SOUTER, and GINSBURG joined; an opinion with respect to Parts III and V, in which Justices KENNEDY, SOUTER, and GINSBURG joined; an opinion with respect to Part VI, in which Justices KENNEDY, THOMAS, and GINSBURG joined; and an opinion with respect to Part IV, in which Justices KENNEDY and GINSBURG joined.*

■ III

Advertising has been a part of our culture throughout our history. Even in colonial days, the public relied on "commercial speech" for vital information about the market. Early newspapers displayed advertisements for goods and services on their front pages, and town criers called out prices in public squares. Indeed, commercial messages played such a central role in public life prior to the Founding that Benjamin Franklin authored his early defense of a free press in support of his decision to print, of all things, an advertisement for voyages to Barbados.

It was not until the 1970's, however, that this Court held that the First Amendment protected the dissemination of truthful and nonmisleading commercial messages about lawful products and services. In *Bigelow v. Virginia*, 421 U.S. 809 (1975), we held that it was error to assume that commercial speech was entitled to no First Amendment protection or that it was without value in the marketplace of ideas. The following Term in *Virginia Bd. of Pharmacy v. Virginia Citizens Consumer Council, Inc.*, 425 U.S. 748 (1976), we expanded on our holding in *Bigelow* and held that the State's blanket ban on advertising the price of prescription drugs violated the First Amendment. *Virginia Pharmacy Bd.* reflected the conclusion that the same interest that supports regulation of potentially misleading advertising, namely the public's interest in receiving accurate commercial information, also supports an interpretation of the First Amendment that provides constitutional protection for the dissemination of accurate and nonmisleading commercial messages. . . . The opinion further explained that a State's paternalistic assumption that the public will use truthful, nonmisleading commercial information unwisely cannot justify a decision to suppress it. . . .

At the same time, our early cases recognized that the State may regulate some types of commercial advertising more freely than other forms of protected speech. Specifically, we explained that the State may require commercial messages to "appear in such a form, or include such additional information, warnings, and disclaimers, as are necessary to prevent its being deceptive," *Virginia Pharmacy Bd.*, and that it may restrict some forms of aggressive sales practices that have the potential to exert "undue influence" over consumers. See *Bates v. State Bar of Ariz.*, 433 U.S. 350 (1977). . . .

In *Central Hudson Gas & Electric Corp. v. Public Service Commission of New York*, 447 U.S. 557 (1980), we took stock of our developing commercial speech jurisprudence. In that case, we considered a regulation "completely" banning all promotional advertising by electric utilities. Our decision acknowledged the special features of commercial speech but identified the serious First Amendment concerns that attend blanket advertising prohibitions that do not protect consumers from commercial harms. . . . In reaching its conclusion, the majority explained that although the special nature of commercial speech may require less than strict review of its regulation, special concerns arise from "regulations that entirely suppress commercial speech in order to pursue a nonspeech-related policy." In those circumstances, "a ban on speech could screen from public view the underlying governmental policy." As a result, the Court concluded that "special care" should attend the review of such blanket bans, and it pointedly remarked that "in recent years this Court has not approved a blanket ban on commercial speech unless the speech itself was flawed in some way, either because it was deceptive or related to unlawful activity."

■ IV

When a State regulates commercial messages to protect consumers from misleading, deceptive, or aggressive sales practices, or requires the disclosure of beneficial consumer information, the purpose of its regulation is consistent with the reasons for according constitutional protection to commercial speech and therefore justifies less than strict review. However, when a State entirely prohibits the dissemination of truthful, nonmisleading commercial messages for reasons unrelated to the preservation of a fair bargaining process, there is far less reason to depart from the rigorous review that the First Amendment generally demands.

Sound reasons justify reviewing the latter type of commercial speech regulation more carefully. Most obviously, complete speech bans, unlike content-neutral restrictions on the time, place, or manner of expression are particularly dangerous because they all but foreclose alternative means of disseminating certain information. . . .

It is the State's interest in protecting consumers from "commercial harms" that provides "the typical reason why commercial speech can be subject to greater governmental regulation than noncommercial speech." *Cincinnati v. Discovery Network, Inc., Inc.*, 507 U.S. 410 (1993). Yet bans that target truthful, nonmisleading commercial messages rarely protect consumers from such harms. Instead, such bans often serve only to obscure an "underlying governmental policy" that could be implemented without regulating speech. *Central Hudson.* In this way, these commercial speech bans not only hinder consumer choice, but also impede debate over central issues of public policy.

Precisely because bans against truthful, nonmisleading commercial speech rarely seek to protect consumers from either deception or overreaching, they usually rest solely on the offensive assumption that the public will respond "irrationally" to the truth. The First Amendment directs us to be especially skeptical of regulations that seek to keep people in the dark for what the government perceives to be their own good. That teaching applies equally to state attempts to deprive consumers of accurate information about their chosen products: "The commercial market-place, like other spheres of our social and cultural life, provides a forum where ideas and information flourish. Some of the ideas and information are vital, some of slight worth. But the general rule is that the speaker and the audience, not the government, assess the value of the information presented." . . .

■ V

The State argues that the price advertising prohibition should nevertheless be upheld because it directly advances the State's substantial interest in promoting temperance, and because it is no more extensive than necessary. Although there is some confusion as to what Rhode Island means by temperance, we assume that the State asserts an interest in reducing alcohol consumption. . . .

Although the record suggests that the price advertising ban may have some impact on the purchasing patterns of temperate drinkers of modest means, the State has presented no evidence to suggest that its speech prohibition will significantly reduce market-wide consumption. . . . In addition, as the District Court noted, the State has not identified what price level would lead to a significant reduction in alcohol consumption, nor has it identified the amount that it believes prices would decrease without the ban. Thus, the State's own showing reveals that any connection between the ban and a significant change in alcohol consumption would be purely fortuitous. . . .

The State also cannot satisfy the requirement that its restriction on speech be no more extensive than necessary. It is perfectly obvious that alternative forms of regulation that would not involve any restriction on speech would be more likely to achieve the State's goal of promoting temperance. As the State's own expert conceded, higher prices can be maintained either by direct regulation or by increased taxation. Per capita purchases could be limited as is the case with prescription drugs. Even educational campaigns focused on the problems of excessive, or even moderate, drinking might prove to be more effective.

As a result, even under the less than strict standard that generally applies in commercial speech cases, the State has failed to establish a "reasonable fit" between its abridgment of speech and its temperance goal. It necessarily follows that the price advertising ban cannot survive the more stringent constitutional review that *Central Hudson* itself concluded was appropriate for the complete suppression of truthful, nonmisleading commercial speech.

■ VI

The State responds by arguing that it merely exercised appropriate "legislative judgment" in determining that a price advertising ban would best promote temperance. Relying on the *Central Hudson* analysis set forth in *Posadas de Puerto Rico Associates v. Tourism Co. of P.R.*, 478 U.S. 328 (1986), and *United States v. Edge Broadcasting Co.*, 509 U.S. 418 (1993), Rhode Island first argues that, because expert opinions as to the effectiveness of the price advertising ban "go both ways," the Court of Appeals correctly concluded that the ban constituted a "reasonable choice" by the legislature. The State next contends that precedent requires us to give particular deference to that legislative choice because the State could, if it chose, ban the sale of alcoholic beverages outright. Finally, the State argues that deference is appropriate because alcoholic beverages are so-called "vice" products. We consider each of these contentions in turn.

The State's first argument fails to justify the speech prohibition at issue. Our commercial speech cases recognize some room for the exercise of legislative judgment. However, Rhode Island errs in concluding that *Edge* and *Posadas* establish the degree of deference that its decision to impose a price advertising ban warrants. . . . [In] *Posadas*, a five-Member majority held that, under the *Central Hudson* test, it was "up to the legislature" to choose to reduce gambling by suppressing in-state casino advertising rather than engaging in educational speech. Rhode Island argues that this logic demonstrates the constitutionality of its own decision to ban price advertising in lieu of raising taxes or employing some other less speech-restrictive means of promoting temperance.

The reasoning in *Posadas* does support the State's argument, but, on reflection, we are now persuaded that *Posadas* erroneously performed the First Amendment analysis. The casino advertising ban was designed to keep truthful, nonmisleading speech from members of the public for fear that they would be more likely to gamble if they received it. As a result, the advertising ban served to shield the State's antigambling policy from the public scrutiny that more direct, nonspeech regulation would draw.

Given our longstanding hostility to commercial speech regulation of this type, *Posadas* clearly erred in concluding that it was "up to the legislature" to choose suppression over a less speech-restrictive policy. The *Posadas* majority's conclusion on that point cannot be reconciled with the unbroken line of prior cases striking down similarly broad regulations on truthful, nonmisleading advertising when non-speech-related alternatives were available.

Because the 5-to-4 decision in *Posadas* marked such a sharp break from our prior precedent, and because it concerned a constitutional question about which this Court is the final arbiter, we decline to give force to its highly deferential approach. Instead, in keeping with our prior holdings, we conclude that a state legislature does not have the broad discretion to suppress truthful, nonmisleading information for paternalistic purposes that the *Posadas* majority was willing to tolerate. We also cannot accept the State's second contention, which is premised entirely on the "greater-includes-the-lesser" reasoning endorsed toward the end of the majority's opinion in *Posadas*. There, the majority stated that "the greater power to completely ban casino gambling necessarily includes the lesser power to ban advertising of casino gambling." . . .

In *Rubin v. Coors Brewing Co.*, [514 U.S. 476] (1995), the United States advanced a similar argument as a basis for supporting a statutory prohibition against revealing the alcoholic content of malt beverages on product labels. We rejected the argument, noting that the statement in the *Posadas* opinion was made only after the majority had concluded that the Puerto Rican regulation "survived the *Central Hudson* test." Further consideration persuades us that the "greater-includes-the-lesser" argument should be rejected for the additional and more important reason that it is inconsistent with both logic and well-settled doctrine.

Although we do not dispute the proposition that greater powers include lesser ones, we fail to see how that syllogism requires the conclusion that the State's power to regulate commercial activity is "greater" than its power to ban truthful, nonmisleading commercial speech. Contrary to the assumption made in *Posadas*, we think it quite clear that banning speech may sometimes prove far more intrusive than banning conduct. As a venerable proverb teaches, it may prove more injurious to prevent people from teaching others how to fish than to prevent fish from being sold. Similarly, a local ordinance banning bicycle lessons may curtail freedom far more than one that prohibits bicycle riding within city limits. In short, we reject the assumption that words are necessarily less vital to freedom than actions, or that logic somehow proves that the power to prohibit an activity is necessarily "greater" than the power to suppress speech about it. . . .

Finally, we find unpersuasive the State's contention that, under *Posadas* and *Edge*, the price advertising ban should be upheld because it targets commercial speech that pertains to a "vice" activity. The appellees premise their request for a so-called "vice" exception to our commercial speech doctrine on language in *Edge* which characterized gambling as a "vice". The respondents misread our precedent. Our decision last Term striking down an alcohol-related advertising restriction effectively rejected the very contention respondents now make. See *Rubin v. Coors Brewing Co.*

Moreover, the scope of any "vice" exception to the protection afforded by the First Amendment would be difficult, if not impossible, to define. Almost any product that poses some threat to public health or public morals might reasonably be characterized by a state legislature as relating to "vice activity". Such characterization, however, is anomalous when applied to products such as alcoholic beverages, lottery tickets, or playing cards, that may be lawfully purchased on the open market. . . . For these reasons, a "vice" label that is unaccompanied by a corresponding prohibition against the commercial behavior at issue fails to provide a principled justification for the regulation of commercial speech about that activity.

▪ VII

As is clear, the text of the Twenty-first Amendment supports the view that, while it grants the States authority over commerce that might otherwise be reserved to the Federal Government, it places no limit whatsoever on other constitutional provisions. Nevertheless, Rhode Island argues, and the Court of Appeals agreed, that in this case the Twenty-first Amendment tilts the First Amendment analysis in the State's favor.

In reaching its conclusion, the Court of Appeals relied on our decision in *California v. LaRue*, 409 U.S. 109 (1972). In *LaRue*, five Members of the Court relied on the Twenty-first Amendment to buttress the conclusion that the First Amendment did not invalidate California's prohibition of certain grossly sexual exhibitions in premises licensed to serve alcoholic beverages. Specifically, the opinion stated that the Twenty-first Amendment required that the prohibition be given an added presumption in favor of its validity. We are now persuaded that the Court's analysis in *LaRue* would have led to precisely the same result if it had placed no reliance on the Twenty-first Amendment.

Without questioning the holding in *LaRue*, we now disavow its reasoning insofar as it relied on the Twenty-first Amendment. As we explained in a case decided more than a decade after *LaRue*, although the Twenty-first Amendment limits the effect of the dormant Commerce Clause on a State's regulatory power over the delivery or use of intoxicating beverages within its borders, "the Amendment does not license the States to ignore their obligations under other provisions of the Constitution." *Capital Cities Cable, Inc. v. Crisp*, 467 U.S. 691 (1984). That general conclusion reflects our specific holdings that the Twenty-first Amendment does not in any way diminish the force of the Supremacy Clause. We see no reason why the First Amendment should not also be included in that list. Accordingly, we now hold that the Twenty-first Amendment does not qualify the constitutional prohibition against laws abridging the freedom of speech embodied in the First Amendment. The Twenty-first Amendment, therefore, cannot save Rhode Island's ban on liquor price advertising.

▪ VIII

Because Rhode Island has failed to carry its heavy burden of justifying its complete ban on price advertising, we conclude that [the state's restrictions on liquor advertising] abridge speech in violation of the First Amendment as made applicable to the States by the Due Process Clause of the Fourteenth Amendment. The judgment of the Court of Appeals is therefore reversed.

☐ *Justice SCALIA, concurring in part and concurring in the judgment.*

Since I do not believe we have before us the wherewithal to declare *Central Hudson* wrong—or at least the wherewithal to say what ought to replace it—I must resolve this case in accord with our existing jurisprudence, which all except Justice THOMAS agree would prohibit the challenged regulation. I am not disposed to develop new law, or reinforce old, on this issue, and accordingly I merely concur in the judgment of the Court. I believe, however, that Justice STEVENS' treatment of the application of the Twenty-First Amendment to this case is correct, and accordingly join Parts I, II, VII, and VIII of Justice STEVENS' opinion.

☐ *Justice THOMAS, concurring in Parts I, II, VI, and VII, and concurring in the judgment.*

In cases such as this, in which the government's asserted interest is to keep legal users of a product or service ignorant in order to manipulate their choices in the marketplace, the balancing test adopted in *Central Hudson* should not be applied, in my view. Rather, such an "interest" is per se illegitimate and can no more justify regulation of "commercial" speech than it can justify regulation of "noncommercial" speech. . . .

I do not see a philosophical or historical basis for asserting that "commercial" speech is of "lower value" than "noncommercial" speech. Nor do I believe that the only explanations that the Court has ever advanced for treating "commercial" speech differently from other speech can justify restricting "commercial" speech in order to keep information from legal purchasers so as to thwart what would otherwise be their choices in the marketplace.

I do not join the principal opinion's application of the *Central Hudson* balancing test because I do not believe that such a test should be applied to a restriction of "commercial" speech, at least when, as here, the asserted interest is one that is to be achieved through keeping would-be recipients of the speech in the dark. Application of the advancement-of-state-interest prong of *Central Hudson* makes little sense to me in such circumstances. Faulting the State for failing to show that its price advertising ban decreases alcohol consumption "significantly," seems to imply that if the State had been more successful at keeping consumers ignorant and thereby decreasing their consumption, then the restriction might have been upheld. This contradicts *Virginia Pharmacy Bd.*'s rationale for protecting "commercial" speech in the first instance. . . .

Although the Court took a sudden turn away from *Virginia Pharmacy Bd.* in *Central Hudson*, it has never explained why manipulating the choices of consumers by keeping them ignorant is more legitimate when the ignorance is maintained through suppression of "commercial" speech than when the same ignorance is maintained through suppression of "noncommercial" speech. The courts, including this Court, have found the *Central Hudson* "test" to be, as a general matter, very difficult to apply with any uniformity. . . . Moreover, the second prong of *Central Hudson*, as applied to the facts of that case and to those here, apparently requires judges to delineate those situations in which citizens cannot be trusted with information, and invites judges to decide whether they themselves think that consumption of a product is harmful enough that it should be discouraged. In my view, the *Central Hudson* test asks the courts to weigh incommensurables—the value of knowledge versus the value of ignorance—and to apply contradictory premises—that informed adults are the best judges of their own interests, and that they are not. Rather than continuing to apply a test that makes no sense to me when the asserted state interest is of the type involved here, I would return to the reasoning and holding of *Virginia Pharmacy Bd*. Under that decision, these restrictions fall.

☐ *Justice O'CONNOR, with whom the CHIEF JUSTICE, Justice SOUTER, and Justice BREYER join, concurring in the judgment.*

I agree with the Court that Rhode Island's price-advertising ban is invalid. I would resolve this case more narrowly, however, by applying our established *Central Hudson* test to determine whether this commercial-speech regulation survives First Amendment scrutiny.

Under that test, we first determine whether the speech at issue concerns lawful activity and is not misleading, and whether the asserted governmental interest is substantial. If both these conditions are met, we must decide whether the regulation "directly advances the governmental interest asserted, and whether it is not more extensive than is necessary to serve that interest." *Central Hudson*. . . . Rhode Island's regulation fails the final prong; that is, its ban is more extensive than necessary to serve the State's interest. . . .

Rhode Island offers one, and only one, justification for its ban on price advertising. Rhode Island says that the ban is intended to keep alcohol prices high as a way to keep consumption low. . . .

The fit between Rhode Island's method and this particular goal is not reasonable. If the target is simply higher prices generally to discourage consumption, the regulation imposes too great, and unnecessary, a prohibition on speech in order to achieve it. The State has other methods at its disposal—methods that would more directly accomplish this stated goal without intruding on sellers' ability to provide truthful, nonmisleading information to customers. . . .

Respondents point for support to *Posadas de Puerto Rico Associates*, where, applying the *Central Hudson* test, we upheld the constitutionality of a Puerto Rico law that prohibited the advertising of casino gambling aimed at residents of Puerto Rico, but permitted such advertising aimed at tourists. . . . It is true that *Posadas* accepted as reasonable, without further inquiry, Puerto Rico's assertions that the regulations furthered the government's interest and were no more extensive than necessary to serve that interest. Since *Posadas*, however, this Court has examined more searchingly the State's professed goal, and the speech restriction put into place to further it, before accepting a State's claim that the speech restriction satisfies First Amendment scrutiny. The closer look that we have required since *Posadas* comports better with the purpose of the analysis set out in *Central Hudson*, by requiring the State to show that the speech restriction directly advances its interest and is narrowly tailored. Under such a closer look, Rhode Island's price-advertising ban clearly fails to pass muster. Because Rhode Island's regulation fails even the less stringent standard set out in *Central Hudson*, nothing here requires adoption of a new analysis for the evaluation of commercial speech regulation. . . . Because we need go no further, I would not here undertake the question whether the test we have employed since *Central Hudson* should be displaced. . . .

Lorillard Tobacco Co. v. Reilly

533 U.S. 525, 121 S.CT. 2404 (2001)

In 1999, Massachusetts enacted comprehensive regulations on the advertising and sale of tobacco products, which in turn were challenged by Lorillard Tobacco Company and other tobacco producers and retailers who contended that the regulations were preempted by federal law and violated the First Amendment. Among the regulations, outdoor advertising was restricted, including a ban on advertising within a 1,000-foot radius of any public playground or school, and the indoor display of tobacco products was restricted. A federal district court upheld the regulations, and the Court of Appeals for the First Circuit concluded that the regulations were not preempted by federal law and did not violate the First Amendment.

The lower court's decision was reversed and affirmed in part by a five to four vote of different justices. In Justice O'Connor's opinion for the Court, Parts I, II-C, and II-D were joined unanimously; Parts III-A, III-C, and III-D were joined by Chief Justice Rehnquist and Justices Scalia, Kennedy, Souter, and Thomas; Part III-B-1 was joined by Chief Justice Rehnquist and Justices Stevens, Souter, Ginsburg, and Breyer; and Parts II-A, II-B, III-B-2, and IV were joined by Chief Justice Rehnquist and Justices Scalia, Kennedy, and Thomas. Justice Kennedy filed an opinion concurring in part and concurring in the judgment, in which Justice Scalia joined. Justice Thomas filed an opinion concurring in part and concurring in the judgment. Justice Souter filed an opinion concurring in part and dissenting in part. Justice Stevens filed an opinion concurring in part and dissenting in part, which Justices Ginsburg and Breyer joined, and in Part I of which Justice Souter joined.

☐ *Justice O'CONNOR delivered the opinion of the Court.*

■ II

Before reaching the First Amendment issues, we must decide to what extent federal law preempts the Attorney General's regulations. The cigarette petitioners contend that the [Federal Cigarette Labeling and Advertising Act] FCLAA preempts the [Massachusetts] Attorney General's cigarette advertising regulations. . . .

■ A

In the FCLAA, Congress has crafted a comprehensive federal scheme governing the advertising and promotion of cigarettes. The FCLAA's preemption provision provides:

"(b) State regulations

"No requirement or prohibition based on smoking and health shall be imposed under State law with respect to the advertising or promotion of any cigarettes the packages of which are labeled in conformity with the provisions of this chapter."

The FCLAA's preemption provision does not cover smokeless tobacco or cigars. . . .

In the preemption provision, Congress unequivocally precludes the requirement of any additional statements on cigarette packages beyond those provided in Section 1333. Congress further precludes States or localities from imposing any requirement or prohibition based on smoking and health with respect to the advertising and promotion of cigarettes. . . .

[W]e fail to see how the FCLAA and its preemption provision permit a distinction between the specific concern about minors and cigarette advertising and the more general concern about smoking and health in cigarette advertising, especially in light of the fact that Congress crafted a legislative solution for those very concerns. We also conclude that a distinction between state regulation of the location as opposed to the content of cigarette advertising has no foundation in the text of the preemption provision. Congress preempted state cigarette advertising regulations like the Attorney General's because they would upset federal legislative choices to require specific warnings and to impose the ban on cigarette advertising in electronic media in order to address concerns about smoking and health. Accordingly, we hold that the Attorney General's outdoor and point-of-sale advertising regulations targeting cigarettes are preempted by the FCLAA.

■ C

Although the FCLAA prevents States and localities from imposing special requirements or prohibitions "based on smoking and health" "with respect to the advertising or promotion" of cigarettes, that language still leaves significant power in the hands of States to impose generally applicable zoning regulations and to regulate conduct.

For instance, the FCLAA does not restrict a State or locality's ability to enact generally applicable zoning restrictions. . . . The FCLAA also does not foreclose all state regulation of conduct as it relates to the sale or use of cigarettes. The FCLAA's preemption provision explicitly governs state regulations of "advertising or promotion." Accordingly, the FCLAA does not pre-empt state laws prohibiting cigarette sales to minors. . . .

■ III

By its terms, the FCLAA's preemption provision only applies to cigarettes. Accordingly, we must evaluate the smokeless tobacco and cigar petitioners' First Amendment challenges to the State's outdoor and point-of-sale advertising regulations. . . .

■ A

For over 25 years, the Court has recognized that commercial speech does not fall outside the purview of the First Amendment. See, e.g., *Virginia Bd. of Pharmacy* [*Virginia Citizens Consumer Council, Inc.*, 425 U.S. 748 (1976)]. Instead, the Court has afforded commercial speech a measure of First Amendment protection " 'commensurate' " with its position in relation to other constitutionally guaranteed expression. In recognition of the "distinction between speech proposing a commercial transaction, which occurs in an area traditionally subject to government regulation, and other varieties of speech," *Central Hudson* [*Gas & Electric Corp. v. Public Service Commission of New York*, 447 U.S. 557 (1980)], we developed a framework for analyzing regulations of commercial speech that is "substantially similar" to the test for time, place, and manner restrictions. The analysis contains four elements: "At the outset, we must determine whether the expression is protected by the First Amendment. For commercial speech to come within that provision, it at least must concern lawful activity and not be misleading. Next, we ask whether the asserted governmental interest is substantial. If both inquiries yield positive answers, we must determine whether the regulation directly advances the governmental interest asserted, and whether it is not more extensive than is necessary to serve that interest."

Only the last two steps of *Central Hudson*'s four-part analysis are at issue here. The Attorney General has assumed for purposes of summary judgment that petitioners' speech is entitled to First Amendment protection. With respect to the second step, none of the petitioners contests the importance of the State's interest in preventing the use of tobacco products by minors.

The third step of *Central Hudson* concerns the relationship between the harm that underlies the State's interest and the means identified by the State to advance that interest. . . .

We do not, however, require that "empirical data come . . . accompanied by a surfeit of background information. . . . [W]e have permitted litigants to justify speech restrictions by reference to studies and anecdotes pertaining to different locales altogether, or even, in a case applying strict scrutiny, to justify restrictions based solely on history, consensus, and 'simple common sense.' "

The last step of the *Central Hudson* analysis "complements" the third step, "asking whether the speech restriction is not more extensive than necessary to serve the interests that support it." We have made it clear that "the least restrictive means" is not the standard; instead, the case law requires a reasonable " 'fit between the legislature's ends and the means chosen to accomplish those ends, . . . a means narrowly tailored to achieve the desired objective.' " Focusing on the third and fourth steps of the *Central Hudson* analysis, we first address the outdoor advertising and point-of-sale advertising regulations for smokeless tobacco and cigars. We then address the sales practices regulations for all tobacco products.

▪ B

The outdoor advertising regulations prohibit smokeless tobacco or cigar advertising within a 1,000-foot radius of a school or playground. . . .

▪ 2

Whatever the strength of the Attorney General's evidence to justify the outdoor advertising regulations, however, we conclude that the regulations do not satisfy the fourth step of the *Central Hudson* analysis. The final step of the *Central Hudson* analysis, the "critical inquiry in this case," requires a reasonable fit between the means and ends of the regulatory scheme. The Attorney General's regulations do not meet this standard. The broad sweep of the regulations indicates that the Attorney General did not "carefully calculat[e] the costs and benefits associated with the burden on speech imposed" by the regulations. *Cincinnati v. Discovery Network, Inc.*, 507 U.S. 410 (1993).

The outdoor advertising regulations prohibit any smokeless tobacco or cigar advertising within 1,000 feet of schools or playgrounds. . . . The substantial geographical reach of the Attorney General's outdoor advertising regulations is compounded by other factors. "Outdoor" advertising includes not only advertising located outside an establishment, but also advertising inside a store if that advertising is visible from outside the store. The regulations restrict advertisements of any size and the term advertisement also includes oral statements.

In some geographical areas, these regulations would constitute nearly a complete ban on the communication of truthful information about smokeless tobacco and cigars to adult consumers. The breadth and scope of the regulations, and the process by which the Attorney General adopted the regulations, do not demonstrate a careful calculation of the speech interests involved.

First, the Attorney General did not seem to consider the impact of the 1,000-foot restriction on commercial speech in major metropolitan areas. The Attorney General apparently selected the 1,000-foot distance based on the FDA's decision to impose an identical 1,000-foot restriction when it attempted to regulate cigarette and smokeless tobacco advertising. But the FDA's 1,000-foot regulation was not an adequate basis for the Attorney General to tailor the Massachusetts regulations. The degree to which speech is suppressed—or alternative avenues for speech remain available—under a particular regulatory scheme tends to be case-specific. And a case-specific analysis makes sense, for although a State or locality may have common interests and concerns about underage smoking and the effects of tobacco advertisements, the impact of a restriction on speech will undoubtedly vary from place to place. The FDA's regulations would have had widely disparate effects nationwide. Even in Massachusetts, the effect of the Attorney General's speech regulations will vary based on whether a locale is rural, suburban, or urban. The uniformly broad sweep of the geographical limitation demonstrates a lack of tailoring.

In addition, the range of communications restricted seems unduly broad. For instance, it is not clear from the regulatory scheme why a ban on oral communications is necessary to further the State's interest. Apparently that restriction means that a retailer is unable to answer inquiries about its tobacco products if that communication occurs outdoors. Similarly, a ban on all signs of any size seems ill suited to target the problem of highly visible billboards, as opposed to smaller signs. . . .

We conclude that the Attorney General has failed to show that the outdoor advertising regulations for smokeless tobacco and cigars are not more extensive than necessary to advance the State's substantial interest in preventing underage tobacco use. . . .

■ C

Massachusetts has also restricted indoor, point-of-sale advertising for smokeless tobacco and cigars. Advertising cannot be "placed lower than five feet from the floor of any retail establishment which is located within a one thousand foot radius of" any school or playground. . . .

We conclude that the point-of-sale advertising regulations fail both the third and fourth steps of the *Central Hudson* analysis. A regulation cannot be sustained if it "provides only ineffective or remote support for the government's purpose," or if there is "little chance" that the restriction will advance the State's goal. . . .

■ D

The Attorney General also promulgated a number of regulations that restrict sales practices by cigarette, smokeless tobacco, and cigar manufacturers and retailers. Among other restrictions, the regulations bar the use of self-service displays and require that tobacco products be placed out of the reach of all consumers in a location accessible only to salespersons. . . .

Assuming that petitioners have a cognizable speech interest in a particular means of displaying their products, cf. *Cincinnati v. Discovery Network, Inc.,* 507 U.S. 410 (1993) (distribution of a magazine through newsracks), these regulations withstand First Amendment scrutiny.

Massachusetts' sales practices provisions regulate conduct that may have a communicative component, but Massachusetts seeks to regulate the placement of tobacco products for reasons unrelated to the communication of ideas. We conclude that the State has demonstrated a substantial interest in preventing access to tobacco products by minors and has adopted an appropriately narrow means of advancing that interest.

Unattended displays of tobacco products present an opportunity for access without the proper age verification required by law. Thus, the State prohibits self-service and other displays that would allow an individual to obtain tobacco products without direct contact with a salesperson. It is clear that the regulations leave open ample channels of communication. The regulations do not significantly impede adult access to tobacco products. Moreover, retailers have other means of exercising any cognizable speech interest in the presentation of their products. We presume that vendors may place empty tobacco packaging on open display, and display actual tobacco products so long as that display is only accessible to sales personnel. . . .

We conclude that the sales practices regulations withstand First Amendment scrutiny. The means chosen by the State are narrowly tailored to prevent access to tobacco products by minors, are unrelated to expression, and leave open alternative avenues for vendors to convey information about products and for would-be customers to inspect products before purchase. . . .

■ IV

To the extent that federal law and the First Amendment do not prohibit state action, States and localities remain free to combat the problem of underage tobacco use by appropriate means. The judgment of the United States Court of Appeals for the First Circuit is therefore affirmed in part and reversed in part, and the cases are remanded for further proceedings consistent with this opinion.

☐ *Justice THOMAS, concurring in part and concurring in the judgment.*

I join the opinion of the Court (with the exception of Part III-B-1) because I agree that the Massachusetts cigarette advertising regulations are preempted by the Federal Cigarette Labeling and Advertising Act. I also agree with the Court's disposition of the First Amendment challenges to the other regulations at issue here, and I share the Court's view that the regulations fail even the intermediate scrutiny of *Central Hudson Gas & Elec. Corp. v. Public Serv. Comm'n of N.Y.*, 447 U.S. 557 (1980). At the same time, I continue to believe that when the government seeks to restrict truthful speech in order to suppress the ideas it conveys, strict scrutiny is appropriate, whether or not the speech in question may be characterized as "commercial." See *44 Liquormart, Inc. v. Rhode Island*, 517 U.S. 484 (1996) (THOMAS, J., concurring in part and concurring in judgment). I would subject all of the advertising restrictions to strict scrutiny and would hold that they violate the First Amendment. . . .

☐ *Justice STEVENS, with whom Justice GINSBURG and Justice BREYER join, and with whom Justice SOUTER joins as to Part I, concurring in part, concurring in the judgment in part, and dissenting in part.*

Because I strongly disagree with the Court's conclusion that the Federal Cigarette Labeling and Advertising Act of 1965 (FCLAA or Act) precludes States and localities from regulating the location of cigarette advertising, I dissent from Parts II-A and II-B of the Court's opinion. On the First Amendment questions, I agree with the Court both that the outdoor advertising restrictions imposed by Massachusetts serve legitimate and important state interests and that the record does not indicate that the measures were properly tailored to serve those interests. Because the present record does not enable us to adjudicate the merits of those claims on summary judgment, I would vacate the decision upholding those restrictions and remand for trial on the constitutionality of the outdoor advertising regulations. Finally, because I do not believe that either the point-of-sale advertising restrictions or the sales practice restrictions implicate significant First Amendment concerns, I would uphold them in their entirety. . . .

E | *Freedom of the Press*

The Supreme Court articulated constitutional principles for freedom of the press based on the recognition that "speech concerning public affairs . . . is the essence of self-government."[1] Consistent with "the assumption that the widest possible dissemination of information from diverse and antagonistic sources is essential to the welfare of the public," in *Associated Press v. United States*, 326 U.S. 1 (1945), the Court reaffirmed that "Any system of prior restraint of expression . . . [bears] a heavy presumption against its constitutional validity" in *New York Times v. United States*, 403 U.S. 713 (1971).

At the same time, First Amendment protection for the press also extends to various modes of disseminating information—pamphlets, leaflets, signs, magazines, advertisements, books, motion pictures, and radio and television broadcasts.[2] Accordingly, the "lonely pamphleteer" and the "citizen-critic" are protected along with the "institutional press." This is because the speech and press clauses have traditionally been viewed as inseparable, coterminous, and thus a constitutional redundancy. As the Court in *Thornhill v. Alabama*, 310 U.S. 88 (1940), observed,

> The freedom of speech and of the press guaranteed by the Constitution embraces at least the liberty to discuss publicly and truthfully all matters of public concern without previous restraint or fear of subsequent punishment. The exigencies of the colonial period and the efforts to secure freedom from oppressive administration developed a broadened conception of these liberties as adequate to supply the public need for information and education with respect to the significant issues of the times. . . . Freedom of discussion, if it would fulfill its historical function in this nation, must embrace all issues about which information is needed or appropriate to enable the members of society to cope with the exigencies of their period.

In the last two decades, though, there has been a movement ostensibly to further enlarge the scope of the First Amendment by recognizing the "institutional status" of the press, such recognition to include affirmative rights to acquire information and special press privileges shielding reporters from indirect restraints on their freedom. Justice

Stewart, among others, argued that the First Amendment "is, in essence, a *structural* provision of the Constitution" that confers preferred constitutional status on "the organized press" and "the daily newspapers and other established news media." The "primary purpose" of the amendment, in his words, "was to create a fourth institution outside the Government as an additional check on the three official branches. . . . The publishing business is, in short, the only organized private business that is given explicit constitutional protection."[3]

Contrary to Justice Stewart's interpretation, however, *New York Times* contributor Anthony Lewis lamented, "The Press does itself no good when it claims special privileges under the Constitution" and the strategy of the press to use the politics of constitutional adjudication to secure "different and better treatment under the Constitution [is a] fundamental mistake."[4]

A dilemma posed by a structuralist interpretation of the First Amendment and special privileges for the institutional press lies in how to define *the press*. As Justice White notes in *Branzburg v. Hayes* (1972) (excerpted below), press privileges "present practical and conceptual difficulties of a high order." The Court could fashion constitutional press privileges by following the lines drawn by some legislatures in drafting press shield laws (which, in some instances, protect reporters from having to reveal their sources), either defining members of the institutional press according to their employer, work schedule, or publication record. Alternatively, immunity could be given for all who write professionally. But both approaches threaten to deny constitutional protection for the citizen-critic, and broader definitions of "the press" might prove so overinclusive as to render meaningless special privileges carved out for the press in the first place.

Is the First Amendment guarantee against "abridging the freedom of speech, or of the press" redundant? Should the press be accorded special constitutional status? These are some of the underlying issues confronting the Court in cases arising from direct and indirect restraints on press freedom.

NOTES

1. *Garrison v. Louisiana*, 379 U.S. 64 (1964).

2. See *Lovell v. City of Griffin*, 303 U.S. 444 (1938) (pamphlets); *Schneider v. New Jersey*, 308 U.S. 147 (1939) (leaflets); *Thornhill v. Alabama*, 310 U.S. 88 (1940) (signs); *Roth v. United States*, 354 U.S. 376 (1957) (*dicta*, books); *Joseph Burstyn, Inc. v. Wilson*, 343 U.S. 495 (1952) (motion pictures); *New York Times Co. v. Sullivan*, 376 U.S. 254 (1964) (noncommercial advertisements); *Virginia State Board of Pharmacy v. Virginia Citizens Consumer Council*, 425 U.S. 748 (1976) (commercial advertisements); *Greenbelt Cooper-*

ative Publishing Association v. Bresler, 398 U.S. 6 (1970) (newspapers); *Time, Inc. v. Hill,* 385 U.S. 374 (1967) (magazines); *Red Lion Broadcasting Co. v. Federal Communications Commission,* 395 U.S. 367 (1969) (radio); and *Estes v. Texas,* 381 U.S. 532 (1965) (*dicta,* television).

3. Potter Stewart, "Or of the Press," 26 *Hastings Law Journal* 631 (1975). See also Randall Bezanson, "The New Free Press Guarantee," 63 *Virginia Law Review* 731 (1977); John Paul Stevens, "Some Thoughts about a General Rule," 21 *Arizona Law Review* 599 (1979); and Floyd Abrams, "The Press *Is* Different: Reflections on Justice Stewart and the Autonomous Press," 7 *Hofstra Law Review* 559 (1979).

4. Anthony Lewis, "A Preferred Position for Journalism," 7 *Hofstra Law Review* 595 (1979). See also Anthony Lewis, "A Public Right to Know about Public Institutions: The First Amendment as Sword," in *The Supreme Court Review,* Vol. 1, ed. Philip Kurland and Gerhard Casper (Chicago: University of Chicago Press, 1981).

■ (1) THE DOCTRINE OF NO PRIOR RESTRAINT

The doctrine of no prior restraint was the touchstone for freedom of the press in English common law and generally assumed to be incorporated into the First Amendment. As Justice Holmes, *Patterson v. Colorado,* 205 U.S. 452 (1907), observed, "[T]he main purpose of [the Free Speech and Press] provisions is to 'prevent all such *previous restraints* upon publications as had been practiced by other governments,' and they do not prevent the subsequent punishment of such as may be deemed contrary to the public welfare."

In *Near v. State of Minnesota ex rel. Olson* (1931) (excerpted below), Chief Justice Hughes wrote the doctrine into the developing law of the First Amendment. Subsequently, *Grosjean v. American Press Company,* 297 U.S. 233 (1936), held that taxes may not impose a discriminatory burden on newspapers. There, Governor Huey Long and his political machine in the Louisiana legislature passed a license tax of 2 percent of the gross income of newspapers selling more than 2,000 copies a week, to stifle their opponents. The principle that taxes may not operate as a prior restraint was reaffirmed in *Minneapolis Star and Tribune v. Minneapolis Commissioner of Revenue,* 460 U.S. 575 (1983) and, again, in the Court's striking down a law imposing a sales tax on magazines, but not newspapers, in *Arkansas Writers' Project v. Ragland,* 481 U.S. 221 (1987).

Notably, in *Simon & Schuster, Inc. v. Members of the New York State Crime Victims Board,* 502 U.S. 105 (1991), the Rehnquist Court struck down New York's "Son-of-Sam" law. The law was adopted in order to prevent criminals from profiting from their notoriety and the sale of stories of their criminal activities. In 1977, David Berkowitz, a serial killer popularly known as the "Son of Sam," murdered five women and later agreed to have his story of terror published for a substantial advance on royalties. New York's legislature immediately responded by passing its "Son-of-Sam" law, requiring publishers to deposit with the Victims Control Board all royalties and earnings from its contracts with accused or convicted criminals. The board in turn was authorized to hold the money for five years, during which time victims could bring civil actions against a convicted defendant, and to make payments to victims of a crime. The act also covered individuals who were not criminally charged, tried, and convicted but who admitted committing crimes in a book or other commercial communications. In 1987, the Victims Control Board notified Simon & Schuster that it had violated the law by not turning over its contract with and the royalties owed Henry Hill, who retold his life in organized crime in *Wiseguy*. Attorneys for Simon & Schuster and Hill countered that New York's law violated the First Amendment's guarantee of freedom of speech and press.

Writing for the Court in *Simon & Schuster*, Justice O'Connor struck down New York's law as "presumptively inconsistent with the First Amendment" for imposing "a financial burden on speakers because of the content of their speech." "In the context of financial regulation," O'Connor underscored, "the Government's ability to impose content-based burdens on speech raises the specter that the Government may effectively drive certain ideas or viewpoints from the marketplace. The First Amendment presumptively places this sort of discrimination beyond the power of the Government." Nor did the Court find New York's statute either to serve a "compelling state interest" or to have been "narrowly drawn to achieve that end."

Under the doctrine of no prior restraint, *Mills v. Alabama*, 384 U.S. 214 (1966), invalidated a law barring editorial comments on election days. In *Landmark Communications, Inc. v. Virginia*, 435 U.S. 829 (1978), the Court struck down a Virginia law forbidding the disclosure of confidential information about the proceedings of the state's Judicial Inquiry and Review Commission. So too in *Smith v. Daily Mail Publishing Company*, 443 U.S. 97 (1979), a statute barring the disclosure of the names of juveniles arrested by police was struck down as a prior restraint. And *Butterworth v. Smith*, 494 U.S. 624 (1990), overturned a Florida statute barring witnesses before grand juries from later disclosing their testimony.

Further underscoring the First Amendment's outweighing of interests in personal privacy and law enforcement, *Bartnicki v. Vopper*, 532 U.S. 514 (2001), held that the amendment protects lawfully obtained information even when the original source acquired the information through unlawful means. At issue was the reach of federal and state wiretapping laws aimed at preventing people from intercepting private communications versus the First Amendment's protection for the dissemination of information. The case stemmed from heated contract negotiations between a teachers' union and a school board, when the union's president on her cell phone angrily told the union's chief negotiator that if the school board members did not accept its offer, the teachers were going to "blow off the front porches" of their homes. An opponent of the union said that he found a recording of that conversation in his mailbox and turned it over to a local radio station, which broadcast it. Yet, in balancing the government's interests, in deterring unlawful wiretapping and protecting the privacy of personal communications, against the communication of matters of public importance and criticisms of public officials, Justice Stevens concluded that the government's interests were not so great as to override the First Amendment's protection for the dissemination of information lawfully obtained, even though the original acquisition of the information was unlawful. Chief Justice Rehnquist and Justice Scalia and Thomas dissented.

Notice that Chief Justice Hughes in *Near v. Minnesota* does not deny that "a government might prevent actual obstruction of the sailing dates of transports or the number or location of troops," implying that there might be a "national security" exception to the First Amendment doctrine of no prior restraint. "On similar grounds," he also notes that "the primary requirements of decency may be enforced against obscene publications" and "[t]he security of the community life may be protected against incitements to acts of violence." In these areas there remains controversy over the application of the doctrine of no prior restraint. In *New York Times Co. v. United States*, 403 U.S. 713 (1971) (see excerpt below) the Court denied as a prior restraint the government's attempt to enjoin the publication of the "Pentagon Papers." In *Southeastern Promotions v. Conrad*, 420 U.S. 546 (1975), the Court required the municipal board of Chattanooga, Tennessee, to make its city Memorial Auditorium available for the stage production of *Hair*, a theatrical performance that includes nudity, simulated sex, and vulgar language. Over Rehnquist's dissent that there was no real issue of prior restraint (because scheduling limitations for the auditorium precluded the presentation of every production), the majority concluded that denying the use of the facility constituted a prior restraint. In reaffirming that "a system of prior restraint 'avoids constitutional infirmity only if it takes place under procedural safeguards designed to obviate the dangers of a censorship system,'" the Court indicated that local governments bear a burden of instituting judicial proceedings and of proving that materials or productions are unprotected expression under the First Amendment.

Selected Bibliography

Ellsberg, Daniel. *Secrets: A Memoir of Vietnam and the Pentagon Papers.* New York: Viking, 2003.

Friendly, Fred. *Minnesota Rag: The Dramatic Story of the Landmark Supreme Court That Gave New Meaning to Freedom of the Press.* New York: Random House, 1981.

Gleason, Timothy. *The Watchdog Concept.* Ames: Iowa State University Press, 1990.

Levy, Leonard. *Emergence of a Free Press.* New York: Oxford University Press, 1985.

O'Brien, David. *The Public's Right to Know: The Supreme Court and the First Amendment.* New York: Praeger, 1981.

Prados, John, and Porter, Margaret P., eds. *Inside the Pentagon Papers.* Lawrence: University Press of Kansas, 2004.

Rudenstine, David. *The Day the Presses Stopped: A History of the Pentagon Papers Case.* Berkeley: University of California Press, 1996.

Smith, Jeffrey. *Printers and Press Freedom.* New York: Oxford University Press, 1988.

Snepp, Frank. *Irreparable Harm: A First Hand Account of How One Agent Took on the CIA in an Epic Battle over Secrecy and Free Speech.* New York: Random House, 1999.

Near v. State of Minnesota ex rel. Olson
283 U.S. 697, 51 S.Ct. 625 (1931)

Jay Near was the editor of a muckraking newspaper, the *Saturday Press*, that gave vent to his anti-Semitic, antiblack, anti-Catholic, and antilabor views. In 1927, his newspaper was closed under a 1925 Minnesota abatement statute for any newspaper, magazine, or periodical creating a public nuisance by "malicious, scandalous and defamatory" publication. Under the law, Near could be permanently enjoined from publishing, with a penalty of $1,000 as a fine or a year in jail for violating the injunction against publishing. Near contended the law was unconstitutional, but the state supreme court disagreed, and subsequently a district court and the state supreme court upheld the closing of Near's newspaper. But Near's case came to be championed by Colonel Robert McCormick, the publisher of the Chicago *Tribune*, who paid for an appeal to the Supreme Court.

The Court's decision was five to four, and the majority's opinion was announced by Chief Justice Hughes. Dissent was by Justice Butler, who was joined by Justices Van Devanter, McReynolds, and Sutherland.

☐ *Chief Justice HUGHES delivered the opinion of the Court.*

Chapter 285 of the Session Laws of Minnesota for the year 1925 provides for the abatement, as a public nuisance, of a "malicious, scandalous and defamatory newspaper, magazine or other periodical." Section 1 of the act is as follows:

> "Section 1. Any person who, as an individual, or as a member or employee of a firm, or association or organization, or as an officer, director, member or employee of a corporation, shall be engaged in the business of regularly or customarily producing, publishing or circulating, having in possession, selling or giving away
>
> "(a) an obscene, lewd and lascivious newspaper, magazine, or other periodical, or
>
> "(b) a malicious, scandalous and defamatory newspaper, magazine or other periodical,
>
> —is guilty of a nuisance, and all persons guilty of such nuisance may be enjoined, as hereinafter provided." . . .

Under this statute (section 1, clause (b), the county attorney of Hennepin county brought this action to enjoin the publication of what was described as a "malicious, scandalous and defamatory newspaper, magazine or other periodical," known as the *Saturday Press*, published by the defendants in the city of Minneapolis. . . .

Without attempting to summarize the contents of the voluminous exhibits attached to the complaint, we deem it sufficient to say that the articles charged, in substance, that a Jewish gangster was in control of gambling, bootlegging, and racketeering in Minneapolis, and that law enforcing officers and agencies were not energetically performing their duties. . . .

If we cut through mere details of procedure, the operation and effect of the statute in substance is that public authorities may bring the owner or publisher of a newspaper or periodical before a judge upon a charge of conducting a business of publishing scandalous and defamatory matter—in particular that the matter consists of charges against public officers of official dereliction—and, unless the owner or publisher is able and disposed to bring competent evidence to satisfy the judge that the charges are true and are published with good motives and for justifiable ends, his newspaper or periodical is suppressed and further publication is made punishable as a contempt. This is of the essence of censorship.

The question is whether a statute authorizing such proceedings in restraint of publication is consistent with the conception of the liberty of the press as historically conceived and guaranteed. In determining the extent of the constitutional protection, it has been generally, if not universally, considered that it is the chief purpose of the guaranty to prevent previous restraints upon publication. The struggle in England, directed against the legislative power of the licenser, resulted in renunciation of the censorship of the press. The liberty deemed to be established was thus described by Blackstone: "The liberty of the press is indeed essential to the nature of a free state; but this consists in laying no *previous* restraints upon publications, and not in freedom from censure for criminal matter when published. Every freeman has an undoubted right to lay what sentiments he pleases before the public; to forbid this, is to destroy the freedom of the press; but if he publishes what is improper, mischievous or illegal, he must take the consequence of his own temerity." 4 Bl. Com. 151, 152. See *Story on the Constitution*, §§ 1884, 1889. The distinction was early pointed out between the extent of the freedom with respect to censorship under our constitutional system and that enjoyed in England. Here, as Madison said, "the great and essential rights of the people are secured against legislative as well as against executive ambition. They are secured, not by laws paramount to prerogative, but by constitutions paramount to laws. This security of the freedom of the press requires that it should be exempt not only from previous restraint by the Executive, as in Great Britain, but from legislative restraint also." Report on the Virginia Resolutions, Madison's Works, vol. IV, p. 543. . . .

The criticism upon Blackstone's statement has not been because immunity from previous restraint upon publication has not been regarded as deserving of special emphasis, but chiefly because that immunity cannot be deemed to exhaust the conception of the liberty guaranteed by State and Federal Constitutions. . . . [I]t is recognized that punishment for the abuse of the liberty accorded to the press is essential to the protection of the public, and that the common-law rules that subject the libeler to responsibility for the public offense, as well as for the private injury, are not abolished by the protection extended in our Constitutions. The law of criminal libel rests upon that secure foundation. There is also the conceded authority of courts to punish for contempt when publications directly tend to prevent the proper discharge of judicial functions. In the present case, we have no occasion to inquire as to the permissible scope of subsequent punishment. For whatever wrong the appellant has committed or may commit, by his publications, the state appropriately affords both public and private redress by its libel laws. As has been noted, the statute in question does not deal with punishments; it provides for no punishment, except in case of contempt for violation of the court's order, but for suppression and injunction—that is, for restraint upon publication.

The objection has also been made that the principle as to immunity from previous restraint is stated too broadly, if every such restraint is deemed to be prohibited. That is undoubtedly true; the protection even as to previous restraint is not absolutely unlimited. But the limitation has been recognized only in exceptional cases. "When a nation is at war many things that might be said in time of peace are such a hindrance to its effort that their utterance will not be endured so long as men fight and that no Court could regard them as protected by any constitutional right." *Schenck v. United States.* [249 U.S. 47 (1919)]. No one would question but that a government might prevent actual obstruction to its recruiting service or the publication of the sailing dates of transports or the number and location of troops. On similar grounds, the primary requirements of decency may be enforced against obscene publications. The security of the community life may be protected against incitements to acts of violence and the overthrow by force of orderly government. The constitutional guaranty of free speech does not "protect a man from an injunction against uttering words that may have all the effect of force. *Gompers v. Buck's Stove & Range Co.*, 221 U.S. 418

[(1911)]. . . ." *Schenck v. United States, supra.* These limitations are not applicable here. . . .

The fact that for approximately one hundred and fifty years there has been almost an entire absence of attempts to impose previous restraints upon publications relating to the malfeasance of public officers is significant of the deep-seated conviction that such restraints would violate constitutional right. Public officers, whose character and conduct remain open to debate and free discussion in the press, find their remedies for false accusations in actions under libel laws providing for redress and punishment, and not in proceedings to restrain the publication of newspapers and periodicals. The general principle that the constitutional guaranty of the liberty of the press gives immunity from previous restraints has been approved in many decisions under the provisions of state constitutions. . . .

For these reasons we hold the statute, so far as it authorized the proceedings in this action under clause (b) of section 1, to be an infringement of the liberty of the press guaranteed by the Fourteenth Amendment.

     ☐ *Justice BUTLER, with whom Justices VAN DEVANTER, McREYNOLDS, and SUTHERLAND join, dissenting.*

The decision of the Court in this case . . . gives to freedom of the press a meaning and a scope not heretofore recognized, and construes "liberty" in the due process clause of the Fourteenth Amendment to put upon the states a federal restriction that is without precedent. . . .

The Minnesota statute does not operate as a *previous* restraint on publication within the proper meaning of that phrase. It does not authorize administrative control in advance such as was formerly exercised by the licensers and censors, but prescribes a remedy to be enforced by a suit in equity. In this case there was previous publication made in the course of the business of regularly producing malicious, scandalous, and defamatory periodicals. The business and publications unquestionably constitute an abuse of the right of free press. The statute denounces the things done as a nuisance on the ground, as stated by the state Supreme Court, that they threaten morals, peace, and good order. There is no question of the power of the state to denounce such transgressions. The restraint authorized is only in respect of continuing to do what has been duly adjudged to constitute a nuisance.

***

New York Times Company v. United States
403 U.S. 670, 91 S.Ct. 2140 (1971)

In 1971, amid growing opposition to the undeclared Vietnam War, the Nixon administration sought to enjoin the *New York Times* and the *Washington Post* from publishing a series of articles based on a forty-seven-volume study, *History of U.S. Decision-Making Process on Vietnam Policy.* The study was prepared in 1968 and was classified "Top Secret—Sensitive." The *New York Times* received copies of the study from Daniel

Ellsberg, who had secretly copied them while working for a think tank and after his unsuccessful efforts to persuade leading politicians to publicize the study.

After several months of reviewing the documents, the *New York Times* commenced publication of selected items on June 13, 1971. Following the third installment the Department of Justice sought an injunction against publication of the balance of the series and obtained a temporary restraining order prohibiting further publication until June 19. On June 18 the *Washington Post* also printed two articles based on the study and by five o'clock that day the government had filed a similar suit against its further publication of the material.

The next morning a district court denied the government's request for a preliminary injunction, but later in the day a circuit court judge extended the temporary restraining order until noon, June 21, to give a panel of the circuit court the opportunity to consider the government's application. On June 22, the circuit court remanded the case to the district court to determine whether any of the other materials posed such grave and immediate danger to the security of the country as to warrant prior restraint and a continued stay on publication until June 25. The *New York Times* promptly appealed to the Supreme Court to vacate the stay on publication and to expedite consideration of the case. On June 25 the Court granted *certiorari* and heard arguments the next day. Remarkably, four days later the Court issued no fewer than ten opinions.

The Court's decision was six to three, and the opinion was announced *per curiam.* There were concurrences by Justices Black, Douglas, Brennan, Stewart, White, and Marshall and dissents by Chief Justice Burger and Justices Harlan and Blackmun.

PER CURIAM.

We granted *certiorari* in these cases in which the United States seeks to enjoin the *New York Times* and the *Washington Post* from publishing the contents of a classified study entitled "*History of U.S. Decision-Making Process on Vietnam Policy.*"

"Any system of prior restraints of expression comes to this Court bearing a heavy presumption against its constitutional validity." *Bantam Books, Inc. v. Sullivan,* 372 U.S. 58 (1963); see also *Near v. Minnesota ex rel. Olson,* 283 U.S. 697 (1931). The Government "thus carries a heavy burden of showing justification for the imposition of such a restraint." *Organization for a Better Austin v. Keefe,* 402 U.S. 415 (1971). The District Court for the Southern District of New York in the *New York Times* case, 328 F.Supp. 324, and the District Court for the District of Columbia and the Court of Appeals for the District of Columbia Circuit, 446 F.2d 1327, in the *Washington Post* case held that the Government had not met that burden. We agree.

The judgment of the Court of Appeals for the District of Columbia

Circuit is therefore affirmed. The order of the Court of Appeals for the Second Circuit is reversed and the case is remanded with directions to enter a judgment affirming the judgment of the District Court for the Southern District of New York. The stays entered June 25, 1971, by the Court are vacated.

☐ *Justice BLACK, with whom Justice DOUGLAS joins, concurring.*

I believe that every moment's continuance of the injunctions against these newspapers amounts to a flagrant, indefensible, and continuing violation of the First Amendment. . . . In my view it is unfortunate that some of my Brethren are apparently willing to hold that the publication of news may sometimes be enjoined. Such a holding would make a shambles of the First Amendment. . . .

In seeking injunctions against these newspapers and in its presentation to the Court, the Executive Branch seems to have forgotten the essential purpose and history of the First Amendment. When the Constitution was adopted, many people strongly opposed it because the document contained no Bill of Rights to safeguard certain basic freedoms. They especially feared that the new powers granted to a central government might be interpreted to permit the government to curtail freedom of religion, press, assembly, and speech. . . . Madison and the other Framers of the First Amendment, able men that they were, wrote in language they earnestly believed could never be misunderstood: "Congress shall make no law . . . abridging the freedom . . . of the press. . . ." Both the history and language of the First Amendment support the view that the press must be left free to publish news, whatever the source, without censorship, injunctions, or prior restraints. . . .

In other words, we are asked to hold that despite the First Amendment's emphatic command, the Executive Branch, the Congress, and the Judiciary can make laws enjoining publication of current news and abridging freedom of the press in the name of "national security." The Government does not even attempt to rely on any act of Congress. Instead it makes the bold and dangerously farreaching contention that the courts should take it upon themselves to "make" a law abridging freedom of the press in the name of equity, presidential power and national security. . . . To find that the President has "inherent power" to halt the publication of news by resort to the courts would wipe out the First Amendment and destroy the fundamental liberty and security of the very people the Government hopes to make "secure." No one can read the history of the adoption of the First Amendment without being convinced beyond any doubt that it was injunctions like those sought here that Madison and his collaborators intended to outlaw in this Nation for all time.

The word "security" is a broad, vague generality whose contours should not be invoked to abrogate the fundamental law embodied in the First Amendment. The guarding of military and diplomatic secrets at the expense of informed representative government provides no real security for our Republic. The Framers of the First Amendment, fully aware of both the need to defend a new nation and the abuses of the English and Colonial Governments, sought to give this new society strength and security by providing that freedom of speech, press, religion, and assembly should not be abridged.

☐ *Justice DOUGLAS, with whom Justice BLACK joins, concurring.*

The Government says that it has inherent powers to go into court and obtain an injunction to protect the national interest, which in this case is alleged to be national security.

Near v. Minnesota ex rel. Olson, 283 U.S. 697 [(1931)], repudiated that expansive doctrine in no uncertain terms. . . .

Secrecy in government is fundamentally anti-democratic, perpetuating bureaucratic errors. Open debate and discussion of public issues are vital to our national health. On public questions there should be "uninhibited, robust, and wide-open" debate.

☐ *Justice BRENNAN, concurring.*

I write separately in these cases only to emphasize what should be apparent that our judgments in the present cases may not be taken to indicate the propriety, in the future, of issuing temporary stays and restraining orders to block the publication of material sought to be suppressed by the Government. So far as I can determine, never before has the United States sought to enjoin a newspaper from publishing information in its possession. The relative novelty of the questions presented, the necessary haste with which decisions were reached, the magnitude of the interests asserted, and the fact that all the parties have concentrated their arguments upon the question whether permanent restraints were proper may have justified at least some of the restraints heretofore imposed in these cases. . . . But even if it be assumed that some of the interim restraints were proper in the two cases before us, that assumption has no bearing upon the propriety of similar judicial action in the future. . . . More important, the First Amendment stands as an absolute bar to the imposition of judicial restraints in circumstances of the kind presented by these cases.

☐ *Justice STEWART, with whom Justice WHITE joins, concurring.*

In the governmental structure created by our Constitution, the Executive is endowed with enormous power in the two related areas of national defense and international relations. This power, largely unchecked by the Legislative and Judicial branches, has been pressed to the very hilt since the advent of the nuclear missile age. For better or for worse, the simple fact is that a President of the United States possesses vastly greater constitutional independence in these two vital areas of power than does, say, a prime minister of a country with a parliamentary form of government.

In the absence of the governmental checks and balances present in other areas of our national life, the only effective restraint upon executive policy and power in the areas of national defense and international affairs may lie in an enlightened citizenry—in an informed and critical public opinion which alone can here protect the values of democratic government. For this reason, it is perhaps here that a press that is alert, aware, and free most vitally serves the basic purpose of the First Amendment. For without an informed and free press there cannot be an enlightened people.

Yet it is elementary that the successful conduct of international diplomacy and the maintenance of an effective national defense require both confidentiality and secrecy. Other nations can hardly deal with this Nation in an atmosphere of mutual trust unless they can be assured that their confidences will be kept. And within our own executive departments, the development of considered and intelligent international policies would be impossible if those charged with their formulation could not communicate with each other freely, frankly, and in confidence. In the area of basic national defense the frequent need for absolute secrecy is, of course, self-evident.

I think there can be but one answer to this dilemma, if dilemma it be. The responsibility must be where the power is. If the Constitution gives the Executive a large degree of unshared power in the conduct of foreign affairs and the maintenance of our national defense, then under the Constitution the Executive must have the largely unshared duty to determine and preserve the degree of internal security necessary to exercise that power successfully. It is an awesome responsibility, requiring judgment and wisdom of a high order. I should suppose that moral, political, and practical considerations would dictate that a very first principle of that wisdom would be an insistence upon avoiding secrecy for its own sake. For when everything is classified, then nothing is classified, and the system becomes one to be disregarded by the cynical or the careless, and to be manipulated by those intent on self-protection or self-promotion. I should suppose, in short, that the hallmark of a truly effective internal security system would be the maximum possible disclosure, recognizing that secrecy can best be preserved only when credibility is truly maintained. But be that as it may, it is clear to me that it is the constitutional duty of the Executive—as a matter of sovereign prerogative and not as a matter of law as the courts know law—through the promulgation and enforcement of executive regulations, to protect the confidentiality necessary to carry out its responsibilities in the fields of international relations and national defense.

This is not to say that Congress and the courts have no role to play. Undoubtedly Congress has the power to enact specific and appropriate criminal laws to protect government property and preserve government secrets. . . . Moreover, if Congress should pass a specific law authorizing civil proceedings in this field, the courts would likewise have the duty to decide the constitutionality of such a law as well as its applicability to the facts proved.

But in the cases before us we are asked neither to construe specific regulations nor to apply specific laws. We are asked, instead, to perform a function that the Constitution gave to the Executive, not the Judiciary. We are asked, quite simply, to prevent the publication by two newspapers of material that the Executive Branch insists should not, in the national interest, be published. I am convinced that the Executive is correct with respect to some of the documents involved. But I cannot say that disclosure of any of them will surely result in direct, immediate, and irreparable damage to our Nation or its people. That being so, there can under the First Amendment be but one judicial resolution of the issues before us. I join the judgments of the Court.

☐ *Justice WHITE, with whom Justice STEWART joins, concurring.*

I concur in today's judgments, but only because of the concededly extraordinary protection against prior restraints enjoyed by the press under our constitutional system. I do not say that in no circumstances would the First Amendment permit an injunction against publishing information about government plans or operations. Nor, after examining the materials the Government characterizes as the most sensitive and destructive, can I deny that revelation of these documents will do substantial damage to public interests. Indeed, I am confident that their disclosure will have that result. But I nevertheless agree that the United States has not satisfied the very heavy burden that it must meet to warrant an injunction against publication in these cases, at least in the absence of express and appropriately limited congressional authorization for prior restraints in circumstances such as these.

The Government's position is simply stated: The responsibility of the Executive for the conduct of the foreign affairs and for the security of the Nation is so basic that the President is entitled to an injunction against publication of a newspaper story whenever he can convince a court that the information to be revealed threatens "grave and irreparable" injury to the public interest; and the injunction should issue whether or not the material to be published is classified, whether or not publication would be lawful under relevant criminal statutes enacted by Congress, and regardless of the circumstances by which the newspaper came into possession of the information.

At least in the absence of legislation by Congress, based on its own investigations and findings, I am quite unable to agree that the inherent powers of the Executive and the courts reach so far as to authorize remedies having such sweeping potential for inhibiting publications by the press. Much of the difficulty inheres in the "grave and irreparable danger" standard suggested by the United States. If the United States were to have judgment under such a standard in these cases, our decision would be of little guidance to other courts in other cases, for the material at issue here would not be available from the Court's opinion or from public records, nor would it be published by the press. Indeed, even today where we hold that the United States has not met its burden, the material remains sealed in court records and it is properly not discussed in today's opinions. Moreover, because the material poses substantial dangers to national interests and because of the hazards of criminal sanctions, a responsible press may choose never to publish the more sensitive materials. To sustain the Government in these cases would start the courts down a long and hazardous road that I am not willing to travel, at least without congressional guidance and direction.

☐ *Justice MARSHALL, concurring.*

The problem here is whether in these particular cases the Executive Branch has authority to invoke the equity jurisdiction of the courts to protect what it believes to be the national interest. See *In re Debs*, 158 U.S. 564 (1895). The Government argues that in addition to the inherent power of any government to protect itself, the President's power to conduct foreign affairs and his position as Commander in Chief give him authority to impose censorship on the press to protect his ability to deal effectively with foreign nations and to conduct the military affairs of the country. Of course, it is beyond cavil that the President has broad powers by virtue of his primary responsibility for the conduct of our foreign affairs and his position as Commander in Chief. . . .

It would, however, be utterly inconsistent with the concept of separation of powers for this Court to use its power of contempt to prevent behavior that Congress has specifically declined to prohibit. There would be a similar damage to the basic concept of these co-equal branches of Government if when the Executive Branch has adequate authority granted by Congress to protect "national security" it can choose instead to invoke the contempt power of a court to enjoin the threatened conduct. The Constitution provides that Congress shall make laws, the President execute laws, and courts interpret laws. It did not provide for government by injunction in which the courts and the Executive Branch can "make law" without regard to the action of Congress. It may be more convenient for the Executive Branch if it need only convince a judge to prohibit conduct rather than ask the Congress to pass a law, and it may be more convenient to enforce a contempt order than to seek a criminal conviction in a jury trial. Moreover, it may be considered politically wise to get a court to share the responsibility for arresting those who the Executive Branch has probable cause to believe are violating the law. But convenience and political considerations of the moment do not justify a basic departure from the principles of our system of government.

☐ *Chief Justice BURGER, dissenting.*

I suggest . . . these cases have been conducted in unseemly haste. . . .

Here, moreover, the frenetic haste is due in large part to the manner in which the Times proceeded from the date it obtained the purloined documents. It seems reasonably clear now that the haste precluded reasonable and deliberate judicial treatment of these cases and was not warranted. . . .

☐ *Justice HARLAN, with whom the Chief Justice and Justice BLACKMUN join, dissenting.*

With all respect, I consider that the Court has been almost irresponsibly feverish in dealing with these cases.

Both the Court of Appeals for the Second Circuit and the Court of Appeals for the District of Columbia Circuit rendered judgment on June 23. The *New York Times'* petition for *certiorari*, its motion for accelerated consideration thereof, and its application for interim relief were filed in this Court on June 24 at about 11 A.M. The application of the United States for interim relief in the *Post* case was also filed here on June 24 at about 7:15 P.M. This Court's order setting a hearing before us on June 26 at 11 A.M., a course which I joined only to avoid the possibility of even more peremptory action by the Court, was issued less than 24 hours before. The record in the *Post* case was filed with the Clerk shortly before 1 P.M. on June 25; the record in the *Times* case did not arrive until 7 or 8 o'clock that same night. The briefs of the parties were received less than two hours before argument on June 26.

This frenzied train of events took place in the name of the presumption against prior restraints created by the First Amendment. Due regard for the extraordinarily important and difficult questions involved in these litigations should have led the Court to shun such a precipitate timetable. In order to decide the merits of these cases properly, some or all of the following questions should have been faced:

1. Whether the Attorney General is authorized to bring these suits in the name of the United States. . . .

2. Whether the First Amendment permits the federal courts to enjoin publication of stories which would present a serious threat to national security. . . .

3. Whether the threat to publish highly secret documents is of itself a sufficient implication of national security to justify an injunction on the theory that regardless of the contents of the documents harm enough results simply from the demonstration of such a breach of secrecy.

4. Whether the unauthorized disclosure of any of these particular documents would seriously impair the national security.

5. What weight should be given to the opinion of high officers in the Executive Branch of the Government with respect to questions 3 and 4.

6. Whether the newspapers are entitled to retain and use the documents notwithstanding the seemingly uncontested facts that the documents, or the originals of which they are duplicates, were purloined from the Government's possession and that the newspapers received them with knowledge that they had been feloniously acquired. . . .

7. Whether the threatened harm to the national security or the Government's possessory interest in the documents justifies the issuance of an injunction against publication in light of—

a. The strong First Amendment policy against prior restraints on publication;

b. The doctrine against enjoining conduct in violation of criminal statutes; and

c. The extent to which the materials at issue have apparently already been otherwise disseminated.

These are difficult questions of fact, of law, and of judgment: the potential consequences of erroneous decision are enormous. The time which has been available to us, to the lower courts, and to the parties has been wholly inadequate for giving these cases the kind of consideration they deserve. It is a reflection on the stability of the judicial process that these great issues—as important as any that have arisen during my time on the Court—should have been decided under the pressures engendered by the torrent of publicity that has attended these litigations from their inception.

Forced as I am to reach the merits of these cases, I dissent from the opinion and judgments of the Court. . . .

It is plain to me that the scope of the judicial function in passing upon the activities of the Executive Branch of the Government in the field of foreign affairs is very narrowly restricted. This view is, I think, dictated by the concept of separation of powers upon which our constitutional system rests.

In a speech on the floor of the House of Representatives, Chief Justice John MARSHALL, then a member of that body, stated:

> "The President is the sole organ of the nation in its external relations, and its sole representative with foreign nations." 10 Annals of Cong. 613.

From that time, shortly after the founding of the Nation, to this, there has been no substantial challenge to this description of the scope of executive power. . . . I agree that, in performance of its duty to protect the values of the First Amendment against political pressures, the judiciary must review the initial Executive determination to the point of satisfying itself that the subject matter of the dispute does lie within the proper compass of the President's foreign relations power. Constitutional considerations forbid "a complete abandonment of judicial control." Moreover the judiciary may properly insist that the determination that disclosure of the subject matter would irreparably impair the national security be made by the head of the Executive Department concerned—here the Secretary of State or the Secretary of Defense—after actual personal consideration by that officer. This safeguard is required in the analogous area of executive claims of privilege for secrets of state. . . .

But in my judgment the judiciary may not properly go beyond these two inquiries and redetermine for itself the probable impact of disclosure on the national security.

☐ *Justice BLACKMUN, dissenting.*

The country would be none the worse off were the cases tried quickly, to be sure, but in the customary and properly deliberative manner. The most recent of the material, it is said, dates no later than 1968, already about three years ago, and the Times itself took three months to formulate its plan of procedure and, thus, deprived its public for that period.

The First Amendment, after all, is only one part of an entire Constitution. Article II of the great document vests in the Executive Branch primary power over the conduct of foreign affairs and places in that branch the responsibility for the Nation's safety. Each provision of the Constitution is important, and I cannot subscribe to a doctrine of unlimited absolutism for the First Amendment at the cost of downgrading other provisions. First Amendment absolutism has never commanded a majority of this Court. . . .

What is needed here is a weighing, upon properly developed standards, of the broad right of the press to print and of the very narrow right of the Government to prevent.

■ (2) INDIRECT PRIOR RESTRAINTS

Besides direct prior restraints, the press may be subject to indirect restraints and requirements that arguably have a chilling effect on the exercise of free speech and press. In *Snepp v. United States*, 444 U.S. 507 (1980), for example, the Court summarily dismissed a First Amendment challenge to the Central Intelligence Agency's requiring employees and former employees to submit any (fiction or nonfiction) writings for prepublication review. In *Meese v. Keene*, 481 U.S. 465 (1987), over the objections of three dissenters (Justices Blackmun, Brennan, and Marshall), the Rehnquist Court upheld the labeling as "political propaganda" of three documentary films (dealing with acid rain and the environment) under the Foreign Agents Registration Act.

In three companion cases in 1972, *Branzburg v. Hayes*, *In re Pappas*, and *United States v. Caldwell* (see excerpt below), a bare majority of the Court rejected reporters' claims that the First Amendment guarantees them a testimonial privilege against discussing their sources before grand juries and at trials. Compare Justice White's opinion announcing the decision of the Court with the views expressed in the two dissenting opinions filed by Justice Stewart (with whom Justices Brennan and Marshall joined) and Justice Douglas. Justice White, again, wrote for the Court in *Zurcher v. The Stanford Daily*, 436 U.S. 547 (1978) rejecting the dissenters' interpretation of the First Amendment, in holding that newspaper offices are not exempt from searches by police for photographs and other mere evidence of crime. The ruling in *Zurcher*, however, was undercut by Congress's passing the Privacy Protection Act of 1980, which prohibits the unannounced searches of newsrooms by federal, state, and local law enforcement officers, except in certain narrowly defined circumstances. As discussed in section B of this chapter, the Rehnquist Court has also substantially cut back on the First Amendment freedoms of students and student newspapers in cases such as *Hazelwood School District v. Kuhlmeier*, 484 U.S. 260 (1988).

In the 1970s, members of the press also unsuccessfully sought to have the Court vindicate a First Amendment right of access to acquire information. In *dicta* in a number of rulings the Court had suggested that the amendment conveys a "right to receive" as a corollary of the freedom to disseminate information.[1] But a bare majority of the Court rebuffed a further expansion of the First Amendment when members of the press pushed for an "affirmative right of access" in challenging prohibitions of personal interviews between reporters and inmates in state and federal prisons, in *Pell v. Procunier*, 417 U.S. 817 (1974), and *Saxbe v. Washington Post*, 417 U.S. 843 (1974). There Justice Stewart reaffirmed that "the First Amendment does not guarantee the press a constitutional right of special access to information not available to the public generally." In dissent with Justices Brennan and Marshall, Justice Douglas argued that the First Amendment confers special privileges on the press so it may vindicate the public's interests in information about the operation of government. Justice Powell also dissented, finding that the prohibition "significantly impairs the right of the people to a free flow of information and ideas on the conduct of Government" and explained, "The underlying right is the right of the public generally. The press is the necessary representative of the public's interests in this context and the instrumentality which effects the public's rights." When the issue again arose in *Houchins v. KQED, Inc.* (1978) (see excerpt below), the Court remained sharply divided. However, see and compare *Globe Newspaper Co. v. Superior Court for the County of Norfolk* (1982) (excerpted in Section G of this chapter).

Cohen v. Cowles Media Co., 501 U.S. 663 (1991), raised an issue bearing on indirect prior restraints on the press. *Cohen* posed the question of whether newspapers may be sued for disclosing the names of their confidential sources. Dan Cohen, a political consultant, was fired from his job after two newspapers identified him as the confidential source of damaging information about the criminal record of another candidate. He had been promised anonymity by reporters, but their editors overrode their objections to naming him and revised their stories so as to point up the fact that Cohen was the source of the damaging information. Cohen sued for breach of contract, and a jury awarded him $700,000. The Minnesota Supreme Court, however, overturned that award when holding that the First Amendment's guarantee for freedom of the press outweighed "the common law interest in protecting a promise of anonymity."

By a five-to-four vote, the Court held that the First Amendment does not provide a shield against suits for damages, under state promissory estoppel law, for a newspaper's breach of a promise of confidentiality. Writing for the bare majority, Justice White observed that

> generally applicable laws do not offend the First Amendment simply because their enforcement against the press has incidental effect on its ability to gather and report the news. . . . [T]ruthful information sought to be published must have been lawfully acquired. The press may not with impunity break and enter an office or dwelling to gather news. Neither does the First Amendment relieve a newspaper reporter of the obligation shared by all citizens to respond to a grand jury subpoena and answer questions relevant to a criminal investigation, even though the reporter might be required to reveal a confidential source. . . . It is therefore beyond dispute that "[t]he publisher of a newspaper has no special immunity from the application of general laws. He has no special privilege to invade the rights and liberties of others." Accordingly, enforcement of such general laws against the press is not subject to stricter scrutiny than would be applied to enforcement against other persons or organizations.

Finally, in *United States v. National Treasury Employees Union*, 513 U.S. 432 (1995), the Court struck down provisions of the Ethics Reform Act of 1989 that banned federal employees from receiving honoraria for giving speeches and publishing articles and books. Writing for the Court, Justice Stevens explained that

> Federal employees who write for publication in their spare time have made significant contributions to the marketplace of ideas. They include literary giants like Nathaniel Hawthorne and

Herman Melville, who were employed by the Customs Service; Walt Whitman, who worked for the Departments of Justice and Interior; and Bret Harte, an employee of the mint. . . .

The large-scale disincentive to Government employees' expression also imposes a significant burden on the public's right to read and hear what the employees would otherwise have written and said. We have no way to measure the true cost of that burden, but we cannot ignore the risk that it might deprive us of the work of a future Melville or Hawthorne. The honoraria ban imposes the kind of burden that abridges speech under the First Amendment.

By contrast, Chief Justice Rehnquist, joined by Justices Scalia and Thomas, dissented because the Court's majority, in the words of the chief justice, "understates the weight which should be accorded to the governmental justifications for the honoraria ban and overstates the amount of speech which actually will be deterred." In a separate opinion, Justice O'Connor dissented in part but concurred in the judgment.

NOTE

1. See *Martin v. City of Struthers*, 319 U.S. 141, 143 (1943); *Thomas v. Collins*, 323 U.S. 516 (1945); *Procunier v. Martinez*, 416 U.S. 396 (1974); and *Kleindienst v. Mandel*, 408 U.S. 753 (1972).

SELECTED BIBLIOGRAPHY

Cross, Harold. *The People's Right to Know*. New York: Columbia University Press, 1953.

O'Brien, David M. *The Public's Right to Know: The First Amendment and the Supreme Court*. New York: Praeger, 1981.

Van Gerpen, Maurice. *Privileged Communication and the Press*. Westport, CT: Greenwood Press, 1979.

Branzburg v. Hayes, In re Pappas, and *United States v. Caldwell*
408 U.S. 665, 92 S.CT. 2646 (1972)

Paul Branzburg, Paul Pappas, and Earl Caldwell were reporters working for different newspapers and television stations on unrelated stories involving the production of hashish and the activities of the Black Panthers and other black militant groups. Each refused to reveal the sources of his story and claimed a First Amendment reporter's privilege of confidentiality, for which each was found in contempt by a judge. On appeal to the Supreme Court, their cases were consolidated for oral argument and decided in a plurality opinion announcing the decision of the Court, and in which Justice White further discusses the facts in each case.

The Court's decision was five to four, and the majority's opinion was announced by Justice White. Justice Powell concurred; dissents were by Justices Douglas and Stewart, who were joined by Justices Brennan and Marshall.

☐ *Justice WHITE delivered the opinion of the Court.*

The issue in these cases is whether requiring newsmen to appear and testify before state or federal grand juries abridges the freedom of speech and press guaranteed by the First Amendment. We hold that it does not.

The writ of *certiorari* in No. 70-85, *Branzburg v. Hayes and Meigs*, brings before us two judgments of the Kentucky Court of Appeals, both involving petitioner Branzburg, a staff reporter for the *Courier-Journal*, a daily newspaper published in Louisville, Kentucky.

On November 15, 1969, the *Courier-Journal* carried a story under petitioner's by-line describing in detail his observations of two young residents of Jefferson County synthesizing hashish from marihuana, an activity which, they asserted, earned them about $5,000 in three weeks. The article included a photograph of a pair of hands working above a laboratory table on which was a substance identified by the caption as hashish. The article stated that petitioner had promised not to reveal the identity of the two hashish makers. Petitioner was shortly subpoenaed by the Jefferson County grand jury; he appeared, but refused to identify the individuals he had seen possessing marihuana or the persons he had seen making hashish from marihuana. A state trial court judge ordered petitioner to answer these questions and rejected his contention that the Kentucky reporters' privilege statute, the First Amendment of the United States Constitution, or §§ 1, 2 and 8 of the Kentucky Constitution authorized his refusal to answer. . . .

In re Pappas, No. 70-94, originated when petitioner Pappas, a television newsman-photographer working out of the Providence, Rhode Island, office of a New Bedford, Massachusetts, television station, was called to New Bedford on July 30, 1970, to report on civil disorders there which involved fires and other turmoil. He intended to cover a Black Panther news conference at that group's headquarters in a boarded-up store. Petitioner found the streets around the store barricaded, but he ultimately gained entrance to the area and recorded and photographed a prepared statement read by one of the Black Panther leaders at about 3 P.M. . . . As a condition of entry, Pappas agreed not to disclose anything he saw or heard inside the store except an anticipated police raid, which Pappas, "on his own," was free to photograph and report as he wished. . . . Two months later, petitioner was summoned before the Bristol County Grand Jury and appeared, answered questions as to his name, address, employment, and what he had seen and heard outside Panther headquarters, but refused to answer any questions about what had taken place inside headquarters while he was there, claiming that the First Amendment afforded him a privilege to protect confidential informants and their information. . . .

United States v. Caldwell, No. 70-57, arose from subpoenas issued by a federal grand jury in the Northern District of California to respondent Earl Caldwell, a reporter for the *New York Times* assigned to cover the Black Panther Party and other black militant groups. . . . [Caldwell maintained that even to appear before a grand jury investigating violations of law would destroy his relationship with the Panthers and violate his First Amendment rights.]

Petitioners Branzburg and Pappas and respondent Caldwell press First Amendment claims that may be simply put: that to gather news it is often necessary to agree either not to identify the source of information published or to publish only part of the facts revealed, or both; that if the reporter is nevertheless forced to reveal these confidences to a grand jury, the source so identified and other confidential sources of other reporters will be measurably deterred from furnishing publishable information, all to the detriment of the free flow of information protected by the First Amendment. Although the newsmen in these cases do not claim an absolute privilege against official interrogation in all circumstances, they assert that the reporter should not be forced either to appear or to testify before a grand jury or at trial until and unless sufficient grounds are shown for believing that the reporter possesses information relevant to a crime the grand jury is investigating, that the information the reporter has is unavailable from other sources, and that the need for the information is sufficiently compelling to override the claimed invasion of First Amendment interests occasioned by the disclosure. . . .

The heart of the claim is that the burden on news gathering resulting from compelling reporters to disclose confidential information outweighs any public interest in obtaining the information.

We do not question the significance of free speech, press, or assembly to the country's welfare. Nor is it suggested that news gathering does not qualify for First Amendment protection; without some protection for seeking out the news, freedom of the press could be eviscerated. But these cases involve no intrusions upon speech or assembly, no prior restraint or restriction on what the press may publish, and no express or implied command that the press publish what it prefers to withhold. . . .

The sole issue before us is the obligation of reporters to respond to grand jury subpoenas as other citizens do and to answer questions relevant to an investigation into the commission of crime. Citizens generally are not constitutionally immune from grand jury subpoenas; and neither the First Amendment nor any other constitutional provision protects the average citizen from disclosing to a grand jury information that he has received in confidence. . . .

It is clear that the First Amendment does not invalidate every incidental burdening of the press that may result from the enforcement of civil or criminal statutes of general applicability. . . .

It has generally been held that the First Amendment does not guarantee the press a constitutional right of special access to information not available to the public generally. In *Zemel v. Rusk*, [381 U.S. 1 (1965)] for example, the Court sustained the Government's refusal to validate passports to Cuba even though that restriction "render[ed] less than wholly free the flow of information concerning that country." The ban on travel was held constitutional, for "[t]he right to speak and publish does not carry with it the unrestrained right to gather information."

Despite the fact that news gathering may be hampered, the press is regularly excluded from grand jury proceedings, our own conferences, the meetings of other official bodies gathered in executive session, and the meetings of private organizations. Newsmen have no constitutional right of access to the scenes of crime or disaster when the general public is excluded, and they may be prohibited from attending or publishing information about trials if such restrictions are necessary to assure a defendant a fair trial before an impartial tribunal. . . .

The prevailing constitutional view of the newsman's privilege is very much rooted in the ancient role of the grand jury that has the dual function of determining if there is probable cause to believe that a crime has been committed and of protecting citizens against unfounded criminal prosecutions. . . . Because its task is to inquire into the existence of possible criminal conduct and to return only well-founded indictments, its investigative powers are necessarily broad. . . .

Until now the only testimonial privilege for unofficial witnesses that is rooted in the Federal Constitution is the Fifth Amendment privilege against compelled self-incrimination. We are asked to create another by interpreting the First Amendment to grant newsmen a testimonial privilege that other citizens do not enjoy. This we decline to do. Fair and effective law enforcement aimed at providing security for the person and property of the individual is a fundamental function of government, and the grand jury plays an important, constitutionally mandated role in this process. On the records now before us, we perceive no basis for holding that the public interest in law enforcement and in ensuring effective grand jury proceedings is insufficient to override the consequential, but uncertain, burden on news gathering that is said to result from insisting that reporters, like other citizens, respond to relevant questions put to them in the course of a valid grand jury investigation or criminal trial.

This conclusion itself involves no restraint on what newspapers may publish or on the type or quality of information reporters may seek to acquire, nor does it threaten the vast bulk of confidential relationships between reporters and their sources. . . . Only where news sources themselves are implicated in crime or possess information relevant to the grand jury's task need they or the reporter be concerned about grand jury subpoenas. Nothing before us indicates that a large number or percentage of *all* confidential news sources falls into either category and would in any way be deterred by our holding that the Constitution does not, as it never has, exempt the newsman from performing the citizen's normal duty of appearing and furnishing information relevant to the grand jury's task. . . .

☐ *Justice STEWART, with whom Justice BRENNAN and Justice MARSHALL join, dissenting.*

The Court's crabbed view of the First Amendment reflects a disturbing insensitivity to the critical role of an independent press in our society. The question whether a reporter has a constitutional right to a confidential relationship with his source is of first impression here, but the principles that should guide our decision are as basic as any to be found in the Constitution. While Justice POWELL's enigmatic concurring opinion gives some hope of a more flexible view in the future, the Court in these cases holds that a newsman has no First Amendment right to protect his sources when called before a grand jury. The Court thus invites state and federal authorities to undermine the historic independence of the press by attempting to annex the journalistic profession as an investigative arm of government. . . .

The reporter's constitutional right to a confidential relationship with his source stems from the broad societal interest in a full and free flow of information to the public. It is this basic concern that underlies the Constitution's protection of a free press, because the guarantee is "not for the benefit of the press so much as for the benefit of all of us." *Time, Inc. v. Hill* [385 U.S. 374 (1967)].

The right to gather news implies, in turn, a right to a confidential relationship between a reporter and his source. This proposition follows as a matter of simple logic once three factual predicates are recognized: (1) newsmen require informants to gather news; (2) confidentiality—the promise or understanding that names or certain aspects of communications will be kept off the record—is essential to the creation and maintenance of a news-gathering relationship with informants; and (3) an unbridled subpoena power—the absence of a constitutional right protecting, in *any* way, a confidential relationship from compulsory process—will either deter sources from divulging information or deter reporters from gathering and publishing information. . . .

The impairment of the flow of news cannot, of course, be proved with scientific precision, as the Court seems to demand. . . . But we have never before demanded that First Amendment rights rest on elaborate empirical studies demonstrating beyond any conceivable doubt that deterrent effects exist; we have never before required proof of the exact number of people potentially affected by governmental action, who would actually be dissuaded from engaging in First Amendment activity.

Rather, on the basis of common sense and available information, we have asked, often implicitly, (1) whether there was a rational connection between the cause (the governmental action) and the effect (the deterrence or impairment of First Amendment activity), and (2) whether the effect would occur with some regularity, *i.e.*, would not be *de minimis*. . . . Once this threshold inquiry has been satisfied, we have then examined the competing interests in determining whether there is an unconstitutional infringement of First Amendment freedoms. . . .

To require any greater burden of proof is to shirk our duty to protect values securely embedded in the Constitution. We cannot await an unequivocal—and therefore unattainable—imprimatur from empirical studies. We can and must accept the evidence developed in the record, and elsewhere, that overwhelmingly supports the premise that deterrence will occur with regularity in important types of news-gathering relationships. . . .

In striking the proper balance between the public interest in the efficient administration of justice and the First Amendment guarantee of the fullest flow of information, we must begin with the basic proposition that because of their "delicate and vulnerable" nature, and their transcendent importance for the just functioning of our society, First Amendment rights require special safeguards. . . .

Thus, when an investigation impinges on First Amendment rights, the government must not only show that the inquiry is of "compelling and overriding importance" but it must also "convincingly" demonstrate that the investigation is "substantially related" to the information sought.

Governmental officials must, therefore, demonstrate that the information sought is *clearly* relevant to a *precisely* defined subject of governmental inquiry. They must demonstrate that it is reasonable to think the witness in question has that information. And they must show that there is not any means of obtaining the information less destructive of First Amendment liberties. . . .

I believe the safeguards developed in our decisions involving governmental investigations must apply to the grand jury inquiries in these cases. Surely the function of the grand jury to aid in the enforcement of the law is no more important than the function of the legislature, and its committees, to make the law. . . .

Accordingly, when a reporter is asked to appear before a grand jury and reveal confidences, I would hold that the government must (1) show that there is probable cause to believe that the newsman has information that is clearly relevant to a specific probable violation of law; (2) demonstrate that the information sought cannot be obtained by alternative means less destructive of First Amendment rights; and (3) demonstrate a compelling and overriding interest in the information.

☐ *Justice DOUGLAS, dissenting.*

Today's decision will impede the wide-open and robust dissemination of ideas and counterthought which a free press both fosters and protects and which is essential to the success of intelligent self-government. Forcing a reporter before a grand jury will have two retarding effects upon the ear and the pen of the press. Fear of exposure will cause dissidents to communicate less openly to trusted reporters. And, fear of accountability will cause editors and critics to write with more restrained pens. . . .

When we deny newsmen that protection, we deprive the people of the information needed to run the affairs of the Nation in an intelligent way.

Madison said:

> "A popular Government, without popular information, or the means of acquiring it, is but a Prologue to a Farce or a Tragedy; or, perhaps both. Knowledge will forever govern ignorance: And a people who mean to be their own Governors, must arm themselves with the power which knowledge gives." (To W. T. Barry, Aug. 4, 1822). 9 Writings of James Madison 103. (G. Hunt ed. 1910).

Today's decision is more than a clog upon news gathering. It is a signal to publishers and editors that they should exercise caution in how they use whatever information they can obtain. Without immunity they may be summoned to account for their criticism. Entrenched officers have been quick to crash their powers down upon unfriendly commentators. . . .

The intrusion of government into this domain is symptomatic of the disease of this society. As the years pass the power of government becomes more and more pervasive. It is a power to suffocate both people and causes. Those in power, whatever their politics, want only to perpetuate it. Now that the fences of the law and the tradition that has protected the press are broken down, the people are the victims. The First Amendment, as I read it, was designed precisely to prevent that tragedy.

Houchins v. KQED, Inc.
438 U.S. 1, 98 S.Ct. 2588 (1978)

This case involves the claim of a radio station, KQED, to have a "right of access," under the First Amendment, to interview particular prisoners in a jail. Chief Justice Burger further discusses the facts in this case in his plurality opinion announcing the decision of the Court.

The Court's decision was four to three, with the plurality's opinion announced by Chief Justice Burger and with Justices Marshall and Blackmun not participating. Concurrence was by Justice Stewart; dissent was by Justice Stevens, who was joined by Justices Brennan and Powell.

☐ *Chief Justice BURGER, with whom Justice WHITE and Justice REHNQUIST join, delivered the opinion of the Court.*

The question presented is whether the news media have a constitutional right of access to a county jail, over and above that of other persons, to interview inmates and make sound recordings, films, and photographs for publication and broadcasting by newspapers, radio and television.

Petitioner Houchins, as Sheriff of Alameda County, Cal., controls all access to the Alameda County Jail at Santa Rita. Respondent KQED operates licensed television and radio broadcasting stations which have frequently reported newsworthy events relating to penal institutions in the San Francisco Bay Area. On March 31, 1975, KQED reported the suicide of a prisoner in the Greystone portion of the Santa Rita Jail. The report included a statement by a psychiatrist that the conditions at the Greystone facility were responsible for the illnesses of his patient-prisoners there, and a statement from petitioner denying that prison conditions were responsible for the prisoners' illnesses.

KQED requested permission to inspect and take pictures within the Greystone facility. After permission was refused, KQED and the Alameda and Oakland Branches of the National Association for the Advancement of Colored People (NAACP) filed suit under 42 U.S.C. § 1983. They alleged that petitioner had violated the First Amendment by refusing to permit media access and failing to provide any effective means by which the public could be informed of conditions prevailing in the Greystone facility or learn of the prisoners' grievances. Public access to such information was essential, they asserted, in order for NAACP members to participate in the public debate on jail conditions in Alameda County. They further asserted that television coverage of the conditions in the cells and facilities was the most effective way of informing the public of prison conditions. . . .

From the right to gather news and the right to receive information [the respondents] argue for an implied special right of access to government controlled sources of information. This right, they contend, compels access as a *constitutional* matter. . . . Respondents contend that public access to penal institutions is necessary to prevent officials from concealing prison conditions from the voters and impairing the public's right to discuss and criticize the prison system and its administration. . . .

Beyond question, the role of the media is important; acting as the "eyes and ears" of the public, they can be a powerful and constructive force, contributing to remedial action in the conduct of public business. They have served that function since the beginning of the Republic, but like all other components of our society media representatives are subject to limits. . . .

The public importance of conditions in penal facilities and the media's role of providing information afford no basis for reading into the Constitution a right of the public or the media to enter these institutions, with camera equipment, and take moving and still pictures of inmates for broadcast purposes. This Court has never intimated a First Amendment guarantee of a right of access to all sources of information within government control. Nor does the rationale of the decisions upon which respondents rely lead to the implication of such a right. . . .

The respondents' argument is flawed, not only because it lacks precedential support and is contrary to statements in this Court's opinions, but also because it invites the Court to involve itself in what is clearly a legislative task which the Constitution has left to the political processes. Whether the government should open penal institutions in the manner sought by respondents is a question of policy which a legislative body might appropriately resolve one way or the other.

☐ *Justice STEWART, concurring.*

The First and Fourteenth Amendments do not guarantee the public a right of access to information generated or controlled by government, nor do they guarantee the press any basic right of access superior to that of the public generally. The Constitution does no more than assure the public and the press equal access once government has opened its doors. Accordingly, I agree substantially with what the opinion of the CHIEF JUSTICE has to say on that score.

We part company, however, in applying these abstractions to the facts of this case. Whereas he appears to view "equal access" as meaning access that is identical in all respects, I believe that the concept of equal access must be accorded more flexibility in order to accommodate the practical distinctions between the press and the general public.

When on assignment, a journalist does not tour a jail simply for his own edification. He is there to gather information to be passed on to others, and his mission is protected by the Constitution for very specific reasons. . . .

That the First Amendment speaks separately of freedom of speech and freedom of the press is no constitutional accident, but an acknowledgement of the critical role played by the press in American society. The Constitution requires sensitivity to that role and to the special needs of the press in performing it effectively. A person touring Santa Rita Jail can grasp its reality with his own eyes and ears. But if a television reporter is to convey the jail's sights and sounds to those who cannot personally visit the place, he must use cameras and sound equipment. In short, terms of access that are reasonably imposed on individual members of the public may, if they impede effective reporting without sufficient justification, be unreasonable as applied to journalists who are there to convey to the general public what the visitors see.

Under these principles, KQED was clearly entitled to some form of preliminary injunctive relief. At the time of the District Court's decision, members of the public were permitted to visit most parts of the Santa Rita Jail, and the First and Fourteenth Amendments required the Sheriff to give members of the press *effective* access to the same areas. The Sheriff evidently assumed that he could fulfill this obligation simply by allowing reporters to sign up for tours on the same terms as the public. I think he was mistaken in this assumption, as a matter of constitutional law. . . .

In two respects, however, the District Court's preliminary injunction was overbroad. It ordered the Sheriff to permit reporters into the Little Greystone facility and it required him to let them interview randomly encountered inmates. In both these respects, the injunction gave the press access to areas and sources of information from which persons on the public tours had been excluded, and thus enlarged the scope of what the Sheriff and Supervisors had opened to public view. The District Court erred in concluding that the First and Fourteenth Amendments compelled this broader access for the press.

☐ *Justice STEVENS, with whom Justice BRENNAN and Justice POWELL join, dissenting.*

The Court holds that the scope of press access to the Santa Rita jail required by the preliminary injunction issued against petitioner is inconsistent with the holding in *Pell v. Procunier,* [417 U.S. 817 (1974)], that "newsmen have no constitutional right of access to prisons or their inmates beyond that afforded the general public" and therefore the injunction was an abuse of the District Court's discretion. I respectfully disagree. . . .

For two reasons, which shall be discussed separately, the decisions in *Pell* and *Saxbe* [*v. Washington Post,* 417 U.S. 843 (1974)] do not control the propriety of the District Court's preliminary injunction. First, the unconstitutionality of petitioner's policies which gave rise to this litigation does not rest on the premise that the press has a greater right of access to information regarding prison conditions than do other members of the public. Second, relief tailored to the needs of the press may properly be awarded to a representative of the press which is successful in proving that it has been harmed by a constitutional violation and need not await the grant of relief to members of the general public who may also have been injured by petitioner's unconstitutional access policy but have not yet sought to vindicate their rights. . . .

In *Pell v. Procunier,* the Court stated that "newsmen have no constitutional right of access to prisons or their inmates beyond that afforded the general public." But the Court has never intimated that a nondiscriminatory policy of excluding entirely both the public and the press from access to information about prison conditions would avoid constitutional scrutiny. . . .

The preservation of a full and free flow of information to the general public has long been recognized as a core objective of the First Amendment to the Constitution. It is for this reason that the First Amendment protects not only the dissemination but also the receipt of information and ideas. . . .

The reasons which militate in favor of providing special protection to the flow of information to the public about prisons relate to the unique function they perform in a democratic society. Not only are they public institutions, financed with public funds and administered by public servants; they are an integral component of the criminal justice system. The citizens confined therein are temporarily, and sometimes permanently, deprived of their liberty as a result of a trial which must conform to the dictates of the Constitution. By express command of the Sixth Amendment the proceeding must be a "public trial." It is important not only that the trial itself be fair, but also that the community at large have confidence in the integrity of the proceeding. That public interest survives the judgment of conviction and appropriately carries over to an interest in how the convicted person is treated during his period of punishment and hoped-for rehabilitation. While a ward of the State and subject to its stern discipline, he retains constitutional protections against cruel and unusual punishment, a protection which may derive more practical support from access to information about prisons by the public than by occasional litigation in a busy court. . . .

In this case, the record demonstrates that both the public and the press had been consistently denied any access to the inner portions of the Santa Rita jail, that there had been excessive censorship of inmate correspondence, and that there was no valid justification for these broad restraints on the flow of information. An affirmative answer to the question whether respondent established a likelihood of prevailing on the merits did not depend, in final analysis, on any right of the press to special treatment beyond that accorded the public at large. Rather, the probable existence of a constitutional violation rested upon the special importance of allowing a democratic community access to knowledge about how its servants were treating some of its members who have been committed to their custody. An official prison policy of concealing such knowledge from the public by arbitrarily cutting off the flow of information at its source abridges the freedom of speech and of the press protected by the First and Fourteenth Amendments to the Constitution.

F | *Regulating the Broadcast and Cable Media and the Internet*

Radio, television, cable, and other electronic media have posed special First Amendment problems. This is because they were considered a scarce public resource that should be licensed and regulated in "the public interest." In 1934, the Federal Communications Commission (FCC) was created to regulate broadcast and telecommunications systems based on considerations of "public interest, convenience and necessity." While the FCC is forbidden from exercising censorship per se, it has the authority to license every radio and television station, subject to renewal every three years, and to revoke or suspend those licenses for violations of its rules or other statutory requirements, including antitrust laws. Among the regulations imposed are those requiring "equal time" for opponents of political candidates who are given air time and a "family hour" on television (during which programs are shown that have little or no violence and suggestive sexual material), bans against broadcasting obscene and indecent language, and limitations on the co-ownership of newspapers and broadcasting systems.

In the past several decades, however, regulations were gradually cut back. This was partially in response to technological developments, such as cable television and satellite transmissions. These advances increased the multiplicity of channels and held the potential for greater public access. This, in turn, undermined the traditional rationale for regulating radio and television as a scarce public resource, and exempted from First Amendment protection. In addition, beginning in Jimmy Carter's presidency and throughout that of Ronald Reagan and George Bush, there was a movement toward deregulation to promote economic competition and efficiency. Because the radio market, for example, had grown and competition increased since the 1930s, the FCC relaxed some of its regulations and did away with others—such as requiring maximum time limits for commercials and minimum requirements for news and public affairs programming.

One of the most controversial requirements imposed on the broadcast media in 1949, and finally eliminated in 1987, was the "fairness doctrine" requiring stations to notify and provide air time for individuals personally attacked or made the subject of political editorials. When upholding the fairness doctrine in *Red Lion Broadcasting Co., Inc. v. Federal Communications Commission* (1969) (see excerpt below), Justice White reviews the rationales for treating the broadcast media differently from the print media in terms of the First Amendment. *Red Lion's* distinctions were underscored by the Court's striking down Florida's "right to reply" law, requiring newspapers to print the reply of any political candidate who was subject to a personal attack by a newspaper. In *Miami Herald Publishing Company v. Tornillo*, 418 U.S. 241 (1974), Justice White explained that "this [right to reply] law runs afoul of the elementary First Amendment proposition that government may not force a newspaper to print copy which, in its journalistic discretion, it chooses to leave on the newspaper floor."

In *Columbia Broadcasting System v. Democratic National Committee*, 412 U.S. 94 (1973), the Court also ruled that the FCC was not required to ensure a "private right of access to the broadcast media," when sustaining CBS's policy of refusing paid editorial advertisements. In *CBS, Inc. v. FCC*, 453 U.S. 367 (1981), however, the Court affirmed a "right of access" for legally qualified candidates for federal office when ruling that CBS should not have refused to sell air time in 1979 to the Democratic National Committee for President Carter's reelection bid because it deemed it too early for the presidential campaign of 1980 to begin.

While the FCC abandoned the fairness doctrine, in 1987 it also moved to enforce more strictly its regulations against "indecent" broadcasts. This followed the ruling in *Federal Communications Commission v. Pacifica Foundation*, (1978) (see excerpt in Section B), and from a change in the views of a majority of the commissioners, who were appointed by President Reagan. As a result, some new First Amendment controversies have arisen over the reading on the radio of literary works, such as Allen Ginsberg's poem "Howl."

The Court upheld as well the FCC's rules banning the acquisition of radio and television stations by newspapers in *FCC v. National Citizens Committee*, 436 U.S. 775 (1978), and the FCC's decision not to consider changes in the entertainment format of radio stations when reviewing applications for renewal or transfer of broadcasting licenses in *FCC v. WNCN Listeners Guild*, 450 U.S. 582 (1981).

The Court accorded greater First Amendment protection to electronic media because of the multiplicity of channels and greater access brought about by the development of cable television and more satellite and telecommunications systems. In *United States v. Midwest Video Corporation*, 406 U.S. 649 (1972), the justices (five to four) upheld the FCC's regulation of television antennae and cable systems. But in *FCC v. Midwest Video Corporation*, 440 U.S. 689 (1979), the Court (six to three) struck down the FCC's regulations requiring major cable systems (with twenty or more channel capacities) to provide up to four channels for free public expression and public affairs programming. "Under the [FCC's] rules," Justice White observed, "cable operators [were] deprived of all discretion regarding who may exploit their access channels and what may be transmitted over such channels."

Due to the Court's ruling in *Midwest Video Corporation* (II), the FCC has less jurisdiction over cable television systems than over radio and broadcast television. The Court, though, held the FCC's technical standards governing the quality of cable television signals to preempt those of states and localities. *City of New York v. FCC*, 486 U.S. 57 (1988). The powers of states and localities over cable television were also sharply limited in *Capital Cities Cable, Inc. v. Crisp*, 467 U.S. 691

(1984), overturning an Oklahoma law barring the broadcasting of advertisements for alcoholic beverages as applied to cable television operators. Without hearing oral arguments or issuing a written opinion, the Court also affirmed a lower federal court ruling striking down Utah's law restricting cable telecasts of nudity, sex acts, and other "indecent" images in *Wilkinson v. Jones*, 480 U.S. 926 (1987). But in *Leathers v. Medlock*, 499 U.S. 439 (1991), the Court upheld a state's 4 percent tax on cable television, though not on similar communications services. In her opinion for the Court, Justice O'Connor reaffirmed that states may neither single out the press as a whole for special taxes nor discriminate among different kinds of media on the basis of content or for the purpose of censorship. Nonetheless, O'Connor held that states may apply general taxes to some kinds of media, and not others, so long as the taxes do not discriminate "on the basis of ideas."

Finally, in *Turner Broadcasting System, Inc. v. Federal Communications Commission*, 512 U.S. 622 (1994) (*Turner Broadcasting I*), the Court held for the first time that the First Amendment extends some protection to the cable industry and requires heightened judicial scrutiny of any regulation or restriction, in light of the differences between broadcast and cable technologies. In 1992, Congress overrode a presidential veto to enact the Cable Television Consumer Protection and Competition Act. That legislation subjects the cable industry to rate regulation by the Federal Communications Commission (FCC) and by municipal franchising authorities; prohibits municipalities from awarding exclusive franchises to cable operators; imposes various restrictions on cable programmers; and directs the FCC to develop and promulgate regulations imposing minimum technical standards for cable operators. Turner Broadcasting System challenged two "must-carry provisions" of the law as a violation of the First Amendment. Section 4 of the act requires cable companies to carry "local commercial television stations," other than those qualifying as "noncommercial educational" stations under Section 5, that operate within the same television market as the cable system. Cable systems with more than twelve active channels, and more than three hundred subscribers, are required to set aside up to one-third of their channels for commercial broadcast stations that request carriage. Cable systems with more than three hundred subscribers, but only twelve or fewer active channels, must carry the signals of three commercial broadcast stations. Section 5 of the act imposes similar requirements regarding the carriage of local public broadcasting television stations.

Writing for the Court in *Turner Broadcasting I*, Justice Kennedy held that the First Amendment extends protection to the cable industry. On that issue, the justices were unanimous. However, Justice

Kennedy commanded only four other votes—those of the chief justice and Justices Blackmun, Souter, and Stevens—on the central issue of the constitutionality of the "must-carry provisions." On that issue a bare majority declined to strike down the regulations and remanded the case back to the lower court for reconsideration. In an opinion, dissenting in part, and joined by Justices Ginsburg, Scalia, and Thomas, Justice O'Connor countered that the "must-carry provisions" were content-based and thus "an impermissible restraint on cable operators' editorial discretion as well as on the cable programmers' speech."

But, subsequently in *Turner Broadcasting System, Inc. v. Federal Communications Commissions*, 520 U.S. 180 (1997) (*Turner Broadcasting II*), Justice Kennedy commanded a bare majority for upholding the must-carry provisions. The provisions, according to Justice Kennedy, were "content neutral" and therefore had to pass only an intermediate level of scrutiny, namely, do the regulations advance an "important government interest" without unnecessarily burdening speech. Turning to the economic theory advanced in *Turner Broadcasting I* as a justification for the provisions, Justice Kennedy ruled that it was reasonable for Congress to conclude that local broadcast stations needed special protection. In his words: "Congress has an independent interest in preserving a multiplicity of broadcasters to ensure that all households have access to information and entertainment on an equal footing with those who subscribe to cable."

The Court, then, further extended First Amendment protection for cable television when striking down two restrictions on the programming of "indecent material" that Congress had imposed in the Cable Television Consumer Protection and Competition Act of 1992. Although upholding the act's authorization for cable operators to forbid the programmers of privately "leased cable channels" from programming "patently offensive" material, the Court invalidated the act's similar authorization for cable operators with respect to "public, educational, and governmental channels." The Court also invalidated another provision that required cable operators to isolate "patently offensive" programming on a single channel and require viewers to request access in advance and in writing. See *Denver Area Educational Telecommunications Consortium, Inc. v. Federal Communications Commissions*, 518 U.S. 727 (1996) (excerpted below).

In a related controversy over Congress's regulation of indecent and obscene material on cable, the Court struck down a provision of the Telecommunications Act of 1966, in *United States v. Playboy Entertainment Group, Inc.*, 529 U.S. 803 (2000). That act required, in part, cable television operators providing channels "primarily dedicated to sexually-oriented programming" to either fully scramble those channels or limit their transmission to hours between 10 P.M. and 6 A.M., when children viewers were unlikely. Scrambling proved inexact, however, and audio or visual portions could often be heard or viewed in what is known as "signal bleed." As a result, most cable operators adopted the "time channeling" approach, which in turn meant that for two-thirds of the day no viewers in their service could watch sexually oriented programming. Writing for the Court, Justice Kennedy ruled that that section of the act could not survive strict scrutiny because it was content-based and therefore had to advance a compelling governmental interest in the least restrictive way. Here, Justice Kennedy emphasized the key difference between broadcast and cable television: Cable television may block unwanted channels on a household-by-household basis and, thus, time-channeling on cable television sweeps too broadly. Chief Justices Rehnquist and Justices Breyer, O'Connor, and Scalia dissented.

Finally, in its first major ruling on free speech and the Internet, in *Reno v. American Civil Liberties Union* (1997) (excerpted in Section B of this chapter), the Court unanimously struck down provisions of the Communications Decency Act of 1996, which had made a federal crime the transmission of "obscene or indecent" messages to anyone under the age of 18. In doing so, the Court also held that the Internet is a unique medium unlike broadcast and cable communications. Subsequently, the Court, in *Ashcroft v. American Civil Liberties Union* (2004) (excerpted below), affirmed lower court orders enjoining the enforcement of the Child Online Protection Act of 1998, which Congress enacted in response to the ruling in *Reno v. ACLU*. However, in *United States v. American Library Association* (2003) (excerpted below), it upheld the Children's Internet Protection Act of 2001, authorizing public libraries to install pornography filters on computers that provide public access to the internet.

SELECTED BIBLIOGRAPHY

Biegel, Stuart. *Beyond Our Control? Confronting the Limits of Our Legal System in the Age of Cyberspace.* Cambridge, MA: MIT Press, 2001.

Collins, Ronald, and Skouer, David, *The Death of Discourse.* 2d ed. Boulder, CO: Westview, 2004.

Friendly, Fred W. *The Good Guys, the Bad Guys and the First Amendment.* New York: Random House, 1976.

Godwin, Mike. *Cyber Rights: Defending Free Speech in the Digital Age.* Cambridge, MA: MIT Press, 2003.

Lane, Frederick S. *Obscene Profits: The Entrepreneurs of Pornography in the Cyber Age.* New York: Routledge, 2000.

Lessig, Lawrence. *Code and Other Laws of Cyberspace.* New York: Basic Books, 2000.

Powe, Lucas. *American Broadcasting and the First Amendment*. Berkeley: University of California Press, 1987.

Sunstein, Cass. *Republic.com*. Princeton, NJ: Princeton University Press, 2001.

Vaidhyanathan, Siva. *The Anarchist Library: How the Clash between Freedom of Control is Leaving Cyberspace and Entering the Real World*. New York: Basic Books, 2004.

Red Lion Broadcasting Co., Inc. v. Federal Communications Commission

395 U.S. 367, 89 S.Ct. 1794 (1969)

Justice White states the facts in this case, upholding the FCC's fairness doctrine, at the outset of his opinion for the Court. Although the FCC abandoned the fairness doctrine in 1987, Justice White's opinion remains important for its articulation of the traditional rationales for treating the print and broadcast media differently for First Amendment purposes.

The Court's decision was unanimous, and the opinion was announced by Justice White, with Justice Douglas not participating.

☐ *Justice WHITE delivered the opinion of the Court.*

The Red Lion Broadcasting Company is licensed to operate a Pennsylvania radio station, WGCB. On November 27, 1964, WGCB carried a 15-minute broadcast by the Reverend Billy James Hargis as part of a "Christian Crusade" series: A book by Fred J. Cook entitled "Goldwater—Extremist on the Right" was discussed by Hargis, who said that Cook had been fired by a newspaper for making false charges against city officials; that Cook had then worked for a Communist-affiliated publication; that he had defended Alger Hiss and attacked J. Edgar Hoover and the Central Intelligence Agency; and that he had now written a "book to smear and destroy Barry Goldwater." When Cook heard of the broadcast he concluded that he had been personally attacked and demanded free reply time, which the station refused. After an exchange of letters among Cook, Red Lion, and the FCC, the FCC declared that the Hargis broadcast constituted a personal attack on Cook; that Red Lion had failed to meet its obligation under the fairness doctrine. . . . On review in the Court of Appeals for the District of Columbia Circuit, the FCC's position was upheld as constitutional and otherwise proper. . . .

The broadcasters challenge the fairness doctrine and its specific manifestations in the personal attack and political editorial rules on conventional First Amendment grounds, alleging that the rules abridge their freedom of speech and press. Their contention is that the First Amendment protects their desire to use their allotted frequencies continuously to broadcast whatever they choose, and to exclude whomever they choose from ever using that frequency. No man may be prevented from saying or publishing what he thinks, or from refusing in his speech or other utterances to give equal weight to the views of his opponents. This right, they say, applies equally to broadcasters.

Although broadcasting is clearly a medium affected by a First Amendment interest, differences in the characteristics of new media justify differences in the First Amendment standards applied to them. . . .

Where there are substantially more individuals who want to broadcast than there are frequencies to allocate, it is idle to posit an unabridgeable First Amendment right to broadcast comparable to the right of every individual to speak, write, or publish. If 100 persons want broadcast licenses but there are only 10 frequencies to allocate, all of them may have the same "right" to a license; but if there is to be any effective communication by radio, only a few can be licensed and the rest must be barred from the airwaves. It would be strange if the First Amendment, aimed at protecting and furthering communications, prevented the Government from making radio communication possible by requiring licenses to broadcast and by limiting the number of licenses so as not to overcrowd the spectrum. . . .

By the same token, as far as the First Amendment is concerned those who are licensed stand no better than those to whom licenses are refused. A license permits broadcasting, but the licensee has no constitutional right to be the one who holds the license or to monopolize a radio frequency to the exclusion of his fellow citizens. There is nothing in the First Amendment which prevents the Government from requiring a licensee to share his frequency with others and to conduct himself as a proxy or fiduciary with obligations to present those views and voices which are representative of his community and which would otherwise, by necessity, be barred from the airwaves. . . .

Nor can we say that it is inconsistent with the First Amendment goal of producing an informed public capable of conducting its own affairs to require a broadcaster to permit answers to personal attacks occurring in the course of discussing controversial issues, or to require that the political opponents of those endorsed by the station be given a chance to communicate with the public. Otherwise, station owners and a few networks would have unfettered power to make time available only to the highest bidders, to communicate only their own views on public issues, people and candidates, and to permit on the air only those with whom they agreed. There is no sanctuary in the First Amendment for unlimited private censorship operating in a medium not open to all. . . .

It is strenuously argued, however, that if political editorials or personal attacks will trigger an obligation in broadcasters to afford the opportunity for expression to speakers who need not pay for time and whose views are unpalatable to the licensees, then broadcasters will be irresistibly forced to self-censorship and their coverage of controversial public issues will be eliminated or at least rendered wholly ineffective. Such a result would indeed be a serious matter, for should licensees actually eliminate their coverage of controversial issues, the purposes of the doctrine would be stifled.

At this point, however, as the Federal Communications Commission has indicated, that possibility is at best speculative. The communications industry, and in particular the networks, have taken pains to present controversial issues in the past, and even now they do not assert that they intend to abandon their efforts in this regard. It would be better if the FCC's encouragement were never necessary to induce the broadcasters to meet their responsibility. And if experience with the administration of those doctrines indicates that they have the net effect of reducing rather than enhancing the volume and quality of coverage, there will be time enough to reconsider the constitutional implications. The fairness doctrine in the past has had no such overall effect.

That this will occur now seems unlikely, however, since if present licensees should suddenly prove timorous, the Commission is not powerless to insist that they give adequate and fair attention to public issues. It does not violate the First Amendment to treat licensees given the privilege of using scarce radio frequencies as proxies for the entire community, obligated to give suitable time and attention to matters of great public concern. To condition the granting or renewal of licenses on a willingness to present representative community views on controversial issues is consistent with the ends and purposes of those constitutional provisions forbidding the abridgment of freedom of speech and freedom of the press. . . .

[T]he fact remains that existing broadcasters have often attained their present position because of their initial government selection in competition with others before new technological advances opened new opportunities for further uses. Long experience in broadcasting, confirmed habits of listeners and viewers, network affiliation, and other advantages in program procurement give existing broadcasters a substantial advantage over new entrants, even where new entry is technologically possible. These advantages are the fruit of a preferred position conferred by the Government. Some present possibility for new entry by competing stations is not enough, in itself, to render unconstitutional the Government's effort to assure that a broadcaster's programming ranges widely enough to serve the public interest.

In view of the scarcity of broadcast frequencies, the Government's role in allocating those frequencies, and the legitimate claims of those unable without governmental assistance to gain access to those frequencies for expression of their views, we hold the regulations and ruling at issue here are both authorized by statute and constitutional.

Federal Communications Commission v. Pacifica Foundation
438 U.S. 726, 98 S.CT. 3026 (1978)

In this case, the Court upheld the FCC's power to ban indecent language on the radio. The case is reprinted in part in Section B of this chapter.

Denver Area Educational Telecommunications Consortium, Inc. v. Federal Communications Commission

518 U.S. 727, 116 S.Ct. 2374 (1996)

In 1992, Congress enacted, and the President signed into law, the Cable Television Consumer Protection and Competition Act. Subsequently, three of its provisions, regulating "patently offensive" sex-related material, were challenged by cable programmers. Section 10(a), which applies to privately "leased cable channels," permits cable operators to prohibit programmers from programming material that the "operator reasonably believes describes or depicts sexual or excretory activities or organs in a patently offensive way." Section 10(c) does the same with respect to "public, educational, or governmental channels." Section 10(b), furthermore, required cable operators to isolate "patently offensive" programming on a single channel and to block access to the channel unless a viewer requested access in advance and in writing. A federal appellate court upheld all three provisions and the cable programmers appealed to the Supreme Court.

The Court's decision was announced by Justice Breyer, but his opinion was joined in parts by only pluralities of other justices. Justices Stevens and Souter filed concurring opinions. Justice O'Connor filed an opinion in part concurring and dissenting. Justice Kennedy filed an opinion concurring in part and dissenting in part, which Justice Ginsburg joined. Justice Thomas filed an opinion concurring in the judgment in part and dissenting in part, which Chief Justice Rehnquist and Justice Scalia joined.

   □ *Justice BREYER announced the judgment of the Court and delivered the opinion of the Court with respect to Part III, an opinion with respect to Parts I, II, and V, in which Justice STEVENS, Justice O'CONNOR, and Justice SOUTER join, and an opinion with respect to Parts IV and VI, in which Justice STEVENS and Justice SOUTER join.*

We conclude that the first provision—that permits the operator to decide whether or not to broadcast such programs on leased access channels—is consistent with the First Amendment. The second provision, that requires leased channel operators to segregate and to block that programming, and the third provision, applicable to public, educational, and governmental channels, violate the First Amendment, for they are not appropriately tailored to achieve the basic, legitimate objective of protecting children from exposure to "patently offensive" material.

■ II

We turn initially to the provision that permits cable system operators to prohibit "patently offensive" (or "indecent") programming transmitted over leased access channels. Section 10(a). . . .

We recognize that the First Amendment, the terms of which apply to governmental action, ordinarily does not itself throw into constitutional doubt the decisions of private citizens to permit, or to restrict, speech—and this is so ordinarily even where those decisions take place within the framework of a regulatory regime such as broadcasting. Were that not so, courts might have to face the difficult, and potentially restrictive, practical task of deciding which, among any number of private parties involved in providing a program (for example, networks, station owners, program editors, and program producers), is the "speaker" whose rights may not be abridged, and who is the speech-restricting "censor." Furthermore, as this Court has held, the editorial function itself is an aspect of "speech," see *Turner* [*Broadcasting System, Inc. v. Federal Communications Commission,* 114 512 U.S. 622 (1994)], and a court's decision that a private party, say, the station owner, is a "censor," could itself interfere with that private "censor's" freedom to speak as an editor. . . .

Like the petitioners, Justices KENNEDY and THOMAS would have us decide this case simply by transferring and applying literally categorical standards this Court has developed in other contexts. For Justice KENNEDY, leased access channels are like a common carrier, cablecast is a protected medium, strict scrutiny applies, Section 10(a) fails this test, and, therefore, Section 10(a) is invalid. For Justice THOMAS, the case is simple because the cable operator who owns the system over which access channels are broadcast, like a bookstore owner with respect to what it displays on the shelves, has a predominant First Amendment interest. Both categorical approaches suffer from the same flaws: they import law developed in very different contexts into a new and changing environment, and they lack the flexibility necessary to allow government to respond to very serious practical problems without sacrificing the free exchange of ideas the First Amendment is designed to protect.

The history of this Court's First Amendment jurisprudence, however, is one of continual development, as the Constitution's general command . . . has been applied to new circumstances requiring different adaptations of prior principles and precedents. The essence of that protection is that Congress may not regulate speech except in cases of extraordinary need and with the exercise of a degree of care that we have not elsewhere required. . . . At the same time, our cases have not left Congress or the States powerless to address the most serious problems. See, e.g., *Chaplinsky v. New Hampshire,* 315 U.S. 568 (1942); *Young v. American Mini Theaters, Inc.,* 427 U.S. 50 (1976); *FCC v. Pacific Foundation,* 438 U.S. 726 (1978). . . .

[We decide this case] narrowly, by closely scrutinizing Section 10(a) to assure that it properly addresses an extremely important problem, without imposing, in light of the relevant interests, an unnecessarily great restriction on speech. The importance of the interest at stake here—protecting children from exposure to patently offensive depictions of sex; the accommodation of the interests of programmers in maintaining access channels and of cable operators in editing the contents of their channels; the similarity of the problem and its solution to those at issue in *Pacifica*; and the flexibility inherent in an approach that permits private cable operators to make editorial decisions, lead us to conclude that Section 10(a) is a sufficiently tailored response to an extraordinarily important problem.

First, the provision before us comes accompanied with an extremely important justification, one that this Court has often found compelling—the need to protect children from exposure to patently offensive sex-related material. *Ginsberg v. New York*, 390 U.S. 629 (1968); *New York v. Ferber*, 458 U.S. 747 (1982).

Second, the provision arises in a very particular context—congressional permission for cable operators to regulate programming that, but for a previous Act of Congress, would have had no path of access to cable channels free of an operator's control....

Third, the problem Congress addressed here is remarkably similar to the problem addressed by the FCC in *Pacifica*, and the balance Congress struck is commensurate with the balance we approved there. . . . Cable television broadcasting, including access channel broadcasting, is as "accessible to children" as over-the-air broadcasting, if not more so. Cable television systems, including access channels, "have established a uniquely pervasive presence in the lives of all Americans." "Patently offensive" material from these stations can "confront the citizen" in the "privacy of the home," *Pacifica*, with little or no prior warning. There is nothing to stop "adults who feel the need" from finding similar programming elsewhere, say, on tape or in theaters. In fact, the power of cable systems to control home program viewing is not absolute. Over-the-air broadcasting and direct broadcast satellites already provide alternative ways for programmers to reach the home, and are likely to do so to a greater extent in the near future.

Fourth, the permissive nature of Section 10(a) means that it likely restricts speech less than, not more than, the ban at issue in *Pacifica*. The provision removes a restriction as to some speakers—namely, cable operators. Moreover, although the provision does create a risk that a program will not appear, that risk is not the same as the certainty that accompanies a governmental ban. . . .

For the reasons discussed, we conclude that Section 10(a) is consistent with the First Amendment.

■ III

The statute's second provision significantly differs from the first, for it does not simply permit, but rather requires, cable system operators to restrict speech—by segregating and blocking "patently offensive" sex-related material appearing on leased channels (but not on other channels). Section 10(b). In particular, as previously mentioned, this provision and its implementing regulations require cable system operators to place "patently offensive" leased channel programming on a separate channel; to block that channel; to unblock the channel within 30 days of a subscriber's written request for access; and to reblock the channel within 30 days of a subscriber's request for reblocking. Also, leased channel programmers must notify cable operators of an intended "patently offensive" broadcast up to 30 days before its scheduled broadcast date.

These requirements have obvious restrictive effects. The several up-to-30-day delays, along with single channel segregation, mean that a subscriber cannot decide to watch a single program without considerable advance planning and without letting the "patently offensive" channel in its entirety invade his household for days, perhaps weeks, at a time. These restrictions will prevent programmers from broadcasting to viewers who select programs day by day (or, through "surfing," minute by minute); to viewers who would like occasionally to watch a few, but not many, of the programs on the "patently offensive" channel; and to viewers who simply tend to judge a program's value through channel reputation, i.e., by the company it keeps. Moreover, the "written notice" requirement will further restrict viewing by subscribers who fear for their reputations should the operator, advertently or inadvertently, disclose the list of those who wish to watch the "patently offensive" channel. Further, the added costs and burdens that these requirements impose upon a cable system operator may encourage that operator to ban programming that the operator would otherwise permit to run, even if only late at night. . . .

We agree with the Government that protection of children is a "compelling interest." But we do not agree that the "segregate and block" requirements properly accommodate the speech restrictions they impose and the legitimate objective they seek to attain. Nor need we here determine whether, or the extent to which, *Pacifica* does, or does not, impose some lesser standard of review where indecent speech is at issue. . . .

The record's description and discussion of a different alternative—the "lockbox"—leads, through a different route, to a similar conclusion. The Cable Communications Policy Act of 1984 required cable operators to provide "upon the request of a subscriber, a device by which the subscriber can prohibit viewing of a particular cable service during periods selected by the subscriber." This device—the "lockbox"—would help protect children by permitting their parents to "lock out" those programs or channels that they did not want their children to see. . . .

Consequently, we cannot find that the "segregate and block" restrictions on speech are a narrowly, or reasonably, tailored effort to protect children. Rather, they are overly restrictive, "sacrificing" important First Amendment interests for too "speculative a gain." For that reason they are not consistent with the First Amendment.

■ IV

The statute's third provision, as implemented by FCC regulation, is similar to its first provision, in that it too permits a cable operator to prevent transmission of "patently offensive" programming, in this case on public access channels. But there are four important differences.

The first is the historical background. As Justice KENNEDY points out, cable operators have traditionally agreed to reserve channel capacity for public, governmental, and educational channels as part of the consideration they give municipalities that award them cable franchises. . . .

The second difference is the institutional background that has developed as a result of the historical difference. When a "leased channel" is made available by the operator to a private lessee, the lessee has total control of programming during the leased time slot. Public access channels, on the other hand, are normally subject to complex supervisory systems of various sorts, often with both public and private elements. . . .

Third, the existence of a system aimed at encouraging and securing programming that the community considers valuable strongly suggests that a "cable operator's veto" is less likely necessary to achieve the statute's basic objective, protecting children, than a similar veto in the context of leased channels. Of course, the system of access managers and supervising boards can make mistakes, which the operator might in some cases correct with its veto power. Balanced against this potential benefit, however, is the risk that the veto itself may be mistaken; and its use, or threatened use, could prevent the presentation of programming, that, though borderline, is not "patently offensive" to its targeted audience. And this latter threat must bulk large within a system that already has publicly accountable systems for maintaining responsible programs.

Finally, our examination of the legislative history and the record before us is consistent with what common sense suggests, namely that the public/nonprofit programming control systems now in place would normally avoid, minimize, or eliminate any child-related problems concerning "patently offensive" programming. . . .

The upshot, in respect to the public access channels, is a law that could radically change present programming-related relationships among local community and nonprofit supervising boards and access managers, which relationships are established through municipal law, regulation, and contract. In doing so, it would not significantly restore editorial rights of cable operators, but would greatly increase the risk that certain categories of programming (say, borderline offensive programs) will not appear. At the same time, given present supervisory mechanisms, the need for this particular provision, aimed directly at public access channels, is not obvious. Having carefully reviewed the legislative history of the Act, the proceedings before the FCC, the record below, and the submissions of the parties and amici here, we conclude that the Government cannot sustain its burden of showing that Section 10(c) is necessary to protect children or that it is appropriately tailored to secure that end. Consequently, we find this third provision violates the First Amendment. . . .

☐ *Justice SOUTER, concurring.*

Justice KENNEDY's separate opinion . . . sees no warrant in this case for anything but a categorical and rule-based approach applying a fixed level of scrutiny, the strictest, to judge the content-based provisions of Sections 10(a), (b), and (c), and he accordingly faults the plurality opinion for declining to decide the precise doctrinal categories that should govern the issue at hand. The value of the categorical approach generally to First Amendment security prompts a word to explain why I join the Court's unwillingness to announce a definitive categorical analysis in this case. . . .

I cannot guess how much time will go by until the technologies of communication before us today have matured and their relationships become known. But until a category of indecency can be defined both with reference to the new technology and with a prospect of durability, the job of the courts will be just what Justice BREYER does today: recognizing established First Amendment interests through a close analysis that constrains the Congress, without wholly incapacitating it in all matters of the significance apparent here, maintaining the high value of open communication, measuring the costs of regulation by exact attention to fact, and compiling a pedigree of experience with the changing subject. These are familiar judicial responsibilities in times when we know too little to risk the finality of precision, and attention to them will probably take us through the communications revolution. Maybe the judicial obligation to shoulder these responsibilities can itself be captured by a much older rule, familiar to every doctor of medicine: "First, do no harm."

☐ *Justice O'CONNOR, concurring in part and dissenting in part.*

I agree that Section 10(a) is constitutional and that Section 10(b) is unconstitutional, and I join Parts I, II, III, and V, and the judgment in part. I am not persuaded, however, that the asserted "important differences" between Sections 10(a) and 10(c) are sufficient to justify striking down Section 10(c). I find the features shared by Section 10(a), which covers leased access channels, and Section 10(c), which covers public access channels, to be more significant than the differences. For that reason, I would find that Section 10(c) too withstands constitutional scrutiny. . . .

☐ *Justice KENNEDY, with whom Justice GINSBURG joins, concurring in part, concurring in the judgment in part, and dissenting in part.*

Though I join Part III of the opinion (there for the Court) striking down Section 10(b) of the Act, and concur in the judgment that Section 10(c) is unconstitutional, with respect I dissent from the remainder. . . .

Sections 10(a) and (c) present a classic case of discrimination against speech based on its content. There are legitimate reasons why the Government might wish to regulate or even restrict the speech at issue here, but Sections 10(a) and 10(c) are not drawn to address those reasons with the precision the First Amendment requires. . . .

☐ *Justice THOMAS, joined by the CHIEF JUSTICE and Justice SCALIA, concurring in the judgment in part and dissenting in part.*

I agree with the plurality's conclusion that Section 10(a) is constitutionally permissible, but I disagree with its conclusion that Section 10(b) and (c) violate the First Amendment. For many years, we have failed to articulate how and to what extent the First Amendment protects cable operators, programmers, and viewers from state and federal regulation. I think it is time we did so, and I cannot go along with the plurality's assiduous attempts to avoid addressing that issue openly. . . .

Reno v. American Civil Liberties Union

521 U.S. 844, 117 S.CT. 2329 (1997)

This case is excerpted in Section B of this chapter.

Ashcroft v. American Civil Liberties Union

124 S. CT. 2783 (2004)

Following the Supreme Court's invalidation of the Communications Decency Act (CDA) of 1996 in *Reno v. American Civil Liberties Union*, 521 U.S. 844 (1997), (excerpted in Ch. 5), in 1998 Congress enacted the Child Online Protection Act (COPA), prohibiting any person from "knowingly and with knowledge of the character of the material, in interstate or foreign commerce by means of the World Wide Web, making any communication for commercial purposes that is available to any minor and that includes any material that is harmful to minors." Compared with the CDA, Congress limited COPA's scope in three ways. First, while the CDA applied to communications over the Internet as a whole, including e-mail messages, COPA applies only to material displayed on the web. Second, unlike the CDA, COPA covers only communications made "for commercial purposes." And third, whereas the CDA prohibited "indecent" and "patently offensive" communications, the COPA restricts only the narrower category of "material harmful to minors."

Drawing on the three-part test for obscenity set forth in *Miller v. California*, 413 U.S. 15 (1973) (excerpted in Ch. 5), COPA defines "material that is harmful to minors" as "any communication, picture, image, graphic image file, article, recording, writing, or other matter of any kind that is obscene or that—(A) the average person, applying contemporary community standards, would find, taking the material as a whole and with respect to minors, is designed to appeal to, or is designed to pander to, the prurient interest; (B) depicts, describes, or represents, in a manner patently offensive with respect to minors, an actual or simulated sexual act or sexual contact, an actual or simulated normal or perverted sexual act, or a lewd exhibition of the genitals or post-pubescent female breast; and (C) taken as a whole, lacks serious literary, artistic, political, or scientific value for minors." For each violation of the statute, a civil penalty of up to $50,000 and criminal penalties of up to six months in prison may be imposed.

One month before COPA was scheduled to go into effect, the American Civil Liberties Union (ACLU) challenged the constitutionality of the act. A federal district court granted a motion for a preliminary injunction, barring the enforcement of the act. Subsequently, the district court concluded that the ACLU was likely to establish at trial that COPA could not withstand strict scrutiny because, among other reasons, it had not been shown to be the least restrictive means of preventing minors from accessing harmful materials. Attorney General John Ashcroft appealed that decision and the Court of Appeals for the Third Circuit affirmed the lower court. On appeal, in *Ashcroft v. American Civil Liberties Union*, 535 U.S. 564 (2002) (*Ashcroft I*), the Court held that the law's use of "community standards" to define what material in cyberspace is "harmful to minors" did not necessarily violate the First Amendment. However, the Court also allowed the law to remain enjoined from going into effect until questions about its impact on free speech were resolved. On the remand, the appellate court again affirmed the lower court and found that the COPA was not narrowly tailored and was not the least restrictive means of preventing minors from using the Internet to obtain access to harmful materials. Ashcroft appealed that decision and the Supreme Court granted review.

The appellate court's decision was affirmed by a five-to-four vote. Justice Kennedy delivered the opinion for the Court, holding that the appellate court correctly affirmed the order enjoining enforcement of the statute. Justice Stevens filed a concurring opinion. Justices Scalia and Breyer filed dissenting opinions; the latter's dissent was joined by Chief Justice Rehnquist and Justice O'Connor.

☐ *Justice KENNEDY delivered the opinion of the Court.*

Content-based prohibitions, enforced by severe criminal penalties, have the constant potential to be a repressive force in the lives and thoughts of a free people. To guard against that threat the Constitution demands that content-based restrictions on speech be presumed invalid, *R. A. V. v. St. Paul*, 505 U.S. 377 (1992), and that the Government bear the burden of showing their constitutionality. *United States v. Playboy Entertainment Group, Inc.*, 529 U.S. 803 (2000). This is true even when Congress twice has attempted to find a constitutional means to restrict, and punish, the speech in question. . . .

The Government has failed, at this point, to rebut the plaintiffs' contention that there are plausible less restrictive alternatives to the statute. Substantial practical considerations, furthermore, argue in favor of upholding the injunction and allowing the case to proceed to trial. For those reasons, we affirm the decision of the Court of Appeals upholding the preliminary injunction, and we remand the case so that it may be returned to the District Court for trial on the issues presented.

[T]he District Court concluded that respondents were likely to prevail. That conclusion was not an abuse of discretion, because on this record there are a number of plausible, less restrictive alternatives to the statute.

The primary alternative considered by the District Court was blocking and filtering software. Blocking and filtering software is an alternative that is less restrictive than COPA, and, in addition, likely more effective as a means of restricting children's access to materials harmful to them. The District Court, in granting the preliminary injunction, did so primarily because the plaintiffs had proposed that filters are a less restrictive alternative to COPA and the Government had not shown it would be likely to disprove the plaintiffs' contention at trial.

Filters are less restrictive than COPA. They impose selective restrictions on speech at the receiving end, not universal restrictions at the source. Under a filtering regime, adults without children may gain access to speech they have a right to see without having to identify themselves or provide their credit card information. Even adults with children may obtain access to the same speech on the same terms simply by turning off the filter on their home computers. Above all, promoting the use of filters does not condemn as criminal any category of speech, and so the potential chilling effect is eliminated, or at least much diminished. All of these things are true, moreover, regardless of how broadly or narrowly the definitions in COPA are construed.

Filters also may well be more effective than COPA. First, a filter can prevent minors from seeing all pornography, not just pornography posted to the Web from America. [F]ilters also may be more effective because they can be applied to all forms of Internet communication, including e-mail, not just communications available via the World Wide Web.

That filtering software may well be more effective than COPA is confirmed by the findings of the Commission on Child Online Protection, a blue-ribbon commission created by Congress in COPA itself. . . .

There are also important practical reasons to let the injunction stand pending a full trial on the merits. First, the potential harms from reversing the injunction outweigh those of leaving it in place by mistake. Where a prosecution is a likely possibility, yet only an affirmative defense is available, speakers may self-censor rather than risk the perils of trial. There is a potential for extraordinary harm and a serious chill upon protected speech. The harm done from letting the injunction stand pending a trial on the merits, in contrast, will not be extensive. No prosecutions have yet been undertaken under the law, so none will be disrupted if the injunction stands. Further, if the injunction is upheld, the Government in the interim can enforce obscenity laws already on the books.

Second, there are substantial factual disputes remaining in the case. As mentioned above, there is a serious gap in the evidence as to the effectiveness of filtering software. For us to assume, without proof, that filters are less effective than COPA would usurp the District Court's factfinding role. . . .

Third, and on a related point, the factual record does not reflect current technological reality—a serious flaw in any case involving the Internet. The technology of the Internet evolves at a rapid pace. Yet the factfindings of the District Court were entered in February 1999, over five years ago. Since then, certain facts about the Internet are known to have changed. It is reasonable to assume that other technological developments important to the First Amendment analysis have also occurred during that time. More and better filtering alternatives may exist than when the District Court entered its findings. Indeed, we know that after the District Court entered its factfindings, a congressionally appointed commission issued a report that found that filters are more effective than verification screens. . . .

On a final point, it is important to note that this opinion does not hold that Congress is incapable of enacting any regulation of the Internet designed to prevent minors from gaining access to harmful materials. The parties, because of the conclusion of the Court of Appeals that the statute's definitions rendered it unconstitutional, did not devote their attention to the question whether further evidence might be introduced on the relative restrictiveness and effectiveness of alternatives to the statute. On remand, however, the parties will be able to introduce further evidence on this point. This opinion does not foreclose the District Court from concluding, upon a proper showing by the Government that meets the Government's constitutional burden as defined in this opinion, that COPA is the least restrictive alternative available to accomplish Congress' goal.

On this record, the Government has not shown that the less restrictive alternatives proposed by respondents should be disregarded. Those alternatives, indeed, may be more effective than the provisions of COPA. The District Court did not abuse its discretion when it entered the preliminary injunction. The judgment of the Court of Appeals is affirmed, and the case is remanded for proceedings consistent with this opinion.

It is so ordered.

☐ *Justice SCALIA, dissenting.*

I agree with Justice BREYER's conclusion that the Child Online Protection Act (COPA) is constitutional. Both the Court and Justice BREYER err, however, in subjecting COPA to strict scrutiny. Nothing in the First Amendment entitles the type of material covered by COPA to that exacting standard of review. "We have recognized that commercial entities which engage in 'the sordid business of pandering' by 'deliberately emphasiz[ing] the sexually provocative aspects of [their nonobscene products], in order to catch the salaciously disposed,' engage in constitutionally unprotected behavior." *United States v. Playboy Entertainment Group, Inc.*, 529 U.S. 803 (2000) (SCALIA, J., dissenting) (quoting *Ginzburg v. United States*, 383 U.S. 463 [1966]).

There is no doubt that the commercial pornography covered by COPA fits this description. The statute applies only to a person who, "as a regular course of such person's trade or business, with the objective of earning a profit," and "with knowledge of the character of the material" communicates material that depicts certain specified sexual acts and that "is designed to appeal to, or is designed to pander to, the prurient interest." Since this business could, consistent with the First Amendment, be banned entirely, COPA's lesser restrictions raise no constitutional concern.

☐ *Justice BREYER, with whom THE CHIEF JUSTICE and Justice O'CONNOR join, dissenting.*

[M]y examination of (1) the burdens the Act imposes on protected expression, (2) the Act's ability to further a compelling interest, and (3) the proposed "less restrictive alternatives" convinces me that the Court is wrong. I cannot accept its conclusion that Congress could have accomplished its statutory objective—protecting children from commercial pornography on the Internet—in other, less restrictive ways.

The Act's definitions limit the material it regulates to material that does not enjoy First Amendment protection, namely legally obscene material, and very little more. . . .

[T]he statute, read literally, insofar as it extends beyond the legally obscene, could reach only borderline cases. And to take the words of the statute literally is consistent with Congress' avowed objective in enacting this law; namely, putting material produced by professional pornographers behind screens that will verify the age of the viewer. . . .

The Act does not censor the material it covers. Rather, it requires providers of the "harmful to minors" material to restrict minors' access to it by verifying age. They can do so by inserting screens that verify age using a credit card, adult personal identification number, or other similar technology. In this way, the Act requires creation of an internet screen that minors, but not adults, will find difficult to bypass.

I recognize that the screening requirement imposes some burden on adults who seek access to the regulated material, as well as on its providers. The cost is, in part, monetary. The parties agreed that a Web site could store card numbers or passwords at between 15 and 20 cents per number. . . .

In addition to the monetary cost, and despite strict requirements that identifying information be kept confidential, the identification requirements inherent in age-screening may lead some users to fear embarrassment. Both monetary costs and potential embarrassment can deter potential viewers and, in that sense, the statute's requirements may restrict access to a site. But this Court has held that in the context of congressional efforts to protect children, restrictions of this kind do not automatically violate the Constitution. And the Court has approved their use. See, e.g., *United States v. American Library Assn., Inc.*, 539 U.S. 194 (2003).

In sum, the Act at most imposes a modest additional burden on adult access to legally obscene material, perhaps imposing a similar burden on access to some protected borderline obscene material as well.

I turn next to the question of "compelling interest," that of protecting minors from exposure to commercial pornography. No one denies that such an interest is "compelling." Rather, the question here is whether the Act, given its restrictions on adult access, significantly advances that interest. In other words, is the game worth the candle?

The majority argues that it is not, because of the existence of "blocking and filtering software." The majority refers to the presence of that software as a "less restrictive alternative." But that is a misnomer—a misnomer that may lead the reader to believe that all we need do is look to see if the blocking and filtering software is less restrictive; and to believe that, because in one sense it is (one can turn off the software), that is the end of the constitutional matter.

But such reasoning has no place here. Conceptually speaking, the presence of filtering software is not an alternative legislative approach to the problem of protecting children from exposure to commercial pornography. Rather, it is part of the status quo, i.e., the backdrop against which Congress enacted the present statute. It is always true, by definition, that the status quo is less restrictive than a new regulatory law. It is always less restrictive to do nothing than to do something. But "doing nothing" does not address the problem Congress sought to address—namely that, despite the availability of filtering software, children were still being exposed to harmful material on the Internet. . . .

Filtering software, as presently available, does not solve the "child protection" problem. It suffers from four serious inadequacies that prompted Congress to pass legislation instead of relying on its voluntary use. First, its filtering is faulty, allowing some pornographic material to pass through without hindrance. . . .

Second, filtering software costs money. Not every family has the $40 or so necessary to install it. By way of contrast, age screening costs less.

Third, filtering software depends upon parents willing to decide where their children will surf the Web and able to enforce that decision. As to millions of American families, that is not a reasonable possibility. More than 28 million school age children have both parents or their sole parent in the work force, at least 5 million children are left alone at home without supervision each week, and many of those children will spend afternoons and evenings with friends who may well have access to computers and more lenient parents.

Fourth, software blocking lacks precision, with the result that those who wish to use it to screen out pornography find that it blocks a great deal of material that is valuable. . . .

In sum, a "filtering software status quo" means filtering that underblocks, imposes a cost upon each family that uses it, fails to screen outside the home, and lacks precision. Thus, Congress could reasonably conclude that a system that relies entirely upon the use of such software is not an effective system. And a law that adds to that system an age-verification screen requirement significantly increases the system's efficacy. That is to say, at a modest additional cost to those adults who wish to obtain access to a screened program, that law will bring about better, more precise blocking, both inside and outside the home. . . .

My conclusion is that the Act, as properly interpreted, risks imposition of minor burdens on some protected material—burdens that adults wishing to view the material may overcome at modest cost. At the same time, it significantly helps to achieve a compelling congressional goal, protecting children from exposure to commercial pornography. There is no serious, practically available "less restrictive" way similarly to further this compelling interest. Hence the Act is constitutional. . . . For these reasons, I dissent.

United States v. American Library Association
539 U.S. 126, 123 S. Ct. 2297 (2003)

Congress authorized federal funding for public libraries to acquire and to provide access to the Internet under an E-rate program under the Telecommunications Act of 1996 and the Library Services and Technology Act (LSTA). Subsequently, Congress was lobbied to enact the

Children's Internet Protection Act (CIPA) of 2001. Under that law, public libraries may not receive federal funding for Internet access unless they install software to block obscene or pornographic images and prevent minors from assessing such materials. The statute authorizes, but does not require, librarians to unblock Internet sites at the request of adult users. It also neither specifies what kinds of filters libraries should install nor provides standards and procedures for unblocking Internet sites at the request of adult users. The American Library Association and a number of other organizations and individuals challenged the constitutionality of the law. A federal district court ruled that the law ran afoul of the First Amendment and blocked its enforcement. The government appealed.

The lower court's decision was reversed by a six-to-three vote. Chief Justice Rehnquist delivered the opinion of the Court, which only Justices O'Connor, Scalia, and Thomas joined. Justices Kennedy and Breyer filed opinions concurring in the judgment. Justices Stevens and Souter filed dissenting opinions, which Justice Ginsburg joined.

   ☐ *CHIEF JUSTICE REHNQUIST announced the judgment of the Court and delivered an opinion, in which Justice O'CONNOR, Justice SCALIA, and Justice THOMAS joined.*

By connecting to the Internet, public libraries provide patrons with a vast amount of valuable information. But there is also an enormous amount of pornography on the Internet, much of which is easily obtained. The accessibility of this material has created serious problems for libraries, which have found that patrons of all ages, including minors, regularly search for online pornography. Some patrons also expose others to pornographic images by leaving them displayed on Internet terminals or printed at library printers.

Upon discovering these problems, Congress became concerned that the E-rate and LSTA programs were facilitating access to illegal and harmful pornography. Congress learned that adults "us[e] library computers to access pornography that is then exposed to staff, passersby, and children," and that "minors acces[s] child and adult pornography in libraries."

But Congress also learned that filtering software that blocks access to pornographic Web sites could provide a reasonably effective way to prevent such uses of library resources. By 2000, before Congress enacted CIPA, almost 17% of public libraries used such software on at least some of their Internet terminals, and 7% had filters on all of them. A library can set such software to block categories of material, such as "Pornography" or "Violence." When a patron tries to view a site that falls within such a category, a screen appears indicating that the site is blocked. But a filter set to block pornography may sometimes block other sites that present neither obscene nor pornographic material, but that nevertheless trigger the filter. To minimize this problem, a library can set its software to prevent the blocking of material that falls into categories like "Education," "History," and "Medical."

A library may also add or delete specific sites from a blocking category, and anyone can ask companies that furnish filtering software to unblock particular sites. Responding to this information, Congress enacted CIPA. . . .

Congress has wide latitude to attach conditions to the receipt of federal assistance in order to further its policy objectives. *South Dakota v. Dole*, 483 U. S. 203 (1987). But Congress may not "induce" the recipient "to engage in activities that would themselves be unconstitutional." To determine whether libraries would violate the First Amendment by employing the filtering software that CIPA requires, we must first examine the role of libraries in our society.

Public libraries pursue the worthy missions of facilitating learning and cultural enrichment. To this end, libraries collect only those materials deemed to have "requisite and appropriate quality."

We have held in two analogous contexts that the government has broad discretion to make content-based judgments in deciding what private speech to make available to the public. In *Arkansas Ed. Television Comm'n v. Forbes*, 523 U. S. 666 (1998), we held that public forum principles do not generally apply to a public television station's editorial judgments regarding the private speech it presents to its viewers. Recognizing a broad right of public access "would [also] risk implicating the courts in judgments that should be left to the exercise of journalistic discretion."

Similarly, in *National Endowment for Arts v. Finley*, 524 U. S. 569 (1998), we upheld an art funding program that required the National Endowment for the Arts (NEA) to use content-based criteria in making funding decisions. We explained that "[a]ny content-based considerations that may be taken into account in the grant-making process are a consequence of the nature of arts funding."

The principles underlying *Forbes* and *Finley* also apply to a public library's exercise of judgment in selecting the material it provides to its patrons. Just as forum analysis and heightened judicial scrutiny are incompatible with the role of public television stations and the role of the NEA, they are also incompatible with the discretion that public libraries must have to fulfill their traditional missions. Public library staffs necessarily consider content in making collection decisions and enjoy broad discretion in making them.

The public forum principles on which the District Court relied are out of place in the context of this case. Internet access in public libraries is neither a "traditional" nor a "designated" public forum. First, this resource—which did not exist until quite recently—has not "immemorially been held in trust for the use of the public and, time out of mind, . . . been used for purposes of assembly, communication of thoughts between citizens, and discussing public questions."

Nor does Internet access in a public library satisfy our definition of a "designated public forum." To create such a forum, the government must make an affirmative choice to open up its property for use as a public forum.

The situation here is very different. A public library does not acquire Internet terminals in order to create a public forum for Web publishers to express themselves, any more than it collects books in order to provide a public forum for the authors of books to speak. It provides Internet access, not to "encourage a diversity of views from private speakers," but for the same reasons it offers other library resources: to facilitate research, learning, and recreational pursuits by furnishing materials of requisite and appropriate quality. . . .

Moreover, because of the vast quantity of material on the Internet and the rapid pace at which it changes, libraries cannot possibly segregate, item by item, all the Internet material that is appropriate for inclusion from all that is not. While a library could limit its Internet collection to just those sites it found worthwhile, it could do so only at the cost of excluding an enormous amount of valuable information that it lacks the capacity to review. Given that tradeoff, it is entirely reasonable for public libraries to reject that approach and instead exclude certain categories of content, without making individualized judgments that everything they do make available has requisite and appropriate quality. . . .

Because public libraries' use of Internet filtering software does not violate their patrons' First Amendment rights, CIPA does not induce libraries to violate the Constitution, and is a valid exercise of Congress' spending power. Nor does CIPA impose an unconstitutional condition on public libraries.

☐ *Justice KENNEDY, concurring in the judgment.*

If, on the request of an adult user, a librarian will unblock filtered material or disable the Internet software filter without significant delay, there is little to this case. The Government represents this is indeed the fact. . . .

If some libraries do not have the capacity to unblock specific Web sites or to disable the filter or if it is shown that an adult user's election to view constitutionally protected Internet material is burdened in some other substantial way, that would be the subject for an as-applied challenge, not the facial challenge made in this case. . . .

☐ *Justice STEVENS, dissenting.*

The plurality incorrectly argues that the statute does not impose "an unconstitutional condition on public libraries." On the contrary, it impermissibly conditions the receipt of Government funding on the restriction of significant First Amendment rights. . . .

☐ *Justice SOUTER, with whom Justice GINSBURG joins, dissenting.*

Like the other Members of the Court, I have no doubt about the legitimacy of governmental efforts to put a barrier between child patrons of public libraries and the raw offerings on the Internet otherwise available to them there, and if the only First Amendment interests raised here were those of children, I would uphold application of the Act. We have said that the governmental interest in "shielding" children from exposure to indecent material is "compelling," *Reno v. American Civil Liberties Union*, 521 U. S. 844 (1997), and I do not think that the awkwardness a child might feel on asking for an unblocked terminal is any such burden as to affect constitutionality. . . .

The question for me, then, is whether a local library could itself constitutionally impose these restrictions on the content otherwise available to an adult patron through an Internet connection, at a library terminal provided for public use. The answer is no. A library that chose to block an adult's

Internet access to material harmful to children (and whatever else the undiscriminating filter might interrupt) would be imposing a content-based restriction on communication of material in the library's control that an adult could otherwise lawfully see. This would simply be censorship. True, the censorship would not necessarily extend to every adult, for an intending Internet user might convince a librarian that he was a true researcher or had a "lawful purpose" to obtain everything the library's terminal could provide. But as to those who did not qualify for discretionary unblocking, the censorship would be complete and, like all censorship by an agency of the Government, presumptively invalid owing to strict scrutiny in implementing the Free Speech Clause of the First Amendment. . . .

G | *Fair Trial/Free Press Controversies*

Television, along with newspapers, and their coverage of sensational trials led to a series of "fair trial/free press" controversies. Adverse, prejudicial pretrial and trial publicity ostensibly creates a conflict between the defendant's Sixth Amendment right to a fair trial and the First Amendment freedoms of speech and press, as well as the public's interest in information about the operation of the criminal justice system. But because constitutional rights are assertable only against the government, not other individuals, fair trial/free press controversies actually involve determining what process is due and how to reconcile governmental attempts to limit publicity or access to judicial proceedings with First Amendment principles.

The Sixth Amendment specifically provides that "in all criminal prosecutions the accused shall enjoy the right to a speedy and *public trial*" (emphasis added). A presumption of openness is rooted in common-law practice, stemming from earlier Anglo-Saxon customs. Open, public trials have traditionally been viewed as an essential safeguard against judicial abuse of power and miscarriages of justice. Also, publicity may both educate people about the operation of the judiciary and provide an opportunity for members of the public to scrutinize the administration of justice.

Despite the language of the Sixth Amendment and generally accepted practice of having open trials, neither the press nor the public could compel openness. While acknowledging the public's interests in open trials, the Court maintained that the Sixth Amendment guarantees only the rights of the accused, not the public. However, the Court also noted that "although a defendant can, under some circumstances, waive his constitutional right to a public trial, he has no absolute right to compel a private trial" in *Singer v. United States*, 380 U.S. 24 (1965). In short, under the Sixth Amendment, members of the public have no constitutional claim to compel open trials, but neither do defendants have a right to a closed trial.

Because the Sixth Amendment guarantees an accused person's rights, and only secondarily the public's interests, judges may restrict public access and publicity to ensure due process and procedural fairness.[1] But as judges began increasingly to restrict media coverage of judicial proceedings, lawyers turned to the First Amendment claiming, as Justice Douglas once put it, "The trial is a public event. What transpires in the courtroom is public property."[2] Because the First Amendment, unlike the Sixth Amendment, comprehends the public's broad interests in freedom of information, it provides a basis for challenging restraints on publicity and access to trials.

Prior to the 1960s, the Court tended to overturn contempt charges of the press for editorials and news stories concerning pretrial and trial proceedings.[3] But extensive publicity and, in one case, the videotaping and playing of a confession on television prior to the accused's trial, led to the Court's reconsideration and insistence that judges exercise their powers to ensure fair trials.[4] Then in *Estes v. Texas*, 381 U.S. 532 (1965), when the Court first tackled the controversy over televising of criminal trials, the justices were deeply split. Justice Stewart's initial draft failed to command a majority. He was relegated to writing a dissenting opinion, joined by three others. Justice Tom Clark wrote the majority's opinion holding that cameras in the courtroom were too disruptive and denied the defendant's right to a fair trial.

The year after *Estes*, with an even more controversial ruling, in *Sheppard v. Maxwell*, 385 U.S. 333 (1966), the Warren Court overturned the conviction of Dr. Sam Sheppard for murdering his wife because the trial judge failed to ensure the decorum essential to a fair trial. There the press had what Justice Clark characterized as "a Roman holiday," with live broadcasting of the coroner's inquest from a high-school gymnasium. During the trial, the judge reserved three of the four rows of benches in the courtroom for news reporters and permitted the erection of a press table inside the bar of the courtroom, which allowed journalists to overhear all of Sheppard's conversations with his attorneys.

In *Sheppard*, Justice Clark's opinion for the Court suggested that in sensational trials judges should adopt rules governing reporters' access to the courtroom and insulating witnesses from journalists, as well as issue gag orders barring police, witnesses, and counsel from talking with reporters about trial proceedings. But this ruling only intensified the fair trial/free press controversy. Immediately, the American Bar Association adopted as part of its Canons of Professional Ethics rules limiting attorneys' permissible statements about pending trials and recommendations that judges use their contempt power to inhibit prejudicial publicity. The American Newspaper Publishers Association countered that such interference with news reporting constituted a prior restraint.

Following *Sheppard*, trial courts' increasing reliance on gag orders was vigorously contested by the press as a prior restraint in violation of the First Amendment. The Court finally addressed the constitutionality of gag orders in *Nebraska Press Association v. Stuart*, 427 U.S. 539 (1976). In striking down the gag order there, Chief Justice Burger's opinion did not hold gag orders unconstitutional per se, which prompted Justice Brennan's concurring opinion expressing the view that all gag orders run afoul of the First Amendment. Chief Justice Burger indicated alternatives to issuing gag orders, including changes of venue (that is, moving a trial to another locality where there is less public interest in or publicity about the trial), postponing trials to permit adverse publicity to die down, permitting rigorous examination of potential jurors to check against prejudice, instructing juries emphatically of their responsibility to consider admitted evidence only, and even sequestering juries. In addition, mistrials for adverse publicity may be granted and convictions overturned on appeal.

Although the Court in *Nebraska Press Association* did not rule out gag orders in all circumstances, it made them extremely difficult to defend against First Amendment challenges.[5] As a result, when confronted with the difficulties of controlling for prejudicial publicity, trial judges simply closed pretrial hearings and trials. That generated a new controversy over the right of the press and the public to attend judicial proceedings under the First and Sixth Amendments.

When the Court initially confronted the issue of closed judicial proceedings in *Gannett Co. v. DePasquale*, 443 U.S. 368 (1979), involving the closure of a pretrial hearing, the justices split five to four, and even those in the majority were not in agreement on interpreting the First and Sixth Amendments. Justice Stewart's opinion announcing the decision upholding the closure there, moreover, further fueled the controversy, prompting five justices later publicly to try to explain the ruling.[6] Stewart expressly rejected the view that the Sixth Amendment embodies a right of the public to attend criminal trials and declined to decide "in the abstract . . . whether there is any such constitutional right" under the First Amendment. But because he also stated twelve times in his opinion that the public and press have no constitutional right of access to *either pretrial hearings or trials*, there was confusion over the scope of the Court's ruling.

Gannett's ambiguity and confusion had considerable impact on public and press access to judicial proceedings. In the year following the ruling, defendants, prosecutors, witnesses, and judges sought to close proceedings in 13 federal courts and 259 state courts. One year after *Gannett*, the Court tried to clear up some of the confusion, but a majority of the justices still could not agree on the rationale for and scope of the Court's ruling in *Richmond Newspapers, Inc. v. Virginia*, 488 U.S. 555 (1980). Only Justices Stevens and White joined Chief Justice Burger's opinion announcing the Court's overturning the closure of a criminal trial. Both the First and Sixth Amendments, according to Burger, run together to make trials analogous to other "public forums" in which members of the press and public have historically enjoyed access, and distinguishable from places not generally recognized as open to the public (such as prisons, jails, and military bases). For this reason, Burger held that the press and public enjoy a "right of visitation" that precludes, except in extraordinary circumstances, the closing of criminal trials in contrast with pretrial hearings. But Burger did not go far enough for concurring Justices Brennan, Marshall, and Stevens, who contended that the First Amendment has an "affirmative side" requiring public access to pretrial hearings and trials in every circumstance.

Three years after *Gannett*, Justice Brennan was able to mass a solid majority behind his opinion in *Globe Newspaper Company v. Superior Court for the County of Norfolk* (1982) (see excerpt below), holding that the First Amendment guarantees the press and the public access to pretrial hearings and trials. Subsequently, the Court reaffirmed the principle of openness when overturning the closure of *voir dire* examinations, in *Press-Enterprise Co. v. Superior Court of California*, 464 U.S. 501 (1984). In *Waller v. Georgia*, 467 U.S. 39 (1984), Justice Powell held, for a unanimous Court, that the entire closure of pretrial hearings on the suppression of evidence violated the Sixth Amendment. Finally, *Press-Enterprise Co. v. Superior Court of California*, 477 U.S. 648 (1986), reaffirmed the First Amendment right of the press and the public to attend pretrial hearings in virtually all cases; Chief Justice Burger's opinion for the Court there was so sweeping that dissenting Justices Rehnquist and Stevens warned that the ruling could lead to the opening up of grand jury proceedings.

Controversies over ensuring both fair trials and freedom of the press evolved with the struggles within the Court over reaching agreement on the scope of the First Amendment. At the same time, though, television coverage of trials became more responsible, and television technology became more sophisticated and less intrusive. In the 1970s, a number of states began once again allowing television coverage of state criminal trials. The Court reconsidered *Estes* and *Sheppard* in

Chandler v. Florida, 449 U.S. 560 (1981), and upheld television coverage of criminal trials over the objections of the defendants.

The most recent ruling bearing on the "fair trial/free press" controversy came in *Mu'Min v. Virginia*, 500 U.S. 415 (1991) (further discussed in Ch. 9). Writing for a bare majority, Chief Justice Rehnquist held that in a murder case that had received substantial pretrial publicity the Sixth Amendment does not require judges to question potential jurors about what information each has seen or read about the crime. As the chief justice explained:

> Undoubtedly, if counsel were allowed to see individual jurors answer questions about exactly what they have read, a better sense of the jurors' general outlook on life might be revealed, and such a revelation would be of some use in exercising peremptory challenges. But, since peremptory challenges are not required by the Constitution, *Ross v. Oklahoma*, 487 U.S. 81 (1988), this benefit cannot be a basis for making "content" questions about pretrial publicity a constitutional requirement.

NOTES

1. *Illinois v. Allen*, 397 U.S. 337 (1970).

2. *Craig v. Harney*, 331 U.S. 367 (1947).

3. See *Pennekamp v. Florida*, 328 U.S. 331 (1946); and *Craig v. Harney*, 331 U.S. 367 (1947).

4. See *Irvin v. Dowd*, 366 U.S. 717 (1961); and *Rideau v. Louisiana*, 373 U.S. 723 (1963) (videotaping and televising of confessions denied due process).

5. See *Oklahoma Press Publishing Company v. District Court*, 430 U.S. 308 (1977) (striking down gag orders); and *Seattle Times Co. v. Rhinehart*, 467 U.S. 20 (1984) (upholding a protective order on pretrial discovery proceedings so long as it did not preclude dissemination of the same information gathered from other sources).

6. See David M. O'Brien, "The Trials and Tribulations of Courtroom Secrecy and Judicial Craftsmanship: Reflections on *Gannett* and *Richmond Newspapers*," 3 *Communications and the Law* 3–33 (1981).

SELECTED BIBLIOGRAPHY

O'Brien, David, M. *The Public's Right to Know* (New York: Praeger, 1981).

Siebert, Fredrick. *Free Press and Fair Trial*. Athens: University of Georgia Press, 1970.

Globe Newspaper Company v. Superior Court for the County of Norfolk
457 U.S. 596, 102 S.CT. 2613 (1982)

Under a Massachusetts statute, trial courts were required to exclude members of the press and public from the courtroom in cases involving certain sexual offenses and during the testimony of victims under the age of eighteen. Citing the statute, a trial judge excluded reporters from Globe Newspapers at a preliminary hearing for a person charged with raping three minor girls and ordered the trial closed. The newspaper moved to have the court revoke its order. When that failed, the newspaper immediately sought injunctive relief from the Supreme Judicial Court of Massachusetts, which was denied. Attorneys for Globe Newspapers, then, filed an appeal to the full court, but before its decision came down, the rape trial proceeded and the defendant was acquitted. Nine months later, the Supreme Judicial Court found the case moot but nevertheless proceeded to rule that the statute did not require the closure of entire trials, only the exclusion of the press and public during the testimony of a minor rape victim. Globe Newspapers Company appealed that ruling to the Supreme Court.

The Court's decision was six to three, and the majority's opinion was announced by Justice Brennan. Justice O'Connor concurred. Dissents were by Justice Stevens and Chief Justice Burger, who was joined by Justice Rehnquist.

□ *Justice BRENNAN delivered the opinion of the Court.*

Section 16A of Chapter 278 of the Massachusetts General Laws, as construed by the Massachusetts Supreme Judicial Court, requires trial judges, at trials for specified sexual offenses involving a victim under the age of 18, to exclude the press and general public from the courtroom during the testimony of that victim. The question presented is whether the statute thus construed violates the First Amendment as applied to the States through the Fourteenth Amendment. . . .

The Court's recent decision in *Richmond Newspapers* [*Inc. v. Virginia*, 488 U.S. 555 (1980)], firmly established for the first time that the press and general public have a constitutional right of access to criminal trials. Although there was no opinion of the Court in that case, seven Justices recognized that this right of access is embodied in the First Amendment, and applied to the States through the Fourteenth Amendment. . . .

Two features of the criminal justice system, emphasized in the various opinions in *Richmond Newspapers*, together serve to explain why a right of access to *criminal trials* in particular is properly afforded protection by the

First Amendment. First, the criminal trial historically has been open to the press and general public. "[A]t the time when our organic laws were adopted, criminal trials both here and in England had long been presumptively open." *Richmond Newspapers, Inc. v. Virginia, supra.* . . .

Second, the right of access to criminal trials plays a particularly significant role in the functioning of the judicial process and the government as a whole. Public scrutiny of a criminal trial enhances the quality and safeguards the integrity of the factfinding process, with benefits to both the defendant and to society as a whole. Moreover, public access to the criminal trial fosters an appearance of fairness, thereby heightening public respect for the judicial process. And in the broadest terms, public access to criminal trials permits the public to participate in and serve as a check upon the judicial process— an essential component in our structure of self-government. In sum, the institutional value of the open criminal trial is recognized in both logic and experience.

Although the right of access to criminal trials is of constitutional stature, it is not absolute. See *Richmond Newspapers, Inc. v. Virginia* (plurality opinion); *Nebraska Press Assn. v. Stuart,* 427 U.S. [539 (1976)]. But the circumstances under which the press and public can be barred from a criminal trial are limited; the State's justification in denying access must be a weighty one. Where, as in the present case, the State attempts to deny the right of access in order to inhibit the disclosure of sensitive information, it must be shown that the denial is necessitated by a compelling governmental interest, and is narrowly tailored to serve that interest. . . .

The state interests asserted to support § 16A, though articulated in various ways, are reducible to two: the protection of minor victims of sex crimes from further trauma and embarrassment; and the encouragement of such victims to come forward and testify in a truthful and credible manner. We consider these interests in turn.

We agree with appellee that the first interest—safeguarding the physical and psychological well-being of a minor—is a compelling one. But as compelling as that interest is, it does not justify a *mandatory* closure rule, for it is clear that the circumstances of the particular case may affect the significance of the interest. . . .

Nor can § 16A be justified on the basis of the Commonwealth's second asserted interest—the encouragement of minor victims of sex crimes to come forward and provide accurate testimony. The Commonwealth has offered no empirical support for the claim that the rule of automatic closure contained in § 16A will lead to an increase in the number of minor sex victims coming forward and cooperating with state authorities. Not only is the claim speculative in empirical terms, but it is also open to serious question as a matter of logic and common sense. Although § 16A bars the press and general public from the courtroom during the testimony of minor sex victims, the press is not denied access to the transcript, court personnel, or any other possible source that could provide an account of the minor victim's testimony. Thus § 16A cannot prevent the press from publicizing the substance of a minor victim's testimony, as well as his or her identity. . . .

For the foregoing reasons, we hold that § 16A, as construed by the Massachusetts Supreme Judicial Court, violates the First Amendment to the

Constitution. Accordingly, the judgment of the Massachusetts Supreme Judicial Court is
Reversed.

□ *Chief Justice BURGER, with whom Justice REHNQUIST joins, dissenting.*

Historically our society has gone to great lengths to protect minors *charged* with crime, particularly by prohibiting the release of the names of offenders, barring the press and public from juvenile proceedings, and sealing the records of those proceedings. Yet today the Court holds unconstitutional a state statute designed to protect not the *accused*, but the minor *victims* of sex crimes. In doing so, it advances a disturbing paradox. Although states are permitted, for example, to mandate the closure of all proceedings in order to protect a 17-year-old charged with rape, they are not permitted to require the closing of part of criminal proceedings in order to protect an innocent child who has been raped or otherwise sexually abused. . . .

I cannot agree with the Court's expansive interpretation of our decision in *Richmond Newspapers, Inc. v. Virginia* (1980), or its cavalier rejection of the serious interests supporting Massachusetts' mandatory closure rule. Accordingly, I dissent. . . .

H | *Symbolic Speech and Speech-Plus-Conduct*

Besides the First Amendment protection accorded pure speech (except, as discussed above, for those categories of unprotected speech), the Supreme Court has extended protection to "symbolic speech"—symbols, signs, and other means of expression—and to "speech-plus-conduct"—activities such as sit-ins, picketing, and demonstrating. The Court has done so because symbolic speech and speech-plus-conduct are, in Justice Harlan's words, in *Garner v. Louisiana,* 368 U.S. 157 (1961):

> as much a part of the "free trade in ideas" . . . as in verbal expression, more commonly thought of as "speech." It, like speech, appeals to good sense and to "the power of reason as applied through public discussion" . . . just as much as, if not more than, a public oration delivered from a soapbox at a street corner. This Court has never limited the right to speak, a protected "liberty" under the Fourteenth Amendment . . . to mere verbal expression.

Justice Harlan, however, also pointed out that it is often necessary to weigh these First Amendment claims against the competing interests and rights of property owners, for example, and the government's interests in preserving the public safety and order in public streets, parks, and buildings. In these cases, the Court must determine whether symbols or conduct in fact serve to express or communicate ideas; whether the government's interests in regulating or prohibiting expression is content neutral, rather than an effort to suppress particular ideas; and how great an inhibition particular ordinances and statutes impose on the exercise of First Amendment freedoms. By extending First Amendment protection in these and other areas, the Court has created a complex "system of freedom of expression."

SELECTED BIBLIOGRAPHY

Cleary, Edward. *Beyond the Burning Cross: The First Amendment and the Landmark R.A.V. Case.* New York: Random House, 1994.

Downs, D. A. *Nazis in Skokie: Freedom, Communication, and the First Amendment.* Notre Dame, IN: Notre Dame University Press, 1985.

Emerson, Thomas. *The System of Freedom of Expression.* New York: Random House, 1970.

Goldstein, Justin. *Burning the Flag: The Great 1989–1990 American Flag Desecration Controversy.* Kent, OH: Kent State University Press, 1996.

Kalven, Harry, Jr. *The Negro and the First Amendment.* Chicago: University of Chicago Press, 1965.

Shiffrin, Steve. *The First Amendment, Democracy, and Romance.* Cambridge, MA: Harvard University Press, 1990.

Strum, Philippa. *When the Nazis Came to Skokie.* Lawrence: University Press of Kansas, 1999.

■ (1) SYMBOLIC SPEECH

The Court initially acknowledged that symbols and symbolic speech may receive First Amendment protection in *Stromberg v. California*, 283 U.S. 359 (1931). There Chief Justice Hughes struck down a state law prohibiting the display of a red flag as a symbol of opposition to the government and overturned the conviction of a director of a Communist youth camp who raised a red flag every morning as part of the camp's daily activities.

In *West Virginia State Board of Education v. Barnette* (1943) (excerpted below), striking down a state law compelling schoolchildren to salute the American flag, the Court reaffirmed that nonverbal expressions receive First Amendment protection and that an individual may not be forced to participate in symbolic activities. In this case, compare Justice Jackson's interpretation of the First Amendment with Justice Frankfurter's impassioned dissenting opinion.

The Court underscored the principles announced in *Barnette* in *Wooley v. Maynard*, 430 U.S. 705 (1977), when striking down New Hampshire's statute requiring passenger cars to carry license plates inscribed with the state's motto, Live Free or Die. Writing for the Court, Chief Justice Burger found the state's justifications not sufficiently compelling to override First Amendment interests. Specifically, he rejected the state's arguments that requiring the motto on the license plates of passengers cars, but not commercial vehicles, was an aid to police; and that the state had an interest in inculcating respect for history and authority. But dissenting Justice Rehnquist countered that the state had not compelled Maynard to do anything and that there were other ways for him to express his views. Moreover, he questioned how far protection for free speech principles should extend: should the First Amendment protect an atheist's objections to the motto "In God We Trust" on coins and currency?

First Amendment protection for other symbols and nonverbal expression has been extended as well. *Tinker v. Des Moines Independent Community School District* (1969) (see excerpt below) upheld the right of children to wear black armbands to school when protesting America's involvement in the Vietnam War. But compare the Court's opinion there with the ruling and opinions in *Bethel School District No. 403 v. Fraser* (1986) (in Section B).

The Court also found, in *Brown v. Louisiana*, 383 U.S. 131 (1966), that the protest of a group of black students standing silently in a "whites-only" library to be constitutionally protected symbolic speech. But in *Clark v. Community for Creative Non-Violence*, 468 U.S. 288 (1984), over the objections of Justices Brennan and Marshall, the Court held that the National Park Service's regulations against camping in national parks not designated as campsites do not violate the First Amendment as applied to demonstrators who erected and slept in a tent city in Lafayette Park, Washington, D.C., as a way of dramatizing the plight of the needy and homeless. In reaffirming there that not all forms of symbolic speech and nonverbal expression are protected, the Court applied a test created in *United States v. O'Brien*, 391 U.S. 367 (1968).

In *United States v. O'Brien*, the Court held that burning draft cards at protest rallies against the Vietnam War was not protected symbolic speech. There Chief Justice Earl Warren set out certain guidelines for differentiating between protected and unprotected symbolic speech. Those guidelines are often referred to as the *O'Brien* four-prong test: (1) Is the regulation within Congress's authority to enact? (2) Does the regulation further a legitimate governmental interest? (3) Is the regulation unrelated to the suppression of speech? And (4) Is the regulation only an incidental restriction on speech? Chief Justice Warren concluded that the ban on draft card burning survived all of those concerns. Congress had the authority because it has the power to raise an army, and the ban promoted the efficiency of the system. He also deemed the regulation to be unrelated to the suppression of speech per se, and to be only a minor incidental restriction, since antiwar protests could be expressed in other ways. He further explained:

> [w]e cannot accept the view that an apparently limitless variety of conduct can be labelled "speech" whenever the person engaging in the conduct intends thereby to express an idea. . . . This Court has held that when "speech" and "nonspeech" elements are combined in the same course of conduct, a sufficiently important governmental interest in regulating the nonspeech element can justify incidental limitations on First Amendment freedoms. To characterize the quality of the governmental interest which must appear, the Court has employed a variety of descriptive terms: compelling; substantial; subordinating; paramount; cogent; strong. Whatever imprecision inheres in these terms, we think it clear that a government regulation is sufficiently justified if it is within the constitutional power of the Government; if it furthers an important or substantial governmental interest; if the governmental interest is unrelated to the suppression of free expression; and if the incidental restriction on alleged First Amendment freedoms is no greater than is essential to the furtherance of that interest.

One of the most potent national political symbols is the American flag, and the Court has often faced controversies over not just the government's forcing individuals to participate in symbolic acts honoring the flag, as in *Barnette*, but over punishing individuals who use and abuse the flag as a way of expressing their political views. In *Street v. New York*, 394 U.S. 576 (1969), the justices split five to four when overturning the conviction of a protestor who burned the flag, in violation of a law making it a misdemeanor publicly to mutilate, deface, or cast contempt on the flag "by words or act." There Chief Justice Warren and Justices Black, Fortas, and White dissented. Over the dissent of Chief Justice Burger and Justices Blackmun and Rehnquist, the Court, in *Smith v. Groguen*, 415 U.S. 566 (1974), overturned the conviction of an individual wearing a small United States flag on the seat of his pants. With those three justices in dissent again, *Spence v. Washington*, 418 U.S. 405 (1974), held that the First Amendment protected a student who hung the American flag upside down with a peace symbol attached on the window of his dormitory room.

In another surprising and controversial five-to-four decision, the Court once again upheld the First Amendment protection for symbolic speech in *Texas v. Johnson* (1989) (see excerpt below), prompting President George H. W. Bush and numerous congressmen to call for a constitutional amendment overturning that decision. Congress, however, passed instead the Federal Flag Protection Act of 1989, authorizing the prosecution of those who desecrate the American flag. That law was immediately challenged and was overturned by the Court in *United States v. Eichman*, 496 U.S. 310 (1990). As in *Johnson*, the justices split five to four in holding that the federal statute "suffer[ed] from the same fundamental flaw" as the earlier state laws in aiming at "suppressing expression." Following that ruling, a further attempt to overturn *Texas v. Johnson* by passing a constitutional amendment failed. The Senate in March 2000 rejected, again, a proposed constitutional amendment giving Congress the power to ban flag desecration by a vote of 67 to 37, four votes short of the two-thirds majority required.

However, in *Virginia v. Black* (2003) (excerpted in Section B) the Court held that states may criminalize cross burning, unlike burning the American flag. Although striking down Virginia's law making it a crime to burn a cross, a majority of the Court indicated that a properly drawn statute criminalizing cross burning would survive First Amendment scrutiny because of the unique history and intimidation associated with cross burning.

West Virginia State Board of Education v. Barnette
319 U.S. 624, 63 S.Ct. 1178 (1943)

During World War I and throughout World War II, patriotism and fear of communism, socialism, and fascism led states and localities to enact statutes requiring, among other things, students to salute the flag and recite the pledge of allegiance. When Jehovah's Witnesses challenged the constitutionality of a small Pennsylvania town's 1914 ordinance compelling students to salute the American flag (in a manner similar to that in Nazi Germany, with right arm extended and the palm of the hand pointing upward), the Court upheld the flag-salute statute in *Minersville School District v. Gobitis*, 310 U.S. 586 (1940), with an opinion by Justice Frankfurter and only Justice Stone dissenting.

Following *Gobitis*, the West Virginia state legislature enacted a law requiring all schools to offer history and civics courses, and pursuant to that legislation the State Board of Education directed all teachers and students to salute the flag as part of the daily activities of the school. Failure to comply with this requirement could lead to students being expelled, and parents were liable for prosecution with a penalty of thirty days in jail and a $50 fine.

Walter Barnette, a Jehovah's Witness, sought in federal district court an injunction against the enforcement of compulsory flag salutes in school on the grounds that it violated his and his children's religious belief that they should not worship any graven image and the First Amendment free exercise clause. The State Board of Education moved to dismiss the complaint, but a federal district judge granted the injunction. The State Board of Education appealed that decision to the Supreme Court.

By the time the justices heard *Barnette*, the Court's composition had changed from that when *Gobitis* was decided three years earlier. Chief Justice Hughes and Justice McReynolds retired in 1941, and President Franklin Roosevelt elevated Justice Stone to chief justice, appointed his attorney general, Robert Jackson, to fill Stone's seat as associate justice and named James Byrnes to replace McReynolds. Justice Byrnes served only one year and was succeeded by FDR's last appointee, Wiley Rutledge. Moreover, FDR's three earlier appointees, Justices Black, Douglas, and Murphy, who had voted with the majority in *Gobitis*, switched their positions and voted with FDR's last three appointees in *Barnette*. Chief Justice Stone assigned Jackson to write the opinion for the Court striking down compulsory flag salutes as a violation of the First Amendment guarantee for free speech, instead of on the free exercise clause. Justices Black, Douglas, and Murphy wrote separate concurring opinions explaining their reversing of positions. Justice Frankfurter wrote an impassioned dissenting opinion and, along with Justices Reed and Roberts, maintained the views expressed in *Gobitis*.

The Court's decision was six to three, and the majority's opinion was announced by Justice Jackson. Concurrences were by Justices Murphy and Black, who was joined by Justice Douglas. Justices Reed and Roberts dissented without opinion. There was also a dissent by Justice Frankfurter.

☐ *Justice JACKSON delivered the opinion of the Court.*

The freedom asserted by these appellees does not bring them into collision with rights asserted by any other individual. It is such conflicts which most frequently require intervention of the State to determine where the rights of one end and those of another begin. But the refusal of these persons to participate in the ceremony does not interfere with or deny rights of others to do so. Nor is there any question in this case that their behavior is peaceable and orderly. The sole conflict is between authority and rights of the individual. The State asserts power to condition access to public education on making a prescribed sign and profession and at the same time to coerce attendance by punishing both parent and child. The latter stand on a right of self-determination in matters that touch individual opinion and personal attitude.

As the present CHIEF JUSTICE said in dissent in the *Gobitis* case, the State may "require teaching by instruction and study of all in our history and in the structure and organization of our government, including the guaranties of civil liberty which tend to inspire patriotism and love of country." Here, however, we are dealing with a compulsion of students to declare a belief. They are not merely made acquainted with the flag salute so that they may be informed as to what it is or even what it means. The issue here is whether this slow and easily neglected route to aroused loyalties constitutionally may be short-cut by substituting a compulsory salute and slogan. . . .

There is no doubt that, in connection with the pledges, the flag salute is a form of utterance. Symbolism is a primitive but effective way of communicating ideas. The use of an emblem or flag to symbolize some system, idea, institution, or personality is a short cut from mind to mind. Causes and nations, political parties, lodges and ecclesiastical groups seek to knit the loyalty of their followings to a flag or banner, a color or design. The State announces rank, function, and authority through crowns and maces, uniforms and black robes; the church speaks through the Cross, the Crucifix, the altar and shrine, and clerical raiment. Symbols of State, often convey political ideas just as religious symbols come to convey theological ones. Associated with many of these symbols are appropriate gestures of acceptance or respect: a salute, a bowed or bared head, a bended knee. A person gets from a symbol the meaning he puts into it, and what is one man's comfort and inspiration is another's jest and scorn.

Over a decade ago Chief Justice HUGHES led this Court in holding that the display of a red flag as a symbol of opposition by peaceful and legal means to organized government was protected by the free speech guaranties of the Constitution. *Stromberg v. California*, 283 U.S. 359 [(1931)]. Here it is the State that employs a flag as a symbol of adherence to government as presently organized. It requires the individual to communicate by word and sign his acceptance of the political ideas it thus bespeaks. Objection to this form of communication when coerced is an old one, well known to the framers of the Bill of Rights. . . .

[H]ere the power of compulsion is invoked without any allegation that remaining passive during a flag salute ritual creates a clear and present danger that would justify an effort even to muffle expression. To sustain the compulsory flag salute we are required to say that a Bill of Rights which guards the individual's right to speak his own mind, left it open to public authorities to compel him to utter what is not in his mind.

Whether the First Amendment to the Constitution will permit officials to order observance of ritual of this nature does not depend upon whether as a voluntary exercise we would think it to be good, bad or merely innocuous. . . .

Nor does the issue as we see it turn on one's possession of particular religious views or the sincerity with which they are held. While religion supplies appellees' motive for enduring the discomforts of making the issue in this case, many citizens who do not share these religious views hold such a compulsory rite to infringe constitutional liberty of the individual. It is not necessary to inquire whether non-conformist beliefs will exempt from the duty to salute unless we first find power to make the salute a legal duty.

The *Gobitis* decision, however, *assumed*, as did the argument in that case and in this, that power exists in the State to impose the flag salute discipline upon school children in general. The Court only examined and rejected a claim based on religious beliefs of immunity from an unquestioned general rule. The question which underlies the flag salute controversy is whether such a ceremony so touching matters of opinion and political attitude may be imposed upon the individual by official authority under powers committed to any political organization under our Constitution. We examine rather than assume existence of this power and, against this broader definition of issues in this case, re-examine specific grounds assigned for the *Gobitis* decision.

1. It was said that the flag-salute controversy confronted the Court with "the problem which Lincoln cast in memorable dilemma: 'Must a government of necessity be too *strong* for the liberties of its people, or too *weak* to maintain its own existence?' " and that the answer must be in favor of strength. . . .

We think these issues may be examined free of pressure or restraint growing out of such considerations.

It may be doubted whether Mr. Lincoln would have thought that the strength of government to maintain itself would be impressively vindicated by our confirming power of the state to expel a handful of children from school. Such oversimplification, so handy in political debate, often lacks the precision necessary to postulates of judicial reasoning. If validly applied to this problem, the utterance cited would resolve every issue of power in favor of those in authority and would require us to override every liberty thought to weaken or delay execution of their policies. . . .

2. It was also considered in the *Gobitis* case that functions of educational officers in states, counties and school districts were such that to interfere with their authority "would in effect make us the school board for the country." . . .

The Fourteenth Amendment, as now applied to the States, protects the citizen against the State itself and all of its creatures—Boards of Education not excepted. These have, of course, important, delicate, and highly discretionary functions, but none that they may not perform within the limits of the Bill of Rights. That they are educating the young for citizenship is reason for scrupulous protection of constitutional freedoms of the individual, if we are not to strangle the free mind at its source and teach youth to discount important principles of our government as mere platitudes. . . .

3. The *Gobitis* opinion reasoned that this is a field "where courts possess no marked and certainly no controlling competence," that it is committed to the legislatures as well as the courts to guard cherished liberties and that it is constitutionally appropriate to "fight out the wise use of legislative authority in the forum of public opinion and before legislative assemblies rather than to transfer such a contest to the judicial arena," since all the "effective means of inducing political changes are left free." . . .

The very purpose of a Bill of Rights was to withdraw certain subjects from the vicissitudes of political controversy, to place them beyond the reach of majorities and officials and to establish them as legal principles to be applied by the courts. One's right to life, liberty, and property, to free speech, a free press, freedom of worship and assembly, and other fundamental rights may not be submitted.

4. Lastly, and this is the very heart of the *Gobitis* opinion, it reasons that

"National unity is the basis of national security," that the authorities have "the right to select appropriate means for its attainment," and hence reaches the conclusion that such compulsory measures toward "national unity" are constitutional. Upon the verity of this assumption depends our answer in this case.

Struggles to coerce uniformity of sentiment in support of some end thought essential to their time and country have been waged by many good as well as by evil men. Nationalism is a relatively recent phenomenon but at other times and places the ends have been racial or territorial security, support of a dynasty or regime, and particular plans for saving souls. As first and moderate methods to attain unity have failed, those bent on its accomplishment must resort to an ever-increasing severity. As governmental pressure toward unity becomes greater, so strife becomes more bitter as to whose unity it shall be. Probably no deeper division of our people could proceed from any provocation than from finding it necessary to choose what doctrine and whose program public educational officials shall compel youth to unite in embracing. Ultimate futility of such attempts to compel coherence is the lesson of every such effort from the Roman drive to stamp out Christianity as a disturber of its pagan unity, the Inquisition, as a means to religious and dynastic unity, the Siberian exiles as a means to Russian unity, down to the fast failing efforts of our present totalitarian enemies. Those who begin coercive elimination of dissent soon find themselves exterminating dissenters. Compulsory unification of opinion achieves only the unanimity of the graveyard.

It seems trite but necessary to say that the First Amendment to our Constitution was designed to avoid these ends by avoiding these beginnings. There is no mysticism in the American concept of the State or of the nature or origin of its authority. We set up government by consent of the governed, and the Bill of Rights denies those in power any legal opportunity to coerce that consent. Authority here is to be controlled by public opinion, not public opinion by authority. . . .

If there is any fixed star in our constitutional constellation, it is that no official, high or petty, can prescribe what shall be orthodox in politics, nationalism, religion, or other matters of opinion or force citizens to confess by word or act their faith therein. If there are any circumstances which permit an exception, they do not now occur to us.

We think the action of the local authorities in compelling the flag salute and pledge transcends constitutional limitations on their power and invades the sphere of intellect and spirit which it is the purpose of the First Amendment to our Constitution to reserve from all official control.

☐ *Justice ROBERTS and Justice REED adhere to the views expressed by the Court in* Minersville School District v. Gobitis, *and are of the opinion that the judgment below should be reversed.*

☐ *Justice BLACK and Justice DOUGLAS, concurring.*

We are substantially in agreement with the opinion just read, but since we originally joined with the Court in the *Gobitis* case, it is appropriate that we make a brief statement of reasons for our change of view.

Reluctance to make the Federal Constitution a rigid bar against state regulation of conduct thought inimical to the public welfare was the controlling influence which moved us to consent to the *Gobitis* decision. Long reflection convinced us that although the principle is sound, its application in the particular case was wrong. We believe that the statute before us fails to accord full scope to the freedom of religion secured to the appellees by the First and Fourteenth Amendments. . . .

No well-ordered society can leave to the individuals an absolute right to make final decisions, unassailable by the State, as to everything they will or will not do. The First Amendment does not go so far. Religious faiths, honestly held, do not free individuals from responsibility to conduct themselves obediently to laws which are either imperatively necessary to protect society as a whole from grave and pressingly imminent dangers or which, without any general prohibition, merely regulate time, place or manner of religious activity. Decision as to the constitutionality of particular laws which strike at the substance of religious tenets and practices must be made by this Court. The duty is a solemn one, and in meeting it we cannot say that a failure, because of religious scruples, to assume a particular physical position and to repeat the words of a patriotic formula creates a grave danger to the nation. Such a statutory exaction is a form of test oath, and the test oath has always been abhorrent in the United States.

□ *Justice FRANKFURTER, dissenting.*

One who belongs to the most vilified and persecuted minority in history is not likely to be insensible to the freedoms guaranteed by our Constitution. Were my purely personal attitude relevant I should wholeheartedly associate myself with the general libertarian views in the Court's opinion, representing as they do the thought and action of a lifetime. But as judges we are neither Jew nor Gentile, neither Catholic nor agnostic. We owe equal attachment to the Constitution and are equally bound by our judicial obligations whether we derive our citizenship from the earliest or the latest immigrants to these shores. As a member of this Court I am not justified in writing my private notions of policy into the Constitution, no matter how deeply I may cherish them or how mischievous I may deem their disregard. The duty of a judge who must decide which of two claims before the Court shall prevail, that of a State to enact and enforce laws within its general competence or that of an individual to refuse obedience because of the demands of his conscience, is not that of the ordinary person. It can never be emphasized too much that one's own opinion about the wisdom or evil of a law should be excluded altogether when one is doing one's duty on the bench. The only opinion of our own even looking in that direction that is material is our opinion whether legislators could in reason have enacted such a law. In the light of all the circumstances, including the history of this question in this Court, it would require more daring than I possess to deny that reasonable legislators could have taken the action which is before us for review. Most unwillingly, therefore, I must differ from my brethren with regard to legislation like this. I cannot bring my mind to believe that the "liberty" secured by the Due Process Clause gives this Court authority to deny to the State of West Virginia the attainment of that which we all recognize as a legitimate legislative end, namely, the promotion of good citizenship, by employment of the means here chosen.

Not so long ago we were admonished that "the only check upon our own exercise of power is our own sense of self-restraint. For the removal of unwise laws from the statute books appeal lies, not to the courts, but to the ballot and to the processes of democratic government." We have been told that generalities do not decide concrete cases. But the intensity with which a general principle is held may determine a particular issue, and whether we put first things first may decide a specific controversy.

The admonition that judicial self-restraint alone limits arbitrary exercise of our authority is relevant every time we are asked to nullify legislation. The Constitution does not give us greater veto power when dealing with one phase of "liberty" than with another, or when dealing with grade school regulations than with college regulations that offend conscience, as was the case in *Hamilton v. Regents*, 293 U.S. 245 [(1934)]. In neither situation is our function comparable to that of a legislature or are we free to act as though we were a super-legislature. Judicial self-restraint is equally necessary whenever an exercise of political or legislative power is challenged. There is no warrant in the constitutional basis of this Court's authority for attributing different roles to it depending upon the nature of the challenge to the legislation. Our power does not vary according to the particular provision of the Bill of Rights which is invoked. The right not to have property taken without just compensation has, so far as the scope of judicial power is concerned, the same constitutional dignity as the right to be protected against unreasonable searches and seizures, and the latter has no less claim than freedom of the press or freedom of speech or religious freedom. In no instance is this Court the primary protector of the particular liberty that is invoked. . . .

When Justice HOLMES, speaking for this Court, wrote that "it must be remembered that legislatures are ultimate guardians of the liberties and welfare of the people in quite as great a degree as the courts," he went to the very essence of our constitutional system and the democratic conception of our society. He did not mean that for only some phases of civil government this Court was not to supplant legislatures and sit in judgment upon the right or wrong of a challenged measure. He was stating the comprehensive judicial duty and role of this Court in our constitutional scheme whenever legislation is sought to be nullified on any ground, namely, that responsibility for legislation lies with legislatures, answerable as they are directly to the people, and this Court's only and very narrow function is to determine whether within the broad grant of authority vested in legislatures they have exercised a judgment for which reasonable justification can be offered.

The framers of the federal Constitution might have chosen to assign an active share in the process of legislation to this Court. . . . But the framers of the Constitution denied such legislative powers to the federal judiciary. They chose instead to insulate the judiciary from the legislative function. They did not grant to this Court supervision over legislation.

The reason why from the beginning even the narrow judicial authority to nullify legislation has been viewed with a jealous eye is that it serves to prevent the full play of the democratic process. The fact that it may be an undemocratic aspect of our scheme of government does not call for its rejection or its disuse. But it is the best of reasons, as this Court has frequently recognized, for the greatest caution in its use.

The precise scope of the question before us defines the limits of the constitutional power that is in issue. The State of West Virginia requires all pupils to share in the salute to the flag as part of school training in citizenship. The present action is one to enjoin the enforcement of this requirement by those in school attendance. We have not before us any attempt by the State to punish disobedient children or visit penal consequences on their parents. All that is in question is the right of the state to compel participation in this exercise by those who choose to attend the public schools.

We are not reviewing merely the action of a local school board. The flag salute requirement in this case comes before us with the full authority of the State of West Virginia. We are in fact passing judgment on "the power of the State as a whole." Practically we are passing upon the political power of each of the forty-eight states. Moreover, since the First Amendment has been read into the Fourteenth, our problem is precisely the same as it would be if we had before us an Act of Congress for the District of Columbia. To suggest that we are here concerned with the heedless action of some village tyrants is to distort the augustness of the constitutional issue and the reach of the consequences of our decision. . . .

We are told that symbolism is a dramatic but primitive way of communicating ideas. Symbolism is inescapable. Even the most sophisticated live by symbols. But it is not for this Court to make psychological judgments as to the effectiveness of a particular symbol in inculcating concededly indispensable feelings, particularly if the state happens to see fit to utilize the symbol that represents our heritage and our hopes. And surely only flippancy could be responsible for the suggestion that constitutional validity of a requirement to salute our flag implies equal validity of a requirement to salute a dictator. The significance of a symbol lies in what it represents. To reject the swastika does not imply rejection of the Cross. And so it bears repetition to say that it mocks reason and denies our whole history to find in the allowance of a requirement to salute our flag on fitting occasions the seeds of sanction for obeisance to a leader. To deny the power to employ educational symbols is to say that the state's educational system may not stimulate the imagination because this may lead to unwise stimulation. . . .

The flag salute exercise has no kinship whatever to the oath tests so odious in history. For the oath test was one of the instruments for suppressing heretical beliefs. Saluting the flag suppresses no belief nor curbs it. Children and their parents may believe what they please, avow their belief and practice it. It is not even remotely suggested that the requirement for saluting the flag involves the slightest restriction against the fullest opportunity on the part both of the children and of their parents to disavow as publicly as they choose to do so the meaning that others attach to the gesture of salute. All channels of affirmative free expression are open to both children and parents. Had we before us any act of the state putting the slightest curbs upon such free expression, I should not lag behind any member of this Court in striking down such an invasion of the right to freedom of thought and freedom of speech protected by the Constitution. . . .

One's conception of the Constitution cannot be severed from one's conception of a judge's function in applying it. The Court has no reason for existence if it merely reflects the pressures of the day. Our system is built on the faith that men set apart for this special function, freed from the influences of immediacy and from the deflections of worldly ambition, will become able to take a view of longer range than the period of responsibility entrusted to Congress and legislatures. We are dealing with matters as to which legislators and voters have conflicting views. Are we as judges to impose our strong convictions on where wisdom lies? That which three years ago had seemed to five successive Courts to lie within permissible areas of legislation is now outlawed by the deciding shift of opinion of two Justices. What reason is there to believe that they or their successors may not have another view a few years hence? Is that which was deemed to be of so fundamental a nature as to be written into the Constitution to endure for all times to be the sport of shifting winds of doctrine? Of course, judicial opinions, even as to questions of constitutionality, are not immutable. As has been true in the past, the Court will from time to time reverse its position. But I believe that never before these Jehovah's Witnesses cases (except for minor deviations subsequently retraced) has this Court overruled decisions so as to restrict the powers of democratic government. Always heretofore, it has withdrawn narrow views of legislative authority so as to authorize what formerly it had denied.

In view of this history it must be plain that what thirteen Justices found to be within the constitutional authority of a state, legislators can not be deemed unreasonable in enacting. Therefore, in denying to the states what heretofore has received such impressive judicial sanction, some other tests of unconstitutionality must surely be guiding the Court than the absence of a rational justification for the legislation. But I know of no other test which this Court is authorized to apply in nullifying legislation.

In the past this Court has from time to time set its views of policy against that embodied in legislation by finding laws in conflict with what was called the "spirit of the Constitution." Such undefined destructive power was not conferred on this Court by the Constitution. Before a duly enacted law can be judicially nullified, it must be forbidden by some explicit restriction upon political authority in the Constitution. Equally inadmissible is the claim to strike down legislation because to us as individuals it seems opposed to the "plan and purpose" of the Constitution. That is too tempting a basis for finding in one's personal views the purposes of the Founders.

The uncontrollable power wielded by this Court brings it very close to the most sensitive areas of public affairs. As appeal from legislation to adjudication becomes more frequent, and its consequences more far-reaching, judicial self-restraint becomes more and not less important, lest we unwarrantably enter social and political domains wholly outside our concern. I think I appreciate fully the objections to the law before us. But to deny that it presents a question upon which men might reasonably differ appears to me to be intolerance. And since men may so reasonably differ, I deem it beyond my constitutional power to assert my view of the wisdom of this law against the view of the State of West Virginia.

Jefferson's opposition to judicial review has not been accepted by history, but it still serves as an admonition against confusion between judicial and political functions. As a rule of judicial self-restraint, it is still as valid as Lincoln's admonition. For those who pass laws not only are under duty to pass laws. They are also under duty to observe the Constitution. And even though legislation relates to civil liberties, our duty of deference to those who have the responsibility for making the laws is no less relevant or less exacting. And this is so especially when we consider the accidental contingencies by which one man may determine constitutionality and thereby confine the political power of the Congress of the United States and the legislatures of forty-eight states. The attitude of judicial humility which these considerations enjoin is not an abdication of the judicial function. It is a due observance of its limits. Moreover, it is to be borne in mind that in a question like this we are not passing on the proper distribution of political power as between the states and the central government. We are not discharging the basic function of this Court as the mediator of powers within the federal system. To strike down a law like this is to deny a power to all government.

Of course patriotism cannot be enforced by the flag salute. But neither can the liberal spirit be enforced by judicial invalidation of illiberal legislation. Our constant preoccupation with the constitutionality of legislation rather than with its wisdom tends to preoccupation of the American mind with a false value. The tendency of focusing attention on constitutionality is to make constitutionality synonymous with wisdom, to regard a law as all right if it is constitutional. Such an attitude is a great enemy of liberalism. Particularly in legislation affecting freedom of thought and freedom of speech much which should offend a free-spirited society is constitutional. Reliance for the most precious interests of civilization, therefore, must be found outside of their vindication in courts of law. Only a persistent positive translation of the faith of a free society into the convictions and habits and actions of a community is the ultimate reliance against unabated temptations to fetter the human spirit.

Tinker v. Des Moines Independent Community School District
393 U.S. 503, 89 S.Ct. 733 (1969)

In December 1965, a group of adults and students in Des Moines, Iowa, held a meeting and decided to publicize their objections to the war in Vietnam by wearing black armbands during the holiday season. The principals of the Des Moines schools became aware of the plan and promptly adopted a policy forbidding the wearing of armbands in school and suspending any student who refused to comply.

John Tinker, a fifteen-year-old high-school student, and his sister, Mary Beth, a thirteen-year-old junior-high-school student, wore black armbands to school and were immediately sent home and suspended until they agreed no longer to wear the armbands. They and their parents asked a federal district court for an injunction restraining school officials from enforcing the policy against wearing black armbands. The court, however, upheld the school's authority. On appeal to the Court

In 1965, in support of Senator Robert Kennedy's call for an extension of a Christ-mas truce in Vietnam, several public schoolchildren in Des Moines, Iowa, decided to wear black armbands with peace symbols to school in order to mourn the war casu-alties and to protest the war. The students were suspended and allowed to return to school without the armbands. John and Mary Beth Tinker, shown here, became the name parties in the case testing the constitutional rights of children in school. (Photo Source: Library of Congress, 1965.)

of Appeals for the Eighth Circuit, the judges were evenly divided and accordingly upheld the lower court's ruling without issuing an opinion. The Tinkers, thereupon, appealed to the Supreme Court, which granted *certiorari*.

The Court's decision was seven to two, and the majority's opinion was announced by Justice Fortas. Justices Stewart and White concurred; Justices Black and Harlan dissented.

☐ *Justice FORTAS delivered the opinion of the Court.*

[T]he wearing of an armband for the purpose of expressing certain views is the type of symbolic act that is within the Free Speech Clause of the First Amendment. . . . It [is] closely akin to "pure speech" which, we have repeatedly held, is entitled to comprehensive protection under the First Amendment.

First Amendment rights, applied in light of the special characteristics of the school environment, are available to teachers and students. It can hardly be argued that either students or teachers shed their constitutional rights to free-dom of speech or expression at the schoolhouse gate. This has been the un-mistakable holding of this Court for almost 50 years. In *Meyer v. Nebraska*, 262 U.S. 390 (1923), and *Bartels v. Iowa*, 262 U.S. 404 (1923), this Court, in opinions by Justice McREYNOLDS, held that the Due Process Clause of the Fourteenth Amendment prevents States from forbidding the teaching of a foreign language to young students. Statutes to this effect, the Court held, unconstitutionally interfere with the liberty of teacher, student, and parent. . . .

The problem posed by the present case does not relate to regulation of the length of skirts or the type of clothing, to hair style, or deportment. It does not concern aggressive, disruptive action or even group demonstrations. Our problem involves direct, primary First Amendment rights akin to "pure speech."

The school officials banned and sought to punish petitioners for a silent, passive expression of opinion, unaccompanied by any disorder or disturbance on the part of petitioners. There is here no evidence whatever of petitioners' interference, actual or nascent, with the schools' work or of collision with the rights of other students to be secure and to be let alone. Accordingly, this case does not concern speech or action that intrudes upon the work of the schools or the rights of other students. . . .

[T]he school authorities did not purport to prohibit the wearing of all symbols of political or controversial significance. The record shows that students in some of the schools wore buttons relating to national political campaigns, and some even wore the Iron Cross, traditionally a symbol of Nazism. The order prohibiting the wearing of armbands did not extend to these. Instead, a particular symbol—black armbands worn to exhibit opposition to this Nation's involvement in Vietnam—was singled out for prohibition. Clearly, the prohibition of expression of one particular opinion, at least without evidence that it is necessary to avoid material and substantial interference with schoolwork or discipline, is not constitutionally permissible. . . .

We reverse and remand for further proceedings consistent with this opinion.

☐ *Justice BLACK, dissenting.*

Even a casual reading of the record shows that this armband did divert students' minds from the regular lessons, and that talk, comments, etc., made John Tinker "self-conscious" in attending school with his armband. While the absence of obscene remarks or boisterous and loud disorder perhaps justifies the Court's statement that the few armband students did not actually "disrupt" the classwork, I think the record overwhelmingly shows that the armbands did exactly what the elected school officials and principals foresaw they would, that is, took the students' minds off their classwork and diverted them to thoughts about the highly emotional subject of the Vietnam war. And I repeat that if the time has come when pupils of state-supported schools, kindergartens, grammar schools, or high schools, can defy and flout orders of school officials to keep their minds on their own schoolwork, it is the beginning of a new revolutionary era of permissiveness in this country fostered by the judiciary.

☐ *Justice HARLAN, dissenting.*

I would, in cases like this, cast upon those complaining the burden of showing that a particular school measure was motivated by other than legitimate school concerns—for example, a desire to prohibit the expression of an unpopular point of view, while permitting expression of the dominant opinion.

Finding nothing in this record which impugns the good faith of respondents in promulgating the armband regulation, I would affirm the judgment below.

Texas v. Johnson

491 U.S. 397, 109 S.Ct. 2533 (1989)

During the 1984 Republican National Convention, Gregory Johnson participated in a political demonstration in Dallas, Texas, to protest the policies of the Reagan administration. After a march through the streets, Johnson burned the American flag while protesters chanted. No one was physically injured or threatened with injury. Johnson was arrested, tried, and convicted of flag desecration in violation of a Texas statute, and a state appeals court affirmed. However, the Texas Court of Criminal Appeals reversed, holding that Johnson's flag burning was expressive conduct protected by the First Amendment. The state appealed that decision to the Supreme Court.

The Court's decision was five to four, and the majority's opinion was announced by Justice Brennan. Justice Kennedy concurred; dissents were by Justice Stevens and Chief Justice Rehnquist, who was joined by Justices White and O'Connor.

☐ *Justice BRENNAN delivered the opinion of the Court.*

Johnson was convicted of flag desecration for burning the flag rather than for uttering insulting words. This fact somewhat complicates our consideration of his conviction under the First Amendment. We must first determine whether Johnson's burning of the flag constituted expressive conduct, permitting him to invoke the First Amendment in challenging his conviction. If his conduct was expressive, we next decide whether the State's regulation is related to the suppression of free expression. See, *e.g.*, *United States v. O'Brien*, 391 U.S. 367 (1968). If the State's regulation is not related to expression, then the less stringent standard we announced in *United States v. O'Brien* for regulations of noncommunicative conduct controls. If it is, then we are outside of *O'Brien's* test, and we must ask whether this interest justifies Johnson's conviction under a more demanding standard. A third possibility is that the State's asserted interest is simply not implicated on these facts, and in that event the interest drops out of the picture. . . .

The First Amendment literally forbids the abridgement only of "speech," but we have long recognized that its protection does not end at the spoken or written word. While we have rejected "the view that an apparently

Gregory Johnson being arrested after setting fire to the American flag during a protest at the Republican party's 1984 national convention. His arrest and conviction were appealed and overturned in *Texas v. Johnson* (1989). (*John Keating*)

limitless variety of conduct can be labeled 'speech' whenever the person engaging in the conduct intends thereby to express an idea," *United States v. O'Brien*, we have acknowledged that conduct may be "sufficiently imbued with elements of communication to fall within the scope of the First and Fourteenth Amendments." . . .

Especially pertinent to this case are our decisions recognizing the communicative nature of conduct relating to flags. Attaching a peace sign to the flag, *Spence* [*v. Washington*, 418 U.S. 405 (1974)], saluting the flag, [*West Virginia State Board of Education v. Barnette*, 319 U.S. 624 (1943)], and displaying a red flag, *Stromberg v. California*, 283 U.S. 359 (1931), we have held, all may find shelter under the First Amendment. See also *Smith v. Grogen*, 415 U.S. 566 (1974) (WHITE, J., concurring in judgment) (treating flag "contemptuously" by wearing pants with small flag sewn into their seat is expressive conduct). That we have had little difficulty identifying an expressive element in conduct relating to flags should not be surprising. The very purpose of a national flag is to serve as a symbol of our country; it is, one might say, "the one visible manifestation of two hundred years of nationhood." Thus, we have observed:

> "[T]he flag salute is a form of utterance. Symbolism is a primitive but effective way of communicating ideas. The use of an emblem or flag to symbolize some system, idea, institution, or personality, is a short cut from mind to mind. Causes and nations, political parties, lodges and ecclesiastical groups seek to knit the loyalty of their followings to a flag or banner, a color or design." *Barnette*. . . .

We have not automatically concluded, however, that any action taken with respect to our flag is expressive. Instead, in characterizing such action for First Amendment purposes, we have considered the context in which it occurred. . . .

The State of Texas conceded for purposes of its oral argument in this case that Johnson's conduct was expressive conduct. . . . Johnson burned an American flag as part—indeed, as the culmination—of a political demonstration that coincided with the convening of the Republican Party and its renomination of Ronald Reagan for President. The expressive, overtly political nature of this conduct was both intentional and overwhelmingly apparent. At his trial, Johnson explained his reasons for burning the flag as follows: "The American Flag was burned as Ronald Reagan was being renominated as President. And a more powerful statement of symbolic speech, whether you agree with it or not, couldn't have been made at that time. It's quite a just position [juxtaposition]. We had new patriotism and no patriotism." In these circumstances, Johnson's burning of the flag was conduct "sufficiently imbued with elements of communication," to implicate the First Amendment.

The Government generally has a freer hand in restricting expressive conduct than it has in restricting the written or spoken word. . . . It may not, however, proscribe particular conduct *because* it has expressive elements. . . . It is, in short, not simply the verbal or nonverbal nature of the expression, but the governmental interest at stake, that helps to determine whether a restriction on that expression is valid.

Thus, although we have recognized that where " 'speech' and 'non-speech' elements are combined in the same course of conduct, a sufficiently important governmental interest in regulating the nonspeech element can justify incidental limitations on First Amendment freedoms," *O'Brien*, we have limited the applicability of *O'Brien*'s relatively lenient standard to those cases in which "the governmental interest is unrelated to the suppression of free expression." . . .

In order to decide whether *O'Brien*'s test applies here, therefore, we must decide whether Texas has asserted an interest in support of Johnson's conviction that is unrelated to the suppression of expression. If we find that an interest asserted by the State is simply not implicated on the facts before us, we need not ask whether *O'Brien*'s test applies. The State offers two separate interests to justify this conviction: preventing breaches of the peace, and preserving the flag as a symbol of nationhood and national unity. We hold that the first interest is not implicated on this record and that the second is related to the suppression of expression.

Texas claims that its interest in preventing breaches of the peace justifies Johnson's conviction for flag desecration. However, no disturbance of the peace actually occurred or threatened to occur because of Johnson's burning of the flag. Although the State stresses the disruptive behavior of the protestors during their march toward City Hall, it admits that "no actual breach of the peace occurred at the time of the flagburning or in response to the flagburning." . . .

The State also asserts an interest in preserving the flag as a symbol of nationhood and national unity. In *Spence*, we acknowledged that the Government's interest in preserving the flag's special symbolic value "is directly related to expression in the context of activity" such as affixing a peace symbol to a flag. We are equally persuaded that this interest is related to expression in the case of Johnson's burning of the flag. The State, apparently, is concerned that such conduct will lead people to believe either that the flag does not stand for nationhood and national unity, but instead reflects other, less positive concepts, or that the concepts reflected in the flag do not in fact exist, that is, we do not enjoy unity as a Nation. These concerns blossom only when a person's treatment of the flag communicates some message, and thus are related "to the suppression of free expression" within the meaning of *O'Brien*. We are thus outside of *O'Brien's* test altogether.

It remains to consider whether the State's interest in preserving the flag as a symbol of nationhood and national unity justifies Johnson's conviction. . . .

Whether Johnson's treatment of the flag violated Texas law thus depended on the likely communicative impact of his expressive conduct. Our decision in *Boos v. Barry*, [485 U.S. 312 (1988)], tells us that this restriction on Johnson's expression is content-based. In *Boos*, we considered the constitutionality of a law prohibiting "the display of any sign within 500 feet of a foreign embassy if that sign tends to bring that foreign government into 'public odium' or 'public disrepute.' " Rejecting the argument that the law was content-neutral because it was justified by "our international law obligation to shield diplomats from speech that offends their dignity," we held that "[t]he emotive impact of speech on its audience is not a 'secondary effect' " unrelated to the content of the expression itself.

According to the principles announced in *Boos*, Johnson's political expression was restricted because of the content of the message he conveyed. We must therefore subject the State's asserted interest in preserving the special symbolic character of the flag to "the most exacting scrutiny." *Boos v. Barry*. . . .

The State's argument is not that it has an interest simply in maintaining the flag as a symbol of *something*, no matter what it symbolizes; indeed, if that were the State's position, it would be difficult to see how that interest is endangered by highly symbolic conduct such as Johnson's. Rather, the State's claim is that it has an interest in preserving the flag as a symbol of *nationhood* and *national unity*, a symbol with a determinate range of meanings. According to Texas, if one physically treats the flag in a way that would tend to cast doubt on either the idea that nationhood and national unity are the flag's referents or that national unity actually exists, the message conveyed thereby is a harmful one and therefore may be prohibited.

If there is a bedrock principle underlying the First Amendment, it is that the Government may not prohibit the expression of an idea simply because society finds the idea itself offensive or disagreeable. . . .

We have not recognized an exception to this principle even where our flag has been involved. In *Street v. New York*, 394 U.S. 576 (1969), we held that a State may not criminally punish a person for uttering words critical of the flag. Rejecting the argument that the conviction could be sustained on the ground that Street had "failed to show the respect for our national symbol which may properly be demanded of every citizen," we concluded that "the constitutionally guaranteed 'freedom to be intellectually . . . diverse or even contrary,' and the 'right to differ as to things that touch the heart of the existing order,' encompass the freedom to express publicly one's opinions about our flag, including those opinions which are defiant or contemptuous." Nor may the Government, we have held, compel conduct that would evince respect for the flag. "To sustain the compulsory flag salute we are required to say that a Bill of Rights which guards the individual's right to speak his own mind, left it open to public authorities to compel him to utter what is not in his mind." . . .

In short, nothing in our precedents suggests that a State may foster its own view of the flag by prohibiting expressive conduct relating to it. To bring its argument outside our precedents, Texas attempts to convince us that even if its interest in preserving the flag's symbolic role does not allow it to prohibit words or some expressive conduct critical of the flag, it does permit it to forbid the outright destruction of the flag. The State's argument cannot depend here on the distinction between written or spoken words and nonverbal conduct. That distinction, we have shown, is of no moment where the nonverbal conduct is expressive, as it is here, and where the regulation of that conduct is related to expression, as it is here. . . .

There is, moreover, no indication—either in the text of the Constitution or in our cases interpreting it—that a separate juridical category exists for the American flag alone. Indeed, we would not be surprised to learn that the persons who framed our Constitution and wrote the Amendment that we now construe were not known for their reverence for the Union Jack. The First Amendment does not guarantee that other concepts virtually sacred to our Nation as a whole—such as the principle that discrimination on the basis of race is odious and destructive—will go unquestioned in the marketplace of ideas. See *Brandenburg v. Ohio*, 395 U.S. 444 (1969). We decline, therefore, to create for the flag an exception to the joust of principles protected by the First Amendment.

It is not the State's ends, but its means, to which we object. It cannot be gainsaid that there is a special place reserved for the flag in this Nation, and thus we do not doubt that the Government has a legitimate interest in making efforts to "preserv[e] the national flag as an unalloyed symbol of our country." . . . To say that the Government has an interest in encouraging proper treatment of the flag, however, is not to say that it may criminally punish a person for burning a flag as a means of political protest. . . .

The way to preserve the flag's special role is not to punish those who feel differently about these matters. It is to persuade them that they are wrong. . . .

Johnson was convicted for engaging in expressive conduct. The State's interest in preventing breaches of the peace does not support his conviction because Johnson's conduct did not threaten to disturb the peace. Nor does the State's interest in preserving the flag as a symbol of nationhood and national unity justify his criminal conviction for engaging in political expression. The judgment of the Texas Court of Criminal Appeals is therefore

Affirmed.

☐ *Justice KENNEDY, concurring.*

I write not to qualify the words Justice BRENNAN chooses so well, for he says with power all that is necessary to explain our ruling. I join his opinion without reservation, but with a keen sense that this case, like others before us from time to time, exacts its personal toll. This prompts me to add to our pages these few remarks. . . .

The hard fact is that sometimes we must make decisions we do not like. We make them because they are right, right in the sense that the law and the Constitution, as we see them, compel the result. And so great is our commitment to the process that, except in the rare case, we do not pause to express distaste for the result, perhaps for fear of undermining a valued principle that dictates the decision. This is one of those rare cases.

Our colleagues in dissent advance powerful arguments why respondent may be convicted for his expression, reminding us that among those who will be dismayed by our holding will be some who have had the singular honor of carrying the flag in battle. And I agree that the flag holds a lonely place of honor in an age when absolutes are distrusted and simple truths are burdened by unneeded apologetics.

With all respect to those views, I do not believe the Constitution gives us the right to rule as the dissenting members of the Court urge, however painful this judgment is to announce. Though symbols often are what we ourselves make of them, the flag is constant in expressing beliefs Americans share, beliefs in law and peace and that freedom which sustains the human spirit. The case here today forces recognition of the costs to which those beliefs commit us. It is poignant but fundamental that the flag protects those who hold it in contempt. . . .

☐ *Chief Justice REHNQUIST, with whom Justice WHITE and Justice O'CONNOR join, dissenting.*

For more than 200 years, the American flag has occupied a unique position as the symbol of our Nation, a uniqueness that justifies a governmental prohibition against flag burning in the way respondent Johnson did here. . . .

No other American symbol has been as universally honored as the flag. In 1931, Congress declared "The Star Spangled Banner" to be our national anthem. In 1949, Congress declared June 14th to be Flag Day. In 1987, John Philip Sousa's "The Stars and Stripes Forever" was designated as the national march. Congress has also established "The Pledge of Allegiance to the Flag" and the manner of its deliverance. The flag has appeared as the principal symbol on approximately 33 United States postal stamps and in the design of at least 43 more, more times than any other symbol.

Both Congress and the States have enacted numerous laws regulating misuse of the American flag. Until 1967, Congress left the regulation of misuse of the flag up to the States. Now, however, Title 18 U.S.C. § 700(a), provides that:

> "Whoever knowingly casts contempt upon any flag of the United States by publicly mutilating, defacing, defiling, burning, or trampling upon it shall be fined not more than $1,000 or imprisoned for not more than one year, or both."

Congress has also prescribed detailed rules for the design of the flag, the time and occasion of flag's display, the position and manner of its display, respect for the flag, and conduct during hoisting, lowering and passing of the flag. With the exception of Alaska and Wyoming, all of the States now have statutes prohibiting the burning of the flag. . . .

The American flag, then, throughout more than 200 years of our history, has come to be the visible symbol embodying our Nation. It does not represent the views of any particular political party, and it does not represent any particular political philosophy. The flag is not simply another "idea" or "point of view" competing for recognition in the marketplace of ideas. Millions and millions of Americans regard it with an almost mystical reverence regardless of what sort of social, political, or philosophical beliefs they may have. I cannot agree that the First Amendment invalidates the Act of Congress, and the laws of 48 of the 50 States, which make criminal the public burning of the flag. . . .

Here it may equally well be said that the public burning of the American flag by Johnson was no essential part of any exposition of ideas, and at the same time it had a tendency to incite a breach of the peace. Johnson was free to make any verbal denunciation of the flag that he wished; indeed, he was free to burn the flag in private. He could publicly burn other symbols of the Government or effigies of political leaders. He did lead a march through the streets of Dallas, and conducted a rally in front of the Dallas City Hall. He engaged in a "die-in" to protest nuclear weapons. He shouted out various slogans during the march, including: "Reagan, Mondale which will it be? Either one means World War III"; "Ronald Reagan, killer of the hour, Perfect example of U.S. power"; and "red, white and blue, we spit on you, you stand for plunder, you will go under." For none of these acts was he arrested or prosecuted; it was only when he proceeded to burn publicly an American flag stolen from its rightful owner that he violated the Texas statute. . . .

The result of the Texas statute is obviously to deny one in Johnson's frame of mind one of many means of "symbolic speech." Far from being a case of "one picture being worth a thousand words," flag burning is the equivalent of an inarticulate grunt or roar that, it seems fair to say, is most likely to be indulged in not to express any particular idea, but to antagonize others. . . .

☐ *Justice STEVENS, dissenting.*

The Court is . . . quite wrong in blandly asserting that respondent "was prosecuted for his expression of dissatisfaction with the policies of this country, expression situated at the core of our First Amendment values." Respondent was prosecuted because of the method he chose to express his dissatisfaction with those policies. Had he chosen to spray paint—or perhaps convey with a motion picture projector—his message of dissatisfaction on the facade of the Lincoln Memorial, there would be no question about the power of the Government to prohibit his means of expression. The prohibition would be supported by the legitimate interest in preserving the quality of an important national asset. Though the asset at stake in this case is intangible, given its unique value, the same interest supports a prohibition on the desecration of the American flag.

■ (2) SPEECH-PLUS-CONDUCT

Speech-plus-conduct includes activities such as peaceful picketing, boycotts, and demonstrations. Individuals engaged in these activities may receive some First Amendment protection, but it depends on the circumstances and they do not enjoy the same freedom as those "who communicate ideas by pure speech."[1] Moreover, individuals remain subject to laws making it illegal to trespass onto private property without the owner's permission, for example, and laws forbidding the "breach of the peace," disorderly conduct, blocking traffic, resisting arrest, and inciting to riot.

The Court extended First Amendment protection to speech-plus-conduct initially by developing the "public forum" doctrine in recognition of the importance of discussion of public affairs in public streets, parks, and facilities. The concept of a public forum was introduced into constitutional law by Justice Roberts in *Hague v. Committee for Industrial Organization* (*CIO*), 307 U.S. 496 (1937). There the CIO was denied permission to use public halls for a rally in Jersey City, New Jersey, and its members were arrested and removed from the city for publicly discussing and distributing leaflets on the labor movement. When striking down the city's ordinance prohibiting assemblies "in or upon the public streets, highways, public parks or public buildings" without a permit from the director of public safety, Justice Roberts observed,

> Wherever the title of streets and parks may rest, they have immemorially been held in trust for the use of the public and, time out of mind, have been used for purposes of assembly, communicating thoughts between citizens, and discussing public questions. Such use of the streets and public places has, from ancient times, been a part of the privileges, immunities, rights and liberties of citizens. The privilege of a citizen of the United States to use the streets and parks for communication of views on national questions may be regulated in the interest of all; it is not absolute, but relative, and must be exercised in consonance with peace and good order; but it must not, in the guise of regulation, be abridged or denied.

Subsequently, the concept of a public forum was expanded to include municipal auditoriums, sidewalks, shopping centers, criminal trials, and the public areas surrounding schools, courthouses, embassies, and state capitol buildings. In *Forsyth County v. The Nationalist Movement*, 505 U.S. 123 (1992), a bare majority struck down an ordinance imposing a fee of up to $1,000 per day for parades, which was adopted after a clash between civil rights demonstrators and Klu Klux Klan members. Writing for the majority, Justice Blackmun found the ordinance to (1) give "unbridled discretion" to city administrators; (2) discriminate against groups on the basis of the content of their speech, since unpopular groups had to pay higher fees; and (3) impose a $1,000 ceiling on fees that was irrelevant in light of the competing First Amendment values.

Access to a public forum, however, is conditional. States and localities may impose reasonable "time, place, and manner" restrictions governing the use of public streets, parks, and other public facilities. They may also require permits for parades, marches, and demonstrations, so long as those restrictions are evenly applied and not overly broad so as to allow local officials to censor particular groups. In *Cox v. New Hampshire*, 312 U.S. 569 (1941), for example, the Court unanimously upheld the convictions of a group of Jehovah's Witnesses who marched single file along a downtown street, carrying placards, without first obtaining a special permit for "parades or processions."[2] Moreover, in *Ward v. Rock Against Racism*, 491 U.S. 781 (1989), the Rehnquist Court indicated that it was prepared to give states and localities greater leeway in imposing time, place, and manner restrictions. By a vote of six to three, New York's ordinance requiring concerts in Central Park to use a city-owned sound system and engineer to operate the system was upheld. And the majority ruled that time, place, and manner restrictions do not have to meet the least restrictive alternative test that the Court applies in other areas of regulation imposing on First Amendment freedoms. Subsequently, *United States v. Kokinda*, 497 U.S. 720 (1990), held that post offices may ban all solicitations on their property. Four members of the Court—Chief Justice Rehnquist and Justices O'Connor, White, and Scalia—also held that a sidewalk on postal property was not a public forum, and thus solicitations could be banned there as well. Justice Kennedy, casting the crucial fifth vote, however, concluded that the Court need not address the public forum issue, because the post office's ban on solicitations was a reasonable time, place, and manner restriction. By contrast, dissenting Justices Brennan, Marshall, Blackmun, and Stevens contended that the public sidewalks outside of post offices constituted public forums entitled to First Amendment protection.

It bears emphasizing that the concept of public forum and time, place, and manner restrictions apply only to public streets and other public places not otherwise restricted to the public. Generally, individuals have no First Amendment rights to intrude on private property and may be prosecuted for trespass or nuisance.[3] However, in *Amalgamated Food Employees Union v. Logan Valley Plaza*, 391 U.S. 308 (1968), the Court (six to three) upheld the right of a labor union to picket outside a store in a privately owned shopping center on the grounds that the Logan Valley Plaza was the only shopping center in the community and, hence, was functionally equivalent for First Amendment

■ THE DEVELOPMENT OF LAW

Rulings Extending the Concept of a Public Forum

CASE	RULING
Hague v. CIO, 307 U.S. 496 (1937)	Public streets and meeting halls.
Edwards v. South Carolina, 371 U.S. 229 (1963)	Steps of state capitol building.
Cox v. Louisiana, 379 U.S. 536 (1965)	Streets surrounding state capitol.
Cox v. Louisiana, 379 U.S. 559 (1965)	Streets and sidewalk near courthouse.
Police Department of City of Chicago v. Mosley, 408 U.S. 92 (1972)	Sidewalks and streets in front of school.
Chief of the Capitol Police v. Jeanette Rankin Brigade, 409 U.S. 972 (1972)	Peaceful protests in Lafayette Park.
Southeastern Promotions v. Conrad, 420 U.S. 546 (1975)	Municipal auditorium.
Richmond Newspapers, Inc. v. Virginia, 448 U.S. 358 (1980)	Criminal trials.
Widmar v. Vincent, 454 U.S. 263 (1981)	State university facilities that have been established as an open forum cannot be denied to religious groups.
United States v. Grace, 461 U.S. 171 (1982)	Steps of the Supreme Court of the United States.
Board of Airport Commissioners of Los Angeles v. Jews for Jesus, Inc., 482 U.S. 569 (1987)	Struck down a "First Amendment free zone," which banned all First Amendment expression, solicitations, and canvassing in central airport terminal.
Boos v. Barry, 485 U.S. 312 (1988)	Struck down statute prohibiting protests within 500 feet of an embassy.

■ THE DEVELOPMENT OF LAW

Places That Have Been Held Not to Be Public Forums

CASE	RULING
Lehman v. City of Shaker Heights, 418 U.S. 298 (1974)	Bus placards.
Adderly v. Florida, 385 U.S. 39 (1966)	Area surrounding jails.
Flower v. United States, 407 U.S. 197 (1972)	Army bases.
Greer v. Spock, 424 U.S. 828 (1976)	Military bases.
United States v. Kokinda, 497 U.S. 720 (1990)	Sidewalks on property of U.S. post offices (plurality holding).
International Society for Krishna Consciousness v. Lee, 505 U.S. 830 (1992)	Airports (bare majority holding).
Arkansas Educational Television Commission v. Forbes, 523 U.S. 666 (1998)	Public televisions may exclude "marginal" candidates from televised debates of major candidates for political office. In refusing to extend the con-

cept of a "public forum" to such debates, Justice Kennedy ruled that the televised debate was a "nonpublic forum" and that the decision to exclude Steve Forbes, an independent candidate, was under the circumstances a reasonable, viewpoint-neutral exercise of journalistic discretion consistent with the First Amendment. Justices Stevens, Ginsburg, and Souter dissented.

| *United States v. American Library Association*, 539 U.S. 126 (2003) | In upholding the Children's Internet Protection Act of 2001, which authorizes public libraries that receive |

federal funding to install pornography filters on computers providing Internet access, Chief Justice Rehnquist held that providing Internet access does not turn a library into a public forum.

purposes to a downtown business district and the only forum available for the union to publicize its labor dispute. But after Nixon's four appointees joined the Court, the justices five to four (with Justices Brennan, Douglas, Marshall, and Stewart dissenting) held that a privately owned shopping center could prohibit the distribution of handbills protesting the draft and the Vietnam War. In *Lloyd Corporation v. Tanner*, 407 U.S. 551 (1972), Justice Powell, writing for the majority, thought that there were "adequate alternative avenues of communication" available. Then in *Hudgens v. National Labor Relations Board*, 424 U.S. 507 (1976), involving another labor picketing dispute, the justices (voting six to two) rejected the *Logan Valley* ruling, and Justice Stewart's opinion for the Court contended that the First Amendment guarantee for freedom of expression was inapplicable to shopping centers. But, finally, in *PruneYard Shopping Center v. Robins*, 447 U.S. 74 (1980), the Court unanimously held that California could under its own state constitution permit the distribution of pamphlets and petitions in shopping malls and confer greater freedom of expression than the Court does when interpreting and applying the First Amendment.

In addition to time, place, and manner restrictions, as well as required parade permits, the courts may issue injunctions against or limiting demonstrations, marches, and parades. The Court in *Walker v. City of Birmingham*, 388 U.S. 307 (1967), arising from Martin Luther King's defiance of a court order against a march in Birmingham, Alabama, upheld the power of courts to enjoin particular marches and to find those who fail to comply with their orders in contempt of court.

In an important ruling on freedom of speech and speech-plus-conduct, growing out of the continuing controversy over abortion, the Rehnquist Court confronted the issue of anti-abortion protesters' First Amendment rights in *Madsen v. Women's Health Center*, 512 U.S. 735 (1994). *Madsen* presented the issue of whether a Florida trial judge's injunction against anti-abortion protesters constituted a suppression of their message or, as the Florida state supreme court held, aimed at protecting constitutionally guaranteed interests in medical care and patients' privacy.

Splitting six to three and five to four on different parts of the ruling in *Madsen*, the Court held that injunctions restraining anti-abortion protesters must be evaluated for "content neutrality" and must not burden protesters' speech more than necessary to achieve the government's legitimate interests, as well as be framed in the narrowest possible terms to achieve its pinpoint objective. Writing for the majority, Chief Justice Rehnquist upheld the thirty-six-foot buffer zone around the clinic's entrances and driveway, along with the limitations on noise around the clinic during surgery and recovery periods. However, he rejected as too broad and as an infringement on First Amendment freedoms the injunction's (1) thirty-six-foot buffer zone as applied to private property, (2) blanket ban on "observable images" on pickets, and (3) three-hundred-foot-no-approach zone around the clinic. Justice Souter filed a brief concurring opinion, and Justice Stevens filed an opinion in part concurring and dissenting. In a bitter dissent, joined by Justices Kennedy and Thomas, Justice Scalia took strong exception to the majority's upholding any part of the injunction and criticized it for sanctioning the suppression of a particular message, the views of anti-abortion advocates.

Subsequently, in *Schenck v. Pro-Choice Network of Western New York,* 519 U.S. 357 (1997), the Court upheld a lower court's creation of a "fifteen-foot fixed buffer zone" around doorways and parking lot entrances to an abortion clinic, but also permitting two anti-abortion counselors to enter the zone at any one time. The problem of anti-abortion protests and clinic blockades diminished following the enactment of the Freedom of Access to Clinic Entrances Act (FACE) in 1994, which makes it a federal crime to obstruct access to clinics and imposes stiff prison sentences for doing so. Nonetheless, returning to the issue of restrictions on anti-abortion protesters, the Court upheld Colorado's law making it unlawful for a person within 100 feet of a health care facility's entrance to "knowingly approach" within eight feet another person, without permission, in order to pass out leaflets or engage in oral protest. Writing for the Court in *Hill v. Colorado,* 530 U.S. 703 (2000), Justice Stevens found the statute to be a "narrowly tailored" time, place, and manner regulation, under *Ward v. Rock Against Racism,* 491 U.S. 781 (1989). Justice Scalia, along with Justices Kennedy and Thomas, dissented.

Finally, in *Hurley v. Irish-American Gay, Lesbian, and Bisexual Group of Boston,* 515 U.S. 557 (1995), the justices unanimously reversed a Massachusetts state court decision holding that the veteran groups organizing Boston's St. Patrick Day parade could not exclude gay, lesbian, and bisexual marchers. The state court had ruled that the parade's organizers could not discriminate on the basis of sexual orientation and that the parade, although privately organized, was nonetheless subject to the state's public accommodations law. Writing for the Court, Justice Souter explained that

> [T]he Massachusetts law has been applied in a peculiar way. Its enforcement does not address any dispute about the participation of openly gay, lesbian, or bisexual individuals in various units admitted to the parade. The petitioners disclaim any intent to exclude homosexuals as such, and no individual member of GLIB claims to have been excluded from parading as a member of any group that the

Council has approved to march. Instead, the disagreement goes to the admission of GLIB as its own parade unit carrying its own banner. Since every participating unit affects the message conveyed by the private organizers, the state court's application of the statute produced an order essentially requiring petitioners to alter the expressive content of their parade. . . . Under this approach any contingent of protected individuals with a message would have the right to participate in petitioners' speech, so that the communication produced by the private organizers would be shaped by all those protected by the law who wished to join in with some expressive demonstration of their own. But this use of the State's power violates the fundamental rule of protection under the First Amendment, that a speaker has the autonomy to choose the content of his own message. . . .

Rather like a composition, the Council selects the expressive units of the parade from potential participants, and though the score may not produce a particularized message, each contingent's expression in the Council's eyes comports with what merits celebration on that day. Even if this view gives the Council credit for a more considered judgment than it actively made, the Council clearly decided to exclude a message it did not like from the communication it chose to make, and that is enough to invoke its right as a private speaker to shape its expression by speaking on one subject while remaining silent on another. The message it disfavored is not difficult to identify. . . . But whatever the reason, it boils down to the choice of a speaker not to propound a particular point of view, and that choice is presumed to lie beyond the government's power to control.

NOTES

1. *Cox v. Louisiana*, 379 U.S. 536 (1965).

2. See also *Niemotko v. Maryland*, 340 U.S. 268 (1951); *Poulos v. New Hampshire*, 345 U.S. 395 (1951); *Kunz v. New York*, 290 U.S. 36 (1951); and *Cameron v. Johnson*, 381 U.S. 741 (1965).

3. But see *Gregory v. Chicago*, 394 U.S. 111 (1969) (upholding the picketing by black activists on the sidewalk outside of the home of Chicago's Mayor Richard Daley).

I | *Freedom of Association*

The First Amendment's provision for "the right of the people to peaceably assemble, and to petition the Government for a redress of grievances" provides the textual basis for the Court's recognition of a right of association and associational privacy. But the Court also recognized that the freedom of association is implicit in the very structure of the First Amendment's guarantees for a "system of freedom of expression" and the Constitution's framework for the operation of free government. In *Sweezy v. New Hampshire*, 354 U.S. 234 (1957), the Court thus observed that "[o]ur form of government is built on the premise that every citizen shall have the right to engage in political expression and association. This right was enshrined in the First Amendment of the Bill of Rights." More than a century before, Alexis de Tocqueville found that in "no country in the world has the principle of association been more successfully used or more unsparingly applied to a multitude of different objects, than in America," when proclaiming, "The most natural privilege of a man next to the right of acting for himself, is that of combining his exertions with those of his fellow creatures and of acting in common with them. The right of association therefore appears to be as almost inalienable in its nature as the right of personal liberty. No legislator can attack it without impairing the foundations of society."[1]

The Court formally proclaimed a First Amendment right of association and associational privacy in *National Association for the Advancement of Colored People v. Alabama* (1958) (see excerpt below), when unanimously reversing a contempt citation for the NAACP's refusal to turn over lists of members to Alabama's state attorney general. The Court in the 1950s and 1960s, however, remained divided over the scope of freedom of association, especially when confronted with First Amendment challenges to congressional investigations (see Vol. 1, Ch. 5) and state and federal prosecutions of members of the Communist party and other "subversive" organizations (see section A, in this chapter). The year after *NAACP v. Alabama*, for example, the justices split five to four in *Uphaus v. Wyman*, 260 U.S. 72 (1959), holding that New Hampshire could compel the production of membership lists of "Communist front" organizations. But the next year in *Bates v. City of Little Rock*, 364 U.S. 479 (1960), and *Sheldon v. Tucker*, 364 U.S. 516 (1960), the Court reaffirmed that compelled disclosure of membership lists denies individuals' freedom of association and associational privacy. *Sheldon* struck down as overly broad an Arkansas statute requiring teachers to file affidavits listing all organizations to which they had belonged in the preceding five years. There Stewart pointed out that "to compel a teacher to disclose his every associational tie is to impair that teacher's right of free association, a right closely allied to freedom of speech, and a right which, like free speech, lies at the foundation of a free society." Still, the justices, divided five to four as in *Uphaus*, upheld the provisions of the Internal Security Act of 1950, making it unlawful to be a member of the Communist Party and requiring members of subversive organizations to register with the Subversive Activities Control Board, in *Communist Party v. Subversive Activities Con-*

trol Board (*SACB*), 367 U.S. 1 (1961), and *Scales v. United States*, 367 U.S. 203 (1961).[2]

The Warren Court's rulings in the 1950s and early 1960s extended First Amendment protection to groups and organizations formed or associated for lawful purposes, but not to those, such as the Communist party, which were deemed to have subversive purposes. In *NAACP v. Alabama*, the Court thus distinguished an earlier ruling, *Bryant v. Zimmerman*, 278 U.S. 63 (1928), upholding a New York anti-Klu Klux Klan statute requiring oath-bound organizations to submit membership lists on the basis of the Klan's illegal activities. This was the basis for the Court's denial of First Amendment claims whenever associations were found or deemed to have unlawful purposes. As the Court explained, in *DeJonge v. Oregon*, 299 U.S. 353 (1937), "The right of peaceable assembly is a right cognate to those of free speech and free press and is equally fundamental," but it did not extend to associations that "incite[d] violence and crime," which could also be prosecuted under laws punishing criminal conspiracies, among other illegal activities.

The Court's dichotomy between nonsubversive and subversive organizations was problematic because organizations may have both legal and illegal goals, and thus individual members might be punished for knowing but guiltless behavior; their only crime being guilt by association. In addition, states could thwart the activities of organizations, such as the NAACP, by claiming they were subversive or infiltrated by other subversive organizations.

The balance on the Warren Court, though, shifted in 1962 when Justice Goldberg, a prominent union lawyer and a successful labor negotiator, was named to the bench. He sided with Chief Justice Warren and Justices Black, Brennan, and Douglas in forming a solid majority for extending greater First Amendment protection, which held even after Goldberg's resignation in 1965 with President Johnson's appointments of Justices Fortas (in 1965) and Marshall (in 1967). *Gibson v. Florida Legislative Investigation Committee*, 372 U.S. 539 (1963) (see Vol. 1, Ch. 5), signaled that the Court would no longer presume the validity of governmental inquiries but require that the government establish an "immediate, substantial, and subordinating state interest necessary to sustain its right of inquiry into the membership lists of a nonsubversive organization." Along with that ruling, in *NAACP v. Button*, 371 U.S. 415 (1963), the Court held that the NAACP's litigation activities aimed at forcing desegregation were protected under the First Amendment. In Justice Brennan's words, litigation is a "form of political expression" and "for such a group association for litigation may be the most effective form of political association." Subsequently, the Court held that the Subversive Activities Control Board (SACB) could not revoke the passports of individuals who registered, as required under the Internal Security Act of 1950, as members of the Communist party.[3] And the SACB's ordering all Communists to register with the federal government was overturned in *American Committee for Protection of Foreign Born v. SACB*, 380 U.S. 503 (1965). Finally, in *United States v. Robel*, 389 U.S. 258 (1967), a section of the Internal Security Act making it unlawful for a member of a Communist-action organization to work in a defense facility was held to violate the First Amendment. The statute, in the Court's view, swept too broadly and "indiscriminately across all types of associations with Communist-action groups, without regard to the quality or degree of membership. . . . The statute quite literally establishes guilt by association alone, without any need to establish that an individual's association poses the threat feared by the Government in proscribing it."

The scope of First Amendment protection for freedom of association and expression was also expanded in cases challenging the constitutionality of loyalty oaths and the firing of public employees for their political beliefs, associations, and activities. However, over First Amendment objections the Court approved restrictions on political activities imposed on federal career civil servants under the Hatch Act or Federal Lobbying Act, forbidding active participating in political campaigns. The law was upheld in *United States v. Harris*, 347 U.S. 612 (1954), and again in *United States Civil Service Commission v. National Association of Letter Carriers*, 413 U.S. 548 (1973). In the words of Justice White, who authored the majority's opinion in the latter six-to-three ruling, "It is in the best interest of the country, indeed essential, that federal service should depend upon meritorious performance rather than political service, and that the political influence of federal employees on others and on the electoral process should be limited." In *Lyng v. International Union, United Automobile, Aerospace and Agricultural Workers of America*, 485 U.S. 360 (1988), the Court upheld over the First Amendment objections of the union a 1981 amendment to the Food Stamp Act, which makes households ineligible for food stamps if a member of the household is on a strike.

In another highly controversial ruling in *Elrod v. Burns*, 427 U.S. 347 (1976), the justices (voting five to three and with Stevens not participating), struck down the practice of patronage dismissals as an unconstitutional restriction on city employees' First Amendment freedoms. The controversy and struggle within the Court over systems of political patronage and dismissal of public employees continued in *Branti v. Finkel*, 445 U.S. 507 (1980). In that case, the justices, six to three (with Justices Stewart, Powell, and Rehnquist in dissent), held that the First Amendment protects district attorneys from being discharged for expressing their political views. After Stewart retired and was re-placed by O'Connor, however, the Court held (five to four, with Justices Brennan, Blackmun, Marshall, and Stevens now in dissent) that the firing of state attorneys general for political reasons does not violate the First Amendment.[4] But then Justice Brennan marshaled a bare majority, in *Rutan v. Republican Party of Illinois*, 497 U.S. 62 (1990), for eliminating political patronage in the hiring and firing of most public employees (see Vol. 1, Ch. 8).

The protection accorded freedom of association extends to a broad range of groups, associations and organizations, including public interest groups,[5] unions,[6] political parties,[7] and married couples.[8] But the right of association and associational privacy does not extend to individuals' claims to anonymity. In *Laird v. Tatum*, 408 U.S. 1 (1972), the Burger Court, over the sharp dissents of Justices Douglas, Brennan, Marshall, and Stewart, upheld the army's surveillance of political protesters at rallies, demonstrations, and marches against America's involvement in the Vietnam War.

Nor does the First Amendment right of association present a barrier to state and federal laws prohibiting invidious discrimination in privately owned businesses serving the public or private associations and clubs. The freedom of association is basically the freedom to discriminate— the freedom to choose with whom one associates and in what context and for what purpose. But the Court has held that not all private associations and discriminations receive First Amendment protection; those associations discriminating against racial minorities and women may not find a haven in the First Amendment right of association.

While the Warren Court broadened the First Amendment to include a right of association and associational privacy in cases such as *NAACP v. Alabama*, it was reluctant to tackle the competing First Amendment claims of those who protested segregation with sit-ins, and those who discriminated against blacks in their private businesses and associations. Over the objections of dissenting Justices Black and Douglas, the Court upheld a lower court's ordering the integration of the Wisconsin state bar association in *Lathrop v. Donahue*, 367 U.S. 820 (1961). But when it came to cases challenging the convictions for trespass of blacks who demonstrated with sit-ins at racially segregated lunch counters, and raising the claim of owners of segregated restaurants that they had a right to decide whom to serve, the Court split three ways. In *Bell v. Maryland*, 378 U.S. 226 (1964), Justice Brennan's opinion for the Court simply declined to confront the issue when it remanded the case back to the Maryland Supreme Court. Justices Douglas and Goldberg, along with Chief Justice Warren, however, were prepared to hold that individuals have no First Amendment right to discriminate racially in their accommodations open to the public. They were unable to forge a majority, though, because Justices Clark and Stewart were unwilling to go that far and joined Brennan instead. Dissenting Justices Black, Harlan, and White agreed that individuals could associate and racially discriminate in their private affairs, but they did not think that either the Fourteenth Amendment's equal protection clause forbade private discrimination in public accommodations or that the First Amendment protected the protesters of segregated lunch counters. In Black's words:

> The right to freedom of expression is a right to express views—not a right to force other people to supply a platform or a pulpit. It is argued that this supposed constitutional right to invade other people's property would not mean that a man's home, his private club, or his church could be forcibly entered or used against his will— only his store or place of business which he has himself "opened to the public" by selling goods or services for money. . . . But the whole quarrel . . . [here is] that instead of being open to all, the restaurant refused service to Negroes.

Times change, and the Warren Court was at a great turning point in the history of constitutional politics. In 1964, Congress passed the Civil Rights Act, or Public Accommodations Act, banning racial discrimination or segregation in public accommodations. The Court upheld that legislation in *Heart of Atlanta Motel v. United States*, 379 U.S. 241 (1964) (see Vol. 1, Ch. 6), and avoided becoming further entangled with the remaining issues of discrimination in private clubs and associations. Exempted from the Civil Rights Act are boarding houses renting fewer than five rooms, and private clubs and other enterprises not open to the general public.

As times change, so does the Court. With states and localities pushing to eliminate discrimination based on race and gender, the Court finally confronted the issue of whether freedom of association extended to private clubs discriminating racially or against women. In *Roberts v. United States Jaycees* (1984) (see excerpt below), the First Amendment freedom of association argument of the Jaycees was rejected by the Court in upholding a Minnesota human rights law, compelling the Jaycees to accept women as regular members.

On the basis of the analysis in *United States Jaycees*, the Court subsequently upheld state laws barring all-male clubs from discriminating against women, in *Board of Directors of Rotary International v. Rotary Club of Duarte*, 481 U.S. 537 (1987), and *New York State Club Association, Inc. v. City of New York*, 487 U.S. 1 (1988). In *City of Dallas v. Stanglin*, 490 U.S. 1591 (1989), Chief Justice Rehnquist further ruled that an ordinance limiting certain dance halls to only fourteen-through-eighteen-year-olds did not deny adults' freedom of association under the First Amendment. The Court further held in *Boy Scouts of America v. Dale* (2000) (excerpted below) that homosexuals may be excluded from the Boy Scouts; otherwise, the latter's First Amendment right to "expressive association" would be violated. Justices Stevens, Souter, Ginsburg, and Breyer dissented.

Notes

1. Alexis de Tocqueville, *Democracy in America*, Vol. 2, ed. Phillips Bradley (New York: Vintage Books, 1954), 196.

2. In *Camp v. Board of Public Education*, 368 U.S. 278 (1961), the Court also upheld a state regulation requiring an affidavit for public employees that they are not members of a subversive organization.

3. *Aptheker v. United States*, 378 U.S. 500 (1964).

4. *Connick v. Myers*, 461 U.S. 138 (1983).

5. See *NAACP v. Button*, 371 U.S. 415 (1963).

6. In *International Association of Machinists v. Street*, 367 U.S. 740 (1961), the Court upheld closed union shops. See also *Brotherhood of Railway Trainmen v. Virginia State Bar*, 377 U.S. 1 (1964). In *Jones v. North Carolina Prisoners' Labor Union, Inc.*, 433 U.S. 119 (1977), however, the Court upheld restrictions on a prison inmate's "labor union" mailings for membership and solicitations. In *Minnesota State Board for Community Colleges v. Knight*, 465 U.S. 271 (1984), the Court held that a state's requiring public employees to engage in official exchanges of views only through their professional representatives did not violate the First Amendment.

7. In *Cousins v. Wigoda*, 419 U.S. 477 (1975), the Court upheld the national political party's power to specify how delegates from a state political party will be selected. In *Democratic Party of the United States v. Wisconsin*, 442 U.S. 107 (1981), Wisconsin's rule on binding primaries was found to violate the First Amendment. In *Brown v. Socialist Workers 74 Campaign Committee*, 459 U.S. 87 (1982), the Court held that disclosure of membership lists of the Socialist Workers party violated the First Amendment. However, the Court upheld the disclosure provisions of the Federal Election Campaign Act in *Buckley v. Valeo*, 424 U.S. 1 (1976), which is reprinted in part in Volume 1, Chapter 8.

8. See *Griswold v. Connecticut*, 381 U.S. 479 (1965) (see Chapters 2 and 11).

Selected Bibliography

Abernathy, Glen. *The Right of Assembly and Association*, 2d ed. Columbia: University of South Carolina Press, 1981.

Fellman, David. *The Constitutional Right of Association*. Chicago: University of Chicago Press, 1963.

Gutmann, Amy, ed. *Freedom of Association*. Princeton: Princeton University Press, 1998.

Kalven, Harry, Jr. *The Negro and The First Amendment*. Chicago: University of Chicago Press, 1965.

Karst, Kenneth. *Belonging to America: Equal Citizenship and the Constitution*. New York: Oxford University Press, 1989.

Levinson, Sanford. *Constitutional Faith*, Princeton, NJ: Princeton University Press, 1988.

National Association for the Advancement of Colored People v. Alabama

357 U.S. 449, 78 S.Ct. 1163 (1958)

The National Association for the Advancement of Colored People (NAACP) encountered bitter opposition in the South for bringing litigation challenging racial discrimination. Hostility mounted following its victory in the landmark school desegregation ruling in *Brown v. Board of Education*, 347 U.S. 483 (1954) (see Vol. 2, Ch. 12). As the NAACP sought to force compliance with *Brown*, southern hostility led to efforts by the states to prevent the NAACP from bringing more litigation. In 1956, Alabama's state attorney general sought to enjoin the NAACP from conducting business in the state under a law requiring out-of-state corporations to register and satisfy certain reporting requirements before doing business in the state. The NAACP was incorporated in New York and considered itself exempt from Alabama's law requiring, among other things, filing with the state certain records and membership lists, including the names and addresses of all members residing in the state. While filing the registration forms, the NAACP refused to give up its membership lists. For that it was found in contempt and fined $100,000. The state supreme court declined to review an appeal, and the NAACP appealed to the Supreme Court.

The court's decision was unanimous, and the opinion was announced by Justice Harlan.

    □ *Justice HARLAN delivers the opinion of the Court.*

We review from the standpoint of its validity under the Federal Constitution a judgment of civil contempt entered against petitioner, the National Association for the Advancement of Colored People, in the courts of Alabama. The question presented is whether Alabama, consistently with the Due Process Clause of the Fourteenth Amendment, can compel petitioner to reveal to the State's Attorney General the names and addresses of all its Alabama members and agents, without regard to their positions or functions in

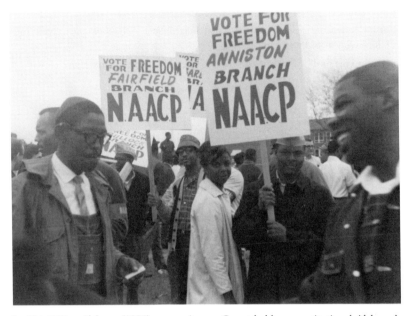

In *NAACP v. Alabama* (1958), a unanimous Court held unconstitutional Alabama's demand that the NAACP reveal the names and addresses of all its members and agents in the state. The decision markedly broadened the horizons of the First Amendment. (*Library of Congress*)

the Association. The judgment of contempt was based upon petitioner's refusal to comply fully with a court order requiring in part the production of membership lists. . . .

Alabama has a statute similar to those of many other States which requires a foreign corporation, except as exempted, to qualify before doing business by filing its corporate charter with the Secretary of State and designating a place of business and an agent to receive service of process. . . . [The NAACP] has never complied with the qualification statute, from which it considered itself exempt.

In 1956 the Attorney General of Alabama brought an equity suit in the State Circuit Court, Montgomery County, to enjoin the Association from conducting further activities within, and to oust it from, the State. . . .

[T]he State moved for the production of a large number of the Association's records and papers, including bank statements, leases, deeds, and records containing the names and addresses of all Alabama "members" and "agents" of the Association. It alleged that all such documents were necessary for adequate preparation for the hearing, in view of petitioner's denial of the conduct of intrastate business within the meaning of the qualification statute. Over petitioner's objections, the court ordered the production of a substantial part of the requested records, including the membership lists. . . .

Thereafter petitioner . . . produced substantially all the data called for by the production order except its membership lists, as to which it contended that Alabama could not constitutionally compel disclosure, and moved to modify or vacate the contempt judgment, or stay its execution pending appellate review. This motion was denied. While a similar stay application, which was later denied, was pending before the Supreme Court of Alabama, the Circuit Court made a further order adjudging petitioner in continuing contempt and increasing the fine already imposed to $100,000. . . .

It is beyond debate that freedom to engage in association for the advancement of beliefs and ideas is an inseparable aspect of the "liberty" assured by the Due Process Clause of the Fourteenth Amendment, which embraces freedom of speech. . . .

The fact that Alabama, so far as is relevant to the validity of the contempt judgment presently under review, has taken no direct action, to restrict the right of petitioner's members to associate freely, does not end inquiry into the effect of the production order. In the domain of these indispensable liberties; whether of speech, press, or association, the decisions of this Court recognize that abridgement of such rights, even though unintended, may inevitably follow from varied forms of governmental action. . . .

It is hardly a novel perception that compelled disclosure of affiliation with groups engaged in advocacy may constitute as effective a restraint on freedom of association as the forms of governmental action in the cases above were thought likely to produce upon the particular constitutional rights there involved. This Court has recognized the vital relationship between freedom to associate and privacy in one's associations. . . . Inviolability of privacy in group association may in many circumstances be indispensable to preservation of freedom of association, particularly where a group espouses dissident beliefs.

We think that the production order, in the respects here drawn in question, must be regarded as entailing the likelihood of a substantial restraint upon the exercise by petitioner's members of their right to freedom of association. Petitioner has made an uncontroverted showing that on past occasions revelation of the identity of its rank-and-file members has exposed these members to economic reprisal, loss of employment, threat of physical coercion, and other manifestations of public hostility. Under these circumstances, we think it apparent that compelled disclosure of petitioner's Alabama membership is likely to affect adversely the ability of petitioner and its members to pursue their collective effort to foster beliefs which they admittedly have the right to advocate, in that it may induce members to withdraw from the Association and dissuade others from joining it because of fear of exposure of their beliefs shown through their associations and of the consequences of this exposure. . . .

We turn to the final question whether Alabama has demonstrated an interest in obtaining the disclosures it seeks from petitioner which is sufficient to justify the deterrent effect which we have concluded these disclosures may well have on the free exercise by petitioner's members of their constitutionally protected right of association. Such a ". . . subordinating interest of the State must be compelling," *Sweezy v. New Hampshire*, 354 U.S. 234 [(1957)] (concurring opinion). . . .

Whether there was "justification" in this instance turns solely on the substantiality of Alabama's interest in obtaining the membership lists. . . . The exclusive purpose was to determine whether petitioner was conducting intrastate business in violation of the Alabama foreign corporation registration statute, and the membership lists were expected to help resolve this question. . . . Without intimating the slightest view upon the merits of these issues, we are unable to perceive that the disclosure of the names of petitioner's rank-and-file members has a substantial bearing. As matters stand in the state court, petitioner (1) has admitted its presence and conduct of activities in Alabama since 1918; (2) has offered to comply in all respects with the state qualification statute, although preserving its contention that the statute does not apply to it; and (3) has apparently complied satisfactorily with the production order, except for the membership lists, by furnishing the Attorney General with varied business records, its charter and statement of purposes, the names of all of its directors and officers, and with the total number of its Alabama members and the amount of their dues. . . .

We hold that the immunity from state scrutiny of membership lists which the Association claims on behalf of its members is here so related to the right of the members to pursue their lawful private interests privately and to associate freely with others in so doing as to come within the protection of the Fourteenth Amendment. And we conclude that Alabama has fallen short of showing a controlling justification for the deterrent effect on the free enjoyment of the right to associate which disclosure of membership lists is likely to have. Accordingly, the judgment of civil contempt and the $100,000 fine which resulted from petitioner's refusal to comply with the production order in this respect must fall.

Roberts v. United States Jaycees
468 U.S. 609, 104 S.Ct. 3244 (1984)

The United States Jaycees is a nonprofit organization devoted to promoting the growth and development of young men's civic organizations. According to its bylaws, regular membership was limited to men between the ages of eighteen and thirty-five, while women and older men could be associate members. The latter could not vote or hold local or national office, however. Two local chapters in Minnesota had been violating the bylaws for several years by admitting women as regular members. After imposing a number of sanctions, including denying their members eligibility for state and national offices, the United States Jaycees revoked charters of these two chapters. That prompted members of the two chapters to file a discrimination claim with the Minnesota Department of Human Rights alleging that the exclusion of women from full membership violated the Minnesota Human Rights Act, which makes it "an unfair discriminatory practice . . . [t]o deny any person the full and equal enjoyment of the goods, services, facilities, privileges, advantages, and accommodations of a place of public accommodation because of race, color, creed, religion, disability, national origin or sex." Before a hearing took place, however, the Jaycees brought a lawsuit against Kathryn Roberts, the acting commissioner of the state's Department of Human Rights, to prevent enforcement of the law. The Jaycees claimed that requiring it to accept women as regular members would violate its male members' First Amendment rights of free speech and association. A federal district court ruled against the Jaycees, but the Court of Appeals for the Eighth Circuit found the application of the state's law to the Jaycees would produce a "direct and substantial" interference with its members' First Amendment freedoms. Roberts and the state of Minnesota appealed that decision to the Supreme Court.

The Court's decision was unanimous, and the opinion was announced by Justice Brennan, with Chief Justice Burger and Justice Blackmun not participating. Concurring opinions were delivered by Justices Rehnquist and O'Connor.

☐ *Justice BRENNAN delivered the opinion of the Court.*

This case requires us to address a conflict between a State's efforts to eliminate gender-based discrimination against its citizens and the constitutional freedom of association asserted by members of a private organization. . . .

The Court has long recognized that, because the Bill of Rights is designed to secure individual liberty, it must afford the formation and preservation of certain kinds of highly personal relationships a substantial measure of sanctuary from unjustified interference by the State. Without precisely identifying every consideration that may underlie this type of constitutional protection, we have noted that certain kinds of personal bonds have played a critical role in the culture and traditions of the Nation by cultivating and transmitting shared ideals and beliefs; they thereby foster diversity and act as critical buffers between the individual and the power of the State. Moreover, the constitutional shelter afforded such relationships reflects the realization that individuals draw much of their emotional enrichment from close ties with others. . . .

The personal affiliations that exemplify these considerations, and that therefore suggest some relevant limitations on the relationships that might be entitled to this sort of constitutional protection, are those that attend the creation and sustenance of a family—marriage, childbirth, the raising and education of children, and cohabitation with one's relatives. . . . Conversely, an association lacking these qualities—such as a large business enterprise— seems remote from the concerns giving rise to this constitutional protection. Accordingly, the Constitution undoubtedly imposes constraints on the State's power to control the selection of one's spouse that would not apply to regulations affecting the choice of one's fellow employees. . . .

Between these poles, of course, lies a broad range of human relationships that may make greater or lesser claims to constitutional protection from particular incursions by the State. Determining the limits of state authority over an individual's freedom to enter into a particular association therefore unavoidably entails a careful assessment of where that relationship's objective characteristics locate it on a spectrum from the most intimate to the most attenuated of personal attachments. We need not mark the potentially significant points on this terrain with any precision. We note only that factors that may be relevant include size, purpose, policies, selectivity, congeniality, and other characteristics that in a particular case may be pertinent. In this case, however, several features of the Jaycees clearly place the organization outside of the category of relationships worthy of this kind of constitutional protection. . . .

The undisputed facts reveal that the local chapters of the Jaycees are large and basically unselective groups. At the time of the state administrative hearing, the Minneapolis chapter had approximately 430 members, while the St. Paul chapter had about 400. . . .

In short, the local chapters of the Jaycees are neither small nor selective. Moreover, much of the activity central to the formation and maintenance of the association involves the participation of strangers to that relationship. Accordingly, we conclude that the Jaycees chapters lack the distinctive characteristics that might afford constitutional protection to the decision of its members to exclude women. . . .

[W]e have long understood as implicit in the right to engage in activities protected by the First Amendment a corresponding right to associate with others in pursuit of a wide variety of political, social, economic, educational, religious, and cultural ends. . . .

The right to associate for expressive purposes is not, however, absolute. Infringements on that right may be justified by regulations adopted to serve compelling state interests, unrelated to the suppression of ideas, that cannot be achieved through means significantly less restrictive of associational freedoms. . . . We are persuaded that Minnesota's compelling interest in eradicating discrimination against its female citizens justifies the impact that application of the statute to the Jaycees may have on the male members' associational freedoms.

On its face, the Minnesota Act does not aim at the suppression of speech, does not distinguish between prohibited and permitted activity on the basis of viewpoint, and does not license enforcement authorities to administer the statute on the basis of such constitutionally impermissible criteria. Nor does the Jaycees contend that the Act has been applied in this case for the purpose of hampering the organization's ability to express its views. Instead, as the Minnesota Supreme Court explained, the Act reflects the State's strong historical commitment to eliminating discrimination and assuring its citizens equal access to publicly available goods and services. That goal, which is unrelated to the suppression of expression, plainly serves compelling state interests of the highest order. . . .

In applying the Act to the Jaycees, the State has advanced those interests through the least restrictive means of achieving its ends. Indeed, the Jaycees has failed to demonstrate that the Act imposes any serious burdens on the male members' freedom of expressive association. . . .

There is . . . no basis in the record for concluding that admission of women as full voting members will impede the organization's ability to engage in these protected activities or to disseminate its preferred views. The Act requires no change in the Jaycees' creed of promoting the interests of young men, and it imposes no restrictions on the organization's ability to exclude individuals with ideologies or philosophies different from those of its existing members. . . . Moreover, the Jaycees already invites women to share the group's views and philosophy and to participate in much of its training and community activities. Accordingly, any claim that admission of women as full voting members will impair a symbolic message conveyed by the very fact that women are not permitted to vote is attenuated at best. . . .

In the absence of a showing far more substantial than that attempted by the Jaycees, we decline to indulge in the sexual stereotyping that underlies appellee's contention that, by allowing women to vote, application of the Minnesota Act will change the content or impact of the organization's speech. . . .

The judgment of the Court of Appeals is Reversed.

Boy Scouts of America v. Dale

530 U.S. 640, 120 S.Ct. 2446 (2000)

Founded in 1910, the Boy Scouts of America is a federally chartered corporation that, as of 1992, included more than 4 million youths and 1 million adults as active members in more than 44,000 Boy Scout troops throughout the country. In 1991 the New Jersey legislature amended its Law Against Discrimination (LAD) to include protection from discrimination based on "affectional or sexual orientation." Subsequently, the Boy Scouts revoked James Dale's Boy Scout Adult membership, upon learning that he was a homosexual, and he sued the Boy Scouts for violating the provisions of LAD.

In 1978, at the age of eight, James Dale joined a Cub Scout Pack and remained a member until 1981, when he became a member of a Boy Scout Troop. He remained a youth member until he reached age 18 in 1988. During that time he earned more than 25 merit badges. In 1989 he sought and received adult membership and became an Assistant Scoutmaster, a position that he held for about a year and a half. About that time, he left home to attend Rutgers University and, while at college, acknowledged for the first time that he was gay. Shortly thereafter Dale became copresident of the Rutgers University Lesbian/Gay Alliance. Then, in July 1990, while attending a seminar on the health needs of lesbian and gay teenagers, Dale was interviewed by the *Star-Ledger,* which subsequently published an article that included

Dale's photograph and identified him as the "co-president of the Rutgers University Lesbian/Gay Alliance." Later that month, Dale received from the Boy Scouts a letter revoking his membership and asking him to "sever any relations [he] may have with the Boy Scouts of America." Dale appealed unsuccessfully, and finally, in 1992, he filed a lawsuit in state court against the Boy Scouts of America for discriminating against him in violation of LAD.

The trial court concluded that Dale was "a sexually active homosexual" and the Boy Scouts had always excluded "active homosexual[s]." The court also ruled that the provisions of LAD did not apply to the Boy Scouts because it was not a "public accommodation." A state appellate court reversed and remanded upon concluding that the Boy Scouts were a "public accommodation." The state supreme court affirmed that decision, and the Boy Scouts appealed to the Supreme Court, which granted review.

The decision of the state supreme court was reversed in a five-to-four decision, and the opinion for the Court was delivered by Chief Justice Rehnquist. Justices Stevens and Souter each filed dissenting opinions, and were joined by Justices Ginsburg and Breyer.

☐ *Chief Justice REHNQUIST delivered the opinion of the Court.*

In *Roberts v. United States Jaycees,* 468 U.S. 609 (1984), we observed that "implicit in the right to engage in activities protected by the First Amendment" is "a corresponding right to associate with others in pursuit of a wide variety of political, social, economic, educational, religious, and cultural ends." This right is crucial in preventing the majority from imposing its views on groups that would rather express other, perhaps unpopular, ideas. Government actions that may unconstitutionally burden this freedom may take many forms, one of which is "intrusion into the internal structure or affairs of an association" like a "regulation that forces the group to accept members it does not desire." Forcing a group to accept certain members may impair the ability of the group to express those views, and only those views, that it intends to express. Thus, "[f]reedom of association plainly presupposes a freedom not to associate."

The forced inclusion of an unwanted person in a group infringes the group's freedom of expressive association if the presence of that person affects in a significant way the group's ability to advocate public or private viewpoints. *New York State Club Assn., Inc. v. City of New York,* 487 U.S. 1 (1988). But the freedom of expressive association, like many freedoms, is not absolute. We have held that the freedom could be overridden "by regulations adopted to serve compelling state interests, unrelated to the suppression of ideas, that cannot be achieved through means significantly less restrictive of associational freedoms." *Roberts.*

To determine whether a group is protected by the First Amendment's expressive associational right, we must determine whether the group engages in "expressive association." The First Amendment's protection of expressive association is not reserved for advocacy groups. But to come within its ambit, a group must engage in some form of expression, whether it be public or private.

Because this is a First Amendment case where the ultimate conclusions of law are virtually inseparable from findings of fact, we are obligated to independently review the factual record to ensure that the state court's judgment does not unlawfully intrude on free expression. The record reveals the following. The Boy Scouts is a private, nonprofit organization. According to its mission statement: "It is the mission of the Boy Scouts of America to serve others by helping to instill values in young people and, in other ways, to prepare them to make ethical choices over their lifetime in achieving their full potential." "The values we strive to instill are based on those found in the Scout Oath and Law." . . .

Thus, the general mission of the Boy Scouts is clear: "[T]o instill values in young people." The Boy Scouts seeks to instill these values by having its adult leaders spend time with the youth members, instructing and engaging them in activities like camping, archery, and fishing. During the time spent with the youth members, the scoutmasters and assistant scoutmasters inculcate them with the Boy Scouts' values—both expressly and by example. It seems indisputable that an association that seeks to transmit such a system of values engages in expressive activity.

Given that the Boy Scouts engages in expressive activity, we must determine whether the forced inclusion of Dale as an assistant scoutmaster would significantly affect the Boy Scouts' ability to advocate public or private viewpoints. This inquiry necessarily requires us first to explore, to a limited extent, the nature of the Boy Scouts' view of homosexuality.

The values the Boy Scouts seeks to instill are "based on" those listed in the Scout Oath and Law. The Boy Scouts explains that the Scout Oath and Law provide "a positive moral code for living; they are a list of do's rather than don'ts." The Boy Scouts asserts that homosexual conduct is inconsistent with the values embodied in the Scout Oath and Law, particularly with the values represented by the terms "morally straight" and "clean."

Obviously, the Scout Oath and Law do not expressly mention sexuality or sexual orientation. And the terms "morally straight" and "clean" are by no means self-defining. Different people would attribute to those terms very different meanings. For example, some people may believe that engaging in homosexual conduct is not at odds with being "morally straight" and "clean." And others may believe that engaging in homosexual conduct is contrary to being "morally straight" and "clean." The Boy Scouts says it falls within the latter category. . . .

The Boy Scouts asserts that it "teach[es] that homosexual conduct is not morally straight," Brief for Petitioners, and that it does "not want to promote homosexual conduct as a legitimate form of behavior." We accept the Boy Scouts' assertion. We need not inquire further to determine the nature of the Boy Scouts' expression with respect to homosexuality. . . .

The Boy Scouts publicly expressed its views with respect to homosexual conduct by its assertions in prior litigation. For example, throughout a California case with similar facts filed in the early 1980's, the Boy Scouts consistently asserted the same position with respect to homosexuality that it asserts today. We cannot doubt that the Boy Scouts sincerely holds this view.

We must then determine whether Dale's presence as an assistant scoutmaster would significantly burden the Boy Scouts' desire to not "promote homosexual conduct as a legitimate form of behavior." As we give deference to an association's assertions regarding the nature of its expression, we must also give deference to an association's view of what would impair its expression. That is not to say that an expressive association can erect a shield against antidiscrimination laws simply by asserting that mere acceptance of a member from a particular group would impair its message. But here Dale, by his own admission, is one of a group of gay Scouts who have "become leaders in their community and are open and honest about their sexual orientation." Dale was the copresident of a gay and lesbian organization at college and remains a gay rights activist. Dale's presence in the Boy Scouts would, at the very least, force the organization to send a message, both to the youth members and the world, that the Boy Scouts accepts homosexual conduct as a legitimate form of behavior.

Hurley [*v. Irish-American Gay, Lesbian, and Bisexual Group of Boston*, 515 U.S. 557 (1995)], is illustrative on this point. There we considered whether the application of Massachusetts' public accommodations law to require the organizers of a private St. Patrick's Day parade to include among the marchers an Irish-American gay, lesbian, and bisexual group, GLIB, violated the parade organizers' First Amendment rights. We noted that the parade organizers did not wish to exclude the GLIB members because of their sexual orientations, but because they wanted to march behind a GLIB banner. We observed: "[A] contingent marching behind the organization's banner would at least bear witness to the fact that some Irish are gay, lesbian, or bisexual, and the presence of the organized marchers would suggest their view that people of their sexual orientations have as much claim to unqualified social acceptance as heterosexuals. The parade's organizers may not believe these facts about Irish sexuality to be so, or they may object to unqualified social acceptance of gays and lesbians or have some other reason for wishing to keep GLIB's message out of the parade. But whatever the reason, it boils down to the choice of a speaker not to propound a particular point of view, and that choice is presumed to lie beyond the government's power to control." Here, we have found that the Boy Scouts believes that homosexual conduct is inconsistent with the values it seeks to instill in its youth members; it will not "promote homosexual conduct as a legitimate form of behavior." As the presence of GLIB in Boston's St. Patrick's Day parade would have interfered with the parade organizers' choice not to propound a particular point of view, the presence of Dale as an assistant scoutmaster would just as surely interfere with the Boy Scouts' choice not to propound a point of view contrary to its beliefs. . . .

Having determined that the Boy Scouts is an expressive association and that the forced inclusion of Dale would significantly affect its expression, we inquire whether the application of New Jersey's public accommodations law to require that the Boy Scouts accept Dale as an assistant scoutmaster runs afoul of the Scouts' freedom of expressive association. We conclude that it does.

State public accommodations laws were originally enacted to prevent discrimination in traditional places of public accommodation—like inns and trains. Many on the list are what one would expect to be places where the public is invited. For example, the statute includes as places of public accommodation taverns, restaurants, retail shops, and public libraries. But the statute also includes places that often may not carry with them open invitations to the public, like summer camps and roof gardens. In this case, the New Jersey Supreme Court went a step further and applied its public accommodations law to a private entity without even attempting to tie the term "place" to a physical location. As the definition of "public accommodation" has expanded from clearly commercial entities, such as restaurants, bars, and hotels, to membership organizations such as the Boy Scouts, the potential for conflict between state public accommodations laws and the First Amendment rights of organizations has increased.

We recognized in cases such as *Roberts* and *Duarte* that States have a compelling interest in eliminating discrimination against women in public accommodations. But in each of these cases we went on to conclude that the enforcement of these statutes would not materially interfere with the ideas that the organization sought to express. In *Roberts*, we said "[i]ndeed, the Jaycees has failed to demonstrate any serious burden on the male members' freedom of expressive association." We thereupon concluded in each of these cases that the organizations' First Amendment rights were not violated by the application of the States' public accommodations laws.

In *Hurley*, we said that public accommodations laws "are well within the State's usual power to enact when a legislature has reason to believe that a given group is the target of discrimination, and they do not, as a general matter, violate the First or Fourteenth Amendments." But we went on to note that in that case "the Massachusetts [public accommodations] law has been applied in a peculiar way" because "any contingent of protected individuals with a message would have the right to participate in petitioners' speech, so that the communication produced by the private organizers would be shaped by all those protected by the law who wish to join in with some expressive demonstration of their own." And in the associational freedom cases such as *Roberts, Duarte,* and *New York State Club Assn.,* after finding a compelling state interest, the Court went on to examine whether or not the application of the state law would impose any "serious burden" on the organization's rights of expressive association. So in these cases, the associational interest in freedom of expression has been set on one side of the scale, and the State's interest on the other. . . .

The judgment of the New Jersey Supreme Court is reversed, and the cause remanded for further proceedings not inconsistent with this opinion.

☐ *Justice STEVENS, with whom Justice SOUTER, Justice GINSBURG, and Justice BREYER join, dissenting.*

The majority holds that New Jersey's law violates BSA's right to associate and its right to free speech. But that law does not "impos[e] any serious burdens" on BSA's "collective effort on behalf of [its] shared goals," *Roberts v. United States Jaycees,* 468 U.S. 609 (1984), nor does it force BSA to communicate any message that it does not wish to endorse. New Jersey's law, therefore, abridges no constitutional right of the Boy Scouts. . . .

In light of BSA's self-proclaimed ecumenism, furthermore, it is even more difficult to discern any shared goals or common moral stance on homosexuality. Insofar as religious matters are concerned, BSA's bylaws state that it is "absolutely nonsectarian in its attitude toward religious training." "The BSA does not define what constitutes duty to God or the practice of religion. This is the responsibility of parents and religious leaders." In fact, many diverse religious organizations sponsor local Boy Scout troops. Because a number of religious groups do not view homosexuality as immoral or wrong and reject discrimination against homosexuals, it is exceedingly difficult to believe that BSA nonetheless adopts a single particular religious or moral philosophy when it comes to sexual orientation. This is especially so in light of the fact that Scouts are advised to seek guidance on sexual matters from their religious leaders (and Scoutmasters are told to refer Scouts to them); BSA surely is aware that some religions do not teach that homosexuality is wrong.

The Court seeks to fill the void by pointing to a statement of "policies and procedures relating to homosexuality and Scouting" signed by BSA's President and Chief Scout Executive in 1978 and addressed to the members of the Executive Committee of the national organization. [However, four] aspects of the 1978 policy statement are relevant to the proper disposition of this case. First, at most this letter simply adopts an exclusionary membership policy. But simply adopting such a policy has never been considered sufficient, by itself, to prevail on a right to associate claim.

Second, the 1978 policy was never publicly expressed—unlike, for example, the Scout's duty to be "obedient." It was an internal memorandum, never circulated beyond the few members of BSA's Executive Committee. It remained, in effect, a secret Boy Scouts policy.

Third, it is apparent that the draftsmen of the policy statement foresaw the possibility that laws against discrimination might one day be amended to protect homosexuals from employment discrimination. Their statement clearly provided that, in the event such a law conflicted with their policy, a Scout's duty to be "obedient" and "obe[y] the laws," even if "he thinks [the laws] are unfair" would prevail in such a contingency. In 1978, however, BSA apparently did not consider it to be a serious possibility that a State might one day characterize the Scouts as a "place of public accommodation" with a duty to open its membership to all qualified individuals. The portions of the statement dealing with membership simply assume that membership in the Scouts is a "privilege" that BSA is free to grant or to withhold. The statement does not address the question whether the publicly proclaimed duty to obey the law should prevail over the private discriminatory policy if, and when, a conflict between the two should arise—as it now has in New Jersey. At the very least, then, the statement reflects no unequivocal view on homosexuality. . . .

Fourth, the 1978 statement simply says that homosexuality is not "appropriate." It makes no effort to connect that statement to a shared goal or expressive activity of the Boy Scouts. Whatever values BSA seeks to instill in Scouts, the idea that homosexuality is not "appropriate" appears entirely unconnected to, and is mentioned nowhere in, the myriad of publicly declared values and creeds of the BSA. That idea does not appear to be among any of the principles actually taught to Scouts. Rather, the 1978 policy appears to be no more than a private statement of a few BSA executives that the organization wishes to exclude gays—and that wish has nothing to do with any expression BSA actually engages in. . . .

It is clear, then, that nothing in these policy statements supports BSA's claim. The only policy written before the revocation of Dale's membership was an equivocal, undisclosed statement that evidences no connection between the group's discriminatory intentions and its expressive interests. The later policies demonstrate a brief—though ultimately abandoned—attempt to tie BSA's exclusion to its expression, but other than a single sentence, BSA fails to show that it ever taught Scouts that homosexuality is not "morally straight" or "clean," or that such a view was part of the group's collective efforts to foster a belief. Furthermore, BSA's policy statements fail to establish any clear, consistent, and unequivocal position on homosexuality. . . .

BSA's claim finds no support in our cases. We have recognized "a right to associate for the purpose of engaging in those activities protected by the First Amendment—speech, assembly, petition for the redress of grievances, and the exercise of religion." *Roberts*. And we have acknowledged that "when the State interferes with individuals' selection of those with whom they wish to join in a common endeavor, freedom of association may be implicated." But "[t]he right to associate for expressive purposes is not absolute"; rather, "the nature and degree of constitutional protection afforded freedom of association may vary depending on the extent to which the constitutionally protected liberty is at stake in a given case." Indeed, the right to associate does not mean "that in every setting in which individuals exercise some discrimination in choosing associates, their selective process of inclusion and exclusion is protected by the Constitution." *New York State Club Assn., Inc. v. City of New York*, 487 U.S. 1 (1988). . . .

Several principles are made perfectly clear by *Jaycees* and [*Board of Directors of Rotary Int'l v.*] *Rotary Club*. First, to prevail on a claim of expressive association in the face of a State's antidiscrimination law, it is not enough simply to engage in some kind of expressive activity. Both the Jaycees and the Rotary Club engaged in expressive activity protected by the First Amendment, yet that fact was not dispositive. Second, it is not enough to adopt an openly avowed exclusionary membership policy. Both the Jaycees and the Rotary Club did that as well. Third, it is not sufficient merely to articulate some connection between the group's expressive activities and its exclusionary policy. The Rotary Club, for example, justified its male-only membership policy by pointing to the "aspect of fellowship that is enjoyed by the [exclusively] male membership" and by claiming that only with an exclusively male membership could it "operate effectively" in foreign countries.

Rather, in *Jaycees*, we asked whether Minnesota's Human Rights Law requiring the admission of women "impose[d] any serious burdens" on the group's "collective effort on behalf of [its] shared goals." Notwithstanding the group's obvious publicly stated exclusionary policy, we did not view the inclusion of women as a "serious burden" on the Jaycees' ability to engage in the protected speech of its choice. . . . The relevant question is whether the mere inclusion of the person at issue would "impose any serious burden," "affect in any significant way," or be "a substantial restraint upon" the organization's "shared goals," "basic goals," or "collective effort to foster beliefs." Accordingly, it is necessary to examine what, exactly, are BSA's shared goals and the degree to which its expressive activities would be burdened, affected, or restrained by including homosexuals.

The evidence before this Court makes it exceptionally clear that BSA has, at most, simply adopted an exclusionary membership policy and has no shared goal of disapproving of homosexuality. BSA's mission statement and federal charter say nothing on the matter; its official membership policy is silent; its Scout Oath and Law—and accompanying definitions—are devoid of any view on the topic; its guidance for Scouts and Scoutmasters on sexuality declare that such matters are "not construed to be Scouting's proper area," but are the province of a Scout's parents and pastor; and BSA's posture respecting religion tolerates a wide variety of views on the issue of homosexuality. Moreover, there is simply no evidence that BSA otherwise teaches anything in this area, or that it instructs Scouts on matters involving homosexuality in ways not conveyed in the Boy Scout or Scoutmaster Handbooks. In short, Boy Scouts of America is simply silent on homosexuality. There is no shared goal or collective effort to foster a belief about homosexuality at all—let alone one that is significantly burdened by admitting homosexuals. . . .

Equally important is BSA's failure to adopt any clear position on homosexuality. BSA's temporary, though ultimately abandoned, view that homosexuality is incompatible with being "morally straight" and "clean" is a far cry from the clear, unequivocal statement necessary to prevail on its claim. Despite the solitary sentences in the 1991 and 1992 policies, the group continued to disclaim any single religious or moral position as a general matter and actively eschewed teaching any lesson on sexuality. It also continued to define "morally straight" and "clean" in the Boy Scout and Scoutmaster Handbooks without any reference to homosexuality. As noted earlier, nothing in our cases suggests that a group can prevail on a right to expressive association if it, effectively, speaks out of both sides of its mouth. A State's antidiscrimination law does not impose a "serious burden" or a "substantial restraint" upon the group's "shared goals" if the group itself is unable to identify its own stance with any clarity. . . .

The majority's argument relies exclusively on *Hurley v. Irish-American Gay, Lesbian and Bisexual Group of Boston, Inc.*, 515 U.S. 557 (1995). In that case, petitioners John Hurley and the South Boston Allied War Veterans Council ran a privately operated St. Patrick's Day parade. Respondent, an organization known as "GLIB," represented a contingent of gays, lesbians, and bisexuals who sought to march in the petitioners' parade "as a way to express pride in their Irish heritage as openly gay, lesbian, and bisexual individuals." When the parade organizers refused GLIB's admission, GLIB brought suit under Massachusetts' antidiscrimination law. That statute, like New Jersey's law, prohibited discrimination on account of sexual orientation in any place of public accommodation, which the state courts interpreted to include the parade. Petitioners argued that forcing them to include GLIB in their parade would violate their free speech rights.

We agreed. We first pointed out that the St. Patrick's Day parade—like most every parade—is an inherently expressive undertaking. Next, we reaffirmed that the government may not compel anyone to proclaim a belief with which he or she disagrees. We then found that GLIB's marching in the parade would be an expressive act suggesting the view "that people of their sexual orientations have as much claim to unqualified social acceptance as heterosexuals." Finally, we held that GLIB's participation in the parade "would likely be perceived" as the parade organizers' own speech—or at least as a view which they approved—because of a parade organizer's customary control over who marches in the parade. Though *Hurley* has a superficial similarity to the present case, a close inspection reveals a wide gulf between that case and the one before us today. . . .

Dale's inclusion in the Boy Scouts is nothing like the case in *Hurley*. His participation sends no cognizable message to the Scouts or to the world. Unlike GLIB, Dale did not carry a banner or a sign; he did not distribute any fact sheet; and he expressed no intent to send any message. If there is any kind of message being sent, then, it is by the mere act of joining the Boy Scouts. Such an act does not constitute an instance of symbolic speech under the First Amendment. . . .

Furthermore, it is not likely that BSA would be understood to send any message, either to Scouts or to the world, simply by admitting someone as a member. Over the years, BSA has generously welcomed over 87 million young Americans into its ranks. In 1992 over one million adults were active BSA members. The notion that an organization of that size and enormous prestige implicitly endorses the views that each of those adults may express in a non-Scouting context is simply mind-boggling. . . .

Unfavorable opinions about homosexuals "have ancient roots." *Bowers v. Hardwick,* 478 U.S. 186 (1986). Like equally atavistic opinions about certain racial groups, those roots have been nourished by sectarian doctrine. Over the years, however, interaction with real people, rather than mere adherence to traditional ways of thinking about members of unfamiliar classes, have modified those opinions. A few examples: The American Psychiatric Association's and the American Psychological Association's removal of "homosexuality" from their lists of mental disorders; a move toward greater understanding within some religious communities; Justice BLACKMUN's classic opinion in *Bowers*; Georgia's invalidation of the statute upheld in *Bowers*; and New Jersey's enactment of the provision at issue in this case.

That such prejudices are still prevalent and that they have caused serious and tangible harm to countless members of the class New Jersey seeks to protect are established matters of fact that neither the Boy Scouts nor the Court disputes. That harm can only be aggravated by the creation of a constitutional shield for a policy that is itself the product of a habitual way of thinking about strangers. As Justice BRANDEIS so wisely advised, "we must be ever on our guard, lest we erect our prejudices into legal principles."

If we would guide by the light of reason, we must let our minds be bold. I respectfully dissent.

6

FREEDOM FROM AND OF
RELIGION

Religious freedom is guaranteed in the two opening clauses of the
First Amendment: "Congress shall make no law respecting an establishment of religion, or prohibiting the free exercise thereof." Together, the clauses guarantee freedom from and of religion by pointing
in opposite directions. The establishment clause points toward a principle of the separation of government from religion; neither should involve itself with the other. The free exercise clause suggests a principle
of voluntarism—freedom from coercion in choosing a religion or no
religion.

Religious freedom has never been absolute, however. The First
Amendment, as the Court observed in *Cantwell v. Connecticut*, 310 U.S.
296 (1940), "embraces two concepts—freedom to believe and freedom
to act. The first is absolute but, in the nature of things, the second cannot be. Conduct remains subject to regulation of society." Drawing on
the distinction between belief and action, the Court thus wrote into
constitutional law a third principle of religious freedom that runs back
to Thomas Jefferson, who, in his *Bill for Establishing Religious Freedom* for
the state of Virginia in 1779, observed that "the acts of the body," unlike "the operations of the mind, are subject to the coercion of the
laws."[1]

Nor does the text and historical record of the First Amendment
provide simple interpretive solutions for the continuing controversies
in constitutional politics over religious freedom. What is "an establishment of religion," for example, and what is a "law respecting" the establishment of religion? What is and who defines *religion*? Many of the
contemporary disputes over the separation of government and religion,

moreover, could not have been foreseen during the founding period; there was no controversy over school prayer because there was no system of public education.

The traditions and aspirations of religious freedom from the colonial through the revolutionary period and to the time the First Amendment was adopted and ratified in 1791 were complex and occasionally conflicting. Although populated by many escaping religious persecution in England or on the European continent, colonial settlements remained religious enclaves, discriminating against those of other faiths. In Massachusetts, the established Congregational Church taxed and harassed Quakers, Baptists, and others. In Virginia and four other southern colonies, the (Anglican) Church of England was established.

As the colonies developed and their leaders moved toward the Declaration of Independence, religious freedom grew and began to take on new meaning. With that conceptual change came a rejection of the European understanding of established church-states. England, Scotland, and Germany had established churches, while the Roman Catholic Church was established in Italy, Spain, and elsewhere. But in 1774 when the British Parliament passed a statute establishing both Anglicanism and Catholicism in Canada, the Continental Congress protested with "astonishment, that a British Parliament should ever consent to establish in that country a religion that has deluged [England] in blood, and dispersed bigotry, persecution, murder and rebellion through every part of the world."[2]

By the 1770s, the original thirteen colonies, always predominantly Protestant, were on their way to a new form of establishmentism, unlike the European single state-church denomination. Christianity or Protestantism, in contrast with Judaism, Islam, and Hinduism (as well as, for some colonists, Catholicism), was established in the northern colonies, but allowed for multiple churches and denominations. Maryland's "declaration of rights" in 1776, for instance, recognized the religious freedom of "persons professing the Christian religion." In 1778, South Carolina's constitution proclaimed that "the Christian Protestant religion shall be deemed . . . the established religion of this state." Notably, four colonies (Rhode Island, Pennsylvania, Delaware, and New Jersey) never established a state religion.[3] In the 1770s, Patrick Henry reflected these changes and championed *nonpreferentialism*, that is, no governmental aid for particular religions but support for all religions. Nonpreferentialism, however, fell out of favor in the 1790s and early nineteenth century as states abandoned established churches and religions as well as religious qualifications for holding state office.

Religious freedom found expression in Article VI of the Constitu-

tion, providing that "no religious Test shall ever be required as a Qualification to any Office or public Trust under the United States." But that
was not enough to silence critics pressing for the addition of a bill of
rights. When defending the Constitution during Virginia's ratifying
convention on June 12, 1788, Madison sought to reassure those fearing
government would deny religious freedom:

> If there were a majority of one sect, a bill of rights would be a
> poor protection for liberty. Happily for the states, they enjoy the ut-
> most freedom of religion. This freedom arises from that multiplicity
> of sects, which pervades America, and which is the best and only
> security for religious liberty in any society. For where there is such
> a variety of sects, there cannot be a majority of any one sect to op-
> press and persecute the rest. . . . A particular state might concur in
> one religious project. But the United States abound in such a vari-
> ety of sects, that it is a strong security against religious persecution,
> and it is sufficient to authorize a conclusion, that no one sect will
> ever be able to outnumber or depress the rest.[4]

Madison failed to dissuade those seeking further protection for religious freedom. While ratifying the Constitution, the Virginia convention proposed the addition of a bill of rights, including the following:

> That religion or the duty which we owe to our Creator, and the
> manner of discharging it can be directed only by reason and con-
> viction, not by force or violence, and therefore all men have an
> equal, natural and unalienable right to the free exercise of religion
> according to the dictates of conscience, and that no particular reli-
> gious sect or society ought to be favored or established by Law in
> preference to others.[5]

Defenders of religious freedom, however, were not of one mind.
Some maintained that disestablishment of church and state was neces-
sary to safeguard religion from the corrosive influence of politics.
When celebrating the purity of evangelical faith in 1644, Roger
Williams proclaimed that God commanded that "the most Paganish,
Jewish, Turkish, or Antichristian consciences and worships, be granted
to all men in all Nations and Countries." And he invoked the metaphor
of a "wall of separation" in defense of the integrity of religion.

> First, the faithful labors of many witnesses of Jesus Christ, extant to
> the world, abundantly proving that the church of the Jews under
> the Old Testament in the antitype were both separate from the
> world; and that when they have opened a gap in the hedge or *wall
> of separation* between the garden of the church and the wilderness
> of the world, God hath ever broke down the wall itself, removed
> the candlestick, and made His garden a wilderness, as at this day.

And that therefore if He will ever please to restore His garden and paradise again, it must of necessity be walled in peculiarly unto Himself from the world; and that all that shall be saved out of the world are to be transplanted out of the wilderness of the world, and added unto His church or garden.[6]

More than 150 years later, President Jefferson again relied on the metaphor of a wall of separation in his famous letter to the Danbury Baptist Association in 1802:

Believing with you that religion is a matter which lies solely between man and his God, that he owes account to none other for his faith or his worship, that the legislative powers of government reach actions only, and not opinions, I contemplate with sovereign reverence that act of the whole American people which declared that their legislature should "make no law respecting an establishment of religion, or prohibiting the free exercise thereof," thus building a wall of separation between Church and State.[7]

Unlike those who shared Roger Williams's view, Jefferson was more concerned about insulating government from the influences of religion and religious fervor. In his home state of Virginia, Jefferson had fought for religious freedom—freedom not just for Protestants or Christians. As he reflected about the opposition in 1779 to his "Bill for Establishing Religious Freedom":

Where the preamble declares, that coercion is a departure from the plan of the holy author of our religion, an amendment was proposed, by inserting the word "Jesus Christ," that it should read, "a departure from the plan of Jesus Christ, the holy author of our religion;" the insertion was rejected by a great majority, in proof that they meant to comprehend, within the mantle of its protection, the Jew and the Gentile, the Christian and Mohometan, the Hindoo, and Infidel of every denomination.[8]

James Madison agreed that a wall of separation would help preserve the integrity of government, but he also thought that it might benefit religion as well. Madison, along with Jefferson, opposed proposals to establish religious taxes in Virginia. In his famous "Memorial and Remonstrance against Religious Assessments" in 1785, he persuasively argued against government support of religion. Governmental assistance to religious establishments, Madison maintained, tended to divide society into factions and produce "pride and indolence in the clergy; ignorance and servility in the laity; in both, superstition, bigotry and persecution." Nor did Madison think government depended on the support of religion. "That is not a just government," he wrote in 1792, in which "a man's religious rights are violated by penalties, or fettered by tests, or taxes by a hierarchy."[9]

But Madison proved unsuccessful in persuading the First Congress that the states as well as the federal government should be barred from passing laws respecting the establishment of religion and religious freedom. On June 8, 1789, in the House of Representatives, Madison introduced a series of proposed amendments to the Constitution, among them: "The civil rights of none shall be abridged on account of religious belief or worship, nor shall any national religion be established, nor shall the full and equal rights of conscience be in any manner, or on any pretext, infringed." And another: "No State shall violate the equal rights of conscience, or the freedom of the press, or the trial by jury in criminal cases."[10]

Without debate, Madison's proposals were referred to a special committee, of which he was a member. Within a week, the committee reported back to the full House. Madison's proposals remained intact, except for some editing: the words "civil rights" and "national" were deleted. The House devoted a single day to considering the amendment. As a result of a motion by Fisher Ames, and further stylistic changes, the revised amendment read: "Congress shall make no law establishing religion, or prohibiting the free exercise thereof, nor shall the rights of conscience be infringed."

The House's proposed amendments were debated in secret by the Senate in September. The *Senate Journal*, however, records three unsuccessful motions to change the amendment on September 3. All would have narrowed the amendment to ban establishments preferring "one religious sect or society," or "any particular denomination of religion in preference to another." But six weeks later, the Senate voted to amend the House's version to read: "Congress shall make no law establishing articles of faith or a mode of worship, or prohibiting the free exercise of religion." This change narrowed the religion clauses to barring Congress only from endorsing a single denomination or national religion. Under it, Congress could provide nondiscriminatory government aid to all religions (something Baptists bitterly opposed).

The Senate's changes provoked opposition in the House. A joint conference committee, chaired by Madison, was created to resolve the differences between the House and Senate versions of the proposed amendments. Finally, on September 24, the House agreed to accept the Senate's version of other amendments on the condition that the amendment on religion be changed to its present form: "Congress shall make no laws respecting an establishment of religion, or prohibiting the free exercise thereof." The Senate agreed; Congress adopted the religion clauses.

Madison's efforts to guarantee "the full and equal rights of conscience" and to forbid the states from violating "the equal rights of conscience" nevertheless failed. States continued vestiges of establishment and restrictions on religious freedom. Massachusetts, for one, denied Jews the right to hold public office until 1828 and did not remove its final vestiges of establishment until 1833.

Not until *Cantwell v. Connecticut*, 310 U.S. 296 (1940), did the Hughes Court hold the free exercise clause applicable to the states. In Justice Roberts's words, "The Fourteenth Amendment has rendered the legislatures of the states as incompetent as Congress to enact" laws denying the free exercise of religion. Seven years later, the Vinson Court made the establishment clause applicable to the states in *Everson v. Board of Education of Ewing Township* (1947) (excerpted below), in which Justice Black, for a bare majority, wrote the high-wall theory of the separation of government from religion into constitutional law but upheld the reimbursement of the costs of transporting children to private religious schools.

Since *Cantwell* and *Everson*, controversy has infused and surrounded the Court's interpretation of the religion clauses. But before turning to the Court's rulings and rival interpretations of the religion clauses, it may be helpful to consider two different theoretical approaches to religious freedom that have animated constitutional politics: nonpreferentialism and the high-wall theory of the separation of government and religion.

President Ronald Reagan's attorney general, Edwin Meese III, championed the nonpreferentialism position, advocated over 200 years ago by Patrick Henry, when he wrote,

> the First Amendment forbade the establishment of a particular religion or a particular church. It also precluded the federal government from favoring one church, or one church group over another. That's what the First Amendment did, but it did not go further. It did not, for example, preclude federal aid to religious groups so long as that assistance furthered a public purpose and so long as it did not discriminate in favor of one religious group against another.[11]

Chief Justices Burger and Rehnquist, along with other justices, shared this view, as well as political scientist Walter Berns. "There was no dispute with respect to the principles on which the Constitution was built," Berns claims, when observing that "stated in its most radical form, [the Framers] all agreed that our institutions do *not* presuppose a providential Supreme Being." But, he adds, "whereas our institutions do not presuppose a Supreme Being, their preservation does." And on that basis Berns reasons that "[l]iberal democracy must preserve what it cannot itself generate, and it must do this without jeopardizing the private character of religion." Thus *Everson*, from Berns's perspective, wrongly launched "an interpretation under which the First Amendment forbids precisely what many a man in the First Congress went to such pains to protect—namely, public support of religion, albeit on a nondiscriminatory basis."[12] However, Justice Black's opinion, although writing the high-wall theory into constitutional law, allowed reimbursement for the cost of busing children to private religious schools on a "child benefit" theory. In short, nonpreferentialism holds that government may aid religion, but not support or endorse any particular religion.

By contrast, the four dissenters in *Everson* argued for a "strict neutrality" interpretation of Jefferson's high-wall theory of separation of government and religion. Historian Leonard Levy supports this interpretation when attacking the nonpreferentialist's approach to the religion clauses:

> The fundamental defect of the nonpreferential interpretation is that it results in the unhistorical contention that the First Amendment augmented a nonexistent congressional power to legislate in the field of religion [since Article I does not give Congress any legislative powers over religion]. . . . Preferring 'religion over irreligion' is a red herring; the question of such a preference was not an issue. The government possessed no power to aid irreligion or religion. . . .
>
> Nonpreferentialism, unfortunately, is but a pose for those who think that religion needs to be patronized and promoted by government. When they speak of nonpreferential aid, they speak euphemistically as if they are not partisan. In fact they really are preferentialists. . . . Nonpreferentialists prefer government sponsorship and subsidy of religion rather than allow it to compete on its merits against irreligion and indifference. They prefer government nurture of religion because they mistakenly dread government neutrality as too risky, and so they condemn it as hostility. They prefer what they call, again euphemistically, accommodation.[13]

Conflicts in constitutional politics over religious freedom, however, involve not only deciding between and applying the nonpreferentialist or accommodationist approach versus the high-wall theory of separation of government and religion. In the contemporary administrative state, laws and exemptions from laws may be challenged for violating either the establishment clause or the free exercise clause. There is an essential tension between these two guarantees. Exemption from the draft for conscientious (religious) objection to killing and war, for instance, may be defended by claiming the free exercise clause, but attacked under the establishment clause for aiding religion. Scholarships, grants, tax credits, or reimbursements have, likewise, been viewed as infringing on, alternatively, one or the other religion clauses. In *Witters v. Washington Department of Services for the Blind*, 474 U.S. 481 (1986), for example, the Court confronted a controversy over the denial of aid for vocational rehabilitation, available under state law, to Larry Witters by the Washington State Commission for the Blind. Witters's application for financial aid was denied because he wanted to pursue a Bible studies degree at a private Christian college. The commission's denial of financial aid might have been viewed as infringing on Witters's free exercise of religion, but the Washington State Supreme Court ruled that giving assistance to Witters would have the primary effect of advancing religion and so violated the establishment clause. On appeal, the Supreme Court reversed that decision and held that such assistance does not violate the establishment clause. Subsequently, a bare majority of the Rehnquist Court extended that ruling in *Zobrest v. Catalina Foothills School District*, 509 U.S. 1 (1993) (excerpted in Section A), when upholding public funding for a sign-language interpreter for a deaf high school student who attended a religious school. And by a six-to-three vote the Court, then, extended *Witters* and *Zobrest* to uphold the loan of computer software and hardware to private religious schools, in *Mitchell v. Helms*, 530 U.S. 793 (2000); and in *Zelman v. Simmons-Harris* (2003) (excerpted below in Section A) upheld vouchers for public school students to attend religious schools.

The Court drew a line, however, and addressed the tensions between the (dis)establishment and free exercise clauses in *Locke v. Davey* (2004) (excerpted below in Section B). There, the Court held that a student awarded a scholarship who wanted to earn a degree in theology could be barred from using it for that purpose, under Washington state's constitutional bar against public expenditures for religion, over his objections that that violated the First Amendment guarantee for the free exercise of religion. Writing for the Court, Chief Justice Rehnquist distinguished *Zelman* and other (dis)establishment clause rulings permitting indirect aid for religious schools, whether through vouchers, computer software, or scholarships, on the ground that those programs directly benefit students and turned on individual student choices. Thus, although in *Witters v. Washington Department of Services for the Blind*, the Court held that the (dis)establishment clause was not violated by permitting Witters to use a state scholarship to pursue biblical studies, Witters never received the scholarship because on remand state courts held that the state constitution imposed a more strict separation of government from religion than the federal constitution. When Joshua Davey subsequently argued that the state's constitutional provision barring his use of a scholarship to pursue a pastoral degree violated the First Amendment free exercise clause in *Locke v. Davey*, the Court ruled that the free exercise clause does not compel what the (dis)establishment clause would permit. In *Locke* Justices Scalia and Thomas dissented and objected to the majority's permitting states to discriminate against religion.

Notes

1. Thomas Jefferson, in *The Writings of Thomas Jefferson*, Vol. 2, ed. Paul Ford (New York: Putnam's Sons, 1892–1899), 237–239.

2. "Continental Congress to the People of Great Britain, October 21, 1774," in *The Founders' Constitution*, Vol. 5, ed. Philip Kurland and Ralph Lerner (Chicago: University of Chicago Press, 1987), 61.

3. See Leonard Levy, *The Establishment Clause: Religion and the First Amendment* (New York: Macmillan, 1986), 61.

4. James Madison, in *The Founders' Constitution*, Vol. 5, ed. Kurland and Lerner, 88.

5. "Virginia Ratifying Convention," in *The Founders' Constitution*, Vol. 5, ed. Kurland and Lerner, 89.

6. Quoted in Levy, *The Establishment Clause*, 184.

7. Thomas Jefferson, "Letter to Danbury Baptist Association, January 1, 1802," in *The Founders' Constitution*, Vol. 5, ed. Kurland and Lerner, 96.

8. Thomas Jefferson, in *The Founders' Constitution*, Vol. 5, ed. Kurland and Lerner, 85.

9. James Madison, *The Papers of James Madison*, Vol. 14, ed. Robert Rutland (Chicago: University of Chicago Press, 1983), 266–267.

10. Joseph Gales and W. W. Seaton, *The Debates and Proceedings in the Congress of the United States*, Vol. 1 (Washington, DC: Gales and Seaton, 1834–1856), 451–452.

11. Edwin Meese III, "Address before the Christian Legal Society," given in San Diego, CA, Sept. 29, 1985.

12. Walter Berns, *The First Amendment and the Future of American Democracy* (New York: Basic Books, 1976), 10, 12, 34, and 60. For similar positions, see Edward S. Corwin, "The Supreme Court as a National School Board," 14 *Law and Contemporary Problems* 3 (1949); and Michael Malbin, *Religion and Politics: The Intentions of the Authors of the First Amendment* (Washington, DC: American Enterprise Institute, 1978).

13. Levy, *The Establishment Clause*, 93–94 and 118. See also Jesse Choper, "The Establishment Clause and Aid to Parochial Schools," 56 *California Law Review* 260 (1968); and J. Choper, "Religion in the Public Schools: A Proposed Constitutional Standard," 47 *University of Minnesota Law Review* 329 (1963).

Selected Bibliography

Berns, Walter. *The First Amendment and the Future of American Democracy*. New York: Basic Books, 1976.

Steven P. Brown, *Trumping Religion: The New Christian Right, The Free Speech Clause, and the Courts*. Tuscaloosa: University of Alabama Press, 2002.

Curry, Thomas. *The First Freedoms: Church and State in America to the Passage of the First Amendment.* New York: Oxford University Press, 1986.

Howe, Mark DeWolfe. *The Garden and the Wilderness: Religion and Government in American Constitutional History.* Chicago: University of Chicago Press, 1965.

Kramnick, Isaac, and Moore, Laurence. *The Godless Constitution: The Case against Religious Correctness.* New York: W. W. Norton, 1996.

Levy, Leonard. *The Establishment Clause: Religion and the First Amendment.* New York: Macmillan, 1986.

Noonan, John T. *The Lustre of Our Country: The American Experience of Religious Freedom.* Berkeley: University of California Press, 1998.

———. *Religion, State, and the Burger Court.* New York: Prometheus Books, 1985.

Rosenblum, Nancy, ed. *Obligations of Citizenship and Demands of Faith: Religious Accommodation in Pluralistic Democracies.* Princeton, NJ: Princeton University Press, 2000.

A | *The (Dis)Establishment of Religion*

In the constitutional politics of interpreting and applying the establishment clause, the Court has been divided over three rival interpretative principles and tests for the separation of government from religion: (1) "strict separation" requires state neutrality and a secular purpose for legislation but may permit some benefits or indirect support for religion; (2) "strict neutrality" requires not merely a secular purpose for legislation but bars all laws that either aid or hinder religion (directly or indirectly); and, alternatively, (3) an "accommodationist" approach, while maintaining that laws must have a secular purpose, allows for governmental accommodation of religion in ways that further religious freedom without endorsing a particular religion.

Strict separation of government and religion holds "that government can do nothing which involves governmental support of religion or which is favorable to the cultivation of religious interests."[1] In *Everson v. Board of Education of Ewing Township* (1947) (see excerpt below), the Vinson Court embraced this theory and wrote Jefferson's metaphor of a wall of separation into constitutional law. However, the justices split five to four because the majority decided to construe New Jersey's program of reimbursing parents for the cost of busing children to private schools, including parochial schools, as a "subsidy to parents not churches." Justice Black's opinion for the majority suggested that strict separation need not preclude "child benefits" or a state's "benevolent neutrality" toward religion. So too, in *Corporation of Presiding Bishops v. Amos*, 483 U.S. 327 (1987), the Rehnquist Court ruled that the establishment clause was not violated by allowing nonprofit (Mormon) industries to hire only religiously faithful employees.

The four dissenters in *Everson* agreed that the establishment clause embodies a high-wall principle of separation, but viewed the majority's holding as a breach of the wall. In their view, strict neutrality was required; that is, religion "may not be used as a basis for classification for purposes of governmental action, whether that action be the conferring of rights or privileges or the imposition of duties or obligations."[2]

A year after *Everson*, the Court struck down a "released-time program," allowing public-school children to attend religious instruction on campus grounds, in *McCollum v. Board of Education*, 333 U.S. 203 (1948). The religious instructors were not paid by the city, but the use of the classrooms in public schools was held to violate the establishment clause. In a second case, involving students going off campus for religious instruction, however, the Court upheld the released-time program on the grounds that the religious instruction did not occur on school property, and did not involve the expenditure of public funds and there was no evidence that the students were being compelled to attend the off-campus classes on religion. In *Zorach v. Clauson*, 343 U.S. 306 (1952), dissenting Justices Black, Jackson, and Frankfurter contended that even this released-time program breached the high wall of separation between government and religion.

The Vinson Court thus agreed that the establishment clause requires state neutrality and that governmental programs must have a secular purpose, but disagreed over whether religion might indirectly benefit or receive assistance from government. As the Court's composition changed, the Warren Court moved constitutional law in the direction of a "strict neutrality" version of the high wall of separation, and then the Burger and Rehnquist Courts swung back toward a nonpreferentialist position, allowing governmental accommodation of religion. Since *Everson*, though, the justices have remained split on the tests for determining whether public-school facilities may be used for religious purposes and in what other ways government may accommodate religion.

In *Widmar v. Vincent*, 454 U.S. 263 (1981), the Burger Court struck down a Missouri statute prohibiting the use of university buildings and grounds "for purposes of religious worship," which had been used to deny a student religious group access to the facilities of a state university. There, the Court observed that "[u]niversity students are . . . less impressionable than younger students and should be able to appreciate that the university's policy is one of neutrality towards religion." The Court's holding in *Widmar* that an equal access policy at the level of universities did not violate the establishment clause encouraged Congress to extend that principle to primary and secondary schools. Congress did so with the passage of the Equal Access Act of 1984, which bars public schools from discriminating against meetings of student activity groups on school grounds on the basis of "religious, political, philosophical or other content of the speech at such meetings."

When the constitutionality of the Equal Access Act was challenged in *Board of Education of the Westside Community Schools v. Mergens*, 496 U.S. 226 (1990), the Rehnquist Court upheld the law, with only Justice Stevens dissenting. In that case, the school board had prohibited a Christian Bible club from meeting on school grounds. The board contended that if the religious club was allowed to meet it would have to have a faculty sponsor, which in turn would violate the establishment clause. But, writing for the Court, Justice O'Connor held that the school board had violated the provisions of the Equal Access Act and that those provisions did not violate the establishment clause. In her view, the act neither had a primary effect of advancing religion nor excessively entangled government and religion, even though the student religious meetings would be held on school grounds and under the school's aegis.

Subsequently, in *Lamb's Chapel v. Center Moriches Union Free School District*, 508 U.S. 384 (1993), the Court unanimously held that a school district's denial of a religious group's use of school facilities for meetings after school hours violated the First Amendment's guarantee of free speech. Although resting the decision on free speech grounds, Justice White's opinion for the Court also held that permitting religious groups access to school grounds did not run afoul of the First Amendment's (dis)establishment clause. *Lamb's Chapel*, then, was reaffirmed and extended in *Good News Club v. Milford Central School*, 533 U.S. 98 (2001).

The Warren Court generated a continuing storm of controversy when holding that public school systems may not require children to recite either nondenominational prayers or the Lord's Prayer, in *Engel v. Vitale* (1962) (excerpted below) and *Abington School District v. Schempp* (1963) (excerpted below). In *Schempp*, the Court drew on its earlier rationale, in *McGowan v. State of Maryland*, 366 U.S. 420 (1961), for upholding blue laws, or Sunday closing laws, and formulated a two-part test for laws under the establishment clause: whether laws have "a secular legislative purpose and a primary effect that neither advances nor inhibits religion."

By the end of the Warren Court era, the wall of separation appeared firmly entrenched in constitutional law. In charting the boundaries between religion and government, the Warren Court had pushed constitutional law in the direction of strict neutrality when applying

■ Constitutional History
Religious Displays in Public Places and the Establishment Clause

Alabama Supreme Court Chief Justice Roy Moore created a nationwide controversy in 2003 when he refused to comply with a federal appellate court order directing him to remove a two-and-a-half ton granite Ten Commandments monument he had installed in the entry way inside the building of the state supreme court. Years earlier he had stirred a similar controversy by hanging a plaque of the Ten Commandments behind his bench in a trial court. In 2000, he ran for election as chief justice on the slogan "Roy Moore: Still the Ten Commandments Judge." When the federal court threatened a fine of $5,000 a day he still refused to comply, and his colleagues on the supreme court voted to order the removal of the monument as well as his suspension from the bench. Subsequently, Chief Justice Moore made an unsuccessful appeal to the Supreme Court, which denied review.

Because not all public displays of religious symbols aim at endorsing particular religions or religion but have other purposes, federal courts have often rendered seemingly conflicting rulings. Above the justices' bench in the U.S. Supreme Court, for example, is a frieze depicting the world's great lawgivers, including Moses holding two tablets with the roman numerals I to X, representing the Ten Commandments. In *Stone v. Graham*, 449 U.S. 39 (1980), however, the Court split five to four in striking down a Kentucky law requiring the posting of the Ten Commandments in classrooms of all public schools. There, the Court concluded, the Kentucky legislature aimed to promote a particular religion by requiring the posting of the Ten Commandments in classrooms. But the constitutionality of public displays of such religious symbols depends largely on the context and whether the government aims to endorse religion or a particular religion.

In *County of Allegheny v. American Civil Liberties Union Greater Pittsburgh Chapter*, 492 U.S. 573 (1989), the Court sought to clarify the matter but the justices again split five to four and only a plurality joined Justice Blackmun's opinion for the Court. At issue were two religious displays erected during Christmas time on public property in the city of Pittsburgh and Allegheny county. The Court held that one of the displays was impermissible, but upheld the other over First Amendment objections.

The Court held that the establishment clause barred the display of a crèche, put up by the Holy Name Society, a Roman Catholic organization, on the Grand Staircase inside the Allegheny County Courthouse. In front of the crèche was a plaque stating "This Display Donated by the Holy Name Society," and next to it was an angel, presented as saying "Glory to God in the Highest!" Given its prominence, standing alone inside the courthouse, and historical religious significance, Justice Blackmun ruled that the display of the crèche constituted an impermissible governmental endorsement of religion.

By contrast, the Court ruled that the First Amendment was not violated by the display of an eighteen-foot menorah, a Chanukah lamp, alongside a forty-five-foot Christmas tree and a sign saluting liberty *outside* the Pittsburgh and Allegheny city-county office building, a block away from the county courthouse. Within that context, the display of religious symbols was deemed constitutionally permissible, not an endorsement of particular religions but instead a celebration of religious liberty and alternative traditions.

Schempp's secular purpose–secular effect test, much as the dissenters in *Everson* had urged. In Chief Justice Warren's last term, the Court unanimously struck down Arkansas's law forbidding the teaching of evolution in public schools in *Epperson v. Arkansas*, 393 U.S. 97 (1968).

The direction of constitutional law, however, began to shift when Chief Justice Burger was appointed and came to the Court in 1969. As the composition of the bench further changed with the appointees of Republican Presidents Nixon, Reagan, and George H. W. Bush, the balance on the Court moved toward greater accommodation of government support of religion. Burger took an activist role in redirecting the interpretation and application of the establishment clause. He signaled his disagreement with the Warren Court's strict interpretation in *Walz v. Tax Commission of City of New York*, 397 U.S. 664 (1971). There the Court rejected a challenge to New York's tax exemption for "real or personal property used exclusively for religious, educational or charitable purposes." And Burger found occasion to stress that *Everson's* majority upheld governmental benevolent neutrality, as well as to advance his accommodationist interpretation of the religion clauses. "[T]here is room for play in the joints productive of a benevolent neutrality which will permit religious exercise to exist without sponsorship and without interference," Burger claimed, when explaining that

> [i]n attempting to articulate the scope of the two Religion Clauses, the Court's opinions reflect the limitations inherent in formulating general principles on a case-by-case basis. The considerable internal inconsistency in the opinions of the Court derives from what, in retrospect, may have been too sweeping utterances on aspects of these clauses that seemed clear in relation to the particular cases but have limited meaning as general principles. . . .
>
> The course of constitutional neutrality in this area cannot be an absolutely straight line; rigidity could well defeat the basic purpose of these provisions, which is to insure that no religion be sponsored or

The display of the crèche inside a courthouse building was held to run afoul of the First Amendment. (*Courtesy of Allegheny County Law Department*)

The display of a menorah, a Christmas tree, and a sign saluting liberty, outside a city-county office building was deemed constitutionally permissible. (*Andy Stanes*)

favored, none commanded, and none inhibited. The general principle deducible from the First Amendment and all that has been said
by the Court is this: that we will not tolerate either governmentally
established religion or governmental interference with religion.

Chief Justice Burger, however, went a step further by suggesting that
government support of religion was permissible so long as there was
"no excessive governmental entanglement with religion."

When introducing the idea of "excessive governmental entanglement with religion" in *Walz*, Burger failed to mention the Warren
Court's *Schempp* test. But the following year in *Lemon v. Kurtzman*
(1971) (excerpted below), which involves reimbursement of the cost of
teachers' salaries and instructional materials in secular subjects for private religious schools, he turned *Schempp's* two-prong test (whether a
statute has a secular purpose and its primary effect neither advances nor
inhibits religion) into a three-prong test by adding that a "statute must
not foster 'an excessive government entanglement with religion.' "

The *Lemon* test allowed the Burger Court to move in the direction
of permitting governmental accommodation of religion. But the
Lemon test requires the Court to distinguish sharply between the level
of educational institutions (primary and secondary schools versus institutions of higher education) and the particular kinds of assistance, services, and benefits extended by the government. At the same time, the
line of separation between government and religion became less clear,
turning on the degree of entanglement, and thus the particular facts of
and kind of entanglement presented in each case. Reliance on *Lemon*
also meant that whether governmental support of religion survives establishment clause objections depends on the policy goals of the majority on the Court. In a companion ruling handed down with *Lemon*,
for example, the justices voted five to four in upholding a federal program providing construction grants to colleges and universities. The
majority in *Tilton v. Richardson*, 403 U.S. 672 (1971), had no problem
with these grants going to religiously affiliated schools and, in contrast
to *Lemon*, held that the program survived *Lemon's* three-prong test as
follows: (1) The buildings to be constructed had a secular purpose and
were to be used only for nonreligious purposes. (2) Unlike the primary
and secondary schools in *Lemon*, in the view of the majority, church-
related colleges are not "permeated" with religion and students are "less
impressionable and less susceptible to church indoctrination." Finally,
(3) the grants were on a one-time basis and, hence, did not give rise to
excessive government entanglement with religion.

The difficulties in and disagreements about applying *Lemon* further
divided the Court over whether *Lemon* should be abandoned in favor

of another accommodationist approach or in favor of returning to a strict interpretation of the wall of separation between government and religion. In *Wolman v. Walter*, 433 U.S. 229 (1977), for example, when upholding certain diagnostic and therapeutic testing services to be provided to primary and secondary schools affiliated with particular religions in Ohio, the justices could not agree on the application of the *Lemon* test, and Blackmun's opinion for the Court simply failed to mention it. Only Burger, Powell, and Stewart continued (although not always wholeheartedly) to support *Lemon*. Rehnquist, O'Connor, White, and Scalia, although inclined toward an accommodationist approach to the establishment clause, have criticized the *Lemon* tests. Brennan, Marshall, and Stevens, while relying on *Lemon* in some of their opinions for the Court, also suggested abandoning *Lemon* to return to a strict separation of government from religion. Dissenting in *Committee for Public Education and Religious Liberty v. Regan*, 444 U.S. 646 (1980), Stevens observed that

> the entire enterprise of trying to justify various types of subsidies to nonpublic schools should be abandoned. Rather than continuing with the Sisyphean task of trying to patch together the "blurred, indistinct, and variable barrier" described in *Lemon v. Kurtzman*, ... I would resurrect the "high and impregnable" wall between church and state constructed by the Framers of the First Amendment. See *Everson v. Board of Education*.

As a result of the Court's failure to agree on an interpretative approach and test for applying the establishment clause, the justices sometimes invoke *Lemon*'s three-prong test[3] and at other times pay little or no attention to it.[4] *Stone v. Graham*, 449 U.S. 41 (1980), is illustrative. There in a *per curiam* opinion for a bare majority, the *Lemon* tests were recited verbatim, but the Court struck down Kentucky's law requiring the posting of the Ten Commandments in school classrooms simply because it lacked a secular purpose. *Stone v. Graham* also underscores the importance of whether the justices construe the legislative purpose of a law to be secular or religious. In *Stone*, the majority held that posting the Ten Commandments "serves no ... educational function."

The continuing struggle within the Court is registered in several important rulings. Splitting five to four in *Lynch v. Donnelly*, 465 U.S. 668 (1984), the Burger Court upheld the Pawtucket, Rhode Island, display of the crèche during the Christmas holiday season. Notably, the majority interpreted the crèche to be a secular, not a religious, symbol and found no excessive government entanglement with religion. The following year, then, the justices divided six to three in *Wallace v. Jaffree* (1985) (see excerpt below) in striking down Alabama's law requiring a moment of silence in public schools for meditation or voluntary prayer. Along with Stevens's opinion for the Court, relying on *Lemon,* compare O'Connor's concurring opinion and Burger's dissenting opinion, both criticizing reliance on and application of *Lemon.* The dissenting opinion of Rehnquist is also notable in attacking not only *Lemon* but the Court's understanding of the establishment clause since *Everson.*

In *Edwards v. Aguillard,* 482 U.S. 578 (1987), Justice Brennan forged a seven-to-two ruling overturning Louisiana's law requiring the teaching of creationism. And in *County of Allegheny v. American Civil Liberties Union Greater Pittsburgh Chapter,* 492 U.S. 573 (1989), the Rehnquist Court reconsidered under what circumstances local governments may display the crèche and menorah. There, again splitting five to four, the justices held that the display of a crèche inside a city building violated the establishment clause and limited *Lynch v. Donnelly,* as well as rejected Chief Justice Burger's analysis there. At the same time, the Court upheld the display of the menorah next to a Christmas tree outside a city/county office building. In both *Lynch* and *County of Allegheny,* Justice O'Connor cast the crucial vote in determining the outcome and drawing the Court's line between religion and government.

In *Lee v. Weisman,* 505 U.S. 577 (1992) (excerpted below), a bare majority of the Court held that the First Amendment forbids school-sponsored invocations and benedictions at graduation ceremonies. Justice Kennedy announced the decision because he cast the deciding vote in a ruling that otherwise split the justices four to four. The school district's supervision of graduation ceremonies, according to Kennedy, "places public pressure, as well as peer pressure, on attending students to stand as a group or, at least, maintain respectful silence during the Invocation and Benediction." Yet, in suggesting a "governmental coercion" test, his opinion held out the possibility that government may endorse religion in other ways. In that regard, Justice Kennedy conceded too much for the four other justices—Justices Souter, O'Connor, Blackmun, and Stevens—in the majority. In separate concurrences, those four justices emphasized that in their view government may no more endorse religion than, as in *Lee,* coerce participation in a religious practice. By contrast, the four dissenters—Chief Justice Rehnquist and Justices Scalia, Thomas, and White—derided Justice Kennedy's analysis of the psychological coercion of students forced to attend benedictions as "psychology practiced by amateurs."

The ruling in *Lee v. Weisman* provoked considerable protest, including school-sponsored prayers at the outset of high school football games. When that practice was challenged in *Santa Fe Independent School District v. Doe,* 530 U.S. 290 (2000), the Court reaffirmed *Weisman* by a six-to-three vote in holding that schools may not sponsor prayers at football games. Chief Justice Rehnquist and Justice Scalia and Thomas dissented from Justice Steven's opinion for the Court.

In sum, despite bitter disagreements, the Court continues to rely on the *Lemon* test and expressly declined to overrule it in *Lee v. Weisman.* Moreover, in *Board of Education of Kiryas Joel v. Grumet*, 512 U.S. 687 (1994) (excerpted below), the Court's majority again declined to jettison *Lemon.* Dividing six to three when striking down New York's law creating a special school district for Kiryas Joel, a community inhabited solely by Hasidic Jews, Justice Souter's opinion for the Court approvingly cited *Lemon* twice. Justice Blackmun's concurrence strongly supported the *Lemon* test, while Justice O'Connor's concurrence called for abandoning *Lemon,* as did dissenting Justice Scalia, whose dissent was joined by Chief Justice Rehnquist and Justice Thomas.

In addition, the Court has recently grappled with the issue of the interrelationship among First Amendment doctrines for free speech, the (dis)establishment of religion, and the free exercise of religion. During the past decade, a number of Christian groups have challenged a variety of public schools' policies based on the (dis)establishment clause and the Court's interpretations of that clause. They have argued that those policies restrict their freedom of religious expression and that violates their First Amendment right of free speech; in other words, in order to achieve their free exercise goals, they have sued on the basis of the First Amendment's guarantee for free speech and press. In the so-called "*Wide Awake*" case, *Rosenberger v. The Rector and Visitors of the University of Virginia*, 515 U.S. 819 (1995) (excerpted below), the editor of a university Christian student group's magazine sued the university over its policy, based on the (dis)establishment clause's prohibition of governmental sponsorship of religion, denying student–activity funds for the magazine. Rosenberger contended that the policy was discriminatory and a violation of the First Amendment guarantee for free speech. Writing for the Court, Justice Kennedy agreed, holding that discrimination against the expression of religious viewpoints violates the First Amendment's guarantee for free speech and that the amendment's (dis)establishment clause did not compel or justify the university's policy. By contrast, Justice Souter, joined by Justices Breyer, Ginsburg, and Stevens, countered that for the first time the Court had approved direct government expenditures for religious activities, which ran afoul of the First Amendment's (dis)establishment clause and "strict neutrality."

Following *Rosenberger*, some New Christian Right students objected to the use of their student fees to support gay and lesbian organizations at the University of Wisconsin. They contended that the expenditures violated their beliefs protected by the First Amendment and, thus, they should be exempt from portions of the fee. Writing for the Court in *Board of Regents of the University of Wisconsin System v. Southworth*, 529 U. S. 217 (2000), Justice Kennedy upheld the requiring of mandatory student activity fees, but ruled that here the allocation of those funds for extracurricular activities based on a student referendum mechanism was not viewpoint neutral and thus ran afoul of the First Amendment.

In another case, *Capitol Square Review Board v. Pinette*, 515 U.S. 753 (1995), a majority of the Court upheld the display of a cross in a public park as private religious expression protected by the First Amendment's free speech clause. This case appealed lower court decisions rejecting Columbus, Ohio's argument that it could, on the basis of the (dis)establishment clause, deny permission for the Ku Klux Klan (KKK) to display at Christmas time a ten-foot cross in a public park across from the state capitol. The KKK, represented by the American Civil Liberties Union, argued that the lower courts correctly enforced the First Amendment guarantee for free speech. By contrast, the American Jewish Congress sided with Cleveland's review board in contending that free speech claims should not automatically defeat all arguments in support of government policies based on the (dis)establishment clause. The latter's arguments, however, were rejected by Justice Scalia in his opinion for the Court, holding that, "Religious expression cannot violate the Establishment Clause where it (1) is purely private and (2) occurs in a traditional or designated public forum, publicly announced and open to all on equal terms." In a separate opinion joined by Justices Souter and Breyer, Justice O'Connor reasserted her "endorsement test" for determining the application of the (dis)establishment clause and that, based on the facts and that test, the clause was not abridged here. Dissenting Justices Ginsburg and Stevens, however, defended the view that the (dis)establishment clause compels a strict neutrality in the separation of the state from religion.

The Court's continuing reassessment of its (dis)establishment clause jurisprudence is underscored by the bare majority's ruling in *Agostini v. Felton*, 521 U.S. 203 (1997) (excerpted below), overruling two twelve-year-old precedents set in *Aguilar v. Felton*, 473 U.S. 402 (1985) and *School District of Grand Rapids v. Ball*, 473 U.S. 373 (1985); both of those decisions were also decided by bare majorities. In *Aguilar v. Felton*, the Court held impermissible New York's providing teachers for handicapped students in parochial schools. As a result, New York instituted a program whereby the students walked from their classrooms to state vans parked on the street, outside of the parochial school grounds, and were given remedial education by public school teachers. In light of the Rehnquist Court's rulings and evolving jurisprudence, however, a district court held that those two 1985 rulings had been effectively overruled. An appellate court reversed that decision but in turn was reversed by a bare majority of the Court in *Agostini v. Felton.*

Underscoring the Court's reassessment of prior decisions in the area, by a six-to-three vote the justices overruled two other rulings, *Meek v. Pittenger,* 421 U.S. 349 (1975), and *Wolman v. Walter,* 433 U.S. 229 (1977), in *Mitchell v. Helms* 530 U.S. 793 (2000). Relying on *Agostini v. Felton* and extending *Witters v. Washington Department of Services for the Blind,* 474 U.S. 481 (1986), and *Zobrest v. Catalina Foothills School District,* 509 U.S. 1 (1993), Justice Thomas held that public school districts may lend computer software, as well as other forms of aid, to private religious schools. Notably, Justice Thomas also wrote for the Court in the six-to-three decision in *Good News Club v. Milford Central School* 533 U.S. 98 (2001), holding that when public schools establish limited public forums they may not deny access to religious groups seeking to use their facilities for after-school meetings, thereby reaffirming and extending the prior rulings in *Lamb's Chapel v. Center Moriches Union Free School Disrict* and *Rosenberger v. The Rector and Visitors of the University of Virginia.* Moreover, in *Zelman v. Simmons-Harris* (2003) (excerpted below) a bare majority of the Court, extended *Witters, Agostini,* and *Zobrest* in upholding public-funded vouchers for students to attend private religious schools. Although in those cases the Court held that governmental aid to religious schools in the form of student scholarships, remedial teachers, sign interpreters, and vouchers does not violate the (dis)establishment clause, in *Locke v. Davey* (2004) (excerpted in Section B of this chapter) the Court held that the free exercise clause does not provide a basis for compelling a state to allow a student to use a scholarship to pursue a pastoral degree when the state's constitution forbids such aid and imposes a more rigorous separation of government from religion than the Court's interpretation of the First Amendment. In sum, such aid to religion is permitted under the (dis)establishment clause but not required and cannot be compelled under the free exercise clause.

Finally, the Court avoided the heated controversy over whether requiring school children to recite the Pledge of Allegiance violates the First Amendment by denying standing to raise the issue in *Elk Grove Unified School District v. Newdow* (2004) (excerpted in Chapter 2). Writing for the Court, Justice Stevens held that Michael A. Newdow, who challenged the policy on behalf of his daughter, though he was not her legal custodian, lacked "prudential standing" to bring the suit. In other words, when legal claims are made on behalf of another person based on domestic relations law, a field largely left to states, "the prudent course is for the federal court to stay its hand rather than reach out to resolve a weighty question of federal constitutional law." But in separate concurring opinions Chief Justice Rehnquist and Justices O'Connor and Thomas would have granted standing and rejected Newdow's claims, though for different reasons. Chief Justice Rehnquist contended that *Lee v. Weisman*, invalidating school-sponsored prayer at graduation 1ceremonies, could be distinguished and that the words "under God" are "not endorsement of any religion." Justice O'Connor agreed; however, she deemed teacher-led recitations of "under God" as simply "ceremonial deism." By contrast, Justice Thomas would have upheld the school district's policy because *Lee v. Weisman* and other prior decisions applying the (dis)establishment clause to the states were wrongly decided and should be overruled. Justice Scalia recused himself because in off-the-bench remarks he had criticized the lower court for ruling that the First Amendment had been violated. The controversy over the Pledge and the motto "In God We Trust" is certain to continue and to return to the Court in another case.

Notes

1. Paul Kauper, *Religion and the Constitution* (Baton Rouge: Louisiana State University Press, 1964), 59.

2. Philip Kurland, "Of Church and State and the Supreme Court," 29 *University of Chicago Law Review* 5 (1961).

3. See, for example, *Stone v. Graham*, 449 U.S. 39 (1980); *Committee for Public Education and Religious Liberty v. Regan*, 444 U.S. 646 (1980); *Larkin v. Grendel's Den, Inc.*, 459 U.S. 116 (1982); *Aguilar v. Felton*, 473 U.S. 402 (1985); and *Texas Monthly, Inc. v. Bullock*, 489 U.S. 1 (1989).

4. See, for example, *Larson v. Valente*, 456 U.S. 228 (1982); and *Marsh v. Chambers*, 463 U.S. 783 (1983).

Selected Bibliography

Curry, Thomas. *The First Freedoms: Church and State in America to the Passage of the First Amendment.* New York: Oxford University Press, 1986.

Dreisbach, Daniel. *Thomas Jefferson and the Wall of Separation between Church and State.* New York: New York University Press, 2002.

Feldman, Stephen. *Please Don't Wish Me a Merry Christmas: A Critical History of the Separation of Church and State.* New York: New York University Press, 1997.

Feldman, Stephen, ed. *Law and Religion: A Critical Anthology.* New York: New York University Press, 2000.

Fisher, Louis. *Religious Liberty in America: Political Safeguards.* Lawrence: University Press of Kansas, 2003.

Guliuzza, Frank. *Over the Wall: Protecting Religious Expression in the Public Square.* Albany: State University Press of New York, 2000.

Hamburger, Philip. *Separation of Church and State.* Cambridge, MA: Harvard University Press, 2002.

Howe, Mark De Wolfe. *The Garden and the Wilderness: Religion and Government in American Constitutional History.* Chicago: University of Chicago Press, 1965.

Ivers, Gregg. *To Build a Wall: American Jews and the Separation of Church and State.* Charlottesville: University Press of Virginia, 1995.

Kauper, Paul. *Religion and the Constitution.* Baton Rouge: Louisiana State University Press, 1964.

Larson, Edward. *Summer for the Gods: The Scopes Trial and America's Continuing Debate over Science and Religion.* New York: Basic Books, 1997.

Levy, Leonard. *The Establishment Clause: Religion and the First Amendment.* New York: Macmillan, 1986.

Peters, Shawn F. *Judging Jehovah's Witnesses.* Lawrence: University Press of Kansas, 2000.

Pfeffer, Leo. *God, Caesar and the Constitution.* Boston: Beacon Press, 1975.

Ravitch, Frank. *School Prayer and Discrimination: The Civil Rights of Religious Minorities.* Northeastern University Press, 1999.

Sheffer, Martin. *God versus Caesar: Belief, Worship, and Proselytizing under the First Amendment.* Albany: State University Press of New York, 2000.

Stokes, Anson, and Pfeffer, Leo. *Church and State in the United States.* New York: Harper and Row, 1965.

Sullivan, Winnifred Fallers. *Paying the Words Extra: Religious Discourse in the Supreme Court of the United States.* Cambridge, MA: Harvard University Press, 1995.

■ The Development of Law

Major Rulings Upholding Governmental Aid or Support of Religion over Establishment Clause Objections

CASE	VOTE	KIND OF AID/SUPPORT FOR RELIGION UPHELD
Everson v. Board of Education of Ewing Township, New Jersey, 330 U.S. 1 (1947)	5:4	Bus fare reimbursement for parents of children attending private religious schools
Zorach v. Clauson, 343 U.S. 306 (1952)	6:3	Released-time program for religious instruction in class held off campus.
Waltz v. Tax Commission of the City of New York, 397 U.S. 664 (1970)	7:1	Tax exemption for property used solely for religious purposes as permissible benevolent neutrality.

CASE	VOTE	KIND OF AID/SUPPORT FOR RELIGION UPHELD
Tilton v. Richardson, 403 U.S. 672 (1971)	5:4	Most of a $240 million federal funding program for the construction of academic buildings

on private sectarian and secular colleges; not enough entanglement of church and state to violate establishment clause.

Hunt v. McNair, 413 U.S. 734 (1973)	6:3	South Carolina's state bond issue for construction of academic buildings for non-religious purposes by private religious schools.
Meek v. Pittenger, 413 U.S. 349 (1973)	6:3	Loan of secular textbooks from public schools to private and parochial schools.
Roemer v. Maryland Public Works Board, 426 U.S. 736 (1976)	5:4	General-purpose funds for non-sectarian purposes to colleges and universities with religious affiliations.
Wolman v. Walter, 433 U.S. 229 (1977)	8:1	Diagnostic and therapeutic testing services provided to private primary and secondary schools affiliated with particular religions.
Committee for Public Education and Religious Liberty v. Regan, 444 U.S. 646 (1980)	5:4	Reimbursement for certain expenses for record keeping and testing incurred by private schools due to state regulations.
Mueller v. Allen, 463 U.S. 388 (1983)	5:4	Annual tax deduction of $700 for parents of children in elementary and secondary schools run by religious organizations: a neutral accommodation.
Marsh v. Chambers, 463 U.S. 783 (1983)	5:4	State practice of a chaplain opening sessions of legislature.
Lynch v. Donnelly, 465 U.S. 688 (1984)	5:4	City-sponsored display of crèche as part of Christmas display in park; accommodation and crèche viewed as a secular symbol.
Bowen v. Kendrick, 487 U.S. 589 (1988)	5:4	Authorization of federal funds for public and private organizations under Adolescent Family

CASE	VOTE	KIND OF AID/SUPPORT FOR RELIGION UPHELD

Life Act for premarital counseling services by organizations affiliated with established churches.

County of Allegheny v. American Civil Liberties Union Greater Pittsburgh Chapter, 492 U.S. 573 (1989) — 5:4 — Writing for the majority, Justice Blackmun held that the display of a crèche inside a city building violated the (dis)establishment clause and limited the earlier ruling in *Lynch v. Donnelly*, 465 U.S. 688 (1984), which had upheld a city-sponsored display of a crèche as part of a Christmas exhibit in a park. At the same time, Justice Blackmun upheld the display of the menorah next to a Christmas tree outside of a city-county office building. Justice O'Connor cast the deciding vote and issued a concurring opinion. Separate opinions, in part concurring and dissenting, were filed by Justices Brennan and Stevens, and joined by Justice Marshall. Justice Kennedy also issued a separate opinion, concurring and dissenting in part, and was joined by Chief Justice Rehnquist and Justices Scalia and White.

Board of Education of the Westside Community Schools v. Mergens, 496 U.S. 226 (1990) — 8:1 — Upheld the Equal Access Act of 1984, which bars public schools from discriminating against meetings on school grounds of student activity groups on the basis of "religious, political, philosophical or other content of the speech at such meetings."

Zobrest v. Catalina Foothills School District, 509 U.S. 1 (1993) — 5:4 — Upheld public funding for a sign-language interpreter for a deaf student attending a private religious high school.

Lamb's Chapel v. Center Moriches Union Free School District, 508 U.S. 384 (1993) — 9:0 — Held that public schools that provide after-hours access to other groups may not deny access to facilities to religious groups.

Rosenberger v. The Rector and Visitors of the University of Virginia, 515 U.S. 819 (1995) — 5:4 — Writing for the majority, Justice Kennedy held the University of Virginia's policy, of denying student-activities funds to groups that advocate particular religions, discriminated against the expression of religious viewpoints in violation of the First Amendment's guarantee for free speech, and that the amendment's (dis)establishment clause did not compel or justify the university's policy. The four dissenters—Justices Breyer, Ginsburg, Souter, and Stevens—thought otherwise.

CASE	VOTE	KIND OF AID/SUPPORT FOR RELIGION UPHELD
Agostini v. Felton, 521 U. S. 203 (1997)	5:4	Overruling two precedents, *Aguilar v. Felton*, 473 U.S. 402 (1985), and *School District of*

Grand Rapids v. Ball, 473 U.S. 373 (1985), in an opinion delivered by Justice O'Connor, the Court held that public school teachers could be sent into parochial schools to provide remedial education. Justices Souter and Ginsburg filed dissenting opinions, which were joined by Justices Stevens and Breyer.

Mitchell v. Helms, 530 U.S. 793 (2000)	6:3	Overturning *Meek v. Pittenger*, 421 U.S. 349 (1975), and *Wolman v. Walter*, 433 U.S. 229

(1977), Justice Thomas held that the First Amendment does not bar public schools from lending computer software and hardware to private religious schools. Justices Souter, Stevens, and Ginsburg dissented.

Good News Club v. Milford Central School, 533 U.S. 98 (2001)	6:3	Writing for the Court, Justice Thomas held that when public schools established limited public forums they may not

deny access to religious groups seeking to use their facilities for after-school meetings.

Zelman v. Simmons-Harris, 536 U.S. 639 (2002)	5:4	Writing for the Court, Chief Justice Rehnquist upheld Ohio's voucher program permitting stu-

students of Cleveland's inner-city schools to attend private religious schools over First Amendment objections. Justices Stevens, Souter, Ginsburg, and Breyer dissented.

■ THE DEVELOPMENT OF LAW

Major Rulings Striking Down Laws and Policies for Violating the Establishment Clause

CASE	VOTE	ACTIVITY/ASSISTANCE HELD UNCONSTITUTIONAL
McCollum v. Board of Education, 333 U.S. 203 (1948)	8:1	Released-time program for religious instruction held on school grounds.

CASE	VOTE	ACTIVITY/ASSISTANCE HELD UNCONSTITUTIONAL
Engel v. Vitale, 370 U.S. 421 (1962)	6:1	A twenty-two-word non-denominational prayer written for students in public school.
Abington School District v. Schempp and *Murray v. Curlett*, 374 U.S. 203 (1963)	8:1	Reading of the Lord's Prayer and Bible verses in public schools.
Epperson v. Arkansas, 393 U.S. 97 (1968)	9:0	Arkansas's "monkey law," forbidding the teaching of evolutionary theory.
Lemon v. Kurtzman, 403 U.S. 602 (1971)	8:0	Direct aid to parochial schools, including use of public funds to pay salaries of parochial teachers.
Levitt v. Commission for Public Education and Religious Liberty, 413 U.S. 472 (1973); *Committee for Public Education and Religious Liberty v. Nyquist*, 413 U.S. 756 (1973); *Sloan v. Lemon*, 413 U.S. 825 (1973)	6:3	Financial aid for parochial schools, including tuition reimbursement, tax exemptions, and special counseling services and loan of educational equipment.
Meek v. Pittenger, 421 U.S. 349 (1975)	6:3	Counseling, testing, remedial classes, equipment, and other auxiliary services given to schools affiliated with religious organizations. Overruled by *Mitchell v. Helms*, 530 U.S. 793 (2000).
Wolman v. Walter, 433 U.S. 229 (1977)	5:4	Financial aid for field trips and class paraphernalia provided to private schools affiliated with religious organizations. Overruled by *Mitchell v. Helms*, 530 U.S. 793 (2000).
New York v. Cathedral Academy, 434 U.S. 125 (1977)	6:3	Direct reimbursement to parochial schools for record keeping and testing services.
Stone v. Graham, 449 U.S. 39 (1980)	5:4	Kentucky law requiring the posting of the Ten Commandments in classrooms.
Widmar v. Vincent, 454 U.S. 263 (1981)	8:1	Missouri's prohibition of the use of state university buildings for "religious worship."

CASE	VOTE	ACTIVITY/ASSISTANCE HELD UNCONSTITUTIONAL
Larkin v. Grendel's Den, 454 U.S. 1140 (1982)	5:4	Law giving churches veto over issuance of liquor licenses.
Wallace v. Jaffree, 472 U.S. 38 (1985)	6:3	Alabama law authorizing one minute of silence in public schools for meditation or voluntary prayer.
Aguilar v. Felton, 473 U.S. 402 (1985)	5:4	Instructional services given and provided on grounds of parochial schools. Overruled by *Agostini v. Felton*, 521 U.S. 203 (1997).
School District of Grand Rapids v. Ball, 473 U.S. 373 (1985)	5:4	Invalidated a "shared time" program that provided remedial classes, at public expense,

to students attending religious schools. This ruling, along with *Aguilar v. Felton* (above) was overruled in *Agostini v. Felton*, 521 U.S. 203 (1997).

Edwards v. Aguillard, 482 U.S. 578 (1987)	7:2	Louisiana law requiring the teaching of creationism to balance the teaching of evolution.
Texas Monthly, Inc. v. Bullock, 489 U.S. 1 (189)	6:3	Texas law giving tax exemption to religious periodicals.
County of Allegheny v. American Civil Liberties Union Greater Pittsburgh Chapter, 492 U.S. 573 (1989)	5:4	Writing for the majority, Justice Blackmun held that the display of a crèche inside a city building violated the (dis)establishment clause and

limited the earlier ruling in *Lynch v. Donnelly*, 465 U.S. 688 (1984), which had upheld a city-sponsored display of a creche as part of a Christmas exhibit in a park. At the same time, Justice Blackmun upheld the display of the menorah next to a Christmas tree outside of a city-county office building. Justice O'Connor cast the deciding vote and issued a concurring opinion. Separate opinions, in part concurring and dissenting, were filed by Justices Brennan and Stevens, and joined by Justice Marshall. Justice Kennedy also issued a separate opinion, concurring and dissenting in part, and was joined by Chief Justice Rehnquist and Justices Scalia and White.

Lee v. Weisman, 505 U.S. 577 (1992)	5:4	Invocations and benedictions at public school graduation ceremonies supervised by school authorities.

CASE	VOTE	ACTIVITY/ASSISTANCE HELD UNCONSTITUTIONAL

Board of Education of Kiryas Joel v. Grumet, 512 U.S. 687 (1994) — 6:3 — Writing for the Court, Justice Souter struck down New York's law creating a special school district in Kiryas Joel, a community inhabited solely by Hasidic Jews of the Satmar sect, one of the most orthodox and conservative Jewish sects. That law was passed after the Court, in *Aguilar v. Felton*, 473 U.S. 402 (1985), prohibited New York from paying for remedial classes for handicapped children attending private religious schools. Notably, Justice Souter's opinion declined to jettison the three-prong test set forth in *Lemon v. Kurtzman*, 403 U.S. 602 (1971) and commanded only a plurality in parts. Justice Blackmun concurred, in an opinion strongly supporting *Lemon*, while Justice O'Connor's concurrence suggested that *Lemon* should be abandoned. Joined by Chief Justice Rehnquist and Justice Thomas, Justice Scalia rejected the majority's analysis and decision, as well as renewed his call for discarding *Lemon*.

Santa Fe Independent School District v. Doe, 530 U.S. 790 (2000) — 6:3 — Writing for the Court and reaffirming *Lee v. Weisman*, 505 U.S. 577 (1992), Justice Stevens held that having school-sponsored prayers prior to high school football games violates the First Amendment. Chief Justice Rehnquist and Justices Scalia and Thomas dissented.

Everson v. Board of Education of Ewing Township
330 U.S. 1, 67 S.Ct. 504 (1947)

Arch Everson filed a suit challenging the constitutionality of an authorization for reimbursement to parents with children in private schools for the cost of busing their children. The Board of Education of Ewing Township had adopted the plan under a New Jersey statute permitting local school districts to make their own rules for the transportation of children to and from schools. Most of the private schools in the area were Catholic parochial schools. A state court struck down the program. The New Jersey Court of Errors and Appeals reversed, holding that neither the state law nor the school board's resolution violated the state or federal Constitution. Everson then turned to the Supreme Court, which granted review.

The Court's decision was five to four, and the majority's opinion was announced by Justice Black. A dissent by Justice Rutledge was joined by Justices Jackson, Frankfurter, and Burton.

☐ *Justice BLACK delivered the opinion of the Court.*

The New Jersey statute is challenged as a "law respecting an establishment of religion." . . . These words of the First Amendment reflected in the minds of early Americans a vivid mental picture of conditions and practices which they fervently wished to stamp out in order to preserve liberty for themselves and for their posterity. Doubtless their goal has not been entirely reached; but so far has the Nation moved toward it that the expression "law respecting an establishment of religion," probably does not so vividly remind present-day Americans of the evils, fears, and political problems that caused that expression to be written into our Bill of Rights. Whether this New Jersey law is one respecting the "establishment of religion" requires an understanding of the meaning of that language, particularly with respect to the imposition of taxes. Once again, therefore, it is not inappropriate briefly to review the background and environment of the period in which that constitutional language was fashioned and adopted.

A large proportion of the early settlers of this country came here from Europe to escape the bondage of laws which compelled them to support and attend government favored churches. The centuries immediately before and contemporaneous with the colonization of America had been filled with turmoil, civil strife, and persecutions, generated in large part by established sects determined to maintain their absolute political and religious supremacy. With the power of government supporting them, at various times and places, Catholics had persecuted Protestants, Protestants had persecuted Catholics, Protestant sects had persecuted other Protestant sects, Catholics of one shade of belief had persecuted Catholics of another shade of belief, and all of these had from time to time persecuted Jews. In efforts to force loyalty to whatever religious group happened to be on top and in league with the government of a particular time and place, men and women had been fined, cast in jail, cruelly tortured, and killed. . . .

These practices of the old world were transplanted to and began to thrive in the soil of the new America. The very characters granted by the English Crown to the individuals and companies designated to make the laws which would control the destinies of the colonials authorized these individuals and companies to erect religious establishments which all, whether believers or non-believers, would be required to support and attend. An exercise of this authority was accompanied by a repetition of many of the old world practices and persecutions. Catholics found themselves hounded and proscribed because of their faith; Quakers who followed their conscience went to jail; Baptists were peculiarly obnoxious to certain dominant Protestant sects; men and women of varied faiths who happened to be in a minority in a particular locality were persecuted because they steadfastly persisted in worshipping God only as their own consciences dictated. And all of these dissenters were compelled to pay tithes and taxes to support government-sponsored churches whose ministers preached inflammatory sermons designed to strengthen and consolidate the established faith by generating a burning hatred against dissenters.

These practices became so commonplace as to shock the freedom-loving colonials into a feeling of abhorrence. The imposition of taxes to pay ministers' salaries and to build and maintain churches and church property aroused their indignation. It was these feelings which found expression in the First Amendment. No one locality and no one group throughout the Colonies can rightly be given entire credit for having aroused the sentiment that culminated in adoption of the Bill of Rights' provisions embracing religious liberty. But Virginia, where the established church had achieved a dominant influence in political affairs and where many excesses attracted wide public attention, provided a great stimulus and able leadership for the movement. The people there, as elsewhere, reached the conviction that individual religious liberty could be achieved best under a government which was stripped of all power to tax, to support, or otherwise to assist any or all religions, or to interfere with the beliefs of any religious individual or group.

The movement toward this end reached its dramatic climax in Virginia in 1785–86 when the Virginia legislative body was about to renew Virginia's tax levy for the support of the established church. Thomas Jefferson and James Madison led the fight against this tax. Madison wrote his great Memorial and Remonstrance against the law. In it, he eloquently argued that a true religion did not need the support of law; that no person, either believer or non-believer, should be taxed to support a religious institution of any kind; that the best interest of a society required that the minds of men always be wholly free; and that cruel persecutions were the inevitable result of government-established religions. Madison's Remonstrance received strong support throughout Virginia, and the Assembly postponed consideration of the proposed tax measure until its next session. When the proposal came up for consideration at that session, it not only died in committee, but the Assembly enacted the famous "Virginia Bill for Religious Liberty" originally written by Thomas Jefferson. The preamble to that Bill stated among other things that

> "Almighty God hath created the mind free; that all attempts to influence it by temporal punishments, or burthens, or by civil incapacitations, tend only to beget habits of hypocrisy and meanness, and are a departure from the plan of the Holy author of our religion who being Lord both of body and mind, yet chose not to propagate it by coercions on either; . . . that to compel a man to furnish contributions of money for the propagation of opinions which he disbelieves, is sinful and tyrannical; that even the forcing him to support this or that teacher of his own religious persuasion, is depriving him of the comfortable liberty of giving his contributions to the particular pastor, whose morals he would make his pattern. . . ."

And the statute itself enacted

> "[t]hat no man shall be compelled to frequent or support any religious worship, place, or ministry whatsoever, nor shall be enforced, restrained, molested, or burthened, in his body or goods, nor shall otherwise suffer on account of his religious opinions or belief. . . ."

This Court has previously recognized that the provisions of the First Amendment, in the drafting and adoption of which Madison and Jefferson played such leading roles, had the same objective and were intended to provide the same protection against governmental intrusion on religious liberty as the Virginia statute.

Prior to the adoption of the Fourteenth Amendment, the First Amendment did not apply as a restraint against the states. Most of them did soon provide similar constitutional protections for religious liberty. But some states persisted for about half a century in imposing restraints upon the free exercise of religion and in discriminating against particular religious groups. In recent years, so far as the provision against the establishment of a religion is concerned, the question has most frequently arisen in connection with proposed state aid to church schools and efforts to carry on religious teachings in the public schools in accordance with the tenets of a particular sect. Some churches have either sought or accepted state financial support for their schools. Here again the efforts to obtain state aid or acceptance of it have not been limited to any one particular faith. The state courts, in the main, have remained faithful to the language of their own constitutional provisions designed to protect religious freedom and to separate religious and governments. Their decisions, however, show the difficulty in drawing the line between tax legislation which provides funds for the welfare of the general public and that which is designed to support institutions which teach religion.

The meaning and scope of the First Amendment, preventing establishment of religion or prohibiting the free exercise thereof, in the light of its history and the evils it was designed forever to suppress, have been several times elaborated by the decisions of this Court prior to the application of the First Amendment to the states by the Fourteenth. The broad meaning given the Amendment by these earlier cases has been accepted by this Court in its decisions concerning an individual's religious freedom rendered since the Fourteenth Amendment was interpreted to make the prohibitions of the First applicable to state action abridging religious freedom. There is every reason to give the same application and broad interpretation to the "establishment of religion" clause. . . .

The "establishment of religion" clause of the First Amendment means at least this: Neither a state nor the Federal Government can set up a church. Neither can pass laws which aid one religion, aid all religions, or prefer one religion over another. Neither can force nor influence a person to go to or to remain away from church against his will or force him to profess a belief or disbelief in any religion. No person can be punished for entertaining or professing religious beliefs or disbeliefs, for church attendance or non-attendance. No tax in any amount, large or small, can be levied to support any religious activities or institutions, whatever they may be called, or whatever form they may adopt to teach or practice religion. Neither a state nor the Federal Government can, openly or secretly, participate in the affairs of any religious organizations or groups and vice versa. In the words of Jefferson, the clause against establishment of religion by law was intended to erect "a wall of separation between Church and State."

We must consider the New Jersey statute in accordance with the foregoing limitations imposed by the First Amendment. But we must not strike that state statute down if it is within the state's constitutional power even though it approaches the verge of that power. New Jersey cannot consistently with the "establishment of religion" clause of the First Amendment contribute tax-raised funds to the support of an institution which teaches the tenets and faith of any church. On the other hand, other language of the amendment commands that New Jersey cannot hamper its citizens in the free exercise of their own religion. Consequently, it cannot exclude individual Catholics, Lutherans, Mohammedans, Baptists, Jews, Methodists, Non-believers, Presbyterians, or the members of any other faith, *because of their faith, or lack of it*, from receiving the benefits of public welfare legislation. While we do not mean to intimate that a state could not provide transportation only to children attending public schools, we must be careful, in protecting the citizens of New Jersey against state-established churches, to be sure that we do not inadvertently prohibit New Jersey from extending its general State law benefits to all its citizens without regard to their religious belief.

Measured by these standards, we cannot say that the First Amendment prohibits New Jersey from spending tax-raised funds to pay the bus fares of parochial school pupils as a part of a general program under which it pays the fares of pupils attending public and other schools. It is undoubtedly true that children are helped to get to church schools. There is even a possibility that some of the children might not be sent to the church schools if the parents were compelled to pay their children's bus fares out of their own pockets when transportation to a public school would have been paid for by the State. The same possibility exists where the state requires a local transit company to provide reduced fares to school children including those attending parochial schools, or where a municipally owned transportation system undertakes to carry all school children free of charge. Moreover, state-paid policemen, detailed to protect children going to and from church schools from the very real hazards of traffic, would serve much the same purpose and accomplish much the same result as state provisions intended to guarantee free transportation of a kind which the state deems to be best for the school children's welfare. And parents might refuse to risk their children to the serious danger of traffic accidents going to and from parochial schools, the approaches to which were not protected by policemen. Similarly, parents might be reluctant to permit their children to attend schools which the state had cut off from such general government services as ordinary police and fire protection, connections for sewage disposal, public highways and sidewalks. Of course, cutting off church schools from these services, so separate and so indisputably marked off from the religious function, would make it far more difficult for the schools to operate. But such is obviously not the purpose of the First Amendment. That Amendment requires the state to be a neutral in its relations with groups of religious believers and non-believers; it does not require the state to be their adversary. State power is no more to be used so as to handicap religions, than it is to favor them. . . .

The First Amendment has erected a wall between church and state. That wall must be kept high and impregnable. We could not approve the slightest breach. New Jersey has not breached it here.

Affirmed.

☐ *Justice RUTLEDGE, with whom Justice FRANKFURTER, Justice JACKSON, and Justice BURTON join, dissenting.*

The Amendment's purpose was not to strike merely at the official establishment of a single sect, creed or religion, outlawing only a formal relation such as had prevailed in England and some of the colonies. Necessarily it was to uproot all such relationships. But the object was broader than separating church and state in this narrow sense. It was to create a complete and permanent separation of the spheres of religious activity and civil authority by comprehensively forbidding every form of public aid or support for religion. In proof the Amendment's wording and history unite with this Court's consistent utterances whenever attention has been fixed directly upon the question.

"Religion" appears only once in the Amendment. But the word governs two prohibitions and governs them alike. It does not have two meanings, one narrow to forbid "an establishment" and another, much broader, for securing "the free exercise thereof." "Thereof" brings down "religion" with its entire and exact content, no more and no less, from the first into the second guaranty, so that Congress and now the states are as broadly restricted concerning the one as they are regarding the other. . . .

Compulsory attendance upon religious exercises went out early in the process of separating church and state, together with forced observance of religious forms and ceremonies. Test oaths and religious qualification for office followed later. These things none devoted to our great tradition of religious liberty would think of bringing back. Hence today, apart from efforts to inject religious training or exercises and sectarian issues into the public schools, the only serious surviving threat to maintaining that complete and permanent separation of religion and civil power which the First Amendment commands is through use of the taxing power to support religion, religious establishments, or establishments having a religious foundation whatever their form or special religious function.

Does New Jersey's action furnish support for religion by use of the taxing power? Certainly it does, if the test remains undiluted as Jefferson and Madison made it, that money taken by taxation from one is not to be used or given to support another's religious training or belief, or indeed one's own. Today as then the furnishing of "contributions of money for the propagation of opinions which he disbelieves" is the forbidden exaction; and the prohibition is absolute for whatever measure brings that consequence and whatever mount may be sought or given to that end.

The funds used here were raised by taxation. The Court does not dispute nor could it that their use does in fact give aid and encouragement to religious instruction. It only concludes that this aid is not "support" in law. But Madison and Jefferson were concerned with aid and support in fact not as a legal conclusion "entangled in precedents." Remonstrance. Here parents pay money to send their children to parochial schools and funds raised by taxation are used to reimburse them. This not only helps the children to get to school and the parents to send them. It aids them in a substantial way to get the very thing which they are sent to the particular school to secure, namely, religious training and teaching. . . .

To say that New Jersey's appropriation and her use of the power of taxation for raising the funds appropriated are not for public purposes but are for private ends, is to say that they are for the support of religion and religious teaching. Conversely, to say that they are for public purposes is to say that they are not for religious ones.

This is precisely for the reason that education which includes religious training and teaching, and its support, have been made matters of private right and function not public, by the very terms of the First Amendment. That is the effect not only in its guaranty of religion's free exercise, but also in the prohibition of establishments. . . .

The reasons underlying the Amendment's policy have not vanished with time or diminished in force. Now as when it was adopted the price of religious freedom is double. It is that the church and religion shall live both within and upon that freedom. There cannot be freedom of religion, safeguarded by the state, and intervention by the church or its agencies in the state's domain or dependency on its largesse. Madison's Remonstrance. The great condition of religious liberty is that it be maintained free from sustenance, as also from other interferences, by the state. For when it comes to rest upon that secular foundation it vanishes with the resting. Public money devoted to payment of religious costs, educational or other, brings the quest for more. It brings too the struggle of sect against sect for the larger share or for any. Here one by numbers alone will benefit most, there another. That is precisely the history of societies which have had an established religion and dissident groups. It is the very thing Jefferson and Madison experienced and sought to guard against, whether in its blunt or in its more screened forms. . . .

No one conscious of religious values can be unsympathetic toward the burden which our constitutional separation puts on parents who desire religious instruction mixed with secular for their children. They pay taxes for others' children's education, at the same time the added cost of instruction for their own. Nor can one happily see benefits denied to children which others receive, because in conscience they or their parents for them desire a different kind of training others do not demand.

But if those feelings should prevail, there would be an end to our historic constitutional policy and command. No more unjust or discriminatory in fact is it to deny attendants at religious schools the cost of their transportation than it is to deny them tuitions, sustenance for their teachers, or any other educational expense which others receive at public cost. Hardship in fact there is which none can blink. But, for assuring to those who undergo it the greater, the most comprehensive freedom, it is one written by design and firm intent into our basic law. . . .

That policy necessarily entails hardship upon persons who forego the right to educational advantages the state can supply in order to secure others it is precluded from giving. Indeed this may hamper the parent and the child forced by conscience to that choice. But it does not make the state unneutral to withhold what the Constitution forbids it to give. On the contrary it is only by observing the prohibition rigidly that the state can maintain its neutrality and avoid partisanship in the dissensions inevitable when sect opposes sect over demands for public moneys to further religious education, teaching or training in any form or degree, directly or indirectly. . . .

Now as in Madison's day it is one of principle, to keep separate the separate spheres as the First Amendment drew them; to prevent the first experiment upon our liberties; and to keep the question from becoming entangled in corrosive precedents. We should not be less strict to keep strong and untarnished the one side of the shield of religious freedom than we have been of the other.

The judgment should be reversed.

Engel v. Vitale
370 U.S. 421, 82 S.Ct. 1261 (1962)

Steven Engel and several other parents of school-age children sued the principal and the Board of Education of Union Free School District No. 9, in New Hyde Park, New York, for requiring students to recite at the beginning of each school day a nondenominational prayer. The prayer, written by the State Board of Regents, was as follows: "Almighty God, we acknowledge our dependence upon Thee, and we beg Thy blessings upon us, our parents, our teachers and our country." An order upholding the power of New York to adopt and require children to recite this prayer was issued by a state court and affirmed by the New York Court of Appeals. Engel made a final appeal to the Supreme Court.

The Court's decision was six to one, and the majority's opinion was announced by Justice Black, with Justices Frankfurter and White not participating. Concurrence was by Justice Douglas and dissent by Justice Stewart.

☐ *Justice BLACK delivered the opinion of the Court.*

We think that by using its public school system to encourage recitation of the Regents' prayer, the State of New York has adopted a practice wholly inconsistent with the Establishment Clause. There can, of course, be no doubt that New York's program of daily classroom invocation of God's blessings as prescribed in the Regents' prayer is a religious activity. . . .

The petitioners contend among other things that the state laws requiring or permitting use of the Regents' prayer must be struck down as a violation of the Establishment Clause because that prayer was composed by governmental officials as a part of a governmental program to further religious beliefs. For this reason, petitioners argue, the State's use of the Regents' prayer in its public school system breaches the constitutional wall of separation between Church and State. We agree with that contention since we think that the constitutional prohibition against laws respecting an establishment of religion must at least mean that in this country it is no part of the business of government to compose official prayers for any group of the American people to recite as a part of a religious program carried on by government.

It is a matter of history that this very practice of establishing governmentally composed prayers for religious services was one of the reasons which caused many of our early colonists to leave England and seek religious freedom in America. *The Book of Common Prayer*, which was created under governmental direction and which was approved by Acts of Parliament in 1548 and 1549, set out in minute detail the accepted form and content of prayer and other religious ceremonies to be used in the established, tax-supported Church of England. . . .

[G]roups, lacking the necessary political power to influence the Government on the matter, decided to leave England and its established church and seek freedom in America from England's governmentally ordained and supported religion.

It is an unfortunate fact of history that when some of the very groups which had most strenuously opposed the established Church of England found themselves sufficiently in control of colonial governments in this country to write their own prayers into law, they passed laws making their own religion the official religion of their respective colonies. Indeed, as late as the time of the Revolutionary War, there were established churches in at least eight of the thirteen former colonies and established religions in at least four of the other five. But the successful Revolution against English political domination was shortly followed by intense opposition to the practice of establishing religion by law. This opposition crystallized rapidly into an effective political force in Virginia where the minority religious groups such as Presbyterians, Lutherans, Quakers and Baptists had gained such strength that the adherents to the established Episcopal Church were actually a minority themselves. In 1785–1786, those opposed to the established Church, led by James Madison and Thomas Jefferson, who, though themselves not members of any of these dissenting religious groups, opposed all religious establishments by law on grounds of principle, obtained the enactment of the famous "Virginia Bill for Religious Liberty" by which all religious groups were placed on an equal footing so far as the State was concerned. Similar though less far-reaching legislation was being considered and passed in other States.

By the time of the adoption of the Constitution, our history shows that there was a widespread awareness among many Americans of the dangers of a union of Church and State. These people knew, some of them from bitter personal experience, that one of the greatest dangers to the freedom of the individual to worship in his own way lay in the Government's placing its official stamp of approval upon one particular kind of prayer or one particular form of religious services. They knew the anguish, hardship and bitter strife that could come when zealous religious groups struggled with one another to obtain the Government's stamp of approval from each King, Queen, or Protector that came to temporary power. The Constitution was intended to avert a part of this danger by leaving the government of this country in the hands of the people rather than in the hands of any monarch. But this safeguard was not enough. Our Founders were no more willing to let the content of their prayers and their privilege of praying whenever they pleased be influenced by the ballot box than they were to let these vital matters of personal conscience depend upon the succession of monarchs. The First Amendment was added to the Constitution to stand as a guarantee that neither the power nor the prestige of the Federal Government would be used to control, support or influence the kinds of prayer the American people can say—that the people's religions must not be subjected to the pressures of government for change each time a new political administration is elected to office. Under that Amendment's prohibition against governmental establishment of religion, as reinforced by the provisions of the Fourteenth Amendment, government in this country, be it state or federal, is without power to prescribe by law any particular form of prayer which is to be used as an official prayer in carrying on any program of governmentally sponsored religious activity.

There can be no doubt that New York's state prayer program officially establishes the religious beliefs embodied in the Regents' prayer. The respondents' argument to the contrary, which is largely based upon the contention that the Regents' prayer is "nondenominational" and the fact that the program, as modified and approved by state courts, does not require all pupils to recite the prayer but permits those who wish to do so to remain silent or be excused from the room, ignores the essential nature of the program's constitutional defects. Neither the fact that the prayer may be denominationally neutral nor the fact that its observance on the part of the students is voluntary can serve to free it from the limitations of the Establishment Clause, as it might from the Free Exercise Clause, of the First Amendment, both of which are operative against the States by virtue of the Fourteenth Amendment. Although these two clauses may in certain instances overlap, they forbid two quite different kinds of governmental encroachment upon religious freedom. The Establishment Clause, unlike the Free Exercise Clause, does not depend upon any showing of direct governmental compulsion and is violated by the enactment of laws which establish an official religion whether those laws operate directly to coerce nonobserving individuals or not. This is not to say, of course, that laws officially prescribing a particular form of religious worship do not involve coercion of such individuals. When the power, prestige and financial support of government is placed behind a particular religious belief, the indirect coercive pressure upon religious minorities to conform to the prevailing officially approved religion is plain. But the purposes underlying the Establishment Clause go much further than that. Its first and most immediate purpose rested on the belief that a union of government and religion tends to destroy government and to degrade religion. The history of governmentally established religion, both in England and in this country, showed that whenever government had allied itself with one particular form of religion, the inevitable result had been that it had incurred the hatred, disrespect and even contempt of those who held contrary beliefs. That same history showed that many people had lost their respect for any religion that had relied upon the support of government to spread its faith. The Establishment Clause thus stands as an expression of principle on the part of the Founders of our Constitution that religion is too personal, too sacred, too holy, to permit its "unhallowed perversion" by a civil magistrate. Another purpose of the Establishment Clause rested upon an awareness of the historical fact that governmentally established religions and religious persecutions go hand in hand. . . . The New York laws officially prescribing the Regents' prayer are inconsistent both with the purposes of the Establishment Clause and with the Establishment Clause itself.

It has been argued that to apply the Constitution in such a way as to prohibit state laws respecting an establishment of religious services in public schools is to indicate a hostility toward religion or toward prayer. Nothing, of course, could be more wrong. . . . It is neither sacrilegious nor antireligious to say that each separate government in this country should stay out of the business of writing or sanctioning official prayers and leave that purely religious function to the people themselves and to those the people choose to look to for religious guidance. . . .

To those who may subscribe to the view that because the Regents' official prayer is so brief and general there can be no danger to religious freedom in its governmental establishment, however, it may be appropriate to say in the words of James Madison, the author of the First Amendment:

"[I]t is proper to take alarm at the first experiment on our liberties. . . . Who does not see that the same authority which can establish Christianity, in exclusion of all other Religions, may establish with the same ease any particular sect of Christians, in exclusion of all other Sects? That the same authority which can force a citizen to contribute three pence only of his property for the support of any one establishment, may force him to conform to any other establishment in all cases whatsoever?"

The judgment of the Court of Appeals of New York is reversed and the cause remanded for further proceedings not inconsistent with this opinion.

Reversed and remanded.

☐ *Justice DOUGLAS, concurring.*

As I read this regulation, a child is free to stand or not stand, to recite or not recite, without fear of reprisal or even comment by the teacher or any other school official.

In short, the only one who need utter the prayer is the teacher; and no teacher is complaining of it. Students can stand mute or even leave the classroom, if they desire. . . .

The question presented by this case is therefore an extremely narrow one. It is whether New York oversteps the bounds when it finances a religious exercise.

What New York does on the opening of its public schools is what we do when we open court. Our Crier has from the beginning announced the convening of the Court and then added "God save the United States and this Honorable Court." That utterance is a supplication, a prayer in which we, the judges, are free to join, but which we need not recite any more than the students need recite the New York prayer.

What New York does on the opening of its public schools is what each House of Congress does at the opening of each day's business. . . .

In New York the teacher who leads in prayer is on the public payroll; and the time she takes seems minuscule as compared with the salaries appropriated by state legislatures and Congress for chaplains to conduct prayers in the legislative halls. Only a bare fraction of the teacher's time is given to reciting this short 22-word prayer, about the same amount of time that our Crier spends announcing the opening of our sessions and offering a prayer for this Court. Yet for me the principle is the same, no matter how briefly the prayer is said, for in each of the instances given the person praying is a public official on the public payroll, performing a religious exercise in a governmental institution. It is said that the element of coercion is inherent in the giving of this prayer. If that is true here, it is also true of the prayer with which this Court is convened, and of those that open the Congress. Few adults, let alone children, would leave our courtroom or the Senate or the House while those prayers are being given. Every such audience is in a sense a "captive" audience.

At the same time I cannot say that to authorize this prayer is to establish a religion in the strictly historic meaning of those words. A religion is not established in the usual sense merely by letting those who choose to do so say the prayer that the public school teacher leads. Yet once government finances a religious exercise it inserts a divisive influence into our communities. . . .

By reason of the First Amendment government is commanded "to have no interest in theology or ritual" for on those matters "government must be neutral." The First Amendment leaves the Government in a position not of hostility to religion but of neutrality. The philosophy is that the atheist or agnostic—the non-believer—is entitled to go his own way. The philosophy is that if government interferes in matters spiritual, it will be a divisive force. The First Amendment teaches that a government neutral in the field of religion better serves all religious interests. . . .

I therefore join the Court in reversing the judgment below.

☐ *Justice STEWART, dissenting.*

With all respect, I think the Court has misapplied a great constitutional principle. I cannot see how an "official religion" is established by letting those who want to say a prayer say it. On the contrary, I think that to deny the wish of these school children to join in reciting this prayer is to deny them the opportunity of sharing in the spiritual heritage of our nation. . . .

At the opening of each day's Session of this Court we stand, while one of our officials invokes the protection of God. Since the days of JOHN MARSHALL our Crier has said, "God save the United States and this Honorable Court." Both the Senate and the House of Representatives open their daily Sessions with prayer. . . .

Countless similar examples could be listed, but there is no need to belabor the obvious. It was all summed up by this Court just ten years ago in a single sentence: "We are a religious people whose institutions presuppose a Supreme Being." *Zorach v. Clauson*, 343 U.S. 306 [(1952)].

I do not believe that this Court, or the Congress, or the President has by the actions and practices I have mentioned established an "official religion" in violation of the Constitution. And I do not believe the State of New York has done so in this case.

Abington School District v. Schempp
and Murray v. Curlett
374 U.S. 203, 83 S.CT. 1560 (1963)

The Supreme Court granted and consolidated these two cases. Each involved disputes arising from state laws requiring schools to begin each day with readings from the Bible. Edward Schempp challenged Pennsylvania's law, which declared that "at least ten verses from the Holy Bible shall be read, without comment, at the opening of each public school day. Any child shall be excused from such Bible reading, or attending such Bible reading, upon written request of his parent or guardian." A three-judge federal district court struck down the state's law as a violation of the First Amendment, and the school board appealed directly to the Supreme Court. The companion case was brought by Madalyn Murray and her son, both professed atheists. They challenged the constitutionality of a rule of the school board of Baltimore, Maryland, requiring students to recite the Lord's Prayer at the opening of each school day. A state court and the Maryland Court of Appeals had upheld the school board.

The Court's decision was eight to one, and the majority's opinion was announced by Justice Clark. Concurrences were by Justices Douglas, Brennan, and Goldberg, who was joined by Justice Harlan. Justice Stewart dissented.

☐ *Justice CLARK delivered the opinion of the Court.*

The wholesome "neutrality" of which this Court's cases speak . . . stems from a recognition of the teachings of history that powerful sects or groups might bring about a fusion of governmental and religious functions or a concert or dependency of one upon the other to the end that official support of the State or Federal Government would be placed behind the tenets of one or of all orthodoxies. This the Establishment Clause prohibits. And a further reason for neutrality is found in the Free Exercise Clause, which recognizes the value of religious training, teaching and observance and, more particularly, the right of every person to freely choose his own course with reference thereto, free of any compulsion from the state. This the Free Exercise Clause guarantees. Thus . . . the two clauses may overlap. . . . [T]he Establishment Clause has been directly considered by this Court eight times in the past score of years and, with only one Justice dissenting on the point, it has consistently held that the clause withdrew all legislative power respecting religious belief or the expression thereof. The test may be stated as follows: what are the purpose and the primary effect of the enactment? If either is the advancement or inhibition of religion then the enactment exceeds the scope of legislative power as circumscribed by the Constitution. That is to say that to withstand the strictures of the Establishment Clause there must be a secular legislative purpose and a primary effect that neither advances nor inhibits religion. The Free Exercise Clause, likewise considered many times here, withdraws from legislative power, state and federal, the exertion of any restraint on the free exercise of religion. Its purpose is to secure religious liberty in the individual by prohibiting any invasions thereof by civil authority. Hence it is necessary in a free exercise case for one to show the coercive effect of the enactment as it operates against him in the practice of his religion. The distinction between the two clauses is apparent—a violation of the Free Exercise Clause is predicated on coercion while the Establishment Clause violation need not be so attended.

Applying the Establishment Clause principles to the cases at bar we find that the States are requiring the selection and reading at the opening of the school day of verses from the Holy *Bible* and the recitation of the Lord's Prayer by the students in unison. These exercises are prescribed as part of the curricular activities of students who are required by law to attend school. They are held in the school buildings under the supervision and with the participation of teachers employed in those schools. . . . The trial court in [*Schempp*] has found that such an opening exercise is a religious ceremony and was intended by the State to be so. We agree with the trial court's finding as to the religious character of the exercises. Given that finding, the exercises and the law requiring them are in violation of the Establishment Clause.

There is no such specific finding as to the religious character of the exercises in [*Murray*] and the State contends (as does the State in [*Schempp*]) that the program is an effort to extend its benefits to all public school children without regard to their religious belief. Included within its secular purposes, it says, are the promotion of moral values, the contradiction to the materialistic trends of our times, the perpetuation of our institutions and the teaching of literature. The case came up on demurrer, of course, to a petition which alleged that the uniform practice under the rule had been to read from the King James version of the Bible and that the exercise was sectarian. The short answer, therefore, is that the religious character of the exercise was admitted by the State. But even if its purpose is not strictly religious, it is sought to be accomplished through readings, without comment, from the Bible. Surely the place of the Bible as an instrument of religion cannot be gainsaid, and the State's recognition of the pervading religious character of the ceremony is evident from the rule's specific permission of the alternative use of the Catholic Douay version as well as the recent amendment permitting nonattendance at the exercises. None of these factors is consistent with the contention that the Bible is here used either as an instrument for nonreligious moral inspiration or as a reference for the teaching of secular subjects.

The conclusion follows that in both cases the laws require religious exercises and such exercises are being conducted in direct violation of the rights of the appellees and petitioners. Nor are these required exercises mitigated by the fact that individual students may absent themselves upon parental request, for that fact furnishes no defense to a claim of unconstitutionality under the Establishment Clause. . . . Further, it is no defense to urge that the religious practices here may be relatively minor encroachments on the First Amendment. The breach of neutrality that is today a trickling stream may all too soon become a raging torrent and, in the words of Madison, "it is proper to take alarm at the first experiment on our liberties.". . .

It is insisted that unless these religious exercises are permitted a "religion of secularism" is established in the schools. We agree of course that the State may not establish a "religion of secularism" in the sense of affirmatively opposing or showing hostility to religion, thus "preferring those who believe in no religion over those who do believe." We do not agree, however, that this decision in any sense has that effect. In addition, it might well be said that one's education is not complete without a study of comparative religion or the history of religion and its relationship to the advancement of civilization. It certainly may be said that the Bible is worthy of study for its literary and historic qualities. Nothing we have said here indicates that such study of the Bible or of religion, when presented objectively as part of a secular program of education, may not be effected consistently with the First Amendment. But the exercises here do not fall into those categories. They are religious exercises, required by the States in violation of the command of the First Amendment that the Government maintain strict neutrality, neither aiding nor opposing religion.

Finally, we cannot accept that the concept of neutrality, which does not permit a State to require a religious exercise even with the consent of the majority of those affected, collides with the majority's right to free exercise of religion. While the Free Exercise Clause clearly prohibits the use of state action to deny the rights of free exercise to *anyone*, it has never meant that a majority could use the machinery of the State to practice its beliefs. Such a contention was effectively answered by Justice JACKSON for the Court in *West Virginia Board of Education v. Barnette*, 319 U.S. 624 (1943). . . .

The place of religion in our society is an exalted one, achieved through a long tradition of reliance on the home, the church and the inviolable citadel of the individual heart and mind. We have come to recognize through bitter experience that it is not within the power of government to invade that citadel, whether its purpose or effect be to aid or oppose, to advance or retard. In the relationship between man and religion, the State is firmly committed to a position of neutrality. Though the application of that rule requires interpretation of a delicate sort, the rule itself is clearly and concisely stated in the words of the First Amendment.

☐ *Justice DOUGLAS, concurring.*

I join the opinion of the Court and add a few words in explanation. . . .

In these cases we have no coercive religious exercise aimed at making the students conform. The prayers announced are not compulsory, though some may think they have that indirect effect because the nonconformist student may be induced to participate for fear of being called an "oddball." But that coercion, if it be present, has not been shown: so the vices of the present regimes are different.

These regimes violate the Establishment Clause in two different ways. In each case the State is conducting a religious exercise; and, as the Court holds, that cannot be done without violating the "neutrality" required of the State by the balance of power between individual, church and state that has been struck by the First Amendment. But the Establishment Clause is not limited to precluding the State itself from conducting religious exercises. It also forbids the State to employ its facilities or funds in a way that gives any church, or all churches, greater strength in our society than it would have by relying on its members alone. Thus, the present regimes must fall under that clause for the additional reason that public funds, though small in amount, are being used to promote a religious exercise. Through the mechanism of the State, all of the people are being required to finance a religious exercise that only some of the people want and that violates the sensibilities of others.

The most effective way to establish any institution is to finance it; and this truth is reflected in the appeals by church groups for public funds to finance their religious schools. Financing a church either in its strictly religious activities or in its other activities is equally unconstitutional, as I understand the Establishment Clause. Budgets for one activity may be technically separable from budgets for others. But the institution is an inseparable whole, a living organism, which is strengthened in proselytizing when it is strengthened in any department by contributions from other than its own members.

☐ *Justice BRENNAN, concurring.*

[T]he history which our prior decisions have summoned to aid interpretation of the Establishment Clause permits little doubt that its prohibition was designed comprehensively to prevent those official involvements of religion which would tend to foster or discourage religious worship or belief.

But an awareness of history and an appreciation of the aims of the Founding Fathers do not always resolve concrete problems. The specific question before us has, for example, aroused vigorous dispute whether the architects of the First Amendment—James Madison and Thomas Jefferson particularly—understood the prohibition against any "law respecting an establishment of religion" to reach devotional exercises in the public schools. . . .

A too literal quest for the advice of the Founding Fathers upon the issues of these cases seems to me futile and misdirected for several reasons: First, on our precise problem the historical record is at best ambiguous, and statements can readily be found to support either side of the proposition. The ambiguity of history is understandable if we recall the nature of the problems uppermost in the thinking of the statesmen who fashioned the religious guarantees; they were concerned with far more flagrant intrusions of government into the realm of religion than any that our century has witnessed. While it is clear to me that the Framers meant the Establishment Clause to prohibit more than the creation of an established federal church such as existed in England, I have no doubt that, in their preoccupation with the imminent question of established churches, they gave no distinct consideration to the particular question whether the clause also forbade devotional exercises in public institutions.

Second, the structure of American education has greatly changed since the First Amendment was adopted. In the context of our modern emphasis upon public education available to all citizens, any views of the eighteenth century as to whether the exercises at bar are an "establishment" offer little aid to decision. Education, as the Framers knew it, was in the main confined to private schools more often than not under strictly sectarian supervision. Only gradually did control of education pass largely to public officials. It would, therefore, hardly be significant if the fact was that the nearly universal devotional exercises in the schools of the young Republic did not provoke criticism; even today religious ceremonies in church-supported private schools are constitutionally unobjectionable.

Third, our religious composition makes us a vastly more diverse people than were our forefathers. They knew differences chiefly among Protestant sects. Today the Nation is far more heterogeneous religiously, including as it does substantial minorities not only of Catholics and Jews but as well of those who worship according to no version of the Bible and those who worship no God at all. In the face of such profound changes, practices which may have been objectionable to no one in the time of Jefferson and Madison may today be highly offensive to many persons, the deeply devout and the nonbelievers alike.

Whatever Jefferson or Madison would have thought of Bible reading or the recital of the Lord's Prayer in what few public schools existed in their day, our use of the history of their time must limit itself to broad purposes, not specific practices. By such a standard, I am persuaded, as is the Court, that the devotional exercises carried on in the Baltimore and Abington schools offend the First Amendment because they sufficiently threaten in our day those substantive evils the fear of which called forth the Establishment Clause of the First Amendment. . . .

Fourth, the American experiment in free public education available to all children has been guided in large measure by the dramatic evolution of the religious diversity among the population which our public schools serve. The interaction of these two important forces in our national life has placed in bold relief certain positive values in the consistent application to public institutions generally, and public schools particularly, of the constitutional decree against official involvements of religion which might produce the evils the Framers meant the Establishment Clause to forestall. The public schools are supported entirely, in most communities, by public funds—funds exacted not only from parents, nor alone from those who hold particular religious views, nor indeed from those who subscribe to any creed at all. It is implicit in the history and character of American public education that the public schools serve a uniquely *public* function: the training of American citizens in an atmosphere free of parochial, divisive, or separatist influences of any sort—an atmosphere in which children may assimilate a heritage common to all American groups and religions. . . .

Attendance at the public schools has never been compulsory; parents remain morally and constitutionally free to choose the academic environment in which they wish their children to be educated. The relationship of the Establishment Clause of the First Amendment to the public school system is preeminently that of reserving such a choice to the individual parent, rather than vesting it in the majority of voters of each State or school district. The choice which is thus preserved is between a public secular education with its uniquely democratic values, and some form of private or sectarian education, which offers values of its own. In my judgment the First Amendment forbids the State to inhibit that freedom of choice by diminishing the attractiveness of either alternative—either by restricting the liberty of the private schools to inculcate whatever values they wish, or by jeopardizing the freedom of the public schools from private or sectarian pressures. The choice between these very different forms of education is one—very much like the choice of whether or not to worship, which our Constitution leaves to the individual parent. It is no proper function of the state or local government to influence or restrict that election.

Lemon v. Kurtzman, Earley v. DiCenso, and *Robinson v. DiCenso*
403 U.S. 602, 91 S.Ct. 2105 (1971)

These three cases brought controversies over laws in Pennsylvania and Rhode Island that provided for direct and indirect financial support of private primary and secondary schools, some of which were run by religious organizations. The cases were consolidated for oral argument and decision. Chief Justice Burger discusses the programs of each state at the outset of his opinion for the Court.

The Court's decision was unanimous, and the opinion was announced by Chief Justice Burger, with Justice Marshall not participating in *Lemon.* Justice Douglas concurred and was joined by Justice Black.

☐ *Chief Justice BURGER delivered the opinion of the Court.*

Pennsylvania has adopted a statutory program that provides financial support to nonpublic elementary and secondary schools by way of reimbursement for the cost of teachers' salaries, textbooks, and instructional materials in specified secular subjects. Rhode Island has adopted a statute under which the State pays directly to teachers in nonpublic elementary schools a supplement of 15% of their annual salary. Under each statute state aid has been given to church-related educational institutions. We hold that both statutes are unconstitutional.

■ I

The Rhode Island Statute The Rhode Island Salary Supplement Act was enacted in 1969. It rests on the legislative finding that the quality of education available in nonpublic elementary schools has been jeopardized by the rapidly rising salaries needed to attract competent and dedicated teachers. The Act authorizes state officials to supplement the salaries of teachers of secular subjects in nonpublic elementary schools by paying directly to a teacher an amount not in excess of 15% of his current annual salary. As supplemented, however, a nonpublic school teacher's salary cannot exceed the maximum paid to teachers in the State's public schools, and the recipient must be certified by the state board of education in substantially the same manner as public school teachers.

In order to be eligible for the Rhode Island salary supplement, the recipient must teach in a nonpublic school at which the average per-pupil expenditure on secular education is less than the average in the State's public schools during a specified period. Appellant State Commissioner of Education also requires eligible schools to submit financial data. If this information indicates a per-pupil expenditure in excess of the statutory limitation, the records of the school in question must be examined in order to assess how much of the expenditure is attributable to secular education and how much to religious activity.

The Act also requires that teachers eligible for salary supplements must teach only those subjects that are offered in the State's public schools. They must use "only teaching materials which are used in the public schools." Finally, any teacher applying for a salary supplement must first agree in writing "not to teach a course in religion for so long as or during such time as he or she receives any salary supplements" under the Act. . . .

A three-judge federal court found that Rhode Island's nonpublic elementary schools accommodated approximately 25% of the State's pupils. About 95% of these pupils attended schools affiliated with the Roman Catholic church. To date some 250 teachers have applied for benefits under the Act. All of them are employed by Roman Catholic schools. . . .

The District Court concluded that the Act violated the Establishment Clause, holding that it fostered "excessive entanglement" between government and religion. In addition two judges thought that the Act had the impermissible effect of giving "significant aid to a religious enterprise." We affirm.

The Pennsylvania Statute Pennsylvania has adopted a program that has some but not all of the features of the Rhode Island program. The Pennsylvania Nonpublic Elementary and Secondary Education Act was passed in 1968 in response to a crisis that the Pennsylvania Legislature found existed in the State's nonpublic schools due to rapidly rising costs. . . .

The statute authorizes appellee state Superintendent of Public Instruction to "purchase" specified "secular educational services" from nonpublic schools. Under the "contracts" authorized by the statute, the State directly reimburses nonpublic schools solely for their actual expenditures for teachers' salaries, textbooks, and instructional materials. A school seeking reimbursement must maintain prescribed accounting procedures that identify the "separate" cost of the "secular educational service." These accounts are subject to state audit. . . .

There are several significant statutory restrictions on state aid. Reimbursement is limited to courses "presented in the curricula of the public schools." It is further limited "solely" to courses in the following "secular" subjects: mathematics, modern foreign languages, physical science, and physical education. Textbooks and instructional materials included in the program must be approved by the state Superintendent of Public Instruction. Finally, the statute prohibits reimbursement for any course that contains "any subject matter expressing religious teaching, or the morals or forms of worship of any sect." . . .

It appears that some $5 million has been expended annually under the

Act. The State has now entered into contracts with some 1,181 nonpublic elementary and secondary schools with a student population of some 535,215 pupils—more than 20% of the total number of students in the State. More than 96% of these pupils attend church-related schools, and most of these schools are affiliated with the Roman Catholic church. . . .

A three-judge federal court . . . held that the Act violated neither the Establishment nor the Free Exercise Clause. . . . We reverse. . . .

■ II

The language of the Religion Clauses of the First Amendment is at best opaque, particularly when compared with other portions of the Amendment. Its authors did not simply prohibit the establishment of a state church or a state religion, an area history shows they regarded as very important and fraught with great dangers. Instead they commanded that there should be "no law *respecting* an establishment of religion." A law may be one "respecting" the forbidden objective while falling short of its total realization. A law "respecting" the proscribed result, that is, the establishment of religion, is not always easily identifiable as one violative of the Clause. A given law might not *establish* a state religion but nevertheless be one "respecting" that end in the sense of being a step that could lead to such establishment and hence offend the First Amendment. . . .

Every analysis in this area must begin with consideration of the cumulative criteria developed by the Court over many years. Three such tests may be learned from our cases. First, the statute must have a secular legislative purpose; second, its principal or primary effect must be one that neither advances or inhibits religion; finally, the statute must not foster "an excessive government Entanglement with religion." . . .

Inquiry into the legislative purposes of the Pennsylvania and Rhode Island statutes affords no basis for a conclusion that the legislative intent was to advance religion. On the contrary, the statutes themselves clearly state that they are intended to enhance the quality of the secular education in all schools covered by the compulsory attendance laws. There is no reason to believe the legislatures meant anything else. . . .

The legislatures of Rhode Island and Pennsylvania have concluded that secular and religious education are identifiable and separable. In the abstract we have no quarrel with this conclusion.

The two legislatures, however, have also recognized that church-related elementary and secondary schools have a significant religious mission and that a substantial portion of their activities is religiously oriented. They have therefore sought to create statutory restrictions designed to guarantee the separation between secular and religious educational functions and to ensure that State financial aid supports only the former. All these provisions are precautions taken in candid recognition that these programs approached, even if they did not intrude upon, the forbidden areas under the Religion Clauses. We need not decide whether these legislative precautions restrict the principal or primary effect of the programs to the point where they do not offend the Religion Clauses, for we conclude that the cumulative impact of the entire relationship arising under the statutes in each State involves excessive entanglement between government and religion.

■ III

In *Walz v. Tax Commission*, [397 U.S. 664 (1970)], the Court upheld state tax exemptions for real property owned by religious organizations and used for religious worship. That holding, however, tended to confine rather than enlarge the area of permissible state involvement with religious institutions by calling for close scrutiny of the degree of entanglement involved in the relationship. The objective is to prevent, as far as possible, the intrusion of either into the precincts of the other.

Our prior holdings do not call for total separation between church and state; total separation is not possible in an absolute sense. Some relationship between government and religious organizations is inevitable. . . . Fire inspections, building and zoning regulations, and state requirements under compulsory school-attendance laws are examples of necessary and permissible contacts. . . . Judicial caveats against entanglement must recognize that the line of separation, far from being a "wall," is a blurred, indistinct, and variable barrier depending on all the circumstances of a particular relationship.

This is not to suggest, however, that we are to engage in a legalistic minuet in which precise rules and forms must govern. A true minuet is a matter of pure form and style, the observance of which is itself the substantive end. Here we examine the form of the relationship for the light that it casts on the substance.

In order to determine whether the government entanglement with religion is excessive, we must examine the character and purposes of the institutions that are benefited, the nature of the aid that the State provides, and the resulting relationship between the government and the religious authority. . . . Here we find that both statutes foster an impermissible degree of entanglement.

(a) *Rhode Island program* The church schools involved in the program are located close to parish churches. . . . The school buildings contain identifying religious symbols such as crosses on the exterior and crucifixes, and religious paintings and statutes either in the classrooms or hallways. Although only approximately 30 minutes a day are devoted to direct religious instruction, there are religiously oriented extracurricular activities. Approximately two-thirds of the teachers in these schools are nuns of various religious orders. Their dedicated efforts provide an atmosphere in which religious instruction and religious vocations are natural and proper parts of life in such schools. . . .

This process of inculcating religious doctrine is, of course, enhanced by the impressionable age of the pupils, in primary schools particularly. In short, parochial schools involve substantial religious activity and purpose.

The substantial religious character of these church-related schools gives rise to entangling church-state relationships of the kind the Religion Clauses sought to avoid. . . .

The dangers and corresponding entanglements are enhanced by the particular form of aid that the Rhode Island Act provides. Our decisions from *Everson* to *Allen* have permitted the States to provide church-related schools with secular, neutral, or nonideological services, facilities, or materials. Bus transportation, school lunches, public health services, and secular textbooks supplied in common to all students were not thought to offend the Establishment Clause. . . .

In [*Board of Education v. Allen*, 392 U.S. 236 (1968)] the Court refused to make assumptions, on a meager record, about the religious content of the textbooks that the State would be asked to provide. We cannot, however, refuse here to recognize that teachers have a substantially different ideological character from books. In terms of potential for involving some aspect of faith or morals in secular subjects, a textbook's content is ascertainable, but a teacher's handling of a subject is not. We cannot ignore the danger that a teacher under religious control and discipline poses to the separation of the religious from the purely secular aspects of precollege education. The conflict of functions inheres in the situation.

In our view the record shows these dangers are present to a substantial degree. . . .

The schools are governed by the standards set forth in a "Handbook of School Regulations," which has the force of synodal law in the diocese. It emphasizes the role and importance of the teacher in parochial schools: "The prime factor for the success or the failure of the school is the spirit and personality, as well as the professional competency, of the teacher. . . ." The Handbook also states that: "Religious formation is not confined to formal courses; nor is it restricted to a single subject area." . . .

Several teachers testified, however, that they did not inject religion into their secular classes. . . . But what has been recounted suggests the potential if not actual hazards of this form of state aid. The teacher is employed by a religious organization, subject to the direction and discipline of religious authorities, and works in a system dedicated to rearing children in a particular faith. These controls are not lessened by the fact that most of the lay teachers are of the Catholic faith. Inevitably some of a teacher's responsibilities hover on the border between secular and religious orientation.

We need not and do not assume that teachers in parochial schools will be guilty of bad faith or any conscious design to evade the limitations imposed by the statute and the First Amendment. We simply recognize that a dedicated religious person, teaching in a school affiliated with his or her faith and operated to inculcate its tenets, will inevitably experience great difficulty in remaining religiously neutral. Doctrines and faith are not inculcated or advanced by neutrals. With the best of intentions such a teacher would find it hard to make a total separation between secular teaching and religious doctrine. What would appear to some to be essential to good citizenship might well for others border on or constitute instruction in religion. Further difficulties are inherent in the combination of religious discipline and the possibility of disagreement between teacher and religious authorities over the meaning of the statutory restrictions. . . .

The Rhode Island Legislature has not, and could not, provide state aid on the basis of a mere assumption that secular teachers under religious discipline can avoid conflicts. The State must be certain, given the Religion Clauses, that subsidized teachers do not inculcate religion—indeed the State here has undertaken to do so. To ensure that no trespass occurs, the State has therefore carefully conditioned its aid with pervasive restrictions. . . .

A comprehensive, discriminating, and continuing state surveillance will inevitably be required to ensure that these restrictions are obeyed and the First Amendment otherwise respected. Unlike a book, a teacher cannot be inspected once so as to determine the extent and intent of his or her personal beliefs and subjective acceptance of the limitations imposed by the

First Amendment. These prophylactic contacts will involve excessive and enduring entanglement between state and church.

There is another area of entanglement in the Rhode Island program that gives concern. The statute excludes teachers employed by nonpublic schools whose average per-pupil expenditures on secular education equal or exceed the comparable figures for public schools. In the event that the total expenditures of an otherwise eligible school exceed this norm, the program requires the government to examine the school's records in order to determine how much of the total expenditures is attributable to secular education and how much to religious activity. This kind of state inspection and evaluation of the religious content of a religious organization is fraught with the sort of entanglement that the Constitution forbids. It is a relationship pregnant with dangers of excessive government direction of church schools and hence of churches. . . .

(b) *Pennsylvania program* As we noted earlier, the very restrictions and surveillance necessary to ensure that teachers play a strictly nonideological role give rise to entanglements between church and state. The Pennsylvania statute, like that of Rhode Island, fosters this kind of relationship. . . .

The Pennsylvania statute, moreover, has the further defect of providing state financial aid directly to the church-related schools. This factor distinguishes both *Everson* and *Allen*, for in both those cases the Court was careful to point out that state aid was provided to the student and his parents—not to the church-related school. . . . The history of government grants of a continuing cash subsidy indicates that such programs have almost always been accompanied by varying measures of control and surveillance. The government cash grants before us now provide no basis for predicting that comprehensive measures of surveillance and controls will not follow. . . .

■ IV

A broader base of entanglement of yet a different character is presented by the devisive political potential of these state programs. In a community where such a large number of pupils are served by church-related schools, it can be assumed that state assistance will entail considerable political activity. Partisans of parochial schools, understandably concerned with rising costs and sincerely dedicated to both the religious and secular educational missions of their schools, will inevitably champion this cause and promote political action to achieve their goals. Those who oppose state aid, whether for constitutional, religious, or fiscal reasons, will inevitably respond and employ all of the usual political campaign techniques to prevail. Candidates will be forced to declare and voters to choose. . . .

Ordinarily political debate and division, however vigorous or even partisan, are normal and healthy manifestations of our democratic system of government, but political division along religious lines was one of the principal evils against which the First Amendment was intended to protect. The potential divisiveness of such conflict is a threat to the normal political process. It conflicts with our whole history and tradition to permit questions of the Religion Clauses to assume such importance in our legislatures and in our elections that they could divert attention from the myriad issues and problems that confront every level of government. The highways of church and state relationships are not likely to be one-way streets, and the Constitution's authors sought to protect religious worship from the pervasive power of government. The history of many countries attests to the hazards of religion's intruding into the political arena or of political power intruding into the legitimate and free exercise of religious belief. . . .

The potential for political divisiveness related to religious belief and practice is aggravated in these two statutory programs by the need for continuing annual appropriations and the likelihood of larger and larger demands as costs and populations grow. The Rhode Island District Court found that the parochial school system's "monumental and deepening financial crisis" would "inescapably" require larger annual appropriations subsidizing greater percentages of the salaries of lay teachers. Although no facts have been developed in this respect in the Pennsylvania case, it appears that such pressures for expanding aid have already required the state legislature to include a portion of the state revenues from cigarette taxes in the program.

We have no long history of state aid to church-related educational institutions comparable to 200 years of tax exemption for churches. Indeed, the state programs before us today represent something of an innovation. We have already noted that modern governmental programs have self-perpetuating and self-expanding propensities. These internal pressures are only enhanced when the schemes involve institutions whose legitimate needs are growing and whose interests have substantial political support. Nor can we fail to see that in constitutional adjudication some steps, which when taken were thought to approach "the verge," have become the platform for yet further steps. A certain momentum develops in constitutional theory and it can be a "downhill thrust" easily set in motion but difficult to retard or stop. Development by momentum is not invariably bad; indeed, it is the way the common law has grown, but it is a force to be recognized and reckoned with. The dangers are increased by the difficulty of perceiving in advance exactly where the "verge" of the precipice lies. As well as constituting an independent evil against which the Religion Clauses were intended to protect, involvement or entanglement between government and religion serves as a warning signal. . . .

The merit and benefits of these schools . . . are not the issue before us in these cases. The sole question is whether state aid to these schools can be squared with the dictates of the Religion Clauses. Under our system the choice has been made that government is to be entirely excluded from the area of religious instruction and churches excluded from the affairs of government. The Constitution decrees that religion must be a private matter for the individual, the family, and the institutions of private choice, and that while some involvement and entanglement are inevitable, lines must be drawn.

☐ *Justice DOUGLAS, whom Justice BLACK joins, concurring.*

We said in unequivocal words in *Everson v. Board of Education*, 330 U.S. 1 [(1947)], "No tax in any amount, large or small, can be levied to support any religious activities or institutions, whatever they may be called, or whatever form they may adopt to teach or practice religion." We reiterated the same idea in *Zorach v. Clauson*, [343 U.S. 306 (1952)]; and in *McGowan v. Maryland*, [366 U.S. 420 (1961)]; and in *Torcaso v. Watkins*, [367 U.S. 488 (1961)]. We repeated the same idea in *McCollum v. Board of Education*, and added that a

State's tax-supported public schools could not be used "for the dissemination of religious doctrines" nor could a State provide the church "pupils for their religious classes through use of the state's compulsory public school machinery." . . .

Yet in spite of this long and consistent history there are those who have the courage to announce that a State may nonetheless finance the *secular* part of a sectarian school's educational program. That, however, makes a grave constitutional decision turn merely on cost accounting and bookkeeping entries. A history class, a literature class, or a science class in a parochial school is not a separate institute; it is part of the organic whole which the State subsidizes. The funds are used in these cases to pay or help pay the salaries of teachers in parochial schools; and the presence of teachers is critical to the essential purpose of the parochial school, *viz.*, to advance the religious endeavors of the particular church. It matters not that the teacher receiving taxpayers' money only teaches religion a fraction of the time. Nor does it matter that he or she teaches no religion. The school is an organism living on one budget. What the taxpayers give for salaries of those who teach only the humanities or science without any trace of proseletyzing enables the school to use all of its own funds for religious training. . . .

In my view the taxpayers' forced contribution to the parochial schools in the present cases violates the First Amendment.

Wallace v. Jaffree
472 U.S. 38, 105 S.Ct. 2479 (1985)

The pertinent facts in this controversy, involving a challenge to Alabama's law requiring that each school day begin with a moment of silent prayer or meditation, are stated by Justice Stevens in his opinion for the Court. (Excerpts from the lower court's opinion are reprinted in Ch. 2.)

The Court's decision was six to three, and the majority's opinion was announced by Justice Stevens. Concurrences were by Justices Powell and O'Connor, dissents by Chief Justice Burger and Justices White and Rehnquist.

□ *Justice STEVENS delivered the opinion of the Court.*

Appellee Ishmael Jaffree is a resident of Mobile County, Alabama. On May 28, 1982, he filed a complaint on behalf of three of his minor children; two of them were second-grade students and the third was then in kindergarten. The complaint named members of the Mobile County School Board, various school officials, and the minor plaintiffs' three teachers as defendants. The complaint alleged that the appellees brought the action "seeking principally a declaratory judgment and an injunction restraining the

Defendants and each of them from maintaining or allowing the maintenance of regular religious prayer services or other forms of religious observances in the Mobile County Public Schools in violation of the First Amendment as made applicable to states by the Fourteenth Amendment to the United States Constitution." The complaint further alleged that two of the children had been subjected to various acts of religious indoctrination "from the beginning of the school year in September, 1981"; that the defendant teachers had "on a daily basis" led their classes in saying certain prayers in unison; that the minor children were exposed to ostracism from their peer group class members if they did not participate; and that Ishmael Jaffree had repeatedly but unsuccessfully requested that the devotional services be stopped. . . .

The District Court found that during that academic year each of the minor plaintiffs' teachers had led classes in prayer activities, even after being informed of appellees' objections to these activities.

In its lengthy conclusions of law, the District Court reviewed a number of opinions of this Court interpreting the Establishment Clause of the First Amendment, and then embarked on a fresh examination of the question whether the First Amendment imposes any barrier to the establishment of an official religion by the State of Alabama. After reviewing at length what it perceived to be newly discovered historical evidence, the District Court concluded that "the establishment clause of the first amendment to the United States Constitution does not prohibit the state from establishing a religion." In a separate opinion, the District Court dismissed appellees' challenge to the three Alabama statutes because of a failure to state any claim for which relief could be granted. The court's dismissal of this challenge was also based on its conclusion that the Establishment Clause did not bar the States from establishing a religion.

The Court of Appeals . . . , not surprisingly, reversed. . . .

Our unanimous affirmance of the Court of Appeals' judgment . . . makes it unnecessary to comment at length on the District Court's remarkable conclusion that the Federal Constitution imposes no obstacle to Alabama's establishment of a state religion. Before analyzing the precise issue that is presented to us, it is nevertheless appropriate to recall how firmly embedded in our constitutional jurisprudence is the proposition that the several States have no greater power to restrain the individual freedoms protected by the First Amendment than does the Congress of the United States. . . .

When the Court has been called upon to construe the breadth of the Establishment Clause, it has examined the criteria developed over a period of years. Thus, in *Lemon v. Kurtzman*, 403 U.S. 602 (1972), we wrote:

> "Every analysis in this area must begin with consideration of the cumulative criteria developed by the Court over many years. Three such tests may be gleaned from our cases. First, the statute must have a secular legislative purpose; second, its principal or primary effect must be one that neither advances nor inhibits religion . . . finally, the statute must not foster 'an excessive government entanglement with religion.' " . . . It is the first of these three criteria that is most plainly implicated by this case. As the District Court correctly recognized, no consideration of the second or third crite-

ria is necessary if a statute does not have a clearly secular purpose. For even though a statute that is motivated in part by a religious purpose may satisfy the first criterion, see, *e.g., Abington School Dist. v. Schempp,* . . . the First Amendment requires that a statute must be invalidated if it is entirely motivated by a purpose to advance religion."

In applying the purpose test, it is appropriate to ask "whether government's actual purpose is to endorse or disapprove of religion." In this case, the answer to that question is dispositive. For the record not only provides us with an unambiguous affirmative answer, but it also reveals that the enactment of [the Alabama law] was not motivated by any clearly secular purpose—indeed, the statute had *no* secular purpose.

The sponsor of the bill that became [law], Senator Donald Holmes, inserted into the legislative record—apparently without dissent—a statement indicating that the legislation was an "effort to return voluntary prayer" to the public schools. Later Senator Holmes confirmed this purpose before the District Court. In response to the question whether he had any purpose for the legislation other than returning voluntary prayer to public schools, he stated, "No, I did not have no other purpose in mind." The State did not present evidence of *any* secular purpose. . . .

We must, therefore, conclude that the Alabama Legislature intended to change existing law and that it was motivated by the same purpose that the Governor's Answer to the Second Amended Complaint expressly admitted; that the statement inserted in the legislative history revealed; and that Senator Holmes' testimony frankly described. The Legislature enacted [the statute authorizing teachers to lead students in a moment of "silent meditation or voluntary prayer"] despite the existence of [an earlier law permitting teachers to begin each school day with a period of silence "for meditation"] for the sole purpose of expressing the State's endorsement of prayer activities for one minute at the beginning of each school day. The addition of "or voluntary prayer" indicates that the State intended to characterize prayer as a favored practice. Such an endorsement is not consistent with the established principle that the Government must pursue a course of complete neutrality toward religion.

The importance of that principle does not permit us to treat this as an inconsequential case involving nothing more than a few words of symbolic speech on behalf of the political majority. For whenever the State itself speaks on a religious subject, one of the questions that we must ask is "whether the Government intends to convey a message of endorsement or disapproval of religion." The well-supported concurrent findings of the District Court and the Court of Appeals—that [the Alabama statute] was intended to convey a message of State-approval of prayer activities in the public schools—make it unnecessary, and indeed inappropriate, to evaluate the practical significance of the addition of the words "or voluntary prayer" to the statute. Keeping in mind, as we must, "both the fundamental place held by the Establishment Clause in our constitutional scheme and the myriad, subtle ways in which Establishment Clause values can be eroded," we conclude that [the statute] violates the First Amendment.

The judgment of the Court of Appeals is affirmed. . . .

☐ *Justice O'CONNOR, concurring.*

I write separately to identify the peculiar features of the Alabama law that render it invalid, and to explain why moment of silence laws in other States do not necessarily manifest the same infirmity. . . .

It once appeared that the Court had developed a workable standard by which to identify impermissible government establishments of religion. See *Lemon v. Kurtzman* (1971). Under the now familiar *Lemon* test, statutes must have both a secular legislative purpose and a principal or primary effect that neither advances nor inhibits religion, and in addition they must not foster excessive government entanglement with religion. Despite its initial promise, the *Lemon* test has proven problematic: The required inquiry into "entanglement" has been modified and questioned, see *Mueller v. Allen*, 463 U.S. 388 (1983), and in one case we have upheld state action against an Establishment Clause challenge without applying the *Lemon* test at all. *Marsh v. Chambers*, 463 U.S. 783 (1983). . . .

I am not ready to abandon all aspects of the *Lemon* test. I do believe, however, that the standards announced in *Lemon* should be reexamined and refined in order to make them more useful in achieving the underlying purpose of the First Amendment. We must strive to do more than erect a constitutional "signpost," to be followed or ignored in a particular case as our predilections may dictate. Instead, our goal should be "to frame a principle for constitutional adjudication that is not only grounded in the history and language of the first amendment, but one that is also capable of consistent application to the relevant problems." . . .

[R]eligious liberty protected by the Establishment Clause is infringed when the government makes adherence to religion relevant to a person's standing in the political community. Direct government action endorsing religion or a particular religious practice is invalid under this approach because it "sends a message to nonadherents that they are outsiders, not full members of the political community, and an accompanying message to adherents that they are insiders, favored members of the political community." Under this view, *Lemon's* inquiry as to the purpose and effect of a statute requires courts to examine whether government's purpose is to endorse religion and whether the statute actually conveys a message of endorsement.

The endorsement test is useful because of the analytic content it gives to the *Lemon*-mandated inquiry into legislative purpose and effect. In this country, church and state must necessarily operate within the same community. Because of this co-existence, it is inevitable that the secular interests of Government and the religious interests of various sects and their adherents will frequently intersect, conflict, and combine. A statute that ostensibly promotes a secular interest often has an incidental or even a primary effect of helping or hindering a sectarian belief. Chaos would ensue if every such statute were invalid under the Establishment Clause. For example, the State could not criminalize murder for fear that it would thereby promote the Biblical command against killing. The task for the Court is to sort out those statutes and government practices whose purpose and effect go against the grain of religious liberty protected by the First Amendment.

The endorsement test does not preclude government from acknowledging religion or from taking religion into account in making law and policy. It does preclude government from conveying or attempting to convey a message that religion or a particular religious belief is favored or preferred. Such an endorsement infringes the religious liberty of the nonadherent, for "[w]hen the power, prestige and financial support of government is placed behind a particular religious belief, the indirect coercive pressure upon religious minorities to conform to the prevailing officially approved religion is plain." *Engel v. Vitale*, [370 U.S. 421 (1962)]. At issue today is whether state moment of silence statues in general, and Alabama's moment of silence statute in particular, embody an impermissible endorsement of prayer in public schools.

Twenty-five states permit or require public school teachers to have students observe a moment of silence in their classrooms. A few statutes provide that the moment of silence is for the purpose of meditation alone. The typical statute, however, calls for a moment of silence at the beginning of the school day during which students may meditate, pray, or reflect on the activities of the day. . . .

Relying on this Court's decisions disapproving vocal prayer and Bible reading in the public schools, see *Abington School District v. Schempp*, [374 U.S. 203 (1963)]; [and] *Engel v. Vitale*, the courts that have struck down the moment of silence statutes generally conclude that their purpose and effect is to encourage prayer in public schools.

The *Engel* and *Abington* decisions are not dispositive on the constitutionality of moment of silence laws. In those cases, public school teachers and students led their classes in devotional exercises. . . . The Court reviewed the purpose and effect of the statutes, concluded that they required religious exercises, and therefore found them to violate the Establishment Clause. . . .

A state sponsored moment of silence in the public schools is different from state sponsored vocal prayer or Bible reading. First, a moment of silence is not inherently religious. Silence, unlike prayer or Bible reading, need not be associated with a religious exercise. Second, a pupil who participates in a moment of silence need not compromise his or her beliefs. During a moment of silence, a student who objects to prayer is left to his or her own thoughts, and is not compelled to listen to the prayers or thoughts of others. For these simple reasons, a moment of silence statute does not stand or fall under the Establishment Clause according to how the Court regards vocal prayer or Bible reading. . . . It is difficult to discern a serious threat to religious liberty from a room of silent, thoughtful schoolchildren. . . .

The analysis above suggests that moment of silence laws in many States should pass Establishment Clause scrutiny because they do not favor the child who chooses to pray during a moment of silence over the child who chooses to meditate or reflect. [The Alabama statute] does not stand on the same footing. However deferentially one examines its text and legislative history, however objectively one views the message attempted to be conveyed to the public, the conclusion is unavoidable that the purpose of the statute is to endorse prayer in public schools. I accordingly agree . . . that the Alabama statute has a purpose which is in violation of the Establishment Clause, and cannot be upheld. . . .

☐ *Justice REHNQUIST, dissenting.*

Thirty-eight years ago this Court, in *Everson v. Board of Education* [330 U.S. 1] (1947) summarized its exegesis of Establishment Clause doctrine thus:

"In the words of Jefferson, the clause against establishment of religion by law was intended to erect 'a wall of separation between church and State.' *Reynolds v. United States*, [98 U.S. 145 (1879).]"

This language from *Reynolds*, a case involving the Free Exercise Clause of the First Amendment rather than the Establishment Clause, quoted from Thomas Jefferson's letter to the Danbury Baptist Association the phrase "I contemplate with sovereign reverence that act of the whole American people which declared that their legislature should 'make no law respecting an establishment of religion, or prohibiting the free exercise thereof,' thus building a wall of separation between church and State."

It is impossible to build sound constitutional doctrine upon a mistaken understanding of constitutional history, but unfortunately the Establishment Clause has been expressly freighted with Jefferson's misleading metaphor for nearly forty years. Thomas Jefferson was of course in France at the time the constitutional amendments known as the Bill of Rights were passed by Congress and ratified by the states. His letter to the Danbury Baptist Association was a short note of courtesy, written fourteen years after the amendments were passed by Congress. He would seem to any detached observer as a less than ideal source of contemporary history as to the meaning of the Religion Clauses of the First Amendment.

Jefferson's fellow Virginian James Madison, with whom he was joined in the battle for the enactment of the Virginia Statute of Religious Liberty of 1786, did play as large a part as anyone in the drafting of the Bill of Rights. He had two advantages over Jefferson in this regard: he was present in the United States, and he was a leading member of the First Congress. But when we turn to the record of the proceedings in the First Congress leading up to the adoption of the Establishment Clause of the Constitution, including Madison's significant contributions thereto, we see a far different picture of its purpose than the highly simplified "wall of separation between church and State." . . .

On the basis of the record of these proceedings in the House of Representatives, James Madison was undoubtedly the most important architect among the members of the House of the amendments which became the Bill of Rights, but it was James Madison speaking as an advocate of sensible legislative compromise, not as an advocate of incorporating the Virginia Statute of Religious Liberty into the United States Constitution. During the ratification debate in the Virginia Convention, Madison had actually opposed the idea of any Bill of Rights. His sponsorship of the amendments in the House was obviously not that of a zealous believer in the necessity of the Religion Clauses, but of one who felt it might do some good, could do no harm, and would satisfy those who had ratified the Constitution on the condition that Congress propose a Bill of Rights. His original language "nor shall any national religion be established" obviously does not conform to the "wall of separation" between church and State idea which latter day commentators have ascribed to him. His explanation on the floor of the meaning of his language—"that Congress should not establish a religion, and enforce the legal observation of it by law" is of the same ilk. When he replied to Huntington in the debate over the proposal which came from the Select Committee of the House, he urged that the language "no religion shall be established by law" should be amended by inserting the word "national" in front of the word "religion."

It seems indisputable from these glimpses of Madison's thinking, as reflected by actions on the floor of the House in 1789, that he saw the amendment as designed to prohibit the establishment of a national religion, and perhaps to prevent discrimination among sects. He did not see it as requiring neutrality on the part of government between religion and irreligion. Thus the Court's opinion in *Everson*—while correct in bracketing Madison and Jefferson together in their exertions in their home state leading to the enactment of the Virginia Statute of Religious Liberty—is totally incorrect in suggesting that Madison carried these views onto the floor of the United States House of Representatives when he proposed the language which would ultimately become the Bill of Rights.

The repetition of this error in the Court's opinion in [*McCollum v. Board of Education* (1948) and *Engel v. Vitale* (1962)] does not make it any sounder historically. Finally, in *Abington School Board District v. Schempp* [(1963)], the Court made the truly remarkable statement that "the views of Madison and Jefferson, preceded by Roger Williams came to be incorporated not only in the Federal Constitution but likewise in those of most of our States" (footnote omitted). On the basis of what evidence we have, this statement is demonstrably incorrect as a matter of history. And its repetition in varying forms in succeeding opinions of the Court can give it no more authority than it possesses as a matter of fact; *stare decisis* may bind courts as to matters of law, but it cannot bind them as to matters of history. . . .

The actions of the First Congress, which re-enacted the Northwest Ordinance for the governance of the Northwest Territory in 1789, confirm the view that Congress did not mean that the Government should be neutral between religion and irreligion. The House of Representatives took up the Northwest Ordinance on the same day as Madison introduced his proposed amendments which became the Bill of Rights; while at that time the Federal Government was of course not bound by draft amendments to the Constitution which had not yet been proposed by Congress, say nothing of ratified by the States, it seems highly unlikely that the House of Representatives would simultaneously consider proposed amendments to the Constitution and enact an important piece of territorial legislation which conflicted with the intent of those proposals. The Northwest Ordinance, 1 Stat. 50, reenacted the Northwest Ordinance of 1787 and provided that "[r]eligion, morality, and knowledge, being necessary to good government and the happiness of mankind, schools and the means of education shall forever be encouraged." . . .

As the United States moved from the 18th into the 19th century, Congress appropriated time and again public moneys in support of sectarian Indian education carried on by religious organizations. Typical of these was Jefferson's treaty with the Kaskaskia Indians, which provided annual cash support for the Tribe's Roman Catholic priest and church. It was not until 1897, when aid to sectarian education for Indians had reached $500,000 annually, that Congress decided thereafter to cease appropriating money for education in sectarian schools. . . . This history shows the fallacy of the notion found in *Everson* that "no tax in any amount" may be levied for religious activities in any form. . . .

Notwithstanding the absence of an historical basis for this theory of rigid separation, the wall idea might well have served as a useful albeit misguided analytical concept, had it led this Court to unified and principled results in Establishment Clause cases. The opposite, unfortunately, has been true; in the 38 years since *Everson* our Establishment Clause cases have been neither principaled nor unified. Our recent opinions, many of them hopelessly divided pluralities, have with embarassing candor conceded that the "wall of separation" is merely a "blurred, indistinct, and variable barrier," which "is not wholly accurate" and can only be "dimly perceived." . . .

Whether due to its lack of historical support or its practical workability, the *Everson* "wall" has proven all but useless as a guide to sound constitutional adjudication. . . .

But the greatest injury of the "wall" notion is its mischievous diversion of judges from the actual intentions of the drafters of the Bill of Rights. The "crucible of litigation," is well adapted to adjudicating factual disputes on the basis of testimony presented in court, but no amount of repetition of historical errors in judicial opinions can make the errors true. The "wall of separation between church and State" is a metaphor based on bad history, a metaphor which has proved useless as a guide to judging. It should be frankly and explicitly abandoned.

The Court has more recently attempted to add some mortar to *Everson's* wall through the three-part test of *Lemon*, which served at first to offer a more useful test for purposes of the Establishment Clause than did the "wall" metaphor. Generally stated, the *Lemon* test proscribes state action that has a sectarian purpose or effect, or causes an impermissible governmental entanglement with religion. . . .

Lemon cited *Board of Education v. Allen*, [392 U.S. 236] (1968), as the source of the "purpose" and "effect" prongs of the three-part test. The *Allen* opinion explains, however, how it inherited the purpose and effect elements from *Schempp* and *Everson*, both of which contain the historical errors described above. Thus the purpose and effect prongs have the same historical deficiencies as the wall concept itself: they are in no way based on either the language or intent of the drafters.

The secular purpose prong has proven mercurial in application because it has never been fully defined, and we have never fully stated how the test is to operate. If the purpose prong is intended to void those aids to sectarian institutions accompanied by a stated legislative purpose to aid religion, the prong will condemn nothing so long as the legislature utters a secular purpose and says nothing about aiding religion. Thus the constitutionality of a statute may depend upon what the legislators put into the legislative history and, more importantly, what they leave out. The purpose prong means little if it only requires the legislature to express any secular purpose and omit all sectarian references, because legislators might do just that. Faced with a valid legislative secular purpose, we could not properly ignore that purpose without a factual basis for doing so.

However, if the purpose prong is aimed to void all statutes enacted with the intent to aid sectarian institutions, whether stated or not, then most statutes providing any aid, such as textbooks or bus rides for sectarian school children, will fail because one of the purposes behind every statute, whether stated or not, is to aid the target of its largesse. In other words, if the purpose prong requires an absence of *any* intent to aid sectarian institutions, whether or not expressed, few state laws in this area could pass the test, and we would be required to void some state aids to religion which we have already upheld.

The entanglement prong of the *Lemon* test came from *Walz v. Tax Commission*. . . . We have not always followed *Walz's* reflective inquiry into entanglement, however. One of the difficulties with the entanglement prong is that, when divorced from the logic of *Walz*, it creates an "insoluable paradox" in school aid cases: we have required aid to parochial schools to be closely watched lest it be put to sectarian use, yet this close supervision itself will create an entanglement. . . .

The entanglement test . . . also ignores the myriad state administrative regulations properly placed upon sectarian institutions such as curriculum, attendance, and certification requirements for sectarian schools, or fire and safety regulations for churches. Avoiding entanglement between church and State may be an important consideration in a case like *Walz*, but if the entanglement prong were applied to all state and church relations in the automatic manner in which it has been applied to school aid cases, the State could hardly require anything of church-related institutions as a condition for receipt of financial assistance.

These difficulties arise because the *Lemon* test has no more grounding in the history of the First Amendment than does the wall theory upon which it rests. The three-part test represents a determined effort to craft a workable rule from an historically faulty doctrine; but the rule can only be as sound as the doctrine it attempts to service. The three-part test has simply not provided adequate standards for deciding. Establishment Clause cases, as this Court has slowly come to realize. Even worse, the *Lemon* test has caused this Court to fracture into unworkable plurality opinions, depending upon how each of the three factors applies to a certain state action. The reults from our school services cases show the difficulty we have encountered in making the *Lemon* test yield principled results. . . .

These results violate the historically sound principle "that the Establishment Clause does not forbid governments . . . to [provide] general welfare under which benefits are distributed to private individuals, even though many of those individuals may elect to use those benefits in ways that 'aid' religious instruction or worship."

The true meaning of the Establishment Clause can only be seen in its history. As drafters of our Bill of Rights, the Framers inscribed the principles that control today. Any deviation from their intentions frustrates the permanence of that Charter and will only lead to the type of unprincipled decisionmaking that has plagued our Establishment Clause cases since *Everson*.

The Framers intended the Establishment Clause to prohibit the designation of any church as a "national" one. The Clause was also designed to stop the Federal Government from asserting a preference for one religious denomination or sect over others. Given the "incorporation" of the Establishment Clause as against the States via the Fourteenth Amendment in *Everson*, States are prohibited as well from establishing a religion or discriminating between sects. As its history abundantly shows, however, nothing in the Establishment Clause requires government to be strictly neutral between religion and irreligion, nor does that Clause prohibit Congress or the States from pursuing legitimate secular ends through nondiscriminatory sectarian means. . . .

The State surely has a secular interest in regulating the manner in which public schools are conducted. Nothing in the Establishment Clause of the First Amendment, properly understood, prohibits any such generalized "endorsement" of prayer. I would therefore reverse the judgment of the Court of Appeals in *Wallace v. Jaffree.*

■ INSIDE THE COURT

Justice Kennedy Switches Positions and the Outcome in Lee v. Weisman

On Wednesday, November 6, 1991, oral arguments were heard in *Lee v. Weisman,* challenging the constitutionality of school-sponsored prayers at graduation ceremonies. Two days later at their Friday conference, the justices split five to four to reverse the lower court decision holding that the First Amendment (dis)establishment clause bars state-sponsored prayers in schools.

Chief Justice Rehnquist led the discussion, observing that there was "no harm here" and that the case was simply "an extension of *Marsh*" v. *Chambers,* 463 U.S. 783 (1983), which by a five-to-four vote upheld the practice of chaplains opening sessions of state legislatures with a prayer. He voted to reverse, as did Justice White who emphasized that the practice survived the three-prong test set down in *Lemon v. Kurtzman* (1971) (excerpted in this chapter). Justices Marshall and Blackmun disagreed and voted to affirm the lower court. Justice Stevens then emphasized that when interpreting the First Amendment, to rely on history "is a dangerous policy" because of the problem of "holy wars" in Ireland and the Near East. He stressed the need for religious tolerance and for him the close connection between the case and prior rulings forbidding state-sponsored prayers in public schools; see *Engel v. Vitale* (1962) (excerpted in this chapter). Justice O'Connor spoke next and shared the concerns about "encouraging a practice of tolerance," as expressed by Blackmun and Stevens. She also thought that the appellate court had "applied *Lemon* faithfully," even though she disagreed with the test set forth there. In short, O'Connor was inclined to reverse. Justice Scalia came down firmly on the chief's side. He said he respected "evolving traditions," but insisted that the issue here was not remotely establishing religion. He also reminded the others that "the country went bananas when [the Court] took prayer out of the schools." And he rejected the suggestion that psychological coercion has "anything to do with the Establishment Clause," and would leave that as consideration solely for free exercise claims. Justice Kennedy followed by emphasizing his coercion test but indicating that he did not find benedictions at graduation ceremonies coercive. In his view, the lower court could be reversed on the basis of either *Marsh* or *Lemon.* Finally, the most recent appointee, Justice Souter, spoke. In his view, the practice failed the

Lemon test and, in any event, the case should be resolved in a way that did not "undermine *Engel.*" He voted to affirm.

With the justices so closely divided, Chief Justice Rehnquist subsequently assigned the opinion for the Court to Justice Kennedy, who appeared inclined to his view and was pivotal to holding on to a bare majority. Almost immediate thereafter Souter wrote Blackmun, telling him that he would write a dissent and, as the newest justice on the bench, "stake out my ground" on the First Amendment. Blackmun, however, urged him to wait until he circulated his own dissenting opinion and Souter agreed to let that opinion serve as "the flagship on our side."

Over the next three months Justice Kennedy and his law clerks worked on drafting an opinion for the Court. In the process, though, he changed his mind and produced a draft affirming, rather than reversing, the lower court, based on the psychological coercion of students forced to observe school-sponsored prayers. On Friday, March 27, 1992, he met with the chief justice and told him his draft reached a result contrary to the opinion assignment. Rehnquist nonetheless agreed to his circulating it to the other justices. The following Monday, March 30, Kennedy sent Blackmun a note giving him advance notice and explaining his change in course:

> Dear Harry:
>
> After writing to reverse in the high school graduation prayer case, my draft looked quite wrong. So I have written it to rule in favor of the objecting student, both at middle school and high school exercises. The Chief said to go ahead and circulate, and I thought as the senior member of those who voted for this result you should have brief advance notice. I will accompany the draft with a memo confirming that I circulate with the Chief's consent, though he had desired a different result. . . . I thought it most important to write something that you and I and the others who voted this way can join. That is why this took me a longer [sic] than it should have and, of course, I will be most attentive to your criticisms. . . .
> Sincerely,
> Tony

The next day Chief Justice Rehnquist gave the opinion assignment to Blackmun, the senior associate now in the new majority, and he reassigned the opinion to Kennedy. During the next two months, Kennedy circulated six drafts and accommodated changes suggested by Blackmun, Stevens, and O'Connor. The latter, in particular, urged him to tone down his reliance on *Lemon.* Justice Scalia in turn drafted a scathing dissent, which Chief Justice Rehnquist and Justices White and Thomas joined. The decision announced from the bench on June 24, 1992, thus, reached a result contrary to the vote originally cast at conference.

Source: Docket book pages and memos in Box 586, Justice Harry A. Blackmun Papers, Library of Congress.

Lee v. Weisman

505 U.S. 577, 112 S.Ct. 2649 (1992)

Daniel Weisman, who is Jewish and the father of two school students in Providence, Rhode Island, initially objected to the middle and high schools' allowing prayers during their commencement ceremonies when his first daughter graduated. He renewed his complaints when his second daughter graduated. At that graduation ceremony, Rabbi Leslie Gutterman offered an invocation thanking God "for the legacy of America where diversity is celebrated" and a benediction in which he observed, "O God, we are grateful for the learning which we have celebrated on this joyous commencement. . . . We give thanks to you, Lord, for keeping us alive, sustaining us and allowing us to reach this special, happy occasion." Subsequently, Weisman sued school officials, and federal district and appellate courts ruled that mentioning God during public-school graduation ceremonies violates the First Amendment establishment clause. In appealing that decision, attorneys for the school board countered that such prayers do not constitute governmental endorsement or promotion of religion. Moreover, in a brief supporting the school board, the Bush administration asked the justices to abandon the three-prong test established in *Lemon v. Kurtzman*. Under that test, laws and government practices run afoul of the establishment clause if they (1) fail to have a secular purpose or (2) have the primary effect of advancing religion or (3) promote "an excessive government entanglement with religion." The district and appellate courts concluded that the graduation prayers constituted an "advancement of religion." And the Bush administration urged the Court to "jettison the framework erected by *Lemon* in circumstances where, as here, the practice under assault is a non-coercive, ceremonial acknowledgement of the heritage of a deeply religious people."

The Court's decision was five to four. The majority's opinion was announced by Justice Kennedy. Justices Blackmun and Souter's concurrences were joined by Justices Stevens and O'Connor. Justice Scalia's dissent was joined by Chief Justice Rehnquist and Justices White and Thomas.

☐ *Justice KENNEDY delivered the opinion of the court.*

This case does not require us to revisit the difficult questions dividing us in recent cases, questions of the definition and full scope of the principles governing the extent of permitted accommodation by the State for the religious beliefs and practices of many of its citizens. See *Allegheny County v.*

Greater Pittsburgh ACLU, 492 U.S. 573 (1989); *Wallace v. Jaffree*, 472 U.S. 38 (1985); *Lynch v. Donnelly*, 465 U.S. 668 (1984). For without reference to those principles in other contexts, the controlling precedents as they relate to prayer and religious exercise in primary and secondary public schools compel the holding here that the policy of the city of Providence is an unconstitutional one. We can decide the case without reconsidering the general constitutional framework by which public schools' efforts to accommodate religion are measured. Thus we do not accept the invitation of petitioners and *amicus* of the United States to reconsider our decision in *Lemon v. Kurtzman*, [403 U.S. 602 (1971)]. The government involvement with religious activity in this case is pervasive, to the point of creating a state-sponsored and state-directed religious exercise in a public school. Conducting this formal religious observance conflicts with settled rules pertaining to prayer exercises for students, and that suffices to determine the question before us.

The principle that government may accommodate the free exercise of religion does not supersede the fundamental limitations imposed by the establishment Clause. It is beyond dispute that, at a minimum, the Constitution guarantees that "government may not coerce anyone to support or participate in religion or its exercise, or otherwise act in a way which establishes a [state] religion or religious faith, or tends to do so." *Lynch*. The State's involvement in the school prayers challenged today violates these central principles. . . .

We need not look beyond the circumstances of this case to see the phenomenon at work. The undeniable fact is that the school district's supervision and control of a high school graduation ceremony places public pressure, as well as peer pressure, on attending students to stand as a group or, at least, maintain respectful silence during the Invocation and Benediction. This pressure, though subtle and indirect, can be as real as any overt compulsion. Of course, in our culture standing or remaining silent can signify adherence to a view or simple respect for the views of others. And no doubt some persons who have no desire to join a prayer have little objection to standing as a sign of respect for those who do. But for the dissenter of high school age, who has a reasonable perception that she is being forced by the State to pray in a manner her conscience will not allow, the injury is no less real. There can be no doubt that for many, if not most, of the students at the graduation, the act of standing or remaining silent was an expression of participation in the Rabbi's prayer. That was the very point of the religious exercise. It is of little comfort to a dissenter, then, to be told that for her the act of standing or remaining in silence signifies mere respect, rather than participation. What matters is that, given our social conventions, a reasonable dissenter in this milieu could believe that the group exercise signified her own participation or approval of it. . . .

The injury caused by the government's action, and the reason why Daniel and Deborah Weisman object to it, is that the State, in a school setting, in effect required participation in a religious exercise. It is, we concede, a brief exercise during which the individual can concentrate on joining its message, meditate on her own religion, or let her mind wander. But the embarrassment and the intrusion of the religious exercise cannot be refuted by arguing that these prayers, and similar ones to be said in the future, are of a de minimis character. To do so would be an affront to the Rabbi who offered them and to all those for whom the prayers were an essential and profound recognition of divine authority. And for the same reason, we think that the intrusion is greater than the two minutes or so of time consumed for prayers like these. . . .

Inherent differences between the public school system and a session of a State Legislature distinguish this case from *Marsh v. Chambers*, 463 U.S. 783 (1983). The considerations we have raised in objection to the invocation and benediction are in many respects similar to the arguments we considered in *Marsh*. But there are also obvious differences. The atmosphere at the opening of a session of a state legislature where adults are free to enter and leave with little comment and for any number of reasons cannot compare with the constraining potential of the one school event most important for the student to attend. The influence and force of a formal exercise in a school graduation are far greater than the prayer exercise we condoned in *Marsh*. The *Marsh* majority in fact gave specific recognition to this distinction and placed particular reliance on it in upholding the prayers at issue there. Today's case is different. At a high school graduation, teachers and principals must and do retain a high degree of control over the precise contents of the program, the speeches, the timing, the movements, the dress, and the decorum of the students. In this atmosphere the state-imposed character of an invocation and benediction by clergy selected by the school combine to make the prayer a state-sanctioned religious exercise in which the student was left with no alternative but to submit. . . .

For the reasons we have stated, the judgment of the Court of Appeals is Affirmed.

☐ *Justice BLACKMUN, with whom Justice STEVENS and Justice O'CONNOR join, concurring.*

[I]t is not enough that the government restrain from compelling religious practices: it must not engage in them either. The Court repeatedly has recognized that a violation of the Establishment Clause is not predicated on coercion. The Establishment Clause proscribes public schools from "conveying or attempting to convey a message that religion or a particular religious belief is favored or preferred," *County of Allegheny v. ACLU* (1989), even if the schools do not actually "impose pressure upon a student to participate in a religious activity." *Westside Community Bd. of Ed. v. Mergens*, 496 U.S. 226 (1990) (KENNEDY, J., concurring). . . .

Our decisions have gone beyond prohibiting coercion, however, because the Court has recognized that "the fullest possible scope of religious liberty," *Schempp*, entails more than freedom from coercion. The Establishment Clause protects religious liberty on a grand scale; it is a social compact that guarantees for generations a democracy and a strong religious community—both essential to safeguarding religious liberty. . . .

☐ *Justice SOUTER, with whom Justice STEVENS and Justice O'CONNOR join, concurring.*

That government must remain neutral in matters of religion does not foreclose it from ever taking religion into account. The State may "accommodate" the free exercise of religion by relieving people from generally applicable rules that interfere with their religious callings. See, e.g., *Corporation of Presiding Bishop of Church of Jesus Christ of Latter-Day Saints v. Amos*, 483 U.S. 327 (1987); see also *Sherbert v. Verner*, 374 U.S. 398 (1963). Contrary to the views of some, such accommodation does not necessarily signify an official endorsement of religious observance over disbelief. . . .

Whatever else may define the scope of accommodation permissible under the Establishment Clause, one requirement is clear: accommodation must lift a discernible burden on the free exercise of religion. Concern for the position of religious individuals in the modern regulatory state cannot justify official solicitude for a religious practice unburdened by general rules; such gratuitous largesse would effectively favor religion over disbelief. By these lights one easily sees that, in sponsoring the graduation prayers at issue here, the State has crossed the line from permissible accommodation to unconstitutional establishment.

☐ *Justice SCALIA, with whom the CHIEF JUSTICE, Justice WHITE, and Justice THOMAS join, dissenting.*

From our Nation's origin, prayer has been a prominent part of governmental ceremonies and proclamations. The Declaration of Independence, the document marking our birth as a separate people, "appealed to the Supreme Judge of the world for the rectitude of our intentions" and avowed "a firm reliance on the protection of divine Providence." In his first inaugural address, after swearing his oath of office on a *Bible*, George Washington deliberately made a prayer a part of his first official act as President. . . . Such supplications have been a characteristic feature of inaugural addresses ever since. . . .

[A] tradition of Thanksgiving Proclamations—with their religious theme of prayerful gratitude to God—has been adhered to by almost every President. . . .

The Court presumably would separate graduation invocations and benedictions from other instances of public "preservation and transmission of religious beliefs" on the ground that they involve "psychological coercion." I find it a sufficient embarrassment that our Establishment Clause jurisprudence regarding holiday displays, has come to "require scrutiny more commonly associated with interior decorators than with the judiciary." *American Jewish Congress v. Chicago*, 827 F. 2d 120 (Easterbrook, J., dissenting). But interior decorating is a rock-hard science compared to psychology practiced by amateurs. A few citations of "research in psychology" that have no particular bearing upon the precise issue here, cannot disguise the fact that the Court has gone beyond the realm where judges know what they are doing. The Court's argument that state officials have "coerced" students to take part in the invocation and benediction at graduation ceremonies is, not to put too fine a point on it, incoherent.

The Court identifies two "dominant facts" that it says dictate its ruling that invocations and benedictions at public-school graduation ceremonies violate the Establishment Clause. Neither of them is in any relevant sense true.

The Court declares that students' "attendance and participation in the [invocation and benediction] are in a fair and real sense obligatory." But what exactly is this "fair and real sense"? According to the Court, students at graduation who want "to avoid the fact or appearance of participation," in the invocation and benediction are psychologically obligated by "public pressure, as well as peer pressure, . . . to stand as a group or, at least, maintain respectful silence" during those prayers. This assertion—the very linchpin of the Court's opinion—is almost as intriguing for what it does not say as for what it says. It does not say, for example, that students are psychologically coerced to bow their heads, place their hands in a Dürer-like prayer position, pay attention to the prayers, utter "Amen," or in fact pray. (Perhaps further intensive psychological research remains to be done on these matters.) It claims only that students are psychologically coerced "to stand . . . or, at least, maintain respectful silence." Both halves of this disjunctive (both of which must amount to the fact or appearance of participation in prayer if the Court's analysis is to survive on its own terms) merit particular attention.

To begin with the latter: The Court's notion that a student who simply sits in "respectful silence" during the invocation and benediction (when all others are standing) has somehow joined—or would somehow be perceived as having joined—in the prayers is nothing short of ludicrous. We indeed live in a vulgar age. But surely "our social conventions," have not coarsened to the point that anyone who does not stand on his chair and shout obscenities can reasonably be deemed to have assented to everything said in his presence. Since the Court does not dispute that students exposed to prayer at graduation ceremonies retain (despite "subtle coercive pressures") the free will to sit, there is absolutely no basis for the Court's decision. It is fanciful enough to say that "a reasonable dissenter," standing head erect in a class of bowed heads, "could believe that the group exercise signified her own participation or approval of it." It is beyond the absurd to say that she could entertain such a belief while pointedly declining to rise.

But let us assume the very worst, that the nonparticipating graduate is "subtly coerced" . . . to stand! Even that half of the disjunctive does not remotely establish a "participation" (or an "appearance of participation") in a religious exercise. The Court acknowledges that "in our culture standing . . . can signify adherence to a view or simple respect for the views of others." (Much more often the latter than the former, I think, except perhaps in the proverbial town meeting, where one votes by standing.) But if it is a permissible inference that one who is standing is doing so simply out of respect for the prayers of others that are in progress, then how can it possibly be said that a "reasonable dissenter . . . could believe that the group exercise signified her own participation or approval"? Quite obviously, it cannot. I may add, moreover, that maintaining respect for the religious observances of others is a fundamental civic virtue that government (including the public schools) can and should cultivate—so that even if it were the case that the displaying of such respect might be mistaken for taking part in the prayer, I would deny that the dissenter's interest in avoiding even the false appearance of participation constitutionally trumps the government's interest in fostering respect for religion generally.

The opinion manifests that the Court itself has not given careful consideration to its test of psychological coercion. For if it had, how could it observe, with no hint of concern or disapproval, that students stood for the Pledge of Allegiance, which immediately preceded Rabbi Gutterman's invocation? The government can, of course, no more coerce political orthodoxy than religious orthodoxy. *West Virginia Board of Education v. Barnette*, 319 U.S. 624 (1943). Moreover, since the Pledge of Allegiance has been revised since *Barnette* to include the phrase "under God," recital of the Pledge would appear to raise the same Establishment Clause issue as the invocation and benediction. If students were psychologically coerced to remain standing during the invocation, they must also have been psychologically coerced, moments before, to stand for (and thereby, in the Court's view, take part in or appear to take part in) the Pledge. Must the Pledge therefore be barred from the public schools (both from graduation ceremonies and from the classroom)? In *Barnette* we held that a public-school student could not be compelled to recite the Pledge; we did not even hint that she could not be compelled to observe respectful silence—indeed, even to stand in respectful silence—when those who wished to recite it did so. Logically, that ought to be the next project for the Court's bulldozer. . . .

The deeper flaw in the Court's opinion does not lie in its wrong answer to the question whether there was state-induced "peer-pressure" coercion; it lies, rather, in the Court's making violation of the Establishment Clause hinge on such a precious question. The coercion that was a hallmark of historical establishments of religion was coercion of religious orthodoxy and of financial support by force of law and threat of penalty. Typically, attendance at the state church was required; only clergy of the official church could lawfully perform sacraments; and dissenters, if tolerated, faced an array of civil disabilities. . . .

Our religion-clause jurisprudence has become bedeviled (so to speak) by reliance on formulaic abstractions that are not derived from, but positively conflict with, our long-accepted constitutional traditions. Foremost among these has been the so-called *Lemon* test, see *Lemon v. Kurtzman*, 403 U.S. 602 (1971), which has received well-earned criticism from many members of this Court. The Court today demonstrates the irrelevance of *Lemon* by essentially ignoring it, and the interment of that case may be the one happy byproduct of the Court's otherwise lamentable decision. Unfortunately, however, the Court has replaced *Lemon* with its psychological coercion test, which suffers the double disability of having no roots whatever in our people's historic practice, and being as infinitely expandable as the reasons for psychotherapy itself. . . . For the foregoing reasons, I dissent.

Zobrest v. Catalina Foothills School District
509 U.S. 1, 113 S.Ct. 2462 (1993)

The parents of James Zobrest, a deaf child, sued the Catalina Foothills School District after it refused to provide a sign-language interpreter to accompany James Zobrest to classes at a Roman Catholic high school. They alleged that the Individuals with Disabilities Education Act (IDEA) and the First Amendment's free exercise clause required the school district to provide the interpreter and that the amendment's (dis)establishment clause did not present an insurmountable barrier. After a federal district and appellate court disagreed, the Zobrests appealed to the Supreme Court, which granted *certiorari*.

The Court's decision was five to four; the majority's opinion was announced by Chief Justice Rehnquist. Justice Blackmun's dissent was joined by Justice Souter and in part by Justices Stevens and O'Connor. Justice O'Connor, joined by Justice Stevens, also delivered a dissenting opinion.

☐ *Chief Justice REHNQUIST delivered the opinion of the Court.*

We have never said that "religious institutions are disabled by the First Amendment from participating in publicly sponsored social welfare programs." *Bowen v. Kendrick*, 487 U.S. 589 (1988). For if the Establishment Clause did bar religious groups from receiving general government benefits, then "a church could not be protected by the police and fire departments, or have its public sidewalk kept in repair." *Widmar v. Vincent*, 454 U.S. 263 (1981). Given that a contrary rule would lead to such absurd results, we have consistently held that government programs that neutrally provide benefits to a broad class of citizens defined without reference to religion are not readily subject to an Establishment Clause challenge just because sectarian institutions may also receive an attenuated financial benefit. Nowhere have we stated this principle more clearly than in *Mueller v. Allen*, 463 U.S. 388 (1983), and *Witters v. Washington Dept. of Services for Blind*, 474 U.S. 481 (1986), two cases dealing specifically with government programs offering general educational assistance.

In *Mueller*, we rejected an Establishment Clause challenge to a Minnesota law allowing taxpayers to deduct certain educational expenses in computing their state income tax, even though the vast majority of those deductions (perhaps over 90%) went to parents whose children attended sectarian schools. Two factors, aside from States' traditionally broad taxing authority, informed our decision. We noted that the law "permits all parents—whether their children attend public school or private—to deduct their children's educational expenses." We also pointed out that under Minnesota's scheme, public funds become available to sectarian schools "only as a result of numerous private choices of individual parents of school-age children," thus distinguishing *Mueller* from our other cases involving "the direct transmission of assistance from the State to the schools themselves."

Witters was premised on virtually identical reasoning. In that case, we upheld against an Establishment Clause challenge the State of Washington's extension of vocational assistance, as part of a general state program, to a blind person studying at a private Christian college to become a pastor, missionary, or youth director. Looking at the statute as a whole, we observed that "any aid provided under Washington's program that ultimately flows to religious institutions does so only as a result of the genuinely independent and private choices of aid recipients." The program, we said, "creates no financial incentive for students to undertake sectarian education." We also remarked that, much like the law in *Mueller*, "Washington's program is 'made available generally without regard to the sectarian-nonsectarian, or public-nonpublic nature of the institution benefited.' " In light of these factors, we held that Washington's program—even as applied to a student who sought state assistance so that he could become a pastor—would not advance religion in a manner inconsistent with the Establishment Clause.

That same reasoning applies with equal force here. . . . Respondent contends, however, that this case differs from *Mueller* and *Witters*, in that petitioners seek to have a public employee physically present in a sectarian school to assist in James' religious education. In light of this distinction, respondent argues that this case more closely resembles *Meek v. Pittenger*, 421 U.S. 349 (1975), and *School Dist. of Grand Rapids v. Ball*, 473 U.S. 373 (1985). In *Meek*, we struck down a statute that provided "massive aid" to private schools—more than 75% of which were church related—through a direct loan of teaching material and equipment. The material and equipment covered by the statute included maps, charts, and tape recorders. . . . *Ball* similarly involved two public programs that provided services on private school premises; there, public employees taught classes to students in private school classrooms. We found that those programs likewise violated the Constitution, relying largely on *Meek*. According to respondent, if the government could not provide educational services on the premises of sectarian schools in *Meek* and *Ball*, then it surely cannot provide James with an interpreter on the premises of Salpointe.

Respondent's reliance on *Meek* and *Ball* is misplaced for two reasons. First, the programs in *Meek* and *Ball*—through direct grants of government aid—relieved sectarian schools of costs they otherwise would have borne in educating their students. For example, the religious schools in *Meek* received teaching material and equipment from the State, relieving them of an otherwise necessary cost of performing their educational function. "This kind of direct aid," we determined, "is indistinguishable from the provision of a direct cash subsidy to the religious school." The extension of aid to petitioners, however, does not amount to "an impermissible 'direct subsidy' " of Salpointe. For Salpointe is not relieved of an expense that it otherwise would have assumed in educating its students. . . .

Second, the task of a sign-language interpreter seems to us quite different from that of a teacher or guidance counselor. . . . Nothing in this record suggests that a sign-language interpreter would do more than accurately interpret whatever material is presented to the class as a whole. . . . James' parents have chosen of their own free will to place him in a pervasively sectarian environment. The sign-language interpreter they have requested will neither add to nor subtract from that environment, and hence the provision of such assistance is not barred by the Establishment Clause. . . .

☐ *Justice BLACKMUN, with whom Justice SOUTER joins, and with whom Justice STEVENS and Justice O'CONNOR join as to Part I, dissenting.*

I disagree both with the Court's decision to reach this question and with its disposition on the merits. I therefore dissent. . . .

At Salpointe [High School, a private Roman Catholic school], where the secular and the sectarian are "inextricably intertwined," governmental assistance to the educational function of the school necessarily entails governmental participation in the school's inculcation of religion. A state-employed sign-language interpreter would be required to communicate the material covered in religion class, the nominally secular subjects that are taught from a religious perspective, and the daily Masses at which Salpointe encourages attendance for Catholic students. In an environment so pervaded by discussions of the divine, the interpreter's every gesture would be infused with religious significance. Indeed, petitioners willingly concede this point: "That the interpreter conveys religious messages is a given in the case." Brief for Petitioners. By this concession, petitioners would seem to surrender their constitutional claim.

The majority attempts to elude the impact of the record by offering three reasons why this sort of aid to petitioners survives Establishment Clause scrutiny. First, the majority observes that provision of a sign-language interpreter occurs as "part of a general government program that distributes benefits neutrally to any child qualifying as 'handicapped' under the IDEA, without regard to the 'sectarian-nonsectarian, or public-nonpublic' nature of the school the child attends." Second, the majority finds significant the fact that aid is provided to pupils and their parents, rather than directly to sectarian schools. And, finally, the majority opines that "the task of a sign-language interpreter seems to us quite different from that of a teacher or guidance counselor."

But the majority's arguments are unavailing. As to the first two, even a general welfare program may have specific applications that are constitutionally forbidden under the Establishment Clause. For example, a general program granting remedial assistance to disadvantaged school-children attending public and private, secular and sectarian schools alike would clearly offend the Establishment Clause insofar as it authorized the provision of teachers. See *Aguilar v. Felton*, 473 U.S. 402 (1985); *Grand Rapids School District v. Ball*, 473 U.S. 373 (1985); *Meek v. Pittenger*, 421 U.S. 349 (1975). Such a program would not be saved simply because it supplied teachers to secular as well as sectarian schools. Nor would the fact that teachers were furnished to pupils and their parents, rather than directly to sectarian schools, immunize such a program from Establishment Clause scrutiny. The majority's decision must turn, then, upon the distinction between a teacher and a sign-language interpreter. . . .

[O]ur cases make clear that government crosses the boundary when it furnishes the medium for communication of a religious message. If petitioners receive the relief they seek, it is beyond question that a state-employed sign-language interpreter would serve as the conduit for petitioner's religious education, thereby assisting Salpointe in its mission of religious indoctrination. But the Establishment Clause is violated when a sectarian school enlists "the machinery of the State to enforce a religious orthodoxy." *Lee v. Weisman*, [505 U.S. 577] (1992). . . .

[The majority's] distinction between the provision of funds and the provision of a human being is not merely one of form. It goes to the heart of the principles animating the Establishment Clause. As Amicus Council on Religious Freedom points out, the provision of a state-paid sign-language interpreter may pose serious problems for the church as well as for the state. Many sectarian schools impose religiously based rules of conduct, as Salpointe has in this case. A traditional Hindu school would be likely to instruct its students and staff to dress modestly, avoiding any display of their bodies. And an orthodox Jewish yeshiva might well forbid all but kosher food upon its premises. To require public employees to obey such rules would impermissibly threaten individual liberty, but to fail to do so might endanger religious autonomy. For such reasons, it long has been feared that "a union of government and religion tends to destroy government and to degrade religion." *Engel v. Vitale*, 370 U.S. 421 (1962). The Establishment Clause was designed to avert exactly this sort of conflict.

Board of Education of Kiryas Joel Village School District v. Grumet

512 U.S. 687, 114 S.Ct. 2481 (1994)

In response to a ruling by a bare majority of the Supreme Court in *Aguilar v. Felton*, 473 U.S. 402 (1985), forbidding public school teachers from offering remedial classes for handicapped children attending religious schools, the New York legislature created a special school district, governed by the Board of Education of Kiryas Joel, in Orange County, New York. Kiryas Joel is a community inhabited solely by Hasidic Jews of the Satmar sect, one of the most orthodox and conservative Jewish sects. All other Jewish children in the district attended private religious schools. But Kiryas Joel did not want to send two hundred handicapped children to public schools in the county because that might expose them to stress and possible ridicule for their clothes, use of Yiddish, and other traditional practices. In 1989, the state legislature created a special public school district for Kiryas Joel's handicapped children. The following year, Louis Grumet, the director of the New York State School Boards, challenged the constitutionality of the special school district as a violation of the First Amendment's (dis)establishment clause. Lower state courts and the New York Court of Appeals agreed that the special district failed to pass the tests set forth in *Lemon v. Kurtzman*, 403 U.S. 602 (1971), specifically, those requiring that legislation have a primary effect that neither advances nor inhibits religion. The school district thereupon appealed to the Supreme Court.

The Court's decision was six to three. Justice Souter announced the majority's opinion, which Justices Blackmun, Stevens, O'Connor, and Ginsburg joined in Parts I, II-B, II-C, and III, and which Justices Blackmun, Stevens, and Ginsburg joined in Part II-A. Justices Blackmun, Stevens, Kennedy, and O'Connor filed separate concurring opinions. Justice Scalia filed a dissenting opinion, which Chief Justice Rehnquist and Justice Thomas joined.

☐ *Justice SOUTER delivered the opinion of the Court.*

The question is whether the Act creating the separate school district violates the Establishment Clause of the First Amendment, binding on the States through the Fourteenth Amendment. Because this unusual act is tantamount to an allocation of political power on a religious criterion and neither presupposes nor requires governmental impartiality toward religion, we hold that it violates the prohibition against establishment. . . .

■ II

"A proper respect for both the Free Exercise and the Establishment Clauses compels the State to pursue a course of 'neutrality' toward religion," *Committee for Public Ed. & Religious Liberty v. Nyquist*, 413 U.S. 756 (1973), favoring neither one religion over others nor religious adherents collectively over nonadherents. Chapter 748, the statute creating the Kiryas Joel Village School District, departs from this constitutional command by delegating the State's discretionary authority over public schools to a group defined by its character as a religious community, in a legal and historical context that gives no assurance that governmental power has been or will be exercised neutrally.

Larkin v. Grendel's Den, Inc., 459 U.S. 116 (1982), provides an instructive comparison with the litigation before us. There, the Court was requested to strike down a Massachusetts statute granting religious bodies veto power over applications for liquor licenses. Under the statute, the governing body of any church, synagogue, or school located within 500 feet of an applicant's premises could, simply by submitting written objection, prevent the Alcohol Beverage Control Commission from issuing a license. In spite of the State's valid interest in protecting churches, schools, and like institutions from " 'the hurly-burly' associated with liquor outlets," the Court found that in two respects the statute violated "the wholesome 'neutrality' of which this Court's cases speak," *School Dist. of Abington v. Schempp*, 374 U.S. 203 (1963). The Act brought about a " 'fusion of governmental and religious functions' " by delegating "important, discretionary governmental powers" to religious bodies, thus impermissibly entangling government and religion. And it lacked "any 'effective means of guaranteeing' that the delegated power '[would] be used exclusively for secular, neutral, and nonideological purposes;' " this, along with the "significant symbolic benefit to religion" associated with "the mere appearance of a joint exercise of legislative authority by Church and State," led the Court to conclude that the statute had a " 'primary' and 'principal' effect of advancing religion." Comparable constitutional problems inhere in the statute before us.

■ A

Larkin presented an example of united civic and religious authority, an establishment rarely found in such straightforward form in modern America. The Establishment Clause problem presented by Chapter 748 is more subtle, but it resembles the issue raised in *Larkin* to the extent that the earlier case teaches that a State may not delegate its civic authority to a group chosen according to a religious criterion. Authority over public schools belongs to the State, and cannot be delegated to a local school district defined by the

State in order to grant political control to a religious group. What makes this litigation different from *Larkin* is the delegation here of civic power to the "qualified voters of the village of Kiryas Joel," as distinct from a religious leader such as the village rov, or an institution of religious government like the formally constituted parish council in *Larkin*. In light of the circumstances of this case, however, this distinction turns out to lack constitutional significance.

It is, first, not dispositive that the recipients of state power in this case are a group of religious individuals united by common doctrine, not the group's leaders or officers. Although some school district franchise is common to all voters, the State's manipulation of the franchise for this district limited it to Satmars, giving the sect exclusive control of the political subdivision. In the circumstances of this case, the difference between thus vesting state power in the members of a religious group as such instead of the officers of its sectarian organization is one of form, not substance. It is true that religious people (or groups of religious people) cannot be denied the opportunity to exercise the rights of citizens simply because of their religious af-filiations or commitments, for such a disability would violate the right to religious free exercise, see *McDaniel v. Paty*, 435 U.S. 618 (1978), which the First Amendment guarantees as certainly as it bars any establishment. But *McDaniel*, which held that a religious individual could not, because of his religious activities, be denied the right to hold political office, is not in point here. That individuals who happen to be religious may hold public office does not mean that a state may deliberately delegate discretionary power to an individual, institution, or community on the ground of religious identity. . . .

It is undisputed that those who negotiated the village boundaries when applying the general village incorporation statute drew them so as to exclude all but Satmars, and that the New York Legislature was well aware that the village remained exclusively Satmar in 1989 when it adopted Chapter 748. The significance of this fact to the state legislature is indicated by the further fact that carving out the village school district ran counter to customary districting practices in the State. Indeed, the trend in New York is not toward dividing school districts but toward consolidating them. . . .

The origin of the district in a special act of the legislature, rather than the State's general laws governing school district reorganization, is likewise anomalous. . . . Because the district's creation ran uniquely counter to state practice, following the lines of a religious community where the customary and neutral principles would not have dictated the same result, we have good reasons to treat this district as the reflection of a religious criterion for identifying the recipients of civil authority. Not even the special needs of the children in this community can explain the legislature's unusual Act, for the State could have responded to the concerns of the Satmar parents without implicating the Establishment Clause, as we explain in some detail further on. We therefore find the legislature's Act to be substantially equivalent to defining a political subdivision and hence the qualification for its franchise by a religious test, resulting in a purposeful and forbidden "fusion of governmental and religious functions." *Larkin v. Grendel's Den.*

■ B

The fact that this school district was created by a special and unusual Act of the legislature also gives reason for concern whether the benefit received by the Satmar community is one that the legislature will provide equally to other religious (and nonreligious) groups. This is the second malady the *Larkin* Court identified in the law before it, the absence of an "effective means of guaranteeing" that governmental power will be and has been neutrally employed. But whereas in *Larkin* it was religious groups the Court thought might exercise civic power to advance the interests of religion (or religious adherents), here the threat to neutrality occurs at an antecedent stage. . . .

■ C

In finding that Chapter 748 violates the requirement of governmental neutrality by extending the benefit of a special franchise, we do not deny that the Constitution allows the state to accommodate religious needs by alleviating special burdens. Our cases leave no doubt that in commanding neutrality the Religion Clauses do not require the government to be oblivious to impositions that legitimate exercises of state power may place on religious belief and practice. Rather, there is "ample room under the Establishment Clause for 'benevolent neutrality which will permit religious exercise to exist without sponsorship and without interference,'" *Corporation of Presiding Bishop of Church of Jesus Christ of Latter-day Saints v. Amos*, 483 U.S. 327 (1987). The fact that Chapter 748 facilitates the practice of religion is not what renders it an unconstitutional establishment.

But accommodation is not a principle without limits, and what petitioners seek is an adjustment to the Satmars' religiously grounded preferences that our cases do not countenance. Prior decisions have allowed religious communities and institutions to pursue their own interests free from governmental interference, but we have never hinted that an otherwise unconstitutional delegation of political power to a religious group could be saved as a religious accommodation. Petitioners' proposed accommodation singles out a particular religious sect for special treatment, and whatever the limits of permissible legislative accommodations may be, compare *Texas Monthly, Inc. v. Bullock* (striking down law exempting only religious publications from taxation), with *Corporation of Presiding Bishop v. Amos*, (upholding law exempting religious employers from Title VII), it is clear that neutrality as among religions must be honored.

This conclusion does not, however, bring the Satmar parents, the Monroe-Woodbury school district, or the State of New York to the end of the road in seeking ways to respond to the parents' concerns. Just as the Court in *Larkin* observed that the State's interest in protecting religious meeting places could be "readily accomplished by other means," there are several alternatives here for providing bilingual and bicultural special education to Satmar children. Such services can perfectly well be offered to village children through the Monroe-Woodbury Central School District. Since the Satmars do not claim that separatism is religiously mandated, their children may receive bilingual and bicultural instruction at a public school already run by the Monroe-Woodbury district. Or if the educationally appropriate offering by Monroe-Woodbury should turn out to be a separate program of bilingual and bicultural education at a neutral site near one of the village's parochial schools, this Court has already made it clear that no Establishment Clause difficulty would inhere in such a scheme, administered in accordance with neutral principles that would not necessarily confine special treatment to Satmars. . . .

■ III

Justice CARDOZO once cast the dissenter as "the gladiator making a last stand against the lions." B. CARDOZO, *Law and Literature* 34 (1931). Justice SCALIA's dissent is certainly the work of a gladiator, but he thrusts at lions of his own imagining. We do not disable a religiously homogeneous group from exercising political power conferred on it without regard to religion. Unlike the states of Utah and New Mexico (which were laid out according to traditional political methodologies taking account of lines of latitude and longitude and topographical features), the reference line chosen for the Kiryas Joel Village School District was one purposely drawn to separate Satmars from non-Satmars. Nor do we impugn the motives of the New York Legislature, which no doubt intended to accommodate the Satmar community without violating the Establishment Clause; we simply refuse to ignore that the method it chose is one that aids a particular religious community, as such, rather than all groups similarly interested in separate schooling. . . .

Our job, of course would be easier if the dissent's position had prevailed with the Framers and with this Court over the years. An Establishment Clause diminished to the dimensions acceptable to Justice SCALIA could be enforced by a few simple rules, and our docket would never see cases requiring the application of a principle like neutrality toward religion as well as among religious sects. But that would be as blind to history as to precedent, and the difference between Justice SCALIA and the Court accordingly turns on the Court's recognition that the Establishment Clause does comprehend such a principle and obligates courts to exercise the judgment necessary to apply it.

In this case we are clearly constrained to conclude that the statute before us fails the test of neutrality. It delegates a power this Court has said "ranks at the very apex of the function of a State," *Wisconsin v. Yoder*, 406 U.S. 205 (1972), to an electorate defined by common religious belief and practice, in a manner that fails to foreclose religious favoritism. It therefore crosses the line from permissible accommodation to impermissible establishment. The judgment of the Court of Appeals of the State of New York is accordingly Affirmed.

☐ *Justice O'CONNOR, concurring in part and concurring in the judgment.*

Experience proves that the Establishment Clause, like the Free Speech Clause, cannot easily be reduced to a single test. There are different categories of Establishment Clause cases, which may call for different approaches. Some cases, like this one, involve government actions targeted at particular individuals or groups, imposing special duties or giving special benefits. Cases involving government speech on religious topics, seem to me to fall into a different category and to require an analysis focusing on whether the speech endorses or disapproves of religion, rather than on whether the government action is neutral with regard to religion. Another category encompasses cases in which the government must make decisions about matters of religious doctrine and religious law. These cases, which often arise in the application of otherwise neutral property or contract principles to religious institutions, involve complicated questions not present in other situations. Government delegations of power to religious bodies may make up yet another category. As *Larkin* itself suggested, government impartiality towards religion may not be enough in such situations: A law that bars all alcohol sales within some distance of a church, school, or hospital may be valid, but an equally evenhanded law that gives each institution discretionary power over the sales may not be. Of course, there may well be additional categories, or more opportune places to draw the lines between the categories.

As the Court's opinion today shows, the slide away from *Lemon's* unitary approach is well under way. A return to *Lemon*, even if possible, would likely be futile, regardless of where one stands on the substantive Establishment Clause questions. I think a less unitary approach provides a better structure for analysis. If each test covers a narrower and more homogeneous area, the tests may be more precise and therefore easier to apply. There may be more opportunity to pay attention to the specific nuances of each area. There might also be, I hope, more consensus on each of the narrow tests than there has been on a broad test. And abandoning the *Lemon* framework need not mean abandoning some of the insights that the test reflected, nor the insights of the cases that applied it. . . .

☐ *Justice SCALIA, with whom the CHIEF JUSTICE and Justice THOMAS join, dissenting.*

The Court today finds that the Powers That Be, up in Albany, have conspired to effect an establishment of the Satmar Hasidim. I do not know who would be more surprised at this discovery: the Founders of our Nation or Grand Rebbe Joel Teitelbaum, founder of the Satmar. The Grand Rebbe would be astounded to learn that after escaping brutal persecution and coming to America with the modest hope of religious toleration for their ascetic form of Judaism, the Satmar had become so powerful, so closely allied with Mammon, as to have become an "establishment" of the Empire State. And the Founding Fathers would be astonished to find that the Establishment Clause—which they designed "to insure that no one powerful sect or combination of sects could use political or governmental power to punish dissenters," *Zorach v. Clauson*, 343 U.S. 306 (1952) (BLACK, J., dissenting)—has been employed to prohibit characteristically and admirably American accommodation of the religious practices (or more precisely, cultural peculiarities) of a tiny minority sect. I, however, am not surprised. Once this Court has abandoned text and history as guides, nothing prevents it from calling religious toleration the establishment of religion. . . .

For his thesis that New York has unconstitutionally conferred governmental authority upon the Satmar sect, Justice SOUTER relies extensively, and virtually exclusively, upon *Larkin v. Grendel's Den, Inc.*, 459 U.S. 116 (1982). Justice SOUTER believes that the present case "resembles" *Grendel's*

Den because that case "teaches that a state may not delegate its civic authority to a group chosen according to a religious criterion." That misdescribes both what that case taught (which is that a state may not delegate its civil authority to a church), and what this case involves (which is a group chosen according to cultural characteristics). The statute at issue there gave churches veto power over the State's authority to grant a liquor license to establishments in the vicinity of the church. The Court had little difficulty finding the statute unconstitutional.

Justice SOUTER concedes that *Grendel's Den* "presented an example of united civic and religious authority, an establishment rarely found in such straightforward form in modern America." The uniqueness of the case stemmed from the grant of governmental power directly to a religious institution, and the Court's opinion focused on that fact, remarking that the transfer of authority was to "churches" (10 times), the "governing body of churches" (twice), "religious institutions" (twice) and "religious bodies" (once). Astonishingly, however, Justice SOUTER dismisses the difference between a transfer of government power to citizens who share a common religion as opposed to "the officers of its sectarian organization"—the critical factor that made *Grendel's Den* unique and "rare"—as being "one of form, not substance."

Justice SOUTER's steamrolling of the difference between civil authority held by a church, and civil authority held by members of a church, is breathtaking. To accept it, one must believe that large portions of the civil authority exercised during most of our history were unconstitutional, and that much more of it than merely the Kiryas Joel School District is unconstitutional today. The history of the populating of North America is in no small measure the story of groups of people sharing a common religious and cultural heritage striking out to form their own communities. It is preposterous to suggest that the civil institutions of these communities, separate from their churches, were constitutionally suspect. And if they were, surely Justice SOUTER cannot mean that the inclusion of one or two nonbelievers in the community would have been enough to eliminate the constitutional vice. If the conferral of governmental power upon a religious institution as such (rather than upon American citizens who belong to the religious institution) is not the test of *Grendel's Den* invalidity, there is no reason why giving power to a body that is overwhelmingly dominated by the members of one sect would not suffice to invoke the Establishment Clause. That might have made the entire States of Utah and New Mexico unconstitutional at the time of their admission to the Union, and would undoubtedly make many units of local government unconstitutional today. [A census taken in 1906, 10 years after statehood was granted to Utah, and 6 years before it was granted to New Mexico, showed that in Utah 87.7% of all church members were Mormon, and in New Mexico 88.7% of all church members were Roman Catholic.]

Justice SOUTER's position boils down to the quite novel proposition that any group of citizens (say, the residents of Kiryas Joel) can be invested with political power, but not if they all belong to the same religion. Of course such disfavoring of religion is positively antagonistic to the purposes of the Religion Clauses, and we have rejected it before. In *McDaniel v. Paty*, 435 U.S. 618 (1978), we invalidated a state constitutional amendment that would have permitted all persons to participate in political conventions, except ministers. We adopted James Madison's view that the State could not " 'punish a religious profession with the privation of a civil right.' " I see no reason why it is any less pernicious to deprive a group rather than an individual of its rights simply because of its religious beliefs. . . .

I turn, next, to Justice SOUTER's second justification for finding an establishment of religion: his facile conclusion that the New York Legislature's creation of the Kiryas Joel School District was religiously motivated. But in the Land of the Free, democratically adopted laws are not so easily impeached by unelected judges. To establish the unconstitutionality of a facially neutral law on the mere basis of its asserted religiously preferential (or discriminatory) effects—or at least to establish it in conformity with our precedents—Justice SOUTER "must be able to show the absence of a neutral, secular basis" for the law. *Gillette v. United States*, 401 U.S. 437 (1971). . . .

Since the obvious presence of a neutral, secular basis renders the asserted preferential effect of this law inadequate to invalidate it, Justice SOUTER is required to come forward with direct evidence that religious preference was the objective. His case could scarcely be weaker. It consists, briefly, of this: The People of New York created the Kiryas Joel Village School District in order to further the Satmar religion, rather than for any proper secular purpose, because (1) they created the district in an extraordinary manner—by special Act of the legislature, rather than under the State's general laws governing school-district reorganization; (2) the creation of the district ran counter to a State trend towards consolidation of school districts; and (3) the District includes only adherents of the Satmar religion. On this indictment, no jury would convict.

One difficulty with the first point is that it is not true. There was really nothing so "special" about the formation of a school district by an Act of the New York Legislature. The State has created both large school districts, and small specialized school districts for institutionalized children, through these special Acts. But in any event all that the first point proves, and the second point as well (countering the trend toward consolidation), is that New York regarded Kiryas Joel as a special case, requiring special measures. I should think it obvious that it did, and obvious that it should have. But even if the New York Legislature had never before created a school district by special statute (which is not true), and even if it had done nothing but consolidate school districts for over a century (which is not true), how could the departure from those past practices possibly demonstrate that the legislature had religious favoritism in mind? It could not. To be sure, when there is no special treatment there is no possibility of religious favoritism; but it is not logical to suggest that when there is special treatment there is proof of religious favoritism.

Justice SOUTER's case against the statute comes down to nothing more, therefore, than his third point: the fact that all the residents of the Kiryas Joel Village School District are Satmars. But all its residents also wear unusual dress, have unusual civic customs, and have not much to do with people who are culturally different from them. The Court recognizes that "the Satmars prefer to live together 'to facilitate individual religious observance and maintain social, cultural and religious values,' but that it is not 'against their religion' to interact with others." On what basis does Justice SOUTER conclude that it is the theological distinctiveness rather than the cultural distinctiveness that was the basis for New York State's decision? The normal assumption would be that it was the latter, since it was not theology but dress, language, and cultural alienation that posed the educational problem for the children. Justice SOUTER not only does not adopt the logical assumption, he does not even give the New York Legislature the benefit of the doubt. . . . In other words, we know the legislature must have been motivated by the desire to favor the Satmar Hasidim religion, because it could have met the needs of these children by a method that did not place the Satmar Hasidim in a separate school district. This is not a rational argument proving religious favoritism; it is rather a novel Establishment Clause principle to the effect that no secular objective may be pursued by a means that might also be used for religious favoritism if some other means is available. . . .

When a legislature acts to accommodate religion, particularly a minority sect, "it follows the best of our traditions." The Constitution itself contains an accommodation of sorts. Article VI, cl. 3, prescribes that executive, legislative and judicial officers of the Federal and State Governments shall bind themselves to support the Constitution "by Oath or Affirmation." Although members of the most populous religions found no difficulty in swearing an oath to God, Quakers, Moravians, and Mennonites refused to take oaths based on Matthew 5:34's injunction "swear not at all." The option of affirmation was added to accommodate these minority religions and enable their members to serve in government. Congress, from its earliest sessions, passed laws accommodating religion by refunding duties paid by specific churches upon the importation of plates for the printing of Bibles, vestments, and bells. Congress also exempted church property from the tax assessments it levied on residents of the District of Columbia; and all 50 States have had similar laws. . . .

In today's opinion, however, the Court seems uncomfortable with this aspect of our constitutional tradition. Although it acknowledges the concept of accommodation, it quickly points out that it is "not a principle without limits," and then gives reasons why the present case exceeds those limits, reasons which simply do not hold water. "We have never hinted," the Court says, "that an otherwise unconstitutional delegation of political power to a religious group could be saved as a religious accommodation." Putting aside the circularity inherent in referring to a delegation as "otherwise unconstitutional" when its constitutionality turns on whether there is an accommodation, if this statement is true, it is only because we have never hinted that delegation of political power to citizens who share a particular religion could be unconstitutional. This is simply a replay of the argument we rejected in Part II.

The second and last reason the Court finds accommodation impermissible is, astoundingly, the mere risk that the State will not offer accommodation to a similar group in the future, and that neutrality will therefore not be preserved. . . .

Contrary to the Court's suggestion, I do not think that the Establishment Clause prohibits formally established "state" churches and nothing more. I have always believed, and all my opinions are consistent with the view, that the Establishment Clause prohibits the favoring of one religion over others. In this respect, it is the Court that attacks lions of straw. What I attack is the Court's imposition of novel "up front" procedural requirements on state legislatures. Making law (and making exceptions) one case at a time, whether through adjudication or through highly particularized rulemaking or legislation, violates, *ex ante*, no principle of fairness, equal protection, or neutrality, simply because it does not announce in advance how all future cases (and all future exceptions) will be disposed of. If it did, the manner of proceeding of this Court itself would be unconstitutional. It is presumptuous for this Court to impose—out of nowhere—an unheard-of prohibition against proceeding in this manner upon the Legislature of New York State. I never heard of such a principle, nor has anyone else, nor will it ever be heard of again. Unlike what the New York Legislature has done, this is a special rule to govern only the Satmar Hasidim. . . .

Rosenberger v. The Rector and Visitors of the University of Virginia
515 U.S. 819, 115 S.Ct. 2510 (1995)

In 1990, Ronald Rosenberger and several other undergraduates at the University of Virginia formed Wide Awake Productions (WAP) and qualified under the university's guidelines as a "Contracted Independent Organization" (CIO), which entitled it to access to the university's facilities, including computer terminals. WAP was established "to publish a magazine of philosophical and religious expression," "to facilitate discussion which fosters an atmosphere of sensitivity to and tolerance of Christian viewpoints," and "to provide a unifying focus for Christians of multicultural backgrounds." In particular, WAP published *Wide Awake: A Christian Perspective*, a paper devoted to offering "a Christian perspective on both personal and community issues, especially those relevant to college students at the University of Virginia." The editors committed the paper to a twofold mission: "to challenge Christians to live, in word and deed, according to the faith they proclaim and to encourage students to consider what a personal relationship with Jesus Christ means."

Under the university's guidelines, some CIOs are also entitled to apply for funds from the Student Activities Fund (SAF). Funded by a mandatory fourteen-dollar fee per semester from each student, the purpose of the SAF is to support a broad range of extracurricular student activities that "are related to the educational purpose of the University." Under the guidelines, the SAF must be administered "in a manner consistent with the educational purpose of the University as well as with state and federal law." The SAF, for instance, may not pay for "religious activities." The Student Council has the initial authority to disburse the funds, but its actions are subject to review by a faculty body.

The university's guidelines recognize eleven categories of student groups that may seek payment to third-party contractors because they "are related to the educational purpose of the University of Virginia." One category includes "student news, information, opinion, entertainment, or academic communications media groups." The guidelines also specify, however, that the costs of certain activities of CIOs that are otherwise eligible for funding will not be reimbursed by the SAF. The student activities which are excluded from SAF support are religious activities, philanthropic contributions and activities, political activities, activities that would jeopardize the university's tax-exempt status, those which involve payment of honoraria or similar fees, or social entertainment or related expenses. The prohibition on "political activities" is defined so that it is limited to electioneering and lobbying. The guidelines provide that "these restrictions on funding political activities are not intended to preclude funding of any otherwise eligible student organization which . . . espouses particular positions or ideological viewpoints, including those that may be unpopular or are not generally accepted." A "religious activity," by contrast, is defined as any activity that "primarily promotes or manifests a particular belief in or about a deity or an ultimate reality."

A few months after receiving CIO status, WAP requested the SAF to pay its printer $5,862 for the costs of printing *Wide Awake.* The appropriations committee of the Student Council denied WAP's request on the ground that *Wide Awake* was a "religious activity" within the meaning of the university's guidelines; that is, *Wide Awake* "promoted or manifested a particular belief in or about a deity or an ultimate reality." WAP appealed to the full Student Council, but that appeal was denied.

Rosenberger and other editors of *Wide Awake* subsequently filed a suit in federal district court. They alleged that refusal to fund *Wide Awake* on the basis of its religious editorial viewpoint violated their rights to freedom of speech and press, to the free exercise of religion, and to equal protection of the law. The district court, however, disagreed and ruled that the university's funding the newspaper would violate the First Amendment's (dis)establishment clause. The Court of Appeals for the Fourth Circuit affirmed, upon concluding that the university had a "compelling interest in maintaining strict separation of church and state," whereupon Rosenberger appealed to the Supreme Court, which granted review.

The Court's decision was five to four and the opinion was delivered by Justice Kennedy. Justices O'Connor and Thomas filed separate concurrences. Justice Souter filed a dissenting opinion, which was joined by Justices Stevens, Ginsburg, and Breyer.

☐ *Justice KENNEDY delivered the opinion of the Court.*

It is axiomatic that the government may not regulate speech based on its substantive content or the message it conveys. Other principles follow from this precept. In the realm of private speech or expression, government regulation may not favor one speaker over another. Discrimination against speech because of its message is presumed to be unconstitutional. These rules informed our determination that the government offends the First Amendment when it imposes financial burdens on certain speakers based on the content of their expression. *Simon & Schuster, Inc. v. Members of N.Y. State Crime Victims Bd.*, 502 U.S. 105 (1991). When the government targets not subject matter but particular views taken by speakers on a subject, the violation of the First Amendment is all the more blatant. See *R.A.V. v. St. Paul*, 505 U.S. 377 (1992). Viewpoint discrimination is thus an egregious form of content discrimination. The government must abstain from regulating speech when the specific motivating ideology or the opinion or perspective of the speaker is the rationale for the restriction.

These principles provide the framework forbidding the State from exercising viewpoint discrimination, even when the limited public forum is one of its own creation. In a case involving a school district's provision of school facilities for private uses, we declared that "there is no question that the District, like the private owner of property, may legally preserve the property under its control for the use to which it is dedicated." *Lamb's Chapel v. Center Moriches Union Free School Dist.*, [508 U.S. 384] (1993). The necessities of confining a forum to the limited and legitimate purposes for which it was created may justify the State in reserving it for certain groups or for the discussion of certain topics. Once it has opened a limited forum, however, the State must respect the lawful boundaries it has itself set. The State may not exclude speech where its distinction is not "reasonable in light of the purpose served by the forum," nor may it discriminate against speech on the basis of its viewpoint. Thus, in determining whether the State is acting to preserve the limits of the forum it has created so that the exclusion of a class of speech is legitimate, we have observed a distinction between, on the one hand, content discrimination, which may be permissible if it preserves the purposes of that limited forum, and, on the other hand, viewpoint discrimination, which is presumed impermissible when directed against speech otherwise within the forum's limitations. . . .

The University does acknowledge (as it must in light of our precedents) that "ideologically driven attempts to suppress a particular point of view are presumptively unconstitutional in funding, as in other contexts," but insists that this case does not present that issue because the Guidelines draw lines based on content, not viewpoint. As we have noted, discrimination against one set of views or ideas is but a subset or particular instance of the more general phenomenon of content discrimination. And, it must be acknowledged, the distinction is not a precise one. It is, in a sense, something of an understatement to speak of religious thought and discussion as just a viewpoint, as distinct from a comprehensive body of thought. The nature of our origins and destiny and their dependence upon the existence of a divine being have been subjects of philosophic inquiry throughout human history. We conclude, nonetheless, that here, as in *Lamb's Chapel*, viewpoint discrimination is the proper way to interpret the University's objections to *Wide Awake*. By the very terms of the SAF prohibition, the University does not exclude religion as a subject matter but selects for disfavored treatment those student journalistic efforts with religious editorial viewpoints. Religion may be a vast area of inquiry, but it also provides, as it did here, a specific premise, a perspective, a standpoint from which a variety of subjects may be discussed and considered. The prohibited perspective, not the general subject matter, resulted in the refusal to make third-party payments, for the subjects discussed were otherwise within the approved category of publications. . . .

The University's denial of WAP's request for third-party payments in the present case is based upon viewpoint discrimination not unlike the discrimination the school district relied upon in *Lamb's Chapel* and that we found invalid. The church group in *Lamb's Chapel* would have been qualified as a social or civic organization, save for its religious purposes. Furthermore, just as the school district in *Lamb's Chapel* pointed to nothing but the religious views of the group as the rationale for excluding its message, so in this case the University justifies its denial of SAF participation to WAP on the ground that the contents of *Wide Awake* reveal an avowed religious perspective. . . .

The University tries to escape the consequences of our holding in *Lamb's Chapel* by urging that this case involves the provision of funds rather than access to facilities. The University begins with the unremarkable proposition that the State must have substantial discretion in determining how to allocate scarce resources to accomplish its educational mission. Citing our decisions in *Rust v. Sullivan*, 500 U.S. 173 (1991), *Regan v. Taxation with Representation of Wash.*, 461 U.S. 540 (1983), and *Widmar v. Vincent*, 454 U.S. 263 (1981), the University argues that content-based funding decisions are both inevitable and lawful. . . .

To this end the University relies on our assurance in *Widmar v. Vincent*. There, in the course of striking down a public university's exclusion of religious groups from use of school facilities made available to all other student groups, we stated: "Nor do we question the right of the University to make academic judgments as to how best to allocate scarce resources." The quoted language in *Widmar* was but a proper recognition of the principle that when the State is the speaker, it may make content-based choices. When the University determines the content of the education it provides, it is the University speaking, and we have permitted the government to regulate the content of what is or is not expressed when it is the speaker or when it enlists private entities to convey its own message. In the same vein, in *Rust v. Sullivan*, we upheld the government's prohibition on abortion-related advice applicable to recipients of federal funds for family planning counseling. There, the government did not create a program to encourage private speech but instead used private speakers to transmit specific information pertaining to its own program. We recognized that when the government appropriates public funds to promote a particular policy of its own it is entitled to say what it wishes. When the government disburses public funds to private entities to convey a governmental message, it may take legitimate and appropriate steps to ensure that its message is neither garbled nor distorted by the grantee.

It does not follow, however, and we did not suggest in *Widmar*, that viewpoint-based restrictions are proper when the University does not itself speak or subsidize transmittal of a message it favors but instead expends funds to encourage a diversity of views from private speakers. A holding that the University may not discriminate based on the viewpoint of private persons whose speech it facilitates does not restrict the University's own speech, which is controlled by different principles. . . .

The distinction between the University's own favored message and the private speech of students is evident in the case before us. The University itself has taken steps to ensure the distinction in the agreement each CIO must sign. The University declares that the student groups eligible for SAF support are not the University's agents, are not subject to its control, and are not its responsibility. Having offered to pay the third-party contractors on behalf of private speakers who convey their own messages, the University may not silence the expression of selected viewpoints.

The University urges that, from a constitutional standpoint, funding of speech differs from provision of access to facilities because money is scarce and physical facilities are not. Beyond the fact that in any given case this proposition might not be true as an empirical matter, the underlying premise that the University could discriminate based on viewpoint if demand for space exceeded its availability is wrong as well. The government cannot justify viewpoint discrimination among private speakers on the economic fact of scarcity. . . .

The Guideline invoked by the University to deny third-party contractor payments on behalf of WAP effects a sweeping restriction on student thought and student inquiry in the context of University-sponsored publications. The prohibition on funding on behalf of publications that "primarily promote or manifest a particular belief in or about a deity or an ultimate reality," in its ordinary and commonsense meaning, has a vast potential reach. The term "promotes" as used here would comprehend any writing advocating a philosophic position that rests upon a belief in a deity or ultimate reality. And the term "manifests" would bring within the scope of the prohibition any writing that is explicable as resting upon a premise which presupposes the existence of a deity or ultimate reality. Were the prohibition applied with much vigor at all, it would bar funding of essays by hypothetical student contributors named Plato, Spinoza, and Descartes. And if the regulation covers, as the University says it does, those student journalistic efforts which primarily manifest or promote a belief that there is no deity and no ultimate reality, then undergraduates named Karl Marx, Bertrand Russell, and Jean-Paul Sartre would likewise have some of their major essays excluded from student publications. If any manifestation of beliefs in first principles disqualifies the writing, as seems to be the case, it is indeed difficult to name renowned thinkers whose writings would be accepted, save perhaps for articles disclaiming all connection to their ultimate philosophy.

Plato could contrive perhaps to submit an acceptable essay on making pasta or peanut butter cookies, provided he did not point out their (necessary) imperfections.

Based on the principles we have discussed, we hold that the regulation invoked to deny SAF support, both in its terms and in its application to these petitioners, is a denial of their right of free speech guaranteed by the First Amendment. It remains to be considered whether the violation following from the University's action is excused by the necessity of complying with the Constitution's prohibition against state establishment of religion. We turn to that question. . . .

A central lesson of our decisions is that a significant factor in upholding governmental programs in the face of Establishment Clause attack is their neutrality towards religion. We have decided a series of cases addressing the receipt of government benefits where religion or religious views are implicated in some degree. The first case in our modern Establishment Clause jurisprudence was *Everson v. Board of Ed. of Ewing*, 330 U.S. 1 (1947). There we cautioned that in enforcing the prohibition against laws respecting establishment of religion, we must "be sure that we do not inadvertently prohibit [the government] from extending its general state law benefits to all its citizens without regard to their religious belief." We have held that the guarantee of neutrality is respected, not offended, when the government, following neutral criteria and evenhanded policies, extends benefits to recipients whose ideologies and viewpoints, including religious ones, are broad and diverse. More than once have we rejected the position that the Establishment Clause even justifies, much less requires, a refusal to extend free speech rights to religious speakers who participate in broad-reaching government programs neutral in design. See *Lamb's Chapel*, [*Board of Ed. of Westside Community Schools v.*] *Mergens* [496 U.S. 226 (1990)], *Widmar*.

The governmental program here is neutral toward religion. . . . The University's SAF Guidelines have a separate classification for, and do not make third-party payments on behalf of, "religious organizations," which are those "whose purpose is to practice a devotion to an acknowledged ultimate reality or deity." The category of support here is for "student news, information, opinion, entertainment, or academic communications media groups," of which *Wide Awake* was 1 of 15 in the 1990 school year. WAP did not seek a subsidy because of its Christian editorial viewpoint; it sought funding as a student journal, which it was. . . .

It does not violate the Establishment Clause for a public university to grant access to its facilities on a religion-neutral basis to a wide spectrum of student groups, including groups which use meeting rooms for sectarian activities, accompanied by some devotional exercises. This is so even where the upkeep, maintenance, and repair of the facilities attributed to those uses is paid from a student activities fund to which students are required to contribute. The government usually acts by spending money. Even the provision of a meeting room, as in *Mergens* and *Widmar*, involved governmental expenditure, if only in the form of electricity and heating or cooling costs. . . . There is no difference in logic or principle, and no difference of constitutional significance, between a school using its funds to operate a facility to which students have access, and a school paying a third-party contractor to operate the facility on its behalf. The latter occurs here. The University provides printing services to a broad spectrum of student newspapers qualified as CIOs by reason of their officers and membership. Any benefit to religion is incidental to the government's provision of secular services for secular purposes on a religion-neutral basis. Printing is a routine, secular, and recurring attribute of student life.

To obey the Establishment Clause, it was not necessary for the University to deny eligibility to student publications because of their viewpoint. The neutrality commanded of the State by the separate Clauses of the First Amendment was compromised by the University's course of action. The viewpoint discrimination inherent in the University's regulation required public officials to scan and interpret student publications to discern their underlying philosophic assumptions respecting religious theory and belief. That course of action was a denial of the right of free speech and would risk fostering a pervasive bias or hostility to religion, which could undermine the very neutrality the Establishment Clause requires. There is no Establishment Clause violation in the University's honoring its duties under the Free Speech Clause.

The judgment of the Court of Appeals must be, and is, reversed.

☐ *Justice O'CONNOR, concurring.*

When two bedrock principles so conflict, understandably neither can provide the definitive answer. Reliance on categorical platitudes is unavailing. Resolution instead depends on the hard task of judging—sifting through the details and determining whether the challenged program offends the Establishment Clause. Such judgment requires courts to draw lines, sometimes quite fine, based on the particular facts of each case. . . .

So it is in this case. The nature of the dispute does not admit of categorical answers, nor should any be inferred from the Court's decision today. Instead, certain considerations specific to the program at issue lead me to conclude that by providing the same assistance to *Wide Awake* that it does to other publications, the University would not be endorsing the magazine's religious perspective.

First, the student organizations, at the University's insistence, remain strictly independent of the University. . . . Second, financial assistance is distributed in a manner that ensures its use only for permissible purposes. A student organization seeking assistance must submit disbursement requests; if approved, the funds are paid directly to the third-party vendor and do not pass through the organization's coffers. . . . Third, assistance is provided to the religious publication in a context that makes improbable any perception of government endorsement of the religious message. *Wide Awake* does not exist in a vacuum. It competes with 15 other magazines and newspapers for advertising and readership. The widely divergent viewpoints of these many purveyors of opinion, all supported on an equal basis by the University, significantly diminishes the danger that the message of any one publication is perceived as endorsed by the University. . . .

Finally, although the question is not presented here, I note the possibility that the student fee is susceptible to a Free Speech Clause challenge by an objecting student that she should not be compelled to pay for speech with which she disagrees. While the Court does not resolve the question here, the existence of such an opt-out possibility not available to citizens generally provides a potential basis for distinguishing proceeds of the student fees in this case from proceeds of the general assessments in support of religion that lie at the core of the prohibition against religious funding, and from government funds generally. Unlike monies dispensed from state or federal treasuries, the Student Activities Fund is collected from students who themselves administer the fund and select qualifying recipients only from among those who originally paid the fee. . . . The Student Activities Fund, then, represents not government resources, whether derived from tax revenue, sales of assets, or otherwise, but a fund that simply belongs to the students.

The Court's decision today therefore neither trumpets the supremacy of the neutrality principle nor signals the demise of the funding prohibition in Establishment Clause jurisprudence. . . . When bedrock principles collide, they test the limits of categorical obstinacy and expose the flaws and dangers of a Grand Unified Theory that may turn out to be neither grand nor unified. The Court today does only what courts must do in many Establishment Clause cases—focus on specific features of a particular government action to ensure that it does not violate the Constitution. By withholding from *Wide Awake* assistance that the University provides generally to all other student publications, the University has discriminated on the basis of the magazine's religious viewpoint in violation of the Free Speech Clause. . . .

☐ *Justice SOUTER, with whom Justice STEVENS, Justice GINSBURG and Justice BREYER join, dissenting.*

The Court today, for the first time, approves direct funding of core religious activities by an arm of the State. It does so, however, only after erroneous treatment of some familiar principles of law implementing the First Amendment's Establishment and Speech Clauses, and by viewing the very funds in question as beyond the reach of the Establishment Clause's funding restrictions as such. Because there is no warrant for distinguishing among public funding sources for purposes of applying the First Amendment's prohibition of religious establishment, I would hold that the University's refusal to support petitioners' religious activities is compelled by the Establishment Clause. I would therefore affirm. . . .

The Court's difficulties will be all the more clear after a closer look at *Wide Awake* than the majority opinion affords. The character of the magazine is candidly disclosed on the opening page of the first issue, where the editor-in-chief announces *Wide Awake*'s mission in a letter to the readership signed, "Love in Christ": it is "to challenge Christians to live, in word and deed, according to the faith they proclaim and to encourage students to consider what a personal relationship with Jesus Christ means." The masthead of every issue bears St. Paul's exhortation, that "the hour has come for you to awake from your slumber, because our salvation is nearer now than when we first believed. Romans 13:11."

Each issue of *Wide Awake* contained in the record makes good on the editor's promise and echoes the Apostle's call to accept salvation. . . . Even featured essays on facially secular topics become platforms from which to call readers to fulfill the tenets of Christianity in their lives. . . .

This writing is . . . [a] straightforward exhortation to enter into a relationship with God as revealed in Jesus Christ, and to satisfy a series of moral obligations derived from the teachings of Jesus Christ. These are not the words of "student news, information, opinion, entertainment, or academic communication . . ." (in the language of the University's funding criterion), but the words of "challenge [to] Christians to live, in word and deed, according to the faith they proclaim and . . . to consider what a personal relationship with Jesus Christ means" (in the language of *Wide Awake*'s founder). The subject is not the discourse of the scholar's study or the seminar room, but of the evangelist's mission station and the pulpit. It is nothing other than the preaching of the word, which (along with the sacraments) is what most branches of Christianity offer those called to the religious life.

Using public funds for the direct subsidization of preaching the word is categorically forbidden under the Establishment Clause, and if the Clause was meant to accomplish nothing else, it was meant to bar this use of public money. Evidence on the subject antedates even the Bill of Rights itself, as may be seen in the writings of Madison, whose authority on questions about the meaning of the Establishment Clause is well settled. Four years before the First Congress proposed the First Amendment, Madison gave his opinion on the legitimacy of using public funds for religious purposes, in the Memorial and Remonstrance Against Religious Assessments, which played the central role in ensuring the defeat of the Virginia tax assessment bill in 1786 and framed the debate upon which the Religion Clauses stand: "Who does not see that . . . the same authority which can force a citizen to contribute three pence only of his property for the support of any one establishment, may force him to conform to any other establishment in all cases whatsoever?" James Madison, Memorial and Remonstrance Against Religious Assessments. . . .

The principle against direct funding with public money is patently violated by the contested use of today's student activity fee. Like today's taxes generally, the fee is Madison's threepence. The University exercises the power of the State to compel a student to pay it, and the use of any part of it for the direct support of religious activity thus strikes at what we have repeatedly held to be the heart of the prohibition on establishment.

The Court, accordingly, has never before upheld direct state funding of the sort of proselytizing published in *Wide Awake* and, in fact, has categorically condemned state programs directly aiding religious activity, *School Dist. v. Ball*, [413 U.S. 756 (1973)] (striking programs providing secular instruction to nonpublic school students on non-public school premises because they are "indistinguishable from the provision of a direct cash subsidy to the religious school that is most clearly prohibited under the Establishment Clause"); *Wolman v. Walter*, 433 U.S. 229 (1977) (striking field trip aid program because it constituted "an impermissible direct aid to sectarian education"); *Meek v. Pittenger*, 421 U.S. 349 (1975) (striking material and equipment loan program to nonpublic schools because of the inability to "channel aid to the secular without providing direct aid to the sectarian"); *Committee for Public Education v. Nyquist*, [413 U.S. 756 (1973),] (striking aid to non-public schools for maintenance and repair of facilities because "no attempt is made to restrict payments to those expenditures related to the upkeep of facilities used exclusively for secular purposes"); *Levitt v. Committee for Public Ed. & Religious Liberty*, 413 U.S. 472 (1973) (striking aid to non-public schools for state-mandated tests because the state had failed to "assure that the state-supported activity is not being used for religious indoctrination"); *Tilton v. Richardson*, 403 U.S. 672 (1971) (striking as insufficient a 20-year limit on prohibition for religious use in federal construction program for university facilities because unrestricted use even after 20 years "is in effect a contribution of some value to a religious body"). . . .

Why does the Court not apply this clear law to these clear facts and conclude, as I do, that the funding scheme here is a clear constitutional violation? The answer must be in part that the Court fails to confront the evidence set out in the preceding section. Throughout its opinion, the Court refers uninformatively to *Wide Awake*'s "Christian viewpoint," or its "religious perspective," and in distinguishing funding of *Wide Awake* from the funding of a church, the Court maintains that "[*Wide Awake*] is not a religious institution, at least in the usual sense." The Court does not quote the magazine's adoption of Saint Paul's exhortation to awaken to the nearness of salvation, or any of its articles enjoining readers to accept Jesus Christ, or the religious verses, or the religious textual analyses, or the suggested prayers. And so it is easy for the Court to lose sight of what the University students and the Court of Appeals found so obvious, and to blanch the patently and frankly evangelistic character of the magazine by unrevealing allusions to religious points of view. . . .

At the heart of the Establishment Clause stands the prohibition against direct public funding, but that prohibition does not answer the questions that occur at the margins of the Clause's application. . . . In the doubtful cases (those not involving direct public funding), where there is initially room for argument about a law's effect, evenhandedness serves to weed out those laws that impermissibly advance religion by channelling aid to it exclusively. Evenhandedness is therefore a prerequisite to further enquiry into the constitutionality of a doubtful law, but evenhandedness goes no further. It does not guarantee success under Establishment Clause scrutiny. . . .

Evenhandedness as one element of a permissibly attenuated benefit is, of course, a far cry from evenhandedness as a sufficient condition of constitutionality for direct financial support of religious proselytization, and our cases have unsurprisingly repudiated any such attempt to cut the Establishment Clause down to a mere prohibition against unequal direct aid. And nowhere has the Court's adherence to the preeminence of the no-direct-funding principle over the principle of evenhandedness been as clear as in *Bowen v. Kendrick* [487 U.S. 589 (1988)].

Bowen involved consideration of the Adolescent Family Life Act (AFLA), a federal grant program providing funds to institutions for counseling and educational services related to adolescent sexuality and pregnancy. At the time of the litigation, 141 grants had been awarded under the AFLA to a broad array of both secular and religiously affiliated institutions. In an Establishment Clause challenge to the Act brought by taxpayers and other interested parties, the District Court resolved the case on a pre-trial motion for summary judgment, holding the AFLA program unconstitutional both on its face and also insofar as religious institutions were involved in receiving grants under the Act. When this Court reversed on the issue of facial constitutionality under the Establishment Clause, we said that there was "no intimation in the statute that at some point, or for some grantees, religious uses are permitted." On the contrary, after looking at the legislative history and applicable regulations, we found safeguards adequate to ensure that grants would not be "used by . . . grantees in such a way as to advance religion." . . .

Bowen was no sport; its pedigree was the line of *Everson v. Board of Ed.*, *Board of Ed. v. Allen*, *Tilton v. Richardson*, *Hunt v. McNair*, and *Roemer v. Board of Pub. Works of Md.* Each of these cases involved a general aid program that provided benefits to a broad array of secular and sectarian institutions on an evenhanded basis, but in none of them was that fact dispositive. . . . Instead, the central enquiry in each of these general aid cases, as in *Bowen*, was whether secular activities could be separated from the sectarian ones sufficiently to ensure that aid would flow to the secular alone.

Witters, *Mueller*, and *Zobrest* expressly preserve the standard thus exhibited so often. Each of these cases explicitly distinguished the indirect aid in issue from contrasting examples in the line of cases striking down direct aid, and each thereby expressly preserved the core constitutional principle that direct aid to religion is impermissible. . . .

If the Court's suggestion is that this feature of the funding program brings this case into line with *Witters*, *Mueller*, and *Zobrest*, the Court has misread those cases, which turned on the fact that the choice to benefit religion was made by a non-religious third party standing between the government and a religious institution. Here there is no third party standing between the government and the ultimate religious beneficiary to break the circuit by its independent discretion to put state money to religious use. The printer, of course, has no option to take the money and use it to print a secular journal instead of *Wide Awake*. It only gets the money because of its contract to print a message of religious evangelism at the direction of *Wide Awake*, and it will receive payment only for doing precisely that. The formalism of distinguishing between payment to *Wide Awake* so it can pay an approved bill and payment of the approved bill itself cannot be the basis of a decision of Constitutional law. . . .

Given the dispositive effect of the Establishment Clause's bar to funding the magazine, there should be no need to decide whether in the absence of this bar the University would violate the Free Speech Clause by limiting funding as it has done. But the Court's speech analysis may have independent application, and its flaws should not pass unremarked. . . .

There is no viewpoint discrimination in the University's application of its Guidelines to deny funding to *Wide Awake*. Under those Guidelines, a "religious activity," which is not eligible for funding is "an activity which primarily promotes or manifests a particular belief(s) in or about a deity or an ultimate reality." It is clear that this is the basis on which Wide Awake Productions was denied funding. The discussion of *Wide Awake*'s content shows beyond any question that it "primarily promotes or manifests a particular belief(s) in or about a deity . . . ," in the very specific sense that its manifest function is to call students to repentance, to commitment to Jesus Christ, and to particular moral action because of its Christian character.

If the Guidelines were written or applied so as to limit only such Christian advocacy and no other evangelical efforts that might compete with it, the discrimination would be based on viewpoint. But that is not what the regulation authorizes; it applies to Muslim and Jewish and Buddhist advocacy as well as to Christian. And since it limits funding to activities promoting or manifesting a particular belief not only "in" but "about" a deity or ultimate reality, it applies to agnostics and atheists as well as it does to deists and theists (as the University maintained at oral argument, and as the Court recognizes). The Guidelines, and their application to *Wide Awake*, thus do not skew debate by funding one position but not its competitors. As understood by their application to *Wide Awake*, they simply deny funding for hortatory speech that "primarily promotes or manifests" any view on the merits of religion; they deny funding for the entire subject matter of religious apologetics.

The Court, of course, reads the Guidelines differently, but while I believe the Court is wrong in construing their breadth, the important point is that even on the Court's own construction the Guidelines impose no viewpoint discrimination. . . .

Even if the Court were indeed correct about the funding restriction's categorical breadth, the stringency of the restriction would most certainly not work any impermissible viewpoint discrimination under any prior understanding of that species of content discrimination. If a University wished to fund no speech beyond the subjects of pasta and cookie preparation, it surely would not be discriminating on the basis of someone's viewpoint, at least absent some controversial claim that pasta and cookies did not exist. The upshot would be an instructional universe without higher education, but not a universe where one viewpoint was enriched above its competitors. . . .

To put the point another way, the Court's decision equating a categorical exclusion of both sides of the religious debate with viewpoint discrimination suggests the Court has concluded that primarily religious and antireligious speech, grouped together, always provides an opposing (and not merely a related) viewpoint to any speech about any secular topic. Thus, the Court's reasoning requires a university that funds private publications about any primarily nonreligious topic also to fund publications primarily espousing adherence to or rejection of religion. But a university's decision to fund a magazine about racism, and not to fund publications aimed at urging repentance before God does not skew the debate either about racism or the desirability of religious conversion. The Court's contrary holding amounts to a significant reformulation of our viewpoint discrimination precedents and will significantly expand access to limited-access forums. . . .

I respectfully dissent.

Agostini v. Felton

521 U.S. 203, 117 S.Ct. 1997 (1997)

In *Aguilar v. Felton*, 473 U.S. 402 (1985), the Burger Court held that New York City's program, pursuant to Title I of the Elementary and Secondary Education Act of 1965, of sending public school teachers into parochial schools to provide remedial education to disadvantaged children constituted an excessive entanglement of government with religion in violation of the First Amendment's Establishment Clause. On remand, the District Court entered a permanent injunction reflecting that ruling. As a result, instead of sending teachers onto parochial school grounds, teachers and mobile classrooms were sent to the schools, parked on the streets, and children were brought to the vans for remedial instruction. A decade later, the Board of Education of the City of New York and a group of parents of parochial schoolchildren filed motions in the District Court seeking relief from the injunction's operation under Federal Rule of Civil Procedure 60(b) (5). They emphasized the significant costs, approximately $6 million a year, of complying with *Aguilar*. They also contended that *Aguilar* was no longer good law because, in *Board of Education of Kiryas Joel Village School District v. Grumet*, 512 U.S. 687 (1994), five justices on the Rehnquist Court indicated that *Aguilar* should be reconsidered. The District Court denied the motion, declaring that *Aguilar's* demise has "not yet occurred," and an appellate court agreed. Subsequently, the Supreme Court granted a petition for *certiorari* and the Clinton administration filed a friend-of-the-court brief, contending that "hundreds of millions of dollars . . . which otherwise could have been used for instructional services have been spent on administrative costs made necessary only because of the need to comply" with the Court's 1985 ruling.

The Court's decision was five to four and its opinion announced by Justice O'Connor. Justices Souter and Ginsburg filed dissenting opinions, which were joined by Justices Stevens and Breyer.

☐ *Justice O'CONNOR delivered the opinion of the Court.*

Petitioners maintain that *Aguilar v. Felton*, 473 U.S. 402 (1985), cannot be squared with our intervening Establishment Clause jurisprudence and ask that we explicitly recognize what our more recent cases already dictate: *Aguilar* is no longer good law. We agree with petitioners that *Aguilar* is not consistent with our subsequent Establishment Clause decisions and further conclude that, on the facts presented here, petitioners are entitled under Federal Rule of Civil Procedure 60(b) (5) to relief from the operation of the District Court's prospective injunction. . . .

In order to evaluate whether *Aguilar* has been eroded by our subsequent Establishment Clause cases, it is necessary to understand the rationale upon which *Aguilar*, as well as its companion case, *School Dist. of Grand Rapids v. Ball*, 473 U.S. 373 (1985), rested.

In *Ball*, the Court evaluated two programs implemented by the School District of Grand Rapids, Michigan. The district's Shared Time program, the one most analogous to Title I, provided remedial and "enrichment" classes, at public expense, to students attending nonpublic schools. The classes were taught during regular school hours by publicly employed teachers, using materials purchased with public funds, on the premises of nonpublic schools.

The Court conducted its analysis by applying the three-part test set forth in *Lemon v. Kurtzman*, 403 U.S. 602 (1971). . . .

The Court found that the program violated the Establishment Clause's prohibition against "government-financed or government-sponsored indoctrination into the beliefs of a particular religious faith" in at least three ways. . . .

Distilled to essentials, the Court's conclusion that the Shared Time program in *Ball* had the impermissible effect of advancing religion rested on three assumptions: (i) any public employee who works on the premises of a religious school is presumed to inculcate religion in her work; (ii) the presence of public employees on private school premises creates a symbolic union between church and state; and (iii) any and all public aid that directly aids the educational function of religious schools impermissibly finances religious indoctrination, even if the aid reaches such schools as a consequence of private decision-making. Additionally, in *Aguilar* there was a fourth assumption: that New York City's Title I program necessitated an excessive government entanglement with religion because public employees who teach on the premises of religious schools must be closely monitored to ensure that they do not inculcate religion.

Our more recent cases have undermined the assumptions upon which *Ball* and *Aguilar* relied. To be sure, the general principles we use to evaluate whether government aid violates the Establishment Clause have not changed since *Aguilar* was decided. For example, we continue to ask whether the government acted with the purpose of advancing or inhibiting religion, and the nature of that inquiry has remained largely unchanged. Likewise, we continue to explore whether the aid has the "effect" of advancing or inhibiting religion. What has changed since we decided *Ball* and *Aguilar* is our understanding of the criteria used to assess whether aid to religion has an impermissible effect.

As we have repeatedly recognized, government inculcation of religious beliefs has the impermissible effect of advancing religion. Our cases subsequent to *Aguilar* have, however, modified in two significant respects the approach we use to assess indoctrination. First, we have abandoned the presumption erected in *Meek* and *Ball* that the placement of public employees on parochial school grounds inevitably results in the impermissible effect of state-sponsored indoctrination or constitutes a symbolic union between government and religion. In *Zobrest v. Catalina Foothills School Dist.*, 509 U.S. 1 (1993), we examined whether the IDEA [Individuals with Disabilities Education Act] was constitutional as applied to a deaf student who sought to bring his state-employed sign-language interpreter with him to his Roman Catholic high school. We held that this was permissible, expressly disavowing the notion that "the Establishment Clause [laid] down [an] absolute bar to the placing of a public employee in a sectarian school." . . . *Zobrest* therefore expressly rejected the notion—relied on in *Ball* and *Aguilar*—that, solely because of her presence on private school property, a public employee will be presumed to inculcate religion in the students. *Zobrest* also implicitly repudiated another assumption on which *Ball* and *Aguilar* turned: that the presence of a public employee on private school property creates an impermissible "symbolic link" between government and religion. . . .

Second, we have departed from the rule relied on in *Ball* that all government aid that directly aids the educational function of religious schools is invalid. In *Witters v. Washington Dept. of Servs. for Blind*, 474 U.S. 481 (1986), we held that the Establishment Clause did not bar a State from issuing a vocational tuition grant to a blind person who wished to use the grant to attend a Christian college and become a pastor, missionary, or youth director. Even though the grant recipient clearly would use the money to obtain religious education, we observed that the tuition grants were " 'made available generally without regard to the sectarian-nonsectarian, or public-nonpublic nature of the institution benefited.' " . . .

Zobrest and *Witters* make clear that, under current law, the Shared Time program in *Ball* and New York City's Title I program in *Aguilar* will not, as a matter of law, be deemed to have the effect of advancing religion through indoctrination. Indeed, each of the premises upon which we relied in *Ball* to reach a contrary conclusion is no longer valid. First, there is no reason to presume that, simply because she enters a parochial school classroom, a full-time public employee such as a Title I teacher will depart from her assigned duties and instructions and embark on religious indoctrination, any more than there was a reason in *Zobrest* to think an interpreter would inculcate religion by altering her translation of classroom lectures. . . .

As discussed above, *Zobrest* also repudiates *Ball*'s assumption that the presence of Title I teachers in parochial school classroom will, without more, create the impression of a "symbolic union" between church and state. Justice SOUTER maintains that *Zobrest* is not dispositive on this point because *Aguilar*'s implicit conclusion that New York City's Title I program created a "symbolic union" rested on more than the presence of Title I employees on parochial school grounds. . . . We do not see any perceptible (let alone dispositive) difference in the degree of symbolic union between a student receiving remedial instruction in a classroom on his sectarian school's campus and one receiving instruction in a van parked just at the school's curbside.

Nor under current law can we conclude that a program placing full-time public employees on parochial campuses to provide Title I instruction would impermissibly finance religious indoctrination. In all relevant respects, the provision of instructional services under Title I is indistinguishable from the provision of sign-language interpreters under the IDEA. Both programs make aid available only to eligible recipients. That aid is provided to students at whatever school they choose to attend. . . .

We are also not persuaded that Title I services supplant the remedial instruction and guidance counseling already provided in New York City's sectarian schools. Although Justice SOUTER maintains that the sectarian schools provide such services and that those schools reduce those services once their students begin to receive Title I instruction, his claims rest on speculation about the impossibility of drawing any line between supplemental and general education, and not on any evidence in the record that the Board is in fact violating Title I regulations by providing services that supplant those offered in the sectarian schools.

What is most fatal to the argument that New York City's Title I program directly subsidizes religion is that it applies with equal force when those services are provided off-campus, and *Aguilar* implied that providing the services off-campus is entirely consistent with the Establishment Clause. . . . Justice SOUTER does not explain why a sectarian school would not have the same incentive to "make patently significant cut-backs" in its curriculum no matter where Title I services are offered, since the school would ostensibly be excused from having to provide the Title I-type services itself. Because the incentive is the same either way, we find no logical basis upon which to conclude that Title I services are an impermissible subsidy of religion when offered on-campus, but not when offered off-campus. Accordingly, contrary to our conclusion in *Aguilar*, placing full-time employees on parochial school campuses does not as a matter of law have the impermissible effect of advancing religion through indoctrination. . . .

We turn now to *Aguilar*'s conclusion that New York City's Title I program resulted in an excessive entanglement between church and state. Whether a government aid program results in such an entanglement has consistently been an aspect of our Establishment Clause analysis. We have considered entanglement both in the course of assessing whether an aid program has an impermissible effect of advancing religion, *Walz v. Tax Comm'n of City of New York*, 397 U.S. 664 (1970), and as a factor separate and apart from "effect," *Lemon v. Kurtzman*. Regardless of how we have characterized the issue, however, the factors we use to assess whether an entanglement is "excessive" are similar to the factors we use to examine "effect." . . .

Not all entanglements, of course, have the effect of advancing or inhibiting religion. Interaction between church and state is inevitable, and we have always tolerated some level of involvement between the two. Entanglement must be "excessive" before it runs afoul of the Establishment Clause. . . .

In *Aguilar*, the Court presumed that full-time public employees on parochial school grounds would be tempted to inculcate religion, despite the ethical standards they were required to uphold. Because of this risk pervasive monitoring would be required. But after *Zobrest* we no longer presume that public employees will inculcate religion simply because they happen to be in a sectarian environment. Since we have abandoned the assumption that properly instructed public employees will fail to discharge their duties faithfully, we must also discard the assumption that pervasive monitoring of Title I teachers is required. There is no suggestion in the record before us that unannounced monthly visits of public supervisors are insufficient to prevent or to detect inculcation of religion by public employees. Moreover, we have not found excessive entanglement in cases in which States imposed far more onerous burdens on religious institutions than the monitoring system at issue here.

To summarize, New York City's Title I program does not run afoul of any of three primary criteria we currently use to evaluate whether government aid has the effect of advancing religion: it does not result in governmental indoctrination; define its recipients by reference to religion; or create an excessive entanglement. We therefore hold that a federally funded program providing supplemental, remedial instruction to disadvantaged children on a neutral basis is not invalid under the Establishment Clause when such instruction is given on the premises of sectarian schools by government employees pursuant to a program containing safeguards such as those present here. The same considerations that justify this holding require us to conclude that this carefully constrained program also cannot reasonably be viewed as an endorsement of religion. Accordingly, we must acknowledge that *Aguilar*, as well as the portion of *Ball* addressing Grand Rapids' Shared Time program, are no longer good law. . . .

For these reasons, we reverse the judgment of the Court of Appeals and remand to the District Court with instructions to vacate its September 26, 1985, order.

It is so ordered.

☐ *Justice SOUTER, with whom Justice STEVENS and Justice GINSBURG join, and with whom Justice BREYER joins as to Part II, dissenting.*

■ I

I believe *Aguilar* was a correct and sensible decision, and my only reservation about its opinion is that the emphasis on the excessive entanglement produced by monitoring religious instructional content obscured those facts that independently called for the application of two central tenets of Establishment Clause jurisprudence. The State is forbidden to subsidize religion directly and is just as surely forbidden to act in any way that could reasonably be viewed as religious endorsement.

As is explained elsewhere, the flat ban on subsidization antedates the Bill of Rights and has been an unwavering rule in Establishment Clause cases, qualified only by the conclusion two Terms ago that state exactions from college students are not the sort of public revenues subject to the ban. See *Rosenberger v. Rector and Visitors of Univ. of Va.*, [515 U. S. 819] (1995) (SOUTER, J., dissenting; and O'CONNOR, J., concurring). The rule expresses the hard lesson learned over and over again in the American past and in the experiences of the countries from which we have come, that religions supported by governments are compromised just as surely as the religious freedom of dissenters is burdened when the government supports religion. . . .

These principles were violated by the programs at issue in *Aguilar* and *Ball*. . . . [E]ach provided classes on the premises of the religious schools, covering a wide range of subjects including some at the core of primary and secondary education, like reading and mathematics; while their services were termed "supplemental," the programs and their instructors necessarily assumed responsibility for teaching subjects that the religious schools would otherwise have been obligated to provide. . . .

What, therefore, was significant in *Aguilar* and *Ball* about the placement of state-paid teachers into the physical and social settings of the religious schools was not only the consequent temptation of some of those teachers to reflect the schools' religious missions in the rhetoric of their instruction, with a resulting need for monitoring and the certainty of entanglement. What was so remarkable was that the schemes in issue assumed a teaching responsibility indistinguishable from the responsibility of the schools themselves. The obligation of primary and secondary schools to teach reading necessarily extends to teaching those who are having a hard time at it, and the same is true of math. Calling some classes remedial does not distinguish their subjects from the schools' basic subjects, however inadequately the schools may have been addressing them.

What was true of the Title I scheme as struck down in *Aguilar* will be just as true when New York reverts to the old practices with the Court's approval after today. There is simply no line that can be drawn between the instruction paid for at taxpayers' expense and the instruction in any subject that is not identified as formally religious. While it would be an obvious sham, say, to channel cash to religious schools to be credited only against the expense of "secular" instruction, the line between "supplemental" and general education is likewise impossible to draw. If a State may constitutionally enter the schools to teach in the manner in question, it must in constitutional principle be free to assume, or assume payment for, the entire cost of instruction provided in any ostensibly secular subject in any religious school. This Court explicitly recognized this in *Ball*, and although in *Aguilar* the Court concentrated on entanglement it noted the similarity to *Ball*, and Judge Friendly's opinion for the Second Circuit made it expressly clear that there was no stopping place in principle once the public teacher entered the religious schools to teach their secular subjects.

In sum, if a line is to be drawn short of barring all state aid to religious schools for teaching standard subjects, the *Aguilar-Ball* line was a sensible one capable of principled adherence. It is no less sound, and no less necessary, today.

■ II

The Court today ignores this doctrine and claims that recent cases rejected the elemental assumptions underlying *Aguilar* and much of *Ball*. But the Court errs. Its holding that *Aguilar* and the portion of *Ball* addressing the Shared Time program are "no longer good law" rests on mistaken reading. . . .

It is . . . puzzling to find the Court insisting that the aid scheme administered under Title I and considered in *Aguilar* was comparable to the programs in *Witters* and *Zobrest*. Instead of aiding isolated individuals within a school system, New York City's Title I program before *Aguilar* served about 22,000 private school students, all but 52 of whom attended religious schools. Instead of serving individual blind or deaf students, as such, Title I as administered in New York City before *Aguilar* (and as now to be revived) funded instruction in core subjects (remedial reading, reading skills, remedial mathematics, English as a second language) and provided guidance services. Instead of providing a service the school would not otherwise furnish, the Title I services necessarily relieved a religious school of "an expense that it otherwise would have assumed," *Zobrest*, and freed its funds for other, and sectarian uses.

Finally, instead of aid that comes to the religious school indirectly in the sense that its distribution results from private decision making, a public educational agency distributes Title I aid in the form of programs and services directly to the religious schools. In *Zobrest* and *Witters*, it was fair to say that individual students were themselves applicants for individual benefits on a scale that could not amount to a systemic supplement. But under Title I, a local educational agency (which in New York City is the Board of Education) may receive federal funding by proposing programs approved to serve individual students who meet the criteria of need, which it then uses to provide such programs at the religious schools; students eligible for such programs may not apply directly for Title I funds. The aid, accordingly, is not even formally aid to the individual students (and even formally individual aid must be seen as aid to a school system), when so many individuals receive it that it becomes a significant feature of the system.

In sum, nothing since *Ball* and *Aguilar* and before this case has eroded the distinction between "direct and substantial" and "indirect and incidental." That principled line is being breached only here and now. . . .

Zelman v. Simmons-Harris

536 U.S. 639, 122 S.Ct. 2460 (2002)

In 1995, Cleveland, Ohio's low-income inner-city schools were declared to be in crisis and placed under state control. Subsequently, Ohio adopted a "Pilot Project Scholarship Program," providing school vouchers for inner-city residents, to pay up to $2,250 of the tuition costs of sending their children to schools outside the Cleveland school district. About 96 percent of the money went to religious schools and a group of taxpayers challenged the constitutionality of the program for violating the First Amendment's separation of government from religion. A federal district held the voucher program unconstitutional and the Court of Appeals for the Sixth Circuit affirmed that decision.

The appellate court's decision was reversed on a vote of five to four. Chief Justice Rehnquist delivered the opinion of the Court. Justices O'Connor and Thomas issued concurring opinions. Justices Stevens, Breyer, and Souter filed dissenting opinions, and Justice Ginsburg joined the latter's dissent.

☐ *CHIEF JUSTICE REHNQUIST delivered the opinion of the Court.*

The Establishment Clause of the First Amendment, applied to the States through the Fourteenth Amendment, prevents a State from enacting laws that have the "purpose" or "effect" of advancing or inhibiting religion. *Agostini v. Felton*, 521 U.S. 203 (1997). There is no dispute that the program challenged here was enacted for the valid secular purpose of providing educational assistance to poor children in a demonstrably failing public school system. Thus, the question presented is whether the Ohio program nonetheless has the forbidden "effect" of advancing or inhibiting religion.

To answer that question, our decisions have drawn a consistent distinction between government programs that provide aid directly to religious schools, *Mitchell v. Helms*, 530 U.S. 793 (2000); *Agostini; Rosenberger v. Rector and Visitors of Univ. of Va.*, 515 U.S. 819 (1995), and programs of true private choice, in which government aid reaches religious schools only as a result of the genuine and independent choices of private individuals, *Mueller v. Allen*, 463 U.S. 388 (1983); *Witters v. Washington Dept. of Servs. for Blind*, 474 U.S. 481 (1986); *Zobrest v. Catalina Foothills School Dist.*, 509 U.S. 1 (1993). While our jurisprudence with respect to the constitutionality of direct aid programs has "changed significantly" over the past two decades, our jurisprudence with respect to true private choice programs has remained consistent and unbroken. Three times we have confronted Establishment Clause challenges to neutral government programs that provide aid directly to a broad class of individuals, who, in turn, direct the aid to religious schools or institutions of their own choosing. Three times we have rejected such challenges.

In *Mueller*, we rejected an Establishment Clause challenge to a Minnesota program authorizing tax deductions for various educational expenses, including private school tuition costs, even though the great majority of the program's beneficiaries (96%) were parents of children in religious schools. . . .

In *Witters*, we used identical reasoning to reject an Establishment Clause challenge to a vocational scholarship program that provided tuition aid to a student studying at a religious institution to become a pastor. . . .

Finally, in *Zobrest*, we applied *Mueller* and *Witters* to reject an Establishment Clause challenge to a federal program that permitted sign-language interpreters to assist deaf children enrolled in religious schools. Reviewing our earlier decisions, we stated that "government programs that neutrally provide benefits to a broad class of citizens defined without reference to religion are not readily subject to an Establishment Clause challenge." Looking once again to the challenged program as a whole, we observed that the program "distributes benefits neutrally to any child qualifying as 'disabled.' " Its "primary beneficiaries," we said, were "disabled children, not sectarian schools." . . .

Mueller, Witters, and *Zobrest* thus make clear that where a government aid program is neutral with respect to religion, and provides assistance directly to a broad class of citizens who, in turn, direct government aid to religious schools wholly as a result of their own genuine and independent private choice, the program is not readily subject to challenge under the Establishment Clause. A program that shares these features permits government aid to reach religious institutions only by way of the deliberate choices of numerous individual recipients. The incidental advancement of a religious mission, or the perceived endorsement of a religious message, is reasonably attributable to the individual recipient, not to the government, whose role ends with the disbursement of benefits.

We believe that the program challenged here is a program of true private choice, consistent with *Mueller, Witters,* and *Zobrest,* and thus constitutional. . . .

Respondents suggest that even without a financial incentive for parents to choose a religious school, the program creates a "public perception that the State is endorsing religious practices and beliefs." But we have repeatedly recognized that no reasonable observer would think a neutral program of private choice, where state aid reaches religious schools solely as a result of the numerous independent decisions of private individuals, carries with it the imprimatur of government endorsement. The argument is particularly misplaced here since "the reasonable observer in the endorsement inquiry must be deemed aware" of the "history and context" underlying a challenged program. *Good News Club v. Milford Central School*, 533 U.S. 98 (2001). Any objective observer familiar with the full history and context of the Ohio program would reasonably view it as one aspect of a broader undertaking to assist poor children in failed schools, not as an endorsement of religious schooling in general. . . .

Respondents and Justice SOUTER claim that even if we do not focus on the number of participating schools that are religious schools, we should attach constitutional significance to the fact that 96% of scholarship recipients have enrolled in religious schools. They claim that this alone proves parents lack genuine choice, even if no parent has ever said so. We need not consider this argument in detail, since it was flatly rejected in *Mueller*, where we found it irrelevant that 96% of parents taking deductions for tuition expenses paid tuition at religious schools. Indeed, we have recently found it irrelevant even to the constitutionality of a direct aid program that a vast majority of program benefits went to religious schools. . . .

Respondents finally claim that we should look to *Committee for Public Ed. & Religious Liberty v. Nyquist*, 413 U.S. 756 (1973), to decide these cases. We disagree for two reasons. First, the program in *Nyquist* was quite different from the program challenged here. *Nyquist* involved a New York program that gave a package of benefits exclusively to private schools and the parents of private school enrollees. Although the program was enacted for ostensibly secular purposes, we found that its "function" was "unmistakably to provide desired financial support for nonpublic, sectarian institutions." Its genesis, we said, was that private religious schools faced "increasingly grave fiscal problems." The program thus provided direct money grants to religious schools.

Second, were there any doubt that the program challenged in *Nyquist* is far removed from the program challenged here, we expressly reserved judgment with respect to "a case involving some form of public assistance (e.g., scholarships) made available generally without regard to the sectarian-nonsectarian, or public-nonpublic nature of the institution benefited." That, of course, is the very question now before us, and it has since been answered, first in *Mueller*. To the extent the scope of *Nyquist* has remained an open question in light of these later decisions, we now hold that *Nyquist* does not govern neutral educational assistance programs that, like the program here, offer aid directly to a broad class of individual recipients defined without regard to religion.

In sum, the Ohio program is entirely neutral with respect to religion. It provides benefits directly to a wide spectrum of individuals, defined only by financial need and residence in a particular school district. It permits such individuals to exercise genuine choice among options public and private, secular and religious. The program is therefore a program of true private choice. In keeping with an unbroken line of decisions rejecting challenges to similar programs, we hold that the program does not offend the Establishment Clause. The judgment of the Court of Appeals is reversed. It is so ordered.

☐ *Justice O'CONNOR, concurring.*

While I join the Court's opinion, I write separately for two reasons. First, although the Court takes an important step, I do not believe that today's decision, when considered in light of other longstanding government programs that impact religious organizations and our prior Establishment Clause jurisprudence, marks a dramatic break from the past. Second, given the emphasis the Court places on verifying that parents of voucher students in religious schools have exercised "true private choice," I think it is worth elaborating on the Court's conclusion that this inquiry should consider all reasonable educational alternatives to religious schools that are available to parents. To do otherwise is to ignore how the educational system in Cleveland actually functions.

These cases are different from prior indirect aid cases in part because a significant portion of the funds appropriated for the voucher program reach religious schools without restrictions on the use of these funds. The share of public resources that reach religious schools is not, however, as significant as respondents suggest. Data from the 1999–2000 school year indicate that 82 percent of schools participating in the voucher program were religious and that 96 percent of participating students enrolled in religious schools (46 of 56 private schools in the program are religiously-affiliated; 3,637 of 3,765 voucher students attend religious private schools), but these data are incomplete. These statistics do not take into account all of the reasonable educational choices that may be available to students in Cleveland public schools. When one considers the option to attend community schools, the percentage of students enrolled in religious schools falls to 62.1 percent. If magnet schools are included in the mix, this percentage falls to 16.5 percent.

Even these numbers do not paint a complete picture. The Cleveland program provides voucher applicants from low-income families with up to $2,250 in tuition assistance and provides the remaining applicants with up to $1,875 in tuition assistance. In contrast, the State provides community schools $4,518 per pupil and magnet schools, on average, $7,097 per pupil. Even if one assumes that all voucher students came from low-income families and that each voucher student used up the entire $2,250 voucher, at most $8.2 million of public funds flowed to religious schools under the voucher program in 1999–2000. Although just over one-half as many students attended community schools as religious private schools on the state fisc, the State spent over $1 million more—$9.4 million—on students in community schools than on students in religious private schools because per-pupil aid to community schools is more than double the per-pupil aid to private schools under the voucher program. Moreover, the amount spent on religious private schools is minor compared to the $114.8 million the State spent on students in the Cleveland magnet schools.

Although $8.2 million is no small sum, it pales in comparison to the amount of funds that federal, state, and local governments already provide religious institutions. Religious organizations may qualify for exemptions from the federal corporate income tax; the corporate income tax in many States; and property taxes in all 50 States; and clergy qualify for a federal tax break on income used for housing expenses. In addition, the Federal Government provides individuals, corporations, trusts, and estates a tax deduction for charitable contributions to qualified religious groups. See §§170, 642 (c). Finally, the Federal Government and certain state governments provide tax credits for educational expenses, many of which are spent on education at religious schools. . . .

Based on the reasoning in the Court's opinion, which is consistent with the realities of the Cleveland educational system, I am persuaded that the Cleveland voucher program affords parents of eligible children genuine non-religious options and is consistent with the Establishment Clause.

☐ *Justice THOMAS, concurring.*

Frederick Douglass once said that "[e]ducation . . . means emancipation. It means light and liberty. It means the uplifting of the soul of man into the glorious light of truth, the light by which men can only be made free." Today many of our inner-city public schools deny emancipation to urban minority students. Despite this Court's observation nearly 50 years ago in *Brown v. Board of Education* that "it is doubtful that any child may reasonably be expected to succeed in life if he is denied the opportunity of an education," urban children have been forced into a system that continually fails them. These cases present an example of such failures. Besieged by escalating financial problems and declining academic achievement, the Cleveland City School District was in the midst of an academic emergency when Ohio enacted its scholarship program.

The dissents and respondents wish to invoke the Establishment Clause of the First Amendment, as incorporated through the Fourteenth, to constrain a State's neutral efforts to provide greater educational opportunity for underprivileged minority students. Today's decision properly upholds the program as constitutional, and I join it in full. . . .

☐ *Justice STEVENS, dissenting.*

Is a law that authorizes the use of public funds to pay for the indoctrination of thousands of grammar school children in particular religious faiths a "law respecting an establishment of religion" within the meaning of the First Amendment? In answering that question, I think we should ignore three factual matters that are discussed at length by my colleagues.

First, the severe educational crisis that confronted the Cleveland City School District when Ohio enacted its voucher program is not a matter that should affect our appraisal of its constitutionality. . . .

Second, the wide range of choices that have been made available to students within the public school system has no bearing on the question whether the State may pay the tuition for students who wish to reject public education entirely and attend private schools that will provide them with a sectarian education. The fact that the vast majority of the voucher recipients who have entirely rejected public education receive religious indoctrination at state expense does, however, support the claim that the law is one "respecting an establishment of religion." The State may choose to divide up its public schools into a dozen different options and label them magnet schools, community schools, or whatever else it decides to call them, but the

State is still required to provide a public education and it is the State's decision to fund private school education over and above its traditional obligation that is at issue in these cases.

Third, the voluntary character of the private choice to prefer a parochial education over an education in the public school system seems to me quite irrelevant to the question whether the government's choice to pay for religious indoctrination is constitutionally permissible. Today, however, the Court seems to have decided that the mere fact that a family that cannot afford a private education wants its children educated in a parochial school is a sufficient justification for this use of public funds.

For the reasons stated by Justice SOUTER and Justice BREYER, I am convinced that the Court's decision is profoundly misguided. Admittedly, in reaching that conclusion I have been influenced by my understanding of the impact of religious strife on the decisions of our forbears to migrate to this continent, and on the decisions of neighbors in the Balkans, Northern Ireland, and the Middle East to mistrust one another. Whenever we remove a brick from the wall that was designed to separate religion and government, we increase the risk of religious strife and weaken the foundation of our democracy.

I respectfully dissent.

Justice BREYER, with whom Justice STEVENS and Justice SOUTER join, dissenting.

I do not believe that the "parental choice" aspect of the voucher program sufficiently offsets the concerns I have mentioned. Parental choice cannot help the taxpayer who does not want to finance the religious education of children. It will not always help the parent who may see little real choice between inadequate nonsectarian public education and adequate education at a school whose religious teachings are contrary to his own. It will not satisfy religious minorities unable to participate because they are too few in number to support the creation of their own private schools. It will not satisfy groups whose religious beliefs preclude them from participating in a government-sponsored program, and who may well feel ignored as government funds primarily support the education of children in the doctrines of the dominant religions. And it does little to ameliorate the entanglement problems or the related problems of social division. Consequently, the fact that the parent may choose which school can cash the government's voucher check does not alleviate the Establishment Clause concerns associated with voucher programs.

The Court, in effect, turns the clock back. It adopts, under the name of "neutrality," an interpretation of the Establishment Clause that this Court rejected more than half a century ago. In its view, the parental choice that offers each religious group a kind of equal opportunity to secure government funding overcomes the Establishment Clause concern for social concord. An earlier Court found that "equal opportunity" principle insufficient; it read the Clause as insisting upon greater separation of church and state, at least in respect to primary education. See *Nyquist*. In a society composed of many different religious creeds, I fear that this present departure from the Court's earlier understanding risks creating a form of religiously based conflict potentially harmful to the Nation's social fabric. Because I believe the Establishment Clause was written in part to avoid this kind of conflict, and for reasons set forth by Justice SOUTER and Justice STEVENS, I respectfully dissent.

⬜ *Justice SOUTER, with whom Justice STEVENS, Justice GINSBURG, and Justice BREYER join, dissenting.*

The applicability of the Establishment Clause to public funding of benefits to religious schools was settled in *Everson v. Board of Ed. of Ewing*, 330 U.S. 1 (1947), which inaugurated the modern era of establishment doctrine. The Court stated the principle in words from which there was no dissent: "No tax in any amount, large or small, can be levied to support any religious activities or institutions, whatever they may be called, or whatever form they may adopt to teach or practice religion." The Court has never in so many words repudiated this statement, let alone, in so many words, overruled *Everson.* . . .

How can a Court consistently leave *Everson* on the books and approve the Ohio vouchers? The answer is that it cannot. It is only by ignoring *Everson* that the majority can claim to rest on traditional law in its invocation of neutral aid provisions and private choice to sanction the Ohio law. It is, moreover, only by ignoring the meaning of neutrality and private choice themselves that the majority can even pretend to rest today's decision on those criteria.

The majority's statements of Establishment Clause doctrine cannot be appreciated without some historical perspective on the Court's announced limitations on government aid to religious education, and its repeated repudiation of limits previously set. . . .

Viewed with the necessary generality, the cases can be categorized in three groups. In the period from 1947 to 1968, the basic principle of no aid to religion through school benefits was unquestioned. Thereafter for some 15 years, the Court termed its efforts as attempts to draw a line against aid that would be divertible to support the religious, as distinct from the secular, activity of an institutional beneficiary. Then, starting in 1983, concern with divertibility was gradually lost in favor of approving aid in amounts unlikely to afford substantial benefits to religious schools, when offered evenhandedly without regard to a recipient's religious character, and when channeled to a religious institution only by the genuinely free choice of some private individual. Now, the three stages are succeeded by a fourth, in which the substantial character of government aid is held to have no constitutional significance, and the espoused criteria of neutrality in offering aid, and private choice in directing it, are shown to be nothing but examples of verbal formalism. . . .

Although it has taken half a century since *Everson* to reach the majority's twin standards of neutrality and free choice, the facts show that, in the majority's hands, even these criteria cannot convincingly legitimize the Ohio scheme.

Consider first the criterion of neutrality. As recently as two Terms ago, a majority of the Court recognized that neutrality conceived of as evenhandedness toward aid recipients had never been treated as alone sufficient to satisfy the Establishment Clause, *Mitchell [v. Helms]*. But at least in its limited significance, formal neutrality seemed to serve some purpose. Today, however, the majority employs the neutrality criterion in a way that renders it impossible to understand.

Neutrality in this sense refers, of course, to evenhandedness in setting eligibility as between potential religious and secular recipients of public money. Thus, for example, the aid scheme in *Witters* provided an eligible recipient with a scholarship to be used at any institution within a practically unlimited universe of schools; it did not tend to provide more or less aid depending on which one the scholarship recipient chose, and there was no indication that the maximum scholarship amount would be insufficient at secular schools. Neither did any condition of *Zobrest's* interpreter's subsidy favor religious education.

In order to apply the neutrality test, then, it makes sense to focus on a category of aid that may be directed to religious as well as secular schools, and ask whether the scheme favors a religious direction. Here, one would ask whether the voucher provisions, allowing for as much as $2,250 toward private school tuition (or a grant to a public school in an adjacent district), were written in a way that skewed the scheme toward benefiting religious schools.

This, however, is not what the majority asks. The majority looks not to the provisions for tuition vouchers, but to every provision for educational opportunity: "The program permits the participation of all schools within the district, [as well as public schools in adjacent districts], religious or nonreligious." The majority then finds confirmation that "participation of all schools" satisfies neutrality by noting that the better part of total state educational expenditure goes to public schools, thus showing there is no favor of religion.

The illogic is patent. If regular, public schools (which can get no voucher payments) "participate" in a voucher scheme with schools that can, and public expenditure is still predominantly on public schools, then the majority's reasoning would find neutrality in a scheme of vouchers available for private tuition in districts with no secular private schools at all. "Neutrality" as the majority employs the term is, literally, verbal and nothing more. This, indeed, is the only way the majority can gloss over the very nonneutral feature of the total scheme covering "all schools": public tutors may receive from the State no more than $324 per child to support extra tutoring (that is, the State's 90% of a total amount of $360), whereas the tuition voucher schools (which turn out to be mostly religious) can receive up to $2,250.

Why the majority does not simply accept the fact that the challenge here is to the more generous voucher scheme and judge its neutrality in relation to religious use of voucher money seems very odd. It seems odd, that is, until one recognizes that comparable schools for applying the criterion of neutrality are also the comparable schools for applying the other majority criterion, whether the immediate recipients of voucher aid have a genuinely free choice of religious and secular schools to receive the voucher money. And in applying this second criterion, the consideration of "all schools" is ostensibly helpful to the majority position.

The majority addresses the issue of choice the same way it addresses neutrality, by asking whether recipients or potential recipients of voucher aid have a choice of public schools among secular alternatives to religious schools. Again, however, the majority asks the wrong question and misapplies the criterion. The majority has confused choice in spending scholarships with choice from the entire menu of possible educational placements, most of them open to anyone willing to attend a public school. I say "confused" because the majority's new use of the choice criterion, which it frames negatively as "whether Ohio is coercing parents into sending their children to religious schools" ignores the reason for having a private choice enquiry in the first place. Cases since *Mueller* have found private choice relevant under a rule that aid to religious schools can be permissible so long as it first passes through the hands of students or parents. The majority's view that all educational choices are comparable for purposes of choice thus ignores the whole point of the choice test: it is a criterion for deciding whether indirect aid to a religious school is legitimate because it passes through private hands that can spend or use the aid in a secular school. The question is whether the private hand is genuinely free to send the money in either a secular direction or a religious one. The majority now has transformed this question about private choice in channeling aid into a question about selecting from examples of state spending (on education) including direct spending on magnet and community public schools that goes through no private hands and could never reach a religious school under any circumstance. When the choice test is transformed from where to spend the money to where to go to school, it is cut loose from its very purpose.

Defining choice as choice in spending the money or channeling the aid is, moreover, necessary if the choice criterion is to function as a limiting principle at all. If "choice" is present whenever there is any educational alternative to the religious school to which vouchers can be endorsed, then there will always be a choice and the voucher can always be constitutional, even in a system in which there is not a single private secular school as an alternative to the religious school. And because it is unlikely that any participating private religious school will enroll more pupils than the generally available public system, it will be easy to generate numbers suggesting that aid to religion is not the significant intent or effect of the voucher scheme.

That is, in fact, just the kind of rhetorical argument that the majority accepts in these cases. In addition to secular private schools (129 students), the majority considers public schools with tuition assistance (roughly 1,400 students), magnet schools (13,000 students), and community schools (1,900 students), and concludes that fewer than 20% of pupils receive state vouchers to attend religious schools. . . .

If, contrary to the majority, we ask the right question about genuine choice to use the vouchers, the answer shows that something is influencing choices in a way that aims the money in a religious direction: of 56 private schools in the district participating in the voucher program (only 53 of which accepted voucher students in 1999–2000), 46 of them are religious; 96.6% of all voucher recipients go to religious schools, only 3.4% to non-religious ones. Unfortunately for the majority position, there is no explanation for this that suggests the religious direction results simply from free choices by parents. One answer to these statistics, for example, which would be consistent with the genuine choice claimed to be operating, might be that 96.6% of families choosing to avail themselves of vouchers choose to educate their children in schools of their own religion. This would not, in my view, render the scheme constitutional, but it would speak to the majority's choice criterion. Evidence shows, however, that almost two out of three families using vouchers to send their children to religious schools did not embrace the religion of those schools. The families made it clear they had not chosen the schools because they wished their children to be proselytized in a religion not their own, or in any religion, but because of educational opportunity.

Even so, the fact that some 2,270 students chose to apply their vouchers to schools of other religions might be consistent with true choice if the students "chose" their religious schools over a wide array of private non-religious options, or if it could be shown generally that Ohio's program had no effect on educational choices and thus no impermissible effect of advancing religious education. But both possibilities are contrary to fact. First, even if all existing nonreligious private schools in Cleveland were willing to accept large numbers of voucher students, only a few more than the 129 currently enrolled in such schools would be able to attend, as the total enrollment at all nonreligious private schools in Cleveland for kindergarten through eighth grade is only 510 children, and there is no indication that these schools have many open seats. Second, the $2,500 cap that the program places on tuition for participating low-income pupils has the effect of curtailing the participation of nonreligious schools: "nonreligious schools with higher tuition (about $4,000) stated that they could afford to accommodate just a few voucher students." By comparison, the average tuition at participating Catholic schools in Cleveland in 1999–2000 was $1,592, almost $1,000 below the cap.

Of course, the obvious fix would be to increase the value of vouchers so that existing nonreligious private and non-Catholic religious schools would be able to enroll more voucher students, and to provide incentives for educators to create new such schools given that few presently exist. Private choice, if as robust as that available to the seminarian in *Witters*, would then be "true private choice" under the majority's criterion. But it is simply unrealistic to presume that parents of elementary and middle schoolchildren in Cleveland will have a range of secular and religious choices even arguably comparable to the statewide program for vocational and higher education in *Witters*. And to get to that hypothetical point would require that such massive financial support be made available to religion as to disserve every objective of the Establishment Clause even more than the present scheme does.

There is, in any case, no way to interpret the 96.6% of current voucher money going to religious schools as reflecting a free and genuine choice by the families that apply for vouchers. The 96.6% reflects, instead, the fact that too few nonreligious school desks are available and few but religious schools can afford to accept more than a handful of voucher students. And contrary to the majority's assertion, public schools in adjacent districts hardly have a financial incentive to participate in the Ohio voucher program, and none has. For the overwhelming number of children in the voucher scheme, the only alternative to the public schools is religious. And it is entirely irrelevant that the State did not deliberately design the network of private schools for the sake of channeling money into religious institutions. The criterion is one of genuinely free choice on the part of the private individuals who choose, and a Hobson's choice is not a choice, whatever the reason for being Hobsonian.

I do not dissent merely because the majority has misapplied its own law, for even if I assumed arguendo that the majority's formal criteria were satisfied on the facts, today's conclusion would be profoundly at odds with the Constitution. Proof of this is clear on two levels. The first is circumstantial, in the now discarded symptom of violation, the substantial dimension of the aid. The second is direct, in the defiance of every objective supposed to be served by the bar against establishment. . . .

It is virtually superfluous to point out that every objective underlying the prohibition of religious establishment is betrayed by this scheme, but something has to be said about the enormity of the violation. I anticipated these objectives earlier in discussing *Everson*, which cataloged them, the first being respect for freedom of conscience. Jefferson described it as the idea that no one "shall be compelled to . . . support any religious worship, place, or ministry whatsoever," A Bill for Establishing Religious Freedom.

As for the second objective, to save religion from its own corruption, Madison wrote of the " 'experience . . . that ecclesiastical establishments, instead of maintaining the purity and efficacy of Religion, have had a contrary operation.' " Memorial and Remonstrance. . . .

The risk is already being realized. In Ohio, for example, a condition of receiving government money under the program is that participating religious schools may not "discriminate on the basis of . . . religion," which means the school may not give admission preferences to children who are members of the patron faith; children of a parish are generally consigned to the same admission lotteries as non-believers. . . .

For perspective on this foot-in-the-door of religious regulation, it is well to remember that the money has barely begun to flow. Prior examples of aid, whether grants through individuals or in-kind assistance, were never significant enough to alter the basic fiscal structure of religious schools; state aid was welcome, but not indispensable. . . .

When government aid goes up, so does reliance on it; the only thing likely to go down is independence. . . .

Justice BREYER has addressed this issue in his own dissenting opinion, which I join, and here it is enough to say that the intensity of the expectable friction can be gauged by realizing that the scramble for money will energize not only contending sectarians, but taxpayers who take their liberty of conscience seriously. Religious teaching at taxpayer expense simply cannot be cordoned from taxpayer politics, and every major religion currently espouses social positions that provoke intense opposition. Not all taxpaying Protestant citizens, for example, will be content to underwrite the teaching of the Roman Catholic Church condemning the death penalty. Nor will all of America's Muslims acquiesce in paying for the endorsement of the religious Zionism taught in many religious Jewish schools, which combines "a nationalistic sentiment" in support of Israel with a "deeply religious" element. . . .

If the divisiveness permitted by today's majority is to be avoided in the short term, it will be avoided only by action of the political branches at the state and national levels. Legislatures not driven to desperation by the problems of public education may be able to see the threat in vouchers negotiable in sectarian schools. Perhaps even cities with problems like Cleveland's will perceive the danger, now that they know a federal court will not save them from it.

My own course as a judge on the Court cannot, however, simply be to hope that the political branches will save us from the consequences of the majority's decision. *Everson's* statement is still the touchstone of sound law, even though the reality is that in the matter of educational aid the Establishment Clause has largely been read away. True, the majority has not approved vouchers for religious schools alone, or aid earmarked for religious instruction. But no scheme so clumsy will ever get before us, and in the cases that we may see, like these, the Establishment Clause is largely silenced. I do not have the option to leave it silent, and I hope that a future Court will reconsider today's dramatic departure from basic Establishment Clause principle.

Elk Grove Unified School District v. Newdow
124 S.Ct. 2301 (2004)

This decision, denying standing to challenge the constitutionality of requiring the reciting of "under God" in the Pledge of Allegiance, is excerpted in Chapter 2.

B | *Free Exercise of Religion*

The free exercise clause embodies the principle of freedom from governmental coercion in choosing a religion or no religion. That guarantee is not absolute, however. Individuals may be prosecuted for certain religious practices (handling poisonous snakes or taking illegal drugs) and compelled to comply with regulations and laws (such as Sunday closing laws) that contravene their religious beliefs. Still, the Court has interpreted the free exercise clause to require state neutrality with regard to religion. A law may not discriminate on the basis of religion or have a religious purpose. On this basis, in *Toracso v. Watkins*, 367 U.S. 488 (1961), the Court struck down Maryland's law requiring that individuals take an oath declaring their "belief in the existence of God" as a condition of holding public office. In *McDaniel v. Paty*, 435 U.S. 618 (1978), a Tennessee statute forbidding ministers and priests from serving as delegates to state constitutional conventions was overturned. Over free exercise objections, the Court has also upheld laws that have a secular purpose but which forbid Mormons from practicing polygamy, *Reynolds v . United States*, 98 U.S. 145 (1890); required smallpox vaccinations, *Jacobson v. Massachusetts*, 197 U.S. 11 (1905); required the closing of businesses on Sundays, *Braunfeld v. Brown*, 366 U.S. 599 (1961); and prohibited the distribution of handbills and solicitations on fairgrounds, *Heffron v. International Society for Krishna Consciousness*, 455 U.S. 252 (1981).

State neutrality and rigid enforcement of the secular regulation principle, however, has been criticized for being too harsh, taking little or no account of the impact of coercive laws on individuals' religious lives. As an alternative, or exception to strict state neutrality, the Court invented the "least drastic means test," when striking down a South Carolina law denying unemployment compensation to a Seventh Day Adventist who refused to work on the Sabbath, in *Sherbert v. Verner* (1963) (see excerpt below). On this test, the Court considers whether states might achieve their objectives through other, less drastic means.

In *Wisconsin v. Yoder* (1972) (see excerpt below), Chief Justice Burger advanced his accommodationist approach in carving out an exception for the Amish from compulsory school attendance beyond the eighth grade. When accommodating free exercise claims the Court basically balances those claims against competing governmental interests, taking into consideration the nature of the regulation, the centrality of a religious belief, and the equality in treatment of religion. In *Cruz v. Beto*, 405 U.S. 319 (1972), for instance, the Court ruled that where Catholic, Protestant, and Jewish prison inmates were allowed to hold religious services, the state could not deny the same right of free exercise to Buddhists. By contrast, in *O'Lone v. Shabazz*, 482 U.S. 342 (1987), a bare majority of the Rehnquist Court held that Islamic prisoners could be denied the right to attend services in jail for security reasons.

The Court also held that governmental interests may simply outweigh free exercise claims, despite their coercive effect on religious beliefs and practices. In *Goldman v. Weinberger*, 475 U.S. 503 (1986), the justices (six to three) upheld the air force's prohibition of wearing yarmulkes by Orthodox Jewish officers. The following year, however, Congress passed a law permitting members of the military to wear religious apparel indoors, while on duty, so long as it does not interfere with their military duties and is "neat and conservative." In *Lyng v. Northwest Indian Cemetery Protective Association*, 485 U.S. 439 (1988), the Court upheld the forest service's permitting road constructions and timber harvests in areas of the national forest that were traditionally used for religious purposes by Indian tribes.

When confronted with free exercise claims, the Court may not be able to avoid the issue of what is religion. And who should define *religious beliefs*—the government, the Court, or the individual? When upholding a congressional statute banning and punishing polygamy, which

Mormons practiced as a religious belief, in *Reynolds v. United States*, 98 U.S. 145 (1879), Chief Justice Waite observed, "The word 'religion' is not defined in the Constitution. We must go elsewhere, therefore, to ascertain its meaning, and nowhere more appropriately, we think, than to the history of the times in the midst of which the provision was adopted." After surveying the founding period, Waite found no religious support for the practice of polygamy (the Mormon Church was not established until the late nineteenth century) and found support for the statute, which had the secular purpose of enforcing the standards of "civilized society," in Jefferson's "Bill for Establishing Religious Freedom," allowing government to "interfere when [religious] principles break out into overt acts against peace and good order." But dissenting in *Everson*, Justice Rutledge cautioned against the Court's trying to define religion for free exercise purposes, while refusing to do so under the establishment clause:

> "Religion" appears only once in the [First] Amendment. But the word governs two prohibitions and governs them alike. It does not have two meanings, one narrow to forbid "an establishment" and another, much broader, for securing "the free exercise thereof." "Thereof" brings down "religion" with its entire and exact content, no more and no less, from the first into the second guaranty, so that Congress and now the states are broadly restricted concerning the one as they are regarding the other.

The Court, once again, confronted the problem in *United States v. Ballard*, 322 U.S. 78 (1944), involving the prosecution of the leaders of the "I Am" religion for mail fraud. Guy Ballard, the founder of the religion, claimed to be the messenger of a Master Saint Germain and to have powers to cure diseases. Ballard's widow and son were charged with making claims about curing diseases, which they knew were false. But the Court held that at their trial the jury could not be allowed to determine the truth or falsity of the Ballards' claims; it could determine only whether the Ballards sincerely believed their claims, or instead were deceitful and guilty of misrepresentations. "Men may believe what they cannot prove," Justice Douglas wrote, adding, "They may not be put to the proof of their religious doctrines or beliefs. . . . The First Amendment does not select any one group or any one type of religion for preferred treatment." The majority did not go far enough for dissenting Justice Jackson, who argued:

> In the first place, as a matter of either practice or philosophy I do not see how we can separate an issue as to what is believed from considerations as to what is believable. . . . In the second place, any

inquiry into intellectual honesty in religion raises profound psychological problems. . . . And then I do not know what degree of skepticism or disbelief in a religious representation amounts to actionable fraud.

In a dissenting opinion, Chief Justice Stone found it hard "to say that freedom of thought and worship includes freedom to procure money by making knowingly false statements about one's religious experiences" and explained that

> if it were shown that a defendant in this case had asserted as a part of the alleged fraudulent scheme, that he had physically shaken hands with St. Germain in San Francisco on a day named, or that, as the indictment here alleges, by the exertion of his spiritual power he "had in fact cured . . . hundreds of persons afflicted with diseases and ailments:, I should not doubt that it would be open to the Government to submit to the jury proof that he had never been in San Francisco and that no such cures had ever been effected.

Stone and Jackson agreed that the Ballards could have been prosecuted for misrepresenting "that funds are being used to build a church when in fact they are being used for personal purposes." (In 1987–1988, televangelists Jim and Tammy Bakker were prosecuted for tax evasion and misappropriation of monies given by their disciples.)

While the government may prosecute religious leaders and their followers for crimes such as tax evasion, fraud, misrepresentations, and child abuse, the Court has suggested that it may be futile for the government to try to define religion for free exercise purposes. At least the Court gave an expansive reading to religion in the conscientious objector cases arising from a federal statute allowing exemptions from military service for an individual "who, by reason of religious training or belief, is conscientiously opposed to participation in war in any form." *Religious training and belief* was defined by Congress as "an individual's belief in relation to a Supreme Being involving duties superior to those arising from any human relation, but . . . not any essentially political, sociological, or philosophical views or a merely personal moral code." When hearing an appeal of three men who did not subscribe to a traditional religion but claimed not to be "irreligious or aetheists," in *United States v. Seeger*, 380 U.S. 163 (1965), the Court unanimously held that they were entitled to conscientious exemption because the test of one's religious belief "in relation to a Supreme Being" is "whether a given belief that is sincere and meaningful occupies a place in the life of its possessor parallel to that filled by the orthodox belief in God of one who clearly qualifies for the exemption. Where such beliefs have parallel positions in the lives of their respective holders we cannot say that one is 'in relation to a Supreme Being' and the other is not." Congress responded to *Seeger* by deleting the language "in relation to a Supreme Being." But the Court went even farther in *Welsh v. United States*, 398 U.S. 333 (1970), holding that an individual who denied that his beliefs opposing war were religious was, nonetheless, entitled to conscientious objector status because his ethical and moral beliefs were parallel to and just as strong as religious convictions.

Finally, the Court applied *Sherbert's* balancing test in several cases to prohibit the denial of unemployment compensation to individuals who lost their jobs because of their religious beliefs. See THE DEVELOPMENT OF LAW box in this section. However, in *Employment Division, Department of Human Resources of Oregon v. Smith* (1990) (see excerpt below), Justice Scalia rejected further application of *Sherbert's* balancing test and its requirement that states show a compelling interest in regulations to justify overriding free exercise claims.

The ruling in *Oregon v. Smith* was sharply criticized from within and without the Court. Moreover, compare *Smith* with the so-called animal sacrifice case, *Church of the Lukumi Babalu Aye v. City of Hialeah*, 508 U.S. 520 (1993) (excerpted below), in which the Court unanimously rejected the City of Hialeah's arguments that its ban on animal sacrifices was a "generally applicable law" that satisfied the analysis and test set forth in *Smith*; instead the Court held that the ordinances targeted a specific religion and violated the principle of religious nondiscrimination. Subsequently, Congress sought to override *Smith* and to reestablish the *Sherbert v. Verner* test with the enactment of the Religious Freedom Restoration Act of 1993. But, when that act was challenged in *City of Boerne v. Flores*, 521 U.S. 507 (1997) (excerpted below), the Court ruled that Congress did not have the power, under the Fourteenth Amendment's enforcement power in Section 5, to enforce constitutional rights broader than previously interpreted by the Court.

In sum, in several recent rulings the Court has attempted to clarify the contours of the free exercise clause and to address the tensions between it and the (dis)establishment clause. On the one hand, under *Oregon v. Smith*, religious minorities are not protected under the free exercise clause from otherwise neutral and generally applicable laws that indirectly burden their religious faith and practices. On the other hand, under *Church of the Lukumi Babalu Aye v. City Hialeah*, the free exercise clause protects religious minorities from overt discrimination and bars legislation that specifically targets them with penalties for their religious practices. Finally, *Locke v. Davey* (2004) (excerpted below), held that the free exercise clause does not override state constitutional provisions barring governmental aid to religion and compel such support, even though such aid would be permissible under the Court's interpretation of the (dis)establishment clause. In other words, the free exercise clause does not exempt religious minorities from neutral and generally applicable laws that impose indirect burdens, but only forbids direct religious discrimination, while providing no basis for compelling governmental support for religion even when such support has be allowed over (dis)establishment clause objections, in cases like *Witters v. Washington Department of Services for the Blind*, 474 U.S. 481 (1986); *Zobrest v. Catalina Foothills School District* (1993) (excerpted in Section A); and *Zelman v. Simmons-Harris* (2002) (excerpted in Section A of this chapter).

SELECTED BIBLIOGRAPHY

Brown, Steven P. *Trumping Religion: The New Christian Right, the Free Speech Clause, and the Courts.* Tuscaloosa: University of Alabama Press, 2002.

Choper, Jesse. *Securing Religious Liberty: Principles for Judicial Interpretation of the Religion Clauses.* Chicago: University of Chicago Press, 1995.

Cookson, Catharine. *Regulating Religion: The Courts and the Free Exercise Clause.* New York: Oxford University Press, 2001.

Epps, Garrett. *To an Unknown God: Religious Freedom on Trial.* New York: St. Martin's, 2001.

Long, Carolyn. *Religious Freedom and Indian Rights: The Case of Oregon v. Smith.* Lawrence: University of Kansas Press, 2000.

Manwaring, David. *Render unto Caesar: The Flag Salute Controversy.* Chicago: University of Chicago Press, 1962.

O'Brien, David M. *Animal Sacrifice and Religious Freedom: Church of Lukumi Babalu Aye, Inc. v. City of Hialeah.* Lawrence: University Press of Kansas, 2004.

Peters, Shawn Francis, *Judging Jehovah's Witnesses: Religious Persecution and the Dawn of the Rights Revolution.* Lawrence: University of Kansas Press, 2000.

Peters, Shawn Francis. *The Yoder Case.* Lawrence: University Press of Kansas, 2003.

Pfeffer, Leo. *God, Caesar and the Constitution.* Boston: Beacon Press, 1975.

Smith, Steven. *Foreordained Failure: The Quest for a Constitutional Principle of Religious Freedom.* New York: Oxford University Press, 1995.

■ THE DEVELOPMENT OF LAW

Major Rulings Denying Free Exercise Claims

CASE	VOTE	RULING
Reynolds v. United States, 90 U.S. 145 (1879)	9:0	Upheld a congressional statute banning polygamy over the religious objections of Mormons.

CASE	VOTE	RULING
Hamilton v. Regents of the University of California, 293 U.S. 245 (1934)	9:0	Upheld compulsory courses in military science over the religious objections of religious students.
Minersville v. Gobitis, 310 U.S. 587 (1940)	8:1	Upheld compulsory flag salute over the objections of Jehovah's Witnesses.
Prince v. Massachusetts, 321 U.S. 158 (1944)	8:1	Upheld statute forbidding minors from selling newspapers on streets over the objections of Jehovah's Witnesses.
McGowan v. Maryland, 366 U.S. 420 (1961); *Braunfeld v. Brown*, 366 U.S. 599 (1961)	6:3 7:2	Upheld Sunday closing laws over the objections of Orthodox Jews who recognize Saturday as the Sabbath.
Garber v. Kansas, 389 U.S. 51 (1967)	6:3	Rejected Amish claim of a right to refuse to send children to public schools.
Gillette v. United States and Negre v. Larsen, 401 U.S. 437 (1971)	8:1	Denied conscientious objection status to those opposing *certain* wars and "unjust" wars.
Heffron v. International Society for Krishna Consciousness, 452 U.S. 640 (1981)	5:4	Upheld law banning sales and solicitations at fairground by a religious group.
United States v. Lee, 455 U.S. 252 (1982)	8:0	Amish employers must pay social security taxes, even though Congress exempted self-employed Amish from paying the taxes.
Bob Jones University and Goldsboro Christian School v. United States, 461 U.S. 574 (1983)	8:1	Upheld IRS's withdrawing of tax-exempt status for educational institutions that discriminate racially.
Tony and Susan Alamo Foundation v. Secretary of Labor, 471 U.S. 290 (1985)	9:0	Religious organizations must comply with federal minimum wage laws.
Goldman v. Weinberger, 475 U.S. 503 (1986)	5:4	Orthodox Jewish rabbi and air force captain may not wear yarmulke contrary to military dress code.

CASE	VOTE	RULING
Bowen v. Roy, 476 U.S. 693 (1986)	8:1	Government may use social security numbers despite religious objections.
O'Lone v. Shabazz, 482 U.S. 342 (1987)	5:4	For security reasons, Islamic prisoners may be denied right to attend religious services.
Lyng v. Northwest Indian Cemetery Protective Association, 485 U.S. 439 (1988)	5:3	With Scalia not participating, Court held that the forest service may permit road construction and timber harvesting in areas of national parks traditionally used for religious purposes by Indian tribes.
Hernandez v. Commissioner of Internal Revenue, 490 U.S. 680 (1989)	5:2	Upheld IRS decision that fixed donations to Church of Scientology by members are not tax-deductible contributions.
Swaggart v. Board of Equalization of California, 493 U.S. 378 (1990)	9:0	Upheld California's 6 percent sales tax as applied to sales of religious materials sold by Jimmy Swaggart Ministries at "evangelistic crusades" in the state and through mail-order sales to state residents.
Employment Division, Department of Human Resources of Oregon v. Smith, 494 U.S. 872 (1990)	6:3	Held that the free exercise clause does not prohibit the application of Oregon's drug laws to the ceremonial use of peyote by members of the Native American Church and that members of the church could be denied unemployment compensation after they were fired from their jobs as drug-rehabilitation counselors because of their ceremonial use of peyote.
Minnesota v. Hershberger, 495 U.S. 901 (1990)	7:2	Vacated a decision of the Minnesota Supreme Court that exempted the Amish from complying with highway safety laws.
City of Boerne v. Flores, 521 U.S. 507 (1997)	6:3	Writing for the Court, Justice Kennedy invalidated the Religious Freedom Restoration Act of 1993, which sought to reestablish the test, set forth in *Sherbert v. Verner*, 374 U.S. 398 (1963), for balancing claims to religious freedom against govern-

CASE	VOTE	RULING

mental interests in generally applicable laws, which the Court discarded in *Employment Division, Dept. of Human Resources of Oregon v. Smith*, 492 U.S. 872 (1990). Justices O'Connor, Souter, and Breyer dissented.

Sherbert v. Verner
374 U.S. 398, 83 S.Ct. 1790 (1963)

In his opinion announcing the decision of the Court, Justice Brennan discusses the facts in this case, involving a claim that the denial of unemployment benefits to an individual who refused to work on her Sabbath violated the free exercise clause.

The Court's decision was seven to two, and the majority's opinion was announced by Justice Brennan. Concurrences were by Justices Douglas and Stewart and dissent was by Justice Harlan, who was joined by Justice White.

 ☐ *Justice BRENNAN delivered the opinion of the Court.*

 Appellant, a member of the Seventh-day Adventist Church was discharged by her South Carolina employer because she would not work on Saturday, the Sabbath Day of her faith. When she was unable to obtain other employment because from conscientious scruples she would not take Saturday work, she filed a claim for unemployment compensation benefits under the South Carolina Unemployment Compensation Act. . . .

 The appellee Employment Security Commission, in administrative proceedings under the statute, found that appellant's restriction upon her availability for Saturday work brought her within the provision disqualifying for benefits insured workers who fail, without good cause, to accept "suitable work when offered . . . by the employment office or the employer. . . ." The Commission's finding was sustained by the Court of Common Pleas for Spartanburg County. That court's judgment was in turn affirmed by the South Carolina Supreme Court, which rejected appellant's contention that, as applied to her, the disqualifying provisions of the South Carolina statute abridged her right to the free exercise of her religion secured under the Free Exercise Clause of the First Amendment through the Fourteenth Amendment. . . . We reverse the judgment of the South Carolina Supreme Court and remand for further proceedings not inconsistent with this opinion. . . .

 We turn first to the question whether the disqualification for benefits imposes any burden on the free exercise of appellant's religion. We think it is clear that it does. In a sense the consequences of such a disqualification to religious principles and practices may be only an indirect result of welfare legislation within the State's general competence to enact; it is true that no criminal sanctions directly compel appellant to work a six-day week. But this is only the beginning, not the end, of our inquiry. For "[i]f the purpose or effect of a law is to impede the observance of one or all religions or is to discriminate invidiously between religions, that law is constitutionally invalid even though the burden may be characterized as being only indirect." *Braunfeld v. Brown.* Here not only is it apparent that appellant's declared ineligibility for benefits derives solely from the practice of her religion, but the pressure upon her to forego that practice is unmistakable. The ruling forces her to choose between following the precepts of her religion and forfeiting benefits, on the one hand, and abandoning one of the precepts of her religion in order to accept work, on the other hand. Governmental imposition of such a choice puts the same kind of burden upon the free exercise of religion as would a fine imposed against appellant for her Saturday worship.

Nor may the South Carolina court's construction of the statute be saved from constitutional infirmity on the ground that unemployment compensation benefits are not appellant's "right" but merely a "privilege." It is too late in the day to doubt that the liberties of religion and expression may be infringed by the denial of or placing of conditions upon a benefit or privilege. . . .

■ III

We must next consider whether some compelling state interest enforced in the eligibility provisions of the South Carolina statute justifies the substantial infringement of appellant's First Amendment right. It is basic that no showing merely of a rational relationship to some colorable state interest would suffice; in this highly sensitive constitutional area, "[o]nly the gravest abuses, endangering paramount interests, give occasion for permissible limitation," *Thomas v. Collins*, 323 U.S. 516 [(1945)]. No such abuse or danger has been advanced in the present case. The appellees suggest no more than a possibility that the filing of fraudulent claims by unscrupulous claimants feigning religious objections to Saturday work might not only dilute the unemployment compensation fund but also hinder the scheduling by employers of necessary Saturday work. But that possibility is not apposite here because no such objection appears to have been made before the South Carolina Supreme Court, and we are unwilling to assess the importance of an asserted state interest without the views of the state court. Nor, if the contention had been made below, would the record appear to sustain it. . . . For even if the possibility of spurious claims did threaten to dilute the fund and disrupt the scheduling of work, it would plainly be incumbent upon the appellees to demonstrate that no alternative forms of regulation would combat such abuses without infringing First Amendment rights.

In these respects, then, the state interest asserted in the present case is wholly dissimilar to the interests which were found to justify the less direct burden upon religious practices in *Braunfeld v. Brown*, [366 U.S. 599 (1961)]. The Court recognized that the Sunday closing law which that decision sustained undoubtedly served "to make the practice of [the Orthodox Jewish merchants'] religious beliefs more expensive." But the statute was nevertheless saved by a countervailing factor which finds no equivalent in the instant case—a strong state interest in providing one uniform day of rest for all workers. That secular objective could be achieved, the Court found, only by declaring Sunday to be that day of rest. Requiring exemptions for Sabbatarians, while theoretically possible, appeared to present an administrative problem of such magnitude, or to afford the exempted class so great a competitive advantage, that such a requirement would have rendered the entire statutory scheme unworkable. In the present case no such justifications underlie the determination of the state court that appellant's religion makes her ineligible to receive benefits.

■ IV

In holding as we do, plainly we are not fostering the "establishment" of the Seventh-day Adventist religion in South Carolina, for the extension of unemployment benefits to Sabbatarians in common with Sunday worshippers reflects nothing more than the governmental obligation of neutrality in the face of religious differences, and does not represent that involvement of religious with secular institutions which it is the object of the Establishment Clause to forestall. See School District of *Abington Township v. Schempp*, 374 U.S. 203 [(1963)]. Nor does the recognition of the appellant's right to unemployment benefits under the state statute serve to abridge any other person's religious liberties. Nor do we, by our decision today, declare the existence of a constitutional right to unemployment benefits on the part of all persons whose religious convictions are the cause of their unemployment. This is not a case in which an employee's religious convictions serve to make him a nonproductive member of society. Finally, nothing we say today constrains the States to adopt any particular form or scheme of unemployment compensation. Our holding today is only that South Carolina may not constitutionally apply the eligibility provisions so as to constrain a worker to abandon his religious convictions respecting the day of rest.

☐ *Justice DOUGLAS, concurring.*

This case is resolvable not in terms of what an individual can demand of government, but solely in terms of what government may not do to an individual in violation of his religious scruples. The fact that government cannot exact from me a surrender of one iota of my religious scruples does not, of course, mean that I can demand of government a sum of money, the better to exercise them. For the Free Exercise Clause is written in terms of what the government cannot do to the individual, not in terms of what the individual can exact from the government.

Those considerations, however, are not relevant here. If appellant is otherwise qualified for unemployment benefits, payments will be made to her not as a Seventh-day Adventist, but as an unemployed worker. Conceivably these payments will indirectly benefit her church, but no more so than does the salary of any public employee. Thus, this case does not involve the problems of direct or indirect state assistance to a religious organization—matters relevant to the Establishment Clause, not in issue here.

☐ *Justice HARLAN with whom Justice WHITE joins, dissenting.*

In the present case all that the state court has done is to apply . . . accepted principles. Since virtually all of the mills in the Spartanburg area were operating on a six-day week, the appellant was "unavailable for work," and thus ineligible for benefits, when personal considerations prevented her from accepting employment on a full-time basis in the industry and locality in which she had worked. The fact that these personal considerations sprang from her religious convictions was wholly without relevance to the state court's application of the law. Thus in no proper sense can it be said that the State discriminated against the appellant on the basis of her religious beliefs or that she was denied benefits *because* she was a Seventh-day Adventist. She was denied benefits just as any other claimant would be denied benefits who was not "available for work" for personal reasons.

With this background, this Court's decision comes into clearer focus. What the Court is holding is that if the State chooses to condition unemployment compensation on the applicant's availability for work, it is constitutionally compelled to *carve out an exception*—and to provide benefits—for those whose unavailability is due to their religious convictions. Such a holding has particular significance in two respects.

First. Despite the Court's protestations to the contrary, the decision necessarily overrules *Braunfeld v. Brown*, which held that it did not offend the "Free Exercise" Clause of the Constitution for a State to forbid a Sabbatarian to do business on Sunday. The secular purpose of the statute before us today is even clearer than that involved in *Braunfeld*. And just as in *Braunfeld*—where exceptions to the Sunday closing laws for Sabbatarians would have been inconsistent with the purpose to achieve a uniform day of rest and would have required case-by-case inquiry into religious beliefs—so here, an exception to the rules of eligibility based on religious convictions would necessitate judicial examination of those convictions and would be at odds with the limited purpose of the statute to smooth out the economy during periods of industrial instability. Finally, the indirect financial burden of the present law is far less than that involved in *Braunfeld*. . . .

Second. The implications of the present decision are far more troublesome than its apparently narrow dimensions would indicate at first glance. The meaning of today's holding, as already noted, is that the State must furnish unemployment benefits to one who is unavailable for work if the unavailability stems from the exercise of religious convictions. The State, in other words, must *single out* for financial assistance those whose behavior is religiously motivated, even though it denies such assistance to others whose identical behavior (in this case, inability to work on Saturdays) is not religiously motivated.

It has been suggested that such singling out of religious conduct for special treatment may violate the constitutional limitations on state action. My own view, however, is that at least under the circumstances of this case it would be a permissible accommodation of religion for the State, if it *chose* to do so, to create an exception to its eligibility requirements for persons like the appellant. The constitutional obligation of "neutrality," see *School District of Abington Township v. Schempp*, is not so narrow a channel that the slightest deviation from an absolutely straight course leads to condemnation. . . .

The State violates its obligation of neutrality when, for example, it mandates a daily religious exercise in its public schools, with all the attendant pressures on the school children that such an exercise entails. See *Engel v. Vitale*, 370 U.S. 421 [(1962)]. *School District of Abington Township v. Schempp, supra*. But there is, I believe, enough flexibility in the Constitution to permit a legislative judgment accommodating an unemployment compensation law to the exercise of religious beliefs such as appellant's.

For very much the same reasons, however, I cannot subscribe to the conclusion that the State is constitutionally *compelled* to carve out an exception to its general rule of eligibility in the present case. Those situations in which the Constitution may require special treatment on account of religion are, in my view, few and far between, and this view is amply supported by the course of constitutional litigation in this area.

■ The Development of Law
Major Rulings Upholding Free Exercise Claims

CASE	VOTE	RULING
Cantwell v. Connecticut, 310 U.S. 296 (1940)	9:0	Struck down permit requirement for soliciting funds on public streets challenged by Jehovah's Witnesses.
Murdock v. Commonwealth of Pennsylvania, 319 U.S. 105 (1943)	5:4	Struck down license tax on canvassing and soliciting as applied to Jehovah's Witnesses.
Martin v. Struthers, 319 U.S. 141 (1943)	5:4	Overturned ordinance forbidding door-to-door solicitations as applied to Jehovah's Witnesses.
Douglas v. City of Jeanette, 319 U.S. 157 (1943)	9:0	After citizens' complaints, police may not stop Jehovah's Witnesses from proselytizing on Sundays.
West Virginia State Board of Education v. Barnette, 319 U.S. 624 (1943)	6:3	Overturned compulsory flag salute statute.
Jamison v. Texas, 318 U.S. 413 (1943)	8:0	Overturned statute barring handbill distributions as related to religious activities.
United States v. Ballard, 322 U.S. 78 (1944)	5:4	The truth of religious beliefs may not be judged by jury at trials.

CASE	VOTE	RULING
Girouard v. United States, 328 U.S. 61 (1946)	5:3	Naturalization may not be denied to conscientious objectors.
Marsh v. Alabama, 326 U.S. 501 (1946)	5:3	Distribution of religious literature cannot be banned in private company town.
Niemotko v. Maryland, 340 U.S. 268 (1951)	9:0	Use of public parks may not be denied to Jehovah's Witnesses.
Torcaso v. Watkins, 367 U.S. 488 (1961)	9:0	Struck down required oath declaring belief in God for public office.
Sherbert v. Verner, 374 U.S. 398 (1963)	7:2	Overturned denial of unemployment compensation to Seventh Day Adventist who was fired for refusing to work on Sabbath.
United States v. Seeger, 380 U.S. 380 (1965)	9:0	Broadly interpreted religious training and belief in according conscientious objector status.
Wisconsin v. Yoder, 406 U.S. 205 (1972)	6:1	Amish are exempt from sending children to school beyond the eighth grade.
Wooley v. Maynard, 430 U.S. 705 (1977)	7:2	Upheld claim of Jehovah's Witnesses that they could not be compelled to bare license plates with the motto Live Free or Die.
McDaniel v. Paty, 435 U.S. 618 (1978)	8:0	Religious leaders may not be disqualified from serving as delegates to state constitutional conventions.
Thomas v. Review Board of Indiana Employment Security-Division, 450 U.S. 707 (1981)	8:1	State may not deny unemployment compensation to individual who terminated employment because of religious objection to working in the production of armaments.
Hobbie v. Unemployment Appeals Commission of Florida, 480 U.S. 136 (1987)	8:1	Applied *Sherbert* in holding that denial of unemployment compensation benefits must withstand strict scrutiny and that it

CASE	VOTE	RULING

is immaterial that claimant had a religious conversion during course of employment. Chief Justice Rehnquist dissented.

Frazee v. Illinois Department of Employment Security, 489 U.S. 829 (1989)	9:0	Held that denial of unemployment compensation to worker who refused to work on Sabbath violated the free exercise

clause, even though refusal was not based on a religious sect's doctrines.

Church of the Lukumi Babalu Aye v. City of Hialeah, 508 U.S. 520 (1993)	9:0	Struck down a ban on animal sacrifice as impermissibly religiously motivated and infringing on the free exercise of religion.

Watchtower Bible & Tract Society of New York, Inc. v. Village of Stratton, 536 U.S. 150 (2002)	8:1	Reaffirming a line of rulings, from *Murdock v. Commonwealth of Pennsylvania*, 319 U.S. 105 (1943), extending First Amend-

ment to the door-to-door canvassing of Jehovah's Witnesses, the Court struck down an ordinance requiring a permit for solicitations on private property. Chief Justice Rehnquist dissented.

Wisconsin v. Yoder

406 U.S. 208, 92 S.Ct. 1527 (1972)

Jonas Yoder and Wallace Miller, members of the Old Order Amish religion, and Adin Yutzy, a member of the Conservative Amish Mennonite Church, were charged, tried, and convicted of violating the compulsory school-attendance law in Green County Court, Wisconsin, and fined $5 each. Under Wisconsin's compulsory school-attendance law, children were required to attend public or private school until reaching the age of sixteen. Yoder, Miller, and Yutzy, however, refused to send their children, ages fourteen and fifteen, to public school after they completed the eighth grade. And when defending their actions, they claimed the compulsory-attendance law violated their free exercise of religion under the First and Fourteenth Amendments. A state appeals court affirmed their convictions, but the Wisconsin Supreme Court reversed and found that the application of the law denied the Amish's First Amendment rights. The state of Wisconsin appealed to the Supreme Court.

The Court's decision was six and one-half to one-half, and the majority's opinion was announced by Chief Justice Burger, with Justices Powell and Rehnquist not participating. The concurrence by Justice Stewart was joined by Justice Brennan. There was a separate opinion, in part dissenting, by Justice Douglas.

☐ *Chief Justice BURGER delivered the opinion of the Court.*

Amish objection to formal education beyond the eighth grade is firmly grounded in these central religious concepts. They object to the high school, and higher education generally, because the values they teach are in marked variance with Amish values and the Amish way of life; they view secondary school education as an impermissible exposure of their children to a "worldly" influence in conflict with their beliefs. The high school tends to emphasize intellectual and scientific accomplishments, self-distinction, competitiveness, worldly success, and social life with other students. Amish society emphasizes informal learning-through-doing; a life of "goodness," rather than a life of intellect; wisdom, rather than technical knowledge, community welfare, rather than competition; and separation from, rather than integration with, contemporary worldly society.

Formal high school education beyond the eighth grade is contrary to Amish beliefs, not only because it places Amish children in an environment hostile to Amish beliefs with increasing emphasis on competition in class work and sports and with pressure to conform to the styles, manners, and ways of the peer group, but also because it takes them away from their community, physically and emotionally, during the crucial and formative adolescent period of life. During this period, the children must acquire Amish attitudes favoring manual work and self-reliance and the specific skills needed to perform the adult role of an Amish farmer or housewife. They must learn to enjoy physical labor. Once a child has learned basic reading, writing, and elementary mathematics, these traits, skills, and attitudes admittedly fall within the category of those best learned through example and "doing" rather than in a classroom. And, at this time in life, the Amish child must also grow in his faith and his relationship to the Amish community if he is to be prepared to accept the heavy obligations imposed by adult baptism. . . .

The Amish do not object to elementary education through the first eight grades as a general proposition because they agree that their children must have basic skills in the "three R's" in order to read the Bible, to be good farmers and citizens, and to be able to deal with non-Amish people when necessary in the course of daily affairs. They view such a basic education as acceptable because it does not significantly expose their children to worldly values or interfere with their development in the Amish community during the crucial adolescent period. While Amish accept compulsory elementary education generally, wherever possible they have established their own elementary schools in many respects like the small local schools of the past. In the Amish belief higher learning tends to develop values they reject as influences that alienate man from God. . . .

There is no doubt as to the power of a State, having a high responsibility for education of its citizens, to impose reasonable regulations for the control and duration of basic education. . . .

[A] State's interest in universal education, however highly we rank it, is not totally free from a balancing process when it impinges on fundamental rights and interests, such as those specifically protected by the Free Exercise Clause of the First Amendment, and the traditional interest of parents with respect to the religious upbringing of their children. . . .

It follows that in order for Wisconsin to compel school attendance beyond the eighth grade against a claim that such attendance interferes with the practice of a legitimate religious belief, it must appear either that the State does not deny the free exercise of religious belief by its requirement, or that there is a state interest of sufficient magnitude to override the interest claiming protection under the Free Exercise Clause. . . .

The essence of all that has been said and written on the subject is that only those interests of the highest order and those not otherwise served can overbalance legitimate claims to the free exercise of religion. We can accept it as settled, therefore, that, however strong the State's interest in universal compulsory education, it is by no means absolute to the exclusion or subordination of all other interests. . . .

We come then to the quality of the claims of the respondents concerning the alleged encroachment of Wisconsin's compulsory school-attendance statute on their rights and the rights of their children to the free exercise of the religious beliefs they and their forbears have adhered to for almost three centuries. In evaluating those claims we must be careful to determine whether the Amish religious faith and their mode of life are, as they claim, inseparable and interdependent. A way of life, however virtuous and admirable, may not be interposed as a barrier to reasonable state regulation of education if it is based on purely secular considerations; to have the protection of the Religion Clauses, the claims must be rooted in religious belief. Although a determination of what is a "religious" belief or practice entitled to constitutional protection may present a most delicate question, the very concept of ordered liberty precludes allowing every person to make his own standards on matters of conduct in which society as a whole has important interests. Thus, if the Amish asserted their claims because of their subjective evaluation and rejection of the contemporary secular values accepted by the majority, much as Thoreau rejected the social values of his time and isolated himself at Walden Pond, their claims would not rest on a religious basis. Thoreau's choice was philosophical and personal rather than religious, and such belief does not rise to the demands of the Religion Clauses.

Giving no weight to such secular considerations, however, we see that the record in this case abundantly supports the claim that the traditional way of life of the Amish is not merely a matter of personal preference, but one of deep religious conviction, shared by an organized group, and intimately related to daily living. . . .

We turn, then, to the State's broader contention that its interest in its system of compulsory education is so compelling that even the established religious practices of the Amish must give way. Where fundamental claims of religious freedom are at stake, however, we cannot accept such a sweeping claim; despite its admitted validity in the generality of cases, we must searchingly examine the interests that the State seeks to promote by its requirement for compulsory education to age 16, and the impediment to those objectives that would flow from recognizing the claimed Amish exemption. . . .

The State advances two primary arguments in support of its system of compulsory education. It notes, as Thomas Jefferson pointed out early in our history, that some degree of education is necessary to prepare citizens to participate effectively and intelligently in our open political system if we are to preserve freedom and independence. Further, education prepares individuals to be self-reliant and self-sufficient participants in society. We accept these propositions.

However, the evidence adduced by the Amish in this case is persuasively to the effect that an additional one or two years of formal high school for Amish children in place of their long-established program of informal vocational education would do little to serve those interests. Respondents' experts testified at trial, without challenge, that the value of all education must be assessed in terms of its capacity to prepare the child for life. It is one thing to say that compulsory education for a year or two beyond the eighth grade may be necessary when its goal is the preparation of the child for life in modern society as the majority live, but it is quite another if the goal of education be viewed as the preparation of the child for life in the separated agrarian community that is the keystone of the Amish faith. . . .

Our holding in no way determines the proper resolution of possible competing interests of parents, children, and the State in an appropriate state court proceeding in which the power of the State is asserted on the theory that Amish parents are preventing their minor children from attending high school despite their expressed desires to the contrary. Recognition of the claim of the State in such a proceeding would, of course, call into question traditional concepts of parental control over the religious upbringing and education of their minor children recognized in this Court's past decisions. It is clear that such an intrusion by a State into family decisions in the area of religious training would give rise to grave questions of religious freedom. . . . On this record we neither reach nor decide those issues. . . .

For the reasons stated we hold, with the Supreme Court of Wisconsin, that the First and Fourteenth Amendments prevent the State from compelling respondents to cause their children to attend formal high school to age 16. . . .

☐ *Justice DOUGLAS, dissenting in part.*

Religion is an individual experience. It is not necessary, nor even appropriate, for every Amish child to express his views on the subject in a prosecution of a single adult. Crucial, however, are the views of the child whose parent is the subject of the suit. Frieda Yoder has in fact testified that her own religious views are opposed to high-school education. I therefore join the judgment of the Court as to respondent Jonas Yoder. But Frieda Yoder's views may not be those of Vernon Yutzy or Barbara Miller. I must dissent, therefore, as to respondents Adin Yutzy and Wallace Miller as their motion to dismiss also raised the question of their children's religious liberty. . . .

On this important and vital matter of education, I think the children should be entitled to be heard. While the parents, absent dissent, normally speak for the entire family, the education of the child is a matter on which the child will often have decided views. He may want to be a pianist or an astronaut or an ocean geographer. To do so he will have to break from the Amish tradition.

It is the future of the student, not the future of the parents, that is imperilled in today's decision. If a parent keeps his child out of school beyond the grade school, then the child will be forever barred from entry into the new and amazing world of diversity that we have today. The child may decide that that is the preferred course, or he may rebel. It is the student's judgment, not his parent's, that is essential if we are to give full meaning to what we have said about the Bill of Rights and of the right of students to be masters of their own destiny. If he is harnessed to the Amish way of life by those in authority over him and if his education is truncated, his entire life may be stunted and deformed. The child, therefore, should be given an opportunity to be heard before the State gives the exemption which we honor today.

Employment Division, Department of Human Resources of Oregon v. Smith

494 U.S. 872, 110 S.CT. 1595 (1990)

Two Native Americans, Alfred Smith and Galen Black, were fired from their jobs with a private drug rehabilitation organization because they took peyote (an intoxicating drug produced from mescal cacti). Both were members of the Native American Church and ingested peyote for sacramental purposes in religious ceremonies. When they later applied for unemployment compensation, Oregon's Employment Division denied them benefits on the grounds that their discharge was for work-related "misconduct." A state appellate court reversed that decision, holding that the denial of benefits violated Smith's and Black's rights under the First Amendment free exercise clause. The state then appealed to the Oregon Supreme Court, which affirmed the lower court. It did so, however, on construing the purpose of the misconduct provision, under which Smith was denied benefits, to be one of preserving the financial integrity of the state's compensation fund and not that of enforcing the state's criminal laws against drug usage. Citing *Sherbert v. Verner* (1963) (see excerpt above), the Oregon Supreme Court concluded that Smith was entitled to unemployment benefits because the state's interest in the compensation fund did not outweigh the burden imposed on Smith's religious beliefs and practices.

In 1987, Oregon appealed the ruling of its state's supreme court to the U.S. Supreme Court, contending that its criminal laws against peyote consumption were relevant to balancing the state's interests in denying benefits and Smith's First Amendment claims. In *Employment Division, Department of Human Resources of Oregon v. Smith*, 485 U.S. 660 (1988) (*Smith I*), a majority of the Court agreed, when vacating the decision and remanding the case back to the Oregon Supreme Court. But when doing so, the Court noted that the state supreme court had not decided whether the sacramental use of peyote was in fact proscribed under state law. Until the state court ruled on that issue, the Supreme Court declined to address the question of "whether the practice is protected by the Federal Constitution." On remand, the Oregon Supreme Court held that its state laws made no exception for the sacramental use of peyote but interpreted the First Amendment to protect such usage and reaffirmed its previous ruling that Smith was entitled to unemployment benefits. The state, again, appealed to the U.S. Supreme Court, which granted *certiorari*.

The Court's decision was six to three, and the majority's opinion was announced by Justice Scalia. Justice O'Connor concurred, agreeing with the majority's result but rejecting its reasoning and abandonment of *Sherbert*'s analysis. Justices Brennan and Marshall concurred in her reasoning but disagreed with her conclusion that Smith was not entitled to benefits. Justice Blackmun dissented and was joined by Justices Brennan and Marshall.

☐ *Justice SCALIA delivered the opinion of the Court.*

This case requires us to decide whether the Free Exercise Clause of the First Amendment permits the State of Oregon to include religiously inspired peyote use within the reach of its general criminal prohibition on use of that drug, and thus permits the State to deny unemployment benefits to persons dismissed from their jobs because of such religiously inspired use. . . .

Respondents' claim for relief rests on our decisions in *Sherbert v. Verner*, [374 U.S. 398 (1963)]; *Thomas v. Review Board, Indiana Employment Security Div.*, [450 U.S. 707 (1981)]; and *Hobbie v. Unemployment Appeals Comm'n of Florida*, 480 U.S. 136 (1987), in which we held that a State could not condition the availability of unemployment insurance on an individual's willingness to forgo conduct required by his religion. As we observed in *Smith I*, however, the conduct at issue in those cases was not prohibited by law. We held that distinction to be critical, for "if Oregon does prohibit the religious use of peyote, and if that prohibition is consistent with the Federal Constitution, there is no federal right to engage in that conduct in Oregon," and "the State is free to withhold unemployment compensation from respondents for engaging in work-related misconduct, despite its religious motivation." Now that the Oregon Supreme Court has confirmed that Oregon does prohibit the religious use of peyote, we proceed to consider whether that prohibition is permissible under the Free Exercise Clause. . . .

The free exercise of religion means, first and foremost, the right to believe and profess whatever religious doctrine one desires. Thus, the First Amendment obviously excludes all "governmental regulation of religious *beliefs* as such." *Sherbert v. Verner*, supra. . . .

But the "exercise of religion" often involves not only belief and profession but the performance of (or abstention from) physical acts: assembling with others for a worship service, participating in sacramental use of bread and wine, proselytizing, abstaining from certain foods or certain modes of transportation. It would be true, we think (though no case of ours has involved the point), that a state would be "prohibiting the free exercise [of religion]" if it sought to ban such acts or abstentions only when they are engaged in for religious reasons, or only because of the religious belief that they display. It would doubtless be unconstitutional, for example, to ban the casting of "statues that are to be used for worship purposes," or to prohibit bowing down before a golden calf.

Respondents in the present case, however, seek to carry the meaning of "prohibiting the free exercise [of religion]" one large step further. They contend that their religious motivation for using peyote places them beyond the reach of a criminal law that is not specifically directed at their religious practice, and that is concededly constitutional as applied to those who use the drug for other reasons. They assert, in other words, that "prohibiting the free exercise [of religion]" includes requiring any individual to observe a generally applicable law that requires (or forbids) the performance of an act that his religious belief forbids (or requires). As a textual matter, we do not think the words must be given that meaning. It is no more necessary to regard the collection of a general tax, for example, as "prohibiting the free exercise [of religion]" by those citizens who believe support of organized government to be sinful, than it is to regard the same tax as "abridging the freedom . . . of the press" of those publishing companies that must pay the tax as a condition of staying in business. It is a permissible reading of the text, in the one case as in the other, to say that if prohibiting the exercise of religion (or burdening the activity of printing) is not the object of the tax but merely the incidental effect of a generally applicable and otherwise valid provision, the First Amendment has not been offended. . . .

Our decisions reveal that the latter reading is the correct one. We have never held that an individual's religious beliefs excuse him from compliance with an otherwise valid law prohibiting conduct that the State is free to regulate. [Citing *Minersville School District Bd. of Ed. v. Gobitis*, 310 U.S. 586 (1940), *Reynolds v. United States*, 98 U.S. 145 (1879), *Prince v. Massachusetts*, 321 U.S. 158 (1944), *Braunfeld v. Brown*, 366 U.S. 599 (1961), and *Gillette v. United States*, 410 U.S. 437 (1971).] . . .

The only decisions in which we have held that the First Amendment bars application of a neutral, generally applicable law to religiously motivated action have involved not the Free Exercise Clause alone, but the Free Exercise Clause in conjunction with other constitutional protections, such as freedom of speech and of the press, see *Cantwell v. Connecticut*, [310 U.S. 296 (1940)], (invalidating a licensing system for religious and charitable solicitations under which the administrator had discretion to deny a license to any cause he deemed nonreligious); *Murdock v. Pennsylvania*, 319 U.S. 105 (1943) (invalidating a flat tax on solicitation as applied to the dissemination of religious ideas); *Follett v. McCormick*, 321 U.S. 573 (1944) (same), or the right of parents, acknowledged in *Pierce v. Society of Sisters*, 268 U.S. 510 (1925), to direct the education of their children, see *Wisconsin v. Yoder*, 406 U.S. 208 (1972) (invalidating compulsory school-attendance laws as applied to Amish parents who refused on religious grounds to send their children to school).

Some of our cases prohibiting compelled expression, decided exclusively upon free speech grounds, have also involved freedom of religion, cf. *Wooley v. Maynard*, 430 U.S. 705 (1977) (invalidating compelled display of a license plate slogan that offended individual religious beliefs); *West Virginia Board of Education v. Barnette*, 319 U.S. 624 (1943) (invalidating compulsory flag salute statute challenged by religious objectors). . . .

The present case does not present such a hybrid situation, but a free exercise claim unconnected with any communicative activity or parental right. Respondents urge us to hold, quite simply, that when otherwise prohibitable conduct is accompanied by religious convictions, not only the convictions but the conduct itself must be free from governmental regulation. . . .

Respondents argue that even though exemption from generally applicable criminal laws need not automatically be extended to religiously motivated actors, at least the claim for a religious exemption must be evaluated under the balancing test set forth in *Sherbert v. Verner* (1963). Under the *Sherbert* test, governmental actions that substantially burden a religious practice must be justified by a compelling governmental interest. . . . Applying that test we have, on three occasions, invalidated state unemployment compensation rules that conditioned the availability of benefits upon an applicant's willingness to work under conditions forbidden by his religion. See *Sherbert v. Verner, supra; Thomas v. Review Board, Indiana Employment Div.* (1981); *Hobbie v. Unemployment Appeals Comm'n of Florida* (1987). We have never invalidated any governmental action on the basis of the *Sherbert* test except the denial of unemployment compensation. . . .

Even if we were inclined to breathe into *Sherbert* some life beyond the unemployment compensation field, we would not apply it to require exemptions from a generally applicable criminal law. . . .

We conclude today that the sounder approach, and the approach in accord with the vast majority of our precedents, is to hold the test inapplicable to such challenges. The government's ability to enforce generally applicable prohibitions of socially harmful conduct, like its ability to carry out other aspects of public policy, "cannot depend on measuring the effects of a governmental action on a religious objector's spiritual development." *Lyng* [*v. Northwest Indian Cemetery Association*, 485 U.S. 439 (1988)]. To make an individual's obligation to obey such a law contingent upon the law's coincidence with his religious beliefs, except where the State's interest is "compelling"—permitting him, by virtue of his beliefs, "to become a law unto himself," *Reynolds v. United States*—contradicts both constitutional tradition and common sense.

The "compelling government interest" requirement seems benign, because it is familiar from other fields. But using it as the standard that must be met before the government may accord different treatment on the basis of race, see, *e.g., Palmore v. Sidoti*, 466 U.S. 429 (1984), or before the government may regulate the content of speech, see, *e.g., Sable Communications of California v. FCC*, 492 U.S. 115 (1989), is not remotely comparable to using it for the purpose asserted here. What it produces in those other fields—equality of treatment, and an unrestricted flow of contending speech—are constitutional norms; what it would produce here—a private right to ignore generally applicable laws—is a constitutional anomaly.

Nor is it possible to limit the impact of respondents' proposal by requiring a "compelling state interest" only when the conduct prohibited is "central" to the individual's religion. It is no more appropriate for judges to determine the "centrality" of religious beliefs before applying a "compelling interest" test in the free exercise field, than it would be for them to determine the "importance" of ideas before applying the "compelling interest" test in the free speech field. What principle of law or logic can be brought to bear to contradict a believer's assertion that a particular act is "central" to his personal faith? . . .

If the "compelling interest" test is to be applied at all, then, it must be applied across the board, to all actions thought to be religiously commanded. Moreover, if "compelling interest" really means what it says (and watering it down here would subvert its rigor in the other fields where it is applied), many laws will not meet the test. Any society adopting such a system would be courting anarchy, but that danger increases in direct proportion to the society's diversity of religious beliefs, and its determination to coerce or suppress none of them. . . .

Values that are protected against government interference through enshrinement in the Bill of Rights are not thereby banished from the political process. Just as a society that believes in the negative protection accorded to the press by the First Amendment is likely to enact laws that affirmatively foster the dissemination of the printed word, so also a society that believes in the negative protection accorded to religious belief can be expected to be solicitous of that value in its legislation as well. It is therefore not surprising that a number of States have made an exception to their drug laws for sacramental peyote use. But to say that a nondiscriminatory religious-practice exemption is permitted, or even that it is desirable, is not to say that it is constitutionally required, and that the appropriate occasions for its creation can be discerned by the courts. It may fairly be said that leaving accommodation to the political process will place at a relative disadvantage those religious practices that are not widely engaged in; but that unavoidable consequence of democratic government must be preferred to a system in which each conscience is a law unto itself or in which judges weigh the social importance of all laws against the centrality of all religious beliefs. . . .

Because respondents' ingestion of peyote was prohibited under Oregon law, and because that prohibition is constitutional, Oregon may, consistent with the Free Exercise Clause, deny respondents unemployment compensation when their dismissal results from use of the drug. The decision of the Oregon Supreme Court is accordingly reversed.

It is so ordered.

☐ *Justice O'CONNOR, with whom Justice BRENNAN, Justice MARSHALL, and Justice BLACKMUN join in parts I and II, concurring.*

Although I agree with the result the Court reaches in this case, I cannot join its opinion. In my view, today's holding dramatically departs from well-settled First Amendment jurisprudence, appears unnecessary to resolve the question presented, and is incompatible with our Nation's fundamental commitment to individual religious liberty. . . .

■ II

The Court today extracts from our long history of free exercise precedents the single categorical rule that "if prohibiting the exercise of religion . . . is . . . merely the incidental effect of a generally applicable and otherwise valid provision, the First Amendment has not been offended." Indeed, the Court holds that where the law is a generally applicable criminal prohibition, our usual free exercise jurisprudence does not even apply. To reach this sweeping result, however, the Court must not only give a strained reading of the First Amendment but must also disregard our consistent application of free exercise doctrine to cases involving generally applicable regulations that burden religious conduct. . . .

The Court today . . . interprets the Clause to permit the government to prohibit, without justification, conduct mandated by an individual's religious beliefs, so long as that prohibition is generally applicable. But a law that prohibits certain conduct—conduct that happens to be an act of worship for someone—manifestly does prohibit that person's free exercise of his religion. A person who is barred from engaging in religiously motivated conduct is barred from freely exercising his religion. Moreover, that person is barred from freely exercising his religion regardless of whether the law prohibits the conduct only when engaged in for religious reasons, only by members of that religion, or by all persons. It is difficult to deny that a law that prohibits religiously motivated conduct, even if the law is generally applicable, does not at least implicate First Amendment concerns.

The Court responds that generally applicable laws are "one large step" removed from laws aimed at specific religious practices. The First Amendment, however, does not distinguish between laws that are generally applicable and laws that target particular religious practices. Indeed, few States would be so naive as to enact a law directly prohibiting or burdening a religious practice as such. Our free exercise cases have all concerned generally applicable laws that had the effect of significantly burdening a religious practice. If the First Amendment is to have any vitality, it ought not be construed to cover only the extreme and hypothetical situation in which a State directly targets a religious practice. . . .

To say that a person's right to free exercise has been burdened, of course, does not mean that he has an absolute right to engage in the conduct. Under our established First Amendment jurisprudence, we have recognized that the freedom to act, unlike the freedom to believe, cannot be absolute. Instead, we have respected both the First Amendment's express textual mandate and the governmental interest in regulation of conduct by requiring the Government to justify any substantial burden on religiously motivated conduct by a compelling state interest and by means narrowly tailored to achieve that interest. . . .

The compelling interest test effectuates the First Amendment's command that religious liberty is an independent liberty, that it occupies a preferred position, and that the Court will not permit encroachments upon this liberty, whether direct or indirect, unless required by clear and compelling governmental interests "of the highest order," [*Wisconsin v.*] *Yoder* [406 U.S. 208 (1972)]. . . .

In my view, however, the essence of a free exercise claim is relief from a burden imposed by government on religious practices or beliefs, whether the burden is imposed directly through laws that prohibit or compel specific religious practices, or indirectly through laws that, in effect, make abandonment of one's own religion or conformity to the religious beliefs of others the price of an equal place in the civil community. . . .

Indeed, we have never distinguished between cases in which a State conditions receipt of a benefit on conduct prohibited by religious beliefs and cases in which a State affirmatively prohibits such conduct. The *Sherbert* compelling interest test applies in both kinds of cases. . . .

Finally, the Court today suggests that the disfavoring of minority religions is an "unavoidable consequence" under our system of government and that accommodation of such religions must be left to the political process. In my view, however, the First Amendment was enacted precisely to protect the rights of those whose religious practices are not shared by the majority and may be viewed with hostility. The history of our free exercise doctrine amply demonstrates the harsh impact majoritarian rule has had on unpopular or emerging religious groups such as the Jehovah's Witnesses and the Amish. . . .

■ III

The Court's holding today not only misreads settled First Amendment precedent; it appears to be unnecessary to this case. I would reach the same result applying our established free exercise jurisprudence. . . .

[T]he critical question in this case is whether exempting respondents from the State's general criminal prohibition "will unduly interfere with fulfillment of the governmental interest." Although the question is close, I would conclude that uniform application of Oregon's criminal prohibition is "essential to accomplish," its overriding interest in preventing the physical harm caused by the use of a Schedule I controlled substance. Oregon's criminal prohibition represents that State's judgment that the possession and use of controlled substances, even by only one person, is inherently harmful and dangerous. Because the health effects caused by the use of controlled substances exist regardless of the motivation of the user, the use of such substances, even for religious purposes, violates the very purpose of the laws that prohibit them. . . .

For these reasons, I believe that granting a selective exemption in this case would seriously impair Oregon's compelling interest in prohibiting possession of peyote by its citizens. Under such circumstances, the Free Exercise Clause does not require the State to accommodate respondents' religiously motivated conduct. . . .

☐ *Justice BLACKMUN, with whom Justice BRENNAN and Justice MARSHALL join, dissenting.*

This Court over the years painstakingly has developed a consistent and exacting standard to test the constitutionality of a state statute that burdens the free exercise of religion. Such a statute may stand only if the law in general, and the State's refusal to allow a religious exemption in particular, are justified by a compelling interest that cannot be served by less restrictive means.

Until today, I thought this was a settled and inviolate principle of this Court's First Amendment jurisprudence. The majority, however, perfunctorily dismisses it as a "constitutional anomaly." As carefully detailed in Justice O'CONNOR's concurring opinion . . . the majority is able to arrive at this view only by mischaracterizing this Court's precedents. The Court discards leading free exercise cases such as *Cantwell v. Connecticut* (1940), and *Wisconsin v. Yoder* (1972), as "hybrid." . . . The Court views traditional free exercise analysis as somehow inapplicable to criminal prohibitions (as opposed to conditions on the receipt of benefits), and to state laws of general applicability (as opposed, presumably, to laws that expressly single out religious practices). The Court cites cases in which, due to various exceptional circumstances, we found strict scrutiny inapposite, to hint that the Court has repudiated that standard altogether. In short, it effectuates a wholesale overturning of settled law concerning the Religion Clauses of our Constitution. One hopes that the Court is aware of the consequences, and that its result is not a product of overreaction to the serious problems the country's drug crisis has generated.

This distorted view of our precedents leads the majority to conclude that strict scrutiny of a state law burdening the free exercise of religion is a "luxury" that a well-ordered society cannot afford, and that the repression of minority religions is an "unavoidable consequence of democratic government." I do not believe the Founders thought their dearly bought freedom from religious persecution a "luxury," but an essential element of liberty—and they could not have thought religious intolerance "unavoidable," for they drafted the Religion Clauses precisely in order to avoid that intolerance.

For these reasons, I agree with Justice O'CONNOR's analysis of the applicable free exercise doctrine, and I join parts I and II of her opinion. As she points out, "the critical question in this case is whether exempting respondents from the State's general criminal prohibition: 'will unduly interfere with fulfillment of the governmental interest.' " I do disagree, however, with her specific answer to that question.

The State's interest in enforcing its prohibition, in order to be sufficiently compelling to outweigh a free exercise claim, cannot be merely abstract or symbolic. The State cannot plausibly assert that unbending application of a criminal prohibition is essential to fulfill any compelling interest, if it does not, in fact, attempt to enforce that prohibition. In this case, the State actually has not evinced any concrete interest in enforcing its drug laws against religious users of peyote. Oregon has never sought to prosecute respondents, and does not claim that it has made significant enforcement efforts against other religious users of peyote. The State's asserted interest thus amounts only to the symbolic preservation of an unenforced prohibition. . . .

The State proclaims an interest in protecting the health and safety of its citizens from the dangers of unlawful drugs. It offers, however, no evidence that the religious use of peyote has ever harmed anyone. . . .

The fact that peyote is classified as a Schedule I controlled substance does not, by itself, show that any and all uses of peyote, in any circumstance, are inherently harmful and dangerous. The Federal Government, which created the classifications of unlawful drugs from which Oregon's drug laws are derived, apparently does not find peyote so dangerous as to preclude an exemption for religious use. . . .

The carefully circumscribed ritual context in which respondents used peyote is far removed from the irresponsible and unrestricted recreational use of unlawful drugs. The Native American Church's internal restrictions on, and supervision of, its members' use of peyote substantially obviate the State's health and safety concerns. . . .

Moreover, just as in *Yoder*, the values and interests of those seeking a religious exemption in this case are congruent, to a great degree, with those the State seeks to promote through its drug laws. . . . Not only does the Church's doctrine forbid nonreligious use of peyote; it also generally advocates self-reliance, familial responsibility, and abstinence from alcohol. . . . Far from promoting the lawless and irresponsible use of drugs. Native American Church members' spiritual code exemplifies values that Oregon's drug laws are presumably intended to foster. . . .

Finally, although I agree with Justice O'CONNOR that courts should refrain from delving into questions of whether, as a matter of religious doctrine, a particular practice is "central" to the religion, I do not think this means that the courts must turn a blind eye to the severe impact of a State's restrictions on the adherents of a minority religion. . . .

If Oregon can constitutionally prosecute them for this act of worship, they, like the Amish, may be "forced to migrate to some other and more tolerant region." *Yoder*. This potentially devastating impact must be viewed in light of the federal policy—reached in reaction to many years of religious persecution and intolerance—of protecting the religious freedom of Native Americans. See, American Indian Religious Freedom Act, 92 Stat. 469 (1978). . . .

The American Indian Religious Freedom Act, in itself, may not create rights enforceable against government action restricting religious freedom, but this Court must scrupulously apply its free exercise analysis to the religious claims of Native Americans, however unorthodox they may be. Otherwise, both the First Amendment and the stated policy of Congress will offer to Native Americans merely an unfulfilled and hollow promise.

For these reasons, I conclude that Oregon's interest in enforcing its drug laws against religious use of peyote is not sufficiently compelling to outweigh respondents' right to the free exercise of their religion. Since the State could not constitutionally enforce its criminal prohibition against respondents, the interests underlying the State's drug laws cannot justify its denial of unemployment benefits. Absent such justification, the State's regulatory interest in denying benefits for religiously motivated "misconduct," is indistinguishable from the state interests this Court has rejected in *Frazee, Hobbie, Thomas*, and *Sherbert*. The State of Oregon cannot, consistently with the Free Exercise Clause, deny respondents unemployment benefits.

I dissent.

Church of the Lukumi Babalu Aye v. City of Hialeah

508 U.S. 520, 113 S.Ct. 2217 (1993)

In 1987, the Church of the Lukumi Babalu Aye leased land in Hialeah, Florida, and announced plans to establish a church, school, and cultural center there, which would bring its practice of Santeria, including the ritual sacrifice of animals, into the open. Santeria originated with the Yoruba people of eastern Africa who were brought as slaves to Cuba and other parts of the Caribbean. Santeria teaches that individuals have a destiny from God, but a destiny only fulfilled with the aid of spirits, or orishas, symbolized through the iconography of Catholic saints and who depend for survival on animal sacrifice. The practice of animal sacrifice is part of rituals performed at birth, marriage, and death rites; for the cure of the sick; at initiation ceremonies, and at an annual celebration. Chickens, pigeons, doves, ducks, guinea pigs, goats, sheep, and turtles are sacrificed by the cutting of the carotid arteries in the neck. The animals are then cooked and eaten, except after healing and death rituals.

The church's announcement sparked immediate controversy and public outcry over the sacrifice of animals. As a result, Hialeah's city council passed several ordinances prohibiting animal sacrifice, including:

> "Resolution 87-66, expressing 'concern' over religious practices inconsistent with public morals, peace, or safety, and declaring the city's 'commitment' to prohibiting such practices;

> "Ordinance 87-40, punishing 'whoever . . . unnecessarily or cruelly . . . kills any animal';

> "Ordinance 87-52, which defines 'sacrifice' as 'to unnecessarily kill . . . an animal in a . . . ritual . . . not for the primary purpose of food consumption,' and prohibits the 'possession, sacrifice, or slaughter' of an animal if it is killed in 'any type of ritual' and there is an intent to use it for food, but exempts 'any licensed [food] establishment' if the killing is otherwise permitted by law;

> "Ordinance 87-71, prohibiting the sacrifice of animals; and

> "Ordinance 87-72, which defines 'slaughter' as 'the killing of animals for food,' and prohibits slaughter outside of areas zoned for slaughterhouses, but includes an exemption for 'small numbers of hogs and/or cattle' when exempted by state law."

Church attorneys immediately attacked the constitutionality of the ordinances for abrogating the First Amendment's guarantee of free exercise of religion. After a federal district and appellate court upheld the ordinances, the church appealed to the Supreme Court.

The Court's decision was unanimous, with Justice Kennedy announcing the opinion. Concurring opinions were delivered by Justice Scalia, who was joined by Chief Justice Rehnquist; by Justice Souter; and by Justice Blackmun, who was joined by Justice O'Connor.

> ☐ *Justice KENNEDY delivered the opinion for the Court with respect to Parts I, III, and IV, which Chief Justice REHNQUIST and Justices WHITE, STEVENS, SCALIA, SOUTER, and THOMAS join; Part II-B, which Chief Justice REHNQUIST and Justices WHITE, STEVENS, SCALIA, and THOMAS join; Parts II-A-1 and II-A-3, which Chief Justice REHNQUIST and Justices STEVENS, SCALIA, and THOMAS join; and Part II-A-2, which Justice STEVENS joins.*

We invalidate the challenged enactments and reverse the judgment of the Court of Appeals. . . .

■ II

In addressing the constitutional protection for free exercise of religion, our cases establish the general proposition that a law that is neutral and of general applicability need not be justified by a compelling governmental interest even if the law has the incidental effect of burdening a particular religious practice. *Employment Div., Dept. of Human Resources of Oregon v. Smith,* [492 U.S. 872 (1992)]. Neutrality and general applicability are interrelated, and, as becomes apparent in this case, failure to satisfy one requirement is a likely indication that the other has not been satisfied. A law failing to satisfy these requirements must be justified by a compelling governmental interest and must be narrowly tailored to advance that interest. These ordinances fail to satisfy the *Smith* requirements. We begin by discussing neutrality.

[A] At a minimum, the protections of the Free Exercise Clause pertain if the law at issue discriminates against some or all religious beliefs or regulates or prohibits conduct because it is undertaken for religious reasons. See, e.g., *Braunfeld v. Brown,* 366 U.S. 599 (1961). . . .

[1] Although a law targeting religious beliefs as such is never permissible, if the object of a law is to infringe upon or restrict practices because of their religious motivation, the law is not neutral, *Smith;* and it is invalid unless it is justified by a compelling interest and is narrowly tailored to advance that interest. There are, of course, many ways of demonstrating that the object or purpose of a law is the suppression of religion or religious conduct. To determine the object of a law, we must begin with its text, for the minimum requirement of neutrality is that a law not discriminate on its face. A law lacks facial neutrality if it refers to a religious practice without a secular meaning discernable from the language or context. Petitioners contend that three of the ordinances fail this test of facial neutrality because they use the words "sacrifice" and "ritual," words with strong religious connotations. We agree that these words are consistent with the claim of facial discrimination, but the argument

is not conclusive. The words "sacrifice" and "ritual" have a religious origin, but current use admits also of secular meanings. The ordinances, furthermore, define "sacrifice" in secular terms, without referring to religious practices.

We reject the contention advanced by the city that our inquiry must end with the text of the laws at issue. Facial neutrality is not determinative. The Free Exercise Clause, like the Establishment Clause, extends beyond facial discrimination. The Clause "forbids subtle departures from neutrality," *Gillette v. United States*, 401 U.S. 437 (1971), and "covert suppression of particular religious beliefs." Official action that targets religious conduct for distinctive treatment cannot be shielded by mere compliance with the requirement of facial neutrality. . . .

The record in this case compels the conclusion that suppression of the central element of the Santeria worship service was the object of the ordinances. First, though use of the words "sacrifice" and "ritual" does not compel a finding of improper targeting of the Santeria religion, the choice of these words is support for our conclusion. There are further respects in which the text of the city council's enactments discloses the improper attempt to target Santeria. Resolution 87-66, adopted June 9, 1987, recited that "residents and citizens of the City of Hialeah have expressed their concern that certain religions may propose to engage in practices which are inconsistent with public morals, peace of safety," and "reiterated" the city's commitment to prohibit "any and all [such] acts of any and all religious groups." No one suggests, and on this record it cannot be maintained, that city officials had in mind a religion other than Santeria.

It becomes evident that these ordinances target Santeria sacrifice when the ordinances' operation is considered. . . . It is a necessary conclusion that almost the only conduct subject to [Hialeah's] Ordinances is the religious exercise of Santeria church members. The texts show that they were drafted in tandem to achieve this result. . . .

The legitimate governmental interests in protecting the public health and preventing cruelty to animals could be addressed by restrictions stopping far short of a flat prohibition of all Santeria sacrificial practice. If improper disposal, not the sacrifice itself, is the harm to be prevented, the city could have imposed a general regulation on the disposal of organic garbage. It did not do so. . . .

Under similar analysis, narrower regulation would achieve the city's interest in preventing cruelty to animals. With regard to the city's interest in ensuring the adequate care of animals, regulation of conditions and treatment, regardless of why an animal is kept, is the logical response to the city's concern, not a prohibition on possession for the purpose of sacrifice. The same is true for the city's interest in prohibiting cruel methods of killing. . . . If the city has a real concern that other methods are less humane, however, the subject of the regulation should be the method of slaughter itself, not a religious classification that is said to be some general relation to it. . . .

[B] We turn next to a second requirement of the Free Exercise Clause, the rule that laws burdening religious practice must be of general applicability. *Smith*. . . .

The principle that government, in pursuit of legitimate interests, cannot in a selective manner impose burdens only on conduct motivated by religious belief is essential to the protection of the rights guaranteed by the Free Exercise Clause. The principle underlying the general applicability requirement has parallels in our First Amendment jurisprudence. In this case we need not define with precision the standard used to evaluate whether a prohibition is of general application, for these ordinances fall well below the minimum standard necessary to protect First Amendment rights.

Respondent claims that Ordinances 87-40, 87-52, and 87-71 advance two interests: protecting the public health and preventing cruelty to animals. The ordinances are underinclusive for those ends. They fail to prohibit nonreligious conduct that endangers these interests in a similar or greater degree than Santeria sacrifice does. The underinclusion is substantial, not inconsequential. Despite the city's proffered interest in preventing cruelty to animals, the ordinances are drafted with care to forbid few killings but those occasioned by religious sacrifice. Many types of animal deaths or kills for nonreligious reasons are either not prohibited or approved by express provision. For example, fishing—which occurs in Hialeah—is legal. Extermination of mice and rats within a home is also permitted. . . .

The ordinances are also underinclusive with regard to the city's interest in public health, which is threatened by the disposal of animals carcasses in open public places and the consumption of uninspected meat. Neither interest is pursued by respondent with regard to conduct that is not motivated by religious conviction. The health risks posed by the improper disposal of animal carcasses are the same whether Santeria sacrifice or some nonreligious killing preceded it. The city does not, however, prohibit hunters from bringing their kill to their houses, nor does it regulate disposal after their activity. Despite substantial testimony at trial that the same public health hazards result from improper disposal of garbage by restaurants, restaurants are outside the scope of the ordinances. Improper disposal is a general problem that causes substantial health risks, but which respondent addresses only when it results from religious exercise.

The ordinances are underinclusive as well with regard to the health risk posed by consumption of uninspected meat. Under the city's ordinances, hunters may eat their kill and fishermen may eat their catch without undergoing governmental inspection. Likewise, state law requires inspection of meat that is sold but exempts meat from animals raised for the use of the owner and "members of his household and nonpaying guests and employees." The asserted interest in inspected meat is not pursued in contexts similar to that of religious animal sacrifice. . . .

We conclude, in sum, that each of Hialeah's ordinances pursues the city's governmental interests only against conduct motivated by religious belief. The ordinances "have every appearance of a prohibition that society is prepared to impose upon [Santeria worshippers] but not upon itself." *The Florida Star v. B.J.F.*, 491 U.S. 524 (1989) (SCALIA, J., concurring in part and concurring in judgment). This precise evil is what the requirement of general applicability is designed to prevent.

■ III

A law burdening religious practice that is not neutral or not of general application must undergo the most rigorous of scrutiny. To satisfy the commands of the First Amendment, a law restrictive of religious practice must advance " 'interests of the highest order' " and must be narrowly tailored in pursuit of those interests. The compelling interest standard that we apply once a law fails to meet the *Smith* requirements is not "watered . . . down" but "really means what it says." *Smith.* A law that targets religious conduct for distinctive treatment or advances legitimate governmental interests only against conduct with a religious motivation will survive strict scrutiny only in rare cases. It follows from what we have already said that these ordinances cannot withstand this scrutiny.

First, even were the governmental interests compelling, the ordinances are not drawn in narrow terms to accomplish those interests. . . . Respondent has not demonstrated, moreover, that, in the context of these ordinances, its governmental interests are compelling. . . . The laws here in question were enacted contrary to these constitutional principles, and they are void.

☐ *Justice SCALIA, with whom Chief Justice REHNQUIST joins, concurring in part and concurring in the judgment.*

The Court analyzes the "neutrality" and the "general applicability" of the Hialeah ordinances in separate sections (Parts II-A and II-B, respectively), and allocates various invalidating factors to one or the other of those sections. If it were necessary to make a clear distinction between the two terms, I would draw a line somewhat different from the Court's. But I think it is not necessary, and would frankly acknowledge that the terms are not only "interrelated," but substantially overlap. . . .

In my view, the defect of lack of neutrality applies primarily to those laws that by their terms impose disabilities on the basis of religion (e.g., a law excluding members of a certain sect from public benefits); whereas the defect of lack of general applicability applies primarily to those laws which, though neutral in their terms, through their design, construction, or enforcement target the practices of a particular religion for discriminatory treatment. But certainly a law that is not of general applicability (in the sense I have described) can be considered "nonneutral"; and certainly no law that is nonneutral (in the relevant sense) can be thought to be of general applicability. Because I agree with most of the invalidating factors set forth in Part II of the Court's opinion, and because it seems to me a matter of no consequence under which rubric ("neutrality," Part II-A, or "general applicability," Part II-B) each invalidating factor is discussed, I join the judgment of the Court and all of its opinion except section 2 of Part II-A.

I do not join that section because it departs from the opinion's general focus on the object of the laws at issue to consider the subjective motivation of the lawmakers, i.e., whether the Hialeah City Council actually intended to disfavor the religion of Santeria. As I have noted elsewhere, it is virtually impossible to determine the singular "motive" of a collective legislative body, and this Court has a long tradition of refraining from such inquiries. . . .

☐ *Justice SOUTER, concurring in part and concurring in the judgment.*

This case turns on a principle about which there is no disagreement, that the Free Exercise Clause bars government action aimed at suppressing religious belief or practice. The Court holds that Hialeah's animal-sacrifice laws violate that principle, and I concur in that holding without reservation.

Because prohibiting religious exercise is the object of the laws at hand, this case does not present the more difficult issue addressed in our last free-exercise case, *Smith*, which announced the rule that a "neutral, generally applicable" law does not run afoul of the Free Exercise Clause even when it prohibits religious exercise in effect. The Court today refers to that rule in *dicta*, and despite my general agreement with the Court's opinion I do not join Part II, where the *dicta* appear, for I have doubts about whether the *Smith* rule merits adherence. I write separately to explain why the *Smith* rule is not germane to this case and to express my view that, in a case presenting the issue, the Court should re-examine the rule *Smith* declared. . . .

[T]his is far from a representative free-exercise case. While, as the Court observes, the Hialeah City Council has provided a rare example of a law actually aimed at suppressing religious exercise, *Smith* was typical of our free-exercise cases, involving as it did a formally neutral, generally applicable law. The rule *Smith* announced, however, was decidedly untypical of the cases involving the same type of law. Because *Smith* left those prior cases standing, we are left with a free-exercise jurisprudence in tension with itself, a tension that should be addressed, and that may legitimately be addressed, by re-examining the *Smith* rule in the next case that would turn upon its application. . . .

The *Smith* rule, in my view, may be reexamined consistently with principles of *stare decisis*. To begin with, the *Smith* rule was not subject to "full-dress argument" prior to its announcement. . . . The *Smith* rule's vitality as precedent is limited further by the seeming want of any need of it in resolving the question presented in that case. Justice O'CONNOR reached the same result as the majority by applying, as the parties had requested, "our established free exercise jurisprudence," and the majority never determined that the case could not be resolved on the narrower ground, going instead straight to the broader constitutional rule. But the Court's better practice, one supported by the same principles of restraint that underlie the rule of *stare decisis*, is not to " 'formulate a rule of constitutional law broader than is required by the precise facts to which it is to be applied.' " *Ashwander v. TVA*, 297 U.S. 288 (1936) (BRANDEIS, J., concurring). I am not suggesting that the *Smith* Court lacked the power to announce its rule, I think a rule of law unnecessary to the outcome of a case, especially one not put into play by the parties, approaches without more the sort of "*dicta* . . . which may be followed if sufficiently persuasive but which are not controlling." *Humphrey's Executor v. United States*, 295 U.S. 602 (1935). . . .

The considerations of full-briefing, necessity, and novelty thus do not exhaust the legitimate reasons for reexamining prior decisions, or even for reexamining the *Smith* rule. One important further consideration warrants mention here, however, because it demands the reexamination I have in mind. *Smith* presents not the usual question of whether to follow a constitutional rule, but the question of which constitutional rule to follow, for *Smith* refrained from overruling prior free-exercise cases that contain a free-exercise rule fundamentally at odds with the rule *Smith* declared. *Smith*, indeed, announced its rule by relying squarely upon the precedent of prior cases. Since that precedent is nonetheless at odds with the *Smith* rule, as I have discussed above, the result is an intolerable tension in free-exercise law which may be resolved, consistently with principles of *stare decisis*, in a case in which the tension is presented and its resolution pivotal.

While the tension on which I rely exists within the body of our extant case law, a rereading of that case law will not, of course, mark the limits of any inquiry directed to reexamining the *Smith* rule, which should be reviewed in light not only of the precedent on which it was rested but also of the text of the Free Exercise Clause and its origins. As for text, *Smith* did not assert that the plain language of the Free Exercise Clause compelled its rule, but only that the rule was "a permissible reading" of the Clause. Suffice it to say that a respectable argument may be made that the pre-*Smith* law comes closer to fulfilling the language of the Free Exercise Clause than the rule *Smith* announced. . . .

Nor did *Smith* consider the original meaning of the Free Exercise Clause, though overlooking the opportunity was no unique transgression. Save in a handful of passing remarks, the Court has not explored the history of the Clause since its early attempts in 1879 and 1890, see *Reynolds v. United States*, 98 U.S. [245(1879)], attempts that recent scholarship makes clear were incomplete. The curious absence of history from our free-exercise decisions creates a stark contrast with our cases under the Establishment Clause, where historical analysis has been so prominent. . . .

Our cases now present competing answers to the question when government, while pursuing secular ends, may compel disobedience to what one believes religion commands. The case before us is rightly decided without resolving the existing tension, which remains for another day when it may be squarely faced.

☐ *Justice BLACKMUN, with whom Justice O'CONNOR joins, concurring.*

I write separately to emphasize that the First Amendment's protection of religion extends beyond those rare occasions on which the government explicitly targets religion (or a particular religion) for disfavored treatment, as is done in this case. In my view, a statute that burdens the free exercise of religion "may stand only if the law in general, and the State's refusal to allow a religious exemption in particular, are justified by a compelling interest that cannot be served by less restrictive means." *Smith* (dissenting opinion). The Court, however, applies a different test. It applies the test announced in *Smith*, under which "a law that is neutral and of general applicability need not be justified by a compelling governmental interest even if the law has the incidental effect of burdening a particular religious practice." I continue to believe that *Smith* was wrongly decided, because it ignored the value of religious freedom as an affirmative individual liberty and treated the Free Exercise Clause as no more than an antidiscrimination principle. Thus, while I agree with the result the Court reaches in this case, I arrive at that result by a different route.

When a law discriminates against religion as such, as do the ordinances in this case, it automatically will fail strict scrutiny under *Sherbert v. Verner*, 374 U.S. 398 (1963) [holding that governmental regulation that imposes a burden upon religious practice must be narrowly tailored to advance a compelling state interest]. This is true because a law that targets religious practice for disfavored treatment both burdens the free exercise of religion and, by definition, is not precisely tailored to a compelling governmental interest.

Thus, unlike the majority, I do not believe that "[a] law burdening religious practice that is not neutral or not of general application must undergo the most rigorous of scrutiny." In my view, regulation that targets religion in this way, ipso facto, fails strict scrutiny. It is for this reason that a statute that explicitly restricts religious practices violates the First Amendment. . . .

City of Boerne v. Flores
521 U.S. 507, 117 S.Ct. 2157 (1997)

Situated on a hill in the city of Boerne, Texas, is St. Peter Catholic Church, built in 1923 and replicating the mission style of the region's earlier history. The church seats about 230 worshippers, but in the 1990s became too small to accommodate the growing number of parishioners. Accordingly, the Archbishop of San Antonio gave permission to the parish to enlarge the building. Shortly afterward, however, the Boerne City Council passed an ordinance authorizing the city's Historic Landmark Commission to prepare a preservation plan with proposed historic landmarks and districts. Under the ordinance, the Commission must preapprove construction affecting historic landmarks or buildings in a historic district. When the Archbishop applied for a building permit so construction could proceed, city authorities, relying on the ordinance and the designation of the church as a historic landmark, denied the application. The Archbishop in turn challenged that decision in federal district court, claiming that the city violated the church's religious freedom as guaranteed by the Religious Freedom Restoration Act of 1993 (RFRA). Congress enacted that law following the Supreme Court's ruling in *Employment Division, Department of Human Resources of Oregon v. Smith*, 492 U.S. 872 (1990) and established as a matter of federal statutory law the pre-*Smith* test for balancing claims to religious freedom against governmental interests in otherwise generally applicable laws, like Boerne's zoning ordinance. And in defending the decision to deny the church a building permit, attorneys for the city countered that Congress had exceeded its enforcement powers under Section 5 of the Fourteenth Amendment in enacting the RFRA. The district court held the RFRA unconstitutional as a violation of the separation of powers. When the Court of Appeals for the Fifth Circuit reversed, the city of Boerne appealed to the Supreme Court, which granted *certiorari*.

The Court's decision was six to three and its opinion delivered by Justice Kennedy. Justices Stevens and Scalia filed concurring opinions.

Justice O'Connor filed a dissenting opinion, which Justices Souter and Breyer joined in part. In a brief dissent omitted here, Justice Souter reiterated his doubts, expressed in *Church of Lukumi Babalu Aye, Inc. v. Hialeah*, 492 U.S. 872 (1990), about the precedential value of *Smith*, and indicated that the Court here should have either reconsidered the soundness of the *Smith* rule or dismissed this case as improvidently granted. In another brief dissent, Justice Breyer expressed agreement with Justice O'Connor's dissent except for her views of Congress' enforcement power under Section 5 of the Fourteenth Amendment, an issue which he would not have reached in this case.

> ☐ *Justice KENNEDY delivered the opinion of the Court, in which Chief Justice REHNQUIST and Justices STEVENS, THOMAS, and GINSBURG joined, and in all but Part III-A-1 of which Justice SCALIA joined.*

A decision by local zoning authorities to deny a church a building permit was challenged under the Religious Freedom Restoration Act of 1993 (RFRA). The case calls into question the authority of Congress to enact RFRA. We conclude the statute exceeds Congress' power. . . .

■ II

Congress enacted RFRA in direct response to the Court's decision in *Employment Div., Dept. of Human Resources of Ore. v. Smith*, 494 U.S. 872 (1990). There we considered a Free Exercise Clause claim brought by members of the Native American Church who were denied unemployment benefits when they lost their jobs because they had used peyote. In evaluating the claim, we declined to apply the balancing test set forth in *Sherbert v. Verner*, 374 U.S. 398 (1963), under which we would have asked whether Oregon's prohibition substantially burdened a religious practice and, if it did, whether the burden was justified by a compelling government interest. . . . The application of the *Sherbert* test, the *Smith* decision explained, would have produced an anomaly in the law, a constitutional right to ignore neutral laws of general applicability. The anomaly would have been accentuated, the Court reasoned, by the difficulty of determining whether a particular practice was central to an individual's religion. . . .

Many criticized the Court's reasoning, and this disagreement resulted in the passage of RFRA. Congress announced:

> "(1) The framers of the Constitution, recognizing free exercise of religion as an unalienable right, secured its protection in the First Amendment to the Constitution;
>
> "(2) laws 'neutral' toward religion may burden religious exercise as surely as laws intended to interfere with religious exercise;
>
> "(3) governments should not substantially burden religious exercise without compelling justification;
>
> "(4) in *Employment Division v. Smith*, 494 U.S. 872 (1990), the Supreme Court virtually eliminated the requirement that the gov-

ernment justify burdens on religious exercise imposed by laws neutral toward religion; and

"(5) the compelling interest test as set forth in prior Federal court rulings is a workable test for striking sensible balances between religious liberty and competing prior governmental interests."

The Act's stated purposes are:

"(1) to restore the compelling interest test as set forth in *Sherbert v. Verner*, 374 U.S. 398 (1963) and *Wisconsin v. Yoder*, 406 U.S. 205 (1972) and to guarantee its application in all cases where free exercise of religion is substantially burdened; and

"(2) to provide a claim or defense to persons whose religious exercise is substantially burdened by government."

RFRA prohibits "government" from "substantially burdening" a person's exercise of religion even if the burden results from a rule of general applicability unless the government can demonstrate the burden "(1) is in furtherance of a compelling governmental interest; and (2) is the least restrictive means of furthering that compelling governmental interest." The Act's mandate applies to any "branch, department, agency, instrumentality, and official (or other person acting under color of law) of the United States," as well as to any "State, or . . . subdivision of a State." . . .

■ III (A)

The parties disagree over whether RFRA is a proper exercise of Congress' Section 5 power "to enforce" by "appropriate legislation" the constitutional guarantee that no State shall deprive any person of "life, liberty, or property, without due process of law" nor deny any person "equal protection of the laws." . . .

All must acknowledge that Section 5 is "a positive grant of legislative power" to Congress, *Katzenbach v. Morgan*, 384 U.S. 641 (1966). In *Ex parte Virginia*, 100 U.S. 339 (1880), we explained the scope of Congress' Section 5 power in the following broad terms: "Whatever legislation is appropriate, that is, adapted to carry out the objects the amendments have in view, whatever tends to enforce submission to the prohibitions they contain, and to secure to all persons the enjoyment of perfect equality of civil rights and the equal protection of the laws against State denial or invasion, if not prohibited, is brought within the domain of congressional power." Legislation which deters or remedies constitutional violations can fall within the sweep of Congress' enforcement power even if in the process it prohibits conduct which is not itself unconstitutional and intrudes into "legislative spheres of autonomy previously reserved to the States." *Fitzpatrick v. Bitzer*, 427 U.S. 445 (1976). For example, the Court upheld a suspension of literacy tests and similar voting requirements under Congress' parallel power to enforce the provisions of the Fifteenth Amendment, see U.S. Const., Amdt. 15, Sec. 2, as a measure to combat racial discrimination in voting, *South Carolina v. Katzenbach*, 383 U.S. 301 (1966), despite the facial constitutionality of the tests under *Lassiter v. Northampton County Bd. of Elections*, 360 U.S. 45 (1959). We have also concluded that other measures protecting voting rights are within Congress' power to enforce the Fourteenth and Fifteenth Amendments, despite the burdens those measures placed on the States. . . .

It is also true, however, that "as broad as the congressional enforcement power is, it is not unlimited." *Oregon v. Mitchell*, 400 U.S. 112 (1970). In assessing the breadth of Section 5's enforcement power, we begin with its text. Congress has been given the power "to enforce" the "provisions of this article." We agree with respondent, of course, that Congress can enact legislation under Section 5 enforcing the constitutional right to the free exercise of religion. The "provisions of this article," to which Section 5 refers, include the Due Process Clause of the Fourteenth Amendment. Congress' power to enforce the Free Exercise Clause follows from our holding in *Cantwell v. Connecticut*, 310 U.S. 296 (1940), that the "fundamental concept of liberty embodied in [the Fourteenth Amendment's Due Process Clause] embraces the liberties guaranteed by the First Amendment."

Congress' power under Section 5, however, extends only to "enforcing" the provisions of the Fourteenth Amendment. The Court has described this power as "remedial," *South Carolina v. Katzenbach*. The design of the Amendment and the text of Section 5 are inconsistent with the suggestion that Congress has the power to decree the substance of the Fourteenth Amendment's restrictions on the States. Legislation which alters the meaning of the Free Exercise Clause cannot be said to be enforcing the Clause. Congress does not enforce a constitutional right by changing what the right is. It has been given the power "to enforce," not the power to determine what constitutes a constitutional violation. Were it not so, what Congress would be enforcing would no longer be, in any meaningful sense, the "provisions of [the Fourteenth Amendment]."

While the line between measures that remedy or prevent unconstitutional actions and measures that make a substantive change in the governing law is not easy to discern, and Congress must have wide latitude in determining where it lies, the distinction exists and must be observed. There must be a congruence and proportionality between the injury to be prevented or remedied and the means adopted to that end. Lacking such a connection, legislation may become substantive in operation and effect. History and our case law support drawing the distinction, one apparent from the text of the Amendment.

■ 1

The Fourteenth Amendment's history confirms the remedial, rather than substantive, nature of the Enforcement Clause. The Joint Committee on Reconstruction of the 39th Congress began drafting what would become the Fourteenth Amendment in January 1866. The objections to the Committee's first draft of the Amendment, and the rejection of the draft, have a direct bearing on the central issue of defining Congress' enforcement power. In February, Republican Representative John Bingham of Ohio reported the following draft amendment to the House of Representatives on behalf of the Joint Committee: "The Congress shall have power to make all laws which shall be necessary and proper to secure to the citizens of each State all privileges and immunities of citizens in the several States, and to all persons in the several States equal protection in the rights of life, liberty, and property."

The proposal encountered immediate opposition, which continued through three days of debate. Members of Congress from across the political spectrum criticized the Amendment, and the criticisms had a common theme: The proposed Amendment gave Congress too much legislative power at the expense of the existing constitutional structure. Democrats and conservative Republicans argued that the proposed Amendment would give Congress a power to intrude into traditional areas of state responsibility, a power inconsistent with the federal design central to the Constitution. Typifying these views, Republican Representative Robert Hale of New York labeled the Amendment "an utter departure from every principle ever dreamed of by the men who framed our Constitution," and warned that under it "all State legislation, in its codes of civil and criminal jurisprudence and procedures ... may be overridden, may be repealed or abolished, and the law of Congress established instead." ...

As a result of these objections having been expressed from so many different quarters, the House voted to table the proposal until April. The Amendment in its early form was not again considered. Instead, the Joint Committee began drafting a new article of Amendment, which it reported to Congress on April 30, 1866.

Section 1 of the new draft Amendment imposed self-executing limits on the States. Section 5 prescribed that "the Congress shall have power to enforce, by appropriate legislation, the provisions of this article." The revised Amendment proposal did not raise the concerns expressed earlier regarding broad congressional power to prescribe uniform national laws with respect to life, liberty, and property. After revisions not relevant here, the new measure passed both Houses and was ratified in July 1868 as the Fourteenth Amendment. ...

■ 2

The remedial and preventive nature of Congress' enforcement power, and the limitation inherent in the power, were confirmed in our earliest cases on the Fourteenth Amendment. In the *Civil Rights Cases*, 109 U.S. 3 (1883), the Court invalidated sections of the Civil Rights Act of 1875 which prescribed criminal penalties for denying to any person "the full enjoyment of" public accommodations and conveyances, on the grounds that it exceeded Congress' power by seeking to regulate private conduct. The Enforcement Clause, the Court said, did not authorize Congress to pass "general legislation upon the rights of the citizen, but corrective legislation; that is, such as may be necessary and proper for counteracting such laws as the States may adopt or enforce, and which, by the amendment, they are prohibited from making or enforcing. ...." Although the specific holdings of these early cases might have been superseded or modified, see, e.g., *Heart of Atlanta Motel, Inc. v. United States*, 379 U.S. 241 (1964), their treatment of Congress' Section 5 power as corrective or preventive, not definitional, has not been questioned. ...

■ 3

Any suggestion that Congress has a substantive, non-remedial power under the Fourteenth Amendment is not supported by our case law. In *Oregon v.*

Mitchell, a majority of the Court concluded Congress had exceeded its enforcement powers by enacting legislation lowering the minimum age of voters from 21 to 18 in state and local elections. The five Members of the Court who reached this conclusion explained that the legislation intruded into an area reserved by the Constitution to the States. . . .

If Congress could define its own powers by altering the Fourteenth Amendment's meaning, no longer would the Constitution be "superior paramount law, unchangeable by ordinary means." It would be "on a level with ordinary legislative acts, and, like other acts, . . . alterable when the legislature shall please to alter it." *Marbury v. Madison.* Under this approach, it is difficult to conceive of a principle that would limit congressional power. Shifting legislative majorities could change the Constitution and effectively circumvent the difficult and detailed amendment process contained in Article V.

We now turn to consider whether RFRA can be considered enforcement legislation under Section 5 of the Fourteenth Amendment.

■ III (B)

While preventive rules are sometimes appropriate remedial measures, there must be a congruence between the means used and the ends to be achieved. The appropriateness of remedial measures must be considered in light of the evil presented. Strong measures appropriate to address one harm may be an unwarranted response to another, lesser one. . . .

Regardless of the state of the legislative record, RFRA cannot be considered remedial, preventive legislation, if those terms are to have any meaning. RFRA is so out of proportion to a supposed remedial or preventive object that it cannot be understood as responsive to, or designed to prevent, unconstitutional behavior. It appears, instead, to attempt a substantive change in constitutional protections. Preventive measures prohibiting certain types of laws may be appropriate when there is reason to believe that many of the laws affected by the congressional enactment have a significant likelihood of being unconstitutional. Remedial legislation under Section 5 "should be adapted to the mischief and wrong which the [Fourteenth] Amendment was intended to provide against." *Civil Rights Cases.*

RFRA is not so confined. Sweeping coverage ensures its intrusion at every level of government, displacing laws and prohibiting official actions of almost every description and regardless of subject matter. RFRA's restrictions apply to every agency and official of the Federal, State, and local Governments. RFRA has no termination date or termination mechanism. Any law is subject to challenge at any time by any individual who alleges a substantial burden on his or her free exercise of religion.

The reach and scope of RFRA distinguish it from other measures passed under Congress' enforcement power, even in the area of voting rights. In *South Carolina v. Katzenbach*, the challenged provisions were confined to those regions of the country where voting discrimination had been most flagrant and affected a discrete class of state laws, i.e., state voting laws. Furthermore, to ensure that the reach of the Voting Rights Act was limited to those cases in which constitutional violations were most likely (in order to reduce the possibility of overbreadth), the coverage under the Act would terminate "at the behest of States and political subdivisions in which the danger of substantial voting discrimination has not materialized during the preceding five years." . . .

The stringent test RFRA demands of state laws reflects a lack of proportionality or congruence between the means adopted and the legitimate end to be achieved. If an objector can show a substantial burden on his free exercise, the State must demonstrate a compelling governmental interest and show that the law is the least restrictive means of furthering its interest. Claims that a law substantially burdens someone's exercise of religion will often be difficult to contest. Laws valid under *Smith* would fall under RFRA without regard to whether they had the object of stifling or punishing free exercise. . . .

The substantial costs RFRA exacts, both in practical terms of imposing a heavy litigation burden on the States and in terms of curtailing their traditional general regulatory power, far exceed any pattern or practice of unconstitutional conduct under the Free Exercise Clause as interpreted in *Smith*. Simply put, RFRA is not designed to identify and counteract state laws likely to be unconstitutional because of their treatment of religion. In most cases, the state laws to which RFRA applies are not ones which will have been motivated by religious bigotry. If a state law disproportionately burdened a particular class of religious observers, this circumstance might be evidence of an impermissible legislative motive. RFRA's substantial burden test, however, is not even a discriminatory effects or disparate impact test. It is a reality of the modern regulatory state that numerous state laws, such as the zoning regulations at issue here, impose a substantial burden on a large class of individuals. When the exercise of religion has been burdened in an incidental way by a law of general application, it does not follow that the persons affected have been burdened any more than other citizens, let alone burdened because of their religious beliefs. In addition, the Act imposes in every case a least restrictive means requirement—a requirement that was not used in the pre-*Smith* jurisprudence RFRA purported to codify—which also indicates that the legislation is broader than is appropriate if the goal is to prevent and remedy constitutional violations. . . .

Broad as the power of Congress is under the Enforcement Clause of the Fourteenth Amendment, RFRA contradicts vital principles necessary to maintain separation of powers and the federal balance. The judgment of the Court of Appeals sustaining the Act's constitutionality is reversed.

☐ *Justice STEVENS, concurring.*

In my opinion, the Religious Freedom Restoration Act of 1993 (RFRA) is a "law respecting an establishment of religion" that violates the First Amendment to the Constitution. . . .

☐ *Justice SCALIA, with whom Justice STEVENS joins, concurring in part.*

I write to respond briefly to the claim of Justice O'CONNOR's dissent (hereinafter "the dissent") that historical materials support a result contrary to the one reached in *Employment Div., Dept. of Human Resources of Ore. v. Smith*, 494 U.S. 872 (1990). The material that the dissent claims is at odds with *Smith* either has little to say about the issue or is in fact more consistent with *Smith* than with the dissent's interpretation of the Free Exercise Clause. . . .

The dissent first claims that *Smith*'s interpretation of the Free Exercise

Clause departs from the understanding reflected in various statutory and con-stitutional protections of religion enacted by Colonies, States, and Territories in the period leading up to the ratification of the Bill of Rights. But the pro-tections afforded by those enactments are in fact more consistent with *Smith's* interpretation of free exercise than with the dissent's understanding of it. [T]he early "free exercise" enactments cited by the dissent protect only against action that is taken "for" or "in respect of " religion; or action taken "on ac-count of " religion; or "discriminatory" action; or, finally (and unhelpfully for purposes of interpreting "free exercise" in the Federal Constitution), action that interferes with the "free exercise" of religion. It is eminently arguable that application of neutral, generally applicable laws of the sort the dissent refers to—such as zoning laws—would not constitute action taken "for," "in respect of," or "on account of " one's religion, or "discriminatory" action.

Assuming, however, that the affirmative protection of religion accorded by the early "free exercise" enactments sweeps as broadly as the dissent's theory would require, those enactments do not support the dissent's view, since they contain "provisos" that significantly qualify the affirmative protection they grant. According to the dissent, the "provisos" support its view because they would have been "superfluous" if "the Court was correct in *Smith* that generally applicable laws are enforceable regardless of religious conscience." I disagree. In fact, the most plausible reading of the "free exercise" enactments (if their affirmative provisions are read broadly, as the dissent's view requires) is a virtual restatement of *Smith*: Religious exercise shall be permitted so long as it does not violate general laws governing conduct. The "provisos" in the enactments negate a license to act in a manner "unfaithfull to the Lord Pro-prietary" (Maryland Act Concerning Religion of 1649), or "behave" in other than a "peaceable and quiet" manner (Rhode Island Charter of 1663), or "disturb the public peace" (New Hampshire Constitution), or interfere with the "peace [and] safety of the State" (New York, Maryland, and Georgia Con-stitutions), or "demean" oneself in other than a "peaceable and orderly manner" (Northwest Ordinance of 1787). At the time these provisos were en-acted, keeping "peace" and "order" seems to have meant, precisely, obeying the laws. "Every breach of law is against the peace." Even as late as 1828, when Noah Webster published his *American Dictionary of the English Language*, he gave as one of the meanings of "peace": "8. Public tranquillity; that quiet, order and security which is guaranteed by the laws; as, to keep the peace; to break the peace." This limitation upon the scope of religious exercise would have been in accord with the background political philosophy of the age (as-sociated most prominently with John Locke), which regarded freedom as the right "to do only what was not lawfully prohibited." And while, under this in-terpretation, these early "free exercise" enactments support the Court's judg-ment in *Smith*, I see no sensible interpretation that could cause them to support what I understand to be the position of Justice O'CONNOR, or any of *Smith's* other critics. No one in that camp, to my knowledge, contends that their favored "compelling state interest" test conforms to any possible inter-pretation of "breach of peace and order"—i.e., that only violence or force, or any other category of action (more limited than "violation of law") which can possibly be conveyed by the phrase "peace and order," justifies state pro-hibition of religiously motivated conduct.

Apart from the early "free exercise" enactments of Colonies, States, and

Territories, the dissent calls attention to those bodies', and the Continental Congress's, legislative accommodation of religious practices prior to ratification of the Bill of Rights. This accommodation—which took place both before and after enactment of the state constitutional protections of religious liberty—suggests (according to the dissent) that "the drafters and ratifiers of the First Amendment . . . assumed courts would apply the Free Exercise Clause similarly." But that legislatures sometimes (though not always) found it "appropriate" to accommodate religious practices does not establish that accommodation was understood to be constitutionally mandated by the Free Exercise Clause. As we explained in *Smith*, "To say that a nondiscriminatory religious-practice exemption is permitted, or even that it is desirable, is not to say that it is constitutionally required."

The dissent's final source of claimed historical support consists of statements of certain of the Framers in the context of debates about proposed legislative enactments or debates over general principles (not in connection with the drafting of State or Federal Constitutions). Those statements are subject to the same objection as was the evidence about legislative accommodation: There is no reason to think they were meant to describe what was constitutionally required (and judicially enforceable), as opposed to what was thought to be legislatively or even morally desirable. . . .

☐ *Justice O'CONNOR, with whom Justice BREYER joins except as to a portion of Part I, dissenting.*

I dissent from the Court's disposition of this case. I agree with the Court that the issue before us is whether the Religious Freedom Restoration Act (RFRA) is a proper exercise of Congress' power to enforce Section 5 of the Fourteenth Amendment. But as a yardstick for measuring the constitutionality of RFRA, the Court uses its holding in *Employment Div., Dept. of Human Resources of Ore. v. Smith*, 494 U.S. 872 (1990), the decision that prompted Congress to enact RFRA as a means of more rigorously enforcing the Free Exercise Clause. I remain of the view that *Smith* was wrongly decided, and I would use this case to reexamine the Court's holding there. . . . If the Court were to correct the misinterpretation of the Free Exercise Clause set forth in *Smith*, it would simultaneously put our First Amendment jurisprudence back on course and allay the legitimate concerns of a majority in Congress who believed that *Smith* improperly restricted religious liberty. We would then be in a position to review RFRA in light of a proper interpretation of the Free Exercise Clause. . . .

■ II

I shall not restate what has been said in other opinions, which have demonstrated that *Smith* is gravely at odds with our earlier free exercise precedents. See *Church of Lukumi Babalu Aye, Inc. v. Hialeah*, 508 U.S. 520 (1993) (SOUTER, J., concurring); *Smith* (O'CONNOR, J., concurring). Rather, I examine here the early American tradition of religious free exercise to gain insight into the original understanding of the Free Exercise Clause—an inquiry the Court in *Smith* did not undertake. We have previously recognized the importance of interpreting the Religion Clauses in light of their history.

The historical evidence casts doubt on the Court's current interpretation of the Free Exercise Clause. The record instead reveals that its drafters and ratifiers more likely viewed the Free Exercise Clause as a guarantee that government may not unnecessarily hinder believers from freely practicing their religion, a position consistent with our pre-*Smith* jurisprudence. . . .

The practice of the colonies and early States bears out the conclusion that, at the time the Bill of Rights was ratified, it was accepted that government should, when possible, accommodate religious practice. . . . Nevertheless, tension between religious conscience and generally applicable laws, though rare, was not unknown in pre-Constitutional America. Most commonly, such conflicts arose from oath requirements, military conscription, and religious assessments. The ways in which these conflicts were resolved suggest that Americans in the colonies and early States thought that, if an individual's religious scruples prevented him from complying with a generally applicable law, the government should, if possible, excuse the person from the law's coverage. For example, Quakers and certain other Protestant sects refused on Biblical grounds to subscribe to oaths or "swear" allegiance to civil authority. Without accommodation, their beliefs would have prevented them from participating in civic activities involving oaths, including testifying in court. Colonial governments created alternatives to the oath requirement for these individuals. In early decisions, for example, the Carolina proprietors applied the religious liberty provision of the Carolina Charter of 1665 to permit Quakers to enter pledges in a book. Similarly, in 1691, New York enacted a law allowing Quakers to testify by affirmation, and in 1734, it permitted Quakers to qualify to vote by affirmation. By 1789, virtually all of the States had enacted oath exemptions. . . .

■ III

The Religion Clauses of the Constitution represent a profound commitment to religious liberty. Our Nation's Founders conceived of a Republic receptive to voluntary religious expression, not of a secular society in which religious expression is tolerated only when it does not conflict with a generally applicable law. As the historical sources discussed above show, the Free Exercise Clause is properly understood as an affirmative guarantee of the right to participate in religious activities without impermissible governmental interference, even where a believer's conduct is in tension with a law of general application. Certainly, it is in no way anomalous to accord heightened protection to a right identified in the text of the First Amendment. . . .

Accordingly, I believe that it is essential for the Court to reconsider its holding in *Smith*—and to do so in this very case. I would therefore direct the parties to brief this issue and set the case for reargument.

Locke v. Davey

124 S.Ct. 1307 (2004)

Washington created a Promise Scholarship Program to assist academically gifted students, from low-income families, with postsecondary education expenses of up to $1,125 per year. In accord with the state constitution, students could not use such a scholarship to pursue a degree in theology. Article I, Section 11 of the state constitution goes beyond the First Amendment in providing that "No public money or property shall be appropriated for or applied to any religious worship, exercise or instruction, or the support of any religious establishment."

Joshua Davey was awarded a Promise Scholarship and chose to attend Northwest College, a church-affiliated institution, in order to pursue a double major in pastoral ministries and business administration. But he was told that he could not use his scholarship to pursue a pastoral degree, and he sued Governor Gary Locke and other state officials. Davey argued that the denial of the scholarship violated the First Amendment's Free Exercise. A federal district court rejected Davey's claims, but the Court of Appeals for the Ninth Circuit reversed, concluding that the state had singled out religion for unfavorable treatment and its exclusion of theology majors ran afoul of the ruling in *Church of Lukumi Babalu Aye, Inc. v. Hialeah*, 508 U. S. 520 (1993) (excerpted in this chapter), as well as declared the program unconstitutional. Locke appealed that decision to the Supreme Court.

The appellate court's decision was reversed by a seven-to-two vote. Chief Justice Rehnquist delivered the opinion for the Court. Justices Scalia and Thomas each delivered dissenting opinions.

☐ *CHIEF JUSTICE REHNQUIST delivered the opinion of the Court.*

The Religion Clauses of the First Amendment . . . are frequently in tension. Yet we have long said that "there is room for play in the joints" between them. *Walz v. Tax Comm'n of City of New York*, 397 U. S. 664 (1970). In other words, there are some state actions permitted by the Establishment Clause but not required by the Free Exercise Clause.

This case involves that "play in the joints" described above. Under our Establishment Clause precedent, the link between government funds and religious training is broken by the independent and private choice of recipients. See *Zelman v. Simmons-Harris*, 536 U. S. 639 (2002); *Zobrest v. Catalina Foothills School Dist.*, 509 U. S. 1 (1993); *Witters v. Washington Dept. of Servs. for Blind*, 474 U. S. 481 (1986); *Mueller v. Allen*, 463 U. S. 388 (1983). As such, there is no doubt that the State could, consistent with the Federal Constitution, permit Promise Scholars to pursue a degree in devotional theology, *Witters*, and the State does not contend otherwise. The question before us, however, is whether Washington, pursuant to its own constitution, which has been authoritatively interpreted as prohibiting even indirectly funding religious instruction that will prepare students for the ministry, see *Witters v. State Comm'n for the Blind*, 112 Wash. 2d 363 (1989), can deny them such funding without violation the Free Exercise Clause.

Davey urges us to answer that question in the negative. He contends that under the rule we enunciated in *Church of Lukumi Babalu Aye, Inc. v. Hialeah* the program is presumptively unconstitutional because it is not facially neutral with respect to religion. We reject his claim of presumptive unconstitutionality, however; to do otherwise would extend the *Lukumi* line of cases well beyond not only their facts but their reasoning. In *Lukumi*, the city of Hialeah made it a crime to engage in certain kinds of animal slaughter. . . . In the present case, the State's disfavor of religion (if it can be called that) is of a far milder kind. It imposes neither criminal nor civil sanctions on any type of religious service or rite. And it does not require students to choose between their religious beliefs and receiving a government benefit. *Sherbert v. Verner*, 374 U.S. 398 (1963). The State has merely chosen not to fund a distinct category of instruction. . . .

Even though the differently worded Washington Constitution draws a more stringent line than that drawn by the United States Constitution, the interest it seeks to further is scarcely novel. . . . Most States that sought to avoid an establishment of religion around the time of the founding placed in their constitutions formal prohibitions against using tax funds to support the ministry [citing the constitutions of Georgia, Pennsylvania, Delaware, Kentucky, Vermont, Tennessee, and Ohio]. The plain text of these constitutional provisions prohibited any tax dollars from supporting the clergy. We have found nothing to indicate, as Justice SCALIA contends, that these provisions would not have applied so long as the State equally supported other professions or if the amount at stake was *de minimis*. That early state constitutions saw no problem in explicitly excluding only the ministry from receiving state dollars reinforces our conclusion that religious instruction is of a different ilk.

Far from evincing the hostility toward religion which was manifest in *Lukumi*, we believe that the entirety of the Promise Scholarship Program goes a long way toward including religion in its benefits. The program permits students to attend pervasively religious schools, so long as they are accredited. As Northwest advertises, its "concept of education is distinctly Christian in the evangelical sense." . . .

In short, we find neither in the history or text of Article I, Sec. 11 of the Washington Constitution, nor in the operation of the Promise Scholarship Program, anything that suggests animus towards religion. Given the historic and substantial state interest at issue, we therefore cannot conclude that the denial of funding for vocational religious instruction alone is inherently constitutionally suspect. . . .

The judgment of the Court of Appeals is therefore reversed.

☐ *Justice SCALIA, with whom Justice THOMAS joins, dissenting.*

In *Church of Lukumi Babalu Aye, Inc. v. Hialeah*, 508 U.S. 520 (1993), the majority opinion held that "[a] law burdening religious practice that is not neutral . . . must undergo the most rigorous of scrutiny," and that "the minimum requirement of neutrality is that a law not discriminate on its face." [That decision is] irreconcilable with today's decision, which sustains a public benefits program that facially discriminates against religion.

We articulated the principle that governs this case more than 50 years ago in *Everson v. Board of Ed. of Ewing*, 330 U.S. 1 (1947). . . . When the State makes a public benefit generally available, that benefit becomes part of the baseline against which burdens on religion are measured; and when the State withholds that benefit from some individuals solely on the basis of religion, it violates the Free Exercise Clause no less than if it had imposed a special tax.

That is precisely what the State of Washington has done here. It has created a generally available public benefit, whose receipt is conditioned only on academic performance, income, and attendance at an accredited school. It has then carved out a solitary course of study for exclusion: theology. No field of study but religion is singled out for disfavor in this fashion. Davey . . . seeks only equal treatment—the right to direct his scholarship to his chosen course of study, a right every other Promise Scholar enjoys.

The Court's reference to historical "popular uprisings against procuring taxpayer funds to support church leaders" is therefore quite misplaced. That history involved not the inclusion of religious ministers in public benefits programs like the one at issue here, but laws that singled them out for financial aid. One can concede the Framers' hostility to funding the clergy specifically, but that says nothing about whether the clergy had to be excluded from benefits the State made available to all. No one would seriously contend, for example, that the Framers would have barred ministers from using public roads on their way to church.

The Court does not dispute that the Free Exercise Clause places some constraints on public benefits programs, but finds none here, based on a principle of " 'play in the joints.' " I use the term "principle" loosely, for that is not so much a legal principle as a refusal to apply any principle when faced with competing constitutional directives. There is nothing anomalous about constitutional commands that abut. A municipality hiring public contractors may not discriminate against blacks or in favor of them; it cannot discriminate a little bit each way and then plead "play in the joints" when haled into court. If the Religion Clauses demand neutrality, we must enforce them, in hard cases as well as easy ones. . . .

In any case, the State already has all the play in the joints it needs. There are any number of ways it could respect both its unusually sensitive concern for the conscience of its taxpayers and the Federal Free Exercise Clause. It could make the scholarships redeemable only at public universities (where it sets the curriculum), or only for select courses of study. Either option would replace a program that facially discriminates against religion with one that just happens not to subsidize it. The State could also simply abandon the scholarship program altogether. If that seems a dear price to pay for freedom of conscience, it is only because the State has defined that freedom so broadly that it would be offended by a program with such an incidental, indirect religious effect.

What is the nature of the State's asserted interest here? [T]he interest to which the Court defers is not fear of a conceivable Establishment Clause violation, budget constraints, avoidance of endorsement, or substantive neutrality—none of these. It is a pure philosophical preference: the State's opinion that it would violate taxpayers' freedom of conscience not to discriminate against candidates for the ministry. This sort of protection of "freedom of conscience" has no logical limit and can justify the singling out of religion for exclusion from public programs in virtually any context. . . .

The Court has not approached other forms of discrimination this way. When we declared racial segregation unconstitutional, we did not ask whether the State had originally adopted the regime, not out of "animus" against blacks, but because of a well-meaning but misguided belief that the races would be better off apart. It was sufficient to note the current effect of segregation on racial minorities. Similarly, the Court does not excuse statutes that facially discriminate against women just because they are the vestigial product of a well-intentioned view of women's appropriate social role. . . .

It may be that Washington's original purpose in excluding the clergy from public benefits was benign, [b]ut those singled out for disfavor can be forgiven for suspecting more invidious forces at work. Let there be no doubt: This case is about discrimination against a religious minority. Most citizens of this country identify themselves as professing some religious belief, but the State's policy poses no obstacle to practitioners of only a tepid, civic version of faith. Those the statutory exclusion actually affects—those whose belief in their religion is so strong that they dedicate their study and their lives to its ministry—are a far narrower set. One need not delve too far into modern popular culture to perceive a trendy disdain for deep religious conviction. In an era when the Court is so quick to come to the aid of other disfavored groups, see, *Romer v. Evans*, 517 U. S. 620 (1996), its indifference in this case, which involves a form of discrimination to which the Constitution actually speaks, is exceptional. . . . I respectfully dissent.

■ IN COMPARATIVE PERSPECTIVE

The Self-Defense Forces Enshrinement Case, *the Supreme Court of Japan, and Religious Minorities*

Before the end of World War II, the Japanese government established State Shinto based on the worship of the Emperor as a living *kami* (god or deity) and the glorification of soldiers who died fighting in wars as "country-protecting deities." Shinto is the ancient indigenous religion of Japan, centered neither on a founder or a doctrine but instead on rites and rituals revolving around purification and animistic folkways. Following the Meiji Revolution in 1868, Shinto and Buddhist rites and rituals were separated and the great *Yasukuni Jinja* (Shrine) was built in Tokyo to enshrine the souls of soldiers who died in battle and to give legitimacy to the government. As branches of *Yasukuni*, each prefecture was required to have a *Gokoku Jinja* (country-protecting shrine), at which soldiers were enshrined and worshiped. School children were required to worship the Emperor and were taught that dying for the country was the highest honor, rewarded with enshrinement in *Yasukuni*, which now enshrines the souls of over 2.5 million soldiers.

Following the end of World War II, U.S. Occupation Forces disestablished State Shinto and wrote into Japan's 1947 Constitution provisions, modeled after the First Amendment to the U.S. Constitution, for the separation of government from religion and for the free exercise of religion in Article 20.

The separation of government from religion was reinforced by the stipulation in Article 89 that "No public money or other property shall be expended or appropriated for the use, benefit or maintenance of any religious institution or association, . . ." *Yasukuni* and other religious organizations became private institutions, entitled to tax exemptions and freedom from interference by the government.

As Japan's economic prosperity grew and its military—the Land, Air, and Sea Self-Defense Forces (SDF)—expanded in the 1970s and 1980s, conservatives in the Liberal Democratic Party and the SDF pushed to renew some of the symbols and institutions of prewar State Shinto. In particular, SDF leaders began encouraging the enshrinement of soldiers who died after the war, during peacetime, in order to build public support for military expansion. Many survivors of the war strongly objected and argued that the government was running afoul of the Constitution. The controversy intensified when the SDF participated in the enshrinement of the soul of the husband of a Christian woman, Mrs. Yasuko Nakaya, who in turn sued the government. The Supreme Court's controversial ruling in the so-called *Self-Defense Forces Enshrinement* case, *Japan v. Nakaya*, 12 Minshu 277 (S.Ct., Grand Bench, June 1, 1988), remains a watershed decision that illustrates both the more communitarian approach to religious freedom taken by the Japanese judiciary and the subtleties of constitutional interpretation in Japan.

When the *Gokoku* Shrine in Yamaguchi prefecture notified Mrs. Nakaya that her husband's soul would be enshrined, along with several other SDF soldiers, she became deeply depressed. She had refused several times to give her permission for the enshrinement. In her view, the unauthorized enshrining of his soul was a sacrilege, a blasphemy of her Christian beliefs. Besides claiming that the government had impermissibly become involved in a religious activity, Mrs. Nakaya's attorneys argued that she had a right to freedom of religious beliefs under Article 20.

On March 22, 1979, the Yamaguchi District Court ruled in favor of Mrs. Nakaya, though it declined to issue an order rescinding the enshrinement. On an appeal, the Hiroshima High Court reaffirmed the district court's holding on Mrs. Nakaya's claim against the state. And the government promptly appealed to the highest court in the land. Almost five years passed before Mrs. Nakaya's attorneys learned that the government's appeal was granted. Subsequently, on June 1, 1988, the Supreme Court's Grand Bench handed down its ruling. By a vote of fourteen-to-one the justices rejected all of Mrs. Nakaya's claims and overruled the lower courts' decisions.

Contrary to the two lower courts' finding that the SDF had supported a particular religion when assisting the SDF Friendship Association in its application for a joint enshrinement, Chief Justice Koichi Yaguchi held that the application was made solely in the name of the association and mainly due to its efforts. The critical factual link between the SDF and the association was severed. Aware of his distortion of the record, Chief Justice Yaguchi stressed that no SDF officer had directly contacted Yamaguchi's *Gokoku* Shrine. Whatever assistance the officers had given to the association was dismissed as merely administrative. As to whether the SDF's cooperation with the SDF Friendship Association formed a constitutionally prohibited religious activity, Chief Justice Yaguchi said that the Court had to weigh a number of factors. It had to "judge objectively the place where the said activity is done, public religious appreciation, the intent and aim of those who act, the existence or nonexistence and the extent of their religious consciousness, and the effect and influence which the activity has on the public." The decision to perform the enshrinement, according to the chief justice, had been solely that of the Shrine's priests. In that light, the enshrinement application was of secondary importance, not a necessary prerequisite. The enshrinement application was thus said to have little legal significance. Moreover, the chief justice asserted that the SDF's collaboration with the SDF Friendship Association did not constitute engaging in a religious activity. Falling back on the purpose and effect test laid down in the *Tsu City Ground-Purification Ceremony, Kakunaga v. Sekiguchi*, 31 Minshu 533 (S.Ct., G.B., July 13, 1977), which drew on the test set forth by the U.S. Supreme Court in *Lemon v. Kurtzman*, 403 U.S. 602 (1971), he ruled that the SDF had not transcended the "proper limits" of entanglement of the state and religion. The SDF's actions were accordingly deemed to have been "indirectly related to religion. Its intent and aim were supposed to raise the social status and morale of the SDF members." The SDF's activities, he concluded, were therefore not unconstitutional.

The lower courts' recognition of Mrs. Nakaya's free exercise claim was also rejected out-of-hand. Moreover, the Supreme Court's majority held that the Shrine's enshrinement of Takafumi Nakaya was protected by the very guarantee for religious freedom in Article 20 that Mrs. Nakaya had claimed. Besides turning that issue around, Chief Justice Yaguchi emphasized the importance of "a mutually generous attitude" on the part of all religious believers. He also stressed that Mrs. Nakaya had not been personally compelled or coerced into doing anything. She remained free to mourn her late husband according to her Christian beliefs, but she also needed to be tolerant of others' religious beliefs.

The *SDF Enshrinement* case was a "hard case." One measure of how hard the case was for the Grand Bench is the extraordinary number of concurring opinions. Separate opinions are rarely filed by justices of the Supreme Court of Japan. Besides the opinion delivered by the chief justice, four separate concurring opinions were signed or joined by seven justices, along with a solo dissent. The separate concurring opinions were more critical of the SDF, even though joining the Court's ruling. In his concurrence Justice Atsushi Nagashima emphasized that religious adherents need to be tolerant of each other, but then proceeded to criticize the SDF for its actions. Still sharper criticism came in an opinion filed by Justices Masuo Takashima, Iwao Yot-suya, and Hisayuki Okuno. The SDF's failure to "exercise self-control" was, again, criticized. In particular, they took issue with the SDF officers' saying that *Yasukuni* and *Gokoku* Shrines were an "official religion." Yet, these justices did not go as far as two other concurring justices, Rokuro Shimatani and Tetsuro Sato. In their view and that of dissenting Justice Itoh, the SDF had unconstitutionally engaged in a religious activity. However, unlike Justice Itoh, they rejected Mrs. Nakaya's claims to a substantive right of religious liberty. Justices Shimatani and Sato, therefore, concluded that, in spite of the SDF's having engaged in activities that violated the Constitution, the SDF had not interfered with any legally recognizable interest on Mrs. Nakaya's part.

The final concurrence was issued by Justice Toshio Sakaue. He, too, thought that the SDF should have exercised more self-control and that the enshrinement violated Mrs. Nakaya's religious interest. However, the bottom line for Justice Sakaue was that he saw no reason that her feelings and claim to religious liberty should have priority over Takafumi's father and others in the SDF Friendship Association. Hence, he concurred in the judgment, though not the reasoning, of the Court.

Dissenting Justice Masami Itoh was the sole member of the Court to agree with all of Mrs. Nakaya's claims. As the lower courts had concluded, Justice Itoh found the actions of Yamaguchi's SDF branch to have gone beyond "simple practical cooperation" and to have run afoul of the Constitution's separation of religion and the state.

The ruling in the *SDF Enshrinement* case provoked an immediate outcry from Christian groups and liberals. Largely missed in press reports and scholarly criticisms, however, was the fact that a majority of the Supreme Court's fifteen justices had rather sharply and uncharacteristically criticized the SDF for its lack of self-control and involvement with the enshrinement of SDF servicemen. Besides dissenting Justice Itoh, concurring Justices Shimatani and Sato had found the SDF's cooperation with the SDF Friendship Association to have been unconstitutional. When those three justices are added to the five other justices signing concurring opinions also critical of the SDF, a total of eight justices—a bare majority of the Court—had censored the SDF. In sum, the SDF's enshrinements had become too controversial. A majority of the highest court in the land disapproved. That was the crucial message of the *SDF Enshrinement* case. And it hit home in the headquarters of the SDF. Following the decision, branches of the SDF did not again engage in the enshrinement of deceased SDF servicemen.

Subsequently, in the related controversy over governmental financial contributions to *Yasukuni* and *Gokoku* shrines, the Supreme Court of Japan held that those contributions by public officials violate Articles 20 and 89 of the postwar Constitution. Whereas only a bare majority in the 1988 *SDF Enshrinement* case rebuffed governmental support for the institutions of pre-war State Shinto, in 1997 a 13-to-2 majority of the Grand Bench rebuked the government's actions and reaffirmed the Constitution's separation of religion from the state in *Anzai v. Shiraishi, Governor of Ehime Prefecture*, 1601 Hanrei jiho 47 (S.Ct., Grand Bench, April 2, 1997). In 2004, the Fukuoka District Court, likewise, ruled that Prime Minister Junichiro Koizumi's 2001 visit to the *Yasukuni* shrine was unconstitutional.

Excerpted from David M. O'Brien with Yasuo Ohkoshi, *To Dream of Dreams: Religious Freedom and Constitutional Politics in Post-War Japan* (Honolulu: University of Hawaii Press, 1996). For further readings see Hiroshi Oda, *Japanese Law* (New York: Oxford University Press, 1999).

7

The Fourth Amendment Guarantee against Unreasonable Searches and Seizures

The fourth amendment guarantees individuals the freedom from unreasonable searches and seizures in providing that "[t]he right of the people to be secure in their persons, houses, papers, and effects, against unreasonable searches and seizures, shall not be violated, and no Warrants shall issue, but upon probable cause, supported by Oath or affirmation, and particularly describing the place to be searched, and the persons or things to be seized." Although the most detailed guarantee in the Bill of Rights, its key elements are not self-explanatory. The Supreme Court, moreover, has often been divided over whether the unreasonable searches and seizures clause is an independent standard, or whether it stands in conjunction with the second, warrant clause, allowing searches and seizures on (1) the issuance of a warrant by a judge or magistrate, (2) based on police showing "probable cause" for an arrest or for a search and seizure, and (3) "particularly describing the place to be searched," and the specific "persons or things to be seized."

The central purpose of the amendment was to deny the government the power to make general searches. The English Parliament permitted "writs of assistance" or general searches in granting police, and even innkeepers in port towns, the authority to search and seize luggage for illegally imported monies and other goods. General warrants were also used against political and religious dissidents. In 1662, Parliament codified writs of assistance, allowing royalist judges to authorize police and customs inspectors to make general searches of all houses for contraband and other illegal items.

By the 1760s, there was strong resistance in the colonies to writs of assistance and general searches. In a famous Massachusetts case, *Paxton's Case*, Quincy's *Mass. Rpts.* 51 (1761), when unsuccessfully arguing that writs of assistance were contrary to the Magna Carta of 1215 (the first great English charter expressing the ideas of the supremacy of law and that there are fundamental rights that the state may not deny), James Otis invoked the principle that "[a] man's house is his castle; and while he is quiet, he is well guarded as a prince in castle." That view was even more eloquently expressed by William Pitt, the Elder, who explained, "The Poorest man may in his cottage bid defiance to all the force of the Crown. It may be frail—its roof may shake—the wind may blow through it—the storm may enter—the rain may enter—but the King of England cannot enter—all his force dares not cross the threshold of the ruined tenement."[1]

The outcry of colonists against the Crown's use of general searches led to states sharply limiting searches and seizures in their constitutions. General warrants were denounced as "grievous and oppressive" in Virginia's Declaration of Rights in 1776. Later at that state's convention on ratifying the Constitution, Patrick Henry pressed for the adoption of a bill of rights and argued that

> [t]he officer of Congress may come upon you now, fortified with all the terrors of paramount federal authority. Excisemen may come in multitudes; for the limitations of their numbers no man knows. They may, unless the general government be restrained by a bill of rights, or some similar restrictions, go into your cellars and rooms, and search, ransack, and measure, everything you eat, drink, and wear. They ought to be restrained within proper bounds.

Subsequently, in the First Congress, James Madison introduced the initial proposal for limiting searches and seizures by the government. It read, "The right of the people to be secured in their persons, houses, papers, and effects, shall not be violated by warrants issuing without probable cause, supported by an oath or affirmation, and not particularly describing the place to be searched or the persons or things to be seized."[2] At Elbridge Gerry's suggestion, the word *secured* was changed to *secure* and the clause "against unreasonable searches and seizures" was inserted; another stylistic change rendered "by warrants issuing" to "and no warrants shall issue." No further changes were made, and after the adoption and ratification of the Bill of Rights, Madison's revised proposal became the Fourth Amendment.

Despite the aim of foreclosing the possibility of general searches, the strictures of the amendment have an open texture and inescapable ambiguity. What constitutes, for example, "probable cause" for issuing a warrant? Is a warrantless search or seizure automatically "unreasonable" if not supported by probable cause? Does every arrest or search require prior judicial approval? How is the right against unreasonable searches and seizures to be enforced? Must illegally obtained evidence by police be excluded from use at trial? And does the amendment only restrict the police? What about other law-enforcement and administrative officials? These and other questions arise in interpreting the Fourth Amendment and led the Supreme Court to develop a complex set of sometimes cross-cutting and confusing rulings. Together, those rulings enforcing the key elements of the amendment and allowing for exceptions to the warrant requirement define the boundaries between reasonable and unreasonable searches and seizures.

NOTES

1. Quoted in *Frank v. Maryland*, 359 U.S. 360, 378 (1959), by Justice Douglas in a dissenting opinion.

2. Quoted in Jonathan Elliot, ed., *The Debates in the Several Conventions on the Adoption of the Federal Constitution*, Vol. 3 (New York: Burt Franklin Reprints, 1974), 448–449.

SELECTED BIBLIOGRAPHY

Allen, Francis. *The Habits of Legality: Criminal Justice and the Rule of Law.* New York: Oxford University Press, 1996.

Amar, Akhil Reed. *The Constitution and Criminal Procedure.* New Haven, CT: Yale University Press, 1997.

Cole, David. *No Equal Justice: Race and Class in the American Criminal Justice System.* New York: New Press, 1999.

Dash Samuel. *The Intruders: Unreasonable Searches and Seizures from King John to John Ashcroft.* Piscataway, NJ: Rutgers University Press, 2004.

Diffie, Whitfield, and Landau, Susan. *Privacy on Line: The Politics of Wiretapping and Encryption.* Boston: MIT Press, 1998.

Flaherty, David. *Privacy in Colonial New England.* Charlottesville: University Press of Virginia, 1974.

Gilliom, John. *Surveillance, Privacy, and the Law: Employee Drug Testing and the Politics of Social Control.* Ann Arbor: University of Michigan Press, 1994.

Heuman, Milton, and Cassak, Lance. *Good Cop, Bad Cop: Racial Profiling and Competing Views of Justice.* New York: Peter Lang, 2003.

Kennedy, Randall. *Race, Crime, and the Law.* New York: Pantheon, 1997.

Landynski, Jacob W. *Search and Seizure and the Supreme Court.* Baltimore, MD: Johns Hopkins University Press, 1966.

Lasson, Nelson B. *The History and Development of the Fourth Amendment to the United States Constitution.* Baltimore, MD: Johns Hopkins University Press, 1937.

Levy, Leonard W. *Against the Law: The Nixon Court and Criminal Justice.* New York: Harper & Row, 1974.

Rosen, Jeffrey. *The Naked Crowd: Redefining Security and Freedom in an Anxious Age.* New York: Random House, 2004.

Schaver, Frederick. *Profiles, Probabilities, and Stereotypes.* Cambridge, MA: Belknap Press, 2003.

Shapiro, B. J. *"Beyond Reasonable Doubt" and "Probable Cause": Historical Perspectives on the Anglo-American Law of Evidence.* Berkeley: University of California Press, 1991.

A | *Requirements for a Warrant and Reasonable Searches and Seizures*

As a general rule (subject to the exceptions discussed in section B, in this chapter), police must obtain search and arrest warrants from a "neutral and detached magistrate." The Court made this requirement applicable to the states in *Wolf v. Colorado*, 338 U.S. 25 (1949). In *Coolidge v. New Hampshire*, 403 U.S. 443 (1971), the Court underscored the importance of judicial approval of warrants when holding invalid a warrant issued by an attorney general;[1] and in *Connelly v. Georgia*, 429 U.S. 245 (1977), declined to permit a justice of the peace to issue warrants when his salary was paid in part by warrant fees.

When obtaining warrants, police must demonstrate probable cause that a person has committed a crime if they are to obtain an arrest warrant, and show probable cause to believe that contraband or the instrumentalities of crime will be found in a particular place when they are seeking a search warrant. Although the Fourth Amendment does not specify the basis for warrantless searches and seizures by police, they too must be based on probable cause.[2] Regardless of whether police seek an arrest or a search warrant, they must supply the same quantum of evidence when establishing probable cause.[3] Probable cause for making an arrest turns on "whether at that moment [of arrest] the facts and circumstances within [the officers'] knowledge and of which they [have] reasonably trustworthy information [are] sufficient to warrant a prudent man in believing that the [suspect] had committed or was committing an offense."[4] And the test is objective in the sense that a judge (or "reasonable" person) would agree that enough evidence exists to support a police officer's determination; in other words, the subjective judgment of an officer alone does not support a finding of probable cause.

In determining whether probable cause has been reasonably established, judges consider the *specificity* of what is to be searched and the *particularity* of what is to be seized. The Court reaffirmed that core principle in *Groh v. Ramirez*, 124 S.Ct. 1284 (2004), in holding that a search warrant that failed to identify the items to be seized, and only described the defendant's house as the place to be searched, violated the Fourth Amendment. Because police often rely on informants, the Court also demands that police show that their information is *reliable*, not vague, and sufficient for judges to draw their own conclusions about.[5] Hearsay evidence may be used,[6] yet police must attest to the reliability of informants, although they need not demonstrate their credibility.[7]

The Warren Court established a two-prong test for determining probable cause when holding that police failed to establish this in an affidavit for a warrant that simply claimed "reliable information from a credible person" indicated "narcotics and narcotics paraphernalia" were kept at certain location. In that case, *Aguilar v. Texas*, 378 U.S. 108 (1964), the Court held that police must explain (1) how it is that an informant knows what he claims to know and (2) why they believe the information to be accurate and reliable. The more conservative Burger and Rehnquist Courts, however, abandoned that test. *Illinois v. Gates*, 462 U.S. 213 (1983), held that the *Aguilar* factors—showing the basis and veracity of informers' tips—were "relevant considerations" but no longer independent requirements. "[A] deficiency in one may be compensated for," Rehnquist held, "by a strong showing as to the other." In *Gates* and *Massachusetts v. Upton*, 466 U.S. 727 (1984), the Court ruled that judges may determine whether "the totality of the circumstances" presented by police justifies a finding of probable cause.[8]

Although search warrants authorize police to search only particular locations and to seize specific items, police had long been allowed to conduct searches when making arrests, with or without arrest warrants. Until the Warren Court era, moreover, police were permitted to undertake rather sweeping searches when armed with only an arrest warrant. *Harris v. United States*, 331 U.S. 145 (1947), for instance, allowed the search of a four-room apartment based only on an arrest warrant for the occupant. The Warren Court, however, signaled a change in *Chapman v. United States*, 365 U.S. 610 (1961), when disapproving of a warrantless search of a rented house, which police entered through an unlocked window with the owner's (but not the renter's) consent. There, Justice Charles Whittaker observed that

> [n]o reason is offered for not obtaining a search warrant except the inconvenience of the officers and some slight delay necessary to

prepare papers and present the evidence to a magistrate. These are never very convincing reasons and, in these circumstances, certainly are not enough to by-pass the constitutional requirement. No suspect was fleeing or likely to take flight. The search was of a permanent premises, not of a movable vehicle. No evidence or contraband was threatened with removal or destruction.

Harris was finally expressly overruled in *Chimel v. California* (1969) (see excerpt below).

Chimel's ruling that police, armed with only an arrest warrant or when they have probable cause to make an arrest, are constrained in searching only what is in "plain view" and in "the immediate area" surrounding an arrestee has been repeatedly reaffirmed. But the Court's rulings usually turn on the particular circumstances of each case.[9]

As *Arizona v. Hicks* (1987) (excerpted below), indicates, the Court, although occasionally sharply split, continues to draw a line limiting the scope of warrantless searches made in connection with arrests. In *Yabarra v. Illinois*, 444 U.S. 85 (1979), the Court also held that a warrant authorizing police to search a small tavern and the bartender for narcotics did not justify a pat-down search of patrons of the bar. In *Payton v. New York*, 445 U.S. 573 (1980), the justices struck down a state statute authorizing police to enter private residences without a warrant to make routine felony arrests. In *Steagald v. United States*, 451 U.S. 204 (1981), the Court held that police needed a search warrant to enter the home of a third party when attempting to arrest a person for whom they had a valid arrest warrant. And in *Welsh v. Wisconsin*, 466 U.S. 470 (1984), the Court rejected a warrantless nighttime entry into a house by police to arrest an individual for driving under the influence of alcohol. But in *Horton v. California*, 496 U.S. 128 (1990), the Court ruled that a warrantless search and seizure was permissible under the plain view doctrine, because the defendant's criminal conduct was immediately apparent to police officers. Justices Brennan and Marshall dissented.

In *Maryland v. Buie*, 494 U.S. 325 (1990), the Court gave police authority to make "protective sweeps" of the premises when arresting a person in his home if they reasonably believe (although do not have probable cause to believe) that the area may harbor another individual who poses a danger to them. Here, police had arrest warrants for Jerome Buie and a suspected accomplice in the robbery of a Godfather's Pizza restaurant by two men, one of whom wore a red running suit. They had a secretary call his home to see if he was there before they arrived. When the police arrived at Buie's house, they quickly entered and fanned out through the first and second floors. Failing to find Buie, the police shouted down to the basement and ordered anyone there to come out. Buie soon appeared. And an officer then went down into the basement to see if "there was someone else" there, whereupon he discovered a red running suit. At his trial, Buie's attorney argued that the running suit had been seized pursuant to an illegal search and should be excluded as evidence. The trial court and state appellate court disagreed. On appeal to the Supreme Court, writing for the majority, Justice White upheld such protective searches, observing,

> To reach our conclusion today, . . . we need not disagree with the Court's statement in *Chimel* that "the invasion of privacy that results from a top-to-bottom search of a man's house [cannot be characterized] as 'minor,'" . . . The type of search we authorize today is far removed from the "top-to-bottom" search involved in *Chimel*; moreover, it is decidedly not "automati[c]" but may be conducted only when justified by a reasonable, articulable suspicion that the house is harboring a person posing a danger to those on the arrest scene.

But dissenting Justice Brennan, joined by Justice Marshall, countered that the Court had extended the holding in *Terry v. Ohio* (1968) (excerpted below) "into the home, dispensing with the Fourth Amendment's general requirements of a warrant and probable cause and carving a 'reasonable suspicion' exception for protective sweeps in private dwellings."

When executing an arrest warrant on private property, however, police may not invite members of the media to come along and film or photograph the arrest. The Court drew the line on that practice in recognition of homeowners' Fourth Amendment protection for privacy interests in *Wilson V. Layne*, 526 U.S. 603 (1999).

The obligation of police to obtain a search warrant (if circumstances permit and when a search is not incident to an arrest) holds. But the more conservative Burger and Rehnquist Courts have tended to be less tough on law enforcement interests (as further discussed in the next section). The Warren Court held in *Jones v. United States*, 382 U.S. 36 (1960), for instance, that to search the house of a man arrested two blocks away was not permissible as a search incident to arrest. In *Hill v. California*, 40 U.S. 797 (1974), the Burger Court held that the arrest of the wrong man permitted a search of the immediate area surrounding him as a search incident to his arrest. In *Mincey v. Arizona*, 437 U.S. 385 (1978), the Court disallowed a warrantless search of the murder scene in an accused's apartment four days after his arrest. That decision was unanimously reaffirmed in *Flippo v. West Virginia*, 528 U.S. 11 (1999), again rejecting a "murder crime scene" exception for warrantless searches. But in *United States v. Edwards*, 415 U.S. 800 (1974), a bare majority of the Court allowed the warrantless search of an accused's bodily clothing ten hours after his arrest and substitute clothing had been given to him. The Court also permits warrantless searches of individuals arrested and taken into custody,[10] as well as delayed searches of automobiles that are impounded after the drivers' arrest.[11] In *Soldal v. Cook County*, 506 U.S. 56 (1992), however, the Court upheld the application of the Fourth Amendment to the seizure and removal of a mobile home from a trailer park by the landowner, who removed the mobile home without an eviction order, while police prevented the homeowner from interfering with the eviction. In an appellate court's view, Edward Soldal's home had not been "seized" for the purposes of the Fourth Amendment because the police had not seized his mobile home, and Soldal's privacy interests were not invaded since his home had not been entered and "the privacy of its interior [remained] uncompromised and undisturbed." Unanimously reversing the lower court, the Court rejected such a narrow reading of the amendment's protection for private property. Writing for the Court, Justice White observed that

> [a] "seizure" of property . . . occurs when "there is some meaningful interference with an individual's possessory interests in that property." *United States v. Jacobsen.* 466 U.S. 109 (1984). In addition, we have emphasized that "at the very core" of the Fourth Amendment "stands the right of a man to retreat into his own home." *Silverman v. United States*, 365 U.S. 505 (1961). As a result of the state action in this case, the Soldals' domicile was not only seized, it literally was carried away, giving a new meaning to the term "mobile home." We fail to see how being unceremoniously dispossessed of one's home in the manner alleged to have occurred here can be viewed as anything but a seizure invoking the protection of the Fourth Amendment.

NOTES

1. However, *Shadwick v. City of Tampa*, 407 U.S. 345 (1972), permitted the delegation of responsibility for issuing warrants to municipal county clerks.

2. See *Wong Sun v. United States*, 371 U.S. 471 (1963).

3. See *Spinelli v. United States*, 393 U.S. 410 (1969), and *Draper v. United States*, 358 U.S. 307 (1959).

4. *Beck v. Ohio*, 362 U.S. 309 (1960).

5. *Jones v. United States*, 362 U.S. 725 (1960).

6. See *McCray v. Illinois*, 386 U.S. 300 (1967).

7. See *United States v. Harris*, 403 U.S. 513 (1971), and *Adams v. Williams*, 407 U.S. 143 (1972).

8. At the same time, the Court holds that, notwithstanding its totality of circumstances approach to determining probable cause, the balance between individual rights and law enforcement interests that is struck in determining probable cause is not drawn on a case-by-case basis. See *Dunaway v. New York*, 442 U.S. 200 (1979).

9. See *Ker v. California*, 374 U.S. 23 (1963) (upholding an arrest for possession of marijuana based on police seeing the plants in a kitchen window); *Vale v. Louisiana*, 399 U.S. 30 (1970) (overturning a warrantless search of a house of a man arrested on its entry steps); and *Lo-Ji Sales v. New York*, 442 U.S. 319 (1979) (reaffirming that the Fourth Amendment forbids open-ended searches of a retail store).

10. *Gustafson v. Florida*, 414 U.S. 260 (1973) (allowing full-body search of a man arrested for traffic violation and taken into custody). In *United States v. Montoya de Hernandez*, 473 U.S. 531 (1985), the Court held that it was not unreasonable to detain a suspected smuggler for sixteen hours.

11. See *Chambers v. Maroney*, 399 U.S. 42 (1970) (upholding search of a car taken to the police station by police who had probable cause to stop the car and believed it contained stolen guns and money); and *South Dakota v. Opperman*, 428 U.S. 543 (1976) (upheld a routine inventory search of a locked car that was impounded).

Chimel v. California
395 U.S. 752, 89 S.Ct. 2034 (1969)

Late one afternoon in September 1965, three police officers arrived at Ted Chimel's home in Santa Ana, California. They had a warrant to arrest him for burglary of a coin shop. Chimel was not at home, but his wife allowed the police to wait in the house until he returned from work. When he arrived, police handed him the arrest warrant and asked whether they could look around his house. Chimel objected but was told that "on the basis of a lawful arrest" the police could conduct a search. The police searched the entire three-bedroom house, including the attic, the garage, and a small workshop. They seized numerous coins, medals, and tokens, which were later used as evidence against Chimel at trial. Following his conviction, Chimel unsuccessfully appealed to a state appellate court and the California Supreme Court, contending that the police had unlawfully searched his house. Failing in those efforts, Chimel appealed to the Supreme Court, which granted review.

The Court's decision was seven to two, and the majority's opinion was announced by Justice Stewart. Justice Harlan concurred, and Justice White, joined by Justice Black, dissented.

☐ *Justice STEWART delivered the opinion of the Court.*

This case raises basic questions concerning the permissible scope under the Fourth Amendment of a search incident to a lawful arrest. . . .

In 1950, [the Court handed down] *United States v. Rabinowitz*, 339 U.S. 56 [(1950)], the decision upon which California primarily relies in the case now before us. In *Rabinowitz*, federal authorities had been informed that the defendant was dealing in stamps bearing forged overprints. On the basis of that information they secured a warrant for his arrest, which they executed at his one-room business office. At the time of the arrest, the officers "searched the desk, safe, and file cabinets in the office for about an hour and a half," and seized 573 stamps with forged overprints. The stamps were admitted into evidence at the defendant's trial, and this Court affirmed his conviction, rejecting the contention that the warrantless search had been unlawful. The Court held that the search in its entirety fell within the principle giving law enforcement authorities "[t]he right 'to search the place where the arrest is made in order to find and seize things connected with the crime. . . .' " The test, said the Court, "is not whether it is reasonable to procure a search warrant, but whether the search was reasonable." . . .

Rabinowitz has come to stand for the proposition, *inter alia*, that a warrantless search "incident to a lawful arrest" may generally extend to the area that is considered to be in the "possession" or under the "control" of the person arrested. And it was on the basis of that proposition that the California courts upheld the search of the petitioner's entire house in this case. That doctrine, however, at least in the broad sense in which it was applied by the California courts in this case, can withstand neither historical nor rational analysis.

Even limited to its own facts, the *Rabinowitz* decision was, as we have seen, hardly founded on an unimpeachable line of authority. [Justice STEWART, after reviewing cases following *Rabinowitz*, concluded that the Fourth] Amendment was in large part a reaction to the general warrants and warrantless searches that had so alienated the colonists and had helped speed the movement for independence. In the scheme of the Amendment, therefore, the requirement that "no Warrants shall issue, but upon probable cause," plays a crucial part. . . .

A similar analysis underlies the "search incident to arrest" principle, and marks its proper extent. When an arrest is made, it is reasonable for the arresting officer to search the person arrested in order to remove any weapons that the latter might seek to use in order to resist arrest or effect his escape. Otherwise, the officer's safety might well be endangered, and the arrest itself frustrated. In addition, it is entirely reasonable for the arresting officer to search for and seize any evidence on the arrestee's person in order to prevent its concealment or destruction. And the area into which an arrestee might reach in order to grab a weapon or evidentiary items must, of course, be governed by a like rule. A gun on a table or in a drawer in front of one who is arrested can be as dangerous to the arresting officer as one concealed in the clothing of the person arrested. There is ample justification, therefore, for a search of the arrestee's person and the area "within his immediate control"—construing that phrase to mean the area from within which he might gain possession of a weapon or destructible evidence.

There is no comparable justification, however, for routinely searching any room other than that in which an arrest occurs—or, for that matter, for searching through all the desk drawers or other closed or concealed areas in that room itself. Such searches, in the absence of well-recognized exceptions, may be made only under the authority of a search warrant. The "adherence to judicial processes" mandated by the Fourth Amendment requires no less. . . .

It is argued in the present case that it is "reasonable" to search a man's house when he is arrested in it. But that argument is founded on little more than a subjective view regarding the acceptability of certain sorts of police conduct, and not on considerations relevant to Fourth Amendment interests. Under such an unconfined analysis, Fourth Amendment protection in this area would approach the evaporation point. It is not easy to explain why, for instance, it is less subjectively "reasonable" to search a man's house when he is arrested on his front lawn—or just down the street—than it is when he happens to be in the house at the time of arrest. . . .

The petitioner correctly points out that one result of decisions such as *Rabinowitz* and *Harris* [v. *United States*, 331 U.S. 14 (1947)], is to give law enforcement officials the opportunity to engage in searches not justified by probable cause, by the simple expedient of arranging to arrest suspects at home rather than elsewhere. We do not suggest that the petitioner is necessarily correct in his assertion that such a strategy was utilized here, but the fact remains that had he been arrested earlier in the day, at his place of employment rather than at home, no search of his house could have been made without a search warrant. . . .

Application of sound Fourth Amendment principles to the facts of this case produces a clear result. The search here went far beyond the petitioner's person and the area from within which he might have obtained either a weapon or something that could have been used as evidence against him. There was no constitutional justification, in the absence of a search warrant, for extending the search beyond that area. The scope of the search was, therefore, "unreasonable" under the Fourth and Fourteenth Amendments and the petitioner's conviction cannot stand.

Reversed.

☐ *Justice HARLAN, concurring.*

The only thing that has given me pause in voting to overrule *Harris* and *Rabinowitz* is that as a result of *Mapp v. Ohio*, [367 U.S. 643] (1961), and *Ker v. California*, [372 U.S. 23] (1963), every change in Fourth Amendment law must now be obeyed by state officials facing widely different problems of local law enforcement. We simply do not know the extent to which cities and towns across the Nation are prepared to administer the greatly expanded warrant system which will be required by today's decision; nor can we say with assurance that in each and every local situation, the warrant requirement plays an essential role in the protection of those fundamental liberties protected against state infringement by the Fourteenth Amendment. . . .

This federal-state factor has not been an easy one for me to resolve, but in the last analysis I cannot in good conscience vote to perpetuate bad Fourth Amendment law.

Arizona v. Hicks

480 U.S. 321, 107 S.Ct. 1149 (1987)

Justice Antonin Scalia presents the pertinent facts in his opinion for the Court in this case, involving a police search and the application of the plain view doctrine.

The Court's decision was six to three, and the majority's opinion was announced by Justice Scalia. Justice White concurred, and Justice O'Connor, joined by Chief Justice Rehnquist and Justice Powell, dissented.

☐ *Justice SCALIA delivered the opinion of the Court.*

In *Coolidge v. New Hampshire*, 403 U.S. 43 (1971), we said that in certain circumstances a warrantless seizure by police of an item that comes within plain view during their lawful search of a private area may be reasonable under the Fourth Amendment. . . . We granted *certiorari* . . . in the present case to decide whether this "plain view" doctrine may be invoked when the police have less than probable cause to believe that the item in question is evidence of a crime or is contraband.

On April 18, 1984, a bullet was fired through the floor of respondent's apartment, striking and injuring a man in the apartment below. Police officers arrived and entered respondent's apartment to search for the shooter, for other victims, and for weapons. They found and seized three weapons, including a sawed-off rifle, and in the course of their search also discovered a stocking-cap mask.

One of the policemen, Officer Nelson, noticed two sets of expensive stereo components, which seemed out of place in the squalid and otherwise ill-appointed four-room apartment. Suspecting that they were stolen, he read and recorded their serial numbers—moving some of the components, including a Bang and Olufsen turntable, in order to do so—which he then reported by phone to his headquarters. On being advised that the turntable had been taken in an armed robbery, he seized it immediately. It was later determined that some of the other serial numbers matched those on other stereo equipment taken in the same armed robbery, and a warrant was obtained and executed to seize that equipment as well. Respondent was subsequently indicted for the robbery.

The state trial court granted respondent's motion to suppress the evidence that had been seized. The Court of Appeals of Arizona affirmed. It was conceded that the initial entry and search, although warrantless, were justified by the exigent circumstance of the shooting. The Court of Appeals viewed the obtaining of the serial numbers, however, as an additional search, unrelated to that exigency. . . . Both courts—the trial court explicitly and the Court of Appeals by necessary implication—rejected the State's contention that Officer Nelson's actions were justified under the "plain view" doctrine of *Coolidge v. New Hampshire, supra.* The Arizona Supreme Court denied review, and the State filed this petition.

Officer Nelson's moving of the equipment . . . constitute[d] a "search" separate and apart from the search for the shooter, victims, and weapons that was the lawful objective of his entry into the apartment. Merely inspecting those parts of the turntable that came into view during the latter search would not have constituted an independent search, because it would have produced no additional invasion of respondent's privacy interest. But taking action, unrelated to the objectives of the authorized intrusion, which exposed to view concealed portions of the apartment or its contents, did produce a new invasion of respondent's privacy unjustified by the exigent circumstance that validated the entry. . . . It matters not that the search uncovered nothing of any great personal value to the respondent—serial numbers rather than (what might conceivably have been hidden behind or under the equipment) letters or photographs. A search is a search, even if it happens to disclose nothing but the bottom of a turntable.

The remaining question is whether the search was "reasonable" under the Fourth Amendment.

On this aspect of the case we reject, at the outset, the apparent position of the Arizona Court of Appeals that because the officers' action directed to the stereo equipment was unrelated to the justification for their entry into respondent's apartment, it was *ipso facto* unreasonable. That lack of relationship *always* exists with regard to action validated under the "plain view" doctrine; where action is taken for the purpose of justifying the entry, invocation of the doctrine is superfluous. . . .

We turn, then, to application of the doctrine to the facts of this case. "It is well established that under certain circumstances the police may *seize* evidence in plain view without a warrant," *Coolidge.* Those circumstances include situations "[w]here the initial intrusion that brings the police within plain view of such [evidence] is supported . . . by one of the recognized exceptions to the warrant requirement," such as the exigent-circumstances intrusion here. It would be absurd to say that an object could lawfully be seized and taken from the premises, but could not be moved for closer examination. It is clear, therefore, that the search here was valid if the "plain view" doctrine would have sustained a seizure of the equipment.

There is no doubt it would have done so if Officer Nelson had probable cause to believe that the equipment was stolen. The State has conceded, however, that he had only a "reasonable suspicion," by which it means something less than probable cause. . . .

We now hold that probable cause is required. To say otherwise would be to cut the "plain view" doctrine loose from its theoretical and practical moorings. The theory of that doctrine consists of extending to nonpublic places such as the home, where searches and seizures without a warrant are presumptively unreasonable, the police's longstanding authority to make warrantless seizures in public places of such objects as weapons and contraband. And the practical justification for that extension is the desirability of sparing police, whose viewing of the object in the course of a lawful search is as legitimate as it would have been in a public place, the inconvenience and the risk—to themselves or to preservation of the evidence—of going to obtain a warrant. . . . Dispensing with the need for a warrant is worlds apart from permitting a lesser standard of *cause* for the seizure than a warrant would require, *i.e.*, the standard of probable cause. No reason is apparent why an object should routinely be seizable on lesser grounds, during an unrelated search and seizure, than would have been needed to obtain a warrant for that same object if it had been known to be on the premises.

We do not say, of course, that a seizure can never be justified on less than probable cause. We have held that it can—where, for example, the seizure is minimally intrusive and operational necessities render it the only practicable means of detecting certain types of crime. See, *e.g., United States v. Cortez*, 449 U.S. 411 (1981) (investigative detention of vehicle suspected to be transporting illegal aliens); *United States v. Place*, 462 U.S. 696 [(1983)] (seizure of suspected drug dealer's luggage at airport to permit exposure to specially trained dog). No special operational necessities are relied on here, however—but rather the mere fact that the items in question came lawfully within the officer's plain view. That alone cannot supplant the requirement of probable cause. . . .

Justice O'CONNOR's dissent suggests that we uphold the action here on the ground that it was a "cursory inspection" rather than a "full-blown search," and could therefore be justified by reasonable suspicion instead of probable cause. As already noted, a truly cursory inspection—one that involves merely looking at what is already exposed to view, without disturbing it—is not a "search" for Fourth Amendment purposes, and therefore does not even require reasonable suspicion. We are unwilling to send police and judges into a new thicket of Fourth Amendment law, to seek a creature of uncertain description that is neither a plain-view inspection nor yet a "full-blown search." Nothing in the prior opinions of this Court supports such a distinction. . . .

For the reasons stated, the judgment of the Court of Appeals of Arizona is

Affirmed.

☐ *Justice O'CONNOR, with whom the CHIEF JUSTICE and Justice POWELL join, dissenting.*

The Court today gives the right answer to the wrong question. The Court asks whether the police must have probable cause before either seizing an object in plain view or conducting a full-blown search of that object, and concludes that they must. I agree. In my view, however, this case presents a different question: whether police must have probable cause before conducting a cursory inspection of an item in plain view. Because I conclude that such an inspection is reasonable if the police are aware of facts or circumstances that justify a reasonable suspicion that the item is evidence of a crime, I would reverse the judgment of the Arizona Court of Appeals, and therefore dissent. . . .

B | *Exceptions to the Warrant Requirement*

There are a number of exceptions to the Fourth Amendment's command that police obtain a warrant prior to conducting a search. Besides conducting searches incident to an arrest and after taking a person into custody (as discussed in section A of this chapter), police may undertake *consent searches*—searches of persons and their property after being given their consent. While it seems obvious that individuals may waive their rights, whose and what kind of consent is necessary for a police search has proven problematic.

The Court maintains that police may not conduct a warrantless search of an apartment or hotel room without the occupant's consent and despite having the owner's permission.[1] However, *Illinois v. Rodriguez*, 497 U.S. 177 (1990), held that incriminating evidence may be used at trial even though it was seized during a warrantless entry into a home by police officers who were let in by a person they mistakenly thought was authorized to consent to a search. "What we hold today does not suggest that law enforcement officers may always accept a person's invitation to enter," wrote Justice Scalia, when holding that "consent to enter must be judged against an objective standard: would the facts available to the officer . . . warrant a man of reasonable caution in the belief that the consenting party had authority over the premises?" In addition, in *Minnesota v. Carter* (1998) (excerpted in Section E of this chapter), the Court held that temporary visitors in homes (unlike homeowners, apartment renters, and even overnight guests) have no "reasonable expectations of privacy" and Fourth Amendment protection.

Traditionally, consent searches were justified on the theory that individuals could waive their Fourth Amendment rights. But in *Schneckloth v. Bustamonte*, 412 U.S. 218 (1973), the Burger Court appeared to dismiss that theory in holding that the underlying issue is whether consent may be reasonably deemed to be "voluntary" based on the circumstances surrounding a particular search. There the Court ruled that, when a suspect is not in custody but police make a consent search, the state must show only that the consent was voluntarily given, even though the suspect had no knowledge that he could refuse to agree to the search. The next year, *United States v. Matlock*, 415 U.S. 164 (1974), held that police could search a bedroom inhabited by two persons so long as they obtained the consent of one of the two. When distinguishing earlier rulings denying consent searches based on a landlord's consent, Justice White explained that "it is reasonable to recognize that any of the co-inhabitants has the right to permit the inspection in his own common area to be searched." In *Illinois v. Batchelder*, 463 U.S. 1112 (1983), the Court also upheld implied consent laws requiring drivers to submit to breathalyzer tests or have their licenses automatically revoked.

Notably, when police make a warrantless arrest, *Gerstein v. Pugh*, 420 U.S. 103 (1975), held that authorities must provide their arrestees "promptly" with a fair and reliable determination of the probable cause for their arrest. However, in *County of Riverside v. McLaughlin*, 500 U.S. 44 (1991) (excerpted below), a bare majority of the Rehnquist Court reinterpreted *Gerstein* and held that states may hold individuals who have been arrested without a warrant for up to forty-eight hours without a hearing to determine whether police had probable cause to make an arrest and incarcerate an individual. Notably, in dissent Justice Scalia sharply criticized the majority for its reinterpretation of *Gerstein* and departure from the common law and constitutional jurisprudence underlying the adoption of the Fourth Amendment in 1791. In a separate opinion, Justices Blackmun, Marshall, and Stevens also dissented.

Another exception is the so-called *open fields doctrine*—allowing police to search and seize illegal items that are in open public view—announced in *Hester v. United States*, 265 U.S. 57 (1924). On this doctrine, the Court upheld a warrantless search of land on which marijuana was growing in *Oliver v. United States*, 466 U.S. 170 (1984). Two years later, in *California v. Ciraolo* (1986) (see excerpt below), the justices rejected the Fourth Amendment arguments of Dow Chemical Company, which objected to the Environmental Protection Agency's aerial photography of its site when inspecting for pollution violations in *Dow Chemical Company v. United States*, 476 U.S. 227 (1986). In *United States v. Dunn*, 480 U.S. 294 (1987), the Rehnquist Court further extended the open fields doctrine when permitting a search of a barn in an open field at night by police armed with a flashlight but no warrant. And in *Florida v. Riley*, 488 U.S. 445 (1988), by a five-to-four vote the Court again rejected Fourth Amendment privacy claims when holding that police do not need a search warrant for searches of private property by helicopters flying 400 feet above ground.

More controversial is the exception the Warren Court carved out in *Terry v. Ohio* (1968) (excerpted below), allowing police without either a warrant or probable cause to *stop and frisk* individuals who look suspicious. There the Court explicitly balanced Fourth Amendment interests against those of law enforcement. Notice, though, Chief Justice Warren approved of such searches only to the extent that they were "limited to outer clothing . . . in an attempt to discover weapons which might be used to assault [a police officer]." A companion ruling, *Sibron v. New York*, 392 U.S. 40 (1968), underscored *Terry's* limited holding in refusing to permit the search of a drug suspect who police had no reason to believe was armed or dangerous; as Chief Justice Warren emphasized, "the police officer is not entitled to seize and search every person whom he sees on the street."

The *Terry* exception has been enlarged by the Burger and Rehnquist Courts to allow greater leeway for police to stop and search suspicious individuals. In *Adams v. Williams*, 407 U.S. 590 (1972), the Court permitted the stopping and frisking of an individual by an officer, who had no personal knowledge of him and merely relied on a tip from a known informant that he was carrying narcotics and had a gun. The officer went to a vehicle in which the man was sitting and, as the man rolled down the door window, the officer reached in and grabbed the man's loaded gun. However, in *Florida v. J.L.*, 529 U.S. 266 (2000), the Court held unconstitutional the stopping and frisking of an individual for a gun based on a police officer's receiving an anonymous tip that a young black male wearing a plaid shirt at a bus stop was carrying a gun. Justice Ginsburg ruled that anonymous tips, unless accompanied by other specific indicators of reliability, fall short of providing a basis for reasonable suspicion to justify the stopping and frisking of individuals.

United States v. Sokolow (1989) (excerpted below) nonetheless underscores that the police no longer need have probable cause to stop and frisk suspicious individuals. When upholding law enforcement officers' investigative stop of a suspected drug courier at an airport, Chief Justice Rehnquist ruled that there need be only a "reasonable suspicion" for stopping a suspect—something more than a "hunch" and considerably less than probable cause.[2] The ruling in *Sokolow* permitting "drug courier profiles" has not been followed by some state supreme courts when construing their state constitutions (see THE DEVELOPMENT OF LAW box in Chapter 2), and civil rights groups complained that it encourages racial profiling. In response, in 2003 President George W. Bush issued guidelines governing seventy federal law enforcement agencies that bar the use of race and ethnicity in routine investigations. Under the policy federal agents may not focus, for example, on specific neighborhoods because of their racial composition; however, the policy does not cover state police and permits the use of race and ethnicity to "identify terrorist threats and stop potential catastrophic attacks."

In a series of rulings, the Rehnquist Court has pushed even further a narrow reading of the Fourth Amendment's proscription against "unreasonable searches and seizures." *California v. Hodari D.*, 499 U.S. 621 (1991), for example, posed an inexorable question given the Court's prior rulings on the permissibility of police officers stopping and frisking individuals whom they have probable cause to believe are engaged or a reasonable suspicion that they are engaged in criminal activities. Specifically, here the question presented was whether police made an unlawful "seizure" when they chased a man who ran away at the sight of them, and then recovered abandoned evidence (drugs) which was used at trial. By a seven-to-one vote, however, the Rehnquist Court held that even though police did not have a "reasonable suspicion" for them to question or detain Hodari D. that did not matter.

Writing for the Court in *Hodari D.*, Justice Scalia held that Hodari D. had not been "seized" within the meaning of the Fourth Amendment. In his view, criminal suspects are "seized" for Fourth Amendment purposes only at the point at which officers either use physical force or the suspect complies with their "show of authority." "We do not think it desirable," as he put it, "to stretch the Fourth Amendment beyond its words. . . . Street pursuits always place the public at some risk, and compliance with police orders to stop should therefore be encouraged. . . . Since policemen do not command 'Stop!' expecting to be ignored, or give chase hoping to be outrun, it fully suffices to apply deterrent to their genuine, successful seizures."

In a footnote, Scalia further added that states need not bother to show that police even had a "reasonable suspicion" to justify their pursuit of an individual fleeing from them, since they need not meet that standard within the context of an individual fleeing their presence. "That it would be unreasonable to stop, for brief inquiry, young men who scatter in panic upon the mere sighting of the police is not self-evident, and arguably contradicts proverbial common sense," he noted, quoting the biblical saying, "The wicked flee when no man pursueth."

The facts in *Hodari D.* are important because they are replayed virtually every day in urban areas of the country. Hodari D., a teenager, was standing with several other youths around a car in a high-crime area of Oakland, California. At some point, they spotted an unmarked police car approaching, and they started running away. With the police in chase, Hodari D. tossed away a small rock of crack cocaine, which the police subsequently recovered. Seconds later Hodari was tackled to the ground by a police officer; he was found to be also carrying a pager and $130 in cash. At a preliminary hearing, Hodari D.'s attorney argued that the cocaine had to be excluded at his trial because it was obtained in violation of the Fourth Amendment. The trial judge disagreed but was overturned by a state appellate court, which relied on the Court's previous rulings that police must have "reasonable suspicion" to stop and question people.

The ruling in *Hodari D.* was subsequently underscored by a bare majority of the Court in upholding the search and seizure of an individual who held an opaque bag and fled upon seeing a police caravan in *Illinois v. Wardlow* (2000) (excerpted below).

In recent years, the Court has also confronted the issue of how far police may go when conducting *suspicionless searches of passengers' belongings on public buses and trains.* In *Florida v. Bostick*, 501 U.S. 429 (1991), by a six-to-three vote the justices upheld random police questioning of bus and train passengers. *Bostick* originated with the "war on drugs" as waged in Broward County, Florida. There, sheriff's department officers routinely board buses at scheduled stops and ask passengers for permission to search their luggage. As it happened, two officers boarded a bus on which Terrance Bostick was traveling and, without reasonable suspicion or probable cause, questioned him and other passengers at a scheduled bus stop. They asked for his consent to search two of his bags and advised him of his right to deny consent, but he contested both that he was in a position to deny their request and that he in fact consented to their search. In any event, police searched his bags, and upon finding some cocaine, they arrested him. At a pretrial hearing he unsuccessfully moved to suppress the introduction of the cocaine as evidence on the grounds that it had been seized in violation of his Fourth Amendment rights. And Bostick later pleaded guilty but reserved the right to appeal the trial court's denial of his motion to suppress the contraband.

Writing for the Court in *Bostick*, Justice O'Connor reaffirmed that "the Fourth Amendment permits police officers to approach individuals at random in airport lobbies and other public places to ask them questions and to request consent to search their luggage, so long as a reasonable person would understand that he or she could refuse to cooperate." And O'Connor found no basis for distinguishing random searches and seizures in airport terminals from those in buses and trains. In her words:

> Our cases make it clear that a seizure does not occur simply because a police officer approaches an individual and asks a few questions. So long as a reasonable person would feel free "to disregard the police and go about his business," *California v. Hodari D.*, 499 U.S. 621 (1991), the encounter is consensual and no reasonable suspicion is required. The encounter will not trigger Fourth Amendment scrutiny unless it loses its consensual nature. The Court made precisely this point in *Terry v. Ohio*, 392 U.S. 1 (1968).

> Since *Terry*, we have held repeatedly that mere police questioning does not constitute a seizure. . . . There is no doubt that if this same encounter had taken place before Bostick boarded the bus or in the lobby of the bus terminal, it would not rise to the level of a seizure. The Court has dealt with similar encounters in airports and has found them to be "the sort of consensual encounter[s] that implicat[e] no Fourth Amendment interest." *Florida v. Rodriguez*, 469 U.S. 1 (1984). We have stated that even when officers have no basis for

suspecting a particular individual, they may generally ask questions of that individual, see *INS v. Delgado*, 466 U.S. 210, 216 (1984); ask to examine the individual's identification, *United States v. Mendenhall*, 446 U.S. 544 (1980); and request consent to search his or her luggage—as long as the police do not convey a message that compliance with their requests is required. . . .

[T]he mere fact that Bostick did not feel free to leave the bus does not mean that the police seized him. Bostick was a passenger on a bus that was scheduled to depart. He would not have felt free to leave the bus even if the police had not been present. Bostick's movements were "confined" in a sense, but this was the natural result of his decision to take the bus; it says nothing about whether or not the police conduct at issue was coercive. . . .

Concluding, Justice O'Connor also rejected Bostick's claim that he was "seized" because no reasonable person would freely consent to a search of luggage that he or she knows contains drugs. That argument, observed O'Connor, could not prevail because the "reasonable person" test presupposes "an innocent person." But dissenting in *Bostick*, Justices Marshall, Blackmun, and Stevens countered that "the Fourth Amendment clearly condemns the suspicionless, dragnet-style sweep of intrastate or interstate buses."

The Court, finally, drew a line on searches of passengers' luggage on public transport in *Bond v. United States* (2000) (excerpted below), with only Justice Breyer and Scalia dissenting from Chief Justice Rehnquist's opinion for the Court. However, in *United States v. Drayton*, 536 U.S. 194 (2002), the Court reaffirmed three earlier interrelated rulings bearing on searches of people in public places: (1) that the "consent" of a passenger on a bus to a request by an officer to a pat-down search for contraband (*Minnesota v. Dickerson*, 508 U.S. 366 [1993] [excerpted below]) (2) "presupposes an innocent person" would consent (*Florida v. Bostick*, 501 U.S. 429 [1991]), and (3) that the officers are not required to inform citizens of their right to refuse to consent (*Ohio v. Robinette*, 519 U.S. 33 [1996]). In *Drayton*, three law enforcement officers boarded a bus in Tallahassee, Florida, which was bound for Detroit, Michigan. One sat in the driver's seat, another in the back of the bus, and the third questioned passengers. Two young men wearing jackets and baggy pants, in the summer, were questioned and consented to pat downs, which revealed plastic bags of cocaine under their clothing. Writing for the Court in *Drayton*, Justice Kennedy observed:

Law enforcement officers do not violate the Fourth Amendment's prohibition of unreasonable seizures merely by approaching individuals on the street or in other public places and putting questions to them if they are willing to listen. Even when law enforcement officers have no basis for suspecting a particular individual, they may pose questions, ask for identification, and request consent to search luggage—provided they do not induce cooperation by coercive means. See *Florida v. Bostick*, 501 U.S. [429 (1991)]. If a reasonable person would feel free to terminate the encounter, then he or she has not been seized. . . .

Bostick first made it clear that for the most part per se rules are inappropriate in the Fourth Amendment context. The proper inquiry necessitates a consideration of "all the circumstances surrounding the encounter." The Court noted next that the traditional rule, which states that a seizure does not occur so long as a reasonable person would feel free "to disregard the police and go about his business," *California v. Hodari D.*, 499 U.S. 621 (1991), is not an accurate measure of the coercive effect of a bus encounter. A passenger may not want to get off a bus if there is a risk it will depart before the opportunity to reboard. A bus rider's movements are confined in this sense, but this is the natural result of choosing to take the bus; it says nothing about whether the police conduct is coercive. The proper inquiry "is whether a reasonable person would feel free to decline the officers' requests or otherwise terminate the encounter." Finally, the Court rejected Bostick's argument that he must have been seized because no reasonable person would consent to a search of luggage containing drugs. The reasonable person test, the Court explained, is objective and "presupposes an innocent person."

The Rehnquist Court also broadened *Terry*'s stop-and-frisk exception in *Minnesota v. Dickerson*, 508 U.S. 366 (1993) (excerpted below). In this case the Court was invited to approve yet another exception—a *"plain feel" exception*—to the Fourth Amendment's warrant requirement. In appealing a ruling of its state supreme court that rejected that exception, Minnesota argued that a "plain feel" exception was analogous to the "plain view" exception and a logical extension of *Terry v. Ohio*. Although partially rejecting the state's arguments and finding that here police went too far in *squeezing* a small object in the suspect's jacket pocket, the Court nevertheless expanded *Terry*'s stop-and-frisk exception to include searches and seizures of "nonthreatening contraband," as well as weapons (which was the basis for *Terry*'s exception), that are identifiable by touch during a police patdown.

A bare majority also ruled, in *Hiibel v. Sixth Judicial District of Nevada*, 124 S.Ct. 2451 (2004), that neither the Fourth nor Fifth Amendment is violated by the arrest of a person who refuses to identify himself or herself during a *Terry*-stop by police. Justices Stevens, Souter, Ginsburg and Breyer dissented.

In addition, in a broad holding in *United States v. Verdugo-Urquidez*, 494 U.S. 259 (1990), Chief Justice Rehnquist announced that the Fourth

Amendment does not forbid warrantless searches and seizures by government agents of the property in foreign countries of aliens who have been arrested and are jailed in the United States. He reasoned that, unlike the Fifth Amendment, which applies to criminal trials, the Fourth Amendment does not apply to aliens or their property outside of the United States. He did so by construing the Fourth Amendment right "of the people to be secure in their persons, houses, papers, and effects" to carve out for constitutional protection only those persons who are part of the national community and to exclude those who are aliens outside of U.S. territory.

Still another exception pertains to when police conduct a search within the context of *hot pursuit* and other *exigent circumstances* to prevent the destruction of evidence. *United States v. Santana* (1976) (excerpted below) indicates how fine a line the Court sometimes draws in permitting the warrantless entry into private homes and in distinguishing prior rulings allowing for warrantless arrests in exigent situations[3] and where police are in hot pursuit chasing an automobile.[4] Along with *Santana* the Court held, in *United States v. Watson*, 423 U.S. 411 (1976), that an arrest may be made in a public place without a warrant, even if police have time to obtain one. But subsequently the Court limited *Santana* and *Watson* in ruling that except where there are truly exigent circumstances, police must obtain a warrant before entering private premises to make an arrest.[5] However, in *Illinois v. McArthur*, 531 U.S. 326 (2001), the Court ruled that police, while waiting for a search warrant, may secure a dwelling and not allow the resident to enter unaccompanied, without violating the Fourth Amendment, if they have probable cause to believe that there is contraband on the premises and the resident would destroy it if allowed unrestricted entry.

In addition, in *Wilson v. Arkansas*, 514 U.S. 927 (1995), the Court reaffirmed that when police enter a home armed with search and arrest warrants, they must generally announce their presence and entry. Writing for the Court, however, Justice Thomas declined to set forth a rigid bright-line rule and instead left it for the lower courts to determine under what circumstances police may reasonably enter a house without first knocking and announcing their entry. Subsequently, in *Richards v. Wisconsin*, 520 U.S. 385 (1997), Justice Stevens held that exceptions for drug-related cases may be made to the knock-and-announce requirement, if police have a "reasonable suspicion" that announcing their entry would result in the destruction of drugs or otherwise inhibit their investigation. In *United States v. Ramirez*, 523 U.S. 65 (1998), then, the Court unanimously ruled that police armed with a search warrant do not need extra justification to enter a home without knocking first, even if the entry results in property damage. The Court reaffirmed its view that police have flexibility, because of potential physical harm and the risk that suspects may destroy evidence, when announcing their presence and entry into the home of suspected drug dealers, in *United States v. Banks*, 124 U.S. 521 (2003). Writing for a unanimous Court, Justice Souter held that the reasonableness of a forced entry under the "knock and announce" rule depends on the "totality of the circumstances," not how long police wait; here, police entered a house fifteen to twenty seconds after announcing. The Court reaffirmed its view that police have flexibility, because of the circumstances of their presence.

Finally, the Court once maintained, but no longer does, that police could not seize, with or without a warrant, *mere evidence*—clothing, private papers, and the like—but only illegal items, such as weapons, contraband, etc. In *Gould v. United States*, 255 U.S. 298 (1921), the Court ruled that unlawfully seized papers could be suppressed at trial on the grounds that the Fourth Amendment permitted the government to seize only that property over which it could also assert a property interest at common law, as with the seizure of stolen goods. The mere evidence rule was an "attempt by the Supreme Court to strike a Fourth Amendment balance between the government's interest in gathering evidence of criminal activity and the individual's reasonable expectations of privacy."[6] Applications of the rule, however, led to inconsistent, sometimes illogical, results,[7] and eventually to the Court's reconsideration of the rule.[8] The mere evidence rule was finally abandoned in *Warden v. Hayden*, 387 U.S. 294 (1967), in which the Court explained that

> [t]he premise that property interests control the right of the Government to search and seize has been discredited. Searches and seizures may be "unreasonable" within the Fourth Amendment even though the Government asserts a superior property interest at common law. We have recognized that the principal object of the Fourth Amendment is the protection of privacy rather than property, and have increasingly discarded fictional and procedural barriers rested on property concepts.

Ironically, the Court's abandonment of the mere evidence rule resulted in less Fourth Amendment protection for individuals' privacy interests in their private papers. The Court subsequently held that the Fourth Amendment does not bar the government from obtaining through a subpoena *duces tecum* (an order requiring the production of papers and documents) individuals' private papers held by their accountants, attorneys, and banks.[9]

The Court also recognizes exceptions for *automobile searches* (examined in Section C) and *administrative searches* (examined in Section D).

NOTES

1. *Chapman v. United States*, 365 U.S. 610 (1961) (landlord's consent for search of tenant's room was not enough); *Stoner v. California*, 376 U.S. 483 (1964) (striking down a search of a hotel room without the consent of the occupant, although the hotel clerk gave permission for the search).

2. In *United States v. Mendenhall*, 446 U.S. 544 (1980), the Court also upheld the stopping and search of a woman at an airport based on her fitting a "drug courier profile." A bare majority found that her agreeing to accompany agents to their office was voluntary, and thus she had not been "seized" for the purposes of the Fourth Amendment. However, in *Florida v. Royer*, 460 U.S. 492 (1983), the Court rejected the arrest of a person based on a drug courier profile as unreasonable, observing "that a person has been 'seized' within the meaning of the Fourth Amendment only if, in view of all the circumstances surrounding the incident, a reasonable person would have believed that he was not free to leave."

3. See *Warden v. Hayden*, 387 U.S. 294 (1967).

4. See *Johnson v. United States*, 333 U.S. 10 (1948).

5. *Payton v. New York*, 445 U.S. 573 (1980).

6. Note, "Papers, Privacy and the Fourth and Fifth Amendments: A Constitutional Analysis," 69 *Northwestern University Law Review* 633 (1974).

7. Compare *Marron v. United States*, 275 U.S. 192 (1927), with *United States v. Lefkowitz*, 285 U.S. 452 (1932).

8. See *Jones v. United States*, 362 U.S. 257 (1960).

9. See *Couch v. United States*, 409 U.S. 322 (1973); *United States v. Miller*, 425 U.S. 564 (1976); *California Bankers Association v. Shultz*, 416 U.S. 21 (1974); and David M. O'Brien, "Reasonable Expectations of Privacy: Principles and Policies of Fourth Amendment-Protected Privacy," 13 *New England Law Review* 662 (1978).

■ INSIDE THE COURT

Memorandum from Justice William J. Brennan to Chief Justice Earl Warren on Terry v. Ohio

March 14, 1968

RE: *The "Stop and Frisk" Cases*

Dear Chief:

I have heard from Bill [Douglas] and Abe [Fortas] something of their comments upon your opinions, and other suggestions for changes. I've read also, of course, the views stated by Hugo [Black], John [Harlan] and Byron [White] in their circulations. All of this has prompted me to do some extended and hard thinking which I hope I may share with you.

I'm attaching a rather extensive suggested revision of your *Terry* opinion with explanatory notes outlining my reasons, and also a rather extensively foot-noted memorandum stating my reasons for the conviction I've reached (contrary to my previous view) that we should not handle this question as a matter of "probable cause" and the Warrant Clause, but as a matter of the Reasonableness Clause. I hope you won't think me presumptuous to submit my thoughts in this form. I do it only because I think it's the best way for me to state them. . . .

I've become acutely concerned that the mere fact of our affirmance in *Terry* will be taken by police all over the country as our license to them to carry on, indeed widely expand, present "aggressive surveillance" techniques which the press tells us are being deliberately employed in Miami, Chicago, Detroit and other ghetto cities. This is happening, of course, in response to the "crime in the streets" alarums [*sic*] being sounded in this election year in the Congress, the White House and every Governor's office. Much of what I suggest be omitted from your opinion strikes me as susceptible to being read as sounding the same note. This seems to me to be particularly unfortunate since our affirmance surely does this: from here on out, it becomes entirely unnecessary for the police to establish "probable cause to *arrest*" to support weapons charges; an officer can move against anyone he *suspects* has a weapon and get a conviction if he "frisks" him and finds one. In this lies the terrible risk that police will conjure up "suspicious circumstances," and courts will credit their versions. It will not take much of this to aggravate the already white heat resentment of ghetto Negroes against the police—and the Court will become the scapegoat.

The alternative would of course mean a reversal of this conviction—a holding that there is no constitutional authority to frisk for weapons unless the officer has probable cause to *arrest* for the crime of carrying a weapon. I recognize that police will frisk anyway and try to make a case that the frisk was incident to an arrest for public drunkenness, vagrancy, loitering, breach of the peace, etc.—but at times I think these abuses would be more tolerable than those I apprehend may follow our legitimating of frisks on the basis of suspicious circumstances.

This states frankly my worries. But if we are to affirm *Terry*, I think the tone of our opinion may be even more important than what we say. If I have exceeded the proprieties, I hope you will forgive me—I am truly worried.

Sincerely,
Bill [Brennan]

Source: Library of Congress, Papers of Chief Justice Earl Warren, Manuscripts Room.

Terry v. Ohio

392 U.S. 1, 88 S.Ct. 1868 (1968)

Chief Justice Earl Warren discusses the facts in this case, upholding a police officer's stopping and frisking of individuals who he had a reasonable suspicion might be contemplating a robbery, at the outset of his opinion for the Court.

The Court's decision was eight to one, and the majority's opinion was announced by Chief Justice Warren. Concurrences were by Justices Black, Harlan, and White. Justice Douglas dissented.

☐ *Chief Justice WARREN delivered the opinion of the Court.*

This case presents serious questions concerning the role of the Fourth Amendment in the confrontation on the street between the citizen and the policeman investigating suspicious circumstances.

Petitioner Terry was convicted of carrying a concealed weapon and sentenced to the statutorily prescribed term of one to three years in the penitentiary. Following the denial of a pretrial motion to suppress, the prosecution introduced in evidence two revolvers and a number of bullets seized from Terry and a codefendant, Richard Chilton, by Cleveland Police Detective Martin McFadden. At the hearing on the motion to suppress this evidence, Officer McFadden testified that while he was patrolling in plain clothes in downtown Cleveland at approximately 2:30 in the afternoon of October 31, 1963, his attention was attracted by two men, Chilton and Terry, standing on the corner of Huron Road and Euclid Avenue. He had never seen the two men before, and he was unable to say precisely what first drew his eye to them. However, he testified that he had been a policeman for 39 years and a detective for 35 and that he had been assigned to patrol this vicinity of downtown Cleveland for shoplifters and pickpockets for 30 years. He explained that he had developed routine habits of observation over the years and that he would "stand and watch people or walk and watch people at many intervals of the day." He added: "Now, in this case when I looked over they didn't look right to me at the time."

His interest aroused, Officer McFadden took up a post of observation in the entrance to a store 300 to 400 feet away from two men. . . . He saw one of the men leave the other one and walk southwest on Huron Road, past some stores. The man paused for a moment and looked in a store window, then walked on a short distance, turned around and walked back toward the corner, pausing once again to look in the same store window. He rejoined his companion at the corner, and the two conferred briefly. Then the second man went through the same series of motions, strolling down Huron Road, looking in the same window, walking on a short distance, turning back, peering in the store window again, and returning to confer with the first man at the corner. The two men repeated this ritual alternately between five and six times apiece—in all, roughly a dozen trips. At one point, while the two were standing together on the corner, a third man approached them and engaged them briefly in conversation. This man then left the two others and walked west on Euclid Avenue. Chilton and Terry resumed their measured pacing, peering and conferring. After this had gone on for 10 to 12 minutes, the two men walked off together, heading west on Euclid Avenue, following the path taken earlier by the third man.

By this time Officer McFadden had become thoroughly suspicious. He . . . suspected the two men of "casing a job, a stick-up," and . . . he considered it his duty as a police officer to investigate further. . . . Thus, Officer McFadden followed Chilton and Terry and saw them stop in front of Zucker's store to talk to the same man who had conferred with them earlier on the street corner. Deciding that the situation was ripe for direct action, Officer McFadden approached the three men, identified himself as a police officer and asked for their names. At this point his knowledge was confined to what he had observed. . . . When the men "mumbled something" in response to his inquiries, Officer McFadden grabbed petitioner Terry, spun him around so that they were facing the other two, with Terry between McFadden and the others, and patted down the outside of his clothing. In the left breast pocket of Terry's overcoat Officer McFadden felt a pistol. He reached inside the overcoat pocket, but was unable to remove the gun. At this point, keeping Terry between himself and the others, the officer ordered all three men to enter Zucker's store. As they went in, he removed Terry's overcoat completely, removed a .38-caliber revolver from the pocket and ordered all three men to face the wall with their hands raised. Officer McFadden proceeded to pat down the outer clothing of Chilton and the third man, Katz. He discovered another revolver in the outer pocket of Chilton's overcoat, but no weapons were found on Katz. The officer testified that he only patted the men down to see whether they had weapons, and that he did not put his hands beneath the outer garments of either Terry or Chilton until he felt their guns. . . .

On the motion to suppress the guns the prosecution took the position that they had been seized following a search incident to a lawful arrest. The trial court rejected this theory, stating that it "would be stretching the facts beyond reasonable comprehension" to find that Officer McFadden had had probable cause to arrest the men before he patted them down for weapons. However, the court denied the defendants' motion on the ground that Officer McFadden, on the basis of his experience, "had reasonable cause to believe . . . that the defendants were conducting themselves suspiciously, and some interrogation should be made of their action." Purely for his own protection, the court held, the officer had the right to pat down the outer clothing of these men, who he had reasonable cause to believe might be armed. . . . We granted *certiorari* to determine whether the admission of the revolvers in evidence violated petitioner's rights under the Fourth Amendment, made applicable to the States by the Fourteenth. We affirm the conviction.

[Here,] the question is whether in all the circumstances of this on-the-street encounter, [the individual's] right to personal security was violated by an unreasonable search and seizure. . . .

Our first task is to establish at what point in this encounter the Fourth Amendment becomes relevant. That is, we must decide whether and when Officer McFadden "seized" Terry and whether and when he conducted a "search." . . . It is quite plain that the Fourth Amendment governs "seizures" of the person which do not eventuate in a trip to the station house and prosecution for crime—"arrests" in traditional terminology. It must be recognized that whenever a police officer accosts an individual and restrains his freedom to walk away, he has "seized" that person. And it is nothing less than sheer torture of the English language to suggest that a careful exploration of the outer surfaces of a person's clothing all over his or her body in an attempt to find weapons is not a "search." Moreover, it is simply fantastic to urge that such a procedure performed in public by a policeman while the citizen stands helpless, perhaps facing a wall with his hands raised, is a "petty indignity." It is a serious intrusion upon the sanctity of the person, which may inflict great indignity and arouse strong resentment, and it is not to be undertaken lightly.

The danger in the logic which proceeds upon distinctions between a "stop" and an "arrest," or "seizure" of the person, and between a "frisk" and a "search" is twofold. It seeks to isolate from constitutional scrutiny the initial stages of the contact between the policeman and the citizen. And by suggesting a rigid all-or-nothing model of justification and regulation under the Amendment, it obscures the utility of limitations upon the scope, as well as the initiation, of police action as a means of constitutional regulation. . . .

The distinctions of classical "stop-and-frisk" theory thus serve to divert attention from the central inquiry under the Fourth Amendment—the reasonableness in all the circumstances of the particular governmental invasion of a citizen's personal security. "Search" and "seizure" are not talismans. We therefore reject the notions that the Fourth Amendment does not come into play at all as a limitation upon police conduct if the officers stop short of something called a "technical arrest" or a "full-blown search." . . .

The crux of this case . . . is not the propriety of Officer McFadden's taking steps to investigate petitioner's suspicious behavior, but rather, whether there was justification for McFadden's invasion of Terry's personal security by searching him for weapons in the course of that investigation. We are now concerned with more than the governmental interest in investigating crime; in addition, there is the more immediate interest of the police officer in taking steps to assure himself that the person with whom he is dealing is not armed with a weapon that could unexpectedly and fatally be used against him. Certainly it would be unreasonable to require that police officers take unnecessary risks in the performance of their duties. American criminals have a long tradition of armed violence, and every year in this country many law enforcement officers are killed in the line of duty, and thousands more are wounded. Virtually all of these deaths and a substantial portion of the injuries are inflicted with guns and knives.

In view of these facts, we cannot blind ourselves to the need for law enforcement officers to protect themselves and other prospective victims of violence in situations where they may lack probable cause for an arrest. When an officer is justified in believing that the individual whose suspicious behavior he is investigating at close range is armed and presently dangerous to the officer or to others, it would appear to be clearly unreasonable to deny the officer the power to take necessary measures to determine whether the person is in fact carrying a weapon and to neutralize the threat of physical harm. . . .

We conclude that the revolver seized from Terry was properly admitted in evidence against him. At the time he seized petitioner and searched him for weapons, Officer McFadden had reasonable grounds to believe that petitioner was armed and dangerous, and it was necessary for the protection of himself and others to take swift measures to discover the true facts and neutralize the threat of harm if it materialized. The policeman carefully restricted his search to what was appropriate to the discovery of the particular items which he sought. Each case of this sort will, of course, have to be decided on its own facts. We merely hold today that where a police officer observes unusual conduct which leads him reasonably to conclude in light of his experience that criminal activity may be afoot and that the persons with whom he is dealing may be armed and presently dangerous, where in the course of investigating this behavior he identifies himself as a policeman and makes reasonable inquiries, and where nothing in the initial stages of the encounter serves to dispel his reasonable fear for his own or others' safety, he is entitled for the protection of himself and others in the area to conduct a carefully limited search of the outer clothing of such persons in an attempt to discover weapons which might be used to assault him.

Such a search is a reasonable search under the Fourth Amendment, and any weapons seized may properly be introduced in evidence against the person from whom they were taken.

Affirmed.

☐ *Justice HARLAN, concurring.*

While I unreservedly agree with the Court's ultimate holding in this case, I am constrained to fill in a few gaps, as I see them, in its opinion. I do this because what is said by this Court today will serve as initial guidelines for law enforcement authorities and courts throughout the land as this important new field of law develops.

A police officer's right to make an on-the-street "stop" and an accompanying "frisk" for weapons is of course bounded by the protections afforded by the Fourth and Fourteenth Amendments. The Court holds, and I agree, that while the right does not depend upon possession by the officer of a valid warrant, nor upon the existence of probable cause, such activities must be reasonable under the circumstances as the officer credibly relates them in court. Since the question in this and most cases is whether evidence produced by a frisk is admissible, the problem is to determine what makes a frisk reasonable. . . .

In the first place, if the frisk is justified in order to protect the officer during an encounter with a citizen, the officer must first have constitutional grounds to insist on an encounter, to make a *forcible* stop. Any person, including a policeman, is at liberty to avoid a person he considers dangerous. If and when a policeman has a right instead to disarm such a person for his own protection, he must first have a right not to avoid him but to be in his presence. That right must be more than the liberty (again, possessed by every citizen) to address questions to other persons, for ordinarily the person addressed has an equal right to ignore his interrogator and walk away; he certainly need not submit to a frisk for the questioner's protection. I would make it perfectly clear that the right to frisk in this case depends upon the reasonableness of a forcible stop to investigate a suspected crime.

Where such a stop is reasonable, however, the right to frisk must be immediate and automatic if the reason for the stop is, as here, an articulable suspicion of a crime of violence. Just as a full search incident to a lawful arrest requires no additional justification, a limited frisk incident to a lawful stop must often be rapid and routine. There is no reason why an officer, rightfully but forcibly confronting a person suspected of a serious crime, should have to ask one question and take the risk that the answer might be a bullet. . . .

Officer McFadden's right to interrupt Terry's freedom of movement and invade his privacy arose only because circumstances warranted forcing an encounter with Terry in an effort to prevent or investigate a crime. Once that forced encounter was justified, however, the officer's right to take suitable measures for his own safely followed automatically.

☐ *Justice DOUGLAS, dissenting.*

I agree that petitioner was "seized" within the meaning of the Fourth Amendment. I also agree that frisking petitioner and his companions for guns was a "search." But it is a mystery how that "search" and that "seizure" can be constitutional by Fourth Amendment standards, unless there was "probable cause" to believe that (1) a crime had been committed or (2) a crime was in the process of being committed or (3) a crime was about to be committed.

The opinion of the Court disclaims the existence of "probable cause." If loitering were in issue and that was the offense charged, there would be "probable cause" shown. But the crime here is carrying concealed weapons; and there is no basis for concluding that the officer had "probable cause" for believing that that crime was being committed. Had a warrant been sought, a magistrate would, therefore, have been unauthorized to issue one, for he can act only if there is a showing of "probable cause." We hold today that the police have greater authority to make a "seizure" and conduct a "search" than a judge has to authorize such action. We have said precisely the opposite over and over again. . . .

The infringement on personal liberty of any "seizure" of a person can only be "reasonable" under the Fourth Amendment if we require the police to possess "probable cause" before they seize him. Only that line draws a meaningful distinction between an officer's mere inkling and the presence of facts within the officer's personal knowledge which would convince a reasonable man that the person seized has committed, is committing, or is about to commit a particular crime. . . .

To give the police greater power than a magistrate is to take a long step down the totalitarian path. Perhaps such a step is desirable to cope with modern forms of lawlessness. But if it is taken, it should be the deliberate choice of the people through a constitutional amendment.

United States v. Sokolow

490 U.S. 1, 109 S.Ct. 1581 (1989)

Chief Justice William H. Rehnquist reviews the circumstances giving rise to this case, involving a warrantless search and seizure of Andrew Sokolow at the Honolulu, Hawaii, airport by drug enforcement agents, in his opinion for the Court.

The Court's decision was seven to two, and the majority's opinion was announced by Chief Justice Rehnquist. The dissent by Justice Marshall was joined by Justice Brennan.

☐ *Chief Justice REHNQUIST delivered the opinion of the Court.*

Respondent Andrew Sokolow was stopped by Drug Enforcement Administration (DEA) agents upon his arrival at Honolulu International Airport. The agents found 1,063 grams of cocaine in his carry-on luggage. When respondent was stopped, the agents knew, *inter alia*, that (1) he paid $2,100 for two airplane tickets from a roll of $20 bills; (2) he traveled under a name that did not match the name under which his telephone number was listed; (3) his original destination was Miami, a source city for illicit drugs; (4) he stayed in Miami for only 48 hours, even though a round-trip flight from Honolulu to Miami takes 20 hours; (5) he appeared nervous during his trip; and (6) he checked none of his luggage. A divided panel of the United States Court of Appeals for the Ninth Circuit held that the DEA agents did not have a reasonable suspicion to stop respondent, as required by the Fourth Amendment. We take the contrary view.

This case involves a typical attempt to smuggle drugs through one of the Nation's airports. On a Sunday in July 1984, respondent went to the United Airlines ticket counter at Honolulu Airport, where he purchased two round-trip tickets for a flight to Miami leaving later that day. The tickets were purchased in the names of "Andrew Kray" and "Janet Norian," and had open return dates. Respondent paid $2,100 for the tickets from a large roll of $20 bills, which appeared to contain a total of $4,000. He also gave the ticket agent his home telephone number. The ticket agent noticed that respondent seemed nervous; he was about 25 years old; he was dressed in a black jumpsuit and wore gold jewelry; and he was accompanied by a woman, who turned out to be Janet Norian. Neither respondent nor his companion checked any of their four pieces of luggage.

After the couple left for their flight, the ticket agent informed Officer John McCarthy of the Honolulu Police Department of respondent's cash purchase of tickets to Miami. Officer McCarthy determined that the telephone number respondent gave to the ticket agent was subscribed to a "Karl Herman," who resided at 348-A Royal Hawaiian Avenue in Honolulu. Unbeknownst to McCarthy (and later to the DEA agents), respondent was Herman's roommate. The ticket agent identified respondent's voice on the answering machine at Herman's number. Officer McCarthy was unable to find any listing under the name "Andrew Kray" in Hawaii. McCarthy subsequently learned that return reservations from Miami to Honolulu had been made in the names of Kray and Norian, with their arrival scheduled for July 25, three days after respondent and his companion had left. He also learned that Kray and Norian were scheduled to make stopovers in Denver and Los Angeles.

On July 25, during the stopover in Los Angeles, DEA agents identified respondent. He "appeared to be very nervous and was looking all around the waiting area." . . . Later that day, at 6:30 P.M., respondent and Norian arrived in Honolulu. As before, they had not checked their luggage. Respondent was still wearing a black jumpsuit and gold jewelry. The couple proceeded directly to the street and tried to hail a cab, where Agent Richard Kempshall and three other DEA agents approached them. Kempshall displayed his credentials, grabbed respondent by the arm and moved him back onto the sidewalk. Kempshall asked respondent for his airline ticket and identification; respondent said that he had neither. He told the agents that his name was "Sokolow," but that he was traveling under his mother's maiden name, "Kray."

Respondent and Norian were escorted to the DEA office at the airport. There, the couple's luggage was examined by "Donker," a narcotics detector dog, which alerted to respondent's brown shoulder bag. The agents arrested respondent. He was advised of his constitutional rights and declined to make any statements. The agents obtained a warrant to search the shoulder bag. They found no illicit drugs, but the bag did contain several suspicious documents indicating respondent's involvement in drug trafficking. The agents had Donker reexamine the remaining luggage, and this time the dog alerted to a medium sized Louis Vuitton bag. By now, it was 9:30 P.M., too late for the agents to obtain a second warrant. They allowed respondent to leave for the night, but kept his luggage. The next morning, after a second dog confirmed Donker's alert, the agents obtained a warrant and found 1,063 grams of cocaine inside the bag.

Respondent was indicted for possession with the intent to distribute cocaine in violation of 21 U.S.C. § 841(a)(1). The United States District Court for Hawaii denied his motion to suppress the cocaine and other evidence seized from his luggage, finding that the DEA agents had a reasonable suspicion that he was involved in drug trafficking when they stopped him at the airport. Respondent then entered a conditional plea of guilty to the offense charged.

The United States Court of Appeals for the Ninth Circuit reversed respondent's conviction by a divided vote, holding that the DEA agents did not have a reasonable suspicion to justify the stop. . . .

The Court of Appeals held that the DEA agents seized respondent when they grabbed him by the arm and moved him back onto the sidewalk. The Government does not challenge that conclusion, and we assume—without deciding—that a stop occurred here. Our decision, then, turns on whether the agents had a reasonable suspicion that respondent was engaged in wrongdoing when they encountered him on the sidewalk. In *Terry v. Ohio*, [392 U.S. 1] (1968), we held that the police can stop and briefly detain a person for investigative purposes if the officer has a reasonable suspicion supported by articulable facts that criminal activity "may be afoot," even if the officer lacks probable cause.

The officer, of course, must be able to articulate something more than an "inchoate and unparticularized suspicion or 'hunch'." The Fourth Amendment requires "some minimal level of objective justification" for making the stop. *INS v. Delgado*, 466 U.S. 210 (1984). That level of suspicion is considerably less than proof of wrongdoing by a preponderance of the evidence. We have held that probable cause means "a fair probability that contraband or evidence of a crime will be found," *Illinois v. Gates*, 462 U.S. 213 (1983), and the level of suspicion required for a *Terry* stop is obviously less demanding than that for probable cause. See *United States v. Montoya de Hernandez*, 473 U.S. 531 (1985).

The concept of reasonable suspicion like probable cause is not readily or even usefully, reduced to a neat set of legal rules." *Gates, supra.* We think the Court of Appeals' effort to refine and elaborate the requirements of "reasonable suspicion" in this case create unnecessary difficulty in dealing with one of the relatively simple concepts embodied in the Fourth Amendment. In evaluating the validity of a stop such as this, we must consider "the totality of the circumstances—the whole picture." *United States v. Cortez*, 449 U.S. 411 [1981]. As we said in *Cortez*:

> "The process does not deal with hard certainties, but with probabilities. Long before the law of probabilities was articulated as such, practical people formulated certain common-sense conclusions about human behavior; jurors as fact-finders are permitted to do the same—and so are law enforcement officers." . . .

We hold that the agents had a reasonable basis to suspect that respondent was transporting illegal drugs on these facts. The judgment of the Court of Appeals is therefore reversed and the case remanded for further proceedings consistent with our decision.

☐ *Justice MARSHALL, with whom Justice BRENNAN joins, dissenting.*

Because the strongest advocates of Fourth Amendment rights are frequently criminals, it is easy to forget that our interpretations of such rights apply to the innocent and the guilty alike. *Illinois v. Gates*, 462 U.S. 213 (1983) (BRENNAN, J., dissenting). In the present case, the chain of events set in motion when respondent Andrew Sokolow was stopped by Drug Enforcement Administration (DEA) agents at Honolulu International Airport led to the discovery of cocaine and, ultimately, to Sokolow's conviction for drug trafficking. But in sustaining this conviction on the ground that the agents reasonably suspected Sokolow of ongoing criminal activity, the Court diminishes the rights of *all* citizens to "to be secure in their persons," U.S. Const., Amdt. IV, as they traverse the Nation's airports. Finding this result constitutionally impermissible, I dissent.

The Fourth Amendment cabins government's authority to intrude on personal privacy and security by requiring that searches and seizures usually be supported by a showing of probable cause. The reasonable-suspicion standard is a derivation of the probable cause command, applicable only to those brief detentions which fall short of being full-scale searches and seizures and which are necessitated by law-enforcement exigencies such as the need to stop ongoing crimes, to prevent imminent crimes, and to protect law-enforcement officers in highly charged situations. *Terry v. Ohio* (1968). By requiring reasonable suspicion as a prerequisite to such seizures, the Fourth Amendment protects innocent persons from being subjected to "overbearing or harassing" police conduct carried out solely on the basis of imprecise stereotypes of what criminals look like, or on the basis of irrelevant personal characteristics such as race. . . .

To deter such egregious police behavior, we have held that a suspicion is not reasonable unless officers have based it on "specific and articulable facts." [See *Terry* and] see also *United States v. Brignoni-Ponce*, 422 U.S. 873 (1975). It is not enough to suspect that an individual has committed crimes in the past, harbors unconsummated criminal designs, or has the propensity to commit crimes. On the contrary, before detaining an individual, law enforcement officers must reasonably suspect that he is engaged in, or poised to commit, a criminal act *at that moment.*

The rationale for permitting brief, warrantless seizures is, after all, that it is impractical to demand strict compliance with the Fourth Amendment's ordinary probable-cause requirement in the face of ongoing or imminent criminal activity demanding "swift action predicated upon the on-the-spot observations of the officer on the beat." *Terry, supra.* Observations raising suspicions of past criminality demand no such immediate action, but instead should appropriately trigger routine police investigation, which may ultimately generate sufficient information to blossom into probable cause.

Evaluated against this standard, the facts about Andrew Sokolow known to the DEA agents at the time they stopped him fall short of reasonably indicating that he was engaged at the time in criminal activity. It is highly significant that the DEA agents stopped Sokolow because he matched one of the DEA's "profiles" of a paradigmatic drug courier. In my view, a law enforcement officer's mechanistic application of a formula of personal and behavioral traits in deciding whom to detain can only dull the officer's ability and determination to make sensitive and fact-specific inferences "in light of his experience," *Terry,* particularly in ambiguous or borderline cases. Reflexive reliance on a profile of drug courier characteristics runs a far greater risk than does ordinary, case-by-case police work, of subjecting innocent individuals to unwarranted police harassment and detention. . . .

The fact is that, unlike the taking of patently evasion action, *Flroida v. Rodriguez*, 469 U.S. 1 (1984), the use of an alias, *Florida v. Royer*, 460 U.S. 491 (1983), the casing of a store, *Terry,* or the provision of a reliable report from an informant that wrongdoing is imminent, *Illinois v. Gates,* nothing about the characteristics shown by airport traveler Sokolow reasonably suggests that criminal activity is afoot. The majority's hasty conclusion to the contrary serves only to indicate its willingness, when drug crimes or anti-drug policies are at issues, to give short shrift to constitutional rights.

Illinois v. Wardlow

528 U.S. 119, 120 S.CT. 673 (2000)

Around noon in an area of Chicago known for drug trafficking, two uniformed police officers were riding in the last of a four-car police caravan when they noticed William Wardlow holding an opaque bag. After looking in their direction, Wardlow fled down an alley and the officers followed, eventually cornering him. During a pat-down search for weapons, one of the officers squeezed the bag and felt a heavy object, which turned out to be a .38-caliber handgun. At his trial, Wardlow's attorney moved to suppress the use of the gun as evidence on the ground that the officer did not have a "reasonable suspicion" to justify the search and seizure under *Terry v. Ohio*, 392 U.S. 1 (1968). The trial court disagreed, but a state appellate court reversed Wardlow's conviction and the Illinois Supreme Court affirmed, concluding that a sudden flight from police, even in a high crime area, does not create a "reasonable suspicion" to justify a *Terry* stop. The state appealed and the Supreme Court granted review.

The state supreme court's decision was reversed in a five-to-four decision, with the opinion delivered by Chief Justice Rehnquist. Justice Stevens filed an opinion in part concurring and dissenting, which Justices Breyer, Ginsburg, and Souter joined.

☐ *Chief Justice REHNQUIST delivered the opinion of the Court.*

This case, involving a brief encounter between a citizen and a police officer on a public street, is governed by the analysis we first applied in *Terry* [*v. Ohio*]. In *Terry*, we held that an officer may, consistent with the Fourth Amendment, conduct a brief, investigatory stop when the officer has a reasonable, articulable suspicion that criminal activity is afoot. While "reasonable suspicion" is a less demanding standard than probable cause and requires a showing considerably less than preponderance of the evidence, the Fourth Amendment requires at least a minimal level of objective justification for making the stop.

An individual's presence in an area of expected criminal activity, standing alone, is not enough to support a reasonable, particularized suspicion that the person is committing a crime. But officers are not required to ignore the relevant characteristics of a location in determining whether the circumstances are sufficiently suspicious to warrant further investigation. . . .

In this case, moreover, it was not merely respondent's presence in an area of heavy narcotics trafficking that aroused the officers' suspicion but his unprovoked flight upon noticing the police. Our cases have also recognized that nervous, evasive behavior is a pertinent factor in determining reasonable suspicion. Headlong flight—wherever it occurs—is the consummate act of evasion: it is not necessarily indicative of wrongdoing, but it is certainly suggestive of such. In reviewing the propriety of an officer's conduct, courts do not have available empirical studies dealing with inferences drawn from suspicious behavior, and we cannot reasonably demand scientific certainty from judges or law enforcement officers where none exists. Thus, the determination of reasonable suspicion must be based on commonsense judgments and inferences about human behavior. We conclude Officer Nolan was justified in suspecting that Wardlow was involved in criminal activity, and, therefore, in investigating further. . . .

☐ *Justice STEVENS, with whom Justice SOUTER, Justice GINSBURG, and Justice BREYER join, concurring in part and dissenting in part.*

Guided by that totality-of-the-circumstances test, the Court concludes that Officer Nolan had reasonable suspicion to stop respondent. In this respect, my view differs from the Court's. The entire justification for the stop is articulated in the brief testimony of Officer Nolan. Some facts are perfectly clear; others are not. This factual insufficiency leads me to conclude that the Court's judgment is mistaken.

Nolan was part of an eight-officer, four-car caravan patrol team. The officers were headed for "one of the areas in the 11th District [of Chicago] that's high [in] narcotics traffic." The reason why four cars were in the caravan was that "[n]ormally in these different areas there's an enormous amount of people, sometimes lookouts, customers." Officer Nolan testified that he was in uniform on that day, but he did not recall whether he was driving a marked or an unmarked car.

Officer Nolan and his partner were in the last of the four patrol cars that "were all caravaning eastbound down Van Buren." Nolan first observed respondent "in front of 4035 West Van Buren." Wardlow "looked in our direction and began fleeing." Nolan then "began driving southbound down the street observing [respondent] running through the gangway and the alley southbound," and observed that Wardlow was carrying a white, opaque bag under his arm. After the car turned south and intercepted respondent as he "ran right towards us," Officer Nolan stopped him and conducted a "protective search," which revealed that the bag under respondent's arm contained a loaded handgun.

This terse testimony is most noticeable for what it fails to reveal. Though asked whether he was in a marked or unmarked car, Officer Nolan could not recall the answer. He was not asked whether any of the other three cars in the caravan were marked, or whether any of the other seven officers were in uniform. Though he explained that the size of the caravan was because "[n]ormally in these different areas there's an enormous amount of people, sometimes lookouts, customers," Officer Nolan did not testify as to whether anyone besides Wardlow was nearby 4035 West Van Buren. Nor is it clear that that address was the intended destination of the caravan. As the Appellate Court of Illinois interpreted the record, "it appears that the officers were simply driving by, on their way to some unidentified location, when they noticed defendant standing at 4035 West Van Buren." Officer Nolan's testimony also does not reveal how fast the officers were driving. It does not indicate whether he saw respondent notice the other patrol cars. And it does not say whether the caravan, or any part of it, had already passed Wardlow by before he began to run. . . .

No other factors sufficiently support a finding of reasonable suspicion. . . . Officer Nolan did testify that he expected to find "an enormous amount of people," including drug customers or lookouts, and the Court points out that "[i]t was in this context that Officer Nolan decided to investigate Wardlow after observing him flee." This observation, in my view, lends insufficient weight to the reasonable suspicion analysis; indeed, in light of the absence of testimony that anyone else was nearby when respondent began to run, this observation points in the opposite direction. . . .

It is the State's burden to articulate facts sufficient to support reasonable suspicion. In my judgment, Illinois has failed to discharge that burden. I am not persuaded that the mere fact that someone standing on a sidewalk looked in the direction of a passing car before starting to run is sufficient to justify a forcible stop and frisk.

Bond v. United States
529 U.S. 334, 120 S.CT. 1462 (2000)

The facts are stated by Chief Justice Rehnquist in the opinion of the Court, reversing the appellate court's decision. Justice Breyer filed a dissenting opinion, which Justice Scalia joined.

◻ *Chief Justice REHNQUIST delivered the opinion of the Court.*

Petitioner Steven Dewayne Bond was a passenger on a Greyhound bus that left California bound for Little Rock, Arkansas. The bus stopped, as it was required to do, at the permanent Border Patrol checkpoint in Sierra Blanca, Texas. Border Patrol Agent Cesar Cantu boarded the bus to check the immigration status of its passengers. After reaching the back of the bus, having satisfied himself that the passengers were lawfully in the United States, Agent Cantu began walking toward the front. Along the way, he squeezed the soft luggage which passengers had placed in the overhead storage space above the seats.

As Agent Cantu inspected the luggage in the compartment above petitioner's seat, he squeezed a green canvas bag and noticed that it contained a "brick-like" object. Petitioner admitted that the bag was his and agreed to allow Agent Cantu to open it. Upon opening the bag, Agent Cantu discovered a "brick" of methamphetamine. The brick had been wrapped in duct tape until it was oval-shaped and then rolled in a pair of pants.

Petitioner was indicted for conspiracy to possess, and possession with intent to distribute, methamphetamine. He moved to suppress the drugs, arguing that Agent Cantu conducted an illegal search of his bag. Petitioner's motion was denied, and the District Court found him guilty on both counts and sentenced him to 57 months in prison. On appeal, he conceded that other passengers had access to his bag, but contended that Agent Cantu manipulated the bag in a way that other passengers would not. The Court of Appeals rejected this argument. . . . We granted *certiorari*, and now reverse.

[T]he Government asserts that by exposing his bag to the public, petitioner lost a reasonable expectation that his bag would not be physically manipulated. The Government relies on our decisions in *California v. Ciraolo,* [476 U.S. 207 (1986)], and *Florida v. Riley,* 488 U.S. 445 (1989), for the proposition that matters open to public observation are not protected by the Fourth Amendment. In *Ciraolo,* we held that police observation of a back-yard from a plane flying at an altitude of 1,000 feet did not violate a reasonable expectation of privacy. Similarly, in *Riley,* we relied on *Ciraolo* to hold that police observation of a greenhouse in a home's curtilage from a helicopter passing at an altitude of 400 feet did not violate the Fourth Amendment. We reasoned that the property was "not necessarily protected from inspection that involves no physical invasion," and determined that because any member of the public could have lawfully observed the defendants' property by flying overhead, the defendants' expectation of privacy was "not reasonable and not one 'that society is prepared to honor.' "

But *Ciraolo* and *Riley* are different from this case because they involved only visual, as opposed to tactile, observation. Physically invasive inspection is simply more intrusive than purely visual inspection. For example, in *Terry v. Ohio,* 392 U.S. 1 (1968), we stated that a "careful [tactile] exploration of the outer surfaces of a person's clothing all over his or her body" is a "serious intrusion upon the sanctity of the person, which may inflict great indignity and arouse strong resentment, and is not to be undertaken lightly." Although Agent Cantu did not "frisk" petitioner's person, he did conduct a probing tactile examination of petitioner's carry-on luggage. Obviously, petitioner's bag was not part of his person. But travelers are particularly concerned about their carry-on luggage; they generally use it to transport personal items that, for whatever reason, they prefer to keep close at hand. . . .

Our Fourth Amendment analysis embraces two questions. First, we ask whether the individual, by his conduct, has exhibited an actual expectation of privacy; that is, whether he has shown that "he [sought] to preserve [something] as private." Here, petitioner sought to preserve privacy by using an opaque bag and placing that bag directly above his seat. Second, we inquire whether the individual's expectation of privacy is "one that society is prepared to recognize as reasonable." When a bus passenger places a bag in an overhead bin, he expects that other passengers or bus employees may move it for one reason or another. Thus, a bus passenger clearly expects that his bag may be handled. He does not expect that other passengers or bus employees will, as a matter of course, feel the bag in an exploratory manner. But this is exactly what the agent did here. We therefore hold that the agent's physical manipulation of petitioner's bag violated the Fourth Amendment.

☐ *Justice BREYER, with whom Justice SCALIA joins, dissenting.*

Does a traveler who places a soft-sided bag in the shared overhead storage compartment of a bus have a "reasonable expectation" that strangers will not push, pull, prod, squeeze, or otherwise manipulate his luggage? Unlike the majority, I believe that he does not. . . .

[A]n individual cannot reasonably expect privacy in respect to objects or activities that he "knowingly exposes to the public." Indeed, the Court has said that it is not objectively reasonable to expect privacy if "[a]ny member of the public could have" used his senses to detect "everything that th[e] officers observed." *California v. Ciraolo.* Thus, it has held that the fact that strangers may look down at fenced-in property from an aircraft or sift through garbage bags on a public street can justify a similar police intrusion. Consider, too, the accepted police practice of using dogs to sniff for drugs hidden inside luggage. . . .

Of course, the agent's purpose here—searching for drugs—differs dramatically from the intention of a driver or fellow passenger who squeezes a bag in the process of making more room for another parcel. But in determining whether an expectation of privacy is reasonable, it is the effect, not the purpose, that matters. . . .

If we are to depart from established legal principles, we should not begin here. At best, this decision will lead to a constitutional jurisprudence of "squeezes," thereby complicating further already complex Fourth Amendment law, increasing the difficulty of deciding ordinary criminal matters, and hindering the administrative guidance (with its potential for control of unreasonable police practices) that a less complicated jurisprudence might provide. . . .

Minnesota v. Dickerson

508 U.S. 366, 113 S.CT. 2130 (1993)

One evening in 1989 two Minneapolis police officers patrolling the city in an unmarked squad car noticed Timothy Dickerson leaving an apartment building. They had previously responded to complaints of drug sales in the building and considered it a "crack house." Dickerson was walking toward the police but upon spotting the squad car abruptly turned in the opposite direction. One of the police officers watched as Dickerson entered an alley and, based upon his seemingly evasive actions and the fact that he had just left a building known for cocaine traffic, the officers decided to stop him. Pulling their squad car into the alley, they ordered Dickerson to stop and submit to a patdown search. That search revealed no weapons, but the officer conducting the search felt a small lump in Dickerson's nylon jacket, reached into a pocket, and retrieved a small plastic bag containing one-fifth of one gram of crack cocaine. Dickerson was immediately arrested and charged with the possession of a controlled substance.

Before trial Dickerson's attorney moved to suppress the cocaine, but the trial judge, after concluding that the officers were justified under *Terry v. Ohio*, 392 U.S. 1 (1968), in stopping and frisking Dickerson, rejected the motion on the grounds that the officers' search of Dickerson's pocket was analogous to the "plain-view" exception. The trial court's decision, however, was reversed by an appellate court, and that decision was affirmed by the state supreme court, which agreed that the police overstepped *Terry* in seizing the cocaine and "declined to adopt the plain feel exception" to the Fourth Amendment's warrant requirement. Minnesota appealed to the Supreme Court, which granted review and affirmed the state supreme court's ruling.

The Court's decision was six to three, with Justice White announcing the majority's opinion. Justice Scalia concurred. In a separate opinion Chief Justice Rehnquist, joined by Justices Blackmun and Thomas, in part concurred and in part dissented.

☐ *Justice WHITE delivered the opinion of the Court.*

Terry [*v. Ohio*, 392 U.S. 1 (1968)] held that "when an officer is justified in believing that the individual whose suspicious behavior he is investigating at close range is armed and presently dangerous to the officer or to others," the officer may conduct a patdown search "to determine whether the person is in fact carrying a weapon." Rather, a protective search—permitted without a warrant and on the basis of reasonable suspicion less than probable cause—must be strictly "limited to that which is necessary for the discovery of weapons which might be used to harm the officer or others nearby." If the protective search goes beyond what is necessary to determine if the suspect is armed, it is no longer valid under *Terry* and its fruits will be suppressed. *Sibron v. New York*, 392 U.S. 40 (1968).

These principles were settled 25 years ago when, on the same day, the Court announced its decisions in *Terry* and *Sibron*. The question presented today is whether police officers may seize nonthreatening contraband detected during a protective patdown search of the sort permitted by *Terry*. We think the answer is clearly that they may, so long as the officers' search stays within the bounds marked by *Terry*.

We have already held that police officers, at least under certain circumstances, may seize contraband detected during the lawful execution of a *Terry* search. In *Michigan v. Long* [463 U.S. 1032 (1983)], for example, police approached a man who had driven his car into a ditch and who appeared to be under the influence of some intoxicant. As the man moved to reenter the car from the roadside, police spotted a knife on the floorboard. The officers stopped the man, subjected him to a patdown search, and then inspected the interior of the vehicle for other weapons. During the search of the passenger compartment, the police discovered an open pouch containing marijuana and seized it. This Court upheld the validity of the search and seizure under *Terry*. The Court held first that, in the context of a roadside encounter, where police have reasonable suspicion based on specific and articulate facts to believe that a driver may be armed and dangerous, they may conduct a protective search for weapons not only of the driver's person but also of the passenger compartment of the automobile. Of course, the protective search of the vehicle, being justified solely by the danger that weapons stored there could be used against the officers or bystanders, must be "limited to those areas in which a weapon may be placed or hidden." The Court then held: "If, while conducting a legitimate *Terry* search of the interior of the automobile, the officer should, as here, discover contraband other than weapons, he clearly cannot be required to ignore the contraband, and the Fourth Amendment does not require its suppression in such circumstances."

The Court in *Long* justified this latter holding by reference to our cases under the "plain-view" doctrine. If, however, the police lack probable cause to believe that an object in plain view is contraband without conducting some further search of the object—i.e., if "its incriminating character [is not] 'immediately apparent' "—the plain-view doctrine cannot justify its seizure. *Arizona v. Hicks*, 480 U.S. 321 (1987).

We think that this doctrine has an obvious application by analogy to cases in which an officer discovers contraband through the sense of touch during an otherwise lawful search. The rationale of the plain-view doctrine is that if contraband is left in open view and is observed by a police officer from a lawful vantage point, there has been no invasion of a legitimate expectation of privacy and thus no "search" within the meaning of the Fourth Amendment—or at least no search independent of the initial intrusion that gave the officers their vantage point. The warrantless seizure of contraband that presents itself in this manner is deemed justified by the realization that resort to a neutral magistrate under such circumstances would often be impracticable and would do little to promote the objectives of the Fourth Amendment. The same can be said of tactile discoveries of contraband. If a police officer lawfully pats down a suspect's outer clothing and feels an object whose contour or mass makes its identity immediately apparent, there has been no invasion of the suspect's privacy beyond that already authorized by the officer's search for weapons; if the object is contraband, its warrantless seizure would be justified by the same practical considerations that inhere in the plain view context. . . .

It remains to apply these principles to the facts of this case. Respondent has not challenged the finding made by the trial court and affirmed by both the Court of Appeals and the State Supreme Court that the police were justified under *Terry* in stopping him and frisking him for weapons. Thus, the dispositive question before this Court is whether the officer who conducted the search was acting within the lawful bounds marked by *Terry* at the time he gained probable cause to believe that the lump in respondent's jacket was contraband. . . . The Minnesota Supreme Court, after "a close examination of the record," held that the officer's own testimony "belies any notion that he 'immediately' " recognized the lump as crack cocaine. Rather, the court concluded, the officer determined that the lump was contraband only after "squeezing, sliding and otherwise manipulating the contents of the defendant's pocket"—a pocket which the officer already knew contained no weapon.

Under the State Supreme Court's interpretation of the record before it, it is clear that the court was correct in holding that the police officer in this case overstepped the bounds of the "strictly circumscribed" search for weapons allowed under *Terry*. Where, as here, "an officer who is executing a valid search for one item seizes a different item," this Court rightly "has been sensitive to the danger . . . that officers will enlarge a specific authorization, furnished by a warrant or an exigency, into the equivalent of a general warrant to rummage and seize at will." *Texas v. Brown*, 460 U.S. [730 (1983)]

(STEVENS, J., concurring in judgment). Here, the officer's continued exploration of respondent's pocket after having concluded that it contained no weapon was unrelated to "the sole justification of the search [under *Terry:*] . . . the protection of the police officer and others nearby." It therefore amounted to the sort of evidentiary search that *Terry* expressly refused to authorize, and that we have condemned in subsequent cases. . . .

☐ *Justice SCALIA, concurring.*

My problem with the present case is that I am not entirely sure that the physical search—the "frisk"—that produced the evidence at issue here complied with [the Fourth Amendment's] constitutional standard. The decision of ours that gave approval to such searches, *Terry v. Ohio*, 392 U.S. 1 (1968), made no serious attempt to determine compliance with traditional standards, but rather, according to the style of this Court at the time, simply adjudged that such a search was "reasonable" by current estimations.

There is good evidence, I think, that the "stop" portion of the *Terry* "stop-and-frisk" holding accords with the common law—that it had long been considered reasonable to detain suspicious persons for the purpose of demanding that they give an account of themselves.

I am unaware, however, of any precedent for a physical search of a person thus temporarily detained for questioning. Sometimes, of course, the temporary detention of a suspicious character would be elevated to a full custodial arrest on probable cause—as, for instance, when a suspect was unable to provide a sufficient accounting of himself. At that point, it is clear that the common law would permit not just a protective "frisk," but a full physical search incident to the arrest. When, however, the detention did not rise to the level of a full-blown arrest (and was not supported by the degree of cause needful for that purpose), there appears to be no clear support at common law for physically searching the suspect. I frankly doubt, moreover, whether the fiercely proud men who adopted our Fourth Amendment would have allowed themselves to be subjected, on mere suspicion of being armed and dangerous, to such indignity. . . .

On the other hand, even if a "frisk" prior to arrest would have been considered impermissible in 1791, perhaps it was considered permissible by 1868, when the Fourteenth Amendment (the basis for applying the Fourth Amendment to the States) was adopted. Or perhaps it is only since that time that concealed weapons capable of harming the interrogator quickly and from beyond arm's reach have become common—which might alter the judgment of what is "reasonable" under the original standard. But technological changes were no more discussed in *Terry* than was the original state of the law.

If I were of the view that *Terry* was (insofar as the power to "frisk" is concerned) incorrectly decided, I might—even if I felt bound to adhere to that case—vote to exclude the evidence incidentally discovered, on the theory that half a constitutional guarantee is better than none. I might also vote to exclude it if I agreed with the original-meaning-is-irrelevant, good-policy-is-constitutional-law school of jurisprudence that the *Terry* opinion represents. As a policy matter, it may be desirable to permit "frisks" for weapons, but not to encourage "frisks" for drugs by admitting evidence other than weapons.

I adhere to original meaning, however. And though I do not favor the mode of analysis in *Terry*, I cannot say that its result was wrong. Constitutionality of the "frisk" in the present case was neither challenged nor argued. Assuming, therefore, that the search was lawful, I agree with the Court's premise that any evidence incidentally discovered in the course of it would be admissible, and join the Court's opinion in its entirety.

United States v. Santana

427 U.S. 38, 96 S.Ct. 2406 (1976)

The facts in this case are given by Justice William Rehnquist in his opinion announcing the ruling of the Court, upholding the warrantless search and seizure of Ms. Santana in her home based on the fact police were in hot pursuit of her and had probable cause to suspect her of dealing drugs.

The Court's decision was seven to two, and the majority's opinion was announced by Justice Rehnquist. Concurrences were by Justices White and Stevens, who was joined by Justice Stewart. Justice Marshall's dissent was joined by Justice Brennan.

☐ *Justice REHNQUIST delivered the opinion of the Court.*

Michael Gilletti, an undercover officer with the Philadelphia Narcotics Squad arranged a heroin "buy" with one Patricia McCafferty (from whom he had purchased narcotics before). McCafferty told him it would cost $115 "and we will go down to Mom Santana's for the dope."

Gilletti notified his superiors of the impending transaction, recorded the serial numbers of $110 [*sic*] in marked bills, and went to meet McCafferty at a prearranged location. She got in his car and directed him to drive to 2311 North Fifth Street, which, as she had previously informed him, was respondent Santana's residence.

McCafferty took the money and went inside the house, stopping briefly to speak to respondent Alejandro who was sitting on the front steps. She came out shortly afterwards and got into the car. Gilletti asked for the heroin; she thereupon extracted from her bra several glassine envelopes containing a brownish-white powder and gave them to him.

Gilletti then stopped the car, displayed his badge, and placed McCafferty under arrest. He told her that the police were going back to 2311 North Fifth Street and that he wanted to know where the money was. She said, "Mom has the money." At this point Sergeant Pruitt and other officers came up to the car. Gilletti showed them the envelope and said "Mom Santana has the money." Gilletti then took McCafferty to the police station.

Pruitt and the others then drove approximately two blocks back to 2311 North Fifth Street. They saw Santana standing in the doorway of the house with a brown paper bag in her hand. They pulled up to within 15 feet of

Santana and got out of their van, shouting "police," and displaying their identification. As the officers approached, Santana retreated into the vestibule of her house.

The officers followed through the open door, catching her in the vestibule. As she tried to pull away, the bag tilted and "two bundles of glazed paper packets with a white powder" fell to the floor. Respondent Alejandro tried to make off with the dropped envelopes but was forcibly restrained. When Santana was told to empty her pockets she produced $135, $70 of which could be identified as Gilletti's marked money. The white powder in the bag was later determined to be heroin. . . .

In *United States v. Watson*, 423 U.S. 411 (1976), we held that the warrantless arrest of an individual in a public place upon probable cause did not violate the Fourth Amendment. Thus the first question we must decide is whether, when the police first sought to arrest Santana, she was in a public place.

While it may be true that under the common law of property the threshold of one's dwelling is "private," as is the yard surrounding the house, it is nonetheless clear that under the cases interpreting the Fourth Amendment Santana was in a "public" place. She was not in an area where she had any expectation of privacy. . . . She was not merely visible to the public but was as exposed to public view, speech, hearing, and touch as if she had been standing completely outside her house. Thus, when the police, who concededly had probable cause to do so, sought to arrest her, they merely intended to perform a function which we have approved in *Watson*.

The only remaining question is whether her act of retreating into her house could thwart an otherwise proper arrest. We hold that it could not. In *Warden v. Hayden*, 387 U.S. 294 (1967), we recognized the right of police, who had probable cause to believe that an armed robber had entered a house a few minutes before, to make a warrantless entry to arrest the robber and to search for weapons. This case, involving a true "hot pursuit," is clearly governed by *Warden*; the need to act quickly here is even greater than in that case while the intrusion is much less. The District Court was correct in concluding that "hot pursuit" means some sort of a chase, but it need not be an extended hue and cry "in and about [the] public streets." The fact that the pursuit here ended almost as soon as it began did not render it any the less a "hot pursuit" sufficient to justify the warrantless entry into Santana's house. Once Santana saw the police, there was likewise a realistic expectation that any delay would result in destruction of evidence. Once she had been arrested the search, incident to that arrest, which produced the drugs and money was clearly justified. . . .

We thus conclude that a suspect may not defeat an arrest which has been set in motion in a public place, and is therefore proper under *Watson*, by the expedient of escaping to a private place. The judgment of the Court of Appeals is

Reversed.

□ *Justice MARSHALL, with whom Justice BRENNAN joins, dissenting.*

[I]f I correctly read the Court's citation to the "open fields" doctrine . . . the Court holds that the police may enter upon private property to make warrantless arrests of persons who are in plain view and outdoors; and the Court applies that doctrine today to persons who are arguably within their homes but who are "as exposed" to the public as if they were outside. But . . . if plain view were the touchstone, Santana would have been just as liable to warrantless arrest as she retreated several feet inside her open door as she was when standing in the doorway.

The Court's doctrine, then, appears *sui generis*, useful only in arresting persons who are "as exposed to public view, speech, hearing, and touch," as though in the unprotected outdoors. Narrow though it may be, however, the Court's approach does not depend on whether exigency justifies an arrest on private property, and thus I cannot join it.

Justice STEVENS focuses on what I believe to be the right question in this case—whether there were exigent circumstances—and reaches an affirmative answer because he finds a "significant risk that the marked money would no longer be in Santana's possession if the police waited until a warrant could be obtained." I agree that there were exigent circumstances in this case. . . .

I do not believe, however, that these exigent circumstances automatically validate Santana's arrest. The exigency that justified the entry and arrest was solely a product of police conduct. Had Officer Gilletti driven McCafferty to a more remote location before arresting her, it appears that no exigency would have been created by the arrest; in such an event a warrant would have been necessary, in my view, before Santana could have been arrested. It is not apparent on this record why Officer Gilletti arrested McCafferty so close to Santana's home when the arresting officers were clearly aware that such a nearby arrest would necessitate the prompt arrest of Santana. While a police decision that the time is right to arrest a suspect should properly be given great deference, the power to arrest is an awesome one and is subject to abuse. An arrest may permit a search of premises incident to the arrest, a search that otherwise could be carried out only upon probable cause and pursuant to a search warrant. Likewise, an arrest in circumstances such as those presented here may create exigency that may justify a search or another arrest. When an arrest is so timed that it is no more than an attempt to circumvent the warrant requirement, I would hold the subsequent arrest or search unlawful.

County of Riverside v. McLaughlin
500 U.S. 44, 111 S.Ct. 1661 (1991)

Donald McLaughlin was arrested without a warrant and imprisoned for two days in the Riverside County Jail without a hearing before a judge to establish the probable cause for his arrest. He later filed a class action suit in federal district court seeking injunctive and declaratory relief. McLaughlin charged that the county of Riverside ran afoul of *Gerstein v. Pugh*, 420 U.S. 103 (1975), in failing to provide "prompt" judicial hearings and determinations of the probable cause for arresting, without a warrant, persons like himself. And he requested an order requiring the County of Riverside to provide "arrestees, arrested without warrants, prompt probable cause, bail and arraignment hearings." Riverside combined such determinations with arraignment proceedings, which it required to be conducted within two days of arrest, excluding weekends and holidays. The district court subsequently issued a preliminary injunction requiring all persons arrested without a warrant in the county to be provided with a probable cause determination within thirty-six hours of their arrest, unless there were exigent circumstances. The Court of Appeals for the Ninth Circuit affirmed, and the County of Riverside appealed to the Supreme Court.

The Court's decision was five to four, with Justice O'Connor delivering the majority's opinion. Dissenting opinions were delivered by Justice Marshall, who was joined by Justices Blackmun and Stevens, and by Justice Scalia.

□ *Justice O'CONNOR delivered the opinion of the Court.*

In *Gerstein v. Pugh*, 420 U.S. 103 (1975), this Court held that the Fourth Amendment requires a prompt judicial determination of probable cause as a prerequisite to an extended pretrial detention following a warrantless arrest.

This case requires us to define what is "prompt" under *Gerstein*. . . .

In *Gerstein*, this Court held unconstitutional Florida procedures under which persons arrested without a warrant could remain in police custody for 30 days or more without a judicial determination of probable cause. In reaching this conclusion we attempted to reconcile important competing interests. On the one hand, States have a strong interest in protecting public safety by taking into custody those persons who are reasonably suspected of having engaged in criminal activity, even where there has been no opportunity for a prior judicial determination of probable cause. On the other hand, prolonged detention based on incorrect or unfounded suspicion may unjustly "imperil [a] suspect's job, interrupt his source of income, and impair his family relationships." We sought to balance these competing concerns by holding that States "must provide a fair and reliable determination of probable cause as a condition for any significant pretrial restraint of liberty, and this determination must be made by a judicial officer either before or promptly after arrest." Id. . . .

Gerstein held that probable cause determinations must be prompt—not immediate. The Court explained that "flexibility and experimentation" were "desirab[le]"; that "[t]here is no single preferred pretrial procedure"; and that "the nature of the probable cause determination usually will be shaped to accord with a State's pretrial procedure viewed as a whole." The Court of Appeals and the dissent disregard these statements, relying instead on selective quotations from the Court's opinion. As we have explained, *Gerstein* struck a balance between competing interests; a proper understanding of the decision is possible only if one takes into account both sides of the equation. . . .

In our view, the Fourth Amendment permits a reasonable postponement of a probable cause determination while the police cope with the everyday problems of processing suspects through an overly burdened criminal justice system.

But flexibility has its limits; *Gerstein* is not a blank check. . . .

Our task in this case is to articulate more clearly the boundaries of what is permissible under the Fourth Amendment. Although we hesitate to announce that the Constitution compels a specific time limit, it is important to provide some degree of certainty so that States and counties may establish procedures with confidence that they fall within constitutional bounds. Taking into account the competing interests articulated in *Gerstein*, we believe that a jurisdiction that provides judicial determinations of probable cause within 48 hours of arrest will, as a general matter, comply with the promptness requirement of *Gerstein*. For this reason, such jurisdictions will be immune from systemic challenges.

This is not to say that the probable cause determination in a particular case passes constitutional muster simply because it is provided within 48 hours. Such a hearing may nonetheless violate *Gerstein* if the arrested individual can prove that his or her probable cause determination was delayed unreasonably. Examples of unreasonable delay are delays for the purpose of gathering additional evidence to justify the arrest, a delay motivated by ill will against the arrested individual, or delay for delay's sake. In evaluating whether the delay in a particular case is unreasonable, however, courts must allow a substantial degree of flexibility. . . .

Where an arrested individual does not receive a probable cause determination within 48 hours, the calculus changes. In such a case, the arrested individual does not bear the burden of proving an unreasonable delay. Rather, the burden shifts to the government to demonstrate the existence of a bona fide emergency or other extraordinary circumstance.

The fact that in a particular case it may take longer than 48 hours to consolidate pretrial proceedings does not qualify as an extraordinary circumstance. Nor, for that matter, do intervening weekends. A jurisdiction that chooses to offer combined proceedings must do so as soon as is reasonably feasible, but in no event later than 48 hours after arrest.

☐ *Justice SCALIA, dissenting.*

It was the purpose of the Fourth Amendment to put this matter beyond time, place and judicial predilection, incorporating the traditional common-law guarantees against unlawful arrest. . . .

In my view, absent extraordinary circumstances, it is an "unreasonable seizure" within the meaning of the Fourth Amendment for the police, having arrested a suspect without a warrant, to delay a determination of probable cause for the arrest either (1) for reasons unrelated to arrangement of the probable-cause determination or completion of the steps incident to arrest, or (2) beyond 24 hours after the arrest. Like the Court, I would treat the time limit as a presumption; when the 24 hours are exceeded the burden shifts to the police to adduce unforeseeable circumstances justifying the additional delay.

C | *The Special Problems of Automobiles in a Mobile Society*

Automobiles pose special Fourth Amendment problems. This is because of their mobility and the possibility of criminal suspects escaping and destroying evidence. The Court's rulings have made automobile searches and seizures not just another exception to the warrant require-ment, but virtually a "whole new ball game" as to what is an unreason-able search and seizure.

The leading case distinguishing automobiles from "houses, papers, and effects" for Fourth Amendment purposes is *Carroll v. United States*, 267 U.S. 132 (1925). There Chief Justice William Howard Taft observed that

> [t]he guaranty of freedom from unreasonable searches and seizures by the Fourth Amendment has been construed, practically since the beginning of government, as recognizing a necessary difference be-tween a search of a store, dwelling house, or other structure in re-spect of which a proper official warrant readily may be obtained and a search of a ship, motor boat, wagon, or automobile for con-traband goods, where it is not practicable to secure a warrant, be-cause the vehicle can be quickly moved out of the locality or jurisdiction in which the warrant must be sought.

But in finding warrantless searches and seizures of automobiles permis-sible, Taft added,

> It would be intolerable and unreasonable if [police] were author-ized to stop every automobile on the chance of finding [illegal goods], and thus subject all persons lawfully using the highways to the inconvenience and indignity of such a search. Travelers may be so stopped in crossing an international boundary because of na-tional self-protection reasonably requiring one entering the country to identify himself as entitled to come in, and his belongings as ef-fects which may be lawfully brought in. But those lawfully within the country, entitled to use the public highways, have a right to free passage without interruption or search unless there is known to a competent official, authorized to search, probable cause for believing that their vehicles are carrying contraband or illegal merchandise.

Subsequently, in *Chambers v. Maroney*, 399 U.S. (1970), the Court re-affirmed that warrantless searches of automobiles and their contents are permissble under the Fourth Amendment on the rationale given in *Carroll*.

Following the *Carroll-Chambers* doctrine, controversy revolved around how far police could go in stopping and searching vehicles and their occupants. In *United States v. Robinson* (1968) (excerpted below), the Court held that police, without a warrant but based on probable cause, could conduct a rather extensive search of a driver arrested for a traffic offense. A companion case, *Gustafson v. Florida*, 414 U.S. 260 (1973), upheld the full-body search of a driver who was arrested and taken into custody. In *Pennsylvania v. Mimms*, 434 U.S. 106 (1977), the justices (six to three) also upheld an officer's frisking a driver who, after stopping a car with an expired license plate, asked the driver to step out of his car and produce his driver's license. At that point, the officer noticed that the driver had a large "bulge" in his sports jacket and patted him down. In two other rulings on drivers and passengers, the Court held, first, that police, after making a routine traffic stop and ticketing the driver, do not have to inform the driver that he or she is "legally free to go," before engaging in further questioning. The Ohio Supreme Court had held contrariwise but the Court reversed in *Ohio v. Robinette*, 519 U.S. 33 (1996). Second, *Maryland v. Wilson*, 519 U.S. 409 (1997), extended the ruling in *Pennsylvania v. Mimms* to permit police to order both drivers and passengers out of a car stopped for routine traffic violations.

In *Delaware v. Prouse*, 440 U.S. 648 (1978), the Court drew a line at police making routine stops of vehicles for the purpose of checking drivers' licenses and car registrations, holding that police must have probable cause or a reasonable suspicion to believe that a vehicle or its occupants have violated some law. However, in *Alabama v. White*, 496 U.S. 325 (1990), the Rehnquist Court held that police may stop and question individuals traveling in their automobiles based on anonymous tips and if they obtain some corroboration that establishes a reasonable suspicion of the occupants' criminal activity. Justices Stevens, Marshall, and Brennan dissented from that ruling, as they also did in *Michigan State Police v. Sitz*, 496 U.S. 444 (1990). In *Sitz*, the Court ruled that highway sobriety checkpoints were permissible, even though police had no reasonable suspicion to believe that drivers were intoxicated. Unlike *Prouse*, Chief Justice Rehnquist emphasized that this case did not involve random highway stops, and statistical evidence showed that about 1.5 percent of the drivers stopped were arrested for alcohol impairment. "The balance of the state's interest in preventing drunken driving," he concluded, "and the degree of intrusion upon individual motorists who are briefly stopped weighs in favor of the state program."

■ THE DEVELOPMENT OF LAW

Automobiles and Border Patrol Searches

CASE	VOTE	RULING
Almeida-Sanchez v. United States, 413 U.S. 266 (1973)	5:4	Warrantless search of cars, without probable cause by roving border patrol agents twenty miles north of the border violated the Fourth Amendment.
United States v. Brignoni-Ponce, 422 U.S. 873 (1975)	9:0	Except at the border, roving border patrol agents may stop cars only if they have reasonable suspicion and specific and articulable facts indicating that a vehicle contains illegal aliens; Mexican ancestry of occupants alone is not grounds for reasonable suspicion.
United States v. Ortiz, 422 U.S. 891 (1975)	9:0	Fourth Amendment forbids order patrol searches at fixed checkpoints distantly removed from the border and requires probable cause for searches.
United States v. Martinez-Fuerte, 428 U.S. 543 (1976)	7:2	Vehicles may be stopped at a fixed checkpoint for brief questioning of occupants, and vehicles may be directed selectively to a secondary inspection point, even when the basis for doing so is the "apparent Mexican ancestry" of occupants of the vehicle.
United States v. Arvizu, 534 U.S. 161 (2002)	9:0	Writing for the Court, Chief Justice Rehnquist held that under *Terry v. Ohio*, 392 U.S. 1 (1968), based on "the totality of the circumstances" an experienced border patrol officer had "reasonable suspicion" to stop on an unpaved road in a remote area of Arizona an otherwise innocuous automobile, which in turn led to a search that uncovered over 100 pounds of marijuana.
United States v. Flores-Montano, 124 S.Ct. 1582 (2004)	9:0	International border customs officers may, without reasonable suspicion, search, remove, disassemble, and reassemble a vehicle's gas tank in order to search for drugs or other contraband. Writing for the Court, Chief Justice Rehnquist held that the government's interests in protecting the border is at its "zenith" at international borders and paramount to any privacy interests in an automobile.

The Court, nonetheless, refused to extend *Sitz* and *United States v. Martinez-Fuerte*, 428 U.S. 543 (1976), upholding border patrol checkpoints, in *Indianapolis v. Edmond*, 531 U.S. 32 (2000). Writing for the Court, Justice O'Connor struck down the use of fixed checkpoints to interdict unlawful drugs on the ground that they lacked individualized suspicion of the drivers' criminal activity and aimed only to advance states' "general interest in crime control," in contrast with sobriety checkpoints. However, *Edmond* was subsequently distinguished and limited in *Illinois v. Lidster* (2004) (excerpted below), in which the Court upheld "informational checkpoints"—checkpoints at which all cars are stopped in order to inquire whether drivers have information pertaining to a recent crime, such as the location of a missing person or the identity of the perpetrator of a crime.

Once police stop a vehicle, they may search the area in plain view around the driver, and if they have a reasonable suspicion of finding illegal items or make a protective search to discover weapons, they may search the entire interior of the vehicle.[1] In *New York v. Class*, 475 U.S. 106 (1986), for example, voting 5 to 4 the justices upheld a search of a car based on an officer's spotting a gun under the front seat, when looking through the front window to see the vehicle identification number on the dashboard. The Court underscored how far police may go in *California v. Carney*, 471 U.S. 386 (1985), upholding a warrantless search of the entire interior of a mobile home that was parked in a public parking lot, where police had probable cause to believe that the occupant was selling marijuana. Warrantless searches of the exterior of vehicles[2] and inventory searches of impounded automobiles are also permissible.[3]

A series of cases presented the Court with another line-drawing problem, however, namely, how far police may go in searching containers found in a vehicle. Initially, in *United States v. Chadwick*, 433 U.S. 1 (1977), the Court held that a locked footlocker that had been loaded into the trunk of an automobile could not be searched without a warrant. On Joseph Chadwick's arrival by train in Boston from San Diego, he was arrested at a waiting vehicle by federal agents, who had been alerted that he was a possible drug trafficker. They arrested Chadwick and seized the automobile and the footlocker, which they had probable cause to believe contained narcotics. At a federal building an hour and half after the arrest, the agents opened the footlocker without Chadwick's consent or a search warrant. The Court disallowed that search, observing that "[b]y placing personal effects inside a double-locked footlocker, [Chadwick] manifested an expectation that the contents would remain free from public examination. No less than one who locks the doors of his home against intruders, one who safeguards his personal possessions in this manner is due the protection of the Fourth Amendment Warrant Clause."

Two years later, *Arkansas v. Sanders*, 442 U.S. 753 (1979), again addressed the issue of whether luggage could be searched without a warrant along with the rest of a vehicle. There, Little Rock, Arkansas, police had a tip that Lonnie Sanders would arrive at the airport carrying a green suitcase, holding marijuana. After he arrived, police watched him retrieve the suitcase from the baggage claim area and place it in the trunk of a taxi. The officers followed the taxi a short distance and then stopped it. Without Sanders's permission, they opened the suitcase containing marijuana. The issue in *Sanders*, as Justice Powell observed, was "whether the warrantless search of [Sanders's] suitcase falls on the *Chadwick* or the *Chambers-Carroll* side of the Fourth Amendment line." When holding that *Chadwick* was controlling there, Justice Powell explained that

> In sum, we hold that the warrant requirement of the Fourth Amendment applies to personal luggage taken from an automobile to the same degree it applies to such luggage in other locations. Thus, insofar as the police are entitled to search such luggage without a warrant, their actions must be justified under some exception to the warrant requirement other than that applicable to automobiles stopped on the highway. Where—as in the present case—the police, without endangering themselves or risking loss of the evidence, lawfully have detained one suspected of criminal activity and secured his suitcase, they should delay the search thereof until after judicial approval has been obtained. In this way, the constitutional right of suspects to prior judicial review of searches will be fully protected.

Justices Blackmun and Rehnquist dissented, contending that the Court had undercut the *Carroll-Chambers* doctrine and invited litigation over all kinds of articles that might be found in vehicles—"the briefcase, the wallet, the package, the paper bag, and every other kind of container."

In *Robbins v. California*, 453 U.S. 420 (1981), the Court then held that an opaque container in the trunk of a car could not be searched without a warrant, even though police had probable cause to search the vehicle and the container. In this case, police had stopped a station wagon that was being driven erratically, and when the driver opened the door of the vehicle they smelled marijuana. A search of the passenger compartment yielded some marijuana. After arresting Jeffrey Robbins, the police then opened the tailgate of the station wagon and searched a recessed luggage compartment, where they found two green garbage bags containing marijuana.

But in *United States v. Ross*, 456 U.S. 798 (1982), following Justice O'Connor's appointment, the Burger Court overturned *Robbins*. Notably, in his opinion for the Court Justice Stevens maintained that *Chadwick* and *Sanders* remained valid, although the dissenters disagreed. Subsequently, as the composition of the bench changed further in the late 1980s and 1990s, the Rehnquist Court incrementally broadened the scope of police searches of automobile occupants and their belongings.[4] Finally, *California v. Acevedo*, 500 U.S. 565 (1991) (excerpted below), expressly overruled *Chadwick* and *Arkansas v. Sanders*.

After over a decade of rulings cutting back on the scope of the Fourth Amendment's application to automobile searches, however, the Court held that police may not conduct full searches of cars stopped for minor traffic violations and whose drivers are issued citations, rather than arrested. That 1998 ruling in *Knowles v. Iowa* (excerpted below) was unanimous and handed down by Chief Justice Rehnquist, who drew a "bright line" limiting automobile searches in a short opinion for the Court.

Nonetheless, the Court underscored in a brief *per curiam* opinion, in *Maryland v. Dyson*, 527 U.S. 465 (1999), that the automobile exception to the Fourth Amendment's warrant requirement does not require police to obtain a warrant to search a car when they have probable cause to believe that it contains contraband. By a six-to-three vote in *Wyoming v. Houghton*, 526 U.S. 295 (1999), the Court also reaffirmed that police may search the belongings of passengers in cars if they have probable cause for doing so. In *Florida v. White*, 526 U.S. 559 (1999), the Court held that the Fourth Amendment does not require police to obtain a warrant before seizing an automobile from a public place when they have probable cause to believe that it is forfeitable contraband. Moreover, in *Atwater v. Lago Vista* (2001) (excerpted below) a bare majority held that police may arrest and hold drivers stopped for routine misdemeanor traffic violations, which are punishable only by fines. The Court also reaffirmed and extended its ruling in *New York v. Belton*, 453 U.S. 454 (1981), holding that after police make a custodial arrest of a driver, they may search the car as a contemporaneous incident of the arrest. In *Thorton v. United States*, 124 S.Ct. 2127 (2004), Chief Justice Rehnquist held that under *Belton* police may permissibly search the passenger compartment of a car after the driver got out and a pat down revealed drugs in his pocket, for which he was arrested. A subsequent search of the car revealed a handgun under the driver's seat, for which Thorton was also prosecuted. Justices Stevens and Souter dissented.

NOTES

1. *New York v. Belton*, 453 U.S. 454 (1981); *Michigan v. Long*, 463 U.S. 1032 (1983); and *Whren and Brown v. United States*, 116 S. Ct. 1769 (1996).

2. *Cardwell v. Lewis*, 417 U.S. 583 (1964) (with probable cause, warrantless inspection of exterior of car is permissible). *Harris v. United States*, 390 U.S. 234 (1968) upheld the use of an automobile registration card found in plain view in an impounded car. See *Texas v. Brown*, 460 U.S. 730 (1983).

3. In *Preston v. United States*, 376 U.S. 364 (1964), however, the Warren Court held that a search of a car, after the driver's arrest and the car was taken to a garage, was too remote to be a search incident to an arrest. But *Chambers v. Maroney*, 399 U.S. 42 (1970), upheld the search of a car in a police station, and *South Dakota v. Opperman*, 428 U.S. 543 (1976), upheld routine inventory searches of locked cars impounded by police.

4. See *United States v. Johns*, 469 U.S. 478 (1985); and *Colorado v. Bertine*, 479 U.S. 367 (1987); but see *Florida v. Wells*, 495 U.S. 1 (1990). Also in *United States v. Jacobsen*, 466 U.S. 109 (1984), the Court found no Fourth Amendment violation where employees of a private freight company opened a damaged package to note its contents, found white powder wrapped in plastic bags, and notified federal agents who seized and tested the powder.

United States v. Robinson
414 U.S. 218, 94 S.Ct. 467 (1973)

Justice William Rehnquist discusses the facts in his opinion for the Court in this case that involves a search incident to the arrest of the driver of an automobile.

The Court's decision was six to three, and the majority's opinion was announced by Justice Rehnquist. The dissent was by Justice Marshall, who was joined by Justices Brennan and Douglas.

☐ *Justice REHNQUIST delivered the opinion of the Court.*

Respondent Robinson was convicted in United States District Court for the District of Columbia of the possession and facilitation of concealment of heroin. He was sentenced to concurrent terms of imprisonment for these offenses. On his appeal to the Court of Appeals for the District of Columbia Circuit, that court first remanded the case to the District Court for an evidentiary hearing concerning the scope of the search of respondent's person which had occurred at the time of his arrest. The District Court made findings of fact and conclusions of law adverse to respondent, and he again appealed. This time the Court of Appeals en banc reversed the judgment of conviction, holding that the heroin introduced in evidence against respondent had been obtained as a result of a search which violated the Fourth Amendment to the United States Constitution. . . .

[A]t approximately 11 P.M., Officer Richard Jenks, a 15-year veteran of the District of Columbia Metropolitan Police Department, observed the respondent driving a 1965 Cadillac near the intersection of 8th and C Streets, N.E., in the District of Columbia. Jenks, as a result of previous investigation following a check of respondent's operator's permit four days earlier, determined there was reason to believe that respondent was operating a motor vehicle after the revocation of his operator's permit. . . .

Jenks signaled respondent to stop the automobile, which respondent did, and all three of the occupants emerged from the car. At that point Jenks informed respondent that he was under arrest for "operating after revocation and obtaining a permit by misrepresentation." It was assumed by the Court of Appeals, and is conceded by the respondent here, that Jenks had probable cause to arrest respondent, and that he effected a full-custody arrest.

In accordance with procedures prescribed in police department instructions, Jenks then began to search respondent. He explained at a subsequent hearing that he was "face-to-face" with the respondent, and "placed [his] hands on [the respondent], my right-hand to his left breast like this (demonstrating) and proceeded to pat him down thus [with the right hand]." During this patdown, Jenks felt an object in the left breast pocket of the heavy coat respondent was wearing, but testified that he "couldn't tell what it was" and also that he "couldn't actually tell the size of it." Jenks then reached into the pocket and pulled out the object, which turned out to be a "crumpled up cigarette package." Jenks testified that at this point he still did not know what was in the package:

> "As I felt the package I could feel objects in the package but I couldn't tell what they were. . . . I knew they weren't cigarettes."

The officer then opened the cigarette pack and found 14 gelatin capsules of white powder which he thought to be, and which later analysis proved to be, heroin. Jenks then continued his search of respondent to completion, feeling around his waist and trouser legs, and examining the remaining pockets. The heroin seized from the respondent was admitted into evidence at the trial which resulted in his conviction in the District Court. . . .

We conclude that the search conducted by Jenks in this case did not offend the limits imposed by the Fourth Amendment, and we therefore reverse the judgment of the Court of Appeals.

It is well settled that a search incident to a lawful arrest is a traditional exception to the warrant requirement of the Fourth Amendment. This general exception has historically been formulated into two distinct propositions. The first is that a search may be made of the *person* of the arrestee by virtue of the lawful arrest. The second is that a search may be made of the area within the control of the arrestee. . . .

In its decision of this case, the Court of Appeals decided that even after a police officer lawfully places a suspect under arrest for the purpose of taking him into custody, he may not ordinarily proceed to fully search the prisoner. He must, instead, conduct a limited frisk of the outer clothing and remove such weapons that he may, as a result of that limited frisk, reasonably believe and ascertain that the suspect has in his possession. While recognizing that *Terry v. Ohio*, [392 U.S. 1 (1968)], dealt with a permissible "frisk" incident to an investigative stop based on less than probable cause to arrest, the Court of Appeals felt that the principles of that case should be carried over to this probable-cause arrest for driving while one's license is revoked. Since there would be no further evidence of such a crime to be obtained in a search of the arrestee, the court held that only a search for weapons could be justified.

Terry v. Ohio did not involve an arrest for probable cause, and it made quite clear that the "protective frisk" for weapons which it approved might be conducted without probable cause. This Court's opinion explictly recognized that there is a "distinction in purpose, character, and extent between a search incident to an arrest and a limited search for weapons." . . . *Terry*, therefore, affords no basis to carry over to a probable-cause arrest the limitations this Court placed on a stop-and-frisk search permissible without probable cause. . . .

Virtually all of the statements of this Court affirming the existence of an unqualified authority to search incident to a lawful arrest are dicta. We would not, therefore, be foreclosed by principles of *stare decisis* from further examination into history and practice in order to see whether the sort of qualifications imposed by the Court of Appeals in this case were in fact intended by the Framers of the Fourth Amendment or recognized in cases decided prior to *Weeks* [*v. United States*, 232 U.S. 383 (1914)]. Unfortunately such authorities as exist are sparse. Such common-law treatises as Blackstone's *Commentaries* and HOLMES' *Common Law* are simply silent on the subject. . . .

It is scarcely open to doubt that the danger to an officer is far greater in the case of the extended exposure which follows the taking of a suspect into custody and transporting him to the police station than in the case of the relatively fleeting contact resulting from the typical *Terry*-type stop. This is an adequate basis for treating all custodial arrests alike for purposes of search justification.

The search of respondent's person conducted by Officer Jenks in this case and the seizure from him of the heroin, were permissible under established Fourth Amendment law. While thorough, the search partook of none of the extreme or patently abusive characteristics which were held to violate the Due Process Clause of the Fourteenth Amendment in *Rochin v. California*, 342 U.S. 165 (1952). Since it is the fact of custodial arrest which gives rise to the authority to search, it is of no moment that Jenks did not indicate any subjective fear of the respondent or that he did not himself suspect that respondent was armed. Having in the course of a lawful search come upon the crumpled package of cigarettes, he was entitled to inspect it; and when his inspection revealed the heroin capsules, he was entitled to seize them as "fruits, instrumentalities, or contraband" probative of criminal conduct.

☐ *Justice MARSHALL, with whom Justice DOUGLAS and Justice BRENNAN join, dissenting.*

Certain fundamental principles have characterized this Court's Fourth Amendment jurisprudence over the years. Perhaps the most basic of these was expressed by Justice BUTLER, speaking for a unanimous Court in *Go-Bart Co. v. United States*, 282 U.S. 344 (1931): "There is no formula for the determination of reasonableness. Each case is to be decided on its own facts and circumstances." . . .

In the present case, however, the majority turns its back on these principles, holding that "the fact of the lawful arrest" always establishes the authority to conduct a full search of the arrestee's person, regardless of whether in a particular case "there was present one of the reasons supporting the authority for a search of the person incident to a lawful arrest." The majority's approach represents a clear and marked departure from our long tradition of case-by-case adjudication of the reasonableness of searches and seizures under the Fourth Amendment. I continue to believe that "[t]he scheme of the Fourth Amendment becomes meaningful only when it is assured that at some point the conduct of those charged with enforcing the laws can be subjected to the more detached, neutral scrutiny of a judge who must evaluate the reasonableness of a particular search or seizure in light of the particular circumstances." *Terry v. Ohio*, 392 U.S. 1 (1968). Because I find the majority's reasoning to be at odds with these fundamental principles, I must respectfully dissent. . . .

No question is raised here concerning the lawfulness of the patdown of respondent's coat pocket. . . .

In the present case, however, Officer Jenks had no reason to believe and did not in fact believe that the object in respondent's coat pocket was a weapon. He admitted later that the object did not feel like a gun. . . .

Since the removal of the object from the pocket cannot be justified as part of a limited *Terry* weapons frisk, the question arises whether it is reasonable for a police officer, when effecting an in-custody arrest of a traffic offender, to make a fuller search of the person than is permitted pursuant to *Terry*.

The underlying rationale of a search incident to arrest of a traffic offender initially suggests as reasonable a search whose scope is similar to the protective weapons frisk permitted in *Terry*. A search incident to arrest, as the majority indicates, has two basic functions: the removal of weapons the arrestee might use to resist arrest or effect an escape, and the seizure of evidence or fruits of the crime for which the arrest is made, so as to prevent their concealment or destruction. . . .

The Government does not now contend that the search of respondent's pocket can be justified by any need to find and seize evidence in order to prevent its concealment or destruction, for, as the Court of Appeals found, there is no evidence or fruits of the offense with which respondent was charged. The only rationale for a search in this case, then, is the removal of weapons which the arrestee might use to harm the officer and attempt an escape. This rationale, of course, is identical to the rationale of the search permitted in *Terry*. . . . Since the underlying rationale of a *Terry* search and the search of a traffic violator are identical, the Court of Appeals held that the scope of the searches must be the same. And in view of its conclusion that the removal of the object from respondent's coat pocket exceeded the scope of a lawful *Terry* frisk, a conclusion not disputed by the Government or challenged by the majority here, the plurality of the Court of Appeals held that the removal of the package exceeded the scope of a lawful search incident to arrest of a traffic violator.

The problem with this approach, however, is that it ignores several significant differences between the context in which a search incident to arrest for a traffic violation is made, and the situation presented in *Terry*. Some of these differences would appear to suggest permitting a more thorough search in this case than was permitted in *Terry*; other differences suggest a narrower, more limited right to search than was there recognized.

The most obvious difference between the two contexts relates to whether the officer has cause to believe that the individual he is dealing with possesses weapons which might be used against him. *Terry* did not permit an officer to conduct a weapons frisk of anyone he lawfully stopped on the street, but rather, only where "he has reason to believe that he is dealing with an armed and dangerous individual. . . ."

Nor was there any particular reason in this case to believe that respondent was dangerous. He had not attempted to evade arrest, but had quickly complied with the police both in bringing his car to a stop after being signaled to do so and in producing the documents Officer Jenks requested. In fact, Jenks admitted that he searched respondent face to face rather than in spread-eagle fashion because he had no reason to believe respondent would be violent. . . .

The majority opinion [also] fails to recognize that the search conducted by Officer Jenks did not merely involve a search of respondent's person. It also included a separate search of effects found on his person. And even were we to assume, *arguendo*, that it was reasonable for Jenks to remove the object he felt in respondent's pocket, clearly there was no justification consistent with the Fourth Amendment which would authorize his opening the package and looking inside. . . .

The Government argues that it is difficult to see what constitutionally protected "expectation of privacy" a prisoner has in the interior of a cigarette pack. One wonders if the result in this case would have been the same were respondent a businessman who was lawfully taken into custody for driving without a license and whose wallet was taken from him by the police. Would it be reasonable for the police officer, because of the possibility that a razor blade was hidden somewhere in the wallet, to open it, remove all the contents, and examine each item carefully? Or suppose a lawyer lawfully arrested for a traffic offense is found to have a sealed envelope on his person. Would it be permissible for the arresting officer to tear open the envelope in order to make sure that it did not contain a clandestine weapon—perhaps a pin or a razor blade? . . .

I, for one, cannot characterize any of these intrusions into the privacy of an individual's papers and effects as being negligible incidents to the more serious intrusion into the individual's privacy stemming from the arrest itself. Nor can any principled distinction be drawn between the hypothetical searches I have posed and the search of the cigarette package in this case. The only reasoned distinction is between warrantless searches which serve legitimate protective and evidentiary functions and those that do not.

Illinois v. Lidster

124 S.CT. 885 (2004)

Shortly after midnight in Lombard, Illinois, a seventy-year-old bicyclist was killed in a hit-and-run accident. A week later, at about the same time and same place, police set up a highway checkpoint. Drivers were stopped, asked whether they had witnessed the incident, and given a flyer requesting assistance in identifying the vehicle and driver. As Robert Lidster approached the checkpoint, his van swerved, nearly hitting an officer, and subsequently he failed a sobriety test. Following his arrest and conviction for driving under the influence of alcohol, his attorney challenged the lawfulness of the arrest and conviction on the ground that the informational checkpoint stop violated the Fourth Amendment. The trial court dismissed the challenge, but the Illinois state supreme court disagreed and held that, under *Indianapolis v. Edmond*, 431 U.S. 32 (2000), such informational checkpoint stops lack individual suspicion and, hence, run afoul of the Fourth Amendment.

The state supreme court's decision was reversed by a vote of six to three. Justice Breyer delivered the opinion for the Court. Justice Stevens, joined by Justices Souter and Ginsburg, filed an opinion in part concurring and dissenting.

☐ *Justice BREYER delivered the opinion of the Court.*

This Fourth Amendment case focuses upon a highway checkpoint where police stopped motorists to ask them for information about a recent hit-and-run accident. We hold that the police stops were reasonable, hence, constitutional.

The Illinois Supreme Court basically held that our decision in [*Indianapolis v.*] *Edmond*, [531 U.S. 32 (2000)] governs the outcome of this case. We do not agree. *Edmond* involved a checkpoint at which police stopped vehicles to look for evidence of drug crimes committed by occupants of those vehicles. After stopping a vehicle at the checkpoint, police would examine (from outside the vehicle) the vehicle's interior; they would walk a drug-sniffing dog around the exterior; and, if they found sufficient evidence of drug (or other) crimes, they would arrest the vehicle's occupants. We found that police had set up this checkpoint primarily for general "crime control" purposes, i.e., "to detect evidence of ordinary criminal wrongdoing." We noted that the stop was made without individualized suspicion. And we held that the Fourth Amendment forbids such a stop, in the absence of special circumstances.

The checkpoint stop here differs significantly from that in *Edmond*. The stop's primary law enforcement purpose was not to determine whether a vehicle's occupants were committing a crime, but to ask vehicle occupants, as members of the public, for their help in providing information about a crime in all likelihood committed by others. The police expected the information elicited to help them apprehend, not the vehicle's occupants, but other individuals.

Edmond's language, as well as its context, makes clear that the constitutionality of this latter, information-seeking kind of stop was not then before the Court. . . . We concede that *Edmond* describes the law enforcement objective there in question as a "general interest in crime control," but it specifies that the phrase "general interest in crime control" does not refer to every "law enforcement" objective. We must read this and related general language in *Edmond* as we often read general language in judicial opinions—as referring in context to circumstances similar to the circumstances then before the Court and not referring to quite different circumstances that the Court was not then considering.

Neither do we believe, *Edmond* aside, that the Fourth Amendment would have us apply an *Edmond*-type rule of automatic unconstitutionality to brief, information-seeking highway stops of the kind now before us. For one thing, the fact that such stops normally lack individualized suspicion cannot by itself determine the constitutional outcome. The Fourth Amendment does not treat a motorist's car as his castle. And special law enforcement concerns will sometimes justify highway stops without individualized suspicion. See *Michigan Dept. of State Police v. Sitz*, 496 U.S. 444 (1990) (sobriety checkpoint); [*United States v.*] *Martinez-Fuerte*, [428 U.S. 543 (1976)] (Border Patrol checkpoint). Moreover, unlike *Edmond*, the context here (seeking information from the public) is one in which, by definition, the concept of individualized suspicion has little role to play. Like certain other forms of police activity, say, crowd control or public safety, an information-seeking stop is not the kind of event that involves suspicion, or lack of suspicion, of the relevant individual.

For another thing, information-seeking highway stops are less likely to provoke anxiety or to prove intrusive. The stops are likely brief. The police are not likely to ask questions designed to elicit self-incriminating information. . . .

Finally, we do not believe that an *Edmond*-type rule is needed to prevent an unreasonable proliferation of police checkpoints. Practical considerations—namely, limited police resources and community hostility to related traffic tie-ups—seem likely to inhibit any such proliferation. And, of course, the Fourth Amendment's normal insistence that the stop be reasonable in context will still provide an important legal limitation on police use of this kind of information-seeking checkpoint. . . .

We now consider the reasonableness of the checkpoint stop before us in light of the factors just mentioned. . . . We hold that the stop was constitutional.

The relevant public concern was grave. Police were investigating a crime that had resulted in a human death. . . . The stop advanced this grave public concern to a significant degree. Most importantly, the stops interfered only minimally with liberty of the sort the Fourth Amendment seeks to protect. Viewed objectively, each stop required only a brief wait in line—a very few minutes at most. . . . Viewed subjectively, the contact provided little reason for anxiety or alarm. The police stopped all vehicles systematically. And there is no allegation here that the police acted in a discriminatory or otherwise unlawful manner while questioning motorists during stops.

For these reasons we conclude that the checkpoint stop was constitutional.

☐ *Justice STEVENS, with whom Justice SOUTER and Justice GINSBURG join, concurring in part and dissenting in part.*

There is a valid and important distinction between seizing a person to determine whether she has committed a crime and seizing a person to ask whether she has any information about an unknown person who committed a crime a week earlier. I therefore join [p]arts of the Court's opinion explaining why our decision in *Indianapolis v. Edmond* is not controlling in this case. However, I find the issue . . . closer than the Court does and believe it would be wise to remand the case to the Illinois state courts to address that issue in the first instance.

In contrast to pedestrians, who are free to keep walking when they encounter police officers handing out flyers or seeking information, motorists who confront a roadblock are required to stop, and to remain stopped for as long as the officers choose to detain them. Such a seizure may seem relatively innocuous to some, but annoying to others who are forced to wait for several minutes when the line of cars is lengthened—for example, by a surge of vehicles leaving a factory at the end of a shift. Still other drivers may find an unpublicized roadblock at midnight on a Saturday somewhat alarming.

On the other side of the equation, the likelihood that questioning a random sample of drivers will yield useful information about a hit-and-run accident that occurred a week earlier is speculative at best. To be sure, the sample in this case was not entirely random: The record reveals that the police knew that the victim had finished work at the Post Office shortly before the fatal accident, and hoped that other employees of the Post Office or the nearby industrial park might work on similar schedules and, thus, have been driving the same route at the same time the previous week. That is a plausible theory, but there is no evidence in the record that the police did anything to confirm that the nearby businesses in fact had shift changes at or near midnight on Saturdays, or that they had reason to believe that a roadblock would be more effective than, say, placing flyers on the employees' cars.

In short, [w]e should be especially reluctant to abandon our role as a court of review in a case in which the constitutional inquiry requires analysis of local conditions and practices more familiar to judges closer to the scene. I would therefore remand the case to the Illinois courts to undertake the initial analysis of the issue that the Court resolves in . . . its opinion. To that extent, I respectfully dissent.

■ Inside the Court

Memorandum from Justice Sandra Day O'Connor on California v. Acevedo

Supreme Court of the United States
Washington, D. C. 20543

CHAMBERS OF
JUSTICE SANDRA DAY O'CONNOR

May 14, 1990

MEMORANDUM TO THE CONFERENCE:

Re: A-783: California v. Acevedo

California has applied for an order staying enforcement of a judgment of the California Court of Appeal pending disposition of its petition for certiorari (No. 89-1690). I have entered a stay to allow consideration of the petition.

In this case, respondent was arrested and charged with offenses arising from possession of marijuana for sale. The police observed respondent place a brown paper lunch bag, which they had probable cause to believe contained illegal drugs, in his car. The police stopped the car and searched the bag, which contained one-quarter to one-half pound of marijuana.

Respondent moved to suppress the evidence on the ground that the search violated his rights under the Fourth Amendment. The trial court denied the motion to suppress, but the California Court of Appeal reversed. The Court of Appeal noted that our decisions in United States v. Chadwick, 433 U.S. 1 (1977), and United States v. Ross, 456 U.S. 798 (1982), established the following rule: If the police have probable cause to search a vehicle, they may make a warrantless search of every container within the vehicle; if the police have probable cause only to search a particular container within the vehicle, they must obtain a search warrant before searching it. Because the police here only had probable cause to search the brown bag, the Court of Appeal determined that the warrantless search violated respondent's Fourth Amendment rights.

In its application, California asks this Court to determine that this case is governed by Ross and its predecessors, which established an automobile exception to the Fourth Amendment warrant requirement. California also notes that the issue presented in the petition for certiorari is the question this Court deadlocked on in Oklahoma v. Castleberry, 471 U.S. 146 (1985).

I have granted the stay to allow the Court to consider the cert petition in the usual course. Because I think the issue raised by this cert petition--whether police may make a warrantless search of a container contained in a motor vehicle even though they have probable cause only to search the container--warrants plenary review, I plan to vote to grant the petition.

Sincerely,

Sandra

Source: Papers of Justice Thurgood Marshall, Library of Congress.

California v. Acevedo

500 U.S. 565, 111 S.CT. 1982 (1991)

In October 1987, police in Santa Ana, California, received a telephone call from a federal drug-enforcement agent in Hawaii, informing them that he had seized a package of marijuana that was to have been delivered by Federal Express to a house in Santa Ana. It was decided that the agent would send the package to the police instead and they would take it to the local Federal Express office and arrest the person who claimed it. A few days later, Jamie Daza claimed the package and then drove to his apartment, taking the package in with him. While still staked out at his apartment an hour later, police observed Daza leave to throw away the box and paper that had contained the marijuana into a trash bin. At that point, one of the officers left the scene to get a search warrant, but before the officer returned police saw Richard St. George leave the apartment carrying a blue knapsack that appeared to be half full. The officers stopped him as he was driving off, searched the knapsack, and found twelve pounds of marijuana. A little later, Charles Acevedo arrived at the apartment and, after about ten minutes, reappeared carrying a brown paper bag that looked full. Acevedo walked to a silver Honda in the parking lot and placed the bag in the trunk of the car and started the car's engine. Fearing the loss of evidence, officers in a marked police car stopped him and subsequently, without a warrant, opened the trunk and the bag and found marijuana.

Acevedo was charged with possession of marijuana. At his trial he moved to suppress the introduction of the marijuana as evidence against him on the grounds that it was obtained in violation of his Fourth Amendment rights. After his motion was denied, he pleaded guilty and, after his conviction and sentence, appealed the court's denial of his motion to suppress the marijuana as evidence. A state appellate court concluded that the marijuana should have been suppressed on the grounds that the officers had probable cause to believe that the paper bag contained drugs but lacked probable cause to suspect that Acevedo's car, itself, otherwise contained contraband. Because the officers' probable cause was directed specifically at the bag, the court held that the case was controlled by *United States v. Chadwick*, 433 U.S. 1 (1977), which held that under similar circumstances police needed a warrant to search a large trunk placed in the back of a car, rather than by *United States v. Ross*, 456 U.S. 798 (1982), which had upheld a warrantless search of containers in the trunk of a car that police had probable cause to believe was being used by a drug dealer. Although the court agreed that the officers could seize the paper bag, it held that, under *Chadwick*, they could not open the bag without first obtaining a warrant for that purpose. Subsequently, the state of California appealed that ruling to the state supreme court, which denied review, and to the Supreme Court, which granted review.

The Court's decision was six to three. Justice Blackmun announced the majority opinion, with which Justice Scalia concurred. Justice White delivered a dissenting opinion, as did Justice Stevens, who was joined by Justice Marshall.

☐ *Justice BLACKMUN delivered the opinion of the Court.*

In *Carroll, v. United States*, 267 U.S. 132 (1925) this Court . . . held that a warrantless search of an automobile based upon probable cause to believe that the vehicle contained evidence of crime in the light of an exigency arising out of the likely disappearance of the vehicle did not contravene the Warrant Clause of the Fourth Amendment.

The Court refined the exigency requirement in *Chambers v. Maroney*, 399 U.S. 42 (1970), when it held that the existence of exigent circumstances was to be determined at the time the automobile is seized. . . . Following *Chambers*, if the police have probable cause to justify a warrantless seizure of an automobile on a public roadway, they may conduct either an immediate or a delayed search of the vehicle.

In *United States v. Ross*, 456 U.S. 798, decided in 1982, we held that a warrantless search of an automobile under the *Carroll* doctrine could include a search of a container or package found inside the car when such a search was supported by probable cause. . . . In *Ross*, therefore, we clarified the scope of the *Carroll* doctrine as properly including a "probing search" of compartments and containers within the automobile so long as the search is supported by probable cause.

In addition to this clarification, *Ross* distinguished the *Carroll* doctrine from the separate rule that governed the search of closed containers. The Court had announced this separate rule, unique to luggage and other closed packages, bags, and containers, in *United States v. Chadwick*, 433 U.S. 1 (1977). In *Chadwick*, federal narcotics agents had probable cause to believe that a 200-pound double-locked footlocker contained marijuana. The agents tracked the locker as the defendants removed it from a train and carried it through the station to a waiting car. As soon as the defendants lifted the locker into the trunk of the car, the agents arrested them, seized the locker, and searched it. In this Court . . . the United States urged that the search of movable luggage could be considered analogous to the search of an automobile. The Court rejected this argument because, it reasoned, a person expects more privacy in his luggage and personal effects than he does in his automobile. . . .

In *Arkansas v. Sanders*, 442 U.S. 753 (1979), the Court extended *Chadwick*'s rule to apply to a suitcase actually being transported in the trunk of a car. In *Sanders*, the police had probable cause to believe a suitcase contained marijuana. They watched as the defendant placed the suitcase in the trunk of a taxi and was driven away. The police pursued the taxi for several blocks, stopped it, found the suitcase in the trunk, and searched it. Although the Court had applied the *Carroll* doctrine to searches of integral parts of the automobile itself, indeed, in *Carroll*, contraband whiskey was in the upholstery of the seats, it did not extend the doctrine to the warrantless search of personal luggage "merely because it was located in an automobile lawfully stopped by the police." Again, the *Sanders* majority stressed the heightened privacy expectation in personal luggage and concluded that the presence of luggage in an automobile did not diminish the owner's expectation of privacy in his personal items.

In *Ross*, the Court endeavored to distinguish between *Carroll*, which governed the *Ross* automobile search, and *Chadwick*, which governed the *Sanders* automobile search. It held that the *Carroll* doctrine covered searches of automobiles when the police had probable cause to search an entire vehicle but that the *Chadwick* doctrine governed searches of luggage when the officers had probable cause to search only a container within the vehicle. Thus, in a *Ross* situation, the police could conduct a reasonable search under the Fourth Amendment without obtaining a warrant, whereas in a *Sanders* situation, the police had to obtain a warrant before they searched. . . .

The facts in this case closely resemble the facts in *Ross*. . . . This Court in *Ross* rejected *Chadwick*'s distinction between containers and cars. . . . [But w]e now must decide the question deferred in *Ross*: whether the Fourth Amendment requires the police to obtain a warrant to open the sack in a movable vehicle simply because they lack probable cause to search the entire car. We conclude that it does not. . . .

We now agree that a container found after a general search of the automobile and a container found in a car after a limited search for the container are equally easy for the police to store and for the suspect to hide or destroy. In fact, we see no principled distinction in terms of either the privacy expectation or the exigent circumstances between the paper bag found by the police in *Ross* and the paper bag found by the police here. Furthermore, by attempting to distinguish between a container for which the police are specifically searching and a container which they come across in a car, we have provided only minimal protection for privacy and have impeded effective law enforcement. . . .

We conclude that it is better to adopt one clear-cut rule to govern automobile searches and eliminate the warrant requirement for closed containers set forth in *Sanders*. The interpretation of the *Carroll* doctrine set forth in *Ross* now applies to all searches of containers found in an automobile. In other words, the police may search without a warrant if their search is supported by probable cause.

☐ *Justice STEVENS, with whom Justice MARSHALL joins, dissenting.*

In its opinion today, the Court recognizes that the police did not have probable cause to search respondent's vehicle and that a search of anything but the paper bag that respondent had carried from Daza's apartment and placed in the trunk of his car would have been unconstitutional. Moreover, as I read the opinion, the Court assumes that the police could not have made a warrantless inspection of the bag before it was placed in the car. Finally, the Court also does not question the fact that, under our prior cases, it would have been lawful for the police to seize the container and detain it (and respondent) until they obtained a search warrant. Thus, all of the relevant facts that governed our decisions in *Chadwick* and *Sanders* are present here whereas the relevant fact that justified the vehicle search in *Ross* is not present. The Court does not attempt to identify any exigent circumstances that would justify its refusal to apply the general rule against warrantless searches. Instead, it advances these three arguments: First, the rules identified in the foregoing cases are confusing and anomalous. Second, the rules do not protect any significant interest in privacy. And, third, the rules impede effective law enforcement. None of these arguments withstands scrutiny.

THE "CONFUSION"

In the nine years since *Ross* was decided, the Court has considered three cases in which the police had probable cause to search a particular container and one in which they had probable cause to search two vehicles. The decisions in all four of those cases were perfectly straightforward and provide no evidence of confusion in the state or lower federal courts.

In *United States v. Place*, 462 U.S. 696 (1983), we held that, although reasonable suspicion justifies the temporary detention of an airline passenger's luggage, the seizure in that particular case was unreasonable because of the prolonged delay in ascertaining the existence of probable cause. . . . In *Oklahoma v. Castleberry*, 471 U.S. 146 (1985), police officers had probable cause to believe the defendant carried narcotics in blue suitcases in the trunk of his car. After arresting him, they opened the trunk, seized the suitcases, and searched them without a warrant. The state court held that the search was invalid. . . . This Court affirmed by an equally divided court. In the case the Court decides today, the California Court of Appeal also had no difficulty applying the critical distinction. . . .

In the case in which the police had probable cause to search two vehicles, *United States v. Johns*, 469 U.S. 478 (1985), we rejected the respondent's reliance on *Chadwick* with a straightforward explanation of why that case, unlike *Ross*, did not involve an exception to the warrant requirement. We first expressed our agreement with the Court of Appeals that the Customs officers who had conducted the search had probable cause to search the vehicles. We then explained:

> "Under the circumstances of this case, respondents' reliance on *Chadwick* is misplaced. . . . *Chadwick*. . . . did not involve the exception to the warrant requirement recognized in *Carroll v. United States*, because the police had no probable cause to believe that the automobile, as contrasted to the footlocker, contained contraband. This point is underscored by our decision in *Ross*, which held that notwithstanding *Chadwick* police officers may conduct a warrantless search of containers discovered in the course of a lawful vehicle search. Given our conclusion that the Customs officers had probable cause to believe that the pickup trucks contained contraband, *Chadwick* is simply inapposite."

The decided cases thus provide no support for the Court's concern about "confusion." The Court instead relies primarily on predictions that were made by Justice BLACKMUN in his dissenting opinions in *Chadwick* and *Sanders*. The Court, however, cites no evidence that these predictions have in fact materialized or that anyone else has been unable to understand the "inherent opaqueness," of this uncomplicated issue. . . .

To the extent there was any "anomaly" in our prior jurisprudence, the Court has "cured" it at the expense of creating a more serious paradox. For, surely it is anomalous to prohibit a search of a briefcase while the owner is carrying it exposed on a public street yet to permit a search once the owner has placed the briefcase in the locked trunk of his car. . . .

THE PRIVACY ARGUMENT

The Court's statement that *Chadwick* and *Sanders* provide only "minimal protection to privacy," is also unpersuasive. Every citizen clearly has an interest in the privacy of the contents of his or her luggage, briefcase, handbag or any other container that conceals private papers and effects from public scrutiny. That privacy interest has been recognized repeatedly in cases spanning more than a century. Under the Court's holding today, the privacy interest that protects the contents of a suitcase or a briefcase from a warrantless search when it is in public view simply vanishes when its owner climbs into a taxicab. . . .

THE BURDEN ON LAW ENFORCEMENT

In the years since *Ross* was decided, the Court has heard argument in 30 Fourth Amendment cases involving narcotics. In all but one, the government was the petitioner. All save two involved a search or seizure without a warrant or with a defective warrant. And, in all except three, the Court upheld the constitutionality of the search or seizure. In the meantime, the flow of narcotics cases through the courts has steadily and dramatically increased. . . . No impartial observer could criticize this Court for hindering the progress of the war on drugs. On the contrary, decisions like the one the Court makes today will support the conclusion that this Court has become a loyal foot soldier in the Executive's fight against crime. Even if the warrant requirement does inconvenience the police to some extent, that fact does not distinguish this constitutional requirement from any other procedural protection secured by the Bill of Rights. It is merely a part of the price that our society must pay in order to preserve its freedom. . . .

I respectfully dissent.

Knowles v. Iowa

525 U.S. 113, 119 S.Ct. 484 (1998)

The facts are discussed the Court's opinion reversing the decision of the Iowa Supreme Court. The Court's decision was unanimous and opinion delivered by Chief Justice Rehnquist.

☐ *Chief Justice REHNQUIST delivered the opinion of the Court.*

An Iowa police officer stopped petitioner Knowles for speeding, but issued him a citation rather than arresting him. The question presented is whether such a procedure authorizes the officer, consistently with the Fourth Amendment, to conduct a full search of the car. We answer this question "no."

Knowles was stopped in Newton, Iowa, after having been clocked driving 43 miles per hour on a road where the speed limit was 25 miles per hour. The police officer issued a citation to Knowles, although under Iowa law he might have arrested him. The officer then conducted a full search of the car, and under the driver's seat he found a bag of marijuana and a "pot pipe." Knowles was then arrested and charged with violation of state laws dealing with controlled substances.

Before trial, Knowles moved to suppress the evidence so obtained. He argued that the search could not be sustained under the "search incident to arrest" exception recognized in *United States v. Robinson*, 414 U.S. 218 (1973), because he had not been placed under arrest. At the hearing on the motion to suppress, the police officer conceded that he had neither Knowles's consent nor probable cause to conduct the search. . . .

In *Robinson*, we noted the two historical rationales for the "search incident to arrest" exception: (1) the need to disarm the suspect in order to take him into custody, and (2) the need to preserve evidence for later use at trial. But neither of these underlying rationales for the search incident to arrest exception is sufficient to justify the search in the present case.

We have recognized that the first rationale—officer safety—is " 'both legitimate and weighty,' " *Maryland v. Wilson*, 519 U.S. 408 (1997). The threat to officer safety from issuing a traffic citation, however, is a good deal less than in the case of a custodial arrest. In *Robinson*, we stated that a custodial arrest involves "danger to an officer" because of "the extended exposure which follows the taking of a suspect into custody and transporting him to the police station." We recognized that "the danger to the police officer flows from the fact of the arrest, and its attendant proximity, stress, and uncertainty, and not from the grounds for arrest." *Id.* A routine traffic stop, on the other hand, is a relatively brief encounter and "is more analogous to a so-called '*Terry* stop' . . . than to a formal arrest." *Berkemer v. McCarty*, 468 U.S. 420 (1984).

This is not to say that the concern for officer safety is absent in the case of a routine traffic stop. It plainly is not. But while the concern for officer safety in this context may justify the "minimal" additional intrusion of ordering a driver and passengers out of the car, it does not by itself justify the often considerably greater intrusion attending a full field-type search. Even without the search authority Iowa urges, officers have other, independent bases to search for weapons and protect themselves from danger. For example, they may order out of a vehicle both the driver, [*Pennsylvania v.*] *Mimns*, [434 U.S. 106 (1977)], and any passengers, *Wilson*; perform a "patdown" of a driver and any passengers upon reasonable suspicion that they may be armed and dangerous, *Terry v. Ohio*, 392 U.S. 1 (1968); conduct a "*Terry* patdown" of the passenger compartment of a vehicle upon reasonable suspicion that an occupant is dangerous and may gain immediate control of a weapon, *Michigan v. Long*, 463 U.S. 1032 (1983); and even conduct a full search of the passenger compartment, including any containers therein, pursuant to a custodial arrest, *New York v. Belton*, 453 U.S. 454 (1981).

Nor has Iowa shown the second justification for the authority to search incident to arrest—the need to discover and preserve evidence. Once Knowles was stopped for speeding and issued a citation, all the evidence necessary to prosecute that offense had been obtained. No further evidence of excessive speed was going to be found either on the person of the offender or in the passenger compartment of the car.

Iowa nevertheless argues that a "search incident to citation" is justified because a suspect who is subject to a routine traffic stop may attempt to hide or destroy evidence related to his identity (e.g., a driver's license or vehicle registration), or destroy evidence of another, as yet undetected crime. As for the destruction of evidence relating to identity, if a police officer is not satisfied with the identification furnished by the driver, this may be a basis for arresting him rather than merely issuing a citation. As for destroying evidence of other crimes, the possibility that an officer would stumble onto evidence wholly unrelated to the speeding offense seems remote.

In *Robinson*, we held that the authority to conduct a full-field search as incident to an arrest was a "bright-line rule," which was based on the concern for officer safety and destruction or loss of evidence, but which did not depend in every case upon the existence of either concern. Here we are asked to extend that "bright-line rule" to a situation where the concern for officer safety is not present to the same extent and the concern for destruction or loss of evidence is not present at all. We decline to do so. The judgment of the Supreme Court of Iowa is reversed, and the case remanded for further proceedings not inconsistent with this opinion.

It is so ordered.

Atwater v. Lago Vista

532 U.S. 318, 121 S.Ct. 1536 (2001)

In Texas, if a car is equipped with safety belts, a front-seat passenger must wear one and the driver must secure any small child riding in front. Violation of either provision is "a misdemeanor punishable by a fine not less than $25 or more than $50." Texas law expressly authorizes "[a]ny peace officer [to] arrest without warrant a person found committing a violation" of these seatbelt laws, although it permits police to issue citations in lieu of arrest.

In March 1997, Gail Atwater was driving her pickup truck in Lago Vista, Texas, with her 3-year-old son and 5-year-old daughter in the front seat. None of them was wearing a seatbelt. A Lago Vista police officer observed the seatbelt violations and pulled Atwater over. According to Atwater, the officer approached the truck and "yell[ed]" something to the effect of "[w]e've met before" and "[y]ou're going to jail." He then called for backup and asked to see Atwater's driver's license and insurance documentation, which state law required her to carry. When Atwater told him that she did not have the papers because her purse had been stolen the day before, the officer said that he had "heard that story two-hundred times." Atwater asked to take her "frightened, upset, and crying" children to a friend's house nearby, but the officer told her, "[y]ou're not going anywhere." As it turned out, Atwater's friend learned what was going on and soon arrived to take charge of the children. The officer then handcuffed Atwater and drove her to the local police station, where booking officers had her remove her shoes, jewelry, and eyeglasses, and empty her pockets. Officers took Atwater's "mug shot" and placed her in a jail cell for an hour, after which she was taken before a magistrate and released on $310 bond. Atwater was charged with driving without her seatbelt fastened, failing to secure her children in seatbelts, driving without a license, and failing to provide proof of insurance. She pleaded no contest to the misdemeanor seatbelt offenses and paid a $50 fine.

Subsequently, Atwater filed suit in a state court against the officer and the city of Lago Vista, alleging that her "right to be free from unreasonable seizure" had been violated. The city moved the suit to a federal district court, which deemed the Fourth Amendment claim "meritless." On appeal, a panel of the Court of Appeals for the Fifth Circuit reversed, concluding that "an arrest for a first-time seat belt offense" was an unreasonable seizure within the meaning of the Fourth Amendment. But sitting *en banc*, the Court of Appeals vacated that decision and affirmed the district court's judgment for the city. Atwater appealed to the Supreme Court, which granted *certiorari*.

The appellate court's decision was affirmed by a five-to-four vote. Justice Souter delivered the opinion for the Court. Justice O'Connor filed a dissenting opinion, which Justices Stevens, Ginsburg, and Breyer joined.

☐ *Justice SOUTER delivered the opinion of the Court.*

The question is whether the Fourth Amendment forbids a warrantless arrest for a minor criminal offense, such as a misdemeanor seatbelt violation punishable only by a fine. We hold that it does not.

We begin with the state of pre-founding English common law and find that, even after making some allowance for variations in the common-law usage of the term "breach of the peace," the "founding-era common-law rules" were not nearly as clear as Atwater claims; on the contrary, the common-law commentators (as well as the sparsely reported cases) reached divergent conclusions with respect to officers' warrantless misdemeanor arrest power.

Atwater's historical argument begins with our quotation from Halsbury in *Carroll v. United States*, 267 U.S. 132 (1925), that " '[i]n cases of misdemeanor, a peace officer like a private person has at common law no power of arresting without a warrant except when a breach of the peace has been committed in his presence or there is reasonable ground for supposing that a breach of peace is about to be committed or renewed in his presence.' " But the isolated quotation tends to mislead. In *Carroll* itself we spoke of the common-law rule as only "sometimes expressed" that way and, indeed, in the very same paragraph, we conspicuously omitted any reference to a breach-of-the-peace limitation in stating that the "usual rule" at common law was that "a police officer [could] arrest without warrant . . . one guilty of a misdemeanor if committed in his presence." Thus, what *Carroll* illustrates, and what others have recognized, is that statements about the common law of warrantless misdemeanor arrest simply are not uniform. Rather, "[a]t common law there is a difference of opinion among the authorities as to whether this right to arrest [without a warrant] extends to all misdemeanors." American Law Institute, Code of Criminal Procedure. . . .

We thus find disagreement, not unanimity, among both the common-law jurists and the text-writers who sought to pull the cases together and summarize accepted practice. Having reviewed the relevant English decisions, as well as English and colonial American legal treatises, legal dictionaries, and procedure manuals, we simply are not convinced that Atwater's is the correct, or even necessarily the better, reading of the common-law history.

A second, and equally serious, problem for Atwater's historical argument is posed by the "divers Statutes," enacted by Parliament well before this Republic's founding that authorized warrantless misdemeanor arrests without reference to violence or turmoil. Quite apart from Hale and Blackstone, the legal background of any conception of reasonableness the Fourth Amendment's Framers might have entertained would have included English statutes, some centuries old, authorizing peace officers (and even private persons) to make warrantless arrests for all sorts of relatively minor offenses unaccompanied by violence. . . .

An examination of specifically American evidence is to the same effect. Neither the history of the framing era nor subsequent legal development indicates that the Fourth Amendment was originally understood, or has traditionally been read, to embrace Atwater's position.

To begin with, Atwater has cited no particular evidence that those who framed and ratified the Fourth Amendment sought to limit peace officers' warrantless misdemeanor arrest authority to instances of actual breach of the peace, and our own review of the recent and respected compilations of framing-era documentary history has likewise failed to reveal any such design. Nor have we found in any of the modern historical accounts of the Fourth Amendment's adoption any substantial indication that the Framers intended such a restriction. Indeed, to the extent the modern histories address the issue, their conclusions are to the contrary.

The evidence of actual practice also counsels against Atwater's position. During the period leading up to and surrounding the framing of the Bill of Rights, colonial and state legislatures, like Parliament before them, regularly authorized local peace officers to make warrantless misdemeanor arrests without conditioning statutory authority on breach of the peace. . . .

Nor does Atwater's argument from tradition pick up any steam from the historical record as it has unfolded since the framing, there being no indication that her claimed rule has ever become "woven . . . into the fabric" of American law. The story, on the contrary, is of two centuries of uninterrupted (and largely unchallenged) state and federal practice permitting warrantless arrests for misdemeanors not amounting to or involving breach of the peace. . . .

Small wonder, then, that today statutes in all 50 States and the District of Columbia permit warrantless misdemeanor arrests by at least some (if not all) peace officers without requiring any breach of the peace, as do a host of congressional enactments. . . .

If we were to derive a rule exclusively to address the uncontested facts of this case, Atwater might well prevail. She was a known and established resident of Lago Vista with no place to hide and no incentive to flee, and common sense says she would almost certainly have buckled up as a condition of driving off with a citation. In her case, the physical incidents of arrest were merely gratuitous humiliations imposed by a police officer who was (at best) exercising extremely poor judgment. Atwater's claim to live free of pointless indignity and confinement clearly outweighs anything the City can raise against it specific to her case.

But we have traditionally recognized that a responsible Fourth Amendment balance is not well served by standards requiring sensitive, case-by-case determinations of government need, lest every discretionary judgment in the field be converted into an occasion for constitutional review. Often enough, the Fourth Amendment has to be applied on the spur (and in the heat) of the moment, and the object in implementing its command of reasonableness is to draw standards sufficiently clear and simple to be applied with a fair prospect of surviving judicial second-guessing months and years after an arrest or search is made. Courts attempting to strike a reasonable Fourth Amendment balance thus credit the government's side with an essential interest in readily administrable rules.

At first glance, Atwater's argument may seem to respect the values of clarity and simplicity, so far as she claims that the Fourth Amendment generally forbids warrantless arrests for minor crimes not accompanied by violence or some demonstrable threat of it (whether "minor crime" be defined as a fine-only traffic offense, a fine-only offense more generally, or a misdemeanor). But the claim is not ultimately so simple, nor could it be, for complications arise the moment we begin to think about the possible applications of the several criteria Atwater proposes for drawing a line between minor crimes with limited arrest authority and others not so restricted.

One line, she suggests, might be between "jailable" and "fine-only" offenses, between those for which conviction could result in commitment and those for which it could not. The trouble with this distinction, of course, is that an officer on the street might not be able to tell. It is not merely that we cannot expect every police officer to know the details of frequently complex penalty schemes, but that penalties for ostensibly identical conduct can vary on account of facts difficult (if not impossible) to know at the scene of an arrest. Is this the first offense or is the suspect a repeat offender? Is the weight of the marijuana a gram above or a gram below the fine-only line? Where conduct could implicate more than one criminal prohibition, which one will the district attorney ultimately decide to charge? And so on. . . .

There is no need for more examples to show that Atwater's general rule and limiting proviso promise very little in the way of administrability. . . . Atwater's rule therefore would not only place police in an almost impossible spot but would guarantee increased litigation over many of the arrests that would occur. . . .

Accordingly, we confirm today what our prior cases have intimated: the standard of probable cause "applie[s] to all arrests, without the need to 'balance' the interests and circumstances involved in particular situations." *Dunaway v. New York*, 442 U.S. 200 (1979). If an officer has probable cause to believe that an individual has committed even a very minor criminal offense in his presence, he may, without violating the Fourth Amendment, arrest the offender. . . .

☐ *Justice O'CONNOR, with whom Justice STEVENS, Justice GINSBURG, and Justice BREYER join, dissenting.*

A full custodial arrest, such as the one to which Ms. Atwater was subjected, is the quintessential seizure. See *Payton v. New York*, 445 U.S. 573 (1980). When a full custodial arrest is effected without a warrant, the plain language of the Fourth Amendment requires that the arrest be reasonable. It is beyond cavil that "[t]he touchstone of our analysis under the Fourth Amendment is always 'the reasonableness in all the circumstances of the particular governmental invasion of a citizen's personal security.' " *Pennsylvania v. Mimms*, 434 U.S. 106 (1977).

We have "often looked to the common law in evaluating the reasonableness, for Fourth Amendment purposes, of police activity." *Tennessee v. Garner*, 471 U.S. 1 (1985). But history is just one of the tools we use in conducting the reasonableness inquiry. And when history is inconclusive, as the majority amply demonstrates it is in this case, we will "evaluate the search or seizure under traditional standards of reasonableness by assessing, on the one hand, the degree to which it intrudes upon an individual's privacy and, on the other, the degree to which it is needed for the promotion of legitimate governmental interests." *Wyoming v. Houghton*, [526 U.S. 295 (1999)].

[W]e have held that the existence of probable cause is a necessary condition for an arrest. And in the case of felonies punishable by a term of imprisonment, we have held that the existence of probable cause is also a sufficient condition for an arrest. See *United States v. Watson*, 423 U.S. 411 (1976). In *Watson*, however, there was a clear and consistently applied common law rule permitting warrantless felony arrests. Accordingly, our inquiry ended there and we had no need to assess the reasonableness of such arrests by weighing individual liberty interests against state interests.

Here, however, we have no such luxury. The Court's thorough exegesis makes it abundantly clear that warrantless misdemeanor arrests were not the subject of a clear and consistently applied rule at common law. We therefore must engage in the balancing test required by the Fourth Amendment. While probable cause is surely a necessary condition for warrantless arrests for fine-only offenses, any realistic assessment of the interests implicated by such arrests demonstrates that probable cause alone is not a sufficient condition. . . .

A custodial arrest exacts an obvious toll on an individual's liberty and privacy, even when the period of custody is relatively brief. The arrestee is subject to a full search of her person and confiscation of her possessions. If the arrestee is the occupant of a car, the entire passenger compartment of the car, including packages therein, is subject to search as well. The arrestee may be detained for up to 48 hours without having a magistrate determine whether there in fact was probable cause for the arrest. See *County of Riverside v. McLaughlin*, 500 U.S. 44 (1991). Because people arrested for all types of violent and nonviolent offenses may be housed together awaiting such review, this detention period is potentially dangerous. And once the period of custody is over, the fact of the arrest is a permanent part of the public record. *Paul v. Davis*, 424 U.S. 693 (1976). . . .

Because a full custodial arrest is such a severe intrusion on an individual's liberty, its reasonableness hinges on "the degree to which it is needed for the promotion of legitimate governmental interests." *Wyoming v. Houghton.* In light of the availability of citations to promote a State's interests when a fine-only offense has been committed, I cannot concur in a rule which deems a full custodial arrest to be reasonable in every circumstance. Giving police officers constitutional carte blanche to effect an arrest whenever there is probable cause to believe a fine-only misdemeanor has been committed is irreconcilable with the Fourth Amendment's command that seizures be reasonable. Instead, I would require that when there is probable cause to believe that a fine-only offense has been committed, the police officer should issue a citation unless the officer is "able to point to specific and articulable facts which, taken together with rational inferences from those facts, reasonably warrant [the additional] intrusion" of a full custodial arrest. *Terry v. Ohio*, 392 U.S. [1 (1968)].

The majority insists that a bright-line rule focused on probable cause is necessary to vindicate the State's interest in easily administrable law enforcement rules. Probable cause itself, however, is not a model of precision. The rule I propose—which merely requires a legitimate reason for the decision to escalate the seizure into a full custodial arrest—thus does not undermine an otherwise "clear and simple" rule.

While clarity is certainly a value worthy of consideration in our Fourth Amendment jurisprudence, it by no means trumps the values of liberty and privacy at the heart of the Amendment's protections. What the *Terry* rule lacks in precision it makes up for in fidelity to the Fourth Amendment's command of reasonableness and sensitivity to the competing values protected by that Amendment. Over the past 30 years, it appears that the *Terry* rule has been workable and easily applied by officers on the street. . . .

The Court's error, however, does not merely affect the disposition of this case. The per se rule that the Court creates has potentially serious consequences for the everyday lives of Americans. A broad range of conduct falls into the category of fine-only misdemeanors. In Texas alone, for example, disobeying any sort of traffic warning sign is a misdemeanor punishable only by fine, as is failing to pay a highway toll, and driving with expired license plates. Nor are fine-only crimes limited to the traffic context. In several States, for example, littering is a criminal offense punishable only by fine.

To be sure, such laws are valid and wise exercises of the States' power to protect the public health and welfare. My concern lies not with the decision to enact or enforce these laws, but rather with the manner in which they may be enforced. Under today's holding, when a police officer has probable cause to believe that a fine-only misdemeanor offense has occurred, that officer may stop the suspect, issue a citation, and let the person continue on her way. Or, if a traffic violation, the officer may stop the car, arrest the driver, search the driver, search the entire passenger compartment of the car including any purse or package inside, and impound the car and inventory all of its contents. Although the Fourth Amendment expressly requires that the latter course be a reasonable and proportional response to the circumstances of the offense, the majority gives officers unfettered discretion to choose that course without articulating a single reason why such action is appropriate.

Such unbounded discretion carries with it grave potential for abuse. The majority takes comfort in the lack of evidence of "an epidemic of unnecessary minor-offense arrests." But the relatively small number of published cases dealing with such arrests proves little and should provide little solace. Indeed, as the recent debate over racial profiling demonstrates all too clearly, a relatively minor traffic infraction may often serve as an excuse for stopping and harassing an individual. After today, the arsenal available to any officer extends to a full arrest and the searches permissible concomitant to that arrest. . . .

The Court neglects the Fourth Amendment's express command in the name of administrative ease. In so doing, it cloaks the pointless indignity that Gail Atwater suffered with the mantle of reasonableness. I respectfully dissent.

D | *Other Governmental Searches in the Administrative State*

The Supreme Court permits a lower standard than probable cause for the issuance of warrants for *administrative searches*—searches by public officials other than police, such as housing, health, safety, and welfare inspectors. The Court also allows for some types of warrantless administrative searches, depending on the kind of search and the manner in which it is conducted. Whether an administrative warrant is required turns on the Court's balancing of individuals' privacy interests against competing governmental interests in conducting various types of searches—housing inspections, for example, welfare visitations, or inspections for violation of health, safety, and environmental regulations.

Initially, in *Frank v. Maryland*, 359 U.S. 360 (1959), the Court held that administrative searches were outside the purview of the Fourth Amendment, when permitting warrantless housing inspections conducted at reasonable times and aimed at enforcing health regulations. Justice Felix Frankfurter held that only searches aimed at obtaining evidence of criminal activity required prior judicial approval. But dissenting Chief Justice Warren and Justices Black, Douglas, and Brennan complained that the majority's distinction between criminal and civil searches diluted Fourth Amendment-protected privacy interests. The amendment, in Justice Douglas's words, was designed to protect the citizen against uncontrolled invasion of his privacy. It does not make the home a place of refuge from the law. It only requires the sanction of the judiciary rather than the executive before that privacy may be invaded. History shows that all officers tend to be officious; and health inspectors, making out a case for criminal prosecution of the citizen are no exception. . . . One invasion of privacy by an official of the government can be as oppressive as another. . . . It would seem that the public interest in protecting privacy is equally as great in one case as another.

Frank's dissenters continued objecting to the formalistic dichotomy between criminal and civil searches, but they could not win a majority over to their side until the Court's composition changed. Finally, they were joined by Justices Byron White and Abe Fortas, who had replaced on the bench two members of the *Frank* majority. In two companion 1967 cases—*Camara v. Municipal Court*, 387 U.S. 523 (1967), and *See v. City of Seattle*, 387 U.S. 541 (1967)—the Court held that a search warrant was required when an owner denies permission for entry and search of his premises by housing and safety inspectors.

Writing for the Court in *Camera*, Justice White ruled, on the one hand, that the Fourth Amendment bars prosecution of a person for refusing to permit administrative officials to conduct warrantless inspections and, on the other hand, that administrative warrants may be issued on showing less than probable cause, as required in criminal cases. The standard for issuing administrative warrants, he explained,

will vary with the municipal program being enforced, may be based upon the passage of time, the nature of the building (e.g., a multifamily apartment house), or the condition of the entire area, but they will not necessarily depend upon specific knowledge of the conditions of the particular dwelling. It has been suggested that to so vary the probable cause test from the standard applied in criminal cases would be to authorize a "synthetic search warrant" and thereby to lessen the overall protections of the Fourth Amendment. . . . But we do not agree. The warrant procedure is designed to guarantee that a decision to search private property is justified by a reasonable governmental interest. But reasonableness is still the ultimate standard. If a valid public interest justifies the intrusion contemplated, there is probable cause to issue a suitably restricted search warrant.

Probable cause remains required for search warrants aimed at uncovering evidence of criminal activity, but administrative searches may be based "balancing the need to search against the invasions which the search entails."

Whether an administrative warrant is required depends on the government's interests and the type and manner of the search, as well as the competing interests in personal privacy. In *Marshall v. Barlow's Inc.*, 436 U.S. 307 (1978), for example, the Court struck down a provision in the Occupational Safety and Health Act authorizing warrantless inspections of workplaces for safety violations. When holding that the businessman's right of privacy included the right to have a magistrate determine the reasonableness of a search according to an "administrative plan containing neutral criteria," Justice White emphasized that "[i]f the government intrudes on a person's property, the privacy interest suffers whether the government's motivation is to investigate violations of criminal laws or breaches of other statutory or regulatory standards."

Warrantless searches of mines and heavily regulated commercial business are permissible, however. In *New York v. Burger*, 482 U.S. 691 (1987), the Court upheld the warrantless search of an automobile junkyard. There Justice Blackmun explained:

> An owner or operator of a business thus has an expectation of privacy in commercial property, which society is prepared to consider to be reasonable, see *Katz v. United States*, 389 U.S. 347 (1967) (HARLAN, J., concurring). . . . An expectation of privacy in commercial premises, however, is different from, and indeed less than, a similar expectation in an individual's home. . . . Because the owner or operator of commercial premises in a "closely regulated" industry has a reduced expectation of privacy, the warrant and probable-cause requirements, which fulfill the traditional Fourth Amendment standard of reasonableness for a government search . . . have lessened application in this context. Rather, we conclude that, as in other situations of "special need," see *New Jersey v. T.L.O.*, 469 U.S. 325 (1985) [holding that a high school principal may search the belongings of students], where the privacy interests of the owner are weakened and the government interests in regulating particular businesses are concomitantly heightened, a warrantless inspection of commercial premises may well be reasonable within the meaning of the Fourth Amendment.

Blackmun proceeded to hold that warrantless administrative searches would "be deemed to be reasonable only so long as three criteria are met":

> First, there must be a "substantial" government interest that informs the regulatory scheme pursuant to which the inspection is made. . . . Second, the warrantless inspections must be "necessary to further [the] regulatory scheme." . . . Finally, "the statute's inspection program, in terms of the certainty and regularity of its application, [must] provid[e] a constitutionally adequate substitute for a warrant." . . . In other words, the regulatory scheme must perform the

two basic functions of a warrant: it must advise the owner of the commercial premises that the search is being made pursuant to the law and has a properly limited scope, and it must limit the discretion of the inspecting officers.

The Court has also been sharply split on according Fourth Amendment protection for the privacy interests of public employees. In *O'Connor v. Ortega*, 480 U.S. 709 (1987), the justices voted five to four to uphold a state hospital supervisor's warrantless search of an employee's office for work-related items.

Even more controversial for the Court and the country is the issue of drug and alcohol testing of public employees. In *National Treasury Employees Union v. Von Raab* (1989) (see excerpt below), the Rehnquist Court split five to four when upholding the U.S. Customs Service's drug-testing program for employees. In another ruling, in *Skinner v. Railway Labor Executives' Association*, 489 U.S. 602 (1989), the justices divided six to three over allowing mandatory drug and alcohol tests for railroad workers involved in serious accidents. Following those rulings, more than forty federal agencies began conducting drug tests under an executive order for a drug-free federal workplace. Carl Willner, an attorney in the antitrust division of the Department of Justice (DoJ), challenged the DoJ's drug-testing requirement as a violation of his Fourth-Amendment guarantee against unreasonable searches and seizures. In 1990, a federal district court ruled that "suspicionless testing" of employees was unconstitutional and should be limited to only public employees in jobs "affecting public safety, and those working directly with aspects of drug enforcement." But a three-judge panel of the Court of Appeals for the District of Columbia Circuit reversed, and the Rehnquist Court denied review to an appeal of that ruling in *Willner v. Barr*, 502 U.S. 1020 (1992).

Subsequently, in *Vernonia School District 47J v. Acton*, 515 U.S. 646 (1995), the Court upheld a public school district's policy requiring all students signing up for interscholastic sports to submit to a drug test and to remain subject to random tests throughout the year. Notably, Justice Scalia, who had dissented from the decision upholding the Custom Service's drug-testing policy for employees in *Von Raab* six years earlier, announced the Court's opinion in *Vernonia*. However, the Court drew the line in *Chandler v. Miller*, 520 U.S. 305 (1997), when striking down Georgia's law requiring candidates for political office to submit the results of a drug test in order to qualify to run in an election, and in *Ferguson v. Charleston* (2001) (excerpted below), striking down a state policy of testing pregnant women for cocaine use, without their consent, and informing police of those who tested positive. Writing for the Court, Justice Stevens refused to extend the "special needs" exception to the Fourth Amendment that had been applied in prior decisions upholding drug testing. However, splitting five to four in *Board of Education of Independent School District 92 of Pottawatomie City v. Earls* (2002) (excerpted below) the Court extended *Vernonia* to uphold the random drug testing of all middle and high school students who participate in extracurricular activities.

■ The Development of Law

Searches by Government Officials in the Administrative State

CASE	VOTE	RULING
Frank v. Maryland, 359 U.S. 360 (1959)	5:4	Warrant requirement does not apply to housing and health inspections, if conducted at reasonable times.
Abel v. United States, 362 U.S. 217 (1960)	5:4	Immigration officers may seize allegedly forged birth certificates without warrant.
Ohio ex. rel. Eaton v. Price, 364 U.S. 263 (1960)	4:4	Affirmed by an equally divided Court a lower court ruling upholding an ordinance authorizing housing inspectors to enter homes without warrants.
Camara v. Municipal Court, 387 U.S. 523 (1967); and *See v. City of Seattle*, 387 U.S. 541 (1967)	6:3	Search warrant required for housing and safety inspections.
Colonnade Catering Corporation v. United States, 397 U.S. 72 (1970)	6:3	Inspection for liquor license by IRS agents did not justify breaking and entering locked storeroom.
Wyman v. James, 400 U.S. 309 (1971)	6:3	Social workers may make warrantless searches of welfare recipients' homes.

CASE	VOTE	RULING
United States v. Biswell, 406 U.S. 311 (1972)	8:1	Upheld warrantless search of gun dealer's locked storeroom during business hours under Gun Control Act of 1968.
Air Pollution Variance Board of State of Colorado v. Western Alfalfa Corporation, 416 U.S. 861 (1974)	9:0	Upheld health inspector's entry of outdoor premises without consent of owner to observe smoke plumes.
California Bankers Association v. Schultz, 416 U.S. 21 (1974)	6:3	Upheld the record keeping and mandatory reporting of depositors' financial transactions under the Bank Secrecy Act.
United States v. Bisceglia, 420 U.S. 141 (1975)	7:2	The IRS has the power to issue "John Doe" summons to banks to identify depositors who filed fraudulent tax returns.
United States v. Miller, 425 U.S. 435 (1976)	7:2	Held depositors have no Fourth Amendment-protected interests in bank deposits.
United States v. Ramsey, 431 U.S. 606 (1977)	6:3	Customs officials may open mail without a warrant in search for narcotics.
Marshall v. Barlow's, Inc., 436 U.S. 307 (1978)	5:3	Struck down section of the Occupational Safety and Health Act authorizing agents to make warrantless inspections for safety violations.
Michigan v. Tyler, 436 U.S. 499 (1978)	6:3	Firefighters need no warrant to enter premises to fight a fire, but thereafter must obtain a warrant when investigating cause of fire.
Donovan v. Dewey, 452 U.S. 594 (1981)	8:1	Upheld warrantless inspection of mines.
Michigan v. Clifford, 464 U.S. 387 (1984)	5:4	Administrative warrant required for a postfire search; criminal warrant necessary if the object of search is evidence of criminal activity.

CASE	VOTE	RULING
Hudson v. Palmer, 468 U.S. 517 (1984)	6:3	Prison inmates have no reasonable expectation of privacy in prison cells from searches by guards.
New Jersey v. T.L.O., 469 U.S. 325 (1985)	6:3	Upheld principal's search of student's purse.
United States v. Jones, 469 U.S. 478 (1985); and *United States v. Sharpe*, 470 U.S. 675 (1985)	7:2	U.S. Customs officials may search a trunk with probable cause but no warrant; and a drug enforcement agent may delay a passenger at the airport without a warrant.
O'Connor v. Ortega, 480 U.S. 709 (1987)	5:4	State hospital supervisor's warrantless search of employee's office for work-related items upheld.
New York v. Burger, 482 U.S. 691 (1987)	6:3	Warrantless administrative search of "heavily regulated" commercial premises—here, a junkyard—permissible.
Griffin v. Wisconsin, 868 U.S. 483 (1987)	5:4	Upheld warrantless search of probationer's home on "reasonable grounds," rather than probable cause, for search.
National Treasury Employees Union v. Von Raab, 489 U.S. 656 (1989)	5:4	Upheld U.S. Customs Service's drug-testing program for employees.
Skinner v. Railway Labor Executives' Association, 489 U.S. 602 (1989)	6:3	Mandatory drug and alcohol testing for employees involved in accidents upheld.
Vernonia School District 47J v. Acton, 515 U.S. 646 (1995)	6:3	Upheld a public school district's policy requiring all students signing up for interscholastic sports to submit to a drug test

and to remain subject to random tests throughout the year.

| *Chandler v. Miller*, 520 U.S. 305 (1997) | 8:1 | Writing for the Court, Justice Ginsburg struck down Georgia's 1990 law requiring candidates |

for public office to submit to drug testing or to certify that they are drug free. Chief Justice Rehnquist dissented.

CASE	VOTE	RULING
Ferguson v. Charleston, 532 U.S. 67 (2001)	6:3	Held that a hospital's drug testing of pregnant women without their consent for law enforcement purposes was an unreasonable search and seizure. Chief Justice Rehnquist and Justices Scalia and Thomas dissented.
Board of Education of Independent School District No. 92 of Pottawatomie City v. Earls, 536 U.S. 822 (2002)	6:3	Upheld a school district's policy of requiring all students who participate in any extracurricular program to submit to random drug tests. Justices O'Connor, Stevens, and Souter dissented.

National Treasury Employees Union v. Von Raab

489 U.S. 656, 109 S.CT. 1384 (1989)

Justice Anthony Kennedy discusses the facts in this case, arising from a challenge to the U.S. Customs Service's mandatory drug-testing program, at the outset of his opinion for the Court.

The Court's decision was five to four, and the majority's opinion was announced by Justice Kennedy. Justices Marshall and Scalia dissented and were joined by Justices Brennan and Stevens.

☐ *Justice KENNEDY delivered the opinion of the Court.*

We granted *certiorari* to decide whether it violates the Fourth Amendment for the United States Customs Service to require a urinalysis test from employees who seek transfer or promotion to certain positions. The United States Customs Service, a bureau of the Department of the Treasury, is the federal agency responsible for processing persons, carriers, cargo, and mail into the United States, collecting revenue from imports, and enforcing customs and related laws. An important responsibility of the Service is the interdiction and seizure of contraband, including illegal drugs. . . . In the routine discharge of their duties, many Customs employees have direct contact with those who traffic in drugs for profit. Drug import operations, often directed by sophisticated criminal syndicates, *United States v. Mendenhall*, 446 U.S. 544 (1980) (POWELL, J., concurring), may be effected by violence or its threat. As a necessary response, many Customs operatives carry and use firearms in connection with their official duties. . . .

In December 1985, respondent, the Commissioner of Customs, established a Drug Screening Task Force to explore the possibility of implementing a drug screening program within the Service. After extensive research and consultation with experts in the field, the Task Force concluded "that drug screening through urinalysis is technologically reliable, valid and accurate." Citing this conclusion, the Commissioner announced his intention to require drug tests of employees who applied for, or occupied, certain positions within the Service. . . .

In May 1986, the Commissioner announced implementation of the drug-testing program. Drug tests were made a condition of placement or employment for positions that meet one or more of three criteria. The first is direct involvement in drug interdiction or enforcement of related laws, an activity the Commissioner deemed fraught with obvious dangers to the mission of the agency and the lives of Customs agents. The second criterion is a requirement that the incumbent carry firearms, as the Commissioner concluded that "[p]ublic safety demands that employees who carry deadly arms and are prepared to make instant life or death decisions be drug free." The third criterion is a requirement for the incumbent to handle "classified" material, which the Commissioner determined might fall into the hands of smugglers if accessible to employees who, by reason of their own illegal drug use, are susceptible to bribery or blackmail. . . .

After an employee qualifies for a position covered by the Customs testing program, the Service advises him by letter that his final selection is contingent upon successful completion of drug screening. An independent contractor contacts the employee to fix the time and place for collecting the sample. On reporting for the test, the employee must produce photographic identification and remove any outer garments, such as a coat or a jacket, and personal belongings. The employee may produce the sample behind a partition, or in the privacy of a bathroom stall if he so chooses. To ensure against adulteration of the specimen, or substitution of a sample from another person, a monitor of the same sex as the employee remains close at hand to listen for the normal sounds of urination. Dye is added to the toilet water to prevent the employee from using the water to adulterate the sample. . . .

The laboratory tests the sample for the presence of marijuana, cocaine, opiates, amphetamines, and phencyclidine. Two tests are used. An initial screening test uses the enzyme-multiplied-immunoassay technique (EMIT). Any specimen that is identified as positive on this initial test must then be confirmed using gas chromatography/mass spectrometry (GC/MS). Confirmed positive results are reported to a "Medical Review Officer," "[a] licensed physician . . . who has knowledge of substance abuse disorders and has appropriate medical training to interpret and evaluate the individual's positive test result together with his or her medical history and any other relevant biomedical information." After verifying the positive result, the Medical Review Officer transmits it to the agency.

Customs employees who test positive for drugs and who can offer no satisfactory explanation are subject to dismissal from the Service. Test results may not, however, be turned over to any other agency, including criminal prosecutors, without the employee's written consent.

Petitioners, a union of federal employees and a union official, commenced this suit in the United States District Court for the Eastern District of Louisiana on behalf of current Customs Service employees who seek covered positions. Petitioners alleged that the Custom Service drug-testing program violated the Fourth Amendment. The District Court agreed. . . . The court enjoined the drug testing program, and ordered the Customs Service not to require drug tests of any applicants for covered positions.

A divided panel of the United States Court of Appeals for the Fifth Circuit vacated the injunction. The court agreed with petitioners that the drug screening program, by requiring an employee to produce a urine sample for chemical testing, effects a search within the meaning of the Fourth Amendment. . . . [But] the court further found that the Government has a strong interest in detecting drug use among employees who meet the criteria of the Customs program. It reasoned that drug use by covered employees casts substantial doubt on their ability to discharge their duties honestly and vigorously, undermining public confidence in the integrity of the Service and concomitantly impairing the Service's efforts to enforce the drug laws. . . .

We now affirm so much of the judgment of the court of appeals as upheld the testing of employees directly involved in drug interdiction or required to carry firearms. We vacate the judgment to the extent it upheld the testing of applicants for positions requiring the incumbent to handle classified materials, and remand for further proceedings. . . .

We have recognized before that requiring the Government to procure a warrant for every work-related intrusion "would conflict with 'the common-sense realization that government offices could not function if every employment decision became a constitutional matter.'" *O'Connor v. Ortega*, [480 U.S. 709 (1987)]; *New Jersey v. T.L.O.*, [469 U.S. 325 (1985)] (noting that "[t]he warrant requirement . . . is unsuited to the school environment: requiring a teacher to obtain a warrant before searching a child suspected of an infraction of school rules (or of the criminal law) would unduly interfere with the maintenance of the swift and informal disciplinary procedures needed in the schools"). Even if Customs Service employees are more likely to be familiar with the procedures required to obtain a warrant than most other Government workers, requiring a warrant in this context would serve only to divert valuable agency resources from the Service's primary mission. The Customs Service has been entrusted with pressing responsibilities, and its mission would be compromised if it were required to seek search warrants in connection with routine, yet sensitive, employment decisions.

Furthermore, a warrant would provide little or nothing in the way of additional protection of personal privacy. A warrant serves primarily to advise the citizen that an intrusion is authorized by law and limited in its permissible scope and to interpose a neutral magistrate between the citizen and the law enforcement officer "engaged in the often competitive enterprise of ferreting out crime." *Johnson v. United States*, 333 U.S. 10 (1948). But in the present context, "the circumstances justifying toxicological testing and the permissible limits of such intrusions are defined narrowly and specifically . . . and doubtless are well known to covered employees." Under the Customs program, every employee who seeks a transfer to a covered position knows that he must take a drug test, and is likewise aware of the procedures the Service must follow in administering the test. A covered employee is simply not subject "to the discretion of the official in the field." *Camara v. Municipal Court*, 387 U.S. 523 (1967). The process becomes automatic when the employee elects to apply for, and thereafter pursue, a covered position. Because the Service does not make a discretionary determination to search based on a judgment that certain conditions are present, there are simply "no special facts for a neutral magistrate to evaluate." . . .

Even where it is reasonable to dispense with the warrant requirement in the particular circumstances, a search ordinarily must be based on probable cause. Our cases teach, however, that the probable-cause standard " 'is peculiarly related to criminal investigations.' " In particular, the traditional probable-cause standard may be unhelpful in analyzing the reasonableness of routine administrative functions especially where the Government seeks to *prevent* the development of hazardous conditions or to detect violations that rarely generate articulable grounds for searching any particular place or person. . . . Our precedents have settled that, in certain limited circumstances, the Government's need to discover such latent or hidden conditions, or to prevent their development, is sufficiently compelling to justify the intrusion on privacy entailed by conducting such searches without any measure of individualized suspicion. We think the Government's need to conduct the suspicionless searches required by the Customs program outweighs the privacy interests of employees engaged directly in drug interdiction, and of those who otherwise are required to carry firearms.

The Customs Service is our Nation's first line of defense against one of the greatest problems affecting the health and welfare of our population. . . .

It is readily apparent that the Government has a compelling interest in ensuring that front-line interdiction personnel are physically fit, and have unimpeachable integrity and judgment. Indeed, the Government's interest here is at least as important as its interest in searching travelers entering the country. We have long held that travelers seeking to enter the country may be stopped and required to submit to a routine search without probable cause, or even founded suspicion, "because of national self protection reasonably requiring one entering the country to identify himself as entitled to come in, and his belongings as effects which may be lawfully brought in." *Carroll v. United States*, 267 U.S. 132 (1925). This national interest in self protection could be irreparably damaged if those charged with safeguarding it were, because of their own drug use, unsympathetic to their mission of interdicting narcotics. A drug user's indifference to the Service's basic mission or, even worse, his active complicity with the malefactors, can facilitate importation of sizable drug shipments or block apprehension of dangerous criminals. The public interest demands effective measures to bar drug users from positions directly involving the interdiction of illegal drugs. . . .

Against these valid public interests we must weigh the interference with individual liberty that results from requiring these classes of employees to undergo a urine test. The interference with individual privacy that results from the collection of a urine sample for subsequent chemical analysis could be substantial in some circumstances. We have recognized, however, that the "operational realities of the workplace" may render entirely reasonable certain work-related intrusions by supervisors and co-workers that might be viewed as unreasonable in other contexts. See *O'Connor v. Ortega*. While these operational realities will rarely affect an employee's expectations of privacy with respect to searches of his person, or of personal effects that the employee may bring to the workplace, it is plain that certain forms of public employment may diminish privacy expectations even with respect to such personal searches. . . .

We think Customs employees who are directly involved in the interdiction of illegal drugs or who are required to carry firearms in the line of duty likewise have a diminished expectation of privacy in respect to the intrusions occasioned by a urine test. Unlike most private citizens or government employees in general, employees involved in drug interdiction reasonably should expect effective inquiry into their fitness and probity. Much the same is true of employees who are required to carry firearms. Because successful performance of their duties depends uniquely on their judgment and dexterity, these employees cannot reasonably expect to keep from the Service personal information that bears directly on their fitness. . . . While reasonable tests designed to elicit this information doubtless infringe some privacy expectations, we do not believe these expectations outweigh the Government's compelling interests in safety and in the integrity of our borders. . . .

In sum, we believe the Government has demonstrated that its compelling interests in safeguarding our borders and the public safety outweigh the privacy expectations of employees who seek to be promoted to positions that directly involve the interdiction of illegal drugs or that require the incumbent to carry a firearm. We hold that the testing of these employees is reasonable under the Fourth Amendment.

We are unable, on the present record, to assess the reasonableness of the Government's testing program insofar as it covers employees who are required "to handle classified material." . . . We readily agree that the Government has a compelling interest in protecting truly sensitive information from those who, "under compulsion of circumstances or for other reasons, . . . might compromise [such] information." *Department of the Navy v. Egan*, 484 U.S. 518 (1988). . . .

We also agree that employees who seek promotions to positions where they would handle sensitive information can be required to submit to a urine test under the Service's screening program, especially if the positions covered under this category require background investigations, medical examinations, or other intrusions that may be expected to diminish their expectations of privacy in respect of a urinalysis test. . . .

It is not clear, however, whether the category defined by the Service's testing directive encompasses only those Customs employees likely to gain access to sensitive information. Employees who are tested under the Service's scheme include those holding such diverse positions as "Accountant," "Accounting Technician," "Animal Caretaker," "Attorney (All)," "Baggage Clerk," "Co-op Student (All)," "Electric Equipment Repairer," "Mail Clerk/Assistant," and "Messenger." We assume these positions were selected for coverage under the Service's testing program by reason of the incumbent's access to "classified" information, as it is not clear that they would fall under either of the two categories we have already considered. Yet it is not evident that those occupying these positions are likely to gain access to sensitive information, and this apparent discrepancy raises in our minds the question whether the Service has defined this category of employees more broadly than necessary to meet the purposes of the Commissioner's directive.

We cannot resolve this ambiguity on the basis of the record before us, and we think it is appropriate to remand the case to the court of appeals for such proceedings as may be necessary to clarify the scope of this category of employees subject to testing. Upon remand the court of appeals should examine the criteria used by the Service in determining what materials are classified and in deciding whom to test under this rubric. In assessing the reasonableness of requiring tests of these employees, the court should also consider pertinent information bearing upon the employees' privacy expectations, as well as the supervision to which these employees are already subject.

Where the Government requires its employees to produce urine samples to be analyzed for evidence of illegal drug use, the collection and subsequent chemical analysis of such samples are searches that must meet the reasonableness requirement of the Fourth Amendment. Because the testing program adopted by the Customs Service is not designed to serve the ordinary needs of law enforcement, we have balanced the public interest in the Service's testing program against the privacy concerns implicated by the tests, without reference to our usual presumption in favor of the procedures specified in the Warrant Clause, to assess whether the tests required by Customs are reasonable.

We hold that the suspicionless testing of employees who apply for promotion to positions directly involving the interdiction of illegal drugs, or to positions which require the incumbent to carry a firearm, is reasonable. The Government's compelling interests in preventing the promotion of drug users to positions where they might endanger the integrity of our Nation's borders or the life of the citizenry outweigh the privacy interests of those who seek promotion to these positions, who enjoy a diminished expectation of privacy by virtue of the special, and obvious, physical and ethical demands of those positions. We do not decide whether testing those who apply for promotion to positions where they would handle "classified" information is reasonable because we find the record inadequate for this purpose.

The judgment of the Court of Appeals for the Fifth Circuit is affirmed in part and vacated in part, and the case is remanded for further proceedings consistent with this opinion.

It is so ordered.

☐ *Justice MARSHALL, with whom Justice BRENNAN joins, dissenting.*

For the reasons stated in my dissenting opinion in *Skinner v. Railway Labor Executives Association,* [489 U.S. 602 (1989)], I also dissent from the Court's decision in this case. Here, as in *Skinner,* the Court's abandonment of the Fourth Amendment's express requirement that searches of the person rest on probable cause is unprincipled and unjustifiable. But even if I believed that balancing analysis was appropriate under the Fourth Amendment, I would still dissent from today's judgment, for the reasons stated by Justice SCALIA in his dissenting opinion.

☐ *Justice SCALIA, with whom Justice STEVENS joins, dissenting.*

The issue in this case is not whether Customs Service employees can constitutionally be denied promotion, or even dismissed, for a single instance of unlawful drug use, at home or at work. They assuredly can. The issue here is what steps can constitutionally be taken to *detect* such drug use. . . .

Until today this Court had upheld a bodily search separate from arrest and without individualized suspicion of wrongdoing only with respect to prison inmates, relying upon the uniquely dangerous nature of that environment. See *Bell v. Wolfish*, 441 U.S. 520 (1979). Today, in *Skinner*, we allow a less intrusive bodily search of railroad employees involved in train accidents. I joined the Court's opinion there because the demonstrated frequency of drug and alcohol use by the targeted class of employees, and the demonstrated connection between such use and grave harm, rendered the search a reasonable means of protecting society. I decline to join the Court's opinion in the present case because neither frequency of use nor connection to harm is demonstrated or even likely. In my view the Customs Service rules are a kind of immolation of privacy and human dignity in symbolic opposition to drug use.

The Fourth Amendment protects the "right of the people to be secure in their persons, houses, papers, and effects, against unreasonable searches and seizures." While there are some absolutes in Fourth Amendment law, as soon as those have been left behind and the question comes down to whether a particular search has been "reasonable," the answer depends largely upon the social necessity that prompts the search. . . .

The Court's opinion in the present case, however, will be searched in vain for real evidence of a real problem that will be solved by urine testing of Customs Service employees. Instead, there are assurances that "[t]he Customs Service is our Nation's first line of defense against one of the greatest problems affecting the health and welfare of our population," that "[m]any of the Service's employees are often exposed to [drug smugglers] and to the controlled substances they seek to smuggle into the country," that "Customs officers have been the targets of bribery by drug smugglers on numerous occasions, and several have been removed from the Service for accepting bribes and other integrity violations." . . .

What is absent in the Government's justifications—notably absent, revealingly absent, and as far as I am concerned dispositively absent—is the recitation of *even a single instance* in which any of the speculated horribles actually occurred: an instance, that is, in which the cause of bribe-taking, or of poor aim, or of unsympathetic law enforcement, or of compromise of classified information, was drug use. . . .

The Court's response to this lack of evidence is that "[t]here is little reason to believe that American workplaces are immune from [the] pervasive social problem" of drug abuse. Perhaps such a generalization would suffice if the workplace at issue could produce such catastrophic social harm that no risk whatever is tolerable—the secured areas of a nuclear power plant, for example. But if such a generalization suffices to justify demeaning bodily searches, without particularized suspicion, to guard against the bribing or blackmailing of a law enforcement agent, or the careless use of a firearm, then the Fourth Amendment has become frail protection indeed. . . .

Today's decision would be wrong, but at least of more limited effect, if its approval of drug testing were confined to that category of employees assigned specifically to drug interdiction duties. Relatively few public employees fit that description. But in extending approval of drug testing to that category consisting of employees who carry firearms, the Court exposes vast numbers of public employees to this needless indignity. . . .

There is only one apparent basis that sets the testing at issue here apart from all these other situations—but it is not a basis upon which the Court is willing to rely. I do not believe for a minute that the driving force behind these drug-testing rules was any of the feeble justifications put forward by counsel here and accepted by the Court. The only plausible explanation, in my view, is what the Commissioner himself offered in the concluding sentence of his memorandum to Customs Service employees announcing the program: "Implementation of the drug screening program would set an important example in our country's struggle with this most serious threat to our national health and security." Or as respondent's brief to this Court asserted: "if a law enforcement agency and its employees do not take the law seriously, neither will the public on which the agency's effectiveness depends." What better way to show that the Government is serious about its "war on drugs" than to subject its employees on the front line of that war to this invasion of their privacy and affront to their dignity? To be sure, there is only a slight chance that it will prevent some serious public harm resulting from Service employee drug use, but it will show to the world that the Service is "clean," and—most important of all—will demonstrate the determination of the Government to eliminate this scourge of our society! I think it obvious that this justification is unacceptable; that the impairment of individual liberties cannot be the means of making a point; that symbolism, even symbolism for so worthy a cause as the abolition of unlawful drugs, cannot validate an otherwise unreasonable search.

Vernonia School District 47J v. Acton
515 U.S. 646, 115 S.Ct. 2386 (1995)

The parents of James Acton, a twelve-year-old seventh-grader with no indication of drug use, challenged the constitutionality of the Vernonia School District's drug-testing policy for students participating in school athletic programs. Teachers and school officials in Vernonia, a small logging community in Oregon, noticed a sharp increase in drug use and disciplinary problems in the late 1980s. Between 1988 and 1989, for instance, the number of disciplinary referrals doubled that reported in the early 1980s. In addition, school officials later testified during the trial that student athletes were not only among the drug users but were leaders of the drug culture. As a result, in the fall of 1989, the school board approved a drug-testing policy under which athletes had to sign a form consenting to drug testing and obtain the written consent of their parents. At the beginning of each season, every student athlete was tested for drugs. Throughout the season, then, 10 percent of the student athletes were randomly tested each week.

A federal district court rejected the Actons' claim that the school district's policy of random drug testing violated the Fourth Amendment's guarantee against "unreasonable searches and seizures." But the Court of Appeals for the Ninth Circuit reversed and school officials appealed to the Supreme Court.

The Court's decision was six to three and the opinion was delivered by Justice Scalia. Justice O'Connor filed a dissenting opinion, which was joined by Justices Stevens and Souter.

☐ *Justice SCALIA delivered the opinion of the Court.*

The Fourth Amendment to the United States Constitution provides that the Federal Government shall not violate "the right of the people to be secure in their persons, houses, papers, and effects, against unreasonable searches and seizures. . . ." We have held that the Fourteenth Amendment extends this constitutional guarantee to searches and seizures by state officers, including public school officials, *New Jersey v. T. L. O.*, 469 U.S. 325 (1985). In *Skinner v. Railway Labor Executives' Assn.*, 489 U.S. 602 (1989), we held that state-compelled collection and testing of urine, such as that required by the Student Athlete Drug Policy, constitutes a "search" subject to the demands of the Fourth Amendment. See also [*National Treasury Employees Union*] *v. Von Raab*, 489 U.S. 656 (1989).

As the text of the Fourth Amendment indicates, the ultimate measure of the constitutionality of a governmental search is "reasonableness." At least in a case such as this, where there was no clear practice, either approving or disapproving the type of search at issue, at the time the constitutional provision was enacted, whether a particular search meets the reasonableness standard "is judged by balancing its intrusion on the individual's Fourth Amendment interests against its promotion of legitimate governmental interests.' " *Skinner.* . . . A search unsupported by probable cause can be constitutional, we have said, "when special needs, beyond the normal need for law enforcement, make the warrant and probable-cause requirement impracticable." *Griffin v. Wisconsin*, 483 U.S. 868 (1987).

We have found such "special needs" to exist in the public-school context. There, the warrant requirement "would unduly interfere with the maintenance of the swift and informal disciplinary procedures [that are] needed," and "strict adherence to the requirement that searches be based upon probable cause" would undercut "the substantial need of teachers and administrators for freedom to maintain order in the schools." *T. L. O.* The school search we approved in *T. L. O.*, while not based on probable cause, was based on individualized suspicion of wrongdoing. As we explicitly acknowledged, however, "the Fourth Amendment imposes no irreducible requirement of such suspicion." We have upheld suspicionless searches and seizures to conduct drug testing of railroad personnel involved in train accidents, *Skinner*; to conduct random drug testing of federal customs officers who carry arms or are involved in drug interdiction, *Von Raab*; and to maintain automobile checkpoints looking for illegal immigrants and contraband, and drunk drivers, *Michigan Dept. of State Police v. Sitz*, 496 U.S. 444 (1990).

The first factor to be considered is the nature of the privacy interest upon which the search here at issue intrudes. The Fourth Amendment does not protect all subjective expectations of privacy, but only those that society recognizes as "legitimate." What expectations are legitimate varies, of course, with context, depending, for example, upon whether the individual asserting the privacy interest is at home, at work, in a car, or in a public park. In addition, the legitimacy of certain privacy expectations vis-a-vis the State may depend upon the individual's legal relationship with the State. . . . Central, in our view, to the present case is the fact that the subjects of the policy are (1) children, who (2) have been committed to the temporary custody of the State as schoolmaster. . . .

Fourth Amendment rights, no less than First and Fourteenth Amendment rights, are different in public schools than elsewhere; the "reasonableness" inquiry cannot disregard the schools' custodial and tutelary responsibility for children. For their own good and that of their classmates, public school children are routinely required to submit to various physical examinations, and to be vaccinated against various diseases. . . .

Legitimate privacy expectations are even less with regard to student athletes. School sports are not for the bashful. They require "suiting up" before each practice or event, and showering and changing afterwards. Public school locker rooms, the usual sites for these activities, are not notable for the privacy they afford. The locker rooms in Vernonia are typical: no individual dressing rooms are provided; shower heads are lined up along a wall, unseparated by any sort of partition or curtain; not even all the toilet stalls have doors. . . .

There is an additional respect in which school athletes have a reduced expectation of privacy. By choosing to "go out for the team," they voluntarily subject themselves to a degree of regulation even higher than that imposed on students generally. In Vernonia's public schools, they must submit to a preseason physical exam (James testified that his included the giving of a urine sample), they must acquire adequate insurance coverage or sign an insurance waiver, maintain a minimum grade point average, and comply with any "rules of conduct, dress, training hours and related matters as may be established for each sport by the head coach and athletic director with the principal's approval." . . .

Finally, we turn to consider the nature and immediacy of the governmental concern at issue here, and the efficacy of this means for meeting it. In both *Skinner* and *Von Raab*, we characterized the government interest motivating the search as "compelling." . . . It is a mistake, however, to think that the phrase "compelling state interest," in the Fourth Amendment context, describes a fixed, minimum quantum of governmental concern, so that one can dispose of a case by answering in isolation the question: Is there a compelling state interest here? Rather, the phrase describes an interest which appears important enough to justify the particular search at hand, in light of other factors which show the search to be relatively intrusive upon a genuine expectation of privacy. Whether that relatively high degree of government concern is necessary in this case or not, we think it is met.

That the nature of the concern is important—indeed, perhaps compelling—can hardly be doubted. Deterring drug use by our Nation's schoolchildren is at least as important as enhancing efficient enforcement of the Nation's laws against the importation of drugs, which was the governmental concern in *Von Raab*, or deterring drug use by engineers and trainmen, which was the governmental concern in *Skinner*. . . .

Taking into account all the factors we have considered above—the decreased expectation of privacy, the relative unobtrusiveness of the search, and the severity of the need met by the search—we conclude Vernonia's Policy is reasonable and hence constitutional. . . .

☐ *Justice O'CONNOR, with whom Justice STEVENS and Justice SOUTER join, dissenting.*

The population of our Nation's public schools, grades 7 through 12, numbers around 18 million. By the reasoning of today's decision, the millions of these students who participate in interscholastic sports, an overwhelming majority of whom have given school officials no reason whatsoever to suspect they use drugs at school, are open to an intrusive bodily search.

In justifying this result, the Court dispenses with a requirement of individualized suspicion on considered policy grounds. First, it explains that precisely because every student athlete is being tested, there is no concern that school officials might act arbitrarily in choosing who to test. Second, a broad-based search regime, the Court reasons, dilutes the accusatory nature of the search. In making these policy arguments, of course, the Court sidesteps powerful, countervailing privacy concerns. Blanket searches, because they can involve "thousands or millions" of searches, "pose a greater threat to liberty" than do suspicion-based ones, which "affect one person at a time," *Illinois v. Krull*, 480 U.S. 340 (1987) (O'CONNOR, J., dissenting). Searches based on individualized suspicion also afford potential targets considerable control over whether they will, in fact, be searched because a person can avoid such a search by not acting in an objectively suspicious way. And given that the surest way to avoid acting suspiciously is to avoid the underlying wrongdoing, the costs of such a regime, one would think, are minimal.

But whether a blanket search is "better" than a regime based on individualized suspicion is not a debate in which we should engage. In my view, it is not open to judges or government officials to decide on policy grounds which is better and which is worse. For most of our constitutional history, mass, suspicionless searches have been generally considered per se unreasonable within the meaning of the Fourth Amendment. And we have allowed exceptions in recent years only where it has been clear that a suspicion-based regime would be ineffectual. Because that is not the case here, I dissent.

In *Carroll v. United States*, 267 U.S. 132 (1925), the Court explained that "the Fourth Amendment does not denounce all searches or seizures, but only such as are unreasonable." Applying this standard, the Court first held that a search of a car was not unreasonable merely because it was warrantless; because obtaining a warrant is impractical for an easily movable object such as a car, the Court explained, a warrant is not required. The Court also held, however, that a warrantless car search was unreasonable unless supported by some level of individualized suspicion, namely probable cause. Significantly, the Court did not base its conclusion on the express probable cause requirement contained in the

Warrant Clause, which, as just noted, the Court found inapplicable. Rather, the Court rested its views on "what was deemed an unreasonable search and seizure when [the Fourth Amendment] was adopted" and "[what] will conserve public interests as well as the interests and rights of individual citizens." . . .

The *Carroll* Court's view that blanket searches are "intolerable and unreasonable" is well-grounded in history. . . . [W]hat the Framers of the Fourth Amendment most strongly opposed, with limited exceptions wholly inapplicable here, were general searches—that is, searches by general warrant, by writ of assistance, by broad statute, or by any other similar authority. . . .

The view that mass, suspicionless searches, however evenhanded, are generally unreasonable remains inviolate in the criminal law enforcement context, see *Ybarra v. Illinois*, 444 U.S. 85 (1979) (invalidating evenhanded, nonaccusatory patdown for weapons of all patrons in a tavern in which there was probable cause to think drug dealing was going on), at least where the search is more than minimally intrusive, see *Michigan Dept. of State Police v. Sitz*, 496 U.S. 444 (1990) (upholding the brief and easily avoidable detention, for purposes of observing signs of intoxication, of all motorists approaching a roadblock). . . .

Thus, it remains the law that the police cannot, say, subject to drug testing every person entering or leaving a certain drug-ridden neighborhood in order to find evidence of crime. And this is true even though it is hard to think of a more compelling government interest than the need to fight the scourge of drugs on our streets and in our neighborhoods. Nor could it be otherwise, for if being evenhanded were enough to justify evaluating a search regime under an open-ended balancing test, the Warrant Clause, which presupposes that there is some category of searches for which individualized suspicion is non-negotiable would be a dead letter. . . .

One searches today's majority opinion in vain for recognition that history and precedent establish that individualized suspicion is "usually required" under the Fourth Amendment (regardless of whether a warrant and probable cause are also required) and that, in the area of intrusive personal searches, the only recognized exception is for situations in which a suspicion-based scheme would be likely ineffectual. Far from acknowledging anything special about individualized suspicion, the Court treats a suspicion-based regime as if it were just any run-of-the-mill, less intrusive alternative—that is, an alternative that officials may bypass if the lesser intrusion, in their reasonable estimation, is outweighed by policy concerns unrelated to practicability. . . .

The great irony of this case is that most (though not all) of the evidence the District introduced to justify its suspicionless drug-testing program consisted of first- or secondhand stories of particular, identifiable students acting in ways that plainly gave rise to reasonable suspicion of in-school drug use— and thus that would have justified a drug-related search under our *T. L. O.* decision. Small groups of students, for example, were observed by a teacher "passing joints back and forth" across the street at a restaurant before school and during school hours. Another group was caught skipping school and using drugs at one of the student's houses. Several students actually admitted their drug use to school officials (some of them being caught with marijuana pipes). . . .

In light of all this evidence of drug use by particular students, there is a substantial basis for concluding that a vigorous regime of suspicion-based testing would have gone a long way toward solving Vernonia's school drug problem while preserving the Fourth Amendment rights of James Acton and others like him. . . .

I recognize that a suspicion-based scheme, even where reasonably effective in controlling in-school drug use, may not be as effective as a mass, suspicionless testing regime. In one sense, that is obviously true—just as it is obviously true that suspicion-based law enforcement is not as effective as mass, suspicionless enforcement might be. "But there is nothing new in the realization" that Fourth Amendment protections come with a price. *Arizona v. Hicks*, 480 U.S. 321 (1987). . . .

I find unpersuasive the Court's reliance on the widespread practice of physical examinations and vaccinations, which are both blanket searches of a sort. . . . [I]t is worth noting that a suspicion requirement for vaccinations is not merely impractical; it is nonsensical, for vaccinations are not searches for anything in particular and so there is nothing about which to be suspicious. . . . It might also be noted that physical exams (and of course vaccinations) are not searches for conditions that reflect wrongdoing on the part of the student, and so are wholly nonaccusatory and have no consequences that can be regarded as punitive. These facts may explain the absence of Fourth Amendment challenges to such searches. By contrast, . . . any testing program that searches for conditions plainly reflecting serious wrongdoing can never be made wholly nonaccusatory from the student's perspective, the motives for the program notwithstanding; and for the same reason, the substantial consequences that can flow from a positive test, such as suspension from sports, are invariably—and quite reasonably—understood as punishment. . . .

I do not believe that suspicionless drug testing is justified on these facts. But even if I agreed that some such testing were reasonable here, I see two other Fourth Amendment flaws in the District's program. First, and most serious, there is virtually no evidence in the record of a drug problem at the Washington Grade School, which includes the 7th and 8th grades, and which Acton attended when this litigation began. . . . Second, even as to the high school, I find unreasonable the school's choice of student athletes as the class to subject to suspicionless testing—a choice that appears to have been driven more by a belief in what would pass constitutional muster than by a belief in what was required to meet the District's principal disciplinary concern. Reading the full record in this case, as well as the District Court's authoritative summary of it, it seems quite obvious that the true driving force behind the District's adoption of its drug-testing program was the need to combat the rise in drug-related disorder and disruption in its classrooms and around campus. I mean no criticism of the strength of that interest. On the contrary, where the record demonstrates the existence of such a problem, that interest seems self-evidently compelling. . . . The evidence of a drug-related sports injury problem at Vernonia, by contrast, was considerably weaker.

On this record, then, it seems to me that the far more reasonable choice would have been to focus on the class of students found to have violated published school rules against severe disruption in class and around campus—disruption that had a strong nexus to drug use, as the District established at trial. Such a choice would share two of the virtues of a suspicion-based regime: testing dramatically fewer students, tens as against

hundreds, and giving students control, through their behavior, over the likelihood that they would be tested. . . .

Having reviewed the record here, I cannot avoid the conclusion that the
District's suspicionless policy of testing all student-athletes sweeps too
broadly, and too imprecisely, to be reasonable under the Fourth Amendment.

Ferguson v. Charleston
532 U.S. 67, 121 S.CT. 1281 (2001)

Staff members at the public hospital operated in the city of Charleston
by the Medical University of South Carolina (MUSC) became concerned about an apparent increase in the use of cocaine by patients who
were receiving prenatal treatment. In response, MUSC began ordering
drug screens to be performed on urine samples from maternity patients
who were suspected of using cocaine. If a patient tested positive, she was
then referred by MUSC staff to the county substance abuse commission
for counseling and treatment. Subsequently, a nurse for the MUSC ob-
stetrics department heard a news report that the police in Greenville,
South Carolina, were arresting pregnant users of cocaine on the theory
that such use harmed the fetus and was therefore child abuse. And she
discussed the story with MUSC's general counsel, who in turn contacted Charleston Solicitor Charles Condon in order to offer MUSC's
cooperation in prosecuting mothers whose children tested positive for
drugs at birth. Condon, then, adopted a policy of prosecuting women
who tested positive for cocaine while pregnant. Under the policy, patients who tested positive were promptly arrested. In 1990, however, the
policy was modified to give the patient who tested positive during labor, like the patient who tested positive during a prenatal care visit, an
opportunity to avoid arrest by consenting to substance abuse treatment.

Ten women who received obstetrical care at MUSC and who were
arrested after testing positive for cocaine challenged the constitutionality of the drug testing policy. They challenged the validity of the policy
under various theories, including the claim that warrantless and nonconsensual drug tests conducted for criminal investigatory purposes
were unconstitutional searches. Attorneys for the city of Charleston
countered that (1) as a matter of fact, petitioners had consented to
the searches; and (2) as a matter of law, the searches were reasonable,
even absent consent, because they were justified by special non-law-
enforcement purposes. A federal district court rejected the second defense because the searches in question "were not done by the medical
university for independent purposes. [Instead,] the police came in and

there was an agreement reached that the positive screens would be shared with the police." Accordingly, the district court submitted the factual defense to the jury with instructions that required a verdict in favor of petitioners unless the jury found consent. The jury found for the city and the women appealed. The Court of Appeals for the Fourth Circuit affirmed, finding that the searches were reasonable as a matter of law under precedents recognizing that "special needs" may, in certain exceptional circumstances, justify such searches, *Treasury Employees v. Von Raab*, 489 U.S. 656 (1989), and *Vernonia School Dist. 47J v. Acton*, 515 U.S. 646 (1995). The women appealed that decision and the Supreme Court granted *certiorari*.

The appellate court was reversed by a vote of six to three in an opinion for the Court delivered by Justice Stevens. Justice Kennedy filed a concurring opinion and Justice Scalia filed a dissenting opinion, which Chief Justice Rehnquist and Justice Thomas joined.

☐ *Justice STEVENS delivered the opinion of the Court.*

In this case, we must decide whether a state hospital's performance of a diagnostic test to obtain evidence of a patient's criminal conduct for law enforcement purposes is an unreasonable search if the patient has not consented to the procedure. More narrowly, the question is whether the interest in using the threat of criminal sanctions to deter pregnant women from using cocaine can justify a departure from the general rule that an official nonconsensual search is unconstitutional if not authorized by a valid warrant. . . .

[T]he urine tests conducted by those staff members were indisputably searches within the meaning of the Fourth Amendment. Neither the District Court nor the Court of Appeals concluded that any of the . . . criteria used to identify the women to be searched provided either probable cause to believe that they were using cocaine, or even the basis for a reasonable suspicion of such use. Rather, the District Court and the Court of Appeals viewed the case as one involving MUSC's right to conduct searches without warrants or probable cause. Furthermore, given the posture in which the case comes to us, we must assume for purposes of our decision that the tests were performed without the informed consent of the patients.

Because the hospital seeks to justify its authority to conduct drug tests and to turn the results over to law enforcement agents without the knowledge or consent of the patients, this case differs from the four previous cases in which we have considered whether comparable drug tests "fit within the closely guarded category of constitutionally permissible suspicionless searches." *Chandler v. Miller*, 520 U.S. 305 (1997). In three of those cases, we sustained drug tests for railway employees involved in train accidents, *Skinner v. Railway Labor Executives' Assn.*, 489 U.S. 602 (1989), for United States Customs Service employees seeking promotion to certain sensitive positions, *Treasury Employees, v. Von Raab*, 489 U.S. 656 (1989), and for high school students participating in interscholastic sports, *Vernonia School Dist. 47J v. Acton*, 515 U.S. 646 (1995). In the fourth case, we struck down such testing for candidates for designated state offices as unreasonable. *Chandler v. Miller*, 520 U.S. 305 (1997).

In each of those cases, we employed a balancing test that weighed the intrusion on the individual's interest in privacy against the "special needs" that supported the program. As an initial matter, we note that the invasion of privacy in this case is far more substantial than in those cases. In the previous four cases, there was no misunderstanding about the purpose of the test or the potential use of the test results, and there were protections against the dissemination of the results to third parties. The use of an adverse test result to disqualify one from eligibility for a particular benefit, such as a promotion or an opportunity to participate in an extracurricular activity, involves a less serious intrusion on privacy than the unauthorized dissemination of such results to third parties. The reasonable expectation of privacy enjoyed by the typical patient undergoing diagnostic tests in a hospital is that the results of those tests will not be shared with nonmedical personnel without her consent. In none of our prior cases was there any intrusion upon that kind of expectation.

The critical difference between those four drug-testing cases and this one, however, lies in the nature of the "special need" asserted as justification for the warrantless searches. In each of those earlier cases, the "special need" that was advanced as a justification for the absence of a warrant or individualized suspicion was one divorced from the State's general interest in law enforcement. In this case, however, the central and indispensable feature of the policy from its inception was the use of law enforcement to coerce the patients into substance abuse treatment. This fact distinguishes this case from circumstances in which physicians or psychologists, in the course of ordinary medical procedures aimed at helping the patient herself, come across information that under rules of law or ethics is subject to reporting requirements, which no one has challenged here.

Respondents argue in essence that their ultimate purpose—namely, protecting the health of both mother and child—is a beneficent one. In *Chandler*, however, we did not simply accept the State's invocation of a "special need." Instead, we carried out a "close review" of the scheme at issue before concluding that the need in question was not "special," as that term has been defined in our cases. In this case, a review of the M-7 policy plainly reveals that the purpose actually served by the MUSC searches "is ultimately indistinguishable from the general interest in crime control." *Indianapolis v. Edmond*, 531 U.S. 32 (2000). . . .

While the ultimate goal of the program may well have been to get the women in question into substance abuse treatment and off of drugs, the immediate objective of the searches was to generate evidence for law enforcement purposes in order to reach that goal. The threat of law enforcement may ultimately have been intended as a means to an end, but the direct and primary purpose of MUSC's policy was to ensure the use of those means. In our opinion, this distinction is critical. Because law enforcement involvement always serves some broader social purpose or objective, under respondents' view, virtually any nonconsensual suspicionless search could be immunized under the special needs doctrine by defining the search solely in terms of its ultimate, rather than immediate, purpose. Such an approach is inconsistent with the Fourth Amendment. Given the primary purpose of the Charleston program, which was to use the threat of arrest and prosecution in order to force women into treatment, and given the extensive involvement of law enforcement officials at every stage of the policy, this case simply does not fit within the closely guarded category of "special needs."

The fact that positive test results were turned over to the police does not merely provide a basis for distinguishing our prior cases applying the "special needs" balancing approach to the determination of drug use. It also provides an affirmative reason for enforcing the strictures of the Fourth Amendment. While state hospital employees, like other citizens, may have a duty to provide the police with evidence of criminal conduct that they inadvertently acquire in the course of routine treatment, when they undertake to obtain such evidence from their patients for the specific purpose of incriminating those patients, they have a special obligation to make sure that the patients are fully informed about their constitutional rights, as standards of knowing waiver require. *Miranda v. Arizona*, 384 U.S. 436 (1966).

While respondents are correct that drug abuse both was and is a serious problem, "the gravity of the threat alone cannot be dispositive of questions concerning what means law enforcement officers may employ to pursue a given purpose." *Indianapolis v. Edmond.* The Fourth Amendment's general prohibition against nonconsensual, warrantless, and suspicionless searches necessarily applies to such a policy.

☐ *Justice KENNEDY, concurring in the judgment.*

In my view, it is necessary and prudent to be explicit in explaining the limitations of today's decision. The beginning point ought to be to acknowledge the legitimacy of the State's interest in fetal life and of the grave risk to the life and health of the fetus, and later the child, caused by cocaine ingestion. Infants whose mothers abuse cocaine during pregnancy are born with a wide variety of physical and neurological abnormalities. Prenatal exposure to cocaine can also result in developmental problems which persist long after birth. There can be no doubt that a mother's ingesting this drug can cause tragic injury to a fetus and a child. There should be no doubt that South Carolina can impose punishment upon an expectant mother who has so little regard for her own unborn that she risks causing him or her lifelong damage and suffering. The State, by taking special measures to give rehabilitation and training to expectant mothers with this tragic addiction or weakness, acts well within its powers and its civic obligations.

The holding of the Court, furthermore, does not call into question the validity of mandatory reporting laws such as child abuse laws which require teachers to report evidence of child abuse to the proper authorities, even if arrest and prosecution is the likely result. That in turn highlights the real difficulty. As this case comes to us, we must accept the premise that the medical profession can adopt acceptable criteria for testing expectant mothers for cocaine use in order to provide prompt and effective counseling to the mother and to take proper medical steps to protect the child. If prosecuting authorities then adopt legitimate procedures to discover this information and prosecution follows, that ought not to invalidate the testing. One of the ironies of the case, then, may be that the program now under review, which gives the cocaine user a second and third chance, might be replaced by some more rigorous system. We must, however, take the case as it comes to us; and the use of handcuffs, arrests, prosecutions, and police assistance in designing and implementing the testing and rehabilitation policy cannot be sustained under our previous cases concerning mandatory testing.

An essential, distinguishing feature of the special needs cases is that the person searched has consented, though the usual voluntariness analysis is altered because adverse consequences (e.g., dismissal from employment or disqualification from playing on a high school sports team) will follow from refusal. The person searched has given consent, as defined to take into account that the consent was not voluntary in the full sense of the word. The consent, and the circumstances in which it was given, bear upon the reasonableness of the whole special needs program. Here, on the other hand, the question of consent, even with the special connotation used in the special needs cases, has yet to be decided. . . .

☐ *Justice SCALIA, with whom THE CHIEF JUSTICE and Justice THOMAS join, dissenting.*

The Constitution does not resolve all difficult social questions, but leaves the vast majority of them to resolution by debate and the democratic process—which would produce a decision by the citizens of Charleston, through their elected Representatives, to forbid or permit the police action at issue here. The question before us is a narrower one: whether, whatever the desirability of this police conduct, it violates the Fourth Amendment's prohibition of unreasonable searches and seizures. In my view, it plainly does not. . . .

I think it clear . . . that there is no basis for saying that obtaining of the urine sample was unconstitutional. The special-needs doctrine is thus quite irrelevant, since it operates only to validate searches and seizures that are otherwise unlawful. In the ensuing discussion, however, I shall assume (contrary to legal precedent) that the taking of the urine sample was (either because of the patients' necessitous circumstances, or because of failure to disclose that the urine would be tested for drugs, or because of failure to disclose that the results of the test would be given to the police) coerced. Indeed, I shall even assume (contrary to common sense) that the testing of the urine constituted an unconsented search of the patients' effects. On those assumptions, the special-needs doctrine would become relevant; and, properly applied, would validate what was done here. . . .

The cocaine tests started in April 1989, neither at police suggestion nor with police involvement. Expectant mothers who tested positive were referred by hospital staff for substance-abuse treatment—an obvious health benefit to both mother and child. Thus, in their origin—before the police were in any way involved—the tests had an immediate, not merely an "ultimate," purpose of improving maternal and infant health. Several months after the testing had been initiated, a nurse discovered that local police were arresting pregnant users of cocaine for child abuse, the hospital's general counsel wrote the county solicitor to ask "what, if anything, our Medical Center needs to do to assist you in this matter," the police suggested ways to avoid tainting evidence, and the hospital and police in conjunction used the testing program as a means of securing what the Court calls the "ultimate" health benefit of coercing drug-abusing mothers into drug treatment. Why would there be any reason to believe that, once this policy of using the drug tests for their "ultimate" health benefits had been adopted, use of them for their original, immediate, benefits somehow disappeared, and testing somehow became in its entirety nothing more than a "pretext" for obtaining grounds for arrest? On the face of it, this is incredible. The only evidence of the exclusively arrest-related purpose of the testing adduced by the Court is that the police-cooperation policy itself does not describe how to care for cocaine-exposed infants. But of course it does not, since that policy, adopted months after the cocaine testing was initiated, had as its only health object the "ultimate" goal of inducing drug treatment through threat of arrest. Does the Court really believe (or even hope) that, once invalidation of the program challenged here has been decreed, drug testing will cease? In sum, there can be no basis for the Court's purported ability to "distinguis[h] this case from circumstances in which physicians or psychologists, in the course of ordinary medical procedures aimed at helping the patient herself, come across information that . . . is subject to reporting requirements," unless it is this: That the addition of a law-enforcement-related purpose to a legitimate medical purpose destroys applicability of the "special-needs" doctrine. But that is quite impossible, since the special-needs doctrine was developed, and is ordinarily employed, precisely to enable searches by law enforcement officials who, of course, ordinarily have a law enforcement objective. . . .

As I indicated at the outset, it is not the function of this Court—at least not in Fourth Amendment cases—to weigh petitioners' privacy interest against the State's interest in meeting the crisis of "crack babies" that developed in the late 1980's. I cannot refrain from observing, however, that the outcome of a wise weighing of those interests is by no means clear. The initial goal of the doctors and nurses who conducted cocaine-testing in this case was to refer pregnant drug addicts to treatment centers, and to prepare for necessary treatment of their possibly affected children. When the doctors and nurses agreed to the program providing test results to the police, they did so because (in addition to the fact that child abuse was required by law to be reported) they wanted to use the sanction of arrest as a strong incentive for their addicted patients to undertake drug-addiction treatment. And the police themselves used it for that benign purpose, as is shown by the fact that only 30 of 253 women testing positive for cocaine were ever arrested, and only 2 of those prosecuted. It would not be unreasonable to conclude that today's judgment, authorizing the assessment of damages against the county solicitor and individual doctors and nurses who participated in the program, proves once again that no good deed goes unpunished. But as far as the Fourth Amendment is concerned: There was no unconsented search in this case. And if there was, it would have been validated by the special-needs doctrine. For these reasons, I respectfully dissent.

Board of Education of Independent School District No. 92 of Pottawatomie City v. Earls

536 U.S. 822, 122 S.CT. 2559 (2002)

Following the Court's upholding of random drug testing of high school athletes, in *Vernonia School District No. 47J v. Acton*, 515 U.S. 646 (1995), in 1998 the school district of Tecumseh, Oklahoma, a rural community about forty miles from Oklahoma City, adopted a policy of requiring all middle and high school students who participate in any extracurricular activities to consent to random drug testing. Lindsay Earls, a member of the choir and the marching band, challenged the constitutionality of the policy for violating the Fourth Amendment guarantee against unreasonable searches and seizures. A federal district court rejected her claim, but the Court of Appeals for the Tenth Circuit reversed and the school board appealed.

The appellate court's decision was reversed by a five-to-four vote. Justice Thomas delivered the opinion of the Court. Justice Breyer filed a concurring opinion. Justices O'Connor and Ginsburg filed dissenting opinions, which Justices Stevens and Souter joined.

> *Justice THOMAS delivered the opinion of the Court.*

The Fourth Amendment to the United States Constitution protects "[t]he right of the people to be secure in their persons, houses, papers, and effects, against unreasonable searches and seizures." Searches by public school officials, such as the collection of urine samples, implicate Fourth Amendment interests. See *Vernonia; New Jersey v. T. L. O.*, 469 U.S. 325 (1985). We must therefore review the School District's Policy for "reasonableness," which is the touchstone of the constitutionality of a governmental search.

In the criminal context, reasonableness usually requires a showing of probable cause. See, e.g., *Skinner v. Railway Labor Executives' Assn.*, 489 U.S. 602 (1989). The probable-cause standard, however, "is peculiarly related to criminal investigations" and may be unsuited to determining the reasonableness of administrative searches where the "Government seeks to prevent the development of hazardous conditions." *Treasury Employees v. Von Raab*, 489 U.S. 656 (1989).

Given that the School District's Policy is not in any way related to the conduct of criminal investigations, respondents do not contend that the School District requires probable cause before testing students for drug use. Respondents instead argue that drug testing must be based at least on some level of individualized suspicion. It is true that we generally determine the reasonableness of a search by balancing the nature of the intrusion on the individual's privacy against the promotion of legitimate governmental interests. But we have long held that "the Fourth Amendment imposes no irreducible requirement of [individualized] suspicion." *United States v. Martinez-Fuerte*, 428 U.S. 543 (1976).

Significantly, this Court has previously held that "special needs" inhere in the public school context. While schoolchildren do not shed their constitutional rights when they enter the schoolhouse, see *Tinker v. Des Moines Independent Community School Dist.*, 393 U.S. 503 (1969), "Fourth Amendment rights . . . are different in public schools than elsewhere; the 'reasonableness' inquiry cannot disregard the schools' custodial and tutelary responsibility for children." *Vernonia.* In particular, a finding of individualized suspicion may not be necessary when a school conducts drug testing.

In *Vernonia*, this Court held that the suspicionless drug testing of athletes was constitutional. Applying the principles of *Vernonia* to the somewhat different facts of this case, we conclude that Tecumseh's Policy is also constitutional.

We first consider the nature of the privacy interest allegedly compromised by the drug testing. . . . A student's privacy interest is limited in a public school environment where the State is responsible for maintaining discipline, health, and safety. Schoolchildren are routinely required to submit to physical examinations and vaccinations against disease. Securing order in the school environment sometimes requires that students be subjected to greater controls than those appropriate for adults.

Respondents argue that because children participating in nonathletic extracurricular activities are not subject to regular physicals and communal undress, they have a stronger expectation of privacy than the athletes tested in *Vernonia.* This distinction, however, was not essential to our decision in *Vernonia*, which depended primarily upon the school's custodial responsibility and authority.

In any event, students who participate in competitive extracurricular activities voluntarily subject themselves to many of the same intrusions on their privacy as do athletes. Some of these clubs and activities require occasional off-campus travel and communal undress. All of them have their own rules and requirements for participating students that do not apply to the student body as a whole.

Next, we consider the character of the intrusion imposed by the Policy. Urination is "an excretory function traditionally shielded by great privacy." *Skinner.* But the "degree of intrusion" on one's privacy caused by collecting a urine sample "depends upon the manner in which production of the urine sample is monitored." *Vernonia.*

Under the Policy, a faculty monitor waits outside the closed restroom stall for the student to produce a sample and must "listen for the normal sounds of urination in order to guard against tampered specimens and to insure an accurate chain of custody." The monitor then pours the sample into two bottles that are sealed and placed into a mailing pouch along with a consent form signed by the student. This procedure is virtually identical to that reviewed in *Vernonia*, except that it additionally protects privacy by allowing male students to produce their samples behind a closed stall. Given that we considered the method of collection in *Vernonia* a "negligible" intrusion, the method here is even less problematic. . . .

Finally, this Court must consider the nature and immediacy of the government's concerns and the efficacy of the Policy in meeting them. This

Court has already articulated in detail the importance of the governmental concern in preventing drug use by schoolchildren. The drug abuse problem among our Nation's youth has hardly abated since *Vernonia* was decided in 1995. In fact, evidence suggests that it has only grown worse. As in *Vernonia*, "the necessity for the State to act is magnified by the fact that this evil is being visited not just upon individuals at large, but upon children for whom it has undertaken a special responsibility of care and direction." The health and safety risks identified in *Vernonia* apply with equal force to Tecumseh's children. Indeed, the nationwide drug epidemic makes the war against drugs a pressing concern in every school. . . .

Given the nationwide epidemic of drug use, and the evidence of increased drug use in Tecumseh schools, it was entirely reasonable for the School District to enact this particular drug testing policy. We reject the Court of Appeals' novel test that "any district seeking to impose a random suspicionless drug testing policy as a condition to participation in a school activity must demonstrate that there is some identifiable drug abuse problem among a sufficient number of those subject to the testing, such that testing that group of students will actually redress its drug problem." Among other problems, it would be difficult to administer such a test. As we cannot articulate a threshold level of drug use that would suffice to justify a drug testing program for schoolchildren, we refuse to fashion what would in effect be a constitutional quantum of drug use necessary to show a "drug problem." . . .

We also reject respondents' argument that drug testing must presumptively be based upon an individualized reasonable suspicion of wrongdoing because such a testing regime would be less intrusive. In this context, the Fourth Amendment does not require a finding of individualized suspicion. And we decline to impose such a requirement on schools attempting to prevent and detect drug use by students. Moreover, we question whether testing based on individualized suspicion in fact would be less intrusive. Such a regime would place an additional burden on public school teachers who are already tasked with the difficult job of maintaining order and discipline. A program of individualized suspicion might unfairly target members of unpopular groups. The fear of lawsuits resulting from such targeted searches may chill enforcement of the program, rendering it ineffective in combating drug use.

Finally, we find that testing students who participate in extracurricular activities is a reasonably effective means of addressing the School District's legitimate concerns in preventing, deterring, and detecting drug use. . . . Accordingly, we reverse the judgment of the Court of Appeals. It is so ordered.

❏ *Justice O'CONNOR, with whom Justice SOUTER joins, dissenting.*

I dissented in *Vernonia School Dist. 47J v. Acton, 515 U.S. 646 (1995)*, and continue to believe that case was wrongly decided. Because *Vernonia* is now this Court's precedent, and because I agree that petitioners' program fails even under the balancing approach adopted in that case, I join Justice GINSBURG's dissent.

☐ *Justice GINSBURG, with whom Justice STEVENS, Justice O'CONNOR, and Justice SOUTER join, dissenting.*

This case presents circumstances dispositively different from those of *Vernonia*. True, as the Court stresses, Tecumseh students participating in competitive extracurricular activities other than athletics share two relevant characteristics with the athletes of *Vernonia*. First, both groups attend public schools. "[O]ur decision in *Vernonia*," the Court states, "depended primarily upon the school's custodial responsibility and authority." Concern for student health and safety is basic to the school's caretaking, and it is undeniable that "drug use carries a variety of health risks for children, including death from overdose."

Those risks, however, are present for all schoolchildren. *Vernonia* cannot be read to endorse invasive and suspicionless drug testing of all students upon any evidence of drug use, solely because drugs jeopardize the life and health of those who use them. Many children, like many adults, engage in dangerous activities on their own time; that the children are enrolled in school scarcely allows government to monitor all such activities. If a student has a reasonable subjective expectation of privacy in the personal items she brings to school, surely she has a similar expectation regarding the chemical composition of her urine. Had the *Vernonia* Court agreed that public school attendance, in and of itself, permitted the State to test each student's blood or urine for drugs, the opinion in *Vernonia* could have saved many words.

The second commonality to which the Court points is the voluntary character of both interscholastic athletics and other competitive extracurricular activities. "By choosing to 'go out for the team,' [school athletes] voluntarily subject themselves to a degree of regulation even higher than that imposed on students generally." Comparably, the Court today observes, "students who participate in competitive extracurricular activities voluntarily subject themselves to" additional rules not applicable to other students. . . .

The comparison is enlightening. While extracurricular activities are "voluntary" in the sense that they are not required for graduation, they are part of the school's educational program; for that reason, the petitioner (hereinafter School District) is justified in expending public resources to make them available. Participation in such activities is a key component of school life, essential in reality for students applying to college, and, for all participants, a significant contributor to the breadth and quality of the educational experience.

Voluntary participation in athletics has a distinctly different dimension: Schools regulate student athletes discretely because competitive school sports by their nature require communal undress and, more important, expose students to physical risks that schools have a duty to mitigate. For the very reason that schools cannot offer a program of competitive athletics without intimately affecting the privacy of students, *Vernonia* reasonably analogized school athletes to "adults who choose to participate in a closely regulated industry." Industries fall within the closely regulated category when the nature of their activities requires substantial government oversight. Interscholastic athletics similarly require close safety and health regulation; a school's choir, band, and academic team do not.

In short, *Vernonia* applied, it did not repudiate, the principle that "the legality of a search of a student should depend simply on the reasonableness, under all the circumstances, of the search." *T. L. O.* Enrollment in a public school, and election to participate in school activities beyond the bare minimum that the curriculum requires, are indeed factors relevant to reasonableness, but they do not on their own justify intrusive, suspicionless searches. *Vernonia,* accordingly, did not rest upon these factors; instead, the Court performed what today's majority aptly describes as a "fact-specific balancing." Balancing of that order, applied to the facts now before the Court, should yield a result other than the one the Court announces today. . . .

Nationwide, students who participate in extracurricular activities are significantly less likely to develop substance abuse problems than are their less-involved peers. Even if students might be deterred from drug use in order to preserve their extracurricular eligibility, it is at least as likely that other students might forgo their extracurricular involvement in order to avoid detection of their drug use. Tecumseh's policy thus falls short doubly if deterrence is its aim: It invades the privacy of students who need deterrence least, and risks steering students at greatest risk for substance abuse away from extracurricular involvement that potentially may palliate drug problems.

To summarize, this case resembles *Vernonia* only in that the School Districts in both cases conditioned engagement in activities outside the obligatory curriculum on random subjection to urinalysis. The defining characteristics of the two programs, however, are entirely dissimilar. The *Vernonia* district sought to test a subpopulation of students distinguished by their reduced expectation of privacy, their special susceptibility to drug-related injury, and their heavy involvement with drug use. The Tecumseh district seeks to test a much larger population associated with none of these factors. It does so, moreover, without carefully safeguarding student confidentiality and without regard to the program's untoward effects. A program so sweeping is not sheltered by *Vernonia;* its unreasonable reach renders it impermissible under the Fourth Amendment. . . . For the reasons stated, I would affirm the judgment of the Tenth Circuit declaring the testing policy at issue unconstitutional.

E | *Wiretapping, Bugging, and Police Surveillance*

Advances in science and technology often generate controversies that the Framers never envisioned and that challenge established constitutional doctrine. The telephone and radio were such a technological change, for with them came the possibility of eavesdropping on private conversations at great distances. Governmental intrusions by means of wiretapping and other electronic monitoring devices eventually led to a new interpretative approach to the Fourth Amendment.

Fourth Amendment protection for personal privacy was initially discussed in *Boyd v. United States,* 116 U.S. 616 (1886). When declaring unconstitutional a statute allowing the government to order individuals to produce private papers and invoices as mere evidence of illegally imported goods, the Court laid the basis for a liberal construction of the Fourth Amendment. In *Boyd*, the Court observed that "constitutional provisions for the security of person and property should be liberally construed. A close and literal construction deprives them of half their efficacy, and leads to gradual depreciation of the right." In his opinion for the Court, Justice Joseph Bradley reasoned that individuals have an "indefeasible" right of private property in the common law and under the Fourth Amendment, which renders "unreasonable" any governmental search or seizure of private papers and other property as mere evidence of criminal activities. In an often-quoted passage, he explained that

> [t]he principles laid down in *Entrick v. Carrington* [19 Howard State Records 1029 (K.B. 1765), holding general warrants to be illegal] affect the very essence of constitutional liberty and security. They reach farther than the concrete form of the case then before the court, with its adventitious circumstances; they apply to all invasions on the part of the government and its employees of the sanctity of a man's home and the privacies of life. It is not the breaking of his doors, and the rummaging of his drawers, that constitutes the essence of the offence; but it is the invasion of his indefeasible right of personal security, personal liberty and private property, where that right has never been forfeited by his conviction of some public offense,—it is the invasion of this sacred right which underlies and constitutes the essence of Lord Camden's judgment. Breaking into a house and opening boxes and drawers are circumstances of aggravation; but any forcible and compulsory extortion of a man's own testimony or of his private papers to be used as evidence to convict him of crime or to forfeit his goods, is within the condemnation of that judgment. In this regard, the Fourth and Fifth Amendments run almost into each other.

Boyd stood as a watershed ruling for not only laying the basis for a liberal construction of Fourth Amendment-protected privacy but also in defining constitutionally protected privacy interests in terms of common-law property rights. As a result, the scope of Fourth Amendment protection extended beyond "persons, houses, papers, and effects" to include other "constitutionally protected areas"—business offices,[1] stores,[2] hotel rooms,[3] apartments,[4] automobiles,[5] and taxicabs.[6]

The Court's analysis in *Boyd* and other cases of constitutionally protected areas greatly expanded protection for privacy interests and did so on an objective standard: Individuals' privacy interests were protected against unreasonable searches and seizures in those areas where they had proprietary interests as well. But by linking privacy interests to common-law property rights, the Court created an obstacle for dealing with Fourth Amendment challenges to governmental intrusions by means of wiretaps and electronic surveillance. Traditionally, common law recognized no "search" unless there was an actual physical trespass on private property and no "seizure" unless tangible items were taken. Wiretapping, of course, involves neither a physical trespass nor the taking of tangible property.

When first confronted with the issue of wiretapping in *Olmstead v. United States* (1928) (excerpted below), the justices split five to four on holding that because the interception of telephone conversations occurs without entry into private premises there is no "search" of a constitutionally protected area, and further that conversations are not things that can be "seized" under the Fourth Amendment. But compare Chief Justice Taft's strict construction and application of the underlying property principles of the Fourth Amendment with the interpretations offered in the dissenting opinions of Justices Pierce Butler and Louis Brandeis. Attempting to combine a strict construction with a liberal application of common-law principles, Butler finds proprietary interests in the wire violated by the tap. By contrast, Brandeis advances both a liberal construction and application of the Fourth Amendment in contending that constitutionally protected privacy interests should not be confined to traditional categories of searches involving physical trespass and seizures of tangible materials.

Olmstead stood for almost forty years. For a time, the Court evaded ruling again on the constitutionality of wiretaps by treating the issue as a matter of interpreting the Federal Communications Act of 1934, which prohibited the interception and divulgence of telephone and telegraph communications.[7] In 1942, however, the Court extended *Olmstead*'s trespass theory to the use of detectaphones—devices placed against a wall that detect sounds on the other side. In *Goldman v. United States*, 316 U.S. 129 (1942), federal agents without a warrant entered a suspect's office and planted a dictaphone with wires leading to an office next door, but the next day the dictaphone broke and the agents used a detectaphone instead. The Court held that evidence obtained by the use of detectaphone was admissible because no physical trespass was involved; whereas, evidence gathered from the dictaphone would have been inadmissible.

Although still relying on *Olmstead-Goldman*'s trespass theory in 1961, the Court rejected *Olmstead*'s holding that conversations per se have no Fourth Amendment protection because they are not tangible objects that may be seized. In *Silverman v. United States*, 365 U.S. 505 (1961), federal agents without a warrant drove a "spike mike" into a wall to overhear conversations. They made contact with a heating duct serving the house and, thereby, were able to monitor conversations throughout the house. The mike's penetration of the duct, the Court held, constituted "an actual intrusion of a constitutionally protected area." The Court remained unwilling, though, to overturn *Olmstead*. Writing for the majority, Justice Potter Stewart claimed to "find no occasion to re-examine *Goldman* here, but we decline to go beyond it, by even a fraction of an inch." Concurring Justice Douglas urged abandonment of *Olmstead's* trespass theory of Fourth Amendment protection:

> The depth of the penetration of the electronic device—even the degree of its remoteness from the inside of the house—is not the measure of the injury. . . . Our concern should not be with the trivialities of the local law of trespass, as the opinion of the Court indicates. But neither should the command of the Fourth Amendment be limited by nice distinctions turning on the kind of electronic equipment employed. Rather the sole concern should be with whether the privacy of the home is invaded.

Finally, in the landmark ruling *Katz v. United States* (1967) (excerpted below), *Olmstead's* trespass theory was overturned. In holding that police must first obtain a warrant before undertaking a wiretap, even of a public telephone, Justice Stewart advanced a new standard for triggering the guarantees of the Fourth Amendment: whether individuals have "reasonable expectations of privacy." Notice that this standard is more subjective than that in *Boyd* and *Olmstead*, which made proprietary rights the basis for defining "constitutionally protected areas" under the Fourth Amendment. For that reason, concurring Justice John Harlan endeavored to clarify and qualify the majority's holding by proposing a two-prong test—"first that a person have exhibited an actual (subjective) expectation of privacy and, second, that the expectation be one that society is prepared to recognize as 'reasonable.' "

Katz's theory of "reasonable expectations of privacy" and Harlan's two-prong test for applying that standard made the reasonableness of searches context dependent. As the Court in *Terry v. Ohio* (1968) (excerpted in Section B of this chapter) observed, "wherever an individual may harbor a reasonable 'expectation of privacy,' . . . he is entitled to be free from unreasonable governmental intrusion" but "the specific content and incidents of this right [of privacy] must be shaped by the context in which it is asserted." As a result, the Court faces the task of deciding whether an expectation of privacy is "reasonable" and one "society is prepared to recognize as 'reasonable.' " While the Warren Court tended to expand Fourth Amendment protection along these lines, the more conservative Burger and Rehnquist Courts have cut back by narrowly construing "reasonable expectations of privacy" under the Fourth Amendment. In cases like *Santana* (excerpted in Section B), warrantless arrests and searches were upheld, despite individuals being in their homes or areas in which they have proprietary interests, because the Court found no "reasonable expectation of privacy."[8] So too, the Court contracted the scope of Fourth Amendment protection by denying that individuals have reasonable expectations of privacy against warrantless searches of private papers held by their attorneys[9] and bank records.[10] "*Katz* has not eliminated property considerations—ownership, possession, occupancy—but has changed their role from legal touchstones for the Fourth Amendment to standards by which expectations of privacy are evaluated."[11]

California v. Ciraolo (1986) (excerpted below) illustrates the Court's analysis in holding that people have no reasonable expectation of privacy against warrantless police surveillance by helicopters. In other rulings, the Court has denied that individuals have Fourth Amendment–protected expectations of privacy against police placing beepers on packages being transported[12] and against warrantless searches of their garbage left in containers for collection.[13] Underscoring the Rehnquist Court's use of the Warren Court's liberal standard of "reasonable expectations of privacy" for determining the scope of the Fourth Amendment is *Minnesota v. Carter* (1998) (excerpted below). There, by a vote of six to three the Court held that temporary visitors in a home, unlike the homeowner, do not have "reasonable expectations of privacy" or Fourth Amendment protection, when they sought to exclude incriminating evidence that was discovered as a result of a police officer's observing them, from a sidewalk, through gaps in an apartment's closed window blind.

However, in an unusual lineup in a five-to-four decision in *Kyllo v. United States* (2001) (excerpted below), the Court held that the use by federal agents of thermal imagers, in order to detect heat radiations from a house that was suspected of being used to grow marijuana, without a warrant violated the Fourth Amendment.

Along with *Katz*, in *Berger v. State of New York*, 388 U.S. 41 (1967), the Court decided the question left unanswered by *Silverman's* holding that conversations receive Fourth Amendment protection: namely, what constitutes a reasonable search and seizure by electronic eavesdropping. When striking down New York's eavesdropping statute and acknowledging that "eavesdropping involves an intrusion on privacy that is broad in scope," the Court established specific constitutional requirements: Police may be authorized by a judge to eavesdrop only on (1) showing probable cause, (2) describing with specificity the object to be seized, and (3) giving notice to the subject of the search; (4) authorization must be for a limited time only; and (5) police are required to return to the magistrate the specific items seized.

As to government informants and secret agents, the Court maintains that individuals simply assume the risk that they are dealing with undercover police and that their conversations are being recorded.[14] In *United States v. White*, 401 U.S. 745 (1971), for example, the Court adhered to its *assumption of risk rule* when upholding a conviction based on evidence obtained by an informer who carried an electronic transmitter. Justice White, for the majority, found no constitutionally significant difference between electronically equipped and non-equipped informers, explaining that

> [o]ur problem is not what the privacy expectations of particular defendants in particular situations may be or the extent to which they may in fact have relied on the discretion of their companions. Very probably, individual defendants neither know nor suspect that their colleagues have gone or will go to the police or are carrying recorders or transmitters. Otherwise, conversation would cease and our problem with these encounters would be nonexistent or far different from those now before us. Our problem, in terms of the principles announced in *Katz*, is what expectations of privacy are constitutionally "justifiable"—what expectations the Fourth Amendment will protect in the absence of a warrant. So far, the law permits the frustration of actual expectations of privacy by permitting authorities to use the testimony of those associates who for one reason or another have determined to turn to the police, as well as by authorizing the use of informants. . . . If the law gives no protection to the wrongdoer whose trusted accomplice is or becomes a police agent, neither should it protect him when that same agent has recorded or transmitted the conversations which are later offered in evidence to prove the State's case.

But dissenting Justice Harlan countered that the majority "ignored the differences occasioned by third-party monitoring and recording which insures full and accurate disclosure of all that is said," and warned that

> [i]t is too easy to forget—and, hence, too often forgotten—that the issue here is whether to interpose a search warrant procedure between law enforcement agencies engaging in electronic eavesdropping and the public generally. By casting its "risk analysis" solely in terms of the expectations and risks that "wrongdoers" or "one contemplating illegal activities" ought to bear, the plurality opinion, I think, misses the mark entirely. . . . Interposition of a warrant requirement is designed not to shield "wrongdoers," but to secure a measure of privacy and a sense of personal security throughout our society.

Justices Marshall and Douglas agreed. In the latter's words:

> The issue in this case is clouded and concealed by the very discussion of it in legalistic terms. What the ancients knew as "eaves-

dropping," we now call "electronic surveillance"; but to equate the two is to treat man's first gun powder on the same level as the nuclear bomb. Electronic surveillance is the greatest leveler of human privacy ever known. How most forms of it can be held "reasonable" within the meaning of the Fourth Amendment is a mystery. To be sure, the Constitution and Bill of Rights are not to be read as covering only the technology known in the 18th century. Otherwise its concept of "commerce" would be hopeless when it comes to the management of modern affairs. At the same time the concepts of privacy which the Founders enshrined in the Fourth Amendment vanish completely when we slavishly allow an all-powerful government, proclaiming law and order, efficiency, and other benign purposes, to penetrate all the walls and doors which men need to shield them from the pressures of a turbulent life around them and give them the health and strength to carry on.

NOTES

1. *Silverthorne Lumber Co. v. United States*, 251 U.S. 385 (1920).

2. *Amos v. United States*, 255 U.S. 313 (1921).

3. *Stoner v. California*, 376 U.S. 483 (1964); *United States v. Jeffers*, 342 U.S. 48 (1951); and *Lustig v. United States*, 338 U.S. 74 (1949).

4. *Jones v. United States*, 362 U.S. 257 (1960).

5. *Henry v. United States*, 361 U.S. 98 (1959).

6. *Rios v. United States*, 364 U.S. 253 (1960).

7. *Nardone v. United States*, 302 U.S. 379 (1937). However, in *Schwartz v. Texas*, 344 U.S. 199 (1952), the Court held, assuming that Congress had not preempted the area of wiretap legislation, that wiretapped evidence could be "divulged" in state courts if obtained by state agents. Five years later the Court nevertheless extended the act to exclude illegally state-gathered wiretap evidence in federal courts. *Benanti v. United States*, 355 U.S. 96 (1957). Finally, in *Lee v. Florida*, 392 U.S. 378 (1968), the Court overturned *Schwartz* when holding that the Act prohibited the admission of state-gathered evidence even in state courts.

8. See *Rakas v. Illinois*, 439 U.S. 128 (1978), holding that passengers in an automobile have no valid Fourth Amendment claims or legitimate expectations of privacy against searches of automobiles or seizures of evidence therein. See also *Brown v. United States*, 411 U.S. 223 (1973).

9. See *United States v. Miller*, 425 U.S. 435 (1976).

10. *California Bankers Association v. Shultz*, 416 U.S. 21 (1974).

11. Comment, "Government Access to Bank Records," 83 *Yale Law Journal* 1461 (1974).

12. *United States v. Knotts*, 460 U.S. 276 (1983).

13. *California v. Greenwood*, 486 U.S. 35 (1988).

14. See *On Lee v. United States*, 343 U.S. 747 (1952); *Hoffa v. United States*, 385 U.S. 293 (1966); *Lewis v. United States*, 385 U.S. 206 (1966); and *Osborn v. United States*, 385 U.S. 323 (1966).

■ INSIDE THE COURT

Letter from Chief *Justice* Taft *on* Olmstead v. United States, *Holmes, Prohibition, and the Supreme Court*

On June 12, 1928, Chief Justice William Howard Taft sent his brother, Horace Taft, the following letter:

> I am interested in what you say as to the comment on our decision and opinion in the wiretapping case. Holmes has written the nastiest opinion in dissent and Brandeis is fuller of eloquence and idealism. Someone sent me an editorial from The World [a newspaper], I think it is. The truth is that Holmes wrote it the other way till Brandeis got after him and induced him to change on the ground that a state law in Washington forbids wiretapping. Holmes in his opinion really admits that the Fourth Amendment does not cover wiretapping. If it does not, then the law is all against his conclusion on which he rests his case, but he is a law unto himself if Brandeis says yes. It has an element of humor for me that the public seemed to be affected by the fact that it is against the bootleggers and assumes that it was that which carried the day. Of course that had nothing to do with the conclusion. The telephone might just as well have been used to carry on a conspiracy to rob, to murder, to commit treason. The truth is we have to face the problems presented by new inventions. Many of them are most useful to the criminals in their war against society and are at once availed of, and these idealist gentlemen urge a conclusion which facilitates the crime by their use and furnishes immunity from conviction by seeking to bring its use by government officers within the obstruction of the Bill of Rights and the Fourth Amendment. I have a very violent attack on me this morning from Mississippi by someone who only signs Alexander Hamilton and Patrick Henry. I fear he is a bootlegger. I have some supporting letters, but on the whole I look most for condemnation. Holmes says the misdemeanor of the State of Washington is a crime but he does not realise or consider that the admissibility of evidence in the federal courts is determined not by a statute but by the common law. More than this, a large majority of the state supreme courts refuse to follow the *Weeks* case [proclaiming the exclusionary rule, prohibiting the use of illegally obtained evidence in federal courts] decided by our Court as to the inadmissibility of evidence secured in violation of the Fourth Amendment. Chief Judge Cardozo speaking for the Court of Appeals of New York writes an opinion showing that 31 state supreme courts are against it and only 14 for it. They have had in New York a case decided by their Appellate Division following

the same principle in which the evidence of the policemen who listened in by wiretapping was held to be admissible although the law of New York forbids wiretapping as a misdemeanor. Of course one does not like to be held up as one who favors the worst morals, but we have to put up with such attacks in our efforts to follow the old time common law recognized by all authorities, English and American, that if evidence is pertinent it is admissible however obtained. Cardozo argues that this view is the proper one in defense of society. We have hard enough time to convict without presenting immunity to worst advanced and progressive criminals. I shall continue to be worried by attacks from all the academic lawyers who write college law journals, but I suppose it is not a basis for impeachment. We pointed out that Congress can change the rule if it sees fit. It will be of interest to see whether Congress will do it. Here it may be that the Prohibitionists in Congress will oppose such legislation not because of their sensitiveness to the scope of the Fourth Amendment but just because they are in favor of convicting bootleggers. Indeed most of the opposing views are due and will be due to that issue solely.

In 1934, Congress passed the Federal Communications Act, prohibiting the interception and divulgence of telephone and telegraph communications.

Source: Justice Oliver Wendell Holmes Papers, Manuscripts Room, Harvard Law School.

Olmstead v. United States
277 U.S. 438, 48 S.Ct. 564 (1928)

Roy Olmstead was indicted and convicted in federal district court of illegally importing and selling liquor in violation of the National Prohibition Act. At his trial, prosecutors introduced incriminating evidence obtained by wiretaps on telephone lines between his home and office. Olmstead challenged the constitutionality of using this evidence on the grounds that it was obtained in violation of the Fourth Amendment guarantee against unreasonable searches and seizures and the Fifth Amendment guarantee against being compelled to testify against oneself. But an appellate court affirmed his conviction, and Olmstead appealed to the Supreme Court.

The Court's decision was five to four, and the majority's opinion was announced by Chief Justice Taft. Justices Brandeis, Holmes, Stone, and Butler dissented.

☐ *Chief Justice TAFT delivered the opinion of the Court.*

There is no room in the present case for applying the Fifth Amendment, unless the Fourth Amendment was first violated. There was no evidence of compulsion to induce the defendants to talk over their many telephones. They were continually and voluntarily transacting business without knowledge of the interception. Our consideration must be confined to the Fourth Amendment. . . .

The well-known historical purpose of the Fourth Amendment, directed against general warrants and writs of assistance, was to prevent the use of governmental force to search a man's house, his person, his papers, and his effects, and to prevent their seizure against his will. . . .

The amendment itself shows that the search is to be of material things—the person, the house, his papers, or his effects. The description of the warrant necessary to make the proceeding lawful is that it must specify the place to be searched and the person or *things* to be seized. . . .

The amendment does not forbid what was done here. There was no searching. There was no seizure. The evidence was secured by the use of the sense of hearing and that only. There was no entry of the houses or offices of the defendants. . . .

The language of the amendment cannot be extended and expanded to include telephone wires, reaching to the whole world from the defendant's house or office. The intervening wires are not part of his house or office, any more than are the highways along which they are stretched. . . .

Congress may, of course, protect the secrecy of telephone messages by making them, when intercepted, inadmissible in evidence in federal criminal trials, by direct legislation, and thus depart from the common law of evidence. But the courts may not adopt such a policy by attributing an enlarged and unusual meaning to the Fourth Amendment. The reasonable view is that one who installs in his house a telephone instrument with connecting wires intends to project his voice to those quite outside, and that the wires beyond his house, and messages while passing over them, are not within the protection of the Fourth Amendment. Here those who intercepted the projected voices were not in the house of either party to the conversation. . . .

We think, therefore, that the wire tapping here disclosed did not amount to a search or seizure within the meaning of the Fourth Amendment.

☐ *Justice BRANDEIS, dissenting.*

The government makes no attempt to defend the methods employed by its officers. Indeed, it concedes that, if wire tapping can be deemed a search and seizure within the Fourth Amendment, such wire tapping as was practiced in the case at bar was an unreasonable search and seizure, and that the evidence thus obtained was inadmissible. But it relies on the language of the amendment, and it claims that the protection given thereby cannot properly be held to include a telephone conversation. . . .

When the Fourth and Fifth Amendments were adopted, "the form that evil had theretofore taken" had been necessarily simple. Force and violence were then the only means known to man by which a government could directly effect self-incrimination. It could compel the individual to testify—a compulsion effected, if need be, by torture. It could secure possession of his papers and other articles incident to his private life—a seizure effected, if need be, by breaking and entry. Protection against such invasion of "the sanctities of a man's home and the privacies of life" was provided in the Fourth and Fifth Amendments by specific language. *Boyd v. United States,* 116 U.S. 616 [(1886)]. But "time works changes, brings into existence new conditions and purposes." Subtler and more far-reaching means of invading privacy have become available to the government. Discovery and invention have made it possible for the government, by means far more effective than stretching upon the rack, to obtain disclosure in court of what is whispered in the closet.

Moreover, "in the application of a Constitution, our contemplation cannot be only of what has been, but of what may be." The progress of science in furnishing the government with means of espionage is not likely to stop with wire tapping. Ways may some day be developed by which the government, without removing papers from secret drawers, can reproduce them in court, and by which it will be enabled to expose to a jury the most intimate occurrences of the home. Advances in the psychic and related sciences may bring means of exploring unexpressed beliefs, thoughts and emotions. . . . Can it be that the Constitution affords no protection against such invasions of individual security? . . .

Time and again this Court, in giving effect to the principle underlying the Fourth Amendment, has refused to place an unduly literal construction upon it. . . .

The protection guaranteed by the amendments is much broader in scope. The makers of our Constitution undertook to secure conditions favorable to the pursuit of happiness. They recognized the significance of man's spiritual nature, of his feelings and of his intellect. They knew that only a part of the pain, pleasure and satisfactions of life are to be found in material things. They sought to protect Americans in their beliefs, their thoughts, their emotions and their sensations. They conferred, as against the government, the right to be let alone—the most comprehensive of rights and the right most valued by civilized men. To protect that right, every unjustifiable intrusion by the government upon the privacy of the individual, whatever the means employed, must be deemed a violation of the Fourth Amendment. And the use, as evidence in a criminal proceeding, of facts ascertained by such intrusion must be deemed a violation of the Fifth.

Applying to the Fourth and Fifth Amendments the established rule of construction, the defendants' objections to the evidence obtained by wire tapping must, in my opinion, be sustained. It is, of course, immaterial where the physical connection with the telephone wires leading into the defendants' premises was made. And it is also immaterial that the intrusion was in aid of law enforcement. Experience should teach us to be most on our guard to protect liberty when the government's purposes are beneficent. Men born to freedom are naturally alert to repel invasion of their liberty by evil-minded rulers. The greatest dangers to liberty lurk in insidious encroachment by men of zeal, well-meaning but without understanding. . . .

Decency, security, and liberty alike demand that government officials shall be subjected to the same rules of conduct that are commands to the citizen. In a government of laws, existence of the government will be imperiled if it fails to observe the law scrupulously. Our government is the potent, the omnipresent teacher. For good or for ill, it teaches the whole people by its example. Crime is contagious. If the government becomes a lawbreaker, it breeds contempt for law; it invites every man to become a law unto himself; it invites anarchy. To declare that in the administration of the criminal law the end justifies the means—to declare that the government may commit crimes in order to secure the conviction of a private criminal— would bring terrible retribution. Against that pernicious doctrine this court should resolutely set its face.

☐ *Justice BUTLER, dissenting.*

The single question for consideration is this: May the government, consistently with that clause, have its officers whenever they see fit, tap wires, listen to, take down, and report the private messages and conversations transmitted by telephones? . . .

Telephones are used generally for transmission of messages concerning official, social, business and personal affairs including communications that are private and privileged—those between physician and patient, lawyer and client, parent and child, husband and wife. The contracts between telephone companies and users contemplate the private use of the facilities employed in the service. The communications belong to the parties between whom they pass. During their transmission the exclusive use of the wire belongs to the persons served by it. Wire tapping involves interference with the wire while being used. Tapping the wires and listening in by the officers literally constituted a search for evidence. As the communications passed, they were heard and taken down. . . .

This Court has always construed the Constitution in the light of the principles upon which it was founded. The direct operation or literal meaning of the words used do not measure the purpose or scope of its provisions. Under the principles established and applied by this court, the Fourth Amendment safeguards against all evils that are like and equivalent to those embraced within the ordinary meaning of its words. . . .

When the facts in these cases are truly estimated, a fair application of that principle decides the constitutional question in favor of the petitioners. With great deference, I think they should be given a new trial.

Katz v. United States

389 U.S. 347, 88 S.Ct. 507 (1967)

Charles Katz was convicted in federal district court of violating federal law for placing bets and wagers from a public telephone booth in Los Angeles to bookies in Boston and Miami. Federal Bureau of Investigation agents had recorded his conversations with an electronic listening device placed outside the booth, and those recorded conversations were used against him at trial. After a federal appellate court rejected an appeal of his conviction, Katz appealed to the Supreme Court.

The Court's decision was seven to one, and the majority's opinion was announced by Justice Stewart. There were concurrences by Justices White, Harlan, and Douglas, who was joined by Justice Brennan. Justice Black dissented.

☐ *Justice STEWART delivered the opinion of the Court.*

The petitioner was convicted in the District Court for the Southern District of California under an eight-count indictment charging him with transmitting wagering information by telephone from Los Angeles to Miami and Boston in violation of a federal statute. At trial the Government was permitted, over the petitioner's objection, to introduce evidence of the petitioner's end of telephone conversations, overheard by FBI agents who had attached an electronic listening and recording device to the outside of the public telephone booth from which he had placed his calls. In affirming his conviction, the Court of Appeals rejected the contention that the recordings had been obtained in violation of the Fourth Amendment. . . .

We granted *certiorari* in order to consider the constitutional questions thus presented.

The petitioner has phrased those questions as follows:

"A. Whether a public telephone booth is a constitutionally protected area so that evidence obtained by attaching an electronic listening recording device to the top of such a booth is obtained in violation of the right to privacy of the user of the booth.

"B. Whether physical penetration of a constitutionally protected area is necessary before a search and seizure can be said to be violative of the Fourth Amendment to the United States Constitution."

We decline to adopt this formulation of the issues. In the first place the correct solution of Fourth Amendment problems is not necessarily promoted by incantation of the phrase "constitutionally protected area." Secondly, the Fourth Amendment cannot be translated into a general constitutional "right to privacy." That Amendment protects individual privacy against certain kinds of governmental intrusion, but its protections go further, and often have nothing to do with privacy at all. Other provisions of the Constitution protect personal privacy from other forms of governmental invasion. But the protection of a person's *general* right to privacy—his right to be let alone by other people—is, like the protection of his property and of his very life, left largely to the law of the individual States.

Because of the misleading way the issues have been formulated, the parties have attached great significance to the characterization of the telephone booth from which the petitioner placed his calls. The petitioner has strenuously argued that the booth was a "constitutionally protected area." The Government has maintained with equal vigor that it was not. But this effort to decide whether or not a given "area," viewed in the abstract, is "constitutionally protected" deflects attention from the problem presented by this case. For the Fourth Amendment protects people, not places. What a person knowingly exposes to the public, even in his own home or office, is not a subject of Fourth Amendment protection. But what he seeks to preserve as private, even in an area accessible to the public, may be constitutionally protected. . . .

The Government stresses the fact that the telephone booth from which the petitioner made his calls was constructed partly of glass, so that he was as visible after he entered it as he would have been if he had remained outside. But what he sought to exclude when he entered the booth was not the intruding eye—it was the uninvited ear. He did not shed his right to do so simply because he made his calls from a place where he might be seen. . . . One who occupies it, shuts the door behind him, and pays the toll that permits him to place a call is surely entitled to assume that the words he utters into the mouthpiece will not be broadcast to the world. To read the Constitution more narrowly is to ignore the vital role that the public telephone has come to play in private communication. . . .

We conclude that the underpinnings of *Olmstead* and *Goldman* have been so eroded by our subsequent decisions that the "trespass" doctrine there enunciated can no longer be regarded as controlling. The Government's activities in electronically listening to and recording the petitioner's words violated the privacy upon which he justifiably relied while using the telephone booth and thus constituted a "search and seizure" within the meaning of the Fourth Amendment. The fact that the electronic device employed to achieve that end did not happen to penetrate the wall of the booth can have no constitutional significance.

The question remaining for decision, then, is whether the search and seizure conducted in this case complied with constitutional standards. In that regard, the Government's position is that its agents acted in an entirely defensible manner: They did not begin their electronic surveillance until investigation of the petitioner's activities had established a strong probability that he was using the telephone in question to transmit gambling information to persons in other States, in violation of federal law. Moreover, the surveillance was limited, both in scope and in duration, to the specific purpose of establishing the contents of the petitioner's unlawful telephonic communications. The agents confined their surveillance to the brief periods during which he used the telephone booth, and they took great care to overhear only the conversations of the petitioner himself. . . .

It is apparent that the agents in this case acted with restraint. Yet the inescapable fact is that this restraint was imposed by the agents themselves, not by a judicial officer. They were not required, before commencing the search to present their estimate of probable cause for detached scrutiny by a neutral magistrate. They were not compelled during the conduct of the search itself, to observe precise limits established in advance by a specific court order. Nor were they directed, after the search had been completed, to notify the authorizing magistrate in detail of all that had been seized. In the absence of such safeguards, this Court has never sustained a search upon the sole ground that officers reasonably expected to find evidence of a particular crime and voluntarily confined their activities to the least intrusive means consistent with that end. . . .

Wherever a man may be, he is entitled to know that he will remain free from unreasonable searches and seizures. The government agents here ignored "the procedure of antecedent justification . . . that is central to the Fourth Amendment," a procedure that we hold to be a constitutional precondition of the kind of electronic surveillance involved in this case. Because the surveillance here failed to meet that condition, and because it led to the petitioner's conviction, the judgment must be reversed.

☐ *Justice HARLAN, concurring.*

I join the opinion of the Court, which I read to hold only (a) that an enclosed telephone booth is an area where, like a home, *Weeks v. United States*, 232 U.S. 383 (1914), and unlike a field, *Hester v. United States*, 265 U.S. 57 (1924), a person has a constitutionally protected reasonable expectation of privacy; (b) that electronic as well as physical intrusion into a place that is in this sense private may constitute a violation of the Fourth Amendment; and (c) that the invasion of a constitutionally protected area by federal authorities is, as the Court has long held, presumptively unreasonable in the absence of a search warrant.

As the Court's opinion states, "the Fourth Amendment protects people, not places." The question, however, is what protection it affords to those people. Generally, as here, the answer to that question requires reference to a "place." My understanding of the rule that has emerged from prior decisions is that there is a twofold requirement, first that a person have exhibited an actual (subjective) expectation of privacy and, second, that the expectation be one that society is prepared to recognize as "reasonable." Thus a man's home is, for most purposes, a place where he expects privacy, but objects, activities, or statements that he exposes to the "plain view" of outsiders are not "protected" because no intention to keep them to himself has been exhibited. On the other hand, conversations in the open would not be protected against being overheard, for the expectation of privacy under the circumstances would be unreasonable.

☐ *Justice BLACK, dissenting.*

My basic objection is twofold: (1) I do not believe that the words of the Amendment will bear the meaning given them by today's decision, and (2) I do not believe that it is the proper role of this Court to rewrite the Amendment in order "to bring it into harmony with the times" and thus reach a result that many people believe to be desirable. . . .

The Fourth Amendment says that

> "The right of the people to be secure in their persons, houses, papers, and effects, against unreasonable searches and seizures, shall not be violated, and no Warrants shall issue, but upon probable cause, supported by Oath or affirmation, and particularly describing the place to be searched, and the persons or things to be seized."

The first clause protects "persons, houses, papers, and effects, against unreasonable searches and seizures. . . ." These words connote the idea of tangible things with size, form, and weight, things capable of being searched, seized, or both. The second clause of the Amendment still further establishes its Framers' purpose to limit its protection to tangible things by providing that no warrants shall issue but those "particularly describing the place to be searched, and the persons or things to be seized." A conversation overheard by eavesdropping, whether by plain snooping or wiretapping, is not tangible and, under the normally accepted meanings of the words, can neither be searched nor seized. . . .

Tapping telephone wires, of course, was an unknown possibility at the time the Fourth Amendment was adopted. But eavesdropping (and wiretapping is nothing more than eavesdropping by telephone) was. . . . There can be no doubt that the Framers were aware of this practice, and if they had desired to outlaw or restrict the use of evidence obtained by eavesdropping, I believe that they would have used the appropriate language to do so in the Fourth Amendment. They certainly would not have left such a task to the ingenuity of language-stretching judges.

Since I see no way in which the word of the Fourth Amendment can be construed to apply to eavesdropping, that closes the matter for me. In interpreting the Bill of Rights, I willingly go as far as a liberal construction of the language takes me, but I simply cannot in good conscience give a meaning to words which they have never before been thought to have and which they certainly do not have in common ordinary usage. I will not distort the words of the Amendment in order to "keep the Constitution up to date" or "to bring it into harmony with the times." It was never meant that this Court have such power, which in affect would make us a continuously functioning constitutional convention.

California v. Ciraolo

476 U.S. 207, 106 S.Ct. 1809 (1986)

Chief Justice Warren Burger discusses the facts of this case, involving a warrantless search for marijuana plants by police helicopter, at the outset of his opinion for the Court.

The Court's decision was five to four, and the majority's opinion was announced by Chief Justice Burger. Justice Powell's dissent was joined by Justices Brennan, Marshall, and Blackmun.

☐ *Chief Justice BURGER delivered the opinion of the Court.*

We granted *certiorari* to determine whether the Fourth Amendment is violated by aerial observation without a warrant from an altitude of 1,000 feet of a fenced-in backyard within the curtilage of a home.

On September 2, 1982, Santa Clara Police received an anonymous telephone tip that marijuana was growing in respondent's backyard. Police were unable to observe the contents of respondent's yard from ground level because of a 6-foot outer fence and a 10-foot inner fence completely enclosing the yard. Later that day, Officer Shutz, who was assigned to investigate, secured a private plane and flew over respondent's house at an altitude of 1,000 feet, within navigable airspace; he was accompanied by Officer Rodriguez. Both officers were trained in marijuana identification. From the overflight, the officers readily identified marijuana plants 8 feet to 10 feet in height growing in a 15-by-25 foot plot in respondent's yard; they photographed the area with a standard 35mm camera.

On September 8, 1982, Officer Shutz obtained a search warrant on the basis of an affidavit describing the anonymous tip and their observations; a photograph depicting respondent's house, the backyard, and neighboring homes was attached to the affidavit as an exhibit. The warrant was executed the next day and 73 plants were seized; it is not disputed that these were marijuana.

After the trial court denied respondent's motion to suppress the evidence of the search, respondent pleaded guilty to a charge of cultivation of marijuana. The California Court of Appeals reversed, however, on the ground that the warrantless aerial *observation* of respondent's yard which led to the issuance of the warrant violated the Fourth Amendment. That court held first that respondent's backyard marijuana garden was within the "curtilage" of his home, under *Oliver v. United States*, 466 U.S. 170 (1984). The court emphasized that the height and existence of the two fences constituted "objective criteria from which we may conclude he manifested a reasonable expectation of privacy by any standard." . . .

The touchstone of Fourth Amendment analysis is whether a person has a "constitutionally protected reasonable expectation of privacy." *Katz v. United States*, 389 U.S. 347 (1967) (HARLAN, J., concurring). *Katz* posits a two-part inquiry: first, has the individual manifested a subjective expectation of privacy in the object of the challenged search? Second, is society willing to recognize that expectation as reasonable?

Clearly—and understandably—respondent has met the test of manifesting his own subjective intent and desire to maintain privacy as to his unlawful agricultural pursuits. . . . It can reasonably be assumed that the 10-foot fence was placed to conceal the marijuana crop from at least street level views. . . .

Yet a 10-foot fence might not shield these plants from the eyes of a citizen or a policeman perched on the top of a truck or a 2-level bus. Whether respondent therefore manifested a subjective expectation of privacy from *all* observations of his backyard, or whether instead he manifested merely a hope that no one would observe his unlawful gardening pursuits, is not entirely clear in these circumstances. . . .

We turn, therefore, to the second inquiry under *Katz, i.e.*, whether that expectation is reasonable. In pursuing this inquiry, we must keep in mind that "[t]he test of legitimacy is not whether the individual chooses to conceal assertedly 'private' activity," but instead "whether the government's intrusion infringes upon the personal and societal values protected by the Fourth Amendment." . . .

Respondent argues that because his yard was in the curtilage of his home, no governmental aerial observation is permissible under the Fourth Amendment without a warrant. . . . The protection afforded the curtilage is essentially a protection of families and personal privacy in an area intimately linked to the home, both physically and psychologically, where privacy expectations are most heightened. The claimed area here was immediately adjacent to a suburban home, surrounded by high double fences. This close nexus to the home would appear to encompass this small area within the curtilage. . . .

That the area is within the curtilage does not itself bar all police observation. The Fourth Amendment protection of the home has never been extended to require law enforcement officers to shield their eyes when passing by a home on public thoroughfares. Nor does the mere fact that an individual has taken measures to restrict some views of his activities preclude an officer's observations from a public vantage point where he has a right to be and which renders the activities clearly visible. . . .

The observations by Officers Shutz and Rodriquez in this case took place within public navigable airspace in a physically nonintrusive manner; from this point they were able to observe plants readily discernable to the naked eye as marijuana. That the observation from aircraft was directed at identifying the plants and the officers were trained to recognize marijuana is irrelevant. Such observation is precisely what a judicial officer needs to provide a basis for a warrant. Any member of the public flying in this airspace who glanced down could have seen everything that these officers observed. On this record, we readily conclude that respondent's expectation that his garden was protected from such observation is unreasonable and is not an expectation that society is prepared to honor.

☐ *Justice POWELL, with whom Justice BRENNAN, Justice MAR-SHALL, and Justice BLACKMUN join, dissenting.*

Concurring in *Katz v. United States*, 389 U.S. 347 (1967), Justice HAR-LAN warned that any decision to construe the Fourth Amendment as proscribing only physical intrusions by police onto private property "is, in the present day, bad physics as well as bad law, for reasonable expectations of privacy may be defeated by electronic as well as physical invasion." Because the Court today ignores that warning in an opinion that departs significantly from the standard developed in *Katz* for deciding when a Fourth Amendment violation has occurred, I dissent. . . .

Our decisions following the teaching of *Katz* illustrate that this inquiry "normally embraces two discrete questions." "The first is whether the individual, by his conduct, has 'exhibited an actual (subjective) expectation of privacy.' "The second is whether that subjective expectation "is 'one that society is prepared to recognize as "reasonable." ' " . . .

While the Court today purports to reaffirm this analytical framework, its conclusory rejection of respondent's expectation of privacy in the yard of his residence as one that "is unreasonable," represents a turning away from the principles that have guided our Fourth Amendment inquiry. . . .

The Court begins its analysis of the Fourth Amendment issue posed here by deciding that respondent had an expectation of privacy in his backyard. I agree with that conclusion because of the close proximity of the yard to the house, the nature of some of the activities respondent conducted there, and because he had taken steps to shield those activities from the view of passersby. The Court then implicitly acknowledges that society is prepared to recognize his expectation as reasonable with respect to ground-level sur-veillance, holding that the yard was within the curtilage, an area in which privacy interests have been afforded the "most heightened" protection. . . . Since Officer Shutz could not see into this private family area from the street, the Court certainly would agree that he would have conducted an un-reasonable search had he climbed over the fence, or used a ladder to peer into the yard without first securing a warrant.

The Court concludes, nevertheless, that Shutz could use an airplane—a product of modern technology—to intrude visually into respondent's yard. The Court argues that respondent had no reasonable expectation of privacy from aerial observation. It notes that Shutz was "within public navigable air-space," when he looked into and photographed respondent's yard. It then relies on the fact that the surveillance was not accompanied by a physical invasion of the curtilage. Reliance on the *manner* of surveillance is directly contrary to the standard of *Katz*, which identifies a constitutionally protected privacy right by focusing on the interests of the individual and of a free society. Since *Katz*, we have consistently held that the presence or absence of physical trespass by po-lice is constitutionally irrelevant to the question whether society is prepared to recognize an asserted privacy interest as reasonable. . . .

The Court's holding, therefore, must rest solely on the fact that mem-bers of the public fly in planes and may look down at homes as they fly over them. The Court does not explain why it finds this fact to be significant. One may assume that the Court believes that citizens bear the risk that air travelers will observe activities occurring within backyards that are open to the sun and air. This risk, the Court appears to hold, nullifies expectations of privacy in those yards even as to purposeful police surveillance from the air. . . .

This line of reasoning is flawed. First, the actual risk to privacy from commercial or pleasure aircraft is virtually nonexistent. . . . The risk that a passenger on such a plane might observe private activities, and might con-nect those activities with particular people, is simply too trivial to protect against. It is no accident that, as a matter of common experience, many peo-ple build fences around their residential areas, but few build roofs over their backyards. Therefore, contrary to the Court's suggestion, people do not " 'knowingly expos[e]' " their residential yards " 'to the public' " merely by failing to build barriers that prevent aerial surveillance. . . .

The only possible basis for this holding is a judgment that the risk to privacy posed by the remote possibility that a private airplane passenger will notice outdoor activities is equivalent to the risk of official aerial surveil-lance. But the Court fails to acknowledge the qualitative difference between police surveillance and other uses made of the air space. Members of the public use the air space for travel, business, or pleasure, not for the purpose of observing activities taking place within residential yards. Here, police con-ducted an overflight at low altitude solely for the purpose of discovering evidence of crime within a private enclave into which they were constitu-tionally forbidden to intrude at ground level without a warrant. It is not easy to believe that our society is prepared to force individuals to bear the risk of this type of warrantless police intrusion into their residential areas. . . .

[T]his Court recognized long ago that the essence of a Fourth Amend-ment violation is "not the breaking of [a person's] doors, and the rummag-ing of his drawers," but rather is "the invasion of his indefeasible right of personal security, personal liberty and private property." Rapidly advancing technology now permits police to conduct surveillance in the home itself, an area where privacy interests are most cherished in our society, without any physical trespass. While the rule in *Katz* was designed to prevent silent and unseen invasions of Fourth Amendment privacy rights in a variety of settings, we have consistently afforded heightened protection to a person's right to be left alone in the privacy of his house. The Court fails to enforce that right or to give any weight to the long-standing presumption that warrantless intrusions into the home are unreasonable. I dissent.

Minnesota v. Carter

525 U.S. 83, 119 S.CT. 469 (1998)

After arriving from Chicago in Twin Cities, Minnesota, Wayne Carter and Melvin Johns went to Kimberly Thompson's apartment. Acting on an informer's tip, a police officer also went to her apartment and, through a gap in a closed window blind, observed them bagging white powder cocaine. He called headquarters, which began preparing affidavits for a search warrant. But, when Carter and Johns left the apartment and got into their car, the officer stopped them and asked them to get out. When the door opened, the officer noticed a black zippered pouch and a handgun, whereupon Carter and Johns were arrested. A subsequent search of the car yielded 47 grams of cocaine.

At their trial for drug possession, attorneys for Carter and Johns moved to suppress the evidence on the ground that the officer's initial observation of their activities in the apartment was an unreasonable search in violation of the Fourth Amendment. The trial court rejected that motion, reasoning that Carter and Johns were only temporary visitors and, thus, not entitled to the protection of the Fourth Amendment. A state appellate court agreed but the Minnesota Supreme Court reversed, holding that Carter and Johns had a "legitimate expectation of privacy" protected by the Fourth Amendment. On appeal, the Supreme Court granted review and reversed the State Supreme Court.

The Court's decision was six to three and opinion delivered by Chief Justice Rehnquist. Justices Scalia, Kennedy, and Breyer filed concurring opinions. Justice Ginsburg filed a dissent, joined by Justices Stevens and Souter.

☐ *Chief Justice REHNQUIST delivered the opinion of the Court.*

The Minnesota courts analyzed whether respondents had a legitimate expectation of privacy under the rubric of "standing" doctrine, an analysis which this Court expressly rejected 20 years ago in *Rakas* [*v. Illinois*, 439 U.S. 128 (1978)]. In that case, we held that automobile passengers could not assert the protection of the Fourth Amendment against the seizure of incriminating evidence from a vehicle where they owned neither the vehicle nor the evidence. Central to our analysis was the idea that in determining whether a defendant is able to show the violation of his (and not someone else's) Fourth Amendment rights, the "definition of those rights is more properly placed within the purview of substantive Fourth Amendment law than within that of standing." Thus, we held that in order to claim the protection of the Fourth Amendment, a defendant must demonstrate that he personally has an expectation of privacy in the place searched, and that his expectation is reasonable; i.e., one which has "a source outside of the Fourth Amendment, either by reference to concepts of real or personal property law or to understandings that are recognized and permitted by society." . . .

The [Fourth] Amendment protects persons against unreasonable searches of "their persons [and] houses" and thus indicates that the Fourth Amendment is a personal right that must be invoked by an individual. See *Katz v. United States*, 389 U.S. 347 (1967). But the extent to which the Fourth Amendment protects people may depend upon where those people are. We have held that "capacity to claim the protection of the Fourth Amendment depends upon whether the person who claims the protection of the Amendment has a legitimate expectation of privacy in the invaded place." *Rakas.* The text of the Amendment suggests that its protections extend only to people in "their" houses. But we have held that in some circumstances a person may have a legitimate expectation of privacy in the house of someone else. In *Minnesota v. Olson*, 495 U.S. 91 (1990), for example, we decided that an overnight guest in a house had the sort of expectation of privacy that the Fourth Amendment protects. . . .

In *Jones v. United States*, 362 U.S. 257 (1960), the defendant seeking to exclude evidence resulting from a search of an apartment had been given the use of the apartment by a friend. He had clothing in the apartment, had slept there "maybe a night," and at the time was the sole occupant of the apartment. But while the holding of *Jones* that a search of the apartment violated the defendant's Fourth Amendment rights is still valid, its statement that "anyone legitimately on the premises where a search occurs may challenge its legality" was expressly repudiated in *Rakas v. Illinois.* Thus an overnight guest in a home may claim the protection of the Fourth Amendment, but one who is merely present with the consent of the householder may not.

Respondents here were obviously not overnight guests, but were essentially present for a business transaction and were only in the home a matter of hours. There is no suggestion that they had a previous relationship with Thompson, or that there was any other purpose to their visit. Nor was there anything similar to the overnight guest relationship in *Olson* to suggest a degree of acceptance into the household. While the apartment was a dwelling place for Thompson, it was for these respondents simply a place to do business.

Property used for commercial purposes is treated differently for Fourth Amendment purposes than residential property. "An expectation of privacy in commercial premises, however, is different from, and indeed less than, a similar expectation in an individual's home." *New York v. Burger*, 482 U.S. 691

(1987). And while it was a "home" in which respondents were present, it was not their home. Similarly, the Court has held that in some circumstances a worker can claim Fourth Amendment protection over his own workplace. See, e.g., *O'Connor v. Ortega*, 480 U.S. 709 (1987). But there is no indication that respondents in this case had nearly as significant a connection to Thompson's apartment as the worker in *O'Connor* had to his own private office.

Because we conclude that respondents had no legitimate expectation of privacy in the apartment, we need not decide whether the police officer's observation constituted a "search." The judgment of the Supreme Court of Minnesota is accordingly reversed, and the cause is remanded for proceedings not inconsistent with this opinion.

☐ *Justice SCALIA, with whom Justice THOMAS joins, concurring.*

I write separately to express my view that [the Court] . . . leaps to apply the fuzzy standard of "legitimate expectation of privacy"—a consideration that is often relevant to whether a search or seizure covered by the Fourth Amendment is "unreasonable"—to the threshold question whether a search or seizure covered by the Fourth Amendment has occurred. If that latter question is addressed first and analyzed under the text of the Constitution as traditionally understood, the present case is not remotely difficult.

The Fourth Amendment protects "[t]he right of the people to be secure in their persons, houses, papers, and effects, against unreasonable searches and seizures." It must be acknowledged that the phrase "their . . . houses" in this provision is, in isolation, ambiguous. It could mean "their respective houses," so that the protection extends to each person only in his own house. But it could also mean "their respective and each other's houses," so that each person would be protected even when visiting the house of someone else. As today's opinion for the Court suggests, however, it is not linguistically possible to give the provision the latter, expansive interpretation with respect to "houses" without giving it the same interpretation with respect to the nouns that are parallel to "houses"—"persons, papers, and effects"—which would give me a constitutional right not to have your person unreasonably searched. This is so absurd that it has to my knowledge never been contemplated. The obvious meaning of the provision is that each person has the right to be secure against unreasonable searches and seizures in his own person, house, papers, and effects.

The Founding-era materials that I have examined confirm that this was the understood meaning. . . . That "their houses" was understood to mean "their respective houses" would have been clear to anyone who knew the English and early American law of arrest and trespass that underlay the Fourth Amendment. The people's protection against unreasonable search and seizure in their "houses" was drawn from the English common-law maxim, "A man's home is his castle." . . .

The dissent may be correct that a person invited into someone else's house to engage in a common business (even common monkey-business, so to speak) ought to be protected against government searches of the room in which that business is conducted; and that persons invited in to deliver milk or pizza (whom the dissent dismisses as "classroom hypotheticals," as opposed, presumably, to flesh-and-blood hypotheticals) ought not to be protected against government searches of the rooms that they occupy. I am not sure of the answer to those policy questions. But I am sure that the answer is not remotely contained in the Constitution, which means that it is left—as many, indeed most, important questions are left—to the judgment of state and federal legislators. We go beyond our proper role as judges in a democratic society when we restrict the people's power to govern themselves over the full range of policy choices that the Constitution has left available to them.

☐ *Justice BREYER, concurring in the judgment.*

I agree with Justice GINSBURG that respondents can claim the Fourth Amendment's protection. Petitioner, however, raises a second question, whether under the circumstances Officer Thielen's observation made "from a public area outside the curtilage of the residence" violated respondents' Fourth Amendment rights. In my view, it did not.

I would answer the question on the basis of the following factual assumptions, derived from the evidentiary record presented here: (1) On the evening of May 15, 1994, an anonymous individual approached Officer Thielen, telling him that he had just walked by a nearby apartment window through which he had seen some people bagging drugs; (2) the apartment in question was a garden apartment that was partly below ground level; (3) families frequently used the grassy area just outside the apartment's window for walking or for playing; (4) members of the public also used the area just outside the apartment's window to store bicycles; (5) in an effort to verify the tipster's information, Officer Thielen walked to a position about one to one and one-half feet in front of the window; (6) Officer Thielen stood there for about 15 minutes looking down through a set of Venetian blinds; (7) what he saw, namely, people putting white powder in bags, verified the account he had heard; and (8) he then used that information to help obtain a search warrant. . . .

For these reasons, while agreeing with Justice GINSBURG, I also concur in the Court's judgment reversing the Minnesota Supreme Court.

☐ *Justice GINSBURG, with whom Justice STEVENS and Justice SOUTER join, dissenting.*

The Court's decision undermines not only the security of short-term guests, but also the security of the home resident herself. In my view, when a homeowner or lessor personally invites a guest into her home to share in a common endeavor, whether it be for conversation, to engage in leisure activities, or for business purposes licit or illicit, that guest should share his host's shelter against unreasonable searches and seizures. . . .

A homedweller places her own privacy at risk, the Court's approach indicates, when she opens her home to others, uncertain whether the duration of their stay, their purpose, and their "acceptance into the household" will earn protection. It remains textbook law that "[s]earches and seizures inside a home without a warrant are presumptively unreasonable absent exigent circumstances." [*United States v.*] *Karo*, [468 U.S. 705 (1984).] The law in practice is less secure. Human frailty suggests that today's decision will tempt police to pry into private dwellings without warrant, to find evidence incriminating guests who do not rest there through the night. *Rakas* tolerates that temptation with respect to automobile searches. I see no impelling reason to extend this risk into the home. As I see it, people are not genuinely "secure in their 'houses' against unreasonable searches and seizures," if their invitations to others increase the risk of unwarranted governmental peering and prying into their dwelling places.

In sum, when a homeowner chooses to share the privacy of her home and her company with a short-term guest, the twofold requirement "emerg[ing] from prior decisions" has been satisfied: Both host and guest "have exhibited an actual (subjective) expectation of privacy"; that "expectation [is] one [our] society is prepared to recognize as 'reasonable.' " *Katz v. United States*, 389 U.S. 347 (1967) (HARLAN, J., concurring). . . .

For the reasons stated, I dissent from the Court's judgment, and would retain judicial surveillance over the warrantless searches today's decision allows.

■ THE DEVELOPMENT OF LAW

Other Important Rulings on Governmental Wiretapping and Electronic Surveillance

CASE	VOTE	RULING
United States v. United States District Court, 407 U.S. 297 (1972)	8:0	Rejects claim of the Nixon administration that there was a national security exception to the requirement that judges approve

warrants for wiretaps upon the request of the attorney general, as required by the Omnibus Crime Control and Safe Streets Act (OCCSS Act) of 1968.

United States v. Kahn, 415 U.S. 143 (1974)	6:3	Upheld use of wiretapped evidence, obtained pursuant to a wiretap as authorized by the

OCCSS Act, against the wife of a man who was the subject of a warrant for wiretapping.

United States v. Giordano, 416 U.S. 505 (1974)	5:4	Authority for issuing wiretaps under the OCCSS Act cannot be delegated from the attorney general to the assistant attorney general.

United States v. Donovan, 429 U.S. 413 (1977)	6:3	Under the OCCSS Act, police must identify all persons for whom they have probable cause

to obtain a wiretap warrant, but failure to do so did not trigger suppression of evidence under the statute.

CASE	VOTE	RULING
United States v. New York Telephone Company, 434 U.S. 159 (1977)	5:4	OCCSS Act does not cover "pen registers"—devices that record the numbers dialed from a phone.
Scott v. United States, 436 U.S. 128 (1978)	7:2	Upheld wiretapping of all phone calls under a warrant issued pursuant to OCCSS Act.
Dalia v. United States, 441 U.S. 238 (1979)	6:3	No need to obtain separate warrant to make a covert entry to plant an authorized wiretap.
Smith v. Maryland, 442 U.S. 735 (1979)	6:3	Upheld use of pen registers.
United States v. Kaio, 468 U.S. 705 (1984)	6:3	Planting of beepers does not require authorization of search warrant.

Kyllo v. United States

533 U.S. 27, 121 S.CT. 2038 (2001)

In 1992, federal agents suspected Danny Kyllo of growing marijuana in his home and decided to use an Agema Thermovision 210 thermal imager to scan his house. The imagers detect infrared radiation, which virtually all objects emit, and converts the radiation into images based on their relative warmth. From the passenger's seat of their car across the street from the house, the agents scanned the house and found that the roof over the garage and a side wall of the house were relatively hot. The agents concluded that Kyllo was using halide, high-intensity lights to grow marijuana and on that basis, along with an informant's tip and utility bills, obtained a warrant to search the house, where they found more than 100 marijuana plants. Kyllo sought to suppress that evidence on the ground that the use of the thermal imager consistuted a warrantless search in violation of the Fourth Amendment. A federal district court rejected that motion and its decision was affirmed by an appellate court.

The appellate court's decision was reversed by a five-to-four vote and the opinion for the Court was delivered by Justice Scalia. Justice

Stevens filed a dissenting opinion, which Chief Justice Rehnquist and Justice O'Connor and Kennedy joined.

☐ *Justice SCALIA delivered the opinion of the Court.*

This case presents the question whether the use of a thermal-imaging device aimed at a private home from a public street to detect relative amounts of heat within the home constitutes a "search" within the meaning of the Fourth Amendment.

"At the very core" of the Fourth Amendment "stands the right of a man to retreat into his own home and there be free from unreasonable governmental intrusion." *Silverman v. United States,* 365 U.S. 505 (1961). . . . On the other hand, the antecedent question of whether or not a Fourth Amendment "search" has occurred is not so simple under our precedent. The permissibility of ordinary visual surveillance of a home used to be clear because, well into the 20th century, our Fourth Amendment jurisprudence was tied to common-law trespass. See, e.g., *Goldman v. United States,* 316 U.S. 129 (1942); *Olmstead v. United States,* 277 U.S. 438 (1928). Visual surveillance was unquestionably lawful because " 'the eye cannot by the laws of England be guilty of a trespass.' " *Boyd v. United States,* 116 U.S. 616 (1886). We have since decoupled violation of a person's Fourth Amendment rights from trespassory violation of his property, see *Rakas v. Illinois,* 439 U.S. 128 (1978), but the lawfulness of warrantless visual surveillance of a home has still been preserved. As we observed in *California v. Ciraolo,* 476 U.S. 207 (1986), "[t]he Fourth Amendment protection of the home has never been extended to require law enforcement officers to shield their eyes when passing by a home on public thoroughfares."

One might think that the new validating rationale would be that examining the portion of a house that is in plain public view, while it is a "search" despite the absence of trespass, is not an "unreasonable" one under the Fourth Amendment. But in fact we have held that visual observation is no "search" at all—perhaps in order to preserve somewhat more intact our doctrine that warrantless searches are presumptively unconstitutional. See *Dow Chemical Co. v. United States,* 476 U.S. 227 (1986). In assessing when a search is not a search, we have applied somewhat in reverse the principle first enunciated in *Katz v. United States,* 389 U.S. 347 (1967) . . . that a Fourth Amendment search does not occur—even when the explicitly protected location of a house is concerned—unless "the individual manifested a subjective expectation of privacy in the object of the challenged search," and "society [is] willing to recognize that expectation as reasonable." *Ciraolo.* . . .

The present case involves officers on a public street engaged in more than naked-eye surveillance of a home. We have previously reserved judgment as to how much technological enhancement of ordinary perception from such a vantage point, if any, is too much. While we upheld enhanced aerial photography of an industrial complex in *Dow Chemical,* we noted that we found "it important that this is not an area immediately adjacent to a private home, where privacy expectations are most heightened."

It would be foolish to contend that the degree of privacy secured to citizens by the Fourth Amendment has been entirely unaffected by the advance of technology. For example, as the cases discussed above make clear, the technology enabling human flight has exposed to public view (and hence, we have said, to official observation) uncovered portions of the house and its curtilage that once were private. The question we confront today is what limits there are upon this power of technology to shrink the realm of guaranteed privacy.

The *Katz* test—whether the individual has an expectation of privacy that society is prepared to recognize as reasonable—has often been criticized as circular, and hence subjective and unpredictable. While it may be difficult to refine *Katz* when the search of areas such as telephone booths, automobiles, or even the curtilage and uncovered portions of residences are at issue, in the case of the search of the interior of homes—the prototypical and hence most commonly litigated area of protected privacy—there is a ready criterion, with roots deep in the common law, of the minimal expectation of privacy that exists, and that is acknowledged to be reasonable. To withdraw protection of this minimum expectation would be to permit police technology to erode the privacy guaranteed by the Fourth Amendment. We think that obtaining by sense-enhancing technology any information regarding the interior of the home that could not otherwise have been obtained without physical "intrusion into a constitutionally protected area," *Silverman*, constitutes a search—at least where (as here) the technology in question is not in general public use. This assures preservation of that degree of privacy against government that existed when the Fourth Amendment was adopted. On the basis of this criterion, the information obtained by the thermal imager in this case was the product of a search.

The Government maintains, however, that the thermal imaging must be upheld because it detected "only heat radiating from the external surface of the house." The dissent makes this its leading point, contending that there is a fundamental difference between what it calls "off-the-wall" observations and "through-the-wall surveillance." But just as a thermal imager captures only heat emanating from a house, so also a powerful directional microphone picks up only sound emanating from a house—and a satellite capable of scanning from many miles away would pick up only visible light emanating from a house. We rejected such a mechanical interpretation of the Fourth Amendment in *Katz*, where the eavesdropping device picked up only sound waves that reached the exterior of the phone booth. Reversing that approach would leave the homeowner at the mercy of advancing technology—including imaging technology that could discern all human activity in the home. While the technology used in the present case was relatively crude, the rule we adopt must take account of more sophisticated systems that are already in use or in development. . . .

We have said that the Fourth Amendment draws "a firm line at the entrance to the house," *Payton*. That line, we think, must be not only firm but also bright—which requires clear specification of those methods of surveillance that require a warrant. While it is certainly possible to conclude from the videotape of the thermal imaging that occurred in this case that no "significant" compromise of the homeowner's privacy has occurred, we must take the long view, from the original meaning of the Fourth Amendment forward. Where, as here, the Government uses a device that is not in general public use, to explore details of the home that would previously have been unknowable without physical intrusion, the surveillance is a "search" and is presumptively unreasonable without a warrant.

Since we hold the Thermovision imaging to have been an unlawful search, it will remain for the District Court to determine whether, without the evidence it provided, the search warrant issued in this case was supported by probable cause—and if not, whether there is any other basis for supporting admission of the evidence that the search pursuant to the warrant produced.

☐ *Justice STEVENS, with whom The CHIEF JUSTICE, Justice O'CONNOR, and Justice KENNEDY join, dissenting.*

There is, in my judgment, a distinction of constitutional magnitude between "through-the-wall surveillance" that gives the observer or listener direct access to information in a private area, on the one hand, and the thought processes used to draw inferences from information in the public domain, on the other hand. The Court has crafted a rule that purports to deal with direct observations of the inside of the home, but the case before us merely involves indirect deductions from "off-the-wall" surveillance, that is, observations of the exterior of the home. Those observations were made with a fairly primitive thermal imager that gathered data exposed on the outside of petitioner's home but did not invade any constitutionally protected interest in privacy. Moreover, I believe that the supposedly "bright-line" rule the Court has created in response to its concerns about future technological developments is unnecessary, unwise, and inconsistent with the Fourth Amendment.

There is no need for the Court to craft a new rule to decide this case, as it is controlled by established principles from our Fourth Amendment jurisprudence. One of those core principles, of course, is that "searches and seizures inside a home without a warrant are presumptively unreasonable." *Payton v. New York,* 445 U.S. 573 (1980). But it is equally well settled that searches and seizures of property in plain view are presumptively reasonable. Whether that property is residential or commercial, the basic principle is the same: " 'What a person knowingly exposes to the public, even in his own home or office, is not a subject of Fourth Amendment protection.' " *California v. Ciraolo,* 476 U.S. 207 (1986).

[T]he notion that heat emissions from the outside of a dwelling is a private matter implicating the protections of the Fourth Amendment is not only unprecedented but also quite difficult to take seriously. Heat waves, like aromas that are generated in a kitchen, or in a laboratory or opium den, enter the public domain if and when they leave a building. A subjective expectation that they would remain private is not only implausible but also surely not "one that society is prepared to recognize as 'reasonable.' " *Katz* (HARLAN, J., concurring).

To be sure, the homeowner has a reasonable expectation of privacy concerning what takes place within the home, and the Fourth Amendment's protection against physical invasions of the home should apply to their functional equivalent. But the equipment in this case did not penetrate the walls of petitioner's home, and while it did pick up "details of the home" that were exposed to the public, it did not obtain "any information regarding the interior of the home." In the Court's own words, based on what the thermal imager "showed" regarding the outside of petitioner's home, the officers "concluded" that petitioner was engaging in illegal activity inside the home.

It would be quite absurd to characterize their thought processes as "searches," regardless of whether they inferred (rightly) that petitioner was growing marijuana in his house, or (wrongly) that "the lady of the house [was taking] her daily sauna and bath." In either case, the only conclusions the officers reached concerning the interior of the home were at least as indirect as those that might have been inferred from the contents of discarded garbage, see *California v. Greenwood,* 486 U.S. 35 (1988), or pen register data, see *Smith v. Maryland,* 442 U.S. 735 (1979). . . .

Since what was involved in this case was nothing more than drawing inferences from off-the-wall surveillance, rather than any "through-the-wall" surveillance, the officers' conduct did not amount to a search and was perfectly reasonable. . . .

Despite the Court's attempt to draw a line that is "not only firm but also bright," the contours of its new rule are uncertain because its protection apparently dissipates as soon as the relevant technology is "in general public use." Yet how much use is general public use is not even hinted at by the Court's opinion, which makes the somewhat doubtful assumption that the thermal imager used in this case does not satisfy that criterion. In any event, putting aside its lack of clarity, this criterion is somewhat perverse because it seems likely that the threat to privacy will grow, rather than recede, as the use of intrusive equipment becomes more readily available. . . .

The two reasons advanced by the Court as justifications for the adoption of its new rule are both unpersuasive. First, the Court suggests that its rule is compelled by our holding in *Katz,* because in that case, as in this, the surveillance consisted of nothing more than the monitoring of waves emanating from a private area into the public domain. Yet there are critical differences between the cases. In *Katz,* the electronic listening device attached to the outside of the phone booth allowed the officers to pick up the content of the conversation inside the booth, making them the functional equivalent of intruders because they gathered information that was otherwise available only to someone inside the private area; it would be as if, in this case, the thermal imager presented a view of the heat-generating activity inside petitioner's home. By contrast, the thermal imager here disclosed only the relative amounts of heat radiating from the house; it would be as if, in *Katz,* the listening device disclosed only the relative volume of sound leaving the booth, which presumably was discernible in the public domain. Surely, there is a significant difference between the general and well-settled expectation that strangers will not have direct access to the contents of private communications, on the one hand, and the rather theoretical expectation that an occasional homeowner would even care if anybody noticed the relative amounts of heat emanating from the walls of his house, on the other. It is pure hyperbole for the Court to suggest that refusing to extend the holding of *Katz* to this case would leave the homeowner at the mercy of "technology that could discern all human activity in the home."

Second, the Court argues that the permissibility of "through-the-wall surveillance" cannot depend on a distinction between observing "intimate details" such as "the lady of the house [taking] her daily sauna and bath," and noticing only "the nonintimate rug on the vestibule floor" or "objects no smaller than 36 by 36 inches." This entire argument assumes, of course, that the thermal imager in this case could or did perform "through-the-wall surveillance" that could identify any detail "that would previously have been unknowable without physical intrusion." In fact, the device could not and did not enable its user to identify either the lady of the house, the rug on the vestibule floor, or anything else inside the house. . . .

Although the Court is properly and commendably concerned about the threats to privacy that may flow from advances in the technology available to the law enforcement profession, it has unfortunately failed to heed the tried and true counsel of judicial restraint. Instead of concentrating on the rather mundane issue that is actually presented by the case before it, the Court has endeavored to craft an all-encompassing rule for the future. It would be far wiser to give legislators an unimpeded opportunity to grapple with these emerging issues rather than to shackle them with prematurely devised constitutional constraints.

I respectfully dissent.

■ THE DEVELOPMENT OF LAW

The USA PATRIOT Act of 2001, Wiretaps, and the Foreign Intelligence Surveillance Court★

Enacted in response to the terrorist attacks of September 11, 2001, the USA PATRIOT Act authorizes sweeping changes in law enforcement, notably lowering the standards for searching and seizing individuals suspected of terrorism, for example, as well as expanding investigatory powers. Among the changes, the law authorizes

- Roving wiretaps—wiretaps on any telephone used by a person suspected of terrorism—and the use of key-logger devices, which register every stroke made on a computer, and Internet wiretaps.
- Police searches of private property without prior notification of the owners and without a search warrant.
- A lower standard for judicial approval of wiretaps for individuals suspected of terrorist activities.
- The attorney general to designate domestic groups as terrorist organizations and to block the entry into the country of foreigners aligned with them.
- The Central Intelligence Agency to investigate Americans suspected of having connections to terrorism.
- The Department of Treasury to monitor financial transactions—bank accounts, mutual funds, and brokerage deals—and to obtain medical and other electronic records on individuals.
- The detention and deportation of foreigners suspected of having connections to terrorist organizations.

One of the most controversial provisions of the USA PATRIOT Act removes restrictions on information sharing and foreign intelligence gathering. Section 203 requires the attorney general to disclose to the director of the Central Intelligence Agency (CIA) "foreign intelligence" obtained from a federal criminal investigation, including wiretaps and grand jury hearings. The CIA may also share information with domestic law enforcement agencies.

Critics charge that the broad language of the act's disclosure requirements permits the Department of Justice (DoJ) to give the CIA all information related to a foreigner or to a citizen's contacts with a foreign government or organization, not merely pertaining to international terrorism. Moreover, the act does not establish any standards or safeguards for restricting the disclosure of "foreign intelligence information." Critics therefore contend that the intelligence community may collect information about individuals who have committed no crimes but who are involved in lawful protests of American foreign policies.

Furthermore, the USA PATRIOT Act changed the Foreign Intelligence Surveillance (FIS) Act of 1978, which created a special FIS court, staffed by sitting federal judges on special assignments, to approve wiretaps and to ensure that "the sole purpose" of domestic intelligence gathering was to obtain foreign intelligence information. That law was enacted because of abuses in domestic surveillance of anti-Vietnam war protesters and leaders of the civil rights movement in the 1960s and 1970s. Section 218 of the USA PATRIOT Act, however, changed the law so the DoJ need only show that the collection of foreign intelligence information has "a significant purpose," instead of being "the sole purpose" of an investigation.

Based on those provisions in 2002, Attorney General John Ashcroft issued new guidelines allowing federal prosecutors to consult with law enforcement agents conducting foreign intelligence surveillance. Those guidelines were in turn challenged as a violation of the Fourth Amendment and for permitting the use of special FIS wiretaps for investigating and prosecuting ordinary criminals, and not just spies and terrorists. In May 2002, the U.S. Foreign Intelligence Surveillance Court unanimously rejected the new guidelines and for the first time in the history of the court released a published opinion, *In re: All Matters Submitted to the Foreign Intelligence Surveillance Court*, No. Multiple 02-429 F. Supp. 2d C (U.S. Foreign Intel. Surv. Ct., 17 May 2002). Emphasizing the special and intrusive nature of FIS Act surveillance, the seven judges on the court maintained that the "walls" prohibiting criminal prosecutors from conducting investigations of suspected foreign spies and terrorists should not be torn down and that the DoJ's new guidelines were not "reasonably designed."

However, the DoJ successfully appealed that decision to a special three-judge court of appeals, as authorized by the FIS Act and whose judges are assigned from other federal appellate courts by the chief justice of the Supreme Court. Subsequently, the FIS appellate court upheld the DoJ's new guidelines, in *In re: Sealed Case* (U.S. Foreign Intelligence Surveillance Court of Review No. 02-001 and 02-002), available at *http://www.cadc.uscourts.gov/common/newsroom/02001.pdf*. In doing so, the appellate court stressed that the USA PATRIOT Act aimed to eliminate "walls" between foreign intelligence and domestic law enforcement agencies, and explained: "Effective counterintelligence, as we have learned, requires the whole-hearted cooperation of all the government's personnel who can be brought to the task. A standard which punishes such cooperation could well be thought dangerous to national security." As a result, federal criminal prosecutors may use information against citizens obtained from wiretaps authorized by the FIS court, based on less than probable cause and on more searching surveillance than permitted under traditional wiretaps.

*The full title of the law is Uniting and Strengthening America by Providing Appropriate Tools Required to Intercept and Obstruct Terrorism (USA PATRIOT) Act of 2001. For the text and other information go to *http://personalinfomediary.com/*USA PATRIOTACT Text.htm.

F | *The Exclusionary Rule*

If police do not honor the commands of the Fourth Amendment and make an unreasonable search and seizure, what is to be done? In England and some other countries, illegally obtained evidence may be used against a defendant and is not grounds for appealing a conviction. But he or she has the right to sue for civil damages or call for criminal proceedings against the officers who violated the law.[1] In *Weeks v. United States*, 232 U.S. 383 (1914), however, the Court adopted the exclusionary rule—prohibiting the admission of illegally seized evidence at the trial.

The basis for and application of the exclusionary rule has been a source of continuing controversy. Some justices and scholars defend the rule as a *constitutional principle* essential to the rights guaranteed by the Fourth Amendment. But this rationale has been criticized for "making the tail of the exclusionary rule wag the dog of the Fourth Amendment."[2] Others claim that the rule is simply an *evidentiary rule* that should be limited or eliminated based on considerations of public policy. One policy argument for the exclusionary rule is that it preserves *judicial integrity*; the judiciary's prestige would be damaged if judges were complacent about allowing the use of illegally obtained evidence by prosecutors in convicting defendants for breaking the law. Critics of the constitutional status of the exclusionary rule more often argue that the rule is defensible only if it succeeds in promoting a policy of deterring police from illegal searches and seizures.[3] The *deterrence rationale*, in turn, has generated debate over whether the exclusionary rule indeed deters police, whether it has a direct or indirect effect on police misconduct, and how significant empirical studies are and should be for determining the fate of the exclusionary rule.[4]

Writing for the majority in *Weeks v. United States*, Justice William Day refused to distinguish between the seizure and introduction at trial of illegally obtained evidence, but he was ambiguous about whether the exclusionary rule was a constitutional requirement or simply an evidentiary rule that could be expanded or contracted depending on public policy considerations. To allow the use of illegally seized evidence, Day observed, "would be to affirm by judicial decision a manifest neglect if not an open defiance of the prohibitions . . . of the Constitution." And he suggested that the exclusionary rule was essential to the personal rights secured by the Fourth Amendment, observing that without it claims against unreasonable "invasions of the home and privacy of the citizens" would have little practical feasibility; "[i]f letters and private documents can thus be seized and held and used in evidence against a citizen accused of an offense, the protection of the Fourth Amendment declaring his right to be secure against such searches and seizures is of no value, and, so far as those thus placed are concerned, might as well be stricken from the Constitution." Yet Day also noted that the exclusionary rule expressed the Court's disapproval of illegal police conduct and recognition of the need to preserve the integrity of the judicial system. In his words, "The tendency of those who execute the criminal laws of the country to obtain conviction by means of unlawful seizures and enforced confessions . . . should find no sanction in the judgments of the courts . . . charged at all times with the support of the Constitution." As a result of Day's ambiguous opinion, it was debatable whether the exclusionary rule expressed a constitutional principle or simply registered a policy aimed at enhancing judicial integrity and deterring police misconduct.

The status of the exclusionary rule remained problematic thirty-five years later when the Court made the Fourth Amendment but not the exclusionary rule applicable to the states under the Fourteenth Amendment. (For further discussion of federal-state relations and the Court's nationalization of the Bill of Rights, see Chapter 4, in this volume, and Vol. 1, Ch. 7.) In *Wolf v. Colorado*, 338 U.S. 25 (1949), Justice Felix Frankfurter observed that "[t]he security of one's privacy against arbitrary intrusion by the police—which is at the core the Fourth Amendment—is basic to a free society. It is therefore implicit in 'the concept of ordered liberty' and as such enforceable against the states through the Due Process Clause." But he held the exclusionary rule to be a nonconstitutional remedy and took a dim view of Justice Day's rationale for the rule, terming it a mere "judicial implication" without foundation in the Fourth Amendment. Likewise, Justice Hugo Black reiterated that the "federal exclusionary rule is not a command of the Fourth Amendment but is a judicially created rule of evidence which Congress might negate."

Wolf 's dissenters (Justices Douglas, Murphy, and Rutledge) had quite a different interpretation. They contended that the Fourth Amendment's guarantee of a right of privacy required the exclusion of illegally obtained evidence and that the exclusionary rule was the only means of giving "content to the commands of the Fourth Amendment."

As a consequence of *Wolf* 's holding that the Fourth Amendment but not the exclusionary rule applied to the states, the Court had to decide on a case-by-case basis whether illegal searches and seizures by state police violated the due process clause of the Fourteenth Amendment.[5] In addition, because the exclusionary rule applied only if federal agents were guilty of unlawful searches and seizures, state police who illegally obtained evidence could turn it over on a "silver platter" to federal prosecutors for use in federal courts. The Warren Court finally abandoned what became known as "the silver platter doctrine" in *Elkins v. United States*, 364 U.S. 206 (1960).

In *Elkins*, a bare majority agreed with *Wolf* 's dissenters on the application of the exclusionary rule, but not its underlying rationale. The distinction drawn in *Wolf* between the Fourth Amendment's requirements imposed on the federal government and those of the due process clause of the Fourteenth Amendment imposed on the states was finally eliminated. And the Court held that evidence illegally seized by state police could no longer be turned over to federal agents and used in federal courts. But the majority declined to make the exclusionary rule fully applicable to the states and accepted *Wolf* 's reasoning that "[t]he rule is calculated to prevent, not repair. Its purpose is to deter—to compel respect for the constitutional guaranty in the only effectively available way—by removing the incentive to disregard it."

Two years after *Elkins*, the Warren Court nevertheless held in a landmark ruling in *Mapp v. Ohio* (1961) (excerpted below) that the exclusionary rule limits the states as well as the federal government. Notice that Justice Tom Clark's opinion for the majority rationalized the exclusionary rule in terms of constitutional principles, including the right of privacy, as well as the policies of preserving judicial integrity and deterring police misconduct. However, in *Linkletter v. Walker* (see Ch. 2), the Court identified deterrence as the principal rationale for the exclusionary rule, when denying retroactivity to its holding in *Mapp*.

There, Justice Clark observed that "[w]e cannot say that this purpose [deterrence] would be advanced by making the rule retrospective. . . . Nor would it add harmony to the delicate state-federal relationship of which we have spoken as part and parcel of the purpose of *Mapp*. Finally, the ruptured privacy of the victims' homes and effects cannot be restored. Reparation comes too late."

Subsequent rulings have not only focused on deterrence as the rationale for the rule but also on that basis criticized the rule and limited its scope. In *United States v. Calandra*, 414 U.S. 338 (1974), for example, the Court held that the exclusionary rule did not apply to questions asked of a grand jury witness that were based on evidence obtained by an illegal search and seizure of his papers. By divorcing the exclusionary rule from its rationale as a safeguard for Fourth Amendment rights, the rule's role in safeguarding privacy interests diminished. As Justice Powell viewed it in his opinion for the Court: "[T]he rule is a judicially created remedy designed to safeguard Fourth Amendment rights generally through its deterrent effect, rather than a personal constitutional right of the party aggrieved."

The Burger and Rehnquist Courts cut back on the application of the exclusionary rule in a number of other ways as well. In *United States v. Janis*, 428 U.S. 433 (1976), the Court held that illegally obtained evidence may be used in civil trials; there, in a suit to recover unpaid federal income taxes. And in a sweeping ruling in *Stone v. Powell*, 428 U.S. 465 (1976), the Court ruled that state prisoners may no longer petition for a writ of *habeas corpus* in federal district courts to review their convictions, when they already have had the opportunity on direct appeal to argue that their Fourth Amendment rights were violated. Writing for the majority, Justice Powell held that the costs of overturning convictions in cases where illegally obtained evidence was used at trial simply outweighed whatever benefits the exclusionary rule has in deterring police misconduct. And he stressed that the exclusionary rule

deflects the truthfinding process and often frees the guilty. The disparity in particular cases between the error committed by the police and the windfall afforded a guilty defendant by application of the rule is contrary to the idea of proportionality that is essential to the concept of justice. Thus, although the rule is thought to deter unlawful police activity in part through the nurturing of respect for Fourth Amendment values, if applied indiscriminately it may well have the opposite effect of generating disrespect for the law and administration of justice. These long-recognized costs of the rule persist when a criminal conviction is sought to be overturned on collateral review on the ground that a search-and-seizure claim was erroneously rejected by two or more tiers of state courts.

Although the Court has not expressly overturned *Mapp* or abandoned the exclusionary rule, it has carved out exceptions to the application of the rule. One long-standing exception to the exclusionary rule, however, permits prosecutors to introduce at trial illegally obtained evidence for the purpose of discrediting the defendant's *own* testimony.[6] In *United States v. Havens*, 446 U.S. 620 (1980), the Burger Court expanded this exception to allow prosecutors to use illegally obtained evidence to impeach the testimony during cross-examination of an accomplice called to testify for the defendant. But a bare majority of the Court in *James v. Illinois*, 493 U.S. 307 (1990), barred further expansion of this exception to the exclusionary rule. In this case, Justice Brennan held that the prosecution may not introduce illegally obtained evidence to impeach the testimony of *any* witness called by a defendant.

In *Nix v. Williams* (1984) (excerpted below), the Court upheld an "inevitable discovery" exception to the exclusionary rule. In a companion ruling, *Segura v. United States*, 468 U.S. 796 (1984), the justices split five to four on holding that the exclusionary rule does not prohibit the use of illegally obtained evidence that police would have later found as a result of other independent sources.

In still two more 1984 rulings, *United States v. Leon* and *Massachusetts v. Sheppard* (excerpted below), the Court legitimized a "good faith" exception to the exclusionary rule. Subsequently, in *Arizona v. Evans*, 514 U.S. 1 (1995) (excerpted below), the Rehnquist Court expanded the "good faith" exception to the exclusionary rule to include police reliance on mistaken computer records of outstanding arrest warrants, and invited angry dissents from Justices Stevens and Ginsburg. *Pennsylvania Board of Probation and Parole v. Scott*, 524 U.S. 357 (1998), held that the exclusionary rule does not apply to parole revocation hearings and that evidence illegally obtained may be used against a parolee suspected of violating the conditions of parole.

NOTES

1. See J. David Hirschel, "What Can We Learn from the English Approach to the Problem of Illegally Obtained Evidence?" 67 *Judicature* 9 (Apr. 1984). In his dissenting opinion in *Bivens v. Six-Unknown Named Agents*, 403 U.S. 388 (1971), Chief Justice Burger urged that the exclusionary rule be abandoned and that in its place a system of tort remedies be established, permitting defendants to sue police for unlawful searches and seizures while allowing illegally obtained evidence to be used.

2. Anthony Amsterdam, "Perspectives on the Fourth Amendment," 58 *Minnesota Law Review* 369 (1974).

3. See Dallin Oaks, "Studying the Exclusionary Rule in Search and Seizure," 37 *University of Chicago Law Review* 665 (1970); and Stephen Schlesinger, *Exclusionary Injustice: The Problem of Illegally Obtained Evidence* (New York: Dekker, 1977).

4. See Stephen Schlesinger, "The Exclusionary Rule: Have Proponents Proven That It Is a Deterrent to Police?" 62 *Judicature* 404 (1979); Bradley Canon, "The Exclusionary Rule: Have Critics Proven That It Doesn't Deter Police?" 62 *Judicature* 398 (1979); Note, "The Exclusionary Rule and Deterrence: An Empirical Study of Chicago Narcotics Officers," 54 *University of Chicago Law Review* 1016 (1987); Note, "On the Limitations of Empirical Evaluations of the Exclusionary Rule," 69 *Northwestern University Law Review* 740 (1974).

5. See *Rochin v. California* (1952), in Volume 2, Chapter 4.

6. See *Walder v. United States*, 347 U.S. 62 (1954).

Selected Bibliography

Amar, Akhil R. *The Constitution and Criminal Procedure*. New Haven:, CT: Yale University Press, 1997.

Amsterdam, Anthony. *Perspectives on the Fourth Amendment*. St. Paul: Minnesota Law Review Foundation, 1974.

Griswold, Erwin. *Search and Seizure*. Lincoln: University of Nebraska Press, 1975.

Schlesinger, Stephen. *Exclusionary Injustice*. New York: Dekker, 1977.

Wilkey, Malcolm. *Enforcing the Fourth Amendment by Alternatives to the Exclusionary Rule*. Washington, DC: National Legal Center for the Public Interest, 1982.

Mapp v. Ohio
367 U.S. 643, 81 S.Ct. 1684 (1961)

Justice Tom Clark discusses the facts in his opinion for the Court, which made the Fourth Amendment exclusionary rule applicable in state as well as federal courts.

The Court's decision was six to three, and the majority's opinion was announced by Justice Clark. Concurrences were by Justices Black and Douglas. Justice Stewart issued a memorandum. Justice Harlan dissented and was joined by Justices Frankfurter and Whittaker.

☐ *Justice CLARK delivered the opinion of the Court.*

Appellant stands convicted of knowingly having had in her possession and under her control certain lewd and lascivious books, pictures, and photographs in violation of §2905.34 of Ohio's Revised Code. . . .

On May 23, 1957, three Cleveland police officers arrived at appellant's residence in that city pursuant to information that "a person [was] hiding out in the home, who was wanted for questioning in connection with a recent

Dollree Mapp. (*Reprinted with permission from* The Plain Dealer)

bombing, and that there was a large amount of policy paraphernalia being hidden in the home." Miss Mapp and her daughter by a former marriage lived on the top floor of the two-family dwelling. Upon their arrival at that house, the officers knocked on the door and demanded entrance but appellant, after telephoning her attorney, refused to admit them without a search warrant. They advised their headquarters of the situation and undertook a surveillance of the house.

The officers again sought entrance some three hours later when four or more additional officers arrived on the scene. When Miss Mapp did not come to the door immediately, at least one of the several doors to the house was forcibly opened and the policemen gained admittance. Meanwhile Miss Mapp's attorney arrived, but the officers, having secured their own entry, and continuing in their defiance of the law, would permit him neither to see Miss Mapp nor enter the house. It appears that Miss Mapp was halfway down the stairs from the upper floor to the front door when the officers, in this highhanded manner, broke into the hall. She demanded to see the search warrant. A paper, claimed to be a warrant, was held up by one of the officers. She grabbed the "warrant" and placed it in her bosom. A struggle ensued in which the officers recovered the piece of paper and as a result of which they handcuffed appellant because she had been "belligerent" in resisting their official rescue of the "warrant" from her person. Running roughshod over appellant, a policeman "grabbed" her, "twisted [her] hand," and she "yelled [and] pleaded with him" because "it was hurting." Appellant, in handcuffs, was then forcibly taken upstairs to her bedroom where the officers searched a dresser, a chest of drawers, a closet and some suitcases. They also looked into a photo album and through personal papers belonging to the appellant. The search spread to the rest of the second floor including the child's bedroom, the living room, the kitchen and a dinette. The basement of

■ INSIDE THE COURT

Letter from Justice Stewart to Justice Clark on Mapp v. Ohio

Supreme Court of the United States
Washington 25, D. C.

CHAMBERS OF
JUSTICE POTTER STEWART

May 1, 1961

No. 236 - Mapp v. Ohio

Dear Tom,

As I am sure you anticipated, your proposed opinion in this case came as quite a surprise. In all honesty, I seriously question the wisdom of using this case as a vehicle to overrule an important doctrine so recently established and so consistently adhered to. Without getting into the merits, I point out only that the idea of overruling <u>Wolf</u> was urged in the brief and oral argument only by amicus curiae and was not even discussed at the Conference, where we all agreed, as I recollect it, that the judgment should be reversed on First Amendment grounds. If <u>Wolf</u> is to be reconsidered, I myself would much prefer to do so only in a case that required it, and only after argument of the case by competent counsel and a full Conference discussion.

Sincerely yours,

P.S.

Mr. Justice Clark

Source: Justice Tom C. Clark Papers, Rare Books and Special Collections, Tarlton Law Library, University of Texas at Austin.

the building and a trunk found therein were also searched. The obscene materials for possession of which she was ultimately convicted were discovered in the course of that widespread search. . . .

The State says that even if the search were made without authority, or otherwise unreasonably, it is not prevented from using the unconstitutionally seized evidence at trial, citing *Wolf v. People of State of Colorado*, [338 U.S. 25], 1949, in which this Court did indeed hold "that in a prosecution in a State court for a State crime the Fourteenth Amendment does not forbid the admission of evidence obtained by an unreasonable search and seizure." . . .

[I]t is urged once again that we review that holding.

■ I

Seventy-five years ago, in *Boyd v. United States*, [116 U.S. 616], 1886 considering the Fourth and Fifth Amendments as running "almost into each other" on the facts before it, this Court held that the doctrines of those Amendments

> "apply to all invasions on the part of the government and its employees of the sanctity of a man's home and the privacies of life. It is not the breaking of his doors, and the rummaging of his drawers, that constitutes the essence of the offence; but it is the invasion of his indefeasible right of personal security, personal liberty and private property. . . . Breaking into a house and opening boxes and drawers are circumstances of aggravation; but any forcible and compulsory extortion of a man's own testimony or of his private papers to be used as evidence to convict him of crime or to forfeit his goods, is within the condemnation . . . [of those Amendments]."

The Court noted that

> "constitutional provisions for the security of person and property should be liberally construed. . . . It is the duty of courts to be watchful for the constitutional rights of the citizen, and against any stealthy encroachments thereon." . . .

In this jealous regard for maintaining the integrity of individual rights, the Court gave life to Madison's prediction that "independent tribunals of justice . . . will be naturally led to resist every encroachment upon rights expressly stipulated for in the Constitution by the declaration of rights." I Annals of Cong. 439 (1789). . . .

Less than 30 years after *Boyd*, this Court, in *Weeks v. United States*, [232 U.S. 383], 1914, stated that

> "the 4th Amendment, . . . put the courts of the United States and Federal officials, in the exercise of their power and authority, under limitations and restraints [and] . . . forever secure[d] the people, their persons, houses, papers, and effects, against all unreasonable searches and seizures under the guise of law . . . and the duty of giving to it force and effect is obligatory upon all entrusted under our Federal system with the enforcement of the laws." . . .

[T]he Court in that case clearly stated that use of the seized evidence involved "a denial of the constitutional rights of the accused." Thus, in the year 1914, in the *Weeks* case, this Court "for the first time" held that "in a federal prosecution the Fourth Amendment barred the use of evidence secured through an illegal search and seizure." This Court has ever since required of federal law officers a strict adherence to that command which this Court has held to be a clear, specific, and constitutionally required—even if judicially implied—deterrent safeguard without insistence upon which the Fourth Amendment would have been reduced to "a form of words." . . .

In 1949, 35 years after *Weeks* was announced, this Court, in *Wolf v. People of State of Colorado*, again for the first time, discussed the effect of the Fourth Amendment upon the States through the operation of the Due Process Clause of the Fourteenth Amendment. It said:

> "[W]e have no hesitation in saying that were a State affirmatively to sanction such police incursion into privacy it would run counter to the guaranty of the Fourteenth Amendment."

Nevertheless, after declaring that the "security of one's privacy against arbitrary intrusion by the police" is "implicit in 'the concept of ordered liberty' and as such enforceable against the States through the Due Process Clause," cf. *Palko v. State of Connecticut*, [302 U.S. 319], 1937, and announcing that it "stoutly adhere[d]" to the *Weeks* decision, the Court decided that the *Weeks* exclusionary rule would not then be imposed upon the States as "an essential ingredient of the right." The Court's reasons for not considering essential to the right to privacy, as a curb imposed upon the States by the Due Process Clause, that which decades before had been posited as part and parcel of the Fourth Amendment's limitation upon federal encroachment of individual privacy, were bottomed on factual considerations.

While they are not basically relevant to a decision that the exclusionary rule is an essential ingredient of the Fourth Amendment as the right it embodies is vouchsafed against the States by the Due Process Clause, we will consider the current validity of the factual grounds upon which *Wolf* was based.

The Court in *Wolf* first stated that "[t]he contrariety of views of the States" on the adoption of the exclusionary rule of *Weeks* was "particularly impressive," and, in this connection, that it could not "brush aside the experience of States which deem the incidence of such conduct by the police too slight to call for a deterrent remedy . . . by overriding the [States'] relevant rules of evidence." While in 1949, prior to the *Wolf* case, almost two-thirds of the States were opposed to the use of the exclusionary rule, now, despite the *Wolf* case, more than half of those since passing upon it, by their own legislative or judicial decision, have wholly or partly adopted or adhered to the *Weeks* rule. . . . Significantly, among those now following the rule is California, which, according to its highest court, was "compelled to reach that conclusion because other remedies have completely failed to secure compliance with the constitutional provisions. . . ." In connection with this California case, we note that the second basis elaborated in *Wolf* in support of its failure to enforce the exclusionary doctrine against the States was that "other means of protection" have been afforded "the right to privacy." The experience of California that such other remedies have been worthless and futile is buttressed by the experience of other States. . . .

[Notably,] the force of [the] reasoning [in *Wolf*] has been largely vitiated by later decisions of this Court. These include the recent discarding of the "silver platter" doctrine which allowed federal judicial use of evidence seized in violation of the Constitution by state agents, *Elkins v. United States*, [364 U.S. 206 (1960)], the relaxation of the formerly strict requirements as to standing to challenge the use of evidence thus seized, so that now the procedure of exclusion, "ultimately referable to constitutional safeguards," is available to anyone even "legitimately on [the] premises" unlawfully searched, *Jones v. United States*, [362 U.S. 257], 1960; and finally, the formulation of a method to prevent state use of evidence unconstitutionally seized by federal agents, *Rea v. United States*, [350 U.S. 214], 1956. . . .

It, therefore, plainly appears that the factual considerations supporting the failure of the *Wolf* Court to include the *Weeks* exclusionary rule when it recognized the enforceability of the right to privacy against the States in 1949, while not basically relevant to the constitutional consideration, could not, in any analysis, now be deemed controlling.

Today we once again examine *Wolf*'s constitutional documentation of the right to privacy free from unreasonable state intrusion, and, after its dozen years on our books, are led by it to close the only courtroom door remaining open to evidence secured by official lawlessness in flagrant abuse of that basic right, reserved to all persons as a specific guarantee against that very same unlawful conduct. We hold that all evidence obtained by searches and seizures in violation of the Constitution is, by that same authority, inadmissible in a state court.

Since the Fourth Amendment's right of privacy has been declared enforceable against the States through the Due Process Clause of the Fourteenth, it is enforceable against them by the same sanction of exclusion as is used against the Federal Government. Were it otherwise, then just as without the *Weeks* rule the assurance against unreasonable federal searches and seizures would be "a form of words," valueless and undeserving of mention in a perpetual charter of inestimable human liberties, so too, without that rule the freedom from state invasions of privacy would be so ephemeral and so neatly severed from its conceptual nexus with the freedom from all brutish means of coercing evidence as not to merit this Court's high regard as a freedom "implicit in 'the concept of ordered liberty.' " At the time that the Court held in *Wolf* that the Amendment was applicable to the States through the Due Process Clause, the cases of this Court, as we have seen, have steadfastly held that as to federal officers the Fourth Amendment included the exclusion of the evidence seized in violation of its provisions. Even *Wolf* "stoutly adhered" to that proposition. The right to privacy, when conceded operatively enforceable against the States, was not susceptible of destruction by avulsion of the sanction upon which its protection and enjoyment had always been deemed dependent under the *Boyd, Weeks* and *Silverthorne* [*Lumber Co. v. United States*, 251 U.S. 385 (1920)], cases. Therefore, in extending the substantive protections of due process to all constitutionally unreasonable searches—state or federal—it was logically and constitutionally necessary that the exclusion doctrine—an essential ingredient of the right newly recognized by the *Wolf* case. In short, the admission of the new constitutional right by *Wolf* could not consistently tolerate denial of its most important constitutional privilege, namely, the exclusion of the evidence which an accused had been forced to give by reason of the unlawful seizure. To hold otherwise is to grant the right but in reality to withhold its privilege and enjoyment. Only last year the Court itself recognized that the purpose of the exclusionary rule "is to deter—to compel respect for the constitutional guarantee in the only effectively available way—by removing the incentive to disregard it in *Elkins v. United States.* . . ."

Indeed, we are aware of no restraint, similar to that rejected today conditioning the enforcement of any other basic constitutional right. The right to privacy, no less important than any other right carefully and particularly reserved to the people, would stand in marked contrast to all other rights declared as "basic to a free society." *Weeks v. People of State of Colorado.* This Court has not hesitated to enforce as strictly against the States as it does against the Federal Government the rights of free speech and of a free press, the rights to notice and to a fair, public trial, including, as it does, the right not to be convicted by use of a coerced confession, however logically relevant it be, and without regard to its reliability. And nothing could be more certain than that when a coerced confession is involved, "the relevant rules of evidence" are overridden without regard to "the incidence of such conduct by the police," slight or frequent. Why should not the same rule apply to what is tantamount to coerced testimony by way of unconstitutional seizure of goods, papers, effects, documents, etc.? . . .

Moreover, our holding that the exclusionary rule is an essential part of both the Fourth and Fourteenth Amendments is not only the logical dictate of prior cases, but it also makes very good sense. There is no war between the Constitution and common sense. Presently, a federal prosecutor may make no use of evidence illegally seized, but a State's attorney across the street may, although he supposedly is operating under the enforceable prohibitions of the same Amendment. Thus the State, by admitting evidence unlawfully seized, serves to encourage disobedience to the Federal Constitution which it is bound to uphold. . . .

In non-exclusionary States, federal officers, being human, were by it invited to and did, as our cases indicate, step across the street to the State's attorney with their unconstitutionally seized evidence. Prosecution on the basis of that evidence was then had in a state court in utter disregard of the enforceable Fourth Amendment. If the fruits of an unconstitutional search had been inadmissible in both state and federal courts, this inducement to evasion would have been sooner eliminated. . . .

There are those who say, as did Justice (then Judge) CARDOZO, that under our constitutional exclusionary doctrine "[t]he criminal is to go free because the constable has blundered." *People v. Defore,* [242 N.Y. 13 (1926)]. In some cases this will undoubtedly be the result. But, as was said in *Elkins,* "there is another consideration—the imperative of judicial integrity." The criminal goes free, if he must, but it is the law that sets him free. Nothing can destroy a government more quickly than its failure to observe its own laws, or worse, its disregard of the character of its own existence. . . .

The ignoble shortcut to conviction left open to the State tends to destroy the entire system of constitutional restraints on which the liberties of the people rest. Having once recognized that the right to privacy embodied in the Fourth Amendment is enforceable against the States, and that the right to be secure against rude invasions of privacy by state officers is, therefore, constitutional in origin, we can no longer permit that right to remain an empty promise. Because it is enforceable in the same manner and to like effect as other basic rights secured by the Due Process Clause, we can no longer permit it to be revocable at the whim of any police officer who, in the name of law enforcement itself, chooses to suspend its enjoyment. Our decision, founded on reason and truth, gives to the individual no more than that which the Constitution guarantees him, to the police officer no less than that to which honest law enforcement is entitled, and, to the courts, that judicial integrity so necessary in the true administration of justice.

The judgment of the Supreme Court of Ohio is reversed and the cause remanded for further proceedings not inconsistent with this opinion.

Reversed and remanded.

☐ *Justice BLACK, concurring.*

I am still not persuaded that the Fourth Amendment, standing alone, would be enough to bar the introduction into evidence against an accused of papers and effects seized from him in violation of its commands. For the Fourth Amendment does not itself contain any provision expressly precluding the use of such evidence, and I am extremely doubtful that such a provision could properly be inferred from nothing more than the basic command against unreasonable searches and seizures. Reflection on the problem, however, in the light of cases coming before the Court since *Wolf*, has led me to conclude that when the Fourth Amendment's ban against unreasonable searches and seizures is considered together with the Fifth Amendment's ban against compelled self-incrimination, a constitutional basis emerges which not only justifies but actually requires the exclusionary rule.

☐ *Justice HARLAN, with whom Justice FRANKFURTER and Justice WHITTAKER join, dissenting.*

I would not impose upon the States this federal exclusionary remedy. The reasons given by the majority for now suddenly turning its back on *Wolf* seem to me notably unconvincing.

First, it is said that "the factual grounds upon which *Wolf* was based" have since changed, in that more States now follow the *Weeks* exclusionary rule than was so at the time *Wolf* was decided. While that is true, a recent survey indicates that at present one-half of the States still adhere to the common-law non-exclusionary rule, and one, Maryland, retains the rule as to felonies. But in any case surely all this is beside the point, as the majority itself indeed seems to recognize. Our concern here, as it was in *Wolf*, is not with the desirability of that rule but only with the question whether the States are Constitutionally free to follow it or not as they may themselves determine, and the relevance of the disparity of views among the States on this point lies simply in the fact that the judgment involved is a debatable one. Moreover, the very fact on which the majority relies, instead of lending support to what is now being done, points away from the need of replacing voluntary state action with federal compulsion.

The preservation of a proper balance between state and federal responsibility in the administration of criminal justice demands patience on the part of those who might like to see things move faster among the States in this respect. Problems of criminal law enforcement vary widely from State to State. . . . For us the question remains, as it has always been, one of state power, not one of passing judgment on the wisdom of one state course or another. In my view this Court should continue to forbear from fettering the States with an adamant rule which may embarrass them in coping with their own peculiar problems in criminal law enforcement. . . .

I regret that I find so unwise in principle and so inexpedient in policy a decision motivated by the high purpose of increasing respect for constitutional rights. But in the last analysis I think this Court can increase respect for the Constitution only if it rigidly respects the limitations which the Constitution places upon it, and respects as well the principles inherent in its own processes. In the present case I think we exceed both, and that our voice becomes only a voice of power, not of reason.

Nix v. Williams
467 U.S. 431, 104 S.CT. 2501 (1984)

Chief Justice Warren Burger discusses the facts in his opinion for the Court, upholding an inevitable discovery exception to the application of the exclusionary rule.

The Court's decision was seven to two, and the majority's opinion was announced by Chief Justice Burger. Concurrences were by Justices White and Stevens. Justice Brennan dissented and was joined by Justice Marshall.

☐ *Chief Justice BURGER delivers the opinion of the Court.*

We granted *certiorari* to consider whether, at respondent Williams' second murder trial in state court, evidence pertaining to the discovery and condition of the victim's body was properly admitted on the ground that it would ultimately or inevitably have been discovered even if no violation of any constitutional or statutory provision had taken place.

■ I

A. On December 24, 1968, 10-year-old Pamela Powers disappeared from a YMCA building in Des Moines, Iowa, where she had accompanied her parents to watch an athletic contest. Shortly after she disappeared, Williams was seen leaving the YMCA carrying a large bundle wrapped in a blanket; a 14-year-old boy who had helped Williams open his car door reported that he had seen "two legs in it and they were skinny and white."

Williams' car was found the next day 160 miles east of Des Moines in Davenport, Iowa. Later several items of clothing belonging to the child, some of Williams' clothing, and an army blanket like the one used to wrap the bundle that Williams carried out of the YMCA were found at a rest stop on Interstate 80 near Grinnell, between Des Moines and Davenport. A warrant was issued for Williams' arrest.

Police surmised that Williams had left Pamela Powers or her body somewhere between Des Moines and the Grinnell rest stop where some of the young girl's clothing had been found. On December 26, the Iowa Bureau of Criminal Investigation initiated a large-scale search. . . . Meanwhile, Williams surrendered to local police in Davenport, where he was promptly arraigned. Williams contacted a Des Moines attorney who arranged for an attorney in Davenport to meet Williams at the Davenport police station. Des Moines police informed counsel they would pick Williams up in Davenport and return him to Des Moines without questioning him. Two Des Moines detectives then drove to Davenport, took Williams into custody, and proceeded to drive him back to Des Moines.

During the return trip, one of the policemen, Detective Leaming, began a conversation with Williams, saying:

> "I want to give you something to think about while we're traveling down the road. . . . They are predicting several inches of snow for tonight, and I feel that you yourself are the only person that knows where this little girl's body is . . . and if you get a snow on top of it you yourself may be unable to find it. And since we will be going right past the area [where the body is] on the way into Des Moines, I feel that we could stop and locate the body, that the parents of this little girl should be entitled to a Christian burial for the little girl who was snatched away from them on Christmas [E]ve and murdered. . . . [A]fter a snow storm [we may not be] able to find it at all."

Leaming told Williams he knew the body was in the area of Mitchellville—a town they would be passing on the way to Des Moines. He concluded the conversation by saying "I do not want you to answer me. . . . Just think about it. . . ."

Later, as the police car approached Grinnell, Williams asked Leaming whether the police had found the young girl's shoes. After Leaming replied that he was unsure, Williams directed the police to a point near a service station where he said he had left the shoes; they were not found. As they continued to drive to Des Moines, Williams asked whether the blanket had been found and then directed the officers to a rest area in Grinnell where he said he had disposed of the blanket; they did not find the blanket. At this point Leaming and his party were joined by the officers in charge of the search. As they approached Mitchellville, Williams, without any further conversation, agreed to direct the officers to the child's body.

The officers directing the search had called off the search at 3 P.M., when they left the Grinnell Police Department to join Leaming at the rest area. At that time, one search team near the Jasper County-Polk County line was only two and one-half miles from where Williams soon guided Leaming and his party to the body. The child's body was found next to a culvert in a ditch beside a gravel road in Polk County, about two miles south of Interstate 80, and essentially within the area to be searched.

B. First Trial: In February 1969 Williams was indicted for first-degree murder. Before trial in the Iowa court, his counsel moved to suppress evidence of the body and all related evidence including the condition of the body as shown by the autopsy. The ground for the motion was that such evidence was the "fruit" or product of Williams' statements made during the automobile ride from Davenport to Des Moines and prompted by Leaming's statements. The motion to suppress was denied.

The jury found Williams guilty of first-degree murder; the judgment of conviction was affirmed by the Iowa Supreme Court. Williams then sought release on *habeas corpus* in the United States District Court for the Southern District of Iowa. That court concluded that the evidence in question had been wrongly admitted at Williams' trial, a divided panel of the Court of Appeals for the Eighth Circuit agreed. . . .

We granted *certiorari*, and a divided Court affirmed, holding that Detective Leaming had obtained incriminating statements from Williams by what was viewed as interrogation in violation of his right to counsel. *Brewer v. Williams*, 430 U.S. 387 (1977). This Court's opinion noted, however, that although Williams' incriminating statements could not be introduced into evidence at a second trial, evidence of the body's location and condition "might well be admissible on the theory that the body would have been discovered in any event, even had incriminating statements not been elicited from Williams."

C. Second Trial: At Williams' second trial in 1977 in the Iowa court, the prosecution did not offer Williams' statements into evidence, nor did it seek to show that Williams had directed the police to the child's body. However, evidence of the condition of her body as it was found, articles and photographs of her clothing, and the results of post mortem medical and chemical tests on the body were admitted. The trial court concluded that the State had proved by a preponderance of the evidence that, if the search had not been suspended and Williams had not led the police to the victim, her body would have been discovered "*within a short time*" in essentially the same condition as it was actually found. . . .

On appeal, the Supreme Court of Iowa again affirmed. That court held that there was in fact a "hypothetical independent source" exception to the exclusionary rule:

> "After the defendant has shown unlawful conduct on the part of the police, the State has the burden to show by a preponderance of the evidence that (1) the police did not act in bad faith for the purpose of hastening discovery of the evidence in question, and (2) that the evidence in question would have been discovered by lawful means." . . .

In 1980 Williams renewed his attack on the state-court conviction by seeking a writ of habeas corpus in the United States District Court for the Southern District of Iowa. The District Court conducted its own independent review of the evidence and concluded, as had the state courts, that the body would inevitably have been found by the searchers in essentially the same condition it was in when Williams led police to its discovery. The District Court denied Williams' petition. . . .

The Court of Appeals for the Eighth Circuit reversed. . . .

We granted the State's petition for *certiorari*, and we reverse.

■ II

A The Iowa Supreme Court correctly stated that the "vast majority" of all courts, both state and federal, recognize an inevitable discovery exception to the exclusionary rule. We are now urged to adopt and apply the so-called ultimate or inevitable discovery exception to the exclusionary rule. . . .

Williams contends that evidence of the body's location and condition is "fruit of the poisonous tree," *i.e.*, the "fruit" or product of Detective Leaming's plea to help the child's parents give her "a Christian burial," which this Court had already held equated to interrogation. He contends that admitting the challenged evidence violated the Sixth Amendment whether it would have been inevitably discovered or not. Williams also contends that, if the inevitable discovery doctrine is constitutionally permissible, it must include a threshold showing of police good faith.

B The doctrine requiring courts to suppress evidence as the tainted "fruit" of unlawful governmental conduct had its genesis in *Silverthorne Lumber Co. v. United States*, 251 U.S. 385 (1920); there, the Court held that the exclusionary rule applies not only to the illegally obtained evidence itself, but also to other incriminating evidence derived from the primary evidence. . . .

The core rationale consistently advanced by this Court for extending the exclusionary rule to evidence that is the fruit of unlawful police conduct has been that this admittedly drastic and socially costly course is needed to deter police from violations of constitutional and statutory protections. This Court has accepted the argument that the way to ensure such protections is to exclude evidence seized as a result of such violations notwithstanding the high social cost of letting persons obviously guilty go unpunished for their crimes. On this rationale, the prosecution is not to be put in a better position than it would have been in if no illegality had transpired.

By contrast, the derivative evidence analysis ensures that the prosecution is not put in a *worse* position simply because of some earlier police error or misconduct. The independent source doctrine allows admission of evidence that has been discovered by means wholly independent of any constitutional violation. That doctrine, although closely related to the inevitable discovery doctrine, does not apply here; Williams' statements to Leaming indeed led police to the child's body, but that is not the whole story. The independent source doctrine teaches us that the interest of society in deterring unlawful police conduct and the public interest in having juries receive all probative evidence of a crime are properly balanced by putting the police in the same, not a *worse*, position than they would have been in if no police error or misconduct had occurred. When the challenged evidence has an independent source, exclusion of such evidence would put the police in a worse position than they would have been in absent any error or violation. There is a functional similarity between these two doctrines in that exclusion of evidence that would inevitably have been discovered would also put the government in a worse position, because the police would have obtained that evidence if no misconduct had taken place. Thus, while the independent source exception would not justify admission of evidence in this case, its rationale is wholly consistent with and justifies our adoption of the ultimate or inevitable discovery exception to the exclusionary rule. . . .

The requirement that the prosecution must prove the absence of bad faith, imposed here by the Court of Appeals, would place courts in the position of withholding from juries relevant and undoubted truth that would have been available to police absent any unlawful police activity. Of course, that view would put the police in a *worse* position than they would have been in if no unlawful conduct had transpired. And, of equal importance, it wholly fails to take into account the enormous societal cost of excluding truth in the search for truth in the administration of justice. Nothing in this court's prior holdings supports any such formalistic, pointless, and punitive approach....

Exclusion of physical evidence that would inevitably have been discovered adds nothing to either the integrity or fairness of a criminal trial. The Sixth Amendment right to counsel protects against unfairness by preserving the adversary process in which the reliability of proffered evidence may be tested in cross-examination. Here, however, Detective Leaming's conduct did nothing to impugn the reliability of the evidence in question— the body of the child and its condition as it was found, articles of clothing found on the body, and the autopsy. No one would seriously contend that the presence of counsel in the police car when Leaming appealed to Williams' decent human instincts would have had any bearing on the reliability of the body as evidence. Suppression, in these circumstances, would do nothing whatever to promote the integrity of the trial process, but would inflict a wholly unacceptable burden on the administration of criminal justice....

C On this record it is clear that the search parties were approaching the actual location of the body, and we are satisfied, along with three courts earlier, that the volunteer search teams would have resumed the search had Williams not earlier led the police to the body and the body inevitably would have been found. The evidence asserted by Williams as newly discovered, *i.e.*, certain photographs of the body and deposition testimony of Agent Ruxlow made in connection with the federal habeas proceeding, does not demonstrate that the material facts were inadequately developed in the suppression hearing in state court or that Williams was denied a full, fair, and adequate opportunity to present all relevant facts at the suppression hearing.

The judgment of the Court of Appeals is reversed, and the case is remanded for further proceedings consistent with this opinion.

It is so ordered.

☐ *Justice BRENNAN, with whom Justice MARSHALL joins, dissenting.*

I agree that in these circumstances the "inevitable discovery" exception to the exclusionary rule is consistent with the requirements of the Constitution.

In its zealous efforts to emasculate the exclusionary rule, however, the Court loses sight of the crucial difference between the "inevitable discovery" doctrine and the "independent source" exception from which it is derived. When properly applied, the "independent source" exception allows the prosecution to use evidence only if it was, in fact, obtained by fully lawful means. It therefore does no violence to the constitutional protections that the exclusionary rule is meant to enforce. The "inevitable discovery" exception is likewise compatible with the Constitution, though it differs in one key respect from its next of kin: specifically, the evidence sought to be introduced at trial has not actually been obtained from an independent source, but rather would have been discovered as a matter of course if independent investigations were allowed to proceed.

In my view, this distinction should require that the government satisfy a heightened burden of proof before it is allowed to use such evidence. The inevitable discovery exception necessarily implicates a hypothetical finding that differs in kind from the factual finding that precedes application of the independent source rule. To ensure that this hypothetical finding is narrowly confined to circumstances that are functionally equivalent to an independent source, and to protect fully the fundamental rights served by the exclusionary rule, I would require clear and convincing evidence before concluding that the government had met its burden of proof on this issue.

United States v. Leon
468 U.S. 902, 104 S.Ct. 3405 (1984)

and

Massachusetts v. Sheppard
468 U.S. 981, 104 S.Ct. 3424 (1984)

In August 1981, a confidential informant told a police officer in Burbank, California, that two persons he knew as "Armando" and "Patsy" were selling cocaine and methaqualone at their home. The informant gave the police their address but also claimed that they generally kept only small quantities of drugs there, and stored the rest at another location. On the basis of this information, police initiated an extensive investigation focusing on the residence of Armando Sanchez, who had previously been arrested for possessing marijuana, and Patsy Stewart, who had no prior criminal record. Later, two other residences were also staked out.

In the course of the investigation, officers observed a car belonging to Richardo Del Castillo, who had previously been arrested for possessing fifty pounds of marijuana, arriving at Sanchez's house. The driver entered the house, leaving shortly thereafter carrying a small paper bag. A check of Del Castillo's probation records led police to Alberto Leon. Leon had been arrested in 1980 on drug charges, and one of his companions informed police that Leon was heavily involved with importing drugs into the country. Police in Burbank also learned from police in Glendale, California, that Leon was living in a house on South Sunset Canyon in Burbank.

One day during their surveillance of Sanchez and Stewart, police observed them board separate flights for Miami, Florida, and later return to Los Angeles together. At the airport, Sanchez and Stewart were stopped and agreed to a search of their luggage. A small amount of marijuana was discovered, but they were allowed to leave the airport.

Based on these and other observations, officer Cyril Rombach applied for a warrant to search the residences of Sanchez, Stewart, and Leon for a long list of items related to drug trafficking. A warrant was issued in September 1981 by a judge, and the ensuing search produced a large quantity of drugs. All three were indicted by a grand jury and charged with conspiracy to possess and distribute cocaine and other drugs.

Leon and the other filed motions to suppress the evidence seized pursuant to the warrant. A district court judge granted part of their motions to suppress on concluding that the police had failed to establish probable cause in their application for a warrant. In response to a request from the government, the court made clear that Officer Rombach had acted in good faith, but rejected the government's argument that the Fourth Amendment exclusionary rule should not apply where evidence is seized by police who reasonably and in good faith rely on a search warrant.

Subsequently, a divided panel of the Court of Appeals for the Ninth Circuit affirmed, finding that Officer Rombach's affidavit failed to meet the two-prong test for establishing probable cause as required in *Aguilar v. Texas*, 378 U.S. 108 (1964), and *Spinelli v. United States*, 393 U.S. 410 (1969), but that test and those rulings were overturned in *Illinois v. Gates*, 462 U.S. 213 (1983) (as discussed in section A of this chapter).

The Reagan administration appealed the appellate court's decision and asked the Supreme Court to decide "[w]hether the Fourth Amendment exclusionary rule should be modified so as not to bar the admission of evidence seized in reasonable, good-faith reliance on a search warrant that is subsequently held to be defective."

The Court granted *certiorari* in this case, along with another, *Massachusetts v. Sheppard*, and upheld the good-faith exception to the exclusionary rule. In the *Massachusetts* case, police relied in good faith on a warrant usually issued for searches for controlled substances, instead of an arrest warrant, when making an arrest. A judge signed the wrong warrant after finding that police had established probable cause in their application, even though they used the wrong application form because their office had run out of (and on Sunday they could not obtain) the proper warrant forms.

The Court's decision was six to three in *Leon* and seven to two in *Sheppard*, and the majority's opinion was announced by Justice White. Justice Blackmun concurred, and Justice Brennan, joined by Justice Marshall, dissented. In a separate opinion, Justice Stevens dissented in *Leon* and concurred in *Sheppard*.

☐ *Justice WHITE delivered the opinion of the Court.*

This case presents the question whether the Fourth Amendment exclusionary rule should be modified so as not to bar the use in the prosecution's case in chief of evidence obtained by officers acting in reasonable reliance on a search warrant issued by a detached and neutral magistrate but ultimately found to be unsupported by probable cause. To resolve this question, we must consider once again the tension between the sometimes competing goals of, on the one hand, deterring official misconduct and removing inducements to unreasonable invasions of privacy and, on the other, establishing procedures under which criminal defendants are "acquitted or convicted on the basis of all the evidence which exposes the truth." . . .

The Fourth Amendment contains no provision expressly precluding the use of evidence obtained in violation of its commands, and an examination of its origin and purposes makes clear that the use of fruits of a past unlawful search or seizure "work[s] no new Fourth Amendment wrong." *United States v. Calandra*, 414 U.S. 338 (1974). The wrong condemned by the Amendment is "fully accomplished" by the unlawful search or seizure itself, and the exclusionary rule is neither intended nor able to "cure the invasion of the defendant's rights which he has already suffered." *Stone v. Powell*, [428 U.S. 465 (1976)] (WHITE, J., dissenting). The rule thus operates as "a judicially created remedy designed to safeguard Fourth Amendment rights generally through its deterrent effect, rather than a personal constitutional right of the party aggrieved." *United States v. Calandra*. . . .

The substantial social costs exacted by the exclusionary rule for the vindication of Fourth Amendment rights have long been a source of concern. "Our cases have consistently recognized that unbending application of the exclusionary sanction to enforce ideals of governmental rectitude would impede unacceptably the truth-finding functions of judge and jury." *United States v. Payne*, 447 U.S. 727 (1980). An objectionable collateral consequence of this interference with the criminal justice system's truth-finding function is that some guilty defendants may go free or receive reduced sentences as a result of favorable plea bargains. Particularly when law enforcement officers have acted in objective good faith or their transgressions have been minor, the magnitude of the benefit conferred on such guilty defendants offends basic concepts of the criminal justice system. Indiscriminate application of the exclusionary rule, therefore, may well "generat[e] disrespect for the law and administration of justice." Accordingly, "[a]s with any remedial device, the application of the rule has been restricted to those areas where its remedial objectives are thought most efficaciously served." . . .

Close attention to those remedial objectives has characterized our recent decisions concerning the scope of the Fourth Amendment exclusionary rule. The Court has, to be sure, not seriously questioned, "in the absence of a more efficacious sanction, the continued application of the rule to suppress evidence from the [prosecution's] case where a Fourth Amendment violation has been substantial and deliberate. . . ." *Franks v. Delaware*, 438 U.S. 154 (1978); *Stone v. Powell, supra.* Nevertheless, the balancing approach that has evolved in various contexts—including criminal trials—"forcefully suggest[s] that the exclusionary rule be more generally modified to permit the introduction of evidence obtained in the reasonable good-faith belief that a search or seizure was in accord with the Fourth Amendment." *Illinois v. Gates* . . . (WHITE, J., concurring in judgment). . . .

As yet, we have not recognized any form of good-faith exception to the Fourth Amendment exclusionary rule. But the balancing approach that has evolved during the years of experience with the rule provides strong support for the modification currently urged upon us. As we discuss below, our evaluation of the costs and benefits of suppressing reliable physical evidence seized by officers reasonably relying on a warrant issued by a detached and neutral magistrate leads to the conclusion that such evidence should be admissible in the prosecution's case in chief.

Because a search warrant "provides the detached scrutiny of a neutral magistrate, which is a more reliable safeguard against improper searches than the hurried judgment of a law enforcement officer 'engaged in the often competitive enterprise of ferreting out crime,' " *United States v. Chadwick*, 433 U.S. 1 (1977) (quoting *Johnson v. United States*, 333 U.S. 10 (1948)), we have expressed a strong preference for warrants and declared that "in a doubtful or marginal case a search under a warrant may be sustainable where without one it would fall." *United States v. Ventresca*, 380 U.S. 102 (1965). Reasonable minds frequently may differ on the question whether a particular affidavit establishes probable cause, and we have thus concluded that the preference for warrants is most appropriately effectuated by according "great deference" to a magistrate's determination.

Deference to the magistrate, however, is not boundless. It is clear, first, that the deference accorded to a magistrate's finding of probable cause does not preclude inquiry into the knowing or reckless falsity of the affidavit on which that determination was based. Second, the courts must also insist that the magistrate purport to "perform his 'neutral and detached' function and not serve merely as a rubber stamp for the police." A magistrate failing to "manifest that neutrality and detachment demanded of a judicial officer when presented with a warrant application" and who acts instead as "an adjunct law enforcement officer" cannot provide valid authorization for an otherwise unconstitutional search.

Third, reviewing courts will not defer to a warrant based on an affidavit that does not "provide the magistrate with a substantial basis for determining the existence of probable cause." *Illinois v. Gates.* "Sufficient information must be presented to the magistrate to allow that official to determine probable cause; his action cannot be a mere ratification of the bare conclusions of others." Even if the warrant application was supported by more than a "bare bones" affidavit, a reviewing court may properly conclude that, notwithstanding the deference that magistrates deserve, the warrant was invalid because the magistrate's probable-cause determination reflected an improper analysis of the totality of the circumstances, or because the form of the warrant was improper in some respect.

Only in the first of these three situations, however, has the Court set forth a rationale for suppressing evidence obtained pursuant to a search warrant; in the other areas, it has simply excluded such evidence without considering whether Fourth Amendment interests will be advanced. To the extent that proponents of exclusion rely on its behavioral effects on judges and magistrates in these areas, their reliance is misplaced. First, the exclusionary rule is designed to deter police misconduct rather than to punish the errors of judges and magistrates. Second, there exists no evidence suggesting that judges and magistrates are inclined to ignore or subvert the Fourth Amendment or that lawlessness among these actors requires application of the extreme sanction of exclusion.

Third, and most important, we discern no basis, and are offered none, for believing that exclusion of evidence seized pursuant to a warrant will have a significant deterrent effect on the issuing judge or magistrate. Many of the factors that indicate that the exclusionary rule cannot provide an effective "special" or "general" deterrent for individual offending law enforcement officers apply as well to judges or magistrates. And, to the extent that the rule is thought to operate as a "systemic" deterrent on a wider audience, it clearly can have no such effect on individuals empowered to issue search warrants. Judges and magistrates are not adjuncts to the law enforcement team; as neutral judicial officers, they have no stake in the outcome of particular criminal prosecutions. The threat of exclusion thus cannot be expected significantly to deter them. Imposition of the exclusionary sanction is not necessary meaningfully to inform judicial officers of their errors, and we cannot conclude that admitting evidence obtained pursuant to a warrant while at the same time declaring that the warrant was somehow defective will in any way reduce judicial officers' professional incentives to comply with the Fourth Amendment, encourage them to repeat their mistakes, or lead to the granting of all colorable warrant requests.

If exclusion of evidence obtained pursuant to a subsequently invalidated warrant is to have any deterrent effect, therefore, it must alter the behavior of individual law enforcement officers or the policies of their departments. One could argue that applying the exclusionary rule in cases where the police failed to demonstrate probable cause in the warrant application deters future inadequate presentations or "magistrate shopping" and thus promotes the ends of the Fourth Amendment. Suppressing evidence obtained pursuant to a technically defective warrant supported by probable cause also might encourage officers to scrutinize more closely the form of the warrant and to point out suspected judicial errors. We find such arguments speculative and conclude that suppression of evidence obtained pursuant to a warrant should be ordered only on a case-by-case basis and only in those unusual cases in which exclusion will further the purposes of the exclusionary rule.

We have frequently questioned whether the exclusionary rule can have any deterrent effect when the offending officers acted in the objectively reasonable belief that their conduct did not violate the Fourth Amendment. "No empirical researcher, proponent or opponent of the rule, has yet been able to establish with any assurance whether the rule has a deterrent effect. . . ." *United States v. Janis* [428 U.S. 433 (1976)]. But even assuming that the rule effectively deters some police misconduct and provides incentives for the law enforcement profession as a whole to conduct itself in accord with the Fourth Amendment, it cannot be expected, and should not be applied, to deter objectively reasonable law enforcement activity. . . .

In short, where the officer's conduct is objectively reasonable, "excluding the evidence will not further the ends of the exclusionary rule in any appreciable way; for it is painfully apparent that . . . the officer is acting as a reasonable officer would and should act in similar circumstances. Excluding the evidence can in no way affect his future conduct unless it is to make him less willing to do his duty." *Stone v. Powell* (WHITE, J., dissenting).

This is particularly true, we believe, when an officer acting with objective good faith has obtained a search warrant from a judge or magistrate and acted within its scope. In most such cases, there is no police illegality and thus nothing to deter. It is the magistrate's responsibility to determine whether the officer's allegations establish probable cause and, if so, to issue a warrant comporting in form with the requirements of the Fourth Amendment. In the ordinary case, an officer cannot be expected to question the magistrate's probable-cause determination or his judgment that the form of the warrant is technically sufficient. Penalizing the officer for the magistrate's error, rather than his own, cannot logically contribute to the deterrence of Fourth Amendment violations.

We conclude that the marginal or nonexistent benefits produced by suppressing evidence obtained in objectively reasonable reliance on a subsequently invalidated search warrant cannot justify the substantial costs of exclusion. We do not suggest, however, that exclusion is always inappropriate in cases where an officer has obtained a warrant and abided by its terms. . . . [T]he officer's reliance on the magistrate's probable-cause determination and on the technical sufficiency of the warrant he issues must be objectively reasonable, and it is clear that in some circumstances the officer will have no reasonable grounds for believing that the warrant was properly issued.

Suppression therefore remains an appropriate remedy if the magistrate or judge in issuing a warrant was misled by information in an affidavit that the affiant knew was false or would have known was false except for his reckless disregard of the truth. . . . The exception we recognize today will also not apply in cases where the issuing magistrate wholly abandoned his judicial role in the manner condemned in *Lo-Ji Sales, Inc. v. New York*, 442 U.S. 319 (1979); in such circumstances, no reasonably well trained officer should rely on the warrant. Nor would an officer manifest objective good faith in relying on a warrant based on an affidavit "so lacking in indicia of probable cause as to render official belief in its existence entirely unreasonable." Finally, depending on the circumstances of the particular case, a warrant may be so facially deficient—*i.e.*, in failing to particularize the place to be searched or the things to be seized—that the executing officers cannot reasonably presume it to be valid. . . .

In so limiting the suppression remedy, we leave untouched the probable-cause standard and the various requirements for a valid warrant. Other objections to the modification of the Fourth Amendment exclusionary rule we consider to be insubstantial. The good-faith exception for searches conducted pursuant to warrants is not intended to signal our unwillingness strictly to enforce the requirements of the Fourth Amendment, and we do not believe that it will have this effect. As we have already suggested, the good-faith exception, turning as it does on objective reasonableness, should not be difficult to apply in practice. . . .

When the principles we have enunciated today are applied to the facts of this case, it is apparent that the judgment of the Court of Appeals cannot stand. The Court of Appeals applied the prevailing legal standards to Officer

Rombach's warrant application and concluded that the application could not support the magistrate's probable-cause determination. In so doing, the court clearly informed the magistrate that he had erred in issuing the challenged warrant. This aspect of the court's judgment is not under attack in this proceeding.

Having determined that the warrant should not have issued, the Court of Appeals understandably declined to adopt a modification of the Fourth Amendment exclusionary rule that this Court had not previously sanctioned. Although the modification finds strong support in our previous cases, the Court of Appeals' commendable self-restraint is not to be criticized. We have now reexamined the purposes of the exclusionary rule and the propriety of its application in cases where officers have relied on a subsequently invalidated search warrant. Our conclusion is that the rule's purposes will only rarely be served by applying it in such circumstances.

In the absence of an allegation that the magistrate abandoned his detached and neutral role, suppression is appropriate only if the officers were dishonest or reckless in preparing their affidavit or could not have harbored an objectively reasonable belief in the existence of probable cause. Only respondent Leon has contended that no reasonably well trained police officer could have believed that there existed probable cause to search his house; significantly, the other respondents advance no comparable argument. Officer Rombach's application for a warrant clearly was supported by much more than a "bare bones" affidavit. The affidavit related the results of an extensive investigation and, as the opinions of the divided panel of the Court of Appeals make clear, provided evidence sufficient to create disagreement among thoughtful and competent judges as to the existence of probable cause. Under these circumstances, the officers' reliance on the magistrate's determination of probable cause was objectively reasonable, and application of the extreme sanction of exclusion is inappropriate.

Accordingly, the judgment of the Court of Appeals is
Reversed.

☐ *Justice BLACKMUN, concurring.*

As the Court's opinion in this case makes clear, the Court has narrowed the scope of the exclusionary rule because of an empirical judgment that the rule has little appreciable effect in cases where officers act in objectively reasonable reliance on search warrants. Because I share the view that the exclusionary rule is not a constitutionally compelled corollary of the Fourth Amendment itself, I see no way to avoid making an empirical judgment of this sort, and I am satisfied that the Court has made the correct one on the information before it. . . .

If a single principle may be drawn from this Court's exclusionary rule decisions, from *Weeks* through *Mapp v. Ohio*, 367 U.S. 643 (1961), to the decisions handed down today, it is that the scope of the exclusionary rule is subject to change in light of changing judicial understanding about the effects of the rule outside the confines of the courtroom. It is incumbent on the Nation's law enforcement officers, who must continue to observe the Fourth Amendment in the wake of today's decisions, to recognize the double-edged nature of that principle.

☐ *Justice BRENNAN, with whom Justice MARSHALL joins, dissenting.*

Ten years ago in *United States v. Calandra*, 414 U.S. 338 (1974), I ex-pressed the fear that the Court's decision "may signal that a majority of my colleagues have positioned themselves to reopen the door [to evidence se-cured by official lawlessness] still further and abandon altogether the ex-clusionary rule in search-and-seizure cases." Since then, in case after case, I have witnessed the Court's gradual but determined strangulation of the rule. It now appears that the Court's victory over the Fourth Amendment is com-plete. That today's decisions represent the *pièce de résistance* of the Court's past efforts cannot be doubted, for today the Court sanctions the use in the pros-ecution's case in chief of illegally obtained evidence against the individual whose rights have been violated—a result that had previously been thought to be foreclosed.

The Court seeks to justify this result on the ground that the "costs" of adhering to the exclusionary rule in cases like those before us exceed the "benefits." But the language of deterrence and of cost/benefit analysis, if used indiscriminately, can have a narcotic effect. It creates an illusion of technical precision and ineluctability. It suggests that not only constitutional principle but also empirical data support the majority's result. When the Court's analy-sis is examined carefully, however, it is clear that we have not been treated to an honest assessment of the merits of the exclusionary rule, but have instead been drawn into a curious world where the "costs" of excluding illegally ob-tained evidence loom to exaggerated heights and where the "benefits" of such exclusion are made to disappear with a mere wave of the hand.

The majority ignores the fundamental constitutional importance of what is at stake here. While the machinery of law enforcement and indeed the nature of crime itself have changed dramatically since the Fourth Amendment became part of the Nation's fundamental law in 1791, what the Framers understood then remains true today—that the task of combating crime and convicting the guilty will in every era seem of such critical and pressing concern that we may be lured by the temptations of expediency into forsaking our commitment to protecting individual liberty and privacy. It was for that very reason that the Framers of the Bill of Rights insisted that law enforcement efforts be permanently and unambiguously restricted in or-der to preserve personal freedoms. In the constitutional scheme they or-dained, the sometimes unpopular task of ensuring that the government's enforcement efforts remain within the strict boundaries fixed by the Fourth Amendment was entrusted to the courts. . . .

A proper understanding of the broad purposes sought to be served by the Fourth Amendment demonstrates that the principles embodied in the exclusionary rule rest upon a far firmer constitutional foundation than the shifting sands of the Court's deterrence rationale. But even if I were to ac-cept the Court's chosen method of analyzing the question posed by these cases, I would still conclude that the Court's decision cannot be justified. . . .

At bottom, the Court's decision turns on the proposition that the ex-clusionary rule is merely a " 'judicially created remedy' designed to safeguard Fourth Amendment rights generally through its deterrent effect, rather than a personal constitutional right." . . .

The essence of this view, as expressed initially in the *Calandra* opinion and as reiterated today, is that the sole "purpose of the Fourth Amendment is to prevent unreasonable governmental intrusions into the privacy of one's person, house, papers, or effects. The wrong condemned is the unjustified governmental invasion of these areas of an individual's life. That wrong . . . is *fully accomplished* by the original search without probable cause" (emphasis added). This reading of the Amendment implies that its proscriptions are directed solely at those government agents who may actually invade an individual's constitutionally protected privacy. The courts are not subject to any direct constitutional duty to exclude illegally obtained evidence, because the question of the admissibility of such evidence is not addressed by the Amendment. This view of the scope of the Amendment relegates the judiciary to the periphery. Because the only constitutionally cognizable injury has already been "fully accomplished" by the police by the time a case comes before the courts, the Constitution is not itself violated if the judge decides to admit the tainted evidence. Indeed, the most the judge *can* do is wring his hands and hope that perhaps by excluding such evidence he can deter future transgressions by the police.

Such a reading appears plausible, because, as critics of the exclusionary rule never tire of repeating, the Fourth Amendment makes no express provision for the exclusion of evidence secured in violation of its commands. A short answer to this claim, of course, is that many of the Constitution's most vital imperatives are stated in general terms and the task of giving meaning to these precepts is therefore left to subsequent judicial decisionmaking in the context of concrete cases. . . .

A more direct answer may be supplied by recognizing that the Amendment, like other provisions of the Bill of Rights, restrains the power of the government as a whole; it does not specify only a particular agency and exempt all others. The judiciary is responsible, no less than the executive, for ensuring that constitutional rights are respected.

When that fact is kept in mind, the role of the courts and their possible involvement in the concerns of the Fourth Amendment comes into sharper focus. Because seizures are executed principally to secure evidence, and because such evidence generally has utility in our legal system only in the context of a trial supervised by a judge, it is apparent that the admission of illegally obtained evidence implicates the same constitutional concerns as the initial seizure of that evidence. Indeed, by admitting unlawfully seized evidence, the judiciary becomes a part of what is in fact a single governmental action prohibited by the terms of the Amendment. Once that connection between the evidence-gathering role of the police and the evidence-admitting function of the courts is acknowledged, the plausibility of the Court's interpretation becomes more suspect. Certainly nothing in the language or history of the Fourth Amendment suggests that a recognition of this evidentiary link between the police and the courts was meant to be foreclosed. It is difficult to give any meaning at all to the limitations imposed by the Amendment if they are read to proscribe only certain conduct by the police but to allow other agents of the same government to take advantage of evidence secured by the police in violation of its requirements. The Amendment therefore must be read to condemn not only the initial unconstitutional invasion of privacy—which is done, after all, for the purpose of securing evidence—but also the subsequent use of any evidence so obtained.

The Court evades this principle by drawing an artificial line between the constitutional rights and responsibilities that are engaged by actions of the police and those that are engaged when a defendant appears before the courts. According to the Court, the substantive protections of the Fourth Amendment are wholly exhausted at the moment when police unlawfully invade an individual's privacy and thus no substantive force remains to those protections at the time of trial when the government seeks to use evidence obtained by the police.

I submit that such a crabbed reading of the Fourth Amendment casts aside the teaching of those Justices who first formulated the exclusionary rule, and rests ultimately on an impoverished understanding of judicial responsibility in our constitutional scheme. For my part, "[t]he right of the people to be secure in their persons, houses, papers, and effects, against unreasonable searches and seizures" comprises a personal right to exclude all evidence secured by means of unreasonable searches and seizures. The right to be free from the initial invasion of privacy and the right of exclusion are coordinate components of the central embracing right to be free from unreasonable searches and seizures.

Such a conception of the rights secured by the Fourth Amendment was unquestionably the original basis of what has come to be called the exclusionary rule when it was first formulated in *Weeks v. United States*, 232 U.S. 383 (1914). . . . As the Court in *Weeks* clearly recognized, the obligations cast upon government by the Fourth Amendment are not confined merely to the police. In the words of Justice HOLMES: "If the search and seizure are unlawful as invading personal rights secured by the Constitution those rights would be infringed yet further if the evidence were allowed to be used." *Dodge v. United States*, 272 U.S. 530 (1926).

That conception of the rule, in my view, is more faithful to the meaning and purpose of the Fourth Amendment and to the judiciary's role as the guardian of the people's constitutional liberties. In contrast to the present Court's restrictive reading, the Court in *Weeks* recognized that, if the Amendment is to have any meaning, police and the courts cannot be regarded as constitutional strangers to each other; because the evidence-gathering role of the police is directly linked to the evidence-admitting function of the courts, an individual's Fourth Amendment rights may be undermined as completely by one as by the other. . . .

Even if I were to accept the Court's general approach to the exclusionary rule, I could not agree with today's result. There is no question that in the hands of the present Court the deterrence rationale has proved to be a powerful tool for confining the scope of the rule. In *Calandra*, for example, the Court concluded that the "speculative and undoubtedly minimal advance in the deterrence of police misconduct," was insufficient to outweigh the "expense of substantially impeding the role of the grand jury." In *Stone v. Powell*, the Court found that "the additional contribution, if any, of the consideration of search-and-seizure claims of state prisoners on collateral review is small in relation to the costs." . . .

Thus, in this bit of judicial stagecraft, while the sets sometimes change, the actors always have the same lines. Given this well-rehearsed pattern, one might have predicted with some assurance how the present case would unfold. First there is the ritual incantation of the "substantial social costs" exacted by the exclusionary rule, followed by the virtually foreordained conclusion that, given the marginal benefits, application of the rule in the circumstances of these cases is not warranted. Upon analysis, however, such a result cannot be justified even on the Court's own terms.

At the outset, the Court suggests that society has been asked to pay a high price—in terms either of setting guilty persons free or of impeding the proper functioning of trials—as a result of excluding relevant physical evidence in cases where the police, in conducting searches and seizing evidence, have made only an "objectively reasonable" mistake concerning the constitutionality of their actions. . . . But what evidence is there to support such a claim?

Significantly, the Court points to none, and, indeed, as the Court acknowledges . . . recent studies have demonstrated that the "costs" of the exclusionary rule—calculated in terms of dropped prosecutions and lost convictions—are quite low. Contrary to the claims of the rule's critics that exclusion leads to "the release of countless guilty criminals," *Bivens v. Six Unknown Federal Narcotics Agents*, 403 U.S. 388 (1971) (BURGER, C.J., dissenting), these studies have demonstrated that federal and state prosecutors very rarely drop cases because of potential search and seizure problems. For example, a 1979 study prepared at the request of Congress by the General Accounting Office reported that only 0.4% of all cases actually declined for prosecution by federal prosecutors were declined primarily because of illegal search problems. . . .

Of course, these data describe only the costs attributable to the exclusion of evidence in all cases; the costs due to the exclusion of evidence in the narrower category of cases where police have made objectively reasonable mistakes must necessarily be even smaller. The Court, however, ignores this distinction and mistakenly weighs the aggregated costs of exclusion in *all* cases, irrespective of the circumstances that led to exclusion, against the potential benefits associated with only those cases in which evidence is excluded because police reasonably but mistakenly believe that their conduct does not violate the Fourth Amendment. When such faulty scales are used, it is little wonder that the balance tips in favor of restricting the application of the rule.

What then supports the Court's insistence that this evidence be admitted? Apparently, the Court's only answer is that even though the costs of exclusion are not very substantial, the potential deterrent effect in these circumstances is so marginal that exclusion cannot be justified. The key to the Court's conclusion in this respect is its belief that the prospective deterrent effect of the exclusionary rule operates only in those situations in which police officers, when deciding whether to go forward with some particular search, have reason to know that their planned conduct will violate the requirements of the Fourth Amendment. If these officers in fact understand (or reasonably should understand because the law is well settled) that their proposed conduct will offend the Fourth Amendment and that, consequently, any evidence they seize will be suppressed in court, they will refrain from conducting the planned search. In those circumstances, the incentive system created by the exclusionary rule will have the hoped-for deterrent effect. But in situations where police officers reasonably (but mistakenly) believe that their planned conduct satisfies Fourth Amendment requirements—presumably either (a) because they are acting on the basis of an apparently valid warrant, or (b) because their conduct is only later determined to be invalid as a result of a subsequent change in the law or the resolution of an unsettled question of law—then such officers will have no reason to refrain from conducting the search and the exclusionary rule will have no effect.

At first blush, there is some logic to this position. Undoubtedly, in the situation hypothesized by the Court, the existence of the exclusionary rule cannot be expected to have any deterrent effect on the particular officers at the moment they are deciding whether to go forward with the search. Indeed, the subsequent exclusion of any evidence seized under such circumstances appears somehow "unfair" to the particular officers involved. As the Court suggests, these officers have acted in what they thought was an appropriate and constitutionally authorized manner, but then the fruit of their efforts is nullified by the application of the exclusionary rule.

The flaw in the Court's argument, however, is that its logic captures only one comparatively minor element of the generally acknowledged deterrent purposes of the exclusionary rule. To be sure, the rule operates to some extent to deter future misconduct by individual officers who have had evidence suppressed in their own cases. But what the Court overlooks is that the deterrence rationale for the rule is not designed to be, nor should it be thought of as, a form of "punishment" of individual police officers for their failures to obey the restraints imposed by the Fourth Amendment. Instead, the chief deterrent function of the rule is its tendency to promote institutional compliance with Fourth Amendment requirements on the part of law enforcement agencies generally. Thus, as the Court has previously recognized, "over the long term, [the] demonstration [provided by the exclusionary rule] that our society attaches serious consequences to violation of constitutional rights is thought to encourage those who formulate law enforcement policies, and the officers who implement them, to incorporate Fourth Amendment ideals into their value system." *Stone v. Powell.* It is only through such an institutionwide mechanism that information concerning Fourth Amendment standards can be effectively communicated to rank-and-file officers.

If the overall educational effect of the exclusionary rule is considered, application of the rule to even those situations in which individual police officers have acted on the basis of a reasonable but mistaken belief that their conduct was authorized can still be expected to have a considerable long-term deterrent effect. If evidence is consistently excluded in these circumstances, police departments will surely be prompted to instruct their officers to devote greater care and attention to providing sufficient information to establish probable cause when applying for a warrant, and to review with some attention the form of the warrant that they have been issued, rather than automatically assuming that whatever document the magistrate has signed will necessarily comport with Fourth Amendment requirements.

After today's decisions, however, that institutional incentive will be lost. Indeed, the Court's "reasonable mistake" exception to the exclusionary rule will tend to put a premium on police ignorance of the law. Armed with the assurance provided by today's decisions that evidence will always be admissible whenever an officer has "reasonably" relied upon a warrant, police departments will be encouraged to train officers that if a warrant has simply been signed, it is reasonable, without more, to rely on it. Since in close cases there will no longer be any incentive to err on the side of constitutional behavior, police would have every reason to adopt a "let's-wait-until-it's-decided" approach in situations in which there is a question about a warrant's validity or the basis for its issuance.

Although the Court brushes these concerns aside, a host of grave consequences can be expected to result from its decision to carve this new exception out of the exclusionary rule. A chief consequence of today's decisions will be to convey a clear and unambiguous message to magistrates that their decisions to issue warrants are now insulated from subsequent judicial review. Creation of this new exception for good-faith reliance upon a warrant implicitly tells magistrates that they need not take much care in reviewing warrant applications, since their mistakes will from now on have virtually no consequence: If their decision to issue a warrant was correct, the evidence will be admitted; if their decision was incorrect but the police relied in good faith on the warrant, the evidence will also be admitted. Inevitably, the care and attention devoted to such an inconsequential chore will dwindle. Although the Court is correct to note that magistrates do not share the same stake in the outcome of a criminal case as the police, they nevertheless need to appreciate that their role is of some moment in order to continue performing the important task of carefully reviewing warrant applications. Today's decisions effectively remove that incentive.

Arizona v. Evans

514 U.S. 1, 115 S.Ct. 1185 (1995)

After stopping the driver of a car going in the wrong direction on a one-way street, the Phoenix police checked their squad car computer and found that the driver had an outstanding arrest warrant, which in fact had been canceled seventeen days earlier but not entered into the police department's computerized records. Based on that mistaken finding of an outstanding warrant for the driver's arrest, the police searched the car and discovered marijuana. Subsequently, the Arizona supreme court held that the marijuana could not be introduced as evidence and refused to apply the "good faith" exception to the exclusionary rule. In the state supreme court's words, "As automation increasingly invades modern life, the potential for Orwellian mischief grows. Under such circumstances, the exclusionary rule is a 'cost' we cannot afford to be without." The state subsequently appealed that ruling and the Supreme Court granted review.

The Court's decision was seven to two and the opinion was written by Chief Justice Rehnquist. Justices O'Connor and Souter filed concurring opinions, which Justice Breyer joined. Justices Stevens and Ginsburg filed dissenting opinions.

☐ *Chief Justice REHNQUIST delivered the opinion of the Court.*

"The question whether the exclusionary rule's remedy is appropriate in a particular context has long been regarded as an issue separate from the question whether the Fourth Amendment rights of the party seeking to invoke the rule were violated by police conduct." *Illinois v. Gates*, 462 U.S. 213 (1983). The exclusionary rule operates as a judicially created remedy designed to safeguard against future violations of Fourth Amendment rights through the rule's general deterrent effect. As with any remedial device, the rule's application has been restricted to those instances where its remedial objectives are thought most efficaciously served. Where "the exclusionary rule does not result in appreciable deterrence, then, clearly, its use . . . is unwarranted." *United States v. Janis*, 428 U.S. 433 (1976).

In [*United States v.*] *Leon*, [468 U.S. 897 (1984)], we applied these principles to the context of a police search in which the officers had acted in objectively reasonable reliance on a search warrant, issued by a neutral and detached Magistrate, that later was determined to be invalid. On the basis of three factors, we determined that there was no sound reason to apply the exclusionary rule as a means of deterring misconduct on the part of judicial officers who are responsible for issuing warrants. *Illinois v. Krull*, 480 U.S. 340 (1987). First, we noted that the exclusionary rule was historically designed "to deter police misconduct rather than to punish the errors of judges and magistrates." Second, there was "no evidence suggesting that judges and magistrates are inclined to ignore or subvert the Fourth Amendment or that lawlessness among these actors requires the application of the extreme sanction of exclusion." Third, and of greatest importance, there was no basis for believing that exclusion of evidence seized pursuant to a warrant would have a significant deterrent effect on the issuing judge or magistrate. . . .

Applying the reasoning of *Leon* to the facts of this case, we conclude that the decision of the Arizona Supreme Court must be reversed. The Arizona Supreme Court['s] . . . holding is contrary to the reasoning of *Leon*. If court employees were responsible for the erroneous computer record, the exclusion of evidence at trial would not sufficiently deter future errors so as to warrant such a severe sanction. First, as we noted in *Leon*, the exclusionary rule was historically designed as a means of deterring police misconduct, not mistakes by court employees. Second, respondent offers no evidence that court employees are inclined to ignore or subvert the Fourth Amendment or that lawlessness among these actors requires application of the extreme sanction of exclusion. To the contrary, the Chief Clerk of the Justice Court testified at the suppression hearing that this type of error occurred once every three or four years.

Finally, and most important, there is no basis for believing that application of the exclusionary rule in these circumstances will have a significant effect on court employees responsible for informing the police that a warrant has been quashed. Because court clerks are not adjuncts to the law enforcement team engaged in the often competitive enterprise of ferreting out crime, they have no stake in the outcome of particular criminal prosecutions. The threat of exclusion of evidence could not be expected to deter such individuals from failing to inform police officials that a warrant had been quashed. . . .

☐ *Justice STEVENS, dissenting.*

The Court seems to assume that the Fourth Amendment—and particularly the exclusionary rule, which effectuates the Amendment's commands—has the limited purpose of deterring police misconduct. Both the constitutional text and the history of its adoption and interpretation identify a more majestic conception. . . . The Fourth Amendment's Warrant Clause provides the fundamental check on official invasions of the individual's right to privacy. *Leon* stands for the dubious but limited proposition that courts should not look behind the face of a warrant on which police have relied in good faith. . . .

The Phoenix Police Department was part of the chain of information that resulted in petitioner's unlawful, warrantless arrest. We should reasonably presume that law enforcement officials, who stand in the best position to monitor such errors as occurred here, can influence mundane communication procedures in order to prevent those errors. That presumption comports with the notion that the exclusionary rule exists to deter future police misconduct systemically. The deterrent purpose extends to law enforcement as a whole, not merely to "the arresting officer." Consequently, the Phoenix officers' good faith does not diminish the deterrent value of invalidating their arrest of petitioner. . . .

[O]ne consequence of the Court's holding seems immediately obvious. Its most serious impact will be on the otherwise innocent citizen who is stopped for a minor traffic infraction and is wrongfully arrested based on erroneous information in a computer data base. . . . [I]f courts are to have any power to discourage official error of this kind, it must be through application of the exclusionary rule. . . . I respectfully dissent.

8

The Fifth Amendment Guarantee against Self-Accusation

The fifth amendment's provision that "[n]o person . . . shall be compelled in any criminal case to be a witness against himself" gave constitutional effect to an old common-law maxim: "No man is bound to betray [accuse] himself."[1] That maxim can be traced to Englishman John Lambert, an obdurate heretic, who in 1537, while chained to a stake, protested the inquisitorial practices of ecclesiastical courts. Not until the middle of the seventeenth century, however, did the principle that no man is bound to accuse himself become firmly embedded in English common law. Yet by the close of that century, the principle had become part of the legal systems in the colonies. Six of the original thirteen states included the guarantee in their state constitutions or bills of rights, and in the remaining it was recognized by their courts.

Although the common-law maxim provided the historical basis for the Fifth Amendment, the drafters of the Bill of Rights were apparently unsure of its precise scope. Initially, George Mason, as author of the Virginia Declaration of Rights, urged the constitutionality of this rule of evidence as part of accepted accusatorial criminal procedure:

> That in all capital or criminal prosecutions a man hath a right to demand the cause and nature of his accusation, to be confronted with the accusers and witnesses, to call for evidence in favor, and to a speedy trial by an impartial jury of twelve men of his vicinage, without whose unanimous consent he cannot be found guilty; *nor can he be compelled to give evidence against himself;* that no man be deprived of his liberty, except by the law of the land or the judgment of his peers.[2]

Mason's formulation, however, fell short of the common-law protection for witnesses as well as for the accused.

By comparison, James Madison's draft of the proposed amendment embraced the broad scope of the traditional common-law maxim: "No person shall be subject, except in cases of impeachment, to more than one punishment or trial for the same offense; *nor shall be compelled to be a witness against himself*; nor be deprived of life, liberty, or property, without due process of law; nor be obliged to relinquish his property, where it may be necessary for public use, without just compensation."

Madison's proposal broadly applied to civil and criminal proceedings as well as to all stages of the legal process, including both legislative and judicial inquiries. Indeed, because Madison collapsed the maxim "No man is bound to accuse himself" with another—"No man should be a witness in his own case"—his formulation would have applied "to any testimony that fell short of making one vulnerable, but that nevertheless exposed him to public disgrace or obloquy, or other injury to name of reputation," and would have extended protection to third-party witnesses in civil and criminal proceedings.[3]

In the House committee assigned to finalize the Bill of Rights, John Lawrence suggested that the clause constituted "a general declaration in some degree contrary to laws passed" and should be "confined to criminal cases." The clause was amended without discussion and adopted unanimously.[4] Inclusion of the phrase "in any criminal case" limited the scope of the guarantee, ostensibly precluding invocation of the right during police interrogations and by parties and witnesses in civil and equity suits as well as in nonjudicial proceedings, such as grand jury and legislative investigations.

But the Supreme Court has interpreted the guarantee to be "as broad as the mischief against which it seeks to guard."[5] The scope of the amendment extends beyond criminal trials to grand jury proceedings;[6] to legislative investigations;[7] and, in some circumstances, to witnesses in civil and criminal cases where truthful assertions might result in forfeiture, penalty, or criminal prosecution.[8] The Warren Court's landmark ruling in *Miranda v. Arizona* (1966) (excerpted in section A) "expanded the right beyond all precedent, yet not beyond its historical spirit and purpose"[9] in extending the guarantee to police interrogations. As a consequence, the Fifth Amendment's guarantee applies from the time police begin "to focus on a particular suspect" through "custodial interrogation"[10] to the trial itself as well as to other quasi-judicial and nonjudicial proceedings.[11] In addition, individuals may not be disbarred or lose their jobs simply because they plead their Fifth Amendment right to remain silent.[12] In *United States v. Aloyzas Balsys*, 524 U.S. 666 (1998), however, the Court held that individuals may not claim the privilege simply because of a fear that incriminating statements may result in deportation and prosecution by a foreign nation.

Although, historically, rejecting a strict construction of the amendment, the Court has imposed two crucial restrictions by loosely construing the guarantee to confer "a privilege against self-incrimination." First, the inference that the amendment grants only a *privilege* rather than a *right* has great jurisprudential significance. Privileges differ from rights: whereas privileges are granted (and revocable) by the government, rights do not derive from the government and limit the exercise of governmental power. As the prominent historian Leonard W. Levy observes, "to speak of the 'privilege' against self-incrimination, degrades it, inadvertently, in comparison to other constitutional rights."[13] Second, the amendment literally does not protect merely self-incrimination. As Levy points out:

> [T]o speak of a right against self-incrimination stunts the wide right not to give evidence against oneself. . . . The "right against self-incrimination" is a shorthand gloss of modern origin that implies a restriction not in the constitutional clause. The right not to be witness against oneself imports a principle of wider reach, applicable at least in criminal cases, to the self-production of any adverse evidence, including evidence that made one the herald of his own infamy, thereby publicly disgracing him. The clause extended, in other words, to all the injurious as well as incriminating consequences of disclosures.[14]

In sum, the shorthand version of the guarantee as a privilege against self-incrimination unnecessarily limits the scope of the Fifth Amendment.

The primary effect of the Fifth Amendment remains that in criminal trials the accused cannot be compelled to take the witness stand. It is also improper for judges to comment on a defendant's refusal to testify.[15] Witnesses must explicitly claim the right to remain silent; otherwise, they are considered to have tacitly waived it.[16] Judges ultimately decide whether a claim to exercise the right is valid.[17] Even in criminal cases, the accused may refuse to answer only questions tantamount to admissions of guilt but not when self-incrimination is "of an imaginary and unsubstantial character, having reference to some extraordinary and barely possible contingency, so improbable that no reasonable man would suffer it to influence his conduct."[18]

The scope of the Fifth Amendment, however, depends on the Supreme Court's construction of the purposes and policies behind the amendment, which in turn depends on the politics of the Court and its composition. *Murphy v. Waterfront Commission*, 387 U.S. 52 (1964), concisely elucidated the "complex of values" underlying the right against self-accusation:

- CONSTITUTIONAL HISTORY

The Accusatorial and Inquisitorial Systems in the Medieval Period Compared

Common Law Safeguards: Accusatorial System	Civil and Canon Law: Inquisitorial System
Charges are screened by grand jury, which issues detailed indictment	No provision is made for specification and revelation of charges
Proceedings are substantially public	Proceedings are shrouded in secrecy
Accused and accusors confront one another in court with sworn testimony before a jury	Proceedings are nonconfrontational—names of witnesses against the accused are not revealed
Accused is presumed innocent; prosecution must prove its case	Accused is forced to submit to self-incriminating oath
Accused cannot give sworn testimony, even if he wants to testify	Accused is tried by secret interrogations
Accused is tried by public evidence	Judge functions as official prosecutor
Judge presides over trial—an oral combat before jury of peers of the accused	Judge decides guilt or innocence
Conviction is based on jury verdict	Torture is routinely used
Torture is regarded as illegal	Suspects can be retried indefinitely
There is no double jeopardy	

It reflects many of our fundamental values and most noble aspirations: our unwillingness to subject those suspected of crime to the cruel trilemma of self-accusation, perjury, or contempt; our preference for an accusatorial rather than an inquisitorial system of criminal justice; our fear that self-incrimination will be elicited by inhumane treatment and abuses; our sense of fair play which dictates a "fair state-individual balance by requiring the government . . . in its contest with the individual to shoulder the entire load," . . . our respect for the inviolability of the human personality and of the right of each individual "to a private enclave where he may lead a private life," . . . our distrust of self-deprecatory statements; and our realization that the privilege while "a shelter to the guilty," has often [been] "a protection to the innocent."

From this complex of values, three basic rationales stand out: the guarantee's role in (1) maintaining a responsible accusatorial system, (2) preventing cruel and inhumane treatment of suspects, and (3) offering protection for personal privacy. Each implies a different interpretative approach toward the amendment. Together, they define the jurisprudential basis for the struggle within the Court over defining the scope of the Fifth Amendment.

The "fox hunter's reason" was how Jeremy Bentham, an eighteenth-century English philosopher and legal reformer, characterized the basis for the privilege against self-incrimination. Just as in a fox hunt certain rules govern the ways by which fox hunters may capture the fox, so too evidentiary rules define an acceptable process for prosecuting suspects of criminal activity in an accusatorial system. Both the rules of fox hunting and of the criminal justice system are predicated on the notion of fairness—fair treatment of the fox and the criminal suspect. In Bentham's words, "[I]t consists in introducing upon the carpet of legal procedure the ideal of *fairness*, in the sense in which the word is used by sportsmen. The fox is to have a fair chance for his life: he must have (so close is the analogy) what is called *law*: leave to run a certain length of way, for the express purpose of giving him a chance for escape."[19]

How does the Fifth Amendment's guarantee serve the ideal of justice as fair treatment in accusatory systems? Justice Abe Fortas explained that

> [t]o maintain a "fair state-individual balance," to require the government "to shoulder the entire load," . . . to respect the inviolability of the human personality, our accusatory system of criminal justice demands that the government seeking to punish an individual produce the evidence by its own independent labors, rather than by the cruel, simple expedient of compelling it from his own mouth. . . . The principle that a man is not obliged to furnish the state with ammunition to use against him is basic to this conception. Equals, meeting in battle, owe no such duty to one another, regardless of the obligations that they may be under prior to battle. A sovereign state has the right to defend itself, and within the limits of accepted

procedure, to punish infractions of the rules that govern its relationships with its sovereign individual to surrender or impair his right of self-defense.[20]

On this interpretation, the Fifth Amendment has instrumental value in securing a "fair fight" and a "fair state-individual balance"; the right against compelled self-incrimination is not an end in itself. But if the amendment has only instrumental value, then its scope is limited to those contexts in which individuals face the threat of prosecution. And the government is forbidden from only exerting "genuine compulsion" in securing a suspect's self-incriminating statements. Where disclosures are not incriminating (merely embarrassing) or when incriminating testimony is given in exchange for a grant of immunity, the amendment offers no protection. This was the view taken in *United States v. Washington*, 431 U.S. 181 (1977): "Absent some officially coerced self-accusation the Fifth Amendment privilege is not violated by even the most damning admissions. . . . The constitutional guarantee is only that the witness be not *compelled* to give self-incriminating testimony. The test is whether, considering the totality of the circumstances, the free will of the witness was overborne."

A rival interpretation is grounded in what Bentham termed "an old woman's reason"; namely, the belief that it is cruel and inhumane to force a person to partake in his own undoing. From this perspective, the Fifth Amendment embodies an end in itself—respect for the moral dignity of the individual—and confers a right to remain silent. "The essence of [the old woman's] reason," as Bentham put it, "is contained in the word *hard*: 'tis hard upon a man to be obliged to criminate himself.' " And Bentham viewed dimly "this plea of tenderness, this double-distilled and treble-refined sentimentality," claiming that it served only the guilty: "Hard it is upon a man, it must be confessed, to be obliged to do anything that he does not like. That he should not much like to do what is meant by his [in]criminating himself, is natural enough; for what it leads to, is, his being punished. What is not less hard is in a man's being punished, that, and no more, is there in his thus being made to incriminate himself."

History, however, shows that respect for human dignity played an important role in the development of a right against self-accusation. In the late sixteenth century, Puritan leaders attacked the *ex officio* oath on the grounds that "[m]uch more is it equall that a mans owne private faults should remayne private to God and himselfe till the Lord discover them. And in regard of this righte consider howe the Lord ordained wittnesses where by the magistrate should seeke into the offences of his subjects and not by oathe rifle the secrets of theare hearts."[21] Colonial common law also offered protection "against physical compulsion and against the moral compulsion that an oath to a revengeful God commands of a pious soul."[22] It is to this history and interpretation that Justice Douglas appealed when dissenting, in *Ullmann v. United States*, 350 U.S. 422 (1956), from the Court's upholding the constitutionality of grants of immunity:

> The guarantee against self-incrimination contained in the Fifth Amendment is not only a protection against conviction and prosecution but a safeguard of conscience and human dignity and freedom of expression as well. . . . [T]he Framers put it well beyond the power of Congress to *compel* anyone to confess his crimes. The evil to be guarded against was partly self-accusation under legal compulsion. But that was only a part of the evil. The conscience and dignity of man were also involved.

Notwithstanding the moral appeal of the old woman's rationale, critics charge that it "confronts the clear fact that the rule against self-incrimination is psychologically and morally unacceptable as a general governing principle in human relations."[23] Court of Appeals Judge Henry J. Friendly, for one, argued that "[n]o parent would teach such a doctrine to his children; the lesson parents preach is that a misdeed, even a serious one, will generally be forgiven; a failure to make a clean breast of it will not be. Every day people are being asked to explain their conduct to parents, employers, and teachers."[24] However, there is a vast difference between the state's compelling a person to incriminate himself and a person's revelations to his or her lover, parents, friends, or employer, as well as between the kinds of sanctions that may result from those self-revelations.

Finally, "the hermit's rationale" draws attention to the amendment's protection for personal privacy. This view of the amendment was often advanced during the Warren Court era. In particular, in *Warden v. Hayden*, 387 U.S. 294 (1967), Justice Douglas observed that "[p]rivacy involves the choice of the individual to disclose or to reveal what he believes, what he thinks, what he possesses. . . . That dual aspect of privacy means that the individual should have the freedom to select for himself the time and circumstances when he will share his secrets with others and decide the extent of that sharing. This is his prerogative, not the State's."

The hermit's rationale invited sharp criticism, however. Judge Friendly charged that

> [f]ar from being a moral doctrine, the privacy justification is about as immoral as one could imagine. To be sure, there may be offenses,

for example, fornication and adultery, where the individual's right to be left alone may transcend the state's interest. . . . [But] can it be seriously argued that when a murder or rape or kidnapping has been committed, a citizen is morally justified in withholding his aid simply because he does not want to be bothered and prefers to remain in a "private enclave" from which the state has cause to believe he departed in order to do violence to another?[25]

Friendly, though, may simply take the privacy rationale too far, for as political scientist Robert Gerstein points out, "The right of privacy cannot be understood as embodying the rule that 'privacy may be never violated.' The alternative is to look at the right of privacy not as an absolute rule but as a principle that would establish privacy as a value of great significance, not to be interfered with lightly by governmental authority." Also, "[t]he case for allowing the privilege [may be] strongest when all these purposes"—the fox hunter's, the old woman's, and the hermit's rationales—are "served by its application."[26]

The importance of these competing rationales is underscored by Justice John Harlan's observation, dissenting in *Garrity v. New Jersey*, 385 U.S. 493 (1967): "The Constitution contains no formulae within which we can calculate the areas . . . to which the privilege should extend, and the Court has therefore been obliged to fashion for itself standards for the application of the privilege." Consider how these competing rationales enter into the Court's rulings on coerced confessions and police interrogations, grants of immunity, and its distinction between "real" and "testimonial" evidence, as well as on claims to Fifth Amendment protection for required records and private papers, in the following sections of this chapter.

NOTES

1. See Leonard Levy, *The Origins of the Fifth Amendment* (New York: Oxford University Press, 1968).

2. "Virginia Declaration of Rights," in *The Federal and State Constitutions, Colonial Charters, and Other Organic Laws*, ed. F. Thorpe (New York: Harper & Brothers, 1898). Emphasis added.

3. Levy, *The Origins of the Fifth Amendment*, 243–244.

4. "Amendments Reported by the House Select Committee, July 28, 1789," in *Documentary History of the Constitution of the United States*, Vol. 5, 186.

5. *Counselman v. Hitchcock*, 142 U.S. 547 (1892).

6. See *Lefkowitz v. Cunningham*, 429 U.S. 893 (1970); *California v. Byers*, 402 U.S. 424 (1971); *United States v. Kordel*, 397 U.S. 1 (1970); and *Marbury v. Madison*, 5 U.S. 137 (1803).

7. See *Watkins v. United States*, 354 U.S. 178 (1957); and *Bart v. United States*, 349 U.S. 219 (1955).

8. *McCarthy v. Arndstein*, 266 U.S. 34 (1924). But see *Chavez v. Martinez*, 538 U.S. 760 (2003), holding that violations of *Miranda* do not apply to civil suits for damages.

9. Levy, *The Origins of the Fifth Amendment*, 38.

10. *Escobedo v. Illinois*, 378 U.S. 478 (1964).

11. See *Miranda v. Arizona*, 384 U.S. 436 (police interrogations); *Emspack v. United States*, 349 U.S. 190 (1955), and *Quinn v. United States*, 349 U.S. 155 (1955) (legislative investigations); *McCarthy v. Arndstein*, 266 U.S. 34 (1924) (civil proceedings); *ICC v. Brimson*, 154 U.S. 447 (1894) (administrative investigations); *Counselman v. Hitchcock*, 142 U.S. 547 (1892) (grand jury proceedings).

12. See *Regan v. New York*, 349 U.S. 105 (1954); *Slochower v. Board of Education*, 350 U.S. 551 (1956); *Spavack v. Klein*, 385 U.S. 511 (1967); *Gardson v. Broderick*, 392 U.S. 273 (1968); *Uniform Sanitation Men's Association v. Commissioner of Sanitation of the City of New York*, 392 U.S. 280 (1968); *Lefkowitz v. Turley*, 414 U.S. 70 (1973); and *Lefkowitz v. Cunningham*, 431 U.S. 801 (1977).

13. Leonard W. Levy, "The Right against Self-Incrimination," 29 *Journal of Politics* 3 (1969).

14. Levy, *The Origins of the Fifth Amendment*, 425–427.

15. See *Griffin v. California*, 380 U.S. 609 (1965). But also see *United States v. Young*, 470 U.S. 1 (1985) (a five-to-four ruling upholding a prosecutor's statements that the defendant was guilty and urging the jury to do its job).

16. *California v. Byers*, 402 U.S. 424 (1971); *Rogers v. United States*, 340 U.S. 367 (1951); and *United States v. Monia*, 317 U.S. 434 (1943).

17. *Mackey v. United States*, 401 U.S. 667 (1971); *Hoffman v. United States*, 341 U.S. 479 (1955); and *Mason v. United States*, 244 U.S. 362 (1917).

18. *Emspack v. United States*, 349 U.S. 190 (1955).

19. Jeremy Bentham, *A Rationale of Judicial Evidence* (1827), 238–239. The discussion in this section draws on David M. O'Brien, "The Fifth Amendment: Fox Hunters, Old Women, Hermits, and the Burger Court," 54 *Notre Dame Lawyer* 26 (1978).

20. Abe Fortas, "The Fifth Amendment: *Nemo Tenetur Prodere Seipsum*," 25 *Cleveland Bar Association Journal* 95 (1954).

21. Quoted in Levy, *The Origins of the Fifth Amendment*, 177.

22. R. Carter Pittman, "The Colonial and Constitutional History of the Privilege against Self-Incrimination," 21 *Virginia Law Review* 783 (1935).

23. David Louisell, "Criminal Discovery and Self-Incrimination," 53 *California Law Review* 95 (1965). See also Sidney Hook, *Common Sense and the Fifth Amendment* (New York: Criterion, 1959).

24. Henry J. Friendly, "The Fifth Amendment Tomorrow: The Case for Constitutional Change," 37 *Cincinnati Law Review* 673 (1968).

25. Friendly, "The Fifth Amendment Tomorrow," 689.

26. Robert Gerstein, "Privacy and Self-Incrimination," 80 *Ethics* 87 (1970).

SELECTED BIBLIOGRAPHY

Baker, Liva. *Miranda: Crime, Law and Politics.* New York: Atheneum, 1983.

Bradley, Craig. *The Failure of the Criminal Procedure Revolution.* Philadelphia: University of Pennsylvania Press, 1993.

Brooks, Peter. *Troubling Confessions: Speaking Guilt in Law and Literature.* Chicago: University of Chicago Press, 2000.

Fletcher, George P. *Basic Concepts of Criminal Law.* New York: Oxford University Press, 1998.

Grano, Joseph. *Confessions, Truth, and the Law.* Ann Arbor: University of Michigan Press, 1993.

Kamisar, Yale. *Police Interrogation and Confessions: Essays in Law and Policy.* Ann Arbor: University of Michigan Press, 1980.

Levy, Leonard W. *Origins of the Fifth Amendment.* New York: Oxford University Press, 1968.

Packer, Herbert L. *The Limits of the Criminal Sanction.* Stanford, CA: Stanford University Press, 1968.

Shuy, Roger. *The Language of Confession, Interrogation and Deception.* Thousand Oaks, CA: Sage Publications, 1998.

White, Welsh S. *Miranda's Waning Protections.* Ann Arbor: University of Michigan Press, 2003.

A | *Coerced Confessions and Police Interrogations*

The issues that arise with police interrogations and coerced confessions were long avoided by the Court until the Fifth Amendment was applied to the states in *Malloy v. Hogan*, 378 U.S. 1 (1964). However, in the 1930s and 1940s the Court confronted police practices and the rights of the accused under the due process clause of the Fourteenth Amendment. In *Brown v. Mississippi*, 297 U.S. 278 (1936), for example, police physically tortured a suspect, and Chief Justice Charles Evans Hughes responded with a unanimous opinion warning that "the freedom of constitutional government . . . is limited by the requirement of due process of law. Because a State may dispense with a jury trial, it does not follow that it may substitute trial by ordeal. The rack and torture chamber may not be substituted for the witness stand." Subsequently, *Ashcraft v. Tennessee*, 322 U.S. 143 (1944), held that the use of some confessions violates the due process clause because they are the result of "inherently coercive" police interrogations; here, Ashcraft's confession came after thirty-six hours of continuous police questioning under electrical lights. On a case-by-case basis in the 1950s, the Court found a number of police interrogations so psychologically coercive as to run afoul of the due process clause.[1] And in *Mallory v. United States*, 354 U.S. 449 (1957), the Court held that a confession was improper when the defendant had not been properly arraigned first.

The problem with the Court's looking at the "totality of the circumstances" in each case to determine whether a confession was coerced and for a violation of a suspect's Fifth Amendment rights (and the Sixth Amendment right to counsel) was that it provided little guidance for police and lower courts. In the 1940s and 1950s police in many areas of the country were still not required to be high school graduates and the quality of state court judges was much lower than today. Still, the Court remained reluctant to establish a "bright line" ruling on how far police could go when interrogating suspects. In *Crooker v. California*, 357 U.S. 433 (1958), for instance, the justices split five to four in holding that the denial of the presence of an attorney during police questioning did not violate the rights of an accused man who had a college degree and some law school training. Yet in the following year the Court unanimously held that the presence of counsel was required when the defendant confessed during a three-o'clock-in-the-morning interrogation by police in *Spano v. New York*, 360 U.S. 315 (1959).

A solid majority on the Warren Court (after the appointment of Justice Arthur Goldberg in 1962) finally came together in establishing a bright line rule for police interrogations.[2] In *Massiah v. United States*, 377 U.S. 201 (1964), the Court held that a defendant's Fifth and Sixth Amendment rights were violated by a prosecutor's use as evidence of his incriminating statements made to a codefendant after being indicted and which were overheard by police on a radio with the codefendant's permission. Splitting five to four in *Escobedo v. Illinois*, 378 U.S. 478 (1964), the Court went even further. For a bare majority, Justice Goldberg held that no "meaningful distinction" could be drawn between police interrogations before and after a suspect's formal indictment. Individuals have the right to the presence of an attorney at the time they become suspects and the focus of police investigations. In Justice Goldberg's words:

> We hold, therefore, that where, as here, the investigation is no longer a general inquiry into an unsolved crime but has begun to focus on a particular suspect, the suspect has been taken into police custody, the police carry out a process of interrogations that lends itself to eliciting incriminating statements, the suspect has requested and been denied an opportunity to consult with his lawyer, and the police have not effectively warned him of his absolute constitu-

tional right to remain silent, the accused has been denied "the assistance of counsel" in violation of the Sixth Amendment of the Constitution . . . [and] no statement elicited by the police during the interrogation may be used against him at a criminal trial.

Escobedo laid the basis for the five-to-four ruling in *Miranda v. Arizona* (1966) (excerpted below) in which Chief Justice Earl Warren set down a code of conduct for police interrogations, requiring police to inform suspects of their rights to remain silent and to have an attorney present during police questioning. As a result, the totality of circumstances standard was replaced by *Miranda*'s bright line rule.

The year after *Miranda*, the Court carried its protection for the rights of the accused even further when holding that the requirements of the due process clause apply to juvenile courts.[3] Historically, juveniles were treated differently from adults on the theory that the state is not an adversary but rather represents parental authority (*parens patriae*) in bringing civil (not criminal) proceedings against them.[4] *In re Gault* (1967) (excerpted below) extended to juvenile courts the rights of notification of charges, timely hearings, representation by counsel, and the right to confront accusors, as well as the Fifth Amendment's right to remain silent.

In re Gault spearheaded a number of other rulings ensuring juveniles of the rights of the accused. Subsequently, the Court ruled that the same standard of proof for guilt must apply in juvenile courts as in other criminal proceedings[5] and that the prohibition against double jeopardy also applies.[6] But *Fare v. Michael C.*, 442 U.S. 707 (1979), held that whether a juvenile's confession may be used as evidence in court, when he asked to see his probation officer rather than an attorney, depends on the totality of circumstances. *Schall v. Martin*, 467 U.S. 253 (1984), upheld the pretrial detention of juveniles deemed by a judge to be a "serious risk."

Miranda ignited a long-running political controversy. Congress responded in the Crime Control and Safe Streets Act of 1968 by providing that in federal courts confessions are admissible based on the totality of circumstances rule (not *Miranda*, which still applies in state courts). Although *Miranda* has not been overturned, the Burger and Rehnquist Courts sharply cut back on its application. The Court has not abandoned *Miranda*'s premise that "interrogation of persons suspected or accused of crime contains inherently compelling pressures which work to undermine the individual's will to resist and to compel him to speak where he would not otherwise do so freely." But as the Court became more conservative (with the addition of appointees of presidents Richard Nixon, Ronald Reagan, and George H. W. Bush), the justices have reevaluated the necessity of full *Miranda* warnings in every circumstance and distinguished *Miranda* requirements as mere "prophylactic rules" from the Fifth Amendment's guarantee, thereby limiting the contexts and circumstances in which police must honor *Miranda*.

Because the Court construes *Miranda* to be basically a procedural ruling, it allows prosecutorial use of incriminating statements made without the benefit of full *Miranda* warnings and without a "knowing and intelligent" waiver of a defendant's Fifth Amendment rights.[7] *Harris v. New York*, 401 U.S. 222 (1971), for example, held that statements, otherwise inadmissible against the defendant because of the failure to satisfy *Miranda*, may be used to impeach the defendant's testimony at trial. In *Oregon v. Hass*, 420 U.S. 714 (1975), *Harris* was extended to permit the defendant's impeachment by use of statements obtained while he was in police custody and after he requested an attorney but before the lawyer arrived. And *Michigan v. Tucker*, 417 U.S. 433 (1975), held that the Fifth Amendment was not violated by the prosecution's use of testimony of a witness discovered as the result of the defendant's statements to police given in the absence of *Miranda* warnings. Again, in *Michigan v. Mosely*, 423 U.S. 96 (1975), the Court sustained a police interrogation, after a two-hour interval, of a suspect who had earlier claimed his right to remain silent.

More recently, in *Yarborough v. Alvarado*, 124 S.Ct. 2140 (2004), a juvenile was brought by parents to the police station where, in a two-hour-long interview, he made incriminating statements about a robbery and murder; he was allowed to leave, then a month later, was arrested and charged. The Court held that for the purposes of *Miranda*, he had not been in police custody. Reaffirming earlier rulings that *Miranda* applies only when a person is in police custody, but not when questioned or interviewed by police, the Court held that Alvarado's incriminating statements could be used against him even though he was not given the *Miranda* warning. Moreover, according to Justice Kennedy's opinion for the Court, Alvarado's being a juvenile and other psychological considerations were not relevant to whether he was in police custody for the purposes of *Miranda*. Justices Stevens, Souter, Ginsburg, and Breyer dissented. (See also other rulings listed in THE DEVELOPMENT OF LAW box in this section). Finally, a bare majority held, in *Hiibel v. Sixth Judicial District of Nevada*, 124 S.Ct. 2451 (2004), that the Fifth Amendment does not bar the arrest of individuals who refuse to identify themselves when stopped and questioned by police when the police have a reasonable suspicion that they are involved in criminal activity. Some twenty states have so-called stop and identify laws permitting such arrests; dissenting Justices Stevens, Souter, Ginsburg and Breyer deemed the laws to violate the Fourth and Fifth Amendments.

Although not overruling *Miranda*, the Court significantly limited its application by distinguishing the circumstances in which it applies on a case-by-case basis. In doing so, the Court redefined the nature of personal compulsion that triggers the Fifth Amendment's protection and returned to the pre-*Miranda* standard of "considering the totality of circumstances, [whether] the free will of the witness is overbore."[8] Three cases—*Rhode Island v. Innis* (1980), *Duckworth v. Eagan* (1989), and *McNeil v. Wisconsin* (1991) (all excerpted below)—illustrate the Court's analysis.

Still, even though the Burger and Rehnquist Courts recognized exceptions to *Miranda*'s application, a majority of the Court remains committed to upholding *Miranda*. In a six-to-two ruling (with Justice David Souter not participating and Chief Justice Rehnquist and Justice Scalia in dissent) in *Minnick v. Mississippi*, 498 U.S. 146 (1990), the Court reinforced *Miranda*'s protections by reaffirming that once an accused person in police custody requests an attorney, police may not initiate further questioning until an attorney is available and present during the questioning. In an earlier decision, *Edwards v. Arizona*, 451 U.S. 477 (1981), the Burger Court held that under *Miranda*, once an accused asks for an attorney, he may not be subjected to another round of questioning "until counsel has been made available to him." But subsequently, the Mississippi State Supreme Court narrowly interpreted *Edwards* to permit the use at trial of incriminating statements obtained during a police interrogation from Robert Minnick in the absence of his lawyer. The Rehnquist Court, however, overturned that ruling in *Minnick v. Mississippi*. Writing for the majority, Justice Anthony Kennedy explained that

> [t]o protect the privilege against self-incrimination guaranteed by the Fifth Amendment, we have held that police must terminate interrogation of an accused in custody if the accused requests the assistance of counsel. *Miranda v. Arizona*, 384 U.S. 436 (1966). We reinforced the protections of *Miranda* in *Edwards v. Arizona*, 451 U.S. 477 (1981), which held that once the accused requests counsel, officials may not reinitiate questioning "until counsel has been made available" to him. The issue in the case before us is whether *Edwards*'s protection ceases once the suspect has consulted with an attorney. . . .
>
> *Edwards* is "designed to prevent police from badgering a defendant into waiving his previously asserted *Miranda* rights." *Michigan v. Harvey*, [494 U.S. 344] (1990). The rule ensures that any statement made in subsequent interrogation is not the result of coercive pressures. *Edwards* conserves judicial resources which would otherwise be expended in making difficult determinations of voluntariness, and implements the protections of *Miranda* in practical and straightforward terms.

The merit of the *Edwards* decision lies in the clarity of its command and the certainty of its application. . . .

We consider our ruling to be an appropriate and necessary application of the *Edwards* rule. A single consultation with an attorney does not remove the suspect from persistent attempts by officials to persuade him to waive his rights, or from the coercive pressures that accompany custody and that may increase as custody is prolonged. . . . We decline to remove protection from police-initiated questioning based on isolated consultations with counsel who is absent when the interrogation resumes.

Still, as *McNeil v. Wisconsin*, 501 U.S. 171 (1991), the Court remains unlikely to broaden *Miranda*'s application. At issue in *McNeil* was whether police violate a suspect's Fifth Amendment-*Miranda* right if they question him about a crime when his court-appointed lawyer in another criminal case is not present. Here, Paul McNeil was in police custody and had previously appeared in court with his attorney on another charge when he was subsequently questioned about a different crime without the presence of his attorney. The narrow question posed, thus, was whether a suspect's Sixth Amendment right to counsel implicitly carries with it the Fifth Amendment right, as construed in *Miranda*, not to be questioned about any other crime in the absence of a suspect's attorney. By a six-to-three vote the Court held that the Sixth Amendment does not convey *Miranda*'s guarantee against being questioned by police about another crime while in police custody and in the absence of a suspect's attorney. A decade later, a bare majority extended the holding in *McNeil v. Wisconsin* in *Texas v. Cobb*, 532 U.S. 162 (2001). Cobb was arrested on burglary charges and confessed to that crime in 1994, but denied any knowledge of the disappearance of the mother and child at the residence. Counsel was appointed to represent him on that charge. But subsequently in 1995 while in custody in response to police questioning, Cobb waived his *Miranda* rights and confessed to the murders. He was later convicted and sentenced to death. Chief Justice Rehnquist held that, pursuant to *McNeil*, the Sixth Amendment right to counsel is offense specific and cannot be invoked for all future prosecutions. In addition, Chief Justice Rehnquist reasoned that because burglary and murder are separate offenses, the Sixth Amendment did not prohibit the police from interrogating Cobb about the murders and, therefore, his confession was admissible. However, in *Fellers v. United States*, 124 S.Ct. 1019 (2004), a unanimous Court reaffirmed that the Sixth Amendment bars the use of incriminating statements elicited by police from an accused after he has waived his *Miranda* rights and after he has been indicted for an offense. Writing for the Court, Justice O'Connor reaffirmed that the Sixth Amendment right to counsel bars interrogations or the deliberate elicitation of information, out of the presence of counsel, once judicial proceedings have begun, whether by a formal charge, preliminary hearing, indictment, or arraignment.

The Court has also cut back on the basis for federal appellate courts to review alleged *Miranda* violations. In *Arizona v. Fulminante*, 499 U.S. 279 (1991) (excerpted below), the Rehnquist Court, with newly appointed Justice Souter casting the crucial vote, significantly undercut a 1967 Warren Court ruling in *Chapman v. California*, 386 U.S. 18 (1967). *Chapman* drew a line on the extension of the so-called harmless error doctrine—under which appellate courts will not reverse the judgments of trial courts on the ground that minor procedural errors were made during a trial. In *Chapman*, adverse comments by the prosecutor and trial judge about a defendant's refusal to testify in his own defense at trial were held not to be constitutionally "harmless errors." Writing for the Court, Justice Black also ruled that "before a federal constitutional error can be held harmless, [an appellate court] must be able to declare a belief that it was harmless beyond a reasonable doubt." Moreover, Justice Black noted that three kinds of constitutional errors were not subject to the "harmless error" doctrine; namely, when a defendant submits to a coerced confession, faces a criminal trial without the assistance of counsel, and is tried before a biased judge. As a result of *Chapman*, prosecutorial use of coerced confessions was not considered a "harmless error" and invariably resulted in reversals of defendants' convictions. But, five members of the Rehnquist Court held otherwise in *Fulminante*.

In *Withrow v. Williams*, 507 U.S. 680 (1993), however, a bare majority declined to extend the ruling in *Stone v. Powell*, 428 U.S. 465 (1976) (see Ch. 7) so as to withdraw federal *habeas corpus* jurisdiction from cases involving state prisoners' claims of *Miranda* violations. In *Stone v. Powell*, the Court held that the landmark ruling on the Fourth Amendment's exclusionary rule, in *Mapp v. Ohio*, 367 U.S. 643 (1961) (see Ch. 7), did not recognize "a personal constitutional right," rather merely a prudential rule geared toward deterring illegal searches and seizures. On that basis, *Stone* held that prisoners could no longer file for a writ of *habeas corpus* in federal courts for review of convictions in state courts that they claimed were based on illegally obtained evidence. Notably, writing for the majority in *Withrow*, Justice Souter refused to extend *Stone*'s reasoning and ruled that *Miranda* guarantees "a fundamental trial right" justifying federal *habeas* review. *Withrow* thus underscores the Court's differing evaluation of *Mapp*'s exclusionary rule and *Miranda's* safeguards, as well as the continuing division within the Court over *Miranda*; in *Withrow*, Chief Justice Rehnquist and Justices O'Connor, Scalia, and Thomas dissented.

Finally, and most important, when faced with a direct challenge to the constitutional status of *Miranda* by a seven-to-two vote the Court affirmed the constitutionality of *Miranda* in *Dickerson v. United States* (2000) (excerpted below). However, subsequently a majority of the Court continued to limit the scope of *Miranda*. In *Chavez v. Martinez*, 538 U.S. 760 (2003), for example, the Court held that violations of *Miranda* do not run afoul of the Fifth Amendment in civil cases seeking an award for damages as a result of persistent police questioning. Writing for the Court, Justice Thomas observed that "a violation of the constitutional right against self-incrimination occurs only if one has been compelled to be a witness against himself in a criminal case." Justices Stevens, O'Connor, and Kennedy dissented. In addition, in two sharply divided rulings on *Miranda*, the Court held, on the one hand, in *Missouri v. Seibert* (2004) (excerpted below) that the practice of police first questioning suspects without reading them their *Miranda* rights and obtaining confessions, then giving them the *Miranda* warnings and again obtaining incriminating statements is unconstitutional. Such mid-interrogation warnings are invalid under *Miranda*; the first confession must be excluded because the suspect was not read the *Miranda* rights, and the second must be excluded because it was obtained by police using the first confession. On the other hand, *United States v. Patane* (2004) (excerpted below) held that, notwithstanding the ruling in *Dickerson v. United States*, holding that *Miranda* was constitutionally based, the *Miranda* warnings are merely prophylactic rules, and if a suspect during police questioning without being given the *Miranda* warnings makes statements that lead police to incriminating physical evidence, that evidence may be used at trial and its introduction does not violate the Fifth Amendment. In short, the plurality held that the failure to provide *Miranda* warnings is not itself a constitutional violation and there was no reason to fashion a "fruit of the poisonous tree" doctrine in order to deter un-*Mirandized* police questioning.

Notes

1. See *Leyra v. Denno*, 347 U.S. 556 (1954); *Fikes v. Alabama*, 352 U.S. 191 (1957); and *Payne v. Arizona*, 356 U.S. 560 (1958).

2. See *Haynes v. Washington*, 373 U.S. 503 (1963) (holding that a written confession was involuntary because the accused had been held incommunicado); and *Jackson v. Denno*, 378 U.S. 368 (1964).

3. In *Gallegos v. Colorado*, 370 U.S. 49 (1962), the Court held that the due process

clause was violated by a confession of a fourteen-year-old boy held by police for five days before his parents were sent for.

4. Relying on the theory of *parens patriae* in according juveniles less protection under the Bill of Rights than adults, the Court in *Ingraham v. Wright*, 430 U.S. 651 (1977), upheld corporal punishment in public schools. The Court also upheld laws permitting parents to admit their minor children to mental hospitals without a hearing. *O'Connor v. Donaldson*, 422 U.S. 563 (1975), held that adults may not be committed to a mental institution under the due process clause without a hearing on their commitment at which time they may contest their institutionalization. But see *Secretary of Public Welfare v. Institutionalized Juveniles*, 422 U.S. 640 (1979); and *Parham v. J.R.*, 422 U.S. 584 (1979).

5. *In re Winship*, 397 U.S. 358 (1970).

6. *Breed v. Jones*, 421 U.S. 519 (1975).

7. See *Harris v. New York*, 401 U.S. 222 (1971); *Michigan v. Tucker*, 417 U.S. 433 (1974); *Michigan v. Mosley*, 423 U.S. 96 (1975); *Oregon v. Hass*, 420 U.S. 714 (1975); *Doyle v. New York*, 426 U.S. 610 (1976); *Oregon v. Mathiason*, 429 U.S. 492 (1977); and *United States v. Wong*, 431 U.S. 174 (1977).

8. *United States v. Wong*, 431 U.S. 174 (1977).

■ INSIDE THE COURT

Chief Justice Earl Warren, Miranda v. Arizona, *and the Attack on the Court*

The Warren Court was sharply criticized for "being soft on criminals" because of its rulings on the rights of the accused. During the 1968 presidential election, Richard Nixon made law and order a campaign issue, promising if elected to appoint strict constructionists to the Court who would overturn the controversial rulings of the Warren Court. Warren and Nixon knew each other from the 1950s, when Warren was the popular governor of California and Nixon was a young Republican congressman from that state. Fearing that Nixon would win the election, Warren offered to retire in 1968 so Democratic President Lyndon Johnson could appoint his successor. But LBJ's nomination of Justice Abe Fortas to be chief justice met opposition in the Senate, and Fortas was forced to withdraw from consideration. Warren stayed on the Court until after the election, and then President Nixon nominated Warren E. Burger to become chief justice in 1969.

Years later in his memoirs, Chief Justice Warren reflected on the campaign against the Court and *Miranda*, observing that the

> attack centered on the case of *Miranda v. Arizona.* . . . [But there] was really nothing new in this except to require police and prosecutors to advise the poor, the ignorant, and the unwary of a basic constitutional right in a manner which had been followed by the Federal

Bureau of Investigation procedures for many years. It was of no assistance to hardened underworld types because they already know what their rights are and demand them. And so it is with all sophisticated criminals and affluent prisoners who had ready access to their lawyers. However, because so many people who are arrested are poor and illiterate, short-cut methods and often cruelties are perpetrated to obtain convictions.*

Before going to the Court in 1953, Warren had worked his way up in politics by serving as California's attorney general. And he had a keen understanding of law enforcement practices that influenced the drafting of his opinion in *Miranda*. When working on *Miranda*, Warren specifically recalled a controversy involving a law professor's seminar for Minneapolis-area police and Minnesota's state attorney general (and later senator and vice president) Walter Mondale. At the seminar, police were told how to adhere to the Court's decisions and still maintain past interrogation practices. "For instance, you're supposed to arraign a prisoner before a magistrate without unreasonable delay," the law professor advised. "But if the magistrate goes hunting for the weekend on a Friday afternoon at 3:00 P.M., you can arrange to arrest your suspect at 3:30. That way you've got the whole weekend." Mondale took the law professor to task at a news conference, responding, "Some persons claim the Supreme Court has gone too far. Others claim to know how constitutional protections may be avoided by tricky indirection. Both viewpoints are wrong—this [seminar] was called to assist us in better fulfilling our sworn duty to uphold the Constitution. It was not called to second guess the Supreme Court." Warren, though, knew full well that not all state attorneys general and police would support the Court's rulings. He, therefore, strove to outline in *Miranda* a code for police procedures governing the interrogation of criminal suspects that police could not easily evade.

After Warren circulated his draft of *Miranda* to the other justices, his trusted ally on the Court, William Brennan, responded with a twenty-one-page list of suggested revisions. At the outset, Brennan emphasized the importance of careful drafting in *Miranda*. "[T]his will be one of the most important opinions of our time," Brennan explained when making "one major suggestion": "It goes to the basic trust of the approach to be taken. In your very first sentence you state that the root problem is 'the *role* society must *assume*, consistent with the federal Constitution, in prosecuting individuals for crime.' I would suggest that the root issue is 'the *restraints* society must *observe*, consistent with the federal Constitution, in prosecuting individuals for crime.' " Warren made that and numerous other changes before handing down the opinion for the Court in *Miranda v. Arizona*.

Sources: Library of Congress, Materials in the Earl Warren Papers and William J. Brennan, Jr., Papers, Manuscripts Room.

*Earl Warren, *The Memoirs of Earl Warren* (Garden City, NY: Doubleday, 1977), 316–317.

Miranda v. Arizona

384 U.S. 436, 86 S.CT. 1602 (1966)

On March 3, 1963, an eighteen-year-old girl was kidnapped and raped on the outskirts of Phoenix, Arizona. Ten days later, police arrested Ernesto A. Miranda, a twenty-three-year-old indigent with a ninth-grade education. (A doctor who later examined Miranda diagnosed him as schizophrenic, although "alert and oriented as to time, place, and person" and competent to stand trial.) At the police station, the rape victim identified Miranda standing in a police lineup as her attacker. Two officers subsequently took Miranda to a separate room and interrogated him. At first denying his guilt, Miranda eventually confessed later and wrote out and signed a brief statement admitting and describing the crime. Following Miranda's trial and conviction, his attorneys appealed on the grounds that Miranda's confession had been coerced and that police had violated his Fifth Amendment rights. The Supreme Court granted review, along with three other cases raising the issue of the admissibility into evidence of confessions obtained during police interrogations.

The Court's decision was five and one-half to three and one-half, and the majority's opinion was announced by Chief Justice Warren. There was a separate opinion, in part concurring and dissenting, by Justice Clark. Justices Harlan and White, joined by Justice Stewart, dissented.

☐ *Chief Justice WARREN delivered the opinion of the Court.*

The cases before us raise questions which go to the roots of our concepts of American criminal jurisprudence: the restraints society must observe consistent with the Federal Constitution in prosecuting individuals for crime. More specifically, we deal with the admissibility of statements obtained from an individual who is subjected to custodial police interrogation and the necessity for procedures which assure that the individual is accorded his privilege under the Fifth Amendment to the Constitution not to be compelled to incriminate himself.

We dealt with certain phases of this problem recently in *Escobedo v. State of Illinois*, 378 U.S. 478 (1964). There, as in the four cases before us, law enforcement officials took the defendant into custody and interrogated him in a police station for the purpose of obtaining a confession. The police did not effectively advise him of his right to remain silent or of his right to consult with his attorney. Rather, they confronted him with an alleged accomplice who accused him of having perpetrated a murder. When the defendant denied the accusation and said "I didn't shoot Manuel, you did it," they handcuffed him and took him to an interrogation room. There, while handcuffed and standing, he was questioned for four hours until he confessed. During this interrogation, the police denied his request to speak to his attorney, and they prevented his retained attorney, who had come to the police station, from consulting with him. At his trial, the State, over his objection, introduced the confession against him. We held that the statements thus made were constitutionally inadmissible. . . .

We granted *certiorari* in these cases in order further to explore some facets of the problems, thus exposed, of applying the privilege against self-incrimination to in-custody interrogation, and to give concrete constitutional guidelines for law enforcement agencies and courts to follow.

We start here, as we did in *Escobedo*, with the premise that our holding is not an innovation in our jurisprudence, but is an application of principles long recognized and applied in other settings. We have undertaken a thorough re-examination of the *Escobedo* decision and the principles it announced, and we reaffirm it. That case was but an explication of basic rights that are enshrined in our Constitution—that "No person . . . shall be compelled in any criminal case to be a witness against himself," and that "the accused shall . . . have the Assistance of Counsel"—rights which were put in jeopardy in that case through official overbearing. . . .

Our holding will be spelled out with some specificity in the pages which follow but briefly stated it is this: the prosecution may not use statements, whether exculpatory or inculpatory, stemming from custodial interrogation of the defendant unless it demonstrates the use of procedural safeguards effective to secure the privilege against self-incrimination. By custodial interrogation, we mean questioning initiated by law enforcement officers after a person has been taken into custody or otherwise deprived of his freedom of action in any significant way. As for the procedural safeguards to be employed, unless other fully effective means are devised to inform accused persons of their right of silence and to assure a continuous opportunity to exercise it, the following measures are required. Prior to any questioning, the person must be warned that he has a right to remain silent, that any statement he does make may be used as evidence against him, and that he has a right to the presence of an attorney, either retained or appointed. The defendant may waive effectuation of these rights, provided the waiver is made voluntarily, knowingly and intelligently. If, however, he indicates in any manner and at any stage of the process that he wishes to consult with an attorney before speaking there can be no questioning. Likewise, if the individual is alone and indicates in any manner that he does not wish to be interrogated, the police may not question him. The mere fact that he may have answered some questions or volunteered some statements on his own does not deprive him of the right to refrain from answering any further inquiries until he has consulted with an attorney and thereafter consents to be questioned.

The constitutional issue we decide in each of these cases is the admissibility of statements obtained from a defendant questioned while in custody or otherwise deprived of his freedom of action in any significant way. In each, the defendant was questioned by police officers, detectives, or a prosecuting attorney in a room in which he was cut off from the outside world. In none of these cases was the defendant given a full and effective warning of his rights at the outset of the interrogation process. In all the cases, the questioning elicited oral admissions, and in three of them, signed statements as well which were admitted at their trials. They all thus share salient features—incommunicado interrogation of individuals in a police-dominated atmosphere, resulting in self-incriminating statements without full warnings of constitutional rights.

An understanding of the nature and setting of this in-custody interrogation is essential to our decisions today. The difficulty in depicting what transpires at such interrogations stems from the fact that in this country they have largely taken place incommunicado. From extensive factual studies undertaken in the early 1930's, including the famous Wickersham Report to Congress by a Presidential Commission, it is clear that police violence and the "third degree" flourished at that time. In a series of cases decided by this Court long after these studies, the police resorted to physical brutality—beatings, hanging, whipping—and to sustained and protracted questioning incommunicado in order to extort confessions. The Commission on Civil Rights in 1961 found much evidence to indicate that "some policemen still resort to physical force to obtain confessions." . . .

Unless a proper limitation upon custodial interrogation is achieved—such as these decisions will advance—there can be no assurance that practices of this nature will be eradicated in the foreseeable future. . . .

[W]e stress that the modern practice of in-custody interrogation is psychologically rather than physically oriented. As we have stated before, "Since *Chambers v. State of Florida*, 309 U.S. 227, [(1940)], this Court has recognized that coercion can be mental, as well as physical, and that the blood of the accused is not the only hallmark of an unconstitutional inquisition." *Blackburn v. State of Alabama*, 361 U.S. 199 (1960). Interrogation still takes place in privacy. Privacy results in secrecy and this in turn results in a gap in our knowledge as to what in fact goes on in the interrogation rooms. A valuable source of information about present police practices, however, may be found in various police manuals and texts which document procedures employed with success in the past, and which recommend various other effective tactics. These texts are used by law enforcement agencies themselves as guides. . . .

[T]he setting prescribed by the manuals and observed in practice [is] clear. In essence, it is this: To be alone with the subject is essential to prevent distraction and to deprive him of any outside support. The aura of confidence in his guilt undermines his will to resist. He merely confirms the preconceived story the police seek to have him describe. Patience and persistence, at times relentless questioning, are employed. To obtain a confession, the interrogator must "patiently maneuver himself or his quarry into a position from which the desired objective may be attained." When normal procedures fail to produce the needed result, the police may resort to deceptive stratagems such as giving false legal advice. It is important to keep the subject off balance, for example, by trading on his insecurity about himself or his surroundings. The police then persuade, trick, or cajole him out of exercising his constitutional rights.

Even without employing brutality, the "third degree" or the specific stratagems described above, the very fact of custodial interrogation exacts a heavy toll on individual liberty and trades on the weakness of individuals. . . .

The potentiality for compulsion is forcefully apparent, for example, in *Miranda*, where the indigent Mexican defendant was a seriously disturbed individual with pronounced sexual fantasies. . . . To be sure, the records do not evince overt physical coercion or patent psychological ploys. The fact remains that in none of these cases did the officers undertake to afford appropriate safeguards at the outset of the interrogation to insure that the statements were truly the product of free choice.

It is obvious that such an interrogation environment is created for no purpose other than to subjugate the individual to the will of his examiner. This atmosphere carries its own badge of intimidation. To be sure, this is not physical intimidation, but it is equally destructive of human dignity. The current practice of incommunicado interrogation is at odds with one of our Nation's most cherished principles—that the individual may not be compelled to incriminate himself. Unless adequate protective devices are employed to dispel the compulsion inherent in custodial surroundings, no statement obtained from the defendant can truly be the product of his free choice. . . .

[T]he constitutional foundation underlying the privilege is the respect a government—state or federal—must accord to the dignity and integrity of its citizens. To maintain a "fair state-individual balance," to require the government "to shoulder the entire load," to respect the inviolability of the human personality, our accusatory system of criminal justice demands that the government seeking to punish an individual produce the evidence against him by its own independent labors, rather than by the cruel, simple expedient of compelling it from his own mouth. In sum, the privilege is fulfilled only when the person is guaranteed the right "to remain silent unless he chooses to speak in the unfettered exercise of his own will." . . .

The question in these cases is whether the privilege is fully applicable during a period of custodial interrogation. . . . We are satisfied that all the principles embodied in the privilege apply to informal compulsion exerted by law-enforcement officers during in-custody questioning. An individual swept from familiar surroundings into police custody, surrounded by antagonistic forces, and subjected to the techniques of persuasion described above cannot be otherwise than under compulsion to speak. As a practical matter, the compulsion to speak in the isolated setting of the police station may well be greater than in courts or other official investigations, where there are often impartial observers to guard against intimidation or trickery. . . .

Today, then, there can be no doubt that the Fifth Amendment privilege is available outside of criminal court proceedings and serves to protect persons in all settings in which their freedom of action is curtailed in any significant way from being compelled to incriminate themselves. We have concluded that without proper safeguards the process of in-custody interrogation of persons suspected or accused of crime contains inherently compelling pressures which work to undermine the individual's will to resist and to compel him to speak where he would not otherwise do so freely. In order to combat these pressures and to permit a full opportunity to exercise the privilege against self-incrimination, the accused must be adequately and effectively apprised of his rights and the exercise of those rights must be fully honored.

It is impossible for us to foresee the potential alternatives for protecting the privilege which might be devised by Congress or the States in the exercise of their creative rule-making capacities. Therefore we cannot say that the Constitution necessarily requires adherence to any particular solution for the inherent compulsions of the interrogation process as it is presently conducted. Our decision in no way creates a constitutional straitjacket which will handicap sound efforts at reform, nor is it intended to have this effect. We encourage Congress and the States to continue their laudable search for increasingly effective ways of protecting the rights of the individual while promoting efficient enforcement of our criminal laws. However, unless we are shown other procedures which are at least as effective in apprising accused persons of their right of silence and in assuring a continuous opportunity to exercise it, the following safeguards must be observed.

At the outset, if a person in custody is to be subjected to interrogation, he must first be informed in clear and unequivocal terms that he has the right to remain silent. For those unaware of the privilege, the warning is needed simply to make them aware of it—the threshold requirement for an intelligent decision as to its exercise. More important, such a warning is an absolute prerequisite in overcoming the inherent pressures of the interrogation atmosphere. It is not just the subnormal or woefully ignorant who succumb to an interrogator's imprecations, whether implied or expressly stated, that the interrogation will continue until a confession is obtained or that silence in the face of accusation is itself damning and will bode ill when presented to a jury. Further, the warning will show the individual that his interrogators are prepared to recognize his privilege should he choose to exercise it. . . .

The warning of the right to remain silent must be accompanied by the explanation that anything said can and will be used against the individual in court. This warning is needed in order to make him aware not only of the privilege, but also of the consequences of forgoing it. It is only through an awareness of these consequences that there can be any assurance of real understanding and intelligent exercise of the privilege. . . .

[T]he right to have counsel present at the interrogation is indispensable to the protection of the Fifth Amendment privilege under the system we delineate today. Our aim is to assure that the individual's right to choose between silence and speech remains unfettered throughout the interrogation process. . . . Thus, the need for counsel to protect the Fifth Amendment privilege comprehends not merely a right to consult with counsel prior to questioning, but also to have counsel present during any questioning if the defendant so desires. . . .

If an individual indicates that he wishes the assistance of counsel before any interrogation occurs, the authorities cannot rationally ignore or deny his request on the basis that the individual does not have or cannot afford a retained attorney. The financial ability of the individual has no relationship to the scope of the rights involved here. The privilege against self-incrimination secured by the Constitution applies to all individuals. . . . The cases before us as well as the vast majority of confession cases with which we have dealt in the past involve those unable to retain counsel. While authorities are not required to relieve the accused of his poverty, they have the obligation not to take advantage of indigence in the administration of justice. . . .

In order fully to apprise a person interrogated of the extent of his rights under this system then, it is necessary to warn him not only that he has the right to consult with an attorney, but also that if he is indigent a lawyer will be appointed to represent him. Without this additional warning, the admonition of the right to consult with counsel would often be understood as meaning only that he can consult with a lawyer if he has one or has the funds to obtain one. The warning of a right to counsel would be hollow if not couched in terms that would convey to the indigent—the person most often subjected to interrogation—the knowledge that he too has a right to have counsel present. . . .

Once warnings have been given, the subsequent procedure is clear. If the individual indicates in any manner, at any time prior to or during questioning, that he wishes to remain silent, the interrogation must cease. At this point he has shown that he intends to exercise his Fifth Amendment privilege; any statement taken after the person invokes his privilege cannot be other than the product of compulsion, subtle or otherwise. Without the right to cut off questioning, the setting of in-custody interrogation operates on the individual to overcome free choice in producing a statement after the privilege has been once invoked. If the individual states that he wants an attorney, the interrogation must cease until an attorney is present. At that time, the individual must have an opportunity to confer with the attorney and to have him present during any subsequent questioning. If the individual cannot obtain an attorney and he indicates that he wants one before speaking to police, they must respect his decision to remain silent. . . .

The principles announced today deal with the protection which must be given to the privilege against self-incrimination when the individual is first subjected to police interrogation while in custody at the station or otherwise deprived of his freedom of action in any significant way. It is at this point that our adversary system of criminal proceedings commences, distinguishing itself at the outset from the inquisitorial system recognized in some countries. Under the system of warnings we delineate today or under any other system which may be devised and found effective, the safeguards to be erected about the privilege must come into play at this point.

Our decision is not intended to hamper the traditional function of police officers in investigating crime. When an individual is in custody on probable cause, the police may, of course, seek out evidence in the field to be used at trial against him. Such investigation may include inquiry of persons not under restraint. General on-the-scene questioning as to facts surrounding a crime or other general questioning of citizens in the fact-finding process is not affected by our holding. It is an act of responsible citizenship for individuals to give whatever information they may have to aid in law enforcement. In such situations the compelling atmosphere inherent in the process of in-custody interrogation is not necessarily present.

In dealing with statements obtained through interrogation, we do not purport to find all confessions inadmissible. Confessions remain a proper element in law enforcement. Any statement given freely and voluntarily without any compelling influences is, of course, admissible in evidence. The fundamental import of the privilege while an individual is in custody is not whether he is allowed to talk to the police without the benefit of warnings and counsel, but whether he can be interrogated. There is no requirement that police stop a person who enters a police station and states that he wishes to confess to a crime, or a person who calls the police to offer a confession or any other statement he desires to make. Volunteered statements of any kind are not barred by the Fifth Amendment and their admissibility is not affected by our holding today.

To summarize, we hold that when an individual is taken into custody or otherwise deprived of his freedom by the authorities in any significant way and is subjected to questioning, the privilege against self-incrimination is jeopardized. Procedural safeguards must be employed to protect the privilege and unless other fully effective means are adopted to notify the person of his right of silence and to assure that the exercise of the right will be scrupulously honored, the following measures are required. He must be warned prior to any questioning that he has the right to remain silent, that anything he says can be used against him in a court of law, that he has the right to the presence of an attorney, and that if he cannot afford an attorney one will be appointed for him prior to any questioning if he so desires. Opportunity to exercise these rights must be afforded to him throughout the interrogation. After such warnings have been given, and such opportunity afforded him, the individual may knowingly and intelligently waive these rights and agree to answer questions or make a statement. But unless and until such warnings and waiver are demonstrated by the prosecution at trial, no evidence obtained as a result of interrogation can be used against him. . . .

In announcing these principles, we are not unmindful of the burdens which law enforcement officials must bear, often under trying circumstances. We also fully recognize the obligation of all citizens to aid in enforcing the criminal laws. This Court, while protecting individual rights, has always given ample latitude to law enforcement agencies in the legitimate exercise of their duties. The limits we have placed on the interrogation process should not constitute an undue interference with a proper system of law enforcement. . . .

Over the years the Federal Bureau of Investigation has compiled an exemplary record of effective law enforcement while advising any suspect or arrested person, at the outset of an interview, that he is not required to make a statement, that any statement may be used against him in court, that the individual may obtain the services of an attorney of his own choice and, more recently, that he has a right to free counsel if he is unable to pay. A letter received from the Solicitor General in response to a question from the Bench makes it clear that the present pattern of warnings and respect for the rights of the individual followed as a practice by the FBI is consistent with the procedure which we delineate today. . . .

Because of the nature of the problem and because of its recurrent significance in numerous cases, we have to this point discussed the relationship of the Fifth Amendment privilege to police interrogation without specific concentration on the facts of the cases before us. We turn now to these facts to consider the application to these cases of the constitutional principles discussed above. In each instance, we have concluded that statements were obtained from the defendant under circumstances that did not meet constitutional standards for protection of the privilege.

☐   *Justice CLARK, concurring and dissenting in part.*

I am unable to join the majority because its opinion goes too far on too little, while my dissenting brethren do not go quite far enough. Nor can I join in the Court's criticism of the present practices of police and investigatory agencies as to custodial interrogation. The materials it refers to as "police manuals" are, as I read them, merely writings in this field by professors and some police officers. Not one is shown by the record here to be the official manual of any police department, much less in universal use in crime detection. Moreover the examples of police brutality mentioned by the Court are rare exceptions to the thousands of cases that appear every year in the law reports. The police agencies—all the way from municipal and state forces to the federal bureaus—are responsible for law enforcement and public safety in this country. I am proud of their efforts, which in my view are not fairly characterized by the Court's opinion. . . .

The rule prior to today—as Justice GOLDBERG, the author of the Court's opinion in *Escobedo*, stated it in *Haynes v. Washington*, [373 U.S. 503 (1963)]—depended upon "a totality of circumstances evidencing an involuntary . . . admission of guilt." . . .

I would continue to follow that rule. Under the "totality of circumstances" rule of which my Brother GOLDBERG spoke in *Haynes*, I would consider in each case whether the police officer prior to custodial interrogation added the warning that the suspect might have counsel present at the interrogation and, further, that a court would appoint one at his request if he was too poor to employ counsel. In the absence of warnings, the burden would be on the State to prove that counsel was knowingly and intelligently waived or that in the totality of the circumstances, including the failure to give the necessary warnings, the confession was clearly voluntary. . . .

☐ *Justice HARLAN, with whom Justice STEWART and Justice WHITE join, dissenting.*

Without at all subscribing to the generally black picture of police conduct painted by the Court, I think it must be frankly recognized at the outset that police questioning allowable under due process precedents may inherently entail some pressure on the suspect and may seek advantage in his ignorance or weaknesses. The atmosphere and questioning techniques, proper and fair though they be, can in themselves exert a tug on the suspect to confess, and in this light "[t]o speak of any confessions of crime made after arrest as being 'voluntary' or 'uncoerced' is somewhat inaccurate, although traditional. A confession is wholly and incontestably voluntary only if a guilty person gives himself up to the law and becomes his own accuser." *Ashcraft v. State of Tennessee*, 322 U.S. 143 [(1944)] (JACKSON, J., dissenting). Until today, the role of the Constitution has been only to sift out *undue* pressure, not to assure spontaneous confessions. . . .

What the Court largely ignores is that its rules impair, if they will not eventually serve wholly to frustrate, an instrument of law enforcement that has long and quite reasonably been thought worth the price paid for it. There can be little doubt that the Court's new code would markedly decrease the number of confessions. To warn the suspect that he may remain silent and remind him that his confession may be used in court are minor obstructions. To require also an express waiver by the suspect and an end to questioning whenever he demurs must heavily handicap questioning. And to suggest or provide counsel for the suspect simply invites the end of the interrogation. . . .

In conclusion: Nothing in the letter or the spirit of the Constitution or in the precedents squares with the heavy-handed and one-sided action that is so precipitously taken by the Court in the name of fulfilling its constitutional responsibilities.

☐ *Justice WHITE, with whom Justice HARLAN and Justice STEWART join, dissenting.*

That the Court's holding today is neither compelled nor even strongly suggested by the language of the Fifth Amendment, is at odds with American and English legal history, and involves a departure from a long line of precedent does not prove either that the Court has exceeded its powers or that the Court is wrong or unwise in its present reinterpretation of the Fifth Amendment. It does, however, underscore the obvious—that the Court has not discovered or found the law in making today's decision, nor has it derived it from some irrefutable sources; what it has done is to make new law and new public policy in much the same way that it has in the course of interpreting other great clauses of the Constitution. This is what the Court historically has done. Indeed, it is what it must do and will continue to do until and unless there is some fundamental change in the constitutional distribution of governmental powers.

But if the Court is here and now to announce new and fundamental policy to govern certain aspects of our affairs, it is wholly legitimate to examine the mode of this or any other constitutional decision in this Court and to inquire into the advisability of its end product in terms of the long-range interest of the country. At the very least, the Court's text and reasoning should withstand analysis and be a fair exposition of the constitutional provision which its opinion interprets. Decisions like these cannot rest alone on syllogism, metaphysics or some ill-defined notions of natural justice, although each will perhaps play its part. In proceeding to such constructions as it now announces, the Court should also duly consider all the factors and interests bearing upon the cases, at least insofar as the relevant materials are available; and if the necessary considerations are not treated in the record or obtainable from some other reliable source, the Court should not proceed to formulate fundamental policies based on speculation alone.

First, we may inquire what are the textual and factual bases of this new fundamental rule. To reach the result announced on the grounds it does, the Court must stay within the confines of the Fifth Amendment, which forbids self-incrimination only if *compelled*. Hence the core of the Court's opinion is that because of the "compulsion inherent in custodial surroundings, no statement obtained from [a] defendant [in custody] can truly be the product of his free choice," absent the use of adequate protective devices as described by the Court. However, the Court does not point to any sudden inrush of new knowledge requiring the rejection of 70 years' experience. . . . Rather than asserting new knowledge, the Court concedes that it cannot truly know what occurs during custodial questioning, because of the innate secrecy of such proceedings. It extrapolates a picture of what it conceives to be the norm from police investigatorial manuals, published in 1959 and 1962 or earlier, without any attempt to allow for adjustments in police practices that may have occurred in the wake of more recent decisions of state appellate tribunals or this Court. . . . Insofar as appears from the Court's opinion, it has not examined a single transcript of any police interrogation, let alone the interrogation that took place in any one of these cases which it decides today. Judged by any of the standards for empirical investigation utilized in the social sciences the factual basis for the Court's premise is patently inadequate. . . .

[E]ven if one assumed that there was an adequate factual basis for the conclusion that all confessions obtained during in-custody interrogation are the product of compulsion, the rule propounded by the Court will still be irrational, for, apparently, it is only if the accused is also warned of his right to counsel and waives both that right and the right against self-incrimination that the inherent compulsiveness of interrogation disappears. But if the defendant may not answer without a warning a question such as "Where were you last night?" without having his answer be a compelled one, how can the Court ever accept his negative answer to the question of whether he wants to consult his retained counsel or counsel whom the court will appoint? And why if counsel is present and the accused nevertheless confesses, or counsel tells the accused to tell the truth, and that is what the accused does, is the situation any less coercive insofar as the accused is concerned? The Court apparently realizes its dilemma of foreclosing questioning without the necessary warnings but at the same time permitting the accused, sitting in the same chair in front of the same policemen, to waive his right to consult an attorney. It expects, however, that the accused will not often waive the right; and if it is claimed that he has, the State faces a severe, if not impossible burden of proof.

All of this makes very little sense in terms of the compulsion which the Fifth Amendment proscribes. That amendment deals with compelling the accused himself. It is his free will that is involved. Confessions and incriminating admissions, as such, are not forbidden evidence; only those which are compelled are banned. I doubt that the Court observes these distinctions today. By considering any answers to any interrogation to be compelled regardless of the content and course of examination and by escalating the requirements to prove waiver, the Court not only prevents the use of compelled confessions but for all practical purposes forbids interrogation except in the presence of counsel. . . .

Criticism of the Court's opinion, however, cannot stop with a demonstration that the factual and textual bases for the rule it propounds are, at best, less than compelling. Equally relevant is an assessment of the rule's consequences measured against community values. The Court's duty to assess the consequences of its action is not satisfied by the utterance of the truth that a value of our system of criminal justice is "to respect the inviolability of the human personality" and to require government to produce the evidence against the accused by its own independent labors. More than the human dignity of the accused is involved; the human personality of others in the society must also be preserved. . . .

The rule announced today . . . is a deliberate calculus to prevent interrogations, to reduce the incidence of confessions and pleas of guilty and to increase the number of trials. . . .

In some unknown number of cases the Court's rule will return a killer,

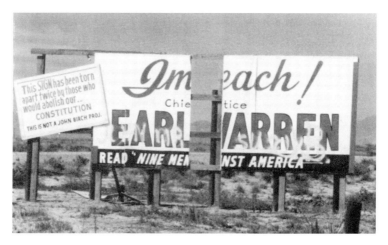

An early "Impeach Earl Warren" sign in 1960. The sign was constructed by those who thought the Warren Court had gone too far in defending civil rights and liberties. (*Paul Conklin*)

a rapist or other criminal to the streets and to the environment which produced him, to repeat his crime whenever it pleases him. As a consequence, there will not be a gain, but a loss, in human dignity. The real concern is not the unfortunate consequences of this new decision on the criminal law as an abstract, disembodied series of authoritative proscriptions, but the impact on those who rely on the public authority for protection and who without it can only engage in violent self-help with guns, knives and the help of their neighbors similarly inclined. . . .

Much of the trouble with the Court's new rule is that it will operate indiscriminately in all criminal cases, regardless of the severity of the crime or the circumstances involved. It applies to every defendant, whether the professional criminal or one committing a crime of momentary passion who is not part and parcel of organized crime. It will slow down the investigation and the apprehension of confederates in those cases where time is of the essence, such as kidnapping; those involving national security; and some of those involving organized crime. . . .

At the same time, the Court's *per se* approach may not be justified on the ground that it provides a "bright line" permitting the authorities to judge in advance whether interrogation may safely be pursued without jeopardizing the admissibility of any information obtained as a consequence. Nor can it be claimed that judicial time and effort, assuming that is a relevant consideration, will be conserved because of the ease of application of the new rule. Today's decision leaves open such questions as whether the accused was in custody, whether his statements were spontaneous or the product of interrogation, whether the accused has effectively waived his rights, and whether nontestimonial evidence introduced at trial is the fruit of statements made during a prohibited interrogation, all of which are certain to prove productive of uncertainty during investigation and litigation during prosecution.

For all these reasons, if further restrictions on police interrogation are desirable at this time, a more flexible approach makes much more sense than the Court's constitutional straitjacket.

In re Gault

387 U.S. 1, 87 S.Ct. 1428 (1967)

Police arrested Gerald Gault, a fifteen-year-old, after a neighbor, Mrs. Cook, complained that he had made lewd remarks to her over the telephone. Gault's parents were neither notified by the police nor given a copy of the affidavit they filed for a court hearing. Gault was not advised of his rights to remain silent and to have the assistance of counsel. Moreover, Mrs. Cook was never called as a witness and no record was made of the court proceedings. Gault was found to be a juvenile delinquent and sentenced to a state industrial school for a maximum of six years (until he reached the age of twenty-one). Because under Arizona law there was no appeal in juvenile cases, the Gaults filed a petition for a writ of *habeas corpus* in state court. They challenged the constitutionality of Arizona's Juvenile Code for failing to afford juveniles numerous procedural guarantees that applied to adult criminal trials under the Fourteenth Amendment. A state superior court dismissed the writ and the Arizona Supreme Court affirmed. The Gaults then appealed to the Supreme Court, which granted *certiorari*.

The Court's decision was seven and one-half to one and one-half, and the majority's opinion was announced by Justice Fortas, Concurrences were by Justices Black and White. Justice Harlan delivered a separate opinion, in part concurring and dissenting. Justice Stewart dissented.

     ☐ *Justice FORTAS delivered the opinion of the Court.*

[A]ppellants . . . urge that we hold the Juvenile Code of Arizona invalid on its face or as applied in this case because, contrary to the Due Process Clause of the Fourteenth Amendment, the juvenile is taken from the custody of his parents and committed to a state institution pursuant to proceedings in which the Juvenile Court has virtually unlimited discretion, and in which the following basic rights are denied:

1. Notice of the charges;
2. Right to counsel;
3. Right to confrontation and cross-examination;
4. Privilege against self-incrimination;

5. Right to a transcript of the proceedings; and
6. Right to appellate review. . . .

From the inception of the juvenile court system, wide differences have been tolerated—indeed insisted upon—between the procedural rights accorded to adults and those of juveniles. In practically all jurisdictions, there are rights granted to adults which are withheld from juveniles. In addition to the specific problems involved in the present case, for example, it has been held that the juvenile is not entitled to bail, to indictment by grand jury, to a public trial or to trial by jury. It is frequent practice that rules governing the arrest and interrogation of adults by the police are not observed in the case of juveniles.

The history and theory underlying this development are well-known, but a recapitulation is necessary for purposes of this opinion. The Juvenile Court movement began in this country at the end of the last century. From the juvenile court statute adopted in Illinois in 1899, the system has spread to every State in the Union, the District of Columbia, and Puerto Rico. . . .

The early reformers were appalled by adult procedures and penalties, and by the fact that children could be given long prison sentences and mixed in jails with hardened criminals. They were profoundly convinced that society's duty to the child could not be confined by the concept of justice alone. They believed that society's role was not to ascertain whether the child was "guilty" or "innocent," but "What is he, how has he become what he is, and what had best be done in his interest and in the interest of the state to save him from a downward career." The child—essentially good, as they saw it— was to be made "to feel that he is the object of [the state's] care and solicitude," not that he was under arrest or on trial. The rules of criminal procedure were therefore altogether inapplicable. The apparent rigidities, technicalities, and harshness which they observed in both substantive and procedural criminal law were therefore to be discarded. The idea of crime and punishment was to be abandoned. The child was to be "treated" and "rehabilitated" and the procedures, from apprehension through institutionalization, were to be "clinical" rather than punitive.

These results were to be achieved, without coming to conceptual and constitutional grief, by insisting that the proceedings were not adversary, but that the state was proceeding as *parens patriae*. The Latin phrase proved to be a great help to those who sought to rationalize the exclusion of juveniles from the constitutional scheme; but its meaning is murky and its historic credentials are of dubious relevance. The phrase was taken from chancery practice, where, however, it was used to describe the power of the state to act *in loco parentis* for the purpose of protecting the property interests and the person of the child. But there is no trace of the doctrine in the history of criminal jurisprudence. At common law, children under seven were considered incapable of possessing criminal intent. Beyond that age, they were subjected to arrest, trial, and in theory to punishment like adult offenders. In these old days, the state was not deemed to have authority to accord them fewer procedural rights than adults.

The right of the state, as *parens patriae*, to deny to the child procedural rights available to his elders was elaborated by the assertion that a child, unlike an adult, has a right "not to liberty but to custody." He can be made to attorn to his parents, to go to school, etc. If his parents default in effectively performing their custodial functions—that is, if the child is "delinquent"—the state may intervene. In doing so, it does not deprive the child of any rights, because he has none. It merely provides the "custody" to which the child is entitled. On this basis, proceedings involving juveniles were described as "civil" not "criminal" and therefore not subject to the requirements which restrict the state when it seeks to deprive a person of his liberty.

Accordingly, the highest motives and most enlightened impulses led to a peculiar system for juveniles, unknown to our law in any comparable context. The constitutional and theoretical basis for this peculiar system is—to say the least—debatable. . . . In 1937, Dean Pound wrote: "The powers of the Star Chamber were a trifle in comparison with those of our juvenile courts. . . ." The absence of substantive standards has not necessarily meant that children receive careful, compassionate, individualized treatment. The absence of procedural rules based upon constitutional principle has not always produced fair, efficient, and effective procedures. . . .

Failure to observe the fundamental requirements of due process has resulted in instances, which might have been avoided, of unfairness to individuals and inadequate or inaccurate findings of fact and unfortunate prescriptions of remedy. Due process of law is the primary and indispensable foundation of individual freedom. It is the basic and essential term in the social compact which defines the rights of the individual and delimits the powers which the state may exercise. . . .

Further, it is urged that the juvenile benefits from informal proceedings in the court. The early conception of the Juvenile Court proceeding was one in which a fatherly judge touched the heart and conscience of the erring youth by talking over his problems, by paternal advice and admonition, and in which, in extreme situations, benevolent and wise institutions of the State provided guidance and help "to save him from a downward career." Then, as now, goodwill and compassion were admirably prevalent. But recent studies have, with surprising unanimity, entered sharp dissent as to the validity of this gentle conception. They suggest that the appearance as well as the actuality of fairness, impartiality and orderliness—in short, the essentials of due process—may be a more impressive and more therapeutic attitude so far as the juvenile is concerned. . . .

Ultimately, however, we confront the reality of that portion of the Juvenile Court process with which we deal in this case. A boy is charged with misconduct. The boy is committed to an institution where he may be restrained of liberty for years. It is of no constitutional consequence—and of limited practical meaning—that the institution to which he is committed is called an Industrial School. The fact of the matter is that, however euphemistic the title, a "receiving home" or an "industrial school" for juveniles is an institution of confinement in which the child is incarcerated for a greater or lesser time. His world becomes "a building with whitewashed walls, regimented routine and institutional hours. . . ." Instead of mother and father and sisters and brothers and friends and classmates, his world is peopled by guards, custodians, state employees, and "delinquents" confined with him for anything from waywardness to rape and homicide.

In view of this, it would be extraordinary if our Constitution did not require the procedural regularity and the exercise of care implied in the phrase "due process." Under our Constitution, the condition of being a boy does not justify a kangaroo court. The traditional ideas of Juvenile Court procedure, indeed, contemplated that time would be available and care would be used to establish precisely what the juvenile did and why he did it—was it a prank of adolescence or a brutal act threatening serious consequences to himself or society unless corrected? Under traditional notions, one would assume that in a case like that of Gerald Gault, where the juvenile appears to have a home, a working mother and father, and an older brother, the Juvenile Judge would have made a careful inquiry and judgment as to the possibility that the boy could be disciplined and dealt with at home, despite his previous transgressions. Indeed, so far as appears in the record before us, except for some conversation with Gerald about his school work and his "wanting to go to the . . . Grand Canyon with his father," the points to which the judge directed his attention were little different from those that would be involved in determining any charge of violation of a penal statute. The essential difference between Gerald's case and a normal criminal case is that safeguards available to adults were discarded in Gerald's case. The summary procedure as well as the long commitment was possible because Gerald was 15 years of age instead of over 18. . . .

[Justice FORTAS concluded by holding that in juvenile proceedings: (1) due process requires adequate and timely notice of the charges against an individual, (2) there is a right to counsel, (3) the privilege against self-incrimination is applicable, and (4) "absent a valid confession, a determination of delinquency and an order to a state institution cannot be sustained in the absence of sworn testimony subjected to the opportunity for cross-examination." Justice FORTAS did not rule on whether juveniles have a right to a transcript of their proceedings or on their right to appellate review.]

Rhode Island v. Innis

446 U.S. 291, 100 S.Ct. 1682 (1980)

In his opinion for the Court, Justice Potter Stewart discusses the facts, involving the issue of what is a police interrogation and when a confession compelled by police is in violation of *Miranda*.

The Court's decision was six to three, and the majority's opinion was announced by Justice Stewart. Concurrences were by Chief Justice Burger and Justice White. Dissents were by Justices Stevens and Marshall; Justice Brennan joined Justice Marshall's dissent.

☐ *Justice STEWART delivered the opinion of the Court.*

On the night of January 12, 1975, John Mulvaney, a Providence, R.I., taxicab driver, disappeared after being dispatched to pick up a customer. His body was discovered four days later buried in a shallow grave in Coventry, R.I. He had died from a shotgun blast aimed at the back of his head.

On January 17, 1975, shortly after midnight, the Providence police received a telephone call from Gerald Aubin, also a taxicab driver, who reported that he had just been robbed by a man wielding a sawed-off shotgun. Aubin further reported that he had dropped off his assailant near Rhode Island College in a section of Providence known as Mount Pleasant. While at the Providence police station waiting to give a statement, Aubin noticed a picture of his assailant on a bulletin board. Aubin so informed one of the police officers present. The officer prepared a photo array, and again Aubin identified a picture of the same person. That person was the respondent. Shortly thereafter, the Providence police began a search of the Mount Pleasant area.

At approximately 4:30 A.M. on the same date, Patrolman Lovell, while cruising the streets of Mount Pleasant in a patrol car, spotted the respondent standing in the street facing him. When Patrolman Lovell stopped his car, the respondent walked towards it. Patrolman Lovell then arrested the respondent, who was unarmed, and advised him of his so-called *Miranda* rights. While the two men waited in the patrol car for other police officers to arrive, Patrolman Lovell did not converse with the respondent other than to respond to the latter's request for a cigarette.

Within minutes, Sergeant Sears arrived at the scene of the arrest, and he also gave the respondent the *Miranda* warnings. Immediately thereafter, Captain Leyden and other police officers arrived. Captain Leyden advised the respondent of his *Miranda* rights. The respondent stated that he understood those rights and wanted to speak with a lawyer. Captain Leyden then directed that the respondent be placed in a "caged wagon," a four-door police car with a wire screen mesh between the front and rear seats, and be driven to the central police station. . . .

While en route to the central station, Patrolman Gleckman initiated a conversation with Patrolman McKenna concerning the missing shotgun. . . . Patrolman McKenna apparently shared his fellow officer's concern. . . . While Patrolman Williams said nothing, he overheard the conversation between the two officers:

> "A. He [Gleckman] said it would be too bad if the little—I believe he said a girl—would pick up the gun, maybe kill herself."

The respondent then interrupted the conversation, stating that the officers should turn the car around so he could show them where the gun was located. At this point, Patrolman McKenna radioed back to Captain Leyden that they were returning to the scene of the arrest and that the respondent would inform them of the location of the gun. At the time the respondent indicated that the officers should turn back, they had traveled no more than a mile, a trip encompassing only a few minutes.

The police vehicle then returned to the scene of the arrest where a search for the shotgun was in progress. There, Captain Leyden again advised the respondent of his *Miranda* rights. The respondent replied that he understood those rights but that he "wanted to get the gun out of the way because of the kids in the area in the school." The respondent then led the police to a nearby field, where he pointed out the shotgun under some rocks by the side of the road. . . .

It was the view of the state appellate court that, even though the police officers may have been genuinely concerned about the public safety and even though the respondent had not been addressed personally by the police officers, the respondent nonetheless had been subjected to "subtle coercion" that was the equivalent of "interrogation" within the meaning of the *Miranda* opinion. . . .

We granted *certiorari* to address for the first time the meaning of "interrogation" under *Miranda v. Arizona*. . . .

In the present case, the parties are in agreement that the respondent was fully informed of his *Miranda* rights and that he invoked his *Miranda* right to counsel when he told Captain Leyden that he wished to consult with a lawyer. It is also uncontested that the respondent was "in custody" while being transported to the police station.

The issue, therefore, is whether the respondent was "interrogated" by the police officers in violation of the respondent's undisputed right under *Miranda* to remain silent until he had consulted with a lawyer. In resolving this issue, we first define the term "interrogation" under *Miranda* before turning to a consideration of the facts of this case.

The starting point for defining "interrogation" in this context is, of course, the Court's *Miranda* opinion. There the Court observed that "[b]y custodial interrogation, we mean *questioning* initiated by law enforcement officers after a person has been taken into custody or otherwise deprived of his freedom of action in any significant way." (emphasis added). This passage and other references throughout the opinion to "questioning" might suggest that the *Miranda* rules were to apply only to those police interrogation practices that involve express questioning of a defendant while in custody.

We do not, however, construe the *Miranda* opinion so narrowly. The concern of the Court in *Miranda* was that the "interrogation environment" created by the interplay of interrogation and custody would "subjugate the individual to the will of his examiner" and thereby undermine the privilege against compulsory self-incrimination. The police practices that evoked this concern included several that did not involve express questioning. For example, one of the practices discussed in *Miranda* was the use of line-ups in which a coached witness would pick the defendant as the perpetrator. . . .

This is not to say, however, that all statements obtained by the police after a person has been taken into custody are to be considered the product of interrogation. As the Court in *Miranda* noted:

> "Confessions remain a proper element in law enforcement. Any statement given freely and voluntarily without any compelling influences is, of course, admissible in evidence. *The fundamental import of the privilege while an individual is in custody is not whether he is allowed to talk to the police without the benefit of warnings and counsel, but whether he can be interrogated*. . . . Volunteered statements of any kind are not barred by the Fifth Amendment and their admissibility is not affected by our holding today." (emphasis added).

It is clear therefore that the special procedural safeguards outlined in *Miranda* are required not where a suspect is simply taken into custody, but rather where a suspect in custody is subjected to interrogation. "Interrogation," as conceptualized in the *Miranda* opinion, must reflect a measure of compulsion above and beyond that inherent in custody itself.

We conclude that the *Miranda* safeguards come into play whenever a person in custody is subjected to either express questioning or its functional equivalent. That is to say, the term "interrogation" under *Miranda* refers not only to express questioning, but also to any words or actions on the part of the police (other than those normally attendant to arrest and custody) that the police should know are reasonably likely to elicit an incriminating response from the suspect. . . .

Turning to the facts of the present case, we conclude that the respondent was not "interrogated" within the meaning of *Miranda*. It is undisputed that the first prong of the definition of "interrogation" was not satisfied, for the conversation between Patrolmen Gleckman and McKenna included no express questioning of the respondent. Rather, that conversation was, at least in form, nothing more than a dialogue between the two officers to which no response from the respondent was invited.

Moreover, it cannot be fairly concluded that the respondent was subjected to the "functional equivalent" of questioning. It cannot be said, in short, that Patrolmen Gleckman and McKenna should have known that their conversation was reasonably likely to elicit an incriminating response from the respondent. There is nothing in the record to suggest that the officers were aware that the respondent was peculiarly susceptible to an appeal to his conscience concerning the safety of handicapped children. Nor is there anything in the record to suggest that the police knew that the respondent was unusually disoriented or upset at the time of his arrest.

The case thus boils down to whether, in the context of a brief conversation, the officers should have known that the respondent would suddenly be moved to make a self-incriminating response. Given the fact that the entire conversation appears to have consisted of no more than a few offhand remarks, we cannot say that the officers should have known that it was reasonably likely that Innis would so respond. . . .

For the reasons stated, the judgment of the Supreme Court of Rhode Island is vacated, and the case is remanded to that court for further proceedings not inconsistent with this opinion.

It is so ordered.

☐ *Justice MARSHALL, with whom Justice BRENNAN joins, dissenting.*

I am substantially in agreement with the Court's definition of "interrogation" within the meaning of *Miranda v. Arizona*. . . . In my view, the *Miranda* safeguards apply whenever police conduct is intended or likely to produce a response from a suspect in custody. As I read the Court's opinion, its definition of "interrogation" for *Miranda* purposes is equivalent, for practical purposes, to my formulation, since it contemplates that "where a police practice is designed to elicit an incriminating response from the accused, it is unlikely that the practice will not also be one which the police should have known was reasonably likely to have that effect." Thus, the Court requires an objective inquiry into the likely effect of police conduct on a typical individual, taking into account any special susceptibility of the suspect to certain kinds of pressure of which the police know or have reason to know.

I am utterly at a loss, however, to understand how this objective standard as applied to the facts before us can rationally lead to the conclusion that there was no interrogation. . . .

The Court attempts to characterize Gleckman's statements as "no more than a few off hand remarks" which could not reasonably have been expected to elicit a response. If the statements had been addressed to respondent, it would be impossible to draw such a conclusion. The simple message of the "talking back and forth" between Gleckman and McKenna was that they had to find the shotgun to avert a child's death.

One can scarcely imagine a stronger appeal to the conscience of a suspect—*any* suspect—than the assertion that if the weapon is not found an innocent person will be hurt or killed. And not just any innocent person, but an innocent child—a little girl—a helpless, handicapped little girl on her way to school. The notion that such an appeal could not be expected to have any effect unless the suspect were known to have some special interest in handicapped children verges on the ludicrous. As a matter of fact, the appeal to a suspect to confess for the sake of others, to "display some evidence of decency and honor," is a classic interrogation technique. . . . This is not a case where police officers speaking among themselves are accidentally overheard by a suspect. These officers were "talking back and forth" in close quarters with the handcuffed suspect, traveling past the very place where they believed the weapon was located. They knew petitioner would hear and attend to their conversation, and they are chargeable with knowledge of and responsibility for the pressures to speak which they created.

I firmly believe that this case is simply an aberration, and that in future cases the Court will apply the standard adopted today in accordance with its plain meaning.

Duckworth v. Eagan

492 U.S. 195, 109 S.Ct. 2875 (1989)

When first questioned by police about the stabbing of a woman, Gary Eagan made an exculpatory statement after being read and signing a waiver form that provided that if he could not afford a lawyer, one would be appointed for him "if and when you go to court." But a day later when being questioned again and after signing a different waiver form, Eagan confessed to the stabbing and led officers to a site where they recovered pertinent physical evidence. Over Eagan's attorney's objections, his two statements were admitted into evidence during trial. Following his conviction, Eagan unsuccessfully appealed to the Indiana Supreme Court and then applied for a writ of *habeas corpus* in federal district court. Eagan claimed, among other things, that his confession was inadmissible because the first waiver form did not comply with the requirements of *Miranda v. Arizona* (see excerpt above). The court denied his petition, holding that the record showed adherence to *Miranda*.

But the Court of Appeals for the Seventh Circuit reversed on the grounds that the police informing Eagan that counsel would be appointed "if and when you go to court" was constitutionally defective, since it failed to make a clear and unequivocal warning that Eagan had a right to an appointed attorney before interrogation and because the police warning linked the right to counsel to a future event. The state appealed that ruling to the Supreme Court, which granted review.

The Court's decision was five to four, and the majority's opinion was announced by Chief Justice Rehnquist. Justice O'Connor's concurrence was joined by Justice Scalia. Justice Marshall dissented and was joined by Justices Brennan, Blackmun, and Stevens.

☐ *Chief Justice REHNQUIST delivered the opinion of the Court.*

[C]*ertiorari* . . . [was granted] to resolve a conflict among the lower courts as to whether informing a suspect that an attorney would be appointed for him "if and when you go to court" renders *Miranda* warnings inadequate. We agree with the majority of the lower courts that it does not.

In *Miranda v. Arizona*, 384 U.S. 436 (1966), the Court established certain procedural safeguards that require police to advise criminal suspects of their rights under the Fifth and Fourteenth Amendments before commencing custodial interrogation. In now-familiar words, the Court said that the suspect must be told that "he has the right to remain silent, that anything he says can be used against him in a court of law, that he has the right to the presence of an attorney, and that if he cannot afford an attorney one will be appointed for him prior to any questioning if he so desires." The Court in *Miranda* "presumed that interrogation in certain custodial circumstances is inherently coercive and . . . that statements made under those circumstances are inadmissible unless the suspect is specifically warned of his *Miranda* rights and freely decides to forgo those rights." *New York v. Quarles*, 467 U.S. 649 (1984). . . .

We have never insisted that *Miranda* warnings be given in the exact form described in that decision. In *Miranda* itself, the Court said that "[t]he warnings required and the waiver necessary in accordance with our opinion today are, *in the absence of a fully effective equivalent*, prerequisites to the admissibility of any statement made by a defendant." . . .

Miranda has not been limited to stationhouse questioning, see *Rhode Island v. Innis*, [446 U.S. 291 (1980)] (police car), and the officer in the field may not always have access to printed *Miranda* warnings, or he may inadvertently depart from routine practice, particularly if a suspect requests an elaboration of the warnings. The prophylactic *Miranda* warnings are "not themselves rights protected by the Constitution but [are] instead measures to insure that the right against compulsory self-incrimination [is] protected." *Michigan v. Tucker*, 417 U.S. 433 (1974). Reviewing courts therefore need not examine *Miranda* warnings as if construing a will or defining the terms of an easement. The inquiry is simply whether the warnings reasonably "convey[y] to [a suspect] his rights as required by *Miranda*." [*California v.*] *Prysock*, [453 U.S. 355 (1981)] . . .

We think the initial warnings given to respondent touched all of the bases required by *Miranda*. The police told respondent that he had the right to remain silent, that anything he said could be used against him in court, that he had the right to speak to an attorney before and during questioning, that he had "this right to the advice and presence of a lawyer even if [he could] not afford to hire one," and that he had the "right to stop answering at any time until [he] talked to a lawyer." . . . [T]he police also added that they could not provide respondent with a lawyer, but that one would be appointed "if and when you go to court." The Court of Appeals thought this "if and when you go to court" language suggested that "only those accused who can afford an attorney have the right to have one present before answering any questions," and "implie[d] that if the accused does not 'go to court,' *i.e.*[,] the government does not file charges, the accused is not entitled to [counsel] at all." . . .

In our view, the Court of Appeals misapprehended the effect of the inclusion of "if and when you go to court" language in *Miranda* warnings. First, this instruction accurately described the procedure for the appointment of counsel in Indiana. . . . We think it must be relatively commonplace for a suspect, after receiving *Miranda* warnings, to ask *when* he will obtain counsel. The "if and when you go to court" advice simply anticipates that question. Second, *Miranda* does not require that attorneys be producible on call, but only that the suspect be informed, as here, that he has the right to an attorney before and during questioning, and that an attorney would be appointed for him if he could not afford one. The Court in *Miranda* emphasized that it was not suggesting that "each police station must have a 'station house lawyer' present at all times to advise prisoners." If the police cannot provide appointed counsel, *Miranda* requires only that the police not question a suspect unless he waives his right to counsel. Here, respondent did just that.

The judgment of the Court of Appeals is accordingly reversed, and the case is remanded for further proceedings not inconsistent with our decision.

It is so ordered.

☐ *Justice MARSHALL, with whom Justice BRENNAN joins, and with whom Justice BLACKMUN and Justice STEVENS join as to Part I, dissenting.*

■ I

The majority holds today that a police warning advising a suspect that he is entitled to an appointed lawyer only "if and when he goes to court" satisfies the requirements of *Miranda v. Arizona*, 384 U.S. 436 (1966). The majority reaches this result by seriously mischaracterizing that decision. Under *Miranda*, a police warning must "*clearly infor[m]*" a suspect taken into custody "that if he cannot afford an attorney one will be appointed for him *prior to any questioning* if he so desires." A warning qualified by an "if and when you go to court" caveat does nothing of the kind; instead, it leads the suspect to believe that a lawyer will not be provided until some indeterminate time in the future *after questioning*. I refuse to acquiesce in the continuing debasement of this historic precedent, and therefore dissent. I also write to express my disagreement with Justice O'CONNOR's uninvited suggestion that the rationale of *Stone v. Powell*, 428 U.S. 465 (1976), should be extended to bar federal *habeas* review of *Miranda* claims.

In concluding that the first warning given to respondent Eagan satisfies the dictates of *Miranda*, the majority makes a mockery of that decision. Eagan was initially advised that he had the right to the presence of counsel before and during questioning. But in the very next breath, the police informed Eagan that, if he could not afford a lawyer, one would be appointed to represent him only "if and when" he went to court. As the Court of Appeals found, Eagan could easily have concluded from the "if and when" caveat that only "those accused who can afford an attorney have the right to have one present before answering any questions; those who are not so fortunate must wait." Eagan was, after all, never told that questioning would be *delayed* until a lawyer was appointed "if and when" Eagan did, in fact, go to court. Thus, the "if and when" caveat may well have had the effect of negating the initial promise that counsel could be present. At best, a suspect like Eagan "would not know . . . whether or not he had a right to the services of a lawyer."

In lawyer-like fashion, the CHIEF JUSTICE parses the initial warnings given Eagan and finds that the most plausible interpretation is that Eagan would not be questioned until a lawyer was appointed when he later appeared in court. What goes wholly overlooked in the CHIEF JUSTICE's analysis is that the recipients of police warnings are often frightened suspects unlettered in the law, not lawyers or judges or others schooled in interpreting legal or semantic nuance. Such suspects can hardly be expected to interpret, in as facile a manner as the CHIEF JUSTICE, "the pretzel-like warnings here—intertwining, contradictory, and ambiguous as they are." The majority thus refuses to recognize that "[t]he warning of a right to counsel would be hollow if not couched in terms that would convey to the indigent—the person most often subjected to interrogation—the knowledge that he too has the right to have counsel present." *Miranda*. . . .

Even if the typical suspect could draw the inference the majority does—that questioning will not commence until a lawyer is provided at a later court appearance—a warning qualified by an "if and when" caveat still fails to give a suspect any indication of *when* he will be taken to court. Upon hearing the warnings given in this case, a suspect would likely conclude that no lawyer would be provided until trial. In common parlance, "going to court" is synonymous with "going to trial." Furthermore, the negative implication of the caveat is that, if the suspect is never taken to court, he "is not entitled to an attorney at all." An unwitting suspect harboring uncertainty on this score is precisely the sort of person who may feel compelled to talk "voluntarily" to the police, without the presence of counsel, in an effort to extricate himself from his predicament. . . .

Miranda, it is true, does not require the police to have a "station house lawyer" ready at all times to counsel suspects taken into custody. But if a suspect does not understand that a lawyer will be made available within a reasonable period of time after he has been taken into custody and advised of his rights, the suspect may decide to talk to the police *for that reason alone*. The threat of an indefinite deferral of interrogation, in a system like Indiana's, thus constitutes an effective means by which the police can pressure a suspect to speak without the presence of counsel. . . .

The majority's misreading of *Miranda*—stating that police warnings need only "touc[h] all of the bases required by *Miranda*," that *Miranda* warnings need only be "reasonably conve[yed]" to a suspect, and that *Miranda* warnings are to be measured not point by point but "in their totality"—is exacerbated by its interpretation of *California v. Prysock*, 453 U.S. 355 (1981) (*per curiam*), a decision that squarely supports Eagan's claim in this case. The juvenile suspect in *Prysock* was initially told that he had the right to have a lawyer present before and during questioning. He then was told that he had the right to have his parents present as well. At this point the suspect was informed that a lawyer would be appointed to represent him at no cost if he could not afford one. The California Court of Appeal ruled these warnings insufficient because the suspect was not expressly told of his right to an appointed attorney before and during questioning. This Court reversed, finding that "nothing in the warnings given respondent suggested any limitation on the right to the presence of appointed counsel." . . .

In reaching this result, the *Prysock* Court pointedly distinguished a series of lower court decisions that had found inadequate warnings in which "the reference to the right to appointed counsel was linked with some future point in time." . . .

It poses no great burden on law enforcement officers to eradicate the confusion stemming from the "if and when" caveat. Deleting the sentence containing the offending language is all that needs to be done. Purged of this language, the warning tells the suspect in a straightforward fashion that he has the right to the presence of a lawyer before and during questioning, and that a lawyer will be appointed if he cannot afford one. The suspect is given no reason to believe that the appointment of an attorney may come after interrogation. . . .

■ **II**

Not content with disemboweling *Miranda* directly, Justice O'CONNOR seeks to do so indirectly as well, urging that federal courts be barred from considering *Miranda* claims on habeas corpus review. In *Stone v. Powell*, 428 U.S. 465 (1976), the Court held that a state prisoner may not seek federal *habeas corpus* relief on the ground that evidence was obtained in violation of his Fourth Amendment rights if the state courts had provided a full and fair opportunity for litigation of that claim. I joined Justice BRENNAN's dissenting opinion in that case, in which he warned that the majority's rationale "portends substantial evisceration of federal *habeas corpus* jurisdiction." . . . Today, however, Justice O'CONNOR seeks to extend *Stone* beyond the Fourth Amendment even though this issue was not raised by petitioner Duckworth below or in his petition for *certiorari*. Her concurring opinion evinces such a palpable distaste for collateral review of state court judgments that it can only be viewed as a harbinger of future assaults on federal *habeas corpus*.

Stone was wrong when it was decided and it is wrong today. I have read and reread the federal *habeas corpus* statute, but I am unable to find any statement to the effect that certain federal claims are unworthy of collateral protection, or that certain federal claims are more worthy of collateral protection than others. Congress did not delineate "second class" claims when it created federal *habeas* jurisdiction. On the contrary, Congress deemed *all* federal claims worthy of collateral protection when it extended the writ to any person "in custody pursuant to the judgment of a State Court . . . in violation of the Constitution or laws or treaties of the United States." At a time when plain language is supposed to count for something, Justice O'CONNOR's suggestion that the Court carve out an exception that has no rooting in the text of the *habeas* statute is difficult to justify.

Under Article III of the Constitution, Congress—not this Court—determines the scope of jurisdiction of the inferior federal courts. Congress is undoubtedly aware that federal *habeas* review of state criminal convictions might disserve interests of comity and finality and might make the enforcement of state criminal laws more difficult. Congress has determined, however, that the individual's interest in vindicating his federal rights in a federal forum outweighs these concerns. Federal courts, not state courts, thus have the "last say."

It is not only disapprobation for federal *habeas* review that pervades Justice O'CONNOR's concurring opinion, but also a profound distaste for *Miranda*. How else to explain the remarkable statement that "*no* significant federal values are at stake" when *Miranda* claims are raised in federal *habeas corpus* proceedings? But irrespective of one's view of the merits of *Miranda*, the critical point is that *Miranda* is *still good law*. . . .

In any event, I vehemently oppose the suggestion that it is for the Court to decide, based on our own vague notions of comity, finality, and the intrinsic value of particular constitutional rights, which claims are worthy of collateral federal review and which are not. Congress already engaged in that balancing process when it created *habeas* review and extended the federal courts' jurisdiction to all claims based on a violation of federal law. The federal courts have been reviewing *Miranda* claims on federal *habeas* for 23 years and Congress has never even remotely indicated that they have been remiss in doing so. To the extent Justice O'CONNOR is unhappy with *Miranda*, she should address that decision head-on. But an endrun through the *habeas* statute is judicial activism at its worst.

Arizona v. Fulminante

499 U.S. 279, 111 S.CT. 1246 (1991)

While serving time in a federal prison for another crime, Oreste C. Fulminante made an incriminating confession to a fellow inmate, Anthony Sarivola, who was actually an informer for the Federal Bureau of Investigation (FBI). He did so because the informer offered to protect him from violence in the prison, but only on the condition that he give him a full account of the murder of Fulminante's eleven-year-old stepdaughter. Fulminante agreed and told Sarivola how he had murdered his stepdaughter. His confession to Sarivola, along with another, less detailed confession made to Sarivola's wife after his release from prison, was later introduced as evidence against him in a trial for murdering his stepdaughter. Following his conviction, Fulminante's attorney appealed to the Arizona Supreme Court, which overturned the conviction. Based on rulings of the Supreme Court of the United States, the state supreme court found that Fulmininate's confession was involuntary and coerced, that the use of the confession at his trial was not a harmless error, and thus Fulminante was entitled to a retrial. The state then appealed that decision to the Supreme Court, which granted review.

The Court's decision was five to four and five to three. The justices were extraordinarily divided on the opinion announced by Justice White, who commanded only a bare majority on just two of the three issues presented. A separate opinion by Chief Justice Rehnquist, in part dissenting and commanding another majority on the central issue, was joined by Justice O'Connor and in parts by Justices Kennedy, Souter, and Scalia. Justice White's opinion held (1) that Fulminante's confession was coerced and (2) that its use as evidence against him at trial was not harmless beyond a reasonable doubt. His opinion on both of those issues was joined by Justices Blackmun, Marshall, and Stevens. And White commanded a bare majority by picking up the vote of Justice Scalia on (1) and the vote of Justice Kennedy on (2). On the latter issue, Chief Justice Rehnquist and Justices O'Connor and Scalia dissented, and Justice Souter failed to indicate how or even whether he voted on that issue. The separate opinion by Chief Justice Rehnquist in turn commanded four votes (O'Connor, Kennedy, Souter, and Scalia) for another bare majority holding that (3) the admission at trial of coerced confessions may be excused as a harmless error if there is other evidence that adequately supports a guilty verdict.

☐ *Justice WHITE delivered the opinion of the Court.*

Although the question is a close one, we agree with the Arizona Supreme Court's conclusion that Fulminante's confession was coerced. . . . Accepting the Arizona court's finding, permissible on this record, that there was a credible threat of physical violence, we agree with its conclusion that Fulminante's will was overborne in such a way as to render his confession the product of coercion.

Four of us, Justices MARSHALL, BLACKMUN, STEVENS, and myself, would affirm the judgment of the Arizona Supreme Court on the ground that the harmless-error rule is inapplicable to erroneously admitted coerced confessions. We thus disagree with the Justices who have a contrary view.

The majority today abandons what until now the Court has regarded as the "axiomatic [proposition] that a defendant in a criminal case is deprived of due process of law if his conviction is founded, in whole or in part, upon an involuntary confession, without regard for the truth or falsity of the confession, and even though there is ample evidence aside from the confession to support the conviction." *Jackson v. Denno*, 378 U.S. 368 (1964). . . .

In extending to coerced confessions the harmless-error rule of *Chapman v. United States*, 386 U.S. 18 (1967), the majority declares that because the Court has applied that analysis to numerous other "trial errors," there is no reason that it should not apply to an error of this nature as well. The four of us remain convinced, however, that we should abide by our cases that have refused to apply the harmless-error rule to coerced confessions, for a coerced confession is fundamentally different from other types of erroneously admitted evidence to which the rule has been applied. . . .

Chapman specifically noted three constitutional errors that could not be categorized as harmless error: using a coerced confession against a defendant in a criminal trial, depriving a defendant of counsel, or trying a defendant before a biased judge. The majority attempts to distinguish the use of a coerced confession from the other two errors listed in *Chapman* first by distorting the decision in *Payne v. Arkansas* [356 U.S. 560 (1958)] and then by drawing a meaningless dichotomy between "trial errors" and "structural defects" in the trial process. . . .

The search for truth is indeed central to our system of justice, but "certain constitutional rights are not, and should not be, subject to harmless-error analysis because those rights protect important values that are unrelated to the truth-seeking function of the trial." *Rose v. Clark*, 478 U.S. 570 (1986). The right of a defendant not to have his coerced confession used against him is among those rights, for using a coerced confession "abort[s] the fair trial process and "render[s] a trial fundamentally unfair." *Id.*

For the foregoing reasons the four of us would adhere to the consistent line of authority that has recognized as a basic tenet of our criminal justice system, before and after both *Miranda* and *Chapman*, the prohibition against using a defendant's coerced confession against him at his criminal trial. *Stare decisis* is "of fundamental importance to the rule of law." *Welch v. Texas Highways and Public Transp.*, 483 U.S. 468 (1987); the majority offers no convincing reason for overturning our long line of decisions requiring the exclusion of coerced confessions.

Since five Justices have determined that harmless-error analysis applies to coerced confessions, it becomes necessary to evaluate under that ruling the admissibility of Fulminante's confession to Sarivola. . . . Five of us are of the view that the State has not carried its burden and accordingly affirm the judgment of the court below reversing petitioner's conviction. . . .

Our review of the record leads us to conclude that the State has failed to meet its burden of establishing, beyond a reasonable doubt, that the admission of Fulminante's confession to Anthony Sarivola was harmless error. Three considerations compel this result.

First, the transcript discloses that both the trial court and the State recognized that a successful prosecution depended on the jury believing the two confessions. Absent the confessions, it is unlikely that Fulminante would have been prosecuted at all. . . .

Second, the jury's assessment of the confession to Donna Sarivola could easily have depended in large part on the presence of the confession to Anthony Sarivola. Absent the admission at trial of the first confession, the jurors might have found Donna Sarivola's story unbelievable. . . .

Third, the admission of the first confession led to the admission of other evidence prejudicial to Fulminante. For example, the State introduced evidence that Fulminante knew of Sarivola's connections with organized crime in an attempt to explain why Fulminante would have been motivated to confess to Sarivola in seeking protection. Absent the confession, this evidence would have no relevance and would have been inadmissible at trial. . . .

In declaring that Fulminante "acted with an especially heinous and depraved state of mind," the sentencing judge relied solely on the two confessions. Although the sentencing judge might have reached the same conclusions even without the confession to Anthony Sarivola, it is impossible to say so beyond a reasonable doubt. . . . Because a majority of the Court has determined that Fulminante's confession to Anthony Sarivola was coerced and because a majority has determined that admitting this confession was not harmless beyond a reasonable doubt, we agree with the Arizona Supreme Court's conclusion that Fulminante is entitled to a new trial at which the confession is not admitted. Accordingly the judgment of the Arizona Supreme Court is

Affirmed.

☐ *Chief Justice REHNQUIST, with whom Justice O'CONNOR joins, Justice KENNEDY and Justice SOUTER join as to parts I and II, and Justice SCALIA joins as to parts II and III, concurring as to part II, and dissenting as to parts I and III.*

■ II

Since this Court's landmark decision in *Chapman v. California*, 386 U.S. 18 (1967), in which we adopted the general rule that a constitutional error does not automatically require reversal of a conviction, the Court has applied harmless-error analysis to a wide range of errors and has recognized that most constitutional errors can be harmless. . . .

The admission of an involuntary confession—a classic "trial error"—is markedly different from the other two constitutional violations referred to in the *Chapman* footnote as not being subject to harmless-error analysis. One of those cases, *Gideon v. Wainwright*, 372 U.S. 335 (1963), involved the total deprivation of the right to counsel at trial. The other, *Turney v. Ohio*, 273 U.S. 510 (1927), involved a judge who was not impartial. These are structural defects in the constitution of the trial mechanism, which defy analysis by "harmless-error" standards. The entire conduct of the trial from beginning to end is obviously affected by the absence of counsel for a criminal defendant, just as it is by the presence on the bench of a judge who is not impartial. Since our decision in *Chapman*, other cases have added to the category of constitutional errors which are not subject to harmless error the following: unlawful exclusion of members of the defendant's race from a grand jury, *Vasquez v. Hillery*, 474 U.S. 254 (1986); the right to self-representation at trial, *McKaskle v. Wiggins*, 465 U.S. 168 (1984); and the right to public trial, *Waller v. Georgia*, 467 U.S. 39 (1984). Each of these constitutional deprivations is a similar structural defect affecting the framework within which the trial proceeds, rather than simply an error in the trial process itself. . . .

It is evident from a comparison of the constitutional violations which we have held subject to harmless error, and those which we have held not, that involuntary statements or confessions belong in the former category. The admission is a "trial error," similar in both degree and kind to the erroneous admission of other types of evidence. The evidentiary impact of an involuntary confession, and its effect upon the composition of the record, is indistinguishable from that of a confession obtained in violation of the Sixth Amendment—of evidence seized in violation of the Fourth Amendment—or [as in *Chapman*] of a prosecutor's improper comment on a defendant's silence at trial in violation of the Fifth Amendment.

■ III

I would agree with the finding of the Supreme Court of Arizona in its initial opinion—in which it believed harmless-error analysis was applicable to the admission of involuntary confessions—that the admission of Fulminante's confession was harmless. Indeed, this seems to me to be a classic case of harmless error; a second confession giving more details of the crime than the first was admitted in evidence and found to be free of any constitutional objection.

Dickerson v. United States

530 U.S. 428, 120 S.CT. 2326 (2000)

In *Miranda v. Arizona*, 384 U.S. 436 (1966), the Supreme Court held that before police question criminal suspects, they must warn them of their Fifth and Sixth Amendment rights to remain silent and to have an attorney present; otherwise, any incriminating statements are considered involuntary and excluded at trial. That decision applied to all state courts and remains controversial. Two years later, Congress enacted the Crime Control and Safe Streets Act of 1968, in which Section 3501 specified that the pre-*Miranda* standard of "the totality of circumstances" for determining the voluntariness of a confession would apply in federal courts, not whether a defendant had been given the *Miranda* warnings. Subsequently, the Department of Justice, in both Republican and Democratic administrations, except in a couple of cases during the administration of Republican president Ronald Reagan, maintained the position that *Miranda* governed in both state and federal criminal prosecutions.

In 1997 Thomas Dickerson was arrested and indicted for bank robbery. At a pretrial hearing, his attorney moved to suppress an incriminating statement made at a Federal Bureau of Investigation office on the ground that the agents failed to read Dickerson his *Miranda* rights.

A federal district court agreed that *Miranda* applied, but the Court of Appeals for the Fourth Circuit reversed, holding that *Miranda* was not a constitutional ruling and therefore Congress could determine the standard for voluntary confessions admitted into evidence in federal courts. That decision was appealed, and the Supreme Court granted review.

The appellate court's decision was reversed in a seven-to-two decision, and opinion for the Court was delivered by Chief Justice Rehnquist. Justice Scalia filed a dissenting opinion, which Justice Thomas joined.

☐ *Chief Justice REHNQUIST delivered the opinion of the Court.*

We hold that *Miranda*, being a constitutional decision of this Court, may not be in effect overruled by an Act of Congress, and we decline to overrule *Miranda* ourselves. We therefore hold that *Miranda* and its progeny in this Court govern the admissibility of statements made during custodial interrogation in both state and federal courts. . . .

In *Miranda*, we noted that the advent of modern custodial police interrogation brought with it an increased concern about confessions obtained by coercion. Because custodial police interrogation, by its very nature, isolates and pressures the individual, we stated that "[e]ven without employing brutality, the 'third degree' or [other] specific stratagems, custodial interrogation exacts a heavy toll on individual liberty and trades on the weakness of individuals." We concluded that the coercion inherent in custodial interrogation blurs the line between voluntary and involuntary statements, and thus heightens the risk that an individual will not be "accorded his privilege under the Fifth Amendment not to be compelled to incriminate himself." Accordingly, we laid down "concrete constitutional guidelines for law enforcement agencies and courts to follow." Those guidelines established that the admissibility in evidence of any statement given during custodial interrogation of a suspect would depend on whether the police provided the suspect with four warnings. These warnings (which have come to be known colloquially as "*Miranda* rights") are: a suspect "has the right to remain silent, that anything he says can be used against him in a court of law, that he has the right to the presence of an attorney, and that if he cannot afford an attorney one will be appointed for him prior to any questioning if he so desires."

Two years after *Miranda* was decided, Congress enacted Section 3501. Given Section 3501's express designation of voluntariness as the touchstone of admissibility, its omission of any warning requirement, and the instruction for trial courts to consider a nonexclusive list of factors relevant to the circumstances of a confession, we agree with the Court of Appeals that Congress intended by its enactment to overrule *Miranda*. Because of the obvious conflict between our decision in *Miranda* and Section 3501, we must address whether Congress has constitutional authority to thus supersede *Miranda*. If Congress has such authority, Section 3501's totality-of-the-circumstances approach must prevail over *Miranda*'s requirement of warnings; if not, that section must yield to *Miranda*'s more specific requirements.

The law in this area is clear. This Court has supervisory authority over the federal courts, and we may use that authority to prescribe rules of evidence and procedure that are binding in those tribunals. However, the power to judicially create and enforce nonconstitutional "rules of procedure and evidence for the federal courts exists only in the absence of a relevant Act of Congress." Congress retains the ultimate authority to modify or set aside any judicially created rules of evidence and procedure that are not required by the Constitution.

But Congress may not legislatively supersede our decisions interpreting and applying the Constitution. See, e.g., *City of Boerne v. Flores*, 521 U.S. 507 (1997). This case therefore turns on whether the *Miranda* Court announced a constitutional rule or merely exercised its supervisory authority to regulate evidence in the absence of congressional direction. Recognizing this point, the Court of Appeals surveyed *Miranda* and its progeny to determine the constitutional status of the *Miranda* decision. Relying on the fact that we have created several exceptions to *Miranda*'s warnings requirement and that we have repeatedly referred to the *Miranda* warnings as "prophylactic," *New York v. Quarles*, 467 U.S. 649 (1984), and "not themselves rights protected by the Constitution," *Michigan v. Tucker*, 417 U.S. 433 (1974), the Court of Appeals concluded that the protections announced in *Miranda* are not constitutionally required.

We disagree with the Court of Appeals' conclusion, although we concede that there is language in some of our opinions that supports the view taken by that court. But first and foremost of the factors on the other side—that *Miranda* is a constitutional decision—is that both *Miranda* and two of its companion cases applied the rule to proceedings in state courts—to wit, Arizona, California, and New York. Since that time, we have consistently applied *Miranda*'s rule to prosecutions arising in state courts. It is beyond dispute that we do not hold a supervisory power over the courts of the several States.

The *Miranda* opinion itself begins by stating that the Court granted *certiorari* "to explore some facets of the problems of applying the privilege against self-incrimination to in-custody interrogation, and to give concrete constitutional guidelines for law enforcement agencies and courts to follow." In fact, the majority opinion is replete with statements indicating that the majority thought it was announcing a constitutional rule. Indeed, the Court's ultimate conclusion was that the unwarned confessions obtained in the four cases before the Court in *Miranda* "were obtained from the defendant under circumstances that did not meet constitutional standards for protection of the privilege." . . .

Whether or not we would agree with *Miranda*'s reasoning and its resulting rule, were we addressing the issue in the first instance, the principles of *stare decisis* weigh heavily against overruling it now.

We do not think there is such justification for overruling *Miranda*. *Miranda* has become embedded in routine police practice to the point where the warnings have become part of our national culture. See *Mitchell v. United States*, 526 U.S. 314 (1999) (SCALIA, J., dissenting) (stating that the fact that a rule has found "wide acceptance in the legal culture" is "adequate reason not to overrule" it). While we have overruled our precedents when subsequent cases have undermined their doctrinal underpinnings, we do not believe that this has happened to the *Miranda* decision. If anything, our subsequent cases have reduced the impact of the *Miranda* rule on legitimate law enforcement while reaffirming the decision's core ruling that unwarned statements may not be used as evidence in the prosecution's case in chief. . . .

In sum, we conclude that *Miranda* announced a constitutional rule that Congress may not supersede legislatively. Following the rule of *stare decisis*, we decline to overrule *Miranda* ourselves. The judgment of the Court of Appeals is therefore Reversed.

☐ *Justice SCALIA, with whom Justice THOMAS joins, dissenting.*

Those to whom judicial decisions are an unconnected series of judgments that produce either favored or disfavored results will doubtless greet today's decision as a paragon of moderation, since it declines to overrule *Miranda v. Arizona*. Those who understand the judicial process will appreciate that today's decision is not a reaffirmation of *Miranda*, but a radical revision of the most significant element of *Miranda* (as of all cases): the rationale that gives it a permanent place in our jurisprudence.

Marbury v. Madison, 1 Cranch 137 (1803), held that an Act of Congress will not be enforced by the courts if what it prescribes violates the Constitution of the United States. That was the basis on which *Miranda* was decided. One will search today's opinion in vain, however, for a statement (surely simple enough to make) that what Section 3501 prescribes—the use at trial of a voluntary confession, even when a *Miranda* warning or its equivalent has failed to be given—violates the Constitution. The reason the statement does not appear is not only (and perhaps not so much) that it would be absurd, inasmuch as Section 3501 excludes from trial precisely what the Constitution excludes from trial, *viz.*, compelled confessions; but also that Justices whose votes are needed to compose today's majority are on record as believing that a violation of *Miranda* is not a violation of the Constitution. And so, to justify today's agreed-upon result, the Court must adopt a significant new, if not entirely comprehensible, principle of constitutional law. As the Court chooses to describe that principle, statutes of Congress can be disregarded, not only when what they prescribe violates the Constitution, but when what they prescribe contradicts a decision of this Court that "announced a constitutional rule." As I shall discuss in some detail, the only thing that can possibly mean in the context of this case is that this Court has the power, not merely to apply the Constitution but to expand it, imposing what it regards as useful "prophylactic" restrictions upon Congress and the States. That is an immense and frightening antidemocratic power, and it does not exist.

It takes only a small step to bring today's opinion out of the realm of power-judging and into the mainstream of legal reasoning: The Court need only go beyond its carefully couched iterations that "*Miranda* is a constitutional decision," that "*Miranda* is constitutionally based," that *Miranda* has "constitutional underpinnings," and come out and say quite clearly: "We reaffirm today that custodial interrogation that is not preceded by *Miranda* warnings or their equivalent violates the Constitution of the United States." It cannot say that, because a majority of the Court does not believe it. The Court therefore acts in plain violation of the Constitution when it denies effect to this Act of Congress.

It was once possible to characterize the so-called *Miranda* rule as resting (however implausibly) upon the proposition that what the statute here before us permits—the admission at trial of un-Mirandized confessions—violates the Constitution. That is the fairest reading of the *Miranda* case itself. The Court began by announcing that the Fifth Amendment privilege against self-incrimination applied in the context of extrajudicial custodial interrogation—itself a doubtful proposition as a matter both of history and precedent. Having extended the privilege into the confines of the station house, the Court liberally sprinkled throughout its sprawling 60-page opinion suggestions that, because of the compulsion inherent in custodial interrogation, the privilege was violated by any statement thus obtained that did not conform to the rules set forth in *Miranda*, or some functional equivalent. . . .

Miranda was objectionable for innumerable reasons, not least the fact that cases spanning more than 70 years had rejected its core premise that, absent the warnings and an effective waiver of the right to remain silent and of the (thitherto unknown) right to have an attorney present, a statement obtained pursuant to custodial interrogation was necessarily the product of compulsion. Moreover, history and precedent aside, the decision in *Miranda*, if read as an explication of what the Constitution requires, is preposterous. There is, for example, simply no basis in reason for concluding that a response to the very first question asked, by a suspect who already knows all of the rights described in the *Miranda* warning, is anything other than a volitional act. And even if one assumes that the elimination of compulsion absolutely requires informing even the most knowledgeable suspect of his right to remain silent, it cannot conceivably require the right to have counsel present. There is a world of difference, which the Court recognized under the traditional voluntariness test but ignored in *Miranda*, between compelling a suspect to incriminate himself and preventing him from foolishly doing so of his own accord. Only the latter (which is not required by the Constitution) could explain the Court's inclusion of a right to counsel and the requirement that it, too, be knowingly and intelligently waived. Counsel's presence is not required to tell the suspect that he need not speak; the interrogators can do that. The only good reason for having counsel there is that he can be counted on to advise the suspect that he should not speak.

Preventing foolish (rather than compelled) confessions is likewise the only conceivable basis for the rules that courts must exclude any confession elicited by questioning conducted, without interruption, after the suspect has indicated a desire to stand on his right to remain silent, see *Michigan v. Mosley*, 423 U.S. 96 (1975), or initiated by police after the suspect has expressed a desire to have counsel present, see *Edwards v. Arizona*, 451 U.S. 477 (1981). Nonthreatening attempts to persuade the suspect to reconsider that initial decision are not, without more, enough to render a change of heart the product of anything other than the suspect's free will. Thus, what is most remarkable about the *Miranda* decision—and what made it unacceptable as a matter of straightforward constitutional interpretation in the *Marbury* tradition—is its palpable hostility toward the act of confession per se, rather than toward what the Constitution abhors, compelled confession.

For these reasons, and others more than adequately developed in the *Miranda* dissents and in the subsequent works of the decision's many critics, any conclusion that a violation of the *Miranda* rules necessarily amounts to a violation of the privilege against compelled self-incrimination can claim no support in history, precedent, or common sense, and as a result would at least presumptively be worth reconsidering even at this late date. But that is unnecessary, since the Court has (thankfully) long since abandoned the notion that failure to comply with *Miranda*'s rules is itself a violation of the Constitution.

As the Court today acknowledges, since *Miranda* we have explicitly, and repeatedly, interpreted that decision as having announced, not the circumstances in which custodial interrogation runs afoul of the Fifth or Fourteenth Amendment, but rather only "prophylactic" rules that go beyond the right against compelled self-incrimination. Of course the seeds of this "prophylactic" interpretation of Miranda were present in the decision itself. In subsequent cases, the seeds have sprouted and borne fruit: The Court has squarely concluded that it is possible—indeed not uncommon—for the police to violate *Miranda* without also violating the Constitution. [See *Michigan v. Tucker*, 417 U.S. 433 (1974); *Oregon v. Hass*, 420 U.S. 714 (1975); *New York v. Quarles*, 467 U.S. 649 (1984); and *Oregon v. Elstad*, 470 U.S. 298 (1985).]

In light of these cases, and our statements to the same effect in others, it is simply no longer possible for the Court to conclude, even if it wanted to, that a violation of *Miranda*'s rules is a violation of the Constitution. But as I explained at the outset, that is what is required before the Court may disregard a law of Congress governing the admissibility of evidence in federal court. The Court today insists that the decision in *Miranda* is a "constitutional" one; that it has "constitutional underpinnings"; "constitutional basis" and a "constitutional origin"; that it was "constitutionally based"; and that it announced a "constitutional rule." It is fine to play these word games; but what makes a decision "constitutional" in the only sense relevant here—in the sense that renders it impervious to supersession by congressional legislation such as Section 3501—is the determination that the Constitution requires the result that the decision announces and the statute ignores. By disregarding congressional action that concededly does not violate the Constitution, the Court flagrantly offends fundamental principles of separation of powers, and arrogates to itself prerogatives reserved to the representatives of the people. . . .

Finally, I am not convinced by petitioner's argument that *Miranda* should be preserved because the decision occupies a special place in the "public's consciousness." As far as I am aware, the public is not under the illusion that we are infallible. I see little harm in admitting that we made a mistake in taking away from the people the ability to decide for themselves what protections (beyond those required by the Constitution) are reasonably affordable in the criminal investigatory process. And I see much to be gained by reaffirming for the people the wonderful reality that they govern themselves—which means that "[t]he powers not delegated to the United States by the Constitution" that the people adopted, "nor prohibited to the States" by that Constitution, "are reserved to the States respectively, or to the people," U.S. Const., Amdt. 10. . . .

I dissent from today's decision, and, until Section 3501 is repealed, will continue to apply it in all cases where there has been a sustainable finding that the defendant's confession was voluntary.

Missouri v. Seibert

124 S.CT. 2601 (2004)

Patrice Seibert's 12-year-old son Jonathan had cerebral palsy, and when he died in his sleep she feared charges of neglect because of bedsores on his body. In her presence, two of her teenage sons and two of their friends devised a plan to conceal the facts surrounding Jonathan's death by incinerating his body in the course of burning the family's mobile home, in which they planned to leave Donald Rector, a mentally ill teenager living with the family, to avoid any appearance that Jonathan was unattended. Seibert's son Darian and a friend set the fire, and Donald died. Five days later, the police woke Seibert at 3 A.M. at a hospital where Darian was being treated for burns. When arresting her, officer Kevin Clinton followed instructions from officer Richard Hanrahan not to give *Miranda* warnings. After Seibert had been taken to the police station and left alone in an interview room for fifteen to twenty minutes, Hanrahan questioned her without *Miranda* warnings for about a half an hour, squeezing her arm and repeating "Donald was also to die in his sleep." After Seibert finally admitted she knew Donald was meant to die in the fire, she was given a twenty-minute coffee and cigarette break. Hanrahan then turned on a tape recorder, gave Seibert the *Miranda* warnings, and obtained a signed waiver of rights from her. He resumed the questioning with "Ok, 'trice, we've been talking for a little while about what happened on Wednesday the twelfth, haven't we?," and confronted her with her prewarning statements:

Hanrahan: "Now, in discussion you told us, you told us that there was a[n] understanding about Donald."

Seibert: "Yes."

Hanrahan : "Did that take place earlier that morning?"

Seibert : "Yes."

Hanrahan : "And what was the understanding about Donald?"

Seibert : "If they could get him out of the trailer, to take him out of the trailer."

Hanrahan : "And if they couldn't?"

Seibert : "I, I never even thought about it. I just figured they would."

Hanrahan : " 'Trice, didn't you tell me that he was supposed to die in his sleep?"

Seibert : "If that would happen, 'cause he was on that new medicine, you know . . ."

Hanrahan : "The Prozac? And it makes him sleepy. So he was supposed to die in his sleep?"

Seibert : "Yes."

After being charged with first-degree murder, Seibert sought to exclude both her prewarning and postwarning statements. At the suppression hearing, Hanrahan testified that he made a "conscious decision" to withhold *Miranda* warnings, thus resorting to an interrogation technique he had been taught: question first, then give the warnings, and then repeat the question "until I get the answer that she's already provided once." He acknowledged that Seibert's ultimate statement was "largely a repeat of information . . . obtained" prior to the warning.

The trial court suppressed the prewarning statement but admitted the responses given after the *Miranda* recitation. A jury convicted Seibert of second-degree murder. On appeal, the Missouri Court of Appeals affirmed, treating the case as indistinguishable from *Oregon v. Elstad*, 470 U.S. 298 (1985). The Supreme Court of Missouri reversed, holding that "[i]n the circumstances here, where the interrogation was nearly continuous, . . . the second statement, clearly the product of the invalid first statement, should have been suppressed." The court distinguished *Elstad* on the ground that warnings had not intentionally been withheld there. The state appealed and the Supreme Court granted review.

The state supreme court's decision was affirmed by a five-to-four vote. Justice Souter delivered the opinion for the Court, Justices Kennedy and Breyer filed concurring opinions. Justice O'Connor filed a dissenting opinion, which Chief Justice Rehnquist and Justices Scalia and Thomas joined.

☐ *Justice SOUTER announced the judgment of the Court and delivered an opinion, in which Justice STEVENS, Justice GINSBURG, and Justice BREYER join.*

This case tests a police protocol for custodial interrogation that calls for giving no warnings of the rights to silence and counsel until interrogation has produced a confession. Although such a statement is generally inadmissible, since taken in violation of *Miranda v. Arizona*, 384 U. S. 436 (1966), the interrogating officer follows it with *Miranda* warnings and then leads the suspect to cover the same ground a second time. The question here is the admissibility of the repeated statement. Because this midstream recitation of warnings after interrogation and unwarned confession could not effectively comply with *Miranda*'s constitutional requirement, we hold that a statement repeated after a warning in such circumstances is inadmissible. . . .

"In criminal trials, in the courts of the United States, wherever a question arises whether a confession is incompetent because not voluntary, the issue is controlled by that portion of the Fifth Amendment . . . commanding that no person 'shall be compelled in any criminal case to be a witness against himself.' " *Bram v. United States*, 168 U.S. 532 (1897). A parallel rule governing the admissibility of confessions in state courts emerged from the Due Process Clause of the Fourteenth Amendment, see *Brown v. Mississippi*, 297 U.S. 278 (1936), which governed state cases until we concluded in *Malloy v. Hogan*, 378 U.S. 1 (1964), that "[t]he Fourteenth Amendment secures against state invasion the same privilege that the Fifth Amendment guarantees against federal infringement—the right of a person to remain silent unless he chooses to speak in the unfettered exercise of his own will, and to suffer no penalty . . . for such silence." In unifying the Fifth and Fourteenth Amendment voluntariness tests, *Malloy* "made clear what had already become apparent—that the substantive and procedural safeguards surrounding admissibility of confessions in state cases had become exceedingly exacting, reflecting all the policies embedded in the privilege" against self-incrimination.

In *Miranda*, we explained that the "voluntariness doctrine in the state Cases . . . encompasses all interrogation practices which are likely to exert such pressure upon an individual as to disable him from making a free and rational choice." We appreciated the difficulty of judicial enquiry post hoc into the circumstances of a police interrogation, *Dickerson v. United States*, 530 U.S. 428 (2000), and recognized that "the coercion inherent in custodial interrogation blurs the line between voluntary and involuntary statements, and thus heightens the risk" that the privilege against self-incrimination will not be observed. Hence our concern that the "traditional totality-of-the-circumstances" test posed an "unacceptably great" risk that involuntary custodial confessions would escape detection.

Accordingly, "to reduce the risk of a coerced confession and to implement the Self-Incrimination Clause," this Court in *Miranda* concluded that "the accused must be adequately and effectively apprised of his rights and the exercise of those rights must be fully honored." *Miranda* conditioned the admissibility at trial of any custodial confession on warning a suspect of his rights: failure to give the prescribed warnings and obtain a waiver of rights before custodial questioning generally requires exclusion of any statements obtained. Conversely, giving the warnings and getting a waiver has generally produced a virtual ticket of admissibility; maintaining that a statement is involuntary even though given after warnings and voluntary waiver of rights requires unusual stamina, and litigation over voluntariness tends to end with the finding of a valid waiver. To point out the obvious, this common consequence would not be common at all were it not that *Miranda* warnings are customarily given under circumstances allowing for a real choice between talking and remaining silent. . . .

The technique of interrogating in successive, unwarned and warned phases raises a new challenge to *Miranda*. Although we have no statistics on the frequency of this practice, it is not confined to Rolla, Missouri. An officer of that police department testified that the strategy of withholding *Miranda* warnings until after interrogating and drawing out a confession was promoted not only by his own department, but by a national police training organization and other departments in which he had worked. Consistently with the officer's testimony, the Police Law Institute, for example, instructs that "officers may conduct a two-stage interrogation. . . . At any point during the pre-*Miranda* interrogation, usually after arrestees have confessed, officers may then read the *Miranda* warnings and ask for a waiver. If the arrestees waive their *Miranda* rights, officers will be able to repeat any subsequent incriminating statements later in court. The upshot of all this advice is a question-first practice of some popularity, as one can see from the reported cases describing its use, sometimes in obedience to departmental policy.

When a confession so obtained is offered and challenged, attention must be paid to the conflicting objects of *Miranda* and question-first. *Miranda* addressed "interrogation practices . . . likely . . . to disable [an individual] from making a free and rational choice" about speaking, and held that a suspect must be "adequately and effectively" advised of the choice the Constitution guarantees. The object of question-first is to render *Miranda* warnings ineffective by waiting for a particularly opportune time to give them, after the suspect has already confessed. . . .

By any objective measure, applied to circumstances exemplified here, it is likely that if the interrogators employ the technique of withholding warnings until after interrogation succeeds in eliciting a confession, the warnings will be ineffective in preparing the suspect for successive interrogation, close in time and similar in content. After all, the reason that question-first is catching on is as obvious as its manifest purpose, which is to get a confession the suspect would not make if he understood his rights at the outset; the sensible underlying assumption is that with one confession in hand before the warnings, the interrogator can count on getting its duplicate, with trifling additional trouble. Upon hearing warnings only in the aftermath of interrogation and just after making a confession, a suspect would hardly think he had a genuine right to remain silent, let alone persist in so believing once the police began to lead him over the same ground again. . . .

Strategists dedicated to draining the substance out of *Miranda* cannot accomplish by training instructions what *Dickerson* held Congress could not do by statute. Because the question-first tactic effectively threatens to thwart *Miranda*'s purpose of reducing the risk that a coerced confession would be admitted, and because the facts here do not reasonably support a conclusion that the warnings given could have served their purpose, Seibert's postwarning statements are inadmissible. The judgment of the Supreme Court of Missouri is affirmed.

☐ *Justice O'CONNOR, with whom THE CHIEF JUSTICE, Justice SCALIA, and Justice THOMAS join, dissenting.*

On two preliminary questions I am in full agreement with the plurality. First, the plurality appropriately follows *Elstad* in concluding that Seibert's statement cannot be held inadmissible under a "fruit of the poisonous tree" theory. Second, the plurality correctly declines to focus its analysis on the subjective intent of the interrogating officer. . . .

The plurality's adherence to *Elstad*, and mine to the plurality, end there. . . . I would analyze the two-step interrogation procedure under the voluntariness standards central to the Fifth Amendment and reiterated in *Elstad*. *Elstad* commands that if Seibert's first statement is shown to have been involuntary, the court must examine whether the taint dissipated through the passing of time or a change in circumstances. In addition, Seibert's second statement should be suppressed if she showed that it was involuntary despite the *Miranda* warnings. . . .

I respectfully dissent.

United States v. Patane

124 S.CT. 2620 (2004)

Samuel Francis Patane was arrested for harassing his ex-girlfriend, Linda O'Donnell, and released on bond, subject to a temporary restraining order that prohibited him from contacting O'Donnell. Patane subsequently violated the restraining order by attempting to telephone O'Donnell, and officer Tracy Fox began an investigation of the matter. At the same time, a county probation officer informed an agent of the Bureau of Alcohol, Tobacco, and Firearms (ATF), that Patane, a convicted felon, illegally possessed a pistol. The ATF relayed this information to detective Josh Benner. Benner and Fox went to Patane's residence and arrested him for violating the restraining order. Benner attempted to advise respondent of his *Miranda* rights but got no further than the right to remain silent, when Patane interrupted and said he knew his rights. Benner then asked about the pistol and Patane stated "I am not sure I should tell you anything about the [pistol] because I don't want you to take it away from me." Benner persisted and Patane told him that the pistol was in his bedroom, and gave Benner permission to retrieve it. A grand jury indicted Patane for possession of a firearm by a convicted felon. A federal district court, however, granted Patane's motion to suppress the firearm on the ground that the officers lacked probable cause to arrest him for violating the restraining order. On appeal, an appellate court reversed the district court's ruling with respect to probable cause, but affirmed the suppression order. The appellate court rejected the government's argument that Supreme Court precedents, in *Oregon v. Elstad*, 470 U.S. 298 (1985), and *Michigan v. Tucker*, 417 U.S. 433 (1974), foreclosed application of the fruit of "the poisonous tree doctrine" of *Wong Sun v. United States*, 371 U.S. 471 (1963), requiring the exclusion of evidence obtained in violation of constitutional rights. Those rulings were, according to the court of appeals, based on the view that *Miranda* announced a prophylactic rule, a position that it found to be incompatible with this Court's decision in *Dickerson v. United States*, 530 U.S. 428 (2000). The court of appeals equated *Dickerson*'s announcement that *Miranda* is a constitutional rule with the proposition that a failure to warn pursuant to *Miranda* is a vi-

olation of the Fifth Amendment. The government appealed that decision and the Supreme Court granted review.

The appellate court was reversed by a five-to-four vote. Justice
Thomas delivered the opinion of the Court. Justice Kennedy filed a
concurring opinion. Justices Souter and Breyer filed dissenting opinion,
which Justices Stevens and Ginsburg joined.

> ☐ *Justice THOMAS announced the judgment of the Court and delivered an
> opinion, in which THE CHIEF JUSTICE and Justice SCALIA join.*

In this case we must decide whether a failure to give a suspect the warnings prescribed by *Miranda v. Arizona*, 384 U.S. 436 (1966), requires
suppression of the physical fruits of the suspect's unwarned but voluntary
statements. . . . Although we believe that the Court's decisions in *Oregon v.
Elstad*, 470 U.S. 298 (1985), and *Michigan v. Tucker*, 417 U.S. 433 (1974), are
instructive, the Courts of Appeals have split on the question after our decision in *Dickerson v. United States*, 530 U.S. 428 (2000). Because the *Miranda*
rule protects against violations of the Self-Incrimination Clause, which, in
turn, is not implicated by the introduction at trial of physical evidence resulting from voluntary statements, we answer the question presented in the
negative.

[T]he *Miranda* rule is a prophylactic employed to protect against violations of the Self-Incrimination Clause. The Self-Incrimination Clause, however, is not implicated by the admission into evidence of the physical fruit of
a voluntary statement. Accordingly, there is no justification for extending the
Miranda rule to this context. And just as the Self-Incrimination Clause primarily focuses on the criminal trial, so too does the *Miranda* rule. The *Miranda* rule is not a code of police conduct, and police do not violate the
Constitution (or even the *Miranda* rule, for that matter) by mere failures to
warn. For this reason, the exclusionary rule articulated in cases such as *Wong
Sun* does not apply. Accordingly, we reverse the judgment of the Court of
Appeals and remand the case for further proceedings consistent with this
opinion.

[T]he core protection afforded by the Self-Incrimination Clause is a
prohibition on compelling a criminal defendant to testify against himself at
trial. See, e.g., *Chavez v. Martinez*, 538 U.S. 760 (2003). The Clause cannot be
violated by the introduction of nontestimonial evidence obtained as a result
of voluntary statements.

[S]tatements taken without *Miranda* warnings (though not actually compelled) can be used to impeach a defendant's testimony at trial, see *Elstad;
Harris v. New York*, 401 U.S. 222 (1971), though the fruits of actually compelled testimony cannot, see *New Jersey v. Portash*, 440 U.S. 450 (1979). More
generally, the *Miranda* rule "does not require that the statements [taken without complying with the rule] and their fruits be discarded as inherently
tainted," *Elstad*. Such a blanket suppression rule could not be justified by reference to the "Fifth Amendment goal of assuring trustworthy evidence" or
by any deterrence rationale, and would therefore fail our close-fit requirement.

Furthermore, the Self-Incrimination Clause contains its own exclusionary rule. It provides that "[n]o person . . . shall be compelled in any criminal case to be a witness against himself." Unlike the Fourth Amendment's bar on unreasonable searches, the Self-Incrimination Clause is self-executing. We have repeatedly explained "that those subjected to coercive police interrogations have an automatic protection from the use of their involuntary statements (or evidence derived from their statements) in any subsequent criminal trial." *Chavez*. This explicit textual protection supports a strong presumption against expanding the *Miranda* rule any further.

Finally, nothing in *Dickerson*, including its characterization of *Miranda* as announcing a constitutional rule, changes any of these observations. . . .

Our cases also make clear the related point that a mere failure to give *Miranda* warnings does not, by itself, violate a suspect's constitutional rights or even the *Miranda* rule. So much was evident in many of our pre-*Dickerson* cases, and we have adhered to this view since *Dickerson*. See *Chavez*. . . .

It follows that police do not violate a suspect's constitutional rights (or the *Miranda* rule) by negligent or even deliberate failures to provide the suspect with the full panoply of warnings prescribed by *Miranda*. Potential violations occur, if at all, only upon the admission of unwarned statements into evidence at trial. And, at that point, "[t]he exclusion of unwarned statements . . . is a complete and sufficient remedy" for any perceived *Miranda* violation.

Thus, unlike unreasonable searches under the Fourth Amendment or actual violations of the Due Process Clause or the Self-Incrimination Clause, there is, with respect to mere failures to warn, nothing to deter. There is therefore no reason to apply the "fruit of the poisonous tree" doctrine of *Wong Sun*. . . .

Accordingly, we reverse the judgment of the Court of Appeals and remand the case for further proceedings consistent with this opinion.

☐ *Justice SOUTER, with whom Justice STEVENS and Justice GINS-BURG join, dissenting.*

The majority repeatedly says that the Fifth Amendment does not address the admissibility of nontestimonial evidence, an overstatement that is beside the point. The issue actually presented today is whether courts should apply the fruit of the poisonous tree doctrine lest we create an incentive for the police to omit *Miranda* warnings before custodial interrogation. In closing their eyes to the consequences of giving an evidentiary advantage to those who ignore *Miranda*, the majority adds an important inducement for interrogators to ignore the rule in that case.

Miranda rested on insight into the inherently coercive character of custodial interrogation and the inherently difficult exercise of assessing the voluntariness of any confession resulting from it. Unless the police give the prescribed warnings meant to counter the coercive atmosphere, a custodial confession is inadmissible, there being no need for the previous time-consuming and difficult enquiry into voluntariness. That inducement to forestall involuntary statements and troublesome issues of fact can only atrophy if we turn around and recognize an evidentiary benefit when an unwarned statement leads investigators to tangible evidence. There is, of course, a price for excluding evidence, but the Fifth Amendment is worth a price, and in the absence of a very good reason, the logic of *Miranda* should be followed: a *Miranda* violation raises a presumption of coercion, *Oregon v. Elstad*, and the Fifth Amendment privilege against compelled self-incrimination extends to the exclusion of derivative evidence, see *United States v. Hubbell*, 530 U.S. 27 (2000) (recognizing "the Fifth Amendment's protection against the prosecutor's use of incriminating information derived directly or indirectly from . . . [actually] compelled testimony"); *Kastigar v. United States*, 406 U.S. 441 (1972). That should be the end of this case. . . .

There is no way to read this case except as an unjustifiable invitation to law enforcement officers to flout *Miranda* when there may be physical evidence to be gained. The incentive is an odd one, coming from the Court on the same day it decides *Missouri v. Seibert*. I respectfully dissent.

■ The Development of Law

Other Court Rulings on Coerced Confessions and Limiting Miranda

CASE	VOTE	RULING
Parker v. North Carolina, 397 U.S. 790 (1970)	6:3	Defendant's guilty plea was voluntary where, after an allegedly coercive interrogation, it was
given one month later and he testified at trial that it was voluntary.		
Harris v. New York, 401 U.S. 222 (1971)	5:4	Incriminating statements without being given *Miranda* warnings may be used to impeach accused's testimony at trial.
Lego v. Twomey, 404 U.S. 477 (1972)	4:3	Preponderance of evidence is the standard for proving that a confession is voluntary.
Michigan v. Tucker, 417 U.S. 433 (1974)	8:1	Upheld the use of a witness at trial who was discovered as a result of questioning of defendant who had not received *Miranda* warnings.
Oregon v. Hass, 420 U.S. 714 (1975)	6:2	Upheld use of incriminating statements made by defendant in police car after being given *Mi-*
randa warnings and requesting the presence of counsel, but where defendant was told that counsel could not be telephoned until they reached police station.		

CASE	VOTE	RULING
Michigan v. Mosley, 423 U.S. 96 (1975)	7:2	Once *Miranda* warnings are given and accused indicates desire to remain silent, any police

questioning must be in presence of an attorney. But here, questioning stopped and was resumed two hours later, and the incriminating statements that were thereby elicited could be used at trial.

Oregon v. Mathiason, 429 U.S. 711 (1977)	6:3	*Miranda* is not violated where a person on parole voluntarily goes to police station at officer's

request, agrees to a thirty-minute interview, and is allowed to leave but is later arrested based on incriminating statements made in the interview.

United States v. Washington, 431 U.S. 181 (1977); and *United States v. Wong*, 431 U.S. 174 (1977)	7:2	Held that prosecutors may use at trial incriminating statements made by a witness before a grand jury even though the witness was not told that he was in

danger of being indicted; as a result, perjured testimony before grand jury may be used at trial even though defendant had not received an effective warning of his rights.

North Carolina v. Butler, 441 U.S. 369 (1979)	6:3	Held that it is not necessary for a suspect to expressly waive rights during a custodial interrogation.
Rhode Island v. Innis, 446 U.S. 291 (1980)	6:3	*Miranda* comes into operation at time of actual police "interrogation."
California v. Prysock, 453 U.S. 355 (1981)	6:3	Precise language of *Miranda* warning is not necessary when informing suspects of their rights.
Oregon v. Bradshaw, 462 U.S. 1039 (1983)	5:4	Held that the initiation of a conversation with the police by a defendant amounts to a waiver of *Miranda* rights.
California v. Beheler, 463 U.S. 1121 (1983)	6:3	*Miranda* is not required when the suspect voluntarily goes to the police station for question-

ing and is allowed to leave and later is arrested.

Minnesota v. Murphy, 465 U.S. 420 (1984)	6:3	Probation officer who obtained incriminating information from parolee was not obliged to give *Miranda* warnings.

CASE	VOTE	RULING
Oregon v. Elstad, 470 U.S. 298 (1985)	6:3	Upheld the use of an initial culpatory statement, made in violation of *Miranda*, because it was voluntarily given by the defendant in his home.
Allen v. Illinois, 478 U.S. 364 (1986)	5:4	Fifth Amendment does not apply to incriminating statements made in proceedings to commit to a psychiatric prison a person said to be sexually dangerous.
Colorado v. Connelly, 479 U.S. 157 (1986)	7:2	Fifth Amendment not violated by the confession of a mentally ill man who told police that the "voice of God" told him to confess to a murder.
Arizona v. Mauro, 481 U.S. 520 (1987)	5:4	*Miranda* not violated when defendant was informed of rights, requested an attorney, and was allowed to have a telephone conversation with his wife, which the police recorded and later introduced as evidence against the defendant.
Pennsylvania v. Burder, 488 U.S. 9 (1988)	7:2	Held that ordinary traffic stops are not custodial stops for the purposes of *Miranda*, and police do not have to read drivers their *Miranda* rights.
Duckworth v. Eagan, 492 U.S. 195 (1989)	5:4	When advising suspects of their rights, the police may depart from the actual wording of the rights set down in *Miranda*.
Illinois v. Perkins, 496 U.S. 292 (1990)	8:1	The Court held that a defendant, who was jailed but not yet arraigned, had no right to be informed of his *Miranda* rights by an undercover police agent seeking to elicit his incriminating statements by posing as a fellow inmate; Justice Marshall dissented.
McNeil v. Wisconsin, 501 U.S. 171 (1991)	6:3	Held that the Sixth Amendment right to counsel does not convey *Miranda*'s guarantees nor bar police from questioning a defendant about a separate crime in the absence of his attorney.
Arizona v. Fulminante, 499 U.S. 279 (1991)	5:4	Although Justice White delivered an opinion for the Court, Chief Justice Rehnquist com-

CASE	VOTE	RULING

manded four other votes for holding that the admission at trial of coerced confessions may be excused as a harmless error if it can be shown that other evidence, obtained independently of the confession, was also used at trial and was adequate to support a guilty verdict. Justice Souter provided the key vote to form a majority on that issue. But the lineup of the justices changed and was complicated by their stands on the other questions presented in the case as well. Notably, Justice White's opinion commanded a majority on the two other issues in the case. White deemed the circumstances of Fulminante's confession to constitute a coerced confession, whereas Rehnquist, O'Connor, Kennedy, and Souter disagreed. On that issue, Scalia joined White's opinion, along with Blackmun, Marshall, and Stevens. On the third issue of whether the use of Fulminante's confession was harmless beyond a reasonable doubt, White commanded a majority for affirming the state supreme court's judgment that Fulminante's confession may not be used against him. On that issue, White was joined by Blackmun, Marshall, Stevens, and Kennedy; Rehnquist, O'Connor, and Scalia dissented; and Souter gave no indication of whether or how he voted.

Brecht v. Abrahamson, 507 U.S. 619 (1993)	5:4	Held that on *habeas corpus* review federal courts may set aside convictions that are challenged

for alleged trial errors in violation of *Miranda* only when the errors have a "substantial and injurious effect or influence" that results in "actual prejudice" against the defendant.

Stansbury v. California, 511 U.S. 318 (1994)	9:0	Held that when trial courts determine whether a person was "in custody" for *Miranda* pur-

poses, the objective circumstances of the police interrogation should be controlling, not the officers' subjective views as to whether the suspect should be given *Miranda* warnings.

Davis v. United States, 512 U.S. 452 (1994)	9:0	Upheld the use of incriminating statements made by a suspect who said, "Maybe I should talk

to a lawyer," during a police interrogation that then continued. Writing for the Court, Justice O'Connor observed, "If the suspect effectively waives his right to counsel after receiving *Miranda* warnings, law enforcement officers are free to question him. . . . We decline the petitioner's invitation to extend *Edwards* [*v. Arizona*, 451 U.S. 477 (1981)] and require law enforcement officers to cease questioning immediately upon the making of an ambiguous or equivocal reference to an attorney."

Yarborough v. Alvarado, 124 S.Ct. 2140 (2004)	5:4	Writing for the Court, Justice Kennedy held that a juvenile, who was brought by his parents

to the police station and who made in a two-hour-long interview made incriminating statements about a robbery and murder, but who was allowed to leave, and a month later was arrested and charged, was not in police custody for the purposes of *Miranda* and his incriminating statements could be used against him even though he had not been given the *Miranda* warning about his rights. According to Justice Kennedy, the fact that he was a juvenile and other psychological considerations was deemed not relevant to whether he was in police custody. Justices Stevens, Souter, Ginsburg, and Breyer dissented.

■ In Comparative Perspective

The Right to Remain Silent and the Exclusion of Incriminating Statements in England, France, Germany, and Italy

The right against self-incrimination was recognized in English courts by the seventeenth century as a legacy of medieval legal commentaries. In *Miranda v. Arizona*, 384 U.S. 436 (1966), the Supreme Court claimed to derive from the English common law right against self-incrimination, as embodied in the Fifth Amendment, a right to remain silent at the time of police interrogations that included the exclusion at trial of incriminating statements in the absence of a police warning to suspects of their right to remain silent.

In England, however, Parliament and the courts have rejected an exclusionary rule for the failure to give *Miranda*-like warnings, as well as rejected the exclusionary rule for evidence obtained from illegal searches that the U.S. Supreme Court proclaimed in *Mapp v. Ohio*, 367 U.S. 643 (1961). Confessions obtained by police coercion were held inadmissible in England, *Regina v. Rennie*, 1 W.L.R. 64 (1982), but besides such exceptions the methods by which police obtain incriminating evidence are otherwise irrelevant, *Regina v. Sang* [1980] App. Cases 402 (1979). Evidence that is stolen, *Kurma v. The Queen*, [1955] App. Cases 197 (1954), or obtained by an illegal search, *Jeffrey v. Black*, [1978] 1 A11 E.R. 555 (1977), remains admissible.

Parliament further removed many of the protections afforded by the right to remain silent, when passing the Criminal Justice and Public Order Act, which went into effect in 1995. Notably, the act authorizes prosecutors and judges to infer the criminality of suspects who refuse to testify in their own behalf. The act also provides for reduced sentences for those who plead guilty to a crime.

France, Germany, and Italy are all civil law countries, in which police, prosecutors, and judges have extensive investigatory powers. Still, in the second half of the twentieth century, each country recognized, to different degrees, an exclusionary rule for the failure of police and judges to warn criminal suspects of the right to remain silent, as indicated below:

Exclusion for Failure to Warn Suspects of the Right to Remain Silent

INVESTIGATOR	FRANCE	GERMANY	ITALY
Police	Yes	Discretionary	Not Applicable
Investigating Magistrate	Yes	Undecided	Yes
Trial Judge	No	Yes	No

In France, since 1897, courts have held that suspects charged with a crime must be warned of the rights to remain silent and to counsel at their first appearance before a magistrate, rather than at the earlier stage of police interrogations. A decade before *Miranda*, in *Fesch* (Judgment of June 16, 1955, Cass. crim., Fr., 1955 J.C.P. II No. 8851) the Court of Cassation sought to extend similar rights to uncharged suspects because police and magistrates could continue their interrogation of suspects without warning them of the right to remain silent, so long as they did not charge them with a crime. There were therefore, long delays prior to the indictment of an accused. *Fesch* held that incriminating statements should be excluded as evidence if the delay in charging a suspect "had the result of evading the protection guaranteed by the Law of 1897." However, law enforcement officials strongly protested that ruling and in 1960 the French Assembly replaced *Fesch* with a "good faith" test and limited exclusion to only those instances in which there is proof of an intentional delay in indicting an accused. As a result, suspects and detainees are not warned about the right to remain silent during preliminary police interrogations, and police and magistrates need not advise them of that right until they have a strong case against the suspect. Once a suspect receives a warning of the right to remain silent, however, any incriminating statements made afterward are excluded as evidence.

In Germany, a right to silence warning was guaranteed, but only in limited circumstances, under the Code of Criminal Procedure of 1877. That code provided that "[t]he accused is to be asked whether he wishes to respond to charges" and required judges to give suspects that warning, but did not require police or prosecutors to do so. In 1964, the German legislature revised those provisions, along the line of French law, to require that the accused be informed of the rights to remain silent and to counsel at the first hearing before police, prosecutors, and a judge. Initially, these provisions were deemed merely advisory and in 1968 the German Supreme Court (*Bundesgerichtshof*) ruled that, because the legislation failed to provide for the exclusion of incriminating statements made in the absence of a right to silence warning, an in-court confession should be automatically excluded [Judgment of May 31, 1968, BGHSt, W.Ger., 22 Entscheidungen des BGHSt 170 (1969)]. That decision was sharply criticized and in 1974 the *Bundesgerichtshof* held that a fair trial requires giving the accused the right to decide whether to remain silent, and thus the right to silence warning is required at the judicial phase of criminal proceedings [Judgment of May 14, 1974, BGHSt, W. Ger., 25 Entscheidungen des BGHSt 325 (1975)]. In 1983, however, the *Bundesgerichtshof* refused to extend the requirement for a right to silence warning to police interrogations, and held that the failure of police to warn suspects did not require the automatic exclusion at trial of their incriminating statements [Judgment of June 7, 1983, BGHSt, W. Ger., 31 Entscheidungen des BGHSt 395 (1983)]. Instead, trial judges have discretion in deciding issues of exclusion based on the circumstances of the confession. In the words of the *Bundesgerichtshof*, "the trial judge is not prevented from evaluating, especially critically, the circumstances and the content of a statement made without the previous warning."

In Italy, a right to silence warning is required at every stage of the criminal process in order to protect the right against self-incrimination. Even a suspect who is summoned, but not arrested, is entitled to the rights of silence and counsel, although suspects need not receive a warning of their right to remain silent. Italian courts also require the exclusion as evidence not only of statements obtained prior to the warning of a right to silence but also for other types of evidence obtained illegally by police.

For further reading see Mirjan Damaska, *The Faces of Justice and State Authority* (New Haven, CT: Yale University Press, 1986); James Whitman, *Harsh Justice: Criminal Punishment and the Widening Divide between America and Europe* (New York: Oxford University Press, 2003); and Mireille Delmas-Marty, and J.R. Spencer, eds., *European Criminal Procedures* (New York: Cambridge University Press, 2002).

B | *Grants of Immunity*

Grants of immunity—immunizing a person from prosecution in exchange for incriminating testimony—have been upheld since *Brown v. United States*, 161 U.S. 591 (1896). There the Court ruled that the primary function of the Fifth Amendment is "to secure the witness against prosecution which might be aided directly or indirectly by his disclosure." Consequently, individuals may be forced to forgo their Fifth Amendment rights when offered immunity, even though their testimony opens them to infamy and disgrace; see *Ullmann v. United States*, 350 U.S. 422 (1956). Refusing to testify after being granted immunity constitutes contempt of court for which a person may be punished.

Traditionally, individuals received complete immunity, or "transactional immunity," barring prosecution for crimes related to their testimony. In *Ullmann v. United States*, 350 U.S. 422 (1956), the Court upheld the Federal Immunity Act of 1954 and subsequently held that grants of immunity are as broad as the privilege against self-incrimination that individuals forfeit. The Court also held, in *Murphy v. Waterfront Commission*, 378 U.S. 52 (1964), that defendants granted immunity by states may not later be prosecuted under federal law on the basis of their incriminating testimony.

Congress, however, cut back on the scope of immunity grants in the Omnibus Crime Control and Safe Streets Act of 1968 by providing for only "use" or "testimonial" immunity. Transactional immunity accords full immunity from prosecution for an offense about which an individual testifies. By contrast, use immunity does not foreclose the possibility of prosecution based on other independently obtained evidence. Use or testimonial immunity was upheld in *Kastigar v. United States*, 406 U.S. 441 (1972). Most recently, the Court split five to four in *McKune v. Lile*, 536 U.S. 24 (2002), in upholding Kansas's Sexual Abuse Treatment Program, which requires sexual offenders to sign a form taking responsibility for their sexual offenses as part of their treatment, without also granting them immunity from further prosecution.

C | *Real Versus Testimonial Evidence*

The Supreme Court has limited the scope of the Fifth Amendment by drawing a distinction between "real" and "testimonial" evidence. No protection is afforded real or physical evidence, such as blood, handwriting, or voice samples. Only testimonial evidence (oral testimony) receives protection. As the Court observed, in *Fisher v. United States*, 425 U.S. 391 (1976), the amendment "prohibits compelling a person to *speak* and incriminate himself but it does not prohibit compelled revelation of *written* thoughts."

The distinction between real and testimonial evidence derives from a 1910 ruling that a suspect may be compelled to cooperate with police by putting on a blouse to determine whether it fits. In *Holt v. United States*, 218 U.S. 245 (1910), the Court explained that "the prohibition of compelling a man to be a witness against himself is a prohibition of physical or moral compulsion to *extort communications* from him, not an exclusion of his body as evidence when it may be material." The distinction was not further elaborated until *Schmerber v. State of California*, 384 U.S. 757 (1966), upholding the taking of blood samples from a driver at the time of his arrest following an automobile accident. Since

Schmerber, handwriting samples, voice samples, and scrapings from under a suspect's fingernails, among other physical evidence, have been held not to violate the Fifth Amendment.

■ THE DEVELOPMENT OF LAW
Rulings on Real versus Testimonial Evidence[a]

CASE	VOTE	RULING
Breithaupt v. Abram, 352 U.S. 432 (1957)	6:3	Upheld police taking blood sample from a driver involved in an automobile accident.
Schmerber v. California, 384 U.S. 757 (1966)	5:4	Upheld taking blood sample in a hospital from a driver who apeared intoxicated.
United States v. Wade, 388 U.S. 218 (1967)	5:4	Held that compelling suspect to voice the words of a bank robber in a postindictment lineup was permissible.
Gilbert v. California, 388 U.S. 263 (1967)	5:4	Upheld taking of handwriting sample from suspect in absence of counsel.
United States v. Dionisio, 410 U.S. 1 (1973)	6:3	Upheld use of voice samples presented to grand jury.
Cupp v. Murphy, 412 U.S. 291 (1973)	9:0	Upheld police taking a sample of scraping from fingernails of individual who was not under
arrest and who had voluntarily gone to police station house.		
Estelle v. Williams, 425 U.S. 501 (1976)	7:2	Accused cannot be compelled to stand trial dressed in prison clothes; but here, the failure to
raise an objection negated any compulsion that would have violated the Fifth Amendment.		
Wyrick v. Fields, 459 U.S. 42 (1982)	8:1	A defendant who agrees, on advice of counsel, to submit to polygraph test may be subsequently questioned about results.
Pennsylvania v. Muniz, 496 U.S. 929 (1990)	8:1	Upheld the admissibility at trial of videotapes of suspects answering questions of police at

CASE	VOTE	RULING

the time of their booking. Writing for the majority, Justice Brennan said that the videotapes, showing slurred speech and other signs of intoxication, were physical—not testimonial—evidence and, therefore, not covered by the Fifth Amendment's privilege against self-incrimination; Justice Marshall dissented.

Hiibel v. Sixth Judicial District of Nevada, 124 S.Ct. 2451 (2004)	5:4	Writing for the Court, Justice Kennedy held that individuals may be arrested for refusing to identify themselves to police

during a *Terry*-stop and questioning. Justices Stevens, Souter, Ginsburg, and Breyer dissented on the ground that this violates the Fourth and Fifth Amendments.

[a]See also the drug testing cases in Chapter 7.

D | *Required Records, Private Papers, and Custodial Possession*

Another limitation on the Fifth Amendment is the "required records" doctrine—that is, records required to be kept to provide information for regulatory agencies receive no Fifth Amendment protection. *Shapiro v. United States*, 335 U.S. 1 (1948), held that required records have "public aspects" that foreclose protection for personal information also contained therein. Twenty years later, in *Grosso v. United States*, 390 U.S. 62 (1968), the Court clarified the doctrine:

> The premises of the doctrine, as it is described in *Shapiro*, are evidently these: first, the purpose of the United States's inquiry must be essentially regulatory; second, information is to be obtained by requiring the preservation of records of a kind which the regulated party has customarily kept; and third, the records themselves must have issued "public aspects" which render them analogous to public documents.

Income tax returns are required records, according to *United States v. Sullivan*, 274 U.S. 259 (1927), and the Fifth Amendment is no defense against prosecution for failing to file tax returns. The problem posed by illegal-income earners and the reporting requirements in filing tax returns, however, continued to be presented to the Court. In *United States v. Murdock*, 284 U.S. 141 (1931), a taxpayer filed a return claiming certain deductions but refused on Fifth Amendment grounds to answer questions concerning them, for which he was prosecuted for willful failure to supply necessary information. Although the taxpayer's Fifth Amendment claim was invalid, the Court held that a good faith claim of the amendment bars conviction for willfully failing to answer the IRS's questions. But in *Marchetti v. United States*, 390 U.S. 39 (1968), the Court struck down an IRS regulation requiring gamblers to register and to submit monthly information concerning their wagering activities. It did so on the grounds that the information was not customarily kept, the reports had no public records aspects, and the requirements were directed at a "select group inherently suspect of criminal activities."

A series of rulings on claims to Fifth Amendment protection for private papers firmly established that "a party is privileged from producing . . . evidence, but not from its production," *Johnson v. United States*, 228 U.S. 457 (1919). Individuals may claim Fifth Amendment privacy interests and, for example, quash an administrative subpoena directing them to produce papers or documents in which they have privacy interests. But they have no Fifth Amendment protection against the government subpoenaing their papers held by a bank, accountant, or attorney.

In *Couch v. United States*, 409 U.S. 322 (1973), for instance, Mrs. Couch was denied any reasonable expectation of privacy under the Fifth Amendment to intervene with an IRS summons of her accountant to turn over her business records. There the Court stressed that "no Fourth or Fifth Amendment claim can prevail where . . . there exists no legitimate expectation of privacy and no semblance of governmental compulsion against the person of the accused. . . . The criterion for Fifth Amendment immunity remains not the ownership of property, but the 'physical or moral compulsion exerted.' "

Two dissenters in *Couch* took quite a different view of the Fifth Amendment's protection for privacy. Justice Douglas urged that a "Fifth Amendment claim [is] valid *even in the absence of personal compulsion* so long as [the] accused has a reasonable expectation of privacy in [the] articles subpoenaed."

A majority of the Court, however, rejected such a broad interpretation of the Fifth Amendment. Three years after *Couch*, *Fisher v. United States*, 425 U.S. 391 (1976), held that individuals have no valid Fifth Amendment claims against their attorneys turning over documents related to their tax returns to the IRS, because that does "not 'compel' the taxpayer to do anything—and certainly [does] not compel him to be a 'witness against himself.' "

Following *Couch* and *Fisher*, in *United States v. Doe*, 465 U.S. 605

(1984), the Court reached the same conclusion with respect to an individual's own papers. Concurring Justice O'Connor emphasized that "the Fifth Amendment provides absolutely no protection for the contents of private papers of any kind. The notion that the Fifth Amendment protects the privacy of papers originated in *Boyd v. United States* . . . but our decision in *Fisher v. United States* . . . sounded the death knell for *Boyd*." In short, the amendment protects only testimonial components of an individual's actual production of personal materials; thus, in his investigation of President Clinton, independent prosecutor Kenneth Starr was not barred from obtaining the personal writings on the computer of White House intern Monica Lewinsky.

In *Baltimore City Department of Social Services v. Bouknight*, 493 U.S. 549 (1990), the Rehnquist Court further extended the *Schmerber* line of cases on real versus testimonial evidence (as discussed in Section C) and those dealing with the production of required records and private papers. There, the Court held that a mother could not invoke the Fifth Amendment when resisting a juvenile court order to produce a child who was in her custody. Maurice Bouknight was an abused child who was taken for a time by social workers from his mother, Jacqueline Bouknight. After a subsequent hearing in juvenile court, the child was returned to her custody on certain conditions, including that she attend a parental training program, and under a protective supervision order. Eight months later, after determining that Mrs. Bouknight was violating the conditions for custody of her child and that the child might be dead, social workers filed petitions to remove the child and to force Mrs. Bouknight to produce her child in court. Mrs. Bouknight in turn claimed that her Fifth Amendment guarantee against self-incrimination barred the juvenile court from compelling her to produce her child in court.

Writing for the majority in *Bouknight*, Chief Justice Rehnquist conceded that the order to produce the child compelled Mrs. Bouknight to make testimonial assertions, but that here, in a civil proceeding, she could not rely on the Fifth Amendment. The guarantee against self-incrimination was inapplicable because (1) Mrs. Bouknight had assumed custodial duties related to the child's production analogous to those assumed with the production of required records; and (2) the production was part of a noncriminal proceeding. As Chief Justice Rehnquist put it, "In assuming the obligation attending [child] custody, Bouknight 'had accepted the incident obligation to permit inspection.' "

In dissent, Justice Marshall, joined by Justice Brennan, rejected the majority's reasoning and reliance on earlier cases. On the one hand, Marshall argued that Mrs. Bouknight's custodial obligations were mis-analogized to those of custodians of corporate entities. Bouknight was "not acting as a custodian in the traditional sense of that word because she is not acting *on behalf of the State*." On the other hand, prior cases upholding diminished Fifth Amendment protection for the production of required records and private papers dealt with purely civil regulatory systems and regulations aimed at the general public. But here, Marshall contended that the civil proceeding against Mrs. Bouknight "*inevitably* intersects with criminal sanctions" for child abuse and "unambiguously indicates that Bouknight's Fifth Amendment privilege must be respected to protect her from the serious risk of self-incrimination."

■ THE DEVELOPMENT OF LAW

Rulings on Required Records and Private Papers

CASE	VOTE	RULING
United States v. Sullivan, 274 U.S. 259 (1927)	9:0	Rejected Fifth Amendment objection to filing federal income tax return.
Shapiro v. United States, 335 U.S. 1 (1948)	5:4	Records required to be kept under the regulatory powers of Congress acquire a "public aspect" and have no Fifth Amendment protection.
Marchetti v. United States, 390 U.S. 39 (1968) and *Grosso v. United States,* 390 U.S. 62 (1968)	8:1	Internal Revenue Service requirement that individuals register as gamblers violates Fifth Amendment since gambling is illegal.
Haynes v. United States, 390 U.S. 6 (1968)	8:1	Fifth Amendment not violated by requirement that gun owners register their guns.
Leary v. United States, 395 U.S. 6 (1969)	9:0	No Fifth Amendment protection against registering and tax on importation of marijuana.
Minor v. United States, 396 U.S. 87 (1969)	7:2	Narcotic seller's rights were not violated by requirement to register and pay sales tax.

CASE	VOTE	RULING
United States v. U.S. Coin and Currency, 401 U.S. 715 (1971)	5:4	Upheld *Marchetti*; Fifth Amendment bars IRS from requiring gamblers to register with federal government.
California v. Byers, 402 U.S. 424 (1971)	5:4	Upheld "hit-and-run" statute requiring drivers who hit a parked car to stop and leave name and driver's license number.
Bellis v. United States, 417 U.S. 85 (1974)	8:1	Fifth Amendment applies to only personal production of private papers—papers held by
third parties (accountants, lawyers, etc.) are not protected, even if they incriminate the custodian of the papers.		
California Bankers Association Shultz, 416 *v.* U.S. 21 (1974)	6:3	Upheld the Bank Secrecy Act giving the IRS access to individuals' bank records.
Garner v. United States, 424 U.S. 648 (1976)	9:0	Held that an individual who could have but failed to raise a Fifth Amendment objection on
a tax return was foreclosed from subsequently invoking the amendment.		
Braswell v. United States, 487 U.S. 99 (1988)	5:4	The president (and sole shareholder) of a corporation cannot claim the Fifth Amendment in refusing to turn over corporate documents.
Doe v. United States, 487 U.S. 201 (1988)	8:1	Contents of foreign bank accounts are not protected by the Fifth Amendment.

9

The Rights to Counsel and Other Procedural Guarantees

Along with the Fourth Amendment and the Fifth Amendment's right against self-accusation and the due process clause, a number of other guarantees of the Fifth, Sixth, Seventh, and Eighth Amendments protect the rights of the accused. The Fifth Amendment provides for indictment by a grand jury and forbids holding defendants in double jeopardy. The Sixth Amendment guarantees an accused the assistance of counsel, the rights to be informed of charges and to confront accusers, as well as a right to a speedy and public trial by an impartial jury in all criminal cases. The Seventh Amendment guarantees a jury trial in civil cases where the controversy exceeds $20. The Eighth Amendment prohibits the imposition of excessive bail and fines, besides banning cruel and unusual punishments (see Ch. 10).

A | *The Right to Counsel*

The Sixth Amendment guarantees the accused "the assistance of counsel for his defense." Literally, the guarantee confers a right of which one may avail himself but which the government is not obliged to ensure in all criminal cases. The year after the adoption and before the ratification of the Bill of Rights, Congress further indicated that the assistance of counsel was not mandatory in all criminal cases. The Federal Crimes Act of 1790 imposed a statutory duty on courts to assign counsel to represent defendants only in capital cases. In noncapital cases, the accused had a right to hire counsel but, if too poor to afford one, the government was not obligated to appoint one for his defense.

In *Johnson v. Zerbst*, 304 U.S. 458 (1938), the Hughes Court fundamentally changed the right to counsel in federal courts. There, in an appeal from a conviction for counterfeiting, the Court noted that the "right to be heard would be, in many cases, of little avail if it did not comprehend the right to be heard by counsel" and ruled that "the Sixth Amendment withholds from federal courts, in all criminal proceedings, the power and authority to deprive an accused of his life or liberty unless he has or waives the assistance of counsel."

The Court remained reluctant to impose the right to counsel on state courts, however. In its first confrontation with that issue in the famous *Scottsboro* case—*Powell v. Alabama* (1932) (see excerpt below)—the Hughes Court declined to apply the Sixth Amendment to state criminal courts. The Court did hold that under the circumstances of the case the due process clause of the Fifth Amendment required the trial court "to make an effective appointment of counsel." In this case, the "Scottsboro boys," as the several young black defendants were known, were accused of the capital offense of raping a white girl. They were tried before an all-white jury, without the assistance of counsel, in a small southern town, Scottsboro, Alabama.

In the 1940s and 1950s, the Stone and Vinson Courts continued to defer to the states but ruled on a case-by-case basis that some defendants had to be retried and given the assistance of counsel. In *Betts v. Brady*, 316 U.S. 455 (1942), the Stone Court interpreted *Powell* to require the appointment of counsel only in "special circumstances" and in capital cases. There, Betts, an indigent white man, was indicted for robbery and requested but was denied counsel. Conceding that a layman might encounter difficulties with courtroom procedures when defending himself, Justice Owen Roberts nonetheless held that Betts was "of ordinary intelligence and ability to take care of his own interests on the trial of [a] narrow issue." Three dissenters, Justices Black, Douglas, and Murphy, protested the refusal to extend the right to counsel to all indigents. "[A]ny other practice seems to me to defeat the promise of our democratic society to provide equal justice under the law," charged Justice Black. "A practice cannot be reconciled with 'common and fundamental ideas of fairness and right,' which subjects innocent men to increased dangers of conviction merely because of their poverty."

Although adhering to the special circumstances rule and upholding several convictions obtained without the defendant's assistance of counsel,[1] the Vinson Court held that counsel was required in capital cases;[2] when the conduct of a trial judge was questionable;[3] where defendants were young, ignorant, or otherwise handicapped;[4] and in legally complex cases.[5]

Finally, in *Gideon v. Wainwright* (1963) (excerpted below), the Warren Court overturned *Betts* and extended the right to counsel to the accused in all states in all criminal cases. *Argersinger v. Hamlin* (1972) (excerpted below) then applied the right to counsel to all offenses involving the possibility of imprisonment, regardless of whether they were petty, misdemeanor, or felony offenses. As a result of a series of rulings, the right to counsel now extends to virtually every stage of the criminal justice system: from when police make a quasi-arrest or arrest, to preindictment preliminary hearings and confessions before and after indictment, as well as to preliminary hearings, arraignment proceedings, police lineups, the trial, and subsequent proceedings on sentencing, appeals, and probation hearings. In addition, *Faretta v. California*, 422 U.S. 806 (1975), held that defendants may waive the right to counsel and represent themselves, if a trial judge finds them competent to do so.[6]

The Burger and Rehnquist Courts qualified the application of the right to counsel in a number of areas. Besides the exceptions for

The Scottsboro boys with their attorney Samuel S. Leibowitz. The Scottsboro boys were initially tried before an all-white jury, without the assistance of counsel in a small town, Scottsboro, Alabama, for allegedly raping a white girl. They were sentenced to death, but their convictions were appealed and led to the Supreme Court's important ruling in *Powell v. Alabama* (1932). (*Brown Brothers*)

■ THE DEVELOPMENT OF LAW

Rulings Extending the Right to Counsel throughout the Criminal Justice System

Stage of Criminal Justice System	Case
Quasi-arrest	*Orozco v. Texas*, 394 U.S. 324 (1969)
Arrest	*Miranda v. Arizona*, 384 U.S. 436 (1966)
Preindictment preliminary hearing	*Coleman v. Alabama*, 399 U.S. 1 (1970)
Preindictment confession	*Escobedo v. Illinois*, 378 U.S. 478 (1964)
Postindictment	*Massiah v. United States*, 377 U.S. 201 (1964)
Preliminary hearings	*White v. Maryland*, 373 U.S. 59 (1963)
Arraignment	*Hamilton v. Alabama*, 368 U.S. 52 (1961)
Lineups	*United States v. Wade*, 388 U.S. 218 (1967); and *Gilbert v. California*, 388 U.S. 263 (1967)
Trials	*Gideon v. Wainwright*, 372 U.S. 335 (1963), as modified by *Argersinger v. Hamlin*, 407 U.S. 25 (1972), and *Scott v. Illinois*, 440 U.S. 367 (1979)
Appeals	*Douglas v. California*, 372 U.S. 535 (1963)
Probation hearings	*Mempa v. Rhay*, 389 U.S. 128 (1967)
Revocation of probation or parole	*Gagnon v. Scarpelli*, 411 U.S. 778 (1973)

the presence of counsel during police questioning and interrogation (see Ch. 8), counsel is not required during hearings on the competency of witnesses testifying against the defendant,[7] nor need counsel be present at preindictment lineups[8] or at photo-identification hearings.[9] *Scott v. Illinois*, 440 U.S. 367 (1979), limited *Argersinger* to require court-appointed attorneys only in cases where defendants are in fact sentenced to jail terms.[10] The right to counsel on appeal was limited in *Ross v. Moffitt*, 417 U.S. 600 (1974), holding that the assistance of counsel applies only to the first appeal and not to further discretionary appeals. *Pennsylvania v. Finley*, 481 U.S. 551 (1987), further ruled that defendants have no right to court-appointed attorneys in postconviction proceedings or to insist that a court-appointed lawyer follow certain procedures when withdrawing from their appeals because the lawyer deems further appeals "frivolous."[11] And there is no right to counsel at disciplinary hearings in prison[12] and proceedings on revoking parole.[13] Finally, in *McNeil v. Wisconsin*, 501 U.S. 171 (1991), the Rehnquist Court held that the Sixth Amendment right to counsel does not convey the same protection as *Miranda*'s guarantee of counsel and that an accused who is in police custody may be questioned about another crime in the absence of his attorney without violating the Sixth Amendment, even though such questioning would be in violation of *Miranda*. However, in *Fellers v. United States*, 124 S.Ct. 1019 (2004), a unanimous Court reaffirmed that the Sixth Amendment bars the use of incriminating statements elicited by police from an accused, after waiving his *Miranda* rights, and after he has been indicted for an offense. Writing for the Justice O'Connor reaffirmed that the Sixth Amendment right to counsel bars interrogations or the deliberate elicitation of information, out of the presence of counsel, once judicial proceedings have begun, whether by a formal charge, preliminary hearing, indictment, or arraignment.

NOTES

1. See *Canizio v. New York*, 327 U.S. 82 (1946); and *Bute v. Illinois*, 333 U.S. 640 (1945).

2. *Tomkins v. Missouri*, 323 U.S. 485 (1945).

3. *Townsend v. Burke*, 334 U.S. 736 (1948); and *White v. Ragen*, 324 U.S. 760 (1945).

4. *De Meerleer v. Michigan*, 329 U.S. 663 (1947); *Marino v. Ragen*, 332 U.S. 561 (1947); *Moore v. Michigan*, 355 U.S. 155 (1957); *Massey v. Moorer*, 348 U.S. 105 (1954); *Hudson v. North Carolina*, 363 U.S. 697 (1960); and *Culombe v. Connecticut*, 367 U.S. 568 (1961).

5. *Cash v. Culver*, 358 U.S. 633 (1959).

6. *McKasle v. Wiggins*, 465 U.S. 168 (1984), however, held that the defendant's right to counsel in his own defense was not violated by the unsolicited participation of a standby counsel.

7. *Kentucky v. Stincer*, 482 U.S. 730 (1987), holding that the Sixth Amendment was not violated by denial of attendance of counsel during competency hearings for two minor victims whom the defendant was accused of sodomizing.

8. *Kirby v. Illinois*, 405 U.S. 951 (1972).

9. *United States v. Ash*, 413 U.S. 300 (1973). *Moore v. Illinois*, 434 U.S. 220 (1977), however, held that counsel must be present during a one-on-one corporeal identification of the defendant.

10. Notably, in *Herring v. New York*, 422 U.S. 853 (1975), the Court held that judges may not deny the right to counsel in nonjury trials.

11. In *Anders v. California*, 386 U.S. 738 (1967), the Court held that a court-appointed attorney who seeks to withdraw from a case because he deems further appeals frivolous must file a brief explaining the meritlessness of an appeal as well as anything that might be arguable on appeal, and a court must then determine that there are no nonfrivolous issues. *Penson v. Ohio*, 488 U.S. 75 (1988), reaffirmed that a defendant's attorney after making a first appeal must file an *Anders* brief showing that further appeals are frivolous and justifying the attorney's request to withdraw.

12. *Baxter v. Palmigiano*, 425 U.S. 308 (1976).

13. *Gagnon v. Scarpelli*, 411 U.S. 778 (1973).

Selected Bibliography

Cole, David. *No Equal Justice*. New York: The New Press, 1999.

Garcia, David. *The Sixth Amendment in Modern American Jurisprudence*. Westport, CT: Greenwood Press, 1992.

Goodman, James. *Stories of Scottsboro*. New York: Pantheon, 1994.

Graham, Fred. *The Self-Inflicted Wound*. New York: Macmillan, 1970.

Heller, F. *The Sixth Amendment to the Constitution of the United States*. Lawrence: University of Kansas Press, 1951.

Lewis, Anthony. *Gideon's Trumpet*. New York: Random House, 1964.

Miller, Jerome. *Search and Destroy: African-American Males in the Criminal Justice System*. New York: Cambridge University Press, 1996.

Norris, C., and Washington, S. *The Last of the Scottsboro Boys*. New York: Putnam, 1979.

Powell v. Alabama
287 U.S. 45, 53 S.Ct. 55 (1932)

In Scottsboro, Alabama, Ozie Powell and eight other black youths were arrested, charged, and tried before an all-white jury for raping two white girls traveling on a train. Each was tried separately without the assistance of counsel, and on conviction they were sentenced to death.

Their trials and convictions received wide publicity, and lawyers affiliated with the International Labor Defense, a Communist-front organization in New York, volunteered to represent them on appeal. After the Alabama Supreme Court affirmed their convictions, an appeal was made to the Supreme Court, which granted review. Justice George Sutherland's opinion for the majority discusses some additional facts in the case.

The Court's decision was seven to two, with Justices Butler and McReynolds dissenting.

☐ *Justice SUTHERLAND delivered the opinion of the Court.*

Before the train reached Scottsboro, Ala., a sheriff's posse seized the defendants and two other negroes. Both girls and the negroes then were taken to Scottsboro, the county seat. Word of their coming and of the alleged assault had preceded them, and they were met at Scottsboro by a large crowd. It does not sufficiently appear that the defendants were seriously threatened with, or that they were actually in danger of, mob violence; but it does appear that the attitude of the community was one of great hostility. The sheriff thought it necessary to call for the militia to assist in safeguarding the prisoners. Chief Justice ANDERSON pointed out in his opinion that every step taken from the arrest and arraignment to the sentence was accompanied by the military. Soldiers took the defendants to Gadsden for safe-keeping, brought them back to Scottsboro for arraignment, returned them to Gadsden for safe-keeping while awaiting trial, escorted them to Scottsboro for trial a few days later, and guarded the courthouse and grounds at every stage of the proceedings. It is perfectly apparent that the proceedings, from beginning to end, took place in an atmosphere of tense, hostile, and excited public sentiment. During the entire time, the defendants were closely confined or were under military guard. The record does not disclose their ages, except that one of them was nineteen; but the record clearly indicates that most, if not all, of them were truthful, and they are constantly referred to as "the boys." They were ignorant and illiterate. All of them were residents of other states, where alone members of their families or friends resided. . . .

[W]e confine ourselves . . . to the inquiry whether the defendants were in substance denied the right of counsel, and if so, whether such denial infringes the due process clause of the Fourteenth Amendment.

First. The record shows that immediately upon the return of the indictment defendants were arraigned and pleaded not guilty. Apparently they were not asked whether they had, or were able to employ, counsel, or wished to have counsel appointed; or whether they had friends or relatives who might assist in that regard if communicated with. That it would not have been an idle ceremony to have given the defendants reasonable opportunity to communicate with their families and endeavor to obtain counsel is demonstrated by the fact that very soon after conviction, able counsel appeared in their behalf. . . .

It is hardly necessary to say that the right to counsel being conceded, a defendant should be afforded a fair opportunity to secure counsel of his own choice. Not only was that not done here, but such designation of counsel as was attempted was either so definite or so close upon the trial as to amount to a denial of effective and substantial aid in that regard. . . .

[U]ntil the very morning of the trial no lawyer had been named or definitely designated to represent the defendants. Prior to that time, the trial judge had "appointed all the members of the bar" for the limited "purpose of arraigning the defendants." Whether they would represent the defendants thereafter, if no counsel appeared in their behalf, was a matter of speculation only, or, as the judge indicated, of mere anticipation on the part of the court. Such a designation, even if made for all purposes, would, in our opinion, have fallen far short of meeting, in any proper sense, a requirement for the appointment of counsel. How many lawyers were members of the bar does not appear; but, in the very nature of things, whether many or few, they would not, thus collectively named, have been given that clear appreciation of responsibility or impressed with that individual sense of duty which should and naturally would accompany the appointment of a selected member of the bar, specifically named and assigned.

That this action of the trial judge in respect of appointment of counsel was little more than an expansive gesture, imposing no substantial or definite obligation upon any one. . . . [D]uring perhaps the most critical period of the proceedings against these defendants, that is to say, from the time of their arraignment until the beginning of their trial, when consultation, thoroughgoing investigation and preparation were vitally important, the defendants did not have the aid of counsel in any real sense, although they were as much entitled to such aid during that period as at the trial itself. . . .

The defendants, young, ignorant, illiterate, surrounded by hostile sentiment, haled back and forth under guard of soldiers, charged with an atrocious crime regarded with especial horror in the community where they were to be tried, were thus put in peril of their lives within a few moments after counsel for the first time charged with any degree of responsibility began to represent them. . . .

Under the circumstances disclosed, we hold that defendants were not accorded the right of counsel in any substantial sense. To decide otherwise, would simply be to ignore actualities. . . .

Second. The Constitution of Alabama provides that in all criminal prosecutions the accused shall enjoy the right to have the assistance of counsel; and a state statute requires the court in a capital case, where the defendant is unable to employ counsel, to appoint counsel for him. The state Supreme Court held that these provisions had not been infringed, and with that holding we are powerless to interfere. The question, however, which it is our duty, and within our power, to decide, is whether the denial of the assistance of counsel contravenes the due process clause of the Fourteenth Amendment to the Federal Constitution. . . .

In the light of the facts outlined in the forepart of this opinion—the ignorance and illiteracy of the defendants, their youth, the circumstances of public hostility, the imprisonment and the close surveillance of the defendants by the military forces, the fact that their friends and families were all in other states and communication with them necessarily difficult, and above all that they stood in deadly peril of their lives—we think the failure of the trial court to give them reasonable time and opportunity to secure counsel was a clear denial of due process.

But passing that, and assuming their inability, even if opportunity had been given, to employ counsel, as the trial court evidently did assume, we are of the opinion that, under the circumstances just stated, the necessity of counsel was so vital and imperative that the failure of the trial court to make an effective appointment of counsel was likewise a denial of due process within the meaning of the Fourteenth Amendment. Whether this would be so in other criminal prosecutions, or under other circumstances, we need not determine. All that it is necessary now to decide, as we do decide, is that in a capital case, where the defendant is unable to employ counsel, and is incapable adequately of making his own defense because of ignorance, feeble-mindedness, illiteracy, or the like, it is the duty of the court, whether requested or not, to assign counsel for him as a necessary requisite of due process of law; and that duty is not discharged by an assignment at such a time or under such circumstances as to preclude the giving of effective aid in the preparation and trial of the case. To hold otherwise would be to ignore the fundamental postulate, already adverted to, "that there are certain immutable principles of justice which inhere in the very idea of free government which no member of the Union may disregard."

Gideon v. Wainwright

372 U.S. 335, 83 S.CT. 792 (1963)

Clarence Earl Gideon, a fifty-one-year-old rambler who was in and out of jails for most of his life, was convicted of breaking and entering into the Bay Harbor Poolroom in Panama City, Florida. At his trial, he claimed he was too poor to afford an attorney and requested that one be provided. The judge refused, and Gideon was convicted and sentenced. But Gideon persisted. While serving a five-year sentence for petty larceny in the Florida State Prison, he mailed a petition, printed on lined paper obtained from a prison guard, to the Supreme Court.

Gideon did not know that he was asking the Court to reverse itself. In *Betts v. Brady* (1942), the Court had held that only in special circumstances, like those in the *Scottsboro* case, was counsel required. Justice Hugo Black, along with Justices Douglas and Murphy, had dissented in *Betts*. Only three members of the Court that decided *Betts*, however, remained when Gideon's petition was granted: two of the dissenters—Black and Douglas—and Felix Frankfurter, who was eighty years old, ill, and in his last year on the bench. They had been joined by Tom Clark and President Eisenhower's appointees—Warren, Harlan, Brennan, Whittaker, and Stewart. By the time *Gideon* was handed

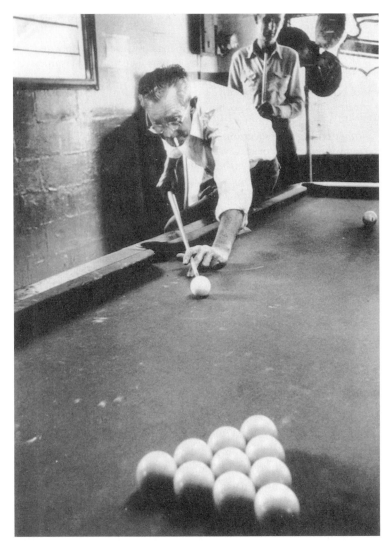

Clarence Gideon in 1964. This photograph was taken two years after the land-mark ruling by the Supreme Court holding that all defendants accused of seri-ous crimes have a right to representation by counsel. (*Flip Schulke/1964 Time Warner Inc.*)

down, Frankfurter and Whittaker had retired. They had been replaced by President Kennedy's appointees—Arthur Goldberg and Byron White.

Gideon fit the agenda of the Warren Court. In fact, Chief Justice Warren had told his law clerks to look for a case that would enable the Court to overrule *Betts*'s special circumstance rule for when the assis-tance of counsel was required for defendants in criminal cases. After granting Gideon's case, Warren asked prominent Washington, D.C., lawyer (and later Supreme Court justice) Abe Fortas to act as counsel for Gideon on his appeal. Because of Justice Black's long-standing interest in overturning *Betts*, Warren assigned him to write the opinion announcing the Court's decision.

The Court's decision was unanimous; the opinion was announced by Justice Black. Concurrences were by Justices Douglas, Clark, and Harlan.

☐ *Justice BLACK delivered the opinion of the Court.*

Since 1942, when *Betts v. Brady*, 316 U.S. 455, was decided by a divided Court, the problem of a defendant's federal constitutional right to counsel in a state court has been a continuing source of controversy and litigation in both state and federal courts. To give this problem another review here, we granted *certiorari*. Since Gideon was proceeding *in forma pauperis*, we appointed counsel to represent him and requested both sides to discuss in their briefs and oral arguments the following: "Should this Court's holding in *Betts v. Brady*, be reconsidered?"

The facts upon which Betts claimed that he had been unconstitutionally denied the right to have counsel appointed to assist him are strikingly like the facts upon which Gideon here bases his federal constitutional claim. . . . Treating due process as "a concept less rigid and more fluid than those envisaged in other specific and particular provisions of the Bill of Rights," the Court held that refusal to appoint counsel under the particular facts and circumstances in the *Betts* case was not so "offensive to the common and fundamental ideas of fairness" as to amount to a denial of due process. Since the facts and circumstances of the two cases are so nearly indistinguishable, we think the *Betts v. Brady* holding if left standing would require us to reject Gideon's claim that the Constitution guarantees him the assistance of counsel. Upon full reconsideration we conclude that *Betts v. Brady* should be overruled. . . .

We accept *Betts v. Brady*'s assumption, based as it was on our prior cases, that a provision of the Bill of Rights which is "fundamental and essential to a fair trial" is made obligatory upon the States by the Fourteenth Amendment. We think the Court in *Betts* was wrong, however, in concluding that the Sixth Amendment's guarantee of counsel is not one of these fundamental rights. Ten years before *Betts v. Brady*, this Court, after full consideration of all the historical data examined in *Betts*, had unequivocally declared that "the right to the aid of counsel is of this fundamental character." *Powell v. Alabama*. . . . While the Court at the close of its *Powell* opinion did by its language, as this Court frequently does, limit its holding to the particular facts and circumstances of that case, its conclusions about the fundamental nature of the right to counsel are unmistakable.

In light of these and many other prior decisions of this Court, it is not surprising that the *Betts* Court, when faced with the contention that "one charged with crime, who is unable to obtain counsel, must be furnished counsel by the state," conceded that "[e]xpressions in the opinions of this court lend color to the argument. . . ." The fact is that in deciding as it did— that "appointment of counsel is not a fundamental right, essential to a fair

DIVISION OF CORRECTIONS
CORRESPONDENCE REGULATIONS

MAIL WILL NOT BE DELIVERED WHICH DOES NOT CONFORM WITH THESE RULES

No. 1 -- Only 2 letters each week, not to exceed 2 sheets letter-size 8 1/2 x 11" and written *on one side only*, and if ruled paper, do not write between lines. *Your complete name* must be signed at the close of your letter. *Clippings, stamps, letters* from other people, *stationery* or *cash* must not be enclosed in your letters.

No. 2 -- All *letters* must be addressed in the complete prison name of the inmate. *Cell number*, where applicable, and *prison number* must be placed in lower left corner of envelope, with your complete name and address in the upper left corner.

No. 3 -- *Do not send any packages without a Package Permit.* Unauthorized *packages* will be destroyed.

No. 4 -- *Letters* must be written in English only.

No. 5 -- *Books, magazines, pamphlets,* and *newspapers* of reputable character will be delivered *only if* mailed direct from the publisher.

No. 6 -- *Money* must be sent in the form of *Postal Money Orders* only, in the inmate's complete prison name and prison number.

INSTITUTION _____ CELL NUMBER _____

NAME _____ NUMBER _____

In The Supreme Court of The United States
Washington D.C.
Clarence Earl Gideon
Petitioner — | Petition for a writ
vs. | of Certiorari Directed
H.G. Cochran, Jr, as | To The Supreme Court
Director, Divisions | State of Florida.
of corrections State | No. 890 Misc.
of Florida — | OCT. TERM 1961
U.S. Supreme Court

To. The Honorable Earl Warren, Chief
Justice of the United States
Comes now The petitioner, Clarence
Earl Gideon, a citizen of The United States
of America, in proper person, and appearing
as his own counsel. Who petitions this
Honorable Court for a Writ of Certiorari
directed To The Supreme Court of The State
of Florida, To review the order and Judge-
ment of the court below denying The
petitioner a Writ of Habeus Corpus.
*   Petitioner submits That The Supreme*
Court of The United States has The authority
and jurisdiction to review The final Judge-
ment of The Supreme Court of The State
of Florida The highest court of The State.
Under sec. 344 (B) Title 28 U.S.C.A. and
Because The "Due process clause" of the

Clarence Gideon's petition to the Supreme Court, which led to the Warren Court's landmark ruling on the right to counsel. (*Collection of the Supreme Court of the United States*)

trial"—the Court in *Betts v. Brady* made an abrupt break with its own well-considered precedents. In returning to these old precedents, sounder we believe than the new, we but restore constitutional principles established to achieve a fair system of justice. Not only these precedents but also reason and reflection require us to recognize that in our adversary system of criminal justice, any person haled into court, who is too poor to hire a lawyer, cannot be assured a fair trial unless counsel is provided for him. This seems to us to be an obvious truth. Governments, both state and federal, quite properly spend vast sums of money to establish machinery to try defendants accused of crime. Lawyers to prosecute are everywhere deemed essential to protect the public's interest in an orderly society. Similarly, there are few defendants charged with crime, few indeed, who fail to hire the best lawyers they can get to prepare and present their defenses. That government hires lawyers to prosecute and defendants who have the money hire lawyers to defend are the strongest indications of the widespread belief that lawyers in criminal courts are necessities, not luxuries. The right of one charged with crime to counsel may not be deemed fundamental and essential to fair trials in some countries, but it is in ours. From the very beginning, our state and national constitutions and laws have laid great emphasis on procedural and substantive safeguards designed to assure fair trials before impartial tribunals in which every defendant stands equal before the law. This noble ideal cannot be realized if the poor man charged with crime has to face his accusers without a lawyer to assist him. . . . The Court in *Betts v. Brady* departed from the sound wisdom upon which the Court's holding in *Powell v. Alabama* rested. Florida, supported by two other States, has asked that *Betts v. Brady* be left intact. Twenty-two States, as friends of the Court, argue that *Betts* was "an anachronism when handed down" and that it should now be overruled. We agree.

☐ *Justice CLARK, concurring.*

The Court's decision today . . . does no more than erase a distinction which has no basis in logic and an increasingly eroded basis in authority. . . .

I [also think] that the Constitution makes no distinction between capital and noncapital cases. The Fourteenth Amendment requires due process of law for the deprival of "liberty" just as for deprival of "life," and there cannot constitutionally be a difference in the quality of the process based merely upon a supposed difference in the sanction involved. How can the Fourteenth Amendment tolerate a procedure which it condemns in capital cases on the ground that deprival of liberty may be less onerous than deprival of life—a value judgment not universally accepted—or that only the latter deprival is irrevocable? I can find no acceptable rationalization for such a result, and I therefore concur in the judgment of the Court.

Argersinger v. Hamlin
407 U.S. 25, 92 S.Ct. 2006 (1972)

In his opinion for the Court, Justice William O. Douglas discusses the pertinent facts involving the appeal of an individual's conviction for carrying a concealed weapon, a crime that was punishable by imprisonment for up to six months, in holding that defendants accused of petty offenses that carry punishments of six months or more imprisonment are entitled to representation by counsel.

The Court's decision was unanimous; the opinion was announced by Justice Douglas. Chief Justice Burger and Justices Brennan and Powell concurred, with whom Justice Rehnquist joined.

☐ *Justice DOUGLAS delivered the opinion of the Court.*

Petitioner, an indigent, was charged in Florida with carrying a concealed weapon, an offense punishable by imprisonment up to six months, a $1,000 fine, or both. The trial was to a judge, and petitioner was unrepresented by counsel. He was sentenced to serve 90 days in jail, and brought this habeas corpus action in the Florida Supreme Court, alleging that, being deprived of his right to counsel, he was unable as an indigent layman properly to raise and present to the trial court good and sufficient defenses to the charge for which he stands convicted. The Florida Supreme Court by a four-to-three decision, in ruling on the right to counsel, followed the line we marked out in *Duncan v. Louisiana*, 391 U.S. 145 [(1968)], as respects the right to trial by jury and held that the right to court-appointed counsel extends only to trials "for non-petty offenses punishable by more than six months imprisonment." . . .

We reverse. . . .

Both *Powell* [*v. Alabama*, 287 U.S. 45 (1932)] and *Gideon* [*v. Wainwright*, 372 U.S. 335 (1963)] involved felonies. But their rationale has relevance to any criminal trial, where an accused is deprived of his liberty. *Powell* and *Gideon* suggest that there are certain fundamental rights applicable to all such criminal prosecutions. . . .

The requirement of counsel may well be necessary for a fair trial even in a petty-offense prosecution. We are by no means convinced that legal and constitutional questions involved in a case that actually leads to imprisonment even for a brief period are any less complex than when a person can be sent off for six months or more. . . .

The trial of vagrancy cases is illustrative. While only brief sentences of imprisonment may be imposed, the cases often bristle with thorny constitutional questions. . . .

In addition, the volume of misdemeanor cases, far greater in number than felony prosecutions, may create an obsession for speedy dispositions, regardless of the fairness of the result. . . .

That picture is seen in almost every report. "The misdemeanor trial is characterized by insufficient and frequently irresponsible preparation on the part of the defense, the prosecution, and the court. Everything is rush, rush." . . .

There is evidence of the prejudice which results to misdemeanor defendants from this "assembly-line justice." One study concluded that "[m]isdemeanants represented by attorneys are five times as likely to emerge from police court with all charges dismissed as are defendants who face similar charges without counsel." American Civil Liberties Union, Legal Counsel for Misdemeanants, Preliminary Report 1 (1970). . . .

We hold, therefore, that absent a knowing and intelligent waiver, no person may be imprisoned for any offense, whether classified as petty, misdemeanor, or felony, unless he was represented by counsel at his trial.

☐ *Justice POWELL, with whom Justice REHNQUIST joins, concurring.*

There is a middle course, between the extremes of Florida's six-month rule and the Court's rule, which comports with the requirements of the Fourteenth Amendment. I would adhere to the principle of due process that requires fundamental fairness in criminal trials, a principle which I believe encompasses the right to counsel in petty cases whenever the assistance of counsel is necessary to assure a fair trial.

I am in accord with the Court that an indigent accused's need for the assistance of counsel does not mysteriously evaporate when he is charged with an offense punishable by six months or less. . . . [But, t]his is not to say that due process requires the appointment of counsel in all petty cases, or that assessment of the possible consequences of conviction is the sole test for the need for assistance of counsel. The flat six-month rule of the Florida court and the equally inflexible rule of the majority opinion apply to *all* cases within their defined areas regardless of circumstances. It is precisely because of this mechanistic application that I find these alternatives unsatisfactory. Due process, perhaps the most fundamental concept in our law, embodies principles of fairness rather than immutable line drawing as to every aspect of a criminal trial. . . .

I would hold that the right to counsel in petty-offense cases is not absolute but is one to be determined by the trial courts exercising a judicial discretion on a case-by-case basis. The determination should be made before the accused formally pleads; many petty cases are resolved by guilty pleas in which the assistance of counsel may be required. If the trial court should conclude that the assistance of counsel is not required in any case, it should state its reasons so that the issue could be preserved for review. The trial court would then become obligated to scrutinize carefully the subsequent proceedings for the protection of the defendant. If an unrepresented defendant sought to enter a plea of guilty, the Court should examine the case against him to insure that there is admissible evidence tending to support the elements of the offense. If a case went to trial without defense counsel, the court should intervene, when necessary, to insure that the defendant adequately brings out the facts in his favor and to prevent legal issues from being overlooked. Formal trial rules should not be applied strictly against unrepresented defendants. Finally, appellate courts should carefully scrutinize all decisions not to appoint counsel and the proceedings which follow.

It is impossible, as well as unwise, to create a precise and detailed set of guidelines for judges to follow in determining whether the appointment of counsel is necessary to assure a fair trial. Certainly three general factors should be weighed. First, the court should consider the complexity of the offense charged. . . .

Second, the court should consider the probable sentence that will follow if a conviction is obtained. The more serious the likely consequences, the greater is the probability that a lawyer should be appointed. . . .

Third, the court should consider the individual factors peculiar to each case. These, of course, would be the most difficult to anticipate. One relevant factor would be the competency of the individual defendant to present his own case. The attitude of the community toward a particular defendant or particular incident would be another consideration. But there might be other reasons why a defendant would have a peculiar need for a lawyer which would compel the appointment of counsel in a case where the court would normally think this unnecessary. Obviously, the sensitivity and diligence of individual judges would be crucial to the operation of a rule of fundamental fairness requiring the consideration of the varying factors in each case.

B | *Plea Bargaining and the Right to Effective Counsel*

Plea bargaining is the practice of prosecutors and defense attorneys agreeing to terms on which the defendant agrees to plead guilty to a lesser charge than the one originally charged in exchange for a reduced sentence. Over 90 percent of all guilty pleas are the result of this practice. The advantage for the government is that it cuts the time and costs of attorneys, trials, and other resources of the criminal justice system. While the defendant receives a reduced sentence, he forgoes several constitutional rights, including, among others, the Fifth Amendment right against self-accusation and the Sixth Amendment rights to a public trial and to confront one's accusers as well as the presumption of innocence.

Brady v. United States, 397 U.S. 742 (1970), upheld the constitutionality of plea bargaining as having a "mutuality of advantage." The state, observed Justice White in his opinion for the Court, conserves "scarce judicial and prosecutorial resources" and achieves "more promptly imposed punishment;" while for the defendant, "his exposure is reduced, the correctional process can begin immediately, and the practical burdens of a trial are eliminated."

Critics of plea bargaining, though, question the constitutionality of defendants forgoing their constitutional rights and whether they are compelled to do so. The five-to-four ruling in *Bordenkircher v. Hayes* (1978) (excerpted below) illustrates the issue and how it has divided the Court.

Another issue arising with plea bargaining (and more generally with court-appointed attorneys) is whether defendants have a right to *effective* counsel. In *McMann v. Richardson*, 397 U.S. 759 (1970), three defendants claimed that their confessions were coerced and their court-appointed attorney had incompetently represented them. But the Court held that their attorney was "reasonably competent" and they must assume the risk of "ordinary error" by their attorneys. *Henderson v. Morgan*, 426 U.S. 637 (1976), however, set aside a conviction because the defendant pled guilty to second-degree murder without being informed of the consequences. The Court, nonetheless, remains reluctant to find attorneys incompetent, even when they have little or no time to confer with their clients[1] and when they misinform their clients on plea bargaining.[2]

The right to counsel includes a right to effective counsel, as Justice Stevens explained in *United States v. Cronic*, 466 U.S. 640 (1984), because competent counsel is essential to the accusatory system and "the reliability of the trial process."[3] Accordingly, public defenders do not enjoy absolute immunity from being sued for incompetent representation.[4] The test for determining when the right to effective counsel has been denied was set forth by Justice O'Connor in *Strickland v. Washington*, 466 U.S. 668 (1984):

> A convicted defendant's claim that counsel's assistance was so defective as to require reversal of a conviction or death sentence has two components. First, the defendant must show that counsel's per-for-mance was deficient. This requires showing that counsel made errors so serious that counsel was not functioning as the "counsel" guaranteed the defendant by the Sixth Amendment. Second, the defendant must show that the deficient performance prejudiced the defense. This requires showing that counsel's errors were so serious as to deprive the defendant of a fair trial, a trial whose result is reliable. Unless a defendant makes both showings, it cannot be said that the conviction or death sentence resulted from a breakdown in the adversary process that renders the result unreliable. . . .

> More specific guidelines are not appropriate. The Sixth Amendment refers simply to "counsel," not specifying particular requirements of effective assistance. It relies instead on the legal profession's maintenance of standards sufficient to justify the law's presumption that counsel will fulfill the role in the adversary process that the Amendment envisions. . . . The proper measure of attorney performance remains simply reasonableness under prevailing professional norms. . . .

O'Connor concluded by emphasizing the Court's deference to counsel in cases challenging their competence and effectiveness:

> Judicial scrutiny of counsel's performance must be highly deferential. It is all too tempting for a defendant to second-guess counsel's assistance after conviction or adverse sentence, and it is all too easy for a court, examining counsel's defense after it has proved unsuccessful, to conclude that a particular act or omission of counsel was unreasonable. . . . A fair assessment of attorney performance requires that every effort be made to eliminate the distorting effects of hindsight, to reconstruct the circumstances of counsel's challenged conduct, and to evaluate the conduct from counsel's perspective at the time. Because of the difficulties inherent in making the evaluation, a court must indulge a strong presumption that counsel's conduct falls within the wide range of reasonable professional assistance; that is, the defendant must overcome the presumption that,

under the circumstances, the challenged action "might be considered sound trial strategy." . . . There are countless ways to provide effective assistance in any given case. Even the best criminal defense attorneys would not defend a particular client in the same way.

Subsequently, the Court held that defendants have a right to effective counsel on their first appeal, *Evitts v. Lucey*, 469 U.S. 830 (1985). But when defendants tell their attorneys that they are going to lie on the witness stand, attorneys may withdraw from their cases without denying the right to effective counsel.[5] In *Mallard v. U.S. District Court*, 490 U.S. 296 (1989), the Court also held that a judge may not compel a lawyer to serve as a defendant's court-appointed counsel.

NOTES

1. See *Morris v. Slappy*, 461 U.S. 1 (1983); and *Chambers v. Maroney*, 399 U.S. 42 (1970).

2. See *North Carolina v. Alford*, 400 U.S. 25 (1970); and *Tollett v. Henderson*, 411 U.S. 258 (1976).

3. See also *Entsminger v. Iowa*, 386 U.S. 748 (1967), holding that defendant was denied the right to effective counsel when the court-appointed attorney failed to file the entire record on appeal.

4. *Ferri v. Ackerman*, 444 U.S. 193 (1979).

5. *Nix v. Whiteside*, 475 U.S. 157 (1986).

SELECTED BIBLIOGRAPHY

Fisher, George. *Plea Bargaining's Triumph: A History of Plea Bargaining in America.* Palo Alto, CA: Stanford University Press, 2003.

McCoy, Candace. *Politics and Plea Bargaining: Victims' Rights in California.* Philadelphia: University of Pennsylvania Press, 1993.

Nardulli, Peter, Eisenstein, James, and Flemming, Roy. *The Tenor of Justice: Criminal Courts and the Guilty Plea Process.* Urbana: University of Illinois Press, 1988.

Packer, Herbert. *The Limits of the Criminal Sanction.* Stanford, CA: Stanford University Press, 1968.

Vogel, Mary. *Coercion to Compromise: Social Conflict and the Emergence of Plea Bargaining.* New York: Oxford University Press, 2001.

■ The Development of Law

Rulings on Plea Bargaining and Effective Counsel

CASE	VOTE	RULING
McCarthy v. United States, 394 U.S. 459 (1969)	9:0	Held that guilty pleas must be personally presented to a judge and the latter must assess their voluntariness.
McMann v. Richardson, 397 U.S. 759 (1970)	6:3	A defendant who enters a guilty plea is not compelled to plead guilty under the Fifth Amendment merely because the plea was a way of avoiding the death penalty.
North Carolina v. Alford, 400 U.S. 25 (1970)	6:3	A guilty plea prevents a defendant from subsequently making a *habeas corpus* claim that his confession was coerced.
Santobello v. New York, 404 U.S. 257 (1971)	6:3	Once a state agrees to a plea bargain it must be honored; here, the state reneged on a bargain struck due to a change in prosecutors.
Rummell v. Estelle, 445 U.S. 263 (1980)	5:4	The Eighth Amendment ban on cruel and unusual punishment was not violated when a

prosecutor threatened a defendant, who insisted on his right to a jury trial, that if he did not agree to a plea bargain he would be indicted and tried under the state's criminal recidivist statute for having committed three prior felonies, and the defendant was sentenced to lifetime imprisonment.

Ricketts v. Adamson, 483 U.S. 1 (1987)	5:4	Held that the Fifth Amendment guarantee against double jeopardy was not violated by the

prosecution of a defendant on the original charge of murder because he breached a plea-bargain agreement to testify against codefendants.

Alabama v. Smith, 490 U.S. 794 (1989)	8:1	Held there is no presumption of unfairness when a judge imposes a harsher sentence on a criminal

defendant who is convicted after a trial, and after backing out of a plea-bargain agreement that had called for a lighter sentence.

CASE	VOTE	RULING
Keeney v. Tampayo-Reyes, 504 U.S. 1 (1992)	5:4	A bare majority held that a Cuban immigrant, who pleaded no-contest to a murder charge but later claimed that the Span-

ish translation of his plea was so poor that he did not understand the basics of his plea-bargain agreement, had forfeited the opportunity for federal *habeas corpus* review because his lawyer failed to spell out adequately the important facts supporting that claim in state court proceedings.

Lockhart v. Fretwell, 506 U.S. 364 (1993)	7:2	Held that a *habeas corpus* petitioner was not denied his Sixth and Fourteenth Amendment

rights to effective counsel during the sentencing phase of a capital felony-murder trial.

Parke v. Raley, 506 U.S. 20 (1992)	8:0	Rejected a claim by a three-time convicted felon who was sentenced to five years for rob-

bery and an additional ten years under Kentucky's "persistent felony offender" statute that he had been denied due process because his first two convictions were the result of plea bargains and that records of those proceedings were not introduced and thus the state had not shown that his pleas were made knowingly and voluntarily.

Godinez v. Moran, 509 U.S. 389 (1993)	7:2	Writing for the Court, Justice Thomas held that the competency standard for pleading

guilty or waiving the right to counsel at trial is the same for standing trial: whether the defendant has "sufficient present ability to consult with his lawyer with a reasonable degree of rational understanding" and a "rational as well as factual understanding of the proceedings against him."

Roe v. Flores-Ortega, 528 U.S. 470 (2000)	6:3	Writing for the Court, Justice O'Connor reaffirmed the holding in *Strickland v. Washington*,

466 U. S. 668 (1984), that a defendant claiming ineffective counsel must show (1) that the counsel's representation fell below an objective standard of reasonableness and (2) that the deficient performance prejudiced the defendant. It was further held that counsel has a constitutionally imposed duty to consult with the defendant about appeals when there is reason to think either that a rational defendant would want to appeal or that the defendant indicated an interest in appealing.

Williams v. Taylor, 529 U.S. 362 (2000)	6:3 & 5:4	Writing for the Court, Justice Stevens held that Terry Williams was denied his constititionally

CASE	VOTE	RULING

guaranteed right to effective counsel, as defined in *Strickland v. Washington*, 466 U.S. 668 (1984), because his attorney failed to investigate and to present substantial mitigating evidence to the jury. Justices O'Connor, Kennedy, Souter, Ginsburg, and Breyer joined portions of that opinion. Justice O'Connor delivered an opinion for the Court holding that the Antiterrorism and Effective Death Penalty Act of 1996 places a new constraint on federal courts in granting writs of *habeas corpus* review; they may grant review only if the state court's adjudication was "contrary to" or "involved an unreasonable application of clearly established federal law." Chief Justice Rehnquist and Justices Kennedy, Scalia, and Thomas joined that opinion.

Mickens v. Taylor, 535 U.S. 162 (2002) — 5:4 — Rejected a death row inmate's claim that his Sixth Amendment right to effective counsel was violated because his court-appointed attorney had previously represented the murder victim.

Wiggins v. Smith, 539 U.S. 510 (2003) — 7:2 — Overturned a death sentence upon finding that the defendant's attorney failed to investigate and to introduce mitigating factors related to sexual abuse and that the failure to do so violated the Sixth Amendment right to effective counsel under *Strickland v. Washington*, 466 U.S. 668 (1984).

Iowa v. Tovar, 124 S.Ct. 1379 (2004) — 9:0 — Writing for the Court, Justice Ginsburg held that the Sixth Amendment right to counsel is not violated by an accused pleading guilty in a plea bargain without the assistance of an attorney, because he waived the right, was informed of the consequences of pleading guilty, and made a knowing and intelligent act.

United States v. Dominguez Benitez, 124 S.Ct. 2333 (2004) — 9:0 — Justice Souter rejected a claim that a sentence should be overturned because a federal district court judge failed to warn the defendant that if the court did not accept a plea bargain he could not withdraw his guilty plea, since it was stipulated in the signed agreement and made no difference in the outcome.

Bordenkircher v. Hayes

434 U.S. 357, 98 S.CT. 663 (1978)

Justice Potter Stewart discusses the facts in his opinion for the Court, upholding a prosecutor's threat of indictment and conviction of Paul Hayes under Kentucky's Habitual Criminal Act because Mr. Hayes refused to agree to a plea bargain and insisted on a trial when he was charged with forging a check in the amount of $88.30.

The Court's decision was five to four, and the majority's opinion was announced by Justice Stewart. Dissents were by Justices Powell and Blackmun, who was joined by Justices Brennan and Marshall.

☐ *STEWART delivered the opinion of the Court.*

The question in this case is whether the Due Process Clause of the Fourteenth Amendment is violated when a state prosecutor carries out a threat made during plea negotiations to reindict the accused on more serious charges if he does not plead guilty to the offense with which he was originally charged.

The respondent, Paul Lewis Hayes, was indicted by a Fayette County, Ky., grand jury on a charge of uttering a forged instrument in the amount of $88.30, an offense then punishable by a term of two to ten years in prison. Ky.Rev.Stat. § 434.130 (repealed 1974). After arraignment, Hayes, his retained counsel, and the Commonwealth's attorney met in the presence of the clerk of the court to discuss a possible plea agreement. During these conferences the prosecutor offered to recommend a sentence of five years in prison if Hayes would plead guilty to the indictment. He also said that if Hayes did not plead guilty and "save the court the inconvenience and necessity of a trial," he would return to the grand jury to seek an indictment under the Kentucky Habitual Criminal Act, then Ky.Rev.Stat. § 431.190 (repealed 1975), which would subject Hayes to a mandatory sentence of life imprisonment by reason of his two prior felony convictions. Hayes chose not to plead guilty, and the prosecutor did obtain an indictment charging him under the Habitual Criminal Act. . . .

A jury found Hayes guilty on the principal charge of uttering a forged instrument and, in a separate proceeding, further found that he had twice before been convicted of felonies. As required by the habitual offender statute, he was sentenced to a life term in the penitentiary. . . .

It may be helpful to clarify at the outset the nature of the issue in this case. While the prosecutor did not actually obtain the recidivist indictment until after the plea conferences had ended, his intention to do so was clearly put forth at the outset of the plea negotiations. Hayes was thus fully informed of the true terms of the offer when he made his decision to plead not guilty. This is not a situation, therefore, where the prosecutor without notice brought an additional and more serious charge after plea negotiations relating only to the original indictment had ended with the defendant's insistence on pleading not guilty. As a practical matter, in short, this case would be no different if the grand jury had indicted Hayes as a recidivist from the outset, and the prosecutor had offered to drop that charge as part of the plea bargain.

The Court of Appeals nonetheless drew a distinction between "concessions relating to prosecution under an existing indictment," and threats to bring more severe charges not contained in the original indictment—a line it thought necessary in order to establish a prophylactic rule to guard against the evil of prosecutorial vindictiveness. . . .

We have recently had occasion to observe that "[w]hatever might be the situation in an ideal world, the fact is that the guilty plea and the often concomitant plea bargain are important components of this country's criminal justice system. Properly administered, they can benefit all concerned." *Blackledge v. Allison*, 431 U.S. 63 [(1977)]. The open acknowledgment of this previously clandestine practice has led this Court to recognize the importance of counsel during plea negotiations, *Brady v. United States*, 397 U.S. 742 [(1970)]. The need for a public record indicating that a plea was knowingly and voluntarily made, *Boykin v. Alabama*, 395 U.S. 238 [(1969)]. And the requirement that a prosecutor's plea bargaining promise must be kept, *Santobello v. New York*, 404 U.S. 257 [(1971)]. . . .

Plea bargaining flows from "the mutuality of advantage" to defendants and prosecutors, each with his own reasons for wanting to avoid trial. *Brady v. United States*. Defendants advised by competent counsel and protected by other procedural safeguards are presumptively capable of intelligent choice in response to prosecutorial persuasion, and unlikely to be driven to false self-condemnation. Indeed, acceptance of the basic legitimacy of plea bargaining necessarily implies rejection of any notion that a guilty plea is involuntary in a constitutional sense simply because it is the end result of the bargaining process. By hypothesis, the plea may have been induced by promises of a recommendation of a lenient sentence or a reduction of charges, and thus by fear of the possibility of a greater penalty upon conviction after a trial. . . .

While confronting a defendant with the risk of more severe punishment clearly may have a "discouraging effect on the defendant's assertion of his trial rights, the imposition of these difficult choices [is] an inevitable"—and permissible—"attribute of any legitimate system which tolerates and encourages the negotiation of pleas." It follows that, by tolerating and encouraging the negotiation of pleas, this Court has necessarily accepted as constitutionally legitimate the simple reality that the prosecutor's interest at the bargaining table is to persuade the defendant to forego his right to plead not guilty.

It is not disputed here that Hayes was properly chargeable under the recidivist statute, since he had in fact been convicted of two previous felonies. In our system, so long as the prosecutor has probable cause to believe that the accused committed an offense defined by statute, the decision whether or not to prosecute, and what charge to file or bring before a grand jury, generally rests entirely in his discretion. . . .

There is no doubt that the breadth of discretion that our country's legal system vests in prosecuting attorneys carries with it the potential for both individual and institutional abuse. And broad though that discretion may be, there are undoubtedly constitutional limits upon its exercise. We hold only that the course of conduct engaged in by the prosecutor in this case, which no more than openly presented the defendant with the unpleasant alternatives of foregoing trial or facing charges on which he was plainly subject to prosecution, did not violate the Due Process Clause of the Fourteenth Amendment.

Accordingly, the judgment of the Court of Appeals is

Reversed.

□ *Justice BLACKMUN, with whom Justice BRENNAN and Justice MARSHALL join, dissenting.*

Prosecutorial vindictiveness, it seems to me, in the present narrow context, is the fact against which the Due Process Clause ought to protect. I perceive little difference between vindictiveness after what the Court describes, as the exercise of a "legal right to attack his original conviction," and vindictiveness in the "give-and-take negotiation common in plea bargaining." Prosecutorial vindictiveness in any context is still prosecutorial vindictiveness. The Due Process Clause should protect an accused against it, however it asserts itself.

□ *Justice POWELL, dissenting.*

Although I agree with much of the Court's opinion, I am not satisfied that the result in this case is just or that the conduct of the plea bargaining met the requirements of due process.

Respondent was charged with the uttering of a single forged check in the amount of $88.30. Under Kentucky law, this offense was punishable by a prison term of from two to 10 years, apparently without regard to the amount of the forgery. During the course of plea bargaining, the prosecutor offered respondent a sentence of five years in consideration of a guilty plea. I observe, at this point, that five years in prison for the offense charged hardly could be characterized as a generous offer. Apparently respondent viewed the offer in this light and declined to accept it; he protested that he was innocent and insisted on going to trial. . . .

The prosecutor's initial assessment of respondent's case led him to forego an indictment under the habitual criminal statute. The circumstances of respondent's prior convictions are relevant to this assessment and to my view of the case. Respondent was 17 years old when he committed his first offense. He was charged with rape but pled guilty to the lesser included offense of "detaining a female." One of the other participants in the incident was sentenced to life imprisonment. Respondent was sent not to prison but to a reformatory where he served five years. Respondent's second offense was robbery. This time he was found guilty by a jury and was sentenced to five years in prison, but he was placed on probation and served no time. Although respondent's prior convictions brought him within the terms of the Habitual Criminal Act, the offenses themselves did not result in imprisonment; yet the addition of a conviction on a charge involving $88.30 subjected respondent to a mandatory sentence of imprisonment for life. Persons convicted of rape and murder often are not punished so severely. . . .

It seems to me that the question to be asked under the circumstances is whether the prosecutor reasonably might have charged respondent under the

Habitual Criminal Act in the first place. The deference that courts properly accord the exercise of a prosecutor's discretion perhaps would foreclose judicial criticism if the prosecutor originally had sought an indictment under that act, as unreasonable as it would have seemed. But here the prosecutor evidently made a reasonable, responsible judgment not to subject an individual to a mandatory life sentence when his only new offense had societal implications as limited as those accompanying the uttering of a single $88 forged check and when the circumstances of his prior convictions confirmed the inappropriateness of applying the habitual criminal statute. I think it may be inferred that the prosecutor himself deemed it unreasonable and not in the public interest to put this defendant in jeopardy of a sentence of life imprisonment. . . .

In most cases a court could not know why the harsher indictment was sought, and an inquiry into the prosecutor's motive would neither be indicated nor likely to be fruitful. In those cases, I would agree with the majority that the situation would not differ materially from one in which the higher charge was brought at the outset.

But this is not such a case. Here, any inquiry into the prosecutor's purpose is made unnecessary by his candid acknowledgement that he threatened to procure and in fact procured the habitual criminal indictment because of respondent's insistence on exercising his constitutional rights. . . .

The plea-bargaining process, as recognized by this Court, is essential to the functioning of the criminal-justice system. It normally affords genuine benefits to defendants as well as to society. And if the system is to work effectively, prosecutors must be accorded the widest discretion, within constitutional limits, in conducting bargaining. This is especially true when a defendant is represented by counsel and presumably is fully advised of his rights. Only in the most exceptional case should a court conclude that the scales of the bargaining are so unevenly balanced as to arouse suspicion. In this case, the prosecutor's actions denied respondent due process because their admitted purpose was to discourage and then to penalize with unique severity his exercise of constitutional rights. Implementation of a strategy calculated solely to deter the exercise of constitutional rights is not a constitutionally permissible exercise of discretion. I would affirm the opinion of the Court of Appeals on the facts of this case.

C | *Indictment by a Grand Jury*

Embedded in the colonies as part of the English common law was the right to a jury trial. But in the 1760s and 1770s, colonists deeply resented royalist judges and were hostile to the legal profession that defended the system. The institution of indictment by a grand jury grew out of colonial hostility toward royalist courts. Prosecuting officers had to make a prima facie case to a body of laymen that an individual violated criminal law, and if the grand jury was persuaded it would vote for an indictment on the charges presented. The original thirteen states, however, varied in the power given to juries. As Alexander Hamilton noted in *The Federalist*, No. 83, "no general rule could have been fixed by the Convention which would have corresponded with the circumstances of all the States."

The Fifth Amendment provides that "no person shall be held to answer for a capital [crime, which carries the death penalty] or otherwise infamous crime, unless on a presentment or indictment of a Grand Jury." This guarantee applies to only the national government because the Court has never reversed *Hurtado v. California*, 110 U.S. 516 (1884) (see Ch. 4), which ruled that the guarantee for an indictment by a grand jury does not apply to the states under the Fourteenth Amendment's due process clause. A grand jury consists of twelve to twenty-three laymen—typically selected by lot from voting rolls or chosen by local officials. The district attorney meets with the grand jury in secret sessions and has the power to inquire into any alleged offense as directed by the district attorney or as charged by a judge.

The Rehnquist Court's conservatism when dealing with the rights of the accused and its eagerness to reach out to address issues of interest to its controlling majority was further underscored by a five-to-four ruling on grand jury indictments. Writing for a bare majority in *United States v. Williams*, 504 U.S. 6 (1992), Justice Scalia held that when seeking a grand jury's indictment charging an accused with a criminal offense, federal prosecutors need not present exculpatory evidence—facts favorable to the accused and which might result in the grand jury's refusal to hand down an indictment. In holding that federal courts have no power to dismiss an indictment because prosecutors withheld "substantially exculpatory evidence" from a grand jury, Scalia emphasized that the role of a grand jury—unlike a trial jury—is to "assess whether there is adequate basis for bringing a criminal charge," not to determine an accused's ultimate guilt or innocence. "Imposing on the prosecutor a legal obligation to present exculpatory evidence in his possession would be incompatible with this system," claimed Scalia, even though prosecutors must turn over such exculpatory evidence to a defendant's attorney before going to trial.

SELECTED BIBLIOGRAPHY

Frankel, Marvin, and Naftails, Gary. *The Grand Jury on Trial.* New York: Hill & Wang, 1975.

Scigliano, Robert. *The Michigan One-Man Grand Jury.* East Lansing: Michigan State University, 1957.

Younger, R. D. *The People's Panel: The Grand Jury in the United States, 1634–1941.* Providence, RI: Brown University, 1963.

Hurtado v. California

110 U.S. 516, 4 S.Ct. 111 (1884)

The pertinent sections of this case are reprinted in Chapter 4.

D | *The Right to an Impartial Jury Trial*

The jury is a fact-finding institution that determines the guilt or innocence of defendants. Because juries are composed of laypeople or "peers" drawn from the community of the accused, juries also represent the democratic subculture within the judicial system. Juries, as Justice White observed in *Duncan v. Louisiana*, 391 U.S. 145 (1968) (see Ch. 4), "prevent oppression by the Government . . . [and] safeguard against the corrupt or overzealous prosecutor and against the complient, biased, or eccentric judge."

The Sixth Amendment (and Article III, section 2 of the Constitution) provides that the accused "shall enjoy the right" to a jury trial in criminal cases. The Seventh Amendment guarantees a jury trial in civil cases "where the value in controversy shall exceed twenty dollars." *Granfianciera v. Nordberg*, 492 U.S. 33 (1989), extended the Seventh Amendment right to a jury trial to defendants charged with bankruptcy fraud. The right to jury trials may be waived but "the consent of the government counsel and the sanction of the court must be had, in addition to the express and intelligent consent of the defendant."[1]

In federal courts, the right to a jury trial is limited to those cases subject to the Fifth Amendment's provision for a grand jury indictment. Consequently, jury trials are not required for some petty crimes.[2] Nor may jury trials be required on charges of being in contempt of court,[3] on petitions for the writ of *habeas corpus*, and in certain other civil and administrative proceedings, such as those for disbarment and deportation. Neither does the Sixth Amendment's guarantee apply to courts-martial.[4]

Duncan v. Louisiana made the right to a jury trial in all nonpetty cases applicable to the states. Nonpetty cases were defined in *Baldwin v. New York*, 399 U.S. 66 (1970), as those carrying a potential sentence of six months or more imprisonment. However, in *Lewis v. United States*, 518 U.S. 322 (1996), the Court held that a defendant has no Sixth

Amendment right to a jury trial when prosecuted in a single proceeding for multiple petty offenses—offenses that each carry a maximum of six or fewer months—even though the aggregate prison term exceeds six months. Writing for the Court, Justice O'Connor held that "[t]he Sixth Amendment's guarantee of the right to a jury trial does not extend to petty offenses, and its scope does not change where a defendant faces a potential aggregate prison term in excess of six months for petty offenses charged."

The requirement that a jury be "impartial" has given rise to numerous questions. In addition to the fair trial/free press controversy (discussed in Ch. 5), the composition and method of selecting of juries has often been contested. In the "second *Scottsboro* case," *Norris v. Alabama*, 294 U.S. 587 (1935), the Hughes Court held that the due process and equal protection clauses of the Fourteenth Amendment do not permit the exclusion of blacks from juries.[5] But in *Fay v. New York*, 322 U.S. 261 (1947), the Vinson Court ruled that the Sixth Amendment does not require proportional representation of a community when upholding "blue ribbon" juries selected from "the upper economic and social stratum" and excluding manual workers.

The basic protection against racial, economic, and gender bias is the principle that juries must reflect a "cross-section of the community." In *Smith v. Texas*, 311 U.S. 128 (1940), the Court observed that "it is part of the established tradition in the use of juries as instruments of public justice that the jury be a body truly representative of the community." When holding that women could not be excluded as potential jurors in *Taylor v. Louisiana*, 419 U.S. 522 (1975), the fair cross-section requirement was reaffirmed "as fundamental to the jury trial guaranteed by the Sixth Amendment." Accordingly, the Court has struck down various methods for selecting jurors because they worked toward "the total exclusion" of blacks and women,[6] but also maintained that there is no right to include the presence of blacks or women on juries.[7] The principle of a fair cross-section of the community in jury selection is also included in the Federal Jury Selection and Service Act of 1974, barring the exclusion of potential jurors on account of race, color, religion, gender, national origin, and economic status.[8]

Defense attorneys may use their peremptory challenges to exclude potential jurors who they believe might harbor racial prejudice. During *voir dire* examination of potential jurors, when the victim and the defendant are members of different racial groups, defense attorneys may also ask potential jurors questions about whether they have any racial bias.[9] Specifically, *Turner v. Murray*, 476 U.S. 28 (1986), held that where a black man was sentenced to death for murdering a white jeweler, the defendant had a right to have prospective jurors informed of the victim's race and questioned about racial bias. *Batson v. Kentucky* (1986) (excerpted below) held that the Fourteenth Amendment forbids prosecutors from challenging potential jurors solely on the basis of race to secure an all-white jury. However, in *Holland v. Illinois*, 493 U.S. 474 (1990), writing for a bare majority, Justice Scalia held that a prosecutor's use of peremptory challenges so as to exclude all potential black jurors from a jury did not deny a white defendant's right to an impartial jury trial under the Sixth Amendment. But then in *Powers v. Ohio*, 499 U.S. 400 (1991), Justice Kennedy held that prosecutors' use of peremptory challenges to exclude blacks from juries trying white defendants violates the equal protection clause. In so doing, he distinguished *Holland* on the basis that the Fourteenth Amendment "prohibits a prosecutor from using the State's peremptory challenges to exclude otherwise qualified and unbiased persons from the . . . jury solely by reason of their race, a practice that forecloses a significant opportunity to participate in civil life." "The suggestion," added Kennedy, "that racial classifications may survive when visited upon all persons is no more authoritative today than the case which advanced the theorem, *Plessy v. Ferguson*, 163 U.S. 537 (1896). The idea has no place in our modern equal protection jurisprudence." Still, Justice Scalia, dissenting along with Chief Justice Rehnquist, claimed that he was "unmoved" by white defendants' claims that their rights are violated when they are tried by all-white juries.

Subsequently, by a six-to-three vote in *Edmonson v. Leesville Concrete Co.*, 500 U.S. 614 (1991) (further discussed in Ch. 12), the Court also extended *Batson* to the use of peremptory challenges to exclude blacks from juries in civil trials. And the Court again revisited in *Georgia v. McCollum*, 505 U.S. 42 (1992), the issue of using race as a basis for excluding potential jurors from criminal trials and further extended the *Batson*, *Powers*, and *Edmunson* line of rulings. *Batson* barred prosecutors from disqualifying jurors on the basis of race and, as noted above, *Powers* held that criminal defendants of any race may challenge prosecutors' racially based peremptory challenges, while *Edmonson* held that lawyers in civil trials may not exclude potential jurors on the basis of race either. *Georgia v. McCollum*, thus, raised the issue of whether two white defendants charged with criminally assaulting two blacks could exclude blacks from serving on the jury.

Writing for the majority in *McCollum*, Justice Blackmun concluded that it was unconstitutional in criminal trials for defendants' attorneys, no less than for prosecutors, to exclude jurors solely on the basis of their race. In his words, it is "an affront to justice to argue that a fair trial includes the right to discriminate against a group of citizens on the basis of their race." As a result, all-white juries in racially charged cases, such as that of the white police officers tried for beating motorist Rodney King in Los Angeles, will be much more difficult to obtain. At the same time, *McCollum* also makes it more difficult for minority defendants to exclude white jurors in order to secure some minorities on their juries. Only Justices O'Connor and Scalia dissented. Subsequently, with Justices Scalia and Thomas dissenting, the Court further extended the *Batson* line of cases in *Campbell v. Louisiana*, 523 U.S. 392 (1998), holding that the selection process for grand jury forepersons could be challenged for racial bias.

The issue of juror bias has posed special problems in jury selection for capital cases. Historically, potential jurors having constitutional objections to the death penalty were excluded from capital cases. But *Witherspoon v. Illinois*, 391 U.S. 510 (1968), held that jurors opposed to the death penalty were impermissibly excluded; otherwise, in Justice Potter Stewart's words, every jury would be a "hanging jury." *Maxwell v. Bishop*, 398 U.S. 262 (1970), ruled that the death penalty may not be imposed when prospective jurors are removed due to their opposition to capital punishment. But the Burger and Rehnquist Courts have reconsidered the issue. In *Darden v. Wainwright*, 477 U.S. 168 (1986), the justices held five to four that potential jurors who have religious objections to the death penalty may be excluded, and *A. L. Lockhart v. McCree* (1986) (excerpted below) held that "death qualified" juries are permissible.[10] Indeed, in *Morgan v. Illinois*, 504 U.S. 719 (1992) (see Ch. 10), the Court held that defendants' attorneys in capital cases during *voir dire* examinations must be allowed to ask whether a potential juror would automatically vote to impose a death sentence upon the defendant's conviction. Denial of such questioning during jury selection, the Court ruled, violates the Fourteenth Amendment's due process clause.

Traditionally, a common-law jury was composed of twelve persons, and *Thompson v. Utah*, 170 U.S. 343 (1898), held that the Sixth Amendment jury was "constituted, as it was in common law, of twelve persons, neither more nor less." *Duncan v. Louisiana* implicitly posed the issue of whether states had to adhere to twelve-member juries as well, or whether they were still free to experiment with jury size. In 1967, Florida enacted a law providing for six-member juries in all criminal cases, except for capital crimes. That law was immediately challenged and upheld in *Williams v. Florida* (1970) (excerpted below). In federal district courts, six-member juries had been used in *civil* cases, even before *Williams*. This was so despite the fact that the Seventh Amendment specifically refers to the common-law jury in providing for jury trials in civil cases. A bare majority of the Court in *Colegrove v. Battin*, 413 U.S. 149 (1973), nevertheless, upheld six-member juries in civil cases. Writing for the majority, Justice Brennan deemed the common-law jury to be not frozen into the Constitution. Justices Douglas, Marshall, Stewart, and Powell dissented from what Marshall termed the majority's upholding of a "six-man mutation . . . a different institution which functions differently, produces different results, and was wholly unknown to the Framers of the Seventh Amendment."

Once the Court abandoned the history and principle of twelve-member juries, it faced the question of where to draw a line on jury size. *Ballew v. Georgia*, 635 U.S. 223 (1978), finally drew the line at six when rejecting Georgia's use of five-member juries in criminal cases.

A related controversy arose with *Johnson v. Louisiana*, 406 U.S. 356 (1972), and *Apodaco v. Oregon*, 406 U.S. 404 (1972), holding that nonunanimous jury verdicts in criminal cases did not violate the Fourteenth Amendment's due process and equal protection clauses. In *Johnson*, a bare majority approved Louisiana's law permitting convictions based on a vote of nine out of twelve jurors. *Apodaco* upheld an Oregon statute under which two defendants were found guilty by jury votes of eleven to one and ten to two. In both, Justice White dismissed the history of unanimous verdicts and applied his *Williams* analysis of the function of juries in concluding that nonunanimous and unanimous juries were "functionally equivalent." His opinion was so sweeping in rejecting the history of unanimity, dating back to 1367 and an accepted part of federal jury trials, that Justice Powell, although joining the majority, was moved to point out in a concurring opinion that unanimity in federal courts was "mandated by history."

Together, *Williams v. Florida*, *Johnson*, and *Apodaco* presented the issue of where the Court would draw the line on the permissibility of nonunanimous verdicts rendered by juries composed of less than twelve members. That issue was met in *Burch v. Louisiana* (1979) (see excerpt below), holding that unanimous verdicts are required in six-member juries.

In *Sullivan v. Louisiana*, 508 U.S. 275 (1993), the Court unanimously reaffirmed that in criminal cases juries must find the accused guilty beyond a reasonable doubt. Although the Rehnquist Court has expanded the "harmless error doctrine" in other areas—for example, *Arizona v. Fulminante* (1991) (in Ch. 8)—here it declined to hold that a judge's instructions to a jury that it must find the defendant "probably guilty" constituted merely a harmless error. Writing for the Court, Justice Scalia observed, "the Fifth Amendment requirement of proof beyond a reasonable doubt and the Sixth Amendment requirement of a jury verdict are interrelated. It would not satisfy the Sixth Amendment to have a jury determine that the defendant is probably guilty. . . . In other words, the jury verdict required by the Sixth Amendment is a jury verdict of guilty beyond a reasonable doubt."

Finally, in the Court's recent interpretation of the Sixth Amendment, the Court casts increasing doubt about the constitutional permissibility of federal and state mandatory sentencing guidelines. In *Apprendi v. New Jersey*, 536 U.S. 466 (2000), the Court struck down New Jersey's law permitting judges to hand down longer sentences for "hate crimes" based on the "preponderance of evidence" standard. A bare majority ruled that enhanced sentences may be imposed only by a jury and on the basis of the stricter "beyond a reasonable doubt" standard." In *Ring v. Arizona*, 536 U.S. 584 (2002), the Court applied the *Apprendi* principle to require juries, not judges, to determine the aggravating circumstances for imposing death sentences. Then, in *Blakely v. Washington*, 124 S.Ct. 2531 (2004), a bare majority struck down Washington's sentencing system for permitting judges to make findings that increase a convicted defendant's sentence beyond the ordinary range for violating the right to trial by a jury. Writing for the Court, Justice Scalia reaffirmed that "any fact that increases the penalty for a crime beyond the prescribed statutory maximum must be submitted to a jury and proved beyond a reasonable doubt." Although Scalia added that "the federal guidelines are not before us, and we express no opinion on them," dissenting Justice O'Connor warned, "Over 20 years of sentencing reform are all but lost, and tens of thousands of criminal judgments are in jeopardy." Chief Justice Rehnquist and Justices Kennedy and Breyer also dissented.

NOTES

1. *Patton v. United States*, 281 U.S. 276 (1980). See also *Singer v. United States*, 380 U.S. 24 (1965).

2. See *Cheff v. Schnackenberg*, 384 U.S. 373 (1966).

3. But see also *United States v. Barnett*, 376 U.S. 681 (1964); and *Cheff v. Schnackenberg*, 384 U.S. 373 (1966).

4. See *Ex parte Milligan*, 4 Wall. 2 (1866) (see Vol. 1, Ch. 3).

5. *Hernandez v. Texas*, 347 U.S. 475 (1954), extended the ruling in *Norris* to prohibit states from excluding Hispanics from juries. *Eubanks v. Louisiana*, 356 U.S. 584 (1958) overturned the conviction of a black man by an all-white jury.

6. See *Turner v. Fouche*, 396 U.S. 346 (1970); *Avery v. Georgia*, 345 U.S. 559 (1952); *Whitus v. Georgia* U.S. (1967); and *Turner v. Fouche*, 396 U.S. 346 (1970).

7. See *Swain v. Alabama*, 380 U.S. 202 (1965); *Carter v. Jury Commission of Greene County*, 396 U.S. 320 (1970).

8. See *Test v. United States*, 420 U.S. 28 (1975), allowing a defendant to inspect jury lists to determine whether a disproportionate number of people with Hispanic surnames have been excluded.

9. See *Ham v. South Carolina*, 409 U.S. 524 (1973); *Ristanino v. Ross*, 424 U.S. 589 (1976); and *Rosales-Lopez v. United States*, 451 U.S. 182 (1981).

10. See also *Wainwright v. Witt*, 469 U.S. 412 (1985). *Buchanan v. Kentucky*, 483 U.S. 1044 (1987), further upheld the use of death-qualified juries in a joint trial where a death sentence was sought for only one of the codefendants.

SELECTED BIBLIOGRAPHY

Abramson, Jeffrey. *We, The Jury: The Jury System and the Ideal of Democracy: With a New Preface*. Cambridge, MA: Harvard University Press, 2000.

Brill, Steven. *Trial by Jury*. New York: Touchstone, 1989.

Bodenhamer, David. *Fair Trial: Rights of the Accused in American History*. New York: Oxford University Press, 1992.

Burnett, D. Graham. *A Trial by Jury*. New York: Knopf, 2001.

Burns, Robert P. *A Theory of the Trial*. Princeton, NJ: Princeton University Press, 1999.

Finkel, Norman. *Commonsense Justice: Jurors' Notions of the Law*. Cambridge, MA: Harvard University Press, 1995.

Jonakait, Randolph. *The American Jury System*. New Haven, CT: Yale University Press, 2003.

Kalven, Harry, and Zeizel, Hans. *The American Jury*. Chicago: University of Chicago Press, 1966.

Levy, Leonard W. *The Palladium of Justice: Origins of Trial by Jury*. Chicago: Ivan R. Dee, 1999.

Vidmar, Neil, ed., *World Jury Systems*. New York: Oxford University Press, 2000.

Wolf, Robert V., and Sarat, Austin, eds. *The Jury System*. New York: Chelsea House, 1998.

Duncan v. Louisiana

391 U.S. 145, 88 S.CT. 1444 (1968).

This case was reprinted in part in Chapter 4.

Batson v. Kentucky

476 U.S. 79, 106 S.CT. 1712 (1986)

James Kirkland Batson, a black man, was tried for second-degree burglary and receiving stolen goods. Before his trial, the judge conducted a *voir dire* examination of the jury venire and excused certain potential jurors. The prosecutor then used his peremptory challenges to strike all four black persons in the venire to secure an all-white jury. Batson's attorney moved to dismiss the jury for violating his client's Sixth and Fourteenth Amendments guarantees of a jury drawn from a cross-section of the community. The trial judge denied the motion and Batson was tried and convicted. The Kentucky Supreme Court affirmed and Batson's attorney made a further appeal to the Supreme Court of the United States.

The Court's decision was seven to two, and the majority's opinion was announced by Justice Powell. Justices White, Stevens, and O'Connor concurred; Chief Justice Burger and Justice Rehnquist dissented.

☐ *Justice POWELL delivered the opinion of the Court.*

In *Swain v. Alabama*, [380 U.S. 202 (1965)], this Court recognized that a "State's purposeful or deliberate denial to Negroes on account of race of participation as jurors in the administration of justice violates the Equal Protection Clause." This principle has been "consistently and repeatedly" reaffirmed in numerous decisions of this Court both preceding and following *Swain*. We reaffirm the principle today.

More than a century ago, the Court decided that the State denies a black defendant equal protection of the laws when it puts him on trial before a jury from which members of his race have been purposefully excluded. *Strauder v. West Virginia*, 100 U.S. 303 (1880). . . .

In holding that racial discrimination in jury selection offends the Equal Protection Clause, the Court in *Strauder* recognized, however, that a defendant has no right to a "petit jury composed in whole or in part of persons of his own race." "The number of our races and nationalities stands in the way of evolution of such a conception" of the demand of equal protection. *Akins v. Texas*, 325 U.S. 398 (1945). But the defendant does have the right to be tried by a jury whose members are selected pursuant to nondiscriminatory criteria. The Equal Protection Clause guarantees the defendant that the State will not exclude members of his race from the jury venire on account of race, *Strauder*, or on the false assumption that members of his race as a group are not qualified to serve as jurors. . . .

The harm from discriminatory jury selection extends beyond that inflicted on the defendant and the excluded juror to touch the entire community. Selection procedures that purposefully exclude black persons from juries undermine public confidence in the fairness of our system of justice. . . .

In *Strauder*, the Court invalidated a state statute that provided that only white men could serve as jurors. We can be confident that no state now has such a law. The Constitution requires, however, that we look beyond the face of the statute defining juror qualifications and also consider challenged selection practices to afford "protection against action of the State through its administrative officers in effecting the prohibited discrimination." . . .

Accordingly, the component of the jury selection process at issue here, the State's privilege to strike individual jurors through peremptory challenges, is subject to the commands of the Equal Protection Clause. Although a prosecutor ordinarily is entitled to exercise permitted peremptory challenges "for any reason at all, as long as that reason is related to his view concerning the outcome" of the case to be tried, the Equal Protection Clause forbids the prosecutor to challenge potential jurors solely on account of their race or on the assumption that black jurors as a group will be unable impartially to consider the State's case against a black defendant.

The principles announced in *Strauder* never have been questioned in any subsequent decision of this Court. Rather, the Court has been called upon repeatedly to review the application of those principles to particular facts." A recurring question in these cases, as in any case alleging a violation of the Equal Protection Clause, was whether the defendant had met his burden of proving purposeful discrimination on the part of the State. . . .

The showing necessary to establish a prima facie case of purposeful discrimination in selection of the venire may be discerned in this Court's decisions. The defendant initially must show that he is a member of a racial group capable of being singled out for differential treatment. In combination with that evidence, a defendant may then make a prima facie case by proving that in the particular jurisdiction members of his race have not been summoned for jury service over an extended period of time. Proof of systematic exclusion from the venire raises an inference of purposeful discrimination because the "result bespeaks discrimination."

Since the ultimate issue is whether the State has discriminated in selecting the defendant's venire, however, the defendant may establish a prima facie case "in other ways than by evidence of long-continued unexplained absence" of members of his race "from many panels." In cases involving the venire, this Court has found a prima facie case on proof that members of the defendant's race were substantially underrepresented on the venire from which his jury was drawn and that the venire was selected under a practice providing "the opportunity for discrimination." This combination of factors raises the necessary inference of purposeful discrimination because the Court has declined to attribute to chance the absence of black citizens on a particular jury array where the selection mechanism is subject to abuse. When circumstances suggest the need, the trial court must undertake a "factual inquiry" that "takes into account all possible explanatory factors" in the particular case. . . .

While we recognize, of course, that the peremptory challenge occupies an important position in our trial procedures, we do not agree that our decision today will undermine the contribution the challenge generally makes to the administration of justice. The reality of practice, amply reflected in many state and federal court opinions, shows that the challenge may be, and unfortunately at times has been, used to discriminate against black jurors. By requiring trial courts to be sensitive to the racially discriminatory use of peremptory challenges, our decision enforces the mandate of equal protection and furthers the ends of justice. In view of the heterogeneous population of our nation, public respect for our criminal justice system and the rule of law will be strengthened if we ensure that no citizen is disqualified from jury service because of his race.

☐ *Chief Justice BURGER, with whom Justice REHNQUIST joins, dissenting.*

Today the Court sets aside the peremptory challenge, a procedure which has been part of the common law for many centuries and part of our jury system for nearly 200 years. It does so on the basis of a constitutional argument that was rejected, without a single dissent, in *Swain v. Alabama*, 380 U.S. 202 (1965). . . .

The Court's opinion, in addition to ignoring the teachings of history, also contrasts with *Swain* in its failure to even discuss the rationale of the peremptory challenge. *Swain* observed:

> "The function of the challenge is not only to eliminate extremes of partiality on both sides, but to assure the parties that the jurors before whom they try the case will decide on the basis of the evidence placed for them, and not otherwise. In this way the peremptory satisfies the rule that 'to perform its high function in the best way, justice must satisfy the appearance of justice.' "

Permitting unexplained peremptories has long been regarded as a means to strengthen our jury system in other ways as well. . . .

Instead of even considering the history or function of the peremptory challenge, the bulk of the Court's opinion is spent recounting the well-established principle that intentional exclusion of racial groups from jury venires is a violation of the Equal Protection Clause. I too reaffirm that principle, which has been a part of our constitutional tradition since at least *Strauder v. West Virginia*. But if today's decision is nothing more than mere "application" of the "principles announced in *Strauder*," as the Court maintains, some will consider it curious that the application went unrecognized for over a century. The Court in *Swain* had no difficulty in unanimously concluding that cases such as *Strauder* did not require inquiry into the basis for a peremptory challenge. . . .

Unwilling to rest solely on jury venire cases such as *Strauder*, the Court also invokes general equal protection principles in support of its holding. But peremptory challenges are often lodged, of necessity, for reasons "normally thought irrelevant to legal proceedings or official action, namely, the race, religion, nationality, occupation or affiliations of people summoned for jury duty." *Swain*. Moreover, in making peremptory challenges, both the prosecutor and defense attorney necessarily act on only limited information or hunch. The process can not be indicted on the sole basis that such decisions are made on the basis of "assumption" or "intuitive judgment." As a result, undulterated equal protection analysis is simply inapplicable to peremptory challenge exercised in any particular case.

A. L. Lockhart v. McCree
476 U.S. 162, 106 S.CT. 1758 (1986)

A. L. Lockhart, the director of the Arkansas Department of Correction, appealed the Court of Appeals for the Eighth Circuit's affirmance of a federal district court's ruling. The district court had held that Ardia Mc-

Cree's Sixth and Fourteenth Amendments' rights were violated in a capital case by a state trial judge's removal, over McCree's objections, of prospective jurors who stated that they would not under any circumstance vote to impose the death penalty. The Supreme Court granted review.

The Court's decision was six to three, and the majority's opinion was announced by Justice Rehnquist. Justice Blackmun delivered a concurring opinion. Justice Marshall dissented and was joined by Justices Brennan and Stevens.

☐ *Justice REHNQUIST delivered the opinion of the Court.*

In this case we address the question left open by our decision nearly 18 years ago in *Witherspoon v. Illinois*, 391 U.S. 510 (1968): Does the Constitution prohibit the removal for cause, prior to the guilt phase of a bifurcated capital trial, of prospective jurors whose opposition to the death penalty is so strong that it would prevent or substantially impair the performance of their duties as jurors at the sentencing phase of the trial? We hold that it does not. . . .

Before turning to the legal issues in the case, we are constrained to point out what we believe to be several serious flaws in the evidence upon which the courts below reached the conclusion that "death qualification" produces "conviction-prone" juries. McCree introduced into evidence some fifteen social science studies in support of his constitutional claims, but only six of the studies even purported to measure the potential effects on the guilt-innocence determination of the removal from the jury of "*Witherspoon* excludables." . . .

Of the six studies introduced by McCree that at least purported to deal with the central issue in this case, namely, the potential effects on the determination of guilt or innocence of excluding "*Witherspoon* excludables" from the jury, three were also before this Court when it decided *Witherspoon, supra*. There, this Court reviewed the studies and concluded:

> "The data adduced by the petitioner . . . are too tentative and fragmentary to establish that jurors not opposed to the death penalty tend to favor the prosecution in the determination of guilt. We simply cannot conclude, either on the basis of the record now before us or as a matter of judicial notice, that the exclusion of jurors opposed to capital punishment results in an unrepresentative jury on the issue of guilt or substantially increases the risk of conviction. In light of the presently available information, we are not prepared to announce a *per se* constitutional rule requiring the reversal of every conviction returned by a jury selected as this one was." . . .

It goes almost without saying that if these studies were "too tentative and fragmentary" to make out a claim of constitutional error in 1968, the same studies, unchanged but for having aged some eighteen years, are still insufficient to make out such a claim in this case.

Nor do the three post-*Witherspoon* studies introduced by McCree on the "death qualification" issue provide substantial support for the "*per se* constitutional rule" McCree asks this Court to adopt. All three of the "new" studies were based on the responses of individuals randomly selected from some segment of the population, but who were not actual jurors sworn under oath to apply the law to the facts of an actual case involving the fate of an actual capital defendant. We have serious doubts about the value of these studies in predicting the behavior of actual jurors.

Finally, and most importantly, only one of the six "death qualification" studies introduced by McCree even attempted to identify and account for the presence of so-called "nullifiers," or individuals who, because of their deep-seated opposition to the death penalty, would be unable to decide a capital defendant's guilt or innocence fairly and impartially. McCree concedes, as he must, that "nullifiers" may properly be excluded from the guilt-phase jury, and studies that fail to take into account the presence of such "nullifiers" thus are fatally flawed. Surely a "*per se* constitutional rule" as far-reaching as the one McCree proposes should not be based on the results of the lone study that avoids this fundamental flaw.

Having identified some of the more serious problems with McCree's studies, however, we will assume for purposes of this opinion that the studies are both methodologically valid and adequate to establish that "death qualification" in fact produces juries somewhat more "conviction-prone" than "non-death-qualified" juries. We hold, nonetheless, that the Constitution does not prohibit the States from "death qualifying" juries in capital cases. . . .

Even if we were willing to extend the fair cross-section requirement to petit juries, we would still reject the Eighth Circuit's conclusion that "death qualification" violates that requirement. The essence of a "fair cross-section" claim is the systematic exclusion of "a 'distinctive' group in the community." . . .

We have never attempted to precisely define the term "distinctive group," and we do not undertake to do so today. But we think it obvious that the concept of "distinctiveness" must be linked to the purposes of the fair cross-section requirement. In *Taylor* [*v. Louisiana*, 419 U.S. 522 (1975)] we identified those purposes as (1) "guard[ing] against the exercise of arbitrary power" and ensuring that the "commonsense judgment of the community" will act as "a hedge against the overzealous or mistaken prosecutor," (2) preserving "public confidence in the fairness of the criminal justice system," and (3) implementing our belief that "sharing in the administration of justice is a phase of civic responsibility." . . .

Our prior jury-representativeness cases, whether based on the fair cross-section component of the Sixth Amendment or the Equal Protection Clause of the Fourteenth Amendment, have involved such groups as blacks, see *Peters v. Kiff*, 407 U.S. 493 (1972) (plurality opinion) (equal protection), women, see *Taylor, supra* (same), and Mexican-Americans, see *Castaneda v. Partida*, 430 U.S. 482 (1977) (equal protection). The wholesale exclusion of these large groups from jury service clearly contravened all three of the aforementioned purposes of the fair cross-section requirement. Because these groups were excluded for reasons completely unrelated to the ability of members of the group to serve as jurors in a particular case, the exclusion raised at least the possibility that the composition of juries would be arbitrarily skewed in such a way as to deny criminal defendants the benefit of the common-sense judgment of the community. In addition, the exclusion from jury service of large groups of individuals not on the basis of their inability to serve as jurors, but on the basis of some immutable characteristic such as race, gender, or ethnic background, undeniably gave rise to an "appearance of unfairness." Finally, such exclusion improperly deprived members of these often historically disadvantaged groups of their right as citizens to serve on juries in criminal cases.

The group of "*Witherspoon* excludables" involved in the case at bar differs significantly from the groups we have previously recognized as "distinctive." "Death qualification," unlike the wholesale exclusion of blacks, women, or Mexican-Americans from jury service, is carefully designed to serve the State's concededly legitimate interest in obtaining a single jury that can properly and impartially apply the law to the facts of the case at both the guilt and sentencing phases of a capital trial. There is very little danger, therefore, and McCree does not even argue, that "death qualification" was instituted as a means for the State to arbitrarily skew the composition of capital-case juries.

Furthermore, unlike blacks, women, and Mexican-Americans, "*Witherspoon* excludables" are singled out for exclusion in capital cases on the basis of an attribute that is within the individual's control. It is important to remember that not all who oppose the death penalty are subject to removal for cause in capital cases; those who firmly believe that the death penalty is unjust may nevertheless serve as jurors in capital cases so long as they state clearly that they are willing to temporarily set aside their own beliefs in deference to the rule of law. Because the group of "*Witherspoon* excludables" includes only those who cannot and will not conscientiously obey the law with respect to one of the issues in a capital case, "death qualification" hardly can be said to create an "appearance of unfairness."

Finally, the removal for cause of "*Witherspoon* excludables" in capital cases does not prevent them from serving as jurors in other criminal cases, and thus leads to no substantial deprivation of their basic rights of citizenship. They are treated no differently than any juror who expresses the view that he would be unable to follow the law in a particular case. . . .

In our view, it is simply not possible to define jury impartiality, for constitutional purposes, by reference to some hypothetical mix of individual viewpoints. Prospective jurors come from many different backgrounds, and have many different attitudes and predispositions. But the Constitution presupposes that a jury selected from a fair cross-section of the community is impartial, regardless of the mix of individual viewpoints actually represented on the jury, so long as the jurors can conscientiously and properly carry out their sworn duty to apply the law to the facts of the particular case. We hold that McCree's jury satisfied both aspects of this constitutional standard.

☐ *Justice MARSHALL, with whom Justice BRENNAN and Justice STEVENS join, dissenting.*

Respondent contends here that the "death-qualified" jury that convicted him, from which the State, as authorized by *Witherspoon*, had excluded all venire persons unwilling to consider imposing the death penalty, was in effect "organized to return a verdict" of guilty. In support of this claim; he has presented overwhelming evidence that death-qualified juries are substantially more likely to convict or to convict on more serious charges than juries on which unalterable opponents of capital punishment are permitted to serve. Respondent does not challenge the application of *Witherspoon* to the jury in the sentencing stage of bifurcated capital cases. Neither does he demand that individuals unable to assess culpability impartially ("nullifiers") be permitted to sit on capital juries. All he asks is the chance to have his guilt or innocence determined by a jury like those that sit in non-capital cases—one whose composition has not been tilted in favor of the prosecution by the exclusion of a group of prospective jurors uncommonly aware of an accused's constitutional rights but quite capable of determining his culpability without favor or bias. . . .

In the wake of *Witherspoon*, a number of researchers set out to supplement the data that the Court had found inadequate in that case. The results of these studies were exhaustively analyzed by the District Court in this case, and can be only briefly summarized here. The data strongly suggest that death qualification excludes a significantly large subset—at least 11% to 17%—of potential jurors who could be impartial during the guilt phase of trial. Among the members of this excludable class are a disproportionate number of blacks and women.

The perspectives on the criminal justice system of jurors who survive death qualification are systematically different from those of the excluded jurors. Death-qualified jurors are, for example, more likely to believe that a defendant's failure to testify is indicative of his guilt, more hostile to the insanity defense, more mistrustful of defense attorneys, and less concerned about the danger of erroneous convictions. This pro-prosecution bias is reflected in the greater readiness of death-qualified jurors to convict or to convict on more serious charges. And, finally, the very process of death qualification—which focuses attention on the death penalty before the trial has even begun—has been found to predispose the jurors that survive it to believe that the defendant is guilty. . . .

Faced with the near unanimity of authority supporting respondent's claim that death qualification gives the prosecution a particular advantage in the guilt phase of capital trials, the majority here makes but a weak effort to contest that proposition. Instead, it merely assumes for the purposes of this opinion "that 'death-qualification' in fact produces juries somewhat more 'conviction-prone' than 'non-death-qualified' juries," and then holds that this result does not offend the Constitution. This disregard for the clear import of the evidence tragically misconstrues the settled constitutional principles that guarantee a defendant the right to a fair trial and an impartial jury whose composition is not biased toward the prosecution. . . .

One need not rely on the analysis and assumptions of . . . *Witherspoon* to demonstrate that the exclusion of opponents of capital punishment capable of impartially determining culpability infringes a capital defendant's constitutional right to a fair and impartial jury. For the same conclusion is compelled by the analysis that in *Ballew v. Georgia*, 435 U.S. 223 (1978) led a majority of this Court to hold that a criminal conviction rendered by a five-person jury violates the Sixth and Fourteenth Amendments. . . .

The principle of "impartiality" invoked in *Witherspoon* is thus not the only basis for assessing whether the exclusion of jurors unwilling to consider the death penalty but able impartially to determine guilt infringes a capital defendant's constitutional interest in a fair trial. By identifying the critical concerns that are subsumed in that interest, the *Ballew* Court pointed to an alternative approach to the issue, drawing on the very sort of empirical data that respondent has presented here. And viewed in light of the concerns articulated in *Ballew*, the evidence is sufficient to establish that death qualification constitutes a substantial threat to a defendant's Sixth and Fourteenth Amendment right to a fair jury trial—a threat constitutionally acceptable only if justified by a sufficient state interest. . . .

Williams v. Florida

399 U.S. 78, 90 S.CT. 1893 (1970)

Johnny Williams was tried by a six-member jury and convicted of robbery in Dade County, Florida. His attorneys appealed the conviction, but a state appellate court affirmed. They made an appeal to the Supreme Court, which granted *certiorari*.

The Court's decision was five to three, and the majority's opinion was announced by Justice White, with Justice Blackmun not participating. Chief Justice Burger concurred. A separate opinion, in part dissenting and concurring, was delivered by Justice Black and joined by Justice Douglas. Justice Marshall dissented, in part.

☐ *Justice WHITE delivered the opinion of the Court.*

In *Duncan v. Louisiana*, 391 U.S. 79 (1968), we held that the Fourteenth Amendment guarantees a right to trial by jury in all criminal cases that— were they to be tried in a federal court—would come within the Sixth Amendment's guarantee. Petitioner's trial for robbery . . . clearly falls within the scope of that holding. The question in this case then is whether the constitutional guarantee of a trial by "jury" necessarily requires trial by exactly 12 persons, rather than some lesser number—in this case six. We hold that the 12-man panel is not a necessary ingredient of "trial by jury," and that respondent's refusal to impanel more than the six members provided for by Florida law did not violate petitioner's Sixth Amendment rights as applied to the States through the Fourteenth.

We had occasion in *Duncan v. Louisiana*, to review briefly the oft-told history of the development of trial by jury in criminal cases. That history revealed a long tradition attaching great importance to the concept of relying on a body of one's peers to determine guilt or innocence as a safeguard against arbitrary law enforcement. That same history, however, affords little insight into the considerations that gradually led the size of that body to be generally fixed at 12. . . . [W]hile sometime in the 14th century the size of the jury at common law came to be fixed generally at 12, that particular feature of the jury system appears to have been a historical accident, unrelated to the great purposes which gave rise to the jury in the first place. The question before us is whether this accidental feature of the jury has been immutably codified into our Constitution. . . .

While "the intent of the Framers" is often an elusive quarry, the relevant constitutional history casts considerable doubt on the easy assumption in our past decisions that if a given feature existed in a jury at common law in 1789, then it was necessarily preserved in the Constitution. Provisions for jury trial were first placed in the Constitution in Article III's provision that "[t]he Trial of all Crimes . . . shall be by Jury; and such Trial shall be held in the State where the said Crimes shall have been committed." The "very scanty history [of this provision] in the records of the Constitutional Convention" sheds little light either way on the intended correlation between Article III's "jury" and the features of the jury at common law. . . .

We do not pretend to be able to divine precisely what the word "jury" imported to the Framers, the First Congress, or the States in 1789. It may well be that the usual expectation was that the jury would consist of 12, and that hence, the most likely conclusion to be drawn is simply that little thought was actually given to the specific question we face today. But there is absolutely no indication in "the intent of the Framers" of an explicit decision to equate the constitutional and common-law characteristics of the jury. Nothing in this history suggests, then, that we do violence to the letter of the Constitution by turning to other than purely historical considerations to determine which features of the jury system, as it existed at common law, were preserved in the Constitution. The relevant inquiry, as we see it, must be the function that the particular feature performs and its relation to the purposes of the jury trial. Measured by this standard, the 12-man requirement cannot be regarded as an indispensable component of the Sixth Amendment.

The purpose of the jury trial, as we noted in *Duncan*, is to prevent oppression by the Government. . . . Given this purpose, the essential feature of a jury obviously lies in the interposition between the accused and his accuser of the commonsense judgment of a group of laymen, and in the community participation and shared responsibility that results from that group's determination of guilt or innocence. The performance of this role is not a function of the particular number of the body that makes up the jury. To be sure, the number should probably be large enough to promote group deliberation, free from outside attempts at intimidation, and to provide a fair possibility for obtaining a representative cross-section of the community. But we find little reason to think that these goals are in any meaningful sense less likely to be achieved when the jury numbers six, than when it numbers 12—particularly if the requirement of unanimity is retained. And, certainly the reliability of the jury as a factfinder hardly seems likely to be a function of its size. . . .

We conclude, in short, as we began: the fact that the jury at common law was composed of precisely 12 is a historical accident, unnecessary to effect the purposes of the jury system and wholly without significance "except to mystics." *Duncan v. Louisiana* (HARLAN, J., dissenting). To read the Sixth Amendment as forever codifying a feature so incidental to the real purpose of the Amendment is to ascribe a blind formalism to the Framers which would require considerably more evidence than we have been able to discover in the history and language of the Constitution or in the reasoning of our past decisions. . . . Legislatures may well have their own views about the relative value of the larger and smaller juries, and may conclude that, wholly apart from the jury's primary function, it is desirable to spread the collective responsibility for the determination of guilt among the larger group. In capital cases, for example, it appears that no State provides for less than 12 jurors—a fact that suggests implicit recognition of the value of the larger body as a means of legitimating society's decision to impose the death penalty. Our holding does no more than leave these considerations to Congress and the States, unrestrained by an interpretation of the Sixth Amendment that would forever dictate the precise number that can constitute a jury. Consistent with this holding, we conclude that petitioner's Sixth Amendment rights, as applied to the States through the Fourteenth Amendment, were not violated by Florida's decision to provide a six-man rather than a 12-man jury. . . .

☐ *Justice MARSHALL dissenting in part.*

I adhere to the decision of the Court in *Thompson v. Utah*, 170 U.S. 343 (1898), that the jury guaranteed by the Sixth Amendment consists "of twelve persons, neither more nor less." As I see it, the Court has not made out a convincing case that the Sixth Amendment should be read differently than it was in *Thompson* even if the matter were now before us *de novo*—much less that an unbroken line of precedent going back over 70 years should be overruled.

Burch v. Louisiana

441 U.S. 130, 99 S.Ct. 1623 (1979)

Daniel Burch was tried for exhibiting two obscene motion pictures. The six-member jury found him guilty by a five-to-one vote. He was sentenced to two consecutive seven-month prison terms, which were suspended, and fined $1,000. Burch's attorney appealed the constitutionality of nonunanimous six-member jury verdicts. The Louisiana Supreme Court affirmed and Burch's attorney appealed to the Supreme Court.

The Court's decision was six to three, and the majority's opinion was announced by Justice Rehnquist. Justice Stevens concurred. A separate opinion, in part dissenting and concurring, was delivered by Justice Brennan and joined by Justices Stewart and Marshall.

☐ *Justice REHNQUIST delivered the opinion of the Court.*

[W]e believe that conviction by a nonunanimous six-member jury in a state criminal trial for a nonpetty offense deprives an accused of his constitutional right to trial by jury.

Only in relatively recent years has this Court had to consider the practices of the several States relating to jury size and unanimity. . . .

The Court in *Duncan* [*v. Louisiana*, 391 U.S. 145 (1968)], held that because trial by jury in "serious" criminal cases is "fundamental to the American scheme of justice" and essential to due process of law, the Fourteenth Amendment guarantees a state criminal defendant the right to a jury trial in any case, which, if tried in a federal court, would require a jury under the Sixth Amendment. . . .

Two terms later in *Williams v. Florida*, 399 U.S. 78 (1970), the Court held that this constitutional guarantee of trial by jury did not require a State to provide an accused with a jury of 12 members and that Florida did not violate the jury trial rights of criminal defendants charged with nonpetty offenses by affording them jury panels comprised of only six persons. . . .

[I]n *Apodaca v. Oregon* 106 U.S. 404 (1972), we upheld a state statute providing that only 10 members of a 12-person jury need concur to render a verdict in certain noncapital cases. In terms of the role of the jury as a safeguard against oppression, the plurality opinion perceived no difference between those juries required to act unanimously and those permitted to act by votes of 10 to two. . . . Nor was unanimity viewed by the plurality as contributing materially to the exercise of the jury's commonsense judgment or as a necessary precondition to effective application of the requirement that jury panels represent a fair cross-section of the community. . . .

[I]n *Ballew v. Georgia*, 135 U.S. 223 (1978), we held that conviction by a unanimous five-person jury in a trial for a nonpetty offense deprives an accused of his right to trial by jury. While readily admitting that the line between six members and five was not altogether easy to justify, at least five Members of the Court believed that reducing a jury to five persons in nonpetty cases raised sufficiently substantial doubts as to the fairness of the proceeding and proper functioning of the jury to warrant drawing the line at six. . . .

[T]his case lies at the intersection of our decisions concerning jury size and unanimity. As in *Ballew*, we do not pretend the ability to discern *a priori* a bright line below which the number of jurors participating in the trial or in the verdict would not permit the jury to function in the manner required by our prior cases. But having already departed from the strictly historical requirements of jury trial, it is inevitable that lines must be drawn somewhere if the substance of the jury trial right is to be preserved. . . . [M]uch the same reasons that led us in *Ballew* to decide that use of a five-member jury threatened the fairness of the proceeding and the proper role of the jury, lead us to conclude now that conviction for a nonpetty offense by only five members of a six-person jury presents a similar threat to preservation of the substance of the jury trial guarantee and justifies our requiring verdicts rendered by six-person juries to be unanimous. We are buttressed in this view by the current jury practices of the several States. It appears that of those States that utilize six-member juries in trials of nonpetty offenses, only two, including Louisiana, also allow nonunanimous verdicts. We think that this near uniform judgment of the Nation provides a useful guide in delimiting the line between those jury practices that are constitutionally permissible and those that are not. . . .

[O]n this record, any benefits that might accrue by allowing five members of a six-person jury to render a verdict, as compared with requiring unanimity of a six-member jury, are speculative, at best. More importantly, we think that when a State has reduced the size of its juries to the minimum number of jurors permitted by the Constitution, the additional authorization of nonunanimous verdicts by such juries sufficiently threatens the constitutional principles that led to the establishment of the size threshold that any countervailing interest of the State should yield.

E | *A Speedy and Public Trial*

A "speedy and public trial" is also a guarantee of the Sixth Amendment, which was made applicable to the states in *Klopfer v. North Carolina*, 386 U.S. 213 (1967). But what is a *speedy* trial? In *Dickey v. Florida*, 398 U.S. 30 (1970), the Court found that a defendant was denied the right to a speedy trial when his trial took place eight years after an alleged offense, and he was available in the state for prosecution during that time. *Barker v. Wingo*, 407 U.S. 514 (1972), however, held that a five-year delay between arrest and trial did not violate the Sixth Amendment. Congress responded with the federal Speedy Trial Act of 1974, requiring persons arrested to be charged within thirty days, arraigned ten days later, and tried within two months of arraignment. Charges may be dismissed if a defendant moves for dismissal after the speedy-trial period has elapsed and no trial has commenced.[1] Finally, *Doggett v. United States*, 505 U.S. 647 (1992), held that the Sixth Amendment right to a speedy trial was violated by the prosecution of an individual who had been indicted eight and one-half years earlier for importing cocaine, but who had left the country before he could be arrested. Based on the facts in the case, the Court chided the federal government for failing to pursue the accused vigorously and accord him a speedy trial.

The Sixth Amendment also embodies a presumption against trials *in absentia* of the defendant, although the Federal Rules of Criminal Procedure permit a waiver of the accused's right to be present at the trial "whenever a defendant initially present is voluntarily absent after the trial has commenced." And in *Crosby v. United States*, 506 U.S. 255 (1993), involving an appeal of the government's trial of a defendant *in absentia*, the Rehnquist Court unanimously ruled that Rule 43 of the Federal Rules of Criminal Procedure forbids the federal government's trying a defendant who is absent at the trial's beginning.

NOTE

1. See *Dillingham v. United States*, 423 U.S. 64 (1975); and *United States v. MacDonald*, 456 U.S. 1 (1982).

SELECTED BIBLIOGRAPHY

Bodenhamer, David. *Fair Trial: Rights of the Accused in American History.* New York: Oxford University Press, 1992.

Misner, R. *Speedy Trial: Federal and State Practices.* Charlottesville, VA: Michie, 1983.

F | *The Rights to Be Informed of Charges and to Confront Accusers*

The accused has a right "to be informed of the nature and cause of the accusation against" him under the Sixth Amendment. This provision aims at ensuring defendants the opportunity to prepare adequate defenses. More often, though, defense attorneys challenge the constitutionality of criminal statutes for being "void for vagueness" under the due process clause. This principle—that a statute must specifically define and give notice of the kind of activity proscribed—was well-stated in *Connally v. General Construction Co.*, 269 U.S. 385 (1926):

> That the terms of a penal statute ... must be sufficiently explicit to inform those who are subject to it what conduct on their part will render them liable to its penalties, is a well-recognized requirement, consonant alike with ordinary notions of fair play and the settled rules of law. And a statute which either forbids or requires the doing of an act in terms so vague that men of common intelligence must necessarily guess at its meaning and differ as to its application, violates the first essential of due process of law.

The accused also has, under the Sixth Amendment, the right "to be confronted with the witnesses against him." This provision was made applicable to the states in *Pointer v. Texas*, 380 U.S. 400 (1965), where a transcript of a witness's testimony made at a preliminary hearing was introduced at trial because the witness had left the state. The accused also has the right to compel witnesses to appear in his favor in federal and state courts.[1] *Lee v. Illinois*, 476 U.S. 530 (1986), held five to four that the use of a codefendant's confession as evidence of a defendant's guilt violated the confrontation clause and was presumptively unreliable because the confession was given after the codefendant was told that the defendant had implicated her in criminal activity. In *Olden v. Kentucky*, 488 U.S. 227 (1988), the Court held that a trial judge's refusal to permit a black defendant in a kidnapping, rape, and sodomy trial to cross-examine the white victim regarding her cohabitation with a black boyfriend violated the defendant's Sixth Amendment right to a confrontation of witnesses. So too, in *Gray v. Maryland*, 521 U.S. 185 (1998), the Court ruled that the Sixth Amendment right to confront witnesses was violated by the introduction of an edited confession of a codefendant as evidence without giving the defendant an opportunity to cross-examine. The Court in *Crawford v. Washington*, 124 S.Ct. 1354 (2004), also overturned the ruling in *Ohio v. Roberts*, 448 U.S. 56 (1980), that statements from a witness who was not available for cross-examination could nevertheless be admitted at trial if the judge deemed them reliable. Writing for a unanimous Court, Justice Scalia held that the standard of "reliability" was too subjective and amorphous. In his words: "Dispensing with confrontation because testimony is obviously reliable is akin to dispensing with jury trial because a defendant is obviously guilty. This is not what the Sixth Amendment prescribes." Under the Court's new rule, the prosecution may use statements of absent witnesses only if they were previously cross-examined by the defense at a deposition or in a prior trial.

In two bitterly divided five-to-four decisions involving the right of defendants to confront accusers in cases involving alleged child abuse, Justice O'Connor held the balance. Writing for a bare majority in *Maryland v. Craig*, 497 U.S. 836 (1990), Justice O'Connor held that individuals charged with child abuse have no constitutional right to confront, at least once, their young accusers. In that case, O'Connor upheld the state's allowing four children to testify out of the presence of the defendant over a one-way, closed-circuit television. In her words, "A state's interest in the physical and psychological well-being of child-abuse victims may be sufficiently important to outweigh, at least in some cases, a defendant's right to face his or her accusers in court." But Justice Scalia countered in a dissenting opinion, joined by Justices Brennan, Marshall, and Stevens, that "[t]o say that a defendant loses his right to confront a witness when that would cause the witness not to testify is rather like saying that the defendant loses his right to counsel when counsel would save him."

In the second case, however, the four dissenters from *Craig* joined Justice O'Connor for another bare majority ruling in *Idaho v. Wright*, 497 U.S. 805 (1990). In that case, Justice O'Connor rejected as hearsay evidence the testimony of a doctor who had interviewed a two-and-a-half-year-old child about alleged sexual abuse. Although O'Connor refused to establish a bright-line rule for when such testimony, in the absence of the victim's own testimony, could be introduced, she emphasized that such hearsay evidence must be so trustworthy as to render a cross-examination of the victim of marginal utility.

Left unanswered by *Craig* and *Wright*, however, was whether judges may exclude all testimony by alleged victims who are capable of testifying, thereby allowing juries to determine a defendant's guilt entirely on the basis of hearsay testimony of those who questioned the children out of court. And the following term after deciding *Wright*, *White v. Illinois*, 502 U.S. 346 (1992), unanimously held that the Sixth Amendment's confrontation clause permits, in a trial of a defendant accused of sexually abusing a four-year-old child, the introduction as testimony of the victim's "spontaneous declaration" made to police and doctors, along with the results of a medical examination. The Court also rejected the claim that an accused's right to confront witnesses against him requires the prosecution either to produce the victim at trial or establish the victim's unavailability.[2] Writing for the Court, Chief Justice Rehnquist explained that

> [g]iven the evidentiary value of such statements, their reliability, and that establishing a generally applicable unavailability rule would have few practical benefits while imposing pointless litigation costs, we see no reason to treat the out-of-court statements in this case differently from those we found admissible in [cases not involving child abuse]. . . . We therefore see no basis . . . for excluding from trial, under the aegis of the Confrontation Clause, evidence embraced within such exceptions to the hearsay rule as those for spontaneous declarations and statements made for medical treatment.

In addition, in *Michigan v. Lucas*, 500 U.S. 145 (1991), the Court upheld Michigan's rape-shield law, which mandates that evidence of past sexual conduct be barred at trial if a defendant fails to give notice of its introduction at least ten days prior to the trial. Writing for the Court in *Lucas*, Justice O'Connor held that a defendant's right to confront accusers does not permit courts to adopt per se rules barring trial courts from allowing the introduction at trial of evidence of rape victims' prior sexual relationship with criminal defendants. Nor are states precluded from requiring defendants to give notification, within ten days of their arraignment, of their plans to present evidence about the alleged victim's past sexual conduct and on that basis ban in some cases the introduction of such evidence at trial. Michigan's ten-day deadline for such notification is the shortest in the country; the federal rape-shield law requires such notice 15 days before a trial commences.

NOTES

1. See *Washington v. Texas*, 388 U.S. 14 (1967). See also *Smith v. Illinois*, 390 U.S. 129 (1968); and *Barber v. Page*, 390 U.S. 719 (1968).

2. In *Tome v. United States*, 513 U.S. 150 (1995), however, the Court limited the introduction of third-party testimony in prosecutions for child abuse under the Federal Rules of Evidence.

SELECTED BIBLIOGRAPHY

Goldstein, Abraham. *The Passive Judiciary: Prosecutorial Discretion and the Guilty Plea.* Baton Rouge: Louisiana State University Press, 1981.

McGough, Lucy. *Child Witness: Fragile Voices in the American Legal System.* New Haven, CT: Yale University Press, 1994.

Walker, Samuel. *Sense and Nonsense about Crime.* 2d. ed. Pacific Grove, CA: Brooks/Cole, 1989.

G | *The Guarantee against Double Jeopardy*

The Fifth Amendment provides that defendants may not be twice held "in jeopardy of life or limb" for the same offense. The purpose of this guarantee, Justice Hugo Black explained in *Green v. United States*, 355 U.S. 184 (1957), is that "the State with all its resources and power should not be allowed to make repeated attempts to convict an individual for an alleged offense, thereby subjecting him to embarrassment, expense and ordeal and compelling him to live in a continuing state of anxiety and insecurity, as well as enhancing the possibility that even though innocent he may be found guilty."

The double jeopardy clause, however, was not deemed to be "fundamental" to the "concept of ordered liberty" so as to apply to the states in *Palko v. Connecticut* (1937) (see Ch. 4). But a solid majority of the Warren Court made the states bound by the double jeopardy clause in *Benton v. Maryland*, 395 U.S. 784 (1969). *Crist v. Bretz*, 437 U.S. 28 (1978) further held that states must observe the federal rule that the jeopardy clause is triggered once a jury is empaneled, and thus the defendant may not be retried for the same offense.

Like some other guarantees, the double jeopardy clause is not self-explanatory; much depends on how *jeopardy* is interpreted in the context of a legal proceeding and how the *same offense* is viewed. Defendants who have been acquitted or convicted and then retried by the same court, of course, have been placed in double jeopardy. *Waller v. Florida*, 397 U.S. 387 (1970), also held that defendants may not be retried for a different crime based on the same evidence. If a jury fails to reach a verdict and is dismissed, a second trial is permissible as a continuation of the first trial.[1] But the government may not appeal an acquittal, even if egregious errors led to the acquittal.[2] The government may, though, retry a defendant who wins a motion for mistrial,[3] except when a mistrial is declared by a judge on his own, due to improper procedures.[4] An accused may waive the right against being held in double jeopardy when requesting a new trial or appealing a guilty verdict, but if the conviction is set aside on appeal a retrial for the same offense is permissible.[5]

Whether defendants are tried for the same offense depends on whether the trial takes place in the same jurisdiction and based on the same evidence. In *United States v. Lara*, 124 S.Ct. 1628 (2004), for instance, the Court held that the federal government may prosecute a Native-American Indian in federal court, even after a conviction in a tribal court for virtually the same offense, assaulting a federal officer. Writing for the Court, Justice Breyer held that the double jeopardy clause does not bar prosecutions by two sovereign governments, and reaffirmed "the inherent power of Indian tribes . . . to exercise criminal jurisdiction over all Indians." Justices Scalia and Souter dissented.

If two charges grow out of the same evidence, retrial on separate charges other than that litigated at the first trial is permissible.[6] *United States v. Halper*, 490 U.S. 435 (1989), unanimously held that civil fines may not be placed on top of criminal penalties for the same offense. However, almost a decade later in *Hudson v. United States*, 522 U. S. 93 (1998), a bare majority overturned *Halper* and held that individuals may face criminal prosecution for banking violations for which they have already been fined. In holding that fines are civil, not criminal, and therefore do not trigger the double jeopardy clause, Chief Justice Rehnquist reaffirmed an earlier rule, set forth in *United States v. Ward*, 448 U.S. 242 (1980), that the threshold question in such cases is whether the legislature intended a successive punishment to be "civil" or "criminal."

The test for whether the double jeopardy clause is violated remains whether the same evidence is introduced in both trials.[7] Under *Blockburger v. United States*, 284 U.S. 299 (1932), successive prosecutions of criminal conduct under different statutes is forbidden, if they include identical statutory elements or lesser included offenses. In *Grady v. Corbin*, 495 U.S. 508 (1990), a bare majority of the Court expanded the scope of the double jeopardy clause to bar a subsequent prosecution under a different statute when the government must show that the defendant's conduct constituted an offense for which the defendant had already been prosecuted under another statute.

In *United States v. Felix*, 503 U.S. 378 (1992), the Court then held that the Fifth Amendment's double jeopardy clause is not violated by two separate federal prosecutions of a defendant for the crime of manufacturing illegal drugs and then for conspiracy to manufacture and distribute the same illegal drugs in a different jurisdiction. The Rehnquist Court unanimously agreed that the two prosecutions were not for "the same offense," despite the use of some of the same evidence against the defendant in both trials.

Following the retirements of Justices Brennan and Marshall, a bare majority was finally mustered to overturn the Court's 1990 ruling in *Grady v. Corbin*. In *United States v. Dixon*, 509 U.S. 688 (1993), another bare majority held that the double jeopardy clause does not bar the prosecution of an individual who has already been subject to prosecution for contempt for defying a judge's order for conduct that led to conviction for contempt of court in the first place. Writing for the Court, Justice Scalia, who had dissented in *Grady*, reaffirmed the test set forth in *Blockburger v. United States*, 284 U.S. 299 (1932), which inquires whether each offense contains an element not contained in the other; and, if not, whether they are the "same offense" for the purposes of the double jeopardy clause. However, he also overruled *Grady*'s "same conduct" test as inconsistent with earlier precedents and the history of the double jeopardy clause. *Dixon* thus reestablished the traditional view that under the double jeopardy clause the question is not whether two prosecutions require proof of the same conduct but, instead, whether the two offenses have the same "elements."

Moreover, *Dowling v. United States*, 493 U.S. 342 (1990), held that prosecutors may introduce at trial evidence relating to crimes for which the defendant in a prior trial had been acquitted. Notably, the double jeopardy clause does not bar defendants from receiving a more severe sentence on retrial.[8] Nor does it forbid both federal and state governments to prosecute the same offense.[9] *Poland v. Arizona*, 476 U.S. 147 (1986), construed the double jeopardy clause not to bar defendants from being retried and given capital punishment after they appealed their first conviction for first-degree murder and where an appellate court had reversed and ordered their retrial because of evidentiary problems even though it found that sufficient evidence had been presented for imposing a death sentence. But the Rehnquist Court split five to four in *Quinn v. Millsap*, 491 U.S. 95 (1989). There, a defendant was sentenced to prison for two crimes—fifteen years for attempted robbery and life imprisonment for felony murder—stemming from the same offense. By the time a state court held invalid the multiple sentences for the same offense, the robbery sentence had been commuted and the time served credited to the life sentence. But a federal court of appeals threw out the life sentence on appeal. Writing for a bare majority, Justice Kennedy reversed, observing that "[n]either the Double Jeopardy Clause nor any other constitutional provision exists to provide unjustified windfalls." Siding with Justices Brennan, Marshall, and Stevens in dissent, Justice Scalia countered that "[a] technical rule with equitable exceptions is no rule at all. Three strikes is out. The state broke the rules here, and must abide by the result."

In *Department of Revenue of Montana v. Kurth Ranch*, 511 U.S. 747 (1994), however, a bare majority of the Rehnquist Court struck down Montana's tax on illegal drugs as a violation of the double jeopardy clause, because it imposed an additional penalty inflicted on those convicted of possessing illegal drugs and thus unconstitutionally punished people twice for the same offense. Along with more than twenty other states, Montana imposed a tax on illegal drugs confiscated in drug raids. But, writing for the majority, Justice Stevens rejected the state's claim that the tax was simply a revenue-raising measure, and observed, "This tax, imposed on criminals and no others, departs so far from normal revenue laws as to become a form of punishment."

Finally, in *United States v. Ursery*, 518 U.S. 267 (1996), the Court nevertheless held that civil forfeiture proceedings, which since the 1980s have become common for defendants who have been criminally convicted for drug trafficking, do not violate the Double Jeopardy Clause when the defendant has also been tried for the same offense on criminal charges. Writing for the Court, Chief Justice Rehnquist held simply that civil forfeitures "do not constitute 'punishment' for purposes of the Double Jeopardy Clause."

Notes

1. *United States v. Perez*, 9 Wheat. 579 (1824).

2. *Sanabria v. United States*, 437 U.S. 54 (1978); and *Oregon v. Washington*, 434 U.S. 497 (1978).

3. See *United States v. Dinitz*, 424 U.S. 600 (1971); and *Oregon v. Kennedy*, 456 U.S. 667 (1987).

4. Compare *United States v. Jorn*, 400 U.S. 470 (1971) with *Illinois v. Somerville*, 410 U.S. 458 (1973).

5. See *United States v. Ball*, 163 U.S. 662 (1896) and compare *Burks v. United States*, 437 U.S. 1 (1978); *Hudson v. Louisiana*, 450 U.S. 40 (1981); and *Tibbs v. Florida*, 457 U.S. 31 (1982).

6. See *Morgan v. Devine*, 237 U.S. 632 (1915); and *United States v. Ewell*, 383 U.S. 116 (1966).

7. See *Hoag v. New York*, 356 U.S. 464 (1958); *Ashe v. Swenson*, 397 U.S. 436 (1978); and *United States v. Halper*, 490 U.S. 435 (1989). *Lockhart v. Nelson*, 488 U.S. 33 (1988) held that the double jeopardy clause does not bar retrial after an appellate court has determined that evidence at the first trial was erroneously admitted.

8. See *United States v. DiFrancesco*, 449 U.S. 117 (1980); and *Chaffin v. Stynchcombem*, 412 U.S. 17 (1973). But compare *North Carolina v. Pierce*, 395 U.S. 711 (1964); and *Bullington v. Missouri*, 451 U.S. 430 (1981). See also *Witte v. United States*, 515 U.S. 389 (1994) (holding that the double jeopardy clause does not bar prosecution for a crime even though the same criminal conduct was previously used to raise the defendant's prison sentence for a different offense).

9. See *United States v. Lanza*, 260 U.S. 377 (1922); *Abbate v. United States*, 359 U.S. 187 (1959); *Bartkus v. Illinois*, 359 U.S. 121 (1959). The Court, however, has overturned the prosecution by local and state governments in the same jurisdiction of a defendant based on the same evidence. See *Waller v. Florida*, 397 U.S. 387 (1970); and *Missouri v. Hunter*, 459 U.S. 359 (1983).

Selected Bibliography

Dickens, James. *Double Jeopardy and Civil Penalties: The Impact of United States v. Halper*. Chapel Hill: Institute of Government, University of North Carolina, 1992.

Friedland, M. *Double Jeopardy.* New York: Oxford University Press, 1969.

Sigler, Jay. *Double Jeopardy: The Development of a Legal and Social Policy.* Ithaca, NY: Cornell University Press, 1969.

Thomas, George C. *Double Jeopardy: The History, the Law.* New York: New York University Press, 1999.

H | *The Guarantee against Excessive Bail and Fines*

The Eighth Amendment's provisions that "excessive bail shall not be required, nor excessive fines imposed" gave constitutional effect to rights dating back to the English Bill of Rights in 1689. Bail is a pledge of money or property by an accused that ostensibly guarantees his appearance at trial; it enables the accused to remain free while awaiting trial. The provision limits both Congress and federal courts in setting bail. Under the Bail Reform Act of 1966, those accused of noncapital federal offenses may be released on their own recognizance or on an unsecured bond, unless a judge deems that release would "not reasonably assure" their appearance in court.

Because of the concern over the number of crimes committed by repeat offenders while on bail and the battle against importers of drugs and narcotics, Congress passed the Bail Reform Act of 1984. It authorizes the pretrial detention of defendants who are deemed to pose a threat to the community. By a vote of six to three in *United States v. Salerno*, 481 U.S. 739 (1987), the Court upheld pretrial detention as "regulatory, not penal." Chief Justice Rehnquist's opinion for the Court explained,

> The Bail Reform Act . . . operates only on individuals who have been arrested for a specific category of extremely serious offenses. Congress specifically found that these individuals are far more likely to be responsible for dangerous acts in the community after arrest. . . . While the government's general interest in preventing is compelling, even this interest is heightened when the government musters convincing proof that the arrestee, already indicted or held to answer for a serious crime, presents a demonstrable danger to the community. Under these narrow circumstances, society's interest in crime prevention is at its greatest.
>
> On the other side of the scale, of course, is the individual's strong interest in liberty. We do not minimize the importance and fundamental nature of this right. But, as our cases hold, this right may, in circumstances where the government's interest is sufficiently weighty, be subordinated to the greater needs of society.

Two years later, in *Caplin & Drysdale v. United States* and *United States v. Monsanto*, 491 U.S. 617 (1989), the Rehnquist Court held five to four that the Department of Justice may seize the money and property illegally acquired by criminal defendants who are facing trial even if they claim that those assets would be used to pay the costs of their defense at trial. In Justice White's words for the majority: "A defendant has no Sixth Amendment right to spend another person's money for services rendered by an attorney, even if those funds are the only way that the defendant will be able to retain the attorney of his choice."

In recent years, the Court has faced a series of challenges to state and federal laws authorizing the seizure and forfeiture of property of individuals who have been convicted of criminal activities. Forfeiture has become a major weapon in the federal government's so-called drug war. But in two Eighth Amendment challenges to forfeitures as constituting "excessive fines," in *Alexander v. United States*, 509 U.S. 544 (1993), and *Austin v. United States*, 509 U.S. 602 (1993), the Court rebuffed the federal government's argument that forfeiture is not punitive but "remedial" and that the guilt or innocence of the property owner is "constitutionally irrelevant."

Notably, in *Austin v. United States*, the Court unanimously held that the guarantee against excessive fines requires the government to show a relationship between the seriousness of the offense and the forfeiture of property. Richard Austin, after having been convicted of selling cocaine, argued that the government's filing of a civil forfeiture complaint against his mobile home and auto-body shop abridged the Eighth Amendment. The government, however, countered that the amendment applies only to criminal proceedings and not civil actions, like forfeiture, even though related to a criminal conviction. In rejecting the government's arguments for the Court, Justice Blackmun observed that

> Fundamentally, even assuming that [the forfeiture provisions here] serve some remedial purpose, the Government's argument fails. . . . In light of the historical understanding of forfeiture as punishment, the clear focus of [the forfeiture provisions] on the culpability of the owner, and the evidence that Congress understood those provisions as serving to deter and to punish, we cannot conclude that forfeiture under Sections 881(a)(4) and (a)(7) [of the U.S. Code] serves solely a remedial purpose. We therefore conclude that forfeiture under these provisions constitutes "payment to a sovereign as punishment for some offense," and, as such, is subject to the limitations of the Eighth Amendment's Excessive Fines Clause.

In *Austin*, Justice Blackmun nevertheless declined to lay down guidelines for when the government's seizure of property is unconstitutionally excessive. Instead, the Court remanded *Austin* back to the lower courts for reconsideration. Consequently, that issue will percolate in the lower federal courts, allowing them to develop their own rules, and allow the Court eventually to revisit the issue of when forfeitures constitute "excessive fines" under the Eighth Amendment.

I | *Indigents and the Criminal Justice System*

Beginning in the 1950s, the Warren Court held in a number of cases that the Fourteenth Amendment due process and equal protection clauses require states to provide indigents with certain resources for their defense at trial and on appeal. *Griffin v. Illinois*, 351 U.S. 12 (1956), is the leading case in which the Court struck down a statute granting free trial transcripts to indigents only for review of constitutional questions and where the defendant was given a death sentence. There, the Court held that the right of indigents to meaningful appellate review was denied unless they were furnished trial transcripts in any appeals. *Gideon v. Wainwright* (1963) (excerpted in Section A), of course, extended the right to counsel to indigents at trial. However, the Burger and Rehnquist Courts have upheld constraints on indigents' access to the judicial system in several, although not all, rulings. Some of the major rulings on the rights of indigents are summarized in THE DEVELOPMENT OF LAW box following.

SELECTED BIBLIOGRAPHY

Allen, Francis. *The Habits of Legality: Criminal Justice and the Rule of Law.* New York: Oxford University Press, 1996.

Lawrence, Susan. *The Poor in Court.* Princeton, NJ: Princeton University Press, 1990.

Lefstein, Norman. *Criminal Defense Services for the Poor.* Chicago: American Bar Association, 1982.

Miller, Jerome. *Search and Destroy: African-American Males in the Criminal Justice System.* Cambridge, UK: Cambridge University Press, 1996.

Smith, Christopher. *Courts and the Poor.* Chicago: Nelson-Hall, 1991.

■ THE DEVELOPMENT OF LAW

Other Rulings on Indigents and the Judicial System

CASE	VOTE	RULING
Burns v. Ohio, 360 U.S. 252 (1959)	7:2	Indigents have the right to file an appeal.
Lane v. Brown, 372 U.S. 477 (1963)	9:0	Right to have trial transcript on appeal.
Hardy v. United States, 375 U.S. 277 (1964)	8:1	Court-appointed attorney is entitled to trial transcript.
Long v. District Court of Iowa, 385 U.S. 143 (1966)	9:0	Transcripts must be provided for *habeas corpus* proceedings on appeal.
Roberts v. LaVallee, 389 U.S. 40 (1967)	8:1	Indigents have a right to transcripts even after exhaustion of state appeals.
Gardner v. California, 393 U.S. 367 (1969)	6:3	Right to free trial transcript for preparation of *habeas corpus* petition.

CASE	VOTE	RULING
Williams v. Oklahoma City, 395 U.S. 458 (1969)	9:0	States that permit appeals for any conviction may not deny right of appeal to indigents.
Williams v. Illinois, 399 U.S. 235 (1970)	9:0	Fourteenth Amendment forbids states from converting fines into prison sentences.
Mayer v. City of Chicago, 404 U.S. 189 (1971)	9:0	Struck down Illinois's law providing trial transcripts only in felony cases as constituting an "unreasonable distinction"; required transcripts in felony and nonfelony cases.
Tate v. Short, 401 U.S. 395 (1971)	9:0	An indigent convicted of traffic offenses may not be committed to a municipal prison farm because of inability to pay fine.
Boddie v. Connecticut, 401 U.S. 371 (1971)	8:1	Struck down filing fee required to have access to divorce court.
Schilb v. Kuebel, 404 U.S. 357 (1971)	6:3	States may require an accused to pay 10 percent of a bail bond or $25, whichever is greater, to secure a pretrial release from jail.
United States v. Kras, 409 U.S. 434 (1973)	5:4	Upheld a $50 filing fee for access to bankruptcy court.
Ortwein v. Schwab, 410 U.S. 656 (1973)	5:4	Upheld Oregon's $25 filing fee for those seeking an appeal of an adverse welfare benefits decision.
Fuller v. Oregon, 417 U.S. 40 (1974)	7:2	Upheld a probationary system requiring reimbursement of the state for fees and the expenses of attorneys.
Ross v. Moffitt, 417 U.S. 600 (1974)	6:3	Held that after the first appeal as of right, indigents have no right to a court-appointed attorney on further appeals to a state's highest court or to the United States Supreme Court.
Bounds v. Smith, 430 U.S. 817 (1977)	6:3	Prisons must provide adequate law libraries for prisoners who want to make a "meaningful appeal."

CASE	VOTE	RULING
Ake v. Oklahoma, 470 U.S. 68 (1985)	8:1	If sanity is an issue at a defendant's trial, the state must provide a psychiatrist.
Pennsylvania v. Finley, 481 U.S. 551 (1987)	5:4	There is no constitutional right to a court-appointed attorney in postconviction proceedings.
Murray v. Giarratano, 492 U.S. 1 (1989)	5:4	States are not required to furnish lawyers for indigents on death row who have lost initial rounds of appeals.
In re Amendment to Rule 34, 500 U.S. 13 (1991)	6:3	Amended the Supreme Court's rules to authorize the denial of *in forma pauperis* petitions if a

majority deems them "frivolous or malicious." Justices Blackmun, Marshall, and Stevens dissented.

Lewis v. Casey, 518 U.S. 343 (1996)	8:1	Writing for the Court, Justice Scalia reinterpreted the ruling in *Bounds v. Smith*, 430 U.S. 817 (1977) to limit the standing to

sue of prison inmates, and the remedial powers of federal courts in ordering changes in prison law libraries and legal assistance programs so as to facilitate inmates' "right of access to the courts."

IO

CRUEL AND UNUSUAL PUNISHMENT

The ban on "cruel and unusual punishments" is another guarantee of the Bill of Rights rooted in the history of English common law. In 1583, the Archbishop of Canterbury turned the High Commission into an Ecclesiastical Court for punishing heretics and critics of the Crown. Torture was used to extract confessions, and death was imposed for a large number of crimes. Opposition gradually mounted and led to the English Bill of Rights of 1689. Among those rights, the ban on "cruel and unusual punishments" registered not only opposition to the practices of the High Commission but also the imposition of punishments unauthorized by statute and disproportionate to the offense. The phrasing of the English guarantee against "cruel and unusual punishments" reappeared in the United States in Virginia's Declaration of Rights in 1776. It was later incorporated verbatim in the Eighth Amendment.

Prior to the 1960s, the Supreme Court had little occasion to interpret the guarantee against "cruel and unusual punishments." But in the 1960s there was an organized legal attack on the constitutionality of capital punishment orchestrated by the American Civil Liberties Union and the National Association for the Advancement of Colored People (NAACP) Legal Defense Fund, among other organizations. In response to these pressures and litigation in the 1970s the Court began erecting barriers to the imposition of the death sentence. But that in turn made capital punishment a major political issue and invited the mobilization of forces pushing for a renewal of executions. With changes in the composition of the high bench, the Court again responded and shifted direction.

Certain themes in the Court's initial interpretation of the guarantee against cruel and unusual punishments, however, laid the basis for its eventual application of the amendment in the area of capital punishment. First, the Court indicated that the amendment does not ban unusual punishments but rather those that are barbaric in their cruelty. The Court's initial encounters with Eighth Amendment claims involved whether novel methods of execution ran afoul of the amendment. *Wilkerson v. Utah*, 99 U.S. 130 (1878), unanimously upheld public execution by musketry, and *In re Kemmler*, 136 U.S. 436 (1890), upheld electrocution, which though unusual at the time was more "humane" than hanging and other forms of execution. As Justice Stephen Field, in *O'Neil v. Vermont*, 144 U.S. 323 (1892), summarized:

> That designation [cruel and unusual punishments], it is true, is usually applied to punishments which inflict torture, such as the rack, the thumbscrew, the iron boot, the stretching of limbs and the like, which are attended with acute pain and suffering. . . . The inhibition is directed, not only against punishments of the character mentioned, but against all punishments which by their excessive length or severity are greatly disproportionate to the offenses charged. The whole inhibition is against that which is excessive.

Second, the Court indicated that the intentions of those who carry out executions may not be controlling in applying the amendment. In the case of Willy Francis, a mechanical failure of the electric chair frustrated the state's first attempt to put him to death. And Francis appealed to the Court, contending that a second trip to the electric chair constituted cruel and unusual punishment. The justices by a vote of five to four rejected his claim, finding the unsuccessful execution an "unforseeable accident" but not intentional cruelty. *Louisiana ex rel. Francis v. Resweber*, 329 U.S. 459 (1947).

Finally, the Court indicated that punishments that are grossly disproportionate to the offense might violate the Eighth Amendment. The first ruling overturning a punishment under the amendment, in *Weems v. United States*, 217 U.S. 349 (1910), involved a Coast Guard officer, stationed in the Philippine Islands, who was convicted of falsifying public documents and sentenced to twelve years of incarceration, chained, and put under perpetual surveillance, as well as stripped of all civil liberties. *Trop v. Dulles*, 356 U.S. 86 (1958), held that the loss of citizenship as a result of a court-martial for wartime desertion constituted cruel and unusual punishment. In controversial although often-cited *dicta*, Chief Justice Warren added that "[t]he amendment must draw its meaning from evolving standards of decency that mark the progress of a maturing society."

SELECTED BIBLIOGRAPHY

Abu-Jamal, Mumia. *Live from Death Row.* Reading, MA: Addison-Wesley, 1995.

Banner, Stuart. *The Death Penalty: An American History.* Cambridge, MA; Harvard University Press, 2002.

Bedau, Hugo, ed., *The Death Penalty in America.* 3rd ed. New York: Oxford University Press, 1982.

Bedau, Hugo, and Cassell, Paul, eds. *Debating the Death Penalty.* New York: Oxford University Press, 2004.

Berger, Raoul. *Death Penalties: The Supreme Court's Obstacle Course.* Cambridge, MA: Harvard University Press, 1982.

Berns, Walter. *For Capital Punishment.* New York: Basic Books, 1979.

Black, Jr., Charles. *Capital Punishment: The Inevitability of Caprice and Mistake.* New York: Norton, 1974.

Bowers, William J. et al. *Legal Homicide: Death as Punishment in America, 1864–1982.* Boston: Northeastern University Press, 1984.

Epstein, Lee, and Kobylka, Joseph. *The Supreme Court and Legal Change: Abortion and the Death Penalty.* Chapel Hill: University of North Carolina Press, 1992.

Garvey, Stephen P., ed. *Beyond Repair? America's Death Penalty.* Durham, NC: Duke University Press, 2003.

Hirsch, James. *Hurricane: The Miraculous Journey of Rubin Carter.* Boston: Houghton Mifflin, 2000.

Hood, Roger. *The Death Penalty: A World Wide Perspective.* 3rd ed. New York: Oxford University Press, 2002.

Lifton, Robert, and Mitchell, Grey. *Who Owns Death?* New York: HarperCollins, 2000.

Masur, Louis. *Rites of Execution: Capital Punishment and the Transformation of American Culture, 1776–1865.* New York: Oxford University Press, 1989.

McFeely, William S. *Proximity to Death.* New York: Norton, 1999.

Mello, Michael. *Dead Wrong: A Death Row Lawyer Speaks Out against Capital Punishment.* Madison: University of Wisconsin Press, 1997.

Miller, Arthur S., and Bowman, J. H. *Death by Installments: The Ordeal of Willie Francis.* Westport, CT: Greenwood Press, 1988.

Moran, Richard. *Executioner's Current: Thomas Edison, George Westinghouse, and Invention of the Electric Chair.* New York: Knopf, 2002.

Parloff, Roger. *Triple Jeopardy.* Boston: Little, Brown, 1996.

Prettyman, Barrett, Jr. *Death and the Supreme Court.* New York: Harcourt, Brace & World, 1961.

Sarat, Austin, ed. *The Killing State: Capital Punishment in Law, Politics, and Culture.* New York: Oxford University Press, 1998.

Scheck, Barry, Neufeld, Peter, and Dwyer, Jim. *Actual Innocence: Five Days to Execution, and Other Dispatches from the Wrongly Convicted.* New York: Doubleday, 2000.

White, Welsh. *The Death Penalty in the Nineties.* Ann Arbor: University of Michigan Press, 1991.

Zimring, Franklin. *The Contradictions of American Capital Punishment.* New York: Oxford University Press, 2003.

A | *Noncapital Punishment*

In *Robinson v. California*, 370 U.S. 660 (1962), the Warren Court struck down a statute making narcotics addiction per se a criminal offense, with at least a mandatory ninety-day jail sentence. Besides finding the punishment disproportionate, the Warren Court indicated that the amendment might have broader application outside of the area of capital punishment. However, a bare majority of the Court refused to extend *Robinson* when upholding a conviction for public drunkenness of an ex-alcoholic and finding alcoholism not to be a "disease," in *Powell v. Texas*, 392 U.S. 514 (1968). The Burger and Rehnquist Courts subsequently held that the conditions of prison isolation cells and prison officials' indifference to the illness of inmates may violate the Eighth Amendment,[1] but also refused to apply the amendment to corporal punishment in public schools,[2] and to the shooting without warning of a prisoner during the quelling of a prison riot.[3] In addition, the Court has been reluctant to strike down noncapital punishments as disproportionate to the crime. *Hutto v. Davis*, 454 U.S. 370 (1982), for instance, upheld a sentence of forty years' imprisonment for the possession and distribution of nine ounces of marijuana. By a vote of five to four in *Rummel v. Estelle*, 445 U.S. 263, (1980), Texas's habitual criminal offenders act was upheld as applied to a man convicted of three thefts totaling $289. The following year, however, Justice Blackmun, who cast the crucial fifth vote in *Rummel*, joined *Rummel's* four dissenters in *Solem v. Helm*, 463 U.S. 277 (1983), striking down as cruel and unusual punishment a life sentence imposed on a defendant convicted for writing a $100 bad check and who had six prior nonviolent offenses. However, a bare majority in *Harmelin v. Michigan*, 501 U.S. 957 (1991), rejected the claim that a lifetime sentence, without the possibility of parole, for possessing 650 grams of cocaine violated the Eighth Amendment. And in *Ewing v. California* (2003) (excerpted below), a bare majority upheld California's "three-strikes-and-you're-out" law, imposing sentences of twenty-five years to life for those convicted of three felonies and, unlike such laws in other states, permits counting certain misdemeanors as felonies. Gary Ewing, who had previous convictions for burglary and robbery, received a twenty-five year to life sentence for stealing three golf clubs, each valued at $399. Writing for the Court, Justice O'Connor held that Ewing's sentence was not grossly disproportionate and therefore did not violate the Eighth Amendment. Justices Scalia and Thomas, concurring, disagreed that disproportionate analysis has any place in Eighth Amendment jurisprudence. Justices Stevens, Souter, Ginsburg, and Breyer dissented.

The issue of the Eighth Amendment's applicability to the confinement and treatment of prison inmates is one area that has continued to haunt and split the Rehnquist Court. In *Wilson v. Seiter*, 501 U.S. 294 (1991), the justices confronted the question of whether unfit prison living conditions, even in the absence of evidence that prison officials acted maliciously, constitute cruel and unusual punishment. There, Ohio prison officials were accused of being indifferent to miserable prison conditions, ranging from overcrowding to rat-infested kitchens. Writing for the majority, Justice Scalia held that prisoners claiming that the conditions of their confinement violate the Eighth Amendment must show "a culpable state of mind on the part of prison officials," since the concept of "intent" is implicit in the amendment's ban against "cruel and unusual punishments." For prisoners to prevail with claims of an Eighth Amendment violation, Scalia ruled that they must show "deliberate indifference" of prison officials to the conditions of their confinement.

In *Hudson v. McMillian*, 503 U.S. 1 (1992), however, the Rehnquist Court went the other way, splitting seven to two in holding that a prison inmate's Eighth Amendment rights were violated by prison guards' use of excessive force. Keith Hudson was punched and kicked by two guards while he remained handcuffed and a supervisor instructed the guards not to "have too much fun." He sustained loosened teeth and a split lip but no "significant injury." After initially winning $800 in damages, Hudson's claims were dismissed by an appellate court on the grounds that he failed to show a "significant injury" from "objectively and clearly unnecessary" use of excessive force aimed at "an unnecessary and wanton infliction of pain."

When reversing the lower court's ruling in *Hudson*, Justice O'Connor ruled that the touchstone for the Court's analysis in such cases was "whether force was applied in a good-faith effort to maintain or restore discipline, or maliciously and sadistically to cause harm." O'Connor thereupon distinguished *Whitley v. Albers*, 475 U.S. 312 (1986), which held that an inmate's Eighth Amendment rights were not violated by a prison guard's shooting him during a prison riot. The settled rule, in O'Connor's view, was whether guards "unnecessarily and wanton[ly]" inflict pain. O'Connor, though, rejected the argument that inmates must also show a "significant injury" and refused to extend Justice Scalia's analysis in *Wilson v. Seiter*, requiring alleged wrongdoing to be "objectively harmful enough" to constitute a constitutional violation.

The "objective component" of the Eighth Amendment's guarantee against "cruel and unusual punishment," Justice O'Connor observed in *Hudson*, was (1) contextually dependent on the kind of claim raised and (2) draws "its meaning from evolving standards of decency that mark the progress of a maturing society," citing *Trop v. Dulles*, 356 U.S. 86 (1958). On that basis, O'Connor distinguished *Wilson* and other cases involving conditions-of-confinement claims and whether the denial of inmates' medical needs constituted "cruel and unusual punishment." In such cases, inmates must show "deliberate indifference" of prison authorities and that the inmates' deprivations or injuries are "serious." By contrast, inmates claiming constitutional deprivations due to excessive force must show that "prison officials maliciously and sadistically use[d] force to cause harm," though not that the inmates suffered "significant harm." To further require a showing of "significant harm," O'Connor reasoned, would permit "any physical punishment, no matter how diabolic or inhuman, inflicting less than some arbitrary quantity of injury" under the Eighth Amendment.

In a sharply worded dissenting opinion in *Hudson*, which Scalia joined, Justice Thomas not only took strong exception to the majority's reliance on the *dicta* in *Trop v. Dulles* that the Eighth Amendment "draw[s] its meaning from evolving standards of decency." He also rejected the Court's conclusions that inmates need not show "a significant injury" and that the ban against "cruel and unusual punishments" applies in cases such as *Hudson*, rather than only those challenging prison sentences or other official "punishment." Justice Thomas's opinion underscored that his approach to constitutional interpretation strongly resists expansive readings and relies heavily on the history of constitutional guarantees. As Justice Thomas explained:

> Until recent years, the Cruel and Unusual Punishment Clause was not deemed to apply at all to deprivations that were not inflicted as part of the sentence for a crime. For generations, judges and commentators regarded the Eighth Amendment as applying only to torturous punishments meted out by statutes or sentencing judges, and not generally to any hardship that might befall a prisoner during incarceration. . . . Surely prison was not a more congenial place in the early years of the Republic than it is today; nor were our judges and commentators so naive as to be unaware of the often harsh conditions of prison life. Rather, they simply did not conceive of the Eighth Amendment as protecting inmates from harsh treatment. . . .

A majority of the Court, nonetheless, buttressed the ruling in *Hudson v. McMillian*, with Justices Thomas and Scalia again dissenting, in *Helling v. McKinney*, 509 U.S. 25 (1993). There, Justice White held that a prison inmate could raise an Eighth Amendment claim against prison authorities who Donald Helling said showed "deliberate indifference" to his objections to being housed with another cell mate who smoked five packs of cigarettes a day and, thus, involuntarily exposed Helling to health risks. As to the amendment's applicability to such conditions of imprisonment, Justice White observed:

> Contemporary standards of decency require no less. In *Estelle* [*v. Gamble*, 429 U.S. 97 (1976)], we concluded that although accidental or inadvertent failure to provide adaquate medical care to a prisoner would not violate the Eighth Amendment, "deliberate indifference to serious medical needs of prisoners" violates the Amendment because it constitutes the unnecessary and wanton infliction of pain contrary to contemporary standards of decency. . . .

For the same reasons expressed in their dissenting opinion in *Hudson*, Justices Thomas and Scalia dissented in *Helling*. However, the justices unanimously reinstated a suit for damages brought by a transsexual prison inmate in *Farmer v. Brennan*, 511 U.S. 825 (1994). Dee Farmer, who is serving a twenty-year sentence for credit card fraud, was born male but underwent estrogen therapy, had breast implants, and had unsuccessful surgery to remove his testicles. In prison, Farmer was raped and subsequently claimed that prison officials should not have put him with the general prison population because they should have known that a transsexual "who projects feminine characteristics" would be vulnerable to sexual assaults. In holding for the Court that Farmer could sue for damages based on showing that prison officials exhibited "deliberate indifference" to his safety, Justice Souter observed, "Being violently assaulted in prison is simply not part of the penalty that criminal offenders pay for their offenses against society." Although concurring in the judgment in a separate opinion, Justice Thomas maintained his position that the Eighth Amendment does not extend to brutality among prisoners or inflicted by guards. As Justice Thomas put it, "Punishment, from the time of the founding through the present day, has always meant a fine, penalty or confinement inflicted upon a person by the authority of the law and the judgment and sentence of a court, for some crime or offense committed by him. . . . Because the unfortunate attack that befell the petitioner was not part of his sentence, it did not constitute 'punishment' under the Eighth Amendment."

In sum, the Eighth Amendment applies to the conditions and treatment of prison inmates. But the standard varies depending on the nature of the case. In conditions of imprisonment cases, like *Wilson v. Seiter* and *Farmer v. Brennan*, the standard is whether prison officials showed a "deliberate indifference" to the conditions and safety of inmates. In cases involving prison officials' use of excessive force, as in

Hudson v. McMillian, the standard is whether "prison officials maliciously and sadistically use[d] force to cause harm."

NOTES

1. *Hutto v. Finney*, 437 U.S. 679 (1978); and *Estelle v. Gamble*, 429 U.S. 97 (1976).
2. *Ingraham v. Wright*, 430 U.S. 651 (1977).
3. *Whitley v. Albers*, 475 U.S. 312 (1986).

Ewing v. California
538 U.S. 11, 123 S. Ct. 1179 (2003)

In the 1990s, about half the states enacted "three-strikes-and-you're-out" laws, requiring mandatory sentences, including life imprisonment, for individuals convicted of three felonies. California's 1994 law provides that a defendant who has two or more prior felony convictions must receive "an indeterminate term of life imprisonment," with the possibility of parole after twenty-five years of imprisonment. In addition, the law gives prosecutors and judges the discretion to treat certain offenses—known as "wobblers"—as either felonies or misdemeanors, and some crimes that would otherwise be misdemeanors may become wobblers and counted as felonies under the law. For example, a petty theft, a misdemeanor, may become a wobbler and treated as a felony when the defendant previously served prison time for committing a theft-related crime.

In 2000, when on parole from serving a nine-year prison term for committing three burglaries and a robbery, Gary Ewing walked into a pro golf shop and walked out with three golf clubs, priced at $399 each, concealed in his pants leg. An employee observed him limp out of the shop and called the police. The police apprehended him in the parking lot and arrested him. Ewing was charged with and convicted of one count of a felony grand theft of personal property in excess of $400. As required under California's three-strikes law, the prosecutor sought a life-time prison sentence. At sentencing, Ewing asked the court to reduce the conviction for grand theft, a "wobbler," to a misdemeanor so as to avoid a three-strikes sentence. The trial judge, however, determined that the theft of the golf clubs should remain a felony and that the four prior strikes for burglary and robbery should stand. Ewing was sentenced to twenty-five years to life in prison. A state appellate court affirmed and the Supreme Court of California denied review, whereupon Ewing appealed to the Supreme Court.

The judgment was affirmed by a five-to-four vote. Justice O'Connor delivered the opinion for the Court, which Chief Justice Rehnquist and Justice Kennedy joined. Justices Scalia and Thomas filed concurring opinions. Justices Stevens and Breyer filed dissenting opinions, which Justices Souter and Ginsburg joined.

☐ *Justice O'CONNOR announced the judgment of the Court and delivered an opinion in which THE CHIEF JUSTICE and Justice KENNEDY join.*

The Eighth Amendment, which forbids cruel and unusual punishments, contains a "narrow proportionality principle" that "applies to noncapital sentences." *Harmelin v. Michigan*, 501 U.S. 957 (1991). We have most recently addressed the proportionality principle as applied to terms of years in a series of cases beginning with *Rummel v. Estelle*, [445 U.S. 263 (1980)].

In *Rummel*, we held that it did not violate the Eighth Amendment for a State to sentence a three-time offender to life in prison with the possibility of parole. Like Ewing, Rummel was sentenced to a lengthy prison term under a recidivism statute. Rummel's two prior offenses were a 1964 felony for "fraudulent use of a credit card to obtain $80 worth of goods or services," and a 1969 felony conviction for "passing a forged check in the amount of $28.36." His triggering offense was a conviction for felony theft—"obtaining $120.75 by false pretenses."

This Court ruled that "having twice imprisoned him for felonies, Texas was entitled to place upon *Rummel* the onus of one who is simply unable to bring his conduct within the social norms prescribed by the criminal law of the State." The recidivism statute "is nothing more than a societal decision that when such a person commits yet another felony, he should be subjected to the admittedly serious penalty of incarceration for life, subject only to the State's judgment as to whether to grant him parole." . . .

In *Hutto v. Davis*, 454 U.S. 370 (1982), the defendant was sentenced to two consecutive terms of 20 years in prison for possession with intent to distribute nine ounces of marijuana and distribution of marijuana. We held that such a sentence was constitutional: "In short, *Rummel* stands for the proposition that federal courts should be reluctant to review legislatively mandated terms of imprisonment, and that successful challenges to the proportionality of particular sentences should be exceedingly rare."

Three years after *Rummel*, in *Solem v. Helm*, 463 U.S. 277 (1983), we held that the Eighth Amendment prohibited "a life sentence without possibility of parole for a seventh nonviolent felony." The triggering offense in *Solem* was "uttering a 'no account' check for $100." We specifically stated that the Eighth Amendment's ban on cruel and unusual punishments "prohibits . . . sentences that are disproportionate to the crime committed," and that the "constitutional principle of proportionality has been recognized explicitly in this Court for almost a century." The *Solem* Court then explained that three factors may be relevant to a determination of whether a sentence is so disproportionate that it violates the Eighth Amendment: "(i) the gravity of the offense and the harshness of the penalty; (ii) the sentences imposed on other criminals in the same jurisdiction; and (iii) the sentences imposed for commission of the same crime in other jurisdictions."

Applying these factors in *Solem*, we struck down the defendant's sentence of life without parole. We specifically noted the contrast between that sentence and the sentence in *Rummel*, pursuant to which the defendant was eligible for parole. . . .

The proportionality principles in our cases . . . guide our application of the Eighth Amendment in the new context that we are called upon to consider.

For many years, most States have had laws providing for enhanced sentencing of repeat offenders. Yet between 1993 and 1995, three strikes laws effected a sea change in criminal sentencing throughout the Nation. These laws responded to widespread public concerns about crime by targeting the class of offenders who pose the greatest threat to public safety: career criminals. . . .

Throughout the States, legislatures enacting three strikes laws made a deliberate policy choice that individuals who have repeatedly engaged in serious or violent criminal behavior, and whose conduct has not been deterred by more conventional approaches to punishment, must be isolated from society in order to protect the public safety. Though three strikes laws may be relatively new, our tradition of deferring to state legislatures in making and implementing such important policy decisions is longstanding.

Our traditional deference to legislative policy choices finds a corollary in the principle that the Constitution "does not mandate adoption of any one penological theory." A sentence can have a variety of justifications, such as incapacitation, deterrence, retribution, or rehabilitation. Some or all of these justifications may play a role in a State's sentencing scheme. Selecting the sentencing rationales is generally a policy choice to be made by state legislatures, not federal courts.

When the California Legislature enacted the three strikes law, it made a judgment that protecting the public safety requires incapacitating criminals who have already been convicted of at least one serious or violent crime. Nothing in the Eighth Amendment prohibits California from making that choice. . . .

Against this backdrop, we consider Ewing's claim that his three strikes sentence of 25 years to life is unconstitutionally disproportionate to his offense of "shoplifting three golf clubs." We first address the gravity of the offense compared to the harshness of the penalty. At the threshold, we note that Ewing incorrectly frames the issue. The gravity of his offense was not merely "shoplifting three golf clubs." Rather, Ewing was convicted of felony grand theft for stealing nearly $1,200 worth of merchandise after previously having been convicted of at least two "violent" or "serious" felonies. Even standing alone, Ewing's theft should not be taken lightly. His crime was certainly not "one of the most passive felonies a person could commit." To the contrary, the Supreme Court of California has noted the "seriousness" of grand theft in the context of proportionality review. That grand theft is a "wobbler" under California law is of no moment. Though California courts have discretion to reduce a felony grand theft charge to a misdemeanor, it remains a felony for all purposes "unless and until the trial court imposes a misdemeanor sentence." . . .

Ewing's sentence is justified by the State's public-safety interest in incapacitating and deterring recidivist felons, and amply supported by his own long, serious criminal record. Ewing has been convicted of numerous misdemeanor and felony offenses, served nine separate terms of incarceration, and committed most of his crimes while on probation or parole. His prior "strikes" were serious felonies including robbery and three residential burglaries. To be sure, Ewing's sentence is a long one. But it reflects a rational legislative judgment, entitled to deference, that offenders who have committed serious or violent felonies and who continue to commit felonies must be incapacitated. . . .

We hold that Ewing's sentence of 25 years to life in prison, imposed for the offense of felony grand theft under the three strikes law, is not grossly disproportionate and therefore does not violate the Eighth Amendment's prohibition on cruel and unusual punishments. The judgment of the California Court of Appeal is affirmed.

☐ *Justice SCALIA, concurring in the judgment.*

In my concurring opinion in *Harmelin v. Michigan,* I concluded that the Eighth Amendment's prohibition of "cruel and unusual punishments" was aimed at excluding only certain modes of punishment, and was not a "guarantee against disproportionate sentences." Out of respect for the principle of *stare decisis,* I might nonetheless accept the contrary holding of *Solem v. Helm* —that the Eighth Amendment contains a narrow proportionality principle— if I felt I could intelligently apply it. This case demonstrates why I cannot.

Proportionality—the notion that the punishment should fit the crime —is inherently a concept tied to the penological goal of retribution. "It becomes difficult even to speak intelligently of 'proportionality,' once deterrence and rehabilitation are given significant weight," *Harmelin*—not to mention giving weight to the purpose of California's three strikes law: incapacitation. In the present case, the game is up once the plurality has acknowledged that "the Constitution does not mandate adoption of any one penological theory," and that a "sentence can have a variety of justifications, such as incapacitation, deterrence, retribution, or rehabilitation." That acknowledgment having been made, it no longer suffices merely to assess "the gravity of the offense compared to the harshness of the penalty;" that classic description of the proportionality principle (alone and in itself quite resistant to policy-free, legal analysis) now becomes merely the "first" step of the inquiry. Having completed that step (by a discussion which, in all fairness, does not convincingly establish that 25-years-to-life is a "proportionate" punishment for stealing three golf clubs), the plurality must then add an analysis to show that "Ewing's sentence is justified by the State's public-safety interest in incapacitating and deterring recidivist felons."

Which indeed it is—though why that has anything to do with the principle of proportionality is a mystery. Perhaps the plurality should revise its terminology, so that what it reads into the Eighth Amendment is not the unstated proposition that all punishment should be reasonably proportionate to the gravity of the offense, but rather the unstated proposition that all punishment should reasonably pursue the multiple purposes of the criminal law. That formulation would make it clearer than ever, of course, that the plurality is not applying law but evaluating policy.

Because I agree that petitioner's sentence does not violate the Eighth Amendment's prohibition against cruel and unusual punishments, I concur in the judgment.

☐ *Justice THOMAS, concurring in the judgment.*

I agree with Justice SCALIA's view that the proportionality test announced in *Solem v. Helm* is incapable of judicial application. Even were *Solem's* test perfectly clear, however, I would not feel compelled by *stare decisis* to apply it. In my view, the Cruel and Unusual Punishments Clause of the Eighth Amendment contains no proportionality principle. See *Harmelin v. Michigan* (opinion of SCALIA, J.). . . .

☐ *Justice STEVENS, with whom Justice SOUTER, Justice GINSBURG and Justice BREYER join, dissenting.*

The concurrences prompt this separate writing to emphasize that proportionality review is not only capable of judicial application but also required by the Eighth Amendment.

"The Eighth Amendment succinctly prohibits 'excessive' sanctions." *Atkins v. Virginia*, 536 U.S. 304 (2002). It "would be anomalous indeed" to suggest that the Eighth Amendment makes proportionality review applicable in the context of bail and fines but not in the context of other forms of punishment, such as imprisonment. *Solem v. Helm.* Rather, by broadly prohibiting excessive sanctions, the Eighth Amendment directs judges to exercise their wise judgment in assessing the proportionality of all forms of punishment.

The absence of a black-letter rule does not disable judges from exercising their discretion in construing the outer limits on sentencing authority that the Eighth Amendment imposes. After all, judges are "constantly called upon to draw . . . lines in a variety of contexts," and to exercise their judgment to give meaning to the Constitution's broadly phrased protections. For example, the Due Process Clause directs judges to employ proportionality review in assessing the constitutionality of punitive damages awards on a case-by-case basis. See, e.g., *BMW of North America, Inc. v. Gore*, 517 U.S. 559 (1996). . . . Throughout most of the Nation's history—before guideline sentencing became so prevalent—federal and state trial judges imposed specific sentences pursuant to grants of authority that gave them uncabined discretion within broad ranges. Likewise, I think it clear that the Eighth Amendment's prohibition of "cruel and unusual punishments" expresses a broad and basic proportionality principle that takes into account all of the justifications for penal sanctions. It is this broad proportionality principle that would preclude reliance on any of the justifications for punishment to support, for example, a life sentence for overtime parking. Accordingly, I respectfully dissent.

☐ *Justice BREYER, with whom Justice STEVENS, Justice SOUTER, and Justice GINSBURG join, dissenting.*

The constitutional question is whether the "three strikes" sentence imposed by California upon repeat-offender Gary Ewing is "grossly disproportionate" to his crime. The sentence amounts to a real prison term of at least 25 years. The sentence-triggering criminal conduct consists of the theft of three golf clubs priced at a total of $1,197. The offender has a criminal history that includes four felony convictions arising out of three separate burglaries (one armed). In *Solem v. Helm*, the Court found grossly disproportionate a somewhat longer sentence imposed on a recidivist offender for triggering criminal conduct that was somewhat less severe. In my view, the differences are not determinative, and the Court should reach the same ultimate conclusion here. . . .

Justice SCALIA and Justice THOMAS argue that we should not review for gross disproportionality a sentence to a term of years. Otherwise, we make it too difficult for legislators and sentencing judges to determine just when their sentencing laws and practices pass constitutional muster. I concede that a bright-line rule would give legislators and sentencing judges more guidance. But application of the Eighth Amendment to a sentence of a term of years requires a case-by-case approach. And, in my view, like that of the plurality, meaningful enforcement of the Eighth Amendment demands that application—even if only at sentencing's outer bounds.

A case-by-case approach can nonetheless offer guidance through example. Ewing's sentence is, at a minimum, 2 to 3 times the length of sentences that other jurisdictions would impose in similar circumstances. That sentence itself is sufficiently long to require a typical offender to spend virtually all the remainder of his active life in prison. . . .

In sum, even if I accept for present purposes the plurality's analytical framework, Ewing's sentence (life imprisonment with a minimum term of 25 years) is grossly disproportionate to the triggering offense conduct—stealing three golf clubs—Ewing's recidivism notwithstanding. For these reasons, I dissent.

B | *Capital Punishment*

Social forces and litigation aimed at persuading the Court to declare capital punishment unconstitutional under the Eighth Amendment and the Fourteenth Amendment's equal protection clause finally reached the justices in the early 1970s. There had been a steady decline in the number of executions since the 1930s, when more than 165 convicts were annually put to death. Between 1960 and 1967, there were fewer than fifty-two executions per year, and after 1967, when most states adopted a moratorium on carrying out death sentences, there were no executions until 1977, when Gary Gilmore was executed by shooting. The moratorium and growing controversy over capital punishment were largely due to the pressures of the NAACP Legal Defense Fund, the American Civil Liberties Union (ACLU), and the American Bar Association (ABA). These groups pointed out the fact that black convicts disproportionately received death sentences, especially when convicted for rape. Variations among state laws and the absence of standards for imposing capital punishment raised the issue of whether executions violated the Fourteenth Amendment equal protection clause as well as whether they constituted cruel and unusual punishment under the Eighth Amendment. These concerns have been underscored with a number of states instituting moratoriums on executions because in recent years more death row inmates were released from prison (often because new DNA evidence proved their innocence) than were executed. Opposition to the death penalty is also growing among a wide range of organizations, including the American Bar Association and the Conference of Catholic Bishops, and Christian Coalition head Pat Robertson.

The controversy over capital punishment proved divisive for the Court. Initially, in *McGautha v. California* and *Crampton v. Ohio*, 502 U.S. 183 (1971), the justices split six to three when holding that states need not specify in their statutes the factors that juries must consider when imposing death sentences. The Court also indicated that bifurcated trials—that is, a two-stage trial in which juries first determine a defendant's guilt and second decide on a sentence—are preferable to single trials in which juries simultaneously convict and sentence, but held that bifurcated trials are not constitutionally required. In Justice John Harlan's words: "To identify before the fact those characteristics of criminal homicides and their perpetrators which call for the death penalty, and to express those characteristics in language which can be fairly understood and applied by the sentencing authority, appear to be tasks which are beyond present human ability."

Despite the rulings in *McGautha* and *Crampton* just the year before, the imposition of capital punishment in one murder and two rape cases was held to violate the Eighth and Fourteenth Amendments in *Furman v. Georgia* (1972) (excerpted below) and two companion cases. The justices were sharply divided, however. The opinion announcing the Court's decision was a brief *per curiam* opinion followed by 231 pages of separate opinions filed by all nine justices, five concurring and four dissenting. Notice in the excerpts reprinted here that even those justices in the majority could not agree on the basis for the Court's ruling. Justices Douglas, Stewart, and White take an analytical approach, interpreting the Eighth Amendment in light of the commands of the Fourteenth Amendment's due process and equal protection clauses. Only Justices Brennan and Marshall address the normative question in maintaining that capital punishment is unconstitutional due to its severity, finality, excessiveness, and denial of human dignity. By contrast, the four dissenters question the role of the Court in overturning capital punishment laws and contend that it should defer to the states on the matter. Rehnquist's dissenting opinion, though, also takes up the normative question and justifies capital punishment on a theory of society's retribution.

Furman immediately escalated the controversy over capital punishment. Thirty-five states enacted new legislation specifying the factors that juries must consider when issuing death sentences. Georgia, Florida, Texas, and twenty-two other states adopted laws requiring juries to consider specific *aggravating factors* (justifying the imposition of capital punishment) and *mitigating factors* (justifying the imposition of an alternative sentence to the death penalty). Louisiana, North Carolina, Oklahoma, and seven other states mandated capital punishment for particular crimes.

By 1976 there were over 600 people on death row under the post-*Furman* laws, and the Court faced numerous challenges to their constitutionality. In a batch of rulings handed down in 1976, the Court squarely ruled that capital punishment is not unconstitutional. In the leading case, *Gregg v. Georgia*, 428 U.S. 153 (1976), with only Brennan and Marshall dissenting, the Court upheld Georgia's statute specifying the aggravating and mitigating circumstances for imposing the death penalty and providing for bifurcated trials.

Woodson v. North Carolina, 428 U.S. 280 (1976), and *Roberts v. Louisiana*, 428 U.S. 325 (1976), however, on a five-to-four vote struck down laws requiring mandatory death sentences for certain crimes. There, a plurality of justices (Stewart, Powell, and Stevens) were joined by Brennan and Marshall (who continued to maintain their position that capital punishment is unconstitutional per se). Stewart's plurality opinion struck down mandatory death sentences for four reasons: (1) there was evidence that juries often fail to convict under mandatory death sentence statutes; (2) these laws provide no standards for guiding juries in their sentencing and fail to allow them to show mercy; (3) the laws also fail to provide for the "particularized consideration" of the accused and the circumstances of the crime, and, (4) because capital punishment is different from every other form of punishment (in its finality), its imposition requires individualized sentencing.

The Court's insistence on individualized sentencing was further underscored in *Lockett v. Ohio* (1978) (see excerpt below), holding that states may not limit the kinds of mitigating factors that juries may consider when deciding whether to impose the death penalty.

While the Court continued to confront numerous procedural challenges to the execution of death sentences, the 1976 rulings made clear that there was not a majority on the Court for striking down capital punishment per se. In what was widely regarded as the last major broadside attack on the wholesale imposition of the death penalty in *McCleskey v. Kemp* (1987) (excerpted below), the justices split five to four in holding that statistics showing that blacks who murder whites receive the death penalty more often than whites who kill blacks did not prove racial bias in the imposition of capital punishment.

Along with numerous other recent rulings on capital punishment (see THE DEVELOPMENT OF LAW: Post-*Furman* Rulings on Capital Punishment), the Rehnquist Court held in *Morgan v. Illinois*, 504 U.S. 719 (1992) (excerpted below) that under the Fourteenth Amendment's guarantee of due process, defendants' attorneys must be permitted to ask potential jurors whether, on the defendant's conviction, they would automatically vote to impose the death penalty.

One particularly controversial practice in the imposition of capital punishment was prosecutorial use during sentencing of so-called victim-impact statements (describing the victim and the impact of his or her murder on relatives). By a five-to-four vote, *Booth v. Maryland*, 482 U.S. 66 (1987), disapproved of the use of victim-impact statements. Justice Powell, the author of the Court's opinion, cast the deciding vote. When he retired at the end of the 1986 term, there was speculation that his replacement, Justice Anthony Kennedy, would tip the balance on the Court toward reconsidering and upholding victim-impact statements. Yet, Justice White, who dissented in *Booth*, switched sides in *South Carolina v. Gathers*, 490 U.S. 805 (1989), joining a bare majority for again disallowing the use of victim-impact statements. But, following Justice Brennan's retirement in 1990, the balance on the high bench shifted further. And in *Payne v. Tennessee*, 501 U.S. 808 (1991) (excerpted below), the Rehnquist Court overturned both *Booth* and *Gathers* in deciding to permit the use of victim-impact statements at the sentencing stage of capital trials.

Two other recurrent issues were the execution of minors and mentally retarded persons. A bare majority vacated the death sentence of a sixteen-year-old in *Eddings v. Oklahoma*, 455 U.S. 104 (1982). Then, six to three in *Thompson v. Oklahoma*, 487 U.S. 815 (1988), the Court held that the Eighth Amendment forbids the execution of convicted murderers who are fifteen years old or younger at the time of their crimes. But with Justice O'Connor casting the deciding vote in *Stanford v. Kentucky*, 492 U.S. 361 (1989), the Rehnquist Court held that the death penalty may be imposed on those who are sixteen or older. The execution of mentally impaired convicts was first confronted in *Ford v. Wainwright*, 477 U.S. 399 (1986). There, the Eighth Amendment was held to bar the execution of convicts who are (or have gone while on death row) insane. However, in another five-to-four ruling in *Penry v. Lynaugh*, 492 U.S. 302 (1989), the execution of convicted murderers who are mildly or moderately retarded was upheld. But the Court reversed that decision in *Atkins v. Virginia* (2002) (excerpted below).

In sum, the Rehnquist Court has pressed in the direction of reduc-

- CONSTITUTIONAL HISTORY

The Imposition and Execution of Capital Punishment

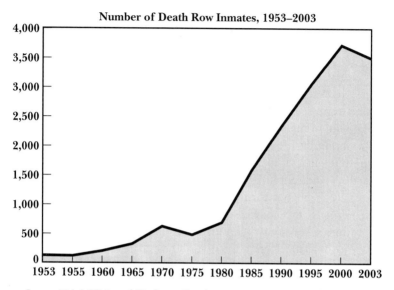

Number of Death Row Inmates, 1953–2003

Source: NAACP Legal Defense Fund

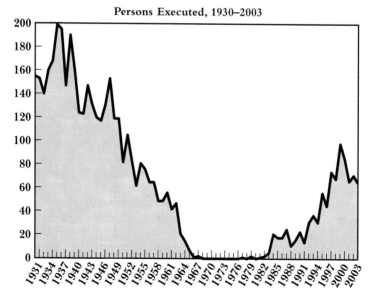

Persons Executed, 1930–2003

Source: Death Penalty Information Center; data through 2003 ing the number of opportunities for appealing death sentences and toward removing procedural obstacles to executions. Long lamenting and criticizing procedural barriers to the imposition of capital punishment and conducting executions, Chief Justice Rehnquist, as the Court's composition changed, came to command a fairly solid majority for expediting the executions of death-row inmates. In a major ruling affecting death-penalty appeals, for instance, the Court sharply curtailed opportunities for death-row inmates and other state prisoners to file multiple challenges to the constitutionality of their sentences. Over the strong objections of three dissenters in *McCleskey v. Zant*, 499 U.S. 467 (1991), the Court handed down a new standard for lower federal courts under which a prisoner's second or subsequent *habeas corpus* petition must be dismissed except only in exceptional circumstances.

The importance of *McCleskey v. Zant* lies in the fact that death-row inmates typically file several successive writ of *habeas corpus* petitions, raising different constitutional claims, in their efforts to overturn their convictions and sentences. Approximately 40 percent of all death sentences have been overturned by lower courts upon finding constitutional errors in the conviction and sentencing of death-row inmates. By limiting lower courts' consideration of successive petitions in *McCleskey v. Zant*, the Rehnquist Court thus enabled states to carry out death sentences more quickly; under federal law, though, there is no limit on the number of *habeas corpus* petitions that may be filed by inmates in federal prisons.

Writing for the majority in *McCleskey v. Zant*, Justice Kennedy redefined the "abuse of the writ" doctrine so as to make it easier for state prosecutors to contest as an "abuse of the writ" all *habeas corpus* petitions filed after a prisoner's initial one. Under the Court's new definition of "abuse of the writ," second and subsequent petitions raising new constitutional claims may be dismissed as abusive unless inmates show (1) that there was "cause" for not raising the claim earlier and (2) that the inmate suffered "actual prejudice" from the constitutional error that he claimed occurred in his trial, conviction, and sentencing. Under the Court's previous approach, dating from the mid-1960s, second and subsequent petitions were considered abusive only if they contained arguments that an attorney, for strategic or other reasons, deliberately refrained from making earlier, or that were previously omitted due to an attorney's "inexcusable neglect." By contrast, Justice Kennedy held that the failure of an inmate's lawyer to raise a constitutional claim, whether mistakenly or not, would not constitute "cause" for saving the petition from automatic dismissal unless the attorney's representation was so deficient as to amount to "constitutionally ineffective assistance of counsel," a very difficult standard to meet (as set forth in *Strickland v. Washington*, 466 U.S.

■ IN COMPARATIVE PERSPECTIVE
Capital Punishment around the World

Countries and Territories That Have Abolished the Death Penalty for All Crimes (N = 79)

Andorra	Dominican	Malta	San Marino
Angola	Republic	Marshall Islands	São-Tomé and Príncipe
Australia	Ecuador	Mauritius	Seychelles
Austria	Estonia	Micronesia	Slovak Republic
Azerbaijan	Finland	Moldova	Slovenia
Belgium	France	Monaco	Solomon Islands
Bosnia-Herzegovina	Georgia	Mozambique	South Africa
Bhutan	Germany	Namibia	Spain
Bulgaria	Guinea-Bissau	Nepal	Sweden
Cambodia	Haiti	Netherlands	Switzerland
Canada	Honduras	New Zealand	Timor-Leste
Cape Verde	Hungary	Nicaragua	Turkmenistan
Colombia	Iceland	Norway	Tuvalu
Costa Rica	Ireland	Palau	Ukraine
Côte d'Ivoire	Italy	Panama	United Kingdom
Croatia	Kiribati	Paraguay	Uruguay
Cyprus	Lichtenstein	Poland	Vanuatu
Czech Republic	Lithuania	Portugal	Vatican City State
Denmark	Luxembourg	Romania	Venezuela
Djibouti	Macedonia	Samoa	Yugoslavia

Countries and Territories That Have Abolished the Death Penalty for Ordinary Crimes (N = 15)

Albania	Brazil	Fiji	Mexico
Argentina	Chile	Greece	Peru
Armenia	Cook Island	Israel	Turkey
Bolivia	El Salvador	Latvia	

Countries and Territories That Have *De Facto* Abolished the Death Penalty (N = 23)

Algeria	Gambia	Mauritania	Sri Lanka
Benin	Grenada	Nauru	Suriname
Brunei	Kenya	Niger	Togo
Burkina Faso	Madagascar	Papua New Guinea	Tonga
Central African Republic	Maldives	Russian Federation	Tunisia
Congo	Mali	Senegal	

CRUEL AND UNUSUAL PUNISHMENT

Countries and Territories That Retain the Death Penalty (N = 78)				
Afghanistan	Congo	Japan	Pakistan	Taiwan
Antigua and	Cuba	Jordan	Palestinian	Tajikistan
Barbuda	Dominica	Kazakhstan	Authority	Tanzania
Bahamas	Egypt	Kuwait	Philippines	Thailand
Bahrain	Ethiopia	Kyrgyzstan	Qatar	Trinidad and
Bangladesh	Eritrea	Laos	Rwanda	Tobago
Barbados	Equatorial	Lebanon	Saint Kitts and	Uganda
Belarus	Guinea	Lesotho	Nevis	United Arab
Belize	Gabon	Liberia	Saint Lucia	Emirates
Botswana	Ghana	Libyan Arab	Saint Vincent	United States
Bulgaria	Guatemala	Jamahiriya	Saudi Arabia	of America
Burma	Guinea	Malawi	Sierra Leone	Uzbekistan
(Myanmar)	Guyana	Malaysia	Singapore	Vietnam
Burundi	India	Mongolia	Somalia	Yemen
Cameroon	Indonesia	Morocco	South Korea	Yugoslavia
Chad	Iran	Nigeria	Sudan	Zambia
China	Iraq	North Korea	Swaziland	Zimbabwe
Comoros	Jamaica	Oman	Syria	

Source: Amnesty International, "The Death Penalty: List of Abolitionist and Retentionist Countries," April 30, 2004, available at http://www.amnesty.org/pages/death penalty-countries-eng.

■ INSIDE THE COURT

Justice Arthur Goldberg's Role in the Controversy over Capital Punishment and Opinion in Rudolph v. Alabama

At the end of his first term on the Court (1962–1963), Justice Arthur Goldberg circulated to the other members of the Warren Court an unpublished twenty-page "Memorandum to the Conference from Mr. Justice Goldberg." In it he pointed out that a number of cases on the Court's docket involved capital punishment, but not one challenged its constitutionality per se. The "petitioners' failure to urge [the unconstitutionality of the death penalty] should not preclude this Court from considering this matter," observed Goldberg at the outset, pointing out that

[t]his Court has never explicitly considered whether, and under what circumstances, the Eighth and Fourteenth Amendments to the United States Constitution proscribe the imposition of the death penalty. The Court has, of course, implicitly decided (in every case affirming a capital conviction) that the death penalty is constitutional. But in light of the worldwide trend toward abolition, I think this Court should now request argument and explicitly consider this constantly recurring issue.

Citing various studies on the imposition of capital punishment in the states and in other countries, Goldberg tried to persuade his brethren to adopt his position on capital punishment: "I am convinced that whatever may be said of times past, 'the evolving standards of decency that mark the progress of [our] maturing society' now condemn as barbaric and inhuman the deliberate institutionalized taking of human life by the state." But, except for Justice Brennan, no other member of the Warren Court yet wanted to confront the issue of capital punishment, nor strike it down as unconstitutional.

Failing to persuade other justices to reach out and tackle the constitutionality of capital punishment, Goldberg filed the following dissent from the denial of *certiorari* in *Rudolph v. Alabama*, 375 U.S. 889 (1963), a case appealing a death sentence imposed on a convicted rapist. This opinion is generally credited with sending a signal to lawyers around the country to challenge the constitutionality of capital punishment in their appeals and thereby force the Court's hand. Goldberg left the Court in 1965, but his position became championed by Justice Brennan in Furman v. Georgia (1972) (excerpted below) and in his subsequent opinions on capital punishment.

SUPREME COURT OF THE UNITED STATES

No. 308, Misc.—October Term, 1963.

Frank Lee Rudolph, Petitioner. *v.* State of Alabama.	On Petition for Writ of Certiorari and Affidavit In Forma Pauperis to the Supreme Court of Alabama.

[October 21, 1963.]

Mr. Justice Goldberg, with whom Mr. Justice Douglas and Mr. Justice Brennan join, dissenting.

I would grant certiorari in this case and in *Snider* v. *Cunningham*, 169, Misc., to consider whether the Eighth and Fourteenth Amendments to the United States Constitution permit the imposition of the death penalty on

RUDOLPH *v.* ALABAMA.

a convicted rapist who has neither taken nor endangered human life.

The following questions, *inter alia*, seem relevant and worthy of argument and consideration:

(1) In light of the trend both in this country and throughout the world against punishing rape by death,[1] does the imposition of the death penalty by those States which retain it for rape violate "evolving standards of decency that mark the progress of [our] maturing society." [2] or "standards of decency more or less universally accepted?" [3]

(2) Is the taking of human life to protect a value other than human life consistent with the constitutional proscription against "punishments which by their exces-

---

[1] The United Nations recently conducted a survey on the laws, regulations and practices relating to capital punishment throughout the world. In addition to the United States, 65 countries and territories responded. All but five—Nationalist China, Northern Rhodesia, Nyasaland, Republic of South Africa, and the United States—reported that their laws no longer permit the imposition of the death penalty for rape.

The following of the United States reported that their laws no longer permit the imposition of the death penalty for rape: Alaska, Arizona, California, Colorado, Connecticut, Delaware, Hawaii, Idaho, Illinois, Indiana, Iowa, Kansas, Maine, Massachusetts, Michigan, Minnesota, Montana, Nebraska, New Hampshire, New Jersey, New Mexico, New York, North Dakota, Ohio, Oregon, Pennsylvania, South Dakota, Tennessee, Utah, Vermont, Washington, Wisconsin and Wyoming. The laws of the remaining States permit the imposition of the death penalty for rape, but some States do not, in fact, impose it. United Nations, Capital Punishment (prepared by Mr. Marc Ancel, Justice of the French Supreme Court) (N. Y. 1962) 38, 71–75.

[2] *Trop* v. *Dulles*, 356 U. S. 86, 101 (opinion of WARREN, C. J., joined by Justices BLACK, DOUGLAS, and Whittaker).

[3] *Francis* v. *Resweber*, 329 U. S. 495, 469 (Frankfurter, J., concurring). See *Weems* v. *United States*, 217 U. S. 349, 373:

"Legislation, both statutory and constitutional, is enacted, it is true, from an experience of evils, but its general language should not, therefore, be necessarily confined to the form that evil had theretofore taken. Time works changes, brings into existence new conditions and purpose. Therefore, a principle to be vital must be capable of wider application than the mischief which gave it birth. This is peculiarly true of constitutions. They are not ephemeral enactments, designed to meeting passing occasions. They are, to use the words of Chief Justice Marshall, 'designed to approach immortality as nearly as human institutions can approach it.' The future is their care and provision for events of good and bad tendencies of which no prophecy can be made. In the application of a constitution, therefore, our contemplation cannot be only of what has been but of what may be. Under any other rule a constitution would indeed be as

RUDOLPH *v.* ALABAMA.

sive . . . severity are greatly disproportioned to the offenses charged?"[4]

(3) Can the permissible aims of punishment (*e. g.*, deterrence, isolation, rehabilitation)[5] be achieved as effectively by punishing rape less severely than by death (*e. g.*, by life imprisonment);[6] if so, does the imposition of the death penalty for rape constitute "unnecessary cruelty?"[7]

---

easy of application as it would be deficient in efficacy and power. Its general principles would have little value and be converted by precedent into impotent and lifeless formulas. Rights declared in words might be lost in reality."

Also see *Ex parte Wilson*, 114 U. S. 417, 427–428:

"What punishments may be considered as infamous may be affected by the changes of opinions from one age to another. In former times, being put in the stocks was not considered as necessarily infamous . . . . But at the present day [it] might be thought an infamous punishment."

[4] *Weems* v. *United States*, 217 U. S. 349, 371. Cf. *Lambert* v. *California*, 355 U. S. 225, 231 (dissenting opinion of Frankfurter, J.).

[5] See, *e. g.*, *Williams* v. *New York*, 337 U. S. 241; *Trop* v. *Dulles*, 356 U. S. 86, 111 (concurring opinion of BRENNAN, J.); *Blyew* v. *United States*, 13 Wall. 581, 600.

[6] The United Nations Report on Capital Punishment noted: "In Canada, rape ceased to be punishable with death in 1954: it is reported that there were 37 convictions for rape in 1950, 44 in 1953 and only 27 in 1954, the year of abolition; from 1957 to 1959 a steady decrease in convictions was noted (from 56 to 44), while in the same period the population of Canada increased by 27 per cent." United Nations, Capital Punishment, *supra*, note 1, at 54–55.

Such statistics must of course be regarded with caution. See, *e. g.*, Royall Commission Report on Capital Punishment (1953) 24; Hart, Murder and Its Punishment, 12 N. W. L. Rev. 433, 457 (1957); Allen, Review, 10 Stan. L. Rev. 595, 600 (1958). In Canada, for example, the death sentence was rarely imposed for rape even prior to its formal abolition in 1954. In 1961 there was a slight increase in the number of convictions for rape. See United Nations, Capital Punishment, *supra*, note 1, at 55.

[7] *Weems* v. *United States*, 217 U. S. 349, 370. See *Robinson* v. *California*, 370 U. S. 660, 677 (concurring opinion of DOUGLAS, J.).

(Collection of the Supreme Court of the United States)

668 (1984) and discussed in Chapter 9). Kennedy also added that there must be a "showing of some external impediment preventing counsel from construing or raising a claim" to excuse the failure to do so in an earlier petition. And he predicted that the newly reformulated "abuse of the writ" standard "should curtail the abusive petitions that in recent years have threatened to undermine the integrity of the *habeas corpus* process."

Dissenting in *McCleskey v. Zant*, Justice Marshall, joined by Justices Blackmun and Stevens, sharply criticized the majority for achieving what Chief Justice Rehnquist had unsuccessfully tried to persuade the Court in 1981 and Congress in 1990 to do. As the titular head of the federal judiciary, in 1989 Chief Justice Rehnquist appointed a committee, chaired by retired Justice Powell, that made recommendations to the Judicial Conference and Congress for limiting the number of *habeas corpus* petitions that an inmate may file. That effort, however, eventually resulted in the enactment of the Antiterrorism and Effective Death Penalty Act of 1996, which basically limits state death row inmates to one *habeas corpus* review in federal courts unless new claims are presented and which was upheld in *Felker v. Turpin,* 518 U.S. 651 (1996).

Furman v. Georgia,
Jackson v. Georgia,
and
Branch v. Texas
408 U.S. 238, 92 S.CT. 2726 (1972)

William Furman was convicted and sentenced to death for murder. Lucious Jackson was sentenced to death after being convicted for rape. And Elmer Branch was sentenced to death on his conviction for rape. After unsuccessful appeals in the Georgia and Texas supreme courts, their attorneys appealed to the Supreme Court, which granted review and consolidated the cases for decision. The Court struck down Georgia's and Texas's laws for imposing capital punishment. Excerpts from the concurring and dissenting opinions are reprinted here.

The Court's decision was five to four, and the majority's opinion *per curiam.* Justices Douglas, Brennan, Stewart, White, and Marshall concurred; Chief Justice Burger and Justices Blackmun, Powell, and Rehnquist dissented.

☐ *Justice DOUGLAS, concurring.*

That the requirements of due process ban cruel and unusual punishment is now settled. *Louisiana ex rel. Francis v. Resweber*, 329 U.S. 459 [(1947)] (BURTON, J., dissenting): *Robinson v. California*, 370 U.S. 660 [(1962)]. It is also settled that the proscription of cruel and unusual punishments forbids the judicial imposition of them as well as their imposition by the legislature. *Weems v. United States*, 217 U.S. 349 [(1910)].

It has been assumed in our decisions that punishment by death is not cruel, unless the manner of execution can be said to be inhuman and barbarous. *In re Kemmler*, 136 U.S. 436 [(1890)]. It is also said in our opinions that the proscription of cruel and unusual punishments "is not fastened to the obsolete, but may acquire meaning as public opinion becomes enlightened by a humane justice." *Weems v. United States,* supra. A like statement was made in *Trop v. Dulles*, 356 U.S. 86 [(1958)], that the Eighth Amendment "must draw its meaning from the evolving standards of decency that mark the progress of a maturing society." . . .

It would seem to be incontestable that the death penalty inflicted on one defendant is "unusual" if it discriminates against him by reason of his race, religion, wealth, social position, or class, or if it is imposed under a procedure that gives room for the play of such prejudices. . . .

The words "cruel and unusual" certainly include penalties that are barbaric. But the words, at least when read in light of the English proscription against selective and irregular use of penalties, suggest that it is "cruel and unusual" to apply the death penalty—or any other penalty—selectively to minorities whose numbers are few, who are outcasts of society, and who are unpopular, but whom society is willing to see suffer though it would not countenance general application of the same penalty across the board. . . .

In a Nation committed to equal protection of the laws there is no permissible "caste" aspect of law enforcement. Yet we know that the discretion of judges and juries in imposing the death penalty enables the penalty to be selectively applied, feeding prejudices against the accused if he is poor and despised, and lacking political clout, or if he is a member of a suspect or unpopular minority, and saving those who by social position may be in a more protected position. In ancient Hindu law a Brahman was exempt from capital punishment, and under that law, "[g]enerally, in the law books, punishment increased in severity as social status diminished." We have, I fear, taken in practice the same position, partially as a result of making the death penalty discretionary and partially as a result of the ability of the rich to purchase the services of the most respected and most resourceful legal talent in the Nation.

The high service rendered by the "cruel and unusual" punishment clause of the Eighth Amendment is to require legislatures to write penal laws that are evenhanded, nonselective, and nonarbitrary, and to require judges to see to it that general laws are not applied sparsely, selectively, and spottily to unpopular groups. . . .

Any law which is nondiscriminatory on its face may be applied in such a way as to violate the Equal Protection Clause of the Fourteenth Amendment. *Yick Wo v. Hopkins*, 118 U.S. 356 [(1886)]. Such conceivably might be the fate of a mandatory death penalty, where equal or lesser sentences were imposed on the elite, a harsher one on the minorities or members of the lower castes. Whether a mandatory death penalty would otherwise be constitutional is a question I do not reach.

I concur in the judgments of the Court.

☐ *Justice BRENNAN, concurring.*

Ours would indeed be a simple task were we required merely to measure a challenged punishment against those that history has long condemned. That narrow and unwarranted view of the Clause, however, was left behind with the 19th century. Our task today is more complex. We know "that the words of the [Clause] are not precise, and that their scope is not static." We know, therefore, that the Clause "must draw its meaning from the evolving standards of decency that mark the progress of a maturing society." That knowledge, of course, is but the beginning of the inquiry.

In *Trop v. Dulles*, it was said that "[t]he question is whether [a] penalty subjects the individual to a fate forbidden by the principle of civilized treatment guaranteed by the [Clause]." It was also said that a challenged punishment must be examined "in light of the basic prohibition against inhuman treatment" embodied in the Clause. It was said, finally, that:

> "The basic concept underlying the [Clause] is nothing less than the dignity of man. While the State has the power to punish, the [Clause] stands to assure that this power be exercised within the limits of civilized standards."

At bottom, then, the Cruel and Unusual Punishments Clause prohibits the infliction of uncivilized and inhuman punishments. The State, even as it punishes, must treat its members with respect for their intrinsic worth as human beings. A punishment is "cruel and unusual," therefore, if it does not comport with human dignity.

This formulation, of course, does not of itself yield principles for assessing the constitutional validity of particular punishments. Nevertheless, even though "[t]his Court has had little occasion to give precise content to the [Clause]," there are principles recognized in our cases and inherent in the Clause sufficient to permit a judicial determination whether a challenged punishment comports with human dignity.

The primary principle is that a punishment must not be so severe as to be degrading to the dignity of human beings. Pain, certainly, may be a factor in the judgment. The infliction of an extremely severe punishment will often entail physical suffering. See *Weems v. United States.* Yet the Framers also knew "that there could be exercises of cruelty by laws other than those which inflicted bodily pain or mutilation." Even though "[t]here may be involved no physical mistreatment, no primitive torture," *Trop v. Dulles*, supra, severe mental pain may be inherent in the infliction of a particular punishment. See *Weems v. United States, supra,* . . . That, indeed, was one of the conclusions underlying the holding of the plurality in *Trop v. Dulles* that the punishment of expatriation violates the Clause. And the physical and mental suffering inherent in the punishment of *cadena temporal*, was an obvious basis for the Court's decision in *Weems v. United States* that the punishment was "cruel and unusual."

More than the presence of pain, however, is comprehended in the judgment that the extreme severity of a punishment makes it degrading to the dignity of human beings. The barbaric punishments condemned by history, "punishments which inflict torture, such as the rack, the thumb-screw, the iron boot, the stretching of limbs, and the like," are, of course, "attended with acute pain and suffering." *O'Neil v. Vermont*, 144 U.S. 323 (1892) (FIELD, J., dissenting). When we consider why they have been condemned, however, we realize that the pain involved is not the only reason. The true significance of these punishments is that they treat members of the human race as nonhumans, as objects to be toyed with and discarded. They are thus inconsistent with the fundamental premise of the Clause that even the vilest criminal remains a human being possessed of common human dignity. . . .

In determining whether a punishment comports with human dignity, we are aided also by a second principle inherent in the Clause—that the State must not arbitrarily inflict a severe punishment. This principle derives from the notion that the State does not respect human dignity when, without reason, it inflicts upon some people a severe punishment that it does not inflict upon others. Indeed, the very words "cruel and unusual punishments" imply condemnation of the arbitrary infliction of severe punishments. And, as we now know, the English history of the Clause reveals a particular concern with the establishment of a safeguard against arbitrary punishments. . . .

A third principle inherent in the Clause is that a severe punishment must not be unacceptable to contemporary society. Rejection by society, of course, is a strong indication that a severe punishment does not comport with human dignity. In applying this principle, however, we must make certain that the judicial determination is as objective as possible. Thus, for example, *Weems v. United States*, and *Trop v. Dulles*, suggest that one factor that may be considered is the existence of the punishment in jurisdictions other than those before the Court. *Wilkerson v. Utah, supra*, suggests that another factor to be considered is the historic usage of the punishment. *Trop v. Dulles, supra*, combined present acceptance with past usage by observing that "the death penalty has been employed throughout our history, and, in a day when it is still widely accepted, it cannot be said to violate the constitutional concept of cruelty." In *Robinson v. California*, [370 U.S. 660 (1962)], which involved the infliction of punishment for narcotics addiction, the Court went a step further, concluding simply that "in the light of contemporary human knowledge, a law which made a criminal offense of such a disease would doubtless be universally thought to be an infliction of cruel and unusual punishment." . . .

The final principle inherent in the Clause is that a severe punishment must not be excessive. A punishment is excessive under this principle if it is unnecessary: The infliction of a severe punishment by the State cannot comport with human dignity when it is nothing more than the pointless infliction of suffering. If there is a significantly less severe punishment adequate to achieve the purposes for which the punishment is inflicted, cf. *Robinson v. California, supra*, (DOUGLAS, J., concurring); *Trop v. Dulles, supra*, (BRENNAN, J., concurring), the punishment inflicted is unnecessary and therefore excessive. . . .

Thus, although "the death penalty has been employed throughout our history," *Trop v. Dulles* . . . in fact the history of this punishment is one of successive restriction. What was once a common punishment has become, in the context of a continuing moral debate, increasingly rare. The evolution of this punishment evidences, not that it is an inevitable part of the American scene, but that it has proved progressively more troublesome to the national conscience. The result of this movement is our current system of administering the punishment, under which death sentences are rarely imposed and death is even more rarely inflicted. It is, of course, "We, the People" who are responsible for the rarity both of the imposition and the carrying out of this punishment. Juries, "express[ing] the conscience of the community on the ultimate question of life or death," *Witherspoon v. Illinois*, [391 U.S. 510 (1968)], have been able to bring themselves to vote for death in a mere 100 or so cases among the thousands tried each year where the punishment is available. Governors, elected by and acting for us, have regularly commuted a substantial number of those sentences. And it is our society that insists upon due process of law to the end that no person will be unjustly put to death, thus ensuring that many more of those sentences will not be carried out. In sum, we have made death a rare punishment today.

The progressive decline in, and the current rarity of, the infliction of death demonstrate that our society seriously questions the appropriateness of this punishment today. The States point out that many legislatures authorize death as the punishment for certain crimes and that substantial segments of the public, as reflected in opinion polls and referendum votes, continue to support it. Yet the availability of this punishment through statutory authorization, as well as the polls and referenda, which amount simply to approval of that authorization, simply underscores the extent to which our society has in fact rejected this punishment. When an unusually severe punishment is authorized for wide-scale application but not, because of society's refusal, inflicted save in a few instances, the inference is compelling that there is a deep-seated reluctance to inflict it. Indeed, the likelihood is great that the punishment is tolerated only because of its disuse. The objective indicator of society's view of an unusually severe punishment is what society does with it, and today society will inflict death upon only a small sample of the eligible criminals. Rejection could hardly be more complete without becoming absolute. At the very least, I must conclude that contemporary society views this punishment with substantial doubt. . . .

In sum, the punishment of death is inconsistent with all four principles: Death is an unusually severe and degrading punishment; there is a strong probability that it is inflicted arbitrarily; its rejection by contemporary society is virtually total; and there is no reason to believe that it serves any penal purpose more effectively than the less severe punishment of imprisonment. The function of these principles is to enable a court to determine whether a punishment comports with human dignity. Death, quite simply, does not.

☐ *Justice STEWART, concurring.*

The penalty of death differs from all other forms of criminal punishment, not in degree but in kind. It is unique in its total irrevocability. It is unique in its rejection of rehabilitation of the convict as a basic purpose of criminal justice. And it is unique, finally, in its absolute renunciation of all that is embodied in our concept of humanity.

For these and other reasons, at least two of my Brothers have concluded that the infliction of the death penalty is constitutionally impermissible in all circumstances under the Eighth and Fourteenth Amendments. Their case is a strong one. But I find it unnecessary to reach the ultimate question they would decide. See *Ashwander v. Tennessee Valley Authority*, 297 U.S. 288 [(1936)] (BRANDEIS, J., concurring). . . .

Legislatures—state and federal—have sometimes specified that the penalty of death shall be the mandatory punishment for every person convicted of engaging in certain designated criminal conduct. . . .

These death sentences are cruel and unusual in the same way that being struck by lightning is cruel and unusual. For, of all the people convicted of rapes and murders in 1967 and 1968, many just as reprehensible as these, the petitioners are among a capriciously selected random handful upon whom the sentence of death has in fact been imposed. My concurring Brothers have demonstrated that, if any basis can be discerned for the selection of these few to be sentenced to die, it is the constitutionally impermissible basis of race. See *McLaughlin v. Florida*, 379 U.S. 184 [(1964)]. But racial discrimination has not been proved, and I put it to one side. I simply conclude that the Eighth and Fourteenth Amendments cannot tolerate the infliction of a sentence of death under legal systems that permit this unique penalty to be so wantonly and so freakishly imposed.

□ *Justice WHITE, concurring.*

In joining the Court's judgments . . . I do not at all intimate that the death penalty is unconstitutional *per se* or that there is no system of capital punishment that would comport with the Eighth Amendment. That question, ably argued by several of my Brethren, is not presented by these cases and need not be decided. . . .

I add only that past and present legislative judgment with respect to the death penalty loses much of its force when viewed in light of the recurring practice of delegating sentencing authority to the jury and the fact that a jury, in its own discretion and without violating its trust or any statutory policy, may refuse to impose the death penalty no matter what the circumstances of the crime. Legislative "policy" is thus necessarily defined not by what is legislatively authorized but by what juries and judges do in exercising the discretion so regularly conferred upon them. In my judgment what was done in these cases violated the Eighth Amendment.

I concur in the judgments of the Court.

□ *Justice MARSHALL, concurring.*

In order to assess whether or not death is an excessive or unnecessary penalty, it is necessary to consider the reasons why a legislature might select it as punishment for one or more offenses, and examine whether less severe penalties would satisfy the legitimate legislative wants as well as capital punishment. If they would, then the death penalty is unnecessary cruelty, and, therefore, unconstitutional.

There are six purposes conceivably served by capital punishment: retribution, deterrence, prevention of repetitive criminal acts, encouragement of guilty pleas and confessions, eugenics, and economy. . . .

[After examining and rejecting each rationale for capital punishment,

Justice MARSHALL concluded:] [E]ven if capital punishment is not excessive, it nonetheless violates the Eighth Amendment because it is morally unacceptable to the people of the United States at this time in their history.

In judging whether or not a given penalty is morally acceptable, most courts have said that the punishment is valid unless "it shocks the conscience and sense of justice of the people."

Judge Frank once noted the problems inherent in the use of such a measuring stick:

> "[The court,] before it reduces a sentence as 'cruel and unusual,' must have reasonably good assurances that the sentence offends the 'common conscience.' And, in any context, such a standard—the community's attitude—is usually an unknowable. It resembles a slithery shadow, since one can seldom learn, at all accurately, what the community, or a majority, actually feels. Even a carefully-taken 'public opinion poll' would be inconclusive in a case like this."

While a public opinion poll obviously is of some assistance in indicating public acceptance or rejection of a specific penalty, its utility cannot be very great. This is because whether or not a punishment is cruel and unusual depends, not on whether its mere mention "shocks the conscience and sense of justice of the people," but on whether people who were fully informed as to the purposes of the penalty and its liabilities would find the penalty shocking, unjust, and unacceptable.

In other words, the question with which we must deal is not whether a substantial proportion of American citizens would today, if polled, opine that capital punishment is barbarously cruel, but whether they would find it to be so in the light of all information presently available.

This is not to suggest that with respect to this test of unconstitutionality people are required to act rationally; they are not. With respect to this judgment, a violation of the Eighth Amendment is totally dependent on the predictable subjective, emotional reactions of informed citizens.

It has often been noted that American citizens know almost nothing about capital punishment. Some of the conclusions arrived at in the preceding section and the supporting evidence would be critical to an informed judgment on the morality of the death penalty: *e.g.*, that the death penalty is no more effective a deterrent than life imprisonment, that convicted murderers are rarely executed, but are usually sentenced to a term in prison; that convicted murderers usually are model prisoners, and that they almost always become law-abiding citizens upon their release from prison; that the costs of executing a capital offender exceed the costs of imprisoning him for life; that while in prison, a convict under sentence of death performs none of the useful functions that life prisoners perform; that no attempt is made in the sentencing process to ferret out likely recidivists for execution; and that the death penalty may actually stimulate criminal activity.

This information would almost surely convince the average citizen that the death penalty was unwise, but a problem arises as to whether it would convince him that the penalty was morally reprehensible. This problem arises from the fact that the public's desire for retribution, even though this is a goal that the legislature cannot constitutionally pursue as its sole justification for capital punishment, might influence the citizenry's view of the morality of capital punishment. The solution to the problem lies in the fact that no one has ever seriously advanced retribution as a legitimate goal of our society. Defenses of capital punishment are always mounted on deterrent or other similar theories. This should not be surprising. It is the people of this country who have urged in the past that prison rehabilitate as well as isolate offenders, and it is the people who have injected a sense of purpose into our penology. I cannot believe that at this stage in our history, the American people would ever knowingly support purposeless vengeance. Thus, I believe that the great mass of citizens would conclude on the basis of the material already considered that the death penalty is immoral and therefore unconstitutional.

But, if this information needs supplementing, I believe that the following facts would serve to convince even the most hesitant of citizens to condemn death as a sanction: capital punishment is imposed discriminatorily against certain identifiable classes of people; there is evidence that innocent people have been executed before their innocence can be proved; and the death penalty wreaks havoc with our entire criminal justice system. . . .

Assuming knowledge of all the facts presently available regarding capital punishment, the average citizen would, in my opinion, find it shocking to his conscience and sense of justice. For this reason alone capital punishment cannot stand.

☐ *Chief Justice BURGER, with whom Justice BLACKMUN, Justice POWELL, and Justice REHNQUIST join, dissenting.*

I view these cases as turning on the single question whether capital punishment is "cruel" in the constitutional sense. The term "unusual" cannot be read as limiting the ban on "cruel" punishments or as somehow expanding the meaning of the term "cruel." For this reason I am unpersuaded by the facile argument that since capital punishment has always been cruel in the everyday sense of the word, and has become unusual due to decreased use, it is, therefore, now "cruel and unusual." . . .

Today the Court has not ruled that capital punishment is *per se* violative of the Eighth Amendment: nor has it ruled that the punishment is barred for any particular class or classes of crimes. The substantially similar concurring opinions of Justice STEWART and Justice WHITE, which are necessary to support the judgment setting aside petitioners' sentences, stop short of reaching the ultimate question. . . .

The critical factor in the concurring opinions of both Justice STEWART and Justice WHITE is the infrequency with which the penalty is imposed. This factor is taken not as evidence of society's abhorrence of capital punishment—the inference that petitioners would have the Court draw—but as the earmark of a deteriorated system of sentencing. It is concluded that petitioners' sentences must be set aside, not because the punishment is impermissibly cruel, but because juries and judges have failed to exercise their sentencing discretion in acceptable fashion. . . .

While I would not undertake to make a definitive statement as to the parameters of the Court's ruling, it is clear that if state legislatures and the Congress wish to maintain the availability of capital punishment, significant statutory changes will have to be made. Since the two pivotal concurring opinions turn on the assumption that the punishment of death is now meted out in a random and unpredictable manner, legislative bodies may seek to bring their laws into compliance with the Court's ruling by providing standards for juries and judges to follow in determining the sentence in capital cases or by more narrowly defining the crimes for which the penalty is to be imposed. If such standards can be devised or the crimes more meticulously defined, the result cannot be detrimental. . . .

Since there is no majority of the Court on the ultimate issue presented in these cases, the future of capital punishment in this country has been left in an uncertain limbo. Rather than providing a final and unambiguous answer on the basic constitutional question, the collective impact of the majority's ruling is to demand an undetermined measure of change from the various state legislatures and the Congress. While I cannot endorse the process of decision making that has yielded today's result and the restraints that that result imposes on legislative action, I am not altogether displeased that legislative bodies have been given the opportunity, and indeed unavoidable responsibility, to make a thorough re-evaluation of the entire subject of capital punishment. If today's opinions demonstrate nothing else, they starkly show that this is an area where legislatures can act far more effectively than courts.

The legislatures are free to eliminate capital punishment for specific crimes or to carve out limited exceptions to a general abolition of the penalty, without adherence to the conceptual strictures of the Eighth Amendment. The legislatures can and should make an assessment of the deterrent influence of capital punishment, both generally and as affecting the commission of specific types of crimes. If legislatures come to doubt the efficacy of capital punishment, they can abolish it, either completely or on a selective basis. If new evidence persuades them that they have acted unwisely, they can reverse their field and reinstate the penalty to the extent it is thought warranted. An Eighth Amendment ruling by judges cannot be made with such flexibility or discriminating precision.

☐ *Justice BLACKMUN, dissenting.*

I join the respective opinions of the CHIEF JUSTICE, Justice POWELL, and Justice REHNQUIST, and add only the following, somewhat personal, comments.

Cases such as these provide for me an excruciating agony of the spirit. I yield to no one in the depth of my distaste, antipathy, and, indeed, abhorrence, for the death penalty, with all its aspects of physical distress and fear and of moral judgment exercised by finite minds. That distaste is buttressed by a belief that capital punishment serves no useful purpose that can be demonstrated. For me, it violates childhood's training and life's experiences, and is not compatible with the philosophical convictions I have been able to develop. It is antagonistic to any sense of "reverence for life." Were I a legislator, I would vote against the death penalty for the policy reasons argued by counsel for the respective petitioners and expressed and adopted in the several opinions filed by the Justices who vote to reverse these judgments. . . .

To reverse the judgments in these cases is, of course, the easy choice. It is easier to strike the balance in favor of life and against death. It is comforting to relax in the thoughts—perhaps the rationalizations—that this is the compassionate decision for a maturing society; that this is the moral and the "right" thing to do; that thereby we convince ourselves that we are moving down the road toward human decency; that we value life even though that life has taken another or others or has grievously scarred another or others and their families; and that we are less barbaric than we were in 1879, or in 1890, or in 1910, or in 1947, or in 1958, or in 1963, or a year ago, in 1971, when *Wilkerson, Kemmler, Weems, Francis, Trop, Rudolph*, and *McGautha* were respectively decided.

This, for me, is good argument, and it makes some sense. But it is good argument and it makes sense only in a legislative and executive way and not as a judicial expedient. As I have said above, were I a legislator, I would do all I could to sponsor and to vote for legislation abolishing the death penalty. And were I the chief executive of a sovereign State, I would be sorely tempted to exercise executive clemency as Governor Rockefeller of Arkansas did recently just before he departed from office. There—on the Legislative Branch of the State or Federal Government, and secondarily, on the Executive Branch—is where the authority and responsibility for this kind of action lies. The authority should not be taken over by the judiciary in the modern guise of an Eighth Amendment issue.

I do not sit on these cases, however, as a legislator, responsive, at least in part, to the will of constituents. Our task here, as must so frequently be emphasized and re-emphasized, is to pass upon the constitutionality of legislation that has been enacted and that is challenged. This is the sole task for judges. We should not allow our personal preferences as to the wisdom of legislative and congressional action, or our distaste for such action, to guide our judicial decision in cases such as these. The temptations to cross that policy line are very great. In fact, as today's decision reveals, they are almost irresistible.

☐ *Justice POWELL, with whom the CHIEF JUSTICE, Justice BLACKMUN, and Justice REHNQUIST join, dissenting.*

With deference and respect for the views of the Justices who differ, it seems to me that all these studies—both in this country and elsewhere—suggest that, as a matter of policy and precedent, this is a classic case for the exercise of our oft-announced allegiance to judicial restraint. I know of no case in which greater gravity and delicacy have attached to the duty that this Court is called on to perform whenever legislation—state or federal—is challenged on constitutional grounds. It seems to me that the sweeping judicial action undertaken today reflects a basic lack of faith and confidence in the democratic process. Many may regret, as I do, the failure of some legislative bodies to address the capital punishment issue with greater frankness or effectiveness. Many might decry their failure either to abolish the penalty entirely or selectively, or to establish standards for its enforcement. But impatience with the slowness, and even the unresponsiveness, of legislatures is no justification for judicial intrusion upon their historic powers. Rarely has there been a more appropriate opportunity for this Court to heed the philosophy of Justice OLIVER WENDELL HOLMES. As Justice FRANKFURTER reminded the Court in *Trop* [*v. Dulles* (1958)]:

"[T]he whole of [Justice HOLMES'] work during his thirty years of service on this Court should be a constant reminder that the power to invalidate legislation must not be exercised as if, either in constitutional theory or in the art of government, it stood as the sole bulwark against unwisdom or excesses of the moment." . . .

☐ *Justice REHNQUIST, with whom the CHIEF JUSTICE, Justice BLACKMUN, and Justice POWELL join, dissenting.*

Whatever its precise rationale, today's holding necessarily brings into sharp relief the fundamental question of the role of judicial review in a democratic society. How can government by the elected representatives of the people co-exist with the power of the federal judiciary, whose members are constitutionally insulated from responsiveness to the popular will, to declare invalid laws duly enacted by the popular branches of government?

The answer, of course, is found in Hamilton's *Federalist* Paper No. 78 and in Chief Justice MARSHALL's classic opinion in *Marbury v. Madison*, 1 Cranch 137, (1803). An oft-told story since then, it bears summarization once more. Sovereignty resides ultimately in the people as a whole and, by adopting through their States a written Constitution for the Nation and subsequently adding amendments to that instrument, they have both granted certain powers to the National Government, and denied other powers to the National and the State Governments. Courts are exercising no more than the judicial function conferred upon them by Art. III of the Constitution when they assess, in a case before them, whether or not a particular legislative enactment is within the authority granted by the Constitution to the enacting body, and whether it runs afoul of some limitation placed by the Constitution on the authority of that body. For the theory is that the people themselves have spoken in the Constitution, and therefore its commands are superior to the commands of the legislature, which is merely an agent of the people.

The Founding Fathers thus wisely sought to have the best of both worlds, the undeniable benefits of both democratic self-government and individual rights protected against possible excesses of that form of government.

The courts in cases properly before them have been entrusted under the Constitution with the last word, short of constitutional amendment, as to whether a law passed by the legislature conforms to the Constitution. But just because courts in general, and this Court in particular, do have the last word, the admonition of Justice STONE dissenting in *United States v. Butler*, [297 U.S. 1 (1936)], must be constantly borne in mind:

"[W]hile unconstitutional exercise of power by the executive and legislative branches of the government is subject to judicial restraint, the only check upon our own exercise of power is our own sense of self-restraint." . . .

The very nature of judicial review, as pointed out by Justice STONE in his dissent in the *Butler* case, makes the courts the least subject to Madisonian check in the event that they shall, for the best of motives, expand judicial authority beyond the limits contemplated by the Framers. It is for this reason that judicial self-restraint is surely an implied, if not an expressed, condition of the grant of authority of judicial review. The Court's holding in these cases has been reached, I believe, in complete disregard of that implied condition.

Lockett v. Ohio

438 U.S. 586, 98 S.Ct. 2954 (1978)

Chief Justice Warren Burger discusses the facts in his opinion for the Court, striking down that portion of Ohio's capital punishment law that restricted the mitigating factors to be considered when imposing the death penalty.

The Court's decision was seven and one-half to one-half, and the majority's opinion was announced by Chief Justice Burger, with Justice Brennan not participating. Concurrences were by Justices Blackmun and Marshall. A separate opinion, in part concurring and in part dissenting, was delivered by Justice Rehnquist.

☐ *Chief Justice BURGER delivered the opinion of the Court.*

Lockett was charged with aggravated murder with the aggravating specifications (1) that the murder was "committed for the purpose of escaping detection, apprehension, trial, or punishment" for aggravated robbery, and (2) that the murder was "committed . . . while committing, attempting to commit, or fleeing immediately after committing or attempting to commit aggravated robbery." That offense was punishable by death in Ohio. . . .

Lockett became acquainted with Parker and Nathan Earl Dew while she and a friend, Joanne Baxter, were in New Jersey. Parker and Dew then accompanied Lockett, Baxter, and Lockett's brother back to Akron, Ohio, Lockett's home town. After they arrived in Akron, Parker and Dew needed money for the trip back to New Jersey. Dew suggested that he pawn his ring. Lockett overheard his suggestion, but felt that the ring was too beautiful to pawn, and suggested instead that they could get some money by robbing a grocery store and a furniture store in the area. . . .

The next day Parker, Dew, Lockett, and her brother gathered at Baxter's apartment. Lockett's brother asked if they were "still going to do it," and everyone, including Lockett, agreed to proceed. The four then drove by the pawnshop several times and parked the car. Lockett's brother and Dew entered the shop. Parker then left the car and told Lockett to start it again in two minutes. The robbery proceeded according to plan until the pawnbroker grabbed the gun when Parker announced the "stickup." The gun went off with Parker's finger on the trigger firing a fatal shot into the pawnbroker.

Parker went back to the car where Lockett waited with the engine running. While driving away from the pawnshop, Parker told Lockett what had happened. She took the gun from the pawnshop and put it into her purse.

Lockett and Parker drove to Lockett's aunt's house and called a taxicab. Shortly thereafter, while riding away in a taxicab, they were stopped by the police. . . .

[At the conclusion of her trial, the judge] instructed the jury that, before it could find Lockett guilty, it had to find that she purposely had killed the pawnbroker while committing or attempting to commit aggravated robbery. The jury was further charged that one who

> "purposely aids, helps, associates himself or herself with another for the purpose of committing a crime is regarded as if he or she were the principal offender and is just as guilty as if the person performed every act constituting the offense." . . .

The jury found Lockett guilty as charged.

Once a verdict of aggravated murder with specifications had been returned, the Ohio death penalty statute required the trial judge to impose a death sentence unless, after "considering the nature and circumstances of the offense" and Lockett's "history, character, and condition," he found by a preponderance of the evidence that (1) the victim had induced or facilitated the offense, (2) it was unlikely that Lockett would have committed the offense but for the fact that she "was under duress, coercion, or strong provocation," or (3) the offense was "primarily the product of [Lockett's] psychosis or mental deficiency." . . .

In accord with the Ohio statute, the trial judge requested a presentence report as well as psychiatric and psychological reports. The reports contained detailed information about Lockett's intelligence, character, and background. The psychiatric and psychological reports described her as a 21-year-old with low average or average intelligence, and not suffering from a mental deficiency. . . .

After considering the reports and hearing argument on the penalty issue, the trial judge concluded that the offense had not been primarily the product of psychosis or mental deficiency. Without specifically addressing the other two statutory mitigating factors, the judge said that he had "no alternative, whether [he] like[d] the law or not" but to impose the death penalty. He then sentenced Lockett to death. . . .

Prior to *Furman v. Georgia*, 408 U.S. 238 (1972), every State that authorized capital punishment had abandoned mandatory death penalties, and instead permitted the jury unguided and unrestrained discretion regarding the imposition of the death penalty in a particular capital case. Mandatory death penalties had proved unsatisfactory, as the plurality noted in *Woodson v. North Carolina*, 428 U.S. 280 (1976), in part because juries, "with some regularity, disregarded their oaths and refused to convict defendants where a death sentence was the automatic consequence of a guilty verdict."

This Court had never intimated prior to *Furman* that discretion in sentencing offended the Constitution. See *Pennsylvania ex rel. Sullivan v. Ashe*, 302 U.S. 51 (1937); *Williams v. New York*, 337 U.S. 241 (1949); *Williams v. Oklahoma*, 358 U.S. 576 (1959). As recently as *McGautha v. California*, 402 U.S. 183 (1971), the Court had specifically rejected the contention that discretion in imposing the death penalty violated the fundamental standards of fairness embodied in Fourteenth Amendment due process . . . and had asserted that States were entitled to assume that "jurors confronted with the truly awesome responsibility of decreeing death for a fellow human [would] act with due regard for the consequences of their decision." . . .

The constitutional status of discretionary sentencing in capital cases changed abruptly, however, as a result of the separate opinions supporting the judgment in *Furman*. The question in *Furman* was whether "the imposition and carrying out of the death penalty [in the cases before the Court] constitute[d] cruel and unusual punishment in violation of the Eighth and Fourteenth Amendments." Two Justices concluded that the Eighth Amendment prohibited the death penalty altogether and on that ground voted to reverse the judgments sustaining the death penalties. *Id.* (BRENNAN, J., concurring); *id.* (MARSHALL, J., concurring). Three Justices were unwilling to hold the death penalty *per se* unconstitutional under the Eighth and Fourteenth Amendments, but voted to reverse the judgments on other grounds. In separate opinions, the three concluded that discretionary sentencing, unguided by legislatively defined standards, violated the Eighth Amendment because it was "pregnant with discrimination," *id.* (DOUGLAS, J., concurring), because it permitted the death penalty to be "wantonly" and "freakishly" imposed, *id.* (STEWART, J., concurring), and because it imposed the death penalty with "great infrequency" and afforded "no meaningful basis for distinguishing the few cases in which it [was] imposed from the many cases in which it [was] not," *id.* (WHITE, J., concurring). Thus, what had been approved under the Due Process Clause of the Fourteenth Amendment in *McGautha* became impermissible under the Eighth and Fourteenth Amendments by virtue of the judgment in *Furman*. See, *Gregg v. Georgia*, 428 U.S. 153 (1976) (opinion of STEWART, POWELL, and STEVENS, JJ.).

Predictably, the variety of opinions supporting the judgment in *Furman* engendered confusion as to what was required in order to impose the death penalty in accord with the Eighth Amendment. Some States responded to what was thought to be the command of *Furman* by adopting mandatory death penalties for a limited category of specific crimes thus eliminating all discretion from the sentencing process in capital cases. Other States attempted to continue the practice of individually assessing the culpability of each individual defendant convicted of a capital offense and, at the same time, to comply with *Furman*, by providing standards to guide the sentencing decision.

Four years after *Furman*, we considered Eighth Amendment issues posed by five of the post-*Furman* death penalty statutes. Four Justices took the position that all five statutes complied with the Constitution; two Justices took the position that none of them complied. Hence, the disposition of each case varied according to the votes of three Justices who delivered a joint opinion in each of the five cases upholding the constitutionality of the statutes of Georgia, Florida, and Texas, and holding those of North Carolina and Louisiana unconstitutional.

The joint opinion reasoned that, to comply with *Furman*, sentencing procedures should not create "a substantial risk that the [death penalty will] be inflicted in an arbitrary and capricious manner." *Gregg v. Georgia, supra.* In the view of the three Justices, however, *Furman* did not require that all sentencing discretion be eliminated, but only that it be "directed and limited," so that the death penalty would be imposed in a more consistent and rational manner and so that there would be a "meaningful basis for distinguishing the . . . cases in which it is imposed from . . . the many cases in which it is not." The plurality concluded, in the course of invalidating North Carolina's mandatory death penalty statute, that the sentencing process must permit consideration of the "character and record of the individual offender and the circumstances of the particular offense as a constitutionally indispensable part of the process of inflicting the penalty of death." *Woodson v. North Carolina*. In order to ensure the reliability, under Eighth Amendment standards, of the determination that "death is the appropriate punishment in a specific case." . . .

In the last decade, many of the States have been obliged to revise their death penalty statutes in response to the various opinions supporting the judgments in *Furman* and *Gregg* and its companion cases. The signals from this Court have not, however, always been easy to decipher. The States now deserve the clearest guidance that the Court can provide; we have an obligation to reconcile previously differing views in order to provide that guidance.

With that obligation in mind we turn to Lockett's attack on the Ohio statute. . . .

We begin by recognizing that the concept of individualized sentencing in criminal cases generally, although not constitutionally required, has long been accepted in this country. . . .

Although legislatures remain free to decide how much discretion in sentencing should be reposed in the judge or jury in non-capital cases, the plurality opinion in *Woodson*, after reviewing the historical repudiation of mandatory sentencing in capital cases concluded that

> "in capital cases the fundamental respect for humanity underlying the Eighth Amendment . . . requires consideration of the character and record of the individual offender and the circumstances of the particular offense as a constitutionally indispensable part of the process of inflicting the penalty of death."

That declaration rested "on the predicate that the penalty of death is qualitatively different" from any other sentence. We are satisfied that this qualitative difference between death and other penalties calls for a greater degree of reliability when the death sentence is imposed. The mandatory death penalty statute in *Woodson* was held invalid because it permitted *no* consideration of "relevant facets of the character and record of the individual offender or the circumstances of the particular offense." The plurality did not attempt to indicate, however, which facets of an offender or his offense it deemed "relevant" in capital sentencing or what degree of consideration of "relevant facets" it would require.

We are now faced with those questions and we conclude that the Eighth and Fourteenth Amendments require that the sentencer, in all but the rarest kind of capital case, not be precluded from considering, *as a mitigating factor*, any aspect of a defendant's character or record and any of the circumstances of the offense that the defendant proffers as a basis for a sentence less than death. We recognize that, in noncapital cases, the established practice of individualized sentences rests not on constitutional commands, but on public policy enacted into statutes. The considerations that account for the wide acceptance of individualization of sentences in noncapital cases surely cannot be thought less important in capital cases. Given that the imposition of death by public authority is so profoundly different from all other penalties, we cannot avoid the conclusion that an individualized decision is essential in capital cases. The need for treating each defendant in a capital case with that degree of respect due the uniqueness of the individual is far more important than in noncapital cases. A variety of flexible techniques—probation, parole, work furloughs, to name a few—and various postconviction remedies may be available to modify an initial sentence of confinement in noncapital cases. The nonavailability of corrective or modifying mechanisms with respect to an executed capital sentence underscores the need for individualized consideration as a constitutional requirement in imposing the death sentence.

There is no perfect procedure for deciding in which cases governmental authority should be used to impose death. But a statute that prevents the sentencer in all capital cases from giving independent mitigating weight to aspects of the defendant's character and record and to circumstances of the offense proffered in mitigation creates the risk that the death penalty will be imposed in spite of factors which may call for a less severe penalty. When the choice is between life and death, that risk is unacceptable and incompatible with the commands of the Eighth and Fourteenth Amendments.

■ II

The Ohio death penalty statute does not permit the type of individualized consideration of mitigating factors we now hold to be required by the Eighth and Fourteenth Amendments in capital cases. . . .

[Under the statute now before us, once] a defendant is found guilty of aggravated murder with at least one of seven specified aggravating circumstances, the death penalty must be imposed unless, considering "the nature and, circumstances of the offense and the history, character, and condition of the offender," the sentencing judge determines that at least one of the following mitigating circumstances is established by a preponderance of the evidence:

> "(1) The victim of the offense induced or facilitated it.
> "(2) It is unlikely that the offense would have been committed, but for the fact that the offender was under duress, coercion, or strong provocation.
> "(3) The offense was primarily the product of the offender's psychosis or mental deficiency, though such condition is insufficient to establish the defense of insanity." Ohio Rev. Code Ann. § 2929.04(B) (1975). . . .

We see, therefore, that once it is determined that the victim did not induce or facilitate the offense, that the defendant did not act under duress or coercion, and that the offense was not primarily the product of the defendant's mental deficiency, the Ohio statute mandates the sentence of death. The absence of direct proof that the defendant intended to cause the death of the victim is relevant for mitigating purposes only if it is determined that it sheds some light on one of the three statutory mitigating factors. Similarly, consideration of a defendant's comparatively minor role in the offense, or age, would generally not be permitted, as such, to affect the sentencing decision.

The limited range of mitigating circumstances which may be considered by the sentencer under the Ohio statute is incompatible with the Eighth and Fourteenth Amendments. To meet constitutional requirements, a death penalty statute must not preclude consideration of relevant mitigating factors.

Accordingly, the judgment under review is reversed to the extent that it sustains the imposition of the death penalty; the case is remanded for further proceedings.

☐ *Justice REHNQUIST, concurring in part and dissenting in part.*

The CHIEF JUSTICE states: "We do not write on a 'clean slate.' " But it can scarcely be maintained that today's decision is the logical application of a coherent doctrine first espoused by the opinions leading to the Court's judgment in *Furman,* and later elaborated in the *Woodson* series of cases decided two Terms ago. Indeed, it cannot even be responsibly maintained that it is a principled application of the plurality and lead opinions in the *Woodson* series of cases, without regard to *Furman.* The opinion strives manfully to appear as a logical exegesis of those opinions, but I believe that it fails in the effort. We are now told, in effect, that in order to impose a death sentence the judge or jury must receive in evidence whatever the defense attorney wishes them to hear. I do not think the CHIEF JUSTICE's effort to trace this quite novel constitutional principle back to the plurality and lead opinions in the *Woodson* cases succeeds.

It seems to me indisputably clear from today's opinion that while we may not be writing on a clean slate, the Court is scarcely faithful to what has been written before. Rather, it makes a third distinct effort to address the same question, an effort which derives little support from any of the various opinions in *Furman* or from the prevailing opinions in the *Woodson* cases. As a practical matter, I doubt that today's opinion will make a great deal of difference in the manner in which trials in capital cases are conducted, since I would suspect that it has been the practice of most trial judges to permit a defendant to offer virtually any sort of evidence in his own defense as he wished. But as my Brother WHITE points out in his dissent, the theme of today's opinion; far from supporting those views expressed in *Furman* which did appear to be carried over to the *Woodson* cases, tends to undercut those views. If a defendant as a matter of constitutional law is to be permitted to offer as evidence in the sentencing hearing any fact, however bizarre, which he wishes, even though the most sympathetically disposed trial judge could conceive of no basis upon which the jury might take it into account in imposing a sentence, the new constitutional doctrine will not eliminate arbitrariness or freakishness in the imposition of sentences, but will codify and institutionalize it. By encouraging defendants in capital cases, and presumably sentencing judges and juries, to take into consideration anything under the sun as a "mitigating circumstance," it will not guide sentencing discretion but will totally unleash it. . . .

I continue to view *McGautha* as a correct exposition of the limits of our authority to revise state criminal procedures in capital cases under the Eighth and Fourteenth Amendments. Sandra Lockett was fairly tried, and was found guilty of aggravated murder. I do not think Ohio was required to receive any sort of mitigating evidence which an accused or his lawyer wishes to offer, and therefore I disagree with [that part] of the plurality's opinion [which holds contrariwise].

McCleskey v. Kemp

481 U.S. 279, 107 S.Ct. 1756 (1987)

Justice Lewis F. Powell discusses the facts in his opinion announcing the decision of a majority of the Court. The Court rejected the argument that statistical studies—showing that black defendants who murder white victims are more likely to receive the death penalty than white defendants charged with murdering white or black victims—establish the basis for declaring the death sentence imposed on Warren Mc-Cleskey, a black man, unconstitutional under the Eighth and Four-teenth Amendments.

The Court's decision was five to four, and the majority's opinion was announced by Justice Powell. Dissents were by Justices Brennan, Blackmun, and Stevens and joined by Justice Marshall.

☐ *Justice POWELL delivered the opinion of the Court.*

This case presents the question whether a complex statistical study that indicates a risk that racial considerations enter into capital sentencing deter-minations proves that petitioner McCleskey's capital sentence is unconstitu-tional under the Eighth or Fourteenth Amendment.

■ I

McCleskey, a black man, was convicted of two counts of armed robbery and one count of murder. . . .

On appeal, the Supreme Court of Georgia affirmed the convictions and sentences. . . .

McCleskey next filed a petition for a writ of *habeas corpus* in the federal District Court for the Northern District of Georgia. His petition raised 18 claims, one of which was that the Georgia capital sentencing process is ad-ministered in a racially discriminatory manner in violation of the Eighth and Fourteenth Amendments to the United States Constitution. In support of his claim, McCleskey proffered a statistical study performed by Professors David C. Baldus, George Woodworth, and Charles Pulaski (the Baldus study) that purports to show a disparity in the imposition of the death sentence in Geor-gia based on the race of the murder victim and, to a lesser extent, the race of the defendant. The Baldus study is actually two sophisticated statistical studies that examine over 2,000 murder cases that occurred in Georgia during the

■ INSIDE THE COURT:

Justice Scalia's Unpublished Memorandum on McCleskey v. Kemp, *indicating that statistics show racial prejudice in death penalty sentencing*

Supreme Court of the United States
Washington, D. C. 20543

CHAMBERS OF
JUSTICE ANTONIN SCALIA

January 6, 1987

Re: No. 84-6811 - McCleskey v. Kemp

MEMORANDUM TO THE CONFERENCE:

I plan to join Lewis's opinion in this case, with two reservations. I disagree with the argument that the inferences that can be drawn from the Baldus study are weakened by the fact that each jury and each trial is unique, or by the large number of variables at issue. And I do not share the view, implicit in the opinion, that an effect of racial factors upon sentencing, if it could only be shown by sufficiently strong statistical evidence, would require reversal. Since it is my view that the unconscious operation of irrational sympathies and antipathies, including racial, upon jury decisions and (hence) prosecutorial decisions is real, acknowledged in the decisions of this court, and ineradicable, I cannot honestly say that all I need is more proof. I expect to write separately to make these points, but not until I see the dissent.

Sincerely,

[signature]

(*Library of Congress, Justice Thurgood Marshall Papers*) For a further discussion, see Denis D. Dorin, "Far Right of the Mainstream: Racism, Right, and Remedies from the Perspective of Justice Antonin Scalia's *McCleskey* Memorandum," 45 *Mercer Law Review* 1035 (1994).

1970s. The raw numbers collected by Professor Baldus indicate that defendants charged with killing white persons received the death penalty in 11% of the cases, but defendants charged with killing blacks received the death penalty in only 1% of the cases. The raw numbers also indicate a reverse racial disparity according to the race of the defendant: 4% of the black defendants received the death penalty, as opposed to 7% of the white defendants.

Baldus also divided the cases according to the combination of the race of the defendant and the race of the victim. He found that the death penalty was assessed in 22% of the cases involving black defendants and white victims; 8% of the cases involving white defendants and white victims; 1% of the cases involving black defendants and black victims; and 3% of the cases involving white defendants and black victims. Similarly, Baldus found that prosecutors sought the death penalty in 70% of the cases involving black defendants and white victims; 32% of the cases involving white defendants and white victims; 15% of the cases involving black defendants and black victims; and 19% of the cases involving white defendants and black victims.

Baldus subjected his data to an extensive analysis, taking account of 230 variables that could have explained the disparities on nonracial grounds. One of his models concludes that, even after taking account of 39 nonracial variables, defendants charged with killing white victims were 4.3 times as likely to receive a death sentence as defendants charged with killing blacks. According to this model, black defendants were 1.1 times as likely to receive a death sentence as other defendants. Thus, the Baldus study indicates that black defendants, such as McCleskey, who kill white victims have the greatest likelihood of receiving the death penalty. . . .

McCleskey's first claim is that the Georgia capital punishment statute violates the Equal Protection Clause of the Fourteenth Amendment. He argues that race has infected the administration of Georgia's statute in two ways: persons who murder whites are more likely to be sentenced to death than persons who murder blacks, and black murderers are more likely to be sentenced to death than white murderers. As a black defendant who killed a white victim, McCleskey claims that the Baldus study demonstrates that he was discriminated against because of his race and because of the race of his victim. . . .

We agree with the Court of Appeals, and every other court that has considered such a challenge, that this claim must fail.

Our analysis begins with the basic principle that a defendant who alleges an equal protection violation has the burden of proving "the existence of purposeful discrimination." A corollary to this principle is that a criminal defendant must prove that the purposeful discrimination "had a discriminatory effect" on him. Thus, to prevail under the Equal Protection Clause, McCleskey must prove that the decisionmakers in *his* case acted with discriminatory purpose. He offers no evidence specific to his own case that would support an inference that racial considerations played a part in his sentence. Instead, he relies solely on the Baldus study. . . .

The Court has accepted statistics as proof of intent to discriminate in certain limited contexts. First, this Court has accepted statistical disparities as proof of an equal protection violation in the selection of the jury venire in a particular district. Although statistical proof normally must present a "stark" pattern to be accepted as the sole proof of discriminatory intent under the Constitution, *Arlington Heights v. Metropolitan Housing Dev. Corp.*, 429

U.S. 252 (1977), "[b]ecause of the nature of the jury-selection task, we have permitted a finding of constitutional violation even when the statistical pattern does not approach [such] extremes." . . . Second, this Court has accepted statistics in the form of multiple regression analysis to prove statutory violations under Title VII. *Bazemore v. Friday*, [478 U.S. 385 (1986)] (opinion of BRENNAN. J., concurring in part).

But the nature of the capital sentencing decision, and the relationship of the statistics to that decision, are fundamentally different from the corresponding elements in the venire-selection or Title VII cases. Most importantly, each particular decision to impose the death penalty is made by a petit jury selected from a properly constituted venire. Each jury is unique in its composition, and the Constitution requires that its decision rest on consideration of innumerable factors that vary according to the characteristics of the individual defendant and the facts of the particular capital offense. Thus, the application of an inference drawn from the general statistics to a specific decision in a trial and sentencing simply is not comparable to the application of an inference drawn from general statistics to a specific venire-selection or Title VII case. In those cases, the statistics relate to fewer entities, and fewer variables are relevant to the challenged decisions. . . .

Finally, McCleskey's statistical proffer must be viewed in the context of his challenge. McCleskey challenges decisions at the heart of the State's criminal justice system. . . .

Implementation of these laws necessarily requires discretionary judgments. Because discretion is essential to the criminal justice process, we would demand exceptionally clear proof before we would infer that the discretion has been abused. The unique nature of the decisions at issue in this case also counsel against adopting such an inference from the disparities indicated by the Baldus study. Accordingly, we hold that the Baldus study is clearly insufficient to support an inference that any of the decisionmakers in McCleskey's case acted with discriminatory purpose.

McCleskey also suggests that the Baldus study proves that the State as a whole has acted with a discriminatory purpose. He appears to argue that the State has violated the Equal Protection Clause by adopting the capital punishment statute and allowing it to remain in force despite its allegedly discriminatory application. But " '[d]iscriminatory purpose' . . . implies more than intent as volition or intent as awareness of consequences. It implies that the decisionmaker, in this case a state legislature, selected or reaffirmed a particular course of action at least in part 'because of,' not merely 'in spite of,' its adverse effects upon an identifiable group." . . .

For this claim to prevail, McCleskey would have to prove that the Georgia Legislature enacted or maintained the death penalty statute *because of* an anticipated racially discriminatory effect. In *Gregg v. Georgia*, 428 U.S. 153 (1976), this Court found that the Georgia capital sentencing system could operate in a fair and neutral manner. There was no evidence then, and there is none now, that the Georgia Legislature enacted the capital punishment statute to further a racially discriminatory purpose. . . .

McCleskey also argues that the Baldus study demonstrates that the Georgia capital sentencing system violates the Eighth Amendment. . . .

Two principal decisions guide our resolution of McCleskey's Eighth Amendment claim. In *Furman v. Georgia*, 408 U.S. 238 (1972), the Court concluded that the death penalty was so irrationally imposed that any particular death sentence could be presumed excessive. Under the statutes at issue in *Furman*, there was no basis for determining in any particular case whether the penalty was proportionate to the crime: "the death penalty [was] exacted with great infrequency even for the most atrocious crimes and . . . there [was] no meaningful basis for distinguishing the few cases in which it [was] imposed from the many cases in which it [was] not." . . .

In *Gregg*, the Court specifically addressed the question left open in *Furman*—whether the punishment of death for murder is "under all circumstances, 'cruel and unusual' in violation of the Eighth and Fourteenth Amendments of the Constitution." We noted that the imposition of the death penalty for the crime of murder "has a long history of acceptance both in the United States and in England." During the 4-year period between *Furman* and *Gregg*, at least 35 states had reenacted the death penalty, and Congress had authorized the penalty for aircraft piracy. . . .

The second question before the Court in *Gregg* was the constitutionality of the particular procedures embodied in the Georgia capital punishment statute. We explained the fundamental principle of *Furman*, that "where discretion is afforded a sentencing body on a matter so grave as the determination of whether a human life should be taken or spared, that discretion must be suitably directed and limited so as to minimize the risk of wholly arbitrary and capricious action." Numerous features of the then new Georgia statute met the concerns articulated in *Furman*. The Georgia system bifurcates guilt and sentencing proceedings so that the jury can receive all relevant information for sentencing without the risk that evidence irrelevant to the defendant's guilt will influence the jury's consideration of that issue. The statute narrows the class of murders subject to the death penalty to cases in which the jury finds at least one statutory aggravating circumstance beyond a reasonable doubt. Conversely, it allows the defendant to introduce any relevant mitigating evidence that might influence the jury not to impose a death sentence. The procedures also require a particularized inquiry into " 'the circumstances of the offense together with the character and propensities of the offender.' " Thus, "while some jury discretion still exists, 'the discretion to be exercised is controlled by clear and objective standards so as to produce non-discriminatory application.' " Moreover, the Georgia system adds "an important additional safeguard against arbitrariness and caprice" in a provision for automatic appeal of a death sentence to the State Supreme Court. The statute requires that court to review each sentence to determine whether it was imposed under the influence of passion or prejudice, whether the evidence supports the jury's finding of a statutory aggravating circumstance, and whether the sentence is disproportionate to sentences imposed in generally similar murder cases. To aid the court's review, the trial judge answers a questionnaire about the trial, including detailed questions as to "the quality of the defendant's representation [and] whether race played a role in the trial." . . .

In the cases decided after *Gregg*, the Court has imposed a number of requirements on the capital sentencing process to ensure that capital sentencing decisions rest on the individualized inquiry contemplated in *Gregg*. . . .

In contrast to the carefully defined standards that must narrow a sentencer's discretion to to *impose* the death sentence, the Constitution limits a

State's ability to narrow a sentencer's discretion to consider relevant evidence that might cause it to *decline to impose* the death sentence. . . .

Although our constitutional inquiry has centered on the procedures by which a death sentence is imposed, we have not stopped at the face of a statute, but have probed the application of statutes to particular cases. For example, in *Godfrey v. Georgia*, 446 U.S. 420 (1980), the Court invalidated a Georgia Supreme Court interpretation of the statutory aggravating circumstance that the murder be "outrageously or wantonly vile, horrible or inhuman in that it involved torture, depravity of mind, or an aggravated battery to the victim." . . . Although that court had articulated an adequate limiting definition of this phrase, we concluded that its interpretation in *Godfrey* was so broad that it may have vitiated the role of the aggravating circumstance in guiding the sentencing jury's discretion.

Finally, where the objective indicia of community values have demonstrated a consensus that the death penalty is disproportionate as applied to a certain class of cases, we have established substantive limitations on its application. In *Coker v. Georgia*, 433 U.S. 584 (1977), the Court held that a State may not constitutionally sentence an individual to death for the rape of an adult woman. . . .

In sum, our decisions since *Furman* have identified a constitutionally permissible range of discretion in imposing the death penalty. First, there is a required threshold below which the death penalty cannot be imposed. In this context, the State must establish rational criteria that narrow the decisionmaker's judgment as to whether the circumstances of a particular defendant's case meet the threshold. Moreover, a societal consensus that the death penalty is disproportionate to a particular offense prevents a State from imposing the death penalty for that offense. Second, States cannot limit the sentencer's consideration of any relevant circumstance that could cause it to decline to impose the penalty. In this respect, the State cannot channel the sentencer's discretion, but must allow it to consider any relevant information offered by the defendant.

In light of our precedents under the Eighth Amendment, McCleskey cannot argue successfully that his sentence is "disproportionate to the crime in the traditional sense." See *Pulley v. Harris*, 465 U.S. 37 (1984). He does not deny that he committed a murder in the course of a planned robbery, a crime for which this Court has determined that the death penalty constitutionally may be imposed. *Gregg v. Georgia*. . . . His disproportionality claim "is of a different sort." *Pulley v. Harris*. McCleskey argues that the sentence in his case is disproportionate to the sentences in other murder cases.

On the one hand, he cannot base a constitutional claim on an argument that his case differs from other cases in which defendants *did* receive the death penalty. On automatic appeal, the Georgia Supreme Court found that McCleskey's death sentence was not disproportionate to other death sentences imposed in the State. . . .

On the other hand, absent a showing that the Georgia capital punishment system operates in an arbitrary and capricious manner, McCleskey cannot prove a constitutional violation by demonstrating that other defendants who may be similarly situated did *not* receive the death penalty. In *Gregg*, the Court confronted the argument that "the opportunities for discretionary action that are inherent in the processing of any murder case under Georgia law," specifically the opportunities for discretionary leniency, rendered the capital sentences imposed arbitrary and capricious. We rejected this contention. . . .

Because McCleskey's sentence was imposed under Georgia sentencing procedures that focus discretion "on the particularized nature of the crime and the particularized characteristics of the individual defendant," we lawfully may presume that McCleskey's death sentence was not "wantonly and freakishly" imposed and thus that the sentence is not disproportionate within any recognized meaning under the Eighth Amendment.

Although our decision in *Gregg* as to the facial validity of the Georgia capital punishment statute appears to foreclose McCleskey's disproportionality argument, he further contends that the Georgia capital punishment system is arbitrary and capricious in *application*, and therefore his sentence is excessive, because racial considerations may influence capital sentencing decisions in Georgia. We now address this claim.

To evaluate McCleskey's challenge, we must examine exactly what the Baldus study may show. Even Professor Baldus does not contend that his statistics *prove* that race enters into any capital sentencing decisions or that race was a factor in McCleskey's particular case. Statistics at most may show only a likelihood that a particular factor entered into some decisions. There is, of course, some risk of racial prejudice influencing a jury's decision in a criminal case. There are similar risks that other kinds of prejudice will influence other criminal trials. . . .

McCleskey asks us to accept the likelihood allegedly shown by the Baldus study as the constitutional measure of an unacceptable risk of racial prejudice influencing capital sentencing decisions. This we decline to do. . . .

At most, the Baldus study indicates a discrepancy that appears to correlate with race. Apparent disparities in sentencing are an inevitable part of our criminal justice system. The discrepancy indicated by the Baldus study is "a far cry from the major systemic defects identified in *Furman*." As this Court has recognized, any mode for determining guilt or punishment "has its weaknesses and the potential for misuse." . . . Despite these imperfections, our consistent rule has been that constitutional guarantees are met when "the mode [for determining guilt or punishment] itself has been surrounded with safeguards to make it as fair as possible." Where the discretion that is fundamental to our criminal process is involved, we decline to assume that what is unexplained is invidious. In light of the safeguards designed to minimize racial bias in the process, the fundamental value of jury trial in our criminal justice system, and the benefits that discretion provides to criminal defendants, we hold that the Baldus study does not demonstrate a constitutionally significant risk of racial bias affecting the Georgia capital-sentencing process.

Two additional concerns inform our decision in this case. First, McCleskey's claim, taken to its logical conclusion, throws into serious question the principles that underlie our entire criminal justice system. The Eighth Amendment is not limited in application to capital punishment, but applies to all penalties. Thus, if we accepted McCleskey's claim that racial bias has impermissibly tainted the capital sentencing decision, we could soon be faced with similar claims as to other types of penalty. Moreover, the claim that his sentence rests on the irrelevant factor of race easily could be extended to apply to claims based on unexplained discrepancies that correlate to membership in other minority groups, and even to gender. . . . Also, there is no logical reason that such a claim need be limited to racial or sexual bias. If arbitrary and capricious punishment is the touchstone under the Eighth Amendment, such a claim could—at least in theory—be based upon any arbitrary variable, such as the defendant's facial characteristics, or the physical attractiveness of the defendant or the victim, that some statistical study indicates may be influential in jury decisionmaking. As these examples illustrate, there is no limiting principle to the type of challenge brought by McCleskey. . . .

Second, McCleskey's arguments are best presented to the legislative bodies. It is not the responsibility—or indeed even the right—of this Court to determine the appropriate punishment for particular crimes. It is the legislatures, the elected representatives of the people, that are "constituted to respond to the will and consequently the moral values of the people." Legislatures also are better qualified to weigh and "evaluate the results of statistical studies in terms of their own local conditions and with a flexibility of approach that is not available to the courts." Capital punishment is now the law in more than two thirds of our States. It is the ultimate duty of courts to determine on a case-by-case basis whether these laws are applied consistently with the Constitution. Despite McCleskey's wide ranging arguments that basically challenge the validity of capital punishment in our multi-racial society, the only question before us is whether in his case, the law of Georgia was properly applied. We agree with the District Court and the Court of Appeals for the Eleventh Circuit that this was carefully and correctly done in this case.

☐ *Justice BRENNAN, with whom Justice MARSHALL joins, and with whom Justice BLACKMUN and Justice STEVENS join in part, dissenting.*

Adhering to my view that the death penalty is in all circumstances cruel and unusual punishment forbidden by the Eighth and Fourteenth Amendments, I would vacate the decision below insofar as it left undisturbed the death sentence imposed in this case. . . .

At some point in this case, Warren McCleskey doubtless asked his lawyer whether a jury was likely to sentence him to die. A candid reply to this question would have been disturbing. First, counsel would have to tell McCleskey that few of the details of the crime or of McCleskey's past criminal conduct were more important than the fact that his victim was white. Furthermore, counsel would feel bound to tell McCleskey that defendants charged with killing white victims in Georgia are 4.3 times as likely to be sentenced to death as defendants charged with killing blacks. Petitioner's Exhibit DB 82. In addition, frankness would compel the disclosure that it was more likely than not that the race of McCleskey's victim would determine whether he received a death sentence: 6 of every 11 defendants convicted of killing a white person would not have received the death penalty if their victims had been black, while, among defendants with aggravating and mitigating factors comparable to McCleskey, 20 of every 34 would not have been sentenced to die if their victims had been black. Finally, the assessment would not be complete without the information that cases involving black defendants and white victims are more likely to result in a death sentence than cases featuring any other racial combination of defendant and victim. The story could be told in a variety of ways, but McCleskey could not fail to grasp its essential narrative line: there was a significant chance that race would play a prominent role in determining if he lived or died.

The Court today holds that Warren McCleskey's sentence was constitutionally imposed. It finds no fault in a system in which lawyers must tell their clients that race casts a large shadow on the capital sentencing process. The Court arrives at this conclusion by stating that the Baldus Study cannot "*prove* that race enters into any capital sentencing decisions or that race was a factor in McCleskey's particular case." Since, according to Professor Baldus, we cannot say "to a moral certainty" that race influenced a decision, we can identify only "a likelihood that a particular factor entered into some decisions," and "a discrepancy that appears to correlate with race." This likelihood" and "discrepancy," holds the Court, is insufficient to establish a constitutional violation. The Court reaches this conclusion by placing four factors on the scales opposite McCleskey's evidence: the desire to encourage sentencing discretion, the existence of "statutory safeguards" in the Georgia scheme, the fear of encouraging wide spread challenges to other sentencing decisions, and the limits of the judicial role. The Court's evaluation of the significance of petitioner's evidence is fundamentally at odds with our consistent concern for rationality in capital sentencing, and the considerations that the majority invokes to discount that evidence cannot justify ignoring its force.

[O]ur inquiry under the Eighth Amendment has not been directed to the validity of the individual sentences before us. In *Godfrey*, for instance, the Court struck down the petitioner's sentence because the vagueness of the statutory definition of heinous crimes created a *risk* that prejudice or other impermissible influences *might have infected* the sentencing decision. In vacating the sentence, we did not ask whether it was likely that Godfrey's own sentence reflected the operation of irrational considerations. Nor did we demand a demonstration that such considerations had actually entered into other sentencing decisions involving heinous crimes. . . .

Defendants challenging their death sentences thus never have had to prove that impermissible considerations have actually infected sentencing decisions. We have required instead that they establish that the system under which they were sentenced posed a significant risk of such an occurrence. McCleskey's claim does differ, however, in one respect from these earlier cases: it is the first to base a challenge not on speculation about how a system *might* operate, but on empirical documentation of how it *does* operate.

The Court assumes the statistical validity of the Baldus study and acknowledges that McCleskey has demonstrated a risk that racial prejudice plays a role in capital sentencing in Georgia. Nonetheless, it finds the probability of prejudice insufficient to create constitutional concern. Close analysis of the Baldus study, however, in light of both statistical principles and human experience, reveals that the risk that race influenced McCleskey's sentence is intolerable by any imaginable standard.

The Baldus study indicates that, after taking into account some 230 nonracial factors that might legitimately influence a sentencer, the jury *more likely than not* would have spared McCleskey's life had his victim been black. The study distinguishes between those cases in which (1) the jury exercises virtually no discretion because the strength or weakness of aggravating factors usually suggests that only one outcome is appropriate; and (2) cases reflecting an "intermediate" level of aggravation, in which the jury has considerable discretion in choosing a sentence. McCleskey's case falls into the intermediate range. In such cases, death is imposed in 34% of white-victim crimes and 14% of black-victim crimes, a difference of 139% in the rate of imposition of the death penalty. In other words, just under 59%—almost 6 in 10—defendants comparable to McCleskey would not have received the death penalty if their victims had been black.

Furthermore, even examination of the sentencing system as a whole, factoring in those cases in which the jury exercises little discretion, indicates the influence of race on capital sentencing. For the Georgia system as a whole, race accounts for a six percentage point difference in the rate at which capital punishment is imposed. Since death is imposed in 11% of all white-victim cases, the rate in comparably aggravated black-victim cases is 5%. The rate of capital sentencing in a white-victim case is thus 120% greater than the rate in a black-victim case. Put another way, over half— 55%—of defendants in white-victim crimes in Georgia would not have been sentenced to die if their victims had been black. Of the more than 200 variables potentially relevant to a sentencing decision, race of the victim is a powerful explanation for variation in death sentence rates—as powerful as nonracial aggravating factors such as a prior murder conviction or acting as the principal planner of the homicide.

These adjusted figures are only the most conservative indication of the risk that race will influence the death sentences of defendants in Georgia. Data unadjusted for the mitigating or aggravating effect of other factors show an even more pronounced disparity by race. The capital sentencing rate for all white-victim cases was almost *11 times* greater than the rate for black-victim cases. Supp. Exh. 47. Furthermore, blacks who kill whites are sentenced to death at nearly *22 times* the rate of blacks who kill blacks, and more than *7 times* the rate of whites who kill blacks. *Ibid.* In addition, prosecutors seek the death penalty for 70% of black defendants with white victims, but for only 15% of black defendants with black victims, and only 19% of white defendants with black victims. Since our decision upholding the Georgia capital-sentencing system in *Gregg*, the State has executed 7 persons. All of the 7 were convicted of killing whites, and 6 of the 7 executed were black. Such execution figures are especially striking in light of the fact that, during the period encompassed by the Baldus study, only 9.2% of Georgia homicides involved black defendants and white victims, while 60.7% involved black victims.

McCleskey's statistics have particular force because most of them are the product of sophisticated multiple-regression analysis. Such analysis is designed precisely to identify patterns in the aggregate, even though we may not be able to reconstitute with certainty any individual decision that goes to make up that pattern. Multiple-regression analysis is particularly well-suited to identify the influence of impermissible considerations in sentencing, since it is able to control for permissible factors that may explain an apparent arbitrary pattern. While the decision-making process of a body such as a jury may be complex, the Baldus study provides a massive compilation of the details that are most relevant to that decision. . . .

The statistical evidence in this case thus relentlessly documents the risk that McCleskey's sentence was influenced by racial considerations. This evidence shows that there is a better than even chance in Georgia that race will influence the decision to impose the death penalty: a majority of defendants in white-victim crimes would not have been sentenced to die if their victims had been black. In determining whether this risk is acceptable, our judgment must be shaped by the awareness that "[t]he risk of racial prejudice infecting a capital sentencing proceeding is especially serious in light of the complete finality of the death sentence." . . .

Evaluation of McCleskey's evidence cannot rest solely on the numbers themselves. We must also ask whether the conclusion suggested by those numbers is consonant with our understanding of history and human experience. Georgia's legacy of a race-conscious criminal justice system, as well as this Court's own recognition of the persistent danger that racial attitudes may affect criminal proceedings, indicate that McCleskey's claim is not a fanciful product of mere statistical artifice.

For many years, Georgia operated openly and formally precisely the type of dual system the evidence shows is still effectively in place. The criminal law expressly differentiated between crimes committed by and against blacks and whites, distinctions whose lineage traced back to the time of slavery. During the colonial period, black slaves who killed whites in Georgia, regardless of whether in self-defense or in defense of another, were automatically executed. . . .

By the time of the Civil War, a dual system of crime and punishment was well established in Georgia. The state criminal code contained separate sections for "Slaves and Free Persons of Color," and for all other persons. . . .

Formal dual criminal laws may no longer be in effect, and intentional discrimination may no longer be prominent. Nonetheless, "subtle, less consciously held racial attitudes" continue to be of concern, and the Georgia system gives such attitudes considerable room to operate. The conclusions drawn from McCleskey's statistical evidence are therefore consistent with the lessons of social experience.

The majority thus misreads our Eighth Amendment jurisprudence in concluding that McCleskey has not demonstrated a degree of risk sufficient to raise constitutional concern. The determination of the significance of his evidence is at its core an exercise in human moral judgment, not a mechanical statistical analysis. It must first and foremost be informed by awareness of the fact that death is irrevocable, and that as a result "the qualitative difference of death from all other punishments requires a greater degree of scrutiny of the capital sentencing determination." For this reason, we have demanded a uniquely high degree of rationality in imposing the death penalty. A capital-sentencing system in which race more likely than not plays a role does not meet this standard. It is true that every nuance of decision cannot be statistically captured, nor can any individual judgment be plumbed with absolute certainty. Yet the fact that we must always act without the illumination of complete knowledge cannot induce paralysis when we confront what is literally an issue of life and death. Sentencing data, history, and experience all counsel that Georgia has provided insufficient assurance of the heightened rationality we have required in order to take a human life. . . .

Warren McCleskey's evidence confronts us with the subtle and persistent influence of the past. His message is a disturbing one to a society that has formally repudiated racism, and a frustrating one to a Nation accustomed to regarding its destiny as the product of its own will. Nonetheless, we ignore him at our peril, for we remain imprisoned by the past as long as we deny its influence in the present.

It is tempting to pretend that minorities on death row share a fate in no way connected to our own, that our treatment of them sounds no echoes beyond the chambers in which they die. Such an illusion is ultimately corrosive, for the reverberations of injustice are not so easily confined. "The destinies of the two races in this country are indissolubly linked together," and the way in which we choose those who will die reveals the depth of moral commitment among the living.

The Court's decision today will not change what attorneys in Georgia tell other Warren McCleskeys about their chances of execution. Nothing will soften the harsh message they must convey, nor alter the prospect that race undoubtedly will continue to be a topic of discussion. McCleskey's evidence will not have obtained judicial acceptance, but that will not affect what is said on death row. However many criticisms of today's decision may be rendered, these painful conversations will serve as the most eloquent dissents of all.

Payne v. Tennessee
501 U.S. 808, 111 S.Ct. 2597 (1991)

Pervis Payne, a borderline retarded man with no previous criminal record, was tried and convicted of stabbing to death a twenty-eight-year-old woman and her two-year-old daughter, as well as attempting to murder her three-year-old son. During closing arguments at his trial, the prosecutor asked the jury to impose the death sentence and told them, "There obviously is nothing you can do for Charisse or Lacie. But there is something you can do for Nicholas. . . . He is going to want to know what type of justice was done." Payne was sentenced to death and his attorney immediately appealed the sentence on the grounds that the trial judge impermissibly allowed the prosecution's use of victim-impact statements and failed to comply with the Court's rulings in *Booth v. Maryland*, 482 U.S. 496 (1987), and *South Carolina v. Gathers*, 490 U.S. 805 (1989). But when the Court granted review, it directed the attorneys specifically to address the question of whether *Booth* and *Gathers* should be overturned, even though neither party had raised that question in the original petitions and briefs.

The Court's decision was six to three. Chief Justice Rehnquist announced the majority's opinion, with which Justices O'Connor, Scalia, and Souter each concurred. Justice Blackmun joined dissents by Justices Marshall and Stevens.

☐ *Chief Justice REHNQUIST delivered the opinion of the Court.*

In this case we reconsider our holdings in *Booth v. Maryland*, 482 U.S. 496 (1987), and *South Carolina v. Gathers*, 490 U.S. 805 (1989), that the Eighth Amendment bars the admission of victim impact evidence during the penalty phase of a capital trial. . . .

Booth and *Gathers* were based on two premises: that evidence relating to a particular victim or to the harm that a capital defendant causes a victim's family do not in general reflect on the defendant's "blameworthiness," and that only evidence relating to "blameworthiness" is relevant to the capital sentencing decision. However, the assessment of harm caused by the defendant as a result of the crime charged has understandably been an important concern of the criminal law, both in determining the elements of the offense and in determining the appropriate punishment. Thus, two equally blameworthy criminal defendants may be guilty of different offenses solely because their acts cause differing amounts of harm. . . .

Payne echoes the concern voiced in Booth's case that the admission of victim impact evidence permits a jury to find that defendants whose victims were assets to their community are more deserving of punishment than those whose victims are perceived to be less worthy. As a general matter, however, victim impact evidence is not offered to encourage comparative judgments of this kind—for instance, that the killer of a hardworking, devoted parent deserves the death penalty, but that the murderer of a reprobate does not. It is designed to show instead each victim's "uniqueness as an individual human being," whatever the jury might think the loss to the community resulting from his death might be. . . .

Under our constitutional system, the primary responsibility for defining crimes against state law, fixing punishments for the commission of these crimes, and establishing procedures for criminal trials rests with the States. The state laws respecting crimes, punishments, and criminal procedure are of course subject to the overriding provisions of the United States Constitution. Where the State imposes the death penalty for a particular crime, we have held that the Eighth Amendment imposes special limitations upon that process.

First, there is a required threshold below which the death penalty cannot be imposed. In this context, the State must establish rational criteria that narrow the decisionmaker's judgment as to whether the circumstances of a particular defendant's case meet the threshold. Moreover, a societal consensus that the death penalty is disproportionate to a particular offense prevents a State from imposing the death penalty for that offense.

Second, States cannot limit the sentencer's consideration of any relevant circumstance that could cause it to decline to impose the penalty. In this respect, the State cannot challenge the sentencer's discretion, but must allow it to consider any relevant information offered by the defendant." *McCleskey v. Kemp*, 481 U.S. 279 (1987). But, as we noted in *California v. Ramos*, 463 U.S. 992 (1983), "[b]eyond these limitations . . . the Court has deferred to the State's choice of substantive factors relevant to the penalty determination." . . .

The States remain free, in capital cases, as well as others, to devise new procedures and new remedies to meet felt needs. Victim impact evidence is simply another form or method of informing the sentencing authority about the specific harm caused by the crime in question, evidence of a general type long considered by sentencing authorities. We think the *Booth* Court was wrong in stating that this kind of evidence leads to the arbitrary imposition of the death penalty. In the majority of cases, and in this case, victim impact evidence serves entirely legitimate purposes. In the event that evidence is introduced that is so unduly prejudicial that it renders the trial fundamentally unfair, the Due Process Clause of the Fourteenth Amendment provides a mechanism for relief. . . .

We thus hold that if the State chooses to permit the admission of victim impact evidence and prosecutional argument on that subject, the Eighth Amendment erects no per se bar. . . .

Stare decisis is not an inexorable command; rather, it "is a principle of policy and not a mechanical formula of adherence to the latest decision." *Helvering v. Hallock*, 309 U.S. 106 (1940). This is particularly true in constitutional cases, because in such cases "correction through legislative action is practically impossible." *Burnet v. Coronado Oil & Gas Co.*, [285 U.S. 393 (1932)] (BRANDEIS, J., dissenting). Considerations in favor of *stare decisis* are at their acme in cases involving property and contract rights, where reliance interests are involved, see *Swift & Co. v. Wickham*, 382 U.S. 111 (1965); *Burnet v. Coronado Oil & Gas Co., supra*; the opposite is true in cases such as the present one involving procedural and evidentiary rules.

Booth and *Gathers* were decided by the narrowest of margins, over spirited dissents challenging the basic underpinnings of those decisions. . . . Reconsidering these decisions now, we conclude for the reasons heretofore stated, that they were wrongly decided and should be, and now are, overruled. We accordingly affirm the judgment of the Supreme Court of Tennessee.

Affirmed.

☐ *Justice MARSHALL, with whom Justice BLACKMUN joins, dissenting.*

Power, not reason, is the new currency of this Court's decisionmaking. . . . Neither the law nor the facts supporting *Booth* and *Gathers* underwent any change in the last four years. Only the personnel of this Court did.

In dispatching *Booth* and *Gathers* to their graves, today's majority ominously suggests that an even more extensive upheaval of this Court's precedents may be in store. Renouncing this Court's historical commitment to a conception of "the judiciary as a source of impersonal and reasoned judgments," *Moragne v. States Marine Lines*, 398 U.S. 375 (1970), the majority declares itself free to discard any principle of constitutional liberty which was recognized or reaffirmed over the dissenting votes of four Justices and with which five or more Justices now disagree. The implications of this radical new exception to the doctrine of *stare decisis* are staggering. The majority today sends a clear signal that scores of established constitutional liberties are now ripe for reconsideration, thereby inviting the very type of open defiance of our precedents that the majority rewards in this case. Because I believe that this Court owes more to its constitutional precedents in general and to *Booth* and *Gathers* in particular, I dissent. . . .

[T]his Court has never departed from precedent without "special justification." *Arizona v. Rumsey*, 467 U.S. 203 (1984). Such justifications include the advent of "subsequent changes or development in the law" that undermine a decision's rationale, *Patterson v. McLean Credit Union*, [491 U.S. 164 (1989)]; the need "to bring [a decision] into agreement with experience and with facts newly ascertained," *Burnet, supra*; and a showing that a particular precedent has become a "detriment to coherence and consistency in the law," *Patterson*.

The majority cannot seriously claim that any of these traditional bases for overruling a precedent applies to *Booth* or *Gathers*. The majority does not suggest that the legal rationale of these decisions has been undercut by changes or developments in doctrine during the last two years. Nor does the majority claim that experience over that period of time has discredited the principle that "any decision to impose the death sentence be, and appear to be, based on reason rather than caprice or emotion," *Gardner v. Florida*, 430 U.S. 349 (1977) (plurality opinion), the larger postulate of political morality on which *Booth* and *Gathers* rest. . . .

It takes little real detective work to discern just what has changed since this Court decided *Booth* and *Gathers*: this Court's own personnel. . . .

In addition, the majority points out, "*Booth* and *Gathers* were decided by the narrowest of margins, over spirited dissents" and thereafter were "questioned by members of the Court." Taken together, these considerations make it legitimate, in the majority's view, to elevate the position of the *Booth* and *Gathers* dissenters into the law of the land.

This truncation of the Court's duty to stand by its own precedents is astonishing. By limiting full protection of the doctrine of *stare decisis* to "cases involving property and contract rights," the majority sends a clear signal that essentially all decisions implementing the personal liberties protected by the Bill of Rights and the Fourteenth Amendment are open to reexamination. Taking into account the majority's additional criterion for overruling—that a case either was decided or reaffirmed by a 5–4 margin "over spirited dissen[t],"—the continued vitality of literally scores of decisions must be understood to depend on nothing more than the proclivities of the individuals who now comprise a majority of this Court.* See, e.g., *Metro Broadcasting v. FCC*, [497 U.S. 547] (1990) (authority of Federal government to set aside broadcast licenses for minority applicants); *Grady v. Corbin*, [495 U.S. 508] (1990) (right under Double Jeopardy Clause not to be subjected twice

---

* Based on the majority's new criteria for overruling, these decisions, too, must be included on the "endangered precedents" list: *Rutan v. Republican Party of Illinois*, [497 U.S. 547] (1990) (First Amendment right not to be denied public employment on the basis of party affiliation); *Peel v. Attorney Registration and Disciplinary Comm'n*, [496 U.S. 91] (1990) (First Amendment right to advertise legal specialization); *Zinermon v. Burch*, 494 U.S. 113 (1990) (due process right to procedural safeguards aimed at assuring voluntariness of decision to commit oneself to mental hospital); *James v. Illinois*, 493 U.S. 307 (1990) (Fourth Amendment right to exclusion of illegally obtained evidence introduced for impeachment of defense witness); *Rankin v. McPherson*, 483 U.S. 378 (1987) (First Amendment right of public employee to express views on matter of public importance); *Rock v. Arkansas*, 483 U.S. 44 (1987) (Fifth Amendment and Sixth Amendment right of criminal defendant to provide hypnotically refreshed testimony on his own behalf); *Gray v. Mississippi*, 481 U.S. 648 (1987) (rejecting applicability of harmless error analysis to Eighth Amendment right not to be sentenced to death by "death qualified" jury); *Maine v. Moulton*, 474 U.S. 159 (1985) (Sixth Amendment right to counsel violated by introduction of statements made to government informant-codefendant in course of preparing defense strategy); *Garcia v. San Antonio Metropolitan Transit Auth.*, 469 U.S. 528 (1985) (rejecting theory that Tenth Amendment provides immunity to states from federal regulation); *Pulliam v. Allen*, 466 U.S. 522 (1984) (right to obtain injunctive relief from constitutional violations committed by judicial officials).

to prosecution for same criminal conduct); *Mills v. Maryland, supra* (Eighth Amendment right to jury instructions that do not preclude consideration of nonunanimous mitigating factors in capital sentencing); *United States v. Paradise*, 480 U.S. 149 (1987) (right to promotions as remedy for racial discrimination in government hiring); *Ford v. Wainwright*, 477 U.S. 399 (1986) (Eighth Amendment right not to be executed if insane); *Thornburgh v. American College of Obstetricians and Gynecologists*, 476 U.S. 747 (1986) (reaffirming right to abortion recognized in *Roe v. Wade*, 410 U.S. 113 (1973)); *Aguilar v. Felton*, 473 U.S. 402 (1985) (Establishment Clause bar on governmental financial assistance to parochial schools).

In my view, this impoverished conception of *stare decisis* cannot possibly be reconciled with the values that inform the proper judicial function. Contrary to what the majority suggests, *stare decisis* is important not merely because individuals rely on precedent to structure their commercial activity but because fidelity to precedent is part and parcel of a conception of "the judiciary as a source of impersonal and reasoned judgments."

Morgan v. Illinois

504 U.S. 719, 112 S.CT. 2222 (1992)

Derrick Morgan was convicted in Cook County, Illinois, of first-degree murder and sentenced to death. Prior to his trial, three separate venires were called before the jury was finally chosen. In accordance with Illinois law, the trial court, rather than the attorneys, conducted *voir dire* examination of the potential jurors. The prosecution in seeking capital punishment requested the judge to determine whether any potential juror would in all instances refuse to impose the death penalty upon conviction of the offense. The trial judge, over opposition from the defense, questioned each venire whether any member had moral or religious principles so strong that he or she could not impose the death penalty "regardless of the facts." Seventeen potential jurors were excused when they expressed substantial doubts about their ability to follow Illinois law in deciding whether to impose a sentence of death. All of the jurors eventually empaneled were also asked individually: "Would you automatically vote against the death penalty no matter what the facts of the case were?" After seven members of the first venire had been questioned, including three who eventually became jurors, petitioner's counsel requested the trial court to ask all prospective jurors the following question: "If you found Derrick Morgan guilty, would you automatically vote to impose the death penalty no matter what the facts are?" The trial court refused this request. Morgan was subsequently convicted and sentenced to death. On appeal, the Illinois Supreme Court affirmed his conviction and sentence, rejecting Morgan's claim that, pursuant to *Ross v. Oklahoma*, 487 U.S. 81 (1988), *voir dire* must include the "life qualifying" or "reverse-*Witherspoon*" question on the request of counsel. (In *Witherspoon v. Illinois*, 391 U.S. 510 (1968), the Court held that it was impermissible to exclude from capital cases potential jurors who opposed the imposition of capital punishment.) Morgan's attorney appealed that ruling to the Supreme Court of the United States.

The Court's decision was six to three; Justice White announced the majority's opinion. Justice Scalia's dissent was joined by Chief Justice Rehnquist and Justice Thomas.

☐ *Justice WHITE delivered the opinion of the Court.*

We decide here whether, during *voir dire* for a capital offense, a state trial court may, consistent with the Due Process Clause of the Fourteenth Amendment, refuse inquiry into whether a potential juror would automatically impose the death penalty upon conviction of the defendant. . . .

We have emphasized previously that there is not "any one right way for a State to set up its capital sentencing scheme," *Spaziano v. Florida*, 468 U.S. 447 (1984), and that no State is constitutionally required by the Sixth Amendment or otherwise to provide for jury determination of whether the death penalty shall be imposed on a capital defendant. Illinois has chosen, however, to delegate to the jury this task in the penalty phase of capital trials in addition to its duty to determine guilt or innocence of the underlying crime. The issue, therefore, is whether petitioner is entitled to relief under the Due Process Clause of the Fourteenth Amendment. We conclude that he is. . . .

[O]ur decisions dealing with capital sentencing juries and presenting issues most analogous to that which we decide here today, e.g., *Witherspoon v. Illinois*, 391 U.S. [510 (1968)]; *Adams v. Texas*, 448 U.S. 38 (1980); *Wainwright v. Witt*, 469 U.S. 412 (1985); *Ross v. Oklahoma*, 487 U.S. 81 (1988), have relied on the strictures dictated by the Sixth and Fourteenth Amendments to ensure the impartiality of any jury that will undertake capital sentencing.

Witt held that "the proper standard for determining when a prospective juror may be excused for cause because of his or her views on capital punishment . . . is whether the juror's views would 'prevent or substantially impair the performance of his duties as a juror in accordance with his instructions and his oath.' " Under this standard, it is clear from *Witt* and *Adams*, the progeny of *Witherspoon*, that a juror who in no case would vote for capital punishment, regardless of his or her instructions, is not an impartial juror and must be removed for cause.

Thereafter, in *Ross v. Oklahoma*, a state trial court refused to remove for cause a juror who declared he would vote to impose death automatically if the jury found the defendant guilty. That juror, however, was removed by the defendant's use of a peremptory challenge, and for that reason the death sentence could be affirmed. But in the course of reaching this result, we announced our considered view that because the Constitution guarantees a defendant on trial for his life the right to an impartial jury, the trial court's failure to remove the juror for cause was a constitutional error under the standard enunciated in *Witt*. . . .

We reiterate this view today. A juror who will automatically vote for the death penalty in every case will fail in good faith to consider the evidence of aggravating and mitigating circumstances as the instructions require him to do. Indeed, because such a juror has already formed an opinion on the merits, the presence or absence of either aggravating or mitigating circumstances is entirely irrelevant to such a juror. Therefore, based on the requirement of impartiality embodied in the Due Process Clause of the Fourteenth Amendment, a capital defendant may challenge for cause any prospective juror who maintains such views. If even one such juror is empaneled and the death sentence is imposed, the State is disentitled to execute the sentence. . . .

☐ *Justice SCALIA, with whom the CHIEF JUSTICE and Justice THOMAS join, dissenting.*

The Court today holds that a juror who will always impose the death penalty for capital murder is not "impartial" in the sense required by the Sixth Amendment; that the Constitution requires that voir dire directed to this specific "bias" be provided upon the defendant's request; and that the more general questions about "fairness" and ability to "follow the law" that were asked during voir dire in this case were inadequate. Because these conclusions seem to me jointly and severally wrong, I dissent. . . .

Even if I agreed with the Court . . . that jurors who will always advocate a death sentence for capital murder are not "impartial" and must be excused for cause, I would not agree with the further conclusion that the Constitution requires a trial court to make specific inquiries on this subject during *voir dire.* . . .

Atkins v. Virginia

536 U.S. 304, 122 S.CT. 2242 (2002)

In *Ford v. Wainwright,* 477 U.S. 399 (1986), the Court held that the Eighth Amendment bars the execution of death-row inmates who are (or who have gone while on death row) insane. However, in *Penry v. Lynaugh,* 492 U.S. 302 (1989), a bare majority upheld the execution of an individual who was mentally retarded. In her opinion for Court, Justice O'Connor emphasized that at the time only one state banned the execution of the mentally retarded and that even when added to the fourteen states that had rejected capital punishment that did "not provide sufficient evidence at present of a national consensus" against executing mentally retarded convicts. Subsequently, seventeen other states of the thirty-eight states that impose the death penalty enacted laws barring executions of the mentally retarded. And opponents of the death penalty continued to raise the issue in an effort to persuade the Court to reconsider the matter.

In 1998, Daryl Renard Atkins, who has an IQ of 59—that of a nine- to twelve-year-old—was convicted and sentenced to death for participating in the robbery and murder of a U.S. airman in Virginia. The Virginia Supreme Court affirmed his sentence and an appeal was made to the Supreme Court. Notably, a number of friend of court briefs highlighted the controversy and urged the Court to abandon its earlier ruling; among those filing *amicus* briefs were the European Union, the U.S. Catholic Conference, and the American Psychological Association.

The state supreme court's decision was reversed on a six-to-three vote and Justice Stevens delivered the opinion of the Court. Chief Justice Rehnquist and Justice Scalia filed dissenting opinions, which Justice Thomas joined.

☐ *Justice STEVENS delivers the opinion of the Court.*

Those mentally retarded persons who meet the law's requirements for criminal responsibility should be tried and punished when they commit crimes. Because of their disabilities in areas of reasoning, judgment, and control of their impulses, however, they do not act with the level of moral culpability that characterizes the most serious adult criminal conduct. Moreover, their impairments can jeopardize the reliability and fairness of capital proceedings against mentally retarded defendants. Presumably for these reasons, in the 13 years since we decided *Penry v. Lynaugh*, 492 U.S. 302 (1989), the American public, legislators, scholars, and judges have deliberated over the question whether the death penalty should ever be imposed on a mentally retarded criminal. The consensus reflected in those deliberations informs our answer to the question presented by this case: whether such executions are "cruel and unusual punishments" prohibited by the Eighth Amendment to the Federal Constitution. . . .

The Eighth Amendment succinctly prohibits "excessive" sanctions. . . . A claim that punishment is excessive is judged not by the standards that prevailed in 1685 when Lord Jeffreys presided over the "Bloody Assizes" or when the Bill of Rights was adopted, but rather by those that currently prevail. As CHIEF JUSTICE WARREN explained in his opinion in *Trop v. Dulles*, 356 U.S. 86 (1958): "The basic concept underlying the Eighth Amendment is nothing less than the dignity of man. . . . The Amendment must draw its meaning from the evolving standards of decency that mark the progress of a maturing society."

Proportionality review under those evolving standards should be informed by " 'objective factors to the maximum possible extent.' " We have pinpointed that the "clearest and most reliable objective evidence of contemporary values is the legislation enacted by the country's legislatures." *Penry*. Relying in part on such legislative evidence, we have held that death is an impermissibly excessive punishment for the rape of an adult woman, *Coker v. Georgia*, 433 U.S. 584 (1977), or for a defendant who neither took life, attempted to take life, nor intended to take life, *Enmund v. Florida*, 458 U.S. 782 (1982). In *Coker*, we focused primarily on the then-recent legislation that had been enacted in response to our decision 10 years earlier in *Furman v. Georgia*, 408 U.S. 238 (1972) (*per curiam*), to support the conclusion that the "current judgment," though "not wholly unanimous," weighed very heavily on the side of rejecting capital punishment as a "suitable penalty for raping an adult woman." The "current legislative judgment" relevant to our decision in *Enmund* was less clear than in *Coker* but "nevertheless weigh[ed] on the side of rejecting capital punishment for the crime at issue." . . .

Guided by our approach in these cases, we shall first review the judgment of legislatures that have addressed the suitability of imposing the death penalty on the mentally retarded and then consider reasons for agreeing or disagreeing with their judgment.

The parties have not called our attention to any state legislative consideration of the suitability of imposing the death penalty on mentally retarded offenders prior to 1986. In that year, the public reaction to the execution of a mentally retarded murderer in Georgia apparently led to the enactment of the first state statute prohibiting such executions. In 1988, when Congress enacted legislation reinstating the federal death penalty, it expressly provided that a "sentence of death shall not be carried out upon a person who is mentally retarded." In 1989, Maryland enacted a similar prohibition. It was in that year that we decided *Penry*, and concluded that those two state enactments, "even when added to the 14 States that have rejected capital punishment completely, do not provide sufficient evidence at present of a national consensus."

Much has changed since then. [S]tate legislatures across the country began to address the issue. In 1990 Kentucky and Tennessee enacted statutes similar to those in Georgia and Maryland, as did New Mexico in 1991, and Arkansas, Colorado, Washington, Indiana, and Kansas in 1993 and 1994. In 1995, when New York reinstated its death penalty, it emulated the Federal Government by expressly exempting the mentally retarded. Nebraska followed suit in 1998. There appear to have been no similar enactments during the next two years, but in 2000 and 2001 six more States—South Dakota, Arizona, Connecticut, Florida, Missouri, and North Carolina—joined the procession. The Texas Legislature unanimously adopted a similar bill, and bills have passed at least one house in other States, including Virginia and Nevada.

It is not so much the number of these States that is significant, but the consistency of the direction of change. Given the well-known fact that anti-crime legislation is far more popular than legislation providing protections for persons guilty of violent crime, the large number of States prohibiting the execution of mentally retarded persons (and the complete absence of States passing legislation reinstating the power to conduct such executions) provides powerful evidence that today our society views mentally retarded offenders as categorically less culpable than the average criminal. . . .

To the extent there is serious disagreement about the execution of mentally retarded offenders, it is in determining which offenders are in fact retarded. In this case, for instance, the Commonwealth of Virginia disputes that Atkins suffers from mental retardation. Not all people who claim to be mentally retarded will be so impaired as to fall within the range of mentally retarded offenders about whom there is a national consensus. As was our approach in *Ford v. Wainwright*, with regard to insanity, "we leave to the State[s] the task of developing appropriate ways to enforce the constitutional restriction upon its execution of sentences." . . .

[O]ur death penalty jurisprudence provides two reasons consistent with the legislative consensus that the mentally retarded should be categorically excluded from execution. First, there is a serious question as to whether either justification that we have recognized as a basis for the death penalty applies to mentally retarded offenders. *Gregg v. Georgia*, 428 U.S. 153 (1976), identified "retribution and deterrence of capital crimes by prospective offenders" as the social purposes served by the death penalty. Unless the imposition of the death penalty on a mentally retarded person "measurably contributes to one or both of these goals, it 'is nothing more than the purposeless and needless imposition of pain and suffering,' and hence an unconstitutional punishment." *Enmund.*

With respect to retribution—the interest in seeing that the offender gets his "just deserts"—the severity of the appropriate punishment necessarily depends on the culpability of the offender. Since Gregg, our jurisprudence has consistently confined the imposition of the death penalty to a narrow category of the most serious crimes. For example, in *Godfrey v. Georgia*, 446 U.S. 420 (1980), we set aside a death sentence because the petitioner's crimes did not reflect "a consciousness materially more 'depraved' than that of any person guilty of murder." If the culpability of the average murderer is insufficient to justify the most extreme sanction available to the State, the lesser culpability of the mentally retarded offender surely does not merit that form of retribution. Thus, pursuant to our narrowing jurisprudence, which seeks to ensure that only the most deserving of execution are put to death, an exclusion for the mentally retarded is appropriate.

With respect to deterrence—the interest in preventing capital crimes by prospective offenders—"it seems likely that 'capital punishment can serve as a deterrent only when murder is the result of premeditation and deliberation,'" *Enmund*. Exempting the mentally retarded from that punishment will not affect the "cold calculus that precedes the decision" of other potential murderers. Indeed, that sort of calculus is at the opposite end of the spectrum from behavior of mentally retarded offenders. . . . Nor will exempting the mentally retarded from execution lessen the deterrent effect of the death penalty with respect to offenders who are not mentally retarded. Such individuals are unprotected by the exemption and will continue to face the threat of execution. Thus, executing the mentally retarded will not measurably further the goal of deterrence. . . .

The judgment of the Virginia Supreme Court is reversed and the case is remanded for further proceedings not inconsistent with this opinion. It is so ordered.

□ *Justice SCALIA, with whom the CHIEF JUSTICE and Justice THOMAS join, dissenting.*

Today's decision is the pinnacle of our Eighth Amendment death-is-different jurisprudence. Not only does it, like all of that jurisprudence, find no support in the text or history of the Eighth Amendment; it does not even have support in current social attitudes regarding the conditions that render an otherwise just death penalty inappropriate. Seldom has an opinion of this Court rested so obviously upon nothing but the personal views of its members. . . .

The Court makes no pretense that execution of the mildly mentally retarded would have been considered "cruel and unusual" in 1791. Only the severely or profoundly mentally retarded, commonly known as "idiots," enjoyed any special status under the law at that time. They, like lunatics, suffered a "deficiency in will" rendering them unable to tell right from wrong. W. Blackstone, *Commentaries on the Laws of England* (1769). Due to their incompetence, idiots were "excuse[d] from the guilt, and of course from the punishment, of any criminal action committed under such deprivation of the senses." Instead, they were often committed to civil confinement or made wards of the State, thereby preventing them from "go[ing] loose, to the terror of the king's subjects." Mentally retarded offenders with less severe impairments—those who were not "idiots"—suffered criminal prosecution and punishment, including capital punishment.

The Court is left to argue, therefore, that execution of the mildly retarded is inconsistent with the "evolving standards of decency that mark the progress of a maturing society." *Trop v. Dulles*. Before today, our opinions consistently emphasized that Eighth Amendment judgments regarding the existence of social "standards" "should be informed by objective factors to the maximum possible extent" and "should not be, or appear to be, merely the subjective views of individual Justices." *Coker v. Georgia*.

The Court pays lipservice to these precedents as it miraculously extracts a "national consensus" forbidding execution of the mentally retarded from the fact that 18 States—less than half (47%) of the 38 States that permit capital punishment (for whom the issue exists)—have very recently enacted legislation barring execution of the mentally retarded. Even that 47% figure is a distorted one. If one is to say, as the Court does today, that all executions of the mentally retarded are so morally repugnant as to violate our national "standards of decency," surely the "consensus" it points to must be one that has set its righteous face against all such executions. Not 18 States, but only seven—18% of death penalty jurisdictions—have legislation of that scope. Eleven of those that the Court counts enacted statutes prohibiting execution of mentally retarded defendants convicted after, or convicted of crimes committed after, the effective date of the legislation; those already on death row, or consigned there before the statute's effective date, or even (in those States using the date of the crime as the criterion of retroactivity) tried in the future for murders committed many years ago, could be put to death. That is not a statement of absolute moral repugnance, but one of current preference between two tolerable approaches. . . .

But let us accept, for the sake of argument, the Court's faulty count. That bare number of States alone—18—should be enough to convince any reasonable person that no "national consensus" exists. How is it possible that agreement among 47% of the death penalty jurisdictions amounts to "consensus"? Our prior cases have generally required a much higher degree of agreement before finding a punishment cruel and unusual on "evolving standards" grounds. . . .

Moreover, a major factor that the Court entirely disregards is that the legislation of all 18 States it relies on is still in its infancy. The oldest of the statutes is only 14 years old; five were enacted last year; over half were enacted within the past eight years. Few, if any, of the States have had sufficient experience with these laws to know whether they are sensible in the long term. . . .

The Court's thrashing about for evidence of "consensus" includes reliance upon the margins by which state legislatures have enacted bans on execution of the retarded. Presumably, in applying our Eighth Amendment "evolving-standards-of-decency" jurisprudence, we will henceforth weight not only how many States have agreed, but how many States have agreed by how much. Of course if the percentage of legislators voting for the bill is significant, surely the number of people represented by the legislators voting for the bill is also significant: the fact that 49% of the legislators in a State with a population of 60 million voted against the bill should be more impressive than the fact that 90% of the legislators in a state with a population of 2 million voted for it. (By the way, the population of the death penalty States that exclude the mentally retarded is only 44% of the population of all death penalty States.) This is quite absurd. . . .

But the Prize for the Court's Most Feeble Effort to fabricate "national consensus" must go to its appeal (deservedly relegated to a footnote) to the views of assorted professional and religious organizations, members of the so-called "world community," and respondents to opinion polls. I agree with the CHIEF JUSTICE that the views of professional and religious organizations and the results of opinion polls are irrelevant. Equally irrelevant are the practices of the "world community," whose notions of justice are (thankfully) not always those of our people. . . .

Today's opinion adds one more to the long list of substantive and procedural requirements impeding imposition of the death penalty imposed under this Court's assumed power to invent a death-is-different jurisprudence. None of those requirements existed when the Eighth Amendment was adopted, and some of them were not even supported by current moral consensus. . . .

This newest invention promises to be more effective than any of the others in turning the process of capital trial into a game. One need only read the definitions of mental retardation adopted by the American Association of Mental Retardation and the American Psychiatric Association to realize that the symptoms of this condition can readily be feigned. And whereas the capital defendant who feigns insanity risks commitment to a mental institution until he can be cured (and then tried and executed), *Jones v. United States*, 463 U.S. 354 (1983), the capital defendant who feigns mental retardation risks nothing at all. The mere pendency of the present case has brought us petitions by death row inmates claiming for the first time, after multiple *habeas* petitions, that they are retarded. . . .

☐ *CHIEF JUSTICE REHNQUIST, with whom Justice SCALIA and Justice THOMAS join, dissenting.*

I agree with Justice SCALIA that the Court's assessment of the current legislative judgment regarding the execution of defendants like petitioner more resembles a post hoc rationalization for the majority's subjectively preferred result rather than any objective effort to ascertain the content of an evolving standard of decency. I write separately, however, to call attention to the defects in the Court's decision to place weight on foreign laws, the views of professional and religious organizations, and opinion polls in reaching its conclusion. The Court's suggestion that these sources are relevant to the constitutional question finds little support in our precedents and, in my view, is antithetical to considerations of federalism, which instruct that any "permanent prohibition upon all units of democratic government must [be apparent] in the operative acts (laws and the application of laws) that the people have approved." *Stanford v. Kentucky*, 492 U.S. 361 (1989).

[T]wo sources—the work product of legislatures and sentencing jury determinations—ought to be the sole indicators by which courts ascertain the contemporary American conceptions of decency for purposes of the Eighth Amendment. They are the only objective indicia of contemporary values firmly supported by our precedents. More importantly, however, they can be reconciled with the undeniable precepts that the democratic branches of government and individual sentencing juries are, by design, better suited than courts to evaluating and giving effect to the complex societal and moral considerations that inform the selection of publicly acceptable criminal punishments.

In reaching its conclusion today, the Court . . . adverts to the fact that other countries have disapproved imposition of the death penalty for crimes committed by mentally retarded offenders (citing the Brief for The European Union as *Amicus Curiae* in *McCarver v. North Carolina*, O. T. 2001, No. 00-8727). I fail to see, however, how the views of other countries regarding the punishment of their citizens provide any support for the Court's ultimate determination. While it is true that some of our prior opinions have looked to "the climate of international opinion," *Coker*, to reinforce a conclusion regarding evolving standards of decency; we have since explicitly rejected the idea that the sentencing practices of other countries could "serve to establish the first Eighth Amendment prerequisite, that [a] practice is accepted among our people." *Stanford* (emphasizing that "American conceptions of decency . . . are dispositive"). . . .

There are strong reasons for limiting our inquiry into what constitutes an evolving standard of decency under the Eighth Amendment to the laws passed by legislatures and the practices of sentencing juries in America. Here, the Court goes beyond these well-established objective indicators of contemporary values. It finds "further support to [its] conclusion" that a national consensus has developed against imposing the death penalty on all mentally retarded defendants in international opinion, the views of professional and religious organizations, and opinion polls not demonstrated to be reliable. Believing this view to be seriously mistaken, I dissent.

■ THE DEVELOPMENT OF LAW

*Other Post-*Furman *Rulings on Capital Punishment*

CASE	VOTE	RULING
Gregg v. Georgia, 428 U.S. 153 (1976) *Jurek v. Texas*, 428 U.S. 262 (1976) *Profflitt v. Florida*, 428 U.S. 242 (1976)	7:2	Capital punishment not *per se* unconstitutional, but statutes must specify the aggravating factors (for which juries may impose death sentences) and the mitigating factors (which juries must consider in deciding whether or not to impose a death sentence); bifurcated trials were upheld.
Woodson v. North Carolina, 428 U.S. 280 (1976), and *Roberts v. Louisiana*, 428 U.S. 325 (1976)	5:4 6:3	Mandatory death sentences for certain crimes held impermissible.
Roberts v. Louisiana, 431 U.S. 633 (1977)	6:3	Held unconstitutional mandatory death sentences for the crime of killing a police officer where juries are not permitted to consider mitigating circumstances.
Coker v. Georgia, 433 U.S. 548 (1977)	6:3	Held that capital punishment is disproportionate for the crime of rape.
Lockett v. Ohio, 438 U.S. 586 (1978), and *Bell v. Ohio*, 438 U.S. 637 (1978)	6:3 7:2	Held that states may not limit the mitigating factors juries consider in imposing the death sentence; must allow for individualized sentencing.
Enmund v. Florida, 458 U.S. 782 (1982)	5:4	Held that the Eighth Amendment forbids the imposition of capital punishment on those who aid and abet, but do not commit, a felony in which a murder is also committed.
Barefoot v. Estelle, 463 U.S. 880 (1983)	6:3	Held that federal courts may use special, speeded-up procedures for handling appeals by death-row inmates.

CASE	VOTE	RULING
Pulley v. Harris, 465 U.S. 37 (1984)	7:2	Held that the Eighth Amendment does not require state appellate courts to review for proportionality the imposition of capital punishment.
Ford v. Wainwright, 477 U.S. 399 (1986)	6:3	Held that Eighth Amendment bars execution of convict who is (or has gone) insane while on death row.
McCleskey v. Kemp, 481 U.S. 279 (1987)	5:4	Held that studies showing that blacks who murder whites receive the death penalty more often than whites who murder blacks does not show that decision makers are racially biased and hence imposition of capital punishment is not unconstitutional.
Sumner v. Shuman, 483 U.S. 66 (1987)	6:3	Struck down statute imposing mandatory death sentences for prison inmates convicted of murder while serving life sentences.
Thompson v. Oklahoma, 487 U.S. 815 (1988)	5:3	Eighth Amendment forbids the execution of convicted murderers who were fifteen years old or younger at the time of their crimes.
Hildwin v. Florida, 490 U.S. 638 (1989)	7:2	States do not have to require juries to specify the aggravating factors for which they impose the death penalty.
Penry v. Lynaugh, 492 U.S. 304 (1989)	5:4	Upheld the imposition of capital punishment of convicted murderers who are mildly or moderately retarded.
Stanford v. Kentucky, 492 U.S. 361 (1989); and *Wilkins v. Missouri*, 492 U.S. 361(1989)	5:4	The death penalty may be imposed on convicted murderers who were sixteen or older at the time of their crimes.
Blystone v. Pennsylvania, 494 U.S. 299	5:4	Upheld Pennsylvania's law mandating the death penalty for certain crimes, when a jury finds no mitigating circumstances and at least one aggravating circumstance for the imposition of a capital punishment sentence.

CASE	VOTE	RULING
Boyde v. California, 494 U.S. 370 (1990)	5:4	Held that the Eighth Amendment was not violated by a state's requiring that juries be

instructed that they "shall impose" the death penalty if they conclude that aggravating circumstances outweigh the mitigating circumstances for the imposition of a death sentence.

McKoy v. North Carolina, 494 U.S. 433 (1990)	6:3	Struck down a state statute allowing juries to weigh only those mitigating factors that

were unanimously agreed to by a jury for impermissibly limiting juries consideration of mitigating factors bearing on its decision to impose the death penalty.

Walton v. Arizona, 497 U.S. 639 (1990)	5:4	Upheld Arizona's law permitting judges, rather than juries, to determine whether the pun-

ishment for first-degree murder should be death or life in prison; Justices Brennan, Marshall, Blackmun, and Stevens dissented.

McCleskey v. Zant, 499 U.S. 467 (1991)	6:3	Set forth a new standard for federal courts' review of successive writ of *habeas corpus* appeals

from death-row inmates by redefining the "abuse of writ" doctrine. After an inmate's first *habeas* petition, subsequent ones may be automatically dismissed as abusive, unless the petitioner shows (1) that there was "cause" for not raising the claim in earlier petitions, and (2) that the inmate suffered "actual prejudice" as a result of the alleged constitutional violation.

Payne v. Tennessee, 501 U.S. 808 (1991)	6:3	Overturned earlier rulings in *Booth v. Maryland*, 482 U.S. 496 (1987), and *South Carolina v.*

Gathers, 490 U.S. 805 (1989), and upheld the use of so-called "victim-impact statements" at the sentencing stage of capital cases. Justices Marshall, Blackmun, and Stevens dissented.

Lankford v. Idaho, 500 U.S. 110 (1991)	5:4	By a five-to-four vote, the Court held that judges may not impose the death sentence after

prosecutors decide not to seek capital punishment.

Morgan v. Illinois, 504 U.S. 719 (1992)	6:3	Held that a defendant's attorney must be permitted to ask prospective jurors whether they

would automatically favor the death penalty, in the event that they convict the defendant. The majority held that the denial of the defendant's request to so question potential jurors violated the Fourteenth Amendment's guarantee

CASE	VOTE	RULING

of due process; Chief Justice Rehnquist and Justices Scalia and Thomas dissented.

Sawyer v. Whitley, 505 U.S. 333   9:0   Held that a defendant bringing
(1992)   a successive *habeas corpus* claim
of "actual innocence" must
show by "clear and convincing evidence" that, but for a constitutional error
at the trial or sentencing, no reasonable juror would have found the defendant eligible for the death sentence.

Herrera v. Collins, 506 U.S. 390   6:3   Held that a defendant who is
(1993)   sentenced to death and belatedly presents new evidence of
his innocence is not ordinarily entitled to a new trial. Writing for the majority, Chief Justice Rehnquist conceded that "truly persuasive" evidence with
an "extraordinarily high" chance of success might warrant in some cases an
exception to that general rule. Rehnquist also rejected Lionel Herrera's argument that Texas's limitation for thirty days for filing for new trials violated
the Fourteenth Amendment's due process clause. That limitation on appeals
for new trials, in Rehnquist's words, does not "transgress a principle of fundamental fairness rooted in the traditions and conscience of our people." By
contrast, dissenting Justice Blackmun, joined by Justices Souter and Stevens,
countered that it "shocks the conscience" and is contrary to "any standard of
decency" to execute someone who can "show that he is probably innocent."

Schlup v. Delo, 513 U.S. 298   5:4   Justice Stevens laid down a new
(1995)   standard for federal courts'
granting *habeas corpus* relief in
cases of death-row inmates claiming "actual innocence." Writing for a bare
majority, Justice Stevens held that inmates who claim their execution would
be a "miscarriage of justice" must show only that "a constitutional violation
has probably resulted in the conviction of one who is actually innocent."
Chief Justice Rehnquist and Justices Kennedy, Scalia, and Thomas dissented.

Kyles v. Whitley, 514 U.S. 419   5:4   Writing for a bare majority, Jus-
(1995)   tice Souter held that death-row
inmates may challenge their
convictions on the ground that the prosecution wrongly suppressed evidence
favorable to their defense when the cumulative effect of the withholding
constitutes a denial of due process and there is a "reasonable probability" that
the disclosure of the exculpatory evidence would have resulted in a different
trial outcome. Chief Justice Rehnquist and Justices Kennedy, Scalia, and
Thomas dissented.

Felker v. Turpin, 518 U.S. 651   9:0   Writing for a unanimous
(1996)   Court, Chief Justice Rehnquist
upheld the provisions of the

CASE	VOTE	RULING

Antiterrorism and Effective Death Penalty Act of 1996. That law limits state prisoners' filing second or successive applications for writs of *habeas corpus* if no new claim is presented. The act also creates a "gatekeeping" mechanism in requiring a three-judge panel to review an inmate's second or successive *habeas* applications and authorizes their denial without the possibility of further appeal.

Calderon v. Coleman, 525 U.S. 141 (1998) 5:4

In an unsigned opinion, a bare majority made it more difficult for federal courts to reverse state death-row inmates' sentences because of a constitutional error. Here, a death-row inmate challenged the constitutionality of his sentence on the ground that the judge failed to instruct jurors that the governor could not reduce a sentence without the approval of four state supreme court justices, but instead told them that the governor had the power to commute a life sentence to a lesser one. The majority emphasized that "the social costs of retrial and resentencing are significant." Justices Breyer, Ginsburg, Souter, and Stevens dissented.

Williams v. Taylor, 529 U.S. 420 (2000) 9:0

Justice Kennedy held that under the Antiterrorism and Effective Death Penalty Act of 1996, limiting federal court *habeas corpus* review, Michael Williams and other death row inmates may raise issues in federal appeals for which they were unable to develop enough information to bring up during state court proceedings, if they were diligent in seeking the information.

Shafer v. South Carolina, 532 U.S. 36 (2001) 7:2

Writing for the Court, Justice Ginsburg held that whenever future dangerousness of the defendant in a capital case is an issue, the defendant has a right to have the sentencing jury informed that he would not be eligible for parole if sentenced to life imprisonment. Justices Scalia and Thomas dissented.

Kelly v. South Carolina, 534 U.S. 246 (2002) 5:4

Writing for the Court, Justice Souter held that, when prosecutors introduce evidence showing future violent propensities of a convict, due process requires a jury instruction that instead of a death sentence, a sentence of life-time imprisonment would be imposed without the possibility of parole.

Ring v. Arizona, 536 U.S. 584 (2002) 7:2

Writing for the Court, Justice Ginsburg struck Arizona's law and those in four other states— Colorado, Idaho, Montana, and Nebraska—permitting judges alone, and not juries, to decide whether "aggravating" factors in a murder warrant the im-

CASE	VOTE	RULING

position of capital punishment. That death-penalty statute was deemed to violate the Sixth Amendment right to a jury trial and to its determination of the facts in a case. In so ruling, the Court extended *Apprendi v. New Jersey*, 530 U.S. 466 (2000), which invalidated a state law permitting judges to hand down longer sentences for "hate crimes," and overturned a prior decision. Chief Justice Rehnquist and Justice O'Connor dissented.

Miller-El v. Cockrell, 537 U.S. 322 (2003)	8:1	Justice Kennedy held that a death row inmate should be allowed to apply for a writ of

habeas corpus based on a claim that the prosecutor's office was historically "suffused with bias" in excluding blacks from juries. Justice Thomas dissented on the ground that evidence of historical bias was "entirely circumstantial" and not "clear and convincing."

Banks v. Dretke, 124 S.Ct. 1256 (2004)	7:2	Writing for the Court, Justice Ginsburg held that a death row inmate was entitled to appeal

his death sentence because at his trial the prosecution withheld evidence that his attorney could have used to discredit a key prosecution witness. Dissenting Justices Scalia and Thomas agreed, but disagreed with the majority's overturning of the death sentence.

Schriro v. Summerlin, 124 S.Ct. 2519 (2004)	5:4	Writing for the Court, Justice Scalia held that the ruling in *Ring v. Arizona*, 536 U.S. 584

(2002), holding that the Sixth Amendment requires juries (not judges) to determine the aggravating circumstances for imposing death sentences, was a new procedural rule and that such rules do not apply retroactively to death sentences that are already final, unless they are fundamental and likely to diminish the chance of an accurate conviction.

■ In Comparative Perspective

The South African Constitutional Court Declares Capital Punishment Unconstitutional

In June 17, 1995, the Constitutional Court of the Republic of South Africa declared capital punishment to violate the provisional 1993 Constitution, which was subsequently superceded by the Constitution of 1996. The decision, in *The State v. T Makwanyane and M Mchunu*, 1995 (3)SA 391

(Const. Ct.), was unanimous, though there were ten concurring opinions filed along with President Chaskalson's opinion for the Court, for a total of 130 pages. In the excerpt below, note President Chaskalson's approach to constitutional interpretation and reliance on comparative constitutional law.

President CHASKALSON:

[2] Section 277(1)(a) of the Criminal Procedure Act No. 51 of 1977 prescribes that the death penalty is a competent sentence for murder. Counsel for the accused was invited by the Appellate Division to consider whether this provision was consistent with the Republic of South Africa Constitution, 1993, which had come into force subsequent to the conviction and sentence by the trial court. He argued that it was not, contending that it was in conflict with the provisions of sections 9 and 11(2) of the Constitution. . . .

[8] Chapter Three of the Constitution sets out the fundamental rights to which every person is entitled under the Constitution and also contains provisions dealing with the way in which the Chapter is to be interpreted by the Courts. It does not deal specifically with the death penalty, but in section 11(2), it prohibits "cruel, inhuman or degrading treatment or punishment." There is no definition of what is to be regarded as "cruel, inhuman or degrading" and we therefore have to give meaning to these words ourselves. . . .

[27] The principal arguments advanced by counsel for the accused in support of their contention that the imposition of the death penalty for murder is a "cruel, inhuman or degrading punishment," were that the death sentence is an affront to human dignity, is inconsistent with the unqualified right to life entrenched in the Constitution, cannot be corrected in case of error or enforced in a manner that is not arbitrary, and that it negates the essential content of the right to life and the other rights that flow from it. The Attorney General argued that the death penalty is recognised as a legitimate form of punishment in many parts of the world, it is a deterrent to violent crime, it meets society's need for adequate retribution for heinous offences, and it is regarded by South African society as an acceptable form of punishment. He asserted that it is, therefore, not cruel, inhuman or degrading within the meaning of section 11(2) of the Constitution. These arguments for and against the death sentence are well known and have been considered in many of the foreign authorities and cases to which we were referred. We must deal with them now in the light of the provisions of our own Constitution. . . .

[33] The death sentence is a form of punishment which has been used throughout history by different societies. It has long been the subject of controversy. As societies became more enlightened, they restricted the offences for which this penalty could be imposed. The movement away from the death penalty gained momentum during the second half of the present century with the growth of the abolitionist movement. . . . According to Amnesty International,

1,831 executions were carried out throughout the world in 1993 as a result of sentences of death, of which 1,419 were in China, which means that only 412 executions were carried out in the rest of the world in that year. Today, capital punishment has been abolished as a penalty for murder either specifically or in practice by almost half the countries of the world including the democracies of Europe and our neighbouring countries, Namibia, Mozambique and Angola. In most of those countries where it is retained, as the Amnesty International statistics show, it is seldom used. . . .

[40] The earliest litigation on the validity of the death sentence seems to have been pursued in the courts of the United States of America. . . . Statutes providing for mandatory death sentences, or too little discretion in sentencing, have been rejected by the Supreme Court because they do not allow for consideration of factors peculiar to the convicted person facing sentence, which may distinguish his or her case from other cases. For the same reason, statutes which allow too wide a discretion to judges or juries have also been struck down on the grounds that the exercise of such discretion leads to arbitrary results. In sum, therefore, if there is no discretion, too little discretion, or an unbounded discretion, the provision authorising the death sentence has been struck down as being contrary to the Eighth Amendment; where the discretion has been "suitably directed and limited so as to minimise the risk of wholly arbitrary and capricious action," the challenge to the statute has failed. . . .

[47] There seems to me to be little difference between the guided discretion required for the death sentence in the United States, and the criteria laid down by the Appellate Division for the imposition of the death sentence. The fact that the Appellate Division, a court of experienced judges, takes the final decision in all cases is, in my view, more likely to result in consistency of sentencing, than will be the case where sentencing is in the hands of jurors who are offered statutory guidance as to how that discretion should be exercised.

[48] The argument that the imposition of the death sentence under section 277 is arbitrary and capricious does not, however, end there. It also focuses on what is alleged to be the arbitrariness inherent in the application of section 277 in practice. Of the thousands of persons put on trial for murder, only a very small percentage are sentenced to death by a trial court, and of those, a large number escape the ultimate penalty on appeal. At every stage of the process there is an element of chance. The outcome may be dependent upon factors such as the way the case is investigated by the police, the way the case is presented by the procurator, how effectively the accused is defended, the personality and particular attitude to capital punishment of the trial judge and, if the matter goes on appeal, the particular judges who are selected to hear the case. Race and poverty are also alleged to be factors. . . .

[58] Under our constitutional order the right to human dignity

is specifically guaranteed. It can only be limited by legislation which passes the stringent test of being 'necessary.' The weight given to human dignity by Justice BRENNAN is wholly consistent with the values of our Constitution and the new order estabished by it. It is also consistent with the approach to extreme punishments followed by courts in other countries.

[59] In Germany, the Federal Constitutional Court has stressed this aspect of punishment. "Respect for human dignity especially requires the prohibition of cruel, inhuman, and degrading punishments. [The state] cannot turn the offender into an object of crime prevention to the detriment of his constitutionally protected right to social worth and respect." [*Life Imprisonment Case* [1977] 45 BverfGE 187]. . . .

[80] The unqualified right to life vested in every person by section 9 of our Constitution is another factor crucially relevant to the question whether the death sentence is cruel, inhuman or degrading punishment within the meaning of section 11(2) of our Constitution. In this respect our Constitution differs materially from the Constitutions of the United States and India. . . .

[95] The carrying out of the death sentence destroys life, which is protected without reservation under section 9 of our Constitution, it annihilates human dignity which is protected under section 10, elements of arbitrariness are present in its enforcement and it is irremediable. Taking these factors into account . . . and giving the words of section 11(2) the broader meaning to which they are entitled at this stage of the enquiry, rather than a narrow meaning, I am satisfied that in the context of our Constitution the death penalty is indeed a cruel, inhuman and degrading punishment. . . .

[144] The rights to life and dignity are the most important of all human rights, and the source of all other personal rights in Chapter Three. By committing ourselves to a society founded on the recognition of human rights we are required to value these two rights above all others. And this must be demonstrated by the State in everything that it does, including the way it punishes criminals. This is not achieved by objectifying murderers and putting them to death to serve as an example to others in the expectation that they might possibly be deterred thereby. . . .

11

THE RIGHT OF PRIVACY

A right of privacy is not specifically provided for in the Constitution or the Bill of Rights. Yet both embody the principle of limited government and hence the idea that individuals in some degree enjoy a "right to be let alone." As Justice Louis Brandeis, dissenting from the Court's initial denial of Fourth Amendment protection against wiretaps in *Olmstead v. United States* (1928) (see Ch. 7), observed:

> The makers of our Constitution undertook to secure conditions favorable to the pursuit of happiness. They recognized the significance of man's spiritual nature, of his feelings and of his intellect. They knew that only part of the pain, pleasure, and satisfactions of life are to be found in material things. They sought to protect Americans in their beliefs, their thoughts, their emotions and their sensations. They conferred as against the Government, the right to be let alone—the most comprehensive of rights and the right most valued by civilized man.

Neither common law nor constitutional law, however, recognized a right of privacy until the late nineteenth century. In his treatise *The Law of Torts* (1888), Judge Thomas Cooley planted the seed for the development of a right of privacy by noting for the first time a right to be let alone. Two years later, writing in the *Harvard Law Review*, Samuel Warren and Louis Brandeis cultivated the idea by arguing that common-law protection for property rights was evolving toward a "recognition of man's spiritual nature."[1] Their analysis of privacy as the right to be let alone sparked the development of a right of privacy in tort law (law dealing with private injuries, such as the public revelations of embarrassing personal facts and the appropriation for commercial purposes of an individual's name or likeness). Between 1890 and 1941, state courts in twelve states recognized a right of privacy; the number increased to eighteen by 1956 and then to more than thirty-one states by 1960.[2]

The Supreme Court initially acknowledged protection for privacy interests under the Fourth and Fifth Amendments in *Boyd v. United States*, 116 U.S. 616 (1886) (see Ch. 7), when holding that those amendments apply "to all invasions on the part of the government and its employees of the sanctity of a man's home and the privacies of life. It is not the breaking of his doors, and the rummaging of his drawers, that constitutes the essence of the offense, but it is the invasion of his indefeasible right of personal security, personal liberty and private property." Subsequently, the Court incorporated an analysis of individuals' "reasonable expectations of privacy" into Fourth Amendment jurisprudence. *Katz v. United States*, 389 U.S. 347 (1967) (see Ch. 7), and *Terry v. Ohio*, 392 U.S. 1 (1968) (see Ch. 7), for example, reaffirmed that "wherever an individual may harbor a reasonable 'expectation of privacy,' . . . he is entitled to be free from unreasonable governmental intrusion," when explaining that "the specific content and incidents of this right [of privacy] must be shaped by the context in which it is asserted."

In a series of other rulings, the Court also acknowledged protection for privacy interests under the Fifth Amendment (see Ch. 8). In addition, by the 1960s the Court had also affirmed First Amendment protection for privacy interests. As early as 1920, Justice Brandeis, dissenting from the Court's upholding of a law forbidding the teaching and advocacy of pacifism in *Gilbert v. Minnesota*, 254 U.S. 352 (1920), contended that the amendment protects "the privacy and freedom of the home. Father and mother may follow the promptings of religious belief, of conscience or of conviction, and teach son or daughter the doctrine of pacifism." When holding that individuals may possess obscenity in their homes in *Stanley v. Georgia* (1969) (see Ch. 5), the Court reaffirmed that individuals have First Amendment–protected privacy interests in their homes.[3] The Court as well formally acknowledged a First Amendment right of associational privacy in *National Association for the Advancement of Colored People v. Alabama* (1958) (see Ch. 5) and extended its protection to a broad range of religious, economic, political, and social activities and associations.

Still, the Warren Court's declaration of a constitutional right of privacy in *Griswold v. Connecticut* (1965) (in Ch. 4) provoked a continuing controversy in constitutional politics. The right of privacy, according to Justice William Douglas, may be found in the penumbras, or shadows, of the First, Third, Fourth, Fifth, and Ninth Amendments and applied to the states under the Fourteenth Amendment due process clause. Dissenting Justices Hugo Black and Potter Stewart countered

that *Griswold's* majority was turning "somersaults with history" and becoming a "super-legislature" by creating a right of privacy out of
whole-constitutional cloth. Notice, however, that at the outset of his
opinion in *Griswold* Justice Douglas disclaims undertaking the kind of
substantive due process analysis associated with the discredited *Lochner*
era. During that era the Court created and enforced a "liberty of contract" and ultimately precipitated the 1937 constitutional crisis over its
invalidation of New Deal and progressive economic legislation (see
Ch. 3). Still, Black and Stewart, and a good number of Court watchers,
remained unpersuaded.

No less controversial, as Justices Black and Stewart suggest, is the
reliance of Justice Douglas and concurring Justice Arthur Goldberg on
the Ninth Amendment. That amendment provides that "[t]he enumeration in the Constitution of certain rights shall not be construed to
deny or disparage others retained by the people." Despite the criticism
of Justices Black and Stewart, though, neither Douglas nor Goldberg
contends that the Ninth Amendment provides an independent basis for
the Court's articulation of unenumerated rights. Instead, they maintain
that the amendment only provides a *rule of construction* for ensuring the
"requisite latitude" of guarantees of the Bill of Rights. As Justice Douglas later explained, "The Ninth Amendment obviously does not create
federally enforceable rights. . . . [b]ut a catalogue of these customary,
traditional, and time-honored rights, amenities, privileges and immunities. . . . Many of them in my view come within the meaning of the
term 'liberty' as used in the Fourteenth Amendment."[4] When defending
this interpretation of the Ninth Amendment, justices and commentators frequently turn to the correspondence between James Madison
and Thomas Jefferson over the adoption of the Bill of Rights. Both initially feared "that a positive declaration of some of the most essential
rights could not be obtained in the requisite latitude" but eventually
agreed that a bill of rights would put "into the hands of the judiciary"
a "legal check" on the exercise of governmental power (see Ch. 4).
When proposing amendments to the Constitution in the first Congress, Madison thus argued:

> It has been objected also against a bill of rights, that, by enumerat-
> ing particular exceptions to the grant of power, it would disparage
> those rights which were not placed in that enumeration; and it
> might follow by implication, that those rights which were not sin-
> gled out, were intended to be assigned into the hands of the Gen-
> eral Government, and were consequently insecure. This is one of
> the most plausible arguments I have ever heard urged against the
> admission of a bill of rights into this system; but, I conceive, that it
> may be guarded against. I have attempted it, as gentlemen may see

by turning to the [proposed amendment that eventually became the Ninth Amendment].[5]

Still, critics counter that there is a difference in kind, rather than simply degree, between the Court's recognition of protection for personal privacy as part of the "requisite latitude," for example, given the Fourth Amendment and the creation of a broad constitutional right of privacy.

The debate sparked by the Warren Court's ruling on the right of privacy in *Griswold* erupted into a major political controversy with the Burger Court's 1973 ruling in *Roe v. Wade*, (1973) (excerpted in Section A of this chapter) striking down a Texas law that sharply limited the availability of abortions. The Burger and Rehnquist Courts limited the application of the right of privacy to areas primarily involving reproductive freedom. While the Rehnquist Court (as indicated in the next section) has been more willing to uphold state laws restricting access to abortions, there has been no indication that the Court would overturn *Griswold*. Moreover, while the Court has generally refused to extend the right of privacy, in *Lawrence v. Texas* (2003) (excerpted in Section B) a majority finally acknowledged that the right of privacy extends to personal autonomy and intimate sexual relations, when striking down Texas's law criminalizing homosexual sodomy.

NOTES

1. S. Warren and L. Brandeis, "The Right of Privacy," 4 *Harvard Law Review* 193 (1890).

2. See William Prosser, "Privacy," 48 *California Law Review* 383 (1960).

3. See also *Cohen v. California* (1971) and *Federal Communications v. Pacific Foundation* (1978), both in Ch. 5.

4. *Doe v. Bolton*, 410 U.S. 179 (1973).

5. James Madison, House of Representatives, in *The Debates and Proceedings in the Congress of the United States*, Vol. 1 (Washington, DC: Gales and Seaton, 1834), 455.

SELECTED BIBLIOGRAPHY

Barnett, Randy, ed. *The Rights Retained by the People: The History and Meaning of the Ninth Amendment.* Fairfax, VA: George Mason University Press, 1989.

Garrow, David J. *Liberty & Sexuality: The Right to Privacy and the Making of Roe v. Wade.* New York: McMillan, 1994.

O'Brien, David M. *Privacy, Law, and Public Policy.* New York: Praeger, 1979.

Westin, Alan F. *Privacy and Freedom.* New York: Atheneum, 1970.

A | *Privacy and Reproductive Freedom*

The Supreme Court initially acknowledged protection under the Fourteenth Amendment due process clause for personal privacy and freedom from governmental intrusions into the areas of marriage, reproduction, and child-rearing in the 1920s, during the height of the *Lochner* era (see Ch. 3). In *Meyer v. Nebraska*, 262 U.S. 390 (1923), the Court struck down a state law, passed shortly after World War I and amid opposition to peace negotiations with Germany, forbidding the teaching of German and modern languages other than English in private and public schools. There, Justice James McReynolds observed,

> Without a doubt, [the Fourteenth Amendment guarantee that "No state . . . shall deprive any person of life, liberty or property without due process of law"] denotes not merely freedom from bodily restraint but also the right of the individual to contract, to engage in any of the common occupations of life, to acquire useful knowledge, to marry, establish a home and bring up children, to worship God according to the dictates of his own conscience, and generally to enjoy these privileges long recognized at common law as essential to the orderly pursuit of happiness by free men.

Two years later, *Pierce v. Society of Sisters*, 268 U.S. 510 (1925), overturned an Oregon law requiring primary and secondary school children to attend public rather than private schools on the grounds that it interfered "with the liberty of parents and guardians to direct the upbringing and education of children under their control." However, in *Buck v. Bell* (1927) (excerpted below) the Court rejected a substantive due process challenge to Virginia's law on the compulsory sterilization of those deemed mentally defective.

The first major ruling extending protection to reproductive freedom, however, came in *Skinner v. Oklahoma*, 316 U.S. 535 (1942). Indeed, in *Buck v. Bell*, 274 U.S. 200 (1927), the Court upheld a Virginia law, passed in response to the eugenics movement, requiring the sterilization of persons confined to state mental health institutions (see Ch. 3). But in *Skinner* the Court unanimously overturned a state law providing for the sterilization of "habitual criminals." Jack Skinner had been convicted of stealing chickens in 1926, of robbery in 1929, and again in 1934. In 1936, the state attorney general instituted proceedings against Skinner under Oklahoma's 1935 Habitual Criminal Sterilization Act, which authorized the sterilization of individuals who had been convicted two or more times of certain "felonies involving moral turpitude." Skinner challenged the constitutionality of Oklahoma's law as a violation of the Fourteenth Amendment due process and equal protection clauses. When striking down the law for running afoul of the equal protection clause because it permitted the sterilization of those convicted of crimes such as embezzlement but not those convicted of larceny, Justice William Douglas explained,

> We are dealing here with legislation which involves one of the basic civil rights of man. Marriage and procreation are fundamental to the very existence and survival of the race. The power to sterilize, if exercised, may have subtle, far-reaching and devastating effects. In evil or reckless hands it can cause races or types which are inimical to the dominant group to wither and disappear. There is no redemption for the individual whom the law touches. Any experiment which the State conducts is to his irreparable injury. He is forever deprived of a basic liberty.

Later, *Loving v. Virginia*, 388 U.S. 1 (1967), struck down a state miscegenation law that criminalized interracial marriages. And when holding that states may not deny parents, who failed to meet child-support obligations, the right to remarry without a court's permission, the Court "reaffirm[ed] the fundamental character of the right to marry" in *Zablocki v. Redhail*, 434 U.S. 374 (1978).

Beginning in the 1940s, individuals began attacking the constitutionality of laws prohibiting the use of contraceptives, but the Court refused to hear their appeals. (See INSIDE THE COURT: Standing and the Connecticut Birth Control Cases, in Ch. 2). Finally, in *Griswold v. Connecticut* (1965) (see Ch. 4) the Court struck down Connecticut's statute as a denial of the right of privacy of married couples. Seven years later, over the dissent of Chief Justice Warren Burger, *Eisenstadt v. Baird*, 405 U.S. 438 (1972) overturned a Massachusetts law forbidding the use of contraceptives by unmarried individuals. In his opinion for the Court, Justice William J. Brennan observed that

> [w]hatever the rights of the individual to access to contraceptives may be, the rights must be the same for the unmarried and the married alike. If under *Griswold* the distribution of contraceptives to married persons cannot be prohibited, a ban on distribution to unmarried persons would be equally impermissible. It is true that in *Griswold* the right of privacy in question inhered in the marital relationship. Yet the marital couple is not an independent entity with a mind and heart of its own, but an association of two individuals each with a separate intellectual and emotional makeup. If the right of privacy means anything, it is the right of the *individual*, married

or single, to be free from unwarranted governmental intrusion into matters so fundamentally affecting a person as the decision whether to bear or beget a child.

A year before *Eisenstadt*, a bare majority of the Burger Court upheld the District of Columbia's law allowing abortions not only to save a woman's life but also to maintain her physical and psychological well-being. But in *United States v. Vuitch*, 402 U.S. 62 (1971), the Court declined to rule on whether a woman's right of privacy included her decision to terminate or carry an unwanted pregnancy to term. Yet the Court could not escape deciding that question. Just one month after deciding *Vuitch*, the Court granted review to abortion cases, *Roe v. Wade* (1973) (see excerpt below) and *Doe v. Bolton*, 410 U.S. 179 (1973). A movement to liberalize abortion laws had grown throughout the turbulent 1960s with demands for women's rights. The legal reforms pushed by women's pro-choice advocates were in some respects little more than a return to the legal status of abortions a century earlier. Until the mid-nineteenth century, most states permitted abortions, except after quickening—the first movement of the fetus—and then an abortion was usually considered only a minor offense. After the Civil War, the American Medical Association, in opposition to the use of midwives, and other antiabortionists persuaded states to toughen their laws, and by 1910 every state, except Kentucky, had made abortion a felony. But by the late 1960s, fourteen states had liberalized laws to permit abortions when the woman's health was in danger, when there was a likelihood of fetal abnormality, and when the woman was a victim of rape or incest. Four states—Alaska, Hawaii, New York, and Washington—had gone so far as to repeal all criminal penalties for abortions performed in early pregnancy.

When handing down *Roe v. Wade* the Court elevated the issue of abortion to the national political agenda and sparked a larger political struggle in the country. States could no longer categorically proscribe abortions or make them unnecessarily difficult to obtain. The promotion of maternal care and the preservation of the life of a fetus were not sufficiently "compelling state interests" to justify restrictive abortion laws. During roughly the first trimester (three months) of a pregnancy, the decision on abortion is that of a woman and her doctor. During the second, the Court ruled, states may regulate abortions, but only in ways reasonably related to its interest in safeguarding the health of women. In the third trimester, states' interests in preserving the life of the unborn become compelling, and they may limit, even ban, abortions, except when necessary to save a woman's life. *Roe* was thus controversial in not only extending the right of privacy in this area, but in Justice

Harry Blackmun's trimester approach to balancing the interests of women seeking abortions and those of the states.

In the years immediately after *Roe*, thirty-four states passed new abortion laws. Some were in conformity with the Court's ruling—requiring, for example, that abortions be performed by licensed physicians—but others sought to limit the impact of *Roe*. States tried to restrict the availability of abortions in several ways: by requiring the informed consent of a husband or that of parents for a minor's abortion, by forbidding the advertising of abortion clinics, and by withholding state funds for abortions not medically necessary. In addition, ten states passed laws or resolutions pledging to ban or severely restrict abortions, and fifteen others left their pre-*Roe* laws on the books, in anticipation of *Roe*'s being eventually overturned.

Initially, the Burger Court basically stood its ground, striking down most state and local attempts to limit the impact of *Roe*. However, in three 1977 decisions the Court (dividing six to three) upheld some state restrictions on the availability of abortions. In *Beal v. Doe*, 432 U.S. 438 (1977), and *Maher v. Roe* (1977) (see excerpt below), a majority of the Court approved restrictions on the public funding of nontherapeutic abortions. In *Poelker v. Doe*, 432 U.S. 59 (1977), the Court upheld a city's policy of refusing nontherapeutic abortions in public hospitals. As the Court's composition further changed in the 1980s, pressure mounted with speculation that *Roe* might be further restricted, if not reversed.

Opposition came not only from the states, but also from Congress and the president. Congress failed to pass a constitutional amendment overturning *Roe* but succeeded in limiting the reach of the Court's ruling in a number of ways. In the decade and a half following *Roe*, Congress enacted over thirty laws restricting the availability of abortions. Among these statutes, Congress barred the use of funds for programs in which abortion is included as a method of family planning; barred government officials from ordering recipients of federal funds to perform abortions; barred lawyers working in federally funded legal aid programs from giving assistance to those seeking "nontherapeutic" abortions; provided that employees are not required to pay health insurance benefits for abortions, except to save a woman's life; prohibited the use of federal employee health benefits to pay for abortions, except when a woman's life is imperiled; prohibited the use of foreign aid funds for abortions; and prohibited federal prisons from paying for pregnant inmates' abortions. In *Harris v. McRae*, 448 U.S. 297 (1980), the Court split five to four when upholding the so-called Hyde Amendment (named after its sponsor, Republican Representative Henry Hyde of Illinois), which forbids federal funding of nontherapeutic abortions under the Medicaid program. Again, voting five to four in *Bowen v. Kendrick*, 487 U.S. 589 (1988), the Court upheld the Adolescent Family Life Act, which prohibits federal funding of organizations involved with abortions, while allowing the funding of religious groups advocating self-discipline as a form of birth control.

By the 1980s, abortion was an issue in presidential politics as well. The 1980, 1984, and 1988 Republican platforms, endorsed by President Reagan, supported a constitutional amendment "to restore protection of the right to life for unborn children." The strategy of the Reagan administration was actually twofold: appoint to the federal bench only those opposed to abortion and initiate litigation that might undercut and ultimately lead to overturning *Roe*. But even after the retirements of Justices William O. Douglas and Potter Stewart—and the appointments of John Paul Stevens in 1975 and Sandra Day O'Connor in 1981—the Court continued to reaffirm its basic ruling in *Roe*. In *City of Akron v. Akron Center for Reproductive Health*, 462 U.S. 416 (1983), for example, the Court struck down several restrictions imposed on women seeking abortions, including requirements that they sign informed consent forms and wait at least twenty-four hours afterward before having an abortion, along with requiring doctors to perform abortions after the first trimester in a hospital and dispose of fetal remains "in a humane and sanitary way."

In *City of Akron*, Reagan's solicitor general, Rex Lee, asked the justices to reconsider *Roe* but stopped short of urging its reversal. Still, only Justice O'Connor, joined by Justices Rehnquist and White (who had dissented in *Roe*), appeared sympathetic in her dissenting opinion suggesting a willingness to reconsider, if not overturn, *Roe*. In her dissenting opinion in *City of Akron*, Justice O'Connor strongly attacked the constitutional theory and trimester-approach of *Roe*, explaining that,

> [t]he trimester or "three-stage" approach adopted by the Court in *Roe*, and, in a modified form, employed by the Court to analyze the state regulations in these cases, cannot be supported as a legitimate or useful framework for accommodating the woman's right and the State's interests. The decision of the Court today graphically illustrates why the trimester approach is a completely unworkable method of accommodating the conflicting personal rights and compelling state interests that are involved in the abortion context.
>
> As the Court indicates today, the State's compelling interest in maternal health changes as medical technology changes, and any health regulation must not "depart from accepted medical practice." . . . In applying this standard, the Court holds that "the safety of second-trimester abortions has increased dramatically" since 1973, when

Roe was decided. . . . Although a regulation such as one requiring that all second-trimester abortions be performed in hospitals "had strong support" in 1973 "as a reasonable health regulation," . . . this regulation can no longer stand because, according to the Court's diligent research into medical and scientific literature, the dilation and evacuation procedure (D & E), used in 1973 only for first-trimester abortions, "is now widely and successfully used for second trimester abortions." Further, the medical literature relied on by the Court indicates that the D & E procedure may be performed in an appropriate non-hospital setting for "at least . . . the early weeks of the second trimester. . . ." The Court then chooses the period of 16 weeks of gestation as that point at which D & E procedures may be performed safely in a non-hospital setting, and thereby invalidates the Akron hospitalization regulation. . . .

Just as improvement in medical technology inevitably will move *forward* the point at which the State may regulate for reasons of maternal health, different technological improvements will move *backwards* the point of viability at which the State may proscribe abortions except when necessary to preserve the life and health of the mother. . . .

The *Roe* framework, then, is clearly on a collision course with itself. As the medical risks of various abortion procedures decrease, the point at which the State may regulate for reasons of maternal health is moved further forward to actual childbirth. As medical science becomes better able to provide for the separate existence of the fetus, the point of viability is moved further back toward conception. . . . The *Roe* framework is inherently tied to the state of medical technology that exists whenever particular litigation ensues. Although legislatures are better suited to make necessary factual judgments in this area, the Court's framework forces legislatures, as a matter of constitutional law, to speculate about what constitutes "accepted medical practice" at any given time. Without the necessary expertise or ability, courts must then pretend to act as science review boards and examine those legislative judgments. . . .

The fallacy inherent in the *Roe* framework is apparent: just because the State has a compelling interest in ensuring maternal safety once an abortion may be more dangerous than childbirth, it simply does not follow that the State has *no* interest before that point that justifies state regulation to ensure that first-trimester abortions are performed as safely as possible.

The state interest in potential human life is likewise extant throughout pregnancy. In *Roe*, the Court held that although the State had an important and legitimate interest in protecting potential life, that interest could not become compelling until the point at which the fetus was viable. The difficulty with this analysis is clear: *potential* life is no less potential in the first weeks of pregnancy than it is at viability or afterward. At any stage in pregnancy, there is the *potential* for human life. Although the Court refused to "resolve the difficult question of when life begins," . . . the Court chose the point of viability—when the fetus is *capable* of life independent of its mother—to permit the complete proscription of abortion. The choice of viability as the point at which the state interest in *potential* life becomes compelling is not less arbitrary than choosing any point before viability or any point afterward. Accordingly, I believe that the State's interest in protecting potential human life exists throughout the pregnancy. . . .

Justice O'Connor also proposed that the Court abandon *Roe*'s trimester-approach and adopt the test of whether state regulations place an "undue burden" on women seeking abortions:

> "*Roe* did not declare an unqualified 'constitutional right to an abortion.' . . . Rather, the right protects the woman from unduly burdensome interference with her freedom to decide whether to terminate her pregnancy." *Maher* . . .
>
> The "undue burden" required in the abortion cases represents the required threshold inquiry that must be conducted before this Court can require a State to justify its legislative actions under the exacting "compelling state interest" standard. . . .
>
> The "unduly burdensome" standard is particularly appropriate in the abortion context because of the *nature* and *scope* of the right that is involved. The privacy right involved in the abortion context "cannot be said to be absolute." *Roe* . . . Rather, the *Roe* right is intended to protect against state action "drastically limiting the availability and safety of the desired service," . . . or against "official interference" and "coercive restraint" imposed on the abortion decision. . . . That a state regulation may "inhibit" abortions to some degree does not require that we find that the regulation is invalid. . . .

In two companion cases handed down along with *City of Akron*, the justices split five to four (with Justice Powell casting the crucial fifth vote) in upholding a Missouri law requiring pathology reports for all abortions, the presence of a second physician during abortions performed after viability, and parental consent for minors seeking abortions. They also sustained the constitutionality of a Virginia statute mandating that second-trimester abortions be performed in licensed outpatient clinics in *Planned Parenthood Association of Kansas City, Missouri v. Ashcroft*, 462 U.S. 476 (1983), and *Simopoulos v. Virginia*, 462 U.S. 506 (1983).

Three years after *City of Akron*, the Reagan administration renewed its attack on *Roe*. This time, Reagan's second solicitor general, Harvard Law School professor Charles Fried, dared to do what his predecessor refused: He questioned the Court's wisdom and argued that *Roe* be

overturned. In support of Pennsylvania's Governor Richard Thornburgh's appeal of a circuit court ruling striking down a state law limiting the availability of abortions, Fried filed an extraordinary *amicus
curiae* ("friend of the court") brief. There, he boldly proclaimed "the
textual, doctrinal and historical basis for *Roe v. Wade* is so far flawed and
. . . a source of such instability in the law that this Court should reconsider that decision and on reconsideration abandon it."

But a majority of the Court again rebuffed the Reagan administration when handing down *Thornburgh v. American College of Obstetricians*,
476 U.S. 747 (1986). A majority of the Court, moreover, appeared impatient with the administration's persistence in trying to undo *Roe*.
When announcing the decision from the bench, Blackmun exclaimed,
"We reaffirm *once again* the general principles of *Roe*." However, Chief
Justice Burger broke with *Roe's* supporters in *Thornburgh*, joining Justices O'Connor, Rehnquist, and White in dissent and indicated that *Roe*
should be "reexamined."

The five-to-four split in *Thornburgh* further escalated speculation
about how another Reagan appointee might affect the Court and *Roe*.
As the Court's composition changed in the 1980s, support for *Roe*
among the justices appeared to decline from seven to two, to six to
three, and to five to four. Then within a week of the ruling on *Thornburgh*, Chief Justice Burger announced that he would step down from
the Court. Reagan immediately responded by shrewdly elevating Justice Rehnquist, one of *Roe's* sharpest critics, to the chief justiceship and
naming Antonin Scalia to his seat on the bench.

As long as Justice Powell remained on the Court, he held the pivotal vote for upholding *Roe*. When he announced his retirement in
June 1987, Reagan's nomination of Judge Robert H. Bork—one of
Roe's harshest critics—set off a political firestorm. After a bitter Senate
battle, Judge Bork's nomination was rejected by the widest margin
(fifty-eight to forty-two) of any Supreme Court nominee. Reagan's
second nominee, Judge Douglas Ginsburg, was forced to withdraw
from consideration, but his third nominee, Judge Anthony Kennedy,
won easy Senate confirmation.

In the final days of the Reagan administration, the Court thus
seemed poised to reconsider, and possibly overturn, *Roe*. Indeed, a
few weeks before the Senate confirmed Justice Kennedy, the justices
split four to four, thereby affirming by an equally divided Court a
lower court's ruling striking down a law requiring parental notification for teenagers seeking abortions. *Hartigan v. Zbaraz*, 484 U.S. 171
(1987). Subsequently, during the summer of 1988 assistant attorney
general William Bradford Reynolds and others in Reagan's Department of Justice talked Missouri's attorney general William Webster into

seizing an opportunity afforded by appealing another appellate court's invalidation of that state's restrictions on abortions. Webster's legal strategy was to defend Missouri's law as "nothing more than regulat[ing] abortions within the parameters allowed by *Roe v. Wade*." But he was persuaded to repeat word for word in his brief filed before the Court the language Fried used in his *Thornburgh* brief demanding *Roe*'s reversal, in *Webster v. Reproductive Health Services*, 492 U.S. 4090 (1989).

Webster badly fragmented the Rehnquist Court. Although a bare majority supported the result, Chief Justice Rehnquist's opinion was joined only by Justices Kennedy and White. Notwithstanding its ruling in *Thornburgh*, just three years earlier, a bare majority of the Court upheld the principal provisions of Missouri's 1986 abortion law (1) decreeing that life begins at conception and that "unborn children have protectable interests in life, health, and well-being," (2) requiring doctors, prior to performing an abortion on a woman believed to be twenty or more weeks pregnant, to test the fetus's "gestational age, weight, and lung maturity," (3) prohibiting public employees and facilities from being used to perform abortions not necessary to save a woman's life, and (4) making it unlawful to use public funds, employees, and facilities for the purpose of "encouraging or counseling" a woman to have an abortion except when her life is in danger. In separate concurring opinions, Justice Scalia decried Justice O'Connor's refusal to vote to overturn *Roe*, while for her part, O'Connor claimed that there would be other occasions to reconsider that ruling.

Following another five-to-four split in *Rust v. Sullivan*, 500 U.S. 173 (1991) (excerpted in Ch. 5), which upheld the Reagan administration's restrictions on organizations that receive federal funding from providing counseling on abortion, and the retirements of two of *Roe*'s staunchest supporters—Justices Brennan and Marshall—speculation again mounted that the Rehnquist Court would overrule *Roe* in *Planned Parenthood of Southeastern Pennsylvania v. Casey*, 505 U.S. 833 (1992) (see excerpt below). Yet, in an extraordinary joint opinion signed by Justices O'Connor, Kennedy, and Souter (and joined in part by Justices Blackmun and Stevens), a controlling majority emerged that claimed to uphold "the essence of *Roe*," while also redefining the standards for reviewing restrictive abortion laws. In caustic dissenting opinions, joined by Justices Thomas and White, Chief Justice Rehnquist and Justice Scalia criticized the plurality's analysis, particularly its refashioning of the doctrine of *stare decisis* in order to justify its refusal to completely jettison *Roe*.

After *Casey* the Court remained bitterly split five to four in striking down so-called partial birth abortion laws that do not provide an exception for the health of women, in *Stenberg v. Carhart* (2000) (excerpted below).

SELECTED BIBLIOGRAPHY

Baer, Judith. *A Historical and Multicultural Encyclopedia of Women's Reproductive Rights in the United States.* Westport, CT: Greenwood Publishing Co., 2001.

Craig, Barbara, and O'Brien, David. *Abortion and American Politics.* Chatham, NJ: Chatham House, 1993.

Dworkin, Ronald. *Life's Dominion.* New York: Knopf, 1993.

Garrow, David. *Liberty & Sexuality: The Right to Privacy and the Making of Roe v. Wade.* New York: Macmillan, 1994.

Graber, Mark. *Rethinking Abortion: Equal Choice, the Constitution, and Reproductive Politics.* Princeton, NJ: Princeton University Press, 1996.

Hull, N.E.H., and Hoffer, Charles. *Roe v. Wade: The Abortion Rights Controversy in American History.* Lawrence: University Press of Kansas, 2001.

Kaplin, Laura. *The Story of Jane: The Legendary Underground Feminist Abortion Service.* New York: Pantheon, 1996.

Mohr, James. *Abortion in America.* New York: Oxford University Press, 1978.

Reagan, Leslie. *When Abortion Was a Crime: Women, Medicine, and Law in the United States, 1867–1973.* Berkeley: University of California Press, 1997.

Saletan, William. *Bearing Right: How Conservatives Won the Abortion War.* Berkeley: University of California Press, 2003.

Tribe, Laurence. *Abortion: The Clash of Absolutes.* New York: W.W. Norton, 1990.

Weddington, Sarah. *A Question of Choice.* New York: Grosset/Putnam, 1992.

Justice William O. Douglas. Justice Douglas was the author of the Court's controversial ruling in *Griswold v. Connecticut* (1965) proclaiming a constitutional right of privacy. (*Corbis/UPI*)

Buck v. Bell

274 U.S. 200, 47 S.CT. 584 (1927)

In 1924, Virginia enacted a law permitting the sterilization of individuals, male and female, who were deemed mentally defective and committed to a State Colony for Epileptics and Feeble Minded. The law, like those in other states, was part of the eugenics movement and a reflection of the late-nineteenth-century philosophy of Social Darwinism. Compulsory sterilization was justified as in the interests of both the individual and society. Subsequently, attorneys challenged the constitutionality of the law as a violation of the Fourteenth Amendment's guarantees for due process and the equal protection of the law. Carrie Buck, an eighteen-year-old "feeble-minded" woman was the daughter of a woman in the same institution. A state court rejected the challenge and Virginia's highest court affirmed, whereupon Buck's attorneys appealed to the Supreme Court.

The Court affirmed the decision below by a vote of eight to one. Justice Holmes delivered the opinion of the Court. Justice Butler dissented without an opinion.

☐ *Justice HOLMES delivered the opinion of the Court.*

An Act of Virginia approved March 20, 1924 recites that the health of the patient and the welfare of society may be promoted in certain cases by the sterilization of mental defectives, under careful safeguard, etc. . . . ; that the Commonwealth is supporting in various institutions many defective persons who if now discharged would become a menace but if incapable of procreating might be discharged with safety and become self-supporting with benefit to themselves and to society; and that experience has shown that heredity plays an important part in the transmission of insanity, imbecility, etc. The statute then enacts that whenever the superintendent of certain institutions including the above named State Colony shall be of the opinion that it is for the best interest of the patients and of society that an inmate under his care should be sexually sterilized, he may have the operation performed upon any patient afflicted with hereditary forms of insanity, imbecility, etc. . . . The superintendent first presents a petition to the special board of directors of his hospital or colony, stating the facts and the grounds for his opinion, verified by affidavit. Notice of the petition and of the time and place of the hearing in the institution is to be served upon the inmate, and also upon his guardian, and if there is no guardian the superintendent is to apply to the Circuit Court of the County to appoint one. . . . The evidence is all to be reduced to writing, and after the board has made its order for or against the operation, the superintendent, or the inmate, or his guardian, may appeal to the Circuit Court of the County. . . . Finally any party may apply to the Supreme Court of Appeals, which, if it grants the appeal, is to hear the case upon the record of the trial in the Circuit Court and may enter such order as it thinks the Circuit Court should have entered. There can be no doubt that so far as procedure is concerned the rights of the patient are most carefully considered. . . .

The attack is not upon the procedure but upon the substantive law. It seems to be contended that in no circumstances could such an order be justified. It certainly is contended that the order cannot be justified upon the existing grounds. The judgment finds the facts that have been recited and that Carrie Buck "is the probable potential parent of socially inadequate offspring, likewise afflicted, that she may be sexually sterilized without detriment to her general health and that her welfare and that of society will be promoted by her sterilization," and thereupon makes the order. In view of the general declarations of the Legislature and the specific findings of the Court obviously we cannot say as a matter of law that the grounds do not exist, and if they exist they justify the result. We have seen more than once that the public welfare may call upon the best citizens for their lives. It would be strange if it could not call upon those who already sap the strength of the State for these lesser sacrifices, often not felt to be such by those concerned, in order to prevent our being swamped with incompetence. It is better for all the world, if instead of waiting to execute degenerate offspring for crime, or to let them starve for their imbecility, society can prevent those who are manifestly unfit from continuing their kind. The principle that sustains compulsory vaccination is broad enough to cover cutting the Fallopian tubes. *Jacobson v. Massachusetts*, 197 U.S. 11 (1905). Three generations of imbeciles are enough. . . .

Griswold v. Connecticut
381 U.S. 479 (1965)

See Chapter 4, where *Griswold v. Connecticut* is reprinted in part. See also INSIDE THE COURT: Standing and the Connecticut Birth Control Cases (in Ch. 2) and INSIDE THE COURT: The Theory and Drafting of Justice Douglas's Opinion in *Griswold v. Connecticut* (in Ch. 4).

■ INSIDE THE COURT
The Oral Argument and Decision-Making Process in Roe v. Wade

On December 13, 1971, the Court heard oral arguments in the case. Sarah Weddington began her argument by pointing out that women like Jane Roe, who were poor and for whom abortions were not necessary to saving their lives, had no real choice. They faced unwanted childbirth or attempting medically unsafe self-abortions that could result in their deaths. But Weddington's argument was diverted when Justice Byron White observed that "so far on the merits, you've told us about the important impact of the law, and you made a very eloquent policy argument against it." But he added, "We cannot here be involved simply with matters of policy, as you know." White wanted to know what was the constitutional basis for a woman's right to have an abortion and for the Court's overturning the Texas law. Appropriate arguments could be drawn from the Ninth Amendment's guarantee of rights retained by the people, Weddington responded, or the protection for rights of persons to life, liberty, and the pursuit of happiness under the Fourteenth Amendment. If *liberty* is meaningful, she concluded, "that liberty to these women would mean liberty from being forced to continue the unwanted pregnancy."

"It's an old joke, but when a man argues against two beautiful ladies like this, they are going to have the last word." There was no laughter in the courtroom, however, at that opening remark by Jay Floyd, the assistant attorney general of Texas who was before the Court to defend the abortion law. This controversy is not one for the courts, he argued, and arguments about freedom of choice are misleading. Floyd pressed the point:

> There are situations in which, of course as the Court knows, no remedy is provided. Now I think she makes her choice prior to the time she becomes pregnant. That is the time of the choice. It's like, more or less, the first three or four years of our life we don't remember anything. But, once a child is born, a woman no longer has a choice, and I think pregnancy then terminates that choice. That's when.

However, one of the justices impatiently shot back, "Maybe she makes her choice when she decides to live in Texas." Laughter almost drowned out Floyd's feeble reply, "There is no restriction on moving."

"What is Texas's interest? What is Texas's interest in the statute?" demanded Justice Marshall. The state has "recognized the humanness of the embryo, or the fetus," Floyd explained, and has "a compelling interest because of the protection of fetal life." Yet, interjected Justice Potter Stewart, "Texas does not attempt to punish a woman who herself performs an abortion on herself." "That is correct," Floyd continued,

> And the matter has been brought to my attention: Why not punish for murder, since you are destroying what you—or what has been said to be a human being? I don't know, except that I will say this. As medical science progresses, maybe the law will progress along with it. Maybe at one time it could be possible, I suppose, statutes could be passed. Whether or not that would be constitutional or not, I don't know.

But, Stewart countered, "we're dealing with the statute as it is. There's no state, is there, that equates abortion with murder? Or is there?" There was none, Floyd admitted and then hastened to emphasize that, although courts had not recognized the unborn as having legal rights, states have a legitimate interest in protecting the unborn. As to a woman's choice on abortion, Floyd reiterated, "we feel that this choice is left up to the woman prior to the time she becomes pregnant. This is the time of choice."

When the justices later discussed *Roe* in private conference, Burger noted that the case had not been argued very well. He also thought because the case presented such a "sensitive issue," it should be set for reargument so that recently appointed Justices Lewis Powell and William Rehnquist could participate and a full Court reach a decision. As chief justice, he led the discussion observing that the Texas law was "certainly arcane," although not unconstitutional. He was inclined but not yet committed to the view that the law should fall for vagueness. Senior Associate Justice Douglas spoke next. He disagreed and had no doubt that the statute was unconstitutional. For Douglas, the Texas law was not merely vague but impinged on a woman's right of privacy. Brennan and Stewart agreed, as later did Marshall. White came out on the other side. He could not go along with the argument that women have a constitutional right of privacy, giving them a choice on abortion. A right of privacy is not specifically mentioned in the Constitution. Blackmun, then the newest member of the Court, spoke last: "Don't think there's an absolute right to do what you will with [your] body." But this statute was poorly drawn, Blackmun observed. It's too restrictive—it "doesn't go as far as it should and impinges too far on [Roe's] Ninth Amendment rights." Blackmun appeared in the middle, but inclined toward the position of Douglas, Brennan, Stewart, and Marshall.

After conference the chief justice, if he is in the majority, by tradition assigns a justice to write the opinion justifying the Court's decision. On the abortion cases Burger appeared to be in the minority, but he nonetheless gave the assignment to Blackmun. When Douglas complained, Burger responded that the issues were so complex and the conference discussion so diverse "that there were, literally, not enough columns to mark up an accurate reflection of the voting" in his docket book. He "therefore marked down no vote and said this was a case that would have to stand or fall on the writing, when it was done."

Assigned to write the Court's opinion in late December 1971, Blackmun did not circulate a first draft until May 18, 1972. Although striking down Texas's law, his draft opinion did so on Burger's view that the law was vague rather than on the majority's view that it violated a woman's constitutional right of privacy. Douglas and Brennan wanted to know why the opinion failed to address the core issue, "which would make reaching the vagueness issue unnecessary." Blackmun claimed that he was "flexible as to results." A freshman in his second year on the Court and assigned to write a very difficult opinion, Blackmun found himself in the middle of the cross-pressures of a growing dispute. Blackmun was himself psychologically and intellectually torn by the dispute. "Although it would prove costly to [him] personally, in the light of energy and hours expended," Blackmun concluded he would move for reargument. He explained that "on an issue so sensitive and so emotional as this one, the country deserves the conclusion of a nine-man, not a seven-man court, whatever the ultimate decision may be." Then Justices Powell and Rehnquist (who had not participated in the case) voted for a rehearing. That made a majority of five for carrying *Roe* over to the next term.

On October 11, 1972, the Court heard rearguments. For a second time Weddington stood before the high bench to ask that it rule that women have a right to choose to continue or terminate a pregnancy. But her arguments were repeatedly interrupted by questions from the bench about the rights of the unborn. Justice White put it bluntly, "Would you lose your case if the fetus was a person?" That would require a balancing of interests, Weddington replied, but that was not at issue here, because it had not been asserted that a fetus has any constitutional rights. The issue was simply a conflict between the constitutional rights of women and the statutory interests of the state. The state would have to establish that the fetus is a "person" under the Fourteenth Amendment or some other part of the Constitution, before it would have a compelling interest in prohibiting abortions and require the Court to strike a balance with the constitutional rights of a woman.

"That's what's involved in this case? Weighing one life against another?" White again asserted toward the end of Weddington's oral argument time. No, she insisted in her concluding exchange with the justices:

STEWART: Well, if—if it were established that an unborn fetus is a person, with the protection of the Fourteenth Amendment, you would have almost an impossible case here, would you not?

WEDDINGTON: I would have a very difficult case.

STEWART: I'm sure you would. So, if you had the same kind of thing, you'd have to say that this would be the equivalent—after the child was born, if the mother thought it bothered her health any having the child around, she could have it killed. Isn't that correct.

WEDDINGTON: That's correct. That—

BURGER: Could Texas constitutionally, in your view, declare that— by statute, that the fetus is a person, for all constitutional purposes, after the third month of gestation?

WEDDINGTON: I do not believe that the State legislature can determine the meaning of the Federal Constitution. It is up to this Court to make that determination.

Chief Justice Burger then called Robert C. Flowers, who had replaced Floyd and as assistant attorney general represented Texas before the Court.

From the outset, Flowers faced a steady barrage of questions about whether a fetus is a "person" under the Constitution. He was driven to concede that no case had recognized the fetus as a person and that the Fourteenth Amendment extends protection only to those born or naturalized in the United States. At the prodding of White, he was forced to agree that the case would be lost if the fetus is not recognized as a person. Yet, Flowers continued to insist that the unborn are entitled to constitutional protection. In response to questions from Justices Marshall and Rehnquist, however, he could not supply any medical evidence that a fetus is a person at the time of conception. Finally, Flowers confessed that he knew of no way "that any court or any legislature or any doctor anywhere can say that here is the dividing line. Here is not a life; and here is a life, after conception."

Whether a fetus is a person, Flowers argued, is an issue that should be left to the state legislatures. But that argument underscored the Court's dilemma and aroused Stewart: "Well, if you're right that an unborn fetus is a person, then you can't leave it to the legislature to play fast and loose dealing with that person. In other words, if you're correct, in your basic submission that an unborn fetus is a person, then abortion laws such as that which New York has are grossly unconstitutional, isn't it?" Liberal abortion laws, Flowers urged, allow "the killing of people."

Weddington had a few minutes to give a final rebuttal, but most of her time was consumed by questions from the bench. "We are not here to advocate abortion." Weddington concluded, stressing that

> [w]e do not ask this Court to rule that abortion is good, or desirable in any particular situation. We are here to advocate that the decision as to whether or not a particular woman will continue to carry or will terminate a pregnancy is a decision that should be made by that individual; that, in fact, she has a constitutional right to make that decision for herself; and that the State has shown no interest in interfering with that decision.

About a month after the Court heard the rearguments, Blackmun had finished a new draft of his opinion for Roe. "It has been an interesting assignment," he observed when circulating the draft that eventually became the Court's final opinion. Justices Douglas, Brennan, Marshall, and Stewart immediately agreed to join. Shortly thereafter, Powell also signed on, commending Blackmun for his "exceptional scholarship." By mid-January Burger had also agreed, although he would add a short concurring opinion, saying that he did not support "abortion on demand." Justices Rehnquist and White were the only dissenters.

Source: Library of Congress, Transcripts of oral arguments and materials in the Papers of Justice William J. Brennan, Jr., and of Justice Harry A. Blackmun.

Roe v. Wade

410 U.S. 113, 93 S.Ct. 705 (1973)

In 1969, a high-school dropout, who was divorced and had a five-year-old daughter and little money, Norma McCorvey, unsuccessfully sought an abortion in Texas. Texas, like most other states at the time, prohibited abortions unless necessary to save a woman's life. McCorvey carried her pregnancy and gave up the child she bore for adoption. The lawyer who arranged for the adoption also introduced McCorvey to two recent graduates of the University of Texas Law School, Sarah Weddington and Linda Coffee. The three women decided to challenge the constitutionality of Texas's law and McCorvey became "Jane Roe" in a test case against Henry Wade, the criminal district attorney for Dallas County, Texas. Wade appealed to the Supreme Court the decision of a three-judge federal district court striking down Texas's law. The Court granted review and heard oral arguments in 1971 and then carried the case over for rearguments in 1972. Justice Blackmun finally handed down the Court's opinion on January 23, 1973.

The Court's decision was seven to two, and the majority's opinion was announced by Justice Blackmun. Chief Justice Burger and Justices Douglas and Stewart concurred; Justices Rehnquist and White dissented.

☐ *Justice BLACKMUN delivers the opinion of the Court.*

This Texas federal appeal . . . present[s] constitutional challenges to state criminal abortion legislation. The Texas statutes under attack here are typical of those that have been in effect in many States for approximately a century. . . .

We forthwith acknowledge our awareness of the sensitive and emotional nature of the abortion controversy, of the vigorous opposing views, even among physicians, and of the deep and seemingly absolute convictions that the subject inspires. . . .

Our task, of course, is to resolve the issue by constitutional measurement, free of emotion and of predilection. We seek earnestly to do this, and, because we do, we have inquired into, and in this opinion place some emphasis upon, medical and medical-legal history and what that history reveals about man's attitudes toward the abortion procedure over the centuries. . . .

The Texas statutes that concern us here make it a crime to "procure an abortion," as therein defined, or to attempt one, except with respect to "an abortion procured or attempted by medical advice for the purpose of saving the life of the mother." Similar statutes are in existence in a majority of the States. . . .

The principal thrust of appellant's attack on the Texas statutes is that they improperly invade a right, said to be possessed by the pregnant woman, to choose to terminate her pregnancy. Appellant would discover this right in the concept of personal "liberty" embodied in the Fourteenth Amendment's Due Process Clause; or in personal, marital, familial, and sexual privacy said to be protected by the Bill of Rights or its penumbras, see *Griswold v. Connecticut*; or among those rights reserved to the people by the Ninth Amendment, *Griswold v. Connecticut*, [381 U.S. 479 (1965)] (GOLDBERG, J., concurring). Before addressing this claim, we feel it desirable briefly to survey, in several aspects, the history of abortion, for such insight as that history may afford us, and then to examine the state purposes and interests behind the criminal abortion laws.

It perhaps is not generally appreciated that the restrictive criminal abortion laws in effect in a majority of States today are of relatively recent vintage. Those laws, generally proscribing abortion or its attempt at any time during pregnancy except when necessary to preserve the pregnant woman's life, are not of ancient or even of common-law origin. Instead, they derive from statutory changes effected, for the most part, in the latter half of the 19th century. . . .

[A]bortion was practiced in Greek times as well as in the Roman Era. . . . Greek and Roman Law afforded little protection to the unborn. . . .

It is undisputed that at common law, abortion performed *before* "quickening"—the first recognizable movement of the fetus *in utero*, appearing usually from the 16th to the 18th week of pregnancy—was not an indictable offense. . . . In this country, the law in effect in all but a few States until mid-19th century was the pre-existing English common law. Connecticut, the first State to enact abortion legislation, adopted in 1821 that part of Lord Ellenborough's Act that related to a woman "quick with child." The death penalty was not imposed. Abortion before quickening was made a crime in that State only in 1860. In 1828, New York enacted legislation that, in two respects, was to serve as a model for early anti-abortion statutes. First, while barring destruction of an unquickened fetus as well as a quick fetus, it made the former only a misdemeanor, but the latter second-degree manslaughter. Second, it incorporated a concept of therapeutic abortion by providing that an abortion was excused if it "shall have been necessary to preserve the life of such mother, or shall have been advised by two physicians to be necessary for such purpose." By 1840, when Texas had received the common law, only eight American States had statutes dealing with abortion. It was not until after the War Between the States that legislation began generally to replace the common law. Most of these initial statutes dealt severely with abortion after quickening but were lenient with it before quickening. . . .

Gradually, in the middle and late 19th century the quickening distinction disappeared from the statutory law of most States and the degree of the offense and the penalties were increased. By the end of the 1950's a large majority of the jurisdictions banned abortion, however and whenever performed, unless done to save or preserve the life of the mother. . . .

It is thus apparent that at common law, at the time of the adoption of our Constitution, and throughout the major portion of the 19th century, abortion was viewed with less disfavor than under most American statutes currently in effect. Phrasing it another way, a woman enjoyed a substantially broader right to terminate a pregnancy than she does in most States today. . . .

Three reasons have been advanced to explain historically the enactment

Norma McCorvey, who became well known as "Jane Roe," the appellant in *Roe v. Wade.* (*Corbis/Bettmann*)

of criminal abortion laws in the 19th century and to justify their continued existence.

It has been argued occasionally that these laws were the product of a Victorian social concern to discourage illicit sexual conduct. Texas, however, does not advance this justification in the present case. . . .

A second reason is concerned with abortion as a medical procedure. When most criminal abortion laws were first enacted, the procedure was a hazardous one for the woman. . . . Thus, it has been argued that a State's real concern in enacting a criminal abortion law was to protect the pregnant woman, that is, to restrain her from submitting to a procedure that placed her life in serious jeopardy.

Modern medical techniques have altered this situation. Appellants and various *amici* refer to medical data indicating that abortion in early pregnancy, that is, prior to the end of the first trimester, although not without its risk, is now relatively safe. Mortality rates for women undergoing early abortions, where the procedure is legal, appear to be as low as or lower than the rates for normal childbirth. Consequently, any interest of the State in protecting the woman from an inherently hazardous procedure, except when it would be equally dangerous for her to forgo it, has largely disappeared. Of course, important state interests in the areas of health and medical standards to remain. The State has a legitimate interest in seeing to it that abortion, like any other medical procedure, is performed under circumstances that insure maximum safety for the patient. This interest obviously extends at least to the performing physician and his staff, to the facilities involved, to the availability of after-care, and to adequate provision for any complication or emergency that might arise. The prevalence of high mortality rates at illegal "abortion mills" strengthens, rather than weakens, the State's interest in regulating the conditions under which abortions are performed. Moreover, the risk to the woman increases as her pregnancy continues. Thus, the State retains a definite interest in protecting the woman's own health and safety when an abortion is proposed at a late stage of pregnancy.

The third reason is the State's interest—some phrase it in terms of duty—in protecting prenatal life. Some of the argument for this justification rests on the theory that a new human life is present from the moment of conception. The State's interest and general obligation to protect life then extends, it is argued, to prenatal life. Only when the life of the pregnant mother herself is at stake, balanced against the life she carries within her, should the interest of the embryo or fetus not prevail. Logically, of course, a legitimate state interest in this area need not stand or fall on acceptance of the belief that life begins at conception or at some other point prior to live birth. In assessing the State's interest, recognition may be given to the less rigid claim that as long as at least *potential* life is involved, the State may assert interests beyond the protection of the pregnant woman alone. . . .

The Constitution does not explicitly mention any right of privacy. In a line of decisions, however, going back perhaps as far as *Union Pacific R. Co. v. Botsford*, 141 U.S. 250 (1891), the Court has recognized that a right of personal privacy, or a guarantee of certain areas or zones of privacy, does exist under the Constitution. In varying contexts, the Court or individual Justices have, indeed, found at least the roots of that right in the First Amendment, *Stanley v. Georgia*, 394 U.S. 557 (1969); in the Fourth and Fifth Amendments, *Terry v. Ohio*, 392 U.S. 1 (1968), *Katz v. United States*, 389 U.S. 347 (1967); *Boyd v. United States*, 116 U.S. 616 (1886), see *Olmstead v. United States*, 277 U.S. 438 (1928) (BRANDEIS, J., dissenting); in the penumbras of the Bill of Rights, *Griswold v. Connecticut*; in the Ninth Amendment, *id.* (GOLDBERG, J., concurring); or in the concept of liberty guaranteed by the first section of the Fourteenth Amendment, see *Meyer v. Nebraska*, 262 U.S. 390 (1923). These decisions make it clear that only personal rights that can be deemed "fundamental" or "implicit in the concept of ordered liberty," *Palko v. Connecticut*, [302 U.S. 319] (1937), are included in this guarantee of personal privacy. They also make it clear that the right has some extension to activities relating to marriage, *Loving v. Virginia*, 388 U.S. 1 (1967); procreation, *Skinner v. Oklahoma*, 316 U.S. 535 (1942); contraception, *Eisenstadt v. Baird*, [405 U.S. 438 (1972)]; family relationships, *Prince v. Massachusetts*, 321 U.S. 158 (1944); and child rearing and education, *Pierce v. Society of Sisters*, 268 U.S. 510 (1925). . . .

This right of privacy, whether it be founded in the Fourteenth Amendment's concept of personal liberty and restrictions upon state action, as we feel it is, or, as the District Court determined, in the Ninth Amendment's reservation of rights to the people, is broad enough to encompass a woman's decision whether or not to terminate her pregnancy. The detriment that the State would impose upon the pregnant woman by denying this choice altogether is apparent. Specific and direct harm medically diagnosable even in early pregnancy may be involved. Maternity, or additional offspring, may force upon the woman a distressful life and future. Psychological harm may be imminent. Mental and physical health may be taxed by child care. There is also the distress, for all concerned, associated with the unwanted child, and there is the problem of bringing a child into a family already unable, psychologically and otherwise, to care for it. In other cases, as in this one, the additional difficulties and continuing stigma of unwed motherhood may be involved. All these are factors the woman and her responsible physician necessarily will consider in consultation.

On the basis of elements such as these, appellant and some *amici* argue that the woman's right is absolute and that she is entitled to terminate her pregnancy at whatever time, in whatever way, and for whatever reason she alone chooses. With this we do not agree. . . . The Court's decisions recognizing a right of privacy also acknowledge that some state regulation in areas protected by that right is appropriate. As noted above, a State may properly assert important interests in safeguarding health, in maintaining medical standards, and in protecting potential life. . . .

We, therefore, conclude that the right of personal privacy includes the abortion decision, but that this right is not unqualified and must be considered against important state interests in regulation. . . .

Where certain "fundamental rights" are involved, the Court has held that regulation limiting these rights may be justified only by a "compelling state interest," and that legislative enactments must be narrowly drawn to express only the legitimate state interests at stake. . . .

The appellee and certain *amici* argue that the fetus is a "person" within the language and meaning of the Fourteenth Amendment. In support of this, they outline at length and in detail the well-known facts of fetal development. If this suggestion of personhood is established, the appellant's case, of course, collapses, for the fetus' right to life would then be guaranteed specifically by the Amendment. The appellant conceded as much on reargument. On the other hand, the appellee conceded on reargument that no case could be cited that holds that a fetus is a person within the meaning of the Fourteenth Amendment.

The Constitution does not define "person" in so many words. Section 1 of the Fourteenth Amendment contains three references to "person." The first, in defining "citizens," speaks of "persons born or naturalized in the United States." The word also appears both in the Due Process Clause and in the Equal Protection Clause. "Person" is used in other places in the Constitution: in the listing of qualifications for Representatives and Senators, Art. I, § 2, cl. 2, and § 3, cl. 3; in the Apportionment Clause, Art. I, § 2, cl. 3; in the Migration and Importation provision, Art. I, § 9, cl. 1; in the Emolument Clause, Art. I, § 9, cl. 8; in the Electors provisions, Art. II, § 1, cl. 2, and the superseded cl. 3; in the provision outlining qualifications for the office of President, Art. II, § 9, cl. 5; in the Extradition provisions, Art. IV, § 2, cl. 2, and the superseded Fugitive Slave Clause 3; and in the Fifth, Twelfth, and Twenty-second Amendments, as well as in §§ 2 and 3 of the Fourteenth Amendment. But in nearly all these instances, the use of the word is such that it has application only postnatally. None indicates, with any assurance, that it has any possible prenatal application.

All this, together with our observation, *supra*, that throughout the major portion of the 19th century prevailing legal abortion practices were far freer than they are today, persuades us that the word "person," as used in the Fourteenth Amendment, does not include the unborn. . . .

This conclusion, however, does not of itself fully answer the contentions raised by Texas, and we pass on to other considerations.

The pregnant woman cannot be isolated in her privacy. She carries an embryo and, later, a fetus, if one accepts the medical definitions of the developing young in the human uterus. The situation therefore is inherently different from marital intimacy, or bedroom possession of obscene material, or marriage, or procreation, or education, with which *Eisenstadt* and *Griswold, Stanley, Loving, Skinner* and *Pierce* and *Meyer* were respectively concerned. As we have intimated above, it is reasonable and appropriate for a State to decide that at some point in time another interest, that of health of the mother or that of potential human life, becomes significantly involved. The woman's privacy is no longer sole and any right of privacy she possesses must be measured accordingly.

Texas urges that, apart from the Fourteenth Amendment, life begins at conception and is present throughout pregnancy, and that, therefore, the State has a compelling interest in protecting that life from and after conception. We need not resolve the difficult question of when life begins. When those trained in the respective disciplines of medicine, philosophy, and theology are unable to arrive at any consensus, the judiciary, at this point in the development of man's knowledge, is not in a position to speculate as to the answer.

It should be sufficient to note briefly the wide divergence of thinking on this most sensitive and difficult question. There has always been strong support for the view that life does not begin until live birth. This was the belief of the Stoics. It appears to be the predominant, though not the unanimous, attitude of the Jewish faith. It may be taken to represent also the position of a large segment of the Protestant community, insofar as that can be ascertained; organized groups that have taken a formal position on the abortion issue have generally regarded abortion as a matter for the conscience of the individual and her family. As we have noted, the common law found greater significance in quickening. Physicians and their scientific colleagues have regarded that event with less interest and have tended to focus either upon conception, upon live birth, or upon the interim point at which the fetus becomes "viable," that is, potentially able to live outside the mother's womb, albeit with artificial aid. Viability is usually placed at about seven months (28 weeks) but may occur earlier, even at 24 weeks. The Aristotelian theory of "mediate animation," that held sway throughout the Middle Ages and the Renaissance in Europe, continued to be official Roman Catholic dogma until the 19th century, despite opposition to this "ensoulment" theory from those in the Church who would recognize the existence of life from the moment of conception. . . .

In areas other than criminal abortion, the law has been reluctant to endorse any theory that life, as we recognize it, begins before live birth or to accord legal rights to the unborn except in narrowly defined situations and except when the rights are contingent upon live birth. . . .

In view of all this, we do not agree that, by adopting one theory of life, Texas may override the rights of the pregnant woman that are at stake. We repeat, however, that the State does have an important and legitimate interest in preserving and protecting the health of the pregnant woman, whether she be a resident of the State or a nonresident who seeks medical consultation and treatment there, and that it has still *another* important and legitimate interest in protecting the potentiality of human life. These interests are separate and distinct. Each grows in substantiality as the woman approaches term and, at a point during pregnancy, each becomes "compelling."

With respect to the State's important and legitimate interest in the health of the mother, the "compelling" point, in the light of present medical knowledge, is at approximately the end of the first trimester. This is so because of the now-established medical fact that until the end of the first trimester mortality in abortion may be less than mortality in normal childbirth. It follows that, from and after this point, a State may regulate the abortion procedure to the extent that the regulation reasonably relates to the preservation and protection of maternal health. Examples of permissible state regulation in this area are requirements as to the qualifications of the person who is to perform the abortion; as to the licensure of that person; as to the facility in which the procedure is to be performed, that is, whether it must be a hospital or may be a clinic or some other place of less-than-hospital status; as to the licensing of the facility; and the like.

This means, on the other hand, that, for the period of pregnancy prior to this "compelling" point, the attending physician, in consultation with his patient, is free to determine, without regulation by the State, that, in his medical judgment, the patient's pregnancy should be terminated. If that decision is reached, the judgment may be effectuated by an abortion free of interference by the State.

With respect to the State's important and legitimate interest in potential life, the "compelling" point is at viability. This is so because the fetus then presumably has the capability of meaningful life outside the mother's womb. State regulation protective of fetal life after viability thus has both logical and biological justifications. If the State is interested in protecting fetal life after viability, it may go so far as to proscribe abortion during that period, except when it is necessary to preserve the life or health of the mother.

Measured against these standards, Art. 1196 of the Texas Penal Code . . . sweeps too broadly. The statute makes no distinction between abortions performed early in pregnancy and those performed later, and it limits to a single reason, "saving" the mother's life, the legal justification for the procedure. The statute, therefore, cannot survive the constitutional attack made upon it here. . . .

To summarize and to repeat:

1. A state criminal abortion statute of the current Texas type, that excepts from criminality only a *life-saving* procedure on behalf of the mother, without regard to pregnancy stage and without recognition of the other interests involved, is violative of the Due Process Clause of the Fourteenth Amendment.

(a) For the stage prior to approximately the end of the first trimester, the abortion decision and its effectuation must be left to the medical judgment of the pregnant woman's attending physician.

(b) For the stage subsequent to approximately the end of the first trimester, the State, in promoting its interest in the health of the mother, may, if it chooses, regulate the abortion procedure in ways that are reasonably related to maternal health.

(c) For the stage subsequent to viability, the State in promoting its interest in the potentiality of human life may, if it chooses, regulate, and even proscribe, abortion except where it is necessary, in appropriate medical judgment, for the preservation of the life or health of the mother. . . .

This holding, we feel, is consistent with the relative weights of the respective interests involved, with the lessons and examples of medical and legal history, with the lenity of the common law, and with the demands of the profound problems of the present day.

☐ *Justice STEWART, concurring.*

[I]t was clear to me then, and it is equally clear to me now, that the *Griswold* decision can be rationally understood only as a holding that the Connecticut statute substantively invaded the "liberty" that is protected by the Due Process Clause of the Fourteenth Amendment. As so understood, *Griswold* stands as one in a long line of . . . cases decided under the doctrine of substantive due process, and I now accept it as such. . . .

[T]he Court today is correct in holding that the right asserted by Jane Roe is embraced within the personal liberty protected by the Due Process Clause of the Fourteenth Amendment. . . .

☐ *Justice REHNQUIST, dissenting.*

I have difficulty in concluding, as the Court does, that the right of "privacy" is involved in this case. Texas, by the statute here challenged, bars the performance of a medical abortion by a licensed physician on a plaintiff such as Roe. A transaction resulting in an operation such as this is not "private" in the ordinary usage of that word. Nor is the "privacy" that the Court finds here even a distant relative of the freedom from searches and seizures protected by the Fourth Amendment to the Constitution, which the Court has referred to as embodying a right to privacy. . . .

If the Court means by the term "privacy" no more than that the claim of a person to be free from unwanted state regulation of consensual transactions may be a form of "liberty" protected by the Fourteenth Amendment, there is no doubt that similar claims have been upheld in our earlier decisions on the basis of that liberty. I agree with the statement of Justice STEWART in his concurring opinion that the "liberty," against deprivation of which without due process the Fourteenth Amendment protects, embraces more than the rights found in the Bill of Rights. But that liberty is not guaranteed absolutely against deprivation, only against deprivation without due process of law. The test traditionally applied in the area of social and economic legislation is whether or not a law such as that challenged has a rational relation to a valid state objective. *Williamson v. Lee Optical Co.*, 348 U.S. 483 (1955).

The Due Process Clause of the Fourteenth Amendment undoubtedly does place a limit, albeit a broad one, on legislative power to enact laws such as this. If the Texas statute were to prohibit an abortion even where the mother's life is in jeopardy, I have little doubt that such a statute would lack a rational relation to a valid state objective under the test stated in *Williamson, supra*. But the Court's sweeping invalidation of any restrictions on abortion during the first trimester is impossible to justify under that standard, and the conscious weighing of competing factors that the Court's opinion apparently substitutes for the established test is far more appropriate to a legislative judgment than to a judicial one. . . .

While the Court's opinion quotes from the dissent of Justice HOLMES in *Lochner v. New York*, 198 U.S. 45 (1905), the result it reaches is more closely attuned to the majority opinion of Justice PECKHAM in that case. As in *Lochner* and similar cases applying substantive due process standards to economic and social welfare legislation, the adoption of the compelling state interest standard will inevitably require this Court to examine the legislative policies and pass on the wisdom of these policies in the very process of deciding whether a particular state interest put forward may or may not be "compelling." The decision here to break pregnancy into three distinct terms and to outline the permissible restrictions the State may impose in each one, for example, partakes more of judicial legislation than it does of a determination of the intent of the drafters of the Fourteenth Amendment.

The fact that a majority of the States reflecting, after all the majority sentiment in those States, have had restrictions on abortions for at least a century is a strong indication, it seems to me, that the asserted right to an abortion is not "so rooted in the traditions and conscience of our people as to be ranked as fundamental." . . .

To reach its result, the Court necessarily has had to find within the Scope of the Fourteenth Amendment a right that was apparently completely unknown to the drafters of the Amendment. As early as 1821, the first state law dealing directly with abortion was enacted by the Connecticut Legislature. By the time of the adoption of the Fourteenth Amendment in 1868, there were at least 36 laws enacted by state or territorial legislatures limiting abortion. . . .

The only conclusion possible from this history is that the drafters did not intend to have the Fourteenth Amendment withdraw from the States the power to legislate with respect to this matter.

□ *Justice WHITE, with whom Justice REHNQUIST joins, dissenting.*

With all due respect, I dissent. I find nothing in the language or history of the Constitution to support the Court's judgment. The Court simply fashions and announces a new constitutional right for pregnant mothers and, with scarcely any reason or authority for its action, invests that right with sufficient substance to override most existing state abortion statutes. The upshot is that the people and the legislatures of the 50 States are constitutionally disentitled to weigh the relative importance of the continued existence and development of the fetus, on the one hand, against a spectrum of possible impacts on the mother, on the other hand. As an exercise of raw judicial power, the Court perhaps has authority to do what it does today; but in my view its judgment is an improvident and extravagant exercise of the power of judicial review that the Constitution extends to this Court.

The Court apparently values the convenience of the pregnant mother more than the continued existence and development of the life or potential life that she carries. Whether or not I might agree with that marshaling of values, I can in no event join the Court's judgment because I find no constitutional warrant for imposing such an order of priorities on the people and legislatures of the States. In a sensitive area such as this, involving as it does issues over which reasonable men may easily and heatedly differ, I cannot accept the Court's exercise of its clear power of choice by interposing a constitutional barrier to state efforts to protect human life and by investing mothers and doctors with the constitutionally protected right to exterminate it. This issue, for the most part, should be left with the people and to the political processes the people have devised to govern their affairs. . . .

Maher v. Roe

432 U.S. 464, 97 S.Ct. 2376 (1977)

Two indigent women, known as Susan Roe and Mary Poe, sued Edward Maher, the commissioner of Connecticut's Department of Social Services, and challenged the constitutionality of a state regulation prohibiting the funding of abortions that are not medically necessary. The state interpreted Title XIX of the Social Security Act, which establishes the Medicaid program under which participating states may provide federally funded medical assistance to needy persons, to forbid the funding of nontherapeutic abortions. Roe, an unmarried mother of three children, was unable to obtain an abortion because her doctor refused to certify that an abortion was medically necessary. Poe, a sixteen-year-old high-school junior, had an abortion but, because she failed to obtain a certificate of medical necessity, the Department of Social Services refused to reimburse the hospital for Poe's $244 hospital bill.

A federal district court rejected Connecticut's interpretation of Title XIX when holding that the Social Security Act not only allowed funding of nontherapeutic abortions but required it. On appeal, the Court of Appeals for the Second Circuit ruled that the Social Security Act permitted (but did not require) state funding of abortions and remanded the case back to the district court, which then overturned Connecticut's regulation forbidding the funding of nontherapeutic abortions.

Maher appealed that ruling to the Supreme Court which granted review. The Court handed down its decision along with *Beal v. Doe*, 432 U.S. 438 (1977), which held that the Social Security Act does not require states to pay for nontherapeutic abortions as a condition of their participating in the Medicaid program.

The Court's decision was six to three, and the majority's opinion was announced by Justice Powell. Chief Justice Burger filed a concurring opinion. Separate dissenting opinions were filed by Justices Brennan, Blackmun, and Marshall.

☐ *Justice POWELL delivers the opinion of the Court.*

[W]e hold today that Title XIX of the Social Security Act does not require the funding of nontherapeutic abortions as a condition of participation in the joint federal-state medicaid program established by that statute. . . .

The Constitution imposes no obligation on the States to pay the pregnancy-related medical expenses of indigent women, or indeed to pay any of the medical expenses of indigents. But when a State decides to alleviate some of the hardships of poverty by providing medical care, the manner in which it dispenses benefits is subject to constitutional limitations. Appellees' claim is that Connecticut must accord equal treatment to both abortion and childbirth, and may not evidence a policy preference by funding only the medical expenses incident to childbirth. This challenge to the classifications established by the Connecticut regulation presents a question arising under the Equal Protection Clause of the Fourteenth Amendment. . . .

This case involves no discrimination against a suspect class. An indigent woman desiring an abortion does not come within the limited category of disadvantaged classes so recognized by our cases. Nor does the fact that the impact of the regulation falls upon those who cannot pay lead to a different conclusion. In a sense, every denial of welfare to an indigent creates a wealth classification as compared to nonindigents who are able to pay for the desired goods or services. But this Court has never held that financial need alone identifies a suspect class for purposes of equal protection analysis. . . . Accordingly, the central question in this case is whether the regulation "impinges upon a fundamental right explicitly or implicitly protected by the Constitution." . . .

At issue in *Roe* [*v. Wade*, 410 U.S. 113 (1973)], was the constitutionality of a Texas law making it a crime to procure or attempt to procure an abortion, except on medical advice for the purpose of saving the life of the mother. . . . [W]e concluded that the Fourteenth Amendment's concept of personal liberty affords constitutional protection against state interference with certain aspects of an individual's personal "privacy," including a woman's decision to terminate her pregnancy. . . .

The Texas law in *Roe* was a stark example of impermissible interference with the pregnant woman's decision to terminate her pregnancy. In subsequent cases, we have invalidated other types of restrictions, different in form but similar in effect, on the woman's freedom of choice. . . .

The Connecticut regulation before us is different in kind from the laws invalidated in our previous abortion decisions. The Connecticut regulation places no obstacles—absolute or otherwise—in the pregnant woman's path to an abortion. An indigent woman who desires an abortion suffers no disadvantage as a consequence of Connecticut's decision to fund childbirth; she continues as before to be dependent on private sources for the service she desires. The State may have made childbirth a more attractive alternative, thereby influencing the woman's decision, but it has imposed no restriction on access to abortions that was not already there. The indigency that may make it difficult—and in some cases, perhaps, impossible—for some women to have abortions is neither created nor in any way affected by the Connecticut regulation. We conclude that the Connecticut regulation does not impinge upon the fundamental right recognized in *Roe.*

Our conclusion signals no retreat from *Roe* or the cases applying it. There is a basic difference between direct state interference with a protected activity and state encouragement of an alternative activity consonant with legislative policy. Constitutional concerns are greatest when the State attempts to impose its will by force of law; the State's power to encourage actions deemed to be in the public interest is necessarily far broader.

The question remains whether Connecticut's regulation can be sustained under the less demanding test of rationality that applies in the absence of a suspect classification or the impingement of a fundamental right. This test requires that the distinction drawn between childbirth and nontherapeutic abortion by the regulation be "rationally related" to a "constitutionally permissible" purpose. We hold that the Connecticut funding scheme satisfies this standard.

Roe itself explicitly acknowledged the State's strong interest in protecting the potential life of the fetus. That interest exists throughout the pregnancy, "grow[ing] in substantiality as the woman approaches term." Because the pregnant woman carries a potential human being she "cannot be isolated in her privacy. . . . [Her] privacy is no longer sole and any right of privacy she possesses must be measured accordingly." . . . The State unquestionably has a "strong and legitimate interest in encouraging normal childbirth," . . . an interest honored over the centuries. Nor can there be any question that the Connecticut regulation rationally furthers that interest. The medical costs associated with childbirth are substantial, and have increased significantly in recent years. As recognized by the District Court in this case, such costs are significantly greater than those normally associated with elective abortions during the first trimester. The subsidizing of costs incident to childbirth is a rational means of encouraging childbirth.

We certainly are not unsympathetic to the plight of an indigent woman who desires an abortion, but "the Constitution does not provide judicial remedies for every social and economic ill."

☐ *Justice BRENNAN, with whom Justice MARSHALL and Justice BLACKMUN join, dissenting.*

[A] distressing insensitivity to the plight of impoverished pregnant women is inherent in the Court's analysis. The stark reality for too many, not just "some," indigent pregnant women is that indigency makes access to competent licensed physicians not merely "difficult" but "impossible." As a practical matter, many indigent women will feel they have no choice but to carry their pregnancies to term because the State will pay for the associated medical services, even though they would have chosen to have abortions if the State had also provided funds for that procedure, or indeed if the State had provided funds for neither procedure. This disparity in funding by the State clearly operates to coerce indigent pregnant women to bear children they would not otherwise choose to have, and just as clearly, this coercion can only operate upon the poor, who are uniquely the victims of this form of financial pressure. . . .

The Court's premise is that only an equal protection claim is presented here. Claims of interference with enjoyment of fundamental rights have, however, occupied a rather protean position in our constitutional jurisprudence. Whether or not the Court's analysis may reasonably proceed under the Equal Protection Clause, the Court plainly errs in ignoring, as it does, the unanswerable argument of appellee, and holding of the District Court, that the regulation unconstitutionally impinges upon her claim of privacy derived from the Due Process Clause.

Roe v. Wade and cases following it hold that an area of privacy invulnerable to the State's intrusion surrounds the decision of a pregnant woman whether or not to carry her pregnancy to term. The Connecticut scheme clearly infringes upon that area of privacy by bringing financial pressures on indigent women that force them to bear children they would not otherwise have. That is an obvious impairment of the fundamental right established by *Roe*. . . .

Until today, I had not thought the nature of the fundamental right established in *Roe* was open to question, let alone susceptible to the interpretation advanced by the Court. The fact that the Connecticut scheme may not operate as an absolute bar preventing all indigent women from having abortions is not critical. What is critical is that the State has inhibited their fundamental right to make that choice free from state interference. . . .

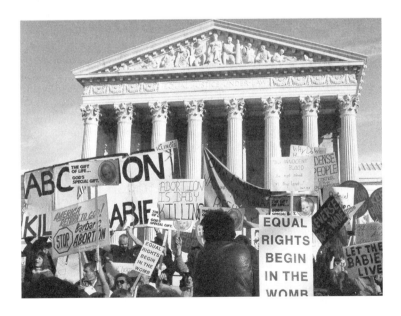

Demonstration on the steps of the Supreme Court Building protesting rulings on abortion. (*Corbis/UPI*)

■ The Development of Law

*Other Post-*Roe *Rulings on Abortion*

CASE	VOTE	RULING
Doe v. Bolton, 410 U.S. 179 (1973)	7:2	A companion case decided along with *Roe v. Wade*, which extended *Roe*, in holding that

states may not criminalize abortions, or make abortions unreasonably difficult to obtain; *Doe* struck down state requirements that abortions be performed in licensed hospitals; that abortions be approved beforehand by a hospital committee; and that two physicians concur in the abortion decision.

Planned Parenthood of Central Missouri v. Danforth, 428 U.S. 552 (1976)	5:4	Ruled that informed consent statutes, requiring doctors to obtain the written consent of a woman after informing her

of the dangers of abortion and possible alternatives, were permissible if the requirements were related to maternal health and not overbearing; the requirements must also be narrowly drawn so as not to unduly interfere with the physician–patient relationship; and in addition, the Court upheld requiring doctors to provide information to states on each abortion performed, so long as the reporting requirements related to maternal health remain confidential and are not overbearing. The Court, however, struck down fetal-protection statutes that pertain only to previable fetuses and require doctors to use available means to save the lives of fetuses; finally, the Court held that "it is not the proper function of the legislature or the courts to place viability, which is essentially a medical concept, at a specific point in the gestation period. The time when viability is achieved may vary with each pregnancy, and the determination of whether a particular fetus is viable is, and must be, a matter for the judgment of the attending physician."

Bellotti v. Baird, 428 U.S. 132 (1976)	9:0	Overturned a law requiring parental consent for minors seeking abortions.

Beal v. Doe, 432 U.S. 438 (1977)	6:3	Held that nothing in the language or history of Title XIX of the Social Security Act re-

quired the funding of nontherapeutic abortions as a condition of a state's participating in the Medicaid program established under the act; the Court indicated that Title XIX left states free to include coverage for nontherapeutic abortions if they choose to do so, but also that they could refuse to fund unnecessary medical services.

CASE	VOTE	RULING

Maher v. Roe, 432 U.S. 464   6:3   Upheld Connecticut's refusal to
(1977)   reimburse Medicaid recipients for abortion expenses except where the attending physician certifies that an abortion is medically or psychiatrically necessary.

Poelker v. Doe, 432 U.S. 59   6:3   Upheld the policy of the city
(1977)   of St. Louis, Missouri, to deny indigent pregnant women access to nontherapeutic abortions in *public* hospitals.

Bellotti v. Baird, 443 U.S. 622   9:0   Ruled that while states may
(1979)   require minors to obtain parental consent, they must provide an alternative judicial procedure for procuring authorization of a minor's abortion, if parental consent is denied or the minor does not want to seek it.

Harris v. McRae, 448 U.S. 297   5:4   Upheld the Hyde Amendment
(1980)   to the Medicaid program that limited federal funding for nontherapeutic abortions; the Court also upheld the right of a state to fund only those medically necessary abortions for which it received federal reimbursement.

H. L. v. Matheson, 450 U.S.   6:3   Upheld a Utah statute requir-
398 (1981)   ing physicians to notify parents, "if possible," prior to performing an abortion on their minor daughter (1) when the girl is living with and dependent on her parents, (2) when she is not emancipated by marriage or otherwise, and (3) when she has made no claim or showing as to her maturity or as to her relationship with her parents.

Akron v. Akron Center for   6:3   Struck down five sections of a
Reproductive Health, 462 U.S.   city ordinance for unduly re-
416 (1983)   stricting a woman's right to obtain an abortion; the sections provided that (1) after the first trimester of a pregnancy, all abortions be performed in a hospital; (2) there be notification of consent by parents before abortions are performed on unmarried minors; (3) the attending physician make certain specified statements to a patient so that the patient's consent for an abortion would amount to "informed consent"; (4) there be a twenty-four-hour waiting period between the time a patient signs the consent form and when an abortion is performed; and (5) fetal remains be disposed of in a "humane and sanitary manner."

CASE	VOTE	RULING
Planned Parenthood Association of Kansas City v. Ashcroft, 462 U.S. 476 (1983)	6:3 & 5:4	Invalidated Missouri's second-trimester hospitalization requirement, but a bare majority struck down the state's require-

ment that after twelve weeks of pregnancy, all abortions be performed in a hospital and (voting five to four) *upheld* three other sections of Missouri's law—they required (1) pathological reports for each abortion performed, (2) the presence of a second doctor during abortions performed after viability, and (3) parental consent or consent from a juvenile court for minors before obtaining an abortion.

Simopoulos v. Virginia, 462 U.S. 506 (1983)	8:1	Upheld Virginia's mandatory hospitalization requirement for abortions performed in the second trimester.

Thornburgh v. American College of Obstetricians & Gynecologists, 476 U.S. 747 (1986)	5:4	Struck down a Pennsylvania law requiring (1) women to be advised of medical assistance and that the natural father is re-

sponsible for child support, (2) physicians to inform women of the detrimental effects and risks of abortion, (3) doctors to report all abortions to the state, (4) a higher degree of care in postviability abortions in an attempt to save the life of the fetus, and (5) the presence of a second physician during the performance of all abortions.

Bowen v. Kendrick, 487 U.S. 589 (1988)	5:4	Upheld the Adolescent Family Life Act, which prohibits federal funding of organizations in-

volved with abortions, while permitting funding of religious groups advocating self-discipline as a form of birth control.

Webster v. Reproductive Health Services, 492 U.S. 490 (1989)	5:4	Upheld the constitutionality of Missouri's 1986 restrictive abortion law, which (1) decreed

that life begins at conception; (2) requires a doctor, before performing an abortion on a woman believed to be twenty or more weeks pregnant, to test the fetus's "gestational age, weight, and lung maturity"; (3) prohibits public employees or facilities from being used to perform abortions not necessary to save a woman's life; and (4) made it unlawful to use public funds, employees, or facilities for the purpose of "encouraging or counseling" a woman to have an abortion, except when her life is endangered. Justices Brennan, Stevens, Marshall, and Blackmun dissented.

CASE	VOTE	RULING
Hodgson v. Minnesota, 497 U.S. 417 (1990)	5:4	With Justice O'Connor casting the crucial vote, a bare majority agreed that, without a judicial

bypass option, the state's requirement that minors notify both parents before obtaining an abortion was unconstitutional—on that issue, Justice O'Connor joined Justices Brennan, Blackmun, Marshall, and Stevens. But O'Connor also joined Chief Justice Rehnquist and Justices Scalia, Kennedy, and White in upholding the constitutionality of the parental consent law.

CASE	VOTE	RULING
Planned Parenthood of Southeastern Pennsylvania v. Casey, 500 U.S. 833 (1992)	5:4	In an unusual opinion for the Court issued by Justices O'Connor, Kennedy, and Souter, and joined in part by

Justices Blackmun and Stevens, the Court upheld most of the provisions of Pennsylvania's 1988 abortion law, requiring (1) doctors to discuss the risks and consequences of abortion and to obtain a woman's written consent for an abortion; (2) women to wait, after giving their informed consent, twenty-four hours before having an abortion; (3) unmarried women under the age of eighteen to obtain the written consent of at least one parent or a judge before having an abortion; and (4) doctors to report to public health authorities on each abortion performed. A bare majority struck down the additional requirement that women, under most circumstances, certify that they have notified their spouses of their intent to have an abortion. That requirement was deemed to constitute an "undue burden" on women, and on that score and the majority's refusal to discard *Roe* the chief justice and Justices Scalia, Thomas, and White dissented.

Rust v. Sullivan

500 U.S. 173, 111 S.CT. 1759 (1991)

In this case, the Supreme Court upheld the Reagan administration's ban on abortion counseling by organizations that receive federal funding. An excerpt of the opinions in the case appears in Chapter 5.

■ INSIDE THE COURT:

Drafting the Opinion for the Court in Planned Parenthood of Southeastern Pennsylvania v. Casey

Planned Parenthood's petition for review asked the Court to rule on whether *Roe's* "holding that a woman's right to choose abortion is a fundamental right" had been overruled by subsequent decisions. But when voting to grant review at conference on January 12, 1992, Justice O'Connor remained in no mood to do so and Souter pushed for a reformulation of the question presented. He followed up by proposing that attorneys brief and direct arguments to whether "the 'undue burden' standard of review [is] the appropriate standard of review" and whether the appellate court correctly applied it. Although agreeing on a rephrasing of the questions, Stevens suggested instead that counsel be asked simply whether the lower court erred in upholding certain provisions and "what weight is due to *stare decisis* in evaluating the constitutional right to abortion." Justice Souter agreed but others disagreed with the latter question, even though it was central to the continuing controversy. As a result, when granting review the Court limited the issues to whether the appellate court erred in upholding provisions of the law and in striking down its requirement for spousal consent.

At the Wednesday conference two days after hearing oral arguments in *Casey* on April 4, Chief Justice Rehnquist led the discussion and voted to uphold all the state's requirements. Justice White agreed, while Stevens thought the requirement for a twenty-four-hour waiting period was "an insult" and the spousal consent requirement was "outrageous." Blackmun would have struck down all of the provisions but "passed." O'Connor remained in no mood to overrule *Roe* but said that the appellate court had "got most [of it] right." Kennedy agreed, while Scalia and Thomas were firmly with the chief justice and would have gone further to overrule *Roe.* Rehnquist thus had a majority and a few days later assigned himself the job of writing the opinion for the Court, as he had done in *Webster v. Reproductive Health Services*, 492 U.S. 490 (1989), and other major cases.

Not quite a month later, on May 27, Chief Justice Rehnquist circulated his draft, upholding all of Pennsylvania's restrictions as having a rational basis. The only concession he made was in noting that women were exempt from the notice and consent requirements when confronted with a "significant threat to [their] life or health," though he also concluded that due process did not require states to include in such a "medical emergency" exception "all insignificant and negligible threats to a woman's health." That outcome, as in *Webster,* had been anticipated and Souter and O'Connor had been privately talking with Kennedy about not following the chief in *Casey* as he had done in *Webster.* They urged him to reaffirm *Roe's* central holding on a woman's right to choose, while upholding most of Pennsylvania's restrictions based on O'Connor's "undue burden" test. Souter had already been working on a draft dealing with *stare decisis* and why *Roe* should be upheld, based on societal expectations and the damage that would be done to the Court's institutional prestige if it were overturned. Kennedy agreed and two days after the chief justice circulated his first draft he sent Blackmun a note telling him that he wanted to talk about some "welcome news."

On June 3, Justices O'Connor, Kennedy, and Souter circulated their draft opinion, concurring and dissenting in part from the chief's draft opinion for the Court. Justice Stevens followed up by joining certain sections of their opinion and urging Blackmun to do the same. Rehnquist circulated a second draft of his opinion for the Court on June 17, which now included a new section taking issue with the analysis of *stare decisis* in the opinion circulated by the "troika," as law clerks referred to O'Connor, Kennedy, and Souter. He dismissed their analysis as "*dicta*" and reaffirmed *Webster's* rejection of a woman's "fundamental right" to abortion and heightened scrutiny analysis. But it proved too late. Stevens and Blackmun agreed to join portions of the O'Connor-Kennedy-Souter draft and thereby formed a new bare majority. Five days later, on June 22, the second draft opinion by O'Connor-Kennedy-Souter circulated but now as the opinion for the Court. Subsequently, on June 26, Rehnquist circulated his third and revised draft, but one that now concurred and dissented in part, rather than spoke for the Court. The next day, the final draft of the opinion for the Court that would come down on June 29 circulated, reaffirming *Roe's* "central holding" while upholding all of Pennsylvania's restrictions except for that requiring spousal consent.

Source: Justice Harry A. Blackmun Papers, Box 151, Manuscripts Room, Library of Congress, Washington, D.C.

Planned Parenthood of Southeastern Pennsylvania v. Casey
505 U.S. 833, 112 S.Ct. 2791 (1992)

In 1988 and 1989, following the Supreme Court's ruling in *Webster v. Reproductive Health Services*, 492 U.S. 490 (1989), Pennsylvania amended its state abortion law by enacting more restrictive provisions conditioning access to abortions. Planned Parenthood of Southeastern Pennsylvania immediately challenged the constitutionality of those provisions. Subsequently, the Court of Appeals for the Third Circuit upheld most of those restrictions, except for a spousal notification provision. In doing so, the Third Circuit adopted Justice O'Connor's undue burden analysis, in her dissenting opinion in *Akron v. Akron Center for Reproductive Health, Inc.*, 462 U.S. 416 (1983). Accordingly, the appellate court gave strict scrutiny to any restriction that unduly burdened women and held that abortion restrictions that do not pose an undue burden are permissible so long as they have a rational basis. And on that basis, the Third Circuit upheld Pennsylvania's requiring women to (1) be informed by doctors about fetal development; (2) give their consent or, if they were minors, obtain parental consent; and (3) wait at least twenty-four hours after giving their informed consent before obtaining an abortion as well as (4) imposing certain reporting and public disclosure requirements on doctors who perform abortions. Despite the fact that virtually identical requirements were struck down by a bare majority of the Burger Court in *Thornburgh v. American College of Obstetricians and Gynecologists*, 476 U.S. 747 (1986), the Third Circuit noted that the Rehnquist Court had substantially altered its analysis and undercut support for a woman's fundamental right to obtain an abortion in *Webster v. Reproductive Health Services*, 492 U.S. 490 (1989). The appellate court, moreover, did not deem any of the above restrictions to constitute an undue burden and, therefore, applied the rational basis test when upholding these requirements. Pennsylvania, however, also required married women to notify their spouses of their desire to obtain an abortion, and the appellate court overturned that requirement as an undue burden on women. When strictly scrutinizing that provision, the Third Circuit concluded that it unduly burdened women by potentially exposing them to spousal abuse, violence, and economic duress at the hands of their husbands. Both sides of the abortion controversy appealed the appellate court's decision.

The Court's decision was five to four, but the justices split three-two-four. The opinion was announced by Justices O'Connor, Kennedy, and Souter. Justices Blackmun and Stevens delivered separate opinions in part concurring and in part dissenting. Chief Justice Rehnquist and Justice Scalia joined each other and were joined by Justices Thomas and White.

> ☐ *Justice O'CONNOR, Justice KENNEDY, and Justice SOUTER announced the judgment of the Court and delivered the opinion of the Court with respect to Parts I, II, III, V-A, V-C, and VI, an opinion with respect to Part V-E, in which Justice STEVENS joins, and an opinion with respect to Parts IV, V-B, and V-D.*

■ I

After considering the fundamental constitutional questions resolved by *Roe* [*v. Wade*, 410 U.S. 113 (1973)], principles of institutional integrity, and the rule of *stare decisis*, we are led to conclude this: the essential holding of *Roe v. Wade* should be retained and once again reaffirmed.

It must be stated at the outset and with clarity that *Roe's* essential holding, the holding we reaffirm, has three parts. First is a recognition of the right of the woman to choose to have an abortion before viability and to obtain it without undue interference from the State. Before viability, the State's interests are not strong enough to support a prohibition of abortion or the imposition of a substantial obstacle to the woman's effective right to elect the procedure. Second is a confirmation of the State's power to restrict abortions after fetal viability, if the law contains exceptions for pregnancies which endanger a woman's life or health. And third is the principle that the State has legitimate interests from the outset of the pregnancy in protecting the health of the woman and the life of the fetus that may become a child. These principles do not contradict one another; and we adhere to each. . . .

■ III

[*A*] [W]hen this Court reexamines a prior holding, its judgment is customarily informed by a series of prudential and pragmatic considerations designed to test the consistency of overruling a prior decision with the ideal of the rule of law, and to gauge the respective costs of reaffirming and overruling a prior case. Thus, for example, we may ask whether the rule has proved to be intolerable simply in defying practical workability; whether the rule is subject to a kind of reliance that would lend a special hardship to the consequences of overruling and add inequity to the cost of repudiation; whether related principles of law have so far developed as to have left the old rule no more than a remnant of abandoned doctrine; or whether facts have so changed, or come to be seen so differently, as to have robbed the old rule of significant application or justification, e.g., *Burnet v. Coronado Oil Gas Co.,* 285 U.S. 393 (1932) (BRANDEIS, J., dissenting). . . .

Although *Roe* has engendered opposition, it has in no sense proven "unworkable," representing as it does a simple limitation beyond which a state law is unenforceable. . . .

We have seen how time has overtaken some of *Roe's* factual assumptions: advances in maternal health care allow for abortions safe to the mother later in pregnancy than was true in 1973, and advances in neonatal care have advanced viability to a point somewhat earlier. But these facts go only to the scheme of time limits on the realization of competing interests, and the divergences from the factual premises of 1973 have no bearing on the validity of *Roe's* central holding, that viability marks the earliest point at which the State's interest in fetal life is constitutionally adequate to justify a legislative ban on nontherapeutic abortions. The soundness or unsoundness of that constitutional judgment in no sense turns on whether viability occurs at approximately 28 weeks, as was usual at the time of *Roe*, at 23 to 24 weeks, as it sometimes does today, or at some moment even slightly earlier in pregnancy, as it may if fetal respiratory capacity can somehow be enhanced in the future. Whenever it may occur, the attainment of viability may continue to serve as the critical fact, just as it has done since *Roe* was decided; which is to say that no change in *Roe's* factual underpinning has left its central holding obsolete, and none supports an argument for overruling it.

[*B*] In a less significant case, *stare decisis* analysis could, and would, stop at the point we have reached. But the sustained and widespread debate *Roe* has provoked calls for some comparison between that case and others of comparable dimension that have responded to national controversies and taken on the impress of the controversies addressed. Only two such decisional lines from the past century present themselves for examination, and in each instance the result reached by the Court accorded with the principles we apply today.

The first example is that line of cases identified with *Lochner v. New York*, 198 U.S. 45 (1905), which imposed substantive limitations on legislation limiting economic autonomy in favor of health and welfare regulation, adopting, in Justice HOLMES' view, the theory of laissez-faire. The *Lochner* decisions were exemplified by *Adkins v. Children's Hospital of D.C.*, 261 U.S. 525 (1923), in which this Court held it to be an infringement of constitutionally protected liberty of contract to require the employers of adult women to satisfy minimum wage standards. Fourteen years later, *West Coast Hotel Co. v. Parrish*, 300 U.S. 379 (1937), signaled the demise of *Lochner* by overruling *Adkins*. In the meantime, the Depression had come and, with it, the lesson that seemed unmistakable to most people by 1937, that the interpretation of contractual freedom protected in *Adkins* rested on fundamentally false factual assumptions about the capacity of a relatively unregulated market to satisfy minimal levels of human welfare. . . .

The second comparison that 20th century history invites is with the cases employing the separate-but-equal rule for applying the Fourteenth Amendment's equal protection guarantee. They began with *Plessy v. Ferguson*, 163 U.S. 537 (1896), holding that legislatively mandated racial segregation in public transportation works no denial of equal protection. . . . The *Plessy* Court considered "the underlying fallacy of the plaintiff's argument to consist in the assumption that the enforced separation of the two races stamps the colored race with a badge of inferiority. If this be so, it is not by reason of anything found in the act, but solely because the colored race chooses to put that construction upon it." Whether, as a matter of historical fact, the Justices in the *Plessy* majority believed this or not, this understanding of the implication of segregation was the stated justification for the Court's opinion. But this understanding of the facts and the rule it was stated to justify were repudiated in *Brown v. Board of Education*, 347 U.S. 483 (1954). . . .

The Court in *Brown* addressed these facts of life by observing that whatever may have been the understanding in *Plessy*'s time of the power of segregation to stigmatize those who were segregated with a "badge of inferiority," it was clear by 1954 that legally sanctioned segregation had just such an effect, to the point that racially separate public educational facilities were deemed inherently unequal. Society's understanding of the facts upon which a constitutional ruling was sought in 1954 was thus fundamentally different from the basis claimed for the decision in 1896. While we think *Plessy* was wrong the day it was decided, we must also recognize that the *Plessy* Court's explanation for its decision was so clearly at odds with the facts apparent to the Court in 1954 that the decision to reexamine *Plessy* was on this ground alone not only justified but required.

West Coast Hotel and *Brown* each rested on facts, or an understanding of facts, changed from those which furnished the claimed justifications for the earlier constitutional resolutions. . . . In constitutional adjudication as elsewhere in life, changed circumstances may impose new obligations, and the thoughtful part of the Nation could accept each decision to overrule a prior case as a response to the Court's constitutional duty.

Because the case before us presents no such occasion it could be seen as no such response. Because neither the factual underpinnings of *Roe*'s central holding nor our understanding of it has changed (and because no other indication of weakened precedent has been shown) the Court could not pretend to be reexamining the prior law with any justification beyond a present doctrinal disposition to come out differently from the Court of 1973. . . .

[C] The examination of the conditions justifying the repudiation of *Adkins* by *West Coast Hotel* and *Plessy* by *Brown* is enough to suggest the terrible price that would have been paid if the Court had not overruled as it did. In the present case, however, as our analysis to this point makes clear, the terrible price would be paid for overruling. Our analysis would not be complete, however, without explaining why overruling *Roe*'s central holding would not only reach an unjustifiable result under principles of *stare decisis*, but would seriously weaken the Court's capacity to exercise the judicial power and to function as the Supreme Court of a Nation dedicated to the rule of law. . . .

The underlying substance of [the Court's] legitimacy is . . . expressed in the Court's opinions, and our contemporary understanding is such that a decision without principled justification would be no judicial act at all. . . . The Court must take care to speak and act in ways that allow people to accept its decisions on the terms the Court claims for them, as grounded truly in principle, not as compromises with social and political pressures having, as such, no bearing on the principled choices that the Court is obliged to make. Thus, the Court's legitimacy depends on making legally principled decisions under circumstances in which their principled character is sufficiently plausible to be accepted by the Nation. . . .

The Court's duty in the present case is clear. In 1973, it confronted the already-divisive issue of governmental power to limit personal choice to undergo abortion, for which it provided a new resolution based on the due process guaranteed by the Fourteenth Amendment. Whether or not a new social consensus is developing on that issue, its divisiveness is no less today than in 1973, and pressure to overrule the decision, like pressure to retain it, has grown only more intense. A decision to overrule *Roe*'s essential holding under the existing circumstances would address error, if error there was, at the cost of both profound and unnecessary damage to the Court's legitimacy, and to the Nation's commitment to the rule of law. It is therefore imperative to adhere to the essence of *Roe*'s original decision, and we do so today.

■ IV

We conclude that the basic decision in *Roe* was based on a constitutional analysis which we cannot now repudiate. The woman's liberty is not so unlimited, however, that from the outset the State cannot show its concern for the life of the unborn, and at a later point in fetal development the State's interest in life has sufficient force so that the right of the woman to terminate the pregnancy can be restricted.

That brings us, of course, to the point where much criticism has been directed at *Roe*, a criticism that always inheres when the Court draws a specific rule from what in the Constitution is but a general standard. . . . And it falls to us to give some real substance to the woman's liberty to determine whether to carry her pregnancy to full term.

We conclude the line should be drawn at viability, so that before that time the woman has a right to choose to terminate her pregnancy. We adhere to this principle for two reasons. First, as we have said, is the doctrine of *stare decisis*. Any judicial act of line-drawing may seem somewhat arbitrary, but *Roe* was a reasoned statement, elaborated with great care. We have twice re-affirmed it in the face of great opposition. Although we must overrule those parts of *Thornburgh* and *Akron I* which, in our view, are inconsistent with *Roe*'s statement that the State has a legitimate interest in promoting the life or potential life of the unborn, the central premise of those cases represents an unbroken commitment by this Court to the essential holding of *Roe*. It is that premise which we reaffirm today.

The second reason is that the concept of viability, as we noted in *Roe*, is the time at which there is a realistic possibility of maintaining and nourishing a life outside the womb, so that the independent existence of the second life can in reason and all fairness be the object of state protection that now overrides the rights of the woman. Consistent with other constitutional norms, legislatures may draw lines which appear arbitrary without the necessity of offering a justification. But courts may not. We must justify the lines we draw. And there is no line other than viability which is more workable. . . .

The woman's right to terminate her pregnancy before viability is the most central principle of *Roe v. Wade*. It is a rule of law and a component of liberty we cannot renounce. . . .

Though the woman has a right to choose to terminate or continue her pregnancy before viability, it does not at all follow that the State is prohibited from taking steps to ensure that this choice is thoughtful and informed. Even in the earliest stages of pregnancy, the State may enact rules and regulations designed to encourage her to know that there are philosophic and social arguments of great weight that can be brought to bear in favor of continuing the pregnancy to full term and that there are procedures and institutions to allow adoption of unwanted children as well as a certain degree of state assistance if the mother chooses to raise the child herself. "The Constitution does not forbid a State or city, pursuant to democratic processes, from expressing a preference for normal childbirth." *Webster v. Reproductive Health Services* [(1989)]. It follows that States are free to enact laws to provide a reasonable framework for a woman to make a decision that has such profound and lasting meaning. This, too, we find consistent with *Roe*'s central premises, and indeed the inevitable consequence of our holding that the State has an interest in protecting the life of the unborn.

We reject the trimester framework, which we do not consider to be part of the essential holding of *Roe*. . . . The trimester framework suffers from these basic flaws: in its formulation it misconceives the nature of the pregnant woman's interest; and in practice it undervalues the State's interest in potential life, as recognized in *Roe*. . . .

Because we set forth a standard of general application to which we in-

tend to adhere, it is important to clarify what is meant by an undue burden.
... We give this summary:

(a) To protect the central right recognized by *Roe v. Wade* while at the same time accommodating the State's profound interest in potential life, we will employ the undue burden analysis as explained in this opinion. An undue burden exists, and therefore a provision of law is invalid, if its purpose or effect is to place a substantial obstacle in the path of a woman seeking an abortion before the fetus attains viability.

(b) We reject the rigid trimester framework of *Roe v. Wade*. To promote the State's profound interest in potential life, throughout pregnancy the State may take measures to ensure that the woman's choice is informed, and measures designed to advance this interest will not be invalidated as long as their purpose is to persuade the woman to choose childbirth over abortion. These measures must not be an undue burden on the right.

(c) As with any medical procedure, the State may enact regulations to further the health or safety of a woman seeking an abortion. Unnecessary health regulations that have the purpose or effect of presenting a substantial obstacle to a woman seeking an abortion impose an undue burden on the right.

(d) Our adoption of the undue burden analysis does not disturb the central holding of *Roe v. Wade*, and we reaffirm that holding. Regardless of whether exceptions are made for particular circumstances, a State may not prohibit any woman from making the ultimate decision to terminate her pregnancy before viability.

(e) We also reaffirm *Roe's* holding that "subsequent to viability, the State in promoting its interest in the potentiality of human life may, if it chooses, regulate, and even proscribe, abortion except where it is necessary, in appropriate medical judgment, for the preservation of the life or health of the mother."

These principles control our assessment of the Pennsylvania statute, and we now turn to the issue of the validity of its challenged provisions.

■ V

[A] Because it is central to the operation of various other requirements, we begin with the statute's definition of medical emergency. Under the statute, a medical emergency is "that condition which, on the basis of the physician's good faith clinical judgment, so complicates the medical condition of a pregnant woman as to necessitate the immediate abortion of her pregnancy to avert her death or for which a delay will create serious risk of substantial and irreversible impairment of a major bodily function."
... We conclude that, as construed by the Court of Appeals, the medical emergency definition imposes no undue burden on a woman's abortion right....

[B] Our prior decisions establish that as with any medical procedure, the

State may require a woman to give her written informed consent to an abortion. In this respect, the statute is unexceptional. Petitioners challenge the statute's definition of informed consent because it includes the provision of specific information by the doctor and the mandatory 24-hour waiting period. The conclusions reached by a majority of the Justices in the separate opinions filed today and the undue burden standard adopted in this opinion require us to overrule in part some of the Court's past decisions, decisions driven by the trimester framework's prohibition of all previability regulations designed to further the State's interest in fetal life. . . .

To the extent *Akron I* and *Thornburgh* find a constitutional violation when the government requires, as it does here, the giving of truthful, non-misleading information about the nature of the procedure, the attendant health risks and those of childbirth, and the "probable gestational age" of the fetus, those cases go too far, are inconsistent with *Roe*'s acknowledgment of an important interest in potential life, and are overruled. . . .

[C] Section 3209 of Pennsylvania's abortion law provides, except in cases of medical emergency, that no physician shall perform an abortion on a married woman without receiving a signed statement from the woman that she has notified her spouse that she is about to undergo an abortion. The woman has the option of providing an alternative signed statement certifying that her husband is not the man who impregnated her; that her husband could not be located; that the pregnancy is the result of spousal sexual assault which she has reported; or that the woman believes that notifying her husband will cause him or someone else to inflict bodily injury upon her. A physician who performs an abortion on a married woman without receiving the appropriate signed statement will have his or her license revoked, and is liable to the husband for damages. . . .

[T]here are millions of women in this country who are the victims of regular physical and psychological abuse at the hands of their husbands. Should these women become pregnant, they may have very good reasons for not wishing to inform their husbands of their decision to obtain an abortion. Many may have justifiable fears of physical abuse, but may be no less fearful of the consequences of reporting prior abuse to the Commonwealth of Pennsylvania. Many may have a reasonable fear that notifying their husbands will provoke further instances of child abuse; these women are not exempt from Section 3209's notification requirement. Many may fear devastating forms of psychological abuse from their husbands, including verbal harassment, threats of future violence, the destruction of possessions, physical confinement to the home, the withdrawal of financial support, or the disclosure of the abortion to family and friends. These methods of psychological abuse may act as even more of a deterrent to notification than the possibility of physical violence, but women who are the victims of the abuse are not exempt from Section 3209's notification requirement. And many women who are pregnant as a result of sexual assaults by their husbands will be unable to avail themselves of the exception for spousal sexual assault, because the exception requires that the woman have notified law enforcement authorities within 90 days of the assault, and her husband will be notified of her report once an investigation begins. . . .

The unfortunate yet persisting conditions we document above will mean that in a large fraction of the cases in which Section 3209 is relevant, it will operate as a substantial obstacle to a woman's choice to undergo an abortion. It is an undue burden, and therefore invalid. . . .

[D] We next consider the parental consent provision. . . .

We have been over most of this ground before. Our cases establish, and we reaffirm today, that a State may require a minor seeking an abortion to obtain the consent of a parent or guardian, provided that there is an adequate judicial bypass procedure. Under these precedents, in our view, the one-parent consent requirement and judicial bypass procedure are constitutional. . . .

[E] In [*Planned Parenthood of Central Missouri v.*] *Danforth*, [428 U.S. 552 (1976)], we held that recordkeeping and reporting provisions "that are reasonably directed to the preservation of maternal health and that properly respect a patient's confidentiality and privacy are permissible." We think that under this standard, all the provisions at issue here except that relating to spousal notice are constitutional. . . .

Subsection (12) of the reporting provision requires the reporting of, among other things, a married woman's "reason for failure to provide notice" to her husband. This provision in effect requires women, as a condition of obtaining an abortion, to provide the Commonwealth with the precise information we have already recognized that many women have pressing reasons not to reveal. Like the spousal notice requirement itself, this provision places an undue burden on a woman's choice, and must be invalidated for that reason.

☐ *Justice BLACKMUN, concurring in part, concurring in the judgment in part, and dissenting in part.*

I join parts I, II, III, V-A, V-C, and VI of the joint opinion of Justice O'CONNOR, KENNEDY, and SOUTER. . . .

Make no mistake, the joint opinion of Justices O'CONNOR, KENNEDY, and SOUTER is an act of personal courage and constitutional principle. In contrast to previous decisions in which Justices O'CONNOR and KENNEDY postponed reconsideration of *Roe v. Wade*, the authors of the joint opinion today join Justice STEVENS and me in concluding that "the essential holding of *Roe* should be retained and once again reaffirmed." In brief, five Members of this Court today recognize that "the Constitution protects a woman's right to terminate her pregnancy in its early stages." . . .

Our precedents and the joint opinion's principles require us to subject all non-*de minimis* abortion regulations to strict scrutiny. Under this standard, the Pennsylvania statute's provisions requiring content-based counseling, a 24-hour delay, informed parental consent, and reporting of abortion-related information must be invalidated. . . .

If there is much reason to applaud the advances made by the joint opinion today, there is far more to fear from the CHIEF JUSTICE's opinion.

The CHIEF JUSTICE's criticism of *Roe* follows from his stunted conception of individual liberty. . . . He argues that the record in favor of a right to abortion is no stronger than the record in *Michael H. v. Gerald D.*, 491 U.S. 110 (1989), where the plurality found no fundamental right to visitation privileges by an adulterous father, or in *Bowers v. Hardwick*, 478 U.S. 186 (1986), where the Court found no fundamental right to engage in homosexual sodomy, or in a case involving the "firing of a gun . . . into another person's body." In the CHIEF JUSTICE's world, a woman considering whether to terminate a pregnancy is entitled to no more protection than adulterers, murderers, and so-called "sexual deviates." Given the CHIEF JUSTICE's exclusive reliance on tradition, people using contraceptives seem the next likely candidate for his list of outcasts. . . .

In one sense, the Court's approach is worlds apart from that of the CHIEF JUSTICE and Justice SCALIA. And yet, in another sense, the distance between the two approaches is short—the distance is but a single vote.

I am 83 years old. I cannot remain on this Court forever, and when I do step down, the confirmation process for my successor well may focus on the issue before us today. That, I regret, may be exactly where the choice between the two worlds will be made.

☐ *Justice STEVENS, in an opinion omitted here, concurred in part and dissented from Parts IV, V-B, and V-D of the joint opinion, voting to uphold the informed consent and reporting requirements, except for the provision for reporting on spousal notification, and voting to strike down as an undue burden the requirements for abortion counseling, a 24-hour waiting period, and spousal notification.*

☐ *Chief Justice REHNQUIST, with whom Justice WHITE, Justice SCALIA, and Justice THOMAS joined, concurring in the judgment in part and dissenting in part.*

We think . . . that the Court was mistaken in *Roe* when it classified a woman's decision to terminate her pregnancy as a "fundamental right" that could be abridged only in a manner which withstood "strict scrutiny." . . .

The joint opinion of Justices O'CONNOR, KENNEDY, and SOUTER cannot bring itself to say that *Roe* was correct as an original matter, but the authors are of the view that "the immediate question is not the soundness of *Roe*'s resolution of the issue, but the precedential force that must be accorded to its holding." Instead of claiming that *Roe* was correct as a matter of original constitutional interpretation, the opinion therefore contains an elaborate discussion of *stare decisis*. This discussion of the principle of *stare decisis* appears to be almost entirely *dicta*, because the joint opinion does not apply that principle in dealing with *Roe*. *Roe* decided that a woman had a fundamental right to an abortion. The joint opinion rejects that view. *Roe* decided that abortion regulations were to be subjected to "strict scrutiny" and could be justified only in the light of "compelling state interests." The joint opinion rejects that view. *Roe* analyzed abortion regulation under a rigid trimester framework, a framework which has guided this Court's decisionmaking for 19 years. The joint opinion rejects that framework. . . .

In our view, authentic principles of *stare decisis* do not require that any portion of the reasoning in *Roe* be kept intact. . . .

The joint opinion discusses several *stare decisis* factors which, it asserts, point toward retaining a portion of *Roe*. Two of these factors are that the main "factual underpinning" of *Roe* has remained the same, and that its doctrinal foundation is no weaker now than it was in 1973. Of course, what might be called the basic facts which gave rise to *Roe* have remained the same—women become pregnant, there is a point somewhere, depending on medical technology, where a fetus becomes viable, and women give birth to children. But this is only to say that the same facts which gave rise to *Roe* will continue to give rise to similar cases. It is not a reason, in and of itself, why those cases must be decided in the same incorrect manner as was the first case to deal with the question. And surely there is no requirement, in considering whether to depart from *stare decisis* in a constitutional case, that a decision be more wrong now than it was at the time it was rendered. If that were true, the most outlandish constitutional decision could survive forever, based simply on the fact that it was no more outlandish later than it was when originally rendered. . . .

In the end, having failed to put forth any evidence to prove any true reliance, the joint opinion's argument is based solely on generalized assertions about the national psyche, on a belief that the people of this country have grown accustomed to the *Roe* decision over the last 19 years and have "ordered their thinking and living around" it. As an initial matter, one might inquire how the joint opinion can view the "central holding" of *Roe* as so deeply rooted in our constitutional culture, when it so casually uproots and disposes of that same decision's trimester framework. Furthermore, at various points in the past, the same could have been said about this Court's erroneous decisions that the Constitution allowed "separate but equal" treatment of minorities, or that "liberty" under the Due Process Clause protected "freedom of contract." The "separate but equal" doctrine lasted 58 years after *Plessy*, and *Lochner's* protection of contractual freedom lasted 32 years. However, the simple fact that a generation or more had grown used to these major decisions did not prevent the Court from correcting its errors in those cases, nor should it prevent us from correctly interpreting the Constitution here.

Apparently realizing that conventional *stare decisis* principles do not support its position, the joint opinion advances a belief that retaining a portion of *Roe* is necessary to protect the "legitimacy" of this Court. . . . [T]he joint opinion goes on to state that when the Court "resolves the sort of intensely divisive controversy reflected in *Roe* and those rare, comparable cases," its decision is exempt from reconsideration under established principles of *stare decisis* in constitutional cases. This is so, the joint opinion contends, because in those "intensely divisive" cases the Court has "called the contending sides of a national controversy to end their national division by accepting a common mandate rooted in the Constitution," and must therefore take special care not to be perceived as "surrendering to political pressure" and continued opposition. This is a truly novel principle. . . . Under this principle, when the Court has ruled on a divisive issue, it is apparently prevented from overruling that decision for the sole reason that it was incorrect, unless opposition to the original decision has died away. . . .

The joint opinion agrees that the Court's stature would have been seriously damaged if in *Brown* and *West Coast Hotel* it had dug in its heels and refused to apply normal principles of *stare decisis* to the earlier decisions. But the opinion contends that the Court was entitled to overrule *Plessy* and *Lochner* in those cases, despite the existence of opposition to the original decisions, only because both the Nation and the Court had learned new lessons in the interim. This is at best a feebly supported, post hoc rationalization for those decisions. . . .

The sum of the joint opinion's labors in the name of *stare decisis* and "legitimacy" is this: *Roe v. Wade* stands as a sort of judicial Potemkin Village, which may be pointed out to passersby as a monument to the importance of adhering to precedent. But behind the facade, an entirely new method of analysis, without any roots in constitutional law, is imported to decide the constitutionality of state laws regulating abortion. Neither *stare decisis* nor "legitimacy" are truly served by such an effort.

For the reasons stated, we therefore would hold that each of the challenged provisions of the Pennsylvania statute is consistent with the Constitution.

☐ *Justice SCALIA, with whom the CHIEF JUSTICE, Justice WHITE, and Justice THOMAS joined, concurring in the judgment in part and dissenting in part.*

My views on this matter are unchanged from those I set forth in my separate opinions in *Webster v. Reproductive Health Services*, 492 U.S. 490 (1989) (SCALIA, J., concurring in part and concurring in judgment), and *Ohio v. Akron Center for Reproductive Health*, 497 U.S. 502 (1990) (*Akron II*) (SCALIA, J., concurring). The States may, if they wish, permit abortion-on-demand, but the Constitution does not require them to do so. The permissibility of abortion, and the limitations upon it, are to be resolved like most important questions in our democracy: by citizens trying to persuade one another and then voting. . . . A State's choice between two positions on which reasonable people can disagree is constitutional even when (as is often the case) it intrudes upon a "liberty" in the absolute sense. Laws against bigamy, for example—which entire societies of reasonable people disagree with—intrude upon men and women's liberty to marry and live with one another. But bigamy happens not to be a liberty specially "protected" by the Constitution.

That is, quite simply, the issue in this case. . . . The issue is whether [a woman's claim to a constitutional right to have an abortion] is liberty protected by the Constitution of the United States. I am sure it is not. I reach that conclusion not because of anything so exalted as my views concerning the "concept of existence, of meaning, of the universe, and of the mystery of human life." Rather, I reach it for the same reason I reach the conclusion that bigamy is not constitutionally protected—because of two simple facts: (1) the Constitution says absolutely nothing about it, and (2) the long-standing traditions of American society have permitted it to be legally proscribed. . . .

The Court's reliance upon *stare decisis* can best be described as contrived. It insists upon the necessity of adhering not to all of *Roe*, but only to what it calls the "central holding." It seems to me that *stare decisis* ought to be applied even to the doctrine of *stare decisis*, and I confess never to have heard of this new, keep-what-you-want-and-throw-away-the-rest version. . . .

I am certainly not in a good position to dispute that the Court has saved the "central holding" of *Roe*, since to do that effectively I would have to know what the Court has saved, which in turn would require me to understand (as I do not) what the "undue burden" test means. I must confess, however, that I have always thought, and I think a lot of other people have always thought, that the arbitrary trimester framework, which the Court today discards, was quite as central to *Roe* as the arbitrary viability test, which the

Court today retains. It seems particularly ungrateful to carve the trimester framework out of the core of *Roe*, since its very rigidity (in sharp contrast to the utter indeterminability of the "undue burden" test) is probably the only reason the Court is able to say, in urging *stare decisis*, that *Roe* "has in no sense proven 'unworkable.' " I suppose the Court is entitled to call a "central holding" whatever it wants to call a "central holding"—which is, come to think of it, perhaps one of the difficulties with this modified version of *stare decisis*. I thought I might note, however, that the following portions of *Roe* have not been saved:

Under *Roe*, requiring that a woman seeking an abortion be provided truthful information about abortion before giving informed written consent is unconstitutional, if the information is designed to influence her choice, *Thornburgh, Akron I*. Under the joint opinion's "undue burden" regime (as applied today, at least) such a requirement is constitutional.

Under *Roe*, requiring that information be provided by a doctor, rather than by nonphysician counselors, is unconstitutional, *Akron I*. Under the "undue burden" regime (as applied today, at least) it is not . . . Under *Roe*, requiring a 24-hour waiting period between the time the woman gives her informed consent and the time of the abortion is unconstitutional, *Akron I*. Under the "undue burden" regime (as applied today, at least) it is not.

Under *Roe*, requiring detailed reports that include demographic data about each woman who seeks an abortion and various information about each abortion is unconstitutional, *Thornburgh*. Under the "undue burden" regime (as applied today, at least) it generally is not.

Roe fanned into life an issue that has inflamed our national politics in general, and has obscured with its smoke the selection of Justices to this Court in particular, ever since. And by keeping us in the abortion-umpiring business, it is the perpetuation of that disruption, rather than of any pax Roeana, that the Court's new majority decrees.

Stenberg v. Carhart

530 U.S. 914, 120 S.Ct. 2597 (2000)

The Court's decision was five to four in affirming the federal appellate court's decision invalidating Nebraska's "partial birth abortion" law. The facts are discussed in the opinion for the Court delivered by Justice Breyer. Justices O'Connor, Ginsburg, and Stevens each filed concurring opinions. Justices Kennedy, Scalia, and Thomas each filed dissenting opinions, and Chief Justice Rehnquist joined the opinions of Justices Kennedy and Thomas.

☐ *Justice BREYER delivered the opinion of the Court.*

We again consider the right to an abortion. We understand the controversial nature of the problem. Millions of Americans believe that life begins at conception and consequently that an abortion is akin to causing the death of an innocent child; they recoil at the thought of a law that would permit it. Other millions fear that a law that forbids abortion would condemn many American women to lives that lack dignity, depriving them of equal liberty and leading those with least resources to undergo illegal abortions with the attendant risks of death and suffering. Taking account of these virtually irreconcilable points of view, aware that constitutional law must govern a society whose different members sincerely hold directly opposing views, and considering the matter in light of the Constitution's guarantees of fundamental individual liberty, this Court, in the course of a generation, has determined and then redetermined that the Constitution offers basic protection to the woman's right to choose. *Roe v. Wade*, 410 U.S. 113 (1973); *Planned Parenthood of Southeastern Pa. v. Casey*, 505 U.S. 833 (1992). We shall not revisit those legal principles. Rather, we apply them to the circumstances of this case.

Three established principles determine the issue before us. We shall set them forth in the language of the joint opinion in *Casey*. First, before "viability the woman has a right to choose to terminate her pregnancy."

Second, "a law designed to further the State's interest in fetal life which imposes an undue burden on the woman's decision before fetal viability" is unconstitutional. An "undue burden is shorthand for the conclusion that a state regulation has the purpose or effect of placing a substantial obstacle in the path of a woman seeking an abortion of a nonviable fetus."

Third, "subsequent to viability, the State in promoting its interest in the potentiality of human life may, if it chooses, regulate, and even proscribe, abortion except where it is necessary, in appropriate medical judgment, for the preservation of the life or health of the mother."

We apply these principles to a Nebraska law banning "partial birth abortion." The statute reads as follows: "No partial birth abortion shall be performed in this state, unless such procedure is necessary to save the life of the mother whose life is endangered by a physical disorder, physical illness, or physical injury, including a life-endangering physical condition caused by or arising from the pregnancy itself." The statute defines "partial birth abortion" as: "an abortion procedure in which the person performing the abortion partially delivers vaginally a living unborn child before killing the unborn child and completing the delivery." It further defines "partially delivers vaginally a living unborn child before killing the unborn child" to mean "deliberately and intentionally delivering into the vagina a living unborn child, or a substantial portion thereof, for the purpose of performing a procedure that the person performing such procedure knows will kill the unborn child and does kill the unborn child." The law classifies violation of the statute as a "Class III felony" carrying a prison term of up to 20 years, and a fine of up to $25,000. It also provides for the automatic revocation of a doctor's license to practice medicine in Nebraska.

We hold that this statute violates the Constitution. . . .

The evidence before the trial court, as supported or supplemented in the literature, indicates the following:

1. About 90% of all abortions performed in the United States take place during the first trimester of pregnancy, before 12 weeks of gestational age. During the first trimester, the predominant abortion method is "vacuum

aspiration," which involves insertion of a vacuum tube (cannula) into the uterus to evacuate the contents. Such an abortion is typically performed on an outpatient basis under local anesthesia. The procedure's mortality rates for first trimester abortion are, for example, 5 to 10 times lower than those associated with carrying the fetus to term. Complication rates are also low. As the fetus grows in size, however, the vacuum aspiration method becomes increasingly difficult to use.

2. Approximately 10% of all abortions are performed during the second trimester of pregnancy (12 to 24 weeks). In the early 1970's, inducing labor through the injection of saline into the uterus was the predominant method of second trimester abortion. Today, however, the medical profession has switched from medical induction of labor to surgical procedures for most second trimester abortions. The most commonly used procedure is called "dilation and evacuation" (D&E). That procedure (together with a modified form of vacuum aspiration used in the early second trimester) accounts for about 95% of all abortions performed from 12 to 20 weeks of gestational age.

3. D&E "refers generically to transcervical procedures performed at 13 weeks gestation or later." . . . There are variations in D&E operative strategy. However, the common points are that D&E involves (1) dilation of the cervix; (2) removal of at least some fetal tissue using nonvacuum instruments; and (3) (after the 15th week) the potential need for instrumental disarticulation or dismemberment of the fetus or the collapse of fetal parts to facilitate evacuation from the uterus.

4. When instrumental disarticulation incident to D&E is necessary, it typically occurs as the doctor pulls a portion of the fetus through the cervix into the birth canal. . . .

5. The D&E procedure carries certain risks. The use of instruments within the uterus creates a danger of accidental perforation and damage to neighboring organs. Sharp fetal bone fragments create similar dangers. And fetal tissue accidentally left behind can cause infection and various other complications. Nonetheless studies show that the risks of mortality and complication that accompany the D&E procedure between the 12th and 20th weeks of gestation are significantly lower than those accompanying induced labor procedures (the next safest mid-second trimester procedures).

6. At trial, Dr. Carhart and Dr. Stubblefield described a variation of the D&E procedure, which they referred to as an "intact D&E." Like other versions of the D&E technique, it begins with induced dilation of the cervix. The procedure then involves removing the fetus from the uterus through the cervix "intact," i.e., in one pass, rather than in several passes. It is used after 16 weeks at the earliest, as vacuum aspiration becomes ineffective and the fetal skull becomes too large to pass through the cervix. . . .

7. The intact D&E procedure can also be found described in certain obstetric and abortion clinical textbooks, where two variations are recognized. The first, as just described, calls for the physician to adapt his method for extracting the intact fetus depending on fetal presentation. A slightly different version of the intact D&E procedure, associated with Dr. Martin Haskell, calls for conversion to a breech presentation in all cases.

8. The American College of Obstetricians and Gynecologists describes

the D&X procedure in a manner corresponding to a breech-conversion intact D&E, including the following steps: "1. deliberate dilatation of the cervix, usually over a sequence of days; 2. instrumental conversion of the fetus to a footling breech; 3. breech extraction of the body excepting the head; and 4. partial evacuation of the intracranial contents of a living fetus to effect vaginal delivery of a dead but otherwise intact fetus." Despite the technical differences we have just described, intact D&E and D&X are sufficiently similar for us to use the terms interchangeably.

9. Dr. Carhart testified he attempts to use the intact D&E procedure during weeks 16 to 20 because (1) it reduces the dangers from sharp bone fragments passing through the cervix, (2) minimizes the number of instrument passes needed for extraction and lessens the likelihood of uterine perforations caused by those instruments, (3) reduces the likelihood of leaving infection-causing fetal and placental tissue in the uterus, and (4) could help to prevent potentially fatal absorption of fetal tissue into the maternal circulation. The District Court made no findings about the D&X procedure's overall safety. The District Court concluded, however, that "the evidence is both clear and convincing that Carhart's D&X procedure is superior to, and safer than, the other abortion procedures used during the relevant gestational period in the 10 to 20 cases a year that present to Dr. Carhart."

10. The materials presented at trial referred to the potential benefits of the D&X procedure in circumstances involving nonviable fetuses, such as fetuses with abnormal fluid accumulation in the brain (hydrocephaly).

11. There are no reliable data on the number of D&X abortions performed annually. Estimates have ranged between 640 and 5,000 per year.

The question before us is whether Nebraska's statute, making criminal the performance of a "partial birth abortion," violates the Federal Constitution, as interpreted in *Planned Parenthood of Southeastern Pa. v. Casey*, and *Roe v. Wade*. We conclude that it does for at least two independent reasons. First, the law lacks any exception "for the preservation of the health of the mother." Second, it "imposes an undue burden on a woman's ability" to choose a D&E abortion, thereby unduly burdening the right to choose abortion itself. We shall discuss each of these reasons in turn. . . .

The fact that Nebraska's law applies both pre- and postviability aggravates the constitutional problem presented. The State's interest in regulating abortion previability is considerably weaker than postviability. Since the law requires a health exception in order to validate even a postviability abortion regulation, it at a minimum requires the same in respect to previability regulation.

The quoted standard also depends on the state regulations "promoting [the State's] interest in the potentiality of human life." The Nebraska law, of course, does not directly further an interest "in the potentiality of human life" by saving the fetus in question from destruction, as it regulates only a method of performing abortion. Nebraska describes its interests differently. It says the law "show[s] concern for the life of the unborn," "prevent[s] cruelty to partially born children," and "preserve[s] the integrity of the medical profession." But we cannot see how the interest-related differences could make any difference to the question at hand, namely, the application of the "health" requirement.

Consequently, the governing standard requires an exception "where it is necessary, in appropriate medical judgment for the preservation of the life or health of the mother," for this Court has made clear that a State may promote but not endanger a woman's health when it regulates the methods of abortion. *Thornburgh v. American College of Obstetricians and Gynecologists,* 476 U.S. 747 (1986); *Colautti v. Franklin,* 439 U.S. 379 (1979); *Doe v. Bolton,* 410 U.S. 179 (1973). . . .

Nebraska responds that the law does not require a health exception unless there is a need for such an exception. . . . Nebraska, along with supporting *amici,* replies that these findings are irrelevant, wrong, or applicable only in a tiny number of instances. It says (1) that the D&X procedure is "little-used," (2) by only "a handful of doctors." It argues (3) that D&E and labor induction are at all times "safe alternative procedures." It refers to the testimony of petitioners' medical expert, who testified (4) that the ban would not increase a woman's risk of several rare abortion complications (disseminated intravascular coagulopathy and amniotic fluid embolus).

The Association of American Physicians and Surgeons et al., *amici* supporting Nebraska, argue (5) that elements of the D&X procedure may create special risks, including cervical incompetence caused by overdilatation, injury caused by conversion of the fetal presentation, and dangers arising from the "blind" use of instrumentation to pierce the fetal skull while lodged in the birth canal.

Nebraska further emphasizes (6) that there are no medical studies "establishing the safety of the partial-birth abortion/D&X procedure," and "no medical studies comparing the safety of partial-birth abortion/D&X to other abortion procedures," (7) an American Medical Association policy statement that "there does not appear to be any identified situation in which intact D&X is the only appropriate procedure to induce abortion." And it points out (8) that the American College of Obstetricians and Gynecologists qualified its statement that D&X "may be the best or most appropriate procedure," by adding that the panel "could identify no circumstances under which [the D&X] procedure would be the only option to save the life or preserve the health of the woman."

We find these eight arguments insufficient to demonstrate that Nebraska's law needs no health exception. For one thing, certain of the arguments are beside the point. The D&X procedure's relative rarity (argument (1)) is not highly relevant. The D&X is an infrequently used abortion procedure; but the health exception question is whether protecting women's health requires an exception for those infrequent occasions. A rarely used treatment might be necessary to treat a rarely occurring disease that could strike anyone—the State cannot prohibit a person from obtaining treatment simply by pointing out that most people do not need it. Nor can we know whether the fact that only a "handful" of doctors use the procedure (argument (2)) reflects the comparative rarity of late second term abortions, the procedure's recent development, the controversy surrounding it, or, as Nebraska suggests, the procedure's lack of utility.

For another thing, the record responds to Nebraska's (and *amici's*) medically based arguments. In respect to argument (3), for example, the District Court agreed that alternatives, such as D&E and induced labor, are "safe" but found that the D&X method was significantly safer in certain circumstances.

In respect to argument (4), the District Court simply relied on different expert testimony—testimony stating that "[a]nother advantage of the Intact D&E is that it eliminates the risk of embolism of cerebral tissue into the woman's blood stream."

In response to *amici's* argument (5), the American College of Obstetricians and Gynecologists, in its own *amici* brief, denies that D&X generally poses risks greater than the alternatives. It says that the suggested alternative procedures involve similar or greater risks of cervical and uterine injury, for "D&E procedures, involve similar amounts of dilatation" and "of course childbirth involves even greater cervical dilatation." The College points out that Dr. Carhart does not reposition the fetus thereby avoiding any risks stemming from conversion to breech presentation, and that, as compared with D&X, D&E involves the same, if not greater, "blind" use of sharp instruments in the uterine cavity.

We do not quarrel with Nebraska's argument (6), for Nebraska is right. There are no general medical studies documenting comparative safety. Neither do we deny the import of the American Medical Association's statement (argument (7))—even though the State does omit the remainder of that statement: "The AMA recommends that the procedure not be used unless alternative procedures pose materially greater risk to the woman."

We cannot, however, read the American College of Obstetricians and Gynecologists panel's qualification (that it could not "identify" a circumstance where D&X was the "only" life- or health-preserving option) as if, according to Nebraska's argument (8), it denied the potential health-related need for D&X. That is because the College writes the following in its *amici* brief: "Depending on the physician's skill and experience, the D&X procedure can be the most appropriate abortion procedure for some women in some circumstances. D&X presents a variety of potential safety advantages over other abortion procedures used during the same gestational period." . . .

The upshot is a District Court finding that D&X significantly obviates health risks in certain circumstances, a highly plausible record-based explanation of why that might be so, a division of opinion among some medical experts over whether D&X is generally safer, and an absence of controlled medical studies that would help answer these medical questions. Given these medically related evidentiary circumstances, we believe the law requires a health exception. . . .

The Eighth Circuit found the Nebraska statute unconstitutional because, in *Casey's* words, it has the "effect of placing a substantial obstacle in the path of a woman seeking an abortion of a nonviable fetus." It thereby places an "undue burden" upon a woman's right to terminate her pregnancy before viability. Nebraska does not deny that the statute imposes an "undue burden" if it applies to the more commonly used D&E procedure as well as to D&X. And we agree with the Eighth Circuit that it does so apply. . . .

The judgment of the Court of Appeals is Affirmed.

☐ *(Justice O'CONNOR, concurring.)*

I write separately to emphasize the following points.

First, the Nebraska statute is inconsistent with *Casey* because it lacks an exception for those instances when the banned procedure is necessary to preserve the health of the mother. . . . Contrary to the assertions of Justice KENNEDY and Justice THOMAS, the need for a health exception does not arise from "the individual views of Dr. Carhart and his supporters." Rather, as the majority explains, where, as here, "a significant body of medical opinion believes a procedure may bring with it greater safety for some patients and explains the medical reasons supporting that view," then Nebraska cannot say that the procedure will not, in some circumstances, be "necessary to preserve the life or health of the mother." Accordingly, our precedent requires that the statute include a health exception.

Second, Nebraska's statute is unconstitutional on the alternative and independent ground that it imposes an undue burden on a woman's right to choose to terminate her pregnancy before viability. Nebraska's ban covers not just the dilation and extraction (D&X) procedure, but also the dilation and evacuation (D&E) procedure, "the most commonly used method for performing previability second trimester abortions." . . . Thus, it is not possible to interpret the statute's language as applying only to the D&X procedure. Moreover, it is significant that both the District Court and the Court of Appeals interpreted the statute as prohibiting abortions performed using the D&E method as well as the D&X method. . . . Indeed, Nebraska conceded at oral argument that "the State could not prohibit the D&E procedure." By proscribing the most commonly used method for previability second trimester abortions, the statute creates a "substantial obstacle to a woman seeking an abortion," and therefore imposes an undue burden on a woman's right to terminate her pregnancy prior to viability.

It is important to note that, unlike Nebraska, some other States have enacted statutes more narrowly tailored to proscribing the D&X procedure alone. Some of those statutes have done so by specifically excluding from their coverage the most common methods of abortion, such as the D&E and vacuum aspiration procedures. . . . By restricting their prohibitions to the D&X procedure exclusively, the Kansas, Utah, and Montana statutes avoid a principal defect of the Nebraska law. . . .

Nebraska's statute, however, does not meet these criteria. It contains no exception for when the procedure, in appropriate medical judgment, is necessary to preserve the health of the mother; and it proscribes not only the D&X procedure but also the D&E procedure, the most commonly used method for previability second trimester abortions, thus making it an undue burden on a woman's right to terminate her pregnancy. For these reasons, I agree with the Court that Nebraska's law is unconstitutional.

□ *Justice GINSBURG, with whom Justice STEVENS joins, concurring.*

I write separately only to stress that amidst all the emotional uproar caused by an abortion case, we should not lose sight of the character of Nebraska's "partial birth abortion" law. As the Court observes, this law does not save any fetus from destruction, for it targets only "a method of performing abortion." Nor does the statute seek to protect the lives or health of pregnant women. Moreover, as Justice STEVENS points out, the most common method of performing previability second trimester abortions is no less distressing or susceptible to gruesome description. . . .

A state regulation that "has the purpose or effect of placing a substantial obstacle in the path of a woman seeking an abortion of a nonviable fetus" violates the Constitution. *Casey.*

☐ *Justice STEVENS, with whom Justice GINSBURG joins, concurring.*

[D]uring the past 27 years, the central holding of *Roe v. Wade* has been endorsed by all but 4 of the 17 Justices who have addressed the issue. That holding—that the word "liberty" in the Fourteenth Amendment includes a woman's right to make this difficult and extremely personal decision—makes it impossible for me to understand how a State has any legitimate interest in requiring a doctor to follow any procedure other than the one that he or she reasonably believes will best protect the woman in her exercise of this constitutional liberty. But one need not even approach this view today to conclude that Nebraska's law must fall. For the notion that either of these two equally gruesome procedures performed at this late stage of gestation is more akin to infanticide than the other, or that the State furthers any legitimate interest by banning one but not the other, is simply irrational.

☐ *Justice SCALIA, dissenting.*

I have joined Justice THOMAS's dissent because I agree that today's decision is an "unprecedented expansio[n]" of our prior cases, "is not mandated" by *Casey*'s "undue burden" test, and can even be called (though this pushes me to the limit of my belief) "obviously irreconcilable with *Casey*'s explication of what its undue-burden standard requires." But I never put much stock in *Casey*'s explication of the inexplicable. In the last analysis, my judgment that *Casey* does not support today's tragic result can be traced to the fact that what I consider to be an "undue burden" is different from what the majority considers to be an "undue burden"—a conclusion that can not be demonstrated true or false by factual inquiry or legal reasoning. It is a value judgment, dependent upon how much one respects (or believes society ought to respect) the life of a partially delivered fetus, and how much one respects (or believes society ought to respect) the freedom of the woman who gave it life to kill it. . . .

While I am in an I-told-you-so mood, I must recall my bemusement, in *Casey*, at the joint opinion's expressed belief that *Roe v. Wade* had "call[ed] the contending sides of a national controversy to end their national division by accepting a common mandate rooted in the Constitution," and that the decision in *Casey* would ratify that happy truce. It seemed to me, quite to the contrary, that "*Roe* fanned into life an issue that has inflamed our national politics in general, and has obscured with its smoke the selection of Justices to this Court in particular, ever since"; and that, "by keeping us in the abortion-umpiring business, it is the perpetuation of that disruption, rather than of any Pax Roeana, that the Court's new majority decrees." Today's decision, that the Constitution of the United States prevents the prohibition of a horrible mode of abortion, will be greeted by a firestorm of criticism—as well it should. I cannot understand why those who acknowledge that, in the opening words of Justice O'CONNOR's concurrence, "[t]he issue of abortion is one of the most contentious and controversial in contemporary

American society," persist in the belief that this Court, armed with neither constitutional text nor accepted tradition, can resolve that contention and controversy rather than be consumed by it. If only for the sake of its own preservation, the Court should return this matter to the people—where the Constitution, by its silence on the subject, left it—and let them decide, State by State, whether this practice should be allowed. *Casey* must be overruled.

☐ *Justice KENNEDY, with whom Chief Justice Rehnquist joins, dissenting.*

The political processes of the State are not to be foreclosed from enacting laws to promote the life of the unborn and to ensure respect for all human life and its potential. The State's constitutional authority is a vital means for citizens to address these grave and serious issues, as they must if we are to progress in knowledge and understanding and in the attainment of some degree of consensus.

The Court's decision today, in my submission, repudiates this understanding by invalidating a statute advancing critical state interests, even though the law denies no woman the right to choose an abortion and places no undue burden upon the right. The legislation is well within the State's competence to enact. Having concluded Nebraska's law survives the scrutiny dictated by a proper understanding of *Casey*, I dissent from the judgment invalidating it. . . .

☐ *Justice THOMAS, with whom Chief Justice Rehnquist and Justice SCALIA join, dissenting.*

Today's decision is so obviously irreconcilable with *Casey's* explication of what its undue-burden standard requires, let alone the Constitution, that it should be seen for what it is, a reinstitution of the pre-*Webster* abortion-on-demand era in which the mere invocation of "abortion rights" trumps any contrary societal interest. If this statute is unconstitutional under *Casey*, then *Casey* meant nothing at all, and the Court should candidly admit it.

To reach its decision, the majority must take a series of indefensible steps. The majority must first disregard the principles that this Court follows in every context but abortion: We interpret statutes according to their plain meaning and we do not strike down statutes susceptible of a narrowing construction. The majority also must disregard the very constitutional standard it purports to employ, and then displace the considered judgment of the people of Nebraska and 29 other States. The majority's decision is lamentable, because of the result the majority reaches, the illogical steps the majority takes to reach it, and because it portends a return to an era I had thought we had at last abandoned. . . .

[Because I interpret] Nebraska's partial birth abortion statute [to] permi[t] doctors to perform D&E abortions, the question remains whether a State can constitutionally prohibit the partial birth abortion procedure without a health exception. Although the majority and Justice O'CONNOR purport to rely on the standard articulated in the *Casey* joint opinion in concluding that a State may not, they in fact disregard it entirely.

Though Justices O'CONNOR, KENNEDY, and SOUTER declined in *Casey*, on the ground of *stare decisis*, to reconsider whether abortion enjoys any constitutional protection, *Casey* professed to be, in part, a repudiation of *Roe* and its progeny. The *Casey* joint opinion expressly noted that prior case law had undervalued the State's interest in potential life, and had invalidated regulations of abortion that "in no real sense deprived women of the ultimate decision." The joint opinion repeatedly recognized the States' weighty interest in this area.

The *Casey* joint opinion therefore adopted the standard: "Only where state regulation imposes an undue burden on a woman's ability to make this decision does the power of the State reach into the heart of the liberty protected by the Due Process Clause." A regulation imposes an "undue burden" only if it "has the effect of placing a substantial obstacle in the path of a woman's choice."

There is no question that the State of Nebraska has a valid interest— one not designed to strike at the right itself—in prohibiting partial birth abortion. *Casey* itself noted that States may "express profound respect for the life of the unborn."

The next question, therefore, is whether the Nebraska statute is unconstitutional because it does not contain an exception that would allow use of the procedure whenever "necessary in appropriate medical judgment, for the preservation of the health of the mother." . . .

The majority and Justice O'CONNOR suggest that their rule is dictated by a straightforward application of *Roe* and *Casey*. But that is simply not true. In *Roe* and *Casey*, the Court stated that the State may "regulate, and even proscribe, abortion except where it is necessary, in appropriate medical judgment, for the preservation of the life or health of the mother." *Casey* said that a health exception must be available if "continuing her pregnancy would constitute a threat" to the woman. Under these cases, if a State seeks to prohibit abortion, even if only temporarily or under particular circumstances, as *Casey* says that it may, the State must make an exception for cases in which the life or health of the mother is endangered by continuing the pregnancy. These cases addressed only the situation in which a woman must obtain an abortion because of some threat to her health from continued pregnancy. But *Roe* and *Casey* say nothing at all about cases in which a physician considers one prohibited method of abortion to be preferable to permissible methods. Today's majority and Justice O'CONNOR twist *Roe* and *Casey* to apply to the situation in which a woman desires—for whatever reason—an abortion and wishes to obtain the abortion by some particular method. In other words, the majority and Justice O'CONNOR fail to distinguish between cases in which health concerns require a woman to obtain an abortion and cases in which health concerns cause a woman who desires an abortion (for whatever reason) to prefer one method over another. . . .

We were reassured repeatedly in *Casey* that not all regulations of abortion are unwarranted and that the States may express profound respect for fetal life. Under *Casey*, the regulation before us today should easily pass constitutional muster. But the Court's abortion jurisprudence is a particularly virulent strain of constitutional exegesis. And so today we are told that 30 States are prohibited from banning one rarely used form of abortion that they believe to border on infanticide. It is clear that the Constitution does not compel this result.

■ The Development of Law

State Laws Regulating Abortion

STATE	REPORTING REQUIREMENT	REQUIRED COUNSELING	WAITING PERIOD	PARENTAL NOTIFICATION AND/OR CONSENT	BANS ON PARTIAL BIRTH ABORTION
ALABAMA	X	X	24 hours	N+C	?
ALASKA	X	X		?	?
ARIZONA	X			N+C	?
ARKANSAS	X	X	24	N	?
CALIFORNIA	?	X		?	
COLORADO	X			N –	
CONNECTICUT	X	X			
DELAWARE	X	X		N –	
DIST OF COLUMBIA	X				
FLORIDA	X	X	?	?	?
GEORGIA	X			N –	★
HAWAII	X				?
IDAHO	X	X	24	N+C	?
ILLINOIS	X			?	
INDIANA	X	X	18	N+C –	<

STATE	REPORTING REQUIREMENT	REQUIRED COUNSELING	WAITING PERIOD	PARENTAL NOTIFICATION AND/OR CONSENT	BANS ON PARTIAL BIRTH ABORTION
IOWA	X			N	?
KANSAS	X		24	N	★
KENTUCKY	X	X	24	N+C	?
LOUISIANA	X	X	24	N+C	?
MAINE	X				
MARYLAND	X			N	
MASSACHUSETTS	X		?	N+C	
MICHIGAN	X	X	24	N+C –	?
MINNESOTA	X	X	24	N	<
MISSISSIPPI	X	X	24	N+C –	?
MISSOURI	X		@	N+C	<
MONTANA	X		?	?	?
NEBRASKA	X	X	24	N	
NEVADA	X	X		?	?
NEW HAMPSHIRE	X			?	?
NEW JERSEY	X			?	?
NEW MEXICO	X			?	★
NEW YORK	X				
NORTH CAROLINA	X			N+C –	
NORTH DAKOTA	X	X	24	N+C –	<

STATE	REPORTING REQUIREMENT	REQUIRED COUNSELING	WAITING PERIOD	PARENTAL NOTIFICATION AND/OR CONSENT	BANS ON PARTIAL BIRTH ABORTION
OHIO	X	X	24	N ~	★
OKLAHOMA	X			~	‹
OREGON	X				
PENNSYLVANIA	X	X	24	N+C –	?
RHODE ISLAND	X	X		N+C	
SOUTH CAROLINA	X	X	1	N+C	
SOUTH DAKOTA	X	X	24	N –	‹
TENNESSEE	X		~	N+C	‹
TEXAS	X	X	24	N –	★
UTAH	X	X	24	N –	
VERMONT	X				?
VIRGINIA	X	X	24	N+C	
WASHINGTON	X				
WEST VIRGINIA	X	X	24	N –	?
WISCONSIN	X	X	24	N+C	?
WYOMING	X			N+C –	?

~ Enjoined by courts.
@ Temporary blocked, pending litigation.
– Do not provide an exception for cases of abuse, incest, or rape.
★ Meets the standards set forth in *Stenberg v. Carhart.*
‹ Does meet standards of *Stenberg v. Carhart* but remains unchallenged.

Source: The Alan Guttmacher Institute, at http://www.agi-usa.org (April 1, 2004).

B | *Privacy and Personal Autonomy*

Griswold v. Connecticut invited further litigation aimed at expanding the right of privacy to include a broad and diverse range of interests in personal autonomy. State and lower federal courts broadly construed the right of privacy, for example, to allow cancer patients to use Laetrile, a drug that had not yet been approved by the Food and Drug Administration;[1] and to outweigh state interests in requiring motor-cyclists to wear helmets.[2]

The Burger and Rehnquist Courts, however, largely declined to broaden the scope of the right of privacy. In *Kelly v. Johnson*, 425 U.S. 238 (1976), for instance, the Court upheld a regulation limiting the length of policemen's hair.[3] In his opinion announcing the decision, Justice Rehnquist distinguished the " 'liberty' interest" claimed in *Kelly* from that in *Griswold* and *Roe* on the grounds that "those cases involved a substantial claim of infringement on the individual's freedom of choice with respect to certain basic matters of procreation, marriage, and family life."

In *Moore v. City of East Cleveland*, 431 U.S. 494 (1977), though, a bare majority overturned a city ordinance limiting the occupancy of any dwelling to members of the same "family" and narrowly defined "family" to include only a "few categories of related individuals." Inex Moore, a grandmother, was convicted of violating the ordinance and sentenced to five days in jail and fined $25, because she lived with her two grandsons, one of whom came to live with her after his mother's death. When striking down the ordinance, Justice Powell explained,

> When a city undertakes such intrusive regulation of the family . . .
> the usual judicial deference to the legislature is inappropriate. "This
> Court has long recognized that freedom of personal choice in mat-
> ters of marriage and family life is one of the liberties protected by
> the Due Process Clause of the Fourteenth Amendment." [Citing
> *Meyer, Pierce, Skinner, Griswold,* and *Roe.*] . . . When government
> intrudes on choices concerning family living arrangements, this
> Court must examine carefully the importance of the governmental
> interests advanced and the extent to which they are served by the
> challenged regulation. When thus examined, this ordinance cannot
> survive. The city seeks to justify it as a means of preventing over-
> crowding, minimizing traffic and parking congestion, and avoiding
> an undue financial burden on the school system. Although these are
> legitimate goals, the ordinance serves them marginally, at best. . . .
>
> Substantive due process has at times been a treacherous field for this
> Court. There *are* risks when the judicial branch gives enhanced pro-

tection to certain substantive liberties without the guidance of the more specific provisions of the Bill of Rights. As the history of the *Lochner* era demonstrates, there is reason for concern lest the only limits to such judicial intervention become the predilections of those who happen at the time to be Members of this Court. That history counsels caution and restraint. But it does not counsel abandonment. . . .

Our decisions establish that the Constitution protects the sanctity of the family precisely because the institution of the family is deeply rooted in this Nation's history and tradition. It is through the family that we inculcate and pass down many of our most cherished values, moral and cultural. . . . The tradition of uncles, aunts, cousins, and especially grandparents sharing a household along with parents has roots equally venerable and equally deserving of constitutional recognition. . . . The choice of relatives in this degree of kinship to live together may not lightly be denied by the State. . . . The Constitution prevents East Cleveland from standardizing its children— and its adults—by forcing all to live in certain narrowly defined family patterns.

But dissenting Chief Justice Burger and Justices Rehnquist, Stewart, and White strongly objected to the majority's broad reading of the Due Process Clause and exercise of judicial review, with Justice White observing:

The ordinance . . . denies appellant the opportunity to live with all her grandchildren in this particular suburb; she is free to do so in other parts of the Cleveland metropolitan area. If there is power to maintain the character of a single-family neighborhood, as there surely is, some limit must be placed on the reach of the "family." Had it been our task to legislate, we might have approached the problem in a different manner than did the drafters of this ordinance; but I have no trouble in concluding that the normal goals of zoning regulation are present here and that the ordinance serves these goals by limiting, in identifiable circumstances, the number of people who can occupy a single household. The ordinance does not violate the Due Process Clause.

Moore v. City of East Cleveland underscores the struggles within the Court and the majority's concern with limiting the application of the right of privacy to matters directly bearing on the "family—marriage; childbirth; the raising and education of children; and cohabitation with one's relatives."[4] Accordingly, the Court has also rejected claims of "informational privacy"—that is privacy interests in "avoiding disclosure of personal matters" in, for example, bank, tax, and medical records; and in "independence in making certain kinds of important decisions" that may be diminished due to developments in computer technology and telecommunications.

Whalen v. Roe 429 U.S. 589 (1976) provided the Court's most comprehensive discussion of claims to informational privacy. There Justice Stevens upheld regulations requiring the reporting and maintaining of computerized records on individuals purchasing certain dangerous drugs. See also the treatment of privacy claims and the First Amendment in *Cox Broadcasting Co. v. Cohn* (1975) (in Ch. 5), *Federal Communications Commission v. Pacifica Foundation* (1978) (in Ch. 5), and Fourth Amendment-protected privacy interests (see Ch. 7), as well as Fifth Amendment-privacy claims with regard to private papers and required records (see Ch. 8). The problems of safeguarding interests in informational privacy remain largely matters for Congress and state legislatures. The Fair Credit Reporting Act of 1970 (regulating consumer reports), the Crime Control Act of 1973 (regulating access to individuals' criminal records), and the Family Educational Rights and Privacy Act of 1974 (regulating access to student educational records), for instance, safeguard specific kinds of interests in informational privacy. The Privacy Act of 1974 embodies the most comprehensive statutory scheme for safeguarding privacy interests by regulating the collection and utilization of personal information by federal agencies.[5]

Both *Moore* and *Whalen v. Roe* indicate the Court's reluctance to expand the right of privacy to provide broader protection for claims of sexual autonomy and personal lifestyle choices. In the 1980s, though, the movement to recognize homosexual rights prompted new legislation and litigation in the courts. Over twenty states repealed laws penalizing sexual activities between consenting adults, and six state supreme courts (in Georgia, Massachusetts, Montana, New York, Pennsylvania, and Tennessee) struck down laws punishing homosexual relations. (See THE DEVELOPMENT OF LAW BOX in Ch. 2.)

The Court avoided directly ruling on claims that the right of privacy includes sexual freedom between consenting adults in the privacy of their homes until *Bowers v. Hardwick*, 478 U.S. 186 (1986). Then the justices split five to four, with Justice Powell casting the controlling vote, for upholding Georgia's law making heterosexual and homosexual sodomy a crime. (See the INSIDE THE COURT box below.) Notably, Justice Powell after he retired publicly regretted his vote in *Bowers*, and some state supreme courts have rejected the Court's analysis as a matter of state constitutional law as well; see, for example, *Commonwealth of Kentucky v. Wasson*, 842 S.W.2d 487 (1992) (excerpted in Ch. 2). *Bowers* was finally reconsidered and overruled in *Lawrence v. Texas* (2003) (excerpted below). There, writing for the Court, Justice Kennedy struck down Texas's law, along with laws in twelve other states, that criminalized homosexual sodomy, holding that such laws violated the substantive privacy interests protected by the Fourteenth Amendment due process clause and implicated by the amendment's equal protection clause. By contrast, concurring Justice O'Connor would not have overturned *Bowers* and would have struck down the law solely on equal protection grounds. Chief Justice Rehnquist and Justices Scalia and Thomas dissented.

The Court will certainly continue to confront claims of personal autonomy. For example, the Court faced for the first time the claim that the right of privacy includes a "right to die" in *Cruzan by Cruzan v. Director, Missouri Department of Health* (1990) (see excerpt below). There, the Court upheld the interests of the state of Missouri over the privacy claims of parents who sued to remove a feeding tube inserted in their daughter, Nancy Cruzan, who is brain injured and who doctors said would remain unconscious for the next thirty years unless the tube is removed and she is allowed to die. Writing for a bare majority, Chief Justice Rehnquist rejected further extension of the right of privacy into this vexing area of social policy. But he ruled as well that the Constitution permits, but does not require, states to demand "clear and convincing" evidence that an incompetent patient would have wanted to discontinue life-support equipment. Chief Justice Rehnquist also construed the Fourteenth Amendment's due process clause to guarantee a liberty interest that protects the right of individuals to terminate unwanted medical treatment, if they are able to express or have clearly expressed (in a living will, for example) their desire to have medical treatment terminated in the event that they become incompetent. With the exception of Justice Scalia, all of the justices (including those in dissent) endorsed this interpretation of the Fourteenth Amendment's protection for individuals' liberty interests.

Subsequently, in two 1997 decisions, *Washington v. Glucksberg* and *Vacco v. Quill* (excerpted below), the Court declined to extend the constitutional protection for the fundamental liberty interest recognized in *Cruzan* to terminally ill patients seeking "physician-assisted suicide"; that is, a right to have doctors prescribe lethal drugs. But note that Chief Justice Rehnquist's opinion for the Court and a number of the other justices' opinions did not completely rule out such a constitutional right, depending on the circumstances and future litigation.

NOTES

1. *Rutherford v. United States*, 438 F.Supp. 1287 (W.D. Oka., 1977), reversed on other grounds, 442 U.S. 544 (1979).

2. *People v. Fries*, 42 Ill. 2d 446, 250 N.E. 2d 149 (1969).

3. See also *Paul v. Davis*, 424 U.S. 693 (1976), rejecting a claim of personal privacy and reputation when upholding the distribution by police of fliers containing mug shot photos captioned "Active Shoplifters" to local merchants.

4. See *Roberts v. United States Jaycees*, 468 U.S. 609 (1984) in Chapter 5.

5. See United States Privacy Protection Study Commission, *Personal Privacy in an Information Society* (Washington, DC: Government Printing Office, 1977).

SELECTED BIBLIOGRAPHY

Behuniak, Susan M., and Svenson, Arthur G. *Physician-Assisted Suicide: The Anatomy of a Constitutional Law Issue*. Lanham, MD: Rowman & Littlefield, 2003).

Diffie, Whitfield. *Privacy on the Line: The Politics of Wiretapping and Encryption*. Cambridge, MA: MIT Press, 1998.

Dworkin, Ronald. *Life's Dominion: An Argument about Abortion, Euthanasia, and Individual Freedom*. New York: Knopf, 1993.

Glick, Henry. *The Right to Die*. New York: Columbia University Press, 1992.

Hendin, Herbert. *Seduced by Death*. New York: W. W. Norton, 1997.

Humphrey, Derek, and Clement, Mary. *People, Politics and the Right-to-Die Movement*. New York: St. Martin's Press, 1998.

Irons, Peter. *The Courage of Their Convictions*. New York: Free Press, 1988, Ch. 16.

Koppleman, Andrew. *The Gay Rights Question in Contemporary American Law*. Chicago: University of Chicago Press, 2002.

Palmer, Larry. *Endings and Beginnings: Law, Medicine, and Society in Assisted Suicide*. Westport, CT: Praeger, 2000.

Pinello, Daniel R. *Gay Rights and American Law*. New York: Cambridge University Press, 2003.

Posner, Richard. *Sex and Reason*. Cambridge, MA: Harvard University Press, 1992.

———, and Silbaugh, Katharine. *A Guide to America's Sex Laws*. Chicago: University of Chicago Press, 1996.

Richards, David A. J. *Identity and the Case for Gay Rights*. Chicago: University of Chicago Press, 1999.

Robb, Graham. *Strangers: Homosexual Love in the Nineteenth Century*. New York: W. W. Norton, 2004.

Rosen, Jeffrey. *The Unwanted Gaze: The Violation of Our Privacy*. New York: Random House, 2000.

Rothstein, Mark. *Genetic Secrets: Protecting Privacy and Confidentiality in the Genetic Era*. New Haven, CT: Yale University Press, 1997.

Schneider, Carl, ed. *Law at the End of Life: The Supreme Court and Assisted Suicide*. Ann Arbor: University of Michigan Press, 2000.

Urofsky, Melvin. *Lethal Judgments: Assisted Suicide and American Law*. Lawrence: University Press of Kansas, 1999.

■ INSIDE THE COURT

Vote Switching in Bowers v. Hardwick *and Justice Powell's April 8, 1986, Memorandum*

When the justices initially discussed *Bowers v. Hardwick* in conference, there were not four votes to grant review of the Court of Appeals for the Eleventh Circuit's ruling striking down Georgia's law proscribing hetero-sexual and homosexual sodomy. Almost a decade earlier, the Court had summarily affirmed a district court decision upholding Virginia's criminal sodomy law, in *Doe v. Commonwealth's Attorney for the City of Richmond*, 425 U.S. 901 (1976). In that case, Justices Brennan, Marshall, and Stevens had voted to grant oral arguments but could not command a fourth vote for do-ing so. Subsequently, when striking down Georgia's sodomy statute, the ap-pellate court held that because *Doe* was a summary affirmance it was not controlling. When the Court then considered that decision at conference in October 1985, Justices Brennan and Marshall still could not find a fourth vote for granting review of constitutional challenges to state sodomy laws.

But, on October 17, 1985, Justice White circulated a proposed four-page dissent from the pending denial of *certiorari* in *Bowers v. Hardwick*. In it he pointed out that the Eleventh Circuit's decision conflicted with circuits' in-terpretations of *Doe* and rejection of claims that the right of privacy extends protection to homosexual activities. Specifically, Justice White noted that a three-judge panel, which included then Judge Antonin Scalia and ill-fated Supreme Court nominee Judge Robert H. Bork, of the District of Colum-bia Circuit, had reached precisely the opposite conclusions in *Dronenburg v. Zech*, 741 F.2d 1388 (CADC 1984).

Justice White's proposed dissent drew quick responses from Justices Brennan and Rehnquist. They both asked to join his dissent. At conference the next day, October 18, there thus emerged four votes to grant review. But, discussions of that and other cases raising similar claims suggested to Justice Brennan that the Court would be sharply divided on the merits. Justice Brennan could count on Marshall, Blackmun, and Stevens to vote with him on affirming the lower court and in recognizing a substantive due process right of privacy extending protection to individuals' sexual autonomy. But Justices White and Rehnquist were steadfastly opposed to stretching the "right of privacy" to protect such activities, as were Chief Justice Burger and Justice O'Connor. And that left Justice Powell in the middle and the likely pivotal vote. On the merits of the case, Justice Brennan worried, a majority might go the other way and reverse.

On further reflection and after discussing the case with his law clerks, Justice Brennan circulated a memorandum on October 23, explaining that he had changed his vote and now voted to deny review. His strategy of vote switching, and thereby possibly minimizing the damage that a majority's rejection of Michael Hardwick's privacy claim might do to developing constitutional law, however, did not go unnoticed. The next day, Chief Justice Burger in turn sent around a memo explaining that he now also would change his conference vote and join the three others in granting the case. At that week's Friday conference there thus remained four votes to grant: Chief Justice Burger and Justices Marshall, Rehnquist, and White voted to grant, while the remaining five voted to deny review. On November 4, the Court announced it would hear oral arguments and, later, scheduled them for March 31, 1986.

When the Court heard oral arguments, Hardwick was represented by Harvard Law School professor Laurence Tribe. Like Justice Brennan, Tribe knew that the Court would be sharply split when deciding the case and guessed that Justice Lewis Powell would likely cast the deciding vote. Just a year earlier, in Justice Powell's absence, the justices split four to four in *Board of Education of Oklahoma City v. National Gay Task Force*, 470 U.S. 903 (1985), leaving intact a lower-court ruling overturning an Oklahoma law providing for the dismissal of teachers who advocate homosexual relations. Tribe thus pitched his arguments for overturning Georgia's law at Justice Powell. "This case is about the limits of government power," he argued, reminding the justices they had held that individuals have constitutionally protected privacy interests in their homes. The question was whether states have a compelling interest in dictating, as Tribe put it, "how every adult, married or unmarried, in every bedroom in Georgia will behave in the closest and most intimate personal association with another adult." But Powell interrupted from the bench to ask whether that meant that states could not proscribe consensual sodomy in "a motel room or the back of an automobile or [public] toilet or wherever." Knowing that a decade earlier the Court had denied, in *Doe v. Commonwealth's Attorney for the City of Richmond*, an appeal of a man's conviction under Virginia's sodomy law for having homosexual relations in a public bathroom, Tribe was evasive. On Justice Powell's persistence and chiding him for avoiding his "public toilet" question, Tribe finally conceded that certain behavior in public places could be outlawed but underscored that "there is something special about a home."

Justice Powell was tentatively persuaded by Tribe's arguments. At the justices' private conference two days later, Chief Justice Burger began discussion of the case and voted to uphold Georgia's law. Justice Brennan countered that such laws violate individuals' privacy rights in their homes and voted to overturn the law. Justice White followed by siding with Burger, while Justices Marshall and Blackmun agreed with Brennan. Powell spoke next. He was troubled by the facts in this case. Powell agreed that individuals enjoy a right of privacy in their homes. But he was torn by two facts pointing in opposite directions. Punishment for sodomy in Georgia carried twenty years imprisonment, which seemed unfair. Still, Powell was concerned about overturning the law since Hardwick had not actually been tried and convicted. He would tentatively vote to strike the law down, but much turned on how the Court's opinion was written. Justice Rehnquist followed, voting to uphold Georgia's law, as did Justice O'Connor. Justice Stevens, then, voted to strike down the law. Since there appeared to be five votes to affirm the lower court's invalidation of Georgia's law, after conference Justice Brennan assigned Blackmun to write an opinion for the majority.

One week after the conference vote, though, Justice Powell circulated the memorandum reproduced below, in which he explains that he has reconsidered his position and would now vote to reverse. As a result, the outcome in the case dramatically changed and, as Brennan had feared, there were five votes to reverse the lower court's decision. Powell's memo obviously troubled the four who had voted to affirm. And Justice Stevens tried to save that outcome by responding to Powell with a letter pointing out that, because Powell had expressed uncertainty about his vote, perhaps the Court ought to affirm with an order explaining that the Court was "equally divided," as the Court had done the year before in *Board of Education of Oklahoma City v. National Gay Task Force*. "Maybe we should follow a similar course in this case," wrote Stevens. But Powell was unmoved and could not in good conscience go along with that suggestion.

The day following Powell's circulation of his memorandum, on April 9, 1986, Chief Justice Burger assigned Justice White to write an opinion for the majority. In late April and May, he circulated three drafts of his proposed opinion. In June, Blackmun circulated his proposed dissent, and Powell circulated his concurring opinion, explaining the importance for him of the fact that Hardwick had not been tried, convicted, and sentenced, as well as explaining his view that, if penalties for sodomy (such as the twenty-year sentence that Hardwick would have faced) were imposed, they might violate the Eighth Amendment's ban against "cruel and unusual punishment."

Commonwealth of Kentucky v. Wasson
842 S.W.2D 487 (1992)

In this case the Kentucky supreme court struck down its state prohibition of homosexual sodomy. In the process the court sharply criticized the U.S. Supreme Court's analysis in *Bowers v. Hardwick*, 478 U.S. 186 (1986), as well as the applicability of that analysis to its decision. Excerpts of the opinion appear in Chapter 2.

Supreme Court of the United States
Washington, D. C. 20543

CHAMBERS OF
JUSTICE LEWIS F. POWELL, JR.

April 8, 1986

85-140 Bowers v. Hardwick

MEMORANDUM TO THE CONFERENCE:

       At Conference last week, I expressed the view that in some cases it would violate the Eighth Amendment to imprison a person for a private act of homosexual sodomy. I continue to think that in such cases imprisonment would constitute cruel and unusual punishment. I relied primarily on Robinson v. California.

       At Conference, given my view as to the Eighth Amendment, my vote was to affirm but on this ground rather than the view of four other Justices that there was a violation of a fundamental substantive constitutional right - as CA11 held. I did not agree that there is a substantive due process right to engage in conduct that for centuries has been recognized as deviant, and not in the best interest of preserving humanity. I may say generally, that I also hesitate to create another substantive due process right.

       I write this memorandum today because upon further study as to exactly what is before us, I conclude that my "bottom line" should be to reverse rather than affirm. The only question presented by the parties is the substantive due process issue, and - as several of you noted at Conference - my Eighth Amendment view was not addressed by the court below or by the parties.

       In sum, my more carefully considered view is that I will vote to reverse but will write separately to explain my view of this case generally. I will not know, until I see the writing, whether I can join an opinion finding no substantive due process right or simply join the judgment.

L.F.P., Jr.

ss

(Library of Congress, Justice Thurgood Marshall Papers; and Washington and Lee Law School, Justice Lewis F. Powell, Jr. Papers.)

Lawrence v. Texas
539 U.S. 558, 123 S.CT. 2472 (2003)

On the night of September 17, 1998, the Harris County Texas police department received a frantic call from someone who claimed that there was a man with a gun "going crazy" in the Houston apartment of

Tyron Garner, left, and John Lawrence were arrested in 1998 under Texas's sodomy law. The appeal of their conviction will be heard by the Supreme Court on Wednesday. (FILE PHOTO/BY DAVID J. PHILLIP—ASSOCIATED PRESS *The Washington Post* Monday March 24, 2003 A2.)

.

John Geddes Lawrence. Officers responded and arrived and entered the apartment. They found no intruder, but instead found Lawrence and Tyron Garner engaged in sodomy. They arrested them for violating the state's "homosexual conduct" law, which made it a misdemeanor for any person to engage "in deviant sexual intercourse with another individual of the same sex." A few weeks later, Lawrence and Garner were tried and found guilty of "deviant homosexual conduct," and each was fined $200. They appealed and challenged the statute's constitutionality. A three-judge appeals panel ruled two to one that the convictions "impermissibly discriminate on the basis of sex," and violated the Equal Rights Amendment of the state constitution. But in March 2001, the full Texas Court of Appeals reversed and upheld the state's "homosexual conduct" law. Lawrence appealed that decision to the Texas Court of Criminal Appeals, which denied review, and subsequently filed an appeal to the U.S. Supreme Court, which granted review.

The state court's decision was reversed by a vote of six to three. Justice Kennedy delivered the opinion of the Court. Justice O'Connor filed a concurring opinion. Justices Scalia and Thomas filed dissenting opinions, which Chief Justice Rehnquist joined.

☐ *Justice KENNEDY delivered the opinion of the Court.*

Liberty protects the person from unwarranted government intrusions into a dwelling or other private places. In our tradition the State is not omnipresent in the home. And there are other spheres of our lives and existence, outside the home, where the State should not be a dominant presence. Freedom extends beyond spatial bounds. Liberty presumes an autonomy of self that includes freedom of thought, belief, expression, and certain intimate conduct. The instant case involves liberty of the person both in its spatial and more transcendent dimensions.

The question before the Court is the validity of a Texas statute making it a crime for two persons of the same sex to engage in certain intimate sexual conduct. . . .

We conclude the case should be resolved by determining whether the petitioners were free as adults to engage in the private conduct in the exercise of their liberty under the Due Process Clause of the Fourteenth Amendment to the Constitution. For this inquiry we deem it necessary to reconsider the Court's holding in *Bowers* [*v. Hardwick*, 478 U.S. 186 (1986)].

There are broad statements of the substantive reach of liberty under the Due Process Clause in earlier cases, including *Pierce v. Society of Sisters*, 268 U. S. 510 (1925), and *Meyer v. Nebraska*, 262 U. S. 390 (1923); but the most pertinent beginning point is our decision in *Griswold v. Connecticut*, 381 U. S. 479 (1965).

In *Griswold* the Court invalidated a state law prohibiting the use of drugs or devices of contraception and counseling or aiding and abetting the use of contraceptives. The Court described the protected interest as a right to privacy and placed emphasis on the marriage relation and the protected space of the marital bedroom.

After *Griswold* it was established that the right to make certain decisions regarding sexual conduct extends beyond the marital relationship. In *Eisenstadt v. Baird*, 405 U. S. 438 (1972), the Court invalidated a law prohibiting the distribution of contraceptives to unmarried persons. The case was decided under the Equal Protection Clause, but with respect to unmarried persons, the Court went on to state the fundamental proposition that the law impaired the exercise of their personal rights.

The opinions in *Griswold* and *Eisenstadt* were part of the background for the decision in *Roe v. Wade*, 410 U. S. 113 (1973). As is well known, the case involved a challenge to the Texas law prohibiting abortions, but the laws of other States were affected as well. Although the Court held the woman's rights were not absolute, her right to elect an abortion did have real and substantial protection as an exercise of her liberty under the Due Process Clause. The Court cited cases that protect spatial freedom and cases that go well beyond it. *Roe* recognized the right of a woman to make certain fundamental decisions affecting her destiny and confirmed once more that the protection of liberty under the Due Process Clause has a substantive dimension of fundamental significance in defining the rights of the person. . . .

This was the state of the law with respect to some of the most relevant cases when the Court considered *Bowers v. Hardwick*. The facts in *Bowers* had some similarities to the instant case. A police officer, whose right to enter seems not to have been in question, observed Hardwick, in his own bedroom, engaging in intimate sexual conduct with another adult male. The conduct was in violation of a Georgia statute making it a criminal offense to engage in sodomy. One difference between the two cases is that the Georgia statute prohibited the conduct whether or not the participants were of the same sex, while the Texas statute, as we have seen, applies only to participants of the same sex. Hardwick was not prosecuted, but he brought an action in federal court to declare the state statute invalid. He alleged he was a practicing homosexual and that the criminal prohibition violated rights guaranteed to him by the Constitution. The Court, in an opinion by Justice WHITE, sustained the Georgia law. Chief Justice BURGER and Justice POWELL joined the opinion of the Court and filed separate, concurring opinions. Four Justices dissented.

The Court began its substantive discussion in *Bowers* as follows: "The issue presented is whether the Federal Constitution confers a fundamental right upon homosexuals to engage in sodomy and hence invalidates the laws of the many States that still make such conduct illegal and have done so for a very long time." That statement, we now conclude, discloses the Court's own failure to appreciate the extent of the liberty at stake. To say that the issue in *Bowers* was simply the right to engage in certain sexual conduct demeans the claim the individual put forward, just as it would demean a married couple were it to be said marriage is simply about the right to have sexual intercourse. The laws involved in *Bowers* and here are, to be sure, statutes that purport to do no more than prohibit a particular sexual act. Their penalties and purposes, though, have more far-reaching consequences, touching upon the most private human conduct, sexual behavior, and in the most private of places, the home. The statutes do seek to control a personal relationship that, whether or not entitled to formal recognition in the law, is within the liberty of persons to choose without being punished as criminals.

This, as a general rule, should counsel against attempts by the State, or a court, to define the meaning of the relationship or to set its boundaries absent injury to a person or abuse of an institution the law protects. It suffices for us to acknowledge that adults may choose to enter upon this relationship in the confines of their homes and their own private lives and still retain their dignity as free persons. When sexuality finds overt expression in intimate conduct with another person, the conduct can be but one element in a personal bond that is more enduring. The liberty protected by the Constitution allows homosexual persons the right to make this choice. . . .

At the outset it should be noted that there is no longstanding history in this country of laws directed at homosexual conduct as a distinct matter. Beginning in colonial times there were prohibitions of sodomy derived from the English criminal laws passed in the first instance by the Reformation Parliament of 1533. The English prohibition was understood to include relations between men and women as well as relations between men and men. Thus early American sodomy laws were not directed at homosexuals as such but instead sought to prohibit nonprocreative sexual activity more generally. This does not suggest approval of homosexual conduct. It does tend to show that this particular form of conduct was not thought of as a separate category from like conduct between heterosexual persons.

Laws prohibiting sodomy do not seem to have been enforced against consenting adults acting in private. A substantial number of sodomy prosecutions and convictions for which there are surviving records were for predatory acts against those who could not or did not consent, as in the case of a minor or the victim of an assault. . . .

The policy of punishing consenting adults for private acts was not much discussed in the early legal literature. We can infer that one reason for this was the very private nature of the conduct. Despite the absence of prosecutions, there may have been periods in which there was public criticism of homosexuals as such and an insistence that the criminal laws be enforced to discourage their practices. But far from possessing "ancient roots," *Bowers*, American laws targeting same-sex couples did not develop until the last third of the 20th century. The reported decisions concerning the prosecution of consensual, homosexual sodomy between adults for the years 1880–1995 are not always clear in the details, but a significant number involved conduct in a public place.

It was not until the 1970's that any State singled out same-sex relations for criminal prosecution, and only nine States have done so. In summary, the historical grounds relied upon in *Bowers* are more complex than the majority opinion and the concurring opinion by Chief Justice BURGER indicate. Their historical premises are not without doubt and, at the very least, are overstated.

It must be acknowledged, of course, that the Court in *Bowers* was making the broader point that for centuries there have been powerful voices to condemn homosexual conduct as immoral. The condemnation has been shaped by religious beliefs, conceptions of right and acceptable behavior, and respect for the traditional family. For many persons these are not trivial concerns but profound and deep convictions accepted as ethical and moral principles to which they aspire and which thus determine the course of their lives. These considerations do not answer the question before us, however. The issue is whether the majority may use the power of the State to enforce these views on the whole society through operation of the criminal law. "Our obligation is to define the liberty of all, not to mandate our own moral code." *Planned Parenthood of Southeastern Pa. v. Casey*, 505 U. S. 833 (1992). . . .

In all events we think that our laws and traditions in the past half century are of most relevance here. These references show an emerging awareness that liberty gives substantial protection to adult persons in deciding how to conduct their private lives in matters pertaining to sex. . . .

In *Bowers* the Court referred to the fact that before 1961 all 50 States had outlawed sodomy, and that at the time of the Court's decision 24 States and the District of Columbia had sodomy laws. Justice POWELL pointed out that these prohibitions often were being ignored, however. Georgia, for instance, had not sought to enforce its law for decades.

The sweeping references by Chief Justice BURGER to the history of Western civilization and to Judeo-Christian moral and ethical standards did not take account of other authorities pointing in an opposite direction. A committee advising the British Parliament recommended in 1957 repeal of laws punishing homosexual conduct. *The Wolfenden Report* (1963). Parliament enacted the substance of those recommendations 10 years later.

Of even more importance, almost five years before *Bowers* was decided the European Court of Human Rights considered a case with parallels to *Bowers* and to today's case. An adult male resident in Northern Ireland alleged he was a practicing homosexual who desired to engage in consensual homosexual conduct. The laws of Northern Ireland forbade him that right. He alleged that he had been questioned, his home had been searched, and he feared criminal prosecution. The court held that the laws proscribing the conduct were invalid under the European Convention on Human Rights. *Dudgeon v. United Kingdom*, 45 Eur. Ct. H. R. (1981). Authoritative in all countries that are members of the Council of Europe (21 nations then, 45 nations now), the decision is at odds with the premise in *Bowers* that the claim put forward was insubstantial in our Western civilization.

In our own constitutional system the deficiencies in *Bowers* became even more apparent in the years following its announcement. The 25 States with laws prohibiting the relevant conduct referenced in the *Bowers* decision are reduced now to 13, of which 4 enforce their laws only against homosexual conduct. In those States where sodomy is still proscribed, whether for same-sex or heterosexual conduct, there is a pattern of nonenforcement with respect to consenting adults acting in private. The State of Texas admitted in 1994 that as of that date it had not prosecuted anyone under those circumstances.

Two principal cases decided after *Bowers* cast its holding into even more doubt. In *Planned Parenthood of Southeastern Pa. v. Casey*, 505 U. S. 833 (1992), the Court reaffirmed the substantive force of the liberty protected by the Due Process Clause. The *Casey* decision again confirmed that our laws and tradition afford constitutional protection to personal decisions relating to marriage, procreation, contraception, family relationships, child rearing, and education. . . . Persons in a homosexual relationship may seek autonomy for these purposes, just as heterosexual persons do. The decision in *Bowers* would deny them this right.

The second post-*Bowers* case of principal relevance is *Romer v. Evans*, 517 U. S. 620 (1996). There the Court struck down class-based legislation directed at homosexuals as a violation of the Equal Protection Clause. *Romer* invalidated an amendment to Colorado's constitution which named as a solitary class persons who were homosexuals, lesbians, or bisexual either by "orientation, conduct, practices or relationships," and deprived them of protection under state antidiscrimination laws. We concluded that the provision was "born of animosity toward the class of persons affected" and further that it had no rational relation to a legitimate governmental purpose. . . .

Equality of treatment and the due process right to demand respect for conduct protected by the substantive guarantee of liberty are linked in important respects, and a decision on the latter point advances both interests. If protected conduct is made criminal and the law which does so remains unexamined for its substantive validity, its stigma might remain even if it were not enforceable as drawn for equal protection reasons. When homosexual conduct is made criminal by the law of the State, that declaration in and of itself is an invitation to subject homosexual persons to discrimination both in the public and in the private spheres. The central holding of *Bowers* has been brought in question by this case, and it should be addressed. Its continuance as precedent demeans the lives of homosexual persons. . . .

The foundations of *Bowers* have sustained serious erosion from our recent decisions in *Casey* and *Romer*. When our precedent has been thus weakened, criticism from other sources is of greater significance. In the United States criticism of *Bowers* has been substantial and continuing, disapproving of its reasoning in all respects, not just as to its historical assumptions. The courts of five different States have declined to follow it in interpreting provisions in their own state constitutions parallel to the Due Process Clause of the Fourteenth Amendment.

To the extent *Bowers* relied on values we share with a wider civilization, it should be noted that the reasoning and holding in *Bowers* have been rejected elsewhere. The European Court of Human Rights has followed not *Bowers* but its own decision in *Dudgeon v. United Kingdom*. Other nations, too, have taken action consistent with an affirmation of the protected right of homosexual adults to engage in intimate, consensual conduct. The right the petitioners seek in this case has been accepted as an integral part of human freedom in many other countries. There has been no showing that in this country the governmental interest in circumscribing personal choice is somehow more legitimate or urgent.

The doctrine of *stare decisis* is essential to the respect accorded to the judgments of the Court and to the stability of the law. It is not, however, an inexorable command. *Payne v. Tennessee*, 501 U. S. 808 (1991). In *Casey* we noted that when a Court is asked to overrule a precedent recognizing a constitutional liberty interest, individual or societal reliance on the existence of that liberty cautions with particular strength against reversing course. The holding in *Bowers*, however, has not induced detrimental reliance comparable to some instances where recognized individual rights are involved. Indeed, there has been no individual or societal reliance on *Bowers* of the sort that could counsel against overturning its holding once there are compelling reasons to do so. *Bowers* itself causes uncertainty, for the precedents before and after its issuance contradict its central holding.

The rationale of *Bowers* does not withstand careful analysis. *Bowers* was not correct when it was decided, and it is not correct today. It ought not to remain binding precedent. *Bowers v. Hardwick* should be and now is overruled.

The present case does not involve minors. It does not involve persons who might be injured or coerced or who are situated in relationships where consent might not easily be refused. It does not involve public conduct or prostitution. It does not involve whether the government must give formal recognition to any relationship that homosexual persons seek to enter. The case does involve two adults who, with full and mutual consent from each other, engaged in sexual practices common to a homosexual lifestyle. The petitioners are entitled to respect for their private lives. The State cannot demean their existence or control their destiny by making their private sexual conduct a crime. Their right to liberty under the Due Process Clause gives them the full right to engage in their conduct without intervention of the government. The Texas statute furthers no legitimate state interest which can justify its intrusion into the personal and private life of the individual. . . .

The judgment of the Court of Appeals for the Texas Fourteenth District is reversed, and the case is remanded for further proceedings not inconsistent with this opinion.

It is so ordered.

☐ *Justice O'CONNOR, concurring in the judgment.*

The Court today overrules *Bowers v. Hardwick*. I joined *Bowers*, and do not join the Court in overruling it. Nevertheless, I agree with the Court that

Texas' statute banning same-sex sodomy is unconstitutional. Rather than relying on the substantive component of the Fourteenth Amendment's Due Process Clause, as the Court does, I base my conclusion on the Fourteenth Amendment's Equal Protection Clause. . . .

This case raises a different issue than *Bowers*: whether, under the Equal Protection Clause, moral disapproval is a legitimate state interest to justify by itself a statute that bans homosexual sodomy, but not heterosexual sodomy. It is not. Moral disapproval of this group, like a bare desire to harm the group, is an interest that is insufficient to satisfy rational basis review under the Equal Protection Clause. Indeed, we have never held that moral disapproval, without any other asserted state interest, is a sufficient rationale under the Equal Protection Clause to justify a law that discriminates among groups of persons. . . .

That this law as applied to private, consensual conduct is unconstitutional under the Equal Protection Clause does not mean that other laws distinguishing between heterosexuals and homosexuals would similarly fail under rational basis review. Texas cannot assert any legitimate state interest here, such as national security or preserving the traditional institution of marriage. Unlike the moral disapproval of same-sex relations—the asserted state interest in this case—other reasons exist to promote the institution of marriage beyond mere moral disapproval of an excluded group.

A law branding one class of persons as criminal solely based on the State's moral disapproval of that class and the conduct associated with that class runs contrary to the values of the Constitution and the Equal Protection Clause, under any standard of review. I therefore concur in the Court's judgment that Texas' sodomy law banning "deviate sexual intercourse" between consenting adults of the same sex, but not between consenting adults of different sexes, is unconstitutional.

☐ *Justice SCALIA, with whom The CHIEF JUSTICE and Justice THOMAS join, dissenting.*

"Liberty finds no refuge in a jurisprudence of doubt." *Planned Parenthood of Southeastern Pa. v. Casey*, 505 U. S. 833 (1992). That was the Court's sententious response, barely more than a decade ago, to those seeking to overrule *Roe v. Wade*, 410 U. S. 113 (1973). The Court's response today, to those who have engaged in a 17-year crusade to overrule *Bowers v. Hardwick*, 478 U. S. 186 (1986), is very different. The need for stability and certainty presents no barrier. . . .

I begin with the Court's surprising readiness to reconsider a decision rendered a mere 17 years ago in *Bowers v. Hardwick*. I do not myself believe in rigid adherence to *stare decisis* in constitutional cases; but I do believe that we should be consistent rather than manipulative in invoking the doctrine. Today's opinions in support of reversal do not bother to distinguish—or indeed, even bother to mention—the paean to *stare decisis* coauthored by three Members of today's majority in *Planned Parenthood v. Casey*. There, when *stare decisis* meant preservation of judicially invented abortion rights, the widespread criticism of *Roe* was strong reason to reaffirm it. Today, however, the widespread opposition to *Bowers*, a decision resolving an issue as "intensely divisive" as the issue in *Roe*, is offered as a reason in favor of overruling it. Gone, too, is any "enquiry" (of the sort conducted in *Casey*) into whether the decision sought to be overruled has "proven 'unworkable,' " *Casey*.

Today's approach to *stare decisis* invites us to overrule an erroneously decided precedent (including an "intensely divisive" decision) if: (1) its foundations have been "eroded" by subsequent decisions; (2) it has been subject to "substantial and continuing" criticism; and (3) it has not induced "individual or societal reliance" that counsels against overturning. The problem is that *Roe* itself—which today's majority surely has no disposition to overrule—satisfies these conditions to at least the same degree as *Bowers*. . . .

What a massive disruption of the current social order, therefore, the overruling of *Bowers* entails. Not so the overruling of *Roe*, which would simply have restored the regime that existed for centuries before 1973, in which the permissibility of and restrictions upon abortion were determined legislatively State-by-State. *Casey*, however, chose to base its *stare decisis* determination on a different "sort" of reliance. "[P]eople," it said, "have organized intimate relationships and made choices that define their views of themselves and their places in society, in reliance on the availability of abortion in the event that contraception should fail." This falsely assumes that the consequence of overruling *Roe* would have been to make abortion unlawful. It would not; it would merely have permitted the States to do so. Many States would unquestionably have declined to prohibit abortion, and others would not have prohibited it within six months (after which the most significant reliance interests would have expired). Even for persons in States other than these, the choice would not have been between abortion and childbirth, but between abortion nearby and abortion in a neighboring State.

To tell the truth, it does not surprise me, and should surprise no one, that the Court has chosen today to revise the standards of *stare decisis* set forth in *Casey*. It has thereby exposed *Casey*'s extraordinary deference to precedent for the result-oriented expedient that it is.

Having decided that it need not adhere to *stare decisis*, the Court still must establish that *Bowers* was wrongly decided and that the Texas statute, as applied to petitioners, is unconstitutional. . . .

Our opinions applying the doctrine known as "substantive due process" hold that the Due Process Clause prohibits States from infringing fundamental liberty interests, unless the infringement is narrowly tailored to serve a compelling state interest. We have held repeatedly, in cases the Court today does not overrule, that only fundamental rights qualify for this so-called "heightened scrutiny" protection—that is, rights which are " 'deeply rooted in this Nation's history and tradition.' "

Bowers held, first, that criminal prohibitions of homosexual sodomy are not subject to heightened scrutiny because they do not implicate a "fundamental right" under the Due Process Clause. Noting that "[p]roscriptions against that conduct have ancient roots," that "[s]odomy was a criminal offense at common law and was forbidden by the laws of the original 13 States when they ratified the Bill of Rights," and that many States had retained their bans on sodomy, *Bowers* concluded that a right to engage in homosexual sodomy was not " 'deeply rooted in this Nation's history and tradition.' "

The Court today does not overrule this holding. Not once does it describe homosexual sodomy as a "fundamental right" or a "fundamental liberty interest," nor does it subject the Texas statute to strict scrutiny. Instead, having failed to establish that the right to homosexual sodomy is " 'deeply rooted in this Nation's history and tradition,' " the Court concludes that the application of Texas's statute to petitioners' conduct fails the rational-basis test, and overrules *Bowers*' holding to the contrary.

I shall address that rational-basis holding presently. First, however, I address some aspersions that the Court casts upon *Bowers*' conclusion that homosexual sodomy is not a "fundamental right"—even though, as I have said, the Court does not have the boldness to reverse that conclusion.

The Court's description of "the state of the law" at the time of *Bowers* only confirms that *Bowers* was right. The Court points to *Griswold v. Connecticut* (1965). But that case expressly disclaimed any reliance on the doctrine of "substantive due process," and grounded the so-called "right to privacy" in penumbras of constitutional provisions other than the Due Process Clause.

Roe v. Wade recognized that the right to abort an unborn child was a "fundamental right" protected by the Due Process Clause. The *Roe* Court, however, made no attempt to establish that this right was " 'deeply rooted in this Nation's history and tradition' "; instead, it based its conclusion that "the Fourteenth Amendment's concept of personal liberty . . . is broad enough to encompass a woman's decision whether or not to terminate her pregnancy" on its own normative judgment that anti-abortion laws were undesirable. . . .

After discussing the history of antisodomy laws, the Court proclaims that, "it should be noted that there is no longstanding history in this country of laws directed at homosexual conduct as a distinct matter." This observation in no way casts into doubt the "definitive [historical] conclusion," on which *Bowers* relied: that our Nation has a longstanding history of laws prohibiting sodomy in general—regardless of whether it was performed by same-sex or opposite-sex couples. It is (as *Bowers* recognized) entirely irrelevant whether the laws in our long national tradition criminalizing homosexual sodomy were "directed at homosexual conduct as a distinct matter." Whether homosexual sodomy was prohibited by a law targeted at same-sex sexual relations or by a more general law prohibiting both homosexual and heterosexual sodomy, the only relevant point is that it was criminalized—which suffices to establish that homosexual sodomy is not a right "deeply rooted in our Nation's history and tradition." The Court today agrees that homosexual sodomy was criminalized and thus does not dispute the facts on which *Bowers* actually relied.

Next the Court makes the claim, again unsupported by any citations, that "[l]aws prohibiting sodomy do not seem to have been enforced against consenting adults acting in private." The key qualifier here is "acting in private"—since the Court admits that sodomy laws were enforced against consenting adults (although the Court contends that prosecutions were "infrequent.") I do not know what "acting in private" means; surely consensual sodomy, like heterosexual intercourse, is rarely performed on stage. . . . There are 203 prosecutions for consensual, adult homosexual sodomy reported in the West Reporting system and official state reporters from the years 1880–1995. There are also records of 20 sodomy prosecutions and 4 executions during the colonial period. *Bowers*' conclusion that homosexual sodomy is not a fundamental right "deeply rooted in this Nation's history and tradition" is utterly unassailable.

Realizing that fact, the Court instead says: "[W]e think that our laws and traditions in the past half century are of most relevance here. These references show an emerging awareness that liberty gives substantial protection to adult persons in deciding how to conduct their private lives in matters pertaining to sex." Apart from the fact that such an "emerging awareness" does not establish a "fundamental right," the statement is factually false. States continue to prosecute all sorts of crimes by adults "in matters pertaining to sex": prostitution, adult incest, adultery, obscenity, and child pornography. Sodomy laws, too, have been enforced "in the past half century," in which there have been 134 reported cases involving prosecutions for consensual, adult, homosexual sodomy. . . .

In any event, an "emerging awareness" is by definition not "deeply rooted in this Nation's history and tradition[s]," as we have said "fundamental right" status requires. Constitutional entitlements do not spring into existence because some States choose to lessen or eliminate criminal sanctions on certain behavior. Much less do they spring into existence, as the Court seems to believe, because foreign nations decriminalize conduct. The *Bowers* majority opinion never relied on "values we share with a wider civilization," but rather rejected the claimed right to sodomy on the ground that such a right was not " 'deeply rooted in this Nation's history and tradition.' " *Bowers*' rational-basis holding is likewise devoid of any reliance on the views of a "wider civilization." The Court's discussion of these foreign views (ignoring, of course, the many countries that have retained criminal prohibitions on sodomy) is therefore meaningless *dicta*.

I turn now to the ground on which the Court squarely rests its holding: the contention that there is no rational basis for the law here under attack. This proposition is so out of accord with our jurisprudence—indeed, with the jurisprudence of any society we know—that it requires little discussion.

The Texas statute undeniably seeks to further the belief of its citizens that certain forms of sexual behavior are "immoral and unacceptable," *Bowers*—the same interest furthered by criminal laws against fornication, bigamy, adultery, adult incest, bestiality, and obscenity. *Bowers* held that this was a legitimate state interest. The Court today reaches the opposite conclusion. The Texas statute, it says, "furthers no legitimate state interest which can justify its intrusion into the personal and private life of the individual." The Court embraces instead Justice STEVENS' declaration in his *Bowers* dissent, that "the fact that the governing majority in a State has traditionally viewed a particular practice as immoral is not a sufficient reason for upholding a law prohibiting the practice." This effectively decrees the end of all morals legislation. If, as the Court asserts, the promotion of majoritarian sexual morality is not even a legitimate state interest, none of the above-mentioned laws can survive rational-basis review.

Finally, I turn to petitioners' equal-protection challenge, which no Member of the Court save Justice O'CONNOR embraces: On its face Section 21.06(a) applies equally to all persons. Men and women, heterosexuals and homosexuals, are all subject to its prohibition of deviate sexual intercourse with someone of the same sex. To be sure, Section 21.06 does distinguish between the sexes insofar as concerns the partner with whom the sexual acts are performed: men can violate the law only with other men, and women only with other women. But this cannot itself be a denial of equal protection, since it is precisely the same distinction regarding partners that is drawn in state laws prohibiting marriage with someone of the same sex while permitting marriage with someone of the opposite sex. . . .

Today's opinion is the product of a Court, which is the product of a law-profession culture, that has largely signed on to the so-called homosexual agenda, by which I mean the agenda promoted by some homosexual activists directed at eliminating the moral opprobrium that has traditionally attached to homosexual conduct. One of the most revealing statements in today's opinion is the Court's grim warning that the criminalization of homosexual conduct is "an invitation to subject homosexual persons to discrimination both in the public and in the private spheres." It is clear from this that the Court has taken sides in the culture war, departing from its role of assuring, as neutral observer, that the democratic rules of engagement are observed. Many Americans do not want persons who openly engage in homosexual conduct as partners in their business, as scoutmasters for their children, as teachers in their children's schools, or as boarders in their home. They view this as protecting themselves and their families from a lifestyle that they believe to be immoral and destructive. The Court views it as "discrimination" which it is the function of our judgments to deter. So imbued is the Court with the law profession's anti-anti-homosexual culture, that it is seemingly unaware that the attitudes of that culture are not obviously "mainstream"; that in most States what the Court calls "discrimination" against those who engage in homosexual acts is perfectly legal; that proposals to ban such "discrimination" under Title VII have repeatedly been rejected by Congress; that in some cases such "discrimination" is mandated by federal statute (mandating discharge from the armed forces of any service member who engages in or intends to engage in homosexual acts); and that in some cases such "discrimination" is a constitutional right, see *Boy Scouts of America v. Dale,* 530 U. S. 640 (2000).

Let me be clear that I have nothing against homosexuals, or any other group, promoting their agenda through normal democratic means. Social perceptions of sexual and other morality change over time, and every group has the right to persuade its fellow citizens that its view of such matters is the best. That homosexuals have achieved some success in that enterprise is attested to by the fact that Texas is one of the few remaining States that criminalize private, consensual homosexual acts. But persuading one's fellow citizens is one thing, and imposing one's views in absence of democratic majority will is something else. I would no more require a State to criminalize homosexual acts—or, for that matter, display any moral disapprobation of them—than I would forbid it to do so. What Texas has chosen to do is well within the range of traditional democratic action, and its hand should not be stayed through the invention of a brand-new "constitutional right" by a Court that is impatient of democratic change. It is indeed true that "later generations can see that laws once thought necessary and proper in fact serve only to oppress," and when that happens, later generations can repeal those laws. But it is the premise of our system that those judgments are to be made by the people, and not imposed by a governing caste that knows best.

□ *Justice THOMAS, dissenting.*

I join Justice SCALIA's dissenting opinion. I write separately to note that the law before the Court today "is . . . uncommonly silly." *Griswold v. Connecticut* (1965) (STEWART, J., dissenting). If I were a member of the Texas Legislature, I would vote to repeal it. Punishing someone for expressing his sexual preference through noncommercial consensual conduct with another adult does not appear to be a worthy way to expend valuable law enforcement resources.

Notwithstanding this, I recognize that as a member of this Court I am not empowered to help petitioners and others similarly situated. My duty, rather, is to "decide cases 'agreeably to the Constitution and laws of the United States.' " And, just like Justice STEWART, I "can find [neither in the Bill of Rights nor any other part of the Constitution a] general right of privacy," or as the Court terms it today, the "liberty of the person both in its spatial and more transcendent dimensions."

Cruzan by Cruzan v. Director, Missouri Department of Health

497 U.S. 261, 110 S.CT. 2841 (1990)

Late in the night of January 11, 1983, Nancy Cruzan, at the age of twenty-five, was thrown from her car as it crashed off the road not far from her home in Catersville, Missouri. By the time police and paramedics arrived and restarted her heart and lungs, her brain had been deprived of oxygen for twelve to fourteen minutes. She never regained consciousness. In the hospital, Miss Cruzan's parents approved the surgical insertion of a feeding tube into her body to keep her alive. Her doctors agreed that she would never regain consciousness and that her cerebral cortex was atrophying. Without removing the feeding tube, they also agreed, Miss Cruzan could persist in a vegetative state for another thirty years.

In early 1987, Miss Cruzan's parents decided to seek permission to have the feeding tube removed. A year later, in 1988 a state trial judge granted the Cruzans permission, but the state appealed to the Missouri Supreme Court. By a vote of four to three, the state supreme court reversed. The majority cited the preamble to the state's 1986 abortion law, which the U.S. Supreme Court upheld in *Webster v. Reproductive Health Services*, 492 U.S. 490 (1989) and which proclaims the state's "unqualified" interest in preserving the "sanctity of human life." The majority also held that the Cruzans could not assert a constitutional right of privacy to make a decision "for an incompetent in the absence of the formalities required under Missouri's Living Will statutes" or without establishing "clear and convincing evidence" that Miss Cruzan would have wanted the feeding tube removed.

The Cruzans appealed the Missouri Supreme Court's decision to the U.S. Supreme Court, which granted *certiorari*. The Bush administration and various antiabortion rights groups filed briefs supporting the state, while the American Civil Liberties Union and other groups supported the Cruzans. In the meantime, while defending the state's decision, Missouri's attorney general, William Webster, endeavored to render the case moot. He drafted a bill, approved by Cruzan's attorneys, that would have allowed the Cruzans to remove the feeding tube from their daughter. The bill would have permitted the removal of life-support systems from patients (1) who were in a "persistent oblivious state" for at least thirty-six months, (2) whose family agreed to the removal of life-support systems, and (3) for which three physicians concurred that there was no likelihood of recovery. In addition, the bill would have provided that a patient's wishes to have such systems discontinued needed to be shown only on a "preponderance of the evidence," rather than the more rigorous standard of "clear and convincing" proof. But the Missouri state legislature refused to enact the bill into law. On June 25, 1990, the Supreme Court handed down its decision.

The Court's decision was five to four, and the majority's opinion was announced by Chief Justice Rehnquist. Justices Scalia and O'Connor delivered concurring opinions. Dissents were by Justices Stevens and Brennan, who were joined by Justices Blackmun and Marshall.

☐ *Chief Justice REHNQUIST delivers the opinion of the Court.*

At common law, even the touching of one person by another without consent and without legal justification was a battery. Before the turn of the century, this Court observed that "[n]o right is held more sacred, or is more carefully guarded, by the common law, than the right of every individual to the possession and control of his own person, free from all restraint or interference of others, unless by clear and unquestionable authority of law." *Union Pacific R. Co. v. Botsford*, 141 U.S. 250, 251 (1891). . . .

The logical corollary of the doctrine of informed consent is that the patient generally possesses the right not to consent, that is, to refuse treatment. Until about 15 years ago and the seminal decision in *In re Quinlan*, 70 N. J. 10 [1976], *cert.* denied *sub nom., Garger v. New Jersey*, 429 U.S. 922 (1976), the number of right-to-refuse-treatment decisions were relatively few. Most of the earlier cases involved patients who refused medical treatment forbidden by their religious beliefs, thus implicating First Amendment rights as well as common law rights of self-determination. More recently, however, with the advance of medical technology capable of sustaining life well past the point where natural forces would have brought certain death in earlier times, cases involving the right to refuse life-sustaining treatment have burgeoned. . . .

[T]he common-law doctrine of informed consent is viewed as generally encompassing the right of a competent individual to refuse medical treatment. Beyond that, these decisions demonstrate both similarity and diversity in their approach to decision of what all agree is a perplexing question with unusually strong moral and ethical overtones. State courts have available to them for decision a number of sources—state constitutions, statutes, and common law—which are not available to us. In this Court, the question is simply and starkly whether the United States Constitution prohibits Missouri from choosing the rule of decision which it did. This is the first case in which we have been squarely presented with the issue of whether the United States Constitution grants what is in common parlance referred to as a "right to die." We follow the judicious counsel of our decision in *Twin City Bank v. Nebeker*, 167 U. S. 196, 202 (1897), where we said that in deciding "a question of such magnitude and importance . . . it is the [better] part of wisdom not to attempt, by any general statement, to cover every possible phase of the subject."

The Fourteenth Amendment provides that no State shall "deprive any person of life, liberty, or property, without due process of law." The principle that a competent person has a constitutionally protected liberty interest in refusing unwanted medical treatment may be inferred from our prior decisions. In *Jacobson v. Massachusetts*, 197 U. S. 11, 24-30 (1905), for instance, the Court balanced an individual's liberty interest in declining an unwanted smallpox vaccine against the State's interest in preventing disease. . . .

But determining that a person has a "liberty interest" under the Due Process Clause does not end the inquiry; "whether respondent's constitutional rights have been violated must be determined by balancing his liberty interests against the relevant state interests." *Youngberg v. Romeo*, 457 U. S. 307 (1982). . . .

[F]or purposes of this case, we assume that the United States Constitution would grant a competent person a constitutionally protected right to refuse lifesaving hydration and nutrition.

Petitioners go on to assert that an incompetent person should possess the same right in this respect as is possessed by a competent person. . . .

The difficulty with petitioners' claim is that in a sense it begs the question: an incompetent person is not able to make an informed and voluntary choice to exercise a hypothetical right to refuse treatment or any other right. Such a "right" must be exercised for her, if at all, by some sort of surrogate. Here, Missouri has in effect recognized that under certain circumstances a surrogate may act for the patient in electing to have hydration and nutrition withdrawn in such a way as to cause death, but it has established a procedural safeguard to assure that the action of the surrogate conforms as best it may to the wishes expressed by the patient while competent. Missouri requires that evidence of the incompetent's wishes as to the withdrawal of treatment be proved by clear and convincing evidence. The question, then, is whether the United States Constitution forbids the establishment of this procedural requirement by the State. We hold that it does not.

Whether or not Missouri's clear and convincing evidence requirement comports with the United States Constitution depends in part on what interests the State may properly seek to protect in this situation. Missouri relies on its interest in the protection and preservation of human life, and there can be no gainsaying this interest. As a general matter, the States—indeed, all civilized nations—demonstrate their commitment to life by treating homicide as serious crime. Moreover, the majority of States in this country have laws imposing criminal penalties on one who assists another to commit suicide. We do not think a State is required to remain neutral in the face of an informed and voluntary decision by a physically-able adult to starve to death.

But in the context presented here, a State has more particular interests at stake. The choice between life and death is a deeply personal decision of obvious and overwhelming finality. We believe Missouri may legitimately seek to safeguard the personal element of this choice through the imposition of heightened evidentiary requirements. It cannot be disputed that the Due Process Clause protects an interest in life as well as an interest in refusing life-sustaining medical treatment. Not all incompetent patients will have loved ones available to serve as surrogate decisionmakers.

In our view, Missouri has permissibly sought to advance these interests through the adoption of a "clear and convincing" standard of proof to govern such proceedings. "The function of a standard of proof, as that concept is embodied in the Due Process Clause and in the realm of factfinding, is to 'instruct the factfinder concerning the degree of confidence our society thinks he should have in the correctness of factual conclusions for a particular type of adjudication.'" *Addington v. Texas*, 441 U.S. 418 (1979) (quoting *In re Winship*, 397 U.S. 358 (1970) (HARLAN, J., concurring))....

We think it self-evident that the interests at stake in the instant proceedings are more substantial, both on an individual and societal level, than those involved in a run-of-the-mill civil dispute. But not only does the standard of proof reflect the importance of a particular adjudication, it also serves as "a societal judgment about how the risk of error should be distributed between the litigants." The more stringent the burden of proof a party must bear, the more that party bears the risk of an erroneous decision. We believe that Missouri may permissibly place an increased risk of an erroneous decision on those seeking to terminate an incompetent individual's life-sustaining treatment. An erroneous decision not to terminate results in a maintenance of the status quo; the possibility of subsequent developments such as advancements in medical science, the discovery of new evidence regarding the patient's intent, changes in the law, or simply the unexpected death of the patient despite the administration of life-sustaining treatment, at least create the potential that a wrong decision will eventually be corrected or its impact mitigated. An erroneous decision to withdraw life-sustaining treatment, however, is not susceptible of correction....

In sum, we conclude that a State may apply a clear and convincing evidence standard in proceedings where a guardian seeks to discontinue nutrition and hydration of a person diagnosed to be in a persistent vegetative state. We note that many courts which have adopted some sort of substituted judgment procedure in situations like this, whether they limit consideration of evidence to the prior expressed wishes of the incompetent individual, or whether they allow more general proof of what the individual's decision would have been, require a clear and convincing standard of proof for such evidence....

The judgment of the Supreme Court of Missouri is
Affirmed.

☐ *Justice O'CONNOR, concurring.*

I agree that a protected liberty interest in refusing unwanted medical treatment may be inferred from our prior decisions, and that the refusal of artificially delivered food and water is encompassed within that liberty interest. I write separately to clarify why I believe this to be so.

As the Court notes, the liberty interest in refusing medical treatment flows from decisions involving the State's invasions into the body. Because our notions of liberty are inextricably entwined with our idea of physical freedom and self-determination, the Court has often deemed state incursions into the body repugnant to the interests protected by the Due Process Clause. . . .

Accordingly, the liberty guaranteed by the Due Process Clause must protect, if it protects anything, an individual's deeply personal decision to reject medical treatment, including the artificial delivery of food and water.

I also write separately to emphasize that the Court does not today decide the issue whether a State must also give effect to the decisions of a surrogate decisionmaker. In my view, such a duty may well be constitutionally required to protect the patient's liberty interest in refusing medical treatment. Few individuals provide explicit oral or written instructions regarding their intent to refuse medical treatment should they become incompetent. States which decline to consider any evidence other than such instructions may frequently fail to honor a patient's intent. Such failures might be avoided if the State considered an equally probative source of evidence: the patient's appointment of a proxy to make health care decisions on her behalf. Delegating the authority to make medical decisions to a family member or friend is becoming a common method of planning for the future. . . .

☐ *Justice SCALIA, concurring.*

While I agree with the Court's analysis today, and therefore join in its opinion, I would have preferred that we announce, clearly and promptly, that the federal courts have no business in this field; that American law has always accorded the State the power to prevent, by force if necessary, suicide—including suicide by refusing to take appropriate measures necessary to preserve one's life; that the point at which life becomes "worthless," and the point at which the means necessary to preserve it become "extraordinary" or "inappropriate," are neither set forth in the Constitution nor known to the nine Justices of this Court any better than they are known to nine people picked at random from the Kansas City telephone directory; and hence, that even when it *is* demonstrated by clear and convincing evidence that a patient no longer wishes certain measures to be taken to preserve her life, it is up to the citizens of Missouri to decide, through their elected representatives, whether that wish will be honored. It is quite impossible (because the Constitution says nothing about the matter) that those citizens will decide upon a line less lawful than the one we would choose; and it is unlikely (because we know no more about "life-and-death" than they do) that they will decide upon a line less reasonable.

The text of the Due Process Clause does not protect individuals against deprivations of liberty *simpliciter*. It protects them against deprivations of liberty "without due process of law." To determine that such a deprivation would not occur if Nancy Cruzan were forced to take nourishment against her will, it is unnecessary to reopen the historically recurrent debate over whether "due process" includes substantive restrictions. . . . It is at least true that no "substantive due process" claim can be maintained unless the claimant demonstrates that the State has deprived him of a right historically and traditionally protected against State interference. *Michael H. v. Gerald D.*, [491 U.S. 110] (1989) (plurality opinion); *Bowers v. Hardwick*, 478 U.S. 186 (1986). . . . That cannot possibly be established here. . . .

I assert only that the Constitution has nothing to say about [a "right to die"]. To raise up a constitutional right here we would have to create out of nothing (for it exists neither in text nor tradition) some constitutional principle whereby, although the State may insist that an individual come in out of the cold and eat food, it may not insist that he take medicine; and although it may pump his stomach empty of poison he has ingested, it may not fill his stomach with food he has failed to ingest. Are there, then, no reasonable and humane limits that ought not to be exceeded in requiring an individual to preserve his own life? There obviously are, but they are not set forth in the Due Process Clause. What assures us that those limits will not be exceeded is the same constitutional guarantee that is the source of most of our protection—what protects us, for example, from being assessed a tax of 100% of our income above the subsistence level, from being forbidden to drive cars, or from being required to send our children to school for 10 hours a day, none of which horribles is categorically prohibited by the Constitution. Our salvation is the Equal Protection Clause, which requires the democratic majority to accept for themselves and their loved ones what they impose on you and me. This Court need not, and has no authority to, inject itself into every field of human activity where irrationality and oppression may theoretically occur, and if it tries to do so it will destroy itself.

☐ *Justice BRENNAN, with whom Justice MARSHALL and Justice BLACKMUN join, dissenting.*

Because I believe that Nancy Cruzan has a fundamental right to be free of unwanted artificial nutrition and hydration, which right is not outweighed by any interests of the State, and because I find that the improperly biased procedural obstacles imposed by the Missouri Supreme Court impermissibly burden that right, I respectfully dissent. Nancy Cruzan is entitled to choose to die with dignity. . . .

The question before this Court is a relatively narrow one: whether the Due Process Clause allows Missouri to require a now-incompetent patient in an irreversible persistent vegetative state to remain on life-support absent rigorously clear and convincing evidence that avoiding the treatment represents the patient's prior, express choice. . . .

The starting point for our legal analysis must be whether a competent person has a constitutional right to avoid unwanted medical care. Earlier this Term, this Court held that the Due Process Clause of the Fourteenth Amendment confers a significant liberty interest in avoiding unwanted medical treatment. *Washington v. Harper*, [494 U.S. 210] (1990). Today, the Court concedes that our prior decisions "support the recognition of a general liberty interest in refusing medical treatment." . . .

But if a competent person has a liberty interest to be free of unwanted medical treatment, as both the majority and Justice O'CONNOR concede, it must be fundamental. "We are dealing here with [a decision] which involves one of the basic civil rights of man." *Skinner v. Oklahoma ex rel. Williamson*, 316 U.S. 535 (1942) (invalidating a statute authorizing sterilization of certain felons).

The right to be free from medical attention without consent, to determine what shall be done with one's own body, *is* deeply rooted in this Nation's traditions, as the majority acknowledges. This right has long been "firmly entrenched in American tort law" and is securely grounded in the earliest common law. See also *Mills v. Rogers*, 457 U.S. 291 (1982) ("the right to refuse any medical treatment emerged from the doctrines of trespass and battery, which were applied to unauthorized touchings by a physician"). . . .

That there may be serious consequences involved in refusal of the medical treatment at issue here does not vitiate the right under our common law tradition of medical self-determination. . . .

There are also affirmative reasons why someone like Nancy might choose to forgo artificial nutrition and hydration under these circumstances. Dying is personal. And it is profound. For many, the thought of an ignoble end, steeped in decay, is abhorrent. A quiet, proud death, bodily integrity intact, is a matter of extreme consequence. . . .

This is not to say that the State has no legitimate interests to assert here. As the majority recognizes, Missouri has a *parens patriae* interest in providing Nancy Cruzan, now incompetent, with as accurate as possible a determination of how she would exercise her rights under these circumstances. Second, if and when it is determined that Nancy Cruzan would want to continue treatment, the State may legitimately assert an interest in providing that treatment. But *until* Nancy's wishes have been determined, the only state interest that may be asserted is an interest in safeguarding the accuracy of that determination.

Accuracy, therefore, must be our touchstone. Missouri may constitutionally impose only those procedural requirements that serve to enhance the accuracy of a determination of Nancy Cruzan's wishes or are at least consistent with an accurate determination. The Missouri "safeguard" that the Court upholds today does not meet that standard. The determination needed in this context is whether the incompetent person would choose to live in a persistent vegetative state on life-support or to avoid this medical treatment. Missouri's rule of decision imposes a markedly asymmetrical evidentiary burden. Only evidence of specific statements of treatment choice made by the patient when competent is admissible to support a finding that the patient, now in a persistent vegetative state, would wish to avoid further medical treatment. Moreover, this evidence must be clear and convincing. No proof is required to support a finding that the incompetent person would wish to continue treatment. . . .

The majority offers several justifications for Missouri's heightened evidentiary standard. First, the majority explains that the State may constitutionally adopt this rule to govern determinations of an incompetent's wishes in order to advance the State's substantive interests, including its unqualified interest in the preservation of human life. Missouri's evidentiary standard, however, cannot rest on the State's own interest in a particular substantive re-

sult. To be sure, courts have long erected clear and convincing evidence standards to place the greater risk of erroneous decisions on those bringing disfavored claims. In such cases, however, the choice to discourage certain
claims was a legitimate, constitutional policy choice. In contrast, Missouri has
no such power to disfavor a choice by Nancy Cruzan to avoid medical treatment, because Missouri has no legitimate interest in providing Nancy with
treatment until it is established that this represents her choice. Just as a State
may not override Nancy's choice directly, it may not do so indirectly
through the imposition of a procedural rule.

The majority claims that the allocation of the risk of error is justified
because it is more important not to terminate life-support for someone who
would wish it continued than to honor the wishes of someone who would
not. An erroneous decision to terminate life-support is irrevocable, says the
majority, while an erroneous decision not to terminate "results in a maintenance of the status quo." But, from the point of view of the patient, an erroneous decision in either direction is irrevocable. An erroneous decision to
terminate artificial nutrition and hydration, to be sure, will lead to failure of
that last remnant of physiological life, the brain stem, and result in complete
brain death. An erroneous decision not to terminate life-support, however,
robs a patient of the very qualities protected by the right to avoid unwanted
medical treatment. His own degraded existence is perpetuated; his family's
suffering is protracted; the memory he leaves behind becomes more and
more distorted. . . .

Even more than its heightened evidentiary standard, the Missouri court's
categorical exclusion of relevant evidence dispenses with any semblance of
accurate factfinding. The court adverted to no evidence supporting its decision, but held that no clear and convincing, inherently reliable evidence had
been presented to show that Nancy would want to avoid further treatment.
In doing so, the court failed to consider statements Nancy had made to family members and a close friend. The court also failed to consider testimony
from Nancy's mother and sister that they were certain that Nancy would
want to discontinue artificial nutrition and hydration, even after the court
found that Nancy's family was loving and without malignant motive. The
court also failed to consider the conclusions of the guardian *ad litem*, appointed by the trial court, that there was clear and convincing evidence that
Nancy would want to discontinue medical treatment and that this was in her
best interests. The court did not specifically define what kind of evidence it
would consider clear and convincing, but its general discussion suggests that
only a living will or equivalently formal directive from the patient when
competent would meet this standard. . . .

Too few people execute living wills or equivalently formal directives for
such an evidentiary rule to ensure adequately that the wishes of incompetent
persons will be honored. While it might be a wise social policy to encourage
people to furnish such instructions, no general conclusion about a patient's
choice can be drawn from the absence of formalities. The probability of becoming irreversibly vegetative is so low that many people may not feel an
urgency to marshal formal evidence of their preferences. Some may not wish
to dwell on their own physical deterioration and mortality. Even someone
with a resolute determination to avoid life-support under circumstances such
as Nancy's would still need to know that such things as living wills exist

and how to execute one. Often legal help would be necessary, especially given the majority's apparent willingness to permit States to insist that a person's wishes are not truly known unless the particular medical treatment is specified. . . .

I do not suggest that States must sit by helplessly if the choices of incompetent patients are in danger of being ignored. Even if the Court had ruled that Missouri's rule of decision is unconstitutional, as I believe it should have, States would nevertheless remain free to fashion procedural protections to safeguard the interests of incompetents under these circumstances. The Constitution provides merely a framework here: protections must be genuinely aimed at ensuring decisions commensurate with the will of the patient, and must be reliable as instruments to that end. Of the many States which have instituted such protections, Missouri is virtually the only one to have fashioned a rule that lessens the likelihood of accurate determinations. In contrast, nothing in the Constitution prevents States from reviewing the advisability of a family decision, by requiring a court proceeding or by appointing an impartial guardian *ad litem.* . . .

Finally, I cannot agree with the majority that where it is not possible to determine what choice an incompetent patient would make, a State's role as *parens patriae* permits the State automatically to make that choice itself. . . .

I respectfully dissent.

Washington v. Glucksberg
521 U.S. 702, 117 S.Ct. 2258 (1997)

and

Vacco v. Quill
521 U.S. 793, 117 S.Ct. 2293 (1997)

These cases arose from the growing controversy over the so-called right to die. In *Cruzan by Cruzan v. Director, Missouri Department of Health,* 497 U.S. 261 (1990), the Court held that individuals have a "fundamental liberty" interest under the Fourteenth Amendment in terminating life-support systems. In 1996, two federal appellate courts extended that ruling to forbid states from passing laws barring physicians from prescribing lethal dosages of drugs at the request of their terminally ill patients. At issue was not whether doctors like Jack Kevorkian may help the terminally ill end their lives, but rather whether they may prescribe lethal drugs to terminally ill patients. The Court of Appeals for the Ninth Circuit struck down Washington's law forbidding physician-assisted suicide on the ground that it violated individuals' "right of privacy" and substantive liberty protected by the due process clause of the Fourteenth Amendment. The Court of Appeals for the Second Circuit invalidated New York's law on the basis of the Fourteenth Amendment's equal protection clause upon rejecting the state's distinction between the terminally ill's right to terminate life-support systems and claim to a right to physician-assisted suicide.

Both appellate court decisions were unanimously reversed by the Supreme Court. Overturning the Second Circuit's decision in his opinion for the Court in *Vacco v. Quill*, Chief Justice Rehnquist rejected its equal protection analysis, observing that

> [t]he Equal Protection Clause commands that no State "deny to any person within its jurisdiction the equal protection of the laws." This provision creates no substantive rights. Instead, it embodies a general rule that States must treat like cases alike but may treat unlike cases accordingly. If a legislative classification or distinction "neither burdens a fundamental right nor targets a suspect class, we will uphold [it] so long as it bears a rational relation to some legitimate end." *Romer v. Evans*, [116 S.Ct. 1620] (1996). . . .
>
> On their faces, neither New York's ban on assisting suicide nor its statutes permitting patients to refuse medical treatment treat anyone differently than anyone else or draw any distinctions between persons. Everyone, regardless of physical condition, is entitled, if competent, to refuse unwanted lifesaving medical treatment; no one is permitted to assist a suicide. Generally speaking, laws that apply evenhandedly to all "unquestionably comply" with the Equal Protection Clause.

Notably, though, in the penultimate paragraph of his opinion in *Vacco*, Chief Justice Rehnquist added a footnote leaving open the possible consideration of future due process claims to a right to physicians' assisted suicide:

> Justice STEVENS [in his opinions in *Vacco* and *Glucksberg*] . . . would not "foreclose the possibility that an individual plaintiff seeking to hasten her death, or a doctor whose assistance was sought, could prevail in a more particularized challenge." Our opinion does not absolutely foreclose such a claim. However, given our holding that the Due Process Clause of the Fourteenth Amendment does not provide heightened protection to the asserted liberty interest in ending one's life with a physician's assistance, such a claim would have been quite different from the ones advanced by respondents here.

The Court's unanimous decision in *Washington v. Glucksberg* was also delivered by Chief Justice Rehnquist but, as in *Vacco v. Quill*, only Justices O'Connor, Scalia, Kennedy, and Thomas joined his opinion for the Court. Moreover, in each case, four justices—Justices O'Connor, Stevens, Souter, and Breyer—issued concurring opinions rejecting some or all of Chief Justice Rehnquist's analysis and indicating that they might be prepared, depending on the particular circumstances of the case, to recognize a right to physician-assisted suicide, which the chief justice's opinion did not entirely rule out. For now, the justices agreed to let the controversy continue to play out in state legislatures and the lower courts.

☐ *Chief Justice REHNQUIST delivered the opinion of the Court.*

The question presented in this case is whether Washington's prohibition against "causing" or "aiding" a suicide offends the Fourteenth Amendment to the United States Constitution. We hold that it does not. . . .

The plaintiffs asserted "the existence of a liberty interest protected by the Fourteenth Amendment which extends to a personal choice by a mentally competent, terminally ill adult to commit physician-assisted suicide." Relying primarily on *Planned Parenthood v. Casey*, 505 U.S. 833 (1992), and *Cruzan by Cruzan v. Director, Missouri Dept. of Health*, 497 U.S. 261 (1990), the District Court agreed and concluded that Washington's assisted-suicide ban is unconstitutional because it "places an undue burden on the exercise of [that] constitutionally protected liberty interest." . . . A panel of the Court of Appeals for the Ninth Circuit reversed, emphasizing that "in the two hundred and five years of our existence no constitutional right to aid in killing oneself has ever been asserted and upheld by a court of final jurisdiction." The Ninth Circuit reheard the case *en banc*, reversed the panel's decision, and affirmed the District Court. . . .

We begin, as we do in all due-process cases, by examining our Nation's history, legal traditions, and practices. In almost every State—indeed, in almost every western democracy—it is a crime to assist a suicide. The States' assisted-suicide bans are not innovations. Rather, they are longstanding expressions of the States' commitment to the protection and preservation of all human life. . . .

Though deeply rooted, the States' assisted-suicide bans have in recent years been reexamined and, generally, reaffirmed. Because of advances in medicine and technology, Americans today are increasingly likely to die in institutions, from chronic illnesses. Public concern and democratic action are therefore sharply focused on how best to protect dignity and independence at the end of life, with the result that there have been many significant changes in state laws and in the attitudes these laws reflect. Many States, for example, now permit "living wills," surrogate health-care decision making, and the withdrawal or refusal of life-sustaining medical treatment. At the same time, however, voters and legislators continue for the most part to reaffirm their States' prohibitions on assisting suicide.

The Washington statute at issue in this case was enacted in 1975 as part of a revision of that State's criminal code. Four years later, Washington passed its Natural Death Act, which specifically stated that the "withholding or withdrawal of life-sustaining treatment . . . shall not, for any purpose, constitute a suicide" and that "nothing in this chapter shall be construed to condone, authorize, or approve mercy killing. . . ." In 1991, Washington voters rejected a ballot initiative which, had it passed, would have permitted a form of physician-assisted suicide. Washington then added a provision to the Natural Death Act expressly excluding physician-assisted suicide.

California voters rejected an assisted-suicide initiative similar to Washington's in 1993. On the other hand, in 1994, voters in Oregon enacted, also through ballot initiative, that State's "Death With Dignity Act," which legalized physician-assisted suicide for competent, terminally ill adults. Since the Oregon vote, many proposals to legalize assisted suicide have been and continue to be introduced in the States' legislatures, but none has been enacted. . . .

Thus, the States are currently engaged in serious, thoughtful examinations of physician-assisted suicide and other similar issues. For example, New York State's Task Force on Life and the Law—an ongoing, blue-ribbon commission composed of doctors, ethicists, lawyers, religious leaders, and interested laymen—was convened in 1984 and commissioned with "a broad mandate to recommend public policy on issues raised by medical advances." Over the past decade, the Task Force has recommended laws relating to end-of-life decisions, surrogate pregnancy, and organ donation. After studying physician-assisted suicide, however, the Task Force unanimously concluded that "legalizing assisted suicide and euthanasia would pose profound risks to many individuals who are ill and vulnerable. . . . The potential dangers of this dramatic change in public policy would outweigh any benefit that might be achieved." . . .

The Due Process Clause guarantees more than fair process, and the "liberty" it protects includes more than the absence of physical restraint. The Clause also provides heightened protection against government interference with certain fundamental rights and liberty interests. In a long line of cases, we have held that, in addition to the specific freedoms protected by the Bill of Rights, the "liberty" specially protected by the Due Process Clause includes the rights to marry, *Loving v. Virginia*, 388 U.S. 1 (1967); to have children, *Skinner v. Oklahoma ex rel. Williamson*, 316 U.S. 535 (1942); to direct the education and upbringing of one's children, *Meyer v. Nebraska*, 262 U.S. 390 (1923); *Pierce v. Society of Sisters*, 268 U.S. 510 (1925); to marital privacy, *Griswold v. Connecticut*, 381 U.S. 479 (1965); to use contraception, *ibid; Eisenstadt v. Baird*, 405 U.S. 438 (1972); to bodily integrity, *Rochin v. California*, 342 U.S. 165 (1952), and to abortion, *Casey*. We have also assumed, and strongly suggested, that the Due Process Clause protects the traditional right to refuse unwanted lifesaving medical treatment. *Cruzan*.

But we "have always been reluctant to expand the concept of substantive due process because guideposts for responsible decision making in this uncharted area are scarce and open-ended." By extending constitutional protection to an asserted right or liberty interest, we, to a great extent, place the matter outside the arena of public debate and legislative action. We must therefore "exercise the utmost care whenever we are asked to break new ground in this field," lest the liberty protected by the Due Process Clause be subtly transformed into the policy preferences of the members of this Court.

Our established method of substantive-due-process analysis has two primary features: First, we have regularly observed that the Due Process Clause specially protects those fundamental rights and liberties which are, objectively, "deeply rooted in this Nation's history and tradition," *Snyder v. Massa-*

chusetts, 291 U.S. 97 (1934) ("so rooted in the traditions and conscience of our people as to be ranked as fundamental"), and "implicit in the concept of ordered liberty," such that "neither liberty nor justice would exist if they were sacrificed," *Palko v. Connecticut*, 302 U.S. 319 (1937). Second, we have required in substantive-due-process cases a "careful description" of the asserted fundamental liberty interest. [*Reno v.*] *Flores* [507 U.S. 292 (1993)]; *Cruzan*. Our Nation's history, legal traditions, and practices thus provide the crucial "guideposts for responsible decision making" that direct and restrain our exposition of the Due Process Clause. As we stated recently in *Flores*, the Fourteenth Amendment "forbids the government to infringe . . . 'fundamental' liberty interests at all, no matter what process is provided, unless the infringement is narrowly tailored to serve a compelling state interest." . . .

We now inquire whether this asserted right has any place in our Nation's traditions. Here, as discussed above, we are confronted with a consistent and almost universal tradition that has long rejected the asserted right, and continues explicitly to reject it today, even for terminally ill, mentally competent adults. To hold for respondents, we would have to reverse centuries of legal doctrine and practice, and strike down the considered policy choice of almost every State. . . .

Respondents contend that in *Cruzan* we "acknowledged that competent, dying persons have the right to direct the removal of life-sustaining medical treatment and thus hasten death," and that "the constitutional principle behind recognizing the patient's liberty to direct the withdrawal of artificial life support applies at least as strongly to the choice to hasten impending death by consuming lethal medication."

The right assumed in *Cruzan*, however, was not simply deduced from abstract concepts of personal autonomy. Given the common-law rule that forced medication was a battery, and the long legal tradition protecting the decision to refuse unwanted medical treatment, our assumption was entirely consistent with this Nation's history and constitutional traditions. The decision to commit suicide with the assistance of another may be just as personal and profound as the decision to refuse unwanted medical treatment, but it has never enjoyed similar legal protection. Indeed, the two acts are widely and reasonably regarded as quite distinct. In *Cruzan* itself, we recognized that most States outlawed assisted suicide—and even more do today—and we certainly gave no intimation that the right to refuse unwanted medical treatment could be somehow transmuted into a right to assistance in committing suicide. . . .

The history of the law's treatment of assisted suicide in this country has been and continues to be one of the rejection of nearly all efforts to permit it. That being the case, our decisions lead us to conclude that the asserted "right" to assistance in committing suicide is not a fundamental liberty interest protected by the Due Process Clause. The Constitution also requires, however, that Washington's assisted-suicide ban be rationally related to legitimate government interests. See *Heller v. Doe*, 509 U.S. 312 (1993); *Flores*. This requirement is unquestionably met here. As the court below recognized, Washington's assisted-suicide ban implicates a number of state interests.

First, Washington has an "unqualified interest in the preservation of human life." *Cruzan*. The State's prohibition on assisted suicide, like all homicide laws, both reflects and advances its commitment to this interest. . . .

Relatedly, all admit that suicide is a serious public-health problem, especially among persons in otherwise vulnerable groups. Those who attempt suicide—terminally ill or not—often suffer from depression or other mental disorders. . . .

The State also has an interest in protecting the integrity and ethics of the medical profession. In contrast to the Court of Appeals' conclusion that "the integrity of the medical profession would [not] be threatened in any way by [physician-assisted suicide]," the American Medical Association, like many other medical and physicians' groups, has concluded that "physician-assisted suicide is fundamentally incompatible with the physician's role as healer."

Next, the State has an interest in protecting vulnerable groups—including the poor, the elderly, and disabled persons—from abuse, neglect, and mistakes. The Court of Appeals dismissed the State's concern that disadvantaged persons might be pressured into physician-assisted suicide as "ludicrous on its face." We have recognized, however, the real risk of subtle coercion and undue influence in end-of-life situations. *Cruzan.* . . . "The risk of harm is greatest for the many individuals in our society whose autonomy and well-being are already compromised by poverty, lack of access to good medical care, advanced age, or membership in a stigmatized social group" [New York Task Force on Life and the Law.] If physician-assisted suicide were permitted, many might resort to it to spare their families the substantial financial burden of end-of-life health-care costs.

The State's interest here goes beyond protecting the vulnerable from coercion; it extends to protecting disabled and terminally ill people from prejudice, negative and inaccurate stereotypes, and "societal indifference." The State's assisted-suicide ban reflects and reinforces its policy that the lives of terminally ill, disabled, and elderly people must be no less valued than the lives of the young and healthy, and that a seriously disabled person's suicidal impulses should be interpreted and treated the same way as anyone else's.

Finally, the State may fear that permitting assisted suicide will start it down the path to voluntary and perhaps even involuntary euthanasia. The Court of Appeals struck down Washington's assisted-suicide ban only "as applied to competent, terminally ill adults who wish to hasten their deaths by obtaining medication prescribed by their doctors." Washington insists, however, that the impact of the court's decision will not and cannot be so limited. If suicide is protected as a matter of constitutional right, it is argued, "every man and woman in the United States must enjoy it." The Court of Appeals' decision, and its expansive reasoning, provide ample support for the State's concerns. The Court noted, for example, that the "decision of a duly appointed surrogate decision maker is for all legal purposes the decision of the patient himself;" that "in some instances, the patient may be unable to self-administer the drugs and . . . administration by the physician . . . may be the only way the patient may be able to receive them;" and that not only physicians, but also family members and loved ones, will inevitably participate in assisting suicide. Thus, it turns out that what is couched as a limited right to "physician-assisted suicide" is likely, in effect, a much broader license, which could prove extremely difficult to police and contain. Washington's ban on assisting suicide prevents such erosion. . . .

Throughout the Nation, Americans are engaged in an earnest and profound debate about the morality, legality, and practicality of physician-assisted suicide. Our holding permits this debate to continue, as it should in a democratic society. The decision of the *en banc* Court of Appeals is reversed, and the case is remanded for further proceedings consistent with this opinion.

☐ *Justice O'CONNOR, concurring.*

Death will be different for each of us. For many, the last days will be spent in physical pain and perhaps the despair that accompanies physical deterioration and a loss of control of basic bodily and mental functions. Some will seek medication to alleviate that pain and other symptoms.

The Court frames the issue in this case as whether the Due Process Clause of the Constitution protects a "right to commit suicide which itself includes a right to assistance in doing so," and concludes that our Nation's history, legal traditions, and practices do not support the existence of such a right. I join the Court's opinions because I agree that there is no generalized right to "commit suicide." But respondents urge us to address the narrower question whether a mentally competent person who is experiencing great suffering has a constitutionally cognizable interest in controlling the circumstances of his or her imminent death. I see no need to reach that question in the context of the facial challenges to the New York and Washington laws at issue here. The parties and *amici* agree that in these States a patient who is suffering from a terminal illness and who is experiencing great pain has no legal barriers to obtaining medication, from qualified physicians, to alleviate that suffering, even to the point of causing unconsciousness and hastening death. In this light, even assuming that we would recognize such an interest, I agree that the State's interests in protecting those who are not truly competent or facing imminent death, or those whose decisions to hasten death would not truly be voluntary, are sufficiently weighty to justify a prohibition against physician-assisted suicide.

Every one of us at some point may be affected by our own or a family member's terminal illness. There is no reason to think the democratic process will not strike the proper balance between the interests of terminally ill, mentally competent individuals who would seek to end their suffering and the State's interests in protecting those who might seek to end life mistakenly or under pressure. . . .

In sum, there is no need to address the question whether suffering patients have a constitutionally cognizable interest in obtaining relief from the suffering that they may experience in the last days of their lives. There is no dispute that dying patients in Washington and New York can obtain palliative care, even when doing so would hasten their deaths. The difficulty in defining terminal illness and the risk that a dying patient's request for assistance in ending his or her life might not be truly voluntary justifies the prohibitions on assisted suicide we uphold here.

☐ *Justice STEVENS, concurring in the judgments.*

The Court ends its opinion with the important observation that our holding today is fully consistent with a continuation of the vigorous debate about the "morality, legality, and practicality of physician-assisted suicide" in a democratic society. I write separately to make it clear that there is also room for further debate about the limits that the Constitution places on the power of the States to punish the practice.

History and tradition provide ample support for refusing to recognize an open-ended constitutional right to commit suicide. Much more than the State's paternalistic interest in protecting the individual from the irrevocable consequences of an ill-advised decision motivated by temporary concerns is at stake. There is truth in John Donne's observation that "No man is an island." The State has an interest in preserving and fostering the benefits that every human being may provide to the community—a community that thrives on the exchange of ideas, expressions of affection, shared memories and humorous incidents as well as on the material contributions that its members create and support. The value to others of a person's life is far too precious to allow the individual to claim a constitutional entitlement to complete autonomy in making a decision to end that life. Thus, I fully agree with the Court that the "liberty" protected by the Due Process Clause does not include a categorical "right to commit suicide which itself includes a right to assistance in doing so."

But just as our conclusion that capital punishment is not always unconstitutional did not preclude later decisions holding that it is sometimes impermissibly cruel, so is it equally clear that a decision upholding a general statutory prohibition of assisted suicide does not mean that every possible application of the statute would be valid. A State, like Washington, that has authorized the death penalty and thereby has concluded that the sanctity of human life does not require that it always be preserved, must acknowledge that there are situations in which an interest in hastening death is legitimate. Indeed, not only is that interest sometimes legitimate, I am also convinced that there are times when it is entitled to constitutional protection. . . .

While I agree with the Court that *Cruzan* does not decide the issue presented by these cases, *Cruzan* did give recognition, not just to vague, unbridled notions of autonomy, but to the more specific interest in making decisions about how to confront an imminent death. Although there is no absolute right to physician-assisted suicide, *Cruzan* makes it clear that some individuals who no longer have the option of deciding whether to live or to die because they are already on the threshold of death have a constitutionally protected interest that may outweigh the State's interest in preserving life at all costs. The liberty interest at stake in a case like this differs from, and is stronger than, both the common-law right to refuse medical treatment and the unbridled interest in deciding whether to live or die. It is an interest in deciding how, rather than whether, a critical threshold shall be crossed. . . .

[A]lthough the differences the majority notes in causation and intent between terminating life-support and assisting in suicide support the Court's rejection of the respondents' facial challenge, these distinctions may be inapplicable to particular terminally ill patients and their doctors. Our holding today in *Vacco v. Quill* that the Equal Protection Clause is not violated by New York's classification, just like our holding in *Washington v. Glucksberg* that the Washington statute is not invalid on its face, does not foreclose the possibility that some applications of the New York statute may impose an intolerable intrusion on the patient's freedom.

There remains room for vigorous debate about the outcome of particular cases that are not necessarily resolved by the opinions announced today.

How such cases may be decided will depend on their specific facts. In my judgment, however, it is clear that the so-called "unqualified interest in the preservation of human life," *Cruzan, Glucksberg,* is not itself sufficient to outweigh the interest in liberty that may justify the only possible means of preserving a dying patient's dignity and alleviating her intolerable suffering.

☐ *Justice SOUTER, concurring in the judgment.*

Three terminally ill individuals and four physicians who sometimes treat terminally ill patients brought this challenge to the Washington statute making it a crime "knowingly . . . [to] aid another person to attempt suicide," claiming on behalf of both patients and physicians that it would violate substantive due process to enforce the statute against a doctor who acceded to a dying patient's request for a drug to be taken by the patient to commit suicide. The question is whether the statute sets up one of those "arbitrary impositions" or "purposeless restraints" at odds with the Due Process Clause of the Fourteenth Amendment. *Poe v. Ullman,* 367 U.S. 497 (1961) (HARLAN, J., dissenting). I conclude that the statute's application to the doctors has not been shown to be unconstitutional, but I write separately to give my reasons for analyzing the substantive due process claims as I do, and for rejecting this one. . . .

Justice HARLAN's *Poe* dissent just cited, the conclusion of which was adopted in *Griswold v. Connecticut,* 381 U.S. 478 (1965), and the authority of which was acknowledged in *Planned Parenthood of Southeastern Pa. v. Casey,* 505 U.S. 833 (1992), . . . is important for three things that point to our responsibilities today. The first is Justice HARLAN's respect for the tradition of substantive due process review itself, and his acknowledgment of the Judiciary's obligation to carry it on. For two centuries American courts, and for much of that time this Court, have thought it necessary to provide some degree of review over the substantive content of legislation under constitutional standards of textual breadth. . . . This enduring tradition of American constitutional practice is, in Justice HARLAN's view, nothing more than what is required by the judicial authority and obligation to construe constitutional text and review legislation for conformity to that text. Like many judges who preceded him and many who followed, he found it impossible to construe the text of due process without recognizing substantive, and not merely procedural, limitations. "Were due process merely a procedural safeguard it would fail to reach those situations where the deprivation of life, liberty or property was accomplished by legislation which by operating in the future could, given even the fairest possible procedure in application to individuals, nevertheless destroy the enjoyment of all three." *Poe.* The text of the Due Process Clause thus imposes nothing less than an obligation to give substantive content to the words "liberty" and "due process of law."

The second of the dissent's lessons is a reminder that the business of such review is not the identification of extratextual absolutes but scrutiny of a legislative resolution (perhaps unconscious) of clashing principles, each quite possibly worthy in and of itself, but each to be weighed within the history of our values as a people. It is a comparison of the relative strengths of opposing claims that informs the judicial task, not a deduction from some first premise. Thus informed, judicial review still has no warrant to substitute one reasonable resolution of the contending positions for another, but authority to supplant the balance already struck between the contenders only when it falls outside the realm of the reasonable. [I deal below] with this second point, and also with the dissent's third, which takes the form of an object lesson in the explicit attention to detail that is no less essential to the intellectual discipline of substantive due process review than an understanding of the basic need to account for the two sides in the controversy and to respect legislation within the zone of reasonableness.

My understanding of unenumerated rights in the wake of the *Poe* dissent and subsequent cases avoids the absolutist failing of many older cases without embracing the opposite pole of equating reasonableness with past practice described at a very specific level. That understanding begins with a concept of "ordered liberty," comprising a continuum of rights to be free from "arbitrary impositions and purposeless restraints." . . . This approach calls for a court to assess the relative "weights" or dignities of the contending interests, and to this extent the judicial method is familiar to the common law. Common law method is subject, however, to two important constraints in the hands of a court engaged in substantive due process review. First, such a court is bound to confine the values that it recognizes to those truly deserving constitutional stature, either to those expressed in constitutional text, or those exemplified by "the traditions from which [the Nation] developed," or revealed by contrast with "the traditions from which it broke." *Poe* (HARLAN, J., dissenting). " 'We may not draw on our merely personal and private notions and disregard the limits . . . derived from considerations that are fused in the whole nature of our judicial process[,] . . . considerations deeply rooted in reason and in the compelling traditions of the legal profession.' " Id. (quoting *Rochin v. California*, 342 U.S. 165 (1952)); see also *Palko v. Connecticut* (looking to " 'principles of justice so rooted in the traditions and conscience of our people as to be ranked as fundamental' ") (quoting *Snyder v. Massachusetts*, 291 U.S. 97 (1934)).

The second constraint, again, simply reflects the fact that constitutional review, not judicial lawmaking, is a court's business here. The weighing or valuing of contending interests in this sphere is only the first step, forming the basis for determining whether the statute in question falls inside or outside the zone of what is reasonable in the way it resolves the conflict between the interests of state and individual. It is no justification for judicial intervention merely to identify a reasonable resolution of contending values that differs from the terms of the legislation under review. It is only when the legislation's justifying principle, critically valued, is so far from being commensurate with the individual interest as to be arbitrarily or pointlessly applied that the statute must give way. Only if this standard points against the statute can the individual claimant be said to have a constitutional right.

The *Poe* dissent thus reminds us of the nature of review for reasonableness or arbitrariness and the limitations entailed by it. But the opinion cautions against the repetition of past error in another way as well, more by its example than by any particular statement of constitutional method: it reminds us that the process of substantive review by reasoned judgment is one of close criticism going to the details of the opposing interests and to their relationships with the historically recognized principles that lend them weight or value. . . .

In my judgment, the importance of the individual interest here, as within that class of "certain interests" demanding careful scrutiny of the State's contrary claim cannot be gainsaid. Whether that interest might in some circumstances, or at some time, be seen as "fundamental" to the degree entitled to prevail is not, however, a conclusion that I need draw here, for I am satisfied that the State's interests . . . are sufficiently serious to defeat the present claim that its law is arbitrary or purposeless. . . .

One must bear in mind that the nature of the right claimed, if recognized as one constitutionally required, would differ in no essential way from other constitutional rights guaranteed by enumeration or derived from some more definite textual source than "due process." An unenumerated right should not therefore be recognized, with the effect of displacing the legislative ordering of things, without the assurance that its recognition would prove as durable as the recognition of those other rights differently derived. To recognize a right of lesser promise would simply create a constitutional regime too uncertain to bring with it the expectation of finality that is one of this Court's central obligations in making constitutional decisions. Legislatures, however, are not so constrained. The experimentation that should be out of the question in constitutional adjudication displacing legislative judgments is entirely proper, as well as highly desirable, when the legislative power addresses an emerging issue like assisted suicide. The Court should accordingly stay its hand to allow reasonable legislative consideration. While I do not decide for all time that respondents' claim should not be recognized, I acknowledge the legislative institutional competence as the better one to deal with that claim at this time.

☐ *Justice BREYER, concurring in the judgments.*

I agree with the Court in *Vacco v. Quill* that the articulated state interests justify the distinction drawn between physician assisted suicide and withdrawal of life support. I also agree with the Court that the critical question in both of the cases before us is whether "the 'liberty' specially protected by the Due Process Clause includes a right" of the sort that the respondents assert. *Washington v. Glucksberg.* I do not agree, however, with the Court's formulation of that claimed "liberty" interest. The Court describes it as a "right to commit suicide with another's assistance." But I would not reject the respondents' claim without considering a different formulation, for which our legal tradition may provide greater support. That formulation would use words roughly like a "right to die with dignity." But irrespective of the exact words used, at its core would lie personal control over the manner of death, professional medical assistance, and the avoidance of unnecessary and severe physical suffering—combined.

As Justice SOUTER points out, Justice HARLAN's dissenting opinion in *Poe v. Ullman* offers some support for such a claim. In that opinion, Justice HARLAN referred to the "liberty" that the Fourteenth Amendment protects as including "a freedom from all substantial arbitrary impositions and purposeless restraints" and also as recognizing that "certain interests require particularly careful scrutiny of the state needs asserted to justify their abridgment." The "certain interests" to which Justice HARLAN referred may well be similar (perhaps identical) to the rights, liberties, or interests that the Court today, as in the past, regards as "fundamental."

Justice HARLAN concluded that marital privacy was such a "special interest." . . . The respondents here essentially ask us to do the same. They argue that one can find a "right to die with dignity" by examining the protection the law has provided for related, but not identical, interests relating to personal dignity, medical treatment, and freedom from state-inflicted pain.

I do not believe, however, that this Court need or now should decide whether or a not such a right is "fundamental." That is because, in my view, the avoidance of severe physical pain (connected with death) would have to comprise an essential part of any successful claim and because, as Justice O'CONNOR points out, the laws before us do not force a dying person to undergo that kind of pain. Rather, the laws of New York and of Washington do not prohibit doctors from providing patients with drugs sufficient to control pain despite the risk that those drugs themselves will kill. And under these circumstances the laws of New York and Washington would overcome any remaining significant interests and would be justified, regardless. . . .

This legal circumstance means that the state laws before us do not infringe directly upon the (assumed) central interest (what I have called the core of the interest in dying with dignity) as, by way of contrast, the state anticontraceptive laws at issue in *Poe* did interfere with the central interest there at stake—by bringing the State's police powers to bear upon the marital bedroom.

Were the legal circumstances different—for example, were state law to prevent the provision of palliative care, including the administration of drugs as needed to avoid pain at the end of life—then the law's impact upon serious and otherwise unavoidable physical pain (accompanying death) would be more directly at issue. And as Justice O'CONNOR suggests, the Court might have to revisit its conclusions in these cases.

12

THE EQUAL PROTECTION OF THE LAWS

A guarantee for "the equal protection of the laws" did not find its way into the Constitution until the ratification of the Fourteenth Amendment in 1868. Then, over a half century lapsed before the Supreme Court began enforcing it as a serious barrier to racial segregation and other kinds of nonracial discrimination as well. The Court, though, never narrowly interpreted the Fourteenth Amendment simply to require the evenhanded application of the laws. On such a view, states could deny blond-haired individuals public employment or benefits so long as they rigorously denied all blond-haired applicants. But such a narrow reading was rejected in *Yick Wo v. Hopkins*, 118 U.S. 356 (1886). When striking down San Francisco's "safety" ordinance, making it illegal to operate laundries in other than stone or brick buildings (and which was used to put Chinese laundries out of business), the Court observed that "[t]hough the law itself be fair on its face and impartial in appearance, yet, if it is applied and administered by public authority with an evil eye and an unjust hand, so as practically to make unjust and illegal discrimination between persons in similar circumstances, material to their rights, the denial of equal justice is . . . within the prohibition of the Constitution." At the same time, the equal protection clause has never been broadly construed to forbid all discrimination or inequities before the law. This is so because all laws—all legislative classifications—discriminate and treat people differently.

The central problem for the Court lies in giving content and application to the principle of *legal equality*—equality before the law. Just as controversial as whether the Fourteenth Amendment aimed to ensure equal voting rights (see Vol. 1, Ch. 8), and whether it applied the guarantees of the Bill of Rights to the states (see Vol. 2, Ch. 4), has been whether the amendment forbids racial segregation, as well as other kinds of nonracial discrimination. Justices, historians, and legal scholars have long debated the legislative history of the Fourteenth Amendment. Some contend that the Thirty-ninth Congress, which drafted and adopted the amendment, aimed to give the federal government broad powers to ensure the rights of blacks and to advance the political ideal of equality.[1] Others marshal evidence that the amendment was not designed to forbid racial segregation;[2] indeed, it neither granted voting rights to blacks nor prohibited racial segregation.[3] Still others conclude that the historical record "is not entirely consistent"[4] and that the amendment is "so broad and general that [it] could be used to support almost anything."[5]

As with other controversies in constitutional politics, the debate over the equal protection clause reflects rival interpretations of politics and the politics of interpretation.[6] Moreover, as historian and Harvard law school professor William Nelson points out, whether the equal protection clause applies to claims of nonracial discrimination that come before the Court in this century is "a question that never occurred to the Reconstruction generation and hence cannot be answered by examining the records of its actual thought." Even issues that Congress extensively debated, such as voting rights for blacks and segregation, went unresolved and inconsistencies remained. As Nelson underscores, "history can never tell us how the founding generation would have resolved inconsistencies that it did not, in fact, resolve."[7]

Once the Supreme Court turned to enforcing the equal protection clause in the twentieth century, it evolved standards for what legislative classifications are permissible and which discriminate in invidious, unconstitutional ways. Shortly after the Court's switch-in-time-that-saved-nine and abandonment of heightened review of economic legislation in 1937 (see Ch. 3), Justice Harlan F. Stone planted the seed for the modern Court's equal protection analysis. He did so in footnote four of *United States v. Carolene Products, Co.*, 304 U.S. 144 (1938), which upheld Congress's power to ban the shipment in interstate commerce of skim milk compounded with fat or other nonmilk products. In his opinion, Justice Stone reaffirmed that no longer would heightened scrutiny be given to legislation regulating economic activities; instead the Court would presume "that it rests upon some rational basis." But at that point he added the following three-paragraph footnote, pointing out that heightened scrutiny might be given to legislation affecting fundamental rights or which singles out racial and other "discrete and insular minorities":

> There may be narrower scope for operation of the presumption of constitutionality when legislation appears on its face to be within a specific prohibition of the Constitution, such as those of the first ten amendments, which are deemed equally specific when held to be embraced within the Fourteenth. See *Stromberg v. California*, 283 U.S. 359 [(1931)]; *Lovell v. Griffin*, 303 U.S. 444 [(*1938*)].

> It is unnecessary to consider now whether legislation which restricts those political processes which can ordinarily be expected to bring about repeal of undesirable legislation is to be subjected to more exacting judicial scrutiny under the general prohibitions of the Fourteenth Amendment than are other types of legislation. On restrictions upon the right to vote, see *Nixon v. Herndon*, 273 U.S. 536 [(1927)]; *Nixon v. Condon*, 286 U.S. 73 [(1932)]; on restrictions upon the dissemination of information, see *Near v. Minnesota*, 283 U.S. 697 [(1931)]; *Grosjean v. American Press Co.*, 297 U.S. 233 [(1936)]; *Lovell v. Griffin* [(1938)]; on interferences with political organizations, see *Stromberg v. California* [(1931)]; *Fiske v. Kansas* [(1927)]; *Whitney v. California*, 274 U.S. 357 [(1927)]; *Herndon v. Lowry* [(1937)]; and see HOLMES, J., in *Gitlow v. New York*, 268 U.S. 652 [(1925)]; as to peaceable assembly, see *De Jonge v. Oregon*, 299 U.S. 353 [(1937)].

> Nor need we inquire whether similar considerations enter into the review of statutes directed at particular religious, *Pierce v. Society of Sisters*, 268 U.S. 510 [(1925)], or national, *Meyer v. Nebraska*, 262 U.S. 390 [(1923)]; *Bartels v. Iowa*, 262 U.S. 404 [(1923)]; *Farrington v. Tokushige*, 273 U.S. 284 [(1927)], or racial minorities, *Nixon v. Herndon* [(1927)]; *Nixon v. Condon* [(1932)]; whether prejudices against discrete and insular minorities may be a special condition, which tends seriously to curtail the operation of those political processes ordinarily thought to be relied upon to protect minorities, and which may call for a correspondingly more searching judicial inquiry. . . .

The third paragraph of Justice Stone's footnote laid the basis for what evolved into a two- (and, later, a three-) tiered set of standards for judicial review under the equal protection clause.[8] By emphasizing the post–1937 Court's presumption of a rational basis for economic legislation, Justice Stone pointed the way toward heightened scrutiny (*strict scrutiny*) of legislation based on "suspect classifications," such as religion and race, or which impinged on "fundamental rights."

Justice Stone, though, used neither the phrase *fundamental rights* nor *strict scrutiny*. Four years later, in *Skinner v. Oklahoma*, 316 U.S. 535 (1942), Justice Douglas made the case for heightened judicial scrutiny of legislation affecting fundamental rights. Striking down a law requiring the forced sterilization of individuals convicted of two or more felonies involving moral turpitude, he observed that "[w]e are dealing here with legislation which involves one of the basic civil rights of man. Marriage and procreation are fundamental to the very existence and survival of the race." Ironically, the strict scrutiny test has its origins in an opinion by Justice Hugo Black, *upholding* the internment of Japanese-Americans during World War II. In *Korematsu v. United States*, 323 U.S. 214 (1944) (see Vol. 1, Ch. 3), Justice Black observed that "all legal restrictions which curtail the civil rights of a single racial group are immediately suspect. That is not to say that all such restrictions are unconstitutional. It is to say that courts must subject them to the most rigid scrutiny."

It remained for the Warren Court (1953–1969) to develop a two-tier approach to judicial review under the equal protection clause. When reviewing economic legislation, the Court gives *minimal scrutiny* and applies the *rational basis test*, asking simply whether legislation is reasonable and has a rational, conceivable basis. Under this test, legislation is invariably upheld. Indeed, only twice since 1937 have economic regulations been found irrational and unconstitutional under the Fourteenth Amendment. In *Morey v. Doud*, 354 U.S. 459 (1957), the Warren Court struck down Illinois's law exempting the American Express Company from licensing requirements for companies issuing money orders. In *Allegheny Pittsburgh Coal Co. v. County Commission*, 488 U.S. 336 (1989), the Rehnquist Court unanimously concluded that the equal protection clause was violated when a West Virginia county tax assessor valued real estate property "on the basis of its recent purchase price, but made only minor modifications in the assessments of land which had not been recently sold," resulting in the property of Allegheny Pittsburgh Coal Company to be "assessed at roughly 8 to 35 times more than comparable neighboring property." The county assessor's practice, in Chief Justice Rehnquist's words, was not "rationally related" to the state's law that property "be taxed at a rate uniform throughout the state according to its estimated market value."

Allegheny Pittsburgh Coal Co. appears to be the exception that proves the Court's predisposition to uphold economic legislation and to apply its minimal scrutiny test. In 1992, for instance, the Rehnquist Court reviewed, in *Nordlinger v. Hahn*, 505 U.S. 1 (1992), an equal protection challenge to California's constitutional amendment—otherwise known as Proposition 13—that limits property-tax rates to 1 percent of assessed value. Under Proposition 13, properties bought before 1978 had their values rolled back to 1975 assessments, and properties purchased after the adoption of the amendment were assessed on the basis of their selling price. The immediate impact was a halt to rapidly rising tax increases, but the long-term consequence has been a growing disparity in the taxes paid by long-term owners and recent purchasers. As a result, some homeowners pay as much as 17 times more taxes than their neighbors who bought homes before 1978. The owner of a $3.8-million, 8,000-square-foot mansion in Beverly Hills who owned the property before 1978 paid about $3,200 in annual taxes, whereas a purchaser of that mansion would pay about $38,000. At the same time, a recent buyer of a 1,000-square-foot bungalow that cost $370,000 pays $3,700 in taxes, or a little more than the owner of the mansion bought before 1978.

Writing for the Court in *Nordlinger*, Justice Blackmun upheld California's Proposition 13 and distinguished *Allegheny Pittsburgh*. In doing so, he underscored that

> [t]he appropriate standard of review is whether the difference in treatment between newer and older owners rationally furthers a legitimate state interest. In general, the Equal Protection Clause is satisfied so long as there is a plausible policy reason for the classification, the legislative facts on which the classification is apparently based rationally may have been considered to be true by the governmental decisionmaker, and the relationship of the classification to its goal is not so attenuated as to render the distinction arbitrary or irrational. This standard is especially deferential in the context of classifications made by complex tax laws. . . .

> We have no difficulty in ascertaining at least two rational or reasonable considerations of difference or policy that justify denying petitioner the benefits of her neighbors' lower assessments. First, the State has a legitimate interest in local neighborhood preservation, continuity, and stability. *Euclid v. Ambler Realty Co.*, 272 U.S. 265 (1926). The State therefore legitimately can decide to structure its tax system to discourage rapid turnover in ownership of homes and businesses, for example, in order to inhibit displacement of lower income families by the forces of gentrification or of established, "mom-and-pop" businesses by newer chain operations. . . .

> Second, the State legitimately can conclude that a new owner at the time of acquiring his property does not have the same reliance interest warranting protection against higher taxes as does an existing owner.

By contrast, the strict scrutiny test applies to "suspect classifications," such as race, and legislation affecting fundamental rights. On this standard of review, legislation is sustained only if there is "a compelling state interest" in the legislative classification. *Korematsu* was the exception rather than the rule; when the Court applies this standard, legislation invariably falls.

■ THE DEVELOPMENT OF LAW

The Supreme Court's Evolving Equal Protection Standards and Tests

TIERS OF ANALYSIS	STANDARD OF JUDICIAL REVIEW	LEGISLATIVE CLASSIFICATIONS	CLAIMS OF FUNDAMENTAL RIGHTS
POST-1937 TWO-TIER ANALYSIS			
Upper Tier Applies to suspect classifications and fundamental rights	Strict Scrutiny Test: Is there a compelling state interest in a legislative classification?	Race See *Brown v. Bd. of Education* (1954)	Right to Vote See Vol. 1, Ch. 8 Right to Travel See *Shapiro v. Thompson* (1969)
Lower Tier Applies to economic regulation and nonsuspect classifications	Minimal Scrutiny/Rational Basis Test: Is there a rational basis for the legislation?	Economic Classifications	
THE BURGER COURT'S (1969–1986) THREE-TIER ANALYSIS			
Upper Tier	Strict Scrutiny Test	Racial classifications that impose burdens on minorities Alienage See *Phyler v. Doe* (1982)	
Intermediate Tier Applies to quasi-suspect categories	Exacting Scrutiny/Strict Rationality Test: Is there a substantial relationship in fact between the means and ends of legislation?	Gender See *Frontiero v. Richardson* (1973); *Craig v. Boren* (1976); *Michael M. v. Superior Court* (1981)	

Lower Tier	Minimal Scrutiny Test/ Rational Basis Test	Affirmative Action See *Regents of the University of California v. Bakke* (1978) Illegitimacy See Section D(3) in this chapter Indigency, Education and Welfare See *San Antonio Independent School District v. Rodriguez* (1973) (excerpted below) Age and Alienage See the DEVELOPMENT OF LAW Box in Section D
THE REHNQUIST COURT'S (1986–) "NEW" TWO-TIER APPROACH*		
Upper Tier	Strict Scrutiny Test	Race and Affirmative Action See *City of Richmond v. J.A. Croson* (1989); *Adarand Constructors v. Pena* (1995); *Gratz v. Bollinger* and *Grutter v. Bollinger* (2003) (excerpted in this chapter)
Lower Tier	Rational Basis Test	Economic Classifications Mental Retardation See *Heller v. Doe* (1993) (excerpted below) Homosexuality See *Roemer v. Evans* (1996) (below); see also *Lawrence v. Texas* (2003) (excerpted in Chapter 11)

*Note that the Court used an intermediate test—"exceedingly persuasive justification"—in striking down gender discrimination in *U.S. v. Virginia* (1996), but there remained no majority for recognizing gender as a "suspect classification."

The Warren Court's two-level analysis of equal protection claims proved as controversial as it was instrumental to forging an "egalitarian revolution" in constitutional law. Conservatives and strict construction-ists criticized the Court for inventing new fundamental rights that they claimed lacked constitutional foundation.[9] Nor was the application of suspect classifications unproblematic. These classifications were "sus-pect" because they discriminated against individuals on the basis of im-mutable characteristics—characteristics, such as race, gender, age, and illegitimacy—which people do not choose and cannot readily, if at all, change (although, sex changes and notice of paternity are possible). By the end of the Warren Court era, the problem facing the justices was one of consistency in determining what classifications were suspect; notably, the Court was also split over whether gender, like race, was a suspect category. In addition, the Court was criticized for encouraging individuals to define their rights in terms of membership in groups and for inviting interest-group litigation. Finally, because legislation was in-variably struck down under the strict scrutiny test and upheld under the rational basis test, the Warren Court's two-tier analysis was criticized for being too rigid, for being "strict in theory and fatal in fact."

By the 1970s and 1980s, the Court and the country were changing in response to the Warren Court's "egalitarian revolution." While litiga-tion brought new claims of nonracial discrimination, the Court's com-position also changed with the appointments of Republican Presidents Richard Nixon, Gerald Ford, and Ronald Reagan. As the high bench became more conservative, the Burger Court (1969–1986) and the Rehnquist Court (1986–) sought retrenchment, refusing to expand the list of fundamental rights, suspect classifications, and quasi-suspect cate-gories like gender. Moreover, the Burger Court evolved a third, *inter-mediate* standard of judicial review: the "exacting scrutiny" or "strict rationality" test.[10] With this test, the Court looks for a "substantial relationship between the means and ends of legislation," and may or may not strike down legislation, for instance, discriminating on the basis of gender (see section D, in this chapter). In addition, the contemporary Court is resistant to attempts to heighten judicial review for new claims of quasi-suspect classifications. Indeed, the Rehnquist Court is inclined to evaluate claims of racial discrimination under the strict scrutiny test and all other equal protection claims under the rational basis test.

Illustrative of the Court's recent equal protection analysis is *City of Cleburne, Texas v. Cleburne Living Center*, 473 U.S. 432 (1985), involving a challenge to a Texas zoning law. The law required a special city per-mit, renewable each year, for the construction of "hospitals for the insane or feeble-minded, or alcoholic or drug addicts, or penal or cor-rectional institutions." The Cleburne Living Center wanted to operate a group home for thirteen mentally retarded men and women but was denied a permit because the city concluded that the home should be classified as a "hospital for the feeble-minded." A federal district court upheld the city's decision. But an appellate court reversed, holding "that mental retardation is a 'quasi-suspect' classification and that the ordinance violated the Equal Protection Clause because it did not substantially further an important governmental purpose." On appeal to the Supreme Court, Justice White held that the lower court erred in finding mental retardation to be a quasi-suspect classification justifying heightened judicial review. Although finding "a lesser standard of scrutiny [to be] appropriate," he nevertheless concluded "that under that standard the ordinance is invalid as applied in this case," explaining that

> where individuals in the group affected by a law have distinguishing characteristics relevant to interests the state has the authority to implement, the courts have been very reluctant, as they should be in our federal system, and with respect for our separation of powers, to closely scrutinize legislative choices as to whether, how and to what extent those interests should be pursued. In such cases, the Equal Protection Clause requires only a rational means to serve a legitimate end.

Heller v. Doe, 509 U.S. 312 (1993) [excerpted in Section D (5)], further illustrates the Rehnquist Court's unwillingness to expand heightened scrutiny beyond the "rational basis" test. That case, however, sharply split the justices over the application of the "rational basis" test. Writing for a bare majority, Justice Kennedy rejected an equal protection and due process challenge to Kentucky's law distinguishing between mentally retarded and mentally ill individuals and providing different procedures for their involuntary commitment. In a dissent, joined by Justices Blackmun, Stevens, and in part by O'Connor, Justice Souter in turn rejected the majority's analysis. Two brief, one-paragraph separate dissenting opinions were also filed by Justices Blackmun and O'Connor. On the one hand, Justice Blackmun reaffirmed his view that cases involving mental retardation require heightened judicial scrutiny; he was the only member on the Court to take that position. Justice O'Connor rejected that view, as did Justices Kennedy and Souter in their opinions. While O'Connor agreed with the three other dissenters that there was no rational basis for differential standards of proof in commitment proceedings for mentally ill and retarded persons, she sided with the majority on allowing guardians and family members to participate in commitment proceedings for retarded, but not for mentally ill, persons.

Three years later, in *Romer v. Evans* (1996) [excerpted in Section D (2)] a majority of the Rehnquist Court affirmed a Colorado supreme court decision striking down a state constitutional amendment forbidding localities from enacting ordinances that outlaw discrimination against homosexuals. Notably, the state supreme court had applied the "strict scrutiny" test, whereas Justice Kennedy's opinion for the Court applies the "rational basis" test. As in *Cleburne Living Center* and *Heller v. Doe*, *Romer v. Evans* underscores the contemporary Court's reluctance, on the one hand, to expand heightened scrutiny under the Fourteenth Amendment and the Court's willingness, on the other hand, both to apply the "rational basis" test and to give that test more of a bite in dealing with challenges to nonracial discriminatory classifications.

The Court's analysis and evolving standards for judicial review under the equal protection clause are examined in this chapter in terms of the political struggles within the Court and the country over the historical quest for equality. The next section examines racial discrimination before and after the ratification of the Fourteenth Amendment and the role the Court played in the constitutional politics of racial segregation and desegregation. Section B turns to the Court's rulings on school desegregation. Section C takes up the controversy over affirmative action and reverse discrimination. Finally, section D considers nonracial classifications and challenges to discrimination based on gender, homosexuality, indigency, illegitimacy, alienage, and age.

NOTES

1. See Horace Flack, *The Adoption of the Fourteenth Amendment* (Baltimore, MD: Johns Hopkins University Press, 1908); Jacobus tenBroek, *The Antislavery Origins of the Fourteenth Amendment* (Berkeley: University of California Press, 1951); William Wiecek, *The Sources of Antislavery Constitutionalism in America* (Ithaca, NY: Cornell University Press, 1977); and Howard Graham, *Everyman's Constitution: Historical Essays on the Fourteenth Amendment, the "Conspiracy Theory," and American Constitutionalism* (Madison: State Historical Society of Wisconsin, 1968).

2. See Alexander Bickel, "The Original Understanding and the Segregation Decision," 69 *Harvard Law Review* 1 (1955).

3. Raoul Berger, *Government by Judiciary: The Transformation of the Fourteenth Amendment* (Cambridge, MA: Harvard University Press, 1977).

4. See Earl Maltz, "The Fourteenth Amendment as Political Compromise—Section One in the Joint Committee on Reconstruction," 45 *Ohio State Law Journal* 933 (1984); and E. Maltz, "The Concept of Equal Protection of the Laws—A Historical Inquiry," 22 *San Diego Law Review* 499 (1985).

5. See Judith Baer, *Equality under the Constitution: Reclaiming the Fourteenth Amendment* (Ithaca, NY: Cornell University Press, 1983), 102–103.

6. See and compare William Brock, *An American Crisis: Congress and the Reconstruction* (New York: St. Martin's Press, 1963); Michael Les Benedict, *A Compromise of Principle: Congressional Republicans and Reconstruction* (New York: W. W. Norton, 1974).

7. William Nelson, *The Fourteenth Amendment* (Cambridge, MA: Harvard University Press, 1988).

8. The footnote was actually initially drafted by Justice Stone's law clerk, Louis Lusky, and revised after Chief Justice Hughes made some suggestions. See Louis Lusky, *By What Right?* (Charlottesville, VA: Michie, 1975).

9. See, for example, the right to travel in *Shapiro v. Thompson* (excerpted in this chapter) and the right to privacy in *Griswold v. Connecticut* (in Ch. 4).

10. See Gerald Gunther, "In Search of Evolving Doctrine on a Changing Court: A Model for a New Equal Protection," 86 *Harvard Law Review* 1 (1972).

SELECTED BIBLIOGRAPHY

Berger, Raoul. *Government by the Judiciary: The Transformation of the Fourteenth Amendment.* Cambridge, MA: Harvard University Press, 1977.

Blight, David. *Race and Reunion: The Civil War in American Memory.* Cambridge, MA: Harvard University Press, 2001.

Brandon, Mark. *Free in the World: American Slavery and Constitutional Failure.* Princeton, NJ: Princeton University Press, 1998.

Devins, Neal, and Davison, Douglas, eds. *Redefining Equality.* New York: Oxford University Press, 1998.

Graham, Hugh. *The Civil Rights Era.* New York: Oxford University Press, 1990.

Hacker, Andrew. *Two Nations.* New York: Scribner's, 1992.

Higginbotham, Jr., A. Leon. *Shades of Freedom: Racial Politics and the Presumptions of the Legal Process.* New York: Oxford University Press, 1996.

Karst, Kenneth. *Belonging to America: Equal Citizenship and the Constitution.* New Haven, CT: Yale University Press, 1989.

———. *Law's Promise, Law's Expression: Visions of Power in the Politics of Race, Gender, and Religion.* New Haven: Yale University Press, 1993.

Klinkner, Philip, and Smith, Rogers. *The Unsteady March: The Rise and Decline of Racial Equality in America.* Chicago: University of Chicago Press, 2000.

Perry, Michael. *We The People: The Fourteenth Amendment and the Supreme Court.* New York: Oxford University Press, 1999.

Richards, David. *Conscience and the Constitution: History, Theory, and Law of the Reconstruction Amendments.* Princeton, NJ: Princeton University Press, 1993.

Scaturro, Frank. *The Supreme Court's Retreat from Reconstruction: A Distortion of Constitutional Jurisprudence.* Westport, CT: Greenwood Press, 2000.

West, Robin. *Progressive Constitutionalism: Reconstructing the Fourteenth Amendment.* Durham, NC: Duke University Press, 1994.

A | *Racial Discrimination and State Action*

"Our Constitution," in the words of Justice John Marshall Harlan dissenting alone in *Plessy v. Ferguson* (1896) (see excerpt below), "is color-blind, and neither knows nor tolerates classes among citizens." However, the history of constitutional politics, both before and after the ratification of the Fourteenth Amendment, belies that noble aspiration and appeal to future generations. While the Declaration of Independence proclaimed that "all men are created equal," the Constitution was far from color-blind.

Opposition to slavery emerged during the Revolutionary War, particularly after slaves served as soldiers in the colonial battle for freedom from the English Crown. After winning independence, laws abolishing slavery were passed in several northern colonies. Still Thomas Jefferson and others won approval of the Northwest Ordinance of 1787, forbidding slavery in western territories north of the Ohio River, only after agreeing that fugitive slaves "may be lawfully reclaimed." And even in New York, the state legislature did not order the mandatory emancipation of slaves until 1828.

The Constitutional Convention compromised on the question of slavery, even though the words *slavery* and *slaves* never appear in the document. Article I, Section 2 provides that, for the purposes of taxation and representation in the House of Representatives, "three fifths of all other [nonfree] Persons" were to be counted. This accommodated southern delegates' twin concerns that when levying taxes the federal government might discriminate against the South in the way it counted slaves and that the South would be underrepresented if slaves were not counted for the purposes of representation. The convention agreed as well to authorize Congress, in Article I, Section 9, to stop the "migration or importation" of slaves, although not before 1808. Finally, without out much debate the convention endorsed (in Article IV, Section 2) the return of fugitive slaves to their owners.

Despite the efforts of some at the Constitutional Convention to limit the perpetuation of slavery, the Constitution registered the prejudices and white supremacy of the country.[1] Over a half century later, Chief Justice Roger Taney wrote those prejudices into constitutional law with his sweeping opinion in *Dred Scott v. Sandford* (1857) (see excerpt below), denying that blacks (not just slaves and temporarily freed slaves, but all blacks) could be citizens, and striking down the Missouri Compromise of 1820, in which Congress had sought to exclude slavery from federal territories north of the line 36°30'. When holding that blacks were excluded from "We the People of the United States," of which the preamble of the Constitution speaks, Chief Justice Taney laid bare the brute fact of white supremacy, explaining that blacks were "a subordinate and inferior class of beings, who had been subjugated by the dominant race, and, whether emancipated or not, yet remained subject to their authority."

Prior to the Civil War, the Court did little to undermine slavery. In *Prigg v. Pennsylvania*, 41 U.S. 539 (1842), though, the Court struck down a state law requiring masters to present to a magistrate proof of ownership of a runaway slave and upheld the federal Fugitive Slave Law of 1793, authorizing federal judges to certify a slaveholder's claim over a fugitive slave. In his opinion for the Court, Justice Joseph Story, however, also noted that states were not compelled by Congress to enforce the 1793 law. As a result, northern states were encouraged not to enforce fugitive slave laws, while southern states pushed for more stringent laws to protect their interests.

Although abolitionists attacked the constitutionality of fugitive slave laws, the Taney Court firmly defended the South's interests in slavery. In *Strader v. Graham*, 51 U.S. 83 (1851), for instance, the Taney Court unanimously upheld Kentucky's law making abettors of fugitive slaves liable for damages to slaveowners, even if slaves had been taken into free territory.[2]

With the outbreak of the Civil War in 1861, *Dred Scott*'s impact was limited. After the war, the ruling was technically overturned by the Thirteenth Amendment (in 1865), which abolished slavery and "involuntary servitude," as well as gave Congress the "power to enforce this article by appropriate legislation." The Reconstruction Congress also considered how to ensure the voting rights and the civil rights of newly freed blacks. In 1862, Congress repealed the District of Columbia's "Black Codes," which limited the property rights of blacks and made certain offenses criminal for blacks only. But in 1865 President Andrew Johnson vetoed the passage of further civil rights legislation, contending that the protection of civil rights was a matter for the states, not the federal government. Congress, however, overrode the veto with a two-thirds vote and enacted the Civil Rights Act of 1866. Because controversy remained over the constitutionality of that legislation, one of the objectives of promoters of the Fourteenth Amendment in 1866 was to ensure the constitutional basis for the Civil Rights Act of 1866. The Fifteenth Amendment later specifically aimed at guaranteeing blacks equal voting rights (see Vol. 1, Ch. 8).

Both the Civil Rights Act of 1866 and the Fourteenth Amendment sought to ensure the citizenship of newly freed blacks and the equal protection of the laws. Congress was very explicit about the legal equality extended to blacks in the Civil Rights Act. It specifically guarantees

> citizens, of every race and color . . . the same right, in every State and Territory . . . to make and enforce contracts, to sue, be parties, and give evidence, to inherit, purchase, lease, sell, hold, and convey real and personal property, and to full and equal benefit of all laws and proceedings for the security of person and property, as is enjoyed by white citizens, and shall be subject to like punishments, pains, and penalties, and to no other.

Although the Fourteenth Amendment's equal protection clause is less detailed, Congress reaffirmed in Section 5 of that amendment its "power to enforce" the amendment with "appropriate legislation," such as the Civil Rights Act of 1866 and the Civil Rights Act of 1875, which barred racial discrimination in public accommodations.

In the face of congressional efforts to legislate away white prejudice, the Court defended and gave constitutional legitimacy to racial segregation. In *The Slaughterhouse Cases* (1873) (see Ch. 3), the Chase Court sharply limited the scope of the Fourteenth Amendment. There and in *Strauder v. West Virginia*, 100 U.S. 303 (1880), the Court gave the amendment narrow scope in eliminating racial discrimination. In *Strauder*, the Waite Court conceded the potential contributions of the Fourteenth Amendment. Strauder, a black, sought to have his case moved from a state to a federal court because West Virginia barred blacks from serving on juries. When affirming his request, the Court observed that

> [t]he words of the amendment . . . contain a necessary implication of a positive immunity, or right, most valuable to the colored race—the right to exemption from unfriendly legislation against them distinctively as colored,—exemption from legal distinctions, implying inferiority in civil society, lessening the security of their enjoyment of the rights which others enjoy, and discriminations which are steps towards reducing them to the condition of a subject race. . . . The very fact that colored people are singled out and expressly denied by statute all right to participate in the administration of the law, as jurors, because of their color, though they are citizens, and may be in other respects fully qualified, is practically a brand upon them, affixed by the law, an assertion of their inferiority, and a stimulant to that race prejudice which is an impediment to securing to individuals of that race that equal justice which the law aims to secure to all others.

That same year in *Ex Parte Virginia*, 100 U.S. 313 (1880), the Waite Court again indicated that practices might be made to conform to the promise "*No state* shall . . . deny to any person . . . the equal protection of the laws." This case involved a Virginia judge charged with violating federal law for excluding blacks from juries. He countered that, because the state had no law excluding blacks from juries, his actions though official did not constitute "state action" in violation of the amendment. Rejecting that argument, the Waite Court held that the amendment barred government "agencies" and "officials" from denying the equal protection of the laws.

Three years later, however, the Waite Court turned state action into a barrier for eliminating racial discrimination. In the *Civil Rights Cases* (1883) (see excerpt below), the Court held that Section 5 of the Fourteenth Amendment only authorized Congress to enact legislation barring racial discrimination that resulted from state action—state laws or actions done "under the color of state laws." Congress, in the Court's view, was not authorized to enact the Civil Rights Act of 1875 or to forbid racial discrimination by individuals and corporations in public accommodations.[3] The state action doctrine thus became a vehicle for perpetuating racial discrimination and segregation.

The *Civil Rights Cases* undercut congressional power and legitimated private racial discrimination. The Fuller Court, then, gave legiti-

Founded in 1866 for the purpose of terrorizing black people, the Ku Klux Klan (KKK) experienced a rebirth in the early twentieth century. Here, in 1925 an estimated 40,000 KKK followers march in the nation's capital in celebration of white supremacy. (Photo Source: Corbis)

macy to the doctrine of "separate but equal" facilities for blacks and whites in *Plessy v. Ferguson* (1896) (see excerpt below). Whereas forty years earlier in *Dred Scott* Chief Justice Taney had no doubts about the inferior status of blacks, in *Plessy* Justice Brown denied that the doctrine of separate but equal implied "the inferiority of either race."

The Court's rulings in the late nineteenth century returned control over race relations to the states. By the turn of the twentieth century, the states of the old Confederacy had largely disenfranchised blacks (see Vol. 1, Ch. 8) and erected a system of racial segregation. Blacks were separated from whites in public schools, government office buildings, public parks, and recreational areas, as well as hotels, restaurants, theaters, and other places of public accommodations.

The Court and the country did not begin to change until well into the twentieth century. In a few early cases, the Court led the way, striking down laws aimed at denying blacks' voting rights,[4] some racial zoning laws,[5] and recognizing the inequities of racially segregated educational facilities.[6] But only after the battle over the New Deal in 1937 and the period surrounding World War II did the federal government undertake the long process of dismantling the system of racial segregation. In 1939, Democratic president Franklin Roosevelt created a Civil Liberties Unit within the Department of Justice and later issued an executive order creating a Committee on Fair Employment Practices with authority over businesses working for the federal government.[7] More significant were the executive orders issued by FDR's successor, President Harry Truman. In 1948, he boldly ordered an end to racial segregation in the military,[8] established the Fair Employment Board, and outlawed racial discrimination in the federal government.

Congress remained unwilling to act, and the actions of FDR and Truman provoked rebellion within the Democratic Party. In 1948 Alabama, Louisiana, Mississippi, and South Carolina left the Democratic Party to form the Dixiecrat Party. But Roosevelt's and Truman's appointments to the Court contributed to the shifting tide in constitutional politics after World War II. FDR elevated Justice Stone to the chief justiceship and named eight justices between 1937 and 1943: Hugo Black in 1937, Stanley Reed in 1938, Felix Frankfurter and William Douglas in 1939, Frank Murphy in 1940, James Byrnes and Robert Jackson in 1941, and Wiley Rutledge in 1943. Truman then appointed Chief Justice Fred Vinson in 1946 and Justices Harold Burton (in 1945) and Thomas Clark and Sherman Minton (in 1949).[9]

In the 1940s and 1950s, litigation brought by the National Association for the Advancement of Colored People (NAACP) pushed the Court into a leading role in the process of ending racial segregation. When striking down restrictive covenants in *Shelley v. Kraemer*

(1948) (see excerpt below), the Court turned the state action doctrine into an instrument for prohibiting private racial discrimination.[10] The state action doctrine, which had supported systems of racial discrimination, became a tool for the Court to reach and ban private racial discrimination.

In the two decades following *Shelley*, the Court never denied relief on the grounds that no state action was present. In *Burton v. Wilmington Parking Authority*, 365 U.S. 715 (1961), for example, the Warren Court applied the state action doctrine to a restaurant denying service to blacks. It did so on the grounds that the restaurant, although privately owned, was located in a publicly owned parking garage and that public property could not be leased in a manner inconsistent with the Fourteenth Amendment. In *Evans v. Newton*, 382 U.S. 296 (1966) (with Justices Black, Harlan, and Stewart dissenting), the Warren Court held that the equal protection clause was violated by Macon, Georgia's "whites only" public park. The land for the park was deeded to the city in 1911 with the stipulation that it be used for a park "for whites only." Although the city resigned as the trustee for the park, and private trustees were appointed, the Court held that the Fourteenth Amendment applied under its new formulation of the state action doctrine. The Court then unanimously struck down Alabama's system of racially segregated prisons in *Lee v. Washington*, 390 U.S. 1 (1967), and, with only Justice Black dissenting, *Hunter v. Erickson*, 393 U.S. 385 (1969), overturned an ordinance barring fair housing practices.

The civil rights movement gathered momentum in the late 1950s and 1960s. Under the leadership of Dr. Martin Luther King, Jr., thousands of protesting blacks defied segregation in restaurants and other public accommodations. When blacks started sit-ins at luncheon counters and restaurants, they were arrested for trespassing on private property or for breach of the peace. Media attention increasingly focused on the struggles of the civil rights movement following the arrest in Montgomery, Alabama, of Rosa Parks. Parks, a forty-two-year-old black woman, was arrested for taking a seat in the section reserved for whites on a public bus and became a symbol for generations. Yet, the Warren Court largely left it to the lower federal courts, the president, and Congress to deal with the controversy over segregated public accommodations. Even in its watershed ruling on school desegregation, in *Brown v. Board of Education of Topeka, Kansas*, 347 U.S. 483 (1954) (excerpted in Section B), the Court neither expressly overruled, nor even mentioned, *Plessy v. Ferguson* (1896) (excerpted below). *Brown*, nonetheless, symbolically and effectively laid to rest *Plessy's* doctrine of "separate but equal" facilities for blacks and whites. Two years after *Brown*, when Montgomery, Alabama's system of segregated seating on buses was challenged, in *Browder v. Gayle*, 142 F.Supp. 707 (M.D. Ala., 1956), a three-judge federal district court split two to one in holding that *Brown* had "impliedly, though not explicitly, overruled" *Plessy*. And when that ruling was appealed in *Gayle v. Browder*, 352 U.S. 903 (1956), the Warren Court simply affirmed the lower court in a one-line *per curiam* opinion, which notably cited *Brown*.

The Warren Court was reluctant to extend the state action doctrine to reach segregated lunch counters and restaurants. Although overturning convictions of civil rights "sitters-in," it did so without relying on the state action doctrine.[11] In *Bell v. Maryland*, 378 U.S. 226 (1964), for example, the convictions of twelve sit-in protesters were overturned on the grounds that Maryland's newly enacted anti-discrimination law might be applied by state courts to abate the prosecutions. Concurring Chief Justice Warren and Justices Douglas and Goldberg also argued that because the restaurant was "property that is serving the public" it could not discriminate against blacks. But dissenting Justice Black, joined by Justices Harlan and White, contended that Congress, not the Court, had the power under the Fourteenth Amendment to ban segregated public accommodations. Justice Black worried about the scope of the state action doctrine and remained unwilling to extend the equal protection clause to the practice of racial discrimination by owners of restaurants.

The controversy within the Warren Court over whether the state action doctrine applied to restaurants and other public accommodations was settled by the president and Congress. Almost a hundred years after the Civil Rights Act of 1875, Congress finally addressed the issue of segregated public accommodations. In response to the massive southern resistance to school desegregation and the violent reactions to the pressures for change brought by the civil rights movement, Democratic president John F. Kennedy proposed new aggressive civil rights legislation.[12] Following Kennedy's assassination, President Lyndon Johnson pushed the Civil Rights Act of 1964 and other legislation through Congress.[13] Besides limiting the use of literacy tests for voters (see Vol. 1, Ch. 8) and authorizing the Department of Justice to challenge segregated public facilities, the Civil Rights Act of 1964 in Title II forbade racial discrimination in public accommodations and in Title VII outlawed discrimination in employment.

Since the *Civil Rights Cases* had held that state action limited congressional power under the Fourteenth Amendment, Congress passed the Civil Rights Act of 1964 on its authority under the commerce clause (see Vol. 1, Ch. 6). When the constitutionality of the Civil Rights Act of 1964 was challenged, the Warren Court upheld it in *Heart of Atlanta Motel, Inc. v. United States* (1964) and *Katzenbach v. McClung* (1964) (both in Vol. 1, Ch. 6). The Court upheld as well the Voting Rights Act of 1965, banning racial discrimination in elections, in *South Carolina v. Katzenbach*, 383 U.S. 301 (1965) (see Vol. 1, Ch. 8). Ironically, in the year that Congress passed the Civil Rights Act of 1968, forbidding discrimination in the sale, rental, financing, and advertising of housing, the Warren Court also construed the Civil Rights Act of 1866 to ban private racial discrimination in housing and affirmed Congress's authority to enact such legislation under the Thirteenth Amendment. In *Jones v. Alfred H. Mayer, Co.*, 392 U.S. 409 (1968), the Court finally accepted the view of Justice Harlan dissenting in the *Civil Rights Cases*, that the Thirteenth Amendment proscribes all "badges and incidents" of slavery. In *McLaughlin v. Florida*, 379 U.S. 184 (1964), and *Loving v. Virginia*, 388 U.S. 1 (1967), the Warren Court struck down state miscegenation laws, which barred interracial marriages.

■ CONSTITUTIONAL HISTORY

Loving v. Virginia and Bans on Interracial Marriage

In *Loving v. Virginia*, 388 U.S. 1 (1967), the Supreme Court struck down bans on interracial marriage; in many states it was a criminal offense. The Court held that states' refusal to recognize interracial marriages violated a fundamental right protected by the Fourteenth Amendment's due process and equal protection clauses.

Notably, in *Loving* the Court made no mention of the "full faith and credit" clause of Article IV of the Constitution, which requires states to honor court decisions of other states. Indeed, prior to the 1967 ruling there was a patchwork of laws on interracial marriages. In 1952, thirty states prohibited interracial marriages. But by the time *Loving* came down fourteen states had repealed their laws against interracial marriage. Moreover, states were not constitutionally compelled to recognize interracial marriages in other states. Some did and some did not, and it often depended on the circumstances and the issues at stake. State courts were almost evenly divided, for example, in recognizing legally married interracial couples in other states when the couple, after years of marriage, moved to a state barring interracial marriages. If a legally married interracial couple in one state, however, sought recognition in another state that barred interracial marriage for the purpose of suing for injuries, damage to property, or inheritance, state courts tended to recognize the interracial marriage, in spite of state laws against such marriages.

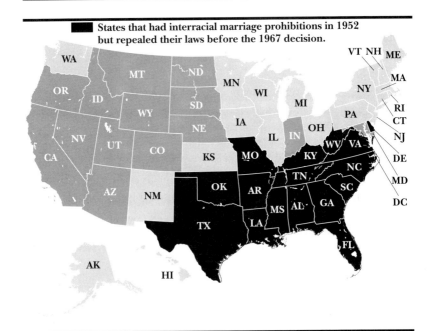

States that had interracial marriage prohibitions in 1952 but repealed their laws before the 1967 decision.

The civil rights revolution forged by the Warren Court, and Democratic presidents and Congresses, embittered southern Democrats and some Republicans. In the 1968 presidential election, Republican candidate Richard Nixon campaigned against the "egalitarian jurisprudence" of the Warren Court, promising to appoint strict constructionists to the bench as part of his "southern strategy" to win the votes of southern white voters. With his election, a brief and dramatic period of social and legal change gradually came to an end. Nixon made his mark by appointing Chief Justice Warren Burger in 1969 and Justices Harry Blackmun in 1971 and Lewis F. Powell and William Rehnquist in 1972.

With the Burger Court (1969–1986) came changes. It drew the line on further extension of earlier rulings, but it also confronted new controversies (involving, for example, affirmative action programs, as examined in section C of this chapter) that would not have arisen were it not for the civil rights revolution of the 1960s. In *James v. Valtierra*, 402 U.S. 137 (1971), for instance, a bare majority upheld a law requiring qualified voters to approve low-cost housing projects, over the objection of the dissenters that that sanctioned racial segregation in housing. However, in *Hills v. Gautreaux*, 425 U.S. 284 (1976), the Court approved a lower court's order for the adoption of a comprehensive metropolitan plan for desegregating Chicago's public housing system.

The state action doctrine was given new twists and limited during the Burger Court years. The Court held that a restaurant's refusal to serve a white woman in the company of blacks was state action.[14] But

Evans v. Abney, 396 U.S. 435 (1970), signaled that the Burger Court would limit the scope of the state action doctrine. There, once again the justices confronted the continuing controversy over Macon, Georgia's all-white park. After the Warren Court's ruling in *Evans v. Newton* (1966), the heirs of the donor of the park reclaimed the land on the grounds that the donor's will was not honored, because it expressly conditioned use of the land for whites only. The Burger Court upheld a state court's decision returning the land and found no state action to trigger the Fourteenth Amendment. In 1971, then, a bare majority of the Burger Court upheld the decision of Jackson, Mississippi, to close, rather than desegregate, the city's public swimming pools. Justices Douglas, Brennan, Marshall, and White dissented from that ruling in *Palmer v. Thompson*, 403 U.S. 217 (1971).

In *Moose Lodge No. 107 v. Irvis*, 407 U.S. 163 (1972), the Burger Court refused to apply the state action doctrine to a private club that refused to serve blacks, even though it had a state liquor license. Writing for the majority, Justice Rehnquist explained that

> [t]he Court has never held, of course, that discrimination by an otherwise private entity would be violative of the equal protection clause if the private entity receives any sort of benefit or service at all from the State, or if it is subject to state regulation in any degree whatever. Since state-furnished services include such necessities of life as electricity, water, and police and fire protection, such a holding would utterly emasculate the distinction between private as distinguished from State conduct set forth in *The Civil Rights Cases* and adhered to in subsequent decisions. Our holdings indicate that where the impetus for the discrimination is private, the State must have "significantly involved itself with invidious discriminations," . . . in order for the discriminatory action to fall within the ambit of the constitutional prohibition.

Dismissing the argument that by licensing the private club the state became implicated in racial discrimination, Justice Rehnquist observed,

> However detailed this type of regulation may be in some particulars, it cannot be said to in any way foster or encourage racial discrimination. Nor can it be said to make the State in any realistic sense a partner or even a joint venturer in the club's enterprise. The limited effect of the prohibition against obtaining additional club licenses when the maximum number of retail licenses allotted to a municipality has been issued, when considered together with the availability of liquor from hotel, restaurant, and retail licensees falls far short of conferring upon club licensees a monopoly in the dispensing of liquor in any given municipality or in the State as a whole. We therefore hold that . . . the operation of the regulatory scheme enforced by the Pennsylvania Liquor Control Board does

---

■ The Development of Law

Other Rulings on State Action

CASE	VOTE	RULING
Jackson v. Metropolitan Edison Co., 419 U.S. 345 (1974)	6:3	Held that a privately owned electric company, operating under a state license, which termi-

nated service to a customer was not covered by the state action doctrine, in a suit brought by the customer, claiming a right to notice, a hearing, and the opportunity to pay past electric bills. Justices Douglas, Brennan, and Marshall dissented.

Blum v. Yaretsky, 457 U.S. 991 (1982)	7:2	The Court rejected the argument that state subsidies to a private institution constituted state

action and made the institution subject to the limitations of the Fourteenth Amendment; here, patients in a nursing home, who were transferred to another without notice or a hearing, claimed they were denied procedural due process; Justices Brennan and Marshall dissented.

San Francisco Arts & Athletics, Inc. v. United States Olympic Committee (USOC), 483 U.S. 522 (1987)	5:4	Held that the USOC was not a government actor, despite Congress's granting it the right to prohibit commercial and promotional uses of the word

Olympic, and rejected the equal protection claims of the petitioner who was barred from calling its athletic competitions the "Gay Olympic Games"; Justices Brennan, Marshall, Blackmun, and O'Connor dissented.

National Collegiate Athletic Association (NCAA) v. Tarkanian, 488 U.S. 179 (1988)	5:4	Upheld the University of Nevada, Las Vegas's disciplinary actions against its head basketball coach in accordance with the

NCAA's rules and ruled that the NCAA recommendations for disciplinary actions were not state action, and hence the NCAA was not liable for violating the coach's civil rights; Justice White, a former football player, was joined by Justices Brennan, Marshall, and O'Connor in dissent, finding the NCAA to be a state actor because it acted jointly with the University of Nevada.

Edmonson v. Leesville Concrete Co., 500 U.S. 614 (1991)	6:3	Held that the state action doctrine precludes the use of peremptory challenges to exclude

blacks from serving on juries in civil cases. Justices O'Connor and Scalia, along with Chief Justice Rehnquist, dissented.

CASE	VOTE	RULING
Brentwood Academy v. Tennessee Secondary School Athletic Association, 531 U.S. 288 (2001)	5:4	Held that the Tennessee Secondary Athletic Association is a "state actor" because of its pervasive entwinement with state school officials. The association

regulates interscholastic sports among Tennessee public and private high schools. Its staff, although not state employees, may join the state retirement system, and the association sets membership standards and student eligibility rules, as well as has the power to penalize schools that violate its rules. When the association penalized Brentwood Academy for violating its recruitment rules, Brentwood Academy sued, claiming that enforcement of the rule constituted state action that violated the First and Fourteenth Amendments. Writing for the Court, Justice Souter reaffirmed that state action may be found when there exists a "close nexus between the state and the challenged action" and when seemingly private behavior "may be fairly treated as that of the state itself," citing *Jackson v. Metropolitan Edison Co.*, 419 U.S. 345 (1974). Chief Justice Rehnquist and Justices Kennedy, Scalia, and Thomas dissented.

---

not sufficiently implicate the State in the discriminatory guest policies of Moose Lodge so as to make the latter "State action" within the ambit of the Equal Protection Clause of the Fourteenth Amendment.

By narrowing the scope of the state action doctrine, the Burger Court enlarged the range of private activities immune from suits under the Fourteenth Amendment. It did so by limiting the public function theory that underlies the doctrine of state action. Whereas the Warren Court looked at the totality of interrelationships between government and private activities, the Burger and Rehnquist Courts tend to scrutinize and then dismiss various arguments for extending the doctrine of state action. With those exceptions already noted, though, the Court has refused to extend the state action doctrine primarily in cases *not* involving claims of racial discrimination.

In one area—that of racially based peremptory challenges in jury selection—however, the Rehnquist Court vigorously enforced the Fourteenth Amendment and the state-action doctrine. In *Batson v. Kentucky*, 476 U.S. 79 (1986), dissenting Justice Rehnquist argued that "there is simply nothing 'unequal' about the State using its peremptory challenges to strike blacks from" juries trying black defendants. Yet, by a seven-to-two vote (with Chief Justice Rehnquist and Justice Scalia dissenting) in *Powers v. Ohio*, 499 U.S. 400 (1991), the Court held that criminal defendants may claim a violation of the Fourteenth Amendment's equal protection when objecting to a prosecutor's race-based exclusion of jurors through the use of peremptory challenges during jury selection. A majority of the Court then went even further in *Edmonson v. Leesville Concrete Co.*, 500 U.S. 614 (1991), holding that parties in civil cases may not use peremptory challenges to exclude blacks from serving on juries. Writing for a six-member majority, Justice Kennedy found that the "state action" doctrine precludes such racial discrimination in civil cases and held that the Fifth Amendment's due process clause incorporated that holding and made it applicable to civil cases filed in federal courts as well. Kennedy reasoned that

> In the ordinary context of civil litigation in which the government is not a party, an adversarial relation does not exist between the government and a private litigant. In the jury-selection process, the government and private litigants work for the same end. . . . [H]ere a private entity becomes a government actor for the limited purpose of using peremptories during jury selection. The selection of jurors represents a unique governmental function delegated to private litigants by the government and attributable to the government for purposes of invoking constitutional protections against discrimination by reason of race.

Subsequently, in *Georgia v. McCollum*, 505 U.S. 42 (1992), the Court extended *Edmonson* to bar the use of peremptory challenges in criminal cases to exclude potential jurors on the basis of race. Once again, Justices O'Connor and Scalia dissented, while Chief Justice Rehnquist and Justice Thomas concurred even though they disagreed with the ruling there and in *Edmonson*. Yet only Justices Scalia and Thomas dissented from the further extension of the *Batson*-line of cases in *Campbell v. Louisiana*, 523 U.S. 392 (1998). There, Justice Kennedy held that a white defendant could challenge the selection process for grand jury forepersons for racial bias, because between 1976 and 1993 no black served as foreperson even though more than 20 percent of the voters in the Parish were black.

Another notable controversy arose in *Bob Jones University v. United States* and *Goldsboro Christian Schools, Inc. v. United States*, 461 U.S. 574 (1983). There the Court upheld the policy decision of the Internal Revenue Service denying tax-exempt status to private schools that racially discriminate. In his opinion for the Court, Chief Justice Burger conceded that the "[d]enial of tax benefits will inevitably have a substantial impact on the operation of private religious schools." But he underscored that

[t]he governmental interest at stake here is compelling. . . . [T]he Government has a fundamental, overriding interest in eradicating racial discrimination in education—discrimination that prevailed, with official approval, for the first 165 years of this Nation's history. That governmental interest substantially outweighs whatever burden denial of tax benefits places on petitioners' exercise of their religious beliefs. The interests asserted by petitioners cannot be accommodated with that compelling governmental interest, . . . and no "less restrictive means," . . . are available to achieve the governmental interest.

However, in *Bazemore v. Friday*, 478 U.S. 385 (1986), speaking for a bare majority Justice White held that the "affirmative duty to desegregate" had no application to 4-H and Homemaker Clubs, which were segregated until 1965 and run by the North Carolina Agricultural Extension Service. He observed that "[w]hile school children must go to school, there is no compulsion to join 4-H or Homemaker Clubs, and . . . there is no statutory or regulatory authority to deny a young person the right to join any Club he or she wishes to join."

The state action doctrine, nevertheless, became less important for striking down private racial discrimination after *Jones v. Alfred H. Mayer Co.*, 392 U.S. 409 (1968), held that Congress intended to forbid private racial discrimination in the Civil Rights Act of 1866 and that it had the authority to do so under the Thirteenth Amendment. The Court, furthermore, extended that ruling and reinforced the Civil Rights Act of 1866 as a barrier to private racial discrimination in housing, schools, and employment,[15] whenever there is proof of intentional discrimination.[16]

After *Alfred H. Mayer Co.*, the Court faced a number of important cases challenging the application of the Civil Rights Act of 1866. In *Runyon v. McCrary*, 427 U.S. 160 (1976), the Burger Court held that the Civil Rights Act of 1866 extended to private schools that refuse to admit blacks. "It is now well established," Justice Stewart observed in his opinion for the Court, that the Civil Rights Act of 1866 "prohibits racial discrimination in the making and enforcement of private contracts." But dissenting Justice White, joined by Justice Rehnquist, countered by rereading the legislative history of the Civil Rights Act and concluded that "the statute means what it says and no more, i.e., that it outlaws any legal rule disabling any person from making or enforcing a contract, but does not prohibit private racially motivated refusals to contract."

Subsequently, the Rehnquist Court extended the protection of the Civil Rights Act of 1866 to Arabians and Jews upon concluding that "Jews and Arabs were among the people [in 1866] then considered to be distinct races and hence within the protection of the statute."[17] In 1987, however, the Rehnquist Court also indicated a move in more conservative directions by suggesting a willingness in *Patterson v. McLean Credit Union* to reconsider *Runyon v. McCrary*. But, ultimately, in *Patterson v. McLean Credit Union*, 491 U.S. 164 (1989), the Rehnquist Court decided that "no special justification has been shown for overruling *Runyon*." In his opinion for the Court, Justice Kennedy explained that

> whether *Runyon*'s interpretation of [the Civil Rights Act of 1866] as prohibiting racial discrimination in the making and enforcement of private contracts is wrong or right as an original matter, it is certain that it is not inconsistent with the prevailing sense of justice in this country. To the contrary, *Runyon* is entirely consistent with our society's deep commitment to the eradication of discrimination based on a person's race or color of his or her skin.

Still, he refused to hold employers liable for racial harassment and discrimination as a condition of employment. The statute, in Justice Kennedy's words, covers "only conduct at the initial formation of the contract and conduct which impairs the right to enforce contract obligations through [the] legal process." Following *Patterson*, Congress expanded coverage of the Civil Rights Act of 1866 to forbid discrimination in all phases of employment and not merely in hiring practices.

NOTES

1. See the excellent collection of writings of the framers of the Constitution on the matter of slavery in Philip Kurland and Ralph Lerner, eds., *The Founders' Constitution*, Vol. 1 (Chicago: University of Chicago Press, 1987), 495–576.

2. See also *Ableman v. Booth*, 62 U.S. 506 (1859).

3. See also *United States v. Cruikshank*, 92 U.S. 542 (1876).

4. See, for example, *Guinn v. United States*, 238 U.S. 347 (1915); and *Lane v. Wilson*, 307 U.S. 268 (1939) (striking down grandfather clauses denying voting rights to most blacks). See also Vol. 1, Ch. 8.

5. See *Missouri ex. rel. Gaines v. Canada*, 305 U.S. 337 (1938).

6. See *Buchanan v. Warley*, 245 U.S. 60 (1917).

7. Exec. Order 8802, *Federal Register*, Vol. VI (1941), 3109.

8. Exec. Order 9981, *Federal Register*, Vol. XII (1948), 4313.

9. For a discussion of FDR's and Truman's appointments, see David M. O'Brien, *Storm Center: The Supreme Court in American Politics*, 7th ed. (New York: W. W. Norton, 2005), Ch. 2.

10. In *Reitman v. Mulkey*, 387 U.S. 369 (1967), a bare majority of the Warren Court struck down California's restrictive covenant law.

11. See *Garner v. Louisiana*, 368 U.S. 157 (1961); *Bouie v. City of Columbia*, 378 U.S. 342 (1964); and *Barr v. City of Columbia*, 378 U.S. 146 (1964).

12. In 1957 and 1960, Congress enacted two other civil rights laws, but both proved ineffective. See Carl Brauer, *John F. Kennedy and the Second Reconstruction* (New York: Columbia University Press, 1977).

13. See James Harvey, *Black Civil Rights during the Johnson Administration* (Jackson: University and College Press of Mississippi, 1973).

14. *Adickes v. S. H. Kress & Co.*, 398 U.S. 144 (1970).

15. In addition to the cases discussed, see *Griffin v. Breckenridge*, 403 U.S. 88 (1971).

16. See *General Building Constructors Association, Inc. v. Pennsylvania*, 451 U.S. 375 (1982).

17. See *St Francis College v. Al-Khazraji*, 481 U.S. 604 (1987); and *Shaare Tefila Congregation v. Cobb*, 481 U.S. 615 (1987).

SELECTED BIBLIOGRAPHY

Barnes, Catherine. *Journey from Jim Crow: The Desegregation of Southern Transit*. New York: Columbia University Press, 1983.

Blight, David W. *Race and Reunion: The Civil War in American Memory*. Cambridge, MA: Harvard University Press, 2001.

Brandon, Mark. *Free in the World: American Slavery and Constitutional Failure*. Princeton, NJ: Princeton University Press, 1998.

Brandwein, Pamela. *Reconstructing Reconstruction: The Supreme Court and the Production of Historical Truth*. Durham, NC: Duke University Press, 1999.

Cortner, Richard C. *Civil Rights and Public Accommodations: The Heart of Atlanta Motel and McClung Cases*. Lawrence: University Press of Kansas, 2001.

Fehrenbacher, Don. *The Dred Scott Case: Its Significance in American Law and Politics*. New York: Oxford University Press, 1978.

Goldman, Robert. *Reconstruction and Black Suffrage: Losing the Vote in Reese and Cruikshank*. Lawrence: University of Kansas Press, 2001.

Hampton, Henry, and Fayer, Steve. *Voices of Freedom: An Oral History of the Civil Rights Movement from the 1960s through the 1980s*. New York: Bantam Books, 1990.

Higginbotham, A. Leon, Jr. *Shades of Freedom: Racial Politics and Presumptions of the American Legal Process*. New York: Oxford University Press, 1996.

Hyman, Harold, and Wiecek, William. *Equal Justice under Law: Constitutional Development 1835–1875*. New York: Harper & Row, 1982.

Kennedy, Randall. *Interracial Intimacies: Sex, Marriage, Identity, and Adoption*. New York: Pantheon, 2003.

Kull, Andrew. *The Color-Blind Constitution*. Cambridge, MA: Harvard University Press, 1994.

Lofgren, Charles. *The Plessy Case*. New York: Oxford University Press, 1987.

Malcomson, Scott. *One Drop of Blood: The American Misadventures of Race*. New York: Farrar, Straus & Giroux, 2000.

Massey, Douglas, and Denton, Nancy. *American Apartheid: Segregation and the Making of the Underclass*. Cambridge, MA: Harvard University Press, 1993.

McWhorter, Diane. *Carry Me Home: Birmingham, Alabama: The Climactic Battle of the Civil Rights Revolution.* New York: Simon & Schuster, 2001.

Sollors, Werner. *Interracialism: Black-White Intermarriage in American History, Literature, and Law.* New York: Oxford University Press, 2000.

tenBroek, Jacobus. *The Antislavery Origins of the Fourteenth Amendment.* Berkeley: University of California Press, 1951.

Tushnet, Mark. *The American Law of Slavery, 1810–1860.* Princeton, NJ: Princeton University Press, 1981.

Dred Scott v. Sandford

19 How. (60 U.S.) 393 (1857)

In 1848, a Missouri slave, Dred Scott, sought to win his freedom in a lawsuit against the widow of John Emerson, his owner and an army medical officer. Scott contended that he had been emancipated as a result of Emerson's having taken him to live on military posts in Illinois and in federal territory north of 36°30' where slavery was outlawed by the Missouri Compromise of 1820. In that legislation, Congress admitted Maine into the Union as a free state and Missouri as a slave state, and banned slavery in all federal territories north of the line 36°30'.

The question Scott raised was whether his residence on free soil had changed his status as a slave. Prior to the 1830s, northern and southern states tried to accommodate each other's interests. Southerners were permitted to travel with their slaves in the North without interference, while southern courts upheld the rule that a slave temporarily domiciled in a free state became permanently free. But under the pressure of abolitionists in the 1830s and 1840s, this accommodation broke down. Northern states began denying southerners the privilege of traveling with their slaves and holding that slaves, who were not fugitives, became free once they were on free soil. Southern states in turn grew increasingly resentful and retaliated by refusing to enforce the antislavery law of other jurisdictions. So it was that after two trials and Scott's temporarily winning his freedom in 1852, the Missouri state supreme court held that it would no longer enforce the antislavery laws of other states and that Scott's residence on free soil did not change his status as a slave.

In a further effort to win Scott's freedom, his attorneys sought review by a federal circuit court in a lawsuit against Mrs. Emerson's brother and agent in the litigation, John Sanford of New York. (Sanford's name was misspelled as Sandford in the official records.) Since Sanford resided in another state than Scott, attorneys claimed that Scott's case fell within the federal court's diversity jurisdiction (jurisdiction over suits brought by citizens of different states). But their legal strategy raised a new issue: to bring a lawsuit in federal court, Scott had to show that he was a citizen. Sanford's attorneys countered that Negroes were not citizens in Missouri and therefore Scott had no standing to sue and the court lacked jurisdiction. The trial judge agreed that Scott's legal status depended on the law in Missouri, not his erstwhile residence in free territory, and a jury decided for Sanford.

Scott's lawyers next appealed to the Supreme Court, which included five southern Democrats, two northern Democrats, one northern Whig, and one Republican. During their oral arguments before the Court in February 1856, Sanford's attorneys raised an additional issue. They argued that not only was Scott a slave, not a citizen, but that he could not have become even temporarily a "freeman" by residing in a free territory because the Missouri Compromise was unconstitutional. That was a hotly debated political question sharply dividing the country, and the Court decided to hold the case over and hear rearguments in its next session.

On March 6, 1857, Chief Justice Roger Taney read from the bench his opinion for the Court: Scott lost. The chief justice held that Scott had no standing to sue in federal courts because he was not and could not be a citizen by virtue of the fact that he was a Negro and a slave. Taney proceeded to declare the antislavery provision of the Missouri Compromise unconstitutional. In sharply worded dissenting opinions, Justices John McLean and Benjamin Curtis took strong exception to the chief justice's sweeping opinion.

Chief Justice Taney's decision contributed to the ongoing struggle that erupted four years later in the Civil War. Despite the Court's ruling, Scott was soon freed by his owners, only to die a year and a half later. Two months after the ruling, Sanford also died, in an insane asylum. The constitutional effect of the ruling was also short lived. In 1862, Congress forbade slavery in all federal territories. Following the Civil War, the Thirteenth Amendment (1865), abolishing slavery, and the Fourteenth Amendment (1868) overturned Chief Justice Taney's ruling.

The Court's decision was seven to two, and the majority's opinion was announced by Chief Justice Taney. Justices Wayne, Nelson, Grier, Campbell, and Catron concurred; and Justices McLean and Curtis dissented.

☐ *Chief Justice TANEY delivered the opinion of the Court.*

[After reviewing the facts, Chief Justice TANEY first addressed the question of whether Scott was a citizen and entitled to bring his lawsuit.]

The question is simply this: can a negro, whose ancestors were imported into this country and sold as slaves, become a member of the political community formed and brought into existence by the Constitution of the United States, and as such become entitled to all the rights, and privileges, and immunities, guarantied by that instrument to the citizen. One of these rights is the privilege of suing in a court of the United States in the cases specified in the Constitution. . . .

The words "people of the United States" and "citizens" are synonymous terms, and mean the same thing. They both describe the political body, who, according to our republican institutions, form the sovereignty, and who hold the power and conduct the government through their representatives. They are what we familiarly call the "sovereign people," and every citizen is one of this people, and a constituent member of this sovereignty. The question before us is, whether the class of persons described in the plea in abatement compose a portion of this people, and are constituent members of this sovereignty. We think they are not, and that they are not included, and were not intended to be included, under the word "citizens" in the Constitution, and can, therefore, claim none of the rights and privileges which that instrument provides for and secures to citizens of the United States. On the contrary, they were at that time considered as a subordinate and inferior class of beings, who had been subjugated by the dominant race, and whether emancipated or not, yet remained subject to their authority, and had no rights or privileges but such as those who held the power and the government might choose to grant them.

It is not the province of the court to decide upon the justice or injustice, the policy or impolicy of these laws. The decision of that question belonged to the political or law-making power; to those who formed the sovereignty and framed the Constitution. The duty of the court is to interpret the instrument they have framed, with the best lights we can obtain on the subject, and to administer it as we find it, according to its true intent and meaning when it was adopted.

In discussing this question, we must not confound the rights of citizenship which a state may confer within its own limits, and the rights of citizenship as a member of the Union. It does not by any means follow, because he has all the rights and privileges of a citizen of a State, that he must be a citizen of the United States. He may have all the rights and privileges of the citizen of a State, and yet not be entitled to the rights and privileges of a citizen in any other State. For, previous to the adoption of the Constitution of the United States, every State had the undoubted right to confer on whomsoever it pleased the character of a citizen, and to endow him with all its rights. But this character, of course, was confined to the boundaries of the State, and gave him no rights or privileges in other States beyond those secured to him by the laws of nations and the comity of States. Nor have the several States surrendered the power of conferring these rights and privileges by adopting the Constitution of the United States. . . . The Constitution has conferred on Congress the right to establish an uniform rule of naturalization, and this right is evidently exclusive, and has always been held by this court to be so. Consequently, no State, since the adoption of the Constitution, can, by naturalizing an alien, invest him with the rights and privileges secured to a citizen of a State under the federal government, although, so far as the State alone was concerned, he would undoubtedly be entitled to the rights of a citizen, and clothed with all the rights and immunities which the Constitution and laws of the State attached to that character.

It is very clear, therefore, that no State can, by any Act or law of its own, passed, since the adoption of the Constitution, introduce a new member into the political community created by the Constitution of the United States. It cannot make him a member of this community by making him a member of its own. And for the same reason it cannot introduce any person, or description of persons, who were not intended to be embraced in this new political family, which the Constitution brought into existence, but were intended to be excluded from it. . . .

In the opinion of the court, the legislation and histories of the times, and the language used in the Declaration of Independence, show, that neither the class of persons who had been imported as slaves, nor their descendants, whether they had become free or not, were then acknowledged as a part of the people, nor intended to be included in the general words used in that memorable instrument.

It is difficult at this day to realize the state of public opinion in relation to that unfortunate race, which prevailed in the civilized and enlightened portions of the world at the time of the Declaration of Independence, and when the Constitution of the United States was framed and adopted. But the public history of every European nation displays it, in a manner too plain to be mistaken.

They had for more than a century before been regarded as beings of an inferior order; and altogether unfit to associate with the white race, either in social or political relations; and so far inferior, that they had no rights which the white man was bound to respect; and that the negro might justly and lawfully be reduced to slavery for his benefit. He was bought and sold, and treated as an ordinary article of merchandise and traffic, whenever a profit could be made by it. This opinion was at that time fixed and universal in the civilized portion of the white race. It was regarded as an axiom in morals as well as in politics, which no one thought of disputing, or supposed to be open to dispute; and men in every grade and position in society daily and habitually acted upon it in their private pursuits, as well as in matters of public concern, without doubting for a moment the correctness of this opinion. . . .

We refer to these historical facts for the purpose of showing the fixed opinions concerning that race, upon which the statesmen of that day spoke and acted. It is necessary to do this, in order to determine whether the general terms used in the Constitution of the United States, as to the rights of man and the rights of the people, was intended to include them, or to give to them or their posterity the benefit of any of its provisions.

The language of the Declaration of Independence is equally conclusive.

It begins by declaring that, "when in the course of human events it becomes necessary for one people to dissolve the political bands which have connected them with another, and to assume among the powers of the earth the separate and equal station to which the laws of nature and nature's God entitle them, a decent respect for the opinions of mankind requires that they should declare the causes which impel them to the separation."

It then proceeds to say: "We hold these truths to be self-evident: that all men are created equal; that they are endowed by their Creator with certain [un]alienable rights; that among them is life, liberty, and pursuit of happiness; that to secure these rights, governments are instituted, deriving their just powers from the consent of the governed."

The general words above quoted would seem to embrace the whole human family, and if they were used in a similar instrument at this day, would be so understood. But it is too clear for dispute, that the enslaved African race were not intended to be included, and formed no part of the people who framed and adopted this Declaration; for if the language, as understood in that day, would embrace them, the conduct of the distinguished men who framed the Declaration of Independence would have been utterly and flagrantly inconsistent with the principles they asserted; and instead of the sympathy of mankind, to which they so confidently appealed, they would have deserved and received universal rebuke and reprobation.

Yet the men who framed this Declaration were great men—high in literary acquirements—high in their sense of honor, and incapable of asserting principles inconsistent with those on which they were acting. They perfectly understood the meaning of the language they used, and how it would be understood by others; and they knew that it would not, in any part of the civilized world, be supposed to embrace the negro race....

This state of public opinion had undergone no change when the Constitution was adopted, as is equally evident from its provisions and language....

[T]here are two clauses in the Constitution which point directly and specifically to the negro race as a separate class of persons, and show clearly that they were not regarded as a portion of the people or citizens of the government then formed.

One of these clauses reserves to each of the thirteen States the right to import slaves until the year 1808, if it thinks proper. And the importation which it thus sanctions was unquestionably of persons of the race of which we are speaking, as the traffic in slaves in the United States had always been confined to them. And by the other provision the States pledge themselves to each other to maintain the right of property of the master, by delivering up to him any slave who may have escaped from his service, and be found within their respective territories. By the first above-mentioned clause, therefore, the right to purchase and hold this property is directly sanctioned and authorized for twenty years by the people who framed the Constitution. And by the second, they pledge themselves to maintain and uphold the right of the master in the manner specified, as long as the government they then formed should endure. And these two provisions show, conclusively, that neither the description of persons therein referred to, nor their descendants, were embraced in any of the other provisions of the Constitution; for certainly these two clauses were not intended to confer on them or their posterity the blessings of liberty, or any of the personal rights so carefully provided for the citizen....

[U]pon a full and careful consideration of the subject, the court is of opinion that, upon the facts stated in the plea in abatement, Dred Scott was not a citizen of Missouri within the meaning of the Constitution of the United States, and not entitled as such to sue in its courts; and, consequently, that the Circuit Court had no jurisdiction of the case, and that the judgment on the plea in abatement is erroneous. . . .

[Chief Justice TANEY then turned to the question of whether Scott remained a slave after his trip into the Louisiana Territory.]

The Act of Congress, upon which the plaintiff relies, declares that slavery and involuntary servitude, except as a punishment for crime, shall be forever prohibited in all that part of that territory ceded by France, under the name of Louisiana, which lies north of thirty-six degrees thirty minutes north latitude, and not included within the limits of Missouri. And the difficulty which meets us at the threshold of this part of the inquiry is, whether Congress was authorized to pass this law under any of the powers granted to it by the Constitution; for if the authority is not given by that instrument, it is the duty of this court to declare it void and inoperative, and incapable of conferring freedom upon one who is held as a slave under the laws of any one of the States. . . .

[T]he power of Congress over the person or property of a citizen can never be a mere discretionary power under our Constitution and form of government. The powers of the government and the rights and privileges of the citizen are regulated and plainly defined by the Constitution itself. And when the territory becomes a part of the United States, the Federal Government enters into possession in the character impressed upon it by those who created it. It enters upon it with its powers over the citizen strictly defined, and limited by the Constitution, from which it derives its own existence, and by virtue of which alone it continues to exist and act as a government and sovereignty. It has no power of any kind beyond it; and it cannot, when it enters a territory of the United States, put off its character, and assume discretionary or despotic powers which the Constitution has denied to it. It cannot create for itself a new character separated from the citizens of the United States, and the duties it owes them under the provisions of the Constitution. The territory being a part of the United States, the government and the citizen both enter it under the authority of the Constitution, with their respective rights defined and marked out; and the Federal Government can exercise no power over his person or property, beyond what that instrument confers, nor lawfully deny any right which it has reserved. . . .

For example, no one, we presume, will contend that Congress can make any law in a territory respecting the establishment of religion or the free exercise thereof, or abridging the freedom of speech or of the press, or the right of the people of the territory peaceably to assemble and to petition the government for the redress of grievances. . . .

These powers, and others in relation to rights of person, which it is not necessary here to enumerate, are, in express and positive terms, denied to the general government; and the rights of private property have been guarded with equal care. Thus the rights of property are united with the rights of person, and placed on the same ground by the fifth amendment to the Constitution, which provides that no person shall be deprived of life, liberty and property, without due process of law. And an Act of Congress which deprives a citizen of the United States of his liberty or property, merely because he came himself or brought his property into a particular Territory of the United States, and who had committed no offense against the laws, could hardly be dignified with the name of due process of law. . . .

Now, as we have already said in an earlier part of this opinion, upon a different point, the right of property in a slave is distinctly and expressly affirmed in the Constitution. The right to traffic in it, like an ordinary article of merchandise and property, was guaranteed to the citizens of the United States, in every State that might desire it, for twenty years. And the government in express terms is pledged to protect it in all future time, if the slave escapes from his owner. This is done in plain words—too plain to be misunderstood. And no word can be found in the Constitution which gives Congress a greater power over slave property, or which entitles property of that kind to less protection than property of any other description. The only power conferred is the power coupled with the duty of guarding and protecting the owner in his rights.

Upon these considerations, it is the opinion of the court that the Act of Congress which prohibited a citizen from holding and owning property of this kind in the territory of the United States north of the line therein mentioned, is not warranted by the Constitution, and is therefore void; and that neither Dred Scott himself, nor any of his family, were made free by being carried into this territory; even if they had been carried there by the owner, with the intention of becoming a permanent resident. . . .

[Finally, Chief Justice TANEY turned to whether Scott was made free by traveling to Illinois, a free state. He held that Scott's status was to be determined by Missouri law, and thus Scott remained a slave.]

☐ *Justice McLEAN, dissenting.*

Being born under our Constitution and laws, no naturalization is required, as one of foreign birth, to make [Scott] a citizen. The most general and appropriate definition of the term citizen is "a freeman." Being a freeman, and having his domicile in a State different from that of the defendant, he is a citizen within the act of Congress, and the courts of the Union are open to him. . . .

It has been argued that, if a colored person be made a citizen of a State, he cannot sue in the Federal court. The Constitution declares that Federal jurisdiction "may be exercised between citizens of different States," and the same is provided in the act of 1789. The above argument is properly met by saying that the Constitution was intended to be a practical instrument; and where its language is too plain to be misunderstood, the argument ends." . . .

In the argument, it was said that a colored citizen would not be an agreeable member of society. This is more a matter of taste than of law. Several of the States have admitted persons of color to the right of suffrage, and in this view have recognized them as citizens; and this has been done in the slave as well as the free States. On the question of citizenship, it must be admitted that we have not been very fastidious. Under the late treaty with Mexico, we have made citizens of all grades, combinations, and colors. The same was done in the admission of Louisiana and Florida. No one ever doubted, and no court ever held, that the people of these Territories did not become citizens under the treaty. They have exercised all the rights of citizens, without being naturalized under the acts of Congress. . . .

I will now consider the relation which the Federal Government bears to slavery in the States: Slavery is emphatically a State institution. In the ninth section of the first article of the Constitution, it is provided "that the migration or importation of such persons as any of the States now existing shall think proper to admit, shall not be prohibited by the Congress prior to the year 1808, but a tax or duty may be imposed on such importation, not exceeding ten dollars for each person." . . .

The provision in regard to the slave trade shows clearly that Congress considered slavery a State institution, to be continued and regulated by its individual sovereignty; and to conciliate that interest, the slave trade was continued twenty years, not as a general measure, but for the "benefit of such States as shall think proper to encourage it." . . .

The only connection which the Federal Government holds with slaves in a State, arises from that provision of the Constitution which declares that "No person held to service or labor in one State, under the laws thereof, escaping into another, shall, in consequence of any law or regulation therein, be discharged from such service or labor, but shall be delivered up, on claim of the party to whom such service or labor may be due."

This being a fundamental law of the Federal Government, it rests mainly for its execution, as has been held, on the judicial power of the Union; and so far as the rendition of fugitives from labor has become a subject of judicial action, the Federal obligation has been faithfully discharged.

In the formation of the Federal Constitution, care was taken to confer no power on the Federal Government to interfere with this institution in the States. In the provision respecting the slave trade, in fixing the ratio of representation, and providing for the reclamation of fugitives from labor, slaves were referred to as persons, and in no other respect are they considered in the Constitution.

We need not refer to the mercenary spirit which introduced the infamous traffic in slaves, to show the degradation of negro slavery in our country. This system was imposed upon our colonial settlements by the mother country, and it is due to truth to say that the commercial colonies and States were chiefly engaged in the traffic. But we know as a historical fact, that James Madison, that great and good man, a leading member in the Federal Convention, was solicitous to guard the language of that instrument so as not to convey the idea that there could be property in man.

I prefer the lights of Madison, Hamilton, and Jay, as a means of construing the Constitution in all its bearings, rather than to look behind that period, into a traffic which is now declared to be piracy, and punished with death by Christian nations. I do not like to draw the sources of our domestic relations from so dark a ground. Our independence was a great epoch in the history of freedom; and while I admit the Government was not made especially for the colored race, yet many of them were citizens of the New England States, and exercised the rights of suffrage when the Constitution was adopted, and it was not doubted by any intelligent person that its tendencies would greatly ameliorate their condition. . . .

The power of Congress to establish Territorial Governments, and to prohibit the introduction of slavery therein, is the next point to be considered. . . .

On the 13th of July, the [Northwest] Ordinance of 1787 was passed, "for the government of the United States territory northwest of the river

Ohio," with but one dissenting vote. This instrument provided there should be organized in the territory not less than three nor more than five States, designating their boundaries. It was passed while the Federal Convention was in session, about two months before the Constitution was adopted by the Convention. The members of the Convention must therefore have been well acquainted with the provisions of the Ordinance. It provided for a temporary Government, as initiatory to the formation of State Governments. Slavery was prohibited in the territory.

Can any one suppose that the eminent men of the Federal Convention could have overlooked or neglected a matter so vitally important to the country, in the organization of temporary Governments for the vast territory northwest of the river Ohio? In the 3d section of the 4th article of the Constitution, they did make provision for the admission of new States, the sale of the public lands, and the temporary Government of the territory. Without a temporary Government, new States could not have been formed, nor could the public lands have been sold. . . .

The sovereignty of the Federal Government extends to the entire limits of our territory. Should any foreign power invade our jurisdiction, it would be repelled. There is a law of Congress to punish our citizens for crimes committed in districts of country where there is no organized Government. Criminals are brought to certain Territories or States, designated in the law, for punishment. Death has been inflicted in Arkansas and in Missouri, on individuals, for murders committed beyond the limit of any organized Territory or State; and no one doubts that such a jurisdiction was rightfully exercised. If there be a right to acquire territory, there necessarily must be an implied power to govern it. When the military force of the Union shall conquer a country, may not Congress provide for the government of such country? This would be an implied power essential to the acquisition of new territory. This power has been exercised, without doubt of its constitutionality, over territory acquired by conquest and purchase.

And when there is a large district of country within the United States, and not within any State Government, if it be necessary to establish a temporary Government to carry out a power expressly vested in Congress— as the disposition of the public lands—may not such Government be instituted by Congress? How do we read the Constitution? Is it not a practical instrument? . . .

The prohibition of slavery north of thirty-six degrees thirty minutes, and of the State of Missouri, contained in the act admitting that State into the Union, was passed by a vote of 134, in the House of Representatives, to 42. Before Mr. Monroe signed the act, it was submitted by him to his Cabinet, and they held the restriction of slavery in a Territory to be within the constitutional powers of Congress. It would be singular, if in 1804 Congress had power to prohibit the introduction of slaves in Orleans Territory from any other part of the Union, under the penalty of freedom to the slave, if the same power, embodied in the Missouri compromise, could not be exercised in 1820. . . .

If Congress may establish a Territorial Government in the exercise of its discretion, it is a clear principle that a court cannot control that discretion. This being the case, I do not see on what ground the act is held to be void.

It did not purport to forfeit property, or take it for public purposes. It only prohibited slavery; in doing which, it followed the ordinance of 1787. . . .

I think the judgment of the court below should be reversed.

☐ *Justice CURTIS, dissenting.*

To determine whether any free persons, descended from Africans held in slavery, were citizens of the United States under the Confederation, and consequently at the time of the adoption of the Constitution of the United States, it is only necessary to know whether any such persons were citizens of either of the States under the Confederation, at the time of the adoption of the Constitution.

Of this there can be no doubt. At the time of the ratification of the Articles of Confederation, all free native-born inhabitants of the States of New Hampshire, Massachusetts, New York, New Jersey, and North Carolina, though descended from African slaves, were not only citizens of those States, but such of them as had the other necessary qualifications possessed the franchise of electors, on equal terms with other citizens. . . .

The fourth of the fundamental articles of the Confederation was as follows: "The free inhabitants of each of these States, paupers, vagabonds, and fugitives from justice, excepted, shall be entitled to all the privileges and immunities of free citizens in the several States." . . .

Did the Constitution of the United States deprive them or their descendants of citizenship?

That Constitution was ordained and established by the people of the United States, through the action, in each State, of those persons who were qualified by its laws to act thereon, in behalf of themselves and all other citizens of that State. In some of the States, as we have seen, colored persons were among those qualified by law to act on this subject. These colored persons were not only included in the body of "the people of the United States," by whom the Constitution was ordained and established, but in at least five of the States they had the power to act, and doubtless did act, by their suffrages, upon the question of its adoption. It would be strange, if we were to find in that instrument anything which deprived of their citizenship any part of the people of the United States who were among those by whom it was established.

I can find nothing in the Constitution which, *proprio vigore*, deprives of their citizenship any class of persons who were citizens of the United States at the time of its adoption, or who should be native-born citizens of any State after its adoption; nor any power enabling Congress to disfranchise persons born on the soil of any State, and entitled to citizenship of such State by its Constitution and laws. And my opinion is, that, under the Constitution of the United States, every free person born on the soil of a State, who is a citizen of that State by force of its Constitution or laws, is also a citizen of the United States. . . .

The conclusions at which I have arrived on this part of the case are:

First. The the free native-born citizens of each State are citizens of the United States.

Second. That as free colored persons born within some of the States are citizens of those States, such persons are also citizens of the United States.

Third. That every such citizen, residing in any State, has the right to sue and is liable to be used in the Federal courts, as a citizen of that State in which he resides.

Fourth. That as the plea to the jurisdiction in this case shows no facts, except that the plaintiff was of African descent, and his ancestors were sold as slaves, and as these facts are not inconsistent with his citizenship of the United States, and his residence in the State of Missouri, the plea to the jurisdiction was bad, and judgment of the Circuit Court overruling it was correct.

I dissent, therefore, from that part of the opinion of the majority of the court, in which it is held that a person of African descent cannot be a citizen of the United States; and I regret I must go further, and dissent both from what I deem their assumption of authority to examine the constitutionality of the act of Congress commonly called the Missouri compromise act, and the grounds and conclusions announced in their opinion. . . .

On what ground can it be denied that all valid laws of the United States, constitutionally enacted by Congress for the government of the Territory, rightfully extended over an officer of the United States and his servant who went into the Territory to remain there for an indefinite length of time, to take part in its civil or military affairs? They were not foreigners, coming from abroad. Dr. Emerson was a citizen of the country which had exclusive jurisdiction over the Territory; and not only a citizen, but he went there in a public capacity, in the service of the same sovereignty which made the laws. Whatever those laws might be, whether, of the kind denominated personal statutes, or not, so far as they were intended by the legislative will, constitutionally expressed, to operate on him and his servant, and on the relations between them, they had a rightful operation, and no other State or country can refuse to allow that those laws might rightfully operate on the plaintiff and his servant, because such a refusal would be a denial that the United States could, by laws constitutionally enacted, govern their own servants, residing on their own Territory, over which the United States had the exclusive control, and in respect to which they are an independent sovereign power. Whether the laws now in question were constitutionally enacted, I repeat once more, is a separate question. But, assuming that they were, and that they operated directly on the status of the plaintiff, I consider that no other State or country could question the rightful power of the United States so to legislate, or, consistently with the settled rules of international law, could refuse to recognise the effects of such legislation upon the status of their officers and servants, as valid everywhere. . . .

What, then, shall we say of the consent of the master, that the slave may contract a lawful marriage, attended with all the civil rights and duties which belong to that relation; that he may enter into a relation which none but a free man can assume—a relation which involves not only the rights and duties of the slave, but those of the other party to the contract, and of their descendants to the remotest generation? In my judgment, there can be no more effectual abandonment of the legal rights of a master over his slave, than by the consent of the master that the slave should enter into a contract of marriage, in a free State, attended by all the civil rights and obligations which belong to that condition. . . .

To avoid misapprehension on this important and difficult subject, I will state, distinctly, the conclusions at which I have arrived. They are:

First. The rules of international law respecting the emancipation of slaves, by the rightful operation of the laws of another State or country upon the status of the slave, while resident in such foreign State or country, are part of the common law of Missouri, and have not been abrogated by any statute law of that State.

Second. The laws of the United States, constitutionally enacted, which operated directly on and changed the status of a slave coming into the Territory of Wisconsin with his master, who went thither to reside for an indefinite length of time, in the performance of his duties as an officer of the United States, had a rightful operation on the status of the slave, and it is in conformity with the rules of international law that this change of status should be recognised everywhere.

Third. The laws of the United States, in operation in the Territory of Wisconsin at the time of the plaintiff's residence there, did act directly on the status of the plaintiff, and change his status to that of a free man.

Fourth. The plaintiff and his wife were capable of contracting, and, with the consent of Dr. Emerson, did contract a marriage in that Territory, valid its laws; and the validity of this marriage cannot be questioned in Missouri, save by showing that it was in fraud of the laws of that State, or of some right derived from them; which cannot be shown in this case, because the master consented to it.

Fifth. That the consent of the master that his slave, residing in a country which does not tolerate slavery, may enter into a lawful contract of marriage, attended with the civil rights and duties which belong to that condition, is an effectual act of emancipation. And the law does not enable Dr. Emerson, or any one claiming under him, to assert a title to the married persons as slaves, and thus destroy the obligation of the contract of marriage, and bastardize their issue, and reduce them to slavery. . . .

In my opinion, the judgment of the Circuit Court should be reversed, and the cause remanded for a new trial.

The Civil Rights Cases
109 U.S. 3, 3 S.Ct. 18 (1883)

At issue in five cases, coming from California, Kansas, Missouri, New Jersey, and Tennessee, which were consolidated and decided together, was the constitutionality of Congress's passage of the Civil Rights Act of 1875. That legislation made it a *federal* crime for owners and operators of any public accommodation—schools, churches, cemeteries, hotels, places of amusement, and common carriers—to "deny the full enjoyment of the accommodations thereof" because of race or religion. Each of the cases involved challenges to the enforcement of the law against innkeepers, theater owners, and a railroad company.

With only Justice John Marshall Harlan dissenting, Justice Joseph Bradley held for the Court that Congress had no authority under the Thirteenth and Fourteenth Amendments to enact the Civil Rights Act of 1875 and had intruded on the powers reserved to the states by the Tenth Amendment. Moreover, Justice Bradley narrowly read the Thirteenth Amendment to only abolish slavery, but not private racial discrimination, and limited the Fourteenth Amendment to bar only racial discrimination backed by state action. By contrast, Justice Harlan pointed out that the Court previously upheld Congress's power to regulate the behavior of private individuals—notably, when upholding fugitive slave laws requiring the return of slaves to their owners. Also, in his view racial discrimination was a badge of servitude abolished by the Thirteenth Amendment and a matter on which Congress could legislate when enforcing the Thirteenth and Fourteenth Amendments. As a result of the majority's ruling, racist attitudes were reinforced and the basis was laid for states to pass Jim Crow laws requiring the separate treatment of blacks and whites in public accommodations.

The Court's decision was eight to one, and the majority's opinion was announced by Justice Bradley. Justice Harlan dissented.

☐ *Justice BRADLEY delivered the opinion of the Court.*

Has Congress constitutional power to make [the Civil Rights Act of 1875]? Of course, no one will contend that the power to pass it was contained in the constitution before the adoption of the last three amendments. The power is sought, first, in the fourteenth amendment, and the views and arguments of distinguished senators, advanced while the law was under consideration, claiming authority to pass it by virtue of that amendment, are the principal arguments adduced in favor of the power. . . .

The first section of the fourteenth amendment,—which is the one relied on,—after declaring who shall be citizens of the United States, and of the several states, is prohibitory in its character, and prohibitory upon the states. It declares that "no state shall make or enforce any law which shall abridge the privileges or immunities of citizens of the United States; nor shall any state deprive any person of life, liberty, or property without due process of law; nor deny to any person within its jurisdiction the equal protection of the laws." It is state action of a particular character that is prohibited. Individual invasion of individual rights is not the subject-matter of the amendment. It has a deeper and broader scope. It nullifies and makes void all state legislation, and state action of every kind, which impairs the privileges and immunities of citizens of the United States, or which injures them in life, liberty, or property without due process of law, or which denies to any of them the equal protection of the laws. It not only does this, but, in order that the national will, thus declared, may not be a mere *brutum fulmen*, the last section of the amendment invests congress with power to enforce it by appropriate legislation. To enforce what? To enforce the prohibition. To adopt appropriate legislation for correcting the effects of such prohibited state law and state acts, and thus to render them effectually null, void, and innocuous. This is the legislative power conferred upon congress, and this is the whole of it. It does not invest congress with power to legislate upon subjects which are within the domain of state legislation; but to provide modes of relief against state legislation, or state action, of the kind referred to. It does not authorize congress to create a code of municipal law for the regulation of private rights; but to provide modes of redress against the operation of state laws, and the action of state officers, executive or judicial, when these are subversive of the fundamental rights specified in the amendment. Positive rights and privileges undoubtedly secured by the fourteenth amendment; but they are secured by way of prohibition against state laws and state proceedings affecting those rights and privileges, and power given to congress to legislate for the purpose of carrying such prohibition into effect; and such legislation must necessarily be predicated upon such supposed state laws or state proceedings, and be directed to the correction of their operation and effect. . . .

And so in the present case, until some state law has been passed, or some state action through its officers or agents has been taken, adverse to the rights of citizens sought to be protected by the fourteenth amendment, no legislation of the United States under said amendment, nor any proceeding under such legislation, can be called into activity, for the prohibitions of the amendment are against state laws and acts done under state authority. Of course, legislation may and should be provided in advance to meet the exigency when it arises, but it should be adapted to the mischief and wrong which the amendment was intended to provide against; and that is, state laws or state action of some kind adverse to the rights of the citizen secured by the amendment. . . . In fine, the legislation which congress is authorized to adopt in this behalf is not general legislation upon the rights of the citizen, but corrective legislation; that is, such as may be necessary and proper for counteracting such laws as the states may adopt or enforce, and which by the amendment they are prohibited from making or enforcing, or such acts and proceedings as the states may commit or take, and which by the amendment they are prohibited from committing or taking. It is not necessary for us to state, if we could, what legislation would be proper for congress to adopt. It is sufficient for us to examine whether the law in question is of that character.

An inspection of the law shows that it makes no reference whatever to any supposed or apprehended violation of the fourteenth amendment on the part of the states. It is not predicated on any such view. It proceeds *ex directo* to declare that certain acts committed by individuals shall be deemed offenses, and shall be prosecuted and punished by proceedings in the courts of the United States. It does not profess to be corrective of any constitutional wrong committed by the states; it does not make its operation to depend upon any such wrong committed. It applies equally to cases arising in states which have the justest laws respecting the personal rights of citizens, and whose authorities are ever ready to enforce such laws as to those which arise in states that may have violated the prohibition of the amendment. In other words, it steps into the domain of local jurisprudence, and lays down rules for the conduct of individuals in society towards each other, and imposes sanctions for the enforcement of those rules, without referring in any manner to any supposed action of the state or its authorities.

If this legislation is appropriate for enforcing the prohibitions of the amendment, it is difficult to see where it is to stop. Why may not congress, with equal show of authority, enact a code of laws for the enforcement and vindication of all rights of life, liberty, and property? If it is supposable that the states may deprive persons of life, liberty, and property without due process of law, (and the amendment itself does suppose this,) why should not congress proceed at once to prescribe due process of law for the protection of every one of these fundamental rights, in every possible case, as well as to prescribe equal privileges in inns, public conveyances, and theaters. The truth is that the implication of a power to legislate in this manner is based upon the assumption that if the states are forbidden to legislate or act in a particular way on a particular subject, and power is conferred upon congress to enforce the prohibition, this gives congress power to legislate generally upon that subject, and not merely power to provide modes of redress against such state legislation or action. The assumption is certainly unsound. It is repugnant to the tenth amendment of the constitution, which declares that powers not delegated to the United States by the constitution, nor prohibited by it to the states, are reserved to the states respectively or to the people. . . .

In this connection it is proper to state that civil rights, such as are guaranteed by the constitution against state aggression, cannot be impaired by the wrongful acts of individuals, unsupported by state authority in the shape of laws, customs, or judicial or executive proceedings. The wrongful act of an individual, unsupported by any such authority, is simply a private wrong, or a crime of that individual; an invasion of the rights of the injured party, it is true, whether they affect his person, his property, or his reputation; but if not sanctioned in some way by the state, or not done under state authority, his rights remain in full force, and may presumably be vindicated by resort to the laws of the state for redress. . . .

But the power of congress to adopt direct and primary, as distinguished from corrective, legislation on the subject in hand, is sought, in the second place, from the thirteenth amendment, which abolishes slavery. This amendment declares "that neither slavery, nor involuntary servitude, except as a punishment for crime, whereof the party shall have been duly convicted, shall exist within the United States, or any place subject to their jurisdiction;" and it gives congress power to enforce the amendment by appropriate legislation.

This amendment, as well as the fourteenth, is undoubtedly self-executing without any ancillary legislation, so far as its terms are applicable to any existing state of circumstances. By its own unaided force and effect it abolished slavery, and established universal freedom. Still, legislation may be necessary and proper to meet all the various cases and circumstances to be affected by it, and to prescribe proper modes of redress for its violation in letter or spirit. And such legislation may be primary and direct in its character; for the amendment is not a mere prohibition of state laws establishing or upholding slavery, but an absolute declaration that slavery or involuntary servitude shall not exist in any part of the United States. . . .

After giving to these questions all the consideration which their importance demands, we are forced to the conclusion that such an act of refusal has nothing to do with slavery or involuntary servitude, and that if it is violative of any right of the party, his redress is to be sought under the laws of the state; or, if those laws are adverse to his rights and do not protect him, his remedy will be found in the corrective legislation which congress has adopted, or may adopt, for counteracting the effect of state laws, or state action, prohibited by the fourteenth amendment. It would be running the slavery argument into the ground to make it apply to every act of discrimination which a person may see fit to make as to the guests he will entertain, or as to the people he will take into his coach or cab or car, or admit to his concert or theater, or deal with in other matters of intercourse or business. Innkeepers and public carriers, by the laws of all the states, so far as we are aware, are bound, to the extent of their facilities, to furnish proper accommodation to all unobjectionable persons who in good faith apply for them. If the laws themselves make any unjust discrimination, amenable to the prohibitions of the fourteenth amendment, congress has full power to afford a remedy under that amendment and in accordance with it. . . .

There were thousands of free colored people in this country before the abolition of slavery, enjoying all the essential rights of life, liberty, and property the same as white citizens; yet no one, at that time, thought that it was any invasion of their personal *status* as freemen because they were not admitted to all the privileges enjoyed by white citizens, or because they were subjected to discriminations in the enjoyment of accommodations in inns, public conveyances, and places of amusement. Mere discriminations on account of race or color were not regarded as badges of slavery. If, since that time, the enjoyment of equal rights in all these respects has become established by constitutional enactment, it is not by force of the thirteenth amendment, (which merely abolishes slavery,) but by force of the fourteenth and fifteenth amendments.

On the whole, we are of opinion that no countenance of authority for the passage of the law in question can be found in either the thirteenth or fourteenth amendment of the constitution; and no other ground of authority for its passage being suggested, it must necessarily be declared void, at least so far as its operation in the several states is concerned.

☐ *Justice HARLAN, dissenting.*

The opinion in these cases proceeds, as it seems to me, upon grounds entirely too narrow and artificial. The substance and spirit of the recent amendments of the constitution have been sacrificed by a subtle and ingenious verbal criticism. "It is not the words of the law but the internal sense of it that makes the law. The letter of the law is the body; the sense and reason of the law is the soul." Constitutional provisions, adopted in the interest of liberty, and for the purpose of securing, through national legislation, if need be, rights inhering in a state of freedom, and belonging to American citizenship, have been so construed as to defeat the ends the people desired to accomplish, which they attempted to accomplish, and which they supposed they had accomplished by changes in their fundamental law. By this I do not mean that the determination of these cases should have been materially controlled by considerations of mere expediency or policy. I mean only, in this form, to express an earnest conviction that the court has departed from the familiar rule requiring, in the interpretation of constitutional provisions, that full effect be given to the intent with which they were adopted. . . .

The thirteenth amendment, my brethren concede, did something more than to prohibit slavery as an *institution*, resting upon distinctions of race, and upheld by positive law. They admit that it established and decreed universal *civil freedom* throughout the United States. But did the freedom thus established involve nothing more than exemption from actual slavery? Was nothing more intended than to forbid one man from owning another as property? Was it the purpose of the nation simply to destroy the institution, and then remit the race, theretofore held in bondage, to the several states for such protection, in their civil rights, necessarily growing out of freedom, as those states, in their discretion, choose to provide? Were the states, against whose solemn protest the institution was destroyed, to be left perfectly free, so far as national interference was concerned, to make or allow discriminations against that race, as such, in the enjoyment of those fundamental rights that inhere in a state of freedom? . . .

That there are burdens and disabilities which constitute badges of slavery and servitude, and that the express power delegated to congress to enforce, by appropriate legislation, the thirteenth amendment, may be exerted by legislation of a direct and primary character, for the eradication, not simply of the institution, but of its badges and incidents, are propositions which ought to be deemed indisputable. They lie at the very foundation of the civil rights act of 1866. Whether that act was fully authorized by the thirteenth amendment alone, without the support which it afterwards received from the fourteenth amendment, after the adoption of which it was re-enacted with some additions, the court, in its opinion, says it is unnecessary to inquire. But I submit, with all respect to my brethren, that its constitutionality is conclusively shown by other portions of their opinion. It is expressly conceded by them that the thirteenth amendment established freedom; that there are burdens and disabilities, the necessary incidents of slavery, which constitute its substance and visible form; that congress, by the act of 1866, passed in view of the thirteenth amendment, before the fourteenth was adopted, undertook to remove certain burdens and disabilities, the necessary incidents of slavery, and to secure to all citizens of every race and color, and without regard to previous servitude, those fundamental rights which are the essence of civil freedom, namely, the same right to make and enforce contracts, to sue, be parties, give evidence, and to inherit, purchase, lease, sell, and convey property as is enjoyed by white citizens; that under the thirteenth amendment congress has to do with slavery and its incidents; and that legislation, so far as necessary or proper to eradicate all forms and incidents of slavery and involuntary servitude, may be direct and primary, operating upon the acts of individuals, whether sanctioned by state legislation or not. These propositions being conceded, it is impossible, as it seems to me, to question the constitutional validity of the civil rights act of 1866. I do not contend that the thirteenth amendment invests congress with authority, by legislation, to regulate the entire body of the civil rights which citizens enjoy, or may enjoy, in the several states. But I do hold that since slavery, as the court has repeatedly declared, was the moving or principal cause of the adoption of that amendment, and since that institution rested wholly upon the inferiority, as a race, of those held in bondage, their freedom necessarily involved immunity from, and protection against, all discrimination against them, because of their race, in respect of such civil rights as belong to freemen of other races. . . .

What has been said is sufficient to show that the power of congress under the thirteenth amendment is not necessarily restricted to legislation against slavery as an institution upheld by positive law, but may be exerted to the extent at least of protecting the race, so liberated, against discrimination, in respect of legal rights belonging to freemen, where such discrimination is based upon race. . . .

I also submit whether it can be said—in view of the doctrines of this court as announced in *Munn* v. *Illinois*, [94 U.S. 113 (1877)], that the management of places of public amusement is a purely private matter, with which government has no rightful concern. In the *Munn Case* the question was whether the state of Illinois could fix, by law, the maximum of charges for the storage of grain in certain warehouses in that state—the *private property of individual citizens*. . . .

The doctrines of *Munn* v. *Illinois* have never been modified by this court, and I am justified, upon the authority of that case, in saying that places of public amusement, conducted under the authority of the law, are clothed with a public interest, because used in a manner to make them of public consequence and to affect the community at large. The law may therefore regulate, to some extent, the mode in which they shall be conducted, and consequently the public have rights in respect of such places which may be vindicated by the law. It is consequently not a matter purely of private concern.

Congress has not, in these matters, entered the domain of state control and supervision. It does not assume to prescribe the general conditions and limitations under which inns, public conveyances, and places of public amusement shall be conducted or managed. It simply declares in effect that since the nation has established universal freedom in this country for all time, there shall be no discrimination, based merely upon race or color, in respect of the legal rights in the accommodations and advantages of public conveyances, inns, and places of public amusement.

I am of the opinion that such discrimination is a badge of servitude, the imposition of which congress may prevent under its power, through appropriate legislation, to enforce the thirteenth amendment; and consequently, without reference to its enlarged power under the fourteenth amendment, the act of March 1, 1875, is not, in my judgment, repugnant to the constitution.

It remains now to consider these cases with reference to the power congress has possessed since the adoption of the fourteenth amendment. . . .

[To begin,] an essential inquiry [is] what, if any, right, privilege, or immunity was given by the nation to colored persons when they were made citizens of the state in which they reside? Did the national grant of state citizenship to that race, of its own force, invest them with any rights, privileges, and immunities whatever? That they became entitled, upon the adoption of the fourteenth amendment, "to all privileges and immunities of citizens in the several states," within the meaning of section 2 of article 4 of the constitution, no one, I suppose, will for a moment question. What are the privileges and immunities to which, by that clause of the constitution, they became entitled? To this it may be answered, generally, upon the authority of the adjudged cases, that they are those which are fundamental in citizenship in a free government, "common to the citizens in the latter states under their constitutions and laws by virtue of their being citizens." Of that provision it has been said, with the approval of this court, that no other one in the constitution has tended so strongly to constitute the citizens of the United States one people. . . .

But what was secured to colored citizens of the United States—as between them and their respective states—by the grant to them of state citizenship? With what rights, privileges, or immunities did this grant from the nation invest them? There is one, if there be no others—exemption from race discrimination in respect of any civil right belonging to citizens of the white race in the same state. That, surely, is their constitutional privilege when within the jurisdiction of other states. And such must be their constitutional right, in their own state, unless the recent amendments be "splendid baubles," thrown out to delude those who deserved fair and generous treatment at the hands of the nation. Citizenship in this country necessarily imports equality of civil rights among citizens of every race in the same state. It is fundamental in American citizenship that, in respect of such rights, there shall be no discrimination by the state, or its officers, or by individuals, or corporations exercising public functions or authority, against any citizen because of his race or previous condition of servitude. . . .

Much light is thrown upon this part of the discussion by the language of this court in reference to the fifteenth amendment. In *U.S.* v. *Cruikshank*, [92 U.S. 542 (1876)], it was said:

> In *U.S.* v. *Reese*, 92 U.S. 214 [(1876)], we held that the fifteenth amendment has invested the citizens of the United States with a new constitutional right, which is exemption from discrimination in the exercise of the elective franchise on account of race, color, or previous condition of servitude. From this it appears that the right of suffrage is not a necessary attribute of national citizenship, but that exemption from discrimination in the exercise of that right on account of race, etc., is. The right to vote in the states comes from the states; but the right of exemption from the prohibited discrimination comes from the United States. The first has not been granted or secured by the constitution of the United States, but the last has been.

Here, in language at once clear and forcible, is stated the principle for which I contend. It can hardly be claimed that exemption from race discrimination, in respect of civil rights, against those to whom state citizenship was granted by the nation, is any less for the colored race a new constitutional right, derived from and secured by the national constitution, than is exemption from such discrimination in the exercise of the elective franchise. It cannot be that the latter is an attribute of national citizenship, while the other is not essential in national citizenship, or fundamental in state citizenship.

If, then, exemption from discrimination in respect of civil rights is a new constitutional right, secured by the grant of state citizenship to colored citizens of the United States, why may not the nation, by means of its own legislation of a primary direct character, guard, protect, and enforce that right? It is a right and privilege which the nation conferred. It did not come from the states in which those colored citizens reside. It has been the established doctrine of this court during all its history, accepted as vital to the national supremacy, that congress, in the absence of a positive delegation of power to the state legislatures, may by legislation enforce and protect any right derived from or created by the national constitution. . . .

But the court says that congress did not, in the act of 1866, assume, under the authority given by the thirteenth amendment, to adjust what may be called the social rights of men and races in the community. I agree that government has nothing to do with social, as distinguished from technically legal, rights of individuals. No government ever has brought, or ever can bring, its people into social intercourse against their wishes. Whether one person will permit or maintain social relations with another is a matter with which government has no concern. I agree that if one citizen chooses not to hold social intercourse with another, he is not and cannot be made amendable to the law for his conduct in that regard; for no legal right of a citizen is violated by the refusal of others to maintain merely social relations with him, even upon grounds of race. What I affirm is that no state, nor the officers of any state, nor any corporation or individual wielding power under state authority for the public benefit or the public convenience, can, consistently either with the freedom established by the fundamental law, or with that equality of civil rights which now belongs to every citizen, discriminate against freemen or citizens, in their civil rights, because of their race, or because they once labored under disabilities imposed upon them as a race. The rights which congress, by the act of 1875, endeavored to secure and protect are legal, not social, rights. The right, for instance, of a colored citizen to use the accommodations of a public highway upon the same terms as are permitted to white citizens is no more a social right than his right, under the law, to use the public streets of a city, or a town, or a turnpike road, or a public market, or a post-office, or his right to sit in a public building with others, of whatever race, for the purpose of hearing the political questions of the day discussed. . . .

Today it is the colored race which is denied, by corporations and individuals wielding public authority, rights fundamental in their freedom and citizenship. At some future time it may be some other race that will fall under the ban. If the constitutional amendments be enforced, according to the intent with which, as I conceive, they were adopted, there cannot be, in this republic, any class of human beings in practical subjection to another class, with power in the latter to dole out to the former just such privileges as they may choose to grant. The supreme law of the land has decreed that no authority shall be exercised in this country upon the basis of discrimination, in respect of civil rights, against freemen and citizens because of their race, color, or previous condition of servitude. To that decree—for the due enforcement of which, by appropriate legislation, congress has been invested with express power—every one must bow, whatever may have been, or whatever now are, his individual views as to the wisdom or policy, either of the recent changes in the fundamental law, or of the legislation which has been enacted to give them effect.

For the reasons stated I feel constrained to withhold my assent to the opinion of the Court.

Plessy v. Ferguson
163 U.S. 537, 3 S.CT. 18 (1896)

Four years after the Supreme Court struck down the Civil Rights Act of 1875 in the *Civil Rights Cases* (1883) (see excerpt above), Florida enacted the first "Jim Crow" law, requiring separate but equal facilities for blacks and whites in railway passenger cars. Louisiana and other states in the Deep South followed with similar laws. Blacks were embittered by the passage of these laws, but the Court adapted the Constitution to support racial discrimination by white legislative majorities. In *Louisville, New Orleans & Texas Pacific Railroad v. Mississippi*, 133 U.S. 587 (1890), the Court ruled that segregated railroad passenger cars traveling in intrastate commerce did not interfere with Congress's power to regulate interstate commerce under the commerce clause.

Louisiana's "Jim Crow" law was challenged in a test case brought by Homer Plessy, who was one-eighth black. When he boarded a railroad train in New Orleans, which was headed for Covington, Louisiana, he refused to sit in the car reserved for "Colored Only" and sat in one reserved for whites instead. He was arrested, convicted, and appealed to the Supreme Court. Plessy's attorneys contended that Louisiana's law violated the Thirteenth and Fourteenth Amendments.

The Supreme Court rejected Plessy's arguments. Note the sharply different interpretations of the Constitution and social attitudes in the majority's opinion by Justice Henry Brown and in the sole dissenting opinion by Justice John Harlan. Whereas Justice Brown dismisses the claim the state's action violates the Thirteenth Amendment as "too clear for argument," Justice Harlan has no doubt that compulsory racial segregation imposed precisely the kind of badge of servitude that the amendment aimed to outlaw. Justice Brown's treatment of the Fourteenth Amendment claim is also far from cogent. Although allowing that the amendment "was undoubtedly to enforce the absolute equality of the two races before the law," he adds that "in the nature of things it could not have been intended to abolish distinctions based on color." For the Court's majority, racial segregation was not discriminatory and did not "necessarily imply the inferiority of either race to the other," but rather a reasonable exercise of state police power "for the promotion of the public good, and not for the annoyance or oppression of a particular class." By contrast, Justice Harlan conceived of all forms of racial discrimination to constitute invidious discrimination under the Fourteenth Amendment.

The Court's decision was seven to one, and the majority's opinion was announced by Justice Brown, with Justice Brewer not participating. Justice Harlan delivered a dissenting opinion.

☐ *Justice BROWN delivered the opinion of the Court.*

This case turns upon the constitutionality of an act of the general assembly of the state of Louisiana, passed in 1890, providing for separate railway carriages for the white and colored races. . . .

The constitutionality of this act is attacked upon the ground that it conflicts both with the thirteenth amendment of the constitution, abolishing slavery, and the fourteenth amendment, which prohibits certain restrictive legislation on the part of the states.

1. That it does not conflict with the thirteenth amendment, which abolished slavery and involuntary servitude, except as a punishment for crime, is too clear for argument. Slavery implies involuntary servitude,—a state of bondage; the ownership of mankind as a chattel, or, at least, the control of the labor and services of one man for the benefit of another, and the absence of a legal right to the disposal of his own person, property, and services. . . .

2. . . . The object of the [Fourteenth] Amendment was undoubtedly to enforce the absolute equality of the two races before the law, but, in the nature of things, it could not have been intended to abolish distinctions based upon color, or to enforce social, as distinguished from political, equality, or a commingling of the two races upon terms unsatisfactory to either. Laws permitting, and even requiring, their separation, in places where they are liable to be brought into contact, do not necessarily imply the inferiority of either race to the other, and have been generally, if not universally, recognized as within the competency of the state legislatures in the exercise of their police power. The most common instance of this is connected with the establishment of separate schools for white and colored children, which have been held to be a valid exercise of the legislative power even by courts of states where the political rights of the colored race have been longest and most earnestly enforced. . . .

In this connection, it is also suggested by the learned counsel for the plaintiff in error that the same argument that will justify the state legislature in requiring railways to provide separate accommodations for the two races will also authorize them to require separate cars to be provided for people whose hair is of a certain color, or who are aliens, or who belong to certain nationalities, or to enact laws requiring colored people to walk upon one side of the street, and white people upon the other, or requiring white men's houses to be painted white, and colored men's black, or their vehicles or business signs to be of different colors, upon the theory that one side of the street is as good as the other, or that a house or vehicle of one color is as good as one of another color. The reply to all this is that every exercise of the police power must be reasonable, and extend only to such laws as are enacted in good faith for the promotion of the public good, and not for the annoyance or oppression of a particular class. . . .

So far, then, as a conflict with the fourteenth amendment is concerned, the case reduces itself to the question whether the statute of Louisiana is a reasonable regulation, and with respect to this there must necessarily be a large discretion on the part of the legislature. In determining the question of reasonableness, it is at liberty to act with reference to the established usages, customs, and traditions of the people, and with a view to the promotion of their comfort, and the preservation of the public peace and good order. Gauged by this standard, we cannot say that a law which authorizes or even requires the separation of the two races in public conveyances is unreasonable, or more obnoxious to the fourteenth amendment than the acts of congress requiring separate schools for colored children in the District of Columbia, the constitutionality of which does not seem to have been questioned, or the corresponding acts of state legislatures.

We consider the underlying fallacy of the plaintiff's argument to consist in the assumption that the enforced separation of the two races stamps the colored race with a badge of inferiority. If this be so, it is not by reason of anything found in the act, but solely because the colored race chooses to put that construction upon it. The argument necessarily assumes that if, as has been more than once the case, and is not unlikely to be so again, the colored race should become the dominant power in the state legislature, and should enact a law in precisely similar terms, it would thereby relegate the white race to an inferior position. We imagine that the white race, at least, would not acquiesce in this assumption. The argument also assumes that social prejudices may be overcome by legislation, and that equal rights cannot be secured to the negro except by an enforced commingling of the two races. We cannot accept this proposition. If the two races are to meet upon terms of social equality, it must be the result of natural affinities, a mutual appreciation of each other's merits, and a voluntary consent of individuals. . . .

Legislation is powerless to eradicate racial instincts, or to abolish distinctions based upon physical differences, and the attempt to do so can only result in accentuating the difficulties of the present situation. If the civil and political rights of both races be equal, one cannot be inferior to the other civilly or politically. If one race be inferior to the other socially, the constitution of the United States cannot put them upon the same plane.

☐ *Justice HARLAN, dissenting.*

In respect of civil rights, common to all citizens, the constitution of the United States does not, I think, permit any public authority to know the race of those entitled to be protected in the enjoyment of such rights. Every true man has pride of race, and under appropriate circumstances, when the rights of others, his equals before the law, are not to be affected, it is his privilege to express such pride and to take such action based upon it as to him seems proper. But I deny that any legislative body or judicial tribunal may have regard to the race of citizens when the civil rights of those citizens are involved. Indeed, such legislation as that here in question is inconsistent not only with that equality of rights which pertains to citizenship, national and state, but with the personal liberty enjoyed by every one within the United States. . . .

It was said in argument that the statute of Louisiana does not discriminate against either race, but prescribes a rule applicable alike to white and colored citizens. But this argument does not meet the difficulty. Every one knows that the statute in question had its origin in the purpose, not so much to exclude white persons from railroad cars occupied by blacks, as to exclude colored people from coaches occupied by or assigned to white persons. . . .

It is one thing for railroad carriers to furnish, or to be required by law to furnish, equal accommodations for all whom they are under a legal duty to carry. It is quite another thing for government to forbid citizens of the white and black races from traveling in the same public conveyance, and to punish officers of railroad companies for permitting persons of the two races to occupy the same passenger coach. If a state can prescribe, as a rule of civil conduct, that whites and blacks shall not travel as passengers in the same railroad coach, why may it not so regulate the use of the streets of its cities and towns as to compel white citizens to keep on one side of a street, and black citizens to keep on the other? Why may it not, upon like grounds, punish whites and blacks who ride together in street cars or in open vehicles on a public road or street? Why may it not require sheriffs to assign whites to one side of a court room, and blacks to the other? And why may it not also prohibit the commingling of the two races in the galleries of legislative halls or in public assemblages convened for the consideration of the political questions of the day? Further, if this statute of Louisiana is consistent with the personal liberty of citizens, why may not the state require the separation in railroad coaches of native and naturalized citizens of the United States, or of Protestants and Roman Catholics?

The answer given at the argument to these questions was that regulations of the kind they suggest would be unreasonable, and could not, therefore, stand before the law. Is it meant that the determination of questions of legislative power depends upon the inquiry whether the statute whose validity is questioned is, in the judgment of the courts, a reasonable one, taking all the circumstances into consideration? A statute may be unreasonable merely because a sound public policy forbade its enactment. But I do not understand that the courts have anything to do with the policy or expediency of legislation. . . .

The white race deems itself to be the dominant race in this country. And so it is, in prestige, in achievements, in education, in wealth, and in power. So, I doubt not, it will continue to be for all time, if it remains true to its great heritage, and holds fast to the principles of constitutional liberty. But in view of the constitution, in the eye of the law, there is in this country no superior, dominant, ruling class of citizens. There is no caste here. Our constitution is color-blind, and neither knows nor tolerates classes among citizens. In respect of civil rights, all citizens are equal before the law. The humblest is the peer of the most powerful. The law regards man as man, and takes no account of his surroundings or of his color when his civil rights as guaranteed by the supreme law of the land are involved. It is therefore to be regretted that this high tribunal, the final expositor of the fundamental law of the land, has reached the conclusion that it is competent for a state to regulate the enjoyment by citizens of their civil rights solely upon the basis of race.

In my opinion, the judgment this day rendered will, in time, prove to be quite as pernicious as the decision made by this tribunal in the *Dred Scott Case*. . . .

The present decision, it may well be apprehended, will not only stimulate aggressions, more or less brutal and irritating, upon the admitted rights of colored citizens, but will encourage the belief that it is possible, by means of state enactments, to defeat the beneficent purposes which the people of the United States had in view when they adopted the recent amendments of the constitution, by one of which the blacks of this country were made citizens of the United States and of the states in which they respectively reside, and whose privileges and immunities, as citizens, the states are forbidden to abridge. Sixty millions of whites are in no danger from the presence here of eight millions of blacks. The destinies of the two races, in this country, are indissolubly linked together, and the interests of both require that the common government of all shall not permit the seeds of race hate to be planted under the sanction of law. What can more certainly arouse race hate, what more certainly create and perpetuate a feeling of distrust between these races, than state enactments which, in fact, proceed on the ground that colored citizens are so inferior and degraded that they cannot be allowed to sit in public coaches occupied by white citizens? That, as all will admit, is the real meaning of such legislation as was enacted in Louisiana. . . .

I am of opinion that the statute of Louisiana is inconsistent with the personal liberty of citizens, white and black, in that state, and hostile to both the spirit and letter of the constitution of the United States. If laws of like character should be enacted in the several states of the Union, the effect would be in the highest degree mischievous. Slavery, as an institution tolerated by law, would, it is true, have disappeared from our country; but there would remain a power in the states, by sinister legislation, to interfere with the full enjoyment of the blessings of freedom, to regulate civil rights, common to all citizens, upon the basis of race, and to place in a condition of legal inferiority a large body of American citizens, now constituting a part of the political community, called the "People of the United States," for whom, and by whom through representatives, our government is administered. Such a system is inconsistent with the guaranty given by the constitution to each state of a republican form of government, and may be stricken down by congressional action, or by the courts in the discharge of their solemn duty to maintain the supreme law of the land, anything in the constitution or laws of any state to the contrary notwithstanding.

For the reason stated, I am constrained to withhold my assent from the opinion.

Shelley v. Kraemer

334 U.S. 1, 68 S.Ct. 836 (1948)

Louis Kraemer and his wife sought and obtained an injunction against J. D. Shelley, a black, from taking possession of a parcel of land in their St. Louis, Missouri, neighborhood. Shelley bought the land from one of Kraemer's neighbors without knowing that it was covered by a restrictive covenant barring owners from selling their land to members of "the Negro or Mongolian race." A state trial court found the covenant technically faulty but was reversed on appeal by the Missouri State Supreme Court, which held that the covenant did not deny Shelley's constitutional rights.

Shelley's appeal to the Supreme Court became a test case for the NAACP Legal Defense Fund and was argued by the NAACP Legal Defense Fund's leading counsel, Charles Houston and Thurgood Marshall. The NAACP sought to persuade the Court to reconsider an earlier ruling, *Corrigan v. Buckley*, 271 U.S. 323 (1926), upholding restrictive covenants. Eighteen *amicus curiae* briefs, including one by Democratic president Harry Truman's solicitor general, supported the NAACP's position.

The Court unanimously held that judicial enforcement of restrictive covenants constituted state action and ran afoul of the Fourteenth Amendment. But note that Chief Justice Fred Vinson neither overrules *Corrigan* nor explains why and how far the state action doctrine extends to bar private racial discrimination not forbidden by the states.

The Court's decision was unanimous; the opinion was announced by Chief Justice Vinson, with Justices Reed, Jackson, and Rutledge not participating.

☐ *Chief Justice VINSON delivered the opinion of the Court.*

These cases present for our consideration questions relating to the validity of court enforcement of private agreements, generally described as restrictive covenants, which have as their purpose the exclusion of persons of designated race or color from the ownership or occupancy of real property. Basic constitutional issues of obvious importance have been raised. . . .

It is well, at the outset, to scrutinize the terms of the restrictive agreements involved in these cases. In the Missouri case, the covenant declares that no part of the affected property shall be "occupied by any person not of the Caucasian race, it being intended hereby to restrict the use of said property . . . against the occupancy as owners or tenants of any portion of said property for resident or other purpose by people of the Negro or Mongolian Race." Not only does the restriction seek to proscribe use and occupancy of the affected properties by members of the excluded class, but as construed by the Missouri courts, the agreement requires that title of any person who uses his property in violation of the restriction shall be divested. . . .

It should be observed that these covenants do not seek to proscribe any particular use of the affected properties. Use of the properties for residential occupancy, as such, is not forbidden. The restrictions of these agreements, rather, are directed toward a designated class of persons and seek to determine who may and who may not own or make use of the properties for residential purposes. The excluded class is defined wholly in terms of race or color; "simply that and nothing more."

It cannot be doubted that among the civil rights intended to be protected from discriminatory state action by the Fourteenth Amendment are the rights to acquire, enjoy, own and dispose of property. Equality in the enjoyment of property rights was regarded by the framers of that Amendment as an essential pre-condition to the realization of other basic civil rights and liberties which the Amendment was intended to guarantee. Thus, § 1978 of the Revised Statutes, derived from § 1 of the Civil Rights Act of 1866 which was enacted by Congress while the Fourteenth Amendment was also under consideration, provides:

> All citizens of the United States shall have the same right, in every State and Territory, as is enjoyed by white citizens thereof to inherit, purchase, lease, sell, hold, and convey real and personal property." . . .

It is likewise clear that restrictions on the right of occupancy of the sort sought to be created by the private agreements in these cases could not be squared with the requirements of the Fourteenth Amendment if imposed by state statute or local ordinance. . . .

But the present cases do not involve action by state legislatures or city councils. Here the particular patterns of discrimination and the areas in which the restrictions are to operate, are determined, in the first instance, by the terms of agreements among private individuals. Participation of the State consists in the enforcement of the restrictions so defined. The crucial issue with which we are here confronted is whether this distinction removes these cases from the operation of the prohibitory provisions of the Fourteenth Amendment.

Since the decision of this Court in the *Civil Rights Cases*, 1883 109 U.S. 3, the principle has become firmly embedded in our constitutional law that the action inhibited by the first section of the Fourteenth Amendment is only such action as may fairly be said to be that of the States. That Amendment erects no shield against merely private conduct, however discriminatory or wrongful.

We conclude, therefore, that the restrictive agreements standing alone cannot be regarded as a violation of any rights guaranteed to petitioners by the Fourteenth Amendment. So long as the purposes of those agreements are effectuated by voluntary adherence to their terms, it would appear clear that there has been no action by the State and the provisions of the Amendment have not been violated. . . .

But here there was more. These are cases in which the purposes of the agreements were secured only by judicial enforcement by state courts of the restrictive teams of the agreement. . . .

That the action of state courts and of judicial officers in their official capacities is to be regarded as action of the State within the meaning of the Fourteenth Amendment, is a proposition which has long been established by decisions of this Court. . . .

We hold that in granting judicial enforcement of the restrictive agreements in these cases, the States have denied petitioners the equal protection of the laws and that, therefore, the action of the state courts cannot stand. We have noted that freedom from discrimination by the States in the enjoyment of property rights was among the basic objectives sought to be effectuated by the framers of the Fourteenth Amendment. That such discrimination has occurred in these cases is clear.

■ CONSTITUTIONAL HISTORY

A Chronology of the Civil Rights Movement and the Court

1909   The National Association for the Advancement of Colored People (NAACP) is founded to protest various forms of racial discrimination, to lobby Congress to enact antilynching laws, and participate in "test cases" challenging practices of racial discrimination.

1932   In a widely publicized case, involving protests at the national capital over the conviction of nine black boys accused of raping a white girl and tried before an all-white jury without the assistance of an attorney in Scottsboro, Alabama, the Court holds that the "Scottsboro Boys" were denied due process and must be given the assistance of counsel in *Powell v. Alabama*, 287 U.S. 32 (1932) (excerpted in ch. 9).

1938   The NAACP finances and supports a challenge to Missouri's law that denies blacks admission to its state law school but provides funding for qualified blacks to attend law schools in other states. *Missouri ex rel. Gaines v. Canada*, 305 U.S. 337 (1938), holds that Missouri's law violates the Fourteenth Amendment guarantee of the equal protection of the law.

1938   The litigation branch of the NAACP is broken off into the NAACP Legal Defense and Educational Fund, Inc., (LDF) and pursues a litigation strategy to persuade the Supreme Court to strike down the doctrine of separate but equal.

1941   A. Philip Randolph, head of the Brotherhood of Sleeping Car Porters, founds the March on Washington Movement to protest discriminatory employment practices in the war industry.

1942   The Congress of Racial Equality (CORE) is founded by pacifists.

1947   CORE initiates the Journey for Reconciliation, sending integrated activists into the South to protest segregation on interstate travel; activists are beaten and arrested.

1948   *Shelley v. Kraemer*, 334 U.S. 1 (1948) (excerpted in Ch. 12), rules that restrictive covenants, barring the sale of property to blacks and other minorities, are unconstitutional. President Harry Truman issues an executive order to desegregate the U.S. armed forces.

1950   The NAACP-LDF wins two major victories in its struggle to overturn the doctrine of separate but equal in public education. *Sweatt v. Painter*, 339 U.S. 629 (1950), and *McLaurin v. Oklahoma State Regents*, 339 U.S. 637 (1950), hold that Texas's separate law school for blacks, and Oklahoma's denial of admission of blacks into its university graduate school program violate the Fourteenth Amendment.

1951   A terrorist bomb kills Henry Tyson Moore, president of the NAACP Florida chapter.

1953   Blacks boycott buses in Baton Rouge, Louisiana.

1954   *Brown v. Board of Education of Topeka, Kansas*, and companion cases, including *Bolling v. Sharpe* (excerpted in Ch. 12), hold that the doctrine of separate but equal is inapplicable to primary and secondary public schools.

1955   *Brown II* (excerpted in Ch. 12) rules that desegregation of public school must proceed with "all deliberate speed." Emmett Till, a 14-year-old, and two other NAACP activists are murdered in Mississippi. The Montgomery, Alabama, boycott of segregated buses begins.

1956   The bus boycott in Montgomery ends. Members of Congress issue the Southern Manifesto (excerpted in Ch. 2) denouncing the ruling in *Brown v. Board of Education*. The White Citizens Council, a middle-class group, is formed to resist desegregation.

1957   The Southern Christian Leadership Conference (SCLC) is founded. The Civil Rights Act of 1957 creates the U.S. Commission on Civil Rights.

1958   *Cooper v. Aaron* (excerpted in Ch. 12) reaffirms the ruling in *Brown*, and President Dwight D. Eisenhower orders federal troops into Little Rock, Arkansas; the "Little Rock Nine" desegregates the Central High School in Little Rock, Arkansas. A number of southern states try to stop the NAACP from bringing lawsuits to force school districts to desegregate by holding that as an out-of-state corporation it could not bring lawsuits in the state. When the NAACP challenged that, Alabama sought the disclosure of the NAACP's membership lists. In *NAACP v. Alabama* (excerpted in Ch. 5), the Court held that the membership lists were protected by the First Amendment guarantee for freedom of association.

1960   The Student Nonviolent Coordinating Committee (SNCC) is founded.

1961   CORE initiates Freedom Rides into the Deep South to resist the segregation in interstate public accommodations. CORE members are beaten and buses burned.

1962   SNCC and CORE activists begin a civil rights campaign in Albany, Georgia, and are met with violence and resistance from local authorities.

1963   SCLC begins a protest movement in Birmingham, Alabama. Over 200,000 assemble with Martin Luther King, Jr., for a historic March on Washington, D.C. King and other ministers apply for a parade permit to hold a march on Good Friday and Easter Sunday but are denied. When they announce plans to proceed, Birmingham officials obtain a court-ordered injunction against the demonstration. The demonstration is nonetheless held, and King and others are arrested, jailed, and found in contempt of court; subsequently the contempt citation is upheld in *Walker v. City of Birmingham*, 388 U.S. 307 (1967). Weeks later the 16th Street Baptist Church is bombed in Birmingham, killing four young girls and injuring others. Medgar Evers, an NAACP leader in Mississippi, is assassinated in his driveway.

1964   Congress enacts the Civil Rights Act of 1964, which is immediately challenged and upheld by the Court in *Heart of Atlanta Motel, Inc. v. United States* and *Katzenbach v. McClung* (excerpted in Vol. 1, Ch. 6). A libel suit against the *New York Times* by a Montgomery, Alabama police commissioner for mistakes in an ad, "Heed Their Rising Voices," soliciting funds for the civil rights movement, results in a landmark ruling in *The New York Times Co. v. Sullivan* (excerpted in Ch. 5). The Mississippi Freedom Summer initiates a grassroots-campaign to expand civil rights.

1965   A voting rights march is held in Selma, Alabama. The Voting Rights Act, barring poll taxes, literacy tests, and other means denying blacks voting rights, is passed. Unrest erupts in south central Los Angeles, popularly known as the Watts Riot.

1966   The SNCC and CORE call for Black Power. The Black Panther Party for Self-Defense is formed in Oakland, California, and the NAACP and the Urban League denounce the Black Power movement. *Brown v. Louisiana*, 383 U.S. 131 (1966), holds that the First Amendment protects the symbolic speech of a group of black students who are arrested for standing silently in a "whites-only" library to protest segregation.

1967   *Loving v. Virginia*, 388 U.S. 1 (1967), strikes down miscegenation laws, barring interracial marriages.

1968   Martin Luther King, Jr., is assassinated and urban unrest and riots take place in over 100 cities. In the last ruling of the Warren Court, *Green v. New Kent County School Board*, 391 U.S. 430 (1968), holds that lower courts should examine "every facet of school operations" in order to achieve integration, including student assignments, faculty, staff, transportation, extracurricular activity opportunities, and school facilities. Republican Richard Nixon wins the 1968 presidential election, after campaigning on a Southern Strategy to win the votes of white Southern Democratic voters based on opposition to the Court's rulings on desegregation and promises to appoint only "strict constructionists" and those opposed to "judicial activism" to the federal judiciary.

B | *Racial Discrimination in Education*

The process of dismantling a century-old system of segregated schools was long and often violent, and could not be achieved by simple judicial decree. At the turn of the twentieth century, in *Cummings v. Richmond County Board of Education*, 175 U.S. 528 (1899), the Fuller Court upheld a Georgia school board's decision to close its all-black high school, because it needed the buildings for an all-black elementary school. Writing for a unanimous Court, Justice Harlan, who had dissented in the *Civil Rights Cases* and *Plessy v. Ferguson*, stressed that public schools were a subject of state, not federal, control. The White Court (1910–1921) and Taft Court (1921–1930) repeatedly avoided the issue of segregated schools.[1]

Not until the Hughes Court (1930–1941) was there a suggestion that racially segregated schools might be constitutionally suspect. In *Missouri ex rel. Gaines v. Canada*, 305 U.S. 337 (1938), Chief Justice Hughes struck down a portion of Missouri's law that denied blacks admission to its law school but provided funding for blacks to attend law schools in other states. Lloyd Gaines, a black citizen of Missouri, qualified for admission into the University of Missouri's law school and argued that as a taxpayer he had a right to attend the law school. By a seven-to-two vote (with Justices McReynolds and Butler dissenting), the Hughes Court held that the equal protection clause was violated because Missouri failed to provide any law school for blacks. Instead, it simply shifted its responsibility to other states. Far from seriously questioning the constitutionality of the separate but equal doctrine as applied to education, Chief Justice Hughes emphasized that states must furnish "equal facilities in separate schools." As a result of the Court's ruling, Missouri established a separate all-black law school at its all-black university, Lincoln University.

The National Association for the Advancement of Colored People (NAACP) financed and argued Gaines's case before the Supreme Court. Encouraged by its small victory, the NAACP mounted a litigation campaign to bring down segregated schools. The NAACP's strategy was twofold. First, it sought to ensure that states in fact provided *equal* educational facilities. Second, it aimed to persuade the Court that "separate but equal" educational facilities were inherently unequal.

A decade after *Gaines*, the NAACP won a first step toward desegregation. In 1948, along with *Shelley v. Kraemer* (excerpted in Section A), in an unsigned *per curiam* opinion, the Vinson Court opinion ordered Oklahoma to provide a qualified black woman with an equal education in the state's law school.[2] Two years later, the NAACP had two more victories. Both rulings were unanimously decided and handed down by Chief Justice Vinson.

In *Sweatt v. Painter*, 339 U.S. 629 (1950), the Court ordered the admission of H. M. Sweatt, a black man, into the University of Texas law school. Sweatt refused to go to the state's separate law school for blacks. And he persuaded the Court that that law school was inferior, and therefore *unequal*, not only in terms of physical facilities but also in the "reputation of the faculty, experience of the administration, position and influence of the alumni, standing in the community, tradition and prestige." In *McLaurin v. Oklahoma State Regents*, 339 U.S. 637 (1950), the Vinson Court went even further. McLaurin, a black, was admitted into the University of Oklahoma's School of Education to work for a Ph.D. But the state legislature mandated that McLaurin, the only black at the university, be treated on a segregated basis; that is, in classes he sat separately from whites, used a special table in the school's library, and

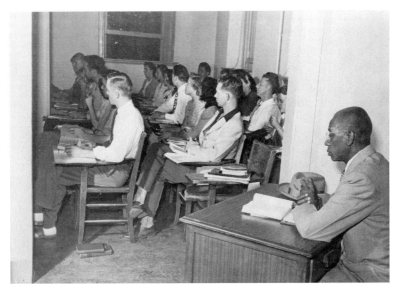

George McLaurin, segregated and required to sit outside of his classroom at the University of Oklahoma in 1948. In *McLaurin v. Oklahoma*, 339 U.S. 637 (1950), the Court held that segregation *within* institutions of higher education was unconstitutional. On the same day, the Court handed down *Sweat v. Painter*, 339 U.S. 629 (1950), holding that Texas's creation of a law school for blacks, instead of admitting them into the University of Texas School of Law at Austin, was unconstitutional and that the Fourteenth Amendment proscribes segregation in *separate institutions*, because of intangible factors such as the number of faculty, the size of the library, and alumni connections, that rendered them unequal. Both decisions undermined, without overruling, the doctrine of "separate but equal" facilities in higher education and set the stage for the landmark ruling on school desegregation in *Brown v. Board of Education of Topeka, Kansas* (1954). (Photo Source: Bettmann/Corbis.)

ate at a designated table at different times from whites in the school cafeteria. McLaurin contended that this treatment denied him the equal protection of the laws, and the Court agreed. In both cases, the Vinson Court acknowledged the intangible elements in education and concluded that separate but equal facilities, at least in higher education, were not equal. But the Court stopped short of overturning the separate but equal doctrine.

The NAACP had prepared the basis for the Court's striking down racially segregated public schools. But when it brought several cases challenging dual educational systems for blacks and whites in 1951, there was no clear indication that the Vinson Court would continue to press ahead. *Sweatt* and *McLaurin* involved only higher education and affected a relatively small number of blacks. Yet they ignited political controversy and strong opposition in the South. The Court knew that striking down segregated primary and secondary schools would affect millions of people, that overturning an educational system in place for close to a hundred years would invite widespread opposition; see Justice Jackson's unpublished memorandum concerning *Brown v. Board of Education of Topeka, Kansas* (excerpted in this section).

Brown v. Board of Education of Topeka, Kansas (1954) (see excerpt below) handed down three years after arriving on the Court's docket and in the first year of Chief Justice Earl Warren's tenure, marked a turning point for the Court and the country. That unanimous ruling striking down segregated public schools was the culmination and the beginning of new political struggles. Along with *Brown I, Bolling v. Sharpe* (1954) (see excerpt below) struck down segregated schools in the District of Columbia. The Fourteenth Amendment only forbids states from denying the equal protection of the laws, and the District of Columbia is under the control of the federal government. In an opinion that would come to have major significance for later rulings on racial and nonracial discrimination, Chief Justice Warren construed the Fifth Amendment's due process clause to incorporate the Fourteenth Amendment's equal protection guarantee and apply it to the federal government.

In *Brown* and *Bolling* the Warren Court did not expressly overrule *Plessy*'s doctrine of separate but equal, nor was anything said about segregation in other public accommodations—hotels, restaurants, and the like. Neither did the Court provide immediate remedial relief. The Court's unanimous rulings were achieved only at the cost of compromise among the justices in the face of certain resistance to their ruling. In order to minimize some of the anticipated opposition, *Brown* was carried over to another term for reargument on the question of remedies—how soon should desegregation take place and what kind of order should the Court issue? One year later in *Brown v. Board of Education of Topeka, Kansas* (*Brown II*) (1955) (see excerpt below), the Warren Court issued its mandate for states and local school boards to proceed "with all deliberate speed" in dismantling segregated schools.

Opposition to the Warren Court's rulings led to bitter, sometimes violent confrontations. In 1956, nineteen U.S. senators and eighty-two members of the House of Representatives denounced *Brown* as unconstitutional in a "Southern Manifesto" (excerpted in Ch. 2). The Republican administration of President Dwight D. Eisenhower did little to enforce compliance with *Brown*. The Warren Court, nevertheless, stood firmly behind its ruling, as registered in the controversy over *Cooper v. Aaron* (1958) (see excerpt below). In subsequent decisions, the Warren Court reaffirmed that school boards had a positive duty to desegregate. In *Griffin v. County School Board of Prince Edward County*, 391 U.S. 430 (1968), for example, the Fourteenth Amendment was interpreted to forbid school boards from closing all public schools rather than desegregating them.[3] Still, given the massive resistance toward *Brown*, the Warren Court effectively placed the burden on lower federal courts to oversee its implementation.[4]

Ten years after *Brown* and massive resistence and continuing litigation, Justice Black complained, "There has been entirely too much deliberation and not enough speed" in complying with *Brown*. "The time for mere 'deliberate speed' has run out."[5] *Brown*'s mandate amounted to a moral appeal and an invitation for delay. At the beginning of the school year in 1964, President Johnson was apprised of the piecemeal progress and continuing resistance:

> *Arkansas*: Desegregation expanded in schools in Little Rock and Fort Smith. About 870 Negroes reported in previously white schools, compared to 390 last year. Twenty-one districts desegregated, compared to 13 last year.

> *Florida*: Four counties integrated, bringing to 21 the number admitting Negroes (State has 67 counties). No trouble. Estimated 8,000 Negroes attending all-white schools.

> *Mississippi: Biloxi*—Seventeen Negro children attended integrated classes in four previously all-white elementary schools, after 10 years of angry resistance. *Canton*—Nineteen Negro students attempted to enroll in the all-white high school but left quietly when rejected by school officials. Civil rights workers said earlier they would not oppose school officials if the youngsters were turned away, but would follow with court action later.

> *Virginia*: Virginia will have 25 newly desegregated districts this year—including Prince Edward County [which had previously closed rather than desegregate its schools]—making 80 of 128 in the State with some integration. About 6,000 Negroes are attending once-white schools.[6]

With no federal leadership, implementation of *Brown* was deliberately slow and uneven. Ruby Martin, an attorney for the U.S. Commission on Civil Rights in the early 1960s, recalls that "the work of the lawyers from 1954 to 1964 resulted in two percent of the Negro kids in the Southern states attending schools with white students."[7] The Department of Justice had little role in ending school segregation before the passage of the Civil Rights Act of 1964. Even after the Department of Justice assumed a role in enforcing school desegregation, little attention was initially given to areas outside of the South or to problems other than ending *de jure* segregation—segregation enforced by laws prohibiting the integration of public schools. The Department of Justice paid almost no attention to *de facto* segregation due to socioeconomic conditions, such as housing patterns, in the North and West. Eventually, the Department of Health, Education and Welfare (HEW) was given responsibility for ending segregated schools. It had authority to issue guidelines and review plans for integration. More important, HEW had the power to cut off federal funding if school districts refused to submit or comply with desegregation plans.

By the mid-1960s the Department of Justice and HEW had assumed leadership in implementing *Brown*. Nevertheless, it took time to build records and evidence of segregation in northern and western school districts, and then to challenge local authorities in the courts. Not until the summer of 1968 did the outgoing Johnson administration initiate the first school desegregation cases in the North and West and try to achieve the national coverage that the Court envisioned in *Brown*. By the end of the decade, the Court was growing impatient. In Justice Black's words, "There is no longer the slightest excuse, reason, or justification for further postponement of the time when every public school system in the United States will be a unitary one."[8] Progress was made, but the Court and the country were also changing.

In Chief Justice Burger's first year on the Court, a brief *per curiam* opinion was handed down in *Alexander v. Holmes County Board of Education*, 396 U.S. 19 (1969). The Court ordered the Fifth Circuit Court of Appeals to deny further requests for delay from southern school districts in ending dual systems of public education and emphasized that the "standard allowing 'all deliberate speed' for desegregation is no longer constitutionally permissible." The message in *Alexander*, like that in *Brown*, remained ambiguous. Justice Thurgood Marshall could not win unanimity on finally setting a cutoff date for school desegregation. Justice Black threatened a dissenting opinion, protesting that "all deliberate speed" connoted delay, not speed. "The duty of this Court and of the others," Black implored, "is too simple to require perpetual litigation and deliberation. That duty is to extirpate all racial discrimination from our system of public schools NOW." But on the bench less than four months, Burger vigorously opposed setting any final cutoff date for desegregation. Justice Brennan sought consensus, yet agreement could not be reached on a more precise order than for proceeding with desegregation here and now. *Alexander*, Justice White lamented in an unpublished memo, "neither says the order is to be entered now, within six months or even with deliberate speed." "Hugo," he added, "is convinced that a mistake was made in 1954–1955 with respect to the deliberate speed formula. I am beginning to understand how mistakes like that happen. Nevertheless, I join, expecting the Court of Appeals to make sure that the shortcomings of this order never come to light."[9]

After two decades the problems of implementing and achieving compliance with *Brown* persisted; some schools remained segregated. Litigation by the NAACP and other civil rights groups forced change, but it was piecemeal, costly, and modest. The judiciary alone could not achieve desegregation. Evasion and resistance were encouraged by the reluctance of presidents and Congress to enforce the mandate. Enforcement and implementation required the cooperation and coordination of all three branches.

But by the 1970s and 1980s, the political controversy touched off by *Brown* primarily revolved around lower courts' ordering of gerrymandered school district lines and the busing of schoolchildren to achieve racial balance and integrated schools. Although *Brown*'s barebones decree ended up encouraging evasion and continued litigation, over the years *Brown*'s mandate was transformed from one of ending racially separated dual school systems into a mandate for *integrated* public schools—a mandate that some members of the Warren Court would never have agreed to in *Brown*.

The Burger Court thus faced the task of providing guidance for lower federal courts and how far they could go in ordering integrated public schools. The Court's two major rulings on the use of busing to achieve school segregation came in *Swann v. Charlotte-Mecklenberg Board of Education* (1971) (excerpted below) and *Milliken v. Bradley* (1974) (excerpted below). In *Swann* Chief Justice Burger established that where all-black schools exist because of present or past *de jure* discrimination, lower courts were to presume intentional segregation. In such situations, the Court upheld court-ordered busing of schoolchildren to achieve integration. But Chief Justice Burger stressed that courts were not to seek exact racial balance in their desegregation orders. Writing for a bare majority in *Milliken*, Chief Justice Burger underscored that the equal protection clause does not reach *de facto* school segregation resulting from housing patterns, and lower courts may not order busing as a remedy for *de facto* segregation where there is no evidence of an "intent" by school boards to discriminate. Throughout the 1970s and 1980s the Court reviewed numerous challenges to court-ordered busing. In the 1980s the Reagan administration strongly opposed the use of busing to achieve integrated schools. But when the administration asked the Court to reconsider its ruling in *Swann*, the Court unanimously declined to do so in *Metropolitan County Board of Education of Nashville v. Kelley*, 459 U.S. 1183 (1983).

Almost forty years after the watershed school desegregation ruling in *Brown v. Board of Education*, there remained about five hundred school desegregation cases in lower federal courts around the country. Most involved either challenges by local school boards to court-ordered remedial plans for achieving and maintaining integrated public schools

"Separate but equal" in West Memphis, Tennessee, in the early 1950s. (*Ed Clark, Life Magazine, Time Inc.*)

or challenges by blacks to changes in school board policies that they claim will perpetuate the vestiges of segregation. At issue are complex questions involving when and how school systems become fully integrated, or "unitary" and free from the vestiges of segregation. Lower courts, moreover, differed over how much proof school boards must show in demonstrating that present *de facto* racial isolation in school districts is unrelated to past *de jure* segregation, as well as what other conditions constitute "vestiges" of prior segregation.

Despite conflicts and confusion in the lower federal courts over when desegregation remedies and judicial supervision should end, for more than a decade the Court provided little guidance. Indeed, the Burger Court declined to review a major case dealing with the fundamentals of school desegregation in the 1980s. But the Rehnquist Court signaled a willingness to tackle the vexing issues of judicial supervision of school districts' implementation of and compliance with *Brown's* mandate in the 1990s. In the 1989 term, a bare majority of the Court upheld the authority of federal judges to order a school board to raise taxes in order to pay for a desegregation plan. Chief Justice Rehnquist and Justices O'Connor and Scalia, however, joined Justice Kennedy's sharp dissenting opinion in that case, *Missouri v. Jenkins*, 495 U.S. 33 (1990) (*Jenkins I*).

The Rehnquist Court also carried over for several terms a number of school desegregation cases, including one appeal by the school board in Topeka, Kansas, which is an offspring of the protracted litigation stemming from the original 1954 ruling in *Brown*. Initially, without Justice Souter's participation, in *Board of Education of Oklahoma City Public Schools v. Dowell*, 498 U.S. 237 (1991), a bare majority held that school districts that were previously required by law to eliminate racial segregation could end the forced busing of students in favor of neighborhood schools, even though that entailed a return to a system of schools attended overwhelmingly by either black or white students.

Writing for the majority in *Dowell*, Chief Justice Rehnquist held that federal judges should end supervision of previously segregated public schools if court-ordered desegregation plans had eliminated "the vestiges of past discrimination" and insisted that the Fourteenth Amendment does not apply to racially isolated schools that are no longer a product of state-imposed segregation. Accordingly, school districts that once intentionally segregated may achieve unitary status, despite the fact that some schools remain overwhelmingly black or white, if (1) they have complied with judicial desegregation orders over a reasonable period of time, (2) they are not likely to return to their former ways, and (3) they have to the extent practicable eliminated "vestiges" of prior discrimination in the operation of their schools. In the chief justice's words:

> [School desegregation] decrees . . . are not intended to operate in perpetuity. Local control over the education of children allows citizens to participate in decisionmaking, and allows innovation so that school programs can fit local needs. . . . Dissolving a desegregation decree after the local authorities have operated in compliance with it for a reasonable period of time properly recognizes that "necessary concern for the important values of local control of public school systems dictates that a federal court's regulatory control of such systems not extend beyond the time required to remedy the effects of past intentional discrimination." . . .
>
> In considering whether the vestiges of *de jure* segregation had been eliminated as far as practicable, the District Court should look not only at student assignments, but "to every facet of school operations—faculty, staff, transportation, extra-curricular activities and facilities." *Green*.

Dissenting Justice Marshall, joined by Justices Blackmun and Stevens, however, took a widely different view of *Brown*'s legacy and the "vestiges" of segregation in public schools. Notably, he would have held that the Oklahoma City school district had not achieved integration and that the persistence of racially identifiable schools necessarily established that the original constitutional violation had not been remedied. In his impassioned dissent, Justice Marshall observed that

> Oklahoma gained statehood in 1907. For the next 65 years, the Oklahoma City School Board maintained segregated schools—initially relying on laws requiring dual school systems; thereafter, by exploiting residential segregation that had been created by legally enforced restrictive covenants. In 1972—18 years after this Court first found segregated schools unconstitutional—a federal court finally interrupted this cycle, enjoining the Oklahoma City School Board to implement a specific plan for achieving actual desegregation of its schools.

> The practical question now before us is whether, 13 years after that injunction was imposed, the same School Board should have been allowed to return many of its elementary schools to their former one-race status. The majority today suggests that 13 years of desegregation was enough. . . .

> By focusing heavily on present and future compliance with the Equal Protection Clause, the majority's standard ignores how the stigmatic harm identified in *Brown I* can persist even after the State ceases actively to enforce segregation. It was not enough in *Green*, for example, for the school district to withdraw its own enforcement of segregation, leaving it up to individual children and their families to "choose" which school to attend. For it was clear under the circumstances that these choices would be shaped by and perpetuate the state-created message of racial inferiority associated with the school district's historical involvement in segregation. In sum, our school-desegregation jurisprudence establishes that the *effects* of past discrimination remain chargeable to the school district regardless of its lack of continued enforcement of segregation, and the remedial decree is required until those effects have been finally eliminated. . . . In a district with a history of state-sponsored school segregation, racial separation, in my view, *remains* inherently unequal.

Dowell, nonetheless, provided little guidance for lower courts and the hundreds of school districts seeking to regain complete autonomy and to escape judicial supervision. Both the majority and the dissenters reaffirmed the holding in *Green v. New Kent County School Board*, 391 U.S. 430 (1968), that lower courts should examine "every facet of school operations," including student assignments, faculty, staff, transportation, extracurricular activities, and facilities. But *Dowell* left unclear the most important issues: whether and how school districts must show that presently racially isolated schools are not related to past intentional discrimination, and what other kinds of conditions may be considered "vestiges" of past *de jure* segregation.

Barely one month after deciding *Dowell* the Rehnquist Court agreed further to address the controversy over judicial supervision of remedial desegregation plans in *Freeman v. Pitts*, 503 U.S. 467 (1992) (excerpted below). Since Justice Thomas had not yet been confirmed by the time the Court heard oral arguments, he did not participate in the Court's decision. Although unanimous in their decision, the justices were not of one mind on how quickly or on what basis lower courts should halt their desegregation efforts. Justice Kennedy's opinion for the Court represented a rough compromise on the closing of the *Brown* era. Kennedy held that lower courts may withdraw from supervising discrete categories of school operations, as identified in *Green*, once school districts show compliance with desegregation orders. Lower courts, moreover, need not wait for a period of years before doing so, nor await desegregation in all areas of a school system before they disengage. Note, however, that Kennedy's opinion did not go far enough for Justice Scalia, who in a concurrence urged an immediate end to all judicial supervision of schools that no longer intentionally discriminate. At the same time, Kennedy's opinion appeared to go too far for Justices Blackmun, Stevens, O'Connor, and Souter. They countered in separate concurrences that lower courts should undertake a probing analysis before abandoning judicial supervision.

Dowell and *Freeman* thus chart a new course, not a dramatic reversal, pointing to a new period of litigation—a period not unlike that immediately after *Brown* but in which lower courts gradually move to relinquish, rather than assert, control over public schools. Along with *Freeman v. Pitts*, the Court also decided *United States v. Fordice*, 505 U.S. 717 (1992) (excerpted below). Whereas *Dowell* and *Freeman* dealt with efforts to achieve integrated primary and secondary public schools, *Fordice* gave the Court the opportunity to revisit, after more than forty years, whether it is enough for colleges and universities simply to end past *de jure* racially discriminatory admissions policies, or whether they must do more than that in order to be free from the vestiges of discrimination. Mississippi's colleges and universities were strictly segregated until a court ordered the admission of James Meredith to the University of Mississippi in 1962. Yet, over two decades later in 1985–1986 approximately 99 percent of the state's white college students were enrolled in historically all-white institutions, while 71 percent of the black students attended historically all-black schools.

Writing for the Court in *Fordice*, Justice White found that Mississippi's admission policies perpetuated the existence of racially isolated colleges and universities. Although symbolic in reaffirming the principles of *Brown*, *Fordice*'s impact is considerably less than that of *Freeman*, because it provides guidance only for courts reviewing challenges to instituions in the fifteen states that once had *de jure* segregated schools, whereas courts supervising integration efforts in hundreds of cases involving primary and secondary schools will look to *Freeman* for guidance.

Finally, the Court continued to grapple with the issue of guidelines for lower courts withdrawing from efforts to force greater integration in public schools in *Missouri v. Jenkins*, 515 U.S. 70 (1995) (*Jenkins II*). Although not laying down new guidelines, a bare majority reiterated its view that lower courts should disengage from desegregation efforts. Writing for the Court, Chief Justice Rehnquist held that a federal district court had exceeded its remedial powers in ordering the state to (1) fund salary increases for virtually all teachers and staff within the Kansas City, Missouri, School District (KCMSD); and (2) to continue to fund remedial "quality education" programs because student achievement scores were still "at or below national norms at many grade levels." In order to eliminate the vestiges of past discrimination and to make the KCMSD's schools, which have over 90 percent black student enrollments, more attractive to white students in surrounding suburbs, the district court also created a magnet school district with expanded educational opportunities and facilities. However, drawing on *Milliken v. Bradley*, 418 U.S. 717 (1974) (excerpted below), Chief Justice Rehnquist ruled that the "*inter*district goal [of encouraging further integration through magnet schools and greater funding] is beyond the scope of the *intra*district violation" of prior racial discrimination. The chief justice also rejected the lower court's use of educational test scores as a legitimate measure of the progress of integration. In remanding the case back to the lower court to determine whether judicial supervision of the school district should be terminated, the chief justice further admonished, "The district court must bear in mind that its end purpose is not only to remedy the violation to the extent practicable, but also to restore state and local authorities to the control of a school system that is operating in compliance with the Constitution."

By contrast, the four dissenters—Justices Souter, Stevens, Ginsburg, and Breyer—countered that the majority had overreached in ruling on issues such as the use of student achievement scores, and firmly rejected the majority's conclusion that lower courts possess no authority to order improvements in school districts so as to make them more attractive to white students. While also joining Justice Souter's opinion for the dissenters, Justice Ginsburg added a few words of her own in a separate dissent. "Given the deep, inglorious history of segregation in Missouri," in her words, "to curtail desegregation at this time and in this manner is an action at once too swift and too soon."

NOTES

1. See *Berea College v. Kentucky*, 211 U.S. 45 (1908); and *Gong Lum v. Rice*, 275 U.S. 78 (1927).

2. See *Spiuel v. Oklahoma*, 322 U.S. 631 (1948); and *Fisher v. Hurst*, 333 U.S. 147 (1948).

3. For other Warren Court rulings, see *Goss v. Board of Education of City of Knoxville*, 373 U.S. 683 (1963) (striking down a transfer plan allowing blacks to go to formally segregated schools); *Green v. County School Board of New Kent County, Virginia*, 391 U.S. 430 (1968) (striking down a freedom of choice plan for desegregation, where no white students attended black schools); and *Monroe v. Board of Commissioners of the City of Jackson, Texas*, 391 U.S. 450 (1968). In *United States v. Montgomery County Board of Education*, 395 U.S. 225 (1969), the Court upheld a lower court's order that schools with fewer than twelve teachers have at least one of a different race and that schools with twelve or more teachers have one teacher of a different race for every six faculty and staff persons.

4. For a fine study of the role of lower federal court judges in implementing *Brown* and the resistance they faced, see Jack Peltason, *Fifty-eight Lonely Men* (New York: Harcourt, Brace & World, 1961).

5. *Griffin v. Prince Edward County School Board*, 377 U.S. 218 (1964).

6. "Memorandum, School Openings and Desegregation," Lee White Papers, Box 5, Johnson Presidential Library.

7. Ruby Martin, Oral History Interview, Johnson Presidential Library.

8. *Alexander v. Holmes County Board of Education*, 396 U.S. 1218 (1969).

9. All quotations in this paragraph are from the justice's memo in John M. Harlan Papers, Boxes 487, 565 and 606, Seeley G. Mudd Library, Princeton University; and William J. Brennan Papers, Box 218, Library of Congress.

SELECTED BIBLIOGRAPHY

Armor, David. *Forced Justice: School Desegregation and the Law*. New York: Oxford University Press, 1995.

Bass, Jack. *Unlikely Heroes*. New York: Simon & Schuster, 1981.

Bell, Derrick. *Silent Covenants: Brown v. Board of Education and the Unfulfilled Hopes for Racial Reform*. New York: Oxford University Press, 2004.

Cottol, Robert, Diamond, Raymond, and Ware, Leland B. *Brown v. Board of Education: Caste, Culture, and the Constitution*. Lawrence: University Press of Kansas, 2004.

Cushman, Clare, and Urofsky, Melvin. *Black, White, and Brown: The Landmark School Desegregation Case*. Washington, DC: C.Q. Press, 2004.

Klarman, Michael. *From Jim Crow to Civil Rights*. New York: Oxford University Press, 2004.

Kluger, Richard. *Simple Justice*. New York: Alfred Knopf, 1976.

Landsberg, Brian K. *Enforcing Civil Rights: Race Discrimination and the Department of Justice*. Lawrence: University Press of Kansas, 1997.

Ogletree, Charles. *All Deliberate Speed*. New York: W. W. Norton, 2004.

Orfield, Gary, and Ashkinaze, Carole. *The Closing Door: Conservative Policy and Black Opportunity*. Chicago: University of Chicago Press, 1991.

Orfield, Gary, and Eaton, Susan. *Dismantling Desegregation: The Quiet Reversal of Brown v. Board of Education*. New York: The New Press, 1996.

Patterson, James. *Brown v. Board of Education: A Civil Rights Milestone and Its Troubled History*. New York: Oxford University Press, 2001.

Peltason, Jack W. *Fifty-eight Lonely Men: Southern Federal Judges and School Desegregation*. New York: Harcourt, Brace & World, 1961.

Samuels, Albert L. *Is Separate Unequal? United States v. Fordice*. Lawrence: University Press of Kansas, 2004.

Sarat, Austin, ed. *Race, Law, and Culture: Reflections on Brown v. Board of Education*. New York: Oxford University Press, 1997.

Schwartz, Bernard. *Swann's Way: The School Busing Case and the Supreme Court*. New York: Oxford University Press, 1980.

Tushnet, Mark V. *The NAACP's Legal Strategy against Segregated Education, 1925–1950*. Chapel Hill: University of North Carolina Press, 1988.

Wasby, Stephen. *Race Relations Litigation in an Age of Complexity*. Charlottesville: University Press of Virginia, 1995.

Wilson, Paul. *A Time to Lose: Representing Kansas*. Lawrence: University Press of Kansas, 1995.

Brown v. Board of Education of Topeka, Kansas (Brown I)
347 U.S. 483, 74 S.Ct. 686 (1954)

This case challenging the constitutionality of racially segregated public schools arrived on the Supreme Court's docket in 1951 and was consolidated with three other cases (from Delaware, South Carolina, and Virginia) and another, *Bolling v. Sharpe* (see excerpt below), attacking the federal government's segregated school system in the District of Columbia. On such a politically explosive issue, Justice Tom Clark recalled, the Court wanted "to get a national coverage, rather than a sectional one."

Oral arguments were heard in December 1952. Instead of the decision coming down as expected in the spring, however, the Court decided to hear rearguments in its next term. The Vinson Court was split and deeply troubled by the prospect of white southern opposition to its striking down racially segregated public schools. Justice Felix Frankfurter persuaded his colleagues to carry the cases over to the next term because 1952 was an election year. "When you have a major social political issue of this magnitude," timing and public reactions are important considerations, and, Frankfurter told a law clerk, "we do not think this is the time to decide it." By holding the cases over, the Court was able to receive the views in an *amicus curiae* brief of the incoming administration of Republican President Dwight Eisenhower.

Rearguments were scheduled for early November 1953. But then came an unexpected turn of events: Chief Justice Fred Vinson died suddenly of a heart attack in the summer, and Eisenhower promptly named as his successor, Earl Warren. Warren, a popular governor of California and that state's favorite-son candidate for the Republican party's 1952 presidential nomination, had impressed Eisenhower as having "unimpeachable integrity," "middle of the road views," and a "splendid record during his years of active law work" as a state attorney general.

Rearguments were, again, put off until December, at which time the new chief justice sat back and listened to the arguments for and against ending segregated schools. At the justices' private conference, though, Warren did two strategic things. First, he firmly expressed his conviction that racially segregated schools denied blacks their rights under the Fourteenth Amendment. Second, because a majority of the justices appeared to support his position, Warren proposed that no vote be taken until the case was fully discussed and considered by all. No formal vote was taken until mid-February.

Chief Justice Warren's opinion for the Court is short and to the point; he wanted a brief opinion that could be printed in newspapers so every citizen could read the decision. Warren also sought a unanimous ruling because *Brown* would inevitably spark widespread resistance, and unanimity might help undercut some of the anticipated opposition. Notably, if *Brown* were decided when it first arrived, the vote would probably have been six to three or even five to four. Vinson was still chief justice and Justice Jackson's notes of conference discussions indicate that Justice Reed would uphold segregation as constitutional, as Vinson might have. Justices Clark and Jackson were also inclined to let segregated schools stand. Yet Warren and Frankfurter managed to persuade all of the justices to join the ruling. At the last minute, Warren got Jackson, who was in the hospital recovering from a heart attack, to suppress a potential concurring opinion (see p. 1401). Jackson had a practice of writing memorandums on cases, with a view to clarifying his thinking and bargaining with the others, and then often withholding their publication when the Court's final draft opinion came along. But as Justice Burton noted in his diary, Warren did a "magnificent job in getting a unanimous Court (This would have been impossible a year ago—probably 6 to 3 with the Chief Justice [Vinson] one of the dissenters)."

☐ *Chief Justice WARREN delivered the opinion of the Court.*

In each of the cases, minors of the Negro race, through their legal representatives, seek the aid of the courts in obtaining admission to the public schools of their community on a nonsegregated basis. In each instance, they have been denied admission to schools attended by white children under laws requiring or permitting segregation according to race. This segregation was alleged to deprive the plaintiffs of the equal protection of the laws under the Fourteenth Amendment. . . .

The plaintiffs contend that segregated public schools are not "equal" and cannot be made "equal," and that hence they are deprived of the equal protection of the laws. Because of the obvious importance of the question presented, the Court took jurisdiction. Argument was heard in the 1952 Term, and reargument was heard this Term on certain questions propounded by the Court.

Reargument was largely devoted to the circumstances surrounding the adoption of the Fourteenth Amendment in 1868. It covered exhaustively consideration of the Amendment in Congress, ratification by the states, then existing practices in racial segregation, and the views of proponents and opponents of the Amendment. This discussion and our own investigation convince us that, although these sources cast some light, it is not enough to resolve the problem with which we are faced. At best, they are inconclusive. The most avid proponents of the post-War Amendments undoubtedly intended them to remove all legal distinctions among "all persons born or naturalized in the United States." Their opponents, just as certainly, were antagonistic to both the letter and the spirit of the Amendments and wished them to have the most limited effect. What others in Congress and the state legislatures had in mind cannot be determined with any degree of certainty.

An additional reason for the inconclusive nature of the Amendment's history, with respect to segregated schools, is the status of public education at that time. In the South, the movement toward free common schools, supported by general taxation, had not yet taken hold. Education of white children was largely in the hands of private groups. Education of Negroes was almost nonexistent, and practically all of the race were illiterate. In fact, any education of Negroes was forbidden by law in some states. Today, in contrast, many Negroes have achieved outstanding success in the arts and sciences as well as in the business and professional world. It is true that public school education at the time of the Amendment had advanced further in the North, but the effect of the Amendment on Northern States was generally ignored in the congressional debates. Even in the North, the conditions of public education did not approximate those existing today. The curriculum was usually rudimentary; ungraded schools were common in rural areas; the school term was but three months a year in many states; and compulsory school attendance was virtually unknown. As a consequence, it is not surprising that there should be so little in the history of the Fourteenth Amendment relating to its intended effect on public education. . . .

In approaching this problem, we cannot turn the clock back to 1868 when the Amendment was adopted, or even to 1896 when *Plessy v. Ferguson*, [163 U.S. 537 (1896)], was written. We must consider public education in the light of its full development and its present place in American life throughout the Nation. Only in this way can it be determined if segregation in public schools deprives these plaintiffs of the equal protection of the laws.

Today, education is perhaps the most important function of state and local governments. Compulsory school attendance laws and the great expenditures for education both demonstrate our recognition of the importance of education to our democratic society. It is required in the performance of our most basic public responsibilities, even service in the armed forces. It is the very foundation of good citizenship. Today it is a principal instrument in awakening the child to cultural values, in preparing him for later professional training, and in helping him to adjust normally to his environment. In these days, it is doubtful that any child may reasonably be expected to succeed in life if he is denied the opportunity of an education. Such an opportunity, where the state has undertaken to provide it, is a right which must be made available to all on equal terms.

We come then to the question presented: Does segregation of children in public schools solely on the basis of race, even though the physical facilities and other "tangible" factors may be equal, deprive the children of the minority group of equal educational opportunities? We believe that it does.

In *Sweatt v. Painter*, 339 U.S. 629 [(1950)], in finding that a segregated law school for Negroes could not provide them equal educational opportunities, this Court relied in large part on "those qualities which are incapable of objective measurement but which make for greatness in a law school." In *McLaurin v. Oklahoma State Regents*, 339 U.S. 637 [(1958)], the Court, in requiring that a Negro admitted to a white graduate school be treated like all other students, again resorted to intangible considerations: ". . . his ability to study, to engage in discussions and exchange views with other students, and, in general, to learn his profession." Such considerations apply with added force to children in grade and high schools. To separate them from others of similar age and qualifications solely because of their race generates a feeling of inferiority as to their status in the community that may affect their hearts and minds in a way unlikely ever to be undone. The effect of this separation on their educational opportunities was well stated by a finding in the Kansas case by a court which nevertheless felt compelled to rule against the Negro plaintiffs:

> "Segregation of white and colored children in public schools has a detrimental effect upon the colored children. The impact is greater when it has the sanction of the law; for the policy of separating the races is usually interpreted as denoting the inferiority of the negro group. A sense of inferiority affects the motivation of a child to learn. Segregation with the sanction of law, therefore, has a tendency to [retard] the educational and mental development of Negro children and to deprive them of some of the benefits they would receive in a racial[ly] integrated school system."

Linda Brown, at age nine in 1952. Her father charged that his state's segregated schools were inherently discriminatory. The case led to a landmark school desegregation ruling. (*AP/Wide World Photos, Inc.*)

Whatever may have been the extent of psychological knowledge at the time of *Plessy v. Ferguson*, this finding is amply supported by modern authority.★ Any language in *Plessy v. Ferguson* contrary to this finding is rejected.

We conclude that in the field of public education the doctrine of "separate but equal" has no place. Separate educational facilities are inherently unequal. Therefore, we hold that the plaintiffs and others similarly situated for whom the actions have been brought are, by reason of the segregation complained of, deprived of the equal protection of the laws guaranteed by the Fourteenth Amendment. This disposition makes unnecessary any discussion whether such segregation also violates the Due Process Clause of the Fourteenth Amendment.

Because these are class actions, because of the wide applicability of this decision, and because of the great variety of local conditions, the formula-

★ [Footnote 11:] K. B. Clark, Effect of Prejudice and Discrimination on Personality Development (Midcentury White House Conference on Children and Youth, 1950); Witmer and Kotinsky, *Personality in the Making* (1952), e. VI; Deutscher and Chein, The Psychological Effects of Enforced Segregation: A Survey of Social Science Opinion, 26 *J.Psychol.* 259 (1948); Chein, What are the Psychological Effects of Segregation under Conditions of Equal Facilities?, 3 *Int. J. Opinion and Attitude Res.* 229 (1949); Brameld, Educational Costs, in *Discrimination and National Welfare* (MacIver, ed., 1949), 44–48; Frazier, *The Negro in the United States* (1949), 674–681. And see generally Myrdal, *An American Dilemma* (1944).

tion of decrees in these cases presents problems of considerable complexity. On reargument, the consideration of appropriate relief was necessarily subordinated to the primary question—the constitutionality of segregation in public education. We have now announced that such segregation is a denial of the equal protection of the laws. In order that we may have the full assistance of the parties in formulating decrees, the cases will be restored to the docket, and the parties are requested to present further argument . . . [on the nature of the remedial decrees this Court should order.] . . .

■ INSIDE THE COURT

William H. Rehnquist's Memorandum to Justice Robert Jackson on Brown v. Board of Education

As a law clerk to Justice Robert Jackson in 1952–1953, William Rehnquist wrote a memorandum to the justice on *Brown v. Board of Education.* Later, at his confirmation hearings on his nomination to the Supreme Court in 1971, Rehnquist claimed that the memo was written at Jackson's request and reflected the justice's views rather than his own. But the content and style of the memo (as well as the fact that Justice Jackson's private papers contain several other memos written by Rehnquist) indicate that the memo reflected Rehnquist's views on the case and the role of the Court.

A Random Thought on the Segregation Cases

One-hundred fifty years ago this Court held that it was the ultimate judge of the restrictions which the Constitution imposed on the various branches of the national and state government. Marbury v. Madison. This was presumably on the basis that there are standards to be applied other than the personal predilections of the Justices.

As applied to questions of inter-state or state-federal relations, as well as to interdepartmental disputes within the federal government, this doctrine of judicial has worked well. Where theoretically co-ordinate bodies of government are disputing, the Court is well suited to its role as arbiter. This is because these problems involve much less emotionally charged subject matter than do those discussed below. In effect, they determine the skeletal relations of the governments to each other without influencing the substantive business of those governments.

As applied to relations between the individual and the state, the system has worked much less well. The Constitution, of course, deals with indivudal rights, particularly in the First Ten and the Fourteenth Amendments. But as I read the history of this Court, it has seldom been out of hot water when attempting to interpret these individual rights. Fletcher v. Peck, in 1810, represented an attempt by Chief Justice Marshall to extend the protection of the contract clause to infant business. Scott v. Sanford was the result of Taney's effort to protect slaveholders from legislative interference.

After the Civil War, business interest came to dominate the Court, and they in turn ventured into the deep water of protecting certain types of individuals against legislative interference. Championed first by Field, then by Peckham and Brewer, the high water mark of the trend in protecting corporations against legislative influence was probably Lochner v. NY. To the majority opinion in that case, Holmes replied that the Fourteenth Amendment did not enact Herbert Spencer's Social Statics. Other cases coming later in a similar vein were Adkins v. Children's Hospital, Hammer v. Dagenhart, Tyson v. Banton, Ribnik v. McBride. But eventually the Court called a halt to this reading of its own economic views into the Constitution. Apparently it recognized that where a legislature was dealing with its own citizens, it was not part of the judicial function to thwart public opinion except in extreme cases.

In these cases now before the Court, the Court is, as Davis suggested, being asked to read its own sociological views into the Constitution. Urging a view palpably at variance with precedent and probably with legislative hsitory, appellants seek to convince the Court of the moral wrongness of the treatment they are receiving. I would suggest that this is a question the Court need never reach; for regardless of the Justice's individual views on the merits of segregation, it quite clearly is not one of those extreme cases which commands intervention from one of any conviction.

If this Court, because its members individually are "liberal" and dislike segregation, now chooses to strike it down, it differs from the McReynolds court only in the kinds of litigants it favors and the kinds of special claims it protects. To those who would argue that"personal" rights are more sacrosanct than "property" rights, the short answer is that the Constitution makes no such distinction. To the argument made by Marshall that a majority may not deprive a minority of its constitutional right, the answer must be made that while this is sound in theory, in the long run it is the majority who will determine what the constitutional rights of the minority are. One hundred and fifty years of attempts on the part of this Court to protect minority rights of any kind—whether those of business, slaveholders, or Jehovah's Witnesses—have all met the same fate. One by one the cases establishing such rights have been sloughed off, and crept silently to rest. If the present Court is unable to profit by this example, it must be prepared to see its work fade in time, too, as embodying only the sentiments of a transient majority of nine men.

I realize that it is an unpopular and unhumanitarian position, for which I have been excoriated by "liberal" colleagues, but I think Plessy v. Ferguson was right and should be re-affirmed. If the Fourteenth Amendment did not enact Spencer's Social Statics, it just as surely did not enact Myrdahl's American Dilemna.

whr

Source: Library of Congress, Justice Robert H. Jackson Papers.

■ INSIDE THE COURT

Justice Robert H. Jackson's Unpublished Memorandum on Brown v. Board of Education

In mid-February, 1954, when the Warren Court finally voted on *Brown v. Board of Education*, Justice Jackson drafted a memorandum to clarify his thoughts and possibly file as a concurring opinion. He never circulated it to the other justices but had it with him when Chief Justice Warren visited him in the hospital in May, shortly before the Court's final opinion was handed down. In his memorandum Justice Jackson probed the social realities and constitutional issues that Chief Justice Warren's opinion for the Court largely glanced over.

Justice Jackson began by pointing out that

[s]ince the close of the Civil War the United States has been "hesitating between two worlds—one dead—the other powerless to be born." War brought an old order to an end but as usual force proved unequal to founding a new one. Neither North nor South has been willing really to adapt its racial practices to its professions. The race problem would be quickly solved if some way could be found to make us all live up to our hypocrisies. . . .

Racial tensions seem to develop wherever the ratio of colored population to white passes a point where the latter vaguely feel themselves, for some reason, insecure. But in the South the Negro not only suffers from racial suspicions and antagonisms present in other states and in other countries, but also I am convinced, has suffered great prejudice from the aftermath of the great American white conflict. The white South retains in historical memory a deep resentment of the forces which, after conquest, imposed a fierce program of reconstruction and the deep humiliation of carpetbag government. The Negro is the visible and reachable beneficiary and symbol of this unhappy experience, on whom many visit their natural desire for retaliation. . . .

Tested by the pace of history, the rise of the Negro in the South, as well as the North, is one of the swiftest and most dramatic advances in the annals of man. Economic and social forces seem to mark discrimination for extinction even faster than legal measures. It is easy, however, to understand that historical process may do the contemporary individual no good for his life moves faster than society. But whether a real abolition of segregation will be accelerated or retarded by what many are likely to regard as a ruthless use of federal judicial power is a question that I cannot and need not answer.

That Negro segregation in the schools has outlived whatever original justification it may have had and is no longer wise or fair public policy is a conclusion congenial to my background and social and political views. Economic, social and political consideration seem to mark it for certain and early, if gradual extinction. Whatever we may say the law is today, I have no doubt that within a generation segregation will be outlawed. As the twin forces of mortality and replacement operate on this bench that seems inevitable unless some dramatic and unforeseeable excess by the Negro and his friends shall cause reversal of present trends.

Jackson then turned to the Court's role in interpreting the Constitution, cautioning that

we cannot oversimplify this decision to be a mere expression of our personal opinion that school segregation is unwise or evil. We have not been chosen as legislators but as judges. Questions of method and standards of constitutional interpretation and of limitation on responsible use of judicial power in our federal system are as far reaching as any that have been before the Court since its establishment. This Court must face the difficulties in the way of honestly saying that the states which have segregated schools have not, until today, been justified in regarding their practice as lawful. And the thoughtful layman, as well as the trained lawyer, must wonder how it is that a supposedly stable organic law of our nation this morning forbids what for three quarters of a century it has allowed. I think we individual justices may not, in justice to this Court as an institution and to our profession, brush off these problems.

Turning to the problems of explaining and justifying the Court's authority to strike down racially segregated schools, Jackson observed:

> Any authority of the judiciary to promulgate this decision has existed in the State cases since 1868 and in the case of the District of Columbia since 1791. The due process and equal protection clauses of the Fourteenth Amendment and the due process clause of the Fifth Amendment are the respective texts for interpretation. Neither of these says anything about education or about segregation. But they are majestic and sweeping generalities which, standing alone can be read to require a full and equal racial partnership. Yet, if these texts had such meaning to the age that wrote them, how could it be that for more than a half century from the adoption of the Fifth Amendment to the Emancipation Proclamation, it was never suggested that the Due Process Clause of the Fifth Amendment even prohibited Negro slavery in the District of Columbia? . . .

> There is controversy as old as the Republic as to whether the courts apply constitutional generalities in the sense that they were understood by the age that framed them or by the later age that reads them. It is implied in our questions on which all of the litigants have bestowed extensive research that the original public will that struggled for expression in these Constitutional phrases is at least relevant to our decision.

> In searching for the original will and purpose expressed in the Fourteenth Amendment, all that I can fairly get from the legislative debates is that it was a passionate, confused, and deplorable era. . . . The majority stopped at conferring upon the freed man very limited civil rights. Most of the leaders and spokesmen for the movement that carried the Civil War Amendments appear never to have reached a point in their thinking where they foresaw either Negro education or Negro segregation as serious or foreseeable problems, let alone any conclusion as to their solution.

> If deeds, rather than words, count as evidence, there is little indeed to show that these Amendments were understood in their own time to condemn the practice here in question. The Congress that proposed the Fourteenth Amendment and all Congresses to this day have established and maintained segregated schools in the District of Columbia. . . .

> This practice of legislators and educators and opinions of the Courts has been reinforced by custom, a powerful lawmaker. Indeed not long ago we decided that custom had nullified the Constitutional plan for independent Presidential electors. But here the custom of segregation is not contrary to any express provision, has prevailed in all Southern and many Northern states, and has been recognized in many judicial decisions. This court, in common with courts everywhere, has recognized the force of long custom and has

been reluctant to use judicial power to try to recast social usages. But we decide today that the unwritten law has long been contrary to a custom deeply anchored in our social system. Thus despite my personal satisfaction with the Court's judgment, I simply cannot find, in surveying all of the usual sources of law, anything which warrants me in saying that it is required by the original purpose and intent of the Fourteenth or Fifth Amendment.

Having reviewed the history and social practices since the adoption of the Fourteenth Amendment, and finding no support for the Court's ruling in a "jurisprudence of original intention," Jackson boldly observed that

> [t]oday's decision can not, with intellectual honesty, be grounded in anything other than the doctrine, of which Judge CAR-DOZO reminded us, that these Constitutional generalities "have a content and a significance that vary from age to age." Certainly no one familiar with his teachings would think this meant, what some people advocate, that we declare new constitutional law with the freedom of a constitutional convention sitting continuously and with no necessity for submitting its innovations for approval of Congress, ratification by the states or approval of the people.

> Of course the Constitution must be a living instrument and cannot be read as if written in a dead language. It is neither novel nor radical doctrine that statutes once constitutional may become invalid by changing conditions and those good in one state of facts may be bad under another. . . .

Still, Jackson was deeply troubled by the fact that the Court's ruling might not appear to have the force of law, and he turned to the sociological evidence that had been presented by the NAACP, and which Chief Justice Warren cited in footnote eleven of his opinion. And he sought to underscore that the Court's ruling rested on the Constitution, not social science or sociological jurisprudence:

> But a good many considerations are urged upon us to decree an end to segregation regardless of what the Amendments originally meant or purposed which I do not think appropriate for judicial appraisal or acceptance. Extralegal criteria from sociological, psychological and political sciences are proposed. Segregation is said to be offensive to the best contemporary opinion here and damaging to our prestige abroad. It is said to be based on a philosophy of inherent inequality of races, and that it creates in young Negro children an inferiority complex which retards their education and embitters their attitudes to life. These are disputed contentions which I have little competence to judge as scientific matters but with which, for purposes of the case, I shall not disagree. . . .

> However that may be, and if all the woes of colored children would be solved by forcing them into white company, I do not

think we should import into the concept of equal protection of the law these elusive psychological and subjective factors. They are not determinable with satisfactory objectivity or mensurable [*sic*] with reasonable certainty. If we adhere to objective criteria the judicial process will still be capricious enough.

Concluding, Jackson observed,

> The real question as I see it is whether the Constitution permits any classification or separation of Negro and White merely on the basis of color or racial descent. If not these policy arguments are superfluous and, if so, they are for consideration of the legislatures not the courts.

> I think the change which warrants our decision is not a change in the Constitution but in the Negro population. Certainly in the 1860's and throughout the nineteenth century the Negro population, as a whole, was a different people than today. Lately freed from bondage, they had no opportunity as yet to show their capacity for education and assimilation, or even a chance to demonstrate that they could be self-supporting or in our public life anything more than a pawn for white exploiters. I cannot say that it was an unreasonable assumption that Negro educational problems were elementary, special and peculiar and their mass teaching an experiment not easily tied in which the education of pupils of more favored background. Nor, when we view the progress that has been made under it, can we honestly say that the practice of each race pursuing its education apart was wholly to the Negro's disadvantage. His progress under these conditions has been spectacular.

> Whatever may have been true at an earlier period, the mere fact that one is in some degree colored no longer creates a presumption that he is inferior, illiterate, retarded or indigent. Moreover, assimilation is under way to a marked extent. Blush or shudder, as many will, mixture of blood has been making inroads on segregation faster than the courtroom. A line of separation between the races has become unclear and blurred and an increasing part of what is called colored population has as much claim to white as to colored blood. This development baffles any just segregation effort.

> Also relevant changes have occurred in the status of the public school. Education, even for the white, was once regarded as a privilege bestowed on those fortunate enough to be able to take advantage of it and often was not compulsory. The concept today has changed. Education is not a privilege but a right and more than that a duty, to be performed not merely for one's own advantage but for the security and stability of the nation. Access to educational facilities has been gradually transformed from a matter of grace into a right which may not be encumbered with unconstitutionally discriminatory or oppressive conditions. And while education was long regarded as at most a local or state concern, far from the reach

of federal authority, the federal judicial power especially, and the appropriative power of Congress has moved in to the local problems and made education a national concern.

The Negro is not free of local educational control. He must meet the prescribed standards of learning, discipline and health. He may be treated on his individual merit as a pupil, attend schools set apart for those of his neighborhood. But he may not be included or excluded merely because he has Negro blood wholly or in part.

Source: Library of Congress, Justice Robert H. Jackson Papers.

Bolling v. Sharpe
347 U.S. 497, 74 S.Ct. 693 (1954)

Handed down with *Brown v. Board of Education* (see excerpt above), this case involved the District of Columbia's segregated schools. The facts are further discussed in the opinion delivered by Chief Justice Earl Warren.

The Court's decision was unanimous; the opinion was announced by Chief Justice Warren.

☐ *Chief Justice WARREN delivered the opinion of the Court.*

This case challenges the validity of segregation in the public schools of the District of Columbia. . . .

We have this day held that the Equal Protection Clause of the Fourteenth Amendment prohibits the states from maintaining racially segregated public schools. The legal problem in the District of Columbia is somewhat different, however. The Fifth Amendment, which is applicable in the District of Columbia, does not contain an equal protection clause as does the Fourteenth Amendment which applies only to the states. But the concepts of equal protection and due process, both stemming from our American ideal of fairness, are not mutually exclusive. The "equal protection of the laws" is a more explicit safeguard of prohibited unfairness than "due process of the law," and, therefore, we do not imply that the two are always interchangeable phrases. But, as this Court has recognized, discrimination may be so unjustifiable as to be violative of due process. . . .

Although the Court has not assumed to define "liberty" with any great precision, that term is not confined to mere freedom from bodily restraint. Liberty under law extends to the full range of conduct which the individual is free to pursue, and it cannot be restricted except for a proper governmental objective. Segregation in public education is not reasonably related to any proper governmental objective, and thus it imposes on Negro children of the District of Columbia a burden that constitutes an arbitrary deprivation of their liberty in violation of the Due Process Clause.

In view of our decision that the Constitution prohibits the states from maintaining racially segregated public schools, it would be unthinkable that the same Constitution would impose a lesser duty on the Federal Government. We hold that racial segregation in the public schools of the District of Columbia is a denial of the due process of law guaranteed by the Fifth Amendment to the Constitution.

Brown v. Board of Education of Topeka, Kansas (Brown II)
349 U.S. 294, 75 S.Ct. 753 (1955)

During the rearguments on what kind of remedial decree the Court should issue to enforce *Brown*, Chief Justice Warren confronted the hard fact of southern resistance. The attorney for South Carolina, S. Emory Rogers, pressed for an open-ended decree—one that would not specify when and how desegregation should take place. He boldly proclaimed:

> Mr. Chief Justice, to say we will conform depends on the decree handed down. I am frank to tell you, right now [in] our district I do not think that we will send—[that] the white people of the district will send their children to the Negro schools. It would be unfair to tell the Court that we are going to do that. I do not think it is. But I do think that something can be worked out. We hope so.

"It is not a question of attitude," Warren shot back, "it is a question of conforming to the decree." Their heated exchange continued:

> Chief Justice Warren: But you are not willing to say here that there would be an honest attempt to conform to this decree, if we did leave it to the district court [to implement]?

> Mr. Rogers: No, I am not. Let us get the word "honest" out of there.

> Chief Justice Warren: No, leave it in.

> Mr. Rogers: No, because I would have to tell you that right now we would not conform—we would not send our white children to the Negro schools.

The exchange reinforced Warren's view "that reasonable attempts to start the integration process is [*sic*] all the court can expect in view of the scope of the problem, and that an order to immediately admit all negroes in white schools would be an absurdity because [it would be] impossible to obey in many areas." Thus while total immediate integration might be a reasonable order for Kansas, it would be unreasonable for Virginia, and the district judge might decide that a grade a year is reasonable compliance in Virginia. Six law clerks were assigned to prepare a Segregation Research Report. They summarized available studies on how school districts in different regions might be desegregated and projected the reactions to various desegregation plans.

The Court's problem, as one of Justice Stanley Reed's law clerks put it, was to frame a decree "so as to allow such divergent results without making it so broad that evasion is encouraged." The clerks agreed that there should be a simple decree but disagreed on whether there should be guidelines for its implementation. One clerk opposed any guidelines. The others thought that "smacks of indecisiveness, and gives the extremists more time to operate." The problem was how precise a guideline should be established. What would constitute good faith compliance? "Although we think a 12-year gradual desegregation plan permissible," they confessed, "we are not certain that the opinion should explicitly sanction it."

At the justices' private conference, Warren repeated these concerns. Justices Black and Minton thought that a simple decree, without an opinion, was enough. As Black explained, "The less we say the better off we are." The others agreed. A short, simple opinion seemed advisable for reaffirming *Brown I* and providing guidance for dealing with the inevitable problems of compliance. Justice John Harlan wanted *Brown II* expressly to recognize that school desegregation was a local problem to be solved by local authorities. The others also insisted on making clear that school boards and lower courts had flexibility in ending segregation. In Justice Harold Burton's view, "neither this Court nor district courts should act as a school board or formulate the program" for desegregation.

Agreement emerged that the Court should issue a short opinion decree. In a memorandum, Chief Justice Warren summarized the main points of agreement. The opinion should simply state that *Brown I* held unconstitutional racially segregated public schools. *Brown II* should acknowledge that "local school authorities have the primary responsibility for assessing and solving these problems; [and] the courts will have to consider these problems in determining whether the efforts of local school authorities" are in good faith compliance. The cases, he concluded, should be remanded to the lower courts "for such proceedings and decree necessary and proper to carry out this Court's decision." The justices agreed, and along these lines Warren drafted the Court's opinion.

The phrase "all deliberate speed" was borrowed from an opinion by Justice Oliver Wendell Holmes, in *Virginia v. West Virginia*, 200 U.S. 1 (1911), a case dealing with how much and when Virginia ought to receive from the state's public debt at the time West Virginia broke off and became a state. It was inserted in the final opinion of *Brown II* at the suggestion of one of Frankfurter's law clerks. Forced integration might lead to lowering educational standards. Immediate, court-ordered desegregation, Frankfurter warned, "would make a mockery of the Constitutional adjudication designed to vindicate a claim to equal treatment to achieve 'integrated' but lower educational standards." The Court, he insisted, "does its duty if it gets effectively under way the righting of a wrong. When the wrong is deeply rooted state policy the court does its duty if it decrees measures that reverse the direction of the unconstitutional policy so as to uproot it 'with all deliberate speed.' " As much an apology for not setting precise guidelines as a recognition of the limitations of judicial power, the phrase symbolized the Court's bold moral appeal to the country.★

The Court's decision was unanimous; the opinion was announced by Chief Justice Warren.

☐ *Chief Justice WARREN delivered the opinion of the Court.*

These cases were decided on May 17, 1954. The opinions of that date, declaring the fundamental principle that racial discrimination in public education is unconstitutional, are incorporated herein by reference. All provisions of federal, state, or local law requiring or permitting such discrimination must yield to this principle. There remains for consideration the manner in which relief is to be accorded.

Because these cases arose under different local conditions and their disposition will involve a variety of local problems, we requested further argument on the question of relief. In view of the nationwide importance of the decision, we invited the Attorney General of the United States and the Attorneys General of all states requiring or permitting racial discrimination in public education to present their views on that question. The parties, the United States, and the States of Florida, North Carolina, Arkansas, Oklahoma, Maryland, and Texas filed briefs and participated in the oral argument. . . .

Full implementation of these constitutional principles may require solution of varied local school problems. School authorities have the primary responsibility for elucidating, assessing, and solving these problems; courts will have to consider whether the action of school authorities constitutes good faith implementation of the governing constitutional principles. Because of their proximity to local conditions and the possible need for further hear-

---

★ Quotations are from materials in the Stanley Reed Papers, University of Kentucky Library; the Harold Burton Papers, Library of Congress; the Tom Clark Papers, University of Texas Law School Library; the Felix Frankfurter Papers, Harvard Law School; and the Earl Warren Papers, Library of Congress.

ings, the courts which originally heard these cases can best perform this judicial appraisal. Accordingly, we believe it appropriate to remand the cases to those courts.

In fashioning and effectuating the decrees, the courts will be guided by equitable principles. Traditionally, equity has been characterized by a practical flexibility in shaping its remedies and by a facility for adjusting and reconciling public and private needs. These cases call for the exercise of these traditional attributes of equity power. At stake is the personal interest of the plaintiffs in admission to public schools as soon as practicable on a non-discriminatory basis. To effectuate this interest may call for elimination of a variety of obstacles in making the transition to school systems operated in accordance with the constitutional principles set forth in our May 17, 1954, decision. Courts of equity may properly take into account the public interest in the elimination of such obstacles in a systematic and effective manner. But it should go without saying that the vitality of these constitutional principles cannot be allowed to yield simply because of disagreement with them.

While giving weight to these public and private considerations, the courts will require that the defendants make a prompt and reasonable start toward full compliance with our May 17, 1954, ruling. Once such a start has been made, the courts may find that additional time is necessary to carry out the ruling in an effective manner. The burden rests upon the defendants to establish that such time is necessary in the public interest and is consistent with good faith compliance at the earliest practicable date. To that end, the courts may consider problems related to administration, arising from the physical condition of the school plant, the school transportation system, personnel, revision of school districts and attendance areas into compact units to achieve a system of determining admission to the public schools on a non-racial basis, and revision of local laws and regulations which may be necessary in solving the foregoing problems. They will also consider the adequacy of any plans the defendants may propose to meet these problems and to effectuate a transition to a racially nondiscriminatory school system. During this period of transition, the courts will retain jurisdiction of these cases.

The judgments below, except that in the Delaware case, are accordingly reversed and the cases are remanded to the District Courts to take such proceedings and enter such orders and decrees consistent with this opinion as are necessary and proper to admit to public schools on a racially non-discriminatory basis with all deliberate speed the parties to these cases.

Cooper v. Aaron

358 U.S. 1, 78 S.CT. 1401 (1958)

In Little Rock, Arkansas, Governor Orval Faubus encouraged disobedience by southern segregationists by calling out the state's National Guard to keep black children from entering Little Rock's Central High School. The attorney general of the United States, Herbert Brownell, got an injunction against the governor's action and eight black children, including John Aaron, were permitted to enter the school. But continued hostility led to the removal of the children and to President Dwight Eisenhower's sending army troops to enforce the court's order and to protect the children.

William Cooper and other members of the Little Rock school board asked a federal district court for a two-and-one-half-year delay in the implementation of its desegregation plans. A federal appellate court, however, reversed the district court's order postponing desegregation. Cooper and the school board immediately appealed that decision to the Supreme Court, which granted review and expedited proceedings. Hearing oral arguments just three days after granting review, the Court handed down the next day a brief order affirming the appellate court's decision. It later published a full opinion (excerpted here).

Justice Brennan's draft of the Court's opinion was worked on by all of the justices in the Court's conference room. Over the strong objections of some of the justices, Justice Felix Frankfurter insisted on writing a concurring opinion because, he said, many of his former students at Harvard Law School were leading members of the southern bar and because ex-Justice (and former governor of South Carolina) James Byrnes had called on the country to curb the Court. Byrnes had published an attack on *Brown* and an article written by one of Frankfurter's favorite former law clerks, Alexander Bickel. As a clerk, Bickel had prepared a lengthy research report on school desegregation when the Court first considered *Brown*. Later, when back at Harvard, Bickel revised and published it in the *Harvard Law Review*. Given Byrnes's attack, Frankfurter felt the need to lecture southern lawyers on the legitimacy of the Court's ruling in *Brown*. But the other justices worried that Frankfurter's opinion might undercut the Court's unanimous decision. For this reason, the justices took the unusual step of noting in the opinion that three—Brennan, Stewart, and Whittaker—were not on the bench when *Brown* was handed down but that they would have joined the unanimous decision if they had been. They also agreed to depart from the practice of one justice signing the opinion for the Court in order to underscore their unanimity and that Frankfurter's opinion was not a "dilution" of the views expressed in the Court's joint opinion."

☐ *Opinion of the Court by the CHIEF JUSTICE, Justice BLACK, Justice FRANKFURTER, Justice DOUGLAS, Justice BURTON, Justice CLARK, Justice HARLAN, Justice BRENNAN, and Justice WHITTAKER.*

As this case reaches us it raises questions of the highest importance to the maintenance of our federal system of government. It necessarily involves a claim by the governor and Legislature of a State that there is no duty on state officials to obey federal court orders resting on this Court's considered interpretation of the United States Constitution. Specifically it involves actions by the Governor and Legislature of Arkansas upon the premise that they are not bound by our holding in *Brown v. Board of Education*, 349 U.S. 483 (1954). That holding was that the Fourteenth Amendment forbids States to use their governmental powers to bar children on racial grounds from attending schools where there is state participation through any arrangement, management, funds or property. We are urged to uphold a suspension of the Little Rock School Board's plan to do away with segregated public schools in Little Rock until state laws and efforts to upset and nullify our holding in *Brown v. Board of Education* have been further challenged and tested in the courts. We reject these contentions. . . .

In affirming the judgment of the Court of Appeals which reversed the District Court we have accepted without reservation the position of the School Board, the Superintendent of Schools, and their counsel that they displayed entire good faith in the conduct of these proceedings and in dealing with the unfortunate and distressing sequence of events which has been outlined. We likewise have accepted the findings of the District Court as to the conditions at Central High School during the 1957–1958 school year, and also the findings that the educational progress of all the students, white and colored, of that school has suffered and will continue to suffer if the conditions which prevailed last year are permitted to continue.

The significance of these findings, however, is to be considered in light of the fact, indisputably revealed by the record before us, that the conditions they depict are directly traceable to the actions of legislators and executive officials of the State of Arkansas, taken in their official capacities, which reflect their own determination to resist this Court's decision in the *Brown* case and which have brought about violent resistance to that decision in Arkansas. In its petition for *certiorari* filed in this Court, the School Board itself describes the situation in this language: "The legislative, executive, and judicial departments of the state government opposed the desegregation of Little Rock schools by enacting laws, calling out troops, making statements villifying federal law and federal courts, and failing to utilize state law enforcement agencies and judicial processes to maintain public peace."

One may well sympathize with the position of the Board in the face of the frustrating conditions which have confronted it, but, regardless of the Board's good faith, the actions of the other state agencies responsible for those conditions compel us to reject the Board's legal position. Had Central High School been under the direct management of the State itself, it could hardly be suggested that those immediately in charge of the school should be heard to assert their own good faith as a legal excuse for delay in implementing the constitutional rights of these respondents, when vindication of those rights was rendered difficult or impossible by the actions of other state officials. The situation here is in no different posture because the members of the School Board and the Superintendent of Schools are local officials; from the point of view of the Fourteenth Amendment, they stand in this litigation as the agents of the State.

The constitutional rights of respondents are not to be sacrificed or yielded to the violence and disorder which have followed upon the actions of the Governor and Legislature. As this Court said some 41 years ago in a unanimous opinion in a case involving another aspect of racial segregation: "It is urged that this proposed segregation will promote the public peace by preventing race conflicts. Desirable as this is, and important as is the preservation of the public peace, this aim cannot be accomplished by laws or ordinances which deny rights created or protected by the federal Constitution." *Buchanan v. Warley*, 245 U.S. 60 [(1917)]. Thus law and order are not here to be preserved by depriving the Negro children of their constitutional rights. The record before us clearly establishes that the growth of the Board's difficulties to a magnitude beyond its unaided power to control is the product of state action. Those difficulties, as counsel for the Board forthrightly conceded on the oral argument in this Court, can also be brought under control by state action.

The controlling legal principles are plain. The command of the Fourteenth Amendment is that no "State" shall deny to any person within its jurisdiction the equal protection of the laws. "A State acts by its legislative, its executive, or its judicial authorities. It can act in no other way. The constitutional provision, therefore, must mean that no agency of the State, or of the officers or agents by whom its powers are exerted, shall deny to any person within its jurisdiction the equal protection of the laws. Whoever, by virtue of public position under a State government . . . denies or takes away the equal protection of the laws, violates the constitutional inhibition; and as he acts in the name and for the State, and is clothed with the State's power, his act is that of the State. This must be so, or the constitutional prohibition has no meaning." *Ex parte Virginia*, 100 U.S. 339 [(1880)]. Thus the prohibitions of the Fourteenth Amendment extend to all action of the State denying equal protection of the laws; whatever the agency of the State taking the action. . . .

In short, the constitutional rights of children not to be discriminated against in school admission on grounds of race or color declared by this Court in the *Brown* case can neither be nullified openly and directly by state legislators or state executive or judicial officers, nor nullified indirectly by them through evasive schemes for segregation whether attempted "ingeniously or ingenuously." *Smith v. Texas*, 311 U.S. 128 [(1940)].

What has been said, in the light of the facts developed, is enough to dispose of the case. However, we should answer the premise of the actions of the Governor and Legislature that they are not bound by our holding in the *Brown* case. It is necessary only to recall some basic constitutional propositions which are settled doctrine.

Article VI of the Constitution makes the Constitution the "supreme Law of the Land." In 1803, Chief Justice MARSHALL, speaking for a unanimous Court, referring to the Constitution as "the fundamental and paramount law of the nation," declared in the notable case of *Marbury v. Madison* 1 Cr. 137 [(1803)], that "It is emphatically the province and duty of the judicial department to say what the law is." This decision declared the basic principle that the federal judiciary is supreme in the exposition of the law of the Constitution, and that principle has ever since been respected by this Court and the Country as a permanent and indispensable feature of our constitutional system. It follows that the interpretation of the Fourteenth Amendment enunciated by this Court in the *Brown* case is the supreme law of the land, and Art.VI of the Constitution makes it of binding effect on the States "any Thing in the Constitution or Laws of any State to the Contrary notwithstanding." Every state legislator and executive and judicial officer is solemnly committed by oath taken pursuant to Art.VI, § 3 "to support this Constitution." Chief Justice TANEY, speaking for a unanimous Court in 1859, said that this requirement reflected the framers' "anxiety to preserve it [the Constitution] in full force, in all its powers, and to guard against resistance to or evasion of its authority, on the part of a State. . . ." *Ableman v. Booth*, 21 How. 506 [(1859)].

No state legislator or executive or judicial officer can war against the Constitution without violating his undertaking to support it. Chief Justice MARSHALL spoke for a unanimous Court in saying that: "If the legislatures of the several states may, at will, annul the judgments of the courts of the United States, and destroy the rights acquired under those judgments, the constitution itself becomes a solemn mockery. . . ." *United States v. Peters*, 5 Cranch 115 [(1809)].

It is, of course, quite true that the responsibility for public education is primarily the concern of the States, but it is equally true that such responsibilities, like all other state activity, must be exercised consistently with federal constitutional requirements as they apply to state action. The Constitution created a government dedicated to equal justice under law. The Fourteenth Amendment embodied and emphasized that ideal. State support of segregated schools through any arrangement, management, funds, or property cannot be squared with the Amendment's command that no State shall deny to any person within its jurisdiction the equal protection of the laws. The right of a student not to be segregated on racial grounds in schools so maintained is indeed so fundamental and pervasive that it is embraced in the concept of due process of law. *Bolling v. Sharpe*, 347 U.S. 497 [(1954)]. The basic decision in *Brown* was unanimously reached by this Court only after the case had been briefed and twice argued and the issues had been given the most serious consideration. Since the first *Brown* opinion three new Justices have come to the Court. They are at one with the Justices still on the Court who participated in that basic decision as to its correctness, and that decision is now unanimously reaffirmed. The principles announced in that decision and the obedience of the States to them, according to the command of the Constitution, are indispensable for the protection of the freedoms guaranteed by our fundamental charter for all of us. Our constitutional ideal of equal justice under law is thus made a living truth.

☐ *Justice FRANKFURTER, concurring.*

While unreservedly participating with my brethren in our joint opinion, I deem it appropriate also to deal individually with the great issue here at stake. . . .

We are now asked to hold that the illegal, forcible interference by the State of Arkansas with the continuance of what the Constitution commands, and the consequences in disorder that it entrained, should be recognized as justification for undoing what the Board of Education had formulated, what the District Court in 1955 had directed to be carried out, and what was in process of obedience. No explanation that may be offered in support of such a request can obscure the inescapable meaning that law should bow to force. To yield to such a claim would be to enthrone official lawlessness and lawlessness if not checked is the precursor of anarchy. On the few tragic occasions in the history of the Nation, North and South, when law was forcibly resisted or systematically evaded, it has signalled the break-down of constitutional processes of government on which ultimately rest the liberties of all. Violent resistance to law cannot be made a legal reason for its suspension without loosening the fabric of our society. What could this mean but to acknowledge that disorder under the aegis of a State has moral superiority over the law of the Constitution. For those in authority thus to defy the law of the land is profoundly subversive not only of our constitutional system but of the presuppositions of a democratic society. The State "must . . . yield to an authority that is paramount to the State." . . .

The duty to abstain from resistance to "the supreme Law of the Land," U.S. Const., Art. VI, § 2, as declared by the organ of our Government for ascertaining it, does not require immediate approval of it nor does it deny the right of dissent. Criticism need not be stilled. Active obstruction or defiance is barred. Our kind of society cannot endure if the controlling authority of the Law as derived from the Constitution is not to be the tribunal specially charged with the duty of ascertaining and declaring what is "the supreme Law of the Land." Particularly is this so where the declaration of what "the supreme Law" commands on an underlying moral issue is not the dubious pronouncement of a gravely divided Court but is the unanimous conclusion of a long-matured deliberative process. The Constitution is not the formulation of the merely personal views of the members of this Court, nor can its authority be reduced to the claim that state officials are its controlling interpreters. Local customs, however hardened by time, are not decreed in heaven. Habits and feelings they engender may be counteracted and moderated. Experience attests that such local habits and feelings will yield, gradually though this be, to law and education. And educational influences are exerted not only by explicit teaching. They vigorously flow from the fruitful exercise of the responsibility of those charged with political official power and from the almost unconsciously transforming actualities of living under law.

The process of ending unconstitutional exclusion of pupils from the common school system—"common" meaning shared alike—solely because of color is no doubt not an easy, overnight task in a few States where a drastic alteration in the ways of communities is involved. Deep emotions have, no doubt, been stirred. They will not be calmed by letting violence loose—violence and defiance employed and encouraged by those upon whom the duty of law observance should have the strongest claim—nor by submitting to it under whatever guise employed. Only the constructive use of time will achieve what an advanced civilization demands and the Constitution confirms. . . .

Swann v. Charlotte-Mecklenberg Board of Education
402 U.S. 1, 91 S.CT. 1267 (1971)

Fifteen years after *Brown*, approximately 60 percent of the black students in Charlotte-Mecklenberg, North Carolina, still attended schools that were 99 percent black, even though 71 percent of all students in the school system were white. James Swann and several others filed a lawsuit in federal district court to modify a 1965 desegregation plan and to achieve further integration. As a result, two proposed desegregation plans were drawn up by the school board and a court-appointed expert, Dr. John Finger, and submitted to district Judge James B. McMillan. He accepted a modified version of the school board's plan for secondary schools but approved Dr. Finger's plans for elementary schools, which provided for more racial balance than acceptable to the school board. On appeal, a federal appellate court vacated that part of Judge McMillan's order dealing with the desegregation of elementary schools and remanded the case. After further proceedings, Judge McMillan issued a sweeping order, incorporating Finger's proposals and requiring district-wide busing.

President Richard Nixon, who appointed Chief Justice Burger in 1969, firmly opposed court-ordered busing. Inside the Court the issue also proved volatile. After oral arguments, Chief Justice Burger led the discussion at conference, suggesting that no votes be taken, just as his predecessor had done when considering *Brown*. At the same time, though, he indicated sympathy with the Nixon administration's opposition to court-ordered busing. Justice Black spoke next and was also unhappy with busing as a judicially fashioned remedy. But then a solid majority emerged for upholding the district court's order; Justices Douglas, Harlan, Brennan, White, and Marshall more or less agreed. Justices Stewart and newly appointed Justice Blackmun were more tentative, but inclined to go along with the majority.

What angered Justice Douglas and troubled some of the others was that Burger decided to draft an opinion for later conference discussion; since Burger had not appeared to be solidly with the views of the majority, the opinion assignment should have gone to Douglas, the senior associate justice in the majority. When Burger later circulated his draft it was indecisive in tone and took a restrictive view of the power of courts to remedy segregated schools, as well as failed to uphold expressly the lower court's order. What happened in the weeks that followed was an exchange of memorandums and various draft opinions, along with threats of dissenting opinions.

In the end, the chief justice incorporated suggestions and revisions put forth by Justices Brennan, Stewart, and Harlan and delivered an opinion for a unanimous Court, approving the lower court's order for district-wide busing.

☐ *Chief Justice BURGER delivered the opinion of the Court.*

This case and those argued with it arose in States having a long history of maintaining two sets of schools in a single school system deliberately operated to carry out a governmental policy to separate pupils in schools solely on the basis of race. That was what *Brown v. Board of Education,* [349 U.S. 294 (1955)], was all about. These cases present us with the problem of defining in more precise terms than heretofore the scope of the duty of school authorities and district courts in implementing *Brown I* and the mandate to eliminate dual systems and establish unitary systems at once. . . .

The objective today remains to eliminate from the public schools all vestiges of state-imposed segregation. . . .

If school authorities fail in their affirmative obligations under these holdings, judicial authority may be invoked. Once a right and a violation have been shown, the scope of a district court's equitable powers to remedy past wrongs is broad, for breadth and flexibility are inherent in equitable remedies. . . .

In seeking to define even in broad and general terms how far this remedial power extends it is important to remember that judicial powers may be exercised only on the basis of a constitutional violation. Remedial judicial authority does not put judges automatically in the shoes of school authorities whose powers are plenary. Judicial authority enters only when local authority defaults.

School authorities are traditionally charged with broad power to formulate and implement educational policy and might well conclude, for example, that in order to prepare students to live in a pluralistic society each school should have a prescribed ratio of Negro to white students reflecting the proportion for the district as a whole. To do this as an educational policy is within the broad discretionary powers of school authorities; absent a finding of a constitutional violation, however, that would not be within the authority of a federal court. As with any equity case, the nature of the violation determines the scope of the remedy. In default by the school authorities of their obligation to proffer acceptable remedies, a district court has broad power to fashion a remedy that will assure a unitary school system. . . .

The central issue in this case is that of student assignment, and there are essentially four problem areas:

(1) to what extent racial balance or racial quotas may be used as an implement in a remedial order to correct a previously segregated system;

(2) whether every all-Negro and all-white school must be eliminated as an indispensable part of a remedial process of desegregation;

(3) what the limits are, if any, on the rearrangement of school districts and attendance zones, as a remedial measure; and

(4) what the limits are, if any, on the use of transportation facilities to correct state-enforced racial school segregation.

(1) RACIAL BALANCES OR RACIAL QUOTAS.

The target of the cases from *Brown I* to the present was the dual school system. The elimination of racial discrimination in public schools is a large task and one that should not be retarded by efforts to achieve broader purposes lying beyond the jurisdiction of school authorities. One vehicle can carry only a limited amount of baggage. It would not serve the important objective of *Brown I* to seek to use school desegregation cases for purposes beyond their scope, although desegregation of schools ultimately will have impact on other forms of discrimination. We do not reach in this case the question whether a showing that school segregation is a consequence of other types of state action, without any discriminatory action by the school authorities, is a constitutional violation requiring remedial action by the school desegregation decree. This case does not present that question and we therefore do not decide it.

   Our objective in dealing with the issues presented by these cases is to see that school authorities exclude no pupil of a racial minority from any school, directly or indirectly, on account of race; it does not and cannot embrace all the problems of racial prejudice, even when those problems contribute to disproportionate racial concentrations in some schools. . . .

   If we were to read the holding of the District Court to require, as a matter of substantive constitutional right, any particular degree of racial balance or mixing, that approach would be disapproved and we would be obliged to reverse. The constitutional command to desegregate schools does not mean that every school in every community must always reflect the racial composition of the school system as a whole. . . .

   [But here] the use made of mathematical ratios was no more than a starting point in the process of shaping a remedy, rather than an inflexible requirement. From that starting point the District Court proceeded to frame a decree that was within its discretionary powers, as an equitable remedy for the particular circumstances. As we said in *Green*, [*v. School Board of New Kent County*, 391 U.S. 430 (1968)], a school authority's remedial plan or a district court's remedial decree is to be judged by its effectiveness. Awareness of the racial composition of the whole school system is likely to be a useful starting point in shaping a remedy to correct past constitutional violations. In sum, the very limited use made of mathematical ratios was within the equitable remedial discretion of the District Court.

(2) ONE-RACE SCHOOLS.

[I]t should be clear that the existence of some small number of one-race, or virtually one-race, schools within a district is not in and of itself the mark of a system that still practices segregation by law. The district judge or school authorities should make every effort to achieve the greatest possible degree of actual desegregation and will thus necessarily be concerned with the elimination of one-race schools. No *per se* rule can adequately embrace all the difficulties of reconciling the competing interests involved; but in a system with a history of segregation the need for remedial criteria of sufficient specificity to assure a school authority's compliance with its constitutional duty warrants a presumption against schools that are substantially disproportionate in their racial composition. Where the school authority's proposed plan for conversion from a dual to a unitary system contemplates the continued existence of some schools that are all or predominantly of one race, they have the burden of showing that such school assignments are genuinely nondiscriminatory. The court should scrutinize such schools, and the burden upon the school authorities will be to satisfy the court that their racial composition is not the result of present or past discriminatory action on their part. . . .

(3) REMEDIAL ALTERING OF ATTENDANCE ZONES.

[O]ne of the principal tools employed by school planners and by courts to break up the dual school system has been a frank—and sometimes drastic—gerrymandering of school districts and attendance zones. An additional step was pairing, "clustering," or "grouping" of schools with attendance assignments made deliberately to accomplish the transfer of Negro students out of formerly segregated Negro schools and transfer of white students to formerly all-Negro schools. More often than not, these zones are neither compact nor contiguous; indeed they may be on opposite ends of the city. As an interim corrective measure, this cannot be said to be beyond the broad remedial powers of a court.

Absent a constitutional violation there would be no basis for judicially ordering assignment of students on a racial basis. All things being equal, with no history of discrimination, it might well be desirable to assign pupils to schools nearest their homes. But all things are not equal in a system that has been deliberately constructed and maintained to enforce racial segregation. The remedy for such segregation may be administratively awkward, inconvenient, and even bizarre in some situations and may impose burdens on some; but all awkwardness and inconvenience cannot be avoided in the interim period when remedial adjustments are being made to eliminate the dual school systems.

No fixed or even substantially fixed guidelines can be established as to how far a court can go, but it must be recognized that there are limits. The objective is to dismantle the dual school system. "Racially neutral" assignment plans proposed by school authorities to a district court may be inadequate; such plans may fail to counteract the continuing effects of past school segregation resulting from discriminatory location of school sites or distortion of school size in order to achieve or maintain an artificial racial separation. When school authorities present a district court with a "loaded game board," affirmative action in the form of remedial altering of attendance zones is proper to achieve truly nondiscriminatory assignments. In short, an assignment plan is not acceptable simply because it appears to be neutral.

In this area, we must of necessity rely to a large extent, as this Court has for more than 16 years, on the informed judgment of the district courts in the first instance and on courts of appeals.

We hold that the pairing and grouping of noncontiguous school zones is a permissible tool and such action is to be considered in light of the objectives sought.

(4) TRANSPORTATION OF STUDENTS.

The scope of permissible transportation of students as an implement of a remedial decree has never been defined by this Court and by the very nature of the problem it cannot be defined with precision. No rigid guidelines as to student transportation can be given for application to the infinite variety of problems presented in thousands of situations. Bus transportation has been an integral part of the public education system for years, and was perhaps the single most important factor in the transition from the one-room school-house to the consolidated school. Eighteen million of the Nation's public school children, approximately 39%, were transported to their schools by bus in 1969–1970 in all parts of the country. . . .

The decree provided that the buses used to implement the plan would operate on direct routes. Students would be picked up at schools near their homes and transported to the schools they were to attend. The trips for elementary school pupils average about seven miles and the District Court found that they would take "not over 35 minutes at the most." This system compares favorably with the transportation plan previously operated in Charlotte under which each day 23,600 students on all grade levels were transported an average of 15 miles one way for an average trip requiring over an hour. In these circumstances, we find no basis for holding that the local school authorities may not be required to employ bus transportation as one tool of school desegregation. Desegregation plans cannot be limited to the walk-in school.

An objection to transportation of students may have validity when the time or distance of travel is so great as to either risk the health of the children or significantly impinge on the educational process. District courts must weigh the soundness of any transportation plan in light of what is said in subdivisions (1), (2), and (3) above. It hardly needs stating that the limits on time of travel will vary with many factors, but probably with none more than the age of the students. The reconciliation of competing values in a desegregation case is, of course, a difficult task with many sensitive facets but fundamentally no more so than remedial measures courts of equity have traditionally employed. . . .

On the facts of this case, we are unable to conclude that the order of the District Court is not reasonable, feasible and workable. However, in seeking to define the scope of remedial power or the limits on remedial power of courts in an area as sensitive as we deal with here, words are poor instruments to convey the sense of basic fairness inherent in equity. Substance, not semantics, must govern, and we have sought to suggest the nature of limitations without frustrating the appropriate scope of equity.

At some point, these school authorities and others like them should have achieved full compliance with this Court's decision in *Brown I*. The systems would then be "unitary" in the sense required by our decisions. . . .

For the reasons herein set forth, the judgment of the Court of Appeals is affirmed as to those parts in which it affirmed the judgment of the District Court. The order of the District Court, dated August 7, 1970, is also affirmed. It is so ordered.

Milliken v. Bradley

418 U.S. 717, 94 S.Ct. 3112 (1974)

In the 1970s, as pressure grew to desegregate urban school systems in the North and West, the school desegregation controversy took a new twist. In some large metropolitan areas, like Detroit, Michigan, "white flight" to the suburbs left inner city school districts overwhelmingly black. In response, federal district courts began ordering *inter*district remedies, requiring the busing of white children from the suburbs to inner city schools and the busing of black students to predominantly white suburban schools. When the first challenge to such court-ordered busing reached the Supreme Court, the justices split four to four. Justice Powell did not participate in that case because it came from Richmond, Virginia, where he had once headed that city's school board. But the next year the Court decided "the Detroit busing case."

Ronald Bradley, along with several other black students and the NAACP, filed a class action suit against Michigan's governor, William Milliken, and other state officials. They charged that school district lines were drawn in racially discriminatory ways. A federal district court agreed, ordering the Detroit school board to draw up a desegregation plan and asking eighty-five surrounding school districts to present evidence relevant to the creation of a comprehensive metropolitan desegregation plan. The court eventually adopted a desegregation proposal, drafted by a panel of experts, mandating the busing of school children to and from Detroit and fifty-three neighboring districts. When a federal appellate court affirmed the substance of that order, Governor Milliken appealed to the Supreme Court.

For a bare majority, Chief Justice Burger ruled that court-ordered *inter*district busing is inappropriate for resolving the *intra*district problems, where suburban districts had not engaged in *de jure* segregation, but were *de facto* segregated due to housing patterns.

The Court's decision was five to four, and the majority's opinion was announced by Chief Justice Burger. Justice Stewart concurred. Dissents were by Justices Douglas, White, and Marshall and joined by Justice Brennan.

□ *Chief Justice BURGER delivered the opinion of the Court.*

We granted *certiorari* in these consolidated cases to determine whether a federal court may impose a multidistrict, areawide remedy to a single-district *de jure* segregation problem absent any finding that the other included school districts have failed to operate unitary school systems within their districts, absent any claim or finding that the boundary lines of any affected school district were established with the purpose of fostering racial segregation in public schools, absent any finding that the included districts committed acts which effected segregation within the other districts, and absent a meaningful opportunity for the included neighboring school districts to present evidence or be heard on the propriety of a multidistrict remedy or on the question of constitutional violations by those neighboring districts. . . .

Viewing the record as a whole, it seems clear that the District Court and the Court of Appeals shifted the primary focus from a Detroit remedy to the metropolitan area only because of their conclusion that total desegregation of Detroit would not produce the racial balance which they perceived as desirable. Both courts proceeded on an assumption that the Detroit schools could not be truly desegregated—in their view of what constituted desegregation—unless the racial composition of the student body of each school substantially reflected the racial composition of the population of the metropolitan area as a whole. The metropolitan area was then defined as Detroit plus 53 of the outlying school districts. . . .

Here the District Court's approach to what constituted "actual desegregation" raises the fundamental question, not presented in *Swann* [*v. Charlotte-Mecklenberg Board of Education*, 402 U.S. 1 (1971)], as to the circumstances in which a federal court may order desegregation relief that embraces more than a single school district. The court's analytical starting point was its conclusion that school district lines are no more than arbitrary lines on a map drawn "for political convenience." Boundary lines may be bridged where there has been a constitutional violation calling for interdistrict relief, but the notion that school district lines may be casually ignored or treated as a mere administrative convenience is contrary to the history of public education in our country. No single tradition in public education is more deeply rooted than local control over the operation of schools; local autonomy has long been thought essential both to the maintenance of community concern and support for public schools and to quality of the educational process. . . . it is obvious from the scope of the interdistrict remedy itself that absent a complete restructuring of the laws of Michigan relating to school districts the District Court will become first, a *de facto* "legislative authority" to resolve these complex questions, and then the "school superintendent" for the entire area. This is a task which few, if any, judges are qualified to perform and one which would deprive the people of control of schools through their elected representatives. . . .

The record before us, voluminous as it is, contains evidence of *de jure* segregated conditions only in the Detroit schools; indeed, that was the theory on which the litigation was initially based and on which the District Court took evidence. With no showing of significant violation by the 53 outlying school districts and no evidence of any interdistrict violation or effect, the court went beyond the original theory of the case as framed by the pleadings and mandated a metropolitan area remedy. To approve the remedy ordered by the court would impose on the outlying districts, not shown to have committed any constitutional violation, a wholly impermissible remedy based on a standard not hinted at in *Brown I* and *II* or any holding of this Court.

In dissent, Justice WHITE and Justice MARSHALL undertake to demonstrate that agencies having statewide authority participated in maintaining the dual school system found to exist in Detroit. They are apparently of the view that once such participation is shown, the District Court should have a relatively free hand to reconstruct school districts outside of Detroit in fashioning relief. Our assumption, *arguendo*, that state agencies did participate in the maintenance of the Detroit system, should make it clear that it is not on this point that we part company. The difference between us arises instead from established doctrine laid down by our cases. *Brown*, *Green* [*v. School Board of New Kent County*, 391 U.S. 430 (1968)], *Swann*, [*United States v.*] *Scotland Neck* [*City Board of Education*, 407 U.S. 484 (1972)], and [*Wright v. City Council of the City of*] *Emporia*, [407 U.S. 451 (1972)], each addressed the issue of constitutional wrong in terms of an established geographic and administrative school system populated by both Negro and white children. In such a context, terms such as "unitary" and "dual" systems, and "racially identifiable schools," have meaning, and the necessary federal authority to remedy the constitutional wrong is firmly established. But the remedy is necessarily designed, as all remedies are, to restore the victims of discriminatory conduct to the position they would have occupied in the absence of such conduct. Disparate treatment of white and Negro students occurred within the Detroit school system, and not elsewhere, and on this record the remedy must be limited to that system. . . .

The constitutional right of the Negro respondents residing in Detroit is to attend a unitary school system in that district. Unless petitioners drew the district lines in a discriminatory fashion, or arranged for white students residing in the Detroit district to attend schools in Oakland and Macomb Counties, they were under no constitutional duty to make provisions for Negro students to do so. The view of the dissenters, that the existence of a dual system in Detroit can be made the basis for a decree requiring cross-district transportation of pupils, cannot be supported on the grounds that it represents merely the devising of a suitably flexible remedy for the violation of rights already established by our prior decisions. It can be supported only by drastic expansion of the constitutional right itself, an expansion without any support in either constitutional principle or precedent.

Accepting, *arguendo*, the correctness of [a] finding of state responsibility for the segregated conditions within the city of Detroit, it does not follow that an interdistrict remedy is constitutionally justified or required. With a single exception, discussed later, there has been no showing that either the State or any of the 85 outlying districts engaged in activity that had a cross-district effect. The boundaries of the Detroit School District, which are coterminous with the boundaries of the city of Detroit, were established over a century ago by neutral legislation when the city was incorporated; there is no evidence in the record, nor is there any suggestion by the respondents, that either the original boundaries of the Detroit School District, or any other school district in Michigan, were established for the purpose of creating, maintaining, or perpetuating segregation of races. There is no claim and there is no evidence hinting that petitioner outlying school districts and their predecessors, or the 30-odd other school districts in the tricounty area—but outside the District Court's "desegregation area"—have ever maintained or operated anything but unitary school systems. Unitary school systems have been required for more than a century by the Michigan Constitution as implemented by state law. Where the schools of only one district have been affected, there is no constitutional power in the courts to decree relief balancing the racial composition of that district's schools with those of the surrounding districts. . . .

We conclude that the relief ordered by the District Court and affirmed by the Court of Appeals was based upon an erroneous standard and was unsupported by record evidence that acts of the outlying districts effected the discrimination found to exist in the schools of Detroit. Accordingly, the judgment of the Court of Appeals is reversed and the case is remanded for further proceedings consistent with this opinion leading to prompt formulation of a decree directed to eliminating the segregation found to exist in Detroit city schools, a remedy which has been delayed since 1970.

Reversed and remanded.

☐ *Justice MARSHALL, with whom Justice DOUGLAS, Justice BRENNAN, and Justice WHITE join, dissenting.*

I cannot subscribe to this emasculation of our constitutional guarantee of equal protection of the laws and must respectfully dissent. Our precedents, in my view, firmly establish that where, as here, state-imposed segregation has been demonstrated, it becomes the duty of the State to eliminate root and branch all vestiges of racial discrimination and to achieve the greatest possible degree of actual desegregation. I agree with both the District Court and the Court of Appeals that, under the facts of this case, this duty cannot be fulfilled unless the State of Michigan involves outlying metropolitan area school districts in its desegregation remedy. Furthermore, I perceive no basis either in law or in the practicalities of the situation justifying the State's interposition of school district boundaries as absolute barriers to the implementation of an effective desegregation remedy. Under established and frequently used Michigan procedures, school district lines are both flexible and permeable for a wide variety of purposes, and there is no reason why they must now stand in the way of meaningful desegregation relief. . . .

Nowhere in the Court's opinion does the majority confront, let alone respond to the District Court's conclusion that a remedy limited to the city of Detroit would not effectively desegregate the Detroit city schools. I, for one, find the District Court's conclusion well supported by the record and its analysis compelled by our prior cases. . . .

Desegregation is not and was never expected to be an easy task. Racial attitudes ingrained in our Nation's childhood and adolescence are not quickly thrown aside in its middle years. But just as the inconvenience of some cannot be allowed to stand in the way of the rights of others, so public opposition, no matter how strident, cannot be permitted to divert this Court from the enforcement of the constitutional principles at issue in this case. Today's holding, I fear, is more a reflection of a perceived public mood that we have gone far enough in enforcing the Constitution's guarantee of equal justice than it is the product of neutral principles of law. In the short run, it may seem to be the easier course to allow our great metropolitan areas to be divided up each into two cities—one white, the other black—but it is a course, I predict, our people will ultimately regret. I dissent.

Freeman v. Pitts

503 U.S. 467, 112 S.CT. 1430 (1992)

Despite the Supreme Court's watershed ruling in *Brown v. Board of Education*, 347 U.S. 483 (1954), and its mandate for desegregation "with all deliberate speed," *Brown v. Board of Education*, 349 U.S. 294 (1955), the DeKalb County, Georgia, public school system (DCSS) made no effort to desegregate for more than a decade. In 1966–1967 the school board finally adopted a "freedom of choice" transfer plan that permitted blacks to go to formerly *de jure* white schools, but that had no impact on desegregating all-black schools. Then in *Green v. New Kent County School Board*, 391 U.S. 430 (1968), the Court struck down a similar "freedom of choice" plan in Virginia. The Court also directed lower courts to examine "every facet of school operations"—including student assignments, faculty, staff, transportation, extracurricular activities, and facilities—in achieving school desegregation.

Within two months of *Green*, Willie Pitts and other black parents and schoolchildren filed a class action against the DCSS to force it to abandon its freedom of choice plan. One year later a federal district court issued a consent order abolishing the freedom of choice plan, closing all formerly *de jure* black schools, and reassigning students to the remaining neighborhood schools. The court retained jurisdiction and continued to supervise the DCSS for more than a decade.

In 1986 Robert Freeman and other members of the DCSS filed a motion to lay the original litigation to rest and to obtain a declaration that "unitary status" according to factors identified in *Green* had been achieved. The district court concluded that the DCSS had achieved unitary status with respect to student assignments, transportation, facilities, and the extracurricular activities of the schools and required no further remedial efforts in these areas. But the court found continued "vestiges" of segregation in teacher and principal assignments, resource allocations, and the quality of education in different schools in the county. And the DCSS was ordered to continue to address these problems.

In appealing the district court's decisions, Pitts and other black parents countered that continuing racial imbalances in the DCSS were a vestige of past discrimination. In the more than thirty years since *Brown*, DeKalb County, along with the rest of the country, had changed. *De jure* segregation had ended, but schools remained segregated. As the DeKalb County school district grew in population from less than 70,000 to over 450,000, the percentage of black students increased from a little more than 5 percent to 47 percent. Demographic changes and the migration of blacks and whites into suburbs resulted in racially identifiable schools. In 1986–1987, as Pitts's attorneys pointed out, 50 percent of the black students attended schools that were over 90 percent black, while almost 30 percent of the white students went to schools enrolling 90 percent whites. The persistence of racially identifiable schools, Pitts's lawyers argued, required continued efforts to integrate and judicial supervision of the DCSS's operations.

The Court of Appeals for the Eleventh Circuit reversed the district court, rejecting its "incremental" approach to determining unitary status and to ending its desegregation orders. According to the appellate court, the district court erred in considering *Green*'s factors as separate and independent categories. Achieving unitary status, it held, required the DCSS to maintain racial equality for at least three years in all six categories. The appellate court also ordered the DCSS to take radical measures to achieve integration, such as pairing and clustering schools, busing, and drastic gerrymandering of school zones. That decision was promptly appealed by Freeman and the DCSS to the Supreme Court, which granted review.

The Court's decision was unanimous; Justice Kennedy announced the opinion. Justices Scalia and Souter each concurred, as did Justice Blackmun, who was joined by Justices Stevens and O'Connor.

☐ *Justice KENNEDY delivered the opinion of the Court.*

Today, we make explicit the rationale that was central in [*Pasadena City Board of Education v.*] *Spangler* [427 U.S. 424 (1976)]. A federal court in a school desegregation case has the discretion to order an incremental or partial withdrawal of its supervision and control. This discretion derives both from the constitutional authority which justified its intervention in the first instance and its ultimate objectives in formulating the decree. The authority of the court is invoked at the outset to remedy particular constitutional violations. In construing the remedial authority of the district courts, we have been guided by the principles that "judicial powers may be exercised only on the basis of a constitutional violation," and that "the nature of the violation determines the scope of the remedy." *Swann* [*v. Charlotte-Mecklenburg Board of Education*, 402 U.S. 1 (1971)]. . . .

We hold that, in the course of supervising desegregation plans, federal courts have the authority to relinquish supervision and control of school districts in incremental stages, before full compliance has been achieved in every area of school operations. While retaining jurisdiction over the case, the court may determine that it will not order further remedies in areas where the school district is in compliance with the decree. That is to say, upon a finding that a school system subject to a court-supervised desegregation plan is in compliance in some but not all areas, the court in appropriate cases may return control to the school system in those areas where compliance has been achieved, limiting further judicial supervision to operations that are not yet in full compliance with the court decree. In particular, the district court may determine that it will not order further remedies in the area of student assignments where racial imbalance is not traceable, in a proximate way, to constitutional violations. . . .

The Court of Appeals' rejection of the District Court's order rests on related premises: first, that given noncompliance in some discrete categories, there can be no partial withdrawal of judicial control; and second, until there is full compliance, heroic measures must be taken to ensure racial balance in student assignments systemwide. Under our analysis and our precedents, neither premise is correct. . . .

That there was racial imbalance in student attendance zones was not tantamount to a showing that the school district was in noncompliance with the decree or with its duties under the law. Racial balance is not to be achieved for its own sake. It is to be pursued when racial imbalance has been caused by a constitutional violation. Once the racial imbalance due to the *de jure* violation has been remedied, the school district is under no duty to remedy imbalance that is caused by demographic factors. . . .

The findings of the District Court that the population changes which occurred in DeKalb County were not caused by the policies of the school district, but rather by independent factors, are consistent with the mobility that is a distinct characteristic of our society. . . . The District Court in this case heard evidence tending to show that racially stable neighborhoods are not likely to emerge because whites prefer a racial mix of 80% white and 20% black, while blacks prefer a 50%–50% mix.

Where resegregation is a product not of state action but of private choices, it does not have constitutional implications. It is beyond the authority and beyond the practical ability of the federal courts to try to counteract these kinds of continuous and massive demographic shifts. To attempt such results would require ongoing and never-ending supervision by the courts of school districts simply because they were once *de jure* segregated. Residential housing choices, and their attendant effects on the racial composition of schools, present an ever-changing pattern, one difficult to address through judicial remedies. . . .

To say, as did the Court of Appeals, that a school district must meet all six *Green* factors before the trial court can declare the system unitary and relinquish its control over school attendance zones, and to hold further that racial balancing by all necessary means is required in the interim, is simply to vindicate a legal phrase. The law is not so formalistic. A proper rule must be based on the necessity to find a feasible remedy that insures systemwide compliance with the court decree and that is directed to curing the effects of the specific violation. . . .

The requirement that the school district show its good faith commitment to the entirety of a desegregation plan so that parents, students and the public have assurance against further injuries or stigma also should be a subject for more specific findings. We stated in *Dowell* that the good faith compliance of the district with the court order over a reasonable period of time is a factor to be considered in deciding whether or not jurisdiction could be relinquished. . . .

The judgment is reversed and the case is remanded to the Court of Appeals.

☐ *Justice SCALIA, concurring.*

At some time, we must acknowledge that it has become absurd to assume, without any further proof, that violations of the Constitution dating from the days when Lyndon Johnson was President, or earlier, continue to have an appreciable effect upon current operation of schools. We are close to that time. While we must continue to prohibit, without qualification, all racial discrimination in the operation of public schools, and to afford remedies that eliminate not only the discrimination but its identified consequences, we should consider laying aside the extraordinary, and increasingly counterfactual, presumption of *Green.* We must soon revert to the ordinary principles of our law, of our democratic heritage, and of our educational tradition: that plaintiffs alleging Equal Protection violations must prove intent and causation and not merely the existence of racial disparity; that public schooling, even in the South, should be controlled by locally elected authorities acting in conjunction with parents; and that it is "desirable" to permit pupils to attend "schools nearest their homes," *Swann.*

☐ *Justice BLACKMUN, with whom Justice STEVENS and Justice O'CONNOR join, concurring.*

Whether a district court must maintain active supervision over student assignment, and order new remedial actions depends on two factors. As the Court discusses, the district court must order changes in student assignment if it "is necessary or practicable to achieve compliance in other facets of the school system." The district court also must order affirmative action in school attendance if the school district's conduct was a "contributing cause" of the racially identifiable schools. . . .

United States v. Fordice

505 U.S. 717, 112 S.Ct. 2727 (1992)

Mississippi's public university system began in 1848 with the establishment of the University of Mississippi, exclusively enrolling whites. In succeeding decades, the state erected additional single-race educational facilities. Two more black institutions were added in 1940 and 1950. Despite the Court's watershed rulings in *Brown I* and *Brown II,* Mississippi's policy of *de jure* segregation continued. The first black student was not admitted to the University of Mississippi until 1962, when under a court order James Meredith enrolled as a student. More than two decades later, in 1985–1986, approximately 99 percent of the state's white college students were enrolled in historically all-white colleges, while 71 percent of the black students attended historically all-black schools.

This case stemmed from a 1975 lawsuit brought by black residents against Mississippi and later joined by the federal government. They charged that the state perpetuated racially separate institutions of higher education through its admissions policies. When reviewing past desegregation cases, as in *Green v. New Kent County School Board*, 391 U.S. 430 (1968), involving elementary and secondary schools, the Supreme Court had rejected school boards' proposals that "freedom of choice" plans were enough. However, in *Bazemore v. Friday*, 478 U.S. 385 (1986), a bare majority of the Burger Court upheld a freedom of choice plan, when ruling that a North Carolina State University had fulfilled its duty to desegregate its 4-H and Homemakers Clubs by simply offering open enrollment, despite the fact that the clubs remain, as a practical matter, racially segregated. Relying on *Bazemore*, a federal district court and the Court of Appeals for the Fifth Circuit held that the more exacting standard, set forth in *Green*, should not apply to institutions of higher education. Instead, the appellate court ruled that the *Bazemore* approach was more appropriate, because college enrollment is voluntary and because students are free to choose which institution they want to attend. The Department of Justice appealed that decision to the Supreme Court of the United States, which granted review.

The Court's decision was eight and one-half to one-half. Justices O'Connor and Thomas each concurred in the opinion, which was announced by Justice White. Justice Scalia delivered a separate opinion in part concurring and in part dissenting.

☐ *Justice WHITE delivered the opinion of the Court.*

Our decisions establish that a State does not discharge its constitutional obligations until it eradicates policies and practices traceable to its prior *de jure* dual system that continue to foster segregation. Thus we have consistently asked whether existing racial identifiability is attributable to the State, and examined a wide range of factors to determine whether the State has perpetuated its formerly *de jure* segregation in any facet of its institutional system. . . .

We deal first with the current admissions policies of Mississippi's public universities. As the District Court found, the three flagship historically white universities in the system—University of Mississippi, Mississippi State University, and University of Southern Mississippi—enacted policies in 1963 requiring all entrants to achieve a minimum composite score of 15 on the American College Testing Program (ACT). The court described the "discriminatory taint" of this policy, an obvious reference to the fact that, at the time, the average ACT score for white students was 18 and the average score for blacks was 7. The District Court concluded, and the en banc Court of Appeals agreed, that present admissions standards derived from policies enacted in the 1970's to redress the problem of student unpreparedness. Obviously, this mid-passage justification for perpetuating a policy enacted originally to discriminate against black students does not make the present admissions standards any less constitutionally suspect.

The present admission standards are not only traceable to the *de jure* system and were originally adopted for a discriminatory purpose, but they also have present discriminatory effects. Every Mississippi resident under 21 seeking admission to the university system must take the ACT. Any applicant who scores at least 15 qualifies for automatic admission to any of the five historically white institutions except Mississippi University for Women, which requires a score of 18 for automatic admission unless the student has a 3.0 high school grade average. Those scoring less than 15 but at least 13 automatically qualify to enter Jackson State University, Alcorn State University, and Mississippi Valley State University. Without doubt, these requirements restrict the range of choices of entering students as to which institution they may attend in a way that perpetuates segregation. Those scoring 13 or 14, with some exceptions, are excluded from the five historically white universities and if they want a higher education must go to one of the historically black institutions or attend junior college with the hope of transferring to a historically white institution. Proportionately more blacks than whites face this choice: in 1985, 72 percent of Mississippi's white high school seniors achieved an ACT composite score of 15 or better, while less than 30 percent of black high school seniors earned that score. It is not surprising then that Mississippi's universities remain predominantly identifiable by race.

The segregative effect of this automatic entrance standard is especially striking in light of the differences in minimum automatic entrance scores among the regional universities in Mississippi's system. The minimum score for automatic admission to Mississippi University for Women (MUW) is 18; it is 13 for the historically black universities. Yet MUW is assigned the same institutional mission as two other regional universities, Alcorn State and Mississippi Valley—that of providing quality undergraduate education. The effects of the policy fall disproportionately on black students who might wish to attend MUW. . . .

We also find inadequately justified by the courts below or by the record before us the differential admissions requirements between universities with dissimilar programmatic missions. . . . [W]e think the 15 ACT test score for automatic admission to the comprehensive universities, as compared with a score of 13 for the regionals, requires further justification in terms of sound educational policy.

Another constitutionally problematic aspect of the State's use of the ACT test scores is its policy of denying automatic admission if an applicant fails to earn the minimum ACT score specified for the particular institution, without also resorting to the applicant's high school grades as an additional factor in predicting college performance. The United States produced evidence that the American College Testing Program ACTP, the administering organization of the ACT, discourages use of ACT scores as the sole admissions criterion on the ground that it gives an incomplete "picture" of the student applicant's ability to perform adequately in college. . . . The record also indicated that the disparity between black and white students' high school grade averages was much narrower than the gap between their average ACT scores, thereby suggesting that an admissions formula which included grades would increase the number of black students eligible for automatic admission to all of Mississippi's public universities. . . .

A second aspect of the present system that necessitates further inquiry is the widespread duplication of programs. "Unnecessary" duplication refers, under the District Court's definition, "to those instances where two or more institutions offer the same nonessential or noncore program. Under this definition, all duplication at the bachelor's level of nonbasic liberal arts and sciences course work and all duplication at the master's level and above are considered to be unnecessary." The District Court found that 34.6 percent of the 29 undergraduate programs at historically black institutions are "unnecessarily duplicated" by the historically white universities, and that 90 percent of the graduate programs at the historically black institutions are unnecessarily duplicated at the historically white institutions. . . .

Because the former *de jure* segregated system of public universities in Mississippi impeded the free choice of prospective students, the State in dismantling that system must take the necessary steps to ensure that this choice now is truly free. The full range of policies and practices must be examined with this duty in mind. That an institution is predominantly white or black does not in itself make out a constitutional violation. But surely the State may not leave in place policies rooted in its prior officially-segregated system that serve to maintain the racial identifiability of its universities if those policies can practicably be eliminated without eroding sound educational policies. . . .

Because the District Court and the Court of Appeals failed to consider the State's duties in their proper light, the cases must be remanded.

☐ *Justice THOMAS, concurring.*

[W]e do not foreclose the possibility that there exists sound "educational justification" for maintaining historically black colleges as such. Despite the shameful history of state-enforced segregation, these institutions have survived and flourished. Indeed, they have expanded as opportunities for blacks to enter historically white institutions have expanded. . . . Although I agree that a State is not constitutionally required to maintain its historically black institutions as such, I do not understand our opinion to hold that a State is forbidden from doing so. It would be ironic, to say the least, if the institutions that sustained blacks during segregation were themselves destroyed in an effort to combat its vestiges.

☐ *Justice SCALIA, concurring in the judgment in part and dissenting in part.*

I reject . . . the effectively unsustainable burden the Court imposes on Mississippi, and all States that formerly operated segregated universities, to demonstrate compliance with *Brown I.* That requirement, which resembles what we prescribed for primary and secondary schools in *Green v. New Kent County School Board,* 391 U.S. 430 (1968), has no proper application in the context of higher education, provides no genuine guidance to States and lower courts, and is as likely to subvert as to promote the interests of those citizens on whose behalf the present suit was brought. . . .

In *Bazemore v. Friday,* we addressed a dispute parallel in all relevant respects to this one. At issue there was state financing of 4-H and Homemaker youth clubs by the North Carolina Agricultural Extension Service, a division of North Carolina State University. . . . We confined *Green* to primary and secondary public schools, where "schoolchildren must go to school" and where "school boards customarily have the power to create school attendance areas and otherwise designate the school that particular students may attend." . . .

Bazemore's standard for dismantling a dual system ought to control here: discontinuation of discriminatory practices and adoption of a neutral admissions policy. To use *Green* nomenclature, modern racial imbalance remains a "vestige" of past segregative practices in Mississippi's universities, in that the previously mandated racial identification continues to affect where students choose to enroll—just as it surely affected which clubs students chose to join in *Bazemore*. We tolerated this vestigial effect in *Bazemore*, squarely rejecting the view that the State was obliged to correct "the racial segregation resulting from [its prior] practices." And we declined to require the State, as the Court has today, to prove that no holdover practices of the *de jure* system, e.g., program offerings in the different clubs, played a role in the students' decisions of which clubs to join. If that analysis was correct six years ago in *Bazemore*, and I think it was, it must govern here as well. . . .

■ THE DEVELOPMENT OF LAW

Other Rulings on School Desegregation

CASE	VOTE	RULING
North Carolina Board of Education v. Swann, 402 U.S. 43 (1971)	9:0	Struck down a state law forbidding the use of busing to achieve school desegregation.
Wright v. City Council of Emporia, 407 U.S. 451 (1972)	5:4	Held that a city, which had been part of a county school system, could not establish a separate school if it impeded efforts to dismantle a dual school system; Chief Justice Burger and Justices Blackmun, Powell, and Rehnquist dissented.
United States v. Scotland Neck City Board of Education, 407 U.S. 484 (1972)	5:4	Struck down a state law providing for some new school districts that were 57 percent white and 43 percent black, while other districts remained over 89 percent black; Chief Justice Burger and Justices Blackmun, Powell, and Rehnquist dissented.
Keyes v. Denver School District, 413 U.S. 189 (1973)	8:1	Found that intentional segregation by a school system created a *prima facie* case for unlawful segregation in the entire school system; Justice Rehnquist dissented.

CASE	VOTE	RULING
Pasadena City Board of Education v. Spangler, 427 U.S. 424 (1976)	6:2	Held that schools need not rearrange attendance zones each year so as to ensure that a racial mix is maintained in perpetuity; Justices Brennan and Marshall dissented.

petuity; Justices Brennan and Marshall dissented.

Columbus Board of Education v. Penick, 443 U.S. 449 (1979); and *Dayton Board of Education v. Brinkman,* 443 U.S. 526 (1979)	7:2 5:4	The Court found intentional discrimination and upheld a lower court's order for massive busing, where in 1976 70 percent of all students attended schools that were either 80 percent

cent black or white; in *Penick,* Justices Powell and Rehnquist dissented, and in *Brinkman* they were joined by Chief Justice Burger and Justice Stewart in dissent.

Board of Education of City School v. Harris, 444 U.S. 130 (1979)	6:3	Found discriminatory impact in the allocation of teachers; Justices Stewart, Powell, and Rehnquist dissented.

Washington v. Seattle School District 1, 458 U.S. 457 (1982)	5:4	Struck down an initiative requiring children to attend schools nearest to their homes; Chief Justice Burger and Jus-

tices O'Connor, Powell, and Rehnquist dissented.

Crawford v. Bd. of Education of the City of Los Angeles, 458 U.S. 527 (1982)	8:1	Upheld California's amendment to its state constitution limiting state court-ordered busing for the purpose of

achieving integrated public schools; Justice Marshall dissented.

Missouri v. Jenkins (Jenkins I), 495 U.S. 33 (1990)	5:4	Justice White upheld the authority of a federal judge to order the Kansas City, Missouri,

school board to raise taxes to pay for a wide-ranging magnet school plan designed to achieve racial integration. But, in so holding, Justice White was joined by only Justices Brennan, Marshall, Stevens, and Blackmun. In a separate concurring opinion, joined by Chief Justice Rehnquist and Justices O'Connor and Scalia, Justice Kennedy declined to join the Court's holding. Simply put, in Justice Kennedy's words, "The power of taxation is one that the federal judiciary does not possess."

CASE	VOTE	RULING
Board of Education of Oklahoma City Public Schools v. Dowell, 498 U.S. 237 (1991)	5:3	Without Justice Souter's participation, the Court held that school districts that were previously required by law to elimi-

nate racial segregation could end forced busing of students in favor of neighborhood schools, even though that entails a return to a system of schools attended overwhelmingly by either black or white students. In terminating local court supervision of school districts' desegregation efforts, lower courts should consider (1) whether school districts have complied with judicial desegregation orders over a reasonable period of time; (2) whether they are likely to return to their former ways; and (3) whether they have to the extent practicable eliminated "vestiges" of prior discrimination. Justices Marshall, Blackmun, and Stevens dissented.

Freeman v. Pitts, 503 U.S. 467 (1992)	9:0	Held that lower courts may withdraw from supervising discrete categories of school oper-

ations, as identified in *Green v. New Kent County School Board,* 391 U.S. 430 (1968) (that is, student assignments, faculty, staff, transportation, extracurricular activities, and facilities), once schools show compliance with a desegregation order, and they need not await desegregation in all areas of a school system before ending judicial supervision. Concurring Justice Scalia urged an immediate end to all judicial supervision of schools that no longer intentionally discriminate, while Justices Blackmun, Stevens, and O'Connor countered that lower courts should make a probing analysis before abandoning their supervision of desegregation efforts.

United States v. Fordice, 503 U.S. 717 (1992)	8½:½	Writing for the Court, Justice White found that Mississippi's admissions policies for its col-

leges and universities perpetuated racial segregation in its institutions of higher education. In a separate opinion concurring and dissenting, Justice Scalia rejected the majority's reasoning and standards for lower courts reviewing desegregation challenges to institutions of higher education.

Missouri v. Jenkins (Jenkins II), 515 U.S. 70 (1995)	5:4	Reiterating that the lower federal courts should disengage from disegregation efforts, Chief

Justice Rehnquist held that a federal district court had exceeded its remedial owners in ordering the state to (1) fund salary increases for teachers, and (2) to continue to fund remedial "quality education" programs because student achievement scores remained "at or below national norms." Dissenting Justices Souter, Stevens, Ginsburg, and Breyer sharply disagreed with the majority's conclusion that lower courts possess no authority to order improvements in school districts so as to make them more attractive to white students.

C | *Affirmative Action and Reverse Discrimination*

In the late 1960s, the federal government took the lead in ending racial segregation and discrimination in education, housing, and employment. Along with state and local governments and private business, the federal government promoted "affirmative action" programs—programs aimed at increasing opportunities for blacks, women, and other minorities in higher education and employment. Affirmative action programs range from aggressive recruiting and remedial training programs, to setting goals and guidelines, and to set-asides and quotas specifying an exact number or percentage of admissions or jobs for blacks, women, and other minorities. Following the enactment of the Civil Rights Act of 1964, President Johnson issued an executive order (No. 11246) encouraging the use of affirmative action programs to overcome the effects of past and present discrimination. In 1967, the Department of Labor adopted a policy of preferential hiring for minorities and women and the Department of Health, Education and Welfare (HEW, now the Department of Education) assumed responsibility for affirmative action in higher education. By the 1970s, HEW issued guidelines and threatened the withholding of federal funding from colleges and universities that failed to meet its hiring and admissions goals for blacks, women, and other minorities.

Affirmative action programs sparked heated political controversy and posed an explosive issue for the Court and the country. Proponents claimed that such programs remedied the effects of past discrimination and would improve the status of blacks, women, and minorities. They pointed out that for a century and a half racial segregation was tolerated; the Constitution had not been color-blind. Moreover, they argued that racial preferences in affirmative action programs were benign; through "positive discrimination" blacks, women, and other minorities would finally achieve an equality of opportunity denied them in the past. As Justice Blackmun, concurring in *Regents of the University of California v. Bakke*, 438 U.S. 265 (1978), put it: "In order to get beyond racism, we must first take account of race. There is no other way."

Opponents of affirmative action programs raised numerous objections. Some argued that racial preferences were not benign for blacks or whites. Just as "Jim Crow" laws stigmatized blacks as inferior, so too race-conscious affirmative action programs implied that blacks were not as meritorious as whites. And racial preferences disadvantaged whites. Other critics conceded that preferential recruitment and special training programs might be appropriately and temporarily used to overcome the effects of past discrimination. But they strongly objected to quotas and set-aside programs. As a matter of public policy, they argued that it was wrong to accord special benefits to members of groups that had suffered past discrimination because those given special advantages may not have actually been victims of discrimination. Moreover, programs setting racial quotas inexorably discriminated against whites and invited charges of *reverse discrimination.* Once again dissenting Justice Harlan's opinion in *Plessy* became poignant, as critics of affirmative action charged that "The Constitution is (or ought to be) color-blind."

White males denied admission to higher education, government contracts, and employment opportunities attacked affirmative action programs for denying their rights under the Fourteenth Amendment's equal protection clause and the Civil Rights Act of 1964. The latter in dealing with federal funding of public and private institutions provides in Title VI that "[n]o person in the United States shall, on the ground of race, color, or national origin, be excluded from participation in, be denied the benefits of, or be subjected to discrimination under any program or activity receiving Federal financial assistance." In Title VII of the Civil Rights Act, Congress sought to end racial discrimination in employment in the private sector and specified that

> [n]othing contained in this subchapter shall be interpreted to require any employer, employment agency, labor organization, or joint labor-management committee subject to this subchapter to grant preferential treatment to any individual or to any group because of the race, color, religion, sex, national origin of such individual or group on account of an imbalance which may exist with respect to the total number or percentage of persons of any race, color, religion, sex, or national origin employed by any employer, referred or classified for employment by any employment agency or labor organization, admitted to membership or classified in any labor organization, or admitted to, or employed in, any apprenticeship or other training program, in comparison with the total number or percentage of such persons of such race, color, religion, sex, or national origin in any community, State, section, or other area, or in the available work force in any community, State, section or other area.

The Burger Court could not escape the constitutional and statutory challenges to affirmative action programs. A bare majority, however, sought to do so in *DeFunis v. Odegaard,* 416 U.S. 312 (1974). Marco DeFunis, Jr., was one of 1,600 applicants for admission to the University of Washington Law School but was denied a place in the first-year entering class of 150 students. He sued Charles Odegaard, president of the university, contending that the law school's admission criteria invidiously discriminated against him in violation of the Fourteenth Amendment. A state trial court agreed and ordered DeFunis's admission. On appeal, the Washington State Supreme Court reversed. By this time DeFunis was in his second year of law school, and he appealed to the Supreme Court. Justice Douglas, as circuit justice for the ninth circuit, stayed the state court's ruling pending "the final disposition of the case by [the Supreme] Court." DeFunis thus remained in school and was in his third year when the Burger Court dismissed his case as moot. A bare majority vacated the state court decision on concluding that because DeFunis would graduate at the end of the academic year the Court should not address the substantive constitutional issue in this case. Justice Brennan, joined by Justices Douglas, Marshall, and White, dissented and criticized the majority for sidestepping the issue, and warned that the controversy would inevitably return to the Court.

In a separate dissenting opinion in *DeFunis*, Justice Douglas addressed the merits of the case. In his view, the Law School Admissions Test (LSAT) may work hardships on members of minority groups, and law schools ought to find other ways to ensure diverse student bodies:

> The key to the problem is the consideration of each application *in a racially neutral way*. Since the LSAT reflects questions touching on cultural backgrounds, the Admissions Committee acted properly in my view in setting minority applications apart for separate processing. These minorities have cultural backgrounds that are vastly different from the dominant Caucasian. Many Eskimos, American Indians, Filipinos, Chicanos, Asian Indians, Burmese, and Africans come from such disparate backgrounds that a test sensitively tuned for most applicants would be wide of the mark for many minorities. . . .
>
> The key to the problem is consideration of such applications *in a racially neutral way*. Abolition of the LSAT would be a start. The invention of substitute tests might be made to get a measure of an applicant's cultural background, perception, ability to analyze, and his or her relation to groups. They are highly subjective, but unlike the LSAT they are not concealed, but in the open. A law school is not bound by any legal principle to admit students by mechanical criteria which are insensitive to the potential of such an applicant which may be realized in a more hospitable environment. It will be necessary under such an approach to put more effort into assessing each individual than is required when LSAT scores and undergraduate grades dominate the selection process. Interviews with the applicant and others who know him is [*sic*] a time-honored test. Some schools currently run summer programs in which potential students who likely would be bypassed under conventional admissions criteria are given the opportunity to try their hand at law

courses, and certainly their performance in such programs could be weighed heavily. There is, moreover, no bar to considering an individual's prior achievements in light of the racial discrimination that barred his way, as a factor. . . . Nor is there any bar to considering on an individual basis, rather than according to racial classifications, the likelihood that a particular candidate will more likely employ his legal skills to service communities that are not now adequately represented than will competing candidates. . . . Certainly such a program would substantially fulfill the Law School's interest in giving a more diverse group access to the legal profession. Such a program might be less convenient administratively than simply sorting students by race, but we have never held administrative convenience to justify racial discrimination.

Although Justice Douglas favored aggressive recruitment of minorities, he staunchly opposed the use of racial classifications and quotas. In his words:

The Equal Protection Clause commands the elimination of racial barriers, not their creation in order to satisfy our theory as to how society ought to be organized. The purpose of the University of Washington cannot be to produce black lawyers for blacks, Polish lawyers for Poles, Jewish lawyers for Jews, Irish lawyers for Irish. It should be to produce good lawyers for Americans and not to place First Amendment barriers against anyone. . . . A segregated admissions process creates suggestions of stigma and caste no less than a segregated classroom, and in the end it may produce that result despite its contrary intentions. One other assumption must be clearly disapproved; that blacks or browns cannot make it on their individual merit. That is a stamp of inferiority that a State is not permitted to place on any lawyer.

Four years after *DeFunis* and three years after Justice Douglas was replaced by Justice Stevens on the bench, the Burger Court handed down its major ruling on affirmative action programs in higher education in *Regents of the University of California v. Bakke* (1978) (see excerpt below). The justices, though, split four to four, and (with the exception of a one-paragraph statement of the facts) no other justice joined Justice Powell's opinion announcing the Court's ruling. Note that Justice Powell held that racial quotas are impermissible, but not affirmative action programs aimed at promoting diverse student bodies. Notably, he relied on an "exacting scrutiny" test, instead of the "strict scrutiny" test, in his narrowly tailored opinion applying only to higher education.

Throughout the 1980s, the Burger Court remained sharply divided over affirmative action programs and claims of reverse discrimination in employment. The justices split five to four and six to three when upholding most programs, and Justice Powell often cast the deciding vote, rebuffing the views pressed by the Reagan administration and opponents of affirmative action. Justices Brennan, Marshall, and Blackmun invariably supported affirmative action programs, while Justices Rehnquist and White generally stood in opposition.

In *United Steelworkers of America v. Weber*, 443 U.S. 193 (1979), with Justices Powell and Stewart not participating, four justices joined Justice Brennan in reading the Civil Rights Act to *permit* (although not require) private voluntary programs designed to achieve racial balance in the workplace through an on-the-job training program set up for blacks. Although Chief Justice Burger and Justice Rehnquist dissented in *Weber*, the following year Burger delivered the Court's opinion in *Fullilove v. Klutznick*, 448 U.S. 448 (1980), upholding Congress's power to set aside 10 percent of all public-works contracts for minority-owned businesses.

In two cases, the Burger Court struck down affirmative action programs. In *Firefighters Local Union No. 1784 v. Stotts*, 467 U.S. 561 (1984), the Court held that under the Civil Rights Act the seniority interests of white workers could not be sacrificed in employment layoffs to preserve jobs for more recently hired blacks. A bare majority in *Wygant v. Jackson Board of Education*, 476 U.S. 267 (1986), then interpreted the Fourteenth Amendment to bar layoffs of white teachers with more seniority than black teachers, where there was no evidence that black teachers had actually suffered past discrimination.

In Chief Justice Burger's last term (1985–1986) on the Court, however, Justice Brennan massed a majority for upholding under the Civil Rights Act a court-ordered affirmative action program setting a "hiring goal" for minority workers, in *Local 28 of the Sheet Metal Workers v. Equal Employment Opportunity Commission*, 478 U.S. 421 (1986), and a judicial consent decree setting hiring goals as a remedy for a union's past discriminatory practices, in *Local No. 93, International Association of Firefighters v. City of Cleveland*, 478 U.S. 501 (1986). Justice Brennan managed to forge majorities in two more 1987 rulings. In *United States v. Paradise*, 480 U.S. 149 (1987), he held that the equal protection clause did not bar a court-ordered quota for the promotion of blacks within the ranks of Alabama's state troopers. And in *Johnson v. Transportation Agency, Santa Clara, California*, 480 U.S. 616 (1987), Justice Brennan upheld a program for promoting minorities and women to positions that were traditionally segregated and where members of those groups had been traditionally underrepresented.

By the end of the 1980s, though, the Rehnquist Court signaled an abrupt shift in analysis and approach toward challenges to affirmative action programs, registering the impact of President Ronald Reagan's appointees to the Court, and in particular Justice Kennedy's appointment in 1988 to the seat previously occupied by Justice Powell. Note that Justice O'Connor's opinion in *City of Richmond v. J. A. Croson* (1989) (see excerpt below), when overturning Richmond's set-aside program for minority-owned businesses (modeled and adopted after the one approved by the Court in *Fullilove*), substitutes the strict scrutiny test for *Bakke's* exacting scrutiny test and indicates that only narrowly tailored affirmative action programs aimed at remedying actual victims of past discrimination will survive constitutional challenge.

One year after *Croson*, however, Justice Brennan managed to forge a bare majority for upholding affirmative action programs adopted by the *federal* government and mandated by Congress, in *Metro Broadcasting, Inc. v. Federal Communications Commission*, 497 U.S. 547 (1990). He and the two other dissenters in *Croson* were joined by Justice White (who voted with the majority in *Croson* but also with the majority in the 1980 *Fullilove* ruling upholding Congress's power to establish affirmative action programs) and Justice Stevens (who concurred in *Croson* yet dissented in *Fullilove*). Chief Justice Rehnquist and Justices O'Connor, Scalia, and Kennedy dissented.

Nonetheless, in 1993 after Justices Brennan and Marshall had left the bench, a solid majority on the Rehnquist Court made it much easier to gain standing to challenge affirmative action programs in *Northeastern Florida Chapter of the Associated Contractors of America v. City of Jacksonville, Florida*, 508 U.S. 679 (1993) (excerpted below). As a result, affirmative action programs are easier to attack in the lower federal courts under *City of Jacksonville* and much more difficult for states and localities to defend under the standards laid down in *Croson*. Subsequently, with the retirements of Justices White and Blackmun, only one justice—Justice Stevens—was left on the bench who had voted with the majority in *Metro Broadcasting*. And a bare majority of the Rehnquist Court expressly overruled that 1990 ruling in *Adarand Constructors, Inc. v. Pena*, 515 U.S. 200 (1995) (excerpted below). As in *Croson*, Justice O'Connor wrote for the majority and held that the "strict scrutiny" test, applied in *Croson* to affirmative action programs adopted by state and local governments, applies no less to federal programs, thereby overturning *Metro Broadcasting*.

A quarter of a century after *Bakke*, the controversy over affirmative action and reverse discrimination remained hotly contested and widely debated. Some states, like California, had abandoned their affirmative action programs and had implemented outreach programs for minorities, as a result of statewide initiative and referendums against affirmative action efforts. Other states, like Texas, had their programs in colleges and universities overturned by federal appellate courts, relying

on the Rehnquist Court's rulings in *J.A. Croson* and *Adarand Construc-*
tors. In order to resolve the growing conflict over the issue in the federal courts and the country, the Court granted and decided two
companion cases challenging the University of Michigan's undergraduate admissions policy based on a "point system" for individual
applicants, in *Gratz v. Bollinger* (2003) (excerpted below); and the University of Michigan Law School's "holistic" approach in student admissions that aimed to achieve diversity in its student body and a "critical
mass" of underrepresented minorities, in *Grutter v. Bollinger* (2003) (excerpted below). Dividing six to three in *Gratz*, the Court struck down
the undergraduate admissions policy. But splitting five to four in *Grut-*
ter, the justices upheld the law school's program. Notably, although
joining the majority in *Gratz*, Justice O'Connor delivered the opinion
for the Court in *Grutter* and declined to overrule *Bakke*. Justice
O'Connor also accepted as permissible the goal of achieving diversity,
rather than remedying past discrimination, in support of affirmative action programs, though she also noted that such programs should be
limited to another twenty-five years. Chief Justice Rehnquist and Justices Scalia, Kennedy, and Thomas dissented.

SELECTED BIBLIOGRAPY

Ball, Howard. *The Bakke Case: Race, Education, and Affirmative Action.* Lawrence: University of Kansas Press, 2000.

Bergmann, Barbara. *In Defense of Affirmative Action.* New York: Basic Books, 1996.

Carter, Stephen. *Reflections of an Affirmative Action Baby.* New York: Basic Books, 1991.

Crosby, Faye, and Van Der Veer, Cheryl, eds. *Sex, Race, and Merit: Debating Affirmative
Action in Education and Employment.* Ann Arbor: University of Michigan Press, 2000.

Eastland, Terry. *Ending Affirmative Action.* New York: Basic Books, 1996.

Edley, Christopher. *Not All Black and White: Affirmative Action, Race, and American Values.* New York: Hill and Wang, 1996.

Kahlenberg, Richard. *The Remedy: Class, Race, and Affirmative Action.* New York: Basic
Books, 1996.

Katznelson, Ira. *When Affirmative Action Was White.* New York: W. W. Norton, 2004.

Kinder, Donald, and Sanders, Lynn. *Divided by Color: Racial Politics and Democratic
Ideals.* Chicago: University of Chicago Press, 1996.

Post, Robert, and Rogan, Michael, eds. *Race and Representation: Affirmative Action.*
New York: Zone Books, 1998.

Rosenfeld, Michel. *Affirmative Action and Justice.* New York: Oxford University Press,
1991.

Sindler, Allan P. *Bakke, Defunis, and Minority Admissions.* New York: Longman, 1978.

Skrentny, John D. *The Ironies of Affirmative Action.* Chicago: University of Chicago
Press, 1996.

Sowell, Thomas. *Affirmative Action around the World*. New Haven, CT: Yale University Press, 2004.

Spann, Girardeau A. *The Law of Affirmative Action: Twenty-five Years of Supreme Court Decisions on Race and Remedies*. New York: New York University Press, 1999.

Thernstrom, Stephan, and Thernstrom, Abigail. *America in Black and White: One Nation, Indivisible*. New York: Simon & Schuster, 1997.

Urofsky, Melvin. *A Conflict of Rights: The Supreme Court and Affirmative Action*. New York: Scribner's, 1991.

Welch, Susan, and Gruhl, John. *Affirmative Action and Minority Enrollments in Medical and Law Schools*. Ann Arbor: University of Michigan Press, 1998.

Regents of the University of California v. Bakke
438 U.S. 265, 98 S.CT. 2733 (1978)

Alan Bakke, a white male, applied but was denied admission to the medical school at the University of California at Davis. There were only 100 openings each year, and sixteen of them were reserved for "disadvantaged" minority students (blacks, Hispanics, Asians, and American Indians). Bakke had been twice denied admission before, even though minorities who had lower grade point averages and lower scores on the Medical College Admission Test were admitted. And he decided to challenge the constitutionality of the admission policy for minorities, contending that he was denied admission on account of his race.

A state superior court held that Davis's program violated Title VI of the Civil Rights Act, the equal protection clause of the Fourteenth Amendment, and a provision of the state constitution. However, the court declined to order Bakke's admission on the grounds that he would not have been admitted even if Davis did not have its affirmative action program. Subsequently, the state supreme court ordered Bakke's admission and reaffirmed that Davis's program impermissibly used race as a factor in its admissions program, and that it could not survive "strict scrutiny" under the Fourteenth Amendment's equal protection clause because the program was not the least restrictive means of advancing the state's interests in an integrated medical profession and increasing the number of doctors serving minority patients.

The Regents of the University of California appealed the state supreme court's decision to the Supreme Court. The controversy over affirmative action programs and claims of reverse discrimination were politically volatile for the Court and the country. At the time, an unprecedented number (120) of organizations joined fifty-eight *amicus* ("friend of the court") briefs: eighty-three for the university, thirty-two for Bakke, and five urging the Court not to decide the case.

The Court's ruling was announced by Justice Lewis F. Powell in an opinion upholding affirmative action programs (but not quota systems like that at Davis), and admitting Bakke to the medical school. Powell delivered the Court's ruling because the other justices were unwilling to bend on their positions and were divided four to four on the statutory and constitutional issues.

Chief Justice Burger and Justices Rehnquist and Stewart accepted the view of Justice Stevens that the Court need not address the question of whether affirmative action programs violate the Constitution. They voted to strike down quota systems as an impermissible racial classification under Title VI of the Civil Rights Act of 1964 and to admit Bakke.

Justices White, Marshall, and Blackmun sided with Brennan in reaching the constitutional question and holding that affirmative action programs, including quotas, are constitutionally permissible remedies for past racial discrimination. They would not have admitted Bakke.

Justice Powell massed the votes, but not the justices' support for his opinion, from each bloc on each of the two key issues. His opinion found that quota systems are invalid and that Bakke should have been admitted, relying on the four votes of the Stevens bloc. At the same time, Powell upheld affirmative action programs in universities and thereby won the vote of the Brennan bloc. Powell, however, refused to accept Brennan's view that past racial discrimination justified racial quotas. Instead, Powell held that affirmative action programs, but not quotas, are permissible because under the First Amendment universities need a diverse student body to ensure academic freedom and the educational process. Powell's pragmatic rationalization for the controversial decision thus had the support of no other justice.

The Court's decision was five to four, but the justices split 1-4-4; the opinion was announced by Justice Powell. A separate opinion, in part concurring and in part dissenting, was delivered by Justice Brennan; Justices White, Marshall, and Blackmun concurred. A separate opinion, in part concurring and in part dissenting, was issued by Justice Stevens, who was joined by Chief Justice Burger and Justices Stewart and Rehnquist.

☐ *Justice POWELL delivered the opinion of the Court.*

For the reasons stated in the following opinion, I believe that so much of the judgment of the California court as holds petitioner's special admissions program unlawful and directs that respondent be admitted to the Medical School must be affirmed. For the reasons expressed in a separate opinion, my Brothers the CHIEF JUSTICE, Justice STEWART, Justice REHN-QUIST and Justice STEVENS concur in this judgment.

I also conclude for the reasons stated in the following opinion that the portion of the court's judgment enjoining petitioner from according any consideration to race in its admissions process must be reversed. For reasons expressed in separate opinions, my Brothers Justice BRENNAN, Justice WHITE, Justice MARSHALL, and Justice BLACKMUN concur in this judgment.

Affirmed in part and reversed in part. . . .

The guarantees of the Fourteenth Amendment extend to all persons. Its language is explicit: "No State shall . . . deny to any person within its jurisdiction the equal protection of the laws." It is settled beyond question that the "rights created by the first section of the Fourteenth Amendment are, by its terms, guaranteed to the individual. The rights established are personal rights." *Shelley v. Kraemer,* 334 U.S. 1 [(1948)]. The guarantee of equal protection cannot mean one thing when applied to one individual and something else when applied to a person of another color. If both are not accorded the same protection, then it is not equal. . . .

The Court has never questioned the validity of those pronouncements. Racial and ethnic distinctions of any sort are inherently suspect and thus call for the most exacting judicial examination.

This perception of racial and ethnic distinctions is rooted in our Nation's constitutional and demographic history. The Court's initial view of the Fourteenth Amendment was that its "one pervading purpose" was "the freedom of the slave race, the security and firm establishment of that freedom, and the protection of the newly-made freeman and citizen from the oppressions of those who had formerly exercised dominion over him." *Slaughter-House Cases,* 16 Wall. 36 (1873). The Equal Protection Clause, however, was "[v]irtually strangled in infancy by post-civil-war judicial reactionism." It was relegated to decades of relative desuetude while the Due Process Clause of the Fourteenth Amendment, after a short germinal period, flourished as a cornerstone in the Court's defense of property and liberty of contract. See, *e.g., Mugler v. Kansas,* 123 U.S. 623 (1887); *Allgeyer v. Louisiana,* 165 U.S. 578, [(1897)]; *Lochner v. New York,* 198 U.S. 45 (1905). In that cause, the Fourteenth Amendment's "one pervading purpose" was displaced. See, *e.g., Plessy v. Ferguson,* 163 U.S. 537 (1896). It was only as the era of substantive due process came to a close, see, *e.g., Nebbia v. New York,* 291 U.S. 502 (1934); *West Coast Hotel Co. v. Parrish,* 300 U.S. 379 (1937), that the Equal Protection Clause began to attain a genuine measure of vitality, see, *e.g., United States v. Carolene Products,* 304 U.S. 144 (1938); *Skinner v. Oklahoma ex rel. Williamson,* [316 U.S. 535 (1942)].

By that time it was no longer possible to peg the guarantees of the Fourteenth Amendment to the struggle for equality of one racial minority. During the dormancy of the Equal Protection Clause, the United States had become a Nation of minorities. Each had to struggle—and to some extent struggles still—to overcome the prejudices not of a monolithic majority, but of a "majority" composed of various minority groups of whom it was said—perhaps unfairly in many cases—that a shared characteristic was a willingness to disadvantage other groups. As the Nation filled with the stock of many lands, the reach of the Clause was gradually extended to all ethnic groups seeking protection from official discrimination. See *Strauder v. West Virginia*, 100 U.S. 303 (1880) (Celtic Irishmen) (*dictum*); *Yick Wo v. Hopkins*, 118 U.S. 356 (1886) (Chinese); *Truax v. Raich*, 239 U.S. 33 (1915) (Austrian resident aliens); *Korematsu*, [*v. United States*, 323 U.S. 214 (1944)] (Japanese); *Hernandez v. Texas*, 347 U.S. 475 (1954) (Mexican-Americans). The guarantees of equal protection, said the Court in *Yick Wo*, "are universal in their application, to all persons within the territorial jurisdiction, without regard to any differences of race, of color, or of nationality; and the equal protection of the laws is a pledge of the protection of equal laws."

Although many of the Framers of the Fourteenth Amendment conceived of its primary function as bridging the vast distance between members of the Negro race and the white "majority," *Slaughter-House Cases, supra*, the Amendment itself was framed in universal terms, without reference to color, ethnic origin, or condition of prior servitude. As this Court recently remarked in interpreting the 1866 Civil Rights Act to extend to claims of racial discrimination against white persons, "the 39th Congress was intent upon establishing in the federal law a broader principle than would have been necessary simply to meet the particular and immediate plight of the newly freed Negro slaves." *McDonald v. Santa Fe Trail Transportation Co.*, 427 U.S. 273 (1976). And that legislation was specifically broadened in 1870 to ensure that "all persons," not merely "citizens," would enjoy equal rights under the law. See *Runyon v. McCrary*, 427 U.S. 160 [(1976)] (WHITE, J., dissenting). Indeed, it is not unlikely that among the Framers were many who would have applauded a reading of the Equal Protection Clause that states a principle of universal application and is responsive to the racial, ethnic, and cultural diversity of the Nation. . . .

Over the past 30 years, this Court has embarked upon the crucial mission of interpreting the Equal Protection Clause with the view of assuring to all persons "the protection of equal laws," *Yick Wo, supra*, in a Nation confronting a legacy of slavery and racial discrimination. . . . Because the landmark decisions in this area arose in response to the continued exclusion of Negroes from the mainstream of American society, they could be characterized as involving discrimination by the "majority" white race against the Negro minority. But they need not be read as depending upon that characterization for their results. It suffices to say that "[o]ver the years, this Court has consistently repudiated '[d]istinctions between citizens solely because of their ancestry' as being 'odious to a free people whose institutions are founded upon the doctrine of equality.' " *Loving v. Virginia*, 388 U.S. 1 (1967), quoting *Hirabayashi* [*v. United States*], 320 U.S. [81 (1943)].

Petitioner urges us to adopt for the first time a more restrictive view of the Equal Protection Clause and hold that discrimination against members of the white "majority" cannot be suspect if its purpose can be characterized as "benign." The clock of our liberties, however, cannot be turned back to 1868. It is far too late to argue that the guarantee of equal protection to *all* persons permits the recognition of special wards entitled to a degree of protection greater than that accorded others. "The Fourteenth Amendment is not directed solely against discrimination due to a 'two-class theory'—that is, based upon differences between 'white' and Negro." *Hernandez* [*v. Texas*, 47 U.S. 475 (1954)].

Once the artificial line of a "two-class theory" of the Fourteenth

Amendment is put aside, the difficulties entailed in varying the level of judicial review according to a perceived "preferred" status of a particular racial or ethnic minority are intractable. The concepts of "majority" and "minority" necessarily reflect temporary arrangements and political judgments. As observed above, the white "majority" itself is composed of various minority groups, most of which can lay claim to a history of prior discrimination at the hands of the State and private individuals. Not all of these groups can receive preferential treatment and corresponding judicial tolerance of distinctions drawn in terms of race and nationality, for then the only "majority" left would be a new minority of white Anglo-Saxon Protestants. There is no principled basis for deciding which groups would merit "heightened judicial solicitude" and which would not. Courts would be asked to evaluate the extent of the prejudice and consequent harm suffered by various minority groups. Those whose societal injury is thought to exceed some arbitrary level of tolerability then would be entitled to preferential classifications at the expense of individuals belonging to other groups. Those classifications would be free from exacting judicial scrutiny. As these preferences began to have their desired effect, and the consequences of past discrimination were undone, new judicial rankings would be necessary. The kind of variable sociological and political analysis necessary to produce such rankings simply does not lie within the judicial competence—even if they otherwise were politically feasible and socially desirable.

Moreover, there are serious problems of justice connected with the idea of preference itself. First, it may not always be clear that a so-called preference is in fact benign. Courts may be asked to validate burdens imposed upon individual members of a particular group in order to advance the group's general interest. Nothing in the Constitution supports the notion that individuals may be asked to suffer otherwise impermissible burdens in order to enhance the societal standing of their ethnic groups. Second, preferential programs may only reinforce common stereotypes holding that certain groups are unable to achieve success without special protection based on a factor having no relationship to individual worth. See *DeFunis v. Odegaard*, 416 U.S. 312 (1974) (DOUGLAS, J., dissenting). Third, there is a measure of inequity in forcing innocent persons in respondent's position to bear the burdens of redressing grievances not of their making.

By hitching the meaning of the Equal Protection Clause to these transitory considerations, we would be holding, as a constitutional principle, that judicial scrutiny of classifications touching on racial and ethnic background may vary with the ebb and flow of political forces. Disparate constitutional tolerance of such classifications well may serve to exacerbate racial and ethnic antagonisms rather than alleviate them. Also, the mutability of a constitutional principle, based upon shifting political and social judgments, undermines the chances for consistent application of the Constitution from one generation to the next, a critical feature of its coherent interpretation. *Pollock v. Farmers' Loan & Trust Co.*, 157 U.S. 429 (1895) (WHITE, J., dissenting). In expounding the Constitution, the Court's role is to discern "principles sufficiently absolute to give them roots throughout the community and continuity over significant periods of time, and to lift them above the level of the pragmatic political judgments of a particular time and place." A. Cox, *The Role of the Supreme Court in American Government* 114 (1976).

If it is the individual who is entitled to judicial protection against classifications based upon his racial or ethnic background because such distinctions impinge upon personal rights, rather than the individual only because of his membership in a particular group, then constitutional standards may be applied consistently. Political judgments regarding the necessity for the particular classification may be weighed in the constitutional balance, *Korematsu v. United States*, 323 U.S. 194 (1944), but the standard of justification will remain constant. This is as it should be, since those political judgments are the product of rough compromise struck by contending groups within the democratic process. When they touch upon an individual's race or ethnic background, he is entitled to a judicial determination that the burden he is asked to bear on that basis is precisely tailored to serve a compelling governmental interest. The Constitution guarantees that right to every person regardless of his background.

Petitioner contends that on several occasions this Court has approved preferential classifications without applying the most exacting scrutiny. Most of the cases upon which petitioner relies are drawn from three areas: school desegregation, employment discrimination, and sex discrimination. Each of the cases cited presented a situation materially different from the facts of this case.

The school desegregation cases are inapposite. Each involved remedies for clearly determined constitutional violations. . . . Racial classifications thus were designed as remedies for the vindication of constitutional entitlement. Moreover, the scope of the remedies was not permitted to exceed the extent of the violations. . . . Here, there was no judicial determination of constitutional violation as a predicate for the formulation of a remedial classification.

The employment discrimination cases also do not advance petitioner's cause. . . .

In this case . . . there has been no determination by the legislature or a responsible administrative agency that the University engaged in a discriminatory practice requiring remedial efforts. Moreover, the operation of petitioner's special admissions program is quite different from the remedial measures approved in those cases. It prefers the designated minority groups at the expense of other individuals who are totally foreclosed from competition for the 16 special admissions seats in every Medical School class. Because of that foreclosure, some individuals are excluded from enjoyment of a state-provided benefit—admission to the Medical School—they otherwise would receive. When a classification denies an individual opportunities or benefits enjoyed by others solely because of his race or ethnic background, it must be regarded as suspect. *E.g., McLaurin v. Oklahoma State Regents*, 339 U.S. [637 (1950)].

We have held that in "order to justify the use of a suspect classification, a State must show that its purpose or interest is both constitutionally permissible and substantial, and that its use of the classification is 'necessary . . . to the accomplishment' of its purpose or the safeguarding of its interest." *In re Griffiths*, 413 U.S. 717 (1973) (footnotes omitted); *Loving v. Virginia*, 388 U.S. [1 (1967)]; *McLaughlin v. Florida*, 379 U.S. 184 (1964). The special admissions program purports to serve the purposes of: (i) "reducing the historic deficit of traditionally disfavored minorities in medical schools and in the medical profession"; (ii) countering the effects of societal discrimination; (iii) increasing the number of physicians who will practice in communities currently underserved; and (iv) obtaining the educational benefits that flow from an ethnically diverse student body. It is necessary to decide which, if any, of these purposes is substantial enough to support the use of a suspect classification.

If petitioner's purpose is to assure within its student body some specified percentage of a particular group merely because of its race or ethnic origin, such a preferential purpose must be rejected not as insubstantial but as facially invalid. Preferring members of any one group for no reason other than race or ethnic origin is discrimination for its own sake. This the Constitution forbids. . . .

The State certainly has a legitimate and substantial interest in ameliorating, or eliminating where feasible, the disabling effects of identified discrimination. The line of school desegregation cases, commencing with *Brown*, attests to the importance of this state goal and the commitment of the judiciary to affirm all lawful means toward its attainment. In the school cases, the States were required by court order to redress the wrongs worked by specific instances of racial discrimination. That goal was far more focused than the remedying of the effects of "societal discrimination," an amorphous concept of injury that may be ageless in its reach into the past.

We have never approved a classification that aids persons perceived as members of relatively victimized groups at the expense of other innocent individuals in the absence of judicial, legislative, or administrative findings of constitutional or statutory violations. After such findings have been made, the governmental interest in preferring members of the injured groups at the expense of others is substantial, since the legal rights of the victims must be vindicated. In such a case, the extent of the injury and the consequent remedy will have been judicially, legislatively, or administratively defined. Also, the remedial action usually remains subject to continuing oversight to assure that it will work the least harm possible to other innocent persons competing for the benefit. Without such findings of constitutional or statutory violations, it cannot be said that the government has any greater interest in helping one individual than in refraining from harming another. Thus, the government has no compelling justification for inflicting such harm.

Petitioner does not purport to have made, and is in no position to make, such findings. Its broad mission is education, not the formulation of any legislative policy or the adjudication of particular claims of illegality. For reasons similar to those stated [above in] this opinion, isolated segments of our vast governmental structures are not competent to make those decisions, at least in the absence of legislative mandates and legislatively determined criteria. . . . Lacking this capability, petitioner has not carried its burden of justification on this issue.

Hence, the purpose of helping certain groups whom the faculty of the Davis Medical School perceived as victims of "societal discrimination" does not justify a classification that imposes disadvantages upon persons like respondent, who bear no responsibility for whatever harm the beneficiaries of the special admissions program are thought to have suffered. To hold otherwise would be to convert a remedy heretofore reserved for violations of legal rights into a privilege that all institutions throughout the Nation could grant at their pleasure to whatever groups are perceived as victims of societal discrimination. That is a step we have never approved. . . .

Petitioner identifies, as another purpose of its program, improving the delivery of health-care services to communities currently underserved. It may be assumed that in some situations a State's interest in facilitating the health care of its citizens is sufficiently compelling to support the use of a suspect classification. But there is virtually no evidence in the record indicating that petitioner's special admissions program is either needed or geared to promote that goal. . . .

Petitioner simply has not carried its burden of demonstrating that it must prefer members of particular ethnic groups over all other individuals in order to promote better health-care delivery to deprived citizens. Indeed, petitioner has not shown that its preferential classification is likely to have any significant effect on the problem.

The fourth goal asserted by petitioner is the attainment of a diverse student body. This clearly is a constitutionally permissible goal for an institution of higher education. Academic freedom, though not a specifically enumerated constitutional right, long has been viewed as a special concern of the First Amendment. The freedom of a university to make its own judgments as to education includes the selection of its student body. . . .

[In] arguing that its universities must be accorded the right to select those students who will contribute the most to the "robust exchange of ideas," petitioner invokes a countervailing constitutional interest, that of the First Amendment. In this light, petitioner must be viewed as seeking to achieve a goal that is of paramount importance in the fulfillment of its mission. . . .

Physicians serve a heterogeneous population. An otherwise qualified medical student with a particular background—whether it be ethnic, geographic, culturally advantaged or disadvantaged—may bring to a professional school of medicine experiences, outlooks, and ideas that enrich the training of its student body and better equip its graduates to render with understanding their vital service to humanity.

Ethnic diversity, however, is only one element in a range of factors a university properly may consider in attaining the goal of a heterogeneous student body. Although a university must have wide discretion in making the sensitive judgments as to who should be admitted, constitutional limitations protecting individual rights may not be disregarded. Respondent urges—and the courts below have held—that petitioner's dual admissions program is a racial classification that impermissibly infringes his rights under the Fourteenth Amendment. As the interest of diversity is compelling in the context of a university's admissions program, the question remains whether the program's racial classification is necessary to promote this interest.

It may be assumed that the reservation of a specified number of seats in each class for individuals from the preferred ethnic groups would contribute to the attainment of considerable ethnic diversity in the student body. But petitioner's argument that this is the only effective means of serving the interest of diversity is seriously flawed. In a most fundamental sense the argument misconceives the nature of the state interest that would justify consideration of race or ethnic background. It is not an interest in simple ethnic diversity, in which a specified percentage of the student body is in effect guaranteed to be members of selected ethnic groups, with the remaining percentage an undifferentiated aggregation of students. The diversity that furthers a compelling state interest encompasses a far broader array of qualifications and characteristics of which racial or ethnic origin is but a single though important element. Petitioner's special admissions program, focused *solely* on ethnic diversity, would hinder rather than further attainment of genuine diversity.

Nor would the state interest in genuine diversity be served by expanding petitioner's two-track system into a multitrack program with a prescribed number of seats set aside for each identifiable category of applicants. Indeed, it is inconceivable that a university would thus pursue the logic of petitioner's two-track program to the illogical end of insulating each category of applicants with certain desired qualifications from competition with all other applicants.

The experience of other university admissions programs, which take race into account in achieving the educational diversity valued by the First Amendment, demonstrates that the assignment of a fixed number of places to a minority group is not a necessary means toward that end. An illuminating example is found in the Harvard College program:

> "In recent years Harvard College has expanded the concept of diversity to include students from disadvantaged economic, racial and ethnic groups. Harvard College now recruits not only Californians or Louisianans but also blacks and Chicanos and other minority students. . . .
>
> "In practice, this new definition of diversity has meant that race has been a factor in some admission decisions. When the Committee on Admissions reviews the large middle group of applicants who are 'admissible' and deemed capable of doing good work in their courses, the race of an applicant may tip the balance in his favor just as geographic origin or a life spent on a farm may tip the balance in other candidates' cases. A farm boy from Idaho can bring something to Harvard College that a Bostonian cannot offer. Similarly, a black student can usually bring something that a white person cannot offer.
>
> "In Harvard College admissions the Committee has not set target-quotas for the number of blacks, or of musicians, football players, physicists or Californians to be admitted in a given year. . . . But that awareness [of the necessity of including more than a token number of black students] does not mean that the Committee sets a minimum number of blacks or of people from west of the Mississippi who are to be admitted. It means only that in choosing among thousands of applicants who are not only 'admissible' academically but have other strong qualities, the Committee, with a number of criteria in mind, pays some attention to distribution among many types and categories of students." App. to Brief for Columbia University, Harvard University, Stanford University, and the University of Pennsylvania, as *Amici Curiae* 2–3.

In such an admissions program, race or ethnic background may be deemed a "plus" in a particular applicant's file, yet it does not insulate the individual from comparison with all other candidates for the available seats. The file of a particular black applicant may be examined for his potential contribution to diversity without the factor of race being decisive when compared, for example, with that of an applicant identified as an Italian-American if the latter is thought to exhibit qualities more likely to promote beneficial educational pluralism. Such qualities could include exceptional personal talents, unique work or service experience, leadership potential, maturity, demonstrated compassion, a history of overcoming disadvantage, ability to communicate with the poor, or other qualifications deemed important. In short, an admissions program operated in that way is flexible enough to consider all pertinent elements of diversity in light of the particular qualifications of each applicant, and to place them on the same footing for consideration, although not necessarily according them the same weight. Indeed the weight attributed to a particular quality may vary from year to year depending upon the "mix" both of the student body and the applicants for the incoming class.

This kind of program treats each applicant as an individual in the admissions process. The applicant who loses out on the last available seat to another candidate receiving a "plus" on the basis of ethnic background will not have been foreclosed from all consideration for that seat simply because he was not the right color or had the wrong surname. It would mean only that his combined qualifications, which may have included similar nonobjective factors, did not outweigh those of the other applicant. His qualifications would have been weighed fairly and competitively, and he would have no basis to complain of unequal treatment under the Fourteenth Amendment....

In summary, it is evident that the Davis special admissions program involves the use of an explicit racial classification never before countenanced by this Court. It tells applicants who are not Negro, Asian, or Chicano that they are totally excluded from a specific percentage of the seats in an entering class. No matter how strong their qualifications, quantitative and extracurricular, including their own potential for contribution to educational diversity, they are never afforded the chance to compete with applicants from the preferred groups for the special admissions seats. At the same time, the preferred applicants have the opportunity to compete for every seat in the class.

The fatal flaw in petitioner's preferential program is its disregard of individual rights as guaranteed by the Fourteenth Amendment. Such rights are not absolute. But when a State's distribution of benefits or imposition of burdens hinges on ancestry or the color of a person's skin, that individual is entitled to a demonstration that the challenged classification is necessary to promote a substantial state interest. Petitioner has failed to carry this burden. For this reason, that portion of the California court's judgment holding petitioner's special admissions program invalid under the Fourteenth Amendment must be affirmed.

In enjoining petitioner from ever considering the race of any applicant, however, the courts below failed to recognize that the State has a substantial interest that legitimately may be served by a properly devised admissions program involving the competitive consideration of race and ethnic origin. For this reason, so much of the California court's judgment as enjoins petitioner from any consideration of the race of any applicant must be reversed.

■ THE DEVELOPMENT OF LAW

Other Rulings on Affirmative Action and Reverse Discrimination

CASE	VOTE	FACTS AND RULING
United Steelworkers of America v. Weber, 443 U.S. 193 (1979)	5:2	The United Steelworkers of America and Kaiser Aluminum Chemical Corporation reached

agreement on an affirmative action plan to overcome racial imbalances in the company's workforce. It required that at least half of the trainees in an on-the-job training program be set aside for blacks. The plan was to remain in effect until the proportion of black workers matched the proportion of blacks in the local labor force. Brian Weber, a white worker excluded from the program, sued and claimed that the plan violated Title VII of the 1964 Civil Rights Act which prohibits "discriminat[ion] . . . because of . . . race." With Justices Powell and Stewart not participating, the majority in an opinion by Justice Brennan held that the affirmative action program was consistent with the spirit, if not the letter, of the Civil Rights Act, despite the wording of Title VII and the legislative history of the act, demonstrating that Congress had not approved of "preferential treatment for any group of citizens. In fact, it specifically forbids it."

Fullilove v. Klutznick, 448 U.S. 448 (1980)	6:3	In the Public Works Employment Act of 1977, Congress required that 10 percent of a

$4 billion public works program be set aside for "minority-controlled businesses" (MCBs), defined as companies in which at least 50 percent interest was held by blacks, Hispanics, Asian-Americans, American Indians, Eskimos, or Aleuts. The program was challenged as unconstitutional under the equal protection component of the Fifth Amendment's due process clause. Chief Justice Burger's plurality opinion adopted the exacting scrutiny test used in *Bakke* and found that Congress had an appropriate objective in remedying past discrimination, holding that "the limited use of racial and ethnic criteria, in the context of the case presented, is a constitutionally permissible *means* for achieving the congressional objectives." He also "reject[ed] the contention that in the remedial context the Congress must act in a wholly 'color-blind' fashion."

Firefighters Local Union No. 1784 v. Stotts, 467 U.S. 561 (1984)	6:3	A black member of the Memphis Fire Department sued the department, claiming that race was a factor in hiring and pro-

motion decisions in violation of Title VII of the Civil Rights Act of 1964.

CASE	VOTE	FACTS AND RULING

That suit resulted in a consent decree requiring that at least 50 percent of all new employees be black until two-fifths of the department was black. But when projected budget deficits in 1981 forced a reduction in the number of city employees, the department announced that it would abide by its "last-hired-is-the-first-fired" seniority system. A newly hired black employee challenged the layoff policy, and a federal district court ordered the department to honor the consent decree and lay off several white firefighters with more seniority than black firefighters. Justice White's opinion for the majority found the consent decree only to bind the parties to remedy past discriminatory hiring and promotion practices, to contain no agreement to set aside seniority in the event of layoffs, and held that setting aside seniority systems as a remedial measure violated Title VII of the Civil Rights Act.

Wygant v. Jackson Board of Education, 476 U.S. 267 (1986) — 5:4 — White teachers with seniority who were laid off sued when minority and less-senior teachers were retained as a result of a collective bargaining agreement between a school district and a teachers' union, which gave preference to members of minority groups and required the laying off of white teachers before black teachers with less seniority.

In a plurality opinion, joined by Chief Justice Burger and Justices Rehnquist and O'Connor, Justice Powell held that the equal protection clause of the Fourteenth Amendment was violated and that the school had not established a compelling interest or narrowly tailored its use of a racial criterion to remedy past discriminatory hiring practices.

Local 28 of the Sheet Metal Workers v. Equal Employment Opportunity Commission, 478 U.S. 421 (1986) — 5:4 — A federal district court found the union in violation of Title VII of the Civil Rights Act of 1964 for discriminating against minority workers. It ordered a 29 percent minority hiring goal (reflecting the percentage of minorities in the local labor force) as a remedy for the union's past discriminatory practices. When the union refused to comply, it was found in civil contempt, and the union appealed the court-imposed affirmative action program on the grounds that it violated Title VII. Justice Brennan found nothing in Section 706(g) of Title VII to forbid courts from imposing remedies such as "hiring goals" and "timetables" even if they "might incidentally benefit individuals who are not the actual victims of [past] discrimination." He concluded that "the relief ordered in this case . . . is narrowly tailored to further the Government's compelling interest in remedying past discrimination."

Local No. 93, International Ass'n of Firefighters v. City of — 6:3 — An independent, nonunion organization of black and His-

CASE	VOTE	FACTS AND RULING
Cleveland, 478 U.S. 501 (1986)		panic firefighters brought a class-action suit alleging discrimination in the hiring, as-

signing, and promoting of the city's firefighters. The union intervened in the suit, but over its objections, the district court handed down a consent decree (between the minority firefighters and the city), which set racial goals and quotas for the hiring and promoting of minority firefighters.

In his opinion for the majority, Justice Brennan observed that "whether or not [Section] 706(g) [of the Civil Rights Act] precludes a court from imposing certain kinds of race-conscious relief after trial, that provision does not apply to relief awarded in a consent decree. . . . [V]oluntary action available to employers and unions seeking to eradicate racial discrimination may include reasonable race-conscious relief that benefits individuals who were not actual victims of discrimination."

| *United States v. Paradise*, 480 U.S. 149 (1987) | 5:4 | Upon finding that not one of Alabama's 232 state troopers with a rank of corporal or |

higher was black, a federal district court ordered that half of all promotions to the rank of corporal go to blacks, if qualified blacks were available. An appellate court affirmed the order, as did a bare majority of the Supreme Court. In a plurality opinion, joined by Justices Marshall, Blackmun, and Powell, Justice Brennan held that the equal protection clause was not violated because the quotas advanced a compelling governmental interest in remedying past and present discrimination, and that the quota was narrowly tailored.

| *Johnson v. Transportation Agency, Santa Clara, California*, 480 U.S. 616 (1987) | 6:3 | A white male passed over for a promotion because an equally qualified female was promoted instead challenged Santa Clara |

County's program for hiring and promoting minorities and women. Under the program, within a traditionally segregated job classification where women were underrepresented, agencies could consider the gender of a qualified candidate as one factor in making its promotion decisions; but no specific quota or goal was set aside. Justice Brennan upheld the program over the claim that it violated Title VII of the 1964 Civil Rights Act. Consistent with *Bakke*, he observed that "[t]he Agency earmarks no positions for anyone; sex is but one of several factors that may be taken into account in evaluating qualified applicants for a position."

| *Martin v. Wilks*, 490 U.S. 754 (1989) | 5:4 | Some white firefighters in Birmingham, Alabama, denied promotion in favor of less- |

CASE	VOTE	FACTS AND RULING

qualified blacks, challenged a consent decree mandating goals for the hiring and promoting of blacks as a violation of Title VII of the Civil Rights Act of 1964. Chief Justice Rehnquist held that white firefighters could challenge the legality of affirmative action programs created by consent decrees because, even though not parties to the original litigation, their interests and employment were affected.

City of Richmond v. J.A. Croson, 6:3
488 U.S. 469 (1989)

Writing for the Court and striking down Richmond, Virginia's minority set-aside program for contractors (which was modeled after the federal set-aside program that was upheld in *Fullilove v. Klutznick,* 448 U.S. 448 [1980]), Justice O'Connor applied the Court's strict scrutiny standard of review in holding that affirmative action programs must be narrowly tailored to remedying actual practices of past discrimination in order to survive judicial scrutiny. Justices Marshall, Brennan, and Blackmun dissented.

Metro Broadcasting, Inc. v. Federal Communications Commission, 497 U.S. 547 (1990)   5:4

In spite of the ruling in *Croson,* Justice Brennan commanded a majority for reaffirming, as in *Fullilove,* that Congress has broader latitude than states and localities when authorizing affirmative-action programs, even without showing a close remedial nexus to past discrimination. Chief Justice Rehnquist and Justices Kennedy, O'Connor, and Scalia dissented.

Northeastern Florida Chapter of the Associated General Contractors of America v. City of Jacksonville, Florida, 508 U.S. 656 (1993)   7:2

Writing for the Court, Justice Thomas held that a building contractors' association had standing to challenge an affirmative action set-aside program, even though during the course of the litigation the city had repealed its program. Moreover, the Court held that the association did not have to show that any of its members, in the absence of the program, would have received building contracts set aside for women and minorities. Justices O'Connor and Blackmun dissented.

Adarand Constructors, Inc. v. Pena, 515 U.S. 200 (1995)   5:4

Writing for the majority, Justice O'Connor overruled *Metro Broadcasting, Inc. v. Federal Communications Commission,* 497 U.S. 547 (1990) and held that the "strict scrutiny" test applies to federal affirmative-action programs, no less than those adopted by state and local governments; Justices Breyer, Ginsburg, Souter, and Stevens dissented.

City of Richmond v. J. A. Croson
488 U.S. 469, 109 S.Ct. 706 (1989)

In 1983, the city of Richmond, Virginia, passed an ordinance requiring nonminority building contractors to subcontract 30 percent of all city-awarded projects to minority-owned businesses, or Minority Business Enterprises (MBEs). This set-aside quota was as much a remedy for past discrimination as a way to help black construction companies penetrate the local building industry. Half of Richmond's population is black, but minority-owned firms had won less than 1 percent of the $25 million awarded in city contracts in the preceding five years. The program was patterned on a federal one that the Supreme Court had upheld in *Fullilove v. Klutznick*, 448 U.S. 448 (1980). There the Burger Court was divided six to three, with Justices Stewart, Rehnquist, and Stevens dissenting. The majority in an opinion by Chief Justice Burger upheld Congress's setting aside 10 percent of all federal contracts for minority-owned businesses. That quota was based on roughly half the difference between percentages of minority contractors and minorities in the country. Likewise, Richmond's quota fell about halfway between the city's black population (50 percent) and the number of minority contractors (fewer than 1 percent) in the city. Opponents, nevertheless, charged that the program created a "racial spoils system." A majority of the city's nine-member council is black and adopted the program six to two, with one abstention.

Before bidding on a $127,000 city contract to install urinals and toilets in the city jail, an Ohio plumbing contractor, J. A. Croson, knew it had to meet the 30 percent quota and that meant finding an MBE subcontractor to supply the fixtures, because their cost alone was 75 percent of the contract. Croson won the contract as the only bidder, despite failing to interest MBE subcontractors in the project. After trying again unsuccessfully to find an MBE subcontractor, Croson sought a waiver of the 30 percent set-aside. On hearing that, an MBE finally made a bid for the subcontract, but it came in $7,000 higher than Croson had estimated. So the company asked the city to raise its contract price accordingly. The city refused and announced it would reopen bidding on the project.

Croson sued. A federal district judge's decision upholding the city's set-aside program was reversed on appeal, and Richmond took its case to the highest court in the land. The composition of the Court, however, had dramatically changed since *Fullilove* was handed down. President Ronald Reagan had elevated Justice Rehnquist to the chief justiceship in 1986 and named to the bench Justices Sandra O'Connor (in 1981), Antonin Scalia (in 1986), and Anthony Kennedy (in 1988). Whereas in *Fullilove* the justices voted six to three to uphold a federal set-aside program, here the justices split six to three in striking down Richmond's program. Justice O'Connor's opinion for the majority, moreover, registers the Rehnquist Court's shift toward a strict scrutiny of affirmative action programs.

The Court's decision was six to three, and the majority's opinion was announced by Justice O'Connor. Concurring opinions were delivered by Justices Stevens, Kennedy, and Scalia. Justices Marshall and Blackmun dissented and were joined by Justice Brennan.

☐ *Justice O'CONNOR delivered the opinion of the Court, with whom the CHIEF JUSTICE, Justice WHITE and Justice KENNEDY join in part.*

■ II

The parties and their supporting *amici* fight an initial battle over the scope of the city's power to adopt legislation designed to address the effects of past discrimination. Relying on our decision in *Wygant* [*v. Jackson Board of Education*, 476 U.S. 267 (1986)], appellee argues that the city must limit any race-based remedial efforts to eradicating the effects of its own prior discrimination. This is essentially the position taken by the Court of Appeals below. Appellant argues that our decision in *Fullilove* [*v. Klutznick*, 448 U.S. 448 (1980)], is controlling, and that as a result the city of Richmond enjoys sweeping legislative power to define and attack the effects of prior discrimination in its local construction industry. We find that neither of these two rather stark alternatives can withstand analysis. . . .

Appellant and its supporting *amici* rely heavily on *Fullilove* for the proposition that a city council, like Congress, need not make specific findings of discrimination to engage in race-conscious relief. Thus, appellant argues "[i]t would be a perversion of federalism to hold that the federal government has a compelling interest in remedying the effects of racial discrimination in its own public works program, but a city government does not."

What appellant ignores is that Congress, unlike any State or political subdivision, has a specific constitutional mandate to enforce the dictates of the Fourteenth Amendment. The power to "enforce" may at times also include the power to define situations which *Congress* determines threaten principles of equality and to adopt prophylactic rules to deal with those situations. . . .

That Congress may identify and redress the effects of society-wide discrimination does not mean that, *a fortiori*, the States and their political subdivisions are free to decide that such remedies are appropriate. Section 1 of the Fourteenth Amendment is an explicit *constraint* on state power, and the States must undertake any remedial efforts in accordance with that provision. To hold otherwise would be to cede control over the content of the Equal Protection Clause to the 50 state legislatures and their myriad political subdivisions. The mere recitation of a benign or compensatory purpose for the use of a racial classification would essentially entitle the States to exercise the full power of Congress under § 5 of the Fourteenth Amendment and insulate any racial classification from judicial scrutiny under § 1. We believe that such a result would be contrary to the intentions of the Framers of the Fourteenth Amendment, who desired to place clear limits on the States' use of race as a criterion for legislative action, and to have the federal courts enforce those limitations. . . .

It would seem equally clear, however, that a state or local subdivision (if delegated the authority from the State) has the authority to eradicate the effects of private discrimination within its own legislative jurisdiction. This authority must, of course, be exercised within the constraints of § 1 of the Fourteenth Amendment. Our decision in *Wygant* is not to the contrary. *Wygant* addressed the constitutionality of the use of racial quotas by local school authorities pursuant to an agreement reached with the local teachers' union. It was in the context of addressing the school board's power to adopt a race-based layoff program affecting its own work force that the *Wygant* plurality indicated that the Equal Protection Clause required "some showing of prior discrimination by the governmental unit involved." *Wygant*. As a matter of state law, the city of Richmond has legislative authority over its procurement policies, and can use its spending powers to remedy private discrimination, if it identifies that discrimination with the particularity required by the Fourteenth Amendment. To this extent, on the question of the city's competence, the Court of Appeals erred in following *Wygant* by rote in a case involving a state entity which has state-law authority to address discriminatory practices within local commerce under its jurisdiction.

Thus, if the city could show that it had essentially become a "passive participant" in a system of racial exclusion practiced by elements of the local construction industry, we think it clear that the city could take affirmative steps to dismantle such a system. It is beyond dispute that any public entity, state or federal, has a compelling interest in assuring that public dollars, drawn from the tax contributions of all citizens, do not serve to finance the evil of private prejudice. . . .

■ III

A. The Richmond Plan denies certain citizens the opportunity to compete for a fixed percentage of public contracts based solely upon their race. To whatever racial group these citizens belong, their "personal rights" to be treated with equal dignity and respect are implicated by a rigid rule erecting race as the sole criterion in an aspect of public decisionmaking.

Absent searching judicial inquiry into the justification for such race-based measures, there is simply no way of determining what classifications are "benign" or "remedial" and what classifications are in fact motivated by illegitimate notions of racial inferiority or simple racial politics. Indeed, the purpose of strict scrutiny is to "smoke out" illegitimate uses of race by assuring that the legislative body is pursuing a goal important enough to warrant use of a highly suspect tool. The test also ensures that the means chosen "fit" this compelling goal so closely that there is little or no possibility that the motive for the classification was illegitimate racial prejudice or stereotype.

Classifications based on race carry a danger of stigmatic harm. Unless they are strictly reserved for remedial settings, they may in fact promote notions of racial inferiority and lead to a politics of racial hostility. See *University of California Regents v. Bakke* [438 U.S. 265 (1978)] (opinion of POWELL, J.) ("[P]referential programs may only reinforce common stereotypes holding that certain groups are unable to achieve success without special protection based on a factor having no relation to individual worth"). We thus reaffirm the view expressed by the plurality in *Wygant* that the standard of review under the Equal Protection Clause is not dependent on the race of those burdened or benefited by a particular classification. . . .

Under the standard proposed by Justice MARSHALL's dissent, "[r]ace-conscious classifications designed to further remedial goals," are forthwith subject to a relaxed standard of review. How the dissent arrives at the legal conclusion that a racial classification is "designed to further remedial goals," without first engaging in an examination of the factual basis for its enactment and the nexus between its scope and that factual basis we are not told. However, once the "remedial" conclusion is reached, the dissent's standard is singularly deferential, and bears little resemblance to the close examination of legislative purpose we have engaged in when reviewing classifications based either on race or gender. . . . The dissent's watered-down version of equal protection review effectively assures that race will always be relevant in American life, and that the "ultimate goal" of "eliminat[ing] entirely from governmental decisionmaking such irrelevant factors as a human being's race," *Wygant* (STEVENS, J., dissenting) will never be achieved.

Even were we to accept a reading of the guarantee of equal protection under which the level of scrutiny varies according to the ability of different groups to defend their interests in the representative process, heightened scrutiny would still be appropriate in the circumstances of this case. One of the central arguments for applying a less exacting standard to "benign" racial classifications is that such measures essentially involve a choice made by dominant racial groups to disadvantage themselves. If one aspect of the judiciary's role under the Equal Protection Clause is to protect "discrete and insular minorities" from majoritarian prejudice or indifference, see *United States v. Carolene Products Co.*, 304 U.S. 144, 153, n. 4 (1938), some maintain that these concerns are not implicated when the "white majority" places burdens upon itself. See J. Ely, Democracy and Distrust 170 (1980).

In this case, blacks comprise approximately 50% of the population of the city of Richmond. Five of the nine seats on the City Council are held by blacks. The concern that a political majority will more easily act to the disadvantage of a minority based on unwarranted assumptions or incomplete facts would seem to militate for, not against, the application of heightened judicial scrutiny in this case.

B. The District Court found the city council's "findings sufficient to ensure that, in adopting the Plan, it was remedying the present effects of past discrimination in the *construction industry*." Like the "role model" theory employed in *Wygant*, a generalized assertion that there has been past discrimination in an entire industry provides no guidance for a legislative body to determine the precise scope of the injury it seeks to remedy. It "has no logical stopping point." *Wygant*, supra. "Relief" for such an ill-defined wrong could extend until the percentage of public contracts awarded to MBEs in

Richmond mirrored the percentage of minorities in the population as a whole.

Appellant argues that it is attempting to remedy various forms of past discrimination that are alleged to be responsible for the small number of minority businesses in the local contracting industry. Among these the city cites the exclusion of blacks from skilled construction trade unions and training programs. This past discrimination has prevented them "from following the traditional path from laborer to entrepreneur." The city also lists a host of nonracial factors which would seem to face a member of any racial group attempting to establish a new business enterprise, such as deficiencies in working capital, inability to meet bonding requirements, unfamiliarity with bidding procedures, and disability caused by an inadequate track record.

While there is no doubt that the sorry history of both private and public discrimination in this country has contributed to a lack of opportunities for black entrepreneurs, this observation, standing alone, cannot justify a rigid racial quota in the awarding of public contracts in Richmond, Virginia. Like the claim that discrimination in primary and secondary schooling justifies a rigid racial preference in medical school admissions, an amorphous claim that there has been past discrimination in a particular industry cannot justify the use of an unyielding racial quota.

It is sheer speculation how many minority firms there would be in Richmond absent past societal discrimination, just as it was sheer speculation how many minority medical students would have been admitted to the medical school at Davis absent past discrimination in educational opportunities. Defining these sorts of injuries as "identified discrimination" would give local governments license to create a patchwork of racial preferences based on statistical generalizations about any particular field of endeavor.

These defects are readily apparent in this case. The 30% quota cannot in any realistic sense be tied to any injury suffered by anyone. The District Court relied upon five predicate "facts" in reaching its conclusion that there was an adequate basis for the 30% quota: (1) the ordinance declares itself to be remedial; (2) several proponents of the measure stated their views that there had been past discrimination in the construction industry; (3) minority businesses received .67% of prime contracts from the city while minorities constituted 50% of the city's population; (4) there were very few minority contractors in local and state contractors' associations; and (5) in 1977, Congress made a determination that the effects of past discrimination had stifled minority participation in the construction industry nationally.

None of these "findings," singly or together, provide the city of Richmond with a "strong basis in evidence for its conclusion that remedial action was necessary." *Wygant.* There is nothing approaching a prima facie case of a constitutional or statutory violation by *anyone* in the Richmond construction industry.

The District Court accorded great weight to the fact that the city council designated the Plan as "remedial." But the mere recitation of a "benign" or legitimate purpose for a racial classification is entitled to little or no weight. . . .

The District Court also relied on the highly conclusionary statement of a proponent of the Plan that there was racial discrimination in the construction industry "in this area, and the State, and around the nation." It also noted that the city manager had related his view that racial discrimination still plagued the construction industry in his home city of Pittsburgh (statement of Mr. Deese). These statements are of little probative value in establishing identified discrimination in the Richmond construction industry. The fact-finding process of legislative bodies is generally entitled to a presumption of regularity and deferential review by the judiciary. But when a legislative body chooses to employ a suspect classification, it cannot rest upon a generalized assertion as to the classification's relevance to its goals. . . .

Reliance on the disparity between the number of prime contracts awarded to minority firms and the minority population of the city of Richmond is similarly misplaced. . . .

In the employment context, we have recognized that for certain entry level positions or positions requiring minimal training, statistical comparisons of the racial composition of an employer's workforce to the racial composition of the relevant population may be probative of a pattern of discrimination. . . . But where special qualifications are necessary, the relevant statistical pool for purposes of demonstrating discriminatory exclusion must be the number of minorities qualified to undertake the particular task. . . .

In this case, the city does not even know how many MBEs in the relevant market are qualified to undertake prime or subcontracting work in public construction projects. . . . Nor does the city know what percentage of total city construction dollars minority firms now receive as subcontractors on prime contracts let by the city.

To a large extent, the set-aside of subcontracting dollars seems to rest on the unsupported assumption that white prime contractors simply will not hire minority firms. . . . Without any information on minority participation in subcontracting, it is quite simply impossible to evaluate overall minority representation in the city's construction expenditures.

The city and the District Court also relied on evidence that MBE membership in local contractors' associations was extremely low. Again, standing alone this evidence is not probative of any discrimination in the local construction industry. There are numerous explanations for this dearth of minority participation, including past societal discrimination in education and economic opportunities as well as both black and white career and entrepreneurial choices. Blacks may be disproportionately attracted to industries other than construction. . . . The mere fact that black membership in these trade organizations is low, standing alone, cannot establish a prima facie case of discrimination.

Finally, the city and the District Court relied on Congress' finding in connection with the set-aside approved in *Fullilove* that there had been nationwide discrimination in the construction industry. The probative value of these findings for demonstrating the existence of discrimination in Richmond is extremely limited. By its inclusion of a waiver procedure in the national program addressed in *Fullilove*, Congress explicitly recognized that the scope of the problem would vary from market area to market area. . . .

Moreover, as noted above, Congress was exercising its powers under § 5 of the Fourteenth Amendment in making a finding that past discrimination would cause federal funds to be distributed in a manner which reinforced prior patterns of discrimination. While the States and their subdivisions may take remedial action when they possess evidence that their own spending practices are exacerbating a pattern of prior discrimination, they must identify that discrimination, public or private, with some specificity before they may use race-conscious relief. Congress has made national findings that there has been societal discrimination in a host of fields. If all a state or local government need do is find a congressional report on the subject to enact a set-aside program, the constraints of the Equal Protection Clause will, in effect, have been rendered a nullity. . . .

In sum, none of the evidence presented by the city points to any identified discrimination in the Richmond construction industry. We, therefore, hold that the city has failed to demonstrate a compelling interest in apportioning public contracting opportunities on the basis of race. To accept Richmond's claim that past societal discrimination alone can serve as the basis for rigid racial preferences would be to open the door to competing claims for "remedial relief" for every disadvantaged group. The dream of a Nation of equal citizens in a society where race is irrelevant to personal opportunity and achievement would be lost in a mosaic of shifting preferences based on inherently unmeasurable claims of past wrongs. . . .

The foregoing analysis applies only to the inclusion of blacks within the Richmond set-aside program. There is *absolutely no evidence* of past discrimination against Spanish-speaking, Oriental, Indian, Eskimo, or Aleut persons in any aspect of the Richmond construction industry. The District Court took judicial notice of the fact that the vast majority of "minority" persons in Richmond were black. It may well be that Richmond has never had an Aleut or Eskimo citizen. The random inclusion of racial groups that, as a practical matter, may never have suffered from discrimination in the construction industry in Richmond, suggests that perhaps the city's purpose was not in fact to remedy past discrimination.

If a 30% set-aside was "narrowly tailored" to compensate black contractors for past discrimination, one may legitimately ask why they are forced to share this "remedial relief" with an Aleut citizen who moves to Richmond tomorrow? The gross overinclusiveness of Richmond's racial preference strongly impugns the city's claim of remedial motivation. . . .

■ IV

As noted by the court below, it is almost impossible to assess whether the Richmond Plan is narrowly tailored to remedy prior discrimination since it is not linked to identified discrimination in any way. We limit ourselves to two observations in this regard.

First, there does not appear to have been any consideration of the use of race-neutral means to increase minority business participation in city contracting. . . . Many of the barriers to minority participation in the construction industry relied upon by the city to justify a racial classification appear to be race neutral. If MBEs disproportionately lack capital or cannot meet bonding requirements, a race-neutral program of city financing for small firms would, *a fortiori*, lead to greater minority participation. The principal opinion in *Fullilove* found that Congress had carefully examined and rejected race-neutral alternatives before enacting the MBE set-aside. . . .

Second, the 30% quota cannot be said to be narrowly tailored to any goal, except perhaps outright racial balancing. It rests upon the "completely unrealistic" assumption that minorities will choose a particular trade in lock-step proportion to their representation in the local population. . . .

Since the city must already consider bids and waivers on a case-by-case basis, it is difficult to see the need for a rigid numerical quota. As noted above, the congressional scheme upheld in *Fullilove* allowed for a waiver of the set-aside provision where an MBE's higher price was not attributable to the effects of past discrimination. Based upon proper findings, such programs are less problematic from an equal protection standpoint because they treat all candidates individually, rather than making the color of an applicant's skin the sole relevant consideration. Unlike the program upheld in *Fullilove*, the Richmond Plan's waiver system focuses solely on the availability of MBEs; there is no inquiry into whether or not the particular MBE seeking a racial preference has suffered from the effects of past discrimination by the city or prime contractors.

Given the existence of an individualized procedure, the city's only interest in maintaining a quota system rather than investigating the need for remedial action in particular cases would seem to be simple administrative convenience. But the interest in avoiding the bureaucratic effort necessary to tailor remedial relief to those who truly have suffered the effects of prior discrimination cannot justify a rigid line drawn on the basis of a suspect classification. . . . Under Richmond's scheme, a successful black, Hispanic, or Oriental entrepreneur from anywhere in the country enjoys an absolute preference over other citizens based solely on their race. We think it obvious that such a program is not narrowly tailored to remedy the effects of prior discrimination.

■ V

Nothing we say today precludes a state or local entity from taking action to rectify the effects of identified discrimination within its jurisdiction. If the city of Richmond had evidence before it that nonminority contractors were systematically excluding minority businesses from subcontracting opportunities it could take action to end the discriminatory exclusion. Where there is a significant statistical disparity between the number of qualified minority contractors willing and able to perform a particular service and the number of such contractors actually engaged by the locality or the locality's prime contractors, an inference of discriminatory exclusion could arise. Under such circumstances, the city could act to dismantle the closed business system by taking appropriate measures against those who discriminate on the basis of race or other illegitimate criteria. In the extreme case, some form of narrowly tailored racial preference might be necessary to break down patterns of deliberate exclusion. . . .

Proper findings in this regard are necessary to define both the scope of the injury and the extent of the remedy necessary to cure its effects. Such findings also serve to assure all citizens that the deviation from the norm of equal treatment of all racial and ethnic groups is a temporary matter, a measure taken in the service of the goal of equality itself. Absent such findings, there is a danger that a racial classification is merely the product of unthinking stereotypes or a form of racial politics. "[I]f there is no duty to attempt either to measure the recovery by the wrong or to distribute that recovery within the injured class in an evenhanded way, our history will adequately support a legislative preference for almost any ethnic, religious, or racial group with the political strength to negotiate 'a piece of the action' for its members." *Fullilove.* (STEVENS, J., dissenting). Because the city of Richmond has failed to identify the need for remedial action in the awarding of its public construction contracts, its treatment of its citizens on a racial basis violates the dictates of the Equal Protection Clause. Accordingly, the judgment of the Court of Appeals for the Fourth Circuit is

Affirmed.

☐ *Justice KENNEDY, concurring in part.*

I join all but Part II of Justice O'CONNOR's opinion and give this further explanation. . . .

The moral imperative of racial neutrality is the driving force of the Equal Protection Clause. Justice SCALIA's opinion underscores that proposition, quite properly in my view. The rule suggested in his opinion, which would strike down all preferences which are not necessary remedies to victims of unlawful discrimination, would serve important structural goals, as it would eliminate the necessity for courts to pass upon each racial preference that is enacted. Structural protections may be necessities if moral imperatives are to be obeyed. His opinion would make it crystal clear to the political branches, at least those of the States, that legislation must be based on criteria other than race.

Nevertheless, given that a rule of automatic invalidity for racial preferences in almost every case would be a significant break with our precedents that require a case-by-case test, I am not convinced we need adopt it at this point. On the assumption that it will vindicate the principle of race neutrality found in the Equal Protection Clause, I accept the less absolute rule contained in Justice O'CONNOR's opinion, a rule based on the proposition that any racial preference must face the most rigorous scrutiny by the courts. My reasons for doing so are as follows. First, I am confident that, in application, the strict scrutiny standard will operate in a manner generally consistent with the imperative of race neutrality, because it forbids the use even of narrowly drawn racial classifications except as a last resort. Second, the rule against race-conscious remedies is already less than an absolute one, for that relief may be the only adequate remedy after a judicial determination that a State or its instrumentality has violated the Equal Protection Clause. I note, in this connection, that evidence which would support a judicial finding of intentional discrimination may suffice also to justify remedial legislative action, for it diminishes the constitutional responsibilities of the political branches to say they must wait to act until ordered to do so by a court. Third, the strict scrutiny rule is consistent with our precedents, as Justice O'CONNOR's opinion demonstrates.

☐ *Justice SCALIA, concurring.*

In my view there is only one circumstance in which the States may act *by race* to "undo the effects of past discrimination": where that is necessary to eliminate their own maintenance of a system of unlawful racial classification. . . . We have stressed each school district's constitutional "duty to *dismantle* its dual system," and have found that "[e]ach instance of a failure or refusal to fulfill this affirmative duty *continues the violation* of the Fourteenth Amendment." *Columbus Board of Education v. Penick* [433 U.S. 449 (1979)].

I agree with the Court's *dictum* that a fundamental distinction must be drawn between the effects of "societal" discrimination and the effects of "identified" discrimination, and that the situation would be different if Richmond's plan were "tailored" to identify those particular bidders who "suffered from the effects of past discrimination by the city or prime contractors." In my view, however, the reason that would make a difference is not, as the Court states, that it would justify race-conscious action but rather that it would enable race-neutral remediation. Nothing prevents Richmond from according a contracting preference to identified victims of discrimination. While most of the beneficiaries might be black, neither the beneficiaries nor those disadvantaged by the preference would be identified *on the basis of their race.* In other words, far from justifying racial classification, identification of actual victims of discrimination makes it less supportable than ever, because more obviously unneeded. . . .

It is plainly true that in our society blacks have suffered discrimination immeasurably greater than any directed at other racial groups. But those who believe that racial preferences can help to "even the score" display, and reinforce, a manner of thinking by race that was the source of the injustice and that will, if it endures within our society, be the source of more injustice still. The relevant proposition is not that it was blacks, or Jews, or Irish who were discriminated against, but that it was individual men and women, "created equal," who were discriminated against. And the relevant resolve is that that should never happen again. Racial preferences appear to "even the score" (in some small degree) only if one embraces the proposition that our society is appropriately viewed as divided into races, making it right that an injustice rendered in the past to a black man should be compensated for by discriminating against a white. Nothing is worth that embrace. Since blacks have been disproportionately disadvantaged by racial discrimination, any race-neutral remedial program aimed at the disadvantaged *as such* will have a disproportionately beneficial impact on blacks. Only such a program, and not one that operates on the basis of race, is in accord with the letter and the spirit of our Constitution.

☐ *Justice MARSHALL, with whom Justice BRENNAN and Justice BLACKMUN join, dissenting.*

[T]oday's decision marks a deliberate and giant step backward in this Court's affirmative action jurisprudence. Cynical of one municipality's attempt to redress the effects of past racial discrimination in a particular industry, the majority launches a grape-shot attack on race-conscious remedies in general. The majority's unnecessary pronouncements will inevitably discourage or prevent governmental entities, particularly States and localities, from acting to rectify the scourge of past discrimination. This is the harsh reality of the majority's decision, but it is not the Constitution's command. . . .

My view has long been that race-conscious classifications designed to further remedial goals "must serve important governmental objectives and must be substantially related to achievement of those objectives" in order to withstand constitutional scrutiny. . . . Analyzed in terms of this two-prong standard, Richmond's set-aside, like the federal program on which it was modeled, is "plainly constitutional." . . .

Turning first to the governmental interest inquiry, Richmond has two powerful interests in setting aside a portion of public contracting funds for minority-owned enterprises. The first is the city's interest in eradicating the effects of past racial discrimination. It is far too late in the day to doubt that remedying such discrimination is a compelling, let alone an important, interest. . . .

Richmond has a second compelling interest in setting aside, where possible, a portion of its contracting dollars. That interest is the prospective one of preventing the city's own spending decisions from reinforcing and perpetuating the exclusionary effects of past discrimination.

When government channels all its contracting funds to a white-dominated community of established contractors whose racial homogeneity is the product of private discrimination, it does more than place its imprimatur on the practices which forged and which continue to define that community. It also provides a measurable boost to those economic entities that have thrived within it, while denying important economic benefits to those entities which, but for prior discrimination, might well be better qualified to receive valuable government contracts. In my view, the interest in ensuring that the government does not reflect and reinforce prior private discrimination in dispensing public contracts is every bit as strong as the interest in eliminating private discrimination—an interest which this Court has repeatedly deemed compelling.

The remaining question with respect to the "governmental interest" prong of equal protection analysis is whether Richmond has proffered satisfactory proof of past racial discrimination to support its twin interests in remediation and in governmental nonperpetuation. Although the Members of this Court have differed on the appropriate standard of review for race-conscious remedial measures, we have always regarded this factual inquiry as a practical one. Thus, the Court has eschewed rigid tests which require the provision of particular species of evidence, statistical or otherwise. At the same time we have required that government adduce evidence that, taken as a whole, is sufficient to support its claimed interest and to dispel the natural concern that it acted out of mere "paternalistic stereotyping, not on a careful consideration of modern social conditions." *Fullilove v. Klutznick.*

Richmond's reliance on localized, industry-specific findings is a far cry from the reliance on generalized "societal discrimination" which the majority decries as a basis for remedial action. But characterizing the plight of Richmond's minority contractors as mere "societal discrimination" is not the only respect in which the majority's critique shows an unwillingness to come to grips with why construction-contracting in Richmond is essentially a whites-only enterprise. The majority also takes the disingenuous approach of disaggregating Richmond's local evidence, attacking it piecemeal, and thereby concluding that no *single* piece of evidence adduced by the city, "standing alone," suffices to prove past discrimination. But items of evidence do not, of course, "stan[d] alone" or exist in alien juxtaposition; they necessarily work together, reinforcing or contradicting each other.

In any event, the majority's criticisms of individual items of Richmond's evidence rest on flimsy foundations. The majority states, for example, that reliance on the disparity between the share of city contracts awarded to minority firms (.67%) and the minority population of Richmond (approximately 50%) is "misplaced." . . . First, considering how minuscule the share of Richmond public construction contracting dollars received by minority-owned businesses is, it is hardly unreasonable to conclude that this case involves a "gross statistical disparit[y]." There are roughly equal numbers of minorities and nonminorities in Richmond—yet minority-owned businesses receive *one-seventy-fifth* the public contracting funds that other businesses receive. . . .

Second, and more fundamentally, where the issue is not present discrimination but rather whether *past* discrimination has resulted in the *continuing exclusion* of minorities from an historically tight-knit industry, a contrast between population and work force is entirely appropriate to help gauge the degree of the exclusion. . . . This contrast is especially illuminating in cases like this, where a main avenue of introduction into the work force—here, membership in the trade associations whose members presumably train apprentices and help them procure subcontracting assignments—is itself grossly dominated by nonminorities. The majority's assertion that the city "does not even know how many MBE's in the relevant market are qualified," is thus entirely beside the point. . . . The city's requirement that prime public contractors set aside 30% of their subcontracting assignments for minority-owned enterprises, subject to the ordinance's provision for waivers where minority-owned enterprises are unavailable or unwilling to participate, is designed precisely to ease minority contractors into the industry.

The majority's perfunctory dismissal of the testimony of Richmond's appointed and elected leaders is also deeply disturbing. . . .

Had the majority paused for a moment on the facts of the Richmond experience, it would have discovered that the city's leadership is deeply familiar with what racial discrimination is. The members of the Richmond City Council have spent long years witnessing multifarious acts of discrimination, including, but not limited to, the deliberate diminution of black residents' voting rights, resistance to school desegregation, and publicly sanctioned housing discrimination. Numerous decisions of federal courts chronicle this disgraceful recent history. . . .

When the legislatures and leaders of cities with histories of pervasive discrimination testify that past discrimination has infected one of their industries, armchair cynicism like that exercised by the majority has no place. . . . Disbelief is particularly inappropriate here in light of the fact that appellee Croson, which had the burden of proving unconstitutionality at trial, *Wygant*, (plurality opinion), has *at no point* come forward with *any* direct evidence that the City Council's motives were anything other than sincere.

Finally, I vehemently disagree with the majority's dismissal of the congressional and Executive Branch findings noted in *Fullilove* as having "extremely limited" probative value in this case. The majority concedes that Congress established nothing less than a "presumption" that minority contracting firms have been disadvantaged by prior discrimination. The majority, inexplicably, would forbid Richmond to "share" in this information, and permit only Congress to take note of these ample findings. In thus requiring that Richmond's local evidence be severed from the context in which it was prepared, the majority would require cities seeking to eradicate the effects of past discrimination within their borders to reinvent the evidentiary wheel and engage in unnecessarily duplicative, costly, and time-consuming factfinding.

No principle of federalism or of federal power, however, forbids a state or local government from drawing upon a nationally relevant historical record prepared by the Federal Government. . . . Of course, Richmond could have built an even more compendious record of past discrimination, one including additional stark statistics and additional individual accounts of past discrimination. But nothing in the Fourteenth Amendment imposes such onerous documentary obligations upon States and localities once the reality of past discrimination is apparent. . . .

Finally, like the federal provision, Richmond's does not interfere with any vested right of a contractor to a particular contract; instead it operates entirely prospectively. . . .

The majority today sounds a full-scale retreat from the Court's long-standing solicitude to race-conscious remedial efforts "directed toward deliverance of the century-old promise of equality of economic opportunity." *Fullilove.* The new and restrictive tests it applies scuttle one city's effort to surmount its discriminatory past, and imperil those of dozens more localities. I, however, profoundly disagree with the cramped vision of the Equal Protection Clause which the majority offers today and with its application of that vision to Richmond, Virginia's, laudable set-aside plan. The battle against pernicious racial discrimination or its effects is nowhere near won. I must dissent.

Northeastern Florida Chapter of the Associated General Contractors of America v. City of Jacksonville, Florida

508 U.S. 656, 113 S.Ct. 2297 (1993)

In 1984 Jacksonville, Florida, adopted a "Minority Business Enterprise Participation" program, under which 10 percent of the city's construction contracts were set aside for "minority business enterprises" (MBEs). An MBE was defined as a business whose ownership was at least 51 percent female or "minority"—minority was in turn defined as black, Spanish-speaking, Oriental, Indian, Eskimo, Aleut, or handicapped. The program was modeled after a federal minority set-aside program, which was upheld by the Burger Court in *Fullilove v. Klutznick*, 448 U.S. 448 (1980).

Five years later, the Northeastern Florida Chapter of the Associated General Contractors of America (AGC), an association of construction companies whose members do business in Jacksonville and do not qualify as MBEs, challenged the constitutionality of the program as a violation of the Fourteenth Amendment's equal protection clause. The AGC claimed that its members "would have . . . bid on . . . designated set aside contracts but for the restrictions imposed" by the city's ordinance. That lawsuit resulted in a federal district court's issuing an injunction restraining the city from further using its set-aside program. But a federal appellate court reversed upon concluding that the AGC failed to show an irreparable injury. Then, on remand in 1990, the district court found that the city's program was inconsistent with the Rehnquist Court's ruling in *City of Richmond v. J. A. Croson*, 488 U.S. 469 (1989), which struck down a minority set-aside program and made affirmative action programs extremely difficult to defend and enforce. Once again Jacksonville appealed, and the Court of Appeals for the Eleventh Circuit held that the AGC lacked standing to sue because it had failed to show that, in the absence of the set-aside program, any of its members would have bid successfully for any of the construction contracts.

The AGC appealed that decision to the Supreme Court, which granted *certiorari*. Subsequently, the city repealed its set-aside ordinance and replaced it with another entitled "African-American and Women's Business Enterprise Participation," which was more narrowly tailored in light of the guidelines laid down in *J. A. Croson*. Unlike its 1984 ordinance, Jacksonville's 1992 ordinance (1) benefited only women and blacks; (2) eliminated the 10 percent set-aside and substituted "participation goals," ranging from 5 to 16 percent, depending on the type of contract; and (3) provided five alternative methods for companies to meet its "participation goals" for women and blacks. The city also filed at the Supreme Court a motion asking that the case be dismissed as moot, since it had abandoned the original set-aside program, but that motion was denied.

The Court's decision was seven to two, with Justice Thomas announcing the majority's opinion. Justice O'Connor's dissent was joined by Justice Blackmun.

☐ *Justice THOMAS delivered the opinion of the Court.*

In their brief on the merits, respondents reassert their claim that the repeal of the challenged ordinance renders the case moot. We decline to disturb our earlier ruling, however; now, as then, the mootness question is controlled by City of *Mesquite v. Aladdin's Castle, Inc.*, 455 U.S. 283 (1982), where we applied the "well settled" rule that "a defendant's voluntary cessation of a challenged practice does not deprive a federal court of its power to determine the legality of the practice." . . .

We hold that the case is not moot, and we now turn to the question on which we granted *certiorari*: whether petitioner has standing to challenge Jacksonville's ordinance.

The doctrine of standing is "an essential and unchanging part of the case-or-controversy requirement of Article III," *Lujan v. Defenders of Wildlife,* [505 U.S. 555] (1992), which itself "defines with respect to the Judicial Branch the idea of separation of powers on which the Federal Government is founded," *Allen v. Wright,* 468 U.S. 737 (1984). It has been established by a long line of cases that a party seeking to invoke a federal court's jurisdiction must demonstrate three things: (1) "injury in fact," by which we mean an invasion of a legally protected interest that is "(a) concrete and particularized, and (b) actual or imminent, not conjectural or hypothetical;" (2) a causal relationship between the injury and the challenged conduct, by which we mean that the injury "fairly can be traced to the challenged action of the defendant," and has not resulted "from the independent action of some third party not before the court," *Simon v. Eastern Kentucky Welfare Rights Org.,* 426 U.S. 26 (1976); and (3) a likelihood that the injury will be redressed by a favorable decision, by which we mean that the "prospect of obtaining relief from the injury as a result of a favorable ruling" is not "too speculative." These elements are the "irreducible minimum," *Valley Forge Christian College v. Americans United for Separation of Church and State, Inc.,* 454 U.S. 464 (1982), required by the Constitution. . . .

The decision that is most closely analogous to this case, however, is *Regents of University of California v. Bakke,* 438 U.S. 265 (1978), where a twice-rejected white male applicant claimed that a medical school's admissions program, which reserved 16 of the 100 places in the entering class for minority applicants, was inconsistent with the Equal Protection Clause. Addressing the argument that the applicant lacked standing to challenge the program, Justice POWELL concluded that the "constitutional requirements of Art. III" had been satisfied, because the requisite "injury" was the medical school's "decision not to permit Bakke to compete for all 100 places in the class, simply because of his race." Thus, "even if Bakke had been unable to prove that he would have been admitted in the absence of the special program, it would not follow that he lacked standing." This portion of Justice POWELL's opinion was joined by four other Justices.

When the government erects a barrier that makes it more difficult for members of one group to obtain a benefit than it is for members of another group, a member of the former group seeking to challenge the barrier need not allege that he would have obtained the benefit but for the barrier in order to establish standing. The "injury in fact" in an equal protection case of this variety is the denial of equal treatment resulting from the imposition of the barrier, not the ultimate inability to obtain the benefit. And in the context of a challenge to a set-aside program, the "injury in fact" is the inability to compete on an equal footing in the bidding process, not the loss of a contract. See [*City of Richmond v. J.A.*] *Croson,* 488 U.S. [469 (1989)]. To establish standing, therefore, a party challenging a set-aside program like Jacksonville's need only demonstrate that it is able and ready to bid on contracts and that a discriminatory policy prevents it from doing so on an equal basis.

In urging affirmance, respondents rely primarily upon *Warth v. Seldin,* 422 U.S. 490 (1975). There the plaintiffs claimed that a town's zoning ordinance, both by its terms and as enforced, violated the Fourteenth Amendment insofar as it had the effect of preventing people of low and moderate income from living in the town. Seeking to intervene in the suit, an association of construction firms alleged that the zoning restrictions had deprived some of its members of business opportunities and profits. We held that the association lacked standing, [because in that case the plaintiffs] . . . "failed to show the existence of any injury to its members of sufficient immediacy and ripeness to warrant judicial intervention."

We think *Warth* is distinguishable. Unlike the other cases that we have discussed, *Warth* did not involve an allegation that some discriminatory classification prevented the plaintiff from competing on an equal footing in its quest for a benefit. In both *Bakke* and this case, the allegation was that the plaintiff (or the plaintiff's membership) was excluded from consideration for a certain portion of benefits—in *Bakke*, places in a medical school class; here, municipal contracts. In *Warth*, by contrast, there was no claim that the construction association's members could not apply for variances and building permits on the same basis as other firms; what the association objected to were the "refusals by the town officials to grant variances and permits." The firms' complaint, in other words, was not that they could not compete equally; it was that they did not win. Thus, while there is undoubtedly some tension between *Warth* and the aforementioned line of cases, this case is governed by the latter. . . .

In its complaint petitioner alleged that its members regularly bid on construction contracts in Jacksonville, and that they would have bid on contracts set aside pursuant to the city's ordinance were they so able. Because those allegations have not been challenged (by way of a motion for summary judgment, for example), we must assume that they are true. Given that assumption, and given the legal standard we have reaffirmed today, it was inappropriate for the Court of Appeals to order that petitioner's complaint be dismissed for lack of standing. The judgment of the Court of Appeals is therefore reversed, and the case is remanded for further proceedings consistent with this opinion.

☐ *Justice O'CONNOR, with whom Justice BLACKMUN joins, dissents in an opinion expressing the view that the case was moot and that the majority should not have addressed the standing issue.*

Adarand Constructors, Inc. v. Peña
515 U.S. 200, 115 S.Ct. 2097 (1995)

Adarand Constructors, Inc., a Colorado-based highway company specializing in guardrail work, submitted a low bid to Mountain Gravel, which had received a contract from the Department of Transportation (DoT) for a construction project. But Gonzales Construction Company, a Hispanic American–owned company, was selected for the work instead. Mountain Gravel picked the latter company over Adarand because the Small Business Act made it a matter of federal policy to encourage subcontracting to "small business concerns owned and controlled by socially and economically disadvantaged individuals." The act defines "socially disadvantaged individuals" as "those who have been subject to racial or ethnic prejudice or cultural bias." The act also established the goal of participation of small businesses "owned or controlled by socially and economically disadvantaged individuals" at "not less than 5 percent of the total value of all prime contract and subcontract awards for each fiscal year." In addition, the Surface Transportation and Uniform Relocation Assistance Act of 1987 (STURAA), a DoT appropriations measure, stipulates that "not less than 10 percent" of appropriated funds "be expended with small business concerns owned and controlled by socially and economically disadvantaged individuals."

After losing the subcontract to Gonzales Construction Company, Adarand filed a suit in federal district court, contending that the federal laws and policy presumptions governing the DoT's subcontracting guidelines violated the Fourteenth Amendment's equal protection clause. The district court rejected Adarand's claims. A federal appellate court affirmed that decision on the basis of *Fullilove v. Klutznick*, 448 U.S. 448 (1980), and *Metro Broadcasting v. Federal Communications Commission*, 497 U.S. 547 (1990), whereupon Adarand appealed to the Supreme Court.

The Court's ruling was five to four and opinion announced by Justice O'Connor. Justices Scalia and Thomas filed concurring opinions. Justices Stevens and Souter filed dissenting opinions, as did Justice Ginsburg, who was joined by Justice Breyer.

> ☐ *Justice O'CONNOR announced the judgment of the Court and delivered an opinion with respect to Parts I, II, III-A, III-B, III-D, and IV, which is for the Court except insofar as it might be inconsistent with the views expressed in Justice SCALIA's concurrence, and an opinion with respect to Part III-C in which Justice KENNEDY joins.*

■ III

Adarand's claim arises under the Fifth Amendment to the Constitution, which provides that "No person shall . . . be deprived of life, liberty, or property, without due process of law." Although this Court has always understood that Clause to provide some measure of protection against arbitrary treatment by the Federal Government, it is not as explicit a guarantee of equal treatment as the Fourteenth Amendment, which provides that "No State shall . . . deny to any person within its jurisdiction the equal protection of the laws." Our cases have accorded varying degrees of significance to the difference in the language of those two Clauses. We think it necessary to revisit the issue here.

■ A

Through the 1940s, this Court had routinely taken the view in non-race-related cases that, "unlike the Fourteenth Amendment, the Fifth contains no equal protection clause and it provides no guaranty against discriminatory legislation by Congress." *Detroit Bank v. United States*, 317 U.S. 329 (1943). When the Court first faced a Fifth Amendment equal protection challenge to a federal racial classification, it adopted a similar approach, with most unfortunate results. In *Hirabayashi v. United States*, 320 U.S. 81 (1943), the Court considered a curfew applicable only to persons of Japanese ancestry. The Court observed—correctly—that "distinctions between citizens solely because of their ancestry are by their very nature odious to a free people whose institutions are founded upon the doctrine of equality," and that "racial discriminations are in most circumstances irrelevant and therefore prohibited." But it also cited *Detroit Bank* for the proposition that the Fifth Amendment "restrains only such discriminatory legislation by Congress as amounts to a denial of due process," and upheld the curfew because "circumstances within the knowledge of those charged with the responsibility for maintaining the national defense afforded a rational basis for the decision which they made." Eighteen months later, the Court again approved wartime measures directed at persons of Japanese ancestry. *Korematsu v. United States*, 323 U.S. 214 (1944), concerned an order that completely excluded such persons from particular areas. . . .

In *Bolling v. Sharpe*, 347 U.S. 497 (1954), the Court for the first time explicitly questioned the existence of any difference between the obligations of the Federal Government and the States to avoid racial classifications. *Bolling* did note that "the 'equal protection of the laws' is a more explicit safeguard of prohibited unfairness than 'due process of law.' " But *Bolling* then concluded that, "in view of [the] decision that the Constitution prohibits the states from maintaining racially segregated public schools, it would be unthinkable that the same Constitution would impose a lesser duty on the Federal Government."

Bolling's facts concerned school desegregation, but its reasoning was not so limited. The Court's observations that "distinctions between citizens solely because of their ancestry are by their very nature odious," *Hirabayashi*, and that "all legal restrictions which curtail the civil rights of a single racial group are immediately suspect," *Korematsu*, carry no less force in the context of federal action than in the context of action by the States—indeed, they first appeared in cases concerning action by the Federal Government. . . . Later cases in contexts other than school desegregation did not distinguish between the duties of the States and the Federal Government to avoid racial classifications. . . .

■ B

Most of the cases discussed above involved classifications burdening groups that have suffered discrimination in our society. In 1978, the Court confronted the question whether race-based governmental action designed to benefit such groups should also be subject to "the most rigid scrutiny." *Regents of Univ. of California v. Bakke*, 438 U.S. 265 [(1978)], involved an equal protection challenge to a state-run medical school's practice of reserving a number of spaces in its entering class for minority students. The petitioners argued that "strict scrutiny" should apply only to "classifications that disadvantage 'discrete and insular minorities.' " *Bakke* did not produce an opinion for the Court, but Justice POWELL's opinion announcing the Court's judgment rejected the argument. In a passage joined by Justice WHITE, Justice POWELL wrote that "the guarantee of equal protection cannot mean one thing when applied to one individual and something else when applied to a person of another color." He concluded that "racial and ethnic distinctions of any sort are inherently suspect and thus call for the most exacting judicial examination." . . .

Two years after *Bakke*, the Court faced another challenge to remedial race-based action, this time involving action undertaken by the Federal Government. In *Fullilove v. Klutznick*, 448 U.S. 448 (1980), the Court upheld Congress' inclusion of a 10% set-aside for minority-owned businesses in the Public Works Employment Act of 1977. As in *Bakke*, there was no opinion for the Court. Chief Justice BURGER, in an opinion joined by Justices WHITE and POWELL, observed that "any preference based on racial or ethnic criteria must necessarily receive a most searching examination to make sure that it does not conflict with constitutional guarantees." That opinion, however, "did not adopt, either expressly or implicitly, the formulas of analysis articulated in such cases as [*Bakke*]." It employed instead a two-part test which asked, first, "whether the objectives of the legislation are within the power of Congress," and second, "whether the limited use of racial and ethnic criteria, in the context presented, is a constitutionally permissible means for achieving the congressional objectives." It then upheld the program under that test, adding at the end of the opinion that the program also "would survive judicial review under either 'test' articulated in the several *Bakke* opinions." . . .

In *Wygant v. Jackson Board of Ed.*, 476 U.S. 267 (1986), the Court considered a Fourteenth Amendment challenge to another form of remedial racial classification. The issue in *Wygant* was whether a school board could adopt race-based preferences in determining which teachers to lay off. Justice POWELL's plurality opinion observed that "the level of scrutiny does not change merely because the challenged classification operates against a group that historically has not been subject to governmental discrimination," and stated the two-part inquiry as "whether the layoff provision is supported by a compelling state purpose and whether the means chosen to accomplish that purpose are narrowly tailored." In other words, "racial classifications of any sort must be subjected to 'strict scrutiny.' " . . .

The Court's failure to produce a majority opinion in *Bakke*, *Fullilove*, and *Wygant* left unresolved the proper analysis for remedial race-based governmental action.

The Court resolved the issue, at least in part, in 1989. [*City of*] *Richmond v. J. A. Croson Co.*, 488 U.S. 469 (1989), concerned a city's determination that 30% of its contracting work should go to minority-owned businesses. A majority of the Court in *Croson* held that "the standard of review under the Equal Protection Clause is not dependent on the race of those burdened or benefited by a particular classification," and that the single standard of review for racial classifications should be "strict scrutiny." The Court also thought it "obvious that [the] program is not narrowly tailored to remedy the effects of prior discrimination."

With *Croson*, the Court finally agreed that the Fourteenth Amendment requires strict scrutiny of all race-based action by state and local governments. But *Croson* of course had no occasion to declare what standard of review the Fifth Amendment requires for such action taken by the Federal Government. . . .

Despite lingering uncertainty in the details, however, the Court's cases through *Croson* had established three general propositions with respect to governmental racial classifications. First, skepticism: "any preference based on racial or ethnic criteria must necessarily receive a most searching examination," *Wygant*. Second, consistency: "the standard of review under the Equal Protection Clause is not dependent on the race of those burdened or benefited by a particular classification," *Croson*. And third, congruence: "equal protection analysis in the Fifth Amendment area is the same as that under the Fourteenth Amendment," *Buckley v. Valeo*, 424 U.S. [1 (1976)]. Taken together, these three propositions lead to the conclusion that any person, of whatever race, has the right to demand that any governmental actor subject to the Constitution justify any racial classification subjecting that person to unequal treatment under the strictest judicial scrutiny. . . .

A year later, however, the Court took a surprising turn. *Metro Broadcasting, Inc. v. [Federal Communications Commission]*, 497 U.S. 547 (1990), involved a Fifth Amendment challenge to two race-based policies of the Federal Communications Commission. In *Metro Broadcasting*, the Court repudiated the long-held notion that "it would be unthinkable that the same Constitution would impose a lesser duty on the Federal Government" than it does on a State to afford equal protection of the laws, *Bolling*. It did so by holding that "benign" federal racial classifications need only satisfy intermediate scrutiny, even though *Croson* had recently concluded that such classifications enacted by a State must satisfy strict scrutiny. "Benign" federal racial classifications, the Court said, "—even if those measures are not 'remedial' in the sense of being designed to compensate victims of past governmental or societal discrimination—are constitutionally permissible to the extent that they serve important governmental objectives within the power of Congress and are substantially related to achievement of those objectives." The Court did not explain how to tell whether a racial classification should be deemed "benign," other than to express "confidence that an 'examination of the legislative scheme and its history' will separate benign measures from other types of racial classifications."

Applying this test, the Court first noted that the FCC policies at issue did not serve as a remedy for past discrimination. Proceeding on the assumption that the policies were nonetheless "benign," it concluded that they served the "important governmental objective" of "enhancing broadcast diversity," and that they were "substantially related" to that objective. It therefore upheld the policies.

By adopting intermediate scrutiny as the standard of review for congressionally mandated "benign" racial classifications, *Metro Broadcasting* departed from prior cases in two significant respects. First, it turned its back on *Croson's* explanation of why strict scrutiny of all governmental racial classifications is essential: "Absent searching judicial inquiry into the justification for such race-based measures, there is simply no way of determining what classifications are 'benign' or 'remedial' and what classifications are in fact motivated by illegitimate notions of racial inferiority or simple racial politics. Indeed, the purpose of strict scrutiny is to 'smoke out' illegitimate uses of race by assuring that the legislative body is pursuing a goal important enough to warrant use of a highly suspect tool. The test also ensures that the means chosen 'fit' this compelling goal so closely that there is little or no possibility that the motive for the classification was illegitimate racial prejudice or stereotype." *Croson.* We adhere to that view today, despite the surface appeal of holding "benign" racial classifications to a lower standard, because "it may not always be clear that a so-called preference is in fact benign," *Bakke.*

Second, *Metro Broadcasting* squarely rejected one of the three propositions established by the Court's earlier equal protection cases, namely, congruence between the standards applicable to federal and state racial classifications, and in so doing also undermined the other two—skepticism of all racial classifications, and consistency of treatment irrespective of the race of the burdened or benefited group. Under *Metro Broadcasting*, certain racial classifications ("benign" ones enacted by the Federal Government) should be treated less skeptically than others; and the race of the benefited group is critical to the determination of which standard of review to apply. *Metro Broadcasting* was thus a significant departure from much of what had come before it.

The three propositions undermined by *Metro Broadcasting* all derive from the basic principle that the Fifth and Fourteenth Amendments to the Constitution protect persons, not groups. . . . Accordingly, we hold today that all racial classifications, imposed by whatever federal, state, or local governmental actor, must be analyzed by a reviewing court under strict scrutiny. In other words, such classifications are constitutional only if they are narrowly tailored measures that further compelling governmental interests. To the extent that *Metro Broadcasting* is inconsistent with that holding, it is overruled. . . .

■ C

It is worth pointing out the difference between the applications of *stare decisis* in this case and in *Planned Parenthood of Southeastern Pa. v. Casey*, [505 U.S. 833] (1992). *Casey* explained how considerations of *stare decisis* inform the decision whether to overrule a long-established precedent that has become integrated into the fabric of the law. Overruling precedent of that kind naturally may have consequences for "the ideal of the rule of law." In addition, such precedent is likely to have engendered substantial reliance, as was true in *Casey* itself. But in this case, as we have explained, we do not face a precedent of that kind, because *Metro Broadcasting* itself departed from our prior cases—and did so quite recently. By refusing to follow *Metro Broadcasting*, then, we do not depart from the fabric of the law; we restore it. . . .

■ D

Our action today makes explicit what Justice POWELL thought implicit in the *Fullilove* lead opinion: federal racial classifications, like those of a State, must serve a compelling governmental interest, and must be narrowly tailored to further that interest. Of course, it follows that to the extent (if any) that *Fullilove* held federal racial classifications to be subject to a less rigorous standard, it is no longer controlling. But we need not decide today whether the program upheld in *Fullilove* would survive strict scrutiny as our more recent cases have defined it. . . .

Finally, we wish to dispel the notion that strict scrutiny is "strict in theory, but fatal in fact." *Fullilove*. The unhappy persistence of both the practice and the lingering effects of racial discrimination against minority groups in this country is an unfortunate reality, and government is not disqualified from acting in response to it. As recently as 1987, for example, every Justice of this Court agreed that the Alabama Department of Public Safety's "pervasive, systematic, and obstinate discriminatory conduct" justified a narrowly tailored race-based remedy. See *United States v. Paradise*, 480 U.S. [149 (1987)]. When race-based action is necessary to further a compelling interest, such action is within constitutional constraints if it satisfies the "narrow tailoring" test this Court has set out in previous cases. . . .

Accordingly, the judgment of the Court of Appeals is vacated, and the case is remanded for further proceedings consistent with this opinion.

☐ *Justice SCALIA, concurring in part and concurring in the judgment.*

I join the opinion of the Court, except Part III-C, and except insofar as it may be inconsistent with the following: In my view, government can never have a "compelling interest" in discriminating on the basis of race in order to "make up" for past racial discrimination in the opposite direction. Individuals who have been wronged by unlawful racial discrimination should be made whole; but under our Constitution there can be no such thing as either a creditor or a debtor race. That concept is alien to the Constitution's focus upon the individual, see Amdt. 14, Sec. 1 ("Nor shall any State . . . deny to any person" the equal protection of the laws), and its rejection of dispositions based on race, see Amdt. 15, Sec. 1 (prohibiting abridgment of the right to vote "on account of race") or based on blood, see Art. III, Sec. 3 ("No Attainder of Treason shall work Corruption of Blood"); Art. I, Sec. 9 ("No Title of Nobility shall be granted by the United States"). To pursue the concept of racial entitlement—even for the most admirable and benign of purposes—is to reinforce and preserve for future mischief the way of thinking that produced race slavery, race privilege and race hatred. In the eyes of government, we are just one race here. It is American. . . .

☐ *Justice STEVENS, with whom Justice GINSBURG joins, dissenting.*

Instead of deciding this case in accordance with controlling precedent, the Court today delivers a disconcerting lecture about the evils of governmental racial classifications. For its text the Court has selected three propositions, represented by the bywords "skepticism," "consistency," and "congruence." I shall comment on each of these propositions, then add a few words about *stare decisis*, and finally explain why I believe this Court has a duty to affirm the judgment of the Court of Appeals.

The Court's concept of skepticism is, at least in principle, a good statement of law and of common sense. Undoubtedly, a court should be wary of a governmental decision that relies upon a racial classification. . . . But, as the opinions in *Fullilove* demonstrate, substantial agreement on the standard to be applied in deciding difficult cases does not necessarily lead to agreement on how those cases actually should or will be resolved. In my judgment, because uniform standards are often anything but uniform, we should evaluate the Court's comments on "consistency," "congruence," and *stare decisis* with the same type of skepticism that the Court advocates for the underlying issue.

The Court's concept of "consistency" assumes that there is no significant difference between a decision by the majority to impose a special burden on the members of a minority race and a decision by the majority to provide a benefit to certain members of that minority notwithstanding its incidental burden on some members of the majority. In my opinion that assumption is untenable. There is no moral or constitutional equivalence between a policy that is designed to perpetuate a caste system and one that seeks to eradicate racial subordination. Invidious discrimination is an engine of oppression, subjugating a disfavored group to enhance or maintain the power of the majority. Remedial race-based preferences reflect the opposite impulse: a desire to foster equality in society. . . .

To illustrate the point, consider our cases addressing the Federal Government's discrimination against Japanese Americans during World War II, *Hirabayashi*, and *Korematsu*. The discrimination at issue in those cases was invidious because the Government imposed special burdens—a curfew and exclusion from certain areas on the West Coast—on the members of a minority class defined by racial and ethnic characteristics. Members of the same racially defined class exhibited exceptional heroism in the service of our country during that War. Now suppose Congress decided to reward that service with a federal program that gave all Japanese-American veterans an extraordinary preference in Government employment. Cf. *Personnel Administrator of Mass. v. Feeney*, 442 U.S. 256 (1979). If Congress had done so, the same racial characteristics that motivated the discriminatory burdens in *Hirabayashi* and *Korematsu* would have defined the preferred class of veterans. Nevertheless, "consistency" surely would not require us to describe the incidental burden on everyone else in the country as "odious" or "invidious" as those terms were used in those cases. We should reject a concept of "consistency" that would view the special preferences that the National Government has provided to Native Americans since 1834 as comparable to the official discrimination against African Americans that was prevalent for much of our history.

The consistency that the Court espouses would disregard the difference between a "No Trespassing" sign and a welcome mat. It would treat a Dixiecrat Senator's decision to vote against Thurgood MARSHALL's confirmation in order to keep African Americans off the Supreme Court as on a par with President Johnson's evaluation of his nominee's race as a positive factor. It would equate a law that made black citizens ineligible for military service with a program aimed at recruiting black soldiers. An attempt by the majority to exclude members of a minority race from a regulated market is fundamentally different from a subsidy that enables a relatively small group of newcomers to enter that market. An interest in "consistency" does not justify treating differences as though they were similarities. . . .

Nothing is inherently wrong with applying a single standard to fundamentally different situations, as long as that standard takes relevant differences into account. For example, if the Court in all equal protection cases were to insist that differential treatment be justified by relevant characteristics of the members of the favored and disfavored classes that provide a legitimate basis for disparate treatment, such a standard would treat dissimilar cases differently while still recognizing that there is, after all, only one Equal Protection Clause. See *Cleburne v. Cleburne Living Center, Inc.*, 473 U.S. 432 (1985). Under such a standard, subsidies for disadvantaged businesses may be constitutional though special taxes on such businesses would be invalid. But a single standard that purports to equate remedial preferences with invidious discrimination cannot be defended in the name of "equal protection."

Moreover, the Court may find that its new "consistency" approach to race-based classifications is difficult to square with its insistence upon rigidly separate categories for discrimination against different classes of individuals. For example, as the law currently stands, the Court will apply "intermediate scrutiny" to cases of invidious gender discrimination and "strict scrutiny" to cases of invidious race discrimination, while applying the same standard for benign classifications as for invidious ones. If this remains the law, then today's lecture about "consistency" will produce the anomalous result that the Government can more easily enact affirmative-action programs to remedy discrimination against women than it can enact affirmative-action programs to remedy discrimination against African Americans—even though the primary purpose of the Equal Protection Clause was to end discrimination against the former slaves. When a court becomes preoccupied with abstract standards, it risks sacrificing common sense at the altar of formal consistency. . . .

The Court's concept of "congruence" assumes that there is no significant difference between a decision by the Congress of the United States to adopt an affirmative-action program and such a decision by a State or a municipality. In my opinion that assumption is untenable. It ignores important practical and legal differences between federal and state or local decision-makers.

These differences have been identified repeatedly and consistently both in opinions of the Court and in separate opinions authored by members of today's majority. Thus, in *Metro Broadcasting*, in which we upheld a federal program designed to foster racial diversity in broadcasting, we identified the special "institutional competence" of our National Legislature. "It is of overriding significance in these cases," we were careful to emphasize, "that the FCC's minority ownership programs have been specifically approved—indeed, mandated—by Congress." We recalled the several opinions in *Fullilove* that admonished this Court to "approach our task with appropriate deference to the Congress, a co-equal branch charged by the Constitution with the power to 'provide for the . . . general Welfare of the United States' and 'to enforce, by appropriate legislation, the equal protection guarantees of the Fourteenth Amendment.' "

The majority in *Metro Broadcasting* and the plurality in *Fullilove* were not alone in relying upon a critical distinction between federal and state programs. . . . In her plurality opinion in *Croson*, Justice O'CONNOR also emphasized the importance of this distinction when she responded to the City's argument that *Fullilove* was controlling. She wrote: "What appellant ignores is that Congress, unlike any State or political subdivision, has a specific constitutional mandate to enforce the dictates of the Fourteenth Amendment. The power to 'enforce' may at times also include the power to define situations which Congress determines threaten principles of equality and to adopt pro-phylactic rules to deal with those situations. The Civil War Amendments themselves worked a dramatic change in the balance between congressional and state power over matters of race."

An additional reason for giving greater deference to the National Legis-lature than to a local law-making body is that federal affirmative-action pro-grams represent the will of our entire Nation's elected representatives, whereas a state or local program may have an impact on nonresident entities who played no part in the decision to enact it. Thus, in the state or local con-text, individuals who were unable to vote for the local representatives who enacted a race-conscious program may nonetheless feel the effects of that program. This difference recalls the goals of the Commerce Clause, U.S. Const., Art. I, Sec. 8, cl. 3, which permits Congress to legislate on certain matters of national importance while denying power to the States in this area for fear of undue impact upon out-of-state residents.

Our opinion in *Metro Broadcasting* relied on several constitutional pro-visions to justify the greater deference we owe to Congress when it acts with respect to private individuals. In the programs challenged in this case, Con-gress has acted both with respect to private individuals and, as in *Fullilove*, with respect to the States themselves. When Congress does this, it draws its power directly from Sec. 5 of the Fourteenth Amendment. That section reads: "The Congress shall have power to enforce, by appropriate legislation, the provisions of this article." One of the "provisions of this article" that Congress is thus empowered to enforce reads: "No State shall make or en-force any law which shall abridge the privileges or immunities of citizens of the United States; nor shall any State deprive any person of life, liberty, or property, without due process of law; nor deny to any person within its jurisdiction the equal protection of the laws." U.S. Const., Amdt. 14, Sec. 1. The Fourteenth Amendment directly empowers Congress at the same time it expressly limits the States. This is no accident. It represents our Nation's consensus, achieved after hard experience throughout our sorry history of race relations, that the Federal Government must be the primary defender of racial minorities against the States, some of which may be inclined to op-press such minorities. A rule of "congruence" that ignores a purposeful "in-congruity" so fundamental to our system of government is unacceptable.

The Court's concept of *stare decisis* treats some of the language we have used in explaining our decisions as though it were more important than our actual holdings. In my opinion that treatment is incorrect. . . . In the Court's view, our decision in *Metro Broadcasting* was inconsistent with the rule an-nounced in *Croson*. But two decisive distinctions separate those two cases. First, *Metro Broadcasting* involved a federal program, whereas *Croson* involved a city ordinance. *Metro Broadcasting* thus drew primary support from *Fullilove*, which predated *Croson* and which *Croson* distinguished on the grounds of the federal-state dichotomy that the majority today discredits. Although members of today's majority trumpeted the importance of that distinction in *Croson*, they now reject it in the name of "congruence." It is therefore quite wrong for the Court to suggest today that overruling *Metro Broadcasting* merely restores the status quo ante, for the law at the time of that decision was entirely open to the result the Court reached. Today's decision is an un-justified departure from settled law.

Second, *Metro Broadcasting*'s holding rested on more than its application of "intermediate scrutiny." Indeed, I have always believed that, labels notwithstanding, the FCC program we upheld in that case would have satisfied any of our various standards in affirmative-action cases—including the one the majority fashions today. What truly distinguishes *Metro Broadcasting* from our other affirmative-action precedents is the distinctive goal of the federal program in that case. Instead of merely seeking to remedy past discrimination, the FCC program was intended to achieve future benefits in the form of broadcast diversity. Reliance on race as a legitimate means of achieving diversity was first endorsed by Justice POWELL in *Bakke*. . . .

The Court's suggestion that it may be necessary in the future to overrule *Fullilove* in order to restore the fabric of the law is even more disingenuous than its treatment of *Metro Broadcasting*. For the Court endorses the "strict scrutiny" standard that Justice POWELL applied in *Bakke*, and acknowledges that he applied that standard in *Fullilove* as well. Moreover, Chief Justice BURGER also expressly concluded that the program we considered in *Fullilove* was valid under any of the tests articulated in *Bakke*, which of course included Justice POWELL's. The Court thus adopts a standard applied in *Fullilove* the same time it questions that case's continued vitality and accuses it of departing from prior law. . . .

The Court's holding in *Fullilove* surely governs the result in this case. The Public Works Employment Act of 1977, which this Court upheld in *Fullilove*, is different in several critical respects from the portions of the Small Business Act (SBA), and the Surface Transportation and Uniform Relocation Assistance Act of 1987 (STURAA), challenged in this case. Each of those differences makes the current program designed to provide assistance to disadvantaged business enterprises (DBE's) significantly less objectionable than the 1977 categorical grant of $400 million in exchange for a 10% set-aside in public contracts to "a class of investors defined solely by racial characteristics." *Fullilove*. In no meaningful respect is the current scheme more objectionable than the 1977 Act. Thus, if the 1977 Act was constitutional, then so must be the SBA and STURAA. Indeed, even if my dissenting views in *Fullilove* had prevailed, this program would be valid.

Unlike the 1977 Act, the present statutory scheme does not make race the sole criterion of eligibility for participation in the program. Race does give rise to a rebuttable presumption of social disadvantage which, at least under STURAA, gives rise to a second rebuttable presumption of economic disadvantage. But a small business may qualify as a DBE, by showing that it is both socially and economically disadvantaged, even if it receives neither of these presumptions. Thus, the current preference is more inclusive than the 1977 Act because it does not make race a necessary qualification.

More importantly, race is not a sufficient qualification. Whereas a millionaire with a long history of financial successes, who was a member of numerous social clubs and trade associations, would have qualified for a preference under the 1977 Act merely because he was an Asian American or an African American, neither the SBA nor STURAA creates any such anomaly. The DBE program excludes members of minority races who are not, in fact, socially or economically disadvantaged. The presumption of social disadvantage reflects the unfortunate fact that irrational racial prejudice—along with its lingering effects—still survives. The presumption of economic disadvantage embodies a recognition that success in the private sector of the economy is often attributable, in part, to social skills and relationships. Unlike the 1977 set-asides, the current preference is designed to overcome the social and economic disadvantages that are often associated with racial characteristics. If, in a particular case, these disadvantages are not present, the presumptions can be rebutted. The program is thus designed to allow race to play a part in the decisional process only when there is a meaningful basis for assuming its relevance. In this connection, I think it is particularly significant that the current program targets the negotiation of subcontracts between private firms. The 1977 Act applied entirely to the award of public contracts, an area of the economy in which social relationships should be irrelevant and in which proper supervision of government contracting officers should preclude any discrimination against particular bidders on account of their race. In this case, in contrast, the program seeks to overcome barriers of prejudice between private parties—specifically, between general contractors and subcontractors. The SBA and STURAA embody Congress' recognition that such barriers may actually handicap minority firms seeking business as subcontractors from established leaders in the industry that have a history of doing business with their golfing partners. Indeed, minority subcontractors may face more obstacles than direct, intentional racial prejudice: they may face particular barriers simply because they are more likely to be new in the business and less likely to know others in the business. Given such difficulties, Congress could reasonably find that a minority subcontractor is less likely to receive favors from the entrenched businesspersons who award subcontracts only to people with whom—or with whose friends—they have an existing relationship. This program, then, if in part a remedy for past discrimination, is most importantly a forward-looking response to practical problems faced by minority subcontractors. . . .

My skeptical scrutiny of the Court's opinion leaves me in dissent. The majority's concept of "consistency" ignores a difference, fundamental to the idea of equal protection, between oppression and assistance. The majority's concept of "congruence" ignores a difference, fundamental to our constitutional system, between the Federal Government and the States. And the majority's concept of *stare decisis* ignores the force of binding precedent. I would affirm the judgment of the Court of Appeals.

□ *Justice GINSBURG, with whom Justice BREYER joins, dissenting.*

The statutes and regulations at issue, as the Court indicates, were adopted by the political branches in response to an "unfortunate reality": "the unhappy persistence of both the practice and the lingering effects of racial discrimination against minority groups in this country." The United States suffers from those lingering effects because, for most of our Nation's history, the idea that "we are just one race" (SCALIA, J.) was not embraced. For generations, our lawmakers and judges were unprepared to say that there is in this land no superior race, no race inferior to any other. In *Plessy v. Ferguson*, 163 U.S. 537 (1896), not only did this Court endorse the oppressive practice of race segregation, but even Justice HARLAN, the advocate of a "color-blind" Constitution, stated: "The white race deems itself to be the dominant race in this country. And so it is, in prestige, in achievements, in education, in wealth and in power. So, I doubt not, it will continue to be for all time, if it remains true to its great heritage and holds fast to the principles of constitutional liberty." (HARLAN, J., dissenting).

Not until *Loving v. Virginia*, 388 U.S. 1 (1967), which held unconstitutional Virginia's ban on interracial marriages, could one say with security that the Constitution and this Court would abide no measure "designed to maintain White Supremacy."

The divisions in this difficult case should not obscure the Court's recognition of the persistence of racial inequality and a majority's acknowledgment of Congress' authority to act affirmatively, not only to end discrimination, but also to counteract discrimination's lingering effects. Those effects, reflective of a system of racial caste only recently ended, are evident in our workplaces, markets, and neighborhoods. Job applicants with identical resumes, qualifications, and interview styles still experience different receptions, depending on their race. White and African-American consumers still encounter different deals. People of color looking for housing still face discriminatory treatment by landlords, real estate agents, and mortgage lenders. Minority entrepreneurs sometimes fail to gain contracts though they are the low bidders, and they are sometimes refused work even after winning contracts. Bias both conscious and unconscious, reflecting traditional and unexamined habits of thought, keeps up barriers that must come down if equal opportunity and nondiscrimination are ever genuinely to become this country's law and practice. Given this history and its practical consequences, Congress surely can conclude that a carefully designed affirmative action program may help to realize, finally, the "equal protection of the laws" the Fourteenth Amendment has promised since 1868. . . .

For a classification made to hasten the day when "we are just one race," however, the lead opinion has dispelled the notion that "strict scrutiny" is " 'fatal in fact.' " Properly, a majority of the Court calls for review that is searching, in order to ferret out classifications in reality malign, but masquerading as benign. The Court's once lax review of sex-based classifications demonstrates the need for such suspicion. Today's decision thus usefully reiterates that the purpose of strict scrutiny "is precisely to distinguish legitimate from illegitimate uses of race in governmental decisionmaking," "to 'differentiate between' permissible and impermissible governmental use of race," to distinguish " 'between a "No Trespassing" sign and a welcome mat.' " . . .

While I would not disturb the programs challenged in this case, and would leave their improvement to the political branches, I see today's decision as one that allows our precedent to evolve, still to be informed by and responsive to changing conditions.

Gratz v. Bollinger
539 U.S. 244, 123 S.Ct. 2411 (2003)

The University of Michigan receives over 13,000 applications for admission into its College of Literature, Science, and Arts, and admits approximately 3,950 students each year. In order to achieve a diverse student body, the college gave preference to applicants from "under-represented minority groups," including African Americans, Hispanics, and Native Americans. In the mid-1990s the college used different admissions criteria and set aside a number of seats in each entering class to achieve a numerical target. In 1998–1999, however, the college changed its policy in favor of a point system. Under that system the college used a "selection index" or ranking on a 150-point scale in three categories: test scores, academic record, and other factors. As many as 110 of those points were based on test scores and academic achievements. A maximum of 40 points were assigned for other factors, including 20 points for students from underrepresented minority groups or from socioeconomically disadvantaged families; 16 points for state residents from rural areas; 4 points for children of alumni. In general, applicants in the range of 100 to 150 points were admitted; those between 95 and 99 were admitted or postponed; 90 to 94 postponed or delayed; 75 to 89 delayed or postponed; and 74 and below delayed or rejected.

In 1995, Jennifer Gratz applied for admission. Her high school grade point average was 3.8 and her ACT standardized test score was 25. The college initially delayed her admission and then placed her on an extended wait list. Under the college's guidelines at the time all underrepresented minority applicants with Ms. Gratz's credentials were admitted, regardless of whether they were in- or out-of-state residents. Ms. Gratz filed a class action lawsuit challenging the constitutionality of the admissions program. In December 2000, a federal district court held that the college's admissions system in 1995–1998 violated the Fourteenth Amendment, but held that its use of a point system was permissible and advanced a compelling governmental interest in promoting diversity in higher education. Ms. Gratz appealed that decision.

The lower court was reversed by a vote of six to three. Chief Justice Rehnquist delivered the opinion of the Court. Justices O'Connor, Breyer, and Thomas filed concurring opinions. Justices Stevens, Souter, and Ginsburg filed dissenting opinions.

□ *CHIEF JUSTICE REHNQUIST delivered the opinion of the Court.*

We granted *certiorari* in this case to decide whether "the University of Michigan's use of racial preferences in undergraduate admissions violate[s] the Equal Protection Clause of the Fourteenth Amendment, Title VI of the Civil Rights Act of 1964." Because we find that the manner in which the University considers the race of applicants in its undergraduate admissions guidelines violates these constitutional and statutory provisions, we reverse that portion of the District Court's decision upholding the guidelines. . . .

Beginning with the 1998 academic year, the OUA [Office of Undergraduate Admissions] dispensed with the Guidelines tables and the SCUGA point system in favor of a "selection index," on which an applicant could score a maximum of 150 points. This index was divided linearly into ranges generally calling for admissions dispositions as follows: 100–150 (admit); 95–99 (admit or postpone); 90–94 (postpone or admit); 75–89 (delay or postpone); 74 and below (delay or reject).

Each application received points based on high school grade point average, standardized test scores, academic quality of an applicant's high school, strength or weakness of high school curriculum, in-state residency, alumni relationship, personal essay, and personal achievement or leadership. Of particular significance here, under a "miscellaneous" category, an applicant was entitled to 20 points based upon his or her membership in an underrepresented racial or ethnic minority group. The University explained that the " 'development of the selection index for admissions in 1998 changed only the mechanics, not the substance of how race and ethnicity were considered in admissions.' " . . .

During 1999 and 2000, the OUA used the selection index, under which every applicant from an underrepresented racial or ethnic minority group was awarded 20 points. Starting in 1999, however, the University established an Admissions Review Committee (ARC), to provide an additional level of consideration for some applications. Under the new system, counselors may, in their discretion, "flag" an application for the ARC to review after determining that the applicant (1) is academically prepared to succeed at the University, (2) has achieved a minimum selection index score, and (3) possesses a quality or characteristic important to the University's composition of its freshman class, such as high class rank, unique life experiences, challenges, circumstances, interests or talents, socioeconomic disadvantage, and underrepresented race, ethnicity, or geography. After reviewing "flagged" applications, the ARC determines whether to admit, defer, or deny each applicant. . . .

It is by now well established that "all racial classifications reviewable under the Equal Protection Clause must be strictly scrutinized." *Adarand Constructors, Inc. v. Peña*, 515 U.S. 200 (1995). This " 'standard of review . . . is not dependent on the race of those burdened or benefited by a particular classification.' " Thus, "any person, of whatever race, has the right to demand that any governmental actor subject to the Constitution justify any racial classification subjecting that person to unequal treatment under the strictest of judicial scrutiny."

To withstand our strict scrutiny analysis, respondents must demonstrate that the University's use of race in its current admission program employs "narrowly tailored measures that further compelling governmental interests." Because "[r]acial classifications are simply too pernicious to permit any but the most exact connection between justification and classification," *Fullilove v. Klutznick*, 448 U.S. 448 (1980), our review of whether such requirements have been met must entail " 'a most searching examination.' " We find that the University's policy, which automatically distributes 20 points, or one-fifth of the points needed to guarantee admission, to every single "underrepresented minority" applicant solely because of race, is not narrowly tailored to achieve the interest in educational diversity that respondents claim justifies their program.

In *Bakke*, Justice POWELL reiterated that "[p]referring members of any one group for no reason other than race or ethnic origin is discrimination for its own sake." He then explained, however, that in his view it would be permissible for a university to employ an admissions program in which "race or ethnic background may be deemed a 'plus' in a particular applicant's file." . . .

Justice POWELL's opinion in *Bakke* emphasized the importance of considering each particular applicant as an individual, assessing all of the qualities that individual possesses, and in turn, evaluating that individual's ability to contribute to the unique setting of higher education. The admissions program Justice POWELL described, however, did not contemplate that any single characteristic automatically ensured a specific and identifiable contribution to a university's diversity. Instead, under the approach Justice POWELL described, each characteristic of a particular applicant was to be considered in assessing the applicant's entire application.

The current LSA policy does not provide such individualized consideration. The LSA's policy automatically distributes 20 points to every single applicant from an "underrepresented minority" group, as defined by the University. The only consideration that accompanies this distribution of points is a factual review of an application to determine whether an individual is a member of one of these minority groups. Moreover, unlike Justice POWELL's example, where the race of a "particular black applicant" could be considered without being decisive, the LSA's automatic distribution of 20 points has the effect of making "the factor of race . . . decisive" for virtually every minimally qualified underrepresented minority applicant. . . .

We conclude, therefore, that because the University's use of race in its current freshman admissions policy is not narrowly tailored to achieve respondents' asserted compelling interest in diversity, the admissions policy violates the Equal Protection Clause of the Fourteenth Amendment. We further find that the admissions policy also violates Title VI. Accordingly, we reverse that portion of the District Court's decision granting respondents summary judgment with respect to liability and remand the case for proceedings consistent with this opinion.

Justice O'CONNOR, concurring.

Unlike the law school admissions policy the Court upholds today in *Grutter v. Bollinger*, the procedures employed by the University of Michigan's (University) Office of Undergraduate Admissions do not provide for a meaningful individualized review of applicants. . . . The selection index thus precludes admissions counselors from conducting the type of individualized consideration the Court's opinion in *Grutter* requires: consideration of each applicant's individualized qualifications, including the contribution each individual's race or ethnic identity will make to the diversity of the student body, taking into account diversity within and among all racial and ethnic groups. . . .

Although the Office of Undergraduate Admissions does assign 20 points to some "soft" variables other than race, the points available for other diversity contributions, such as leadership and service, personal achievement, and geographic diversity, are capped at much lower levels. Even the most outstanding national high school leader could never receive more than five points for his or her accomplishments—a mere quarter of the points automatically assigned to an underrepresented minority solely based on the fact of his or her race. [T]he selection index, by setting up automatic, pre-determined point allocations for the soft variables, ensures that the diversity contributions of applicants cannot be individually assessed. This policy stands in sharp contrast to the law school's admissions plan, which enables admissions officers to make nuanced judgments with respect to the contributions each applicant is likely to make to the diversity of the incoming class. . . .

    ☐ *Justice GINSBURG, with whom Justice SOUTER joins, dissenting.*

In the wake "of a system of racial caste only recently ended" large disparities endure. Unemployment, poverty, and access to health care vary disproportionately by race. Neighborhoods and schools remain racially divided. African-American and Hispanic children are all too often educated in poverty-stricken and underperforming institutions. Adult African-Americans and Hispanics generally earn less than whites with equivalent levels of education. Equally credentialed job applicants receive different receptions depending on their race. Irrational prejudice is still encountered in real estate markets and consumer transactions. "Bias both conscious and unconscious, reflecting traditional and unexamined habits of thought, keeps up barriers that must come down if equal opportunity and nondiscrimination are ever genuinely to become this country's law and practice."

The Constitution instructs all who act for the government that they may not "deny to any person . . . the equal protection of the laws." In implementing this equality instruction, as I see it, government decisionmakers may properly distinguish between policies of exclusion and inclusion.

Our jurisprudence ranks race a "suspect" category, "not because [race] is inevitably an impermissible classification, but because it is one which usually, to our national shame, has been drawn for the purpose of maintaining racial inequality." But where race is considered "for the purpose of achieving equality," no automatic proscription is in order. For, "[t]he Constitution is both color blind and color conscious. "To avoid conflict with the equal protection clause, a classification that denies a benefit, causes harm, or imposes a burden must not be based on race. In that sense, the Constitution is color blind. But the Constitution is color conscious to prevent discrimination being perpetuated and to undo the effects of past discrimination.

The mere assertion of a laudable governmental purpose, of course, should not immunize a race-conscious measure from careful judicial inspection. Close review is needed "to ferret out classifications in reality malign, but masquerading as benign," and to "ensure that preferences are not so large as to trammel unduly upon the opportunities of others or interfere too harshly with legitimate expectations of persons in once-preferred groups."

Examining in this light the admissions policy employed by the University of Michigan's College of Literature, Science, and the Arts (College), and for the reasons well stated by Justice SOUTER, I see no constitutional infirmity. . . .

    ☐ *Justice SOUTER, with whom Justice GINSBURG joins as to Part II, dissenting.*

Grutter reaffirms the permissibility of individualized consideration of race to achieve a diversity of students, at least where race is not assigned a preordained value in all cases. On the other hand, Justice POWELL's opinion in *Regents of Univ. of Cal. v. Bakke*, 438 U.S. 265 (1978), rules out a racial quota or set-aside, in which race is the sole fact of eligibility for certain places in a class. Although the freshman admissions system here is subject to argument on the merits, I think it is closer to what *Grutter* approves than to what *Bakke* condemns, and should not be held unconstitutional on the current record.

The record does not describe a system with a quota like the one struck down in *Bakke*, which "insulate[d]" all nonminority candidates from competition from certain seats. The plan here, in contrast, lets all applicants compete for all places and values an applicant's offering for any place not only on grounds of race, but on grades, test scores, strength of high school, quality of course of study, residence, alumni relationships, leadership, personal character, socioeconomic disadvantage, athletic ability, and quality of a personal essay. A nonminority applicant who scores highly in these other categories can readily garner a selection index exceeding that of a minority applicant who gets the 20-point bonus. . . .

The Court nonetheless finds fault with a scheme that "automatically" distributes 20 points to minority applicants because [t]he only consideration that accompanies this distribution of points is a factual review of an application to determine whether an individual is a member of one of these minority groups." The objection goes to the use of points to quantify and compare characteristics, or to the number of points awarded due to race, but on either reading the objection is mistaken.

The very nature of a college's permissible practice of awarding value to racial diversity means that race must be considered in a way that increases some applicants' chances for admission. Since college admission is not left entirely to inarticulate intuition, it is hard to see what is inappropriate in assigning some stated value to a relevant characteristic, whether it be reasoning ability, writing style, running speed, or minority race. Justice POWELL's plus factors necessarily are assigned some values. The college simply does by a numbered scale what the law school accomplishes in its "holistic review," *Grutter*, the distinction does not imply that applicants to the undergraduate college are denied individualized consideration or a fair chance to compete on the basis of all the various merits their applications may disclose. . . .

Grutter v. Bollinger
539 U.S. 306, 123 S.Ct. 2325 (2003)

In 1992 the University of Michigan Law School adopted an admissions policy based on an index score representing a composite of an applicant's Law School Admissions Test (LSAT) score and undergraduate grade point average. The policy also affirmed the law school's "commitment to racial and ethnic diversity with special reference to the inclusion of students from groups which have been historically discriminated against, like African-Americans, Hispanics, and Native-Americans," who, without some preference, "might not be represented in [the] student body in meaningful numbers." Accordingly, the law school makes "special efforts" to increase the number and achieve a "critical mass" of such students.

Barbara Grutter, an unsuccessful white applicant and a 43-year-old business woman, challenged the constitutionally of the law school's admission program for relying on race and ethnicity as "predominant" factors and for favoring minority groups and giving them "a significantly greater chance of admission than students with similar credentials." A federal district court held that the law school's admissions program violated the Fourteenth Amendment, but the Court of Appeals for the Sixth Circuit reversed and concluded that the school's interest in achieving a diverse student body was compelling under *Regents of the University of California v. Bakke*, 438 U.S. 265 (1978). Ms. Grutter appealed that decision.

The appellate court's decision was affirmed by a vote of five to four. Justice O'Connor delivered the opinion of the Court. Justice Ginsburg filed a concurring opinion. Justices Scalia and Thomas filed opinions concurring and dissenting in part. Chief Justice Rehnquist and Justice Kennedy filed dissenting opinions.

□ *Justice O'CONNOR delivered the opinion of the Court.*

The Law School ranks among the Nation's top law schools. It receives more than 3,500 applications each year for a class of around 350 students. Seeking to "admit a group of students who individually and collectively are among the most capable," the Law School looks for individuals with "substantial promise for success in law school" and "a strong likelihood of succeeding in the practice of law and contributing in diverse ways to the well-being of others." More broadly, the Law School seeks "a mix of students with varying backgrounds and experiences who will respect and learn from each other." In 1992, the dean of the Law School charged a faculty committee with crafting a written admissions policy to implement these goals. In particular, the Law School sought to ensure that its efforts to achieve student body diversity complied with this Court's most recent ruling on the use of race in university admissions. See *Regents of Univ. of Cal. v. Bakke*, 438 U. S. 265 (1978). Upon the unanimous adoption of the committee's report by the Law School faculty, it became the Law School's official admissions policy.

The hallmark of that policy is its focus on academic ability coupled with a flexible assessment of applicants' talents, experiences, and potential "to contribute to the learning of those around them." The policy requires admissions officials to evaluate each applicant based on all the information available in the file, including a personal statement, letters of recommendation, and an essay describing the ways in which the applicant will contribute to the life and diversity of the Law School. In reviewing an applicant's file, admissions officials must consider the applicant's undergraduate grade point average (GPA) and Law School Admissions Test (LSAT) score because they are important (if imperfect) predictors of academic success in law school. The policy stresses that "no applicant should be admitted unless we expect that applicant to do well enough to graduate with no serious academic problems."

The policy makes clear, however, that even the highest possible score does not guarantee admission to the Law School. Nor does a low score automatically disqualify an applicant. Rather, the policy requires admissions officials to look beyond grades and test scores to other criteria that are important to the Law School's educational objectives. So-called " 'soft' variables" such as "the enthusiasm of recommenders, the quality of the undergraduate institution, the quality of the applicant's essay, and the areas and difficulty of undergraduate course selection" are all brought to bear in assessing an "applicant's likely contributions to the intellectual and social life of the institution." . . .

We granted *certiorari* to resolve the disagreement among the Courts of Appeals on a question of national importance: Whether diversity is a compelling interest that can justify the narrowly tailored use of race in selecting applicants for admission to public universities.

We last addressed the use of race in public higher education over 25 years ago. In the landmark *Bakke* case, we reviewed a racial set-aside program that reserved 16 out of 100 seats in a medical school class for members of certain minority groups. The decision produced six separate opinions, none of which commanded a majority of the Court. . . .

Since this Court's splintered decision in *Bakke*, Justice POWELL's opinion announcing the judgment of the Court has served as the touchstone for constitutional analysis of race-conscious admissions policies. Public and private universities across the Nation have modeled their own admissions programs on Justice POWELL's views on permissible race-conscious policies. . . .

We have held that all racial classifications imposed by government "must be analyzed by a reviewing court under strict scrutiny." This means that such classifications are constitutional only if they are narrowly tailored to further compelling governmental interests.

Strict scrutiny is not "strict in theory, but fatal in fact." Although all governmental uses of race are subject to strict scrutiny, not all are invalidated by it. As we have explained, "whenever the government treats any person unequally because of his or her race, that person has suffered an injury that falls squarely within the language and spirit of the Constitution's guarantee of equal protection." But that observation "says nothing about the ultimate validity of any particular law; that determination is the job of the court applying strict scrutiny." When race-based action is necessary to further a compelling governmental interest, such action does not violate the constitutional guarantee of equal protection so long as the narrow-tailoring requirement is also satisfied.

Context matters when reviewing race-based governmental action under the Equal Protection Clause. Not every decision influenced by race is equally objectionable and strict scrutiny is designed to provide a framework for carefully examining the importance and the sincerity of the reasons advanced by the governmental decisionmaker for the use of race in that particular context.

With these principles in mind, we turn to the question whether the Law School's use of race is justified by a compelling state interest. . . . The Law School's educational judgment that such diversity is essential to its educational mission is one to which we defer. The Law School's assessment that diversity will, in fact, yield educational benefits is substantiated by respondents and their *amici*. . . .

As part of its goal of "assembling a class that is both exceptionally academically qualified and broadly diverse," the Law School seeks to "enroll a 'critical mass' of minority students." The Law School's interest is not simply "to assure within its student body some specified percentage of a particular group merely because of its race or ethnic origin." That would amount to outright racial balancing, which is patently unconstitutional. . . .

The Law School's claim of a compelling interest is further bolstered by its *amici*, who point to the educational benefits that flow from student body diversity. In addition to the expert studies and reports entered into evidence at trial, numerous studies show that student body diversity promotes learning outcomes, and "better prepares students for an increasingly diverse workforce and society, and better prepares them as professionals."

These benefits are not theoretical but real, as major American businesses have made clear that the skills needed in today's increasingly global marketplace can only be developed through exposure to widely diverse people, cultures, ideas, and viewpoints. . . .

We have repeatedly acknowledged the overriding importance of preparing students for work and citizenship, describing education as pivotal to "sustaining our political and cultural heritage" with a fundamental role in maintaining the fabric of society. *Plyler v. Doe*, 457 U. S. 202 (1982). This Court has long recognized that "education . . . is the very foundation of good citizenship." *Brown v. Board of Education*, 347 U. S. 483 (1954). For this reason, the diffusion of knowledge and opportunity through public institutions of higher education must be accessible to all individuals regardless of race or ethnicity. The United States, as *amicus curiae*, affirms that "[e]nsuring that public institutions are open and available to all segments of American society, including people of all races and ethnicities, represents a paramount government objective."

Moreover, universities, and in particular, law schools, represent the training ground for a large number of our Nation's leaders. Individuals with law degrees occupy roughly half the state governorships, more than half the seats in the United States Senate, and more than a third of the seats in the United States House of Representatives. The pattern is even more striking when it comes to highly selective law schools. A handful of these schools accounts for 25 of the 100 United States Senators, 74 United States Courts of Appeals judges, and nearly 200 of the more than 600 United States District Court judges. . . .

Even in the limited circumstance when drawing racial distinctions is permissible to further a compelling state interest, government is still "constrained in how it may pursue that end: [T]he means chosen to accomplish the [government's] asserted purpose must be specifically and narrowly framed to accomplish that purpose." *Shaw v. Hunt*, 517 U. S. 899 (1996). The purpose of the narrow tailoring requirement is to ensure that "the means chosen 'fit' . . . th[e] compelling goal so closely that there is little or no possibility that the motive for the classification was illegitimate racial prejudice or stereotype."

Since *Bakke*, we have had no occasion to define the contours of the narrow-tailoring inquiry with respect to race-conscious university admissions programs. That inquiry must be calibrated to fit the distinct issues raised by the use of race to achieve student body diversity in public higher education. . . .

To be narrowly tailored, a race-conscious admissions program cannot use a quota system—it cannot "insulat[e] each category of applicants with certain desired qualifications from competition with all other applicants." Instead, a university may consider race or ethnicity only as a " 'plus' in a particular applicant's file," without "insulat[ing] the individual from comparison with all other candidates for the available seats." In other words, an admissions program must be "flexible enough to consider all pertinent elements of diversity in light of the particular qualifications of each applicant, and to place them on the same footing for consideration, although not necessarily according them the same weight."

We find that the Law School's admissions program bears the hallmarks of a narrowly tailored plan. . . . We are satisfied that the Law School's admissions program, like the Harvard plan described by Justice POWELL, does not operate as a quota. . . . Justice POWELL's distinction between the medical school's rigid 16-seat quota and Harvard's flexible use of race as a "plus" factor is instructive. Harvard certainly had minimum goals for minority enrollment, even if it had no specific number firmly in mind. . . .

Here, the Law School engages in a highly individualized, holistic review of each applicant's file, giving serious consideration to all the ways an applicant might contribute to a diverse educational environment. The Law School affords this individualized consideration to applicants of all races. . . .

What is more, the Law School actually gives substantial weight to diversity factors besides race. The Law School frequently accepts nonminority applicants with grades and test scores lower than underrepresented minority applicants (and other nonminority applicants) who are rejected. This shows that the Law School seriously weighs many other diversity factors besides race that can make a real and dispositive difference for nonminority applicants as well. By this flexible approach, the Law School sufficiently takes into account, in practice as well as in theory, a wide variety of characteristics besides race and ethnicity that contribute to a diverse student body. . . .

We are mindful, however, that "[a] core purpose of the Fourteenth Amendment was to do away with all governmentally imposed discrimination based on race." *Palmore v. Sidoti*, 466 U.S. 429 (1984). Accordingly, race-conscious admissions policies must be limited in time. This requirement reflects that racial classifications, however compelling their goals, are potentially so dangerous that they may be employed no more broadly than the interest demands. . . .

In the context of higher education, the durational requirement can be met by sunset provisions in race-conscious admissions policies and periodic reviews to determine whether racial preferences are still necessary to achieve student body diversity. Universities in California, Florida, and Washington State, where racial preferences in admissions are prohibited by state law, are currently engaged in experimenting with a wide variety of alternative approaches. Universities in other States can and should draw on the most promising aspects of these race-neutral alternatives as they develop. The requirement that all race-conscious admissions programs have a termination point "assure[s] all citizens that the deviation from the norm of equal treatment of all racial and ethnic groups is a temporary matter, a measure taken in the service of the goal of equality itself." *Richmond v. J. A. Croson Co.* . . .

It has been 25 years since Justice POWELL first approved the use of race to further an interest in student body diversity in the context of public higher education. Since that time, the number of minority applicants with high grades and test scores has indeed increased. We expect that 25 years from now, the use of racial preferences will no longer be necessary to further the interest approved today.

In summary, the Equal Protection Clause does not prohibit the Law School's narrowly tailored use of race in admissions decisions to further a compelling interest in obtaining the educational benefits that flow from a diverse student body. Consequently, petitioner's statutory claims based on Title VI also fail. The judgment of the Court of Appeals for the Sixth Circuit, accordingly, is affirmed.

□ *Justice GINSBURG, with whom Justice BREYER joins, concurring.*

However strong the public's desire for improved education systems may be, it remains the current reality that many minority students encounter markedly inadequate and unequal educational opportunities. Despite these inequalities, some minority students are able to meet the high threshold requirements set for admission to the country's finest undergraduate and graduate educational institutions. As lower school education in minority communities improves, an increase in the number of such students may be anticipated. From today's vantage point, one may hope, but not firmly forecast, that over the next generation's span, progress toward nondiscrimination and genuinely equal opportunity will make it safe to sunset affirmative action.

□ *CHIEF JUSTICE REHNQUIST, with whom Justice SCALIA, Justice KENNEDY, and Justice THOMAS join, dissenting.*

As we have explained many times, " '[a]ny preference based on racial or ethnic criteria must necessarily receive a most searching examination.' " *Adarand*. Our cases establish that, in order to withstand this demanding inquiry, respondents must demonstrate that their methods of using race " 'fit' " a compelling state interest "with greater precision than any alternative means." *Bakke*.

Before the Court's decision today, we consistently applied the same strict scrutiny analysis regardless of the government's purported reason for using race and regardless of the setting in which race was being used. We rejected calls to use more lenient review in the face of claims that race was being used in "good faith" because " '[m]ore than good motives should be required when government seeks to allocate its resources by way of an explicit racial classification system.' " . . .

In practice, the Law School's program bears little or no relation to its asserted goal of achieving "critical mass." . . . From 1995 through 2000, the Law School admitted between 1,130 and 1,310 students. Of those, between 13 and 19 were Native American, between 91 and 108 were African-Americans, and between 47 and 56 were Hispanic. If the Law School is admitting between 91 and 108 African-Americans in order to achieve "critical mass," thereby preventing African-American students from feeling "isolated or like spokespersons for their race," one would think that a number of the same order of magnitude would be necessary to accomplish the same purpose for Hispanics and Native Americans. Similarly, even if all of the Native American applicants admitted in a given year matriculate, which the record demonstrates is not at all the case, how can this possibly constitute a "critical mass" of Native Americans in a class of over 350 students? In order for this pattern of admission to be consistent with the Law School's explanation of "critical mass," one would have to believe that the objectives of "critical mass" offered by respondents are achieved with only half the number of Hispanics and one-sixth the number of Native Americans as compared to African-Americans. But respondents offer no race-specific reasons for such disparities. Instead, they simply emphasize the importance of achieving "critical mass," without any explanation of why that concept is applied differently among the three underrepresented minority groups.

These different numbers, moreover, come only as a result of substantially different treatment among the three underrepresented minority groups, as is apparent in an example offered by the Law School and highlighted by the Court: The school asserts that it "frequently accepts nonminority applicants with grades and test scores lower than underrepresented minority applicants (and other nonminority applicants) who are rejected." Specifically, the Law School states that "[s]ixty-nine minority applicants were rejected between 1995 and 2000 with at least a 3.5 [Grade Point Average (GPA)] and a [score of] 159 or higher on the [Law School Admissions Test (LSAT)]" while a number of Caucasian and Asian-American applicants with similar or lower scores were admitted.

Review of the record reveals only 67 such individuals. Of these 67 individuals, 56 were Hispanic, while only 6 were African-American, and only 5 were Native American. This discrepancy reflects a consistent practice. For example, in 2000, 12 Hispanics who scored between a 159-160 on the LSAT and earned a GPA of 3.00 or higher applied for admission and only 2 were admitted. Meanwhile, 12 African-Americans in the same range of qualifications applied for admission and all 12 were admitted. Likewise, that same year, 16 Hispanics who scored between a 151–153 on the LSAT and earned a 3.00 or higher applied for admission and only 1 of those applicants was admitted. Twenty-three similarly qualified African-Americans applied for admission and 14 were admitted. . . .

[T]he correlation between the percentage of the Law School's pool of applicants who are members of the three minority groups and the percentage of the admitted applicants who are members of these same groups is far too precise to be dismissed as merely the result of the school paying "some attention to [the] numbers." [F]rom 1995 through 2000 the percentage of admitted applicants who were members of these minority groups closely tracked the percentage of individuals in the school's applicant pool who were from the same groups. . . . For example, in 1995, when 9.7% of the applicant pool was African-American, 9.4% of the admitted class was African-American. By 2000, only 7.5% of the applicant pool was African-American, and 7.3% of the admitted class was African-American. This correlation is striking. Respondents themselves emphasize that the number of under-represented minority students admitted to the Law School would be signifi-cantly smaller if the race of each applicant were not considered. But, as the examples above illustrate, the measure of the decrease would differ dramati-cally among the groups. The tight correlation between the percentage of ap-plicants and admittees of a given race, therefore, must result from careful race based planning by the Law School. . . .

I do not believe that the Constitution gives the Law School such free rein in the use of race. The Law School has offered no explanation for its ac-tual admissions practices and, unexplained, we are bound to conclude that the Law School has managed its admissions program, not to achieve a "criti-cal mass," but to extend offers of admission to members of selected minority groups in proportion to their statistical representation in the applicant pool. But this is precisely the type of racial balancing that the Court itself calls "patently unconstitutional." . . .

☐ *Justice KENNEDY, dissenting.*

The Court, in a review that is nothing short of perfunctory, accepts the University of Michigan Law School's assurances that its admissions process meets with constitutional requirements. The majority fails to confront the reality of how the Law School's admissions policy is implemented. The dis-senting opinion by the CHIEF JUSTICE, which I join in full, demonstrates beyond question why the concept of critical mass is a delusion used by the Law School to mask its attempt to make race an automatic factor in most in-stances and to achieve numerical goals indistinguishable from quotas. . . . It remains to point out how critical mass becomes inconsistent with individual consideration in some more specific aspects of the admissions process.

About 80 to 85 percent of the places in the entering class are given to applicants in the upper range of Law School Admissions Test scores and grades. An applicant with these credentials likely will be admitted without consideration of race or ethnicity. With respect to the remaining 15 to 20 percent of the seats, race is likely outcome determinative for many members of minority groups. That is where the competition becomes tight and where any given applicant's chance of admission is far smaller if he or she lacks mi-nority status. At this point the numerical concept of critical mass has the real potential to compromise individual review.

The Law School has not demonstrated how individual consideration is, or can be, preserved at this stage of the application process given the instruc-tion to attain what it calls critical mass. In fact the evidence shows otherwise. There was little deviation among admitted minority students during the years from 1995 to 1998. The percentage of enrolled minorities fluctuated only by 0.3%, from 13.5% to 13.8%. The number of minority students to whom offers were extended varied by just a slightly greater magnitude of 2.2%, from the high of 15.6% in 1995 to the low of 13.4% in 1998. . . .

The narrow fluctuation band raises an inference that the Law School subverted individual determination, and strict scrutiny requires the Law School to overcome the inference. Whether the objective of critical mass "is described as a quota or a goal, it is a line drawn on the basis of race and eth-nic status," and so risks compromising individual assessment. . . .

To be constitutional, a university's compelling interest in a diverse student body must be achieved by a system where individual assessment is safeguarded through the entire process. There is no constitutional objection to the goal of considering race as one modest factor among many others to achieve diversity, but an educational institution must ensure, through sufficient procedures, that each applicant receives individual consideration and that race does not become a predominant factor in the admissions decisionmaking. . . .

Justice SCALIA, with whom Justice THOMAS joins, concurring in part and dissenting in part.

Unlike a clear constitutional holding that racial preferences in state educational institutions are impermissible, or even a clear anticonstitutional holding that racial preferences in state educational institutions are OK, today's *Grutter-Gratz* split double header seems perversely designed to prolong the controversy and the litigation. Some future lawsuits will presumably focus on whether the discriminatory scheme in question contains enough evaluation of the applicant "as an individual," and sufficiently avoids "separate admissions tracks" to fall under *Grutter* rather than *Gratz*. Some will focus on whether a university has gone beyond the bounds of a " 'good faith effort' " and has so zealously pursued its "critical mass" as to make it an unconstitutional de facto quota system, rather than merely " 'a permissible goal.' " Other lawsuits may focus on whether, in the particular setting at issue, any educational benefits flow from racial diversity. Still other suits may challenge the bona fides of the institution's expressed commitment to the educational benefits of diversity that immunize the discriminatory scheme in *Grutter*. And still other suits may claim that the institution's racial preferences have gone below or above the mystical *Grutter*-approved "critical mass." Finally, litigation can be expected on behalf of minority groups intentionally short changed in the institution's composition of its generic minority "critical mass." I do not look forward to any of these cases. The Constitution proscribes government discrimination on the basis of race, and state-provided education is no exception.

Justice THOMAS, with whom Justice SCALIA joins as to Parts I–VII, concurring in part and dissenting in part.

No one would argue that a university could set up a lower general admission standard and then impose heightened requirements only on black applicants. Similarly, a university may not maintain a high admission standard and grant exemptions to favored races. The Law School, of its own choosing, and for its own purposes, maintains an exclusionary admissions system that it knows produces racially disproportionate results. Racial discrimination is not a permissible solution to the self-inflicted wounds of this elitist admissions policy.

The majority upholds the Law School's racial discrimination not by interpreting the people's Constitution, but by responding to a faddish slogan of the cognoscenti. Nevertheless, I concur in part in the Court's opinion. First, I agree with the Court insofar as its decision, which approves of only one racial classification, confirms that further use of race in admissions remains unlawful. Second, I agree with the Court's holding that racial discrimination in higher education admissions will be illegal in 25 years. I respectfully dissent from the remainder of the Court's opinion and the judgment, however, because I believe that the Law School's current use of race violates the Equal Protection Clause and that the Constitution means the same thing today as it will in 300 months. . . .

D | *Nonracial Classifications and the Equal Protection of the Laws*

As noted in the beginning of this chapter, in the 1970s, 1980s, and 1990s the Court sought retrenchment from further expansion of the application of the Warren Court's "two-tiered" approach to the equal protection clause. When confronted with challenges to nonracial classifications, the Burger Court evolved a third, intermediate standard of judicial review—the *exacting scrutiny* or *strict rationality test*—for *quasi-suspect categories* like gender and illegitimacy, as well as refused to extend heightened review to claims of discrimination based on wealth and age. As noted earlier in this chapter, the Rehnquist Court in turn has cut back on its use of heightened judicial scrutiny, reserving the strict scrutiny test and heightened review for primarily race-based classifications, and declined to further expand the number of suspect and quasi-suspect categories.

■ (1) GENDER-BASED DISCRIMINATION

Social and economic conditions did not make it possible until the mid-twentieth century for political movements and legal developments to push toward guaranteeing equal rights for women. Only in the 1970s did the Supreme Court begin to question gender-based discrimination. For more than a century, the Fourteenth Amendment offered little promise for women as the Court reinforced the second-class status and sexual stereotypes of women in constitutional law. *Bradwell v. State of Illinois*, 83 U.S. 130 (1873), for example, upheld Illinois's denial of women the right to practice law, and *Minor v. Happersett*, 88 U.S. 162 (1875) dismissed out of hand the claim that women had a constitutional right to vote. Even after the Nineteenth Amendment (1920), extending the right to vote to women, the Court held that neither that amendment nor the Fourteenth Amendment secured legal equality for women.[1] Sexual stereotypes of women as the "weaker sex," who "looks to her brother and depends on him" in Justice David Brewer's words, undergirded even progressive legislation and rulings, like *Muller v. Oregon*, 208 U.S. 412 (1908). In *Muller*, Justice Brewer upheld Oregon's law limiting the hours women could work in factories upon taking notice of the fact that

> [t]he two sexes differ in structure of body, in the functions to be performed by each, in the amount of physical strength, in the capacity for long-continued labor, particularly when done standing, ... [in] the self-reliance which enables one to assert full rights, and in the capacity to maintain the struggle for subsistence. This difference justifies a difference in legislation and upholds that which is designed to compensate for some of the burdens which rest upon her.

On much the same basis the Warren Court unanimously concluded that the equal protection clause did not bar Florida from excluding women from jury service, in *Hoyt v. Florida*, 368 U.S. 57 (1961).

World War II brought about changes in the workforce. An unprecedented number of women worked in industries and factories as a result of wartime mobilization. After the war, economic expansion provided expanded employment opportunities. By the 1960s, the women's movement was revitalized and feminist groups pushed for political and legal changes. Congress responded to that political pressure. In 1963, the Equal Pay Act amended the Fair Labor Standards Act to require equal pay for equal work. The Civil Rights Act of 1964 prohibited sex discrimination by employers, labor organizations, and employment agencies. In 1972, the Civil Rights Act was amended to authorize in Title V the denial of federal funding for public and private programs that discriminated against women, and Title IX specifically requires equal athletic facilities and opportunities for women. Congress also passed in 1972 the Equal Rights Amendment, which after a decade-long battle failed to win ratification by three-fourths of the states as required under the Constitution.

The Supreme Court signaled that it would take seriously challenges to gender-based classification in *Reed v. Reed*, 404 U.S. 71 (1971). Writing for a unanimous Court, Chief Justice Burger overturned Idaho's statute giving preference to males over females in intestate proceedings. While finding the statute lacked a rational basis for distinguishing between men and women, he declined to address the claim that gender is a "suspect" category requiring strict scrutiny. Less than two years later, in *Frontiero v. Richardson* (1973) (excerpted below), Justice Brennan could persuade only three other justices that gender was a suspect category.

Despite the fact that the Court came within one vote of declaring gender a suspect category, *Reed* and *Frontiero* indicated that gender was a quasi-suspect category to which the Court would give heightened, if not strict, scrutiny. In *Craig v. Boren* (1976) (excerpted below), the Court further developed its "heightened or 'intermediate' level of scrutiny test." In applying this test the Court considered whether a gender-based distinction bears a substantial relationship to an important governmental interest. As the following boxes in this section show, the Court has tended to promote gender-neutral classifications, striking down even laws (as in *Craig*) that are defended as "benign" or "compensatory."[2] Note that gender-neutral laws disproportionately affecting one gender, though, typically do not receive the same heightened scrutiny accorded explicit gender-based classifications. Moreover, the Court has upheld some gender-based classifications as illustrated in the five-to-four ruling in *Michael M. v. Superior Court of Sonoma County* (1981) (excerpted below).

The Court has also tended, although not invariably, to affirm claims against gender discrimination under the Civil Rights Act of 1964 and other federal legislation. Notably, in *Meritor Savings Bank, FBD v. Vinson*, 477 U.S. 57 (1986) the Court held that Title VII of the Civil Rights Act of 1964 bars "sexual harassment" in the workplace, and not just gender discrimination in the hiring and firing of employees. Indeed, for over a decade, with the exception of *J.E.B. v. Alabama ex rel. T.B.*, 511 U.S. 127 (1994), which held that the Fourteenth Amendment forbids gender discrimination in the exclusion of potential jurors from jury service, the Court dealt primarily with gender discrimination claims as a matter of statutory interpretation. However, in *United States v. Virginia* (1996) (excerpted below) the Court struck down Virginia's creation of a separate all-female institute as a remedy for a lower court's finding that the state's all-male Virginia Military Institute violated the Fourteenth Amendment.

NOTES

1. See *Fay v. New York*, 332 U.S. 261 (1947). The struggle for women's voting rights is further examined in Vol. 1, Ch. 8.

2. See, for example, *Califano v. Goldfarb*, 430 U.S. 199 (1977), *Orr v. Orr*, 440 U.S. 268 (1979), and *Mississippi University for Women v. Hogan*, 458 U.S. 718 (1982).

SELECTED BIBLIOGRAPHY

Baer, Judith. *Equality under the Constitution: Reclaiming the Fourteenth Amendment.* Ithaca, NY: Cornell University Press, 1983.

Cochran, III, Augustus B. *Sexual Harassment and the Law: The Mechelle Vinson Case.* Lawrence: University Press of Kansas, 2004.

Cushman, Clare, ed. Foreword by Justice Ruth Bader Ginsburg. *Supreme Court Decisions and Women's Rights: Milestones to Equality.* Washington, DC: C.Q. Press, 2000.

Epstein, Cynthia. *Women in Law.* New York: Basic Books, 1981.

Harrison, Cynthia. *On Account of Sex: The Politics of Women's Issues, 1945–1968.* Berkeley: University of California Press, 1988.

Isenberg, Nancy. *Sex and Citizenship in Antebellum America.*Chapel Hill: University of North Carolina Press, 1999.

Mansbridge, Jane. *Why We Lost the ERA.* Chicago: University of Chicago Press, 1986.

Mathews, Donald. *Sex, Gender, and the Politics of the ERA.* New York: Oxford University Press, 1990.

O'Connor, Karen. *Women's Organizations' Use of the Courts.* Lexington, MA: Lexington Books, 1980.

Olson, Lynne. *Freedom's Daughters: The Unsung Heroines of the Civil Rights Movement from 1830 to 1970.* New York: Scribner's.

Rhode, Deborah. *Justice and Gender.* Cambridge, MA: Harvard University Press, 1989.

———. *Theoretical Perspectives on Sexual Differences.* New Haven, CT: Yale University Press, 1990.

———. *Speaking of Sex: The Denial of Gender Inequality.* Cambridge, MA: Harvard University Press, 1997.

Rosen, Ruth. *The World Split Open: How the Modern Women's Movement Changed America.* New York: Viking, 2000.

Schwarzenbach, Sibyl, and Smith, Patricia, eds. *Women and the U.S. Constitution.* New York: Columbia University Press, 2004.

Strum, Philippa. *Women in the Barracks: The VMI Case and Equal Rights.* Lawrence: University Press of Kansas, 2002.

Van Burkleo, Sandra F. *"Belonging to the World": Women's Rights and American Constitutional Culture.* New York: Oxford University Press, 2001.

■ CONSTITUTIONAL HISTORY

The Equal Rights Amendment

During the Progressive era after the turn of the twentieth century, political pressure began to mount for the adoption of a constitutional amendment to guarantee equal rights for women. Indeed, for almost fifty years (from 1923 to 1972) Congress annually considered one proposal or another for an equal rights amendment.

Finally, in response to the women's movement and lobbying of organizations such as the National Organization for Women (NOW) and the National Women's Political Caucus, in 1972 Congress passed the proposed Equal Rights Amendment, providing that

> Section 1. Equality of rights under the law shall not be denied or abridged by the United States or by any State on account of sex.

Section 2. The Congress shall have the power to enforce, by appropriate legislation, the provisions of this article.

Section 3. The Amendment shall take effect two years after the date of ratification.

Within a year of the ERA's proposal, twenty-two states ratified the amendment. But by 1978, one year before the deadline for ratification of the amendment by three-fourths of the states, only thirty-five states had voted for ratification—three votes short of the number needed. Political opposition intensified as organizations such as the National Council of Catholic Women, Mormons, and other religious groups, as well as political activist Phyllis Schlafly's Eagle Forum, mobilized to defeat the ERA's ratification. Three states voted to rescind their earlier support, and faced with the prospect of the ERA's defeat in 1979 Congress voted to extend the ratification deadline for three more years. In 1982, the ERA was defeated; fifteen states refused ratification, and five that had supported the amendment rescinded their votes.

The ERA divided rather than united women politically and culturally. Some women's groups argued that the amendment would not in fact ensure equality in higher education and employment. Others countered that the ERA would do away with protective legislation safeguarding the rights of women in the workplace, requiring marital and child support from divorced husbands, and exempting women from compulsory military registration and service. Still others claimed that the amendment was only symbolic while some ERA supporters maintained that even a symbolic affirmation of the constitutional equality of women was important. By the late 1970s, many gender-based classifications that the ERA was originally intended to outlaw had been rendered illegal by Congress, executive orders, and rulings of the Supreme Court, which applied the equal protection clause, the Civil Rights Act of 1964, and other federal legislation.

■ THE DEVELOPMENT OF LAW

Other Rulings Striking Down Gender-Based Distinctions under the Constitution

CASE	VOTE	RULING
Reed v. Reed, 404 U.S. 71 (1971)	9:0	Chief Justice Burger struck down Idaho's statute giving preference to males in intestate proceedings for lacking a rational basis.

CASE	VOTE	RULING
Weinberger v. Wiesenfeld, 420 U.S. 636 (1975)	8:0	With Justice Douglas not participating, the Court struck down a section of the Social Security Act that granted sur-

vivors' benefits to widows and minor children, but not to widowers because the fact that men are more likely to be employed is not a compelling reason for distinguishing between males and females.

Stanton v. Stanton, 421 U.S. 7 (1975)	8:1	With Justice Rehnquist dissent- ing, the Court overturned as ir- rational a Utah law requiring

child-support payments for males until they reach the age of twenty-one and for females until they reach the age of eighteen.

Califano v. Goldfarb, 430 U.S. 199 (1977)	5:4	Struck down a portion of the Social Security Act which pro- vided benefits for widows based

on the earnings of deceased husbands, but no benefits for widowers unless they had received half of their financial support from their deceased spouses.

Orr v. Orr, 440 U.S. 268 (1979)	6:3	With Chief Justice Burger and Justices Rehnquist and Powell dissenting, the majority struck

down Alabama's law making husbands, but not wives, liable for alimony pay- ments after a divorce.

Caban v. Mohammed, 441 U.S. 380 (1979)	5:4	Overturned New York's law permitting unwed mothers, but not fathers, to withhold consent

from the adoption of their children; Chief Justice Burger and Justices Rehn- quist, Stewart, and Stevens dissented.

Califano v. Westcott, 433 U.S. 2655 (1979)	9:0	Held unconstitutional under the Fifth Amendment due process clause a section of the Social

Security Act that provided benefits to families with dependent children be- cause of father's, but not mother's, unemployment.

Wengler v. Druggists Mutual Insurance Co., 446 U.S. 142 (1980)	8:1	With only Justice Rehnquist dissenting, the Court found in- sufficient support for Missouri's workmen's compensation law,

which denied widowers, but not widows, benefits, unless a widower was "ei- ther mentally or physically incapacitated" or established a dependence on his wife's income.

CASE	VOTE	RULING
Kirchberg v. Fennstra, 450 U.S. 455 (1981)	9:0	Struck down Louisiana's law giving husbands a right to dispose of jointly owned property without wife's consent as unjustified.
Mississippi University for Women v. Hogan, 458 U.S. 718 (1982)	5:4	With Chief Justice Burger and Justices Blackmun, Powell, and Rehnquist dissenting, a bare

majority overturned a nursing school's policy of denying admission to qualified males.

CASE	VOTE	RULING
J.E.B. v. Alabama ex rel. T.B., 511 U.S. 127 (1994)	6:3	Extending its earlier rulings barring the exclusion of jurors from jury service on the basis of

race, Justice Blackmun ruled that the Fourteenth Amendment also precludes such gender discrimination and requires "heightened judicial scrutiny." Chief Justice Rehnquist and Justices Scalia and Thomas dissented.

■ THE DEVELOPMENT OF LAW

Other Rulings Upholding Gender-Based Distinctions under the Constitution

CASE	VOTE	RULING
Kahn v. Shavin, 416 U.S. 351 (1974)	6:3	Justice Douglas's opinion upheld Florida's law giving widows, but not widowers, a $500

property tax exemption as rational, given the greater financial difficulties that women face when their spouses die than those facing men whose spouses die; Justices Brennan, Marshall, and White dissented.

CASE	VOTE	RULING
Schlesinger v. Ballard, 419 U.S. 498 (1975)	5:4	Upheld federal statutes requiring mandatory discharge of women in the Navy after thir-

teen years, if they have not been promoted, and of men after nine years, because it was a rational distinction based on the different opportunities afforded men and women for sea and combat duty.

CASE	VOTE	RULING
Geduldig v. Aiello, 417 U.S. 484 (1974)	6:3	Upheld as rational California's program of allowing disability insurance benefits for private

employees not covered by workmen's compensation laws, except for pregnancy and certain other disabilities because the cost of extending coverage might jeopardize the program.

| *Rostker v. Goldberg*, 453 U.S. 57 (1981) | 6:3 | Upheld the Military Selective Service Act's authorization for the president to require males, |

but not females, to register for potential military service; Justices Brennan, White, and Marshall dissented.

| *Personnel Administrator of Massachusetts v. Fenney*, 442 U.S. 256 (1979) | 7:2 | Upheld a Massachusetts law giving preference in hiring decisions to veterans who qualify for state civil service positions, |

over the objections of a qualified woman who was passed over for a position.

| *Miller v. Albright*, 523 U.S. 420 (1998) | 6:3 | Rejected a challenge to a federal statute that automatically grants citizenship to illegiti- |

mate children born in a foreign country if the mother is a U.S. citizen, but sets a higher standard if the father is a citizen and the mother a foreign natural. Justices Ginsburg, Breyer, and Souter dissented.

| *Tuan Anh Nguyen v. Immigration and Naturalization Service*, 533 U.S. 53 (2001) | 5:4 | Rejected a challenge to a federal statute that makes it more difficult for children born out of wedlock to fathers who are |

U.S. citizens, in contrast to mothers who are U.S. citizens, to become citizens. Children born of mothers who are U.S. citizens are almost automatically made U.S. citizens, whereas those born out of wedlock to mothers who are foreign nationals and whose fathers are U.S. citizens must apply for citizenship before they are 18 years old and present evidence of their paternity. Writing for the Court, Justice Kennedy deemed the law rational and not based on stereotypes, whereas Justice O'Connor in dissent countered that the majority's decision rested on stereotypes of male versus female irresponsibility and violated the Fourteenth Amendment. Justices Souter, Ginsburg, and Breyer joined her dissent.

Frontiero v. Richardson

411 U.S. 677, 93 S.CT. 1764 (1973)

Sharron Frontiero and her husband sued U.S. Secretary of Defense Elliot Richardson and sought an injunction against the enforcement of federal statutes governing the award of benefits for "dependents" of military personnel. Sharron Frontiero was a lieutenant in the U.S. Air Force. She had sought but was denied increased quarters and allowances and health and medical benefits for her husband, who was a full-time student. Because such benefits would automatically be given to the wife of a male military officer, Frontiero argued that the laws unreasonably discriminated against women and violated the due process clause of the Fifth Amendment. Although the Fifth Amendment contains no equal protection clause, *Bolling v. Sharpe* (1954) (excerpted in Section B) and other rulings had held that the amendment bars the discrimination by the federal government that is "so unjustifiable as to be violate of due process."★

On appeal to the Supreme Court, the justices agreed with Frontiero eight to one, with Justice Rehnquist dissenting. However, the majority split four to four on the question of whether gender is a suspect classification and what standard the Court should use when reviewing cases challenging gender-based discrimination. Justice Brennan, joined by three others, contended that gender, like race, is a suspect classification; while Justice Powell, writing for two others, disagreed and contended that it would be wrong for the Court to go that far, because at the time the country was debating the ill-fated Equal Rights Amendment.

☐ *Justice BRENNAN with whom Justice DOUGLAS, Justice WHITE, and Justice MARSHALL join, delivered the opinion of the Court.*

The question before us concerns the right of a female member of the uniformed services to claim her spouse as a "dependent" for the purposes of obtaining increased quarters allowances and medical and dental benefits under 37 U.S.C. §§ 401, 403, and 10 U.S.C. §§ 1072, 1076, on an equal footing with male members. Under these statutes, a serviceman may claim his wife as a "dependent" without regard to whether she is in fact dependent upon him for any part of her support. A servicewoman, on the other hand, may not claim her husband as a "dependent" under these programs unless he is in fact dependent upon her for over one-half of his support. Thus, the question for decision is whether this difference in treatment constitutes an unconstitutional discrimination against servicewomen in violation of the Due Process

★ *Schneider v. Rusk*, 377 U.S. 163 (1964).

Clause of the Fifth Amendment. A three-judge District Court for the Middle District of Alabama, one judge dissenting, rejected this contention and sustained the constitutionality of the provisions of the statutes making this distinction. . . . We reverse. . . .

At the outset, appellants contend that classifications based upon sex, like classifications based upon race, alienage, and national origin, are inherently suspect and must therefore be subjected to close judicial scrutiny. We agree and, indeed, find at least implicit support for such an approach in our unanimous decision only last Term in *Reed v. Reed*, 404 U.S. 71 (1971).

In *Reed*, the Court considered the constitutionality of an Idaho statute providing that, when two individuals are otherwise equally entitled to appointment as administrator of an estate, the male applicant must be preferred to the female. Appellant, the mother of the deceased, and appellee, the father, filed competing petitions for appointment as administrator of their son's estate. Since the parties, as parents of the deceased, were members of the same entitlement class the statutory preference was invoked and the father's petition was therefore granted. Appellant claimed that this statute, by giving a mandatory preference to males over females without regard to their individual qualifications, violated the Equal Protection Clause of the Fourteenth Amendment.

The Court noted that the Idaho statute, "provides that different treatment be accorded to the applicants on the basis of their sex; it thus establishes a classification subject to scrutiny under the Equal Protection Clause." Under "traditional" equal protection analysis, a legislative classification must be sustained unless it is "patently arbitrary" and bears no rational relationship to a legitimate governmental interest.

In an effort to meet this standard, appellee contended that the statutory scheme was a reasonable measure designed to reduce the workload on probate courts by eliminating one class of contests. Moreover, appellee argued that the mandatory preference for male applicants was in itself reasonable since "men [are] as a rule more conversant with business affairs than . . . women." Indeed, appellee maintained that "it is a matter of common knowledge, that women still are not engaged in politics, the professions, business or industry to the extent that men are." And the Idaho Supreme Court, in upholding the constitutionality of this statute, suggested that the Idaho Legislature might reasonably have "concluded that in general men are better qualified to act as an administrator than are women."

Despite these contentions, however, the Court held the statutory preference for male applicants unconstitutional. In reaching this result, the Court implicitly rejected appellee's apparently rational explanation of the statutory scheme, and concluded that, by ignoring the individual qualifications of particular applicants, the challenged statute provide "dissimilar treatment for men and women who are . . . similarly situated." The Court therefore held that, even though the State's interest in achieving administrative efficiency "is not without some legitimacy." "[t]o give a mandatory preference to members of either sex over members of the other, merely to accomplish the elimination of hearings on the merits, is to make the very kind of arbitrary legislative choice forbidden by the [Constitution]. . . ." This departure from "traditional" rational-basis analysis with respect to sex-based classifications is clearly justified.

There can be no doubt that our Nation has had a long and unfortunate history of sex discrimination. Traditionally, such discrimination was rationalized by an attitude of "romantic paternalism" which, in practical effect, put women, not on a pedestal, but in a cage. . . .

As a result of notions such as these, our statute books gradually became laden with gross, stereotyped distinctions between the sexes and, indeed, throughout much of the 19th century the position of women in our society was, in many respects, comparable to that of blacks under the pre-Civil War slave codes. Neither slaves nor women could hold office, serve on juries, or bring suit in their own names, and married women traditionally were denied the legal capacity to hold or convey property or to serve as legal guardians of their own children. . . .

Moreover, since sex, like race and national origin, is an immutable characteristic determined solely by the accident of birth, the imposition of special disabilities upon the members of a particular sex because of their sex would seem to violate "the basic concept of our system that legal burdens should bear some relationship to individual responsibility. . . ." *Weber v. Aetna Casualty & Surety Co.*, 406 U.S. 164, 175 (1972). And what differentiates sex from such nonsuspect statuses as intelligence or physical disability, and aligns it with the recognized suspect criteria, is that the sex characteristic frequently bears no relation to ability to perform or contribute to society. As a result, statutory distinctions between the sexes often have the effect of invidiously relegating the entire class of females to inferior legal status without regard to the actual capabilities of its individual members. . . .

With these considerations in mind, we can only conclude that classifications based upon sex, like classifications based upon race, alienage, or national origin, are inherently suspect, and must therefore be subjected to strict judicial scrutiny. Applying the analysis mandated by that stricter standard of review, it is clear that the statutory scheme now before us is constitutionally invalid.

The sole basis of the classification established in the challenged statutes is the sex of the individuals involved. Thus, under 37 U.S.C. §§ 401, 403, and 10 U.S.C. §§ 2072, 2076, a female member of the uniformed services seeking to obtain housing and medical benefits for her spouse must prove his dependency in fact, whereas no such burden is imposed upon male members. In addition, the statutes operate so as to deny benefits to a female member, such as appellant Sharron Frontiero, who provides less than one-half of her spouse's support, while at the same time granting such benefits to a male member who likewise provides less than one-half of his spouse's support. . . .

The Government offers no concrete evidence, however, tending to support its view that such differential treatment in fact saves the Government any money. In order to satisfy the demands of strict judicial scrutiny, the Government must demonstrate, for example, that it is actually cheaper to grant increased benefits with respect to *all* male members, than it is to determine which male members are in fact entitled to such benefits and to grant increased benefits only to those members whose wives actually meet the dependency requirement. Here, however, there is substantial evidence that, if put to the test, many of the wives of male members would fail to qualify for benefits. And in light of the fact that the dependency determination with respect to the husbands of female members is presently made solely on the basis of affidavits rather than through the more costly hearing process, the Government's explanation of the statutory scheme is, to say the least, questionable.

In any case, our prior decisions make clear that, although efficacious administration of governmental programs is not without some importance, "the Constitution recognizes higher values than speed and efficiency." *Stanley v. Illinois*, 405 U.S. 645 (1972). And when we enter the realm of "strict judicial scrutiny," there can be no doubt that "administrative convenience" is not a shibboleth, the mere recitation of which dictates constitutionality. . . . On the contrary, any statutory scheme which draws a sharp line between the sexes, *solely* for the purpose of achieving administrative convenience, necessarily commands "dissimilar treatment for men and women who are . . . similarly situated," and therefore involves the "very kind of arbitrary legislative choice forbidden by the [Constitution]. . . ." *Reed v. Reed*, [404 U.S. 71 (1971)]. We therefore conclude that, by according differential treatment to male and female members of the uniformed services for the sole purpose of achieving administrative convenience, the challenged statutes violate the Due Process Clause of the Fifth Amendment insofar as they require a female member to prove the dependency of her husband.

Reversed.

☐ *Justice POWELL, with whom the CHIEF JUSTICE and Justice BLACKMUN join, concurring.*

I agree that the challenged statutes constitute an unconstitutional discrimination against servicewomen in violation of the Due Process Clause of the Fifth Amendment, but I cannot join the opinion of Justice BRENNAN, which would hold that all classifications based upon sex, "like classifications based upon race, alienage, and national origin," are "inherently suspect and must therefore be subjected to close judicial scrutiny." It is unnecessary for the Court in this case to characterize sex as a suspect classification, with all of the far-reaching implications of such a holding. . . .

There is another, and I find compelling, reason for deferring a general categorizing of sex classifications as invoking the strictest test of judicial scrutiny. The Equal Rights Amendment, which if adopted will resolve the substance of this precise question, has been approved by the Congress and submitted for ratification by the States. If this Amendment is duly adopted, it will represent the will of the people accomplished in the manner prescribed by the Constitution. By acting prematurely and unnecessarily, as I view it, the Court has assumed a decisional responsibility at the very time when state legislatures, functioning within the traditional democratic process, are debating the proposed Amendment. It seems to me that this reaching out to preempt by judicial action a major political decision which is currently in process of resolution does not reflect appropriate respect for duly prescribed legislative processes.

Craig v. Boren

429 U.S. 190, 97 S.Ct. 451 (1976)

Curtis Craig, a male under twenty-one years old, and a female distributor of alcoholic beverages sought in federal district court declaratory
and injunctive relief against the enforcement of an Oklahoma statute
that forbade the sale of 3.2 beer—beer with low alcohol content—to
males, but not females, under the age of twenty-one. They argued that
the law constituted invidious discrimination against males and violated
the equal protection clause of the Fourteenth Amendment. After a
three-judge district court denied relief, Craig appealed to the Supreme
Court.

The Court's decision was seven to two, and the majority's opinion
was announced by Justice Brennan. Justices Powell, Stevens, and Blackmun, who was joined by Justice Stewart, each concurred. Dissenting
opinions were delivered by Chief Justice Burger and Justice Rehnquist.

☐ *Justice BRENNAN delivered the opinion of the Court.*

The interaction of two sections of an Oklahoma statute, 37 Okla.Stat.
§§ 241 and 245, prohibits the sale of "nonintoxicating" 3.2% beer to males
under the age of 21 and to females under the age of 18. The question to be
decided is whether such a gender-based differential constitutes a denial to
males 18–20 years of age of the Equal Protection of the Laws in violation of
the Fourteenth Amendment. . . .

Analysis may appropriately begin with the reminder that *Reed v. Reed*,
[404 U.S. 71 (1971)], emphasized that statutory classifications that distinguish
between males and females are "subject to scrutiny under the Equal Protection Clause." To withstand constitutional challenge, previous cases establish
that classifications by gender must serve important governmental objectives
and must be substantially related to achievement of those objectives. Thus, in
Reed, the objectives of "reducing the workload on probate courts," . . . and
"avoiding intra-family controversy," were deemed of insufficient importance
to sustain use of an overt gender criterion in the appointment of intestate
administrators. Decisions following *Reed* similarly have rejected administrative ease and convenience as sufficiently important objectives to justify
gender-based classifications. . . .

Reed v. Reed has also provided the underpinning for decisions that have
invalidated statutes employing gender as an inaccurate proxy for other, more
germane bases of classification. Hence, "archaic and overbroad" generalizations, *Schlesinger v. Ballard* [419 U.S. 498 (1975)], concerning the financial position of servicewomen, *Frontiero v. Richardson*, [411 U.S. 677 (1973)], and
working women, *Weinberger v. Wisenfeld*, [420 U.S. 636 (1975)], could not justify use of a gender line in determining eligibility for certain governmental

entitlements. Similarly increasingly outdated misconceptions concerning the role of females in the home rather than in the "marketplace and world of ideas" were rejected as loose-fitting characterizations incapable of supporting state statutory schemes that were premised upon their accuracy. . . .

In this case, too, "*Reed* we feel is controlling. . . ." We turn then to the question whether, under *Reed*, the difference between males and females with respect to the purchase of 3.2% beer warrants the differential in age drawn by the Oklahoma statute. We conclude that it does not. . . .

We accept for purposes of discussion the District Court's identification of the objective underlying §§ 241 and 245 as the enhancement of traffic safety. Clearly, the protection of public health and safety represents an important function of state and local governments. However, appellees' statistics in our view cannot support the conclusion that the gender-based distinction closely serves to achieve that objective and therefore the distinction cannot under *Reed* withstand equal protection challenge.

The appellees introduced a variety of statistical surveys. First, an analysis of arrest statistics for 1973 demonstrated that 18–20-year-old male arrests for "driving under the influence" and "drunkenness" substantially exceeded female arrests for that same age period. Similarly, youths aged 17–21 were found to be over-represented among those killed or injured in traffic accidents, with males again numerically exceeding females in this regard. Third, a random roadside survey in Oklahoma City revealed that young males were more inclined to drive and drink beer than were their female counterparts. Fourth, Federal Bureau of Investigation nationwide statistics exhibited a notable increase in arrests for "driving under the influence." Finally, statistical evidence gathered in other jurisdictions, particularly Minnesota and Michigan, was offered to corroborate Oklahoma's experience by indicating the pervasiveness of youthful participation in motor vehicle accidents following the imbibing of alcohol. . . .

Even were this statistical evidence accepted as accurate, it nevertheless offers only a weak answer to the equal protection question presented here. The most focused and relevant of the statistical surveys, arrests of 18–20-year-olds for alcohol-related driving offenses, exemplifies the ultimate unpersuasiveness of this evidentiary record. Viewed in terms of the correlation between sex and the actual activity that Oklahoma seeks to regulate—driving while under the influence of alcohol—the statistics broadly establish that .18% of females and 2% of males in that age group were arrested for that offense. While such a disparity is not trivial in a statistical sense, it hardly can form the basis for employment of a gender line as a classifying device. Certainly if maleness is to serve as a proxy for drinking and driving, a correlation of 2% must be considered an unduly tenuous "fit." Indeed, prior cases have consistently rejected the use of sex as a decisionmaking factor even though the statutes in question certainly rested on far more predictive empirical relationships than this.

Moreover, the statistics exhibit a variety of other shortcomings that seriously impugn their value to equal protection analysis. Setting aside the obvious methodological problems, the surveys do not adequately justify the salient features of Oklahoma's gender-based traffic-safety law. None purports to measure the use and dangerousness of 3.2% beer as opposed to alcohol generally, a detail that is of particular importance since, in light of its low alcohol level, Oklahoma apparently considers the 3.2% beverage to be "non-intoxicating." . . .

There is no reason to belabor this line of analysis. It is unrealistic to expect either members of the judiciary or state officials to be well versed in the rigors of experimental or statistical technique. But this merely illustrates that proving broad sociological propositions by statistics is a dubious business, and one that inevitably is in tension with the normative philosophy that underlies the Equal Protection Clause. Suffice to say that the showing offered by the appellees does not satisfy us that sex represents a legitimate, accurate proxy for the regulation of drinking and driving. In fact, when it is further recognized that Oklahoma's statute prohibits only the selling of 3.2% beer to young males and not their drinking the beverage once acquired (even after purchase by their 18–20-year-old female companions), the relationship between gender and traffic safety becomes far too tenuous to satisfy *Reed*'s requirement that the gender-based difference be substantially related to achievement of the statutory objective.

We hold, therefore, that under *Reed*, Oklahoma's 3.2% beer statute invidiously discriminates against males 18–20 years of age. . . .

We conclude that the gender-based differential contained in 37 Okla.Stat. § 245 constitutes a denial of the Equal Protection of the Laws to males aged 18–20 and reverse the judgment of the District Court.

☐ *Justice REHNQUIST, dissenting.*

The Court's disposition of this case is objectionable on two grounds. First, is its conclusion that *men* challenging a gender-based statute which treats them less favorably than women may invoke a more stringent standard of judicial review than pertains to most other types of classifications. Second is the Court's enunciation of this standard, without citation to any source, as being that "classifications by gender must serve *important* governmental objectives and must be *substantially* related to achievement of those objectives" (emphasis added). The only redeeming feature of the Court's opinion, to my mind, is that it apparently signals a retreat by those who joined the plurality opinion in *Frontiero v. Richardson*, from their view that sex is a "suspect" classification for purposes of equal protection analysis. I think the Oklahoma statute challenged here need pass only the "rational basis" equal protection analysis, and I believe that it is constitutional under that analysis. . . .

Most obviously unavailable to support any kind of special scrutiny in this case is a history or pattern of past discrimination, such as was relied on by the plurality in *Frontiero* to support its invocation of strict scrutiny. There is no suggestion in the Court's opinion that males in this age group are in any way peculiarly disadvantaged, subject to systematic discriminatory treatment, or otherwise in need of special solicitude from the courts. . . .

I would have thought that if this Court were to leave anything to decision by the popularly elected branches of the Government, where no constitutional claim other than that of equal protection is invoked, it would be the decision as to what governmental objectives to be achieved by law are "important," and which are not. As for the second part of the Court's new test, the Judicial Branch is probably in no worse position than the Legislative or Executive Branches to determine if there is *any* rational relationship between a classification and the purpose which it might be thought to serve. But the introduction of the adverb "substantially" requires courts to make subjective judgments as to operational effects, for which neither their expertise nor their access to data fits them. And even if we manage to avoid both confusion and the mirroring of our own preferences in the development of this new doctrine, the thousands of judges in other courts who must interpret the Equal Protection Clause may not be so fortunate. . . .

The Court "accept[s] for purposes of discussion" the District Court's finding that the purpose of the provisions in question was traffic safety, and proceeds to examine the statistical evidence in the record in order to decide if "the gender-based distinction *closely* serves to achieve that objective. . . . One need not immerse oneself in the fine-points of statistical analysis, however, in order to see the weaknesses in the Court's attempted denigration of the evidence at hand."

One survey of arrest statistics assembled in 1973 indicated that males in the 18–20 age group were arrested for "driving under the influence" almost 18 times as often as their female counterparts, and for "drunkenness" in a ratio of almost ten-to-one. Accepting, as the Court does, appellants' comparison of the total figures with 1973 Oklahoma census data, this survey indicates a 2% arrest rate among males in the age group, as compared to a .18% rate among females. . . .

The rationality of a statutory classification for equal protection purposes does not depend upon the statistical "fit" between the class and the trait sought to be singled out. It turns on whether there may be a sufficiently higher incidence of the trait within the included class than in the excluded class to justify different treatment. Therefore the present equal protection challenge to this gender-based discrimination poses only the question whether the incidence of drunk driving among young men is sufficiently greater than among young women to justify differential treatment. Notwithstanding the Court's critique of the statistical evidence, that evidence suggests clear differences between the drinking and driving habits of young men and women. Those differences are grounds enough for the State reasonably to conclude that young males pose by far the greater drunk driving hazard, both in terms of sheer numbers and in terms of hazard on a per-driver basis. The gender-based difference in treatment in this case is therefore not irrational.

The Court's argument that a 2% correlation between maleness and drunk driving is constitutionally insufficient therefore does not pose an equal protection issue concerning discrimination between males and females. The clearest demonstration of this is the fact that the precise argument made by the Court would be equally applicable to a flat bar on such purchases by *anyone*, male or female, in the 18–20 age group; in fact it would apply *a fortiori* in that case given the even more "tenuous 'fit' " between drunk driving arrests and femaleness. The statistics indicate that about 1% of the age group population as a whole is arrested. What the Court's argument is relevant to is not equal protection, but due process—whether enough persons in the category drive drunk to justify a bar against purchases by all members of the group. . . .

This is not a case where the classification can only be justified on grounds of administrative convenience. There being no apparent way to single out persons likely to drink and drive, it seems plain that the legislature was faced here with the not atypical legislative problem of legislating in terms of broad categories with regard to the purchase and consumption of alcohol. I trust, especially in light of the Twenty-first Amendment, that there would be no due process violation if no one in this age group were allowed to purchase 3.2% beer. Since males drink and drive at a higher rate than the age group as a whole, I fail to see how a statutory bar with regard only to them can create any due process problem.

Michael M. v. Superior Court of Sonoma County

450 U.S. 464, 101 S.Ct. 1200 (1981)

In the summer of 1978, in the Superior Court of Sonoma County, California, a boy of seventeen and a half, Michael M., was tried and convicted for statutory rape. Under California's law, *statutory rape* is defined as unlawful "sexual intercourse accomplished with a female not the wife of the perpetrator, where the female is under the age of 18 years." At his trial and on an unsuccessful appeal of his conviction, Michael M.'s attorneys argued that the law violated the equal protection clause of the Fourteenth Amendment because only males were criminally liable.

The Court's decision was five to four, and the plurality's opinion was announced by Justice Rehnquist. Justices Stewart and Blackmun each delivered concurring opinions. Justices Stevens and Brennan, who was joined by Justices Marshall and White, dissented.

> □ *Justice REHNQUIST, with whom the CHIEF JUSTICE, Justice STEWART, and Justice POWELL join, delivered the opinion of the Court.*

The question presented in this case is whether California's "statutory rape" law, § 261.5 of the Cal.Penal Code Ann. (West Supp. 1981), violates the Equal Protection Clause of the Fourteenth Amendment. Section 261.5 defines unlawful sexual intercourse as "an act of sexual intercourse accomplished with a female not the wife of the perpetrator, where the female is under the age of 18 years." The statute thus makes men alone criminally liable for the act of sexual intercourse.

In July 1978, a complaint was filed in the Municipal Court of Sonoma County, Cal., alleging that petitioner, then a 17½-year-old male, had had unlawful sexual intercourse with a female under the age of 18, in violation of § 261.5. The evidence, adduced at a preliminary hearing showed that at approximately midnight on June 3, 1978, petitioner and two friends approached Sharon, a 16½-year-old female, and her sister as they waited at a bus stop. Petitioner and Sharon, who had already been drinking, moved away from the others and began to kiss. After being struck in the face for rebuffing petitioner's initial advances, Sharon submitted to sexual intercourse with petitioner. . . .

As is evident from our opinions, the Court has had some difficulty in agreeing upon the proper approach and analysis in cases involving challenges to gender-based classifications. . . . [W]e have not held that gender-based classifications are "inherently suspect" and thus we do not apply so-called "strict scrutiny" to those classifications. See *Stanton v. Stanton*, 421 U.S. 7 (1975). Our cases have held, however, that the traditional minimum rationality test takes on a somewhat "sharper focus" when gender-based classifications are challenged. See *Craig v. Boren*, 429 U.S. 190 (1976) (POWELL, J., concurring). In *Reed v. Reed*, 404 U.S. 71 (1971), for example, the Court stated that a gender-based classification will be upheld if it bears a "fair and substantial relationship" to legitimate state ends, while in *Craig v. Boren*, the Court restated the test to require the classification to bear a "substantial relationship" to "important governmental objectives."

Underlying these decisions is the principle that a legislature may not "make overbroad generalizations based on sex which are entirely unrelated to any differences between men and women or which demean the ability or social status of the affected class." *Parham v. Hughes*, 441 U.S. 347 (1979) (plurality opinion of STEWART, J.). But because the Equal Protection Clause does not "demand that a statute necessarily apply equally to all persons" or require " 'things which are different in fact . . . to be treated in law as though they were the same,' " *Rinaldi v. Yeager*, 384 U.S. 305 (1966), quoting *Tigner v. Texas*, 310 U.S. 141 (1940), this Court has consistently upheld statutes where the gender classification is not invidious, but rather realistically reflects the fact that the sexes are not similarly situated in certain circumstances. *Parham v. Hughes*, [441 U.S. 347 (1979)]; *Califano v. Webster*, 430 U.S. 313 (1977); *Schlesinger v. Ballard*, 419 U.S. 498 (1975); *Kahn v. Shevin*, 416 U.S. 351 (1974). As the Court has stated, a legislature may "provide for the special problems of women." *Weinberger v. Wiesenfeld*, 420 U.S. 636 (1975).

Applying those principles to this case, the fact that the California Legislature criminalized the act of illicit sexual intercourse with a minor female is a sure indication of its intent or purpose to discourage that conduct. Precisely why the legislature desired that result is of course somewhat less clear. . . .

The justification for the statute offered by the State, and accepted by the Supreme Court of California, is that the legislature sought to prevent illegitimate teenage pregnancies. . . .

We are satisfied not only that the prevention of illegitimate pregnancy is at least one of the "purposes" of the statute, but also that the State has a strong interest in preventing such pregnancy. At the risk of stating the obvious, teenage pregnancies, which have increased dramatically over the last two decades, have significant social, medical, and economic consequences for both the mother and her child, and the State. Of particular concern to the State is that approximately half of all teenage pregnancies end in abortion. And of those children who are born, their illegitimacy makes them likely candidates to become wards of the State.

We need not be medical doctors to discern that young men and young women are not similarly situated with respect to the problems and the risks of sexual intercourse. Only women may become pregnant, and they suffer disproportionately the profound physical, emotional and psychological consequences of sexual activity. The statute at issue here protects women from sexual intercourse at an age when those consequences are particularly severe.

The question thus boils down to whether a State may attack the problem of sexual intercourse and teenage pregnancy directly by prohibiting a male from having sexual intercourse with a minor female. We hold that such a statute is sufficiently related to the State's objectives to pass constitutional muster.

Because virtually all of the significant harmful and inescapably identifiable consequences of teenage pregnancy fall on the young female, a legislature acts well within its authority when it elects to punish only the participant who, by nature, suffers few of the consequences of his conduct. It is hardly unreasonable for a legislature acting to protect minor females to exclude them from punishment. Moreover, the risk of pregnancy itself constitutes a substantial deterrence to young females. No similar natural sanctions deter males. A criminal sanction imposed solely on males thus serves to roughly "equalize" the deterrents on the sexes. . . .

[W]e cannot say that a gender-neutral statute would be as effective as the statute California has chosen to enact. The State persuasively contends that a gender-neutral statute would frustrate its interest in effective enforcement. Its view is that a female is surely less likely to report violations of the statute if she herself would be subject to criminal prosecution. In an area already fraught with prosecutorial difficulties, we decline to hold that the Equal Protection Clause requires a legislature to enact a statute so broad that it may well be incapable of enforcement.

We similarly reject petitioner's argument that § 261.5 is impermissibly overbroad because it makes unlawful sexual intercourse with prepubescent females, who are, by definition, incapable of becoming pregnant. Quite apart from the fact that the statute could well be justified on the grounds that very young females are particularly susceptible to physical injury from sexual intercourse, see *Rundlett v. Oliver*, 607 F.2d 495 (CA1 1979), it is ludicrous to suggest that the Constitution requires the California Legislature to limit the scope of its rape statute to older teenagers and exclude young girls.

There remains only petitioner's contention that the statute is unconstitutional as it is applied to him because he, like Sharon, was under 18 at the time of sexual intercourse. Petitioner argues that the statute is flawed because it presumes that as between two persons under 18, the male is the culpable aggressor. We find petitioner's contentions unpersuasive. Contrary to his assertions, the statute does not rest on the assumption that males are generally the aggressors. It is instead an attempt by a legislature to prevent illegitimate teenage pregnancy by providing an additional deterrent for men. The age of the man is irrelevant since young men are as capable as older men of inflicting the harm sought to be prevented. . . .

Accordingly, the judgment of the California Supreme Court is Affirmed.

☐ *Justice BRENNAN, with whom Justice WHITE and Justice MAR-SHALL join, dissenting.*

The State of California vigorously asserts that the "important governmental objective" to be served by § 261.5 is the prevention of teenage pregnancy. It claims that its statute furthers this goal by deterring sexual activity by males—the class of persons it considers more responsible for causing those pregnancies. But even assuming that prevention of teenage pregnancy is an important governmental objective and that it is in fact an objective of § 261.5, California still has the burden of proving that there are fewer teenage pregnancies under its gender-based statutory rape law than there would be if the law were gender neutral. To meet this burden, the State must show that because its statutory rape law punishes only males, and not females, it more effectively deters minor females from having sexual intercourse.

The plurality assumes that a gender-neutral statute would be less effective than § 261.5 in deterring sexual activity because a gender-neutral statute would create significant enforcement problems. The plurality thus accepts the State's assertion that

> "a female is surely less likely to report violations of the statute if she herself would be subject to criminal prosecution. In an area already fraught with prosecutorial difficulties, we decline to hold that the Equal Protection Clause requires a legislature to enact a statute so broad that it may well be incapable of enforcement." . . . (footnotes omitted).

However, a State's bare assertion that its gender-based statutory classification substantially furthers an important governmental interest is not enough to meet its burden of proof under *Craig v. Boren*, [429 U.S. 190 (1976)]. Rather, the State must produce evidence that will persuade the court that its assertion is true. See *Craig v. Boren*.

The State has not produced such evidence in this case. Moreover, there are at least two serious flaws in the State's assertion that law enforcement problems created by a gender-neutral statutory rape law would make such a statute less effective than a gender-based statute in deterring sexual activity.

First, the experience of other jurisdictions, and California itself, belies the plurality's conclusion that a gender-neutral statutory rape law "may well be incapable of enforcement." There are now at least 37 States that have enacted gender-neutral statutory rape laws. Although most of these laws protect young persons (of either sex) from the sexual exploitation of older individuals, the laws of Arizona, Florida, and Illinois permit prosecution of both minor females and minor males for engaging in mutual sexual conduct. California has introduced no evidence that those States have been handicapped by the enforcement problems the plurality finds so persuasive. Surely, if those States could provide such evidence, we might expect that California would have introduced it. . . .

The second flaw in the State's assertion is that even assuming that a gender-neutral statute would be more difficult to enforce, the State has still not shown that those enforcement problems would make such a statute less effective than a gender-based statute in deterring minor females from engaging in sexual intercourse. Common sense, however, suggests that a gender-neutral statutory rape law is potentially a *greater* deterrent of sexual activity than a gender-based law, for the simple reason that a gender-neutral law subjects both men and women to criminal sanctions and thus arguably has a deterrent effect on twice as many potential violators. Even if fewer persons were prosecuted under the gender-neutral law, as the State suggests, it would still be true that twice as many persons would be *subject* to arrest. . . .

Until very recently, no California court or commentator had suggested that the purpose of California's statutory rape law was to protect young women from the risk of pregnancy. Indeed, the historical development of § 261.5 demonstrates that the law was initially enacted on the premise that young women, in contrast to young men were to be deemed legally incapable of consenting to an act of sexual intercourse. Because their chastity was considered particularly precious, those young women were felt to be uniquely in need of the State's protection. In contrast, young men were assumed to be capable of making such decisions for themselves; the law therefore did not offer them any special protection. . . .

I would hold that § 261.5 violates the Equal Protection Clause of the Fourteenth Amendment, and I would reverse the judgment of the California Supreme Court.

United States v. Virginia

518 U.S. 515, 116 S.CT. 2264 (1996)

The Virginia Military Institute (VMI) is a state-run, all-male military college, employing an "adversative," military-like training program, aimed at producing "citizen-soldiers, educated and honorable men" suited for leadership in civilian or military life. In 1990, the Bush administration's Department of Justice challenged the all-male policy as a violation of the Fourteenth Amendment's Equal Protection Clause. As a result of that suit, the Court of Appeals for the Fourth Circuit held that, although VMI's single-gender education was pedagogically justifiable, the Fourteenth Amendment required the state to either admit females into VMI or, alternatively, create a similar program for females. Virginia responded by creating a parallel program for women—the Virginia Women's Institute for Leadership (VWIL)—at the private, all-female Mary Baldwin College. A task force determined that the mission of VWIL would be the same as that of VMI, but instead of adopting VMI's "adversative method" it deemphasized harsh military methods and instituted a structured environment emphasizing leadership and training. When this plan was in turn challenged, the district court upheld it and the appellate court affirmed. Whereupon, the Department of Justice appealed to the Supreme Court.

The Court's decision was seven to one and the opinion was delivered by Justice Ginsburg. Chief Justice Rehnquist filed a concurring opinion and Justice Scalia a dissent. Justice Thomas did not participate in the decision.

☐ *Justice GINSBURG delivered the opinion of the Court.*

Virginia's public institutions of higher learning include an incomparable military college, Virginia Military Institute (VMI). The United States maintains that the Constitution's equal protection guarantee precludes Virginia from reserving exclusively to men the unique educational opportunities VMI affords. We agree. . . .

The cross-petitions in this case present two ultimate issues. First, does Virginia's exclusion of women from the educational opportunities provided by VMI—extraordinary opportunities for military training and civilian leadership development—deny to women "capable of all of the individual activities required of VMI cadets," the equal protection of the laws guaranteed by the Fourteenth Amendment? Second, if VMI's "unique" situation—as Virginia's sole single-sex public institution of higher education—offends the Constitution's equal protection principle, what is the remedial requirement?

We note, once again, the core instruction of this Court's pathmarking decisions in *J.E.B. v. Alabama ex rel. T.B.*, 511 U. S. 127 (1994), and *Mississippi Univ. for Women [v. Hogan]*, 458 U. S. [718 (1982)]: Parties who seek to defend gender-based government action must demonstrate an "exceedingly persuasive justification" for that action.

Today's skeptical scrutiny of official action denying rights or opportunities based on sex responds to volumes of history. As a plurality of this Court acknowledged a generation ago, "our Nation has had a long and unfortunate history of sex discrimination." *Frontiero v. Richardson*, 411 U. S. 677 (1973). Through a century plus three decades and more of that history, women did not count among voters composing "We the People"; not until 1920 did women gain a constitutional right to the franchise. And for a half century thereafter, it remained the prevailing doctrine that government, both federal and state, could withhold from women opportunities accorded men so long as any "basis in reason" could be conceived for the discrimination.

In 1971, for the first time in our Nation's history, this Court ruled in favor of a woman who complained that her State had denied her the equal protection of its laws. *Reed v. Reed*, 404 U. S. 71 (holding unconstitutional Idaho Code prescription that, among " 'several persons claiming and equally entitled to administer [a decendent's estate], males must be preferred to females' "). Since *Reed*, the Court has repeatedly recognized that neither federal nor state government acts compatibly with the equal protection principle when a law or official policy denies to women, simply because they are women, full citizenship stature—equal opportunity to aspire, achieve, participate in and contribute to society based on their individual talents and capacities.

Without equating gender classifications, for all purposes, to classifications based on race or national origin, the Court, in post-*Reed* decisions, has carefully inspected official action that closes a door or denies opportunity to women (or to men). To summarize the Court's current directions for cases of official classification based on gender: Focusing on the differential treatment or denial of opportunity for which relief is sought, the reviewing court must determine whether the proffered justification is "exceedingly persuasive." The burden of justification is demanding and it rests entirely on the State. See *Mississippi Univ. for Women*. The State must show "at least that the [challenged] classification serves 'important governmental objectives and that the discriminatory means employed' are 'substantially related to the achievement of those objectives.' " Ibid. The justification must be genuine, not hypothesized or invented post hoc in response to litigation. And it must not rely on overbroad generalizations about the different talents, capacities, or preferences of males and females. See *Weinberger v. Wiesenfeld*, 420 U. S. 636 (1975); *Califano v. Goldfarb*, 430 U. S. 199 (1977) (STEVENS, J., concurring in judgment).

The heightened review standard our precedent establishes does not make sex a proscribed classification. Supposed "inherent differences" are no longer accepted as a ground for race or national origin classifications. See *Loving v. Virginia*, 388 U. S. 1 (1967). Physical differences between men and women, however, are enduring: "The two sexes are not fungible; a community made up exclusively of one [sex] is different from a community composed of both." *Ballard v. United States*, 329 U. S. 187 (1946).

"Inherent differences" between men and women, we have come to appreciate, remain cause for celebration, but not for denigration of the members of either sex or for artificial constraints on an individual's opportunity. Sex classifications may be used to compensate women "for particular economic disabilities [they have] suffered," *Califano v. Webster*, 430 U.S. 313 (1977) (*per curiam*), to "promote equal employment opportunity," see *California Federal Sav. & Loan Assn. v. Guerra*, 479 U.S. 272 (1987), to advance full development of the talent and capacities of our Nation's people. But such classifications may not be used, as they once were, to create or perpetuate the legal, social, and economic inferiority of women.

Measuring the record in this case against the review standard just described, we conclude that Virginia has shown no "exceedingly persuasive justification" for excluding all women from the citizen-soldier training afforded by VMI. We therefore affirm the Fourth Circuit's initial judgment, which held that Virginia had violated the Fourteenth Amendment's Equal Protection Clause. Because the remedy proffered by Virginia—the Mary Baldwin VWIL program—does not cure the constitutional violation, i.e., it does not provide equal opportunity, we reverse the Fourth Circuit's final judgment in this case.

The Fourth Circuit initially held that Virginia had advanced no state policy by which it could justify, under equal protection principles, its determination "to afford VMI's unique type of program to men and not to women." Virginia challenges that "liability" ruling and asserts two justifications in defense of VMI's exclusion of women. First, the Commonwealth contends, "single-sex education provides important educational benefits," and the option of single-sex education contributes to "diversity in educational approaches." Second, the Commonwealth argues, "the unique VMI method of character development and leadership training," the school's adversative approach, would have to be modified were VMI to admit women. We consider these two justifications in turn.

[I]t is not disputed that diversity among public educational institutions can serve the public good. But Virginia has not shown that VMI was established, or has been maintained, with a view to diversifying, by its categorical exclusion of women, educational opportunities within the State. . . .

Mississippi Univ. for Women is immediately in point. There the State asserted, in justification of its exclusion of men from a nursing school, that it

Justices Ruth Bader Ginsburg (left) and Sandra Day O'Connor, the Court's first two female members. *(Collection of the Supreme Court of the United States)*

was engaging in "educational affirmative action" by "compensating for discrimination against women." Undertaking a "searching analysis," the Court found no close resemblance between "the alleged objective" and "the actual purpose underlying the discriminatory classification." Pursuing a similar inquiry here, we reach the same conclusion.

Neither recent nor distant history bears out Virginia's alleged pursuit of diversity through single-sex educational options. In 1839, when the State established VMI, a range of educational opportunities for men and women was scarcely contemplated. Higher education at the time was considered dangerous for women; reflecting widely held views about women's proper place, the Nation's first universities and colleges—for example, Harvard in Massachusetts, William and Mary in Virginia—admitted only men. VMI was not at all novel in this respect: In admitting no women, VMI followed the lead of the State's flagship school, the University of Virginia, founded in 1819. . . .

In 1879, the State Senate resolved to look into the possibility of higher education for women, recognizing that Virginia " 'has never, at any period of her history,' " provided for the higher education of her daughters, though she " 'has liberally provided for the higher education of her sons.' " Despite this recognition, no new opportunities were instantly open to women.

Virginia eventually provided for several women's seminaries and colleges. Farmville Female Seminary became a public institution in 1884. Two women's schools, Mary Washington College and James Madison University, were founded in 1908; another, Radford University, was founded in 1910. By the mid-1970's, all four schools had become coeducational.

Debate concerning women's admission as undergraduates at the main university continued well past the century's midpoint. Familiar arguments were rehearsed. If women were admitted, it was feared, they "would encroach on the rights of men; there would be new problems of government, perhaps scandals; the old honor system would have to be changed; standards would be lowered to those of other coeducational schools; and the glorious reputation of the university, as a school for men, would be trailed in the dust."

Ultimately, in 1970, "the most prestigious institution of higher education in Virginia," the University of Virginia, introduced coeducation and, in 1972, began to admit women on an equal basis with men. A three-judge Federal District Court confirmed: "Virginia may not now deny to women, on the basis of sex, educational opportunities at the Charlottesville campus that are not afforded in other institutions operated by the State."

Virginia describes the current absence of public single-sex higher education for women as "an historical anomaly." But the historical record indicates action more deliberate than anomalous: First, protection of women against higher education; next, schools for women far from equal in resources and stature to schools for men; finally, conversion of the separate schools to coeducation. The state legislature, prior to the advent of this controversy, had repealed "all Virginia statutes requiring individual institutions to admit only men or women." And in 1990, an official commission, "legislatively established to chart the future goals of higher education in Virginia," reaffirmed the policy "of affording broad access" while maintaining "autonomy and diversity." (Report of the Virginia Commission on the University of the 21st Century). . . .

Our 1982 decision in *Mississippi Univ. for Women* prompted VMI to reexamine its male-only admission policy. Virginia relies on that reexamination as a legitimate basis for maintaining VMI's single-sex character. A Mission Study Committee, appointed by the VMI Board of Visitors, studied the problem from October 1983 until May 1986, and in that month counseled against "change of VMI status as a single-sex college." Whatever internal purpose the Mission Study Committee served—and however well-meaning the framers of the report—we can hardly extract from that effort any state policy evenhandedly to advance diverse educational options. As the District Court observed, the Committee's analysis "primarily focused on anticipated difficulties in attracting females to VMI," and the report, overall, supplied "very little indication of how the conclusion was reached."

In sum, we find no persuasive evidence in this record that VMI's male-only admission policy "is in furtherance of a state policy of 'diversity.' " . . . A purpose genuinely to advance an array of educational options, as the Court of Appeals recognized, is not served by VMI's historic and constant plan—a plan to "afford a unique educational benefit only to males." However "liberally" this plan serves the State's sons, it makes no provision whatever for her daughters. That is not equal protection.

Virginia next argues that VMI's adversative method of training provides educational benefits that cannot be made available, unmodified, to women. Alterations to accommodate women would necessarily be "radical," so "drastic," Virginia asserts, as to transform, indeed "destroy," VMI's program. Neither sex would be favored by the transformation, Virginia maintains: Men would be deprived of the unique opportunity currently available to them; women would not gain that opportunity because their participation would "eliminate the very aspects of [the] program that distinguish [VMI] from . . . other institutions of higher education in Virginia." . . .

The United States does not challenge any expert witness estimation on average capacities on preferences of men and women. Instead, the United States emphasizes that time and again since this Court's turning point decision in *Reed v. Reed*, 404 U. S. 71 (1971), we have cautioned reviewing courts to take a "hard look" at generalizations or "tendencies" of the kind pressed by Virginia, and relied upon by the District Court. State actors controlling gates to opportunity, we have instructed, may not exclude qualified individuals based on "fixed notions concerning the roles and abilities of males and females." *Mississippi Univ. for Women.*

It may be assumed, for purposes of this decision, that most women would not choose VMI's adversative method. . . . The issue, however, is not whether "women—or men—should be forced to attend VMI"; rather, the question is whether the State can constitutionally deny to women who have the will and capacity, the training and attendant opportunities that VMI uniquely affords.

The notion that admission of women would downgrade VMI's stature, destroy the adversative system and, with it, even the school, is a judgment hardly proved, a prediction hardly different from other "self-fulfilling prophecies," once routinely used to deny rights or opportunities. When women first sought admission to the bar and access to legal education, concerns of the same order were expressed. For example, in 1876, the Court of Common Pleas of Hennepin County, Minnesota, explained why women were thought ineligible for the practice of law. Women train and educate the young, the court said, which "forbids that they shall bestow that time (early and late) and labor, so essential in attaining to the eminence to which the true lawyer should ever aspire. It cannot therefore be said that the opposition of courts to the admission of females to practice . . . is to any extent the outgrowth of . . . 'old fogyism[.]' . . . It arises rather from a comprehension of the magnitude of the responsibilities connected with the successful practice of law, and a desire to grade up the profession." In *re Application of Martha Angle Dorsett to Be Admitted to Practice as Attorney and Counselor at Law* (Minn. C. P. Hennepin Cty., 1876). . . .

Women's successful entry into the federal military academies, and their participation in the Nation's military forces, indicate that Virginia's fears for the future of VMI may not be solidly grounded. The State's justification for excluding all women from "citizen-soldier" training for which some are qualified, in any event, cannot rank as "exceedingly persuasive," as we have explained and applied that standard.

Virginia and VMI trained their argument on "means" rather than "end," and thus misperceived our precedent. Single-sex education at VMI serves an "important governmental objective," they maintained, and exclusion of women is not only "substantially related," it is essential to that objective. By this notably circular argument, the "straightforward" test *Mississippi Univ. for Women* described, was bent and bowed. . . .

In the second phase of the litigation, Virginia presented its remedial plan—maintain VMI as a male-only college and create VWIL as a separate program for women. The plan met District Court approval. The Fourth Circuit, in turn, deferentially reviewed the State's proposal and decided that the two single-sex programs directly served Virginia's reasserted purposes: single-gender education, and "achieving the results of an adversative method in a military environment." . . . The United States challenges this "remedial" ruling as pervasively misguided.

A remedial decree, this Court has said, must closely fit the constitutional violation; it must be shaped to place persons unconstitutionally denied an opportunity or advantage in "the position they would have occupied in the absence of [discrimination]." See *Milliken v. Bradley*, 433 U. S. 267 (1977). The constitutional violation in this case is the categorical exclusion of women from an extraordinary educational opportunity afforded men. A proper remedy for an unconstitutional exclusion, we have explained, aims to "eliminate [so far as possible] the discriminatory effects of the past" and to "bar like discrimination in the future." *Louisiana v. United States*, 380 U. S. 145 (1965).

Virginia chose not to eliminate, but to leave untouched, VMI's exclusionary policy. For women only, however, Virginia proposed a separate program, different in kind from VMI and unequal in tangible and intangible facilities. Having violated the Constitution's equal protection requirement, Virginia was obliged to show that its remedial proposal "directly addressed and related to" the violation, the equal protection denied to women ready, willing, and able to benefit from educational opportunities of the kind VMI offers. Virginia described VWIL as a "parallel program," and asserted that VWIL shares VMI's mission of producing "citizen-soldiers" and VMI's goals of providing "education, military training, mental and physical discipline, character ". . . and leadership development." If the VWIL program could not "eliminate the discriminatory effects of the past," could it at least "bar like discrimination in the future"? A comparison of the programs said to be "parallel" informs our answer. . . .

VWIL affords women no opportunity to experience the rigorous military training for which VMI is famed. Instead, the VWIL program "de-emphasizes" military education, and uses a "cooperative method" of education "which reinforces self-esteem."

VWIL students participate in ROTC and a "largely ceremonial" Virginia Corps of Cadets, but Virginia deliberately did not make VWIL a military institute. . . . VWIL students receive their "leadership training" in seminars, externships, and speaker series, episodes and encounters lacking the "physical rigor, mental stress, . . . minute regulation of behavior, and indoctrination in desirable values" made hallmarks of VMI's citizen-soldier training. Kept away from the pressures, hazards, and psychological bonding characteristic of VMI's adversative training, VWIL students will not know the "feeling of tremendous accomplishment" commonly experienced by VMI's successful cadets.

Virginia maintains that these methodological differences are "justified pedagogically," based on "important differences between men and women in learning and developmental needs," "psychological and sociological differences" Virginia describes as "real" and "not stereotypes." The Task Force charged with developing the leadership program for women, drawn from the staff and faculty at Mary Baldwin College, "determined that a military model and, especially VMI's adversative method, would be wholly inappropriate for educating and training most women."

As earlier stated, generalizations about "the way women are," estimates of what is appropriate for most women, no longer justify denying opportunity to women whose talent and capacity place them outside the average description. Notably, Virginia never asserted that VMI's method of education suits most men. It is also revealing that Virginia accounted for its failure to make the VWIL experience "the entirely militaristic experience of VMI" on the ground that VWIL "is planned for women who do not necessarily expect to pursue military careers." By that reasoning, VMI's "entirely militaristic" program would be inappropriate for men in general or as a group, for "only about 15% of VMI cadets enter career military service."

In contrast to the generalizations about women on which Virginia rests, we note again these dispositive realities: VMI's "implementing methodology" is not "inherently unsuitable to women;" "some women . . . do well under [the] adversative model;" "some women, at least, would want to attend [VMI] if they had the opportunity;" "some women are capable of all of the individual activities required of VMI cadets," and "can meet the physical standards [VMI] now imposes on men." It is on behalf of these women that the United States has instituted this suit, and it is for them that a remedy must be crafted, a remedy that will end their exclusion from a state-supplied educational opportunity for which they are fit, a decree that will "bar like discrimination in the future." *Louisiana.*

In myriad respects other than military training, VWIL does not qualify as VMI's equal. VWIL's student body, faculty, course offerings, and facilities hardly match VMI's. Nor can the VWIL graduate anticipate the benefits associated with VMI's 157-year history, the school's prestige, and its influential alumni network. . . .

Virginia, in sum, while maintaining VMI for men only, has failed to provide any "comparable single-gender women's institution." Instead, the Commonwealth has created a VWIL program fairly appraised as a "pale shadow" of VMI in terms of the range of curricular choices and faculty stature, funding, prestige, alumni support and influence.

Virginia's VWIL solution is reminiscent of the remedy Texas proposed 50 years ago, in response to a state trial court's 1946 ruling that, given the equal protection guarantee, African Americans could not be denied a legal education at a state facility. See *Sweatt v. Painter,* 339 U.S. 629 (1950). Reluctant to admit African Americans to its flagship University of Texas Law School, the State set up a separate school for Herman Sweatt and other black law students. As originally opened, the new school had no independent faculty or library, and it lacked accreditation. Nevertheless, the state trial and appellate courts were satisfied that the new school offered Sweatt opportunities for the study of law "substantially equivalent to those offered by the State to white students at the University of Texas." . . .

More important than the tangible features, the Court emphasized, are "those qualities which are incapable of objective measurement but which make for greatness" in a school, including "reputation of the faculty, experience of the administration, position and influence of the alumni, standing in the community, traditions and prestige." Facing the marked differences reported in the *Sweatt* opinion, the Court unanimously ruled that Texas had not shown "substantial equality in the [separate] educational opportunities" the State offered. Accordingly, the Court held, the Equal Protection Clause required Texas to admit African Americans to the University of Texas Law School. In line with *Sweatt*, we rule here that Virginia has not shown substantial equality in the separate educational opportunities the State supports at VWIL and VMI. . . .

The Fourth Circuit plainly erred in exposing Virginia's VWIL plan to a deferential analysis, for "all gender-based classifications today" warrant "heightened scrutiny." Valuable as VWIL may prove for students who seek the program offered, Virginia's remedy affords no cure at all for the opportunities and advantages withheld from women who want a VMI education and can make the grade. In sum, Virginia's remedy does not match the constitutional violation; the State has shown no "exceedingly persuasive justification" for withholding from women qualified for the experience premier training of the kind VMI affords. . . .

A generation ago, "the authorities controlling Virginia higher education," despite long established tradition, agreed "to innovate and favorably entertained the [then] relatively new idea that there must be no discrimination by sex in offering educational opportunity." Commencing in 1970, Virginia opened to women "educational opportunities at the Charlottesville campus that [were] not afforded in other [State-operated] institutions." A federal court approved the State's innovation, emphasizing that the University of Virginia "offered courses of instruction . . . not available elsewhere." The court further noted: "There exists at Charlottesville a 'prestige' factor [not paralleled in] other Virginia educational institutions."

VMI, too, offers an educational opportunity no other Virginia institution provides, and the school's "prestige"—associated with its success in developing "citizen-soldiers"—is unequaled. Virginia has closed this facility to its daughters and, instead, has devised for them a "parallel program," with a faculty less impressively credentialed and less well paid, more limited course offerings, fewer opportunities for military training and for scientific specialization. Cf. *Sweatt*. VMI, beyond question, "possesses to a far greater degree" than the VWIL program "those qualities which are incapable of objective measurement but which make for greatness in a . . . school," including "position and influence of the alumni, standing in the community, traditions and prestige." Women seeking and fit for a VMI-quality education cannot be offered anything less, under the State's obligation to afford them genuinely equal protection. . . .

For the reasons stated, the initial judgment of the Court of Appeals is affirmed, the final judgment of the Court of Appeals is reversed, and the case is remanded for further proceedings consistent with this opinion.

It is so ordered.

☐ *Chief Justice REHNQUIST, concurring in the judgment.*

The Court holds first that Virginia violates the Equal Protection Clause by maintaining the Virginia Military Institute's (VMI's) all-male admissions policy, and second that establishing the Virginia Women's Institute for Leadership (VWIL) program does not remedy that violation. While I agree with these conclusions, I disagree with the Court's analysis and so I write separately.

Two decades ago in *Craig v. Boren*, 429 U. S. 190 (1976), we announced that "to withstand constitutional challenge, . . . classifications by gender must serve important governmental objectives and must be substantially related to achievement of those objectives." We have adhered to that standard of scrutiny ever since. While the majority adheres to this test today, it also says that the State must demonstrate an " 'exceedingly persuasive justification' " to support a gender-based classification. It is unfortunate that the Court thereby introduces an element of uncertainty respecting the appropriate test.

While terms like "important governmental objective" and "substantially related" are hardly models of precision, they have more content and specificity than does the phrase "exceedingly persuasive justification." That phrase is best confined, as it was first used, as an observation on the difficulty of meeting the applicable test, not as a formulation of the test itself. To avoid introducing potential confusion, I would have adhered more closely to our traditional, "firmly established," [*Mississippi Univ. for Women v.*] *Hogan; Heckler* [*v. Mathews*], 465 U.S. 728 (1984), standard that a gender-based classification "must bear a close and substantial relationship to important governmental objectives." [*Personnel Administrator of Mass. v.*] *Feeney*, 442 U.S. 256 (1979).

Even if diversity in educational opportunity were the State's actual objective, the State's position would still be problematic. The difficulty with its position is that the diversity benefited only one sex; there was single-sex public education available for men at VMI, but no corresponding single-sex public education available for women. When *Hogan* placed Virginia on notice that VMI's admissions policy possibly was unconstitutional, VMI could have dealt with the problem by admitting women; but its governing body felt strongly that the admission of women would have seriously harmed the institution's educational approach. Was there something else the State could have done to avoid an equal protection violation? Since the State did nothing, we do not have to definitively answer that question. . . .

The dissent criticizes me for "disregarding the four all-women's private colleges in Virginia (generously assisted by public funds)." The private women's colleges are treated by the State exactly as all other private schools are treated, which includes the provision of tuition-assistance grants to Virginia residents. Virginia gives no special support to the women's single-sex education. But obviously, the same is not true for men's education. Had the State provided the kind of support for the private women's schools that it provides for VMI, this may have been a very different case. For in so doing, the State would have demonstrated that its interest in providing a single-sex education for men, was to some measure matched by an interest in providing the same opportunity for women.

Virginia offers a second justification for the single-sex admissions policy: maintenance of the adversative method. I agree with the Court that this justification does not serve an important governmental objective. A State does not have substantial interest in the adversary methodology unless it is pedagogically beneficial. While considerable evidence shows that a single-sex education is pedagogically beneficial for some students, and hence a State may have a valid interest in promoting that methodology, there is no similar evidence in the record that an adversary method is pedagogically beneficial or is any more likely to produce character traits than other methodologies. . . .

In the end, the women's institution Virginia proposes, VWIL, fails as a remedy, because it is distinctly inferior to the existing men's institution and will continue to be for the foreseeable future. VWIL simply is not, in any sense, the institution that VMI is. In particular, VWIL is a program appended to a private college, not a self-standing institution; and VWIL is substantially underfunded as compared to VMI. I therefore ultimately agree with the Court that Virginia has not provided an adequate remedy.

□ *Justice SCALIA, dissenting.*

I shall devote most of my analysis to evaluating the Court's opinion on the basis of our current equal-protection jurisprudence, which regards this Court as free to evaluate everything under the sun by applying one of three tests: "rational basis" scrutiny, intermediate scrutiny, or strict scrutiny. These tests are no more scientific than their names suggest, and a further element of randomness is added by the fact that it is largely up to us which test will be applied in each case. Strict scrutiny, we have said, is reserved for state "classifications based on race or national origin and classifications affecting fundamental rights," *Clark v. Jeter*, 486 U.S. 456 (1988). It is my position that the term "fundamental rights" should be limited to "interests traditionally protected by our society," *Michael H. v. Gerald D.*, 491 U.S. 110 (1989) (plurality opinion of SCALIA, J.); but the Court has not accepted that view, so that strict scrutiny will be applied to the deprivation of whatever sort of right we consider "fundamental." We have no established criterion for "intermediate scrutiny" either, but essentially apply it when it seems like a good idea to load the dice. So far it has been applied to content-neutral restrictions that place an incidental burden on speech, to disabilities attendant to illegitimacy, and to discrimination on the basis of sex.

I have no problem with a system of abstract tests such as rational-basis, intermediate, and strict scrutiny (though I think we can do better than applying strict scrutiny and intermediate scrutiny whenever we feel like it). Such formulas are essential to evaluating whether the new restrictions that a changing society constantly imposes upon private conduct comport with that "equal protection" our society has always accorded in the past. But in my view the function of this Court is to preserve our society's values regarding (among other things) equal protection, not to revise them; to prevent backsliding from the degree of restriction the Constitution imposed upon democratic government, not to prescribe, on our own authority, progressively higher degrees. For that reason it is my view that, whatever abstract tests we may choose to devise, they cannot supersede—and indeed ought to be crafted so as to reflect—those constant and unbroken national traditions that embody the people's understanding of ambiguous constitutional texts. More specifically, it is my view that "when a practice not expressly prohibited by the text of the Bill of Rights bears the endorsement of a long tradition of open, widespread, and unchallenged use that dates back to the beginning of the Republic, we have no proper basis for striking it down." *Rutan v. Republican Party of Ill.*, 497 U. S. 62 (1990) (SCALIA, J., dissenting). The same applies, *mutatis mutandis*, to a practice asserted to be in violation of the post–Civil War Fourteenth Amendment.

The all-male constitution of VMI comes squarely within such a governing tradition. Founded by the Commonwealth of Virginia in 1839 and continuously maintained by it since, VMI has always admitted only men. . . . In other words, the tradition of having government-funded military schools for men is as well rooted in the traditions of this country as the tradition of sending only men into military combat. The people may decide to change the one tradition, like the other, through democratic processes; but the assertion that either tradition has been unconstitutional through the centuries is not law, but politics-smuggled-into-law.

To reject the Court's disposition today, however, it is not necessary to accept my view that the Court's made-up tests cannot displace longstanding national traditions as the primary determinant of what the Constitution means. It is only necessary to apply honestly the test the Court has been applying to sex-based classifications for the past two decades. It is well settled, as Justice O'CONNOR stated some time ago for a unanimous Court, that we evaluate a statutory classification based on sex under a standard that lies "between the extremes of rational basis review and strict scrutiny." *Clark v. Jeter.* We have denominated this standard "intermediate scrutiny" and under it have inquired whether the statutory classification is "substantially related to an important governmental objective."

Before I proceed to apply this standard to VMI, I must comment upon the manner in which the Court avoids doing so. . . .

Only the amorphous "exceedingly persuasive justification" phrase, and not the standard elaboration of intermediate scrutiny, can be made to yield this conclusion that VMI's single-sex composition is unconstitutional because there exist several women (or, one would have to conclude under the Court's reasoning, a single woman) willing and able to undertake VMI's program. Intermediate scrutiny has never required a least-restrictive-means analysis, but only a "substantial relation" between the classification and the state interests that it serves. Thus, in *Califano v. Webster*, 430 U. S. 313 (1977), we upheld a congressional statute that provided higher Social Security benefits for women than for men. We reasoned that "women . . . as such have been unfairly hindered from earning as much as men," but we did not require proof that each woman so benefited had suffered discrimination or that each disadvantaged man had not; it was sufficient that even under the former congressional scheme "women on the average received lower retirement benefits than men." The reasoning in our other intermediate-scrutiny cases has similarly required only a substantial relation between end and means, not a perfect fit. . . . There is simply no support in our cases for the notion that a sex-based classification is invalid unless it relates to characteristics that hold true in every instance. . . .

The question to be answered, I repeat, is whether the exclusion of women from VMI is "substantially related to an important governmental objective."

It is beyond question that Virginia has an important state interest in providing effective college education for its citizens. That single-sex instruction is an approach substantially related to that interest should be evident enough from the long and continuing history in this country of men's and women's colleges. But beyond that, as the Court of Appeals here stated: "That single-gender education at the college level is beneficial to both sexes is a fact established in this case." . . .

The potential of today's decision for widespread disruption of existing institutions lies in its application to private single-sex education. Government support is immensely important to private educational institutions. Mary Baldwin College—which designed and runs VWIL—notes that private institutions of higher education in the 1990–1991 school year derived approximately 19 percent of their budgets from federal, state, and local government funds, not including financial aid to students. Charitable status under the tax laws is also highly significant for private educational institutions, and it is certainly not beyond the Court that rendered today's decision to hold that a donation to a single-sex college should be deemed contrary to public policy and therefore not deductible if the college discriminates on the basis of sex. See *Bob Jones Univ. v. United States*, 461 U.S. 574 (1983). . . .

The only hope for state-assisted single-sex private schools is that the Court will not apply in the future the principles of law it has applied today. That is a substantial hope, I am happy and ashamed to say. After all, did not the Court today abandon the principles of law it has applied in our earlier sex-classification cases? And does not the Court positively invite private colleges to rely upon our ad-hocery by assuring them this case is "unique"? I would not advise the foundation of any new single-sex college (especially an all-male one) with the expectation of being allowed to receive any government support; but it is too soon to abandon in despair those single-sex colleges already in existence. It will certainly be possible for this Court to write a future opinion that ignores the broad principles of law set forth today, and that characterizes as utterly dispositive the opinion's perceptions that VMI was a uniquely prestigious all-male institution, conceived in chauvinism, etc., etc. I will not join that opinion.

■ THE DEVELOPMENT OF LAW

Rulings Dealing with Gender Discrimination and Statutory Interpretation

CASE	VOTE	RULING
General Electric Co. v. Gilbert, 429 U.S. 125 (1976)	6:3	Justice Rehnquist held that the denial of employees' disability benefits for pregnancy disability

leave was permissible under Title VII of the Civil Rights Act; Congress subsequently passed legislation overriding the Court's decision.

CASE	VOTE	RULING

Nashville Gas Co. v. Satty, 434 U.S. 136 (1977) — 9:0 — Justice Rehnquist held that women who take pregnancy leaves may not be denied their seniority in employment on returning to work, under Title VII of the Civil Rights Act.

Dothard v. Rawlinson, 433 U.S. 321 (1977) — 8:1 — With Justices Marshall and Brennan concurring and dissenting in part, and Justice White dissenting, the Court held that the assignment of female prison guards in certain areas of a prison did not violate the Civil Rights Act.

City of Los Angeles, Department of Water & Power v. Manhart, 435 U.S. 702 (1978) — 6:3 — With Chief Justice Burger and Justices Rehnquist and Powell dissenting, the Court struck down under Title VII an ordinance requiring female employees to pay $15 more than male employees into a pension fund, despite evidence that women statistically live longer than men.

Hishon v. King & Spaulding, 467 U.S. 69 (1984) — 9:0 — Held that Title VII does not reach a law firm's decision on the promotion of "associates" to "partners," rejecting the claim of a female lawyer who was denied a partnership.

Grove City College v. Bell, 465 U.S. 555 (1984) — 6:3 — Title IX of the Federal Education Act of 1972 authorizes the withholding of federal funds from institutions that impermissibly engage in gender-based discrimination: here, the Court construed the statute to authorize the withholding of funds only from specific programs that discriminated against women and not from the entire institution—in 1988 Congress passed legislation overriding the Court's ruling.

California Federal Savings & Loan Association v. Guerra, 479 U.S. 272 (1987) — 6:3 — With Justices Rehnquist, White, and Powell dissenting, the Court upheld a California law requiring employers to provide pregnancy disability leaves, even though such leaves are not required under Title VII.

Meritor Savings Bank, FBD v. Vinson, 477 U.S. 57 (1986) — 9:0 — Writing for the Court, Justice Rehnquist held that Title VII of the Civil Rights Act of 1964

CASE	VOTE	RULING

bars sexual harassment in the workplace, and not just gender discrimination in the hiring and firing of employees.

International Union, American   9:0   While unanimously holding
Workers, Aerospace, Agricultural   that the Civil Rights Act of
Implement Workers of America,   1964, as amended by the Preg-
UAW v. Johnson Controls, Inc.,   nancy Discrimination Act of
499 U.S. 187 (1991)   1978, invalidated Johnson Con-
                                             trols's "fetal protection" policy
barring fertile women from certain jobs in its automobile battery factory, the
justices were divided on the extent to which companies are barred from such
discriminatory treatment. Writing for the majority, Justice Blackmun held
that federal laws prohibit such discrimination on the basis of gender and
pregnancy, even for women who are actually pregnant.

Franklin v. Gwinnett County   9:0   Writing for the Court, Justice
Public Schools, **503 U.S. 60**   White held that students in
(1992)   schools receiving federal funds
                                             may sue and win damages for
sexual harassment under Title IX of the Educational Amendments of 1972.
Previously, *Cannon v. University of Chicago*, 441 U.S. 677 (1979), had held that
Title IX implied a private cause of action, entitling individuals to bring lawsuits under the statute. But until *Franklin* the Court had not dealt with
whether victims of sexual harassment may receive damages under Title IX.

Harris v. Forklift Systems, Inc.,   9:0   Addressing an issue left unre-
510 U.S. 17 (1993)   solved by the ruling in *Meritor
                                             Savings Bank v. Vinson,* 477 U.S.
57 (1986), which held that the Civil Rights Act of 1964 forbids sexual harassment in the workplace, along with gender discrimination in hiring and
firing of employees, Justice O'Connor held that individuals need not meet
the high standard of proving "psychological injury." Instead, ruled Justice
O'Connor, judges and juries have substantial leeway in deciding whether
sexual advances, insults, and other offensive conduct constitutes harassment.

Oncale v. Sundowner Offshore   9:0   Writing for a unanimous
Services, **523 U.S. 75 (1998)**   Court, Justice Scalia ruled that
                                             Title VII of the Civil Rights
Act of 1964, forbidding sexual discrimination in the workplace, applies to
same-sex harassment, no less than harassment of employees of different sexes
and sexual orientations.

Gebser v. Lago Vista Independent 5:4   Held that damages may not be
School District, **524 U.S. 274**   recovered for teacher-student
(1998)   sexual harassment in an implied
                                             private right-of-action suit un-

der Title IX, which forbids sex discrimination by schools that receive federal funding and is commonly associated with bringing equality to sports programs. A bare majority ruled that schools are not liable for such misconduct unless school officials with authority to institute corrective measures are "deliberately indifferent" to a teacher's misconduct. Writing for the Court, Justice O'Connor emphasized that Title IX is unlike the Civil Rights Act of 1964, which bans sex discrimination and harassment in the workplace, because it provides for the loss of federal funding when school officials know of and fail to respond to misconduct and Congress, therefore, did not contemplate private cause of action suits for sexual harassment. The four dissenters—Justices Stevens, Souter, Ginsburg, and Breyer—countered that school districts should be liable for teachers' misconduct on the theory that teachers are acting on behalf of the school.

Faragher v. City of Boca Raton,   7:2   Held that under Title VII of the
524 U.S. 775 (1998)   Civil Rights Act an employer is
                                              subject to vicarious liability for
hostile-environment sexual harassment created by a supervisor. Writing for the Court, Justice Souter held that employees need not show that an employer knew or should have known about the sexual harassment and failed to stop it. Even if an employee did not suffer the loss of promotion or employment, a suit may be brought if the sexual harassment or abuse was severe or pervasive. Employers, however, may offer the affirmative defenses (a) that they took reasonable care to prevent or correct sexually harassing behavior and (b) that the employee unreasonably failed to take advantage of corrective opportunities offered by the employer. Here, Justice Souter found that Boca Raton failed to exercise reasonable care in protecting its female lifeguards from a hostile environment of sexual harassment. Justices Scalia and Thomas dissented.

Burlington Industries, Inc. v.   7:2   Writing for the Court, Justice
Ellerth, 524 U.S. 742   Kennedy held that employers
(1998)   are liable, under Title VII of the
                                              Civil Rights Act, for hostile-
environment sexual harassment by supervisors unless they show (a) reasonable care to prevent or correct promptly sexually harassing behavior and (b) that the employee unreasonably failed to take advantage of grievance procedures offered by the employer in order to avoid harm. Justices Scalia and Thomas dissented.

Pennsylvania State Police v.   9:0   Writing for the Court, Justice
Suders, 124 S.Ct. 2342 (2004)   Ginsburg held that under the
                                              Civil Rights Act of 1964 em-
ployers are strictly liable for male supervisors who engage in harassment that creates a hostile environment that forces female employees to quit. Employ-

ers are strictly liable for harassment that amounts to a "constructive discharge" because it "culminates in a tangible employment action, such as discharge, demotion, or undesirable reassignment," and resignation as the only fitting response to intolerable working conditions.

■ (2) Discrimination against Gays and Lesbians

In a ruling that sparked considerable controversy in and outside of the Court, *Romer v. Evans* (excerpted below) struck down a Colorado state constitutional amendment that forbade localities from enacting ordinances outlawing discrimination against homosexuals. However, the Court upheld Georgia's law criminalizing sodomy as applied to homosexuals in *Bowers v. Hardwick*, 478 U.S. 186 (1986), and the First Amendment right of the Boy Scouts of America to exclude homosexuals in *Boy Scouts of America v. Dale*, 530 U.S. 640 (2000) (excerpted in Ch. 5, Sec. I). However, the Court reconsidered and overruled *Bowers* in *Lawrence v. Texas* (2003) (excerpted in Ch. 11).

The controversy over discriminating against gays and lesbians further escalated when in the same month *Lawrence v. Texas* came down, Canadian courts ruled that same-sex marriages could not be discriminated against (see the IN COMPARATIVE PERSPECTIVE box in this section). Subsequently, the Massachusetts state supreme court held that the state could not discriminate against same-sex marriages, and local officials from San Francisco, California, to New Paltz, New York, issued marriage licenses to same-sex couples, in some cases in defiance of state laws. Thirty-nine states prohibit same-sex marriages with laws modeled after the federal Defense of Marriage Act (DOMA) of 1996, which bars federal recognition of same-sex marriages and permits states to ignore those performed in other states. Four of those states (Alaska, Hawaii, Nebraska, and Nevada) amended their state constitutions to bar same-sex marriages. In light of *Lawrence v. Texas* and the Massachusetts state supreme court ruling, state DOMA laws are being challenged in the courts. In response, nineteen states were considering in 2004–2005 amendments to their state constitutions that would ban same-sex marriages. President George W. Bush also called for the passage of a federal constitutional amendment barring same-sex marriages. He did so claiming that states would be required to recognize same-sex marriages performed in other states because of the "full faith and credit" clause of Article IV, Section 1, of the Constitution, which requires state courts to honor the judicial decisions of other states. Indeed, some proponents of same-sex marriage contend that the "full faith and credit" clause compels states banning same-sex marriages to recognize legally married same-sex couples in other states, and draw an analogy between bans on interracial and same-sex marriages. But the history and analogy remains problematic for both opponents and proponents of same-sex marriage (see the box on CONSTITUTIONAL HISTORY: *Loving v. Virginia* and Bans on Interracial Marriages in this chapter, Section A).

SELECTED BIBLIOGRAPHY

Eskridge, William N., *Gay Law: Challenging the Apartheid of the Closet*. Cambridge, MA: Harvard University Press, 2000.

———. *Equality Practice: Civil Unions and the Future of Gay Rights*. New York: Routledge, 2002.

Gerstmann, Evan. *Same-Sex Marriage and the Constitution*. New York: Cambridge University Press, 2004.

Goldberg-Hiller, Jonathan. *The Limits to Union: Same-Sex Marriage and the Politics of Civil Rights*. Ann Arbor: University of Michigan Press, 2002.

Herman, D. *Rights of Passage: Struggles for Lesbian and Gay Equality*. Toronto: University of Toronto Press, 1994.

Keen, Lisa, and Goldberg, Susan. *Strangers to the Law: Gay People on Trial*. Ann Arbor: University of Michigan Press, 1998.

Koppelman, Andrew. *The Gay Rights Question in Contemporary American Law*. Chicago: University of Chicago Press, 2002.

Pinello, Daniel R. *Gay Rights and American Law*. New York: Cambridge University Press, 2003.

Richards, David A. J. *Women, Gays, and the Constitution: The Grounds for Feminism and Gay Rights*. Chicago: University of Chicago Press, 1998.

Robb, Graham. *Strangers: Homosexual Love in the Nineteenth Century*. New York: W. W. Norton, 2004.

Strasser, Mark. *Legally Wed: Same Sex Marriage and the Constitution*. Ithaca, NY: Cornell University Press, 1997.

Romer v. Evans

517 U.S. 620, 116 S.Ct. 1620 (1996)

In November 1992, voters in Colorado approved an amendment to the state constitution that forbade localities from enacting ordinances outlawing discrimination against homosexuals. Known as Amendment 2, the "No Protected Status Based on Homosexual, Lesbian, or Bisexual Orientation Amendment" provides that

[n]either the State of Colorado, through any of its branches or departments, nor any of its agencies, political subdivisions, municipalities or school districts, shall enact, adopt or enforce any statute, regulation, ordinance or policy whereby homosexual, lesbian or bisexual orientation, conduct, practices or relationships shall constitute or otherwise be the basis of or entitle any person or class of persons to have or claim any minority status quota preferences, protected status or claim of discrimination. This Section of the Constitution shall be in all respects self-executing.

Richard G. Evans and several local government officials immediately filed a suit to enjoin the enforcement of the amendment on the grounds that it was unconstitutional. A state trial court subsequently agreed and Governor Roy Romer appealed.

In 1993, the Colorado State Supreme Court interpreted precedents of the U.S. Supreme Court to hold that "the Equal Protection Clause of the United States Constitution protects the fundamental right to participate equally in the political process," and "that any legislation or state constitutional amendment which infringes on this right by 'fencing out' an independently identifiable class of persons must be subject to strict judicial scrutiny." *Evans v. Romer*, 854 P.2d 1270 (Colo. 1993) (*Evans I*). On that basis, the state supreme court affirmed the trial court's decision and remanded the case back to the trial court to determine whether Amendment 2 was supported by a compelling state interest and narrowly tailored to serve that interest. Subsequently, government officials offered six "compelling" state interests for the amendment: (1) deterring factionalism; (2) preserving the integrity of the state's political functions; (3) preserving the ability of the state to remedy discrimination against suspect classes; (4) preventing the government from interfering with personal, familial, and religious privacy; (5) preventing the government from subsidizing the political objectives of a special interest group; and (6) promoting the physical and psychological well-being of Colorado children.

For a second time, however, the trial court rejected most of the rationales given as not compelling state interests, and concluded the government's interests in preventing interference with personal privacy and religious liberty, although compelling, were not narrowly tailored enough. Accordingly, the trial court issued a permanent injunction against the enforcement of Amendment 2. Besides appealing the *Evans I* decision to the U.S. Supreme Court, which denied review, Governor Romer appealed the trial court's second ruling on the amendment to the Colorado State Supreme Court. On appeal in *Evans II*, attorneys for the state argued that (1) the legal standard set forth in *Evans I*, for assessing the constitutionality of Amendment 2, should be reconsidered;

(2) Amendment 2 was supported by several compelling state interests and is narrowly tailored to meet those interests; (3) the unconstitutional provisions of Amendment 2 were severable from the remainder; and (4) Amendment 2 was a valid exercise of state power under the Tenth Amendment to the United States Constitution. However, in 1994 in *Evans II*, the Colorado State Supreme Court rejected those arguments and, once again, held that Amendment 2 was unconstitutional. Subsequently, Colorado's governor, Roy Romer, appealed to the Supreme Court.

The Court's decision was six to three. Justice Kennedy delivered the opinion for the Court and Justice Scalia filed a dissent, which was joined by Chief Justice Rehnquist and Justice Thomas.

□ *Justice KENNEDY delivered the opinion of the Court.*

One century ago, the first Justice HARLAN admonished this Court that the Constitution "neither knows nor tolerates classes among citizens." *Plessy v. Ferguson*, 163 U.S. 537 (1896) (dissenting opinion). Unheeded then, those words now are understood to state a commitment to the law's neutrality where the rights of persons are at stake. The Equal Protection Clause enforces this principle and today requires us to hold invalid a provision of Colorado's Constitution. . . .

The State's principal argument in defense of Amendment 2 is that it puts gays and lesbians in the same position as all other persons. So, the State says, the measure does no more than deny homosexuals special rights. This reading of the amendment's language is implausible. We rely not upon our own interpretation of the amendment but upon the authoritative construction of Colorado's Supreme Court. The state court, deeming it unnecessary to determine the full extent of the amendment's reach, found it invalid even on a modest reading of its implications. The critical discussion of the amendment, set out in *Evans I*, is as follows: "The immediate objective of Amendment 2 is, at a minimum, to repeal existing statutes, regulations, ordinances, and policies of state and local entities that barred discrimination based on sexual orientation. . . .

The change that Amendment 2 works in the legal status of gays and lesbians in the private sphere is far-reaching, both on its own terms and when considered in light of the structure and operation of modern anti-discrimination laws. That structure is well illustrated by contemporary statutes and ordinances prohibiting discrimination by providers of public accommodations. "At common law, innkeepers, smiths, and others who 'made profession of a public employment,' were prohibited from refusing, with good reason, to serve a customer." *Hurley v. Irish-American Gay, Lesbian and Bisexual Group of Boston, Inc.*, [515 U.S. 557 (1995)]. The duty was a general one and did not specify protection for particular groups. The common law rules, however, proved insufficient in many instances, and it was settled early that the Fourteenth Amendment did not give Congress a general power to prohibit discrimination in public accommodations, *Civil Rights Cases*, 109 U.S. 3 (1883). In consequence, most States have chosen to counter discrimination by enacting detailed statutory schemes. Colorado's state and municipal laws typify this emerging tradition of statutory protection and follow a consistent pattern. . . .

These statutes and ordinances also depart from the common law by enumerating the groups or persons within their ambit of protection. Enumeration is the essential device used to make the duty not to discriminate concrete and to provide guidance for those who must comply. . . .

Amendment 2 bars homosexuals from securing protection against the injuries that these public-accommodations laws address. That in itself is a severe consequence, but there is more. Amendment 2, in addition, nullifies specific legal protections for this targeted class in all transactions in housing, sale of real estate, insurance, health and welfare services, private education, and employment. . . .

Amendment 2's reach may not be limited to specific laws passed for the benefit of gays and lesbians. It is a fair, if not necessary, inference from the broad language of the amendment that it deprives gays and lesbians even of the protection of general laws and policies that prohibit arbitrary discrimination in governmental and private settings. At some point in the systematic administration of these laws, an official must determine whether homosexuality is an arbitrary and thus forbidden basis for decision. Yet a decision to that effect would itself amount to a policy prohibiting discrimination on the basis of homosexuality, and so would appear to be no more valid under Amendment 2 than the specific prohibitions against discrimination the state court held invalid. . . .

The Fourteenth Amendment's promise that no person shall be denied the equal protection of the laws must co-exist with the practical necessity that most legislation classifies for one purpose or another, with resulting disadvantage to various groups or persons. We have attempted to reconcile the principle with the reality by stating that, if a law neither burdens a fundamental right nor targets a suspect class, we will uphold the legislative classification so long as it bears a rational relation to some legitimate end. See, e.g., *Heller v. Doe*, 509 U.S. 312 (1993).

Amendment 2 fails, indeed defies, even this conventional inquiry. First, the amendment has the peculiar property of imposing a broad and undifferentiated disability on a single named group, an exceptional and, as we shall explain, invalid form of legislation. Second, its sheer breadth is so discontinuous with the reasons offered for it that the amendment seems inexplicable by anything but animus toward the class that it affects; it lacks a rational relationship to legitimate state interests.

Taking the first point, even in the ordinary equal protection case calling for the most deferential of standards, we insist on knowing the relation between the classification adopted and the object to be attained. The search for the link between classification and objective gives substance to the Equal Protection Clause; it provides guidance and discipline for the legislature, which is entitled to know what sorts of laws it can pass; and it marks the limits of our own authority. In the ordinary case, a law will be sustained if it can be said to advance a legitimate government interest, even if the law seems unwise or works to the disadvantage of a particular group, or if the rationale for it seems tenuous. By requiring that the classification bear a rational relationship to an independent and legitimate legislative end, we ensure that classifications are now drawn for the purpose of disadvantaging the group burdened by the law.

Amendment 2 confounds this normal process of judicial review. It is at once too narrow and too broad. It identifies persons by a single trait and then denies them protection across the board. The resulting disqualification of a class of persons from the right to seek specific protection from the law is unprecedented in our jurisprudence.

It is not within our constitutional tradition to enact laws of this sort. Central both to the idea of the rule of law and to our own Constitution's guarantee of equal protection is the principle that government and each of its parts remain open on impartial terms to all who seek its assistance. " 'Equal protection of the laws is not achieved through indiscriminate imposition of inequalities.' " *Sweatt v. Painter*, 339 U.S. 629 (1950) [quoting *Shelley v. Kraemer*, 334 U.S. 1 (1948)]. Respect for this principle explains why laws singling out a certain class of citizens for disfavored legal status or general hardships are rare. A law declaring that in general it shall be more difficult for one group of citizens than for all others to seek aid from the government is itself a denial of equal protection of the laws in the most literal sense. "The guaranty of 'equal protection of the laws is a pledge of the protection of equal laws.' " *Skinner v. Oklahoma ex rel. Williamson*, 316 U.S. 535 (1942) [quoting *Yick Wo v. Hopkins*, 118 U.S. 356 (1886)].

Davis v. Beason, 133 U.S. 333 (1890), not cited by the parties but relied upon by the dissent, is not evidence that Amendment 2 is within our constitutional tradition, and any reliance upon it as authority for sustaining the amendment is misplaced. In *Davis*, the Court approved an Idaho territorial statute denying Mormons, polygamists, and advocates of polygamy the right to vote and to hold office because, as the Court construed the statue, it "simply excludes from the privilege of voting, or of holding any office of honor, trust or profit, those who have been convicted of certain offenses, and those who advocate a practical resistance to the laws of the Territory and justify and approve the commission of crimes forbidden by it." To the extent *Davis* held that persons advocating a certain practice may be denied the right to vote, it is no longer good law. *Brandenburg v. Ohio*, 395 U.S. 444 (1969) (*per curiam*). To the extent it held that the groups designated in the statute may be deprived of the right to vote because of their status, its ruling could not stand without surviving strict scrutiny, a most doubtful outcome. To the extent *Davis* held that a convicted felon may be denied the right to vote, its holding is not implicated by our decision and is unexceptionable.

A second and related point is that laws of the kind now before us raise the inevitable inference that the disadvantage imposed is born of animosity toward the class of persons affected. Even laws enacted for broad and ambitious purposes often can be explained by reference to legitimate public policies which justify the incidental disadvantages they impose on certain persons. Amendment 2, however, in making a general announcement that gays and lesbians shall not have any particular protections from the law, inflicts on them immediate, continuing, and real injuries that outrun and belie any legitimate justifications that may be claimed for it. We conclude that, in addition to the far-reaching deficiencies of Amendment 2 that we have noted, the principles it offends, in another sense, are conventional and venerable; a law must bear a rational relationship to a legitimate government purpose, and Amendment 2 does not.

The primary rationale the State offers for Amendment 2 is respect for other citizens' freedom of association, and in particular the liberties of landlords or employers who have personal or religious objections to homosexuality. Colorado also cites its interest in conserving resources to fight discrimination against other groups. The breadth of the Amendment is so far removed from these particular justifications that we find it impossible to credit them. We cannot say that Amendment 2 is directed to any identifiable legitimate purpose or discrete objective. It is a status-based enactment divorced from any factual context from which we could discern a relationship to legitimate state interests; it is a classification of persons undertaken for its own sake, something the Equal Protection Clause does not permit. "Class legislation . . . [is] obnoxious to the prohibitions of the Fourteenth Amendment. . . ." *Civil Rights Cases.*

We must conclude that Amendment 2 classifies homosexuals not to further a proper legislative end but to make them unequal to everyone else. This Colorado cannot do. A State cannot so deem a class of persons a stranger to its laws. Amendment 2 violates the Equal Protection Clause, and the judgment of the Supreme Court of Colorado is affirmed.

It is so ordered.

☐ *Justice SCALIA, with whom the CHIEF JUSTICE and Justice THOMAS join, dissenting.*

The Court has mistaken a *Kulturkampf* ["culture war"] for a fit of spite. The constitutional amendment before us here is not the manifestation of a " 'bare . . . desire to harm' " homosexuals, but is rather a modest attempt by seemingly tolerant Coloradans to preserve traditional sexual mores against the efforts of a politically powerful minority to revise those mores through use of the laws. That objective, and the means chosen to achieve it, are not only unimpeachable under any constitutional doctrine hitherto pronounced (hence the opinion's heavy reliance upon principles of righteousness rather than judicial holdings); they have been specifically approved by the Congress of the United States and by this Court.

In holding that homosexuality cannot be singled out for disfavorable treatment, the Court contradicts a decision, unchallenged here, pronounced only 10 years ago, see *Bowers v. Hardwick*, 478 U.S. 186 (1986), and places the prestige of this institution behind the proposition that opposition to homosexuality is as reprehensible as racial or religious bias. Whether it is or not is precisely the cultural debate that gave rise to the Colorado constitutional amendment (and to the preferential laws against which the amendment was directed). Since the Constitution of the United States says nothing about this subject, it is left to be resolved by normal democratic means, including the democratic adoption of provisions in state constitutions. This Court has no business imposing upon all Americans the resolution favored by the elite class from which the Members of this institution are selected, pronouncing that "animosity" toward homosexuality, is evil. I vigorously dissent. . . .

[T]he principle underlying the Court's opinion is that one who is accorded equal treatment under the laws, but cannot as readily as others obtain preferential treatment under the laws, has been denied equal protection of the laws. If merely stating this alleged "equal protection" violation does not suffice to refute it, our constitutional jurisprudence has achieved terminal silliness.

The central thesis of the Court's reasoning is that any group is denied equal protection when, to obtain advantage (or, presumably, to avoid disadvantage), it must have recourse to a more general and hence more difficult level of political decision making than others. The world has never heard of such a principle, which is why the Court's opinion is so long on emotive utterance and so short on relevant legal citation. And it seems to me most unlikely that any multilevel democracy can function under such a principle. For whenever a disadvantage is imposed, or conferral of a benefit is prohibited, at one of the higher levels of democratic decision making (i.e., by the state legislature rather than local government, or by the people at large in the state constitution rather than the legislature), the affected group has (under this theory) been denied equal protection. To take the simplest of examples, consider a state law prohibiting the award of municipal contracts to relatives of mayors or city councilmen. Once such a law is passed, the group composed of such relatives must, in order to get the benefit of city contracts, persuade the state legislature—unlike all other citizens, who need only persuade the municipality. It is ridiculous to consider this a denial of equal protection, which is why the Court's theory is unheard-of.

The Court might reply that the example I have given is not a denial of equal protection only because the same "rational basis" (avoidance of corruption) which renders constitutional the substantive discrimination against relatives (i.e., the fact that they alone cannot obtain city contracts) also automatically suffices to sustain what might be called the electoral-procedural discrimination against them (i.e., the fact that they must go to the state level to get this changed). This is of course a perfectly reasonable response, and would explain why "electoral-procedural discrimination" has not hitherto been heard of: a law that is valid in its substance is automatically valid in its level of enactment. But the Court cannot afford to make this argument, for as I shall discuss next, there is no doubt of a rational basis for the substance of the prohibition at issue here. The Court's entire novel theory rests upon the proposition that there is something special—something that cannot be justified by normal "rational basis" analysis—in making a disadvantaged group (or a nonpreferred group) resort to a higher decision making level. That proposition finds no support in law or logic.

I turn next to whether there was a legitimate rational basis for the substance of the constitutional amendment—for the prohibition of special protection for homosexuals. It is unsurprising that the Court avoids discussion of this question, since the answer is so obviously yes. The case most relevant to the issue before us today is not even mentioned in the Court's opinion: In *Bowers v. Hardwick*, 478 U.S. 186 (1986), we held that the Constitution does not prohibit what virtually all States had done from the founding of the Republic until very recent years—making homosexual conduct a crime. That holding is unassailable, except by those who think that the Constitution changes to suit current fashions. But in any event it is a given in the present case: Respondents' briefs did not urge overruling *Bowers*, and at oral argument respondents' counsel expressly disavowed any intent to seek such overruling. If it is constitutionally permissible for a State to make homosexual conduct criminal, surely it is constitutionally permissible for a State to enact other laws merely disfavoring homosexual conduct. And *a fortiori* it is constitutionally permissible for a State to adopt a provision not even disfavoring homosexual conduct, but merely prohibiting all levels of state government from bestowing special protections upon homosexual conduct. Respondents (who, unlike the Court, cannot afford the luxury of ignoring inconvenient precedent) counter *Bowers* with the argument that a greater-includes-the-lesser rationale cannot justify Amendment 2's application to individuals who do not engage in homosexual acts, but are merely of homosexual "orientation." Some courts of appeals have concluded that, with respect to laws of this sort at least, that is a distinction without a difference.

But assuming that, in Amendment 2, a person of homosexual "orientation" is someone who does not engage in homosexual conduct but merely has a tendency or desire to do so, *Bowers* still suffices to establish a rational basis for the provision. If it is rational to criminalize the conduct, surely it is rational to deny special favor and protection to those with a self-avowed tendency or desire to engage in the conduct. Indeed, where criminal sanctions are not involved, homosexual "orientation" is an acceptable stand-in for homosexual conduct. . . .

Moreover, even if the provision regarding homosexual "orientation" were invalid, respondents' challenge to Amendment 2—which is a facial challenge—must fail. "A facial challenge to a legislative Act is, of course, the most difficult challenge to mount successfully, since the challenger must establish that no set of circumstances exists under which the Act would be valid." *United States v. Salerno*, 481 U.S. 739 (1987). It would not be enough for respondents to establish (if they could) that Amendment 2 is unconstitutional as applied to those of homosexual "orientation"; since, under *Bowers*, Amendment 2 is unquestionably constitutional as applied to those who engage in homosexual conduct, the facial challenge cannot succeed. Some individuals of homosexual "orientation" who do not engage in homosexual acts might successfully bring an as-applied challenge to Amendment 2, but so far as the record indicates, none of the respondents is such a person.

The foregoing suffices to establish what the Court's failure to cite any case remotely in point would lead one to suspect: No principle set forth in the Constitution, nor even any imagined by this Court in the past 200 years, prohibits what Colorado has done here. But the case for Colorado is much stronger than that. What it has done is not only unprohibited, but eminently reasonable, with close, congressionally approved precedent in earlier constitutional practice.

First, as to its eminent reasonableness. The Court's opinion contains grim, disapproving hints that Coloradans have been guilty of "animus" or "animosity" toward homosexuality, as though that has been established as Unamerican. Of course it is our moral heritage that one should not hate any human being or class of human beings. But I had thought that one could consider certain conduct reprehensible—murder, for example, or polygamy, or cruelty to animals—and could exhibit even "animus" toward such conduct. Surely that is the only sort of "animus" at issue here: moral disapproval of homosexual conduct, the same sort of moral disapproval that produced the centuries-old criminal laws that we held constitutional in *Bowers*. The Colorado amendment does not, to speak entirely precisely, prohibit giving favored status to people who are homosexuals; they can be favored for many reasons—for example, because they are senior citizens or members of racial minorities. But it prohibits giving them favored status because of their homosexual conduct—that is, it prohibits favored status for homosexuality. But though Coloradans are, as I say, entitled to be hostile toward homosexual conduct, the fact is that the degree of hostility reflected by Amendment 2 is the smallest conceivable. The Court's portrayal of Coloradans as a society fallen victim to pointless, hate-filled "gay-bashing" is so false as to be comical. Colorado not only is one of the 25 States that have repealed their antisodomy laws, but was among the first to do so. But the society that eliminates criminal punishment for homosexual acts does not necessarily abandon the view that homosexuality is morally wrong and socially harmful; often, abolition simply reflects the view that enforcement of such criminal laws involves unseemly intrusion into the intimate lives of citizens.

There is a problem, however, which arises when criminal sanction of homosexuality is eliminated but moral and social disapprobation of homosexuality is meant to be retained. The Court cannot be unaware of that problem; it is evident in many cities of the country, and occasionally bubbles to the surface of the news, in heated political disputes over such matters as the introduction into local schools of books teaching that homosexuality is an optional and fully acceptable "alternate life style." The problem (a problem, that is, for those who wish to retain social disapprobation of homosexuality) that, because those who engage in homosexual conduct tend to reside in disproportionate numbers in certain communities, and of course care about homosexual-rights issues much more ardently than the public at large, they possess political power much greater than their numbers, both locally and statewide. Quite understandably, they devote this political power to achieving not merely a grudging social toleration, but full social acceptance, of homosexuality.

By the time Coloradans were asked to vote on Amendment 2, their exposure to homosexuals' quest for social endorsement was not limited to newspaper accounts of happenings in places such as New York, Los Angeles, San Francisco, and Key West. Three Colorado cities—Aspen, Boulder, and Denver—had enacted ordinances that listed "sexual orientation" as an impermissible ground for discrimination, equating the moral disapproval of homosexual conduct with racial and religious bigotry. The phenomenon had even appeared statewide: the Governor of Colorado had signed an executive order pronouncing that "in the State of Colorado we recognize the diversity in our pluralistic society and strive to bring an end to discrimination in any form," and directing state agency-heads to "ensure non-discrimination" in hiring and promotion based on, among other things, "sexual orientation." I do not mean to be critical of these legislative successes; homosexuals are as entitled to use the legal system for reinforcement of their moral sentiments as are the rest of society. But they are subject to being countered by lawful, democratic countermeasures as well.

That is where Amendment 2 came in. It sought to counter both the geographic concentration and the disproportionate political power of homosexuals by (1) resolving the controversy at the statewide level, and (2) making the election a single-issue contest for both sides. It put directly, to all the citizens of the State, the question: Should homosexuality be given special protection? They answered no. The Court today asserts that this most democratic of procedures is unconstitutional. Lacking any cases to establish that facially absurd proposition, it simply asserts that it must be unconstitutional, because it has never happened before. . . .

What the Court says is even demonstrably false at the constitutional level. The Eighteenth Amendment to the Federal Constitution, for example, deprived those who drank alcohol not only of the power to alter the policy of prohibition locally or through state legislation, but even of the power to alter it through state constitutional amendment or federal legislation. The Establishment Clause of the First Amendment prevents theocrats from having their way by converting their fellow citizens at the local, state, or federal statutory level; as does the Republican Form of Government Clause prevent monarchists.

But there is a much closer analogy, one that involves precisely the effort by the majority of citizens to preserve its view of sexual morality statewide, against the efforts of a geographically concentrated and politically powerful minority to undermine it. The constitutions of the States of Arizona, Idaho, New Mexico, Oklahoma, and Utah to this day contain provisions stating that polygamy is "forever prohibited." Polygamists, and those who have a polygamous "orientation," have been "singled out" by these provisions for much more severe treatment than merely denial of favored status; and that treatment can only be changed by achieving amendment of the state constitutions. The Court's disposition today suggests that these provisions are unconstitutional, and that polygamy must be permitted in these States on a state-legislated, or perhaps even local-option, basis—unless, of course, polygamists for some reason have fewer constitutional rights than homosexuals.

The United States Congress, by the way, required the inclusion of these antipolygamy provisions in the constitutions of Arizona, New Mexico, Oklahoma, and Utah, as a condition of their admission to statehood. Thus, this "singling out" of the sexual practices of a single group for statewide, democratic vote—so utterly alien to our constitutional system, the Court would have us believe—has not only happened, but has received the explicit approval of the United States Congress.

I cannot say that this Court has explicitly approved any of these state constitutional provisions; but it has approved a territorial statutory provision that went even further, depriving polygamists of the ability even to achieve a constitutional amendment, by depriving them of the power to vote. *Davis v. Beason*, 133 U.S. 333 (1890). To the extent, if any, that this opinion permits the imposition of adverse consequences upon mere abstract advocacy of polygamy, it has of course been overruled by later cases. See *Brandenburg v. Ohio*, 395 U.S. 444 (1969) (*per curiam*). But the proposition that polygamy can be criminalized, and those engaging in that crime deprived of the vote, remains good law. *Beason* rejected the argument that "such discrimination is a denial of the equal protection of the laws." . . .

This Court cited *Beason* with approval as recently as 1993, in an opinion authored by the same Justice who writes for the Court today. That opinion said: "Adverse impact will not always lead to a finding of impermissible targeting. For example, a social harm may have been a legitimate concern of government for reasons quite apart from discrimination. . . . See, e.g., . . . *Davis v. Beason*, 133 U.S. 333 (1890)." *Church of Lukumi Babalu Aye, Inc. v.*

Hialeah, 508 U.S. 520 (1993). It remains to be explained how Section 501 of the Idaho Revised Statutes was not an "impermissible targeting" of polygamists, but (the much more mild) Amendment 2 is an "impermissible targeting" of homosexuals. Has the Court concluded that the perceived social harm of polygamy is a "legitimate concern of government," and the perceived social harm of homosexuality is not?

I strongly suspect that the answer to the last question is yes, which leads me to the last point I wish to make: The Court today, announcing that Amendment 2 "defies . . . conventional [constitutional] inquiry," and "confounds [the] normal process of judicial review," employs a constitutional theory heretofore unknown to frustrate Colorado's reasonable effort to preserve traditional American moral values. The Court's stern disapproval of "animosity" towards homosexuality might be compared with what an earlier Court (including the revered Justices HARLAN and BRADLEY) said in *Murphy v. Ramsey*, 114 U.S. 15 (1885), rejecting a constitutional challenge to a United States statute that denied the franchise in federal territories to those who engaged in polygamous cohabitation:

> "Certainly no legislation can be supposed more wholesome and necessary in the founding of a free, self-governing commonwealth, fit to take rank as one of the co-ordinate States of the Union, than that which seeks to establish it on the basis of the idea of the family, as consisting in and springing from the union for life of one man and one woman in the holy estate of matrimony; the sure foundation of all that is stable and noble in our civilization; the best guaranty of that reverent morality which is the source of all beneficent progress in social and political improvement."

I would not myself indulge in such official praise for heterosexual monogamy, because I think it no business of the courts (as opposed to the political branches) to take sides in this culture war.

But the Court today has done so, not only by inventing a novel and extravagant constitutional doctrine to take the victory away from traditional forces, but even by verbally disparaging as bigotry adherence to traditional attitudes. To suggest, for example, that this constitutional amendment springs from nothing more than " 'a bare . . . desire to harm a politically unpopular group,' " is nothing short of insulting. (It is also nothing short of preposterous to call "politically unpopular" a group which enjoys enormous influence in American media and politics, and which, as the trial court here noted, though composing no more than 4% of the population had the support of 46% of the voters on Amendment 2.)

When the Court takes sides in the culture wars, it tends to be with the knights rather than the villains—and more specifically with the Templars, reflecting the views and values of the lawyer class from which the Court's Members are drawn. How that class feels about homosexuality will be evident to anyone who wishes to interview job applicants at virtually any of the Nation's law schools. The interviewer may refuse to offer a job because the applicant is a Republican; because he is an adulterer; because he went to the wrong prep school or belongs to the wrong country club; because he eats snails; because he is a womanizer; because she wears real-animal fur; or even because he hates the Chicago Cubs. But if the interviewer should wish not to be an associate or partner of an applicant because he disapproves of the applicant's homosexuality, then he will have violated the pledge which the Association of American Law Schools requires all its member-schools to exact from job interviewers: "assurance of the employer's willingness" to hire homosexuals. This law-school view of what "prejudices" must be stamped out may be contrasted with the more plebeian attitudes that apparently still prevail in the United States Congress, which has been unresponsive to repeated attempts to extend to homosexuals the protections of federal civil rights laws, and which took the pains to exclude them specifically from the Americans With Disabilities Act of 1990.

Today's opinion has no foundation in American constitutional law, and barely pretends to. The people of Colorado have adopted an entirely reasonable provision which does not even disfavor homosexuals in any substantive sense, but merely denies them preferential treatment. Amendment 2 is designed to prevent piecemeal deterioration of the sexual morality favored by a majority of Coloradans, and is not only an appropriate means to that legitimate end, but a means that Americans have employed before. Striking it down is an act, not of judicial judgment, but of political will. I dissent.

Lawrence v. Texas

539 U.S. 558, 123 S.Ct. 2472 (2003)

In this case the Court struck down Texas's law criminalizing homosexual sodomy; the case is excerpted in Chapter 11.

■ IN COMPARATIVE PERSPECTIVE

Canadian Courts Forbid Discrimination against Homosexuals and Same-Sex Marriages

---

In *Egan v. Canada*, 2 S.C.R. 513 (1995), the Supreme Court of Canada held, "on the basis historical social, political and economic disadvantage suffered by homosexuals" and the emerging consensus among legislatures, as well as previous judicial decisions, that sexual orientation was embraced by the equality guarantee of Section 15(1) of Canada's Charter of Rights and Freedom, which provides: "Every individual is equal before and under the law and has the right to the equal protection and equal benefit of the law without discrimination and, in particular, without discrimination based on race, national or ethnic origin, colour, religion, sex, age or mental or physical disability."

Later decisions of the Canadian Supreme Court expanded protection for gays and lesbians. In *Vriend v. Alberta*, 1 S.C.R. 493 (1998), for instance, the Court held that Alberta's human rights code must give protection to homosexuals in employment in order to comply with the guarantee of Section 15 (1). See also *M. v. H.*, 2 S.C.R. 3 (1999).

More recently, a lower court judge declared Quebec's prohibition against same-sex marriages invalid, in *Hendricks v. Quebec*, J.Q. No. 3816 (S.C.) (2002). Likewise, the British Columbia Court of Appeal declared the common law definition of marriage unconstitutional and required the substitution of the words "two persons" for "one man and one woman," in *EGALE Canada Inc. v. Attorney General of Canada*, B.C.J. 994 (2003). And in *Halpern v. Attorney General of Canada*, No. C39172 (June 10, 2003), the Court of Appeal for Ontario held that Section 15(1) bars discrimination against same-sex marriages.

Writing for the Court in *Halpern*, Chief Justice Roy McMurtry rejected the government's position against recognizing same-sex marriages, upon reasoning:

> No one is disputing that marriage is a fundamental societal institution. Similarly, it is accepted that, with limited exceptions, marriage has been understood to be a monogamous opposite-sex union. What needs to be determined, however, is whether there is a valid objective to maintaining marriage as an exclusively heterosexual institution. Stating that marriage is heterosexual because it always has been heterosexual is merely an explanation for the opposite-sex requirement of marriage; it is not an objective that is capable of justifying the infringement of a Charter guarantee.
>
> We now turn to the more specific purposes of marriage advanced by the [the government]: (i) uniting the opposite sexes; (ii) encouraging the birth and raising of children of the marriage; and (iii) companionship.
>
> The first purpose, which results in favouring one form of relationship over another, suggests that uniting two persons of the same sex is of lesser importance. . . . [A] purpose that demeans the dignity of same-sex couples is contrary to the values of a free and democratic society and cannot be considered to be pressing and substantial. A law cannot be justified on the very basis upon which it is being attacked.
>
> The second purpose of marriage, as advanced by [the government], is encouraging the birth and raising of children. Clearly, encouraging procreation and childrearing is a laudable goal that is properly regarded as pressing and substantial. However, the [government] must demonstrate that the objective of maintaining marriage as an exclusively heterosexual institution is pressing and substantial: see *Vriend* [*v. Alberta*].
>
> We fail to see how the encouragement of procreation and childrearing is a pressing and substantial objective of maintaining marriage as an exclusively heterosexual institution. Heterosexual

married couples will not stop having or raising children because same-sex couples are permitted to marry. Moreover, an increasing percentage of children are being born to and raised by same-sex couples.

The [government] submits that the union of two persons of the opposite sex is the only union that can "naturally" procreate. In terms of that biological reality, same-sex couples are different from opposite-sex couples. In our view, however, "natural" procreation is not a sufficiently pressing and substantial objective to justify infringing the equality rights of same-sex couples. As previously stated, same-sex couples can have children by other means, such as adoption, surrogacy and donor insemination. A law that aims to encourage only "natural" procreation ignores the fact that same-sex couples are capable of having children.

Similarly, a law that restricts marriage to opposite-sex couples, on the basis that a fundamental purpose of marriage is the raising of children, suggests that same-sex couples are not equally capable of childrearing. The [government] has put forward no evidence to support such a proposition. Neither is the [government] advocating such a view; rather, it takes the position that social science research is not capable of establishing the proposition one way or another. In the absence of cogent evidence, it is our view that the objective is based on a stereotypical assumption that is not acceptable in a free and democratic society that prides itself on promoting equality and respect for all persons.

The third purpose of marriage advanced by the [government] is companionship. We consider companionship to be a laudable goal of marriage. However, encouraging companionship cannot be considered a pressing and substantial objective of the omission of the impugned law. Encouraging companionship between only persons of the opposite sex perpetuates the view that persons in same-sex relationships are not equally capable of providing companionship and forming lasting and loving relationships.

Accordingly, it is our view that the [government] has not demonstrated any pressing and substantial objective for excluding same-sex couples from the institution of marriage. For that reason, we conclude that the violation of the Couples' rights under Section 15(1) of the Charter cannot be saved. . . .

Note: the full text of the opinion in *Halpern v. Attorney General of Canada* is available on the website of the Court of Appeal of Ontario at *www.ontariocourts.on.ca/decisions*.

■ (3) WEALTH, POVERTY, AND ILLEGITIMACY

In *Griffin v. Illinois*, 351 U.S. 12 (1956), when holding that states must provide indigent defendants with transcripts of their trials for appeals on constitutional questions, Justice Black observed that "[i]n criminal trials a State can no more discriminate on account of poverty than on account of religion, race, or color." Justice Black thus suggested that classifications based on wealth might be constitutionally suspect. Subsequently, the Court construed the due process and equal protection clauses to ensure that indigents are not denied the right to vote (see Vol. 1, Ch. 8), and that they have an equal right of access to judicial proceedings (see Vol. 2, Ch. 9).

Nevertheless, the Court applies the "rational basis" test and refuses to scrutinize laws that disadvantage the poor in the overwhelming majority of cases. See, for example, *Maher v. Roe* (1977) (see page 1214) upholding restrictions on Medicaid funding for women seeking elective abortions.

In *Shapiro v. Thompson* (1969) (excerpted below), however, the Court overturned a state residency requirement for indigents seeking public assistance. It did so, though, on the grounds that the residency requirement denied indigents their "fundamental right to interstate travel," rather than a right to welfare benefits. That decision was reaffirmed in *Saenz v. Roe*, 526 U.S. 489 (2000), when striking down California's law limiting welfare benefits of new residents to that paid by the states in which they previously resided. Notably, though, in his opinion for the Court Justice Stevens held that the right to travel is one of the privileges and immunities guaranteed by the Fourteenth Amendment. Chief Justice Rehnquist and Justice Thomas dissented.

Other residency requirements have been similarly struck down, but never on the basis that wealth is a suspect classification. In *Dandridge v. Williams*, 397 U.S. 471 (1970), for instance, the Court rejected the claim of a fundamental right to public assistance, when upholding Maryland's law limiting benefits under the Aid-to-Dependent-Children Social Security program to $250 per month, regardless of the needs and size of a family. So too in *San Antonio Independent School District v. Rodriguez* (1973) (excerpted below), the Court rejected the claim that public education is a fundamental right and that states may not discriminate against indigents in public education.

In contrast to claims of discrimination based on wealth and poverty, the Court gives greater scrutiny to challenges of laws discriminating against illegitimate children. The Court has done so under both the "rational basis" test, as in *Levy v. Louisiana*, 391 U.S. 68 (1968), and the slightly higher standard of review, announced in *Matthews v. Lucas*, 427 U.S. 495 (1976), demanding that classifications based on illegitimacy be "substantially related to a permissible state interest" (see also table on rulings on illegitimate children in THE DEVELOPMENT OF LAW box in this section).

SELECTED BIBLIOGRAPHY

Barber, Sotirios. *Welfare and the Constitution*. Princeton, N.J.: Princeton University Press, 2004.

Bussiere, Elizabeth. *(Dis)Entitling the Poor: The Warren Court, Welfare Rights and the American Political Tradition*. College Station: Pennsylvania State University Press, 1997.

Lawrence, Susan. *The Poor in Court*. Princeton, NJ: Princeton University Press, 1990.

Smith, Christopher. *Courts and the Poor*. Chicago: Nelson-Hall, 1991.

Shapiro v. Thompson
394 U.S. 618, 89 S.Ct. 1322 (1969)

Two months after moving from Massachusetts to Connecticut, Vivian Thompson applied for assistance under the Aid to Families with Dependent Children program. She was nineteen years old, pregnant, and the mother of one child. Thompson was denied assistance because she failed to meet Connecticut's one-year residency requirement for receiving assistance. In federal district court, she sued Bernard Shapiro, Connecticut's welfare commissioner. That court held that the residency requirement had a "chilling effect on the right to travel" and denied Thompson the equal protection of the law as guaranteed by the Fourteenth Amendment. Shapiro then appealed that ruling to the Supreme Court, which granted review and consolidated the case with others, challenging the constitutionality of residency requirements of Pennsylvania and the District of Columbia.

The Court's decision was six to three, and the majority's opinion was announced by Justice Brennan. Justice Stewart concurred. Dissenting opinions were delivered by Justice Harlan and Chief Justice Warren, who was joined by Justice Black.

☐ *Justice BRENNAN delivered the opinion of the Court.*

[This] is an appeal from a decision of a three-judge District Court holding unconstitutional a State or District of Columbia statutory provision which denies welfare assistance to residents of the State or District who have not resided within their jurisdictions for at least one year immediately preceding their applications for such assistance. We affirm. . . .

There is no dispute that the effect of the waiting-period requirement in each case is to create two classes of needy resident families indistinguishable from each other except that one is composed of residents who have resided a year or more, and the second of residents who have resided less than a year, in the jurisdiction. On the basis of this sole difference the first class is granted and the second class is denied welfare aid upon which may depend the ability of the families to obtain the very means to subsist—food, shelter, and other necessities of life. . . . The interests which appellants assert are promoted by the classification either may not constitutionally be promoted by government or are not compelling governmental interests.

Primarily, appellants justify the waiting-period requirement as a protective device to preserve the fiscal integrity of state public assistance programs. It is asserted that people who require welfare assistance during their first year of residence in a State are likely to become continuing burdens on state welfare programs. Therefore, the argument runs, if such people can be deterred from entering the jurisdiction by denying them welfare benefits during the first year, state programs to assist long-time residents will not be impaired by a substantial influx of indigent newcomers. . . .

We do not doubt that the one-year waiting period device is well suited to discourage the influx of poor families in need of assistance. An indigent who desires to migrate, resettle, find a new job, and start a new life will doubtless hesitate if he knows that he must risk making the move without the possibility of falling back on state welfare assistance during his first year of residence, when his need may be most acute. But the purpose of inhibiting migration by needy persons into the State is constitutionally impermissible.

This Court long ago recognized that the nature of our Federal Union and our constitutional concepts of personal liberty unite to require that all citizens be free to travel throughout the length and breadth of our land uninhibited by statutes, rules, or regulations which unreasonably burden or restrict this movement. That proposition was early stated by Chief Justice TANEY in the *Passenger Cases*, 7 How. (48 U.S.) 283 (1849):

> "For all the great purposes for which the Federal government was formed, we are one people, with one common country. We are all citizens of the United States; and, as members of the same community, must have the right to pass and repass through every part of it without interruption, as freely as in our own States."

We have no occasion to ascribe the source of this right to travel interstate to a particular constitutional provision. It suffices that, as Justice STEWART said for the Court in *United States v. Guest*, 383 U.S. 745 (1966):

> "The constitutional right to travel from one State to another . . . occupies a position fundamental to the concept of our Federal Union. It is a right that has been firmly established and repeatedly recognized.
>
> ". . . [The] right finds no explicit mention in the Constitution. The reason, it has been suggested, is that a right so elementary was conceived from the beginning to be a necessary concomitant of the stronger Union the Constitution created. In any event, freedom to travel throughout the United States has long been recognized as a basic right under the Constitution."

Thus, the purpose of deterring the immigration of indigents cannot serve as justification for the classification created by the one-year waiting period, since that purpose is constitutionally impermissible. If a law has "no other purpose . . . than to chill the assertion of constitutional rights by penalizing those who choose to exercise them, then it [is] patently unconstitutional."

Alternatively, appellants argue that even if it is impermissible for a State to attempt to deter the entry of all indigents, the challenged classification may be justified as a permissible state attempt to discourage those indigents who would enter the State solely to obtain larger benefits. . . .

[However,] a State may no more try to fence out those indigents who seek higher welfare benefits than it may try to fence out indigents generally. Implicit in any such distinction is the notion that indigents who enter a State with the hope of securing higher welfare benefits are somehow less deserving than indigents who do not take this consideration into account. But we do not perceive why a mother who is seeking to make a new life for herself and her children should be regarded as less deserving because she considers, among other factors, the level of a State's public assistance. Surely such a mother is no less deserving than a mother who moves into a particular State in order to take advantage of its better educational facilities.

Appellants argue further that the challenged classification may be sustained as an attempt to distinguish between new and old residents on the basis of the contribution they have made to the community through the payment of taxes. [But a]ppellants' reasoning would logically permit the State to bar new residents from schools, parks, and libraries or deprive them of police and fire protection. Indeed it would permit the State to apportion all benefits and services according to the past tax contributions of its citizens. The Equal Protection Clause prohibits such an apportionment of state services.

We recognize that a State has a valid interest in preserving the fiscal integrity of its programs. It may legitimately attempt to limit its expenditures, whether for public assistance, public education, or any other program. But a State may not accomplish such a purpose by inviduous distinctions between classes of its citizens. It could not, for example, reduce expenditures for education by barring indigent children from its schools. Similarly, in the cases before us, appellants must do more than show that denying welfare benefits to new residents saves money. The saving of welfare costs cannot justify an otherwise invidious classification.

Appellants next advance as justification certain administrative and related governmental objectives allegedly served by the waiting-period requirement. They argue that the requirement (1) facilitates the planning of the welfare budget; (2) provides an objective test of residency; (3) minimizes the opportunity for recipients fraudulently to receive payments from more than one jurisdiction; and (4) encourages early entry of new residents into the labor force. . . .

The argument that the waiting-period requirement facilitates budget predictability is wholly unfounded. The records [here] are utterly devoid of evidence that either State or the District of Columbia in fact uses the one-year requirement as a means to predict the number of people who will require assistance in the budget year. . . .

The argument that the waiting period serves as an administratively efficient rule of thumb for determining residency similarly will not withstand scrutiny. The residence requirement and the one-year waiting-period requirement are distinct and independent prerequisites for assistance under these three statutes, and the facts relevant to the determination of each are directly examined by the welfare authorities. Before granting an application, the welfare authorities investigate the applicant's employment, housing, and family situation and in the course of the inquiry necessarily learn the facts upon which to determine whether the applicant is a resident. . . .

Similarly, there is no need for a State to use the one-year waiting period as a safeguard against fraudulent receipt of benefits; for less drastic means are available, and are employed, to minimize that hazard. . . .

[Finally, a] state purpose to encourage employment provides no rational basis for imposing a one-year waiting-period restriction on new residents only.

We conclude therefore that appellants in these cases do not use and have no need to use the one-year requirement for the governmental purposes suggested. Thus, even under traditional equal protection tests a classification of welfare applicants according to whether they have lived in the State for one year would seem irrational and unconstitutional. But, of course, the traditional criteria do not apply in these cases. Since the classification here touches on the fundamental right of interstate movement, its constitutionality must be judged by the stricter standard of whether it promotes a *compelling* state interest. Under this standard, the waiting-period requirement clearly violates the Equal Protection Clause. . . .

☐ *Justice HARLAN, dissenting.*

In upholding the equal protection argument, the Court has applied an equal protection doctrine of relatively recent vintage: the rule that statutory classifications which either are based upon certain "suspect" criteria or affect "fundamental rights" will be held to deny equal protection unless justified by a "compelling" governmental interest.

The "compelling interest" doctrine, which today is articulated more explicitly than ever before, constitutes an increasingly significant exception to the long-established rule that a statute does not deny equal protection if it is rationally related to a legitimate governmental objective. The "compelling interest" doctrine has two branches. The branch which requires that classifications based upon "suspect" criteria be supported by a compelling interest apparently had its genesis in cases involving racial classifications, which have, at least since *Korematsu v. United States*, 323 U.S. 214 (1944), been regarded as inherently "suspect." The criterion of "wealth" apparently was added to the list of "suspects" as an alternative justification for the rationale in *Harper v. Virginia Bd. of Elections*, 383 U.S. 663, (1966), in which Virginia's poll tax was struck down. . . . Today the list apparently has been further enlarged to include classifications based upon recent interstate movement, and perhaps those based upon the exercise of *any* constitutional right. . . . [However,] I do not consider wealth a "suspect" statutory criterion. . . .

The second branch of the "compelling interest" principle is even more troublesome. For it has been held that a statutory classification is subject to the "compelling interest" test if the result of the classification may be to affect a "fundamental right," regardless of the basis of the classification. . . .

I think this branch of the "compelling interest" doctrine particularly unfortunate and unnecessary. It is unfortunate because it creates an exception which threatens to swallow the standard equal protection rule. Virtually every state statute affects important rights. This Court has repeatedly held, for example, that the traditional equal protection standard is applicable to statutory classifications affecting such fundamental matters as the right to pursue a particular occupation, the right to receive greater or smaller wages or to work more or less hours, and the right to inherit property. Rights such as these are in principle indistinguishable from those involved here, and to extend the "compelling interest" rule to all cases in which such rights are affected would go far toward making this Court a "super-legislature." This branch of the doctrine is also unnecessary. When the right affected is one assured by the Federal Constitution, any infringement can be dealt with under the Due Process Clause. But when a statute affects only matters not mentioned in the Federal Constitution and is not arbitrary or irrational, I must reiterate that I know of nothing which entitles this Court to pick out particular human activities, characterize them as "fundamental," and give them added protection under an unusually stringent equal protection test. . . .

If the issue is regarded purely as one of equal protection, then, for the reasons just set forth, this nonracial classification should be judged by ordinary equal protection standards. The applicable criteria are familiar and well established. A legislative measure will be found to deny equal protection only if "it is without any reasonable basis, and therefore is purely arbitrary." . . .

In light of th[e] undeniable relation of residence requirements to valid legislative aims, it cannot be said that the requirements are "arbitrary" or "lacking in rational justification." Hence, I can find no objection to these residence requirements under the Equal Protection Clause of the Fourteenth Amendment or under the analogous standard embodied in the Due Process Clause of the Fifth Amendment. . . .

San Antonio Independent School District v. Rodriguez

411 U.S. 1, 93 S.CT. 1278 (1973)

Demetrio Rodriguez and several other Mexican Americans sued their school district, the state board of education, the state attorney general, and several other government officials. They contended that Texas's system for financing public schools violated the equal protection clause of the Fourteenth Amendment because it discriminated on the basis of wealth. Besides federal funds for education, the state provided for a minimum level of education in all districts by funding a large portion of the cost of teachers' salaries and other operating expenses. In addition, each school district contributed a portion through local property taxes. But because the value of property varied greatly from one school district to another, there were wide disparities in school districts' per-pupil expenditures. At a pretrial conference, the San Antonio Independent School District sided with Rodriguez. But state officials continued to defend the system of financing public schools and appealed to the Supreme Court the ruling of a federal district court, which held that Texas discriminated against students in poor school districts in violation of the Fourteenth Amendment. The Supreme Court split five to four in reversing the lower court, held that wealth is not a suspect classification, and found that the state's system of funding public education was rational and constitutional. In 1989, though, the Texas State Supreme Court ruled contrariwise and found that the state discriminated in violation of a provision of the *state* constitution.

The Court's decision was five to four, and the majority's opinion was announced by Justice Powell. Justice Stewart concurred. Justice Brennan dissented. Justices White and Marshall also dissented and were joined by Justices Douglas and Brennan.

□ *Justice POWELL delivered the opinion of the Court.*

Until recent times, Texas was a predominantly rural State and its population and property wealth were spread relatively evenly across the State. Sizable differences in the value of assessable property between local school districts became increasingly evident as the State became more industrialized and as rural-to-urban population shifts became more pronounced. The location of commercial and industrial property began to play a significant role in determining the amount of tax resources available to each school district. These growing disparities in population and taxable property between districts were responsible in part for increasingly notable differences in levels of local expenditure for education. . . .

The school district in which appellees reside, the Edgewood Independent School District, has been compared throughout this litigation with the Alamo Heights School Independent School District. This comparison between the least and most affluent districts in the San Antonio area serves to illustrate the manner in which the dual system of finance operates and to indicate the extent to which substantial disparities exist despite the State's impressive progress in recent years. Edgewood is one of seven public school districts in the metropolitan area. Approximately 22,000 students are enrolled in its 25 elementary and secondary schools. The district is situated in the core-city sector of San Antonio in a residential neighborhood that has little commercial or industrial property. The residents are predominantly of Mexican-American descent: approximately 90% of the student population is Mexican-American and over 6% is Negro. The average assessed property value per pupil is $5,960—the lowest in the metropolitan area—and the median family income ($4,686) is also the lowest. At an equalized tax rate of $1.05 per $100 of assessed property—the highest in the metropolitan area—the district contributed $26 to the education of each child for the 1967–1968 school year above its Local Fund Assignment for the Minimum

Foundation Program. The Foundation Program contributed $222 per pupil for a state-local total of $248. Federal funds added another $108 for a total of $356 per pupil.

Alamo Heights is the most affluent school district in San Antonio. Its six schools, housing approximately 5,000 students, are situated in a residential community quite unlike the Edgewood District. The school population is predominantly "Anglo," having only 18% Mexican-Americans and less than 1% Negroes. The assessed property value per pupil exceeds $49,000, and the median family income is $8,001. In 1967–1968 the local tax rate of $.85 per $100 of valuation yielded $333 per pupil over and above its contribution to the Foundation Program. Coupled with the $225 provided from that Program, the district was able to supply $558 per student. Supplemented by a $36 per-pupil grant from federal sources, Alamo Heights spent $594 per pupil. . . .

Texas virtually concedes that its historically rooted dual system of financing education could not withstand the strict judicial scrutiny that this Court has found appropriate in reviewing legislative judgments that interfere with fundamental constitutional rights or that involve suspect classifications. . . .

We must decide, first, whether the Texas system of financing public education operates to the disadvantage of some suspect class or impinges upon a fundamental right explicitly or implicitly protected by the Constitution, thereby requiring strict judicial scrutiny. If so, the judgment of the District Court should be affirmed. If not, the Texas scheme must still be examined to determine whether it rationally furthers some legitimate, articulated state purpose and therefore does not constitute an invidious discrimination in violation of the Equal Protection Clause of the Fourteenth Amendment. . . .

[F]or the several reasons that follow, we find neither the suspect-classification nor the fundamental-interest analysis persuasive.

The wealth discrimination discovered by the District Court in this case, and by several other courts that have recently struck down school-financing laws in other States, is quite unlike any of the forms of wealth discrimination heretofore reviewed by this Court. Rather than focusing on the unique features of the alleged discrimination, the courts in these cases have virtually assumed their findings of a suspect classification through a simplistic process of analysis: since, under the traditional systems of financing public schools, some poorer people receive less expensive educations than other more affluent people, these systems discriminate on the basis of wealth. This approach largely ignores the hard threshold questions, including whether it makes a difference for purposes of consideration under the Constitution that the class of disadvantaged "poor" cannot be identified or defined in customary equal protection terms, and whether the relative—rather than absolute—nature of the asserted deprivation is of significant consequence. Before a State's laws and the justifications for the classifications they create are subjected to strict judicial scrutiny, we think these threshold considerations must be analyzed more closely than they were in the court below.

The case comes to us with no definitive description of the classifying facts or delineation of the disfavored class. . . . The Texas system of school financing might be regarded as discriminating (1) against "poor" persons whose incomes fall below some identifiable level of poverty or who might be characterized as functionally "indigent," or (2) against those who are relatively poorer than others, or (3) against all those who, irrespective of their personal incomes, happen to reside in relatively poorer school districts. Our task must be to ascertain whether, in fact, the Texas system has been shown to discriminate on any of these possible bases and, if so, whether the resulting classification may be regarded as suspect.

The precedents of this Court provide the proper starting point. The individuals, or groups of individuals, who constituted the class discriminated against in our prior cases shared two distinguishing characteristics: because of their impecunity they were completely unable to pay for some desired benefit, and as a consequence, they sustained an absolute deprivation of a meaningful opportunity to enjoy that benefit. In *Griffin v. Illinois*, 351 U.S. 12 (1956), and its progeny, the Court invalidated state laws that prevented an indigent criminal defendant from acquiring a transcript, or an adequate substitute for a transcript, for use at several stages of the trial and appeal process. The payment requirements in each case were found to occasion *de facto* discrimination against those who, because of their indigency, were totally unable to pay for transcripts. . . .

Likewise, in *Douglas v. California*, 372 U.S. 353 (1963), a decision establishing an indigent defendant's right to court-appointed counsel on direct appeal, the Court dealt only with defendants who could not pay for counsel from their own resources and who had no other way of gaining representation. *Douglas* provides no relief for those on whom the burdens of paying for a criminal defense are relatively speaking, great but not insurmountable. Nor does it deal with relative differences in the quality of counsel acquired by the less wealthy.

Williams v. Illinois, 399 U.S. 235 (1970), and *Tate v. Short*, 401 U.S. 395 (1971), struck down criminal penalties that subjected indigents to incarceration simply because of their inability to pay a fine. Again, the disadvantaged class was composed only of persons who were totally unable to pay the demanded sum. Those cases do not touch on the question whether equal protection is denied to persons with relatively less money on whom designated fines impose heavier burdens. . . .

Finally, in *Bullock v. Carter*, 405 U.S. 134 (1972), the Court invalidated the Texas filing-fee requirement for primary elections. Both of the relevant classifying facts found in the previous cases were present there. The size of the fee, often running into the thousands of dollars and, in at least one case, as high as $8,900, effectively barred all potential candidates who were unable to pay the required fee. As the system provided "no reasonable alternative means of access to the ballot," inability to pay occasioned an absolute denial of a position on the primary ballot.

Only appellees' first possible basis for describing the class disadvantaged by the Texas school-financing system—discrimination against a class of definably "poor" persons—might arguably meet the criteria established in these prior cases. Even a cursory examination, however, demonstrates that neither of the two distinguishing characteristics of wealth classifications can be found here. First, in support of their charge that the system discriminates against the "poor," appellees have made no effort to demonstrate that it operates to the peculiar disadvantage of any class fairly definable as indigent, or as composed of persons whose incomes are beneath any designated poverty

level. Indeed, there is reason to believe that the poorest families are not necessarily clustered in the poorest property districts. A recent and exhaustive
study of school districts in Connecticut concluded that "[i]t is clearly incorrect . . . to contend that the 'poor' live in 'poor' districts. . . ."

[T]here is no basis on the record in this case for assuming that the poorest people—defined by reference to any level of absolute impecunity—are
concentrated in the poorest districts.

Second, neither appellees nor the District Court addressed the fact that,
unlike each of the foregoing cases, lack of personal resources has not occasioned an absolute deprivation of the desired benefit. The argument here is
not that the children in districts having relatively low assessable property values are receiving no public education; rather, it is that they are receiving a
poorer quality education than that available to children in districts having
more assessable wealth. Apart from the unsettled and disputed question
whether the quality of education may be determined by the amount of
money expended for it, a sufficient answer to appellees' argument is that, at
least where wealth is involved, the Equal Protection Clause does not require
absolute equality or precisely equal advantages. . . .

For these two reasons—the absence of any evidence that the financing
system discriminates against any definable category of "poor" people or that
it results in the absolute deprivation of education—the disadvantaged class is
not susceptible of identification in traditional terms.

As suggested above, appellees and the District Court may have embraced
a second or third approach, the second of which might be characterized as a
theory of relative or comparative discrimination based on family income.
Appellees sought to prove that a direct correlation exists between the wealth
of families within each district and the expenditures therein for education.
That is, along a continuum, the poorer the family the lower the dollar
amount of education received by the family's children. . . .

If, in fact, these correlations could be sustained, then it might be argued that expenditures on education—equated by appellees to the quality of
education—are dependent on personal wealth. Appellees' comparative-
discrimination theory would still face serious unanswered questions, including whether a bare positive correlation or some higher degree of correlation
is necessary to provide a basis for concluding that the financing system is designed to operate to the peculiar disadvantage of the comparatively poor, and
whether a class of this size and diversity could ever claim the special protection accorded "suspect" classes. These questions need not be addressed in this
case, however, since appellees' proof fails to support their allegations or the
District Court's conclusions. . . .

This brings us, then, to the third way in which the classification scheme
might be defined—*district* wealth discrimination. . . . Assuming a perfect correlation between district property wealth and expenditures from top to bottom, the disadvantaged class might be viewed as encompassing every child in
every district except the district that has the most assessable wealth and
spends the most on education. Alternatively, as suggested in Justice MAR-
SHALL's dissenting opinion the class might be defined more restrictively to
include children in districts with assessable property which falls below the
statewide average, or median, or below some other artificially defined level.

However described, it is clear that appellees' suit asks this Court to extend its most exacting scrutiny to review a system that allegedly discriminates against a large, diverse, and amorphous class, unified only by the common factor of residence in districts that happen to have less taxable wealth than other districts. The system of alleged discrimination and the class it defines have none of the traditional indicia of suspectness: the class is not saddled with such disabilities, or subjected to such a history of purposeful unequal treatment, or relegated to such a position of political powerlessness as to command extraordinary protection from the majoritarian political process.

We thus conclude that the Texas system does not operate to the peculiar disadvantage of any suspect class. But in recognition of the fact that this Court has never heretofore held that wealth discrimination alone provides an adequate basis for invoking strict scrutiny, appellees have not relied solely on this contention. They also assert that the State's system impermissibly interferes with the exercise of a "fundamental" right and that accordingly the prior decisions of this Court require the application of the strict standard of judicial review. . . .

We are in complete agreement with the conclusion of the three-judge panel below that "the grave significance of education both to the individual and to our society" cannot be doubted. But the importance of a service performed by the State does not determine whether it must be regarded as fundamental for purposes of examination under the Equal Protection Clause. Justice HARLAN, dissenting from the Court's application of strict scrutiny to a law impinging upon the right of interstate travel, admonished that "[v]irtually every state statute affects important rights." *Shapiro v. Thompson*, 394 U.S. 618 (1969). In his view, if the degree of judicial scrutiny of state legislation fluctuated, depending on a majority's view of the importance of the interest affected, we would have gone "far toward making this Court a 'super-legislature.' " . . .

It is not the province of this Court to create substantive constitutional rights in the name of guaranteeing equal protection of the laws. Thus, the key to discovering whether education is "fundamental" is not to be found in comparisons of the relative societal significance of education as opposed to subsistence or housing. Nor is it to be found by weighing whether education is as important as the right to travel. Rather, the answer lies in assessing whether there is a right to education explicitly or implicitly guaranteed by the Constitution. Education, of course, is not among the rights afforded explicit protection under our Federal Constitution. Nor do we find any basis for saying it is implicitly so protected. . . .

Even if it were conceded that some identifiable quantum of education is a constitutionally protected prerequisite to the meaningful exercise of either right, we have no indication that the present levels of educational expenditures in Texas provide an education that falls short.

We have carefully considered each of the arguments supportive of the District Court's finding that education is a fundamental right or liberty and have found those arguments unpersuasive. . . .

In sum, to the extent that the Texas system of school financing results in unequal expenditures between children who happen to reside in different districts, we cannot say that such disparities are the product of a system that is so irrational as to be invidiously discriminatory.

☐ *Justice WHITE, with whom Justice DOUGLAS and Justice BRENNAN join, dissenting.*

I cannot disagree with the proposition that local control and local decisionmaking play an important part in our democratic system of government. Much may be left to local option, and this case would be quite different if it were true that the Texas system . . . extended a meaningful option to all local districts to increase their per-pupil expenditures and so to improve their children's education to the extent that increased funding would achieve that goal. The system would then arguably provide a rational and sensible method of achieving the stated aim of preserving an area for local initiative and decision.

The difficulty with the Texas system, however, is that it provides a meaningful option to Alamo Heights and like school districts but almost none to Edgewood and those other districts with a low per-pupil real estate tax base. In these latter districts, no matter how desirous parents are of supporting their schools with greater revenues, it is impossible to do so through the use of the real estate property tax. In these districts, the Texas system utterly fails to extend a realistic choice to parents because the property tax, which is the only revenue-raising mechanism extended to school districts, is practically and legally unavailable. . . .

Both the Edgewood and Alamo Heights districts are located in Bexar County, Texas. Student enrollment in Alamo Heights is 5,432, in Edgewood 22,862. The per-pupil market value of the taxable property in Alamo Heights is $49,078, in Edgewood $5,960. In a typical relevant year, Alamo Heights had a maintenance tax rate of $1.20 and a debt service (bond) tax rate of 20¢ per $100 assessed evaluation, while Edgewood had a maintenance rate of 52¢ and a bond rate of 67¢. These rates, when applied to the respective tax bases, yielded Alamo Heights $1,433,473 in maintenance dollars and $236,074 in bond dollars, and Edgewood $223,034 in maintenance dollars and $279,023 in bond dollars. As is readily apparent, because of the variance in tax bases between the districts, results, in terms of revenues, do not correlate with effort, in terms of tax rate. Thus, Alamo Heights, with a tax base approximately twice the size of Edgewood's base, realized approximately six times as many maintenance dollars as Edgewood by using a tax rate only approximately two and one-half times larger. Similarly, Alamo Heights realized slightly fewer bond dollars by using a bond tax rate less than one-third of that used by Edgewood. . . .

Plainly, were Alamo Heights or North East to apply the Edgewood tax rate to its tax base, it would yield far greater revenues than Edgewood is able to yield applying those same rates to its base. Conversely, were Edgewood to apply the Alamo Heights or North East rates to its base, the yield would be far smaller than the Alamo Heights or North East yields. The disparity is, therefore, currently operative and its impact on Edgewood is undeniably serious. It is evident from statistics in the record that show that, applying an equalized tax rate of 85¢ per $100 assessed valuation, Alamo Heights was able to provide approximately $330 per pupil in local revenues over and above the Local Fund Assignment. In Edgewood, on the other hand, with an equalized tax rate of $1.05 per $100 of assessed valuation, $26 per pupil was raised beyond the Local Fund Assignment. As previously noted in Alamo Heights, total per-pupil revenues from local, state, and federal funds was $594 per pupil, in Edgewood $356.

In order to equal the highest yield in any other Bexar County district, Alamo Heights would be required to tax at the rate of 68¢ per $100 of assessed valuation. Edgewood would be required to tax at the prohibitive rate of $5.76 per $100. But state law places a $1.50 per $100 ceiling on the maintenance tax rate, a limit that would surely be reached long before Edgewood attained an equal yield. Edgewood is thus precluded in law, as well as in fact, from achieving a yield even close to that of some other districts.

The Equal Protection Clause permits discriminations between classes but requires that the classification bear some rational relationship to a permissible object sought to be attained by the statute. It is not enough that the Texas system before us seeks to achieve the valid, rational purpose of maximizing local initiative; the means chosen by the State must also be rationally related to the end sought to be achieved. . . .

■ THE DEVELOPMENT OF LAW

Rulings on Residency Requirements, the Right to Interstate Travel, and Indigency

CASE	VOTE	RULING
Dunn v. Blumstein, 405 U.S. 330 (1972)	6:1	Struck down one-year state residency and three-month county residency requirements as a violation of the fundamental right to vote (see also Vol. 1, Ch. 8); Chief Justice Burger dissented.
Valdis v. Kline, 112 U.S. 133 (1973)	6:3	Held as violative of the due process clause Connecticut's presumption that out-of-state students attending the state's colleges retain their status as out-of-state students, for tuition purposes, throughout their attendance in college; Chief Justice Burger and Justices Douglas and Rehnquist dissented.
Memorial Hospital v. Maricopa County, 415 U.S. 250 (1974)	8:1	Found that Arizona's one-year residency requirement for non-emergency medical care at the county's expense to violate the right to travel; Justice Rehnquist dissented.
Sosna v. Iowa, 419 U.S. 393 (1975)	6:3	Upheld a one-year residency requirement for initiating divorce proceedings; Justices Brennan, Marshall, and White dissented.

CASE	VOTE	RULING
Califano v. Aznavorian, 439 U.S. 170 (1978)	9:0	Upheld Congress's withholding of benefits under the Supplemental Security Income program for any month that a recipient spends entirely outside of the United States.

Zobel v. Williams, 457 U.S. 55 (1982) — 8:1 — Struck down Alaska's system for redistributing state income from mineral deposits to each adult resident, based on the number of years of state residency since 1959, upon finding no rational relationship between the residency requirement and the state's goal of prudent management of the fund; Justice Rehnquist dissented.

Supreme Court of New Hampshire v. Piper, 470 U.S. 274 (1985) — 8:1 — Struck down, under the privileges and immunities clause, a state supreme court ruling that only state residents were eligible for admission to the state bar.

Supreme Court of Virginia v. Friedman, 487 U.S. 59 (1988) — 7:2 — Struck down a state supreme court ruling that out-of-state lawyers must become permanent state residents before they may be admitted to the state bar on motion (without taking the state bar examination). The majority found the distinction between resident and nonresident lawyers did not have a close and substantial relationship to the state's interests; Chief Justice Rehnquist and Justice Scalia dissented.

M.L.B. v. S.L.J., 519 U.S. 102 (1996) — 6:3 — Writing for the Court, Justice Ginsburg held that states may not prevent indigents from appealing family court decisions terminating their parental rights by requiring them to purchase trial transcripts before filing an appeal. Chief Justice Rehnquist and Justices Scalia and Thomas dissented.

Saenz v. Roe, 526 U.S. 489 (2000) — 7:2 — Writing for the Court, Justice Stevens stuck down California's law limiting welfare benefits of new residents to that paid by the states in which they previously resided. To deny them California's benefits, which were the sixth highest in the country, Justice Stevens held, infringed on their right to travel and the privileges and immunities guaranteed by the Fourteenth Amendment. Chief Justice Rehnquist and Justice Thomas dissented.

■ The Development of Law

Other Rulings Dealing with Illegitimate Children

CASE	VOTE	RULING
Levy v. Louisiana, 391 U.S. 68 (1968); and *Glona v. American Guarantee*, 391 U.S. 73 (1968)	6:3	Justice Douglas held that illegitimate children are persons within the meaning of the Fourteenth Amendment's equal protection clause and have a right to recover damages for the wrongful death of their mother, striking down Louisiana's law providing that only legitimate surviving children may sue for damages; Justices Harlan, Black, and Stewart dissented.
Labine v. Vincent, 401 U.S. 532 (1971)	5:4	Justice Black held that the equal protection clause was not violated by Louisiana's statute precluding illegitimate children from making claims of inheritance from their natural father's estate; Justices Brennan, Douglas, White, and Marshall dissented.
Gomez v. Perez, 409 U.S. 535 (1973)	7:2	*Per curiam* decision finding the equal protection clause to be violated by a law distinguishing between legitimate and illegitimate children in providing for a father's responsibility for child support; Justices Stewart and Rehnquist dissented.
Weber v. Aetna Casualty, 406 U.S. 164 (1972)	8:1	Justice Powell struck down Louisiana's workers' compensation law that forbade recovery for the wrongful death of a parent by illegitimate children; Justice Rehnquist dissented.
New Jersey Welfare Rights Organization v. Cahill, 411 U.S. 619 (1973)	8:1	A *per curiam* decision holding that the equal protection clause was violated by a state law distinguishing between legitimate and illegitimate children in the award of state welfare benefits; Justice Rehnquist dissented.
Jimenez v. Weinberger, 417 U.S. 628 (1974)	8:1	Chief Justice Burger held that the denial of federal welfare benefits to illegitimate dependents of disabled persons violated the equal protection component of the Fifth Amendment's due process clause; Justice Rehnquist dissented.

CASE	VOTE	RULING
Matthews v. Lucas, 427 U.S. 495 (1976)	6:3	Justice Blackmun upheld the Social Security Act's denial of disability benefits to illegitimate, but not legitimate, children and held that the provision did not require strict judicial scrutiny; Justices Stevens, Marshall, and Brennan dissented.
Trimble v. Gordon, 430 U.S. 762 (1977)	5:4	Justice Powell struck down a statute allowing illegitimate children to inherit only from their mothers, and not fathers, because it was not "substantially related to a permissible state interest"; Chief Justice Burger and Justices Blackmun, Rehnquist, and Stewart dissented.
Lalli v. Lalli, 439 U.S. 259 (1978)	5:4	Despite the ruling in *Trimble*, Justice Powell held for a bare majority that two illegitimate children were not entitled to share in their natural father's estate because during his lifetime he had not obtained a judicial order declaring his paternity; Justices Brennan, Marshall, Stevens, and White dissented.
Fiallo v. Bell, 430 U.S. 787 (1977)	6:3	Justice Powell upheld Congress's denial of preferential status for immigration to the illegitimate children of aliens; Justices Brennan, Marshall, and White dissented.
Quilloin v. Walcott, 434 U.S. 246 (1978)	9:0	Justice Marshall held that a natural father's equal protection claims were not violated by the application of "best interests of a child" standard in adoption proceedings and thus he did not have a veto over the adoption of his child by the natural mother's legal husband.
Parham v. Hughes, 441 U.S. 347 (1979)	5:4	Justice Stevens upheld a Georgia law precluding a father who had not legitimated a child from suing for the child's wrongful death; Justices Brennan, Blackmun, Marshall, and White dissented.
Reed v. Campbell, 476 U.S. 852 (1986)	9:0	Justice Stevens held that illegitimate children are entitled to inherit from the estate of a deceased father.

CASE	VOTE	RULING

Michael H. v. Gerald D., 491   5:4   For a plurality, Justice Scalia
U.S. 110 (1989)   upheld California's law creating
a legal presumption that a child
born to a married woman living with her legal husband is a child of the
marriage and rejected arguments that the natural father, under the Fifth
Amendment's due process clause, had a right to file a filiation suit to establish
paternity and a right to child visitation, as well as dismissed the claim that the
statute violated the child's equal protection rights; Justice Stevens concurred;
Justices Brennan, Blackmun, Marshall, and White dissented.

Miller v. Albright, 523 U.S.   6:3   Rejected a challenge to a fed-
420 (1998)   eral state that automatically grants
citizenship to illegitimate chil-
dren born in a foreign country if the mother is a U.S. citizen, but sets a
higher standard if the father is a citizen and the mother a foreign national.
Justices Ginsburg, Breyer, and Souter dissented.

■ (4) ALIENAGE AND AGE

With the exception of the right to vote, most constitutional rights extend to the "people" or "persons," including citizens and aliens. Aliens, though, do not enjoy the same freedom as citizens when entering the country, and their residency in the United States may be conditioned by the government (as with student visas). In contrast to citizens, aliens may also be deported and the property of enemy aliens confiscated by the government during wartime.

Despite the constitutional rights that aliens share with citizens, and the historic waves of immigrants who built the country, state and federal laws since the Alien and Sedition Act of 1798 have discriminated against aliens, frequently denying them various kinds of public benefits and employment. But in *Graham v. Richardson*, 403 U.S. 365 (1971), the Court announced that alienage was a suspect category and that laws discriminating against aliens must survive strict scrutiny. While a series of subsequent rulings overturned other laws denying aliens benefits and employment opportunities, the Court drew back in *Foley v. Connelie*, 435 U.S. 291 (1979), when it came to New York's law barring aliens from being employed as state police officers. There and in *Ambach v. Norwick*, 441 U.S. 68 (1979), and *Cabell v. Chavez-Salido*, 454 U.S. 432 (1982), the Court held that aliens could be disqualified from positions in public employment that required the exercise of discretion in the performance of important governmental functions, such as law enforcement and education. The Court was also sharply split in *Plyler v. Doe* (1982) (excerpted below), when holding that Texas could not deny undocumented aliens a public education.

While giving heightened scrutiny to classifications based on age, in *Massachusetts Board of Retirement v. Murgia*, 427 U.S. 307 (1976), the Court held that age is not a suspect category under the equal protection clause. There, the Court upheld a state law requiring uniformed police to retire at age fifty. In *Vance v. Bradley*, 440 U.S. 93 (1979), the Court as well upheld under the rational basis test Congress's requiring members of the Foreign Service to retire at age sixty to promote younger members of the service and because of the risks and rigors of overseas service. However, Congress forbade age discrimination in a number of laws; notably, the Age Discrimination in Employment Act of 1967 prohibits employment discrimination against individuals between the ages of forty and seventy. However, in *Gregory v. Ashcroft*, 501 U.S. 452 (1991) (see Vol. 1, Ch. 7), the Rehnquist Court upheld Missouri's constitutional provision mandating that public officials retire at age seventy over the objections of two state judges, who claimed that the provision violated the federal Age Discrimination in Employment Act.

SELECTED BIBLIOGRAPHY

Karst, Kenneth. *Belonging to America: Equal Citizenship and the Constitution.* New Haven, CT: Yale University Press, 1989.

Preston, William, Jr. *Aliens and Dissenters: Federal Suppression of Radicals, 1903–1933.* Cambridge, MA: Harvard University Press, 1963.

■ THE DEVELOPMENT OF LAW
Rulings on the Classification of Aliens

CASE	VOTE	RULING
Graham v. Richardson, 403 U.S. 365 (1971)	9:0	Declared that alienage was a suspect classification and held that Arizona's requirements for state welfare benefits violated the equal protection clause because they conditioned benefits on citizenship and durational residency requirements for aliens.

CASE	VOTE	RULING
In re Griffiths, 413 U.S. 717 (1973)	7:2	Overturned a state law barring aliens from practicing law; Chief Justice Burger and Justice Rehnquist dissented.
Sugerman v. Dougall, 413 U.S. 634 (1973)	9:1	Held that New York's prohibition of aliens from being employed as state civil servants violated the equal protection clause; Justice Rehnquist dissented.
Hampton v. Mow Sun Wong, 426 U.S. 88 (1976)	5:4	Justice Stevens held for a bare majority that the concept of equal justice embodied in the due process clause of the Fifth Amendment forbade the exclusion of all persons who are not citizens of the United States, or natives of Samoa, from being employed in the federal civil service; Chief Justice Burger and Justices Rehnquist, Blackmun, and White dissented.
Mathews v. Diaz, 426 U.S. 67 (1976)	9:0	For a unanimous Court, Justice Stevens upheld the denial of Social Security medicare benefits to aliens who had not resided in the United States for at least five years, observing that the Court should defer to "the strong federal interest in regulating foreign affairs."
Nyquist v. Mauclet, 432 U.S. 1 (1977)	5:4	Struck down a New York law barring resident aliens from eligibility for state financial aid and scholarships; Chief Justice Burger and Justices Powell, Stevens, and Rehnquist dissented.
Foley v. Connelie, 435 U.S. 291 (1978)	6:3	Upheld New York's statute barring aliens from being employed as state police officers on the grounds that police serve important governmental functions; Justices Marshall, Brennan, and Stevens dissented.
Ambach v. Norwick, 441 U.S. 68 (1979)	5:4	Upheld a state law barring aliens from teaching in public schools unless they intended to become citizens of the United States, on the grounds that some state functions are so bound up with the operation of state government as to permit the exclusion of those persons from positions in the government who have not yet become part of the process of government; Justices Blackmun, Brennan, Marshall, and Stevens dissented.

CASE	VOTE	RULING

Cabell v. Chavez-Salido, 454 U.S. 432 (1982) — 5:4 — Extended the state functions analysis in *Ambach* to permit California to bar aliens from working as state probation officers. *Ambach*'s dissenters renewed their opposition.

Bernal v. Fainter, 467 U.S. 216 (1984) — 9:1 — Struck down a Texas law requiring a notary public to be an American citizen, holding that laws that discriminate against aliens must survive the Court's strict scrutiny, unless a state demonstrates that its discrimination against aliens is in the service of an important public function; Justice Rehnquist dissented.

■ THE DEVELOPMENT OF LAW

Recent Rulings on Age Discrimination

CASE	VOTE	RULING

Equal Employment Opportunity Commission v. Arabian American Oil, 499 U.S. 244 (1991) — 6:3 — Held that Title VII of the Civil Rights Act—which bans discrimination in the workplace based on race, gender, religion, and national origins—does *not* apply to companies doing business *outside* of the United States. Justice Scalia concurred, while Justice Marshall, joined by Justices Stevens and Blackmun, dissented.

Gilmer v. Interstate/Johnson Lane Corp., 500 U.S. 20 (1991) — 7:2 — Held that the Age Discrimination in Employment Act of 1967 and the Federal Arbitration Act permit compulsory arbitration, as required under an employment agreement, of employee disputes over alleged dismissals involving age discrimination. Justices Stevens and Marshall dissented.

Astoria Federal Savings and Loan v. Solimino, 501 U.S. 104 (1991) — 9:0 — Held that employees who accuse their employers of age discrimination under the Age Discrimination Act of 1967 may bring suits in federal courts, after state agencies have dismissed their complaints and without further appeals in state courts.

CASE	VOTE	RULING
Gregory v. Ashcroft, 501 U.S. 452 (1991)	6:3	Applied the "rational basis" test to an equal protection chal- lenge to Missouri's state consti-

tutional provision requiring public officials to retire at age seventy. The state's law was deemed to have a rational basis given the undeniable effects of aging and the limited utility in removing judges from office through impeachment and judicial elections. Justices White and Stevens concurred and dissented in part; Justices Blackmun and Marshall dissented.

| *O'Connor v. Consolidated Coin Caterers*, 517 U.S. 308 (1996) | 9:0 | Justice Scalia ruled that a 56- year-old sales manager, who was fired and replaced by a 40- year-old, could bring a suit for |

age discrimination under the federal Age Discrimination in Employment Act. In reversing the lower court's decision dismissing O'Connor's suit, Justice Scalia held that it is not relevant whether an employee's replacement is under 40. Rather, what is relevant in such suits is evidence that an employee was fired because of his or her age. In the words of the justice, "There can be no greater inference of age discrimination when a 40-year-old is replaced by a 39-year-old than when a 56-year-old is replaced by a 40-year-old."

| *Kimel v. Florida Board of Regents*, 528 U.S. 62 (2000) | 5:4 | Writing for the Court, Justice O'Connor held that Congress exceeded its powers under Section 5 of the Fourteenth |

Amendment and violated states' sovereign immunity under the Eleventh Amendment in extending provisions of the Age Discrimination in Employment Act to state employees, and ruled that state employees may not bring suits in federal courts to enforce those provisions. In reaffirming that age discrimination is not a suspect classification under the Fourteenth Amendment, Justice O'Connor emphasized: "Old age also does not define a discrete and insular minority because all persons, if they live out normal life spans, will experience it." Justices Stevens, Souter, Ginsburg, and Breyer dissented.

| *Reeves v. Sanderson Plumbing Products, Inc.*, 530 U.S. 133 (2000) | 9:0 | Writing for the Court, Justice O'Connor ruled that workers need not provide direct evi- dence that employers in- |

tentionally discriminated against them in hiring, promotion, and firing decisions, in a suit brought under the Age Discrimination in Employment Act. Employees need only prove that the employer's stated reason for their dismissal was false, and juries may infer from the evidence presented whether the employer's true motive was discriminatory.

Plyler v. Doe

457 U.S. 202, 102 S.CT. 2382 (1982)

In 1975, two years after the Supreme Court's ruling in *San Antonio Independent School District v. Rodriguez* (1973) (excerpted in section D(3) in this chapter), the Texas state legislature passed legislation authorizing local school districts to exclude children of undocumented aliens from public schools and to withhold school district funds for the education of those children. A class action suit for certain school-age Mexican children who illegally entered and resided in Texas was brought against James Plyler, a school superintendent, and other state officials. A federal district court held that the state had violated the equal protection clause of the Fourteenth Amendment. On appeal to the Supreme Court, the lower court's ruling was affirmed by a bare majority in an opinion delivered by Justice William J. Brennan.

The Court's decision was five to four, and the majority's opinion was announced by Justice Brennan. Justices Marshall, Blackmun, and Powell delivered concurring opinions. Chief Justice Burger dissented and was joined by Justices White, Rehnquist, and O'Connor.

☐ *Justice BRENNAN delivered the opinion of the Court.*

The question presented by these cases is whether, consistent with the Equal Protection Clause of the Fourteenth Amendment, Texas may deny to undocumented school-age children the free public education that it provides to children who are citizens of the United States or legally admitted aliens. . . .

In applying the Equal Protection Clause to most forms of state action, we thus seek only the assurance that the classification at issue bears some fair relationship to a legitimate public purpose.

But we would not be faithful to our obligations under the Fourteenth Amendment if we applied so deferential a standard to every classification. The Equal Protection Clause was intended as a restriction on state legislative action inconsistent with elemental constitutional premises. Thus we have treated as presumptively invidious those classifications that disadvantage a "suspect class," or that impinge upon the exercise of a "fundamental right." With respect to such classifications, it is appropriate to enforce the mandate of equal protection by requiring the State to demonstrate that its classification has been precisely tailored to serve a compelling governmental interest. In addition, we have recognized that certain forms of legislative classification, while not facially invidious, nonetheless give rise to recurring constitutional difficulties; in these limited circumstances we have sought the assurance that the classification reflects a reasoned judgment consistent with the ideal of equal protection by inquiring whether it may fairly be viewed as furthering a substantial interest of the State. We turn to a consideration of the standard appropriate for the evaluation of [the Texas program].

Sheer incapability or lax enforcement of the laws barring entry into this country, coupled with the failure to establish an effective bar to the employment of undocumented aliens, has resulted in the creation of a substantial "shadow population" of illegal migrants—numbering in the millions—within our borders. This situation raises the specter of a permanent caste of undocumented resident aliens, encouraged by some to remain here as a source of cheap labor, but nevertheless denied the benefits that our society makes available to citizens and lawful residents. The existence of such an underclass presents most difficult problems for a Nation that prides itself on adherence to principles of equality under law.

The children who are plaintiffs in these cases are special members of this underclass. Persuasive arguments support the view that a State may withhold its beneficence from those whose very presence within the United States is the product of their own unlawful conduct. These arguments do not apply with the same force to classifications imposing disabilities on the minor *children* of such illegal entrants. At the least, those who elect to enter our territory by stealth and in violation of our law should be prepared to bear the consequences, including, but not limited to, deportation. But the children of those illegal entrants are not comparably situated. Their "parents have the ability to conform their conduct to societal norms," and presumably the ability to remove themselves from the State's jurisdiction; but the children who are plaintiffs in these cases "can affect neither their parents' conduct nor their own status." *Trimble v. Gordon*, 430 U.S. 762 (1977). Even if the State found it expedient to control the conduct of adults by acting against their children, legislation directing the onus of a parent's misconduct against his children does not comport with fundamental conceptions of justice. . . .

Of course, undocumented status is not irrelevant to any proper legislative goal. Nor is undocumented status an absolutely immutable characteristic since it is the product of conscious, indeed unlawful, action. But [Texas's program] is directed against children, and imposes its discriminatory burden on the basis of a legal characteristic over which children can have little control. It is thus difficult to conceive of a rational justification for penalizing these children for their presence within the United States. Yet that appears to be precisely the effect of [the Texas law].

Public education is not a "right" granted to individuals by the Constitution. *San Antonio [Independent] School District, [v. Rodriguez*, 411 U.S. 1 (1973)]. But neither is it merely some governmental "benefit" indistinguishable from other forms of social welfare legislation. Both the importance of education in maintaining our basic institutions, and the lasting impact of its deprivation on the life of the child, mark the distinction. . . . As noted early in our history, "some degree of education is necessary to prepare citizens to participate effectively and intelligently in our open political system if we are to preserve freedom and independence." *Wisconsin v. Yoder*, 406 U.S. 205 (1972). . . . In addition, education provides the basic tools by which individuals might lead economically productive lives to the benefit of us all. In sum, education has a fundamental role in maintaining the fabric of our society. We cannot ignore the significant social costs borne by our Nation when select groups are denied the means to absorb the values and skills upon which our social order rests.

In addition to the pivotal role of education in sustaining our political and cultural heritage, denial of education to some isolated group of children poses an affront to one of the goals of the Equal Protection Clause: the abolition of governmental barriers presenting unreasonable obstacles to advancement on the basis of individual merit. . . . Illiteracy is an enduring disability. The inability to read and write will handicap the individual deprived of a basic education each and every day of his life. The inestimable toll of that deprivation on the social, economic, intellectual and psychological well-being of the individual, and the obstacle it poses to individual achievement, makes it most difficult to reconcile the cost or the principle of a status-based denial of basic education with the framework of equality embodied in the Equal Protection Clause. . . .

These well-settled principles allow us to determine the proper level of deference to be afforded [Texas]. Undocumented aliens cannot be treated as a suspect class because their presence in this country in violation of federal law is not a "constitutional irrelevancy." Nor is education a fundamental right; a State need not justify by compelling necessity every variation in the manner in which education is provided to its population. But more is involved in this case than the abstract question whether [Texas] discriminates against a suspect class, or whether education is a fundamental right. [Texas's program] imposes a lifetime hardship on a discrete class of children not accountable for their disabling status. The stigma of illiteracy will mark them for the rest of their lives. By denying these children a basic education, we deny them the ability to live within the structure of our civic institutions, and foreclose any realistic possibility that they will contribute to even the smallest way to the progress of our Nation. In determining the rationality of [Texas's law] we may appropriately take into account its costs to the Nation and to the innocent children who are its victims. In light of these countervailing costs, the discrimination contained in [Texas's program] can hardly be considered rational unless it furthers some substantial goal of the State.

It is the State's principal argument, and apparently the view of the dissenting Justices, that the undocumented status of these children *vel non* establishes a sufficient rational basis for denying them benefits that a State might choose to afford other residents. The State notes that while other aliens are admitted "on an equality of legal privileges with all citizens under nondiscriminatory laws," the asserted right of these children to an education can claim no implicit congressional imprimatur. Indeed, on the State's view, Congress' apparent disapproval of the presence of these children within the United States, and the evasion of the federal regulatory program that is the mark of undocumented status, provides authority for its decision to impose upon them special disabilities. Faced with an equal protection challenge respecting the treatment of aliens, we agree that the courts must be attentive to congressional policy; the exercise of congressional power might well affect the State's prerogatives to afford differential treatment to a particular class of aliens. But we are unable to find in the congressional immigration scheme any statement of policy that might weigh significantly in arriving at an equal protection balance concerning the State's authority to deprive these children of an education. . . .

To be sure, like all persons who have entered the United States unlawfully, these children are subject to deportation. But there is no assurance that a child subject to deportation will ever be deported. An illegal entrant might be granted federal permission to continue to reside in this country, or even to become a citizen. In light of the discretionary federal power to grant relief from deportation, a State cannot realistically determine that any particular undocumented child will in fact be deported until after deportation proceedings have been completed. . . .

We are reluctant to impute to Congress the intention to withhold from these children, for so long as they are present in this country through no fault of their own, access to a basic education. In other contexts, undocumented status, coupled with some articulable federal policy, might enhance State authority with respect to the treatment of undocumented aliens. But in the area of special constitutional sensitivity presented by this case, and in the absence of any contrary indication fairly discernible in the present legislative record, we perceive no national policy that supports the State in denying these children an elementary education. . . .

Appellants argue that the classification at issue furthers an interest in the "preservation of the state's limited resources for the education of its lawful residents." . . . [But t]he State must do more than justify its classification with a concise expression of an intention to discriminate. Apart from the asserted state prerogative to act against undocumented children solely on the basis of their undocumented status—an asserted prerogative that carries only minimal force in the circumstances of this case—we discern three colorable state interests that might support [Texas's law].

First, appellants appear to suggest that the State may seek to protect the State from an influx of illegal immigrants. . . . [However, t]here is no evidence in the record suggesting that illegal entrants impose any significant burden on the State's economy. To the contrary, the available evidence suggests that illegal aliens under-utilize public services, while contributing their labor to the local economy and tax money to the State fisc. The dominant incentive for illegal entry into the State of Texas is the availability of employment; few if any illegal immigrants come to this country, or presumably to the State of Texas, in order to avail themselves of a free education. . . .

Second. . . . appellants suggest that undocumented children are appropriately singled out for exclusion because of the special burdens they impose on the State's ability to provide high quality public education. But the record in no way supports the claim that exclusion of undocumented children is likely to improve the over-all quality of education in the State. . . . Of course, even if improvement in the quality of education were a likely result of barring some number of children from the schools of the State, the State must support its selection of this group as the appropriate target for exclusion. In terms of educational cost and need, however, undocumented children are "basically indistinguishable" from legally resident alien children.

Finally, appellants suggest that undocumented children are appropriately singled out because their unlawful presence within the United States renders them less likely than other children to remain within the boundaries of the State, and to put their education to productive social or political use within the State. Even assuming that such an interest is legitimate, it is an interest that is most difficult to quantify. The State has no assurance that any child, citizen or not, will employ the education provided by the State within the confines of the State's borders. In any event, the record is clear that many of the undocumented children disabled by this classification will remain in this country indefinitely, and that some will become lawful residents or citizens of the United States. It is difficult to understand precisely what the State hopes to achieve by promoting the creation and perpetuation of a subclass of illiterates within our boundaries, surely adding to the problems and costs of unemployment, welfare, and crime. It is thus clear that whatever savings might be achieved by denying these children an education, they are wholly insubstantial in light of the costs involved to these children, the State, and the Nation.

If the State is to deny a discrete group of innocent children the free public education that it offers to other children residing within its borders, that denial must be justified by a showing that it furthers some substantial state interest. No such showing was made here. Accordingly, the judgment of the Court of Appeals in each of these cases is

Affirmed.

☐ *Justice MARSHALL, concurring.*

While I join the Court's opinion . . . I continue to believe that an individual's interest in education is fundamental, and that this view is amply supported "by the unique status accorded public education by our society, and by the close relationship between education and some of our most basic constitutional values."

☐ *Justice BLACKMUN, concurring.*

[The] Court in *Rodriguez* articulate[d] a firm rule: fundamental rights are those that "explicitly or implicitly [are] guaranteed by the Constitution." It therefore squarely rejected the notion that "an ad hoc determination as to the social or economic importance" of a given interest is relevant to the level of scrutiny accorded classifications involving that interest, and made clear that "[i]t is not the province of this Court to create substantive constitutional rights in the name of guaranteeing equal protection of the laws." . . .

I continue to believe that [*Rodriguez*] provides the appropriate model for resolving most equal protection disputes. . . .

[H]owever, I believe the Court's experience has demonstrated that the *Rodriguez* formulation does not settle every issue of "fundamental rights" arising under the Equal Protection Clause. Only a pedant would insist that there are no meaningful distinctions among the multitude of social and political interests regulated by the States, and *Rodriguez* does not stand for quite so absolute a proposition. To the contrary, *Rodriguez* implicitly acknowledged that certain interests, though not constitutionally guaranteed, must be accorded a special place in equal protection analysis. Thus, the Court's decisions long have accorded strict scrutiny to classifications bearing on the right to vote in state elections, and *Rodriguez* confirmed the "constitutional underpinnings of the right to equal treatment in the voting process." . . . In other words, the right to vote is accorded extraordinary treatment because it is, in equal protection terms, an extraordinary right: a citizen cannot hope to achieve any meaningful degree of individual political equality if granted an inferior right of participation in the political process. Those denied the vote are relegated, by state fiat, in a most basic way to second-class status.

In my view, when the State provides an education to some and denies it to others, it immediately and inevitably creates class distinctions of a type fundamentally inconsistent with those purposes, mentioned above, of the Equal Protection Clause. Children denied an education are placed at a permanent and insurmountable competitive disadvantage, for an uneducated child is denied even the opportunity to achieve. And when those children are members of an identifiable group, that group—through the State's action—will have been converted into a discrete underclass. Other benefits provided by the State, such as housing and public assistance, are of course important; to an individual in immediate need, they may be more desirable than the right to be educated. But classifications involving the complete denial of education are in a sense unique, for they strike at the heart of equal protection values by involving the State in the creation of permanent class distinctions. In a sense, then, denial of an education is the analogue of denial of the right to vote: the former relegates the individual to second-class social status; the latter places him at a permanent political disadvantage.

This conclusion is fully consistent with *Rodriguez*. The Court there reserved judgment on the constitutionality of a state system that "occasioned an absolute denial of educational opportunities to any of its children," noting that "no charge fairly could be made that the system [at issue in *Rodriguez*] fails to provide each child with an opportunity to acquire . . . basic minimal skills." . . .

Because I believe that the Court's carefully worded analysis recognizes the importance of the equal protection and preemption interests I consider crucial, I join its opinion as well as its judgment.

□ Chief Justice BURGER, with whom Justice WHITE, Justice REHNQUIST, and Justice O'CONNOR join, dissenting.

Were it our business to set the Nation's social policy, I would agree without hesitation that it is senseless for an enlightened society to deprive any children—including illegal aliens—of an elementary education. I fully agree that it would be folly—and wrong—to tolerate creation of a segment of society made up of illiterate persons, many having a limited or no command of our language. However, the Constitution does not constitute us as "Platonic Guardians" nor does it vest in this Court the authority to strike down laws because they do not meet our standards of desirable social policy, "wisdom," or "common sense."

The Court's holding today manifests the justly criticized judicial tendency to attempt speedy and wholesale formulation of "remedies" for the failures—or simply the laggard pace—of the political processes of our system of government. The Court employs, and in my view abuses the Fourteenth Amendment in an effort to become an omnipotent and omniscient problem solver. That the motives for doing so are noble and compassionate does not alter the fact that the Court distorts our constitutional function to make amends for the defaults of others. . . .

■ (5) MENTAL ILLNESS AND RETARDATION

Besides *City of Cleburne, Texas v. Cleburne Living Center*, 473 U.S. 432 (1985) (discussed at the outset of this chapter), *Heller v. Doe*, 509 U.S.

Justice William J. Brennan, Jr., in his chambers. During his thirty-four years on the bench (1956–1990), Justice Brennan had a major influence on the Court's interpretation and application of the Fourteenth Amendment. (*Collection of the Supreme Court of the United States*)

312 (1993), underscores the contemporary Court's refusal to expand the categories of nonracial classifications subject to heightened judicial review. Notably, only Justice Blackmun maintained that cases involving mental retardation deserve heightened judicial scrutiny.

Selected Bibliography

Donaldson, Kenneth. *Insanity Inside Out: The Personal Story behind the Landmark Supreme Court Decision*. New York: Crown Publishers, 1976.

Failer, Judith Lynn. *Who Qualifies for Rights? Homelessness, Mental Illness and Civil Commitment*. Ithaca, NY: Cornell University Press, 2002.

Stefan, Susan. *Unequal Rights: Discrimination against People with Mental Disabilities—The Americans with Disabilities Act*. Washington, DC: American Psychological Association, 2001.

Heller v. Doe

509 U.S. 312, 113 S.Ct. 2637 (1993)

A class of involuntarily committed retarded persons challenged the constitutionality of Kentucky's statutes governing the civil commitment of retarded and mentally ill persons. Kentucky distinguishes and provides disparate treatment for those classes of persons in two important ways. At commitment proceedings for the retarded, the burden of proof is whether there is "clear and convincing evidence" that the person poses a danger to himself or others, whereas the "beyond a reasonable doubt" standard applies in proceedings for mentally ill persons. In addition, guardians and family members may participate in proceedings involving retarded, but not mentally ill, persons. Kentucky defended those distinctions on the ground that mental retardation, which is a developmental disability usually well documented in childhood, is easier to diagnose than mental illness, which may appear suddenly in adulthood. A higher burden of proof for the commitment of the latter thus ostensibly offsets the risk of erroneous determinations.

The Court's decision was five to four and six to three; the majority's opinion was announced by Justice Kennedy. Dissenting opinions were delivered by Justice Souter, who was joined by Justice Stevens and in part by Justice O'Connor, and by Justice Blackmun. In a separate opinion Justice O'Connor in part dissented and in part concurred.

    ☐ *Justice KENNEDY delivered the opinion of the Court.*

    We many times have said, and but weeks ago repeated, that rational-basis review in equal protection analysis "is not a license for courts to judge the wisdom, fairness, or logic of legislative choices." *FCC v. Beach Communication, Inc.*, [508 U.S. 307] (1993). For these reasons, a classification neither involving fundamental rights nor proceeding along suspect lines is accorded a strong presumption of validity. Further, a legislature that creates these categories need not "actually articulate at any time the purpose or rationale supporting its classification." A State, moreover, has no obligation to produce evidence to sustain the rationality of a statutory classification. "[A] legislative choice is not subject to courtroom factfinding and may be based on rational speculation unsupported by evidence or empirical data." *Beach Communications.* A statute is presumed constitutional, and "the burden is on the one attacking the legislative arrangement to negative every conceivable basis which might support it," *Lehnhausen v. Lake Shore Auto Parts Co.*, 410 U.S. 356 (1973), whether or not the basis has a foundation in the record. Finally, courts are compelled under rational-basis review to accept a legislature's generalizations even when there is an imperfect fit between means and ends. A classification does not fail rational-basis review because it " 'is not made with mathematical nicety or because in practice it results in some inequality.' " *Dandridge v. Williams*, [397 U.S. 471 (1970)]. . . .

. A statutory classification fails rational-basis review only when it "rests on grounds wholly irrelevant to the achievement of the State's objective.' " *Holt Civic Club v. Tuscaloosa*, 439 U.S. 60 (1978). Because ease of diagnosis [of mental retardation] is relevant . . . it is not "wholly irrelevant" to the achievement of Kentucky's objective, and thus the statutory difference in the applicable burden of proof survives rational-basis review. In any event, it is plausible for Kentucky to have found that, for purposes of determining the acceptable risk of error, diagnosis and dangerousness are the most critical factors in the commitment decision, so the appropriate burden of proof should be tied to them. There is a further, more far-reaching rationale justifying the different burdens of proof: The prevailing methods of treatment for the mentally retarded, as a general rule, are much less invasive than are those given the mentally ill. The mentally ill are subjected to medical and psychiatric treatment which may involve intrusive inquiries into the patient's innermost thoughts, and use of psychotropic drugs. By contrast, the mentally retarded in general are not subjected to these medical treatments. Rather, ". . . mental retardation is . . . a learning disability and training impairment rather than an illness,' " *Youngblood v. Romeo*, 457 U.S. 307 (1982).

It is true that the loss of liberty following commitment for mental illness and mental retardation may be similar in many respects: but the different treatment to which a committed individual is subjected provides a rational basis for Kentucky to decide that a greater burden of proof is needed before a person may be committed for mental illness. . . .

There is a rational basis also for the other distinction challenged by respondents: that Kentucky allows close relatives and guardians to participate as parties in proceedings to commit the mentally retarded but not the mentally ill. By definition, mental retardation has its onset during a person's developmental period. . . . Based on these facts, Kentucky may have concluded that close relatives and guardians, both of whom likely have intimate knowledge of a mentally retarded person's abilities and experiences, have valuable insights which should be considered during the involuntary commitment process.

Mental illness, by contrast, may arise or manifest itself with suddenness only after minority, when the afflicted person's immediate family members have no knowledge of the medical condition and have long ceased to provide care and support. Further, determining the proper course of treatment may be far less dependent upon observations made in a household setting. Indeed, we have noted the severe difficulties inherent in psychiatric diagnosis conducted by experts in the field. In addition, adults previously of sound mental health who are diagnosed as mentally ill may have a need for privacy that justifies the State in confining a commitment proceeding to the smallest group compatible with due process. Based on these facts, Kentucky may have concluded that participation as parties by relatives and guardians of the mentally ill would not in most cases have been of sufficient help to the trier of fact to justify the additional burden and complications of granting party status. . . . As long as Kentucky "rationally advances a reasonable and identifiable governmental objective, we must disregard" the existence of alternative methods of furthering the objective "that we, as individuals, perhaps would have preferred."

□ *Justice SOUTER, with whom Justice BLACKMUN and Justice STEVENS join, and with whom Justice O'CONNOR joins in part, dissenting.*

To begin with, the Court declines to address Doe's argument that we should employ strict or heightened scrutiny in assessing the disparity of treatment challenged here. While I may disagree with the Court's basis for its conclusion that this argument is not "properly presented," I too would decline to address the contention that strict or heightened scrutiny applies. I conclude that the distinctions wrought by the Kentucky scheme cannot survive even that rational-basis scrutiny, requiring a rational relationship between the disparity of treatment and some legitimate governmental purpose, which we have previously applied to a classification on the basis of mental disability, see *Cleburne v. Cleburne Living Center, Inc.*, 473 U.S. 432 (1985) and therefore I need not reach the question of whether scrutiny more searching than *Cleburne*'s should be applied. *Cleburne* was the most recent instance in which we addressed a classification on the basis of mental disability, as we did by inquiring into record support for the State's proffered justifications, and examining the distinction in treatment in light of the purposes put forward to support it. While the Court cites *Cleburne* once, and does not purport to overrule it, neither does the Court apply it, and at the end of the day *Cleburne*'s status is left uncertain. I would follow *Cleburne* here. . . .

Without plausible justification, Kentucky is being allowed to draw a distinction that is difficult to see as resting on anything other than the stereotypical assumption that the retarded are "perpetual children," an assumption that has historically been taken to justify the disrespect and "grotesque mistreatment" to which the retarded have been subjected. As we said in *Cleburne*, the mentally retarded are not "all cut from the same pattern . . . they range from those whose disability is not immediately evident to those who must be constantly cared for." In recent times, at least when imposing the responsibilities of citizenship, our jurisprudence has seemed to reject the analogy between mentally retarded adults and nondisabled children. See, e.g., *Penry v. Lynaugh*, 492 U.S. 302 (1989) (controlling opinion of O'CONNOR, J.) (not "all mentally retarded people . . . —by virtue of their mental retardation alone, and apart from any individualized consideration of their personal responsibility—inevitably lack the cognitive, volitional, and moral capacity to act with the degree of culpability associated with the death penalty"). When the State of Kentucky sets up its respective schemes for institutionalization on the basis of mental illness and mental retardation, it too is obliged to reject that analogy, and to rest any difference in standards for involuntary commitment as between the ill and the retarded on some plausible reason.

□ *Justice BLACKMUN dissented in a separate opinion, expressing his view that the Court should apply a heightened scrutiny test in cases involving the disparate treatment of mentally retarded persons.*

☐ *Justice O'CONNOR concurred and dissented in part, agreeing with Justice SOUTER that Kentucky's differential standard of proof was irrational, but joining the majority in upholding the state's allowing guardians and immediate family members to participate as parties in commitment proceedings.*

Researching Legal Materials

The Internet offers numerous resources for legal research. Conducting legal research on the Internet is similar to researching printed legal documents in libraries. Indeed, most of those legal documents, such as court decisions, may be found on the Internet. Conducting legal research on the Internet, thus, may be more efficient and convenient for those with access to it. But, however legal research is conducted, the researcher must have an understanding of legal sources as well as a research strategy.

I. Conducting Legal Research:

A. LEGAL SOURCES:

Generally, legal research aims to discover *primary* and *secondary* legal authorities to support a legal argument or position (i.e., thesis statement).

1. PRIMARY AUTHORITIES:

Primary authorities are the most persuasive sources because they represent most accurately what the law "is." Examples of primary authorities include federal and state constitutions, statutes, case opinions (written by judges deciding specific cases or controversies), and administrative regulations.

The decisions of the Supreme Court are officially published in the *United States Reports.* In addition, two companies print editions of the Court's decisions. There is the *Lawyers' Edition*, published by the Lawyers' Cooperative, and *The Supreme Court Reporter*, published by West Publishing Company. The decisions of federal courts of appeals are usually found in West's *Federal Reporter* (or *Federal Reporter*, 2d, 3d, or 4th series, respectively). Federal district court decisions may be found in West's *Federal Supplement* series. Most states publish some of the rulings of their courts and West publishes a series of regional reporters that reprint the decisions and opinions of the highest courts in the states. These sources may be found on the Internet (as discussed below) through university and law school Internet servers, or through commercial servers such as *Lexis-Nexis* and *Westlaw.*

Note that primary legal authorities differ in their weight or authoritativeness. The decisions and opinions of the Supreme Court, for instance, are more authoritative than those of lower federal courts. Likewise, the Court's decision usually carries more weight than a concurring or dissenting opinion.

2. SECONDARY AUTHORITIES:

Secondary authorities provide "secondary" perspectives on the law or, more precisely, on how the law may or should be interpreted. Examples of secondary authorities include law review articles (written by law students or scholars), legal treatises and annotations, legal encyclopedias, books, and academic journals (in law, legal history, jurisprudence, and social sciences, like *Judicature* and *The Journal of Supreme Court History*), as well as legal newspapers (such as *Legal Times* and *The National Law Journal*).

B. DEVELOPING A RESEARCH STRATEGY:

While it is impossible to outline a research strategy that would work best for everyone, there are some general considerations in developing one. First, legal research usually involves gaining a broad understanding of the context of a case or controversy, and then moving to the narrower, specific issues presented, as well as to the competing arguments and justifications for resolving those issues one way or the other. In other words, initially consider the historical, philosophical, and political bases for, as well as the subsequent development of, a legal doctrine, such as federalism or free speech, before turning to the specific case or controversy to be addressed. If you know very little about the subject, it is wise to consult secondary authorities *first* about what the law is and how and why it has developed. Second, once you have an understanding of the general legal issues and law involved, then examine the most relevant *primary authorities*, described above. The most critical step in conducting legal research is to read (or re-read) the pertinent provision(s) of the Constitution, statute, or administrative regulation, and then consider *what the Supreme Court has said* about those provisions and the issue presented, carefully analyzing the relevant or governing judicial opinions. Remember that the aim of legal research is to advance a position, a thesis, by persuasively justifying it with an analysis of and arguments drawn from the primary and secondary authorities discussed above.

II. Legal Materials and Law-Related Sources on the Web:

Legal materials, documents, judicial opinions, and other law-related sources on the web are available through a number of legal search engines. One of the most useful is *Findlaw* at **www.findlaw.com**. Another useful site to government links is *Firstgov's* at **www.firstgov.org**. The Supreme Court of the United States maintains a site at **www.supremecourtus.gov**, containing transcripts of oral arguments and opinions in recent cases.

These and other law-related resources are linked and available at the web site that W. W. Norton maintains for the casebook and the annual *Supreme Court Watch* at **www.wwnorton.com/scww/**

The How, Why, and What to Briefing and Citing Court Cases

A. HOW TO BRIEF A CASE:

There is no one "best way" to read and analyze cases. However, an understanding of the decision and opinions may best be acquired by following a prescribed pattern or outline that points up the essential issues of each case. It is suggested that students read the case in its entirety at least once before "briefing" the case along the lines suggested below.

1. TITLE AND CITATION: (*Marbury v. Madison*, 1 Cranch (5 U.S.) 137 (1803).)

2. FACTS OF THE CASE: A brief statement of the circumstances that brought about this case or controversy, identifying the parties and the holding of lower courts.

(Outgoing President Adams commissioned Marbury to serve as a district judge, but the commission went undelivered by his secretary of state, John Marshall. When President Jefferson came into office, he directed his secretary of state, James Madison, not to deliver Marbury's commission. Marbury filed an affidavit requiring Madison to show cause why a writ of mandamus should not be issued directing him to deliver the commission. Section 13 of the Judiciary Act of 1789, Marbury argued, empowered the Court to issue writs of mandamus.)

3. LEGAL QUESTION(S) PRESENTED: The question presented is revealed by the statement of facts, which should indicate the nature of the conflict of interests the Court must resolve. The legal question presented is often concisely stated by the Court at the outset of an opinion or the sections in an opinion dealing with specific questions presented. You should answer each question presented "yes" or "no."

(1. Has Marbury a right to his commission? Yes.

2. If a right has been violated do the laws afford a remedy? Yes.

3. Is the Court the legal body to afford such a remedy? No.

4. Does the Court have the power to declare a law unconstitutional? Yes.)

4. HOLDING: A statement of the Court's ruling and whether it affirmed or reversed the lower court's decision.

(Section 13 of the Judiciary Act of 1789 is unconstitutional.)

5. Opinion for the Court: The opinion refers to the legal reasoning which the Court offers as a justification for its holding. The Court's reasoning should be outlined point by point.

(1-A. Completion of the appointment establishes that Marbury has a legal right to his commission. 2-A. Authorities (Blackstone) show that where there is a legal right there exists a legal remedy. 2-B. Madison violated Marbury's right, and thus a remedy is due Marbury. 3-A. The Court cannot provide the remedy requested, however, since that would require an exercise of its original jurisdiction in violation of Article III of the Constitution. 3-B. Congress cannot alter the Court's original jurisdiction or expand its powers specified there. Section 13 appears to have enlarged the Court's power by giving it the power to issue writs of mandamus in original and appellate cases. 4-A. The Court has the power to declare a law unconstitutional because (1) of the Supremacy Clause of Article VI and (2) Congress may not enlarge the Court's original jurisdiction under Article III. 4-B. It is the duty of the Court "to say what the law is" because (1) judges take an oath to uphold the Constitution and (2) "the Constitution specifies that a law repugnant to the Constitution is void, and courts as well as other departments are bound by it." (3) Since the Court's power extends to all cases and controversies under the Constitution, the Court must declare Section 13 unconstitutional.)

6. Separate Opinions: Both concurring opinions (opinions that agree with the Court's holding but disagree with some or all of its reasoning) and dissenting opinions (opinions that disagree with the Court's result and reasoning) should be noted and their major points emphasized.

(There were no separate opinions filed in this case.)

7. Comments and Evaluation: A statement of the case's legal, history, and political importance, as well as criticisms of the justices' opinions and reasoning.

(1. Chief Justice Marshall should have disqualified himself from participating in the case. 2. The case did not need to be decided; it could have been remanded to a district court, since the Court had no jurisdiction. 3. Marshall's reading of Section 13 is open to criticism. 4. The case is the watershed ruling in which the Court asserted and rationalized the power of judicial review. 5. However, the Court's reasoning is not unassailable—Article III does not expressly provide for judicial review and other officials take an oath to uphold the Constitution as well; *Eakin v. Raub* on triparite or "departmental theory" of constitutional interpretation. 6. *Marbury v. Madison*, however, does not assert "judicial supremacy" as some Court-watchers and justices subsequently claimed.)

B. WHY BRIEF CASES?

Briefing cases has immediate and long-term benefits: the student will have read the case thoroughly and carefully and will have a permanent condensed record of the case. The exercise itself forces the student to come to terms with his or her understanding of the case, prepares the student for lectures and discussion, and will prove an invaluable aid in studying for the midterm and final examination.

C. CASE CITATION: Why, What, Where, and How

1. WHY FOLLOW LEGAL CITATION FORM?

a. Legal writing requires frequent citation of authority and evaluation of that authority depends on proper citation form.

b. In this context, citations in the text greatly aid the reader, eliminating the necessity of moving back and forth between text and footnotes.

2. WHAT TO CITE (in order of their decreasing legal weight):

a. Opinions (majority) for the Supreme Court.
b. Supreme Court plurality, concurring or dissenting opinions.
c. Circuit Court opinions.
d. District Court opinions.
e. Other sources: (1) state court opinions if the issue is one of state law; (2) law review articles *only* if there is no Supreme Court opinion or if the issue involves, for example, economic analysis.
f. Do not cite a lower court opinion or a nonmajority opinion as binding precedent; they are persuasive authority only.

3. WHERE DOES THE CITATION APPEAR?

a. As appositives: In *Brown v. Board of Education*, 347 U.S. 483 (1954), the Court struck down racial segregation of public schools.

b. In citation sentences: Racial segregation of public schools violates the equal protection clause. *Brown v. Board of Education*, 347 U.S. 483 (1954).

4. HOW TO PROPERLY CITE CASES:

a. An opinion for the Supreme Court: *Katzenback v. Morgan*, 384 U.S. 641 (1966), or *Katzenbach v. Morgan*, 384 U.S. 641 (1966) (Brennan, J.).

b. A specific page in the Court's opinion: *Katzenbach v. Morgan*, 384 U.S. 641, 644 (1966).

c. Concurring and dissenting opinions:
Sherbert v. Verner, 374 U.S. 398, 477 (1963) (Stewart, J., con. op.).
Sherbert v. Verner, 374 U.S. 398, 495 (1963) (Harlan and White, J.J., dis. op.).

d. Circuit Court cases: *Yeager v. Estelle*, 489 F.2d 276 (5th Cir., 1973).

e. District Court cases: *Dodd v. Smith*, 389 F. Supp. 154 (D. Mass., 1975).

f. Explanatory phrases and case history: *Jackson v. Metropolitan Edison Co.*, 348 F. Supp. 954 (M.D., Pa., 1972), *aff'd.*, 483 F. 2d 754 (3d Cir., 1974), *rev'd.*, 419 U.S. 345 (1974).

g. Later references to a case previously cited in full:

(1) Use *Id.* (legal version of *Ibid.*) when the later citation immediately follows the full citation: *Id.,* at 427.

(2) Use abbreviated case names, if desired, where other case citations intervene: *Jackson,* at 420 (specific page), or *Jackson, supra.* (full opinion).

5. ADDITIONAL REFERENCES:

See Albert Melone, *Researching Constitutional Law* (New York: Scott, Foresman/Little, Brown, 1990), or the "Blue Book," *A Uniform System of Citation* (Cambridge, MA: The Harvard Law Review Association, 1999).

Members of the Supreme Court of the United States

CHIEF JUSTICES

	APPOINTING PRESIDENT	DATES OF SERVICE
Jay, John	Washington	1789–1795
Rutledge, John	Washington	1795–1795
Ellsworth, Oliver	Washington	1796–1800
Marshall, John	Adams, J.	1801–1835
Taney, Roger Brooke	Jackson	1836–1864
Chase, Salmon Portland	Lincoln	1864–1873
Waite, Morrison Remick	Grant	1874–1888
Fuller, Melville Weston	Cleveland	1888–1910
White, Edward Douglass	Taft	1910–1921
Taft, William Howard	Harding	1921–1930
Hughes, Charles Evans	Hoover	1930–1941
Stone, Harlan Fiske	Roosevelt, F.	1941–1946
Vinson, Frederick Moore	Truman	1946–1953
Warren, Earl	Eisenhower	1953–1969
Burger, Warren Earl	Nixon	1969–1986
Rehnquist, William Hubbs	Reagan	1986–

ASSOCIATE JUSTICES

	APPOINTING PRESIDENT	DATES OF SERVICE
Rutledge, John	Washington	1790–1791
Cushing, William	Washington	1790–1810
Wilson, James	Washington	1789–1798
Blair, John	Washington	1790–1796
Iredell, James	Washington	1790–1799
Johnson, Thomas	Washington	1792–1793
Paterson, William	Washington	1793–1806
Chase, Samuel	Washington	1796–1811
Washington, Bushrod	Adams, J.	1799–1829

	APPOINTING PRESIDENT	DATES OF SERVICE
Moore, Alfred	Adams, J.	1800–1804
Johnson, William	Jefferson	1804–1834
Livingston, Henry Brockholst	Jefferson	1807–1823
Todd, Thomas	Jefferson	1807–1826
Duvall, Gabriel	Madison	1811–1835
Story, Joseph	Madison	1812–1845
Thompson, Smith	Monroe	1823–1843
Trimble, Robert	Adams, J. Q.	1826–1828
McLean, John	Jackson	1830–1861
Baldwin, Henry	Jackson	1830–1844
Wayne, James Moore	Jackson	1835–1867
Barbour, Philip Pendleton	Jackson	1836–1841
Catron, John	Van Buren	1837–1865
McKinley, John	Van Buren	1838–1852
Daniel, Peter Vivian	Van Buren	1842–1860
Nelson, Samuel	Tyler	1845–1872
Woodbury Levi	Polk	1845–1851
Grier, Robert Cooper	Polk	1846–1870
Curtis, Benjamin Robbins	Fillmore	1851–1857
Campbell, John Archibald	Pierce	1853–1861
Clifford, Nathan	Buchanan	1858–1881
Swayne, Noah Haynes	Lincoln	1862–1881
Miller, Samuel Freeman	Lincoln	1862–1890
Davis, David	Lincoln	1862–1877
Field, Stephen Johnson	Lincoln	1863–1897
Strong, William	Grant	1870–1880
Bradley, Joseph P.	Grant	1870–1892
Hunt, Ward	Grant	1873–1882
Harlan, John Marshall	Hayes	1877–1911
Woods, William Burnham	Hayes	1881–1887
Matthews, Stanley	Garfield	1881–1889
Gray, Horace	Arthur	1882–1902
Blatchford, Samuel	Arthur	1882–1893
Lamar, Lucius Quintus C.	Cleveland	1888–1893
Brewer, David Josiah	Harrison	1890–1910
Brown, Henry Billings	Harrison	1891–1906
Shiras, George, Jr.	Harrison	1892–1903
Jackson, Howell Edmunds	Harrison	1893–1895
White, Edward Douglass	Cleveland	1894–1910
Peckham Rufus Wheeler	Cleveland	1896–1909
McKenna, Joseph	McKinley	1898–1925
Holmes, Oliver Wendell	Roosevelt, T.	1902–1932
Day, William Rufus	Roosevelt, T.	1903–1922

ASSOCIATE JUSTICES *(continued)*

	APPOINTING PRESIDENT	DATES OF SERVICE
Moody, William Henry	Roosevelt, T.	1906–1910
Lurton, Horace Harmon	Taft	1910–1914
Hughes, Charles Evans	Taft	1910–1916
Van Devanter, Willis	Taft	1911–1937
Lamar, Joseph Rucker	Taft	1911–1916
Pitney, Mahlon	Taft	1912–1922
McReynolds, James Clark	Wilson	1914–1941
Brandeis, Louis Dembitz	Wilson	1916–1939
Clarke, John Hessin	Wilson	1916–1922
Sutherland, George	Harding	1921–1938
Butler, Pierce	Harding	1923–1939
Sanford, Edward Terry	Harding	1923–1930
Stone, Harlan Fiske	Coolidge	1925–1941
Roberts, Owen Josephus	Hoover	1930–1945
Cardozo, Benjamin Nathan	Hoover	1932–1938
Black, Hugo Lafayette	Roosevelt, F.	1937–1971
Reed, Stanley Forman	Roosevelt, F.	1938–1957
Frankfurter, Felin	Roosevelt, F.	1939–1962
Douglas, William Orville	Roosevelt, F.	1939–1975
Murphy, Frank	Roosevelt, F.	1940–1949
Byrnes, James Francis	Roosevelt, F.	1941–1942
Jackson, Robert Houghwout	Roosevelt, F.	1941–1954
Rutledge, Wiley Blount	Roosevelt, F.	1943–1949
Burton, Harold Hitz	Truman	1945–1958
Clark, Thomas Campbell	Truman	1949–1967
Minton, Sherman	Truman	1949–1956
Harlan, John Marshall	Eisenhower	1955–1971
Brennan, William Joseph, Jr.	Eisenhower	1956–1990
Whittaker, Charles Evans	Eisenhower	1957–1962
Stewart, Potter	Eisenhower	1958–1981
White, Byron Raymond	Kennedy	1962–1993
Goldberg, Arthur Joseph	Kennedy	1962–1965
Fortas, Abe	Johnson, L.	1965–1969
Marshall, Thurgood	Johnson, L.	1967–1991
Blackmun, Harry A.	Nixon	1970–1994
Powell, Lewis Franklin, Jr.	Nixon	1972–1987
Rehnquist, William Hubbs	Nixon	1972–1986
Stevens, John Paul	Ford	1975–
O'Connor, Sandra Day	Reagan	1981–
Scalia, Antonin	Reagan	1986–
Kennedy, Anthony	Reagan	1988–

	APPOINTING PRESIDENT	DATES OF SERVICE
Souter, David Hackett	Bush	1990–
Thomas, Clarence	Bush	1991–
Ginsburg, Ruth Bader	Clinton	1993–
Breyer, Stephen G.	Clinton	1994–

BIOGRAPHIES OF
CURRENT JUSTICES

Chief Justice William Hubbs Rehnquist was born in Milwaukee, Wisconsin, on October 1, 1924. After serving in the military during World War II, he earned a B.A. and an M.A. in political science at Stanford University, as well as a second M.A. in government from Harvard, before attending Stanford Law School, where he graduated first in his class in 1952. Subsequently, he clerked for Justice Robert H. Jackson and then went into private practice in Phoenix, Arizona. There, he also became active in the Republican party and an outspoken critic of liberal legislation and rulings of the Warren Court. In the administration of Republican President Richard M. Nixon, Rehnquist became an assistant attorney general in the Department of Justice. In 1972, Nixon appointed him to the Supreme Court, where he staked out conservative positions on the far right and wrote the largest number of solo dissenting opinions, earning him the nickname of "Lone Ranger." In 1986, Republican president Ronald Reagan elevated him from associate to chief justice to succeed Chief Justice Warren E. Burger. As chief justice, he has won praise for his easygoing manner and sense of humor, as well as for his efficiency in presiding over the justices' private conferences. See U.S. Congress, Senate, Committee on the Judiciary, *Hearings before the Committee on the Judiciary, U.S. Senate, Ninety-ninth Congress, 2d Session, on the Nomination of Justice William Hubbs Rehnquist to the Chief Justice of the United States, July 29, 30, 31, and August 1, 1986* (Washington, DC: Government Printing Office, 1987). Chief Justice Rehnquist has also written a number of books and articles, including *The Supreme Court: A New Edition of the Chief Justice's Classic History* (New York: Knopf, 2001); *The Centennial Crisis: The Disputed Election of 1876* (New York: Knopf, 2004); *All the Laws but One: Civil Liberties in Wartime* (New York: Knopf, 1998); and "The Notion of a Living Constitution," 54 *Texas Law Review* 693 (1976). For examinations of Chief Justice Rehnquist's judicial philosophy, see Sue Davis, *Justice Rehnquist and the Constitution* (Princeton, NJ: Princeton University Press, 1989); David L. Shapiro, "Mr. Justice Rehnquist: A Preliminary View," 90 *Harvard Law Review* 293 (1976); and Jefferson Powell, "The Compleat Jeffersonian: Justice Rehnquist and Federalism," 91 *Yale Law Journal* 91 (1982).

Justice Stephen G. Breyer was born in San Francisco, California, on August 15, 1938. After graduating from Stanford University, he earned a second B.A. as a Marshall Scholar at Oxford University and then received his law degree from Harvard Law School. After clerking for a year with liberal Justice Arthur J. Goldberg, Breyer went into private practice for a few years. In 1970, he went back to Harvard Law School, where he taught administrative law and regulation. During the Watergate investigation of the Nixon administration's illegal activities, he served as an assistant special prosecutor before returning to teaching at Harvard until 1979, when he became chief counsel for the Senate Judiciary Committee. In 1980, Democratic president Jimmy Carter appointed him to the Court of Appeals for the First Circuit, where he served until President Clinton appointed him to the Supreme Court in 1994. See U.S. Congress, Senate, Committee on the Judiciary, *Hearings before the Committee on the Judiciary, U.S. Senate, One Hundred Third Congress, 2nd Session, on the Nomination of Judge Stephen G. Breyer to the Supreme Court of the United States, July 12, 13, 14, and 15, 1994* (Washington, DC: Government Printing Office, 1995). Among Justice Breyer's many publications are "Our Democratic Constitution," 77 *New York University Law Review* 245 (2002); "Judicial Review," 78 *Texas Law Review* 761 (2000); and *Breaking the Vicious Circle: Toward Effective Risk Regulation* (Cambridge, MA: Harvard University Press, 1993). For a discussion of Justice Breyer's judicial philosophy, see Christopher Smith, Joyce A. Baugh, and Thomas R. Hensley, "The First-Term Performance of Justice Stephen Breyer," 79 *Judicature* 74 (1995).

Justice Ruth Bader Ginsburg was born on March 15, 1933, in Brooklyn, New York. After graduating from Cornell University, she attended Harvard Law School but transferred and graduated from Columbia University School of Law. Unable to find a law firm in New York that would hire a female attorney, Ginsburg served for several years as a research associate at Columbia Law School and then joined Rutgers University School of Law, where she rose to the rank of full professor before becoming the first female professor at Columbia Law School. Besides teaching, Ginsburg served as the director of the American Civil Liberties Union's Women's Rights Project and argued six (won five) important gender-based discrimination cases before the Supreme Court. In 1980 she was appointed to the Court of Appeals for the District of Columbia Circuit, and in 1993 she was appointed to the Supreme Court by President Bill Clinton. Justice Ginsburg is the second woman to sit on the high court and the first Jewish justice to sit there since the retirement of Justice Arthur J. Goldberg in 1965. See U.S. Congress, Senate, Committee on the Judiciary, *Hearings before the Committee on the Judiciary, U.S. Senate, One Hundred Third Congress, 1st Session, on the Nomination of Judge Ruth Bader Ginsburg, to Be Associate Justice of the Supreme Court, July 20, 21, 22, and 23, 1993* (Washington, DC: Government Printing Office, 1994), and Amy Leigh Campbell, "Raising the Bar: Ruth Bader Ginsburg and the ACLU Women's Rights Project," 11 *Texas Journal on Women and the Law* 157 (2002). Among Justice Ginsburg's extrajudicial publications are "Speaking in a Judicial Voice" 67 *New York University Law Review*

1185 (1992); "The Progression of Women in the Law," 28 *Valparaiso University Law Review* 1161 (1994); "Some Thoughts on Autonomy and Equality in Relation to *Roe v. Wade*," 63 *North Carolina Law Review* 375 (1985); "Remarks on Writing Separately," 65 *Washington Law Review* 133 (1990); and "Constitutional Adjudication in the United States as a Means of Advancing the Equal Stature of Men and Women under the Law," 83 *Georgetown Law Review* 263 (1997). For a discussion of Justice Ginsburg, see Christopher E. Smith, Joyce A. Baugh, Thomas R. Hensley, and Scott Patrick Johnson, "The First-Term Performance of Justice Ruth Bader Ginsburg," 78 *Judicature* 74 (1994).

Justice Anthony M. Kennedy was born on July 23, 1936, in Sacramento, California, where he grew up in a Roman Catholic family and lived most of his life, prior to his appointment to the Supreme Court by President Ronald Reagan in 1988. After studying at the London School of Economics and Stanford University, where he received his B.A., Kennedy attended Harvard Law School and then went into private practice in Sacramento. In 1965, he began a part-time career teaching constitutional law at the McGeorge School of Law of the University of the Pacific. Based on his activities in the Republican party in California, then Governor Reagan recommended Kennedy for an opening on the Court of Appeals for the Ninth Circuit, to which he was appointed by President Gerald R. Ford in 1974. Following the defeat of President Reagan's nomination in 1987 of Judge Robert H. Bork to fill the seat of Justice Lewis F. Powell, Jr., and the withdrawal of Judge Douglas H. Ginsburg from nomination for that seat, Kennedy, a more moderate conservative than either Judge Bork or Judge Ginsburg, was nominated and confirmed as an associate justice. See U.S. Congress, Senate, Committee on the Judiciary, *Hearings before the Committee on the Judiciary, U.S. Senate, One Hundredth Congress, 1st Session, on the Nomination of Anthony M. Kennedy to Be Associate Justice of the Supreme Court of the United States, December 14, 15, and 16, 1987* (Washington, DC: Government Printing Office, 1989). See also Justice Kennedy, "The Voice of Thurgood Marshall," 44 *Stanford Law Review* 1221 (1992). For discussions of Justice Kennedy's judicial philosophy, see Lawrence Friedman, "The Limitations of Labeling: Justice Kennedy and the First Amendment," 20 *Ohio Northern University Law Review* 225 (1993); and Christopher E. Smith, "Supreme Court Surprise: Justice Anthony Kennedy's Move toward Moderation," 45 *Oklahoma Law Review* 459 (1992).

Justice Sandra Day O'Connor was born in El Paso, Texas, on March 26, 1930. After receiving both her undergraduate and law degrees from Stanford University and unable, as a female attorney, to find private employment, O'Connor became a deputy county attorney in Arizona. Subsequently, she entered private practice, served as assistant attorney general, and was elected as a Republican to the Arizona state senate. In 1974, O'Connor became a state trial judge and later a judge on Arizona's intermediate court of appeals, prior to her appointment to the Supreme Court in 1981 by Republican president Ronald Reagan, who had vowed in his presidential campaign to appoint the first female justice to the Supreme Court. See U.S. Congress, Senate, Committee on the Judiciary, *Hearings before the Committee on the Judiciary, U.S. Senate, Ninety-seventh Congress, 1st Session, on the Nomination of Judge Sandra Day O'Connor, of Arizona, to Serve as an Associate Justice of the Supreme Court of the United States, September 9, 10, and 11, 1981* (Washington, DC: Government Printing Office, 1981). Among her off-the-bench publications are "Portia's Progress," 66 *New York University Law Review* 1546 (1991); "Our Judicial Federalism," 35 *Case Western Reserve Law Review* 1 (1985); and *The Majesty of the Law* (New York: Random House, 2003). For examinations of Justice O'Connor's judicial philosophy, see Sue Davis, "The Voice of Sandra Day O'Connor," 77 *Judicature* 134 (1993); and Nancy Maveety, *Justice Sandra Day O'Connor, Strategist on the Supreme Court.* Lanham, MD: Rowman and Littlefield, 1996.

Justice Antonin Scalia was born in Trenton, New Jersey, on March 11, 1936. The son of an Italian immigrant professor, he became the first Roman Catholic to sit on the Court since the appointment of liberal Justice William J. Brennan, Jr., in 1956. After graduating from Georgetown University, he spent a year studying in Switzerland and then pursued his law degree at Harvard Law School. After working for several years in a leading Cleveland law firm, in 1967 he began teaching at the University of Virginia School of Law. From 1971 to 1977 he served in the administrations of Richard M. Nixon and Gerald R. Ford, after which he spent a year at the American Enterprise Institute, where he wrote articles attacking affirmative action and advocating deregulation. He then moved to the University of Chicago School of Law, where he helped found the Federalist Society, a conservative association of law students, lawyers, and judges. In 1982, President Ronald Reagan appointed him to the Court of Appeals for the District of Columbia Circuit, where he served until his nomination to fill the seat of Associate Justice William H. Rehnquist in 1986. See U.S. Congress, Senate, Committee on the Judiciary, *Hearings before the Committee on the Judiciary, U.S. Senate, Ninety-ninth Congress, 2d Session, on the Nomination of Judge Antonin Scalia, to Be Associate Justice of the Supreme Court of the United States, August 5 and 6, 1986* (Washington, DC: Government Printing Office, 1987). Among Justice Scalia's many off-the-bench publications are "The Dissenting Opinion," *1994 Journal of Supreme Court History* 33 (1994); "Originalism: The Lesser Evil," 57 *University of Cincinnati Law Review* 849 (1989); "The Rule of Law as a Law of Rules," 56 *University of Chicago Law Review* 1175 (1989); "Assorted Canards of Contemporary Legal Analysis," 40 *Case Western Reserve Law Review* 581 (1990); *A Matter of Interpretation* (Princeton, NJ: Princeton University Press, 1997). For discussions of his judicial philosophy, see Richard Brisbin, Jr., *Justice Antonin Scalia and the Conservative Revival* (Baltimore, MD: Johns Hopkins University Press, 1997); and Christopher E. Smith, *Justice Antonin Scalia and the Supreme Court's Conservative Moment* (Westport, CT: Praeger, 1993).

Justice David H. Souter was born in Melrose, Massachusetts, on September 17, 1939. After graduating from Harvard College, he was a Rhodes Scholar for two years at Oxford University and then returned to Harvard for his law degree. He started out in private practice in New Hampshire, but soon thereafter began a career in public service, first, as a state assistant attorney general. In 1971, he became deputy attorney general and in 1976 New Hampshire's state attorney general. Although a Republican, he was never active in party politics and instead pursued interests in mountain climbing, classical music, and history. In 1978, he was named an associate justice of New Hampshire's superior court, the state's trial court of general jurisdiction, and in 1983 he was elevated to the state supreme court. In April 1990, President George Bush, on the advice of his chief of staff and the former governor of New Hampshire, John Sununu, as well as New Hampshire's Republican Senator Warren B. Rudman, named Souter to the Court of Appeals for the First Circuit. Three months later, on July 23, 1990, Bush nominated him to fill the seat of retiring Justice William J. Brennan, Jr. See U.S. Congress, Senate, Committee on the Judiciary, *Hearings on the Nomination of David H. Souter to Be an Associate Justice of the Supreme Court of the United States before the Committee on the Judiciary, U.S. Senate, One Hundred First Congress, 2d Session, September 14, 17, 18, and 19, 1990* (Washington, DC: Government Printing Office, 1991). For discussions of Justice Souter's judicial philosophy, see Robert H. Smith, "Justice Souter Joins the Rehnquist Court: An Empirical Study of Supreme Court Voting Patterns," 41 *University of Kansas Law Review* 11 (1992); and David J. Garrow, "Justice Souter Emerges," *New York Times Magazine* 36 (September 25, 1994).

Justice John Paul Stevens was born in Chicago, Illinois, on April 20, 1920. He graduated from the University of Chicago and then served in the military during World War II, after which he attended the Northwestern University School of Law. Following a clerkship for Justice Wiley Rutledge, he pursued a career in private legal practice, while also teaching part time at both Northwestern and the University of Chicago law schools. In 1970, Republican President Richard M. Nixon appointed him to the Court of Appeals for the Seventh Circuit, and in 1975 he was appointed to the Supreme Court by President Gerald R. Ford. See U.S. Congress, Senate, Committee on the Judiciary, *Hearings on the Nomination of John Paul Stevens to Be an Associate Justice of the Supreme Court of the United States, Ninety-fourth Congress, 1st Session, December 8, 9, and 10, 1975* (Washington, DC: Government Printing Office, 1975). Among Justice Stevens's off-the-bench publications are "The Bill of Rights: A Century of Progress," 59 *University of Chicago Law Review* 13 (1992); "Judicial Restraint," 22 *San Diego Law Review* 437 (1985); "The Life Span of a Judge-Made Rule," 58 *New York University Law Review* 1 (1983); and "Some Thoughts about a General Rule," 21 *Arizona Law Review* 599 (1979); "Freedom of Speech," 102 *Yale Law Journal* 1293 (1997). For discussions of Justice Stevens's judicial philosophy, see Robert Judd Sickels, *John Paul Stevens and the Constitution: The Search for Balance* (University Park: Pennsylvania State University Press, 1988); David M. O'Brien, "The Politics of Professionalism: President Gerald Ford's Appointment of John Paul Stevens," 21 *Presidential Studies Quarterly* 103 (1991); and Note, "Justice Stevens' Equal Protection Jurisprudence," 100 *Harvard Law Review* 1146 (1987).

Justice Clarence Thomas was born in Pin Point, Georgia, on June 23, 1948. Raised as a Catholic, Thomas completed his undergraduate degree at Holy Cross College and then attended Yale Law School. After graduating in 1974, Thomas joined the staff of the attorney general of Missouri, John Danforth, a young Republican who became his political mentor. When Danforth was elected to the Senate, Thomas went into private practice for two years but subsequently rejoined Senator Danforth's staff as a legislative assistant and became active in the movement of conservative blacks opposed to welfare, busing, and affirmative action. Thomas's involvement in the conservative movement within the Republican party brought him to the attention of the administration of President Ronald Reagan. In 1981, he was appointed assistant secretary for civil rights in the Department of Education. Within a year, Reagan promoted him to the position of director of the Equal Employment Opportunity Commission (EEOC). In 1990, he was named to the Court of Appeals for the District of Columbia Circuit, and the following year President George Bush named him to replace retiring Justice Thurgood Marshall. See U.S. Congress, Senate, Committee on the Judiciary, *Hearings before the Committee on the Judiciary, U.S. Senate, 1st Session, on the Nomination of Judge Clarence Thomas to Be Associate Justice of the Supreme Court of the United States* (Washington, DC: Government Printing Office, 1993). See also Justice Thomas's article, "Freedom: A Responsibility, Not a Right," 21 *Ohio Northern University Law Review* 5 (1994); and his publications prior to his appointment to the Supreme Court, such as "Toward a 'Plain Reading' of the Constitution—The Declaration of Independence in Constitutional Interpretation," 30 *Howard Law Journal* 983 (1987); and "The Higher Law Background of the Privileges or Immunities Clause of the Fourteenth Amendment," 12 *Harvard Journal of Law & Public Policy* 63 (1989); "Judging," 45 *Kansas Kaw Review* 1 (1996). For a discussion of Justice Thomas's judicial philosophy, see Scott D. Gerber, *First Principles: The Jurisprudence of Clarence Thomas* (New York: New York University Press, 1999); and Christopher E. Smith and Joyce Baugh, *The Real Clarence Thomas: Confirmation Veracity Meets Performance* (New York: Peter Lang, 2000).

Glossary

Abatement. A reduction or the suspension, in whole or in part, of a continuing charge or activity.

Actual malice. See malice.

Advisory opinion. An opinion or interpretation of law that does not have binding effect. The Court does not give advisory opinions, for example, on hypothetical disputes; it decides only actual cases or controversies.

Affirm. In an appellate court, to reach a decision that agrees with the result reached in a case by the lower court.

Affirmative action programs. Programs required by federal or state laws designed to remedy discriminatory practices by hiring minority-group persons and/or women.

A fortiori. With stronger reason; a term denoting that because a fact exists, another, included in it, though less probable or unusual, must also exist.

Ambulatory retroactivity. The changeable or alterable retroapplication of a constitutional decision, so that the decision applies only to prospective or pending cases.

Amicus curiae. A friend of the court, a person not a party to litigation, who volunteers or is invited by the court to give his views on a case.

Appeal. To take a case to a higher court for review. Generally, a party losing in a trial court may appeal once to an appellate court as a matter of right. If the party loses in the appellate court, appeal to a higher court is within the discretion of the higher court. Most appeals to the Supreme Court are within its discretion to deny or grant a hearing.

Appellant. The party that appeals a lower-court decision to a higher court.

Appellee. One who has an interest in upholding the decision of a lower court and is compelled to respond when the case is appealed to a higher court by the appellant.

Bill of Attainder. A legislative act that inflicts punishment on a named individual or members of a group without a judicial trial.

Brief. A document prepared by counsel to serve as the basis for an argument in court, setting out the facts and legal arguments in support of his case.

Case. A general term for an action, cause, suit, or controversy, at law or equity; a question contested before a court.

Case law. The law as defined by previously decided cases, distinct from statutes and other sources of law.

Certification, writ of. A method of taking a case from appellate court to the Supreme Court in which the lower court asks that some question or interpretation of law be certified, clarified, and made more certain.

Certiorari, **writ of.** A writ issued from the Supreme Court, at its discretion and at the request of a petitioner, to order a lower court to send the record of a case to the Court for its review.

Civil law. The body of law dealing with the private rights of individuals, as distinguished from criminal law.

Class action. A lawsuit brought by one person or group on behalf of all persons similarly situated.

Comity. Courtesy, respect; referring to the deference federal courts pay to state court decisions that are based on state law.

Common law. The collection of principles and rules, particularly from unwritten English law, that derive their authority from long-standing usage and custom or from courts recognizing and enforcing those customs.

Compelling state interest. A test used to uphold state action against First Amendment and equal protection challenges because of the serious need for government action.

Concurring opinion. An opinion by a justice that agrees with the result reached by the Court in a case but disagrees with the Court's rationale or reasoning for its decision.

Contempt (civil and criminal). Civil contempt is the failure to do something for the benefit of another party after being ordered to do so by a court. Criminal contempt occurs when a person exhibits disrespect for a court or obstructs the administration of justice.

Contract. An agreement between two or more persons that creates an obligation to do or not do a particular thing.

Controversies. *See* Justiciable controversy.

Criminal law. The body of law that deals with the enforcement of laws and the punishment of persons who, by breaking laws, commit crimes against the state.

Declaratory judgment. A court pronouncement declaring a legal right or interpretation but not ordering a special action.

De facto. In fact, in reality.

Defendant. In a civil action, the party denying or defending itself against charges brought by a plaintiff. In a criminal action, the person indicted for the commission of an offense.

De jure. As a result of law, as a result of official action.

Delegation of powers. The transfer of authority by one branch of government to another branch or administrative agency.

Dicta. See Obiter dictim.

Discretionary jurisdiction. Jurisdiction that a court may accept or reject in particular cases. The Supreme Court has discretionary jurisdiction in over 90 percent of the cases that come to it.

Dismissal. An order disposing of a case without a hearing or trial.

Dissenting opinion. An opinion by a justice that disagrees with the result reached by the Court in a case.

Docket. All cases filed in a court.

Due process. Fair and regular procedure. The Fifth and Fourteenth Amendments guarantee persons that they will not be deprived of life, liberty, or property by the government until fair and usual procedures have been followed. (see also "substantive due process")

Enemy belligerent/combatant. Citizens who associate with an enemy government or organization in order to perform hostile acts.

Enfranchisement. The act of making free (as from slavery); giving a franchise or freedom; conferring the privilege of voting on a class of people.

Equal protection of the Law. The guarantee that no person or class of persons shall be denied the same protection of the law in their lives, liberty, and property.

Error, writ of. A writ issued from an appeals court to a lower court requiring that it send the record of a case so that it may review it for error.

Exclusionary rule. This rule commands that evidence obtained in violation of the rights guaranteed by the Fourth and Fifth Amendments must be excluded at trial.

Executive agreement. A treaty-like agreement with another country made by the president.

Executive privilege. Exemption from the disclosure requirements for ordinary citizens because of the executive's need for confidentiality in discharging highly important governmental functions.

Ex parte. From, or on, only one side. Application to a court for some ruling or action on behalf of only one party.

Ex post facto. After the fact; by an act or fact occurring after some previous act or fact.

Federalism. The interrelationships among the states and the relationship between the states and the national government.

Federal preemption. The federal government's exclusive power over certain matters such as interstate commerce and sedition to the exclusion of state jurisdiction and law.

Full faith and credit clause. Article IV, Section 1 of the Constitution provides that states must recognize the judicial decisions and laws of other states.

Gerrymander. The process of dividing a state or other division into legal divisions in order to accomplish an ulterior purpose, such as reelecting an incumbent.

Grand jury. A jury of twelve to twenty-three persons that hears in private evidence for serving an indictment.

Habeas corpus. Literally, "you have the body"; a writ issued to inquire whether a person is lawfully imprisoned or detained. The writ demands that the persons holding the prisoner justify his detention or release him.

Immunity. A grant of exemption from prosecution in return for evidence by testimony.

In camera. "In chambers," referring to court hearings in private without spectators.

Indictment. A formal charge of offenses based on evidence presented by a prosecutor from a grand jury.

In forma pauperis. In the manner of a pauper, without liability for the costs of filing cases before a court.

Information. A written set of charges, similar to an indictment, filed by a prosecutor but without a grand jury's consideration of evidence.

Inherent powers. Powers originating from the structure of government or sovereignty that go beyond those expressly granted or which could be construed to have been implied from those expressly granted.

Injunction. A court order prohibiting a person from performing a particular act.

In re. In the affair of, concerning; often used in judicial proceedings where there is no adversary but where the matter (such as a bankrupt's estate) requires judicial action.

Intestate. Without making a will.

Judgment. The official decision of a court.

Judicial review. The power to review and strike down any legislation or other government action that is inconsistent with federal or state constitutions. The Supreme Court reviews government action only under the Constitution of the United States and federal laws.

Jurisdiction. The power of a court to hear a case or controversy, which exists when the proper parties are present and when the point to be decided is among the issues authorized to be handled by a particular court.

Justiciable controversy. A controversy in which a claim of right is asserted against another who has an interest in contesting it. Courts will consider only justiciable controversies, as distinguished from hypothetical disputes.

Malice. The intentional doing of a wrongful act. In libel, "actual malice" is the knowing or reckless disregard of the truth of a statement.

Majority opinion. An opinion in a case that is subscribed to by a majority of the justices who participated in the decision.

Mandamus, writ of. "We command"; an order issued from a superior court directing a lower court or other government authority to perform a particular act.

Mandatory jurisdiction. Jurisdiction that a court must accept. The Supreme Court must decide cases coming under its appellate jurisdiction, though it may avoid giving them plenary consideration.

Moot. Unsettled, undecided. A moot question is also one that is no longer material, or that has already been resolved, and has become hypothetical.

Motion. A written or oral application to a court or judge to obtain a rule or order.

Natural rights. Rights based on the nature of man and independent of those rights secured by positive laws.

Negligence. The failure to do something that a reasonable person would do.

Obiter dictum. A statement by a judge or justices expressing an opinion and included with, but not essential to, an opinion resolving a case before the court. Dicta are not necessarily binding in later cases.

Opinion for the court. The opinion announcing the decision of a court.

Original jurisdiction. The jurisdiction of a court of first instance, or trial court. The Supreme Court has original jurisdiction under Article III of the Constitution.

Per curiam. "By the court"; an unsigned opinion of the court.

Petitioner. One who files a petition with a court seeking action or relief, including the plaintiff or appellant. When a writ of certiorari is granted by the Supreme Court, the party seeking review is called the petitioner, and the party responding is called the respondent.

Petit jury. A trial jury, traditionally a common law jury of twelve persons, but since 1970 the Supreme Court has permitted states to use juries composed of less than twelve persons.

Plea bargaining. The process in which the accused and the prosecutor in a criminal case agree to a mutually acceptable disposition of a case without a trial.

Plenary consideration. Full consideration. When the Supreme Court grants a case review, it may give it full consideration, permitting the parties to submit briefs on the merits of the case and to present oral arguments, before the Court reaches its decision.

Plurality opinion. An opinion announcing the decision of the Court, but which has the support of less than a majority of the Court.

Political question. Questions that courts refuse to decide because they are deemed to be essentially political in nature, or because their determination would involve an intrusion on the powers of the executive or legislature, or because courts could not provide a judicial remedy.

Probable cause. Reasonable cause, having more evidence for, rather than against, when establishing the basis for obtaining a search warrant, for example.

Procedural due process. The safeguards to a person's liberty and property, such as a right to counsel and the right to confrontation.

Rational basis test. A test used by appellate courts to uphold legislation if there is evidence of a rational basis for the law's enactment.

Reapportionment. A realignment or change in electoral districts due to changes in population.

Reasonable and probable cause. The grounds for suspecting a person of crime and placing him in custody, and which would persuade a reasonable person that they are true.

Remand. To send back. After a decision in a case, the case is often sent back by a higher court to the court from which it came for further action in light of its decision.

Republic. A commonwealth; a form of government open to all.

Respondent. The party that is compelled to answer the claims or questions posed in a court by a petitioner.

Reverse. In an appellate court, to reach a decision that disagrees with the result reached in a case by a lower court.

Ripeness. When a case is ready for adjudication and decision; the issues presented must not be hypothetical, and the parties must have exhausted other avenues of appeal.

Search warrant. An order issued by a judge or magistrate directing a law enforcement official to search and seize evidence of the commission of a crime, contraband, the fruits of crime, or things otherwise unlawfully possessed.

Separation of powers. The division of the powers of the national government according to the three branches of government: the legislative, which is empowered to make laws; the executive, which is required to carry out the laws; and the judicial, which has the power to interpret and adjudicate disputes under the law.

Seriatim. Separately, individually, one by one. The Court's practice was once to have each justice give his opinion on a case separately.

Sovereign immunity. The doctrine that precludes a litigant from suing a sovereign without its consent to the suit.

Sovereignty. Supreme political authority; the absolute and uncontrollable power by which an independent nation-state is governed.

Standing. Having the appropriate characteristics to bring or participate in a case; in particular, having a personal interest and stake in the outcome.

Stare decisis. "Let the decision stand." The principle of adherence to settled cases, the doctrine that principles of law established in earlier cases should be accepted as authoritative in similar subsequent cases.

State action. Actions undertaken by a state government and those done "under the color of state law"; that is, those actions required or sanctioned by a state.

Statute. A written law enacted by a legislature.

Stream of commerce. Refers to local goods that for a brief period of time are in interstate commerce.

Subpoena. An order to present oneself before a grand jury, court, or legislative hearing.

Subpoena duces tecum. An order to produce specified documents or papers.

Substantive due process. The interpretation of the Fourteenth Amendment due process clause to extend protection to substantive rights and liberties, and not simply to guarantee procedural safeguards. The process of selectively incorporating guarantees of the Bill of Rights into the Fourteenth Amendment and applying them to the states involved substantive due process analysis, as did the Court's creation and enforcement of the "liberty of contract" and the "right of privacy."

Summary decision. A decision in a case that does not give it full consideration; when the Court decides a case without having the parties submit briefs on the merits of the case or present oral arguments before the Court.

Tort. An injury or wrong to the person or property of another.

Transactional immunity. Immunity granted a person in exchange for evidence or testimony, which protects that person from prosecution, regardless of independent evidence against him; *see* Use immunity.

Treaties. A compact made between two or more independent nations; treaties are made in the United States by the president with the advice and consent of the Senate.

Use immunity. Immunity granted a person in exchange for evidence or testimony but that only protects that person from prosecution based on the use of his own testimony.

Vacate. To make void, annul, or rescind the decision of a lower court.

War power. The power of the national government to wage war; Congress has the power to declare war, while the president, as commander in chief, has authority over the conduct of war.

Writ. An order commanding someone to perform or not perform acts specified in the order.

General Index

abolitionists, 393–394
abortion
   controversy over, 33, 35, 118, 197, 1242, 1254
   liberty of contract and, 75
   presidential influence and, 197
   public opinion and, 188
   right of privacy and, 1228–1235, 1251
   rulings on, 1255–1258
   speech-plus-conduct and, 664–665
   state laws, 1282–1284
access, right of, 180
activism, 425
Act of Settlement (Great Britain), 69
Act to Improve the Administration of Justice (1988), 176
ad hoc balancing, 426–429
administrative searches, 924–954
admiralty cases, 37
Adolescent Family Life Act (1988), 711–712, 778, 1230, 1257
adverseness and advisory opinions, 105–107
advertising, 564
advisory opinions, 105–107, 188
affirmative action
   controversy over, 1344
   equal protection standards and, 1330–1331
   Fourteenth Amendment and, 1334
   mootness of cases and, 118
   reverse discrimination and, 1435–1497
   standing to sue and, 111, 113
age
   discrimination against, 1497, 1564–1574
   equal protection standards and, 1331
Age Discrimination in Employment Act (1967), 1564, 1567–1568
agenda setting, decision-making process and, 103, 171–176
aggravating factors, 1163, 1217–1218
Aid to Families with Dependent Children (AFDC), 354, 1549
Alien and Sedition Acts (1798)
   discrimination and, 1564
   enacting, 43

Jeffersonian-Republicans and, 391–392
judicial review and, 30, 32
libel and, 537
national security and, 380
outcry against, 393
Smith Act and, 401
Alien Registration Act (1940), 401
aliens, 871, 1330, 1564–1574
Al Qaeda, 379, 382, 384
ambulatory-retroactive doctrine, 189, 191
Amendments to Constitution; see also specific amendments by number
American Bar Association (ABA), 631–632, 1161–1162
American Civil Liberties Union (ACLU)
   capital punishment and, 1149, 1161
   freedom of expression and association, 407, 466, 621
   public policy and, 192
   right of privacy, 1306
American College Testing Program, 1429
American Indian Religious Freedom Act (1978), 824
American legal realists, 72
American Library Association, 627
American Medical Association, 1228
American Newspaper Publishers Association, 632
Anti-Federalists
   on Constitution, 305, 307
   government and, 46
   on judiciary powers, 24–25
   on natural rights, 88
Antiterrorism and Effective Death Penalty Act (1996), 1217
appeals
   of capital punishment, 326–327
   circuit riding and, 29
   screening, 126
Appellate Docket, 170
appellate jurisdiction, 51, 104
Article I, U.S. Constitution
   civil liberties and, 304–305
   commerce clause, 78
   contract clause, 222

Article I (*cont.*)
  private property, 220
  standing to sue and, 112
  text of, 1–6
Article II, U.S. Constitution, 7–9
Article III, U.S. Constitution
  on citizens, 76–77
  Federalist interpretation of, 26–27
  on judicial review, 23–24, 31, 104
  on salaries of justices, 195
  text of, 9–10
Article IV, U.S. Constitution
  disposing of property, 137
  full faith and credit clause, 1343
  on government, 119
  private property, 220
  privileges and immunities clause, 252–253, 305
  supremacy clause, 31
  text of, 10–11
Article V, U.S. Constitution, 11, 91
Article VI, U.S. Constitution, 11, 689–690
Article VII, U.S. Constitution, 12
assembly, freedom of, 314, 423
assistance, writs of, 850–851
association, freedom of
  Bill of Rights and, 314
  First Amendment and, 397–430
  overview, 386–397, 666–687
  war time and, 381
assumption of risk rule, 959
attorney, right to, 189, 313–315
attorney general, 188
Austria, 173, 280
Authorization for Use of Military Force
    (2001), 384–385
automobiles, 857, 872, 897–924

"bad tendency" standard, 399
bail, excessive, 1143–1145
Bail Reform Act (1966), 1143–1144
Bank of the United States, 59–62
bankruptcy cases, 38*n*
Bank Secrecy Act, 929
Belgium, 173
Bill of Rights; *see also* specific amendments
  constitutional interpretation of, 77
  cruel and unusual punishment, 1149
  due process and, 304–354
  legal equality and, 1326
  nationalization of, 304–354
  standing to sue and, 112
bills of attainder, 304–305
birth control cases, 120–122, 1230
Black, Hugo, 426–427
blacks; *see also* civil rights; racial discrimina-
    tion; school desegregation
  affirmative action and, 1435
  capital punishment and, 1161–1162,
    1189–1190

citizenship of, 33, 76–77, 196, 252–253,
    1336–1338
  equal protection clause, 84
Blackstone, William, 71, 73, 387–388, 391,
    397
border patrol searches, 899
Brandeis brief, 72, 97, 260, 279
Brandeis, Louis D., 72, 398
broadcast media, 395, 606–630
bugging, *see* wiretapping
Bureau of Alcohol, Tobacco, and Firearms
    (ATF), 1074

Cable Communications Policy Act (1984),
    618
Cable Television Consumer Protection and
    Competition Act (1992), 482, 610, 615
Canada
  constitutional interpretation and, 96–97
  hate speech and pornography, 522–526
  religion and, 689
  same-sex marriages, 1545–1547
capitalism
  communism and, 407
  Court involvement with, 38
  economic rights and, 220–222
  just compensation and, 286–303
  laissez-faire, 194, 255, 258, 262, 311
  liberty of contract and, 252–286
  vested interests in property, 222–252
capital punishment
  appeals of, 326–327
  around the world, 1167–1168
  cruel and unusual punishment, 1150,
    1161–1221
  Eighth Amendment and, 83
  victim impact statements and, 125
caseload
  backlog in, 257
  increasing, 103
  rule of four and, 172
cases
  briefing and citing, 1583–1586
  justiciable controversies, 105
  locating decisions in, 28
  policies for denying, 124–126
  ripeness and mootness of, 116–119
  screening, 170–171
  social forces and, 37
  summarily decided, 176
censorship, 386–387, 394, 433, 586
Central Intelligence Agency (CIA), 112,
    983–985
certification, writ of, 104
certiorari petitions
  defined, 104
  denial of, 172
  indigents and, 105
  institutionalization of, 175
  screening cases and, 170

Child Online Protection Act (1998), 436,
 621–624
Child Pornography Prevention Act (CPPA;
 1996), 474–479
Children's Internet Protection Act (2001),
 436, 611, 627, 663
Christian Coalition, 1162
circuit riding, justices and, 28–29
citizenship
 aliens and, 1564
 of blacks, 33, 76–77, 196, 252–253,
  1336–1338
 constitutional history, 379–385
 dual, 253
 illegitimacy and, 1504, 1564
 privileges and immunities of, 305
 war time and, 381
citizen suits, and standing to sue, 110–111,
 114
civil law, jury trials and, 1117
civil liberties
 Bill of Rights and, 304
 compliance in, 193
 judicial review and, 95
civil rights; *see also* equal protection clause
 Bill of Rights and, 304
 chronology of movement, 1379–1382
 compliance in, 193
 desegregation and, 187
 grassroots campaign, 1381
 judicial review and, 95
 jurisdiction, 106
 presidential influence and, 197
 in wartime, 379–385
Civil Rights Acts
 affirmative action and, 1435, 1439, 1452–
  1455
 congressional power and, 836, 1337, 1339
 desegregation and, 187, 1342–1343,
  1349–1350, 1364, 1386
 discrimination and, 1567
 equal protection and, 1338, 1498
 passage of, 671, 1380–1381
 standing to sue and, 114
 statutory interpretation, 1529–1533
class action suits, 117
Clean Water Act, 114
clear and present danger test, 78, 380, 395,
 398–404, 425–427
coerced confessions, 1027–1083
Cold War, 381
commerce clause
 Article I, 78
 economic rights and, 270
 state sovereignty and, 115–116
commercial speech, 395, 429, 551–578
Committee on Fair Employment Practices,
 1340
Common Cause, 192
common law

Blackstonian principles, 391, 397
 disputes over, 37
 freedom of speech/press and, 388
 on libel, 526
 self-incrimination and, 1081
 wiretapping and, 955–956
 on witnesses, 1019, 1021
Communications Decency Act (1996), 436,
 465–466, 468–473, 621
Communist Control Act (1954), 381
communitarianism, 522–526
comparative constitutional interpretation,
 96–98
Comstock Act (1873), 394
concurring opinions, 183, 185
conference deliberations, 171, 178–182,
 189
Conference of Catholic Bishops, 1162
confronting accusers, 1136–1139
Congress
 judicial review and, 29
 judicial supremacy and, 35
 powers of, 836
 pressuring Court, 194
 religion and, 688
 unconstitutional acts, 36
congressional legislation
 on abortion, 1229
 Court-curbing, 195
 on flag desecration, 90
 interpretation of, 37
 jurisdiction and, 104
 Pledge of Allegiance, 162
 ruling on constitutionality of, 169–170
 standing to sue and, 107–108
Congress of Racial Equality (CORE),
 1380–1382
consensus, 180
consent searches, 864
Conservative Social Darwinism, 260
Constitution
 as bill of rights, 305
 constitutional history, 89–92
 on judicial review, 23
 politics of interpreting, 67–102
 ratifying, 305–307
 on religious freedom, 690–696
 rights of citizenship, 382
 text of, 1–12
 ultimate interpreter of, 35
constitutional amendments
 on abortion, 1229–1230
 Court reversals via, 195–196
 text of, 12–21
 as violations?, 89–92
Constitutional Convention of 1787
 Framers' intent and, 80
 on power of judiciary, 24
 on slavery, 1336
constitutional courts, 173–175

constitutional interpretation
  controversy over, 33
  historical context, 76–86
  noninterpretivism and, 86–102
  politics of, 46, 67–76
  tripartite theory of, 31
constitutions
  of Germany, 89
  of Great Britain, 69
  of Israel, 69–71
consultants, justices as, 107
contraceptives, 75, 120–122, 339, 1227
contract, liberty, *see* liberty of contract
contract clause, 222–252
corporations, as legal persons, 255–256
counsel, right to, 1091–1115
countermajoritarianism, 73–74, 81
Court of Military Appeals, 106
Courts of Appeal, 109
Crime Control Act (1973), 1287
Crime Control and Safe Streets Act (1968), 196, 1029, 1064
criminal justice
  evidence and, 1018
  Fifth Amendment and, 311
  grand juries and, 322
  indigents and, 1145–1148
  jury trials and, 313, 348, 1117
  NAACP and, 312
  reversal of precedent and, 129
  rights of suspects, 189, 196
  right to counsel and, 315
  self-incrimination and, 1019–1020
Critical Legal Studies movement, 74
cruel and unusual punishment
  ban against, 315
  capital punishment, 1161–1221
  Eighth Amendment, 82–83
  noncapital punishment, 1152–1161
  overview, 1149–1152
Czech Republic, 173

Dead List, 181
decisions, *see* Supreme Court decisions
Declaratory Judgment Act, 107
de facto segregation, 1386, 1388–1389
definitional balancing approach, 395, 426–429
de jure segregation, 1386, 1388–1393, 1428
deliberate indifference, 1153, 1155
Democratic Party, 46
desegregation; *see also* racial discrimination; school desegregation
  of armed forces, 1380
  of clubs, 1349
  equal protection and, 1342
  housing and, 1344
discrimination; *see also* civil rights; voting rights
  alienage and age, 1564–1574

equal protection clause and, 1326
  gender-based, 1497–1533
  against homosexuality, 1533–1547
  mental illness and retardation, 1574–1579
  wealth, poverty, and illegitimacy, 1547–1564
  against women, 670, 676
Discuss List, 180–181
dissenting opinions, 183–185
district court jurisdiction, 109
District of Columbia, 109, 282, 291
DNA evidence, 1162
docket, decision-making process, 103, 170–171
dormant commerce clause theory, 113
double jeopardy, 315, 327, 1021, 1139–1143
drugs, 816–817, 866, 927–954
due process clause
  Bill of Rights and, 304–354
  defined, 254
  Fifth Amendment, 254, 313, 382, 1505
  Fourteenth Amendment, 78, 92, 253–256, 270, 282, 285, 310–311, 313, 322, 330, 334, 348, 354, 382, 987, 1027–1028, 1223, 1227, 1236, 1288, 1313
  mentally ill and, 1035*n*
  rise and retreat of, 354–385
  testing, 93

eavesdropping, electronic, *see* wiretapping
economic issues, 260
economic rights, *see* property
education; *see also* schools
  equal protection standards and, 1331
  NAACP and, 312
  racial discrimination in, 1382–1435
  right to privacy and, 1287
Education, Department of, 1435
Eighteenth Amendment, U.S. Constitution, 17, 90; *see also* cruel and unusual punishment
Eighth Amendment, U.S. Constitution, 13, 315–316, 1143–1145
Elementary and Secondary Education Act (1965), 130, 140, 781
Eleventh Amendment, U.S. Constitution, 14, 29, 104, 184, 196
eminent domain, 286, 290, 313; *see also* takings clause
employment; *see also* labor issues
  discrimination in, 1350, 1435
  foreign nationals and, 383
  NAACP and, 312
  procedural guarantees, 355
Endangered Species Act (1973), 111, 114, 141–142
Enemy Alien Act (1798), 380
enemy combatants, 379–385
England, *see* Great Britain
Environmental Defense Fund, 192

environmental issues, 111, 113–114, 141–142
Equal Access Act (1984), 699, 712
Equal Pay Act (1963), 1498
equal protection clause
  affirmative action and reverse discrimination, 1435–1497
  capital punishment, 1162
  constitutional politics, 84
  nonracial classifications and, 1497–1579
  overview, 1325–1336
  racial discrimination and state action, 1336–1382
  racial discrimination in education, 1382–1434
  right of privacy and, 208, 1227, 1236, 1314
Equal Rights Amendment, 1498, 1500–1501
error, writs of, 273
Espionage Act (1917), 380, 395, 396*n,* 399, 405
eugenics movement, 1226
Europe, constitutional courts in, 173–175
European Convention on Human Rights, 69
European Court of Justice on Human Rights, 69
European Union, 69
evidence, 1018, 1084–1086, 1140
exacting scrutiny test, 1330, 1332, 1440
exceedingly persuasive justification, 1331
exclusionary rule, 189, 200, 314, 316, 985–1017
executive branch, 188
executive privilege, 78
ex post facto laws, 304
expression, freedom of; *see also* speech, freedom of
  broadcast media and, 606–630
  Canada and, 523
  commercial speech, 551–578
  defined, 671
  fair trial/fair press controversies, 630–637
  First Amendment and, 397–430
  freedom of the press, 578–606
  libel, 526–551
  obscenity, pornography, offensive speech, 430–526
  overview, 386–397
  symbolic speech, 637–666

Fair Credit Reporting Act (1970), 1287
Fair Labor Standards Act, 1498
fairness, 612, 1022–1023
fair trial, right to, 314, 630–637, 1118
Family Education Rights and Privacy Act (1974), 1287
family planning services, *see* birth control cases

Family Planning Services and Population Research Act (1970), 521
Federal Arbitration Act, 1567
Federal Bureau of Investigation (FBI), 1060
Federal Cigarette Labeling and Advertising Act (FCLAA), 573–574
Federal Communications Act (1934), 956
Federal Communications Commission (FCC), 489, 607–620
federal courts, 29, 37
Federal Crimes Act (1790), 1091
Federal Education Act (1972), 1530
Federal Flag Protection Act (1989), 90, 641
Federal Immunity Act (1954), 1084
federalism, 24, 95
Federalist Papers
  Court use in citations, 81
  No. 44, 241, 249
  No. 78, 25–26, 30, 71, 1182
  No. 83, 1116
  No. 84, 306
Federalists
  on constitutional politics, 68, 71
  court-packing and, 47
  government and, 46
  on natural rights, 88
  on power of judiciary, 26–27, 30
  ratifying Constitution, 307
Federal Jury Selection and Service Act (1974), 1118
Federal Lobbying Act, 669
Federal Property and Administrative Services Act (1949), 140–141
Federal Reporter, 1581
Federal Rules of Civil Procedure, 117, 131, 144, 781–782
feminism, 522–526
Fifteenth Amendment, U.S. Constitution, 16, 184, 313, 1337
Fifth Amendment, U.S. Constitution
  coerced confessions, 1027–1083
  detention and, 384
  double jeopardy and, 327, 1139–1143
  due process clause, 254, 313, 382, 1505
  evidence, 1084–1086
  grand jury indictment, 322, 1115–1117
  immunity, grants of, 1083–1084
  just compensation, 286
  nationalization of, 314–315, 334
  penumbra of, 315–316, 338
  personal reputation and, 110
  police interrogations, 1027–1083
  privacy and, 1223, 1287
  property rights and, 293, 311, 319
  prosecutorial comment and, 330
  public use clause, 290
  "required records" doctrine, 1086–1090
  rights of suspects, 189
  self-incrimination and, 311, 329, 962, 1018–1028, 1030–1032

Fifth Amendment (*cont.*)
  states' rights and, 316
  text of, 13
fighting words, 395, 428–429, 431, 479–526
filings, 105, 171
fines and bails, excessive, 1143–1145
First Amendment, U.S. Constitution; *see also* religion
  Alien and Sedition Acts and, 391
  balancing freedoms in, 78
  citizens and, 382
  commercial speech and, 552–578
  congressional violation of, 30
  establishment of religion, 130, 206
  fair trial/free press, 630–637
  freedom of association, 666–687
  freedom of press and, 43, 392, 395, 407, 578–606
  freedom of religion and, 137, 206
  freedom of speech and, 43, 395, 430–526
  Hamilton on, 390
  judicial approaches to, 397–430
  libel and, 527–551
  media and, 606–630
  nationalization of, 314
  penumbra of, 315–316, 338
  Pledge of Allegiance and, 116, 162, 708
  privacy and, 1223, 1287
  right of access, 180
  right of associational privacy, 337
  standing to sue and, 113
  states' rights and, 313
  symbolic speech and, 637–666
  text of, 12
flag, American
  desecration of, 36*n*, 90–92, 640, 653–654
  saluting, 400, 641–642, 804
Food and Drug Administration, 355
Food Stamp Act, 669
Foreign Agents Registration Act, 594
Foreign Surveillance Intelligence Act (1978), 983–985
Four Horsemen, 263
Fourteenth Amendment, U.S. Constitution; *see also* due process clause
  congressional power and, 35
  contraceptives and, 339
  Court reversals and, 196
  detention and, 384
  dissenting opinions and, 184
  economic rights and, 266
  equal protection clause, 84, 208, 1162, 1227, 1236, 1314, 1325–1579
  fines and, 1147
  juveniles and, 1048
  liberty and, 1224
  life support and, 1313
  nationalization of, 316–317, 327

penumbra of, 338
personal reputation and, 110
privileges or immunities clause, 77–78, 252, 310, 330
property rights and, 293
ratifying, 309
religious freedom and, 693, 802, 832–833
right to life, 375
text of, 15–16
Fourth Amendment, U.S. Constitution
  exclusionary rule, 189, 200, 314, 316
  nationalization of, 314, 334
  penumbra of, 315–316, 338
  privacy and, 1223, 1225
  search warrants and, 316
  self-incrimination and, 1030
  text of, 12–13
  unreasonable searches and seizures, 77, 83–84, 189, 382, 850–1017
Fox Libel Act (1792), 387
Framers' intent, 24, 79–81, 88
France, 173–174, 280, 1081–1083
Freedom of Access to Clinic Entrances Act (FACE; 1994), 665
free exercise clause, *see* religion
Free Speech Coalition, 474
friendly suits, 105–107
frivolous suits, 172
Fugitive Slave Law (1793), 1337
full faith and credit clause, 1343, 1533–1534
"fundamental fairness" doctrine, 93, 314, 317

gays and lesbians, *see* homosexuality
gender-based discrimination, 1330–1331, 1497–1533
Germany
  constitutional courts, 173–174
  constitutional interpretation and, 96
  constitution of, 89
  labor statutes, 280
  self-incrimination, 1081–1083
gerrymandering, 124
glossary, 1597–1603
grand juries, 322, 1115–1117
Granger movement, 270
Great Britain, 69, 280, 689, 1081–1083
Great Depression, 242

habeas corpus, writs of, 105, 195, 305, 1166
Harari Resolutions (Israel), 70
"harmless error" doctrine, 1033
Hatch Act, 669
hate speech, 522–527
Hawaii, land-tenure system, 286, 290
Health, Education, and Welfare, Department of, 517, 1387, 1435
Health and Human Services, Department of, 517–518

hearsay, 854
Hicklin test, 431–432
higher education, *see* education
history, Court use of, 87
Holland, 280
Holmes, Oliver Wendell, 71–72, 398
homosexuality
  comparative constitutional interpretation
    and, 97
  discrimination against, 1334, 1533–
    1547
  equal protection clause, 84, 1331
  expressive association and, 672
  right of privacy and, 208, 679, 1287–
    1288, 1291, 1294
  sodomy and, 193, 1533
Hoover, Herbert, 242
hot pursuit test, 871, 892
House of Representatives, *see* Congress
House Un-American Activities Committee
  (HUAC), 381, 402
housing, racial discrimination in, 1341,
  1344, 1435
Human Rights Act (1998), 69
Hungary, 173
Hyde Amendment, 1229, 1256

illegitimacy, 1331, 1497, 1504, 1547–1564
immigrants, 380–381, 383, 1563
Immigration and Naturalization Act, 36*n*
Immigration and Naturalization Service
  (INS), 364, 383
immunity, grants of, 1083–1084
impeachment, 24, 194
income tax, 196, 1086
indictment, grand jury, 1115–1117
indigents, 105, 1145–1148, 1331, 1560–
  1561
indirect prior restraints, 594–606
Individuals with Disabilities Education Act
  (IDEA), 756, 782
Industrial Revolution, 37–38, 225
in forma pauperis, 105
informational privacy, 1286–1287
informed consent, 1229–1230, 1282–1284
injury tests, for standing to sue, 107–108,
  111, 114
Interest on Lawyers Trust Account (IOLTA)
  programs, 303
Interior, Department of, 141–142
Internal Security Act (1950), 381, 401–402,
  667
Internet, 436, 467, 606–630, 663
internment, 381, 1328
interpretivism, 74, 76–86
interrogations, 189, 196, 313, 1021, 1027–
  1083
interstate commerce, 115–116; *see also* commerce clause
interstate travel, right to, 1560–1561

Israel, Basic Laws, 69–71
Italy, 173–174, 280, 1081–1083

Jackson, Andrew, 33, 59–62
Japan, 96–97, 845–849
Japanese Americans, 381, 1328
Jeffersonian-Republicans
  Alien and Sedition Acts and, 43, 380,
    391–392
  on constitutional politics, 68, 71
  government and, 46, 95
  impeachment and, 194
Jehovah's Witnesses, 192, 641–642, 804,
  810–812
Jim Crow laws, 1372, 1435
John Birch Society, 540
Join-3 vote, 172, 175
judges
  Blackstone on, 71
  power of, 24–27
  as social engineers, 72
Judicial Improvements and Access to Justice
  Act (1988), 175
judicial review
  citizen suits and, 110
  Constitution on, 24
  controversy over, 23, 1286
  equal protection clause and, 1334
  European model, 173–175
  jurisdiction and, 104
  political questions and, 124
  power of, 27–67
  Supreme Court and, 23–27
judicial self-restraint, 169–170
judicial supremacy, 33, 35
Judiciary Act (1789), 23, 29, 47
Judiciary Act (1801), 193–194
Judiciary Act (1925), 104, 126
jurisdiction
  adverseness and advisory opinions, 105–
    107
  Article III on, 24
  defined, 104
  disputes over, 37
  European model, 173–175
  formal rules and practices, 126–127
  justiciable controversies and, 130–170
  over deciding cases, 103
  political questions, 105, 119–124
  reversal of precedent, 128–130
  ripeness and mootness, 116–119
  rule of four, 171–176
  screening cases and, 170–171
  standing to sue, 107–116
  stare decisis and, 124–126
jurisprudence of original intention, 79–80;
  see also Framers' intent
jury trials
  bifurcated, 1162
  constitutional history, 1021

jury trials (*cont.*)
   criminal cases and, 313, 348
   right to, 315–316, 1117–1135
   Sixth Amendment and, 86–87, 348
just compensation, 286–303, 311, 314,
   319
Justice, Department of
   Civil Liberties Unit, 1340
   desegregation and, 187, 1342, 1386–1387
   foreign policies and, 984
   money seizures, 1144
justices
   as advisors, 107
   biographies of, 1591–1596
   discovering consensus, 180
   listed, 1587–1590
   public opinion and, 188
   public policy and, 198
   salaries of, 24, 194–195
   screening cases, 170–171
   self-denying policies of, 124–126
   tentativeness of votes, 180
   voting alignments, 186
   women as, 1520
justiciable controversies, 104–170
juvenile court, 1029, 1048

Kent, James, 30, 40–42
Kentucky Resolutions (1798/1799), 30, 44–
   46, 391
Knesset, 69–71
knock and announce rule, 872
Ku Klux Klan, 422–423, 510–511, 668,
   707, 1339

Labor, Department of, 1435
labor issues, 260, 273, 285
Labor-Management Relations Act (1947),
   401–402
labor relations, *see* employment
labor theory of value, 221
laissez-faire capitalism, 194, 255, 258, 262,
   311
Land, Air, and Sea Self-Defense Forces
   (SDF), 845–849
Land Reform Act (1967), 290
land-use laws, 286–289
Law School Admissions Test (LSAT), 1437,
   1488, 1490
Lawyers' Constitutional Defense Committee (LCDC), 348
Lawyers' Edition, 28, 1581
legal equality principle, 1325–1326
legal persons, 256
legal research, 1581–1582
Legal Services Corporation (LSC), 484
Legal Tender Act (1862), 254
legislation, *see* Congressional legislation;
   state legislation
lesbians and gays, *see* homosexuality

libel
   overview, 526–551
   public opinion on, 394
   seditious, 388, 391, 527
   as unprotected speech, 395, 428–429
liberal jurisprudence, 76
liberal legalism, 74
liberty of contract
   constitutional interpretation, 75
   debates over, 78
   development and demise of, 252–286
   Fourteenth Amendment and, 338
   right of privacy, 1224
Library Services and Technology Act, 626
Licensing Act (1662), 387
life support, 1305–1324
Lincoln, Abraham, 33
Lindh, John Walker, 382
Line Item Veto Act (1996), 114
liquor, 90, 259, 435, 962
literacy tests, 1342, 1381
Locke, John, 221, 223–224, 387–388
lower courts, 23, 104–105, 193

Madisonian system, 74
Magna Carta, 69, 254, 271, 322, 851
mandamus, writ of, 47, 105
marriage
   Bill of Rights and, 337
   discrimination and, 1382
   equal protection and, 1328, 1343
   right of privacy, 1227
   same-sex, 1533–1534, 1545–1547
Maternity Act (1921), 131, 135
McCarran Act (1950), 401–402
McCarthy era, 195, 381, 401
Medicaid, 1230, 1251, 1256
mentally ill and retarded individuals, 1035*n*,
   1200–1213, 1226, 1333, 1574–1579
Military Selective Service Act, 1504
military tribunals, 38*n*, 380–381
minimal scrutiny test, 1328, 1330–1331
minimum-wage laws, 262, 279, 281–282
Minnesota Moratorium Act (1934), 240
minorities; *see also* affirmative action; specific groups
   affirmative action and, 1435–1442
   equal protection standards and, 1330
   equal representation of, 123
   freedom of expression and association,
     670
   religious, 845–849
minority business enterprises (MBEs), 1456,
   1468–1469
Miscellaneous Docket, 170
Missouri Compromise, 1353
mitigating factors, 1163
Mobbs Declaration, 384
mootness of cases, 105, 116–119
Mountain States Legal Foundation, 192

"Nader's Raiders," 192

National Association for the Advancement of Colored People (NAACP)
  Bill of Rights and, 312
  capital punishment and, 1149, 1161, 1165
  on discrimination, 1377
  founding of, 1379
  freedom of expression and association, 603–604, 668, 673–676
  public policy and, 192
  on segregation, 1340, 1383

national banks, 33, 39*n*, 59–62, 95

National Consumers' League (NCL), 279

National Council of Catholic Women, 1501

national defense, 380

National Foundation for the Arts and Humanities Act, 436

National Labor Relations Act (1937), 263

National Organization for Women (NOW), 192, 1500

National Prohibition Act, 962

national security, 395

National Women's Political Caucus, 1500

Native Americans, 816–817

natural justice, 29, 313

natural law, 88, 93

Natural Resources Defense Council, 192

natural rights, 88, 92

New Deal legislation, 62, 194, 263, 1224

Nineteenth Amendment, U.S. Constitution, 18, 90–91, 1497

Ninth Amendment, U.S. Constitution, 14, 316, 338, 1223–1224

noncitizens, constitutional history, 379–385

Nondetention Act (1971), 385

noninterpretivism, 74–75, 86–102

no prior restraint, doctrine of, 580–594

Northwest Ordinance (1787), 1336

obscenity, 394–395, 428–479

Occupational Safety and Health Act, 926, 929

offensive speech, 479–526

Omnibus Crime Control and Safe Streets Act (1968), 195, 977–978, 1084

open fields doctrine, 865

opinion days, 185–186

opinions
  circulating, 182–185
  concurring, 183, 185
  dissenting, 183–185
  published, 183
  unpublished, 117–118

opinions *dicta,* 107, 193, 426

opinion writing, 180, 182–185; *see also* Supreme Court decisions

oral arguments, 171, 176–178

ordered liberty, 313

originalism, 81–82

original jurisdiction, 104, 106, 115–116

Pacific Legal Foundation, 192

packing the Court
  Federalists and, 47
  Roosevelt and, 34, 62–67, 128, 194, 263

Parliament Acts (Great Britain), 69

partial birth abortion law, 1234–1235, 1272, 1282–1284

patronage, political, 669–670

Pentagon Papers, 197

penumbras, 315–316, 1223

per curiam opinions, 176

Petition of Right (1628), 254

plaintiffs, 110

plea bargaining, 1106–1115

Pledge of Allegiance, 116, 161–162, 658, 708

Poland, 173

police
  automobile searches and, 897–924
  exceptions to warrant requirement, 864–896
  interrogations by, 189, 196, 313, 1027–1083
  searches by, 851
  surveillance, 954–985
  wiretapping, 316

political candidates, 607

political jurisprudence, 74

political question doctrine, 105, 118–124, 146, 158

polygamy, 800, 803, 1538, 1543

pornography, 430–479, 522–526; *see also* obscenity

Portugal, 173

positive discrimination, 1435

poverty, 1547–1564

precedent, reversal of, 128–130

Pregnancy Discrimination Act (1978), 1531

presidential powers, 197–198

presidents
  on abortion, 1230
  as chief executive officer, 197
  contesting Court authority, 32–33
  judicial supremacy and, 35

press, freedom of
  censorship and, 387
  fair trial controversies, 630–637
  First Amendment and, 43
  freedom of expression and, 578–606
  liberty and, 388
  nationalization of, 314
  no prior restraint and, 580
  overview, 386–397
  war time and, 381

prior restraint, 580–606

prisoners, 105, 180, 305; *see also* criminal justice

prisoners of war, 379–380
privacy, right of
    administrative searches and, 924–928
    association and, 670
    exclusionary rule and, 985–990
    First Amendment and, 337
    IRS and, 1087
    nationalization of, 315–316
    overview, 1222–1225
    personal autonomy, 1285–1324
    public policy and, 192–193
    reproductive freedom, 1225–1284
    sexual behavior and, 208
    subversive organizations and, 381
    wiretapping and, 954–960
private property, *see* property
privileges or immunities clause, 77–78,
        252–253, 305, 310, 330
prize cases, 37
probable cause, 853–854, 866–867, 899
Progressive Movement, 279
Progressive Party, 194
prohibition, writs of, 105
property
    contract clause, 222–252
    discrimination and, 1377, 1380
    disposing of, 137
    economic rights, 220–222
    Fifth Amendment and, 311
    just compensation and, 319
    standing to sue and, 115
    takings clause, 286–303
    taxation of, 1328
    vested interests in, 222–252
    wiretapping and, 955–956
Proposition 13 (California), 1328
prudential standing, 116, 708
public accommodation, 680
Public Accommodations Act, 671
"public forum" doctrine, 660–666
Public Health Service Act (1970), 517
public policy issues, 192, 196–198
public schools, *see* schools
public use clause, 290
Public Works Employment Act (1977),
        1452, 1481

racial discrimination; *see also* blacks
    in education, 1382–1434
    equal protection standards and, 1330
    Fourteenth Amendment and, 1334
    NAACP and, 312
    state action doctrine and, 1336–1382
    strict scrutiny test and, 1332
radio, *see* broadcast media
rape-shield laws, 635–637
rational basis test, 1328, 1330–1334
reapportionment, 106, 145–147
Reconstruction, 38
redressability of grievances, 314

"Red scare," 380, 405
Reform Social Darwinism, 260
religion
    establishment of, 697–798
    free exercise of, 130, 137, 206, 314, 798–
        849
    overview, 688–697
Religious Freedom Restoration Act
        (RFRA) (1993), 802, 805, 832–
        841
reproductive freedom, 1226–1284; *see also*
        abortion
"required records" doctrine, 1086–1090
residency requirements, 1560–1561
retardation, discrimination against, 1331,
        1333, 1574–1579
reversal of precedent, 128–130
reverse discrimination, 1334, 1435–1497; *see
        also* affirmative action
ripeness of cases, 105, 116–119
Romania, 173
Roosevelt, Franklin D.
    court-packing plans of, 34, 62–67, 128,
        194, 263
    New Deal programs, 263
    radio broadcast, 62–67
rule of construction, 1224
rule of four, 171–176
Russia, 173, 380

salaries, of Supreme Court justices, 24,
        194–195
school desegregation
    controversy over, 33, 35, 197, 1348
    ending, 187, 1341
    equal protection and, 1382–1434
    Fourteenth Amendment and, 1334
    NAACP and, 1381
    presidential influence and, 197
    public opinion and, 188
    separate but equal doctrine and, 1380
    social science and, 88
    standing to sue and, 113
school prayer, 188, 193, 197
schools
    compulsory attendance, 799, 804, 812–
        813
    corporal punishment in, 1035*n*
    freedom of expression and, 395
    religious freedom and, 697–709
search warrants, 316, 334
Second Amendment, U.S. Constitution, 12,
        316, 353–354
seditious libel, 388, 391, 527
segregation, *see* racial discrimination; school
        desegregation
selective incorporation, 313, 316–317
self-incrimination
    coerced confessions, 1027–1083
    evidence, 1084–1086

Fifth Amendment, 311, 329, 962, 1018–1027
    guarantees against, 315
    "required records" doctrine, 1086–1090
self-restraint, 425
Senate, *see* Congress
Senate Permanent Investigations Subcommittee, 381
separate but equal doctrine, 187, 1340–1341, 1379–1380, 1389
separation of church and state
    debates over, 78
    establishment clause and, 688
    Japan and, 845–849
    nationalization of, 314
    overview, 697–798
    suits over, 137
separation of powers, 24
Seventeenth Amendment, U.S. Constitution, 17
Seventh Amendment, U.S. Constitution, 13, 316, 1117–1135
sexual harassment, 1499, 1531–1532
sexual orientation, *see* homosexuality
shaking of hands, 179
shocks the conscience test, 93, 315–316, 367, 379
Sierra Club, 110, 192
silent, right to remain, 189
Sixteenth Amendment, U.S. Constitution, 17, 196
Sixth Amendment, U.S. Constitution
    confronting accusers, 1136–1139
    fair trial/free press, 630–634
    jury trial and, 86–87, 348, 1117–1135
    nationalization of, 314–315
    rights of suspects, 189, 1032–1033
    right to counsel, 1079, 1091–1115
    self-incrimination and, 1028
    "speedy and public trial," 1135–1136
    states' rights and, 313
    text of, 13
slander, 386–387
slavery
    constitutional amendments and, 196
    controversy over, 33, 1336–1337
    freedom of speech about, 393–394
    natural rights and, 92
    property rights and, 254
    self-ownership and, 257
    suits over, 1352–1353
Slovakia, 173
Small Business Act, 1481–1482
Smith Act (1940), 381, 401–402, 412
Social Darwinism, 260, 1236
social forces, and Supreme Court decisions, 103
social science, 88, 260
Social Security Act (1935), 1251, 1255, 1502, 1563

sociological jurisprudence, 72
sodomy, 193, 1287–1288, 1290–1291, 1294, 1533
solicitor general, 188
"Son-of-Sam" law, 580–581
South Africa, 97, 1218–1221
Southern Christian Leadership Conference (SCLC), 1380
Southern Manifesto, 190–191
Spain, 173–174
special interest groups, 192
Special List I, 180
Special List II, 181
speech, freedom of
    censorship and, 387
    clear and present danger test, 380
    First Amendment and, 43
    nationalization of, 314
    overview, 386–397
    religious freedom and, 706–707
    symbolic speech and, 78
    war time and, 381
    Zenger trial and, 389
speech-plus-conduct, 660–666
"speedy and public trial," 1135–1136
Speedy Trial Act (1974), 1135
Stamp and Advertising Act (1711), 387
standing to sue
    birth control cases, 120–122
    contraceptives and, 339
    environmental issues, 142
    jurisdiction and, 105, 107–116
    taxpayers and, 108–110, 130
Star Chamber, 386, 1050
stare decisis, 124–126
state action doctrine, 1336–1382
state courts, 56, 193
state legislation
    on abortion, 1282–1284
    Brandeis brief and, 260
    contract clause and, 224
    interpretation of, 37
    invalidating, 56
    overturned, 36
    powers of, 30
    standing to sue and, 113, 115
states
    Bill of Rights and, 304–305, 309, 316
    contracts and, 222, 224
    disputes with federal government, 38
    Eleventh Amendment and, 29
    First Amendment and, 397
    freedom of religion and, 689
    implementation of rulings and, 188
    judicial review and, 29
    judicial supremacy and, 35
    original jurisdiction and, 106
    religion and, 798
    selective incorporation of, 313

states (*cont.*)
sovereignty of, 29–30, 104, 115–116, 196
Tenth Amendment and, 108
statutory interpretation, 1529–1533
statutory rape, 1513
sterilization, compulsory, 259, 1226–1227, 1236, 1328
strict constructionism, 76–79
strict necessity doctrine, 125
strict rationality test, 1330, 1497
strict scrutiny test, 811, 1327–1328, 1330–1332, 1334, 1440
Student Nonviolent Coordinating Committee (SNCC), 1381–1382
Supplemental Security Income, 1561
supremacy clause, 31
Supreme Court
early years, 27–30, 37
formal rules and practices, 126–127
judicial review and, 23–27
as least dangerous branch, 29
picture shaking hands, 179
purpose of, 37
size of, 194–195
as ultimate interpreter, 35
use of history, 87
web site, 178
Supreme Court decisions
agenda setting, 171–176
circulating drafts of opinions and, 183
communicating, 185–186
conference deliberations, 178–182
constitutional history, 36
docket and, 170–171
impact of, 187–219
locating, 28
opinions and, 182–185
oral argument and, 176–178
reversal of precedent in, 128–130
rule of four, 171–176
screening cases, 170–171
social forces and, 103
summarily decided cases, 176
Supreme Court Reporter, 1581
Supreme Court Reports, 28
Surface Transportation and Uniform Relocation Assistance Act (1987), 1472, 1481–1482
surveillance, police, 380, 954–985
Switzerland, 280
symbolic speech, 78, 637–659

takings clause, 286–303, 314
taxpayer suits, and standing to sue, 108–110, 130
Telecommunications Act (1996), 626
Tenth Amendment, U.S. Constitution, 14, 108
terrorism, war against, 379, 382

Third Amendment, U.S. Constitution, 12, 315–316, 338, 353–354, 1223
Third Geneva Convention, 379
Thirteenth Amendment, U.S. Constitution
Court reversals and, 196
discrimination and, 1343, 1364, 1372
dissenting opinions and, 184
economic rights and, 266
slavery and, 1337, 1353
text of, 15
"three-strikes-and-you're-out" law, 1152, 1156
transactional immunity, 1083–1084
Treasury Department, 254, 983
treaty-making powers, 157
tripartite theory of constitutional interpretation, 31
Twelfth Amendment, U.S. Constitution, 14–15
Twentieth Amendment, U.S. Constitution, 18–19
Twenty-fifth Amendment, U.S. Constitution, 20–21
Twenty-first Amendment, U.S. Constitution, 19, 90, 435
Twenty-fourth Amendment, U.S. Constitution, 20
Twenty-second Amendment, U.S. Constitution, 19
Twenty-seventh Amendment, U.S. Constitution, 21
Twenty-sixth Amendment, U.S. Constitution, 21, 196
Twenty-third Amendment, U.S. Constitution, 20

undue burden test, 1232, 1258, 1260
United States Reports, 28, 1581
unreasonable searches and seizures; *see also* Fourth Amendment; police
administrative searches, 924–954
automobiles and, 897–923
exclusionary rule and, 985–1017
Fourth Amendment, 77, 83–84, 189, 382
right against, 314
warrants and, 850–896
wiretapping and, 954–985
USA PATRIOT ACT, 380, 983–985

Veto Message, 33, 59–62
victim impact statements, 125, 1164
Vietnam War
opposition to, 479, 586, 639, 650–651, 664, 670
standing to sue and, 112
Virginia Resolutions (1798), 30, 43–44
votes
alignments with, 186
conference deliberations and, 182

switching, 180, 263, 749–750, 1290–
    1292
tentativeness of, 180–181, 183
voting rights, 90, 312, 1326, 1337, 1497
Voting Rights Act (1965), 196, 837,
    1343

War of 1812, 380
warrants
    automobiles and, 897–924
    exceptions to, 853–896
    Fourth Amendment and, 850
    search, 316, 334
war time, civil rights in, 379–385
Washington Legal Foundation, 192
wealth, 1497, 1547–1564; *see also* indig-
    ents
Web, *see* Internet
web site, of Supreme Court, 178
wiretapping, 83, 316, 954–985
witch hunts, 381

witnesses
    protection for, 1019–1020
    right to confront, 315, 1021, 1136–1139
women
    affirmative action and, 1435
    discrimination against, 670, 676
    equal protection clause, 84, 1517
    as justices, 1520
    minimum wages and, 262
    Nineteenth Amendment and, 1497
    rights for, 1228
    voting rights and, 90
    working hours, 97, 260, 1498
Women's Legal Education and Action Fund,
    522
World War I, 380, 641
World War II, 380–381, 641

yellow-dog contracts, 260–261, 285

Zenger trial, and free speech, 389

Index of Cases

Note: Cases and page numbers in **boldface** refer to case excerpts.

A. L. Lockhart v. McCree, 1120, **1126– 1131**

Abbate v. United States, 1143n

Abel v. United States, 928

Abington School District v. Schempp, 188, 206, 699, 701, 703, 714, **727–733,** 744, 746, 761, 808, 809

Ableman v. Booth, 1350n, 1414

Abood v. Detroit Board of Education, 559

Abrams v. United States, 380, 396, 399

Adair v. United States, 260, 263, 264, 286

Adamson v. California, 92, 313, 315, 317, **329–334,** 336, 350

Adams v. Texas, 1205

Adams v. Williams, 857n, 866

Adarand Constructors, Inc. v. Pena, 1331, 1440, 1441, 1455, **1471–1483,** 1485

Adderly v. Florida, 663

Addington v. Texas, 356, 1308

Adickes v. S. H. Kress & Co., 1351n

Adkins v. Children's Hospital of D.C., 262, 282, 283, 284, 1263, 1264

Aetna Life Insurance Co. v. Haworth, 127n

Agins v. Tiburon, 293, 301–302

Agostini v. Felton, 707, 708, 713, 715, **781– 787,** 788

Aguilar v. Felton, 707, 709n, 713, 715, 716, 759, 760, 781, 782, 783, 784, 785, 786, 1204

Aguilar v. Texas, 854, 1004

Aikens v. Wisconsin, 406

Air Pollution Variance Board of State of Colorado v. Western Alfalfa Corporation, 929

Ake v. Oklahoma, 1148

Akins v. Texas, 1124

Akron v. Akron Center for Reproductive Health, see City of Akron v. Akron Center for Reproductive Health

Alabama v. Smith, 1109

Alabama v. White, 898

Alberts v. California, 432, **438–442**

Alexander v. Holmes County Board of Education, 1387, 1394n

Alexander v. Sandoval, 114–115

Alexander v. United States, 1144

Allegheny Pittsburgh Coal Co. v. County Commission, 1328, 1329

Allen v. Illinois, 1079

Allen v. Wright, 113, 163, 1470

Allgeyer v. Louisiana, 256, 273, 280, 286, 1444

Almeida-Sanchez v. United States, 899

Amalgamated Food Employees Union v. Logan Valley Plaza, 661, 664

Ambach v. Norwick, 1564, 1566, 1567

American Academy of Pediatricians v. Lungren, 213

American Committee for Protection of Foreign Born v. SACB, 669

American Communications Association v. Douds, 401, 520

American Jewish Congress v. Chicago, 754

Amos v. United States, 960n

Anchorage Police Department Employees Association v. Municipality of Anchorage, 213

Anderson v. Liberty Lobby, Inc., 145, 533

Anders v. California, 1096n

Ankenbrandt v. Richards, 164

Antelope Case, 92

Anzai v. Shiraishi, Governor of Ehime Prefecture, 849

Apodaca v. Oregon, 317, 1121, 1134

Apprendi v. New Jersey, 1122, 1218

Aptheker v. United States, 672n

Arcara v. Cloud Books, Inc., 435

Argersinger v. Hamlin, 315, 318n, 1093, 1094, 1095, **1103–1106**

Arizona v. Evans, 213, 215, 989, **1015–1017**

Arizona v. Fulminante, 1033, **1060–1064,** 1079–1080, 1121

Arizona v. Hicks, 855, **861–863,** 890, 943

Arizona v. Mauro, 1079

Arizona v. Rumsey, 1202

Arkansas Educational Television Commission v. Forbes, 628, 663

Arkansas v. Sanders, 901, 902, 913, 914, 915, 916

Arkansas Writers' Project v. Ragland, 580

Arlington Heights v. Metropolitan Housing Dev. Corp., 1191

Armstrong v. Manzo, 362

Arnett v. Kennedy, 355
ASARCO Inc. v. Kadish, 143
Ashcraft v. Tennessee, 1027, 1044
Ashcroft v. American Civil Liberties Union, 436, 611, **621–626**
Ashcroft v. Free Speech Coalition, 435, 436, **474–479**
Ashe v. Swenson, 1143*n*
Ashton v. Kentucky, 527
Ashwander v. Tennessee Valley Authority, 162, 169, 830, 1177
Associated Press v. United States, 578
Associated Press v. Walker, 528
Astoria Federal Savings and Loan v. Solimino, 1567
Atkins v. Virginia, 97, 1160, 1164, **1206–1213**
Atlantic Coastline Railroad Co. v. City of Goldsboro, 225
Atwater v. Lago Vista, 902, **918–924**
Austin v. Tennessee, 265*n*
Austin v. United States, 1144, 1145
Avery v. Georgia, 1122*n*

Backus v. Fort Street Union Depot Co., 288
Baker v. Carr, 35, 123, 133, 134, **145–157,** 159, 161
Baldwin v. New York, 1117
Ballard v. United States, 1519
Ballew v. Georgia, 1121, 1130, 1134
Baltimore City Department of Social Services v. Bouknight, 1088
Banks v. Dretke, 1218
Bantam Books, Inc. v. Sullivan, 437*n*, 587
Barber v. Page, 1139*n*
Barefoot v. Estelle, 1213
Barenblatt v. United States, 381, 403, 425
Barker v. Wingo, 1135
Barlow v. Collins, 141
Barnes v. Glen Theatre, Inc., 436, 459, 460, 462, 463, 465
Barron v. The Mayor and City of Baltimore, 309, 310, **319–321,** 333
Barr v. City of Columbia, 1351*n*
Barr v. Matteo, 527
Barry v. Barchi, 357
Bartels v. Iowa, 651, 1327
Bartkus v. Illinois, 1143*n*
Bartnicki v. Vopper, 581
Bart v. United States, 1025*n*
Bates v. City of Little Rock, 343, 667
Bates v. State Bar of Arizona, 552, 555, 565
Batson v. Kentucky, 1119, **1123–1126,** 1347, 1348
Baxter v. Palmigiano, 1096*n*
Bazemore v. Friday, 1192, 1349, 1429, 1431, 1432
Beal v. Doe, 1229, 1251, 1255
Beauharnais v. Illinois, 507, 526–527
Beck v. Ohio, 857*n*

Bellis v. United States, 1090
Bellotti v. Baird, 127*n*, 1255, 1256
Bell v. Maryland, 670, 1342
Bell v. Ohio, 1213
Bell v. Wolfish, 937
Benanti v. United States, 960*n*
Bennett v. Spear, 114
Bennis v. Michigan, 303, 365
Benton v. Maryland, 1139
Benyton v. Maryland, 315
Berea College v. Kentucky, 1394*n*
Berger v. State of New York, 958
Berkemer v. McCarty, 917
Berman v. Parker, 265*n*, 287, 291, 292
Bernal v. Fainter, 1567
Bethel School District No. 403 v. Fraser, 483, **495–499,** 639
Betts v. Brady, 376, 1092, 1093, 1099, 1101, 1102, 1103
Bigelow v. Virginia, 552, **559–563,** 565
Bishop v. Wood, 357
Bivens v. Six Unknown Federal Narcotics Agents, 1013
Blackburn v. State of Alabama, 1039
Blackledge v. Allison, 1113
Blakely v. Washington, 1122
Blockburger v. United States, 1140, 1141
Blum v. Yaretsky, 1346
Blyew v. United States, 1171*n*
Blystone v. Pennsylvania, 1214
BMW of North America v. Gore, 289, 363, 366, **369–374,** 1160
Board of Airport Commissioners of Los Angeles v. Jews for Jesus, Inc., 662
Board of Curators of University of Missouri v. Horowitz, 357
Board of Directors of Rotary International v. Rotary Club of Duarte, 671, 683, 685
Board of Education, Island Trees Union Free School District v. Pico, 482
Board of Education of City School v. Harris, 1433
Board of Education of Independent School District 92 of Pottawatomie City v. Earls, 928, 931, **950–954**
Board of Education of Kiryas Joel Village School District v. Grumet, 706, 716, **760–769,** 781
Board of Education of Oklahoma City Public Schools v. Dowell, 1390, 1391, 1392, 1427, 1434
Board of Education of Oklahoma City v. National Gay Task Force, 1291, 1292
Board of Education of the Westside Community Schools v. Mergens, 699, 712
Board of Education v. Allen, 736, 747
Board of Regents of the University of Wisconsin System v. Southworth, 707
Board of Trustees of the State University of New York v. Fox, 556

Bob Jones University and Goldsboro Christian School v. United States, 804, 1348, 1529

Boddie v. Connecticut, 1147

Bolger v. Youngs Drug Products Corp., 435, 471, 555

Bolling v. Sharpe, 1380, 1385, 1395, **1406– 1407,** 1414, 1473, 1475, 1505

Bond v. United States, 869, **886–888**

A Book Named "John Cleland's Memoirs of a Woman of Pleasure" v. Massachusetts, 432

Boos v. Barry, 656, 662

Booth v. Maryland, 1164, 1200, 1201, 1202, 1203, 1215

Bordenkircher v. Hayes, 1106, **1112–1115**

Bose Corporation v. Consumers Union, 533

Boston Beer Co. v. Massachusetts, 225n

Bouie v. City of Columbia, 1351n

Bounds v. Smith, 1147, 1148

Bowen v. Kendrick, 711–712, 757, 778, 779, 1230, 1257

Bowen v. Roy, 805

Bowers v. Hardwick, 180, 193, 208, 209, 210, 211, 213, 214, 687, 1268, 1287, 1288, 1290–1292, 1293, 1295, 1296, 1297, 1298, 1299, 1300, 1301, 1302, 1303, 1310, 1533, 1539, 1540, 1541

Boyde v. California, 1215

Boyd v. United States, 341, 954, 955, 957, 964, 979, 993, 995, 1088, 1223, 1245

Boykin v. Alabama, 1113

Boy Scouts of America v. Dale, 672, **679– 687,** 1304, 1533

Bradwell v. State of Illinois, 1497

Brady v. United States, 1106, 1113

Bram v. United States, 1072

Branch v. Texas, 1172–1183

Brandenburg v. Ohio, 404, 422, **423–426,** 512, 657, 1538, 1543

Branti v. Finkel, 669

Branzburg v. Hayes, 579, 595, **597–603**

Braswell v. United States, 1090

Braunfeld v. Brown, 799, 804, 807, 809, 818, 826

Braxton County Court v. West Virginia, 127n

Breard v. Alexandria, 481

Brecht v. Abrahamson, 1080

Breed v. Jones, 1035n

Breithaupt v. Abram, 1085

Brentwood Academy v. Tennessee Secondary School Athletic Association, 1347

Brewer v. Williams, 1000

Bridges v. California, 404n

Brotherhood of Railway Trainmen v. Virginia State Bar, 672n

Browder v. Gayle, 1342

Brown v. Allen, 175n

Brown v. Board of Education of Topeka, Kansas (Brown I), 34–35, 88, 129, 184, 187, 190, 512, 673, 791, 1263, 1264, 1270, 1330, 1341, 1380, 1384, 1385, 1386, 1387, 1388, 1389, 1390, 1391, 1392, **1395–1406,** 1408, 1411, 1412, 1414, 1416, 1417, 1418, 1420, 1423, 1425, 1428, 1431, 1491

Brown v. Board of Education of Topeka, Kansas (Brown II), 187, 190, 1380, 1385, **1407–1410,** 1425, 1428

Brown v. Louisiana, 639, 1382

Brown v. Mississippi, 313, 1027, 1072

Brown v. Socialist Workers 74 Campaign Committee, 672n

Brown v. State, 212

Brown v. United States, 960n, 1083

Bryant v. Zimmerman, 668

Buchanan v. Kentucky, 1123n

Buchanan v. Warley, 1350n, 1413

Buckley v. Valeo, 672n, 1475

Buck v. Bell, 259, 1226, **1236–1237**

Bullington v. Missouri, 1143n

Bullock v. Carter, 1556

Bunting v. Oregon, 260

Burch v. Louisiana, 1121, **1133–1135**

Burks v. United States, 1142n

Burlington Industries, Inc. v. Ellerth, 1532

Burnet v. Coronado Oil & Gas Co., 127n, 207, 1202, 1262

Burns v. Ohio, 1146

Burton v. Willimington Parking Authority, 1341

Butchers' Benevolent Association v. Cresent City Livestock Landing & Slaughterhouse Co., 253, **266–270;** *see also* Slaughterhouse Cases

Bute v. Illinois, 1095n

Butler v. Michigan, 437n, 477, 494

Butterworth v. Smith, 581

Caban v. Mohammed, 1502

Cabell v. Chavez-Salido, 383, 1564, 1567

Cain v. Kentucky, 433

Calderon v. Coleman, 1217

Calder v. Bull, 29, 88–92, 121

Califano v. Aznavorian, 1561

Califano v. Goldfarb, 1499n, 1502, 1519

Califano v. Webster, 1514, 1519, 1528

Califano v. Westcott, 1502

California Bankers Association v. Shultz, 873n, 929, 960n, 1090

California Federal Sav. & Loan Assn. v. Guerra, 1519, 1530

California v. Acevedo, 902, **911–916**

California v. Beheler, 1078

California v. Byers, 1025n, 1026n, 1090

California v. Carney, 900

California v. Ciraolo, 865, 887, 958, **969– 973,** 979, 981

California v. Greenwood, 216, 960n, 982

California v. Hodari D., 214–215, 866, 867, 868, 870

California v. LaRue, 435, 461, 569

California v. Prysock, 1056, 1059, 1078

California v. Ramos, 1201

Camara v. Municipal Court, 925, 928, 933

Cameron v. Johnson, 666n

Campbell v. Louisiana, 1120, 1348

Camp v. Board of Public Education, 672n

Canizio v. New York, 1095n

Cantrell v. Forest City Publishing Company, 531

Cantwell v. Connecticut, 314, 404n, 500, 688, 693, 810, 818, 823, 835

Capital Cities Cable, Inc. v. Crisp, 569, 608

Capitol Square Review Board v. Pinette, 707

Caplin & Drysdale v. United States, 1144

Cardwell v. Lewis, 903n

Carlisle v. United States, 379

Carroll v. United States, 897, 898, 901, 913, 914, 915, 919, 920, 934, 941, 942

Carter v. Jury Commission of Greene County, 1122n

Cash v. Culver, 1095n

Castaneda v. Partida, 1128

CBS, Inc. v. FCC, 608

Central Hudson Gas & Electric Corp. v. Public Service Commission of New York, 553, 554, 555, 556, 557, 558, 565, 566, 567, 568, 570, 571, 574, 575, 576, 577

Chae Chan Ping v. United States, 383

Chaffin v. Stynchcombem, 1143n

Chambers v. Maroney, 858n, 897, 898, 901, 903n, 913, 1108n

Chambers v. State of Florida, 1039

Chandler v. Florida, 634

Chandler v. Miller, 927, 930, 945

Chaplinsky v. State of New Hampshire, 417, 428, 439, 458, 486, 489, 491, 500, 512, 540, 550, 616

Chapman v. California, 1033, 1063, 1064

Chapman v. United States, 873n, 1062

Charles River Bridge Co. v. Warren Bridge Co., 224, **233–240,** 244

Chavez v. Martinez, 1026n, 1034, 1075, 1076

Cheff v. Schnackenberg, 1122n

Cherokee Nation v. Georgia, 149

Chevron v. Natural Resources Defense Council, 519

Chicago, Burlington & Quincy Railway Co. v. Chicago, 314

Chicago v. Morales, 367

Chief of the Capitol Police v. Jeanette Rankin Brigade, 662

Chimel v. California, 855, 856, **858–860**

Chisholm v. Georgia, 29, 184, 196

Church of Lukumi Babalu Aye, Inc. v. City of Hialeah, 802, 812, **825–832,** 833, 840, 842, 843, 1543–1544

Cincinnati v. Discovery Network, Inc., 566, 575, 576

City of Akron v. Akron Center for Reproductive Health, 1230–1232, 1256, 1261, 1265, 1267, 1272

City of Boerne v. Flores, 35, 196, 802, 805–806, **832–841,** 1066

City of Cleburne, Texas v. Cleburne Living Center, 1332, 1334, 1479, 1574, 1578

City of Dallas v. Stanglin, 671

City of El Paso v. Simmons, 225, **246–249,** 250

City of Erie v. Pap's A. M., 436, **459–465**

City of Houston, Texas v. Hill, 479

City of Ladue v. Gilleo, 557

City of Littleton v. Z. J. Gifts D-4, LLC., 437n

City of Los Angeles Department of Water & Power v. Manhart, 1530

City of Los Angeles v. Alameda Books, Inc., 436

City of Los Angeles v. Lyons, 112

City of Mesquite v. Aladdin's Castle, Inc., 1469

City of Newport, Kentucky v. Iacobucci, 437n

City of New York v. FCC, 608

City of Renton v. Playtime Theatres, Inc., 435

City of Richmond v. J. A. Croson, 1331, 1440, 1441, 1455, **1456–1468,** 1469, 1470, 1474, 1475, 1476, 1493

City of Seattle v. Mesiani, 216

Civil Rights Cases, 836, 837, 1339, 1342, 1343, 1345, **1363–1372,** 1382, 1536, 1539

Clark v. Community for Creative Non-Violence, 639

Clark v. Jeter, 1527, 1528

Cleveland Board of Education v. Loudermill, 357

Codd v. Velger, 357

Cohen v. California, 429n, 431, 480, 481, 482, **485–489,** 491, 493, 512, 1225n

Cohen v. Cowles Media Co., 596

Cohen v. Hurley, 341

Coker v. Georgia, 1194, 1207, 1208, 1210, 1212, 1213

Colautti v. Franklin, 1276

Colegrove v. Battin, 1120

Colegrove v. Green, 119, 146, 147, 148

Coleman v. Alabama, 208, 1094

Coleman v. Miller, 127n, 148, 149, 159, 160

Collins v. Harker Heights, 364, 376, 378, 379

Colonnade Catering Corporation v. United States, 928

Colorado v. Bertine, 903n

Colorado v. Connelly, 1079

Columbia Broadcasting System v. Democratic National Committee, 608

Columbus Board of Education v. Penick, 1433, 1465

Commercial Trust Co. v. Miller, 149

Committee for Public Education & Religious Liberty v. Nyquist, 206, 714, 761, 777, 789, 792

Committee for Public Education & Religious Liberty v. Regan, 704, 709n, 711

Committee to Defend Reproductive Rights v. Meyers, 217

Commonwealth of Kentucky v. Jeffrey Was-
son, 193, **208–212,** 214, 1287, **1292**
Commonwealth of Pennsylvania v. Matos, 214–
215
Commonwealth v. Bonadio, 214
Commonwealth v. Campbell, 210
Commonwealth v. Edmunds, 216
Commonwealth v. Labron, 213
Communist Party v. Subversive Activities Control
Board (SACB), 401, 403, 667–668
Connally v. General Construction Co., 1136
Connecticut Birth Control Cases, 120–122
Connecticut Department of Public Safety v. Doe,
368
Connelly v. Georgia, 853
Connick v. Myers, 672n
Consolidated Edison Company v. Public Service
Commission, 555
Coolidge v. New Hampshire, 853, 861, 862
Cooper Industries, Inc. v. Leatherman Tool Group,
367
Cooper v. Aaron, 35, 1380, 1385, **1410–**
1415
Cooper v. Oklahoma, 365–366
Coppage v. Kansas, 261, 263, 264, 286
Corfield v. Coryell, 121, 253
Corporation of Presiding Bishops of Church of
Jesus Christ of Latter-Day Saints v. Amos,
697, 754, 763
Cotting v. Godard, 265n
Couch v. United States, 873n, 1087
Counselman v. Hitchcock, 1025n, 1026n
County of Allegheny v. American Civil Liberties
Union, Greater Pittsburgh Chapter, 166,
700, 705, 712, 715, 751–752, 753
County of Riverside v. McLaughlin, 865,
894–896, 923
County of Sacramento v. Lewis, see Sacramento
County v. Lewis
Cousins v. Wigoda, 672n
Cox Broadcasting Corporation v. Cohn, 531,
532, **549–551,** 1287
Cox v. Louisiana, 662, 666n
Cox v. New Hampshire, 404n, 661
Craig v. Boren, 1330, 1499, **1509–1513,**
1514, 1516, 1526
Craig v. Harney, 404n, 634n
Crampton v. Ohio, 1162
Crawford v. Bd. of Education of the City of Los
Angeles, 1433
Crawford v. Washington, 1137
Crist v. Bretz, 1139
Crooker v. California, 1028
Crosby v. United States, 1135
Crowell v. Benson, 170
Cruzan by Cruzan v. Director, Missouri De-
partment of Health, 1288, **1305–1313,**
1315, 1317, 1320, 1321
Cruz v. Beto, 799
Culombe v. Connecticut, 1095n

Cummings v. Richmond County Board of Educa-
tion, 1382
Cupp v. Murphy, 1085
Curtis Publishing Company v. Butts, 528
Cusack v. Chicago, 265n

Dalia v. United States, 978
Dames & Moore v. Regan, 286
Dandridge v. Williams, 1548, 1577
Daniels v. Williams, 375
Darden v. Wainwright, 1120
Data Processing Service v. Camp, 127n
Davidson v. Cannon, 363n
Davidson v. New Orleans, 255
Davis v. Bandemer, 124
Davis v. Beason, 1538, 1543
Davis v. Davis, 217
Davis v. State of Texas, 216
Davis v. United States, 1080
Dayton Board of Education v. Brinkman, 1433
Dean v. Commonwealth, Ky., 211
Dean v. Gadsden Times Publishing Corporation,
264
Debs v. United States, 404n, 410
DeFunis v. Odegaard, 118, 1436, 1438, 1446
DeJonge v. Oregon, 314, 328, 668, 1327
Delaware v. Prouse, 898
De Meerleer v. Michigan, 1095n
Democratic Party of the United States v. Wiscon-
sin, 672n
Demore v. Kim, 368–369, 383
Dennis v. United States, 78, 381, 401, 402,
403, **412–423,** 425, 426
Denver Area Education Telecommunications Con-
sortium, Inc. v. Federal Communications
Commission, 482, 610
Department of Revenue of Montana v. Kurth
Ranch, 1142
Department of the Navy v. Egan, 935
Derricott v. Maryland, 216
DeShaney v. Winnebago County Department of
Social Services, 357–358, 520
Desist v. United States, 205
Detroit Bank v. United States, 1473
Detroit Edison Company v. National Labor Rela-
tions Board, 429n
Deutch v. United States, 403
Dickerson v. United States, 1034, **1064–**
1069, 1072, 1073, 1074, 1075, 1076
Dickey v. Florida, 1135
Dillingham v. United States, 1136n
Dixon v. Love, 357
Dodge v. United States, 1012
Doe v. Bolton, 1225n, 1228, 1255, 1276
Doe v. Commonwealth's Attorney for the City of
Richmond, 1290, 1291
Doe v. Director of Michigan Department of Social
Services, 217
Doe v. Maher, 217
Doe v. United States, 1090

Doggett v. United States, 1135

Dolan v. City of Tigard, 302–303

Donovan v. Dewey, 929

Doremus v. Board of Education, 141

Dothard v. Rawlinson, 1530

Douglas v. California, 1094, 1556

Douglas v. City of Jeanette, 404n, 810

Dow Chemical Company v. United States, 865, 979

Dowling v. United States, 1141

Doyle v. New York, 1035n

Draper v. United States, 857n

Dred Scott v. Sandford, 33, 37, 76, 184, 196, 252, 253, 254, 263, 1336, 1337, 1340, **1352–1363**

Dronenburg v. Zech, 1290

Duckworth v. Eagan, 1031, **1055–1060,** 1079

Dudgeon v. United Kingdom, 1298, 1299

Duke Power Co. v. Carolina Environmental Study Group, 127n

Dunaway v. New York, 858n, 922

Dun & Bradstreet, Inc. v. Greenmoss Builders, Inc., 507, 533

Duncan v. Louisiana, 315, 317, **347–353,** 1104, 1117, 1120, **1123,** 1131, 1132, 1134

Dunn v. Blumstein, 1560

Dusenbery v. United States, 367–368

Eakin v. Raub, 31, **56–59**

Earley v. DiCenso, 733–740

Eddings v. Oklahoma, 1164

Edenfield v. Fane, 556

Edgewood Independent School District v. Kirby, 217

Edmonson v. Leesville Concrete Co., 1119, 1346, 1348

Edwards v. Aguillard, 705, 715

Edwards v. Arizona, 1031, 1032, 1068, 1080

Edwards v. South Carolina, 662

EGALE Canada Inc. v. Attorney General of Canada, 1546

Egan v. Canada, 1545

Eisenstadt v. Baird, 122, 1227, 1228, 1245, 1247, 1295, 1316

Eisen v. Carlisle & Jacquelin, 117

Elk Grove Unified School District v. Newdow, 116, **161–169,** 708, **798**

Elkins v. United States, 987, 995, 996

Elrod v. Burns, 669

Employment Division, Department of Human Resources of Oregon v. Smith (Smith I), 214, 802, 805, 806, **816–824,** 826, 829, 830, 831, 832, 833, 838, 839, 840

Emspack v. United States, 1026n

Engel v. Vitale, 166, 188, 206, 699, 714, **723–727,** 744, 749, 750, 760, 809

Enmund v. Florida, 1207, 1209, 1213

Entrick v. Carrington, 955

Entsminger v. Iowa, 1108n

Epperson v. Arkansas, 701, 714

Equal Employment Opportunity Commission v. Arabian American Oil, 1567

Erie R. Co. v. Public Util. Comm'rs., 252

Erzoznik v. City of Jacksonville, 481, 482

Escobedo v. Illinois, 1026n, 1028, 1029, 1037, 1038, 1044, 1094

Estelle v. Gamble, 1155, 1156n

Estelle v. Williams, 1085

Estes v. Texas, 580n, 631, 633

Eubanks v. Louisiana, 1122n

Euclid v. Ambler Realty Co., see Village of Euclid v. Ambler Realty Co.

Evans v. Abney, 1345

Evans v. Newton, 1341, 1345

Evans v. Romer, 1535, 1536

Everson v. Board of Education of Ewing Township, New Jersey, 139, 206, 314, 693, 694, 697, 698, 704, 710, **716–723,** 736, 739, 744, 746, 747, 748, 774, 779, 793, 798, 843

Evitts v. Lucey, 1108

Ewing v. California, 1152, **1156–1161**

Ex parte Baez, 127n

Ex parte Endo, 381

Ex parte McCardle, 194, 195

Ex parte Milligan, 38n, 381, 1122n

Ex parte Quirin, 381, 385

Ex parte Virginia, 834, 1338, 1413

Ex parte Wilson, 1171n

Faragher v. City of Boca Raton, 1532

Faretta v. California, 1093

Fare v. Michael C., 218, 1029

Farmer v. Brennan, 1155

Farrington v. Tokushige, 1327

Fay v. New York, 1118, 1499n

Federal Communications Commission v. Beach Communications, 1576

Federal Communications Commission v. Midwest Video Corporation, 608

Federal Communications Commission v. National Citizens Committee, 608

Federal Communications Commission v. Pacifica Foundation, 429n, 468, 469, 470, 482, **489–494,** 608, **614,** 616, 617, 1225n, 1287

Federal Communications Commission v. WNCN Listeners Guild, 608

Feiner v. New York, 404n

Felker v. Turpin, 1172, 1216–1217

Fellers v. United States, 1032, 1095

Ferguson v. Charleston, 927, 931, **944–949**

Ferguson v. Skrupa, 263

Ferri v. Ackerman, 1108n

Fesch case, 1082

Fiallo v. Bell, 1563

Field v. Clark, 149

Fikes v. Alabama, 1034n
Firefighters Local Union No. 1784 v. Stotts, 1439, 1452–1453
First English Evangelical Lutheran Church v. County of Los Angeles, 287, 288, 302
First National Bank of Boston v. Bellotti, 555
Fisher v. Hunt, 1394n
Fisher v. United States, 1084, 1087, 1088
Fiske v. Kansas, 314
Fitzpatrick v. Bitzer, 834
Flast v. Cohen, 108, 111, **130–137,** 138, 139, 140, 141
Fletcher v. Peck, 222, **226–229,** 251
Flippo v. West Virginia, 856
Florida Bar v. Went For It, 557–558
The Florida Star v. B.J.F., 531, 828
Florida v. Bostick, 868, 869, 870
Florida v. J.L., 866
Florida v. Riley, 865, 887
Florida v. Rodriguez, 868, 883
Florida v. Royer, 873n, 883
Florida v. Wells, 903n
Florida v. White, 215, 902
Flower v. United States, 663
Foley v. Connelie, 383, 1564, 1566
Follett v. Town of McCormick, 404n, 818
Ford v. Wainwright, 1164, 1204, 1206, 1208, 1214
Forsyth County v. The Nationalist Movement, 660
44 Liquormart v. Rhode Island, 554, **564–572,** 577
Foucha v. Louisiana, 362, 364
Francis v. Resweber, 1150, 1170n, 1173, 1181
Franklin v. Gwinnett County Public Schools, 1531
Franks v. Delaware, 1005
Frank v. Maryland, 852n, 924, 925, 928
Frazee v. Illinois Department of Employment Security, 812
Freedman v. Maryland, 437n
Freeman v. Pitts, 1392, **1425–1428,** 1434
Friedman v. Rogers, 555
Friends of the Earth, Inc. v. Laidlaw Environmental Services, 114
Frontiero v. Richardson, 1330, 1498, **1505–1508,** 1509, 1511, 1518
Frothingham v. Mellon, 108, 131, 135, 136, 139
Frowerk v. United States, 404n
Fuller v. Oregon, 1147
Fullilove v. Klutznick, 1439, 1440, 1452, 1455, 1456, 1457, 1461, 1462, 1463, 1464, 1466, 1467, 1468, 1472, 1474, 1477, 1478, 1479, 1480, 1481, 1485
Furman v. Georgia, 1162, 1163, 1164, **1172–1183,** 1184, 1185, 1186, 1188, 1192, 1193, 1194, 1195, 1208

Gagnon v. Scarpelli, 1094, 1096n
Gallegos v. Colorado, 1034n

Gannett Co. v. DePasquale, 632, 633
Garber v. Kansas, 804
Garcia v. San Antonio Metropolitan Transit Authority, 180, 1203n
Gardner v. California, 1146
Gardner v. Florida, 1203
Gardson v. Broderick, 1026n
Garger v. New Jersey, 1306
Garner v. Louisiana, 637, 1351n
Garner v. United States, 1090
Garrison v. Louisiana, 579n
Garrity v. New Jersey, 1025
Gary v. Georgia, 216
Gayle v. Browder, 1342
Gebser v. Lago Vista Independent School District, 1531–1532
Geduldig v. Aiello, 1504
General Building Constructors Association, Inc. v. Pennsylvania, 1351n
General Electric Co. v. Gilbert, 1529
Georgia v. McCollum, 1119, 1120, 1348
German Alliance Insurance Co. v. Lewis, 265n
Gerstein v. Pugh, 865, 894–896
Gertz v. Robert Welch, Inc., 370, 507, 529–530, **540–546,** 548
Gherebi v. Bush, 384
Giboney v. Empire Storage Co., 339
Gibson v. Berryhill, 354–355
Gibson v. Florida Legislative Investigation Committee, 668
Gideon v. Wainwright, 196, 315, 1063, 1093, 1094, **1099–1103,** 1104, 1145
Gilbert v. California, 1085, 1094
Gilbert v. Minnesota, 311, 314, 404n, 1223
Gillette v. United States, 767, 804, 818, 827
Gilmer v. Interstate/Johnson Lane Corp., 1567
Ginsberg v. New York, 433, 468, 469, 472, 473, 477, 492, 617
Ginzburg v. United States, 433, 478, 624
Girouard v. United States, 811
Gitlow v. New York, 312, 314, 381, 399–400, 404n, **406–411,** 414, 425, 1327
Glickman v. Wileman Brothers & Elliott, Inc., 558, 559
Globe Newspaper Co. v. Superior Court for the County of Norfolk, 596, 633, **635–637**
Glona v. American Guarantee, 1562
Go-Bart Co. v. United States, 905
Godfrey v. Georgia, 1194, 1197, 1209
Godinez v. Moran, 1110
Goldberg v. Kelly, 354, 360
Goldman v. United States, 956, 957, 967, 979
Goldman v. Weinberger, 799, 804
Goldwater v. Carter, 123, **157–161**
Gomez v. Perez, 1562
Gomillion v. Lightfoot, 152
Gompers v. Buck's Stove & Range Co., 585
Gong Lum v. Rice, 1394n

Gooding v. Wilson, 484*n*

Good News Club v. Milford Central School, 699, 708, 713, 789

Goss v. Board of Education of City of Knoxville, 1394*n*

Goss v. Lopez, 355

Gould v. United States, 872

Grady v. Corbin, 1140, 1141, 1203

Graham v. Richardson, 383, 1564, 1565

Grand Rapids School District v. Ball, see School District of Grand Rapids v. Ball

Grannis v. Ordean, 362

Gratz v. Bollinger, 1331, 1441, **1483–1488,** 1493

Graves v. O'Keefe, 207

Gray v. Maryland, 1137

Gray v. Mississippi, 1203*n*

Greater New Orleans Broadcasting Association v. United States, 558

Great Northern Ry. v. Clara City, 409

Greenbelt Co-operative Publishing Association v. Bresler, 532*n,* 579*n*–580*n*

Greenholtz v. Inmates, 357

Green v. New Kent County School Board, 1382, 1391, 1394*n,* 1418, 1423, 1425, 1427, 1428, 1429, 1431, 1432, 1434

Green v. United States, 1139

Greer v. Spock, 429*n,* 663

Gregg v. Georgia, 1163, 1185, 1186, 1192, 1193, 1194, 1195, 1198, 1209, 1213

Gregory v. Ashcroft, 1565, 1568

Gregory v. Chicago, 666*n*

Griffin v. Breckenridge, 1351*n*

Griffin v. California, 1026*n*

Griffin v. County School Board of Prince Edward County, 1385, 1394*n*

Griffin v. Illinois, 1145, 1547, 1556

Griffin v. Wisconsin, 930, 939

Griffith v. Kentucky, 191, **204–206**

Griswold v. Connecticut, 93, 122, 192, 315, 316, 317, **336–347,** 354, 359, 376, 450, 672*n,* 1223, 1224, 1225, 1227, 1235, **1237,** 1243, 1245, 1285, 1295, 1302, 1305, 1316, 1321, 1335*n*

Groh v. Ramirez, 854

Grosjean v. American Press Co., 328, 397, 580, 1327

Grosso v. United States, 1086, 1089

Grove City College v. Bell, 1530

Grutter v. Bollinger, 1331, 1441, 1486, 1487, **1488–1497**

Gryczan v. Montana, 214

Guinn v. United States, 1350*n*

Gustafson v. Florida, 858*n,* 898

Gwaltney of Smithfield, Ltd. v. Chesapeake Bay Foundation, 142

H. L. v. Matheson, 1256

Hague v. Committee for Industrial Organization, 660, 662

Halpern v. Attorney General of Canada, 1546, 1547

Hamdi v. Rumsfeld, 385

Hamilton v. Alabama, 1094

Hamilton v. Kentucky Distilleries and Warehouse Co., 265*n*

Hamilton v. Regents of the University of California, 314, 328, 647, 804

Hampton v. Mow Sun Wong, 1566

Ham v. South Carolina, 1122*n*

Handbills Cases, 404*n,* 480, 484*n,* 579*n*

Hardy v. United States, 1146

Harmelin v. Michigan, 1152, 1157, 1159, 1160

Harper v. Virginia Board of Elections, 1552

Harris v. Forklift Systems, Inc., 1531

Harris v. McRae, 215, 219, 520, 1229, 1256

Harris v. New York, 1030, 1035*n,* 1075, 1077

Harris v. United States, 854, 855, 860, 903*n*

Harte-Hanks v. Connaughton, 533

Hartigan v. Zbaraz, 1233

"Hate-Speech" Cases, see R.A.V. v. City of St. Paul, Minnesota

Hawaii Housing Authority v. Midkiff, 287, **290–292**

Haynes v. United States, 1089

Haynes v. Washington, 1034*n,* 1044

Hazelwood School District v. Kuhlmeier, 484*n,* 595

Heart of Atlanta Motel v. United States, 671, 836, 1342, 1381

Heckler v. Mathews, 1526

Heffron v. International Society for Krishna Consciousness, 799, 804

Heller v. Doe, 1317, 1331, 1333, 1334, 1537, 1574, **1576–1579**

Heller v. New York, 437*n*

Helling v. McKinney, 1154

Helvering v. Hallock, 1202

Henderson v. Morgan, 1106

Hendricks v. Quebec, 1546

Henry v. United States, 960*n*

Hepburn v. Griswold, 255

Herbert v. Lando, 530

Hernandez v. Commissioner of Internal Revenue, 805

Hernandez v. Texas, 1122*n,* 1445

Herndon v. Lowry, 1327

Herrera v. Collins, 1216

Herring v. New York, 1096*n*

Hess v. Indiana, 491

Hester v. United States, 865, 968

Hicks v. Arizona, 176

Hiibel v. Sixth Judicial District of Nevada, 870, 1030, 1086

Hildwin v. Florida, 1214

Hills v. Gautreaux, 1344

Hill v. California, 856

Hill v. Colorado, 665

Hirabayashi v. United States, 1445, 1473, 1478

Hishon v. King & Spaulding, 1530

Hoag v. New York, 1143n
Hobbie v. Unemployment Appeals Commission of
 Florida, 811–812, 817, 819
Hodgson v. Minnesota, 1258
Hoffa v. United States, 960n
Hoffman v. United States, 1026n
Holden v. Hardy, 260, 276
Holland v. Illinois, 1119
Holt Civic Club v. Tuscaloosa, 1577
Holt v. United States, 1084
Home Building & Loan Association v. Blais-
 dell, 225, 240–246, 247
Honda Motor Co. v. Oberg, 365
Horton v. California, 855
Houchins v. KQED, Inc., 595, **603–606**
Hoyt v. Florida, 1498
Hoyt v. Minnesota, 433
Hudgens v. National Labor Relations Board, 664
Hudson v. Louisiana, 1142n
Hudson v. McMillian, 1153, 1154, 1155, 1156
Hudson v. North Carolina, 1095n
Hudson v. Palmer, 930
Hudson v. United States, 1140
Humphrey's Executor v. United States, 830
Hunter v. Erickson, 1341
Hunt v McNair, 711, 779
Hurley v. Irish-American Gay, Lesbian, and Bi-
 sexual Group of Boston, Inc., 665, 682,
 683, 686, 687, 1536
Hurtado v. California, 92, 311, 317, **321–**
 326, 327, 330, 375, 1116, **1117**
Hustler Magazine v. Falwell, 533
Hutchinson v. Proxmire, 527
Hutto v. Davis, 1152, 1156n, 1157
Hylton v. United States, 29

Ibanez v. Florida Department of Professional Reg-
 ulation, 557
ICC v. Brimson, 1026n
Idaho v. Wright, 1137, 1138
Illinois v. Allen, 634n
Illinois v. Batchelder, 865
Illinois v. Gates, 218, 854, 882, 883, 1004,
 1006, 1016
Illinois v. Krull, 213, 1016
Illinois v. Lidster, 900
Illinois v. McArthur, 871
Illinois v. Perkins, 1079
Illinois v. Rodriguez, 864
Illinois v. Somerville, 1142n
Illinois v. Wardlow, 868, **884–886**
Illinois v Krull, 941
Immigration and Naturalization Service v.
 Chadha, 36n
Immigration and Naturalization Service v. Del-
 gado, 869, 882
Indianapolis v. Edmond, 900, 908, 909, 910,
 946, 947
Indiana v. Gerschoffer, 212
Ingraham v. Wright, 357, 1035n, 1156n

Ingram v. Commonwealth, Ky., 211
In re: All Matters Submitted to the Foreign Intel-
 ligence Surveillance Court, 984
In re. Sealed Case, 985
In re Amendment to Rule 34, 1148
In re Application of Martha Angle Dorsett to Be
 Admitted to Practice as Attorney and Coun-
 selor at Law, 1522
In re Burrus, 163
In re Debs, 591
In re Gault, 1029, **1048–1051**
In re Griffiths, 1447, 1566
In re Kemmler, 1150, 1173, 1181
In re Oliver, 314
In re Pappas, 595, **597–603**
In re Primus, 552
In re Quinlan, 1306
In re T.W., 217
In re Winship, 1035n, 1308
In re Yamashita, 382
International Association of Machinists v. Street,
 672n
International Society for Krishna Consciousness v.
 Lee, 663
International Union, American Workers, Aerospace
 Agricultural Implement Workers of America
 UAW v. Johnson Controls, Inc., 1531
Iowa v. Gillespie, 213
Iowa v. Tovar, 1111
Irvine v. California, 121, 316
Irvin v. Dowd, 634n

Jackman v. Rosenbaum Co., 157
Jackson v. Denno, 1034n, 1062
Jackson v. Georgia, 1172–1183
Jackson v. Metropolitan Edison Co., 1346, 1347
Jacobellis v. Ohio, 431, 432, 452
Jacobson v. Massachusetts, 259, 276, 798, 1237,
 1307
Jaffree v. Board of School Commissioners of
 Mobile County, 193, **206–208**
James v. Illinois, 989, 1203n
James v. Valtierra, 1344
Jamison v. Texas, 810
Japan v. Nakaya, 846
J.E.B. v. Alabama ex rel. T.B., 1499, 1503, 1518
Jeffrey v. Black, 1081
Jenkins v. Georgia, 434
Jimenez v. Weinberger, 1562
Johnson v. California, 117
Johnson v. Eisentrager, 382, 384
Johnson v. Louisiana, 1121
Johnson v. Transportation Agency, Santa Clara
 California, 1439, 1454
Johnson v. United States, 873n, 933, 1006,
 1087
Johnson v. Zerbst, 1092
Jones v. Alfred H. Mayer Co., 1343, 1349
Jones v. North Carolina Prisoners' Labor Union
 Inc., 672n

Jones v. Opelika, 404n
Jones v. United States, 856, 857n, 873n, 960n, 974, 995, 1211
Joseph Burstyn, Inc. v. Wilson, 579n
Jurek v. Texas, 1213

Kahn v. Shevin, 1503, 1514
Kansas v. Crane, 368
Kansas v. Hendricks, 362, 366–367, 368
Kastigar v. United States, 1077, 1084
Katzenbach v. McClung, 1342, 1381
Katzenbach v. Morgan, 834
Katz v. United States, 84, 926, 957, 958, 959, **965–969**, 970, 971, 972, 974, 977, 979, 980, 981, 982, 1223, 1245
Keeney v. Tampayo-Reyes, 1110
Keeton v. Hustler Magazine, Inc., 532–533
Kelly v. Johnson, 1285
Kelly v. South Carolina, 1217
Kentucky v. Stincer, 1096n
Kentucky v. Wasson, 213
Ker v. California, 858n, 860
Keyes v. School District No. 1, Denver, Colorado, 1432
Keystone Bituminous Coal Association v. DeBenedictis, 302
Kimel v. Florida Board of Regents, 1568
Kingsley Books v. Brown, 437n
Kingsley International Corporation v. Regents of University of New York, 432
Kirby v. Illinois, 1096n
Kirchberg v. Fennstra, 1503
Kleindienst v. Mandel, 597n
Klopfer v. North Carolina, 315, 1135
Knight v. Florida, 98n
Knowles v. Iowa, 902, **916–918**
Korematsu v. United States, 381, 1328, 1329, 1445, 1447, 1473, 1478, 1552
Kovacs v. Cooper, 404n, 481
Kunz v. New York, 666n
Kurma v. The Queen, 1081
Kwong Hai Chew v. Colding, 382
Kyles v. Whitley, 1216
Kyllo v. United States, 958, **978–983**

Labine v. Vincent, 1562
Laird v. Tatum, 110, 670
Lalli v. Lalli, 1563
Lambert v. California, 1171n
Lamb's Chapel v. Center Moriches Union Free School District, 699, 708, 712, 771, 772, 774
Landmark Communications, Inc. v. Virginia, 429n, 581
Lane v. Brown, 1146
Lane v. Wilson, 1350n
Lankford v. Idaho, 1215
Larkin v. Grendel's Den, Inc., 435, 709n, 715, 761, 762, 763, 765, 766
Larson v. Valente, 167, 709n

Lassiter v. Northampton County Bd. of Elections, 834
Lathrop v. Donahue, 670
Lawrence v. Texas, 97, 369, 1225, 1287, **1293–1305**, 1331, 1533, **1545**
Leary v. United States, 1089
Leathers v. Medlock, 609
Lee v. Florida, 960n
Lee v. Illinois, 1136
Lee v. United States, 960n
Lee v. Washington, 1341
Lee v. Weisman, 165, 167, 168, 180, 705, 709, 715, 716, **749–756**, 759
Lefkowitz v. Cunningham, 1025n, 1026n
Lefkowitz v. Turley, 1026n
Legal Services Corporation v. Velazquez, 484
Legal Tender Cases, 296
Lego v. Twomey, 1077
Lehman v. Shaker Heights, 493, 663
Lehnhausen v. Lake Shore Auto Parts Co., 1576
Lemon v. Kurtzman, 703, 704, 705, 706, 714, 716, **733–740**, 741, 743, 747, 748, 749, 750, 751, 752, 756, 760, 765, 782, 784, 847
Leser v. Garnett, 91
Levitt v. Commission for Public Education and Religious Liberty, 714, 778
Levy v. Louisiana, 1548, 1562
Lewis v. Casey, 1148
Lewis v. New Orleans, 479
Lewis v. United States, 960n, 1117
Leyra v. Denno, 1034n
Lies v. Oregon, 437n
Life Imprisonment Case, 1221
Lincoln Federal Labor Union v. Northwestern Iron & Metal Co., 263, **285–286**, 339
Linda R. S. v. Richard D., 110
Linkletter v. Walker, 189, **200–204**, 987
Liverpool, N.Y. & P.S.S. Co. v. Emigration Commissioners, 169
Illinois v. Lidster, **908–910**
Lloyd Corporation v. Tanner, 664
Loan Association v. Topeka, 255
Local No. 93, International Association of Firefighters v. City of Cleveland, 1439, 1453–1454
Local 28 of the Sheet Metal Workers v. EEOC, 1439, 1453
Lochner v. New York, 256, 257, 258, 259, 262, 264, **273–278**, 279, 280, 281, 286, 337–338, 339, 347, 1224, 1226, 1250, 1263, 1270, 1286, 1444
Lockett v. Ohio, 1163, **1183–1189**, 1213
Locke v. Davey, 695, 696, 708, 802, **841–845**
Lockhart v. Fretwell, 1110
Lockhart v. Nelson, 1143n
Lo-Ji Sales v. New York, 858n, 1008
Long v. District Court of Iowa, 1146
Loretto v. Teleprompter Manhattan CATV Corporation, 287, 297, 299, 302

Lorillard Tobacco Co. v. Reilly, 554, 9, **572–578**

Los Angeles Police Department v. United Reporting Publishing Corporation, 558–559

Louisiana ex rel. Francis v. Resweber, 1150, 1170n, 1173, 1181

Louisiana v. United States, 1523

Louisville, New Orleans & Texas Pacific Railroad v. Mississippi, 1372

Lovell v. City of Griffin, 404n, 579n, 1327

Loving v. United States, 98n

Loving v. V, 1247

Loving v. Virginia, 211, 1227, 1245, 1316, 1343, 1382, 1445, 1447, 1483, 1519, 1534

Lucas v. South Carolina Coastal Council, 288, **296–301**

Lujan v. Defenders of Wildlife, 111, 113, **141–145,** 1470

Lujan v. National Wildlife Federation, 142

Lustig v. United States, 960n

Luther v. Borden, 119, 150, 151, 157

Lynch v. Donnelly, 704, 705, 711, 712, 715, 752

Lyng v. International Union, United Automobile, Aerospace and Agricultural Workers of America, 669

Lyng v. Northwest Indian Cemetery Protective Association, 799, 805, 819

M. v. H., 1546

Mackey v. United States, 205, 1026n

Madsen v. Women's Health Center, 664

Maher v. Roe, 519, 520, 1229, 1232, **1251–1254,** 1256, 1548

Maine v. Moulton, 1203n

Maine v. Taylor, 116

Mallard v. U.S. District Court, 1108

Mallory v. United States, 1028

Malloy v. Hogan, 315, 1027, 1072

Manual Enterprises, Inc. v. Day, 432

Mapp v. Ohio, 189, 200, 201, 202, 203, 204, 314, 316, 341, 860, 987, 988, 989, **990–998,** 1009, 1033, 1081

Marbury v. Madison, 31, 32, 34, 35, 37, **46–55,** 56, 119, 145, 342, 837, 1025n, 1067, 1182, 1413

Marchetti v. United States, 1087, 1089, 1090

Marino v. Ragen, 1095n

Marron v. United States, 873n

Marshall v. Barlow's, Inc., 926, 929

Marsh v. Alabama, 404n, 484n, 811

Marsh v. Chambers, 709n, 711, 743, 749, 753

Martin v. City of Struthers, 481, 597n, 810

Martin v. Mott, 149

Martin v. Wilks, 1454–1455

Maryland v. Buie, 855

Maryland v. Craig, 1137, 1138

Maryland v. Dyson, 902

Maryland v. Wilson, 898, 917

Mason v. United States, 1026n

Massachusetts Board of Retirement v. Murgia, 1565

Massachusetts v. Mellon, 156

Massachusetts v. Sheppard, 216, 989, 1004

Massachusetts v. Upton, 854

Massey v. Moorer, 1095n

Massiah v. United States, 1028, 1094

Mason v. The New Yorker Magazine, 530, **546–549**

Mathews v. Diaz, 383, 1566

Mathews v. Elridge, 356, 357

Mathews v. Lucas, 1563

Matthews v. Lucas, 1548

Mattox v. United States, 309

Maxwell v. Bishop, 1120

Maxwell v. Dow, 31

Mayer v. City of Chicago, 1147

McCarthy v. Arndstein, 1026n

McCarthy v. United States, 1109

McCarver v. North Carolina, 1212

McCleskey v. Kemp, 1163, **1189–1200,** 1201, 1214

McCleskey v. Zant, 1166, 1172, 1215

McCollum v. Board of Education, 692, 713, 739, 746

McCray v. Illinois, 857n

McCulloch v. Maryland, 28, 32, 39n, 95, 243, 376

McDaniel v. Paty, 762, 766, 798, 811

McDonald v. Santa Fe Trail Transportation Co., 1445

McGautha v. California, 1162, 1181, 1184, 1188

McGowan v. State of Maryland, 98n, 699, 739, 804

McIntyre v. Ohio Elections Commission, 83, 98n

McKaskle v. Wiggins, 1063, 1095n

McKoy v. North Carolina, 1215

McKune v. Lile, 1084

McLaughlin v. Florida, 1177, 1343, 1447

McLaurin v. Oklahoma State Regents, 1380, 1383, 1384, 1398, 1447

McMann v. Richardson, 1106, 1109

McNeil v. Wisconsin, 1031, 1032, 1079, 1095

Meachum v. Fano, 357

Meek v. Pittenger, 708, 711, 713, 714, 758, 759, 777, 782

Meese v. Keene, 594

Memoirs v. Massachusetts, 446, 452

Memorial Hospital v. Maricopa County, 1560

Mempa v. Rhay, 1094

Memphis Light, Gas & Water Division v. Craft, 357

Meritor Savings Bank, FBD v. Vinson, 1499, 1530–1531

Metro Broadcasting, Inc. v. Federal Communications Commission, 1203, 1440, 1455, 1472, 1475, 1476, 1479, 1480, 1481

Metropolitan County Board of Education of Nashville v. Kelley, 1388

Meyer v. State of Nebraska, 340, 651, 1226, 1245, 1247, 1285, 1295, 1316, 1327

Miami Herald Publishing Co. v. Tornillo, 491, 607

Michael H. v. Gerald D., 358–362, 1268, 1310, 1527, 1564

Michael M. v. Superior Court of Sonoma County, 1330, 1499, **1513–1517**

Michigan Department of State Police v. Sitz, 215, 898, 900, 909, 939, 942

Michigan Organization for Human Rights v. Kelley, 213

Michigan v. Clifford, 929

Michigan v. Harvey, 1031

Michigan v. Long, 219, 889, 890, 903n, 917

Michigan v. Lucas, 1138

Michigan v. Mosley, 1030, 1035n, 1068, 1078

Michigan v. Tucker, 1030, 1035n, 1056, 1066, 1069, 1074, 1075, 1077

Michigan v. Tyler, 927

Mickens v. Taylor, 1111

Milkovich v. Lorain Journal Co., 529, 533

Miller-El v. Cockrell, 1218

Miller v. Albright, 1504, 1564

Miller v. California, 433, 434, 435, **444–449,** 452, 456, 474, 475, 476, 477, 478, 506, 621

Milliken v. Bradley, 1388, 1393, **1421–1424,** 1523

Mills v. Alabama, 581

Mills v. Maryland, 1204

Mills v. Rogers, 1311

Mincey v. Arizona, 856

Minersville School District v. Gobitis, 404n, 641, 642, 643, 644, 645, 804, 818

Minneapolis Star and Tribune v. Minneapolis Commissioner of Revenue, 580

Minnesota State Board for Community Colleges v. Knight, 672n

Minnesota v. Carter, 864, 958, **973–977**

Minnesota v. Dickerson, 869, 870, **888–892**

Minnesota v. Hershberger, 805

Minnesota v. Murphy, 1078

Minnesota v. Olson, 974

Minnick v. Mississippi, 1031

Minor v. Happersett, 1497

Minor v. United States, 1089

Miranda v. Arizona, 189, 195, 196, 947, 1019, 1026n, 1029, 1030, 1031, 1032, 1033, 1034, **1035–1048,** 1051, 1052, 1053, 1054, 1055, 1056, 1057, 1058, 1059, 1060, 1062, 1064, 1065, 1066, 1067, 1068, 1069, 1070, 1071, 1073, 1074, 1075, 1076, 1077, 1078, 1079, 1080, 1081, 1082, 1094, 1095

Mississippi University for Women v. Hogan, 1499n, 1503, 1518, 1519, 1521, 1522, 1523, 1526

Missouri ex rel. Gaines v. Canada, 1350n, 1377, 1383

Missouri Pacific Railway Co. v. Nebraska, 292, 314

Missouri v. Holland, 87, 243

Missouri v. Hunter, 1143n

Missouri v. Jenkins (Jenkins I), 1390, 1393, 1433

Missouri v. Jenkins (Jenkins II), 1434

Missouri v. Seibert, 1034, **1070–1074,** 1077

Mitchell v. Helms, 695, 708, 713, 714, 788, 794

Mitchell v. United States, 1066

M.L.B. v. S.L.J., 1561

Moe v. Secretary of Administration, 217

Monitor Patriot Co. v. Roy, 532n

Monroe v. Board of Commissioners of the City of Jackson, Texas, 1394n

Montana v. Bullock and Peterson, 215

Montana v. Egelhoff, 366

Montana v. Johnson, 218

Montana v. Solis, 218

Moore v. East Cleveland, 362, 1285, 1286, 1287

Moore v. Illinois, 1096n

Moore v. Michigan, 1095n

Moose Lodge No. 107 v. Irvis, 1345

Moragne v. States Marine Lines, 1202

Morehead v. New York ex re. Tipaldo, 262, 282

Morey v. Doud, 1328

Morgan v. Devine, 1142n

Morgan v. Illinois, 1120, 1164, **1204–1206,** 1215–1216

Morrison v. Olson, 83

Morrissey v. Brewer, 354, 366

Morris v. Slappy, 1108n

Mueller v. Allen, 711, 743, 757, 758, 788, 789, 842

Mugler v. Kansas, 258, 297, 409, 1444

Muller v. Oregon, 72, 97, 260, 262, **279–281,** 1498

Mu'Min v. Virginia, 634

Munn v. Illinois, 255, **270–273,** 1369

Murdock v. Commonwealth of Pennsylvania, 404n, 810, 812, 818

Murphy v. Ramsey, 1544

Murphy v. Waterfront Commission of New York Harbor, 1020, 1084

Murray's Lessee v. Hoboken Land & Improvement Company, 254, 323, 325

Murray v. Curlett, 206, 714, **727–733**

Murray v. Giarratano, 1148

Muskrat v. United States, 127n

NAACP v. Alabama, 314, 338, 340, 341, 667, 668, 670, **673–676,** 1223, 1381

NAACP v. Button, 668, 672n

Nardone v. United States, 960n

Nashville Gas Co. v. Satty, 1530

National Collegiate Athletic Association (NCAA) v. Tarkanian, 1346

National Endowment for the Arts v. Finley, 436, 484, 628

National Family Planning and Reproductive Health Association, Inc. v. Sullivan, 518

National Labor Relations Board v. Jones & Laughlin Steel Corporation, 263

National Prohibition Cases, 90

National Treasury Employees Union v. Von Raab, 927, 930, **931–938**, 939, 945, 950

Near v. Minnesota ex rel. Olson, 314, 328, 580, 582, **583–586**, 587, 589, 1327

Nebbia v. New York, 286, 1444

Nebraska Press Association v. Stuart, 429n, 632, 636

Negre v. Larsen, 804

New Jersey v. Hemple and Hemple, 216

New Jersey v. Portash, 1075

New Jersey v. T.L.O., 926, 930, 933, 939, 942, 950, 954

New Jersey v. Wilson, 222

New Jersey Welfare Rights Organization v. Cahill, 1562

New State Ice Co. v. Liebmann, 353

New York Central R. Co. v. White, 225n

New York State Club Association, Inc. v. City of New York, 671, 680, 683, 685

New York State Liquor Authority v. Bellanca, 437n

New York Times Company v. Sullivan, 43, 380, 507, 526, 527–528, **534–539**, 540, 542, 544, 545, 547, 548, 552, 561, 563, 579n, 1381

New York Times Company v. United States, 197, 578, 582, **586–594**

New York v. Belton, 902, 903n, 917

New York v. Burger, 926, 930, 974

New York v. Cathedral Academy, 714

New York v. Class, 900

New York v. Ferber, 435, **455–459**, 474, 477, 478, 617

New York v. P. J. Video, Inc., 218

New York v. Quarles, 1056, 1066, 1069

Niemotko v. Maryland, 404n, 501, 666n, 811

Nixon v. Condon, 1327

Nixon v. Herndon, 1327

Nixon v. United States, 124

Nix v. Whiteside, 1108n

Nix v. Williams, 989, **998–1003**

Nollan v. California Coastal Commission, 286, 288, **293–296**

Nordlinger v. Hahn, 1328, 1329

Norris v. Alabama, 313, 1118, 1122

Norris v. Clymer, 56

North Carolina Board of Education v. Swann, 1432

North Carolina v. Alford, 1108n, 1109

North Carolina v. Butler, 1078

North Carolina v. Pierce, 1143n

Northeastern Florida Chapter of the Associated General Contractors of America v.

City of Jacksonville, Florida, 111, 113, 1440, 1455, **1468–1471**

Northern Pipe Line Construction Co. v. Marathon Pipe Line Co., 38n

Northern Securities Co. v. United States, 276, 416

Nyquist v. Mauclet, 1566

O'Connor v. Consolidated Coin Caterers, 1568

O'Connor v. Donaldson, 355–356, 1035n

O'Connor v. Ortega, 927, 930, 933, 934, 975

O'Donoghue v. United States, 38n

Ogden v. Saunders, 222, 241, 244

Ohio ex. rel. Eaton v. Price, 928

Ohio v. Akron Center for Reproductive Health, 1271

Ohio v. Roberts, 1137

Ohio v. Robinette, 869, 898

Ohralik v. Ohio State Bar Association, 553

Oklahoma Press Publishing Company v. District Court, 634n

Oklahoma v. Castleberry, 911, 915

Old Dominion Co. v. United States, 292

Olden v. Kentucky, 1137

Oliver v. United States, 865, 970

Olmstead v. United States, 83, 956, 957, **961–965**, 967, 979, 1222, 1245

O'Lone v. Shabazz, 799, 805

Olsen v. Nebraska, 265n, 339

Oncale v. Sundowner Offshore Services, 1531

O'Neil v. Vermont, 1150, 1175

Oregon v. Bradshaw, 1078

Oregon v. Elstad, 1069, 1071, 1073, 1074, 1077, 1079

Oregon v. Hass, 1030, 1035n, 1069, 1077

Oregon v. Kennedy, 1142n

Oregon v. Mathiason, 1035n, 1078

Oregon v. Mitchell, 196, 835

Oregon v. Washington, 1142n

Organization for a Better Austin v. Keefe, 587

Orozco v. Texas, 1094

Orr v. Orr, 1499n, 1502

Ortwein v. Schwab, 1147

Osborne v. Ohio, 435

Osborn v. United States, 960n

Otis v. Parker, 276

Overton v. Bazetta, 369

Pacific Gas & Electric v. Public Utilities Commission of California, 555

Pacific Mutual Life Insurance Company v. Haslip, 364, 365, 373

Packer Corporation v. Utah, 265n, 480

Palazzolo v. Rhode Island, 115

Palko v. Connecticut, 313, 317, **326–329,** 330, 335, 344, 352, 994, 1139, 1245, 1317, 1322

Palmer v. Thompson, 1345

Palmore v. Sidoti, 819, 1492

Papish v. Board of Curators, 484n

Parham v. Hughes, 1514, 1563
Parham v. J.R., 363n, 1035n
Paris Adult Theatre I v. Slaton, 434, **449–455**
Parker v. Gladden, 315
Parker v. North Carolina, 1077
Parke v. Raley, 1110
Parratt v. Taylor, 363n
Parrish v. West Coast Hotel Co., 282
Pasadena City Board of Education v. Spangler, 1426, 1433
Passenger Cases, 1550
Patterson v. Colorado, 406, 580
Patterson v. McLean Credit Union, 1203, 1350
Patton v. United States, 1122n
Pauley v. Kelly, 217
Paul v. Davis, 111, 364, 923, 1289n
Paxton's Case, 851
Payne v. Arizona, 1034n
Payne v. Arkansas, 1062
Payne v. Tennessee, 125, 129, 1164, **1200–1204,** 1215, 1299
Payton v. New York, 855, 873n, 922, 980, 981
Peel v. Attorney Registration and Disciplinary Commission of Illinois, 556, 1203n
Pell v. Procunier, 180, 429n, 595, 605
Penn Central Transportation Co. v. New York, 288, 293, 297
Pennekamp v. Florida, 404n, 634n
Pennell v. City of San Jose, 302
Pennsylvania Board of Probation and Parole v. Scott, 989
Pennsylvania Coal Co. v. Mahon, 287, 296, 298
Pennsylvania ex rel. Sullivan v. Ashe, 1184
Pennsylvania State Police v. Suders, 1532–1533
Pennsylvania v. Burder, 1079
Pennsylvania v. Finley, 1095, 1148
Pennsylvania v. Labron, 213
Pennsylvania v. Mimms, 898, 917, 922
Pennsylvania v. Muniz, 1085–1086
Penry v. Lynaugh, 1164, 1206, 1207, 1208, 1214, 1578
Pensacola Telegraph Co. v. Western Union Telegraph, 87
Penson v. Ohio, 1096n
People of California v. Krivda, 216
People v. Bigelow, 216
People v. Croswell, 392
People v. Defore, 996
People v. Fries, 1289n
People v. Long, 219
People v. Onofre, 214
People v. P. J. Video, Inc., 218
People v. Sundling, 216
Permoli v. New Orleans, 309
Personnel Administrator of Massachusetts v. Feeney, 1478, 1504, 1526
Peters v. Kiff, 1128
Philadelphia Newspapers, Inc. v. Hepps, 530, 533
Phillips v. Washington Legal Foundation, 303

Pierce v. Society of Sisters, 108, 340, 818, 1226, 1245, 1247, 1285, 1295, 1316, 1327
Pierce v. United States, 404n
Pinkus v. United States, 434
Pittsburgh Press v. Pittsburgh Commission on Human Rights, 552, 561
Planned Parenthood Association of Kansas City, Missouri v. Ashcroft, 1232, 1257
Planned Parenthood of Central Missouri v. Danforth, 1255, 1268
Planned Parenthood of Southeastern Pennsylvania v. Casey, 126, 129, 187, 217, 1234, 1258, **1259–1272,** 1273, 1275, 1279, 1280, 1281, 1297, 1298, 1299, 1300, 1301, 1315, 1321, 1476
Plessy v. Ferguson, 183–184, 1119, 1263, 1264, 1336, 1340, 1341, 1342, **1372–1376,** 1382, 1398, 1399, 1436, 1444, 1482, 1536
Plyler v. Doe, 382, 1330, 1491, 1565, **1569–1575**
Poelker v. Doe, 1229, 1256
Poe v. Ullman, 120, 132, 339, 340, 344, 1321, 1322, 1323
Pointer v. Texas, 315, 341, 1136
Poland v. Arizona, 1141
Police Department of City of Chicago v. Mosley, 662
Pollock v. Farmers' Loan and Trust Company, 196, 1446
Pope v. Illinois, 434
Posadas de Puerto Rico v. Tourism Company of Puerto Rico, 553, 554, 555–556, 567, 568, 571
Poulos v. New Hampshire, 666n
Powell v. Alabama, 312, 313, 314, 328, 329, 343, 1092, 1093, **1096–1099,** 1101, 1103, 1104, 1379
Powell v. McCormack, 35
Powell v. State of Georgia, 213
Powell v. Texas, 1152
Powers v. Ohio, 1119, 1347
Press-Enterprise Co. v. Superior Court of California, 633
Presser v. Illinois, 353
Preston v. United States, 903n
Prigg v. Pennsylvania, 1337
Prince v. Massachusetts, 804, 818, 1245
Printz v. United States, 97
Procunier v. Martinez, 597n
Profflitt v. Florida, 1213
Prudential Insurance Company v. Cheek, 309
Prune Yard Shopping Center v. Robins, 664
Public Utilities Commission v. Pollak, 481
Pulley v. Harris, 1194, 1214
Pulliam v. Allen, 1203n

A Quantity of Copies of Books v. Kansas, 437n
Quilloin v. Walcott, 1563

Quinn v. Millsap, 1141
Quinn v. United States, 1026n

Rabe v. Washington, 437n
Raines v. Byrd, 114
Rakas v. Illinois, 215, 960n, 974, 976, 979
Rankin v. McPherson, 480, 1203n
Rasul v. Bush, 384
R.A.V. v. City of St. Paul, Minnesota (Hate-Speech Case), 429, 483, **499–507**, 508, 509, 512, 513, 514, 516, 517, 527, 622, 771
Red Lion Broadcasting Co. v. Federal Communications Commission, 491, 580n, 607, **612–614**
Redrup v. New York, 447
Reed v. Campbell, 1563
Reed v. Reed, 1498, 1501, 1506, 1508, 1509, 1510, 1511, 1514, 1518, 1522
Reeves v. Sanderson Plumbing Products, 1568
Regan v. New York, 1026n
Regan v. Taxation with Representation of Wash., 772
Regents of the University of California v. Bakke, 118, 1331, 1435, 1438, 1440, **1442–1451**, 1454, 1459, 1470, 1471, 1473, 1474, 1485, 1488, 1489, 1490, 1492, 1493
Regina v. Butler, 525–526
Regina v. Hicklin, 431, 432, 439
Regina v. Keegstra, 523–525
Regina v. Rennie, 1081
Regina v. Sang, 1081
Reid v. Covert, 382
Reitman v. Mulkey, 1350n
Renne v. Geary, 113
Reno v. American Civil Liberties Union, 436, **465–473**, 611, **620**, 629
Reno v. FlFs, 364
Reno v. Flores, 1317
Renton v. Playtime Theatres, Inc., 460, 461, 464, 468, 469, 501
Reynolds v. United States, 745, 798, 800, 803, 818, 819, 831
Rhode Island v. Innis, 1031, **1051–1055**, 1056, 1078
Richardson v. Wright, 354
Richards v. Wisconsin, 871
Richmond Newspapers, Inc. v. Virginia, 633, 635, 636, 662
Ricketts v. Adamson, 1109
Rick Sitz v. Michigan Department of State Police, 215–216
Rideau v. Louisiana, 634n
Right to Choose v. Byrne, 217, 219
Rinaldi v. Yeager, 1514
Ring v. Arizona, 1217–1218
Rios v. United States, 960n
Ristanino v. Ross, 1122n
Riverside v. McLaughlin, 215

Roaden v. Kentucky, 437n
Robbins v. California, 901, 902
Robertson v. Baldwin, 425
Roberts v. LaVallee, 1146
Roberts v. Louisiana, 1163, 1213
Roberts v. United States Jaycees, 508, 671, **676–679**, 680, 683, 685, 1289n
Robinson v. Cahill, 217
Robinson v. California, 315, 1152, 1171n, 1173, 1175, 1293
Robinson v. DiCenso, 733–740
Rochin v. California, 93, 315, 316, **334–337**, 363, 376, 377, 905, 990n, 1316, 1322
Rock v. Arkansas, 1203n
Roemer v. Maryland Public Works Board, 711, 779
Roe v. Flores-Ortega, 1110
Roe v. Wade, 35, 118, 126, 217, 520, 1225, 1228, 1229, 1230, 1231, 1232, 1233, 1234, **1237–1251**, 1252, 1253, 1254, 1255, 1259, 1260, 1261–1262, 1263, 1264, 1265, 1266, 1267, 1268, 1269, 1270, 1271, 1272, 1273, 1275, 1279, 1281, 1285, 1295, 1300, 1301, 1302
Rogers v. Richmond, 98n
Rogers v. United States, 1026n
Romer v. Evans, 845, 1298, 1314, 1331, 1334, **1534–1545**
Rosales-Lopez v. United States, 1122n
Rosenberger v. The Rector and Visitors of the University of Virginia ("Wide Awake" case), 484, 706, 708, 712, **769–780**, 785, 788
Rosenblatt v. Baer, 528, 541
Rosenbloom v. Metromedia, Inc., 532n, 544, 545
Rose v. Clark, 1062
Rose v. Council for Better Educ., Inc., Ky., 211
Ross v. Moffitt, 1095, 1147
Ross v. Oklahoma, 634, 1205
Rostker v. Goldberg, 1504
Roth v. United States, 432, 433, **438–442**, 444, 445, 447, 448, 452, 454, 486, 491, 494, 503, 579n
Rowan v. U.S. Post Office Department, 435, 487, 492
Rubin v. Coors Brewing Co., 557, 568, 569
Rudolph v. Alabama, 98, **1168–1172**, 1181
Rummel v. Estelle, 1109, 1152, 1157, 1158
Rumsfeld v. Padilla, 385
Rundlett v. Oliver, 1515
Runyon v. McCrary, 1349, 1350, 1445
Rust v. Sullivan, 436, 484, **517–522**, 772, 1234, **1258**
Rutan v. Republican Party of Illinois, 670, 1203n, 1528
Rutherford v. United States, 1288n

Sable Communications v. Federal Communications Commission, 470, 482, 819

Sacramento County v. Lewis, 363, 367, **374–379**

Saenz v. Roe, 1548, 1561

Sanabria v. United States, 1142n

San Antonio Independent School District v. Rodriguez, 211, 217, 1331, 1548, **1553–1560,** 1569, 1570, 1573, 1574

San Diego Gas & Electric Co. v. San Diego, 297

Sandin v. Conner, 365

San Francisco Arts & Athletics, Inc. (SFAA) v. United States Olympics Committee (USOC), 1346

Santa Clara County v. Southern Pacific Railroad Company, 255, 256

Santa Fe Independent School District v. Doe, 705, 716

Santobello v. New York, 1109, 1113

Sawyer v. Whitley, 1216

Saxbe v. Washington Post, 180, 595, 605

Scales v. United States, 403

Schad v. Borough of Mount Ephraim, 435

Schaefer v. United States, 404n

Schall v. Martin, 1029

Schenck v. Pro-Choice Network of Western New York, 665

Schenck v. United States, 380, 399, **405–406,** 410, 412, 414, 416, 425

Schilb v. Kuebel, 1147

Schlesinger v. Ballard, 1503, 1509, 1514

Schlesinger v. Reservists Committee to Stop the War, 112, 138, 141

Schlup v. Delo, 1216

Schmerber v. State of California, 1084, 1085, 1088

Schneckloth v. Bustamonte, 864

Schneider v. New Jersey (Handbills Cases), 404n, 480, 484n, 579n

Schneider v. Rusk, 1505n

School District of Grand Rapids v. Ball, 707, 713, 715, 758, 759, 777, 782, 783, 785, 786

Schriro v. Summerlin, 1218

Schwartz v. Texas, 960n

Scottsboro Boys Case, 312, 313, 1092, 1093

Scottsboro Case II (Norris v. Alabama), 313, 1118, 1122

Scott v. Illinois, 1094, 1095

Scott v. United States, 978

Seattle School Dist. No. 1 v. State, 217

Seattle Times Co. v. Rhinehart, 634n

Secretary of Public Welfare v. Institutionalized Juveniles, 1035n

See v. City of Seattle, 925, 927

Segura v. United States, 989

Self-Defense Forces Enshrinement Case, 845–849

Sell v. United States, 369

Serrano v. Priest, 217

Shaare Tefila Congregation v. Cobb, 1351n

Shadler v. Florida, 213

Shadwick v. City of Tampa, 857n

Shafer v. South Carolina, 1217

Shapero v. Kentucky Bar Association, 553

Shapiro v. Thompson, 1330, 1335n, 1548, **1549–1553,** 1558

Shapiro v. United States, 1086, 1089

Shaughnesy v. United States ex rel Mezei, 383

Shaw v. Hunt, 1491

Sheff v. O'Neill, 214

Sheldon v. Tucker, 667

Shelley v. Kraemer, 1340, 1341, **1377–1379,** 1380, 1383, 1444, 1538

Sheppard v. Maxwell, 631, 633

Sherbert v. Verner, 754, 799, 802, 805, **806–810,** 811, 816, 817, 819, 831, 833, 834, 843

Sibron v. New York, 866, 889

Sierra Club v. Morton, 110, 142

Sigert v. Gilley, 364

Silverman v. United States, 857, 956, 958, 979, 980

Silverthorne Lumber Co. v. United States, 960n, 995, 1001

Simon & Schuster Inc. v. Members of the New York State Crime Victims Board, 501, 580, 581, 771

Simon v. Eastern Kentucky Welfare Rights Organization, 112, 143, 1470

Simopoulos v. Virginia, 1232, 1257

Singer v. United States, 631, 1122n

Skinner v. Oklahoma ex rel. Williamson, 1226, 1245, 1247, 1285, 1311, 1316, 1327, 1444, 1538

Skinner v. Railway Labor Executives' Association, 927, 930, 936, 937, 939, 945, 950

Slaughterhouse Cases, 253, 254, **266–270,** 310, 311, **321,** 1338, 1444, 1445

Sloan v. Lemon, 714

Slochower v. Board of Education, 1026n

Smith v. Collin, 527

Smith v. Daily Mail Publishing Company, 581

Smith v. Fair Employment and Housing Commission, 214

Smith v. Grogen, 640, 654

Smith v. Illinois, 1139n

Smith v. Maryland, 978, 982

Smith v. Texas, 1118, 1413

Snepp v. United States, 594

Snider v. Cunningham, 1169

Snyder v. Com. of Massachusetts, 343, 359, 1316–1317, 1322

Soldal v. Cook County, 857

Solem v. Helm, 1152, 1157, 1159, 1160, 1161

Sosna v. Iowa, 1560

South Carolina v. Gathers, 1164, 1200, 1201, 1202, 1203, 1215

South Carolina v. Katzenbach, 834, 835, 837, 1343

South Dakota v. Dole, 628

South Dakota v. Neville, 218

South Dakota v. Opperman, 858n, 903n

Southeastern Promotions, Ltd. v. Conrad, 437n, 582, 662

Southern Pacific Co. v. Jensen, 75n

Southwest Case, 89, 92n

Spano v. New York, 1028

Spavack v. Klein, 1026n

Spaziano v. Florida, 1205

Speiser v. Randall, 520

Spence v. Washington, 640, 654

Spinelli v. United States, 857n, 1004

Spiuel v. Oklahoma, 1394n

St. Amant v. Thompson, 528

St. Francis College v. Al-Khazraji, 1351n

Stanford v. Kentucky, 1164, 1212, 1214

Stanley v. Georgia, 433, 434, **442–444,** 450, 454, 1223, 1245, 1247

Stanley v. Illinois, 1508

Stansbury v. California, 1080

Stanton v. Stanton, 1502, 1514

State Farm Mutual Automobile Insurance v. Campbell, 368

State of Rhode Island v. Palmer, 90

State Tax Commission of Utah v. Aldrich, 98n

State v. Alosa, 215

State v. Alston, 215

State v. Carter, 216

State v. Cline, 213

State v. Cogshell, 213

State v. Marsala, 216

State v. Novembrino, 216

State v. Oakes, 216

State v. Tanaka, 216

State v. Van Hyem, 218

State v. White, 215

The State v. T. Makwanyane and M. Mchunu, 1218–1221

Steagald v. United States, 855

Stenberg v. Carhart, 1235, **1272–1281**

Stoner v. California, 873n, 960n

Stone v. Graham, 700, 704, 709n, 714

Stone v. Mississippi, 224

Stone v. Powell, 988, 1005, 1008, 1012, 1033, 1058, 1059

"Stop and Frisk" cases, 873–879

Strader v. Graham, 1337

Strauder v. West Virginia, 1124, 1126, 1338, 1445

Street v. New York, 640, 656

Strickland v. Washington, 1107, 1110, 1111, 1166

Stromberg v. California, 638, 643, 654, 1327

Stuart v. Laird, 194

Sturges v. Crowninshield, 68, 222

Sugerman v. Dougall, 1566

Sullivan v. Louisiana, 1121

Sumner v. Shuman, 1214

Supreme Court of New Hampshire v. Piper, 1561

Supreme Court of Virginia v. Friedman, 1561

Swaggart v. Board of Equalization of California, 805

Swain v. Alabama, 1124

Swann v. Charlotte-Mecklenberg Board of Education, 1388, **1416–1420,** 1422, 1423, 1426

Sweatt v. Painter, 1380, 1383, 1384, 1398, 1524, 1525, 1538

Sweezy v. State of New Hampshire, 340, 667, 675

Swift & Co. v. Wickham, 1202

Tahoe-Sierra Preservation Council, Inc. v. Tahoe Regional Planning Agency, 303

Tate v. Short, 1147, 1556

Taylor v. Louisiana, 1118, 1128

Teitel Film Corporation v. Cusack, 437n

Tennessee v. Garner, 922

Tennessee v. Sundquist, 214

Terminello v. Chicago, 404n

Terry v. Ohio, 856, 865, 866, 868, 870, **873–879,** 881, 882, 883, 884, 887, 888, 889, 890, 891, 892, 899, 905, 906, 907, 917, 923, 957, 1223, 1245

Test v. United States, 1122n

Texas Monthly, Inc. v. Bullock, 709n, 715, 763

Texas v. Brown, 890, 903n

Texas v. Cobb, 1032

Texas v. Johnson, 36n, 90, 460, 499, 500, 512, 640, 641, **653–659**

Thomas v. Collins, 597n, 807

Thomas v. Review Board of Indiana Employment Security Division, 811, 817, 819

Thompson v. Consolidated Gas Corp., 292

Thompson v. Oklahoma, 98n, 1164, 1214

Thompson v. Utah, 86, 88, 1120, 1133

Thompson v. Western States Medical Center, 559

Thornburgh v. American College of Obstetricians and Gynecologists, 1204, 1233, 1234, 1257, 1261, 1265, 1267, 1272, 1276

Thornhill v. Alabama, 404n, 578, 579n

Thorton v. United States, 902

Tibbs v. Florida, 1142n

Tigner v. Texas, 1514

Tileston v. Ullman, 120, 339

Tilton v. Richardson, 141, 703, 711, 778, 779

Time, Inc. v. Firestone, 529

Time, Inc. v. Hill, 531, 550, 580n, 601

Times Film Corporation v. City of Chicago, 437n

Tinker v. Des Moines Independent Community School District, 483, 488, 495, 496, 512, 639, **650–653,** 951

Tollett v. Henderson, 1108n

Tome v. United States, 1139n

Tomkins v. Missouri, 1095n

Tony and Susan Alamo Foundation v. Secretary of Labor, 804

Torcaso v. Watkins, 168, 739, 798, 811

Torre Jenkins v. Chief Justice of the District Court Department, 215
Townsend v. Burke, 1095*n*
Townsend v. Yeomans, 265*n*
Transportation Co. v. Chicago, 296
Trial of William Prynn, 386, 396*n*
Trimble v. Gordon, 1563, 1570
Trop v. Dulles, 98*n*, 1150, 1154, 1170*n*, 1171*n*, 1173, 1174, 1175, 1181, 1207, 1210
Troxel v. Granville, 367
Truax v. Raich, 1445
Trustees of Dartmouth College v. Woodward, 222, **229–233**
Tsu City Ground-Purification Ceremony, Kakunaga v. Sekiguchi, 847
Tuan Anh Nguyen v. Immigration and Naturalization Service, 1504
Turner Broadcasting System, Inc. v. Federal Communications Commission (Turner Broadcasting I), 609, 610, 616
Turner Broadcasting System, Inc. v. Federal Communications Commission (Turner Broadcasting II), 610
Turner v. Fouche, 1122*n*
Turner v. Murray, 1118
Turney v. Ohio, 1063
Twin City Bank v. Nebeker, 1307
Twining v. New Jersey, 311, 328, 330, 333, 334
TXO Production Corporation v. Alliance Resources Corporation, 364–365, 370, 373

Ullmann v. United States, 1024, 1083, 1084
Uniform Sanitation Men's Association v. Commissioner of Sanitation of the City of New York, 1026*n*
Union Pacific R. Co. v. Botsford, 1245, 1306
United Mizrachi Bank plc v. Migdal Cooperative Village, 70, 71*n*
United Public Workers of America v. Mitchell, 133
United States Civil Service Commission v. National Association of Letter Carriers, 669
United States Railroad Retirement Board v. Fritz, 264
United States Trust Co. of New York v. State of New Jersey, 225, **249–252**
United States v. Aloyzas Balsys, 1019
United States v. American Library Association, 436, 484, 611, 625, **626–630**, 663
United States v. Armstrong, 366
United States v. Arvizu, 899
United States v. Ash, 1096*n*
United States v. Ball, 1142*n*
United States v. Ballard, 800, 810
United States v. Banks, 872
United States v. Barnett, 1122*n*
United States v. Bisceglia, 929
United States v. Biswell, 929
United States v. Brignoni-Ponce, 883, 899

United States v. Butler, 34, 1182
United States v. Calandra, 988, 1005, 1010, 1012
United States v. Caldwell, 595, **597–603**
United States v. Carolene Products Co., 95, 1326, 1444, 1459
United States v. Causby, 287
United States v. Chadwick, 900, 901, 902, 911, 912, 913, 914, 915, 916, 1006
United States v. Cortez, 863, 882
United States v. Cronic, 1107
United States v. Cruikshank, 1350*n*, 1370
United States v. Curtiss-Wright Corp., 160
United States v. Darby, 347
United States v. DiFrancesco, 1143*n*
United States v. Dinitz, 1142*n*
United States v. Dionisio, 1085
United States v. Dixon, 1141
United States v. Doe, 1087
United States v. Dominguez Benitez, 1111
United States v. Donovan, 977
United States v. Drayton, 869
United States v. Dunn, 865
United States v. Edge Broadcasting Company, 556–557, 558, 567, 568
United States v. Edwards, 856
United States v. Eichman, 90, 641
United States v. Ewell, 1142*n*
United States v. Felix, 1141
United States v. Flores-Montano, 899
United States v. 12-1200 Foot Reels of Super 8Mm Film, 434
United States v. Fordice, 1392, **1428–1432**, 1434
United States v. Giordano, 977
United States v. Grace, 662
United States v. Guest, 1550
United States v. Halper, 1140, 1143*n*
United States v. Harris, 669, 857*n*
United States v. Havens, 989
United States v. Hubbell, 1077
United States v. Hudson and Goodwin, 392
United States v. Jacobsen, 857, 903*n*
United States v. James Daniel Good Real Property, 365
United States v. Janis, 988, 1007, 1016
United States v. Jeffers, 960*n*
United States v. Johns, 903*n*, 915
United States v. Johnson, 204, 205
United States v. Jones, 930
United States v. Jorn, 1142*n*
United States v. Kahn, 977
United States v. Kaio, 976, 978
United States v. Klein, 198*n*
United States v. Knotts, 960*n*
United States v. Kokinda, 661, 663
United States v. Kordel, 1025*n*
United States v. Kras, 1147
United States v. Lanza, 1143*n*
United States v. Lara, 1140

United States v. Lee, 804

United States v. Lefkowitz, 873*n*

United States v. Leon, 213, 989, **1003–1015,** 1016

United States v. MacDonald, 1136*n*

United States v. Martinez-Fuerte, 899, 900, 909, 951

United States v. Matlock, 864

United States v. Mendenhall, 869, 873*n*, 931

United States v. Midwest Video Corporation, 608

United States v. Miller, 354, 873*n*, 929, 960*n*

United States v. Monia, 1026*n*

United States v. Monsanto, 1144

United States v. Montgomery County Board of Education, 1394*n*

United States v. Montoya de Hernandez, 858*n*, 882

United States v. Murdock, 1086

United States v. National Treasury Employees Union, 596

United States v. New York Telephone Company, 978

United States v. Nixon, 197

United States v. O'Brien, 460, 461, 463, 465, 508, 512, 639, 653, 654, 655, 656

United States v. Ortiz, 899

United States v. Paradise, 1204, 1439, 1454, 1477

United States v. Patane, 1034, **1074–1077**

United States v. Payne, 1005

United States v. Perez, 1142*n*

United States v. Peters, 1414

United States v. 37-Photographs, 434

United States v. Place, 863, 915

United States v. Playboy Entertainment Group, 610, 622, 624

United States v. Rabinowitz, 859, 860

United States v. Ramirez, 871

United States v. Ramsey, 929

United States v. Reese, 1370

United States v. Reidel, 435

United States v. Richardson, 112, 141

United States v. Robel, 381, 426, 669

United States v. Robinson, 898, **903–907,** 917, 918

United States v. Ross, 902, 911, 912, 914, 915

United States v. Salerno, 383, 1144, 1541

United States v. Santana, 871, **892–894,** 957

United States v. Scotland Neck City Board of Education, 1423, 1432

United States v. Seeger, 801, 811

United States v. Sharpe, 930

United States v. Sokolow, 216, 866, **880–883**

United States v. Students Challenging Regulatory Agency Procedure (SCRAP), 110

United States v. Sullivan, 1086, 1089

United States v. United Foods, 559

United States v. United States District Court, 977

United States v. Ursery, 1142

United States v. U.S. Coin and Currency, 1090

United States v. Ventresca, 1006

United States v. Verdugo-Urquidez, 870

United States v. Virginia, 1331, 1499, **1517–1529**

United States v. Vuitch, 1228

United States v. Wade, 1085, 1094

United States v. Ward, 1140

United States v. Washington, 1023, 1078

United States v. Watson, 871, 893, 922

United States v. White, 218, 959

United States v. Williams, 1116

United States v. Wong, 1035*n*, 1078

United States v. Young, 1026*n*

United Steelworkers of America v. Weber, 1439, 1452

Uphaus v. Wyman, 667

Vacco v. Quill, 1288, **1313–1324**

Valdis v. Kline, 1560

Valentine v. Chrestensen, 536, 551, 552, 561

Vale v. Louisiana, 858*n*

Valley Forge Christian College v. Americans United for Separation of Church and State, Inc., 111, **137–141,** 1470

Vance v. Bradley, 1565

Vance v. Universal Amusement Co., 437*n*

Vasquez v. Hillery, 1063

Vernonia School District 47J v. Acton, 213, 927, 930, **938–944,** 945, 950, 951, 952, 953, 954

Vieth v. Juderlirer, 124

Village of Euclid v. Ambler Realty Co., 265*n*, 293, 301, 492, 1329

Virginia State Board of Pharmacy v. Virginia Citizens Consumer Council, Inc., 501, 553, 555, 565, 570, 571, 574, 579*n*

Virginia v. Black, 404, 429, 484, **510–517,** 641

Virginia v. West Virginia, 1409

Vitek v. Jones, 357, 363*n*

Vriend v. Alberta, 1546

Wainwright v. Witt, 1123*n*, 1205

Walder v. United States, 990*n*

Walker v. City of Birmingham, 664, 1381

Walker v. Ohio, 433

Wallace v. Jaffree, 193, 206, 318*n*, 704, 715, **740–749,** 752

Waller v. Florida, 1140, 1143*n*

Waller v. Georgia, 633, 1063

Walton v. Arizona, 1215

Waltz v. Tax Commission of the City of New York, 710

Walz v. Tax Commission of City of New York, 701, 703, 736, 748, 784, 842

Warden v. Hayden, 872, 873*n*, 893, 1024

Ward v. Rock Against Racism, 464, 500, 661, 665

Ware v. Hylton, 29

Warth v. Seldin, 112, 142, 1470, 1471
Washakie County School Dist. No. 1 v. Herschler, 217
Washington v. Chrisman, 219
Washington v. Glucksberg, 97, 375, 378, 379, 1288, **1313–1324**
Washington v. Harper, 362, 1310
Washington v. Seattle School District 1, 1433
Washington v. Texas, 315, 1139*n*
Watchtower Bible & Tract Society of New York, Inc. v. Village of Stratton, 481, 812
Watkins v. United States, 381, 1025*n*
Watts v. United States, 479, 512
Webb's Fabulous Pharmacies, Inc. v. Beckwith, 300
Weber v. Aetna Casualty & Surety Co., 1507, 1562
Webster v. Reproductive Health Services, 520, 1234, 1257, 1259, 1260, 1261, 1265, 1271, 1280, 1305
Weeks v. United States, 201, 203, 905, 961, 968, 985, 986, 993, 994, 995, 996, 997, 1009, 1012
Weems v. United States, 1150, 1170*n*, 1171*n*, 1173, 1174, 1175, 1181
Weinberger v. Hynson, Westcott & Dunning, Inc., 355
Weinberger v. Wiesenfeld, 1502, 1509, 1514, 1519
Welch v. Swasey, 265*n*
Welch v. Texas Highways and Public Transp., 1062
Welsh v. United States, 802, 855
Wengler v. Druggists Mutual Insurance Co., 1502
West Coast Hotel Co. v. Parrish, 263, **281–284,** 339, 347, 1263, 1264, 1270, 1444
West River Bridge Co. v. Dix, 244
Westside Community Bd. of Ed. v. Mergens, 753, 774
West Virginia State Board of Education v. Barnette, 95, 168, 340, 404*n*, 638, 639, 640, **641–650,** 654, 730, 756, 810, 819
Whalen v. Roe, 1287
White v. Illinois, 1138
White v. Maryland, 1094
White v. Ragen, 1095*n*
Whitley v. Albers, 1153, 1156*n*
Whitney v. California, 400, 404*n*, 414, 422, 425
Whitus v. Georgia, 1122*n*
Whren and Brown v. United States, 903*n*
"Wide Awake" case, 706, 708, 712, **769–780,** 785, 788
Widmar v. Vincent, 662, 698, 714, 757, 772, 774
Wiggins v. Smith, 1111
Wilkerson v. Utah, 1150, 1175, 1181
Wilkinson v. Jones, 609

Wilkins v. Missouri, 1214
Williamson v. Lee Optical of Oklahoma, 265*n*, 339, 1249, 1250
Williams v. Florida, 88, 317, 1120, 1121, **1131–1133,** 1134
Williams v. Illinois, 1147, 1556
Williams v. New York, 1171*n*, 1184
Williams v. Oklahoma City, 1147, 1184
Williams v. Taylor, 1110–1111, 1217
Williams v. United States, 198*n*
Willner v. Barr, 927
Wilson v. Arkansas, 871
Wilson v. Layne, 856
Wilson v. Seiter, 1153, 1155
Wisconsin v. Constantineau, 354
Wisconsin v. Mitchell, 483, **508–510**
Wisconsin v. Yoder, 764, 799, 811, **812–816,** 818, 821, 823, 834, 1570
Witherspoon v. Illinois, 1120, 1127, 1128, 1129, 1130, 1176, 1205
Withrow v. Williams, 1033, 1034
Witters v. Washington Commission for the Blind, 217, 842
Witters v. Washington Department of Services for the Blind, 217, 695, 708, 757, 758, 783, 786, 787, 788, 794, 803, 842
Witte v. United States, 1143*n*
Wolff v. McDonnell, 375
Wolf Packing Co. v. Court of Industrial Relations, 262
Wolf v. People of State of Colorado, 200, 201, 202, 314, 853, 986, 987, 993, 994, 995, 996, 997
Wolman v. Walter, 704, 708, 711, 713, 714, 777
Wolston v. Reader's Digest, 532*n*
Women of Minnesota v. Gomez, 215
Wong Sun v. United States, 857*n*, 1074, 1075
Woodson v. North Carolina, 1163, 1184, 1186, 1188, 1213
Wooley v. Maynard, 639, 811, 819
Worcester v. Georgia, 32, 197
Wright v. City Council of Emporia, 1423, 1432
Wygant v. Jackson Board of Education, 1439, 1453, 1457, 1458, 1459, 1460, 1467, 1474, 1475
Wyman v. James, 928
Wynehamer v. New York, 254
Wyoming v. Houghton, 902, 922
Wyoming v. Oklahoma, 111, 113
Wyrick v. Fields, 1085

Yamataya v. Fisher, 383
Yarborough v. Alvarado, 1030, 1080–1081
Yates v. United States, 402
Yazoo case, 222
Ybarra v. Illinois, 855, 942
Yee v. The City of Escondido, California, 289*n*
Yick Wo v. Hopkins, 382, 1173, 1325, 1445, 1538

Youngberg v. Romeo, 356, 1307, 1577

Younger v. Harris, 429n

Youngstown Sheet & Tube Co. v. Sawyer, 160, 385

Young v. American Mini Theatres, 435, 461, 464, 616

Young v. Harper, 366

Zablocki v. Redhail, 1227

Zacchini v. Scripps-Howard Broadcasting Corporation, 532n

Zadvydas v. Davis, 382, 383

Zauderer v. Office of Disciplinary Counsel of Supreme Court of Ohio, 553

Zelman v. Simmons-Harris, 695, 708, 713, **787–798,** 803, 842

Zemel v. Rusk, 599

Zobel v. Williams, 1561

Zobrest v. Catalina Foothills School District, 695, 708, 712, **756–760,** 782, 783, 784, 786, 787, 788, 794, 803, 842

Zorach v. Clauson, 698, 710, 727, 739, 765

Zurcher v. The Stanford Daily, 595